INTERNATIONAL MONETARY FUND

International
Financial Statistics

Yearbook 2005

INTERNATIONAL FINANCIAL STATISTICS

Vol. LVIII, 2005
Prepared by the IMF Statistics Department
Robert W. Edwards, Director

For information related to this publication, please:
   fax the Statistics Department at (202) 623-6460,
   or write Statistics Department
      International Monetary Fund
      Washington, D.C. 20431
   or telephone (202) 623-6180.
For copyright inquiries, please fax the Editorial Division at (202) 623-6579.
For purchases only, please contact Publication Services (see information below).

International Financial Statistics (IFS) is a standard source of statistics on all aspects of international and domestic finance. *IFS* publishes, for most countries of the world, current data on exchange rates, international liquidity, international banking, money and banking, interest rates, prices, production, international transactions (including balance of payments and international investment position), government finance, and national accounts. Information is presented in tables for specific countries and in tables for area and world aggregates. *IFS* is published monthly and annually.

Address orders to:
International Monetary Fund
Attention: Publication Services
Washington, D.C. 20431
U.S.A.
Telephone: (202) 623-7430
Telefax: (202) 623-7201
E-mail: publications@imf.org
Internet: http://www.imf.org

ISSN 0250-7463
ISBN 1-58906-459-3

POSTMASTER: Send address changes to International Financial Statistics, Publication Services, 700 19th St., N.W., Washington, D.C. 20431. Postage for periodicals paid at Washington, D.C. USPS 049-610

Recycled paper

CONTENTS

"Country" in this publication does not always refer to a territorial entity that is a state as understood by international law and practice; the term also covers the euro area, the Eastern Caribbean Currency Union, and some nonsovereign territorial entities, for which statistical data are provided internationally on a separate basis.

SELECTION OF STATISTICAL PUBLICATIONS

International Financial Statistics (IFS)

Acknowledged as a standard source of statistics on all aspects of international and domestic finance, *IFS* publishes, for most countries of the world, current data on exchange rates, international liquidity, international banking, money and banking, interest rates, prices, production, international transactions (including balance of payments and international investment position), government finance, and national accounts. Information is presented in tables for specific countries and in tables for area and world aggregates. *IFS* is published monthly and annually. *Price:* Subscription price is US$495 a year (US$247 to university faculty and students) for twelve monthly issues and the yearbook. Single copy price is US$65 for a monthly issue and US$95 for a yearbook issue.

Balance of Payments Statistics Yearbook (BOPSY)

Issued in three parts, this annual publication contains balance of payments and international investment position data. Part 1 provides detailed tables on balance of payments statistics for approximately 167 countries and international investment position data for 93 countries. Part 2 presents tables of regional and world totals of major balance of payments components. Part 3 contains descriptions of methodologies, compilation practices, and data sources used by reporting countries Price: US$98.

Direction of Trade Statistics (DOTS)

Quarterly issues of this publication provide, for about 156 countries, tables with current data (or estimates) on the value of imports from and exports to their most important trading partners. In addition, similar summary tables for the world, industrial countries, and developing countries are included. The yearbook provides, for the most recent seven years, detailed trade data by country for approximately 186 countries, the world, and major areas. *Price:* Subscription price is US$155 a year (US$129 to university faculty and students) for the quarterly issues and the yearbook. Price for a quarterly issue only is US$25, the yearbook only is US$70, and a guide only is US$12.50.

Government Finance Statistics Yearbook (GFSY)

This annual publication provides detailed data on transactions in revenue, expense, net acquisition of assets and liabilities, other economic flows, and balances of assets and liabilities of general government and its subsectors. The data are compiled according to the framework of the 2001 *Government Finance Statistics Manual,* which provides for several summary measures of government fiscal performance. *Price:* US$80.

CD-ROM Subscriptions

International Financial Statistics (IFS), Balance of Payments Statistics (BOPS), Direction of Trade Statistics (DOTS), and *Government Finance Statistics (GFS)* are available on CD-ROM by annual subscription. The CD-ROMs incorporate a Windows-based browser facility, as well as a flat file of the database in scientific notation. *Price of each subscription:* US$450 a year for single-user PC license (US$225 for university faculty and students). Network and redistribution licenses are negotiated on a case-by-case basis. Please contact Publication Services for information.

Subscription Packages

Combined Subscription Package

The combined subscription package includes all issues of *IFS, DOTS, BOPSY, GFSY,* and *Staff Papers,* the Fund's economic journal. *Combined subscription price:* US$749 a year. Airspeed delivery available at additional cost; please inquire.

Combined Statistical Yearbook Subscription

This subscription comprises *BOPSY, GFSY, IFSY,* and *DOTSY* at a combined rate of US$265. Because of different publication dates of the four yearbooks, it may take up to one year to service an order. Airspeed delivery available at additional cost; please inquire.

IFS on the Internet

The Statistics Department of the Fund is pleased to make available to subscribers the *International Financial Statistics (IFS)* database through an easy-to-use online service. The *IFS* database contains time series data beginning in 1948. The browser software provides a familiar and easy-to-use Windows interface for browsing the database, selecting series of interest, displaying the selected series in a spreadsheet format, and saving the selected series for transfer to other software systems, such as Microsoft Excel®. Single user license price for the *IFS Online Service* is $495, and $247 for academic users. Dependent on certain criteria, a range of scaled discounts is available. For full details of qualification for these discounts and online payment, please visit http://www.imfstatistics.org or email us directly at publications@imf.org.

Address orders to

Publication Services, IMF, Washington, DC 20431, USA
Telephone: (202) 623-7430   Telefax: (202) 623-7201   E-mail: publications@imf.org
Internet: http://www.imf.org

Note: Prices include the cost of delivery by surface mail. Enhanced delivery is available for an additional charge.

INTRODUCTION

Table of Contents

1. Overview

The Fund's principal statistical publication, *International Financial Statistics (IFS)*, has been published monthly since January 1948. In 1961, the monthly was supplemented by a yearbook, and in 1991 and 2000, respectively, *IFS* was introduced on CD-ROM and the Internet.

IFS contains country tables for most Fund members, as well as for Anguilla, Aruba, the Central African Economic and Monetary Community (CEMAC), the Eastern Caribbean Currency Union (ECCU), the euro area, Montserrat, the Netherlands Antilles, the West African Economic Monetary Union (WAEMU), and some nonsovereign territorial entities for which statistics are provided internationally on a separate basis. Also, selected series are drawn from the country tables and published in area and world tables. The country tables normally include data on a country's exchange rates, Fund position, international liquidity, money and banking accounts, interest rates, prices, production, labor, international transactions, government accounts, national accounts, and population. Selected series, including data on Fund accounts, international reserves, and international trade, are drawn from the country tables and published in world tables as well.

The monthly printed issue of *IFS* reports current monthly, quarterly, and annual data, while the yearbook reports 30 observations of annual data. Most annual data on the CD-ROM and Internet begin in 1948; quarterly and monthly data generally begin in 1957; most balance of payments data begin in 1970.

The following sections describe conceptual and technical aspects of various data published in *IFS*. The reader will find more detailed descriptions—about coverage, deviations from the standard methodologies, and discontinuities in the data—in the footnotes in the individual country and world tables in the monthly and yearbook issues of *IFS*, in the Print_Me file on the CD-ROM, and in the PDF pages on the Internet. (Where references are made in this introduction to notes in monthly issues, they refer to notes files on the CD-ROM and Internet as well.)

2. Exchange Rates and Exchange Rate Arrangements

Exchange rates in *IFS* are classified into three broad categories, reflecting the role of the authorities in determining the rates and/or the multiplicity of the exchange rates in a country. The three categories are the **market rate**, describing an exchange rate determined largely by market forces; the **official rate**, describing an exchange rate determined by the authorities—sometimes in a flexible manner; and the **principal**, **secondary**, or **tertiary rate**, for countries maintaining multiple exchange arrangements.

In *IFS*, exchange rates are expressed in time series of national currency units per SDR (the unit of account for the Fund) and national currency units per U.S. dollar, or vice versa.

The exchange rates in SDRs are classified and coded as follows:

Series **aa** shows the end-of-period national currency value of the SDR, and series **ac** shows the end-of-period SDR value of the national currency unit.

Series **sa, sb, sc,** and **sd**—provided on the country table for the United States—show the SDR value of U.S. dollars. Series **sa** and **sc** refer to end-of-period values of U.S. dollars per SDR and SDRs per U.S. dollar, respectively, while series **sb** and **sd** are geometric averages of values within the period.

The exchange rates in U.S. dollars are classified and coded as follows:

Series **ae** shows end-of-period national currency units per U.S. dollar, and series **ag** shows end-of-period U.S. dollars per unit of national currency.

Series **rf** shows period-average national currency units per U.S. dollar, and series **rh** shows period-average U.S. dollars per unit of national currency. Series **rf** and **rh** data are the monthly average of market rates or official rates of the reporting country. If those are not available, they are the monthly average rates in New York. Or if the latter are not available, they are estimates based on simple averages of the end-of-month market rates quoted in the reporting country.

The country tables contain two of the U.S. dollar series—either **ae** and **rf** or **ag** and **rh**—depending on the form in which the exchange rate is quoted.

Reciprocal relationships are the following:

The end-of-period rates **aa** and **ac, ae** and **ag,** and **sa** and **sc** are reciprocals of each other. The period-average SDR rates in terms of the U.S. dollar (**sb** and **sd**) are also reciprocals of each other, because they are calculated as geometric averages. Other period average rates (**rf** and **rh**) are calculated as arithmetic averages and are not reciprocals.

The relationship between trade figures in *IFS* and exchange rates is the following:

All trade figures in *IFS* are converted from national currency values to U.S. dollars and from U.S. dollar values to national currency, using series **rf**. Conversions are based on the data available for the shortest period, and these data are summed to obtain data for longer periods. Conversion is based on longer period rates of only the difference, if any, between the longer period data and the sum of the shorter period data. The country table notes in the monthly issues identify the exchange rates used.

For members maintaining dual or multiple exchange rate systems, which often reflect wide ranges of exchange rates in effect in a country, lines **w**, **x**, and **y** are presented. Notes on the tables in the monthly issues for these countries describe the current exchange rate systems and identify the exchange rates shown.

European Currency Unit (ECU) and the Euro

For periods before January 1999, the exchange rate sections in tables for members of the European Union (EU)—Austria, Belgium, Denmark, Finland, France, Germany, Greece, Ireland, Italy, Luxembourg, the Netherlands, Portugal, Spain, Sweden, and the United Kingdom—Norway and the United States contain a time series on the value of the European currency unit (ECU).

The ECU was issued by the European Monetary Institute (EMI)—successor to the European Monetary Cooperation Fund on January 1, 1994—against gold and foreign exchange deposits by the central banks of the EU member states. The ECU was defined as a basket of currencies of the EU member countries. The share of each currency in the basket was based on the gross national product and foreign trade of the country issuing that currency. The equivalent of the ECU was calculated—first in U.S. dollars and then in the currencies of the member countries—by using representative market exchange rates for the U.S. dollar, as reported by the member countries. In *IFS*, series **ea** and **ec** refer to end-of-period values of national currency units per ECU and ECUs per unit of national currency, respectively; series **eb** and **ed** are the arithmetic averages of values within the period.

On January 1, 1999, the euro replaced the ECU, at a rate of one euro per one ECU. Irrevocable conversion factors for the euro, adopted for the eleven countries in the euro area, fixed the central rates between the euro and the currencies participating in the exchange rate mechanism. The irrevocable fixed factors, legally mandated to have six significant digits, are the following: Austria (S 13.7603), Belgium (BF 40.3399), Finland (Fmk 5.94573), France (F 6.55957), Germany (DM 1.95583), Ireland (IR£0.787564), Italy (Lit 1936.27), Luxembourg (Lux F 40.3399), the Netherlands (f. 2.20371), Portugal (Esc 200.482), and Spain (Pta 166.386).

An accord established compulsory intervention rates for the Danish krone (± 2.25 percent around the euro central rate) and the Greek drachma (± 15 percent around the euro central rate) from January 1, 1999 onwards. Greece joined the euro area on January 1, 2001, adopting the euro as its currency, with a conversion factor of 340.750 drachmas per euro.

In addition, from January 1, 1999 onwards, the member countries of the Bank of Central African States and the Central Bank of West African States changed the peg of their currencies from the French franc to the euro, at a rate of CFAF 655.957 per euro. A few other countries also have pegged their currencies to the euro.

On January 1, 2002, euro banknotes and coins were issued. National currencies continued to be accepted in trade for a short transition period that ended in all member countries by the end of February 2002. The statistical treatment of euro banknotes and coins and outstanding national currencies is described in the section *European Economic and Monetary Union* in Section 5—Money and Banking.

Effective Exchange Rates

The country tables, euro area tables, and world tables provide measures of effective exchange rates, compiled by the IMF's Research Department, Policy Development and Review Department, Statistics Department, and area departments.

A **nominal** effective exchange rate index represents the ratio (expressed on the base 2000=100) of an index of a currency's period-average exchange rate to a weighted geometric average of exchange rates for the currencies of selected countries and the euro area. A **real effective** exchange rate index represents a nominal effective exchange rate index adjusted for relative movements in national price or cost indicators of the home country, selected countries, and the euro area.

Line ahx

For ease of comparison between the nominal effective exchange rate index and the real effective exchange rate index, the average exchange rate expressed in terms of U.S. dollars per unit of each of the national currencies (line **ah**) is also given as an index form based on 2000=100 (line **ahx**). In both cases of the indices, an increase in the index reflects an appreciation. Because of certain data-related limits, particularly where Fund estimates have been used, data users need to exercise considerable caution in interpreting movements in nominal and real effective exchange rates.

The Fund publishes calculated effective exchange rates data only for countries that have given their approval. Please note that similar indices that are calculated by country authorities could cause different results.

Lines neu and reu

The nominal effective exchange rate index (line **neu**) and the real effective exchange rate index (line **reu**) are published in the country tables for approximately 18 industrial countries and the euro area, for which data are available for normalized unit labor costs in manufacturing.

For the nominal effective exchange rate index, weights are derived from trade in manufactured goods among industrial countries over the period 1989–91. For the real effective exchange rate index for these countries (excluding Australia and New Zealand) and the euro area (excluding Ireland and Portugal), data are compiled from the nominal effective exchange rate index and from a cost indicator of relative normalized unit labor costs in manufacturing. The **reu** and **neu** indices are discussed more fully in the world table section of this introduction.

A selection of other measures of real effective exchange rates for these countries and the euro area, using alternative measures of costs and prices, is shown in the world table *Real Effective Exchange Rates Indices*.

Lines nec and rec

The country tables for selected other countries include a nominal effective exchange rate index in line **nec**. This index is based on a methodology that takes account of each country's trade in both *manufactured* goods and *primary* products with its partner, or competitor, countries.

For *manufactured* goods, trade by type of good and market is distinguished in the database. So it is possible to allow at a disaggregated level for competition among various exporters in a foreign market (i.e., third-market competition) as well as that arising from bilateral trade links.

For *primary* products, the weights assigned depend principally on a country's role as a global supplier or buyer of the product. Trade in crude petroleum, petroleum, and other energy products is excluded. For some countries that depend heavily on tourism, bilateral exports of tourism services averaged over 1988–90 are also included in calculating the competitiveness weights.

From January 1990 onwards, the line **nec** index is weighted based on disaggregate trade data for manufactured goods and primary products covering the three-year period 1988–90. Before that, the weights are for the three-year span 1980–82. The series based on the old weights and the new weights are linked by splicing at December 1989, and the reference base is shifted to 2000=100.

The real effective exchange rate index in line **rec** is derived from the nominal effective exchange rate index, adjusted for relative changes in consumer prices. Consumer price indices, often available monthly, are used as a measure of domestic costs and prices for these countries. This practice typically reflects the use of consumer prices by the reference and partner, or competitor, countries in compiling these indices.

For countries where multiple exchange rates are in effect, Fund staff estimates of weighted average exchange rates are used in many cases. A weighted average exchange rate is constructed as an average of the various exchange rates, with the weights reflecting the share of trade transacted at each rate. For countries where a weighted average exchange rate cannot be calculated, the principal rate, generally line **ahx**, is used.

The notes to the country tables in the monthly issues provide information about exceptions in the choice of the consumer price index (generally line 64) and the period average exchange rate index (generally line **ahx**). For a relatively small number of countries, notes in the country tables in the monthly issues indicate 1) where alternative price indices, such as the wholesale/producer price index or a weighted average of several price indices, are used; 2) where data constraints have made it necessary to use weighting schemes based on aggregate bilateral non-oil trade data; and 3) where trade in services (such as tourism) has been taken into account.

The world table section of this introduction provides a description of the effective exchange rates tables. In addition, a Fund working paper entitled "A Primer on the IMF's Information Notice System" (WP/97/71), distributed in May 1997, provides background on the concepts and methodology underlying the effective exchange rates.

SDR Value

Before July 1974, the value of the SDR (unit of account for the Fund) was fixed in terms of U.S. dollars. Over time, the value changed as follows: SDR 1 = U.S. dollar 1 through November 1971; SDR 1 = U.S. dollar 1.08571 from December 1971 through January 1973; and SDR 1 = U.S. dollar 1.20635 from February 1973 through June 1974.

Since July 1974, the Fund has determined the value of the SDR daily on the basis of a basket of currencies, with each currency being assigned a weight in the determination of that value. The currencies in the basket are valued at their market exchange rates for the U.S. dollar. The U.S. dollar equivalents of each currency are summed to yield the rate of the SDR in terms of the U.S. dollar. The rates for the SDR in terms of other currencies are derived from the market exchange rates of these currencies for the U.S. dollar and the U.S. dollar rate for the SDR.

Although the method of calculating the U.S. dollar/SDR exchange rate has remained the same, the currencies' number and weight have changed over time. Their amount in the SDR basket is reviewed every five years.

From July 1974 through June 1978, the currencies in the basket were of the countries that averaged more than 1 percent share in world exports of goods and services from 1968–72. This established a basket of 16 currencies. Each currency's relative weight was broadly proportionate to the country's exports but modified for the U.S. dollar to reflect its real weight in the world economy. To preserve the continuity of valuation, the amount of each of the 16 currencies was such that on June 28, 1974 the value of SDR 1 = U.S. dollar 1.20635.

From July 1978 through December 1980, the composition of the basket was changed on the basis of updated data for 1972–76. The weights of some currencies were also changed. The amount of each of the 16 currencies in the revised basket was such as to ensure that the value of the SDR in terms of any currency on June 30, 1978 was exactly the same in the revised valuation as in the previous valuation.

Since January 1, 1981, the value of the SDR has been determined based on the currencies of the five member countries having the largest exports of goods and services during the five-year period ending one year before the date of the latest revision to the valuation basket. Broadly reflecting the currencies' relative importance in international trade and finance, the weights are based on the value of the exports of goods and services of the members issuing these currencies and the balances of their currencies officially held by members of the Fund.

From January 1981 through December 1985, the currencies and currency weights of the five members having the largest exports of goods and services during 1975–79 were the U.S. dollar, 42 percent; deutsche mark, 19 percent; French franc, Japanese yen, and pound sterling, 13 percent each.

From January 1986 through December 1990, reflecting the period 1980–84, the weights had changed to U.S. dollar, 42 percent; deutsche mark, 19 percent; Japanese yen, 15 percent; French franc and pound sterling, 12 percent each.

From January 1991 through December 1995, reflecting the period 1985–89, the weights were U.S. dollar, 40 percent; deutsche mark, 21 percent; Japanese yen, 17 percent; French franc and pound sterling, 11 percent each.

On January 1, 1996, the weights were U.S. dollar, 39 percent; deutsche mark, 21 percent; Japanese yen, 18 percent; French franc and pound sterling, 11 percent each.

On January 1, 1999, the currency amount of deutsche mark and French francs were replaced with equivalent amounts of euros, based on the fixed conversion rates between those currencies and the euro, announced on December 31, 1998 by the European Council. The weights in the SDR basket were changed to U.S. dollar, 39 percent; euro, 32 percent (in replacement of the 21 percent for the deutsche mark and 11 percent for the French franc), Japanese yen, 18 percent; and pound sterling, 11 percent.

As of January 1, 2001, the SDR valuation basket weights are the sum of the values of the amounts of each currency in the following amounts: U.S. dollar, 45 percent; euro, 29 percent; Japanese yen, 15 percent; and pound sterling, 11 percent.

World Tables on Exchange Rates

Tables A, B, C, and D on exchange rates, described below, are presented in *IFS*. Daily exchange rates are not yet provided on the CD-ROM or Internet.

Table A of exchange rates gives the monthly, quarterly, and annual SDR rates in terms of U.S. dollars and reciprocals of these rates.

Table B reports for the latest available month the daily rates and the monthly averages, both in terms of currency units per U.S. dollar (**af**) and U.S. dollars per currency unit (**ah**) of (1) 16 major currencies, other than the U.S. dollar, as quoted in the markets of these countries, (2) the SDR, and (3) the euro.

Table C gives daily rates of currencies in terms of national currency units per SDR for the latest available month.

Table D provides, in terms of national currency units per SDR, end-of-period rates for the currencies of Fund members—including Hong Kong (Special Administrative Region as of 1997)—and the Netherlands Antilles.

Method of Deriving IFS Exchange Rates

For countries that have introduced new currencies, the rates shown in *IFS* for the period before the introduction of the most recent currency may be used as conversion factors—they may be used to convert national currency data in *IFS* to U.S. dollar or SDR data. In such cases, the factors are constructed by chain linking the exchange rates of the old and the new currencies. The basis used is the value of the new currency relative to the old currency, as established by the issuing agency at the time the new currency was introduced. Footnotes about the introduction of new currencies are to be found on individual country tables in the monthly issues of *IFS*.

For countries that are members of the euro area, the exchange rates shown are expressed in national currency units per SDR or per U.S. dollar through 1998, and in euros per SDR or per U.S. dollar thereafter.

A detailed description of the derivation of the exchange rates in *IFS*, as well as technical issues associated with these rates, is contained in the *IFS Supplement on Exchange Rates*, No. 9 (1985).

3. Fund Accounts

Data on members' Fund accounts are presented in the Fund Position section in the country tables and in 12 world tables. Details about Fund Accounts terms and concepts and the time series in the country and world tables follow:

Terms and Concepts in Fund Accounts

Quota

When a country joins the Fund, it is assigned a quota that fits into the structure of existing quotas. Quotas are considered in the light of the member's economic characteristics relative to those of other members of comparable size. The size of the member's quota determines, among other things, the member's voting power, the size of its potential access to Fund resources, and its share in allocations of SDRs.

Quotas are reviewed at intervals of not more than five years. The reviews take account of changes in the relative economic positions of members and the growth of the world economy. Initial subscriptions, and normally subscriptions associated with increases in quotas, are paid mainly in the member's own currency, and a smaller portion, not exceeding 25 percent, is paid in reserve assets (SDRs or other members' currencies that are acceptable to the Fund).

General Resources Account

The General Resources Account (GRA) resources consist of the currencies of Fund member countries, SDRs, and gold. These resources are received in the form of subscriptions (which are equal to quotas), borrowings, charges on the use of the Fund's resources, income from investments, and interest on the Fund's holdings of SDRs. Subscriptions are the main source of funds.

Borrowing Arrangements

Borrowings are regarded as a temporary source of funds. The Fund has the authority to borrow the currency of any member from any source with the consent of the issuer.

General Arrangements to Borrow

The Fund's first borrowings were made under the General Arrangements to Borrow (GAB). The Arrangements were established in 1962 initially for four years but, through successive extensions, have been continuously in force since then. The original Arrangements

permitted the Fund to borrow the currencies of ten industrial country members (those forming the Group of Ten) to finance purchases by any of these ten countries.

The Fund also had an agreement with Switzerland, under which Switzerland undertook to consider making loans to the Fund to finance additional purchases by members that made purchases financed by the GAB.

The revised GAB, that became effective in December 1983, permits the Fund under certain circumstances to extend GAB resources to members that are not GAB participants, authorizes participation of the Swiss National Bank, and permits certain borrowing arrangements between the Fund and nonparticipating members to be associated with the GAB. The GAB decision was amended on December 22, 1992 to take account of Switzerland's membership in the Fund.

Temporary Arrangements

The Fund has also entered into borrowing arrangements to finance purchases under its temporary lending facilities.

Oil Facilities: The Fund arranged in 1974 and 1975 to borrow from the principal oil exporting countries and other countries with strong external positions to finance two special facilities—the 1974 and 1975 Oil Facilities. Under these facilities, repayments were completed in May 1983.

Supplementary Financing Facility: In 1977 the Fund initiated bilateral borrowing arrangements with 14 countries or their institutions to finance commitments under the Supplementary Financing Facility. This facility was established in 1979, and its funds were fully committed by March 1981.

Policy on Enlarged Access: The first borrowing agreement under the Policy on Enlarged Access to the Fund's resources was reached in March 1981 between the Fund and the Saudi Arabian Monetary Agency.

Others: Since then, additional agreements have been entered into with central banks and official agencies of a number of countries, and with international agencies. In December 1986 the Fund entered into a borrowing arrangement with the government of Japan, under which resources were made available for use by the Fund in support of members' adjustment programs, including under the Enlarged Access Policy.

All of the above borrowing arrangements were disbursed and used by December 1991, except for the GAB, which remains intact. Meanwhile, in December 1987 the Fund, as "Trustee," was authorized to enter into borrowing arrangements with official lenders from a wide range of countries to finance loans under the Enhanced Structural Adjustment Facility, renamed Poverty Reduction and Growth Facility in November 1999.

New Arrangements to Borrow

The New Arrangements to Borrow (NAB), which became effective on November 17, 1998, is a set of credit arrangements between the Fund and 25 members and institutions to provide supplementary resources to the Fund. These resources are to forestall or cope with an impairment of the international monetary system or to deal with an exceptional situation that poses a threat to the stability of that system. The NAB does not replace the GAB, which remains in force.

The total amount of resources available to the Fund under the NAB and GAB combined will be up to SDR 34 billion, double the amount available under the GAB alone. By strengthening the Fund's ability to support the adjustment efforts of its members and to address their balance of payments difficulties, the NAB is an important element of the Fund's capacity to respond to potential systemic problems. The NAB will be in effect for five years, beginning on November 17, 1998, and may be renewed.

Financing Policies and Facilities

Purchases (.2kk.)

The principal way the Fund makes its resources available to members is to sell to them currencies of other members or SDRs in exchange for their own currencies. Such transactions change the composition, but not the overall size, of the Fund's resources. A member to whom the Fund sells currencies or SDRs is said to make "purchases" (also referred to as "drawings") from the Fund.

The purpose of making the Fund's resources available to members is to meet their balance of payments needs. The Fund's resources are provided through permanent policies for general balance of payments purposes (the tranche policies), permanent facilities for specific purposes (the Buffer Stock Financing Facility, the Extended Fund Facility, the Compensatory and Contingency Financing Facility, and the Supplemental Reserve Facility (SRF)), and temporary facilities (the Oil Facilities, the Supplementary Financing Facility, the Policy on Enlarged Access to the Fund's resources, and the Systemic Transformation Facility (STF)).

Permanent Policies

Reserve Tranche: A member's reserve tranche is the excess of its quota in the Fund over the adjusted Fund holdings of its currency in the GRA. Adjusted Fund holdings of a member's currency are equal to the actual holdings of the currency less holdings arising from outstanding purchases under the Fund's policies and facilities, which are subject to exclusion under Article XXX(c). Reserve tranche purchases, like all other purchases, may be made only to meet a balance of payments need. However, for reserve tranche purchases the Fund does not challenge a member's statement of need. As the reserve tranche is considered a reserve deposit in the Fund, a member using its reserve tranche is not considered to be using Fund credit.

Credit Tranche Policy: The credit tranche policy is often referred to as the Fund's basic financing policy. Credit under this policy is viewed as being available in tranches, each tranche being equivalent to 25 percent of quota. Credit tranche purchases may be made outright or under a stand-by arrangement. The latter, which is like a line of credit, assures the member that during a given period it will be able to use the Fund's resources up to a specified amount, so long as it is observing the terms of the arrangement.

Permanent Facilities

Buffer Stock Financing Facility: The Buffer Stock Financing Facility, established in June 1969, is to assist members with a balance of payments need related to their participation in arrangements to finance approved international buffer stocks of primary products.

Extended Fund Facility (EFF): The EFF, established in September 1974, is to make resources available for longer periods and in larger amounts than under the credit tranche policies. It is to assist members that are experiencing balance of payments difficulties owing to structural imbalances in production, trade, and prices, or that are unable to pursue active development policies because of their weak balance of payments positions.

Compensatory and Contingency Financing Facility (CCFF): The CCFF superseded the Compensatory Financing Facility (CFF) in August 1988. The CCFF keeps the essential elements of the CFF and adds a mechanism for contingency financing to support adjustment programs approved by the Fund.

The CFF, established in February 1963, was to assist members, particularly primary producing countries, experiencing balance of payments difficulties attributable to shortfalls in earnings from merchandise exports. Such difficulties were also attributable to invisibles both temporary and due largely to factors beyond their control.

In May 1981 the Fund decided to extend financial assistance to members facing balance of payments difficulties produced by an excess in the cost of their cereal imports. This assistance was integrated with support available under the compensatory financing facility for temporary shortfalls in export receipts.

Supplemental Reserve Facility (SRF): The SRF, established in December 1997, is to financially assist a member country experiencing exceptional balance of payments difficulties caused by a large short-term financing need. This need resulted from a sudden and disruptive loss of market confidence reflected in pressure on the capital account and the member's reserves.

Financing under the SRF, available in the form of additional resources under a Stand-By or Extended Arrangement, may be committed for up to one year and be generally available in two or more tranches. Purchases under the SRF are included as part of either the Stand-By or the Extended Fund Facility, as indicated in the footnote to the world table "Financing Components of Members' Outstanding Obligations to the Fund."

Access

Under the present guidelines on access limits, adopted on October 24, 1994, member access to the Fund's general resources in the credit tranches and the Extended Facility is subject to an annual limit of 100 percent of quota, and a cumulative limit of 300 percent of quota. This is net of scheduled repurchases and excluding purchases under the Compensatory Financing Facility and the Buffer Stock Financing Facility.

Within these limits, the amount of access in individual cases will vary according to the circumstances of the member. In exceptional circumstances, the Fund may approve Stand-By or Extended Arrangements that provide for amounts over these access limits. The guidelines and access limits are intended to be temporary and are reviewed periodically.

Temporary Facilities

Oil Facilities: The oil facilities, set up in June 1974 and April 1975, were to assist members with balance of payments difficulties owing to the rise in oil prices. Purchases under the facilities were completed in May 1976.

Supplementary Financing Facility (SFF): The SFF, established in February 1979, was to assist members facing payments difficulties that were large in relation to their economies and their Fund quotas. Resources under the facility, which were borrowed and therefore not part of the Fund's ordinary resources, were made available only in connection with an upper credit tranche stand-by arrangement and an extended arrangement. The facility was fully committed by March 1981.

Enlarged Access Policy: The Policy on Enlarged Access to the Fund's resources, which continued the policies of the Supplementary Financing Facility following the full commitment of the latter's resources, became operational in May 1981. Under this policy, resources were provided only under stand-by and extended arrangements. The amount of assistance available to a member under the policy was determined according to guidelines adopted by the Fund from time to time. The policy was discontinued in November 1992 because of the effectiveness of the increases in quotas under the

Ninth Review, which increased the Fund's ordinary resources by 50 percent.

Systemic Transformation Facility (STF): The STF could be accessed between April 1993 and December 1995. It was to help member countries facing balance of payments difficulties owing to severe disruptions of their traditional trade and payments arrangements. The disruptions had arisen during a shift from significant reliance on trading at nonmarket prices to multilateral, market-based trade. Countries eligible to draw on the STF included most of those belonging to the former Council for Mutual Economic Assistance, the Baltic countries, Russia, and other countries of the former Soviet Union (BRO), and a number of other countries experiencing similar transformation.

Access

Except for access to the credit tranches and the Extended Facility, which are now subject to common ceilings, access to resources under one policy or facility is independent of access under any other policies or facilities.

All requests for purchases other than those in the reserve tranche are subject to examination by the Fund to determine whether the proposed use of purchases would be consistent with the provisions of the Articles of Agreement and Fund policies. These provisions call for adequate safeguards to ensure that the member will adopt the policies, take measures to overcome its balance of payments difficulties, and meet scheduled repurchases, thereby ensuring the revolving nature of the Fund's resources.

Repurchases

Because the Fund's resources revolve to finance temporary balance of payments deficits, members that purchase from the Fund must subsequently repurchase their currencies with the currencies of other members or SDRs. A member is required to repurchase Fund holdings of its currency that are subject to charges. These holdings include those that result from purchases of currencies or SDRs, other than reserve tranche purchases, and all adjusted Fund holdings that are more than 100 percent of the member's quota.

Members may repurchase at any time the Fund's holdings of their currencies that are subject to charges. However, if their balance of payments and reserve positions improve, they are expected to repurchase the Fund's holdings of their currencies from purchases.

In any event, they must make repurchases—irrespective of their balance of payments positions—in installments within limits of 3 1/4 to 5 years for purchases under the credit tranche policies, the Compensatory Financing Facility, and the Buffer Stock Financing Facility; 4 1/2 to 10 years for purchases under the Extended Facility and Systemic Transformation Facility financed by ordinary resources; and 3 1/2 to 7 years for purchases under the Policy on Enlarged Access to resources.

Positions in the Fund

The Fund normally determines the currencies that are used in transactions and operations with members. Each quarter, the Fund prepares a financial transactions plan, in which it indicates the amounts of particular currencies and SDRs to be used during the relevant period. The Fund selects the currencies of members with strong balance of payments and reserve positions. It also seeks to promote, over time, balanced "**positions in the Fund**."

The effects of Fund transactions and operations are summarized in the Fund's **holdings of members' currencies** and in two other measures, namely, **reserve position in the Fund** and total **Fund credit and loans outstanding**. (See world table in the monthly printed copy of *IFS* and the yearbook, entitled Fund Accounts: Position to Date, and also the Fund Position section in the country tables.)

These measures are defined as follows:

The Fund's **holdings of a member's currency** reflect, among other things, the transactions and operations of the Fund in that currency. This concept is used in calculating the amounts that a member can draw on the Fund under tranche policies and in respect to certain of its obligations to the Fund.

A member's **reserve position in the Fund** (time series .1c.s), which has the characteristics of a reserve asset, comprises the reserve tranche position and creditor position under the various borrowing arrangements. A reserve tranche position arises from (1) the payment of part of a member's subscription in reserve assets and (2) the Fund's net use of the member's currency. Normally, a member's reserve tranche position is equal to its quota less the adjusted Fund holdings of its currency, less subscriptions receivable, less the balances held in the administrative accounts of the Fund to the extent they are not above 0.1 percent of a member's quota, if positive.

Total Fund credit and loans outstanding (.2tl.) represents the sum of (1) the use of Fund credit within the GRA and (2) outstanding loans under the SAF, PRGF, and the Trust Fund.

Use of Fund credit within the General Resources Account (.2egs) is the sum of a member's outstanding purchases and the Fund's net operational receipts and expenditures in that currency that increase the adjusted Fund holdings above quota. It measures the amount that a member is obligated to repurchase.

Outstanding purchases (.2kk.) are equal to purchases other than reserve tranche purchases, less repurchases, less other members' purchases of that member's currency, and less any other use by the Fund of that member's currency (except administrative expenditures) that the member wishes to attribute to specific outstanding purchases.

Use of Fund credit within the Special Disbursement Account (SDA) relates to outstanding loans under the structural adjustment facility (SAF) and that portion of the enhanced structural adjustment facility (ESAF) loans not financed from the ESAF Trust Account. The SDA is the vehicle for receiving and investing profits from the sale of the IMF's gold (i.e., the net proceeds in excess of the book value of SDR 35 a fine ounce), and for making transfers to other accounts for special purposes authorized in the Articles, in particular for financial assistance to low-income members of the IMF.

Structural Adjustment Facility and Poverty Reduction and Growth Facility

The Structural Adjustment Facility (SAF), established in March 1986, provides additional balance of payments assistance in the form of loans on concessional terms. This assistance is for low-income developing countries that were eligible for International Development Association (IDA) resources, that face protracted balance of payments problems, and that are in need of such assistance.

Resources of the SAF comprise Trust Fund reflows, the interest income on SAF loans, investment income from the resources available for the facility, and amounts not used for the Supplementary Financing Facility (SFF) Subsidy Account, which may be transferred back to the SDA.

The Enhanced Structural Adjustment Facility (ESAF) was established in December 1987 and renamed Poverty Reduction and Growth Facility (PRGF), effective November 22, 1999. It provides additional assistance in the form of loans on concessional terms to low-income developing countries that were eligible for assistance from the SAF.

In contrast to the uniform access limit of 70 percent of quota for SAF loans, individual access limits for PRGF loans are determined on the basis of balance of payments need and the strength of adjustment efforts. The maximum access limit is set at 250 percent of quota, with a provision for higher access in exceptional cases. Repayment of each loan must be made in 10 equal semiannual installments starting 5 1/2 years and finishing 10 years after the date of the disbursement. Outstanding SAF and PRGF loans do not affect a member's access to the Fund's general resources, which remain available under the terms of those policies.

Resources available for disbursement under PRGF arrangements include (1) the resources of the PRGF Trust (previously the ESAF Trust, established in December 1987), which comprise special loans and contributions and are held separately from the property and assets of all other accounts of the Fund, including other administered accounts, (2) amounts available from the SDA that have not been used under SAF arrangements, and (3) amounts made available by associated lenders.

Trust Fund and Supplementary Financing Facility Subsidy Account

The Fund is Trustee for two additional accounts, whose resources are legally separate from the resources of the Fund. These are the Trust Fund and the Supplementary Financing Facility (SFF) Subsidy Account.

The Trust Fund, established in May 1976, provides balance of payments assistance on concessional terms to eligible members and also distributes funds directly to developing members. The resources of the Trust Fund are derived from profits from the sale of about 25 million ounces of the Fund's gold holdings during 1976–80, from income on the investment of these profits, from contributions by members, and from low-interest borrowings.

The SFF Subsidy Account, established in December 1980, reduced the cost for low-income developing countries for using the supplementary financing facility. The SFF Subsidy Account consists of transfers from reflows of Trust Fund loans, donations, loans, and the interest income received from investment of resources held pending disbursement.

SDRs

SDRs are unconditional reserve assets created by the Fund to supplement existing reserve assets. SDRs are allocated to Fund members that participate in the Fund's Operations Division for SDRs and Administered Accounts in proportion to their quotas. Six SDR allocations totaling SDR 21.4 billion have been made by the Fund (in January 1970, January 1971, January 1972, January 1979, January 1980, and January 1981).

The Fund cannot allocate SDRs to itself but receives them from members through various financial transactions and operations. Entities authorized to conduct transactions in SDRs are the Fund itself, participants in the Fund's Operations Division for SDRs and Administered Accounts, and prescribed "other holders."

The SDR can be used for a wide range of transactions and operations, including for acquiring other members' currencies, settling financial obligations, making donations, and extending loans. SDRs may also be used in swap arrangements and as security for the performance of financial obligations. Forward as well as spot transactions may be conducted in SDRs.

World Tables on Fund Accounts

Twelve world tables on Fund Accounts are presented in *IFS*, as described below. The tables on Fund accounts arrangements, position

to date, financing components, and borrowing agreements are not yet available on the CD-ROM or Internet.

The world table Fund Accounts: Arrangements reports the current status of stand-by, extended, and poverty reduction and growth (previously, the enhanced structural adjustment) arrangements.

The table Fund Accounts: Position to Date reports latest monthly data on members' Fund positions, including quota, reserve position in the Fund, total Fund credit and loans outstanding, Fund holdings of currencies, and positions in the SDR Department.

The table Financing Components of Members' Outstanding Obligations to the Fund reports latest monthly data on the sources of financing of Fund credit and loans outstanding.

The tables Purchases (.2kk.) and Repurchases (.2lk.) relate to transactions within the General Resources Account (GRA). Purchases exclude reserve tranche purchases.

The table Fund Accounts: Borrowing Agreements reports the current status of the Fund's borrowing activities.

The tables Loan Disbursements (.2kl.) and Repayments of Loans (.2ll.) relate to the Structural Adjustment Facility (SAF), Poverty Reduction and Growth Facility (PRGF; which was previously named Enhanced Structural Adjustment Facility-ESAF), and Trust Fund loans.

The table Total Fund Credit and Loans Outstanding (.2tl.) relates to the outstanding use of Fund resources under the GRA and to outstanding loans under the SAF, PRGF, and Trust Fund.

The table Use of Fund Credit: GRA (.2egs) relates to the outstanding use of the Fund resources under the GRA.

The table SDRs (.1b.s) shows holdings of SDRs by members and includes a foot table showing SDR holdings by all participants, the IMF, other holders, and the world.

The table Reserve Position in the Fund (.1c.s) relates to members' claims on the Fund.

Pamphlet on Fund Accounts

A more detailed description of the Fund accounts is contained in the IMF's *Financial Organization and Operations of the IMF*, Pamphlet No. 45, sixth edition, 2001.

4. International Liquidity

Data on international liquidity are presented in the country tables and in world tables on reserves. The international liquidity section in the country tables comprises lines for total reserves minus gold, gold holdings, other foreign assets and foreign liabilities of the monetary authorities, and foreign accounts of other financial institutions. The euro area section for international liquidity covers assets of the European Central Bank (ECB) and the national central banks (NCBs) of the countries that have adopted the euro (details below).

Total Reserves (Minus Gold) and Gold Holdings

Total Reserves Minus Gold (line 1 l.d) is the sum of the items Foreign Exchange, Reserve Position in the Fund, and the U.S. dollar value of SDR holdings by monetary authorities. Monetary authorities comprise central banks and, to the extent that they perform monetary authorities' functions, currency boards, exchange stabilization funds, and treasuries.

Official Gold Holdings (lines 1ad and 1and) are expressed in millions of fine troy ounces and valued, according to national practice, in U.S. dollars.

Under Total Reserves Minus Gold, the line for Foreign Exchange (1d.d) includes monetary authorities' claims on nonresidents in the form of foreign banknotes, bank deposits, treasury bills, short- and long-term government securities, ECUs (for periods before January 1999), and other claims usable in the event of balance of payments need.

For *IFS* yearbook users, this background information on foreign exchange is particularly useful: Before December 1971, when the U.S. dollar was at par with the SDR, foreign exchange data were compiled and expressed in terms of U.S. dollars at official par values. Conversions from national currencies to U.S. dollars from December 1971 through January 1973 were calculated at the cross rates reflecting the parities and central rates agreed to in December 1971. From February 1973 through June 1974, foreign exchange was valued at the cross rates of parities or central rates for countries having effective parities or central rates, and at market rates for the Canadian dollar, Irish pound, Italian lira, Japanese yen, and pound sterling. Beginning in July 1974, foreign exchange is valued at end-of-month market rates or, in the absence of market rate quotations, at other prevailing official rates.

Total Reserves for the Euro Area

Until December 31, 1998, member countries of the European Union (Austria, Belgium, Denmark, Finland, France, Germany, Greece, Ireland, Italy, Luxembourg, the Netherlands, Portugal, Spain, Sweden, and the United Kingdom) held ECU deposits with the European Monetary Cooperation Fund (EMCF) and/or its successor, the European Monetary Institute. The reserves data for each country excluded, from gold and foreign exchange holdings, the deposits of gold and foreign exchange with the EMCF, but the data included, in foreign exchange holdings, the equivalent amounts of ECU deposits.

These deposits were transferred from the EMCF to the EMI upon its creation on January 1, 1994, and to the European Central Bank (ECB) when it succeeded the EMI on June 1, 1998. Each national central bank (NCB) deposited gold and foreign exchange with the ECB. On January 1, 1999, the euro replaced the ECU at a rate of one euro per one ECU.

Total reserves for the euro area and individual euro area countries are based on the statistical definition of international reserves adopted by the ECB's Statistics Committee in December 1998. Defined on a euro area-wide residency basis, they include reserve assets denominated only in currencies of non-euro area countries. All positions with residents of other euro area countries and with the ECB are excluded from reserve assets.

For the euro area countries, Total Reserves minus Gold (line 1 l.d) is defined in broad accordance with the fifth edition of the *Balance of Payments Manual*. It includes the monetary authorities' holdings of SDRs, reserve position in the Fund, and foreign exchange, including financial derivative claims on non-euro area countries. It excludes claims among euro area countries and all euro-denominated claims on non-euro area countries. Total reserves of the euro area comprise the reserve holdings of the NCBs and ECB. Definitions of reserves at the national and euro area levels are harmonized.

Other Foreign Assets, Foreign Liabilities

Time series, where significant, are also provided in international liquidity sections on other foreign assets and foreign liabilities of the monetary authorities.

Other Assets (line 3..d) usually comprises claims on nonresidents that are of limited usability in the event of balance of payments need, such as balances under bilateral payments agreements and holdings of inconvertible currencies. (Claims on nonresidents under Other Assets (line 3..d) are included in line 11.)

Other Liabilities (line 4..d) comprises foreign liabilities of the monetary authorities other than use of Fund credit (GRA), SAF, PRGF, and Trust Fund loans outstanding. Positions with the Fund are reported separately, in SDRs, in the Fund position section of the country tables.

Foreign Accounts of Other Financial Institutions

Where significant, foreign accounts of financial institutions other than the monetary authorities are reported. The measures provided are normally U.S. dollar equivalents of time series reported in the appropriate money and banking sections as follows: line 7a.d is derived from line 21; line 7b.d is derived from line 26c plus line 26cl; line 7e.d is derived from line 41; and line 7f.d is derived from line 46c plus line 46cl. Sometimes the measures are reported directly in U.S. dollars and may differ slightly in coverage.

In addition for some countries, summary data are provided on the foreign accounts of special or international license banks that operate locally but are not presently covered in the money and banking section. Their foreign assets are reported as line 7k.d, and their foreign liabilities as line 7m.d, when available (although 7m.d is not shown separately if it is equal to line 7k.d).

World Tables on Reserves

World tables on reserves report all country table time series on reserves, other than gold at national valuation, and present totals for countries, country groups, and the world.

Also provided is a table on total reserves, with gold valued at SDR 35 per ounce. A foot table to that table reports total reserves of all countries, including gold valued both at SDR 35 per ounce and at market prices. And the yearbook includes a world table on the ratio of nongold reserves (line 1 l.d) to imports (line 71..d), expressed in terms of the number of weeks of imports covered by the stock of nongold reserves.

Except for the world table on gold holdings in physical terms, world tables on reserves are expressed in SDRs. Foreign exchange holdings are expressed in SDRs by converting the U.S. dollar values shown in the country tables on the basis of the end-period U.S. dollar/SDR rate.

Similarly, a foot table to the world table on gold indicates gold holdings valued at SDR 35 per ounce and at market prices for all countries, the IMF, the ECB, the Bank for International Settlements (BIS), and the world. A simple addition of the gold held by all of these holders would involve double-counting, because most of the gold deposited with the BIS is also included in countries' official gold reserves. *IFS* therefore reports BIS gold holdings net of gold deposits, and negative figures for BIS gold holdings are balanced by forward operations. This foot table also provides data on the U.S. dollar price of gold on the London market, the U.S. dollar/SDR rate, and the end-period derived market price of gold in terms of SDRs.

5. Money and Banking

Statistics on the accounts of monetary and other financial institutions are given in money and banking sections 10 through 50 in the country tables and in world tables, described in the world table section of this introduction.

Monetary Authorities

Monetary authorities' data (section 10) in *IFS* generally consolidate the accounts of the central bank with the accounts of other institutions that undertake monetary functions. These functions include issuing currency, holding international reserves, and conducting Fund account transactions. Data on monetary authorities measure the stock of reserve money comprising currency in circulation, deposits of the deposit money banks, and deposits of other residents, apart from the central government, with the monetary authorities.

Major aggregates of the accounts on the asset side are foreign assets (line 11) and domestic assets (line 12*). Domestic assets are broken down into Claims on Central Government (line 12a), Claims on Deposit Money Banks (line 12e), and, if sizable, Claims on State and Local Governments (line 12b); Claims on Nonfinancial Public Enterprises (line 12c); Claims on the Private Sector (line 12d); Claims on Other Banking Institutions (line 12f), and Claims on Nonbank Financial Institutions (line 12g).

In some countries, where insufficient data are available to provide disaggregations of claims on governmental bodies other than the central government, a classification of Claims on Official Entities (line 12bx) is used. In addition, in countries where insufficient data are available to provide disaggregations of claims on other banking institutions and nonbank financial institutions, a classification of Claims on Other Financial Institutions (line 12f) is used.

The principal liabilities of monetary authorities consist of Reserve Money (line 14); Other Liabilities to Deposit Money Banks (line 14n), comprising liabilities of the central bank to deposit money banks that are excluded from Reserve Money; Liabilities of the Central Bank: Securities (line 16ac); Foreign Liabilities (line 16c); Central Government Deposits (line 16d); and Capital Accounts (line 17a).

Deposit Money Banks

Deposit money banks comprise commercial banks and other financial institutions that accept transferable deposits, such as demand deposits. Deposit money banks' data (section 20) measure the stock of deposit money.

Major aggregates of the accounts on the assets side are Reserves (line 20), comprising domestic currency holdings and deposits with the monetary authorities; Claims on Monetary Authorities: Securities (line 20c), comprising holdings of securities issued by the central bank; Other Claims on Monetary Authorities (line 20n), comprising claims on the central bank that are excluded from Reserves; Foreign Assets (line 21); and Claims on Other Resident Sectors (lines 22*), as described in the preceding section on monetary authorities (lines 12*).

The principal liabilities consist of Demand Deposits (line 24); Time, Savings, and Foreign Currency Deposits (line 25); Money Market Instruments (line 26aa); Bonds (line 26ab); Foreign Liabilities (line 26c); Central Government Deposits (line 26d); Credit from Monetary Authorities (line 26g); Liabilities to Other Banking Institutions (line 26i); Liabilities to Nonbank Financial Institutions (line 26j); and Capital Accounts (line 27a).

Monetary Survey

Monetary authorities' and deposit money banks' data are consolidated into a monetary survey (section 30). The survey measures the stock of narrow Money (line 34), comprising transferable deposits and currency outside deposit money banks, and the Quasi-Money (line 35) liabilities of these institutions, comprising time, savings, and foreign currency deposits.

Standard relationships between the monetary survey lines and the component lines in sections 10 and 20 are as follows:

Foreign Assets (Net) (line 31n) equals the sum of foreign asset lines 11 and 21, less the sum of foreign liability lines 16c and 26c.

Claims on Central Government (Net) (line 32an) equals claims on central government (the sum of lines 12a and 22a), less central government deposits (the sum of lines 16d and 26d), plus, where applicable, the counterpart entries of lines 24..i and 24..r (private sector demand deposits with the postal checking system and with the Treasury).

Claims on State and Local Governments (line 32b) equals the sum of lines 12b and 22b. Note that, for some countries, lack of sufficient data to perform the standard classifications of claims on governmental bodies excluding the central government has resulted in the use of the alternative classification "claims on official entities" (line 32bx), which is the sum of lines 12bx and 22bx. These series may therefore include state and local governments, public financial institutions, and nonfinancial public enterprises.

Claims on Nonfinancial Public Enterprises (line 32c) equals the sum of lines 12c and 22c.

Claims on Private Sector (line 32d) equals the sum of lines 12d and 22d.

Claims on Other Banking Institutions (line 32f) equals the sum of lines 12f and 22f.

Claims on Nonbank Financial Institutions (line 32g) equals the sum of lines 12g and 22g.

Domestic Credit (line 32) is the sum of lines 32an, 32b, 32c, 32d, 32f, and 32g even when, owing to their small size, data for lines 32b, 32c, 32f, and 32g are not published separately. Thus, the data for line 32 may be larger than the sum of its published components.

Money (line 34) equals the sum of currency outside deposit money banks (line 14a) and demand deposits other than those of the central government (lines 14d, 14e, 14f, 14g, and 24) plus, where applicable, lines 24..i and 24..r.

Quasi-Money (line 35) equals the sum of lines 15 and 25, comprising time, savings, and foreign currency deposits of resident sectors other than central government.

The data in line 34 are frequently referred to as M1, while the sum of lines 34 and 35 gives a broader measure of money similar to that which is frequently called M2.

Money Market Instruments (line 36aa) equals the sum of lines 16aa and 26aa.

Bonds (line 36ab) equals the sum of lines 16ab and 26ab.

Liabilities of Central Bank: Securities (line 36ac) equals the outstanding stock of securities issued by the monetary authorities (line 16ac) less the holdings of these securities by deposit money banks (line 20c).

Restricted Deposits (line 36b) equals the sum of lines 16b and 26b.

Long-Term Foreign Liabilities (line 36cl) equals the sum of lines 16cl and 26cl.

Counterpart Funds (line 36e) equals the sum of lines 16e and 26e.

Central Government Lending Funds (line 36f) equals the sum of lines 16f and 26f.

Liabilities to Other Banking Institutions (line 36i) is equal to line 26i.

Liabilities to Nonbank Financial Institutions (line 36j) is equal to line 26j.

Capital Accounts (line 37a) equals the sum of lines 17a and 27a.

These monetary survey lines give the full range of *IFS* standard lines. Some of them are not applicable to every country, whereas others may not be published separately in sections 10 and 20, because the data are small. Unpublished lines are included in Other Items (Net) (lines 17r and 27r) but are classified in the appropriate monetary survey aggregates in section 30.

Exceptions to the standard calculations of monetary survey aggregates are indicated in the notes to the country tables in the monthly issues. Exceptions also exist in the standard presentation of the consolidation of financial institutions, e.g., for Japan, Nicaragua, the United Kingdom, and the United States.

Other Banking Institutions

Section 40 contains data on the accounts of other banking institutions. This subsector comprises institutions that do not accept transferable deposits but that perform financial intermediation by accepting other types of deposits or by issuing securities or other liabilities that are close substitutes for deposits. This subsector covers such institutions as savings and mortgage loan institutions, post-office savings institutions, building and loan associations, finance companies that accept deposits or deposit substitutes, development banks, and offshore banking institutions.

The major aggregates in this section are claims on the various sectors of the economy (lines 42*), as described in the preceding paragraphs, and quasi-monetary liabilities (line 45), largely in the form of time and savings deposits.

Banking Survey

Where reasonably complete data are available for other banking institutions, a banking survey (section 50) is published. It consolidates data for other banking institutions with the monetary survey and thus provides a broader measure of monetary liabilities.

The sectoral classification of assets in the banking survey follows the classification used in the monetary survey, as outlined in the description for that section.

Nonbank Financial Institutions

For a few countries, data are shown on the accounts of nonbank financial institutions, such as insurance companies, pension funds, and superannuation funds. Given the nature of their liabilities, these institutions generally exert minimal impact on the liquidity of a given economy. However, they can play a significant role in distributing credit from the financial sector to the rest of the economy.

European Economic and Monetary Union (Euro Area)

Stage Three of the European Economic and Monetary Union (EMU), beginning in January 1999, created a monetary union among European countries. New definitions of statistics aggregates were created, resulting in a major break in data series for all participating countries. The euro area, an official descriptor of the monetary union, is defined by its membership as of a specified date. The 11 original members were Austria, Belgium, Finland, France, Germany, Ireland, Italy, Luxembourg, Netherlands, Portugal, and Spain. Greece joined in January 2001. In 2002, euro banknotes and coins were issued, and national currency banknotes and coins withdrawn.

The main features of the euro area monetary statistics are described as follows:

Creation of the Eurosystem

In Stage Three of the EMU, the "Eurosystem"—the European Central Bank (ECB) and the national central banks (NCBs) of the euro area member states—executes a single monetary policy for the euro area. The new common currency unit is the euro. Until 2002, national currency circulated, and various types of transactions were denominated in either euros or national currency.

The monetary statistics standards for the euro area countries underwent comprehensive revisions. The revisions permitted compilation of consolidated monetary accounts for the euro area and provided the data needed to execute the single monetary policy. Statistical standards are based on the *European System of Accounts 1995 (1995 ESA)* and additional standards prescribed by ECB regulation. Statistics are collected under a "layered approach," whereby monetary statistics compiled at the country level are forwarded to the ECB for consolidation into euro area totals. NCBs are required to compile monetary statistics according to a single set of standards and a common format for submission of data to the ECB.

Denomination in Euros

Beginning with data for 1999, monetary data for euro area countries presented in *IFS* are denominated in euros, except for Greece whose data are denominated in euros beginning in January 2001. Data for the consolidated euro area table are in euros for all time periods.

Residency Principles

Statistics are compiled on the basis of both national residency criteria, described in the fifth edition of the *Balance of Payments Manual*, and euro area-wide residency criteria, based on the EU membership as of a specified date.

In the application of the latter criteria, all institutional units located in euro area countries are treated as resident, and all units outside the euro area as nonresident. For example, claims on government under the national criteria include only claims on the government of the country, whereas claims on government under the euro area-wide residency criteria include claims on the governments of all euro area countries. Under the euro area-wide residency criteria, the ECB is a resident unit, whereas under the national residency criteria, it is a foreign unit for all countries. Under ECB statistical reporting requirements—concerning the consolidated balance sheet of the monetary financial institutions sector—the ECB is to be classified as a resident unit of the country where it is physically located (Germany).

The monetary statistics in the tables for each euro area country are presented on both national and euro area-wide residency bases.

Euro Banknotes and Coins

On January 1, 2002, euro banknotes and coins were issued. The existing national currencies continued to be accepted in trade for a short transition period that ended in all member countries by the end of February 2002, at the latest. The national currencies and coins can be redeemed with the national authorities for extended periods, or indefinitely, as set by national policy. The changeover to euro banknotes and coins was smooth, and the stock of outstanding national currencies rapidly decreased by 86 percent between January 1 and February 28, 2002. The national currencies still outstanding at the end of each reporting period remained part of the euro area monetary aggregates until year-end 2002. Euro area monetary aggregates are net of banknotes and coins held by monetary financial institutions (other depository corporations) in the euro area.

The euro banknotes are issued by the Eurosystem as a whole, comprising the ECB and the national central banks of the euro area countries. Banknotes are put into circulation by each NCB as demanded and are physically identical regardless of the issuing NCB. According to the accounting regime chosen by the Eurosystem, although the ECB does not put banknotes into circulation, a share of 8 percent of the total value of euro banknotes put into circulation is allocated to the balance sheet of the ECB each month. The balance of the remaining 92 percent is allocated among the NCBs on a monthly basis, whereby each NCB of the Eurosystem records on its balance sheet as "banknotes issued" a share proportional to its share in the ECB's capital. This allocation procedure is referred to as the capital share mechanism–CSM.

For each NCB, the difference between the value of the euro banknotes allocated according to the CSM and the value of euro banknotes it puts into circulation is classified as an "Intra-Eurosystem claim/liability related to banknote issue." Each NCB will have a single claim/liability vis-à-vis the Eurosystem, calculated monthly. Similarly, the ECB will always have an Intra-Eurosystem claim equal to its 8 percent share of banknotes issued.

On the country pages for the euro area countries, Intra-Eurosystem claims/liabilities related to banknote issue are classified by the IMF as part of monetary authorities' Claims on Banking Institutions (line 12e.u)/Liabilities to Banking Institutions (line 14c.u). Intra-Eurosystem claims/liabilities related to banknote issue are also recorded within the memo item Net Claims on Eurosystem (line 12e.s). In contrast, in the Monetary Authorities (Eurosystem) section on the euro area page, the Intra-Eurosystem claims/liabilities of the Eurosystem members are recorded as part of Other Items (Net) (line 17r), where they effectively net to zero.

Euro coins are issued by national authorities. The ECB approves the volume of coins to be issued by each country. All have a common design on the obverse and a national design on the reverse. All revenues associated with coin issuance are retained by national authorities without application to an accounting allocation mechanism such as is used for banknotes.

The euro also has been adopted officially by several small jurisdictions within Europe—Andorra, Monaco, San Marino, and the Vatican. It is also used as the principal currency in several areas that were formerly part of Yugoslavia.

TARGET

Effective with data beginning end-November 2000, changes in the operating procedures of the TARGET (Trans-European Automated Real-Time Gross Settlement Express Transfer) euro clearing system affect monetary authorities' Foreign Assets (line 11), Foreign Liabilities (line 16c), Claims on Banking Institutions (line 12e.u), and Liabilities to Banking Institutions (line 14c.u). (See Recording of TARGET System Positions in the following section.)

Monetary Authorities—Euro Area

In *IFS* country tables, the term monetary authorities refers to the national central bank and other institutional units that perform monetary authorities' functions and are included in the central bank subsector (currency boards, exchange stabilization funds, etc). For the euro area member countries, upon joining the union, the monetary authority consists of the NCB, as defined by its membership within the Eurosystem.

At the Eurosystem level, monetary authority refers to the ECB and the NCBs of the euro area member countries, based on the actual date of membership.

For purposes of comparison with pre-euro area data, "of which" lines show positions with residents of the country.

Beginning in January 1999, Foreign Assets (line 11) and Foreign Liabilities (line 16c) include only positions with non-euro area countries. All positions with residents of other euro area countries, including the ECB, are classified as domestic positions in the data based on euro area residency.

Claims on General Government (line 12a.u) includes claims on the central government and other levels of government, including the

social security system. It also includes claims on general government in other euro area countries.

Claims on Banking Institutions (NCBs and Other Monetary Financial Institutions or MFIs) (line 12e.u) and Liabilities to Banking Institutions (NCBs and Other MFIs) (line 14c.u) include all positions with NCBs and Other MFIs in all euro area countries. Before January 1999, positions with NCBs and Other MFIs in other euro area countries were in Foreign Assets and Foreign Liabilities. Other MFIs are monetary institutions other than the NCB and ECB. Other MFIs were previously called deposit money banks (DMBs) and other banking institutions (OBIs). Beginning in January 1999, other MFIs is defined to include money market funds.

Claims on Other Resident Sectors (line 12d) comprises claims on nonbank financial institutions, public nonfinancial corporations, and the private sector.

Net Claims on Eurosystem (line 12e.s) equals gross claims on, less gross liabilities to, the ECB and other NCBs within the Eurosystem. This item comprises euro-denominated claims equivalent to the transfer of foreign currency reserves to the ECB, Intra-Eurosystem claims/liabilities related to banknote issuance, net claims or liabilities within the TARGET clearing system (see description below), and other positions such as contra-entries to the NCBs' holdings of assets acquired in conjunction with open-market or intervention operations. NCBs' issues of securities other than shares and money market paper held by other NCBs, which are not separately identifiable, are included in Liabilities to Banking Institutions (line 14c.u). Before January 1999, positions with the EMI or ECB and other euro area NCBs are included in Foreign Assets and Foreign Liabilities.

Currency Issued (line14a): Until 2002, this line covers national currency in circulation. Beginning in 2002, this series is redefined to include euro banknotes issued by each NCB, euro coins issued by each euro area country, and national currency not yet withdrawn. The amount of euro banknotes recorded as issued by each NCB is the legal allocation recorded on its balance sheet according to the accounting regime (CSM) described above in **Euro Banknotes and Coins.** That amount does not correspond to either the actual amount of euro banknotes put into circulation by the NCB or the actual circulation of euro banknotes within the domestic territory. The actual amount of euro banknotes put into circulation by the NCB is included within Memo: Currency Put into Circulation (line 14m). In addition, this item includes euro coin issued and the national currency not yet withdrawn.

Capital Accounts (line 17a) includes general provisions.

Recording of TARGET System Positions

Effective November 2000, external positions of members of the TARGET (Trans-European Automated Real-Time Gross Settlement Express Transfer) euro clearing system with each other are affected by changes in TARGET's operating procedures. Previously, from January 1999 to October 2000, TARGET positions are on a gross bilateral basis between all members, which results in large external asset and liability positions between the TARGET members. From November 2000 onward, multilateral netting by novation procedures results in each member recording only a single TARGET position vis-à-vis the ECB, which is generally a much smaller value than recorded under the previous arrangement.

This change affects Monetary Authorities' Foreign Assets (line 11) and Foreign Liabilities (line 16c) of all TARGET members. It also affects Monetary Authorities' Claims on Banking Institutions (line 12e.u) and Liabilities to Banking Institutions (line 14c.u) of the euro area TARGET members. The non-euro area TARGET members are not permitted to hold a net liability position against TARGET as a whole; therefore, after November 2000, they do not have any TARGET-related Foreign Liabilities.

Banking Institutions—Euro Area

For comparison with pre-euro area data, "of which" lines show positions with residents of the country.

Beginning in January 1999, this section covers the accounts of other MFIs (monetary financial institutions)—monetary institutions other than the NCB and ECB. Other MFIs were previously called deposit money banks (DMBs) and other banking institutions (OBIs). Beginning in January 1999, other MFIs is defined to include money market funds.

Claims on Monetary Authorities (line 20) comprises banking institutions' holdings of euro banknotes and coins, holdings of national currency, deposits with the NCB, and loans to the NCB.

Claims on Banking Institutions (including ECB) in Other Euro Area Countries (line 20b.u) and Liabilities to Banking Institutions (including ECB) in Other Euro Area Countries (line 26h.u) comprise all positions with the ECB, NCBs, and Other MFIs in other euro area countries. These positions are classified as domestic under the euro area residency criteria. Before January 1999, these accounts were classified under Foreign Assets and Foreign Liabilities. Claims include holdings of currencies issued in other euro area countries.

Beginning in January 1999, Foreign Assets (line 21) and Foreign Liabilities (line 26c) include only positions with non-euro area countries. All positions with residents of other euro area countries, including the ECB, are classified as domestic positions.

Claims on General Government (line 22a.u) includes claims on central government and other levels of government in all euro area countries.

Claims on Other Resident Sectors (line 22d.u) comprises claims on nonbank financial institutions, public nonfinancial corporations, and the private sectors in all euro area countries.

Demand Deposits (line 24.u) includes demand deposits in all currencies by other resident sectors in all euro area countries.

Other Deposits (line 25.u) includes deposits with fixed maturity, deposits redeemable at notice, securities repurchase agreements, and subordinated debt in the form of deposits by other resident sectors of all euro area countries. Before January 1999, subordinated debt was included in Other Items (Net) (line 27r).

Money Market Fund Shares (line 26m.u) include shares/units issued by money market funds.

Bonds and Money Market Instruments (line 26n.u) include subordinated debt in the form of securities, other bonds, and money market paper.

Credit from Monetary Authorities (line 26g) comprises banking institutions' borrowing from the NCBs.

Other Items (Net) (line 27r) includes holdings of shares issued by other MFIs.

Banking Survey (Based on National Residency)—Euro Area

This section consolidates the accounts of the monetary authorities and banking institutions based on national residency criteria.

Foreign Assets (Net) (line 31n) includes positions with nonresidents of the country. Positions with the ECB for all euro area countries are classified in Foreign Assets under the national residency criteria.

Claims on General Government (Net) (line 32an) includes claims on general government minus deposits of central government.

Deposits of other levels of government are included in liabilities to other resident sectors.

Until 2002, Currency Issued (line 34a.n) covers national currency in circulation. Beginning in 2002, this series is redefined to include euro banknotes issued by each NCB, euro coins issued by each euro area country, and the amount of national currency not yet withdrawn. Under the accounting regime used by the Eurosystem, the allocation of euro banknotes issued by each NCB is the legal allocation recorded on its balance sheet according to the accounting regime (CSM) described above in **Euro Banknotes and Coins**. The allocation does not correspond to either the actual amount of euro banknotes placed in circulation by the NCB or the actual circulation of banknotes within the domestic territory.

Other Items (Net) (line 37r) includes other MFIs' holdings of shares issued by other MFIs.

Banking Survey (Based on Euro Area-Wide Residency)

This section consolidates the accounts of the monetary authorities and banking institutions based on euro area-wide residency criteria.

Foreign Assets (Net) (line 31n.u) includes all positions with nonresidents of the euro area. Positions with residents of all euro area countries, including the ECB, are classified as domestic positions.

Claims on General Government (Net) (line 32anu) includes claims on central government and all other levels of government of all euro area countries minus deposits of central government of all euro area countries. Deposits of other levels of government are included in liabilities to other resident sectors.

Until 2002, Currency Issued (line 34a.u) covers national currency in circulation. Beginning in 2002, this series is redefined to include euro banknotes issued by each NCB, euro coins issued by each euro area country, and the amount of national currency not yet withdrawn. Under the accounting regime used by the Eurosystem, the allocation of euro banknotes issued by each NCB is the legal allocation recorded on its balance sheet according to the accounting regime (CSM) described above in **Euro Banknotes and Coins.** The allocation does not correspond to either the actual amount of euro banknotes placed in circulation by the NCB or the actual circulation of banknotes within the domestic territory.

Other Items (Net) (line 37r.u) includes other MFIs' holdings of shares issued by other MFIs.

6. Interest Rates

Data are presented in the Interest Rates section in the country tables and in the world tables on national and international interest rates.

Discount Rate/Bank Rate (line 60) is the rate at which the central banks lend or discount eligible paper for deposit money banks, typically shown on an end-of-period basis.

Money Market Rate (line 60b) is the rate on short-term lending between financial institutions.

Treasury Bill Rate (line 60c) is the rate at which short-term securities are issued or traded in the market.

Deposit Rate (line 60l) usually refers to rates offered to resident customers for demand, time, or savings deposits. Often, rates for time and savings deposits are classified according to maturity and amounts deposited. In addition, deposit money banks and similar deposit-taking institutions may offer short- and medium-term instruments at specified rates for specific amounts and maturities; these are frequently termed "certificates of deposit." For countries where savings deposits are important, a Savings Rate (line 60k) is also published.

Lending Rate (line 60p) is the bank rate that usually meets the short- and medium-term financing needs of the private sector. This rate is normally differentiated according to creditworthiness of borrowers and objectives of financing.

Government Bond Yield (line 61*) refers to one or more series representing yields to maturity of government bonds or other bonds that would indicate longer term rates.

Interest rates for foreign-currency-denominated instruments are also published for countries where such instruments are important.

Quarterly and annual interest rate data are arithmetic averages of monthly interest rates reported by the countries.

The country notes in the monthly issues carry a brief description of the nature and characteristics of the rates reported and of the financial instrument to which they relate.

A typical series from each of these groups is included in the world tables on national interest rates.

Euro Area Interest Rates

The Eurosystem Marginal Lending Facility Rate (line 60) is the rate at which other monetary financial institutions (MFIs) obtain overnight liquidity from NCBs, against eligible assets. The terms and conditions of the lending are identical throughout the euro area. The Eurosystem Refinancing Rate (line 60r), Interbank Rate (Overnight) (line 60a), and Interbank Rate (Three-Month) (line 60b) are also provided on the euro area table.

A new set of harmonized MFI interest rate statistics is compiled for the euro area and its member countries. Rates for household and corporate customers' deposits and lending, both for stock and new business, are compiled by reporting MFIs in accordance with Regulation ECB/2001/18, as described in the ECB *Manual on MFI Interest Rate Statistics* (ECB: October 2003).

Deposit Rate (Households) (line 60lhs) is MFI weighted average interest rate paid on outstanding amounts of euro-denominated deposits from households with an agreed maturity up to and including two years; Deposit Rate (Corporations) (line 60lcs) is MFI weighted average interest rate paid on outstanding amounts of euro-denominated deposits from nonfinancial corporations with an agreed maturity up to and including two years.

Lending Rate (Households) (line 60phm) is MFI weighted average interest rate charged on outstanding amounts of euro-denominated loans to households for house purchases with over five years maturity; Lending Rate (Corporations) (line 60pcs) is MFI weighted average interest rate on outstanding amounts of euro-denominated loans to nonfinancial corporations with a maturity up to and including one year.

World Table on International Interest Rates

The world table on international interest rates reports London interbank offer rates on deposits denominated in SDRs, U.S. dollars, euros, French francs, deutsche mark, Japanese yen, and Swiss francs and Paris interbank offer rates on deposits denominated in pounds sterling. Monthly data are averages of daily rates. The table includes the premium or discount on three-month forward rates of currencies of the major industrial countries against the U.S. dollar.

This table also reports the SDR interest rate and the rate of remuneration. Monthly data are arithmetic averages of daily rates. Interest is paid on holdings of SDRs, and charges are levied on participants' cumulative allocations. Interest and charges accrue daily at the same rate and are settled quarterly in SDRs. As a result, participants who have SDR holdings above their net cumulative allocations receive net interest, and those with holdings below their

net cumulative allocations pay net charges. Other official holders of SDRs—including the Fund's General Resources Account—receive interest on their holdings and pay no charges because they receive no allocations.

The Fund also pays quarterly remuneration to members on their creditor positions arising from the use of their currencies in Fund transactions and operations. This is determined by the positive difference between the remuneration norm and the average daily balances of the member's currency in the General Resources Account.

Effective August 1, 1983, the weekly SDR interest rate has been based on the combined market interest rate. That rate is calculated by applying to the specific amounts of the five currencies included in the SDR valuation basket, converted into SDR equivalents, the market rates on specified short-term money market instruments quoted in the five countries.

As of January 1, 1991, the interest rates used in this calculation are market yield for three-month U.S. treasury bills, three-month interbank deposit rate (line 60bs) in Germany, three-month rate for treasury bills (line 60cs) in France, three-month rate on certificates of deposit (line 60bs) in Japan, and market yield for three-month U.K. treasury bills (line 60cs). These series are shown in the table.

The combined market rate is calculated each Friday and enters into effect each Monday. The interest rate on the SDR is 100 percent of the combined market rate, rounded to two nearest decimal places. The rate of remuneration, effective February 2, 1987, is 100 percent of the rate of interest on the SDR.

7. Prices, Production, and Labor

This section (lines 62 through 67) covers domestic prices, production, and labor market indicators. A more detailed discussion of major price indicators is provided in the *IFS Supplement on Price Statistics*, No. 12 (1986).

The index series are compiled from reported versions of national indices and, for some production and labor series, from absolute data.

There is a wide variation between countries and over time in the selection of base years, depending upon the availability of comprehensive benchmark data that permit an adequate review of weighting patterns. The series are linked by using ratio splicing at the first annual overlap, and the linked series are shifted to a common base period 2000=100.

For industrial production, the data are seasonally adjusted if an appropriate adjusted series is available. Seasonally adjusted series are indicated in the descriptor and also described in the country notes in the monthly issues.

Share Prices

Indices shown for Share Prices (line 62) generally relate to common shares of companies traded on national or foreign stock exchanges. Monthly indices are obtained as simple arithmetic averages of the daily or weekly indices, although in some cases mid-month or end-of-month quotations are included.

All reported indices are adjusted for changes in quoted nominal capital of companies. Indices are, in general, base-weighted arithmetic averages with market value of outstanding shares as weights.

Producer Price Index or Wholesale Price Index

Indices shown for Producer or Wholesale Prices (line 63) are designed to monitor changes in prices of items at the first important commercial transaction. Where a choice is available, preference is given to the Producer Price Index (PPI), because the concept, weighting pattern, and coverage are likely to be more consistent with national accounts and industrial production statistics. In principle, the PPI should include service industries, but in practice it is limited to the domestic agricultural and industrial sectors. The prices should be farm-gate prices for the agricultural sector and ex-factory prices for the industrial sector.

The Wholesale Price Index (WPI), when used, covers a mixture of prices of agricultural and industrial goods at various stages of production and distribution, inclusive of imports and import duties. Preference is given to indices that provide broad coverage of the economy. The indices are computed using the Laspeyres formula, unless otherwise indicated in the country notes in the monthly issues.

Subindices are occasionally included for the PPI or the WPI.

Consumer Price Index

Indices shown for Consumer Prices (line 64) are the most frequently used indicators of inflation and reflect changes in the cost of acquiring a fixed basket of goods and services by the average consumer. Preference is given to series having wider geographical coverage and relating to all income groups, provided they are no less current than more narrowly defined series.

Because the weights are usually derived from household expenditure surveys (which may be conducted infrequently), information on the year to which the weights refer is provided in the country table notes in the monthly issues. The notes also provide information on any limitations in the coverage of commodities for pricing, income groups, or their expenditures in the chosen index. The Laspeyres formula is used unless otherwise indicated in the country notes.

For the European Union (EU) countries, a harmonized index of consumer prices (HICP) (line 64h) is shown. It is compiled according to methodological and sampling standards set by the European Commission. Owing to institutional differences among the EU member countries, the HICP excludes expenditure on certain types of goods and services. Examples are medical care and services of owner-occupied dwellings.

Wage Rates or Earnings

Indices shown for Wages Rates or Earnings (line 65) represent wage rates or earnings per worker employed per specified time period. Where establishment surveys are the source, the indices are likely to have the same coverage as the Industrial Production Index (line 66) and the Industrial Employment Index (line 67). Preference is given to data for earnings that include payments in kind and family allowances and that cover salaried employees as well as wage earners. The indices either are computed from absolute wage data or are as reported directly to the Fund.

Industrial Production

Indices shown for Industrial Production (line 66) are included as indicators of current economic activity. For some countries the indices are supplemented by indicators (such as data on tourism) relevant to a particular country.

Generally, the coverage of industrial production indices comprises mining and quarrying, manufacturing and electricity, and gas and water, according to the UN International Standard Industrial Classification (ISIC). The indices are generally compiled using the Laspeyres formula.

For many developing countries the indices refer to the production of a major primary commodity, such as crude petroleum. For most of the OECD countries, Industrial Production data are sourced from the OECD database, as indicated in the country notes. It should be noted that there may be differences for annual data between seasonal adjusted and unadjusted series. These differences are the result of OECD calculation methodology, which is based on two different calculation methods, namely the frequency method and the proxy method. The frequency method is the annual average of the adjusted 12 months data while the proxy method uses the annual data of the unadjusted series for the seasonally adjusted series.

Labor

Labor market indicators refer to the levels of the Labor Force (line 67d), Employment (line 67e), Unemployment (line 67c), and the Unemployment Rate (line 67r). Data on labor market statistics cover the economically active civilian population. They are provided by the International Labor Organization (ILO), which publishes these data in its *Yearbook of Labour Statistics* and its quarterly *Bulletin of Labour Statistics* and supplements. The concept of employment and unemployment conforms to the recommendations adopted by the ILO: Thirteenth International Conference of Labor Statisticians, Geneva, 1992. In addition, indices of employment in the industrial sector (line 67) are provided for 49 countries. For the euro area, EUROSTAT provides the data. Supplemental sources are also available on the industrial countries' websites.

8. International Transactions

Summary statistics on the international transactions of a country are given in lines 70 through 79. A section on external trade statistics (lines 70 through 76) provides data on the values (lines 70 and 71), volumes (lines 72 and 73), unit values (lines 74 and 75), and prices (line 76) for exports and imports. A section follows on balance of payments statistics (lines 78 through 79).

External Trade

Merchandise Exports f.o.b. (line 70) and Imports c.i.f. (line 71) are, in general, customs statistics reported under the general trade system, in accordance with the recommendations of the UN International Merchandise Trade Statistics: Concepts and Definitions, 1998. For some countries, data relate to the special trade system. The difference between general and special trade lies mainly in the treatment of the recording of the movement of goods through customs-bonded storage areas (warehouses, free areas, etc.).

Many countries use customs data on exports and imports as the primary source for the recording of exports and imports of goods in the balance of payments. However, customs data and the entries for goods in the balance of payments may not be equal, owing to differences in definition. These differences may relate to the following:

- the coverage of transactions (e.g., the goods item in the balance of payments often includes adjustments for certain goods transactions that may not be recorded by customs authorities, e.g., parcel post),
- the time of recording of transactions (e.g., in the balance of payments, transactions are to be recorded when change of ownership occurs, rather than the moment goods cross the customs border, which generally determines when goods are recorded in customs based trade statistics), and
- some classification differences (e.g., in the balance of payments, repair on goods is part of goods transactions).

The data for Merchandise Imports f.o.b. (line 71.v) are obtained directly from statistical authorities.

Details of commodity exports are presented for commodities that are traded in the international markets and have an impact on world market prices.

Data for petroleum exports are presented only for 12 oil exporting countries. For a number of these countries, data estimated by Fund staff are derived from available data for the volume of production. They are also derived from estimates for prices that are, in part, taken from *Petroleum Intelligence Weekly* and other international sources. The country table notes in the monthly issues provide details of these estimates.

For a number of countries where data are uncurrent or unavailable, additional lines show data, converted from U.S. dollars to national currency, from the Fund's *Direction of Trade Statistics* quarterly publication (*DOTS*). Exports and imports data published in *DOTS* include reported data, updated where necessary with estimates for the current periods. The introduction of *DOTS* gives a description of the nature of the estimates.

Indices for Volume of Exports (line 72) and Volume of Imports (line 73) are either Laspeyres or Paasche. For nine countries, as indicated in the country notes, export volume indices are calculated from reported volume data for individual commodities weighted by reported values.

Indices for Unit Value of Exports (line 74) and Unit Value of Imports (line 75) are Laspeyres, with weights derived from the data for transactions. For about seven countries, also as indicated in the country notes, export unit values are calculated from reported value and volume data for individual commodities. The country indices are unit value indices, except for a few, which are components of wholesale price indices or based on specific price quotations.

Indices for export and import prices are compiled from survey data for wholesale prices or directly from the exporter or importer (called "direct pricing"). They are shown in line 76, where available. Indices based on direct pricing are generally considered preferable to unit value indices, because problems of unit value bias are reduced.

A more detailed presentation of trade statistics is presented in the *IFS Supplement on Trade Statistics,* No. 15 (1988).

Balance of Payments Statistics

The balance of payments lines are presented on the basis of the methodology and presentation of the fifth edition of the *Balance of Payments Manual (BPM5)*. Published by the IMF in 1993, the *BPM5* was supplemented and amended by the *Financial Derivatives, a Supplement to the Fifth Edition (1993) of the Balance of Payments Manual,* published in 2000. Before 1995, issues of the *IFS Yearbook* presented balance of payments data based on the fourth edition of the manual (*BPM4*).

Lines for Balance of Payments Statistics

In *IFS*, balance of payments data are shown in an analytic presentation (i.e., the components are classified into five major data categories, which the Fund regards as useful for analyzing balance of payments developments in a uniform manner). In the analytic presentation, the components are arrayed to highlight the financing items (the reserves and related items). The standard presentation, as described in the *BPM5*, provides structural framework within which balance of payments statistics are compiled. Both analytic and standard presentations are published in the *Balance of Payments Statistics Yearbook*.

Current Account, n.i.e. (line 78ald) is the sum of the balance on goods, services and income (line 78aid), plus current transfers, n.i.e.: credit (line 78ajd), plus current transfers: debit (line 78akd) (i.e., line 78aid, plus line 78ajd, plus line 78akd).

Goods: Exports f.o.b. (line 78aad) and Goods: Imports f.o.b. (line 78abd) are both measured on the "free-on-board" (f.o.b.) basis—that is, by the value of the goods at the border of the exporting economy.

For imports, this excludes the cost of freight and insurance incurred beyond the border of the exporting economy. The goods item covers general merchandise, goods for processing, repairs on goods, goods procured in ports by carriers, and nonmonetary gold.

Trade Balance (line 78acd) is the balance of exports f.o.b. and imports f.o.b. (line 78aad plus line 78abd). A positive trade balance shows that merchandise exports are larger than merchandise imports, whereas a negative trade balance shows that merchandise imports are larger than merchandise exports.

Services: Credit (line 78add) and Services: Debit (line 78aed) comprise services in transportation, travel, communication, construction, insurance, finance, computer and information, royalties and license fees, other business, personal, cultural and recreational, and government, n.i.e.

Balance on Goods and Services (line 78afd) is the sum of the balance on goods (line 78acd), plus services: credit (line 78add), plus services: debit (line 78aed) (i.e., line 78acd, plus line 78add, plus line 78aed).

Income: Credit (line 78agd) and Income: Debit (line 78ahd) comprise (1) investment income (consisting of direct investment income, portfolio investment income, and other investment income), and (2) compensation of employees.

Balance on Gds., Serv., & Inc. (i.e., Balance on Goods, Services, and Income) (line 78aid) is the sum of the balance on goods and services (line 78afd), plus income: credit (line 78agd), plus income: debit (line 78ahd) (i.e., line 78afd, plus line 78agd, plus line 78ahd).

Current Transfers, n.i.e.: Credit (line 78ajd) comprise all current transfers received by the reporting economy, except those made to the economy to finance its "overall balance" (see line 78cbd description below); therefore, the label "n.i.e." The latter are included in Exceptional Financing (line 79ded) (see below). (Note: Some of the capital and financial account lines shown below are also labeled "n.i.e." This means that Exceptional Financing items have been excluded from specific capital and financial account components.) Current transfers comprise (1) general government transfers and (2) other sector transfers, including workers' remittances.

Current Transfers: Debit (line 78akd) comprise all current transfers paid by the reporting economy.

Capital Account, n.i.e. (line 78bcd) is the balance on the capital account (capital account, n.i.e.: credit, plus capital account: debit). Capital account, n.i.e.: credit (line 78bad) covers (1) transfers linked to the acquisition of a fixed asset and (2) the disposal of nonproduced, nonfinancial assets. It does not include debt forgiveness, which is classified under Exceptional Financing. Capital account: debit (line 78bbd) covers (1) transfers linked to the disposal of fixed assets, and (2) acquisition of nonproduced, nonfinancial assets.

Financial Account, n.i.e. (line 78bjd) is the net sum of direct investment (line 78bdd plus line 78bed), portfolio investment (line 78bfd plus line 78bgd), financial derivatives (line 78bwd plus line 78bxd), and other investment (line 78bhd plus line 78bid).

Direct Investment Abroad (line 78bdd) and Direct Investment in Rep. Econ., n.i.e. (Direct Investment in the Reporting Economy, n.i.e.) (line 78bed) represent the flows of direct investment capital out of the reporting economy and those into the reporting economy, respectively. Direct investment includes equity capital, reinvested earnings, other capital, and financial derivatives associated with various intercompany transactions between affiliated enterprises. Excluded are flows of direct investment capital into the reporting economy for exceptional financing, such as debt-for-equity swaps. Direct investment abroad is usually shown with a negative figure, reflecting an increase in net outward investment by residents, with a corresponding net payment outflow from the reporting economy. Direct investment in the reporting economy is generally shown with a positive figure, reflecting an increase in net inward investment by nonresidents, with a corresponding net payment inflow into the reporting economy.

Portfolio Investment Assets (line 78bfd) and Portfolio Investment Liab., n.i.e. (Portfolio Investment Liabilities) (line 78bgd) include transactions with nonresidents in financial securities of any maturity (such as corporate securities, bonds, notes, and money market instruments) other than those included in direct investment, exceptional financing, and reserve assets.

Equity Securities Assets (line 78bkd) and Equity Securities Liabilities (line 78bmd) include shares, stocks, participation, and similar documents (such as American depository receipts) that usually denote ownership of equity.

Debt Securities Assets (line 78bld) and Debt Securities Liabilities (line 78bnd) cover (1) bonds, debentures, notes, etc., and (2) money market or negotiable debt instruments.

Financial Derivatives Assets (line 78bwd) and Financial Derivatives Liabilities (line 78bxd) cover financial instruments that are linked to other specific financial instruments, indicators, or commodities, and through which specific financial risks (such as interest rate risk, foreign exchange risk, equity and commodity price risks, credit risk, etc.) can, in their own right, be traded in financial markets. The *IFS* presents gross asset and liability information. However, owing to the unique nature of financial derivatives, and the manner in which some institutions record transactions, some countries can provide only net transactions data. While such net data could be included under assets, in the *IFS* it has been decided to include these net transactions, and net positions when reported, under liabilities, because one common source of demand for these instruments is from entities that are hedging cash flows associated with debt liabilities.

Other Investment Assets (line 78bhd) and Other Investment Liabilities, n.i.e. (line 78bid) include all financial transactions not covered in direct investment, portfolio investment, financial derivatives, or reserve assets. Major categories are transactions in currency and deposits, loans, and trade credits.

Net Errors and Omissions (line 78cad) is a residual category needed to ensure that all debit and credit entries in the balance of payments statement sum to zero. It reflects statistical inconsistencies in the recording of the credit and debit entries. In the *IFS* presentation, net errors and omissions is equal to, and opposite in sign to, the total value of the following items: the current account balance (line 78ald), the capital account balance (line 78bcd), the financial account balance (line 78bjd), and reserves and reserve related items (line 79dad). The item is intended as an offset to the overstatement or understatement of the recorded components. Thus, if the balance of those components is a credit, the item for net errors and omissions will be shown as a debit of equal value, and vice versa.

Overall Balance (line 78cbd) is the sum of the balances on the current account (line 78ald), the capital account (line 78bcd), the financial account (line 78bjd), and net errors and omissions (line 78cad) (i.e., line 78ald, plus line 78bcd, plus line 78bjd, plus line 78cad).

Reserves and Related Items (line 79dad) is the sum of transactions in reserve assets (line 79dbd), exceptional financing (line 79ded), and use of Fund credit and loans (line 78dcd) (i.e., line 79dbd, plus line 79ded, plus line 79dcd).

Reserve Assets (line 79dbd) consists of external assets readily available to and controlled by monetary authorities primarily for direct financing of payments imbalances and for indirect regulating of the magnitude of such imbalances through exchange market intervention. Reserve assets comprise monetary gold, special drawing rights, reserve position in the Fund, foreign exchange assets (consisting of currency and deposits and securities), and other claims.

Use of Fund Credit and Loans (line 79dcd) includes purchases and repurchases in the credit tranches of the Fund's General Resource Account, and net borrowings under the Structural Adjustment Facility (SAF), the Poverty Reduction and Growth Facility (PRGF), which was previously named the Enhanced Structural Adjustment Facility (ESAF), and the Trust Fund.

Exceptional Financing (line 79ded) includes any other transactions undertaken by the authorities to finance the "overall balance," as an alternative to, or in conjunction with, the use of reserve assets and the use of Fund credit and loans from the Fund.

A more detailed presentation of balance of payments data for use in cross-country comparisons is published in the *Balance of Payments Statistics Yearbook*.

Lines for International Investment Position

The international investment position (IIP) data are presented in lines 79aad through 79ljd. An economy's IIP is a balance sheet of the stock of external financial assets and liabilities. The coverage of the various components of IIP is similar to that of the corresponding components under the balance of payments. The IIP at the end of a specific period reflects not only the sum of balance of payments transactions over time, but also price changes, exchange rate changes, and other adjustments.

Countries in the early stages of IIP compilation are encouraged to submit partial IIP statements. In general, these partial statements include data on the monetary authorities (including international reserves) and at least one other sector. No totals are shown for partial IIP statements.

9. Government Finance

Section 80 presents summary statistics on government finance. The summary statistics cover operations of the budgetary central government or of the consolidated central government (i.e., operations of budgetary central government, extrabudgetary units, and social security funds). The coverage of consolidated central government may not necessarily include all existing extrabudgetary units and/or social security funds.

Unless otherwise stated in individual country notes in the monthly issues, data are as reported for *IFS*. In some cases, data are derived from unpublished worksheets and are therefore not attributed to a specific source.

Quarterly and monthly data, when available, may not add up to the annual data, owing to differences in coverage and/or methodology. The country notes in the monthly issues will indicate these differences.

More extensive data for use in cross-country comparisons are published in the *Government Finance Statistics Yearbook (GFSY)* and are based on *A Manual on Government Finance Statistics*. When countries do not report data for *IFS* but provide data for the *GFSY*, these data are published in *IFS*.

The data for lines 80 through 87 are flows and are on a cash basis, as follows:

The Deficit or Surplus (line 80) is calculated as the difference between Revenue and, if applicable, Grants Received (lines 81 and 81z) on the one hand and Expenditure and Lending Minus Repayments (lines 82 and 83) on the other. The deficit/surplus is also equal, with the opposite sign, to the sum of the net borrowing by the government plus the net decrease in government cash, deposits, and securities held for liquidity purposes.

Revenue (line 81) comprises all nonrepayable government receipts, whether requited or unrequited, other than grants; revenue is shown net of refunds and other adjustment transactions.

Grants Received (line 81z) comprises all unrequited, nonrepayable, noncompulsory receipts from other governments—domestic or foreign—and international institutions. Grants are grouped with revenue because, like revenue, they provide the means whereby expenditure can be made without incurring a debt for future repayment.

Expenditure (line 82) comprises all nonrepayable payments by government, whether requited or unrequited and whether for current or capital purposes.

Lending Minus Repayments (line 83) comprises government acquisition of claims on others—both loans and equities—for public policy purposes and is net of repayments of lending and sales of equities previously purchased. Line 83 includes both domestic and foreign lending minus repayments. In determining the deficit or surplus, lending minus repayments is grouped with expenditure, because it is presumed to represent a means of pursuing government policy objectives and not to be an action undertaken to manage government liquidity.

The total of the financing items equals the deficit or surplus with a reverse sign. Total Financing is classified according to the residence of the lender. Where this information is not available, the distinction is based on the currency in which the debt instruments are denominated.

For some countries, Total Financing is broken down between Net Borrowing and Use of Cash Balances. Net Borrowing covers the net change in government liabilities to all other sectors. It represents mainly other sectors' direct loans or advances to government or their holding of government securities acquired from the government itself or in transactions with others. Where possible, data for Domestic and Foreign Net Borrowing are classified according to the residence of the lender.

Use of Cash Balances (line 87) is intended to measure changes over a period—resulting from transactions but not revaluations—in government holdings of currency and deposits with the monetary system. It corresponds to changes in *IFS* lines 16d and 26d. All currency issues are regarded as liabilities of the monetary authorities, rather than government debt. And any proceeds reaching the government are regarded as coming from the monetary authorities.

Data for outstanding Debt (lines 88 and 89) relate to the direct and assumed debt of the central government and exclude loans guaranteed by the government. The distinction between Domestic and Foreign Debt (lines 88a and 89a) is based on residence of the lender, where possible, but otherwise on the currency in which the debt instruments are denominated (lines 88b and 89b).

The euro area table and the tables of the individual euro area countries also present Deficit or Surplus (line 80g) and Debt (line 88g) data for the general government, expressed as percent of harmonized Gross Domestic Product. Both indicators are defined according to the convergence criteria on public finance as laid down in the Maastricht Treaty. Deficit or Surplus corresponds to net lending/borrowing. The data are not comparable with central government Deficit or Surplus (line 80) and Debt (line 88), owing to differences in coverage as well as in definition.

10. National Accounts and Population

The summary data for national accounts are compiled according to the *System of National Accounts (SNA)*. Gross Domestic Product (GDP) is presented in *IFS* as the sum of final expenditures, following the presentation of the *1993 SNA*, as well as the *European System of Accounts (1995 ESA)*.

The national accounts lines shown in the country tables are as follows:

Household Consumption Expenditure, including Nonprofit Institutions Serving Households (NPISHs) (line 96f), Government Consumption Expenditure (line 91f), Gross Fixed Capital Formation (line 93e), Changes in Inventories (line 93i) (formerly Increase/Decrease(-) in Stocks), Exports of Goods and Services (line 90c), and Imports of Goods and Services (line 98c).

Household Consumption Expenditure, including Nonprofit Institutions Serving Households (NPISHs) (line 96f) consists of the expenditure incurred by resident households and resident NPISHs on individual consumption goods and services. Government Consumption Expenditure (line 91f) consists of expenditure incurred by general government on both individual-consumption goods and services and collective-consumption services.

Gross Fixed Capital Formation (line 93e) is measured by the total value of a producer's acquisitions, less disposals, of fixed assets during the accounting period, plus certain additions to the value of nonproduced assets (such as subsoil assets or major improvements in the quantity, quality, or productivity of land). Changes in Inventories (line 93i) (including work-in-progress) consist of changes in (1) stocks of outputs that are still held by the units that produced them before the outputs are further processed, sold, delivered to other units, or used in other ways and (2) stocks of products acquired from other units that are intended to be used for intermediate consumption or for resale without further processing.

Exports of Goods and Services (line 90c) consist of sales, barter, gifts, or grants of goods and services from residents to nonresidents. Imports of Goods and Services (line 98c) consist of purchases, barter, or receipts of gifts or grants of goods and services by residents from nonresidents. Gross Domestic Product (GDP) (line 99b) is the sum of consumption expenditure (of households, NPISHs, and general government), gross fixed capital formation, changes in inventories, and exports of goods and services, less the value of imports of goods and services.

Net Primary Income from Abroad (line 98.n) is the difference between the total values of the primary incomes receivable from, and payable to, nonresidents. Gross National Income (line 99a) is derived by adding net primary income from abroad to GDP.

Gross National Income (GNI) (line 99a) is derived by adding Net Primary Income from Abroad (line 98.n) to GDP. Gross National Disposable Income (GNDI) (line 99i) is derived by adding Net Current Transfers from Abroad (line 98t) to GNI, and Gross Saving (line 99s) is derived by deducting final consumption expenditure (lines 96f + 91f) from GNDI. Consumption of Fixed Capital (line 99cf) is shown for countries that provide these data.

The country table notes in the monthly issues provide information on which countries have implemented the *1993 SNA* or the *1995 ESA*.

The national accounts lines generally do not explicitly show the statistical discrepancies between aggregate GDP compiled from expenditure flows as against GDP compiled from the production or income accounts (or from a mixture of these accounts). Hence, in some cases, the components of GDP that are shown in *IFS* may not add up exactly to the total.

For countries that publish quarterly seasonally adjusted data, the data in *IFS* in the monthly issues are also on a seasonally adjusted basis (codes ending with c or r). For the United States, Japan, Australia, South Africa, Argentina, and Mexico, quarterly data are shown at annual rates, which the country authorities provide as such.

Lines 99b.p and 99b.r are measures of GDP volume at reference year value levels. In the past, these series used a common reference year (e.g., 1990) for publication. With the June 1999 issue, these series are published on the same reference year(s) as reported by the national compilers. The code *p* indicates data that are not seasonally adjusted, whereas code *r* indicates data that are seasonally adjusted.

Lines 99bvp and 99bvr are GDP volume indices that are presented on a standard 2000 reference year and are derived from the GDP volume series reported by national compilers. For this calculation the data series provided by national compilers are linked together (if there is more than one series) to form a single time series. The earliest overlapping year from the different reference year series is used to calculate the link factors.

The GDP Deflator (lines 99bip or 99bir) are not direct measurements of prices but are derived implicitly: the GDP series at current prices is divided by constant price GDP series referenced to 2000. The latter series is constructed by multiplying the 2000 current price GDP level by the GDP volume index (2000=100). The deflator is expressed in index form with 2000=100.

Data on Population are provided by the Population Division of the Department of Economic and Social Affairs of the United Nations. These data represent mid-year estimates and are revised every two years.

11. World Tables

Besides the world tables on exchange rates, members' Fund positions and transactions, international reserves, and interest rates—discussed earlier in this introduction—*IFS* also brings together country data on money, consumer prices, values and unit values of countries' exports and imports, and wholesale prices and unit values (expressed in U.S. dollars) of principal world trade commodities. Tables on balance of payments may be found in the *IFS* yearbook and also in the *Balance of Payments Statistics Yearbook, Part 2*.

Tables showing totals or averages of country series may report data for selected countries only.

Country Groups

Countries whose data are included in **world/all countries'** totals and averages are arrayed into two main groups—industrial countries and developing countries. The **industrial** countries' group also shows separate data for the euro area. The **developing** countries group is further subdivided into area subgroups for Africa, Asia, Europe, the Middle East, and the Western Hemisphere.

The country composition of the world is all countries for which the topic series are available in the *IFS* files. Consequently, the country coverage of some areas, mainly Africa and Asia, differs from topic to topic, and area and world totals or averages may be biased to some extent toward the larger reporting countries.

Data for subgroups oil exporting countries and non-oil developing countries are shown as memorandum items. Oil exporting countries are defined as those countries whose oil exports (net of any imports of crude oil) both represent a minimum of two thirds of their total exports and are at least equivalent to approximately 1 percent of world exports of oil. The calculations presently used to determine which countries meet the above criteria are based on 1976–78 averages.

Area and World Indices

Area and world indices are obtained as weighted averages of country indices. For the area and world indices on unit values of exports and imports—where the country indices are expressed in U.S. dollars—arithmetic means are used. For consumer prices and industrial production, geometric means are used because, unlike arithmetic means, geometric means are not unduly influenced by data for the few countries with extreme growth rates. Geometric means assure that, if all series have constant although different rates of increase, their average will have a constant rate of increase.

The weights are as follows: For the area averages for consumer prices, the country series are weighted by the 2000 purchasing power parity (PPP) value of GDP. (A comparison of PPP-based GDP weights and exchange rate-based GDP weights is presented in *World Economic Outlook*, May 1993, Annex IV.) For the industrial production table, the country series are weighted by value added in industry, as derived from individual countries' national accounts, expressed in U.S. dollars. And for the export unit values and import unit values tables, the country series are weighted by the 2000 value of exports and imports (both in U.S. dollars), respectively.

Weights are normally updated at about five-year intervals—following international practice—to reflect changes in the importance of each country's data with the data of all other countries. The standard weight base years used are 1953, 1958, 1963, 1970, 1975, 1980, 1984–86, 1990, 1995, and 2000. The corresponding time spans to which the weights are applied are 1948–55, 1955–60, 1960–68, 1968–73, 1973–78, 1978–83, 1983–88, 1988–93, 1993–98, and 1998 onward.

Separate averages are calculated for each time span, and the index series are linked by the splicing at overlap years and shifted to the reference base 2000=100.

Calculation of Area Totals and Averages

The calculation of area totals and averages in the world tables takes account of the problem that data for some countries do not run through the end of the period for which world and area data should be calculable. If country data are known that contribute at least 60 percent of the area total or index aggregate during recent periods for which data of all countries of an area are available, then area totals and averages for most topics are estimated for current and for earlier periods.

Area totals or averages are estimated by assuming that the rate of change in the unreported country data is the same as the rate of change in the weighted total or average of the reported country data for that area. These estimates are made for the area totals and averages only; separate country estimates are not calculated.

Except for import unit values, the world totals and averages are made from the calculated and estimated data for the two main groups—industrial countries and developing countries. A world total or average will only be calculated when totals or averages are available for both these country groups.

For import unit values, world data are calculated directly from country data. This is because the number of countries for which the series are available and current is insufficient to allow calculation or estimation of the area averages and because the variability of import unit value indices among countries is judged to be less than that for other topics. World estimates are made when data are available for countries whose combined weights represent at least 80 percent of the total country weights.

For the terms of trade index numbers in the yearbook, the world and area data for export unit values are divided by the corresponding series for import unit values, where possible. Thus terms of trade averages are available only for areas with both export and import unit values. The country coverage within the areas for the export and import unit values is not identical, leading to a small degree of asymmetry in the terms of trade calculation.

Calculation of Individual World Tables

International Reserves: Country series on international reserves begin generally with their appropriate dates and are complete monthly time series; therefore, earlier period estimates are not required. When current data of a few countries of an area are not reported, the area total is estimated by carrying forward the last reported country figure.

Money (and Reserve Money and Money plus Quasi-Money, which are available in the yearbook): Percent changes are based on end-of-year data (over a 12-month period for Money). When there is more than one version or definition of money over time, different time series are chained through a ratio splicing technique. When actual stock data needed for the growth rate calculation are missing, no percent change is shown in the world table.

Ratio of Reserve Money to Money plus Quasi-Money (available in the yearbook): The measures of money used in calculating this ratio are end-of-year data.

Income Velocity of Money plus Quasi-Money: The measure of income in this table is *IFS* data on GDP. The data for money plus quasi-money are annual averages of the highest frequency data available. The ratio is then converted into an index number with a base year of 1995.

Real Effective Exchange Rate Indices: This table shows three real effective exchange rate indices for industrial countries. Two of these comprise alternative measures of costs and prices derived from Relative Unit Labor Costs (line 65um) and Relative Normalized Unit Labor Costs (line reu). They have been applied to the weighting scheme, based on aggregated data for trade in manufactured goods, averaged over the period 1989–91. The weights reflect both the relative importance of a country's trading partners in its direct bilateral trade relations and that resulting from competition in third markets. The measure is expressed as an index 2000=100 in accord with all indices published in *IFS*.

One of the two indices—the index Based on Relative Normalized Unit Labor Costs (line reu)—is also shown in the country tables (except for Ireland), with the Nominal Effective Exchange Rate Index (line neu) from which the measures are drawn.

The third real effective exchange rate index—Based on Relative Consumer Prices (line rec)—is provided as a measure of domestic cost and price developments. It covers trade in manufactured goods and primary products for trading partners—and competitors. It uses the same methodology used to compile nominal and real effective exchange rates for nonindustrial countries, as discussed in the exchange rate and exchange rate arrangements section of this introduction.

Beginning with the October 1992 issue of *IFS*, the data published are from a revised database. The database underwent a comprehensive review and update of the underlying data sources and a change in the method of normalization of output per hour. The method uses the Hodrick-Prescott filter, which smoothes a time series by removing short-run fluctuations while retaining changes of a larger amplitude.

The footnotes to this world table in the monthly issues discuss the data sources used to derive the cost and price indicators for the real effective exchange rates.

Producer/Wholesale Prices (world table available in the yearbook): Data are those prices reported in lines 63* in the country tables. The percent changes are calculated from the index number series.

Consumer Prices: Data are those prices reported in lines 64* in the country tables. The percent changes are calculated from the index number series.

Industrial Production: This table presents non-seasonally adjusted indices on industrial production for 22 industrial countries, together with an aggregate index for the group. The data are those shown in the country tables as either Industrial Production (lines 66..*) or Manufacturing Production (lines 66ey*), the asterisk representing a wildcard.

Wages (world table available in the yearbook): This table presents indices computed either from absolute wage data or from the wage indices reported to the Fund for the industrial sector for 22 industrial countries. The data are those shown in the country tables as Wage Rates or Earnings (line 65).

Employment (world table available in the yearbook): This table presents indices computed from indices of employment or number of persons employed as reported by the countries for the industrial sector for 20 industrial countries. The data are those shown in the country tables as Employment (lines 67 or 67ey).

Exports and *Imports:* Data are published in U.S. dollars, as reported, if available, by the countries. Otherwise, monthly data in national currency, published in the country tables (lines 70... and 71...), are converted to U.S. dollars using the exchange rate **rf**. For quarterly and annual data, conversions are made using the trade-weighted average of the monthly exchange rates.

Export Unit Values/Export Prices and *Import Unit Values/Import Prices:* Data are the index numbers reported in the country tables expressed in U.S. dollars at rate **rf**. The country indices are typically unit value data (lines 74 and 75). However, for some countries, they are components of wholesale price indices or are derived from specific price quotations (lines 76, 76.x, and 76aa).

Terms of Trade (world table available in the yearbook): Data are index numbers computed from the export and import unit value indices and shown in the appropriate world table. The percent changes are calculated from the index number series.

Balance of Payments (world tables available in the yearbook): For a precise definition of the concepts used in these tables, the reader is referred to the section in this introduction on international transactions. The concepts and definitions are further described in the fifth edition of the *Balance of Payments Manual,* as supplemented and amended by *Financial Derivatives, a Supplement to the Fifth Edition of the Balance of Payments Manual.*

Trade Balance is the series reported in line 78acd of the country tables. Current Account Balance, Excluding Exceptional Financing is the series reported in line 78ald of the country tables. Capital and Financial Account, Including Net Errors and Omissions but Excluding Reserve Assets, Use of Fund Credit, and Exceptional Financing are the sum of the series reported in lines 78bcd, 78bjd, and 78cad of the country tables. Overall Balance Excluding Reserve Assets, Use of Fund Credit, and Exceptional Financing is the series reported in line 78cbd (calculated as the sum of lines 78ald, 78bcd, 78bjd, and 78cad) of the country tables. Note that in some cases, data published in the country pages may be more current than those in the Balance of Payments world tables due to an earlier cutoff date for calculating these world tables.

GDP Volume Measures (world table available in the yearbook): Data are derived from those series reported in lines 99bvp and 99bvr in the country tables. The percent changes are calculated from index numbers.

GDP Deflator (world table available in the yearbook): Data are derived from those series reported in lines 99bip in the country tables. The percent changes are calculated from index numbers.

Gross Capital Formation as Percentage of GDP (world table available in the yearbook): Data are the percent share of gross capital formation in GDP at current market prices. Gross capital formation comprises Gross Fixed Capital Formation and Increase/Decrease (-) in Stocks (lines 93e and 93i, respectively).

Final Consumption Expenditure as a Percentage of GDP (world table available in the yearbook): Data are the percent share of final consumption expenditure in GDP at current market prices, which comprises Government Consumption and Private Consumption (91f and 96f, respectively).

Commodity Prices: Data are obtained primarily from the Commodities and Special Issues Division of the IMF's Research Department, from *Commodity Price Data* of the World Bank, from *Monthly Commodity Price Bulletin* of the UNCTAD, and from a number of countries that produce commodities that are significantly traded in the international markets. Data derived from the last source are reported in the country tables. The market price series (lines 76) are expressed as U.S. dollars per quantity units and refer to values often used in the respective commodity markets. For comparison purposes, indices of unit values (lines 74) at base 2000=100 are provided. The accompanying notes to the table (located in the back of the printed copies) provide information specific to each commodity series, including data sources, grades, and quotation frequency.

12. Country Codes and *IFS* Line Numbers

Each *IFS* time series carries a unique identification code. For publication purposes, the code has been truncated to a three-digit country code and to a five-digit subject code, referred to as the *IFS* line number.

Line numbers apply uniformly across countries—that is, a given line number measures the same economic variable for each country, subject to data availability. The line numbers take the form of two numerics followed by three alphabetic codes (NNaaa). The two numerics are the section and subsection codes, the first two alphabetic codes are the classification codes, and the last alphabetic code is the qualification code. Any of these positions may be blank: for publication purposes, blanks in the first or final positions are omitted, whereas embedded blanks are represented by a period. The line numbers are part of the descriptor stub in the country tables.

Data expressed in units of money (values or prices) are ordinarily expressed in national currency and in natural form, that is, without seasonal adjustment. For these data the qualification code is blank.

Transformation of these data is denoted by various qualification codes. For data that are not seasonally adjusted, qualification codes are *d* for U.S. dollar values, *s* for SDR values, and *p* for constant national currency values. For data that are seasonally adjusted for *IFS*, codes are *f* for U.S. dollar values, *u* for SDR values, and *b* for national currency values. For data that are seasonally adjusted by national compilers, codes are *c* for national currency values and *r* for constant national currency values.

The qualification codes are also used to distinguish separate groups of deposit money banks or other financial institutions when data for separate groups are given.

13. Symbols, Conventions, and Abbreviations

The abbreviation "ff.," often used on the title page of the printed copies of *IFS*, means "following."

Entries printed in bold on the country pages of the monthly book refer to updates and revisions made since the publication of the preceding issue of *IFS*.

Italic midheadings in the middle of the pages of the monthly book and yearbook identify the units in which data are expressed and whether data are stocks (end of period), flows (transactions during a period), or averages (for a period).

(—) Indicates that a figure is zero or less than half a significant digit or that data do not exist.

(....) Indicates a lack of statistical data that can be reported or calculated from underlying observations.

(†) Marks a break in the comparability of data, as explained in the relevant notes in the monthly and yearbook. In these instances, data after the symbol do not form a consistent series with those for earlier dates. The break symbols not explained in the country table notes can show a point of splice, where series having different base years are linked. A case would be the series described in the section of this introduction on prices, production, and labor. They can also point out a change in magnitude for high-inflation countries, as described in the section on electronic products.

(e) In superscript position after the figure marks an observation that is an estimate.

(f) In superscript position after the figure marks an observation that is forecast.

(p) In superscript position after the figure marks that data are in whole or in part provisional or preliminary.

Standard source codes, listed in the footnotes, refer with some exceptions to the following data sources:

(A) Annual report of the central bank

(B) Bulletin of the central bank

(C) Customs department of a country

(E) OECD

(L) International Labor Organization

(M) Ministry or other national source

(N) National bureau or other national source

(S) Statistical office

(U) United Nations

(V) Eurostat

The CD-ROM supports text messages to indicate breaks in the data. The time series observations with footnotes are highlighted in bold blue type within the *IFS* Data Viewer. When the cursor is moved over the footnoted cell, a small window will be displayed with the footnoted text. These footnotes/comments provide meaningful information about the specific observation, e.g., butt splicing, ratio splicing, extrapolation, estimations, etc.

Because of space limits in the phototypesetting of descriptor stubs on the country tables and table headings of world tables, abbreviations are sometimes necessary. While most are self-explanatory, the following abbreviation in the descriptors and table headings should be noted:

n.i.e. = Not included elsewhere.

Of which: Currency Outside DMBs = Of which: Currency Outside Deposit Money Banks.

Househ.Cons.Expend.,incl.NPISHs = Household Consumption Expenditure, including Nonprofit Institutions Serving Households.

Use of Fund Credit (GRA) = Use of Fund Credit (General Resources Account).

Data relating to fiscal years are allocated to calendar years to which most of their months refer. Fiscal years ending June 30 are allocated to that calendar year. For instance, the fiscal year from July 1, 1999 to June 30, 2000 is shown as calendar year 2000.

For countries that have reported semiannual transactions data, the data for the first half of a year may be given in the monthly book in the column for the second quarter of that year. And those for the second half may be given in the column for the fourth quarter. In these instances, no data are shown in the columns for the first and third quarters.

14. CD-ROM and Internet Account Subscriptions

The *IFS* is available on CD-ROM and the Internet. It contains:

(1) all time series appearing on *IFS* country tables;

(2) all series published in the *IFS* world tables, except for the daily exchange rates appearing in the Exchange Rates tables;

(3) the following exchange rate series as available for all Fund members, plus Aruba and the Netherlands Antilles: aa, ac, ae, af, ag, ah, b, c, de, dg, ea, eb, ec, ed, g, rb, rd, rf, rh, sa, sb, sc, sd, wa, wc, we, wf, wg, wh, xe, xf, ye, yf, nec, rec, aat, aet, rbt, rft, neu, reu, and ahx

(for an explanation of series af, ah, de, dg, rb, and rd, see *IFS Supplement on Exchange Rates,* No. 9 (1985));

(4) Fund accounts time series, denominated in SDR terms, for all countries for which data are available, though some series are not published in the *IFS* monthly book (2af, 2al , 2ap, 2aq, 2as, 2at 2ej, 2ek, 2en, 2eo, 2f.s, 1c.s, 2tl, 2egs, 2eb, 2h.s, 1bd, 1b.s, 2dus, 2krs, 2ees, 2kxs, 2eu, 2ey, 2eg, 2ens, 2ehs, 2eqs, 2ers, 2ets, 2kk, 2lk, 2kl, 2ll, 1ch, and 1cj) and in percentages (2tlp, 2fz, and 1bf); and

(5) balance of payments series (78aad to 79ded) for all countries for which data are available, though some series are not published in the *IFS* monthly book.

All series in *IFS* contain publication code F except for the euro data lines that contain the code W.

A partner country code may sometimes be included in the control field. When it exists, it usually is shown in the *IFS* printed copy either in the italic midheading (see Real Effective Exchange Rate Indices table) or in the notes (see Commodity Prices table notes). Occasionally, the partner country code attached to a commodity price refers to a market (e.g., the London Metals Exchange) rather than the country of origin.

In the yearbook, data expressed in national currency for countries that have undergone periods of high inflation (e.g., Brazil, Democratic Republic of Congo, and Turkey) are presented in different magnitudes on the same printed line. Users may refer to midheaders on country pages for an indication of the magnitude changes. The practice of expressing different magnitudes on the same line was adopted to prevent early-period data from disappearing from the printed tables. On the CD-ROM and the Internet (CSV format), the data are stored in a scientific notation with six significant digits for all time periods. Therefore, historical as well as current data may be viewed when using the display choices available on the CD-ROM and the Internet.

WORLD
and
AREA TABLES

Exchange Rates

SDR Rates: 1988–2005

	Jan.	Feb.	Mar.	Apr.	May	June	July	Aug.	Sep.	Oct.	Nov.	Dec.	I	II	III	IV	Year
sa US Dollars per SDR (End of Period)																	
1988	1.36642	1.36101	1.38729	1.38417	1.36483	1.31061	1.29648	1.28818	1.29039	1.34592	1.36637	1.34570	1.38729	1.31061	1.29039	1.34570	1.34570
1989	1.31093	1.32150	1.29271	1.29566	1.24362	1.24639	1.28749	1.24652	1.27981	1.27782	1.28771	1.31416	1.29271	1.24639	1.27981	1.31416	1.31416
1990	1.32559	1.31681	1.30083	1.30247	1.31200	1.32388	1.36564	1.38595	1.39256	1.43078	1.42677	1.42266	1.30083	1.32388	1.39256	1.42266	1.42266
1991	1.43476	1.42053	1.34632	1.34081	1.34084	1.31452	1.33400	1.33698	1.36800	1.36652	1.38072	1.43043	1.34632	1.31452	1.36800	1.43043	1.43043
1992	1.39733	1.38091	1.37174	1.36976	1.39632	1.43117	1.44416	1.48286	1.47284	1.40595	1.37896	1.37500	1.37174	1.43117	1.47284	1.37500	1.37500
1993	1.38188	1.37610	1.39773	1.42339	1.42847	1.40360	1.39072	1.40758	1.41840	1.39293	1.38389	1.37356	1.39773	1.40360	1.41840	1.37356	1.37356
1994	1.38067	1.39930	1.41260	1.42138	1.41733	1.44837	1.44327	1.44770	1.46738	1.48454	1.45674	1.45985	1.41260	1.44837	1.46738	1.45985	1.45985
1995	1.47670	1.49440	1.56050	1.57303	1.57591	1.56876	1.55954	1.49249	1.50632	1.49455	1.48615	1.48649	1.56050	1.56876	1.50632	1.48649	1.48649
1996	1.45169	1.46868	1.46121	1.45006	1.44219	1.44334	1.46554	1.45766	1.43937	1.44623	1.44462	1.43796	1.46121	1.44334	1.43937	1.43796	1.43796
1997	1.39466	1.38494	1.38689	1.36553	1.39179	1.38814	1.35862	1.36358	1.36521	1.38362	1.36184	1.34925	1.38689	1.38814	1.36521	1.34925	1.34925
1998	1.34536	1.35023	1.33589	1.34666	1.33536	1.33154	1.32949	1.34222	1.37132	1.40835	1.38017	1.40803	1.33589	1.33154	1.37132	1.40803	1.40803
1999	1.38977	1.36556	1.35784	1.35123	1.34196	1.33587	1.36421	1.36986	1.38769	1.38072	1.36963	1.37251	1.35784	1.33587	1.38769	1.37251	1.37251
2000	1.35288	1.33928	1.34687	1.31921	1.32002	1.33728	1.31335	1.30480	1.29789	1.27934	1.28197	1.30291	1.34687	1.33728	1.29789	1.30291	1.30291
2001	1.29779	1.29248	1.26065	1.26579	1.25423	1.24565	1.25874	1.28823	1.28901	1.27808	1.26608	1.25673	1.26065	1.24565	1.28901	1.25673	1.25673
2002	1.24204	1.24163	1.24691	1.26771	1.29066	1.33046	1.32248	1.32751	1.32269	1.32163	1.32408	1.35952	1.24691	1.33046	1.32269	1.35952	1.35952
2003	1.37654	1.37085	1.37379	1.38391	1.41995	1.40086	1.39195	1.37727	1.42979	1.43178	1.44878	1.48597	1.37379	1.40086	1.42979	1.48597	1.48597
2004	1.48131	1.48007	1.48051	1.45183	1.46882	1.46622	1.45776	1.46073	1.46899	1.49878	1.53590	1.55301	1.48051	1.46622	1.46899	1.55301	1.55301
2005	1.52484	1.53199	1.51083	1.51678	1.47495	1.45661	1.45186						1.51083	1.45661			
sb US Dollars per SDR (Period Average, geometric)																	
1988	1.37723	1.35556	1.37141	1.38197	1.37595	1.34654	1.30514	1.29206	1.29368	1.31949	1.35659	1.35588	1.36804	1.36807	1.29695	1.34387	1.34392
1989	1.32525	1.31652	1.30486	1.29975	1.26560	1.24062	1.27158	1.26166	1.24703	1.27221	1.27724	1.30191	1.31552	1.26843	1.26005	1.28372	1.28176
1990	1.31850	1.32659	1.30170	1.30135	1.31832	1.31442	1.34402	1.37719	1.39049	1.42846	1.44481	1.42654	1.31556	1.31134	1.37042	1.43325	1.35675
1991	1.42291	1.44058	1.38077	1.35123	1.34351	1.31934	1.32155	1.33571	1.35355	1.36201	1.38487	1.40799	1.41453	1.33796	1.33687	1.38483	1.36816
1992	1.40925	1.39042	1.36599	1.37060	1.38810	1.41173	1.44375	1.45645	1.45767	1.43476	1.38701	1.38883	1.38844	1.39004	1.45261	1.40336	1.40838
1993	1.37705	1.37168	1.38045	1.41266	1.41561	1.40969	1.39025	1.40151	1.41756	1.40746	1.38903	1.38404	1.37639	1.41265	1.40306	1.39347	1.39633
1994	1.37343	1.38750	1.40197	1.40425	1.41500	1.42736	1.45706	1.45439	1.46377	1.47720	1.47121	1.45201	1.38759	1.41550	1.45840	1.46676	1.43170
1995	1.46580	1.47826	1.53602	1.57620	1.55819	1.56369	1.55763	1.51069	1.48396	1.49828	1.49474	1.48532	1.49305	1.56601	1.51712	1.49277	1.51695
1996	1.46779	1.46625	1.46181	1.45086	1.44464	1.44290	1.45003	1.45830	1.44811	1.43968	1.45295	1.43817	1.46528	1.44613	1.45214	1.44359	1.45176
1997	1.41537	1.38421	1.37811	1.37150	1.38518	1.39032	1.37726	1.35396	1.35939	1.36989	1.37399	1.35418	1.39256	1.38231	1.36350	1.36599	1.37602
1998	1.34310	1.35002	1.34421	1.34312	1.34373	1.33354	1.33092	1.32668	1.36482	1.40747	1.39199	1.40211	1.34577	1.34013	1.34070	1.40051	1.35654
1999	1.40441	1.38073	1.36265	1.35485	1.34869	1.34004	1.33924	1.36415	1.37613	1.38943	1.37626	1.37280	1.38249	1.34785	1.35975	1.37948	1.36732
2000	1.37068	1.34485	1.34286	1.33915	1.31082	1.33062	1.32348	1.30836	1.29409	1.28650	1.28276	1.29440	1.35274	1.32681	1.30859	1.28788	1.31879
2001	1.30203	1.29353	1.27989	1.26764	1.26217	1.25028	1.25125	1.27495	1.28593	1.27882	1.26827	1.26279	1.29179	1.26001	1.27062	1.26995	1.27304
2002	1.25276	1.24463	1.25009	1.25669	1.27713	1.30065	1.33033	1.32103	1.32182	1.31765	1.33109	1.34003	1.24915	1.27803	1.32269	1.32960	1.29484
2003	1.36538	1.37045	1.37004	1.36908	1.40825	1.41481	1.39832	1.38494	1.39628	1.43198	1.43391	1.46743	1.36861	1.39658	1.39042	1.43959	1.39883
2004	1.49108	1.49645	1.47301	1.46088	1.45118	1.46565	1.47273	1.46495	1.46450	1.47952	1.51377	1.54036	1.48982	1.46100	1.46620	1.51103	1.48201
2005	1.52868	1.51752	1.52527	1.51043	1.49728	1.46737	1.44970						1.52222	1.49169			
sc SDRs per US Dollar (End of Period)																	
1988	.73184	.73475	.72083	.72245	.73269	.76300	.77132	.77629	.77496	.74299	.73187	.74311	.72083	.76300	.77496	.74311	.74311
1989	.76282	.75672	.77357	.77181	.80410	.80232	.77670	.80223	.78137	.78258	.77657	.76094	.77357	.80232	.78137	.76094	.76094
1990	.75438	.75941	.76874	.76777	.76219	.75536	.73226	.72153	.71810	.69892	.70089	.70291	.76874	.75536	.71810	.70291	.70291
1991	.69698	.70396	.74277	.74582	.74580	.76074	.74962	.74795	.73100	.73179	.72426	.69909	.74277	.76074	.73100	.69909	.69909
1992	.71565	.72416	.72900	.73006	.71617	.69873	.69244	.67437	.67896	.71127	.72518	.72727	.72900	.69873	.67896	.72727	.72727
1993	.72365	.72669	.71545	.70255	.70005	.71245	.71905	.71044	.70502	.71791	.72260	.72804	.71545	.71245	.70502	.72804	.72804
1994	.72429	.71465	.70792	.70354	.70555	.69043	.69287	.69075	.68149	.67361	.68646	.68500	.70792	.69043	.68149	.68500	.68500
1995	.67719	.66916	.64082	.63572	.63455	.63745	.64121	.67002	.66387	.66910	.67288	.67273	.64082	.63745	.66387	.67273	.67273
1996	.68885	.68088	.68436	.68963	.69339	.69284	.68234	.68603	.69475	.69145	.69222	.69543	.68436	.69284	.69475	.69543	.69543
1997	.71702	.72205	.72104	.73232	.71850	.72039	.73604	.73336	.73249	.72274	.73430	.74115	.72104	.72039	.73249	.74115	.74115
1998	.74330	.74061	.74856	.74258	.74886	.75101	.75217	.74503	.72922	.71005	.72455	.71021	.74856	.75101	.72922	.71021	.71021
1999	.71954	.73230	.73646	.74007	.74518	.74857	.73303	.73000	.72062	.72426	.73013	.72859	.73646	.74857	.72062	.72859	.72859
2000	.73917	.74667	.74246	.75803	.75757	.74779	.76141	.76640	.77048	.78165	.78005	.76751	.74246	.74779	.77048	.76751	.76751
2001	.77054	.77371	.79324	.79002	.79731	.80280	.79445	.77626	.77579	.78243	.78984	.79572	.79324	.80280	.77579	.79572	.79572
2002	.80513	.80403	.80198	.78883	.77480	.75162	.75615	.75329	.75603	.75664	.75524	.73555	.80198	.75162	.75603	.73555	.73555
2003	.72646	.72947	.72791	.72259	.70425	.71385	.71842	.72608	.70614	.69843	.69024	.67296	.72791	.71385	.70614	.67296	.67296
2004	.67508	.67564	.67544	.68879	.68082	.68203	.68599	.68459	.68074	.66721	.65108	.64391	.67544	.68203	.68074	.64391	.64391
2005	.65581	.65275	.66189	.65929	.67799	.68652	.68877						.66189	.68652			
sd SDRs per US Dollar (Period Average, geometric)																	
1988	.72609	.73770	.72918	.72361	.72677	.74264	.76620	.77396	.77299	.75787	.73714	.73753	.73098	.73096	.77104	.74412	.74409
1989	.75458	.75958	.76637	.76938	.79014	.80605	.78642	.79261	.80191	.78603	.78294	.76810	.76016	.78838	.79362	.77899	.78018
1990	.75844	.75381	.76823	.76843	.75854	.76079	.74404	.72612	.71917	.70006	.69213	.70100	.76014	.76258	.72970	.69772	.73706
1991	.70279	.69417	.72423	.74007	.74432	.75795	.75669	.74867	.73880	.73421	.72209	.71023	.70694	.74741	.74802	.72211	.73091
1992	.70960	.71921	.73207	.72961	.72041	.70835	.69264	.68660	.68603	.69698	.72098	.72003	.72024	.71940	.68842	.71258	.71004
1993	.72619	.72903	.72440	.70788	.70641	.70938	.71930	.71352	.70544	.71050	.71993	.72252	.72654	.70789	.71276	.71763	.71616
1994	.72810	.72072	.71328	.71213	.70671	.70059	.68631	.68757	.68317	.67696	.67971	.68870	.72068	.70646	.68568	.68177	.69847
1995	.68222	.67647	.65104	.63444	.64177	.63951	.64200	.66195	.67387	.66743	.66901	.67326	.66977	.63857	.65914	.66990	.65922
1996	.68130	.68201	.68408	.68925	.69221	.69305	.68964	.68573	.69056	.69460	.68825	.69533	.68246	.69150	.68864	.69272	.68882
1997	.70653	.72243	.72563	.72913	.72193	.71926	.72608	.73857	.73562	.72999	.72781	.73845	.71810	.72344	.73341	.73207	.72673
1998	.74455	.74073	.74393	.74453	.74420	.74988	.75136	.75376	.73270	.71114	.71840	.71321	.73431	.74620	.74588	.71424	.73722
1999	.71204	.72425	.73387	.73809	.74146	.74624	.74669	.73306	.72668	.71972	.72661	.72844	.72333	.74192	.73543	.72491	.73136
2000	.72957	.74358	.74468	.74674	.76288	.75153	.75559	.76431	.77275	.77730	.77957	.77256	.73924	.75369	.76418	.77647	.75827
2001	.76803	.77308	.78132	.78887	.79229	.79982	.79920	.78435	.77765	.78197	.78847	.79189	.77412	.79364	.78702	.78744	.78552
2002	.79824	.80345	.79994	.79574	.78301	.76885	.75169	.75698	.75653	.75893	.75127	.74625	.80054	.78245	.75506	.75213	.77230
2003	.73239	.72969	.72990	.73042	.71010	.70681	.71515	.72205	.71619	.69833	.69739	.68146	.73067	.71618	.71922	.69467	.71517
2004	.67066	.66825	.67888	.68452	.68909	.68229	.67901	.68262	.68283	.67589	.66060	.64920	.67123	.68449	.68204	.66198	.67494
2005	.65416	.65897	.65562	.66206	.66788	.68149	.68980						.65694	.67048			

Exchange Rates

		1993	1994	1995	1996	1997	1998	1999	2000	2001	2002	2003	2004
							Market, Official, or Principal Rate						
						National Currency Units per SDR: End of Period (aa)							

Industrial Countries

		1993	1994	1995	1996	1997	1998	1999	2000	2001	2002	2003	2004
US dollar	111	1.3736	1.4599	1.4865	1.4380	1.3493	1.4080	1.3725	1.3029	1.2567	1.3595	1.4860	1.5530
Canadian dollar	156	1.8186	2.0479	2.0294	1.9694	1.9282	2.1550	1.9809	1.9546	2.0015	2.1475	1.9205	1.8692
Australian dollar	193	2.0286	1.8793	1.9953	1.8053	2.0672	2.2936	2.0993	2.3518	2.4613	2.4011	1.9813	1.9936
Japanese yen	158	153.63	145.61	152.86	166.80	175.34	162.77	140.27	149.70	165.64	163.01	159.15	161.70
New Zealand dollar	196	2.4581	2.2721	2.2754	2.0368	2.3195	2.6723	2.6364	2.9598	3.0246	2.5822	2.2861	2.1618
EMU Euro	163	....	....	....	....	....	....	1.36623	1.40023	1.42600	1.29639	1.17654	1.14016
Austrian schilling	122	16.679	16.013	14.996	15.751	17.045	16.540	....	....	....	....	....	....
Belgium franc	124	49.599	46.478	43.725	46.022	49.814	48.682	....	....	....	....	....	....
Finnish markka	172	7.9454	6.9244	6.4790	6.6777	7.3139	7.1753	....	....	....	....	....	....
French franc	132	8.0978	7.8044	7.2838	7.5306	8.0794	7.9161	....	....	....	....	....	....
Deutsche mark	134	2.3712	2.2610	2.1309	2.2357	2.4180	2.3556	....	....	....	....	....	....
Greek drachma	174	342.32	350.51	352.36	355.20	381.31	397.87	450.79	476.37	....	....	....	....
Irish pound	178	.97360	.94360	.92587	.85537	.94327	.94670	....	....	....	....	....	....
Italian lira	136	2,340.5	2,379.2	2,355.7	2,200.9	2,373.6	2,327.6	....	....	....	....	....	....
Luxembourg franc	137	49.599	46.478	43.725	46.022	49.814	48.682	....	....	....	....	....	....
Netherlands guilder	138	2.6659	2.5330	2.3849	2.5072	2.7217	2.6595	....	....	....	....	....	....
Portuguese escudo	182	242.86	232.25	222.10	224.88	247.35	241.94	....	....	....	....	....	....
Spanish peseta	184	195.34	192.32	180.47	188.77	204.68	200.79	....	....	....	....	....	....
Danish krone	128	9.302	8.880	8.244	8.548	9.210	8.992	10.155	10.450	10.568	9.628	8.853	8.491
Icelandic krona	176	99.899	99.708	96.964	96.185	97.389	97.605	99.576	110.356	129.380	109.550	105.489	94.796
Norwegian krone	142	10.3264	9.8715	9.3931	9.2641	9.8707	10.7010	11.0343	11.5288	11.3251	9.4700	9.9263	9.3802
Swedish krona	144	11.4054	10.8927	9.8973	9.8802	10.6280	11.3501	11.7006	12.4232	13.4062	11.9978	10.6829	10.2725
Swiss franc	146	2.0322	1.9146	1.7102	1.9361	1.9636	1.9382	2.1955	2.1322	2.1079	1.8854	1.8380	1.7574
Pound sterling	112	.92733	.93430	.95903	.84686	.81585	.84643	.84912	.87315	.86647	.84348	.83262	.80409

Developing Countries

Africa

		1993	1994	1995	1996	1997	1998	1999	2000	2001	2002	2003	2004
Algerian dinar	612	33.1344	62.6166	77.5576	80.7931	78.8150	84.9790	95.1346	98.1649	97.7982	108.3856	107.9004	112.7698
Angolan kwanza	614	.0089	.7434	.0085	.2905	.3540	.9807	† 7.6585	21.9121	40.1517	79.7581	117.5127	133.5399
Benin, CFA franc	638	404.89	† 780.44	728.38	753.06	807.94	791.61	† 896.19	918.49	935.39	850.37	771.76	747.90
Botswana pula	616	3.5229	3.9670	4.1944	5.2404	5.1400	6.2774	6.3572	6.9861	8.7760	7.4331	6.6014	6.6482
Burkina Faso, CFA franc	748	404.89	† 780.44	728.38	753.06	807.94	791.61	† 896.19	918.49	935.39	850.37	771.76	747.90
Burundi franc	618	362.99	360.78	413.37	462.63	551.56	710.64	860.83	1,014.76	1,090.92	1,451.07	1,618.31	1,717.35
Cameroon, CFA franc	622	404.89	† 780.44	728.38	753.06	807.94	791.61	† 896.19	918.49	935.39	850.37	771.76	747.90
Cape Verde escudo	624	118.12	118.45	115.14	122.46	129.85	132.71	150.65	154.40	157.24	142.95	129.74	125.73
Cent.African Rep.,CFA franc	626	404.89	† 780.44	728.38	753.06	807.94	791.61	† 896.19	918.49	935.39	850.37	771.76	747.90
Chad, CFA franc	628	404.89	† 780.44	728.38	753.06	807.94	791.61	† 896.19	918.49	935.39	850.37	771.76	747.90
Comorian franc	632	404.89	† 585.32	546.28	564.79	605.95	593.70	672.14	688.87	701.54	637.78	578.82	560.92
Congo, Dem.Rep., congo franc	636	.481	47.445	.220	1.662	1.430	† 3.450	6.176	65.146	394.111	519.527	549.200	703.638
Congo, Rep., CFA franc	634	404.89	† 780.44	728.38	753.06	807.94	791.61	† 896.19	918.49	935.39	850.37	771.76	747.90
Côte d'Ivoire,CFA franc	662	404.89	† 780.44	728.38	753.06	807.94	791.61	† 896.19	918.49	935.39	850.37	771.76	747.90
Djibouti franc	611	244.11	259.45	264.18	255.56	239.79	250.24	243.92	231.55	223.35	241.62	264.09	276.00
Eq. Guinea, CFA franc	642	404.89	† 780.44	728.38	753.06	807.94	791.61	† 896.19	918.49	935.39	850.37	771.76	747.90
Eritrean nafka	643	6.8678	8.6861	9.3946	9.2403	† 9.6134	10.6967	13.1761	13.2897	17.3397	19.2117	20.4878	21.4121
Ethiopian birr	644	6.8678	8.6861	9.3946	9.2403	9.2613	10.5644	11.1640	10.8324	10.7555	11.6659	12.8100	13.4365
Gabon, CFA franc	646	404.89	† 780.44	728.38	753.06	807.94	791.61	† 896.19	918.49	935.39	850.37	771.76	747.90
Gambian dalasi	648	13.096	13.983	14.330	14.225	14.207	15.476	15.849	19.397	21.279	31.802	46.005	46.083
Ghanaian cedi	652	1,125.87	1,536.68	2,154.33	2,522.74	3,066.48	3,274.49	4,852.02	9,182.45	9,201.70	11,472.74	13,154.28	14,061.36
Guinean franc	656	1,335.67	1,432.15	1,483.49	1,494.23	1,544.82	1,827.67	2,382.68	2,452.43	2,498.79	2,620.18	2,964.24	3,516.29
Guinea-Bissau, CFA franc	654	242.25	345.18	501.49	772.88	807.94	791.61	896.19	918.49	935.39	850.37	771.76	747.90
Kenya shilling	664	93.626	65.458	83.153	79.118	84.568	87.165	100.098	101.674	98.779	104.781	113.140	120.117
Lesotho loti	666	4.6667	5.1730	5.4220	6.7332	6.5675	8.2511	8.4471	9.8611	15.2397	11.7463	9.8668	8.7434
Liberian dollar	668	1.3736	1.4599	1.4865	1.4380	1.3493	† 60.8973	54.2141	55.6994	62.2081	88.3688	75.0415	84.6390
Malagasy ariary	674	539.2	1,130.2	1,017.6	1,244.8	1,426.1	1,521.3	1,796.1	1,706.9	1,666.7	1,749.6	1,812.3	2,903.2
Malawi kwacha	676	6.1733	22.3337	22.7479	22.0340	28.6416	61.7894	63.7362	104.3318	84.5705	118.4665	161.3258	169.1899
Mali, CFA franc	678	404.89	† 780.44	728.38	753.06	807.94	791.61	† 896.19	918.49	935.39	850.37	771.76	747.90
Mauritanian ouguiya	682	170.54	187.40	203.81	204.84	227.15	289.74	308.81	328.72	331.93	365.32	394.67	...
Mauritian rupee	684	25.625	26.077	26.258	25.842	30.041	34.896	34.955	36.327	38.197	39.694	38.766	43.802
Moroccan dirham	686	13.257	13.080	12.589	12.653	13.107	13.031	13.845	13.836	14.528	13.822	13.002	12.762
Mozambique, metical	688	7,339.2	9,709.5	16,187.9	16,359.7	15,574.4	17,411.7	18,254.4	† 22,332.5	29,307.5	32,430.4	35,450.3	29,350.8
Namibia dollar	728	4.66667	5.17298	5.42197	6.73325	6.56747	8.25106	8.44711	9.86107	15.23974	11.74625	9.86684	8.74345
Niger, CFA franc	692	404.89	† 780.44	728.38	753.06	807.94	791.61	† 896.19	918.49	935.39	850.37	771.76	747.90
Nigerian naira	694	30.056	32.113	32.534	31.471	29.530	† 30.816	134.437	142.734	141.948	171.843	202.835	205.541
Rwanda franc	714	201.39	201.39	445.67	437.37	411.31	450.75	479.24	560.67	572.84	695.88	849.07	878.35
São Tomé & Príncipe dobra	716	709.72	1,730.37	2,611.58	4,074.04	9,403.91	9,694.29	10,019.32	11,218.90	11,335.34	12,496.49	14,051.18	15,485.06
Senegal, CFA franc	722	404.89	† 780.44	728.38	753.06	807.94	791.61	† 896.19	918.49	935.39	850.37	771.76	747.90
Seychelles rupee	718	7.2345	7.2345	7.2345	7.2345	6.9218	7.6699	7.3671	8.1642	7.2226	6.8474	8.1434	8.5131
Sierra Leonean leone	724	793.41	894.90	1,402.35	1,307.24	1,799.00	2,239.84	3,123.90	2,171.52	2,716.13	2,979.70	3,807.32	4,442.37
South African rand	199	4.6667	5.1730	5.4220	6.7332	6.5675	8.2511	8.4471	9.8611	15.2397	11.7463	9.8668	8.7434
Sudanese pound	732	29.8600	58.3940	78.2363	208.4000	232.3489	334.8307	353.6958	335.3039	328.5469	355.7592	386.5900	389.2309
Swaziland lilangeni	734	4.6667	5.1730	5.4220	6.7332	6.5675	8.2511	8.4471	9.8611	15.2397	11.7463	9.8668	8.7434
Tanzanian shilling	738	659.13	764.16	818.10	856.51	842.70	958.87	1,094.34	1,046.58	1,151.54	1,327.30	1,580.51	1,619.73
Togo, CFA franc	742	404.89	780.44	728.38	753.06	807.94	791.61	† 896.19	918.49	935.39	850.37	771.76	747.90
Tunisian dinar	744	1.4376	1.4470	1.4134	1.4358	1.5483	1.5502	1.7191	1.8049	1.8453	1.8137	1.7955	1.8627
Uganda shilling	746	1,552.3	1,352.9	1,500.5	1,480.5	1,538.3	1,918.7	2,067.1	2,301.8	2,170.9	2,518.6	2,875.8	2,700.0
Zambian kwacha	754	686.780	993.095	1,421.278	1,844.457	1,908.973	3,236.948	3,612.707	5,417.278	4,813.779	5,892.703	6,903.044	7,409.892
Zimbabwe dollar	698	9.53	12.24	13.84	15.59	25.11	52.62	52.35	71.75	69.17	74.82	1,224.03	8,897.61

Asia

		1993	1994	1995	1996	1997	1998	1999	2000	2001	2002	2003	2004
Afghanistan,afghani	512	69.502	729.925	1,486.490	† 4,313.880	4,047.750	4,224.090	4,117.530	3,908.730	3,770.190	4,078.560	4,457.910	4,659.030
Bangladesh taka	513	54.736	58.759	60.574	61.041	61.323	68.289	69.998	70.357	71.634	78.716	87.348	94.333
Bhutan,ngultrum	514	43.102	45.810	52.295	51.666	52.999	59.813	59.690	60.911	60.549	65.298	67.768	67.688
Cambodian riel	522	3,166.1	3,759.1	3,754.9	3,901.2	4,657.6	5,308.3	5,174.4	5,087.9	4,895.0	5,342.9	5,920.1	6,254.0

Exchange Rates

		1993	1994	1995	1996	1997	1998	1999	2000	2001	2002	2003	2004
						Market, Official, or Principal Rate							
						National Currency Units per SDR: End of Period (aa)							
Asia(Cont.)													
Chinese yuan	924	7.9666	† 12.3302	12.3637	11.9325	11.1715	11.6567	11.3637	10.7847	10.4017	11.2532	12.2989	12.8535
Fiji dollar	819	2.1164	2.0570	2.1248	1.9900	2.0902	2.7965	2.6981	2.8479	2.9017	2.8072	2.5589	2.5547
Hong Kong dollar	532	10.6121	11.2963	11.4935	11.1241	10.4513	10.9066	10.6658	10.1575	9.7987	10.6015	11.5356	12.0723
Indian rupee	534	43.102	45.810	52.295	51.666	52.999	59.813	59.690	60.911	60.549	65.298	67.768	67.688
Indonesian rupiah	536	2,898.2	3,211.7	3,430.8	3,426.7	6,274.0	11,299.4	9,724.2	12,501.4	13,070.0	12,154.1	12,578.7	14,427.5
Kiribati, Aust.dollar	826	2.0286	1.8793	1.9953	1.8053	2.0672	2.2936	2.0993	2.3518	2.4613	2.4011	1.9813	1.9936
Korean won	542	1,110.0	1,151.4	1,151.6	1,213.9	2,287.0	1,695.3	1,561.9	1,647.5	1,650.7	1,612.7	1,772.2	1,607.5
Lao P.D. Rep., kip	544	986.22	1,049.63	† 1,372.03	1,344.49	3,554.60	6,017.92	10,431.08	10,707.31	11,926.37	14,519.67	15,553.65	16,114.81
Macao pataca	546	10.9283	11.6352	11.8391	11.4571	10.7690	11.2359	10.9868	10.4672	10.0932	10.9208	11.8832	12.4388
Malaysian ringgit	548	3.71067	3.73722	3.77866	3.63660	5.25115	5.35051	5.21554	4.95106	4.77557	5.16618	5.64669	5.90144
Maldivian rufiyaa	556	15.253	17.182	17.496	16.925	15.881	16.573	16.154	15.335	16.086	17.402	19.020	19.879
Mongolian togrog	948	† 544.630	604.509	704.031	997.240	1,097.156	1,270.043	1,471.839	1,429.292	1,384.916	1,529.460	1,735.613	1,877.589
Myanmar kyat	518	8.5085	8.5085	8.5085	8.5085	8.5085	8.5085	8.5085	8.5085	8.5085	8.5085	8.5085	8.5085
Nepalese rupee	558	67.634	72.817	83.243	82.007	85.408	95.288	94.326	96.806	96.108	106.450	110.021	111.506
Pakistan rupee	564	41.372	44.963	50.912	57.691	59.434	64.608	† 71.075	75.607	76.489	79.578	85.020	91.820
Papua New Guinea kina	853	1.3479	1.7205	1.9846	1.9366	2.3630	2.9518	3.6995	4.0028	4.7281	5.4643	4.9532	4.8532
Philippine peso	566	38.046	35.647	38.967	37.801	53.936	54.996	55.330	65.143	64.601	72.185	82.574	87.383
Samoa tala	862	3.5816	3.5789	3.7566	3.5004	3.7324	4.2385	4.1428	4.3532	4.4628	4.3729	4.1277	4.1513
Singapore dollar	576	2.2087	2.1324	2.1023	2.0129	2.2607	2.3380	2.2866	2.2560	2.3262	2.3608	2.5273	2.5373
Solomon Islands dollar	813	4.4611	4.8597	5.1668	5.2081	6.4067	6.8417	6.9671	6.6441	6.9935	10.1381	11.1309	11.6592
Sri Lanka rupee	524	68.076	72.963	80.341	81.540	82.689	96.164	99.054	107.594	117.075	131.500	143.750	162.453
Thai baht	578	35.081	36.628	37.445	36.826	† 63.748	51.662	51.428	56.374	55.575	58.665	58.831	60.662
Tongan pa'anga	866	1.8946	1.8371	1.8883	1.7438	1.8377	2.2749	2.2066	2.5754	2.7736	3.0299	3.0020	2.9689
Vanuatu vatu	846	165.93	163.62	169.07	159.28	167.73	182.73	176.90	186.07	184.41	181.05	166.15	165.44
Vietnamese dong	582	14,892.8	16,132.8	16,373.7	16,031.8	16,585.0	19,557.5	19,253.6	18,910.4	18,956.5	20,940.7	23,249.5	24,501.8
Europe													
Albanian lek	914	135.570	139.547	140.087	148.211	201.227	197.941	185.454	185.847	171.606	181.822	158.375	143.871
Armenian dram	911	103.02	591.98	597.57	625.61	667.85	735.03	718.88	719.44	706.04	795.17	841.06	754.51
Azerbaijan manat	912	162.08	6,105.09	6,600.02	5,892.76	5,245.88	5,477.24	6,008.85	5,947.78	6,000.89	6,652.13	7,315.43	7,614.41
Belarusian rubel	913	.960	15.474	17.095	22.288	41.476	309.767	439.203	1,537.434	1,985.633	2,610.278	3,203.751	3,370.032
Bosnia & Herzegovina conv.marka.	963	....	....	....	....	2.418	2.356	2.672	2.739	2.789	2.536	2.301	2.230
Bulgarian lev	918	.0449	.0964	.1051	.7008	2.3969	2.3586	2.6721	2.7386	2.7891	2.5627	2.3012	2.2300
Croatian kuna	960	9.01316	8.21706	7.90233	7.96572	8.50446	8.79667	10.49648	10.62568	10.50129	9.71478	9.09192	8.75414
Cyprus pound	423	.71398	.69523	.67867	.67567	.70935	.70152	.78862	.80357	.81712	.74344	.69134	.66004
Czech Republic koruna	935	41.145	40.947	39.544	39.302	46.733	42.037	49.382	49.267	45.568	40.977	38.121	34.733
Estonian kroon	939	19.062	18.088	17.038	17.888	19.343	18.882	21.359	21.915	22.234	20.306	18.440	17.815
Georgian lari	915	....	....	1.8284	1.8348	1.7594	2.5345	2.6489	2.5732	2.5889	2.8414	3.0834	2.8432
Hungarian forint	944	138.317	161.591	207.321	237.163	274.572	308.401	346.586	370.978	350.665	306.110	308.963	279.992
Kazakhstani tenge	916	8.67	79.21	95.06	105.40	101.94	117.99	189.68	188.27	188.76	210.18	214.31	201.89
Kyrgyz som	917	11.03	15.55	16.65	24.01	23.44	41.36	62.35	62.94	59.97	62.67	65.67	64.64
Latvian lats	941	.81727	.80000	.79825	.79951	.79606	.80117	.80017	.79868	.80179	.80755	.80391	.80135
Lithuanian litas	946	5.357	5.839	5.946	5.752	5.397	5.632	5.490	5.212	5.027	4.502	4.104	3.936
Macedonian denar	962	61.062	59.264	56.456	59.547	74.776	72.987	82.816	86.420	86.930	79.665	72.887	69.990
Maltese lira	181	.54272	.53738	.52384	.51712	.52717	.53141	.56558	.57038	.56812	.54220	.50895	.49472
Moldovan leu	921	4.9998	6.2336	6.6877	6.7215	6.2882	11.7185	15.9077	16.1343	16.4517	18.7913	19.6445	19.3522
Polish zloty	964	2.9317	3.5579	3.6687	4.1349	4.7467	4.9337	5.6936	5.3982	5.0097	5.2189	5.5587	4.6441
Romanian leu	968	1,752.7	2,579.6	3,832.2	5,802.2	10,825.0	15,419.3	25,055.2	33,779.2	39,708.9	45,543.9	48,435.2	45,141.3
Russian ruble	922	1.7128	5.1825	6.8973	7.9951	8.0415	† 29.0758	37.0578	36.6899	37.8778	43.2115	43.7685	43.0940
Slovak koruna	936	45.605	45.660	43.954	45.864	46.930	51.975	58.011	61.744	60.910	54.430	49.000	44.255
Slovenian tolar	961	181.093	184.609	187.283	203.443	228.266	226.974	270.069	296.252	315.371	300.550	281.394	273.707
Tajik somoni	923	.019	.058	.436	.472	1.008	1.377	1.971	† 2.866	3.205	4.079	4.393	4.716
Turkish new lira	186	.0199	.0565	.0887	.1550	.2774	.4428	.7431	.8774	1.8224	2.2346	2.0754	2.0803
Ukrainian hryvnia	926	.1732	1.5212	2.6668	† 2.7163	2.5622	4.8253	7.1594	7.0807	6.6588	7.2495	7.9224	8.2393
Middle East													
Bahrain, Kingdom of, dinar	419	.51646	.54890	.55892	.54067	.50732	.52942	.51606	.48989	.47253	.51118	.55873	.58393
Egyptian pound	469	4.6314	4.9504	5.0392	4.8718	4.5713	4.7704	4.6734	4.8077	5.6427	6.1178	9.1435	9.5221
Iranian rial	429	2,415.49	2,534.26	2,597.64	2,515.19	2,366.94	2,465.36	2,405.04	2,948.39	2,200.47	† 10,810.87	12,292.11	13,655.62
Iraqi dinar	433	.42698	.45381	.46209	.44700	.41942	.43770	.42665	.40502	.39066	.42262	....	....
Israeli new sheqel	436	4.1015	4.4058	4.6601	4.6748	4.7709	5.8588	5.7000	5.2651	5.5497	6.4400	6.5071	6.6904
Jordan dinar	439	.96699	1.02336	1.05392	1.01951	.95662	.99829	.97311	.92376	.89102	.96390	1.05355	1.10108
Kuwaiti dinar	443	.40990	.43813	.44436	.43123	.41139	.42461	.41749	.39793	.38691	.40726	.43792	.45767
Lebanese pound	446	2,350.2	2,404.4	2,372.4	2,231.7	2,060.3	2,123.3	2,069.1	1,964.1	1,894.5	2,049.5	2,240.1	2,341.2
Libyan dinar	672	.44643	.63412	.63412	.63412	.63412	.63412	.63412	.70403	.81699	1.64474	1.93237	1.93237
Rial Omani	449	.52813	.56131	.57156	.55290	.51879	.54139	.52773	.50097	.48321	.52274	.57136	.59713
Qatar riyal	453	4.9998	5.3139	5.4108	5.2342	4.9113	5.1252	4.9999	4.7426	4.5754	4.9487	5.4089	5.6530
Saudi Arabian riyal	456	5.1509	5.4744	5.5743	5.3924	5.0597	5.2801	5.1469	4.8859	4.7127	5.0982	5.5724	5.8238
Syrian pound	463	15.418	16.387	16.686	16.141	15.145	15.805	15.406	14.625	14.107	15.261	16.680	17.433
U.A.Emirates dirham	466	5.0423	5.3591	5.4569	5.2788	4.9551	5.1710	5.0405	4.7849	4.6153	4.9928	5.4572	5.7034
Yemen,Rep.,Yemeni rial	474	16.496	17.533	† 74.384	† 182.492	176.023	199.447	218.366	215.749	217.754	243.368	273.879	288.658
Western Hemisphere													
Anguilla, E.Caribbean dollar	312	3.7086	3.9416	4.0135	3.8825	3.6430	3.8017	3.7058	3.5179	3.3932	3.6707	4.0121	4.1931
Antigua & Barbuda,E.Car.dollar	311	3.7086	3.9416	4.0135	3.8825	3.6430	3.8017	3.7058	3.5179	3.3932	3.6707	4.0121	4.1931
Argentine peso	213	1.37150	1.45912	1.48649	1.43724	1.34858	1.40733	1.37182	1.30226	1.25610	4.51361	4.31674	4.59536
Aruban florin	314	2.4587	2.6131	2.6608	2.5739	2.4152	2.5204	2.4568	2.3322	2.2495	2.4335	2.6599	2.7799
Bahamian dollar	313	1.3736	1.4599	1.4865	1.4380	1.3493	1.4080	1.3725	1.3029	1.2567	1.3595	1.4860	1.5530
Barbados dollar	316	2.7471	2.9197	2.9730	2.8759	2.6985	2.8161	2.7450	2.6058	2.5135	2.7190	2.9719	3.1060
Belize dollar	339	2.7471	2.9197	2.9730	2.8759	2.6985	2.8161	2.7450	2.6058	2.5135	2.7190	2.9719	3.1060
Bolivia, boliviano	218	6.14668	6.85400	7.33583	7.45582	7.23873	7.94833	8.22133	8.32559	8.57090	10.18280	11.63515	12.50173
Brazilian real	223	.16288	† 1.23503	1.44635	1.49462	1.50630	1.70189	2.45542	2.54667	2.91612	4.80250	4.29208	4.12107
Chilean peso	228	592.06	589.91	605.19	611.09	593.41	667.08	727.53	746.15	824.67	968.49	890.72	869.42
Colombian peso	233	1,260.01	1,213.53	1,468.13	1,445.62	1,745.36	2,122.63	2,571.77	2,849.49	2,892.15	3,894.74	4,132.22	3,746.02
Costa Rican colon	238	208.01	240.98	289.72	316.51	329.61	382.17	409.27	414.35	429.39	514.88	621.92	712.23

Exchange Rates

		1993	1994	1995	1996	1997	1998	1999	2000	2001	2002	2003	2004
						Market, Official, or Principal Rate							
						National Currency Units per SDR: End of Period (aa)							
Western Hemisphere(Cont.)													
Dominica, E.Caribbean dollar.........	321	3.7086	3.9416	4.0135	3.8825	3.6430	3.8017	3.7058	3.5179	3.3932	3.6707	4.0121	4.1931
Dominican peso...........................	243	17.536	19.071	20.015	20.220	19.383	22.230	22.014	21.725	21.551	28.813	55.352	48.313
Ecuadoran sucre...........................	248	2,807.3	3,312.4	4,345.8	5,227.0	5,974.5	9,609.8	27,783.7	32,572.8	31,418.3	33,988.0	37,149.3	38,825.3
Salvadoran colon.........................	253	11.9088	12.7737	13.0142	12.5893	11.8127	12.3273	12.0163	11.4070	10.9964	11.8958	13.0022	13.5888
Grenada, E.Caribbean dollar.........	328	3.7086	3.9416	4.0135	3.8825	3.6430	3.8017	3.7058	3.5179	3.3932	3.6707	4.0121	4.1931
Guatemalan quetzal......................	258	7.9876	8.2460	8.9810	8.5782	8.3342	9.6425	10.7342	10.0731	10.0544	10.6140	11.9482	12.0334
Guyana dollar..............................	336	179.593	208.029	208.852	203.112	194.292	228.453	247.738	240.713	238.150	260.688	288.650	310.214
Haitian gourde.............................	263	17.5884	18.9001	24.0215	21.7028	23.3569	23.2390	24.6577	29.3470	33.1009	51.1305	62.5369	57.8214
Honduran lempira.........................	268	9.9720	13.7227	15.3751	18.5057	17.6673	19.4415	19.9067	19.7270	20.0068	23.0076	26.3733	28.9369
Jamaica dollar.............................	343	44.6057	48.4692	58.8894	50.1351	49.0326	52.1744	56.6719	59.1715	59.4257	69.0115	89.9266	95.4325
Mexican peso...............................	273	4.2661	7.7737	11.3605	11.2893	10.9064	13.8902	13.0585	12.4717	11.4894	14.0201	16.6964	17.4943
Montserrat, E.Caribbean dollar......	351	3.7086	3.9416	4.0135	3.8825	3.6430	3.8017	3.7058	3.5179	3.3932	3.6707	4.0121	4.1931
Netherlands Antilles guilder...........	353	2.4587	2.6131	2.6608	2.5739	2.4152	2.5204	2.4568	2.3322	2.2495	2.4335	2.6599	2.7799
Nicaraguan gold córdoba..............	278	8.722	10.382	11.840	12.832	13.486	15.761	16.907	17.012	17.394	19.946	23.109	25.359
Panamanian balboa......................	283	1.3736	1.4599	1.4865	1.4380	1.3493	1.4080	1.3725	1.3029	1.2567	1.3595	1.4860	1.5530
Paraguayan guarani......................	288	2,582.3	2,809.8	2,942.7	3,033.6	3,184.2	3,999.1	4,568.9	4,595.2	5,884.0	9,657.5	9,086.6	9,706.3
Peruvian new sol..........................	293	2.96689	3.18247	3.43379	3.73870	3.68345	4.44937	4.81751	4.59536	4.32818	4.77735	5.14591	5.09620
St.Kitts & Nevis, E.C. dollar...........	361	3.7086	3.9416	4.0135	3.8825	3.6430	3.8017	3.7058	3.5179	3.3932	3.6707	4.0121	4.1931
St.Lucia, E.Caribbean dollar...........	362	3.7086	3.9416	4.0135	3.8825	3.6430	3.8017	3.7058	3.5179	3.3932	3.6707	4.0121	4.1931
St. Vinc. & Grens., E. Carib. dollar..	364	3.7086	3.9416	4.0135	3.8825	3.6430	3.8017	3.7058	3.5179	3.3932	3.6707	4.0121	4.1931
Surinamese dollar........................	366	.002	† .598	.605	.577	.541	.565	1.355	2.838	2.738	3.419	† 3.901	† 4.216
Trinidad & Tobago dollar...............	369	7.9860	8.6616	8.9146	8.9074	8.5001	9.2881	8.6467	8.2078	7.9051	8.5648	9.3615	9.7838
Uruguayan peso............................	298	† 6.0656	8.1766	10.5704	12.5289	13.5465	15.2307	15.9417	16.3059	18.5594	36.9789	43.5389	40.9218
Venezuelan bolivar.......................	299	145.102	† 248.175	431.082	685.188	680.359	794.833	889.730	911.711	958.885	1,905.027	2,374.580	2,978.673

Fund Accounts: Position to Date

(As of July 31, 2005 and Expressed in Millions of SDRs)

		Quota	Reserve Position in the Fund	Total Fund Credit and Loans Outstanding				Fund Holdings of Currency		SDR Department		
				Total Amount	Percent of Quota	Outstanding Purchases (GRA)	Outstanding Loans	Amount	Percent of Quota	Net Cumulative Allocation	Holdings of SDR	
											Amount	Percent of Allocation
		(1)	(2)	(3)	(4)	(5)	(6)	(7)	(8)	(9)	(10)	(11)
All Countries	010	**213,478.4**	**43,108.7**	**49,802.6**	**23.3**	**43,229.5**	**6,573.2**	**213,602.1**	**100.1**	**21,433.3**	**20,681.7**	**96.5**
Industrial Countries	110	**130,566.6**	**32,322.2**	—	—	—	—	**98,244.6**	**75.2**	**14,595.3**	**14,165.7**	**97.1**
United States	111	37,149.3	9,255.7	—	—	—	—	27,892.7	75.1	4,899.5	7,718.7	157.5
Canada	156	6,369.2	1,447.4	—	—	—	—	4,921.8	77.3	779.3	613.2	78.7
Australia	193	3,236.4	854.7	—	—	—	—	2,381.8	73.6	470.5	131.5	27.9
Japan	158	13,312.8	3,122.9	—	—	—	—	10,190.6	76.5	891.7	1,800.8	201.9
New Zealand	196	894.6	245.1	—	—	—	—	649.5	72.6	141.3	23.2	16.4
Austria	122	1,872.3	516.7	—	—	—	—	1,355.6	72.4	179.0	100.9	56.4
Belgium	124	4,605.2	1,086.7	—	—	—	—	3,518.5	76.4	485.2	196.2	40.4
Denmark	128	1,642.8	433.5	—	—	—	—	1,209.3	73.6	178.9	26.5	14.8
Finland	172	1,263.8	330.4	—	—	—	—	933.4	73.9	142.7	94.7	66.4
France	132	10,738.5	2,892.5	—	—	—	—	7,846.0	73.1	1,079.9	590.0	54.6
Germany	134	13,008.2	2,843.6	—	—	—	—	10,164.7	78.1	1,210.8	1,327.0	109.6
Greece	174	823.0	242.6	—	—	—	—	580.4	70.5	103.5	19.0	18.3
Iceland	176	117.6	18.6	—	—	—	—	99.0	84.2	16.4	—	.2
Ireland	178	838.4	220.7	—	—	—	—	617.8	73.7	87.3	59.6	68.3
Italy	136	7,055.5	1,783.5	—	—	—	—	5,272.1	74.7	702.4	137.1	19.5
Luxembourg	137	279.1	73.5	—	—	—	—	205.6	73.7	17.0	10.7	62.8
Netherlands	138	5,162.4	1,235.5	—	—	—	—	3,926.9	76.1	530.3	501.3	94.5
Norway	142	1,671.7	496.2	—	—	—	—	1,175.5	70.3	167.8	202.3	120.6
Portugal	182	867.4	228.6	—	—	—	—	638.9	73.7	53.3	69.2	129.7
San Marino	135	17.0	4.1	—	—	—	—	12.9	75.9	—	.6	—
Spain	184	3,048.9	764.3	—	—	—	—	2,284.6	74.9	298.8	224.7	75.2
Sweden	144	2,395.5	657.5	—	—	—	—	1,738.0	72.6	246.5	101.9	41.3
Switzerland	146	3,458.5	1,029.8	—	—	—	—	2,428.6	70.2	—	15.2	—
United Kingdom	112	10,738.5	2,538.1	—	—	—	—	8,200.5	76.4	1,913.1	201.6	10.5
Developing Countries	200	**82,911.8**	**10,786.5**	**49,802.6**	**60.1**	**43,229.5**	**6,573.2**	**115,357.5**	**139.1**	**6,838.1**	**6,515.9**	**95.3**
Africa	605	**11,498.1**	**293.7**	**4,769.5**	**41.5**	**1,086.8**	**3,682.7**	**12,291.7**	**106.9**	**1,382.5**	**433.0**	**31.3**
Algeria	612	1,254.7	85.1	295.4	23.5	295.4	—	1,465.1	116.8	128.6	8.5	6.6
Angola	614	286.3	—	—	—	—	....	286.4	100.1	—	.1	—
Benin	638	61.9	2.2	37.8	61.0	—	37.8	59.7	96.5	9.4	.1	1.1
Botswana	616	63.0	16.3	—	—	—	—	46.7	74.1	4.4	35.0	802.4
Burkina Faso	748	60.2	7.3	74.4	123.6	—	74.4	52.9	87.8	9.4	.1	.5
Burundi	618	77.0	.4	33.6	43.6	—	33.6	76.6	99.5	13.7	.1	.9
Cameroon	622	185.7	.7	202.1	108.8	—	202.1	185.0	99.6	24.5	.3	1.2
Cape Verde	624	9.6	—	8.6	90.0	—	8.6	9.6	100.0	.6	—	2.5
Central African Rep.	626	55.7	.2	25.1	45.1	5.6	19.5	61.1	109.7	9.3	.1	1.6
Chad	628	56.0	.3	60.5	108.0	—	60.5	55.7	99.5	9.4	1.5	16.0
Comoros	632	8.9	.5	—	—	—	—	8.4	93.9	.7	—	.2
Congo, Dem. Rep. of	636	533.0	—	526.8	98.8	—	526.8	533.0	100.0	86.3	1.9	2.2
Congo, Republic of	634	84.6	.5	13.3	15.7	2.6	10.6	86.7	102.5	9.7	.1	1.0
Côte d'Ivoire	662	325.2	.6	166.7	51.3	—	166.7	324.6	99.8	37.8	.3	.9
Djibouti	611	15.9	1.1	13.4	84.0	—	13.4	14.8	93.1	1.2	.3	27.8
Equatorial Guinea	642	32.6	—	—	—	—	—	32.6	100.0	5.8	.4	7.6
Eritrea	643	15.9	—	—	—	—	—	15.9	100.0	—	—	—
Ethiopia	644	133.7	7.2	115.0	86.0	—	115.0	126.5	94.6	11.2	.1	.9
Gabon	646	154.3	.2	54.3	35.2	54.3	—	208.5	135.1	14.1	.8	5.5
Gambia, The	648	31.1	1.5	14.9	48.0	—	14.9	29.6	95.2	5.1	.2	3.1
Ghana	652	369.0	—	307.1	83.2	—	307.1	369.0	100.0	63.0	1.4	2.2
Guinea	656	107.1	.1	69.7	65.1	—	69.7	107.0	99.9	17.6	—	—
Guinea-Bissau	654	14.2	—	8.7	61.3	—	8.7	14.2	100.0	1.2	.4	35.5
Kenya	664	271.4	12.7	113.6	41.9	—	113.6	258.7	95.3	37.0	.5	1.2
Lesotho	666	34.9	3.6	24.5	70.2	—	24.5	31.3	89.8	3.7	.4	10.4
Liberia	668	71.3	—	223.7	313.7	200.8	22.9	272.1	381.6	21.0	—	—
Madagascar	674	122.2	—	151.3	123.9	—	151.3	122.2	100.0	19.3	.2	1.1
Malawi	676	69.4	2.3	54.4	78.5	17.4	37.1	84.5	121.7	11.0	.4	4.1
Mali	678	93.3	9.1	84.7	90.8	—	84.7	84.2	90.3	15.9	.3	1.6
Mauritania	682	64.4	—	52.0	80.7	—	52.0	64.4	100.0	9.7	.1	1.1
Mauritius	684	101.6	22.9	—	—	—	—	78.7	77.5	15.7	17.7	112.6
Morocco	686	588.2	70.4	—	—	—	—	517.8	88.0	85.7	63.5	74.2
Mozambique	688	113.6	—	121.0	106.5	—	121.0	113.6	100.0	—	.1	—
Namibia	728	136.5	.1	—	—	—	—	136.4	100.0	—	.1	—
Niger	692	65.8	8.6	81.4	123.7	—	81.4	57.2	87.0	9.4	.2	1.6
Nigeria	694	1,753.2	.1	—	—	—	—	1,753.1	100.0	157.2	1.2	.7
Rwanda	714	80.1	—	56.6	70.7	—	56.6	80.1	100.0	13.7	18.5	135.4
São Tomé & Príncipe	716	7.4	—	1.9	25.7	—	1.9	7.4	100.0	.6	—	.9
Senegal	722	161.8	1.6	111.2	68.7	—	111.2	160.3	99.0	24.5	.5	2.1
Seychelles	718	8.8	—	—	—	—	—	8.8	100.0	.4	—	1.0
Sierra Leone	724	103.7	—	137.2	132.3	—	137.2	103.7	100.0	17.5	23.3	133.4
Somalia	726	44.2	—	112.0	253.4	96.7	15.3	140.9	318.8	13.7	—	—
South Africa	199	1,868.5	.6	—	—	—	—	1,867.9	100.0	220.4	222.8	101.1
Sudan	732	169.7	—	369.9	218.0	310.6	59.2	480.4	283.1	52.2	.4	.8
Swaziland	734	50.7	6.6	—	—	—	—	44.1	87.1	6.4	2.5	38.5
Tanzania	738	198.9	10.0	257.0	129.2	—	257.0	188.9	95.0	31.4	.2	.8
Togo	742	73.4	.3	10.9	14.8	—	10.9	73.1	99.5	11.0	.1	.8
Tunisia	744	286.5	20.2	—	—	—	—	266.3	92.9	34.2	1.3	3.8
Uganda	746	180.5	—	106.7	59.1	—	106.7	180.5	100.0	29.4	.5	1.6
Zambia	754	489.1	—	493.4	100.9	—	493.4	489.1	100.0	68.3	26.5	38.8
Zimbabwe	698	353.4	.3	178.5	50.5	103.3	75.2	456.4	129.1	10.2	.1	.7

Fund Accounts: Position to Date

(As of July 31, 2005 and Expressed in Millions of SDRs)

		Quota	Reserve Position in the Fund	Total Fund Credit and Loans Outstanding				Fund Holdings of Currency		SDR Department	Holdings of SDR	
				Total Amount	Percent of Quota	Outstanding Purchases (GRA)	Outstanding Loans	Amount	Percent of Quota	Net Cumulative Allocation	Amount	Percent of Allocation
		(1)	(2)	(3)	(4)	(5)	(6)	(7)	(8)	(9)	(10)	(11)
Asia	**505**	**22,046.8**	**4,189.8**	**8,033.2**	**36.4**	**6,483.8**	**1,549.4**	**24,341.3**	**110.4**	**2,043.7**	**1,461.8**	**71.5**
Afghanistan, I.S. of.	512	161.9	—	—	—	—	—	161.9	100.0	26.7	.2	.7
Bangladesh	513	533.3	.2	215.8	40.5	—	215.8	533.1	100.0	47.1	.4	.8
Bhutan	514	6.3	1.0	—	—	—	—	5.3	83.8	—	.3	—
Brunei Darussalam	516	215.2	58.3	—	—	—	—	157.1	73.0	—	9.5	—
Cambodia	522	87.5	—	59.1	67.5	—	59.1	87.5	100.0	15.4	.1	.9
China,P.R.: Mainland	924	6,369.2	1,641.3	—	—	—	—	4,727.9	74.2	236.8	841.5	355.4
China,P.R.:Hong Kong	532	....		....	....	....	—	....	....	....	....	....
Fiji	819	70.3	15.3	—	—	—	—	55.0	78.3	7.0	5.5	78.5
India	534	4,158.2	982.4	—	—	—	—	3,175.8	76.4	681.2	2.9	.4
Indonesia	536	2,079.3	145.5	5,849.6	281.3	5,849.6	—	7,783.4	374.3	239.0	64.0	26.8
Kiribati	826	5.6	—	—	—	—	....	5.6	100.0	—	—	—
Korea	542	1,633.6	463.3	—	—	—	—	1,170.3	71.6	72.9	25.8	35.4
Lao People's Dem.Rep.	544	52.9	—	22.2	42.0	—	22.2	52.9	100.0	9.4	9.9	105.3
Malaysia	548	1,486.6	390.9	—	—	—	—	1,095.7	73.7	139.0	132.9	95.6
Maldives	556	8.2	1.6	4.1	50.0	4.1	—	10.7	131.1	.3	.3	111.7
Marshall Islands,Rep.	867	3.5	—	—	—	—	—	3.5	100.0	—	—	—
Micronesia, Fed.Sts.	868	5.1	—	—	—	—	—	5.1	100.0	—	1.2	—
Mongolia	948	51.1	.1	26.2	51.3	—	26.2	51.0	99.7	—	—	—
Myanmar	518	258.4	—	—	—	—	—	258.4	100.0	43.5	.3	.8
Nepal	558	71.3	—	14.3	20.0	—	14.3	71.3	100.0	8.1	6.2	76.6
Pakistan	564	1,033.7	—	1,087.8	105.2	74.7	1,013.1	1,108.3	107.2	170.0	155.3	91.4
Palau	565	3.1	.1	—	—	—	—	3.1	100.0	—	—	—
Papua New Guinea	853	131.6	.4	4.7	3.6	4.7	—	135.9	103.3	9.3	.2	2.1
Philippines	566	879.9	87.5	322.3	36.6	322.3	—	1,114.7	126.7	116.6	4.7	4.1
Samoa	862	11.6	.7	—	—	—	—	10.9	94.1	1.1	2.4	213.9
Singapore	576	862.5	226.9	—	—	—	—	635.7	73.7	16.5	193.7	1,175.8
Solomon Islands	813	10.4	.6	—	—	—	—	9.9	94.7	.7	—	.9
Sri Lanka	524	413.4	47.9	266.8	64.5	228.4	38.4	593.9	143.7	70.9	2.0	2.9
Thailand	578	1,081.9	121.6	—	—	—	—	960.3	88.8	84.7	.5	.5
Timor-Leste	537	8.2	—	—	—	—	—	8.2	100.0	—	—	—
Tonga	866	6.9	1.7	—	—	—	—	5.2	75.2	—	.3	—
Vanuatu	846	17.0	2.5	—	—	—	—	14.5	85.3	—	1.0	—
Vietnam	582	329.1	—	160.4	48.8	—	160.4	329.1	100.0	47.7	.7	1.5
Europe	**170**	**17,270.1**	**1,199.1**	**15,336.2**	**88.8**	**14,614.2**	**722.0**	**30,685.4**	**177.7**	**374.1**	**464.0**	**124.0**
Albania	914	48.7	3.4	62.6	128.6	—	62.6	45.4	93.1	—	65.7	—
Armenia	911	92.0	—	131.1	142.5	—	131.1	92.0	100.0	—	—	—
Azerbaijan, Republic of	912	160.9	—	122.8	76.3	28.3	94.5	189.2	117.6	—	2.3	—
Belarus	913	386.4	—	—	—	—	—	386.4	100.0	—	—	—
Bosnia & Herzegovina	963	169.1	—	57.3	33.9	57.3	—	226.4	133.9	20.5	.9	4.2
Bulgaria	918	640.2	32.9	683.3	106.7	683.3	—	1,290.5	201.6	—	7.9	—
Croatia	960	365.1	.2	—	—	—	—	364.9	100.0	44.2	.6	1.4
Cyprus	423	139.6	37.0	—	—	—	—	102.6	73.5	19.4	2.7	14.1
Czech Republic	935	819.3	215.4	—	—	—	—	603.9	73.7	—	5.9	—
Estonia	939	65.2	—	—	—	—	—	65.2	100.0	—	.1	—
Georgia	915	150.3	—	165.7	110.3	—	165.7	150.3	100.0	—	7.3	—
Hungary	944	1,038.4	299.8	—	—	—	—	738.6	71.1	—	41.1	—
Kazakhstan	916	365.7	—	—	—	—	—	365.7	100.0	—	.8	—
Kyrgyz Republic	917	88.8	—	132.1	148.7	—	132.1	88.8	100.0	—	11.5	—
Latvia	941	126.8	.1	—	—	—	—	126.8	100.0	—	.1	—
Lithuania	946	144.2	—	—	—	—	—	144.2	100.0	—	.1	—
Macedonia, FYR	962	68.9	—	36.3	52.7	21.0	15.4	89.9	130.4	8.4	1.2	13.9
Malta	181	102.0	40.3	—	—	—	—	61.7	60.5	11.3	31.4	278.1
Moldova	921	123.2	—	70.7	57.4	43.0	27.7	166.2	134.9	—	.1	—
Poland	964	1,369.0	360.6	—	—	—	—	1,008.4	73.7	—	50.0	—
Romania	968	1,030.2	—	223.1	21.7	223.1	—	1,253.3	121.7	76.0	3.2	4.2
Russia	922	5,945.4	33.0	—	—	—	—	5,912.5	99.4	—	3.9	—
Serbia & Montenegro	965	467.7	—	660.5	141.2	660.5	—	1,128.2	241.2	56.7	15.0	26.5
Slovak Republic	936	357.5	—	—	—	—	—	357.5	100.0	—	.9	—
Slovenia	961	231.7	63.6	—	—	—	—	168.1	72.6	25.4	7.7	30.2
Tajikistan	923	87.0	—	92.9	106.8	—	92.9	87.0	100.0	—	14.9	—
Turkey	186	964.0	112.8	11,978.9	1,242.6	11,978.9	—	12,830.2	1,330.9	112.3	179.3	159.6
Turkmenistan	925	75.2	—	—	—	—	—	75.2	100.0	—	—	—
Ukraine	926	1,372.0	—	914.7	66.7	914.7	—	2,286.7	166.7	—	9.4	—
Uzbekistan	927	275.6	—	4.2	1.5	4.2	—	279.8	101.5	—	.1	—
Middle East	**405**	**16,162.9**	**3,435.8**	**705.4**	**4.4**	**514.2**	**191.2**	**13,242.1**	**81.9**	**986.5**	**1,745.5**	**176.9**
Bahrain, Kingdom of	419	135.0	71.2	—	—	—	—	63.8	47.3	6.2	.9	14.5
Egypt	469	943.7	—	—	—	—	—	943.7	100.0	135.9	65.6	48.3
Iran, I.R. of	429	1,497.2	—	—	—	—	—	1,497.2	100.0	244.1	274.3	112.4
Iraq	433	1,188.4	171.1	297.1	25.0	297.1	—	1,314.4	110.6	68.5	295.5	431.7
Israel	436	928.2	262.2	—	—	—	—	666.0	71.8	106.4	11.6	10.9
Jordan	439	170.5	.1	187.0	109.6	187.0	—	357.4	209.6	16.9	2.2	13.1
Kuwait	443	1,381.1	382.8	—	—	—	—	998.3	72.3	26.7	122.9	459.5
Lebanon	446	203.0	18.8	—	—	—	—	184.2	90.7	4.4	21.6	490.9
Libya	672	1,123.7	395.5	—	—	—	—	728.2	64.8	58.8	484.4	824.2
Oman	449	194.0	51.7	—	—	—	—	142.3	73.4	6.3	9.7	154.3
Qatar	453	263.8	74.1	—	—	—	—	189.7	71.9	12.8	24.4	190.6
Saudi Arabia	456	6,985.5	1,841.3	—	—	—	—	5,144.2	73.6	195.5	359.6	183.9

Fund Accounts: Position to Date

(As of July 31, 2005 and Expressed in Millions of SDRs)

		Quota	Reserve Position in the Fund	Total Fund Credit and Loans Outstanding				Fund Holdings of Currency		SDR Department		
				Total Amount	Percent of Quota	Outstanding Purchases (GRA)	Outstanding Loans	Amount	Percent of Quota	Net Cumulative Allocation	Holdings of SDR	
											Amount	Percent of Allocation
		(1)	(2)	(3)	(4)	(5)	(6)	(7)	(8)	(9)	(10)	(11)
Middle East(Cont.)												
Syrian Arab Republic	463	293.6	—	—	—	—	—	293.6	100.0	36.6	36.6	100.0
United Arab Emirates	466	611.7	167.0	—	—	—	—	445.3	72.8	38.7	5.2	13.3
Yemen, Republic of	474	243.5	—	221.3	90.9	30.2	191.2	273.7	112.4	28.7	31.1	108.1
Western Hemisphere	**205**	**15,933.9**	**1,668.1**	**20,958.3**	**131.5**	**20,530.4**	**427.9**	**34,797.0**	**218.4**	**2,051.3**	**2,411.6**	**117.6**
Antigua and Barbuda	311	13.5	—	—	—	—	—	13.5	100.0	—	—	—
Argentina	213	2,117.1	.2	7,594.6	358.7	7,594.6	—	9,711.5	458.7	318.4	1,559.4	489.8
Bahamas, The	313	130.3	6.3	—	—	—	—	124.0	95.2	10.2	.1	1.1
Barbados	316	67.5	5.3	—	—	—	—	62.3	92.3	8.0	.1	.8
Belize	339	18.8	4.2	—	—	—	—	14.6	77.5	—	1.7	—
Bolivia	218	171.5	8.9	190.2	110.9	106.1	84.1	268.8	156.7	26.7	27.0	101.1
Brazil	223	3,036.1	—	10,789.1	355.4	10,789.1	—	13,825.7	455.4	358.7	204.8	57.1
Chile	228	856.1	228.4	—	—	—	—	627.7	73.3	121.9	35.5	29.1
Colombia	233	774.0	285.8	—	—	—	—	488.2	63.1	114.3	117.6	102.9
Costa Rica	238	164.1	20.0	—	—	—	—	144.1	87.8	23.7	.1	.6
Dominica	321	8.2	—	7.2	87.5	3.0	4.2	11.2	136.2	.6	—	7.4
Dominican Republic	243	218.9	—	183.9	84.0	183.9	—	402.8	184.0	31.6	2.4	7.7
Ecuador	248	302.3	17.2	98.0	32.4	98.0	—	383.1	126.7	32.9	1.6	4.9
El Salvador	253	171.3	—	—	—	—	—	171.3	100.0	25.0	25.0	100.0
Grenada	328	11.7	—	5.9	50.1	5.9	—	17.6	150.1	.9	—	1.7
Guatemala	258	210.2	—	—	—	—	—	210.2	100.0	27.7	4.9	17.6
Guyana	336	90.9	—	58.8	64.7	—	58.8	90.9	100.0	14.5	1.7	11.8
Haiti	263	81.9	.1	14.8	18.0	10.2	4.6	92.1	112.4	13.7	.1	1.1
Honduras	268	129.5	8.6	126.2	97.5	—	126.2	120.9	93.3	19.1	.2	1.1
Jamaica	343	273.5	—	—	—	—	—	273.5	100.0	40.6	.5	1.3
Mexico	273	2,585.8	631.0	—	—	—	—	1,954.9	75.6	290.0	304.8	105.1
Nicaragua	278	130.0	—	150.0	115.4	—	150.0	130.0	100.0	19.5	2.0	10.4
Panama	283	206.6	11.9	20.0	9.7	20.0	—	214.8	103.9	26.3	.6	2.3
Paraguay	288	99.9	21.5	—	—	—	—	78.4	78.5	13.7	87.1	635.5
Peru	293	638.4	—	53.5	8.4	53.5	—	691.9	108.4	91.3	1.2	1.3
St. Kitts and Nevis	361	8.9	.1	—	—	—	—	8.8	99.1	—	—	—
St. Lucia	362	15.3	—	—	—	—	—	15.3	100.0	.7	1.5	204.1
St. Vincent & Grens	364	8.3	.5	—	—	—	—	7.8	94.0	.4	—	.9
Suriname	366	92.1	6.1	—	—	—	—	86.0	93.4	7.8	1.1	14.8
Trinidad and Tobago	369	335.6	90.3	—	—	—	—	245.3	73.1	46.2	2.2	4.9
Uruguay	298	306.5	—	1,666.3	543.6	1,666.3	—	1,972.8	643.6	50.0	23.8	47.7
Venezuela, Rep. Bol.	299	2,659.1	321.9	—	—	—	—	2,337.2	87.9	316.9	4.5	1.4
Memorandum Items												
Oil Exporting Ctys	**999**	**20,991.7**	**3,636.1**	**6,442.1**	**30.7**	**6,442.1**	**—**	**23,798.5**	**113.4**	**1,493.0**	**1,654.1**	**110.8**
Non-Oil Develop.Ctys.	**201**	**61,920.1**	**7,150.4**	**43,360.5**	**70.0**	**36,787.3**	**6,573.2**	**91,559.0**	**147.9**	**5,345.1**	**4,861.9**	**91.0**

Financing Components of Members' Outstanding Obligations to the Fund

(As of July 31, 2005 and Expressed in Millions of SDRs)

		Total Fund Credit and Loans Outstanding	Outstanding Purchases (GRA)									SAF Arrangements	PRGF Arrangements		Trust Fund
			Total Amount	Ordinary Resources				Borrower Resources				SDA Resources	SDA Resources	PRGF Trust Resources	Administered Accounts
				CCFF	STF	Stand-by/ Credit Tranche	Extended Fund Facility	SFF	EAR	GAB	NAB				
		(1)	(2)	(3)	(4)	(5)	(6)	(7)	(8)	(9)	(10)	(11)	(12)	(13)	(14)
All Countries	010	49,802.6	43,229.5	82.8	6.6	33,695.5	9,072.6	99.8	272.6	—	—	27.0	—	6,457.6	88.6
Industrial Countries	110	—	—	—	....	—	—	—	—	—	—	—	....	....	—
Developing Countries	200	49,802.6	43,229.5	82.8	6.6	33,695.5	9,072.6	99.8	272.6	—	—	27.0	—	6,457.6	88.6
Africa	605	4,769.5	1,086.8	82.8	....	219.1	412.9	99.8	272.6	—	—	27.0	—	3,567.1	88.6
Algeria	612	295.4	295.4	—	....	—	295.4	....	....	—	—	—	....	—	....
Angola	614	—	—	—	....	—	—	....	....	—	—	—	....	—	....
Benin	638	37.8	—	....	....	—	—	....	....	—	—	—	—	37.8	—
Botswana	616	—	—	—	....	—	—	....	....	—	—	—	....	—	....
Burkina Faso	748	74.4	—	....	....	—	—	....	....	—	—	—	—	74.4	—
Burundi	618	33.6	—	—	....	—	—	....	....	—	—	—	—	33.6	—
Cameroon	622	202.1	—	—	....	—	—	....	....	—	—	—	—	202.1	—
Cape Verde	624	8.6	—	—	....	—	—	....	....	—	—	—	—	8.6	—
Central African Rep.	626	25.1	5.6	—	....	5.6	....	....	....	—	—	—	....	19.5	—
Chad	628	60.5	—	—	....	—	—	....	....	—	—	—	—	60.5	—
Comoros	632	—	—	....	....	—	—	....	....	—	—	—	—	—	....
Congo, Dem. Rep. of	636	526.8	—	—	....	—	—	....	....	—	—	—	—	526.8	—
Congo, Republic of	634	13.3	2.6	—	....	2.6	—	....	....	—	—	—	—	10.6	—
Côte d'Ivoire	662	166.7	—	—	....	—	—	....	....	—	—	—	—	166.7	—
Djibouti	611	13.4	—	....	....	—	—	....	....	—	—	—	....	13.4	....
Equatorial Guinea	642	—	—	—	....	—	—	....	....	—	—	—	—	—	....
Eritrea	643	—	—	....	....	—	—	....	....	—	—	—	—	—	....
Ethiopia	644	115.0	—	—	....	—	—	....	....	—	—	—	—	115.0	—
Gabon	646	54.3	54.3	—	....	43.3	11.0	—	—	—	—	—	—	—	—
Gambia, The	648	14.9	—	—	....	—	—	....	....	—	—	—	—	14.9	....
Ghana	652	307.1	—	—	....	—	—	....	....	—	—	—	—	307.1	—
Guinea	656	69.7	—	—	....	—	—	....	....	—	—	—	—	69.7	—
Guinea-Bissau	654	8.7	—	—	....	—	—	....	....	—	—	—	—	8.7	....
Kenya	664	113.6	—	—	....	....	....	....	....	—	—	—	—	113.6	—
Lesotho	666	24.5	—	—	....	—	—	....	....	—	—	—	—	24.5	—
Liberia	668	223.7	200.8	34.7	....	45.5	....	36.3	84.3	—	—	—	....	—	22.9
Madagascar	674	151.3	—	—	....	—	—	....	....	—	—	—	—	151.3	—
Malawi	676	54.4	17.4	—	....	17.4	—	....	....	—	—	—	—	37.1	—
Mali	678	84.7	—	—	....	—	—	....	....	—	—	—	—	84.7	—
Mauritania	682	52.0	—	—	....	—	—	....	....	—	—	—	—	52.0	—
Mauritius	684	—	—	—	....	—	—	....	....	—	—	—	—	—	—
Morocco	686	—	—	—	....	—	—	....	....	—	—	—	—	—	—
Mozambique	688	121.0	—	....	....	—	—	....	....	—	—	—	—	121.0	—
Namibia	728	—	—	—	....	—	—	....	....	—	—	—	—	—	....
Niger	692	81.4	—	—	....	—	—	....	....	—	—	—	—	81.4	—
Nigeria	694	—	—	....	....	....	....	....	....	—	—	—	—	—	....
Rwanda	714	56.6	—	—	....	....	....	....	....	—	—	—	....	56.6	....
São Tomé & Príncipe	716	1.9	—	....	....	....	....	....	....	—	—	—	—	1.9	—
Senegal	722	111.2	—	—	....	—	—	....	....	—	—	—	—	111.2	—
Seychelles	718	—	—	....	....	—	—	....	....	—	—	—	—	—	—
Sierra Leone	724	137.2	—	—	....	—	—	....	....	—	—	....	—	137.2	....
Somalia	726	112.0	96.7	28.5	....	12.6	....	—	55.5	—	—	8.8	—	—	6.5
South Africa	199	—	—	—	....	—	—	....	....	—	—	—	—	—	—
Sudan	732	369.9	310.6	19.6	....	28.2	67.1	63.5	132.8	—	—	—	—	—	59.2
Swaziland	734	—	—	—	....	....	....	....	....	—	—	—	—	—	—
Tanzania	738	257.0	—	—	....	—	—	—	—	—	—	—	—	257.0	—
Togo	742	10.9	—	—	....	—	—	....	....	—	—	—	—	10.9	—
Tunisia	744	—	—	—	....	—	—	....	....	—	—	—	—	—	—
Uganda	746	106.7	—	—	....	—	—	....	....	—	—	—	—	106.7	....
Zambia	754	493.4	—	—	....	—	—	....	....	—	—	18.2	—	475.3	—
Zimbabwe	698	178.5	103.3	—	....	63.9	39.4	—	—	—	—	—	—	75.2	—
Asia	505	8,033.2	6,483.8	—	—	259.4	6,224.4	—	—	—	—	—	—	1,549.4	—
Afghanistan, I.S. of	512	—	—	—	....	—	—	....	....	—	—	—	....	....	....
Bangladesh	513	215.8	—	—	....	—	—	....	....	—	—	—	—	215.8	....
Bhutan	514	—	—	....	....	—	—	....	....	—	—	—	—	—	—
Brunei Darussalam	516	—	—	—	....	—	—	....	....	—	—	—	—	—	—
Cambodia	522	59.1	—	—	....	—	—	....	....	—	—	—	—	59.1	—
China, People's Rep.	924	—	—	—	....	—	—	....	....	—	—	—	....	....	—
Fiji	819	—	—	—	....	—	—	....	....	—	—	—	—	—	—
India	534	—	—	—	....	—	—	....	....	—	—	—	—	—	—
Indonesia	536	5,849.6	5,849.6	—	—	—	5,849.6	....	....	—	—	—	—	—	—
Kiribati	826	—	—	—	....	—	—	....	....	—	—	—	—	—	—
Korea	542	—	—	—	....	—	—	....	....	—	—	—	—	—	—
Lao People's Dem.Rep.	544	22.2	—	—	....	—	—	....	....	—	—	—	—	22.2	—
Malaysia	548	—	—	—	....	—	—	....	....	—	—	—	—	—	—
Maldives	556	4.1	4.1	....	....	4.1	....	....	....	—	—	—	—	—	—
Marshall Islands,Rep.	867	—	—	....	....	—	—	....	....	—	—	—	—	—	—
Micronesia, Fed.Sts.	868	—	—	—	....	—	—	....	....	—	—	—	—	—	—
Mongolia	948	26.2	—	—	....	—	—	....	....	—	—	—	—	26.2	—
Myanmar	518	—	—	—	....	—	—	....	....	—	—	—	....	....	—
Nepal	558	14.3	—	—	....	—	—	....	....	—	—	—	....	14.3	—
Pakistan	564	1,087.8	74.7	—	....	13.1	61.6	—	—	—	—	—	—	1,013.1	—

Financing Components of Members' Outstanding Obligations to the Fund

(As of July 31, 2005 and Expressed in Millions of SDRs)

Country	Code	Total Fund Credit and Loans Outstanding (1)	Ordinary Resources – Total Amount (2)	CCFF (3)	STF (4)	Stand-by/ Credit Tranche (5)	Extended Fund Facility (6)	SFF (7)	EAR (8)	GAB (9)	NAB (10)	SAF – SDA Resources (11)	PRGF – SDA Resources (12)	PRGF Trust Resources (13)	Trust Fund – Administered Accounts (14)
Asia(Cont.)															
Palau	565	—	—	—	....	—	—	—	—	—	—	....	....	—	—
Papua New Guinea	853	4.7	4.7	—	....	4.7	—	....	—	—	—	....	....	—	—
Philippines	566	322.3	322.3	—	....	29.7	292.6	—	—	—	—	—	—	—	—
Samoa	862	—	—	—	....	—	—	—	—	—	—	—	....	....	—
Singapore	576	—	—	....	....	....	....	....	—	—	—	....	....	....	....
Solomon Islands	813	—	—	—	....	—	—	....	—	—	—	—	—	—	—
Sri Lanka	524	266.8	228.4	—	....	207.7	20.6	—	—	—	—	—	—	38.4	—
Thailand	578	—	—	—	....	—	—	—	—	—	—	....	....	....	—
Tonga	866	—	—	—	....	—	—	—	—	—	—	....	....	....	—
Vanuatu	846	—	—	....	....	....	....	—	—	—	—	—	....	....	—
Vietnam	582	160.4	—	—	—	—	....	—	—	—	—	—	—	160.4	—
Europe	170	15,336.2	14,614.2	—	6.6	12,543.0	2,064.6	—	—	—	—	—	—	722.0	—
Albania	914	62.6	—	—	—	—	—	—	—	—	—	—	—	62.6	—
Armenia	911	131.1	—	—	—	—	—	—	—	—	—	—	....	131.1	—
Azerbaijan, Republic of	912	122.8	28.3	—	2.4	—	25.9	—	—	—	—	—	—	94.5	—
Belarus	913	—	—	—	—	—	....	....	—	—	—	—	....	—	—
Bosnia & Herzegovina	963	57.3	57.3	—	—	57.3	—	—	—	—	—	—	—	—	—
Bulgaria	918	683.3	683.3	—	—	190.8	492.5	—	—	—	—	—	—	—	—
Croatia	960	—	—	—	—	—	—	—	—	—	—	—	....	—	....
Cyprus	423	—	—	....	....	—	—	....	—	—	—	....	....	....	....
Czech Republic	935	—	—	—	....	—	—	—	—	—	—	....	....	—	—
Estonia	939	—	—	—	....	—	—	—	—	—	—	—	....	—	—
Georgia	915	165.7	—	—	—	—	—	—	—	—	—	—	....	165.7	—
Hungary	944	—	—	—	—	—	—	—	—	—	—	—	....	....	—
Kazakhstan	916	—	—	—	....	—	—	....	—	—	—	—	—	—	—
Kyrgyz Republic	917	132.1	—	—	—	—	—	—	—	—	—	—	—	132.1	—
Latvia	941	—	—	—	—	—	—	—	—	—	—	—	—	—	—
Lithuania	946	—	—	—	....	—	—	—	—	—	—	—	—	—	—
Macedonia, FYR	962	36.3	21.0	—	—	20.0	1.0	—	—	—	—	—	—	15.4	—
Malta	181	—	—	....	....	....	....	....	—	—	—	....	....	....	....
Moldova	921	70.7	43.0	—	—	—	43.0	—	—	—	—	—	—	27.7	—
Poland	964	—	—	—	....	—	—	—	—	—	—	....	....	....	....
Romania	968	223.1	223.1	—	—	223.1	—	—	—	—	—	—	—	—	—
Russia	922	—	—	—	—	—	—	—	—	—	—	—	....	....	—
Serbia & Montenegro	965	660.5	660.5	—	—	73.0	587.5	—	—	—	—	—	....	—	—
Slovak Republic	936	—	—	—	—	—	—	—	—	—	—	—	....	—	—
Slovenia	961	—	—	—	—	—	—	—	—	—	—	—	—	—	—
Tajikistan	923	92.9	—	—	....	—	—	—	—	—	—	—	—	92.9	—
Turkey	186	11,978.9	11,978.9	—	—	11,978.9	....	—	—	—	—	—	....	—	—
Turkmenistan	925	—	—	—	—	—	—	—	—	—	—	....	....	....	—
Ukraine	926	914.7	914.7	—	—	—	914.7	—	—	—	—	—	....	—	—
Uzbekistan	927	4.2	4.2	—	4.2	—	—	—	—	—	—	—	....	—	—
Middle East	405	705.4	514.2	—	....	302.4	211.8	....	....	—	—	—	—	—	191.2
Bahrain, Kingdom of	419	—	—	....	....	—	—	....	—	—	—	—	....	....	....
Egypt	469	—	—	....	....	—	—	....	—	—	—	—	....	....	....
Iran, I.R. of	429	—	—	....	....	—	—	....	—	—	—	—	....	....	....
Iraq	433	297.1	297.1	—	....	297.1	....	—	—	—	—	—	—	....	—
Israel	436	—	—	—	....	—	—	—	—	—	—	—	....	....	....
Jordan	439	187.0	187.0	—	....	5.3	181.6	—	—	—	—	—	—	....	—
Kuwait	443	—	—	....	....	....	....	—	—	—	—	—	....	....	....
Lebanon	446	—	—	....	....	—	—	—	—	—	—	—	....	....	....
Libya	672	—	—	....	....	—	—	....	—	—	—	—	....	....	....
Oman	449	—	—	....	....	—	—	—	—	—	—	—	....	....	....
Qatar	453	—	—	....	....	....	....	—	—	—	—	—	....	....	....
Saudi Arabia	456	—	—	....	....	....	....	—	—	—	—	—	....	....	....
Syrian Arab Republic	463	—	—	....	....	—	—	—	—	—	—	—	....	....	....
United Arab Emirates	466	—	—	....	....	—	—	—	—	—	—	—	....	....	....
Yemen, Republic of	474	221.3	30.2	—	....	—	30.2	—	—	—	—	—	....	191.2	—
Western Hemisphere	205	20,958.3	20,530.4	—	....	20,371.6	158.9	—	—	—	—	—	—	—	427.9
Antigua and Barbuda	311	—	—	....	....	—	—	....	—	—	—	....	....	....	....
Argentina	213	7,594.6	7,594.6	—	....	7,509.2	85.4	—	—	—	—	—	—	—	....
Bahamas, The	313	—	—	....	....	....	....	—	—	—	—	—	....	....	....
Barbados	316	—	—	—	....	—	—	....	—	—	—	—	....	....	....
Belize	339	—	—	—	....	—	—	....	—	—	—	....	....	....	....
Bolivia	218	190.2	106.1	—	....	106.1	....	—	—	—	—	—	—	84.1	....
Brazil	223	10,789.1	10,789.1	—	....	10,789.1	—	—	—	—	—	—	—	—	....
Chile	228	—	—	—	....	—	—	....	—	—	—	—	....	....	....
Colombia	233	—	—	—	....	—	—	....	—	—	—	—	....	....	....
Costa Rica	238	—	—	—	....	—	—	....	—	—	—	—	....	....	....
Dominica	321	7.2	3.0	—	—	3.0	—	—	—	—	—	—	—	4.2	—
Dominican Republic	243	183.9	183.9	—	....	183.9	—	—	—	—	—	—	—	—	—
Ecuador	248	98.0	98.0	—	....	98.0	—	—	—	—	—	—	....	....	....
El Salvador	253	—	—	—	....	—	—	....	—	—	—	—	....	....	—
Grenada	328	5.9	5.9	—	....	5.9	—	—	—	—	—	—	—	....	....
Guatemala	258	—	—	—	....	—	—	....	—	—	—	....	....	....	....

Financing Components of Members' Outstanding Obligations to the Fund

(As of July 31, 2005 and Expressed in Millions of SDRs)

		Outstanding Purchases (GRA)									Outstanding Loans			
	Total Fund Credit and Loans Outstanding	Ordinary Resources					Borrower Resources				SAF Arrangements	PRGF Arrangements		Trust Fund
		Total Amount	CCFF	STF	Stand-by/ Credit Tranche	Extended Fund Facility	SFF	EAR	GAB	NAB	SDA Resources	SDA Resources	PRGF Trust Resources	Administered Accounts
	(1)	(2)	(3)	(4)	(5)	(6)	(7)	(8)	(9)	(10)	(11)	(12)	(13)	(14)
Western Hemisphere(C														
Guyana 336	58.8	—	—	....	—	—	—	—	—	—	—	—	58.8	—
Haiti 263	14.8	10.2	—	....	10.2	—	—	—	—	—	—	....	4.6	—
Honduras 268	126.2	—	—	....	—	—	—	—	—	—	....	—	126.2	—
Jamaica 343	—	—	—	....	—	—	—	—	—	—	....	....	....	....
Mexico 273	—	—	—	—	—	—	—	—	—	—	....	....	....	....
Nicaragua 278	150.0	—	—	—	—	....	....	....	—	—	....	....	150.0	....
Panama 283	20.0	20.0	—	....	—	20.0	—	—	—	—	....	....	....	....
Paraguay 288	—	—	....	....	—	—	....	....	—	—	....	....	....	....
Peru 293	53.5	53.5	—	....	—	53.5	—	—	—	—	....	....	....	....
St. Kitts and Nevis .. 361	—	—	....	....	—	—	—	—	—	—	....	....	....	....
St. Lucia 362	—	—	—	....	—	....	....	—	—	—	....	....	....	....
St. Vincent & Grens .. 364	—	—	....	....	—	....	....	—	—	—	....	....	....	....
Suriname 366	—	—	....	....	....	....	—	—	—	—	....	....	....	....
Trinidad and Tobago .. 369	—	—	—	....	....	....	—	—	—	—	....	....	....	....
Uruguay 298	1,666.3	1,666.3	—	....	1,666.3	....	—	—	—	—	....	....	....	....
Venezuela, Rep. Bol .. 299	—	—	....	....	—	....	—	—	—	—	....	....	....	....
Memorandum Items														
Oil Exporting Ctys 999	6,442.1	6,442.1	—	—	297.1	6,145.0	....	—	—	—	—	....	....	....
Non-Oil Develop.Ctys. 201	43,360.5	36,787.3	82.8	6.6	33,398.4	2,927.6	99.8	272.6	—	—	27.0	—	6,457.6	88.6

Purchases

		1993	1994	1995	1996	1997	1998	1999	2000	2001	2002	2003	2004
						Expressed in Millions of SDRs							
World	001	5,042.2	4,979.5	16,967.9	5,271.0	16,112.9	20,586.2	10,010.1	7,178.0	23,761.6	25,237.0	20,323.1	4,170.7
Developing Countries	200	5,042.2	4,979.5	16,967.9	5,271.0	16,112.9	20,586.2	10,010.1	7,178.0	23,761.6	25,237.0	20,323.1	4,170.7
Africa	605	678.8	761.5	1,038.5	556.9	370.1	313.6	266.9	35.6	—	27.0	9.6	47.2
Algeria	612	—	587.5	312.8	512.2	337.6	253.3	223.5	—	—	—	—	—
Angola	614	—	—	—	—	—	—	—	—	—	—	—	—
Benin	638	—	—	—	—	—	—	—	—	—	—	—	—
Burkina Faso	748	—	—	—	—	—	—	—	—	—	—	—	—
Burundi	618	—	—	—	—	—	—	—	—	—	9.6	9.6	—
Cameroon	622	—	21.9	8.5	19.7	—	—	—	—	—	—	—	—
Cape Verde	624	—	—	—	—	—	—	—	—	—	—	—	—
Central African Rep	626	—	10.7	—	—	—	—	—	—	—	—	—	5.6
Chad	628	—	10.3	—	—	—	—	—	—	—	—	—	—
Comoros	632	—	—	—	—	—	—	—	—	—	—	—	—
Congo, Dem. Rep. of	636	—	—	—	—	—	—	—	—	—	—	—	—
Congo, Republic of	634	—	12.5	—	—	—	7.2	—	10.6	—	—	—	—
Côte d'Ivoire	662	—	—	—	—	—	—	—	—	—	—	—	—
Djibouti	611	—	—	—	2.9	1.1	2.3	1.0	—	—	—	—	—
Equatorial Guinea	642	—	—	—	—	—	—	—	—	—	—	—	—
Ethiopia	644	—	—	—	—	—	—	—	—	—	—	—	—
Gabon	646	—	44.7	37.5	22.1	16.6	—	—	13.2	—	—	—	41.7
Gambia, The	648	—	—	—	—	—	—	—	—	—	—	—	—
Ghana	652	47.0	—	—	—	—	—	—	—	—	—	—	—
Guinea	656	—	—	—	—	—	—	—	—	—	—	—	—
Guinea-Bissau	654	—	—	—	—	—	—	2.1	1.4	—	—	—	—
Kenya	664	—	—	—	—	—	—	—	—	—	—	—	—
Lesotho	666	—	—	—	—	—	—	—	—	—	—	—	—
Liberia	668	—	—	—	—	—	—	—	—	—	—	—	—
Madagascar	674	—	—	—	—	—	—	—	—	—	—	—	—
Malawi	676	—	12.7	—	—	—	—	—	—	—	17.4	—	—
Mali	678	—	—	—	—	—	—	—	—	—	—	—	—
Mauritania	682	—	—	—	—	—	—	—	—	—	—	—	—
Mauritius	684	—	—	—	—	—	—	—	—	—	—	—	—
Morocco	686	—	—	—	—	—	—	—	—	—	—	—	—
Mozambique	688	—	—	—	—	—	—	—	—	—	—	—	—
Niger	692	—	11.1	—	—	—	—	—	—	—	—	—	—
Nigeria	694	—	—	—	—	—	—	—	—	—	—	—	—
Rwanda	714	—	—	8.9	—	14.9	—	—	—	—	—	—	—
São Tomé & Príncipe	716	—	—	—	—	—	—	—	—	—	—	—	—
Senegal	722	—	30.9	—	—	—	—	—	—	—	—	—	—
Seychelles	718	—	—	—	—	—	—	—	—	—	—	—	—
Sierra Leone	724	—	—	—	—	—	11.6	15.6	10.4	—	—	—	—
Somalia	726	—	—	—	—	—	—	—	—	—	—	—	—
South Africa	199	614.4	—	—	—	—	—	—	—	—	—	—	—
Sudan	732	—	—	—	—	—	—	—	—	—	—	—	—
Swaziland	734	—	—	—	—	—	—	—	—	—	—	—	—
Tanzania	738	—	—	—	—	—	—	—	—	—	—	—	—
Togo	742	—	—	—	—	—	—	—	—	—	—	—	—
Tunisia	744	—	—	—	—	—	—	—	—	—	—	—	—
Uganda	746	—	—	—	—	—	—	—	—	—	—	—	—
Zambia	754	—	—	651.7	—	—	—	—	—	—	—	—	—
Zimbabwe	698	17.4	19.1	19.1	—	—	39.2	24.7	—	—	—	—	—
Asia	505	755.3	220.2	167.3	109.2	12,801.7	11,259.8	2,236.4	1,267.6	784.7	1,197.6	1,396.9	—
Afghanistan, I.S. of	512	—	—	—	—	—	—	—	—	—	—	—	—
Bangladesh	513	—	—	—	—	—	98.1	—	—	—	—	—	—
Bhutan	514	—	—	—	—	—	—	—	—	—	—	—	—
Cambodia	522	6.3	—	—	—	—	—	—	—	—	—	—	—
China, People's Rep	924	—	—	—	—	—	—	—	—	—	—	—	—
Fiji	819	—	—	—	—	—	—	—	—	—	—	—	—
India	534	462.0	—	—	—	—	—	—	—	—	—	—	—
Indonesia	536	—	—	—	—	2,201.5	4,254.3	1,011.0	851.2	309.7	1,101.0	1,376.2	—
Kiribati	826	—	—	—	—	—	—	—	—	—	—	—	—
Korea	542	—	—	—	—	8,200.0	5,850.0	362.5	—	—	—	—	—
Lao People's Dem.Rep	544	—	—	—	—	—	—	—	—	—	—	—	—
Malaysia	548	—	—	—	—	—	—	—	—	—	—	—	—
Maldives	556	—	—	—	—	—	—	—	—	—	—	—	—
Micronesia, Fed.Sts	868	—	—	—	—	—	—	—	—	—	—	—	—
Mongolia	948	—	—	—	—	—	—	—	—	—	—	—	—
Myanmar	518	—	—	—	—	—	—	—	—	—	—	—	—
Nepal	558	—	—	—	—	—	—	—	—	—	—	—	—
Pakistan	564	88.0	123.2	134.0	107.2	91.5	19.0	409.6	150.0	315.0	—	—	—
Palau	565	—	—	—	—	—	—	—	—	—	—	—	—
Papua New Guinea	853	—	—	33.3	2.0	—	—	—	28.9	56.7	—	—	—
Philippines	566	126.6	36.5	—	—	508.8	538.3	253.3	237.6	—	—	—	—
Samoa	862	—	—	—	—	—	—	—	—	—	—	—	—
Solomon Islands	813	—	—	—	—	—	—	—	—	—	—	—	—
Sri Lanka	524	—	—	—	—	—	—	—	—	103.4	96.7	20.7	—
Thailand	578	—	—	—	—	1,800.0	500.0	200.0	—	—	—	—	—
Vietnam	582	72.5	60.5	—	—	—	—	—	—	—	—	—	—
Europe	170	1,700.0	3,177.1	5,337.2	3,488.2	2,272.3	5,312.9	1,944.9	3,253.3	9,456.6	10,327.5	1,696.3	1,028.3
Albania	914	3.4	—	—	—	8.8	—	—	—	—	—	—	—
Armenia	911	—	16.9	30.4	—	—	—	—	—	—	—	—	—
Azerbaijan, Republic of	912	—	—	67.9	53.8	20.5	15.8	68.6	—	—	—	—	—
Belarus	913	70.1	—	120.1	—	—	—	—	—	—	—	—	—

Purchases

Europe(Cont.)		1993	1994	1995	1996	1997	1998	1999	2000	2001	2002	2003	2004
						Expressed in Millions of SDRs							
Bosnia & Herzegovina	963	—	—	30.3	—	—	24.2	29.0	27.2	14.0	31.6	24.0	12.0
Bulgaria	918	31.0	232.5	—	80.0	355.2	228.9	209.2	209.2	104.6	84.0	104.0	52.0
Croatia	960	—	78.5	65.4	—	28.8	—	—	—	—	—	—	—
Cyprus	423	—	—	—	—	—	—	—	—	—	—	—	—
Czech Republic	935	70.0	—	—	—	—	—	—	—	—	—	—	—
Estonia	939	34.1	—	20.9	—	—	—	—	—	—	—	—	—
Georgia	915	—	27.8	50.0	—	—	—	—	—	—	—	—	—
Hungary	944	56.7	—	—	—	—	—	—	—	—	—	—	—
Kazakhstan	916	61.9	136.1	92.8	92.8	—	154.7	—	—	—	—	—	—
Kyrgyz Republic	917	43.9	—	—	—	—	—	—	—	—	—	—	—
Latvia	941	52.6	32.0	—	—	—	—	—	—	—	—	—	—
Lithuania	946	70.7	46.6	41.4	31.1	41.4	—	—	—	—	—	—	—
Macedonia, FYR	962	—	12.4	24.8	9.9	—	—	13.8	1.1	—	—	12.0	8.0
Moldova	921	63.0	49.5	42.4	22.5	15.0	—	50.0	—	—	—	—	—
Poland	964	—	640.3	—	—	—	—	—	—	—	—	—	—
Romania	968	—	245.1	37.7	—	120.6	—	53.0	86.8	52.0	82.7	165.3	—
Russia	922	1,078.3	1,078.3	3,594.3	2,587.9	1,467.3	4,600.0	471.4	—	—	—	—	—
Serbia & Montenegro	965	—	—	—	—	—	—	—	116.9	100.0	200.0	200.0	162.5
Slovak Republic	936	64.4	96.5	—	—	—	—	—	—	—	—	—	—
Tajikistan	923	—	—	—	15.0	7.5	7.5	—	—	—	—	—	—
Turkey	186	—	235.5	225.0	—	—	—	583.2	2,622.1	8,895.2	9,929.2	1,191.0	793.8
Ukraine	926	—	249.3	788.0	536.0	207.3	281.8	466.6	190.1	290.8	—	—	—
Uzbekistan	927	—	—	106.0	59.3	—	—	—	—	—	—	—	—
Middle East	**405**	**11.1**	**65.6**	**75.8**	**166.2**	**154.0**	**32.7**	**77.4**	**15.2**	**37.0**	**71.6**	**—**	**297.1**
Bahrain, Kingdom of	419	—	—	—	—	—	—	—	—	—	—	—	—
Egypt	469	—	—	—	—	—	—	—	—	—	—	—	—
Iran, I.R. of	429	—	—	—	—	—	—	—	—	—	—	—	—
Iraq	433	—	—	—	—	—	—	—	—	—	—	—	297.1
Israel	436	—	—	—	—	—	—	—	—	—	—	—	—
Jordan	439	11.1	65.6	75.8	82.2	96.7	23.7	55.4	15.2	30.5	71.6	—	—
Lebanon	446	—	—	—	—	—	—	—	—	—	—	—	—
Syrian Arab Republic	463	—	—	—	—	—	—	—	—	—	—	—	—
Yemen, Republic of	474	—	—	—	84.0	57.4	9.0	22.0	—	6.5	—	—	—
Western Hemisphere	**205**	**1,896.9**	**755.1**	**10,349.1**	**950.6**	**514.7**	**3,667.2**	**5,484.5**	**2,606.3**	**13,483.5**	**13,613.3**	**17,220.2**	**2,798.0**
Antigua and Barbuda	311	—	—	—	—	—	—	—	—	—	—	—	—
Argentina	213	1,154.8	612.0	1,559.0	548.2	321.0	—	—	1,587.8	8,168.5	—	4,004.5	2,341.0
Barbados	316	—	—	—	—	—	—	—	—	—	—	—	—
Belize	339	—	—	—	—	—	—	—	—	—	—	—	—
Bolivia	218	—	—	—	—	—	—	—	—	—	—	64.3	37.5
Brazil	223	—	—	—	—	—	3,419.0	4,450.1	—	5,277.2	12,274.0	12,635.4	—
Chile	228	—	—	—	—	—	—	—	—	—	—	—	—
Colombia	233	—	—	—	—	—	—	—	—	—	—	—	—
Costa Rica	238	—	—	—	—	—	—	—	—	—	—	—	—
Dominica	321	—	—	—	—	—	—	—	—	—	2.1	.9	—
Dominican Republic	243	53.3	—	—	—	—	39.7	—	—	—	—	87.6	43.8
Ecuador	248	—	98.9	—	—	—	—	—	113.3	37.8	75.6	60.4	—
El Salvador	253	—	—	—	—	—	—	—	—	—	—	—	—
Grenada	328	—	—	—	—	—	—	—	—	—	—	2.9	2.9
Guatemala	258	—	—	—	—	—	—	—	—	—	—	—	—
Guyana	336	—	—	—	—	—	—	—	—	—	—	—	—
Haiti	263	—	—	16.4	—	—	15.2	—	—	—	—	—	—
Honduras	268	—	—	—	—	—	47.5	—	—	—	—	—	—
Jamaica	343	36.4	34.4	7.0	—	—	—	—	—	—	—	—	—
Mexico	273	—	—	8,758.0	—	—	—	1,034.4	905.1	—	—	—	—
Nicaragua	278	—	—	—	—	—	—	—	—	—	—	—	—
Panama	283	9.9	9.9	8.7	52.4	33.2	30.0	—	—	—	—	—	—
Paraguay	288	—	—	—	—	—	—	—	—	—	—	—	—
Peru	293	642.7	—	—	—	160.5	—	—	—	—	—	—	—
St. Kitts and Nevis	361	—	—	—	—	—	1.6	—	—	—	—	—	—
St. Lucia	362	—	—	—	—	—	—	—	—	—	—	—	—
St. Vincent & Grens	364	—	—	—	—	—	—	—	—	—	—	—	—
Suriname	366	—	—	—	—	—	—	—	—	—	—	—	—
Trinidad and Tobago	369	—	—	—	—	—	—	—	—	—	—	—	—
Uruguay	298	—	—	—	—	—	114.2	—	—	—	1,261.7	364.2	372.8
Venezuela, Rep. Bol	299	—	—	—	350.0	—	—	—	—	—	—	—	—
Memorandum Items													
Oil Exporting Ctys	999	—	587.5	312.8	862.2	2,539.1	4,507.6	1,234.5	851.2	309.7	1,101.0	1,376.2	297.1
Non-Oil Develop.Ctys	201	5,042.2	4,392.0	16,655.1	4,408.7	13,573.8	16,078.6	8,775.6	6,326.9	23,452.0	24,136.0	18,946.9	3,873.6

Repurchases

		1993	1994	1995	1996	1997	1998	1999	2000	2001	2002	2003	2004
		Expressed in Millions of SDRs											
World...............................	001	3,814.0	4,572.0	6,650.9	5,071.9	5,681.3	6,694.2	19,398.8	15,249.4	13,274.9	15,113.1	18,892.1	13,829.0
Developing Countries...............	200	3,814.0	4,572.0	6,650.9	5,071.9	5,681.3	6,694.2	19,398.8	15,249.4	13,274.9	15,113.1	18,892.1	13,829.0
Africa.................................	605	626.5	423.3	1,522.4	269.2	730.0	827.9	407.3	198.2	241.1	426.4	348.1	318.7
Algeria................................	612	235.4	136.5	112.5	93.8	254.6	320.8	262.8	70.2	110.5	229.6	313.7	250.8
Burkina Faso.........................	748	—	—	—	—	—	—	—	—	—	—	—	—
Burundi...............................	618	—	—	—	—	—	—	—	—	—	—	—	19.3
Cameroon............................	622	33.8	3.9	4.0	4.0	8.2	12.0	13.3	14.1	2.5	—	—	—
Central African Rep...............	626	.6	.4	—	—	2.7	5.6	2.4	—	—	—	—	—
Chad..................................	628	—	—	—	—	3.9	5.2	1.3	—	—	—	—	—
Comoros..............................	632	—	—	—	—	—	—	—	—	—	—	—	—
Congo, Dem. Rep. of...............	636	—	3.0	.9	22.7	—	.4	.7	—	—	157.1	—	—
Congo, Republic of.................	634	.5	2.0	1.5	—	1.6	7.8	3.1	—	.9	3.6	2.7	5.3
Côte d'Ivoire........................	662	36.5	53.5	56.8	32.8	16.1	—	—	—	—	—	—	—
Djibouti..............................	611	—	—	—	—	—	—	.7	1.7	1.6	1.8	1.3	.1
Equatorial Guinea..................	642	—	—	—	—	—	—	—	—	—	—	—	—
Ethiopia..............................	644	—	—	—	—	—	—	—	—	—	—	—	—
Gabon.................................	646	25.7	16.1	34.5	3.8	2.6	16.7	17.9	7.4	8.7	10.1	10.1	16.7
Gambia, The.........................	648	—	—	—	—	—	—	—	—	—	—	—	—
Ghana.................................	652	39.3	27.1	13.1	16.8	34.5	24.6	—	—	—	—	—	—
Guinea................................	656	—	—	—	—	—	—	—	—	—	—	—	—
Guinea-Bissau.......................	654	—	—	—	—	—	—	—	—	—	.3	1.6	1.5
Kenya.................................	664	41.5	—	—	—	—	—	—	—	—	—	—	—
Lesotho...............................	666	—	—	—	—	—	—	—	—	—	—	—	—
Liberia................................	668	—	—	.1	—	—	—	—	.2	.3	.2	—	—
Madagascar..........................	674	7.4	4.5	.6	—	—	—	—	—	—	—	—	—
Malawi................................	676	4.2	1.2	—	—	—	6.4	6.4	—	—	—	—	—
Mali...................................	678	6.3	4.8	1.0	—	—	—	—	—	—	—	—	—
Mauritania...........................	682	1.0	—	—	—	—	—	—	—	—	—	—	—
Mauritius............................	684	—	—	—	—	—	—	—	—	—	—	—	—
Morocco..............................	686	112.0	106.1	66.2	32.5	2.3	—	—	—	—	—	—	—
Niger..................................	692	3.5	2.0	—	—	4.2	5.6	1.4	—	—	—	—	—
Nigeria................................	694	—	—	—	—	—	—	—	—	—	—	—	—
Rwanda...............................	714	—	—	—	—	—	—	4.5	6.7	7.4	5.2	—	—
Senegal...............................	722	11.0	2.5	—	—	11.6	15.5	3.9	—	—	—	—	—
Sierra Leone.........................	724	5.9	42.6	—	—	—	—	—	—	—	37.5	—	—
Somalia...............................	726	—	—	—	—	—	—	—	—	—	—	—	—
South Africa.........................	199	—	—	—	—	307.2	307.2	—	—	—	—	—	—
Sudan.................................	732	—	—	23.0	24.5	25.5	42.2	27.6	41.1	41.1	17.0	18.7	21.1
Swaziland............................	734	—	—	—	—	—	—	—	—	—	—	—	—
Tanzania..............................	738	—	—	—	—	—	—	—	—	—	—	—	—
Togo..................................	742	5.2	2.4	2.0	.2	—	—	—	—	—	—	—	—
Tunisia................................	744	3.8	—	10.2	32.1	36.6	36.6	36.6	30.4	24.7	—	—	—
Uganda...............................	746	3.1	—	—	—	—	—	—	—	—	—	—	—
Zambia................................	754	49.8	14.6	1,196.2	—	—	—	—	—	—	—	—	—
Zimbabwe............................	698	—	—	—	5.9	18.5	21.6	24.8	26.4	5.9	1.5	—	3.9
Asia...................................	505	369.7	1,066.0	1,113.8	1,262.8	831.0	2,514.2	8,330.4	375.5	6,943.9	3,419.1	2,110.8	1,417.5
Afghanistan, I.S. of................	512	—	—	—	—	—	—	—	—	—	—	—	—
Bangladesh...........................	513	35.9	—	—	—	—	—	—	—	—	49.1	49.1	—
Bhutan................................	514	—	—	—	—	—	—	—	—	—	—	—	—
Cambodia.............................	522	6.3	—	—	—	—	1.0	1.0	1.0	1.0	1.0	1.0	—
China, People's Rep................	924	—	—	—	—	—	—	—	—	—	—	—	—
Fiji.....................................	819	—	—	—	—	—	—	—	—	—	—	—	—
India..................................	534	137.5	821.7	796.5	881.4	495.5	304.9	246.4	38.5	—	—	—	—
Indonesia.............................	536	—	—	—	—	—	—	—	—	1,375.9	1,834.6	979.3	678.1
Korea.................................	542	—	—	—	—	—	2,050.0	7,900.0	—	4,462.5	—	—	—
Lao People's Dem.Rep.............	544	—	—	—	—	—	—	—	—	—	—	—	—
Malaysia..............................	548	—	—	—	—	—	—	—	—	—	—	—	—
Mongolia.............................	948	—	—	6.3	6.9	.6	—	—	—	—	—	—	—
Myanmar.............................	518	—	—	—	—	—	—	—	—	—	—	—	—
Nepal..................................	558	—	—	—	—	—	—	—	—	—	—	—	—
Pakistan..............................	564	91.4	34.1	61.2	167.0	138.8	39.7	107.6	161.2	80.8	167.4	351.7	309.4
Papua New Guinea..................	853	10.7	21.4	10.7	—	—	3.0	16.7	14.7	1.0	—	3.8	40.4
Philippines...........................	566	46.0	188.7	239.1	207.5	156.9	58.2	39.5	6.1	6.1	313.0	434.4	318.8
Samoa................................	862	—	—	—	—	—	—	—	—	—	—	—	—
Solomon Islands.....................	813	—	—	—	—	—	—	—	—	—	—	—	—
Sri Lanka.............................	524	13.6	—	—	—	—	—	—	—	—	—	—	69.8
Thailand..............................	578	—	—	—	—	—	—	—	150.0	1,012.5	1,050.0	287.5	—
Vietnam..............................	582	28.4	—	—	—	39.3	57.4	19.2	4.0	4.0	4.0	4.0	1.0
Europe................................	170	244.1	1,325.2	2,010.7	1,047.8	687.5	1,522.7	4,309.1	3,841.5	4,763.9	6,767.4	3,120.3	4,981.4
Albania...............................	914	—	—	.8	5.7	5.8	.9	—	—	4.4	4.4	—	—
Armenia..............................	911	—	—	—	—	—	.4	9.6	12.0	5.6	5.6	7.0	5.6
Azerbaijan, Republic of...........	912	—	—	—	—	—	—	11.7	39.0	30.9	35.8	45.3	25.7
Belarus...............................	913	—	—	—	—	—	17.9	42.5	42.1	23.4	23.4	23.4	11.7
Bosnia & Herzegovina.............	963	—	—	18.4	1.4	.7	—	15.2	15.2	6.1	17.6	36.3	32.1
Bulgaria..............................	918	—	48.0	162.3	154.9	64.4	134.7	90.7	105.3	236.2	195.2	76.6	89.2
Croatia...............................	960	17.2	6.2	3.9	3.1	1.6	6.5	22.9	21.8	24.2	97.2	—	—
Cyprus................................	423	—	—	—	—	—	—	—	—	—	—	—	—
Czech Republic......................	935	70.0	780.7	—	—	—	—	—	—	—	—	—	—
Estonia...............................	939	—	—	1.0	7.7	14.1	18.7	2.9	3.9	3.9	10.7	—	—
Georgia...............................	915	—	—	—	—	—	.7	15.7	19.7	9.3	9.3	11.6	9.3
Hungary..............................	944	36.2	114.7	522.9	140.0	—	118.7	—	—	—	—	—	—
Kazakhstan...........................	916	—	—	—	—	4.6	70.0	128.5	335.1	—	—	—	—
Kyrgyz Republic.....................	917	—	—	—	2.7	7.1	8.5	5.4	5.4	5.4	5.4	4.0	—

Repurchases

		1993	1994	1995	1996	1997	1998	1999	2000	2001	2002	2003	2004
							Expressed in Millions of SDRs						
Europe(Cont.)													
Latvia	941	—	—	1.9	17.5	26.7	18.3	11.1	7.6	7.6	7.6	7.6	3.8
Lithuania	946	—	—	—	16.9	31.1	20.6	12.1	20.7	26.7	31.1	59.1	13.4
Macedonia, FYR	962	2.2	1.2	.7	.6	.3	1.7	12.4	14.7	6.0	5.9	11.0	8.3
Moldova	921	—	—	—	5.1	14.6	47.2	47.9	18.6	11.3	13.8	15.8	14.6
Poland	964	98.9	219.4	918.6	—	—	—	—	—	—	—	—	—
Romania	968	—	89.6	245.8	245.4	98.4	92.3	102.0	72.9	91.7	75.7	79.6	115.3
Russia	922	—	—	—	359.5	359.5	673.9	3,101.1	2,189.5	2,997.9	1,147.6	1,356.1	1,117.4
Serbia & Montenegro	965	—	—	—	—	—	—	—	—	—	—	—	158.5
Slovak Republic	936	—	61.9	132.3	85.6	37.6	49.8	38.1	96.5	—	—	—	—
Slovenia	961	9.9	3.6	2.2	1.8	.9	—	—	—	—	—	—	—
Tajikistan	923	—	—	—	—	—	—	3.8	7.5	9.4	7.5	1.9	—
Turkey	186	—	—	—	—	20.1	164.6	210.2	65.6	867.6	4,916.4	1,223.9	3,158.2
Ukraine	926	—	—	—	—	—	77.3	407.0	643.5	361.2	140.7	144.5	201.8
Uzbekistan	927	—	—	—	—	—	—	18.4	49.4	35.1	16.6	16.6	16.6
Middle East	405	**33.1**	**48.4**	**135.2**	**163.2**	**49.4**	**6.8**	**50.7**	**77.9**	**81.7**	**74.6**	**76.3**	**72.8**
Egypt	469	—	22.5	62.7	58.6	10.9	—	—	—	—	—	—	—
Iran, I.R. of	429	—	—	—	—	—	—	—	—	—	—	—	—
Iraq	433	—	—	—	—	—	—	—	—	—	—	—	—
Israel	436	—	—	67.0	89.3	22.3	—	—	—	—	—	—	—
Jordan	439	33.1	25.9	5.6	15.3	16.2	6.8	26.0	23.8	40.2	61.0	71.4	66.1
Syrian Arab Republic	463	—	—	—	—	—	—	—	—	—	—	—	—
Yemen, Republic of	474	—	—	—	—	—	—	24.8	54.1	41.4	13.6	4.8	6.7
Western Hemisphere	205	**2,540.5**	**1,709.2**	**1,868.8**	**2,329.0**	**3,383.4**	**1,822.5**	**6,301.3**	**10,756.2**	**1,244.3**	**4,425.6**	**13,236.7**	**7,038.6**
Argentina	213	275.1	289.7	319.3	296.5	347.8	484.2	602.5	970.2	927.6	573.6	4,105.8	3,714.1
Barbados	316	—	—	11.9	18.4	6.5	—	—	—	—	—	—	—
Belize	339	—	—	—	—	—	—	—	—	—	—	—	—
Bolivia	218	17.0	—	—	—	—	—	—	—	—	—	—	—
Brazil	223	360.4	93.5	32.3	48.2	23.7	15.5	1,445.9	5,074.2	—	3,588.3	8,898.6	2,939.8
Chile	228	178.5	147.0	199.5	—	—	—	—	—	—	—	—	—
Colombia	233	—	—	—	—	—	—	—	—	—	—	—	—
Costa Rica	238	—	13.8	29.1	15.8	.5	—	—	—	—	—	—	—
Dominica	321	.1	—	—	—	—	—	—	—	—	—	—	—
Dominican Republic	243	7.2	5.6	22.4	41.0	45.3	21.1	—	—	—	19.9	19.9	—
Ecuador	248	20.8	14.9	19.0	15.8	2.0	49.5	49.5	—	—	—	24.8	75.6
El Salvador	253	—	—	—	—	—	—	—	—	—	—	—	—
Grenada	328	—	—	—	—	—	—	—	—	—	—	—	—
Guatemala	258	22.4	—	—	—	—	—	—	—	—	—	—	—
Guyana	336	2.4	15.3	15.6	8.1	6.7	1.4	—	—	—	—	—	—
Haiti	263	—	14.8	.3	—	—	6.0	8.2	2.2	—	7.6	7.6	—
Honduras	268	2.1	11.2	28.8	26.1	6.4	—	—	—	—	23.8	23.8	—
Jamaica	343	51.9	60.9	62.9	49.5	25.1	12.5	13.9	14.5	14.5	14.5	11.4	5.4
Mexico	273	841.7	841.0	754.1	1,413.6	2,499.2	783.7	3,726.7	4,164.3	—	—	—	—
Nicaragua	278	—	2.1	8.5	6.4	—	—	—	—	—	—	—	—
Panama	283	7.3	.9	25.6	35.8	18.8	9.9	17.2	39.3	26.2	6.2	6.7	6.7
Paraguay	288	—	—	—	—	—	—	—	—	—	—	—	—
Peru	293	458.7	—	—	—	53.6	107.1	107.1	107.1	120.5	133.9	80.3	26.8
St. Kitts and Nevis	361	—	—	—	—	—	—	—	—	—	.8	.8	—
St. Lucia	362	—	—	—	—	—	—	—	—	—	—	—	—
St. Vincent & Grens	364	—	—	—	—	—	—	—	—	—	—	—	—
Trinidad and Tobago	369	92.5	50.4	28.7	17.3	13.3	3.1	—	—	—	—	—	—
Uruguay	298	10.2	7.4	6.5	8.0	6.0	—	—	—	—	57.1	57.1	270.3
Venezuela, Rep. Bol.	299	192.0	140.6	304.2	328.5	328.5	328.5	330.3	384.4	155.6	—	—	—
Memorandum Items													
Oil Exporting Ctys	999	**427.5**	**277.1**	**416.7**	**422.3**	**583.2**	**649.3**	**593.1**	**454.7**	**1,642.0**	**2,064.2**	**1,292.9**	**928.8**
Non-Oil Develop.Ctys	201	**3,386.5**	**4,295.0**	**6,234.2**	**4,649.6**	**5,098.1**	**6,044.9**	**18,805.7**	**14,794.7**	**11,633.0**	**13,048.9**	**17,599.2**	**12,900.1**

Loan Disbursements

		1993	1994	1995	1996	1997	1998	1999	2000	2001	2002	2003	2004
		Expressed in Millions of SDRs											
World	001	271.7	910.4	1,431.4	708.6	730.6	896.0	736.8	492.5	872.6	1,344.5	848.4	812.4
Developing Countries	200	271.7	910.4	1,431.4	708.6	730.6	896.0	736.8	492.5	872.6	1,344.5	848.4	812.4
Africa	605	142.1	467.1	1,247.8	404.3	348.3	532.6	334.8	364.8	467.0	922.9	275.5	399.5
Benin	638	15.7	18.1	9.1	13.6	4.5	—	7.2	6.8	8.1	4.0	6.7	1.4
Burkina Faso	748	8.8	17.7	17.7	6.6	13.3	13.3	12.2	5.6	16.8	11.2	3.4	3.4
Burundi	618	—	—	—	—	—	—	—	—	—	—	—	26.4
Cameroon	622	—	—	—	—	27.0	54.0	45.0	52.0	15.9	31.8	15.9	—
Cape Verde	624	—	—	—	—	—	—	—	—	—	2.5	2.5	1.2
Central African Rep.	626	—	—	—	—	—	8.2	8.2	—	8.0	—	—	—
Chad	628	—	—	8.3	16.5	8.3	8.3	8.3	10.4	13.4	13.4	5.2	—
Comoros	632	—	1.4	—	—	—	—	—	—	—	—	—	—
Congo, Dem. Rep. of	636	—	—	—	—	—	—	—	—	—	420.0	53.4	53.4
Congo, Republic of	634	—	—	—	13.9	—	—	—	—	—	—	—	7.9
Côte d'Ivoire	662	—	119.1	119.1	95.3	—	123.9	—	—	—	58.5	—	—
Djibouti	611	—	—	—	—	—	—	2.7	2.7	3.6	4.5	—	—
Ethiopia	644	21.2	14.1	—	14.7	—	14.7	—	—	34.8	34.2	10.4	20.9
Gambia, The	648	—	—	—	—	—	3.4	3.4	6.9	6.9	2.9	—	—
Ghana	652	—	—	27.4	27.4	—	82.2	44.3	26.8	52.6	52.6	52.7	26.4
Guinea	656	—	8.7	20.3	—	23.6	23.6	7.9	—	20.7	12.9	—	—
Guinea-Bissau	654	—	—	1.6	2.1	4.5	2.4	—	5.1	—	—	—	—
Kenya	664	22.6	22.6	—	24.9	—	—	—	33.6	—	—	25.0	—
Lesotho	666	6.8	3.8	—	—	—	—	—	—	7.0	7.0	3.5	7.0
Liberia	668	—	—	—	—	—	—	—	—	—	—	—	—
Madagascar	674	—	—	—	13.6	13.6	—	13.6	38.0	22.7	11.3	11.3	34.9
Malawi	676	—	5.6	7.6	15.3	7.6	12.8	7.6	6.4	—	—	6.4	—
Mali	678	10.2	29.5	29.5	20.7	20.7	10.3	17.1	6.8	18.2	6.8	12.9	1.3
Mauritania	682	8.5	17.0	14.3	14.3	14.3	—	6.1	6.1	18.2	12.1	.9	—
Mauritius	684	—	—	—	—	—	—	—	—	—	—	—	—
Morocco	686	—	—	—	—	—	—	—	—	—	—	—	—
Mozambique	688	15.3	14.7	—	12.6	25.2	25.2	21.0	45.2	8.4	8.4	8.4	1.6
Niger	692	—	—	—	9.7	19.3	19.3	—	8.5	8.5	16.9	16.9	8.4
Rwanda	714	—	—	—	—	—	11.9	21.4	19.0	9.5	.6	.6	1.1
São Tomé & Príncipe	716	—	—	—	—	—	—	—	1.9	—	—	—	—
Senegal	722	—	16.7	54.7	23.8	35.7	35.7	14.3	14.3	23.3	9.0	3.5	3.5
Sierra Leone	724	—	95.6	13.1	10.2	5.1	—	—	—	46.8	28.0	14.0	28.0
Somalia	726	—	—	—	—	—	—	—	—	—	—	—	—
Sudan	732	—	—	—	—	—	—	—	—	—	—	—	—
Swaziland	734	—	—	—	—	—	—	—	—	—	—	—	—
Tanzania	738	—	—	—	25.7	61.4	35.7	58.8	40.0	40.0	40.0	17.8	5.6
Togo	742	—	10.9	21.7	—	10.9	10.9	—	—	—	—	—	—
Uganda	746	—	36.7	36.8	43.5	43.5	36.8	25.7	8.9	8.9	1.5	4.0	2.0
Zambia	754	—	—	833.4	—	10.0	—	10.0	20.0	74.8	132.7	—	165.1
Zimbabwe	698	30.4	33.4	33.4	—	—	—	—	—	—	—	—	—
Asia	505	105.5	358.9	100.1	132.2	125.2	113.7	52.2	14.3	194.3	325.6	460.6	278.4
Afghanistan, I.S. of	512	—	—	—	—	—	—	—	—	—	—	—	—
Bangladesh	513	28.8	—	—	—	—	—	—	—	—	—	49.5	99.0
Cambodia	522	—	14.0	28.0	—	—	—	8.4	8.4	16.7	16.7	8.4	—
China,P.R.: Mainland	924	—	—	—	—	—	—	—	—	—	—	—	—
India	534	—	—	—	—	—	—	—	—	—	—	—	—
Lao People's Dem.Rep.	544	5.9	5.9	11.7	5.9	5.9	—	—	—	4.5	9.1	4.5	—
Maldives	556	—	—	—	—	—	—	—	—	—	—	—	—
Mongolia	948	9.3	14.8	—	5.6	5.6	—	5.9	5.9	4.1	—	8.1	—
Myanmar	518	—	—	—	—	—	—	—	—	—	—	—	—
Nepal	558	5.6	5.6	—	—	—	—	—	—	—	—	7.1	7.1
Pakistan	564	—	202.2	—	—	113.7	113.7	37.9	—	86.2	258.4	344.6	172.3
Papua New Guinea	853	—	—	—	—	—	—	—	—	—	—	—	—
Philippines	566	—	—	—	—	—	—	—	—	—	—	—	—
Samoa	862	—	—	—	—	—	—	—	—	—	—	—	—
Solomon Islands	813	—	—	—	—	—	—	—	—	—	—	—	—
Sri Lanka	524	56.0	56.0	—	—	—	—	—	—	—	—	38.4	—
Thailand	578	—	—	—	—	—	—	—	—	—	—	—	—
Vietnam	582	—	60.4	60.4	120.8	—	—	—	—	82.8	41.4	—	—
Europe	170	8.5	25.0	37.4	105.4	178.4	146.2	107.7	58.9	87.4	83.5	83.0	79.7
Albania	914	8.5	15.5	7.1	—	—	5.9	15.5	14.3	9.4	4.0	8.0	8.0
Armenia	911	—	—	—	33.8	16.9	37.8	20.9	—	10.0	20.0	20.0	19.0
Azerbaijan, Republic of	912	—	—	—	—	55.6	14.6	11.7	—	8.1	8.1	25.7	—
Georgia	915	—	—	—	55.5	55.5	27.8	33.3	—	27.0	22.5	—	14.0
Kyrgyz Republic	917	—	9.5	30.3	16.1	32.3	10.8	19.6	14.3	11.7	11.7	21.3	19.1
Macedonia, FYR	962	—	—	—	—	18.2	9.1	—	1.7	—	—	—	—
Moldova	921	—	—	—	—	—	—	—	9.2	9.2	9.2	—	—
Tajikistan	923	—	—	—	—	—	40.3	6.7	19.3	12.0	8.0	8.0	19.6
Middle East	405	—	—	—	—	44.0	44.0	62.0	—	88.8	—	—	—
Egypt	469	—	—	—	—	—	—	—	—	—	—	—	—
Yemen, Republic of	474	—	—	—	—	44.0	44.0	62.0	—	88.8	—	—	—
Western Hemisphere	205	15.6	59.4	46.1	66.8	34.8	59.4	180.1	54.5	35.2	12.5	29.2	54.8
Bolivia	218	—	30.4	16.8	33.7	16.8	33.6	16.8	11.2	19.0	—	—	—
Dominica	321	—	—	—	—	—	—	—	—	—	—	2.4	.6
El Salvador	253	—	—	—	—	—	—	—	—	—	—	—	—
Grenada	328	—	—	—	—	—	—	—	—	—	—	—	—
Guyana	336	8.9	9.0	9.0	17.9	17.9	9.0	9.0	7.0	—	5.6	6.0	6.0

Loan Disbursements

		1993	1994	1995	1996	1997	1998	1999	2000	2001	2002	2003	2004
						Expressed in Millions of SDRs							
Western Hemisphere(Cont.)													
Haiti..	263	—	—	—	15.2	—	—	—	—	—	—	—	—
Honduras..	268	6.8	—	20.3	—	—	—	76.0	16.2	16.2	—	—	20.3
Nicaragua.......................................	278	—	20.0	—	—	—	16.8	78.3	20.2	—	7.0	20.9	27.9
Memorandum Items													
Non-Oil Develop.Ctys..............	201	271.7	910.4	1,431.4	708.6	730.6	896.0	736.8	492.5	872.6	1,344.5	848.4	812.4

Repayments of Loans

		1993	1994	1995	1996	1997	1998	1999	2000	2001	2002	2003	2004
						Expressed in Millions of SDRs							
World.........................	001	133.4	223.4	373.8	484.5	606.0	620.9	595.2	605.1	789.6	906.6	842.2	933.3
Developing Countries..............	200	133.4	223.4	373.8	484.5	606.0	620.9	595.2	605.1	789.6	906.6	842.2	933.3
Africa.........................	605	51.5	145.2	230.6	300.0	338.4	350.0	324.5	320.6	501.5	625.9	532.6	593.4
Benin..........................	638	—	.6	1.3	1.3	3.1	3.9	6.5	9.5	11.4	11.3	11.4	8.5
Burkina Faso..................	748	—	—	—	.6	1.3	2.1	3.9	7.5	10.1	10.8	12.6	13.5
Burundi........................	618	3.0	4.3	6.0	6.0	6.0	6.8	5.6	3.8	3.8	2.1	—	—
Cameroon......................	622	—	—	—	—	—	—	—	—	—	—	8.1	18.9
Central African Rep...........	626	.7	2.9	4.9	4.3	2.7	3.9	1.2	.6	—	—	—	1.6
Chad...........................	628	1.2	1.2	4.6	4.3	4.3	3.1	2.1	.6	2.5	5.8	12.4	9.5
Comoros.......................	632	—	—	—	—	.2	.2	.3	.5	.5	.3	.3	.1
Congo, Dem. Rep. of..........	636	—	—	—	2.4	—	.2	—	—	—	142.9	—	—
Congo, Republic of...........	634	—	—	—	—	—	—	—	—	—	2.8	2.8	2.8
Côte d'Ivoire.................	662	—	—	—	—	—	—	6.0	29.8	52.4	66.7	75.0	85.5
Djibouti.......................	611	—	—	—	—	—	—	—	—	—	—	—	—
Equatorial Guinea.............	642	—	.4	.7	.8	2.2	2.1	1.8	2.0	2.0	.9	.6	.2
Ethiopia.......................	644	—	—	—	—	—	2.8	7.1	9.9	9.9	12.8	10.0	8.7
Gambia, The..................	648	1.7	2.7	4.1	5.1	5.1	4.1	3.1	1.7	.7	—	—	7.6
Ghana.........................	652	8.2	30.5	57.8	69.4	85.9	77.7	55.4	28.1	51.4	11.0	15.1	29.6
Guinea.........................	656	2.3	4.1	5.8	5.8	7.5	6.9	5.2	6.1	9.3	8.7	10.5	13.2
Guinea-Bissau.................	654	.3	.3	.8	.8	.8	.5	.5	.2	.5	.9	1.9	2.1
Kenya..........................	664	2.8	9.7	25.8	41.9	48.9	46.1	43.7	32.2	18.6	14.0	14.0	9.5
Lesotho........................	666	—	1.1	1.8	2.3	3.1	3.6	4.3	3.9	3.4	2.9	1.8	.4
Liberia.........................	668	—	.7	—	—	—	.4	.4	.3	.2	—	—	—
Madagascar....................	674	2.7	3.9	9.1	11.6	12.9	10.3	9.0	3.8	1.3	2.7	5.4	5.4
Malawi.........................	676	—	2.8	6.5	10.2	12.3	12.3	10.0	6.9	5.5	5.7	7.2	9.2
Mali...........................	678	—	2.0	3.6	5.1	5.1	8.1	8.6	13.0	16.9	21.0	21.1	21.7
Mauritania....................	682	3.4	4.2	5.9	6.8	5.4	5.1	6.8	8.3	10.3	12.5	13.6	12.0
Mauritius......................	684	—	—	—	—	—	—	—	—	—	—	—	—
Morocco.......................	686	—	—	—	—	—	—	—	—	—	—	—	—
Mozambique...................	688	4.3	7.3	9.5	22.5	11.0	18.1	22.8	22.2	21.0	17.1	14.8	15.3
Niger...........................	692	3.4	5.1	6.7	8.1	6.7	4.7	3.0	1.3	1.0	2.9	6.8	9.7
Rwanda........................	714	—	—	—	.9	1.8	1.8	1.8	1.8	.9	—	1.2	3.6
São Tomé & Príncipe..........	716	—	.1	.2	.2	.2	.2	.1	—	—	—	—	—
Senegal........................	722	8.5	17.4	26.8	30.6	34.0	28.9	20.0	17.1	21.1	20.8	27.9	33.3
Sierra Leone...................	724	—	13.8	2.3	2.3	—	—	9.1	19.1	21.7	24.3	24.8	15.7
Somalia........................	726	—	—	—	—	—	—	—	—	—	—	—	—
Sudan..........................	732	—	—	3.0	—	5.2	—	—	—	—	—	—	—
Swaziland......................	734	—	—	—	—	—	—	—	—	—	—	—	—
Tanzania.......................	738	4.3	10.7	12.8	15.0	22.5	27.8	21.4	19.3	17.1	17.3	17.4	27.5
Togo...........................	742	.8	2.3	5.4	7.7	8.4	8.4	6.9	7.1	8.1	7.3	9.8	10.9
Uganda.........................	746	4.0	17.1	18.8	34.1	41.8	45.8	37.6	37.1	32.4	31.7	34.1	37.5
Zambia.........................	754	—	—	6.6	—	—	—	—	—	166.7	167.7	168.7	169.7
Zimbabwe......................	698	—	—	—	—	—	14.0	20.4	27.0	1.0	.9	3.2	10.2
Asia...........................	505	77.8	62.0	123.6	152.1	230.4	224.9	222.7	226.5	223.3	169.9	171.4	151.2
Afghanistan, I.S. of...........	512	—	—	—	—	—	—	—	—	—	—	—	—
Bangladesh.....................	513	28.8	38.4	40.3	58.9	86.3	77.6	70.9	69.0	50.3	17.3	2.9	—
Cambodia......................	522	—	—	—	—	—	1.4	4.2	8.4	8.4	8.4	7.0
China, People's Rep...........	924	—	—	—	—	—	—	—	—	—	—	—	—
India...........................	534	—	—	—	—	—	—	—	—	—	—	—	—
Lao People's Dem.Rep.........	544	—	—	1.2	2.1	3.5	4.7	5.9	5.9	7.3	7.0	6.5	5.3
Mongolia.......................	948	—	—	—	—	—	.9	2.8	4.8	5.4	5.9	6.1	4.9
Myanmar.......................	518	—	—	—	—	—	—	—	—	—	—	—	—
Nepal...........................	558	1.5	3.7	5.2	5.2	5.2	4.8	4.3	3.4	3.4	3.4	2.2	.6
Pakistan........................	564	—	10.9	54.6	54.6	87.4	76.5	64.7	62.3	62.3	40.4	74.6	79.6
Papua New Guinea.............	853	—	—	—	—	—	—	—	—	—	—	—	—
Philippines.....................	566	—	—	—	—	—	—	—	—	—	—	—	—
Samoa..........................	862	—	—	—	—	—	—	—	—	—	—	—	—
Solomon Islands...............	813	—	—	—	—	—	—	—	—	—	—	—	—
Sri Lanka.......................	524	4.5	8.9	22.3	31.2	48.0	60.4	72.7	64.9	56.0	39.2	22.4	5.6
Thailand........................	578	—	—	—	—	—	—	—	—	—	—	—	—
Vietnam........................	582	43.1	—	—	—	—	—	—	12.1	30.2	48.3	48.3	48.3
Europe.........................	170	—	—	—	—	—	—	2.5	8.8	18.6	63.3	82.2	101.7
Albania.........................	914	—	—	—	—	—	—	2.5	5.5	6.2	6.2	6.8	6.4
Armenia........................	911	—	—	—	—	—	—	—	—	1.7	8.4	11.8	17.7
Azerbaijan, Republic of.......	912	—	—	—	—	—	—	—	—	—	2.0	11.1	14.6
Georgia........................	915	—	—	—	—	—	—	—	—	2.8	13.9	22.2	27.8
Kyrgyz Republic...............	917	—	—	—	—	—	—	—	3.3	8.0	12.8	17.6	21.7
Macedonia, FYR...............	962	—	—	—	—	—	—	—	—	—	.9	4.5	5.5
Tajikistan.......................	923	—	—	—	—	—	—	—	—	—	19.0	8.1	8.1
Middle East....................	405	—	—	—	—	—	—	—	—	—	—	8.8	21.2
Egypt..........................	469	—	—	—	—	—	—	—	—	—	—	—	—
Yemen, Republic of...........	474	—	—	—	—	—	—	—	—	—	—	8.8	21.2
Western Hemisphere..............	205	4.0	16.3	19.6	32.4	37.2	46.0	45.5	49.1	46.2	47.5	47.1	65.7
Bolivia..........................	218	3.6	10.4	17.2	21.8	24.9	29.9	24.5	22.4	22.9	21.2	20.5	27.4
Dominica.......................	321	.4	.5	.6	.6	.4	.2	—	—	—	—	—	—
El Salvador.....................	253	—	—	—	—	—	—	—	—	—	—	—	—
Grenada........................	328	—	—	—	—	—	—	—	—	—	—	—	—
Guyana.........................	336	—	—	—	8.3	11.9	14.5	16.3	19.0	12.5	12.5	12.5	13.4
Haiti............................	263	—	5.3	1.8	1.8	—	—	—	—	—	3.0	3.0	3.0
Honduras.......................	268	—	—	—	—	—	1.4	2.7	3.7	6.8	6.8	5.4	10.1
Nicaragua......................	278	—	—	—	—	—	—	2.0	4.0	4.0	4.0	5.7	11.9

Repayments of Loans

	1993	1994	1995	1996	1997	1998	1999	2000	2001	2002	2003	2004
						Expressed in Millions of SDRs							
Western Hemisphere(Cont.)												
Memorandum Items												
Non-Oil Develop.Ctys.............	201	133.4	223.4	373.8	484.5	606.0	620.9	595.2	605.1	789.6	906.6	842.2	933.3

Total Fund Credit & Loans Outstdg.

		1993	1994	1995	1996	1997	1998	1999	2000	2001	2002	2003	2004
						Expressed in Millions of SDRs							
World	001	29,159.1	30,260.9	41,636.1	42,058.6	52,614.7	66,781.7	57,534.1	49,350.2	59,920.0	70,481.7	71,918.9	62,139.8
Developing Countries	200	29,159.1	30,260.9	41,636.1	42,058.6	52,614.7	66,781.7	57,534.1	49,350.2	59,920.0	70,481.7	71,918.9	62,139.8
Africa	605	5,871.5	6,531.6	7,065.3	7,457.3	7,107.3	6,775.7	6,645.5	6,527.1	6,251.5	6,149.0	5,553.4	5,088.1
Algeria	612	342.7	793.8	994.1	1,412.5	1,495.5	1,428.0	1,388.7	1,318.5	1,208.0	978.4	664.7	414.0
Angola	614												
Benin	638	31.3	48.8	56.6	68.9	70.3	66.4	67.1	64.4	61.1	53.9	49.2	42.0
Burkina Faso	748	15.2	32.8	50.5	56.5	68.5	79.6	87.9	86.1	92.7	93.0	83.9	73.8
Burundi	618	44.4	40.1	34.2	28.2	22.2	15.4	9.8	6.0	2.1	9.6	19.3	26.4
Cameroon	622	11.9	29.9	34.4	50.1	68.9	110.9	142.7	180.5	194.0	225.8	233.6	214.7
Cape Verde	624										2.5	4.9	6.2
Central African Rep.	626	21.0	28.3	23.5	19.2	13.8	12.5	17.1	16.5	24.5	24.5	24.5	28.4
Chad	628	20.2	29.3	33.0	45.2	45.3	45.3	50.2	60.0	70.9	78.5	71.3	61.8
Comoros	632	.9	2.3	2.3	2.3	2.1	1.9	1.6	1.1	.7	.4	.1	—
Congo, Dem. Rep. of	636	330.3	327.3	326.4	301.3	301.3	300.7	300.0	300.0	300.0	420.0	473.4	526.8
Congo, Republic of	634	3.5	14.0	12.5	26.4	24.8	24.3	21.1	31.7	30.8	24.4	18.9	18.7
Côte d'Ivoire	662	159.1	224.8	287.1	349.6	333.5	457.3	451.4	421.6	369.2	361.1	286.0	200.5
Djibouti	611	—	—	—	2.9	4.0	6.3	9.3	10.3	12.3	15.1	13.8	13.6
Equatorial Guinea	642	12.0	13.4	12.7	11.9	9.8	7.6	5.8	3.8	1.7	.8	.2	—
Ethiopia	644	35.3	49.4	49.4	64.2	64.2	76.1	69.0	59.1	84.0	105.4	105.8	118.0
Gabon	646	32.9	61.4	65.0	83.3	97.2	80.5	62.6	68.4	59.6	49.5	39.4	64.4
Gambia, The	648	26.7	23.9	19.8	14.7	9.6	8.9	9.3	14.4	20.6	23.5	23.5	15.9
Ghana	652	537.3	479.7	436.2	377.3	257.0	236.9	225.8	224.5	225.7	267.3	304.9	301.6
Guinea	656	44.0	48.6	63.1	57.3	73.4	90.0	92.7	86.6	98.1	102.2	91.7	78.5
Guinea-Bissau	654	3.5	3.2	4.0	5.3	9.0	11.0	12.6	19.0	18.4	17.2	13.8	10.2
Kenya	664	264.3	277.3	251.5	234.5	185.6	139.5	95.8	97.2	78.6	64.6	75.6	66.1
Lesotho	666	24.9	27.6	25.8	23.5	20.4	16.8	12.5	8.5	12.1	16.2	17.9	24.5
Liberia	668	226.5	225.8	225.7	225.7	225.7	225.3	224.8	224.4	223.9	223.7	223.7	223.7
Madagascar	674	67.0	58.6	48.9	50.8	51.5	41.2	45.8	80.0	101.4	110.0	115.9	145.4
Malawi	676	62.6	76.9	78.0	83.1	78.4	72.6	63.8	63.4	57.9	69.6	68.8	59.5
Mali	678	51.4	74.1	99.0	114.6	130.2	132.4	140.9	134.7	136.0	121.8	113.6	93.2
Mauritania	682	46.1	58.8	67.1	74.6	83.4	78.3	77.6	75.4	83.2	82.9	70.2	58.2
Mauritius	684	—	—	—	—	—	—	—	—	—	—	—	—
Morocco	686	207.2	101.1	34.8	2.3	—	—	—	—	—	—	—	—
Mozambique	688	137.9	145.2	135.8	125.9	140.1	147.2	145.4	168.5	155.9	147.2	140.8	127.0
Namibia	728	—	—	—	—	—	—	—	—	—	—	—	—
Niger	692	37.7	41.8	35.0	36.6	45.0	54.1	49.6	56.8	64.3	78.3	88.4	87.2
Nigeria	694	—	—	—	—	—	—	—	—	—	—	—	—
Rwanda	714	8.8	8.8	17.7	16.8	29.9	40.1	55.3	65.9	67.1	62.5	61.8	59.4
São Tomé & Príncipe	716	.8	.7	.6	.4	.2	.1	—	1.9	1.9	1.9	1.9	1.9
Senegal	722	177.8	205.4	233.3	226.5	216.5	207.8	198.2	195.4	197.6	185.8	161.3	131.5
Seychelles	718	—	—	—	—	—	—	—	—	—	—	—	—
Sierra Leone	724	61.0	100.2	110.9	118.8	123.9	135.4	142.0	133.2	120.8	124.5	113.8	126.0
Somalia	726	112.0	112.0	112.0	112.0	112.0	112.0	112.0	112.0	112.0	112.0	112.0	112.0
South Africa	199	614.4	614.4	614.4	614.4	307.2	—	—	—	—	—	—	—
Sudan	732	671.6	671.6	645.7	621.2	590.5	548.4	520.8	479.7	438.6	421.6	402.9	381.7
Swaziland	734	—	—	—	—	—	—	—	—	—	—	—	—
Tanzania	738	156.2	145.5	132.7	143.4	182.4	190.2	227.6	248.3	271.2	293.9	294.3	272.3
Togo	742	49.9	56.0	70.4	62.5	64.9	67.4	60.4	53.3	45.3	38.0	28.2	17.4
Tunisia	744	207.3	207.3	197.1	165.0	128.4	91.8	55.2	24.7	—	—	—	—
Uganda	746	243.0	262.6	280.6	290.1	291.7	282.7	270.8	242.6	219.1	188.9	158.8	123.3
Zambia	754	565.8	551.2	833.4	833.4	843.4	843.4	853.4	873.4	781.6	746.6	577.9	573.3
Zimbabwe	698	205.0	257.5	310.0	304.1	285.5	289.2	268.8	215.4	208.4	206.1	202.9	188.8
Asia	505	6,365.7	5,816.8	4,846.9	3,673.4	15,538.9	24,173.2	17,908.7	18,588.5	12,400.3	10,334.5	9,909.9	8,619.6
Afghanistan, I.S. of	512												
Bangladesh	513	511.8	473.4	433.1	374.2	287.9	308.4	237.6	168.6	118.3	51.9	49.5	148.5
Bhutan	514												
Cambodia	522	6.3	20.3	48.3	48.3	48.3	47.2	53.1	56.2	63.5	70.8	69.7	62.7
China, People's Rep.	924	—	—	—	—	—	—	—	—	—	—	—	—
Fiji	819												
India	534	3,584.9	2,763.2	1,966.6	1,085.3	589.8	284.9	38.5	—	—	—	—	—
Indonesia	536	—	—	—	—	2,201.5	6,455.8	7,466.8	8,318.0	7,251.7	6,518.1	6,915.1	6,237.0
Kiribati	826	—	—	—	—	—	—	—	—	—	—	—	—
Korea	542	—	—	—	—	8,200.0	12,000.0	4,462.5	4,462.5	—	—	—	—
Lao People's Dem.Rep.	544	26.4	32.2	42.8	46.6	49.0	44.3	38.4	32.5	29.7	31.8	29.9	24.6
Malaysia	548	—	—	—	—	—	—	—	—	—	—	—	—
Maldives	556	—	—	—	—	—	—	—	—	—	—	—	—
Mongolia	948	23.0	37.9	31.6	30.3	35.2	34.3	37.5	38.6	37.3	31.3	33.4	28.5
Myanmar	518	—	—	—	—	—	—	—	—	—	—	—	—
Nepal	558	35.8	37.7	32.5	27.2	22.0	17.2	12.9	9.5	6.2	2.8	7.7	14.3
Pakistan	564	816.5	1,096.8	1,115.0	1,000.5	979.5	996.0	1,271.2	1,197.7	1,455.8	1,506.4	1,424.6	1,207.9
Palau	565												
Papua New Guinea	853	32.1	10.7	33.3	35.3	35.3	32.4	15.7	29.9	85.5	85.5	81.8	41.4
Philippines	566	880.7	728.6	489.5	281.9	633.8	1,114.0	1,327.7	1,559.2	1,553.1	1,240.2	805.8	486.9
Samoa	862	—	—	—	—	—	—	—	—	—	—	—	—
Solomon Islands	813	—	—	—	—	—	—	—	—	—	—	—	—
Sri Lanka	524	375.7	422.8	400.5	369.2	321.2	260.8	188.1	123.2	170.6	228.0	264.7	189.3
Thailand	578	—	—	—	—	1,800.0	2,300.0	2,500.0	2,350.0	1,337.5	287.5	—	—
Tonga	866	—	—	—	—	—	—	—	—	—	—	—	—
Vietnam	582	72.5	193.4	253.8	374.6	335.3	277.9	258.7	242.6	291.2	280.2	227.9	178.6

Total Fund Credit & Loans Outstdg.

		1993	1994	1995	1996	1997	1998	1999	2000	2001	2002	2003	2004
						Expressed in Millions of SDRs							
Europe	170	6,159.5	8,036.4	11,400.3	13,945.3	15,708.5	19,644.9	17,385.4	16,847.3	21,608.7	25,189.0	23,765.9	19,790.8
Albania	914	21.6	37.1	43.4	37.7	40.7	45.8	58.7	67.5	66.3	59.6	60.8	62.4
Armenia	911	—	16.9	47.3	81.0	97.9	135.3	146.6	134.7	137.4	143.3	144.4	140.1
Azerbaijan, Republic of	912	—	—	67.9	121.7	197.7	228.1	296.7	257.7	234.9	205.1	174.5	134.2
Belarus	913	70.1	70.1	190.2	190.2	190.2	172.3	129.7	87.6	64.3	40.9	17.5	5.8
Bosnia & Herzegovina	963	—	—	32.5	31.0	30.3	54.5	68.4	80.4	88.4	102.4	90.1	70.0
Bulgaria	918	459.9	644.4	482.1	407.2	698.0	792.3	910.7	1,014.6	883.0	771.8	799.2	762.0
Croatia	960	14.8	87.1	148.6	145.4	172.7	166.1	143.2	121.4	97.2	—	—	—
Cyprus	423	—	—	—	—	—	—	—	—	—	—	—	—
Czech Republic	935	780.7	—	—	—	—	—	—	—	—	—	—	—
Estonia	939	41.9	41.9	61.8	54.2	40.0	21.3	18.4	14.5	10.7	—	—	—
Georgia	915	—	27.8	77.7	133.2	188.7	215.8	233.3	213.7	228.7	228.0	194.3	171.3
Hungary	944	896.3	781.6	258.7	118.7	118.7	—	—	—	—	—	—	—
Kazakhstan	916	61.9	198.0	290.8	383.6	379.0	463.7	335.1	—	—	—	—	—
Kyrgyz Republic	917	43.9	53.3	83.6	97.1	122.2	124.4	138.7	144.3	142.7	136.3	135.9	133.2
Latvia	941	77.8	109.8	107.9	90.4	63.7	45.4	34.3	26.7	19.1	11.4	3.8	—
Lithuania	946	88.0	134.6	176.0	190.1	200.5	179.8	167.8	147.1	120.3	89.3	30.2	16.8
Macedonia, FYR	962	2.8	14.0	38.1	47.4	65.3	72.7	74.1	62.3	56.3	49.6	46.0	40.3
Moldova	921	63.0	112.5	154.9	172.3	172.7	125.6	127.7	118.3	116.3	111.8	95.9	81.4
Poland	964	497.7	918.6	—	—	—	—	—	—	—	—	—	—
Romania	968	750.9	906.4	698.3	453.0	475.2	382.8	333.8	347.7	308.0	314.9	400.6	285.4
Russia	922	1,797.3	2,875.6	6,469.8	8,698.2	9,805.9	13,732.0	11,102.3	8,912.8	5,914.8	4,767.3	3,411.2	2,293.8
Serbia & Montenegro	965	—	—	—	—	—	—	—	116.9	216.9	416.9	616.9	621.0
Slovak Republic	936	405.2	439.8	307.5	222.0	184.4	134.6	96.5	—	—	—	—	—
Slovenia	961	8.5	4.9	2.7	.9	—	—	—	—	—	—	—	—
Tajikistan	923	—	—	—	15.0	22.5	70.3	73.2	85.0	87.7	69.2	67.2	78.7
Turkey	186	—	235.5	460.5	460.5	440.4	275.8	648.8	3,205.3	11,232.9	16,245.7	16,212.8	13,848.3
Ukraine	926	—	249.3	1,037.3	1,573.3	1,780.6	1,985.0	2,044.6	1,591.2	1,520.7	1,380.0	1,235.5	1,033.7
Uzbekistan	927	—	—	106.0	165.2	165.2	165.2	146.8	97.5	62.3	45.7	29.1	12.5
Middle East	405	385.0	409.7	350.3	353.3	502.0	571.8	660.5	597.8	641.8	638.8	553.7	756.8
Bahrain, Kingdom of	419	—	—	—	—	—	—	—	—	—	—	—	—
Egypt	469	147.2	132.2	69.5	10.9	—	—	—	—	—	—	—	—
Iran, I.R. of	429	—	—	—	—	—	—	—	—	—	—	—	—
Iraq	433	—	—	—	—	—	—	—	—	—	—	—	297.1
Israel	436	178.6	178.6	111.7	22.3	—	—	—	—	—	—	—	—
Jordan	439	59.2	98.9	169.2	236.1	316.6	333.4	362.9	354.3	344.5	355.0	283.6	217.5
Syrian Arab Republic	463	—	—	—	—	—	—	—	—	—	—	—	—
Yemen, Republic of	474	—	—	—	84.0	185.4	238.4	297.6	243.5	297.3	283.8	270.1	242.2
Western Hemisphere	205	10,377.5	9,466.4	17,973.3	16,629.2	13,758.1	15,616.2	14,934.0	6,789.5	19,017.6	28,170.4	32,136.0	27,884.5
Antigua and Barbuda	311	—	—	—	—	—	—	—	—	—	—	—	—
Argentina	213	2,562.4	2,884.7	4,124.4	4,376.0	4,349.3	3,865.1	3,262.6	3,880.3	11,121.1	10,547.5	10,446.2	9,073.0
Barbados	316	36.8	36.8	24.9	6.5	—	—	—	—	—	—	—	—
Belize	339	—	—	—	—	—	—	—	—	—	—	—	—
Bolivia	218	160.5	180.5	180.1	192.0	183.9	187.6	180.0	168.8	164.8	143.7	187.5	197.7
Brazil	223	221.0	127.5	95.2	47.0	23.3	3,426.8	6,431.0	1,356.8	6,633.9	15,319.6	19,056.5	16,116.7
Chile	228	346.5	199.5	—	—	—	—	—	—	—	—	—	—
Colombia	233	—	—	—	—	—	—	—	—	—	—	—	—
Costa Rica	238	59.3	45.5	16.3	.5	—	—	—	—	—	—	—	—
Dominica	321	2.3	1.7	1.1	.6	.2	—	—	—	—	2.1	5.3	5.9
Dominican Republic	243	135.5	129.9	107.5	66.5	21.1	39.7	39.7	39.7	39.7	19.9	87.6	131.3
Ecuador	248	51.8	135.7	116.7	100.9	98.9	49.5	—	113.3	151.1	226.7	262.3	186.8
El Salvador	253	—	—	—	—	—	—	—	—	—	—	—	—
Grenada	328	—	—	—	—	—	—	—	—	—	—	2.9	5.9
Guatemala	258	—	—	—	—	—	—	—	—	—	—	—	—
Guyana	336	128.6	122.3	115.6	117.1	116.4	109.5	102.2	90.1	77.7	70.7	64.2	56.7
Haiti	263	23.8	3.8	18.2	31.6	31.6	40.8	32.6	30.4	30.4	19.7	9.1	6.1
Honduras	268	86.0	74.8	66.4	40.3	33.9	80.0	153.3	165.8	175.1	144.6	115.4	125.7
Jamaica	343	244.2	217.6	161.7	112.2	87.1	74.7	60.8	46.3	31.9	17.4	6.0	.6
Mexico	273	3,485.2	2,644.2	10,648.1	9,234.5	6,735.2	5,951.5	3,259.2	—	—	—	—	—
Nicaragua	278	17.0	34.9	26.4	20.0	20.0	36.8	113.2	129.3	125.3	128.3	143.5	159.5
Panama	283	82.3	91.3	74.4	91.0	105.4	125.5	108.3	69.1	42.9	36.7	30.0	23.3
Paraguay	288	—	—	—	—	—	—	—	—	—	—	—	—
Peru	293	642.7	642.7	642.7	642.7	749.6	642.5	535.4	428.3	307.8	173.9	93.6	66.9
St. Kitts and Nevis	361	—	—	—	—	—	1.6	1.6	1.6	1.6	.8	—	—
St. Lucia	362	—	—	—	—	—	—	—	—	—	—	—	—
St. Vincent & Grens	364	—	—	—	—	—	—	—	—	—	—	—	—
Suriname	366	—	—	—	—	—	—	—	—	—	—	—	—
Trinidad and Tobago	369	112.8	62.4	33.8	16.5	3.1	—	—	—	—	—	—	—
Uruguay	298	27.9	20.5	14.0	6.0	—	114.2	114.2	114.2	114.2	1,318.8	1,625.9	1,728.4
Venezuela, Rep. Bol.	299	1,950.7	1,810.2	1,506.0	1,527.4	1,198.9	870.4	540.0	155.6	—	—	—	—
Memorandum Items													
Oil Exporting Ctys	999	2,293.5	2,603.9	2,500.0	2,940.0	4,895.9	8,754.2	9,395.6	9,792.1	8,459.7	7,496.5	7,579.8	6,948.1
Non-Oil Develop.Ctys	201	26,865.6	27,657.0	39,136.1	39,118.6	47,718.8	58,027.5	48,138.5	39,558.2	51,460.3	62,985.2	64,339.1	55,191.7

Use of Fund Credit (GRA)

		1993	1994	1995	1996	1997	1998	1999	2000	2001	2002	2003	2004
							Expressed in Millions of SDRs						
World.................................	001	25,196.8	25,611.7	35,929.2	36,127.5	46,559.0	60,451.0	51,061.9	42,990.5	53,477.2	63,601.1	65,032.1	55,373.8
Developing Countries...............	200	25,196.8	25,611.7	35,929.2	36,127.5	46,559.0	60,451.0	51,061.9	42,990.5	53,477.2	63,601.1	65,032.1	55,373.8
Africa..................................	605	3,525.7	3,863.9	3,380.4	3,668.1	3,308.2	2,793.9	2,653.5	2,490.9	2,249.7	1,850.3	1,511.8	1,240.3
Algeria.................................	612	342.7	793.8	994.1	1,412.5	1,495.5	1,428.0	1,388.7	1,318.5	1,208.0	978.4	664.7	414.0
Burkina Faso.........................	748	—	—	—	—	—	—	—	—	—	—	—	—
Burundi................................	618	—	—	—	—	—	—	—	—	—	9.6	19.3	—
Cameroon.............................	622	11.9	29.9	34.4	50.1	41.9	29.9	16.6	2.5	—	—	—	—
Central African Rep................	626	.4	10.7	10.7	10.7	8.0	2.4	—	—	—	—	—	5.6
Chad...................................	628	—	10.3	10.3	10.3	6.5	1.3	—	—	—	—	—	—
Comoros...............................	632	—	—	—	—	—	—	—	—	—	—	—	—
Congo, Dem. Rep. of...............	636	184.8	181.8	180.9	158.2	158.2	157.8	157.1	157.1	157.1	—	—	—
Congo, Republic of..................	634	3.5	14.0	12.5	12.5	10.9	10.4	7.2	17.8	16.9	13.3	10.6	5.3
Côte d'Ivoire.........................	662	159.1	105.7	48.9	16.1	—	—	—	—	—	—	—	—
Djibouti................................	611	—	—	—	2.9	4.0	6.3	6.6	4.8	3.2	1.4	.1	—
Equatorial Guinea...................	642	—	—	—	—	—	—	—	—	—	—	—	—
Ethiopia................................	644	—	—	—	—	—	—	—	—	—	—	—	—
Gabon..................................	646	32.9	61.4	65.0	83.3	97.2	80.5	62.6	68.4	59.6	49.5	39.4	64.4
Gambia, The.........................	648	—	—	—	—	—	—	—	—	—	—	—	—
Ghana..................................	652	116.0	89.0	75.9	59.0	24.6	—	—	—	—	—	—	—
Guinea.................................	656	—	—	—	—	—	—	—	—	—	—	—	—
Guinea-Bissau.......................	654	—	—	—	—	—	—	2.1	3.6	3.6	3.3	1.7	.2
Kenya..................................	664	—	—	—	—	—	—	—	—	—	—	—	—
Lesotho................................	666	—	—	—	—	—	—	—	—	—	—	—	—
Liberia..................................	668	201.6	201.6	201.5	201.5	201.5	201.5	201.5	201.3	201.0	200.8	200.8	200.8
Madagascar..........................	674	5.2	.6	—	—	—	—	—	—	—	—	—	—
Malawi.................................	676	1.2	12.7	12.7	12.7	12.7	6.4	—	—	—	17.4	17.4	17.4
Mali....................................	678	5.7	1.0	—	—	—	—	—	—	—	—	—	—
Mauritania............................	682	—	—	—	—	—	—	—	—	—	—	—	—
Mauritius..............................	684	—	—	—	—	—	—	—	—	—	—	—	—
Morocco...............................	686	207.2	101.1	34.8	2.3	—	—	—	—	—	—	—	—
Niger...................................	692	2.0	11.1	11.1	11.1	6.9	1.4	—	—	—	—	—	—
Nigeria.................................	694	—	—	—	—	—	—	—	—	—	—	—	—
Rwanda................................	714	—	—	8.9	8.9	23.8	23.8	19.3	12.6	5.2	—	—	—
Senegal................................	722	2.5	30.9	30.9	30.9	19.3	3.9	—	—	—	—	—	—
Sierra Leone..........................	724	42.6	—	—	—	—	11.6	27.1	37.5	—	—	—	—
Somalia................................	726	96.7	96.7	96.7	96.7	96.7	96.7	96.7	96.7	96.7	96.7	96.7	96.7
South Africa..........................	199	614.4	614.4	614.4	614.4	307.2	—	—	—	—	—	—	—
Sudan..................................	732	604.3	604.2	581.3	556.8	531.3	489.1	461.5	420.4	379.4	362.4	343.6	322.5
Swaziland.............................	734	—	—	—	—	—	—	—	—	—	—	—	—
Tanzania..............................	738	—	—	—	—	—	—	—	—	—	—	—	—
Togo....................................	742	4.6	2.2	.2	—	—	—	—	—	—	—	—	—
Tunisia.................................	744	207.3	207.3	197.1	165.0	128.4	91.8	55.2	24.7	—	—	—	—
Uganda................................	746	—	—	—	—	—	—	—	—	—	—	—	—
Zambia.................................	754	559.2	544.6	—	—	—	—	—	—	—	—	—	—
Zimbabwe.............................	698	119.9	139.0	158.1	152.2	133.6	151.3	151.2	124.9	119.0	117.5	117.5	113.6
Asia.....................................	505	5,024.4	4,178.6	3,232.1	2,078.5	14,049.2	22,794.7	16,700.7	17,592.7	11,433.5	9,212.1	8,498.2	7,080.7
Afghanistan, I.S. of.................	512	—	—	—	—	—	—	—	—	—	—	—	—
Bangladesh...........................	513	—	—	—	—	98.1	98.1	98.1	98.1	49.1	—	—	—
Bhutan.................................	514	—	—	—	—	—	—	—	—	—	—	—	—
Cambodia.............................	522	6.3	6.3	6.3	6.3	6.3	5.2	4.2	3.1	2.1	1.0	—	—
China, People's Rep.................	924	—	—	—	—	—	—	—	—	—	—	—	—
Fiji......................................	819	—	—	—	—	—	—	—	—	—	—	—	—
India....................................	534	3,584.9	2,763.2	1,966.6	1,085.3	589.8	284.9	38.5	—	—	—	—	—
Indonesia..............................	536	—	—	—	—	2,201.5	6,455.8	7,466.8	8,318.0	7,251.7	6,518.1	6,915.1	6,237.0
Korea..................................	542	—	—	—	—	8,200.0	12,000.0	4,462.5	4,462.5	—	—	—	—
Lao People's Dem.Rep..............	544	—	—	—	—	—	—	—	—	—	—	—	—
Malaysia...............................	548	—	—	—	—	—	—	—	—	—	—	—	—
Maldives...............................	556	—	—	—	—	—	—	—	—	—	—	—	—
Mongolia..............................	948	13.8	13.8	7.5	.6	—	—	—	—	—	—	—	—
Myanmar..............................	518	—	—	—	—	—	—	—	—	—	—	—	—
Nepal...................................	558	—	—	—	—	—	—	—	—	—	—	—	—
Pakistan...............................	564	434.1	523.2	595.9	536.1	488.8	468.0	770.0	758.8	993.0	825.6	473.9	164.5
Palau...................................	565	—	—	—	—	—	—	—	—	—	—	—	—
Papua New Guinea..................	853	32.1	10.7	33.3	35.3	35.3	32.4	15.7	29.9	85.5	85.5	81.8	41.4
Philippines............................	566	880.7	728.6	489.5	281.9	633.8	1,114.0	1,327.7	1,559.2	1,553.1	1,240.2	805.8	486.9
Samoa..................................	862	—	—	—	—	—	—	—	—	—	—	—	—
Solomon Islands.....................	813	—	—	—	—	—	—	—	—	—	—	—	—
Sri Lanka..............................	524	—	—	—	—	—	—	—	—	103.4	200.0	220.7	150.9
Thailand...............................	578	—	—	—	—	1,800.0	2,300.0	2,500.0	2,350.0	1,337.5	287.5	—	—
Vietnam................................	582	72.5	133.0	133.0	133.0	93.7	36.3	17.1	13.1	9.1	5.0	1.0	—
Europe.................................	170	6,151.0	8,002.9	11,329.4	13,769.1	15,353.9	19,144.1	16,779.5	16,191.3	20,883.9	24,444.0	23,020.1	19,067.0
Albania................................	914	13.1	13.1	12.3	6.6	9.7	8.8	8.8	8.8	4.4	—	—	—
Armenia...............................	911	—	16.9	47.3	47.3	47.3	46.8	37.3	25.3	19.7	14.1	7.0	1.4
Azerbaijan, Republic of............	912	—	—	67.9	121.7	142.2	157.9	214.8	175.8	144.9	109.2	63.9	38.2
Belarus................................	913	70.1	70.1	190.2	190.2	190.2	172.3	129.7	87.6	64.3	40.9	17.5	5.8
Bosnia & Herzegovina..............	963	—	—	32.5	31.0	30.3	54.5	68.4	80.4	88.4	102.4	90.1	70.0
Bulgaria...............................	918	459.9	644.4	482.1	407.2	698.0	792.3	910.7	1,014.6	883.0	771.8	799.2	762.0
Croatia.................................	960	14.8	87.1	148.6	145.4	172.7	166.1	143.2	121.4	97.2	—	—	—
Cyprus.................................	423	—	—	—	—	—	—	—	—	—	—	—	—
Czech Republic......................	935	780.7	—	—	—	—	—	—	—	—	—	—	—
Estonia.................................	939	41.9	41.9	61.8	54.2	40.0	21.3	18.4	14.5	10.7	—	—	—
Georgia................................	915	—	27.8	77.7	77.7	77.7	77.0	61.3	41.6	32.4	23.1	11.6	2.3
Hungary...............................	944	896.3	781.6	258.7	118.7	118.7	—	—	—	—	—	—	—

Use of Fund Credit (GRA)

		1993	1994	1995	1996	1997	1998	1999	2000	2001	2002	2003	2004
							Expressed in Millions of SDRs						
Europe(Cont.)													
Kazakhstan	916	61.9	198.0	290.8	383.6	379.0	463.7	335.1	—	—	—	—	—
Kyrgyz Republic	917	43.9	43.9	43.9	41.2	34.1	25.5	20.2	14.8	9.4	4.0	—	—
Latvia	941	77.8	109.8	107.9	90.4	63.7	45.4	34.3	26.7	19.1	11.4	3.8	—
Lithuania	946	88.0	134.6	176.0	190.1	200.5	179.8	167.8	147.1	120.3	89.3	30.2	16.8
Macedonia, FYR	962	2.8	14.0	38.1	47.4	47.1	45.4	46.8	33.3	27.3	21.5	22.4	22.2
Moldova	921	63.0	112.5	154.9	172.3	172.7	125.6	127.7	109.1	97.8	84.1	68.2	53.6
Poland	964	497.7	918.6	—	—	—	—	—	—	—	—	—	—
Romania	968	750.9	906.4	698.3	453.0	475.2	382.8	333.8	347.7	308.0	314.9	400.6	285.4
Russia	922	1,797.3	2,875.6	6,469.8	8,698.2	9,805.9	13,732.0	11,102.3	8,912.8	5,914.8	4,767.3	3,411.2	2,293.8
Serbia & Montenegro	965	—	—	—	—	—	—	—	116.9	216.9	416.9	616.9	621.0
Slovak Republic	936	405.2	439.8	307.5	222.0	184.4	134.6	96.5	—	—	—	—	—
Slovenia	961	8.5	4.9	2.7	.9	—	—	—	—	—	—	—	—
Tajikistan	923				15.0	22.5	30.0	26.3	18.8	9.4	1.9	—	—
Turkey	186	—	235.5	460.5	460.5	440.4	275.8	648.8	3,205.3	11,232.9	16,245.7	16,212.8	13,848.3
Ukraine	926	—	249.3	1,037.3	1,573.3	1,780.6	1,985.0	2,044.6	1,591.2	1,520.7	1,380.0	1,235.5	1,033.7
Uzbekistan	927	—	—	106.0	165.2	165.2	165.2	146.8	97.5	62.3	45.7	29.1	12.5
Middle East	**405**	**385.0**	**409.7**	**350.3**	**353.3**	**458.0**	**483.8**	**510.5**	**447.8**	**403.1**	**400.0**	**323.7**	**548.1**
Egypt	469	147.2	132.2	69.5	10.9	—	—	—	—	—	—	—	—
Iran, I.R. of	429	—	—	—	—	—	—	—	—	—	—	—	—
Iraq	433	—	—	—	—	—	—	—	—	—	—	—	297.1
Israel	436	178.6	178.6	111.7	22.3	—	—	—	—	—	—	—	—
Jordan	439	59.2	98.9	169.2	236.1	316.6	333.4	362.9	354.3	344.5	355.0	283.6	217.5
Syrian Arab Republic	463	—	—	—	—	—	—	—	—	—	—	—	—
Yemen, Republic of	474	—	—	—	84.0	141.4	150.4	147.6	93.5	58.6	45.0	40.2	33.5
Western Hemisphere	**205**	**10,110.8**	**9,156.6**	**17,636.9**	**16,258.5**	**13,389.8**	**15,234.5**	**14,417.7**	**6,267.8**	**18,506.9**	**27,694.7**	**31,678.3**	**27,437.7**
Argentina	213	2,562.4	2,884.7	4,124.4	4,376.0	4,349.3	3,865.1	3,262.6	3,880.3	11,121.1	10,547.5	10,446.2	9,073.0
Barbados	316	36.8	36.8	24.9	6.5	—	—	—	—	—	—	—	—
Belize	339	—	—	—	—	—	—	—	—	—	—	—	—
Bolivia	218	—	—	—	—	—	—	—	—	—	—	64.3	101.8
Brazil	223	221.0	127.5	95.2	47.0	23.3	3,426.8	6,431.0	1,356.8	6,633.9	15,319.6	19,056.5	16,116.7
Chile	228	346.5	199.5	—	—	—	—	—	—	—	—	—	—
Colombia	233	—	—	—	—	—	—	—	—	—	—	—	—
Costa Rica	238	59.3	45.5	16.3	.5	—	—	—	—	—	2.1	3.0	3.0
Dominica	321	—	—	—	—	—	—	—	—	—	—	—	—
Dominican Republic	243	135.5	129.9	107.5	66.5	21.1	39.7	39.7	39.7	39.7	19.9	87.6	131.3
Ecuador	248	51.8	135.7	116.7	100.9	98.9	49.5	—	113.3	151.1	226.7	262.3	186.8
El Salvador	253	—	—	—	—	—	—	—	—	—	—	—	—
Grenada	328	—	—	—	—	—	—	—	—	—	—	2.9	5.9
Guatemala	258	—	—	—	—	—	—	—	—	—	—	—	—
Guyana	336	47.1	31.8	16.2	8.1	1.4	—	—	—	—	—	—	—
Haiti	263	15.0	.3	16.4	16.4	16.4	25.6	17.4	15.2	15.2	7.6	—	—
Honduras	268	72.5	61.3	32.5	6.4	—	47.5	47.5	47.5	47.5	23.8	—	—
Jamaica	343	244.2	217.6	161.7	112.2	87.1	74.7	60.8	46.3	31.9	17.4	6.0	.6
Mexico	273	3,485.2	2,644.2	10,648.1	9,234.5	6,735.2	5,951.5	3,259.2	—	—	—	—	—
Nicaragua	278	17.0	14.9	6.4	—	—	—	—	—	—	—	—	—
Panama	283	82.3	91.3	74.4	91.0	105.4	125.5	108.3	69.1	42.9	36.7	30.0	23.3
Paraguay	288	—	—	—	—	—	—	—	—	—	—	—	—
Peru	293	642.7	642.7	642.7	642.7	749.6	642.5	535.4	428.3	307.8	173.9	93.6	66.9
St. Kitts and Nevis	361	—	—	—	—	—	1.6	1.6	1.6	1.6	.8	—	—
St. Lucia	362	—	—	—	—	—	—	—	—	—	—	—	—
St. Vincent & Grens	364	—	—	—	—	—	—	—	—	—	—	—	—
Trinidad and Tobago	369	112.8	62.4	33.8	16.5	3.1	—	—	—	—	—	—	—
Uruguay	298	27.9	20.5	14.0	6.0	—	114.2	114.2	114.2	114.2	1,318.8	1,625.9	1,728.4
Venezuela, Rep. Bol.	299	1,950.7	1,810.2	1,506.0	1,527.4	1,198.9	870.4	540.0	155.6	—	—	—	—
Memorandum Items													
Oil Exporting Ctys	999	**2,293.5**	**2,603.9**	**2,500.0**	**2,940.0**	**4,895.9**	**8,754.2**	**9,395.6**	**9,792.1**	**8,459.7**	**7,496.5**	**7,579.8**	**6,948.1**
Non-Oil Develop.Ctys	201	**22,903.4**	**23,007.7**	**33,429.1**	**33,187.5**	**41,663.2**	**51,696.8**	**41,666.3**	**33,198.5**	**45,017.5**	**56,104.6**	**57,452.2**	**48,425.7**

Total Reserves minus Gold

2005, International Monetary Fund : *International Financial Statistics Yearbook*

		1993	1994	1995	1996	1997	1998	1999	2000	2001	2002	2003	2004
							Millions of SDRs: End of Period						
All Countries............................	010	799,739	860,302	991,320	1,145,671	1,265,437	1,248,499	1,372,822	1,556,066	1,709,485	1,856,728	2,124,008	2,489,181
Industrial Countries...................	110	413,531	433,940	487,827	548,944	577,832	546,026	590,188	656,131	689,731	730,997	820,185	904,284
United States............................	111	45,395	43,350	50,307	44,536	43,659	50,223	44,080	43,442	45,860	49,990	50,401	48,866
Canada....................................	156	9,087	8,416	10,124	14,202	13,209	16,553	20,493	24,502	27,024	27,204	24,376	22,170
Australia..................................	193	8,083	7,730	8,003	10,073	12,485	10,398	15,455	13,906	14,287	15,218	21,662	23,054
Japan......................................	158	71,729	86,214	123,277	150,663	162,793	153,030	209,045	272,392	314,431	339,227	446,368	536,952
New Zealand.............................	196	2,430	2,540	2,967	4,140	3,299	2,986	3,246	2,556	2,394	2,750	3,302	3,409
Euro Area (incl. ECB)..................	163	....	....	....	....	....	....	187,088	185,988	186,965	181,678	149,879	136,054
Austria....................................	122	10,637	11,523	12,600	15,901	14,628	15,932	† 11,017	10,990	9,954	7,123	5,700	5,060
Belgium...................................	124	8,310	9,505	10,883	11,789	11,999	12,977	† 7,969	7,671	8,965	8,720	7,395	6,672
Finland....................................	172	3,939	7,303	6,753	4,810	6,238	6,885	† 5,989	6,122	6,352	6,830	7,076	7,932
France.....................................	132	16,489	17,986	18,065	18,635	22,922	31,471	† 28,926	28,428	25,263	20,864	20,314	22,739
Germany..................................	134	56,525	52,994	57,185	57,844	57,504	52,573	† 44,472	43,664	40,903	37,639	34,115	31,437
Greece.....................................	174	5,672	9,924	9,943	12,171	9,335	12,399	13,204	10,303	† 4,101	5,945	2,935	767
Ireland....................................	178	4,314	4,189	5,806	5,706	4,837	6,674	† 3,880	4,114	4,445	3,983	2,745	1,823
Italy.......................................	136	20,054	22,102	23,482	31,954	41,311	21,227	† 16,336	19,623	19,431	21,039	20,435	17,939
Luxembourg..............................	137	49	52	50	51	47	....	† 56	59	84	112	188	192
Netherlands..............................	138	22,819	23,655	22,680	18,615	18,429	15,211	† 7,203	7,401	7,189	7,034	7,410	6,505
Portugal...................................	182	11,532	10,627	10,663	11,070	11,606	11,239	† 6,140	6,838	7,692	8,223	3,954	3,332
Spain......................................	184	29,882	28,459	23,199	40,284	50,694	39,245	† 24,127	23,784	23,539	25,403	13,317	7,977
Denmark..................................	128	7,499	6,203	7,411	9,834	14,174	10,841	16,238	11,596	13,615	19,849	24,970	25,166
Iceland....................................	176	310	201	207	316	284	303	349	298	269	324	533	674
Norway....................................	142	14,286	13,033	15,148	18,441	17,343	13,528	17,346	21,181	18,522	23,538	25,048	28,530
San Marino...............................	135	87	121	134	150	136	121	105	104	106	135	170	229
Sweden....................................	144	13,869	15,929	16,180	13,288	8,023	10,013	10,943	11,407	11,122	12,598	13,245	14,249
Switzerland...............................	146	23,760	23,790	24,496	26,727	28,926	29,254	26,463	24,769	25,467	29,536	32,068	35,735
United Kingdom.........................	112	26,775	28,265	28,265	27,745	23,952	22,877	† 26,135	33,687	29,668	28,951	28,164	29,197
Developing Countries................	200	386,208	426,363	503,494	596,727	687,605	702,473	782,634	899,935	1,019,754	1,125,731	1,303,823	1,584,903
Africa......................................	605	13,658	16,201	17,727	22,111	32,254	29,372	30,756	42,153	51,819	53,630	61,802	82,120
CEMAC (Incl. BEAC hqtrs.)............	758	....	....	....	....	....	....	....	965	859	1,177	1,220	2,003
Cameroon.................................	622	2	† 2	3	2	1	1	3	163	264	463	430	534
Central African Republic..............	626	82	144	157	162	132	103	99	102	94	91	89	96
Chad.......................................	628	28	52	96	114	101	85	69	85	97	161	126	143
Congo, Rep. of..........................	634	1	34	40	63	44	1	29	170	55	23	23	77
Equatorial Guinea.......................	642	—	—	—	—	4	1	2	18	56	65	160	608
Gabon.....................................	646	1	120	100	173	209	11	13	146	8	103	132	286
WAEMU (Incl. BCEAO hqtrs.).........	759	....	....	1,708	1,905	2,126	2,247	2,136	2,520	3,008	4,012	4,528	4,668
Benin.......................................	638	178	† 177	133	182	188	186	291	352	460	453	483	412
Burkina Faso..............................	748	278	163	234	235	256	265	215	187	207	231	506	431
Côte d'Ivoire.............................	662	2	140	356	421	458	608	459	513	811	1,371	877	1,091
Guinea Bissau............................	654	10	13	14	8	25	25	26	51	55	76	22	47
Mali..	678	242	† 152	217	300	308	286	255	293	278	437	641	554
Niger.......................................	692	140	76	64	55	39	38	29	62	85	98	175	166
Senegal....................................	722	2	123	183	200	286	306	294	295	356	469	748	893
Togo.......................................	742	114	65	88	62	88	84	89	117	101	151	138	232
Algeria.....................................	612	1,074	1,832	1,349	2,945	5,964	4,862	3,297	9,228	14,388	17,092	22,292	27,847
Angola.....................................	614	....	....	143	384	294	144	361	920	582	276	427	879
Botswana..................................	616	2,983	3,015	3,159	3,496	4,206	4,219	4,589	4,849	4,693	4,026	3,593	3,645
Burundi....................................	618	119	140	141	97	84	47	35	25	14	43	45	42
Cape Verde...............................	624	42	29	25	19	14	6	31	22	36	59	63	90
Comoros...................................	632	28	30	30	35	30	28	27	33	50	59	63	67
Congo, Dem. Rep. of...................	636	34	83	99	57	....	....	....	....	....	....	....	....
Djibouti....................................	611	55	51	49	54	49	47	51	52	56	54	67	60
Eritrea.....................................	643	....	....	27	57	148	16	25	20	32	22	17	22
Ethiopia...................................	644	332	373	519	509	371	363	334	235	345	649	643	964
Gambia, The.............................	648	77	67	71	71	71	76	81	84	84	79	40	54
Ghana......................................	652	298	400	469	576	399	268	331	178	237	397	910	1,047
Guinea.....................................	656	96	60	58	61	90	168	145	114	159	126	....	....
Kenya......................................	664	295	382	238	519	584	556	577	689	847	786	997	978
Lesotho....................................	666	184	255	307	320	424	408	364	321	308	299	310	324
Liberia.....................................	668	2	3	19	—	—	—	—	—	—	2	5	12
Madagascar...............................	674	59	49	73	168	209	122	166	219	317	267	279	324
Malawi.....................................	676	41	29	74	157	120	192	183	190	165	121	85	86
Mauritania................................	682	32	27	57	98	149	144	163	215	226	291	280	....
Mauritius..................................	684	551	512	581	623	514	397	533	689	665	903	1,061	1,034
Morocco...................................	686	2,661	2,981	2,423	2,638	2,959	3,150	4,145	3,702	6,743	7,453	9,321	10,519
Mozambique..............................	688	136	122	131	239	383	432	475	557	569	603	672	728
Namibia....................................	728	97	139	149	135	186	185	223	200	186	238	219	222
Nigeria.....................................	694	999	949	971	2,834	5,619	5,043	3,971	7,607	8,321	5,393	4,797	10,918
Rwanda....................................	714	35	35	67	74	114	120	127	146	169	179	144	203
São Tomé & Príncipe....................	716	....	....	3	3	9	7	8	9	12	13	17	13
Seychelles.................................	718	26	21	18	15	20	15	22	34	30	51	45	22
Sierra Leone..............................	724	21	28	23	18	29	31	29	38	41	62	45	81
South Africa..............................	199	742	1,154	1,897	655	3,557	3,094	4,629	4,669	4,810	4,343	4,371	8,462
Sudan......................................	732	27	54	110	74	60	64	138	† 190	94	324	570	1,047
Swaziland..................................	734	192	203	201	177	219	255	274	270	216	203	187	208
Tanzania...................................	738	148	227	182	306	461	426	565	748	920	1,125	1,372	1,478
Tunisia.....................................	744	622	1,001	1,080	1,320	1,466	1,314	1,648	1,390	1,583	1,685	1,982	2,534

Total Reserves minus Gold

1l s		1993	1994	1995	1996	1997	1998	1999	2000	2001	2002	2003	2004
						Millions of SDRs: End of Period							
Africa(Cont.)													
Uganda	746	107	220	309	367	470	515	556	620	782	687	727	842
Zambia	754	140	184	150	155	177	49	33	188	146	394	167	217
Zimbabwe	698	315	278	401	416	119	93	195	148	51	61	....	....
Asia *	**505**	**221,476**	**262,647**	**291,127**	**343,989**	**384,346**	**413,548**	**482,554**	**548,242**	**631,786**	**717,996**	**840,366**	**1,039,412**
Bangladesh	513	1,755	2,150	1,574	1,276	1,172	1,353	1,168	1,140	1,015	1,238	1,735	2,043
Bhutan	514	71	83	† 88	132	140	182	213	244	257	261	247	257
Cambodia	522	18	81	129	185	221	230	286	385	467	571	549	607
China, P.R.: Mainland	924	16,298	36,246	50,708	74,438	105,809	105,955	114,919	129,155	171,560	214,140	274,670	395,683
China, P.R.: Hong Kong	532	31,295	33,737	37,268	44,374	68,782	63,671	70,117	82,540	88,448	82,306	79,652	79,549
China, P.R.: Macao	546	1,142	1,347	1,518	1,684	1,877	1,749	2,082	2,550	2,792	2,795	2,923	3,500
Fiji	819	196	187	235	297	267	274	312	316	292	264	285	308
India	534	7,425	13,493	12,056	14,027	18,298	19,418	23,801	29,090	36,500	49,772	66,581	81,515
Indonesia	536	8,200	8,311	9,222	12,692	12,293	16,131	19,268	21,876	21,680	22,781	23,528	22,506
Korea	542	14,727	17,563	21,983	23,670	15,096	36,913	53,907	73,781	81,762	89,256	104,500	128,136
Lao P. D. Rep.	544	46e	42e	62	118	83	80	74	107	104	141	140	144
Malaysia	548	19,838	17,415	15,994	18,783	15,407	18,153	22,286	22,659	24,249	25,172	29,957	42,745
Maldives	556	19	21	32	53	73	84	93	94	74	98	107	131
Micronesia, Fed. States of	868	....	....	47	62	64	72	68	87	78	86	60	35
Mongolia	948	43	56	79	75	130	67	99	137	164	257	159	152
Myanmar	518	221	289	377	159	185	224	193	171	319	346	370	433
Nepal	558	466	475	395	397	464	537	616	726	826	749	823	942
Pakistan	564	871	2,007	1,166	381	886	730	1,101	1,162	2,896	5,942	7,363	6,310
Papua New Guinea	853	103	66	176	406	269	137	149	220	336	236	333	407
Philippines	566	3,404	4,136	4,303	6,995	5,409	6,587	9,668	10,047	10,723	9,804	9,189	8,446
Samoa	862	37	35	37	42	48	44	50	49	45	46	56	62
Singapore	576	35,208	39,851	46,213	53,442	52,836	53,215	55,987	61,502	59,977	60,331	64,433	72,267
Solomon Islands	813	15	12	11	23	27	35	37	25	15	13	25	52
Sri Lanka	524	1,186	1,401	1,404	1,364	1,500	1,406	1,192	797	1,024	1,200	1,524	1,373
Thailand	578	17,817	20,093	24,206	26,239	19,403	20,472	24,818	24,573	25,745	27,985	27,643	31,335
Tonga	866	27	24	19	21	20	20	20	21	21	20	29	38
Vanuatu	846	33	30	32	31	28	32	30	30	30	27	29	40
Vietnam	582	....	....	890	1,207	1,472	1,422	2,423	2,622	2,924	3,031	4,189	4,534
*of which:													
Taiwan Province of China	528	60,844	63,331	60,754	61,224	61,888	64,161	77,376	81,926	97,245	118,907	139,055	155,658
Europe	**170**	**25,334**	**30,530**	**57,652**	**61,672**	**71,931**	**72,769**	**78,853**	**97,249**	**111,453**	**138,281**	**169,370**	**213,504**
Albania	914	107	140	162	195	229	273	356	473	589	617	679	874
Armenia	911	10	22	67	108	170	230	232	244	255	313	343	371
Azerbaijan, Republic of	912	—	1	81	147	345	318	490	522	714	531	552	702
Belarus	913	....	69	254	326	292	499	214	269	311	455	400	483
Bosnia & Herzegovina	963	....	....	....	....	60	124	330	381	972	972	1,208	1,550
Bulgaria	918	477	686	832	336	1,565	1,907	2,107	2,421	2,619	3,242	4,234	5,651
Croatia	960	449	962	1,275	1,609	1,882	2,000	2,204	2,705	3,742	4,329	5,512	5,639
Cyprus	423	798	1,003	751	1,072	1,031	980	1,335	1,336	1,804	2,223	2,192	2,518
Czech Republic	935	2,759	4,209	9,312	8,590	7,214	8,908	9,330	9,992	11,412	17,326	18,016	18,196
Estonia	939	281	304	390	443	562	576	622	707	653	736	924	1,151
Georgia	915	....	....	131	131	148	87	96	84	127	145	128	247
Hungary	944	4,878	4,614	8,055	6,760	6,232	6,618	7,981	8,588	8,536	7,612	8,572	10,243
Kazakhstan	916	332	574	764	900	1,258	1,038	1,078	1,224	1,589	1,880	2,851	5,456
Kyrgyz Republic	917	35	18	54	66	126	116	167	183	210	212	245	353
Latvia	941	314	373	340	455	563	569	635	653	914	913	964	1,231
Lithuania	946	255	360	509	537	749	1,001	871	1,007	1,287	1,728	2,269	2,262
Macedonia, FYR	962	76	102	173	167	190	217	313	330	593	531	604	583
Malta	181	992	1,267	1,079	1,126	1,103	1,181	1,303	1,128	1,326	1,625	1,836	1,738
Moldova	921	56	123	173	217	271	102	135	171	182	198	203	303
Poland	964	2,979	4,002	9,939	12,409	15,125	19,407	19,202	20,387	20,409	21,073	21,924	22,745
Romania	968	725	1,429	1,062	1,462	2,819	2,036	1,112	1,896	3,121	4,505	5,411	9,412
Russia	922	4,248	2,727	9,676	7,842	9,557	5,541	6,162	18,623	25,895	32,404	49,244	77,790
Slovak Republic	936	303	1,158	2,263	2,378	2,394	2,037	2,456	3,087	3,295	6,479	7,859	9,284
Slovenia	961	574	1,027	1,225	1,598	2,457	2,584	2,308	2,453	3,445	5,134	5,718	5,662
Tajikistan	923	....	....	....	....	27	38	40	71	74	66	75	101
Turkey	186	4,566	4,911	8,370	11,430	13,829	13,841	17,010	17,260	15,022	19,910	22,875	22,968
Ukraine	926	118	446	707	1,363	1,735	541	762	1,038	2,352	3,120	4,530	5,990
Middle East	**405**	**46,757**	**45,585**	**50,058**	**60,551**	**73,304**	**72,440**	**78,426**	**92,099**	**98,269**	**97,426**	**100,614**	**107,692**
Bahrain, Kingdom of	419	948	801	861	917	956	766	997	1,200	1,340	1,269	1,197	1,250
Egypt	469	9,395	9,234	10,886	12,099	13,833	12,872	10,553	10,068	10,285	9,741	9,145	9,191
Israel	436	4,647	4,653	5,462	7,938	15,069	16,104	16,470	17,869	18,603	17,714	17,709	17,446
Jordan	439	† 1,192	1,159	1,327	1,223	1,631	1,243	1,916	2,557	2,437	2,925	3,496	3,391
Kuwait	443	3,068	2,398	2,395	2,444	2,558	2,803	3,515	5,436	7,875	6,773	5,099	5,307
Lebanon	446	1,646	2,661	3,050	4,125	4,429	4,656	5,665	4,562	3,990	5,328	8,425	7,556
Libya	672	....	....	....	....	....	5,163	5,304	9,564	11,777	10,524	13,179	16,541
Oman	449	1,313	1,128	1,232	1,364	1,534	1,376	2,016	1,827	1,882	2,334	2,418	2,316
Qatar	453	505	451	500	477	608	741	950	889	1,045	1,152	1,981	2,187
Saudi Arabia	456	5,408	5,054	5,800	† 9,959	11,026	10,099	12,384	15,032	14,001	15,160	15,222	17,573
United Arab Emirates	466	4,444	4,561	5,026	5,602	6,205	6,447	7,778	10,379	11,256	11,195	10,154	11,932
Yemen, Republic of	474	106	175	416	707	892	707	1,072	2,226	2,911	3,244	3,356	3,648
Western Hemisphere	**205**	**78,983**	**71,399**	**86,929**	**108,404**	**125,770**	**114,344**	**112,046**	**120,193**	**126,427**	**118,399**	**131,672**	**142,175**
ECCU (incl. ECCB hqtrs.)	309	196	179	211	203	228	256	268	297	357	374	366	408
Anguilla	312	7	6	9	10	12	13	15	16	19	19	22	22
Antigua and Barbuda	311	28	31	40	33	38	42	51	49	63	64	77	77
Dominica	321	14	11	15	16	18	20	23	23	25	33	32	27
Grenada	328	20	21	25	25	32	33	37	44	51	65	56	78
Montserrat	351	4	5	6	6	8	8	10	8	10	11	10	9

Total Reserves minus Gold

Total Reserves minus Gold

		1993	1994	1995	1996	1997	1998	1999	2000	2001	2002	2003	2004
1I s							*Millions of SDRs: End of Period*						
Western Hemisphere(Cont.)													
St. Kitts and Nevis	361	21	22	23	23	27	33	36	35	45	48	44	51
St. Lucia	362	44	40	42	39	45	50	54	61	71	69	72	85
St. Vincent & Grens	364	23	21	20	21	23	28	31	42	49	39	34	48
Argentina	213	10,040	9,814	9,612	12,590	16,542	17,579	19,127	19,301	11,580	7,715	9,525	12,160
Aruba	314	132	122	146	130	128	158	160	160	234	250	199	190
Bahamas, The	313	125	121	121	119	168	246	299	268	254	280	330	434
Barbados	316	110	134	147	201	196	260	220	363	549	492	497	373
Belize	339	28	24	25	41	44	31	52	94	89	84	57	31
Bolivia	218	163	309	444	664	805	674	710	711	705	427	482	562
Brazil	223	22,281	25,393	33,440	40,560	37,670	30,241	25,352	24,935	28,438	27,718	33,050	33,960
Chile	228	7,018	8,965	9,512	10,412	13,024	11,271	10,650	11,539	11,442	11,284	10,659	10,299
Colombia	233	5,774	5,474	5,616	6,846	7,265	6,144	5,834	6,843	8,079	7,894	7,257	8,624
Costa Rica	238	746	612	704	696	935	755	1,064	1,011	1,058	1,101	1,236	1,235
Dominican Republic	243	474	173	246	244	290	356	506	481	875	345	170	514
Ecuador	248	1,005	1,263	1,095	1,292	1,551	1,150	1,197	727	668	526	547	689
El Salvador	253	390	445	510	652	969	1,146	1,460	1,475	1,385	1,194	1,308	1,241
Guatemala	258	632	591	472	605	824	948	866	1,340	1,824	1,691	1,907	2,206
Guyana	336	180	169	181	229	234	196	195	234	229	209	186	149
Haiti	263	23	35	129	150	153	183	192	140	113	60	42	74
Honduras	268	71	117	176	173	430	581	916	1,008	1,126	1,121	962	1,269
Jamaica	343	304	504	458	612	506	504	404	809	1,512	1,210	804	1,189
Mexico	273	18,281	4,301	11,333	13,514	21,343	22,584	23,156	27,253	35,601	37,215	39,675	41,301
Netherlands Antilles	353	170	123	137	131	159	176	193	200	240	299	251	267
Nicaragua	278	40	97	92	137	280	249	371	375	302	330	338	430
Panama	283	435	482	526	603	851	678	600	555	869	870	680	406
Paraguay	288	460	706	735	730	619	614	713	585	568	463	652	752
Peru	293	2,481	4,790	5,531	7,356	8,140	6,794	6,361	6,427	6,900	6,869	6,579	7,841
Suriname	366	13	27	89	67	81	75	28	48	95	78	71	83
Trinidad and Tobago	369	150	241	241	378	524	556	689	1,064	1,517	1,491	1,649	2,040
Uruguay	298	552	663	774	870	1,154	1,472	1,516	1,903	2,464	566	1,402	1,615
Venezuela, Rep. Bol	299	6,709	5,526	4,227	8,198	10,656	8,466	8,945	10,046	7,352	6,243	10,791	11,832
Memorandum Items													
Oil Exporting Countries	999	45,714	43,434	43,740	60,123	70,933	70,503	77,143	102,277	110,344	108,620	118,610	138,196
Non-Oil Developing Countries	201	340,494	382,929	459,754	536,604	616,672	631,969	705,492	797,658	909,410	1,017,111	1,185,213	1,446,706

2005, International Monetary Fund : *International Financial Statistics Yearbook*

Nongold Reserves/Imports

		1993	1994	1995	1996	1997	1998	1999	2000	2001	2002	2003	2004
1rl s							*Weeks of Imports*						
World..	001	**15.0**	**15.1**	**14.7**	**15.7**	**15.7**	**16.4**	**16.9**	**16.1**	**17.7**	**20.0**	**21.4**	**21.6**
Industrial Countries................	110	**11.5**	**11.3**	**11.0**	**11.5**	**11.1**	**10.7**	**10.7**	**10.2**	**10.8**	**12.1**	**12.9**	**12.5**
United States.....................	111	5.4	4.8	5.0	4.1	3.4	3.9	3.0	2.3	2.5	2.9	3.0	2.6
Canada..............................	156	4.7	4.1	4.7	6.1	4.6	5.9	6.6	6.8	7.8	8.5	7.7	6.6
Australia...........................	193	12.7	11.0	10.1	11.5	13.3	11.8	15.9	13.2	14.6	14.8	18.8	17.0
Japan................................	158	21.2	23.8	28.4	32.3	33.7	39.9	47.9	48.6	58.9	71.1	90.1	95.4
New Zealand......................	196	18.0	16.2	16.4	21.0	15.9	17.5	16.2	12.5	11.8	12.9	13.7	11.9
Euro Area													
Austria..............................	122	15.6	15.8	14.7	17.7	15.8	17.1	† 11.3	10.8	9.2	6.9	5.0	3.8
Belgium.............................	124	5.2	5.5	5.3	5.4	5.4	5.8	† 3.5	2.9	3.3	3.1	2.4	1.9
Finland..............................	172	15.6	23.9	18.6	12.3	14.7	15.6	† 13.5	12.2	12.9	14.4	13.1	12.8
France...............................	132	5.8	5.8	5.0	4.9	5.9	7.9	† 7.0	6.2	5.5	4.7	4.2	4.1
Germany............................	134	11.7	10.4	9.5	9.4	9.1	8.2	† 6.7	6.0	5.5	5.4	4.4	3.5
Greece...............................	174	20.1	35.2	28.7	30.7	23.5	30.9	32.8	23.9	† 9.0	13.5	5.1	1.2
Ireland..............................	178	14.0	12.3	13.6	11.9	8.7	10.9	† 5.9	5.4	5.7	5.5	4.0	2.4
Italy..................................	136	9.7	9.9	8.8	11.5	13.8	7.1	† 5.3	5.6	5.4	6.0	5.3	4.1
Luxembourg......................	137	.5	.5	.4	.4	.4	....	† .4	.4	.5	.7	1.1	.9
Netherlands.......................	138	13.1	12.7	9.9	7.7	7.3	5.9	† 2.7	2.5	2.4	2.6	2.5	1.9
Portugal............................	182	33.9	29.5	24.7	23.5	23.2	† 21.4	† 11.0	12.1	12.8	15.2	7.5	5.5
Spain................................	184	26.8	23.4	15.8	24.7	29.0	21.6	† 11.9	10.5	10.0	11.0	4.9	2.5
Denmark............................	128	17.1	12.9	12.5	16.3	22.4	17.1	26.0	17.7	20.2	28.7	34.3	30.5
Iceland..............................	176	16.5	10.3	9.1	11.6	10.0	8.9	9.9	7.8	7.8	10.1	14.8	15.3
Norway..............................	142	42.6	36.2	35.5	38.7	34.1	26.4	36.2	41.7	36.7	47.7	49.0	47.9
Sweden.............................	144	23.2	23.4	19.3	14.8	8.6	10.7	11.4	10.6	11.4	13.4	12.2	11.5
Switzerland........................	146	29.9	28.2	24.6	26.8	28.6	29.0	25.0	22.1	21.6	26.4	26.9	27.1
United Kingdom..................	112	9.3	9.4	8.2	7.2	5.5	5.3	† 5.9	6.8	6.0	6.1	5.7	5.2
Developing Countries................	200	**21.5**	**22.2**	**21.9**	**23.3**	**24.0**	**28.0**	**29.8**	**27.3**	**30.6**	**34.4**	**36.9**	**36.8**
Africa...	605	**12.9**	**14.9**	**13.5**	**16.2**	**21.4**	**20.3**	**22.0**	**27.5**	**31.1**	**33.4**	**34.5**	**38.6**
CEMAC													
Cameroon..........................	622	.1	† .1	.2	.1	—	—	.2	8.6	10.9	11.5	15.5	18.1
Central African Republic.............	626	46.4	78.4	69.8	85.4	66.1	51.7	54.1	59.2	57.7	53.3	58.5	48.7
Chad.................................	628	10.1	22.3	20.3	25.8	21.2	17.5	15.6	18.3	9.4	6.9	11.1	15.5
Congo, Rep. of...................	634	.1	4.1	4.6	3.1	3.4	.1	2.5	24.8	....	....	....	....
Equatorial Guinea...............	642	.4	.5	—	.1	.8	.1	.4	2.7	....	....	....	....
Gabon...............................	646	—	12.0	8.7	13.5	13.3	.7	1.1	9.9	.6	7.8	9.8	16.9
WAEMU													
Benin................................	638	22.2	† 31.1	13.8	20.8	19.3	18.5	27.8	38.9	48.3	44.2	41.9	39.0
Burkina Faso......................	748	39.1	35.4	39.7	27.2	30.5	26.5	27.0	19.4	20.9	23.2	42.3	31.4
Côte d'Ivoire......................	662	.1	5.5	9.4	10.9	11.6	13.3	11.9	14.5	21.9	39.5	20.4	....
Guinea Bissau.....................	654	12.0	5.9	7.9	6.9	19.7	29.7	35.9	70.6	58.5	91.5	24.9	....
Mali..................................	678	27.3	† 19.5	21.7	29.0	29.2	27.5	30.0	33.5	24.8	43.8	50.8	....
Niger.................................	692	26.6	17.5	13.2	9.1	7.4	5.9	6.1	12.9	16.8	18.8	33.0	25.7
Senegal.............................	722	.2	9.1	10.0	10.4	15.0	15.4	15.3	14.9	16.3	20.7	24.5	25.4
Togo.................................	742	45.3	22.1	11.4	6.9	9.6	10.4	13.0	16.3	12.7	18.4	12.6	33.5
Algeria...............................	612	9.6	15.2	10.3	24.2	....	....	....	....	....	101.0	139.1	123.6
Botswana...........................	616	120.7	139.5	127.8	151.7	130.7	129.4	147.9	133.1	169.5	147.7	117.7	....
Burundi..............................	618	43.2	47.4	46.5	57.1	48.4	21.6	21.1	11.6	6.6	23.6	22.2	19.4
Cape Verde........................	624	19.5	10.5	7.6	6.1	4.3	1.9	8.5	6.4	9.5	14.2	....	....
Comoros............................	632	33.8	43.5	37.0	....	....	....	....	....	....	....	....	....
Congo, Dem. Rep. of...........	636	....	....	8.8	3.9	....	....	....	....	....	....	....	....
Djibouti.............................	611	18.5	19.5	21.2	22.4	23.4	21.8	24.1	....	....	....	....	....
Ethiopia.............................	644	30.1	27.4	35.0	27.2	....	17.5	15.5	12.6	12.4	27.5	....	....
Gambia, The......................	648	21.1	24.0	30.3	20.6	28.7	24.2	30.1	30.4	41.0	37.6	....	19.0
Ghana...............................	652	5.4	14.4	19.0	20.4	12.0	7.6	6.8	4.1	....	....	....	....
Guinea..............................	656	9.2	6.8	5.9	7.5	10.9	19.8	18.6	14.4	20.9	10.2	....	....
Kenya................................	664	11.9	13.9	6.1	13.2	12.5	12.7	14.5	15.0	17.3	17.1	20.7	17.4
Lesotho.............................	666	15.1	22.8	24.1	24.0	29.0	34.6	33.2	29.9	29.5	26.9	23.4	....
Madagascar........................	674	9.0	8.5	10.4	24.0	29.4	16.4	20.1	20.3	27.9	37.3	17.8	....
Malawi..............................	676	5.4	4.5	12.1	18.8	10.8	27.2	19.4	24.1	19.1	12.4	8.4	7.4
Mauritania.........................	682	....	5.1	....	....	....	....	....	....	....	....	....	....
Mauritius...........................	684	22.9	20.1	22.7	20.4	16.5	14.0	16.9	22.3	21.9	29.6	34.7	30.1
Morocco............................	686	28.2	27.4	18.7	20.3	21.8	22.4	29.8	21.7	39.9	44.4	....	....
Mozambique.......................	688	....	17.3	14.2	23.1	35.7	39.3	29.2	....	....	....	....	....
Namibia.............................	728	5.2	7.5	7.1	6.0	7.4	8.2	9.9	8.7	7.9	13.4	9.5	8.2
Nigeria..............................	694	12.9	10.9	† 9.1	32.9	41.5	40.1	33.0	59.1	46.9	50.5	34.2	62.2
Rwanda.............................	714	7.4	22.0	21.7	21.6	26.8	30.9	36.3	47.0	44.2	62.5	45.5	57.6
São Tomé & Príncipe...........	716	....	....	9.1	11.7	40.1	....	....	....	....	....	....	....
Seychelles..........................	718	7.8	7.6	6.1	3.0	4.0	2.9	3.6	6.7	4.1	8.6	8.5	3.6
Sierra Leone.......................	724	10.2	14.0	13.5	6.6	21.6	24.1	25.4	17.1	14.7	16.7	11.4	22.7
South Africa.......................	199	2.7	3.8	4.8	1.6	7.6	† 7.7	12.4	10.7	11.1	10.5	8.2	14.2
Sudan................................	732	2.1	3.3	† 7.0	3.6	2.7	2.5	6.9	† 8.3	3.9	9.4	16.1	....
Swaziland..........................	734	17.5	18.4	15.4	12.4	14.4	17.2	18.3	17.5	12.5	14.6	....	....
Tanzania............................	738	7.1	11.5	8.4	16.5	24.2	21.4	25.9	33.3	35.1	47.9	49.9	47.5
Tunisia..............................	744	7.2	11.5	10.6	12.8	12.9	11.5	13.9	11.0	10.9	12.5	14.0	16.1
Uganda.............................	746	12.4	19.1	22.6	23.1	25.0	26.6	29.6	27.3	32.1	43.7	44.9	33.7
Zambia..............................	754	12.4	23.5	16.5	13.9	15.2	3.3	2.7	11.6	....	....	....	....
Zimbabwe.........................	698	12.4	9.4	11.6	8.2	2.7	2.4	6.4	5.5	2.0	....	....	....

Nongold Reserves/Imports

		1993	1994	1995	1996	1997	1998	1999	2000	2001	2002	2003	2004
1rl s							*Weeks of Imports*						
Asia *	505	**22.8**	**24.5**	**22.5**	**24.5**	**25.3**	**34.1**	**35.7**	**30.8**	**36.7**	**41.6**	**44.4**	**44.9**
Bangladesh	513	31.4	35.5	18.7	14.4	11.9	14.2	10.8	9.2	7.9	11.1	14.1	14.6
Bhutan	514	56.6	68.9	† 60.4	77.4	71.6	99.9	83.5	94.3	88.3	93.9	76.6	....
Cambodia	522	....	....	....	....	13.9	14.9	16.4	18.3	21.0	24.1	24.5	....
China, P.R.: Mainland	924	11.2	23.8	29.7	40.1	52.1	55.3	49.5	38.9	46.0	51.3	51.4	57.0
China, P.R.: Hong Kong	532	16.1	15.8	14.9	16.7	23.1	25.3	27.9	26.3	28.7	28.0	26.5	23.7
China, P.R.: Macao	546	40.3	48.1	57.5	63.0	63.3	65.5	72.9	76.6	76.5	78.1	82.0	81.3
Fiji	819	19.5	17.1	20.4	22.5	19.4	27.8	24.7	26.0	24.0	20.8	18.8	19.5
India	534	23.3	38.2	26.9	27.6	31.0	33.1	36.2	38.3	47.3	62.3	72.2	70.0
Indonesia	536	20.7	19.7	17.5	22.1	16.8	33.5	41.3	34.0	37.7	42.0	43.0	34.9
Korea	542	12.6	13.0	12.6	11.8	7.3	29.0	32.1	31.1	37.9	41.5	45.2	46.1
Lao People's Democratic Rep.	544	7.6e	5.6e	8.1	12.8	8.3	10.6	10.0	13.5	12.9	23.1	20.7	23.0
Malaysia	548	31.0	22.2	15.9	17.9	13.7	22.8	24.3	18.7	21.5	22.3	28.2	32.8
Maldives	556	7.1	7.3	9.3	13.1	14.7	17.4	16.4	16.4	12.3	17.7	17.6	16.4
Mongolia	948	8.0	18.5	14.7	12.7	19.5	9.7	13.8	15.1	16.8	26.3	15.3	12.2
Myanmar	518	19.2	24.6	21.6	8.7	6.3	6.1	5.9	4.8	7.2	10.4	13.7	15.7
Nepal	558	37.4	31.2	22.9	21.2	19.2	31.6	30.9	31.2	36.6	37.3	36.2	40.7
Pakistan	564	6.6	17.1	7.9	2.4	5.4	5.7	7.7	7.2	18.6	37.4	43.6	28.4
Papua New Guinea	853	5.7	3.3	9.4	17.4	11.1	8.1	9.0	13.0	20.5	13.5	19.0	19.6
Philippines	566	13.0	13.9	11.7	15.3	9.8	15.3	21.2	18.4	20.1	18.6	18.0	16.1
Samoa	862	25.2	32.4	30.3	31.5	34.5	33.0	30.7	31.3	22.6	24.1	31.8	29.5
Singapore	576	29.5	29.5	28.7	30.4	28.0	37.2	36.0	31.0	33.8	36.6	38.9	35.6
Solomon Islands	813	7.6	6.4	5.4	14.3	12.8	17.0	23.9	17.0	11.2	14.2	23.5	41.8
Sri Lanka	524	21.2	22.3	20.9	18.8	18.0	17.4	14.5	8.6	11.2	13.9	17.7	13.9
Thailand	578	27.6	28.0	26.4	27.1	21.7	34.9	35.2	26.9	27.2	30.6	28.2	26.5
Tonga	866	31.4	26.7	19.3	21.3	19.7	21.7	19.1	20.2	18.7	16.2	23.7	....
Vanuatu	846	30.1	25.3	26.4	23.4	20.7	24.8	22.0	23.3	21.7	21.2	21.7	25.1
Vietnam	582	....	....	....	8.1	8.9	9.1	14.7	11.4	11.9	11.3	13.0	11.8
*of which:													
Taiwan Province of China	528	56.4	56.2	45.3	45.2	38.1	44.8	49.8	39.7	59.2	74.5	84.4	74.8
Europe	170	**9.6**	**10.7**	**15.4**	**13.8**	**14.2**	**15.3**	**18.2**	**18.4**	**19.4**	**23.2**	**24.2**	**24.4**
Albania	914	13.4	17.6	17.6	17.4	24.9	24.1	22.3	29.3	28.9	29.0	28.2	....
Armenia	911	2.8	4.3	7.7	9.5	13.3	18.7	20.7	18.8	19.1	22.3	20.9	22.7
Azerbaijan, Republic of	912	—	.1	9.4	11.4	30.5	21.6	33.8	30.2	32.6	22.5	16.3	16.1
Belarus	913	....	1.7	3.5	3.5	2.4	4.3	2.3	2.1	2.5	3.5	2.7	2.4
Bulgaria	918	7.2	12.2	11.4	3.7	21.0	28.2	27.6	25.2	23.6	28.7	30.0	31.5
Croatia	960	6.9	14.0	13.1	15.5	14.5	17.5	20.2	23.2	26.7	28.6	30.0	27.5
Cyprus	423	22.0	25.2	15.7	20.1	19.6	19.5	26.3	23.5	30.1	38.5	38.0	35.5
Czech Republic	935	† 12.7	† 17.5	† 27.3	21.9	17.6	21.5	22.6	20.0	19.5	28.6	25.9	21.3
Estonia	939	22.5	† 13.8	11.8	10.3	8.9	9.1	10.8	11.3	9.9	10.8	11.0	11.0
Georgia	915	....	....	25.7	14.3	11.0	7.2	11.8	7.9	11.0	12.9	8.7	....
Hungary	944	27.9	24.5	40.5	28.0	20.7	18.9	20.4	18.2	16.5	14.2	13.9	13.9
Kazakhstan	916	6.1	12.2	15.5	15.9	20.5	17.6	21.0	16.4	16.1	20.2	26.2	34.5
Kyrgyz Republic	917	5.8	4.3	8.1	5.9	12.5	10.1	19.9	22.4	29.3	25.6	26.4	30.3
Latvia	941	25.7	22.7	14.5	14.7	14.5	13.1	15.4	13.9	17.0	15.9	14.2	14.3
Lithuania	946	8.0	11.6	13.1	10.3	10.5	13.7	13.4	13.1	13.9	16.2	18.1	14.9
Macedonia, FYR	962	4.5	5.2	7.8	7.7	7.5	8.3	12.6	10.7	22.9	18.8	20.3	16.4
Malta	181	32.6	39.4	28.3	30.1	30.3	32.4	32.7	22.5	31.8	40.5	41.8	36.6
Moldova	921	6.3	13.3	15.9	15.1	16.2	7.3	16.5	14.9	13.3	13.5	11.2	13.8
Poland	964	11.3	14.2	26.4	25.0	25.1	30.6	29.9	28.2	26.5	27.0	24.9	20.9
Romania	968	7.9	15.3	8.0	9.6	17.5	12.6	7.6	9.8	13.1	17.8	17.4	23.3
Russia	922	8.4	† 3.7	10.9	7.8	8.5	6.4	10.1	25.7	28.6	34.2	45.5	59.3
Slovak Republic	936	3.3	12.9	19.0	15.6	15.6	10.9	14.7	15.6	13.9	26.2	25.6	24.6
Slovenia	961	6.3	10.7	10.0	12.7	18.4	18.7	16.3	16.4	22.2	33.2	31.9	26.0
Turkey	186	11.1	16.0	18.1	19.6	20.0	22.1	29.8	21.5	23.7	28.3	26.9	19.2
Ukraine	926	.9	3.1	3.5	5.8	7.1	2.7	4.6	5.0	9.7	13.0	15.2	16.7
Middle East	405	**24.6**	**27.0**	**27.2**	**29.3**	**32.0**	**33.4**	**34.4**	**34.5**	**32.6**	**32.8**	**33.0**	**29.8**
Bahrain	419	17.6	16.2	17.9	16.0	16.7	15.7	19.3	17.6	20.3	17.9	18.1	15.9
Egypt	469	81.7	68.6	71.6	69.4	73.5	58.3	47.0	48.7	52.7	54.9	63.4	57.7
Israel	436	14.7	14.0	14.3	18.8	34.3	40.2	35.4	38.5	34.3	35.3	37.7	32.9
Jordan	439	† 24.1	26.0	27.7	21.3	27.9	23.8	36.8	37.7	32.7	40.7	47.0	33.7
Kuwait	443	31.1	27.2	23.8	21.8	21.8	23.8	32.9	51.5	65.4	53.2	35.9	35.7
Lebanon	446	† 53.1	77.7	43.0	40.9	41.6	48.2	65.1	49.6	35.7	58.4	90.8	65.2
Libya	672	....	....	....	....	....	80.2	91.0	173.6	175.0	169.2	235.2	....
Oman	449	22.8	21.9	22.4	22.3	21.4	17.7	30.8	24.6	21.2	27.5	28.4	21.1
Qatar	453	19.1	17.7	11.4	12.4	12.8	15.9	27.1	....	....	20.1	31.3	29.4
Saudi Arabia	456	13.7	16.5	16.0	† 26.9	27.0	24.7	31.6	33.7	29.3	33.2	31.9	31.9
United Arab Emirates	466	16.3	16.5	18.5	18.5	14.5	19.1	16.7	20.1	19.7	18.6	15.1	....
Yemen, Republic of	474	2.7	6.3	20.4	26.0	31.1	23.9	38.1	64.9	82.3	....	....	....
Western Hemisphere	205	**29.8**	**24.4**	**26.8**	**28.9**	**26.4**	**23.8**	**23.4**	**20.8**	**21.6**	**23.5**	**27.6**	**25.5**
ECCU													
Anguilla	312	13.6	13.1	20.5	12.5	13.8	13.2	11.3	11.2	16.2	19.5		
Antigua and Barbuda	311	6.1	7.0	8.9	6.8	7.1	8.0	8.8	....	....	....	....	....
Dominica	321	11.1	8.3	9.8	9.2	10.0	10.9	11.9	10.3	12.3	20.3	19.8	15.2
Grenada	328	11.8	13.7	15.5	12.2	12.8	12.2	12.9	12.2	....	....	....	....
St. Kitts and Nevis	361	13.0	13.0	13.1	12.9	14.3	18.6	19.1	13.6	17.6	19.3	....	....
St. Lucia	362	10.4	9.9	10.7	9.3	9.5	11.0	10.9	11.5	13.0	15.8	13.8	....
St. Vincent & Grens	364	12.2	12.5	11.4	11.9	8.6	10.5	11.0	17.6	17.2	15.9	13.3	17.1
Argentina	213	42.7	34.5	36.9	39.6	38.1	41.0	53.5	51.7	37.2	60.7	53.2	44.0
Aruba	314	....	....	19.9	16.9	14.6	14.2	14.6	13.0	18.2	21.0	18.1	17.6
Bahamas, The	313	9.4	8.7	7.5	6.5	7.1	9.6	12.1	8.8	8.7	11.5	14.5	22.1
Barbados	316	13.6	16.6	14.8	18.1	13.8	18.8	14.2	21.3	33.0	33.5	33.9	23.1
Belize	339	7.2	6.9	7.6	11.9	10.8	7.8	10.0	12.2	11.3	11.4	8.0	....

28

2005, International Monetary Fund : *International Financial Statistics Yearbook*

Nongold Reserves/Imports

		1993	1994	1995	1996	1997	1998	1999	2000	2001	2002	2003	2004
1rl s							*Weeks of Imports*						
Western Hemisphere(Cont.)													
Bolivia	218	9.6	19.4	24.1	30.4	30.5	24.9	28.9	26.3	27.0	17.1	23.1	24.6
Brazil	223	57.4	53.5	48.1	53.3	40.7	36.5	35.0	28.8	31.8	39.5	50.4	41.6
Chile	228	45.0	57.6	46.2	40.6	43.9	41.5	47.5	42.2	42.9	46.7	42.5	33.4
Colombia	233	41.9	35.0	31.3	37.4	33.1	30.7	39.1	40.2	41.1	43.8	40.4	41.6
Costa Rica	238	15.1	12.3	13.3	12.0	13.2	8.9	12.0	10.7	10.5	10.8	12.5	12.1
Dominican Republic	243	13.9	3.8	5.2	4.4	4.2	4.6	6.0	4.4	....	....	....	....
Ecuador	248	28.0	26.5	20.4	22.6	22.0	15.1	28.3	13.2	8.1	5.8	6.5	7.1
El Salvador	253	14.6	15.0	13.8	18.2	22.8	26.9	33.2	26.3	23.4	21.6	23.1	20.5
Guatemala	258	17.4	16.1	11.1	14.4	15.0	14.9	13.6	17.6	21.3	19.0	21.9	22.8
Guyana	336	26.6	25.4	26.5	28.7	26.0	....	....	....	25.6	26.3	14.1	17.7
Haiti	263	4.7	10.6	15.3	16.9	16.6	16.8	13.4	9.1	7.3	3.8	2.7	4.6
Honduras	268	4.5	8.4	8.3	7.0	14.0	16.8	24.4	23.9	25.0	26.6	22.7	26.2
Jamaica	343	10.2	17.2	12.6	15.4	11.3	12.2	9.9	16.6	29.4	24.2	17.1	25.5
Mexico	273	19.1	3.9	11.5	10.8	13.0	12.6	11.1	10.1	13.2	14.9	17.2	16.1
Netherlands Antilles	353	6.2	5.3	....	....	....	....	....	4.8	5.5	9.3	7.4	....
Nicaragua	278	3.8	8.5	7.3	8.9	13.6	12.2	14.2	14.1	11.1	13.3	13.9	15.7
Panama	283	14.2	15.2	16.2	16.2	19.9	14.6	12.2	11.1	19.2	20.6	17.0	9.1
Paraguay	288	19.4	25.0	20.4	19.1	14.0	18.2	29.5	19.3	18.7	....	....	....
Peru	293	35.8	54.3	46.0	58.3	55.5	50.2	55.7	49.0	....	....	....	....
Suriname	366	.9	4.9	11.8	10.0	10.0	10.0	3.5	6.3	13.5	11.2	7.8	....
Trinidad and Tobago	369	7.3	16.2	10.9	13.2	12.3	13.6	17.9	21.8	27.8	28.9	32.7	....
Uruguay	298	17.0	18.1	20.9	19.6	21.7	28.3	32.2	37.2	52.6	20.4	49.1	44.7
Venezuela, Rep. Bol	299	38.3	45.7	25.8	62.0	51.2	39.2	45.4	42.0	26.2	34.0	90.1	57.3
Memorandum Items													
Oil Exporting Countries	999	**22.9**	**24.9**	**22.1**	**29.1**	**27.9**	**31.8**	**34.6**	**38.8**	**38.4**	**39.8**	**41.5**	**39.4**
Non-Oil Developing Countries.	201	**21.3**	**21.9**	**21.9**	**22.8**	**23.6**	**27.6**	**29.4**	**26.3**	**29.9**	**33.9**	**36.4**	**36.5**

SDRs

1b s

Millions of SDRs: End of Period

		1993	1994	1995	1996	1997	1998	1999	2000	2001	2002	2003	2004
All Countries	010	14,614.3	15,761.5	19,773.2	18,521.4	20,532.2	20,379.7	18,456.7	18,489.0	19,556.8	19,672.7	19,914.6	20,301.5
Industrial Countries	110	11,454.4	12,485.9	14,998.5	14,521.1	15,511.5	15,844.0	14,726.0	14,411.1	15,967.8	15,791.9	15,305.9	15,282.8
United States	111	6,569.42	6,876.43	7,424.77	7,171.50	7,431.46	7,530.17	7,538.96	8,088.47	8,580.44	8,948.51	8,504.64	8,774.97
Canada	156	773.46	786.44	791.85	812.37	834.27	779.52	383.75	440.64	488.96	528.84	563.95	595.19
Australia	193	59.66	49.93	36.77	25.39	13.81	12.59	52.64	71.79	86.80	100.26	114.27	125.50
Japan	158	1,123.39	1,426.99	1,821.07	1,837.31	1,955.05	1,891.04	1,935.45	1,870.15	1,891.67	1,856.76	1,861.31	1,827.75
New Zealand	196	.04	.23	.57	.27	.24	1.23	4.97	10.03	12.82	15.89	18.95	21.99
Euro Area													
Austria	122	160.50	193.81	121.69	135.69	124.77	105.87	105.91	102.74	185.33	136.05	121.94	103.10
Belgium	124	124.71	123.44	331.14	346.49	362.69	433.25	197.10	235.81	375.70	407.85	434.12	225.28
Finland	172	83.77	222.66	241.63	201.58	241.71	247.53	211.33	106.46	186.27	147.03	130.98	106.72
France	132	240.78	248.31	642.76	682.07	719.88	786.19	252.67	308.90	391.74	457.85	512.32	563.26
Germany	134	700.15	763.32	1,346.21	1,326.24	1,324.95	1,326.57	1,427.29	1,352.90	1,426.43	1,456.23	1,307.13	1,326.98
Greece	174	.12	.22	.22	.01	.41	.24	3.76	9.19	7.71	11.13	14.43	17.41
Ireland	178	96.58	101.30	107.16	114.87	123.08	137.14	29.23	36.97	43.46	48.60	52.99	57.33
Italy	136	175.38	85.76	.03	20.44	49.57	78.65	122.49	182.43	236.45	79.32	104.85	93.14
Luxembourg	137	6.98	7.22	7.46	7.75	8.04	8.72	1.78	3.22	5.00	6.72	8.29	9.83
Netherlands	138	424.38	441.92	616.41	566.17	586.49	643.85	742.39	501.12	598.28	512.89	523.45	500.82
Portugal	182	41.93	48.32	56.96	68.19	79.43	95.95	32.12	41.22	49.42	55.82	61.13	66.25
Spain	184	157.38	174.50	276.78	313.87	351.26	408.08	189.78	222.63	279.19	260.06	278.04	213.96
Denmark	128	62.38	124.63	106.76	116.72	248.72	245.96	249.94	50.51	223.49	75.87	54.58	28.77
Iceland	176	.04	.08	.02	.03	.01	.01	.01	.04	.09	.11	.03	.08
Norway	142	288.44	266.73	311.47	247.19	257.87	294.08	297.97	235.35	282.06	232.07	225.42	232.31
San Marino	135	.04	.11	.18	.25	.33	.42	.08	.20	.34	.43	.49	.56
Sweden	144	42.16	46.40	296.83	198.91	276.70	292.37	227.78	165.25	157.08	132.03	133.13	134.80
Switzerland	146	112.82	161.95	181.27	87.84	170.49	192.32	344.72	124.71	225.00	54.24	24.72	45.50
United Kingdom	112	209.95	335.21	278.72	239.48	350.44	332.17	373.87	250.39	234.07	267.29	254.68	211.29
Developing Countries	200	3,159.9	3,275.6	4,774.7	4,000.4	5,020.7	4,535.7	3,730.7	4,077.9	3,589.0	3,880.8	4,608.8	5,018.8
Africa	605	116.3	119.0	134.0	117.1	122.2	280.2	394.4	404.6	463.5	481.7	491.1	468.6
CEMAC (incl. BEAC hqtrs.)	758	1.02	1.13	1.35	.35	.08	.24	6.50	6.19	5.26	4.13	2.32	16.35
Cameroon	622	.06	.03	.03	.11	—	.01	1.90	5.93	.01	.87	.99	.43
Central African Rep.	626	.03	.01	.02	.01	—	.01	.04	—	.01	.01	.01	1.58
Chad	628	.01	—	.02	.16	.01	.01	.02	—	—	.01	—	.04
Congo, Rep. of	634	.01	.03	.02	.01	.01	—	.08	.03	.15	2.38	.43	4.66
Equatorial Guinea	642	.28	.01	.01	.01	—	.01	—	.09	.79	.44	.03	.44
Gabon	646	.03	.17	—	.02	—	.01	—	.05	.04	—	—	4.03
WAEMU (incl. BCEAO hqtrs.)	759	7.28	6.90	10.20	5.78	2.28	1.33	6.62	2.18	8.15	8.94	10.93	6.41
Benin	638	.06	.02	.08	.21	.04	.05	.15	.05	.30	.09	.13	.02
Burkina Faso	748	5.58	5.55	5.52	1.78	1.63	.54	.53	.31	.41	.30	.21	.11
Côte d'Ivoire	662	.77	.11	1.24	.82	.02	.12	2.48	.97	.58	.86	.18	.13
Guinea Bissau	654	.01	—	.01	.01	.04	.02	.06	.03	.16	.30	.80	.44
Mali	678	.09	.14	.31	.21	.05	.06	.42	.08	.30	.03	.61	.40
Niger	692	.41	.29	.20	1.33	.12	.14	.98	.02	.25	.50	1.80	.60
Senegal	722	.30	.75	2.57	1.18	.35	.36	1.83	.71	5.96	6.68	7.10	4.71
Togo	742	.08	.05	.27	.25	.01	.05	.17	—	.18	.19	.10	.01
Algeria	612	4.90	15.66	.78	3.47	.54	1.09	1.38	2.34	9.14	10.18	38.19	.80
Angola	614	.10	.10	.11	.11	.12	.12	.13	.13	.14	.14	.14	.15
Botswana	616	24.03	25.39	27.06	28.71	30.36	32.41	28.05	29.89	31.53	32.63	33.52	34.42
Burundi	618	.51	.14	.05	.08	.05	.07	.07	.03	.04	.12	.09	.23
Cape Verde	624	.02	.05	.02	.04	.02	.04	.01	.04	.01	—	—	.02
Comoros	632	.07	.03	.07	.04	.10	—	.12	.13	.02	.03	—	—
Congo, Dem. Rep. of	636	—	—	—	—	—	—	—	—	—	6.12	5.35	3.54
Djibouti	611	.15	.11	.06	.10	.55	.27	.06	.28	.10	.76	.09	.64
Eritrea	643	—	—	—	—	—	—	—	—	—	—	—	—
Ethiopia	644	.21	.28	.17	.01	.09	.06	.05	—	.15	.11	.06	.33
Gambia, The	648	.23	.18	.09	.20	.09	.30	.49	.17	.01	.01	.02	.48
Ghana	652	.40	2.88	1.64	1.55	2.50	42.41	13.28	.41	3.19	2.71	31.49	13.34
Guinea	656	8.49	3.79	5.01	.54	1.97	1.02	.94	.19	.63	1.22	.15	—
Kenya	664	.82	.47	.19	.54	.50	.42	1.71	.21	.78	.61	1.37	.39
Lesotho	666	.41	.33	.24	.92	.89	.86	.85	.51	.46	.44	.42	.40
Liberia	668	—	—	—	—	—	—	—	—	—	—	—	—
Madagascar	674	.10	.02	.02	.04	.05	.03	.11	.04	.09	.03	.02	.12
Malawi	676	.17	4.25	.59	.94	.07	4.84	.29	.36	.67	.07	.32	.77
Mauritania	682	.10	—	.04	.99	.26	.01	—	.28	.16	.15	.09	.02
Mauritius	684	21.05	21.34	21.68	22.15	22.48	22.84	16.07	16.45	16.81	17.04	17.24	17.53
Morocco	686	25.12	18.04	17.25	5.17	.88	2.34	62.06	91.64	98.14	90.01	75.62	77.41
Mozambique	688	.03	.03	.03	.04	.04	.04	.05	.05	.05	.05	.05	.05
Namibia	728	.01	.01	.01	.01	.01	.01	.02	.02	.02	.02	.02	.02
Nigeria	694	.15	—	.45	.43	.44	.52	.14	.24	.53	.11	.15	.27
Rwanda	714	2.11	1.75	13.65	12.71	19.64	17.36	10.54	.87	9.82	7.48	20.03	19.45
São Tomé & Príncipe	716	.01	.01	.03	.01	—	—	—	—	—	.01	.02	—
Seychelles	718	.01	.02	.02	.02	.03	.03	.03	.01	.02	.01	—	—
Sierra Leone	724	2.79	6.18	11.48	5.32	8.29	7.36	15.17	4.03	.30	17.69	23.20	32.82
Somalia	726	—	—	—	—	—	—	—	—	—	—	—	—
South Africa	199	8.78	.85	3.29	.82	6.81	131.67	209.60	222.40	222.56	222.77	222.79	222.82
Sudan	732	—	—	—	—	—	—	—	—	—	.13	.23	—
Swaziland	734	5.88	5.89	5.90	5.93	5.94	5.96	2.42	2.44	2.45	2.46	2.47	2.47
Tanzania	738	.03	—	.05	.10	.08	.25	.20	.11	.39	.08	.34	.05
Tunisia	744	1.30	1.84	4.72	11.05	12.09	2.07	19.33	2.97	1.34	1.98	1.65	6.01

		1993	1994	1995	1996	1997	1998	1999	2000	2001	2002	2003	2004
1b s							*Millions of SDRs: End of Period*						
Africa(Cont.)													
Uganda	746	.04	2.10	.30	.74	3.98	3.54	1.69	2.72	1.48	2.18	3.22	.43
Zambia	754	—	—	8.17	1.41	.79	.57	.05	17.13	53.25	51.73	.32	16.00
Zimbabwe	698	.62	.05	.52	6.78	.22	.28	.79	.18	—	.01	—	—
Asia	505	**683.4**	**647.5**	**875.4**	**925.4**	**1,530.8**	**1,298.9**	**906.1**	**927.8**	**973.6**	**1,045.2**	**1,226.6**	**1,342.6**
Afghanistan, Islamic State of	512	2.01	.96									.40	.04
Bangladesh	513	16.61	24.64	107.28	76.19	21.65	9.14	.66	.33	.95	1.65	2.16	.80
Bhutan	514	.38	.40	.44	.47	.50	.54	.13	.17	.21	.23	.25	.27
Brunei Darussalam	516	—	—	—	.54	1.58	2.75	3.75	5.04	6.24	6.99	7.85	8.81
Cambodia	522	11.42	10.89	10.21	9.51	8.77	6.95	3.78	.14	.41	.40	.14	.05
China, P.R.: Mainland	924	352.03	369.13	391.58	427.15	446.53	480.10	539.58	612.71	676.82	734.19	741.33	803.01
Fiji	819	6.26	7.39	7.67	7.99	8.29	8.62	4.10	4.47	4.81	5.02	5.18	5.35
India	534	72.85	1.41	93.33	85.12	57.38	59.02	3.04	1.22	4.15	5.03	1.91	3.24
Indonesia	536	.26	.27	.87	1.53	369.98	221.52	.27	24.50	12.64	13.66	2.49	1.58
Kiribati	826	.01	.01	.01	.01	.01	.01	.01	.01	.01	.01	.01	.01
Korea	542	42.29	52.30	65.74	82.34	43.60	8.12	.50	2.70	2.66	8.68	14.18	21.14
Lao P. D. Rep.	544	1.90	7.46	9.49	7.17	9.31	4.32	.05	.07	2.72	4.47	12.87	9.90
Malaysia	548	87.78	92.71	101.64	115.28	129.88	145.77	60.80	80.81	99.58	111.36	119.95	128.18
Maldives	556	.02	.03	.05	.06	.08	.10	.14	.20	.25	.28	.30	.32
Marshall Islands, Rep. of	867	—	—	—	—	—	—	—	—	—	—	—	—
Micronesia, Fed. States of	868	.831	.866	.907	.944	.982	1.024	1.060	1.106	1.149	1.176	1.196	1.217
Mongolia	948	.02	1.98	1.70	.30	.52	.34	.12	.01	.01	.03	.03	.03
Myanmar	518	.21	.10	.06	.06	.06	.23	.12	.11	.44	.06	.07	.03
Nepal	558	.03	.09	.01	.01	.08	.02	.23	.01	.07	.01	.54	6.23
Pakistan	564	.52	.21	9.90	9.18	7.98	.65	.17	10.92	3.09	1.57	166.87	157.76
Palau	565	—	—	—	—	—	—	—	—	—	—	—	—
Papua New Guinea	853	.03	.07	.47	.04	.06	.04	.53	9.34	6.93	4.46	2.48	.47
Philippines	566	7.31	16.65	5.36	1.67	1.28	1.36	5.11	1.48	11.15	7.48	1.19	.65
Samoa	862	1.95	1.99	2.04	2.10	2.14	2.19	2.24	2.29	2.34	2.38	2.40	2.43
Singapore	576	56.92	24.13	33.05	42.48	52.25	64.91	89.23	105.32	119.56	130.19	139.61	188.86
Solomon Islands	813	.03	.01	—	.01	—	—	.01	—	.01	—	—	—
Sri Lanka	524	.28	.24	.62	1.34	.31	.89	.70	.31	.68	1.72	.42	.12
Thailand	578	15.95	21.84	30.46	41.50	357.56	277.86	188.06	63.43	4.19	3.09	.24	.66
Tonga	866	.44	.49	.04	.08	.11	.15	.03	.10	.15	.19	.22	.24
Vanuatu	846	.15	.22	.29	.36	.44	.53	.60	.70	.79	.84	.89	.93
Vietnam	582	4.92	11.03	2.20	11.91	9.44	1.79	1.06	.25	11.59	.03	1.46	.29
Europe	170	**270.1**	**373.6**	**636.8**	**511.5**	**784.2**	**730.0**	**568.0**	**558.1**	**480.8**	**276.4**	**294.6**	**251.4**
Albania	914	.01	.20	.10	.52	.46	43.39	56.06	58.33	64.87	60.02	60.98	64.90
Armenia	911	—	.19	29.82	28.86	27.63	19.89	29.64	16.54	8.15	22.14	12.67	7.70
Azerbaijan, Republic of	912	—	—	.84	14.48	4.14	.08	5.15	5.07	1.98	.51	12.14	9.36
Belarus	913	3.22	.01	3.05	.10	—	.30	.30	.14	.31	.19	.02	.01
Bosnia and Herzegovina	963	—	—	5.05	1.84	—	3.71	5.59	8.18	4.86	2.31	2.29	.32
Bulgaria	918	.83	10.39	20.08	8.31	8.37	21.38	59.53	64.97	1.80	.55	45.54	8.45
Croatia	960	.82	3.09	94.40	87.31	109.00	164.19	138.07	113.01	85.49	1.10	.03	.03
Cyprus	423	.07	.11	.03	.03	.25	.20	.40	.77	1.13	1.53	1.99	2.51
Czech Republic	935	5.98		.12	—	—	—	—	.16	.68	3.36	6.28	3.41
Estonia	939	41.56	1.09	.20	.12	.01	.05	.99	.01	.03	.05	.05	.05
Georgia	915	—	1.61	1.12	.05	.10	3.69	6.13	2.51	3.15	2.13	3.31	7.22
Hungary	944	2.14	1.08	.58	.35	.13	.52	3.19	8.97	16.36	24.07	31.20	37.56
Kazakhstan	916	13.98	69.54	154.87	240.19	327.15	275.08	164.24	.01	—	.76	.78	.79
Kyrgyz Republic	917	9.37	.65	9.59	5.14	.70	.24	3.71	.54	1.05	.47	6.94	12.80
Latvia	941	71.10	.21	1.49	1.56	1.50	.21	2.24	—	.07	.05	.09	.10
Lithuania	946	54.71	10.38	12.22	7.09	7.95	11.50	3.19	1.01	14.67	39.31	.04	.06
Macedonia, FYR	962	.01	.01	.15	.03	.28	.76	.87	.50	1.77	4.50	.19	.49
Malta	181	35.25	35.62	37.64	39.75	41.91	44.36	22.49	24.51	26.39	28.94	29.84	30.77
Moldova	921	25.05	14.62	8.81	5.45	.89	.50	.23	.26	.59	.20	.03	.05
Poland	964	.52	1.02	1.51	3.08	3.99	5.02	8.13	13.60	20.54	29.04	36.89	45.17
Romania	968	1.37	38.14	37.72	2.82	76.95	.83	7.34	.75	5.42	1.69	.18	.36
Russia	922	3.65	2.11	78.53	3.13	90.68	.05	—	.41	2.29	.88	.49	.55
Serbia & Montenegro	965	—	—	—	—	—	—	—	15.22	6.81	.70	.26	.03
Slovak Republic	936	.25	58.89	39.00	11.24	19.59	1.19	.57	.37	.53	.85	.86	.88
Slovenia	961	.03	.04	.04	.09	.05	.17	1.17	2.83	4.00	5.13	6.18	7.18
Tajikistan	923	—	—	—	2.21	9.06	2.05	.04	.02	6.02	3.86	1.34	.57	.85
Turkey	186	.13	.82	1.93	.98	.58	.97	.06	21.88	3.56	23.01	20.46	9.02
Turkmenistan	925	—	—	—	—	—	—	—	—	—	—	—	—
Ukraine	926	—	123.73	97.06	46.72	52.70	129.53	47.86	191.19	199.80	20.81	14.27	.75
Uzbekistan	927	—	—	.81	.03	.09	.16	.41	.30	.67	.79	.07	.02
Middle East	405	**1,014.4**	**1,090.4**	**1,165.0**	**1,397.5**	**1,556.0**	**1,424.9**	**829.9**	**1,041.1**	**1,076.7**	**1,211.3**	**1,316.5**	**1,741.1**
Bahrain, Kingdom of	419	10.77	11.01	11.28	11.68	11.90	12.15	.03	1.03	.84	.77	.68	.58
Egypt	469	50.43	59.19	69.51	85.57	83.92	113.80	30.07	36.94	27.68	67.24	127.01	106.38
Iran, I.R. of	429	104.85	97.91	89.88	239.76	244.62	1.12	101.26	267.49	267.40	267.96	268.41	273.91
Iraq	433												296.12
Israel	436	.39	.24	.38	.95	.03	.20	.11	.83	1.37	3.36	6.39	9.77
Jordan	439	3.99	.46	.82	.57	.14	.55	.19	.47	.93	.63	.75	1.08
Kuwait	443	49.07	55.02	61.28	68.15	74.14	82.51	53.74	69.79	85.90	97.74	107.51	117.07
Lebanon	446	10.51	11.35	12.34	13.34	14.33	15.44	16.38	18.21	19.37	20.10	20.64	21.19
Libya	672	303.46	324.75	349.69	373.87	398.47	425.79	372.59	412.77	441.19	448.87	461.97	475.41
Oman	449	4.96	6.17	7.49	8.84	10.10	11.47	1.33	3.12	5.02	6.53	7.81	8.98
Qatar	453	18.66	19.88	21.21	22.52	23.76	25.11	10.67	15.85	17.90	19.98	21.75	23.45
Saudi Arabia	456	402.69	415.98	448.24	481.28	512.14	545.95	110.45	146.57	192.27	243.89	289.75	334.08
Syrian Arab Rep.	463	.02			.01	.01	.05	.05	.01	.32	.02	.04	36.58
United Arab Emirates	466	54.14	54.99	55.91	57.60	58.36	59.19	4.55	3.08	1.76	1.13	.48	3.49
Yemen, Republic of	474	.47	33.49	37.01	33.34	124.06	131.55	128.48	64.96	14.71	33.04	3.29	33.03

SDRs

1b s		1993	1994	1995	1996	1997	1998	1999	2000	2001	2002	2003	2004
		Millions of SDRs: End of Period											
Western Hemisphere	205	**1,075.7**	**1,045.1**	**1,963.5**	**1,049.0**	**1,027.6**	**801.7**	**1,032.3**	**1,146.4**	**594.5**	**866.3**	**1,279.9**	**1,215.1**
ECCU (incl. ECCB hqtrs.)	309	3.24	3.36	3.47	3.60	3.67	3.80	3.89	3.91	4.02	4.07	4.11	1.56
Antigua and Barbuda	311	—	—	—	—	—	—	.01	.01	.01	.01	.01	.01
Dominica	321	—	—	—	—	—	—	.01	—	—	—	—	.03
Grenada	328	—	.02	.02	.04	—	.03	—	—	—	—	—	.01
St. Kitts and Nevis	361	—	—	—	—	—	—	—	—	.01	—	—	—
St. Lucia	362	1.34	1.36	1.39	1.42	1.45	1.48	1.50	1.43	1.46	1.48	1.49	1.50
St. Vincent & Grens.	364	.09	.09	.08	.07	.07	.07	.06	.06	.03	.02	—	—
Argentina	213	329.45	385.68	362.67	277.42	123.58	187.73	100.34	562.21	8.49	69.28	678.68	564.49
Bahamas, The	313	.01	.01	.02	.01	.02	.02	.02	.09	.09	.08	.01	.02
Barbados	316	.05	.03	.03	.02	.02	.02	.01	.02	.04	.04	.01	.04
Belize	339	.29	.37	.47	.61	.71	.82	1.01	1.20	1.37	1.48	1.56	1.64
Bolivia	218	10.19	16.99	26.88	26.81	26.81	26.81	27.27	27.29	27.32	27.35	27.13	26.56
Brazil	223	1.65	.30	.68	.66	.37	1.24	7.32	.27	8.42	202.07	1.54	2.67
Chile	228	.92	.45	2.07	1.33	.96	5.86	13.48	18.89	23.02	26.87	30.72	33.88
Colombia	233	114.88	116.38	118.83	122.83	127.64	139.34	95.18	103.32	107.81	113.15	115.19	116.51
Costa Rica	238	.12	.12	.04	.01	.02	.05	.59	.33	.07	.06	.04	.09
Dominican Republic	243	10.28	2.53	.35	.29	.23	.19	.21	.27	.35	.21	.09	1.02
Ecuador	248	3.15	2.97	2.11	1.87	.41	.20	1.70	.24	1.85	1.38	.67	36.09
El Salvador	253	.01	.07	24.99	24.99	24.98	24.98	24.98	24.98	24.98	24.98	24.98	24.98
Guatemala	258	11.43	11.38	10.60	10.15	9.44	8.65	8.36	7.52	6.73	6.06	5.53	5.14
Guyana	336	—	.05	.09	.07	.14	.17	.92	7.02	1.96	3.43	3.26	4.60
Haiti	263	—	—	.36	.03	.06	.39	.62	.05	.41	.37	.23	.12
Honduras	268	.11	.15	.10	.06	.06	.05	.68	.08	.25	.35	.08	.06
Jamaica	343	9.06	.02	.31	.05	.17	.46	.53	.07	1.19	.66	.04	.05
Mexico	273	162.65	121.13	1,074.05	178.69	490.13	239.65	575.45	281.23	283.47	288.02	291.64	299.23
Nicaragua	278	.03	.01	—	.02	.03	.15	.16	.05	.26	.02	.04	.32
Panama	283	.09	.03	.55	.03	.37	.10	1.20	.27	1.10	.78	.56	.56
Paraguay	288	65.08	67.63	70.58	73.30	76.08	79.14	74.81	78.49	81.33	83.25	84.63	86.04
Peru	293	.69	.31	.50	.22	.17	1.48	.28	1.15	1.39	.55	.27	.23
Suriname	366	—	—	7.75	8.22	8.23	8.25	2.00	1.77	1.56	1.42	1.32	1.21
Trinidad and Tobago	369	.24	.08	.15	.03	.10	.08	—	.06	.16	.29	.74	1.73
Uruguay	298	.29	.02	2.39	2.75	.03	.53	.71	.36	1.47	4.16	2.52	.78
Venezuela, Rep. Bol.	299	353.61	316.94	255.38	316.98	135.27	73.73	92.89	27.69	7.92	8.41	6.98	5.48
Memorandum Items													
Oil Exporting Countries	999	**1,296.7**	**1,307.6**	**1,291.2**	**1,574.4**	**1,827.8**	**1,448.0**	**749.3**	**973.4**	**1,041.7**	**1,118.5**	**1,205.5**	**1,540.6**
Non-Oil Developing Countries	201	**1,863.1**	**1,968.0**	**3,483.5**	**2,426.0**	**3,192.9**	**3,087.7**	**2,981.4**	**3,104.5**	**2,547.4**	**2,762.4**	**3,403.3**	**3,478.1**

SDR Holdings

		1993	1994	1995	1996	1997	1998	1999	2000	2001	2002	2003	2004
		Millions of SDRs: End of Period											
World	001	21,480.9	21,476.9	21,484.5	21,495.2	21,508.2	21,522.1	21,534.8	21,527.5	21,539.5	21,525.8	21,521.2	21,468.7
All Participants	969	14,614.3	15,761.5	19,773.2	18,521.4	20,532.2	20,379.7	18,456.7	18,489.0	19,556.8	19,672.7	19,914.6	20,301.5
IMF	992	6,687.28	5,510.08	652.47	1,726.32	634.78	687.34	2,459.29	2,413.89	1,543.19	1,201.69	1,087.86	841.50
Other Holders	970	179.36	205.33	1,058.87	1,247.41	341.26	455.05	618.86	624.58	439.53	651.43	518.69	325.66

Reserve Position in the Fund

		1993	1994	1995	1996	1997	1998	1999	2000	2001	2002	2003	2004
							Millions of SDRs: End of Period						
All Countries	010	32,802.2	31,725.6	36,673.2	38,005.3	47,078.0	60,630.9	54,785.6	47,377.7	56,861.3	66,064.6	66,507.8	55,786.2
Industrial Countries	110	28,308.8	27,417.0	31,643.8	32,609.8	41,336.5	53,919.2	46,775.8	39,699.5	46,960.1	53,717.1	52,584.4	43,581.8
United States	111	8,589.0	8,240.8	9,854.7	10,733.8	13,393.4	17,124.1	13,092.9	11,377.3	14,219.0	16,166.5	15,164.9	12,584.7
Canada	156	689.95	629.18	836.15	852.79	1,167.32	1,632.72	2,307.95	1,925.85	2,278.39	2,633.36	2,588.94	2,149.58
Australia	193	400.48	346.86	337.62	334.89	538.98	892.26	1,189.43	953.89	1,123.59	1,422.89	1,381.33	1,098.71
Japan	158	6,014.52	5,912.26	5,448.95	4,639.25	6,777.41	6,813.09	4,773.53	4,032.09	4,018.95	5,298.43	5,204.18	4,371.38
New Zealand	196	103.62	100.82	110.33	126.63	131.92	252.82	308.57	245.68	308.25	337.91	433.07	305.45
Euro Area													
Austria	122	381.49	363.86	458.91	562.40	713.73	969.69	698.68	531.46	662.48	705.16	770.73	602.32
Belgium	124	560.17	556.33	675.81	747.30	875.80	1,348.36	1,668.38	1,303.84	1,631.74	1,759.41	1,812.32	1,478.63
Finland	172	220.39	196.13	259.51	292.84	414.15	594.98	464.32	381.84	438.98	476.83	522.09	405.99
France	132	1,681.77	1,626.73	1,853.88	1,874.51	2,119.18	3,161.79	3,949.93	3,470.99	3,893.91	4,249.92	4,241.98	3,453.00
Germany	134	2,876.62	2,760.48	3,504.97	3,802.51	4,406.90	5,698.26	4,676.60	4,191.00	4,695.84	4,924.84	5,152.31	4,419.30
Greece	174	113.69	113.69	113.69	113.69	113.69	191.49	284.98	227.82	284.31	322.45	334.26	270.60
Ireland	178	155.08	151.93	197.47	226.07	252.15	413.56	302.94	252.37	267.68	345.25	386.68	269.23
Italy	136	1,575.39	1,392.80	1,320.60	1,289.87	1,660.68	3,075.29	2,583.58	2,230.13	2,559.73	2,874.12	2,795.77	2,384.59
Luxembourg	137	23.58	23.61	22.94	23.56	21.75	59.37	54.37	55.47	78.95	104.75	120.26	89.66
Netherlands	138	795.25	802.16	1,169.12	1,275.26	1,625.48	2,112.77	1,879.77	1,524.06	1,871.66	2,095.25	2,055.01	1,717.59
Portugal	182	219.42	230.80	302.98	320.31	313.36	442.12	274.96	242.38	299.42	329.07	360.82	283.34
Spain	184	750.60	759.53	1,064.90	1,110.30	1,409.46	1,557.82	1,111.18	907.54	1,055.08	1,170.75	1,253.37	1,014.29
Denmark	128	309.15	294.59	400.00	421.81	467.92	827.45	582.07	440.12	566.83	721.95	686.33	542.81
Iceland	176	10.48	10.48	10.48	10.49	10.49	10.50	18.58	18.58	18.58	18.58	18.58	18.58
Norway	142	425.50	440.93	636.16	643.80	725.52	899.13	621.23	448.09	577.34	729.81	669.50	559.24
San Marino	135	2.35	2.35	2.35	2.35	2.35	2.35	4.10	4.10	4.10	4.10	4.10	4.10
Sweden	144	451.42	451.42	451.43	451.43	589.10	899.90	862.95	683.33	827.12	1,050.33	988.12	842.47
Switzerland	146	604.54	643.21	981.22	1,064.90	1,407.48	1,828.05	1,218.12	963.67	1,258.68	1,410.04	1,383.44	1,153.85
United Kingdom	112	1,354.4	1,366.1	1,629.5	1,689.1	2,198.2	3,111.3	3,846.7	3,287.9	4,019.5	4,456.4	4,256.3	3,562.4
Developing Countries	200	4,493.4	4,308.6	5,029.4	5,395.4	5,741.5	6,711.7	8,009.8	7,678.1	9,901.1	12,347.5	13,923.4	12,204.4
Africa	605	157.6	157.6	151.0	152.0	150.5	159.4	335.5	290.0	289.5	291.5	306.0	296.5
CEMAC (incl. BEAC hqtrs.)	758	1.23	1.23	1.28	1.35	1.39	1.43	1.52	1.59	1.65	1.70	1.80	1.81
Cameroon	622	.34	.34	.36	.37	.41	.45	.50	.52	.54	.58	.64	.65
Central African Rep.	626	.09	.09	.09	.10	.10	.10	.10	.11	.11	.12	.16	.16
Chad	628	.28	.28	.28	.28	.28	.28	.28	.28	.28	.28	.28	.28
Congo, Rep. of	634	.47	.47	.50	.54	.54	.54	.54	.54	.54	.54	.54	.54
Equatorial Guinea	642	—	—	—	—	—	—	—	—	—	—	—	—
Gabon	646	.05	.05	.05	.07	.07	.07	.11	.15	.18	.18	.18	.18
WAEMU (incl. BCEAO hqtrs.)	759	28.00	28.07	28.19	28.33	28.46	28.54	28.62	28.71	28.86	29.05	29.29	29.49
Benin	638	2.09	2.10	2.13	2.16	2.18	2.18	2.19	2.19	2.19	2.19	2.19	2.19
Burkina Faso	748	7.20	7.20	7.22	7.22	7.22	7.22	7.22	7.22	7.23	7.26	7.28	7.31
Côte d'Ivoire	662	.07	.09	.09	.11	.17	.19	.24	.28	.31	.45	.57	.59
Guinea Bissau	654	—	—	—	—	—	—	—	—	—	—	—	—
Mali	678	8.73	8.73	8.73	8.76	8.76	8.78	8.78	8.78	8.83	8.83	8.88	8.97
Niger	692	8.56	8.56	8.56	8.56	8.56	8.56	8.56	8.56	8.56	8.56	8.56	8.56
Senegal	722	1.10	1.14	1.20	1.27	1.33	1.35	1.37	1.40	1.44	1.45	1.48	1.53
Togo	742	.25	.25	.25	.25	.25	.25	.25	.28	.30	.31	.33	.33
Algeria	612	.01	.01	.01	.01	.01	.01	85.08	85.08	85.08	85.08	85.08	85.08
Angola	614	—	—	—	—	—	—	—	—	—	—	—	—
Botswana	616	16.60	16.34	19.28	19.91	18.13	27.61	22.59	17.74	22.28	23.80	30.32	20.50
Burundi	618	5.86	5.86	5.86	5.86	5.86	5.86	5.86	5.86	.36	.36	.36	.36
Cape Verde	624	—	—	—	—	—	—	—	—	—	—	—	—
Comoros	632	.50	.52	.54	.54	.54	.54	.54	.54	.54	.54	.54	.54
Congo, Dem. Rep. of	636	—	—	—	—	—	—	—	—	—	—	—	—
Djibouti	611	—	—	—	—	—	—	1.10	1.10	1.10	1.10	1.10	1.10
Eritrea	643	—	—	.01	.01	.01	.01	.01	.01	.01	.01	.01	.01
Ethiopia	644	6.99	7.01	7.03	7.05	7.08	7.10	7.10	7.10	7.12	7.17	7.19	7.19
Gambia, The	648	1.49	1.48	1.48	1.48	1.48	1.48	1.48	1.48	1.48	1.48	1.48	1.48
Ghana	652	17.38	17.38	17.38	17.38	17.38	17.38	41.13	—	—	—	—	—
Guinea	656	.07	.07	.07	.08	.08	.08	.08	.08	.08	.08	.08	.08
Kenya	664	12.23	12.31	12.31	12.32	12.36	12.42	12.43	12.45	12.54	12.58	12.68	12.70
Lesotho	666	3.51	3.51	3.51	3.51	3.52	3.53	3.53	3.54	3.54	3.54	3.54	3.56
Liberia	668	.03	.03	.03	.03	.03	.03	.03	.03	.03	.03	.03	.03
Madagascar	674	—	.01	.02	.02	.03	.03	.03	.03	.03	.03	.03	.03
Malawi	676	2.22	2.22	2.22	2.22	2.22	2.24	2.24	2.24	2.27	2.28	2.29	2.29
Mauritania	682	—	—	—	—	—	—	—	—	—	—	—	—
Mauritius	684	7.33	7.33	7.34	7.37	7.37	7.38	14.47	14.47	14.47	14.48	21.88	21.88
Morocco	686	30.31	30.31	30.31	30.32	30.32	30.32	70.44	70.44	70.44	70.44	70.44	70.44
Mozambique	688	.01	.01	.01	.01	.01	.01	.01	.01	.01	.01	.01	.01
Namibia	728	.01	.01	.02	.03	.03	.04	.04	.04	.04	.05	.05	.06
Nigeria	694	.07	.07	.07	.07	.07	.07	.09	.14	.14	.14	.14	.14
Rwanda	714	9.79	9.79	—	—	—	—	—	—	—	—	—	—
São Tomé & Príncipe	716	—	—	—	—	—	—	—	—	—	—	—	—
Seychelles	718	.80	.80	.80	.80	.80	—	—	—	—	—	—	—
Sierra Leone	724	.02	.02	.02	.02	.02	.02	.02	.02	.02	.02	.02	.02
Somalia	726	—	—	—	—	—	—	—	—	—	—	—	—
South Africa	199	.05	.05	.06	.10	.10	.11	.11	.27	.35	.42	.50	.57
Sudan	732	.01	.01	.01	.01	.01	.01	.01	.01	.01	.01	.01	.01
Swaziland	734	3.00	3.00	3.00	3.00	3.00	3.00	6.55	6.55	6.55	6.55	6.55	6.56
Tanzania	738	9.98	9.98	9.98	9.98	9.98	9.98	9.98	9.98	9.98	9.99	10.00	10.00
Tunisia	744	.04	.04	.04	.04	.04	.04	20.17	20.17	20.17	20.17	20.20	20.22
Uganda	746	—	—	—	—	—	—	—	—	—	—	—	—
Zambia	754	.02	.02	.02	.02	.02	.02	.02	.02	.02	.02	.02	.02
Zimbabwe	698	.07	.07	.10	.11	.15	.19	.27	.31	.33	.33	.33	.33

Reserve Position in the Fund

Reserve Position in the Fund

		1993	1994	1995	1996	1997	1998	1999	2000	2001	2002	2003	2004
							Millions of SDRs: End of Period						
Asia	505	**2,056.7**	**2,173.8**	**2,848.4**	**3,142.2**	**3,201.8**	**3,680.0**	**3,643.0**	**3,355.3**	**4,013.9**	**4,910.5**	**5,359.9**	**4,815.8**
Afghanistan, Islamic State of	512	4.93	4.93	4.93	4.93	4.93	4.93	4.93	4.93	4.93	4.93	—	—
Bangladesh	513	.06	.07	.09	.11	.11	.16	.19	.19	.19	.19	.19	.21
Bhutan	514	.57	.57	.57	.57	.57	.57	1.02	1.02	1.02	1.02	1.02	1.02
Brunei Darussalam	516	—	—	—	35.26	35.26	35.26	35.28	35.28	35.28	51.79	58.29	58.29
Cambodia	522	—	—	—	—	—	—	—	—	—	—	—	—
China, P.R.: Mainland	924	512.77	517.31	817.78	970.97	1,682.40	2,523.33	1,684.72	1,462.33	2,060.54	2,738.22	2,555.95	2,138.08
China, P.R.: Hong Kong	532	—	—	—	—	—	31.34	—	—	—	—	—	—
Fiji	819	9.95	9.99	10.00	10.05	10.08	10.12	14.94	14.98	15.00	15.07	15.19	15.26
India	534	212.63	212.63	212.63	212.63	212.63	212.79	488.57	488.64	488.78	488.88	887.01	917.09
Indonesia	536	199.70	213.99	270.00	298.00	—	.05	145.47	145.48	145.48	145.50	145.50	145.50
Kiribati	826	—	—	—	—	—	—	—	—	—	.02	.01	—
Korea	542	339.17	363.61	438.49	474.30	443.72	.06	208.60	208.64	208.83	383.99	507.66	507.68
Lao P. D. Rep.	544	—	—	—	—	—	—	—	—	—	—	—	—
Malaysia	548	229.07	273.70	456.34	478.20	444.68	444.68	608.16	608.16	608.16	581.22	586.19	499.76
Maldives	556	.88	.88	.88	.88	.88	.88	1.55	1.55	1.55	1.55	1.55	1.55
Marshall Islands, Rep. of	867	—	—	—	—	—	—	—	—	—	—	—	—
Micronesia, Fed. States of	868	—	.001	.001	.001	.001	.001	.001	.001	.001	.001	.001	.001
Mongolia	948	.01	—	—	—	—	—	.02	.04	.06	.08	.10	.12
Myanmar	518	—	—	—	—	—	—	—	—	—	—	—	—
Nepal	558	5.73	5.73	5.73	5.73	5.73	5.73	5.73	5.75	5.75	5.75	5.77	—
Pakistan	564	.06	.06	.06	.06	.06	.06	.10	.10	.11	.12	—	—
Palau	565	—	—	—	—	—	—	—	—	—	—	.12	.12
Papua New Guinea	853	.05	.05	.05	.05	.05	.05	.05	.18	.30	.36	.40	.43
Philippines	566	87.10	87.10	87.10	87.10	87.10	87.10	87.10	87.10	87.18	87.28	87.36	87.43
Samoa	862	.66	.66	.67	.67	.68	.68	.68	.68	.68	.69	.69	.69
Singapore	576	157.44	172.84	199.85	204.73	248.42	297.65	303.44	237.71	297.50	351.29	379.27	283.42
Solomon Islands	813	.54	.54	.54	.54	.54	.54	.54	.54	.54	.55	.55	.55
Sri Lanka	524	20.21	20.25	20.25	20.25	20.25	20.25	47.71	47.74	47.79	47.82	47.86	47.86
Thailand	578	271.52	285.15	318.69	333.47	.02	.02	.02	.02	.02	.02	75.02	106.56
Tonga	866	1.19	1.20	1.21	1.21	1.21	1.22	1.70	1.71	1.71	1.71	1.71	1.71
Vanuatu	846	2.49	2.49	2.49	2.49	2.50	2.50	2.50	2.50	2.50	2.50	2.50	2.50
Vietnam	582	.01	.01	.01	.01	.01	.01	.01	.01	.01	.01	.01	.01
Europe	170	**262.9**	**262.8**	**264.6**	**268.2**	**269.2**	**302.8**	**653.1**	**665.3**	**1,099.4**	**1,418.3**	**1,662.6**	**1,377.5**
Albania	914	—	—	—	—	—	—	3.4	3.4	3.4	3.4	3.4	3.4
Armenia	911	.01	.01	.01	.01	—	—	—	—	—	—	—	—
Azerbaijan, Republic of	912	.01	.01	.01	.01	.01	.01	.01	.01	.01	.01	.01	.01
Belarus	913	.02	.02	.02	.02	.02	.02	.02	.02	.02	.02	.02	.02
Bosnia and Herzegovina	963	—	—	—	—	—	—	—	—	—	—	—	—
Bulgaria	918	32.63	32.63	32.63	32.63	32.63	32.63	32.69	32.74	32.78	32.78	32.78	32.85
Croatia	960	—	—	—	.03	.07	.11	.14	.16	.16	.16	.16	.16
Cyprus	423	25.45	25.45	25.45	25.45	25.45	25.45	35.36	35.37	35.37	49.11	66.82	47.28
Czech Republic	935	—	—	—	—	—	—	—	2.35	120.45	173.45	314.61	263.97
Estonia	939	—	.01	.01	.01	.01	.01	.01	.01	.01	.01	.01	.01
Georgia	915	.01	.01	.01	.01	.01	.01	.01	.01	.01	.01	.01	.01
Hungary	944	56.10	56.10	56.10	56.10	56.10	56.10	176.78	201.78	321.95	437.47	454.95	346.26
Kazakhstan	916	.01	.01	.01	.01	.01	.01	.01	.01	.01	.01	.01	.01
Kyrgyz Republic	917	.01	.01	—	—	—	—	—	—	—	—	—	—
Latvia	941	.01	.01	.01	.01	.01	.01	.01	.06	.06	.06	.06	.06
Lithuania	946	.01	.01	.01	.01	.01	.02	.02	.02	.02	.02	.02	.02
Macedonia, FYR	962	—	—	—	—	—	—	—	—	—	—	—	—
Malta	181	25.28	25.44	27.26	30.66	31.64	31.64	40.26	40.26	40.26	40.26	40.26	40.26
Moldova	921	.01	.01	.01	.01	.01	.01	.01	.01	.01	—	.01	.01
Poland	964	77.13	77.13	77.13	77.13	77.13	77.13	172.26	172.26	366.84	478.86	537.97	451.33
Romania	968	—	—	—	—	—	—	—	—	—	—	—	—
Russia	922	1.01	.84	.77	.93	.93	.93	.93	.93	1.14	1.18	1.43	1.83
Serbia & Montenegro	965	—	—	—	—	—	—	—	—	—	—	—	—
Slovak Republic	936	—	—	—	—	—	—	—	—	—	—	—	—
Slovenia	961	12.88	12.87	12.88	12.88	12.88	46.46	78.40	63.19	64.16	88.77	97.34	77.26
Tajikistan	923	—	—	—	—	—	—	—	—	—	—	—	—
Turkey	186	32.28	32.27	32.28	32.28	32.28	32.28	112.77	112.78	112.78	112.78	112.78	112.78
Turkmenistan	925	.01	.01	—	—	—	—	—	—	—	—	—	—
Ukraine	926	.01	.01	—	—	.01	.01	—	—	—	—	—	—
Uzbekistan	927	.01	.01	.01	.01	.01	.01	.01	.01	.01	.01	.01	.01
Middle East	405	**1,703.3**	**1,396.5**	**1,399.0**	**1,401.7**	**1,393.2**	**1,500.1**	**2,325.2**	**2,365.1**	**3,474.4**	**4,345.6**	**4,828.7**	**4,019.9**
Bahrain, Kingdom of	419	40.90	42.19	43.70	45.09	46.70	48.51	62.37	64.86	67.18	68.62	69.70	70.84
Egypt	469	53.75	53.75	53.75	53.75	53.75	53.75	120.08	120.08	—	—	—	—
Iran, I.R. of	429	—	—	—	—	—	—	—	—	—	—	—	—
Iraq	433	—	—	—	—	—	—	—	—	—	—	—	171.10
Israel	436	—	—	—	—	.01	.01	65.51	89.91	157.36	304.01	354.79	298.26
Jordan	439	—	—	—	—	—	.01	.05	.05	.05	.05	.05	.09
Kuwait	443	167.78	142.59	138.95	136.53	167.55	244.76	368.30	373.80	476.07	528.29	522.74	458.94
Lebanon	446	18.83	18.83	18.83	18.83	18.83	18.83	18.83	18.83	18.83	18.83	18.83	18.83
Libya	672	318.98	318.98	318.98	318.98	318.98	318.98	395.51	395.51	395.51	395.51	395.51	395.51
Oman	449	37.84	35.98	34.47	33.97	31.15	31.15	49.80	49.80	64.96	73.41	77.57	63.68
Qatar	453	33.80	30.65	29.73	29.23	26.40	26.40	44.73	44.73	79.11	99.59	103.46	86.36
Saudi Arabia	456	868.6	604.3	574.7	560.9	532.5	523.8	987.5	1,042.7	2,035.5	2,621.4	3,046.8	2,253.1
Syrian Arab Rep.	463	.01	.01	.01	.01	.01	.01	.01	.01	.01	.01	.01	.01
United Arab Emirates	466	162.82	149.12	185.81	204.37	197.37	233.89	212.55	164.82	179.79	235.83	239.30	203.16
Yemen, Republic of	474	.01	.01	.01	.01	.01	.01	.01	.01	.01	.01	.01	.01

Reserve Position in the Fund

		1993	1994	1995	1996	1997	1998	1999	2000	2001	2002	2003	2004
						Millions of SDRs: End of Period							
Western Hemisphere...............	205	313.0	318.0	366.5	431.4	726.8	1,069.3	1,053.0	1,002.5	1,024.0	1,381.6	1,766.2	1,694.7
ECCU (incl. ECCB hqtrs.)............	309	.53	.53	.53	.53	.53	.53	.58	.59	.59	.59	.60	.60
Antigua and Barbuda................	311	—	—	—	—	—	—	—	—	—	—	.01	.01
Dominica............................	321	.01	.01	.01	.01	.01	.01	.01	.01	.01	.01	.01	.01
Grenada............................	328	—	—	—	—	—	—	—	—	—	—	—	—
St. Kitts and Nevis................	361	.02	.01	.01	.01	.01	.01	.07	.08	.08	.08	.08	.08
St. Lucia............................	362	—	—	—	—	—	—	—	—	—	—	.01	.01
St. Vincent & Grens..............	364	.50	.50	.50	.50	.50	.50	.50	.50	.50	.50	.50	.50
Argentina..........................	213	—	—	—	—	—	—	—	—	—	.02	.06	.16
Bahamas, The......................	313	6.24	6.24	6.24	6.24	6.24	6.24	6.24	6.24	6.24	6.24	6.25	6.26
Barbados..........................	316	.03	.03	.03	.03	.03	.03	4.68	4.68	4.71	4.85	5.02	5.15
Belize..............................	339	2.91	2.91	2.91	2.91	2.91	2.91	4.24	4.24	4.24	4.24	4.24	4.24
Bolivia..............................	218	8.88	8.87	8.87	8.87	8.87	8.87	8.87	8.87	8.87	8.87	8.87	8.87
Brazil..............................	223	—	—	—	—	—	—	—	—	—	—	—	—
Chile..............................	228	.01	.02	.02	35.03	232.03	429.63	299.43	248.82	245.66	360.93	392.29	287.04
Colombia..........................	233	79.81	86.75	135.26	165.06	263.41	408.28	285.80	285.80	285.80	285.80	285.80	285.80
Costa Rica........................	238	8.73	8.73	8.73	8.73	8.73	8.73	20.00	20.00	20.00	20.00	20.00	20.00
Dominican Republic..............	243	—	—	—	—	—	—	—	—	—	—	—	—
Ecuador............................	248	17.13	17.13	17.15	17.15	17.15	17.15	17.15	17.15	17.15	17.15	17.15	17.15
El Salvador........................	253	—	—	—	—	—	—	—	—	—	—	—	—
Guatemala........................	258	—	—	—	—	—	—	—	—	—	—	—	—
Guyana............................	336	—	—	—	—	—	—	—	—	—	—	—	—
Haiti..............................	263	.05	.05	.05	.05	.05	.05	.05	.06	.06	.07	.07	.07
Honduras..........................	268	—	—	—	—	—	—	8.63	8.63	8.63	8.63	8.63	8.63
Jamaica............................	343	—	—	—	—	—	—	—	—	—	—	—	—
Mexico............................	273	—	—	.03	.12	.12	.21	.27	.32	.39	226.46	526.53	578.31
Nicaragua..........................	278	—	—	—	—	—	—	—	—	—	—	—	—
Panama............................	283	11.86	11.86	11.86	11.86	11.86	11.86	11.86	11.86	11.86	11.86	11.86	11.86
Paraguay..........................	288	16.48	14.53	14.53	14.53	14.53	14.53	21.48	21.48	21.48	21.48	21.48	21.48
Peru..............................	293	—	—	—	—	—	—	—	—	—	—	—	—
Suriname..........................	366	—	—	—	—	—	—	6.13	6.13	6.13	6.13	6.12	6.12
Trinidad and Tobago..............	369	.01	.01	.01	.01	.01	.02	.02	.02	24.57	76.37	129.32	111.09
Uruguay............................	298	15.38	15.38	15.38	15.38	15.38	15.38	35.68	35.68	35.68	—	—	—
Venezuela, Rep. Bol...............	299	144.95	144.95	144.95	144.95	144.95	144.95	321.90	321.90	321.90	321.90	321.90	321.90
Memorandum Items													
Oil Exporting Countries...........	999	1,934.5	1,640.7	1,697.7	1,727.0	1,418.9	1,524.0	2,610.9	2,623.9	3,783.6	4,506.7	4,938.0	4,184.4
Non-Oil Developing Countries.	201	2,558.9	2,667.9	3,331.8	3,668.4	4,322.6	5,187.6	5,398.9	5,054.2	6,117.6	7,840.8	8,985.5	8,020.0

		1993	1994	1995	1996	1997	1998	1999	2000	2001	2002	2003	2004
1d s							*Millions of SDRs: End of Period*						
All Countries	010	752,320	812,812	934,871	1,089,142	1,197,825	1,167,486	1,299,573	1,490,197	1,633,060	1,770,988	2,037,583	2,413,093
Industrial Countries	110	373,768	394,037	441,184	501,813	520,984	476,263	528,686	602,020	626,803	661,488	752,295	845,419
United States	111	30,237	28,233	33,028	26,631	22,834	25,568	23,448	23,976	23,061	24,875	26,731	27,507
Canada	156	7,623	7,000	8,496	12,537	11,208	14,141	17,801	22,136	24,257	24,042	21,223	19,425
Australia	193	7,623	7,334	7,628	9,713	11,932	9,493	14,213	12,880	13,077	13,694	20,166	21,829
Japan	158	64,591	78,875	116,007	144,187	154,060	144,326	202,336	266,490	308,521	332,072	439,302	530,753
New Zealand	196	2,326	2,439	2,856	4,013	3,167	2,731	2,933	2,300	2,073	2,396	2,850	3,082
Euro Area (incl. ECB)	163	....	....	....	....	....	....	166,111	167,802	165,440	158,741	126,524	116,381
Austria	122	10,095	10,966	12,020	15,203	13,789	14,856	10,212	10,355	9,106	6,281	4,807	4,355
Belgium	124	7,625	8,826	9,876	10,696	10,761	11,195	†6,104	6,131	6,957	6,553	5,149	4,968
Finland	172	3,635	6,885	6,252	4,315	5,582	6,043	5,313	5,634	5,727	6,206	6,423	7,419
France	132	14,567	16,111	15,568	16,078	20,083	27,523	24,724	24,648	20,978	16,156	15,560	18,723
Germany	134	52,948	49,470	52,334	52,716	51,772	45,548	†38,368	38,120	34,781	31,258	27,656	25,691
Greece	174	5,558	9,810	9,829	12,057	9,221	12,207	12,915	10,066	†3,809	5,612	2,586	479
Ireland	178	4,062	3,935	5,501	5,365	4,462	6,123	3,548	3,824	4,134	3,589	2,305	1,496
Italy	136	18,303	20,623	22,161	30,643	39,601	18,073	†13,630	17,210	16,635	18,086	17,534	15,461
Luxembourg	137	18	21	20	20	18	....	—	—	—	—	60	93
Netherlands	138	21,600	22,411	20,895	16,773	16,217	12,455	4,581	5,376	4,719	4,426	4,832	4,286
Portugal	182	11,271	10,348	10,303	10,681	11,214	10,701	†5,833	6,554	7,343	7,838	3,532	2,982
Spain	184	28,974	27,525	21,857	38,860	48,933	37,279	22,826	22,654	22,205	23,972	11,785	6,749
Denmark	128	7,128	5,784	6,904	9,295	13,457	9,767	15,406	11,105	12,825	19,052	24,229	24,595
Iceland	176	300	190	197	305	274	292	330	280	250	305	515	655
Norway	142	13,572	12,325	14,201	17,550	16,360	12,335	16,427	20,498	17,663	22,576	24,153	27,739
San Marino	135	85	118	131	147	133	118	101	99	102	130	165	224
Sweden	144	13,375	15,431	15,432	12,637	7,157	8,820	9,852	10,559	10,137	11,416	12,123	13,272
Switzerland	146	23,042	22,985	23,333	25,574	27,348	27,234	24,900	23,681	23,984	28,072	30,660	34,536
United Kingdom	112	25,210	26,392	26,357	25,816	21,403	19,434	†21,914	30,148	25,414	24,119	23,618	25,423
Developing Countries	200	378,552	418,776	493,686	587,329	676,841	691,223	770,887	888,177	1,006,257	1,109,500	1,285,288	1,567,675
Africa	605	13,384	15,924	17,441	21,842	31,981	28,932	30,021	41,458	51,062	52,857	61,004	81,349
CEMAC (Incl. BEAC hqtrs.)	758	....	....	....	....	....	....	....	957	852	1,172	1,216	1,985
Cameroon	622	1	†1	2	1	—	—	1	156	263	462	429	533
Central African Republic	626	81	144	157	161	132	103	99	102	94	91	89	94
Chad	628	28	52	96	114	100	85	69	85	97	161	126	142
Congo, Rep. of	634	—	34	39	63	44	—	28	170	54	20	22	72
Equatorial Guinea	642	—	—	—	—	4	1	2	18	56	65	160	608
Gabon	646	—	120	100	173	209	11	13	146	8	103	132	281
WAEMU (Incl. BCEAO hqtrs.)	759	....	....	1,669	1,871	2,095	2,217	2,101	2,490	2,971	3,974	4,488	4,632
Benin	638	175	†175	131	180	185	183	289	349	457	451	481	410
Burkina Faso	748	266	150	221	226	247	257	207	179	200	223	499	423
Côte d'Ivoire	662	1	140	355	420	458	607	457	511	810	1,369	877	1,090
Guinea Bissau	654	10	13	14	8	25	25	26	51	55	75	21	47
Mali	678	233	†143	208	291	299	277	246	284	268	428	631	545
Niger	692	131	67	55	45	31	29	19	53	76	89	165	157
Senegal	722	1	121	179	198	285	304	290	293	348	461	739	886
Togo	742	113	64	87	61	88	83	89	117	100	150	137	231
Algeria	612	1,069	1,816	1,348	2,942	5,963	4,861	3,211	9,141	14,293	16,997	22,169	27,761
Angola	614	....	....	143	383	294	144	361	920	582	276	427	879
Botswana	616	2,942	2,973	3,112	3,448	4,158	4,159	4,539	4,802	4,639	3,970	3,530	3,591
Burundi	618	112	134	135	91	78	41	29	19	14	43	45	42
Cape Verde	624	42	29	25	19	14	6	31	22	36	59	63	90
Comoros	632	28	30	29	35	29	27	26	32	49	58	63	66
Congo, Dem. Rep. of	636	34	83	99	57	....	....	....	....	....	....	....	....
Djibouti	611	55	50	48	53	49	47	50	51	55	52	66	59
Eritrea	643	....	....	27	57	148	16	25	20	32	22	17	22
Ethiopia	644	325	366	512	502	364	356	327	228	337	641	636	956
Gambia, The	648	75	65	70	69	70	74	79	82	83	77	38	52
Ghana	652	280	380	450	557	379	208	276	178	234	394	879	1,034
Guinea	656	88	56	53	60	88	167	144	113	159	125	....	....
Kenya	664	282	369	225	506	571	543	563	676	834	772	983	965
Lesotho	666	180	251	304	316	419	404	360	317	304	295	306	320
Liberia	668	2	3	19	—	—	—	—	—	—	2	5	12
Madagascar	674	59	49	73	167	209	122	165	219	317	267	279	324
Malawi	676	39	23	71	154	118	184	180	187	162	119	82	83
Mauritania	682	32	27	57	97	149	144	163	215	226	291	279	....
Mauritius	684	523	483	552	594	484	367	502	658	634	871	1,022	995
Morocco	686	2,605	2,933	2,375	2,603	2,928	3,117	4,013	3,540	6,574	7,293	9,175	10,371
Mozambique	688	136	122	131	239	383	432	475	556	569	602	672	728
Namibia	728	97	139	149	135	186	185	223	200	186	238	219	222
Nigeria	694	999	949	971	2,834	5,619	5,043	3,971	7,606	8,320	5,392	4,797	10,918
Rwanda	714	23	24	53	62	94	102	116	145	159	172	124	183
São Tomé & Príncipe	716	....	....	3	3	9	7	8	9	12	13	17	13
Seychelles	718	25	20	17	14	19	15	22	34	30	51	45	22
Sierra Leone	724	18	22	12	13	20	24	14	34	41	45	22	48
South Africa	199	734	1,153	1,894	654	3,550	2,963	4,419	4,446	4,587	4,120	4,148	8,238
Sudan	732	27	54	110	74	60	64	138	†190	94	324	570	1,047
Swaziland	734	184	195	192	168	210	246	265	261	207	194	178	199
Tanzania	738	138	217	172	296	451	415	555	738	910	1,114	1,361	1,468
Tunisia	744	620	999	1,075	1,309	1,454	1,312	1,608	1,367	1,561	1,662	1,960	2,508

Foreign Exchange

		1993	1994	1995	1996	1997	1998	1999	2000	2001	2002	2003	2004
1d s						*Millions of SDRs: End of Period*							
Africa(Cont.)													
Uganda	746	107	218	308	367	466	512	554	617	781	685	724	842
Zambia	754	140	184	142	153	176	49	33	171	93	342	166	201
Zimbabwe	698	314	277	400	410	118	92	194	148	51	61	....	....
Asia	505	**218,736**	**259,826**	**287,403**	**339,922**	**379,613**	**408,569**	**478,005**	**543,959**	**626,798**	**712,040**	**833,779**	**1,033,253**
Bangladesh	513	1,738	2,125	1,467	1,200	1,150	1,344	1,168	1,140	1,013	1,236	1,732	2,042
Bhutan	514	70	82	† 87	131	139	181	212	243	256	260	245	255
Cambodia	522	6	70	119	175	213	223	283	385	467	570	549	607
China, P.R.: Mainland	924	15,434	35,360	49,498	73,040	103,680	102,952	112,695	127,080	168,823	210,668	271,372	392,742
China, P.R.: Hong Kong	532	31,295	33,737	37,268	44,374	68,782	63,639	70,117	82,540	88,448	82,306	79,652	79,549
China, P.R.: Macao	546	1,142	1,347	1,518	1,684	1,877	1,749	2,082	2,550	2,792	2,795	2,923	3,500
Fiji	819	180	170	217	279	249	255	293	297	272	244	265	287
India	534	7,140	13,279	11,750	13,729	18,028	19,146	23,309	28,601	36,007	49,278	65,692	80,594
Indonesia	536	8,000	8,097	8,951	12,393	11,923	15,910	19,122	21,706	21,522	22,621	23,380	22,359
Korea	542	14,345	17,147	21,479	23,114	14,608	36,905	53,697	73,570	81,551	88,863	103,978	127,607
Lao P. D. Rep.	544	44e	34e	52	111	74	75	74	107	101	136	127	134
Malaysia	548	19,522	17,048	15,436	18,190	14,833	17,562	21,617	21,970	23,541	24,479	29,251	42,118
Maldives	556	18	20	31	52	72	83	91	92	72	96	105	129
Micronesia, Fed. States of	868	....	....	46	61	63	71	66	86	77	85	59	34
Mongolia	948	43	54	77	74	130	66	99	137	164	257	159	152
Myanmar	518	220	289	377	159	185	223	193	171	318	346	370	433
Nepal	558	460	469	389	392	458	531	610	720	820	743	816	935
Pakistan	564	871	2,006	1,156	372	878	729	1,101	1,151	2,893	5,940	7,196	6,152
Papua New Guinea	853	103	66	175	406	269	137	149	211	329	232	330	406
Philippines	566	3,310	4,032	4,211	6,906	5,320	6,498	9,576	9,958	10,625	9,710	9,101	8,358
Samoa	862	34	32	34	40	45	41	47	46	42	43	53	58
Singapore	576	34,994	39,654	45,980	53,194	52,535	52,852	55,595	61,159	59,560	59,849	63,914	71,795
Solomon Islands	813	14	11	10	22	26	34	37	24	15	13	24	51
Sri Lanka	524	1,166	1,381	1,384	1,343	1,480	1,385	1,143	749	975	1,150	1,476	1,325
Thailand	578	17,530	19,786	23,857	25,864	19,045	20,194	24,630	24,509	25,741	27,982	27,568	31,228
Tonga	866	25	23	18	20	19	19	18	19	19	18	27	36
Vanuatu	846	31	27	30	28	25	29	27	27	27	24	26	36
Vietnam	582	....	....	888	1,195	1,462	1,420	2,422	2,622	2,912	3,031	4,187	4,534
Europe	170	**24,801**	**29,893**	**56,750**	**60,892**	**70,878**	**71,736**	**77,632**	**96,025**	**109,873**	**136,586**	**167,412**	**211,875**
Albania	914	107	140	162	195	228	229	296	411	521	554	615	806
Armenia	911	10	22	37	79	142	210	202	228	247	290	331	363
Azerbaijan, Republic of	912	—	1	80	132	341	318	485	517	712	530	540	692
Belarus	913	....	69	251	326	292	499	214	269	311	455	400	483
Bosnia & Herzegovina	963	....	....	....	....	60	120	324	373	967	970	1,206	1,550
Bulgaria	918	444	643	779	295	1,524	1,853	2,015	2,324	2,584	3,208	4,155	5,610
Croatia	960	448	959	1,181	1,522	1,773	1,835	2,066	2,592	3,657	4,327	5,512	5,639
Cyprus	423	773	978	726	1,047	1,006	954	1,300	1,300	1,768	2,172	2,123	2,468
Czech Republic	935	2,753	4,209	9,312	8,590	7,214	8,908	9,330	9,990	11,290	17,150	17,695	17,929
Estonia	939	240	303	390	443	562	576	621	707	653	736	924	1,151
Georgia	915	....	....	129	131	148	84	90	81	124	143	125	239
Hungary	944	4,820	4,557	7,999	6,703	6,175	6,562	7,801	8,377	8,197	7,150	8,086	9,860
Kazakhstan	916	318	504	609	660	931	763	914	1,223	1,589	1,879	2,850	5,455
Kyrgyz Republic	917	26	17	45	61	125	116	164	183	209	212	238	340
Latvia	941	243	373	339	453	562	569	633	653	914	913	964	1,231
Lithuania	946	200	350	497	530	741	989	867	1,006	1,273	1,689	2,269	2,262
Macedonia, FYR	962	76	102	173	167	190	217	312	329	591	527	604	582
Malta	181	931	1,206	1,014	1,056	1,029	1,105	1,240	1,064	1,259	1,556	1,766	1,667
Moldova	921	31	109	164	211	270	101	135	170	181	198	203	303
Poland	964	2,901	3,923	9,860	12,329	15,044	19,325	19,021	20,201	20,021	20,565	21,350	22,249
Romania	968	723	1,391	1,024	1,459	2,742	2,036	1,105	1,895	3,116	4,504	5,410	9,411
Russia	922	4,243	2,724	9,596	7,838	9,465	5,540	6,161	18,622	25,891	32,402	49,242	77,788
Slovak Republic	936	302	1,100	2,224	2,366	2,375	2,036	2,455	3,087	3,295	6,478	7,858	9,283
Slovenia	961	561	1,014	1,212	1,585	2,444	2,537	2,229	2,387	3,377	5,040	5,615	5,578
Tajikistan	923	....	....	....	....	18	36	40	65	70	64	75	101
Turkey	186	4,533	4,878	8,336	11,397	13,796	13,808	16,897	17,126	14,906	19,775	22,741	22,846
Ukraine	926	118	322	610	1,316	1,682	411	715	847	2,152	3,099	4,515	5,989
Middle East	405	**44,040**	**43,098**	**47,494**	**57,752**	**70,355**	**69,515**	**75,271**	**88,693**	**93,718**	**91,869**	**94,469**	**101,931**
Bahrain, Kingdom of	419	896	748	806	860	898	706	935	1,135	1,272	1,200	1,126	1,178
Egypt	469	9,290	9,121	10,762	11,960	13,696	12,704	10,403	9,911	10,258	9,673	9,018	9,084
Israel	436	4,646	4,653	5,462	7,937	15,069	16,103	16,404	17,778	18,444	17,407	17,348	17,138
Jordan	439	† 1,188	1,159	1,326	1,223	1,631	1,243	1,915	2,556	2,436	2,924	3,495	3,390
Kuwait	443	2,851	2,200	2,195	2,240	2,317	2,476	3,092	4,992	7,314	6,147	4,469	4,731
Lebanon	446	1,616	2,630	3,019	4,093	4,396	4,622	5,630	4,525	3,951	5,289	8,386	7,516
Libya	672	....	....	....	....	....	4,418	4,536	8,756	10,940	9,679	12,322	15,670
Oman	449	1,271	1,086	1,190	1,321	1,493	1,334	1,965	1,774	1,812	2,254	2,333	2,244
Qatar	453	453	400	449	425	558	689	895	828	948	1,033	1,856	2,077
Saudi Arabia	456	4,137	4,033	4,777	† 8,917	9,981	9,030	11,286	13,843	11,773	12,295	11,886	14,986
United Arab Emirates	466	4,227	4,357	4,784	5,340	5,949	6,154	7,561	10,211	11,075	10,958	9,914	11,725
Yemen, Republic of	474	105	141	379	674	768	575	944	2,161	2,896	3,211	3,353	3,615
Western Hemisphere	205	**77,592**	**70,034**	**84,597**	**106,922**	**124,014**	**112,471**	**109,958**	**118,042**	**124,806**	**116,148**	**128,623**	**139,265**
ECCU (incl. ECCB hqtrs.)	309	192	175	207	198	224	252	263	292	352	369	361	406
Anguilla	312	7	6	9	10	12	13	15	16	19	19	22	22
Antigua and Barbuda	311	28	31	40	33	38	42	51	49	63	64	77	77
Dominica	321	14	11	15	16	18	20	23	23	25	33	32	27
Grenada	328	20	21	25	25	32	33	37	44	51	65	56	78
Montserrat	351	4	5	6	6	8	18	10	8	10	11	10	9
St. Kitts and Nevis	361	21	22	23	23	27	33	36	35	45	48	44	50
St. Lucia	362	42	38	41	38	44	49	53	59	69	68	70	84

Foreign Exchange

1d s		1993	1994	1995	1996	1997	1998	1999	2000	2001	2002	2003	2004
Western Hemisphere(Cont.)		*Millions of SDRs: End of Period*											
St. Vincent & Grens.....................	364	22	21	19	20	23	27	30	42	48	39	34	48
Argentina.....................................	213	9,711	9,428	9,249	12,313	16,419	17,392	19,027	18,738	11,572	7,646	8,846	11,595
Aruba..	314	132	122	146	130	128	158	160	160	234	250	199	190
Bahamas, The..............................	313	119	115	114	113	162	240	293	262	248	274	324	428
Barbados......................................	316	109	134	147	201	196	260	215	358	545	487	492	368
Belize..	339	25	20	22	37	40	28	47	89	84	79	51	25
Bolivia...	218	144	283	408	628	770	638	674	675	669	391	446	526
Brazil...	223	22,279	25,392	33,439	40,559	37,670	30,239	25,345	24,935	28,430	27,516	33,048	33,957
Chile...	228	7,018	8,965	9,510	10,376	12,791	10,835	10,337	11,272	11,173	10,896	10,236	9,978
Colombia.....................................	233	5,579	5,270	5,362	6,559	6,874	5,596	5,454	6,454	7,686	7,495	6,856	8,222
Costa Rica....................................	238	737	603	695	687	926	746	1,043	991	1,038	1,081	1,216	1,215
Dominican Republic......................	243	464	170	246	243	290	356	505	481	875	344	170	513
Ecuador.......................................	248	984	1,243	1,076	1,273	1,534	1,133	1,178	709	649	507	529	635
El Salvador...................................	253	390	445	485	627	944	1,121	1,435	1,450	1,360	1,169	1,283	1,216
Guatemala...................................	258	620	580	462	595	814	940	858	1,333	1,817	1,685	1,901	2,201
Guyana..	336	180	169	181	229	234	196	195	227	227	206	183	145
Haiti..	263	23	35	128	150	153	183	192	140	112	60	41	73
Honduras.....................................	268	71	117	176	173	430	581	907	999	1,118	1,112	954	1,260
Jamaica..	343	295	504	458	612	505	503	403	809	1,511	1,209	804	1,189
Mexico...	273	18,118	4,179	10,259	13,335	20,853	22,344	22,581	26,972	35,317	36,700	38,857	40,423
Netherlands Antilles......................	353	170	123	137	131	159	176	193	200	240	299	251	267
Nicaragua....................................	278	40	97	92	137	280	249	371	375	302	330	338	430
Panama..	283	423	471	513	591	838	666	587	542	856	857	668	394
Paraguay......................................	288	378	624	650	642	529	520	616	486	465	358	546	645
Peru...	293	2,480	4,790	5,530	7,356	8,139	6,792	6,361	6,426	6,899	6,869	6,579	7,840
Suriname......................................	366	13	27	82	59	73	67	20	40	87	71	64	76
Trinidad and Tobago.....................	369	150	241	241	378	523	556	689	1,064	1,493	1,415	1,519	1,927
Uruguay.......................................	298	536	648	756	852	1,138	1,457	1,480	1,867	2,427	562	1,399	1,614
Venezuela, Rep. Bol......................	299	6,211	5,064	3,826	7,736	10,376	8,247	8,530	9,696	7,022	5,912	10,462	11,505
Memorandum Items													
Oil Exporting Countries...........	999	42,483	40,486	40,751	56,821	67,686	67,531	73,782	98,679	105,518	102,995	112,466	132,471
Non-Oil Developing Countries.	201	336,069	378,290	452,935	530,508	609,155	623,691	697,105	789,497	900,738	1,006,505	1,172,821	1,435,203

Gold (Million Fine Troy Ounces)

1ad

		1993	1994	1995	1996	1997	1998	1999	2000	2001	2002	2003	2004
		Millions of Ounces: End of Period											
All Countries	010	919.72	915.67	907.34	905.51	888.64	968.42	967.07	952.44	942.98	931.18	913.56	900.84
Industrial Countries	110	770.83	768.05	754.97	748.16	732.47	808.67	810.43	796.51	783.55	769.85	754.29	740.60
United States	111	261.79	261.73	261.70	261.66	261.64	261.61	261.67	261.61	262.00	262.00	261.55	261.59
Canada	156	6.05	3.89	3.41	3.09	3.09	2.49	1.81	1.18	1.05	.60	.11	.11
Australia	193	7.90	7.90	7.90	7.90	2.56	2.56	2.56	2.56	2.56	2.56	2.56	2.56
Japan	158	24.23	24.23	24.23	24.23	24.23	24.23	24.23	24.55	24.60	24.60	24.60	24.60
New Zealand	196	—	—	—	—	—	—	—	—	—	—	—	—
Euro Area (incl. ECB)	163	....	....	....	....	....	....	402.76	399.54	401.88	399.02	393.54	390.00
Austria	122	18.60	18.34	11.99	10.75	7.87	9.64	13.10	12.14	11.17	10.21	10.21	9.89
Belgium	124	25.04	25.04	20.54	15.32	15.32	9.52	8.30	8.30	8.30	8.29	8.29	8.29
Finland	172	2.00	2.00	1.60	1.60	1.60	2.00	1.58	1.58	1.58	1.58	1.58	1.58
France	132	81.85	81.85	81.85	81.85	81.89	102.37	97.25	97.25	97.25	97.25	97.25	95.98
Germany	134	95.18	95.18	95.18	95.18	95.18	118.98	111.52	111.52	111.13	110.79	110.58	110.38
Greece	174	3.44	3.45	3.46	3.47	3.64	3.62	4.24	4.26	3.94	3.94	3.45	3.46
Ireland	178	.36	.36	.36	.36	.36	.45	.18	.18	.18	.18	.18	.18
Italy	136	66.67	66.67	66.67	66.67	66.67	83.36	78.83	78.83	78.83	78.83	78.83	78.83
Luxembourg	137	.31	.31	.31	.31	.31	....	.08	.08	.08	.08	.08	.07
Netherlands	138	35.05	34.77	34.77	34.77	27.07	33.83	31.57	29.32	28.44	27.38	25.00	25.00
Portugal	182	16.06	16.07	16.07	16.07	16.07	20.09	19.51	19.51	19.51	19.03	16.63	14.86
Spain	184	15.62	15.62	15.63	15.63	15.63	19.54	16.83	16.83	16.83	16.83	16.83	16.83
Denmark	128	1.64	1.63	1.65	1.66	1.69	2.14	2.14	2.14	2.14	2.14	2.14	2.14
Iceland	176	.05	.05	.05	.05	.05	.06	.06	.06	.06	.06	.06	.06
Norway	142	1.18	1.18	1.18	1.18	1.18	1.18	1.18	1.18	1.18	1.18	1.18	—
San Marino	135	....	—	—	—	—	—	—	—	—	—	—	—
Sweden	144	6.07	6.07	4.70	4.70	4.72	4.72	5.96	5.96	5.96	5.96	5.96	5.96
Switzerland	146	83.28	83.28	83.28	83.28	83.28	83.28	83.28	77.79	70.68	61.62	52.51	43.54
United Kingdom	112	18.45	18.44	18.43	18.43	18.42	23.00	20.55	15.67	11.42	10.09	10.04	10.04
Developing Countries	200	148.90	147.63	152.38	157.35	156.17	159.74	156.64	155.93	159.44	161.33	159.27	160.24
Africa	605	13.28	12.69	13.84	13.49	14.09	13.98	14.01	15.69	15.22	15.34	13.45	13.50
CEMAC (Incl. BEAC hqtrs.)	758	....	....	.23	.23	.23	.23	.23	.23	.23	.23	.23	.23
Cameroon	622	.03	.03	.03	.03	.03	.03	.03	.03	.03	.03	.03	.03
Central African Republic	626	.01	.01	.01	.01	.01	.01	.01	.01	.01	.01	.01	.01
Chad	628	.01	.01	.01	.01	.01	.01	.01	.01	.01	.01	.01	.01
Congo, Rep. of	634	.01	.01	.01	.01	.01	.01	.01	.01	.01	.01	.01	.01
Equatorial Guinea	642	—	—	—	—	—	—	—	—	—	—	—	—
Gabon	646	.01	.01	.01	.01	.01	.01	.01	.01	.01	.01	.01	.01
WAEMU (Incl. BCEAO hqtrs.)	759	....	....	.80	.86	.90	.96	1.01	1.06	1.12	1.17	1.17	1.17
Benin	638	.01	.01	—	—	—	—	—	—	—	—	—	—
Burkina Faso	748	.01	.01	—	—	—	—	—	—	—	—	—	—
Côte d'Ivoire	662	.04	.04	—	—	—	—	—	—	—	—	—	—
Guinea Bissau	654	—	—	—	—	—	—	—	—	—	—	—	—
Mali	678	.02	.02	—	—	—	—	—	—	—	—	—	—
Niger	692	.01	.01	—	—	—	—	—	—	—	—	—	—
Senegal	722	.03	.03	—	—	—	—	—	—	—	—	—	—
Togo	742	.01	.01	—	—	—	—	—	—	—	—	—	—
Algeria	612	5.58	5.58	5.58	5.58	5.58	5.58	5.58	5.58	5.58	5.58	5.58	5.58
Burundi	618	.02	.02	.02	.02	.02	.02	.02	.02				
Cape Verde	624	—	—	—	—	—	—	—	—	—	—	—	—
Comoros	632	—	—	—	—	—	—	—	—	—	—	—	—
Congo, Dem. Rep. of	636	.02	.03	.03	....	.05	....	....	....	....	....	....	....
Eritrea	643	....	....	....	....	.10	.16	.08	.04	.04	....	....	....
Ethiopia	644	.11	.11	.11	.30	.30	.30	.30	.20	.20	.25	—	—
Ghana	652	.27	.28	.28	.28	.28	.28	.28	.28	.28	.28	.28	.28
Guinea	656	....	....	.08	.08	.08	....	....	.07	.03	.27	....	....
Kenya	664	.08	.08	.08	.08	.08	—	—	—	—	—	—	—
Malawi	676	.01	.01	.01	.01	.01	.01	.01	.01	.01	.01	.01	.01
Mauritania	682	.01	.01	.01	.01	.01	.01	.01	.01	.01	.01	.01	....
Mauritius	684	.06	.06	.06	.06	.06	.06	.06	.06	.06	.06	.06	.06
Morocco	686	.70	.70	.70	.70	.70	.70	.70	.71	.71	.71	.71	.71
Mozambique	688	....	....	....	....	.07	.07	.06	.07	.05	.06	.02	.06
Namibia	728	—	—	—	—	—	—	—	—	—	—	—	—
Nigeria	694	.69	.69	.69	.69	.69	.69	.69	.69	.69	.69	.69	.69
Rwanda	714	—	....	—	—	—	—	—	—	—	—	—	—
South Africa	199	4.76	4.20	4.25	3.79	3.99	4.00	3.94	5.90	5.72	5.58	3.98	3.98
Tunisia	744	.22	.22	.22	.22	.22	.22	.22	.22	.22	.22	.22	.22
Zambia	754	....	....	—	—	—	—	—	—	—	—	—	—
Zimbabwe	698	.50	.47	.76	.64	.77	.62	.73	.47	.20	.14	....	....
Asia	505	53.65	53.70	55.38	56.53	56.76	56.41	56.11	57.28	61.62	65.50	65.03	64.04
Bangladesh	513	.09	.09	.09	.09	.10	.11	.11	.11	.11	.11	.11	.11
Cambodia	522	—	—	—	—	—	.40	.40	.40	.40	.40	.40	.40
China, P.R.: Mainland	924	12.70	12.70	12.70	12.70	12.70	12.70	12.70	12.70	16.10	19.29	19.29	19.29
China, P.R.: Hong Kong	532	.07	.07	.07	.07	.07	.07	.07	.07	.07	.07	.07	.07
China, P.R.: Macao	546	—	—	—	—	—	—	—	—	—	—	—	—
Fiji	819	—	—	—	—	—	—	—	—	—	—	—	—
India	534	11.46	11.80	12.78	12.78	12.74	11.49	11.50	11.50	11.50	11.50	11.50	11.50
Indonesia	536	3.10	3.10	3.10	3.10	3.10	3.10	3.10	3.10	3.10	3.10	3.10	3.10
Korea	542	.32	.33	.33	.33	.33	.43	.44	.44	.44	.44	.45	.45
Lao People's Democratic Rep.	544	.02	.02	.02	.02	.02	.02	.12	.02	.07	.07	.12	.12
Malaysia	548	2.39	2.39	2.39	2.39	2.35	2.35	1.18	1.17	1.17	1.17	1.17	1.17
Maldives	556	—	—	—	—	—	—	—	—	—	—	—	—
Micronesia, Fed. States of	868	....	....	—	—	—	—	—	—	—	—	—	—

Gold (Million Fine Troy Ounces)

		1993	1994	1995	1996	1997	1998	1999	2000	2001	2002	2003	2004
1ad						*Millions of Ounces: End of Period*							
Asia(Cont.)													
Mongolia	948	.02	.03	.10	.15	.08	.03	—	.08	.18	.14	.02	.03
Myanmar	518	.25	.25	.23	.23	.23	.23	.23	.23	.23	.23	.23	.23
Nepal	558	.15	.15	.15	.15	.15	.15	.15	.15	.15	.15	.15	.15
Pakistan	564	2.04	2.05	2.05	2.06	2.07	2.08	2.09	2.09	2.09	2.09	2.10	2.10
Papua New Guinea	853	.06	.06	.01	.06	.06	.06	.06	.06	.06	.06	.06	.06
Philippines	566	3.22	2.89	3.58	4.65	4.99	5.43	6.20	7.23	7.98	8.73	8.22	7.12
Sri Lanka	524	.06	.06	.06	.06	.06	.06	.06	† .34	.26	.22	.17	.17
Thailand	578	2.47	2.47	2.47	2.47	2.47	2.47	2.47	2.37	2.48	2.50	2.60	2.70
Europe	170	**23.19**	**22.00**	**23.38**	**28.05**	**30.81**	**31.12**	**30.05**	**29.46**	**30.90**	**29.82**	**29.66**	**29.89**
Albania	914	.05	.05	.06	.12	.12	.12	.12	.11	.11	.08	.07	.07
Armenia	911	—	.01	.03	.03	.04	.04	.04	.04	.04	.04		
Azerbaijan, Republic of	912	—	—	—	.01	—	—	—	—	—	—	—	—
Belarus	913	....	—	—	....	....	....	....	....	....	.20	.10	.20
Bosnia & Herzegovina	963	....	....	....	....	—	—	—	—	—	—	—	—
Bulgaria	918	1.02	1.03	1.03	1.03	1.29	1.29	1.28	1.28	1.29	1.28	1.28	1.28
Croatia	960	—	—	—	—	—	—	—	—	—	—	—	—
Cyprus	423	.46	.46	.46	.44	.46	.46	.46	.46	.46	.46	.47	.47
Czech Republic	935	1.95	2.10	1.99	1.99	1.04	.29	.45	.45	.44	.44	.44	.44
Estonia	939	.01	.01	.01	.01	.01	.01	.01	.01	.01	.01	.01	.01
Georgia	915	....	....										
Hungary	944	.11	.11	.11	.10	.10	.10	.10	.10	.10	.10	.10	.10
Kazakhstan	916	.65	.99	1.36	1.80	1.81	1.75	1.80	1.84	1.84	1.71	1.74	1.83
Kyrgyz Republic	917	....	....	.14	.12	.08	.08	.08	.08	.08	.08	.08	.08
Latvia	941	.24	.25	.25	.25	.25	.25	.25	.25	.25	.25	.25	.25
Lithuania	946	.19	.19	.19	.19	.19	.19	.19	.19	.19	.19	.19	.19
Macedonia, FYR	962	.04	.05	.05	.08	.08	.10	.10	.11	.19	.20	.09	.20
Malta	181	.10	.11	.04	.04	.01	.01	.01	—	.01	—	—	—
Moldova	921	—	—	—	—	—	—	—	—	—	—	—	—
Poland	964	.47	.47	.47	.47	.90	3.31	3.31	3.31	3.31	3.31	3.31	3.31
Romania	968	2.37	2.63	2.70	2.82	3.02	3.22	3.32	3.37	3.38	3.39	3.38	3.38
Russia	922	10.20	8.42	9.41	13.49	16.30	14.74	13.33	12.36	13.60	12.46	12.55	12.44
Slovak Republic	936	1.29	1.29	1.29	1.29	1.29	1.29	1.29	1.29	1.13	1.13	1.13	1.13
Slovenia	961	—	—	—	—	—	—	—	—	.24	.24	.24	.24
Tajikistan	923	....	....	....	....	.01	.01	.01	.01	.01	—	.01	.03
Turkey	186	4.03	3.82	3.75	3.75	3.75	3.75	3.74	3.74	3.73	3.73	3.73	3.73
Ukraine	926	.01	.04	.05	.03	.06	.11	.16	.45	.48	.50	.50	.51
Middle East	405	**31.48**	**31.41**	**30.96**	**31.55**	**31.35**	**35.97**	**35.20**	**35.12**	**35.12**	**34.84**	**34.44**	**34.46**
Bahrain, Kingdom of	419	.15	.15	.15	.15	.15	.15	.15	.15	.15	.15	.15	.15
Egypt	469	2.43	2.43	2.43	2.43	2.43	2.43	2.43	2.43	2.43	2.43	2.43	2.43
Iran, I.R. of	429	4.76	4.74	4.84	....	....	....	....	....	....	....	....	....
Israel	436	.01	.01	.01	.01	.01	—	—	—	—	—	—	—
Jordan	439	.79	.79	.79	.80	.81	.83	.49	.40	.41	.41	.41	.41
Kuwait	443	2.54	2.54	2.54	2.54	2.54	2.54	2.54	2.54	2.54	2.54	2.54	2.54
Lebanon	446	9.22	9.22	9.22	9.22	9.22	9.22	9.22	9.22	9.22	9.22	9.22	9.22
Libya	672	....	....	....	....	....	4.62	4.62	4.62	4.62	4.62	4.62	4.62
Oman	449	.29	.29	.29	.29	.29	.29	.29	.29	.29	—	—	—
Qatar	453	.86	.81	.27	.27	.05	.05	.02	.02	.02	.02	.02	.04
Saudi Arabia	456	4.60	4.60	4.60	4.60	4.60	4.60	4.60	4.60	4.60	4.60	4.60	4.60
Syrian Arab Rep	463	.83	.83	.83	.83	.83	.83	.83	.83	.83	.83	.83	....
United Arab Emirates	466	.80	.80	.80	.80	.80	.80	.40	.40	.40	.40	—	—
Yemen, Republic of	474	.05	.05	.05	.05	.05	.05	.05	.05	.05	.05	.05	.05
Western Hemisphere	205	**27.30**	**27.83**	**28.81**	**27.72**	**23.18**	**22.26**	**21.27**	**18.38**	**16.57**	**15.83**	**16.69**	**18.34**
Argentina	213	4.37	4.37	4.37	4.37	.36	.36	.34	.02	.01	.01	.01	1.77
Aruba	314	.10	.10	.10	.10	.10	.10	.10	.10	.10	.10	.10	.10
Bahamas, The	313	—	—	—	—	—	—	—	—	—	—	—	—
Barbados	316	—	—	—	—	—	—	—	—	—	—	—	—
Bolivia	218	.89	.89	.89	.94	.94	.94	.94	.94	.94	.91	.91	.91
Brazil	223	2.93	3.71	4.58	3.69	3.03	4.60	3.17	1.89	.46	.44	.45	.45
Chile	228	1.87	1.86	1.86	1.86	1.86	1.22	1.22	.07	.07	.01	.01	.01
Colombia	233	.30	.29	.27	.25	.36	.36	.33	.33	.33	.33	.33	.33
Costa Rica	238	.03	.03	.03	—	—	—	—	—	—	—	—	—
Dominican Republic	243	.02	.02	.02	.02	.02	.02	.02	.02	.02	.02	.02	.02
Ecuador	248	.41	.41	.41	.41	.41	.41	† .85	.85	.85	.85	.85	.85
El Salvador	253	.47	.47	.47	.47	.47	.47	.47	.47	.47	.47	.47	.42
Guatemala	258	.21	.21	.21	.21	.21	.22	.22	.22	.22	.22	.22	.22
Haiti	263	.02	.02	.02	.02	.02	.02	—	—	—	—	—	—
Honduras	268	.02	.02	.02	.02	.02	.02	.02	.02	.02	.02	.02	.02
Jamaica	343	—	—	—	—	—	—	—	—	—	—	—	—
Mexico	273	.48	.43	.51	.26	.19	.22	.16	.25	.23	.22	.17	.14
Netherlands Antilles	353	.55	.55	.55	.55	.55	.42	.42	.42	.42	.42	.42	.42
Nicaragua	278	.01	.01	.02	.02	.02	.02	.02	.01	.01	.01	.01	—
Paraguay	288	.03	.03	.03	.03	.03	.03	.03	.03	.03	.03	.03	—
Peru	293	1.30	1.12	1.12	1.11	1.11	1.10	1.10	1.10	1.11	1.11	1.11	1.11
Suriname	366	.05	.05	.09	.13	.19	.13	.25	.26	.27	.02	.02	.02
Trinidad and Tobago	369	.06	.05	.05	.05	.06	.06	.06	.06	.06	.06	.06	.06
Uruguay	298	1.70	1.70	1.72	1.74	1.76	1.78	1.80	1.08	.01	.01	.01	.01
Venezuela, Rep. Bol	299	11.46	11.46	11.46	11.46	11.46	9.76	9.76	10.24	10.94	10.56	11.47	11.49

Gold (Million Fine Troy Ounces)

		1993	1994	1995	1996	1997	1998	1999	2000	2001	2002	2003	2004
1ad						*Millions of Ounces: End of Period*							
Memorandum Items													
Oil Exporting Countries...........	999	**38.82**	**38.75**	**38.31**	**38.89**	**38.67**	**41.59**	**41.16**	**41.64**	**42.34**	**41.67**	**42.18**	**42.23**
Non-Oil Developing Countries.	201	**110.07**	**108.88**	**114.07**	**118.46**	**117.50**	**118.15**	**115.48**	**114.29**	**117.10**	**119.66**	**117.09**	**118.01**
Gold Holdings at SDR 35 per Ounce													
(1a.s)						*Millions of SDRs: End of Period*							
World..	001	39,248	39,059	38,911	38,762	38,072	37,739	37,692	37,180	36,847	36,433	35,813	35,384
All Countries................................	010	32,190	32,049	31,757	31,693	31,103	33,895	33,848	33,335	33,004	32,591	31,975	31,529
of which: ECB..........................	168	....	....	....	....	....	....	841	841	863	863	863	863
IMF...	992	3,620	3,620	3,620	3,620	3,620	3,620	3,620	3,620	3,620	3,620	3,620	3,620
EMI...	977	3,135	3,146	3,278	3,219	3,131	....	....	....	....	....	....	....
BIS...	993	302	244	255	230	218	224	224	224	222	222	218	234
Gold Holdings at Market Prices													
(1ams)						*Millions of SDRs: End of Period*							
World..	001	318,925	292,970	289,248	284,389	233,962	220,395	227,739	223,763	231,623	262,435	287,313	285,128
All Countries................................	010	261,575	240,389	236,070	232,522	191,132	197,943	204,511	200,625	207,471	234,760	256,522	254,067
of which: ECB..........................	168	....	....	....	....	....	....	5,082	5,062	5,425	6,216	6,923	6,954
IMF...	992	29,419	27,156	26,913	26,562	22,248	21,143	21,875	21,789	22,758	26,078	29,045	29,173
EMI...	977	25,478	23,594	24,369	23,618	19,240	....	....	....	....	....	....	....
BIS...	993	2,453	1,831	1,896	1,687	1,343	1,309	1,353	1,349	1,394	1,596	1,746	1,888
Gold Prices and SDR Rates:						*End of Period*							
US Dollars per Oz.(London)(c..)........	112	390.65	383.25	386.75	369.25	290.20	287.80	290.25	274.45	276.50	342.75	417.25	438.00
US Dollars per SDR (sa.)..................	111	1.3736	1.4599	1.4865	1.4380	1.3493	1.4080	1.3725	1.3029	1.2567	1.3595	1.4860	1.5530
SDRs per Ounce (g..).......................	112	284.41	262.53	260.18	256.79	215.08	204.40	211.47	210.64	220.02	252.11	280.79	282.03

Total Reserves

1 s (w/ Gold at SDR 35 per Oz)

Millions of SDRs: End of Period

		1993	1994	1995	1996	1997	1998	1999	2000	2001	2002	2003	2004
All Countries	010	831,929	892,351	1,023,077	1,177,363	1,296,540	1,282,394	1,406,670	1,589,401	1,742,489	1,889,320	2,155,983	2,520,711
Industrial Countries	110	440,510	460,821	514,251	575,129	603,469	574,330	618,553	684,009	717,155	757,942	846,585	930,205
United States	111	54,558	52,510	59,467	53,694	52,817	59,379	53,238	52,598	55,030	59,160	59,555	58,022
Canada	156	9,299	8,552	10,243	14,310	13,317	16,640	20,556	24,544	27,061	27,225	24,380	22,173
Australia	193	8,359	8,007	8,279	10,350	12,575	10,487	15,545	13,996	14,377	15,307	21,751	23,143
Japan	158	72,577	87,062	124,125	151,511	163,641	153,878	209,893	273,251	315,292	340,088	447,229	537,813
New Zealand	196	2,430	2,540	2,967	4,140	3,299	2,986	3,246	2,556	2,394	2,750	3,302	3,409
Euro Area (incl. ECB)	163	....	....	....	....	....	....	201,185	199,971	201,031	195,644	163,653	149,703
Austria	122	11,288	12,165	13,020	16,277	14,903	22,661	† 11,475	11,414	10,345	7,480	6,057	5,406
Belgium	124	9,187	10,382	11,601	12,326	12,535	13,310	† 8,260	7,961	9,255	9,010	7,686	6,962
Finland	172	4,009	7,374	6,809	4,866	6,294	6,955	† 6,044	6,178	6,408	6,885	7,131	7,987
France	132	19,354	20,851	20,930	21,500	25,788	35,054	† 32,330	31,832	28,667	24,268	23,718	26,098
Germany	134	59,856	56,325	60,517	61,176	60,835	56,737	† 48,376	47,567	44,793	41,516	37,986	35,301
Greece	174	5,792	10,045	10,064	12,292	9,462	12,526	13,352	10,452	† 4,239	6,083	3,056	888
Ireland	178	4,326	4,201	5,818	5,719	4,849	6,690	† 3,886	4,120	4,451	3,989	2,751	1,829
Italy	136	22,387	24,435	25,815	34,287	43,644	24,144	† 19,095	22,382	22,190	23,798	23,194	20,698
Luxembourg	137	60	63	61	62	58	....	† 59	61	87	114	191	195
Netherlands	138	24,046	24,872	23,897	19,832	19,376	16,395	† 8,308	8,427	8,184	7,993	8,285	7,380
Portugal	182	12,094	11,189	11,225	11,632	12,169	11,942	† 6,823	7,520	8,375	8,889	4,536	3,852
Spain	184	30,429	29,006	23,746	40,831	51,241	39,929	† 24,716	24,373	24,128	25,992	13,906	8,566
Denmark	128	7,557	6,260	7,468	9,892	14,233	10,916	16,313	11,671	13,690	19,924	25,045	25,241
Iceland	176	312	202	209	317	286	305	351	301	271	326	535	676
Norway	142	14,327	13,074	15,190	18,482	17,385	13,570	17,387	21,223	18,564	23,579	25,089	28,530
San Marino	135	....	121	134	150	136	121	105	104	106	135	170	229
Sweden	144	14,081	16,141	16,344	13,452	8,188	10,178	11,151	11,616	11,330	12,807	13,453	14,458
Switzerland	146	26,674	26,704	27,411	29,642	31,840	32,169	29,378	27,492	27,941	31,693	33,906	37,259
United Kingdom	112	27,420	28,739	28,910	28,390	24,596	23,682	† 26,854	34,235	30,067	29,305	28,516	29,548
Developing Countries	200	391,419	431,529	508,827	602,234	693,071	708,064	788,117	905,393	1,025,334	1,131,378	1,309,398	1,590,511
Africa	605	14,123	16,645	18,212	22,583	32,747	29,862	31,246	42,702	52,352	54,167	62,273	82,592
CEMAC (Incl. BEAC hqtrs.)	758	....	....	....	....	....	....	....	973	867	1,185	1,228	2,011
Cameroon	622	3	† 3	4	3	2	2	4	164	265	464	431	535
Central African Republic	626	82	144	158	162	133	104	100	103	95	91	89	96
Chad	628	29	52	96	115	101	86	70	85	98	161	126	143
Congo, Rep. of	634	1	35	40	64	45	1	29	171	55	24	24	77
Equatorial Guinea	642	—	—	—	—	4	1	2	18	56	65	160	608
Gabon	646	1	120	100	173	210	11	14	146	8	103	133	286
WAEMU (Incl. BCEAO hqtrs.)	759	....	....	1,736	1,935	2,157	2,281	2,172	2,557	3,047	4,053	4,569	4,709
Benin	638	178	† 177	133	182	188	186	291	352	460	453	483	412
Burkina Faso	748	279	163	234	235	256	265	215	187	207	231	506	431
Côte d'Ivoire	662	3	141	356	421	458	608	459	513	811	1,371	877	1,091
Guinea Bissau	654	10	13	14	8	25	25	26	51	55	76	22	47
Mali	678	243	† 152	217	300	308	286	255	293	278	437	641	554
Niger	692	140	76	64	55	39	38	29	62	85	98	175	166
Senegal	722	4	124	183	200	286	306	294	295	356	469	748	893
Togo	742	114	65	88	62	88	84	89	117	101	151	138	232
Algeria	612	1,269	2,027	1,544	3,141	6,159	5,057	3,493	9,424	14,583	17,288	22,487	28,042
Angola	614	....	....	143	384	294	144	361	920	582	276	427	879
Botswana	616	2,983	3,015	3,159	3,496	4,206	4,219	4,589	4,849	4,693	4,026	3,593	3,645
Burundi	618	119	141	142	98	84	47	36	26	14	43	45	42
Cape Verde	624	42	29	25	19	14	6	31	22	36	59	63	90
Comoros	632	28	30	30	35	30	28	27	33	50	59	63	67
Congo, Dem. Rep. of	636	34	84	100	....	....	....	....	....	....	....	....	....
Djibouti	611	55	51	49	54	49	47	51	52	56	54	67	60
Eritrea	643	....	....	....	....	151	22	28	21	33	22	17	22
Ethiopia	644	336	377	523	520	382	374	345	242	352	657	643	964
Gambia, The	648	77	67	71	71	71	76	81	84	84	79	40	54
Ghana	652	308	410	479	586	408	277	340	188	247	407	920	1,057
Guinea	656	96	....	....	....	....	....	....	116	160	135	....	....
Kenya	664	298	385	241	522	587	556	577	689	847	786	997	978
Lesotho	666	184	255	307	320	424	408	364	321	308	299	310	324
Liberia	668	2	3	19	—	—	—	—	—	—	2	5	12
Madagascar	674	59	49	73	168	209	122	166	219	317	267	279	324
Malawi	676	42	30	74	157	121	192	183	190	165	122	86	86
Mauritania	682	33	28	58	99	149	144	164	215	227	292	280	....
Mauritius	684	553	514	583	625	516	399	535	691	667	905	1,064	1,036
Morocco	686	2,686	3,006	2,447	2,663	2,984	3,174	4,170	3,727	6,768	7,478	9,346	10,544
Mozambique	688	....	....	....	....	† 386	435	477	559	571	605	673	730
Namibia	728	97	139	149	135	186	185	223	200	186	238	219	222
Nigeria	694	1,023	973	995	2,858	5,643	5,067	3,995	7,631	8,345	5,417	4,821	10,942
Rwanda	714	35	....	....	74	114	120	127	146	169	179	144	203
São Tomé & Príncipe	716	—	—	3	3	9	7	8	9	12	13	17	13
Seychelles	718	26	21	18	15	20	15	22	34	30	51	45	22
Sierra Leone	724	21	28	23	18	29	31	29	38	41	62	45	81
South Africa	199	909	1,301	2,046	787	3,697	3,234	4,767	4,875	5,011	4,538	4,510	8,601
Sudan	732	27	54	110	74	60	64	138	† 190	94	324	570	1,047
Swaziland	734	192	203	201	177	219	255	274	270	216	203	187	208
Tanzania	738	148	227	182	306	461	426	565	748	920	1,125	1,372	1,478
Tunisia	744	629	1,009	1,087	1,327	1,474	1,322	1,655	1,398	1,590	1,692	1,990	2,542
Uganda	746	107	220	309	367	470	515	556	620	782	687	727	842
Zambia	754	....	....	150	155	177	49	33	188	146	394	167	217
Zimbabwe	698	332	294	427	439	146	115	221	165	58	66	....	....

Total Reserves

1 s (w/ Gold at SDR 35 per Oz)		1993	1994	1995	1996	1997	1998	1999	2000	2001	2002	2003	2004
		Millions of SDRs: End of Period											
Asia *	505	**223,353**	**264,527**	**293,065**	**345,968**	**386,332**	**415,522**	**484,518**	**550,246**	**633,942**	**720,289**	**842,642**	**1,041,653**
Bangladesh	513	1,758	2,153	1,577	1,279	1,176	1,357	1,172	1,144	1,018	1,242	1,739	2,047
Bhutan	514	71	83	† 88	132	140	182	213	244	257	261	247	257
Cambodia	522	18	81	129	185	221	244	300	399	481	585	563	621
China, P.R.: Mainland	924	16,743	36,691	51,152	74,883	106,253	106,400	115,364	129,600	172,124	214,815	275,345	396,358
China, P.R.: Hong Kong	532	31,298	33,739	37,270	44,376	68,784	63,673	70,119	82,542	88,450	82,308	79,654	79,551
China, P.R.: Macao	546	1,142	1,347	1,518	1,684	1,877	1,749	2,082	2,550	2,792	2,795	2,923	3,500
Fiji	819	196	187	235	297	267	274	312	316	292	264	285	308
India	534	7,826	13,907	12,504	14,474	18,744	19,820	24,203	29,493	36,902	50,174	66,984	81,917
Indonesia	536	8,308	8,419	9,330	12,801	12,402	16,240	19,376	21,984	21,789	22,889	23,637	22,615
Korea	542	14,738	17,574	21,995	23,682	15,107	36,928	53,922	73,797	81,778	89,272	104,516	128,152
Lao People's Democratic Rep.	544	46e	42e	62	118	83	80	74	107	104	141	140	144
Malaysia	548	19,922	17,498	16,077	18,867	15,489	18,235	22,328	22,700	24,290	25,213	29,998	42,786
Maldives	556	19	21	32	53	73	84	93	94	74	98	107	131
Micronesia, Fed. States of	868	....	....	47	62	64	72	68	87	78	86	60	35
Mongolia	948	44	57	82	80	133	68	99	140	170	262	159	153
Myanmar	518	229	298	386	167	193	232	202	179	327	354	378	441
Nepal	558	471	480	400	403	469	542	621	731	831	754	828	947
Pakistan	564	943	2,078	1,238	453	958	803	1,174	1,235	2,970	6,015	7,436	6,383
Papua New Guinea	853	105	68	176	408	271	139	152	222	339	239	335	410
Philippines	566	3,517	4,237	4,428	7,158	5,583	6,777	9,885	10,300	11,003	10,110	9,477	8,695
Samoa	862	37	35	37	42	48	44	50	49	45	46	56	62
Singapore	576	35,208	39,851	46,213	53,442	52,836	53,215	55,987	61,502	59,977	60,331	64,433	72,267
Solomon Islands	813	15	12	11	23	27	35	37	25	15	13	25	52
Sri Lanka	524	1,188	1,404	1,407	1,366	1,502	1,408	1,194	† 809	1,033	1,207	1,530	1,379
Thailand	578	17,904	20,179	24,293	26,326	19,490	20,559	24,905	24,655	25,832	28,073	27,734	31,430
Tonga	866	27	24	19	21	20	20	20	21	21	20	29	38
Vanuatu	846	33	30	32	31	28	32	30	30	30	27	29	40
*of which:													
Taiwan Province of China	528	61,319	63,806	61,229	61,699	62,362	64,636	77,851	82,400	97,720	119,381	139,532	156,134
Europe	170	**26,146**	**31,300**	**58,470**	**62,654**	**73,010**	**73,858**	**79,905**	**98,280**	**112,535**	**139,325**	**170,408**	**214,550**
Albania	914	109	142	164	199	233	277	360	476	593	620	682	877
Armenia	911	10	22	68	109	171	232	234	246	257	314	343	371
Azerbaijan, Republic of	912	—	1	81	147	346	318	490	522	714	531	552	702
Belarus	913	....	69	254	....	....	....	....	....	....	462	404	490
Bosnia & Herzegovina	963	....	....	....	....	60	124	330	381	972	972	1,208	1,550
Bulgaria	918	513	722	868	372	1,610	1,952	2,152	2,466	2,664	3,286	4,278	5,696
Croatia	960	449	962	1,275	1,609	1,882	2,000	2,204	2,705	3,742	4,329	5,512	5,639
Cyprus	423	815	1,019	767	1,088	1,048	996	1,352	1,353	1,821	2,239	2,208	2,534
Czech Republic	935	2,827	4,282	9,382	8,659	7,251	8,918	9,346	10,008	11,427	17,342	18,031	18,212
Estonia	939	281	304	390	443	562	576	622	707	653	736	924	1,152
Georgia	915	....	....	131	131	148	87	96	84	127	145	128	247
Hungary	944	4,882	4,618	8,059	6,763	6,235	6,622	7,985	8,592	8,539	7,615	8,575	10,247
Kazakhstan	916	355	608	811	963	1,321	1,099	1,141	1,288	1,654	1,939	2,912	5,520
Kyrgyz Republic	917	....	....	59	70	129	119	170	186	213	215	248	356
Latvia	941	323	382	349	464	572	578	644	662	923	922	973	1,240
Lithuania	946	262	366	516	544	755	1,007	877	1,013	1,294	1,735	2,276	2,268
Macedonia, FYR	962	78	104	175	169	193	221	317	333	600	538	607	590
Malta	181	995	1,271	1,081	1,128	1,103	1,181	1,303	1,129	1,326	1,625	1,836	1,738
Moldova	921	56	123	173	217	271	102	135	171	182	198	203	303
Poland	964	2,996	4,018	9,955	12,426	15,156	19,522	19,318	20,502	20,525	21,189	22,040	22,861
Romania	968	808	1,521	1,157	1,561	2,925	2,149	1,228	2,014	3,240	4,624	5,529	9,530
Russia	922	4,605	3,021	10,005	8,314	10,127	6,056	6,628	19,056	26,370	32,840	49,683	78,226
Slovak Republic	936	348	1,204	2,308	2,423	2,439	2,083	2,501	3,132	3,335	6,519	7,898	9,323
Slovenia	961	574	1,027	1,225	1,598	2,457	2,584	2,308	2,453	3,454	5,143	5,727	5,671
Tajikistan	923	....	....	....	....	27	38	40	71	74	66	76	103
Turkey	186	4,707	5,045	8,501	11,561	13,960	13,972	17,141	17,391	15,153	20,041	23,005	23,098
Ukraine	926	118	447	708	1,364	1,737	545	768	1,054	2,369	3,137	4,547	6,008
Middle East	405	**47,859**	**46,685**	**51,142**	**61,655**	**74,401**	**73,698**	**79,658**	**93,328**	**99,498**	**98,645**	**101,819**	**108,899**
Bahrain, Kingdom of	419	953	806	866	922	962	772	1,003	1,206	1,345	1,275	1,202	1,255
Egypt	469	9,480	9,319	10,971	12,184	13,919	12,957	10,638	10,153	10,370	9,826	9,230	9,276
Israel	436	4,647	4,653	5,462	7,938	15,069	16,104	16,470	17,869	18,603	17,714	17,709	17,446
Jordan	439	† 1,220	1,187	1,355	1,251	1,659	1,272	1,933	2,571	2,451	2,939	3,510	3,406
Kuwait	443	3,157	2,487	2,484	2,533	2,647	2,892	3,603	5,525	7,964	6,862	5,188	5,396
Lebanon	446	1,968	2,983	3,372	4,448	4,752	4,979	5,988	4,885	4,312	5,651	8,748	7,879
Libya	672	....	....	....	....	....	5,325	5,466	9,726	11,939	10,686	13,341	16,703
Oman	449	1,323	1,138	1,242	1,374	1,544	1,386	2,027	1,837	1,892	2,334	2,418	2,316
Qatar	453	535	545	479	528	506	620	752	954	893	1,049	1,157	1,987	2,198
Saudi Arabia	456	5,569	5,214	5,961	† 10,120	11,187	10,260	12,545	15,193	14,162	15,321	15,383	17,734
United Arab Emirates	466	4,472	4,589	5,054	5,630	6,233	6,474	7,792	10,393	11,270	11,209	10,154	11,932
Yemen, Republic of	474	108	176	418	709	893	709	1,074	2,228	2,913	3,246	3,358	3,649
Western Hemisphere	205	**79,938**	**72,373**	**87,938**	**109,374**	**126,581**	**115,123**	**112,790**	**120,837**	**127,007**	**118,953**	**132,256**	**142,817**
ECCU (incl. ECCB hqtrs.)	309	196	179	211	203	228	256	268	297	357	374	366	408
Anguilla	312	7	6	9	10	12	13	15	16	19	19	22	22
Antigua and Barbuda	311	28	31	40	33	38	42	51	49	63	64	77	77
Dominica	321	14	11	15	16	18	20	23	23	25	33	32	27
Grenada	328	20	21	25	25	32	33	37	44	51	65	56	78
Montserrat	351	4	5	6	6	8	18	10	8	10	11	10	9
St. Kitts and Nevis	361	21	22	23	23	27	33	36	35	45	48	44	51
St. Lucia	362	44	40	42	39	45	50	54	61	71	69	72	85
St. Vincent & Grens.	364	23	21	20	21	23	28	31	42	49	39	34	48
Argentina	213	10,193	9,967	9,765	12,743	16,555	17,592	19,139	19,301	11,580	7,716	9,525	12,222
Aruba	314	135	125	149	134	131	161	164	163	237	253	202	194

Total Reserves

1 s (w/ Gold at SDR 35 per Oz) Western Hemisphere(Cont.)		1993	1994	1995	1996	1997	1998	1999	2000	2001	2002	2003	2004
		Millions of SDRs: End of Period											
Bahamas, The	313	125	121	121	119	168	246	299	268	254	280	330	434
Barbados	316	110	134	147	201	196	260	220	363	549	492	497	373
Belize	339	28	24	25	41	44	31	52	94	89	84	57	31
Bolivia	218	194	340	475	697	838	707	743	744	738	459	514	594
Brazil	223	22,383	25,523	33,600	40,689	37,776	30,401	25,463	25,001	28,454	27,734	33,065	33,975
Chile	228	7,084	9,030	9,577	10,477	13,089	11,313	10,692	11,542	11,444	11,284	10,660	10,299
Colombia	233	5,784	5,484	5,626	6,855	7,278	6,157	5,846	6,855	8,091	7,906	7,269	8,636
Costa Rica	238	747	613	705	696	935	755	1,064	1,011	1,058	1,101	1,236	1,235
Dominican Republic	243	475	173	247	244	290	357	506	482	876	345	171	515
Ecuador	248	1,019	1,278	1,109	1,307	1,566	1,165	† 1,226	756	698	555	576	718
El Salvador	253	407	461	527	668	986	1,162	1,476	1,492	1,402	1,210	1,324	1,256
Guatemala	258	639	599	480	612	831	956	874	1,348	1,832	1,699	1,914	2,214
Guyana	336	180	169	181	229	234	196	195	234	229	209	186	149
Haiti	263	24	36	130	151	154	184	192	140	113	60	42	74
Honduras	268	71	118	177	174	431	582	917	1,009	1,127	1,122	963	1,269
Jamaica	343	304	504	458	612	506	504	404	809	1,512	1,210	804	1,189
Mexico	273	18,298	4,316	11,351	13,523	21,350	22,592	23,162	27,262	35,609	37,223	39,681	41,306
Netherlands Antilles	353	190	142	156	151	178	191	208	215	254	314	266	282
Nicaragua	278	40	97	92	138	281	249	372	375	303	330	338	430
Panama	283	435	482	526	603	851	678	600	555	869	870	680	406
Paraguay	288	461	707	736	731	621	615	714	587	569	464	653	752
Peru	293	2,527	4,829	5,570	7,395	8,179	6,832	6,399	6,466	6,939	6,908	6,618	7,880
Suriname	366	15	29	93	72	88	80	37	57	104	79	72	84
Trinidad and Tobago	369	152	243	243	380	526	558	691	1,066	1,520	1,494	1,652	2,042
Uruguay	298	612	723	834	931	1,215	1,535	1,579	1,940	2,465	566	1,402	1,616
Venezuela, Rep. Bol	299	7,111	5,927	4,628	8,599	11,057	8,807	9,287	10,404	7,735	6,612	11,192	12,234
Memorandum Items													
Oil Exporting Countries	999	47,073	44,790	45,081	61,484	72,286	71,959	78,583	103,734	111,826	110,079	120,086	139,674
Non-Oil Developing Countries.	201	344,346	386,739	463,746	540,751	620,785	636,105	709,534	801,658	913,509	1,021,299	1,189,312	1,450,837

(with Gold at SDR 35 per Ounce) (1..s)													
		Millions of SDRs: End of Period											
All Countries	010	831,929	892,351	1,023,077	1,177,363	1,296,540	1,282,394	1,406,670	1,589,401	1,742,489	1,889,320	2,155,983	2,520,711

(with Gold at Market Prices) (1m.s)													
		Millions of SDRs: End of Period											
All Countries	010	1,061,314	1,100,691	1,227,390	1,378,193	1,456,569	1,446,442	1,577,333	1,756,691	1,916,956	2,091,488	2,380,531	2,743,248

Reserve Money

		1993	1994	1995	1996	1997	1998	1999	2000	2001	2002	2003	2004
							Percent Change over Previous Year						
Industrial Countries													
United States	111	9.1	8.6	4.4	4.7	8.0	6.0	20.0	−6.1	7.8	7.5	5.2	4.2
Canada	156	5.5	2.3	1.4	4.3	3.3	6.6	24.3	−7.4	4.2	5.5	1.0	4.6
Australia	193	6.5	8.2	5.0	61.2	−20.3	5.7	−5.1	−.7	18.8	2.2	1.9	3.3
Japan	158	5.8	2.9	7.8	8.5	7.3	3.7	44.5	−19.9	19.4	11.8	12.0	3.8
New Zealand	196	2.9	11.6	7.1	−2.7	4.9	6.3	76.1	−24.4	9.2	8.6	2.1	6.2
Euro Area													
Austria	122	8.1	4.5	−1.0	6.9	−.7	....	....	....	....	....	....	....
Belgium	124	2.9	−6.7	9.2	3.7	2.3	56.2	....	....	....	....	....	....
Finland	172	.6	51.1	1.6	−32.8	−7.7	−1.8	....	....	....	....	....	....
France	132	−3.9	.1	8.7	2.2	3.0	22.4	....	....	....	....	....	....
Germany	134	−1.3	−1.6	2.0	4.8	−.9	1.1	....	....	....	....	....	....
Greece	174	8.5	35.6	3.2	12.1	11.3	34.8	25.1	−16.1	....	....	....	....
Ireland	178	20.5	4.3	26.6	1.1	18.9	....	....	....	....	....	....	....
Italy	136	−8.9	−5.0	−6.3	2.4	7.4	−29.0	....	....	....	....	....	....
Luxembourg	137	70.0	—	−11.5	17.1	−.2	....	....	....	....	....	....	....
Netherlands	138	7.4	6.0	−12.3	−4.4	10.2	5.4	....	....	....	....	....	....
Portugal	182	9.0	−58.8	−2.5	11.2	−1.3	.6	....	....	....	....	....	....
Spain	184	.8	10.1	4.5	3.3	6.8	3.4	....	....	....	....	....	....
Denmark	128	64.2	.7	13.5	33.3	31.1	−22.6	98.8	−22.7	−5.6	10.9	8.7	−7.3
Iceland	176	−8.9	3.0	−18.1	26.4	11.4	2.2	55.7	−11.8	−11.7	13.4	−36.0	140.4
Norway	142	10.7	3.3	5.2	53.0	−11.5	−11.0	50.2	−16.3	−.8	49.2	−28.5	....
Sweden	144	47.7	22.4	−14.9	−33.1	−25.8	3.8	17.0	−5.0	9.6	−.7	.5	1.3
Switzerland	146	−1.3	.6	−2.4	5.1	−2.3	7.7	17.0	−10.6	12.5	−6.8	7.9	−3.1
United Kingdom	112	6.8	5.3	7.0	3.5	7.1	4.5	18.6	−.3	.6	4.4	7.9	14.0
Developing Countries													
Africa													
CEMAC	758	....	....	....	....	....	....	....	....	5.6	14.3	1.3	17.7
Cameroon	622	−23.0	39.3	−21.0	28.3	40.2	10.2	8.2	34.2	22.3	27.7	−11.3	16.5
Central African Republic	626	19.8	84.2	4.5	7.7	−12.4	−20.2	7.7	9.3	−6.2	−6.0	−8.0	15.3
Chad	628	−20.2	23.5	58.2	31.5	−4.2	−10.2	−6.3	16.3	17.4	34.4	−10.3	7.3
Congo, Rep. of	634	−4.3	35.4	8.3	8.6	11.6	−20.7	34.2	103.1	−23.4	−8.6	7.2	20.4
Equatorial Guinea	642	−20.4	78.0	99.1	14.6	9.8	−19.9	95.3	48.9	85.6	4.6	142.5	25.1
Gabon	646	−8.2	129.4	−4.2	28.8	1.7	−8.5	−7.9	36.2	−4.2	1.1	14.4	21.3
WAEMU	759	....	19.5	9.0	2.6	11.2	7.4	3.5	11.6	23.7	20.6	−1.9	1.4
Benin	638	−12.9	1.4	−26.1	9.2	19.9	−4.4	75.7	40.7	23.2	−13.1	2.4	−18.9
Burkina Faso	748	15.4	−.8	24.0	4.7	23.5	−3.6	−14.1	.1	.2	−24.2	170.0	−26.4
Côte d'Ivoire	662	9.1	56.3	11.6	6.7	11.8	19.1	−7.7	2.0	34.3	40.0	−42.0	20.6
Guinea Bissau	654	32.2	32.3	32.1	38.7	125.8	−13.3	34.5	87.5	15.9	30.5	−67.8	58.6
Mali	678	9.1	−19.4	10.3	18.3	7.7	−5.6	12.7	26.5	11.9	46.6	32.0	−15.1
Niger	692	−4.3	−24.0	13.0	−5.9	−21.3	−35.7	32.0	3.9	48.6	−4.7	83.9	11.0
Senegal	722	−30.3	49.2	4.1	−14.2	3.3	6.8	15.9	5.8	34.3	12.2	52.5	10.3
Togo	742	−32.1	2.4	28.8	−12.6	.8	10.9	14.3	21.1	−6.4	5.9	−20.9	31.1
Algeria	612	27.6	−5.3	7.6	19.9	16.6	13.1	11.4	22.4	41.4	25.5	43.6	11.3
Angola	614	....	....	....	3,397.1	92.0	49.8	419.9	217.7	146.6	117.7	76.0	55.9
Botswana	616	−6.7	−.9	3.5	11.8	26.2	23.6	14.2	6.1	13.1	8.3	27.5	−5.7
Burundi	618	4.9	26.5	−.8	19.1	1.9	2.7	35.6	−2.6	11.1	23.2	10.9	37.2
Cape Verde	624	43.4	−38.9	22.7	−6.3	.5	9.3	6.7	15.8	7.6	15.3	2.8	6.9
Comoros	632	40.3	14.0	36.3	−12.4	−10.8	19.1	25.9	70.6	18.9	−1.5	−1.6	
Congo, Dem. Rep. of	636	2,608.4	3,264.3	650.3	524.2	106.5	2,690.2	420.3	−38.5	112.7	21.2	29.3	65.3
Djibouti	611	−7.7	5.5	−12.6	−3.7	−2.1	−2.0	4.4	−.8	5.4	9.0	31.2	−5.1
Eritrea	643	....	....	....	86.1	88.5	−34.8	38.3	7.7	−3.4	16.9	13.5	6.2
Ethiopia	644	4.9	10.3	12.6	−16.5	8.8	−12.2	−4.9	38.7	−9.0	34.8	15.1	89.5
Gambia, The	648	11.2	−3.9	25.4	.5	26.8	7.2	14.5	16.8	21.0	34.1	62.7	11.0
Ghana	652	4.9	78.9	35.1	44.8	33.4	16.7	38.4	54.5	41.0	46.2	28.1	17.9
Guinea	656	18.9	−10.0	12.3	−1.4	27.2	4.9	....	....	14.9	21.7	17.8	35.8
Kenya	664	52.5	22.8	31.0	8.2	2.1	−.4	6.0	−.7	−1.0	11.9	−1.1	14.6
Lesotho	666	21.9	6.6	32.4	5.0	12.3	38.9	32.8	−6.6	−25.4	.3	6.6	6.1
Liberia	668	27.2	5.4	31.3	17.9	8.0	1.9	4.4	41.3	11.8	6.3	8.9	62.3
Madagascar	674	−6.6	71.9	29.7	48.7	1.1	6.5	26.1	11.8	29.5	4.4	−.2	19.0
Malawi	676	62.6	41.3	89.6	38.5	.2	38.6	32.1	5.8	33.8	26.7	27.6	30.7
Mauritania	682	55.1	−3.7	−5.7	−49.5	−13.1	−7.5	4.5	4.9	5.4	3.2	−.3	....
Mauritius	684	18.1	5.1	14.6	−5.2	−2.2	9.4	7.8	11.8	10.4	14.9	9.3	16.4
Morocco	686	8.6	6.2	5.2	7.6	7.9	7.1	13.3	3.2	21.4	3.6	16.2	12.6
Mozambique	688	75.8	66.4	31.7	26.6	16.1	−3.7	17.5	25.7	53.0	17.3	21.9	20.4
Namibia	728	5.2	60.2	11.2	22.3	19.9	3.6	43.6	−6.3	8.3	7.8	19.7	....
Nigeria	694	49.4	31.3	20.5	6.1	4.5	16.7	21.7	48.2	34.1	13.1	42.9	−5.3
Rwanda	714	27.9	9.3	38.7	22.6	11.4	−8.8	14.8	−8.3	22.2	−.9	11.5	32.4
São Tomé and Príncipe	716	....	....	....	81.1	144.9	10.1	−15.2	29.3	74.7	14.3	64.8	−25.6
Seychelles	718	23.1	47.7	20.8	13.7	18.7	−49.3	9.4	3.1	7.2	26.7	−19.4	82.5
Sierra Leone	724	3.7	25.4	12.1	23.9	109.0	−20.4	39.0	9.2	29.4	24.9	22.4	12.6
South Africa	199	−8.5	17.8	29.8	13.6	11.5	5.5	23.3	4.7	14.6	13.3	11.1	23.0
Sudan	732	64.6	39.9	76.7	81.8	34.3	29.4	35.1	46.7	4.5	21.3	27.3	28.2
Swaziland	734	−11.3	17.6	2.5	−7.4	5.4	−8.4	11.6	−4.5	−6.4	27.3	27.1	11.5
Tanzania	738	35.1	48.7	39.1	6.6	8.7	14.7	21.5	9.4	5.0	19.1	12.6	23.5
Tunisia	744	4.8	7.2	9.4	35.8	8.1	−11.8	30.5	−11.4	17.9	−3.1	7.5	16.7
Uganda	746	23.4	48.1	13.7	11.6	9.1	20.0	15.1	21.8	13.4	10.7	11.0	20.5
Zambia	754	....	48.0	−14.6	35.4	48.2	16.8	28.5	53.4	45.7	44.7	14.3	32.3
Zimbabwe	698	52.0	23.6	2.5	65.9	37.8	29.9	60.9	16.0	164.9	171.2	394.8	217.6

Reserve Money

		1993	1994	1995	1996	1997	1998	1999	2000	2001	2002	2003	2004
							Percent Change over Previous Year						
Asia													
Bangladesh	513	24.0	29.6	−9.3	8.7	9.4	13.4	12.7	14.5	24.1	3.3	6.9	8.0
Bhutan	514	53.7	−33.4	67.1	8.3	9.3	55.4	25.7	21.1	2.3	13.3	19.9	10.2
Cambodia	522	....	25.4	10.0	43.0	21.2	47.2	15.9	24.9	17.1	45.7	8.5	23.9
China, P.R.: Mainland	924	36.2	31.0	20.6	29.5	17.0	2.8	7.6	9.0	10.0	12.5	17.6	13.0
China, P.R.: Hong Kong	532	17.1	9.7	3.9	5.0	6.4	2.2	19.6	−8.1	6.7	7.1	18.9	.8
Fiji	819	−2.9	1.7	8.8	1.9	5.0	6.3	56.8	−18.9	19.3	9.5	31.9	−14.3
India	534	21.7	21.7	12.6	9.5	11.2	12.4	11.4	7.7	10.2	9.3	13.8	16.3
Indonesia	536	8.3	25.2	17.8	35.8	38.3	77.8	38.8	24.3	16.0	−.9	12.8	24.3
Korea	542	27.5	9.2	16.3	−12.2	−12.5	−8.1	37.6	−.9	16.3	15.7	7.3	−4.8
Lao People's Democratic Rep.	544	64.5	22.3	13.4	24.0	43.8	87.7	71.0	59.1	7.3	31.2	23.2	16.2
Malaysia	548	−30.6	36.2	24.7	35.2	28.4	−56.4	26.3	−9.4	−3.3	6.4	6.9	10.0
Maldives	556	19.0	14.2	1.6	17.7	15.4	10.9	6.9	4.4	9.7	18.7	−1.7	26.1
Mongolia	948	184.5	103.8	29.0	36.4	23.1	18.3	50.4	20.2	6.8	21.9	14.5	17.0
Myanmar	518	20.7	23.1	27.8	32.0	29.5	26.8	18.7	34.5	51.6	34.9	46.1	29.3
Nepal	558	30.1	11.7	8.6	9.9	61.1	−9.3	10.3	19.3	12.0	−.1	2.9	15.3
Pakistan	564	14.2	15.7	17.9	−3.6	14.3	13.0	13.0	−2.1	28.3	8.8	16.5	20.0
Papua New Guinea	853	17.9	11.3	15.3	91.3	−34.3	20.7	73.3	−16.4	5.5	18.0	12.3	10.6
Philippines	566	18.0	7.9	12.4	32.5	−6.1	2.0	36.7	−10.6	−11.1	16.3	9.3	4.2
Samoa	862	−8.0	3.2	4.4	20.5	19.1	−45.7	21.4	8.8	−4.8	20.3	10.7	15.8
Singapore	576	8.4	6.2	9.4	6.7	5.6	−13.3	28.6	−13.7	8.5	−.3	3.4	5.7
Solomon Islands	813	11.7	30.9	23.0	30.4	−6.2	46.0	−.3	14.6	−3.3	16.5	27.3	72.9
Sri Lanka	524	25.9	20.5	15.5	8.8	−2.1	10.9	8.2	4.7	7.0	12.3	11.9	20.9
Thailand	578	16.1	14.5	22.6	13.5	15.8	−4.5	54.8	−12.9	6.2	2.4	26.5	18.2
Tonga	866	−62.8	−4.5	−17.7	43.0	12.3	10.3	7.5	12.6	29.7	20.7	−9.4	59.6
Vanuatu	846	53.6	−6.8	30.4	−4.2	−.2	5.2	22.3	1.9	−.4	—	8.0	10.3
Vietnam	582	27.8	....	....	20.1	12.5	8.7	50.5	25.0	16.7	12.4	27.4	16.1
Europe													
Albania	914	....	....	28.1	14.0	48.1	−1.1	21.6	17.8	18.1	7.7	−2.0	11.2
Armenia	911	1,375.5	842.0	92.0	42.8	24.8	4.9	—	34.4	11.1	38.4	6.6	12.9
Azerbaijan, Republic of	912	1,375.6	642.9	179.8	17.6	41.4	−24.3	15.9	29.1	1.5	14.0	23.5	64.7
Belarus	913	....	....	287.9	78.1	107.6	162.9	178.5	124.4	103.9	32.1	51.1	41.9
Bosnia and Herzegovina	963	....	....	....	....	....	38.8	241.7	19.2	164.6	−8.9	12.5	24.2
Bulgaria	918	22.0	55.9	52.0	91.5	826.7	10.2	17.6	11.1	30.4	8.0	16.1	40.2
Croatia	960	994.1	109.6	43.1	30.0	18.0	12.3	28.6	15.1	36.6	27.9	24.0	19.9
Cyprus	423	1.6	12.5	−4.3	−8.8	−.8	16.2	14.8	10.8	7.6	24.8	4.8	8.0
Czech Republic	935	....	34.4	53.6	.5	.1	22.5	8.9	6.9	4.9	−49.6	7.3	3.6
Estonia	939	103.3	11.6	19.9	22.2	37.7	6.4	26.7	14.9	−9.8	−1.5	14.6	24.0
Georgia	915	....	....	....	36.3	32.6	−6.3	18.8	27.0	10.4	19.6	14.3	49.8
Hungary	944	2.9	−1.6	17.8	−8.5	29.9	20.6	26.2	17.3	1.7	5.5	10.2	11.7
Kazakhstan	916	....	623.4	113.5	26.8	36.8	−29.4	55.7	6.0	30.6	18.6	52.2	82.4
Kyrgyz Republic	917	....	....	....	23.9	21.1	7.6	30.7	11.7	11.5	42.7	32.6	21.8
Latvia	941	....	19.5	1.6	23.0	31.2	6.7	11.6	7.7	13.3	18.4	6.3	18.6
Lithuania	946	203.7	44.2	35.0	2.2	32.4	28.8	−4.0	−3.3	8.3	20.8	26.6	7.1
Macedonia, FYR	962	....	71.7	30.6	−3.2	22.7	5.6	29.6	46.6	8.1	3.8	7.8	−.3
Malta	181	.2	31.7	−12.2	−4.2	1.5	3.0	6.9	3.5	3.7	4.2	....	....
Moldova	921	391.7	128.9	41.3	9.5	32.9	−6.7	40.3	30.9	27.9	31.1	16.6	39.8
Poland	964	7.6	22.6	45.0	20.5	34.0	16.9	−1.3	−7.8	30.5	−2.6	6.9	4.9
Romania	968	191.5	87.5	56.2	51.4	136.5	20.8	92.4	54.7	59.9	54.7	20.0	72.6
Russia	922	....	203.5	107.8	27.3	27.6	28.1	65.6	67.2	29.1	31.2	54.1	24.4
Slovak Republic	936	....	23.9	30.8	28.7	18.2	−5.6	20.0	4.0	22.6	1.7	−7.3	.8
Slovenia	961	38.2	56.9	25.2	15.6	23.0	19.7	21.3	1.9	35.5	−1.8	5.4	3.9
Turkey	186	67.9	119.5	79.5	91.5	99.9	80.4	97.5	46.2	78.5	17.6	18.6	33.5
Ukraine	926	1,560.0	407.4	132.8	39.9	49.0	16.6	41.3	43.8	42.5	23.8	30.1	37.3
Middle East													
Bahrain	419	−20.1	−4.1	34.5	−11.1	12.6	−21.7	45.5	−.6	14.4	13.9	34.8	4.4
Egypt	469	19.2	12.5	9.3	4.2	11.1	19.3	1.6	18.7	17.0	8.7	39.7	18.6
Iran, I.R. of	429	18.8	34.2	48.0	27.1	23.0	18.0	17.1	16.7	6.4	26.7	14.4	....
Israel	436	28.1	−6.7	−26.8	34.9	119.3	14.4	23.8	.6	.7	−15.8	−7.5	−22.7
Jordan	439	5.2	5.1	6.4	−13.4	−2.8	−4.7	12.1	.8	−5.7	3.9	16.9	3.2
Kuwait	443	−6.3	.1	−6.6	.8	−10.1	5.0	30.0	−8.3	−2.5	13.2	16.9	13.4
Lebanon	446	41.9	76.7	21.2	21.2	50.0	−5.5	5.5	6.6	37.2	10.1	121.7	3.3
Libya	672	−2.4	15.9	7.7	9.0	6.6	−1.0	−5.3	−.9	10.0	2.6	11.2	46.3
Oman	449	−4.8	4.1	3.6	6.4	8.5	7.1	−1.1	8.8	8.8	30.3	5.8	−8.2
Qatar	453	4.5	−6.9	5.0	6.1	9.7	3.1	12.2	6.7	11.6	17.0	14.9	31.1
Saudi Arabia	456	−.2	4.5	−2.3	−1.4	7.6	−1.2	23.5	−4.0	−4.1	9.3	5.1	11.4
Syrian Arab Rep.	463	14.6	8.6	4.7	7.6	4.8	5.0	7.3	15.2	16.9	16.0	10.2	....
United Arab Emirates	466	−3.3	25.7	13.1	8.1	.5	.2	30.5	36.5	6.0	−1.9	12.3	29.5
Yemen, Republic of	474	29.8	35.5	19.8	6.9	−12.5	11.2	20.8	14.0	14.0	9.2	21.1	14.4
Western Hemisphere													
ECCU	309	−5.7	2.8	10.7	−5.9	6.8	17.5	6.4	4.3	13.9	8.3	10.7	13.9
Anguilla	312	12.9	−2.1	33.7	14.6	12.5	12.2	11.2	2.7	28.6	1.3	26.2	3.2
Antigua and Barbuda	311	−18.5	15.0	17.5	−17.3	4.6	13.1	14.0	−2.5	20.1	5.3	27.0	3.4
Dominica	321	−7.5	−9.4	17.4	−.7	2.8	11.6	12.4	−2.7	−.8	42.5	−3.4	−6.7
Grenada	328	−7.4	6.4	8.5	.3	12.5	6.4	6.0	10.4	11.2	18.7	9.0	39.9
Montserrat	351	−1.3	19.5	9.0	3.0	26.1	115.2	−44.0	−24.9	14.9	13.4	6.1	−8.3
St. Kitts and Nevis	361	5.3	7.2	−1.5	−3.3	6.6	19.7	12.9	7.9	10.4	16.4	−2.7	21.9
St. Lucia	362	4.7	−4.6	11.5	−4.4	1.7	13.9	3.3	3.8	16.4	2.1	12.3	19.8
St. Vincent & Grens	364	−10.7	−3.3	−5.4	−2.6	9.1	20.8	16.8	20.6	9.5	−10.6	4.3	6.0
Argentina	213	36.1	8.5	−15.4	2.1	13.6	2.6	.8	−8.8	17.9	69.8	66.3	20.7
Aruba	314	10.7	−6.4	18.0	−14.3	−4.2	40.5	6.3	−11.5	32.4	13.7	−5.7	4.9
Bahamas, The	313	−.4	12.0	2.8	−2.6	14.5	19.7	20.8	−2.2	10.4	11.7	6.4	31.7
Barbados	316	−11.7	−1.9	15.7	34.2	−9.6	9.0	4.2	11.9	15.2	39.2	19.8	−29.0
Belize	339	−.7	−2.0	13.4	2.9	5.2	7.8	21.9	22.7	27.1	−22.9	4.1	12.3

Reserve Money

Western Hemisphere(Cont.)		1993	1994	1995	1996	1997	1998	1999	2000	2001	2002	2003	2004
					Percent Change over Previous Year								
Bolivia	218	32.8	4.3	23.3	15.7	20.1	−20.8	11.3	10.4	12.1	1.5	13.6	17.9
Brazil	223	2,424.4	2,241.7	11.9	22.8	34.2	−11.1	7.8	4.8	19.0	150.0	−4.2	10.8
Chile	228	18.5	17.7	21.3	11.5	7.2	9.8	4.5	−7.0	8.9	5.9	−3.8	19.8
Colombia	233	25.6	28.2	6.8	17.7	16.5	−17.1	39.7	9.1	9.9	20.3	16.4	15.4
Costa Rica	238	9.5	29.6	16.2	21.9	16.9	11.2	7.4	−4.7	−25.9	4.3	29.8	26.4
Dominican Republic	243	28.3	.5	16.4	10.9	18.9	22.4	15.0	10.3	28.9	−8.7	108.2	5.7
Ecuador	248	47.0	2.5	−9.5	7.0	7.2	−3.9	−15.0	−42.7	11.4	−8.8	9.9	14.1
El Salvador	253	51.7	22.2	12.4	10.0	13.3	8.3	10.2	−9.7	−29.2	−22.4	52.7	−19.7
Guatemala	258	23.3	4.5	3.5	12.8	22.9	−3.9	2.8	19.3	16.2	18.4	11.1	18.0
Guyana	336	−23.1	31.4	19.1	5.9	17.1	11.8	−3.9	14.0	10.9	10.0	10.3	9.1
Haiti	263	29.2	23.8	14.7	−4.1	11.1	.3	29.0	25.9	16.9	23.9	31.4	17.9
Honduras	268	6.8	47.0	23.9	43.5	91.9	16.1	11.6	9.3	9.8	26.2	6.6	38.7
Jamaica	343	44.6	34.3	29.7	4.0	15.2	22.1	−4.2	7.8	−6.4	−3.2	24.5	11.8
Mexico	273	10.4	21.2	33.4	23.1	48.4	37.1	38.3	−6.6	23.1	26.6	16.8	17.6
Netherlands Antilles	353	5.5	−6.5	19.9	−14.3	15.6	9.9	−5.9	8.2	36.3	24.9	−6.0	19.8
Nicaragua	278	7.8	52.5	23.6	34.6	32.5	19.7	5.7	4.7	41.7	10.8	19.2	15.7
Panama	283	4.1	−1.8	2.8	39.8	2.8	3.3	−1.5	4.9	.4	−2.0	−.3	4.4
Paraguay	288	13.5	27.3	26.2	−1.9	7.3	6.5	9.1	−1.0	6.1	2.7	50.9	17.4
Peru	293	59.4	31.0	31.2	37.8	38.7	5.7	15.6	2.0	4.6	8.3	−6.2	5.2
Suriname	366	70.0	207.8	227.0	−10.3	−.4	65.0	47.4	155.0	14.5	31.6	−8.3	20.7
Trinidad and Tobago	369	−4.7	56.9	−.7	8.9	16.1	20.9	3.7	3.1	10.7	−1.4	6.4	−3.2
Uruguay	298	42.6	32.4	30.5	32.5	25.0	14.4	21.2	9.4	26.2	.7	60.6	−18.0
Venezuela, Rep. Bol.	299	10.4	64.0	31.7	96.9	73.9	18.2	33.0	14.8	12.0	19.5	47.2	45.3

Money

		1993	1994	1995	1996	1997	1998	1999	2000	2001	2002	2003	2004
							Percent Change over Previous Year						
Industrial Countries													
United States	111	9.7	.1	−.9	1.4	3.5	3.5	10.3	−1.7	11.4	2.9	8.0	7.9
Canada	156	8.3	6.6	10.2	12.7	9.2	5.7	10.9	13.0	12.7	5.8	5.9	9.8
Australia	193	17.8	10.9	6.5	14.0	13.3	6.1	9.8	9.1	21.3	25.7	10.2	5.4
Japan	158	7.0	4.2	13.1	9.7	8.6	5.0	11.7	3.5	13.7	23.5	4.5	4.0
New Zealand	196	7.3	6.1	8.4	2.1	7.2	8.7	18.3	7.2	19.7	6.5	8.4	3.3
Euro Area	163	5.3	4.2	37.1	10.6	12.1	10.1	10.7	5.8	9.2	9.4	11.2	7.8
Austria	122	9.2	8.6	14.8	4.7	4.7	....	....	....	....	....	....	....
Belgium	124	7.5	1.5	4.9	4.2	3.1	....	....	....	....	....	....	....
Finland	172	5.1	8.9	14.0	16.4	5.5	4.8	....	....	....	....	....	....
Germany	134	8.8	4.9	7.1	12.3	2.1	10.4	....	....	....	....	....	....
Greece	174	11.5	23.5	13.6	10.9	14.4	11.9	34.3	−4.0	....	....	....	....
Ireland	178	12.9	12.5	64.1	8.8	−17.4	25.2	....	....	....	....	....	....
Italy	136	6.3	3.9	.4	4.9	6.5	11.1	....	....	....	....	....	....
Netherlands	138	10.5	1.7	13.5	12.1	7.8	....	....	....	....	....	....	....
Portugal	182	10.7	6.6	10.9	12.1	12.9	17.0	....	....	....	....	....	....
Spain	184	3.5	7.1	2.9	7.1	14.0	15.8	....	....	....	....	....	....
Denmark	128	10.5	−1.4	4.6	11.5	5.7	4.8	5.8	1.1	7.5	3.8	8.9	14.4
Iceland	176	5.4	10.7	9.6	8.5	16.4	20.3	21.1	2.6	−2.0	23.9	30.8	20.8
Norway	142	5.2	4.4	1.1	9.5	6.2	19.3	5.6	7.6	16.7	8.2	4.8	
Switzerland	146	5.8	4.0	6.1	27.4	9.0	6.8	9.5	−2.1	8.5	10.2	24.1	−5.6
United Kingdom	112	9.9	.8	16.7	9.3	25.7	9.4	11.1	14.1	11.3	10.1	10.2	12.8
Developing Countries													
Africa													
CEMAC	758	....	....	....	....	....	....	....	....	2.7	14.2	−3.1	12.6
Cameroon	622	−14.1	35.1	−11.6	−1.6	34.9	14.5	10.8	17.4	12.8	14.3	−5.2	7.6
Central African Rep.	626	16.4	74.0	7.6	4.9	−8.1	−18.3	12.6	3.2	−2.6	−4.4	−9.8	14.4
Chad	628	−27.7	31.5	42.7	33.5	−4.7	−8.0	−3.1	17.7	21.8	27.3	−3.1	2.5
Congo, Rep. of	634	−19.7	40.4	.3	13.6	8.7	−13.6	27.8	68.2	−23.1	13.9	−13.3	18.6
Equatorial Guinea	642	−28.6	135.5	58.4	50.1	−4.3	9.7	89.8	34.8	26.0	51.7	56.2	49.0
Gabon	646	−3.4	41.9	12.3	26.0	8.1	−5.1	−5.1	19.3	3.7	4.4	−.5	12.3
WAEMU	759	....	54.9	13.6	6.1	8.4	7.9	4.4	6.5	13.3	15.1	1.1	2.5
Benin	638	−13.2	67.3	−13.2	17.2	2.0	−4.7	46.9	35.0	10.0	−8.6	10.9	−17.2
Burkina Faso	748	11.6	38.9	25.5	7.0	17.5	−2.6	−1.9	5.3	−3.0	−7.1	85.4	−16.3
Côte d'Ivoire	662	.9	61.7	18.2	2.3	11.7	12.9	−1.7	−3.7	14.8	32.1	−34.6	13.6
Guinea Bissau	654	27.3	58.1	46.9	51.0	236.3	−12.1	22.4	63.7	7.8	22.3	−64.8	43.6
Mali	678	8.8	47.9	13.8	21.3	6.5	4.5	−.6	9.4	29.6	28.9	26.4	−7.2
Niger	692	11.1	15.4	9.2	−9.5	−19.4	−18.5	15.4	11.8	35.3	−8.2	56.4	21.7
Senegal	722	−9.0	54.4	3.7	8.5	−.1	15.7	10.8	5.5	14.9	5.8	47.6	6.7
Togo	742	−18.5	104.6	37.7	−7.8	1.9	6.9	9.9	22.2	−8.7	−8.1	4.3	24.7
Algeria	612	19.4	7.8	7.1	13.4	14.6	20.9	8.9	17.3	18.5	15.2	14.6	33.2
Angola	614	....	....	....	3,392.6	107.5	39.8	326.2	342.0	168.1	134.0	106.4	38.7
Botswana	616	14.7	11.1	7.2	14.7	9.1	45.8	17.3	6.9	23.9	7.4	11.8	28.5
Burundi	618	12.0	28.3	−3.3	12.5	10.5	1.3	41.9	−1.0	16.8	25.5	19.0	....
Cape Verde	624	7.0	8.2	16.6	10.6	21.6	−2.0	17.3	11.4	2.6	8.8	1.3	6.0
Comoros	632	4.6	9.8	−5.3	8.1	−18.6	−5.5	16.4	21.0	62.5	10.4	−2.1	−5.7
Congo, Dem. Rep. of	636	2,460.6	5,635.4	407.2	....	....	....	....	....	....	41.0	24.6	62.4
Djibouti	611	4.1	3.3	−1.6	−2.9	−9.6	−9.9	3.5	−7.8	2.6	24.0	20.7	10.7
Eritrea	643	....	....	....	29.9	36.1	18.0	46.4	13.4	28.1	18.8	15.9	12.6
Ethiopia	644	4.4	21.4	2.7	−2.7	20.2	−4.7	14.8	9.6	4.8	19.4	12.3	20.0
Gambia, The	648	6.0	−11.7	15.7	−3.8	38.8	−.5	14.3	37.4	14.4	56.1	63.5	8.2
Ghana	652	27.9	50.3	33.4	31.7	46.0	20.9	15.8	38.2	46.3	59.9	33.2	28.2
Guinea	656	19.4	−3.2	8.5	−.2	21.3	8.7	....	....	12.0	21.6	31.1	28.0
Kenya	664	27.4	5.2	6.6	14.6	17.4	4.5	16.7	8.8	5.9	18.7	29.5	8.4
Lesotho	666	23.4	12.3	10.5	19.3	22.7	24.9	−2.6	8.2	24.7	11.5	6.7	3.4
Liberia	668	59.8	7.6	42.4	6.7	−1.4	128.8	14.9	−11.5	6.7	38.8	16.6	35.3
Madagascar	674	11.9	56.5	15.2	17.3	22.9	10.9	20.2	13.2	30.3	7.5	4.2	19.4
Malawi	676	34.8	50.5	44.0	24.7	16.5	63.4	33.5	38.9	13.5	26.5	27.1	44.8
Mauritania	682	3.6	−5.4	−8.1	−10.9	8.3	5.3	6.3	22.7	14.8	4.3	11.4	....
Mauritius	684	3.0	19.4	8.0	2.7	7.9	9.2	3.6	10.8	16.2	17.5	12.4	15.8
Morocco	686	4.9	11.1	6.0	5.8	7.2	7.8	11.6	7.9	15.3	9.0	9.8	9.9
Mozambique	688	52.0	50.5	35.0	20.0	25.1	14.5	24.6	22.3	17.6	14.5	23.8	16.2
Namibia	728	46.3	14.7	8.3	53.6	3.5	27.0	22.2	28.2	9.5	6.1	17.2	....
Nigeria	694	57.0	43.4	16.3	13.5	16.8	19.0	22.5	62.1	25.7	15.9	29.5	8.6
Rwanda	714	10.7	15.6	41.1	11.7	22.7	−.8	7.0	6.7	1.0	10.4	17.0	....
São Tomé and Príncipe	716	....	....	....	66.5	107.8	−3.3	5.3	23.5	54.3	13.7	49.9	6.2
Seychelles	718	15.3	−3.0	2.9	34.4	44.8	19.3	38.4	−1.1	12.6	17.9	11.7	−21.9
Sierra Leone	724	11.7	10.0	29.5	6.6	57.1	7.3	49.4	4.4	35.4	30.6	18.4	17.6
South Africa	199	6.7	25.1	18.3	32.0	17.4	23.2	21.7	2.4	17.3	14.4	8.2	9.7
Sudan	732	76.1	54.6	66.7	86.2	32.5	29.3	27.8	42.2	15.7	29.8	30.2	31.8
Swaziland	734	14.2	7.3	16.6	16.5	16.2	1.9	32.3	−.3	14.2	9.5	26.9	3.0
Tanzania	738	32.9	33.3	29.9	4.9	9.9	10.5	16.0	9.9	10.2	25.2	16.1	18.2
Tunisia	744	3.6	10.7	9.6	13.0	13.0	7.5	16.0	9.9	10.1	−1.7	5.4	10.6
Uganda	746	25.9	36.5	15.4	10.3	13.7	19.5	12.6	16.8	12.8	21.0	12.3	8.6
Zambia	754	....	44.8	61.1	19.4	31.0	16.8	23.6	51.2	34.2	28.6	28.1	22.9
Zimbabwe	698	94.9	18.2	52.4	23.1	53.7	23.5	34.7	53.3	142.8	170.0	485.1	228.6
Asia													
Bangladesh	513	16.0	24.3	16.7	4.7	7.7	7.4	12.7	18.4	10.7	5.1	7.6	17.8
Bhutan	514	12.1	27.1	26.6	56.8	4.5	21.2	41.7	5.8	23.1	43.8	−2.9	19.0
Cambodia	522	....	−1.1	38.1	18.1	17.0	41.2	−2.1	1.4	13.0	33.4	15.1	23.2
China, P.R.: Mainland	924	21.8	27.2	17.3	19.4	26.3	11.2	21.4	16.1	13.1	17.8	19.0	14.9
China, P.R.: Hong Kong	532	20.9	.1	.3	15.3	−3.8	−4.6	15.4	—	14.3	14.0	34.8	14.9

Money

		1993	1994	1995	1996	1997	1998	1999	2000	2001	2002	2003	2004
						Percent Change over Previous Year							
Asia(Cont.)													
China, P.R.: Macao	546	....	....	....	....	....	....	−2.6	−7.8	19.6	7.3	38.4	52.9
Fiji	819	14.7	−6.0	13.0	18.7	−2.3	10.6	39.8	−13.7	4.6	14.7	26.1	13.4
India	534	18.7	27.4	11.1	14.1	12.6	11.7	16.9	10.6	10.0	12.5	16.2	20.7
Indonesia	536	21.9	23.7	15.6	10.0	32.8	25.3	28.8	37.7	8.8	7.4	17.3	13.9
Korea	542	18.1	11.9	19.6	1.7	−11.4	1.6	24.7	5.9	13.8	18.0	3.7	4.5
Lao People's Dem. Rep.	544	48.6	17.4	9.5	12.5	5.8	111.4	29.6	57.3	8.0	57.9	42.5	44.3
Malaysia	548	35.3	16.8	13.2	23.7	11.8	−29.6	29.3	6.8	3.7	9.3	15.2	8.5
Maldives	556	49.7	22.5	5.7	17.8	12.9	15.8	14.5	11.1	−5.9	13.9	11.6	19.7
Micronesia, Fed.Sts.	868	....	....	....	−1.7	10.2	−1.1	−6.5	−5.5	13.0	−7.3	14.1	4.9
Mongolia	948	142.8	78.2	29.0	42.7	25.1	8.5	39.0	13.9	19.4	20.2	13.4	4.4
Myanmar	518	25.2	33.8	28.1	33.4	31.0	28.2	22.6	34.5	50.8	44.0	17.5	25.4
Nepal	558	23.9	20.6	9.9	5.9	44.2	−11.2	21.1	14.4	....	....	....	....
Pakistan	564	1.7	15.1	12.8	7.5	32.5	4.6	8.6	10.1	10.1	15.9	24.1	21.6
Papua New Guinea	853	35.9	3.4	14.0	52.0	−5.5	10.3	21.0	2.2	3.2	15.0	16.4	22.8
Philippines	566	22.3	11.3	21.7	19.8	14.2	7.4	38.3	−1.3	.4	22.0	8.6	9.2
Samoa	862	14.7	8.1	29.1	−.2	22.5	−10.7	20.7	16.1	−6.9	10.1	23.6	5.7
Singapore	576	23.6	2.3	8.3	6.7	1.7	−1.0	14.2	6.9	8.5	−.7	8.1	14.0
Solomon Islands	813	18.1	31.4	5.0	15.7	7.4	−.2	25.7	−5.8	−1.5	3.5	29.6	12.9
Sri Lanka	524	18.6	18.7	6.7	4.0	9.8	12.1	12.8	9.1	3.2	14.0	16.0	16.6
Thailand	578	18.6	17.0	12.1	9.1	1.5	4.9	64.0	−7.5	−4.9	3.7	28.8	9.3
Tonga	866	20.5	−5.5	−13.9	3.8	2.6	4.7	22.1	10.6	26.2	32.0	12.7	15.7
Vanuatu	846	12.3	.9	10.1	3.5	1.8	14.4	.2	6.1	−.5	44.3	5.7	4.9
Vietnam	582	28.9	....	....	25.1	19.5	13.1	51.2	33.1	23.5	11.5	25.3	26.1
Europe													
Albania	914	....	....	52.8	52.6	1.4	−8.7	23.0	20.4	15.3	6.7	−5.2	19.4
Armenia	911	1,060.1	907.3	124.3	32.4	10.6	19.6	−.9	36.7	8.3	49.2	6.9	7.4
Azerbaijan, Republic of	912	980.1	468.3	130.5	30.4	36.1	−25.6	17.5	12.9	7.6	16.2	27.0	30.6
Belarus	913	....	....	273.2	56.7	115.5	139.1	188.4	117.8	84.7	45.4	63.7	48.0
Bosnia & Herzegovina	963	....	....	....	....	....	11.9	199.4	28.0	89.7	13.1	4.3	15.2
Bulgaria	918	....	....	....	217.1	556.4	13.9	9.0	18.8	25.8	11.0	19.9	28.2
Croatia	960	....	112.2	24.6	37.9	21.0	−1.4	1.7	30.1	31.5	30.2	9.8	2.0
Cyprus	423	8.5	4.9	6.2	6.8	7.8	3.7	42.1	−2.1	−.5	1.1	30.6	7.6
Czech Republic	935	....	50.2	6.7	4.7	−7.3	−3.4	10.8	11.4	17.0	17.0	16.6	6.4
Estonia	939	75.2	20.9	29.8	37.6	24.0	−6.3	32.1	20.5	19.5	9.3	13.0	17.4
Georgia	915	....	....	....	37.3	31.1	−10.0	9.9	33.7	7.2	14.9	14.1	58.5
Hungary	944	11.7	8.0	3.8	22.5	23.5	17.2	19.3	11.3	16.8	18.7	10.3	.4
Kazakhstan	916	....	576.0	108.2	20.9	8.2	−21.3	73.4	14.7	14.3	41.5	25.4	57.7
Kyrgyz Republic	917	....	....	....	16.6	7.8	2.9	31.0	9.6	20.7	38.1	38.3	22.9
Latvia	941	....	31.1	.8	20.3	33.3	6.0	6.3	19.6	13.0	21.3	17.7	22.3
Lithuania	946	....	41.8	40.9	3.5	41.5	9.0	−5.3	7.5	18.9	23.5	26.5	18.4
Macedonia, FYR	962	....	....	....	−3.6	16.2	9.1	32.4	13.1	−50.1	148.2	2.1	2.1
Malta	181	4.0	9.1	7.6	−1.9	—	7.2	10.6	2.6	6.7	7.0	....	....
Moldova	921	304.9	116.5	68.8	12.4	30.6	−18.0	38.9	36.7	23.6	42.4	24.0	38.3
Poland	964	31.3	39.7	36.4	39.8	17.9	16.2	23.1	−6.4	14.0	19.9	18.3	9.4
Romania	968	95.0	107.8	57.7	58.7	66.9	17.7	34.6	55.9	39.0	36.2	28.2	34.2
Russia	922	....	187.0	120.7	27.2	55.6	15.0	53.3	66.9	35.5	25.6	45.6	30.5
Slovak Republic	936	....	6.2	20.9	15.8	−4.4	−11.4	4.2	21.5	21.3	8.5	44.6	14.3
Slovenia	961	41.5	35.1	24.8	18.4	18.1	25.2	26.6	6.1	19.9	47.1	12.8	27.9
Tajikistan	923	....	....	....	....	....	....	17.6	46.9	25.4	34.4	28.3	8.5
Turkey	186	64.8	81.5	68.3	129.5	69.1	63.1	93.6	57.3	46.3	36.7	43.1	26.4
Ukraine	926	1,552.5	444.0	151.7	34.9	43.3	14.1	36.4	47.1	43.1	35.2	31.9	28.3
Middle East													
Bahrain, Kingdom of	419	3.7	−5.5	−3.6	.8	3.7	5.1	16.6	4.6	23.8	17.3	26.9	4.8
Egypt	469	12.1	10.7	8.5	7.2	9.4	20.3	.8	5.3	7.9	13.0	23.4	16.0
Iran, I.R. of	429	30.0	41.6	32.5	33.6	19.9	22.7	21.5	24.7	23.0	23.6	18.9	....
Israel	436	27.9	7.7	15.1	20.4	11.3	12.3	20.4	2.5	21.8	1.5	11.7	23.6
Jordan	439	7.1	1.3	−.2	−11.8	6.1	−.8	9.5	14.2	3.8	8.5	24.5	10.9
Kuwait	443	.5	1.1	5.2	4.9	.4	−8.3	19.9	7.0	11.8	25.9	26.4	21.5
Lebanon	446	−4.7	25.7	8.6	12.4	10.0	6.3	10.2	5.7	−1.0	8.5	10.9	6.4
Libya	672	4.5	13.0	6.2	1.2	5.2	.4	4.7	4.5	1.2	6.0	6.3	21.7
Oman	449	4.3	4.7	−.3	6.8	9.2	−8.0	1.1	7.5	27.7	10.0	4.7	12.8
Qatar	453	4.2	−8.1	−4.9	4.4	6.3	2.1	−.9	6.5	17.3	20.5	79.3	29.4
Saudi Arabia	456	−1.6	3.4	−.2	6.1	6.1	−.6	11.7	5.7	8.4	12.7	10.2	18.2
Syrian Arab Republic	463	22.0	8.2	8.7	8.6	6.7	8.0	11.1	17.7	13.9	17.8	27.0	....
United Arab Emirates	466	21.3	5.6	8.6	6.9	13.9	9.5	8.9	12.6	15.8	19.2	23.8	38.7
Yemen, Republic of	474	31.9	35.1	17.5	−4.5	6.3	8.1	15.2	19.3	14.5	8.2	13.4	12.4
Western Hemisphere													
ECCU	309	2.2	7.5	13.4	−2.5	7.8	14.7	7.9	.4	4.9	7.2	15.7	28.0
Anguilla	312	−21.7	2.8	51.4	−3.8	15.5	5.1	10.7	15.3	−4.3	10.9	9.1	28.4
Antigua and Barbuda	311	−1.8	16.5	28.1	−7.5	2.2	25.1	−1.9	−2.3	8.8	−1.5	18.1	25.6
Dominica	321	−12.7	−5.0	19.6	3.1	1.8	5.8	29.1	−19.9	2.0	25.0	−.1	11.0
Grenada	328	13.5	11.3	5.3	.5	4.9	14.5	4.3	8.4	4.9	16.0	14.8	51.0
Montserrat	351	5.6	20.4	−.4	−6.8	61.9	3.7	−14.3	−15.3	4.1	1.7	28.3	5.3
St. Kitts and Nevis	361	7.9	−3.4	14.0	7.5	−3.9	24.9	4.0	.4	−6.8	20.9	19.3	38.8
St. Lucia	362	4.9	−.2	7.8	−5.0	7.6	7.9	9.8	−1.0	1.2	3.8	23.3	30.7
St. Vincent & Grenadines	364	3.2	18.7	−4.6	7.8	28.0	11.6	22.9	14.9	9.4	1.8	10.3	15.1
Argentina	213	33.0	15.7	1.6	14.6	12.8	—	1.6	−9.1	−20.1	78.4	51.9	30.2
Aruba	314	14.1	16.8	.5	.9	5.7	15.6	7.8	1.1	17.5	20.4	16.7	−2.5
Bahamas, The	313	.4	9.1	6.8	.5	15.7	14.7	26.1	6.7	−3.9	5.7	9.0	18.5
Barbados	316	−5.1	8.3	−17.0	46.4	−1.1	23.4	20.7	23.5	1.3	2.3	31.0	6.5
Belize	339	7.9	5.7	7.8	5.5	1.3	12.3	33.0	15.7	32.1	−13.5	22.4	9.4
Bolivia	218	30.0	29.3	21.1	21.7	19.0	7.1	−5.8	8.8	18.7	−.4	19.3	18.6
Brazil	223	2,017.8	2,195.4	25.7	29.9	22.3	7.5	13.6	18.9	12.1	29.1	4.0	17.6

Money

Western Hemisphere(Cont.)		1993	1994	1995	1996	1997	1998	1999	2000	2001	2002	2003	2004
						Percent Change over Previous Year							
Chile	228	21.1	15.8	22.3	16.4	19.9	−4.6	15.8	7.2	11.4	9.1	11.3	16.3
Colombia	233	28.1	29.0	20.2	23.4	17.4	−7.9	24.2	25.9	9.6	16.9	15.5	16.0
Costa Rica	238	7.0	37.9	−6.0	16.9	54.3	17.1	28.6	19.8	13.2	16.4	15.1	7.9
Dominican Republic	243	13.9	7.5	17.3	22.3	19.3	6.2	21.8	−1.1	16.4	6.1	64.5	5.7
Ecuador	248	45.8	19.0	−19.4	4.8	7.4	−13.6	−24.8	−.9	45.7	−1.1	10.6	26.4
El Salvador	253	18.8	4.0	8.8	14.3	.6	8.0	15.1	−6.7	9.6	−9.0	9.9	4.8
Guatemala	258	20.4	40.1	9.9	13.5	29.9	13.5	13.6	21.8	11.8	8.4	18.0	6.7
Guyana	336	26.6	10.4	16.7	14.5	10.0	−1.6	23.0	10.4	1.2	7.8	14.2	14.0
Haiti	263	22.7	31.8	31.6	−13.1	18.7	.3	26.6	9.5	15.1	27.3	20.2	10.8
Honduras	268	11.9	36.1	21.7	29.4	41.0	12.7	18.2	8.2	3.6	14.8	21.3	16.0
Jamaica	343	26.2	25.7	38.0	14.4	2.8	6.4	22.8	6.3	13.0	9.7	6.1	18.5
Mexico	273	17.9	.8	2.4	38.7	32.2	21.2	25.8	14.2	13.3	13.1	13.8	8.4
Netherlands Antilles	353	6.5	13.8	7.9	−4.3	—	2.6	3.3	2.1	14.3	15.2	−5.3	12.8
Nicaragua	278	−4.6	36.2	13.2	25.9	24.7	23.6	23.5	8.3	32.8	3.1	24.9	14.2
Panama	283	10.8	13.5	1.3	3.3	18.3	13.0	1.6	2.9	10.3	2.0	10.1	10.8
Paraguay	288	16.5	30.0	28.2	.5	10.4	5.2	9.2	18.2	7.1	.6	37.3	26.3
Peru	293	52.6	28.9	34.2	19.7	69.1	26.3	16.2	−5.4	1.8	2.8	−3.2	11.1
Suriname	366	87.6	245.6	178.2	−2.0	20.2	34.6	51.5	104.3	38.2	38.4	4.2	23.2
Trinidad and Tobago	369	16.3	19.5	4.7	6.1	21.1	5.8	12.3	6.6	19.6	15.8	−1.4	8.4
Uruguay	298	57.9	40.4	32.3	24.8	16.7	14.1	3.1	−3.5	−4.2	3.8	34.3	15.9
Venezuela, Rep. Bol.	299	12.0	139.2	38.0	149.2	77.0	4.7	24.5	25.3	15.5	18.2	73.7	46.6

Money plus Quasi-Money

		1993	1994	1995	1996	1997	1998	1999	2000	2001	2002	2003	2004
						Percent Change over Previous Year							
Industrial Countries													
United States	111	1.5	—	5.6	6.1	6.6	10.1	8.2	6.9	14.1	4.3	2.1	3.4
Canada	156	11.6	8.0	6.2	5.0	8.6	2.3	5.7	13.9	6.5	5.6	7.0	10.2
Australia	193	5.7	10.0	8.5	10.6	7.3	8.4	11.7	3.8	13.2	5.6	13.3	11.7
Japan	158	2.2	3.1	2.7	2.3	3.1	4.1	3.4	1.1	2.2	3.4	1.8	1.6
New Zealand	196	7.0	7.6	9.3	16.1	5.2	1.8	5.0	2.3	6.8	7.7	10.6	5.6
Euro Area													
Austria	122	5.5	5.4	5.0	2.8	2.2	....	....	....	....	....	....	....
Belgium	124	7.7	2.8	4.9	6.3	7.1	....	....	....	....	....	....	....
Finland	172	1.5	1.4	6.0	−2.9	2.5	3.7	....	....	....	....	....	....
France	132	.7	3.3	8.7	—	6.6	....	....	....	....	....	....	....
Germany	134	11.1	2.6	4.4	7.4	2.4	5.9	....	....	....	....	....	....
Ireland	178	24.8	10.1	52.8	15.6	19.5	17.8	....	....	....	....	....	....
Italy	136	7.5	1.8	2.3	2.2	−5.8	.6	....	....	....	....	....	....
Netherlands	138	5.7	.3	6.0	5.6	6.7	....	....	....	....	....	....	....
Portugal	182	10.7	9.1	8.3	5.6	6.8	5.9	....	....	....	....	....	....
Spain	184	9.8	7.1	6.6	2.6	1.4	7.1	....	....	....	....	....	....
Denmark	128	19.7	−10.0	6.2	8.1	6.8	3.3	−.9	−5.2	3.6	4.2	6.0	11.0
Iceland	176	6.5	2.0	2.5	6.2	9.4	15.2	17.3	10.7	14.9	15.0	22.4	13.2
Norway	142	−.7	5.0	3.8	6.9	1.4	15.5	1.7	8.7	8.8	7.6	3.4	....
Sweden	144	....	....	....	....	....	....	....	....	....	3.7	4.1	2.4
Switzerland	146	8.9	4.2	4.6	9.6	6.6	5.1	13.3	−16.9	3.9	5.7	8.4	2.9
United Kingdom	112	4.7	7.7	20.3	14.5	25.6	6.7	19.1	11.1	8.6	5.0	9.8	10.3
Developing Countries													
Africa													
CEMAC	758	....	....	....	....	....	....	....	....	6.4	14.9	1.7	10.3
Cameroon	622	−9.2	26.5	−6.2	−10.1	18.6	7.8	13.3	19.1	15.1	15.9	1.3	6.4
Central African Republic	626	12.8	78.5	4.3	4.9	−7.7	−16.1	11.1	2.4	−1.1	−4.3	−8.0	14.2
Chad	628	−28.3	31.4	48.7	27.9	−4.1	−7.7	−2.6	18.5	22.0	26.6	−3.1	3.5
Congo, Rep. of	634	−26.6	28.2	−.1	15.7	9.5	−12.8	19.9	58.5	−22.8	13.1	−2.4	17.4
Equatorial Guinea	642	−25.9	139.5	48.9	42.8	9.3	15.6	68.7	36.2	35.1	53.1	56.7	33.5
Gabon	646	−1.7	37.4	10.1	17.2	11.3	−1.8	−3.0	18.3	7.5	5.7	−1.2	11.4
WAEMU	759	....	39.8	14.1	7.6	7.3	3.5	5.0	7.2	11.8	15.6	3.0	5.2
Benin	638	−3.1	47.9	−1.8	13.0	4.6	−3.6	34.8	26.0	12.2	−7.0	10.8	−9.3
Burkina Faso	748	8.0	29.4	22.3	5.2	17.7	1.0	2.6	6.2	1.6	.6	60.6	−8.3
Côte d'Ivoire	662	−1.4	46.8	18.1	3.9	8.2	6.0	−1.7	−1.9	12.0	30.0	−26.3	9.6
Guinea Bissau	654	40.5	48.5	43.0	48.3	119.4	−11.1	21.5	60.8	7.3	22.8	−64.7	42.8
Mali	678	8.4	39.2	7.3	24.5	8.9	4.2	1.0	12.2	19.6	27.9	26.4	−2.6
Niger	692	.1	6.7	3.8	−6.6	−21.3	−18.5	15.4	12.4	31.4	−.5	42.5	19.7
Senegal	722	−12.6	38.7	7.4	11.7	3.7	8.5	13.1	10.7	13.6	8.2	31.5	12.2
Togo	742	−16.2	44.3	22.3	−6.3	5.3	.1	8.4	15.2	−2.6	−2.2	10.9	18.1
Algeria	612	22.7	13.0	9.2	14.4	18.6	18.9	13.7	13.2	24.8	36.8	16.0	11.3
Angola	614	....	....	....	4,105.6	71.9	57.6	564.8	309.0	160.6	158.6	63.9	35.8
Botswana	616	−14.4	12.8	12.3	18.8	28.6	39.4	26.3	1.4	31.2	−1.1	15.5	16.0
Burundi	618	8.1	33.3	−11.2	24.3	9.4	−3.7	47.3	4.3	15.7	29.5	15.8	....
Cape Verde	624	18.0	12.2	18.2	9.7	10.9	2.8	14.9	13.7	9.9	13.6	9.0	11.1
Comoros	632	3.4	7.3	−6.1	9.8	−4.2	−14.2	18.5	14.5	46.7	9.2	−1.2	−5.0
Congo, Dem. Rep. of	636	2,853.1	6,968.9	357.6	....	....	....	....	....	....	40.0	32.3	72.6
Djibouti	611	.9	3.7	5.3	−7.4	−4.5	−4.1	−3.8	1.1	7.5	15.7	17.8	13.9
Eritrea	643	....	....	....	21.0	28.1	20.5	36.1	17.3	32.6	20.6	15.1	11.6
Ethiopia	644	8.8	23.2	9.0	9.0	19.8	−1.1	13.7	13.1	9.7	15.9	12.4	19.3
Gambia, The	648	12.8	−3.8	14.2	5.8	23.0	10.2	12.1	34.8	19.4	35.3	43.4	18.3
Ghana	652	33.5	52.6	43.2	39.2	44.1	17.5	25.4	54.2	31.7	48.9	34.2	27.4
Guinea	656	22.8	−3.4	11.3	3.6	18.2	6.4	....	....	12.9	19.7	33.2	36.5
Kenya	664	28.0	23.2	29.0	25.3	20.2	2.9	6.5	4.9	2.8	11.7	11.9	13.7
Lesotho	666	29.4	10.9	9.8	17.1	14.8	15.5	−5.1	1.4	17.2	8.8	6.0	3.3
Liberia	668	65.6	11.7	29.5	−11.9	3.5	106.0	11.6	18.3	12.7	4.9	9.5	45.7
Madagascar	674	24.2	52.6	16.2	16.0	20.8	6.2	19.2	17.2	23.8	8.0	8.8	25.2
Malawi	676	39.9	36.5	56.2	40.0	2.1	67.8	28.0	45.5	23.7	22.6	27.5	29.7
Mauritania	682	.7	−.5	−5.1	−5.1	8.0	4.1	2.1	16.1	17.3	8.9	10.5	....
Mauritius	684	17.0	12.3	18.7	7.6	16.4	11.2	15.2	9.2	10.9	12.5	10.9	13.2
Morocco	686	7.9	10.2	7.0	6.6	8.0	6.0	10.2	8.4	14.1	6.4	8.7	7.8
Mozambique	688	67.1	50.4	47.7	19.1	23.9	17.8	31.8	38.3	28.2	21.1	18.3	5.8
Namibia	728	25.7	25.9	24.2	29.0	6.7	11.3	18.4	13.0	4.5	6.9	20.7	....
Nigeria	694	53.8	34.5	19.4	16.2	16.0	22.3	33.1	48.1	27.0	21.6	24.1	14.0
Rwanda	714	2.5	−3.7	69.5	8.6	29.1	3.5	7.9	15.6	11.2	12.6	15.4	....
São Tomé and Príncipe	716	....	....	....	84.5	116.4	2.8	7.7	24.9	40.1	25.0	53.0	2.9
Seychelles	718	23.7	18.8	14.4	14.3	16.2	15.8	18.8	4.6	11.9	11.1	5.9	.9
Sierra Leone	724	21.9	8.8	19.6	29.7	47.1	11.3	37.8	12.1	33.7	29.6	21.9	20.1
South Africa	199	6.3	18.3	16.0	14.3	17.8	13.7	10.9	7.2	16.7	21.9	13.4	13.7
Sudan	732	104.0	51.2	73.3	65.3	37.7	29.9	23.5	37.1	24.7	30.2	30.3	30.8
Swaziland	734	13.6	10.9	3.9	16.3	19.4	12.9	15.6	−6.6	10.7	13.1	14.1	10.4
Tanzania	738	39.2	35.3	33.0	8.4	12.9	10.8	18.6	14.8	17.1	25.1	16.6	19.2
Tunisia	744	6.1	8.1	6.6	13.3	16.5	5.4	18.9	14.1	10.7	4.4	6.4	11.3
Uganda	746	57.2	35.8	13.9	19.3	19.4	22.9	13.6	18.1	9.2	25.0	17.9	11.1
Zambia	754	....	59.2	55.5	35.0	25.1	25.6	27.7	73.8	13.6	31.1	22.7	32.1
Zimbabwe	698	71.3	35.1	25.5	33.3	41.2	11.3	35.9	68.9	128.5	191.7	430.0	229.3
Asia													
Bangladesh	513	10.5	19.3	12.2	10.7	9.8	11.4	15.4	19.3	14.7	13.3	13.1	16.3
Bhutan	514	30.0	23.3	35.6	9.0	58.9	13.9	32.0	17.4	7.9	27.9	1.0	19.9
Cambodia	522	....	35.6	43.6	40.4	16.6	15.7	17.3	26.9	20.4	31.1	14.9	30.4
China, P.R.: Mainland	924	23.7	31.5	29.5	25.3	20.7	14.9	14.7	12.3	15.0	19.4	19.7	14.8

Money plus Quasi-Money

Money plus Quasi-Money

		1993	1994	1995	1996	1997	1998	1999	2000	2001	2002	2003	2004
							Percent Change over Previous Year						
China, P.R.: Hong Kong	532	14.5	11.7	10.6	12.5	8.7	11.1	8.3	9.3	−.3	.5	6.3	7.3
Fiji	819	6.3	2.5	4.5	.9	−8.7	−.5	13.6	−1.5	−3.1	7.8	25.0	10.5
India	534	17.0	20.3	11.0	18.7	17.7	18.2	17.1	15.2	14.3	16.8	13.0	16.7
Indonesia	536	20.1	20.2	27.5	27.1	25.3	62.8	12.2	16.6	12.8	4.5	8.1	8.2
Korea	542	16.6	18.7	15.6	15.8	14.1	27.0	27.4	25.4	13.2	11.0	6.7	−.6
Lao People's Democratic Rep.	544	64.6	31.9	16.4	26.7	65.8	113.3	78.4	46.0	13.7	37.6	20.1	21.6
Malaysia	548	26.6	12.8	20.9	25.5	18.2	−1.5	16.3	11.6	2.4	3.7	9.6	19.3
Maldives	556	36.3	24.2	15.6	26.0	23.1	22.8	3.6	4.1	9.0	19.3	14.6	32.6
Micronesia, Federal States of	868	....	....	....	−5.8	3.8	.7	3.4	−1.0	6.0	−12.0	−3.7	−.1
Mongolia	948	227.6	80.0	32.6	17.2	42.2	−1.7	31.6	17.6	27.9	42.0	49.6	20.5
Myanmar	518	26.9	35.6	36.5	38.9	28.8	34.2	29.7	42.4	43.9	34.6	1.4	32.4
Nepal	558	24.8	18.1	15.6	12.2	29.2	11.1	21.6	18.8	....	....	....	....
Pakistan	564	18.1	17.4	13.8	20.1	19.9	7.9	4.3	12.1	11.7	16.8	17.5	20.5
Papua New Guinea	853	17.8	−1.3	13.7	30.7	.9	7.7	2.5	9.2	5.0	1.6	4.0	−.4	12.4
Philippines	566	28.1	26.7	23.9	23.7	23.1	8.6	16.9	8.1	3.6	10.4	3.6	9.9
Samoa	862	1.4	13.9	24.4	6.3	15.2	2.5	15.7	16.3	6.1	10.2	14.0	8.3
Singapore	576	8.5	14.4	8.5	9.8	10.3	30.2	8.5	−2.0	5.9	−.3	8.1	6.2
Solomon Islands	813	15.6	25.1	9.2	15.3	6.7	2.5	7.0	.6	−13.6	6.0	25.4	17.5
Sri Lanka	524	23.3	19.7	35.8	11.3	15.6	13.2	13.4	12.9	13.6	13.4	15.3	19.6
Thailand	578	18.4	12.9	17.0	12.6	16.5	9.7	5.4	3.4	2.4	1.4	6.6	5.1
Tonga	866	25.0	6.6	.7	5.3	7.8	14.7	11.9	18.8	14.9	7.8	14.4	13.2
Vanuatu	846	5.0	2.9	13.4	10.1	−.4	12.6	−9.2	5.5	5.7	−1.7	−.8	9.9
Vietnam	582	12.3	....	....	25.7	24.3	23.5	66.4	35.4	27.3	13.3	33.1	31.0
Europe													
Albania	914	....	....	51.8	43.8	28.5	20.6	22.3	12.0	19.9	5.9	7.6	13.1
Armenia	911	1,076.8	740.4	64.3	35.1	29.2	36.7	14.0	38.6	4.3	34.0	10.4	22.3
Azerbaijan, Republic of	912	825.8	1,116.5	25.4	17.1	41.4	−17.4	20.1	73.4	−10.6	14.6	30.8	46.1
Belarus	913	....	....	158.4	52.4	111.4	276.0	132.7	219.3	62.2	50.3	56.8	45.6
Bosnia & Herzegovina	963	....	....	....	....	....	22.0	27.5	11.3	90.0	9.4	9.5	22.4
Bulgaria	918	53.9	77.5	40.5	123.9	351.4	11.8	13.4	30.8	26.0	12.3	20.2	24.0
Croatia	960	....	74.6	40.4	49.2	38.4	13.0	−1.8	29.1	45.7	9.6	10.7	8.2
Cyprus	423	16.3	12.5	11.4	10.5	11.0	8.3	20.8	9.7	13.4	9.0	4.0	5.6
Czech Republic	935	....	20.4	29.3	6.4	1.7	3.4	2.6	16.0	11.2	−2.1	7.4	4.4
Estonia	939	42.8	30.4	27.5	36.8	37.8	4.2	23.7	25.7	23.0	11.2	10.9	15.8
Georgia	915	....	....	....	41.4	44.0	−1.1	21.1	39.4	20.5	17.9	22.8	42.4
Hungary	944	17.7	14.2	20.9	22.2	19.7	15.6	15.7	12.6	16.1	14.1	12.5	8.9
Kazakhstan	916	....	576.0	108.2	20.9	8.2	−14.1	84.4	45.0	20.8	30.1	29.5	69.3
Kyrgyz Republic	917	....	....	....	14.8	32.2	17.5	33.7	11.7	11.3	33.9	33.4	32.1
Latvia	941	....	50.3	−21.4	19.6	37.0	6.7	8.3	27.0	19.8	19.9	22.1	26.7
Lithuania	946	....	63.0	28.9	−3.5	34.1	14.5	7.7	16.5	21.4	16.9	18.2	24.1
Macedonia, FYR	962	....	−57.1	11.7	−1.0	23.5	13.0	32.0	21.4	32.1	15.7	15.8	16.1
Malta	181	10.5	14.9	11.8	8.6	8.0	8.1	9.8	4.0	8.4	10.4	....	....
Moldova	921	318.8	115.7	65.3	14.8	34.5	−8.3	42.9	41.7	35.8	38.6	30.4	39.8
Poland	964	36.0	38.2	35.0	31.0	29.1	25.2	19.4	11.8	15.0	−2.8	5.7	6.9
Romania	968	143.3	138.1	70.1	67.4	105.0	48.9	44.9	38.0	46.2	38.2	23.3	39.9
Russia	922	....	216.5	112.6	29.6	28.8	37.6	56.7	58.0	36.3	33.8	38.5	33.7
Slovak Republic	936	....	17.4	18.4	16.2	8.4	2.5	11.6	15.2	11.9	4.0	10.0	6.8
Slovenia	961	62.2	44.7	29.8	23.3	23.3	19.5	15.1	18.0	30.4	12.3	6.2	7.6
Turkey	186	64.4	145.3	103.6	117.3	97.5	89.7	100.3	40.5	86.2	29.1	14.6	22.1
Ukraine	926	1,809.2	567.9	115.5	35.1	33.9	22.2	40.6	44.5	43.0	42.3	46.9	32.8
Middle East													
Bahrain	419	5.7	6.0	7.4	3.1	7.8	16.8	4.1	10.2	9.2	10.3	6.4	4.2
Egypt	469	13.2	11.2	9.9	10.8	10.8	10.8	5.7	11.6	13.2	12.6	21.3	14.4
Iran, I.R. of	429	30.3	33.3	30.1	32.5	23.7	20.4	21.5	22.4	27.6	24.9	24.5	....
Israel	436	22.0	24.6	21.7	25.0	15.0	19.7	15.5	8.0	9.5	6.9	−.1	3.6
Jordan	439	9.3	3.3	5.7	−.9	7.6	6.3	15.5	7.6	8.1	8.6	16.6	10.5
Kuwait	443	5.6	5.4	9.4	−.6	3.9	−.8	1.6	6.3	12.8	4.8	7.8	12.1
Lebanon	446	33.1	25.3	16.4	26.4	19.6	16.1	11.7	9.8	7.5	8.1	13.0	10.1
Libya	672	5.9	14.0	9.6	1.0	−3.7	3.8	7.4	3.1	4.3	1.1	7.8	17.9
Oman	449	3.2	6.7	7.7	8.1	24.5	4.8	6.4	6.0	9.2	5.2	2.5	4.0
Qatar	453	5.8	9.1	1.1	5.6	9.9	8.0	11.4	10.7	—	11.8	15.8	20.5
Saudi Arabia	456	3.4	3.0	3.4	7.3	5.2	3.6	6.8	4.5	5.1	15.2	8.5	17.3
Syrian Arab Rep.	463	30.3	12.2	9.2	10.2	8.2	10.5	13.4	19.0	23.5	18.5	7.8	....
United Arab Emirates	466	−1.6	7.9	10.2	6.9	9.0	4.2	11.5	15.3	23.2	11.0	15.5	23.8
Yemen, Republic of	474	31.1	32.5	50.7	8.1	11.2	11.8	13.8	25.3	18.8	17.5	19.7	14.6
Western Hemisphere													
ECCU	309	7.4	7.7	13.5	2.3	8.5	13.3	13.4	9.3	6.5	7.9	8.8	12.0
Anguilla	312	13.2	11.4	26.2	2.8	9.9	20.2	9.2	17.5	12.9	12.9	8.0	20.8
Antigua and Barbuda	311	7.5	8.3	21.4	−3.6	7.3	15.7	26.9	6.3	5.3	5.9	16.1	6.4
Dominica	321	−2.5	3.6	22.2	6.4	4.1	5.8	10.0	−2.1	6.5	10.2	6.4	5.6
Grenada	328	22.1	12.0	9.7	8.3	10.2	11.9	12.8	15.4	10.8	8.4	6.6	20.5
Montserrat	351	−2.2	20.3	−.7	−8.5	16.3	10.9	−4.3	−7.9	2.8	−.8	11.7	8.8
St. Kitts and Nevis	361	9.4	1.2	14.9	2.3	13.8	11.5	3.5	26.9	1.1	8.5	13.8	17.9
St. Lucia	362	4.2	6.3	8.5	5.0	4.4	11.1	8.1	5.2	5.6	2.6	8.4	8.3
St. Vincent & Grens.	364	9.5	5.5	4.1	6.4	12.6	14.4	16.6	5.6	7.7	4.9	4.5	10.5
Argentina	213	46.5	17.6	−2.8	18.8	25.5	10.5	4.1	1.5	−19.4	19.7	29.6	21.4
Aruba	314	5.7	13.9	4.2	4.3	4.0	13.6	10.2	2.0	6.4	10.5	9.0	2.7
Bahamas, The	313	16.1	8.7	8.5	5.6	23.5	16.2	10.6	9.3	4.9	3.0	3.7	9.2
Barbados	316	2.9	8.9	4.9	19.3	8.8	7.6	12.1	9.4	2.4	15.8	6.8	12.2
Belize	339	3.3	8.4	18.2	7.6	11.5	5.9	15.8	12.4	12.3	−1.7	4.7	8.6
Bolivia	218	33.7	24.2	7.7	24.2	16.7	12.9	5.7	.4	2.2	−6.9	13.9	2.2
Brazil	223	2,854.0	1,279.7	34.6	12.3	19.4	9.8	6.9	3.9	12.5	24.1	3.6	19.4
Chile	228	24.5	11.7	24.3	20.1	9.8	10.3	7.8	6.1	2.3	−.3	8.1	8.3
Colombia	233	37.6	39.7	21.7	24.4	41.9	20.9	13.7	14.7	16.0	13.6	9.9	18.2

Money plus Quasi-Money

Western Hemisphere(Cont.)		1993	1994	1995	1996	1997	1998	1999	2000	2001	2002	2003	2004
							Percent Change over Previous Year						
Costa Rica	238	15.2	22.0	4.8	47.6	16.4	26.3	29.0	18.4	10.4	20.9	16.7	33.8
Dominican Republic	243	21.1	12.1	17.8	18.4	24.2	16.6	23.7	17.4	26.9	10.3	63.1	9.0
Ecuador	248	46.8	39.1	6.8	12.4	9.1	−6.6	−55.2	47.0	31.8	−.7	18.9	24.2
El Salvador	253	33.5	40.4	11.9	13.8	10.6	9.0	8.8	2.0	3.7	−3.1	2.3	1.6
Guatemala	258	15.1	12.0	15.8	13.8	18.4	19.4	12.5	35.5	18.1	11.8	15.0	9.4
Guyana	336	19.7	12.5	24.4	19.4	10.1	6.7	10.8	8.4	8.7	5.7	7.8	8.7
Haiti	263	29.2	31.4	27.1	1.1	24.8	9.7	23.0	20.1	14.1	22.8	39.0	5.2
Honduras	268	10.4	30.3	29.2	41.2	50.5	22.9	24.7	24.4	17.5	13.7	15.8	20.7
Jamaica	343	35.9	40.6	31.8	10.9	13.3	7.7	12.2	13.0	8.6	12.0	10.5	14.0
Mexico	273	16.9	20.1	31.9	27.0	33.0	17.4	18.7	−4.5	12.5	8.3	7.1	10.7
Netherlands Antilles	353	9.4	8.7	7.5	−3.5	2.1	4.0	5.6	2.8	14.8	11.5	7.3	11.5
Nicaragua	278	25.2	65.9	35.1	40.6	52.5	32.1	18.8	9.4	41.0	13.3	12.6	17.2
Panama	283	17.2	15.5	7.9	6.1	15.0	13.0	8.5	10.0	9.6	−.3	4.8	8.4
Paraguay	288	29.0	23.6	15.7	14.1	7.7	9.9	18.2	4.8	16.4	3.1	7.6	14.2
Peru	293	71.8	37.2	29.3	37.2	30.8	17.3	14.5	−.4	2.1	5.1	−2.4	3.1
Suriname	366	65.7	204.7	181.5	38.5	19.0	37.8	37.9	80.5	28.2	116.7	19.9	31.0
Trinidad and Tobago	369	15.3	16.7	4.0	5.8	11.3	14.5	4.2	11.7	6.9	5.7	−.7	14.1
Uruguay	298	37.4	42.1	39.0	36.6	28.4	19.3	13.1	7.2	19.0	28.2	12.5	−1.7
Venezuela, Rep. Bol.	299	25.5	68.9	36.6	70.2	61.1	15.4	20.7	23.1	15.3	15.8	57.6	46.9

Ratio of Reserve Money to Money plus Quasi-Money

		1993	1994	1995	1996	1997	1998	1999	2000	2001	2002	2003	2004
							Percent						
Industrial Countries													
United States	111	10.0	10.8	10.7	10.6	10.7	10.3	11.4	10.0	9.5	9.8	10.1	10.1
Canada	156	7.4	7.0	6.7	6.6	6.3	6.6	7.7	6.3	6.2	6.2	5.8	5.5
Australia	193	64.5	93.5	131.6	284.5	304.2	431.1	548.5	730.0	1,163.0	7.3	6.5	6.0
Japan	158	9.3	9.3	9.7	10.3	10.7	10.7	14.9	11.8	13.8	14.9	16.5	16.8
New Zealand	196	2.7	2.8	2.8	2.3	2.3	2.4	4.0	3.0	3.1	3.1	2.8	2.9
Euro Area													
Austria	122	10.4	10.3	9.7	10.1	9.8	....	....	....	....	....	....	....
Belgium	124	7.7	7.0	7.3	7.1	6.8	....	....	....	....	....	....	....
Finland	172	12.8	19.1	18.3	12.6	11.4	10.8	....	....	....	....	....	....
France	132	18.3	17.8	17.8	18.1	17.5	....	....	....	....	....	....	....
Germany	134	14.2	13.6	13.3	13.0	12.6	12.0	....	....	....	....	....	....
Ireland	178	13.9	13.2	10.9	9.6	9.5	....	....	....	....	....	....	....
Italy	136	18.9	17.6	16.2	16.2	18.5	13.0	....	....	....	....	....	....
Netherlands	138	11.1	11.7	9.7	8.8	9.1	....	....	....	....	....	....	....
Portugal	182	23.3	8.8	7.9	8.3	7.7	7.3	....	....	....	....	....	....
Denmark	128	4.1	4.6	4.9	6.0	7.4	5.5	11.1	9.0	8.2	8.8	9.0	7.5
Iceland	176	12.4	12.5	10.0	11.9	12.1	10.8	14.3	11.4	8.7	8.6	4.5	9.6
Norway	142	8.9	8.7	8.9	12.7	11.1	8.5	12.6	9.7	8.9	12.3	8.5	
Sweden	144	24.2	27.6	21.9	13.7	9.4	9.1	10.0	8.8	9.8	9.4	9.1	9.0
Switzerland	146	9.3	9.0	8.4	8.0	7.4	7.5	7.8	8.4	9.1	8.0	8.0	7.5
United Kingdom	112	5.3	5.2	4.6	4.2	3.6	3.5	3.5	3.1	2.9	2.9	2.8	2.9
Developing Countries													
Africa													
CEMAC	758	....	....	....	....	....	....	....	49.0	48.7	48.4	48.2	51.4
Cameroon	622	23.8	26.2	22.0	31.4	37.1	38.0	36.2	40.8	43.4	47.8	41.8	45.8
Central African Republic	626	81.2	83.8	84.0	86.3	82.0	78.0	75.7	80.8	76.6	75.3	75.3	76.0
Chad	628	80.2	75.4	80.2	82.4	82.3	80.1	77.1	75.6	72.8	77.3	71.6	74.2
Congo, Rep. of	634	51.1	54.0	58.5	54.9	55.9	50.8	56.9	72.9	72.4	58.6	64.3	65.9
Equatorial Guinea	642	75.9	56.4	75.4	60.5	60.8	42.2	48.8	53.4	73.3	50.1	77.5	72.7
Gabon	646	24.6	41.1	35.7	39.3	35.9	33.4	31.7	36.5	32.6	31.2	36.1	39.3
WAEMU	759	49.5	42.3	40.4	38.6	40.0	41.5	40.9	42.6	47.2	49.3	46.9	45.2
Benin	638	63.0	43.2	32.5	31.4	36.0	35.7	46.5	51.9	57.0	53.3	49.2	44.1
Burkina Faso	748	67.5	51.7	52.4	52.2	54.8	52.3	43.8	41.3	40.7	30.7	51.6	41.4
Côte d'Ivoire	662	35.9	38.2	36.1	37.1	38.3	43.0	40.4	42.0	50.4	54.3	42.7	47.0
Guinea Bissau	654	73.3	65.3	60.3	56.4	58.1	56.7	62.7	73.1	79.0	84.0	76.5	85.0
Mali	678	84.4	48.8	50.2	47.7	47.2	42.8	47.7	53.8	50.3	57.7	60.2	52.5
Niger	692	65.9	46.9	51.1	51.5	51.5	40.6	46.4	42.9	48.5	46.4	59.9	55.5
Senegal	722	37.6	40.5	39.2	30.1	30.0	29.5	30.3	28.9	34.2	35.4	41.1	40.4
Togo	742	54.1	38.4	40.5	37.8	36.1	40.1	42.3	44.4	42.7	46.2	33.0	36.6
Algeria	612	38.6	32.3	31.9	33.4	32.8	31.2	30.6	33.1	37.5	34.4	42.6	42.6
Angola	614	....	....	71.9	59.8	66.8	63.5	49.6	38.6	36.5	30.7	33.0	37.9
Botswana	616	18.6	16.4	15.1	14.2	13.9	12.4	11.2	11.7	10.1	11.0	12.2	9.9
Burundi	618	42.2	40.0	44.7	42.8	39.9	42.6	39.2	36.6	35.1	33.4	32.0	....
Cape Verde	624	75.5	41.2	42.7	36.5	33.1	35.2	32.7	33.3	32.6	33.1	31.2	30.0
Comoros	632	49.2	52.4	50.1	62.2	56.9	59.1	59.4	65.3	75.9	82.7	82.4	85.4
Congo, Dem. Rep. of	636	84.7	40.3	66.1	62.1	19.3	81.1	63.6	5.9	64.3	55.7	54.4	52.1
Djibouti	611	19.2	19.6	16.2	16.9	17.3	17.7	19.2	18.9	18.5	17.4	19.4	16.2
Eritrea	643	....	....	41.6	64.0	94.2	51.0	51.8	47.6	34.6	33.6	33.1	31.5
Ethiopia	644	61.7	55.3	57.1	43.7	39.7	35.2	29.5	36.1	30.0	34.9	35.7	56.7
Gambia, The	648	38.4	38.3	42.1	40.0	41.2	40.1	40.9	35.4	35.9	35.6	40.4	37.9
Ghana	652	36.3	42.6	40.2	41.8	38.7	38.4	42.4	42.5	45.5	44.7	42.6	39.4
Guinea	656	62.3	58.1	58.6	55.8	60.1	59.2	....	63.0	64.2	65.2	57.7	57.4
Kenya	664	38.5	38.4	39.0	33.7	28.6	27.7	27.5	26.1	25.1	25.2	22.2	22.4
Lesotho	666	25.0	24.0	29.0	26.0	25.4	30.5	42.8	39.4	25.1	23.1	23.2	23.9
Liberia	668	74.4	70.2	71.2	95.2	99.3	49.1	46.0	54.9	54.5	55.2	54.9	61.2
Madagascar	674	35.1	39.6	44.1	56.6	47.3	47.5	50.2	47.9	50.1	48.5	44.5	42.3
Malawi	676	45.3	46.9	56.9	56.3	55.3	45.7	47.2	34.3	37.1	38.3	38.4	38.7
Mauritania	682	82.7	80.1	79.6	42.4	34.1	30.3	31.0	28.0	25.2	23.8	21.5	....
Mauritius	684	19.7	18.4	17.8	15.7	13.2	12.9	12.1	12.4	12.3	12.6	12.4	12.8
Morocco	686	28.3	27.3	26.8	27.1	27.1	27.4	28.1	26.8	28.5	27.7	29.7	31.0
Mozambique	688	35.0	38.7	34.5	36.7	34.4	28.1	25.0	22.8	27.2	26.3	27.1	30.9
Namibia	728	7.8	9.9	8.9	8.4	9.5	8.8	10.7	8.9	9.2	9.3	9.2	....
Nigeria	694	58.2	56.8	57.3	52.4	47.2	45.0	41.1	41.2	43.5	40.4	46.6	38.7
Rwanda	714	46.7	53.0	43.4	48.9	42.2	37.2	39.6	31.4	34.5	30.3	29.3	....
São Tomé and Príncipe	716	....	....	51.4	50.5	57.1	61.2	48.2	49.9	62.2	56.9	61.3	44.3
Seychelles	718	30.9	38.4	40.6	40.4	41.2	18.1	16.6	16.4	15.7	17.9	13.6	24.6
Sierra Leone	724	49.0	56.5	53.0	50.6	71.9	51.4	51.8	50.5	48.9	47.1	47.3	44.3
South Africa	199	8.2	8.2	9.1	9.1	8.6	8.0	8.9	8.7	8.5	7.9	7.8	8.4
Sudan	732	54.6	50.5	51.5	56.6	55.2	55.0	60.2	64.4	54.0	50.3	49.1	48.1
Swaziland	734	24.0	25.4	25.1	20.0	17.6	14.3	13.8	14.1	11.9	13.4	15.0	15.1
Tanzania	738	36.2	39.7	41.6	40.9	39.4	40.8	41.8	39.8	35.7	34.0	32.8	34.0
Tunisia	744	21.0	20.8	21.4	25.6	23.8	19.9	21.8	16.9	18.0	16.7	16.9	17.7
Uganda	746	41.2	44.9	44.8	41.9	38.3	37.4	37.9	39.1	40.6	35.9	33.8	36.7
Zambia	754	51.2	47.6	26.1	26.2	31.0	28.9	29.0	25.6	32.9	36.3	33.8	33.8
Zimbabwe	698	30.2	27.6	22.5	28.1	27.4	32.0	37.9	26.0	30.1	28.0	26.2	25.2
Asia													
Bangladesh	513	26.7	29.0	23.4	23.0	22.9	23.3	22.8	21.9	23.7	21.6	20.4	18.9
Bhutan	514	99.4	53.7	66.2	65.8	45.2	61.7	58.7	60.6	57.5	51.0	60.4	55.6
Cambodia	522	68.4	63.2	48.5	49.3	51.3	65.2	64.5	63.4	61.7	68.6	64.8	61.5
China, P.R.: Mainland	924	36.8	36.7	34.2	35.3	34.2	30.6	28.7	27.9	26.7	25.1	24.7	24.3
China, P.R.: Hong Kong	532	10.0	9.8	9.2	8.6	8.4	7.7	8.5	7.2	7.7	8.2	9.2	8.6

Ratio of Reserve Money to Money plus Quasi-Money

		1993	1994	1995	1996	1997	1998	1999	2000	2001	2002	2003	2004
							Percent						
Asia(Cont.)													
Fiji	819	16.1	16.0	16.6	16.8	19.3	20.6	28.5	23.5	28.9	29.4	31.0	24.0
India	534	32.3	32.6	33.1	30.5	28.9	27.4	26.1	24.4	23.5	22.0	22.2	22.1
Indonesia	536	12.8	13.3	12.3	13.1	14.5	15.9	19.6	20.9	21.5	20.4	21.2	24.4
Korea	542	20.6	18.9	19.0	14.4	11.1	8.0	8.7	6.8	7.0	7.3	7.4	7.1
Lao People's Democratic Rep.	544	48.2	44.7	43.6	42.6	37.0	32.5	31.2	34.0	32.1	30.6	31.4	30.0
Malaysia	548	21.4	25.9	26.7	28.7	31.2	13.8	15.0	12.2	11.5	11.8	11.5	10.6
Maldives	556	84.0	77.2	67.9	63.5	59.5	53.7	55.5	55.6	56.0	55.7	47.8	45.4
Mongolia	948	33.4	37.8	36.8	42.8	37.0	44.5	50.9	52.0	43.4	37.3	28.6	27.7
Myanmar	518	81.3	73.8	69.1	65.6	66.0	62.3	57.0	53.8	56.8	56.9	82.0	80.0
Nepal	558	41.9	39.6	37.2	36.5	45.5	37.1	33.6	33.8	....	....	....	....
Pakistan	564	40.1	39.6	41.0	32.9	31.4	32.8	35.6	31.1	35.7	33.2	32.9	32.8
Papua New Guinea	853	11.8	13.3	13.5	19.8	12.0	14.2	22.5	17.9	18.6	21.1	23.8	23.4
Philippines	566	33.4	28.4	25.8	27.7	21.1	19.8	23.2	19.2	16.5	17.3	18.3	17.3
Samoa	862	48.0	43.5	36.5	41.4	42.8	22.7	23.8	22.3	20.0	21.8	21.2	22.6
Singapore	576	17.9	16.6	16.7	16.2	15.6	10.3	12.3	10.8	11.1	11.1	10.6	10.5
Solomon Islands	813	18.8	19.7	22.2	25.0	22.0	31.3	29.2	33.3	37.3	41.0	41.6	61.2
Sri Lanka	524	35.4	35.6	30.3	29.6	25.1	24.6	23.5	21.8	20.5	20.3	19.7	19.9
Thailand	578	11.5	11.7	12.2	12.3	12.2	10.7	15.7	13.2	13.7	13.8	16.4	18.4
Tonga	866	29.2	26.2	21.4	29.1	30.3	29.2	28.0	26.6	30.0	33.6	26.6	37.6
Vanuatu	846	12.3	11.1	12.8	11.1	11.2	10.4	14.0	13.6	12.8	13.0	14.1	14.2
Vietnam	582	64.8	....	58.2	55.6	50.3	44.3	40.0	36.9	33.9	33.6	32.2	28.5
Europe													
Albania	914	....	59.4	50.1	39.7	45.8	37.5	37.3	39.2	38.7	39.3	35.8	35.2
Armenia	911	54.6	61.2	71.6	75.7	73.1	56.1	49.2	47.7	50.8	52.5	50.7	46.8
Azerbaijan, Republic of	912	51.1	31.2	69.7	69.9	69.9	64.1	61.8	46.0	52.3	52.0	49.1	55.4
Belarus	913	....	25.3	38.0	44.4	43.6	30.5	36.5	25.7	32.3	28.4	27.3	26.6
Bosnia & Herzegovina	963	....	....	....	....	11.4	12.9	34.7	37.2	51.7	43.1	44.3	44.9
Bulgaria	918	23.1	20.3	21.9	18.8	38.5	38.0	39.4	33.5	34.7	33.3	32.2	36.4
Croatia	960	22.5	27.0	27.5	23.9	20.4	20.3	26.6	23.7	22.2	25.9	29.1	32.2
Cyprus	423	25.9	25.9	22.2	18.4	16.4	17.6	16.7	16.9	16.0	18.4	18.5	18.9
Czech Republic	935	21.8	24.3	28.9	27.3	26.9	31.8	33.8	31.1	29.4	15.1	15.1	15.0
Estonia	939	58.0	49.6	46.7	41.7	41.7	42.5	43.6	39.8	29.2	25.9	26.7	28.6
Georgia	915	....	....	85.0	81.9	75.4	71.5	70.1	63.9	58.5	59.3	55.2	58.1
Hungary	944	31.7	27.3	26.6	19.9	21.6	22.6	24.6	25.7	22.5	20.8	20.4	20.9
Kazakhstan	916	39.5	42.3	43.3	45.5	57.5	47.2	39.9	29.2	31.5	28.8	33.8	36.4
Kyrgyz Republic	917	....	....	73.6	79.5	72.8	66.7	65.2	65.2	65.3	69.6	69.2	63.8
Latvia	941	48.6	38.6	49.9	51.3	49.1	49.2	50.7	43.0	40.6	40.1	34.9	32.7
Lithuania	946	47.0	41.6	43.5	46.1	45.5	51.2	45.6	37.8	33.7	34.8	37.3	32.2
Macedonia, FYR	962	8.6	34.4	40.2	39.4	39.1	36.5	35.9	43.3	35.5	31.8	29.6	25.4
Malta	181	32.5	37.2	29.3	25.8	24.3	23.1	22.5	22.4	21.4	20.2	....	....
Moldova	921	69.0	73.3	62.6	59.7	59.1	60.1	59.0	54.5	51.3	48.5	43.4	43.4
Poland	964	28.6	25.4	27.3	25.1	26.0	24.3	20.1	16.6	18.8	18.8	19.1	18.7
Romania	968	45.4	35.8	32.9	29.7	34.3	27.8	36.9	41.4	45.3	50.7	49.3	60.9
Russia	922	50.1	48.1	47.0	46.2	45.7	42.6	44.9	47.6	45.0	44.2	49.2	45.7
Slovak Republic	936	15.4	16.2	17.9	19.8	21.6	19.4	20.9	18.9	20.7	20.2	17.0	16.1
Slovenia	961	11.9	12.9	12.4	11.6	11.6	11.6	12.3	10.6	11.0	9.6	9.5	9.2
Turkey	186	25.6	22.9	20.2	17.8	18.0	17.1	16.9	17.6	16.8	15.3	15.9	17.3
Ukraine	926	61.6	46.8	50.6	52.3	58.2	55.5	55.8	55.6	55.4	48.2	42.7	44.1
Middle East													
Bahrain	419	14.3	12.9	16.2	13.9	14.5	9.7	13.6	12.3	12.9	13.3	16.8	16.9
Egypt	469	32.0	32.3	32.2	30.2	30.3	32.7	31.4	33.4	34.6	33.4	38.4	39.8
Iran, I.R. of	429	39.8	40.1	45.6	43.8	43.5	42.7	41.1	39.2	32.7	33.1	30.5	....
Israel	436	20.8	15.6	9.4	10.1	19.3	18.4	19.7	18.4	16.9	13.3	12.3	9.2
Jordan	439	51.0	51.9	52.2	45.6	41.2	36.9	35.8	33.5	29.3	28.0	28.1	26.2
Kuwait	443	7.9	7.5	6.4	6.5	5.6	5.9	7.6	6.5	5.7	6.1	6.6	6.7
Lebanon	446	13.8	19.4	20.2	19.4	24.3	19.8	18.7	18.1	23.1	23.6	46.3	43.4
Libya	672	58.9	59.9	58.9	63.6	70.4	67.1	59.2	56.8	60.0	60.8	62.7	77.8
Oman	449	21.6	21.1	20.3	20.0	17.4	17.8	16.6	17.0	16.9	20.9	21.6	19.1
Qatar	453	12.9	11.0	11.4	11.5	11.5	11.0	11.0	10.6	11.9	12.4	12.3	13.4
Saudi Arabia	456	23.7	24.1	22.8	20.9	21.4	20.4	23.6	21.6	19.8	18.7	18.2	17.3
Syrian Arab Rep.	463	58.7	56.9	54.5	53.2	51.6	49.0	46.3	44.9	42.4	41.5	42.5	....
United Arab Emirates	466	19.2	22.4	22.9	23.2	21.4	20.6	24.1	28.5	24.5	21.7	21.1	22.0
Yemen, Republic of	474	88.6	90.6	72.0	71.3	56.1	55.8	59.2	53.9	51.7	48.1	48.7	48.6
Western Hemisphere													
ECCU	309	20.2	19.3	18.8	17.3	17.0	17.7	16.6	15.8	16.9	17.0	17.3	17.6
Anguilla	312	13.9	12.2	13.0	14.4	14.8	13.8	14.1	12.3	14.0	12.6	14.7	12.5
Antigua and Barbuda	311	17.8	18.9	18.3	15.7	15.3	15.0	13.5	12.3	14.1	14.0	15.3	14.9
Dominica	321	21.5	18.8	18.1	16.9	16.7	17.6	18.0	17.9	16.6	21.5	19.5	17.3
Grenada	328	20.6	19.5	19.3	17.9	18.2	17.3	16.3	15.6	15.7	17.2	17.5	20.4
Montserrat	351	20.7	20.6	22.6	25.4	27.6	53.5	31.3	25.5	28.5	32.6	31.0	26.1
St. Kitts and Nevis	361	21.6	22.9	19.7	18.6	17.4	18.7	20.4	17.3	18.9	20.3	17.4	18.0
St. Lucia	362	21.0	18.9	19.4	17.6	17.2	17.6	16.8	16.6	18.3	18.2	18.9	20.9
St. Vincent & Grens.	364	25.4	23.3	21.2	19.4	18.8	19.9	19.9	22.7	23.1	19.7	19.7	18.9
Argentina	213	33.0	30.4	26.5	22.8	20.6	19.1	18.5	16.7	24.4	34.6	44.3	44.0
Aruba	314	23.7	19.5	22.1	18.1	16.7	20.7	19.9	17.3	21.5	22.1	19.1	19.6
Bahamas, The	313	12.8	13.2	12.5	11.5	10.7	11.0	12.0	10.7	11.3	12.3	12.6	15.2
Barbados	316	17.4	15.7	17.3	19.5	16.2	16.4	15.2	15.6	17.5	21.0	23.6	14.9
Belize	339	24.6	22.3	21.4	20.4	19.3	19.6	20.6	22.5	25.5	20.0	19.9	20.6
Bolivia	218	27.3	22.9	26.3	24.5	25.2	17.7	18.6	20.5	22.4	24.5	24.4	28.1
Brazil	223	17.1	29.0	24.1	26.3	29.6	24.0	24.2	24.4	25.8	52.0	48.1	44.6
Chile	228	14.2	15.0	14.6	13.6	13.3	13.2	12.8	11.2	11.9	12.7	11.3	12.5
Colombia	233	48.7	44.7	39.2	37.0	30.4	20.9	25.6	24.4	23.1	24.5	25.9	25.3
Costa Rica	238	48.9	51.9	57.5	47.5	47.7	42.0	34.9	28.1	18.9	16.3	18.1	17.1

Ratio of Reserve Money to Money plus Quasi-Money

Western Hemisphere(Cont.)		1993	1994	1995	1996	1997	1998	1999	2000	2001	2002	2003	2004
							Percent						
Dominican Republic......................	243	46.3	41.5	41.0	38.4	36.8	38.6	35.9	33.7	34.3	28.4	36.2	35.1
Ecuador.............................	248	24.9	18.3	15.6	14.8	14.5	15.0	28.4	11.1	9.3	8.6	7.9	7.3
El Salvador.............................	253	28.1	24.5	24.6	23.8	24.3	24.2	24.5	21.7	14.8	11.9	17.7	14.0
Guatemala.............................	258	53.9	50.3	45.0	44.6	46.3	37.3	34.1	30.0	29.5	31.2	30.2	32.5
Guyana.............................	336	33.4	39.0	37.3	33.1	35.2	36.9	32.0	33.7	34.4	35.8	36.6	36.8
Haiti.............................	263	58.8	55.4	50.0	47.4	42.2	38.6	40.4	42.3	43.4	43.8	41.4	46.3
Honduras.............................	268	28.4	32.0	30.7	31.2	39.8	37.6	33.6	29.5	27.6	30.7	28.2	32.4
Jamaica.............................	343	39.9	38.1	37.5	35.1	35.7	40.5	34.6	33.0	28.4	24.6	27.7	27.1
Mexico.............................	273	12.2	12.3	12.4	12.0	13.4	15.7	18.2	17.9	19.5	22.9	24.9	26.5
Netherlands Antilles....................	353	17.4	14.9	16.7	14.8	16.7	17.7	15.8	16.6	19.7	22.1	19.3	20.8
Nicaragua.............................	278	55.2	50.7	46.4	44.4	38.5	34.9	31.1	29.7	29.9	29.2	30.9	30.5
Panama.............................	283	5.9	5.0	4.8	6.3	5.6	5.1	4.7	4.4	4.1	4.0	3.8	3.7
Paraguay.............................	288	28.5	29.3	32.0	27.5	27.4	26.6	24.5	23.1	21.1	21.0	29.5	30.3
Peru.............................	293	40.7	38.8	39.4	39.5	41.9	37.8	38.2	39.1	40.0	41.3	39.6	40.5
Suriname.............................	366	60.8	61.4	71.3	46.2	38.6	46.3	49.5	69.9	62.4	37.9	29.0	26.7
Trinidad and Tobago....................	369	16.8	22.7	21.6	22.3	23.2	24.5	24.4	22.5	23.3	21.7	23.3	19.8
Uruguay.............................	298	33.9	31.6	29.6	28.8	28.0	26.9	28.8	29.4	31.2	24.5	35.0	29.2
Venezuela, Rep. Bol.....................	299	32.9	31.9	30.8	35.6	38.4	39.4	43.4	40.5	39.3	40.6	37.9	37.5

Income Velocity of Money plus Quasi-Money

		1993	1994	1995	1996	1997	1998	1999	2000	2001	2002	2003	2004
							Index Numbers: 2000=100						
Industrial Countries													
United States	111	103.2	109.6	108.5	108.1	107.7	103.1	101.0	100.0	90.5	89.6	92.0	95.1
Canada	156	108.9	106.8	105.8	104.0	101.1	102.4	104.0	100.0	96.6	95.4	93.8	90.4
Australia	193	8.6	12.2	17.2	24.6	34.8	49.4	69.5	100.0	142.8	.9	.9	.8
Japan	158	115.0	112.9	111.4	111.8	110.8	105.2	100.3	100.0	96.8	92.1	90.5	90.4
New Zealand	196	94.4	66.5	38.7	202.2	124.7	66.0	90.4	100.0	70.4	36.7	31.3	22,719.0
Euro Area													
Austria	122	....	....	....	....	....	....	....	....	....	....	....	....
Belgium	124	....	....	....	....	....	....	....	....	....	....	....	....
Finland	172	....	....	....	....	....	....	....	....	....	....	....	....
France	132	....	....	....	....	....	....	....	....	....	....	....	....
Germany	134	....	....	....	....	....	....	....	....	....	....	....	....
Greece	174	116.1	106.7	106.7	104.1	104.5	106.3	96.1	100.0	....	....	....	....
Ireland	178	....	....	....	....	....	....	....	....	....	....	....	....
Italy	136	....	....	....	....	....	....	....	....	....	....	....	....
Luxembourg	137	....	....	....	....	....	....	....	....	....	....	....	....
Netherlands	138	....	....	....	....	....	....	....	....	....	....	....	....
Portugal	182	....	....	....	....	....	....	....	....	....	....	....	....
Spain	184	....	....	....	....	....	....	....	....	....	....	....	....
Denmark	128	75.5	90.0	88.6	86.0	84.8	84.9	89.6	100.0	99.9	97.8	95.0	89.0
Iceland	176	113.6	118.3	118.8	120.1	115.5	111.5	101.9	100.0	97.5	87.7	74.6	71.0
Norway	142	85.3	85.4	88.3	90.5	96.5	85.2	91.2	100.0	95.5	88.4	87.9	....
Sweden	144	115.2	114.5	114.7	109.6	106.3	103.4	101.5	100.0	105.3	105.3	104.8	106.8
Switzerland	146	108.6	107.0	103.5	94.9	90.6	88.4	79.5	100.0	97.8	94.4	87.6	87.3
United Kingdom	112	177.0	174.3	153.0	142.0	120.1	119.5	105.5	100.0	96.3	96.4	92.6	88.4
Developing Countries													
Africa													
CEMAC	758	....	....	....	....	....	....	....	....	....	....	....	....
Cameroon	622	87.1	83.3	102.4	126.2	115.9	113.8	108.3	100.0	93.8	86.3	....	....
Central African Republic	626	93.1	68.1	76.9	67.9	78.2	101.9	96.7	100.0	106.7	112.3	117.7	102.6
Chad	628	105.7	127.8	94.2	84.3	97.4	116.2	112.2	100.0	101.6	91.3	103.8	....
Congo, Rep. of	634	89.2	89.9	96.7	102.9	98.0	95.3	100.2	100.0	115.8	105.1	106.1	98.0
Equatorial Guinea	642	83.9	47.4	39.7	46.9	94.2	69.1	70.2	100.0	111.4	85.1	61.7	73.7
Gabon	646	95.6	105.8	102.2	102.6	98.4	85.3	95.4	100.0	87.3	....	....	....
WAEMU	759	....	....	95.9	98.1	101.9	107.5	106.0	100.0	96.2	87.4	....	....
Benin	638	99.9	94.1	115.7	115.3	129.1	146.5	115.0	100.0	97.2	111.7	106.6	123.0
Burkina Faso	748	108.2	107.3	98.9	104.4	95.3	108.5	106.3	100.0	111.2	120.3	81.7	96.1
Côte d'Ivoire	662	77.8	76.5	76.0	81.3	92.6	96.3	100.5	100.0	93.1	74.2	100.8	95.4
Guinea Bissau	654	513.0	662.4	457.0	337.5	184.6	155.2	144.9	100.0	88.7	70.2	194.4	145.3
Mali	678	89.5	88.4	114.3	96.7	98.3	103.2	107.3	100.0	97.7	79.2	67.8	71.3
Niger	692	47.4	54.0	62.6	73.1	97.4	135.1	118.8	100.0	83.8	92.2	64.0	61.0
Senegal	722	114.6	101.3	112.4	106.3	109.5	109.3	102.9	100.0	95.5	90.7	74.0	71.2
Togo	742	81.0	86.9	100.1	117.0	130.3	123.6	118.2	100.0	103.7	111.7	104.6	90.9
Algeria	612	74.3	82.2	101.5	113.8	103.8	88.9	89.4	100.0	82.9	63.7	63.1	....
Angola	614	....	....	46.4	67.2	81.9	75.8	76.6	100.0	82.5	70.2	....	....
Botswana	616	126.3	240.2	238.6	228.5	224.0	194.7	168.5	100.0	153.5	98.6	164.2	92.0
Burundi	618	110.3	94.5	98.4	83.3	99.2	120.3	93.0	100.0	93.0	76.3	72.7	....
Congo, Dem. Rep. of	636	—	1,380.2	1,725.2	1,897.7	769.8	148.4	115.9	100.0	2,435.9	2,375.9	2,132.9	1,412.1
Ethiopia	644	114.3	98.6	108.1	111.0	110.5	110.7	105.7	100.0	92.8	....	....	....
Kenya	664	94.9	92.5	83.3	75.5	74.0	80.1	80.6	100.0	103.1	93.5	91.8	90.1
Lesotho	666	81.2	81.6	84.7	86.7	87.9	79.3	94.6	100.0	94.6	102.2	107.0	....
Madagascar	674	90.5	84.0	106.7	110.8	102.0	108.3	104.4	100.0	91.8	85.6	88.8	85.3
Malawi	676	82.3	70.4	91.8	107.3	131.8	99.2	109.8	100.0	96.5	94.2	85.6	....
Mauritius	684	112.6	111.5	103.1	107.8	103.1	104.8	98.2	100.0	99.7	95.8	94.9	93.2
Morocco	686	121.5	123.3	116.4	123.5	113.9	116.1	105.8	100.0	94.8	92.5	89.6	....
Mozambique	688	96.7	106.9	112.3	149.2	146.6	146.5	123.0	100.0	102.3	106.4	109.9	....
Namibia	728	128.1	126.3	111.9	102.5	107.2	108.0	100.5	100.0	109.8	....	....	....
Nigeria	694	73.5	71.3	129.1	158.6	142.3	114.0	98.7	100.0	76.9	72.9	75.3	78.6
Rwanda	714	117.5	71.8	85.9	100.2	102.6	110.4	103.3	100.0	97.2	94.4	92.7	....
Seychelles	718	178.9	152.3	131.0	118.5	115.3	112.7	98.5	100.0	91.5	87.2	....	....
Sierra Leone	724	139.9	157.7	162.1	164.8	107.8	122.1	101.7	100.0	90.0	85.3	82.7	85.8
South Africa	199	115.4	110.4	108.1	106.7	100.5	95.7	94.6	100.0	94.8	88.9	84.2	81.4
Swaziland	734	67.9	74.2	86.9	85.9	83.6	83.5	81.5	100.0	102.8	103.0	107.2	....
Tanzania	738	78.8	77.6	76.6	88.2	97.6	104.3	101.6	100.0	97.2	87.9	86.1	96.3
Tunisia	744	119.7	119.5	120.9	119.2	112.2	114.9	105.7	100.0	97.5	97.1	98.3	....
Uganda	746	149.5	143.7	146.0	133.8	125.0	111.9	109.7	100.0	98.6	84.0	83.3	....
Zimbabwe	698	111.1	108.7	95.5	100.7	88.7	108.0	120.0	100.0	....	....	....	....
Asia													
Bangladesh	513	131.9	119.4	119.9	118.1	116.9	116.3	110.5	100.0	93.3	88.7	86.2	....
Bhutan	514	169.6	164.2	141.8	152.8	116.5	116.7	103.4	100.0	....	....	....	....
Cambodia	522	264.2	204.2	168.8	130.8	123.4	124.7	120.6	100.0	87.4	71.8	65.5	....
China, P.R.: Mainland	924	147.1	151.4	146.6	136.7	124.1	113.9	103.9	100.0	95.9	87.9	82.7	81.0
China, P.R.: Hong Kong	532	141.0	142.3	136.9	134.5	137.3	117.6	105.7	100.0	98.8	96.6	88.0	86.1
Fiji	819	79.0	81.6	81.8	85.8	97.2	104.8	102.9	100.0	113.0	....	....	....
India	534	122.3	119.9	126.6	122.8	116.2	112.4	106.8	100.0	95.1	88.3	87.5	84.5
Indonesia	536	123.3	118.9	110.9	102.3	96.2	90.0	92.3	100.0	107.4	113.7	115.9	120.1
Korea	542	184.9	182.3	184.9	179.6	172.2	133.7	114.8	100.0	95.0	94.1	93.4	101.0
Lao People's Democratic Rep.	544	124.7	110.1	122.1	116.3	89.5	80.8	110.4	100.0	101.0	86.0	79.1	78.8
Malaysia	548	129.7	130.5	122.9	111.7	104.9	107.1	97.8	100.0	95.1	99.2	98.6	93.9
Maldives	556	141.6	133.2	131.2	117.5	107.8	93.3	98.2	100.0	95.5	85.8	80.8	66.4
Nepal	558	143.5	141.2	134.4	136.1	118.7	114.5	107.1	100.0	....	....	....	77.8
Pakistan	564	85.2	85.1	89.3	84.5	80.8	82.6	86.9	100.0	98.2	88.9	82.8	77.8

Income Velocity of Money plus Quasi-Money

		1993	1994	1995	1996	1997	1998	1999	2000	2001	2002	2003	2004
							Index Numbers: 2000=100						
Asia(Cont.)													
Philippines	566	144.2	130.6	118.7	109.4	99.2	100.4	95.9	100.0	104.5	101.2	105.9	108.5
Singapore	576	122.9	122.9	124.9	124.3	122.9	91.5	85.9	100.0	91.0	94.1	88.4	93.4
Solomon Islands	813	97.1	90.6	97.9	98.3	97.3	107.9	107.5	100.0	118.8	117.3	....	....
Sri Lanka	524	120.3	116.5	98.9	102.3	102.6	103.6	99.3	100.0	98.5	97.7	94.3	90.8
Thailand	578	133.1	135.2	133.3	130.5	115.0	102.4	97.4	100.0	101.9	106.5	108.9	114.8
Vietnam	582	221.6	222.7	225.5	213.2	197.7	184.3	122.6	100.0	85.6	84.1	72.4	64.2
Europe													
Albania	914	....	161.0	132.2	125.9	100.3	106.4	100.1	100.0	92.5	93.5	....	....
Armenia	911	4,302.5	112.3	190.8	178.8	168.4	146.3	132.7	100.0	109.3	94.6	102.2	97.5
Belarus	913	....	45.3	119.6	124.0	112.2	57.1	105.8	100.0	115.9	117.3	104.7	97.2
Bosnia & Herzegovina	963	....	....	....	....	109.7	102.3	99.5	100.0	57.4	55.8	53.2	....
Bulgaria	918	46.7	46.2	55.1	49.3	108.0	124.3	116.3	100.0	88.2	85.4	75.9	67.4
Croatia	960	198.8	238.1	190.8	140.3	116.2	114.3	119.8	100.0	74.5	73.6	71.6	71.0
Cyprus	423	127.6	126.5	128.6	120.6	114.3	113.5	100.7	100.0	94.8	90.8	93.3	93.6
Czech Republic	935	98.4	94.7	90.8	96.6	102.2	108.7	110.1	100.0	96.9	103.2	101.7	104.8
Estonia	939	124.8	131.5	141.6	134.3	119.6	130.6	110.6	100.0	91.4	92.0	90.4	86.7
Hungary	944	81.9	88.3	93.9	94.3	97.6	99.7	97.4	100.0	97.1	95.9	93.8	95.1
Kazakhstan	916	45.7	108.6	120.7	128.9	141.2	169.3	116.6	100.0	100.4	90.4	84.6	62.1
Kyrgyz Republic	917	....	....	65.8	83.1	82.4	78.1	83.3	100.0	101.6	77.4	64.6	54.8
Latvia	941	88.9	82.4	132.3	131.9	111.6	114.6	114.5	100.0	92.1	84.5	76.9	70.7
Lithuania	946	99.6	89.1	104.5	136.7	124.4	122.4	111.0	100.0	87.5	79.9	73.6	65.3
Macedonia, FYR	962	26.5	153.2	158.7	166.8	142.4	132.1	107.3	100.0	74.9	67.5	60.6	....
Malta	181	104.9	100.0	99.6	96.2	95.5	93.4	90.9	100.0	93.6	87.3	....	....
Moldova	921	116.3	140.2	116.0	121.6	103.4	115.3	109.0	100.0	87.4	....	....	....
Poland	964	113.3	118.5	128.5	123.4	116.3	108.6	100.7	100.0	91.3	96.5	95.2	96.6
Romania	968	103.1	107.6	91.7	82.7	93.7	93.0	93.7	100.0	99.4	93.3	95.1	85.3
Russia	922	89.9	101.1	111.2	120.7	109.3	89.1	104.3	100.0	89.8	81.3	71.8	67.9
Slovak Republic	936	104.2	106.9	105.0	100.1	103.1	107.6	104.1	100.0	96.6	101.1	100.5	103.9
Slovenia	961	156.5	139.6	137.8	128.4	118.7	110.7	107.6	100.0	85.8	85.3	86.9	87.0
Turkey	186	182.1	144.9	142.8	125.1	123.6	118.0	87.3	100.0	76.9	92.7	104.8	101.7
Ukraine	926	56.4	68.6	144.1	159.4	136.4	122.6	110.9	100.0	84.0	63.8	51.8	51.0
Middle East													
Bahrain	419	110.7	111.8	109.3	110.6	106.7	89.0	91.6	100.0	91.1	87.9	94.0	....
Egypt	469	90.6	90.7	96.2	97.6	98.8	99.6	100.9	100.0	93.2	87.4	79.4	80.6
Iran, I.R. of	429	87.7	85.8	94.0	94.8	90.3	84.3	92.1	100.0	90.7	100.1	96.2	....
Israel	436	131.6	128.2	122.9	115.1	113.1	104.5	98.7	100.0	92.7	89.6	91.2	92.4
Jordan	439	99.9	108.4	111.0	116.7	113.4	116.4	103.6	100.0	97.9	95.3	86.1	....
Kuwait	443	81.3	78.7	79.1	92.5	86.9	75.2	85.8	100.0	81.5	79.7	86.0	....
Libya	672	74.3	69.6	68.1	76.8	92.7	80.4	83.1	100.0	93.9	131.3	....	....
Oman	449	114.9	111.3	110.5	113.1	94.2	80.0	83.8	100.0	91.9	88.9	92.7	....
Qatar	453	68.6	64.8	70.8	74.6	84.7	71.2	77.2	100.0	99.9	99.3	88.9	....
Saudi Arabia	456	97.3	96.0	98.5	101.7	101.1	86.3	89.2	100.0	92.4	82.7	86.7	86.3
Syrian Arab Rep	463	99.7	108.7	112.3	123.4	123.0	118.0	107.8	100.0	85.4	75.5	....	....
Yemen, Republic of	474	59.4	58.2	64.2	84.4	91.0	78.1	95.4	100.0	88.4	83.9	81.0	....
Western Hemisphere													
ECCU	309	132.4	131.3	119.7	122.6	119.3	112.3	104.9	100.0	94.3	88.5	....	....
Anguilla	312	157.8	156.7	123.1	127.6	128.3	115.1	117.3	100.0	89.8	80.4	....	....
Antigua and Barbuda	311	146.3	148.1	120.4	136.8	137.0	126.3	104.6	100.0	....	....	....	....
Dominica	321	118.1	121.8	102.7	103.3	103.0	103.0	96.7	100.0	92.2	80.3	77.5	....
Grenada	328	130.1	122.0	117.0	115.2	111.6	111.1	106.3	100.0	....	....	....	....
Montserrat	351	219.3	191.8	182.6	162.0	118.0	98.4	93.2	100.0	101.2	108.7	....	....
St. Kitts and Nevis	361	114.8	126.7	118.9	124.0	122.6	114.5	117.5	100.0	102.8	97.1	88.7	....
St. Lucia	362	116.1	113.7	111.8	109.5	106.7	104.7	102.8	100.0	90.7	90.7	88.0	....
St. Vincent & Grens	364	131.7	126.0	133.4	132.2	122.9	116.2	104.0	100.0	95.8	95.3	95.0	....
Argentina	213	165.7	153.3	158.1	140.4	120.3	111.2	101.3	100.0	117.4	114.0	105.8	103.7
Aruba	314	....	....	98.5	98.6	105.2	100.7	94.6	100.0	96.0	87.5	....	....
Barbados	316	124.9	120.8	123.7	110.7	112.4	112.5	104.8	100.0	96.8	84.5	....	....
Belize	339	142.4	136.3	123.2	118.4	108.3	107.7	98.9	100.0	92.9	100.8	101.9	99.1
Bolivia	218	109.4	99.5	107.8	101.0	96.1	95.7	93.1	100.0	101.3	114.9	110.0	120.9
Brazil	223	38.9	69.8	96.0	103.0	96.4	92.2	91.9	100.0	96.8	87.5	97.7	92.9
Chile	228	109.7	120.9	116.0	106.6	107.9	103.0	97.1	100.0	104.9	112.0	113.4	118.5
Colombia	233	141.5	130.9	134.4	128.9	109.7	104.8	99.4	100.0	93.0	88.8	91.0	85.8
Costa Rica	238	118.2	117.2	142.1	112.5	117.1	112.7	108.7	100.0	99.5	92.4	91.1	....
Dominican Republic	243	123.4	124.3	124.5	118.9	112.1	108.3	100.8	100.0	88.9	88.6	67.9	96.2
Ecuador	248	105.9	93.9	95.7	89.6	91.3	96.2	153.8	100.0	100.1	116.6	109.8	98.4
El Salvador	253	125.2	104.8	110.1	105.0	102.5	101.5	96.8	100.0	101.3	108.3	110.6	115.3
Guatemala	258	136.4	141.5	139.4	137.3	131.1	126.2	122.4	100.0	93.2	92.1	86.5	85.6
Haiti	263	87.6	103.7	93.0	121.6	112.8	120.0	107.2	100.0	96.8	86.3	79.1	88.0
Honduras	268	173.1	169.0	170.0	153.3	130.8	122.3	107.3	100.0	94.3	90.6	87.2	....
Jamaica	343	112.8	107.4	102.9	110.2	106.0	105.7	100.4	100.0	101.1	99.0	103.1	....
Mexico	273	81.5	76.8	75.3	81.5	77.0	79.4	79.9	100.0	94.1	93.7	96.3	96.3
Nicaragua	278	177.7	199.3	177.2	146.9	109.9	98.3	96.8	100.0	78.3	71.9	69.7	68.9
Panama	283	140.2	129.4	122.6	124.4	117.0	112.3	108.5	100.0	92.7	96.6	96.7	....
Paraguay	288	106.6	107.6	110.0	107.9	105.9	107.9	94.0	100.0	89.7	99.0	111.6	....
Peru	293	159.1	165.0	156.5	129.2	113.5	102.0	93.4	100.0	99.5	99.8	108.6	116.7
Trinidad and Tobago	369	90.8	93.2	96.9	99.9	93.1	86.3	93.2	100.0	100.1	102.5	117.5	....
Uruguay	298	121.7	127.7	127.7	124.8	121.9	116.8	104.6	100.0	85.5	70.4	75.7	92.6
Venezuela, Rep. Bol.	299	74.3	69.9	80.8	102.1	90.3	93.3	91.7	100.0	96.9	101.5	80.1	83.8

2005, International Monetary Fund : *International Financial Statistics Yearbook*

National Interest Rates

		1993	1994	1995	1996	1997	1998	1999	2000	2001	2002	2003	2004
							Central Bank Discount Rates (60) *(End of period in percent per annum)*						
Industrial Countries													
United States	111	3.00	4.75	5.25	5.00	5.00	4.50	5.00	6.00	1.25	.75	† 2.00	3.15
Canada	156	4.11	7.43	5.79	3.25	4.50	5.25	5.00	6.00	2.50	3.00	3.00	2.75
Australia	193	5.83	5.75	5.75	....	....	....	....	....	....	....	....	....
Japan	158	1.75	1.75	.50	.50	.50	.50	.50	.50	.10	.10	.10	.10
New Zealand	196	5.70	9.75	9.80	8.80	9.70	5.60	5.00	6.50	4.75	5.75	5.00	6.50
Euro Area	163	....	....	....	....	....	....	4.00	5.75	4.25	3.75	3.00	3.00
Austria	122	5.25	4.50	3.00	2.50	2.50	2.50	....	....	....	....	....	....
Belgium	124	5.25	4.50	3.00	2.50	2.75	2.75	....	....	....	....	....	....
Finland	172	5.50	5.25	4.88	4.00	4.00	3.50	....	....	....	....	....	....
Germany	134	5.75	4.50	3.00	2.50	2.50	2.50	....	....	....	....	....	....
Greece	174	21.50	20.50	18.00	16.50	14.50	....	† 11.81	8.10	....	....	....	....
Ireland	178	7.00	6.25	6.50	6.25	6.75	4.06	....	....	....	....	....	....
Italy	136	8.00	7.50	9.00	7.50	5.50	3.00	....	....	....	....	....	....
Netherlands	138	5.00	....	....	....	....	....	....	....	....	....	....	....
Portugal	182	11.00	8.88	8.50	6.70	5.31	3.00	....	....	....	....	....	....
Spain	184	9.00	7.38	9.00	6.25	4.75	3.00	....	....	....	....	....	....
Denmark	128	6.25	5.00	4.25	3.25	3.50	3.50	3.00	4.75	3.25	2.86	2.00	2.00
Iceland	176	....	4.70	5.93	5.70	6.55	† 8.50	10.00	12.40	12.00	8.20	7.70	10.25
Norway	142	7.00	6.75	6.75	6.00	5.50	10.00	7.50	9.00	8.50	8.50	4.25	3.75
Sweden	144	5.00	7.00	7.00	3.50	2.50	2.00	1.50	2.00	2.00	† 4.50	3.00	2.00
Switzerland	146	4.00	3.50	1.50	1.00	1.00	1.00	.50	† 3.20	1.59	.50	.11	.54
Developing Countries													
Africa													
CEMAC	758	11.50	† 7.75	8.60	7.75	7.50	7.00	7.30	7.00	6.50	6.30	6.00	6.00
Cameroon	622	11.50	† 7.75	8.60	7.75	7.50	7.00	7.30	7.00	6.50	6.30	6.00	6.00
Central African Rep.	626	11.50	† 7.75	8.60	7.75	7.50	7.00	7.60	7.00	6.50	6.30	6.00	6.00
Chad	628	11.50	† 7.75	8.60	7.75	7.50	7.00	7.60	7.00	6.50	6.30	6.00	6.00
Congo, Republic of	634	11.50	† 7.75	8.60	7.75	7.50	7.00	7.60	7.00	6.50	6.30	6.00	6.00
Equatorial Guinea	642	11.50	† 7.75	8.60	7.75	7.50	7.00	7.60	7.00	6.50	6.30	6.00	6.00
Gabon	646	11.50	† 7.75	8.60	7.75	7.50	7.00	7.60	7.00	6.50	6.30	6.00	6.00
WAEMU	759	....	....	6.00	6.00	6.00	6.00	6.00	6.00	6.00	6.00	4.50	4.00
Benin	638	† 6.00	6.00	6.00	6.00	6.00	6.00	6.00	6.00	6.00	6.00	4.50	4.00
Burkina Faso	748	† 6.00	6.00	6.00	6.00	6.00	6.00	6.00	6.00	6.00	6.00	4.50	4.00
Côte d'Ivoire	662	† 6.00	6.00	6.00	6.00	6.00	6.00	6.00	6.00	6.00	6.00	4.50	4.00
Guinea-Bissau	654	† 6.00	6.00	6.00	6.00	6.00	6.00	6.00	6.00	6.00	6.00	4.50	4.00
Mali	678	† 6.00	6.00	6.00	6.00	6.00	6.00	6.00	6.00	6.00	6.00	4.50	4.00
Niger	692	† 6.00	6.00	6.00	6.00	6.00	6.00	6.00	6.00	6.00	6.00	4.50	4.00
Senegal	722	† 6.00	6.00	6.00	6.00	6.00	6.00	6.00	6.00	6.00	6.00	4.50	4.00
Togo	742	† 6.00	6.00	6.00	6.00	6.00	6.00	6.00	6.00	6.00	6.00	4.50	4.00
Algeria	612	11.50	21.00	† 14.00	13.00	11.00	9.50	8.50	6.00	6.00	5.50	4.50	4.00
Angola	614	....	....	160.00	2.00	48.00	58.00	120.00	150.00	150.00	150.00	150.00	95.00
Botswana	616	14.25	13.50	13.00	13.00	12.00	12.75	13.75	14.25	14.25	15.25	14.25	14.25
Burundi	618	10.00	10.00	10.00	10.00	12.00	12.00	12.00	14.00	14.00	15.50	14.50	14.50
Comoros	632	....	....	....	....	....	....	† 6.36	5.63	5.89	4.79	3.82	3.55
Congo, Dem. Rep. of	636	95.00	145.00	125.00	238.00	13.00	22.00	120.00	120.00	140.00	24.00	8.00	....
Ethiopia	644	12.00	12.00	12.00	....	....	....	....	....	....	....	....	....
Gambia, The	648	13.50	13.50	14.00	14.00	14.00	12.00	10.50	10.00	13.00	18.00	29.00	28.00
Ghana	652	35.00	33.00	45.00	45.00	45.00	37.00	27.00	27.00	27.00	24.50	21.50	18.50
Guinea	656	17.00	17.00	18.00	18.00	15.00	....	....	11.50	16.25	16.25	16.25	16.25
Kenya	664	45.50	21.50	24.50	26.88	32.27	17.07	26.46	....	....	....	....	....
Lesotho	666	13.50	13.50	15.50	17.00	15.60	19.50	19.00	15.00	13.00	16.19	15.00	13.00
Madagascar	674	....	....	....	....	....	....	15.00	....	....	....	....	....
Malawi	676	25.00	40.00	50.00	27.00	23.00	43.00	47.00	50.23	46.80	40.00	35.00	25.00
Mauritius	684	8.30	13.80	11.40	11.82	10.46	17.19	....	....	....	....	....	....
Morocco	686	....	7.17	....	....	....	6.04	5.42	5.00	4.71	3.79	3.25	3.25
Mozambique	688	....	69.70	57.75	32.00	12.95	9.95	9.95	9.95	9.95	9.95	9.95	9.95
Namibia	728	14.50	15.50	17.50	17.75	16.00	18.75	11.50	11.25	9.25	12.75	7.75	7.50
Nigeria	694	26.00	13.50	13.50	13.50	13.50	13.50	18.00	14.00	20.50	16.50	15.00	15.00
Rwanda	714	11.00	11.00	16.00	16.00	10.75	11.38	11.19	11.69	13.00	13.00	14.50	14.50
São Tomé & Príncipe	716	30.00	32.00	50.00	35.00	55.00	29.50	17.00	17.00	15.50	15.50	14.50	14.50
Seychelles	718	13.08	12.50	12.83	11.00	11.00	5.50	5.50	5.50	5.50	5.50	4.67	3.51
South Africa	199	12.00	13.00	15.00	17.00	16.00	† 19.32	12.00	12.00	9.50	13.50	8.00	7.50
Swaziland	734	11.00	12.00	15.00	16.75	15.75	18.00	12.00	11.00	9.50	13.50	8.00	7.50
Tanzania	738	14.50	67.50	47.90	19.00	16.20	17.60	20.20	10.70	8.70	9.18	12.34	14.42
Tunisia	744	8.88	8.88	8.88	7.88	....	....	....	....	....	....	....	....
Uganda	746	24.00	15.00	13.30	15.85	14.08	9.10	15.75	18.86	8.88	13.08	25.62	16.15
Zambia	754	72.50	20.50	40.20	47.00	17.70	....	32.93	25.67	40.10	27.87	14.35	16.68
Zimbabwe	698	28.50	29.50	29.50	27.00	31.50	† 39.50	74.41	57.84	57.20	29.65	300.00	110.00
Asia													
Bangladesh	513	6.00	5.50	6.00	7.00	8.00	8.00	7.00	7.00	6.00	6.00	5.00	5.00
China,P.R.: Mainland	924	10.08	10.08	10.44	9.00	8.55	4.59	3.24	3.24	3.24	2.70	2.70	3.33
China,P.R.:Hong Kong	532	4.00	5.75	6.25	6.00	7.00	6.25	7.00	8.00	3.25	2.75	2.50	3.75
Fiji	819	6.00	6.00	6.00	6.00	1.88	2.50	2.50	8.00	1.75	1.75	1.75	2.25
India	534	12.00	12.00	12.00	12.00	9.00	9.00	8.00	8.00	6.50	6.25	6.00	6.00
Indonesia	536	8.82	12.44	13.99	12.80	20.00	38.44	12.51	14.53	17.62	12.93	8.31	7.43
Korea	542	5.00	5.00	5.00	5.00	5.00	3.00	3.00	3.00	2.50	2.50	2.50	2.00
Lao People's Dem.Rep.	544	25.00	30.00	32.08	35.00	....	35.00	34.89	35.17	35.00	20.00	20.00	20.00
Malaysia	548	5.24	4.51	6.47	7.28	....	....	....	....	....	....	....	....
Mongolia	948	628.80	180.00	150.00	109.00	45.50	23.30	11.40	8.65	8.60	9.90	11.50	15.75
Myanmar	518	11.00	11.00	12.50	15.00	15.00	15.00	12.00	10.00	10.00	10.00	10.00	10.00

National Interest Rates

		1993	1994	1995	1996	1997	1998	1999	2000	2001	2002	2003	2004
							Central Bank Discount Rates (60) *(End of period in percent per annum)*						
Asia(Cont.)													
Nepal	558	11.00	11.00	11.00	11.00	9.00	9.00	9.00	7.50	6.50	5.50	5.50	5.50
Pakistan	564	10.00	†15.00	17.00	20.00	18.00	16.50	13.00	13.00	10.00	7.50	7.50	7.50
Papua New Guinea	853	†6.30	6.55	†18.00	14.86	9.49	17.07	16.66	9.79	11.73	11.71	†15.50	12.67
Philippines	566	9.40	8.30	10.83	11.70	14.64	12.40	7.89	13.81	8.30	4.19	5.53	8.36
Sri Lanka	524	17.00	17.00	17.00	17.00	17.00	17.00	16.00	25.00	....	18.00	15.00	15.00
Thailand	578	9.00	9.50	10.50	10.50	12.50	12.50	4.00	4.00	3.75	3.25	2.75	3.50
Vanuatu	846	....	....	....	....	....	7.00	7.00	7.00	6.50	6.50	6.50	6.50
Vietnam	582	....	....	....	18.90	10.80	12.00	6.00	6.00	4.80	4.80	5.00	5.00
Europe													
Albania	914	34.00	25.00	20.50	24.00	32.00	23.44	18.00	10.82	7.00	8.50	6.50	5.25
Armenia	911	210.00	210.00	77.80	26.00	65.10	....	....	....	....	....	....	....
Azerbaijan, Republic of	912	100.00	200.00	80.00	20.00	12.00	14.00	10.00	10.00	10.00	7.00	7.00	7.00
Belarus	913	210.00	480.00	66.00	8.30	8.90	9.60	23.40	†80.00	48.00	38.00	28.00	17.00
Bulgaria	918	52.00	72.00	34.00	180.00	†6.65	5.08	4.46	4.63	4.65	3.31	2.83	2.37
Croatia	960	34.49	8.50	8.50	6.50	5.90	5.90	7.90	5.90	5.90	4.50	4.50	4.50
Cyprus	423	6.50	6.50	6.50	†7.50	7.00	7.00	7.00	7.00	5.50	5.00	4.50	5.50
Czech Republic	935	8.00	8.50	11.30	12.40	14.75	9.50	5.25	5.25	4.50	2.75	2.00	2.50
Hungary	944	22.00	25.00	28.00	23.00	20.50	17.00	14.50	11.00	9.75	8.50	12.50	9.50
Kazakhstan	916	170.00	230.00	†52.50	35.00	18.50	25.00	18.00	14.00	9.00	7.50	7.00	7.00
Latvia	941	27.00	25.00	24.00	9.50	4.00	4.00	4.00	3.50	3.50	3.00	3.00	4.00
Macedonia, FYR	962	295.00	33.00	15.00	9.20	8.90	8.90	8.90	7.90	10.70	10.70	6.50	6.50
Malta	181	5.50	5.50	5.50	5.50	5.50	5.50	4.75	4.75	4.25	3.75	....	....
Poland	964	29.00	28.00	25.00	22.00	24.50	18.25	19.00	21.50	14.00	7.75	5.75	7.00
Russia	922	....	....	160.00	48.00	28.00	60.00	55.00	25.00	25.00	21.00	16.00	13.00
Slovak Republic	936	12.00	12.00	9.75	8.80	8.80	8.80	8.80	8.80	†7.75	6.50	6.00	4.00
Slovenia	961	19.00	17.00	11.00	11.00	11.00	11.00	9.00	11.00	12.00	10.50	7.25	5.00
Tajikistan	923	....	....	....	....	76.00	36.40	20.10	20.60	20.00	†24.75	†15.00	10.00
Turkey	186	48.00	55.00	50.00	50.00	67.00	67.00	60.00	60.00	60.00	55.00	43.00	38.00
Ukraine	926	240.00	252.00	110.00	40.00	35.00	60.00	45.00	27.00	12.50	7.00	7.00	9.00
Middle East													
Egypt	469	16.50	14.00	13.50	13.00	12.25	12.00	12.00	12.00	11.00	10.00	10.00	10.00
Israel	436	9.78	17.01	14.19	15.30	13.72	13.47	11.20	8.21	5.67	9.18	5.20	3.90
Jordan	439	8.50	8.50	8.50	8.50	7.75	9.00	8.00	6.50	5.00	4.50	2.50	3.75
Kuwait	443	5.75	7.00	7.25	7.25	7.50	7.00	6.75	7.25	4.25	3.25	3.25	4.75
Lebanon	446	20.22	16.49	19.01	25.00	30.00	30.00	25.00	20.00	20.00	20.00	20.00	20.00
Libya	672	5.00	....	....	....	....	3.00	5.00	5.00	5.00	5.00	5.00	4.00
Syrian Arab Republic	463	5.00	5.00	5.00	5.00	5.00	5.00	5.00	5.00	5.00	5.00	....	....
Western Hemisphere													
ECCU	309	....	9.00	9.00	9.00	8.00	8.00	8.00	8.00	7.00	7.00	6.50	6.50
Anguilla	312	....	9.00	9.00	9.00	8.00	8.00	8.00	8.00	7.00	7.00	6.50	6.50
Antigua and Barbuda	311	....	9.00	9.00	9.00	8.00	8.00	8.00	8.00	7.00	7.00	6.50	6.50
Dominica	321	....	9.00	9.00	9.00	8.00	8.00	8.00	8.00	7.00	7.00	6.50	6.50
Grenada	328	....	9.00	9.00	9.00	8.00	8.00	8.00	8.00	7.00	7.00	6.50	6.50
Montserrat	351	....	9.00	9.00	9.00	8.00	8.00	8.00	8.00	7.00	7.00	6.50	6.50
St. Kitts and Nevis	361	....	9.00	9.00	9.00	8.00	8.00	8.00	8.00	7.00	7.00	6.50	6.50
St. Lucia	362	....	9.00	9.00	9.00	8.00	8.00	8.00	8.00	7.00	7.00	6.50	6.50
St. Vincent & Grens	364	....	9.00	9.00	9.00	8.00	8.00	8.00	8.00	7.00	7.00	6.50	6.50
Aruba	314	9.50	9.50	9.50	9.50	9.50	9.50	6.50	6.50	6.50	6.50	5.00	5.00
Bahamas, The	313	7.00	6.50	6.50	6.50	6.50	6.50	5.75	5.75	5.75	5.75	5.75	5.75
Barbados	316	8.00	9.50	12.50	12.50	9.00	9.00	10.00	10.00	7.50	7.50	7.50	7.50
Belize	339	12.00	12.00	12.00	12.00	12.00	12.00	12.00	12.00	12.00	12.00	12.00	12.00
Bolivia	218	....	....	....	16.50	13.25	14.10	12.50	10.00	8.50	12.50	7.50	6.00
Brazil	223	....	....	....	25.34	45.09	39.41	21.37	†18.52	21.43	30.42	23.92	24.55
Chile	228	7.96	13.89	7.96	11.75	7.96	9.12	7.44	8.73	6.50	3.00	2.45	2.25
Colombia	233	33.49	44.90	40.42	35.05	31.32	42.28	23.05	18.28	16.40	12.73	12.95	12.76
Costa Rica	238	35.00	37.75	38.50	35.00	31.00	37.00	34.00	31.50	28.75	31.25	26.00	26.00
Ecuador	248	33.57	44.88	59.41	46.38	37.46	61.84	64.40	†13.16	16.44	14.55	11.19	9.86
Guyana	336	17.00	20.25	17.25	12.00	11.00	11.25	13.25	11.75	8.75	6.25	5.50	6.00
Netherlands Antilles	353	5.00	5.00	6.00	6.00	6.00	6.00	6.00	6.00	6.00	6.00	....	....
Nicaragua	278	11.75	10.50	....	....	....	....	....	....	....	....	....	....
Paraguay	288	27.17	19.15	20.50	15.00	20.00	20.00	20.00	20.00	20.00	20.00	20.00	20.00
Peru	293	28.63	16.08	18.44	18.16	15.94	18.72	17.80	14.00	14.00	4.75	4.25	4.25
Trinidad and Tobago	369	13.00	13.00	13.00	13.00	13.00	13.00	13.00	13.00	13.00	7.25	7.00	7.00
Uruguay	298	164.30	182.30	178.70	160.30	95.50	73.70	66.39	57.26	71.66	316.01	....	....
Venezuela, Rep. Bol.	299	71.25	48.00	49.00	45.00	45.00	60.00	38.00	38.00	37.00	40.00	28.50	28.50

National Interest Rates

		1993	1994	1995	1996	1997	1998	1999	2000	2001	2002	2003	2004
						Money Market Rates (60b) *(Period averages in percent per annum)*							
Industrial Countries													
United States	111	3.02	4.20	5.84	5.30	5.46	5.35	4.97	6.24	3.89	1.67	1.13	1.35
Canada	156	4.62	5.05	6.92	4.32	3.26	4.87	4.74	5.52	4.11	2.45	2.93	2.25
Australia	193	5.11	5.18	† 7.50	7.20	5.50	4.99	† 4.78	5.90	5.06	4.55	4.81	5.25
Japan	158	† 3.06	2.20	1.21	.47	.48	.37	.06	.11	.06	.01	—	—
New Zealand	196	6.25	6.13	8.91	9.38	7.38	6.86	4.33	6.12	5.76	5.40	5.33	5.77
Euro Area	163	....	6.53	6.82	5.09	4.38	3.96	2.97	4.39	4.26	3.32	2.34	2.11
Austria	122	7.22	5.03	4.36	3.19	3.27	3.36	....	....	....	....	....	....
Belgium	124	8.21	5.72	4.80	3.24	3.46	3.58	....	....	....	....	....	....
Finland	172	7.77	5.35	5.75	3.63	3.23	3.57	2.96	4.39	4.26	3.32	2.33	2.11
France	132	8.75	5.69	6.35	3.73	3.24	3.39	....	....	....	....	....	....
Germany	134	7.49	5.35	4.50	3.27	3.18	3.41	2.73	4.11	4.37	3.28	2.32	2.05
Greece	174	....	24.60	16.40	13.80	12.80	13.99	....	....	....	....	....	....
Ireland	178	10.49	† 5.75	5.45	5.74	6.43	3.23	3.14	4.84	3.31	2.88	2.08	2.13
Italy	136	10.20	8.51	10.46	8.82	6.88	4.99	2.95	4.39	4.26	3.32	2.33	2.10
Luxembourg	137	8.09	5.16	4.26	3.29	3.36	3.48	....	....	....	....	....	....
Netherlands	138	7.10	5.14	4.22	2.89	3.07	3.21	....	....	....	....	....	....
Portugal	182	13.25	10.62	8.91	7.38	5.78	4.34	2.71	....	....	....	....	....
Spain	184	12.33	7.81	8.98	7.65	5.49	4.34	2.72	4.11	4.36	3.28	2.31	2.04
Denmark	128	† 11.49	6.30	6.19	3.98	3.71	4.27	3.37	4.98	....	3.56	2.38	2.16
Iceland	176	8.61	4.96	6.58	6.96	7.38	8.12	9.24	11.61	14.51	11.21	5.14	6.09
Norway	142	7.64	5.70	5.54	4.97	3.77	6.03	6.87	6.72	7.38	7.05	4.45	2.17
Sweden	144	9.08	7.36	8.54	6.28	4.21	4.24	3.14	3.81	4.09	4.19	3.29	....
Switzerland	146	4.94	3.85	2.89	1.78	1.35	1.22	.93	† 3.50	1.65	.44	.09	.55
United Kingdom	112	5.91	4.88	6.08	5.96	6.61	7.21	5.20	5.77	5.08	3.89	3.59	4.29
Developing Countries													
Africa													
WAEMU	759	....	....	4.95	4.95	4.95	4.95	4.95	4.95	4.95	4.95	4.95	4.95
Benin	638	4.95	4.95	4.95	4.95	4.95	4.95	4.95	4.95	4.95	4.95	4.95	4.95
Burkina Faso	748	4.95	4.95	4.95	4.95	4.95	4.95	4.95	4.95	4.95	4.95	4.95	4.95
Côte d'Ivoire	662	4.95	4.95	4.95	4.95	4.95	4.95	4.95	4.95	4.95	4.95	4.95	4.95
Guinea-Bissau	654	4.95	4.95	4.95	4.95	4.95	4.95	4.95	4.95	4.95	4.95	4.95	4.95
Mali	678	4.95	4.95	4.95	4.95	4.95	4.95	4.95	4.95	4.95	4.95	4.95	4.95
Niger	692	4.95	4.95	4.95	4.95	4.95	4.95	4.95	4.95	4.95	4.95	4.95	4.95
Senegal	722	4.95	4.95	4.95	4.95	4.95	4.95	4.95	4.95	4.95	4.95	4.95	4.95
Togo	742	4.95	4.95	4.95	4.95	4.95	4.95	4.95	4.95	4.95	4.95	4.95	4.95
Algeria	612	....	19.80	† 19.75	18.09	13.00	10.00	9.99	6.45	2.84	3.13	1.91	1.09
Ghana	652	....	....	....	....	....	....	....	....	....	....	24.71	15.73
Madagascar	674	....	....	29.00	10.00	....	11.24	....	16.00	....	....	10.50	16.50
Mauritius	684	7.73	10.23	10.35	9.96	9.43	8.99	10.01	7.66	7.25	6.20	3.22	1.33
Morocco	686	....	12.29	10.06	8.42	7.89	6.30	5.64	5.41	4.44	2.99	3.22	2.39
Mozambique	688	....	....	....	....	....	....	9.92	16.12	† 25.00	20.40	13.34	9.87
Namibia	728	10.83	10.25	13.08	15.00	15.41	17.14	13.17	9.19	9.53	10.46	10.03	6.93
South Africa	199	10.83	10.24	13.07	15.54	15.59	17.11	13.06	9.54	† 8.49	11.11	10.93	7.15
Swaziland	734	9.73	7.01	8.52	9.77	10.35	10.63	8.86	5.54	5.06	7.31	6.98	4.12
Tunisia	744	10.48	8.81	8.81	8.64	6.88	6.89	5.99	5.88	6.04	5.93	5.14	5.00
Zimbabwe	698	34.18	30.90	29.64	26.18	25.15	37.22	53.13	64.98	21.52	32.35	110.05	130.42
Asia													
China,P.R.:Hong Kong	532	4.00	5.44	6.00	5.13	4.50	5.50	5.75	7.13	2.69	1.50	.07	.13
China,P.R.:Macao	546	3.79	5.91	6.01	5.60	7.54	5.41	5.70	6.29	2.11	1.48	.11	.27
Fiji	819	2.91	4.10	3.95	2.43	1.91	1.27	1.27	2.58	.79	.92	.86	.90
India	534	8.64	7.14	15.57	11.04	5.29	....	....	....	....	....	....	....
Indonesia	536	8.66	9.74	13.64	13.96	27.82	62.79	23.58	10.32	15.03	13.54	7.76	5.38
Korea	542	12.12	12.45	12.57	12.44	13.24	14.98	5.01	5.16	4.69	4.21	4.00	3.65
Malaysia	548	7.10	4.20	5.60	6.92	7.61	8.46	3.38	2.66	2.79	2.73	2.74	2.70
Maldives	556	5.00	5.00	6.80	6.80	6.80	6.80	6.80	6.80	....	....	....	....
Pakistan	564	11.00	8.36	11.52	11.40	12.10	10.76	9.04	8.57	8.49	5.53	2.14	2.70
Philippines	566	13.77	13.99	11.93	12.77	16.16	13.90	10.16	10.84	9.75	7.15	6.97	7.05
Singapore	576	2.50	3.68	2.56	2.93	4.35	5.00	2.04	2.57	1.99	.96	.74	1.04
Sri Lanka	524	25.65	18.54	41.87	24.33	18.42	15.74	16.69	17.30	21.24	12.33	9.68	8.87
Thailand	578	6.54	7.25	10.96	9.23	14.59	13.02	1.77	1.95	2.00	1.76	1.31	1.23
Vanuatu	846	6.00	6.00	6.00	6.00	6.00	8.65	6.99	5.58	5.50	5.50	5.50	5.50
Europe													
Armenia	911	....	....	....	48.56	36.41	27.84	23.65	18.63	19.40	12.29	7.51	4.18
Bulgaria	918	48.07	66.43	53.09	119.88	66.43	2.48	2.93	3.02	3.74	2.47	1.95	1.95
Croatia	960	1,370.50	26.93	21.13	17.60	9.71	11.16	10.21	6.78	3.42	1.75	3.31	5.11
Cyprus	423	....	....	....	6.85	4.82	4.80	5.15	5.96	4.93	3.42	3.35	4.01
Czech Republic	935	8.00	12.65	10.93	12.67	17.50	10.08	5.58	5.42	4.69	2.63	2.08	2.56
Estonia	939	....	5.67	4.94	3.53	6.45	11.66	5.39	† 5.68	5.31	3.88	2.92	2.50
Georgia	915	....	....	....	43.39	26.58	43.26	34.61	18.17	† 17.52	27.69	16.88	11.87
Kyrgyz Republic	917	....	....	....	....	....	43.98	43.71	24.26	11.92	....	....	....
Latvia	941	....	37.18	22.39	13.08	3.76	4.42	4.72	2.97	5.23	3.01	2.86	3.25
Lithuania	946	....	69.48	26.73	20.26	9.55	† 6.12	6.26	3.60	3.37	2.21	1.79	1.53
Moldova	921	....	....	....	....	28.10	30.91	32.60	20.77	11.04	5.13	11.51	13.19
Poland	964	24.51	23.32	25.82	20.63	22.43	20.59	13.58	18.16	16.23	9.39	5.76	6.03
Russia	922	....	....	190.43	47.65	20.97	50.56	14.79	7.14	10.10	8.19	3.77	3.33
Slovak Republic	936	....	....	....	....	....	....	....	8.08	7.76	6.33	6.08	3.82
Slovenia	961	39.15	29.08	12.18	13.98	9.71	7.45	6.87	6.95	6.90	4.93	5.59	4.40
Turkey	186	62.83	136.47	72.30	76.24	70.32	74.60	73.53	56.72	91.95	49.51	36.16	21.57
Ukraine	926	....	....	....	....	22.05	40.41	44.98	18.34	16.57	5.50	7.90	6.34

National Interest Rates

		1993	1994	1995	1996	1997	1998	1999	2000	2001	2002	2003	2004

Money Market Rates (60b)
(Period averages in percent per annum)

		1993	1994	1995	1996	1997	1998	1999	2000	2001	2002	2003	2004
Middle East													
Bahrain, Kingdom of.....................	419	3.53	5.18	6.24	5.69	....	5.69	5.58	6.89	3.85	2.02	1.24	1.74
Jordan...	439	....	....	....	....	....	....	5.19	5.28	4.63	3.49	2.58	2.18
Kuwait...	443	7.43	6.31	7.43	6.98	7.05	7.24	6.32	6.82	4.62	2.99	2.47	2.14
Libya...	672	4.00	....	....	....	....	4.00	4.00	4.00	4.00	4.00	4.00	4.00
Western Hemisphere													
ECCU...	309	5.25	5.25	5.25	5.25	5.25	5.25	5.25	5.25	† 5.64	6.32	6.07	4.67
Anguilla......................................	312	5.25	5.25	5.25	5.25	5.25	5.25	5.25	5.25	† 5.64	6.32	6.07	4.67
Antigua and Barbuda.................	311	5.25	5.25	5.25	5.25	5.25	5.25	5.25	5.25	† 5.64	6.32	6.07	4.67
Dominica....................................	321	5.25	5.25	5.25	5.25	5.25	5.25	5.25	5.25	† 5.64	6.32	6.07	4.67
Grenada......................................	328	5.25	5.25	5.25	5.25	5.25	5.25	5.25	5.25	† 5.64	6.32	6.07	4.67
Montserrat.................................	351	5.25	5.25	5.25	5.25	5.25	5.25	5.25	5.25	† 5.64	6.32	6.07	4.67
St. Kitts and Nevis.....................	361	5.25	5.25	5.25	5.25	5.25	5.25	5.25	5.25	† 5.64	6.32	6.07	4.67
St. Lucia....................................	362	5.25	5.25	5.25	5.25	5.25	5.25	5.25	5.25	† 5.64	6.32	6.07	4.67
St. Vincent & Grens....................	364	5.25	5.25	5.25	5.25	5.25	5.25	5.25	5.25	† 5.64	6.32	6.07	4.67
Argentina......................................	213	6.31	7.66	9.46	6.23	6.63	6.81	6.99	8.15	24.90	41.35	3.74	1.96
Bolivia..	218	....	....	22.42	20.27	13.97	12.57	13.49	7.40	6.99	8.41	4.07	4.05
Brazil..	223	3,284.44	4,820.64	53.37	27.45	25.00	29.50	26.26	17.59	17.47	19.11	23.37	16.24
Chile...	228	....	....	....	....	....	....	....	10.09	6.81	4.08	2.72	1.88
Colombia.......................................	233	....	....	22.40	28.37	23.83	35.00	18.81	10.87	10.43	6.06	6.95	7.01
Dominican Republic.......................	243	....	....	....	14.70	13.01	16.68	15.30	18.28	13.47	14.50	24.24	36.76
El Salvador....................................	253	....	....	....	....	10.43	9.43	10.68	6.93	5.28	4.40	3.86	4.36
Guatemala.....................................	258	....	....	....	....	7.77	6.62	9.23	9.33	10.58	9.11	6.65	6.16
Mexico..	273	17.39	16.47	† 60.92	33.61	21.91	26.89	24.10	16.96	12.89	8.17	6.83	7.15
Panama...	283	....	....	....	....	....	....	....	....	....	2.22	1.50	1.90
Paraguay.......................................	288	22.55	18.64	20.18	16.35	12.48	20.74	17.26	10.70	13.45	13.19	13.02	1.33
Uruguay..	298	....	39.82	36.81	28.47	23.43	20.48	13.96	14.82	22.10	89.37	....	....
Venezuela, Rep. Bol.....................	299	....	....	....	16.70	12.47	18.58	7.48	8.14	13.33	28.87	13.23	4.38

National Interest Rates

		1993	1994	1995	1996	1997	1998	1999	2000	2001	2002	2003	2004
						Treasury Bill Rates (60c) *(Period averages in percent per annum)*							
Industrial Countries													
United States	111	3.02	4.27	5.51	5.02	5.07	4.82	4.66	5.84	3.45	1.61	1.01	1.38
Canada	156	4.84	5.54	6.89	4.21	3.26	4.73	4.72	5.49	3.77	2.59	2.87	2.22
Australia	193	5.00	5.69	† 7.64	7.02	5.29	4.84	4.76	5.98	4.80	....	....	....
New Zealand	196	6.21	6.69	8.82	9.09	7.53	7.10	4.58	6.39	5.56	5.52	5.21	5.85
Belgium	124	8.52	5.57	4.67	3.19	3.38	3.51	2.72	4.02	4.16	3.17	2.23	1.97
France	132	8.41	5.79	6.58	3.84	3.35	3.45	2.72	4.23	4.26	3.28	2.27	....
Germany	134	6.22	5.05	4.40	3.30	3.32	3.42	2.88	4.32	3.66	2.97	1.98	2.00
Greece	174	20.25	17.50	14.20	11.20	11.38	10.30	8.30	† 6.22	4.08	3.50	2.34	2.27
Iceland	176	8.35	4.95	7.22	6.97	7.04	7.40	8.61	11.12	11.03	8.01	4.93	6.04
Ireland	178	† 9.06	5.87	6.19	5.36	6.03	5.37	....	....	....	....	....	....
Italy	136	10.58	9.17	10.85	8.46	6.33	4.59	3.01	4.53	4.05	3.26	2.19	2.08
Portugal	182	....	....	7.75	5.75	4.43	....	....	....	....	....	....	....
Spain	184	10.53	8.11	9.79	7.23	5.02	3.79	3.01	4.61	3.92	3.34	2.21	2.17
Sweden	144	8.35	7.40	8.75	5.79	4.11	4.19	3.12	3.95	....	4.07	3.04	....
Switzerland	146	4.75	3.97	2.78	1.72	1.45	1.32	1.17	2.93	2.68	.94	.16	.37
United Kingdom	112	5.21	5.15	6.33	5.78	6.48	6.82	5.04	5.80	4.77	3.86	3.55	4.43
Developing Countries													
Africa													
Algeria	612	9.50	16.50	....	....	....	† 9.96	10.05	7.95	5.69	1.80	1.25	.15
Ethiopia	644	12.00	12.00	12.00	7.22	3.97	3.48	3.65	2.74	3.06	1.30	† 1.31	.56
Ghana	652	30.95	27.72	35.38	41.64	42.77	34.33	26.37	36.28	40.96	25.11	27.25	16.57
Kenya	664	49.80	23.32	18.29	22.25	22.87	22.83	13.87	12.05	12.60	8.95	3.51	3.17
Lesotho	666	† 10.01	9.44	12.40	13.89	14.83	15.47	12.45	9.06	9.49	11.34	11.96	8.55
Madagascar	674	....	....	....	....	....	....	....	....	10.28	....	11.94	12.95
Malawi	676	23.54	27.68	46.30	30.83	18.31	32.98	42.85	39.52	42.41	41.75	39.32	28.58
Mozambique	688	....	....	....	....	....	....	....	16.97	24.77	29.55	15.31	12.37
Namibia	728	12.16	11.35	13.91	15.25	15.69	17.24	13.28	10.26	9.29	11.00	10.51	7.78
Nigeria	694	24.50	12.87	12.50	12.25	12.00	12.26	17.82	15.50	17.50	19.03	14.79	14.34
Seychelles	718	13.25	12.50	12.28	11.55	10.50	8.13	5.00	5.00	5.00	5.00	4.61	3.17
Sierra Leone	724	28.64	12.19	14.73	29.25	12.71	22.10	32.42	26.22	13.74	15.15	15.68	26.14
South Africa	199	11.31	10.93	13.53	15.04	15.26	16.53	12.85	10.11	9.68	11.16	10.67	7.53
Swaziland	734	8.25	8.35	10.87	13.68	14.37	13.09	11.19	8.30	7.16	8.59	10.61	7.94
Tanzania	738	34.00	35.09	40.33	15.30	9.59	11.83	10.05	9.78	4.14	3.55	6.26	8.35
Uganda	746	† 21.30	12.52	8.75	11.71	10.59	7.77	7.43	13.19	11.00	5.85	16.87	9.02
Zambia	754	124.03	74.21	39.81	52.78	29.48	24.94	36.19	31.37	44.28	34.54	29.97	12.60
Zimbabwe	698	33.04	29.22	27.98	24.53	22.07	32.78	50.48	64.78	17.60	28.51	52.73	125.68
Asia													
China,P.R.:Hong Kong	532	3.17	5.66	5.55	4.45	7.50	5.04	4.94	5.69	1.69	1.35	−.08	.07
Fiji	819	2.91	2.69	3.15	2.98	2.60	2.00	2.00	3.63	1.51	1.66	1.06	1.56
Lao People's Dem.Rep.	544	....	....	20.46	20.46	....	23.66	30.00	29.94	22.70	21.41	24.87	20.37
Malaysia	548	6.48	3.68	5.50	6.41	6.41	6.86	3.53	2.86	2.79	2.73	2.79	2.40
Nepal	558	4.50	6.50	9.90	11.51	2.52	3.70	4.30	5.30	5.00	3.80	3.85	2.40
Pakistan	564	13.03	11.26	12.49	13.61	† 15.74	....	....	8.38	10.71	6.08	1.93	2.48
Papua New Guinea	853	6.25	6.85	† 17.40	14.44	9.94	21.18	22.70	17.00	12.36	10.93	18.69	8.85
Philippines	566	12.45	12.71	11.76	12.34	12.89	15.00	10.00	9.91	9.73	5.49	5.87	7.32
Singapore	576	.92	1.94	1.05	1.38	2.32	2.12	1.12	2.18	1.69	.81	.64	.96
Solomon Islands	813	12.15	11.25	12.50	12.75	12.88	6.00	6.00	7.05	8.23	6.87	5.85	6.00
Sri Lanka	524	16.52	12.68	16.81	† 17.40	....	12.59	12.51	14.02	17.57	12.47	8.09	7.71
Vietnam	582	26.40	....	....	....	....	....	....	5.42	5.49	5.92	5.83	....
Europe													
Albania	914	....	....	13.84	17.81	32.59	27.49	17.54	10.80	7.72	9.49	8.81	6.79
Armenia	911	....	....	37.81	† 43.95	57.54	46.99	55.10	24.40	† 20.59	14.75	11.91	5.27
Azerbaijan, Republic of	912	....	....	....	....	12.23	14.10	18.31	16.73	16.51	14.12	8.00	4.62
Bulgaria	918	45.45	57.72	48.27	114.31	78.35	6.02	5.43	4.21	4.57	4.29	2.81	2.64
Cyprus	423	6.00	6.00	6.00	6.05	5.38	5.59	5.59	6.01	....	....	3.56	....
Czech Republic	935	6.62	6.98	8.99	11.91	11.21	10.51	5.71	5.37	5.06	2.72	2.04	2.57
Georgia	915	....	....	....	....	....	....	....	....	29.93	43.42	44.26	19.16
Hungary	944	17.22	26.93	32.04	23.96	20.13	17.83	14.68	11.03	10.79	8.91	8.22	11.32
Kazakhstan	916	....	214.34	48.98	28.91	15.15	23.59	15.63	6.59	5.28	5.20	5.86	3.28
Kyrgyz Republic	917	....	143.13	34.90	40.10	35.83	43.67	47.19	32.26	19.08	10.15	7.21	4.94
Latvia	941	....	....	28.24	16.27	4.73	5.27	6.23	† 4.85	5.63	3.52	3.24	....
Lithuania	946	....	....	26.82	20.95	8.64	10.69	11.14	† 9.27	5.68	3.72	2.61	....
Malta	181	4.60	4.29	4.65	4.99	5.08	5.41	5.15	4.89	4.93	4.03	....	....
Moldova	921	....	....	52.90	39.01	23.63	30.54	28.49	22.20	14.24	5.89	15.08	11.89
Poland	964	33.16	28.81	25.62	20.32	21.58	19.09	13.14	16.62	....	....	....	....
Romania	968	....	....	....	51.09	85.72	63.99	74.21	51.86	42.18	27.03	....	....
Russia	922	....	....	168.04	86.07	23.43	....	....	12.12	12.45	12.72	5.35	....
Slovenia	961	....	....	....	....	....	....	8.63	10.94	10.88	8.73	6.53	4.17
Turkey	186	....	....	....	....	....	....	....	25.18	85.33	59.50	34.90	21.95
Middle East													
Bahrain, Kingdom of	419	3.33	4.81	6.07	5.49	5.68	5.53	5.46	6.56	3.78	1.75	1.13	1.56
Egypt	469	....	....	....	....	....	8.80	8.80	9.00	9.10	7.20	5.50	6.90	9.90
Israel	436	10.54	11.77	14.37	15.34	13.39	11.33	11.41	8.81	6.50	7.38	7.00	4.78
Kuwait	443	....	6.32	7.35	6.93	6.98	....	....	....	....	....	....	....
Lebanon	446	18.27	15.09	19.40	15.19	13.42	12.70	11.57	11.18	11.18	10.90	....	5.25
Western Hemisphere													
Antigua and Barbuda	311	7.00	7.00	7.00	7.00	7.00	7.00	7.00	7.00	7.00	7.00	7.00	7.00
Bahamas, The	313	3.96	1.88	3.01	4.45	4.35	3.84	1.97	1.03	1.94	2.50	1.78	.56
Barbados	316	5.44	7.26	8.01	6.85	3.61	5.61	5.83	5.29	3.14	2.10	1.41	1.20
Belize	339	4.59	4.27	4.10	3.78	3.51	3.83	5.91	5.91	5.91	4.59	3.22	3.22

National Interest Rates

		1993	1994	1995	1996	1997	1998	1999	2000	2001	2002	2003	2004
							Treasury Bill Rates (60c)						
							(Period averages in percent per annum)						
Western Hemisphere(Cont.)													
Bolivia	218	....	17.89	24.51	19.93	13.65	12.33	14.07	10.99	11.48	12.41	9.92	7.41
Brazil	223	....	....	49.93	25.73	24.79	28.57	26.39	18.51	20.06	19.43	22.10	17.14
Dominica	321	6.40	6.40	6.40	6.40	6.40	6.40	6.40	6.40	6.40	6.40	6.40	6.40
Grenada	328	6.50	6.50	6.50	6.50	6.50	6.50	6.50	6.50	† 7.00	7.00	6.50	6.00
Guyana	336	16.83	17.66	17.51	11.35	8.91	8.33	11.31	9.88	7.78	4.94	3.04	3.62
Haiti	263	....	....	....	....	14.13	16.21	7.71	12.33	13.53	7.56	20.50	12.23
Jamaica	343	28.85	42.98	27.65	37.95	21.14	25.65	20.75	18.24	16.71	15.54	25.94	15.47
Mexico	273	14.99	14.10	48.44	31.39	19.80	24.76	21.41	15.24	11.31	7.09	6.23	6.82
Netherlands Antilles	353	4.83	4.48	5.46	5.66	5.77	5.82	6.15	6.15	6.15	4.96	2.80	3.86
St. Kitts and Nevis	361	6.50	6.50	6.50	6.50	6.50	6.50	6.50	6.50	7.50	7.50	7.17	7.00
St. Lucia	362	7.00	7.00	7.00	7.00	7.00	7.00	7.00	7.00	6.80	6.80	6.33	6.40
St. Vincent & Grens	364	6.50	6.50	6.50	6.50	6.50	6.50	6.50	6.50	7.00	7.00	....	....
Trinidad and Tobago	369	9.45	10.00	8.41	10.44	9.83	11.93	10.40	10.56	8.55	4.83	4.71	4.77
Uruguay	298	....	44.60	39.40	29.20	23.18	....	....	....	....	....	....	....

National Interest Rates

		1993	1994	1995	1996	1997	1998	1999	2000	2001	2002	2003	2004
						Deposit Rates (60l)							
						except for United States (60lc)							
						(Period averages in percent per annum)							

Industrial Countries

		1993	1994	1995	1996	1997	1998	1999	2000	2001	2002	2003	2004
United States	111	3.17	4.63	5.92	5.39	5.62	5.47	5.33	6.46	3.69	1.73	1.15	1.56
Canada	156	3.21	3.98	5.28	3.00	1.90	3.08	2.88	3.48	2.25	.83	1.10	.78
Australia	193	4.90	4.96	6.14	5.74	4.40	3.75	† 3.55	4.16	3.27	3.11	3.31	3.77
Japan	158	2.14	1.70	.90	.30	.30	.27	.12	.07	.06	.04	.04	.08
New Zealand	196	6.24	6.38	8.49	8.49	7.26	6.78	4.56	6.36	5.35	5.33	5.10	5.77
Euro Area	163	....	....	....	4.08	3.41	3.20	2.45	3.45	3.49	2.80	....	....
Austria	122	2.98	2.31	2.19	1.71	1.50	† 2.65	2.21	....	....	....	....	....
Belgium	124	† 7.11	4.86	4.04	2.66	2.88	3.01	2.42	3.58	3.40	2.60	1.65	....
Finland	172	4.75	3.27	3.19	2.35	2.00	....	1.22	1.63	1.94	1.49	....	....
France	132	4.50	4.50	4.50	3.67	3.50	3.21	2.69	2.63	3.00	3.00	2.69	2.25
Germany	134	6.27	4.47	3.85	2.83	2.69	2.88	2.43	3.40	3.56	2.65	....	....
Greece	174	19.33	18.92	15.75	13.51	10.11	10.70	8.69	6.13	3.32	2.76	2.48	2.29
Ireland	178	2.27	.33	.44	.29	.46	.43	.10	.10	.10	.10	.04	.01
Italy	136	† 7.79	6.20	6.45	6.49	4.83	3.16	1.61	1.84	1.96	1.43	.95	....
Luxembourg	137	5.33	5.00	5.00	3.54	3.46	3.31	....	....	....	....	....	....
Netherlands	138	3.11	† 4.70	4.40	3.54	3.18	3.10	2.74	2.89	3.10	2.77	2.49	2.31
Portugal	182	11.06	8.37	8.38	6.32	4.56	3.37	2.40	....	....	....	....	....
Spain	184	9.63	6.70	7.68	6.12	3.96	2.92	1.85	2.95	3.08	2.50	....	....
Denmark	128	6.52	† 3.53	3.85	2.80	2.65	3.08	2.43	3.15	3.30	† 2.40	2.40	....
Iceland	176	6.63	3.03	3.69	4.25	4.72	4.50	4.82	7.11	6.94	4.69	4.81	4.85
Norway	142	5.51	5.21	4.95	4.15	3.63	7.24	5.38	6.73	† 6.43	6.46	2.12	1.48
Sweden	144	5.10	4.91	6.16	2.47	2.50	1.91	1.65	2.15	2.10	2.26	1.51	1.00
Switzerland	146	3.50	3.63	1.28	1.34	1.00	.69	1.24	† 3.00	1.68	.43	.17	.39
United Kingdom	112	3.97	3.66	4.11	3.05	3.63	4.48	....	....	....	....	....	....

Developing Countries
Africa

		1993	1994	1995	1996	1997	1998	1999	2000	2001	2002	2003	2004
CEMAC	758	7.75	5.50	5.50	5.00	5.00	5.00	5.00	5.00	5.00	5.00	5.00	5.00
Cameroon	622	7.75	8.08	5.50	5.38	5.04	5.00	5.00	5.00	5.00	5.00	5.00	5.00
Central African Rep.	626	7.75	8.08	5.50	5.46	5.00	5.00	5.00	5.00	5.00	5.00	5.00	5.00
Chad	628	7.75	8.08	5.50	5.46	5.00	5.00	5.00	5.00	5.00	5.00	5.00	5.00
Congo, Republic of	634	7.75	8.08	5.50	5.46	5.00	5.00	5.00	5.00	5.00	5.00	5.00	5.00
Equatorial Guinea	642	7.75	8.08	5.50	5.46	5.00	5.00	5.00	5.00	5.00	5.00	5.00	5.00
Gabon	646	7.75	8.08	5.50	5.46	5.00	5.00	5.00	5.00	5.00	5.00	5.00	5.00
WAEMU	759	....	....	3.50	3.50	3.50	3.50	3.50	3.50	3.50	3.50	3.50	3.50
Benin	638	3.50	3.50	3.50	3.50	3.50	3.50	3.50	3.50	3.50	3.50	3.50	3.50
Burkina Faso	748	3.50	3.50	3.50	3.50	3.50	3.50	3.50	3.50	3.50	3.50	3.50	3.50
Côte d'Ivoire	662	3.50	3.50	3.50	3.50	3.50	3.50	3.50	3.50	3.50	3.50	3.50	3.50
Guinea-Bissau	654	3.50	3.50	3.50	3.50	3.50	3.50	3.50	3.50	3.50	3.50	3.50	3.50
Mali	678	3.50	3.50	3.50	3.50	3.50	3.50	3.50	3.50	3.50	3.50	3.50	3.50
Niger	692	3.50	3.50	3.50	3.50	3.50	3.50	3.50	3.50	3.50	3.50	3.50	3.50
Senegal	722	3.50	3.50	3.50	3.50	3.50	3.50	3.50	3.50	3.50	3.50	3.50	3.50
Togo	742	3.50	3.50	3.50	3.50	3.50	3.50	3.50	3.50	3.50	3.50	3.50	3.50
Algeria	612	8.00	12.00	† 16.00	14.50	9.75	8.50	7.50	7.50	6.25	5.25	5.25	2.50
Angola	614	....	....	125.92	147.13	29.25	36.88	† 36.57	† 39.58	47.91	48.69	26.17	15.44
Botswana	616	13.49	10.59	9.79	9.68	9.51	8.43	9.10	9.42	10.09	10.45	9.95	9.85
Cape Verde	624	4.00	4.00	† 5.00	5.00	5.04	5.27	4.76	4.34	4.67	4.86	3.93	3.46
Comoros	632	....	....	....	....	....	....	† 11.42	3.00	3.00	3.17	3.50	3.50
Congo, Dem. Rep. of	636	....	60.00	60.00	60.00	....	....	....	....	....	....	....	....
Djibouti	611	....	....	....	....	....	....	....	....	2.81	1.23	.82	.80
Ethiopia	644	11.50	11.50	11.46	9.42	7.00	6.00	6.32	6.00	6.00	3.79	3.35	3.38
Gambia, The	648	13.00	12.58	12.50	12.50	12.50	12.50	12.50	12.50	12.50	12.71	16.42	22.00
Ghana	652	23.63	23.15	28.73	34.50	35.76	32.05	23.56	28.60	30.85	16.21	14.32	13.63
Guinea	656	19.75	18.00	17.50	....	....	6.38	5.67	7.50	8.03	7.40	6.50	8.85
Kenya	664	....	....	13.60	17.59	16.72	18.40	9.55	8.10	6.64	5.49	4.13	† 2.43
Lesotho	666	8.06	8.43	13.34	12.73	11.81	10.73	7.45	4.92	4.83	5.19	5.16	4.24
Liberia	668	....	6.34	6.37	....	6.43	6.22	6.25	6.18	5.94	6.25	5.29	3.84
Madagascar	674	19.50	19.50	18.50	19.00	14.38	8.00	15.33	15.00	12.00	12.00	11.50	....
Malawi	676	21.75	25.00	37.27	26.33	10.21	19.06	33.21	33.25	34.96	28.08	25.13	13.73
Mauritania	682	....	....	....	....	....	....	....	....	....	....	8.00	....
Mauritius	684	8.40	11.04	12.23	10.77	9.08	9.28	10.92	9.61	9.78	9.88	9.53	8.15
Morocco	686	....	....	....	....	....	7.26	6.39	5.16	5.04	4.54	3.78	3.61
Mozambique	688	....	33.38	38.84	18.14	25.43	8.22	7.86	9.70	† 15.01	17.99	12.15	9.91
Namibia	728	9.61	9.18	10.84	12.56	12.70	12.94	10.82	7.39	6.79	7.81	8.76	6.35
Nigeria	694	23.24	13.09	13.53	13.06	7.17	10.11	12.81	11.69	15.26	16.67	14.22	13.70
Rwanda	714	5.00	....	....	10.92	9.46	8.50	7.95	8.94	9.22	8.00	8.14	....
São Tomé & Príncipe	716	35.00	35.00	35.00	31.00	36.75	38.29	27.00	† 21.00	15.00	15.00	12.29	10.55
Seychelles	718	9.37	8.85	9.22	9.90	9.20	7.53	5.13	4.77	4.92	4.93	3.99	3.55
Sierra Leone	724	27.00	11.63	7.03	13.96	9.91	7.12	9.50	9.25	7.67	8.23	8.42	10.14
South Africa	199	11.50	11.11	13.54	14.91	15.38	16.50	12.24	9.20	† 9.37	10.77	9.76	6.55
Swaziland	734	7.89	7.54	9.44	11.08	12.00	11.92	9.86	6.53	6.15	8.02	7.59	4.63
Tanzania	738	....	....	24.63	13.59	7.83	7.75	7.75	† 7.39	4.81	3.29	3.05	4.20
Uganda	746	16.26	9.99	7.61	10.62	11.84	11.36	8.73	9.84	8.47	5.56	9.85	7.74
Zambia	754	....	46.14	30.24	42.13	34.48	13.08	20.27	20.24	23.41	23.33	21.95	11.51
Zimbabwe	698	29.45	26.75	25.92	21.58	18.60	29.06	38.51	50.17	13.95	18.38	35.92	103.21

Asia

		1993	1994	1995	1996	1997	1998	1999	2000	2001	2002	2003	2004
Bangladesh	513	8.18	6.40	6.04	7.28	8.11	8.42	8.74	8.56	8.50	8.17	7.82	7.11
Bhutan	514	8.00	8.00	8.00	8.25	8.25	8.25	8.25	8.25	7.50	7.00	5.00	....
Cambodia	522	....	....	8.71	8.80	8.03	7.80	7.33	6.83	4.36	2.49	2.02	1.79
China, P.R.: Mainland	924	10.98	10.98	10.98	7.47	5.67	3.78	2.25	2.25	2.25	1.98	1.98	2.25

National Interest Rates

		1993	1994	1995	1996	1997	1998	1999	2000	2001	2002	2003	2004
							Deposit Rates (60l) except for United States (60lc) *(Period averages in percent per annum)*						

		1993	1994	1995	1996	1997	1998	1999	2000	2001	2002	2003	2004
Asia(Cont.)													
China,P.R.:Hong Kong	532	2.25	3.54	5.63	4.64	5.98	6.62	4.50	4.80	2.38	.35	.07	.03
China,P.R.:Macao	546	2.75	4.21	5.93	5.23	6.22	7.00	5.30	5.33	2.59	.63	....	....
Fiji	819	3.69	3.15	3.18	3.38	3.08	2.17	1.24	.90	.78	.62	.51	.38
Indonesia	536	14.55	12.53	16.72	17.26	20.01	39.07	25.74	12.50	15.48	15.50	10.59	6.44
Korea	542	8.58	8.50	8.83	7.50	† 10.81	13.29	7.95	7.94	5.79	4.95	4.25	3.87
Lao People's Dem.Rep.	544	13.33	12.00	14.00	16.00	....	17.79	13.42	12.00	6.50	6.00	6.58	7.85
Malaysia	548	7.03	4.89	5.93	7.09	7.78	8.51	4.12	3.36	3.37	3.21	3.07	3.00
Maldives	556	....	....	....	6.80	6.80	6.80	6.93	6.88	6.97	7.50	7.50	6.50
Micronesia, Fed.Sts.	868	....	....	5.33	4.58	4.21	3.98	3.72	4.59	3.17	1.47	1.02	1.02
Mongolia	948	280.20	115.71	74.62	44.75	36.37	27.51	23.42	16.80	14.30	13.22	14.00	14.15
Myanmar	518	9.00	9.00	9.75	12.50	12.50	12.50	11.00	9.75	9.50	9.50	9.50	9.50
Nepal	558	....	8.75	....	9.63	9.79	8.92	7.31	5.96	4.75	....	....	2.71
Papua New Guinea	853	5.03	5.09	† 7.30	7.13	4.13	8.36	8.13	8.46	5.46	3.18	4.38	1.73
Philippines	566	9.61	10.54	8.39	9.68	10.19	12.11	8.17	8.31	8.74	4.61	5.22	6.18
Samoa	862	5.50	5.50	5.50	5.50	5.50	6.50	6.50	6.46	5.53	5.10	5.10	5.10
Singapore	576	2.30	3.00	3.50	3.41	3.47	4.60	1.68	1.71	1.54	.91	.51	.41
Solomon Islands	813	9.77	9.00	8.38	6.46	2.42	2.33	2.88	2.54	1.35	.75	.75	.92
Sri Lanka	524	13.77	13.10	12.13	12.36	11.25	9.56	9.12	9.17	11.01	9.22	6.00	5.07
Thailand	578	8.63	8.46	11.58	10.33	10.52	10.65	4.73	3.29	2.54	1.98	1.33	1.00
Tonga	866	4.25	4.64	4.72	5.53	5.57	5.63	5.42	5.36	5.47	5.47	5.47	5.85
Vanuatu	846	5.00	5.06	3.00	4.50	3.73	3.29	1.60	1.27	1.25	1.00	1.21	1.71
Vietnam	582	22.04	....	....	....	8.51	9.23	7.37	3.65	5.30	6.45	6.62	....
Europe													
Albania	914	† 27.33	19.83	† 15.30	16.78	27.28	22.56	12.95	8.30	7.73	8.54	8.38	6.61
Armenia	911	....	....	63.18	32.19	26.08	24.94	27.35	18.08	14.90	9.60	6.87	4.90
Azerbaijan, Republic of	912	....	....	....	....	....	....	12.08	12.90	8.46	8.66	9.54	9.18
Belarus	913	65.08	89.60	100.82	32.36	15.64	14.33	23.80	37.55	34.18	26.85	17.44	12.72
Bosnia & Herzegovina	963	....	....	....	....	....	51.88	9.07	14.67	....	† 4.53	4.03	3.72
Bulgaria	918	42.56	51.14	35.94	74.68	46.83	3.00	3.21	3.10	2.88	2.77	2.89	3.01
Croatia	960	379.31	6.52	5.53	5.59	4.30	4.62	4.31	3.74	3.23	1.89	1.53	1.87
Cyprus	423	5.75	5.75	5.75	† 7.00	6.50	6.50	6.50	6.50	4.65	4.20	3.30	3.99
Czech Republic	935	7.03	7.07	6.96	6.79	7.71	8.08	4.48	3.42	2.87	2.00	1.33	1.28
Estonia	939	....	11.51	8.74	6.05	6.19	8.07	4.19	3.76	4.03	2.74	2.40	2.16
Georgia	915	....	....	....	31.05	13.73	17.00	14.58	10.17	7.75	9.82	9.28	7.24
Hungary	944	15.65	20.31	† 24.36	18.57	16.94	14.42	11.94	9.49	8.40	7.41	10.98	9.09
Kyrgyz Republic	917	....	....	....	36.73	39.59	35.76	35.58	18.38	12.50	5.91	4.98	6.70
Latvia	941	34.78	31.68	14.79	11.71	5.90	5.33	5.04	4.38	5.24	3.23	3.02	3.27
Lithuania	946	88.29	48.43	20.05	13.95	7.89	5.98	4.94	3.86	3.00	1.70	1.27	1.22
Macedonia, FYR	962	....	117.56	24.07	12.75	11.64	11.68	11.40	11.18	9.97	9.56	7.97	6.54
Malta	181	4.50	4.50	4.50	4.50	4.56	4.64	4.66	4.86	4.84	4.30	....	....
Moldova	921	....	....	....	25.43	23.47	21.68	27.54	24.87	20.93	14.20	12.55	15.12
Poland	964	34.00	† 33.40	26.78	20.02	19.36	18.19	11.22	14.17	11.80	6.21	3.71	3.82
Russia	922	....	....	101.96	55.05	† 16.77	17.05	13.68	6.51	4.85	4.96	4.48	3.79
Slovak Republic	936	8.02	9.32	9.01	9.30	13.44	16.25	14.37	8.45	6.46	6.65	5.33	4.14
Slovenia	961	33.04	28.10	15.38	15.08	13.19	10.54	7.24	10.05	9.81	8.24	5.95	3.82
Tajikistan	923	....	....	....	....	23.93	9.82	5.24	1.26	5.19	† 9.21	9.67	9.75
Turkey	186	64.58	87.79	76.02	80.74	79.49	80.11	78.43	47.16	74.70	50.49	37.68	24.26
Ukraine	926	148.63	208.63	70.29	33.63	18.21	22.25	20.70	13.72	10.99	7.93	6.98	7.80
Middle East													
Bahrain, Kingdom of	419	3.03	4.00	5.70	5.18	5.28	4.74	4.80	5.82	2.71	1.34	....	....
Egypt	469	12.00	11.83	10.92	10.54	9.84	9.36	9.22	9.46	9.46	9.33	8.23	7.73
Israel	436	10.44	12.19	14.08	14.48	13.07	10.99	11.34	8.63	6.18	6.03	6.65	3.62
Jordan	439	6.88	7.09	7.68	8.50	9.10	8.21	8.30	6.97	5.81	4.43	3.14	2.49
Kuwait	443	7.07	5.70	6.53	6.05	5.93	6.32	5.76	5.89	4.47	3.15	2.42	2.65
Lebanon	446	15.56	14.80	16.30	15.54	13.37	13.61	12.50	11.21	10.85	11.03	8.69	7.37
Oman	449	4.17	4.34	6.53	6.85	7.30	8.46	8.12	7.63	4.50	2.89	2.37	2.32
Qatar	453	4.08	4.84	6.19	6.50	6.63	6.56	6.50	....	....	....	....	....
Saudi Arabia	456	3.52	5.10	6.18	5.47	5.79	6.21	6.14	6.67	3.92	2.23	1.63	1.73
Syrian Arab Republic	463	4.00	4.00	4.00	4.00	4.00	4.00	4.00	4.00	4.00	4.00	....	....
Western Hemisphere													
ECCU	309	7.21	† 3.87	4.06	4.16	4.20	4.30	4.35	4.46	4.37	4.04	4.76	4.05
Anguilla	312	2.25	3.47	3.64	3.74	3.77	3.79	3.78	3.52	3.54	3.25	4.59	4.83
Antigua and Barbuda	311	5.01	4.19	4.02	4.33	4.36	4.34	4.45	5.18	4.49	4.36	4.86	4.33
Dominica	321	4.19	4.50	4.20	4.30	4.27	4.23	4.38	3.87	3.98	3.91	3.66	3.26
Grenada	328	3.88	3.61	3.67	3.74	3.93	4.16	4.30	4.24	4.23	3.59	3.39	3.32
Montserrat	351	3.44	3.25	3.24	3.29	3.02	2.74	3.14	3.35	3.35	3.08	3.06	2.29
St. Kitts and Nevis	361	4.39	3.99	4.52	4.27	4.27	4.22	4.31	4.32	4.23	4.01	4.49	4.54
St. Lucia	362	4.04	3.83	4.43	4.50	4.65	4.80	4.76	4.80	4.88	4.27	5.47	3.05
St. Vincent & Grens.	364	3.90	3.89	4.34	4.14	4.21	4.27	4.46	4.54	4.56	4.35	4.56	3.30
Argentina	213	11.34	8.08	11.90	7.36	6.97	7.56	8.05	8.34	16.16	39.25	10.16	2.61
Aruba	314	4.20	4.40	4.30	4.20	4.40	....	† 6.17	6.20	5.84	5.56	5.33	4.26
Bahamas, The	313	5.19	4.30	4.20	5.14	5.23	5.36	4.57	4.08	4.25	4.25	3.95	3.83
Barbados	316	4.39	4.32	5.11	5.20	4.58	4.20	4.40	4.97	4.04	2.70	2.56	2.54
Belize	339	8.13	8.55	9.37	9.08	9.19	8.76	8.12	7.69	6.35	6.28	6.93	7.42
Bolivia	218	22.18	18.43	18.87	19.16	14.73	12.82	12.26	10.98	9.82	9.58	11.41	7.42
Brazil	223	3,293.50	5,175.24	52.25	26.45	24.35	28.00	26.02	17.20	17.86	19.14	21.97	15.42
Chile	228	18.24	15.12	13.73	13.48	12.02	14.92	8.56	9.20	6.19	3.80	2.73	1.94
Colombia	233	25.84	29.42	32.34	31.15	24.13	32.58	21.33	12.15	12.44	8.94	7.80	7.80
Costa Rica	238	16.90	17.72	23.88	17.29	13.03	12.76	14.31	13.38	11.77	11.46	10.41	9.51
Dominican Republic	243	14.04	13.70	14.94	13.91	13.40	17.65	16.07	17.65	15.61	16.54	20.50	21.12
Ecuador	248	31.97	33.65	43.31	41.50	28.09	39.39	† 10.03	8.46	6.58	5.47	5.53	4.08

National Interest Rates

		1993	1994	1995	1996	1997	1998	1999	2000	2001	2002	2003	2004
						Deposit Rates (60l) except for United States (60lc) *(Period averages in percent per annum)*							

Western Hemisphere(Cont.)													
El Salvador	253	15.27	13.57	14.37	13.98	11.77	10.32	10.75	9.31	....	....	....	....
Guatemala	258	12.63	9.69	7.87	7.65	† 5.83	5.44	7.96	10.17	8.75	6.92	4.78	4.19
Guyana	336	12.26	11.42	12.90	10.49	8.56	8.10	9.08	8.71	7.63	4.53	3.18	2.67
Haiti	263	....	....	....	....	10.74	13.06	7.39	11.85	13.66	8.24	13.99	10.79
Honduras	268	11.60	11.56	11.97	16.70	21.28	18.58	19.97	15.93	14.48	13.74	11.48	11.09
Jamaica	343	27.59	36.41	23.21	25.16	13.95	15.61	13.48	11.62	9.64	8.58	8.46	7.98
Mexico	273	16.69	15.03	39.82	26.40	16.36	15.45	11.60	8.26	6.23	3.76	3.09	2.70
Netherlands Antilles	353	4.33	4.05	3.75	3.67	3.66	3.58	3.59	3.63	3.65	3.62	3.48	2.92
Nicaragua	278	11.61	11.70	11.15	12.35	12.41	10.77	† 11.83	10.80	11.56	7.79	5.55	4.72
Panama	283	5.90	6.11	7.18	7.20	7.03	6.76	6.92	7.07	6.83	4.97	3.98	2.23
Paraguay	288	22.10	23.12	21.16	17.16	13.00	15.95	† 19.75	15.72	16.22	22.86	15.83	5.11
Peru	293	44.14	22.35	15.70	14.90	15.01	15.11	16.27	13.29	9.92	4.19	3.83	2.98
Suriname	366	4.75	7.45	21.00	17.83	17.25	16.00	15.60	15.48	11.86	9.00	8.28	8.34
Trinidad and Tobago	369	7.06	6.91	....	....	6.91	7.95	8.51	8.15	7.66	4.76	2.91	2.79
Uruguay	298	40.38	37.92	39.21	28.84	20.10	15.47	14.61	12.41	14.68	† 42.54	19.75	3.19
Venezuela, Rep. Bol.	299	53.75	39.02	24.72	27.58	14.70	34.84	21.28	16.30	15.51	29.00	17.21	12.60

National Interest Rates

		1993	1994	1995	1996	1997	1998	1999	2000	2001	2002	2003	2004
							Lending Rates (60p)						
							(Period averages in percent per annum)						
Industrial Countries													
United States	111	6.00	7.14	8.83	8.27	8.44	8.35	7.99	9.23	6.92	4.68	4.12	4.34
Canada	156	5.94	6.88	8.65	6.06	4.96	6.60	6.44	7.27	5.81	4.21	4.69	4.00
Australia	193	9.42	9.23	10.70	10.50	8.89	8.15	7.99	9.27	8.66	8.16	8.41	8.85
Japan	158	† 4.41	4.13	3.51	2.66	2.45	2.32	2.16	2.07	1.97	1.86	1.82	1.77
New Zealand	196	10.34	9.69	12.09	12.27	11.35	11.22	8.49	10.22	9.88	9.83	9.81	10.38
Euro Area	163	....	....	....	8.88	7.58	6.73	5.65	6.60	6.83	6.14	....	....
Austria	122	....	....	....			6.42	5.64					
Belgium	124	11.81	9.42	8.42	7.17	7.06	7.25	6.71	7.98	8.46	7.71	6.89	6.70
Finland	172	9.92	7.91	7.75	6.16	5.29	5.35	4.71	5.61	5.79	4.82	....	....
France	132	8.90	7.89	8.12	6.77	6.34	6.55	6.36	6.70	6.98	6.60	6.60	6.60
Germany	134	12.85	11.48	10.94	10.02	9.13	9.02	8.81	9.63	10.01	9.70	....	....
Greece	174	28.56	27.44	23.05	20.96	18.92	18.56	15.00	12.32	8.59	7.41	6.79	....
Ireland	178	9.93	6.13	6.56	5.85	6.57	6.22	3.34	4.77	4.84	3.83	2.85	2.57
Italy	136	13.87	11.22	12.47	12.06	9.75	7.88	5.58	6.26	6.53	5.78	5.03	....
Luxembourg	137	7.65	6.58	6.50	5.50	5.50	5.27	....	....	....	....	....	....
Netherlands	138	10.40	8.29	7.21	5.90	6.13	6.50	† 3.46	4.79	5.00	3.96	3.00	2.75
Portugal	182	16.48	15.01	13.80	11.73	9.15	7.24	5.19	....	....	....	....	....
Spain	184	12.78	8.95	10.05	8.50	6.08	5.01	3.95	5.18	5.16	4.31	....	....
Denmark	128	10.46	† 9.95	10.33	8.70	7.73	7.90	7.13	8.08	8.20	† 7.10	....	....
Iceland	176	14.11	10.57	11.58	12.43	12.89	12.78	13.30	16.80	17.95	15.37	11.95	12.02
Norway	142	9.17	8.38	7.60	6.68	6.00	9.80	7.61	8.93	8.69	8.71	4.73	4.04
Sweden	144	11.40	10.64	11.11	7.38	7.01	5.94	5.53	5.83	5.55	5.64	4.79	4.00
Switzerland	146	6.40	5.51	5.48	4.97	4.47	4.07	3.90	4.29	4.30	3.93	3.27	3.20
United Kingdom	112	5.92	5.48	6.69	5.96	6.58	7.21	5.33	5.98	5.08	4.00	3.69	4.40
Developing Countries													
Africa													
CEMAC	758	17.50	16.00	16.00	22.00	22.00	22.00	22.00	22.00	18.00	18.00	18.00	18.00
Cameroon	622	17.46	17.50	16.00	22.00	22.00	22.00	22.00	22.00	20.67	18.00	18.00	18.00
Central African Rep	626	17.46	17.50	16.00	22.00	22.00	22.00	22.00	22.00	20.67	18.00	18.00	18.00
Chad	628	17.46	17.50	16.00	22.00	22.00	22.00	22.00	22.00	20.67	18.00	18.00	18.00
Congo, Republic of	634	17.46	17.50	16.00	22.00	22.00	22.00	22.00	22.00	20.67	18.00	18.00	18.00
Equatorial Guinea	642	17.46	17.50	16.00	22.00	22.00	22.00	22.00	22.00	20.67	18.00	18.00	18.00
Gabon	646	17.46	17.50	16.00	22.00	22.00	22.00	22.00	22.00	20.67	18.00	18.00	18.00
Algeria	612	....	16.00	† 19.00	19.00	12.50	11.00	10.00	10.00	9.50	8.50	8.00	8.00
Angola	614	....	....	206.25	217.88	37.75	45.00	† 80.30	† 103.16	95.97	97.34	96.12	82.33
Botswana	616	14.92	13.92	14.42	14.50	13.95	13.65	14.78	15.48	15.75	16.21	16.33	15.75
Burundi	618	13.77	14.20	15.26	....	....	....	15.24	15.77	16.82	19.47	18.23	18.25
Cape Verde	624	10.00	10.67	12.00	12.00	12.06	12.51	12.03	11.94	12.85	13.17	12.73	12.69
Comoros	632	....	....	....	....	....	....	† 13.67	12.00	12.00	12.00	11.83	11.00
Congo, Dem. Rep. of	636	....	398.25	293.88	247.00	134.58	29.00	124.58	165.00	167.92	66.79	....	....
Djibouti	611	....	....	....	....	....	....	....	....	11.46	11.30	11.30	11.25
Ethiopia	644	14.00	14.33	15.08	13.92	10.50	10.50	10.58	10.89	10.87	8.66	† 7.00	7.00
Gambia, The	648	26.08	25.00	25.04	25.50	25.50	25.38	24.00	24.00	24.00	24.00	29.33	36.50
Guinea	656	24.50	22.00	21.50	....	....	19.56	19.88	19.38	....	....	....	....
Guinea-Bissau	654	63.58	36.33	32.92	51.75	....	....	....	....	....	....	....	....
Kenya	664	29.99	36.24	28.80	33.79	30.25	29.49	22.38	22.34	19.67	18.45	16.57	† 12.53
Lesotho	666	15.83	14.25	16.38	17.71	18.03	20.06	19.06	17.11	16.55	17.11	16.02	12.38
Liberia	668	....	14.53	15.57	....	16.83	† 21.74	16.72	20.53	22.14	20.21	17.06	18.10
Madagascar	674	26.00	30.50	37.50	32.75	30.00	27.00	28.00	26.50	25.25	25.25	24.25	....
Malawi	676	29.50	31.00	47.33	45.33	28.25	37.67	53.58	53.13	56.17	50.54	48.92	36.83
Mauritania	682	....	....	....	....	....	....	....	....	....	21.00	....	....
Mauritius	684	16.58	18.92	20.81	20.81	18.92	19.92	21.63	20.77	21.10	21.00	21.00	21.00
Morocco	686	....	10.00	....	....	....	13.50	13.50	13.31	13.25	13.13	12.56	11.50
Mozambique	688	....	....	....	....	....	24.35	19.63	19.04	† 22.73	26.71	24.69	22.08
Namibia	728	18.02	17.05	18.51	19.16	20.18	20.72	18.48	15.28	14.53	13.84	14.70	11.39
Nigeria	694	31.65	20.48	20.23	19.84	17.80	18.18	20.29	21.27	23.44	24.77	20.71	19.18
Rwanda	714	15.00	....	....	....	....	....	....	....	....	....	....	....
São Tomé & Príncipe	716	37.00	30.00	52.00	38.00	51.50	55.58	40.33	† 39.67	37.00	37.08	33.79	30.00
Seychelles	718	15.71	15.72	15.76	16.22	14.88	14.39	12.01	11.45	11.14	11.09	11.08	10.13
Sierra Leone	724	50.46	27.33	28.83	32.12	23.87	23.83	26.83	26.25	24.27	22.17	20.00	22.08
South Africa	199	16.16	15.58	17.90	19.52	20.00	21.79	18.00	14.50	13.77	15.75	14.96	11.29
Swaziland	734	14.35	14.25	17.05	18.67	19.50	19.50	17.42	14.00	13.25	15.25	14.63	11.29
Tanzania	738	31.00	39.00	42.83	† 33.97	26.27	22.89	21.89	† 21.58	20.26	16.43	14.48	13.92
Uganda	746	....	....	20.16	20.29	21.37	20.86	21.55	22.92	22.66	19.10	18.94	20.60
Zambia	754	113.31	70.56	45.53	53.78	46.69	31.80	40.52	38.80	46.23	45.20	40.57	30.73
Zimbabwe	698	36.33	34.86	34.73	34.23	32.55	42.06	55.39	68.21	38.02	36.48	97.29	278.92
Asia													
Bangladesh	513	15.00	14.50	14.00	14.00	14.00	14.00	14.13	15.50	15.83	16.00	16.00	14.75
Bhutan	514	17.00	16.00	16.00	16.00	16.00	16.00	16.00	16.00	15.75	15.25	15.00	....
Cambodia	522	....	....	18.70	18.80	18.40	18.33	17.56	17.34	16.50	16.23	18.47	17.62
China, P.R.: Mainland	924	10.98	10.98	12.06	10.08	8.64	6.39	5.85	5.85	5.85	5.31	5.31	5.58
China, P.R.: Hong Kong	532	6.50	8.50	8.75	8.50	9.50	9.00	8.50	9.50	5.13	5.00	5.00	5.00
China, P.R.: Macao	546	6.50	7.95	9.90	9.56	9.73	10.97	9.46	9.89	7.99	6.11	6.00	....
Fiji	819	11.74	11.28	11.06	11.33	11.03	9.66	8.77	8.40	8.34	8.05	7.60	7.17
India	534	16.25	14.75	15.46	15.96	13.83	13.54	12.54	12.29	12.08	11.92	11.46	10.92
Indonesia	536	20.59	17.76	18.85	19.22	21.82	32.15	27.66	18.46	18.55	18.95	16.94	14.12
Korea	542	8.58	8.50	9.00	8.84	† 11.88	15.28	9.40	8.55	7.71	6.77	6.24	5.90
Lao People's Dem.Rep	544	† 25.33	24.00	† 25.67	27.00	....	29.28	32.00	32.00	26.17	29.33	30.50	29.25
Malaysia	548	10.03	8.76	8.73	9.94	10.63	12.13	8.56	7.67	7.13	6.53	6.30	6.05
Maldives	556	....	....	....	15.00	15.00	15.00	12.50	13.00	13.00	13.54	14.00	13.17
Micronesia, Fed.Sts	868	....	....	15.00	15.00	15.00	15.00	15.17	15.33	15.33	15.28	15.00	15.38

National Interest Rates

		1993	1994	1995	1996	1997	1998	1999	2000	2001	2002	2003	2004
							Lending Rates (60p)						
							(Period averages in percent per annum)						
Asia(Cont.)													
Mongolia	948	300.00	279.22	134.37	87.91	82.05	46.77	39.29	32.75	30.24	28.38	26.31	25.38
Myanmar	518	....	16.50	16.50	16.50	16.50	16.50	16.13	15.25	15.00	15.00	15.00	15.00
Nepal	558	....	....	....	12.88	14.54	14.00	11.33	9.46	7.67	....	....	8.50
Papua New Guinea	853	11.29	9.16	13.14	13.30	10.45	17.70	18.90	17.54	16.21	13.89	13.36	13.25
Philippines	566	14.68	15.06	14.68	14.84	16.28	16.78	11.78	10.91	12.40	9.14	9.47	10.08
Samoa	862	12.00	12.00	12.00	12.00	12.00	11.50	11.50	11.00	9.93	9.75	9.75	9.75
Singapore	576	5.39	5.88	6.37	6.26	6.32	7.44	5.80	5.83	5.66	5.37	5.31	5.30
Solomon Islands	813	17.80	15.72	16.59	17.78	15.71	14.84	14.50	15.49	15.72	16.42	16.33	16.07
Sri Lanka	524	20.20	18.13	18.04	18.26	14.69	15.03	14.72	16.16	19.39	13.17	10.34	9.47
Thailand	578	11.17	10.90	13.25	13.40	13.65	14.42	8.98	7.83	7.25	6.88	5.94	5.50
Tonga	866	† 9.94	9.48	9.82	10.16	10.02	10.40	10.32	10.35	11.43	11.43	10.15	12.51
Vanuatu	846	16.00	16.00	10.50	10.50	10.50	10.96	10.29	9.85	8.81	7.41	5.90	7.61
Vietnam	582	32.18	....	....	20.10	14.42	14.40	12.70	10.55	9.42	9.06	9.48	....
Europe													
Albania	914	29.58	23.67	† 19.65	23.96	....	....	21.62	22.10	19.65	15.30	14.27	11.76
Armenia	911	....	....	111.86	66.36	54.23	48.49	38.85	31.57	26.69	21.14	20.83	18.63
Azerbaijan, Republic of	912	....	....	....	....	....	....	19.48	19.66	19.71	17.37	15.46	15.72
Belarus	913	71.63	148.50	175.00	62.33	31.80	26.99	51.04	67.67	46.97	36.88	23.98	16.91
Bosnia & Herzegovina	963	....	....	....	....	....	73.50	24.29	30.50	....	† 12.70	10.87	10.28
Bulgaria	918	58.30	72.58	58.98	123.48	83.96	13.30	12.79	11.52	11.11	9.35	8.82	8.77
Croatia	960	1,443.61	22.91	20.24	22.52	15.47	15.75	14.94	12.07	9.55	† 12.84	11.58	11.75
Cyprus	423	9.00	8.83	8.50	8.50	8.08	8.00	8.00	8.00	† 7.52	7.15	6.95	7.66
Czech Republic	935	14.07	13.12	12.80	12.54	13.20	12.81	8.68	7.16	7.20	6.72	5.95	6.03
Estonia	939	33.66	24.65	19.01	14.87	11.76	15.06	11.09	7.43	7.78	6.70	5.51	5.66
Georgia	915	....	....	....	58.24	50.64	46.00	33.42	32.75	27.25	31.83	32.27	31.23
Hungary	944	25.43	27.40	32.61	27.31	21.77	19.28	16.34	12.60	12.12	10.17	9.60	12.82
Kyrgyz Republic	917	....	....	....	65.02	49.38	73.44	60.86	51.90	37.33	24.81	19.13	29.27
Latvia	941	86.36	55.86	34.56	25.78	15.25	14.29	14.20	11.87	11.17	7.97	5.38	7.45
Lithuania	946	91.84	62.30	27.08	21.56	14.39	12.21	13.09	12.14	9.63	6.84	5.84	5.74
Macedonia, FYR	962	....	159.82	45.95	21.58	21.42	21.03	20.45	18.93	19.35	18.36	16.00	12.44
Malta	181	8.50	8.50	† 7.38	7.77	7.99	8.09	7.70	7.28	6.90	6.04	....	....
Moldova	921	....	....	....	36.67	33.33	30.83	35.54	33.78	28.69	23.52	19.29	20.94
Poland	964	35.25	32.83	† 33.45	26.08	24.96	24.49	16.94	20.01	18.36	12.03	7.30	7.56
Russia	922	....	....	320.31	146.81	† 32.04	41.79	39.72	24.43	17.91	15.71	12.98	11.40
Slovak Republic	936	14.41	14.56	16.85	13.92	18.65	21.17	21.07	14.89	11.24	10.25	8.46	9.07
Slovenia	961	48.61	38.87	23.36	22.60	20.02	16.09	12.38	15.77	15.05	13.17	10.75	8.65
Tajikistan	923	....	....	....	....	75.52	50.89	26.24	25.59	21.05	† 14.20	16.57	20.32
Ukraine	926	184.25	250.28	122.70	79.88	49.12	54.50	54.95	41.53	32.28	25.35	17.89	17.40
Middle East													
Bahrain, Kingdom of	419	10.95	10.83	11.83	12.45	12.33	11.92	11.86	11.73	10.81	8.50	....	....
Egypt	469	18.30	16.51	16.47	15.58	13.79	13.02	12.97	13.22	13.29	13.79	13.53	13.38
Israel	436	16.44	17.45	20.22	20.68	18.71	16.18	16.36	12.87	10.03	9.89	10.65	7.44
Jordan	439	10.23	10.45	10.66	11.25	12.25	12.61	12.33	11.80	10.94	10.18	9.30	8.26
Kuwait	443	7.95	7.61	8.37	8.77	8.80	8.93	8.56	8.87	7.88	6.48	5.42	5.64
Lebanon	446	28.53	23.88	24.69	25.21	20.29	....	19.48	18.15	17.19	16.58	13.43	10.81
Libya	672	7.00	....	....	....	....	....	7.00	7.00	7.00	7.00	7.00	6.08
Oman	449	8.49	8.57	9.38	9.23	9.30	10.09	10.32	10.06	9.23	8.55	8.23	7.57
Syrian Arab Republic	463	9.00	9.00	9.00	9.00	9.00	9.00	9.00	9.00	9.00	9.00	....	....
Qatar	453	7.20	8.86	....	....	....	....	....	....	....	....	....	....
Western Hemisphere													
ECCU	309	11.81	11.71	11.94	11.74	11.77	11.60	11.91	11.98	11.55	11.47	13.34	13.49
Anguilla	312	8.29	12.84	12.60	11.95	11.37	11.16	11.31	11.32	10.74	10.35	11.42	10.99
Antigua and Barbuda	311	12.68	13.15	12.70	12.26	11.98	12.20	12.07	12.17	11.62	11.39	12.82	12.39
Dominica	321	11.92	11.61	11.50	11.43	11.17	11.27	11.40	11.68	11.14	10.97	11.50	8.94
Grenada	328	11.83	11.03	11.08	9.99	11.24	11.73	11.62	11.60	10.19	11.31	12.05	10.18
Montserrat	351	13.12	13.06	12.63	12.37	12.37	12.15	11.52	11.52	11.52	11.34	12.10	10.95
St. Kitts and Nevis	361	10.28	10.94	10.89	10.92	11.16	11.42	11.21	11.10	11.08	10.89	12.22	10.25
St. Lucia	362	11.81	11.06	12.68	12.82	12.68	11.40	12.79	13.06	12.97	12.59	15.00	11.07
St. Vincent & Grens	364	11.92	11.73	11.07	11.23	11.29	11.31	11.55	11.46	11.63	11.56	11.83	9.66
Argentina	213	....	10.06	17.85	10.51	9.24	10.64	11.04	11.09	27.71	51.68	19.15	6.78
Aruba	314	10.60	10.60	10.60	10.30	10.00	....	† 13.14	12.07	12.10	13.08	11.50	11.58
Bahamas, The	313	7.46	6.88	6.75	6.75	6.75	6.75	6.38	6.00	6.00	6.00	6.00	6.00
Barbados	316	8.92	9.08	10.00	10.00	9.83	9.75	9.40	10.19	9.58	8.50	8.50	8.33
Belize	339	14.37	14.78	15.69	16.30	16.29	16.50	16.27	16.01	15.45	14.83	14.35	13.94
Bolivia	218	53.88	55.57	51.02	55.97	50.05	39.41	35.37	34.60	20.06	20.63	17.66	14.47
Brazil	223	....	....	....	....	78.19	86.36	80.44	56.83	57.62	62.88	67.08	55.08
Chile	228	24.35	20.34	18.16	17.37	15.67	20.17	12.62	14.84	11.89	7.76	6.18	5.13
Colombia	233	35.81	40.47	42.72	41.99	34.22	42.24	† 25.77	18.79	20.72	16.33	15.19	15.08
Costa Rica	238	30.02	33.03	36.70	26.27	22.48	22.47	25.74	24.89	23.83	26.42	25.58	23.43
Dominican Republic	243	29.89	28.68	30.68	23.73	21.01	25.64	25.05	26.80	24.26	26.06	31.39	32.63
Ecuador	248	47.83	43.99	55.67	54.50	43.02	49.55	† 16.53	16.26	15.46	15.08	13.08	9.65
El Salvador	253	19.42	19.03	19.08	18.57	16.05	14.98	15.46	13.96	....	....	....	....
Guatemala	258	24.73	22.93	21.16	22.72	† 18.64	16.56	19.51	20.88	18.96	16.86	14.98	13.81
Guyana	336	19.36	18.36	19.22	17.79	17.04	16.77	17.11	17.30	17.01	16.33	14.99	14.54
Haiti	263	....	....	....	....	21.00	23.62	22.88	25.09	28.63	25.67	30.58	34.08
Honduras	268	22.06	24.68	26.95	29.74	32.07	30.69	30.15	26.82	23.76	22.69	20.80	19.88
Jamaica	343	43.71	49.46	43.58	39.83	32.86	31.59	27.01	23.35	20.61	18.50	18.89	18.14
Mexico	273	17.73	19.30	59.43	36.39	22.14	26.36	23.74	16.93	12.80	8.20	6.91	7.22
Netherlands Antilles	353	12.59	12.73	12.93	13.21	13.29	13.58	13.60	9.98	10.44	10.14	11.26	10.56
Nicaragua	278	20.23	20.14	19.89	20.72	21.02	21.63	† 17.57	18.14	18.55	18.30	15.55	13.49
Panama	283	10.06	10.15	11.10	10.62	10.63	10.82	10.05	† 10.48	10.97	10.58	9.93	8.82
Paraguay	288	30.78	† 35.47	33.94	31.88	27.79	30.49	30.21	26.78	28.25	38.66	49.99	33.54

National Interest Rates

		1993	1994	1995	1996	1997	1998	1999	2000	2001	2002	2003	2004
							Lending Rates (60p) *(Period averages in percent per annum)*						
Western Hemisphere(Cont.)													
Peru..	**293**	97.37	53.56	27.16	26.07	29.96	30.80	30.79	27.91	20.43	14.73	14.21	14.49
Suriname.......................................	**366**	9.35	15.38	40.18	35.78	33.13	27.50	27.33	28.95	25.73	22.18	21.04	20.44
Trinidad and Tobago......................	**369**	15.50	15.98	15.17	15.79	15.33	17.33	17.04	16.50	15.67	12.48	11.17	9.31
Uruguay...	**298**	90.55	88.46	92.20	85.14	66.57	53.89	49.57	45.63	48.11	† 117.29	79.89	29.58
Venezuela, Rep. Bol........................	**299**	59.90	54.66	39.74	39.41	23.69	46.35	32.13	25.20	22.45	36.58	25.19	18.50

National Interest Rates

		1993	1994	1995	1996	1997	1998	1999	2000	2001	2002	2003	2004
						Government Bond Yields (61)							
						(Average yields to maturity in percent per annum)							
Industrial Countries													
United States	111	5.87	7.08	6.58	6.44	6.35	5.26	5.64	6.03	5.02	4.61	4.02	4.27
Canada	156	7.85	8.63	8.28	7.50	6.42	5.47	5.69	5.89	5.78	5.66	5.28	5.08
Australia	193	7.28	9.04	9.17	8.17	6.89	5.50	6.08	6.26	5.63	5.82	5.36	5.61
Japan	158	3.69	3.71	2.53	2.23	1.69	1.10	† 1.77	1.75	1.33	1.25	1.01	1.50
New Zealand	196	6.69	7.48	7.94	8.04	7.21	6.47	6.13	6.85	6.12	6.28	5.51	5.98
Euro Area	163	....	8.18	8.73	7.23	5.96	4.70	4.65	5.44	5.03	4.92	4.16	4.14
Austria	122	6.64	6.69	6.47	5.30	4.79	4.29	4.09	....	....	....	....	....
Belgium	124	7.19	7.82	7.45	6.45	5.74	4.72	4.81	5.58	5.13	4.96	4.18	4.15
Finland	172	8.84	9.03	8.78	....	....	....	4.72	5.48	5.04	4.98	4.14	4.11
France	132	6.91	7.35	7.59	6.39	5.58	4.72	4.69	5.45	5.05	4.93	4.18	4.15
Germany	134	6.28	6.67	6.50	5.63	5.08	4.39	4.26	5.24	4.70	4.61	3.81	3.75
Greece	174	....	....	....	....	....	8.48	6.30	6.10	5.30	5.12	4.27	4.26
Ireland	178	7.72	8.19	8.30	7.48	6.49	4.99	....	....	....	....	....	....
Italy	136	11.31	10.56	12.21	9.40	6.86	4.90	4.73	5.58	5.19	5.03	4.25	4.26
Luxembourg	137	6.93	6.38	6.05	5.21	5.39	5.29	....	....	....	....	....	....
Netherlands	138	6.51	7.20	7.20	6.49	5.81	4.87	4.92	5.51	5.17	5.00	4.18	4.10
Portugal	182	12.45	10.83	10.34	7.25	5.48	4.09	....	....	....	....	....	....
Spain	184	10.16	9.69	11.04	8.18	5.84	4.55	4.30	5.36	4.87	4.62	3.52	3.59
Denmark	128	7.08	7.41	7.58	6.04	5.08	4.59	4.30	5.54	....	4.57	3.53	3.32
Iceland	176	6.80	5.02	7.18	5.61	5.49	4.73	4.28	5.35	5.33	5.23	4.41	3.88
Norway	142	6.52	7.13	6.82	5.94	5.13	5.35	5.38	6.38	6.31	6.33	4.50	3.60
Sweden	144	8.54	9.52	10.24	8.06	6.61	4.99	4.98	5.37	5.11	5.30	4.63	....
Switzerland	146	4.05	5.23	3.73	3.63	3.08	† 2.71	3.62	3.55	3.56	2.40	2.78	2.38
United Kingdom	112	7.87	8.05	8.26	8.10	7.09	5.45	4.70	4.68	4.78	4.83	4.64	4.77
Developing Countries													
Africa													
Botswana	616	....	....	....	....	....	....	....	....	....	....	10.46	10.07
Ethiopia	644	13.00	13.00	13.00	13.00	....	....	....	....	....	....	† 3.05	4.00
Ghana	652	....	....	....	....	....	....	....	....	....	....	....	21.50
Malawi	676	....	23.50	38.58	42.67	39.25	....	....	....	....	....	....	....
Namibia	728	13.94	14.63	16.11	15.48	14.70	15.10	14.90	13.81	11.39	12.86	12.72	11.88
Seychelles	718	14.40	14.38	13.25	13.25	11.63	8.96	8.58	8.22	8.13	8.25	5.96	6.58
South Africa	199	13.97	14.83	16.11	15.48	14.70	15.12	14.90	13.79	11.41	11.50	9.62	9.53
Asia													
Fiji	819	7.26	6.49	6.69	7.41	7.08	6.49	6.17	5.57	4.79	4.28	3.27	2.56
Korea	542	12.08	12.30	12.40	10.90	11.70	12.80	8.72	8.50	6.66	6.47	4.93	4.45
Malaysia	548	6.35	5.11	6.51	6.39	6.87	7.66	5.63	5.11	3.54	3.47	3.60	4.09
Myanmar	518	....	10.50	10.50	13.13	14.00	14.00	† 11.00	9.00	9.00	9.00	9.00	9.00
Nepal	558	....	9.00	3.00	9.00	9.00	9.00	8.75	8.50	8.50	8.25	7.50	6.63
Pakistan	564	7.40	7.07	6.63	6.06	5.43	4.79	4.16	....	....	....	....	....
Philippines	566	....	13.25	14.25	13.99	13.01	† 17.99	12.33	11.77	13.40	8.69	8.72	10.27
Samoa	862	13.50	13.50	13.50	13.50	13.50	13.50	13.50	13.50	13.50	13.50	13.50	13.50
Solomon Islands	813	13.00	13.00	13.00	11.50	11.75	12.50	12.88	13.00	13.00	13.00	13.00	13.00
Sri Lanka	524	16.25	....	....	....	....	....	....	....	....	....	....	....
Thailand	578	10.75	10.75	10.75	10.75	10.75	10.25	6.69	6.95	5.82	5.07	3.76	5.09
Vanuatu	846	8.00	8.00	8.00	8.00	8.00	8.00	8.50	8.50	8.50	8.50	8.50	8.50
Europe													
Armenia	911	....	....	....	....	....	....	....	25.51	23.15	17.44	15.71	8.21
Bulgaria	918	....	56.86	49.76	....	....	10.10	10.05	7.38	6.70	6.75	....	....
Czech Republic	935	....	....	....	....	....	....	....	6.72	4.84	3.17	3.77	3.33
Slovak Republic	936	....	....	....	....	....	....	....	8.34	8.06	6.91	4.99	5.02
Western Hemisphere													
Honduras	268	10.40	23.11	27.24	35.55	29.59	20.34	16.04	14.79	15.28	11.97	11.26	11.67
Jamaica	343	24.82	26.82	26.85	26.87	26.85	....	....	....	....	....	....	....
Mexico	273	....	....	51.74	32.81	21.44	....	20.11	† 15.81	† 10.28	10.13	8.98	9.54
Netherlands Antilles	353	8.14	7.48	8.02	8.25	8.67	8.60	8.75	8.77	9.00	8.20	6.72	7.09
Venezuela, Rep. Bol	299	41.03	54.73	53.38	49.09	25.41	47.88	† 31.12	21.03	22.12	38.51	32.15	15.57

International Interest Rates

		1993	1994	1995	1996	1997	1998	1999	2000	2001	2002	2003	2004
London Interbank Offer Rates on SDR Deposits (99260lsa, 60lsb, 60lsc) *(Period averages in percent per annum)*													
Three-Month	992	4.74	3.86	4.60	3.72	3.91	....	....	....	....	....	....	....
Six-Month	992	4.64	3.97	4.63	3.79	4.00	....	....	....	....	....	....	....
One-Year	992	4.59	4.22	4.72	3.95	4.14	....	....	....	....	....	....	....
London Interbank Offer Rates on US Dollar Deposits (11160lda, 60ldb, 60ldc, 60ldd, 60lde, 60ldf) *(Period averages in percent per annum)*													
Overnight	111	3.05	4.24	5.90	5.35	5.54	....	....	....	3.98	1.75	1.19	1.40
Seven-Day	111	3.08	4.31	5.93	5.40	5.58	5.53	5.16	6.36	3.95	1.76	1.20	1.44
One-Month	111	3.16	4.46	5.97	5.44	5.64	5.60	5.25	6.41	3.88	1.76	1.21	1.50
Three-Month	111	3.29	4.74	6.04	5.51	5.76	5.59	5.41	6.53	3.78	1.79	1.22	1.62
Six-Month	111	3.41	5.07	6.10	5.59	5.86	5.56	5.53	6.65	3.73	1.87	1.23	1.79
One-Year	111	3.64	5.59	6.24	5.78	6.08	5.53	5.71	6.83	3.86	2.19	1.36	2.12
London Interbank Offer Rates on Three-Month Deposits (60ea) (Pound sterling rates relate to Paris market) *(Period averages in percent per annum)*													
French Franc	132	8.57	5.88	6.68	3.94	3.48	3.64	....	....	....	....	....	....
Deutsche Mark	134	7.30	5.36	4.53	3.31	3.37	3.60	2.96	....	....	....	....	....
Japanese Yen	158	3.00	2.31	1.27	.63	.63	.71	.22	.28	.15	.08	.06	.05
Netherlands Guilder	138	6.85	5.23	4.47	3.03	3.37	3.55	....	....	....	....	....	....
Swiss Franc	146	4.96	4.16	3.09	2.05	1.71	1.60	1.39	3.10	2.94	1.18	.33	.47
Pound Sterling	112	6.05	5.54	6.73	6.09	6.90	7.39	5.54	6.19	5.04	4.06	3.73	4.64
Euro	163	....	....	....	....	....	....	2.96	4.41	4.26	3.32	2.33	2.11
London Interbank Offer Rates on Six-Month Deposits (60eb) (Pound sterling rates relate to Paris market) *(Period averages in percent per annum)*													
French Franc	132	7.92	5.95	6.61	4.02	3.54	3.68	....	....	....	....	....	....
Deutsche Mark	134	6.95	5.35	4.57	3.31	3.42	3.66	3.05	....	....	....	....	....
Japanese Yen	158	2.96	2.36	1.26	.71	.65	.71	.24	.31	.15	.09	.07	.06
Netherlands Guilder	138	6.57	5.25	4.55	3.08	3.46	3.64	....	....	....	....	....	....
Swiss Franc	146	4.76	4.23	3.16	2.09	1.78	1.68	1.55	3.26	2.87	1.24	.38	.59
Pound Sterling	112	5.93	5.80	6.91	6.13	7.04	7.32	5.62	6.31	5.02	4.16	3.76	4.77
Euro	163	....	....	....	....	....	....	3.05	4.54	4.15	3.35	2.30	2.15
Discounts (-) or Premiums (60f) on Three-Month Forward Exchange Rates *(End of period in percent per annum based on end-of-period quotation of the currencies against the US dollar)*													
Canada	156	-3.84	-3.99	-.23	22.78	....	....	....	....	....	....	....	....
Australia	193	....	....	....	....	....	....	....	-.65	-2.13	....	....	....
Japan	158	1.18	3.69	4.86	5.12	5.45	6.25	6.25	5.75	2.78	....	....	....
Austria	122	-2.21	-1.13	-1.67	2.34	1.99	2.32	....	....	....	....	....	....
Belgium	124	-3.54	1.10	1.43	2.44	2.17	1.90	....	....	....	....	....	....
Denmark	128	-3.30	.20	.80	1.85	1.74	.99	2.36	.97	-1.78	-1.72	-1.09	.50
Finland	172	-2.61	.43	1.14	2.32	2.12	1.85	....	....	....	....	....	....
France	132	....	....	....	....	....	....	....	....	....	....	....	....
Germany	134	-2.66	1.24	1.81	2.26	2.10	1.89	....	....	....	....	....	....
Italy	136	-7.10	-.87	-4.64	-1.00	-2.62	.51	....	....	....	....	....	....
Netherlands	138	....	....	....	....	....	....	....	—	—	....	....	....
Norway	142	-2.47	.09	-1.08	.89	1.98	1.12	.32	-.99	-4.44	-4.84	-.60	.66
Spain	184	-.32	-3.67	-7.31	.79	4.81	3.50	....	....	....	....	....	....
Sweden	144	-1.83	-1.66	-.36	-.37	-.58	.84	2.54	4.07	2.36	1.99	-1.71	-.48
Switzerland	146	-.95	1.98	3.30	2.50	4.21	3.34	4.65	3.30	-.17	.81	1.26	1.63
United Kingdom	112	-1.91	-.12	-.86	-.89	-1.77	....	....	....	....	....	....	....
SDR Interest Rate (99260s) and Rate of Remuneration (99260r) *(Period averages in percent per annum)*													
SDR Interest Rate	992	4.6394	4.2858	4.5847	3.8998	4.0719	4.1052	3.4759	4.4397	3.4258	2.2416	1.6491	1.8358
United States (3-Mo.T-Bill Rate)	111	3.06	4.35	5.65	5.14	5.20	4.90	4.77	6.00	3.48	1.63	1.02	1.39
United Kingdom (3-Mo.T-Bill Rate)	112	5.35	5.18	6.40	5.89	6.62	7.23	5.14	5.83	4.79	3.96	3.55	4.44
France (3-Mo.T-Bill Rate)	132	8.41	5.79	6.58	3.84	3.35	3.45	2.72	4.23	4.26	3.28	2.27	....
Germany (3-Mo. Interbank Rate)	134	7.24	5.31	4.48	3.27	3.30	3.52	2.94	4.37	4.25	3.30	2.32	2.09
Japan (3-Mo.Certif. of Deposits)	158	2.97	2.24	1.22	.59	.62	.72	.15	.23	....	....	....	....
Rate of Remuneration	992	4.6394	4.2858	4.5847	3.8998	4.0719	4.1052	3.4759	4.4397	3.4258	2.2416	1.6491	1.8358

Real Effective Exchange Rate Indices

		1993	1994	1995	1996	1997	1998	1999	2000	2001	2002	2003	2004
							(2000=100)						
						Based on Relative Unit Labor Costs (65um.110)							
Industrial Countries													
United States	111	87.1	87.3	81.0	82.0	87.2	90.6	89.7	100.0	104.0	102.4	92.8	85.8
Canada	156	109.7	99.8	99.9	103.6	106.3	103.1	102.5	100.0	99.9	97.7	105.9	113.4
Japan	158	101.3	110.8	111.8	93.4	88.7	85.7	96.3	100.0	92.5	83.3	77.8	76.1
Euro Area	163	125.1	124.9	131.6	131.0	118.5	114.6	110.0	100.0	99.4	103.7	115.9	121.1
Austria	122	126.2	124.1	119.4	114.1	106.5	104.6	100.9	100.0	100.0	99.1	101.5	104.7
Belgium	124	117.5	117.0	120.8	113.4	103.9	104.5	102.5	100.0	101.9	105.4	109.3	113.1
Finland	172	107.0	112.1	127.1	120.2	114.7	114.1	110.0	100.0	104.4	105.6	109.1	111.7
France	132	119.7	116.5	117.0	115.8	108.0	109.9	107.1	100.0	98.2	98.7	106.3	108.0
Germany *	134	108.0	112.5	123.5	121.1	112.1	106.9	106.4	100.0	98.2	100.1	103.3	101.1
Ireland	178	188.0	180.5	165.2	165.7	153.9	128.5	112.8	100.0	103.4	96.1	98.4	101.6
Italy	136	102.7	97.3	89.2	102.0	105.2	104.6	103.8	100.0	102.6	107.7	115.4	122.9
Netherlands	138	112.7	107.7	110.3	106.3	102.8	104.4	103.0	100.0	103.6	107.0	114.2	116.0
Spain	184	102.0	95.3	94.2	98.1	97.1	99.4	100.3	100.0	102.6	105.4	107.9	110.2
Denmark	128	110.7	100.8	103.8	109.2	102.6	103.8	104.6	100.0	99.9	102.7	109.5	113.6
Norway	142	77.8	80.3	85.0	86.4	91.5	92.3	97.0	100.0	103.1	115.4	114.1	111.4
Sweden	144	97.1	93.5	100.2	113.5	105.1	105.7	103.5	100.0	97.6	94.1	94.9	95.0
Switzerland	146	90.6	95.8	101.2	99.1	95.7	100.0	99.0	100.0	104.3	110.0	110.9	113.6
United Kingdom	112	65.9	68.0	68.7	72.8	88.9	96.7	96.7	100.0	96.7	99.0	91.6	94.1
							(2000=100)						
						Based on Relative Consumer Prices (..rec)							
United States	111	83.8	82.7	80.0	83.4	89.5	95.9	95.3	100.0	107.4	107.0	98.0	92.6
Canada	156	114.2	104.0	100.6	102.3	103.7	99.1	98.0	100.0	99.2	98.3	106.7	111.1
Japan	158	98.4	103.3	105.0	88.6	83.6	82.2	93.0	100.0	89.5	82.9	81.4	81.6
Euro Area	163	121.4	120.6	126.7	126.4	114.8	117.6	111.9	100.0	103.8	109.2	122.0	126.4
Austria	122	105.8	106.5	110.5	108.2	104.5	104.5	102.5	100.0	101.1	102.1	104.3	105.6
Belgium	124	107.0	108.8	112.7	110.6	105.4	105.2	103.4	100.0	100.8	101.9	105.4	106.5
Finland	172	98.8	105.2	114.7	110.1	105.7	106.8	104.0	100.0	99.9	102.2	106.5	106.1
France	132	110.3	110.0	113.0	112.8	108.0	108.4	105.2	100.0	100.1	101.6	106.4	107.8
Germany *	134	113.6	113.9	119.0	115.1	109.4	110.0	106.4	100.0	100.8	102.1	106.7	108.1
Ireland	178	108.6	108.9	109.6	111.7	111.4	106.4	103.2	100.0	103.7	108.7	117.4	118.5
Italy	136	102.4	99.4	92.6	103.4	104.0	106.3	104.2	100.0	101.4	103.7	109.3	111.0
Netherlands	138	105.7	106.4	110.9	109.1	104.0	104.9	104.1	100.0	103.3	106.6	111.6	112.0
Spain	184	109.4	104.3	106.1	108.4	103.3	103.3	102.5	100.0	101.9	104.4	109.5	111.6
Denmark	128	103.2	102.6	107.0	106.2	103.1	105.1	104.2	100.0	101.6	103.7	108.5	109.5
Norway	142	103.0	101.1	104.0	103.8	105.1	102.1	101.8	100.0	103.8	112.4	110.2	106.0
Sweden	144	107.0	105.4	105.1	114.0	108.5	104.9	102.0	100.0	92.2	94.5	99.8	100.7
Switzerland	146	102.7	107.4	114.4	111.3	102.9	104.2	102.3	100.0	103.1	106.8	106.4	105.4
United Kingdom	112	78.4	78.5	75.7	77.5	91.2	96.9	96.6	100.0	98.3	98.9	95.4	100.8
							(2000=100)						
						Based on Relative Normalized Unit Labor Costs (..reu)							
United States	111	88.7	87.1	80.3	82.1	86.6	91.8	90.8	100.0	103.6	104.6	95.3	88.0
Canada	156	110.9	104.0	102.9	103.8	107.3	101.2	100.8	100.0	99.5	96.3	102.8	109.5
Japan	158	99.4	105.6	110.7	94.3	89.8	83.7	94.6	100.0	89.3	80.0	76.6	76.2
Euro Area	163	126.3	124.6	132.1	133.3	120.2	117.1	112.2	100.0	101.9	105.4	116.4	119.9
Austria	122	126.4	124.4	121.6	115.8	109.1	107.4	105.3	100.0	99.2	99.4	101.7	103.7
Belgium	124	114.5	114.2	119.4	114.4	109.5	109.5	105.5	100.0	101.5	104.6	108.6	111.3
Finland	172	107.6	113.5	126.7	118.5	111.7	111.0	107.1	100.0	103.0	102.9	106.0	108.3
France	132	116.1	115.2	117.3	113.8	108.0	107.3	105.4	100.0	97.6	98.7	102.7	103.9
Germany *	134	105.4	109.0	118.2	117.0	109.5	107.2	104.7	100.0	99.8	99.2	101.7	100.1
Ireland	178	178.2	165.4	154.8	146.9	137.3	123.6	113.8	100.0	101.6	101.9	105.3	105.4
Italy	136	101.7	96.6	89.9	103.4	105.4	104.2	104.1	100.0	103.5	106.2	112.9	118.4
Netherlands	138	106.2	107.7	111.8	108.4	102.7	104.5	103.6	100.0	103.1	106.1	111.3	113.2
Spain	184	108.8	102.2	101.4	104.2	101.2	103.0	102.6	100.0	103.2	107.4	114.1	117.2
Denmark	128	103.4	103.1	107.4	105.9	102.8	104.9	104.4	100.0	101.9	104.2	109.6	112.0
Norway	142	83.7	83.8	89.0	91.3	94.8	95.8	99.6	100.0	107.1	120.5	119.8	116.0
Sweden	144	96.6	96.1	97.5	110.0	107.0	105.5	101.8	100.0	92.3	91.8	94.3	95.7
Switzerland	146	86.7	94.2	100.9	101.1	97.4	102.9	102.1	100.0	105.6	111.2	112.0	113.3
United Kingdom	112	72.9	74.8	72.8	75.5	89.4	95.0	96.2	100.0	99.5	99.7	94.2	98.7

* Data refer to the former
Federal Republic of Germany

Production and Labor Indices

Industrial Production

Index Numbers (2000=100): (66..i)

		1993	1994	1995	1996	1997	1998	1999	2000	2001	2002	2003	2004
Industrial Countries	110	80.2	83.5	85.9	87.8	92.0	93.2	95.5	100.0	97.0	96.4	97.1	100.5
United States	111	70.0	73.8	77.5	80.8	86.7	91.7	95.9	100.0	96.4	96.2	96.1	100.1
Canada	156	....	....	78.6	79.5	84.0	86.9	92.1	100.0	96.1	97.5	98.3	101.8
Australia	193	81.6	85.8	87.1	90.5	92.1	94.6	95.1	100.0	101.4	104.3	104.6	....
Japan	158	90.8	92.0	95.5	97.7	101.2	94.5	94.8	100.0	93.7	92.6	95.4	100.5
New Zealand	196	71.1	75.4	94.6	96.6	97.0	93.9	95.7	100.0	99.9	104.3	104.9	109.3
Euro Area													
Austria	122	68.2	70.9	74.5	75.2	80.0	86.6	91.8	100.0	102.8	103.6	105.6	112.0
Belgium	124	80.1	81.8	86.5	87.0	91.0	94.1	94.9	100.0	99.0	100.3	101.0	104.3
Finland	172	57.5	64.0	69.1	71.3	77.3	84.3	89.0	100.0	99.8	102.0	103.2	107.6
France	132	† 80.6	84.0	75.1	75.0	78.1	80.9	96.6	100.0	101.2	100.2	85.4	87.4
Germany	134	84.0	86.7	† 87.4	87.6	90.3	93.6	94.7	100.0	100.2	99.2	99.6	102.6
Greece	174	84.7	85.4	† 87.1	86.8	88.8	96.0	95.2	100.0	97.5	97.4	97.0	98.1
Ireland	178	36.8	41.2	† 49.6	53.6	63.0	75.5	86.6	100.0	110.2	118.5	124.3	124.9
Italy	136	83.1	88.0	92.9	91.3	94.9	96.0	95.9	100.0	99.0	97.4	96.9	96.2
Luxembourg	137	75.2	79.7	† 81.3	81.4	86.1	86.0	95.9	100.0	103.1	105.2	110.7	117.8
Netherlands	138	86.3	90.5	90.9	93.1	93.3	95.3	96.6	100.0	100.4	100.1	97.7	100.2
Portugal	182	77.8	77.7	84.7	89.1	91.4	96.6	99.5	100.0	103.1	102.7	102.6	94.6
Spain	184	74.3	80.0	83.9	82.7	88.5	93.4	95.8	100.0	98.5	98.7	100.0	101.6
Denmark	128	75.4	83.2	86.5	87.6	92.0	94.7	94.9	100.0	102.0	103.0	102.3	102.0
Norway	142	79.6	85.2	90.4	95.0	98.4	97.4	97.1	100.0	98.7	99.6	95.5	97.4
Sweden	144	....	....	82.3	83.0	87.1	91.2	94.2	100.0	98.9	99.9	102.2	106.8
Switzerland	146	77.3	80.6	82.2	82.2	86.0	89.1	92.2	100.0	99.3	94.2	94.6	98.4
United Kingdom	112	87.2	91.8	† 93.4	94.7	96.0	97.0	98.1	100.0	98.4	96.0	95.5	96.2

Wages

Index Numbers (2000=100): (65, 65ey, 65..c)

		1993	1994	1995	1996	1997	1998	1999	2000	2001	2002	2003	2004
Industrial Countries	110	84.2	86.5	88.9	91.4	93.7	95.5	97.6	100.0	102.0	103.9	106.0	108.0
United States	111	81.7	84.0	86.2	89.0	91.7	93.9	96.7	100.0	103.1	106.8	109.9	112.7
Canada	156	88.2	89.7	90.9	93.6	94.3	96.2	97.5	100.0	101.6	104.4	107.8	110.6
Australia	193	75.8	78.4	82.4	85.6	89.1	92.8	95.3	100.0	104.9	110.3	116.5	120.9
Japan	158	92.4	94.6	96.5	98.3	99.8	99.5	99.8	100.0	99.5	97.9	97.9	97.9
New Zealand	196	† 89.0	90.0	91.3	93.1	95.2	97.0	98.5	100.0	101.9	104.1	106.5	108.9
Euro Area													
Austria	122	92.1	95.8	100.0	† 90.9	92.9	95.2	98.0	100.0	102.2	104.8	106.8	114.9
Belgium	124	85.4	87.5	89.3	91.1	93.0	95.3	97.9	100.0	102.8	105.4	107.4	109.8
Finland	172	79.5	81.1	84.7	88.2	90.4	93.6	96.1	100.0	104.8	108.9	113.6	118.2
France	132	83.8	86.3	87.0	88.5	91.0	93.6	95.7	100.0	104.5	108.4	112.8	116.1
Germany	134	81.2	83.2	86.9	91.0	92.7	94.6	97.2	100.0	103.3	106.5	108.0	110.0
Greece	174	....	....	....	....	....	....	96.9	100.0	101.5	105.9	124.3	130.4
Ireland	178	75.2	77.4	79.1	81.1	85.0	88.5	93.7	100.0	109.1	115.2	122.6	128.7
Italy	136	81.7	84.6	87.2	90.0	93.2	95.8	98.0	100.0	101.8	104.5	107.2	110.5
Netherlands	138	84.2	85.7	86.6	88.1	90.8	93.7	96.4	100.0	103.9	107.7	110.6	112.3
Spain	184	77.3	80.7	84.6	89.1	92.7	95.3	97.7	100.0	103.8	108.1	112.7	118.8
Denmark	128	....	79.3	82.3	85.4	88.8	92.6	96.5	100.0	104.2	108.3	112.3	115.7
Iceland	176	96.3	96.8	100.0	75.1	81.2	87.5	92.9	100.0	109.6	115.5	121.7	129.0
Norway	142	....	....	....	....	....	91.3	96.1	100.0	104.5	110.0	115.2	120.0
Sweden	144	75.0	78.2	82.4	87.8	91.7	95.0	96.7	100.0	102.9	106.4	109.4	112.3
Switzerland	146	93.5	94.9	96.2	97.4	97.8	98.5	98.8	100.0	102.5	104.3	105.8	106.7
United Kingdom	112	75.2	77.9	80.4	83.2	86.8	91.3	95.7	100.0	104.4	108.1	111.8	116.7

Employment

Index Numbers (2000=100): (67, 67ey, 67..c, 67e, 67eyc)

		1993	1994	1995	1996	1997	1998	1999	2000	2001	2002	2003	2004
Industrial Countries	110	96.7	96.8	97.5	97.6	98.4	99.2	99.5	100.0	99.0	96.8	95.5	95.7
United States	111	84.1	86.7	89.0	90.8	93.2	95.5	97.9	100.0	100.0	98.9	98.6	99.8
Canada	156	82.5	84.2	85.8	87.8	91.0	94.0	96.0	100.0	100.0	100.7	100.4	98.0
Australia	193	94.6	97.8	98.8	99.0	100.5	97.2	95.5	100.0	96.7	97.8	95.8	96.4
Japan	158	116.1	113.5	111.4	109.0	107.8	105.9	102.8	100.0	97.0	92.4	89.4	88.2
New Zealand	196	89.4	100.8	104.7	103.6	100.6	102.8	99.2	100.0	103.1	103.2	99.1	102.5
Euro Area													
Austria	122	97.5	98.0	97.9	97.2	97.5	98.1	99.2	100.0	100.5	100.7	101.6	99.4
Finland	172	85.9	86.4	92.5	93.0	93.8	96.2	98.8	100.0	100.7	99.4	95.2	92.9
France	132	105.5	103.3	102.2	99.4	98.7	99.0	98.7	100.0	101.3	99.3	97.1	94.9
Germany	134	99.4	98.6	98.5	98.3	97.8	98.0	99.4	100.0	100.6	99.8	98.8	106.2
Greece	174	93.5	95.2	96.1	97.3	96.8	100.0	99.7	100.0	99.0	100.7	102.6	108.4
Ireland	178	77.3	80.2	85.1	89.2	94.4	97.1	96.2	100.0	101.0	96.3	92.5	89.8
Italy	136	104.7	102.4	100.7	99.6	98.9	99.8	100.0	100.0	100.8	101.9	103.7	104.5
Luxembourg	137	....	....	....	....	....	....	94.7	100.0	105.6	109.0	111.0	113.9
Netherlands	138	76.4	76.7	86.3	88.4	91.1	94.4	97.6	100.0	103.7	104.4	102.6	102.2
Spain	184	81.8	81.0	83.2	85.6	88.2	91.2	95.5	100.0	102.0	112.3	115.3	118.3
Denmark	128	94.9	93.9	95.8	96.5	98.4	98.8	99.5	100.0	100.1	99.6	98.9	99.9
Norway	142	88.3	89.7	91.6	93.9	96.7	99.1	99.5	100.0	100.4	100.7	100.0	100.3
Sweden	144	96.9	95.6	100.7	101.7	100.4	100.8	100.1	100.0	97.6	93.8	90.7	89.3
Switzerland	146	112.0	107.1	105.7	103.0	100.4	99.9	99.0	100.0	101.4	98.7	95.5	93.8
United Kingdom	112	89.6	90.2	91.3	92.8	94.9	96.7	98.3	100.0	101.1	101.5	101.9	102.6

Producer Prices/Wholesale Prices

		1993	1994	1995	1996	1997	1998	1999	2000	2001	2002	2003	2004
		Percent Change over Previous Year; Calculated from Indices											
World..................	001	**17.1**	**25.9**	**14.9**	**6.4**	**4.7**	**3.7**	**4.7**	**8.0**	**3.7**	**2.4**	**3.8**	**6.1**
Industrial Countries..................	110	**1.0**	**1.2**	**3.3**	**.8**	**.5**	**-1.4**	**.2**	**4.5**	**.9**	**-1.3**	**2.6**	**4.0**
United States..................	111	1.5	1.3	3.6	2.3	-.1	-2.5	.8	5.8	1.1	-2.3	5.3	6.2
Canada..................	156	3.6	6.1	7.4	.4	.9	-.1	1.6	5.1	1.1	.1	-1.1	2.8
Australia..................	193	2.0	.8	4.2	.3	1.2	-4.0	-.9	7.1	3.1	.2	.5	4.0
Japan..................	158	-1.5	-1.7	-.8	-1.6	.7	-1.5	-1.5	.1	-2.3	-2.1	-.8	1.2
New Zealand..................	196	2.4	1.3	.8	.6	.4	.7	1.0	7.6	6.0	.2	-.8	1.7
Euro Area..................	163	....	....	....	.4	1.1	-.8	-.4	5.3	2.2	-.1	1.5	2.1
Austria..................	122	-.4	1.3	.3	—	.4	-.5	-.8	4.0	1.5	-.4	1.6	4.9
Belgium..................	124	-2.5	1.6	3.3	2.2	3.7	-1.9	—	10.6	2.0	-.8	-.4	4.0
Finland..................	172	3.0	1.3	.7	-.9	1.6	-1.4	-.1	8.3	-.3	-1.2	-.1	1.6
France..................	132	-2.8	1.1	6.1	-2.7	-.6	-.9	....	....	....	....	....	....
Germany..................	134	† .2	.6	1.7	-1.2	1.2	-.4	-1.0	3.3	3.0	-.4	1.7	1.6
Greece..................	174	....	....	....	7.8	1.6	2.3	1.5	13.6	3.6	2.3	2.3	3.5
Ireland..................	178	4.7	.9	2.2	.5	-.5	1.5	1.1	6.1	2.9	.2	-5.6	....
Italy..................	136	3.8	3.7	7.9	1.9	1.3	.1	-.3	6.0	1.9	-.2	1.6	2.7
Luxembourg..................	137	-1.3	1.5	3.9	-3.1	1.5	2.4	-3.1	4.8	-.2	-.8	1.2	9.0
Netherlands..................	138	.1	.5	1.5	2.0	1.8	-.2	1.0	4.8	3.0	.8	1.4	3.9
Portugal..................	182	....	....	....	....	....	....	....	....	2.8	.4	.8	2.7
Spain..................	184	2.5	4.3	6.4	1.7	1.0	-.7	.7	5.4	1.7	.7	1.4	3.4
Denmark..................	128	-.5	1.2	2.9	1.1	1.9	-.6	.5	5.9	2.0	.1	.2	2.2
Norway..................	142	-1.0	1.3	2.6	2.2	1.4	.6	3.1	6.9	-4.7	-5.6	3.6	11.8
Sweden..................	144	6.2	4.8	7.7	-1.8	1.2	-.6	1.1	5.8	3.2	.5	-.8	2.3
Switzerland..................	146	.4	-.5	-.1	-1.8	-.7	-1.2	-1.0	.9	.5	-.5	—	1.2
United Kingdom..................	112	3.9	2.5	4.0	2.6	.9	—	.4	1.5	-.3	—	1.5	2.5
Developing Countries..................	200	**63.7**	**87.4**	**39.4**	**17.3**	**12.8**	**13.9**	**12.9**	**14.1**	**8.6**	**9.0**	**5.9**	**9.9**
Africa..................	605	**8.5**	**8.3**	**10.1**	**6.7**	**5.2**	**4.7**	**2.9**	**5.7**	**4.5**	**7.6**	**.5**	**1.2**
Central African Rep..................	626	-1.5	....	....	....	....	—	1.2	6.4	8.9	8.6	3.8	-.5
Morocco..................	686	4.5	2.3	6.5	4.4	-1.6	2.8	-1.7	4.2	-.4	2.2	-4.5	....
South Africa..................	199	6.6	8.3	9.5	6.9	7.1	3.5	5.8	9.2	8.5	14.2	1.7	.7
Tunisia..................	744	4.7	3.4	5.7	3.7	2.4	3.2	.4	3.3	1.8	2.5	2.4	3.8
Zambia..................	754	140.8	70.6	72.0	....	....	....	....	....	....	....	....	....
Zimbabwe..................	698	20.5	22.3	20.8	17.1	12.9	31.5	57.2	....	....	....	....	....
Asia..................	505	**4.0**	**7.3**	**8.8**	**4.6**	**5.1**	**19.1**	**2.2**	**6.5**	**4.8**	**2.0**	**4.5**	**7.6**
China, P.R.: Hong Kong..................	532	.7	2.1	2.7	-.1	-.3	-1.8	-1.6	.2	-1.6	-2.7	-.3	2.3
India..................	534	7.5	10.5	9.3	4.5	4.5	5.9	3.5	6.6	4.8	2.5	5.4	6.6
Indonesia..................	536	3.7	5.4	11.4	7.9	9.0	101.8	10.5	12.5	14.2	2.8	2.1	8.6
Korea..................	542	-2.3	2.7	4.7	3.2	3.8	12.2	-2.1	2.0	-.5	-.3	2.2	6.1
Malaysia..................	548	1.4	4.9	5.5	2.3	2.6	10.8	-3.3	3.1	-5.0	4.5	5.7	9.2
Pakistan..................	564	10.2	19.7	12.8	11.1	11.2	2.3	7.3	4.0	4.6	3.0	6.5	8.4
Philippines..................	566	....	4.1	4.2	4.1	3.5	10.9	7.0	12.5	17.0	2.9	8.1	7.5
Singapore..................	576	-4.4	-.4	—	.1	-1.2	-3.0	2.1	10.1	-1.6	-1.5	2.0	5.1
Sri Lanka..................	524	7.6	5.0	8.8	20.5	6.9	6.2	-.4	1.7	11.7	10.7	3.0	12.6
Thailand..................	578	-.4	4.0	8.2	1.8	5.1	12.2	-4.7	3.9	2.5	1.7	4.0	6.7
Europe..................	170	**43.3**	**199.2**	**130.8**	**42.9**	**33.4**	**17.4**	**39.8**	**35.0**	**20.4**	**13.2**	**-4.5**	**15.9**
Armenia..................	911	....	....	....	....	....	14.6	5.9	-.4	1.1	3.6	8.9	21.0
Belarus..................	913	1,536.3	2,170.8	499.1	34.7	87.5	72.5	355.8	185.6	71.8	40.4	37.5	24.1
Bulgaria..................	918	-82.8	1,146.3	55.7	132.7	971.2	17.0	2.8	17.5	3.7	1.3	4.9	6.0
Croatia..................	960	1,512.4	77.6	.7	1.4	2.3	-1.2	2.6	12.1	1.1	1.8	-.3	3.4
Cyprus..................	423	2.5	3.3	3.6	2.1	2.8	.5	1.2	7.2	1.6	1.4	2.9	4.7
Czech Republic..................	935	9.3	5.3	7.5	4.8	4.9	4.9	1.0	4.9	2.8	-.5	-.3	5.6
Estonia..................	939	....	....	25.6	14.8	8.4	4.2	-1.2	4.9	4.4	.4	.2	2.9
Georgia..................	915	....	....	....	....	....	....	14.3	5.8	3.7	6.0	....	....
Hungary..................	944	13.9	12.3	28.5	21.8	20.3	11.3	5.1	11.7	4.8	-1.4	2.4	3.5
Kazakhstan..................	916	....	....	....	23.9	15.5	.8	18.9	38.0	.3	.2	9.3	16.7
Kyrgyz Republic..................	917	....	215.3	21.8	23.0	26.3	7.9	53.7	30.7	12.0	4.8	4.6	6.1
Latvia..................	941	117.1	16.8	11.9	13.7	4.1	1.9	-4.0	.6	1.7	.9	3.2	8.6
Lithuania..................	946	391.9	44.7	28.3	17.3	4.3	-7.4	1.4	17.5	-3.7	-3.6	-.3	7.7
Poland..................	964	32.2	30.1	25.5	13.2	12.2	7.2	5.5	7.7	1.7	1.2	2.7	7.0
Romania..................	968	165.0	140.5	35.1	49.9	156.9	33.2	44.5	53.4	38.1	23.1	19.5	19.1
Russia..................	922	943.8	337.0	236.5	50.8	15.0	7.0	58.9	46.5	19.2	10.4	16.4	23.4
Slovak Republic..................	936	17.2	10.0	9.0	4.1	4.5	3.3	3.8	9.8	6.6	2.1	8.3	3.4
Slovenia..................	961	21.7	17.7	12.8	6.7	6.1	6.0	2.1	7.6	9.0	5.1	2.5	4.3
Turkey..................	186	58.0	121.3	86.0	75.9	81.8	71.8	53.1	51.4	61.6	50.1	-58.8	14.6
Ukraine..................	926	4,619.3	1,143.8	487.9	51.7	7.7	13.2	31.1	20.9	8.6	3.1	7.8	20.4
Middle East..................	405	**12.0**	**16.0**	**24.6**	**14.3**	**5.5**	**4.5**	**7.9**	**7.4**	**2.2**	**5.3**	**8.0**	**10.0**
Egypt..................	469	8.6	4.6	6.3	8.3	4.2	1.4	.9	1.8	1.0	6.4	14.4	17.1
Iran, I.R. of..................	429	25.6	37.6	60.6	32.9	10.7	11.9	19.2	18.9	5.9	8.2	10.6	12.6
Israel..................	436	8.2	7.9	10.7	8.6	6.3	4.2	7.1	3.6	-.1	3.9	4.3	5.4
Jordan..................	439	3.4	4.8	-2.4	2.0	1.6	.6	-2.4	-3.6	-1.5	1.6	2.6	6.0
Kuwait..................	443	1.8	-.2	1.4	5.2	-1.3	-1.6	-1.2	.4	2.0	3.3	1.9	.4
Saudi Arabia..................	456	.6	1.8	7.3	-.3	—	-1.9	.4	.4	-.1	—	.9	3.1
Syrian Arab Rep..................	463	8.5	14.2	6.9	3.2	2.5	-.6	-1.8	-5.7	-5.0	7.4	....	....
Western Hemisphere..................	205	**289.1**	**246.4**	**35.8**	**18.2**	**11.1**	**8.4**	**12.4**	**13.5**	**7.6**	**17.9**	**18.2**	**9.8**
Argentina..................	213	....	.4	4.3	2.9	-1.1	-3.4	-4.0	13.3	-2.0	78.3	19.6	7.7
Brazil..................	223	2,050.1	2,311.6	57.5	6.3	8.1	3.5	16.6	18.1	12.6	17.8	28.6	10.5
Chile..................	228	8.6	7.7	7.6	6.2	1.6	1.9	5.2	11.4	7.8	6.8	6.6	2.5
Colombia..................	233	14.2	17.2	18.1	15.0	15.4	17.3	9.8	13.2	9.4	5.3	9.1	5.2
Costa Rica..................	238	5.2	13.1	23.9	16.0	11.6	8.8	10.1	11.0	9.3	8.0	10.6	15.5
Ecuador..................	248	....	....	....	31.2	31.2	31.2	102.7	164.3	-.2	6.8	7.3	9.1
El Salvador..................	253	....	....	....	....	....	....	....	6.5	1.0	-2.2	2.5	7.5
Mexico..................	273	7.4	6.1	38.6	33.9	17.5	16.0	14.2	7.8	5.0	5.1	7.5	9.3

Producer Prices/Wholesale Prices

		1993	1994	1995	1996	1997	1998	1999	2000	2001	2002	2003	2004
		Percent Change over Previous Year; Calculated from Indices											
Western Hemisphere(Cont.)													
Panama..................................	283	−.2	2.0	3.0	2.1	−2.2	−3.9	2.7	8.8	−3.2	−3.0	1.7	4.4
Paraguay...............................	288	....	....	....	....	1.2	14.9	5.3	14.7	5.8	19.9	26.5	5.8
Peru......................................	293	47.6	17.9	10.5	9.4	7.4	7.3	4.9	4.3	1.4	−1.0	1.7	5.2
Trinidad and Tobago................	369	5.4	5.4	3.6	2.9	1.9	1.4	1.7	1.3	.9	.6	....	....
Uruguay.................................	298	33.4	34.2	37.7	25.0	16.4	9.3	−.9	6.8	6.6	31.9	38.9	14.7
Venezuela, Rep. Bol..................	299	35.0	78.2	57.7	103.2	29.8	22.2	16.2	15.2	15.5	37.3	51.4	30.5
Memorandum Items													
Oil Exporting Countries...........	999	12.7	20.1	26.7	22.4	10.4	45.0	10.7	11.3	8.7	7.0	8.8	10.4
Non-Oil Developing Countries.	201	75.0	100.6	41.5	16.5	13.2	9.8	13.2	14.6	8.6	9.4	5.5	9.8

Indices

		1993	1994	1995	1996	1997	1998	1999	2000	2001	2002	2003	2004
		Index Numbers: 2000=100											
World...	001	52.9	66.6	76.6	81.4	85.3	88.5	92.6	100.0	103.7	106.2	110.2	117.0
Industrial Countries.................	110	91.5	92.6	95.7	96.5	97.0	95.6	95.7	100.0	100.9	99.5	102.1	106.2
Developing Countries..............	200	19.7	36.9	51.5	60.4	68.2	77.6	87.6	100.0	108.6	118.4	125.4	137.8
Africa..................................	605	65.5	71.0	78.1	83.4	87.7	91.9	94.6	100.0	104.5	112.5	113.1	114.4
Asia.....................................	505	60.2	64.5	70.2	73.4	77.1	91.9	93.9	100.0	104.8	106.9	111.7	120.2
Europe................................	170	3.4	10.3	23.7	33.8	45.1	53.0	74.1	100.0	120.4	136.3	130.2	150.9
Middle East..........................	405	47.4	55.0	68.5	78.3	82.6	86.3	93.1	100.0	102.2	107.6	116.3	127.9
Western Hemisphere..............	205	11.7	40.6	55.1	65.1	72.3	78.4	88.1	100.0	107.6	126.9	150.0	164.7

Consumer Prices

		1993	1994	1995	1996	1997	1998	1999	2000	2001	2002	2003	2004
						Percent Change over Previous Year; Calculated from Indices							
World	001	19.01	26.77	15.42	8.69	6.13	5.78	5.39	4.40	4.09	3.42	3.62	3.56
Industrial Countries	110	2.71	2.35	2.44	2.24	2.04	1.41	1.42	2.38	2.18	1.47	1.89	2.02
United States	111	2.95	2.61	2.81	2.93	2.34	1.55	2.19	3.38	2.83	1.59	2.27	2.68
Canada	156	1.84	.19	2.17	1.58	1.62	.99	1.72	2.75	2.53	2.25	2.77	1.83
Australia	193	1.81	1.89	4.64	2.61	.25	.85	1.47	4.48	4.38	3.00	2.77	2.34
Japan	158	1.28	.71	−.13	.14	1.73	.66	−.34	−.67	−.73	−.92	−.25	−.01
New Zealand	196	1.42	2.40	3.74	2.30	1.17	1.29	−.12	2.62	2.63	2.68	1.75	2.29
Euro Area	163	....	....	....	2.15	1.58	1.09	1.12	2.34	2.11	2.25	2.07	2.14
Austria	122	3.63	2.96	2.25	1.84	1.33	.90	.56	2.35	2.66	1.81	1.36	2.05
Belgium	124	2.75	2.38	1.47	2.06	1.63	.95	1.12	2.55	2.47	1.64	1.59	2.10
Finland	172	2.10	1.09	.99	.62	1.20	1.40	1.16	3.37	2.57	1.58	.86	.19
France	132	2.11	1.66	1.78	2.01	1.20	.67	.50	1.69	1.66	1.92	2.08	2.17
Germany	134	4.43	2.74	1.72	1.45	1.88	.94	.57	1.47	1.98	1.37	1.05	1.67
Greece	174	14.41	10.92	8.94	8.20	5.54	4.77	2.64	3.17	3.40	3.57	3.54	2.89
Ireland	178	1.42	2.37	2.52	1.74	1.40	2.43	1.64	5.56	4.87	4.67	3.48	2.19
Italy	136	4.48	4.03	5.24	3.97	2.04	1.96	1.66	2.54	2.79	2.47	2.67	2.21
Luxembourg	137	3.58	2.20	1.92	1.39	1.37	.96	1.00	3.15	2.67	2.07	2.05	2.23
Netherlands	138	2.58	2.80	2.10	2.02	2.16	1.98	2.21	3.03	4.20	3.26	2.11	1.23
Portugal	182	6.50	5.21	4.12	3.12	2.16	2.72	2.30	2.85	4.39	3.55	3.28	2.36
Spain	184	4.57	4.72	4.67	3.56	1.97	1.83	2.31	3.43	3.59	3.07	3.03	3.03
Denmark	128	1.25	1.99	2.10	2.11	2.20	1.85	2.48	2.92	2.35	2.43	2.09	1.16
Iceland	176	4.08	1.55	1.65	2.30	1.75	1.72	3.22	5.16	6.39	5.17	2.06	2.80
Norway	142	2.27	1.40	2.46	1.26	2.58	2.26	2.33	3.09	3.02	1.29	2.48	.47
Sweden	144	4.73	2.13	2.45	.55	.66	−.27	.47	.89	2.42	2.17	1.91	.38
Switzerland	146	3.27	.86	1.80	.82	.52	.02	.82	1.54	.99	.64	.63	.82
United Kingdom	112	1.56	2.48	3.41	2.45	3.13	3.42	1.56	2.93	1.82	1.63	2.91	2.96
Developing Countries	200	49.92	65.28	33.60	17.26	11.45	11.51	10.19	6.81	6.37	5.75	5.67	5.38
Africa	605	32.68	32.35	32.54	24.12	12.99	8.00	9.72	11.35	12.39	8.91	6.68	4.68
CEMAC	758	....	....	....	....	....	....	....	....	....	....	....	....
Cameroon	622	−3.21	35.09	9.08	3.92	4.78	3.18	1.53	−2.05	4.51	2.80	....	....
Central African Rep.	626	−2.92	24.57	19.19	3.72	1.61	−1.89	−1.41	3.20	3.83	2.33	4.13	−2.07
Chad	628	−7.07	40.43	9.06	12.39	5.62	12.14	−6.80	3.80	12.44	5.19	−1.88	....
Equatorial Guinea	642	3.99	36.42	....	....	....	....	....	....	....	....	....	....
Gabon	646	.53	36.12	9.65	.69	3.97	1.45	−1.94	.50	2.14	.04	2.24	.39
WAEMU	759	1.07	29.97	12.05	3.41	3.00	3.69	.19	1.78	4.03	2.93	1.34	.54
Benin	638	.44	38.53	14.46	4.91	3.47	5.75	.33	4.17	3.98	2.49	1.49	.87
Burkina Faso	748	.55	25.18	7.39	6.17	2.31	5.05	−1.07	−.30	5.01	2.18	2.03	−.40
Côte d'Ivoire	662	2.16	26.08	14.30	2.48	4.02	4.69	.79	2.46	4.28	3.11	3.35	1.44
Guinea Bissau	654	48.11	15.18	45.37	50.73	49.10	6.50	−2.02	8.60	3.17	3.37	−3.52	.86
Mali	678	−.26	23.18	13.44	6.81	−.36	4.14	−1.20	−.68	5.19	5.03	−1.35	−3.10
Niger	692	−1.22	36.04	10.56	5.29	2.93	4.55	−2.30	2.90	4.01	2.63	−1.61	.26
Senegal	722	−.59	32.29	7.86	2.75	1.58	1.16	.83	.73	3.07	2.23	−.03	.51
Togo	742	−1.01	39.16	16.43	4.69	8.25	.97	−.07	1.89	3.91	3.07	−.96	.39
Algeria	612	20.54	29.05	29.78	18.68	5.73	4.95	2.65	.34	4.23	1.42	2.58	3.56
Angola	614	1,379.41	948.81	2,671.79	4,145.11	219.18	107.28	248.20	325.00	169.73	107.96	94.86	37.34
Botswana	616	14.33	10.54	10.51	10.08	8.72	6.66	7.75	8.60	6.56	8.03	9.19	6.95
Burundi	618	9.68	14.85	19.26	26.44	31.11	12.50	3.40	24.31	9.24	−6.34	11.73	13.04
Cape Verde	624	5.79	3.45	8.35	5.96	8.56	4.39	4.36	−2.48	3.35	1.88	1.19	−1.89
Congo, Dem. Rep. of	636	1,987	23,773	542	492	199	29	285	550	314	38	13	4
Ethiopia	644	3.54	7.59	10.02	−5.07	2.40	2.58	7.87	.65	−8.12	1.55	17.78	....
Gambia, The	648	6.46	1.71	6.98	1.10	2.78	3.49	2.16	.19	8.08	4.94	17.02	14.20
Ghana	652	24.96	24.87	59.46	46.56	27.89	14.62	12.41	25.19	32.91	14.82	26.67	12.62
Kenya	664	45.98	28.81	1.55	8.86	11.36	6.72	5.74	9.98	5.74	1.96	9.82	11.62
Lesotho	666	13.14	8.21	9.27	9.33	7.33	7.33	7.33	6.13	−9.62	33.81	6.67	....
Madagascar	674	10.01	38.94	49.06	19.77	4.49	6.21	9.93	12.03	6.94	15.93	−1.22	13.81
Malawi	676	22.77	34.65	83.33	37.60	9.14	29.75	44.80	29.58	22.70	14.74	9.57	11.26
Mauritania	682	9.37	4.13	6.54	4.68	4.63	8.03	4.07	3.25	4.71	3.90	5.15	10.37
Mauritius	684	10.52	7.32	6.03	6.55	6.83	6.81	6.91	4.20	5.39	6.40	3.91	4.72
Morocco	686	5.18	5.14	6.12	2.99	1.04	2.75	.68	1.89	.62	2.80	1.17	....
Mozambique	688	42.20	63.18	54.43	48.49	7.37	1.48	2.86	12.72	9.05	16.78	13.43	11.10
Namibia	728	8.53	10.76	10.02	7.98	8.81	6.17	8.64	8.99	9.54	11.35	7.19	3.91
Nigeria	694	57.17	57.03	72.81	29.29	8.21	10.32	4.76	14.52	12.96	12.88	14.03	15.00
Rwanda	714	12.35	41.04	41.04	7.41	12.02	6.21	−2.41	4.29	2.98	2.25	7.15	11.95
Seychelles	718	1.38	1.74	−.24	−1.10	.62	2.58	6.35	6.27	5.97	.20	3.29	3.84
Sierra Leone	724	22.21	24.20	25.99	23.14	14.95	35.53	34.09	−.84	2.09	−3.29	7.60	14.19
South Africa	199	9.72	8.94	8.68	7.35	8.60	6.88	5.18	5.34	5.70	9.16	5.86	1.39
Sudan	732	101.38	115.40	68.38	132.82	46.65	17.11	15.99	5.69	7.20	8.37	7.77	8.51
Tanzania	738	25.28	33.09	28.38	20.98	16.09	12.80	7.89	5.92	5.13	.98	3.54	.03
Tunisia	744	3.97	4.73	6.24	3.73	3.65	3.13	2.69	2.93	1.98	2.72	2.72	3.57
Uganda	746	6.08	9.73	8.59	7.22	6.93	−.02	6.35	2.83	2.00	−.32	7.83	3.33
Zambia	754	183.31	54.60	34.93	43.07	24.42	24.46	26.79	26.03	21.39	22.23	21.40	17.97
Zimbabwe	698	27.59	22.26	22.59	21.43	18.74	31.82	58.52	55.86	76.71	140.08	....	....
Asia	505	9.20	14.69	11.82	7.65	4.65	8.03	2.16	1.62	2.38	1.95	2.35	3.98
Bangladesh	513	3.01	5.31	10.20	2.38	5.39	8.40	6.11	2.21	2.01	3.33	5.67	3.16
Bhutan	514	11.21	6.99	9.50	8.79	6.51	10.58	6.78	4.01	3.41	2.46	2.10	4.60
Cambodia	522	....	....	1.06	10.07	3.17	14.81	4.01	−.79	−.60	3.23	1.36	3.66
China, P.R.: Mainland	924	14.58	24.24	16.90	8.32	2.81	−.84	−1.41	.26	.46	−.77	1.16	3.99
China, P.R.: Hong Kong	532	8.82	8.78	9.03	6.37	5.78	2.85	−3.96	−3.75	−1.61	−3.04	−2.58	−.43
China, P.R.: Macao	546	....	....	....	....	....	....	−3.20	−1.61	−1.99	−2.64	−1.56	.98
Fiji	819	5.21	.82	2.17	3.05	3.37	5.71	1.97	1.09	4.27	.76	4.17	2.83
India	534	6.36	10.21	10.22	8.98	7.16	13.23	4.67	4.01	3.68	4.39	3.81	3.77
Indonesia	536	9.68	8.52	9.43	7.97	6.23	58.39	20.49	3.72	11.50	11.88	6.59	6.24

Consumer Prices

		1993	1994	1995	1996	1997	1998	1999	2000	2001	2002	2003	2004
						Percent Change over Previous Year; Calculated from Indices							
Asia(Cont.)													
Korea...........................	542	4.80	6.20	4.44	4.98	4.40	7.54	.82	2.25	4.10	2.69	3.55	3.59
Lao People's Dem. Rep.............	544	6.27	6.78	19.59	13.02	27.51	90.98	128.42	25.09	7.81	10.63	15.49	10.46
Malaysia........................	548	3.54	3.72	3.45	3.49	2.66	5.27	2.74	1.53	1.42	1.81	1.06	1.45
Maldives........................	556	20.13	3.38	5.49	6.24	7.58	−1.41	2.95	−1.18	.68	.93	−2.87	6.41
Mongolia........................	948	268.15	87.58	56.76	46.89	36.56	9.36	7.56	11.60	6.28	.92	5.13	8.24
Myanmar........................	518	31.83	24.10	25.19	16.28	29.70	51.49	18.40	−.11	21.10	57.07	36.59	....
Nepal...........................	558	7.51	8.35	7.62	9.22	4.01	11.24	7.45	2.48	2.69	3.03	5.71	2.79
Pakistan........................	564	9.97	12.37	12.34	10.37	11.38	6.23	4.14	4.37	3.15	3.29	2.91	7.44
Papua New Guinea...............	853	4.97	2.85	17.28	11.62	3.96	13.57	14.93	15.60	9.30	11.80	14.71	2.07
Philippines.....................	566	6.88	8.36	6.71	7.51	5.59	9.27	5.95	3.95	6.80	3.00	3.45	5.98
Samoa..........................	862	1.72	12.08	−2.90	5.37	6.86	2.22	.27	.97	3.84	8.05	.12	16.34
Singapore.......................	576	2.29	3.10	1.72	1.38	2.00	−.27	.02	1.36	1.00	−.39	.51	1.66
Solomon Islands.................	813	9.17	13.26	9.63	11.77	8.08	12.40	8.02	7.06	6.89	10.16	9.96	7.12
Sri Lanka.......................	524	11.75	8.45	7.67	15.94	9.57	9.36	4.69	6.18	14.16	9.55	6.31	7.58
Thailand........................	578	3.37	5.09	5.80	5.83	5.60	8.07	.30	1.57	1.64	.62	1.80	2.77
Tonga..........................	866	.96	1.01	1.46	3.00	2.12	3.27	4.46	6.31	8.30	10.36	11.64	10.98
Vanuatu........................	846	3.57	2.30	2.23	.91	2.83	3.28	2.00	2.46	3.65	1.96	3.02	1.44
Vietnam........................	582	....	....	....	5.68	3.21	7.27	4.12	−1.71	−.43	3.83	3.10	7.80
Europe	**170**	**85.07**	**192.81**	**121.90**	**44.69**	**34.17**	**29.30**	**49.69**	**25.09**	**21.05**	**15.24**	**11.27**	**8.46**
Albania.........................	914	85.00	22.57	7.79	12.73	33.18	20.64	.39	.05	3.11	7.77	.48	2.28
Armenia........................	911	....	4,962.22	175.97	18.70	13.91	8.67	.66	−.81	3.14	1.10	4.76	6.93
Azerbaijan, Republic of..........	912	1,129.04	1,664.53	411.74	19.76	3.60	−.69	−8.59	1.77	1.55	2.81	2.23	6.71
Belarus.........................	913	1,190.23	2,221.02	709.35	52.71	63.94	72.87	293.68	168.62	61.13	42.54	28.40	18.11
Bulgaria........................	918	72.88	96.06	62.05	121.61	1,058.37	18.67	2.57	10.32	7.36	5.81	2.16	6.35
Croatia.........................	960	1,500.00	107.33	3.95	4.30	4.17	6.40	3.46	5.27	4.77	1.70	.12	3.72
Cyprus.........................	423	4.85	4.70	2.62	2.98	3.61	2.23	1.63	4.14	1.98	2.80	4.14	2.29
Czech Republic..................	935	....	9.96	9.17	8.80	8.55	10.63	2.14	3.90	4.71	1.79	.10	2.83
Czechoslovakia..................	964	36.87	33.25	28.07	19.82	15.08	11.73	7.28	10.06	5.49	1.90	.79	3.58
Estonia.........................	939	89.81	47.65	28.78	23.05	10.58	8.21	3.30	4.03	5.74	3.57	1.34	3.05
Georgia........................	915	....	....	162.72	39.36	7.09	3.57	19.19	4.06	4.65	5.56	4.78	5.66
Hungary........................	944	22.45	18.87	28.30	23.60	18.28	14.23	10.00	9.80	9.22	5.27	4.64	6.78
Kazakhstan.....................	916	....	1,877.37	176.16	39.18	17.41	7.15	8.30	13.18	8.35	5.84	6.44	6.88
Kyrgyz Republic.................	917	....	....	....	31.95	23.44	10.46	35.90	18.69	6.93	2.13	3.50	8.52
Latvia..........................	941	108.77	35.93	24.98	17.61	8.44	4.66	2.36	2.65	2.49	1.94	2.92	6.19
Lithuania.......................	946	410.24	72.15	39.66	24.62	8.88	5.07	.75	1.01	1.30	.30	−1.18	1.20
Macedonia, FYR.................	962	....	126.58	16.37	2.47	1.29	.54	−1.28	6.61	5.20	2.31	1.11	−.37
Malta..........................	181	4.14	4.13	4.43	2.05	3.11	2.39	2.13	2.37	2.93	2.19	.74	2.79
Moldova........................	921	....	....	12.07	20.89	8.01	6.64	45.94	31.29	9.77	5.30	11.75	12.53
Poland.........................	964	36.87	33.25	28.07	19.82	15.08	11.73	7.28	10.06	5.49	1.90	.79	3.58
Romania........................	968	255.17	136.76	32.24	38.83	154.76	59.10	45.80	45.67	34.47	22.54	15.27	11.88
Russia..........................	922	874.62	307.63	197.47	47.74	14.77	27.67	85.74	20.78	21.46	15.79	13.66	10.88
Slovak Republic.................	936	....	13.41	9.89	5.81	6.11	6.70	10.57	12.04	7.33	3.32	8.55	7.55
Slovenia........................	961	32.86	20.99	13.46	9.79	8.38	7.98	6.11	8.82	8.46	7.48	5.58	3.58
Turkey..........................	186	66.10	106.26	88.11	80.35	85.73	84.64	64.87	54.92	54.40	44.96	25.30	8.60
Ukraine.........................	926	4,734.91	891.19	376.75	80.33	15.94	10.58	22.68	28.20	11.96	.76	5.21	9.04
Middle East.....................	**405**	**11.71**	**13.78**	**21.36**	**12.82**	**7.61**	**7.11**	**7.50**	**4.98**	**3.63**	**5.32**	**6.55**	**7.41**
Bahrain, Kingdom of.............	419	2.54	.82	2.70	−.45	2.43	−.22	−1.43	−.70	.24	1.22	....	....
Egypt...........................	469	12.09	8.15	15.74	7.19	4.63	3.87	3.08	2.68	2.27	2.74	4.51	11.27
Iran, I.R. of.....................	429	21.20	31.45	49.66	28.94	17.35	17.87	20.07	14.48	11.27	14.34	16.47	14.76
Israel...........................	436	10.94	12.34	10.05	11.27	9.00	5.43	5.20	1.14	1.10	5.64	.72	−.41
Jordan..........................	439	3.32	3.52	2.35	6.50	3.04	3.09	.61	.67	1.77	1.83	1.63	3.36
Kuwait.........................	443	.38	2.53	2.69	3.56	.66	.15	2.99	1.81	1.66	1.40	.99	1.14
Lebanon........................	446	15.66	6.80	....	....	....	....	....	....	....	....	....	....
Oman...........................	449	−.31	.41	2.46	.90	−.52	−.83	.43	−1.14	−1.06	−.66	−.42	.36
Qatar...........................	453	−.87	1.32	2.96	7.43	2.75	2.60	2.16	1.68	1.44	.24	2.27	6.80
Saudi Arabia....................	456	1.06	.56	4.87	1.22	.06	−.36	−1.35	−1.13	−1.11	.23	.59	.55
Syrian Arab Republic............	463	13.22	15.33	7.98	8.25	1.89	−.80	−3.70	−3.85	3.00	.97	....	....
Yemen, Republic of..............	474	35.75	49.39	55.08	30.73	2.18	5.98	8.66	4.59	11.91	12.23	10.83	....
Western Hemisphere...............	**205**	**214.73**	**211.30**	**40.34**	**21.34**	**13.09**	**9.88**	**8.95**	**8.15**	**6.33**	**9.09**	**10.81**	**6.74**
ECCU...........................	309	....	....	....	....	....	....	....	....	....	....	....	....
Anguilla.......................	312	4.27	3.51	1.39	3.58	.11	2.64	2.64	−35.82	2.25	.56	....	....
Dominica......................	321	1.57	.02	1.32	1.68	2.44	1.00	1.19	.86	1.52	.24	1.55	2.00
Grenada.......................	328	2.81	3.77	1.87	2.03	1.24	1.41	.57	2.14	1.67	1.07	....	....
St. Kitts and Nevis..............	361	1.79	1.44	2.96	1.98	8.99	3.46	3.45	1.98	2.15	2.05	2.23	....
St. Lucia.......................	362	1.13	2.53	5.63	.92	−.01	3.20	3.41	3.80	.10	1.60	.94	4.66
St. Vincent & Grenadines.........	364	4.29	1.01	1.74	4.41	.44	2.14	1.03	.20	.82	.81	.26	2.94
Argentina.......................	213	10.61	4.18	3.38	.16	.53	.92	−1.17	−.94	−1.07	25.87	13.44	4.42
Aruba..........................	314	5.22	6.31	3.36	3.23	3.00	1.87	2.28	4.04	3.11	3.44	3.29	2.53
Bahamas, The...................	313	2.71	1.41	2.07	1.52	.79	1.86	1.44	1.04	2.92	.90	3.36	.74
Barbados........................	316	1.11	.08	1.88	2.39	7.71	−1.27	1.56	2.44	2.58	.15	1.58	1.43
Belize..........................	339	1.48	2.59	2.89	6.40	1.05	−.87	−1.21	.61	1.16	2.21	2.61	3.09
Bolivia.........................	218	8.53	7.87	10.19	12.43	4.71	7.67	2.16	4.60	1.60	.92	3.34	4.44
Brazil...........................	223	1,927.98	2,075.89	66.01	15.76	6.93	3.20	4.86	7.04	6.84	8.45	14.71	6.60
Chile...........................	228	12.73	11.44	8.24	7.36	6.14	5.11	3.34	3.84	3.57	2.49	2.81	1.05
Colombia.......................	233	22.61	23.84	20.96	20.24	18.47	18.68	10.88	9.22	7.97	6.35	7.13	5.90
Costa Rica......................	238	9.78	13.53	23.19	17.52	13.23	11.67	10.05	10.99	11.23	9.16	9.45	12.32
Dominican Republic..............	243	5.25	8.26	12.54	5.40	8.30	4.83	6.47	7.72	8.88	5.22	27.45	51.46
Ecuador........................	248	45.00	27.44	22.89	24.37	30.64	36.10	52.24	96.09	37.68	12.48	7.93	2.74
El Salvador......................	253	18.51	10.59	10.03	9.79	4.49	2.55	.51	2.27	3.75	1.87	2.12	4.45
Guatemala......................	258	11.82	10.86	8.41	11.06	9.23	6.97	4.86	5.98	7.63	8.03	5.48	7.39
Guyana.........................	336	....	....	12.21	7.09	3.56	4.59	7.54	6.15	2.63	5.34	5.98	4.67
Haiti...........................	263	29.71	39.33	27.61	20.58	20.56	10.63	8.67	13.71	14.18	9.85	39.28	22.81
Honduras.......................	268	10.75	21.73	29.46	23.84	20.17	13.71	11.65	11.06	9.67	7.70	7.67	8.11

Consumer Prices

		1993	1994	1995	1996	1997	1998	1999	2000	2001	2002	2003	2004
					Percent Change over Previous Year; Calculated from Indices								
Western Hemisphere(Cont.)													
Mexico...........................	273	9.75	6.97	35.00	34.38	20.63	15.93	16.59	9.50	6.36	5.03	4.55	4.69
Netherlands Antilles................	353	2.04	1.78	2.80	3.60	3.26	1.13	.37	5.81	1.79	.42	2.03	1.38
Nicaragua........................	278	20.40	6.71	10.94	11.62	9.22	13.04	11.22	11.55	7.36	3.99	5.15	8.44
Panama..........................	283	.45	1.27	.99	1.26	1.32	.56	1.25	1.50	.31	1.01	1.41	.27
Paraguay........................	288	18.21	20.57	13.40	9.81	6.99	11.53	6.75	8.98	7.27	10.51	14.23	4.33
Peru............................	293	48.58	23.74	11.13	11.54	8.56	7.25	3.47	3.76	1.98	.19	2.26	3.66
Suriname........................	366	143.51	368.48	235.56	−.70	7.15	18.98	98.93	59.40	38.59	15.53	22.98	....
Trinidad and Tobago...............	369	10.84	8.81	5.18	3.40	3.63	5.61	3.44	3.56	5.54	4.14	3.81	3.72
Uruguay.........................	298	54.10	44.74	42.25	28.34	19.82	10.81	5.66	4.76	4.36	13.97	19.38	9.16
Venezuela, Rep. Bol................	299	38.12	60.82	59.92	99.88	50.04	35.78	23.57	16.21	12.53	22.43	31.09	21.75
Memorandum Items													
Oil Exporting Countries...........	999	17.10	20.15	25.15	20.44	11.77	27.63	14.31	6.15	8.54	9.76	9.78	8.65
Non-Oil Developing Countries.	201	55.79	71.97	34.68	16.87	11.41	9.66	9.73	6.88	6.14	5.32	5.23	5.02

Indices

		1993	1994	1995	1996	1997	1998	1999	2000	2001	2002	2003	2004
						Index Numbers: 2000=100							
World..........................	001	50.9	64.5	74.5	81.0	85.9	90.9	95.8	100.0	104.1	107.7	111.5	115.5
Industrial Countries..............	110	86.8	88.9	91.0	93.1	95.0	96.3	97.7	100.0	102.2	103.7	105.6	107.8
Developing Countries.............	200	26.4	43.6	58.3	68.4	76.2	85.0	93.6	100.0	106.4	112.5	118.9	125.3
Africa..........................	605	30.8	40.8	54.0	67.1	75.8	81.9	89.8	100.0	112.4	122.4	130.6	136.7
Asia............................	505	61.7	70.8	79.1	85.2	89.2	96.3	98.4	100.0	102.4	104.4	106.8	111.1
Europe.........................	170	3.3	9.6	21.3	30.8	41.3	53.4	79.9	100.0	121.1	139.5	155.2	168.4
Middle East.....................	405	49.3	56.1	68.1	76.9	82.7	88.6	95.3	100.0	103.6	109.1	116.3	124.9
Western Hemisphere.............	205	12.9	40.1	56.3	68.3	77.2	84.9	92.5	100.0	106.3	116.0	128.5	137.2

Exports, f.o.b.

		1993	1994	1995	1996	1997	1998	1999	2000	2001	2002	2003	2004
		Billions of US Dollars											
World	001	3,767.7	4,289.9	5,130.3	5,350.2	5,539.3	5,451.4	5,645.1	6,376.7	6,130.1	6,428.6	7,469.0	9,052.5
Industrial Countries	110	2,597.1	2,917.1	3,473.4	3,565.6	3,644.9	3,673.9	3,739.7	4,003.9	3,872.0	3,990.6	4,569.4	5,364.3
United States	111	465	513	585	625	689	682	696	782	729	693	725	819
Canada	156	145	165	192	202	214	214	238	277	260	252	273	304
Australia	193	43	48	53	60	63	56	56	64	63	65	72	86
Japan	158	362	397	443	411	421	388	419	479	403	417	472	566
New Zealand	196	10.5	12.2	13.6	14.4	14.2	12.0	12.5	13.3	13.7	14.4	16.5	20.4
Euro Area													
Austria	122	40.2	45.0	57.6	57.8	58.6	62.7	† 64.1	64.2	66.7	70.9	87.6	109.0
Belgium	124	126	144	176	175	172	179	† 179	188	190	216	255	306
Finland	172	23.4	29.7	39.6	38.4	39.3	43.0	† 41.8	45.5	42.8	44.6	52.5	60.7
France	132	209	236	287	288	290	306	† 302	300	297	312	366	424
Germany	134	382	430	524	524	512	543	† 543	550	571	615	752	912
Greece	174	9.1	8.8	11.0	11.9	11.1	10.7	10.5	10.7	9.5	10.3	13.2	15.0
Ireland	178	29.3	34.1	44.6	48.7	53.5	64.5	† 71.2	77.1	83.0	87.4	92.4	104.2
Italy	136	169	191	234	252	240	246	† 235	240	244	254	299	354
Luxembourg	137	6	7	8	7	7	8	† 8	8	8	8	10	12
Netherlands	138	139	156	196	197	195	201	† 200	213	216	221	259	318
Portugal	182	15.4	18.0	23.2	24.6	24.0	† 24.8	† 25.2	23.3	24.4	25.5	30.6	33.0
Spain	184	61.0	72.9	91.0	102.0	104.4	109.2	† 110.0	113.3	115.2	123.5	156.0	182.1
Denmark	128	38.2	43.1	51.5	51.5	49.1	48.8	50.4	50.4	51.1	56.3	65.3	75.8
Iceland	176	1.40	1.62	1.80	1.64	1.85	2.05	2.00	1.89	2.02	2.23	2.39	2.90
Norway	142	31.8	34.7	42.0	49.6	48.5	40.4	45.5	60.1	59.2	59.7	67.5	81.8
Sweden	144	49.9	61.3	79.8	84.9	82.9	85.0	84.8	86.9	75.8	81.3	102.4	123.2
Switzerland	146	59	66	78	76	72	75	76	75	78	84	97	114
United Kingdom	112	181	204	242	262	281	272	268	282	267	276	304	342
Developing Countries	200	1,170.62	1,372.79	1,656.88	1,784.61	1,894.41	1,777.45	1,905.40	2,372.86	2,258.07	2,438.00	2,899.54	3,688.14
Africa	605	74.86	79.56	94.52	107.04	108.56	92.03	100.00	123.84	116.76	120.67	150.10	196.73
Algeria	612	10.4	8.9	10.3	13.2	....	....	....	....	....	18.8	24.6	32.3
Angola	614	2.9	3.0	3.7	5.1	5.0	3.5	5.4	7.7	6.4	7.5	9.2	13.0
Benin	638	.38	.40	.42	.65	.42	.41	.42	.39	.20	.24	.27	.30
Botswana	616	1.76	1.85	2.14	2.54	2.84	1.95	....	2.68	2.31	2.32	3.02	....
Burkina Faso	748	.069	.107	.276	.233	.232	.319	.216	.241	.263	.292	.376	.514
Burundi	618	.06	.12	.11	.04	.09	.06	.05	.05	.04	.03	.04	.05
Cameroon	622	1.9	1.5	1.6	1.6	1.7	1.8	1.5	1.5	2.1	2.3	2.3	2.6
Cape Verde	624	—	—	.01	.01	.01	.01	.01	.01	.01	.01	....	....
Central African Rep.	626	.11	.15	.17	.15	.16	.15	.15	.16	.14	.15	.13	.10
Chad	628	.13	.15	.24	.24	.24	.26	.24	.18	.19	.18	.50	1.97
Congo, Rep. of	634	1.07	.96	1.17	1.35	1.67	1.37	1.56	2.49	....	....	....	....
Côte d'Ivoire	662	2.5	2.7	3.8	4.4	4.5	4.6	4.7	3.9	3.9	5.3	5.8	....
Equatorial Guinea	642	.06	.06	.09	.18	.50	.44	.71	1.10	....	....	....	....
Ethiopia	644	.20	.37	.42	.42	.59	.56	.47	.49	.46	.48	....	....
Gabon	646	2.3	2.4	2.7	3.2	3.0	1.9	2.4	2.5	2.6	2.6	3.3	4.2
Gambia, The	648	.067	.035	.016	.021	.015	.021	.005	.015	.003	.002	....	.010
Ghana	652	1.0	1.4	1.7	1.7	1.6	1.8	....	....	....	....	....	....
Guinea	656	....	....	.68	.66	.64	.63	.49	.62	.54	....	.63	.56
Guinea-Bissau	654	.028	.086	.044	.028	.048	.027	.051	.062	.063	.054	.069	....
Kenya	664	1.4	1.6	1.9	2.1	2.1	2.0	1.7	1.7	1.9	2.1	2.4	2.7
Lesotho	666	.13	.14	.16	.19	.20	.19	....	....	....	....	....	....
Madagascar	674	.26	.37	.37	.46	.41	.56	.60	.82	.69	.50	.85	....
Malawi	676	.32	.34	.41	.48	.54	.43	.45	.38	.45	.41	.53	.48
Mali	678	.48	.33	.44	.43	.56	.56	.57	.55	.73	.87	.99	....
Mauritius	684	1.30	1.35	1.54	1.80	1.59	1.65	1.59	1.56	1.63	1.80	1.90	2.00
Morocco	686	3.1	5.6	6.9	6.9	7.0	7.2	7.4	7.0	7.1	7.9	....	....
Namibia	728	1.24	1.31	1.41	1.42	1.34	1.23	1.23	1.32	1.18	1.07	1.26	1.83
Niger	692	.29	.23	.29	.33	.27	.33	.29	.28	.27	.28	.20	.21
Nigeria	694	10	9	† 12	16	15	10	14	21	17	15	20	31
Rwanda	714	.07	.03	.05	.06	.09	.06	.06	.05	.08	.06	.06	.10
Senegal	722	.71	.79	.99	.99	.90	.97	1.03	.92	1.00	1.07	1.13	1.27
Seychelles	718	.05	.05	.05	.14	.11	.12	.15	.19	.22	.23	.21	.18
Sierra Leone	724	.12	.12	.04	.05	.02	.01	.01	.01	.03	.05	.09	.14
South Africa	199	24.2	25.3	27.9	29.2	31.0	† 26.4	26.7	30.0	29.3	29.7	36.5	46.0
Sudan	732	.4	.5	.6	.6	.6	.6	.8	1.8	1.7	1.9	2.5	3.8
Swaziland	734	.68	.79	.87	.86	.96	.97	.94	.91	1.05	.94	....	....
Tanzania	738	.45	.52	.68	.78	.75	.59	.54	.66	.78	.90	1.13	1.34
Togo	742	.14	.33	.38	.44	.42	.42	.39	.36	.36	.43	.62	.37
Tunisia	744	3.7	4.7	5.5	5.5	5.6	5.7	5.9	5.9	6.6	6.9	8.0	9.7
Uganda	746	.18	.41	.46	.59	.55	.50	.52	.46	.46	.44	.56	.88
Zambia	754	.83	.93	1.04	1.04	.92	1.02	.52	.76	....	....	....	....
Zimbabwe	698	1.56	1.88	2.11	2.41	2.39	1.96	1.93	1.83	1.21	....	3.36	1.89
Asia *	505	646.25	768.58	932.78	973.16	1,041.91	987.75	1,054.39	1,269.97	1,183.46	1,300.04	1,538.90	1,934.73
Bangladesh	513	2.3	2.7	3.2	3.3	3.8	3.8	3.9	4.8	4.8	4.6	5.3	6.6
Bhutan	514	.1	.1	.1	.1	.1	.1	.1	.1	.1	.1	.1	....
Cambodia	522	....	....	....	....	1	1	1	1	1	1	2	....
China, P.R.: Mainland	924	92	121	149	151	183	184	195	249	266	326	438	593
China, P.R.: Hong Kong	532	135	151	174	181	188	174	174	202	190	200	224	259
China, P.R.: Macao	546	1.79	1.87	2.00	2.00	2.15	2.14	2.20	2.54	2.30	2.36	2.58	2.81
Fiji	819	.45	.57	.62	.75	.62	.51	.61	.58	.54	.55	.68	....
India	534	21.6	25.0	30.6	33.1	35.0	33.4	35.7	42.4	43.4	49.3	57.1	71.8
Indonesia	536	36.8	40.1	45.4	49.8	56.3	50.4	51.2	65.4	57.4	60.2	64.1	71.3
Korea	542	82	96	125	130	136	132	144	172	150	162	194	254
Lao People's Dem. Rep.	544	.2	.3	.3	.3	.4	.4	.3	.3	.3	.3	.4	.4

Exports, f.o.b.

		1993	1994	1995	1996	1997	1998	1999	2000	2001	2002	2003	2004
							Billions of US Dollars						
Asia *(Cont.)													
Malaysia	548	47.1	58.8	73.9	78.3	78.7	73.3	84.6	98.2	88.0	93.3	99.4	125.7
Maldives	556	—	—	—	.1	.1	.1	.1	.1	.1	.1	.1	.1
Mongolia	948	.4	.4	.5	.4	.6	.3	.5	.5	.5	.5	.6	.9
Myanmar	518	.59	.80	.86	.75	.87	1.08	1.14	1.65	2.38	3.05	2.48	2.53
Nepal	558	.384	.362	.345	.385	.406	.474	.602	.804	.737	.568	.662	.756
Pakistan	564	6.7	7.4	8.0	9.3	8.7	8.5	8.4	9.0	9.2	9.9	11.9	13.4
Papua New Guinea	853	2.5	2.6	2.6	2.5	2.1	1.8	1.9	2.1	1.8	1.6	2.2	2.6
Philippines	566	11.1	13.3	17.5	20.4	24.9	29.4	36.6	39.8	32.7	36.5	37.0	39.7
Samoa	862	.006	.004	.009	.010	.015	.015	.020	.014	.016	.014	.015	.011
Singapore	576	74.0	96.8	118.3	125.0	125.0	109.9	114.7	137.8	121.8	125.2	144.2	179.6
Solomon Islands	813	.129	.142	.168	.162	.157	.118	.126	.065	.024	.030	.077	.074
Sri Lanka	524	2.86	3.21	3.80	4.10	4.64	4.81	4.59	5.43	4.82	4.70	5.13	5.76
Thailand	578	37	45	56	56	57	54	58	69	65	68	80	97
Tonga	866	.0158	.0138	.0141	.0114	.0097	.0075	.0124	.0088	.0067	.0146	.0176	....
Vanuatu	846	.023	.025	.028	.030	.035	.034	.026	.026	.020	.019	.027	.037
Vietnam	582	....	....	....	7	9	9	12	14	15	17	20	26
* of which:													
Taiwan Province of China	528	84.6	92.9	111.6	115.7	121.1	110.5	121.5	147.8	122.5	130.5	143.9	173.9
Europe	170	**157.66**	**201.96**	**255.05**	**276.29**	**285.98**	**280.57**	**279.31**	**340.78**	**359.31**	**396.55**	**510.33**	**686.27**
Albania	914	.1	.1	.2	.2	.1	.2	.3	.3	.3	.3	.5	....
Armenia	911	.16	.22	.27	.29	.23	.22	.23	.29	.34	.51	.68	.71
Azerbaijan, Republic of	912	.7	.7	.6	.6	.8	.6	.9	1.7	2.3	2.2	2.6	3.6
Belarus	913	2	3	5	6	7	7	6	7	7	8	10	14
Bulgaria	918	4	4	5	7	5	4	4	5	5	6	8	10
Croatia	960	3.9	4.3	4.6	4.5	4.2	4.5	4.3	4.4	4.7	4.9	6.2	8.0
Cyprus	423	.87	.97	1.23	1.40	1.10	1.06	1.00	.95	.98	.84	.84	1.15
Czech Republic	935	† 14	† 16	† 22	22	23	26	26	29	33	38	49	67
Estonia	939	.8	† 1.3	1.8	2.1	2.9	3.1	2.9	3.1	3.3	3.4	4.5	5.9
Georgia	915	....	156	151	199	240	191	238	326	317	350	476	....
Hungary	944	8.9	10.4	12.8	15.6	19.0	23.0	25.0	28.0	30.5	34.5	42.5	54.9
Kazakhstan	916	3.3	3.2	5.3	5.9	6.5	5.3	5.9	8.8	8.6	9.7	12.9	20.1
Kyrgyz Republic	917	.3	.3	.4	.5	.6	.5	.5	.5	.5	.5	.6	.7
Latvia	941	1	1	1	1	2	2	2	2	2	2	3	4
Lithuania	946	2	2	2	3	3	3	3	4	4	5	7	9
Macedonia, FYR	962	1.1	1.1	1.2	1.1	1.2	1.3	1.2	1.3	1.2	1.1	1.4	1.7
Malta	181	1.36	1.57	1.91	1.73	1.63	1.83	1.98	2.44	1.96	2.23	2.47	2.64
Moldova	921	—	1	1	1	1	1	—	—	1	1	1	1
Poland	964	14	17	23	24	26	27	27	32	36	41	54	74
Romania	968	4.9	6.2	7.9	8.1	8.4	8.3	8.5	10.4	11.4	13.9	17.6	23.5
Russia	922	44	† 68	83	91	89	75	76	106	102	107	136	183
Slovak Republic	936	5	7	9	9	8	11	10	12	13	14	22	28
Slovenia	961	6	7	8	8	8	9	9	9	9	10	13	16
Turkey	186	15	18	22	23	26	27	27	28	31	35	47	62
Ukraine	926	8	10	13	14	14	13	12	15	16	18	23	33
Middle East	405	**135.33**	**142.99**	**157.75**	**183.87**	**185.92**	**148.57**	**183.38**	**289.77**	**266.47**	**286.40**	**342.20**	**433.23**
Bahrain, Kingdom of	419	3.7	3.6	4.1	4.7	4.4	3.3	4.4	6.2	5.6	5.8	6.4	7.6
Egypt	469	2.3	3.5	3.4	3.5	3.9	3.1	3.6	4.7	4.1	4.7	6.3	7.5
Iran, I.R. of	429	18	19	18	22	18	13	21	28	24	28	34	....
Israel	436	15	17	19	21	23	23	26	31	29	29	32	39
Jordan	439	1.25	1.42	1.77	1.82	1.84	1.80	1.83	1.90	2.29	2.77	3.08	3.95
Kuwait	443	10.2	11.3	12.8	14.9	14.2	9.6	12.2	19.4	16.2	15.4	20.7	28.7
Lebanon	446	.5	.5	.7	.7	.6	.7	.7	.7	.9	1.0	1.5	1.7
Libya	672	8	9	8	8	7	5	8	10	9	8	11	....
Oman	449	5.4	5.5	6.1	7.3	7.6	5.5	7.2	11.3	11.1	11.2	11.7	13.3
Qatar	453	....	3.1	3.5	3.8	3.8	4.9	7.2	....	....	10.8	13.2	....
Qatar	453	....	3.1	3.5	3.8	3.8	4.9	7.2	....	....	10.8	13.2	....
Saudi Arabia	456	42	43	50	61	61	39	51	77	68	72	93	126
Syrian Arab Rep	463	3.1	3.0	3.6	4.0	3.9	2.9	3.5	† 19.3	21.6	28.1	23.6	22.2
United Arab Emirates	466	....	....	....	....	....	....	....	50	49	52	66	....
Yemen, Republic of	474	1	1	2	3	3	1	2	4	3	....	....	....
Western Hemisphere	205	**158.11**	**183.14**	**221.95**	**249.81**	**277.22**	**274.39**	**292.70**	**353.25**	**339.28**	**342.54**	**372.10**	**458.51**
Anguilla	312	.0010	.0009	.0005	.0016	.0016	.0032	.0026	.0040	.0032	.0043	....	....
Argentina	213	13	16	21	24	26	26	23	26	27	26	30	34
Aruba	314	....	....	—	—	—	—	—	.2	.1	.1	.1	.1
Bahamas, The	313	.2	.2	.2	.2	.2	.3	.5	.6	.4	.4	.4	.4
Barbados	316	.19	.18	.24	.28	.28	.25	.26	.27	.26	.21	.21	.22
Belize	339	.14	.15	.16	.17	.18	.17	.19	.22	.17	.17	.20	....
Bolivia	218	.7	1.0	1.1	1.1	1.2	1.1	1.1	1.2	1.3	1.3	1.6	2.1
Brazil	223	39	44	47	48	53	51	48	55	58	60	73	96
Chile	228	9.2	11.6	16.0	15.7	17.9	16.3	17.2	19.2	18.3	18.2	21.5	32.0
Colombia	233	7.1	8.4	10.1	10.6	11.5	10.9	11.6	13.0	12.3	11.9	12.7	16.2
Costa Rica	238	2.6	2.9	3.5	3.8	4.3	5.5	6.7	5.8	5.0	5.3	6.1	6.3
Dominica	321	—	—	—	.1	.1	.1	.1	.1	—	—	—	....
Dominican Republic	243	.51	.64	.87	.95	1.02	.88	.81	.97	.80	.83	1.04	....
Ecuador	248	2.9	3.8	4.3	5.2	5.3	4.2	4.5	4.9	4.7	5.0	6.0	7.7
El Salvador	253	.7	.8	1.0	1.0	1.4	1.3	1.2	1.3	1.2	1.2	1.3	1.5
Grenada	328	.02	.02	.02	.02	.02	.03	....	....	....	....	....	....
Guatemala	258	1.3	1.6	2.0	2.1	2.4	2.6	2.5	2.7	2.5	2.5	2.6	2.9
Guyana	336	.41	.46	.45	.52	.64	.48	.52	.50	.48	.49	.63	.59
Haiti	263	.080	.082	.110	.090	.212	.320	.334	.318	.274	.280	.347	.391
Honduras	268	.8	.8	1.2	1.3	1.4	1.5	1.2	1.4	1.3	1.3	1.3	1.5
Jamaica	343	1.07	1.21	1.43	1.38	1.38	1.31	1.24	1.29	1.22	1.11	1.18	1.39

Exports, f.o.b.

		1993	1994	1995	1996	1997	1998	1999	2000	2001	2002	2003	2004
							Billions of US Dollars						
Western Hemisphere(Cont.)													
Mexico	273	52	61	80	96	110	117	136	166	159	161	165	189
Netherlands Antilles	353	1.3	1.4	....	....	....	....	....	2.0	2.4	1.6	1.2	....
Nicaragua	278	.3	.3	.5	.5	.6	.6	.5	.6	.6	.6	.6	.8
Panama	283	.55	.58	.63	....	.72	.78	.82	.86	.91	.85	.86	.94
Paraguay	288	.7	.8	.9	1.0	1.1	1.0	.7	.9	1.0	1.0	1.2	1.6
Peru	293	3.4	4.4	5.5	5.9	6.8	5.8	6.1	7.0	7.0	7.7	9.1	12.6
St. Lucia	362	.1	.1	.1	.1	.1	.1	.1	—	—	—	.1	....
St. Vincent & Grens	364	.06	.05	.04	.05	.05	.05	.05	.05	.04	.04	.04	.04
Suriname	366	1.19	.45	.48	.54	.56	.51	.46	.51	.40	.47	.64	....
Trinidad and Tobago	369	1.7	1.9	2.5	2.5	2.5	2.3	2.8	4.3	4.3	3.9	5.2	....
Uruguay	298	1.6	1.9	2.1	2.4	2.7	2.8	2.2	2.3	2.1	1.9	2.2	2.9
Venezuela, Rep. Bol	299	15	16	18	23	22	17	20	31	25	26	24	34
Memorandum Items													
Euro Area	163	....	....	....	....	....	791.46	† 884.59	922.63	936.32	1,006.81	1,170.79	1,410.67
Oil Exporting Countries	999	180.75	187.43	209.51	247.84	252.96	199.72	238.66	360.67	318.03	329.84	396.52	517.27
Non-Oil Developing Countries	201	990.30	1,186.36	1,448.92	1,537.98	1,642.89	1,579.71	1,668.45	2,013.27	1,940.62	2,108.58	2,503.56	3,174.63

Imports, c.i.f.

		1993	1994	1995	1996	1997	1998	1999	2000	2001	2002	2003	2004
							Billions of US Dollars						
World	001	3,840.2	4,365.0	5,213.9	5,471.3	5,647.4	5,579.1	5,802.5	6,571.1	6,335.7	6,575.3	7,657.9	9,318.5
Industrial Countries	110	2,558.6	2,906.4	3,436.5	3,559.4	3,636.5	3,739.8	3,931.0	4,339.2	4,159.8	4,262.2	4,925.1	5,842.5
United States	111	603	689	771	822	899	944	1,059	1,259	1,179	1,200	1,303	1,526
Canada	156	139	155	168	175	201	206	220	245	227	227	245	273
Australia	193	46	53	61	65	66	65	69	72	64	73	89	109
Japan	158	242	275	336	349	339	280	311	380	349	337	383	455
New Zealand	196	9.6	11.9	14.0	14.7	14.5	12.5	14.3	13.9	13.3	15.0	18.6	23.2
Euro Area													
Austria	122	48.6	55.3	66.4	67.3	64.8	68.2	† 69.6	69.0	70.4	72.8	88.3	108.9
Belgium	124	114	130	160	164	157	165	† 165	177	179	198	235	285
Finland	172	18.0	23.2	28.1	29.3	29.8	32.3	† 31.6	33.9	32.1	33.6	41.6	50.1
France	132	203	235	281	282	272	290	† 295	311	302	312	371	443
Germany	134	346	385	464	459	446	471	† 474	495	486	490	605	718
Greece	174	20.2	21.4	26.8	29.7	27.9	29.4	28.7	29.2	29.9	31.2	44.4	51.6
Ireland	178	22.0	25.9	33.1	35.9	39.2	44.6	† 47.2	51.5	51.3	51.5	53.3	61.4
Italy	136	148	169	206	208	210	218	† 220	238	236	246	297	355
Luxembourg	137	8	8	10	10	9	10	† 11	11	11	12	14	17
Netherlands	138	125	141	177	181	178	188	† 188	199	196	194	233	284
Portugal	182	24.3	27.3	33.3	35.2	35.1	† 38.5	† 39.8	38.2	39.4	38.3	40.8	49.2
Spain	184	79.7	92.2	113.3	121.8	122.7	133.1	† 144.4	152.9	153.6	163.5	208.5	257.6
Denmark	128	31.3	36.6	45.7	45.0	44.4	46.3	44.5	44.4	44.1	48.9	56.2	66.6
Iceland	176	1.34	1.47	1.76	2.03	1.99	2.49	2.50	2.59	2.25	2.27	2.79	3.55
Norway	142	24.0	27.3	33.0	35.6	35.7	37.5	34.2	34.4	33.0	34.9	39.5	48.1
Sweden	144	42.7	51.7	64.7	66.9	65.7	68.6	68.8	73.0	63.5	66.4	84.2	100.4
Switzerland	146	57	64	77	74	71	74	75	76	77	79	92	107
United Kingdom	112	206	226	265	287	307	314	318	334	321	335	381	452
Developing Countries	200	1,281.69	1,458.60	1,777.38	1,911.91	2,010.86	1,839.31	1,871.50	2,231.93	2,175.91	2,313.14	2,732.74	3,476.00
Africa	605	75.85	82.48	101.36	101.83	105.66	105.95	100.00	103.88	108.73	113.46	138.32	171.76
Algeria	612	8.0	9.2	10.1	9.1	....	....	....	....	....	12.0	12.4	18.2
Benin	638	.57	.43	.75	.65	.68	.74	.75	.61	.62	.72	.89	.85
Botswana	616	1.77	1.64	1.91	1.72	2.26	2.39	2.21	2.47	1.81	1.93	2.36	....
Burkina Faso	748	.51	.35	.45	.65	.59	.73	.57	.65	.65	.70	.92	1.11
Burundi	618	.20	.22	.23	.13	.12	.16	.12	.15	.14	.13	.16	.18
Cameroon	622	1.1	1.1	.9	1.1	1.2	1.5	1.5	1.3	1.6	2.8	2.2	2.4
Cape Verde	624	.15	.21	.25	.23	.23	.23	.26	.23	.25	.29	....	....
Central African Rep.	626	.13	.14	.17	.14	.14	.15	.13	.12	.11	.12	.12	.16
Chad	628	.20	.18	.37	.33	.33	.36	.32	.32	.68	1.65	.87	.74
Congo, Rep. of	634	.58	.63	.67	1.55	.93	.68	.82	.46	....	....	....	....
Côte d'Ivoire	662	2.1	1.9	2.9	2.9	2.8	3.3	2.8	2.4	2.4	2.5	3.3	....
Equatorial Guinea	642	.06	.04	.05	.29	.33	.32	.43	.45	....	....	....	....
Ethiopia	644	.79	1.03	1.15	1.40	....	1.52	1.54	1.26	1.81	1.67	....	....
Gabon	646	.85	.76	.88	.96	1.10	1.10	.84	.99	.86	.94	1.04	1.37
Gambia, The	648	.26	.21	.18	.26	.17	.23	.19	.19	.13	.15	....	.23
Ghana	652	3.9	2.1	1.9	2.1	2.3	2.6	3.5	3.0	....	....	....	....
Guinea-Bissau	654	.061	.164	.133	.087	.089	.063	.051	.049	.062	.058	.069	....
Kenya	664	1.8	2.1	3.0	2.9	3.3	3.2	2.8	3.1	3.2	3.2	3.7	4.6
Lesotho	666	.87	.85	.99	1.00	1.02	.86	.78	.73	.68	.79	1.02	....
Madagascar	674	.47	.44	.54	.52	.50	.54	.59	.73	.74	.51	1.21	....
Malawi	676	.55	.49	.47	.62	.78	.52	.67	.53	.56	.70	.79	.93
Mali	678	.63	.59	.77	.77	.74	.76	.61	.59	.73	.71	.98	....
Mauritius	684	1.72	1.93	1.98	2.29	2.19	2.07	2.25	2.09	1.99	2.16	2.36	2.78
Morocco	686	6.7	8.3	10.0	9.7	9.5	10.3	9.9	11.5	11.0	11.9	....	....
Mozambique	688	....	1	1	1	1	1	1	....	....	....	....	....
Namibia	728	1.33	1.41	1.62	1.67	1.75	1.65	1.61	1.55	1.55	1.26	1.79	2.18
Niger	692	.37	.33	.37	.45	.37	.47	.34	.32	.33	.37	.41	.52
Nigeria	694	5.5	6.6	† 8.2	6.4	9.5	9.2	8.6	8.7	11.6	7.5	10.9	14.2
Rwanda	714	.33	.12	.24	.26	.30	.28	.25	.21	.25	.20	.25	.28
Senegal	722	1.09	1.02	1.41	1.44	1.33	1.46	1.37	1.34	1.43	1.60	2.36	2.84
Seychelles	718	.24	.21	.23	.38	.34	.38	.43	.34	.48	.42	.41	.50
Sierra Leone	724	.15	.15	.13	.21	.09	.09	.08	.15	.18	.26	.30	.29
South Africa	199	20	23	31	30	33	† 29	27	30	28	29	41	48
Sudan	732	.9	1.2	† 1.2	1.5	1.6	1.9	1.4	1.6	1.6	2.4	2.7	....
Swaziland	734	.79	.84	1.01	1.06	1.07	1.08	1.07	1.05	1.13	.98	....	....
Tanzania	738	1.5	1.5	1.7	1.4	1.3	1.5	1.5	1.5	1.7	1.7	2.1	2.5
Togo	742	.18	.22	.59	.66	.65	.59	.49	.48	.52	.58	.84	.56
Tunisia	744	6.2	6.6	7.9	7.7	7.9	8.4	8.5	8.6	9.5	9.5	10.9	12.7
Uganda	746	.61	.87	1.06	1.19	1.32	1.42	1.34	1.54	1.59	1.11	1.25	2.02
Zambia	754	.81	.59	.70	.84	.82	1.09	.88	1.10	....	....	....	....
Zimbabwe	698	1.82	2.24	2.66	3.81	3.11	2.79	2.18	1.84	1.72	....	.69	2.15
Asia *	505	695.17	812.73	999.96	1,050.54	1,066.38	886.65	965.72	1,205.58	1,124.19	1,221.51	1,462.84	1,868.22
Bangladesh	513	4.0	4.6	6.5	6.6	6.9	7.0	7.7	8.4	8.3	7.9	9.5	11.3
Bhutan	514	.1	.1	.1	.1	.1	.1	.2	.2	.2	.2	.2	....
Cambodia	522	....	....	....	....	1	1	1	1	1	2	2	....
China, P.R.: Mainland	924	104	116	132	139	142	140	166	225	244	295	413	561
China, P.R.: Hong Kong	532	139	162	193	199	209	185	180	213	201	208	232	271
China, P.R.: Macao	546	2.03	2.13	2.04	2.00	2.08	1.95	2.04	2.25	2.39	2.53	2.76	3.48
Fiji	819	.72	.83	.89	.99	.97	.72	.90	.83	.79	.90	1.17	1.27
India	534	22.8	26.8	34.7	37.9	41.4	43.0	47.0	51.5	50.4	56.5	71.2	94.1
Indonesia	536	28.3	32.0	40.6	42.9	51.3	35.3	33.3	43.6	37.5	38.3	42.2	52.1
Korea	542	84	102	135	150	145	93	120	160	141	152	179	224
Lao People's Dem. Rep.	544	.4	.6	.6	.7	.7	.6	.5	.5	.5	.4	.5	.5
Malaysia	548	45.7	59.6	77.7	78.4	79.0	58.3	65.4	82.0	73.9	79.9	81.9	105.3

Imports, c.i.f.

		1993	1994	1995	1996	1997	1998	1999	2000	2001	2002	2003	2004
						Billions of US Dollars							
Asia *(Cont.)													
Maldives	556	.2	.2	.3	.3	.3	.4	.4	.4	.4	.4	.5	.6
Mongolia	948	.4	.2	.4	.4	.5	.5	.5	.6	.6	.7	.8	1.0
Myanmar	518	.82	.89	1.35	1.37	2.06	2.69	2.32	2.40	2.88	2.35	2.09	2.23
Nepal	558	.89	1.16	1.33	1.40	1.69	1.25	1.42	1.57	1.47	1.42	1.75	1.87
Pakistan	564	9.5	8.9	11.5	12.1	11.6	9.3	10.2	10.9	10.2	11.2	13.0	17.9
Papua New Guinea	853	1.29	1.52	1.45	1.74	1.70	1.23	1.19	1.15	1.07	1.24	1.36	1.68
Philippines	566	18.7	22.6	28.3	34.1	38.6	31.5	32.6	37.0	34.9	37.2	39.5	42.3
Samoa	862	.105	.081	.095	.100	.097	.097	.115	.090	.120	.128	.129	.155
Singapore	576	85	103	125	131	132	105	111	135	116	116	128	164
Solomon Islands	813	.137	.142	.154	.118	.148	.150	.111	.098	.090	.067	.082	.100
Sri Lanka	524	3.99	4.78	5.19	5.42	5.84	5.93	5.87	6.28	5.97	6.10	6.67	7.97
Thailand	578	46	54	71	72	63	43	50	62	62	65	76	95
Tonga	866	.061	.069	.077	.075	.073	.069	.073	.069	.073	.089	.093	....
Vanuatu	846	.079	.089	.095	.098	.094	.093	.098	.087	.090	.090	.105	.128
Vietnam	582	....	....	....	11	12	12	12	16	16	19	25	31
* of which:													
Taiwan Province of China	528	77.1	85.5	103.7	101.3	113.9	104.9	111.0	139.9	107.3	112.8	127.4	168.1
Europe	170	**188.08**	**216.81**	**289.55**	**333.69**	**354.96**	**349.05**	**309.52**	**358.34**	**374.65**	**422.14**	**540.57**	**707.67**
Albania	914	.6	.6	.7	.8	.6	.8	1.1	1.1	1.3	1.5	1.9	....
Armenia	911	.25	.39	.67	.86	.89	.90	.80	.88	.87	.99	1.27	1.32
Azerbaijan, Republic of	912	.6	.8	.7	1.0	.8	1.1	1.0	1.2	1.4	1.7	2.6	3.5
Belarus	913	3	3	6	7	9	9	7	9	8	9	12	16
Bulgaria	918	5	4	6	7	5	5	5	7	7	8	11	14
Croatia	960	4.7	5.2	7.5	7.8	9.1	8.4	7.8	7.9	9.1	10.7	14.2	16.6
Cyprus	423	2.59	3.02	3.69	3.98	3.70	3.69	3.62	3.85	3.92	4.09	4.46	5.73
Czech Republic	935	† 16	† 18	† 26	29	29	30	29	34	38	43	54	....
Estonia	939	.9	† 1.7	2.5	3.2	4.4	4.6	4.1	4.2	4.3	4.8	6.5	8.5
Georgia	915	....	338	392	687	944	887	585	720	752	794	1,141	....
Hungary	944	12.5	14.3	15.4	18.1	21.1	25.7	27.9	32.0	33.7	37.8	47.6	59.6
Kazakhstan	916	3.9	3.6	3.8	4.2	4.3	4.3	3.7	5.0	6.4	6.6	8.4	12.8
Kyrgyz Republic	917	.4	.3	.5	.8	.7	.8	.6	.6	.5	.6	.7	.9
Latvia	941	1	1	2	2	3	3	3	3	4	4	5	7
Lithuania	946	2	2	3	4	5	5	5	5	6	8	10	12
Macedonia, FYR	962	1.2	1.5	1.7	1.6	1.8	1.9	1.8	2.1	1.7	2.0	2.3	2.9
Malta	181	2.17	2.44	2.94	2.80	2.55	2.67	2.85	3.40	2.73	2.84	3.40	3.83
Moldova	921	1	1	1	1	1	1	1	1	1	1	1	2
Poland	964	19	21	29	37	42	46	46	49	50	55	68	88
Romania	968	6.5	7.1	10.3	11.4	11.3	11.8	10.4	13.1	15.6	17.9	24.0	32.7
Russia	922	36	† 55	69	75	79	64	44	49	59	67	84	106
Slovak Republic	936	7	7	9	11	11	14	12	13	16	17	24	30
Slovenia	961	7	7	9	9	9	10	10	10	11	14	18
Turkey	186	29	23	36	44	49	46	41	55	41	50	66	96
Ukraine	926	10	11	15	18	17	15	12	14	16	17	23	29
Middle East	405	**135.72**	**128.15**	**142.10**	**154.41**	**160.58**	**158.83**	**162.49**	**180.85**	**196.92**	**210.20**	**235.54**	**292.07**
Bahrain, Kingdom of	419	3.9	3.7	3.7	4.3	4.0	3.6	3.7	4.6	4.3	5.0	5.1	6.3
Egypt	469	8.2	10.2	11.8	13.0	13.2	16.2	16.0	14.0	12.8	12.6	11.1	12.9
Iran, I.R. of	429	21	14	12	15	14	14	13	14	18	21	28	....
Israel	436	22.6	25.2	29.6	31.6	30.8	29.3	33.2	31.4	35.4	35.5	36.3	42.9
Jordan	439	3.5	3.4	3.7	4.3	4.1	3.8	3.7	4.6	4.9	5.1	5.7	8.1
Kuwait	443	7.0	6.7	7.8	8.4	8.2	8.6	7.6	7.2	7.9	9.0	11.0	12.0
Lebanon	446	† 2.2	2.6	5.5	7.5	7.5	7.1	6.2	6.2	7.3	6.4	7.2	9.4
Libya	672	5.6	4.3	4.1	4.4	4.6	4.7	4.2	3.7	4.4	4.4	4.3	....
Oman	449	4.11	3.91	4.25	4.58	5.03	5.68	4.67	5.04	5.80	6.01	6.57	8.87
Qatar	453	1.89	1.93	3.40	2.87	3.32	3.41	2.50	....	....	4.05	4.90	6.00
Saudi Arabia	456	28	23	28	28	29	30	28	30	31	32	37	45
Syrian Arab Rep	463	4.1	5.5	4.7	5.4	4.0	3.9	3.8	† 16.7	19.6	21.0	21.1	29.1
United Arab Emirates	466	20	21	21	23	30	25	33	35	37	43	52	....
Yemen, Republic of	474	3	2	2	2	2	2	2	2	2	....	....	....
Western Hemisphere	205	**189.33**	**221.74**	**250.89**	**280.16**	**333.65**	**351.96**	**342.21**	**391.19**	**382.44**	**356.07**	**368.36**	**449.77**
Anguilla	312	.0355	.0364	.0324	.0599	.0616	.0714	.0919	.0945	.0777	.0699	....	....
Argentina	213	17	22	20	24	30	31	26	25	20	9	14	22
Aruba	314	....	....	.6	.6	.6	.8	.8	.8	.8	.8	.8	.9
Bahamas, The	313	1.0	1.1	1.2	1.4	1.7	1.9	1.8	2.1	1.9	1.7	1.8	1.6
Barbados	316	.58	.61	.77	.83	1.00	1.01	1.11	1.16	1.09	1.04	1.13	1.31
Belize	339	.28	.26	.26	.26	.29	.30	.37	.52	.52	.52	.55	....
Bolivia	218	1.2	1.2	1.4	1.6	1.9	2.0	1.8	1.8	1.7	1.8	1.6	1.8
Brazil	223	28	36	54	57	65	61	52	59	58	50	51	66
Chile	228	11.1	11.8	15.9	19.2	20.8	19.9	16.0	18.5	17.4	17.1	19.4	24.9
Colombia	233	9.8	11.9	13.9	13.7	15.4	14.6	10.7	11.5	12.8	12.7	13.9	16.7
Costa Rica	238	3.5	3.8	4.1	4.3	5.0	6.2	6.4	6.4	6.6	7.2	7.7	8.3
Dominica	321	.1	.1	.1	.1	.1	.1	.1	.1	.1	.1	.1	.1
Dominican Republic	243	2.4	3.4	3.6	4.1	4.8	5.6	6.0	7.4	....	....	....	....
Ecuador	248	2.6	3.6	4.2	4.3	5.0	5.6	3.0	3.7	5.4	6.4	6.5	7.9
El Salvador	253	1.9	2.2	2.9	2.7	3.0	3.1	3.1	3.8	3.9	3.9	4.4	4.9
Grenada	328	.12	.12	.12	.15	.17	.20	.20	.25	....	....	....	....
Guatemala	258	2.6	2.8	3.3	3.1	3.9	4.7	4.6	5.2	5.6	6.3	6.7	7.8
Guyana	336	.48	.51	.53	.60	.63	....	....	....	.58	.56	1.02	.68
Haiti	263	.355	.252	.653	.665	.648	.797	1.025	1.036	1.013	1.130	1.188	1.306
Honduras	268	1.1	1.1	1.6	1.8	2.1	2.5	2.7	2.9	2.9	3.0	3.3	3.9
Jamaica	343	2.13	2.22	2.82	2.97	3.13	3.04	2.90	3.30	3.36	3.53	3.64	3.77
Mexico	273	68	83	76	94	115	131	149	183	176	177	179	207
Netherlands Antilles	353	1.9	1.8	....	....	....	....	....	2.9	2.8	2.3	2.6	....

Imports, c.i.f.

		1993	1994	1995	1996	1997	1998	1999	2000	2001	2002	2003	2004
						Billions of US Dollars							
Western Hemisphere(Cont.)													
Nicaragua	278	.8	.9	1.0	1.2	1.4	1.5	1.9	1.8	1.8	1.8	1.9	2.2
Panama	283	2.19	2.40	2.51	2.78	3.00	3.40	3.52	3.38	2.96	2.98	3.09	3.59
Paraguay	288	1.7	2.1	2.8	2.9	3.1	2.5	1.7	2.1	2.0	....	....	....
Peru	293	4.9	6.7	9.3	9.4	10.3	9.9	8.2	8.9	....	....	....	....
St. Lucia	362	.3	.3	.3	.3	.3	.3	.4	.4	.4	.3	.4	....
St. Vincent & Grens	364	.13	.13	.14	.13	.19	.19	.20	.16	.19	.17	.20	.23
Suriname	366	.99	.42	.59	.50	.57	.55	.56	.52	.46	.49	.70	....
Trinidad and Tobago	369	1.5	1.1	1.7	2.1	3.0	3.0	2.7	3.3	3.6	3.6	3.9	....
Uruguay	298	2.3	2.8	2.9	3.3	3.7	3.8	3.4	3.5	3.1	2.0	2.2	2.9
Venezuela, Rep. Bol	299	12.5	9.2	12.6	9.9	14.6	15.8	14.1	16.2	18.3	13.0	9.3	16.7
Memorandum Items													
Euro Area	163	....	....	....	....	....	709.27	† 830.50	911.42	898.96	906.68	1,094.41	1,323.04
Oil Exporting Countries	999	142.67	132.35	153.18	154.57	178.50	162.50	158.98	178.65	187.63	192.73	220.80	283.50
Non-Oil Developing Countries.	201	1,139.27	1,327.22	1,625.60	1,759.13	1,833.90	1,678.22	1,714.10	2,055.43	1,990.09	2,122.49	2,514.61	3,196.50

Export Unit Values/Export Prices

		1993	1994	1995	1996	1997	1998	1999	2000	2001	2002	2003	2004
		Indices of Unit Values (Prices) In Terms of US Dollars: 2000=100											
World	001	107.2	110.2	121.2	119.0	111.6	105.4	103.9	100.0	96.2	96.9	106.9	114.0
Industrial Countries	110	107.8	110.9	122.4	119.8	111.4	108.0	105.6	100.0	97.2	98.1	109.6	117.0
United States	111	96.9	98.9	103.9	104.5	103.1	99.7	98.4	100.0	99.2	98.2	99.7	103.6
Canada	156	91.0	92.1	98.9	100.2	98.2	97.4	105.7	100.0	97.8	95.1	105.6	115.0
Australia	193	102.2	106.8	116.3	117.7	113.6	100.9	96.2	100.0	98.2	100.0	109.9	129.1
Japan	158	109.9	116.3	123.6	111.9	102.5	96.0	99.2	100.0	91.4	87.6	90.9	96.0
New Zealand	196	107.5	113.3	123.3	124.6	116.4	98.6	98.8	100.0	100.7	99.3	111.2	128.3
Euro Area													
Belgium	124	104.2	109.0	125.9	123.0	112.1	110.4	105.2	100.0	99.3	103.5	120.4	135.2
Finland	172	102.1	113.3	145.1	139.1	120.5	117.0	107.1	100.0	92.8	92.3	106.0	117.2
France	132	134.0	† 143.8	158.7	150.0	128.5	123.2	114.0	100.0	107.7	109.0	130.7	102.0
Germany	134	127.0	128.3	148.5	138.4	120.5	118.1	111.5	100.0	99.0	101.5	118.3	128.9
Greece	174	112.8	115.8	133.7	138.3	125.7	118.8	123.1	100.0	104.9	112.3	134.8	153.4
Ireland	178	108.5	109.8	119.8	118.9	113.9	109.8	110.0	100.0	98.3	103.2	114.7	115.4
Italy	136	95.5	96.6	104.5	115.1	107.6	109.1	107.1	100.0	100.6	107.3	129.6	148.8
Netherlands	138	111.8	114.4	131.9	126.0	115.6	110.1	102.8	100.0	99.6	99.4	115.6	126.3
Portugal	182	135.1	133.0	144.2	131.6	119.2	116.3	109.3	100.0	92.9	96.3	112.0	....
Spain	184	116.4	115.3	131.9	131.2	117.2	114.9	108.9	100.0	97.6	101.7	120.1	133.4
Denmark	128	111.0	114.4	130.4	128.4	114.9	111.8	107.9	100.0	98.9	102.4	122.2	135.8
Iceland (1995=100)	176	87.4	88.2	100.0	95.8	90.9	....	....	....	....	....	....	....
Norway	142	78.2	76.1	87.4	92.6	85.6	71.2	77.9	100.0	93.1	93.3	104.3	126.8
Sweden	144	102.2	108.3	130.5	132.0	117.0	111.8	106.5	100.0	90.1	93.8	110.3	121.2
Switzerland	146	107.2	115.0	130.2	125.8	111.1	111.5	109.3	100.0	101.3	106.7	123.6	136.5
United Kingdom	112	104.5	108.8	116.1	115.5	114.9	110.6	105.7	100.0	93.6	97.4	108.0	120.9
Developing Countries	200	104.2	107.4	116.2	115.4	111.3	96.5	98.2	100.0	92.6	92.9	97.5	103.6
Africa	605	104.3	103.8	123.7	118.4	114.9	107.6	101.8	100.0	93.7	96.5	....	....
Burkina Faso (1995=100)	748	114.1	76.3	100.0	95.4	....	....	....	....	....	....	....	....
Kenya	664	92.8	98.6	116.8	111.6	127.2	125.2	100.6	100.0	....	....	....	....
Mauritius	684	104.1	107.0	117.3	126.4	111.3	111.4	105.4	100.0	91.7	97.0	109.8	122.7
Morocco	686	104.7	103.8	124.1	128.5	118.5	114.5	110.2	100.0	94.4	99.1	....	....
South Africa	199	103.7	107.4	123.0	114.5	112.3	103.6	99.9	100.0	93.4	95.6	....	....
Asia	505	109.9	113.4	121.7	118.8	114.3	99.6	98.5	100.0	91.9	89.5	91.0	97.2
China, P.R.: Hong Kong	532	104.9	106.4	109.8	109.6	107.7	103.6	100.6	100.0	97.6	95.0	93.8	94.8
India	534	112.0	113.6	107.5	102.6	116.8	106.8	101.0	100.0	94.3	91.9	....	....
Indonesia	536	91.0	90.3	103.1	109.0	103.6	80.8	64.9	100.0	89.9	95.5	102.7	120.4
Korea	542	146.8	150.6	161.8	140.5	127.9	102.0	99.6	100.0	86.9	83.1	85.1	91.5
Pakistan	564	89.8	96.7	117.7	114.2	115.0	117.2	109.4	100.0	93.9	89.9	96.2	103.0
Papua New Guinea	853	77.4	87.3	99.0	99.4	97.2	81.2	80.3	100.0	89.4	85.5	101.0	126.4
Philippines	566	130.9	134.9	139.7	145.3	134.1	104.6	120.2	100.0	82.8	75.9	....	....
Singapore	576	111.6	113.2	119.9	119.4	111.7	† 97.2	96.2	100.0	92.5	† 90.5	89.7	92.7
Sri Lanka	524	86.9	89.1	98.6	102.1	104.5	109.9	100.6	100.0	96.2	90.7	96.2	101.6
Thailand	578	103.0	106.5	116.4	126.7	122.1	106.2	102.1	100.0	98.6	91.5	98.6	114.3
Europe	170	111.0	112.5	127.0	122.2	115.6	113.5	106.9	100.0	100.1	103.0	115.2	131.5
Hungary	944	111.4	114.9	128.7	125.0	117.3	115.4	108.3	100.0	100.7	106.3	121.7	132.5
Latvia	941	65.5	91.0	112.1	114.1	109.9	108.1	104.9	100.0	99.1	103.4	120.8	145.0
Poland	964	107.8	110.6	125.7	122.1	113.4	115.0	107.9	100.0	101.9	106.8	117.8	138.1
Turkey	186	117.4	† 113.9	128.3	122.6	116.8	112.1	104.5	100.0	97.4	95.7	105.3	† 122.0
Middle East	405	69.6	69.7	76.3	86.3	82.0	59.4	74.5	100.0	89.2	....	....	....
Israel	436	99.5	98.0	102.7	† 102.7	101.8	98.8	99.9	100.0	† 96.4	96.3	100.4	105.8
Jordan	439	92.3	95.9	111.4	117.0	113.6	107.3	104.6	100.0	101.4	101.7	101.9	113.7
Saudi Arabia	456	57.7	58.0	64.2	75.8	71.7	46.3	67.1	100.0	97.5	....	....	....
Western Hemisphere	205	94.5	101.3	108.9	114.7	114.4	100.0	114.6	100.0	94.3	109.2	117.3	112.3
Argentina	213	102.0	105.0	111.0	118.3	114.2	102.3	90.9	100.0	96.6	92.9	101.7	111.4
Bolivia	218	123.0	131.5	141.1	138.4	98.2	86.8	85.4	100.0	91.5	80.5	90.4	121.9
Brazil	223	93.7	99.0	102.9	106.4	112.7	98.6	93.3	100.0	94.8	90.7	101.1	111.8
Colombia	233	77.2	102.9	111.6	104.3	115.0	102.4	95.4	100.0	89.1	85.4	87.3	96.2
Costa Rica (1990=100)	238	68.7	....	....	....	....	....	....	....	....	....	....	....
Ecuador	248	71.4	73.0	75.4	29.1	28.7	21.6	78.1	100.0	87.8	94.3	106.3	117.9
Honduras	268	90.1	98.4	132.4	118.6	135.6	138.2	102.9	100.0	101.0	95.2	83.1	102.2
Peru	293	75.0	88.5	107.2	106.8	103.6	83.9	82.7	100.0	84.8	88.0	98.5	125.6
Memorandum Items													
Oil Exporting Countries	999	70.6	70.6	78.9	88.9	84.5	59.2	69.7	100.0	86.8	....	....	....
Non-Oil Developing Countries	201	109.4	113.1	122.0	119.4	115.3	102.8	102.9	100.0	93.5	93.3	97.4	102.4

Import Unit Values/Import Prices

		1993	1994	1995	1996	1997	1998	1999	2000	2001	2002	2003	2004
		Indices of Unit Values (Prices) In Terms of US Dollars: 2000=100											
World...............................	001	**102.4**	**105.5**	**116.2**	**114.7**	**108.5**	**101.6**	**99.7**	**100.0**	**96.3**	**95.8**	**104.8**	**114.5**
Industrial Countries..................	110	**103.4**	**106.1**	**116.8**	**115.0**	**107.9**	**102.1**	**100.4**	**100.0**	**96.3**	**96.2**	**106.1**	**116.1**
United States.............................	111	94.6	96.2	100.6	101.6	99.1	93.1	93.9	100.0	96.5	94.1	96.9	102.3
Canada.....................................	156	98.2	98.6	101.8	102.1	101.2	94.3	95.7	100.0	98.8	98.2	102.0	107.9
Australia...................................	193	106.1	111.4	117.0	116.9	110.7	101.6	102.0	100.0	94.3	94.5	103.8	111.1
Japan.......................................	158	96.4	99.1	107.6	102.1	98.6	86.7	90.4	100.0	90.9	86.8	93.1	103.9
New Zealand..............................	196	103.6	109.8	121.4	123.9	117.9	99.0	100.0	100.0	93.9	97.0	107.5	116.8
Euro Area													
Belgium....................................	124	98.0	103.3	120.8	119.2	109.5	105.9	102.8	100.0	99.5	102.2	119.8	136.3
Finland.....................................	172	100.6	109.7	131.2	126.6	113.3	106.2	102.3	100.0	94.3	96.3	114.8	130.8
France......................................	132	125.9	† 133.7	149.0	142.7	124.4	118.0	108.6	100.0	99.5	98.9	118.7	127.6
Germany...................................	134	114.4	118.8	138.2	129.0	114.9	110.7	104.2	100.0	97.1	97.2	110.4	120.3
Ireland.....................................	178	103.6	108.8	121.2	119.1	113.4	109.0	106.7	100.0	100.0	101.1	111.1	120.6
Italy...	136	96.5	98.0	108.9	115.1	106.0	102.4	99.5	100.0	99.7	104.4	124.8	143.9
Netherlands...............................	138	110.2	112.6	127.8	122.8	112.6	107.9	103.4	100.0	101.2	101.1	117.1	129.6
Portugal....................................	182	128.3	124.8	137.7	130.0	115.1	109.4	106.0	100.0	88.9	91.0	110.3	....
Spain.......................................	184	112.1	112.7	126.4	124.9	111.9	107.2	102.5	100.0	96.2	98.0	115.9	130.6
Denmark...................................	128	106.6	109.9	127.7	125.7	114.2	112.6	108.1	100.0	98.2	101.6	119.2	132.9
Iceland (1995=100)....................	176	87.0	88.9	100.0	99.9	94.3	....	....	....	....	....	....	....
Norway.....................................	142	127.6	129.4	144.9	141.2	126.5	117.6	109.0	100.0	98.2	102.8	116.1	126.5
Sweden.....................................	144	98.0	103.4	119.2	122.3	109.5	104.2	102.7	100.0	92.7	98.6	116.2	131.2
Switzerland................................	146	116.2	119.5	135.0	129.1	115.9	112.9	106.5	100.0	100.1	105.2	121.2	134.3
United Kingdom..........................	112	100.1	105.6	115.9	114.4	112.0	106.5	103.6	100.0	94.3	95.7	103.5	115.2
Developing Countries...............	200	**98.6**	**103.2**	**113.6**	**113.4**	**110.2**	**99.4**	**96.9**	**100.0**	**96.4**	**93.9**	**99.1**	**108.0**
Africa....................................	605	**106.6**	**111.3**	**121.4**	**112.1**	**110.5**	**101.6**	**102.5**	**100.0**	**92.7**	**94.5**	**....**	**....**
Kenya.......................................	664	86.4	81.8	102.8	101.1	105.0	104.8	97.8	100.0	....	....	....	....
Mauritius..................................	684	102.3	107.7	117.8	122.1	106.5	99.1	100.2	100.0	97.0	98.8	113.2	138.3
Morocco....................................	686	121.1	138.3	146.2	151.6	134.0	116.1	113.6	100.0	91.0	97.4	....	....
South Africa..............................	199	102.8	104.6	116.4	106.9	106.1	98.8	98.2	100.0	93.3	93.2	....	....
Asia.......................................	505	**101.1**	**105.6**	**114.0**	**114.2**	**108.8**	**96.6**	**95.3**	**100.0**	**95.3**	**92.8**	**96.4**	**103.7**
China, P.R.: Hong Kong...............	532	103.1	105.9	111.2	109.8	107.2	101.9	99.6	100.0	96.8	93.0	92.8	95.5
India..	534	99.0	95.6	99.9	104.2	102.7	91.3	96.5	100.0	96.4	103.7	....	....
Korea..	542	111.0	110.1	116.8	112.0	104.7	87.4	87.3	100.0	91.0	87.5	95.6	107.3
Pakistan....................................	564	83.8	90.3	98.5	95.5	96.8	85.8	92.6	100.0	94.0	94.8	108.5	121.8
Philippines.................................	566	167.7	174.0	173.6	178.8	162.1	120.1	117.3	100.0	79.9	83.3	....	....
Singapore..................................	576	101.9	106.7	114.9	114.2	106.8	93.0	93.3	100.0	96.5	95.9	98.9	103.6
Thailand....................................	578	85.8	88.4	99.8	110.8	106.2	97.7	95.1	100.0	108.5	102.3	109.5	124.4
Europe....................................	170	**104.9**	**105.7**	**120.4**	**119.5**	**110.5**	**106.7**	**100.8**	**100.0**	**100.1**	**101.1**	**113.4**	**126.3**
Hungary....................................	944	109.7	112.1	123.4	122.7	113.8	110.5	105.4	100.0	100.9	106.1	122.1	133.9
Poland......................................	964	108.4	109.9	116.4	122.7	114.6	113.8	106.3	100.0	99.6	101.5	116.1	129.2
Turkey......................................	186	98.4	† 105.3	123.0	115.6	105.6	101.2	95.7	100.0	99.7	98.5	106.3	† 119.6
Middle East.............................	405	**100.0**	**102.3**	**110.1**	**109.4**	**104.0**	**102.1**	**99.5**	**100.0**	**97.9**	**94.1**	**99.1**	**107.3**
Israel..	436	100.7	102.8	111.5	† 110.7	105.7	99.9	97.0	100.0	† 98.6	98.5	104.5	111.9
Jordan......................................	439	87.9	84.8	95.7	103.2	100.9	100.1	97.7	100.0	102.3	105.1	115.3	130.2
Western Hemisphere.................	205	**74.4**	**82.8**	**102.4**	**103.9**	**116.3**	**105.5**	**98.5**	**100.0**	**99.6**	**91.5**	**92.7**	**104.6**
Argentina..................................	213	108.2	109.7	115.7	114.3	111.7	106.0	100.0	100.0	97.3	93.8	94.2	101.5
Brazil..	223	54.0	67.6	93.9	98.9	113.6	105.3	95.8	100.0	99.5	86.8	86.2	101.5
Colombia...................................	233	102.1	113.4	121.2	122.5	119.4	110.3	102.4	100.0	98.2	95.7	95.0	103.7
Venezuela, Rep. Bol....................	299	74.5	82.3	104.3	94.4	98.3	101.4	102.2	100.0	104.5	100.1	112.2	123.1
Memorandum Items													
Oil Exporting Countries...........	999	**87.7**	**92.5**	**106.7**	**97.5**	**98.5**	**104.7**	**104.8**	**100.0**	**100.3**	**91.3**	**98.2**	**106.0**
Non-Oil Developing Countries.	201	**98.9**	**103.5**	**113.8**	**113.8**	**110.5**	**99.3**	**96.7**	**100.0**	**96.3**	**94.0**	**99.1**	**108.1**

Terms of Trade

		1993	1994	1995	1996	1997	1998	1999	2000	2001	2002	2003	2004
		Percent Change over Previous Year; Calculated from Indices											
World	001	.4	−.2	−.2	−.6	−.8	1.0	.4	−4.0	−.1	1.3	.9	−2.5
Industrial Countries	110	.7	.1	.3	−.6	−.9	2.4	−.6	−4.9	1.0	.9	1.4	−2.5
United States	111	.8	.4	.5	−.5	1.1	2.9	−2.1	−4.6	2.8	1.5	−1.3	−1.7
Canada	156	−.8	.7	4.1	1.0	−1.1	6.3	7.0	−9.5	−1.0	−2.2	7.0	2.9
Australia	193	−6.3	−.4	3.7	1.3	1.9	−3.2	−5.0	6.1	4.1	1.7	.1	9.7
Japan	158	2.6	2.9	−2.1	−4.5	−5.2	6.5	−.9	−8.9	.6	.3	−3.3	−5.3
New Zealand	196	3.1	−.7	−1.5	−1.0	−1.8	.8	−.7	1.2	7.2	−4.5	.9	6.3
Euro Area													
Belgium	124	....	−.7	−1.2	−1.1	−.8	1.8	−1.8	−2.3	−.2	1.5	−.8	−1.3
Finland	172	−3.2	1.8	7.1	−.7	−3.1	3.6	−5.0	−4.5	−1.6	−2.5	−3.7	−2.9
France	132	1.8	1.0	−1.0	−1.2	−1.8	1.1	.5	−4.7	8.3	1.7	—	−27.5
Germany	134	.9	−2.8	−.4	−.2	−2.2	1.8	.3	−6.6	1.9	2.5	2.6	—
Greece	174	−.7	−.5	3.0	4.8	.8	−3.0	−.1	5.6	−1.2	1.4	−1.0	2.9
Ireland	178	2.2	−3.7	−1.9	.9	.6	.3	2.3	−3.0	−1.7	3.8	1.2	−7.3
Italy	136	−.3	−.4	−2.7	4.3	1.5	5.1	1.0	−7.1	.9	1.8	1.1	−.4
Netherlands	138	3.1	.2	1.6	−.6	.1	−.7	−2.5	.6	−1.5	−.1	.4	−1.2
Portugal	182	−1.3	1.3	−1.7	−3.3	2.3	2.6	−3.0	−2.9	4.4	1.5	−4.2	....
Spain	184	−.1	−1.5	2.0	.7	−.4	2.4	−.8	−6.0	1.5	2.2	−.1	−1.5
Denmark	128	.2	−.1	−1.9	—	−1.6	−1.2	.5	.2	.7	—	1.8	−.3
Iceland	176	−5.2	−1.2	.8	−4.2	.6	....	....	....	....	....	....	....
Norway	142	−1.3	−4.0	2.5	8.8	3.1	−10.5	18.1	39.9	−5.1	−4.4	−1.0	11.6
Sweden	144	−3.4	.4	4.6	−1.4	−1.1	.5	−3.4	−3.6	−2.8	−2.1	−.2	−2.7
Switzerland	146	2.2	4.3	.2	1.0	−1.6	3.1	3.9	−2.6	1.1	.2	.6	−.4
United Kingdom	112	2.1	−1.3	−2.7	.8	1.6	1.2	−1.7	−2.0	−.8	2.5	2.6	.5
Developing Countries	200	−1.4	−1.5	−1.7	−.6	−.7	−3.8	4.3	−1.3	−4.0	3.0	−.6	−2.5
Africa	605	−3.1	−4.6	9.2	3.6	−1.5	1.8	−6.2	.7	1.1	1.0	....	....
Burkina Faso	748	−5.4	−20.3	10.2	−5.7	....	....	....	....	....	....	....	....
Kenya	664	13.4	12.2	−5.7	−2.8	9.7	−1.5	−13.8	−2.8	....	....	....	....
Mauritius	684	−1.8	−2.4	.2	3.9	.9	7.5	−6.4	−4.9	−5.5	3.8	−1.1	−8.5
Morocco	686	−8.9	−13.3	13.1	−.1	4.3	11.6	−1.7	3.1	3.7	−1.9	....	....
South Africa	199	1.8	1.7	2.9	1.4	−1.2	−.9	−3.0	−1.8	.1	2.5	....	....
Togo	742	18.8	18.8	18.8	337.7	−15.5	−13.7	−32.7	3.4	−62.3	−19.3	−20.0	21.2
Asia	505	.1	−1.2	−.6	−2.6	1.1	−1.9	.3	−3.3	−3.5	—	−2.1	−.8
China, P.R.: Hong Kong	532	.2	−1.2	−1.7	1.0	.7	1.2	−.7	−1.0	.9	1.3	−1.1	−1.7
India	534	14.4	5.1	−9.5	−8.4	15.5	2.9	−10.5	−4.5	−2.2	−9.4	....	....
Korea	542	−1.6	3.4	1.3	−9.4	−2.6	−4.5	−2.2	−12.3	−4.5	−.5	−6.3	−4.2
Pakistan	564	2.0	—	11.5	.2	−.8	14.9	−13.5	−15.3	−.1	−5.0	−6.5	−4.6
Philippines	566	−1.0	−.6	3.8	1.0	1.8	5.2	17.6	−2.4	3.6	−12.1	....	....
Singapore	576	−.2	−3.1	−1.7	.2	—	—	−1.5	−2.9	−4.1	−1.6	−3.9	−1.4
Sri Lanka	524	4.2	−1.0	−.6	2.1	4.1	13.4	−4.5	−6.9	−1.6	2.5	....	....
Thailand	578	1.0	.3	−3.2	−2.0	.5	−5.4	−1.2	−6.9	−9.2	−1.6	.6	2.1
Europe	170	4.2	.7	−1.0	−3.1	2.3	1.7	−.3	−5.7	—	1.8	−.3	2.6
Hungary	944	3.1	.9	1.8	−2.3	1.3	1.3	−1.6	−2.7	−.2	.4	−.5	−.7
Poland	964	7.8	1.2	7.2	−7.8	−.5	2.1	.5	−1.5	2.4	2.7	−3.5	5.3
Turkey	186	3.6	−9.4	−3.6	1.7	4.3	.1	−1.3	−8.5	−2.3	−.6	2.0	3.0
Middle East	405	−4.8	−2.0	1.7	13.8	—	−26.2	28.6	33.5	−8.9	....	....	....
Israel	436	3.9	−3.5	−3.3	.7	3.8	2.6	4.2	−2.9	−2.2	−.1	−1.7	−1.6
Jordan	439	−.6	7.7	2.8	−2.5	−.7	−4.8	—	−6.7	−.9	−2.3	−8.7	−1.2
Syrian Arab Rep	463	3.8	−4.8	11.2	−.4	−7.8	....	....	....	....	....	....	....
Western Hemisphere	205	−10.0	−3.7	−13.0	3.8	−11.0	−3.6	22.7	−14.0	−5.3	26.1	6.1	−15.2
Argentina	213	2.9	1.5	.3	7.8	−1.2	−5.5	−5.9	10.0	−.7	−.4	9.2	1.5
Brazil	223	−8.1	−15.6	−25.2	−1.8	−7.8	−5.5	3.9	2.7	−4.7	9.7	12.2	−6.1
Colombia	233	1.2	20.0	1.4	−7.6	13.2	−3.5	.3	7.3	−9.3	−1.6	3.0	1.0
Costa Rica	238	1.8	....	....	....	....	....	....	....	....	....	....	....
Memorandum Items													
Oil Exporting Countries	999	−4.6	−5.2	−3.1	23.3	−5.9	−34.1	17.8	50.3	−13.5	....	....	....
Non-Oil Developing Countries.	201	−.7	−1.2	−2.0	−2.2	−.5	−.8	2.8	−6.1	−2.9	2.2	−1.0	−3.6

Indices

		1993	1994	1995	1996	1997	1998	1999	2000	2001	2002	2003	2004
		Index Numbers: 2000=100											
World	001	104.7	104.5	104.3	103.7	102.8	103.8	104.2	100.0	99.9	101.2	102.1	99.5
Industrial Countries	110	104.3	104.4	104.8	104.2	103.3	105.8	105.1	100.0	101.0	101.9	103.3	100.7
Developing Countries	200	105.7	104.1	102.4	101.8	101.0	97.1	101.3	100.0	96.0	98.9	98.4	95.9
Africa	605	97.8	93.3	101.9	105.6	104.0	105.9	99.3	100.0	101.1	102.1	....	....
Asia	505	108.7	107.4	106.8	104.0	105.1	103.1	103.4	100.0	96.5	96.4	94.4	93.7
Europe	170	105.8	106.5	105.5	102.2	104.6	106.3	106.0	100.0	100.0	101.8	101.6	104.2
Middle East	405	69.5	68.2	69.3	78.9	78.9	58.2	74.9	100.0	91.1	....	....	....
Western Hemisphere	205	127.0	122.3	106.4	110.4	98.3	94.8	116.3	100.0	94.7	119.4	126.6	107.3

Balance of Payments

Trade Balance
Expressed in Millions of US Dollars

		1993	1994	1995	1996	1997	1998	1999	2000	2001	2002	2003	2004
All Countries	010	71,604	95,114	120,255	102,225	117,523	69,617	42,872	18,721	4,394	42,322	67,625	....
Industrial Countries	110	99,908	94,660	122,301	93,398	96,616	26,638	−112,401	−242,408	−208,630	−211,441	−260,216	....
United States	111	−130,551	−163,781	−172,330	−189,100	−196,164	−244,736	−343,716	−449,784	−424,085	−479,405	−544,300	−662,036
Canada	156	10,136	14,834	25,855	31,091	18,565	15,922	28,292	45,047	45,716	36,488	41,076	50,682
Australia	193	−29	−3,277	−4,223	−635	1,849	−5,332	−9,761	−4,841	1,736	−5,517	−15,335	−18,215
Japan	158	139,417	144,191	131,787	83,585	101,600	122,389	123,325	116,716	70,214	93,829	106,395	132,134
New Zealand	196	1,719	1,408	971	523	903	912	−371	680	1,471	166	−456	−1,433
Euro Area													
Austria	122	−6,476	−7,914	−6,656	−7,315	−4,274	−3,684	−3,629	−2,737	−1,269	3,588	1,140	4,205
Belgium	124	....	....	....	....	....	....	....	....	....	8,733	10,234	8,993
Belgium-Luxembourg	126	5,780	6,901	9,555	8,690	7,703	6,981	7,027	2,591	3,707	....	....	....
Finland	172	6,449	7,723	12,437	11,314	11,544	12,490	12,168	13,684	12,659	12,882	12,947	12,821
France	132	7,516	7,249	10,998	14,936	26,899	24,940	16,939	−3,618	2,837	7,638	3,426	−7,944
Germany	134	41,168	51,028	63,910	69,379	70,119	76,913	69,646	57,218	89,197	127,834	147,928	191,784
Greece	174	−10,499	−11,273	−14,425	−15,505	−15,375	....	−17,951	−20,239	−19,087	−21,452	−25,606	....
Ireland	178	8,175	9,366	13,557	15,754	18,625	25,390	23,587	25,010	27,263	33,447	37,807	39,562
Italy	136	28,889	31,568	38,729	54,118	39,878	35,631	23,437	9,549	15,540	13,412	11,477	10,911
Luxembourg	137	....	....	....	....	....	....	....	....	....	−2,099	−2,652	−3,157
Netherlands	138	16,904	18,686	23,812	22,767	20,937	20,430	16,034	17,427	20,840	19,944	26,648	31,041
Portugal	182	−8,050	−8,321	−8,910	−9,722	−10,342	−12,211	−13,714	−13,870	−13,638	−12,677	−13,431	−18,149
Spain	184	−14,999	−14,892	−18,415	−16,283	−13,407	−20,758	−30,339	−34,820	−32,539	−32,841	−42,923	−64,524
Denmark	128	7,719	7,441	6,528	7,532	5,369	3,886	6,658	6,641	7,418	7,662	9,697	....
Iceland	176	181	272	206	19	5	−351	−307	−474	−75	150	−210	−519
Norway	142	6,966	7,496	8,685	12,972	11,648	2,061	10,723	25,975	26,472	24,340	28,269	33,576
Sweden	144	7,548	9,558	15,978	18,636	17,999	17,632	15,714	15,215	13,832	16,631	18,933	....
Switzerland	146	1,592	3,346	3,260	1,869	2,738	933	850	2,071	1,640	6,648	6,961	15,547
United Kingdom	112	−19,648	−16,947	−19,006	−21,228	−20,203	−36,127	−47,012	−49,850	−58,477	−70,843	−78,242	−107,302
Developing Countries	200	−28,304	454	−2,046	8,827	20,907	42,980	155,273	261,130	213,024	253,762	327,841	....
Africa	605	8,498	3,660	3,248	16,660	11,237	−4,722	5,798	32,194	20,651	15,015	21,428	....
Algeria	612	....	....	....	....	....	....	....	....	....	....	....	....
Angola	614	1,438	1,563	2,255	3,055	2,410	1,464	2,047	4,881	3,355	4,568	....	....
Botswana	616	267	510	555	750	895	78	785	902	710	676	....	....
Burundi	618	−99	−92	−63	−60	−9	−59	−42	−59	−69	−74	−93	....
Cape Verde	624	−143	−181	−217	−184	−172	−186	−213	−187	−194	−236	−291	....
Comoros	632	−28	−34	−42	....	....	....	....	....	....	....	....	....
Congo, Dem. Rep. of	636	....	....	....	....	....	....	....	....	....	....	....	....
Djibouti	611	−184	−181	−171	....	....	....	....	....	....	....	....	....
Eritrea	643	−307	−411	−368	−455	−469	−480	−489	−435	....	....	....	....
Ethiopia	644	−507	−554	−670	−585	−413	−799	−920	−645	−1,170	−975	−1,418	....
Gambia, The	648	−57	−57	−40	−98	−87	....	....	....	....	....	....	....
Ghana	652	−664	−342	−257	−381	−654	−901	−1,274	−830	−1,101	−692	−714	−1,513
Guinea	656	−22	−170	−39	111	118	121	54	79	169	40	−35	37
Kenya	664	−247	−238	−750	−515	−886	−1,012	−975	−1,262	−1,347	−996	−1,143	....
Lesotho	666	−734	−667	−825	−812	−828	−673	−607	−516	−400	−381	....	....
Liberia	668	....	....	....	....	....	....	....	....	....	....	....	....
Madagascar	674	−180	−96	−122	−120	−178	−154	−158	−174	−27	−117	−254	....
Malawi	676	−23	−160	−63	−78	−158	39	−127	−59	−44	−151	....	....
Mauritania	682	3	47	184	134	107	40	....	....	....	....	....	....
Mauritius	684	−242	−397	−241	−326	−436	−264	−519	−392	−218	−211	−278	....
Morocco	686	−2,065	−2,107	−2,482	−2,193	−1,864	−2,319	−2,448	−3,235	−3,022	−3,061	−4,345	−6,494
Mozambique	688	−727	−767	−536	−478	−454	−491	−806	−682	−271	−536	−348	....
Namibia	728	−42	−86	−130	−127	−272	−173	−204	−1	−202	−211	−466	....
Nigeria	694	3,248	2,948	3,513	9,679	5,706	−240	4,288	....	....	....	....	....
Rwanda	714	−200	−524	−162	−157	−185	−169	−185	−155	−152	−166	....	....
São Tomé & Príncipe	716	....	....	....	....	....	−12	−18	−22	−21	−23	....	....
Seychelles	718	−165	−135	−161	−170	−190	−212	−224	−117	−205	−140	....	....
Sierra Leone	724	−69	−73	−127	−180	−56	−57	−81	−124	−136	−195	−200	....
Somalia	726	....	....	....	....	....	....	....	....	....	....	....	....
South Africa	199	7,532	4,398	2,379	2,859	2,319	1,991	4,008	4,698	5,255	4,756	3,285	−115
Sudan	732	−227	−522	−510	−719	−828	−1,137	−476	440	304	−345	6	192
Swaziland	734	−104	−50	−197	−204	−104	−106	−131	−136	−77	−79	....	....
Tanzania	738	−857	−790	−657	−449	−449	−776	−872	−704	−784	−609	....	....
Tunisia	744	−2,064	−1,567	−1,989	−1,761	−1,955	−2,152	−2,141	−2,253	−2,369	−2,123	−2,269	−2,434
Uganda	746	−278	−251	−367	−348	−450	−656	−506	−500	−500	−573	−679	−755
Zambia	754	....	....	....	....	54	−153	−98	−221	....	....	....	....
Zimbabwe	698	122	158	....	....	....	....	....	....	....	....	....	....
CEMAC													
Cameroon	622	502	402	627	....	....	....	....	....	....	....	....	....
Central African Rep.	626	−26	15	....	....	....	....	....	....	....	....	....	....
Chad	628	−63	−77	....	....	....	....	....	....	....	....	....	....
Congo, Republic of	634	619	346	632	1,068	1,013	809	1,037	2,037	1,374	1,598	1,011	....
Equatorial Guinea	642	10	25	−31	−117	....	....	....	....	....	....	....	....
Gabon	646	1,481	1,589	1,847	2,373	2,002	744	1,588	....	....	....	....	....
WAEMU													
Benin	638	−168	−54	−203	−32	−153	−158	−214	−124	−180	....	....	....
Burkina Faso	748	−243	−129	....	....	....	....	....	−312	−286	....	....	....
Côte d'Ivoire	662	748	1,289	1,376	1,824	1,793	1,720	1,895	1,486	1,528	2,819	2,524	....
Guinea-Bissau	654	−38	−21	−35	−35	−14	....	....	....	1	−4	—	....

Balance of Payments

		1993	1994	1995	1996	1997	1998	1999	2000	2001	2002	2003	2004
						Trade Balance *Expressed in Millions of US Dollars*							
Africa(Cont.)													
Mali............................	678	−120	−114	−115	−119	16	−2	−35	−47	−10	163	−60	....
Niger............................	692	−12	−44	−18	....	....	....	....	....	....	....	....	....
Senegal............................	722	−350	−203	−250	−276	−271	−313	−346	−417	−425	−537	....	....
Togo............................	742	−111	−37	−129	−127	−108	−133	−98	−123	−159	−151	−157	....
Asia*............................	505	**−10,370**	**−6,535**	**−13,372**	**−21,367**	**31,720**	**138,347**	**137,337**	**118,082**	**115,518**	**141,066**	**155,571**	....
Afghanistan, I.S. of............	512	....	....	....	....	....	....	....	....	....	....	....	....
Bangladesh............................	513	−1,113	−1,416	−2,324	−2,275	−1,711	−1,574	−2,077	−1,654	−2,049	−1,678	−2,442	....
Bhutan............................	514	....	....	....	....	....	....	....	....	....	....	....	....
Brunei Darussalam............	516	....	....	....	....	....	....	....	....	....	....	....	....
Cambodia............................	522	−187	−255	−332	−428	−328	−365	−462	−538	−523	−563	−549	....
China,P.R.: Mainland............	924	−10,654	7,290	18,050	19,535	46,222	46,614	35,982	34,474	34,017	44,167	44,652	....
China,P.R.:Hong Kong............	532	....	....	....	....	....	−7,833	−3,159	−8,193	−8,331	−5,053	−5,779	−9,312
China,P.R.: Macao............	546	....	....	....	....	....	....	....	....	....	−920	−1,093	....
Fiji............................	819	−282	−229	−242	−168	−283	−186	−116	....	....	....	....	....
India............................	534	−2,093	−4,150	−6,719	−10,052	−10,028	−10,752	−8,679	−10,640	−6,418	−3,559	−8,870	....
Indonesia............................	536	8,231	7,901	6,533	5,948	10,075	18,429	20,643	25,042	22,696	23,513	23,708	....
Kiribati............................	826	−25	−21	....	....	....	....	....	....	....	....	....	....
Korea............................	542	2,150	−3,017	−4,365	−15,077	−3,256	41,665	28,463	16,954	13,488	14,777	22,161	38,161
Lao People's Dem.Rep............	544	−150	−214	−316	−321	−283	−165	−190	−205	−217	....	....	....
Malaysia............................	548	3,037	1,577	−103	3,848	3,510	17,505	22,644	20,827	18,383	18,135	25,711	....
Maldives............................	556	−125	−120	−151	−186	−217	−216	−262	−233	−236	−212	−262	....
Mongolia............................	948	21	34	25	−36	115	−62	−56	−73	−101	−156	....	....
Myanmar............................	518	−636	−613	−831	−940	−1,143	−1,401	−887	−504	56	382	578	....
Nepal............................	558	−462	−790	−961	−1,106	−1,278	−757	−882	−814	−765	−793	−988	....
Pakistan............................	564	−2,586	−2,239	−2,891	−3,656	−2,399	−1,984	−1,847	−1,157	−610	−596	−109	−3,382
Papua New Guinea............	853	1,470	1,326	1,408	1,017	677	695	856	1,095	881	....	....	....
Philippines............................	566	−6,222	−7,850	−8,944	−11,342	−11,127	−28	4,959	3,814	−743	407	−5,455	−6,381
Samoa............................	862	−81	−65	−72	−81	−85	−77	−98	....	....	....	....	....
Singapore............................	576	−2,724	1,354	6,452	7,186	6,509	13,411	12,442	12,723	15,709	19,903	29,323	....
Solomon Islands............	813	−8	—	14	11	−28	−18	55	....	....	....	....	....
Sri Lanka............................	524	−742	−1,085	−985	−800	−640	−505	−769	−1,044	−560	−796	−872	....
Thailand............................	578	−4,297	−3,726	−7,968	−9,488	1,572	16,238	14,013	11,701	8,543	9,081	11,175	11,124
Tonga............................	866	−41	....	....	....	....	....	....	....	−57	−55	....	....
Vanuatu............................	846	−47	−50	−51	−51	−44	−42	−59	−50	−58	−58	−65	....
Vietnam............................	582	....	....	....	−2,775	−1,247	−989	972	375	481	−1,054	....	....
*of which:													
Taiwan Prov.of China............	528	11,450	11,849	13,235	17,543	13,882	10,316	14,705	13,674	19,718	24,193	24,891	16,128
Europe............................	170	**−23,029**	**−3,043**	**−15,441**	**−27,497**	**−41,431**	**−44,692**	**−13,566**	**3,590**	**9,447**	**4,978**	**5,379**	....
Albania............................	914	−490	−460	−475	−678	−535	−604	−663	−814	−1,027	−1,155	−1,336	....
Armenia............................	911	−98	−178	−403	−469	−559	−577	−474	−463	−420	−369	−434	−465
Azerbaijan, Republic of............	912	....	....	−373	−694	−567	−1,046	−408	319	614	482	−98	161
Belarus............................	913	−528	−490	−666	−1,149	−1,407	−1,501	−570	−884	−807	−914	−1,256	−2,066
Bosnia & Herzegovina............	963	....	....	....	....	....	−3,116	−3,297	−2,764	−2,958	−3,340	−4,159	−4,569
Bulgaria............................	918	−885	−17	121	188	380	−381	−1,081	−1,176	−1,580	−1,594	−2,478	−3,353
Croatia............................	960	−709	−1,278	−3,228	−3,488	−5,383	−4,072	−3,299	−3,203	−4,101	−5,648	−7,908	−8,346
Cyprus............................	423	−1,507	−1,736	−2,085	−2,183	−2,071	−2,426	−2,309	−2,606	−2,577	−2,847	−3,134	−4,043
Czech Republic............	935	−517	−1,408	−3,685	−5,706	−4,938	−2,647	−1,902	−3,095	−3,078	−2,240	−2,505	....
Estonia............................	939	−145	−356	−666	−1,019	−1,124	−1,115	−878	−768	−789	−1,089	−1,554	−1,966
Faroe Islands............	816	....	....	....	....	....	69	17	−38	37	66	−90	....
Georgia............................	915	....	....	....	....	−786	−695	−534	−512	−550	−483	−636	−916
Hungary............................	944	−4,021	−3,716	−1,459	−1,673	−1,328	−1,885	−2,170	−2,913	−2,237	−2,119	−3,278	−2,922
Kazakhstan............................	916	....	....	114	−335	−276	−801	344	2,168	983	1,987	3,679	6,786
Kyrgyz Republic............	917	−107	−86	−122	−252	−15	−221	−89	4	33	−74	−134	....
Latvia............................	941	3	−301	−580	−798	−848	−1,130	−1,027	−1,044	−1,335	−1,479	−2,003	−2,749
Lithuania............................	946	−155	−205	−698	−896	−1,147	−1,518	−1,405	−1,104	−1,108	−1,315	−1,704	−2,317
Macedonia, FYR............	962	....	....	....	−317	−388	−515	−496	−690	−526	−804	−851	....
Malta............................	181	−568	−603	−810	−838	−721	−673	−663	−754	−566	−357	−697	−871
Moldova............................	921	....	−54	−70	−260	−348	−388	−137	−294	−313	−378	−623	−758
Poland............................	964	−3,505	−575	−1,646	−7,287	−9,822	−12,836	−15,072	−12,307	−7,661	−7,249	−5,725	−5,584
Romania............................	968	−1,128	−411	−1,577	−2,470	−1,980	−2,625	−1,092	−1,684	−2,969	−2,611	−4,537	....
Russia............................	922	....	16,928	19,816	21,591	14,913	16,429	36,012	60,172	48,121	46,335	59,860	87,145
Slovak Republic............	936	−912	61	−229	−2,283	−2,084	−2,351	−1,109	−895	....	−2,166	−649	....
Slovenia............................	961	−154	−336	−954	−826	−775	−792	−1,235	−1,139	−619	−252	−625	−1,044
Tajikistan............................	923	....	....	....	....	....	....	....	....	....	−124	−120	−135
Turkey............................	186	−14,044	−4,134	−13,114	−10,264	−15,048	−14,052	−10,185	−21,959	−3,733	−7,283	−14,010	−23,830
Turkmenistan............................	925	....	....	....	304	−231	....	....	....	....	....	....	....
Ukraine............................	926	....	−2,575	−2,702	−4,296	−4,205	−2,584	244	779	198	710	518	3,741
Uzbekistan............................	927	....	....	....	....	....	....	....	....	....	....	....	....
Middle East............................	405	**7,377**	**22,132**	**24,119**	**40,301**	**38,301**	**−4,402**	**38,691**	**108,918**	**76,271**	**74,793**	**106,863**	....
Bahrain, Kingdom of............	419	107	120	626	665	605	−28	894	1,849	1,610	1,190	1,402	1,485
Egypt............................	469	−6,378	−5,953	−7,597	−8,390	−8,632	−10,214	−9,928	−8,321	−6,935	−5,762	−4,201	−6,576
Iran, I.R. of............	429	−1,207	6,817	5,586	7,402	4,258	−1,168	7,597	13,138	....	....	....	....
Iraq............................	433	....	....	....	....	....	....	....	....	....	....	....	....
Israel............................	436	−5,607	−5,486	−7,196	−6,954	−5,008	−3,051	−4,238	−2,870	−3,047	−3,694	−2,240	−1,888
Jordan............................	439	−1,899	−1,579	−1,518	−2,001	−1,813	−1,602	−1,460	−2,174	−2,007	−1,731	−1,996	−3,378
Kuwait............................	443	3,324	4,685	5,579	6,997	6,534	1,903	5,516	13,027	9,192	7,242	11,912	19,301
Lebanon............................	446	....	....	....	....	....	....	....	....	....	....	....	....
Libya............................	672	113	945	2,302	2,085	2,249	396	2,974	9,379	6,160	2,443	7,464	....
Oman............................	449	1,336	1,849	2,015	3,142	3,012	307	2,938	6,725	5,763	5,536	5,584	....

Balance of Payments

		1993	1994	1995	1996	1997	1998	1999	2000	2001	2002	2003	2004

Trade Balance
Expressed in Millions of US Dollars

Middle East(Cont.)		1993	1994	1995	1996	1997	1998	1999	2000	2001	2002	2003	2004
Qatar	453	....	....	....	....	....	....	....	....	....	....	....	....
Saudi Arabia	456	16,500	21,261	24,358	35,323	34,317	11,272	25,006	49,777	39,366	42,840	59,376	85,222
Syrian Arab Republic	463	−259	−1,275	−146	−338	454	−178	216	1,423	1,424	2,210	1,332	−115
United Arab Emirates	466	....	....	....	....	....	....	....	....	....	....	....	....
West Bank and Gaza	487	....	....	−1,909	−2,364	−2,443	−2,411	−2,618	−2,303	−1,467	....	....	....
Yemen, Republic of	474	−971	274	149	−31	−133	−785	358	1,313	766	689	377	817
Western Hemisphere	205	−10,780	−15,760	−600	730	−18,920	−41,552	−12,987	−1,654	−8,863	17,910	38,599	....
Argentina	213	−2,364	−4,139	2,357	1,760	−2,123	−3,097	−795	2,452	7,385	17,178	16,448	13,239
Aruba	314	−392	−311	−425	−308	−387	−353	−592	−58	55	−530	−334	....
Bahamas, The	313	−738	−815	−931	−1,014	−1,116	−1,374	−1,428	−1,371	−1,340	−1,152	−1,206	....
Barbados	316	−327	−355	−446	−456	−599	−651	−714	−744	−681	−702	−801	....
Belize	339	−119	−75	−66	−58	−90	−105	−124	−191	−214	−190	−209	....
Bolivia	218	−396	−30	−182	−236	−477	−656	−488	−364	−295	−340	75	....
Brazil	223	14,329	10,861	−3,157	−5,453	−6,652	−6,603	−1,261	−698	2,650	13,121	24,794	33,693
Chile	228	−990	732	1,381	−1,072	−1,428	−2,040	2,427	2,119	1,844	2,386	3,522	9,019
Colombia	233	−1,657	−2,229	−2,546	−2,092	−2,638	−2,450	1,775	2,633	579	239	524	1,134
Costa Rica	238	−761	−606	−323	−249	−498	−399	580	−210	−820	−1,267	−1,131	−1,463
Dominican Republic	243	−1,443	−1,451	−1,391	−1,674	−1,995	−2,617	−2,904	−3,742	−3,503	−3,673	−2,444	....
Ecuador	248	214	149	−66	921	491	−1,132	1,588	1,395	−397	−998	−71	....
El Salvador	253	−962	−1,170	−1,462	−1,242	−1,143	−1,306	−1,356	−1,740	−1,933	−1,865	−2,275	−2,619
Guatemala	258	−1,021	−997	−875	−643	−940	−1,409	−1,445	−1,657	−2,282	−2,972	−3,116	−3,760
Guyana	336	−68	−41	−41	−20	−48	−54	−25	−80	−94	−68	−59	....
Haiti	263	−180	−111	−429	−416	−354	−527	−674	−755	−750	−706	−783	....
Honduras	268	−204	−250	−141	−287	−294	−323	−753	−658	−834	−829	−965	−1,267
Jamaica	343	−815	−551	−829	−994	−1,132	−1,131	−1,187	−1,442	−1,618	−1,871	−1,944	....
Mexico	273	−13,481	−18,464	7,089	6,531	623	−7,834	−5,613	−8,337	−9,617	−7,633	−5,780	−8,811
Netherlands Antilles	353	−838	−921	−1,035	−1,129	−975	−1,048	−1,117	−986	−1,114	−1,027	−1,003	....
Nicaragua	278	−392	−429	−385	−527	−728	−749	−1,071	−921	−910	−918	−972	−1,112
Panama	283	−334	−250	−589	−644	−685	−1,296	−1,340	−1,143	−696	−1,035	−1,113	−1,585
Paraguay	288	79	−243	−270	−587	−865	−393	−441	−537	−614	−280	−275	−391
Peru	293	−776	−1,075	−2,241	−1,991	−1,678	−2,437	−655	−411	−195	292	836	2,792
Suriname	366	84	99	123	−2	36	−27	44	153	140	47	30	93
Trinidad and Tobago	369	547	741	588	382	−529	−741	64	969	718	238	....	....
Uruguay	298	−387	−706	−563	−687	−704	−772	−897	−927	−775	48	182	....
Venezuela, Rep. Bol	299	3,275	7,625	7,013	13,770	8,954	952	6,471	16,664	7,456	13,421	16,483	21,430
ECCU													
Anguilla	312	−33	−37	−46	−51	−53	−60	−78	−79	−65	−57	....	....
Antigua and Barbuda	311	−208	−242	−238	−271	−275	−283	−315	−293	−283	−291	....	....
Dominica	321	−43	−47	−53	−64	−65	−53	−66	−76	−71	−59	....	....
Grenada	328	−95	−94	−105	−122	−122	−137	−110	−138	−133	−139	....	....
Montserrat	351	−22	−27	−22	5	−20	−18	−18	−18	−16	−21	....	....
St. Kitts and Nevis	361	−63	−70	−81	−93	−85	−87	−90	−121	−112	−113	....	....
St. Lucia	362	−139	−166	−155	−181	−222	−225	−251	−249	−218	−207	....	....
St. Vincent & Grens	364	−61	−67	−57	−75	−105	−120	−127	−93	−109	−117	....	....
Memorandum Items													
Oil Exporting Ctys	999	44,624	60,101	66,000	100,394	92,797	41,350	96,254	194,825	142,483	139,497	183,618	....
Non-Oil Develop.Ctys	201	−72,928	−59,647	−68,047	−91,567	−71,891	1,630	59,019	66,305	70,541	114,265	144,222	....

Balance of Payments

Current Account Balance
Excluding Exceptional Financing
Expressed in Millions of US Dollars

		1993	1994	1995	1996	1997	1998	1999	2000	2001	2002	2003	2004
All Countries	010	−65,853	−63,982	−60,569	−53,786	−8,560	−89,962	−125,966	−158,872	−147,381	−128,435	−59,907	....
Industrial Countries	110	41,288	5,980	41,671	32,644	71,514	−41,149	−178,920	−297,487	−247,912	−279,829	−305,947	....
United States	111	−81,963	−118,062	−109,472	−120,170	−135,979	−209,532	−296,846	−413,442	−385,699	−473,943	−530,664	−665,939
Canada	156	−21,822	−13,024	−4,328	3,378	−8,233	−7,839	1,765	19,622	16,281	13,456	13,360	22,000
Australia	193	−9,683	−17,145	−19,323	−15,810	−12,384	−18,050	−22,335	−15,412	−8,363	−16,837	−30,354	−40,025
Japan	158	131,637	130,255	111,044	65,792	96,814	118,749	114,604	119,660	87,798	112,447	136,215	172,059
New Zealand	196	−746	−2,384	−3,003	−3,891	−4,304	−2,157	−3,515	−2,462	−1,253	−2,235	−3,357	−6,232
Euro Area													
Austria	122	−1,013	−2,992	−5,448	−4,890	−5,221	−5,258	−6,655	−4,864	−3,636	565	−1,363	988
Belgium	124	....	....	....	....	....	....	....	....	....	14,025	13,780	12,046
Belgium-Luxembourg	126	11,237	12,571	14,232	13,762	13,914	12,168	14,086	11,381	9,392	....	....	....
Finland	172	−1,135	1,110	5,231	5,003	6,633	7,340	8,045	8,975	8,704	10,148	6,497	7,529
France	132	8,990	7,415	10,840	20,561	37,801	37,699	41,509	18,581	28,759	10,997	11,803	−4,833
Germany	134	−13,808	−29,417	−26,960	−13,734	−8,660	−11,651	−25,549	−29,600	3,069	45,643	51,447	104,301
Greece	174	−747	−146	−2,864	−4,554	−4,860	....	−7,295	−9,820	−9,400	−10,405	−11,225	....
Ireland	178	1,765	1,577	1,721	2,049	1,866	1,016	245	−516	−690	−1,399	−2,105	−748
Italy	136	7,802	13,209	25,076	39,999	32,403	19,998	8,111	−5,781	−652	−9,369	−19,406	−15,137
Luxembourg	137	....	....	....	....	....	....	....	....	2,436	2,230	2,828	
Netherlands	138	13,203	17,294	25,773	21,502	25,077	13,031	12,996	6,817	7,836	10,117	16,403	23,172
Portugal	182	233	−2,196	−132	−5,216	−6,465	−7,833	−9,733	−11,080	−11,083	−9,115	−7,937	−12,682
Spain	184	−5,804	−6,389	792	407	2,512	−3,135	−13,761	−19,237	−16,404	−16,044	−23,676	−49,225
Denmark	128	4,832	3,189	1,855	3,090	921	−2,008	3,047	2,262	4,848	3,460	6,963	....
Iceland	176	37	116	52	−131	−128	−555	−589	−847	−336	128	−534	−1,055
Norway	142	3,522	3,760	5,233	10,969	10,036	6	8,378	25,851	26,171	24,473	28,326	34,445
Sweden	144	−4,159	743	4,940	5,892	7,406	4,639	5,982	6,617	6,696	12,784	22,844	....
Switzerland	146	16,875	16,729	20,703	19,916	25,317	25,194	27,879	32,493	21,897	24,721	43,618	50,568
United Kingdom	112	−17,966	−10,234	−14,291	−11,278	−2,952	−6,630	−39,289	−36,684	−31,847	−24,570	−27,501	−41,883
Developing Countries	200	−107,140	−69,962	−102,240	−86,430	−80,073	−48,813	52,954	138,615	100,531	151,394	246,040	....
Africa	605	−4,929	−8,378	−13,459	2,220	−5,235	−18,655	−9,487	11,891	4,457	−2,837	3,660	....
Algeria	612	....	....	....	....	....	....	....	....	....	....	....	....
Angola	614	−669	−340	−295	3,266	−884	−1,867	−1,710	796	−1,431	−150	....	....
Botswana	616	427	222	300	495	721	170	583	545	598	170	....	....
Burundi	618	−28	−17	10	−40	—	−51	−23	−53	−39	−10	−37	....
Cape Verde	624	−24	−46	−62	−35	−30	−59	−74	−58	−56	−72	−77	....
Comoros	632	10	−7	−19	....	....	....	....	....	....	....	....	....
Congo, Dem. Rep. of	636	....	....	....	....	....	....	....	....	....	....	....	....
Djibouti	611	−34	−46	−23	....	....	....	....	....	....	....	....	....
Eritrea	643	107	124	−32	−60	5	−293	−209	−105	....	....	....	....
Ethiopia	644	−50	125	39	80	−40	−333	−465	10	−401	−170	−199	....
Gambia, The	648	−5	8	−8	−48	−24	....	....	....	....	....	....	....
Ghana	652	−559	−255	−144	−307	−403	−522	−964	−387	−325	−32	255	−236
Guinea	656	−57	−248	−216	−177	−91	−184	−214	−155	−102	−200	−188	−175
Kenya	664	71	98	−400	−73	−457	−475	−90	−199	−341	−137	68	....
Lesotho	666	29	108	−323	−303	−269	−280	−221	−151	−95	−119	....	....
Liberia	668	....	....	....	....	....	....	....	....	....	....	....	....
Madagascar	674	−258	−277	−276	−291	−266	−301	−252	−283	−170	−298	−439	....
Malawi	676	−166	−181	−78	−147	−276	−4	−158	−73	−60	−201	....	....
Mauritania	682	−174	−70	22	91	48	77	....	....	....	....	....	....
Mauritius	684	−92	−232	−22	34	−89	3	−124	−37	276	249	122	....
Morocco	686	−521	−723	−1,296	−58	−169	−146	−171	−501	1,606	1,472	1,552	1,063
Mozambique	688	−446	−467	−445	−421	−296	−429	−912	−764	−657	−712	−516	....
Namibia	728	110	85	176	116	90	162	159	255	17	79	271	....
Nigeria	694	−780	−2,128	−2,578	3,507	552	−4,244	506	....	....	....	....	....
Rwanda	714	−129	−72	57	−9	−62	−83	−141	−94	−102	−126	....	....
São Tomé & Príncipe	716	....	....	....	....	....	−10	−16	−19	−21	−23	....	....
Seychelles	718	−7	24	−3	−59	−73	−118	−127	−51	−123	−131	....	....
Sierra Leone	724	−58	−89	−118	−151	−55	−33	−99	−112	−98	−73	−80	....
Somalia	726	....	....	....	....	....	....	....	....	....	....	....	....
South Africa	199	2,803	30	−2,493	−1,678	−2,227	−2,199	−675	−191	153	731	−2,605	−6,982
Sudan	732	−202	−602	−500	−827	−828	−957	−465	−557	−618	−1,008	−955	−871
Swaziland	734	−64	2	−30	−52	−3	−93	−35	−65	−53	−46	....	....
Tanzania	738	−1,048	−711	−646	−511	−630	−920	−835	−499	−480	−251	....	....
Tunisia	744	−1,323	−537	−774	−478	−595	−675	−442	−821	−840	−746	−730	−555
Uganda	746	−224	−208	−339	−252	−367	−503	−711	−825	−368	−411	−389	−254
Zambia	754	....	....	....	....	−383	−573	−447	−584	....	....	....	....
Zimbabwe	698	−116	−425	....	....	....	....	....	....	....	....	....	....
CEMAC													
Cameroon	622	−565	−56	90	....	....	....	....	....	....	....	....	....
Central African Rep.	626	−13	−25	....	....	....	....	....	....	....	....	....	....
Chad	628	−117	−38	....	....	....	....	....	....	....	....	....	....
Congo, Republic of	634	−553	−793	−625	−651	−156	−241	−231	648	−28	−34	−3	....
Equatorial Guinea	642	3	—	−123	−344	....	....	....	....	....	....	....	....
Gabon	646	−49	317	465	889	531	−596	390	....	....	....	....	....
WAEMU													
Benin	638	−101	−23	−207	−57	−170	−151	−191	−111	−160	....	....	....
Burkina Faso	748	−71	15	....	....	....	....	....	−392	−381	....	....	....
Côte d'Ivoire	662	−892	−14	−492	−162	−155	−290	−120	−241	−61	768	353	....

		1993	1994	1995	1996	1997	1998	1999	2000	2001	2002	2003	2004
						Current Account Balance							
						Excluding Exceptional Financing							
						Expressed in Millions of US Dollars							

Africa(Cont.)

		1993	1994	1995	1996	1997	1998	1999	2000	2001	2002	2003	2004
Guinea-Bissau	654	−65	−48	−51	−60	−30	....	....	....	−27	−9	−6	....
Mali	678	−189	−163	−284	−261	−178	−208	−253	−255	−310	−149	−271	....
Niger	692	−97	−126	−152	....	....	....	....	....	....	....	....	....
Senegal	722	−433	−187	−244	−199	−185	−247	−320	−332	−245	−317	....	....
Togo	742	−82	−56	−122	−154	−117	−140	−127	−140	−169	−140	−162	....
Asia*	**505**	**−13,028**	**−3,504**	**−38,560**	**−39,075**	**18,152**	**115,955**	**114,336**	**91,803**	**96,898**	**137,047**	**173,727**	**....**
Afghanistan, I.S. of	512	....	....	....	....	....	....	....	....	....	....	....	....
Bangladesh	513	359	200	−824	−991	−286	−35	−364	−306	−535	739	132	....
Bhutan	514	....	....	....	....	....	....	....	....	....	....	....	....
Brunei Darussalam	516	....	....	....	....	....	....	....	....	....	....	....	....
Cambodia	522	−104	−157	−186	−185	−210	−205	−243	−206	−138	−120	−155	....
China,P.R.: Mainland	924	−11,609	6,908	1,618	7,243	36,963	31,472	21,115	20,518	17,401	35,422	45,875	....
China,P.R.:Hong Kong	532	....	....	....	....	....	2,529	10,248	6,993	9,786	12,412	16,470	16,357
China,P.R.: Macao	546	....	....	....	....	....	....	....	....	....	2,737	3,177	....
Fiji	819	−138	−113	−113	14	−34	−60	13	....	....	....	....	....
India	534	−1,876	−1,676	−5,563	−5,956	−2,965	−6,903	−3,228	−4,702	1,251	6,964	6,718	....
Indonesia	536	−2,106	−2,792	−6,431	−7,663	−4,889	4,097	5,783	7,992	6,901	7,824	7,252	....
Kiribati	826	−4	1	....	....	....	....	....	....	....	....	....	....
Korea	542	821	−4,024	−8,665	−23,210	−8,384	40,371	24,522	12,251	8,033	5,394	12,321	27,613
Lao People's Dem.Rep.	544	−139	−284	−346	−347	−306	−150	−121	−8	−82	....	....	....
Malaysia	548	−2,991	−4,520	−8,644	−4,462	−5,935	9,529	12,604	8,488	7,287	7,190	13,381	....
Maldives	556	−54	−11	−18	−7	−35	−22	−79	−51	−59	−36	−30	....
Mongolia	948	31	46	39	−101	55	−129	−112	−156	−154	−158	....	....
Myanmar	518	−230	−130	−261	−283	−416	−499	−285	−212	−169	10	50	....
Nepal	558	−223	−352	−356	−327	−388	−67	−256	−299	−339	56	110	....
Pakistan	564	−2,901	−1,812	−3,349	−4,436	−1,712	−2,248	−920	−85	1,878	3,854	3,573	−808
Papua New Guinea	853	474	402	492	189	−192	−29	95	345	282	....	....	....
Philippines	566	−3,016	−2,950	−1,980	−3,953	−4,351	1,546	7,219	6,258	1,323	4,383	1,396	2,080
Samoa	862	−39	6	9	12	9	20	−19	....	....	....	....	....
Singapore	576	4,211	11,400	14,708	13,898	14,962	18,578	15,291	13,257	16,086	18,909	28,183	....
Solomon Islands	813	−8	−3	8	15	−38	8	21	....	....	....	....	....
Sri Lanka	524	−382	−757	−770	−683	−395	−228	−561	−1,044	−237	−268	−160	....
Thailand	578	−6,364	−8,085	−13,554	−14,691	−3,021	14,243	12,428	9,313	6,192	7,014	7,953	7,080
Tonga	866	−6	....	....	....	....	....	....	....	−11	−3	....	....
Vanuatu	846	−15	−20	−18	−27	−19	−9	−33	−14	−15	−31	−41	....
Vietnam	582	....	....	....	−2,020	−1,528	−1,074	1,177	1,106	682	−604	....	....

*of which:

		1993	1994	1995	1996	1997	1998	1999	2000	2001	2002	2003	2004
Taiwan Prov.of China	528	7,042	6,498	5,474	10,923	7,051	3,438	7,992	8,901	18,093	25,630	29,258	18,658
Europe	**170**	**−17,671**	**4,665**	**−5,491**	**−14,976**	**−29,997**	**−26,661**	**−3,729**	**14,729**	**15,377**	**4,441**	**−3,250**	**....**
Albania	914	15	−157	−12	−107	−272	−65	−155	−156	−217	−408	−407	....
Armenia	911	−67	−104	−218	−291	−307	−418	−307	−278	−201	−148	−191	−167
Azerbaijan, Republic of	912	....	....	−401	−931	−916	−1,365	−600	−168	−52	−768	−2,021	−2,589
Belarus	913	−435	−444	−458	−516	−859	−1,017	−194	−338	−394	−311	−424	−1,043
Bosnia & Herzegovina	963	....	....	....	....	....	−371	−547	−463	−805	−1,253	−1,745	−1,917
Bulgaria	918	−1,099	−32	−26	16	427	−62	−652	−704	−984	−827	−1,676	−1,813
Croatia	960	625	554	−1,592	−1,049	−2,825	−1,468	−1,408	−471	−727	−1,917	−2,066	−1,668
Cyprus	423	110	74	−205	−468	−418	291	−170	−488	−322	−458	−442	−915
Czech Republic	935	466	−820	−1,374	−4,128	−3,622	−1,308	−1,466	−2,690	−3,273	−4,265	−5,661	....
Estonia	939	22	−166	−158	−398	−562	−478	−295	−294	−339	−717	−1,116	−1,432
Faroe Islands	816	....	....	....	....	....	224	176	99	146	126	−7	....
Georgia	915	....	....	....	....	−514	−276	−198	−269	−212	−221	−375	−426
Hungary	944	−4,262	−4,054	−1,650	−1,766	−2,080	−3,391	−3,775	−4,004	−3,205	−4,693	−7,211	−8,819
Kazakhstan	916	....	....	−213	−751	−799	−1,225	−171	366	−1,390	−1,024	−270	533
Kyrgyz Republic	917	−88	−84	−235	−425	−139	−413	−252	−124	−56	−75	−95	....
Latvia	941	417	201	−16	−280	−345	−650	−654	−355	−626	−621	−917	−1,673
Lithuania	946	−86	−94	−614	−723	−981	−1,298	−1,194	−675	−574	−721	−1,278	−1,590
Macedonia, FYR	962	....	....	....	−288	−275	−270	−32	−72	−244	−358	−279	....
Malta	181	−84	−132	−361	−406	−202	−221	−122	−470	−165	12	−275	−550
Moldova	921	....	−82	−88	−195	−275	−335	−79	−108	−34	−72	−130	−114
Poland	964	−5,788	954	854	−3,264	−5,744	−6,901	−12,487	−9,981	−5,375	−5,011	−4,599	−3,585
Romania	968	−1,231	−455	−1,780	−2,579	−2,104	−2,917	−1,297	−1,355	−2,229	−1,525	−3,311	....
Russia	922	....	7,844	6,965	10,847	−80	216	24,611	46,840	33,795	29,116	35,410	60,109
Slovak Republic	936	−580	671	390	−2,090	−1,961	−2,126	−1,155	−694	....	−1,955	−282	....
Slovenia	961	191	575	−75	55	50	−118	−698	−548	31	325	−99	−275
Tajikistan	923	....	....	....	....	....	....	....	....	....	−15	−5	−57
Turkey	186	−6,433	2,631	−2,338	−2,437	−2,638	1,984	−1,344	−9,819	3,390	−1,521	−7,905	−15,451
Turkmenistan	925	....	....	....	—	−580	....	....	....	....	....	....	....
Ukraine	926	....	−1,163	−1,152	−1,184	−1,335	−1,296	1,658	1,481	1,402	3,174	2,891	6,804
Uzbekistan	927	....	....	....	....	....	....	....	....	....	....	....	....
Middle East	**405**	**−26,022**	**−11,272**	**−6,820**	**5,127**	**3,790**	**−28,236**	**9,320**	**68,032**	**36,775**	**28,787**	**62,935**	**....**
Bahrain, Kingdom of	419	−339	−256	237	260	−31	−777	−37	830	227	−50	201	415
Egypt	469	2,299	31	−254	−192	−711	−2,566	−1,635	−971	−388	622	3,743	3,922
Iran, I.R. of	429	−4,215	4,956	3,358	5,232	2,213	−2,139	6,589	12,645	....	....	....	....
Iraq	433	....	....	....	....	....	....	....	....	....	....	....	....
Israel	436	−2,480	−3,447	−4,647	−5,124	−3,289	−1,149	−1,646	−1,230	−1,580	−1,288	795	1,474
Jordan	439	−629	−398	−259	−222	29	14	405	59	−4	537	1,179	−18
Kuwait	443	2,499	3,243	5,016	7,107	7,935	2,215	5,010	14,672	8,324	4,251	9,416	18,884
Lebanon	446	....	....	....	....	....	....	....	....	....	....	....	....

		1993	1994	1995	1996	1997	1998	1999	2000	2001	2002	2003	2004

Current Account Balance
Excluding Exceptional Financing
Expressed in Millions of US Dollars

		1993	1994	1995	1996	1997	1998	1999	2000	2001	2002	2003	2004
Middle East(Cont.)													
Libya	672	−1,366	26	1,650	1,220	1,550	−351	2,136	7,740	3,417	117	3,642	....
Oman	449	−1,190	−805	−801	243	−166	−3,164	−460	3,263	2,008	1,770	1,446	....
Qatar	453	....	....	....	....	....	....	....	....	....	....	....	....
Saudi Arabia	456	−17,245	−10,473	−5,318	679	305	−13,132	411	14,317	9,353	11,873	28,048	51,488
Syrian Arab Republic	463	−203	−791	263	40	461	58	201	1,061	1,221	1,440	728	360
United Arab Emirates	466	....	....	....	....	....	....	....	....	....	....	....	....
West Bank and Gaza	487	....	....	−984	−1,424	−1,548	−1,213	−1,327	−1,023	−641	....	....	....
Yemen, Republic of	474	−1,275	178	144	39	−69	−472	358	1,337	667	538	149	225
Western Hemisphere	205	**−45,490**	**−51,473**	**−37,910**	**−39,726**	**−66,783**	**−91,216**	**−57,487**	**−47,841**	**−52,975**	**−16,043**	**8,967**	**....**
Argentina	213	−8,163	−11,148	−5,175	−6,822	−12,219	−14,510	−11,948	−8,989	−3,290	8,673	7,658	3,353
Aruba	314	42	81	—	−69	−196	−19	−333	233	333	−327	−140	....
Bahamas, The	313	49	−42	−146	−263	−472	−995	−672	−471	−584	−337	−418	....
Barbados	316	69	134	43	70	−50	−63	−148	−145	−111	−168	−169	....
Belize	339	−49	−40	−17	−7	−32	−60	−78	−139	−185	−163	−181	....
Bolivia	218	−506	−90	−303	−404	−554	−666	−488	−446	−274	−352	36	....
Brazil	223	20	−1,153	−18,136	−23,248	−30,491	−33,829	−25,400	−24,225	−23,215	−7,637	4,177	11,669
Chile	228	−2,555	−1,586	−1,350	−3,083	−3,660	−3,918	99	−898	−1,100	−580	−1,102	1,390
Colombia	233	−2,102	−3,673	−4,527	−4,641	−5,750	−4,857	671	761	−1,094	−1,340	−1,021	−1,110
Costa Rica	238	−620	−244	−358	−264	−481	−521	−666	−707	−713	−916	−929	−831
Dominican Republic	243	−533	−283	−183	−213	−163	−338	−429	−1,027	−741	−798	867	....
Ecuador	248	−849	−898	−1,000	−55	−457	−2,099	918	921	−695	−1,359	−455	....
El Salvador	253	−123	−18	−262	−169	−98	−91	−239	−431	−150	−405	−764	−612
Guatemala	258	−702	−625	−572	−452	−634	−1,039	−1,026	−1,050	−1,253	−1,235	−1,039	−1,188
Guyana	336	−140	−125	−135	−69	−111	−102	−78	−115	−134	−111	−91	....
Haiti	263	−12	−23	−87	−138	−48	29	−60	−85	−95	−48	−13	....
Honduras	268	−309	−343	−201	−335	−272	−395	−625	−262	−339	−264	−314	−413
Jamaica	343	−184	82	−99	−143	−332	−334	−216	−367	−759	−1,074	−761	....
Mexico	273	−23,400	−29,662	−1,576	−2,537	−7,695	−16,017	−13,931	−18,620	−17,342	−13,008	−6,479	−7,409
Netherlands Antilles	353	1	−98	128	−254	−65	−137	−277	−51	−211	−59	7	....
Nicaragua	278	−644	−911	−722	−825	−841	−687	−928	−792	−796	−767	−749	−795
Panama	283	−96	16	−471	−201	−507	−1,016	−1,159	−673	−170	−96	−437	−1,104
Paraguay	288	59	−274	−92	−353	−650	−160	−165	−163	−266	93	132	20
Peru	293	−2,464	−2,701	−4,625	−3,646	−3,367	−3,321	−1,464	−1,526	−1,144	−1,063	−935	−11
Suriname	366	44	59	73	−64	−68	−155	−29	32	−84	−131	−159	−87
Trinidad and Tobago	369	113	218	294	105	−614	−644	31	544	416	76	....	....
Uruguay	298	−244	−438	−213	−233	−287	−476	−508	−566	−488	322	52	....
Venezuela, Rep. Bol.	299	−1,993	2,541	2,014	8,914	3,732	−4,432	2,112	11,853	1,983	7,599	11,448	13,830
ECCU													
Anguilla	312	−13	−11	−9	−20	−19	−19	−51	−54	−36	−35	....	....
Antigua and Barbuda	311	15	−6	−1	−59	−47	−47	−57	−66	−64	−103	....	....
Dominica	321	−27	−38	−41	−51	−42	−23	−36	−53	−49	−38	....	....
Grenada	328	−44	−27	−41	−56	−68	−82	−53	−84	−99	−116	....	....
Montserrat	351	−8	−12	−2	16	−2	3	−1	−7	−6	−8	....	....
St. Kitts and Nevis	361	−29	−24	−45	−65	−62	−46	−82	−66	−106	−124	....	....
St. Lucia	362	−50	−48	−33	−58	−78	−60	−97	−79	−75	−104	....	....
St. Vincent & Grens	364	−44	−57	−41	−36	−84	−92	−73	−29	−41	−42	....	....
Memorandum Items													
Oil Exporting Ctys	999	−22,387	−5,062	−4,163	24,206	18,435	−21,252	26,416	109,334	63,116	50,361	91,206	....
Non-Oil Develop.Ctys	201	−84,754	−64,899	−98,077	−110,636	−98,508	−27,561	26,538	29,281	37,416	101,033	154,834	....

Balance of Payments

		1993	1994	1995	1996	1997	1998	1999	2000	2001	2002	2003	2004

Capital and Financial Account
Including Net Errors and Omissions, but Excluding Reserve Assets,
Use of Fund Credit, and Exceptional Financing
Expressed in Millions of US Dollars

Country	Code	1993	1994	1995	1996	1997	1998	1999	2000	2001	2002	2003	2004
All Countries	010	128,746	124,305	176,998	214,901	73,695	68,202	250,657	316,093	273,104	356,722	535,146	....
Industrial Countries	110	−12,850	29,453	36,460	44,117	−48,027	33,693	218,645	342,778	274,647	346,125	472,259	....
United States	111	83,340	112,712	119,219	113,504	136,991	216,263	288,119	413,737	390,626	477,636	529,135	663,135
Canada	156	22,727	12,632	7,039	2,119	5,840	12,836	4,168	−15,902	−14,109	−13,641	−16,615	−24,835
Australia	193	9,641	16,185	19,719	18,282	15,258	16,010	29,040	14,047	9,458	16,959	37,231	41,191
Japan	158	−104,164	−104,990	−52,433	−30,652	−90,247	−124,914	−38,348	−70,705	−47,311	−66,314	50,938	−11,205
New Zealand	196	672	3,117	3,387	5,663	2,862	1,671	3,704	2,319	1,066	3,322	4,139	6,861
Euro Area													
Austria	122	3,214	3,826	6,839	5,965	2,168	8,740	4,484	4,119	1,748	−2,288	−673	−2,837
Belgium	124	....	....	....	....	....	....	....	....	....	−14,060	−15,505	−13,019
Belgium-Luxembourg	126	−13,359	−12,351	−13,990	−13,169	−12,858	−14,263	−15,954	−12,340	−7,950	....	....	....
Finland	172	1,426	3,603	−5,603	−8,038	−4,329	−7,044	−8,032	−8,624	−8,294	−10,262	−7,006	−6,623
France	132	−13,996	−4,968	−10,128	−20,321	−31,861	−17,883	−42,957	−21,014	−34,325	−14,962	−10,529	8,943
Germany	134	−390	27,381	34,184	12,539	4,908	15,666	11,434	24,378	−8,535	−47,621	−52,130	−106,108
Greece	174	4,186	6,455	2,841	8,769	345	....	9,730	12,393	3,701	12,268	6,503	....
Ireland	178	894	−1,752	618	−2,101	−2,974	2,196	−2,218	477	1,085	1,107	215	−686
Italy	136	−10,938	−11,634	−22,272	−28,092	−19,254	−41,470	−16,162	9,028	64	12,538	20,521	12,294
Luxembourg	137	....	....	....	....	....	....	....	....	....	−2,401	−2,122	−2,820
Netherlands	138	−6,562	−16,794	−27,684	−27,197	−27,786	−15,370	−17,607	−6,597	−8,187	−10,249	−17,323	−24,170
Portugal	182	−3,081	765	−168	5,764	7,438	8,341	9,949	11,451	11,936	10,133	1,482	10,819
Spain	184	600	6,426	−7,206	23,871	9,244	−11,220	−9,090	16,356	15,064	19,734	8,189	42,813
Denmark	128	−5,399	−5,041	643	474	5,611	−2,231	6,517	−7,783	−1,531	2,085	−2,289	....
Iceland	176	−96	−266	−48	284	84	587	674	773	287	−67	840	1,257
Norway	142	4,731	−3,507	−4,658	−4,499	−11,234	−6,390	−2,394	−22,165	−28,517	−18,749	−27,981	−29,218
Sweden	144	6,689	1,639	−6,604	−12,278	−14,118	−1,386	−4,101	−6,446	−7,744	−12,119	−20,768	....
Switzerland	146	−16,390	−15,720	−20,673	−17,394	−23,163	−24,015	−30,564	−36,707	−21,275	−22,172	−40,214	−48,949
United Kingdom	112	23,403	11,735	13,438	10,626	−952	6,373	38,253	41,985	27,391	23,935	24,909	42,290
Developing Countries	200	141,596	94,852	140,538	170,784	121,722	34,510	32,012	−26,685	−1,543	10,598	62,887	....
Africa	605	−4,027	−2,495	−3,574	−10,310	3,499	4,841	1,488	−7,921	−1,078	−1,094	8,036	....
Algeria	612	....	....	....	....	....	....	....	....	....	....	....	....
Angola	614	−651	−688	−944	−505	279	755	1,667	−478	645	−206	....	....
Botswana	616	−30	−86	−93	16	−86	−126	−189	−178	−428	−110	....	....
Burundi	618	44	52	26	5	−40	−27	−26	−42	−35	−37	−64	....
Cape Verde	624	39	68	30	57	30	69	123	30	39	82	21	....
Comoros	632	−2	12	9	....	....	....	....	....	....	....	....	....
Congo, Dem. Rep. of	636	....	....	....	....	....	....	....	....	....	....	....	....
Djibouti	611	23	47	−1	....	....	....	....	....	....	....	....	....
Eritrea	643	−74	−69	29	117	115	133	210	40	....	....	....	....
Ethiopia	644	82	−126	−145	−544	−388	−28	229	−224	−370	−918	−10	....
Gambia, The	648	17	−2	9	62	31	....	....	....	....	....	....	....
Ghana	652	593	508	326	282	481	549	828	17	203	18	248	222
Guinea	656	−40	124	144	117	−40	26	139	92	−14	120	−41	116
Kenya	664	341	−36	259	460	472	558	56	192	351	121	357	....
Lesotho	666	73	13	421	419	410	396	180	169	261	−7	....	....
Liberia	668	....	....	....	....	....	....	....	....	....	....	....	....
Madagascar	674	−76	1	−54	197	250	1	148	123	−83	15	74	....
Malawi	676	190	195	3	26	292	−170	191	165	−8	291	....	....
Mauritania	682	−108	−35	−28	−87	−20	−34	....	....	....	....	....	....
Mauritius	684	99	189	131	14	54	−69	314	268	−328	92	101	....
Morocco	686	958	1,206	−599	−615	−820	−494	102	−665	−746	−1,524	−1,398	−410
Mozambique	688	−200	−99	58	−3	−183	37	586	347	172	−727	551	....
Namibia	728	−19	−10	−152	−93	−23	−106	−362	−449	−409	−312	−596	....
Nigeria	694	−1,131	190	−195	−4,268	−536	1,371	−4,043	....	....	....	....	....
Rwanda	714	79	78	−5	29	93	76	69	−37	32	105	....	....
São Tomé & Príncipe	716	....	....	....	....	....	4	14	14	20	16	....	....
Seychelles	718	−23	−51	−29	−3	28	44	28	−52	76	−58	....	....
Sierra Leone	724	65	30	119	128	75	35	83	122	128	53	51	....
Somalia	726	....	....	....	....	....	....	....	....	....	....	....	....
South Africa	199	−2,845	571	3,112	570	6,818	3,054	4,743	695	2,312	925	10,162	15,498
Sudan	732	244	621	563	864	846	1,030	580	681	467	1,253	1,282	1,653
Swaziland	734	−5	−5	53	44	30	135	38	37	10	46	....	....
Tanzania	738	473	292	288	257	332	410	756	497	611	577	....	....
Tunisia	744	1,390	1,063	871	920	981	538	1,180	616	1,129	886	1,113	1,532
Uganda	746	99	145	288	243	326	462	255	361	459	257	423	376
Zambia	754	....	....	....	....	−549	−98	−207	64	....	....	....	....
Zimbabwe	698	342	339	....	....	....	....	....	....	....	....	....	....
CEMAC													
Cameroon	622	−320	−495	−74	....	....	....	....	....	....	....	....	....
Central African Rep.	626	−1	38	....	....	....	....	....	....	....	....	....	....
Chad	628	69	43	....	....	....	....	....	....	....	....	....	....
Congo, Republic of	634	133	639	45	−665	−527	−788	−425	−891	−652	−679	−159	....
Equatorial Guinea	642	−13	−18	112	339	....	....	....	....	....	....	....	....
Gabon	646	−403	−490	−901	−1,140	−729	−71	−788	....	....	....	....	....
WAEMU													
Benin	638	−56	41	−48	−92	70	65	103	91	114	....	....	....
Burkina Faso	748	74	−22	....	....	....	....	....	200	194	....	....	....

		1993	1994	1995	1996	1997	1998	1999	2000	2001	2002	2003	2004

Capital and Financial Account
Including Net Errors and Omissions, but Excluding Reserve Assets,
Use of Fund Credit, and Exceptional Financing
Expressed in Millions of US Dollars

		1993	1994	1995	1996	1997	1998	1999	2000	2001	2002	2003	2004
Africa(Cont.)													
Côte d'Ivoire	662	−345	−7	238	−686	−322	−359	−588	−367	−25	−1,047	−1,111	....
Guinea-Bissau	654	5	−7	10	17	15	....	....	....	14	15	35	....
Mali	678	91	98	232	290	169	162	240	317	263	287	408	....
Niger	692	73	50	134	....	....	....	....	....	....	....	....	....
Senegal	722	292	210	212	−2	90	−1	52	101	51	70	....	....
Togo	742	−107	−41	−72	129	130	123	159	176	167	170	153	....
Asia*	505	**47,898**	**63,498**	**77,595**	**96,554**	**−12,860**	**−77,187**	**−23,210**	**−34,216**	**−844**	**17,353**	**56,775**	....
Afghanistan, I.S. of	512	....	....	....	....	....	....	....	....	....	....	....	....
Bangladesh	513	338	492	312	577	151	324	175	275	392	−242	757	....
Bhutan	514	....	....	....	....	....	....	....	....	....	....	....	....
Brunei Darussalam	516	....	....	....	....	....	....	....	....	....	....	....	....
Cambodia	522	125	193	212	257	244	206	245	240	167	233	168	....
China,P.R.: Mainland	924	13,378	23,545	20,851	24,462	−1,106	−25,224	−12,463	−9,825	30,046	39,795	70,711	....
China,P.R.:Hong Kong	532	....	....	....	....	....	−9,318	−220	3,051	−5,102	−14,789	−15,476	−13,071
China,P.R.: Macao	546	....	....	....	....	....	....	....	....	....	−2,445	−2,652	....
Fiji	819	125	135	206	65	9	65	−58	....	....	....	....	....
India	534	6,087	12,067	4,831	9,914	8,286	9,974	9,892	10,797	7,073	11,487	19,289	....
Indonesia	536	2,700	3,576	8,004	12,166	−3,248	−7,534	−3,867	−4,066	−6,916	−2,866	−3,605	....
Kiribati	826	−1	−7	....	....	....	....	....	....	....	....	....	....
Korea	542	2,188	8,638	15,704	24,626	−14,596	−14,441	8,738	11,539	5,245	6,375	13,470	11,062
Lao People's Dem.Rep.	544	2	106	196	188	−64	−104	−212	52	79	....	....	....
Malaysia	548	14,341	1,360	6,881	6,975	2,061	489	−7,892	−9,497	−6,287	−3,533	−3,201	....
Maldives	556	52	17	35	36	57	42	88	47	29	76	57	....
Mongolia	948	−17	−40	−7	13	−49	76	93	71	75	171	....	....
Myanmar	518	152	176	229	258	447	560	239	188	349	35	−11	....
Nepal	558	288	414	371	358	557	347	34	222	40	−369	−18	....
Pakistan	564	3,328	3,155	2,145	3,656	2,249	−862	−1,596	−2,542	319	230	−665	−543
Papua New Guinea	853	−727	−572	−531	14	15	−192	30	−241	−153	....	....	....
Philippines	566	3,352	5,277	3,215	8,291	1,257	−267	−3,569	−6,634	−1,027	−4,494	−1,475	−3,667
Samoa	862	29	−10	−7	−5	2	−15	26	....	....	....	....	....
Singapore	576	3,367	−6,664	−6,067	−6,499	−6,848	−15,589	−11,103	−6,507	−16,953	−17,582	−21,509	....
Solomon Islands	813	6	1	−9	3	47	9	−26	....	....	....	....	....
Sri Lanka	524	1,150	1,065	1,009	692	702	451	466	683	396	607	708	....
Thailand	578	10,270	12,254	20,713	16,859	−15,229	−16,938	−11,040	−11,120	−3,916	−1,478	−7,435	−1,370
Tonga	866	4	....	....	....	....	....	....	....	13	10	....	....
Vanuatu	846	18	14	24	22	17	3	10	−5	4	13	30	....
Vietnam	582	....	....	....	2,298	1,856	1,111	133	−996	−476	1,052	....	....
*of which:													
Taiwan Prov.of China	528	−5,501	−1,876	−9,405	−9,821	−7,779	1,389	10,601	−6,424	−740	8,034	7,834	7,937
Europe	170	**5,947**	**−18,319**	**24,466**	**3,544**	**33,491**	**9,072**	**13,515**	**2,376**	**−7,524**	**23,669**	**47,447**	....
Albania	914	34	164	32	163	312	118	262	276	364	443	505	....
Armenia	911	80	101	248	245	357	419	312	295	219	212	263	199
Azerbaijan, Republic of	912	....	....	458	846	1,055	1,305	733	493	125	803	2,145	2,906
Belarus	913	297	127	380	302	924	697	214	464	316	408	342	1,228
Bosnia & Herzegovina	963	....	....	....	....	....	11	−49	199	1,272	693	1,659	2,008
Bulgaria	918	777	−184	470	−754	718	−32	748	841	1,357	1,542	2,408	3,546
Croatia	960	−437	−278	1,632	2,066	3,216	1,629	1,866	1,126	2,125	2,731	3,467	1,736
Cyprus	423	35	173	−158	408	371	−374	809	480	933	847	254	1,286
Czech Republic	935	2,575	4,294	8,827	3,302	1,863	3,199	3,105	3,533	5,060	10,883	6,103	....
Estonia	939	143	184	241	505	778	516	414	422	297	786	1,286	1,703
Faroe Islands	816	....	....	....	....	....	....	....	....	....	....	....	....
Georgia	915	....	....	....	....	452	172	184	275	239	32	326	534
Hungary	944	6,807	3,579	7,033	529	1,906	4,342	6,110	5,056	3,121	2,901	7,546	10,800
Kazakhstan	916	....	....	512	910	1,348	782	424	204	1,774	1,559	1,804	3,466
Kyrgyz Republic	917	58	89	154	405	185	340	203	62	25	76	98	....
Latvia	941	−119	−145	−17	491	447	712	819	358	940	634	996	2,076
Lithuania	946	294	207	783	718	1,206	1,725	1,015	833	933	1,183	1,891	1,485
Macedonia, FYR	962	....	....	....	193	157	313	174	352	329	236	332	....
Malta	181	219	514	54	321	209	412	360	248	420	276	419	343
Moldova	921	....	95	−88	92	87	−18	−37	103	9	25	108	253
Poland	964	2,560	52	8,981	7,088	8,785	12,825	12,643	10,605	4,948	5,659	5,805	4,386
Romania	968	792	626	1,300	1,997	3,563	2,274	1,536	2,263	3,764	3,316	4,324	....
Russia	922	....	−26,957	−15,291	−28,065	−6,440	−21,594	−26,315	−32,918	−22,529	−17,553	−7,648	−13,468
Slovak Republic	936	594	535	1,401	2,460	2,060	1,649	1,932	1,614	....	5,639	1,790	....
Slovenia	961	−66	72	315	535	1,238	276	617	726	1,254	1,492	409	−22
Tajikistan	923	....	....	....	....	....	....	....	....	....	17	33	61
Turkey	186	6,741	−2,428	6,998	6,981	5,981	−1,543	6,698	5,885	−16,278	1,307	11,992	19,759
Turkmenistan	925	....	....	....	8	978	....	....	....	....	....	....	....
Ukraine	926	....	−37	−472	581	632	−2,161	−1,842	−908	−409	−1,943	−718	−4,281
Uzbekistan	927	....	....	....	....	....	....	....	....	....	....	....	....
Middle East	405	**22,751**	**10,436**	**12,258**	**6,478**	**7,204**	**24,360**	**−4,785**	**−50,206**	**−29,482**	**−19,382**	**−50,642**	....
Bahrain, Kingdom of	419	227	208	−68	−267	134	761	62	−630	−104	85	−157	−257
Egypt	469	−2,281	−1,195	−1,573	−1,533	75	1,179	−2,979	−1,059	−956	−1,426	−4,150	−4,506
Iran, I.R. of	429	4,443	−4,048	−572	−2,791	−5,910	1,148	−6,138	−11,562	....	....	....	....
Iraq	433	....	....	....	....	....	....	....	....	....	....	....	....
Israel	436	2,153	1,337	5,127	6,330	10,365	994	1,552	1,495	1,940	350	−1,132	−3,047
Jordan	439	−232	133	87	34	245	−550	347	634	−240	393	170	196

Balance of Payments

Capital and Financial Account
Including Net Errors and Omissions, but Excluding Reserve Assets,
Use of Fund Credit, and Exceptional Financing
Expressed in Millions of US Dollars

		1993	1994	1995	1996	1997	1998	1999	2000	2001	2002	2003	2004
Middle East(Cont.)													
Kuwait	443	−3,976	−3,193	−5,157	−7,132	−7,929	−1,957	−4,092	−12,404	−5,419	−5,224	−11,240	−18,258
Lebanon	446	....	....	....	....	....	....	....	....	....	....	....	....
Libya	672	−351	248	51	1	4	−75	−1,448	−1,282	−2,124	161	−626	....
Oman	449	132	144	369	−55	699	2,393	664	−999	−993	−1,461	−790	....
Qatar	453	....	....	....	....	....	....	....	....	....	....	....	....
Saudi Arabia	456	18,739	10,327	6,533	5,062	342	12,414	2,404	−11,652	−11,262	−9,137	−26,440	−46,990
Syrian Arab Republic	463	507	1,357	576	947	−12	376	58	−247	−201	−390	−33	57
United Arab Emirates	466	....	....	....	....	....	....	....	....	....	....	....	....
West Bank and Gaza	487	....	....	984	1,646	1,706	1,160	1,292	1,107	603	....	....	....
Yemen, Republic of	474	163	−900	−672	−475	4,087	−109	−284	258	−114	−113	182	148
Western Hemisphere	205	69,027	41,732	29,794	74,518	90,388	73,424	45,003	63,281	37,385	−9,949	1,272	....
Argentina	213	19,285	10,474	2,863	10,080	15,549	18,600	13,960	7,813	−18,114	−22,076	−16,736	−10,363
Aruba	314	−8	−84	43	43	177	70	336	−248	−250	367	104	....
Bahamas, The	313	−30	51	143	256	529	1,115	737	410	528	380	322	....
Barbados	316	−49	−96	—	17	54	55	182	324	326	145	237	....
Belize	339	34	36	21	27	33	46	90	96	181	155	170	....
Bolivia	218	472	1	395	672	654	791	515	407	238	9	−97	....
Brazil	223	6,870	7,751	31,105	31,930	22,240	17,527	8,635	32,206	19,797	−3,630	−591	−5,070
Chile	228	2,983	4,737	2,488	5,676	6,979	1,727	−846	1,214	501	765	745	−1,581
Colombia	233	2,567	3,855	4,523	6,370	6,028	3,460	−983	101	2,319	1,479	833	3,579
Costa Rica	238	362	141	574	194	288	16	896	365	577	879	703	798
Dominican Republic	243	−11	−228	329	173	254	350	581	978	1,255	244	−1,321	....
Ecuador	248	167	123	−459	−71	−65	1,314	−1,862	−6,618	437	1,138	526	....
El Salvador	253	181	131	410	334	460	394	447	385	−27	282	1,080	572
Guatemala	258	901	632	420	666	863	1,275	901	1,692	1,727	1,256	1,589	1,797
Guyana	336	104	119	92	81	110	89	100	156	160	125	100	....
Haiti	263	−11	−26	225	87	78	5	86	28	89	−20	8	....
Honduras	268	−25	273	160	257	454	239	436	106	265	245	116	781
Jamaica	343	294	276	126	414	162	378	80	886	1,624	834	326	....
Mexico	273	30,632	12,463	−14,735	13,533	26,857	19,187	18,181	25,746	24,656	20,368	16,297	11,513
Netherlands Antilles	353	43	22	−67	182	59	162	202	−79	429	111	20	....
Nicaragua	278	−375	−608	−242	77	548	285	533	336	304	366	280	398
Panama	283	−212	−378	139	467	850	911	1,350	596	804	240	283	708
Paraguay	288	−16	575	137	306	435	177	−136	−177	216	−218	100	250
Peru	293	2,105	4,254	4,034	4,526	5,421	2,080	602	1,395	1,576	2,073	1,496	2,467
Suriname	366	−31	−24	49	62	87	163	25	−23	162	112	166	163
Trinidad and Tobago	369	45	−32	−210	133	807	724	131	−103	86	39	....	....
Uruguay	298	437	547	440	386	687	831	398	733	792	−4,219	906	....
Venezuela, Rep. Bol.	299	2,117	−3,485	−3,458	−2,676	−638	1,027	−1,054	−5,895	−3,812	−12,027	−5,994	−11,675
ECCU													
Anguilla	312	14	11	9	22	21	21	53	55	40	37	....	....
Antigua and Barbuda	311	−27	14	14	48	50	56	68	60	80	110	....	....
Dominica	321	28	34	49	53	43	27	47	53	53	46	....	....
Grenada	328	44	32	47	56	75	86	58	91	104	147	....	....
Montserrat	351	8	14	3	−16	5	10	−9	3	8	10	....	....
St. Kitts and Nevis	361	32	24	48	64	65	57	85	62	118	134	....	....
St. Lucia	362	55	45	39	52	83	70	101	84	87	109	....	....
St. Vincent & Grens	364	43	58	39	36	85	100	77	43	50	36	....	....
Memorandum Items													
Oil Exporting Ctys	999	19,887	−1,265	548	−7,091	−23,282	7,383	−22,893	−71,735	−50,535	−41,789	−68,392	....
Non-Oil Develop.Ctys	201	121,709	96,117	139,991	177,875	145,004	27,127	54,905	45,049	48,992	52,386	131,279	....

Balance of Payments

		1993	1994	1995	1996	1997	1998	1999	2000	2001	2002	2003	2004

Overall Balance
Excluding Reserves Assets, Use of Fund Credit, and Exceptional Financing
Expressed in Millions of US Dollars

		1993	1994	1995	1996	1997	1998	1999	2000	2001	2002	2003	2004
All Countries	010	62,893	60,323	116,429	161,115	65,136	−21,760	124,691	157,222	125,723	228,288	475,239	....
Industrial Countries	110	28,438	35,433	78,131	76,761	23,487	−7,457	39,725	45,292	26,735	66,296	166,312	
United States	111	1,376	−5,350	9,747	−6,667	1,012	6,731	−8,727	295	4,927	3,692	−1,529	−2,804
Canada	156	904	−392	2,711	5,498	−2,393	4,996	5,933	3,720	2,172	−185	−3,255	−2,836
Australia	193	−42	−960	396	2,471	2,873	−2,040	6,705	−1,365	1,096	122	6,877	1,166
Japan	158	27,473	25,265	58,611	35,141	6,567	−6,164	76,256	48,955	40,487	46,134	187,153	160,854
New Zealand	196	−74	733	384	1,772	−1,442	−486	188	−143	−187	1,086	783	629
Euro Area													
Austria	122	2,201	834	1,391	1,075	−3,053	3,482	−2,172	−746	−1,888	−1,723	−2,036	−1,849
Belgium	124	....	....	....	....	....	....	....	....	....	−35	−1,725	−974
Belgium-Luxembourg	126	−2,122	219	243	593	1,056	−2,095	−1,867	−959	1,442	....	....	....
Finland	172	291	4,714	−372	−3,036	2,304	296	13	351	410	−113	−508	906
France	132	−5,006	2,448	712	239	5,940	19,815	−1,448	−2,433	−5,567	−3,965	1,274	4,111
Germany	134	−14,199	−2,036	7,224	−1,195	−3,751	4,015	−14,115	−5,222	−5,466	−1,979	−684	−1,807
Greece	174	3,439	6,309	−23	4,215	−4,515	....	2,435	2,573	−5,699	1,863	−4,722	....
Ireland	178	2,660	−176	2,339	−52	−1,109	3,212	−1,973	−39	395	−292	−1,890	−1,435
Italy	136	−3,135	1,575	2,804	11,907	13,150	−21,472	−8,051	3,247	−588	3,169	1,115	−2,844
Luxembourg	137	....	....	....	....	....	....	....	....	35	108	8	
Netherlands	138	6,641	500	−1,911	−5,695	−2,709	−2,339	−4,611	219	−351	−132	−920	−998
Portugal	182	−2,848	−1,430	−300	547	974	508	216	371	852	1,017	−6,455	−1,863
Spain	184	−5,203	36	−6,414	24,279	11,756	−14,355	−22,850	−2,881	−1,340	3,690	−15,487	−6,412
Denmark	128	−567	−1,851	2,498	3,563	6,532	−4,239	9,564	−5,521	3,317	5,546	4,674	....
Iceland	176	−59	−150	4	153	−44	32	86	−74	−48	61	307	202
Norway	142	8,253	253	575	6,470	−1,198	−6,384	5,984	3,686	−2,346	5,723	346	5,227
Sweden	144	2,530	2,381	−1,664	−6,386	−6,712	3,254	1,881	170	−1,048	665	2,076	....
Switzerland	146	486	1,009	29	2,521	2,154	1,179	−2,685	−4,214	622	2,549	3,405	1,618
United Kingdom	112	5,437	1,500	−853	−653	−3,904	−257	−1,036	5,300	−4,456	−635	−2,592	407
Developing Countries	200	34,456	24,890	38,298	84,354	41,649	−14,303	84,965	111,930	98,988	161,992	308,927	....
Africa	605	−8,956	−10,873	−17,034	−8,090	−1,736	−13,814	−7,999	3,970	3,378	−3,931	11,696	....
Algeria	612	....	....	....	....	....	....	....	....	....	....	....	....
Angola	614	−1,320	−1,028	−1,239	2,761	−604	−1,112	−43	318	−786	−356	....	....
Botswana	616	397	135	207	511	635	44	394	367	170	61	....	....
Burundi	618	16	35	37	−35	−41	−78	−49	−95	−74	−47	−101	....
Cape Verde	624	15	22	−32	22	—	11	49	−28	−17	10	−56	....
Comoros	632	8	5	−10	....	....	....	....	....	....	....	....	....
Congo, Dem. Rep. of	636	....	....	....	....	....	....	....	....	....	....	....	....
Djibouti	611	−12	1	−24	....	....	....	....	....	....	....	....	....
Eritrea	643	33	54	−3	57	120	−160	1	−64	....	....	....	....
Ethiopia	644	32	—	−105	−465	−429	−360	−236	−214	−771	−1,088	−209	....
Gambia, The	648	11	6	1	15	7	....	....	....	....	....	....	....
Ghana	652	34	253	183	−25	77	28	−136	−369	−121	−14	504	−13
Guinea	656	−97	−124	−72	−60	−131	−158	−76	−63	−117	−80	−229	−59
Kenya	664	412	62	−142	387	15	83	−34	−7	10	−16	425	....
Lesotho	666	102	121	98	117	141	116	−41	18	166	−125	....	....
Liberia	668	....	....	....	....	....	....	....	....	....	....	....	....
Madagascar	674	−334	−276	−330	−94	−16	−299	−104	−160	−253	−283	−365	....
Malawi	676	24	14	−75	−122	16	−174	33	91	−68	90	....	....
Mauritania	682	−282	−105	−6	4	28	43	....	....	....	....	....	....
Mauritius	684	7	−44	109	48	−35	−65	190	231	−52	341	222	....
Morocco	686	436	483	−1,895	−673	−988	−640	−69	−1,166	861	−52	154	653
Mozambique	688	−647	−566	−387	−424	−478	−393	−326	−416	−485	−1,439	35	....
Namibia	728	91	75	24	23	68	56	−203	−194	−393	−232	−326	....
Nigeria	694	−1,911	−1,938	−2,774	−761	15	−2,873	−3,538	....	....	....	....	....
Rwanda	714	−50	6	53	20	31	−7	−72	−131	−70	−21	....	....
São Tomé & Príncipe	716	....	....	....	....	....	−6	−3	−5	−1	−7	....	....
Seychelles	718	−30	−28	−32	−62	−45	−74	−99	−103	−47	−189	....	....
Sierra Leone	724	8	−59	1	−22	20	2	−16	10	30	−20	−29	....
Somalia	726	....	....	....	....	....	....	....	....	....	....	....	....
South Africa	199	−41	601	619	−1,108	4,591	855	4,068	505	2,464	1,655	7,557	8,516
Sudan	732	42	19	63	38	18	73	115	124	−151	245	327	782
Swaziland	734	−69	−4	24	−8	28	41	3	−28	−43	—	....	....
Tanzania	738	−575	−419	−359	−254	−297	−509	−79	−1	131	326	....	....
Tunisia	744	67	527	97	442	386	−138	738	−205	288	140	383	977
Uganda	746	−125	−62	−51	−9	−41	−41	−455	−464	91	−154	34	123
Zambia	754	....	....	....	....	−932	−671	−654	−520	....	....	....	....
Zimbabwe	698	226	−86	....	....	....	....	....	....	....	....	....	....
CEMAC													
Cameroon	622	−885	−551	15	....	....	....	....	....	....	....	....	....
Central African Rep.	626	−14	13	....	....	....	....	....	....	....	....	....	....
Chad	628	−48	6	....	....	....	....	....	....	....	....	....	....
Congo, Republic of	634	−420	−155	−581	−1,316	−682	−1,029	−656	−243	−681	−713	−161	....
Equatorial Guinea	642	−10	−18	−12	−5	....	....	....	....	....	....	....	....
Gabon	646	−452	−173	−436	−251	−197	−667	−398	....	....	....	....	....
WAEMU													
Benin	638	−157	18	−255	−149	−100	−87	−89	−20	−46	....	....	....
Burkina Faso	748	2	−7	....	....	....	....	....	−192	−187	....	....	....
Côte d'Ivoire	662	−1,237	−20	−254	−848	−477	−650	−708	−608	−86	−278	−758	....

Balance of Payments

		1993	1994	1995	1996	1997	1998	1999	2000	2001	2002	2003	2004
Overall Balance													
Excluding Reserves Assets, Use of Fund Credit, and Exceptional Financing													
Expressed in Millions of US Dollars													
Africa(Cont.)													
Guinea-Bissau	654	−61	−55	−41	−43	−15	....	....	....	−13	6	29	....
Mali	678	−97	−65	−52	29	−10	−46	−13	63	−47	138	137	....
Niger	692	−24	−76	−18	....	....	....	....	....	....	....	....	....
Senegal	722	−141	23	−33	−201	−95	−248	−268	−231	−194	−247	....	....
Togo	742	−190	−97	−194	−25	13	−17	32	37	−2	30	−9	....
Asia*	505	34,869	59,994	39,035	57,479	5,292	38,768	91,126	57,588	96,054	154,399	230,502	....
Afghanistan, I.S. of	512	....	....	....	....	....	....	....	....	....	....	....	....
Bangladesh	513	698	691	−512	−414	−135	288	−189	−31	−144	497	889	....
Bhutan	514	....	....	....	....	....	....	....	....	....	....	....	....
Brunei Darussalam	516	....	....	....	....	....	....	....	....	....	....	....	....
Cambodia	522	21	36	26	72	34	1	2	34	29	114	13	....
China,P.R.: Mainland	924	1,769	30,453	22,469	31,705	35,857	6,248	8,652	10,693	47,447	75,217	116,586	....
China,P.R.:Hong Kong	532	....	....	....	....	....	−6,789	10,028	10,044	4,684	−2,377	994	3,286
China,P.R.: Macao	546	....	....	....	....	....	....	....	....	....	293	524	....
Fiji	819	−14	23	93	78	−25	5	−45	....	....	....	....	....
India	534	4,211	10,391	−733	3,958	5,321	3,071	6,664	6,095	8,324	18,451	26,007	....
Indonesia	536	594	784	1,573	4,503	−8,137	−3,437	1,916	3,926	−15	4,958	3,647	....
Kiribati	826	−5	−6	....	....	....	....	....	....	....	....	....	....
Korea	542	3,009	4,614	7,039	1,416	−22,979	25,930	33,260	23,790	13,278	11,769	25,791	38,675
Lao People's Dem.Rep.	544	−137	−178	−151	−158	−369	−254	−333	43	−4	....	....	....
Malaysia	548	11,350	−3,160	−1,763	2,513	−3,875	10,018	4,712	−1,009	1,000	3,657	10,181	....
Maldives	556	−1	5	17	28	22	20	9	−4	−30	40	26	....
Mongolia	948	15	6	32	−87	7	−53	−19	−86	−79	13	....	....
Myanmar	518	−78	46	−32	−25	31	60	−46	−23	180	45	39	....
Nepal	558	66	63	15	31	169	280	−223	−77	−300	−313	93	....
Pakistan	564	428	1,343	−1,204	−780	538	−3,110	−2,516	−2,627	2,197	4,084	2,908	−1,351
Papua New Guinea	853	−253	−170	−39	202	−177	−221	125	104	129	....	....	....
Philippines	566	336	2,327	1,235	4,338	−3,094	1,279	3,650	−376	296	−111	−79	−1,587
Samoa	862	−9	−4	2	7	11	6	7	....	....	....	....	....
Singapore	576	7,578	4,736	8,641	7,399	8,114	2,989	4,188	6,751	−867	1,327	6,675	....
Solomon Islands	813	−2	−2	−1	18	9	17	−5	....	....	....	....	....
Sri Lanka	524	768	308	239	9	307	224	−95	−361	159	339	549	....
Thailand	578	3,907	4,169	7,159	2,167	−18,250	−2,696	1,388	−1,806	2,276	5,537	518	5,710
Tonga	866	−2	....	....	....	....	....	....	....	2	7	....	....
Vanuatu	846	3	−6	5	−5	−2	−7	−23	−19	−10	−18	−11	....
Vietnam	582	....	....	....	278	328	37	1,310	110	206	448	....	....
of which:													
Taiwan Prov.of China	528	1,541	4,622	−3,931	1,102	−728	4,827	18,593	2,477	17,353	33,664	37,092	26,595
Europe	170	−11,724	−13,653	18,975	−11,432	3,493	−17,589	9,787	17,105	7,853	28,110	44,197	....
Albania	914	49	7	21	56	40	52	107	120	147	36	98	....
Armenia	911	13	−3	30	−45	50	1	5	17	19	64	72	32
Azerbaijan, Republic of	912	....	....	58	−85	139	−59	133	326	73	34	124	317
Belarus	913	−138	−317	−78	−214	65	−319	20	125	−79	97	−81	185
Bosnia & Herzegovina	963	....	....	....	....	....	−360	−596	−264	467	−560	−87	91
Bulgaria	918	−322	−216	445	−739	1,145	−94	96	137	373	715	732	1,733
Croatia	960	188	277	40	1,017	390	161	458	656	1,398	815	1,401	68
Cyprus	423	145	247	−363	−60	−47	−83	639	−8	611	389	−188	371
Czech Republic	935	3,041	3,474	7,453	−825	−1,758	1,890	1,639	844	1,787	6,618	442	....
Estonia	939	165	17	84	106	216	37	119	128	−42	69	169	271
Faroe Islands	816	....	....	....	....	....	....	....	....	....	....	....	....
Georgia	915	....	....	....	....	−62	−103	−14	6	28	−190	−49	109
Hungary	944	2,545	−475	5,384	−1,237	−175	951	2,335	1,052	−84	−1,792	336	1,981
Kazakhstan	916	....	....	299	159	548	−443	253	570	385	535	1,534	3,999
Kyrgyz Republic	917	−30	5	−81	−20	46	−73	−50	−62	−30	1	4	....
Latvia	941	298	57	−33	211	102	63	165	3	314	12	80	403
Lithuania	946	208	113	168	−5	224	427	−179	158	359	463	613	−104
Macedonia, FYR	962	....	....	....	−95	−119	43	142	279	86	−122	54	....
Malta	181	135	383	−307	−85	7	191	238	−222	255	288	144	−207
Moldova	921	....	13	−175	−103	−188	−353	−116	−5	−25	−47	−22	139
Poland	964	−3,228	1,006	9,835	3,824	3,041	5,924	156	624	−427	648	1,206	801
Romania	968	−439	171	−480	−582	1,459	−643	239	908	1,535	1,791	1,013	....
Russia	922	....	−19,113	−8,326	−17,218	−6,520	−21,378	−1,704	13,922	11,266	11,563	27,762	46,640
Slovak Republic	936	14	1,205	1,791	370	99	−478	777	920	....	3,684	1,508	....
Slovenia	961	125	647	240	590	1,288	158	−81	178	1,285	1,817	310	−297
Tajikistan	923	....	....	....	....	....	....	....	....	....	2	28	4
Turkey	186	308	203	4,660	4,544	3,343	441	5,354	−3,934	−12,888	−214	4,087	4,308
Turkmenistan	925	....	....	....	8	398	....	....	....	....	....	....	....
Ukraine	926	....	−1,200	−1,624	−603	−703	−3,457	−184	573	993	1,231	2,173	2,523
Uzbekistan	927	....	....	....	....	....	....	....	....	....	....	....	....
Middle East	405	−3,271	−837	5,437	11,605	10,994	−3,876	4,536	17,827	7,293	9,405	12,293	....
Bahrain, Kingdom of	419	−113	−48	169	−6	103	−17	25	200	123	35	44	158
Egypt	469	18	−1,164	−1,827	−1,725	−635	−1,387	−4,614	−2,030	−1,345	−804	−407	−584
Iran, I.R. of	429	228	908	2,786	2,441	−3,697	−991	451	1,083	....	....	....	....
Iraq	433	....	....	....	....	....	....	....	....	....	....	....	....
Israel	436	−327	−2,111	480	1,206	7,077	−155	−94	266	360	−938	−337	−1,573
Jordan	439	−861	−265	−171	−188	275	−536	752	693	−244	930	1,348	179
Kuwait	443	−1,478	50	−141	−25	6	258	918	2,268	2,905	−973	−1,824	626
Lebanon	446	....	....	....	....	....	....	....	....	....	....	....	....

Balance of Payments

		1993	1994	1995	1996	1997	1998	1999	2000	2001	2002	2003	2004
						Overall Balance							
						Excluding Reserves Assets, Use of Fund Credit, and Exceptional Financing							
						Expressed in Millions of US Dollars							
Middle East(Cont.)													
Libya	672	−1,716	274	1,701	1,221	1,553	−426	688	6,458	1,293	278	3,016	....
Oman	449	−1,058	−661	−432	187	533	−771	205	2,263	1,015	309	656	....
Qatar	453	....	....	....	....	....	....	....	....	....	....	....	....
Saudi Arabia	456	1,494	−146	1,215	5,741	647	−718	2,815	2,665	−1,909	2,736	1,608	4,498
Syrian Arab Republic	463	304	566	839	987	449	434	259	814	1,020	1,050	695	417
United Arab Emirates	466	....	....	....	....	....	....	....	....	....	....	....	....
West Bank and Gaza	487	....	....	—	221	158	−53	−35	84	−39	....	....	....
Yemen, Republic of	474	−1,112	−722	−528	−436	4,018	−581	74	1,594	553	425	330	373
Western Hemisphere	205	**23,537**	**−9,741**	**−8,116**	**34,792**	**23,605**	**−17,792**	**−12,484**	**15,441**	**−15,590**	**−25,992**	**10,239**	
Argentina	213	11,122	−675	−2,311	3,258	3,331	4,090	2,013	−1,176	−21,405	−13,402	−9,077	−7,010
Aruba	314	33	−3	43	−26	−18	51	3	−15	83	40	−36	....
Bahamas, The	313	19	9	−3	−8	57	119	65	−61	−56	43	−97	....
Barbados	316	20	38	42	86	4	−7	35	179	215	−23	67	....
Belize	339	−14	−4	4	21	1	−14	13	−43	−3	−8	−11	....
Bolivia	218	−34	−90	92	268	101	125	27	−39	−36	−343	−62	....
Brazil	223	6,890	6,598	12,969	8,682	−8,251	−16,302	−16,765	7,981	−3,418	−11,266	3,586	6,599
Chile	228	428	3,151	1,139	2,593	3,318	−2,191	−747	317	−599	185	−357	−191
Colombia	233	464	182	−4	1,729	278	−1,398	−312	862	1,225	139	−188	2,469
Costa Rica	238	−258	−103	216	−69	−193	−504	230	−341	−136	−37	−226	−34
Dominican Republic	243	−544	−511	146	−40	91	11	151	−48	515	−554	−454	....
Ecuador	248	−682	−775	−1,459	−126	−521	−784	−944	−5,697	−258	−221	70	....
El Salvador	253	59	113	148	165	363	303	208	−45	−178	−123	316	−40
Guatemala	258	200	6	−152	214	230	235	−125	643	474	21	550	608
Guyana	336	−36	−6	−43	12	−2	−13	22	40	26	15	10	....
Haiti	263	−23	−50	138	−50	30	34	26	−57	−5	−68	−5	....
Honduras	268	−333	−70	−41	−79	182	−155	−188	−157	−74	−19	−198	368
Jamaica	343	110	358	27	271	−170	44	−136	518	865	−240	−435	....
Mexico	273	7,232	−17,199	−16,312	10,997	19,162	3,170	4,250	7,126	7,314	7,359	9,817	4,104
Netherlands Antilles	353	44	−76	60	−72	−6	25	−75	−130	218	52	27	....
Nicaragua	278	−1,019	−1,519	−964	−748	−293	−402	−395	−456	−492	−401	−470	−398
Panama	283	−308	−362	−331	267	343	−105	191	−77	634	144	−155	−396
Paraguay	288	43	301	45	−47	−216	17	−301	−339	−50	−126	233	270
Peru	293	−359	1,553	−590	880	2,055	−1,241	−862	−130	432	1,010	561	2,456
Suriname	366	13	34	123	−2	19	8	−4	10	78	−19	7	76
Trinidad and Tobago	369	159	186	84	238	194	80	162	441	502	116	....	....
Uruguay	298	193	109	228	152	400	355	−110	166	304	−3,897	958	....
Venezuela, Rep. Bol	299	124	−944	−1,444	6,238	3,094	−3,405	1,058	5,958	−1,829	−4,428	5,454	2,155
ECCU													
Anguilla	312	1	—	—	1	2	2	2	—	4	2	....	....
Antigua and Barbuda	311	−12	8	14	−11	3	9	10	−6	16	8	....	....
Dominica	321	1	−3	8	2	1	4	11	—	3	8	....	....
Grenada	328	—	5	6	—	7	4	5	7	6	31	....	....
Montserrat	351	—	2	1	—	3	14	−11	−4	2	2	....	....
St. Kitts and Nevis	361	3	−1	2	−1	4	11	3	−4	12	10	....	....
St. Lucia	362	5	−3	6	−6	5	10	4	5	12	5	....	....
St. Vincent & Grens	364	−1		−1		1	8	4	14	9	−6	....	....
Memorandum Items													
Oil Exporting Ctys	999	−2,500	−6,327	−3,615	17,115	−4,847	−13,869	3,522	37,600	12,580	8,572	22,814	....
Non-Oil Develop.Ctys	201	36,955	31,217	41,914	67,239	46,495	−434	81,443	74,330	86,408	153,420	286,113	....

		1993	1994	1995	1996	1997	1998	1999	2000	2001	2002	2003	2004
\multicolumn{14}{c}{**Exports of Goods and Services** *As percent of GDP*}

Industrial Countries													
United States	111	9.7	9.9	10.7	10.9	11.3	10.7	10.4	10.9	9.9	9.3	9.3	9.8
Canada	156	30.0	33.8	37.2	38.2	39.3	41.2	43.0	45.5	43.4	41.3	37.9	38.1
Australia	193	18.4	18.3	19.3	19.5	20.6	19.9	18.8	21.9	22.4	20.8	18.0	18.2
Japan	158	9.3	9.3	9.4	10.0	11.1	11.1	10.4	11.1	10.8	11.6	12.3	13.6
New Zealand	196	30.3	30.7	29.7	28.4	27.8	29.2	29.7	34.4	35.2	33.0	29.2	29.0
Euro Area													
Austria	122	35.3	36.0	37.5	38.9	42.3	43.5	44.9	49.5	52.0	52.4	52.0	54.9
Belgium	124	....	....	....	....	....	....	....	....	....	83.8	81.8	84.1
Belgium-Luxembourg	126	....	....	....	....	....	....	....	....	....	....	....	....
Finland	172	32.5	35.4	37.1	37.5	39.0	38.8	37.9	43.3	40.3	39.0	37.5	37.7
France	132	22.4	22.7	23.3	23.5	26.1	26.7	26.5	28.5	28.5	27.3	26.2	26.3
Germany	134	22.3	23.1	23.9	24.9	27.4	28.7	29.2	33.3	34.8	35.6	35.8	38.4
Greece	174	14.5	14.7	13.2	12.3	12.2	....	19.9	26.0	....	....	....	....
Ireland	178	64.6	69.3	74.5	75.2	76.9	110.5	87.6	97.0	97.9	93.7	83.9	80.3
Italy	136	22.3	23.9	26.9	25.8	26.3	25.9	25.0	27.6	27.8	26.4	25.2	26.0
Luxembourg	137	....	....	....	....	....	....	....	....	....	141.3	137.8	147.5
Netherlands	138	50.9	52.2	58.2	58.8	63.2	62.8	61.5	68.5	66.6	62.8	61.9	65.2
Portugal	182	27.2	28.8	30.8	30.9	32.7	32.2	29.7	32.1	30.9	30.3	30.4	31.0
Spain	184	19.3	22.3	22.9	24.1	26.9	27.4	27.6	29.2	30.1	29.1	28.2	27.2
Denmark	128	35.7	36.5	36.4	36.8	36.8	36.6	40.3	46.6	47.5	47.7	45.3	....
Iceland	176	32.7	34.7	35.7	36.4	37.5	36.0	34.9	35.0	40.8	40.2	36.2	36.9
Norway	142	38.0	38.2	37.9	40.8	41.4	37.6	39.3	46.6	45.4	41.2	41.1	43.6
Sweden	144	31.2	34.6	38.5	37.5	40.8	41.6	42.8	44.9	44.7	44.8	44.0	....
Switzerland	146	40.0	39.2	39.2	40.3	45.9	44.8	45.4	50.3	49.4	47.4	46.7	49.5
United Kingdom	112	25.5	26.6	28.3	29.4	28.8	26.9	26.5	28.1	27.5	26.4	25.7	25.0

Developing Countries													
Africa													
Algeria	612	....	....	....	....	....	....	....	....	....	....	....	....
Angola	614	—	—	76.8	82.2	67.3	56.3	86.3	89.7	75.4	85.7	....	....
Botswana	616	50.8	50.1	54.7	55.7	62.4	48.5	64.2	61.4	54.2	55.7	....	....
Burundi	618	9.1	8.9	12.9	5.9	9.5	7.7	7.4	7.5	6.7	5.9	7.2	....
Cape Verde	624	13.6	15.0	17.0	20.1	27.3	22.7	22.0	27.1	....	....	....	....
Comoros	632	19.7	20.5	20.4	....	....	....	....	....	....	....	....	....
Congo, Dem. Rep. of	636	....	....	....	....	....	....	....	....	....	....	....	....
Djibouti	611	....	....	....	....	....	....	....	....	....	....	....	....
Eritrea	643	....	....	....	....	....	....	....	....	....	....	....	....
Ethiopia	644	8.9	12.9	13.9	13.3	14.5	15.1	15.3	15.7	15.6	....	....	....
Gambia, The	648	85.8	71.5	....	....	....	....	....	....	....	....	....	....
Ghana	652	20.3	25.5	24.5	24.9	24.0	....	....	....	....	....	....	....
Guinea	656	....	....	....	....	....	....	....	....	....	....	....	....
Kenya	664	40.4	37.1	32.6	32.6	28.1	24.8	25.5	21.8	22.8	24.1	23.7	....
Lesotho	666	21.0	21.7	21.3	24.3	27.6	27.7	23.7	29.5	41.6	52.9	....	....
Liberia	668	....	....	....	....	....	....	....	....	....	....	....	....
Madagascar	674	15.5	22.0	23.7	20.1	22.2	22.2	24.5	30.6	28.2	16.1	20.6	....
Malawi	676	17.1	29.1	33.6	23.9	21.7	32.1	28.0	25.1	27.5	24.4	....	....
Mauritania	682	44.8	42.4	47.6	47.3	43.4	....	....	....	....	....	....	....
Mauritius	684	58.2	56.4	58.1	62.9	59.6	62.3	61.5	57.6	62.8	62.2	57.0	....
Morocco	686	26.0	24.9	27.3	26.3	28.5	27.8	30.1	31.4	33.0	33.8	32.6	....
Mozambique	688	15.1	15.4	18.0	16.5	14.7	13.4	14.2	18.0	26.4	25.0	23.9	....
Namibia	728	53.4	48.6	49.5	49.9	47.4	47.2	44.9	44.6	45.3	....	....	....
Nigeria	694	34.8	23.6	13.7	13.1	11.9	7.5	38.5	....	....	....	....	....
Rwanda	714	5.2	4.3	5.8	6.0	7.7	5.6	6.0	7.1	9.2	7.5	....	....
São Tomé & Príncipe	716	....	....	....	....	....	....	....	....	....	....	....	....
Seychelles	718	66.5	62.4	65.4	66.3	65.6	60.9	68.0	79.1	83.0	77.7	....	....
Sierra Leone	724	23.0	23.7	14.7	11.6	5.6	7.5	4.3	8.7	10.1	10.5	17.9	....
Somalia	726	....	....	....	....	....	....	....	....	....	....	....	....
South Africa	199	22.5	22.1	22.8	24.7	24.6	25.8	25.3	27.8	30.1	33.0	27.9	26.7
Sudan	732	7.2	10.3	8.2	8.2	6.2	....	....	....	....	....	....	....
Swaziland	734	75.7	78.9	74.7	71.9	73.4	78.6	73.1	80.5	91.1	90.8	....	....
Tanzania	738	18.0	20.8	24.1	21.1	15.7	13.7	13.2	14.2	15.4	16.2	....	....
Tunisia	744	39.6	44.2	44.3	41.6	43.2	42.8	42.3	44.3	47.7	45.3	43.9	47.2
Uganda	746	9.1	10.2	11.0	12.8	11.5	10.8	11.3	11.6	12.1	11.9	13.3	....
Zambia	754	....	....	....	....	31.2	....	....	....	....	....	....	....
Zimbabwe	698	30.2	34.0	....	....	....	....	....	....	....	....	....	....
CEMAC													
Cameroon	622	17.2	26.2	23.3	....	....	....	....	....	....	....	....	....
Central African Rep.	626	14.2	21.0	....	....	....	....	....	....	....	....	....	....
Chad	628	13.7	16.1	....	....	....	....	....	....	....	....	....	....
Congo, Republic of	634	43.8	58.0	64.9	68.7	75.8	76.2	72.5	81.6	78.7	81.3	43.4	....
Equatorial Guinea	642	40.4	54.6	56.6	65.8	....	....	....	....	....	....	....	....
Gabon	646	48.8	61.7	59.4	62.7	61.3	47.4	59.6	....	....	....	....	....
WAEMU													
Benin	638	25.6	36.1	30.6	29.6	23.8	22.7	24.0	22.4	20.8	....	....	....
Burkina Faso	748	8.9	12.8	....	....	....	....	....	9.2	9.2	....	....	....
Côte d'Ivoire	662	30.7	44.4	43.4	46.2	43.0	40.8	41.8	41.2	42.1	50.1	46.7	....
Guinea-Bissau	654	6.1	6.1	6.6	8.5	20.3	....	....	....	33.8	29.9	29.8	....
Mali	678	17.8	22.9	19.5	18.8	23.7	21.8	23.1	24.1	28.9	31.6	26.8	....

Balance of Payments

		1993	1994	1995	1996	1997	1998	1999	2000	2001	2002	2003	2004
							Exports of Goods and Services *As percent of GDP*						

		1993	1994	1995	1996	1997	1998	1999	2000	2001	2002	2003	2004
Africa(Cont.)													
Niger	692	14.7	18.1	16.9	....	....	....	....	....	....	....	....	....
Senegal	722	21.4	36.7	33.8	29.8	29.7	30.2	30.7	29.9	30.4	30.6	....	....
Togo	742	28.0	40.6	30.2	33.8	30.2	31.3	29.2	31.9	32.9	35.6	38.5	....
Asia*													
Afghanistan, I.S. of	512	....	....	....	....	....	....	....	....	....	....	....	....
Bangladesh	513	9.7	10.5	11.7	11.6	13.4	13.7	13.9	15.9	15.0	14.7	15.6	....
Bhutan	514	....	....	....	....	....	....	....	....	....	....	....	....
Brunei Darussalam	516	....	....	....	....	....	....	....	....	....	....	....	....
Cambodia	522	14.0	19.8	28.6	23.5	26.6	31.6	41.2	50.7	56.3	58.7	62.1	....
China,P.R.: Mainland	924	14.5	22.0	21.0	20.9	22.9	21.7	22.1	25.9	25.1	28.0	33.0	....
China,P.R.:Hong Kong	532	....	....	....	....	....	126.5	130.1	146.0	141.5	152.0	174.2	192.5
China,P.R.: Macao	546	....	....	....	....	....	....	....	....	....	104.3	103.3	....
Fiji	819	52.1	56.1	54.4	60.9	56.8	56.4	57.2	....	....	....	....	....
India	534	9.6	9.8	10.4	10.6	10.7	10.8	11.4	12.9	12.9	13.9	14.0	....
Indonesia	536	25.7	25.5	26.2	25.0	29.3	57.5	39.9	42.8	38.3	32.9	28.7	....
Kiribati	826												
Korea	542	26.2	26.4	28.6	27.5	32.0	45.7	38.6	40.4	37.5	35.1	37.9	44.0
Lao People's Dem.Rep.	544	25.1	25.4	22.9	22.8	24.3	37.9	32.2	29.2	27.2	....	....	....
Malaysia	548	78.7	88.9	93.8	91.3	93.1	115.6	121.3	124.4	116.4	113.8	114.3	....
Maldives	556	66.2	76.6	79.7	81.9	79.1	79.0	73.7	73.2	74.3	77.3	84.5	....
Mongolia	948	69.5	60.1	41.4	40.6	58.9	55.6	58.5	64.8	62.6	64.1	....	....
Myanmar	518	1.5	1.4	1.2	1.0	.8	.7	.5	.5	.5	.3	.2	....
Nepal	558	20.7	23.5	24.4	26.1	26.5	23.0	25.3	24.0	20.7	17.3	17.8	....
Pakistan	564	17.6	17.4	17.3	17.9	16.9	15.6	15.2	14.3	15.8	16.6	17.8	17.2
Papua New Guinea	853	58.5	54.2	65.0	56.8	52.1	55.7	63.7	60.5	60.5	....	....	....
Philippines	566	29.5	31.6	36.2	40.4	49.0	56.7	51.2	54.4	48.3	49.7	49.7	50.6
Samoa	862	26.5	25.1	33.6	35.3	34.4	....	....	....	....	....	....	....
Singapore	576	165.3	171.3	187.5	180.8	174.8	172.5	183.1	193.0	189.8	189.3	204.1	....
Solomon Islands	813	60.7	60.1	57.6	53.2	55.5	54.9	58.1	....	....	....	....	....
Sri Lanka	524	33.1	33.8	35.4	35.0	36.5	36.2	35.5	39.1	39.2	36.1	35.8	....
Thailand	578	38.0	38.9	41.8	39.3	48.0	58.9	58.2	66.6	65.9	64.3	65.7	70.4
Tonga	866	22.1	....	....	....	....	....	....	....	....	....	....	....
Vanuatu	846	44.1	48.1	46.3	50.1	48.1	58.1	56.0	64.2	59.3	43.2	44.0	....
Vietnam	582	....	....	....	38.5	43.6	44.0	48.9	55.0	54.6	56.1	....	....
***of which:**													
Taiwan Prov.of China	528	....	....	....	....	....	....	....	....	....	....	....	....
Europe													
Albania	914	15.4	11.3	12.3	12.4	10.3	10.8	15.8	19.0	20.4	20.4	....	....
Armenia	911	.2	35.3	23.3	23.1	20.2	19.0	20.8	23.4	25.5	29.4	32.2	27.3
Azerbaijan, Republic of	912	....	....	....	....	....	....	....	....	....	....	....	....
Belarus	913	....	....	50.0	46.2	55.6	46.6	52.7	73.3	68.6	63.8	64.9	68.4
Bosnia & Herzegovina	963	....	....	....	....	....	27.1	26.2	33.1	32.2	28.9	30.7	....
Bulgaria	918	45.2	53.5	51.7	63.2	60.6	47.0	44.7	55.6	53.2	51.8	53.2	58.0
Croatia	960	52.4	48.4	35.8	39.6	39.4	39.4	40.8	46.9	48.6	46.4	51.9	52.0
Cyprus	423	48.5	48.6	50.2	51.0	51.7	49.6	51.5	55.0	56.0	51.4	46.9	47.5
Czech Republic	935	54.2	51.4	51.0	49.3	52.3	55.2	56.4	64.4	66.5	61.8	62.4	....
Estonia	939	66.4	72.1	68.5	62.8	73.3	74.9	70.9	88.0	83.9	74.6	75.3	79.6
Faroe Islands	816	....	....	....	....	....	....	....	....	....	....	....	....
Georgia	915	....	....	....	....	16.1	18.3	19.5	21.9	25.3	29.3	....	....
Hungary	944	28.4	25.9	44.2	48.3	54.8	61.8	64.2	74.3	73.5	65.0	63.6	65.3
Kazakhstan	916	....	....	34.7	34.6	36.4	32.1	39.4	56.4	47.3	47.9	49.8	55.1
Kyrgyz Republic	917	....	33.6	30.0	30.8	38.2	36.4	42.2	41.8	36.7	39.9	38.8	....
Latvia	941	73.1	46.0	42.7	46.8	46.8	47.1	40.4	42.1	41.6	41.2	42.3	43.8
Lithuania	946	83.3	55.3	49.9	52.2	53.1	45.7	39.1	44.9	50.0	53.3	52.0	52.8
Macedonia, FYR	962	....	....	....	29.5	35.7	40.2	39.8	45.6	40.7	36.0	36.1	....
Malta	181	94.4	96.0	92.4	85.3	83.1	85.7	88.7	94.3	82.8	86.1	79.3	76.3
Moldova	921	....	....	61.3	54.9	54.8	46.8	52.1	49.8	50.0	....	....	....
Poland	964	20.7	25.3	26.3	25.9	27.5	27.2	23.8	27.8	27.7	29.7	34.5	39.2
Romania	968	21.6	23.9	26.5	27.3	28.2	22.6	27.7	32.7	33.4	35.4	36.0	....
Russia	922	....	27.2	29.7	26.3	24.9	32.0	43.2	44.1	37.0	35.0	35.3	35.0
Slovak Republic	936	55.3	58.0	56.5	52.3	55.7	58.7	59.3	69.7	....	71.3	77.3	....
Slovenia	961	59.0	60.1	51.8	52.0	53.6	53.3	49.3	56.0	57.6	57.8	56.6	59.9
Tajikistan	923	....	....	....	....	....	....	....	....	....	....	....	....
Turkey	186	14.6	22.3	21.6	25.1	27.4	27.2	24.7	25.7	34.6	29.8	29.3	30.3
Turkmenistan	925	....	....	....	....	....	....	....	....	....	....	....	....
Ukraine	926	....	45.3	46.2	45.7	40.6	42.1	54.0	62.4	55.5	56.3	58.6	61.4
Uzbekistan	927	....	....	....	....	....	....	....	....	....	....	....	....
Middle East													
Bahrain, Kingdom of	419	84.1	79.7	82.0	88.0	79.1	64.6	78.9	90.0	83.3	82.3	83.1	....
Egypt	469	24.4	23.4	22.0	20.8	19.6	14.8	16.3	17.2	17.8	19.5	28.1	33.9
Iran, I.R. of	429	24.3	26.6	17.8	16.4	11.7	7.9	8.9	9.0	....	....	....	....
Iraq	433	....	....	....	....	....	....	....	....	....	....	....	....
Israel	436	31.1	31.0	30.7	29.9	30.6	31.5	36.1	39.7	35.2	37.2	38.8	43.8
Jordan	439	50.3	47.9	51.7	52.9	49.3	45.8	43.4	41.9	42.2	48.1	48.4	....
Kuwait	443	48.0	51.1	52.4	52.3	52.9	43.9	45.8	57.5	52.6	48.4	59.7	....
Lebanon	446	....	....	....	....	....	....	....	....	....	....	....	....
Libya	672	28.0	27.1	29.4	28.5	26.7	19.7	24.1	39.9	39.3	53.6	....	....
Oman	449	43.1	43.0	44.0	49.8	50.0	41.9	48.7	59.2	57.3	57.1	55.9	....
Qatar	453	....	....	....	....	....	....	....	....	....	....	....	....

		1993	1994	1995	1996	1997	1998	1999	2000	2001	2002	2003	2004
							Exports of Goods and Services						
							As percent of GDP						
Middle East(Cont.)													
Saudi Arabia	456	34.6	34.2	37.6	40.3	39.4	29.8	34.8	43.7	39.9	41.2	46.1	52.7
Syrian Arab Republic	463	13.2	11.5	11.3	9.7	8.5	6.8	7.5	8.5	8.8	9.2	....	....
United Arab Emirates	466	....	....	....	....	....	....	....	....	....	....	....	....
West Bank and Gaza	487	....	....	....	....	....	....	....	....	....	....	....	....
Yemen, Republic of	474	6.8	7.5	17.1	31.4	36.5	27.0	35.3	42.1	36.9	36.9	37.5	....
Western Hemisphere													
Argentina	213	6.9	7.5	9.7	10.4	10.6	10.4	9.8	11.0	11.6	28.4	26.1	25.9
Aruba	314	....	....	150.9	181.6	166.1	123.5	139.5	190.1	179.7	129.7	....	....
Bahamas, The	313	57.9	56.0	57.6	....	....	....	....	....	....	....	....	....
Barbados	316	53.0	57.6	59.4	60.8	56.6	54.4	52.6	53.1	52.1	49.8	....	....
Belize	339	50.5	47.8	48.0	48.2	50.6	47.4	51.2	46.2	51.7	53.4	54.0	....
Bolivia	218	15.6	19.7	18.4	17.7	17.8	15.9	15.8	17.5	18.7	19.6	23.1	....
Brazil	223	9.9	9.0	7.5	6.8	7.3	7.5	10.3	10.7	13.3	15.2	16.5	18.0
Chile	228	24.6	25.6	27.1	26.7	26.3	25.5	28.8	31.0	32.7	33.5	36.1	40.4
Colombia	233	16.4	13.3	13.3	13.5	13.3	13.6	16.2	18.8	18.3	17.4	19.6	19.6
Costa Rica	238	30.2	31.4	38.0	40.8	41.7	48.8	52.2	48.6	41.6	42.4	46.8	....
Dominican Republic	243	49.4	50.1	48.0	46.5	46.9	47.2	46.0	45.3	38.8	38.1	54.4	....
Ecuador	248	25.0	24.8	25.7	26.4	25.6	21.5	32.1	37.6	26.8	25.2	26.1	....
El Salvador	253	19.8	20.2	21.5	21.3	26.2	25.4	25.5	27.9	26.0	26.6	26.8	27.2
Guatemala	258	17.8	17.3	19.3	17.7	17.9	18.0	19.0	20.0	18.6	17.0	16.6	17.2
Guyana	336	113.8	107.1	101.2	102.2	99.7	....	....	....	....	....	....	....
Haiti	263	7.5	3.3	8.2	6.4	11.7	12.6	13.0	13.7	12.7	13.2	16.6	....
Honduras	268	34.9	39.2	41.3	47.1	46.5	46.1	41.1	41.3	37.9	38.1	38.8	....
Jamaica	343	49.0	62.1	58.6	50.9	45.7	43.7	45.0	45.4	41.3	38.2	43.2	....
Mexico	273	15.2	16.9	31.2	32.1	30.3	30.7	30.8	31.0	27.6	26.8	27.8	29.9
Netherlands Antilles	353	....	....	....	....	....	....	....	....	....	....	....	....
Nicaragua	278	19.2	16.4	20.8	21.8	26.6	26.4	25.7	28.0	27.1	28.4	31.5	33.9
Panama	283	84.5	87.9	87.9	79.5	83.2	75.2	62.3	67.4	67.6	61.9	59.1	....
Paraguay	288	48.0	48.2	53.3	45.7	41.4	48.6	37.3	37.9	35.7	43.4	45.7	....
Peru	293	12.1	12.2	12.3	13.1	14.2	13.3	14.9	16.0	15.8	16.4	17.8	21.2
Suriname	366	5.6	76.5	90.9	69.5	63.6	44.8	55.6	63.7	73.3	49.2	55.3	....
Trinidad and Tobago	369	40.5	42.5	52.5	48.9	52.2	48.5	50.2	59.4	55.3	47.9	....	....
Uruguay	298	18.4	18.6	18.2	18.8	19.4	18.5	17.0	18.2	17.6	21.8	27.3	....
Venezuela, Rep. Bol.	299	26.8	30.3	26.8	35.8	29.3	20.9	22.8	29.6	22.8	29.9	33.6	36.6
ECCU													
Anguilla	312	98.3	102.4	93.0	90.6	94.0	107.0	83.1	80.2	84.3	78.8	....	....
Antigua and Barbuda	311	96.2	87.3	81.4	74.5	76.3	75.1	73.2	70.4	....	....	....	....
Dominica	321	48.8	46.7	50.6	51.6	56.0	58.4	58.6	53.3	45.0	48.0	....	....
Grenada	328	44.2	48.3	44.8	44.7	44.1	47.3	57.6	57.4	....	....	....	....
Montserrat	351	49.4	55.1	71.3	135.8	62.2	43.3	72.3	57.7	48.8	47.9	....	....
St. Kitts and Nevis	361	60.6	56.8	51.6	52.1	50.9	50.5	47.9	45.6	45.0	44.2	....	....
St. Lucia	362	65.9	65.1	68.7	62.1	62.0	61.8	54.9	56.1	51.5	48.8	....	....
St. Vincent & Grens	364	50.0	46.6	51.3	53.3	50.1	49.7	53.1	53.1	50.3	49.0	....	....

Imports of Goods and Services
As percent of GDP

		1993	1994	1995	1996	1997	1998	1999	2000	2001	2002	2003	2004
Industrial Countries													
United States	111	10.7	11.3	12.0	12.2	12.6	12.6	13.3	14.8	13.5	13.3	13.8	15.0
Canada	156	30.1	32.7	34.0	34.3	37.4	39.4	39.4	39.8	37.8	37.0	34.1	34.0
Australia	193	18.9	19.6	20.7	19.7	20.2	21.6	21.5	23.1	22.0	22.2	21.1	21.3
Japan	158	7.1	7.3	7.9	9.5	10.0	9.2	8.9	9.7	10.1	10.3	10.6	11.6
New Zealand	196	27.9	28.8	28.4	28.0	27.4	28.9	30.6	33.4	32.2	32.0	28.7	29.4
Euro Area													
Austria	122	34.8	36.3	38.4	40.0	43.8	44.1	45.7	50.1	51.6	50.5	50.9	52.8
Belgium	124	....	....	....	....	....	....	....	....	....	79.5	77.8	80.9
Belgium-Luxembourg	126	....	....	....	....	....	....	....	....	....	....	....	....
Finland	172	27.6	29.5	29.2	30.0	30.9	30.0	29.3	33.7	31.7	30.4	30.8	32.4
France	132	20.5	20.8	21.5	21.5	23.0	23.8	24.0	27.3	26.4	25.6	25.1	26.1
Germany	134	22.1	22.9	23.5	24.1	26.4	27.5	28.6	33.1	32.9	31.3	31.8	33.3
Greece	174	20.8	20.6	21.0	20.6	21.1	....	28.4	36.8	....	....	....	....
Ireland	178	54.3	59.7	63.5	64.2	64.8	96.0	74.3	84.0	83.0	77.0	68.4	64.8
Italy	136	19.0	20.3	22.8	20.7	22.3	22.6	22.9	26.7	26.3	25.5	24.6	25.2
Luxembourg	137	....	....	....	....	....	....	....	....	....	118.0	115.8	123.0
Netherlands	138	45.7	46.8	52.2	52.8	56.8	57.0	57.5	64.3	61.8	58.3	56.9	59.5
Portugal	182	35.2	36.9	37.8	38.5	41.5	41.9	40.0	43.3	41.0	38.1	36.8	38.8
Spain	184	20.0	22.3	22.8	23.4	25.8	27.2	28.8	31.4	31.6	30.2	29.6	30.5
Denmark	128	28.6	30.5	32.1	31.7	33.4	34.7	35.5	40.8	40.9	41.8	39.1	....
Iceland	176	29.6	29.7	32.0	35.8	36.8	40.6	39.7	42.1	41.6	38.4	39.4	42.9
Norway	142	31.4	32.0	31.7	31.7	33.1	35.8	31.9	29.3	28.4	27.4	27.5	29.4
Sweden	144	27.8	30.6	32.7	31.3	34.3	36.0	37.6	39.9	38.9	37.9	37.1	....
Switzerland	146	35.2	34.2	34.6	36.1	40.6	40.1	40.3	44.0	44.2	40.3	39.7	40.3
United Kingdom	112	26.5	27.3	28.8	29.9	28.6	27.8	28.2	30.1	30.2	29.4	28.5	28.3
Developing Countries													
Africa													
Algeria	612	....	....	....	....	....	....	....	....	....	....	....	....
Angola	614	—	—	70.5	68.4	68.0	72.5	92.7	62.9	74.9	71.1	....	....
Botswana	616	47.3	40.8	46.3	42.4	48.7	52.5	51.4	47.5	43.2	42.7	....	....
Burundi	618	29.5	24.9	25.9	15.9	13.5	18.5	15.2	21.2	22.1	23.6	29.4	....
Cape Verde	624	50.2	56.2	60.0	55.0	58.2	58.9	59.5	60.4	....	....	....	....
Comoros	632	37.3	46.9	46.0	....	....	....	....	....	....	....	....	....
Congo, Dem. Rep. of	636	....	....	....	....	....	....	....	....	....	....	....	....
Djibouti	611	....	....	....	....	....	....	....	....	....	....	....	....
Eritrea	643	....	....	....	....	....	....	....	....	....	....	....	....
Ethiopia	644	18.8	23.8	26.3	22.6	20.7	28.8	30.2	25.6	34.3	....	....	....
Gambia, The	648	104.8	82.5	....	....	....	....	....	....	....	....	....	....
Ghana	652	36.4	36.8	32.8	34.3	37.9	....	....	....	....	....	....	....
Guinea	656	....	....	....	....	....	....	....	....	....	....	....	....
Kenya	664	36.1	34.4	39.1	37.3	35.6	32.4	31.2	29.6	30.7	28.8	28.1	....
Lesotho	666	115.1	104.7	112.2	111.8	106.6	103.2	91.0	89.6	94.8	107.3	....	....
Liberia	668	....	....	....	....	....	....	....	....	....	....	....	....
Madagascar	674	24.2	29.4	31.2	25.1	30.5	30.2	32.2	39.2	32.4	22.8	30.2	....
Malawi	676	29.5	52.6	47.2	33.9	34.5	37.2	42.8	36.1	37.5	41.1	....	....
Mauritania	682	61.7	53.1	48.1	53.4	48.8	....	....	....	....	....	....	....
Mauritius	684	64.2	65.1	60.7	63.8	64.4	63.9	66.5	59.5	58.5	59.1	55.3	....
Morocco	686	32.0	30.9	34.0	29.6	31.8	31.9	33.9	37.6	36.2	36.9	36.5	....
Mozambique	688	54.6	52.6	46.1	35.3	29.4	28.6	36.8	38.9	43.7	43.4	35.9	....
Namibia	728	63.9	57.6	59.9	60.5	59.1	56.1	54.5	49.0	52.4	....	....	....
Nigeria	694	29.5	22.9	14.2	8.7	10.6	10.2	33.5	....	....	....	....	....
Rwanda	714	20.7	63.3	29.1	26.5	25.5	21.1	23.5	23.5	25.1	24.7	....	....
São Tomé & Príncipe	716	....	....	....	....	....	....	....	....	....	....	....	....
Seychelles	718	64.6	55.1	62.5	75.7	76.6	76.7	84.5	78.7	95.7	82.6	....	....
Sierra Leone	724	32.3	32.5	29.9	35.5	14.1	19.0	28.0	39.3	34.3	35.9	40.9	....
Somalia	726	....	....	....	....	....	....	....	....	....	....	....	....
South Africa	199	17.8	19.8	22.1	23.2	23.4	24.5	22.7	24.9	26.2	29.3	26.2	27.2
Sudan	732	12.3	21.9	14.9	18.9	15.7	....	....	....	....	....	....	....
Swaziland	734	101.7	91.0	93.4	97.9	91.3	99.6	91.6	95.9	102.2	99.7	....	....
Tanzania	738	47.5	40.2	40.7	33.4	25.5	28.1	25.6	22.6	23.8	23.0	....	....
Tunisia	744	49.1	48.4	48.9	43.5	46.0	46.1	44.5	47.9	52.1	49.5	47.6	50.0
Uganda	746	23.8	22.3	24.6	27.1	25.9	29.9	23.4	24.6	25.6	26.5	27.5	....
Zambia	754	....	....	....	....	34.1	....	....	....	....	....	....	....
Zimbabwe	698	31.3	36.5	....	....	....	....	....	....	....	....	....	....
CEMAC													
Cameroon	622	15.8	22.7	18.4	....	....	....	....	....	....	....	....	....
Central African Rep	626	22.7	28.7	....	....	....	....	....	....	....	....	....	....
Chad	628	31.0	34.9	....	....	....	....	....	....	....	....	....	....
Congo, Republic of	634	50.1	90.9	63.6	60.0	60.2	72.6	59.1	37.1	54.9	53.6	27.9	....
Equatorial Guinea	642	51.7	50.7	117.9	174.2	....	....	....	....	....	....	....	....
Gabon	646	34.6	38.3	35.7	33.0	37.2	48.0	38.1	....	....	....	....	....
WAEMU													
Benin	638	35.0	42.3	44.5	33.9	33.0	31.1	34.2	30.0	29.8	....	....	....
Burkina Faso	748	20.9	22.7	....	....	....	....	....	25.6	23.0	....	....	....
Côte d'Ivoire	662	29.8	34.2	38.1	37.5	35.3	34.5	33.6	34.2	34.4	34.2	35.9	....
Guinea-Bissau	654	17.7	12.8	20.0	25.7	31.7	....	....	....	46.2	42.2	42.5	....
Mali	678	33.9	43.5	36.4	33.4	33.0	31.1	33.1	34.7	38.1	33.3	34.3	....

Balance of Payments

		1993	1994	1995	1996	1997	1998	1999	2000	2001	2002	2003	2004

Imports of Goods and Services
As percent of GDP

		1993	1994	1995	1996	1997	1998	1999	2000	2001	2002	2003	2004
Africa(Cont.)													
Niger	692	21.8	29.7	24.1	....	....	....	....	....	....	....	....	....
Senegal	722	31.0	45.1	40.9	36.1	36.5	37.4	38.4	39.8	39.9	41.7	....	....
Togo	742	40.5	49.9	43.6	46.8	41.3	44.3	39.3	45.3	49.6	50.1	53.3	....
Asia*													
Afghanistan, I.S. of	512	....	....	....	....	....	....	....	....	....	....	....	....
Bangladesh	513	14.5	16.0	20.0	18.7	19.0	18.6	20.0	21.3	21.3	19.5	21.7	....
Bhutan	514	....	....	....	....	....	....	....	....	....	....	....	....
Brunei Darussalam	516	....	....	....	....	....	....	....	....	....	....	....	....
Cambodia	522	23.9	32.2	40.6	37.4	37.2	44.7	54.4	62.9	65.6	67.0	72.2	....
China,P.R.: Mainland	924	16.4	20.6	19.3	18.8	18.2	17.1	19.1	23.2	22.8	25.2	30.6	....
China,P.R.:Hong Kong	532	....	....	....	....	....	126.3	125.5	142.4	137.5	144.3	165.3	183.7
China,P.R.: Macao	546	....	....	....	....	....	....	....	....	....	63.7	61.3	....
Fiji	819	59.5	59.5	58.3	59.3	57.8	58.5	56.1	....	....	....	....	....
India	534	10.9	11.7	13.2	14.2	13.9	14.1	14.0	15.7	14.8	14.9	15.9	....
Indonesia	536	24.2	24.7	26.9	26.1	29.1	46.1	30.7	33.9	30.8	26.3	23.9	....
Kiribati	826	....	....	....	....	....	....	....	....	....	....	....	....
Korea	542	26.2	27.5	30.0	31.3	33.2	33.3	32.4	37.7	35.5	33.9	35.5	39.7
Lao People's Dem.Rep.	544	35.6	43.5	42.1	41.1	40.7	46.9	39.8	33.4	31.9	....	....	....
Malaysia	548	78.8	90.5	97.8	89.9	92.2	93.5	96.3	104.5	98.0	96.4	93.3	....
Maldives	556	72.9	72.4	78.3	78.5	78.9	76.0	78.4	72.3	73.0	71.2	77.5	....
Mongolia	948	73.0	61.9	42.5	48.6	53.0	69.0	72.5	81.5	81.6	85.7	....	....
Myanmar	518	2.4	2.0	1.9	1.6	1.4	1.1	.7	.6	.5	.3	.2	....
Nepal	558	31.5	36.1	38.5	39.6	39.6	31.5	34.0	33.5	31.0	30.7	32.6	....
Pakistan	564	25.3	23.3	24.1	26.6	22.7	20.3	19.7	17.2	18.0	17.2	18.3	23.5
Papua New Guinea	853	39.0	36.3	41.4	43.9	49.0	49.8	52.7	45.8	46.0	....	....	....
Philippines	566	38.0	40.6	45.0	49.9	61.3	60.8	48.3	52.5	52.2	50.6	59.0	59.7
Samoa	862	78.9	52.4	60.1	58.8	60.3	....	....	....	....	....	....	....
Singapore	576	157.5	156.4	171.5	165.5	161.9	151.4	165.5	177.1	170.6	166.5	171.2	....
Solomon Islands	813	77.0	77.6	63.5	58.5	71.4	59.8	52.0	....	....	....	....	....
Sri Lanka	524	42.6	45.6	45.9	43.9	43.6	42.3	43.3	49.6	45.3	42.8	42.3	....
Thailand	578	42.5	44.1	48.9	45.9	48.0	43.4	45.9	58.4	59.9	58.2	59.5	66.2
Tonga	866	53.5	....	....	....	....	....	....	....	....	....	....	....
Vanuatu	846	48.4	50.4	48.3	48.0	44.9	52.4	62.4	60.1	64.3	52.6	52.9	....
Vietnam	582	....	....	....	50.0	50.6	49.6	47.4	55.6	54.9	61.2	....	....
*of which:													
Taiwan Prov.of China	528	....	....	....	....	....	....	....	....	....	....	....	....
Europe													
Albania	914	62.2	37.6	33.7	36.9	37.4	34.4	32.0	40.6	43.3	46.2	....	....
Armenia	911	.3	67.0	56.4	55.6	58.1	53.6	49.8	50.5	46.2	46.6	50.1	42.4
Azerbaijan, Republic of	912	....	....	....	....	....	....	....	....	....	....	....	....
Belarus	913	....	....	54.6	50.2	61.6	53.3	54.8	77.6	72.7	67.1	68.7	74.4
Bosnia & Herzegovina	963	....	....	....	....	....	98.5	90.2	88.2	87.3	85.1	86.2	....
Bulgaria	918	53.9	53.5	49.6	60.1	55.3	47.0	50.6	60.9	61.9	58.9	62.6	68.2
Croatia	960	48.8	47.1	48.4	49.7	57.5	48.7	49.2	52.1	54.4	57.3	59.7	58.8
Cyprus	423	47.5	47.9	50.5	54.0	53.6	53.1	50.7	56.4	54.4	52.4	48.4	51.1
Czech Republic	935	52.7	53.7	54.4	55.4	58.0	56.4	57.6	67.4	69.1	63.9	64.6	....
Estonia	939	70.5	82.5	76.1	73.6	84.1	84.7	76.4	91.8	87.4	81.7	83.1	87.6
Faroe Islands	816	....	....	....	....	....	....	....	....	....	....	....	....
Georgia	915	....	....	....	....	39.5	36.9	38.9	39.0	40.1	42.4	....	....
Hungary	944	38.2	34.5	44.6	47.9	53.9	63.3	66.9	78.1	75.0	67.4	68.1	68.2
Kazakhstan	916	....	....	35.5	37.6	39.0	37.1	38.4	48.9	49.1	47.9	44.3	45.8
Kyrgyz Republic	917	....	44.9	48.7	56.5	46.2	56.8	56.5	47.9	37.4	44.8	45.4	....
Latvia	941	57.8	44.4	44.8	54.2	54.6	59.6	49.9	49.4	51.6	51.4	55.2	59.6
Lithuania	946	91.2	61.4	61.0	61.8	63.4	57.2	49.2	51.2	55.4	58.8	57.9	59.1
Macedonia, FYR	962	....	....	....	40.2	50.0	56.3	52.2	63.5	56.6	57.8	54.4	....
Malta	181	104.9	106.8	105.5	98.7	91.1	91.8	94.1	104.3	88.1	84.9	84.8	84.2
Moldova	921	....	....	69.8	73.7	74.3	72.4	67.4	75.4	73.7	....	....	....
Poland	964	24.1	23.0	24.9	28.6	32.1	32.6	32.3	34.3	31.4	33.0	36.9	41.2
Romania	968	26.3	25.9	31.9	35.4	34.9	30.3	32.0	37.9	41.1	41.1	43.8	....
Russia	922	....	23.6	26.4	22.1	22.7	27.5	27.0	23.5	24.3	24.4	23.9	22.4
Slovak Republic	936	60.1	53.3	54.9	63.1	65.2	69.2	64.5	71.9	....	78.3	78.5	....
Slovenia	961	57.2	57.9	53.7	53.0	54.4	54.7	53.4	59.6	58.2	56.3	56.7	60.6
Tajikistan	923	....	....	....	....	....	....	....	....	....	....	....	....
Turkey	186	18.6	20.1	23.7	27.1	29.6	27.5	26.2	31.0	30.9	29.5	30.8	34.0
Turkmenistan	925	....	....	....	....	....	....	....	....	....	....	....	....
Ukraine	926	....	49.0	49.4	48.2	43.6	45.0	48.2	57.4	53.9	51.8	56.0	53.8
Uzbekistan	927	....	....	....	....	....	....	....	....	....	....	....	....
Middle East													
Bahrain, Kingdom of	419	80.7	74.0	70.5	76.2	69.5	63.9	63.0	64.4	60.5	66.6	64.6	....
Egypt	469	32.6	30.3	28.5	27.0	27.6	24.9	23.9	23.4	23.3	23.2	27.6	34.4
Iran, I.R. of	429	31.5	21.2	14.2	12.7	10.5	9.1	6.4	5.3	....	....	....	....
Iraq	433	....	....	....	....	....	....	....	....	....	....	....	....
Israel	436	40.0	39.5	39.4	38.0	36.0	34.6	39.3	40.3	38.3	41.1	40.2	44.3
Jordan	439	80.1	70.5	72.8	78.2	71.6	65.6	61.3	68.6	67.4	67.6	70.0	....
Kuwait	443	48.1	44.8	46.5	41.4	42.4	51.1	39.4	30.7	36.4	39.7	39.5	....
Lebanon	446	....	....	....	....	....	....	....	....	....	....	....	....
Libya	672	31.3	26.1	22.6	23.8	21.8	21.3	17.4	14.7	20.6	46.8	....	....
Oman	449	39.5	35.6	36.5	36.4	39.2	50.4	38.3	32.0	36.1	36.8	37.5	....
Qatar	453	....	....	....	....	....	....	....	....	....	....	....	....

		1993	1994	1995	1996	1997	1998	1999	2000	2001	2002	2003	2004

Imports of Goods and Services
As percent of GDP

		1993	1994	1995	1996	1997	1998	1999	2000	2001	2002	2003	2004
Middle East(Cont.)													
Saudi Arabia	456	38.1	29.2	31.5	31.5	31.7	30.4	27.7	28.1	26.2	26.3	25.5	26.5
Syrian Arab Republic	463	13.4	13.8	10.9	9.9	7.7	6.8	7.1	6.7	7.0	7.1	....	....
United Arab Emirates	466	....	....	....	....	....	....	....	....	....	....	....	....
West Bank and Gaza	487	....	....	....	....	....	....	....	....	....	....	....	....
Yemen, Republic of	474	16.0	8.6	19.5	36.6	45.4	48.0	37.7	34.6	36.0	37.7	40.2	....
Western Hemisphere													
Argentina	213	9.3	10.6	10.1	11.1	12.8	13.0	11.6	11.6	10.3	13.1	14.4	18.4
Aruba	314	....	....	152.8	185.5	177.0	124.4	157.8	173.2	156.9	137.1	....	....
Bahamas, The	313	52.5	53.7	58.5	....	....	....	....	....	....	....	....	....
Barbados	316	47.6	49.6	56.3	56.6	58.8	56.9	58.3	58.6	56.5	55.7	....	....
Belize	339	61.3	55.1	52.5	50.0	57.2	56.6	60.8	62.9	70.3	68.1	67.8	....
Bolivia	218	25.0	22.6	23.4	23.4	26.0	25.9	24.0	24.7	24.3	26.1	24.4	....
Brazil	223	8.0	8.0	9.0	8.5	9.3	9.4	11.8	12.0	14.3	13.4	12.6	13.2
Chile	228	27.1	24.6	25.7	28.1	28.2	28.7	26.5	29.1	31.2	31.0	32.1	31.4
Colombia	233	18.8	17.4	17.3	16.9	17.2	17.6	15.5	17.2	19.4	18.8	20.7	20.2
Costa Rica	238	35.7	34.0	40.3	42.7	44.5	50.0	45.5	45.8	42.1	45.8	48.5	....
Dominican Republic	243	57.0	55.7	51.4	51.4	51.7	56.3	53.5	54.9	46.6	46.9	55.7	....
Ecuador	248	26.6	26.4	28.3	24.1	25.8	28.8	25.2	31.5	31.5	32.2	28.9	....
El Salvador	253	34.4	35.2	38.1	34.3	37.8	37.5	37.8	42.9	41.8	41.3	43.2	44.4
Guatemala	258	26.1	24.6	25.4	22.4	23.6	26.0	27.4	28.9	28.9	29.4	29.5	31.6
Guyana	336	135.4	121.9	113.9	108.2	109.4	....	....	....	....	....	....	....
Haiti	263	18.7	11.4	34.3	26.3	27.5	27.7	30.6	36.9	37.0	38.4	48.7	....
Honduras	268	42.7	48.4	46.8	55.2	53.3	53.5	55.5	54.2	53.1	52.1	53.8	....
Jamaica	343	56.8	62.6	64.3	59.3	54.6	52.1	51.9	56.0	56.6	56.6	60.1	....
Mexico	273	19.2	22.0	28.7	30.2	30.5	32.9	32.6	33.0	29.8	28.7	29.5	32.0
Netherlands Antilles	353	....	....	....	....	....	....	....	....	....	....	....	....
Nicaragua	278	42.7	32.8	36.1	41.4	50.6	49.8	57.6	54.5	52.3	53.9	57.5	60.8
Panama	283	84.7	86.9	89.7	80.5	85.8	81.2	67.9	69.9	66.0	62.4	58.0	....
Paraguay	288	49.1	53.4	57.7	52.4	50.4	52.6	41.9	42.6	42.3	44.6	46.1	....
Peru	293	15.9	15.7	17.9	17.8	18.4	18.8	17.5	18.1	17.8	17.5	17.8	18.4
Suriname	366	5.1	64.3	79.4	78.8	72.1	60.9	59.3	60.0	69.6	58.8	66.1	....
Trinidad and Tobago	369	31.0	29.8	39.6	38.0	56.3	53.8	44.4	45.5	44.8	42.6	....	....
Uruguay	298	19.1	19.9	18.5	19.4	20.2	20.0	19.1	20.9	20.0	20.2	24.2	....
Venezuela, Rep. Bol.	299	26.7	22.5	21.8	21.0	21.9	22.8	19.1	18.2	19.4	18.6	17.0	20.2
ECCU													
Anguilla	312	108.0	103.6	122.5	123.6	115.7	130.6	138.1	143.6	122.7	112.9	....	....
Antigua and Barbuda	311	87.3	84.4	88.9	86.5	82.3	79.0	81.4	75.1	....	....	....	....
Dominica	321	63.7	62.4	66.6	69.6	70.5	66.4	67.5	67.5	62.3	61.1	....	....
Grenada	328	63.7	61.2	60.9	65.6	67.1	72.2	69.9	75.1	....	....	....	....
Montserrat	351	68.6	81.3	94.4	127.4	115.7	122.1	137.1	128.5	134.3	140.0	....	....
St. Kitts and Nevis	361	73.9	67.2	75.0	78.9	71.2	67.2	72.3	75.5	70.6	73.4	....	....
St. Lucia	362	71.1	71.3	71.1	68.5	71.6	67.7	67.0	63.8	58.8	59.7	....	....
St. Vincent & Grens.	364	68.2	70.6	65.7	66.5	78.1	78.6	73.5	60.9	61.1	60.2	....	....

Balance of Payments

		1993	1994	1995	1996	1997	1998	1999	2000	2001	2002	2003	2004

Current Account Balance
Excluding Exceptional Financing
As percent of GDP

		1993	1994	1995	1996	1997	1998	1999	2000	2001	2002	2003	2004
Industrial Countries													
United States	111	−1.2	−1.7	−1.5	−1.5	−1.6	−2.4	−3.2	−4.2	−3.8	−4.5	−4.8	−5.7
Canada	156	−3.9	−2.3	−.7	.6	−1.3	−1.3	.3	2.7	2.3	1.8	1.5	2.2
Australia	193	−3.3	−5.1	−5.4	−3.9	−3.1	−5.0	−5.7	−4.1	−2.3	−4.2	−6.0	−6.5
Japan	158	3.0	2.7	2.1	1.4	2.2	3.0	2.6	2.5	2.1	2.8	3.2	3.7
New Zealand	196	−1.7	−4.6	−4.9	−5.8	−6.5	−3.9	−6.1	−4.7	−2.4	−3.7	−4.2	−6.4
Euro Area													
Austria	122	−.5	−1.5	−2.3	−2.1	−2.5	−2.5	−3.1	−2.5	−1.9	.3	−.5	.3
Belgium	124	....	....	....	....	....	....	....	....	....	5.7	4.5	3.4
Belgium-Luxembourg	126	....	....	....	....	....	....	....	....	....			
Finland	172	−1.3	1.1	4.0	3.9	5.4	5.7	6.3	7.5	7.2	7.7	4.0	4.0
France	132	.7	.5	.7	1.3	2.7	2.6	2.9	1.4	2.2	.8	.7	−.2
Germany	134	−.7	−1.4	−1.1	−.6	−.4	−.5	−1.2	−1.6	.2	2.3	2.1	3.8
Greece	174	−.8	−.1	−2.4	−3.7	−4.0	....	−5.8	−8.7				
Ireland	178	3.5	2.9	2.6	2.8	2.3	1.2	.3	−.5	−.7	−1.2	−1.4	−.4
Italy	136	.8	1.3	2.3	3.2	2.8	1.7	.7	−.5	−.1	−.8	−1.3	−.9
Luxembourg	137	....	....	....	....	....	....	....	....	....	11.6	8.5	8.9
Netherlands	138	4.1	4.9	6.2	5.2	6.7	3.3	3.3	1.8	2.0	2.4	3.2	4.0
Portugal	182	.3	−2.5	−.1	−4.8	−6.3	−7.3	−8.5	−10.4	−10.1	−7.5	−5.4	−7.6
Spain	184	−1.2	−1.3	.1	.1	.4	−.5	−2.3	−3.3	−2.8	−2.4	−2.8	−5.0
Denmark	128	3.5	2.1	1.0	1.7	.5	−1.2	1.8	1.4	3.0	2.0	3.3	....
Iceland	176	.6	1.8	.7	−1.8	−1.8	−6.9	−7.0	−10.1	−4.4	1.5	−5.1	−8.6
Norway	142	3.0	3.0	3.5	6.9	6.4	—	5.3	15.5	15.4	12.9	12.8	13.8
Sweden	144	−2.1	.3	2.0	2.2	3.0	1.9	2.4	2.8	3.0	5.3	7.6	....
Switzerland	146	7.0	6.2	6.6	6.6	9.7	9.4	10.5	13.2	8.7	8.9	13.6	14.1
United Kingdom	112	−1.9	−1.0	−1.3	−.9	−.2	−.5	−2.7	−2.6	−2.2	−1.6	−1.5	−2.0
Developing Countries													
Africa													
Algeria	612	....	....	....	....	....	....	....	....	....	....	....	....
Angola	614	—	—	−5.9	50.1	−11.6	−28.7	−27.8	8.7	−16.0	−1.5	....	....
Botswana	616	11.3	5.4	6.8	11.6	14.8	3.6	12.5	11.2	12.2	3.4	....	....
Burundi	618	−2.9	−1.6	1.0	−4.6	—	−5.8	−2.9	−7.5	−5.9	−1.6	−6.3	....
Cape Verde	624	−6.6	−11.2	−12.6	−6.9	−6.0	−11.1	−12.4	−10.8	....	....	....	....
Comoros	632	3.6	−3.7	−8.4	....	....	....	....	....	....	....	....	....
Congo, Dem. Rep. of	636	....	....	....	....	....	....	....	....	....	....	....	....
Djibouti	611	....	....	....	....	....	....	....	....	....	....	....	....
Eritrea	643	....	....	....	....	....	....	....	....	....	....	....	....
Ethiopia	644	−.9	2.4	.7	1.3	−.6	−5.3	−7.6	.2	−6.4	....	....	....
Gambia, The	648	−1.9	2.7	....	....	....	....	....	....	....	....	....	....
Ghana	652	−9.4	−4.7	−2.2	−4.4	−5.9	....	....	....	....	....	....	....
Guinea	656	....	....	....	....	....	....	....	....	....	....	....	....
Kenya	664	1.2	1.4	−4.4	−.8	−4.3	−4.1	−.8	−1.6	−2.6	−1.0	.5	....
Lesotho	666	3.6	12.9	−34.6	−32.1	−26.3	−31.5	−24.2	−17.6	−12.4	−16.1	....	....
Liberia	668	....	....	....	....	....	....	....	....	....	....	....	....
Madagascar	674	−7.7	−9.3	−8.7	−7.3	−7.5	−8.0	−6.8	−7.3	−3.8	−6.8	−8.0	....
Malawi	676	−8.1	−15.1	−5.6	−6.5	−10.4	−.2	−8.9	−4.2	−3.5	−10.4	....	....
Mauritania	682	−18.4	−7.0	2.1	8.4	4.5	....	....	....	....	....	....	....
Mauritius	684	−2.8	−6.5	−.5	.8	−2.1	.1	−2.9	−.8	6.1	5.3	2.2	....
Morocco	686	−1.9	−2.4	−3.9	−.2	−.5	−.4	−.5	−1.5	4.7	4.1	3.5	....
Mozambique	688	−21.6	−21.2	−19.4	−14.5	−8.6	−10.9	−22.4	−19.9	−17.8	−17.5	−10.4	....
Namibia	728	3.9	2.6	5.0	3.3	2.5	4.8	4.7	7.6	.5	....	....	....
Nigeria	694	−2.5	−5.1	−2.9	2.7	.4	−3.2	1.4	....	....	....	....	....
Rwanda	714	−6.6	−6.1	4.5	−.6	−3.3	−4.1	−7.5	−5.2	−5.9	−7.2	....	....
São Tomé & Príncipe	716	....	....	....	....	....	....	....	....	....	....	....	....
Seychelles	718	−1.6	4.9	−.6	−11.8	−12.9	−19.4	−20.5	−8.3	−20.0	−18.7	....	....
Sierra Leone	724	−7.5	−9.8	−13.6	−16.0	−6.5	−4.9	−14.8	−17.7	−12.1	−7.8	−8.1	....
Somalia	726	....	....	....	....	....	....	....	....	....	....	....	....
South Africa	199	2.1	—	−1.6	−1.2	−1.5	−1.6	−.5	−.1	.1	.7	−1.6	−3.3
Sudan	732	−3.9	−10.4	−6.0	−10.1	−8.1	....	....	....	....	....	....	....
Swaziland	734	−6.2	.2	−2.2	−3.9	−.2	−6.9	−2.6	−4.7	−4.2	−3.9	....	....
Tanzania	738	−24.6	−15.8	−12.3	−7.9	−8.2	−11.0	−9.7	−5.5	−5.1	−2.6	....	....
Tunisia	744	−9.1	−3.4	−4.3	−2.4	−3.1	−3.4	−2.1	−4.2	−4.2	−3.5	−2.9	−2.0
Uganda	746	−6.9	−4.0	−5.6	−4.1	−5.6	−7.9	−11.8	−14.4	−6.4	−6.8	−6.0	....
Zambia	754	....	....	....	....	−9.8	....	....	....	....	....	....	....
Zimbabwe	698	−1.8	−6.2	....	....	....	....	....	....	....	....	....	....
CEMAC													
Cameroon	622	−5.1	−.8	1.0	....	....	....	....	....	....	....	....	....
Central African Rep	626	−1.0	−2.9	....	....	....	....	....	....	....	....	....	....
Chad	628	−8.0	−3.2	....	....	....	....	....	....	....	....	....	....
Congo, Republic of	634	−20.6	−44.8	−29.5	−25.6	−6.7	−12.3	−9.8	20.1	−1.0	−1.1	−.1	....
Equatorial Guinea	642	1.6	−.3	−74.2	−125.7	....	....	....	....	....	....	....	....
Gabon	646	−.9	7.6	9.4	15.6	10.0	−13.3	8.4	....	....	....	....	....
WAEMU													
Benin	638	−4.8	−1.5	−10.3	−2.6	−7.5	−6.2	−7.7	−4.7	−6.4	....	....	....
Burkina Faso	748	−2.2	.7	....	....	....	....	....	−15.2	−13.5	....	....	....
Côte d'Ivoire	662	−8.6	−.2	−4.9	−1.5	−1.3	−2.3	−1.0	−2.3	−.6	6.6	2.5	....
Guinea-Bissau	654	−15.5	−7.5	−11.3	−18.0	−10.8	....	....	....	−13.5	−4.3	−2.5	....
Mali	678	−7.5	−9.2	−10.4	−9.3	−6.6	−7.1	−8.6	−9.5	−10.2	−4.5	−6.3	....

Balance of Payments

		1993	1994	1995	1996	1997	1998	1999	2000	2001	2002	2003	2004
						Current Account Balance							
						Excluding Exceptional Financing							
						As percent of GDP							

Africa(Cont.)

Country	Code	1993	1994	1995	1996	1997	1998	1999	2000	2001	2002	2003	2004
Niger	692	−4.3	−8.9	−8.0	....	....	....	....	....	....	....	....	....
Senegal	722	−8.1	−5.6	−5.5	−4.3	−4.3	−5.4	−6.8	−7.6	−5.3	−6.4	....	....
Togo	742	−6.6	−5.7	−7.9	−9.4	−6.9	−8.8	−8.1	−10.5	−13.0	−9.7	−9.0	....

Asia*

Country	Code	1993	1994	1995	1996	1997	1998	1999	2000	2001	2002	2003	2004
Afghanistan, I.S. of	512	....	....	....	....	....	....	....	....	....	....	....	....
Bangladesh	513	1.1	.6	−2.2	−2.5	−.7	−.1	−.8	−.7	−1.2	1.6	.3	....
Bhutan	514	....	....	....	....	....	....	....	....	....	....	....	....
Brunei Darussalam	516	....	....	....	....	....	....	....	....	....	....	....	....
Cambodia	522	−4.2	−5.7	−5.5	−5.4	−6.2	−6.6	−7.0	−5.7	−3.7	−3.0	−3.7	....
China,P.R.: Mainland	924	−1.9	1.3	.2	.9	4.1	3.3	2.1	1.9	1.5	2.7	3.1	....
China,P.R.:Hong Kong	532	....	....	....	....	....	1.5	6.4	4.2	6.0	7.8	10.6	10.0
China,P.R.: Macao	546	....	....	....	....	....	....	....	....	....	40.1	40.1	....
Fiji	819	−8.4	−6.2	−5.7	.6	−1.6	−3.6	.7	....	....	....	....	....
India	534	−.7	−.5	−1.5	−1.5	−.7	−1.6	−.7	−1.0	.3	1.4	1.1	....
Indonesia	536	−1.3	−1.6	−3.2	−3.4	−2.3	4.3	4.1	4.8	4.2	3.9	3.0	....
Kiribati	826	....	....	....	....	....	....	....	....	....	....	....	....
Korea	542	.2	−1.0	−1.7	−4.2	−1.6	11.7	5.5	2.4	1.7	1.0	2.0	4.1
Lao People's Dem.Rep	544	−10.5	−18.4	−19.5	−18.5	−17.5	−11.7	−8.3	−.5	−4.7	....	....	....
Malaysia	548	−4.5	−6.1	−9.7	−4.4	−5.9	13.2	15.9	9.4	8.3	7.6	12.9	....
Maldives	556	−16.7	−3.1	−4.6	−1.7	−6.8	−4.0	−13.4	−8.2	−9.4	−5.6	−4.4	....
Mongolia	948	5.5	6.8	3.2	−8.5	5.2	−13.2	−12.4	−16.5	−15.2	−14.3	....	....
Myanmar	518	−.4	−.2	−.2	−.2	−.2	−.2	−.1	−.1	—	—	—	....
Nepal	558	−6.3	−8.7	−8.4	−7.4	−8.0	−1.5	−5.1	−5.6	−6.2	1.0	1.8	....
Pakistan	564	−6.1	−3.5	−5.7	−7.5	−2.9	−3.8	−1.5	−.1	2.8	5.2	4.3	−.9
Papua New Guinea	853	9.5	7.6	10.7	3.6	−3.9	−.8	2.8	8.9	8.1	....	....	....
Philippines	566	−5.5	−4.6	−2.7	−4.8	−5.3	2.4	9.5	8.2	1.9	5.8	1.8	2.5
Samoa	862	−24.3	3.1	4.9	5.8	3.9	....	....	....	....	....	....	....
Singapore	576	7.2	16.1	17.5	15.1	15.7	22.7	18.6	14.3	18.7	21.4	30.5	....
Solomon Islands	813	−2.7	−1.1	2.3	3.6	−9.3	2.3	5.6	....	....	....	....	....
Sri Lanka	524	−3.7	−6.5	−5.9	−4.9	−2.6	−1.4	−3.6	−6.4	−1.5	−1.6	−.9	....
Thailand	578	−5.1	−5.6	−8.1	−8.1	−2.0	12.7	10.1	7.6	5.4	5.5	5.6	4.3
Tonga	866	−4.1	....	....	....	....	....	....	....	....	....	....	....
Vanuatu	846	−7.6	−9.2	−7.7	−11.0	−7.6	−3.7	−13.2	−5.6	−6.2	−13.3	−14.9	....
Vietnam	582	....	....	....	−8.2	−5.7	−3.9	4.1	3.5	2.1	−1.7	....	....

*of which:

Country	Code	1993	1994	1995	1996	1997	1998	1999	2000	2001	2002	2003	2004
Taiwan Prov.of China	528	....	....	....	....	....	....	....	....	....	....	....	....

Europe

Country	Code	1993	1994	1995	1996	1997	1998	1999	2000	2001	2002	2003	2004
Albania	914	1.2	−8.1	−.5	−3.6	−12.6	−2.4	−4.5	−4.2	−5.3	−9.1	....	....
Armenia	911	−.1	−16.0	−17.0	−18.2	−18.7	−22.1	−16.6	−14.6	−9.5	−6.2	−6.8	−4.7
Azerbaijan, Republic of	912	....	....	....	....	....	....	....	....	....	....	....	....
Belarus	913	....	....	−4.3	−3.6	−6.1	−6.7	−1.6	−3.2	−3.2	−2.1	−2.4	−4.6
Bosnia & Herzegovina	963	....	....	....	....	....	−9.0	−11.2	−9.8	−16.1	−22.4	−24.9	....
Bulgaria	918	−10.1	−.3	−.2	.2	4.1	−.5	−5.0	−5.6	−7.2	−5.3	−8.4	−7.5
Croatia	960	5.3	3.8	−8.5	−5.3	−13.9	−6.8	−7.1	−2.6	−3.7	−8.4	−7.2	−4.9
Cyprus	423	1.7	1.0	−2.2	−5.1	−4.8	3.1	−1.8	−5.3	−3.4	−4.4	−3.4	−5.9
Czech Republic	935	1.3	−2.0	−2.5	−6.7	−6.4	−2.2	−2.5	−4.8	−5.4	−5.8	−6.2	....
Estonia	939	1.3	−6.9	−4.2	−8.6	−11.4	−8.6	−5.3	−5.4	−5.7	−10.2	−12.3	−13.0
Faroe Islands	816	....	....	....	....	....	....	....	....	....	....	....	....
Georgia	915	....	....	....	....	−14.4	−7.6	−7.1	−8.8	−6.6	−6.5	....	....
Hungary	944	−11.0	−9.8	−3.7	−3.9	−4.6	−7.2	−7.9	−8.6	−6.2	−7.2	−8.8	−8.8
Kazakhstan	916	....	....	−1.2	−3.7	−3.8	−5.8	−1.0	2.0	−6.4	−4.2	−.9	1.3
Kyrgyz Republic	917	....	−7.6	−15.7	−23.3	−7.8	−25.1	−20.2	−9.1	−3.6	−4.7	−4.9	....
Latvia	941	19.2	5.5	−.3	−5.0	−5.6	−9.8	−9.1	−4.6	−7.6	−6.8	−8.3	−12.3
Lithuania	946	−3.2	−2.2	−9.6	−9.0	−10.0	−11.7	−11.0	−5.9	−4.7	−5.1	−7.0	−7.1
Macedonia, FYR	962	....	....	....	−6.5	−7.4	−7.5	−.9	−2.0	−7.1	−9.4	−6.0	....
Malta	181	−3.4	−4.8	−11.1	−12.2	−6.1	−6.3	−3.3	−12.4	−4.4	.3	−5.8	−10.3
Moldova	921	....	....	−6.1	−11.5	−14.3	−19.7	−6.7	−8.4	−2.3	....	....	....
Poland	964	−6.7	1.0	.6	−2.3	−4.0	−4.3	−7.7	−6.0	−2.9	−2.6	−2.2	−1.5
Romania	968	−4.7	−1.5	−5.0	−7.3	−6.0	−6.9	−3.6	−3.7	−5.5	−3.3	−5.8	....
Russia	922	....	2.8	2.2	2.8	—	.1	12.6	18.0	11.0	8.4	8.2	10.3
Slovak Republic	936	−4.3	4.3	2.0	−10.0	−9.3	−9.6	−5.7	−3.4	....	−8.1	−.9	....
Slovenia	961	1.5	4.0	−.4	.3	.3	−.6	−3.3	−2.9	.2	1.5	−.4	−.9
Tajikistan	923	....	....	....	....	....	....	....	....	....	....	....	....
Turkey	186	−3.6	2.0	−1.4	−1.3	−1.4	1.0	−.7	−4.9	2.3	−.8	−3.3	−5.1
Turkmenistan	925	....	....	....	....	....	....	....	....	....	....	....	....
Ukraine	926	....	−3.2	−3.1	−2.7	−2.7	−3.1	5.3	4.7	3.7	7.7	5.9	10.5
Uzbekistan	927	....	....	....	....	....	....	....	....	....	....	....	....

Middle East

Country	Code	1993	1994	1995	1996	1997	1998	1999	2000	2001	2002	2003	2004
Bahrain, Kingdom of	419	−6.5	−4.6	4.1	4.3	−.5	−12.6	−.6	10.4	2.9	−.6	2.1	....
Egypt	469	4.9	.1	−.4	−.3	−.9	−3.0	−1.8	−1.0	−.4	.7	5.2	5.0
Iran, I.R. of	429	−5.3	6.6	3.2	3.7	1.3	−1.1	2.6	3.8	....	....	....	....
Iraq	433	....	....	....	....	....	....	....	....	....	....	....	....
Israel	436	−3.7	−4.5	−5.2	−5.2	−3.2	−1.1	−1.6	−1.1	−1.4	−1.2	.7	1.3
Jordan	439	−11.2	−6.4	−3.8	−3.2	.4	.2	5.0	.7	....	5.7	11.8	....
Kuwait	443	10.4	13.0	18.4	22.6	26.1	8.5	16.6	39.6	24.4	12.1	22.6	....
Lebanon	446	....	....	....	....	....	....	....	....	....	....	....	....
Libya	672	−4.5	.1	6.5	4.4	5.0	−1.3	7.0	22.6	12.0	.6	....	....
Oman	449	−9.5	−6.2	−5.8	1.6	−1.0	−22.5	−2.9	16.4	10.1	8.7	6.7	....

Balance of Payments

		1993	1994	1995	1996	1997	1998	1999	2000	2001	2002	2003	2004
					Current Account Balance Excluding Exceptional Financing *As percent of GDP*								
Middle East(Cont.)													
Qatar	453	....	....	....	....	....	....	....	....	....	....	....	....
Saudi Arabia	456	−13.1	−7.8	−3.7	.4	.2	−9.0	.3	7.6	5.1	6.3	13.1	20.5
Syrian Arab Republic	463	−.6	−1.8	.5	.1	.7	.1	.3	1.3	1.4	1.6	....	....
United Arab Emirates	466	....	....	....	....	....	....	....	....	....	....	....	....
West Bank and Gaza	487	....	....	....	....	....	....	....	....	....	....	....	....
Yemen, Republic of	474	−6.4	.7	1.1	.5	−1.0	−7.6	4.8	14.0	7.0	5.2	1.3	....
Western Hemisphere													
Argentina	213	−3.4	−4.3	−2.0	−2.5	−4.2	−4.9	−4.2	−3.2	−1.2	8.5	5.9	2.2
Aruba	314	....	....	—	−5.0	−12.8	−1.1	−19.3	12.5	17.5	−17.1	....	....
Bahamas, The	313	1.7	−1.4	−4.8	....	....	....	....	....	....	....	....	....
Barbados	316	4.2	7.7	2.3	3.5	−2.3	−2.6	−6.0	−5.6	−4.3	−6.5	....	....
Belize	339	−8.7	−6.9	−2.8	−1.0	−4.9	−8.7	−10.6	−16.8	−21.3	−17.6	−18.4	....
Bolivia	218	−8.8	−1.5	−4.5	−5.5	−7.0	−7.8	−5.9	−5.3	−3.4	−4.4	.4	....
Brazil	223	—	−.2	−2.6	−3.0	−3.8	−4.3	−4.7	−4.0	−4.6	−1.7	.8	1.9
Chile	228	−5.4	−2.8	−1.9	−4.1	−4.4	−4.9	.1	−1.2	−1.6	−.9	−1.5	1.5
Colombia	233	−3.5	−4.6	−4.9	−4.8	−5.4	−4.9	.8	.9	−1.3	−1.6	−1.3	−1.1
Costa Rica	238	−6.4	−2.3	−3.1	−2.2	−3.7	−3.7	−4.2	−4.4	−4.3	−5.4	−5.3	....
Dominican Republic	243	−5.5	−2.7	−1.5	−1.6	−1.1	−2.1	−2.5	−5.2	−3.4	−3.7	5.3	....
Ecuador	248	−5.6	−4.8	−5.0	−.3	−1.9	−9.0	5.5	5.8	−3.3	−5.6	−1.7	....
El Salvador	253	−1.8	−.2	−2.8	−1.6	−.9	−.8	−1.9	−3.3	−1.1	−2.8	−5.1	−3.9
Guatemala	258	−6.2	−4.8	−3.9	−2.9	−3.6	−5.4	−5.6	−5.4	−6.0	−5.3	−4.2	−4.4
Guyana	336	−30.1	−22.9	−21.7	−9.8	−15.0	....	....	....	....	....	....	....
Haiti	263	−.8	−1.1	−3.7	−4.6	−1.5	.8	−1.5	−2.3	−2.7	−1.5	−.5	....
Honduras	268	−8.8	−10.0	−5.1	−8.2	−5.8	−7.5	−11.5	−4.4	−5.3	−4.0	−4.5	....
Jamaica	343	−3.8	1.7	−1.7	−2.2	−4.5	−4.3	−2.8	−4.7	−9.4	−12.7	−9.3	....
Mexico	273	−5.8	−7.0	−.6	−.8	−1.9	−3.8	−2.9	−3.2	−2.8	−2.0	−1.0	−1.1
Netherlands Antilles	353	....	....	....	....	....	....	....	....	....	....	....	....
Nicaragua	278	−33.7	−30.6	−22.7	−24.8	−24.8	−19.2	−24.8	−20.1	−19.3	−19.1	−18.1	−17.5
Panama	283	−1.2	.2	−5.4	−2.2	−5.0	−9.3	−10.1	−5.8	−1.4	−.8	−3.4	....
Paraguay	288	.9	−3.5	−1.0	−3.7	−6.8	−1.9	−2.1	−2.1	−3.9	1.7	2.2	....
Peru	293	−7.1	−6.0	−8.6	−6.5	−5.7	−5.9	−2.8	−2.9	−2.1	−1.9	−1.5	—
Suriname	366	.7	12.2	12.8	−8.8	−8.7	−16.4	−3.8	4.2	−12.3	−15.8	−16.1	....
Trinidad and Tobago	369	2.5	4.4	5.5	1.8	−10.7	−10.6	.4	6.7	4.7	.8	....	....
Uruguay	298	−1.6	−2.5	−1.1	−1.1	−1.3	−2.1	−2.4	−2.8	−2.6	2.6	.5	....
Venezuela, Rep. Bol.	299	−3.3	4.3	2.6	12.6	4.3	−4.9	2.2	10.1	1.6	8.2	13.7	12.7
ECCU													
Anguilla	312	−22.6	−18.6	−15.5	−31.1	−26.1	−24.6	−59.2	−63.0	−40.9	−39.9	....	....
Antigua and Barbuda	311	3.3	−1.3	−.1	−11.0	−8.2	−7.5	−8.8	−9.9	....	....	....	....
Dominica	321	−13.7	−17.5	−18.5	−21.7	−17.2	−8.9	−13.4	−19.5	−18.4	−14.9	....	....
Grenada	328	−17.5	−10.3	−14.8	−18.9	−21.6	−23.2	−14.0	−20.5	....	....	....	....
Montserrat	351	−15.2	−22.4	−3.8	37.5	−5.6	10.4	−4.8	−22.2	−18.4	−25.0	....	....
St. Kitts and Nevis	361	−15.4	−11.4	−19.8	−26.6	−22.4	−16.1	−27.1	−20.1	−31.0	−35.4	....	....
St. Lucia	362	−10.1	−9.3	−6.0	−10.2	−13.5	−9.5	−14.5	−11.5	−11.4	−15.4	....	....
St. Vincent & Grens	364	−18.4	−23.8	−15.3	−12.7	−28.7	−29.1	−21.9	−8.8	−11.9	−11.7	....	....

GDP Volume Measures

		1993	1994	1995	1996	1997	1998	1999	2000	2001	2002	2003	2004
		Percent Change over Previous Year; Calculated from Indices											
World	001	2.68	4.66	3.99	4.31	4.18	2.65	3.73	5.14	1.76	1.96	3.20	....
Industrial Countries	110	1.11	3.21	2.44	2.84	3.33	2.81	3.57	3.61	1.24	1.23	1.97	3.29
United States	111	2.67	4.02	2.50	3.70	4.50	4.18	4.45	3.66	.75	1.60	2.70	4.22
Canada	156	2.34	4.80	2.81	1.62	4.22	4.10	5.53	5.26	1.92	3.28	1.71	3.09
Australia	193	3.84	4.83	3.49	4.32	3.86	5.30	4.32	3.17	2.46	3.99	3.37	3.21
Japan	158	.20	1.13	1.88	3.62	1.82	−1.16	.19	2.88	.40	−.49	2.57	3.67
New Zealand	196	6.27	5.14	3.74	3.23	2.74	1.00	5.16	1.84	3.76	4.70	3.58	3.63
Euro Area	163	....	....	....	1.34	2.20	2.74	.45	3.25	3.64	.84	.61	1.75
Austria	122	.33	2.66	1.91	2.62	1.84	3.56	3.32	3.36	.72	1.17	.76	2.18
Belgium	124	−.68	3.31	2.29	.85	3.88	2.08	10.39	3.68	.87	.89	1.27	2.74
Finland	172	−1.15	3.95	3.81	4.01	6.29	5.33	11.96	5.13	1.07	2.20	2.40	3.66
France	132	−.89	1.80	1.88	1.06	1.90	3.48	5.03	4.07	2.05	1.22	.80	2.32
Germany	134	−.80	2.66	1.89	.99	1.80	2.03	2.01	3.21	1.19	.16	—	1.57
Greece	174	−1.60	2.00	2.10	2.36	3.64	3.36	3.60	4.13	4.10	3.88	4.69	4.20
Ireland	178	2.69	5.76	9.73	7.99	10.83	8.61	11.57	9.92	6.01	6.13	3.66	4.87
Italy	136	−.88	2.21	2.92	1.09	2.03	1.81	1.65	3.03	1.76	.38	.25	1.22
Luxembourg	137	....	....	....	3.62	9.09	5.94	5.73	9.49	1.60	....	....	....
Netherlands	138	.64	6.70	3.03	3.05	3.83	3.09	5.27	3.47	1.43	.57	−.88	1.44
Portugal	182	−1.37	2.47	2.92	3.19	3.47	3.49	8.45	3.69	1.64	.43	−1.40	1.01
Spain	184	−1.03	2.38	2.76	2.44	4.03	3.67	4.91	4.40	3.54	2.68	2.91	3.09
Denmark	128	—	5.47	2.75	2.52	2.97	2.47	2.64	2.83	1.31	.50	.70	2.39
Iceland	176	.79	4.03	.08	5.22	4.67	.68	4.41	5.68	2.60	−2.10	4.23	5.19
Norway	142	2.73	5.26	4.36	5.25	5.19	2.63	2.13	2.84	2.73	1.11	.37	2.91
Sweden	144	−2.00	4.16	4.05	1.29	2.44	3.65	4.58	4.33	1.05	1.98	1.47	3.60
Switzerland	146	−.23	1.07	.38	.52	1.91	2.79	1.31	3.61	1.04	.33	−.35	1.68
United Kingdom	112	2.33	4.43	2.85	2.82	3.28	3.09	2.86	3.86	2.30	1.77	2.20	3.08
Developing Countries	200	5.37	6.76	6.24	6.42	5.41	2.42	3.95	7.19	2.45	2.94	4.84	....
Africa	605	−.25	2.84	2.31	5.32	2.60	2.82	1.95	3.02	4.12	3.15	4.05	4.04
Benin	638	3.52	4.37	4.60	5.55	10.14	3.96	5.33	4.87	6.24	4.43	3.88	2.66
Botswana	616	−.21	4.05	3.23	5.54	5.61	8.06	4.13	6.60	8.51	2.08	7.78	5.73
Burkina Faso	748	−1.53	2.09	6.48	9.87	6.83	8.48	3.75	1.59	6.78	4.56	7.97	4.57
Burundi	618	−7.03	−3.08	−7.02	−8.61	.38	4.49	−1.00	−.90	2.10	4.50	−1.20	4.40
Cameroon	622	−3.18	−2.64	3.30	5.00	5.00	....	....	....	....	....	....	....
Congo, Dem. Rep. of	636	−13.53	−3.87	.72	−1.10	−5.43	−1.76	−4.23	−6.97	.94	....	....	....
Congo, Rep. of	634	−.98	−5.47	2.19	4.29	−.47	3.75	−3.22	8.00	....	....	....	....
Côte d'Ivoire	662	−.38	2.05	7.08	6.89	6.62	5.99	....	....	....	....	....	....
Gambia, The	648	6.57	3.65	−4.10	....	....	....	....	....	....	....	....	....
Ghana	652	4.93	3.27	4.02	4.60	4.18	....	....	....	....	....	....	....
Guinea-Bissau	654	2.49	4.97	3.67	4.85	4.80	....	....	....	....	....	....	....
Kenya	664	.35	2.63	4.41	4.15	3.00	.28	−3.60	7.06	4.38	.40	2.77	4.34
Lesotho	666	3.48	3.40	4.39	9.96	8.15	−4.64	.24	1.32	3.21	3.80	....	....
Madagascar	674	2.10	−.07	1.71	2.14	3.69	3.94	4.68	4.74	6.01	−12.67	9.78	5.28
Malawi	676	10.80	−11.61	15.01	8.15	6.35	2.35	1.25	1.58	−4.80	2.67	6.07	....
Mali	678	−3.18	2.65	6.63	3.59	....	....	....	....	....	....	....	....
Mauritius	684	5.03	4.24	4.42	5.56	5.76	6.02	2.90	9.16	5.28	−.80	3.85	4.75
Morocco	686	−1.73	10.64	−6.56	11.80	−2.23	7.67	−.08	.96	6.29	3.19	5.24	3.42
Mozambique	688	6.79	6.98	3.31	6.76	11.07	12.63	7.54	1.94	13.10	8.71	7.94	....
Namibia	728	−2.01	7.32	4.11	3.19	4.23	3.29	3.42	3.27	....	....	....	....
Niger	692	1.02	2.51	1.92	3.92	2.37	16.38	.99	−2.58	6.35	5.85	3.04	....
Nigeria	694	2.63	1.25	2.17	3.86	3.23	2.31	2.82	3.71	4.22	4.09	3.78	....
Rwanda	714	−8.39	−49.66	34.20	14.88	14.34	9.20	6.47	6.66	5.86	9.55	2.39	2.49
Senegal	722	−2.22	2.87	5.17	5.15	3.28	4.44	2.41	6.77	4.73	....	....	....
Seychelles	718	6.18	−.81	−.83	4.92	4.95	5.50	2.90	1.40	.95	....	....	....
Sierra Leone	724	1.38	−1.95	−8.00	6.09	−17.60	−.84	−8.12	3.81	18.17	27.46	9.29	7.36
South Africa	199	1.23	3.23	3.12	4.31	2.65	.52	2.36	4.15	2.74	3.56	2.81	3.71
Swaziland	734	3.26	3.36	3.79	3.89	3.83	3.26	3.53	2.03	1.77	....	....	....
Togo	742	−16.55	16.76	6.94	9.71	4.28	−2.19	2.96	−.89	.63	2.88	....	....
Tunisia	744	2.19	3.18	2.35	7.15	5.44	4.78	6.05	4.72	4.89	1.66	5.56	6.05
Uganda	746	6.78	10.61	9.33	6.18	5.40	9.72	6.53	4.37	6.45	4.73	6.26	....
Zambia	754	6.80	−3.51	−2.27	6.50	3.50	....	....	....	....	....	....	....
Zimbabwe	698	2.11	5.80	.18	9.72	1.40	.78	−4.10	−6.77	....	....	....	....
Asia	505	8.69	9.63	8.83	8.19	6.21	2.26	6.20	9.28	....	....	....	....
Bangladesh	513	4.57	4.08	4.92	4.62	5.39	5.23	4.87	5.95	5.27	4.42	5.33	....
China, P.R.: Mainland	924	13.49	12.66	10.51	9.59	8.80	7.80	7.11	8.00	....	....	....	....
China, P.R.: Hong Kong	532	6.35	5.48	3.89	4.31	5.07	−4.97	3.42	10.16	.46	1.94	3.15	8.15
India	534	5.90	7.25	7.34	7.84	4.80	6.51	6.06	4.37	5.78	3.98	8.22	....
Indonesia	536	6.50	7.54	8.22	7.82	7.00	−13.13	.79	50.12	3.83	4.38	4.88	5.13
Korea	542	5.49	8.54	9.17	7.00	4.65	−6.85	9.49	8.49	3.84	6.97	3.10	4.64
Lao People's Democratic Rep	544	4.57	9.51	7.05	6.89	6.91	3.99	7.28	5.78	5.77	5.87	5.86	5.01
Malaysia	548	9.89	9.21	9.83	10.00	7.32	−7.36	6.14	8.86	.32	4.15	5.31	7.06
Maldives	556	5.42	7.51	7.81	9.09	10.16	8.18	7.41	4.59	2.08	....	....	....
Mongolia	948	−3.00	2.30	36.29	2.35	4.00	3.53	3.22	1.13	.95	3.95	5.00	....
Myanmar	518	6.04	7.48	6.95	6.44	5.74	5.77	10.92	6.23	11.34	12.03	13.84	....
Nepal	558	2.95	8.27	2.73	5.69	5.01	3.34	4.54	6.09	4.74	−.32	2.74	3.48
Pakistan	564	1.91	3.90	5.14	4.99	−.10	2.55	3.66	4.26	1.86	3.22	5.15	6.01
Papua New Guinea	853	18.21	5.95	−3.31	7.72	−3.90	4.38	−.84	−1.24	−3.37	−.56	....	....
Philippines	566	2.12	4.39	4.68	5.85	5.19	−.58	3.40	4.01	3.40	5.54	4.92	5.00
Samoa	862	2.41	−3.72	6.80	6.13	1.60	....	....	....	....	....	....	....
Singapore	576	12.26	11.40	8.04	8.17	8.56	−.76	6.83	9.64	−1.95	3.17	1.36	8.41
Sri Lanka	524	6.95	5.63	5.45	3.76	6.30	4.74	4.33	6.02	−1.54	3.96	6.02	5.36

GDP Volume Measures

		1993	1994	1995	1996	1997	1998	1999	2000	2001	2002	2003	2004
				Percent Change over Previous Year; Calculated from Indices									
Asia(Cont.)													
Thailand	578	8.25	8.99	9.24	5.90	−1.37	−10.51	4.45	4.75	2.17	5.33	6.87	6.05
Tonga	866	−.07	4.79	....	....	....	....	....	....	....	....	....	....
Vanuatu	846	4.49	2.54	3.17	8.74	4.91	4.31	−3.18	2.67	−2.06	−5.54	2.43	....
Europe	170	1.68	.10	7.03	4.53	3.89	2.58	.38	4.91	−.05	4.37	4.64	6.89
Armenia	911	....	....	6.89	5.87	3.32	7.34	3.25	....	....	....	....	....
Belarus	913	−7.64	−11.70	−10.45	2.78	11.43	8.41	3.35	5.80	4.73	5.05	7.04	11.04
Bulgaria	918	−1.50	1.80	2.90	−10.10	−6.90	....	....	....	....	....	....	....
Croatia	960	−.90	.64	1.69	4.26	6.76	2.52	−.86	2.86	3.77	5.23	4.26	4.47
Kazakhstan	916	....	....	−8.17	.50	1.69	−1.86	2.69	9.81	13.53	9.81	9.22	....
Cyprus	423	.70	5.90	9.92	1.80	2.30	4.97	4.81	5.04	4.11	2.11	1.91	3.73
Czech Republic	935	.06	2.22	12.51	4.16	−.73	−1.15	1.21	3.89	2.64	1.49	3.21	4.44
Estonia	939	....	−1.64	4.53	4.40	11.10	4.44	.31	7.85	6.46	7.24	6.69	7.81
Hungary	944	−.58	2.95	1.49	1.32	4.57	4.86	4.15	5.20	3.85	3.49	2.94	4.23
Kyrgyz Republic	917	−15.50	−20.10	−5.40	7.08	9.92	2.12	3.58	5.54	5.32	—	6.99	7.07
Latvia	941	−9.92	2.36	−26.30	3.79	8.28	4.72	3.29	6.89	8.01	6.45	−.71	17.46
Lithuania	946	−16.23	−9.77	3.29	4.68	7.01	7.28	−1.70	3.92	6.38	6.76	9.69	6.69
Malta	181	4.20	3.00	9.33	3.99	4.85	3.43	4.06	6.30	−.42	1.03	−1.89	1.02
Poland	964	3.80	5.20	14.48	6.00	6.80	4.80	4.10	3.95	1.02	1.37	3.85	5.34
Romania	968	1.52	3.93	7.14	3.95	−6.05	−4.82	−1.15	2.15	5.75	5.12	5.16	8.29
San Marino	135	....	....	....	....	....	7.52	9.00	2.20	7.67	−1.67	....	....
Slovak Republic	936	7.18	6.21	5.84	6.15	4.61	4.21	1.47	2.04	3.79	4.62	4.46	5.50
Slovenia	961	2.84	5.33	4.11	3.64	4.76	3.56	5.55	3.89	2.68	3.33	2.52	4.57
Turkey	186	8.04	−5.46	7.19	7.00	7.53	3.09	−4.71	7.15	−7.32	7.79	5.95	8.93
Middle East	405	1.50	2.99	3.48	5.17	4.34	4.07	1.95	5.09	2.62	3.58	5.47	....
Bahrain	419	12.88	−.25	3.93	4.10	3.11	4.78	4.32	5.28	4.64	5.18	6.78	....
Egypt	469	2.90	3.97	4.64	4.99	5.49	7.54	6.11	5.38	3.52	3.19	3.11	4.17
Iran, I.R. of	429	−2.09	1.72	3.29	6.69	5.37	2.74	1.93	5.14	3.67	7.45	6.73	....
Israel	436	3.20	6.76	7.05	5.22	3.49	3.74	2.47	8.02	−.90	−.73	1.29	4.31
Jordan	439	4.48	4.99	6.18	2.07	3.32	3.01	3.06	4.10	4.90	4.82	3.25	....
Kuwait	443	33.75	8.63	1.38	.60	2.49	3.65	−1.79	1.92	.71	−.52	9.71	....
Oman	449	6.14	3.85	4.83	2.89	6.18	2.70	−.23	5.49	9.31	.02	2.47	....
Saudi Arabia	456	.03	.67	.20	3.38	2.59	2.83	−.75	4.86	.55	.13	7.66	5.23
Syrian Arab Rep	463	5.18	7.65	5.75	7.34	2.49	7.60	−2.00	.63	3.37	3.23	....	....
Yemen Republic	474	7.94	3.00	12.19	8.03	6.26	6.83	2.43	4.65	4.66	3.90	4.01	....
Western Hemisphere	205	3.94	4.96	1.66	3.61	5.19	2.16	.27	3.99	.64	−.42	2.95	4.11
ECCU	309	2.55	3.00	.65	2.67	3.24	3.99	4.09	2.82	−1.30	.19	....	....
Antigua and Barbuda	311	5.39	6.33	−4.18	6.60	5.23	3.27	3.66	....	....	....	....	....
Anguilla	312	7.47	7.13	−4.15	3.48	9.20	5.17	8.65	−.32	2.13	−3.24	....	....
Argentina	213	5.72	5.84	−2.85	5.53	8.11	3.85	−3.39	−.79	−4.41	−10.89	8.84	8.98
Bahamas, The	313	−2.06	1.95	1.08	....	....	....	....	....	....	....	....	....
Barbados	316	.82	4.47	2.51	3.14	3.30	4.37	3.61	2.40	−3.43	−.45	2.21	....
Belize	339	6.22	.19	.66	1.42	3.59	3.70	8.74	13.00	4.61	4.72	9.17	4.61
Bolivia	218	4.27	4.67	4.68	4.36	4.96	5.03	.42	2.51	1.69	2.43	2.78	3.58
Brazil	223	4.92	5.85	4.22	2.66	3.27	.13	.81	4.36	1.31	1.93	1.93	1.93
Chile	228	7.00	5.71	10.63	7.40	6.61	3.23	−.76	4.49	3.82	1.75	3.73	6.06
Colombia	233	5.71	5.15	5.20	2.06	3.43	.57	−4.20	2.92	1.47	1.93	4.12	4.10
Costa Rica	238	7.41	4.73	3.92	.89	5.58	8.40	8.22	1.80	1.08	2.92	6.53	....
Dominica	321	−.26	1.43	1.97	3.51	2.51	3.15	.64	.64	−3.75	−4.06	1.96	....
Dominican Republic	243	2.96	4.32	4.67	7.17	8.15	7.43	8.15	8.13	3.63	4.43	−1.87	1.95
Ecuador	248	2.03	4.70	1.75	2.40	4.05	2.12	−6.30	2.80	5.12	3.41	2.66	6.95
El Salvador	253	1.52	7.03	6.46	1.71	4.25	3.75	3.45	2.15	1.65	2.23	1.81	1.54
Guatemala	258	3.91	4.04	4.95	2.94	4.37	5.01	3.84	3.61	2.33	2.25	2.11	2.66
Guyana	336	8.23	....	....	....	....	....	....	....	....	....	....	....
Haiti	263	−2.44	−8.29	4.43	2.70	2.71	2.18	2.71	.87	−1.04	−.55	.48	−3.77
Honduras	268	6.23	−1.30	4.08	3.58	4.99	2.90	−1.89	5.75	2.61	2.72	3.48	....
Jamaica	343	2.46	.98	2.45	.25	−1.08	−1.14	.87	.76	1.47	1.09	2.26	....
Mexico	273	1.95	4.42	−6.17	5.15	6.77	5.03	3.76	6.59	−.03	.77	1.44	4.24
Montserrat	351	2.51	.89	−7.61	−21.43	−19.98	−10.10	−12.57	−3.00	−2.84	4.61	....	....
Nicaragua	278	−.39	3.34	5.91	6.34	3.97	3.71	7.04	4.10	2.96	.75	2.26	5.15
Panama	283	5.46	2.85	1.75	7.37	6.46	7.34	3.92	2.72	.57	2.23	4.32	6.24
Paraguay	288	4.15	3.09	4.71	1.27	2.59	−.41	.48	−.35	2.72	−2.32	2.55	....
Peru	293	4.76	12.82	8.58	2.49	6.84	−.68	.89	2.92	.18	4.85	3.76	5.06
St. Kitts and Nevis	361	6.66	5.10	3.14	6.68	7.41	.95	3.64	4.32	1.99	.95	2.20	....
St. Lucia	362	2.58	1.32	1.66	2.87	−.42	6.17	2.28	−.76	−5.59	1.89	4.32	....
St. Vincent & Grenadines	364	2.37	−2.00	7.57	1.45	3.66	5.12	4.16	1.85	1.06	2.72	4.01	....
Suriname	366	—	—	106.67	3.23	—	3.13	—	....	9.09	2.78	2.70	....
Trinidad and Tobago	369	−1.45	3.56	3.96	5.15	6.87	7.68	10.64	11.28	2.60	....	....	....
Uruguay	298	2.66	7.28	−1.45	5.58	5.05	4.54	−2.85	−1.44	−3.38	−11.03	2.18	12.27
Venezuela, Rep. Bol.	299	.27	−2.35	3.95	−.20	6.37	.17	−6.09	3.24	2.79	−8.88	....	....
Memorandum Items													
Oil Exporting Countries	999	2.69	3.57	4.90	5.44	4.65	−4.54	.09	20.49	3.27	2.68	5.77	....
Non-Oil Developing Countries	201	5.71	7.17	6.41	6.54	5.50	3.34	4.38	5.84	2.32	2.98	4.71	....

GDP Volume Measures

Indices

		1993	1994	1995	1996	1997	1998	1999	2000	2001	2002	2003	2004
							Index Numbers: 2000=100						
World	001	75.5	79.0	82.2	85.7	89.3	91.7	95.1	100.0	101.8	103.8	107.1	....
Industrial Countries	110	80.7	83.3	85.3	87.7	90.6	93.2	96.5	100.0	101.2	102.5	104.5	107.9
Developing Countries	200	68.9	73.5	78.1	83.1	87.6	89.7	93.3	100.0	102.4	105.5	110.6	....
Africa	605	81.5	83.8	85.7	90.3	92.6	95.2	97.1	100.0	104.1	107.4	111.8	116.3
Asia	505	61.5	67.4	73.3	79.3	84.3	86.2	91.5	100.0	....	....	....	....
Europe	170	79.6	79.6	85.2	89.1	92.6	95.0	95.3	100.0	99.9	104.3	109.2	116.7
Middle East	405	76.7	79.0	81.7	86.0	89.7	93.3	95.2	100.0	102.6	106.3	112.1	....
Western Hemisphere	205	80.7	84.7	86.1	89.2	93.9	95.9	96.2	100.0	100.6	100.2	103.2	107.4

2005, International Monetary Fund : *International Financial Statistics Yearbook*

GDP Deflators

		1993	1994	1995	1996	1997	1998	1999	2000	2001	2002	2003	2004
		Percent Change over Previous Year; Calculated from Indices											
World	001	**19.9**	**18.8**	**9.7**	**6.6**	**5.1**	**4.4**	**3.0**	**3.6**	**4.2**	**4.5**	**3.8**	....
Industrial Countries	110	**2.4**	**1.9**	**2.0**	**1.7**	**1.5**	**1.1**	**.7**	**1.6**	**1.8**	**1.6**	**1.5**	**1.7**
United States	111	2.3	2.1	2.0	1.9	1.7	1.1	1.4	2.2	2.4	1.7	2.0	2.6
Canada	156	1.4	1.1	2.3	1.6	1.2	–.4	1.7	4.0	1.0	1.0	3.4	3.0
Australia	193	1.2	.8	1.8	2.2	1.6	.5	.6	4.0	4.0	1.9	3.4	3.6
Japan	158	.6	.1	–.5	–1.0	.3	—	–1.6	–2.0	–1.5	–1.1	–2.6	–2.1
New Zealand	196	1.8	1.7	2.6	1.6	.8	.7	.8	3.8	3.8	–.3	2.7	3.7
Euro Area	163	....	....	....	3.1	–.1	3.1	4.0	1.5	2.8	2.5	1.9	2.2
Austria	122	2.7	2.7	1.9	1.0	—	.3	.6	1.8	1.7	1.3	1.5	1.9
Belgium	124	3.7	2.0	1.3	1.5	1.0	1.6	–5.2	1.5	1.6	1.8	1.9	2.5
Finland	172	2.3	2.0	4.1	–.2	2.1	3.0	–7.6	3.2	3.0	1.0	.2	.7
France	132	1.7	1.8	1.5	1.7	1.4	.9	–1.8	1.4	1.8	2.2	1.6	1.6
Germany	134	3.7	2.4	1.9	.5	.3	.6	.4	–.7	1.3	1.5	.7	.4
Greece	174	14.4	11.2	9.8	7.4	6.8	5.2	2.8	3.7	3.7	3.9	3.5	3.4
Ireland	178	5.2	1.7	3.0	2.0	4.3	5.7	4.2	4.8	5.7	4.5	1.6	3.5
Italy	136	3.9	3.5	5.0	5.3	2.4	2.7	1.6	2.2	2.6	3.1	2.9	2.6
Netherlands	138	2.1	–1.0	1.1	1.2	1.9	2.5	.9	3.9	5.2	3.1	3.0	1.2
Portugal	182	7.0	6.1	5.0	3.1	2.8	3.1	3.8	3.2	4.8	4.6	2.3	2.5
Spain	184	4.5	3.9	4.9	3.5	2.3	3.1	2.1	6.8	4.2	4.4	4.0	4.1
Denmark	128	1.4	1.7	1.8	2.5	2.2	1.0	1.8	3.0	2.1	1.6	2.2	1.6
Iceland	176	2.3	2.1	2.9	2.0	.5	10.4	2.7	2.8	9.2	5.7	–.2	2.4
Norway	142	2.3	–.1	2.9	4.1	2.9	–.7	6.6	15.9	1.1	–1.6	2.4	4.9
Sweden	144	3.0	2.3	3.4	1.2	1.6	.8	.7	1.3	2.3	1.7	2.1	.8
Switzerland	146	2.4	1.5	.8	–.1	–.1	–.3	.7	.8	.6	1.7	.9	.9
United Kingdom	112	2.7	1.5	2.6	3.4	2.8	3.0	2.3	1.4	2.2	3.4	3.2	2.1
Developing Countries	200	**56.1**	**47.8**	**21.7**	**13.9**	**10.6**	**9.2**	**6.2**	**6.2**	**7.6**	**8.4**	**6.9**	....
Africa	605	**15.7**	**16.2**	**31.9**	**23.5**	**12.9**	**6.8**	**14.8**	**18.9**	**11.1**	**5.8**	**8.3**	....
Benin	638	1.2	33.5	15.4	6.7	6.4	5.2	.4	4.5	2.7	2.3	1.7	1.9
Botswana	616	9.1	106.2	8.0	7.8	19.4	12.2	5.0	–43.5	85.7	–37.8	78.3	–38.5
Burkina Faso	748	1.7	25.7	5.8	1.0	.7	6.0	–3.1	–1.7	5.8	4.0	1.1	3.1
Burundi	618	12.7	17.7	–.5	15.2	29.8	11.7	15.0	13.2	5.4	1.7	11.6	11.2
Cameroon	622	1.7	24.4	11.6	5.5	3.7	....	....	....	....	....	....	....
Congo, Dem. Rep. of	636	....	....	467.9	638.7	184.9	30.3	441.7	516.2	369.4	....	....	....
Côte d'Ivoire	662	....	....	....	....	....	....	....	....	....	....	....	....
Ethiopia	644	13.2	2.6	12.7	.9	3.7	10.2	3.3	2.9	–6.3	–7.0	14.5	....
Gambia, The	648	–19.8	10.6	....	....	....	....	....	....	....	....	....	....
Ghana	652	31.7	30.2	43.2	39.8	19.5	....	....	....	....	....	....	....
Guinea-Bissau	654	9.4	82.7	–4.8	4.4	14.5	....	....	....	....	....	....	....
Kenya	664	25.7	17.0	11.3	9.0	14.4	11.1	11.1	21.6	1.6	.9	7.0	6.9
Lesotho	666	9.9	7.6	9.3	9.0	7.7	9.3	12.8	5.8	7.4	13.3	....	....
Madagascar	674	13.0	41.6	45.1	17.8	7.3	8.5	9.8	7.1	7.3	15.3	2.8	14.3
Malawi	676	24.8	32.2	77.2	51.2	17.9	23.3	39.9	30.5	25.4	16.6	9.2	....
Mali	678	2.0	33.9	30.1	1.7	....	....	....	....	....	....	....	....
Mauritius	684	9.2	6.6	5.1	6.6	5.3	6.6	4.9	1.9	5.1	8.9	5.8	6.2
Morocco	686	4.2	1.1	8.1	1.1	1.9	.4	.5	1.5	1.8	.6	—	....
Mozambique	688	48.5	55.4	50.3	48.2	9.6	4.6	2.9	10.3	16.0	15.8	13.2	....
Namibia	728	13.6	15.7	5.7	14.5	7.1	8.6	6.5	8.9	....	....	....	....
Niger	692	3.2	18.6	18.1	4.9	2.4	–2.8	.4	–2.8	3.5	3.5	–4.1	....
Nigeria	694	24.3	28.8	111.6	37.5	.8	–4.2	12.1	44.6	–6.3	10.6	23.7	....
Rwanda	714	14.4	16.8	51.2	10.2	15.6	2.0	–5.2	5.0	2.1	–.1	10.7	....
Senegal	722	–1.4	19.1	13.3	.5	3.4	3.7	4.0	.8	3.6	....	....	....
Seychelles	718	3.1	2.0	–.8	–1.5	8.2	7.2	.9	4.8	1.5	....	....	....
Sierra Leone	724	26.7	25.1	33.6	24.3	16.8	27.0	25.0	6.1	1.8	–3.7	8.2	16.0
South Africa	199	13.1	9.6	10.3	8.1	8.1	7.7	7.1	8.8	7.7	10.3	4.5	5.9
Swaziland	734	16.1	17.2	17.2	16.0	12.0	9.1	9.0	12.4	11.8	....	....	....
Tanzania	738	25.5	31.4	26.9	19.7	20.8	13.9	10.2	7.7	7.7	6.6	8.1	....
Togo	742	–4.8	32.6	31.7	–.2	12.4	–2.9	.7	–1.6	.4	2.4	....	....
Tunisia	744	4.7	4.5	5.4	4.4	4.0	3.0	3.1	3.1	2.9	2.4	1.9	2.9
Uganda	746	1.5	18.0	5.9	3.0	5.8	.3	4.5	3.2	1.2	1.7	10.0	....
Zambia	754	143.6	56.7	36.9	24.3	25.5	....	....	....	....	....	....	....
Zimbabwe	698	21.0	24.9	10.2	28.0	22.7	34.4	57.5	51.0	....	....	....	....
Asia	505	**12.3**	**13.4**	**10.6**	**6.7**	**4.4**	**7.6**	**.9**	**.6**	....	....	....	....
Bangladesh	513	.3	3.8	7.3	4.2	3.1	5.3	4.7	1.9	1.6	3.2	4.4	....
Bhutan	514	6.8	10.7	9.4	12.2	12.0	7.6	9.2	7.9	....	....	....	....
China, P.R.: Mainland	924	17.5	20.1	13.4	6.6	.7	–2.1	–2.3	.1	....	....	....	....
China, P.R.: Hong Kong	532	8.5	7.0	2.5	5.9	5.7	.2	–5.9	–6.2	–1.9	–3.6	–6.2	–2.8
Fiji	819	5.2	.6	2.2	3.1	3.4	5.7	2.0	1.1	4.3	.8	3.3	....
India	534	9.6	9.4	9.0	7.4	6.7	7.9	3.9	3.5	3.4	4.2	3.3	....
Indonesia	536	9.7	7.8	9.9	8.7	12.6	75.3	14.2	–15.8	16.7	6.0	4.7	7.1
Korea	542	12.1	7.8	7.4	5.1	4.6	5.8	–.1	.7	3.5	2.8	2.7	2.7
Lao People's Democratic Rep	544	7.7	6.4	20.6	12.9	19.3	85.2	127.1	25.1	8.6	10.6	4.3	15.5
Malaysia	548	4.0	3.9	3.6	3.7	3.5	8.5	—	4.8	–2.9	3.8	3.5	6.0
Maldives	556	11.3	8.6	5.6	3.5	2.4	–1.8	1.6	1.3	2.0	....	....	....
Mongolia	948	262.3	66.6	42.5	14.8	23.8	–5.2	9.7	8.9	8.5	5.7	5.9	....
Myanmar	518	36.2	22.1	19.6	23.0	33.7	35.9	22.7	9.7	24.8	41.5	20.5	....
Nepal	558	11.4	7.4	7.1	7.5	7.3	3.8	8.8	4.6	3.4	3.1	4.9	5.1
Pakistan	564	8.5	12.7	13.7	8.2	14.6	7.5	5.9	23.8	7.7	2.4	4.2	6.8
Papua New Guinea	853	–2.5	4.4	13.2	8.5	6.8	5.6	13.7	24.0	13.2	14.4	....	....
Philippines	566	6.8	10.0	7.6	7.7	6.2	10.5	8.0	8.3	4.7	1.3	3.3	7.2
Samoa	862	4.3	19.1	–5.2	3.9	11.8	....	....	....	....	....	....	....
Singapore	576	3.4	2.7	2.1	1.0	.4	–2.3	–4.6	4.1	–1.7	–.2	.2	3.5

GDP Deflators

114

		1993	1994	1995	1996	1997	1998	1999	2000	2001	2002	2003	2004
						Percent Change over Previous Year; Calculated from Indices							
Asia(Cont.)													
Sri Lanka	524	9.5	9.3	8.4	12.1	8.6	8.4	4.4	6.7	12.4	8.4	5.0	9.2
Thailand	578	3.3	5.2	5.6	4.0	4.1	9.2	−4.0	1.3	2.1	.7	1.9	4.6
Vanuatu	846	5.6	2.4	3.4	−5.4	3.2	4.8	3.2	1.2	3.4	1.6	.7	....
Europe	170	**98.7**	**61.3**	**52.0**	**37.9**	**54.7**	**34.3**	**30.7**	**26.8**	**23.6**	**17.7**	**10.9**	**7.0**
Armenia	911	....	....	161.2	19.6	17.7	10.7	.1	....	....	....	....	....
Belarus	913	1,054.0	1,945.1	661.9	53.7	71.6	76.6	317.0	185.3	79.5	44.9	30.7	21.8
Bulgaria	918	51.1	72.7	62.8	122.5	963.2	....	....	....	....	....	....	....
Croatia	960	1,506.5	107.7	10.6	5.3	7.4	8.4	3.8	4.7	4.7	2.9	3.2	2.7
Cyprus	423	5.1	5.3	3.0	1.8	2.8	2.4	2.3	3.7	3.2	2.2	4.8	2.2
Czech Republic	935	21.0	13.4	10.2	8.7	8.3	11.2	2.8	1.4	4.9	2.8	2.6	3.0
Estonia	939	....	39.7	31.4	24.3	10.4	8.9	4.5	5.4	5.6	4.4	2.1	3.1
Hungary	944	21.3	19.5	26.7	21.2	18.5	12.6	8.4	9.9	8.6	8.9	6.8	6.0
Kazakhstan	916	....	....	152.1	28.4	16.6	4.9	23.7	13.2	6.8	6.7	10.9	....
Kyrgyz Republic	917	754.9	180.9	42.0	35.3	19.3	9.1	37.7	27.0	7.3	2.0	4.0	4.8
Latvia	941	62.1	36.0	71.4	14.9	7.0	4.6	4.8	3.8	2.1	3.4	11.9	−.9
Lithuania	946	306.2	61.6	46.4	20.6	14.0	5.0	−.6	1.0	−.1	—	−.8	3.3
Malta	181	3.1	6.2	1.9	.8	2.3	2.2	2.7	7.6	1.8	2.0	5.0	2.0
Poland	964	30.6	37.4	27.9	18.6	13.9	11.6	6.4	6.7	4.0	1.3	.5	2.9
Romania	968	227.3	139.0	35.3	45.3	147.2	55.3	47.7	44.2	37.4	23.4	19.5	15.9
San Marino	135	....	....	....	....	....	1.8	1.6	2.6	2.8	2.3	....	....
Slovak Republic	936	15.5	13.4	9.9	4.3	6.7	5.2	6.5	8.5	4.2	4.0	4.7	4.6
Slovenia	961	37.1	22.6	23.0	10.9	8.8	7.6	5.9	5.6	9.1	8.0	5.5	3.0
Turkey	186	67.8	106.5	87.2	77.8	81.5	75.7	55.6	50.2	54.5	44.3	22.3	8.8
Middle East	405	**18.8**	**13.4**	**18.2**	**14.4**	**6.9**	**.2**	**15.0**	**14.7**	**3.6**	**11.5**	**7.8**	**....**
Bahrain	419	−3.0	7.3	1.1	.2	.9	−7.1	2.6	14.4	−4.9	1.3	6.5	....
Egypt	469	9.9	7.0	11.4	7.1	6.3	3.9	.9	4.9	1.9	2.4	6.9	11.5
Iran, I.R. of	429	53.8	28.3	37.9	25.2	11.8	9.5	30.1	26.4	11.6	28.3	12.1	....
Israel	436	12.1	13.8	8.9	11.2	9.2	6.5	6.5	1.4	2.4	4.1	.4	.6
Jordan	439	3.0	6.9	1.9	2.1	1.2	6.0	−.2	−.2	.9	.8	2.0	....
Kuwait	443	−7.2	−6.0	8.5	15.5	−4.7	−17.1	18.1	21.5	−8.7	2.9	6.1	....
Oman	449	−5.5	−.4	1.9	7.6	−2.4	−13.4	11.8	19.9	−8.2	1.8	4.3	....
Saudi Arabia	456	−3.1	1.0	5.8	7.1	2.0	−14.0	11.2	11.6	−3.4	2.9	5.7	11.0
Syrian Arab Rep.	463	5.9	13.6	6.7	12.7	5.3	−1.5	5.7	9.7	2.1	1.5	....	....
Yemen Republic	474	15.1	26.1	48.3	31.4	12.8	−10.1	35.6	25.4	.3	7.4	11.0	....
Western Hemisphere	205	**210.1**	**219.3**	**38.7**	**20.7**	**11.2**	**7.9**	**7.8**	**9.0**	**5.8**	**11.4**	**10.3**	**9.1**
ECCU	309	1.3	3.6	2.8	2.0	2.3	2.5	1.8	1.3	1.8	1.0	....	....
Antigua and Barbuda	311	2.2	3.0	3.0	2.7	2.2	3.3	1.3	....	....	....	....	....
Argentina	213	−1.4	2.8	3.2	−.1	−.5	−1.7	−1.8	1.0	−1.1	30.6	10.5	9.2
Anguilla	312	1.5	3.3	3.3	3.0	1.2	2.5	2.5	.5	−.6	4.5	....	....
Bahamas, The	313	2.0	4.9	−.5	....	....	....	....	....	....	....	....	....
Barbados	316	3.3	.8	4.8	3.5	6.9	3.3	.7	2.0	2.7	1.6	....	....
Belize	339	1.7	3.6	6.1	2.0	−1.5	1.5	−2.2	.6	−.2	1.8	−3.0	.9
Bolivia	218	6.6	8.0	11.4	11.6	5.7	7.0	2.4	5.2	1.9	3.1	6.1	8.5
Brazil	223	1,995.9	2,240.4	77.6	17.4	8.3	4.9	5.7	8.4	7.4	10.2	13.4	11.4
Chile	228	11.7	16.4	7.9	2.7	4.3	1.9	2.4	4.6	3.4	4.6	5.5	6.6
Colombia	233	24.5	22.9	18.9	16.9	16.8	14.8	12.6	12.1	6.2	6.4	8.2	7.1
Costa Rica	238	10.6	15.5	22.2	15.8	14.9	12.1	15.0	7.0	8.6	9.1	8.0	....
Dominica	321	4.8	5.3	1.1	3.5	1.2	2.6	2.5	.6	2.0	.1	.6	....
Dominican Republic	243	5.0	8.3	12.7	5.4	8.3	4.8	6.5	7.7	8.9	5.2	27.4	51.5
Ecuador	248	16.6	17.8	6.9	2.8	6.8	−3.6	−23.5	−7.0	25.5	11.8	9.0	4.1
El Salvador	253	8.5	9.9	10.4	6.8	3.5	3.9	.3	3.2	3.4	1.4	2.5	4.3
Guatemala	258	14.5	11.7	8.7	8.9	8.3	9.5	5.1	6.8	7.6	8.1	5.7	5.5
Guyana	336	16.9	....	....	....	....	....	....	....	....	....	....	....
Haiti	263	35.8	69.6	9.2	28.8	12.7	14.2	7.0	11.1	11.6	10.1	26.9	21.6
Honduras	268	13.6	28.9	24.9	22.9	22.3	11.6	11.6	9.7	8.0	6.3	7.7	....
Jamaica	343	35.8	32.6	23.1	18.5	10.1	8.6	5.7	11.6	8.3	8.4	12.5	....
Montserrat	351	2.8	4.3	2.3	3.4	5.8	2.9	3.7	1.8	7.1	1.8	....	....
Mexico	273	9.5	8.3	37.9	30.7	17.7	15.4	15.1	12.1	5.8	7.0	8.5	6.3
Nicaragua	278	20.4	80.1	13.4	9.6	9.8	14.0	9.2	8.6	7.2	3.2	6.8	10.2
Panama	283	3.6	3.7	.5	.3	1.6	1.0	.8	−1.2	1.0	1.7	.5	....
Paraguay	288	19.1	21.0	13.0	10.5	3.0	12.4	2.5	11.9	1.7	16.4	18.3	....
Peru	293	47.1	26.2	12.9	10.5	7.5	6.2	3.9	3.6	1.4	.6	2.3	5.3
St. Kitts and Nevis	361	2.2	6.3	4.5	—	4.8	3.3	2.4	3.5	1.9	1.5	1.8	....
St. Lucia	362	−2.5	2.8	4.9	—	2.1	2.7	3.7	3.1	1.4	.7	.9	....
St. Vincent & Grenadines	364	—	2.9	2.5	3.9	1.0	2.8	.2	−.4	2.2	1.5	.2	....
Suriname	366	115.7	483.6	90.6	10.9	7.5	17.7	72.2	56.4	32.9	28.4	28.6	....
Trinidad and Tobago	369	7.5	15.6	4.0	3.8	−3.0	−1.5	1.8	7.6	4.4	....	....	....
Uruguay	298	47.9	39.0	41.0	26.4	19.3	9.4	4.2	4.0	5.3	18.7	18.4	7.0
Venezuela, Rep. Bol.	299	31.6	62.9	51.8	115.5	33.9	19.0	26.3	30.0	8.6	33.1	....	....
Memorandum Items													
Oil Exporting Countries	999	**19.8**	**18.0**	**24.9**	**24.2**	**12.0**	**28.2**	**18.8**	**7.1**	**9.0**	**13.9**	**8.4**	**....**
Non-Oil Developing Countries.	201	**61.5**	**52.0**	**21.3**	**12.7**	**10.4**	**7.1**	**4.9**	**6.1**	**7.3**	**7.5**	**6.6**	**....**

2005, International Monetary Fund : *International Financial Statistics Yearbook*

GDP Deflators

Indices

		1993	1994	1995	1996	1997	1998	1999	2000	2001	2002	2003	2004
								Index Numbers: 2000=100					
World............................	001	61.4	73.0	80.1	85.4	89.7	93.7	96.6	100.0	104.2	108.9	113.0	....
Industrial Countries................	110	90.2	91.9	93.7	95.2	96.6	97.7	98.4	100.0	101.8	103.4	105.0	106.8
Developing Countries..............	200	35.8	52.9	64.4	73.4	81.1	88.6	94.2	100.0	107.6	116.6	124.6	....
Africa............................	605	32.1	37.3	49.2	60.7	68.6	73.3	84.1	100.0	111.1	117.6	127.3	....
Asia..............................	505	65.5	74.3	82.2	87.7	91.5	98.5	99.4	100.0	....	....	....	....
Europe...........................	170	8.6	13.9	21.1	29.0	44.9	60.3	78.8	100.0	123.6	145.5	161.4	172.7
Middle East.......................	405	46.2	52.3	61.9	70.8	75.6	75.8	87.2	100.0	103.6	115.5	124.5	....
Western Hemisphere.............	205	13.3	42.4	58.7	70.9	78.8	85.1	91.7	100.0	105.8	117.9	130.0	141.8

Gross Capital Formation as Percentage of GDP

		1993	1994	1995	1996	1997	1998	1999	2000	2001	2002	2003	2004
							Percentages						
World.............................	001	23.74	23.87	24.19	23.83	24.01	23.68	23.44	23.81	23.18	22.68	23.16	....
Industrial Countries...................	110	20.16	20.63	20.77	20.77	21.16	21.39	21.51	21.77	20.66	19.78	19.82	20.45
United States......................	111	17.61	18.64	18.61	19.00	19.77	20.25	20.63	20.78	19.14	18.40	18.46	19.61
Canada............................	156	17.89	18.86	18.74	18.20	20.73	20.48	20.13	20.26	19.38	19.92	20.15	20.63
Australia..........................	193	21.80	23.28	22.73	22.31	21.85	24.04	24.71	23.08	21.79	23.57	25.31	24.82
Japan.............................	158	29.39	28.16	28.24	29.12	28.66	26.89	26.01	26.28	25.76	23.97	23.90	23.92
New Zealand.......................	196	20.23	21.73	22.74	22.30	21.27	19.51	21.53	20.80	21.50	21.10	22.64	23.79
Euro Area..........................	163	19.40	19.98	20.21	19.33	19.62	21.23	21.42	22.54	20.97	19.96	19.90	20.48
Austria..........................	122	22.36	22.81	23.35	22.75	22.98	23.15	23.36	23.38	22.44	21.03	21.86	21.73
Belgium..........................	124	20.22	20.29	20.09	19.56	20.27	20.31	20.70	21.69	20.46	19.19	19.01	20.42
Finland...........................	172	16.91	17.84	18.13	17.10	19.09	20.10	19.56	20.59	20.57	19.34	18.87	19.40
France............................	132	17.58	18.40	18.64	17.72	17.45	18.77	19.24	20.47	20.07	18.97	18.93	19.75
Germany..........................	134	22.17	22.47	22.22	21.11	21.11	21.61	21.49	21.78	19.57	17.41	17.43	17.27
Greece............................	174	19.90	18.75	18.92	19.79	20.08	21.35	22.53	23.91	23.78	23.60	25.66	25.54
Ireland...........................	178	15.11	16.13	18.11	19.59	21.48	23.37	24.71	25.36	23.77	22.73	23.97	25.01
Italy..............................	136	18.37	18.49	19.34	18.68	18.86	19.28	19.65	20.20	19.71	19.97	19.46	19.81
Luxembourg.......................	137	24.25	22.94	21.43	21.63	23.05	23.70	24.53	23.49	23.82	21.17	21.12	19.48
Netherlands.......................	138	19.95	20.29	20.98	21.28	21.73	22.19	22.65	22.21	21.70	20.61	20.20	20.46
Portugal..........................	182	23.23	23.91	24.41	24.39	25.73	26.50	29.35	30.07	28.96	26.72	22.97	....
Spain.............................	184	21.28	21.47	22.33	21.90	22.13	23.27	24.57	26.28	26.33	26.59	27.66	28.27
Denmark..........................	128	16.42	17.60	19.67	18.94	20.76	21.67	19.73	21.03	20.38	20.25	19.66	20.16
Iceland...........................	176	17.92	17.00	17.35	20.18	20.33	24.70	22.26	24.27	22.07	17.66	19.96	21.58
Norway...........................	142	20.76	21.78	22.89	21.49	23.81	27.27	23.73	20.95	19.63	19.25	17.60	19.02
Sweden...........................	144	15.34	16.54	17.19	16.56	16.21	17.23	17.51	18.47	17.69	16.73	16.21	16.14
Switzerland........................	146	22.59	23.60	23.51	22.46	21.67	22.36	22.32	22.87	22.43	20.83	19.98	19.78
United Kingdom....................	112	15.79	16.50	16.94	16.73	17.07	18.18	17.80	17.46	17.42	16.53	16.61	17.22
Developing Countries..............	200	28.66	28.33	28.90	28.05	27.92	26.63	25.94	26.42	26.42	26.41	27.46	....
Africa..............................	605	17.71	19.00	19.37	18.14	17.65	18.41	18.10	17.55	17.85	18.59	19.57	....
Algeria...........................	612	28.26	31.46	31.57	25.08	23.29	27.34	26.25	23.05	27.09	30.42	29.80	....
Benin.............................	638	14.34	18.54	23.51	17.91	19.87	19.03	18.75	19.30	21.13	17.98	21.06	20.64
Botswana.........................	616	30.53	15.43	14.44	13.59	14.72	15.97	19.10	20.45	11.16	26.16	17.50	30.01
Burkina Faso......................	748	17.30	24.30	21.36	22.36	24.65	21.91	20.51	21.11	19.64	18.66	20.98	18.11
Burundi...........................	618	15.72	8.70	9.29	12.28	7.20	6.80	7.53	7.55	7.29	10.06	10.72	11.26
Cameroon.........................	622	16.71	14.08	13.69	15.08	16.15	....	....	....	....	....	....	....
Central African Rep................	626	10.58	11.71	14.12	7.28	10.08	11.96	13.45	11.68	10.80	10.11	6.70	7.67
Congo, Dem. Rep. of...............	636	—	3.46	11.05	14.29	8.15	6.54	9.64	11.04	8.10	9.29	13.80	19.61
Congo, Rep. of....................	634	19.06	46.16	51.68	29.15	24.92	49.79	38.86	23.45	35.78	26.12	26.35	29.47
Côte d'Ivoire......................	662	8.29	12.54	14.95	13.24	13.50	11.58	13.24	10.49	10.91	8.94	9.57	....
Ethiopia..........................	644	14.22	15.16	16.44	19.10	17.00	17.20	16.00	15.35	16.50	....	....	....
Gabon............................	646	22.52	20.77	22.06	22.74	24.46	31.84	....	....	....	....	....	....
Ghana............................	652	22.22	23.95	20.02	21.47	24.55	....	....	....	....	....	....	....
Guinea-Bissau.....................	654	25.06	12.94	18.15	19.77	13.06	38.83	28.58	28.36	15.83	14.73	17.88	....
Kenya.............................	664	17.61	19.29	21.80	20.33	18.50	17.30	16.15	17.41	19.18	16.31	17.41	18.28
Malawi............................	676	14.47	28.66	17.16	11.92	11.33	13.05	14.82	14.50	14.94	11.69	12.47	....
Mali..............................	678	17.36	24.37	25.29	18.70	22.54	19.70	18.54	19.66	24.30	18.45	24.62	....
Mauritania........................	682	18.58	19.12	20.38	17.76	17.26	....	....	....	....	....	....	....
Mauritius..........................	684	30.59	31.93	25.62	24.41	29.33	25.42	26.34	25.65	20.74	22.32	23.23	24.44
Morocco..........................	686	22.39	21.32	20.67	19.58	20.70	22.16	23.13	23.70	22.89	22.70	23.77	....
Mozambique.......................	688	23.76	24.82	30.63	21.83	20.58	24.22	36.68	33.54	25.89	26.80	26.54	....
Namibia...........................	728	16.46	21.71	21.70	23.12	20.17	25.75	23.28	19.92	23.79	....	....	....
Niger.............................	692	8.14	17.06	12.59	15.57	15.88	16.20	10.22	19.09	12.04	19.04	18.65	....
Nigeria............................	694	11.60	9.32	5.81	6.11	7.01	6.72	5.33	5.41	7.66	8.93	12.05	16.16
Rwanda...........................	714	18.22	11.70	13.51	14.30	13.67	14.66	17.55	17.30	16.67	17.44	18.28	....
Senegal...........................	722	13.81	18.45	16.80	17.68	15.20	16.75	20.11	21.63	18.14	18.44	19.52	....
Seychelles.........................	718	28.67	27.08	30.34	32.14	34.36	36.11	....	....	....	....	....	....
Sierra Leone.......................	724	4.08	8.67	5.49	10.02	4.35	5.50	3.48	6.46	5.63	5.84	13.90	....
South Africa.......................	199	15.30	16.81	18.17	17.29	16.64	17.00	16.38	15.91	15.29	16.11	17.17	17.67
Swaziland.........................	734	23.86	21.50	19.95	20.69	20.60	22.36	18.76	19.89	18.09	18.39	12.59	....
Togo..............................	742	4.26	14.90	14.60	12.75	10.97	16.23	11.81	15.40	16.60	16.39	19.45	....
Tunisia............................	744	29.24	24.64	24.70	25.01	26.44	26.90	26.30	27.32	27.92	25.69	25.02	24.27
Uganda...........................	746	16.57	14.53	17.14	17.07	16.77	18.63	19.93	18.94	19.68	20.57	22.05	....
Zambia............................	754	15.04	19.77	30.16	44.91	38.84	....	....	....	....	....	....	....
Zimbabwe.........................	698	17.90	28.98	25.29	17.44	18.83	22.25	17.07	13.50	....	....	....	....
Asia................................	505	34.43	34.19	34.92	33.32	32.46	29.38	29.39	30.01	30.58	30.80	32.24	....
Bangladesh........................	513	17.95	18.40	19.12	19.99	20.72	21.63	22.19	23.02	23.09	23.15	23.21	....
Bhutan............................	514	46.06	47.44	46.84	44.68	34.10	38.22	43.07	43.77	....	....	....	....
China, P.R.: Mainland..............	924	43.47	41.25	40.81	39.32	38.00	37.40	37.14	36.38	38.00	39.21	42.29	....
China, P.R.: Hong Kong.............	532	27.58	31.76	34.66	32.06	34.52	29.15	25.26	28.08	25.91	23.37	22.39	22.41
Fiji...............................	819	15.97	13.49	13.57	11.37	11.50	15.90	14.94	12.64	14.52	....	....	....
India..............................	534	21.25	23.38	26.53	21.77	22.57	21.38	23.66	22.64	22.41	22.13	23.03	....
Indonesia.........................	536	29.48	31.06	31.93	30.69	31.75	16.77	11.37	21.30	23.45	20.63	17.30	21.33
Korea.............................	542	35.73	36.95	37.67	38.87	35.97	25.00	29.12	31.00	29.33	29.08	29.96	30.22
Malaysia..........................	548	39.18	41.20	43.64	41.48	42.97	26.67	22.38	27.30	23.92	23.78	21.37	22.45
Myanmar..........................	518	12.44	12.37	14.24	12.25	12.50	12.38	13.43	12.45	11.57	10.15	10.96	....
Nepal.............................	558	23.14	22.41	25.20	27.33	25.34	24.84	20.48	24.31	24.05	24.08	25.83	26.69
Pakistan...........................	564	20.82	19.54	18.54	18.98	17.92	17.71	15.57	17.37	17.19	16.77	16.74	18.08
Papua New Guinea.................	853	17.63	21.44	22.06	22.68	21.07	17.91	16.39	21.29	21.78	19.81	....	....
Philippines........................	566	23.98	24.06	22.45	24.02	24.78	20.34	18.75	21.17	18.97	18.03	16.99	17.42
Singapore.........................	576	37.39	33.10	34.17	35.81	39.25	32.27	31.98	32.46	26.02	22.75	14.84	18.30

2005, International Monetary Fund : *International Financial Statistics Yearbook*

Gross Capital Formation as Percentage of GDP

		1993	1994	1995	1996	1997	1998	1999	2000	2001	2002	2003	2004
							Percentages						
Asia(Cont.)													
Sri Lanka	524	25.56	27.03	25.73	24.25	24.39	25.14	27.29	28.04	22.01	21.61	22.20	25.00
Thailand	578	40.01	40.25	42.09	41.82	33.66	20.45	20.50	22.84	24.10	23.87	25.01	27.13
Vanuatu	846	27.82	28.84	32.66	24.80	18.84	17.69	20.28	22.15	19.98	21.17	19.89	....
Europe	170	**25.50**	**23.63**	**23.88**	**23.94**	**24.11**	**24.32**	**23.21**	**24.23**	**21.86**	**22.31**	**23.23**	**24.30**
Armenia	911	9.76	23.45	18.42	20.01	19.07	19.14	18.35	18.64	19.76	21.67	24.26	23.93
Belarus	913	41.03	32.94	24.75	23.52	26.84	26.71	23.71	25.40	23.76	22.18	26.61	28.31
Bulgaria	918	15.28	9.39	15.65	8.12	9.88	16.88	17.92	18.29	20.67	19.81	21.74	23.52
Cyprus	423	24.01	25.43	21.80	21.60	19.28	19.23	17.06	18.42	16.51	18.77	17.91	20.72
Czech Republic	935	27.29	29.75	32.52	33.02	30.55	28.55	26.94	28.77	28.88	27.92	27.11	27.56
Estonia	939	26.21	27.05	26.64	27.01	30.43	30.34	24.91	27.79	29.17	31.79	32.00	31.21
Hungary	944	19.95	22.19	22.60	25.50	26.57	28.85	28.72	30.91	26.81	25.23	25.01	24.21
Kazakhstan	916	20.87	26.83	22.55	16.89	16.25	16.58	17.08	18.08	27.63	27.81	26.38	23.85
Kyrgyz Republic	917	11.67	9.01	18.34	25.20	21.45	15.16	17.76	19.76	15.49	17.61	11.83	9.98
Malta	181	29.84	30.66	31.98	28.63	25.57	23.70	24.00	26.17	18.32	15.58	20.52	22.00
Moldova	921	55.80	28.82	24.88	24.25	23.81	25.87	22.88	23.95	20.07	....	....	....
Poland	964	15.55	17.62	18.42	20.47	23.01	24.60	24.87	24.67	20.74	18.85	18.88	19.97
Romania	968	28.93	24.81	24.27	25.85	20.63	17.75	16.08	19.47	22.56	21.68	22.94	23.05
Slovak Republic	936	24.65	20.97	24.84	34.75	34.54	34.00	27.57	26.14	30.00	29.34	25.44	26.34
Slovenia	961	19.35	20.94	22.53	22.38	23.68	24.71	27.27	26.66	23.88	23.76	25.32	26.81
Turkey	186	27.61	21.48	25.47	24.55	25.11	24.18	23.35	24.51	16.78	21.32	22.78	25.68
Ukraine	926	36.29	35.33	26.68	22.67	21.45	20.82	17.44	19.72	21.81	19.07	20.03	18.80
Middle East	405	**25.48**	**21.37**	**23.19**	**24.77**	**24.64**	**25.25**	**23.15**	**23.07**	**23.82**	**24.32**	**25.02**	**....**
Egypt	469	16.21	16.57	17.21	16.61	18.16	21.50	21.62	19.55	18.26	18.26	17.01	16.62
Iran, I.R. of	429	33.28	22.74	29.20	35.88	35.75	32.84	29.74	32.98	35.23	36.49	39.28	....
Iraq	433	15.48	....	....	....	....	....	....	....	....	....	....	....
Israel	436	25.99	25.27	26.47	25.75	24.20	22.56	22.94	21.65	21.13	18.83	16.90	17.63
Jordan	439	36.63	33.30	32.96	30.52	25.73	21.82	21.59	22.16	20.79	20.10	....	....
Kuwait	443	17.19	16.16	14.76	15.11	13.64	18.45	14.56	7.64	8.71	9.16	8.65	....
Libya	672	16.28	16.33	12.16	15.50	12.36	11.96	11.19	13.04	12.98	14.46	....	....
Oman	449	17.53	15.74	14.98	13.70	17.65	23.98	14.85	11.93	12.61	12.77	15.66	....
Qatar	453	19.77	24.52	35.08	35.77	35.43	31.97	18.88	20.15	22.69	....	....	....
Saudi Arabia	456	24.59	19.85	19.79	18.10	18.30	22.42	21.14	18.71	18.88	19.67	19.82	18.93
Syrian Arab Rep	463	25.97	29.96	27.23	23.60	20.85	20.55	18.77	17.27	20.88	20.01	....	....
United Arab Emirates	466	29.34	29.36	28.52	26.41	28.10	30.08	....	....	....	....	....	....
Yemen, Republic of	474	20.18	20.73	21.82	23.29	25.17	32.75	23.75	17.16	17.20	16.20	16.84	....
Western Hemisphere	205	**20.60**	**21.58**	**21.50**	**21.39**	**23.09**	**22.88**	**20.70**	**21.06**	**20.18**	**18.84**	**18.94**	**20.66**
Antigua and Barbuda	311	31.68	32.40	36.91	39.67	41.32	....	....	....	....	....	....	....
Argentina	213	19.69	19.97	18.52	19.64	20.86	21.00	17.88	17.52	15.61	10.98	14.59	18.87
Bahamas, The	313	19.60	21.17	23.21	....	....	....	....	....	....	....	....	....
Barbados	316	12.69	13.31	14.08	12.67	15.32	....	....	....	....	....	....	....
Belize	339	28.37	20.56	21.71	20.36	20.17	19.07	24.60	31.70	24.87	23.99	20.69	19.80
Bolivia	218	16.56	14.37	15.24	16.24	19.63	23.61	18.77	18.14	14.27	16.57	13.35	12.36
Brazil	223	20.85	22.15	22.29	20.92	21.50	21.12	20.16	21.54	21.20	19.76	19.76	21.32
Chile	228	26.93	24.29	26.18	27.38	27.72	26.90	20.90	21.86	22.09	21.66	22.00	21.69
Colombia	233	17.79	25.50	25.72	22.05	20.79	19.61	12.77	13.58	14.14	15.29	....	....
Costa Rica	238	20.88	20.05	18.24	15.96	18.08	20.46	17.03	16.91	20.28	22.52	20.49	....
Dominica	321	25.47	25.69	31.30	28.78	31.35	27.25	27.70	28.06	23.90	20.64	25.06	....
Dominican Republic	243	23.91	21.38	19.48	18.96	19.83	23.47	24.21	23.78	22.88	22.76	23.35	24.27
Ecuador	248	....	....	....	....	....	....	....	....	....	....	....	....
El Salvador	253	18.58	19.69	20.04	15.19	15.12	17.55	16.43	16.93	16.67	16.19	16.67	15.56
Grenada	328	33.09	37.80	33.69	36.75	38.25	37.81	41.42	....	....	....	....	....
Guatemala	258	17.25	15.68	15.05	12.69	13.68	17.40	17.35	17.84	17.78	19.11	18.06	17.80
Honduras	268	33.56	37.63	31.56	31.13	32.17	30.93	34.67	30.72	29.57	25.62	26.88	....
Jamaica	343	28.71	27.15	28.76	29.11	29.25	25.81	24.47	26.79	29.15	31.84	30.01	....
Mexico	273	21.00	21.72	19.82	23.11	25.86	24.32	23.47	23.73	20.88	20.65	20.55	21.75
Nicaragua	278	19.47	20.37	22.00	25.77	31.16	31.03	38.35	30.98	28.25	26.07	26.08	28.41
Panama	283	22.58	24.48	27.65	26.74	25.68	27.21	25.79	24.14	17.64	15.75	19.10	....
Paraguay	288	22.95	23.36	23.93	23.40	23.55	22.93	23.04	21.85	19.78	19.09	19.82	....
Peru	293	19.31	22.25	24.83	22.85	24.13	23.66	21.16	20.24	18.80	18.78	19.88	18.97
St. Vincent & Grenadines	364	25.64	28.51	30.05	28.16	30.81	35.81	34.55	27.28	29.70	30.03	....	....
Suriname	366	23.88	43.17	35.98	80.20	71.88	84.22	66.81	59.83	65.30	74.12	69.16	....
Trinidad and Tobago	369	14.35	20.20	20.78	24.28	30.11	33.38	21.01	17.03	19.44	....	....	....
Uruguay	298	15.64	15.87	15.41	15.24	15.22	15.87	15.14	13.96	13.77	11.52	12.59	13.29
Venezuela, Rep. Bol.	299	18.75	14.16	18.11	16.55	27.67	30.66	26.52	24.17	27.52	21.16	15.56	21.05
Memorandum Items													
Oil Exporting Countries	999	**26.43**	**24.05**	**25.67**	**25.75**	**27.20**	**22.64**	**19.01**	**22.28**	**24.38**	**23.51**	**22.54**	**....**
Non-Oil Developing Countries	201	**28.98**	**28.95**	**29.36**	**28.39**	**28.03**	**27.12**	**26.78**	**26.93**	**26.66**	**26.76**	**28.05**	**....**

Final Consumption Expenditure as Percentage of GDP

		1993	1994	1995	1996	1997	1998	1999	2000	2001	2002	2003	2004
							Percentages						
World............................	001	**76.50**	**76.15**	**75.93**	**76.04**	**75.66**	**75.83**	**76.29**	**75.98**	**76.71**	**76.69**	**76.35**	....
Industrial Countries..................	110	**79.49**	**79.07**	**78.81**	**78.74**	**78.18**	**78.39**	**78.85**	**79.09**	**80.01**	**80.79**	**81.10**	**80.76**
United States........................	111	83.37	82.68	82.62	82.23	81.45	81.58	82.18	83.09	84.49	85.65	86.10	85.71
Canada..............................	156	82.71	80.36	78.42	78.12	77.57	77.73	75.82	73.46	75.01	75.77	75.78	75.17
Australia...........................	193	78.99	77.97	78.79	77.95	77.75	77.73	78.25	77.89	77.65	77.91	77.69	77.66
Japan..............................	158	68.39	69.83	70.36	70.38	70.24	71.28	72.44	72.29	73.61	74.74	74.50	74.17
New Zealand.......................	196	76.85	76.41	76.50	77.16	78.38	80.17	79.27	77.47	76.18	77.32	77.15	77.05
Euro Area...........................	163	78.75	78.00	77.53	77.95	77.31	76.26	76.83	78.91	77.37	77.45	78.01	77.42
Austria............................	122	77.26	77.61	77.15	77.93	76.81	75.59	74.99	74.18	74.40	73.99	74.45	73.56
Belgium...........................	124	76.22	75.67	75.62	76.37	75.32	75.42	74.99	75.23	76.20	76.50	77.12	76.64
Finland............................	172	78.35	76.35	74.01	75.34	72.87	71.08	71.91	70.16	71.09	72.31	74.38	74.10
France.............................	132	81.50	80.73	80.22	80.77	79.65	78.68	78.66	78.63	78.78	79.32	79.96	80.00
Germany...........................	134	77.86	77.38	77.31	77.99	77.64	77.03	77.65	77.87	78.43	78.12	78.57	77.79
Greece.............................	174	87.39	86.73	88.40	88.19	87.27	87.00	86.01	86.55	84.68	84.52	83.05	83.02
Ireland............................	178	75.34	74.97	70.93	69.74	66.67	64.70	61.60	60.68	60.49	59.93	60.96	59.79
Italy...............................	136	78.39	78.02	76.59	76.39	77.09	77.31	78.29	78.82	78.85	79.01	79.95	79.38
Luxembourg.......................	137	66.48	65.64	66.33	66.99	63.48	61.46	59.02	55.62	58.55	59.67	60.15	58.88
Netherlands.......................	138	74.48	73.59	73.08	72.98	72.34	72.39	73.01	72.57	73.07	74.29	74.77	74.13
Portugal...........................	182	87.24	86.55	85.27	85.37	84.95	85.95	82.06	82.06	81.70	81.66	82.85	84.12
Spain..............................	184	79.49	78.68	77.86	77.58	76.85	76.66	76.68	76.85	76.11	75.42	74.59	75.34
Denmark...........................	128	76.77	77.05	76.24	76.14	75.73	76.31	75.48	73.01	73.15	74.06	74.15	74.73
Iceland............................	176	78.88	77.80	79.00	79.19	79.09	79.86	82.56	83.16	78.94	80.55	83.14	84.35
Norway............................	142	72.70	72.04	70.87	69.49	67.90	70.84	68.77	61.71	63.30	67.09	68.84	66.80
Sweden............................	144	80.93	78.93	76.07	76.85	76.54	76.48	76.33	75.71	75.88	76.57	77.05	75.84
Switzerland........................	146	71.69	70.91	71.49	72.35	72.33	71.70	71.95	71.10	72.01	72.15	72.68	72.48
United Kingdom...................	112	85.22	84.22	83.53	83.69	82.85	82.75	83.84	84.50	85.42	86.25	86.52	86.52
Developing Countries..............	200	**72.39**	**72.13**	**71.97**	**72.32**	**72.19**	**72.54**	**73.00**	**71.97**	**72.45**	**71.41**	**70.24**	....
Africa................................	605	**80.30**	**83.18**	**82.52**	**82.01**	**82.93**	**84.74**	**80.27**	**77.91**	**80.99**	**80.78**	**80.92**	**81.03**
Algeria.............................	612	73.16	74.05	72.57	67.72	67.99	72.79	68.38	55.49	58.28	59.57	55.95	....
Benin..............................	638	96.95	90.00	88.87	90.49	85.81	87.20	87.73	85.64	88.87	90.30	89.75	87.09
Botswana..........................	616	64.45	35.23	35.79	35.16	32.05	30.57	32.61	61.60	34.19	62.21	36.69	63.11
Burkina Faso.......................	748	94.24	85.35	89.77	92.93	89.53	91.97	94.31	95.22	94.17	93.93	92.01	93.74
Burundi............................	618	104.52	107.06	105.06	97.61	97.39	104.49	100.86	105.92	103.19	107.37	108.27	107.15
Cameroon..........................	622	82.44	73.86	76.02	75.67	73.47	....	....	....	....	....	....	....
Central African Rep................	626	94.93	89.91	91.91	96.87	91.97	95.47	91.19	93.12	94.45	93.40	98.30	101.12
Congo, Dem. Rep. of..............	636	—	93.36	84.21	77.52	90.34	94.73	90.13	89.16	93.14	87.82	93.31	83.21
Congo, Rep. of....................	634	81.16	71.33	47.89	61.96	59.64	46.73	47.74	31.55	41.00	44.80	42.24	44.23
Côte d'Ivoire.......................	662	90.59	77.64	79.66	76.00	76.79	80.20	77.81	81.18	80.59	75.16	79.69	....
Ethiopia...........................	644	94.40	94.97	93.31	93.50	103.50	92.20	98.80	101.00	99.00	....	....	....
Gabon.............................	646	62.96	53.23	56.98	50.74	54.46	69.34	....	....	....	....	....	....
Ghana.............................	652	93.40	87.40	88.30	88.14	92.19	....	....	....	....	....	....	....
Guinea-Bissau.....................	654	101.50	107.50	102.75	102.79	97.36	92.94	94.36	91.33	96.44	97.53	92.57	....
Kenya..............................	664	77.61	77.57	84.11	83.97	88.87	90.32	89.63	93.34	94.73	95.13	93.84	91.95
Madagascar........................	674	97.85	96.66	96.63	93.65	96.35	95.07	93.11	93.54	89.27	95.64	97.13	92.89
Malawi.............................	676	101.47	94.85	96.82	98.15	100.95	92.35	100.45	95.71	94.19	106.22	110.19	....
Mali...............................	678	96.04	95.73	91.69	95.97	86.81	89.57	91.49	90.93	84.93	83.21	81.74	....
Mauritania.........................	682	98.39	91.61	80.13	88.34	89.50	....	....	....	....	....	....	....
Mauritius..........................	684	75.44	76.79	76.80	76.28	75.56	75.41	77.16	74.92	73.34	74.64	75.48	77.88
Morocco...........................	686	86.61	87.74	89.03	88.06	86.45	86.12	85.43	87.71	87.11	86.69	86.45	....
Mozambique.......................	688	115.01	111.74	109.16	101.83	98.92	93.18	90.97	91.52	82.82	76.48	74.82	....
Namibia............................	728	90.64	83.31	86.79	87.96	90.87	89.10	89.42	90.01	87.64	....	....	....
Niger...............................	692	97.59	92.99	94.32	91.52	91.64	92.81	97.41	88.94	95.68	90.46	92.57	....
Nigeria.............................	694	80.55	85.53	84.25	88.92	88.65	102.78	66.91	54.34	83.17	80.19	82.65	81.40
Rwanda............................	714	97.24	146.79	109.81	106.23	103.99	100.77	99.84	99.15	99.95	102.21	100.12	....
Senegal............................	722	93.25	91.64	91.78	87.48	86.66	86.65	87.55	86.06	90.53	....	....	....
Seychelles.........................	718	80.46	75.30	76.39	77.07	77.71	76.56	....	....	....	....	....	....
Sierra Leone.......................	724	95.42	91.80	95.00	91.65	98.27	94.63	96.10	96.00	103.35	94.34	88.97	....
South Africa........................	199	81.89	81.86	80.91	81.34	82.15	82.10	81.63	81.13	80.99	80.24	81.93	82.84
Swaziland..........................	734	102.18	96.51	98.68	105.31	96.66	96.71	96.08	95.47	95.00	91.00	85.11	....
Tanzania...........................	738	....	....	....	....	....	....	....	....	....	....	....	....
Togo...............................	742	108.23	94.43	98.79	100.15	100.13	96.75	98.36	98.02	100.03	98.13	97.50	....
Tunisia.............................	744	78.28	78.29	79.20	76.49	76.02	76.45	75.96	76.32	76.67	78.58	78.86	78.63
Uganda............................	746	101.82	96.72	98.74	103.40	93.18	91.62	92.50	94.31	94.74	94.88	93.03	....
Zambia.............................	754	86.96	84.63	74.71	68.26	73.67	....	....	....	....	....	....	....
Zimbabwe..........................	698	83.82	72.94	77.38	82.37	87.78	79.44	80.57	87.10	....	....	....	....
Asia..................................	505	**66.84**	**65.85**	**65.82**	**66.68**	**66.20**	**66.34**	**67.88**	**67.32**	**67.10**	**66.30**	**64.71**	....
Bangladesh.........................	513	87.70	86.90	86.87	85.10	84.10	82.59	82.29	82.12	82.00	81.84	81.42	....
Bhutan.............................	514	66.43	62.35	57.91	64.98	75.37	77.31	74.98	72.59	....	....	....	....
China, P.R.: Mainland..............	924	58.50	57.39	57.49	58.54	58.19	58.74	60.14	61.13	59.79	58.20	55.50	....
China, P.R.: Hong Kong.............	532	66.45	67.99	70.87	70.34	69.75	70.60	70.17	68.33	70.40	68.91	68.63	68.73
Fiji.................................	819	83.63	78.68	78.97	78.73	77.63	76.34	70.55	77.11	74.13	....	....	....
India...............................	534	78.27	76.31	75.30	76.70	75.78	77.74	78.62	77.73	77.97	76.20	75.22	....
Indonesia..........................	536	67.54	67.80	69.41	69.92	68.52	73.47	80.55	68.18	68.46	73.21	75.07	74.69
Korea..............................	542	63.33	63.74	63.47	64.27	64.22	62.13	64.23	66.08	68.11	66.98	66.98	64.96
Malaysia...........................	548	60.92	60.40	60.29	57.14	56.11	51.33	52.57	52.75	57.69	57.94	57.66	56.17
Myanmar...........................	518	88.59	88.25	86.63	88.54	88.21	88.25	86.90	87.65	88.49	89.76	89.03	....
Nepal..............................	558	86.48	85.33	85.19	86.17	86.04	86.23	86.39	84.83	85.02	87.98	88.41	87.78
Pakistan...........................	564	85.32	83.21	84.17	85.52	86.77	83.33	86.05	83.88	83.88	83.32	82.66	82.11
Papua New Guinea.................	853	66.67	60.23	58.75	68.96	77.58	77.37	86.68	76.31	87.37	88.31	....	....
Philippines.........................	566	86.24	85.15	85.47	85.40	85.79	87.60	85.69	82.70	82.88	82.61	82.31	81.00
Singapore..........................	576	54.04	52.10	49.77	49.71	48.93	48.63	50.91	51.77	56.03	56.17	55.11	52.88

Final Consumption Expenditure as Percentage of GDP

		1993	1994	1995	1996	1997	1998	1999	2000	2001	2002	2003	2004
							Percentages						
Asia(Cont.)													
Sri Lanka	524	83.99	84.78	84.71	84.68	82.68	80.81	80.49	82.56	84.23	85.52	84.10	84.10
Thailand	578	64.66	63.73	63.07	63.96	64.74	65.21	67.46	67.46	68.61	68.25	67.30	66.58
Vanuatu	846	77.66	76.87	73.94	76.77	79.71	77.57	80.83	80.69	79.45	84.39	85.29	....
Europe	170	**79.25**	**79.02**	**79.79**	**80.38**	**81.07**	**81.43**	**82.42**	**81.37**	**81.78**	**80.66**	**80.70**	**79.78**
Armenia	911	110.56	105.83	117.45	111.65	114.74	111.15	108.28	108.94	104.84	99.07	93.49	94.73
Belarus	913	74.70	79.90	79.64	80.56	77.38	77.71	78.15	76.39	79.18	80.52	78.51	76.62
Bulgaria	918	92.34	91.23	85.94	86.47	85.54	82.89	87.85	87.06	86.90	86.81	87.75	86.82
Cyprus	423	75.69	74.23	78.42	81.44	82.63	82.01	81.49	81.75	81.84	82.45	83.27	83.13
Czech Republic	935	72.23	72.93	71.80	72.94	74.78	72.58	74.25	74.31	73.66	74.13	75.10	72.78
Estonia	939	80.93	84.26	83.03	84.64	81.00	80.35	80.33	77.09	76.55	77.56	77.44	74.77
Hungary	944	88.25	84.28	77.45	74.04	72.40	72.58	74.00	72.94	74.67	77.09	79.49	78.75
Kazakhstan	916	88.35	82.57	81.88	83.88	86.38	88.16	80.67	73.37	73.32	71.28	67.44	68.81
Kyrgyz Republic	917	95.98	97.29	94.55	100.62	86.22	106.10	96.77	85.73	82.30	86.15	94.74	95.97
Malta	181	79.82	79.51	81.68	85.30	82.88	81.85	81.56	83.88	85.69	84.70	84.96	85.82
Moldova	921	55.90	75.43	82.89	94.33	97.35	100.89	90.01	103.02	104.36	....	....	....
Poland	964	83.47	80.23	79.38	80.99	81.03	80.32	81.12	81.87	82.94	84.49	83.60	81.84
Romania	968	76.04	77.26	81.32	82.57	86.44	90.28	88.75	86.16	85.19	84.02	84.85	86.30
Slovak Republic	936	79.66	73.41	72.66	75.76	74.95	76.66	76.78	75.90	77.83	77.68	76.40	76.05
Slovenia	961	79.57	76.87	79.35	78.56	77.05	76.70	76.90	76.89	76.79	74.76	74.71	73.80
Turkey	186	82.12	81.61	81.10	78.84	80.30	81.87	87.42	85.59	86.27	80.25	80.08	80.86
Ukraine	926	64.02	67.83	76.40	79.88	81.61	81.46	77.03	75.25	76.57	76.45	77.24	73.38
Middle East	405	**73.99**	**73.91**	**73.60**	**72.19**	**72.73**	**78.16**	**73.78**	**69.84**	**71.56**	**69.91**	**68.47**	**....**
Egypt	469	83.28	84.86	85.00	87.31	88.10	88.00	86.64	87.06	86.59	86.09	85.65	83.71
Iran, I.R. of	429	59.04	62.15	63.04	59.76	61.16	69.34	64.53	61.53	62.13	57.83	57.66	....
Iraq	433	86.21	....	....	....	....	....	....	....	....	....	....	....
Israel	436	89.10	89.02	87.86	87.72	86.04	85.10	84.95	83.86	86.58	89.72	89.04	88.53
Jordan	439	93.99	89.97	88.18	94.78	96.54	97.66	96.31	104.60	104.38	100.61	....	....
Kuwait	443	79.33	74.97	74.85	71.80	73.10	88.78	78.94	65.54	75.14	82.16	75.49	....
Libya	672	87.02	82.74	81.08	79.74	82.70	89.55	82.16	67.04	75.13	74.11	....	....
Oman	449	77.47	76.04	76.54	72.26	70.88	83.48	73.51	59.96	65.15	66.14	65.99	....
Qatar	453	68.82	64.37	63.92	60.29	52.45	56.90	46.77	34.89	35.75	....	....	....
Saudi Arabia	456	74.50	72.17	70.52	68.43	68.49	74.38	67.32	62.54	65.31	62.92	58.18	53.30
Syrian Arab Rep	463	87.06	82.37	79.66	82.66	80.53	79.82	80.91	75.78	72.59	71.99	....	....
United Arab Emirates	466	62.16	63.06	64.41	61.41	63.10	69.90	....	75.25	81.95	83.35	87.39	....
Yemen Republic	474	107.81	97.34	97.82	85.73	83.69	88.23	78.61	75.25	81.04	79.34	78.51	76.41
Western Hemisphere	205	**79.63**	**80.06**	**79.34**	**79.20**	**78.94**	**80.33**	**80.70**	**79.74**	**81.04**	**79.34**	**78.51**	**76.41**
Antigua and Barbuda	311	62.81	66.07	71.83	74.83	69.61	66.63	63.01	67.17	....	....	....	....
Argentina	213	82.72	83.11	81.91	81.03	81.39	81.55	83.87	83.12	83.07	74.13	74.64	74.00
Bahamas, The	313	83.91	84.02	83.45	....	....	....	....	....	....	....	....	....
Barbados	316	81.56	77.05	81.67	80.28	84.15	83.68	86.14	88.22	86.74	88.93	....	....
Belize	339	83.11	86.23	86.15	88.75	90.55	91.80	90.90	86.90	91.26	93.02	92.24	93.36
Bolivia	218	92.74	91.16	89.39	88.46	88.62	89.28	91.64	90.90	91.02	89.50	87.50	83.32
Brazil	223	77.76	77.50	79.48	80.99	80.87	81.06	81.38	79.97	79.79	78.17	76.64	74.02
Chile	228	75.10	71.98	71.39	74.31	74.40	76.37	76.83	76.28	76.38	75.93	74.00	69.31
Colombia	233	68.15	80.38	80.63	83.49	84.99	86.17	86.58	84.21	86.19	86.22	....	....
Costa Rica	238	85.58	85.52	84.57	87.51	85.76	82.19	77.15	80.23	82.72	82.65	81.29	....
Dominica	321	86.99	90.40	84.70	89.22	83.22	80.68	81.18	86.17	93.28	92.44	87.02	....
Dominican Republic	243	83.63	84.12	83.90	85.89	84.93	85.53	83.24	86.21	85.05	86.15	77.28	75.43
El Salvador	253	96.17	95.55	96.08	97.67	96.54	94.74	95.92	98.11	99.13	98.60	99.68	101.36
Grenada	328	88.37	77.13	84.05	85.68	85.63	89.57	67.73	82.99	....	....	....	....
Guatemala	258	90.77	91.55	91.12	92.09	91.96	90.69	91.00	90.92	92.40	93.24	94.70	96.17
Guyana	336	63.70	63.58	62.30	62.15	65.08	....	....	....	....	....	....	....
Haiti	263	107.29	101.21	121.61	98.80	102.14	99.31	....	....	....	....	....	....
Honduras	268	75.47	72.39	72.82	73.99	73.46	76.73	80.28	83.15	86.83	89.70	89.52	....
Jamaica	343	79.63	79.10	81.53	82.39	83.57	84.16	83.80	84.60	87.17	88.22	88.52	....
Mexico	273	82.93	83.11	77.52	74.83	74.24	77.82	78.15	78.21	81.39	81.21	81.07	80.12
Nicaragua	278	107.96	96.20	93.55	93.46	93.64	92.75	94.23	96.24	97.44	100.23	100.55	99.06
Panama	283	64.99	62.53	61.03	72.01	69.92	74.71	75.40	73.10	75.57	79.08	74.87	....
Paraguay	288	87.99	95.22	92.47	92.81	92.66	94.00	90.70	92.90	96.32	93.81	94.64	....
Peru	293	84.55	81.13	80.85	82.10	80.29	81.72	81.17	81.68	82.89	82.01	81.05	78.54
St. Kitts and Nevis	361	66.12	70.67	77.18	80.81	76.38	73.78	88.81	80.38	71.39	80.08	68.45	....
St. Lucia	362	77.05	77.81	77.80	81.61	76.38	86.49	80.49	84.43	82.04	81.35	88.69	89.12	....
St. Vincent & Grenadines	364	92.20	95.77	84.34	85.08	97.25	93.15	86.07	80.97	81.00	82.67	79.53	....
Suriname	366	47.27	38.63	32.42	71.49	87.66	....	....	....	....	....	....	....
Trinidad and Tobago	369	80.77	66.96	64.70	65.35	73.10	71.94	73.23	69.09	69.98	76.76	67.46	....
Uruguay	298	84.79	84.74	84.70	84.95	84.77	84.86	86.12	87.72	87.92	86.52	85.90	85.01
Venezuela, Rep. Bol.	299	81.47	77.28	76.59	68.26	65.05	71.10	69.73	64.20	69.15	66.55	67.63	62.84
Memorandum Items													
Oil Exporting Countries	999	**70.35**	**70.39**	**70.66**	**68.74**	**68.28**	**75.05**	**72.25**	**63.31**	**66.92**	**67.09**	**66.99**	**65.08**
Non-Oil Developing Countries	201	**72.68**	**72.38**	**72.15**	**72.83**	**72.75**	**72.23**	**73.10**	**73.02**	**73.12**	**71.94**	**70.63**	**....**

Commodity Prices

		1993	1994	1995	1996	1997	1998	1999	2000	2001	2002	2003	2004
Market Prices (lines 76) and Unit Values (lines 74) Country of Origin and, for Market Prices, Pricing Point in Parentheses													
Aluminum (US $/MT)													
All Origins (London) *	156	1,139.93	1,475.64	1,805.02	1,506.81	1,599.28	1,357.58	1,359.99	1,551.50	1,446.74	1,351.08	1,432.83	1,718.52
Bananas (US $/MT)													
Latin America (US Ports) *	248	443.03	439.79	445.10	469.58	522.56	492.19	373.92	422.27	584.70	527.61	375.19	524.84
Barley (US $/MT)													
Canada (Winnepeg) *	156	71.38	72.65	104.01	119.67	97.24	85.05	75.94	77.23	93.94	108.97	104.72	98.99
Beef (US cents/pound)													
Australia-NZ (US Ports) *	193	118.74	105.82	86.50	80.97	84.17	78.30	83.14	87.79	96.54	95.40	89.74	113.91
Argentina (frozen)	213	147.31	111.55	102.34	82.14	87.83	114.38	100.56	99.28	80.58	....	....	....
Butter (US cents/pound)													
New Zealand	196	979.37	337.74	397.17	1,238.31	1,004.72	964.94	827.53	767.92	813.12	685.28	809.60	1,049.83
Coal (US $/MT)													
Australia	193	31.33	32.30	39.37	38.07	35.10	29.23	25.89	26.25	32.31	27.06	27.74	54.70
Australia	193	39.38	37.35	40.08	43.14	41.43	37.37	31.60	29.13	33.32	33.65	32.86	43.49
South Africa	199	26.96	28.56	35.23	33.52	31.35	26.84	24.27	26.57	33.86	26.01	29.97	54.69
Cocoa Beans (US $/MT)													
New York and London *	652	1,111.27	1,395.68	1,432.54	1,455.25	1,618.74	1,676.00	1,135.05	903.91	1,088.38	1,779.04	1,753.07	1,550.74
Coconut Oil (US $/MT)													
Philippines (New York) *	566	452.50	610.82	672.38	769.06	663.21	655.03	758.59	457.73	314.23	414.78	461.75	673.30
Philippines	566	416.21	559.83	616.30	719.91	623.44	598.64	716.07	445.89	294.47	373.28	425.55	602.67
Coffee (US cents/pound)													
Other Milds (New York) *	386	69.94	148.53	149.41	120.25	185.02	132.40	101.67	85.05	61.91	60.37	64.05	80.09
Brazil (New York)	223	66.58	143.32	145.98	120.29	166.80	121.81	88.92	79.80	50.50	45.03	50.78	69.24
Brazil	223	50.08	115.51	123.88	100.21	143.38	106.24	79.56	73.16	43.74	34.95	43.16	56.27
Uganda (New York) *	799	53.50	119.82	126.83	82.84	80.70	83.93	67.65	42.16	27.32	30.82	38.38	37.28
Copper (US $/MT)													
United Kingdom (London) *	112	1,914.96	2,305.53	2,932.04	2,293.39	2,275.19	1,653.71	1,572.53	1,814.52	1,580.17	1,560.29	1,779.36	2,863.47
Copra (US $/MT)													
Philippines (Europ. Ports)	566	295.42	416.84	438.50	488.98	433.75	411.03	462.27	308.92	195.55	265.93	299.45	451.13
Cotton (US cents/pound)													
Liverpool Index *	111	58.02	79.72	98.30	80.54	79.23	65.53	53.13	59.05	48.00	46.26	63.44	62.01
DAP (US $/MT)													
US Gulf Coast	111	129.11	172.79	216.59	213.16	199.92	203.42	177.78	154.22	147.73	157.53	179.41	221.25
Fish (US $/kilogram)													
Norway *	142	5.01	5.01	4.78	4.11	3.73	3.72	3.57	3.65	2.89	2.94	2.99	3.34
Fish Meal (US $/MT)													
Any Origin (Hamburg) *	293	404.53	403.17	521.48	629.27	645.95	709.00	433.11	452.10	530.05	645.54	650.20	692.88
Iceland	176	405.15	452.21	528.38	611.03	673.15	724.26	493.31	468.77	....	....	....	....
Gasoline (US cents/gallon)													
US Gulf Coast	111	50.86	47.90	50.92	59.65	58.53	41.30	51.84	83.37	73.41	72.05	87.17	117.03
Gold (US $/troy ounce)													
United Kingdom (London)	112	359.53	384.12	384.16	387.82	331.00	294.14	278.87	279.17	271.05	310.04	363.53	409.23
Groundnuts (US $/MT)													
Nigeria (London) *	694	927.64	921.03	816.67	810.11	874.21	795.10	762.64	785.51	753.25	654.93	855.90	910.00
Groundnut Oil (US $/MT)													
Any Origin (Europe) *	694	737.88	1,022.64	990.92	897.33	1,010.42	908.58	786.67	712.43	671.80	687.97	1,250.63	1,159.42
Hides (US cents/pound)													
United States (Chicago) *	111	80.03	86.81	88.14	87.32	88.25	76.69	72.15	80.22	84.60	80.75	68.30	67.13
Iron Ore (US cents/DMTU)													
Brazil (North Sea Ports) *	223	29.09	26.47	28.38	30.00	30.15	31.00	27.59	28.79	30.03	29.33	31.95	37.90
Jute (US $/MT)													
Bangladesh (Chitta.-Chalna)	513	271.25	295.67	365.67	454.25	302.00	259.08	275.67	278.83	329.58	290.75	241.96	280.63
Lamb (US cents/pound)													
New Zealand (London) *	196	124.13	125.66	113.26	145.44	150.28	116.00	115.84	112.85	130.25	146.04	159.81	165.77
Lead (US $/MT)													
United Kingdom (London) *	112	407.34	548.72	629.30	774.13	623.06	526.92	501.77	454.17	476.36	452.25	514.21	881.95
Linseed Oil (US $/MT)													
Any Origin	001	448.50	516.74	657.50	565.83	571.24	707.71	512.54	399.39	382.25	520.21	678.20	872.75
Maize (US $/MT)													
United States (US Gulf Pts) *	111	102.04	107.78	123.45	164.52	117.17	101.62	90.29	88.22	89.61	99.33	105.19	111.78
Thailand	578	134.24	162.64	202.15	297.67	280.16	154.60	143.86	313.34	111.89	181.51	184.61	145.85
Natural Gas (US $/000 M³)													
Russian Federation	922	93.54	83.25	97.06	99.00	96.13	80.82	65.05	124.34	139.44	95.99	125.51	135.18
Indonesia	536	75.69	69.12	74.83	82.11	79.13	57.95	70.33	110.14	98.24	93.14	104.80	123.95
United States	111	76.11	68.94	61.36	96.82	88.57	75.16	81.40	155.07	142.53	120.99	197.83	212.69
Newsprint (US $/short ton)													
Finland	172	377.58	401.99	605.05	650.84	470.85	453.66	....	....	....	....	....	....
Nickel (US $/MT)													
United Kingdom(N.Europ.Ports)*	156	5,308.17	6,331.93	8,223.56	7,504.09	6,924.72	4,623.59	6,002.51	8,630.52	5,969.63	6,783.31	9,630.29	13,821.01
Olive Oil (US $/MT)													
United Kingdom *	112	2,703.64	3,148.84	4,499.51	5,965.18	4,236.48	3,227.05	3,650.44	2,980.12	2,667.28	2,900.51	3,796.77	4,630.94
Oranges (US $/MT)													
French Import Price *	132	432.49	411.34	531.47	491.67	458.96	442.40	438.23	363.21	595.50	564.53	683.05	854.55
Palm Kernel Oil(US $/MT)													
Malaysia (Rotterdam)	548	437.84	627.75	677.67	727.97	651.83	686.93	695.03	448.72	308.86	416.47	458.49	640.71
Palm Oil (US $/MT)													
Malaysia (N.W.Europe)*	548	312.14	437.27	537.62	467.15	490.43	600.85	377.28	261.14	238.40	356.75	410.37	434.72
Malaysia	548	383.06	484.21	623.66	509.38	506.51	603.02	424.93	295.36	248.32	359.56	425.80	441.23
Pepper (US cents/pound)													
Singapore	576	104.90	139.41	171.86	167.71	286.88	322.29	309.58	196.93	112.28	104.49	127.71	116.45

Commodity Prices

		1993	1994	1995	1996	1997	1998	1999	2000	2001	2002	2003	2004
		Market Prices (lines 76) and Unit Values (lines 74) Country of Origin and, for Market Prices, Pricing Point in Parentheses											
Petroleum, spot (US$/barrel)													
Average crude price *	001	16.79	15.95	17.20	20.37	19.27	13.07	17.98	28.23	24.33	24.95	28.89	37.76
Dubai Fateh *	466	14.91	14.83	16.13	18.54	18.10	12.09	17.08	26.09	22.71	23.73	26.73	33.46
U.K. Brent *	112	17.00	15.83	17.06	20.45	19.12	12.72	17.70	28.31	24.41	25.00	28.85	38.30
West Texas Intermediate *	111	18.46	17.18	18.43	22.13	20.59	14.42	19.17	30.32	25.87	26.12	31.10	41.45
Phosphate Rock (US $/MT)													
Morocco (Casablanca)	686	33.00	33.00	35.00	39.00	40.83	43.00	44.00	43.75	41.84	41.00	40.50	40.98
Potash (US $/MT)													
Canada (Vancouver)	156	107.42	105.72	117.76	116.93	116.53	116.89	121.64	122.50	118.08	113.32	113.28	124.56
Poultry (US cents/pound)													
United States (Georgia) *	111	54.68	55.29	55.48	62.31	60.99	63.16	59.97	59.45	63.63	63.08	66.21	75.73
Plywood (US cents/sheet)													
Philippines (Tokyo)	566	661.42	599.50	584.44	529.52	484.96	374.56	440.56	448.23	409.65	402.75	436.08	464.83
Pulp (US $/MT)													
Sweden (North Sea Ports)	144	423.91	552.46	853.45	574.12	554.87	508.77	500.14	664.63	518.71	452.21	521.42	634.49
Rice (US $/MT)													
Thailand (Bangkok) *	578	237.25	269.46	320.80	338.06	302.47	305.42	248.97	203.69	172.71	191.83	199.46	245.78
Thailand	578	257.18	484.96	314.85	366.67	216.85	321.01	264.11	265.95	205.82	222.39	248.73	269.76
Rubber (US cents/pound)													
Malaysia (Singapore) *	548	37.71	51.07	71.68	63.59	46.16	32.73	28.83	30.30	26.09	34.70	49.12	59.17
Malaysia	548	40.09	49.75	72.17	64.55	47.04	33.06	29.03	31.38	27.40	32.70	45.22	54.17
Thailand	578	35.07	44.08	63.81	59.04	43.30	30.41	23.79	27.02	23.51	28.28	40.74	47.21
Shrimp (US $/pound)													
United States (U.S. Gulf Ports) *	111	5.16	5.93	15.72	14.39	15.78	16.55	14.93	17.22	12.95	12.06	11.51	10.39
Silver (US cents/troy ounce)													
United States (New York)	111	429.8	528.4	519.2	518.3	489.2	553.4	525.0	499.9	438.6	462.5	491.1	669.1
Sisal (US $/MT)													
East Africa (Europe)	639	615.42	604.58	710.42	868.25	777.50	821.33	695.75	628.67	699.00	659.92	698.42	862.08
Sorghum (US $/MT)													
United States (US Gulf Ports)	111	99.03	103.87	118.97	150.03	109.62	98.04	84.39	88.00	95.23	101.75	106.54	109.80
Soybeans (US $/MT)													
United States (Rotterdam) *	111	230.17	229.58	224.17	277.42	280.67	223.17	174.92	183.00	168.75	188.75	233.25	276.83
Soybean Meal (US $/MT)													
United States (Rotterdam) *	111	216.50	198.83	198.58	266.42	279.83	174.58	152.42	187.08	180.75	183.92	214.58	257.17
Soybean Oil (US $/MT)													
All Origins (Dutch Ports) *	111	503.13	603.04	584.69	544.23	525.84	562.49	392.40	351.81	347.00	409.84	500.29	590.45
Sugar (US cents/pound)													
EU Import Price *	112	28.10	28.20	31.21	31.15	28.38	27.13	26.84	25.16	23.88	24.91	27.09	30.38
Free Market *	001	10.02	12.11	13.28	11.96	11.40	8.92	6.27	8.08	8.23	6.24	6.92	7.55
U.S. Import Price *	111	21.61	22.03	23.06	22.36	21.93	22.06	21.14	19.40	21.34	20.94	21.50	20.57
Philippines	566	14.13	15.36	19.72	19.30	22.28	19.21	21.14	16.14	17.64	18.14	18.99	13.12
Sunflower Oil (US $/MT)													
EU (NW European ports) *	112	682.17	723.53	631.71	560.39	556.89	665.23	466.46	379.33	436.11	605.83	650.00	734.41
Superphosphate (US $/MT)													
United States (US Gulf Ports)	111	111.95	132.11	149.63	175.83	171.91	173.67	154.50	137.72	126.88	133.07	149.34	186.31
Swine Meat (US cents/pound)													
United States (Iowa) *	111	64.52	56.41	62.80	92.49	72.86	45.62	44.41	59.29	61.43	47.26	53.40	71.01
Tea (US cents/kg)													
Average Auction (London) *	112	185.64	183.32	74.46	80.36	107.59	108.21	105.40	112.55	89.87	81.28	88.15	89.88
Sri Lanka	524	188.66	184.77	199.64	252.46	268.48	286.82	229.90	239.43	233.78	226.30	237.99	246.38
Timber (US $/cubic meter)													
Hardwood Logs													
Malaysia, Sarawak *	548	388.98	316.32	257.68	252.15	237.74	162.86	187.02	190.06	159.87	162.40	187.11	197.40
Hardwood Sawnwood													
Malaysia *	548	758.24	821.44	740.19	740.89	662.33	484.16	601.11	599.18	488.26	518.38	550.20	582.77
Softwood Logs													
United States *	111	217.94	201.23	193.84	204.07	185.31	159.10	164.55	180.78	157.73	145.92	145.57	173.68
Softwood Sawnwood													
United States *	111	277.44	299.55	300.62	309.91	294.13	279.81	300.55	284.81	282.83	273.25	284.30	323.98
Tin (US $/MT)													
Any Origin (London) *	112	5,167.55	5,459.98	6,197.36	6,158.88	5,640.48	5,536.23	5,391.40	5,435.90	4,489.44	4,061.00	4,889.65	8,480.94
Malaysia	548	5,342.31	5,318.29	6,180.62	6,168.86	5,339.01	5,517.63	5,374.75	5,549.34	4,446.94	4,135.67	4,931.50	8,313.21
Bolivia	218	5,180.55	5,405.45	6,187.31	6,306.34	3,846.06	3,711.16	3,638.32	3,712.68	3,387.58	2,759.03	3,165.37	5,574.95
Thailand	578	5,122.65	5,479.86	6,091.70	6,143.43	5,632.28	5,470.51	5,259.14	5,337.72	4,298.25	4,065.75	4,806.09	8,455.67
Tobacco (US $/MT)													
United States (All Markets) *	111	2,695.34	2,641.66	2,643.44	3,056.73	3,531.81	3,336.12	3,101.45	2,988.17	2,989.02	2,733.62	....	....
Uranium (US $/pound)													
Restricted *	001	10.08	9.42	11.67	15.60	12.10	10.39	10.02	8.29	8.62	9.83	11.24	18.05
Urea (US $/MT)													
Ukraine	926	....	....	187.21	179.00	114.00	83.08	66.40	101.12	95.32	94.36	138.90	175.29
Wheat (US $/MT)													
Australia	193	136.58	128.75	189.78	214.17	168.79	144.97	129.36	124.72	144.04	152.90	165.55	167.09
United States (US Gulf Pts) *	111	140.21	149.78	176.96	207.14	159.67	126.10	112.05	114.00	126.80	148.53	146.14	156.88
Argentina	213	127.05	129.50	145.46	179.98	153.15	125.12	113.83	110.55	120.56	121.22	152.45	140.04
Wool (US cents/kilogram)													
Australia-NZ(UK) 48's *	112	319.73	399.59	497.14	428.88	442.79	336.39	276.47	280.98	332.43	565.65	658.99	553.20
Australia-NZ(UK) 64's *	112	463.26	745.33	775.31	651.59	759.84	552.81	619.25	733.54	623.44	644.41	702.04	713.28
Australia (greasy wool)	193	240.38	323.18	395.82	325.53	358.97	274.66	238.06	252.51	258.15	373.95	429.00	397.07
Zinc (US $/MT)													
United Kingdom (London) *	112	963.96	998.22	1,031.09	1,024.98	1,314.90	1,024.29	1,075.80	1,127.70	886.82	778.90	827.97	1,048.04
Bolivia	218	962.68	988.05	1,037.23	1,013.71	781.46	603.80	630.35	672.84	549.21	462.51	438.64	614.92

Commodity Prices

		1993	1994	1995	1996	1997	1998	1999	2000	2001	2002	2003	2004
		Indices of Market Prices (lines 76) and of Unit Values (lines 74)											
							2000=100						
All Primary Commodities	001	77.0	79.0	86.0	92.1	88.2	68.3	75.4	100.0	91.2	91.1	103.0	130.4
Non-Fuel Primary Commodities	001	104.2	115.5	125.7	123.8	120.2	102.8	95.7	100.0	95.9	96.7	103.5	122.8
Food	001	115.5	119.2	126.6	137.4	125.6	111.7	97.6	100.0	100.1	103.6	108.9	124.5
Beverages	001	93.3	153.4	154.2	131.4	172.2	149.6	117.8	100.0	83.9	97.7	102.5	105.6
Agricultural Raw Materials	001	108.5	119.7	123.7	119.2	113.5	94.6	95.8	100.0	95.1	96.7	100.4	105.9
Metals	001	86.9	100.9	122.1	108.3	109.6	90.1	89.1	100.0	90.2	87.7	98.4	134.0
Energy	001	61.9	58.8	64.0	74.5	70.4	49.2	64.1	100.0	88.5	88.0	102.8	134.5
World Bank LMICs	200	105.4	128.8	140.8	132.5	135.4	114.2	101.6	100.0	90.9	95.7	105.1	123.7
Aluminum (US $/MT)													
All Origins (London) *	156	73.5	95.1	116.3	97.1	103.1	87.5	87.7	100.0	93.2	87.1	92.4	110.8
Bananas (US $/MT)													
Latin America (US Ports) *	248	104.9	104.1	105.4	111.2	123.7	116.6	88.5	100.0	138.5	124.9	88.9	124.3
Barley (US $/MT)													
Canada (Winnepeg) *	156	92.4	94.1	134.7	154.9	125.9	110.1	98.3	100.0	121.6	141.1	135.6	128.2
Beef (US cents/pound)													
Australia-NZ (US Ports) *	193	135.3	120.5	98.5	92.2	95.9	89.2	94.7	100.0	110.0	108.7	102.2	129.8
Argentina (frozen)	213	148.4	112.4	103.1	82.7	88.5	115.2	101.3	100.0	81.2	....	....	....
Butter (US cents/pound)													
New Zealand	196	127.5	44.0	51.7	161.3	130.8	125.7	107.8	100.0	105.9	89.2	105.4	136.7
Coal (US $/MT)													
Australia	193	119.4	123.0	150.0	145.0	133.7	111.4	98.6	100.0	123.1	103.1	105.7	208.4
Australia	193	135.2	128.2	137.6	148.1	142.2	128.3	108.5	100.0	114.4	115.5	112.8	149.3
South Africa	199	101.5	107.5	132.6	126.1	118.0	101.0	91.4	100.0	127.5	97.9	112.8	205.8
Cocoa Beans (US $/MT)													
New York and London *	652	122.9	154.4	158.5	161.0	179.1	185.4	125.6	100.0	120.4	196.8	193.9	171.6
Coconut Oil (US $/MT)													
Philippines (New York) *	566	98.9	133.4	146.9	168.0	144.9	143.1	165.7	100.0	68.6	90.6	100.9	147.1
Philippines	566	93.3	125.6	138.2	161.5	139.8	134.3	160.6	100.0	66.0	83.7	95.4	135.2
Coffee (US cents/pound)													
Other Milds (New York) *	386	82.2	174.6	175.7	141.4	217.6	155.7	119.6	100.0	72.8	71.0	75.3	94.2
Brazil (New York)	223	83.4	179.6	182.9	150.7	209.0	152.6	111.4	100.0	63.3	56.4	63.6	86.8
Brazil	223	68.5	157.9	169.3	137.0	196.0	145.2	108.8	100.0	59.8	47.8	59.0	76.9
Uganda (New York) *	799	126.9	284.2	300.8	196.5	191.4	199.1	160.5	100.0	64.8	73.1	91.0	88.4
Copper (US $/MT)													
United Kingdom (London) *	112	105.5	127.1	161.6	126.4	125.4	91.1	86.7	100.0	87.1	86.0	98.1	157.8
Copra (US $/MT)													
Philippines (Europ. Ports)	566	95.6	134.9	141.9	158.3	140.4	133.1	149.6	100.0	63.3	86.1	96.9	146.0
Cotton (US cents/pound)													
Liverpool Index *	111	98.3	135.0	166.5	136.4	134.2	111.0	90.0	100.0	81.3	78.3	107.4	105.0
DAP (US $/MT)													
US Gulf Coast	111	83.7	112.0	140.4	138.2	129.6	131.9	115.3	100.0	95.8	102.1	116.3	143.5
Fish (US $/kilogram)													
Norway *	142	137.5	137.5	131.0	112.8	102.2	102.0	97.9	100.0	79.3	80.6	82.1	91.7
Fish Meal (US $/MT)													
Any Origin (Hamburg) *	293	89.5	89.2	115.3	139.2	142.9	156.8	95.8	100.0	117.2	142.8	143.8	153.3
Iceland	176	86.4	96.5	112.7	130.3	143.6	154.5	105.2	100.0	....	....	....	....
Gasoline (US cents/gallon)													
US Gulf Coast	111	61.0	57.5	61.1	71.5	70.2	49.5	62.2	100.0	88.0	86.4	104.6	140.4
Gold (US $/troy ounce)													
United Kingdom (London)	112	128.8	137.6	137.6	138.9	118.6	105.4	99.9	100.0	97.1	111.1	130.2	146.6
Groundnuts (US $/MT)													
Nigeria (London) *	694	118.1	117.3	104.0	103.1	111.3	101.2	97.1	100.0	95.9	83.4	109.0	115.8
Groundnut Oil (US $/MT)													
Any Origin (Europe) *	694	103.6	143.5	139.1	126.0	141.8	127.5	110.4	100.0	94.3	96.6	175.5	162.7
Hides (US cents/pound)													
United States (Chicago) *	111	99.8	108.2	109.9	108.8	110.0	95.6	89.9	100.0	105.5	100.7	85.1	83.7
Iron Ore (US cents/DMTU)													
Brazil (North Sea Ports) *	223	101.0	91.9	98.6	104.2	104.7	107.7	95.8	100.0	104.3	101.9	111.0	131.6
Jute (US $/MT)													
Bangladesh (Chitta.-Chalna)	513	97.3	106.0	131.1	162.9	108.3	92.9	98.9	100.0	118.2	104.3	86.8	100.6
Lamb (US cents/pound)													
New Zealand (London) *	196	110.0	111.3	100.4	128.9	133.2	102.8	102.7	100.0	115.4	129.4	141.6	146.9
Lead (US $/MT)													
United Kingdom (London) *	112	89.7	120.8	138.6	170.4	137.2	116.0	110.5	100.0	104.8	99.6	113.2	194.2
Linseed Oil (US $/MT)													
Any Origin	001	112.3	129.4	164.6	141.7	143.0	177.2	128.3	100.0	95.7	130.3	169.8	218.5
Maize (US $/MT)													
United States (US Gulf Pts) *	111	115.7	122.2	139.9	186.5	132.8	115.2	102.4	100.0	101.6	112.6	119.2	126.7
Thailand	578	42.8	51.9	64.5	95.0	89.4	49.3	45.9	100.0	35.7	57.9	58.9	46.5
Natural Gas (US $/000 M³)													
Russian Federation	922	75.2	67.0	78.1	79.6	77.3	65.0	52.3	100.0	112.1	77.2	100.9	108.7
Indonesia	536	68.7	62.8	67.9	74.5	71.8	52.6	63.8	100.0	89.2	84.6	95.1	112.5
United States	111	49.1	44.5	39.6	62.4	57.1	48.5	52.5	100.0	91.9	78.0	127.6	137.2
Newsprint (US $/short ton)													
Finland (1995=100)	172	62.4	66.4	100.0	107.6	77.8	75.0	....	....	....	....	....	....
Nickel (US $/MT)													
United Kingdom(N.Europ.Ports)*	156	61.5	73.4	95.3	86.9	80.2	53.6	69.5	100.0	69.2	78.6	111.6	160.1
Olive Oil (US $/MT)													
United Kingdom *	112	90.7	105.7	151.0	200.2	142.2	108.3	122.5	100.0	89.5	97.3	127.4	155.4
Oranges (US $/MT)													
French Import Price *	132	119.1	113.3	146.3	135.4	126.4	121.8	120.7	100.0	164.0	155.4	188.1	235.3

Commodity Prices

2005, International Monetary Fund : *International Financial Statistics Yearbook*

		1993	1994	1995	1996	1997	1998	1999	2000	2001	2002	2003	2004
		Indices of Market Prices (lines 76) and of Unit Values (lines 74) 2000=100											
Palm Kernel Oil(US $/MT)													
Malaysia (Rotterdam)	548	97.6	139.9	151.0	162.2	145.3	153.1	154.9	100.0	68.8	92.8	102.2	142.8
Palm Oil (US $/MT)													
Malaysia (N.W.Europe)*	548	119.5	167.4	205.9	178.9	187.8	230.1	144.5	100.0	91.3	136.6	157.1	166.5
Malaysia	548	129.7	163.9	211.1	172.5	171.5	204.2	143.9	100.0	84.1	121.7	144.2	149.4
Pepper (US cents/pound)													
Malaysia (New York)	548	53.4	70.8	87.3	85.2	145.7	163.7	157.2	100.0	57.0	53.1	64.6	59.1
Singapore	576	53.3	70.8	87.3	85.2	145.7	163.7	157.2	100.0	57.0	53.1	64.8	59.1
Petroleum,spot (US$/barrel)													
Average crude price *	001	59.5	56.5	60.9	72.2	68.2	46.3	63.7	100.0	86.2	88.4	102.3	133.7
Dubai Fateh *	466	57.1	56.9	61.8	71.1	69.4	46.3	65.5	100.0	87.1	91.0	102.5	128.3
U.K. Brent *	112	60.0	55.9	60.3	72.3	67.5	44.9	62.5	100.0	86.2	88.3	101.9	135.3
West Texas Intermediate *	111	60.9	56.7	60.8	73.0	67.9	47.6	63.2	100.0	85.3	86.1	102.6	136.7
Phosphate Rock (US $/MT)													
Morocco (Casablanca)	686	75.4	75.4	80.0	89.1	93.3	98.3	100.6	100.0	95.6	93.7	92.6	93.7
Potash (US $/MT)													
Canada (Vancouver)	156	87.7	86.3	96.1	95.5	95.1	95.4	99.3	100.0	96.4	92.5	92.5	101.7
Poultry (US cents/pound)													
United States (Georgia) *	111	92.0	93.0	93.3	104.8	102.6	106.2	100.9	100.0	107.0	106.1	111.4	127.4
Plywood (US cents/sheet)													
Philippines (Tokyo)	566	147.6	133.7	130.4	118.1	108.2	83.6	98.3	100.0	91.4	89.9	97.3	103.7
Pulp (US $/MT)													
Sweden (North Sea Ports)	144	63.8	83.1	128.4	86.4	83.5	76.5	75.3	100.0	78.0	68.0	78.5	95.5
Rice (US $/MT)													
Thailand (Bangkok) *	578	116.5	132.3	157.5	166.0	148.5	149.9	122.2	100.0	84.8	94.2	97.9	120.7
Thailand	578	96.7	182.3	118.4	137.9	81.5	120.7	99.3	100.0	77.4	83.6	93.5	101.4
Rubber (US cents/pound)													
Malaysia (Singapore) *	548	124.4	168.5	236.6	209.9	152.3	108.0	95.2	100.0	86.1	114.5	162.1	195.3
Malaysia	548	127.7	158.5	230.0	205.7	149.9	105.3	92.5	100.0	87.3	104.2	144.1	172.6
Thailand	578	129.8	163.1	236.1	218.5	160.2	112.5	88.1	100.0	87.0	104.7	150.8	174.7
Shrimp (US $/pound)													
United States(U.S. Gulf Ports)*	111	30.0	34.5	91.3	83.6	91.7	96.2	86.7	100.0	75.2	70.1	66.9	60.4
Silver (US cents/troy ounce)													
United States (New York)	111	86.0	105.7	103.9	103.7	97.9	110.7	105.0	100.0	87.7	92.5	98.2	133.8
Sisal (US $/MT)													
East Africa (Europe)	639	97.9	96.2	113.0	138.1	123.7	130.6	110.7	100.0	111.2	105.0	111.1	137.1
Sorghum (US $/MT)													
United States (US Gulf Ports)	111	112.5	118.0	135.2	170.5	124.6	111.4	95.9	100.0	108.2	115.6	121.1	124.8
Soybeans (US $/MT)													
United States (Rotterdam) *	111	125.8	125.5	122.5	151.6	153.4	121.9	95.6	100.0	92.2	103.1	127.5	151.3
Soybean Meal (US $/MT)													
United States (Rotterdam) *	111	115.7	106.3	106.1	142.4	149.6	93.3	81.5	100.0	96.6	98.3	114.7	137.5
Soybean Oil (US $/MT)													
All Origins (Dutch Ports) *	111	143.0	171.4	166.2	154.7	149.5	159.9	111.5	100.0	98.6	116.5	142.2	167.8
Sugar (US cents/pound)													
EU Import Price *	112	111.7	112.1	124.0	123.8	112.8	107.8	106.7	100.0	94.9	99.0	107.6	120.7
Free Market *	001	124.0	149.9	164.4	148.0	141.1	110.4	77.5	100.0	101.9	77.2	85.7	93.4
U.S. Import Price *	111	111.4	113.6	118.9	115.3	113.1	113.8	109.0	100.0	110.0	108.0	110.8	106.1
Philippines	566	87.6	95.1	122.2	119.6	138.0	119.0	130.9	100.0	109.3	112.4	117.6	81.3
Sunflower Oil (US $/MT)													
EU (NW European ports) *	112	179.8	190.7	166.5	147.7	146.8	175.4	123.0	100.0	115.0	159.7	171.4	193.6
Superphosphate (US $/MT)													
United States (US Gulf Ports)	111	81.3	95.9	108.7	127.7	124.8	126.1	112.2	100.0	92.1	96.6	108.4	135.3
Swine Meat (US cents/pound)													
United States (Iowa) *	111	108.8	95.1	105.9	156.0	122.9	76.9	74.9	100.0	103.6	79.7	90.1	119.8
Tea (US cents/kg)													
Average Auction (London) *	112	164.9	162.9	66.2	71.4	95.5	96.1	93.6	100.0	79.9	72.2	78.3	79.9
Sri Lanka	524	78.8	77.2	83.4	105.4	112.1	119.8	96.0	100.0	97.6	94.5	99.4	102.9
Timber (US $/cubic meter)													
Hardwood Logs													
Malaysia, Sarawak *	548	204.7	166.4	135.6	132.7	125.1	85.7	98.4	100.0	84.1	85.4	98.4	103.9
Hardwood Sawnwood													
Malaysia *	548	126.5	137.1	123.5	123.7	110.5	80.8	100.3	100.0	81.5	86.5	91.8	97.3
Softwood Logs													
United States *	111	120.6	111.3	107.2	112.9	102.5	88.0	91.0	100.0	87.2	80.7	80.5	96.1
Softwood Sawnwood													
United States *	111	97.4	105.2	105.6	108.8	103.3	98.2	105.5	100.0	99.3	95.9	99.8	113.8
Tin (US $/MT)													
Any Origin (London) *	112	95.1	100.4	114.0	113.3	103.8	101.8	99.2	100.0	82.6	74.7	90.0	156.0
Malaysia	548	96.3	95.8	111.4	111.2	96.2	99.4	96.9	100.0	80.1	74.5	88.9	149.8
Bolivia	218	139.5	145.6	166.7	169.9	103.6	100.0	98.0	100.0	91.2	74.3	85.3	150.2
Thailand	578	96.0	102.7	114.1	115.1	105.5	102.5	98.5	100.0	80.5	76.2	90.0	158.4
Tobacco (US $/MT)													
United States (All Markets)	111	90.2	88.4	88.5	102.3	118.2	111.6	103.8	100.0	100.0	91.5	. . . .	. . . .
Uranium (US $/pound)													
Restricted *	001	121.6	113.7	140.8	188.3	146.0	125.4	120.9	100.0	104.0	118.6	135.6	217.8
Urea (US $/MT)													
Ukraine	926	. . . .	. . . .	185.1	177.0	112.7	82.2	65.7	100.0	94.3	93.3	137.4	173.4
Wheat (US $/MT)													
Australia	193	109.5	103.2	152.2	171.7	135.3	116.2	103.7	100.0	115.5	122.6	132.7	134.0
United States (US Gulf Pts) *	111	123.0	131.4	155.2	181.7	140.1	110.6	98.3	100.0	111.2	130.3	128.2	137.6
Argentina	213	114.9	117.1	131.6	162.8	138.5	113.2	103.0	100.0	109.1	109.7	137.9	126.7

Commodity Prices

		1993	1994	1995	1996	1997	1998	1999	2000	2001	2002	2003	2004
				Indices of Market Prices (lines 76) and of Unit Values (lines 74)									
						2000=100							
Wool (US cents/kilogram)													
Australia-NZ(UK) 48's *	112	113.8	142.2	176.9	152.6	157.6	119.7	98.4	100.0	118.3	201.3	234.5	196.9
Australia-NZ(UK) 64's *	112	63.2	101.6	105.7	88.8	103.6	75.4	84.4	100.0	85.0	87.8	95.7	97.2
Australia (greasy wool)	193	95.2	128.0	156.8	128.9	142.2	108.8	94.3	100.0	102.2	148.1	169.9	157.2
Zinc (US $/MT)													
United Kingdom (London) *	112	85.5	88.5	91.4	90.9	116.6	90.8	95.4	100.0	78.6	69.1	73.4	92.9
Bolivia	218	143.1	146.8	154.2	150.7	116.1	89.7	93.7	100.0	81.6	68.7	65.2	91.4

COUNTRY TABLES

Albania 914

		1993	1994	1995	1996	1997	1998	1999	2000	2001	2002	2003	2004
Exchange Rates						*Leks per SDR: End of Period*							
Market Rate	aa	135.57	139.55	140.09	148.21	201.23	197.94	185.45	185.85	171.61	181.82	158.37	143.87
						Leks per US Dollar: End of Period (ae) Period Average (rf)							
Market Rate	ae	98.70	95.59	94.24	103.07	149.14	140.58	135.12	142.64	136.55	133.74	106.58	92.64
Market Rate	rf	102.06	94.62	92.70	104.50	148.93	150.63	137.69	143.71	143.48	140.15	121.86	....
Fund Position						*Millions of SDRs: End of Period*							
Quota	2f.s	35.30	35.30	35.30	35.30	35.30	35.30	48.70	48.70	48.70	48.70	48.70	48.70
SDRs	1b.s	.01	.20	.10	.52	.46	43.39	56.06	58.33	64.87	60.02	60.98	64.90
Reserve Position in the Fund	1c.s	.01	.01	.01	.01	.01	.01	3.36	3.36	3.36	3.36	3.35	3.35
Total Fund Cred.&Loans Outstg	2tl	21.60	37.13	43.40	37.70	40.74	45.77	58.69	67.47	66.25	59.63	60.83	62.43
International Liquidity						*Millions of US Dollars Unless Otherwise Indicated: End of Period*							
Total Reserves minus Gold	1l.d	147.42	204.80	241.05	280.86	308.93	384.22	488.30	615.65	739.90	838.78	1,009.42	1,357.68
SDRs	1b.d	.01	.30	.14	.75	.62	61.10	76.95	76.00	81.52	81.60	90.61	100.79
Reserve Position in the Fund	1c.d	.01	.01	.01	.01	.01	.01	4.60	4.37	4.22	4.56	4.99	5.21
Foreign Exchange	1d.d	147.40	204.50	240.90	280.10	308.30	323.12	406.75	535.27	654.17	752.62	913.83	1,251.68
Gold (Million Fine Troy Ounces)	1ad	.05	.05	.06	.12	.12	.12	.12	.11	.11	.08	.07	.07
Gold (National Valuation)	1and	19.41	20.85	24.30	42.50	33.40	33.70	34.50	30.40	30.70	27.68	28.86	30.25
Monetary Authorities						*Billions of Leks: End of Period*							
Foreign Assets	11	....	22.65	46.76	57.02	85.21	91.04	71.08	92.34	104.90	114.63	109.77	127.56
Claims on Central Government	12a	....	69.33	45.69	52.14	85.48	77.56	74.72	82.49	74.14	78.58	74.30	65.63
Claims on Banks	12e	....	3.42	3.31	3.37	7.44	7.00	6.69	6.63	6.73	10.72	.42	.28
Reserve Money	14	....	42.07	53.88	61.39	90.93	89.89	109.31	128.78	152.14	163.89	160.55	178.60
of which: Currency Outside Banks	14a	....	27.63	41.91	47.81	72.73	68.32	81.34	99.24	119.08	130.78	125.19	138.10
Other Liabilities to Banks	14n	....	—	—	—	—	2.44	.79	5.23	—	—	1.21	2.26
Foreign Liabilities	16c	....	59.41	33.65	36.81	53.85	55.11	24.15	20.48	18.94	19.65	11.45	10.53
Central Government Deposits	16d	....	3.75	4.27	3.25	5.62	5.39	5.85	7.62	4.20	5.90	8.82	7.97
Capital Accounts	17a	....	14.26	10.61	16.83	31.43	38.56	14.82	21.52	20.92	27.49	14.31	3.43
Other Items (Net)	17r	....	−24.08	−6.64	−4.99	−3.00	−15.14	−1.85	−2.10	−10.36	−12.98	−11.85	−9.33
Banking Institutions						*Billions of Leks: End of Period*							
Reserves	20	....	11.93	10.30	12.90	16.44	21.57	28.15	30.16	33.81	32.02	35.21	40.69
Other Claims on Monetary Author	20n	....	—	—	—	1.40	2.44	.79	5.15	† —	—	1.20	2.26
Foreign Assets	21	....	16.94	23.47	35.44	38.96	49.97	57.97	65.05	83.36	81.33	77.60	71.38
Claims on Central Government	22a	....	86.55	108.52	142.51	108.30	125.45	147.34	156.15	† 170.30	175.98	205.43	221.68
Claims on Nonfin.Pub.Enterprises	22c	....	3.25	3.09	3.41	2.83	2.83	1.67	1.48	1.68	1.16	1.13	1.24
Claims on Private Sector	22d	....	7.20	8.35	10.89	13.01	14.86	18.22	24.41	34.94	46.17	58.14	76.86
Demand Deposits	24	....	11.14	17.35	42.59	18.94	15.41	21.67	24.81	23.94	21.90	19.54	34.73
Time and Savings Deposits	25a	....	18.70	28.12	30.24	70.55	115.53	136.66	140.46	162.25	171.99	204.78	218.58
Foreign Currency Deposits	25b	....	13.30	20.08	33.91	36.33	40.26	53.21	63.60	88.13	91.96	98.91	115.80
Foreign Liabilities	26c	....	1.82	1.14	1.22	2.02	2.87	4.83	6.83	12.05	15.49	17.22	15.55
Central Government Deposits	26d	....	68.05	75.92	80.41	25.80	1.05	.80	1.46	2.25	.82	.86	.65
Credit from Monetary Authorities	26g	....	.65	—	1.69	3.64	4.73	1.44	5.81	† 1.05	3.98	.66	.83
Capital Accounts	27a	....	10.37	12.01	16.70	21.85	26.46	27.00	34.17	34.43	38.13	38.52	42.83
Other Items (Net)	27r	....	1.84	−.89	−1.60	1.81	10.80	8.52	5.27	−.02	−7.60	−1.77	−14.84
Banking Survey						*Billions of Leks: End of Period*							
Foreign Assets (Net)	31n	....	−21.63	35.44	54.42	68.30	83.03	100.07	130.08	157.28	160.83	158.71	172.86
Domestic Credit	32	....	94.52	85.46	125.30	178.20	214.27	235.30	255.45	† 274.61	295.18	329.32	356.79
Claims on Central Govt. (Net)	32an	....	84.07	74.02	111.00	162.37	196.57	215.41	229.55	† 237.99	247.85	270.05	278.69
Claims on Nonfin.Pub.Enterprises	32c	....	3.25	3.09	3.41	2.83	2.83	1.67	1.48	1.68	1.16	1.13	1.24
Claims on Private Sector	32d	....	7.20	8.35	10.89	13.01	14.86	18.22	24.41	34.94	46.17	58.14	76.86
Money	34	....	38.77	59.25	90.41	91.67	83.73	103.00	124.04	143.03	152.67	144.73	172.83
Quasi-Money	35	....	32.01	48.20	64.15	106.88	155.80	189.87	204.06	250.39	263.94	303.70	334.37
Capital Accounts	37a	....	24.62	22.62	33.53	53.29	65.02	41.83	55.69	55.36	65.62	52.83	46.26
Other Items (Net)	37r	....	−22.50	−9.17	−7.60	−4.63	−6.60	1.25	1.81	† −16.81	−26.23	−13.23	−23.80
Money plus Quasi-Money	35l	....	70.77	107.45	154.55	198.55	239.53	292.87	328.10	393.41	416.62	448.43	507.20
Interest Rates						*Percent Per Annum*							
Bank Rate (End of Period)	60	34.00	25.00	20.50	24.00	32.00	23.44	18.00	10.82	7.00	8.50	6.50	5.25
Treasury Bill Rate	60c	....	....	13.84	17.81	32.59	27.49	17.54	10.80	7.72	9.49	8.81	6.79
Deposit Rate	60l	† 27.33	19.83	† 15.30	16.78	27.28	22.56	12.95	8.30	7.73	8.54	8.38	6.61
Lending Rate	60p	29.58	23.67	† 19.65	23.96	....	....	21.62	22.10	19.65	15.30	14.27	11.76
Prices and Labor						*Index Numbers (2000=100): Period Averages*							
Consumer Prices	64	41.6	51.0	55.0	62.0	82.5	99.6	100.0	100.0	† 103.1	111.1	111.7	114.2
						Number in Thousands: Period Averages							
Employment	67e	1,046	1,162	1,138	1,116	1,108	1,085	1,065	1,068	921	920	926	931
Unemployment	67c	301	262	171	158	194	235	240	215	181	172	166	159
Unemployment Rate (%)	67r	22.0	18.0	12.9	12.3	14.9	17.7	18.4	16.8	16.4	15.8	15.2	14.4
Intl. Transactions & Positions						*Millions of Leks*							
Exports	70	12,499	13,092	18,712	21,603	21,044	30,656	36,369	37,547	43,771	46,193	55,157	61,837
Imports, c.i.f	71	58,536	56,732	66,145	87,995	95,021	124,337	157,424	157,219	190,696	210,436	226,054	235,188

Albania 914

		1993	1994	1995	1996	1997	1998	1999	2000	2001	2002	2003	2004
Balance of Payments		*Millions of US Dollars: Minus Sign Indicates Debit*											
Current Account, n.i.e.	78ald	14.9	−157.3	−11.5	−107.3	−272.2	−65.1	−155.4	−156.3	−217.3	−407.5	−406.8	....
Goods: Exports f.o.b.	78aad	111.6	141.3	204.9	243.7	158.6	208.0	275.0	255.7	304.5	330.2	447.2	....
Goods: Imports f.o.b.	78abd	−601.5	−601.0	−679.7	−922.0	−693.6	−811.7	−938.0	−1,070.0	−1,331.6	−1,485.4	−1,783.5	....
Trade Balance	78acd	−489.9	−459.7	−474.8	−678.3	−535.0	−603.6	−663.0	−814.3	−1,027.1	−1,155.1	−1,336.3	....
Services: Credit	78add	77.6	79.1	98.8	129.2	63.8	86.6	269.4	447.8	534.3	585.0	719.7	....
Services: Debit	78aed	−161.9	−132.5	−156.5	−189.4	−115.2	−129.3	−163.1	−429.3	−444.1	−590.2	−802.6	....
Balance on Goods & Services	78afd	−574.2	−513.1	−532.5	−738.5	−586.4	−646.3	−556.7	−795.8	−936.9	−1,160.3	−1,419.2	....
Income: Credit	78agd	64.9	55.1	72.0	83.7	61.4	86.1	85.5	115.9	162.5	148.3	194.8	....
Income: Debit	78ahd	−31.0	−41.3	−28.4	−11.9	−11.8	−8.7	−10.2	−9.3	−13.5	−20.6	−24.4	....
Balance on Gds, Serv. & Inc	78aid	−540.3	−499.3	−488.9	−666.7	−536.8	−569.0	−481.4	−689.2	−787.9	−1,032.6	−1,248.8	....
Current Transfers, n.i.e.: Credit	78ajd	556.9	347.5	521.2	595.9	299.8	560.8	508.9	629.0	647.5	683.7	924.2	....
Current Transfers: Debit	78akd	−1.7	−5.5	−43.8	−36.5	−35.2	−56.9	−182.9	−96.1	−76.9	−58.6	−82.3	....
Capital Account, n.i.e.	78bcd	—	—	389.4	4.8	2.0	31.0	22.6	78.0	117.7	121.2	157.0	....
Capital Account, n.i.e.: Credit	78bad	—	—	389.4	4.8	2.0	31.0	22.6	78.0	117.7	121.2	157.0	....
Capital Account: Debit	78bbd	—	—	—	—	—	—	—	—	—	—	—	....
Financial Account, n.i.e.	78bjd	44.1	40.2	−411.0	61.5	151.4	15.4	33.7	188.4	110.0	213.4	200.6	....
Direct Investment Abroad	78bdd	—	—	....	....	....	....	....	....	....	....	....	....
Dir. Invest. in Rep. Econ., n.i.e.	78bed	58.0	53.0	70.0	90.1	47.5	45.0	41.2	143.0	207.3	135.0	178.0	....
Portfolio Investment Assets	78bfd	—	—	....	—	—	—	—	−25.0	−23.5	−36.8	−22.5	....
Equity Securities	78bkd	—	—	....	....	....	....	....	—	—	—	—	....
Debt Securities	78bld	—	—	....	....	....	....	....	−25.0	−23.5	−36.8	−22.5	....
Portfolio Investment Liab., n.i.e.	78bgd	—	—	....	—	—	—	—	—	—	—	—	....
Equity Securities	78bmd	—	—	....	....	....	....	....	—	—	—	—	....
Debt Securities	78bnd	—	—	....	....	....	....	....	—	—	—	—	....
Financial Derivatives Assets	78bwd	....	....	....	....	....	....	....	....	....	....	....	....
Financial Derivatives Liabilities	78bxd	....	....	....	....	....	....	....	....	....	....	....	....
Other Investment Assets	78bhd	−78.6	−97.3	−97.0	−138.6	59.8	−126.9	−130.1	−40.2	−197.2	−2.7	−71.6	....
Monetary Authorities	78bod	....	....	—	—	—	—	—	....	−1.8	2.2	.3	....
General Government	78bpd	....	....	....	....	....	....	....	....	....	....	....	....
Banks	78bqd	−25.5	−22.9	−68.4	−110.5	81.5	−91.2	−96.8	−2.5	−132.3	42.2	−45.3	....
Other Sectors	78brd	−53.1	−74.4	−28.6	−28.1	−21.7	−35.7	−33.3	−37.7	−63.1	−47.1	−26.7	....
Other Investment Liab., n.i.e.	78bid	64.7	84.5	−384.0	110.0	44.1	97.3	122.6	110.6	123.4	118.0	116.7	....
Monetary Authorities	78bsd	—	—	−9.1	10.4	16.0	10.4	8.9	−.2	−.3	.5	−1.0	....
General Government	78btd	50.5	74.6	−404.5	61.3	40.3	81.3	97.9	90.8	86.1	118.2	96.6	....
Banks	78bud	3.4	2.6	−3.3	4.0	−.6	3.5	16.0	5.2	42.1	10.9	19.8	....
Other Sectors	78bvd	10.8	7.3	32.9	34.3	−11.6	2.0	−.2	14.8	−4.5	−11.6	1.4	....
Net Errors and Omissions	78cad	−10.3	123.9	53.7	96.9	158.4	71.1	206.2	9.8	136.3	108.5	147.4	....
Overall Balance	78cbd	48.7	6.8	20.6	55.9	39.5	52.4	107.1	119.9	146.7	35.6	98.1	....
Reserves and Related Items	79dad	−48.7	−6.8	−20.6	−55.9	−39.5	−52.4	−107.1	−119.9	−146.7	−35.6	−98.1	....
Reserve Assets	79dbd	−114.9	−55.2	−30.5	−47.6	−43.7	−60.0	−124.7	−132.0	−145.1	−28.6	−99.6	....
Use of Fund Credit and Loans	79dcd	16.6	22.3	9.9	−8.3	4.2	6.8	17.5	12.1	−1.6	−8.5	1.5	....
Exceptional Financing	79ded	49.5	26.1	....	....	....	.8	.1	—	—	1.5	—	....
Government Finance		*Millions of Leks: Year Ending December 31*											
Deficit (-) or Surplus	80	....	....	−20,157	−34,689	−41,053	−38,972	....	....	....	....	....	....
Revenue	81	....	....	49,068	47,551	53,205	89,145	....	....	....	....	....	....
Grants Received	81z	....	....	598	722	2,304	9,005	....	....	....	....	....	....
Expenditure	82	....	....	69,687	83,553	97,472	137,254	....	....	....	....	....	....
Lending Minus Repayments	83	....	....	136	−591	−910	−132	....	....	....	....	....	....
Financing													
Domestic	84a	....	....	15,919	27,680	36,815	27,464	....	....	....	....	....	....
Foreign	85a	....	....	4,238	7,009	4,238	11,509	....	....	....	....	....	....
Debt: Domestic	88a	....	....	53,876	82,654	120,527	149,439	....	....	....	....	....	....
Foreign	89a	....	....	25,434	42,668	55,432	64,405	....	....	....	....	....	....
National Accounts		*Billions of Leks*											
Househ.Cons.Expend.,incl.NPISHs.	96f	....	....	....	211,984	287,801	346,775	334,801	350,038	359,016	363,864	....	....
Government Consumption Expend.	91f	....	....	....	30,539	34,871	40,222	43,703	47,020	56,050	63,666	....	....
Gross Fixed Capital Formation	93e	....	....	....	52,935	49,547	58,184	81,633	112,958	151,327	145,920	....	....
Changes in Inventories	93i	....	....	....	91,343	34,287	64,147	91,067	125,983	141,553	209,787	....	....
Exports of Goods and Services	90c	....	....	....	38,782	33,739	44,376	74,588	93,453	107,524	122,044	....	....
Imports of Goods and Services (-)	98c	....	....	....	110,934	118,365	141,738	151,910	199,036	227,507	276,081	....	....
Gross Domestic Product (GDP)	99b	125,334	184,393	229,793	314,879	322,186	412,327	474,291	530,906	588,664	630,000	....	....
GDP Volume 1986 Prices	99b.p	12,309	13,331	15,107	16,482	15,325	16,547	17,748	19,125	20,180	....	....	....
GDP Volume (2000=100)	99bvp	64.4	69.7	79.0	86.2	80.1	86.5	92.8	100.0	105.5	....	....	....
GDP Deflator (2000=100)	99bip	36.7	49.8	54.8	68.8	75.7	89.8	96.3	100.0	105.1	....	....	....
		Milliions: Midyear Estimates											
Population	99z	3.22	3.17	3.13	3.10	3.08	3.07	3.06	3.06	3.07	3.08	3.09	3.11

Algeria 612

		1993	1994	1995	1996	1997	1998	1999	2000	2001	2002	2003	2004
Exchange Rates		*Dinars per SDR: End of Period*											
Official Rate	aa	33.134	62.617	77.558	80.793	78.815	84.979	95.135	98.165	97.798	108.386	107.900	112.770
		Dinars per US Dollar: End of Period (ae) Period Average (rf)											
Official Rate	ae	24.123	42.893	52.175	56.186	58.414	60.353	69.314	75.343	77.820	79.723	72.613	72.614
Official Rate	rf	23.345	35.059	47.663	54.749	57.707	58.739	66.574	75.260	77.215	79.682	77.395	72.061
		Index Numbers (2000=100): Period Averages											
Nominal Effective Exchange Rate	nec	247.66	174.72	115.32	102.54	109.03	109.93	100.34	100.00	101.61	94.56	84.24	83.34
Real Effective Exchange Rate	rec	128.27	112.30	93.24	96.89	106.36	111.46	102.58	100.00	102.81	94.85	85.30	85.89
Fund Position		*Millions of SDRs: End of Period*											
Quota	2f.s	914	914	914	914	914	914	1,255	1,255	1,255	1,255	1,255	1,255
SDRs	1b.s	5	16	1	3	1	1	1	2	9	10	38	1
Reserve Position in the Fund	1c.s	—	—	—	—	—	—	85	85	85	85	85	85
Total Fund Cred.&Loans Outstg.	2tl	343	794	994	1,413	1,496	1,428	1,389	1,319	1,208	978	665	414
International Liquidity		*Millions of US Dollars Unless Otherwise Indicated: End of Period*											
Total Reserves minus Gold	1l.d	1,475	2,674	2,005	4,235	8,047	6,846	4,526	12,024	18,081	23,238	33,125	43,246
SDRs	1b.d	7	23	1	5	1	2	2	3	11	14	57	1
Reserve Position in the Fund	1c.d	—	—	—	—	—	—	117	111	107	116	126	132
Foreign Exchange	1d.d	1,468	2,651	2,004	4,230	8,046	6,844	4,407	11,910	17,963	23,108	32,942	43,113
Gold (Million Fine Troy Ounces)	1ad	5.58	5.58	5.58	5.58	5.58	5.58	5.58	5.58	5.58	5.58	5.58	5.58
Gold (National Valuation)	1and	268	285	290	281	264	275	268	255	246	266	290	303
Monetary Authorities:Other Assets	3..d	12	1	4	3	9	7	19	9	9	10	10	15
Other Liab	4..d	464	466	363	291	414	387	364	208	182	248	303	240
Deposit Money Banks: Assets	7a.d	683	1,046	638	576	396	456	402	376	416	624	765	1,060
Liabilities	7b.d	5,201	4,200	2,749	2,088	1,216	1,068	1,015	720	767	927	1,111	1,583
Monetary Authorities		*Billions of Dinars: End of Period*											
Foreign Assets	11	38.66	120.39	111.71	252.88	485.04	423.47	329.89	919.47	1,445.97	1,868.63	2,419.76	3,173.29
Claims on Central Government	12a	273.80	255.57	243.40	180.87	177.67	174.59	163.48	168.20	144.67	133.77	141.97	122.11
Claims on Deposit Money Banks	12e	29.39	50.45	188.59	255.13	219.06	226.25	310.80	170.54				
Reserve Money	14	250.41	237.22	255.17	305.91	356.63	403.47	449.46	550.23	777.84	976.36	1,402.27	1,560.07
of which: Currency Outside DMBs	14a	211.31	222.99	249.77	290.88	337.62	390.78	440.26	484.95	577.34	664.69	781.34	874.31
Foreign Liabilities	16c	22.55	69.68	96.06	130.45	142.06	144.70	157.34	145.08	132.30	125.80	93.72	64.12
Central Government Deposits	16d	2.94	9.25	9.80	4.41	21.93	75.32	4.46	324.61	420.96	438.55	606.08	1,037.91
Other Items (Net)	17r	65.96	110.26	182.67	248.11	361.16	200.82	192.89	238.28	259.54	461.70	459.66	633.30
Deposit Money Banks		*Billions of Dinars: End of Period*											
Reserves	20	37.89	7.32	5.58	12.79	18.77	15.85	13.37	42.74	182.94	339.61	624.51	679.40
Foreign Assets	21	16.47	44.88	33.30	32.38	23.11	27.50	27.89	28.32	32.35	49.75	55.53	76.96
Claims on Central Government	22a	300.52	204.63	155.64	141.43	273.15	410.39	459.49	600.38	591.50	841.87	805.90	794.16
Claims on Nonfin.Pub.Enterprises	22c	142.04	208.00	461.00	637.71	632.59	601.86	760.48	530.06	549.31	706.45	791.37	865.19
Claims on Private Sector	22d	77.12	96.75	103.47	137.85	108.56	128.86	173.89	245.31	289.05	559.37	586.56	672.86
Demand Deposits	24	188.93	196.45	210.78	234.03	254.83	334.52	352.71	460.27	551.88	647.57	719.59	1,139.21
Time Deposits	25	198.83	247.68	280.46	325.96	409.95	474.19	578.57	617.87	836.18	1,411.11	1,655.92	1,484.72
Foreign Liabilities	26c	12.94	35.14	22.58	20.79	15.71	25.48	30.87	26.66	35.18	37.28	38.76	65.34
Long-Term Foreign Liabilities	26cl	112.52	145.02	120.88	96.51	55.30	39.00	39.46	27.61	24.50	36.62	41.88	49.63
Central Government Deposits	26d	90.19	38.82	44.53	97.53	84.36	55.74	56.66	33.51	26.90	69.93	51.14	66.51
Central Govt. Lending Funds	26f	13.19	13.61	13.79	12.30	12.90	13.69	13.22	20.95	11.13	36.24	59.76	44.30
Credit from Monetary Authorities	26g	29.39	50.69	190.29	259.13	219.06	226.25	310.80	170.54	—	—	—	—
Other Items (Net)	27r	−71.95	−165.83	−124.31	−84.09	4.07	15.58	52.82	89.39	159.39	258.31	296.81	238.85
Post Office: Checking Deposits	24..i	40.98	48.50	53.74	57.96	71.68	81.05	87.43	89.09	97.00	100.64	117.19	120.33
Treasury: Checking Deposits	24..r	5.68	7.89	4.82	6.22	7.43	7.33	9.38	7.07	9.44	8.80	12.94	37.98
Monetary Survey		*Billions of Dinars: End of Period*											
Foreign Assets (Net)	31n	19.65	60.45	26.37	134.02	350.38	280.79	169.57	776.05	1,310.85	1,755.31	2,342.80	3,120.79
Domestic Credit	32	748.09	774.38	968.93	1,061.39	1,164.93	1,273.45	1,593.76	1,282.87	1,234.07	1,843.47	1,799.73	1,510.78
Claims on Central Govt. (Net)	32an	527.84	468.54	403.29	284.55	423.65	542.30	658.66	506.61	394.74	576.60	420.79	−29.84
Claims on Nonfin.Pub.Enterprises	32c	142.04	208.00	461.00	637.71	632.59	601.86	760.48	530.06	549.31	706.45	791.37	865.19
Claims on Private Sector	32d	77.16	96.79	103.50	137.88	108.63	129.18	174.48	245.99	289.80	560.12	587.25	673.50
Money	34	450.32	485.65	520.29	589.99	675.96	817.26	889.78	1,044.02	1,237.38	1,425.97	1,634.50	2,176.40
Quasi-Money	35	198.83	247.68	280.46	325.96	409.95	474.19	578.57	617.87	836.18	1,411.11	1,655.92	1,484.72
Long-Term Foreign Liabilities	36cl	112.52	145.02	120.88	96.51	55.30	39.00	39.46	27.61	24.50	36.62	41.88	49.63
Central Govt. Lending Funds	36f	13.19	13.61	13.79	12.30	12.90	13.69	13.22	20.95	11.13	36.24	59.76	44.30
Other Items (Net)	37r	−7.12	−57.13	59.89	170.65	361.21	210.10	242.26	348.47	435.72	688.84	750.47	876.52
Money plus Quasi-Money	35l	649.15	733.33	800.74	915.95	1,085.91	1,291.46	1,468.36	1,661.89	2,073.56	2,837.08	3,290.42	3,661.13
Interest Rates		*Percent Per Annum*											
Discount Rate	60	11.50	21.00	† 14.00	13.00	11.00	9.50	8.50	6.00	6.00	5.50	4.50	4.00
Money Market Rate	60b	....	19.80	† 19.75	18.09	13.00	10.00	9.99	6.45	2.84	3.13	1.91	1.09
Treasury Bill Rate	60c	9.50	16.50	....	....	....	† 9.96	10.05	7.95	5.69	1.80	1.25	.15
Deposit Rate	60l	8.00	12.00	† 16.00	14.50	9.75	8.50	7.50	7.50	6.25	5.25	5.25	2.50
Lending Rate	60p	....	16.00	† 19.00	19.00	12.50	11.00	10.00	10.00	9.50	8.50	8.00	8.00
Prices, Production, Labor		*Index Numbers (2000=100): Period Averages*											
Producer Prices	63	....	....	....	97.1	98.8	99.6	100.0	100.3	99.8	100.4	101.9	
Consumer Prices	64	44.0	56.8	73.7	87.5	92.5	97.1	99.7	100.0	104.2	105.7	108.4	112.3
Industrial Production	66	111.2	103.9	102.8	95.2	91.8	98.4	98.7	100.0	99.8	100.9	102.1	....
Crude Petroleum Production	66aa	94.6	92.1	95.3	101.4	104.5	102.0	96.0	100.0	101.4	107.2	143.5	155.5
		Number in Thousands: Period Averages											
Labor Force	67d	6,560	6,810	7,560	7,810	8,070	8,326	8,583	8,850	9,075	9,303	8,762	9,470
Employment	67e	5,042	5,154	5,436	5,625	5,815	5,993	6,077	6,240	6,597	6,900	6,684	7,798
Unemployment	67c	1,518	1,656	2,124	2,185	2,255	2,333	2,506	2,610	2,478	2,403	2,078	1,672
Unemployment Rate (%)	67r	23.2	24.4	28.1	28.0	28.0	28.0	29.2	29.5	27.3	25.9	23.7	17.7

		1993	1994	1995	1996	1997	1998	1999	2000	2001	2002	2003	2004
Intl. Transactions & Positions						*Millions of Dinars*							
Exports...........................	70	239,552	324,339	498,451	740,811	791,591	588,875	848,743	1,545,853	1,414,514	1,476,308	....	....
Imports, c.i.f....................	71	205,035	340,142	513,193	498,326	499,776	550,445	608,489	679,362	752,811	940,941	....	....
Volume of Exports							*2000=100*						
Petroleum....................	72a	81.1	81.5	81.5	90.2	85.4	90.5	93.8	100.0	98.5	108.1	....	....
Crude Petroleum.......................	72aa	70.0	72.2	73.0	85.6	81.0	88.9	90.5	100.0	95.1	118.8	157.8	191.1
Refined Petroleum.....................	72ab	104.4	96.7	95.5	98.3	93.0	93.8	99.9	100.0	104.7	92.4	92.5	74.1
Export Prices						*2000=100: Index of Prices in US Dollars*							
Crude Petroleum........................	76aad	61.5	57.3	61.8	76.2	68.5	45.2	63.2	100.0	87.3	87.5	102.2	135.8
Government Finance						*Millions of Dinars: Year Ending December 31*							
Deficit (-) or Surplus........................	80	....	† −65,354	−28,243	75,258	66,126	−108,134	−16,493	398,856	171,015	10,449	....	....
Revenue.................................	81	....	† 434,199	600,847	825,157	926,668	774,511	950,496	1,578,161	1,505,526	1,603,198	....	....
Expenditure.................................	82	....	† 493,626	625,965	749,009	863,196	875,739	961,682	1,178,122	1,321,028	1,550,646	....	....
Lending Minus Repayments............	83	....	5,927	3,125	890	−2,654	6,906	5,307	1,183	13,483	42,103	....	....
Financing													
Net Borrowing: Domestic..............	84a	....	−120,023	−147,866	−178,249	....	....	....	....	....	....	....	....
Foreign...........................	85a	....	141,376	172,158	100,937	....	....	....	....	....	....	....	....
Use of Cash Balances....................	87	....	44,001	3,951	2,054	....	....	....	....	....	....	....	....
National Accounts						*Billions of Dinars*							
Househ.Cons.Expend.,incl.NPISHs....	96f	649.1	837.5	1,114.8	1,335.0	1,430.3	1,556.7	1,670.7	1,714.2	1,847.7	1,970.6	2,108.8	....
Government Consumption Expend...	91f	221.2	263.9	340.2	405.4	459.8	503.6	543.6	560.1	624.6	683.2	758.2	....
Gross Fixed Capital Formation..........	93e	324.1	407.5	541.8	639.4	638.1	728.8	789.8	879.4	965.5	1,102.2	1,218.7	....
Changes in Inventories....................	93i	12.1	60.4	91.2	5.2	9.3	45.2	60.2	65.6	183.8	253.0	308.2	....
Exports of Goods and Services..........	90c	252.3	342.6	533.0	781.7	837.2	652.3	911.6	1,734.8	1,550.9	1,587.7	1,988.7	....
Imports of Goods and Services (-).....	98c	269.1	424.5	616.1	596.7	594.7	656.1	737.6	855.2	930.7	1,142.6	1,258.6	....
Gross Domestic Product (GDP)..........	99b	1,189.7	1,487.4	2,005.0	2,570.0	2,780.2	2,830.5	3,238.2	4,098.8	4,241.8	4,454.8	5,124.0	....
						Millions: Midyear Estimates							
Population.................................	99z	27.16	27.74	28.27	28.76	29.20	29.62	30.03	30.46	30.91	31.38	31.87	32.36

		1993	1994	1995	1996	1997	1998	1999	2000	2001	2002	2003	2004
Exchange Rates					*Kwanzas per Thousands SDRs through 1994; per SDR Thereafter: End of Period*								
Market Rate	aa	.0089	.7434	.0085	.2905	.3540	.9807	† 7.6585	21.9121	40.1517	79.7581	117.5127	133.5399
					Kwanzas per Thous.US$ through 1994; per US$ Thereafter: End of Period: (ae) Period Average (rf)								
Market Rate	ae	.0065	.5093	.0057	.2020	.2624	.6965	† 5.5799	16.8178	31.9494	58.6664	79.0815	85.9878
Market Rate	rf	.0027	.0595	.0028	.1280	.2290	.3928	2.7907	10.0405	22.0579	43.5302	74.6063	83.5414
Fund Position						*Millions of SDRs: End of Period*							
Quota	2f.s	207.30	207.30	207.30	207.30	207.30	207.30	286.30	286.30	286.30	286.30	286.30	286.30
SDRs	1b.s	.10	.10	.11	.11	.12	.12	.13	.13	.14	.14	.14	.15
Reserve Position in the Fund	1c.s	—	—	—	—	—	—	—	—	—	—	—	—
Total Fund Cred.&Loans Outstg	2tl	—	—	—	—	—	—	—	—	—	—	—	—
International Liquidity					*Millions of US Dollars Unless Otherwise Indicated: End of Period*								
Total Reserves minus Gold	1l.d	....	....	212.83	551.62	396.43	203.45	496.10	1,198.21	731.87	375.55	634.20	1,364.72
SDRs	1b.d	.14	.15	.16	.16	.16	.17	.18	.17	.17	.19	.21	.23
Reserve Position in the Fund	1c.d	—	—	—	—	—	—	—	—	—	—	—	—
Foreign Exchange	1d.d	....	....	212.67	551.46	396.27	203.28	495.93	1,198.04	731.69	375.35	633.99	1,364.50
Monetary Authorities: Other Assets	3..d	....	....	143.95	6.86	1.98	.85	—	—	—	—	1.60	1.59
Other Liab	4..d	....	....	1,901.59	348.01	329.78	444.98	90.53	212.42	247.35	107.88	30.36	30.36
Banking Institutions: Assets	7a.d	....	....	264.62	523.49	833.30	682.25	747.42	878.08	1,168.78	1,453.84	1,283.96	1,364.43
Liabilities	7b.d	....	....	69.68	61.07	137.31	199.46	119.12	49.14	157.42	126.89	90.07	109.17
Monetary Authorities						*Millions of Kwanzas: End of Period*							
Foreign Assets	11	....	....	2.1	112.8	104.0	141.7	† 2,768.2	20,151.3	23,382.7	22,031.9	50,153.4	117,432.5
Claims on Central Government	12a	....	....	4.3	36.2	82.3	330.2	† 4,033.1	1,062.1	559.1	26,425.9	25,528.9	21,686.2
Claims on Nonfin.Pub.Enterprises	12c	....	....	2.9	2.5	3.7	2.5	† 32.4	156.4	272.3	371.3	787.2	823.5
Claims on Private Sector	12d	....	....	—	—	—	—	† 9.0	43.2	247.2	392.2	704.8	968.0
Claims on Banking Institutions	12e	....	....	—	—	48.8	61.5	† 76.7	252.6	330.4	287.2	1.0	1.0
Reserve Money	14	....	....	2.6	89.9	172.6	258.6	† 1,956.0	6,215.2	15,325.7	33,365.3	58,722.7	91,535.0
of which: Currency Outside Banks	14a	....	....	1.2	42.2	101.6	165.7	† 665.4	2,968.6	8,215.3	20,878.5	35,407.9	46,022.5
Time & Foreign Currency Deposits	15	....	....	2.4	58.5	6.8	7.2	† 13.5	41.3	—	146.6	240.7	271.0
Liabs. of Central Bank: Securities	16ac	....	....	—	—	.3	—	† 7.0	190.0	3,292.0	5,277.6	11,778.2	11,225.7
Foreign Liabilities	16c	....	....	10.8	70.3	86.5	309.9	† 505.1	3,572.4	7,902.8	6,328.8	2,401.0	2,610.3
Central Government Deposits	16d	....	....	.3	21.3	—	.2	† 2,878.4	14,251.9	1,213.0	5,717.2	12,592.5	54,525.1
Capital Accounts	17a	....	....	−1.2	18.4	15.1	23.2	† −636.4	−351.9	1,363.0	3,240.8	12,210.7	6,170.7
Other Items (Net)	17r	....	....	−5.6	−106.8	−42.4	−63.3	† 2,195.7	−2,253.3	−4,304.8	−4,567.7	−20,770.5	−25,426.5
Banking Institutions						*Millions of Kwanzas: End of Period*							
Reserves	20	....	....	1.1	47.7	82.3	92.4	† 1,044.9	2,964.2	7,509.5	16,099.8	25,389.6	48,901.0
Claims on Mon.Author.:Securities	20c	....	....	—	—	—	—	† 7.0	175.0	3,292.0	5,277.6	11,778.2	11,073.3
Foreign Assets	21	....	....	1.5	105.7	218.6	475.2	† 4,170.6	14,767.4	37,341.8	85,291.6	101,537.7	117,324.0
Claims on Central Government	22a	....	....	.3	1.0	5.9	55.3	† 12.0	3.3	40.4	2,017.1	15,981.2	47,456.5
Claims on Local Government	22b	....	....	—	—	—	—	† .4	10.0	23.1	3.7	947.6	1,361.9
Claims on Nonfin. Pub. Enterprises	22c	....	....	—	—	—	.2	† 61.1	186.7	601.6	1,061.5	4,126.9	7,484.1
Claims on Private Sector	22d	....	....	.7	26.5	90.6	90.0	† 432.9	1,802.7	7,106.2	22,849.1	52,359.3	85,915.1
Demand Deposits	24	....	....	1.2	51.8	93.3	106.6	† 516.0	2,037.0	5,449.5	10,961.0	33,630.1	49,715.7
Time, Savings,& Fgn.Currency Dep	25	....	....	.4	78.0	194.5	344.9	† 2,720.5	10,741.5	27,697.1	74,981.0	108,606.3	145,610.5
of which: Fgn. Currency Deposits	25b	....	....	.4	67.7	170.1	330.7	† 2,626.3	10,696.1	26,833.9	73,081.0	104,739.3	140,583.9
Money Market Instruments	26aa	....	....	—	—	—	—	† —	—	321.3	649.2	2,361.6	25,552.1
Foreign Liabilities	26c	....	....	.4	12.3	36.0	138.9	† 664.7	826.4	5,029.4	7,444.4	7,123.2	9,387.0
Central Government Deposits	26d	....	....	—	5.2	6.8	28.9	† 462.8	2,538.1	8,856.9	20,633.7	22,841.4	40,187.1
Credit from Monetary Authorities	26g	....	....	—	—	48.0	58.0	† 500.6	1,180.8	—	—	—	—
Capital Accounts	27a	....	....	.2	16.1	23.9	100.6	† 703.7	2,905.2	8,901.6	17,980.4	36,889.9	53,232.7
Other Items (Net)	27r	....	....	1.4	17.7	−5.1	−64.9	† 160.6	−319.7	−341.2	−49.4	667.8	−4,169.2
Banking Survey						*Millions of Kwanzas: End of Period*							
Foreign Assets (Net)	31n	....	....	−7.6	135.9	200.1	168.0	† 5,768.9	30,520.0	47,792.3	93,550.3	142,166.9	222,759.1
Domestic Credit	32	....	....	7.9	39.9	175.7	449.0	† 1,239.7	−13,525.7	−1,220.1	26,769.9	65,001.8	70,983.2
Claims on Central Govt.(Net)	32an	....	....	4.3	10.8	81.4	356.3	† 703.9	−15,724.7	−9,470.4	2,092.1	6,076.2	−25,569.5
Claims on Local Government	32b	....	....	—	—	—	—	† .4	10.0	23.1	3.7	947.6	1,361.9
Claims on Nonfin.Pub.Enterprises	32c	....	....	2.9	2.5	3.7	2.7	† 93.5	343.1	873.9	1,432.8	4,914.1	8,307.6
Claims on Private Sector	32d	....	....	.7	26.5	90.6	90.0	† 441.9	1,845.8	7,353.4	23,241.4	53,064.0	86,883.1
Money	34	....	....	2.7	93.9	194.9	272.4	† 1,206.5	5,332.8	14,298.7	33,459.2	69,074.5	95,778.2
Quasi-Money	35	....	....	2.8	136.5	201.3	352.1	† 2,734.0	10,782.7	27,697.1	75,127.6	108,847.0	145,881.5
Money Market Instruments	36aa	....	....	—	—	—	—	† —	—	321.3	649.2	2,361.6	25,552.1
Liabs. of Central Banks: Securities	36ac	....	....	—	—	.3	—	† —	15.0	—	—	—	152.4
Capital Accounts	37a	....	....	−1.0	34.5	38.9	123.8	† 67.3	2,553.4	10,264.6	21,221.2	49,100.7	59,403.4
Other Items (Net)	37r	....	....	−4.2	−89.1	−59.6	−131.3	† 3,000.8	−1,689.6	−6,009.3	−10,137.0	−22,215.0	−33,025.2
Money plus Quasi-Money	35l	....	....	5.5	230.4	396.2	624.6	† 3,940.5	16,115.5	41,995.8	108,586.8	177,921.5	241,659.6
Interest Rates						*Percent Per Annum*							
Discount Rate (End of Period)	60	....	....	160.00	2.00	48.00	58.00	120.00	150.00	150.00	150.00	150.00	95.00
Deposit Rate	60l	....	....	125.92	147.13	29.25	36.88	† 36.57	† 39.58	47.91	48.69	26.17	15.44
Lending Rate	60p	....	....	206.25	217.88	37.75	45.00	† 80.30	† 103.16	95.97	97.34	96.12	82.33
Prices						*Index Numbers (2000=100): Period Averages*							
Consumer Prices	64	† —	....	† —	1.0	3.3	6.8	23.5	100.0	269.7	560.9	1,093.0	1,501.2
Consumer Prices (2000=1 Million)	64.a	.8	8.7	240.6	10,213.9	32,600.4	....	....	....	....	....	....	....
Intl. Transactions & Positions						*Millions of US Dollars*							
Exports, f.o.b	70..d	2,901.0	3,017.0	3,723.0	5,095.0	5,006.8	3,542.9	5,397.0	7,702.0	6,379.8	7,509.6	9,237.4	12,974.4
Imports, f.o.b	71.vd	1,463.0	1,454.0	1,468.0	2,040.5	2,597.0	2,079.4	3,109.1	3,039.5	3,179.2	....	3,406.8	3,573.2

Angola 614

		1993	1994	1995	1996	1997	1998	1999	2000	2001	2002	2003	2004
Balance of Payments					*Millions of US Dollars: Minus Sign Indicates Debit*								
Current Account, n.i.e.	78ald	−668.5	−339.8	−295.0	3,266.4	−883.5	−1,867.1	−1,710.4	795.7	−1,430.9	−150.1	−719.6	686.2
Goods: Exports f.o.b.	78aad	2,900.5	3,016.6	3,722.7	5,095.0	5,006.8	3,542.9	5,156.5	7,920.7	6,534.3	8,327.9	9,508.2	13,475.0
Goods: Imports f.o.b.	78abd	−1,462.6	−1,454.1	−1,467.7	−2,040.5	−2,597.0	−2,079.4	−3,109.1	−3,039.5	−3,179.2	−3,760.1	−5,480.1	−5,831.8
Trade Balance	78acd	1,437.9	1,562.5	2,255.0	3,054.5	2,409.8	1,463.5	2,047.5	4,881.2	3,355.1	4,567.8	4,028.1	7,643.2
Services: Credit	78add	105.8	150.2	113.1	267.7	138.5	121.8	153.0	267.3	202.5	206.8	201.1	322.8
Services: Debit	78aed	−1,561.9	−1,562.9	−2,051.4	−2,423.3	−2,605.4	−2,635.2	−2,594.6	−2,699.5	−3,518.1	−3,322.0	−3,321.1	−4,802.7
Balance on Goods & Services	78afd	−18.2	149.8	316.7	898.9	−57.1	−1,049.8	−394.1	2,449.0	39.5	1,452.6	908.0	3,163.3
Income: Credit	78agd	11.3	13.0	15.9	43.3	112.1	34.5	24.1	34.4	23.0	17.7	12.3	33.0
Income: Debit	78ahd	−827.4	−747.7	−783.2	−1,516.7	−1,033.1	−1,003.3	−1,396.2	−1,715.2	−1,584.0	−1,652.3	−1,738.7	−2,516.6
Balance on Gds, Serv. & Inc.	78aid	−834.3	−584.9	−450.6	−574.4	−978.1	−2,018.6	−1,766.2	768.2	−1,521.5	−182.1	−818.5	679.6
Current Transfers, n.i.e.: Credit	78ajd	253.4	333.2	312.2	3,949.4	176.4	238.2	154.5	123.5	208.3	142.3	186.2	124.4
Current Transfers: Debit	78akd	−87.6	−88.1	−156.7	−108.6	−81.8	−86.7	−98.7	−96.0	−117.8	−110.3	−87.3	−117.9
Capital Account, n.i.e.	78bcd	—	—	—	—	11.2	8.4	6.8	18.3	3.9	....	....	—
Capital Account, n.i.e.: Credit	78bad	—	—	—	—	11.2	8.4	6.8	18.3	3.9	....	....	—
Capital Account: Debit	78bbd	—	—	—	—	—	—	—	—	—	....	....	....
Financial Account, n.i.e.	78bjd	−274.3	−443.4	−924.8	−654.5	449.9	368.3	1,739.6	−445.6	950.0	−356.7	1,370.5	−628.2
Direct Investment Abroad	78bdd	—	—	—	—	—	—	—	—	—	−28.7	−23.6	−35.2
Dir. Invest. in Rep. Econ., n.i.e.	78bed	302.1	170.3	472.4	180.6	411.7	1,114.0	2,471.5	878.6	2,145.5	1,672.1	3,504.7	1,444.3
Portfolio Investment Assets	78bfd	—	—	—	—	—	—	—	—	....	....	1.0	−2.7
Equity Securities	78bkd	—	—	—	—	—	—	—	—	....	....	....	−3.3
Debt Securities	78bld	—	—	—	—	—	—	—	—	....	....	1.0	.6
Portfolio Investment Liab., n.i.e.	78bgd	—	—	—	—	—	—	—	—	....	....	....	....
Equity Securities	78bmd	—	—	—	—	—	—	—	—	....	....	....	....
Debt Securities	78bnd	—	—	—	—	—	—	—	—	....	....	....	....
Financial Derivatives Assets	78bwd	....	....	....	....	....	....	....	....	....	....	....	....
Financial Derivatives Liabilities	78bxd	....	....	....	....	....	....	....	....	....	....	....	....
Other Investment Assets	78bhd	−92.9	214.1	−168.4	−327.6	−330.7	−40.8	−186.1	−702.1	−516.6	−1,321.0	120.0	−1,951.5
Monetary Authorities	78bod	....	....	....	....	....	....	....	....	....	....	....	....
General Government	78bpd	−156.0	—	—	—	—	—	—	—	—	−1,112.6	75.0	−68.2
Banks	78bqd	10.0	—	−4.4	−48.8	—	—	—	—	—	−208.4	45.0	−1,883.3
Other Sectors	78brd	53.1	214.1	−164.1	−278.8	−330.7	−40.8	−186.1	−702.1	−516.6	−208.4	45.0	−1,883.3
Other Investment Liab., n.i.e.	78bid	−483.5	−827.8	−1,228.8	−507.4	368.9	−704.8	−545.7	−622.1	−678.9	−679.1	−2,231.5	−83.0
Monetary Authorities	78bsd	17.6	−185.9	−114.3	−143.9	—	−303.0	−272.2	17.3	−62.0	−142.7	−38.0	−2.2
General Government	78btd	−583.6	−792.6	−778.1	−202.7	−69.0	−478.6	−180.5	−665.3	−483.1	−352.0	309.5	−161.1
Banks	78bud	.6	—	—	−1.6	4.8	2.4	3.5	—	—	52.1	−10.5	18.4
Other Sectors	78bvd	81.9	150.7	−336.4	−159.2	433.2	74.4	−96.5	25.9	−133.8	−236.6	−2,492.5	61.9
Net Errors and Omissions	78cad	−377.1	−244.5	−19.4	149.2	−181.8	378.5	−78.9	−50.6	−308.6	150.5	−388.2	282.3
Overall Balance	78cbd	−1,319.9	−1,027.7	−1,239.3	2,761.0	−604.3	−1,112.0	−42.9	317.8	−785.6	−356.3	262.8	340.3
Reserves and Related Items	79dad	1,319.9	1,027.7	1,239.3	−2,761.0	604.3	1,112.0	42.9	−317.8	785.6	356.3	−262.8	−340.3
Reserve Assets	79dbd	192.9	14.2	−30.7	−330.3	162.6	318.0	−530.1	−631.3	466.3	356.3	−262.8	−780.3
Use of Fund Credit and Loans	79dcd	—	—	—	—	—	—	—	—	—	....	....	—
Exceptional Financing	79ded	1,127.0	1,013.5	1,270.0	−2,430.7	441.7	794.0	573.0	313.4	319.3	....	....	440.0
National Accounts						*Millions of Kwanzas*							
Gross Domestic Product (GDP)	99b	26.9	620.2	13.7	835.5	1,752.0	2,556.0	17,171.0	91,666.0	197,111.0	433,553.0	....	....
GDP Volume 1992 Prices	99b.p	2.6	2.7	3.0	3.4	3.6	3.8	3.9	4.0	4.2	4.9	....	....
GDP Deflator (2000=100)	99bip	—	1.0	—	1.1	2.1	3.0	19.4	100.0	204.2	388.9	....	....
GDP Volume (2000=100)	99bvp	65.6	67.3	74.4	83.9	89.1	94.0	96.5	100.0	105.3	121.6	....	....
						Millions: Midyear Estimates							
Population	99z	11.57	11.94	12.28	12.60	12.90	13.19	13.50	13.84	14.21	14.62	15.05	15.49

		1993	1994	1995	1996	1997	1998	1999	2000	2001	2002	2003	2004
Exchange Rates		*E. Caribbean Dollars per SDR: End of Period (aa) E. Caribbean Dollars per US Dollar: End of Period (ae)*											
Official Rate	aa	3.7086	3.9416	4.0135	3.8825	3.6430	3.8017	3.7058	3.5179	3.3932	3.6707	4.0121	4.1931
Official Rate	ae	2.7000	2.7000	2.7000	2.7000	2.7000	2.7000	2.7000	2.7000	2.7000	2.7000	2.7000	2.7000
International Liquidity		*Millions of US Dollars Unless Otherwise Indicated: End of Period*											
Total Reserves minus Gold	1l.d	9.33	9.14	12.78	14.45	16.31	18.15	19.91	20.30	24.19	26.20	33.28	34.25
Foreign Exchange	1d.d	9.33	9.14	12.78	14.45	16.31	18.15	19.91	20.30	24.19	26.20	33.28	34.25
Monetary Authorities: Other Liab.	4..d	—	—	—	—	—	—	—	—	—	—	—	—
Deposit Money Banks: Assets	7a.d	39.10	49.34	66.99	74.43	76.65	108.01	89.54	93.14	103.52	129.83	131.97	203.60
Liabilities	7b.d	39.63	38.01	37.47	48.60	49.21	64.12	69.08	75.46	71.52	78.48	90.94	114.14
Monetary Authorities		*Millions of E. Caribbean Dollars: End of Period*											
Foreign Assets	11	25.19	24.69	34.53	39.00	44.05	49.01	53.83	54.89	65.51	70.87	89.92	92.55
Claims on Central Government	12a	—	—	.05	—	—	—	—	—	5.01	.43	—	—
Claims on Deposit Money Banks	12e	.02	.01	.01	.01	.02	.01	.01	.02	.02	.01	.03	.01
Reserve Money	14	25.21	24.69	33.00	37.82	42.56	47.77	53.11	54.53	70.13	71.05	89.65	92.51
of which: Currency Outside DMBs	14a	4.87	5.04	7.06	7.32	7.17	8.45	8.72	8.76	8.98	8.25	8.98	9.51
Foreign Liabilities	16c	—	—	—	—	—	—	—	—	—	—	—	—
Central Government Deposits	16d	—	.01	1.58	1.19	1.51	1.26	.72	.39	.40	.27	.30	.05
Other Items (Net)	17r												
Deposit Money Banks		*Millions of E. Caribbean Dollars: End of Period*											
Reserves	20	20.28	19.20	21.48	30.84	34.40	35.75	44.51	49.27	61.27	62.79	81.50	82.95
Foreign Assets	21	105.56	133.21	180.87	200.95	206.96	291.63	241.76	251.47	279.51	350.54	356.31	549.72
Claims on Central Government	22a	1.34	.73	1.12	.35	1.62	1.76	—	—	—	—	—	.17
Claims on Local Government	22b	.08	—	—	—	—	—	1.85	12.51	16.11	21.68	23.32	53.53
Claims on Nonfin.Pub.Enterprises	22c	—	—	—	—	—	7.90	7.89	7.61	7.38	8.20	5.17	3.45
Claims on Private Sector	22d	196.22	193.34	204.82	219.31	245.12	261.08	337.06	424.83	457.66	479.17	540.38	589.89
Claims on Nonbank Financial Insts	22g	.99	.35	.75	.80	1.63	.82	.65	.63	.93	1.04	1.64	6.95
Demand Deposits	24	5.08	5.19	8.43	7.55	9.40	9.63	11.30	14.34	13.13	16.20	17.78	24.84
Time, Savings,& Fgn.Currency Dep.	25	171.16	191.60	239.14	246.94	270.47	327.55	357.56	420.57	479.01	541.47	584.36	703.73
Foreign Liabilities	26c	107.01	102.62	101.16	131.21	132.86	173.11	186.53	203.74	193.09	211.90	245.53	308.17
Central Government Deposits	26d	21.20	26.32	31.83	38.22	41.06	45.57	45.87	55.34	62.72	69.07	70.78	77.58
Credit from Monetary Authorities	26g	.98	.01	—	.02	—	1.82	.01	3.52	.02	.02	2.22	2.36
Capital Accounts	27a	16.06	21.09	25.82	31.76	37.96	47.13	54.80	62.46	87.72	103.73	110.39	131.63
Other Items (Net)	27r	2.97	—	2.66	−3.44	−2.03	−5.89	−22.34	−13.64	−12.83	−18.97	−22.72	38.35
Monetary Survey		*Millions of E. Caribbean Dollars: End of Period*											
Foreign Assets (Net)	31n	23.74	55.27	114.24	108.74	118.15	167.53	109.06	102.62	151.93	209.51	200.71	334.09
Domestic Credit	32	177.43	168.09	173.32	181.05	205.80	224.72	300.85	389.86	423.97	441.18	499.44	576.36
Claims on Central Govt. (Net)	32an	−19.86	−25.60	−32.25	−39.06	−40.95	−45.06	−46.59	−55.72	−58.11	−68.90	−71.07	−77.46
Claims on Local Government	32b	.08	—	—	—	—	—	1.85	12.51	16.11	21.68	23.32	53.53
Claims on Nonfin.Pub.Enterprises	32c	—	—	—	—	—	7.90	7.89	7.61	7.38	8.20	5.17	3.45
Claims on Private Sector	32d	196.22	193.34	204.82	219.31	245.12	261.08	337.06	424.83	457.66	479.17	540.38	589.89
Claims on Nonbank Financial Inst.	32g	.99	.35	.75	.80	1.63	.82	.65	.63	.93	1.04	1.64	6.95
Money	34	9.96	10.23	15.50	14.90	17.21	18.10	20.03	23.10	22.12	24.53	26.76	34.35
Quasi-Money	35	171.16	191.60	239.14	246.94	270.47	327.55	357.56	420.57	479.01	541.47	584.36	703.73
Capital Accounts	37a	16.06	21.09	25.82	31.76	37.96	47.13	54.80	62.46	87.72	103.73	110.39	131.63
Other Items (Net)	37r	3.99	.44	7.11	−3.81	−1.69	−.53	−22.48	−13.65	−12.95	−19.04	−21.35	40.74
Money plus Quasi-Money	35l	181.12	201.83	254.63	261.84	287.68	345.65	377.59	443.67	501.12	566.00	611.11	738.08
Money (National Definitions)		*Millions of E. Caribbean Dollars: End of Period*											
M1	59ma	10.48	10.77	15.05	15.50	14.85	17.51	18.53	20.13	20.35	19.51	24.48	26.06
M2	59mb	179.35	199.48	249.45	258.80	283.19	340.99	369.78	432.13	484.25	545.58	587.13	697.71
Interest Rates		*Percent Per Annum*											
Discount Rate (End of Period)	60	....	9.00	9.00	9.00	8.00	8.00	8.00	8.00	7.00	7.00	6.50	6.50
Money Market Rate	60b	5.25	5.25	5.25	5.25	5.25	5.25	5.25	5.25	† 5.64	6.32	6.07	4.67
Savings Rate	60k	5.33	4.60	4.96	5.00	5.00	5.00	5.00	5.00	5.00	5.00	† 3.23	3.81
Deposit Rate	60l	2.25	3.47	3.64	3.74	3.77	3.79	3.78	3.52	3.54	3.25	4.59	4.83
Deposit Rate (Fgn. Currency)	60l.f	....	....	....	....	....	....	....	....	....	....	4.65	4.71
Lending Rate	60p	8.29	12.84	12.60	11.95	11.37	11.16	11.31	11.32	10.74	10.35	11.42	10.99
Prices, Tourism, Labor		*Index Numbers (2000=100): Period Averages*											
Consumer Prices	64	135.9	140.7	142.6	147.7	147.9	151.8	155.8	100.0	102.3	102.8	....	....
Number of Tourists	66t	344.0	399.2	352.0	342.5	394.4	400.8	106.8	100.0	36.5	33.5	51.1	....
		Number in Thousands: Period Averages											
Employment	67e	....	....	....	....	....	6.2	....	5.6	5.5	....	....	
Intl. Transactions & Positions		*Millions of E. Caribbean Dollars*											
Exports	70	2.6	2.4	1.4	4.3	4.2	8.6	7.1	10.9	8.6	11.7	....	....
Imports	71	96.0	98.2	87.4	161.8	166.3	192.7	248.1	255.2	209.8	188.7	....	....

		1993	1994	1995	1996	1997	1998	1999	2000	2001	2002	2003	2004
Balance of Payments					*Millions of US Dollars: Minus Sign Indicates Debit*								
Current Account, n.i.e.	78ald	−12.61	−11.46	−9.47	−20.26	−18.74	−19.07	−51.05	−54.47	−35.87	−35.38	....	....
Goods: Exports f.o.b.	78aad	1.14	1.67	1.23	1.76	1.60	3.50	2.90	4.43	3.57	4.38	....	....
Goods: Imports f.o.b.	78abd	−34.36	−39.09	−47.00	−52.86	−54.26	−63.01	−80.86	−83.29	−68.50	−61.63	....	....
Trade Balance	78acd	−33.21	−37.41	−45.78	−51.10	−52.66	−59.51	−77.96	−78.86	−64.93	−57.26	....	....
Services: Credit	78add	53.63	61.43	55.56	57.22	66.01	79.44	68.80	64.94	70.43	65.53	....	....
Services: Debit	78aed	−25.78	−24.78	−27.81	−27.59	−28.96	−38.19	−38.30	−40.86	−39.12	−38.53	....	....
Balance on Goods & Services	78afd	−5.36	−.76	−18.03	−21.47	−15.61	−18.26	−47.46	−54.77	−33.62	−30.26	....	....
Income: Credit	78agd	1.11	1.47	2.06	2.27	3.28	1.56	3.67	3.97	1.86	1.56	....	....
Income: Debit	78ahd	−9.17	−10.78	−9.60	−8.48	−7.07	−5.43	−6.87	−6.67	−5.39	−6.82	....	....
Balance on Gds, Serv. & Inc.	78aid	−13.41	−10.06	−25.57	−27.67	−19.40	−22.13	−50.65	−57.47	−37.14	−35.52	....	....
Current Transfers, n.i.e.: Credit	78ajd	7.28	5.28	21.51	12.63	7.20	9.30	8.25	11.15	9.83	8.54	....	....
Current Transfers: Debit	78akd	−6.48	−6.68	−5.42	−5.22	−6.54	−6.24	−8.64	−8.14	−8.57	−8.40	....	....
Capital Account, n.i.e.	78bcd	5.66	6.80	5.40	5.23	2.51	5.60	7.96	9.75	8.81	6.80	....	....
Capital Account, n.i.e.: Credit	78bad	6.95	8.11	6.71	6.54	3.87	6.95	9.31	11.10	10.11	8.12	....	....
Capital Account: Debit	78bbd	−1.30	−1.31	−1.31	−1.31	−1.35	−1.35	−1.35	−1.35	−1.30	−1.32	....	....
Financial Account, n.i.e.	78bjd	4.44	−1.50	−.95	35.73	19.20	11.60	58.75	41.05	20.23	17.26	....	....
Direct Investment Abroad	78bdd	—											
Dir. Invest. in Rep. Econ., n.i.e.	78bed	6.47	11.14	17.58	33.23	21.24	28.06	38.01	38.18	32.72	36.53		
Portfolio Investment Assets	78bfd	.05	—	−.18	—	—	—	—	—	—	−.85		
Equity Securities	78bkd	....	....	....	....	....	....	....	....	....	....		
Debt Securities	78bld	....	....	....	....	....	....	....	....	....	....		
Portfolio Investment Liab., n.i.e.	78bgd	—	—	—	—	—	−.23	—	—	1.15	.01		
Equity Securities	78bmd	....	....	....	....	....	....	....	....	....	....		
Debt Securities	78bnd	....	....	....	....	....	....	....	....	....	....		
Financial Derivatives Assets	78bwd	....	....	....	....	....	....	....	....	....	....		
Financial Derivatives Liabilities	78bxd	....	....	....	....	....	....	....	....	....	....		
Other Investment Assets	78bid	−.23	−.44	−.75	−1.23	−.61	−.56	−1.29	−.66	−3.49	−.57		
Monetary Authorities	78bod	....	....	....	....	....	....	....	....	....	....		
General Government	78bpd	....	....	....	....	....	....	....	....	....	....		
Banks	78bqd	....	....	....	....	....	....	....	....	....	....		
Other Sectors	78brd	....	....	....	....	....	....	....	....	....	....		
Other Investment Liab., n.i.e.	78bid	−1.84	−12.20	−17.60	3.73	−1.43	−15.67	22.03	3.53	−10.15	−17.86		
Monetary Authorities	78bsd	....	....	....	....	....	....	....	....	....	....		
General Government	78btd	....	....	....	....	....	....	....	....	....	....		
Banks	78bud	....	....	....	....	....	....	....	....	....	....		
Other Sectors	78bvd	....	....	....	....	....	....	....	....	....	....		
Net Errors and Omissions	78cad	3.59	6.16	5.03	−19.26	−1.12	3.70	−13.90	4.05	10.73	13.07		
Overall Balance	78cbd	1.07	—	—	1.44	1.86	1.84	1.76	.39	3.90	1.75		
Reserves and Related Items	79dad	−1.07	—	—	−1.44	−1.86	−1.84	−1.76	−.39	−3.90	−1.75		
Reserve Assets	79dbd	−1.07	—	—	−1.44	−1.86	−1.84	−1.76	−.39	−3.90	−1.75		
Use of Fund Credit and Loans	79dcd	....	....	....	....	....	....	....	....	....	....		
Exceptional Financing	79ded	....	....	....	....	....	....	....	....	....	....		
National Accounts						*Millions of E. Caribbean Dollars*							
Gross Domestic Product (GDP)	99b	150.4	166.5	164.9	175.8	194.2	209.2	233.0	233.4	236.9	239.5	....	....
GDP Volume 1990 Prices	99b.p	139.7	149.6	143.4	148.4	162.1	170.5	185.2	184.6	188.6	182.5	....	....
GDP Volume (2000=100)	99bvp	75.7	81.1	77.7	80.4	87.8	92.3	100.3	100.0	102.1	98.8	....	....
GDP Deflator (2000=100)	99bip	85.2	88.0	90.9	93.7	94.8	97.1	99.5	100.0	99.4	103.8	....	....
						Millions: Midyear Estimates							
Population	99z	.010	.010	.010	.011	.011	.011	.011	.011	.011	.012	.012	.012

Antigua and Barbuda   311

		1993	1994	1995	1996	1997	1998	1999	2000	2001	2002	2003	2004
Exchange Rates		*E. Caribbean Dollars per SDR: End of Period (aa) E. Caribbean Dollars per US Dollar: End of Period (ae)*											
Official Rate	aa	3.7086	3.9416	4.0135	3.8825	3.6430	3.8017	3.7058	3.5179	3.3932	3.6707	4.0121	4.1931
Official Rate	ae	2.7000	2.7000	2.7000	2.7000	2.7000	2.7000	2.7000	2.7000	2.7000	2.7000	2.7000	2.7000
		Index Numbers (2000=100): Period Averages											
Official Rate	ahx	100.0	100.0	100.0	100.0	100.0	100.0	100.0	100.0	100.0	100.0	100.0	100.0
Nominal Effective Exchange Rate	nec	92.2	92.2	89.4	90.7	93.6	94.4	95.3	100.0	102.8	100.9	94.2	89.6
Real Effective Exchange Rate	rec	104.7e	96.3	92.9	94.4	95.5	97.6	98.0	100.0	103.6	103.0	96.9	92.5
Fund Position		*Millions of SDRs: End of Period*											
Quota	2f.s	8.50	8.50	8.50	8.50	8.50	8.50	13.50	13.50	13.50	13.50	13.50	13.50
SDRs	1b.s	—	—	—	—	—	—	.01	.01	.01	.01	.01	.01
Reserve Position in the Fund	1c.s	—	—	—	—	—	—	—	—	—	—	.01	.01
Total Fund Cred.&Loans Outstg	2tl	—	—	—	—	—	—	—	—	—	—	—	—
International Liquidity		*Millions of US Dollars: End of Period*											
Total Reserves minus Gold	1l.d	37.81	45.81	59.44	47.74	50.70	59.37	69.73	63.56	79.72	87.65	113.77	120.14
SDRs	1b.d	.01	.01	.01	.01	.01	.01	.01	.01	.01	.01	.01	.01
Reserve Position in the Fund	1c.d	—	—	—	—	—	—	—	—	—	—	.01	.01
Foreign Exchange	1d.d	37.80	45.80	59.43	47.73	50.69	59.36	69.72	63.55	79.71	87.64	113.75	120.12
Monetary Authorities: Other Liab	4..d	—	—	—	—	—	—	—	—	—	—	—	—
Deposit Money Banks: Assets	7a.d	56.76	77.30	77.54	72.02	58.79	71.34	160.10	172.17	187.34	259.14	297.26	331.97
Liabilities	7b.d	54.04	60.72	46.57	78.47	103.51	114.42	129.49	181.85	148.54	208.93	163.61	181.78
Monetary Authorities		*Millions of E. Caribbean Dollars: End of Period*											
Foreign Assets	11	102.05	123.95	159.27	129.36	137.41	161.22	189.29	172.76	216.59	238.44	309.95	327.27
Claims on Central Government	12a	39.48	39.11	32.68	29.28	28.63	26.74	25.27	36.46	34.90	26.37	26.58	22.17
Claims on Deposit Money Banks	12e	1.46	1.33	1.18	1.03	.95	.90	.74	.62	.49	.40	.33	.26
Reserve Money	14	142.88	164.26	193.00	159.61	166.91	188.77	215.20	209.74	251.86	265.20	336.85	348.42
of which: Currency Outside DMBs	14a	60.78	65.87	77.22	68.06	66.55	79.78	85.01	84.63	78.13	88.20	98.86	113.34
Foreign Liabilities	16c	—	—	—	—	—	—	—	—	—	—	—	—
Central Government Deposits	16d	.12	.12	.13	.06	.09	.09	.09	.10	.11	.01	.01	1.28
Other Items (Net)	17r												
Deposit Money Banks		*Millions of E. Caribbean Dollars: End of Period*											
Reserves	20	91.66	96.82	116.90	93.87	99.01	115.73	130.99	117.01	190.80	172.61	215.82	244.86
Foreign Assets	21	153.24	208.72	209.36	194.46	158.72	192.61	432.28	464.85	505.83	699.67	802.59	896.31
Claims on Central Government	22a	118.31	124.62	162.83	161.20	192.52	224.83	269.28	283.05	270.51	293.64	289.37	291.84
Claims on Local Government	22b	.81	.23	.72	.52	.72	1.43	—	—	.48	.57	.55	.21
Claims on Nonfin.Pub.Enterprises	22c	9.69	9.53	33.78	33.25	32.44	53.94	77.60	87.36	82.26	75.55	75.53	81.36
Claims on Private Sector	22d	625.30	613.83	706.86	850.34	1,027.00	1,103.30	1,196.01	1,308.10	1,348.71	1,413.70	1,491.61	1,514.29
Claims on Nonbank Financial Insts	22g	5.92	21.50	7.78	6.73	6.75	9.34	16.43	8.24	10.13	8.89	47.31	54.72
Demand Deposits	24	125.98	151.77	201.63	189.93	197.19	250.10	238.50	231.42	265.87	250.71	301.33	389.14
Time, Savings,& Fgn.Currency Dep	25	614.08	649.27	773.57	756.28	824.64	929.91	1,274.88	1,382.59	1,444.39	1,554.36	1,798.06	1,836.94
Foreign Liabilities	26c	145.92	163.95	125.73	211.88	279.48	308.92	349.62	491.00	401.05	564.11	441.76	490.82
Central Government Deposits	26d	45.22	53.83	65.10	72.77	71.32	69.60	57.57	54.26	55.31	63.45	58.22	82.41
Credit from Monetary Authorities	26g	1.94	1.29	1.17	1.03	4.31	15.63	13.60	10.97	31.50	3.14	4.70	9.71
Capital Accounts	27a	76.01	99.96	107.12	112.55	130.99	147.70	164.56	157.96	174.91	195.26	194.02	231.51
Other Items (Net)	27r	−4.22	−44.83	−36.09	−4.07	9.24	−20.68	23.87	−59.59	35.70	33.59	124.71	43.06
Monetary Survey		*Millions of E. Caribbean Dollars: End of Period*											
Foreign Assets (Net)	31n	109.37	168.72	242.91	111.94	16.66	44.91	271.95	146.61	321.38	374.00	670.79	732.76
Domestic Credit	32	754.17	754.86	879.42	1,008.49	1,216.65	1,349.89	1,526.93	1,668.85	1,691.55	1,755.25	1,872.73	1,880.89
Claims on Central Govt. (Net)	32an	112.46	109.78	130.28	117.65	149.73	181.88	236.89	265.15	249.99	256.55	257.72	230.31
Claims on Local Government	32b	.81	.23	.72	.52	.72	1.43	—	—	.48	.57	.55	.21
Claims on Nonfin.Pub.Enterprises	32c	9.69	9.53	33.78	33.25	32.44	53.94	77.60	87.36	82.26	75.55	75.53	81.36
Claims on Private Sector	32d	625.30	613.83	706.86	850.34	1,027.00	1,103.30	1,196.01	1,308.10	1,348.71	1,413.70	1,491.61	1,514.29
Claims on Nonbank Financial Inst	32g	5.92	21.50	7.78	6.73	6.75	9.34	16.43	8.24	10.13	8.89	47.31	54.72
Money	34	186.90	217.83	278.95	258.07	263.81	329.93	323.54	316.05	344.00	338.93	400.20	502.48
Quasi-Money	35	614.08	649.27	773.57	756.28	824.64	929.91	1,274.88	1,382.59	1,444.39	1,554.36	1,798.06	1,836.94
Capital Accounts	37a	76.01	99.96	107.12	112.55	130.99	147.70	164.56	157.96	174.91	195.26	194.02	231.51
Other Items (Net)	37r	−13.44	−43.48	−37.31	−6.48	13.87	−12.74	35.90	−41.14	49.64	40.71	151.24	42.72
Money plus Quasi-Money	35l	800.98	867.10	1,052.51	1,014.35	1,088.45	1,259.84	1,598.42	1,698.64	1,788.39	1,893.28	2,198.26	2,339.43
Money (National Definitions)		*Millions of E. Caribbean Dollars: End of Period*											
M1	59ma	174.58	194.92	259.58	233.18	242.39	298.70	302.59	284.33	307.13	308.01	369.52	444.20
M2	59mb	748.45	823.10	998.77	948.94	1,030.10	1,187.53	1,311.71	1,386.99	1,453.58	1,545.09	1,871.10	2,041.30
Interest Rates		*Percent Per Annum*											
Discount Rate (End of Period)	60	....	9.00	9.00	9.00	8.00	8.00	8.00	8.00	7.00	7.00	6.50	6.50
Money Market Rate	60b	5.25	5.25	5.25	5.25	5.25	5.25	5.25	5.25	† 5.64	6.32	6.07	4.67
Treasury Bill Rate	60c	7.00	7.00	7.00	7.00	7.00	7.00	7.00	7.00	7.00	7.00	7.00	7.00
Savings Rate	60k	8.00	8.00	8.00	8.00	8.00	8.00	8.00	8.00	8.00	8.00	† 3.56	3.40
Deposit Rate	60l	5.01	4.19	4.02	4.33	4.36	4.34	4.45	5.18	4.49	4.36	4.86	4.33
Deposit Rate (Fgn. Currency)	60l.f	....	....	....	....	....	....	....	....	....	....	4.64	5.35
Lending Rate	60p	12.68	13.15	12.70	12.26	11.98	12.20	12.07	12.17	11.62	11.39	12.82	12.39
Intl. Transactions & Positions		*Millions of US Dollars*											
Exports	70..d	62.1	44.4	53.1	37.7	37.9	36.2	37.8	....	....	....	....	....
Imports, c.i.f	71..d	323.4	341.5	345.7	365.3	370.4	385.2	414.1	....	....	....	....	....

		1993	1994	1995	1996	1997	1998	1999	2000	2001	2002	2003	2004
Balance of Payments					*Millions of US Dollars: Minus Sign Indicates Debit*								
Current Account, n.i.e.	78ald	15.06	−6.34	−.52	−59.44	−47.37	−46.77	−57.26	−65.78	−64.41	−102.56	....	....
Goods: Exports f.o.b.	78aad	62.08	45.23	53.15	38.88	38.80	37.38	37.43	49.71	38.62	44.80	....	....
Goods: Imports f.o.b.	78abd	−270.43	−287.50	−291.04	−309.94	−313.86	−320.84	−352.70	−342.39	−321.17	−335.64	....	....
Trade Balance	78acd	−208.35	−242.27	−237.89	−271.06	−275.06	−283.46	−315.27	−292.68	−282.55	−290.84	....	....
Services: Credit	78add	377.09	391.23	348.46	363.64	404.49	428.52	439.21	416.39	402.67	391.84	....	....
Services: Debit	78aed	−128.07	−134.42	−147.89	−157.43	−164.43	−169.09	−177.27	−154.32	−171.89	−174.68	....	....
Balance on Goods & Services	78afd	40.67	14.53	−37.32	−64.84	−35.00	−24.02	−53.33	−30.61	−51.77	−73.67	....	....
Income: Credit	78agd	3.11	4.26	5.21	5.79	3.71	12.89	11.70	15.52	18.69	12.56	....	....
Income: Debit	78ahd	−26.05	−30.81	−32.07	−32.01	−25.86	−33.92	−35.14	−60.04	−40.47	−47.06	....	....
Balance on Gds, Serv. & Inc.	78aid	17.73	−12.03	−64.18	−91.06	−57.16	−45.06	−76.77	−75.13	−73.55	−108.17	....	....
Current Transfers, n.i.e.: Credit	78ajd	9.07	15.15	78.04	35.19	19.90	12.42	23.61	18.43	22.52	22.97	....	....
Current Transfers: Debit	78akd	−11.75	−9.47	−14.38	−3.56	−10.12	−14.13	−4.10	−9.09	−13.38	−17.36	....	....
Capital Account, n.i.e.	78bcd	6.81	5.91	6.99	4.36	9.17	156.33	17.62	39.33	11.93	13.92	....	....
Capital Account, n.i.e.: Credit	78bad	6.81	6.53	6.99	4.36	9.17	156.33	17.62	39.33	11.93	13.92	....	....
Capital Account: Debit	78bbd	—	−.62	—	—	—	—	—	—	—	—	....	....
Financial Account, n.i.e.	78bjd	−17.47	−19.88	−10.66	54.98	50.54	−56.72	52.10	42.07	60.05	84.65	....	....
Direct Investment Abroad	78bdd					—		—	—	—	—		
Dir. Invest. in Rep. Econ., n.i.e.	78bed	15.24	24.79	31.49	19.35	22.94	22.77	32.09	28.11	43.93	47.71	....	....
Portfolio Investment Assets	78bfd	—	−1.38	1.19	−.78	—		−.09	−.01	−.05	−2.92	....	....
Equity Securities	78bkd	....	....	....	....	....	....	....	....	....	....	....	....
Debt Securities	78bld	....	....	....	....	....	....	....	....	....	....	....	....
Portfolio Investment Liab., n.i.e.	78bgd	—	—	−1.28	−.81	—	−.29	2.78	2.35	−2.46	.74	....	....
Equity Securities	78bmd	....	....	....	....	....	....	....	....	....	....	....	....
Debt Securities	78bnd	....	....	....	....	....	....	....	....	....	....	....	....
Financial Derivatives Assets	78bwd	....	....	....	....	....	....	....	....	....	....	....	....
Financial Derivatives Liabilities	78bxd	....	....	....	....	....	....	....	....	....	....	....	....
Other Investment Assets	78bhd	−1.17	−23.89	−31.34	−6.68	−2.40	−20.41	74.74	−.39	−3.74	−10.83	....	....
Monetary Authorities	78bod	....	....	....	....	....	....	....	....	....	....	....	....
General Government	78bpd	....	....	....	....	....	....	....	....	....	....	....	....
Banks	78bqd	....	....	....	....	....	....	....	....	....	....	....	....
Other Sectors	78brd	....	....	....	....	....	....	....	....	....	....	....	....
Other Investment Liab., n.i.e.	78bid	−31.54	−19.40	−10.71	43.90	29.99	−58.79	−57.41	12.00	22.36	49.94	....	....
Monetary Authorities	78bsd	—	—	—	—	—	—	—	—	—	—	....	....
General Government	78btd	....	....	....	....	....	....	....	....	....	....	....	....
Banks	78bud	....	....	....	....	....	....	....	....	....	....	....	....
Other Sectors	78bvd	....	....	....	....	....	....	....	....	....	....	....	....
Net Errors and Omissions	78cad	−16.25	28.39	17.78	−11.16	−9.38	−43.96	−2.07	−21.78	8.44	11.72	....	....
Overall Balance	78cbd	−11.84	8.08	13.59	−11.26	2.96	8.88	10.39	−6.16	16.00	7.73	....	....
Reserves and Related Items	79dad	11.84	−8.08	−13.59	11.26	−2.96	−8.89	−10.39	6.16	−16.00	−7.73	....	....
Reserve Assets	79dbd	11.84	−8.08	−13.59	11.26	−2.96	−8.89	−10.39	6.16	−16.00	−7.73	....	....
Use of Fund Credit and Loans	79dcd	—	—	—	—	—	—	—	—	—	—	....	....
Exceptional Financing	79ded	....	....	....	....	....	....	....	....	....	....	....	....
National Accounts						*Millions of E. Caribbean Dollars*							
Househ.Cons.Expend.,incl.NPISHs.	96f	544.1	633.8	672.5	784.0	774.0	750.6	711.3	780.1	....	....	....	....
Government Consumption Expend.	91f	230.2	258.2	284.8	307.7	318.1	364.9	396.4	420.0	....	....	....	....
Gross Fixed Capital Formation	93e	390.6	437.4	491.9	578.8	614.6	720.6	793.8	862.4	....	....	....	....
Exports of Goods and Services	90c	1,186.1	1,190.0	1,084.3	1,086.8	1,190.2	1,245.6	1,259.8	1,260.3	....	....	....	....
Imports of Goods and Services (-)	98c	1,118.2	1,169.2	1,201.0	1,298.3	1,328.1	1,407.5	1,403.3	1,536.2	....	....	....	....
Gross Domestic Product (GDP)	99b	1,232.7	1,350.2	1,332.7	1,459.0	1,568.8	1,674.2	1,758.1	1,786.6	....	....	....	....
Net Primary Income from Abroad	98.n	−61.9	−71.7	−72.5	−70.8	−72.8	−80.6	−80.8	−84.7	....	....	....	....
Gross National Income (GNI)	99a	1,170.7	1,278.6	1,260.2	1,388.2	1,496.0	1,593.6	1,677.3	1,701.9	....	....	....	....
Net Current Transf.from Abroad	98t	−7.2	2.4	187.3	85.4	33.1	−2.0	55.7	1.7	....	....	....	....
Gross Nat'l Disposable Inc.(GNDI)	99i	1,163.5	1,281.0	1,447.5	1,473.6	1,529.1	1,591.7	1,733.0	1,703.6	....	....	....	....
Gross Saving	99s	389.3	389.0	490.0	381.9	437.0	476.2	625.4	503.6	....	....	....	....
GDP Volume 1990 Prices	99b.p	1,146.6	1,219.1	1,168.2	1,245.3	1,310.5	1,353.4	1,403.0	....	....	....	....	....
GDP Volume (1995=100)	99bvp	98.1	104.4	100.0	106.6	112.2	115.9	120.1	....	....	....	....	....
GDP Deflator (1995=100)	99bip	94.2	97.1	100.0	102.7	104.9	108.4	109.8	....	....	....	....	....
						Millions: Midyear Estimates							
Population	99z	.07	.07	.07	.07	.07	.07	.08	.08	.08	.08	.08	.08

		1993	1994	1995	1996	1997	1998	1999	2000	2001	2002	2003	2004
Exchange Rates						*Pesos per SDR: End of Period*							
Official Rate	aa	1.37150	1.45912	1.48649	1.43724	1.34858	1.40733	1.37182	1.30226	1.25610	4.51361	4.31674	4.59536
					Pesos per US Dollar: End of Period (ae) Period Average (rf)								
Official Rate	ae	.99850	.99950	1.00000	.99950	.99950	.99950	.99950	.99950	.99950	3.32000	2.90500	2.95900
Official Rate	rf	.99895	.99901	.99975	.99966	.99950	.99950	.99950	.99950	.99950	3.06326	2.90063	2.92330
Fund Position						*Millions of SDRs: End of Period*							
Quota	2f.s	1,537.1	1,537.1	1,537.1	1,537.1	1,537.1	1,537.1	2,117.1	2,117.1	2,117.1	2,117.1	2,117.1	2,117.1
SDRs	1b.s	329.5	385.7	362.7	277.4	123.6	187.7	100.3	562.2	8.5	69.3	678.7	564.5
Reserve Position in the Fund	1c.s	—	—	—	—	—	—	—	—	—	—	.1	.2
Total Fund Cred.&Loans Outstg	2tl	2,562.4	2,884.7	4,124.4	4,376.0	4,349.3	3,865.1	3,262.6	3,880.3	11,121.1	10,547.5	10,446.2	9,073.0
International Liquidity						*Millions of US Dollars Unless Otherwise Indicated: End of Period*							
Total Reserves minus Gold	1l.d	13,791	14,327	14,288	18,104	22,320	24,752	26,252	25,147	14,553	10,489	14,153	18,884
SDRs	1b.d	453	563	539	399	167	264	138	733	11	94	1,008	877
Reserve Position in the Fund	1c.d	—	—	—	—	—	—	—	—	—	—	—	—
Foreign Exchange	1d.d	13,339	13,764	13,749	17,705	22,153	24,488	26,114	24,414	14,542	10,395	13,145	18,007
Gold (Million Fine Troy Ounces)	1ad	4.373	4.374	4.374	4.374	.361	.360	.338	.019	.009	.009	.009	1.770
Gold (National Valuation)	1and	1,672	1,651	1,679	1,611	120	124	121	7	3	3	4	769
Monetary Authorities:Other Assets	3..d	—	57	22	30	42	30	13	3	—	—	—	—
Other Liab.	4..d	161	—	—	—	—	—	—	—	5	18	34	4
Deposit Money Banks: Assets	7a.d	5,153	5,587	6,302	10,011	17,732	16,895	15,007	17,911	7,179	3,627	3,350	2,878
Liabilities	7b.d	9,051	10,995	13,649	15,820	21,048	21,440	22,831	24,170	16,297	12,717	9,334	7,290
Other Banking Insts.: Assets	7e.d	32	26	31	25	24	17	74	42	35	15	21	8
Liabilities	7f.d	26	39	62	84	148	395	434	405	263	45	17	28
Monetary Authorities						*Millions of Pesos: End of Period*							
Foreign Assets	11	15,448	† 16,035	15,989	19,745	22,806	26,249	27,322	26,925	15,321	35,236	40,733	58,444
Claims on Central Government	12a	11,432	† 8,361	8,499	8,223	7,867	7,170	6,350	7,468	20,495	57,231	62,584	65,538
Claims on Deposit Money Banks	12e	22,527	† 22,463	24,129	2,106	1,794	2,070	2,160	1,930	6,019	24,794	25,098	24,897
Claims on Other Banking Insts	12f	5	† 4	3	3	—	—	—	—	81	91	116	
Reserve Money	14	14,989	† 16,267	13,769	14,060	15,975	16,392	16,524	15,077	17,768	30,165	50,158	60,525
of which: Currency Outside DMBs	14a	10,067	† 11,229	11,161	11,736	13,331	13,503	13,736	12,571	9,081	16,430	26,649	33,872
Foreign Liabilities	16c	3,677	† 4,211	6,131	6,293	5,868	5,442	4,478	5,056	13,982	48,286	45,652	41,915
Central Government Deposits	16d	1,338	† 764	1,677	2,242	325	1,343	935	1,769	4,366	67	259	161
Capital Accounts	17a	7,217	† 3,279	3,583	4,053	4,059	4,604	4,415	4,659	3,542	7,012	5,993	7,206
Other Items (Net)	17r	22,191	† 22,342	23,461	3,430	6,242	7,708	9,480	9,762	2,177	31,811	26,445	39,187
Deposit Money Banks						*Millions of Pesos: End of Period*							
Reserves	20	5,488	† 5,203	2,637	2,358	2,673	2,905	3,101	2,826	8,429	13,507	23,061	26,439
Foreign Assets	21	5,148	† 5,587	6,302	10,011	17,732	16,895	15,007	17,911	7,179	12,196	9,830	8,559
Claims on Central Government	22a	11,657	† 6,094	10,299	13,013	14,513	17,433	18,982	18,859	20,518	82,709	92,425	101,443
Claims on State and Local Govts	22b	—	† 5,008	5,247	5,273	5,950	5,827	8,924	9,585	9,133	11,366	2,503	1,824
Claims on Official Entities	22bx	1,509	† 493	463	565	612	285	276	278	443	259	617	589
Claims on Private Sector	22d	42,600	† 51,372	50,780	54,093	63,131	70,525	68,431	65,843	54,159	47,249	39,926	46,092
Demand Deposits	24	5,052	† 5,133	5,458	7,305	8,151	7,986	8,099	7,267	6,763	11,843	16,292	22,055
Time, Savings,& Fgn.Currency Dep	25	30,334	† 37,109	35,352	42,710	56,038	64,162	67,315	70,677	57,078	59,022	70,224	81,485
Foreign Liabilities	26c	9,042	† 10,995	13,649	15,820	21,048	21,440	22,831	24,170	16,297	42,768	27,392	21,679
Central Government Deposits	26d	5,054	† 3,014	2,467	3,054	3,990	4,525	3,602	4,474	2,150	5,255	8,691	13,491
Credit from Monetary Authorities	26g	22,336	† 2,184	2,650	1,375	409	393	308	78	4,478	28,879	28,352	29,239
Capital Accounts	27a	12,503	† 13,519	13,771	15,065	15,806	16,674	16,437	16,726	15,816	25,033	20,964	23,045
Other Items (Net)	27r	−17,919	† 1,802	2,381	−18	−830	−1,311	−3,868	−8,092	−2,722	−5,513	−3,553	−6,049
Monetary Survey						*Millions of Pesos: End of Period*							
Foreign Assets (Net)	31n	7,877	† 6,416	2,510	7,643	13,623	16,262	15,021	15,610	−7,778	−43,622	−22,481	3,409
Domestic Credit	32	60,811	† 67,554	71,148	75,874	87,759	95,372	98,427	95,790	98,231	193,573	189,196	201,950
Claims on Central Govt. (Net)	32an	16,697	† 10,677	14,654	15,940	18,066	18,735	20,795	20,084	34,496	134,619	146,059	153,328
Claims on State and Local Govts	32b	—	† 5,008	5,247	5,273	5,950	5,827	8,924	9,585	9,133	11,366	2,503	1,824
Claims on Official Entities	32bx	1,509	† 493	463	565	612	285	276	278	443	259	617	589
Claims on Private Sector	32d	42,600	† 51,372	50,780	54,093	63,131	70,525	68,431	65,843	54,159	47,249	39,926	46,092
Claims on Other Banking Insts	32f	5	† 4	3	3	—	—	—	—	—	81	91	116
Money	34	15,119	† 16,362	16,619	19,042	21,482	21,489	21,836	19,838	15,844	28,272	42,940	55,927
Quasi-Money	35	30,334	† 37,109	35,352	42,710	56,038	64,162	67,315	70,677	57,078	59,022	70,224	81,485
Capital Accounts	37a	19,720	† 16,798	17,354	19,118	19,864	21,279	20,852	21,386	19,358	32,045	26,956	30,252
Other Items (Net)	37r	3,515	† 3,701	4,333	2,647	3,997	4,704	3,446	−501	−1,827	30,612	26,594	37,695
Money plus Quasi-Money	35l	45,453	† 53,471	51,971	61,752	77,520	85,651	89,150	90,515	72,922	87,294	113,164	137,412
Other Banking Institutions						*Millions of Pesos: End of Period*							
Reserves	40	20	† 20	14	7	6	7	15	15	89	141	169	79
Foreign Assets	41	32	† 26	31	25	24	17	74	42	35	49	61	25
Claims on Central Government	42a	26	† 35	37	84	96	114	89	56	18	941	677	525
Claims on Local and State Govts	42b	—	† 2	2	—	2	—	—	—	—	6	—	—
Claims on Official Entities	42bx	—	† —	—	—	—	—	—	—	2	—	—	—
Claims on Private Sector	42d	644	† 838	725	846	1,103	1,681	2,147	2,067	1,821	676	532	879
Claims on Deposit Money Banks	42e	5	† 10	13	20	18	22	27	27	22	15	25	27
Time, Savings,& Fgn.Currency Dep	45	412	† 501	284	348	320	333	295	344	223	192	215	203
Foreign Liabilities	46c	26	† 39	62	84	148	395	434	405	263	153	51	82
Credit from Monetary Authorities	46g	5	† 4	3	3	—	—	—	—	—	81	91	116
Capital Accounts	47a	202	† 236	210	190	233	367	468	557	667	1,052	981	834
Other Items (Net)	47r	82	† 151	263	357	547	746	1,155	902	833	351	126	300

Argentina 213

		1993	1994	1995	1996	1997	1998	1999	2000	2001	2002	2003	2004
Banking Survey						*Millions of Pesos: End of Period*							
Foreign Assets (Net).........................	51n	7,883	† 6,403	2,480	7,585	13,499	15,884	14,661	15,247	−8,006	−43,726	−22,472	3,352
Domestic Credit..............................	52	61,476	† 68,424	71,908	76,802	88,959	97,167	100,663	97,913	100,072	195,116	190,315	203,239
Claims on Central Govt. (Net)........	52an	16,723	† 10,711	14,691	16,024	18,163	18,850	20,884	20,140	34,514	135,560	146,736	153,854
Claims on State and Local Govts....	52b	—	† 5,009	5,249	5,273	5,951	5,827	8,924	9,585	9,133	11,372	2,503	1,824
Claims on Official Entities.............	52bx	1,509	† 493	463	565	612	285	276	278	445	259	618	590
Claims on Private Sector................	52d	43,244	† 52,210	51,505	54,939	64,234	72,206	70,578	67,910	55,979	47,924	40,458	46,971
Liquid Liabilities.............................	55l	45,845	† 53,952	52,241	62,094	77,835	85,977	89,430	90,844	73,056	87,345	113,210	137,536
Capital Accounts............................	57a	19,922	† 17,034	17,564	19,308	20,098	21,646	21,320	21,942	20,024	33,098	27,937	31,086
Other Items (Net)............................	57r	3,592	† 3,841	4,584	2,984	4,526	5,428	4,573	374	−1,015	30,947	26,696	37,968
Interest Rates						*Percent Per Annum*							
Money Market Rate........................	60b	6.31	7.66	9.46	6.23	6.63	6.81	6.99	8.15	24.90	41.35	3.74	1.96
Money Market Rate (Fgn. Cur.)........	60b.f	....	....	8.40	5.91	6.39	6.55	6.07	7.53	12.76	13.01	1.64	2.03
Deposit Rate...................................	60l	11.34	8.08	11.90	7.36	6.97	7.56	8.05	8.34	16.16	39.25	10.16	2.61
Deposit Rate (Fgn. Currency)............	60l.f	....	5.68	8.19	6.10	5.87	6.40	6.42	7.03	9.81	4.44	.86	.38
Lending Rate...................................	60p	....	10.06	17.85	10.51	9.24	10.64	11.04	11.09	27.71	51.68	19.15	6.78
Lending Rate (Fgn. Currency)...........	60p.f	....	8.17	13.88	9.12	7.84	8.95	9.07	9.67	17.67	....	....	....
Prices, Production, Labor						*Index Numbers (2000=100): Period Averages*							
Share Prices....................................	62	86.9	114.6	84.0	111.4	149.0	110.6	96.9	100.0	72.6	79.4	145.4	219.6
Producer Prices..............................	63	97.5	97.9	102.1	105.1	104.0	100.5	96.4	100.0	98.0	174.6	208.9	225.0
Consumer Prices.............................	64	93.3	97.2	100.5	† 100.7	101.2	102.1	100.9	100.0	98.9	124.5	141.3	147.5
Wages: Monthly(Mfg)('95=100)......	65ey	95.2	101.7	100.0	100.7	....	....	....	....	....	....	....	....
Manufacturing Prod., Seas.Adj.......	66eyc	95.7	103.0	96.6	99.1	108.4	110.6	101.4	100.0	74.4	67.0	78.6	89.7
Crude Petroleum Production............	66aa	76.9	86.4	93.2	99.5	108.1	109.8	104.1	100.0	100.3	98.0	96.0	90.0
						Number in Thousands: Period Averages							
Labor Force.....................................	67d	11,741	11,923	12,306	12,526	12,971	13,077	13,455	13,780	13,914	14,336	....	....
Employment....................................	67e	10,675	10,520	10,301	10,453	11,231	11,495	11,641	11,760	11,401	11,827	....	....
Unemployment................................	67c	1,066	1,402	2,006	2,074	1,740	1,582	1,814	2,019	2,513	2,509	....	....
Unemployment Rate (%).................	67r	9.0	12.0	16.0	16.6	13.4	12.1	13.5	14.7	18.1	17.5	....	....
Intl. Transactions & Positions						*Millions of US Dollars*							
Exports..	70..d	13,118	15,839	20,963	23,811	26,431	26,434	23,309	26,341	26,543	25,650	29,566	34,453
Wheat...	70d.d	735	657	1,005	1,066	1,347	1,308	1,002	1,218	1,302	1,097	941	1,374
Imports, c.i.f....................................	71..d	16,784	21,590	20,122	23,762	30,450	31,377	25,508	25,280	20,320	8,990	13,834	22,320
Imports, f.o.b..................................	71.vd	15,544	20,077	18,726	22,190	28,554	29,532	24,103	23,889	19,158	8,473	13,118	21,215
						2000=100							
Volume of Exports..........................	72	48.8	57.3	71.7	76.4	87.9	98.1	97.4	100.0	104.3	105.1	110.3	117.8
Wheat...	72d	51.7	47.0	62.5	53.5	78.7	95.5	79.9	100.0	97.9	82.1	55.9	90.4
Volume of Imports..........................	73	61.3	77.8	68.8	82.2	107.8	117.2	100.9	100.0	82.6	37.9	58.1	87.4
						2000=100: Indices of Unit Values in US Dollars							
Unit Value of Exports/Export Prices...	74..d	102.0	105.0	111.0	118.3	114.2	102.3	90.9	100.0	96.6	92.9	101.7	111.4
Frozen Beef..................................	74kad	148.4	112.4	103.1	82.7	88.5	115.2	101.3	100.0	81.2	....	....	....
Corned Beef (1990=100)..............	74kdd	108.7	116.7	....	....	....	....	....	....	....	....	....	....
Wheat..	74d.d	114.9	117.1	131.6	162.8	138.5	113.2	103.0	100.0	109.1	109.7	137.9	126.7
Unit Value of Imports/Import Prices..	75..d	108.2	109.7	115.7	114.3	111.7	106.0	100.0	100.0	97.3	93.8	94.2	101.5

		1993	1994	1995	1996	1997	1998	1999	2000	2001	2002	2003	2004
Balance of Payments		*Millions of US Dollars: Minus Sign Indicates Debit*											
Current Account, n.i.e.	78ald	−8,163	−11,148	−5,175	−6,822	−12,219	−14,510	−11,948	−8,989	−3,290	8,673	7,658	3,353
Goods: Exports f.o.b.	78aad	13,269	16,023	21,162	24,043	26,431	26,434	23,309	26,341	26,543	25,651	29,566	34,550
Goods: Imports f.o.b.	78abd	−15,633	−20,162	−18,804	−22,283	−28,554	−29,531	−24,103	−23,889	−19,158	−8,473	−13,118	−21,311
Trade Balance	78acd	−2,364	−4,139	2,357	1,760	−2,123	−3,097	−795	2,452	7,385	17,178	16,448	13,239
Services: Credit	78add	3,070	3,362	3,817	4,339	4,534	4,756	4,617	4,808	4,627	3,290	4,205	5,151
Services: Debit	78aed	−6,394	−7,138	−7,234	−7,865	−8,942	−9,246	−8,768	−9,130	−8,490	−4,873	−5,601	−6,841
Balance on Goods & Services	78afd	−5,688	−7,915	−1,059	−1,767	−6,531	−7,587	−4,946	−1,871	3,522	15,595	15,052	11,549
Income: Credit	78agd	2,592	3,461	4,385	4,440	5,509	6,151	6,109	7,446	5,847	3,021	3,084	3,495
Income: Debit	78ahd	−5,589	−7,158	−9,054	−9,943	−11,712	−13,538	−13,565	−14,968	−13,085	−10,506	−11,054	−12,379
Balance on Gds, Serv. & Inc.	78aid	−8,685	−11,612	−5,728	−7,270	−12,734	−14,974	−12,402	−9,392	−3,715	8,111	7,081	2,665
Current Transfers, n.i.e.: Credit	78ajd	841	799	823	704	822	790	777	781	856	795	917	1,091
Current Transfers: Debit	78akd	−319	−336	−269	−257	−307	−326	−322	−377	−431	−233	−340	−403
Capital Account, n.i.e.	78bcd	16	18	14	51	66	73	149	106	157	406	70	45
Capital Account, n.i.e.: Credit	78bad	25	27	25	72	112	92	161	121	165	410	77	49
Capital Account: Debit	78bbd	−9	−10	−11	−21	−46	−19	−12	−15	−8	−4	−7	−4
Financial Account, n.i.e.	78bjd	20,328	11,360	4,989	11,713	16,746	18,936	14,448	7,853	−14,971	−20,686	−15,864	−10,424
Direct Investment Abroad	78bdd	−705	−1,013	−1,497	−1,601	−3,653	−2,325	−1,730	−901	−161	627	−774	−351
Dir. Invest. in Rep. Econ., n.i.e.	78bed	2,793	3,635	5,609	6,949	9,160	7,291	23,988	10,418	2,166	2,149	1,652	4,084
Portfolio Investment Assets	78bfd	−1,555	−1,486	−2,882	−2,381	−1,570	−1,906	−2,005	−1,252	212	477	−95	−77
Equity Securities	78bkd	−1,363	−763	−401	−594	−838	−839	167	−1,455	−931	13	−34	−72
Debt Securities	78bld	−192	−723	−2,481	−1,787	−733	−1,067	−2,173	203	1,143	464	−61	−5
Portfolio Investment Liab., n.i.e.	78bgd	35,266	9,843	4,734	12,098	11,666	10,693	−4,780	−1,331	−9,715	−5,117	−7,663	−9,358
Equity Securities	78bmd	4,979	3,116	1,090	990	1,391	−210	−10,773	−3,227	31	−116	65	−86
Debt Securities	78bnd	30,287	6,727	3,643	11,108	10,276	10,903	5,993	1,896	−9,746	−5,001	−7,728	−9,272
Financial Derivatives Assets	78bwd	....	....	....	....	....	....	....	....	....	....	....	....
Financial Derivatives Liabilities	78bxd	....	....	....	....	....	....	....	....	....	....	....	....
Other Investment Assets	78bhd	−4,721	−3,163	−8,123	−5,217	−7,116	−173	−2,862	−1,368	−1,907	−8,896	−4,403	−1,987
Monetary Authorities	78bod	—	—	—	—	—	—	—	—	—	—	—	—
General Government	78bpd	−1,548	442	−686	62	−99	111	−1,553	1,056	232	307	−78	−161
Banks	78bqd	−1,727	−297	−603	−3,039	−5,337	613	995	−2,348	8,960	1,896	447	240
Other Sectors	78brd	−1,446	−3,308	−6,834	−2,240	−1,681	−897	−2,304	−76	−11,099	−11,099	−4,773	−2,066
Other Investment Liab., n.i.e.	78bid	−10,750	3,544	7,148	1,865	8,259	5,356	1,838	2,287	−5,566	−9,925	−4,581	−2,735
Monetary Authorities	78bsd	−3,996	−16	−94	−214	−11	−10	−13	−16	1,130	−341	−634	53
General Government	78btd	−8,709	535	1,903	−151	311	1,924	1,203	440	1,007	−2,207	−98	−1,054
Banks	78bud	1,150	1,098	3,250	443	3,843	621	1,133	898	−6,775	−2,178	−2,917	−916
Other Sectors	78bvd	805	1,927	2,089	1,788	4,116	2,822	−486	964	−928	−5,199	−932	−817
Net Errors and Omissions	78cad	−1,059	−904	−2,140	−1,684	−1,263	−409	−637	−146	−3,300	−1,796	−941	17
Overall Balance	78cbd	11,122	−675	−2,311	3,258	3,331	4,090	2,013	−1,176	−21,405	−13,402	−9,077	−7,010
Reserves and Related Items	79dad	−11,122	675	2,311	−3,258	−3,331	−4,090	−2,013	1,176	21,405	13,402	9,077	7,010
Reserve Assets	79dbd	−4,279	−685	82	−3,875	−3,293	−3,436	−1,186	403	12,070	4,526	−3,497	−5,283
Use of Fund Credit and Loans	79dcd	1,211	455	1,924	367	−38	−654	−826	773	9,335	−739	−151	−2,038
Exceptional Financing	79ded	−8,054	904	305	250	—	—	—	—	—	9,616	12,725	14,330
International Investment Position		*Millions of US Dollars*											
Assets	79aad	86,913	89,673	102,834	117,398	133,241	140,617	150,380	153,633	132,797	131,983	144,833	....
Direct Investment Abroad	79abd	8,086	9,148	10,696	12,374	16,034	18,335	20,118	21,141	21,283	20,618	21,500	....
Portfolio Investment	79acd	20,393	19,154	22,539	26,548	28,900	30,270	34,410	35,190	1,225	843	939	....
Equity Securities	79add	53	68	108	102	217	51	31	43	43	30	64	....
Debt Securities	79aed	20,340	19,087	22,431	26,447	28,683	30,219	34,379	35,147	1,182	813	875	....
Financial Derivatives	79ald	—	—	—	—	—	—	—	—	—	—	—	....
Other Investment	79afd	42,511	44,775	53,097	58,331	65,333	65,498	68,374	69,652	95,365	99,951	107,267	....
Monetary Authorities	79agd	—	—	—	—	—	—	—	—	—	—	—	....
General Government	79ahd	6,593	5,252	6,136	6,091	6,075	5,957	7,524	6,377	6,600	6,108	6,330	....
Banks	79aid	5,079	5,377	5,980	9,019	14,355	13,742	12,747	15,095	5,888	3,141	2,694	....
Other Sectors	79ajd	30,839	34,147	40,981	43,221	44,902	45,799	48,103	48,179	82,877	90,702	98,243	....
Reserve Assets	79akd	15,924	16,595	16,502	20,144	22,974	26,513	27,479	27,651	14,923	10,571	15,127	....
Liabilities	79lad	102,194	119,555	139,918	159,475	188,157	206,760	218,956	221,785	214,009	172,148	190,936	....
Dir. Invest. in Rep. Economy	79lbd	18,520	22,428	27,991	33,589	42,084	47,898	62,088	67,769	69,169	32,394	38,323	....
Portfolio Investment	79lcd	49,516	56,945	60,953	73,299	87,297	94,566	91,776	86,682	75,617	67,630	67,110	....
Equity Securities	79ldd	10,257	10,102	11,597	13,730	19,070	14,297	8,389	3,636	2,206	862	2,127	....
Debt Securities	79led	39,259	46,843	49,356	59,569	68,227	80,269	83,387	83,046	73,411	66,768	64,983	....
Financial Derivatives	79lld	—	—	—	—	—	—	—	—	—	—	—	....
Other Investment	79lfd	34,158	40,182	50,974	52,588	58,777	64,296	65,093	67,333	69,223	72,123	85,504	....
Monetary Authorities	79lgd	3,619	4,281	6,184	6,331	5,898	5,462	4,493	5,067	13,980	14,466	15,513	....
General Government	79lhd	18,706	20,510	23,225	22,054	20,587	22,766	23,334	22,932	23,551	29,977	43,233	....
Banks	79lid	6,891	7,988	11,238	11,681	15,524	16,146	17,279	18,177	11,402	9,111	6,967	....
Other Sectors	79ljd	4,943	7,403	10,327	12,522	16,768	19,923	19,987	21,158	20,289	18,569	19,790	....
Government Finance		*Millions of Pesos: Year Ending December 31*											
Deficit (-) or Surplus	80	−1,574.0	−1,885.7	† −1,426.0	−5,233.6	−4,357.3	−4,148.3	−8,125.7	−6,817.6	−8,739.9	−3,463.8	445.9	9,424.4
Revenue	81	15,555.0	15,591.8	† 38,060.9	35,501.0	41,944.1	42,921.1	41,132.2	42,437.9	39,268.4	42,345.7	57,254.9	73,902.0
Exp. & Lending Minus Repay.	82z	17,129.0	17,477.5	† 39,486.9	40,734.6	46,301.4	47,069.4	49,257.9	49,255.5	48,008.3	45,809.5	56,809.0	64,477.6
Expenditure	82	....	....	40,574.5	41,066.1	46,174.3	47,108.3	49,214.2	49,365.9	48,032.9	45,774.8	56,827.3	63,291.4
Lending Minus Repayments	83	....	....	−1,087.6	−331.5	127.1	−38.9	43.7	−110.4	−24.6	34.7	−18.3	1,186.2
Total Financing	84	1,574.0	1,885.7	† 1,426.0	5,233.6	4,357.3	4,148.2	8,125.7	6,817.6	8,739.9	3,463.8	−445.9	−9,424.4
Net Borrowing: Domestic	84a	1,740.0	863.2	....	−1,622.4	2,008.2	−576.8	−2,276.1	−1,924.6	....	....	....	....
Foreign	85a	1,283.0	1,256.8	....	....	....	....	....	....	....	....	....	....
Use of Cash Balances	87	−1,449.0	−234.3	† −2,371.3	−344.1	1,262.1	−1,585.9	556.5	−533.9	−2,239.6	9,991.0	−532.1	−6,867.6

		1993	1994	1995	1996	1997	1998	1999	2000	2001	2002	2003	2004
National Accounts							*Millions of Pesos*						
Househ.Cons.Expend.,incl.NPISHs....	**96f**	† 163,676	180,007	176,909	186,487	203,029	206,434	198,870	197,044	185,164	193,482	237,567	281,167
Government Consumption Expend...	**91f**	† 31,953	33,948	34,446	34,023	35,325	37,353	38,909	39,175	38,038	38,245	42,997	49,826
Gross Fixed Capital Formation..........	**93e**	† 45,069	51,331	46,285	49,211	56,727	59,595	51,074	46,020	38,099	37,387	56,904	85,652
Changes in Inventories....................	**93i**	† 1,494	79	1,493	4,251	4,350	3,180	−378	3,766	3,854	−3,076	−2,041	−1,262
Exports of Goods and Services.........	**90c**	† 16,341	19,364	24,897	28,301	30,834	31,046	27,751	30,937	30,977	86,553	93,869	113,067
Imports of Goods and Services (-).....	**98c**	† 22,028	27,289	25,998	30,124	37,406	38,659	32,702	32,738	27,435	40,010	53,385	81,142
Gross Domestic Product (GDP).........	**99b**	† 236,505	257,440	258,032	272,150	292,859	298,948	283,523	284,204	268,697	312,580	375,910	447,307
Net Primary Income from Abroad.....	**98.n**	† −2,995	−3,697	−4,669	−5,502	−6,218	−7,406	−7,464	−7,470	−7,744	−19,402	−22,429	....
Gross National Income (GNI)............	**99a**	† 233,510	253,743	253,363	266,648	286,641	291,542	276,059	276,734	260,953	293,179	353,481	....
GDP Vol. 1986 Prices......................	**99b.p**	12	....	....	....	....	....	....	....	....	....	....	....
GDP Vol. 1993 Prices......................	**99b.p**	236,505	250,308	243,186	256,626	277,441	288,123	278,369	276,173	263,997	235,236	256,024	279,020
GDP Volume (2000=100)................	**99bvp**	† 85.6	90.6	88.1	92.9	100.5	104.3	100.8	100.0	95.6	85.2	92.7	101.0
GDP Deflator (2000=100)................	**99bip**	† 97.2	99.9	103.1	103.1	102.6	100.8	99.0	100.0	98.9	129.1	142.7	155.8
							Millions: Midyear Estimates						
Population..............................	**99z**	33.95	34.40	34.83	35.27	35.69	36.10	36.50	36.90	37.27	37.64	38.01	38.37

		1993	1994	1995	1996	1997	1998	1999	2000	2001	2002	2003	2004
Exchange Rates					*Dram per SDR: End of Period*								
Official Rate	aa	103.02	591.98	597.57	625.61	667.85	735.03	718.88	719.44	706.04	795.17	841.06	754.51
					Dram per US Dollar: End of Period (ae) Period Average (rf)								
Official Rate	ae	75.00	405.51	402.00	435.07	494.98	522.03	523.77	552.18	561.81	584.89	566.00	485.84
Official Rate	rf	9.11	288.65	405.91	414.04	490.85	504.92	535.06	539.53	555.08	573.35	578.76	533.45
					Index Numbers (2000=100): Period Averages								
Nominal Effective Exchange Rate	nec	....	16.94	27.37	60.00	58.06	66.34	93.97	100.00	98.63	97.40	93.88	98.98
Real Effective Exchange Rate	rec	....	47.16	86.08	104.19	91.32	98.16	105.38	100.00	90.62	82.73	77.06	80.70
Fund Position					*Millions of SDRs: End of Period*								
Quota	2f.s	67.50	67.50	67.50	67.50	67.50	67.50	92.00	92.00	92.00	92.00	92.00	92.00
SDRs	1b.s	—	.19	29.82	28.86	27.63	19.89	29.64	16.54	8.15	22.14	12.67	7.70
Reserve Position in the Fund	1c.s	.01	.01	.01	.01	—	—	—	—	—	—	—	—
Total Fund Cred.&Loans Outstg	2tl	—	16.88	47.25	81.00	97.88	135.25	146.62	134.66	137.35	143.29	144.44	140.13
International Liquidity					*Millions of US Dollars Unless Otherwise Indicated: End of Period*								
Total Reserves minus Gold	1l.d	13.59	32.28	99.58	155.65	228.75	324.00	318.56	318.32	320.82	425.02	510.19	575.87
SDRs	1b.d	—	.28	44.33	41.50	37.28	28.00	40.68	21.55	10.24	30.10	18.83	11.96
Reserve Position in the Fund	1c.d	.01	.01	.01	.01	.01	.01	—	—	—	—	—	—
Foreign Exchange	1d.d	13.58	31.99	55.24	114.14	191.46	295.99	277.88	296.77	310.58	394.92	491.36	563.90
Gold (Million Fine Troy Ounces)	1ad	—	.0100	.0300	.0340	.0361	.0432	.0436	.0446	.0449	.0449	—	—
Gold (National Valuation)	1and	—	2.44	10.46	12.82	10.72	12.37	12.69	12.17	12.41	15.68	—	—
Monetary Authorities:Other Assets	3..d	2.93	.20	.10	.52	.25	.10	.05	.11	.01	.01	.03	.08
Other Liab	4..d	23.96	2.05	1.19	5.09	5.05	2.54	1.59	2.89	6.51	12.81	15.63	22.90
Deposit Money Banks: Assets	7a.d	22.68	22.03	24.28	18.14	33.28	33.12	70.34	96.07	100.98	125.99	180.76	252.21
Liabilities	7b.d	3.45	12.98	24.59	50.74	73.39	96.10	119.90	105.29	93.10	102.07	128.88	
Monetary Authorities					*Millions of Dram: End of Period*								
Foreign Assets	11	1,239	14,162	44,278	73,523	118,657	175,652	173,521	182,551	187,222	257,770	288,786	279,433
Claims on General Government	12a	1,463	9,536	10,624	27,971	16,491	18,083	18,471	10,296	10,190	3,437	1,047	5,887
Claims on Private Sector	12d	—	—	—	—	—	—	30	179	684	683	38	43
Claims on Deposit Money Banks	12e	286	3,629	3,781	3,346	3,345	3,253	1,698	3,332	3,905	10,392	8,700	12,857
Reserve Money	14	1,593	15,002	28,806	41,140	51,333	53,863	53,853	72,389	80,418	111,272	118,642	133,895
of which: Currency Outside DMBs	14a	881	10,056	24,601	34,784	37,596	41,370	42,610	59,486	65,037	88,553	91,997	98,569
Time,Savings,& Fgn.Currency Dep	15	—	781	556	116	187	491	346	1	1	1	43	155
Foreign Liabilities	16c	1,797	10,823	28,715	52,890	67,863	100,741	106,234	98,480	100,633	121,433	130,334	116,857
General Government Deposits	16d	76	1,433	423	8,733	8,165	9,851	10,165	2,004	1,922	13,148	32,554	42,735
Capital Accounts	17a	121	596	1,691	7,214	13,733	16,609	12,079	21,412	22,026	33,427	19,926	918
Other Items (Net)	17r	−599	−1,309	−1,509	−5,254	−2,788	15,431	11,043	2,073	−2,999	−6,997	−2,928	3,661
Deposit Money Banks					*Millions of Dram: End of Period*								
Reserves	20	529	3,164	3,987	6,083	13,681	12,033	11,082	12,593	14,717	22,092	25,478	34,083
Foreign Assets	21	1,701	8,933	9,759	7,894	16,472	17,287	36,843	53,048	56,732	73,691	102,308	122,534
Claims on General Government	22a	199	335	354	5,865	9,198	15,436	12,268	16,890	18,250	26,313	29,179	33,138
of which: Claims on Local Govts	22ab	—	—	—	—	—	2	5	—	—	—	—	—
Claims on Other Sectors	22d	353	20,718	37,946	37,181	48,486	70,791	86,188	102,406	91,826	93,478	97,088	136,602
Claims on Nonbank Financial Insts	22g	—	—	—	—	—	11,369	4,352	7,137	5,398	4,492	6,559	6,269
Demand Deposits	24	443	3,188	5,375	4,968	6,372	11,216	9,553	11,743	12,073	26,400	30,618	33,283
Time,Savings,& Fgn.Currency Dep	25	1,584	10,310	9,617	14,424	26,005	42,868	56,881	80,258	80,854	96,578	110,503	153,375
Money Market Instruments	26aa	—	—	—	—	—	24	201	—	90	—	562	3,406
Foreign Liabilities	26c	259	5,262	9,884	22,074	36,328	50,168	58,399	66,207	59,151	54,453	57,770	62,616
General Government Deposits	26d	217	1,324	1,748	2,533	2,469	3,662	5,205	15,881	17,121	16,662	12,278	13,540
of which: Local Govt. Deposits	26db	134	790	857	222	577	349	209	70	58	105	—	—
Credit from Monetary Authorities	26g	4	1,367	4,093	3,539	3,710	3,257	1,701	3,342	3,973	10,601	8,870	13,094
Capital Accounts	27a	165	3,646	7,579	12,315	17,835	28,685	36,366	38,151	38,166	35,479	55,148	68,842
Other Items (Net)	27r	112	8,053	13,750	−2,831	−4,882	−12,966	−17,574	−23,507	−24,504	−20,108	−15,137	−15,531
Monetary Survey					*Millions of Dram: End of Period*								
Foreign Assets (Net)	31n	884	7,010	15,438	6,453	30,938	42,030	45,731	70,912	84,171	155,576	202,990	222,494
Domestic Credit	32	1,728	27,832	46,753	59,753	63,544	102,167	105,941	119,023	107,305	98,594	89,080	125,665
Claims on General Govt. (Net)	32an	1,370	7,113	8,807	22,570	15,055	20,005	15,368	9,301	9,396	−60	−14,605	−17,249
Claims on Other Sectors	32d	353	20,718	37,946	37,181	48,486	70,791	86,218	102,586	92,511	94,161	97,126	136,645
Claims on Nonbank Financial Insts.	32g	5	—	—	3	3	11,372	4,354	7,137	5,398	4,492	6,559	6,269
Money	34	1,331	13,410	30,078	39,830	44,055	52,678	52,227	71,395	77,297	115,307	123,272	132,414
Quasi-Money	35	1,584	11,091	10,173	14,540	26,192	43,360	57,227	80,259	80,855	96,579	110,546	153,530
Money Market Instruments	36aa	—	—	—	—	—	24	201	—	90	—	562	3,406
Capital Accounts	37a	286	4,242	9,270	19,530	31,568	45,295	48,445	59,562	60,192	68,906	75,074	69,760
Other Items (Net)	37r	−590	6,099	12,670	−7,694	−7,333	2,840	−6,428	−21,280	−26,958	−26,623	−17,384	−10,951
Money plus Quasi-Money	35l	2,916	24,501	40,251	54,371	70,247	96,037	109,454	151,653	158,151	211,886	233,818	285,943
Interest Rates					*Percent Per Annum*								
Discount Rate (End of Period)	60	210.00	210.00	77.80	26.00	65.10	....	....	....	....	....	....	....
Refinancing Rate (End of Period)	60a	210.00	210.00	52.00	60.00	54.00	39.00	† 43.00	25.00	15.00	13.50	7.00	3.75
Money Market Rate	60b	....	....	....	48.56	36.41	27.84	23.65	18.63	19.40	12.29	7.51	4.18
Treasury Bill Rate	60c	....	....	37.81	† 43.95	57.54	46.99	55.10	24.40	† 20.59	14.75	11.91	5.27
Deposit Rate	60l	....	....	63.18	32.19	26.08	24.94	27.35	18.08	14.90	9.60	6.87	4.90
Lending Rate	60p	....	....	111.86	66.36	54.23	48.49	38.85	31.57	26.69	21.14	20.83	18.63
Government Bond Yield	61	....	....	....	....	....	....	....	25.51	23.15	17.44	15.71	8.21
Prices, Production, Labor					*Index Numbers (2000=100): Period Averages*								
Producer Prices	63	....	....	....	82.7	94.9	100.4	100.0	101.1	104.7	114.0	† 137.9	
Consumer Prices	64	.5	24.7	68.2	80.9	† 92.2	100.2	100.8	100.0	103.1	104.3	109.2	† 116.8
Wages:Avg. Month.Earn	65	....	8.2	28.0	40.8	55.4	73.7	87.8	100.0	111.2	124.5	161.7	199.2
Industrial Production	66	....	....	....	72.5	78.5	93.5	100.0	....	112.5	....	175.4	
					Number in Thousands: Period Averages								
Employment	67e	....	1,487.6	1,476.4	1,435.6	1,372.2	1,337.3	1,298.2	1,277.7	1,264.9	1,106.4	1,111.6	....
Unemployment	67c	....	91.8	131.7	159.3	174.4	133.8	175.0	153.9	138.4	127.3	118.6	....
Unemployment Rate (%)	67r	....	8.5	10.4	15.2	15.1	13.3	15.0	15.7	14.1	13.1	14.2	....

Armenia 911

		1993	1994	1995	1996	1997	1998	1999	2000	2001	2002	2003	2004
Intl. Transactions & Positions						*Millions of US Dollars*							
Exports............................	70..d	156.20	215.50	270.90	290.30	232.55	220.50	232.20	294.20	342.80	507.20	678.08	705.25
Imports, c.i.f......................	71..d	254.20	393.80	673.90	855.80	892.30	902.40	799.70	881.90	874.30	991.00	1,269.44	1,318.19
Imports, f.o.b.....................	71.vd	233.80	343.80	625.40	757.50	779.40	794.10	703.60	776.20	751.90	875.70	1,110.17	1,213.19
Balance of Payments						*Millions of US Dollars: Minus Sign Indicates Debit*							
Current Account, n.i.e...............	78ald	−66.83	−103.78	−218.37	−290.68	−306.51	−417.96	−307.05	−278.34	−199.56	−147.88	−189.44	−161.69
Goods: Exports f.o.b...............	78aad	156.19	215.35	270.90	290.44	233.64	228.89	247.31	309.92	353.11	513.78	696.13	738.31
Goods: Imports f.o.b...............	78abd	−254.18	−393.63	−673.87	−759.63	−793.10	−806.29	−721.35	−773.41	−773.33	−882.54	−1,130.21	−1,196.26
Trade Balance.....................	78acd	−97.99	−178.28	−402.97	−469.19	−559.46	−577.40	−474.04	−463.49	−420.22	−368.76	−434.08	−457.95
Services: Credit...................	78add	17.28	13.67	28.60	77.71	96.60	130.34	135.81	136.94	186.53	183.83	207.36	246.62
Services: Debit....................	78aed	−40.06	−40.70	−52.27	−128.52	−159.38	−208.71	−197.87	−192.75	−204.30	−224.52	−275.70	−317.36
Balance on Goods & Services.......	78afd	−120.77	−205.31	−426.64	−520.00	−622.24	−655.77	−536.10	−519.30	−438.00	−409.45	−502.42	−528.70
Income: Credit....................	78agd	....	....	54.63	78.04	138.95	103.91	93.57	103.74	103.75	136.57	165.97	310.74
Income: Debit.....................	78ahd	−1.30	−4.02	−14.61	−33.31	−40.44	−43.51	−38.64	−50.84	−39.29	−48.36	−71.48	−274.10
Balance on Gds, Serv. & Inc........	78aid	−122.07	−209.33	−386.62	−475.27	−523.73	−595.37	−481.17	−466.40	−373.54	−321.23	−407.93	−492.06
Current Transfers, n.i.e.: Credit......	78ajd	56.29	106.33	169.95	198.99	252.41	203.02	200.57	208.52	200.79	199.68	245.01	389.09
Current Transfers: Debit............	78akd	−1.05	−.78	−1.70	−14.40	−35.19	−25.61	−26.45	−20.46	−26.81	−26.33	−26.53	−58.72
Capital Account, n.i.e...............	78bcd	5.10	5.74	8.05	13.40	10.88	9.74	12.55	28.31	30.12	68.06	89.94	34.30
Capital Account, n.i.e.: Credit.......	78bad	5.10	5.74	8.05	13.40	10.88	9.74	16.85	29.49	32.57	70.18	92.14	40.19
Capital Account: Debit.............	78bbd	....	....	....	....	....	—	−4.30	−1.18	−2.45	−2.12	−2.20	−5.89
Financial Account, n.i.e.............	78bjd	57.82	89.94	227.48	216.76	334.82	390.43	286.18	249.88	175.09	147.82	174.48	161.04
Direct Investment Abroad............	78bdd	....	....	....	....	....	—	....	....	....	—	−.36	−2.25
Dir. Invest. in Rep. Econ., n.i.e.....	78bed	.80	8.00	25.32	17.57	51.94	220.83	122.04	104.19	69.87	110.74	120.87	218.80
Portfolio Investment Assets..........	78bfd	....	....	....	−.01	−.14	.63	.06	−19.10	−5.75	3.38	.05	−.49
Equity Securities...............	78bkd	....	....	....	−.01	−.03	.53	.01	−3.01	−.52	−.86	.05	−.11
Debt Securities.................	78bld	....	....	....	....	−.11	.10	.05	−16.09	−5.23	4.24	—	−.38
Portfolio Investment Liab., n.i.e.....	78bgd	....	....	....	7.23	15.90	−16.57	1.58	.25	−.09	−1.85	.21	−2.39
Equity Securities...............	78bmd	....	....	....	1.88	.46	.72	−.32	.40	.49	−.41	.05	1.37
Debt Securities.................	78bnd	....	....	....	5.35	15.44	−17.29	1.90	−.15	−.58	−1.44	.16	−3.77
Financial Derivatives Assets.........	78bwd	....	....	....	....	....	....	....	....	....	—	—	....
Financial Derivatives Liabilities.......	78bxd	....	....	....	....	....	....	....	....	....	—	—	....
Other Investment Assets.............	78bhd	−44.00	35.89	−8.60	35.34	40.76	19.97	2.97	−9.49	−18.33	−88.04	−63.59	−142.32
Monetary Authorities.................	78bod	−33.40	....	−8.58	−.08	1.36	.07	.06	−.10	.04	.03	−.10	−1.46
General Government.................	78bpd	−10.60	−6.24	....	....	....	−43.27	15.56	11.33	12.76	−6.80	2.18	−19.89
Banks.............................	78bqd	....	.27	−.02	7.33	−17.57	6.17	−34.42	−14.11	−19.69	−38.21	−52.71	−62.90
Other Sectors.....................	78brd	....	41.86	....	28.09	56.97	57.00	21.77	−6.61	−11.43	−43.07	−12.95	−58.07
Other Investment Liab., n.i.e.........	78bid	101.02	46.05	210.76	156.63	226.36	165.57	159.53	174.03	129.39	123.60	117.29	89.69
Monetary Authorities.................	78bsd	28.24	−9.18	.53	4.68	−.04	−2.92	−.93	1.59	3.97	4.43	.24	5.25
General Government.................	78btd	99.05	55.26	151.20	44.21	122.86	35.01	80.16	44.28	62.32	45.14	24.66	38.46
Banks.............................	78bud	−26.27	−.03	.03	26.18	29.04	23.99	11.19	8.78	−3.70	2.72	10.51	32.85
Other Sectors.....................	78bvd	....	....	59.00	81.56	74.50	109.49	69.11	119.38	66.80	71.31	81.88	13.13
Net Errors and Omissions...........	78cad	17.17	4.83	12.35	15.06	10.83	18.39	13.11	17.05	11.07	−4.79	−1.59	−.84
Overall Balance...................	78cbd	13.26	−3.27	29.51	−45.46	50.02	.60	4.79	16.90	16.72	63.20	73.39	32.81
Reserves and Related Items...........	79dad	−13.26	3.27	−29.51	45.46	−50.02	−.60	−4.79	−16.90	−16.72	−63.20	−73.39	−32.81
Reserve Assets....................	79dbd	−13.26	−21.24	−76.22	−60.35	−73.48	−52.13	−20.79	−19.75	−20.06	−82.25	−47.36	−26.40
Use of Fund Credit and Loans.......	79dcd	—	24.50	46.71	49.04	23.46	51.53	16.00	−15.91	3.35	8.07	1.78	−6.41
Exceptional Financing..............	79ded	....	....	....	56.77	....	....	—	—	18.77	—	10.97	−27.81
International Investment Position						*Millions of US Dollars*							
Assets............................	79aad	....	....	....	....	381.90	417.38	489.43	529.42	544.13	685.02	786.85	978.29
Direct Investment Abroad............	79abd	....	....	....	....	—	—	—	.01	.02	.36	.39	2.67
Portfolio Investment...............	79acd	....	....	....	....	.61	.18	.12	19.27	8.90	4.51	4.45	4.62
Equity Securities...............	79add	....	....	....	....	.50	.10	.09	3.09	3.60	4.46	4.39	4.49
Debt Securities.................	79aed	....	....	....	....	.11	.08	.03	16.18	5.30	.04	.06	.14
Financial Derivatives..............	79ald	....	....	....	....	....	....	....	....	....	−.01	....	....
Other Investment.................	79afd	....	....	....	....	141.82	124.09	185.77	196.01	204.06	247.98	277.95	421.04
Monetary Authorities...............	79agd	....	....	....	....	.18	.10	.04	.14	.17	.62	.72	2.49
General Government...............	79ahd	....	....	....	....	18.00	61.27	45.71	35.96	23.19	29.99	27.80	47.69
Banks...........................	79aid	....	....	....	....	37.77	33.85	70.12	83.37	98.52	131.32	180.68	248.52
Other Sectors...................	79ajd	....	....	....	....	85.87	28.87	69.90	76.55	82.18	86.05	68.76	122.34
Reserve Assets...................	79akd	....	....	....	....	239.47	293.10	303.53	314.12	331.15	432.18	504.06	549.96
Liabilities........................	79lad	....	....	....	....	949.92	1,332.15	1,607.72	1,829.73	1,978.23	2,197.46	2,363.71	2,664.63
Dir. Invest. in Rep. Economy..........	79lbd	....	....	....	....	103.44	312.67	421.36	513.10	579.84	684.48	793.38	1,005.09
Portfolio Investment................	79lcd	....	....	....	....	21.18	3.44	4.47	4.79	5.93	5.83	6.37	4.25
Equity Securities...............	79ldd	....	....	....	....	.44	1.09	.75	1.09	1.55	2.93	2.94	4.22
Debt Securities.................	79led	....	....	....	....	20.74	2.35	3.72	3.70	4.38	2.90	3.43	.03
Financial Derivatives..............	79lld	....	....	....	....	—	—	—	....	....	—	—	....
Other Investment.................	79lfd	....	....	....	....	825.30	1,016.04	1,181.90	1,311.84	1,392.46	1,507.15	1,563.96	1,655.30
Monetary Authorities...............	79lgd	....	....	....	....	137.49	192.94	202.80	178.35	179.12	207.69	230.25	240.56
General Government...............	79lhd	....	....	....	....	496.80	538.29	611.83	694.22	757.71	853.16	860.22	937.27
Banks...........................	79lid	....	....	....	....	112.51	96.73	111.51	118.48	114.96	94.83	94.63	129.34
Other Sectors...................	79ljd	....	....	....	....	78.50	188.08	255.75	320.79	340.66	351.47	378.85	348.13
National Accounts						*Millions of Dram*							
Househ.Cons.Expend.,incl.NPISHs...	96f	....	176,885	555,056	664,002	832,638	956,322	951,565	1,001,704	1,100,035	1,213,754	1,353,059	1,593,085
Government Consumption Expend...	91f	....	21,086	58,336	74,265	90,220	105,589	117,591	121,791	132,708	136,071	165,831	203,443
Gross Fixed Capital Formation.........	93e	....	37,855	84,365	118,254	130,336	154,925	162,134	190,130	208,025	287,369	373,615	429,831
Changes in Inventories.............	93i	....	6,012	11,859	14,029	23,015	27,900	19,085	2,149	24,304	7,839	20,490	24,022
Exports of Goods and Services.........	90c	....	73,569	124,965	153,665	163,065	181,552	204,976	241,078	299,477	399,975	522,366	518,981
Imports of Goods and Services (-)......	98c	....	136,747	324,775	370,208	468,722	504,820	491,769	521,272	542,653	634,733	812,890	805,398
Gross Domestic Product (GDP)........	99b	....	187,065	522,256	661,209	804,336	955,385	987,444	1,031,338	1,175,877	1,362,472	1,624,643	1,896,442
Statistical Discrepancy...............	99bs	....	8,404	12,451	7,203	33,783	33,917	23,862	−4,241	−46,020	−47,803	2,172	−67,523
GDP Volume (1995=100)...............	99bvp	....	93.6	100.0	105.9	109.4	117.4	121.2	....	....	....	....	....
GDP Deflator (1995=100)...............	99bip	....	38.3	100.0	119.6	140.8	155.8	156.0	....	....	....	....	....
						Millions: Midyear Estimates							
Population............................	99z	3.37	3.29	3.23	3.18	3.14	3.12	3.10	3.08	3.06	3.05	3.04	3.03

		1993	1994	1995	1996	1997	1998	1999	2000	2001	2002	2003	2004
Exchange Rates					*Aruban Florins per SDR: End of Period*								
Official Rate	aa	2.4587	2.6131	2.6608	2.5739	2.4152	2.5204	2.4568	2.3322	2.2495	2.4335	2.6599	2.7799
					Aruban Florins per US Dollar: End of Period (ae) Period Average (rf)								
Official Rate	ae	1.7900	1.7900	1.7900	1.7900	1.7900	1.7900	1.7900	1.7900	1.7900	1.7900	1.7900	1.7900
Official Rate	rf	1.7900	1.7900	1.7900	1.7900	1.7900	1.7900	1.7900	1.7900	1.7900	1.7900	1.7900	1.7900
International Liquidity					*Millions of US Dollars: End of Period*								
Total Reserves minus Gold	1l.d	181.24	177.59	216.67	187.62	172.33	222.19	219.91	208.01	293.71	339.73	295.22	295.42
Foreign Exchange	1d.d	181.24	177.59	216.67	187.62	172.33	222.19	219.91	208.01	293.71	339.73	295.22	295.42
Gold (Million Fine Troy Ounces)	1ad	.100	.100	.100	.100	.100	.100	.100	.100	.100	.100	.100	.100
Gold (National Valuation)	1and	25.630	25.630	26.307	27.978	27.978	22.878	22.900	22.900	30.751	38.118	46.404	48.663
Deposit Money Banks: Assets	7a.d	213.42	222.37	207.98	233.69	257.38	269.57	280.49	299.19	297.19	303.20	354.35	325.54
Liabilities	7b.d	163.04	150.87	161.08	190.85	217.10	190.79	191.93	221.36	228.81	259.06	302.95	269.85
Monetary Authorities					*Millions of Aruban Florins: End of Period*								
Foreign Assets	11	370.30	363.77	434.93	385.91	358.55	438.67	434.74	417.17	580.79	676.35	611.51	615.92
Reserve Money	14	249.57	233.57	275.54	236.23	226.35	318.08	338.01	299.00	395.80	449.93	424.46	445.26
of which: Currency Outside DMBs	14a	81.66	87.56	93.70	94.87	101.52	104.91	122.44	121.48	125.96	127.84	126.13	130.83
Central Government Deposits	16d	58.57	71.70	99.97	92.55	68.27	65.56	55.64	57.84	96.97	112.16	67.29	48.28
Capital Accounts	17a	58.60	56.02	66.40	70.48	76.12	71.71	65.95	80.62	90.81	124.84	140.68	143.41
Other Items (Net)	17r	3.57	2.48	−6.98	−13.35	−12.19	−16.67	−24.87	−20.28	−2.80	−10.59	−20.92	−21.03
Deposit Money Banks					*Millions of Aruban Florins: End of Period*								
Reserves	20	168.16	147.44	181.48	154.97	119.11	209.55	224.24	181.36	245.95	314.01	293.31	306.95
Foreign Assets	21	382.02	398.05	372.29	418.30	460.71	482.53	502.08	535.55	531.96	542.73	634.29	582.71
Claims on Central Government	22a	43.16	67.94	36.88	59.43	59.50	55.91	61.44	43.47	62.37	65.86	83.70	84.89
Claims on Private Sector	22d	793.09	946.52	1,017.98	1,121.78	1,185.47	1,248.15	1,376.10	1,502.35	1,581.67	1,783.64	2,012.89	2,091.79
Demand Deposits	24	293.14	350.09	343.90	346.37	366.07	433.80	458.88	471.23	553.43	705.49	856.30	826.71
Time and Savings Deposits	25	673.52	755.64	795.31	853.93	881.59	991.61	1,105.88	1,133.42	1,138.99	1,188.42	1,230.30	1,313.76
Bonds	26ab	....	....	....	12.75	—	5.00	5.00	5.00	5.00	5.00	5.00	5.00
Foreign Liabilities	26c	291.84	270.06	288.33	341.61	388.62	341.52	343.55	396.23	409.58	463.71	542.28	483.03
Central Government Deposits	26d	20.90	37.90	22.95	16.33	15.89	11.28	7.93	9.02	6.41	31.19	59.73	65.18
Capital Accounts	27a	56.56	70.34	85.62	105.49	112.89	105.78	109.64	127.57	146.19	135.59	164.04	223.87
Other Items (Net)	27r	50.48	75.91	72.51	78.00	59.73	107.15	133.00	120.26	162.36	176.82	166.54	148.78
Monetary Survey					*Millions of Aruban Florins: End of Period*								
Foreign Assets (Net)	31n	448.02	478.10	517.80	461.50	428.18	578.01	593.16	554.17	700.60	746.91	700.92	714.08
Domestic Credit	32	756.79	904.86	931.93	1,072.33	1,160.81	1,227.22	1,373.97	1,478.96	1,540.66	1,706.14	1,969.56	2,063.22
Claims on Central Govt. (Net)	32an	−36.30	−41.66	−86.05	−49.45	−24.66	−20.93	−2.13	−23.39	−41.01	−77.50	−43.33	−28.56
Claims on Private Sector	32d	793.09	946.52	1,017.98	1,121.78	1,185.47	1,248.15	1,376.10	1,502.35	1,581.67	1,783.64	2,012.89	2,091.79
Money	34	377.89	441.45	443.70	447.47	473.18	547.00	589.73	596.51	701.05	844.41	985.61	960.99
Quasi-Money	35	674.03	756.17	804.74	855.08	881.76	991.78	1,106.06	1,133.60	1,139.18	1,189.11	1,230.99	1,314.45
Bonds	36ab	....	....	....	12.75	—	5.00	5.00	5.00	5.00	5.00	5.00	5.00
Other Items (Net)	37r	152.88	185.34	201.30	218.52	234.04	261.45	266.35	298.02	396.02	414.52	448.88	496.86
Money plus Quasi-Money	35l	1,051.93	1,197.62	1,248.44	1,302.55	1,354.94	1,538.78	1,695.79	1,730.11	1,840.23	2,033.52	2,216.59	2,275.44
Interest Rates					*Percent Per Annum*								
Discount Rate	60	9.5	9.5	9.5	9.5	9.5	9.5	6.5	6.5	6.5	6.5	5.0	5.0
Deposit Rate	60l	4.2	4.4	4.3	4.2	4.4	....	† 6.2	6.2	5.8	5.6	5.3	4.3
Lending Rate	60p	10.6	10.6	10.6	10.3	10.0	....	† 13.1	12.1	12.1	13.1	11.5	11.6
Prices and Tourism					*Index Numbers (2000=100): Period Averages*								
Consumer Prices	64	79.0	83.9	86.8	89.6	92.2	94.0	† 96.1	100.0	103.1	106.7	110.2	113.0
Number of Tourists	66ta	77.8	80.7	85.8	88.9	90.1	89.8	94.7	100.0	95.9	89.1	89.0	101.0
Number of Tourist Nights	66tb	76.7	80.7	85.2	89.5	92.3	93.2	98.0	100.0	98.0	92.7	97.1	107.5
Intl. Transactions & Positions					*Millions of US Dollars*								
Exports	70..d	....	....	14.7	12.5	24.1	29.1	29.2	173.0	148.9	128.4	83.4	79.6
Imports, c.i.f.	71..d	....	....	566.5	578.3	614.5	814.7	782.1	835.2	841.4	841.4	847.8	875.2

Aruba 314

		1993	1994	1995	1996	1997	1998	1999	2000	2001	2002	2003	2004
Balance of Payments					*Millions of US Dollars: Minus Sign Indicates Debit*								
Current Account, n.i.e.	78ald	41.7	81.1	−.3	−69.1	−195.8	−18.8	−421.4	225.1	325.5	−339.3	−135.8	10.4
Goods: Exports f.o.b.	78aad	1,154.4	1,296.8	1,347.2	1,735.7	1,728.7	1,164.8	1,390.4	2,525.9	2,423.9	1,487.9	2,049.5	2,715.2
Goods: Imports f.o.b.	78abd	−1,546.5	−1,607.3	−1,772.5	−2,043.4	−2,115.9	−1,518.2	−1,995.6	−2,582.7	−2,369.2	−2,018.2	−2,378.4	−2,986.2
Trade Balance	78acd	−392.1	−310.6	−425.3	−307.7	−387.2	−353.4	−605.2	−56.8	54.7	−530.3	−328.9	−271.0
Services: Credit	78add	604.1	624.2	645.1	769.9	815.8	892.1	925.0	1,011.2	993.6	996.6	1,045.1	1,239.5
Services: Debit	78aed	−169.1	−228.7	−245.5	−515.9	−596.1	−553.1	−661.2	−642.5	−615.8	−606.9	−728.0	−796.2
Balance on Goods & Services	78afd	42.8	85.0	−25.6	−53.6	−167.5	−14.4	−341.4	312.0	432.5	−140.6	−11.8	172.3
Income: Credit	78agd	13.4	9.6	16.4	19.2	20.7	40.5	41.5	53.1	50.5	34.3	34.2	36.4
Income: Debit	78ahd	−24.6	−22.3	−24.6	−31.0	−37.9	−40.1	−76.7	−68.2	−99.4	−158.1	−74.9	−93.7
Balance on Gds, Serv. & Inc.	78aid	31.6	72.3	−33.8	−65.5	−184.7	−14.0	−376.6	296.9	383.6	−264.4	−52.5	114.9
Current Transfers, n.i.e.: Credit	78ajd	43.4	47.5	71.5	18.4	18.4	29.3	34.5	36.9	40.2	34.9	40.1	40.1
Current Transfers: Debit	78akd	−33.3	−38.7	−37.9	−22.0	−29.5	−34.1	−79.3	−108.7	−98.2	−109.8	−123.3	−144.6
Capital Account, n.i.e.	78bcd	−1.8	−4.1	−.5	28.0	21.0	5.2	1.5	11.3	−1.5	21.3	100.8	18.4
Capital Account, n.i.e.: Credit	78bad	.9	.3	3.1	28.7	21.6	10.2	6.5	16.3	8.5	28.5	122.5	28.7
Capital Account: Debit	78bbd	−2.8	−4.4	−3.6	−.7	−.6	−5.0	−5.0	−5.0	−10.0	−7.2	−21.7	−10.3
Financial Account, n.i.e.	78bjd	−8.4	−75.4	41.6	10.7	158.9	64.2	443.7	−262.8	−230.4	334.9	−10.6	−28.2
Direct Investment Abroad	78bdd	—	—	....	−.3	1.7	−1.4	−3.8	−13.3	−14.6	−2.5	−18.1	.8
Dir. Invest. in Rep. Econ., n.i.e.	78bed	−17.9	−73.2	−5.5	84.5	195.9	83.6	470.7	−117.8	−264.2	306.1	187.7	130.6
Portfolio Investment Assets	78bfd	10.8	16.5	−16.6	−7.8	−1.6	−44.1	−53.7	−45.9	38.4	6.0	−22.8	−24.5
Equity Securities	78bkd	—	—	....	....	....	....	−41.6	−44.9	5.8	−5.0	−18.4	−25.2
Debt Securities	78bld	10.8	16.5	−16.6	−7.8	−1.6	−44.1	−12.1	−1.1	32.6	11.1	−4.4	.7
Portfolio Investment Liab., n.i.e.	78bgd	−14.6	−25.8	....	1.6	−17.4	−3.4	32.3	43.2	17.0	56.8	66.5	63.8
Equity Securities	78bmd	—	—	....	....	....	....	−.1	2.7	−.2	—	.1	....
Debt Securities	78bnd	−14.6	−25.8	....	1.6	−17.4	−3.4	32.5	40.5	17.2	56.8	66.4	63.8
Financial Derivatives Assets	78bwd	....	....	....	....	....	....	....	—	—	—	—	....
Financial Derivatives Liabilities	78bxd	....	....	....	....	....	....	....	—	—	—	—	....
Other Investment Assets	78bhd	−25.8	5.8	12.5	−11.3	−49.7	29.2	6.8	−28.2	−4.9	−33.0	−100.3	−89.2
Monetary Authorities	78bod	....	....	....	....	....	....	....	—	—	—	.2	....
General Government	78bpd	—	−.8	....	....	....	....	....	—	—	—	—	—
Banks	78bqd	−15.7	−3.7	15.6	−17.0	−30.7	−11.5	−3.2	−15.5	−11.0	8.2	−68.4	52.0
Other Sectors	78brd	−10.1	10.4	−3.1	5.7	−19.0	40.7	10.1	−12.6	6.1	−41.2	−32.1	−141.1
Other Investment Liab., n.i.e.	78bid	39.2	1.3	51.2	−55.9	30.0	.4	−8.7	−100.9	−2.1	1.5	−123.7	−109.7
Monetary Authorities	78bsd	—	—	....	....	....	....	....	....	....	....	....	....
General Government	78btd	.6	.4	.6	−10.6	−8.9	22.2	−1.5	−21.5	−1.5	−1.3	−160.1	−12.5
Banks	78bud	18.5	−8.7	10.7	17.0	37.3	−26.4	.4	27.7	6.5	21.8	72.8	−50.2
Other Sectors	78bvd	20.1	9.6	39.9	−62.3	1.6	4.6	−7.6	−107.1	−7.1	−19.1	−36.4	−47.0
Net Errors and Omissions	78cad	2.0	−4.7	2.0	4.3	−2.5	.6	−20.9	11.5	−10.8	23.4	9.2	1.0
Overall Balance	78cbd	33.4	−3.2	42.7	−26.1	−18.4	51.3	2.8	−15.0	82.8	40.2	−36.4	1.6
Reserves and Related Items	79dad	−33.4	3.2	−42.7	26.1	18.4	−51.3	−2.8	15.0	−82.8	−40.2	36.4	−1.6
Reserve Assets	79dbd	−33.4	3.2	−42.7	26.1	18.4	−51.3	−2.8	15.0	−82.8	−40.2	36.4	−1.6
Use of Fund Credit and Loans	79dcd	—	—	....	....	....	....	....	....	....	....	....	....
Exceptional Financing	79ded	....	....	....	....	....	....	....	....	....	....	....	....
National Accounts					*Millions of Aruban Florins*								
Exports of Goods and Services	90c	....	....	2,006.9	2,139.6	2,263.1	2,374.2	2,465.5	2,476.1	2,466.8	2,369.9	....	....
Government Consumption Expend.	91f	....	....	....	....	647.4	655.0	674.0	731.4	804.6	898.5	....	....
Gross Fixed Capital Formation	93e	....	....	....	....	773.6	851.7	899.1	787.0	742.8	765.9	....	....
Changes in Inventories	93i	....	....	....	....	56.0	93.3	53.1	30.8	20.2	32.4	....	....
Houseed.Cons.Expend.,incl.NPISHs.	96f	....	....	....	....	1,367.0	1,499.5	1,602.4	1,664.2	1,712.1	1,799.8	....	....
Imports of Goods and Services	98c	....	....	2,044.0	2,191.4	2,365.0	2,493.1	2,610.2	2,362.6	2,347.9	2,445.3	....	....
Gross Domestic Product (GDP)	99b	....	....	2,363.7	2,470.1	2,742.2	2,980.5	3,083.8	3,326.9	3,398.7	3,421.2	....	....
GDP at 1995 Prices	99b.p	....	....	2,366.6	2,390.0	2,579.2	2,751.7	2,783.8	2,886.3	2,866.3	2,792.4	....	....
GDP Volume (2000=100)	99bvp	....	....	82.0	82.8	89.4	95.3	96.4	100.0	99.3	96.7	....	....
GDP Deflator (2000=100)	99bip	....	....	86.6	89.7	92.2	94.0	96.1	100.0	102.9	106.3	....	....
					Millions: Midyear Estimates								
Population	99z	.08	.08	.08	.09	.09	.09	.09	.09	.09	.10	.10	.10

		1993	1994	1995	1996	1997	1998	1999	2000	2001	2002	2003	2004
Exchange Rates													
		SDRs per Australian Dollar: End of Period											
Market Rate	ac	.4930	.5321	.5012	.5539	.4838	.4360	.4764	.4252	.4063	.4165	.5047	.5016
		US Dollars per Australian Dollar: End of Period (ag) Period Average (rh)											
Market Rate	ag	.6771	.7768	.7450	.7965	.6527	.6139	.6538	.5540	.5106	.5662	.7500	.7790
Market Rate	rh	.6801	.7317	.7415	.7829	.7441	.6294	.6453	.5823	.5176	.5439	.6519	.7366
		Index Numbers (2000=100): Period Averages											
Market Rate	ahx	116.8	125.6	127.3	134.4	127.8	108.1	110.8	100.0	88.9	93.4	111.9	126.5
Nominal Effective Exchange Rate	nec	100.7	110.6	107.1	117.5	119.0	106.1	107.2	100.0	93.9	97.4	107.2	114.4
Real Effective Exchange Rate	rec	104.4	108.5	106.0	116.5	115.9	102.6	104.4	100.0	96.4	102.0	113.7	121.9
Fund Position													
		Millions of SDRs: End of Period											
Quota	2f.s	2,333	2,333	2,333	2,333	2,333	2,333	3,236	3,236	3,236	3,236	3,236	3,236
SDRs	1b.s	60	50	37	25	14	13	53	72	87	100	114	125
Reserve Position in the Fund	1c.s	400	347	338	335	539	892	1,189	954	1,124	1,423	1,381	1,099
of which: Outstg.Fund Borrowing	2c	—	—	—	—	—	75	—	—	—	—	—	—
Total Fund Cred.&Loans Outstg	2tl	—	—	—	—	—	—	—	—	—	—	—	—
International Liquidity													
		Millions of US Dollars Unless Otherwise Indicated: End of Period											
Total Reserves minus Gold	1l.d	11,102	11,285	11,896	14,485	16,845	14,641	21,212	18,118	17,955	20,689	32,189	35,803
SDRs	1b.d	82	73	55	37	19	18	72	94	109	136	170	195
Reserve Position in the Fund	1c.d	550	506	502	482	727	1,256	1,633	1,243	1,412	1,934	2,053	1,706
Foreign Exchange	1d.d	10,470	10,706	11,340	13,967	16,099	13,366	19,507	16,782	16,434	18,618	29,966	33,901
Gold (Million Fine Troy Ounces)	1ad	7.90	7.90	7.90	7.90	2.56	2.56	2.56	2.56	2.56	2.56	2.56	2.56
Gold (National Valuation)	1and	3,086	3,023	3,055	2,918	740	737	743	699	709	878	1,070	1,123
Monetary Authorities: Other Liab	4..d	26	38	67	50	28	66	63	47	78	86	112
Banking Institutions: Assets	7a.d	11,024	13,369	16,808	22,217	23,424	23,148	29,906	28,703	31,014	26,640	45,869	56,152
Liabilities	7b.d	41,840	39,355	49,238	63,521	64,258	73,409	88,291	90,027	98,049	100,915	161,228	203,309
Monetary Authorities													
		Millions of Australian Dollars: Average of Weekly Figures for Last Month of Period											
Foreign Assets	11	21,415	18,344	20,080	22,581	28,325	27,632	38,596	39,820	44,335	44,568	55,222	53,835
Claims on Central Government	12a	14,265	13,446	17,700	30,608	18,374	23,703	14,684	18,834	20,267	21,276	11,871	18,250
Reserve Money	14	22,027	23,835	25,024	40,335	32,160	33,997	32,259	32,019	38,044	38,866	39,590	40,914
of which: Currency Outside Banks	14a	17,279	18,208	19,092	19,628	21,098	22,784	24,604	26,928	28,471	29,703	31,470	32,803
Foreign Liabilities	16c	38	49	90	63	43	108	84	114	92	137	115	143
Central Government Deposits	16d	2,594	941	3,076	4,123	2,703	4,214	9,485	12,076	9,815	9,704	8,529	13,120
Capital Accounts	17a	1,588	1,517	1,573	1,533	3,294	3,948	3,857	3,976	7,350	7,322	7,257	7,263
Other Items (Net)	17r	9,434	5,448	8,017	7,134	8,498	9,068	7,595	10,470	9,302	9,816	11,602	10,644
Banking Institutions													
		Millions of Australian Dollars: Average of Weekly Figures for Last Month of Period											
Reserves	20	4,674	5,498	5,830	13,378	8,789	9,052	5,052	4,228	8,532	† 8,205	7,254	7,305
Foreign Assets	21	16,281	17,210	22,562	27,893	35,887	37,706	45,742	51,810	60,740	† 47,050	61,158	72,083
Claims on Central Government	22a	30,929	28,457	28,072	25,635	19,991	20,182	23,153	13,371	11,756	† 7,421	−1,569	355
Claims on State and Local Govts	22b	—	—	—	—	—	—	—	—	—	† 2,774	4,856	4,906
Claims on Nonfin.Pub. Enterprises	22c	4,419	3,233	3,591	3,909	4,659	6,550	11,104	10,593	12,131	† 2,042	2,488	1,395
Claims on Private Sector	22d	281,109	311,556	345,970	378,196	419,273	466,152	522,657	580,073	625,054	† 690,712	797,130	887,050
Claims on Nonbank Financial Insts	22g	9,124	8,477	9,348	9,930	8,007	11,026	9,779	11,666	14,887	† 51,730	36,708	46,372
Demand Deposits	24	53,719	60,496	64,771	75,801	86,965	91,864	101,179	110,660	138,456	† 180,177	200,008	211,102
Time, Savings,& Fgn.Currency Dep	25	180,265	197,542	215,949	236,124	247,668	271,109	305,051	309,634	339,526	† 324,661	374,291	433,012
Foreign Liabilities	26c	61,793	50,663	66,091	79,750	98,450	119,579	135,043	162,504	192,028	† 178,232	214,970	260,987
Central Government Deposits	26d	3,637	2,988	3,523	3,291	3,578	5,721	5,497	5,197	4,399	† 845	874	804
Capital Accounts	27a	—	—	—	—	—	—	—	—	—	† 69,335	78,829	86,185
Other Items (Net)	27r	47,120	62,741	65,038	63,975	59,947	62,395	70,717	83,746	58,690	† 56,684	39,054	27,377
Banking Survey													
		Millions of Australian Dollars: Average of Weekly Figures for Last Month of Period											
Foreign Assets (Net)	31n	−24,135	−15,158	−23,540	−29,339	−34,282	−54,348	−50,789	−70,988	−87,045	† −86,751	−98,705	−135,213
Domestic Credit	32	333,615	361,238	398,082	440,864	464,024	517,677	566,394	617,263	669,882	† 765,407	842,081	944,405
Claims on Central Govt. (Net)	32an	38,964	37,973	39,173	48,829	32,084	33,949	22,855	14,932	17,809	† 18,148	899	4,681
Claims on State and Local Govts	32b	—	—	—	—	—	—	—	—	—	† 2,774	4,856	4,906
Claims on Nonfin.Pub. Enterprises	32c	4,419	3,233	3,591	3,909	4,659	6,550	11,104	10,593	12,131	† 2,042	2,488	1,395
Claims on Private Sector	32d	281,109	311,556	345,970	378,196	419,273	466,152	522,657	580,073	625,054	† 690,712	797,130	887,050
Claims on Nonbank Financial Insts.	32g	9,124	8,477	9,348	9,930	8,007	11,026	9,779	11,666	14,887	† 51,730	36,708	46,372
Money	34	71,066	78,820	83,954	95,715	108,431	115,011	126,261	137,809	167,126	† 210,120	231,553	243,950
Quasi-Money	35	180,265	197,542	215,949	236,124	247,668	271,109	305,051	309,634	339,526	† 324,661	374,291	433,012
Capital Accounts	37a	1,588	1,517	1,573	1,533	3,294	3,948	3,857	3,976	7,350	† 76,656	86,086	93,448
Other Items (Net)	37r	56,561	68,201	73,067	78,153	70,350	73,261	80,437	94,858	68,835	† 67,218	51,447	38,782
Money plus Quasi-Money	35l	251,331	276,362	299,903	331,839	356,099	386,120	431,312	447,442	506,651	† 534,781	605,844	676,962
Money (National Definitions)													
		Millions of Australian Dollars: Average of Weekly Figures for Last Month of Period											
Money Base	19ma	21,980	23,765	24,958	33,043	29,962	31,926	29,733	31,189	37,017	37,513	38,844	40,109
M1	59ma	71,026	78,762	83,898	95,466	108,137	114,737	125,832	137,621	166,942	151,348	164,456	168,659
M1, Seasonally Adjusted	59mac	68,421	75,987	80,916	92,058	104,062	110,454	121,148	133,856	162,756	147,724	160,591	164,726
M3	59mc	237,660	262,064	286,243	313,435	333,599	358,762	394,886	412,854	473,374	507,434	639,063	621,830
M3, Seasonally Adjusted	59mcc	234,318	258,598	282,588	309,350	328,895	353,878	389,582	409,429	469,664	504,416	633,119	616,316
Broad Money	59md	288,531	313,937	341,112	373,782	402,209	435,837	464,532	494,495	550,672	578,717	638,328	693,850
Broad Money, Seasonally Adjusted	59mdc	285,323	310,421	337,378	370,608	398,697	432,459	461,504	490,934	545,755	573,539	632,387	687,399
Interest Rates													
		Percent Per Annum											
Money Market Rate	60b	5.11	5.18	† 7.50	7.20	5.50	4.99	† 4.78	5.90	5.06	4.55	4.81	5.25
Treasury Bill Rate	60c	5.00	5.69	† 7.64	7.02	5.29	4.84	4.76	5.98	4.80	....	....	....
Deposit Rate	60l	4.90	4.96	6.14	5.74	4.40	3.75	† 3.55	4.16	3.27	3.11	3.31	3.77
Lending Rate	60p	9.42	9.23	10.70	10.50	8.89	8.15	7.99	9.27	8.66	8.16	8.41	8.85
Govt. Bond Yield: Short-Term	61a	6.21	8.19	8.42	7.53	6.00	5.02	5.55	6.18	4.97	5.30	4.90	5.30
Long-Term	61	7.28	9.04	9.17	8.17	6.89	5.50	6.08	6.26	5.63	5.82	5.36	5.61

		1993	1994	1995	1996	1997	1998	1999	2000	2001	2002	2003	2004
Prices, Production, Labor						*Index Numbers (2000=100): Period Averages*							
Share Prices	62	57.3	64.3	63.9	71.6	80.0	83.9	92.7	100.0	103.2	100.2	96.1	111.7
Prices: Manufacturing Output	63	92.0	92.7	96.6	96.9	98.1	94.2	†93.3	100.0	103.1	103.3	103.8	107.9
Consumer Prices	64	85.3	86.9	90.9	93.3	93.5	94.3	95.7	100.0	104.4	107.5	110.5	113.1
Wages, Weekly Earnings	65	75.8	78.4	82.4	85.6	89.1	92.8	95.3	100.0	104.9	110.3	116.5	120.9
Industrial Production	66	81.6	85.8	87.1	90.5	92.1	94.6	95.1	100.0	101.4	104.3	104.6	....
Manufacturing Empl., Seas. Adj	67eyc	94.6	97.8	98.8	99.0	100.5	97.2	95.5	100.0	96.7	97.8	95.8	96.4
						Number in Thousands: Period Averages							
Labor Force	67d	8,613	8,771	8,995	9,115	9,204	9,339	9,466	9,678	9,817	9,983	10,112	....
Employment	67e	7,699	7,942	8,256	8,364	8,444	8,618	8,785	9,043	9,157	9,334	9,481	9,677
Unemployment	67c	914	829	739	751	760	721	658	611	660	629	611	567
Unemployment Rate (%)	67r	10.6	9.5	8.2	8.2	8.3	7.8	7.0	6.3	6.7	6.3	5.9	5.5
Intl. Transactions & Positions						*Millions of Australian Dollars*							
Exports	70	62,839	64,904	71,657	76,978	84,786	88,977	86,895	110,464	122,664	119,483	109,811	117,577
Wheat	70d	2,217	2,283	1,765	3,987	4,407	3,514	3,311	3,813	4,330	4,136	2,426	4,192
Coal	70vr	7,707	6,700	7,380	7,758	8,784	9,823	8,391	9,340	12,482	12,843	10,890	13,302
Greasy Wool	70ha	1,951	2,394	2,242	2,108	2,446	1,715	1,494	2,103	2,304	2,482	1,790	1,973
Imports, c.i.f	71	67,027	72,882	82,673	83,543	88,884	102,905	107,154	123,461	123,539	133,424	136,577	148,744
Imports, f.o.b	71.v	62,385	68,087	77,467	78,402	83,364	96,723	101,446	116,840	117,357	126,457	129,884	140,956
						2000=100							
Volume of Exports	72	61.4	66.6	68.7	76.7	87.5	86.5	91.0	100.0	103.1	103.7	101.4	105.9
Wheat	72d	62.3	73.1	38.9	82.2	109.3	85.9	93.2	100.0	87.7	82.9	53.6	104.1
Coal	72vr	71.3	70.3	73.1	75.4	84.5	88.6	91.8	100.0	103.8	111.2	115.7	120.7
Greasy Wool	72ha	113.8	111.8	86.6	104.5	104.5	81.0	83.5	100.0	95.3	74.4	56.1	75.5
Volume of Imports	73	50.4	58.0	63.5	68.9	77.3	83.7	92.4	100.0	94.6	107.9	117.7	137.5
Export Prices	76	87.1	84.7	90.9	87.2	88.7	93.1	†86.4	100.0	110.0	106.7	98.3	101.8
Wheat (1995=100)	76d	85.2	83.1	100.0	109.0	94.7	92.6	....	....	....	....	....	....
Coal (Unit Value)	74vr	115.8	102.1	108.1	110.2	111.3	118.7	97.9	100.0	128.7	123.7	100.8	118.0
Greasy Wool (Unit Value)	74ha	81.5	101.9	123.1	95.9	111.3	100.6	85.1	100.0	115.0	158.6	151.8	124.3
Import Prices	76.x	90.5	88.3	91.5	86.6	86.4	93.7	†91.6	100.0	105.7	100.8	92.8	87.6
Balance of Payments						*Millions of US Dollars: Minus Sign Indicates Debit*							
Current Account, n.i.e	78ald	−9,683	−17,145	−19,323	−15,810	−12,384	−18,050	−22,335	−15,412	−8,363	−16,837	−30,354	−40,025
Goods: Exports f.o.b	78aad	42,637	47,371	53,220	60,397	64,893	55,884	56,096	64,025	63,625	65,013	70,526	87,063
Goods: Imports f.o.b	78abd	−42,666	−50,648	−57,443	−61,032	−63,044	−61,215	−65,857	−68,866	−61,890	−70,530	−85,861	−105,278
Trade Balance	78acd	−29	−3,277	−4,223	−635	1,849	−5,332	−9,761	−4,841	1,736	−5,517	−15,335	−18,215
Services: Credit	78add	11,942	14,185	16,156	18,531	18,488	16,181	17,399	18,678	16,698	17,880	21,149	25,418
Services: Debit	78aed	−13,412	−15,458	−17,110	−18,606	−18,844	−17,272	−18,330	−18,388	−16,948	−18,107	−21,495	−26,179
Balance on Goods & Services	78afd	−1,500	−4,550	−5,177	−710	1,493	−6,422	−10,692	−4,551	1,486	−5,744	−15,681	−18,976
Income: Credit	78agd	4,179	4,462	5,258	6,027	7,162	6,522	7,404	8,977	8,196	8,523	10,001	13,315
Income: Debit	78ahd	−12,268	−16,829	−19,294	−21,220	−21,000	−17,868	−19,018	−19,791	−18,065	−19,552	−24,514	−34,095
Balance on Gds, Serv. & Inc	78aid	−9,589	−16,917	−19,213	−15,903	−12,345	−17,768	−22,306	−15,365	−8,384	−16,773	−30,194	−39,756
Current Transfers, n.i.e.: Credit	78ajd	2,100	2,204	2,364	2,699	2,765	2,651	3,003	2,622	2,242	2,310	2,767	3,145
Current Transfers: Debit	78akd	−2,193	−2,431	−2,474	−2,606	−2,805	−2,933	−3,032	−2,669	−2,221	−2,373	−2,927	−3,414
Capital Account, n.i.e	78bcd	260	323	558	964	903	670	819	615	591	443	736	784
Capital Account, n.i.e.: Credit	78bad	780	908	1,250	1,674	1,606	1,315	1,535	1,406	1,320	1,298	1,664	1,980
Capital Account: Debit	78bbd	−519	−586	−692	−710	−703	−646	−716	−791	−729	−855	−928	−1,196
Financial Account, n.i.e	78bjd	10,203	15,897	18,632	16,070	16,820	15,204	27,613	12,953	9,063	17,033	35,726	41,186
Direct Investment Abroad	78bdd	−1,942	−2,817	−3,267	−7,052	−6,368	−3,346	422	−3,275	−12,077	−7,816	−16,362	−16,598
Dir. Invest. in Rep. Econ., n.i.e	78bed	4,318	5,001	12,026	6,181	7,631	5,957	3,311	13,618	4,621	15,570	7,151	43,519
Portfolio Investment Assets	78bfd	−3,947	1,503	−2,842	−3,307	−79	−3,794	−10,487	−10,919	−10,306	−16,651	−7,988	−24,514
Equity Securities	78bkd	−2,358	−543	−1,175	−2,416	−567	−2,343	−6,710	−7,346	−5,337	−11,801	−4,318	−11,758
Debt Securities	78bld	−1,589	2,045	−1,668	−892	489	−1,451	−3,778	−3,573	−4,969	−4,851	−3,669	−12,756
Portfolio Investment Liab., n.i.e	78bgd	12,023	14,593	15,200	23,738	13,219	6,959	24,352	14,874	21,041	18,186	49,420	41,261
Equity Securities	78bmd	7,004	8,120	2,585	2,068	8,775	10,777	11,060	−726	11,955	1,167	11,404	−25,233
Debt Securities	78bnd	5,020	6,473	12,615	21,670	4,444	−3,818	13,292	15,601	9,086	17,019	38,016	66,495
Financial Derivatives Assets	78bwd	—	1,004	2,801	974	−470	−382	290	−1,165	161	3,048	7,697	20,348
Financial Derivatives Liabilities	78bxd	—	−632	−2,217	−681	1,092	−636	1,089	291	453	−2,848	−7,235	−20,350
Other Investment Assets	78bhd	−1,008	−1,597	−3,223	−5,613	−6,735	−686	−2,987	−4,887	891	−3,511	−6,070	−7,288
Monetary Authorities	78bod	—	—	—	−246	−414	−180	−327	133	275	411	110	—
General Government	78bpd	17	137	−57	−94	−840	−412	−214	−22	−153	−85	−104	−159
Banks	78bqd	−47	−2,438	−2,824	−4,618	−4,233	−608	−2,442	−1,745	−2,616	−3,733	−6,345	−6,633
Other Sectors	78brd	−978	704	−342	−656	−1,248	513	−5	−3,253	3,385	−104	268	−496
Other Investment Liab., n.i.e	78bid	758	−1,158	154	1,829	8,530	11,131	11,624	4,416	4,280	11,055	9,112	4,808
Monetary Authorities	78bsd	13	−4	27	−29	−3	9	61	−70	3	7	37	7
General Government	78btd	−9	157	133	103	−91	129	−228	75	−125	—	—	−27
Banks	78bud	2,622	−1,375	2,998	2,717	7,207	7,654	7,926	4,924	3,536	10,747	10,368	2,494
Other Sectors	78bvd	−1,868	64	−3,004	−963	1,417	3,339	3,865	−514	867	301	−1,293	2,335
Net Errors and Omissions	78cad	−821	−34	529	1,248	−2,466	136	608	479	−196	−517	769	−780
Overall Balance	78cbd	−42	−960	396	2,471	2,873	−2,040	6,705	−1,365	1,096	122	6,877	1,166
Reserves and Related Items	79dad	42	960	−396	−2,471	−2,873	2,040	−6,705	1,365	−1,096	−122	−6,877	−1,166
Reserve Assets	79dbd	42	960	−396	−2,471	−2,873	2,040	−6,705	1,365	−1,096	−122	−6,877	−1,166
Use of Fund Credit and Loans	79dcd	—	—	—	—	—	—	—	....	....	....	....	....
Exceptional Financing	79ded	....	....	....	....	....	....	....	....	....	....	....	....

		1993	1994	1995	1996	1997	1998	1999	2000	2001	2002	2003	2004
International Investment Position							*Millions of US Dollars*						
Assets...	**79aad**	100,894	119,962	133,885	161,821	173,545	185,349	232,599	231,688	241,036	269,002	380,848	474,894
Direct Investment Abroad..............	**79abd**	40,510	47,774	53,010	66,816	71,936	78,635	89,556	85,385	92,160	93,119	127,075	167,547
Portfolio Investment......................	**79acd**	30,247	29,375	35,658	42,023	42,451	48,651	72,847	75,990	79,666	91,586	128,246	163,194
Equity Securities.........................	**79add**	21,428	22,538	27,029	31,518	32,947	36,652	57,043	59,024	60,032	65,298	93,095	114,511
Debt Securities...........................	**79aed**	8,819	6,837	8,629	10,506	9,504	11,999	15,804	16,966	19,635	26,288	35,151	48,683
Financial Derivatives......................	**79ald**	—	8,924	7,679	6,733	8,058	9,282	10,756	12,593	14,780	19,521	32,918	37,716
Other Investment..........................	**79afd**	15,950	19,581	22,589	28,847	34,006	33,404	37,485	38,903	35,767	43,210	59,351	69,509
Monetary Authorities..................	**79agd**	—	—	—	—	491	766	953	875	536	136	—	—
General Government...................	**79ahd**	1,173	1,201	1,208	1,377	4,044	4,283	4,677	4,223	4,155	4,508	5,682	5,947
Banks......................................	**79aid**	7,099	9,232	11,905	16,989	18,892	18,470	21,626	21,183	22,160	28,505	42,230	51,692
Other Sectors...........................	**79ajd**	7,678	9,148	9,476	10,481	10,578	9,886	10,229	12,622	8,916	10,061	11,439	11,870
Reserve Assets.............................	**79akd**	14,188	14,308	14,949	17,402	17,094	15,377	21,956	18,817	18,664	21,567	33,258	36,927
Liabilities.......................................	**79lad**	264,564	309,880	335,211	388,362	360,313	380,429	451,510	428,585	435,677	513,609	738,909	896,684
Dir. Invest. in Rep. Economy...........	**79lbd**	82,891	95,519	104,074	116,724	101,043	105,944	120,589	111,138	107,913	134,799	186,921	253,629
Portfolio Investment......................	**79lcd**	137,835	162,325	181,223	218,728	203,158	208,590	254,691	241,859	252,672	279,732	410,569	494,017
Equity Securities.........................	**79ldd**	35,916	46,544	51,314	61,123	60,297	72,987	100,761	84,902	94,495	93,291	146,328	154,340
Debt Securities...........................	**79led**	101,919	115,780	129,909	157,605	142,861	135,603	153,930	156,958	158,177	186,442	264,241	339,677
Financial Derivatives......................	**79lld**	—	7,564	7,250	8,275	9,884	9,862	12,550	13,318	12,900	20,919	36,584	38,249
Other Investment..........................	**79lfd**	43,838	44,472	42,665	44,636	46,227	56,034	63,679	62,270	62,192	78,158	104,835	110,789
Monetary Authorities..................	**79lgd**	43	46	71	45	33	36	100	18	19	28	81	91
General Government...................	**79lhd**	202	397	439	573	237	360	153	210	64	71	89	62
Banks......................................	**79lid**	24,229	23,637	25,010	27,883	30,851	37,522	46,949	48,166	48,977	62,845	87,517	90,027
Other Sectors...........................	**79ljd**	19,363	20,392	17,145	16,134	15,106	18,116	16,477	13,875	13,131	15,214	17,149	20,608
Government Finance						*Millions of Australian Dollars: Year Ending June 30*							
Deficit (-) or Surplus........................	**80**	−13,500	−13,637	−11,641	−4,840	2,062	16,368	−3,398	6,801	4,194	−8,297	....	....
Revenue..	**81**	99,204	104,559	114,234	125,092	134,579	142,036	† 151,934	163,767	161,200	164,432	....	....
Expenditure...................................	**82**	115,239	121,561	127,358	135,130	139,857	140,877	† 149,023	156,883	156,296	165,946	....	....
Lending Minus Repayments............	**83**	−2,535	−3,365	−1,483	−5,198	−7,340	−15,209	† 6,309	83	710	6,783	....	
Financing (by Residence of Lender)													
Domestic....................................	**84a**	11,122	10,024	8,349	−3,123	−3,978	−11,213	....	....	....	....		
Foreign.......................................	**85a**	3,325	3,612	3,292	7,963	1,916	−5,155	....	....	....	....		
Debt: Domestic.............................	**88a**	58,025	71,334	79,489	78,892	73,510	60,094	....	....	....	....		
Foreign.......................................	**89a**	21,376	22,869	28,012	36,482	42,610	39,355	....	....	....	....		
National Accounts							*Billions of Australian Dollars*						
Househ.Cons.Expend.,incl.NPISHs....	**96f.c**	260.54	273.29	292.60	307.46	325.12	344.36	364.97	388.68	414.79	440.23	467.96	499.77
Government Consumption Expend...	**91f.c**	83.64	85.79	89.58	95.53	99.18	104.60	109.09	117.88	123.05	131.86	141.69	151.83
Gross Fixed Capital Formation..........	**93e.c**	93.40	105.44	109.36	113.88	123.28	135.57	144.01	148.83	150.95	174.24	192.14	205.93
Changes in Inventories....................	**93i.c**	1.59	1.79	.87	1.45	−4.03	3.25	5.72	1.27	−.01	−1.17	6.49	2.36
Exports of Goods and Services..........	**90c.c**	80.28	84.11	93.71	100.61	112.00	114.78	113.69	142.78	155.55	152.56	140.97	152.65
Imports of Goods and Services (-).....	**98.c.c**	82.41	90.08	100.61	101.66	110.22	124.83	130.27	150.30	152.42	162.45	164.68	178.37
Gross Domestic Product (GDP).........	**99b.c**	435.71	460.55	485.04	516.96	545.72	577.56	605.84	650.32	692.67	734.26	784.73	839.04
Net Primary Income from Abroad.....	**98.nc**	−11.80	−16.92	−18.97	−19.30	−18.72	−18.08	−17.91	−18.86	−19.79	−21.58	−22.45	−27.95
Gross National Income (GNI)............	**99a.c**	423.91	443.63	466.07	497.67	527.00	559.48	587.93	631.47	672.87	712.68	762.28	811.10
Net Current Transf.from Abroad.......	**98t.c**	−.95	1.06	1.18	.80	.41	.27	−1.68	1.82	−.16	.93	−.17	−1.67
Gross Nat'l Disposable Inc.(GNDI)....	**99i.c**	422.96	444.69	467.25	498.46	527.41	559.75	586.25	633.28	672.72	713.61	762.11	809.43
Gross Saving..................................	**99s.c**	78.79	85.62	85.07	95.48	103.12	110.80	112.19	126.73	134.87	141.52	152.46	157.82
Consumption of Fixed Capital..........	**99cfc**	71.81	75.10	77.46	79.24	82.99	88.59	94.43	102.10	110.65	118.24	122.56	130.00
GDP Vol. 2001/02 Ref.,Chained........	**99b.r**	526.77	552.21	571.49	596.20	619.21	652.03	680.21	701.74	718.98	747.67	772.86	797.69
GDP Volume (2000=100)..............	**99bvr**	75.1	78.7	81.4	85.0	88.2	92.9	96.9	100.0	102.5	106.5	110.1	113.7
GDP Deflator (2000=100)..............	**99bir**	89.3	90.0	91.6	93.6	95.1	95.6	96.1	100.0	104.0	106.0	109.6	113.5
							Millions: Midyear Estimates						
Population.................................	**99z**	17.52	17.73	17.94	18.16	18.39	18.62	18.85	19.07	19.29	19.51	19.73	19.94

Austria 122

		1993	1994	1995	1996	1997	1998	1999	2000	2001	2002	2003	2004
Exchange Rates		colspan*Schillings per SDR through 1998, Euros per SDR Thereafter: End of Period*											
Official Rate	aa	16.679	16.013	14.996	15.751	17.045	16.540	1.3662	1.4002	1.4260	1.2964	1.1765	1.1402
		Schillings per US Dollar through 1998, Euros per US Dollar Thereafter: End of Period (ae) Period Average (rf)											
Official Rate	ae	12.143	10.969	10.088	10.954	12.633	11.747	.9954	1.0747	1.1347	.9536	.7918	.7342
Official Rate	rf	11.632	11.422	10.081	10.587	12.204	12.379	.9386	1.0854	1.1175	1.0626	.8860	.8054
		Schillings per ECU: End of Period (ea) Period Average (eb)											
ECU Rate	ea	13.5998	13.4923	13.2581	13.7253	13.9495	13.7058	....	....	....	....	....	....
ECU Rate	eb	13.6360	13.5755	13.1880	13.4234	13.8403	13.8648	....	....	....	....	....	....
		Index Numbers (2000=100): Period Averages											
Official Rate (1995=100)	ahx	86.6	88.4	100.0	95.2	82.6	81.5	....	....	....	....	....	....
Nominal Effective Exchange Rate	neu	105.5	105.9	110.0	107.7	104.1	104.5	103.1	100.0	100.2	101.0	104.1	105.2
Real Effective Exchange Rate	reu	126.4	124.4	121.6	115.8	109.1	107.4	105.3	100.0	99.2	99.4	101.7	103.7
Fund Position		*Millions of SDRs: End of Period*											
Quota	2f.s	1,188	1,188	1,188	1,188	1,188	1,188	1,872	1,872	1,872	1,872	1,872	1,872
SDRs	1b.s	161	194	122	136	125	106	106	103	185	136	122	103
Reserve Position in the Fund	1c.s	381	364	459	562	714	970	699	531	662	705	771	602
of which: Outstg.Fund Borrowing	2c	—	—	—	—	—	38	—	—	—	—	—	—
International Liquidity		*Millions of US Dollars Unless Otherwise Indicated: End of Period*											
Total Res.Min.Gold (Eurosys.Def)	1l.d	14,610	16,822	18,730	22,865	19,736	22,432	† 15,120	14,319	12,509	9,683	8,470	7,858
SDRs	1b.d	220	283	181	195	168	149	145	134	233	185	181	160
Reserve Position in the Fund	1c.d	524	531	682	809	963	1,365	959	692	833	959	1,145	935
Foreign Exchange	1d.d	13,866	16,008	17,867	21,861	18,605	20,918	14,016	13,492	11,444	8,540	7,144	6,763
o/w:Fin.Deriv.Rel.to Reserves	1ddd	....	....	....	....	....	....	—	—	—	—	—	—
Other Reserve Assets	1e.d	....	....	....	....	....	....	—	—	—	—	—	—
Gold (Million Fine Troy Ounces)	1ad	18.60	18.34	11.99	10.75	7.87	9.64	13.10	12.14	11.17	10.21	10.21	9.89
Gold (Eurosystem Valuation)	1and	2,871	3,135	2,223	1,805	1,168	2,795	3,803	3,331	3,089	3,499	4,259	4,330
Memo:Euro Cl. on Non-EA Res.	1dgd	....	....	....	....	....	....						
Non-Euro Cl. on EA Res.	1dhd	....	....	....	....	....	....	2,146	1,453	985	3,588	4,389	3,742
Mon. Auth.: Other Foreign Assets	3..d	....	....	....	....	....	....						
Foreign Liabilities	4..d	9	18	19	8	107	....	† 1,584	845	925	613	472	8
Banking Insts.: Foreign Assets	7a.d	68,418	77,885	92,040	89,538	....	....	† 62,990	69,678	74,777	91,219	122,766	157,517
Foreign Liab.	7b.d	74,089	84,321	99,148	102,739	....	....	† 49,417	49,932	58,520	56,534	70,378	81,780
Monetary Authorities		*Billions of Schillings through 1998; Billions of Euros Beginning 1999: End of Period*											
Fgn. Assets (Cl.on Non-EA Ctys)	11	211.6	217.4	237.0	268.3	263.4	....	21.95	20.48	19.01	16.44	13.69	11.56
Claims on General Government	12a.u	....	....	....	....	....	....	1.43	1.06	1.45	3.19	3.22	4.48
o/w: Claims on Gen.Govt.in Cty	12a	9.2	9.6	9.6	10.6	11.6	....	.22	.26	.40	.43	.59	.57
Claims on Banking Institutions	12e.u	....	....	....	....	....	....	16.20	10.45	6.42	8.81	8.09	15.03
o/w: Claims on Bank.Inst.in Cty	12e	64.0	62.0	47.6	47.2	74.2	....	5.57	7.08	1.73	3.13	3.60	9.38
Claims on Other Resident Sectors	12d.u	....	....	....	....	....	....	2.33	2.42	2.32	2.58	2.43	2.68
o/w: Cl. on Oth.Res.Sect.in Cty	12d	....	....	....	....	....	....	.86	.90	.99	1.13	.94	1.03
Currency Issued	14a	149.8	158.3	168.6	176.7	178.8	....	13.92	14.54	10.69	11.01	12.29	14.11
Liabilities to Banking Insts.	14c.u	....	....	....	....	....	....	16.21	8.76	6.87	11.04	7.40	12.99
o/w: Liabs to Bank.Inst.in Cty	14c	55.2	55.9	43.5	50.1	46.3	....	3.28	3.40	6.56	3.54	4.26	4.00
Demand Dep. of Other Res.Sect.	14d.u	....	....	....	....	....	....	.01	.01	.01	.01	—	—
o/w:D.Dep.of Oth.Res.Sect.in Cty	14d	....	....	....	....	....	....	.01	.01	.01	.01	—	—
Other Dep. of Other Res.Sect.	15..u	....	....	....	....	....	....	—	—	—	—	—	—
o/w:O.Dep.of Oth.Res.Sect.in Cty	15	....	....	....	....	....	....	—	—	—	—	—	—
Bonds & Money Mkt. Instruments	16n.u	....	....	....	....	....	....	....	....	....	....	....	....
o/w: Held by Resid. of Cty	16n	....	....	....	....	....	....	....	....	1.05	.59	.37	.01
Foreign Liab. (to Non-EA Ctys)	16c	.1	.2	.2	.1	1.3	....	1.58	.91	....	....	....	....
Central Government Deposits	16d.u	....	....	....	....	....	....	.01	.01	.03	.02	.02	.01
o/w: Cent.Govt.Dep. in Cty	16d	.3	.3	.2	.3	.2	....	.01	.01	.03	.02	.02	.01
Other Items (Net)	17r	79.5	74.4	81.6	98.9	122.5	....	10.18	10.18	10.56	8.36	7.36	6.64
Memo: Net Claims on Eurosystem	12e.s	....	....	....	....	....	....	−5.55	−3.84	3.04	−3.36	−.35	−4.96
Currency Put into Circ	14m	....	....	....	....	....	....	....	....	....	18.41	15.35	11.23
Banking Institutions		*Billions of Schillings through 1998; Billions of Euros Beginning 1999: End of Period*											
Claims on Monetary Authorities	20	77.4	80.5	74.0	80.1	77.5	....	3.31	3.88	7.98	3.73	4.86	3.82
Claims on Bk.Inst.in Oth.EA Ctys	20b.u	....	....	....	....	....	....	31.09	38.65	44.68	39.15	43.61	47.05
Fgn. Assets (Cl.on Non-EA Ctys)	21	830.8	854.3	928.5	980.8	....	....	62.70	74.88	84.85	86.98	97.20	115.64
Claims on General Government	22a.u	....	....	....	....	....	....	52.90	51.69	48.80	49.72	49.55	55.55
o/w: Claims on Gen.Govt.in Cty	22a	676.8	805.6	† 833.1	823.9	783.4	....	49.85	48.51	43.72	41.85	39.98	42.90
Claims on Other Resident Sectors	22d.u	....	....	....	....	....	....	208.29	227.15	240.55	246.66	253.32	268.45
o/w: Cl. on Oth.Res.Sect.in Cty	22d	2,018.6	2,086.2	† 2,228.8	2,376.9	2,595.9	....	197.09	213.04	224.07	229.50	234.89	247.68
Demand Deposits	24..u	....	....	....	....	....	....	44.60	45.05	51.04	54.07	63.44	68.89
o/w:D.Dep.of Oth.Res.Sect.in Cty	24	181.2	201.1	244.0	255.2	273.5	....	42.15	42.69	48.41	51.45	60.66	66.08
Other Deposits	25..u	....	....	....	....	....	....	130.22	132.01	139.87	137.19	139.75	143.03
o/w:O.Dep.of Oth.Res.Sect.in Cty	25	1,643.1	1,721.0	1,770.9	1,812.1	1,840.7	....	123.21	124.96	132.12	129.78	130.51	132.85
Money Market Fund Shares	26m.u	....	....	....	....	....	....	....	....	....	....	....	....
Bonds & Money Mkt. Instruments	26n.u	....	....	....	....	....	....	94.14	114.39	128.43	135.36	142.45	156.66
o/w: Held by Resid.of Cty	26n	491.9	538.7	596.8	607.9	630.2	....	....	....	....	....	....	....
Foreign Liab. (to Non-EA Ctys)	26c	899.7	924.9	1,000.2	1,125.4	....	....	49.19	53.66	66.40	53.91	55.72	60.04
Central Government Deposits	26d.u	....	....	....	....	....	....	1.61	1.90	3.26	3.36	2.89	4.13
o/w: Cent.Govt.Dep. in Cty	26d	55.2	74.0	77.4	77.7	69.7	....	1.61	1.90	3.25	3.36	2.88	4.08
Credit from Monetary Authorities	26g	64.0	62.0	47.6	47.2	74.2	....	5.19	7.50	1.98	3.41	4.07	10.50
Liab. to Bk.Inst.in Oth. EA Ctys	26h.u	....	....	....	....	....	....	27.81	31.89	28.08	26.98	26.69	26.99
Capital Accounts	27a	211.4	226.6	238.4	254.7	275.7	....	25.50	27.25	29.30	30.93	33.96	38.36
Other Items (Net)	27r	57.0	78.3	89.0	81.6	....	....	−19.96	−17.40	−21.51	−18.98	−20.43	−18.09

		1993	1994	1995	1996	1997	1998	1999	2000	2001	2002	2003	2004
Banking Survey (Nat'l Residency)		*Billions of Schillings through 1998; Billions of Euros Beginning 1999: End of Period*											
Foreign Assets (Net)	31n	142.6	146.6	165.1	123.6	....	....	42.55	56.15	71.50	78.90	93.62	110.31
Domestic Credit	32	2,649.0	2,827.2	† 2,993.8	3,133.4	3,321.0	....	246.41	260.79	265.88	269.53	273.50	288.09
Claims on General Govt. (Net)	32an	630.5	740.9	† 765.0	756.5	725.1	....	48.46	46.85	40.83	38.90	37.68	39.39
Claims on Other Resident Sectors	32d	2,018.6	2,086.2	† 2,228.8	2,376.9	2,595.9	....	197.96	213.94	225.05	230.63	235.83	248.70
Currency Issued	34a.n	149.8	158.3	168.6	176.7	178.8	....	13.92	14.54	10.69	11.01	12.29	14.11
Demand Deposits	34b.n	181.2	201.1	244.0	255.2	273.5	....	42.16	42.70	48.42	51.46	60.66	66.08
Other Deposits	35..n	1,643.1	1,721.0	1,770.9	1,812.1	1,840.7	....	123.21	124.96	132.12	129.78	130.51	132.85
Money Market Fund Shares	36m	....	....	....	....	....	....	....	—	—	—	—	—
Bonds & Money Mkt. Instruments	36n	491.9	538.7	596.8	607.9	630.2	....	94.14	114.39	128.43	135.36	142.45	156.66
o/w: Over Two Years	36na	....	....	....	....	....	....	87.95	104.01	118.57	128.15	135.12	147.76
Other Items (Net)	37r	325.7	354.7	378.6	405.1	....	....	15.54	20.35	17.73	20.82	21.21	28.71
Banking Survey (EA-Wide Residency)						*Billions of Euros: End of Period*							
Foreign Assets (Net)	31n.u	....	....	....	....	....	....	33.88	40.79	36.41	48.93	54.79	67.16
Domestic Credit	32..u	....	....	....	....	....	....	263.33	280.41	289.83	298.77	305.62	327.03
Claims on General Govt. (Net)	32anu	....	....	....	....	....	....	52.72	50.84	46.96	49.53	49.87	55.90
Claims on Other Resident Sect.	32d.u	....	....	....	....	....	....	210.62	229.57	242.87	249.24	255.75	271.13
Currency Issued	34a.u	....	....	....	....	....	....	13.92	14.54	10.69	11.01	12.29	14.11
Demand Deposits	34b.u	....	....	....	....	....	....	44.61	45.06	51.05	54.08	63.44	68.89
Other Deposits	35..u	....	....	....	....	....	....	130.22	132.01	139.87	137.19	139.75	143.03
o/w: Other Dep. Over Two Yrs.	35abu	....	....	....	....	....	....	49.83	50.09	50.65	49.07	51.34	52.92
Money Market Fund Shares	36m.u	....	....	....	....	....	....	....					
Bonds & Money Mkt. Instruments	36n.u	....	....	....	....	....	....	94.14	114.39	128.43	135.36	142.45	156.66
o/w: Over Two Years	36nau	....	....	....	....	....	....	87.95	104.01	118.57	128.15	135.12	147.76
Other Items (Net)	37r.u	....	....	....	....	....	....	14.33	15.21	−3.79	10.05	2.48	11.50
Money (National Definitions)						*Billions of Schillings: End of Period*							
Central Bank Money	19mb	205.24	214.47	212.37	227.13	225.38	....	....	....	....	....	....	....
Extended Monetary Base	19mc	224.39	235.17	250.84	260.35	265.81	....	....	....	....	....	....	....
Money, M1	59ma	334.64	355.58	409.19	431.15	452.30	....	....	....	....	....	....	....
Interest Rates						*Percent Per Annum*							
Discount Rate (End of Period)	60	5.25	4.50	3.00	2.50	2.50	2.50						
Money Market Rate	60b	7.22	5.03	4.36	3.19	3.27	3.36	....	....	....	....	....	....
Deposit Rate	60l	2.98	2.31	2.19	1.71	1.50	† 2.65	2.21				....	....
Deposit Rate (Households)	60lhs	....	....	....	....	....	....	....	....	....	....	1.75	1.72
Deposit Rate (Corporations)	60lcs	....	....	....	....	....	....	....	....	....	....	1.92	2.01
Lending Rate	60p	....	....	....	....	....	6.42	5.64	....	....	....		
Lending Rate (Households)	60phm	....	....	....	....	....	....	....	....	....	....	4.81	4.52
Lending Rate (Corporations)	60pcs	....	....	....	....	....	....	....	....	....	....	4.05	3.72
Government Bond Yield	61	6.64	6.69	6.47	5.30	4.79	4.29	4.09	....	....	....	....	....
Prices, Production, Labor						*Index Numbers (2000=100): Period Averages*							
Share Prices (1995=100)	62	100.9	115.3	100.0	105.2	119.9	135.2	....	....	....	....	....	
Wholesale Prices	63	95.5	96.8	97.1	† 97.1	97.4	96.9	96.1	100.0	† 101.5	101.1	102.7	107.8
Consumer Prices	64	88.6	91.3	93.3	† 95.0	96.3	97.2	97.7	100.0	† 102.7	104.5	105.9	108.1
Harmonized CPI	64h	....	....	94.0	95.7	96.8	97.6	98.1	100.0	102.3	104.0	105.4	107.4
Wages (1996=100)	65a	....	....	....	90.9	92.9	95.2	98.0	100.0	102.2	104.8	106.8	114.9
Industrial Production	66	68.2	70.9	74.5	75.2	80.0	86.6	91.8	100.0	102.8	103.6	105.6	112.0
Employment	67	97.5	98.0	97.9	97.2	97.5	99.2	100.0	100.0	100.5	100.7	101.6	99.4
						Number in Thousands: Period Averages							
Labor Force	67d	3,285	3,286	3,284	3,278	3,292	3,313	3,330	3,328	3,352	3,388	3,425	3,444
Employment	67e	† 3,576	3,742	3,759	3,710	3,719	3,723	3,762	3,777	3,148	3,155	3,185	3,200
Unemployment	67c	222	215	216	231	233	238	222	194	204	224	240	244
Unemployment Rate (%)	67r	6.8	6.5	6.6	7.0	7.1	7.2	6.7	5.8	6.1	6.9	7.0	7.1
Intl. Transactions & Positions					*Billions of Schillings through 1998; Billions of Euros Beginning 1999*								
Exports	70	467.66	511.89	580.01	612.19	715.02	774.74	† 60.27	69.69	74.45	75.05	77.44	87.67
Imports, c.i.f.	71	565.56	629.42	668.03	712.76	790.25	842.13	† 65.32	74.94	78.66	77.19	78.10	87.51
						1990=100							
Volume of Exports	72	108.0	....	....	....	....	....	....	....	....	....	....	....
Volume of Imports	73	105.8	....	....	....	....	....	....	....	....	....	....	....
Export Prices	76	90.6	....	....	....	....	....	....	....	....	....	....	....
Import Prices	76.x	95.5	....	....	....	....	....	....	....	....	....	....	....

		1993	1994	1995	1996	1997	1998	1999	2000	2001	2002	2003	2004
Balance of Payments					*Millions of US Dollars: Minus Sign Indicates Debit*								
Current Account, n.i.e.	78ald	−1,013	−2,992	−5,448	−4,890	−5,221	−5,258	−6,655	−4,864	−3,636	565	−1,363	988
Goods: Exports f.o.b.	78aad	40,271	45,175	57,695	57,937	58,662	63,299	64,422	64,684	66,900	73,667	89,619	111,134
Goods: Imports f.o.b.	78abd	−46,747	−53,089	−64,352	−65,252	−62,936	−66,983	−68,051	−67,421	−68,169	−70,080	−88,479	−106,929
Trade Balance	78acd	−6,476	−7,914	−6,656	−7,315	−4,274	−3,684	−3,629	−2,737	−1,269	3,588	1,140	4,205
Services: Credit	78add	26,725	28,019	32,211	33,977	29,605	29,759	31,306	31,342	33,352	35,386	43,053	48,960
Services: Debit	78aed	−19,186	−20,743	−27,703	−29,331	−28,569	−27,398	−29,421	−29,653	−31,437	−34,996	−41,391	−47,144
Balance on Goods & Services	78afd	1,064	−639	−2,149	−2,669	−3,239	−1,323	−1,745	−1,048	646	3,978	2,802	6,021
Income: Credit	78agd	7,237	7,074	8,900	9,852	10,393	9,957	12,673	11,992	12,031	13,816	16,169	18,939
Income: Debit	78ahd	−8,310	−8,344	−10,498	−10,291	−10,682	−11,958	−15,552	−14,456	−15,111	−15,406	−18,005	−21,259
Balance on Gds, Serv. & Inc.	78aid	−9	−1,909	−3,746	−3,107	−3,527	−3,325	−4,624	−3,512	−2,435	2,389	966	3,701
Current Transfers, n.i.e.: Credit	78ajd	1,266	1,370	2,972	3,145	2,912	2,940	2,925	2,914	3,267	3,815	4,382	5,329
Current Transfers: Debit	78akd	−2,270	−2,453	−4,674	−4,928	−4,605	−4,874	−4,956	−4,267	−4,468	−5,639	−6,712	−8,042
Capital Account, n.i.e.	78bcd	−448	−68	−62	78	26	−347	−265	−432	−529	−378	−12	−341
Capital Account, n.i.e.: Credit	78bad	246	676	540	591	590	483	555	530	483	1,012	878	733
Capital Account: Debit	78bbd	−694	−744	−602	−513	−564	−831	−820	−962	−1,013	−1,390	−891	−1,074
Financial Account, n.i.e.	78bjd	3,970	4,311	7,365	5,325	1,666	9,535	4,789	3,407	1,795	−4,713	−457	−693
Direct Investment Abroad	78bdd	−1,189	−1,256	−1,134	−1,848	−1,984	−2,794	−3,306	−5,599	−3,132	−5,745	−7,061	−7,271
Dir. Invest. in Rep. Econ., n.i.e.	78bed	1,129	2,117	1,901	4,485	2,624	4,661	3,008	8,523	5,906	319	7,276	4,916
Portfolio Investment Assets	78bfd	−1,912	−4,475	−2,836	−8,296	−10,157	−11,210	−29,216	−27,145	−10,955	−22,992	−18,414	−32,747
Equity Securities	78bkd	−618	−842	−545	−1,146	−2,405	−5,280	−5,281	−15,387	35	−3,062	−2,706	−3,935
Debt Securities	78bld	−1,294	−3,633	−2,291	−7,150	−7,752	−5,930	−23,935	−11,757	−10,990	−19,930	−15,708	−28,812
Portfolio Investment Liab., n.i.e.	78bgd	7,912	4,253	12,292	5,607	10,956	17,942	26,364	30,360	16,699	18,790	22,992	32,058
Equity Securities	78bmd	1,182	1,304	1,262	2,652	2,610	1,005	2,131	3,436	−4,538	2,772	2,437	6,972
Debt Securities	78bnd	6,729	2,949	11,030	2,955	8,345	16,937	24,232	26,924	21,237	16,018	20,555	25,086
Financial Derivatives Assets	78bwd	−20	−85	−133	215	−191	303	−517	−441	−143	−495	−668	−131
Financial Derivatives Liabilities	78bxd	....	....	....	....	223	−99	100	254	95	8	−77	−813
Other Investment Assets	78bhd	−5,099	−2,545	−9,923	719	−5,208	−690	−11,592	−16,334	−8,680	11,978	−15,117	−21,676
Monetary Authorities	78bod	....	−17	−131	131	—	−115	−3,561	1,760	538	−139	362	−147
General Government	78bpd	70	−183	−231	324	−647	−512	331	−1,003	−286	775	−242	−540
Banks	78bqd	−5,176	−1,307	−10,848	2,292	−3,873	924	−5,242	−13,593	−6,790	12,057	−12,850	−17,343
Other Sectors	78brd	7	−1,039	1,287	−2,027	−687	−988	−3,121	−3,498	−2,143	−715	−2,387	−3,645
Other Investment Liab., n.i.e.	78bid	3,149	6,303	7,199	4,442	5,403	1,423	19,948	13,790	2,005	−6,576	10,610	24,969
Monetary Authorities	78bsd	—	—	—	—	—	−1	6,684	−647	−6,130	−1,443	959	12,470
General Government	78btd	−492	1,558	467	−715	−319	526	101	157	1,417	−392	53	1,419
Banks	78bud	3,088	4,584	6,077	5,142	5,695	1,695	10,740	11,721	5,812	−9,146	7,572	10,512
Other Sectors	78bvd	553	160	655	15	27	−797	2,422	2,559	905	4,406	2,025	568
Net Errors and Omissions	78cad	−308	−417	−464	562	476	−447	−40	1,143	482	2,803	−203	−1,803
Overall Balance	78cbd	2,201	834	1,391	1,075	−3,053	3,482	−2,172	−746	−1,888	−1,723	−2,036	−1,849
Reserves and Related Items	79dad	−2,201	−834	−1,391	−1,075	3,053	−3,482	2,172	746	1,888	1,723	2,036	1,849
Reserve Assets	79dbd	−2,201	−834	−1,391	−1,075	3,053	−3,482	2,172	746	1,888	1,723	2,036	1,849
Use of Fund Credit and Loans	79dcd	—	—	—	—	—	—	—	—	—	—	—	—
Exceptional Financing	79ded	....	....	....	....	....	....	....	....	....	....	....	....
International Investment Position						*Millions of US Dollars*							
Assets	79aad	122,090	137,955	160,211	161,785	166,135	194,856	225,924	261,554	267,909	335,373	441,931	....
Direct Investment Abroad	79abd	8,112	9,390	11,707	11,868	15,159	18,726	20,458	26,262	29,934	44,076	59,142	....
Portfolio Investment	79acd	17,096	22,673	27,389	33,303	44,051	58,747	93,299	115,680	112,458	152,484	206,807	....
Equity Securities	79add	3,722	4,941	5,868	6,454	11,502	17,225	28,936	42,698	31,190	30,047	44,044	....
Debt Securities	79aed	13,374	17,732	21,521	26,849	32,549	41,522	64,363	72,982	81,268	122,437	162,762	....
Financial Derivatives	79ald	74	109	169	219	201	—	—	—	—	—	—	....
Other Investment	79afd	75,113	82,040	95,054	89,730	84,853	90,959	93,236	101,985	109,906	125,631	163,253	....
Monetary Authorities	79agd	—	—	—	—	12	189	4,355	2,383	1,765	2,220	2,173	....
General Government	79ahd	2,528	1,021	1,209	1,607	2,039	2,828	2,078	2,853	2,934	2,648	3,335	....
Banks	79aid	62,645	70,380	83,267	77,716	73,651	77,267	74,447	80,897	87,993	99,280	130,398	....
Other Sectors	79ajd	9,940	10,639	10,577	10,407	9,150	10,676	12,357	15,852	17,214	21,483	27,347	....
Reserve Assets	79akd	21,695	23,742	25,893	26,666	21,871	26,423	18,931	17,627	15,611	13,181	12,729	....
Liabilities	79lad	133,600	155,538	189,790	189,264	198,918	236,547	262,994	299,033	315,205	379,038	484,508	....
Dir. Invest. in Rep. Economy	79lbd	11,398	13,246	17,536	18,258	19,694	23,837	23,991	31,280	35,164	44,618	60,938	....
Portfolio Investment	79lcd	61,896	69,469	89,473	87,676	97,091	121,674	139,054	161,082	171,393	218,273	279,784	....
Equity Securities	79ldd	3,591	5,379	6,989	9,056	15,662	15,623	14,745	19,569	14,920	17,235	26,483	....
Debt Securities	79led	58,305	64,090	82,484	78,620	81,430	106,052	124,309	141,512	156,473	201,037	253,301	....
Financial Derivatives	79lld	—	119	129	110	12	—	—	—	—	—	—	....
Other Investment	79lfd	60,306	72,705	82,653	83,221	82,121	91,036	99,949	106,672	108,648	116,147	143,786	....
Monetary Authorities	79lgd	—	18	20	9	—	—	6,141	5,639	−562	−2,296	−1,367	....
General Government	79lhd	1,359	3,045	4,074	3,478	2,955	3,719	3,564	3,412	4,319	4,438	5,287	....
Banks	79lid	49,543	57,681	65,385	68,267	68,669	76,438	79,628	84,906	91,597	93,536	113,017	....
Other Sectors	79ljd	9,405	11,961	13,174	11,466	10,496	10,879	10,616	12,715	13,294	17,342	22,808	....
Government Finance													
Federal Government				*Billions of Schillings through 1998; Millions of Euros Beginning 1999: Year Ending December 31*									
Deficit (-) or Surplus	80	−107.14	−128.81	† −119.88	−99.71	....	....	....	....	....	....	....	....
Revenue	81	777.75	815.10	† 845.40	903.40	....	....	....	....	....	....	....	....
Grants Received	81z	3.59	4.03	† 23.93	16.36	....	....	....	....	....	....	....	....
Expenditure	82	875.99	917.14	† 981.20	1,009.89	....	....	....	....	....	....	....	....
Lending Minus Repayments	83	12.49	30.80	† 1.01	5.86	....	....	....	....	....	....	....	....
Financing													
Net Borrowing	84	106.86	121.24	† 113.75	127.56	....	....	....	....	....	....	....	....
Net Borrowing: Domestic	84a	82.11	89.13	....	....	....	....	....	....	....	....	....	....
Net Borrowing: Foreign	85a	25.31	47.25	....	....	....	....	....	....	....	....	....	....
Use of Cash Balances	87	.28	7.57	† 6.13	−27.85	....	....	....	....	....	....	....	....
Debt: Domestic	88a	899.56	975.25	† 1,053.73	1,120.66	1,190.76	† 1,384.46	....	....	....	....	....	....
Debt: Foreign	89a	212.86	260.94	† 296.63	296.47	304.93	† 188.43	....	....	....	....	....	....
General Government					*As Percent of Gross Domestic Product*								
Deficit (-) or Surplus	80g	−4.2	−5.0	−5.1	−3.8	−1.7	−2.4	−2.2	−1.5	.1	....	....	....
Debt	88g	62.7	65.4	69.4	68.3	64.7	63.9	64.9	63.6	61.7	....	....	....

National Accounts		1993	1994	1995	1996	1997	1998	1999	2000	2001	2002	2003	2004
		Billions of Schillings through 1998; Billions of Euros Beginning 1999											
Househ.Cons.Expend.,incl.NPISHs....	96f	1,267.9	1,344.7	† 1,378.1	1,452.8	1,474.6	1,502.9	† 112.0	117.4	121.6	123.9	127.7	131.4
Government Consumption Expend...	91f	436.1	459.5	485.3	497.6	482.2	498.2	† 38.0	38.7	38.8	39.6	40.6	41.8
Gross Fixed Capital Formation..........	93e	495.7	532.4	† 534.1	553.3	568.2	592.2	† 44.2	47.9	47.4	45.9	48.6	51.2
Changes in Inventories....................	93i	−2.6	−2.3	29.9	16.0	17.3	20.8	† 2.5	1.3	1.0	.6	.9	−.1
Exports of Goods and Services..........	90c	730.7	781.1	847.0	897.5	1,012.2	1,104.2	† 85.3	95.6	102.9	107.5	109.1	120.1
Imports of Goods and Services (-).....	98c	715.9	798.8	† 853.8	917.4	1,006.5	1,066.2	† 81.9	92.7	97.8	96.4	100.1	108.7
Gross Domestic Product (GDP)........	99b	2,205.4	2,324.7	† 2,415.3	2,502.6	2,547.6	2,647.3	† 200.0	210.4	215.6	221.0	226.1	235.4
Net Primary Income from Abroad.....	98.n	−15.6	−18.0	−34.7	−17.2	−26.8	−28.7	† −4.2	−4.0	−5.2	−3.5	−3.4	−3.4
Gross National Income (GNI)...........	99a	2,191.7	2,307.3	2,373.8	2,477.3	2,509.7	2,605.6	† 195.8	206.3	210.4	217.5	222.7	232.0
Net Current Transf.from Abroad.......	98t	....	....	....	....	....	....	† −3.4	−4.1	−2.9	−3.4	−3.5	....
Gross Nat'l Disposable Inc.(GNDI)....	99i	....	....	....	....	....	....	† 192.4	202.3	207.6	214.1	219.4	....
Gross Saving.................................	99s	....	....	....	....	....	....	† 41.4	45.1	45.9	49.5	49.7	....
Consumption of Fixed Capital..........	99cf	307.6	319.3	333.1	346.7	356.5	368.6	....	....	....	....	....	....
GDP Volume 1995 Prices................	99b.p	2,394.25	2,457.96	2,504.90	2,570.51	2,617.79	2,711.01	† 203.56	210.39	211.90	214.37	216.00	220.70
GDP Volume (2000=100)................	99bvp	82.7	84.9	86.5	88.8	90.4	93.6	† 96.8	100.0	100.7	101.9	102.7	104.9
GDP Deflator (2000=100)................	99bip	92.1	94.6	† 96.4	97.4	97.3	97.6	† 98.3	100.0	101.7	103.1	104.7	106.7
		Millions: Midyear Estimates											
Population.................................	99z	7.93	8.00	8.05	8.08	8.09	8.09	8.09	8.10	8.11	8.13	8.15	8.17

Azerbaijan, Republic of   912

		1993	1994	1995	1996	1997	1998	1999	2000	2001	2002	2003	2004
Exchange Rates						*Manat per SDR: End of Period*							
Official Rate	aa	162.08	6,105.09	6,600.02	5,892.76	5,245.88	5,477.24	6,008.85	5,947.78	6,000.89	6,652.13	7,315.43	7,614.41
					Manat per US Dollar: End of Period (ae) Period Average (rf)								
Official Rate	ae	118.00	4,182.00	4,440.00	4,098.00	3,888.00	3,890.00	4,378.00	4,565.00	4,775.00	4,893.00	4,923.00	4,903.00
Official Rate	rf	99.98	1,570.23	4,413.54	4,301.26	3,985.38	3,869.00	4,120.17	4,474.15	4,656.58	4,860.82	4,910.73	4,913.48
Fund Position						*Millions of SDRs: End of Period*							
Quota	2f.s	117.00	117.00	117.00	117.00	117.00	117.00	160.90	160.90	160.90	160.90	160.90	160.90
SDRs	1b.s	—	—	.84	14.48	4.14	.08	5.15	5.07	1.98	.51	12.14	9.36
Reserve Position in the Fund	1c.s	.01	.01	.01	.01	.01	.01	.01	.01	.01	.01	.01	.01
Total Fund Cred.&Loans Outstg	2tl	—	—	67.86	121.68	197.73	228.14	296.73	257.73	234.90	205.11	174.47	134.18
International Liquidity						*Millions of US Dollars Unless Otherwise Indicated: End of Period*							
Total Reserves minus Gold	1l.d	.59	2.03	120.88	211.28	466.09	447.33	672.59	679.61	896.70	721.51	820.85	1,089.55
SDRs	1b.d	—	—	1.25	20.82	5.59	.11	7.07	6.60	2.49	.70	18.03	14.53
Reserve Position in the Fund	1c.d	.01	.01	.01	.01	.01	.01	.01	.01	.01	.01	.01	.02
Foreign Exchange	1d.d	.58	2.02	119.62	190.45	460.49	447.20	665.50	672.99	894.20	720.80	802.80	1,075.00
Gold (Million Fine Troy Ounces)	1ad	—	—	—	.01	—	—	—	—	—	—	—	—
Gold (National Valuation)	1and	—	—	—	2.38	1.38	1.37	—	—	—	—	—	—
Monetary Authorities:Other Assets	3..d	54.28	1.93	1.57	1.91	1.53	1.16	1.03	.05		.17	—	—
Other Liab	4..d	63.09	2.87	1.75	1.33	1.37	13.28	12.34	12.01	.30	1.31	.87	.76
Deposit Money Banks: Assets	7a.d	257.48	135.30	167.69	156.17	154.48	97.27	152.11	379.46	193.13	211.78	226.59	204.20
Liabilities	7b.d	152.74	41.05	33.95	75.89	53.16	56.08	69.32	96.54	92.58	110.60	109.46	90.12
Monetary Authorities						*Billions of Manat: End of Period*							
Foreign Assets	11	6.47	16.59	543.70	883.38	1,823.46	† 1,739.58	2,948.81	3,102.63	† 4,270.19	3,549.44	3,954.69	5,274.49
Claims on Central Government	12a	25.73	428.87	333.46	416.73	360.26	† 1,903.93	2,563.34	2,518.48	† 790.17	722.57	652.74	706.87
Claims on Nonfin.Pub.Enterprises	12c	.13	1.02	8.48	8.93	8.76	† 3.50	3.44	—	† —	—	—	—
Claims on Private Sector	12d	—	—	—	—	—	† —	—	—	† —	.37	2.22	2.55
Claims on Deposit Money Banks	12e	23.93	141.69	1,052.40	893.67	865.45	† 750.15	746.24	701.25	† 101.00	86.41	236.58	314.71
Reserve Money	14	43.84	325.69	911.14	1,071.06	1,514.08	† 1,181.57	1,369.42	1,767.31	† 1,797.40	2,049.62	2,530.55	4,168.13
of which: Currency Outside DMBs	14a	43.18	276.13	602.40	865.44	1,170.51	† 926.05	1,135.84	1,349.81	† 1,468.99	1,668.73	2,040.88	2,388.97
Time, Savings,& Fgn.Currency Dep	15	—	.88	—	.03	.04	† —	—	—	† 2.05	10.03	53.46	.40
Foreign Liabilities	16c	7.44	12.02	455.63	722.52	1,042.60	† 1,301.25	1,837.03	1,587.77	† 1,411.05	1,370.81	1,280.56	1,025.41
Central Government Deposits	16d	5.75	235.86	447.68	334.46	367.65	† 1,817.21	2,837.37	2,556.29	† 1,488.12	612.61	590.51	607.24
Capital Accounts	17a	4.08	44.87	405.19	400.30	1,128.62	† 196.15	240.35	333.32	† 368.47	324.18	431.81	480.77
Other Items (Net)	17r	−4.85	−31.14	−281.61	−325.66	−995.06	† −99.02	−22.34	77.67	† 94.28	−8.46	−40.66	16.68
Deposit Money Banks						*Billions of Manat: End of Period*							
Reserves	20	6.65	43.89	303.17	242.76	301.94	204.07	177.85	† 391.51	† 318.49	361.20	491.92	1,750.35
Foreign Assets	21	30.38	565.81	744.55	639.97	600.62	378.37	665.95	† 1,732.24	† 922.21	1,036.26	1,115.49	1,001.18
Claims on Central Government	22a	.33	51.49	12.49	32.03	52.69	30.04	69.44	† 275.99	† 324.61	366.05	333.57	163.17
Claims on Nonfin.Pub.Enterprises	22c	53.43	623.57	1,403.59	1,719.82	1,635.51	1,658.84	1,722.20	† 817.62	† 496.61	468.48	491.92	809.38
Claims on Private Sector	22d	15.08	62.46	126.52	159.32	386.81	530.06	559.69	† 1,391.76	† 1,327.53	1,662.15	2,353.97	3,807.90
Claims on Nonbank Financial Insts	22g	.02	.06	—	—	—	—	—	† 3.24	† 1.97	.56	100.64	103.85
Demand Deposits	24	22.00	93.70	251.29	250.08	323.80	203.02	215.83	† 218.21	† 218.73	292.74	458.18	875.48
Time,Savings,& Fgn.Currency Dep	25	20.59	674.36	455.53	418.73	651.71	662.47	826.07	† 2,273.28	† 1,743.55	1,961.90	2,601.40	4,265.32
Restricted Deposits	26b	—	—	—	—	—	—	—	† —	† 152.01	213.54	167.25	127.34
Foreign Liabilities	26c	18.02	171.66	150.75	311.00	206.69	218.15	303.46	† 440.72	† 442.07	541.17	538.86	441.84
Central Government Deposits	26d	7.19	101.60	98.20	222.31	30.20	82.23	84.95	† 185.40	† 51.27	25.88	62.67	310.43
Credit from Monetary Authorities	26g	27.06	56.53	893.23	782.36	838.02	615.87	592.89	† 654.22	† 96.45	86.31	236.06	314.01
Liab. to Nonbank Financial Insts	26j	.20	.45	2.84	7.44	6.84	5.55	2.17	† —	† 15.87	27.36	105.62	228.15
Capital Accounts	27a	12.84	121.45	355.30	640.98	831.83	1,020.01	1,152.11	† 732.21	† 670.34	790.98	898.05	1,244.65
Other Items (Net)	27r	−2.02	127.51	383.18	160.99	88.51	−5.92	17.67	† 108.32	† 1.15	−45.17	−180.57	−171.39
Monetary Survey						*Billions of Manat: End of Period*							
Foreign Assets (Net)	31n	11.39	398.73	681.87	489.83	1,174.80	† 598.55	1,474.27	† 2,806.39	† 3,339.29	2,673.73	3,250.76	4,808.43
Domestic Credit	32	81.77	830.00	1,338.66	1,780.06	2,046.19	† 2,226.93	1,995.80	† 2,265.39	† 1,401.51	2,581.69	3,281.87	4,676.05
Claims on Central Govt. (Net)	32an	13.12	142.89	−199.93	−108.00	15.11	† 34.53	−289.53	† 52.78	† −424.60	450.13	333.12	−47.63
Claims on Nonfin.Pub.Enterprises	32c	53.56	624.59	1,412.07	1,728.75	1,644.27	† 1,662.34	1,725.64	† 817.62	† 496.61	468.48	491.92	809.38
Claims on Private Sector	32d	15.08	62.46	126.52	159.32	386.81	† 530.06	559.69	† 1,391.76	† 1,327.53	1,662.52	2,356.19	3,810.45
Claims on Nonbank Fin. Insts	32g	.02	.06	—	—	—	† —	—	† 3.24	† 1.97	.56	100.64	103.85
Money	34	65.52	372.38	858.38	1,119.74	1,524.08	† 1,183.26	1,390.08	† 1,569.81	† 1,693.10	1,967.27	2,499.09	3,264.50
Quasi-Money	35	20.59	675.23	455.53	418.76	651.75	† 662.47	826.07	† 2,273.28	† 1,745.60	1,971.93	2,654.85	4,265.72
Restricted Deposits	36b	—	—	—	—	—	† —	—	† —	† 152.01	213.54	167.25	127.34
Liab. to Nonbank Financial Insts	36j	.20	.45	2.84	7.44	6.84	† 5.55	2.17	† —	† 15.87	27.36	105.62	228.15
Capital Accounts	37a	16.92	166.33	760.50	1,041.28	1,960.45	† 1,216.16	1,392.46	† 1,065.53	† 1,038.81	1,115.16	1,329.86	1,725.42
Other Items (Net)	37r	−10.07	14.34	−56.72	−317.33	−922.14	† −241.95	−140.72	† 163.16	† 95.42	−39.84	−224.04	−126.65
Money plus Quasi-Money	35l	86.11	1,047.62	1,313.92	1,538.50	2,175.83	† 1,845.73	2,216.15	† 3,843.09	† 3,438.71	3,939.20	5,153.95	7,530.22
Money (National Definitions)						*Billions of Manat: End of Period*							
Reserve Money	19mb	....	....	736.30	985.40	1,339.30	1,057.10	1,256.60	1,541.90	1,680.60	1,871.90	2,316.00	3,200.20
M1	59ma	....	....	924.99	1,173.68	1,537.82	1,202.45	1,390.04	1,609.50	1,469.00	1,967.40	2,499.10	3,286.30
M2	59mb	....	....	957.59	1,204.18	1,556.27	1,218.50	1,404.32	1,661.10	1,687.50	2,032.10	2,592.20	3,418.00
Interest Rates						*Percent Per Annum*							
Refinancing Rate	60	100.00	200.00	80.00	20.00	12.00	14.00	10.00	10.00	10.00	7.00	7.00	7.00
Treasury Bill Rate	60c	....	....	....	....	12.23	14.10	18.31	16.73	16.51	14.12	8.00	4.62
Deposit Rate	60l	....	....	....	....	....	....	12.08	12.90	8.46	8.66	9.54	9.18
Deposit Rate (Foreign Currency)	60l.f	....	....	....	....	....	....	10.75	11.12	9.51	9.34	8.83	9.09
Lending Rate	60p	....	....	....	....	....	....	19.48	19.66	19.71	17.37	15.46	15.72
Lending Rate (Foreign Currency)	60p.f	....	....	....	....	....	....	16.27	17.98	18.67	18.69	18.64	19.68
Prices and Labor						*Percent Change over Previous Period*							
Consumer Prices	64.xx	1,129.0	1,664.5	411.7	19.8	3.6	−.7	−8.6	1.8	1.5	2.8	2.2	6.7
						Number in Thousands: Period Averages							
Employment	67e	3,714.6	3,631.3	3,613.0	3,686.7	3,694.1	3,701.5	3,702.8	3,704.5	3,715.0	3,726.5	3,747.0	3,764.2
Unemployment	67c	19.5	23.6	28.3	31.9	38.3	42.3	45.2	43.7	48.4	51.0	54.4	55.9
Unemployment Rate (%)	67r	.5	.7	.8	.9	1.0	1.1	1.2	1.2	1.3	1.3	1.4	....

		1993	1994	1995	1996	1997	1998	1999	2000	2001	2002	2003	2004
Intl. Transactions & Positions							*Millions of US Dollars*						
Exports	70..d	724.7	652.7	637.2	631.2	781.3	606.2	929.7	1,745.2	2,314.3	2,167.4	2,590.4	3,615.4
Imports, cif	71..d	628.8	777.9	667.7	960.6	794.3	1,076.5	1,035.9	1,172.1	1,430.9	1,665.5	2,626.2	3,516.0
Balance of Payments							*Millions of US Dollars: Minus Sign Indicates Debit*						
Current Account, n.i.e.	78ald	....	....	−400.7	−931.2	−915.8	−1,364.5	−599.7	−167.8	−51.8	−768.4	−2,020.9	−2,589.2
Goods: Exports f.o.b.	78aad	....	....	612.3	643.7	808.3	677.8	1,025.2	1,858.3	2,078.9	2,304.9	2,624.6	3,743.0
Goods: Imports f.o.b.	78abd	....	....	−985.4	−1,337.6	−1,375.2	−1,723.9	−1,433.4	−1,539.0	−1,465.1	−1,823.3	−2,723.1	−3,581.7
Trade Balance	78acd	....	....	−373.1	−693.9	−566.9	−1,046.2	−408.2	319.3	613.9	481.6	−98.5	161.3
Services: Credit	78add	....	....	172.4	149.3	341.8	331.7	256.8	259.8	289.8	362.1	432.0	492.0
Services: Debit	78aed	....	....	−304.6	−440.9	−726.0	−700.8	−485.1	−484.5	−664.9	−1,297.7	−2,046.5	−2,730.4
Balance on Goods & Services	78afd	....	....	−505.4	−985.6	−951.1	−1,415.2	−636.5	94.6	238.8	−454.0	−1,713.0	−2,077.1
Income: Credit	78agd	....	....	9.9	15.1	22.8	38.3	11.0	55.9	41.5	37.1	52.6	65.3
Income: Debit	78ahd	....	....	−16.0	−27.2	−32.3	−51.6	−56.0	−391.4	−408.7	−421.8	−494.7	−765.9
Balance on Gds, Serv., & Inc.	78aid	....	....	−511.4	−997.7	−960.6	−1,428.5	−681.5	−240.9	−128.4	−838.7	−2,155.0	−2,777.7
Current Transfers, n.i.e.: Credit	78ajd	....	....	129.3	107.2	95.7	145.0	134.5	135.0	176.5	228.2	225.1	262.6
Current Transfers: Debit	78akd	....	....	−18.5	−40.7	−50.9	−80.9	−52.8	−62.0	−99.9	−157.9	−90.9	−74.1
Capital Account, n.i.e.	78bcd	....	....	−1.6	—	−10.2	−.7	....	....	....	−28.7	−23.1	−4.1
Capital Account, n.i.e.: Credit	78bad	....	....	....	....	....	....	....	....	....	18.4	15.0	24.0
Capital Account: Debit	78bbd	....	....	−1.6	—	−10.2	−.7	....	....	....	−47.1	−38.1	−28.1
Financial Account, n.i.e.	78bjd	....	....	400.3	822.5	1,092.1	1,326.0	690.2	493.4	126.0	918.7	2,279.7	2,960.2
Direct Investment Abroad	78bdd	....	....	....	....	....	—	....	−.8	....	....	....	....
Dir. Invest. in Rep. Econ., n.i.e.	78bed	....	....	330.1	627.3	1,114.8	1,023.0	510.3	129.9	226.5	−325.6	−933.3	−1,204.8
Portfolio Investment Assets	78bfd	....	....	−1.7	—	1.1	....	....	....	....	1,392.4	3,285.0	3,556.1
Equity Securities	78bkd	....	....	....	....	....	....	....	....	....	.4	—	−18.1
Debt Securities	78bld	....	....	−1.7	—	1.1	—	....	....	....	....	....	1.9
Portfolio Investment Liab., n.i.e.	78bgd	....	....	—	—	—	.4	....	....	....	.4	—	−20.0
Equity Securities	78bmd	....	....	....	....	....	....	....	....	....	....	....	....
Debt Securities	78bnd	....	....	—	—	—	.4	....	....	....	....	....	....
Financial Derivatives Assets	78bwd	....	....	....	....	....	....	....	....	....	....	....	....
Financial Derivatives Liabilities	78bxd	....	....	....	....	....	....	....	....	....	....	....	....
Other Investment Assets	78bhd	....	....	−22.1	−216.8	−102.6	22.3	−81.0	−114.2	−394.0	−302.9	−169.2	−360.4
Monetary Authorities	78bod	....	....	....	....	....	....	....	....	....	....	....	1.8
General Government	78bpd	....	....	....	....	....	....	....	....	−220.5	−200.7	−109.4	−123.5
Banks	78bqd	....	....	−19.6	−136.9	5.3	62.4	−44.2	7.1	−77.7	−18.3	−16.7	20.1
Other Sectors	78brd	....	....	−2.5	−79.8	−107.9	−40.1	−36.8	−121.2	−95.8	−83.9	−43.2	−258.8
Other Investment Liab., n.i.e.	78bid	....	....	94.1	412.0	78.8	280.4	260.9	478.4	293.5	154.4	97.2	987.4
Monetary Authorities	78bsd	....	....	....	....	....	....	....	....	....	30.3	34.4	....
General Government	78btd	....	....	30.0	—	70.8	75.6	161.6	246.2	138.6	17.2	32.4	34.8
Banks	78bud	....	....	−.3	26.5	−18.8	−1.7	−.1	−22.9	3.0	16.9	−.2	−16.4
Other Sectors	78bvd	....	....	64.3	385.5	26.8	206.5	99.3	255.0	151.9	90.0	30.5	969.0
Net Errors and Omissions	78cad	....	....	59.7	23.6	−27.0	−20.1	42.4	—	−.9	−87.4	−111.8	−49.9
Overall Balance	78cbd	....	....	57.8	−85.0	139.2	−59.2	132.9	325.6	73.4	34.2	123.8	317.0
Reserves and Related Items	79dad	....	....	−57.8	85.0	−139.2	59.2	−132.9	−325.6	−73.4	−34.2	−123.8	−317.0
Reserve Assets	79dbd	....	....	−161.6	7.1	−244.2	18.7	−228.5	−274.2	−44.1	5.0	−82.0	−257.2
Use of Fund Credit and Loans	79dcd	....	....	103.8	77.9	105.0	40.5	95.6	−51.4	−29.3	−39.2	−41.8	−59.8
Exceptional Financing	79ded	....	....	....	....	....	....	....	....	....	....	....	....
International Investment Position							*Millions of US Dollars*						
Assets	79aad	....	....	....	....	....	....	....	....	....	2,084.8	3,185.3	4,993.3
Direct Investment Abroad	79abd	....	....	....	....	....	....	....	....	....	....	....	....
Portfolio Investment	79acd	....	....	....	....	....	....	—	.8	.8	326.4	1,259.7	2,464.5
Equity Securities	79add	....	....	....	....	....	....	—	—	—	.4	.4	18.5
Debt Securities	79aed	....	....	....	....	....	....	....	....	....	—	—	−1.9
Financial derivatives	79ald	....	....	....	....	....	....	—	—	—	.4	.4	20.4
Other Investment	79afd	....	....	....	....	....	....	385.1	282.4	827.5	1,037.5	1,122.4	1,434.3
Monetary Authorities	79agd	....	....	....	....	....	....	—	—	—	—	—	—
General Government	79ahd	....	....	....	....	....	....	....	....	491.5	692.2	801.6	971.8
Banks	79aid	....	....	....	....	....	....	....	....	190.7	209.3	225.6	203.7
Other Sectors	79ajd	....	....	....	....	....	....	....	....	145.3	136.0	95.2	258.8
Reserve Assets	79akd	....	....	....	....	....	....	675.8	950.8	725.4	720.5	802.8	1,076.0
Liabilities	79lad	....	....	....	....	....	....	....	....	....	7,221.9	10,733.7	14,305.5
Dir. Invest. in Rep. Economy	79lbd	....	....	....	....	....	....	3,099.5	3,735.2	3,961.7	5,354.1	8,639.1	11,482.4
Portfolio Investment	79lcd	....	....	....	....	....	....	—	—	—	—	—	—
Equity Securities	79ldd	....	....	....	....	....	....	—	—	—	—	—	—
Debt Securities	79led	....	....	....	....	....	....	—	—	—	—	—	—
Financial Derivatives	79lld	....	....	....	....	....	....	—	—	—	—	—	—
Other Investment	79lfd	....	....	....	....	....	....	1,616.4	1,497.1	1,797.9	1,867.8	2,094.6	2,823.1
Monetary Authorities	79lgd	....	....	....	....	....	....	....	....	446.9	453.9	476.9	455.0
General Government	79lhd	....	....	....	....	....	....	....	....	56.8	87.3	131.4	237.0
Banks	79lid	....	....	....	....	....	....	....	....	98.2	115.2	112.5	96.1
Other Sectors	79ljd	....	....	....	....	....	....	....	....	1,196.0	1,211.4	1,373.8	2,035.0
Government Finance							*Billions of Manat: Year Ending December 31*						
Deficit(-)/ or Surplus	80	....	−209.21	−545.03	−405.89	−341.84	−623.00	−479.46	....	....	....	....	....
Total Revenue and Grants	81y	....	479.70	1,920.25	1,960.77	2,402.03	3,143.02	3,380.17	....	....	....	....	....
Revenue	81	....	479.70	1,920.25	1,881.02	2,350.03	3,076.02	3,316.97	....	....	....	....	....
Grants	81z	....	—	—	79.76	52.00	67.00	63.20	....	....	....	....	....
Exp. & Lending Minus Repay.	82z	....	688.91	2,465.27	2,366.67	2,743.88	3,766.02	3,859.64	....	....	....	....	....
Expenditure	82	....	688.91	2,254.33	2,283.64	3,028.57	3,993.14	4,260.94	....	....	....	....	....
Lending Minus Repayments	83	....	—	210.94	83.03	−284.70	−227.12	−401.31	....	....	....	....	....
Total Financing	80h	....	209.21	545.03	405.90	341.84	623.00	479.46	....	....	....	....	....

Azerbaijan, Republic of   912

		1993	1994	1995	1996	1997	1998	1999	2000	2001	2002	2003	2004
National Accounts							*Billions of Manat*						
Househ.Cons.Expend.,incl.NPISHs....	**96f**	....	....	9,477	12,569	12,742	15,076	15,854	17,367	18,513	19,067	21,428	24,358
Government Consumption Expend...	**91f**	....	....	887	1,053	1,009	1,295	1,396	1,402	1,458	3,760	4,427	4,019
Gross Fixed Capital Formation..........	**93e**	....	....	1,669	3,977	5,841	6,110	5,382	5,458	6,081	10,330	18,895	22,689
Changes in Inventories.....................	**93i**	....	....	868	−15	−435	−369	−380	−581	−586	151	103	126
Exports of Goods and Services..........	**90c**	....	....	3,466	3,406	4,585	3,905	5,279	9,477	11,030	12,964	15,010	14,514
Imports of Goods and Services.........	**98c**	....	....	5,698	7,640	8,377	9,381	7,900	9,054	9,918	15,171	23,421	22,536
Gross Domestic Product (GDP).........	**99b**	....	....	10,669	13,663	15,791	17,203	18,875	23,591	26,578	30,312	35,733	41,873
Statistical Discrepancy....................	**99bs**	....	....	—	314	426	568	−755	−479	—	−788	−710	−1,298
							Millions: Midyear Estimates						
Population.................................	**99z**	7.58	7.69	7.79	7.88	7.96	8.02	8.09	8.14	8.20	8.25	8.30	8.35

		1993	1994	1995	1996	1997	1998	1999	2000	2001	2002	2003	2004
Exchange Rates		*Bahamian Dollars per SDR: End of Period*											
Principal Rate............aa=.........	wa	1.3736	1.4599	1.4865	1.4380	1.3493	1.4080	1.3725	1.3029	1.2567	1.3595	1.4860	1.5530
		Bahamian Dollars per US Dollar: End of Period (we and xe) Period Average (xf)											
Principal Rate............ae=.........	we	1.0000	1.0000	1.0000	1.0000	1.0000	1.0000	1.0000	1.0000	1.0000	1.0000	1.0000	1.0000
Secondary Rate........................	xe	1.2250	1.2250	1.2250	1.2250	1.2250	1.2250	1.2250	1.2250	1.2250	1.2250	1.2250	1.2250
Secondary Rate........................	xf	1.2250	1.2250	1.2250	1.2250	1.2250	1.2250	1.2250	1.2250	1.2250	1.2250	1.2250	1.2250
		Index Numbers (2000=100): Period Averages											
Principal Rate........................	ahx	100.0	100.0	100.0	100.0	100.0	100.0	100.0	100.0	100.0	100.0	100.0	100.0
Nominal Effective Exchange Rate.....	nec	89.8	88.2	87.9	89.8	93.0	94.8	97.2	100.0	102.8	102.0	97.4	94.4
Real Effective Exchange Rate..........	rec	97.7	94.2	91.1	91.5	93.5	95.2	97.4	100.0	102.5	102.8	99.3	95.1
Fund Position		*Millions of SDRs: End of Period*											
Quota................................	2f.s	94.9	94.9	94.9	94.9	94.9	94.9	130.3	130.3	130.3	130.3	130.3	130.3
SDRs..................................	1b.s	—	—	—	—	—	—	—	.1	.1	.1	—	—
Reserve Position in the Fund..........	1c.s	6.2	6.2	6.2	6.2	6.2	6.2	6.2	6.2	6.2	6.2	6.2	6.3
Total Fund Cred.&Loans Outstg........	2tl	—	—	—	—	—	—	—	—	—	—	—	—
International Liquidity		*Millions of US Dollars Unless Otherwise Indicated: End of Period*											
Total Reserves minus Gold..............	1l.d	172.3	176.6	179.2	171.4	227.0	346.5	410.5	349.6	319.3	380.6	491.1	674.4
SDRs...............................	1b.d	—	—	—	—	—	—	—	.1	.1	.1	—	—
Reserve Position in the Fund.........	1c.d	8.6	9.1	9.3	9.0	8.4	8.8	8.6	8.1	7.8	8.5	9.3	9.7
Foreign Exchange...................	1d.d	163.7	167.5	169.9	162.4	218.6	337.7	401.9	341.4	311.3	372.1	481.8	664.7
Deposit Money Banks: Assets..........	7a.d	35,688	42,817	35,144	41,384	41,310	46,329	58,682	77,649	103,669	136,339	89,838	70,339
Liabilities...	7b.d	35,958	43,219	35,542	41,796	41,662	47,053	59,127	78,346	104,136	136,804	90,451	70,878
Other Banking Insts.: Assets............	7e.d	1,911	2,232	2,450	2,646	2,836	2,685	2,785	2,907	2,293	2,490	2,411	2,398
Liabilities.............	7f.d	1,541	1,802	1,881	2,084	2,384	2,498	2,626	2,644	2,036	2,130	2,077	1,825
Branches of US Banks: Assets..........	7k.d	87,620	....	....	....	....	....	....	....	....	....	....	....
Liab........	7m.d	89,058	....	....	....	....	....	....	....	....	....	....	....
Monetary Authorities		*Millions of Bahamian Dollars: End of Period*											
Foreign Assets........................	11	163	170	171	163	219	339	404	343	312	373	484	668
Claims on Central Government........	12a	115	144	149	153	141	62	73	129	190	182	115	150
Claims on Deposit Money Banks......	12e	—	—	—	—	1	—	—	—	—	—	—	—
Claims on Nonbank Financial Insts...	12g	3	3	4	3	4	5	8	9	8	8	8	9
Reserve Money.......................	14	205	230	236	230	264	315	381	373	411	459	489	643
of which: Currency Outside DMBs..	14a	84	89	93	97	110	126	149	152	154	155	160	177
Central Government Deposits..........	16d	3	14	8	8	17	4	14	11	9	12	24	91
Capital Accounts.....................	17a	74	77	78	80	84	87	90	98	95	97	96	96
Other Items (Net).....................	17r	−1	−3	2	2	1	—	—	−1	−5	−5	−2	−4
Deposit Money Banks		*Millions of Bahamian Dollars: End of Period*											
Reserves..............................	20	105	123	128	118	146	183	226	208	250	292	318	457
Foreign Assets........................	21	35,688	42,817	35,144	41,384	41,310	46,329	58,682	77,649	103,669	136,339	89,838	70,339
Claims on Central Government........	22a	330	296	303	313	356	458	489	454	493	547	487	494
Claims on Official Entities................	22bx	89	73	77	82	79	128	158	126	133	203	347	314
Claims on Private Sector................	22d	1,400	1,592	1,777	1,953	2,488	2,767	3,072	3,511	3,782	3,926	3,948	4,200
Claims on Other Banking Insts........	22f	11	20	18	16	27	29	25	33	54	65	65	105
Demand Deposits.....................	24	280	309	336	334	398	460	588	630	605	644	714	860
Time, Savings,& Fgn.Currency Dep...	25	1,221	1,326	1,447	1,551	1,950	2,275	2,423	2,668	2,870	2,934	2,999	3,193
Bonds................................	26ab	20	10	9	8	6	6	8	6	8	9	5	1
Foreign Liabilities.....................	26c	35,958	43,219	35,542	41,796	41,662	47,053	59,127	78,346	104,136	136,804	90,451	70,878
Central Government Deposits..........	26d	30	36	44	59	65	66	68	71	58	72	94	93
Credit from Monetary Authorities.....	26g	—	—	—	—	1	—	1	1	1	1	1	1
Liabilities to Other Banking Insts......	26i	29	27	40	43	43	42	34	37	48	43	43	38
Capital Accounts.....................	27a	71	−20	10	38	250	−28	403	228	624	860	903	1,047
Other Items (Net).....................	27r	13	14	21	38	31	20	−1	−5	32	5	−206	−205
Monetary Survey		*Millions of Bahamian Dollars: End of Period*											
Foreign Assets (Net).....................	31n	−107	−231	−227	−248	−133	−385	−41	−355	−154	−92	−129	128
Domestic Credit.......................	32	1,914	2,078	2,277	2,454	3,014	3,379	3,743	4,180	4,594	4,847	4,852	5,086
Claims on Central Govt. (Net)........	32an	412	390	401	399	415	450	481	501	617	646	485	460
Claims on Official Entities...........	32bx	89	73	77	82	79	128	158	126	133	203	347	314
Claims on Private Sector..............	32d	1,400	1,592	1,777	1,953	2,488	2,767	3,072	3,511	3,782	3,926	3,948	4,200
Claims on Other Banking Insts.......	32f	11	20	18	16	27	29	25	33	54	65	65	105
Claims on Nonbank Financial Inst...	32g	3	3	4	3	4	5	8	9	8	8	8	9
Money................................	34	382	416	445	447	517	593	748	798	767	811	884	1,047
Quasi-Money..........................	35	1,221	1,326	1,447	1,551	1,950	2,275	2,423	2,668	2,870	2,934	2,999	3,193
Bonds................................	36ab	20	10	9	8	6	6	8	6	8	9	5	1
Liabilities to Other Banking Insts......	36i	29	27	40	43	43	42	34	37	48	43	43	38
Capital Accounts.....................	37a	145	57	88	117	334	59	494	326	719	958	999	1,143
Other Items (Net).....................	37r	10	9	22	39	31	19	−5	−9	28	1	−207	−208
Money plus Quasi-Money..............	35l	1,603	1,743	1,892	1,998	2,467	2,868	3,171	3,466	3,637	3,745	3,883	4,241
Other Banking Institutions		*Millions of Bahamian Dollars End of Period*											
Reserves..............................	40	13	13	13	13	3	3	4	5	4	5	6	6
Foreign Assets........................	41	1,911	2,232	2,450	2,646	2,836	2,685	2,785	2,907	2,293	2,490	2,411	2,398
Claims on Central Government........	42a	24	22	22	22	3	3	4	4	3	3	4	4
Claims on Private Sector................	42d	268	267	283	297	63	69	87	108	120	144	147	140
Claims on Deposit Money Banks......	42e	25	27	32	43	45	43	59	32	47	40	46	54
Demand Deposits.....................	44	8	8	11	12	4	5	5	8	8	9	12	10
Time, Savings,& Fgn.Currency Dep...	45	245	243	248	260	39	41	66	78	71	84	97	94
Foreign Liabilities.....................	46c	1,541	1,802	1,881	2,084	2,384	2,498	2,626	2,644	2,036	2,130	2,077	1,825
Central Government Deposits..........	46d	—	—	—	—	—	—	—	—	—	—	—	—
Credit from Monetary Authorities.....	46g	—	—	—	—	10	15	—	10	—	—	—	—
Credit from Deposit Money Banks....	46h	4	13	11	12	23	26	17	25	46	56	48	86
Capital Accounts.....................	47a	316	323	317	285	252	231	253	318	359	404	381	613
Other Items (Net).....................	47r	126	172	333	369	239	−12	−27	−26	−52	−2	−1	−27

		1993	1994	1995	1996	1997	1998	1999	2000	2001	2002	2003	2004
Banking Survey						*Millions of Bahamian Dollars: End of Period*							
Foreign Assets (Net)..................	51n	262	198	343	314	319	−198	119	−92	103	269	205	701
Domestic Credit.......................	52	2,195	2,346	2,564	2,757	3,053	3,423	3,809	4,259	4,663	4,929	4,938	5,126
Claims on Central Govt. (Net).......	52an	435	412	423	421	419	453	485	506	620	649	489	464
Claims on Official Entities.........	52bx	89	73	77	82	79	128	158	126	133	203	347	314
Claims on Private Sector.............	52d	1,668	1,859	2,060	2,250	2,551	2,837	3,159	3,619	3,902	4,070	4,095	4,339
Claims on Nonbank Financial Inst..	52g	3	3	4	3	4	5	8	9	8	8	8	9
Liquid Liabilities....................	55l	1,844	1,981	2,137	2,256	2,507	2,911	3,238	3,547	3,711	3,834	3,986	4,339
Bonds.................................	56ab	20	10	9	8	6	6	8	6	8	9	5	1
Capital Accounts.....................	57a	461	380	405	402	586	290	747	644	1,077	1,362	1,380	1,756
Other Items (Net)....................	57r	133	174	355	404	274	18	−65	−30	−30	−7	−228	−269
Interest Rates							*Percent Per Annum*							
Bank Rate (End of Period)...............	60	7.00	6.50	6.50	6.50	6.50	6.50	5.75	5.75	5.75	5.75	5.75	5.75
Treasury Bill Rate......................	60c	3.96	1.88	3.01	4.45	4.35	3.84	1.97	1.03	1.94	2.50	1.78	.56
Savings Rate...........................	60k	3.79	3.34	3.15	3.30	3.65	3.72	3.31	3.07	3.03	2.77	2.66	2.58
Deposit Rate...........................	60l	5.19	4.30	4.20	5.14	5.23	5.36	4.57	4.08	4.25	4.25	3.95	3.83
Lending Rate...........................	60p	7.46	6.88	6.75	6.75	6.75	6.75	6.38	6.00	6.00	6.00	6.00	6.00
Prices, Production, Labor							*Index Numbers (2000=100): Period Averages*							
Consumer Prices........................	64	90.4	91.7	†93.6	95.0	95.8	97.6	99.0	100.0	102.9	103.8	107.3	108.1
Tourist Arrivals.......................	66t	86.1	82.0	77.1	81.3	82.2	79.6	86.8	100.0	99.5	104.8	109.3	119.0
							Number in Thousands: Period Averages							
Labor Force............................	67d	....	137	....	....	....	296	....	....	....	....	174	....
Employment.............................	67e	119	120	127	130	135	144	145	....	153	153	155	....
Unemployment...........................	67c	18	18	16	17	15	12	12	....	11	15	19	....
Unemployment Rate (%).................	67r	13.1	13.3	10.9	11.5	9.8	7.7	7.8	....	6.9	9.1	10.8	....
Intl. Transactions & Positions							*Millions of Bahamian Dollars*							
Exports................................	70	162	167	176	180	181	300	462	576	423	446	425	357
Imports, c.i.f.........................	71	954	1,056	1,243	1,366	1,666	1,873	1,757	2,074	1,912	1,728	1,762	1,586
Balance of Payments							*Millions of US Dollars: Minus Sign Indicates Debit*							
Current Account, n.i.e................	78ald	48.7	−42.2	−145.9	−263.3	−472.1	−995.4	−671.9	−471.3	−584.1	−336.7	−418.5	....
Goods: Exports f.o.b..................	78aad	192.2	198.5	225.4	273.3	295.0	362.9	379.9	805.3	423.1	446.3	424.7	....
Goods: Imports f.o.b..................	78abd	−930.2	−1,013.8	−1,156.7	−1,287.4	−1,410.7	−1,737.1	−1,808.1	−2,176.4	−1,763.6	−1,598.1	−1,630.2	....
Trade Balance.......................	78acd	−738.0	−815.3	−931.3	−1,014.1	−1,115.7	−1,374.2	−1,428.2	−1,371.1	−1,340.5	−1,151.9	−1,205.6	....
Services: Credit.....................	78add	1,459.0	1,510.6	1,542.3	1,578.2	1,592.9	1,533.0	1,811.2	2,036.6	1,859.8	1,981.4	1,980.3	....
Services: Debit......................	78aed	−567.7	−627.2	−639.1	−715.8	−836.0	−990.9	−953.8	−1,007.2	−969.0	−1,001.2	−1,078.7	....
Balance on Goods & Services.......	78afd	153.3	68.1	−28.1	−151.7	−358.8	−832.1	−570.8	−341.7	−449.6	−171.6	−303.9	....
Income: Credit......................	78agd	112.2	61.2	75.1	84.6	105.7	147.9	229.6	212.0	118.6	57.9	48.2	....
Income: Debit.......................	78ahd	−240.6	−198.8	−210.8	−233.4	−258.3	−345.4	−367.2	−385.0	−294.9	−265.4	−211.4	....
Balance on Gds, Serv. & Inc.......	78aid	24.9	−69.5	−163.8	−300.5	−511.4	−1,029.6	−708.4	−514.7	−625.9	−379.1	−467.2	....
Current Transfers, n.i.e.: Credit......	78ajd	33.1	33.1	25.1	45.9	50.0	45.0	49.0	53.8	52.7	55.4	59.8	....
Current Transfers: Debit.............	78akd	−9.3	−5.8	−7.2	−8.7	−10.7	−10.8	−12.5	−10.5	−10.9	−13.0	−11.1	....
Capital Account, n.i.e...............	78bcd	−9.4	−11.6	−12.5	−24.4	−12.9	−11.7	−14.5	−16.4	−21.3	−24.5	−37.4	....
Capital Account, n.i.e.: Credit.......	78bad	—	—	—	—	—	—	—	—	....	....	....	....
Capital Account: Debit.............	78bbd	−9.4	−11.6	−12.5	−24.4	−12.9	−11.7	−14.5	−16.4	−21.3	−24.5	−37.4	....
Financial Account, n.i.e.............	78bjd	9.3	66.8	104.6	181.1	412.0	817.7	611.4	429.3	239.8	387.7	397.2	....
Direct Investment Abroad..............	78bdd	−.1	.1	−.1	.3	−.4	−1.0	−.2	—	....	....	....	....
Dir. Invest. in Rep. Econ., n.i.e....	78bed	27.1	23.4	106.8	87.8	210.0	146.9	144.6	249.7	102.4	152.8	146.6	....
Portfolio Investment Assets..........	78bfd	....	....	....	....	....	....	....	....	....	....	—	....
Equity Securities.................	78bkd	....	....	....	....	....	....	....	....	....	....	—	....
Debt Securities...................	78bld	....	....	....	....	....	....	....	....	....	....	—	....
Portfolio Investment Liab., n.i.e....	78bgd	....	....	....	....	....	....	....	....	....	....	—	....
Equity Securities.................	78bmd	....	....	....	....	....	....	....	....	....	....	—	....
Debt Securities...................	78bnd	....	....	....	....	....	....	....	....	....	....	—	....
Financial Derivatives Assets.........	78bwd	....	....	....	....	....	....	....	....	....	....	....	....
Financial Derivatives Liabilities.......	78bxd	....	....	....	....	....	....	....	....	....	....	....	....
Other Investment Assets..............	78bhd	−3,009.4	−7,455.9	7,436.6	−6,428.8	−80.7	−4,872.0	−12,487.1	−19,067.2	−25,411.7	−32,840.8	46,576.8	....
Monetary Authorities...............	78bod	—	—	—	—	—	—	—	—	....	....	....	....
General Government..................	78bpd	—	—	—	—	—	—	—	—	....	....	....	....
Banks..............................	78bqd	−3,009.4	−7,455.9	7,436.6	−6,428.8	−80.7	−4,872.0	−12,487.1	−19,067.2	−25,411.7	−32,840.8	46,576.8	....
Other Sectors......................	78brd	—	—	—	—	—	—	—	—	....	....	....	....
Other Investment Liab., n.i.e........	78bid	2,991.7	7,499.2	−7,438.7	6,521.8	283.1	5,543.8	12,954.1	19,246.9	25,549.1	33,075.7	−46,326.3	....
Monetary Authorities...............	78bsd	—	—	—	—	—	—	—	—	....	....	....	....
General Government..................	78btd	−16.4	−5.8	−26.9	−25.2	19.2	−5.9	11.7	−11.2	−47.8	−52.4	178.2	....
Banks..............................	78bud	3,010.7	7,459.6	−7,417.9	6,451.8	141.9	4,901.8	12,578.9	19,039.1	25,533.1	33,024.4	−46,679.2	....
Other Sectors......................	78bvd	−2.6	45.4	6.1	95.2	122.0	647.9	363.5	218.9	63.8	103.8	174.7	....
Net Errors and Omissions.............	78cad	−30.0	−3.9	50.9	99.0	129.5	308.6	140.2	−2.6	309.9	16.3	−38.1	....
Overall Balance.....................	78cbd	18.6	9.1	−2.9	−7.6	56.5	119.2	65.2	−61.0	−55.7	42.8	−96.8	....
Reserves and Related Items............	79dad	−18.6	−9.1	2.9	7.6	−56.5	−119.2	−65.2	61.0	55.7	−42.8	96.8	....
Reserve Assets.....................	79dbd	−18.6	−9.1	2.9	7.6	−56.5	−119.2	−65.2	61.0	29.9	−60.1	−110.1	....
Use of Fund Credit and Loans........	79dcd	—	—	—	—	—	—	—	—	—	—	—	....
Exceptional Financing.................	79ded	....	....	....	....	....	....	....	....	25.8	17.4	206.9	....
Government Finance							*Millions of Bahamian Dollars: Year Ending December 31*							
Deficit (-) or Surplus.................	80	†−85.1	−20.0	−23.2	−64.0	−138.5	−80.4	−51.4	−8.0	−95.2	−134.3	−207.8	−197.0
Revenue...............................	81	†537.1	618.2	660.2	685.8	736.5	761.4	869.1	950.6	920.3	888.9	901.8	960.2
Grants Received.......................	81z	....	....	....	.5	.5	....	....	....	....	....	....	....
Expenditure...........................	82	†584.0	604.5	657.3	720.2	840.0	806.4	885.2	924.8	956.0	1,018.2	1,067.6	1,119.7
Lending Minus Repayments............	83	†38.2	33.7	26.1	30.1	35.5	35.4	35.3	33.8	59.5	5.0	42.0	37.5
Financing														
Net Borrowing: Domestic.............	84a	†93.8	47.3	10.1	95.1	133.4	72.1	38.0	10.4	40.8	42.1	29.5	210.8
Net borrowing: Foreign..............	85a	†−14.6	−9.6	14.8	−13.7	19.4	−3.1	11.6	5.5	32.3	103.4	197.1	−4.4
Use of Cash Balances.................	87	†5.9	−17.7	−1.7	−17.5	−14.3	11.5	1.7	−8.0	22.1	−11.3	−18.8	−9.3
Debt: Domestic.....................	88a	†954.1	1,032.9	1,074.9	1,158.0	1,281.7	1,342.7	1,407.9	1,404.1	1,486.1	1,710.5	1,647.6	1,813.3
Debt: Foreign......................	89a	†110.6	100.4	90.9	77.0	96.4	93.2	104.7	110.2	117.5	96.1	293.2	289.8

National Accounts		1993	1994	1995	1996	1997	1998	1999	2000	2001	2002	2003	2004
							Millions of Bahamian Dollars						
Househ.Cons.Expend.,incl.NPISHs....	96f	1,986.0	2,054.1	2,077.4	....	....	....	....	....	....	....	....	....
Government Consumption Expend...	91f	408.4	511.0	483.9	516.9	578.5	592.4	642.3	680.4	730.4	770.4	785.0	810.5
Gross Fixed Capital Formation..........	93e	526.4	614.0	698.5	....	....	....	....	....	....	....	....	....
Changes in Inventories....................	93i	32.8	32.4	13.8	....	....	....	....	....	....	....	....	....
Exports of Goods and Services.........	90c	1,517.4	1,569.3	1,680.1	1,733.7	1,750.2	1,793.5	2,130.8	2,351.1	2,163.5	2,370.7	2,322.1	2,471.4
Imports of Goods and Services (-).....	98c	1,477.4	1,633.3	1,819.6	2,036.7	2,491.4	2,639.9	2,826.5	3,172.1	3,000.4	2,862.7	2,981.3	3,290.9
Statistical Discrepancy....................	99bs	−140.1	−94.3	−64.7	−168.2	−88.2	−127.6	−195.2	−155.4	−163.0	−150.5	−120.0	−95.6
Gross Domestic Product (GDP)........	99b	2,853.6	3,053.1	3,069.4	....	....	....	....	....	....	....	....	....
Net Primary Income from Abroad.....	98.n	−74.5	−89.3	−96.9	....	....	....	....	....	....	....	....	....
Gross National Income (GNI)..........	99a	2,779.1	2,963.8	2,972.5	....	....	....	....	....	....	....	....	....
Net Current Transf.from Abroad.......	98t	14.5	15.7	5.4	....	....	....	....	....	....	....	....	....
Gross Nat'l Disposable Inc.(GNDI)....	99i	2,793.6	2,979.5	2,977.9	....	....	....	....	....	....	....	....	....
Gross Saving.................................	99s	399.1	423.4	416.6	....	....	....	....	....	....	....	....	....
GDP Volume 1991 Prices................	99b.p	2,664.8	2,716.8	2,746.1	....	....	....	....	....	....	....	....	....
GDP Volume (1995=100)...............	99bvp	97.0	98.9	100.0	....	....	....	....	....	....	....	....	....
GDP Deflator (1995=100)...............	99bip	95.8	100.5	100.0	....	....	....	....	....	....	....	....	....
							Millions: Midyear Estimates						
Population.................................	99z	.27	.27	.28	.28	.29	.29	.30	.30	.31	.31	.31	.32

Bahrain, Kingdom of 419

		1993	1994	1995	1996	1997	1998	1999	2000	2001	2002	2003	2004
Exchange Rates						*SDRs per Dinar: End of Period*							
Official Rate....................	ac	1.9363	1.8218	1.7892	1.8495	1.9711	1.8889	1.9377	2.0413	2.1163	1.9563	1.7898	1.7125
						US Dollars per Dinar: End of Period (ag) Period Average (rh)							
Official Rate....................	ag	2.6596	2.6596	2.6596	2.6596	2.6596	2.6596	2.6596	2.6596	2.6596	2.6596	2.6596	2.6596
Official Rate....................	rh	2.6596	2.6596	2.6596	2.6596	2.6596	2.6596	2.6596	2.6596	2.6596	2.6596	2.6596	2.6596
						Index Numbers (2000=100): Period Averages							
Official Rate....................	ahx	100.0	100.0	100.0	100.0	100.0	100.0	100.0	100.0	100.0	100.0	100.0	100.0
Nominal Effective Exchange Rate.....	nec	90.1	88.3	84.1	86.1	91.4	94.7	94.5	100.0	104.2	101.7	92.7	86.9
Real Effective Exchange Rate...........	rec	99.4	96.0	91.4	91.1	98.5	100.2	97.4	100.0	102.2	101.1	92.6	87.5
Fund Position						*Millions of SDRs: End of Period*							
Quota..........................	2f.s	82.8	82.8	82.8	82.8	82.8	82.8	135.0	135.0	135.0	135.0	135.0	135.0
SDRs..........................	1b.s	10.8	11.0	11.3	11.7	11.9	12.1	—	1.0	.8	.8	.7	.6
Reserve Position in the Fund...........	1c.s	40.9	42.2	43.7	45.1	46.7	48.5	62.4	64.9	67.2	68.6	69.7	70.8
International Liquidity						*Millions of US Dollars Unless Otherwise Indicated: End of Period*							
Total Reserves minus Gold..............	1l.d	1,302.2	1,169.7	1,279.9	1,318.4	1,290.3	1,079.2	1,369.0	1,564.1	1,684.0	1,725.7	1,778.4	1,940.5
SDRs..........................	1b.d	14.8	16.1	16.8	16.8	16.1	17.1	—	1.3	1.1	1.1	1.0	.9
Reserve Position in the Fund..........	1c.d	56.2	61.6	65.0	64.8	63.0	68.3	85.6	84.5	84.4	93.3	103.6	110.0
Foreign Exchange......................	1d.d	1,231.2	1,092.0	1,198.2	1,236.8	1,211.2	993.8	1,283.4	1,478.3	1,598.5	1,631.4	1,673.8	1,829.6
Monetary Agency....................	1dad	980.4	841.5	947.3	985.9	960.5	743.0	1,032.9	1,227.4	1,348.5	1,381.4	1,423.8	1,579.6
Government........................	1dbd	250.8	250.5	250.9	250.9	250.7	250.8	250.5	250.9	250.0	250.0	250.0	250.0
Gold (Million Fine Troy Ounces)........	1ad	.150	.150	.150	.150	.150	.150	.150	.150	.150	.150	.150	.150
Gold (National Valuation)................	1and	6.6	6.6	6.6	6.6	6.6	6.6	6.6	6.6	6.6	6.6	6.6	6.6
Monetary Authorities: Other Liab.....	4..d												
Deposit Money Banks: Assets..........	7a.d	2,272.9	2,761.7	2,592.0	2,557.2	2,863.0	3,164.1	3,410.6	3,419.9	3,327.9	3,387.9	3,719.1	4,238.6
Liabilities....................	7b.d	977.1	1,486.2	1,136.4	1,042.3	1,583.2	1,522.1	2,305.3	1,672.9	1,480.6	1,536.0	1,949.3	2,856.6
OBU: Foreign Assets......................	7k.d	57,673	62,363	61,061	64,435	69,382	....	....	....	....	54,847	....	....
Foreign Liabilities......................	7m.d	57,180	61,875	60,579	64,068	68,644	....	....	....	....	53,458	....	....
Monetary Authorities						*Millions of Dinars: End of Period*							
Foreign Assets..........................	11	433.5	417.2	481.5	478.0	514.7	509.5	518.5	592.1	634.5	653.1	672.8	734.0
Claims on Central Government........	12a	48.4	41.9	14.7	16.7	43.7	40.4	12.4	20.7	41.7	113.5	116.3	127.4
Reserve Money..........................	14	181.5	173.9	234.0	208.0	234.1	183.2	266.5	264.9	303.0	345.1	465.3	485.6
of which: Currency Outside DMBs..	14a	103.8	105.5	103.3	102.9	104.6	93.3	113.0	120.7	122.9	142.0	155.8	173.7
Time and Savings Deposits...............	15	10.0	10.0	20.0	24.5	23.5	35.9	48.4	26.3	40.3	146.1	46.0	44.4
Foreign Liabilities........................	16c	—	—	—	—	—	—	—	—	—	—	—	—
Central Government Deposits...........	16d	118.9	120.3	131.4	124.5	122.2	137.5	124.4	133.0	125.1	128.1	130.6	133.5
Capital Accounts........................	17a	213.3	206.1	240.3	251.0	270.8	291.5	296.5	313.2	332.9	347.1	353.8	367.5
Other Items (Net).......................	17r	−41.8	−51.1	−129.3	−113.0	−92.2	−98.2	−204.9	−124.7	−125.1	−199.8	−206.5	−169.6
Deposit Money Banks						*Millions of Dinars: End of Period*							
Reserves..................................	20	73.3	66.3	124.6	99.0	126.6	89.4	153.7	139.1	177.9	204.1	303.7	296.0
Foreign Assets..........................	21	854.6	1,038.4	974.6	961.5	1,076.5	1,189.7	1,282.4	1,285.9	1,251.3	1,273.9	1,398.4	1,593.7
Claims on Central Government........	22a	132.1	138.5	150.7	166.6	172.1	223.3	323.8	322.3	333.5	311.7	412.7	517.9
Claims on Private Sector................	22d	818.5	915.0	947.8	954.7	1,074.3	1,164.2	1,302.5	1,380.5	1,411.3	1,606.6	1,754.2	2,172.7
Demand Deposits......................	24	261.1	239.2	229.2	232.4	243.1	272.3	313.2	325.1	429.1	505.2	665.6	687.4
Time and Savings Deposits...............	25	896.5	992.7	1,095.0	1,132.6	1,238.3	1,477.7	1,482.1	1,684.6	1,763.7	1,806.3	1,897.4	1,974.1
Foreign Liabilities......................	26c	367.4	558.8	427.3	391.9	595.3	572.3	866.8	629.0	556.7	577.6	732.9	1,074.1
Central Government Deposits...........	26d	337.0	416.7	358.0	433.3	443.1	409.9	431.0	436.7	426.3	439.4	513.2	665.1
Capital Accounts........................	27a	169.1	194.6	185.5	191.5	199.4	254.9	259.6	294.1	312.1	357.5	387.9	463.5
Other Items (Net).......................	27r	−152.8	−243.7	−97.4	−200.0	−269.8	−320.4	−290.2	−241.7	−313.9	−289.7	−328.1	−283.7
Monetary Survey						*Millions of Dinars: End of Period*							
Foreign Assets (Net)....................	31n	920.7	896.8	1,028.8	1,047.6	995.9	1,126.9	934.1	1,249.0	1,329.1	1,349.4	1,338.3	1,253.6
Domestic Credit..........................	32	543.1	558.4	623.8	580.2	724.8	880.5	1,083.3	1,153.8	1,235.1	1,464.2	1,639.4	2,019.4
Claims on Central Govt. (Net)........	32an	−275.4	−356.6	−324.0	−374.5	−349.5	−283.7	−219.2	−226.7	−176.2	−142.3	−114.8	−153.3
Claims on Private Sector..............	32d	818.5	915.0	947.8	954.7	1,074.3	1,164.2	1,302.5	1,380.5	1,411.3	1,606.6	1,754.2	2,172.7
Money....................................	34	364.9	344.7	332.5	335.3	347.7	365.6	426.2	445.8	552.0	647.2	821.4	861.1
Quasi-Money.............................	35	906.5	1,002.7	1,115.0	1,157.1	1,261.8	1,513.6	1,530.5	1,710.9	1,804.0	1,952.4	1,943.4	2,018.5
Other Items (Net).......................	37r	192.2	108.0	205.2	135.6	111.1	128.3	60.8	246.0	208.2	214.0	212.8	393.6
Money plus Quasi-Money................	35l	1,271.4	1,347.4	1,447.5	1,492.4	1,609.5	1,879.2	1,956.7	2,156.7	2,356.0	2,599.6	2,764.8	2,879.6
Other Banking Institutions						*Millions of Dinars: End of Period*							
Reserves..................................	40	....	....	....	....	....	....	....	....	....	....	....	....
Claims on Mon.Author.:Securities....	40c	....	....	....	....	....	....	....	....	....	....	....	....
Foreign Assets..........................	41	21,879.0	23,637.0	23,312.5	24,699.8	26,667.8	32,591.7	32,964.2	34,407.4	32,933.0	22,040.8	31,083.6	36,262.8
Claims on Central Government........	42a	.2	.2	.2	.3	.3	15.5	24.7	24.4	39.4	49.2	106.9	153.8
Claims on Local Government...........	42b	....	....	....	....	....	....	....	....	....	....	....	....
Claims on Private Sector...............	42d	365.8	369.0	313.5	278.1	349.5	299.8	298.4	262.4	273.4	284.1	315.9	471.6
Other Claims on Dep.Money Banks..	42e	....	....	....	....	....	....	....	....	....	....	....	....
Time and Saving Deposits...............	45	....	....	....	....	....	....	....	....	....	....	....	....
Liquid Liabilities.........................	45l	152.3	178.4	206.2	317.8	434.5	439.6	391.6	282.3	229.2	239.8	261.9	267.0
Money Market Instruments..............	46aa	....	....	....	....	....	....	....	....	....	....	....	....
Foreign Liabilities......................	46c	21,371.2	23,613.8	22,799.6	23,993.5	25,852.6	31,798.4	32,042.1	33,712.0	32,206.7	21,286.7	30,244.7	35,282.2
Central Government Deposits...........	46d	103.4	174.5	369.3	375.4	243.7	190.0	177.5	185.6	228.2	197.6	269.2	332.7
Credit from Monetary Authorities.....	46g	....	....	....	....	....	....	....	....	....	....	....	....
Credit from Deposit Money Banks.....	46h	....	....	....	....	....	....	....	....	....	....	....	....
Capital Accounts........................	47a	....	....	....	....	....	....	....	....	....	....	....	....
Other Items (Net).......................	47r	....	....	....	....	....	....	....	....	....	....	....	....

Bahrain, Kingdom of   419

		1993	1994	1995	1996	1997	1998	1999	2000	2001	2002	2003	2004
Banking Survey		*Millions of Dinars: End of Period*											
Foreign Assets (Net)	51n	....	....	....	....	....	....	....	....	....	....	....	....
Domestic Credit	52	....	....	....	....	....	....	....	....	....	....	....	....
Claims on Central Govt. (Net)	52an	....	....	....	....	....	....	....	....	....	....	....	....
Claims on Local Government	52	....	....	....	....	....	....	....	....	....	....	....	....
Claims on Private Sector	52d	....	....	....	....	....	....	....	....	....	....	....	....
Liquid Liabilities	55l	....	....	....	....	....	....	....	....	....	....	....	....
Money Market Instruments	56a	....	....	....	....	....	....	....	....	....	....	....	....
Capital Accounts	57a	....	....	....	....	....	....	....	....	....	....	....	....
Other Items (Net)	57r	....	....	....	....	....	....	....	....	....	....	....	....
Interest Rates		*Percent Per Annum*											
Money Market Rate	60b	3.5	5.2	6.2	5.7	....	5.7	5.6	6.9	3.9	2.0	1.2	1.7
Treasury Bill Rate	60c	3.3	4.8	6.1	5.5	5.7	5.5	5.5	6.6	3.8	1.8	1.1	1.6
Deposit Rate	60l	3.0	4.0	5.7	5.2	5.3	4.7	4.8	5.8	2.7	1.3	....	....
Lending Rate	60p	11.0	10.8	11.8	12.5	12.3	11.9	11.9	11.7	10.8	8.5	....	....
Prices, Production, Labor		*Index Numbers (2000=100): Period Averages*											
Consumer Prices	64	97.0	97.8	100.4	100.0	† 102.4	102.2	100.7	100.0	100.2	101.5	....	....
Refined Petroleum Production	66ab	95.4	96.0	97.3	101.2	97.4	96.4	102.0	100.0	93.2	96.5	98.7	98.9
		Number in Thousands: Period Averages											
Labor Force	67d	239	247	255	264	273	281	291	301	308	....	....	....
Employment	67e	....	....	....	....	....	....	....	....	157	165	....	....
Unemployment	67c	....	....	....	....	....	....	....	....	17	....	....	....
Unemployment Rate (%)	67r	....	....	....	....	....	....	....	....	5.4	....	....	....
Intl. Transactions & Positions		*Millions of Dinars*											
Exports	70	1,400.0	1,359.9	1,546.4	1,768.0	1,648.2	1,229.6	1,640.4	2,329.3	2,096.9	2,178.7	2,393.0	2,843.4
Imports, c.i.f.	71	1,450.6	1,409.2	1,397.1	1,606.6	1,513.6	1,340.9	1,390.3	1,742.2	1,619.0	1,884.7	1,923.7	2,385.9
Balance of Payments		*Millions of US Dollars: Minus Sign Indicates Debit*											
Current Account, n.i.e.	78ald	−339.4	−255.6	237.4	260.4	−31.1	−777.4	−37.0	830.0	227.2	−50.5	200.9	415.3
Goods: Exports f.o.b.	78aad	3,723.4	3,617.0	4,114.4	4,702.1	4,383.0	3,270.2	4,362.8	6,242.6	5,657.2	5,887.3	6,720.9	7,620.7
Goods: Imports f.o.b.	78abd	−3,616.2	−3,497.3	−3,488.3	−4,037.0	−3,778.2	−3,298.7	−3,468.4	−4,393.6	−4,047.1	−4,697.3	−5,319.1	−6,135.4
Trade Balance	78acd	107.2	119.7	626.1	665.2	604.8	−28.5	894.4	1,848.9	1,610.1	1,190.0	1,401.7	1,485.3
Services: Credit	78add	651.9	818.6	683.2	666.2	637.2	724.7	858.9	933.5	950.4	1,068.0	1,260.1	1,558.2
Services: Debit	78aed	−581.9	−621.8	−634.0	−612.8	−634.8	−651.9	−700.5	−738.5	−747.6	−926.6	−885.7	−933.5
Balance on Goods & Services	78afd	177.1	316.5	675.3	718.6	607.2	44.4	1,052.9	2,043.9	1,812.9	1,331.3	1,776.1	2,110.0
Income: Credit	78agd	2,283.8	3,112.5	4,086.9	3,815.1	4,271.0	4,764.0	5,118.5	6,327.9	3,794.4	1,678.9	1,266.6	2,544.3
Income: Debit	78ahd	−2,477.7	−3,355.1	−4,145.8	−3,840.3	−4,507.1	−4,926.0	−5,388.9	−6,551.5	−4,115.9	−2,203.8	−1,759.6	−3,119.1
Balance on Gds, Serv. & Inc.	78aid	−16.8	73.9	616.4	693.4	371.1	−117.6	782.5	1,820.3	1,491.3	806.4	1,283.1	1,535.2
Current Transfers, n.i.e.: Credit	78ajd	73.1	101.1	120.7	126.3	232.7	65.2	36.7	22.4	22.9	14.7	—	—
Current Transfers: Debit	78akd	−395.7	−430.6	−499.7	−559.3	−634.8	−725.0	−856.2	−1,012.7	−1,286.9	−871.5	−1,082.2	−1,119.9
Capital Account, n.i.e.	78bcd	202.1	319.1	156.9	50.0	125.0	100.0	100.0	50.0	100.0	101.6	50.0	50.0
Capital Account, n.i.e.: Credit	78bad	202.1	319.1	156.9	50.0	125.0	100.0	100.0	50.0	100.0	101.6	50.0	50.0
Capital Account: Debit	78bbd	—	—	—	—	—	—	—	—	—	—	—	—
Financial Account, n.i.e.	78bjd	593.9	1,176.9	−1,726.7	−510.2	15.1	22.5	229.9	−29.8	−417.1	−1,234.1	493.1	−390.8
Direct Investment Abroad	78bdd	−38.8	−198.7	16.1	−304.8	−47.6	−180.8	−163.4	−9.6	−216.0	−190.0	−741.4	−1,035.6
Dir. Invest. in Rep. Econ., n.i.e.	78bed	−275.0	208.2	430.6	2,048.2	329.3	179.5	453.7	363.6	80.4	217.0	516.7	865.3
Portfolio Investment Assets	78bfd	−1,335.4	−454.0	−113.3	−779.9	−1,150.9	−1,206.7	−2,105.8	−88.3	−1,448.0	−5,140.0	−3,095.7	−3,892.6
Equity Securities	78bkd	....	....	—	—	—	—	−119.9	−161.1	−389.0	−1,143.5	−489.0	−1,999.0
Debt Securities	78bld	−1,335.4	−454.0	−113.3	−779.9	−1,150.9	−1,206.7	−1,985.9	72.8	−1,059.0	−3,996.5	−2,606.7	−1,893.6
Portfolio Investment Liab., n.i.e.	78bgd	....	....	—	—	—	194.8	112.8	282.5	−30.7	915.2	688.4	387.7
Equity Securities	78bmd	....	....	—	—	—	—	—	—	1.2	366.0	238.5	20.9
Debt Securities	78bnd	....	....	—	—	—	194.8	112.8	282.5	−31.9	549.2	449.9	366.8
Financial Derivatives Assets	78bwd	....	....	....	....	....	....	....	....	....	....	....	....
Financial Derivatives Liabilities	78bxd	....	....	....	....	....	....	....	....	....	....	....	....
Other Investment Assets	78bhd	10,672.3	−4,527.1	1,124.5	−2,579.8	−4,342.1	−14,677.8	966.9	−3,833.9	5,623.2	33,425.4	−20,786.6	−9,779.9
Monetary Authorities	78bod	....	....	....	....	....	....	....	....	....	....	....	....
General Government	78bpd	−5.3	−8.0	−5.3	−8.0	−8.0	−5.1	−7.7	−5.9	−6.9	−7.2	−10.4	−5.1
Banks	78bqd	10,677.7	−4,519.1	1,129.8	−2,571.8	−4,334.1	−14,672.7	974.6	−3,828.0	5,629.1	33,427.2	−20,777.7	−9,777.2
Other Sectors	78brd	....	....	....	....	....	....	....	....	1.0	5.3	1.6	2.3
Other Investment Liab., n.i.e.	78bid	−8,429.3	6,148.4	−3,184.5	1,106.2	5,226.5	15,713.5	965.6	3,255.8	−4,426.0	−30,461.7	23,911.6	13,064.3
Monetary Authorities	78bsd	—	—	—	—	—	—	—	—	....	....	....	....
General Government	78btd	4.5	4.0	11.0	1.4	52.3	44.0	54.8	59.1	34.6	102.7	168.5	24.7
Banks	78bud	−8,660.1	6,268.4	−2,901.9	1,056.3	5,175.5	15,394.5	875.7	3,249.2	−4,289.7	−29,734.7	23,793.4	13,004.7
Other Sectors	78bvd	226.3	−123.9	−293.6	48.4	−1.3	275.0	35.1	−52.4	−170.9	−829.7	−50.3	35.0
Net Errors and Omissions	78cad	−569.2	−1,288.0	1,501.3	193.4	−6.3	638.3	−267.7	−650.1	213.4	1,217.8	−700.3	83.5
Overall Balance	78cbd	−112.5	−47.5	168.9	−6.4	102.8	−16.6	25.3	200.1	123.5	34.8	43.7	157.9
Reserves and Related Items	79dad	112.5	47.5	−168.9	6.4	−102.8	16.6	−25.3	−200.1	−123.5	−34.8	−43.7	−157.9
Reserve Assets	79dbd	112.5	47.5	−168.9	6.4	−102.8	16.6	−25.3	−200.1	−123.5	−34.8	−43.7	−157.9
Use of Fund Credit and Loans	79dcd	—	—	—	—	—	—	—	—	—	—	—	—
Exceptional Financing	79ded	....	....	....	....	....	....	....	....	....	....	....	....

Bahrain, Kingdom of   419

		1993	1994	1995	1996	1997	1998	1999	2000	2001	2002	2003	2004
International Investment Position							*Millions of US Dollars*						
Assets.....................	79aad	61,614.0	66,735.3	65,872.8	69,518.6	75,156.1	91,569.9	92,887.3	97,291.7	93,445.4	65,165.3	89,831.1	104,355.3
Direct Investment Abroad.............	79abd	861.2	1,059.9	1,043.8	1,348.6	1,396.3	1,579.2	1,742.6	1,752.1	1,968.1	2,158.1	2,899.5	3,935.1
Portfolio Investment....................	79acd	6,201.1	6,647.5	6,760.6	7,538.9	8,696.9	10,268.2	12,373.7	12,719.2	14,166.7	19,338.0	22,433.7	25,968.9
Equity Securities..................	79add	....	—	—	—	—	1,342.6	1,462.4	1,840.2	2,229.2	3,372.7	3,861.7	5,502.0
Debt Securities..................	79aed	6,201.1	6,647.5	6,760.6	7,538.9	8,696.9	8,925.6	10,911.3	10,879.0	11,937.4	15,965.3	18,572.0	20,466.9
Financial Derivatives..................	79ald	....	—	—	—	—	—	—	—	—	—	—	—
Other Investment....................	79afd	53,398.6	57,917.8	56,788.0	59,359.8	63,693.9	78,366.6	77,392.1	81,245.7	75,615.6	42,183.1	62,959.2	72,750.0
Monetary Authorities..............	79agd	....	....	....	....	....	....	....	—	....	....	....	....
General Government..............	79ahd	....	....	....	....	....	....	....	—	....	....	....	....
Banks..................	79aid	....	57,917.8	56,788.0	59,359.8	63,693.9	78,366.6	77,392.1	81,220.0	75,590.9	42,163.7	62,941.4	72,718.6
Other Sectors..................	79ajd	....	....	....	....	....	....	....	25.7	24.7	19.4	17.8	31.3
Reserve Assets....................	79akd	1,153.2	1,110.1	1,280.4	1,271.3	1,369.0	1,355.9	1,379.0	1,574.7	1,695.1	1,486.1	1,538.6	1,701.4
Liabilities....................	79lad	58,049.1	64,529.6	62,081.9	65,187.8	70,744.5	86,515.4	88,016.3	92,136.4	87,929.8	59,426.0	84,599.9	98,690.3
Dir. Invest. in Rep. Economy...........	79lbd	1,764.6	1,972.8	2,403.4	4,451.6	4,780.9	4,960.3	5,414.0	5,905.8	5,986.1	6,203.1	6,719.8	7,354.0
Portfolio Investment....................	79lcd	....	—	—	—	—	194.8	307.6	615.9	585.3	1,500.5	2,188.9	2,576.6
Equity Securities..................	79ldd	....	—	—	—	—	—	—	25.8	27.1	393.0	631.5	652.4
Debt Securities..................	79led	....	—	—	—	—	194.8	307.6	590.1	558.2	1,107.4	1,557.4	1,924.2
Financial Derivatives..................	79lld	....	—	—	—	—	—	—	—	—	—	—	—
Other Investment....................	79lfd	56,284.5	62,556.8	59,678.5	60,736.2	65,963.7	81,360.3	82,294.6	85,614.7	81,358.4	51,722.4	75,691.2	88,759.7
Monetary Authorities..................	79lgd	....	—	—	—	—	—	—	—	—	—	—	—
General Government..................	79lhd	....	150.1	173.7	175.1	227.1	229.2	287.8	345.8	378.8	478.3	653.0	694.7
Banks..................	79lid	....	62,406.6	59,504.7	60,561.1	65,736.6	81,131.1	82,006.8	85,256.0	80,966.3	51,231.6	75,025.0	88,029.6
Other Sectors..................	79ljd	....	—	—	—	—	—	—	12.9	13.3	12.4	13.2	35.5
Government Finance						*Millions of Dinars: Year Ending December 31*							
Deficit (-) or Surplus....................	80	−1.9	−58.3	−126.6	−55.0	−125.2	−116.5	−133.6	66.0	−30.9	....	....	....
Revenue....................	81	544.8	476.3	526.6	615.5	633.2	516.6	653.5	1,065.9	969.3	....	....	....
Grants Received....................	81z	18.8	37.6	37.6	18.8	46.9	37.6	37.6	18.8	37.6	....	....	....
Expenditure....................	82	593.4	623.4	594.1	581.3	620.0	644.6	699.3	777.0	826.6	....	....	....
Lending Minus Repayments...........	83	−27.9	−51.2	96.7	108.0	185.3	26.1	125.4	241.7	211.2	....	....	....
Financing													
Total Financing....................	80h	1.9	58.3	126.6	55.0	125.3	116.5	133.6	−66.0	30.9	....	....	....
Domestic....................	84a	−.4	56.6	122.5	54.5	125.1	99.9	113.4	−87.6	19.1	....	....	....
Foreign....................	85a	2.3	1.7	4.1	.5	.2	16.6	20.2	21.6	11.8	....	....	....
Debt: Domestic....................	88a	323.6	318.8	314.0	297.0	319.5	404.5	482.0	747.9	773.6	....	....	....
Foreign....................	89a	54.7	55.5	59.6	65.8	85.4	87.6	107.8	129.4	141.2	....	....	....
National Accounts							*Millions of Dinars*						
Househ.Cons.Expend.,incl.NPISHs....	96f	1,095.3	1,123.4	1,165.5	1,229.3	1,277.4	1,327.6	1,378.4	1,411.8	1,415.7	1,435.1	1,479.7	....
Government Consumption Expend...	91f	435.5	440.0	458.5	464.3	465.1	482.8	518.2	526.0	550.6	588.7	672.3	....
Gross Fixed Capital Formation..........	93e	454.2	417.5	381.3	284.1	285.9	326.2	338.0	404.6	397.7	549.0	699.8	....
Changes in Inventories....................	93i	−96.3	−6.5	−59.8	46.4	130.6	171.9	−141.2	−96.1	−34.2	137.5	114.0	....
Exports of Goods and Services..........	90c	1,645.1	1,667.8	1,803.9	2,018.5	1,887.6	1,502.1	1,963.4	2,680.3	2,454.2	2,580.3	2,883.3	....
Imports of Goods and Services (-)......	98c	1,578.5	1,548.8	1,550.0	1,748.3	1,659.3	1,485.4	1,567.5	1,929.7	1,802.8	2,114.2	2,237.2	....
Gross Domestic Product (GDP).........	99b	1,955.4	2,093.4	2,199.4	2,294.3	2,387.3	2,325.1	2,489.3	2,996.9	2,981.2	3,176.5	3,612.0	....
Net Primary Income from Abroad.....	98.n	−72.9	−91.0	−22.2	−9.5	−88.8	−60.9	−101.6	−84.1	−120.8	−197.3	−196.0	....
Gross National Income (GNI)............	99a	1,882.5	2,002.4	2,177.2	2,284.8	2,298.5	2,264.3	2,387.7	2,912.8	2,860.4	2,979.2	3,416.0	....
Consumption of Fixed Capital..........	99cf	307.5	326.7	332.6	328.6	332.3	343.5	229.0	250.2	245.5	234.9	253.9	....
Net National Income....................	99e	1,575.0	1,675.7	1,844.6	1,956.2	1,966.2	1,920.8	2,158.7	2,662.6	2,614.9	2,744.3	3,162.1	....
GDP Volume 1989 Prices................	99b.p	2,032.5	2,027.4	2,107.0	2,193.4	2,261.5	2,369.7	2,471.9	2,602.5	2,723.2	2,864.3	3,058.5	....
GDP Volume (2000=100)...............	99bvp	78.1	77.9	81.0	84.3	86.9	91.1	95.0	100.0	104.6	110.1	117.5	....
GDP Deflator (2000=100)..............	99bip	83.5	89.7	90.6	90.8	91.7	85.2	87.4	100.0	95.1	96.3	102.6	....
						Millions: Midyear Estimates							
Population................................	99z	.55	.57	.58	.60	.62	.64	.66	.67	.68	.70	.71	.72

		1993	1994	1995	1996	1997	1998	1999	2000	2001	2002	2003	2004
Exchange Rates							Taka per SDR: End of Period						
Official Rate..........aa=..........	wa	54.736	58.759	60.574	61.041	61.323	68.289	69.998	70.357	71.634	78.716	87.348	94.333
						Taka per US Dollar: End of Period (we) Period Average (wf)							
Official Rate..........ae=..........	we	39.850	40.250	40.750	42.450	45.450	48.500	51.000	54.000	57.000	57.900	58.782	60.742
Official Rate..........rf=..........	wf	39.567	40.212	40.278	41.794	43.892	46.906	49.085	52.142	55.807	57.888	58.150	59.513
Fund Position							Millions of SDRs: End of Period						
Quota..........	2f.s	392.5	392.5	392.5	392.5	392.5	392.5	533.3	533.3	533.3	533.3	533.3	533.3
SDRs..........	1b.s	16.6	24.6	107.3	76.2	21.6	9.1	.7	.3	.9	1.7	2.2	.8
Reserve Position in the Fund..........	1c.s	.1	.1	.1	.1	.1	.2	.2	.2	.2	.2	.2	.2
Total Fund Cred.&Loans Outstg.......	2tl	511.8	473.4	433.1	374.2	287.9	308.4	237.6	168.6	118.3	51.9	49.5	148.5
International Liquidity						Millions of US Dollars Unless Otherwise Indicated: End of Period							
Total Reserves minus Gold..........	1l.d	2,410.8	3,138.7	2,339.7	1,834.6	1,581.5	1,905.4	1,603.6	1,486.0	1,275.0	1,683.2	2,577.9	3,172.4
SDRs..........	1b.d	22.8	36.0	159.5	109.6	29.2	12.9	.9	.4	1.2	2.2	3.2	1.2
Reserve Position in the Fund..........	1c.d	.1	.1	.1	.2	.1	.2	.3	.2	.2	.3	.3	.3
Foreign Exchange..........	1d.d	2,387.9	3,102.6	2,180.1	1,724.9	1,552.1	1,892.3	1,602.5	1,485.3	1,273.6	1,680.7	2,574.4	3,170.9
Gold (Million Fine Troy Ounces).......	1ad	.092	.094	.094	.094	.101	.105	.106	.109	.111	.112	.112	.113
Gold (National Valuation)...............	1and	25.9	27.2	26.9	28.0	25.3	22.3	19.6	29.6	30.6	39.2	46.3	49.9
Monetary Authorities: Other Liab.....	4..d	100.2	124.0	171.8	160.9	127.5	257.4	137.6	151.9	289.5	186.6	226.8	307.5
Deposit Money Banks: Assets..........	7a.d	402.5	703.4	730.6	771.6	827.9	794.9	917.0	1,203.4	1,081.0	916.2	772.8	827.3
Liabilities....................	7b.d	241.7	283.7	327.0	399.7	510.7	437.3	463.7	571.4	673.5	633.6	444.8	349.8
Monetary Authorities							Millions of Taka: End of Period						
Foreign Assets..........	11	101,190	130,167	97,949	80,687	73,398	93,361	82,779	81,907	74,715	100,019	154,540	196,090
Claims on Central Government........	12a	5,366	5,697	22,783	38,576	36,371	47,968	72,915	81,529	130,336	86,210	56,217	91,521
Claims on Nonfin.Pub.Enterprises.....	12c	597	594	591	590	590	2,140	2,140	1,570	1,321	1,013	688	149
Claims on Private Sector..........	12d	—	—	—	—	—	—	7,594	7,707	9,324	10,802	12,005	12,593
Claims on Deposit Money Banks.....	12e	24,409	26,275	29,139	34,551	36,220	40,993	48,641	51,472	52,925	55,307	56,468	59,324
Claims on Nonbank Financial Insts...	12g	11,721	13,153	11,555	11,521	11,493	11,724	12,617	12,507	11,477	11,467	8,736	10,898
Reserve Money..........	14	87,967	114,017	103,458	112,457	122,988	139,489	157,166	180,023	223,476	230,752	246,755	266,457
of which: Currency Outside DMBs..	14a	44,987	57,248	64,523	68,195	76,074	80,756	93,819	116,877	127,863	133,895	144,556	169,997
Liabs. of Central Bank: Securities......	16ac	1,450	4,000	2,755	7,361	—	—	—	—	—	—	—	—
Foreign Liabilities..........	16c	32,005	32,807	33,237	29,670	23,454	33,547	23,647	20,063	24,972	14,892	17,654	32,689
Central Government Deposits..........	16d	9,717	4,868	3,986	9	13	14	10	11	10	10	12	142
Central Govt. Lending Funds..........	16f	13,272	18,977	14,128	11,263	8,452	18,209	22,120	10,516	9,129	10,728	10,971	9,457
Capital Accounts..........	17a	6,346	6,726	6,665	9,304	9,998	11,006	21,632	19,138	20,556	25,661	39,097	40,907
Other Items (Net)..........	17r	−7,474	−5,509	2,212	−4,139	−6,833	−6,079	2,111	6,941	1,955	−17,226	−25,834	20,924
Deposit Money Banks							Millions of Taka: End of Period						
Reserves..........	20	46,874	56,221	43,333	45,882	48,678	64,661	63,584	65,494	96,995	94,687	104,787	104,238
Claims on Mon.Author.:Securities.....	20c	1,450	3,994	2,741	7,358	—	—	—	—	—	—	—	—
Foreign Assets..........	21	16,039	28,313	29,770	32,753	37,628	38,554	46,766	64,985	61,619	53,048	45,429	50,250
Claims on Central Government.......	22a	54,135	64,899	64,283	63,790	81,206	99,534	117,884	142,606	130,277	181,397	191,745	213,693
Claims on State & Local Govts..........	22b	455	622	800	816	809	1,388	1,279	1,417	1,392	999	749	581
Claims on Nonfin.Pub.Enterprises.....	22c	45,951	33,731	31,717	39,426	42,900	40,712	40,431	46,111	52,785	60,644	59,831	67,650
Claims on Private Sector..........	22d	191,744	220,332	318,484	359,202	411,731	465,130	509,760	577,077	667,883	779,577	852,312	991,035
Claims on Nonbank Financial Insts...	22g	11,614	14,644	18,114	20,234	19,231	20,312	25,019	26,986	31,433	30,250	35,840	56,124
Demand Deposits..........	24	48,294	58,717	70,819	73,481	76,559	83,214	91,055	102,074	114,572	120,705	129,272	152,019
Time Deposits..........	25	236,578	277,489	305,996	347,091	383,813	433,586	504,965	603,882	701,196	814,259	935,128	1,083,528
Restricted Deposits..........	26b	14	21	23	45	31	38	54	634	364	279	283	252
Foreign Liabilities..........	26c	9,122	11,064	12,993	16,782	23,112	21,115	23,554	30,762	38,299	36,290	25,692	20,812
Central Government Deposits..........	26d	26,845	32,200	34,509	31,250	39,571	50,076	52,881	59,785	54,802	61,510	63,528	81,776
Central Govt. Lending Funds..........	26f	5,341	5,423	6,443	5,869	7,164	7,174	6,391	6,065	5,431	5,832	6,125	5,283
Credit from Monetary Authorities.....	26g	27,192	28,781	30,843	37,623	39,047	43,789	44,463	47,049	48,551	48,137	48,898	54,221
Liab. to Nonbank Finacial Insts..........	26j	—	—	—	—	—	366	50	35	—	—	—	6
Capital Accounts..........	27a	18,515	21,068	27,738	30,511	33,528	35,989	43,684	52,904	60,044	65,477	76,461	89,950
Other Items (Net)..........	27r	−3,639	−12,007	19,878	26,809	39,358	54,944	37,626	21,486	19,125	48,113	5,306	−4,276
Monetary Survey							Millions of Taka: End of Period						
Foreign Assets (Net)..........	31n	76,102	114,609	81,489	66,989	64,460	77,253	82,344	96,067	73,064	101,884	156,624	192,840
Domestic Credit..........	32	285,021	316,604	429,832	502,896	564,747	638,818	736,748	837,714	981,416	1,100,839	1,154,583	1,362,326
Claims on Central Govt. (Net)........	32an	22,939	33,528	48,571	71,107	77,993	97,412	137,908	164,339	205,801	206,087	184,422	223,296
Claims on State & Local Govts..........	32b	455	622	800	816	809	1,388	1,279	1,417	1,392	999	749	581
Claims on Nonfin.Pub.Enterprises.....	32c	46,548	34,325	32,308	40,016	43,490	42,852	42,571	47,681	54,106	61,657	60,519	67,799
Claims on Private Sector..........	32d	191,744	220,332	318,484	359,202	411,731	465,130	517,354	584,784	677,207	790,379	864,317	1,003,628
Claims on Nonbank Financial Insts.	32g	23,335	27,797	29,669	31,755	30,724	32,036	37,636	39,493	42,910	41,717	44,576	67,022
Money..........	34	93,281	115,965	135,342	141,676	152,633	163,970	184,874	218,951	242,437	254,717	274,021	322,898
Quasi-Money..........	35	236,578	277,489	305,996	347,091	383,813	433,586	504,965	603,882	701,196	814,259	935,128	1,083,528
Restriced Deposits..........	36b	14	21	23	45	31	38	54	634	364	279	283	252
Central Govt. Lending Funds..........	36f	18,613	24,400	20,571	17,132	15,616	25,383	28,511	16,581	14,560	16,560	17,096	14,740
Liab. to Nonbank Financial Insts.......	36j	—	—	—	—	—	366	50	35	—	—	—	6
Capital Accounts..........	37a	26,523	29,646	36,340	39,815	43,526	46,995	65,316	72,042	80,600	91,138	115,558	130,857
Other Items (Net)..........	37r	−13,886	−16,307	13,049	24,125	33,588	45,733	35,322	21,656	15,322	25,770	−30,879	2,885
Money plus Quasi-Money..........	35l	329,859	393,454	441,338	488,767	536,446	597,556	689,839	822,833	943,633	1,068,976	1,209,149	1,406,426
Interest Rates							Percent Per Annum						
Discount Rate (End of Period)..........	60	6.00	5.50	6.00	7.00	8.00	8.00	7.00	7.00	6.00	6.00	5.00	5.00
Deposit Rate..........	60l	8.18	6.40	6.04	7.28	8.11	8.42	8.74	8.56	8.50	8.17	7.82	7.11
Lending Rate..........	60p	15.00	14.50	14.00	14.00	14.00	14.00	14.13	15.50	15.83	16.00	16.00	14.75
Prices, Production, Labor							Index Numbers (2000=100): Period Averages						
Share Prices..........	62	68.5	123.2	139.0	251.2	190.5	107.8	89.1	100.0	117.6	138.6	141.8	237.6
Consumer Prices..........	64	67.9	71.5	78.8	80.7	85.1	92.2	97.8	100.0	102.0	105.4	† 111.4	114.9
Industrial Production..........	66	63.6	68.7	73.4	78.0	85.2	88.7	91.8	100.0	102.6	110.1	117.3	124.9
							Number in Thousands: Period Averages						
Labor Force..........	67d	....	....	50,337	....	....	....	53,512	....	....	....	....	....
Employment..........	67e	....	....	....	54,597	....	....	....	51,764	....	....	....	....
Unemployment..........	67c	....	....	....	1,417	....	....	....	1,750	....	....	....	....
Unemployment Rate..........	67r	....	....	....	2.5	....	....	....	3.3	....	....	....	....

		1993	1994	1995	1996	1997	1998	1999	2000	2001	2002	2003	2004
Intl. Transactions & Positions							*Millions of Taka*						
Exports.................................	70	90,183	107,013	127,782	137,944	166,087	179,614	192,571	249,860	269,150	264,295	306,090	392,808
Imports, c.i.f.............................	71	158,123	185,098	261,878	276,838	302,942	327,575	377,496	436,450	465,607	458,119	553,235	671,040
Imports, f.o.b.............................	71.v	142,055	166,246	235,502	248,932	265,565	298,386	342,064	394,340	421,415	....	....	....
Balance of Payments						*Millions of US Dollars: Minus Sign Indicates Debit*							
Current Account, n.i.e.....................	78ald	359.3	199.6	−823.9	−991.4	−286.3	−35.2	−364.4	−305.8	−535.4	739.3	131.6	....
Goods: Exports f.o.b.....................	78aad	2,544.7	2,934.4	3,733.3	4,009.3	4,839.9	5,141.4	5,458.3	6,399.2	6,084.7	6,102.4	7,050.1	....
Goods: Imports f.o.b.....................	78abd	−3,657.3	−4,350.5	−6,057.4	−6,284.6	−6,550.7	−6,715.7	−7,535.5	−8,052.9	−8,133.4	−7,780.1	−9,492.0	....
Trade Balance............................	78acd	−1,112.6	−1,416.1	−2,324.1	−2,275.3	−1,710.8	−1,574.3	−2,077.2	−1,653.7	−2,048.7	−1,677.8	−2,441.9	....
Services: Credit..........................	78add	529.4	589.8	698.2	604.8	687.3	723.9	777.7	815.1	752.2	848.7	1,011.7	....
Services: Debit...........................	78aed	−932.2	−1,025.0	−1,531.2	−1,166.0	−1,283.7	−1,237.1	−1,396.7	−1,620.2	−1,521.5	−1,405.7	−1,711.5	....
Balance on Goods & Services......	78afd	−1,515.3	−1,851.3	−3,157.1	−2,836.5	−2,307.2	−2,087.4	−2,696.3	−2,458.9	−2,818.0	−2,234.8	−3,141.7	....
Income: Credit...........................	78agd	100.1	150.5	270.1	129.4	86.6	91.5	94.3	78.4	76.6	56.8	56.5	....
Income: Debit............................	78ahd	−175.8	−188.7	−201.8	−193.1	−198.0	−206.1	−258.5	−344.8	−361.9	−322.0	−361.3	....
Balance on Gds, Serv. & Inc......	78aid	−1,591.0	−1,889.6	−3,088.8	−2,900.2	−2,418.6	−2,202.1	−2,860.4	−2,725.3	−3,103.3	−2,500.1	−3,446.4	....
Current Transfers, n.i.e.: Credit......	78ajd	1,951.8	2,091.4	2,266.7	1,912.8	2,136.5	2,172.9	2,501.4	2,426.5	2,572.8	3,245.4	3,586.2	....
Current Transfers: Debit...............	78akd	−1.5	−2.2	−1.8	−4.0	−4.3	−5.9	−5.3	−7.0	−4.9	−6.0	−8.2	....
Capital Account, n.i.e....................	78bcd	—	—	—	371.2	366.8	238.7	364.1	248.7	235.4	363.7	386.7	....
Capital Account, n.i.e.: Credit........	78bad	—	—	—	371.2	366.8	238.7	364.1	248.7	235.4	363.7	386.7	....
Capital Account: Debit................	78bbd	—	—	—	—	—	—	—	—	—	....	....	....
Financial Account, n.i.e................	78bjd	268.9	748.8	178.8	92.4	−140.2	−116.0	−446.9	−256.0	262.1	−256.2	289.0	....
Direct Investment Abroad..............	78bdd	—	—	—	—	−3.1	−3.0	−.1	—	....	−2.7	−2.8	....
Dir. Invest. in Rep. Econ., n.i.e......	78bed	14.0	11.1	1.9	13.5	139.4	190.1	179.7	280.4	78.5	52.3	268.3	....
Portfolio Investment Assets..........	78bfd	—	—	—	—	—	—	−.2	—	.1	−1.2	—	....
Equity Securities......................	78bkd	—	—	—	—	—	—	−.2	—	−.2	−1.2	—	....
Debt Securities.........................	78bld	—	—	—	—	—	—	—	—	.3	—	—	....
Portfolio Investment Liab., n.i.e......	78bgd	8.4	105.9	−15.2	−117.0	−9.9	−4.1	−1.1	1.3	−3.5	−1.4	1.6	....
Equity Securities......................	78bmd	8.4	105.9	−15.2	−117.0	−9.9	−4.2	−1.1	1.2	−3.5	−1.4	1.6	....
Debt Securities.........................	78bnd	—	—	—	—	.1	—	.1	....	....	....	—	....
Financial Derivatives Assets..........	78bwd	—	—	—	—	—	—	—	—	....	....	....	....
Financial Derivatives Liabilities......	78bxd	—	—	—	—	—	—	—	—	....	....	....	....
Other Investment Assets..............	78bhd	−178.4	−1.6	−243.9	−426.7	−677.8	−859.7	−1,143.7	−1,246.8	−433.8	−560.4	−693.6	....
Monetary Authorities.................	78bod	....	....	....	—	—	—	—	—	—	—	—	....
General Government..................	78bpd	−.7	−.1	—	—	—	—	—	—	—	—	—	....
Banks..................................	78bqd	−177.7	−1.5	−243.9	−41.1	−70.2	−38.1	−131.4	−315.7	151.7	143.7	136.2	....
Other Sectors.........................	78brd	—	—	—	−385.6	−607.6	−821.6	−1,012.3	−931.0	−585.5	−704.0	−829.8	....
Other Investment Liab., n.i.e.........	78bid	424.8	633.4	436.1	622.6	411.2	560.7	518.4	709.1	620.7	257.1	715.5	....
Monetary Authorities.................	78bsd	−.2	15.0	58.3	−4.3	−25.5	126.6	−118.9	35.2	132.7	−99.9	37.9	....
General Government..................	78btd	379.3	718.5	374.2	511.3	294.1	404.6	524.7	537.9	413.7	138.2	728.2	....
Banks..................................	78bud	—	−116.3	−34.2	83.0	118.4	2.6	30.7	105.7	29.0	58.4	−188.4	....
Other Sectors.........................	78bvd	45.8	16.2	37.9	32.7	24.2	26.9	82.0	30.4	45.3	160.4	137.9	....
Net Errors and Omissions................	78cad	69.4	−257.1	133.3	113.5	−75.5	201.0	258.0	282.4	−106.0	−349.3	81.1	....
Overall Balance........................	78cbd	697.6	691.3	−511.7	−414.3	−135.1	288.5	−189.2	−30.7	−143.9	497.4	888.5	....
Reserves and Related Items.............	79dad	−697.6	−691.3	511.7	414.3	135.1	−288.5	189.2	30.7	143.9	−497.4	−888.5	....
Reserve Assets.........................	79dbd	−647.0	−636.2	572.8	499.9	253.8	−319.1	286.0	121.0	207.9	−411.8	−886.3	....
Use of Fund Credit and Loans........	79dcd	−50.6	−55.1	−61.0	−85.6	−118.7	30.6	−96.8	−90.3	−64.0	−85.6	−2.2	....
Exceptional Financing..................	79ded	—	—	—	—	—	....	....	....	....	....	....	....
International Investment Position						*Millions of US Dollars*							
Assets....................................	79aad	....	....	....	....	....	....	....	2,783.6	2,082.8	2,380.1	3,104.0	....
Direct Investment Abroad..............	79abd	....	....	—	—	—	—	—	68.3	85.3	88.3	95.5	....
Portfolio Investment..................	79acd	....	....	—	—	—	—	—	.6	.7	1.0	1.0	....
Equity Securities......................	79add	....	....	—	—	—	—	—	.6	.7	1.0	1.0	....
Debt Securities........................	79aed	....	....	—	—	—	—	—	—	—	—	—	....
Financial Derivatives..................	79ald	....	....	....	....	....	....	....	—	—	—	—	....
Other Investment......................	79afd	....	....	730.6	771.6	827.9	794.9	917.0	1,203.4	691.1	568.4	383.5	....
Monetary Authorities.................	79agd	....	....	—	—	—	—	—	—	—	—	—	....
General Government..................	79ahd	....	....	—	—	—	—	—	—	—	—	—	....
Banks..................................	79aid	....	....	730.6	771.6	827.9	794.9	917.0	1,203.4	691.1	568.4	383.5	....
Other Sectors.........................	79ajd	....	....	—	—	—	—	—	—	—	—	—	....
Reserve Assets........................	79akd	....	....	2,337.2	1,842.4	1,558.2	1,920.8	1,617.6	1,511.4	1,305.7	1,722.4	2,624.1	....
Liabilities...............................	79lad	....	....	....	....	....	....	....	18,988.4	17,813.2	19,269.7	20,728.4	....
Dir. Invest. in Rep. Economy..........	79lbd	....	....	—	—	—	—	—	2,202.0	2,246.3	2,524.5	2,973.1	....
Portfolio Investment..................	79lcd	....	....	—	—	—	—	—	22.2	17.2	16.7	21.6	....
Equity Securities......................	79ldd	....	....	—	—	—	—	—	19.8	15.2	14.7	19.6	....
Debt Securities........................	79led	....	....	—	—	—	—	—	2.4	2.0	2.0	2.0	....
Financial Derivatives..................	79lld	....	....	....	....	....	....	....	—	—	—	—	....
Other Investment......................	79lfd	....	....	17,018.2	15,509.7	15,462.1	14,569.4	15,267.0	16,764.2	15,549.7	16,728.4	17,733.8	....
Monetary Authorities.................	79lgd	....	....	643.8	538.1	388.5	434.3	326.1	219.6	148.6	70.6	73.6	....
General Government..................	79lhd	....	....	16,055.5	14,576.3	14,565.1	13,699.8	14,479.1	15,974.9	14,926.1	16,205.5	17,400.5	....
Banks..................................	79lid	....	....	318.8	395.3	508.5	435.4	461.8	569.7	475.0	452.3	259.8	....
Other Sectors.........................	79ljd	....	....	—	—	—	—	—	—	—	—	—	....

Bangladesh 513

		1993	1994	1995	1996	1997	1998	1999	2000	2001	2002	2003	2004
National Accounts						*Billions of Taka: Year Ending June 30*							
Househ.Cons.Expend.,incl.NPISHs....	96f	1,037.4	1,110.6	1,254.4	1,342.2	1,440.8	1,558.6	1,707.1	1,838.5	1,964.9	2,099.2	2,297.6	....
Government Consumption Expend...	91f	62.1	66.1	70.6	73.3	78.9	94.7	100.8	108.4	114.3	136.6	149.0	....
Gross Fixed Capital Formation..........	93e	225.0	249.2	291.6	332.5	374.5	433.0	487.6	545.9	585.4	632.4	697.4	....
Changes in Inventories.....................	93i	—	—	—	—	—	—	—	—	—	—	—	....
Exports of Goods and Services..........	90c	113.1	121.9	165.7	184.4	216.7	266.8	289.9	331.5	390.0	390.0	398.2	....
Imports of Goods and Services (-).....	98c	176.8	187.7	263.5	310.9	325.6	365.9	409.9	455.9	545.1	520.4	565.2	....
Gross Domestic Product (GDP)........	99b	1,253.7	1,354.1	1,525.2	1,663.2	1,807.0	2,001.8	2,197.0	2,370.9	2,535.5	2,732.0	3,004.9	....
Net Primary Income from Abroad.....	98.n	34.1	42.3	46.5	49.5	58.5	65.0	75.5	87.1	88.4	125.4	140.4	....
Gross National Income (GNI)............	99a	1,287.8	1,396.5	1,571.7	1,712.8	1,865.5	2,066.7	2,272.5	2,458.0	2,623.9	2,857.4	3,145.3	....
Consumption of Fixed Capital..........	99cf	110.9	120.2	134.1	146.9	158.9	176.0	175.3	187.8	203.0	218.1	239.8	....
GDP Volume 1995/96 Prices............	99b.p	1,455.7	1,515.1	1,589.8	1,663.2	1,752.9	1,844.5	1,934.3	2,049.3	2,157.4	2,252.6	2,372.6	....
GDP Volume (2000=100)...............	99bvp	71.0	73.9	77.6	81.2	85.5	90.0	94.4	100.0	105.3	109.9	115.8	....
GDP Deflator (2000=100)...............	99bip	74.4	77.3	82.9	86.4	89.1	93.8	98.2	100.0	101.6	104.8	109.5	....
						Millions: Midyear Estimates							
Population...............................	99z	111.43	113.95	116.45	118.95	121.43	123.90	126.40	128.92	131.46	134.03	136.62	139.21

162   2005, International Monetary Fund : *International Financial Statistics Yearbook*

Barbados 316

		1993	1994	1995	1996	1997	1998	1999	2000	2001	2002	2003	2004
Exchange Rates		*Barbados Dollars per SDR: End of Period (aa) Barbados Dollars per US Dollar: End of Period (ae)*											
Official Rate	aa	2.7471	2.9197	2.9730	2.8759	2.6985	2.8161	2.7450	2.6058	2.5135	2.7190	2.9719	3.1060
Official Rate	ae	2.0000	2.0000	2.0000	2.0000	2.0000	2.0000	2.0000	2.0000	2.0000	2.0000	2.0000	2.0000
Fund Position		*Millions of SDRs: End of Period*											
Quota	2f.s	48.90	48.90	48.90	48.90	48.90	48.90	67.50	67.50	67.50	67.50	67.50	67.50
SDRs	1b.s	.05	.03	.03	.02	.02	.02	.01	.02	.04	.04	.01	.04
Reserve Position in the Fund	1c.s	.03	.03	.03	.03	.03	.03	4.68	4.68	4.71	4.85	5.02	5.15
Total Fund Cred.&Loans Outstg	2tl	36.84	36.84	24.94	6.52	—	—	—	—	—	—	—	—
International Liquidity		*Millions of US Dollars Unless Otherwise Indicated: End of Period*											
Total Reserves minus Gold	1l.d	150.45	195.77	219.10	289.69	264.92	365.95	301.94	472.69	690.37	668.51	737.94	579.86
SDRs	1b.d	.07	.04	.04	.03	.03	.03	.01	.02	.05	.06	.01	.06
Reserve Position in the Fund	1c.d	.03	.04	.04	.04	.03	.04	6.42	6.09	5.92	6.60	7.46	8.00
Foreign Exchange	1d.d	150.35	195.69	219.02	289.62	264.85	365.88	295.52	466.58	684.40	661.86	730.47	571.80
Monetary Authorities	1dad	143.21	188.28	212.75	280.06	227.62	298.66	226.13	373.25	568.41	515.28	552.37	387.02
Government	1dbd	7.14	7.41	6.27	9.56	37.23	67.22	69.39	93.33	115.99	146.58	178.10	184.78
Gold (Million Fine Troy Ounces)	1ad	—	—	—	—	—	—	—	—	—	—	—	—
Gold (National Valuation)	1and	—	—	—	—	—	—	—	—	—	—	—	—
Monetary Authorities: Other Liab	4..d	56.01	38.33	28.20	16.59	12.02	7.83	6.99	.14	.11	.73	.59	.57
Deposit Money Banks: Assets	7a.d	95.65	126.53	204.00	341.07	309.48	277.73	338.78	263.09	335.70	527.73	617.71	637.98
Liabilities	7b.d	152.56	173.11	274.86	402.14	382.40	400.97	450.04	373.02	440.94	607.94	566.85	623.63
Monetary Authorities		*Millions of Barbados Dollars: End of Period*											
Foreign Assets	11	335.8	442.2	502.6	641.5	592.1	571.8	628.7	967.6	1,396.9	1,342.3	1,468.4	1,171.6
Claims on Central Government	12a	225.3	219.2	117.6	90.3	64.1	50.0	83.1	15.6	.6	.6	.6	52.7
Claims on Deposit Money Banks	12e	5.0		6.0	—	—	23.5	15.0	—	—	—	—	—
Claims on Other Banking Insts	12f	25.3	10.1	10.1	9.0	9.0	9.0	9.0	9.0	9.0	9.0	9.0	9.0
Reserve Money	14	324.6	318.4	368.5	494.4	446.8	486.9	507.4	567.8	654.2	910.8	1,091.2	774.9
of which: Currency Outside DMBs	14a	177.0	189.6	200.3	220.1	239.6	268.2	302.7	310.7	312.4	337.5	329.0	398.7
Foreign Liabilities	16c	213.2	184.2	130.6	51.9	24.0	15.7	14.0	.3	.2	1.5	1.2	1.1
Central Government Deposits	16d	110.1	212.0	197.8	255.5	266.7	244.5	261.6	471.5	757.7	474.4	405.7	471.7
Capital Accounts	17a	34.1	35.5	35.9	35.1	33.7	34.6	34.1	32.9	32.2	33.9	35.9	37.0
Other Items (Net)	17r	−90.7	−78.6	−96.4	−96.1	−106.0	−127.4	−81.3	−80.3	−37.8	−68.6	−56.0	−51.4
Deposit Money Banks		*Millions of Barbados Dollars: End of Period*											
Reserves	20	129.3	114.1	144.9	243.8	166.5	217.2	195.8	255.7	328.1	533.4	748.1	370.9
Foreign Assets	21	191.3	253.1	408.0	682.1	619.0	555.5	677.6	526.2	671.4	1,055.5	1,235.4	1,276.0
Claims on Central Government	22a	594.9	603.4	713.5	915.3	981.6	922.9	880.6	1,067.7	1,169.1	1,346.6	1,567.2	1,728.7
Claims on Private Sector	22d	1,128.9	1,268.1	1,470.6	1,536.1	1,839.1	2,138.1	2,445.4	2,508.2	2,504.3	2,583.9	2,578.1	2,940.1
Claims on Other Banking Insts	22f	83.7	159.3	39.4	41.2	91.6	108.5	94.1	109.2	111.5	178.4	180.6	338.7
Demand Deposits	24	280.8	309.6	208.4	370.0	350.1	493.3	615.6	825.7	837.1	842.3	1,211.7	1,247.7
Time, Savings,& Fgn.Currency Dep	25	1,389.0	1,514.5	1,701.6	1,913.3	2,144.3	2,209.2	2,411.4	2,508.0	2,582.0	3,146.4	3,073.8	3,535.0
Foreign Liabilities	26c	305.1	346.2	549.7	804.3	764.8	801.9	900.1	746.0	881.9	1,215.9	1,133.7	1,247.3
Central Government Deposits	26d	101.3	173.5	215.3	245.8	330.1	287.7	249.8	270.8	391.7	337.3	434.2	501.7
Credit from Monetary Authorities	26g	19.7	10.1	24.7	28.7	12.2	22.5	38.5	19.6	29.6	26.4	25.6	26.5
Capital Accounts	27a	46.5	92.2	101.0	105.4	117.1	117.6	137.4	134.0	154.0	288.4	539.9	566.1
Other Items (Net)	27r	−14.4	−48.2	−24.6	−48.9	−20.8	10.0	−59.4	−37.1	−91.9	−159.0	−109.4	−469.9
Monetary Survey		*Millions of Barbados Dollars: End of Period*											
Foreign Assets (Net)	31n	8.7	164.8	230.3	467.4	422.2	309.7	392.2	747.5	1,186.2	1,180.4	1,568.9	1,199.2
Domestic Credit	32	1,846.5	1,874.6	1,938.0	2,090.7	2,388.7	2,696.3	3,000.8	2,967.4	2,645.1	3,306.7	3,495.7	4,095.9
Claims on Central Govt. (Net)	32an	608.7	437.0	417.9	504.4	449.0	440.8	452.3	341.0	20.4	535.4	728.0	808.0
Claims on Private Sector	32d	1,128.9	1,268.1	1,470.6	1,536.1	1,839.1	2,138.1	2,445.4	2,508.2	2,504.3	2,583.9	2,578.1	2,940.1
Claims on Other Banking Insts	32f	109.0	169.4	49.5	50.2	100.6	117.5	103.1	118.2	120.5	187.4	189.6	347.7
Money	34	476.6	516.3	428.5	627.2	620.6	765.7	924.4	1,141.2	1,156.3	1,182.3	1,549.2	1,650.3
Quasi-Money	35	1,389.0	1,514.5	1,701.6	1,913.3	2,144.3	2,209.2	2,411.4	2,508.0	2,582.0	3,146.4	3,073.8	3,535.0
Capital Accounts	37a	80.5	127.7	136.9	140.5	150.8	152.2	171.5	167.0	186.2	322.2	575.8	603.0
Other Items (Net)	37r	−90.9	−119.1	−98.8	−122.8	−104.7	−121.1	−114.2	−101.3	−93.2	−163.7	−134.1	−493.2
Money plus Quasi-Money	35l	1,865.6	2,030.8	2,130.1	2,540.5	2,764.9	2,974.9	3,335.8	3,649.2	3,738.3	4,328.7	4,623.0	5,185.2
Other Banking Institutions		*Millions of Barbados Dollars: End of Period*											
Claims on Central Government	42a	7.1	.5	5.5	4.9	1.3	1.7	1.9	3.2	3.7	3.7	.6	5.3
Claims on Private Sector	42d	403.5	417.5	424.7	443.0	381.8	433.4	378.6	423.0	446.4	442.3	440.6	451.4
Claims on Deposit Money Banks	42e	8.6	2.1	6.3	14.8	19.5	14.0	13.9	53.6	21.3	57.4	43.5	36.6
Time Deposits	45	339.4	301.8	308.8	326.5	258.8	297.1	241.4	273.2	255.2	340.2	321.7	356.8
Central Government Deposits	46d	26.2	34.5	37.7	44.0	31.5	7.5	40.0	50.2	90.7	76.8	54.8	54.0
Credit from Deposit Money Banks	46h	6.3	46.8	49.2	43.8	70.7	92.6	63.4	94.9	54.3	15.4	52.2	31.7
Capital Accounts	47a	5.0	5.1	5.1	5.1	7.9	10.9	18.9	18.9	18.9	18.9	18.9	18.9
Other Items (Net)	47r	42.4	32.0	35.8	43.3	33.7	40.9	30.7	42.6	52.4	52.1	37.2	32.0
Banking Survey		*Millions of Barbados Dollars: End of Period*											
Foreign Assets (Net)	51n	8.7	164.8	230.3	467.4	422.2	309.8	392.3	747.5	1,186.2	1,180.4	1,568.9	1,199.2
Domestic Credit	52	2,122.0	2,088.7	2,281.0	2,444.5	2,639.6	3,006.4	3,238.1	3,225.1	2,884.0	3,488.6	3,692.5	4,150.9
Claims on Central Govt. (Net)	52an	589.7	403.0	385.7	465.3	418.7	435.0	414.1	294.0	−66.6	462.4	673.8	759.4
Claims on Private Sector	52d	1,532.3	1,685.7	1,895.2	1,979.1	2,220.9	2,571.4	2,824.0	2,931.1	2,950.6	3,026.2	3,018.7	3,391.5
Liquid Liabilities	55l	2,205.0	2,332.5	2,438.9	2,867.0	3,023.6	3,271.9	3,577.0	3,920.1	3,992.9	4,667.7	4,944.5	5,541.9
Capital Accounts	57a	85.5	132.8	142.0	145.6	158.7	163.1	190.4	185.9	205.1	341.1	594.7	622.0
Other Items (Net)	57r	−159.8	−211.8	−69.7	−100.6	−120.4	−118.9	−136.9	−133.4	−127.8	−339.7	−277.8	−813.8
Interest Rates		*Percent Per Annum*											
Bank Rate (End of Period)	60	8.00	9.50	12.50	12.50	9.00	9.00	10.00	10.00	7.50	7.50	7.50	7.50
Treasury Bill Rate	60c	5.44	7.26	8.01	6.85	3.61	5.61	5.83	5.29	3.14	2.10	1.41	1.20
Savings Rate	60k	4.17	4.25	5.00	5.00	4.33	4.00	4.17	4.83	4.38	3.29	3.00	3.63
Deposit Rate	60l	4.39	4.32	5.11	5.20	4.58	4.20	4.40	4.97	4.04	2.70	2.56	2.54
Lending Rate	60p	8.92	9.08	10.00	10.00	9.83	9.75	9.40	10.19	9.58	8.50	8.50	8.33

		1993	1994	1995	1996	1997	1998	1999	2000	2001	2002	2003	2004
Prices, Production, Labor		*Index Numbers (2000=100): Period Averages*											
Consumer Prices	64	86.6	† 86.7	88.3	90.4	97.4	96.1	97.6	100.0	† 102.6	102.7	104.4	105.8
Industrial Production	66	86.7	89.1	90.6	92.1	96.4	102.7	100.8	100.0	93.8	94.4	94.0	94.7
		Number in Thousands: Period Averages											
Labor Force	67d	133	135	137	136	136	136	137	139	145	143	145	....
Employment	67e	101	106	110	115	118	122	125	129	129	129	129	....
Unemployment	67c	31	28	27	21	20	17	14	13	14	15	16	....
Unemployment Rate (%)	67r	27.6	26.4	23.2	19.3	17.8	16.3	13.2	11.4	11.9	12.2	12.6	....
Intl. Transactions & Positions		*Millions of Barbados Dollars*											
Exports	70	374.0	363.0	477.8	561.2	565.9	503.1	527.6	544.7	518.7	412.8	419.9	437.6
Imports, c.i.f.	71	1,154.1	1,228.6	1,541.2	1,667.3	1,991.0	2,019.6	2,216.1	2,312.1	2,173.3	2,078.3	2,266.0	2,615.8
Balance of Payments		*Millions of US Dollars: Minus Sign Indicates Debit*											
Current Account, n.i.e.	78ald	68.8	133.6	42.6	69.7	−50.0	−62.6	−147.8	−145.1	−110.9	−167.9	−169.4	....
Goods: Exports f.o.b.	78aad	187.8	190.0	245.4	286.7	289.0	270.1	275.3	286.4	271.2	253.0	264.2	
Goods: Imports f.o.b.	78abd	−514.3	−544.7	−691.1	−743.0	−887.7	−920.7	−989.4	−1,030.3	−952.3	−955.0	−1,065.6	
Trade Balance	78acd	−326.6	−354.7	−445.8	−456.3	−598.7	−650.6	−714.1	−743.9	−681.1	−702.0	−801.4	
Services: Credit	78add	689.5	813.6	866.6	926.9	959.3	1,023.6	1,029.4	1,090.2	1,068.5	1,041.3	1,165.5	
Services: Debit	78aed	−272.6	−319.0	−363.2	−387.1	−409.5	−432.3	−458.3	−487.4	−498.5	−491.4	−518.8	
Balance on Goods & Services	78afd	90.4	140.0	57.7	83.6	−48.9	−59.2	−143.0	−141.1	−111.1	−152.0	−154.7	
Income: Credit	78agd	40.1	46.1	48.4	54.2	60.5	63.5	66.7	70.2	73.0	72.2	75.1	
Income: Debit	78ahd	−81.0	−86.8	−96.1	−106.3	−108.2	−119.1	−137.7	−152.0	−166.2	−173.8	−182.0	
Balance on Gds, Serv. & Inc.	78aid	49.4	99.3	10.0	31.4	−96.6	−114.8	−214.1	−222.9	−204.3	−253.6	−261.6	
Current Transfers, n.i.e.: Credit	78ajd	41.8	54.5	56.2	64.8	71.7	78.4	94.0	108.9	125.6	120.1	126.5	
Current Transfers: Debit	78akd	−22.5	−20.2	−23.6	−26.6	−25.1	−26.2	−27.7	−31.0	−32.3	−34.3	−34.3	
Capital Account, n.i.e.	78bcd	—	—	—	.4	—	.7	.7	1.8	1.3	—	—	....
Capital Account, n.i.e.: Credit	78bad	—	—	—	.4	—	.7	.7	1.8	1.3	—	—	
Capital Account: Debit	78bbd	—	—	—	—	—	—	—	—	—	—	—	
Financial Account, n.i.e.	78bjd	.6	−5.9	−26.4	−22.8	19.9	55.1	120.2	289.5	285.0	119.7	202.4	....
Direct Investment Abroad	78bdd	−2.6	−1.1	−3.3	−3.6	−1.2	−1.0	−1.3	−1.1	−1.1	−.5	−.5	
Dir. Invest. in Rep. Econ., n.i.e.	78bed	9.4	13.0	11.8	13.3	14.8	15.8	17.4	19.4	18.6	17.4	58.3	
Portfolio Investment Assets	78bfd	−9.9	−1.9	−3.1	−17.4	−17.3	−24.8	−29.8	−28.9	−30.5	−24.6	−22.9	
Equity Securities	78bkd	−9.9	−13.4	−7.6	−9.7	−11.3	−14.0	−16.3	−13.9	−14.8	−21.0	−23.1	
Debt Securities	78bld	—	11.5	4.6	−7.8	−6.0	−10.8	−13.5	−15.0	−15.7	−3.6	.2	
Portfolio Investment Liab., n.i.e.	78bgd	1.5	48.7	40.4	−1.6	−25.5	−25.7	44.8	100.5	150.4	−7.7	84.1	
Equity Securities	78bmd	.9	—	—	—	−.1	−.1	−.1	—	—	1.1	94.7	
Debt Securities	78bnd	.6	48.7	40.4	−1.6	−25.4	−25.6	44.9	100.5	150.4	−8.8	−10.6	
Financial Derivatives Assets	78bwd	....	....	....	....	....	....	....	....	....	....	....	
Financial Derivatives Liabilities	78bxd	....	....	....	....	....	....	....	....	....	....	....	
Other Investment Assets	78bhd	−8.2	−88.9	−167.0	−211.0	−12.2	−16.9	−92.9	52.6	−56.7	−180.9	−83.1	
Monetary Authorities	78bod	....	....	—	—	—	—	—	—	—	—	—	
General Government	78bpd	−1.4	−7.7	−9.3	−7.1	−14.2	−11.0	−4.4	−4.6	−5.4	−5.6	−4.4	
Banks	78bqd	−14.9	−32.6	−87.5	−154.1	24.5	21.5	−72.5	66.9	−83.1	−201.3	−87.9	
Other Sectors	78brd	8.0	−48.6	−70.3	−49.8	−22.5	−27.4	−16.1	−9.7	31.8	26.1	9.3	
Other Investment Liab., n.i.e.	78bid	10.4	24.3	94.9	197.4	61.1	107.6	182.1	146.9	204.4	315.9	166.5	
Monetary Authorities	78bsd	−1.9	−5.2	−8.5	−6.7	−6.7	—	—	—	—	—	—	
General Government	78btd	−25.2	−40.6	−34.3	9.8	7.9	23.8	5.0	18.6	11.5	−2.2	4.8	
Banks	78bud	11.2	16.6	101.4	127.3	−19.8	18.6	49.1	−77.0	67.9	167.0	−41.1	
Other Sectors	78bvd	26.3	53.5	36.3	67.1	79.6	65.3	128.0	205.2	125.0	151.1	202.8	
Net Errors and Omissions	78cad	−49.7	−89.9	25.9	39.1	33.7	−.6	61.6	32.7	40.0	25.0	34.4	
Overall Balance	78cbd	19.6	37.8	42.1	86.4	3.6	−7.5	34.6	178.9	215.3	−23.1	67.4	
Reserves and Related Items	79dad	−19.6	−37.8	−42.1	−86.4	−3.6	7.5	−34.6	−178.9	−215.3	23.1	−67.4	
Reserve Assets	79dbd	−21.1	−59.1	−25.0	−61.1	4.8	6.9	−35.4	−179.4	−215.9	22.6	−68.0	
Use of Fund Credit and Loans	79dcd	—	—	−18.1	−26.8	−9.0	—	—	—	—	—	—	
Exceptional Financing	79ded	1.5	21.3	1.0	1.5	.7	.6	.8	.5	.6	.5	.6	....
Government Finance		*Millions of Barbados Dollars: Year Ending December 31*											
Deficit (-) or Surplus	80	−86.31	−81.17	26.85	−129.65	−39.05	−39.21	−118.39	−76.69	−169.83	−308.41	−185.26	−126.53
Total Revenue and Grants	81y	1,022.79	1,017.43	1,140.52	1,194.44	1,424.53	1,526.78	1,545.31	1,694.00	1,733.33	1,697.69	1,830.41	1,880.26
Revenue	81	1,022.79	1,017.43	1,140.52	1,194.44	1,424.53	1,526.78	1,545.31	1,694.00	1,733.33	1,697.69	1,830.41	1,880.26
Grants	81z	—	—	—	—	—	—	—	—	—	—	—	....
Exp. & Lending Minus Repay.	82z	1,109.10	1,098.60	1,113.67	1,324.09	1,463.58	1,565.99	1,663.70	1,770.69	1,903.16	2,006.10	2,015.67	2,006.79
Expenditure	82	1,103.97	1,070.34	1,125.78	1,324.26	1,458.02	1,573.67	1,660.81	1,767.40	1,882.54	2,004.96	2,013.57	2,005.08
Lending Minus Repayments	83	5.13	28.26	−12.10	−.17	5.56	−7.68	2.89	3.29	20.62	1.14	2.10	1.71
Statistical Discrepancy	80xx	....	−31.82	1.43	−47.48	−10.65	−14.08	28.95	−67.61	15.33	−212.55	−57.49	....
Total Financing	80h	....	112.99	−28.28	177.13	49.70	53.29	89.44	144.30	154.50	520.96	242.75	....
Domestic	84a	....	69.58	−19.30	162.93	83.98	104.99	6.69	−97.41	−163.37	551.49	90.76	....
Foreign	85a	....	43.41	−8.98	14.20	−34.28	−51.70	82.75	237.95	332.13	−30.53	151.99	....
Total Debt by Residence	88	2,322.6	2,492.2	2,479.9	2,721.1	2,737.1	2,796.2	2,897.5	3,232.7	3,692.7	3,950.7	4,043.3	4,091.5
Domestic	88a	1,618.0	1,777.8	1,762.2	1,967.0	2,036.9	2,121.4	2,108.6	2,204.1	2,333.4	2,605.4	2,710.1	2,803.1
Foreign	89a	704.6	714.4	717.7	754.1	700.2	674.9	788.9	1,028.6	1,359.4	1,345.3	1,333.1	1,288.4
National Accounts		*Millions of Barbados Dollars*											
Househ.Cons.Expend.,incl.NPISHs	96f	1,967	1,978	2,305	2,359	2,786	2,998	3,249	3,488	3,316	3,402	....	....
Government Consumption Expend.	91f	732	707	752	848	927	982	1,027	1,084	1,143	1,219	....	....
Gross Capital Formation	93	420	464	527	506	676	....	....	....	....	....	....	....
Exports of Goods and Services	90c	1,727	1,980	2,177	2,380	2,438	2,522	2,546	2,583	2,593	2,480	....	....
Imports of Goods and Services (-)	98c	1,537	1,684	2,059	2,200	2,530	2,620	2,823	2,919	2,735	2,740	....	....
Gross Domestic Product (GDP)	99b	3,309	3,485	3,742	3,995	4,413	4,755	4,963	5,183	5,140	5,197	....	....
GDP Volume 1974 Prices	99b.p	790.5	825.8	846.5	873.1	901.9	941.3	975.3	998.7	964.4	960.1	981.3	....
GDP Volume (2000=100)	99bvp	79.2	82.7	84.8	87.4	90.3	94.3	97.7	100.0	96.6	96.1	98.3	....
GDP Deflator (2000=100)	99bip	80.7	81.3	85.2	88.2	94.3	97.3	98.1	100.0	102.7	104.3	....	....
		Millions: Midyear Estimates											
Population	99z	.26	.26	.26	.26	.26	.26	.27	.27	.27	.27	.27	.27

Belarus 913

		1993	1994	1995	1996	1997	1998	1999	2000	2001	2002	2003	2004
Exchange Rates						*Rubels per SDR: End of Period*							
Official Rate	aa	.960	15.474	17.095	22.288	41.476	309.767	439.203	1,537.434	1,985.633	2,610.278	3,203.751	3,370.032
						Rubels per US Dollar: End of Period (ae) Period Average (rf)							
Official Rate	ae	.699	10.600	11.500	15.500	30.740	106.000	320.000	1,180.000	1,580.000	1,920.000	2,156.000	2,170.000
Official Rate	rf	....	....	11.521	13.230	26.021	46.128	249.295	876.750	1,390.000	1,790.917	2,051.271	2,160.258
Fund Position						*Millions of SDRs: End of Period*							
Quota	2f.s	280.40	280.40	280.40	280.40	280.40	280.40	386.40	386.40	386.40	386.40	386.40	386.40
SDRs	1b.s	3.22	.01	3.05	.10	—	.30	.30	.14	.31	.19	.02	.01
Reserve Position in the Fund	1c.s	.02	.02	.02	.02	.02	.02	.02	.02	.02	.02	.02	.02
Total Fund Cred.&Loans Outstg	2tl	70.10	70.10	190.20	190.20	190.20	172.27	129.74	87.62	64.26	40.89	17.52	5.84
International Liquidity						*Millions of US Dollars Unless Otherwise Indicated: End of Period*							
Total Reserves minus Gold	1l.d	....	100.99	377.02	469.15	393.70	702.76	294.27	350.50	390.68	618.81	594.81	749.37
SDRs	1b.d	4.43	.01	4.54	.14	—	.42	.42	.18	.40	.26	.03	.01
Reserve Position in the Fund	1c.d	.03	.03	.03	.03	.03	.03	.03	.03	.03	.03	.03	.03
Foreign Exchange	1d.d	....	100.95	372.45	468.98	393.67	702.31	293.82	350.29	390.26	618.52	594.75	749.33
Monetary Authorities: Other Liab	4..d		7.53	11.88	144.97	61.87	78.90	77.31	94.29	137.08	253.69	275.63	75.80
Dep.Money Banks: Assets Conv	7axd	....	280.29	261.71	246.78	276.63	290.03	308.20	280.54	249.61	215.34	272.12	378.33
Assets Nonconv	7ayd		40.66	27.90	82.98	93.25	18.54	28.73	49.55	47.20	48.47	61.54	76.96
Dep.Money Banks: Liab. Conv	7bxd		51.69	88.05	84.25	89.30	134.49	108.07	99.16	142.17	202.86	329.25	536.17
Liab. Nonconv	7byd		36.49	31.68	58.55	70.10	4.71	7.78	14.90	45.92	70.48	66.34	79.92
Monetary Authorities						*Billions of Rubels: End of Period*							
Foreign Assets	11	....	1.23	4.59	7.41	12.33	76.46	98.36	423.56	706.18	1,439.90	1,946.82	2,056.50
Claims on Central Government	12a	....	1.68	4.88	8.59	14.45	54.93	153.75	302.80	504.35	190.42	643.26	432.56
Claims on Local Government	12b		—	—	—	—	—	—	—	—	8.17	12.07	15.07
Claims on Nonfin.Pub.Enterprises	12c	....	.01	.09	.11	.10	.02	.04	.02	—	8.17	12.07	15.07
Claims on Private Sector	12d	....	.01	.04	.03	.07	.34	2.04	7.52	12.58	8.85	11.45	41.38
Claims on Banks	12e	....	1.43	2.32	6.72	17.05	51.23	60.23	107.08	180.56	255.45	332.13	564.54
Reserve Money	14	....	1.76	6.82	12.14	25.21	66.30	184.68	414.33	844.96	1,116.29	1,686.79	2,394.21
of which: Currency Outside DMBs	14a	....	.74	3.78	6.20	12.30	27.07	86.85	238.80	512.21	650.02	926.44	1,339.44
Time, Savings,& Fgn.Currency Dep	15	....	.02	.02	.02	.02	.08	.14	.31	.76	—	.19	
Foreign Liabilities	16c	....	1.26	3.39	6.49	9.79	70.72	81.72	245.98	344.17	593.81	650.39	184.16
Central Government Deposits	16d	....	.38	.34	1.11	2.01	6.49	15.07	41.74	35.10	22.57	126.68	233.75
Capital Accounts	17a	....	.30	.64	1.40	3.69	5.97	24.90	129.19	185.69	311.87	474.98	488.11
Other Items (Net)	17r	....	.64	.72	1.71	3.27	33.43	7.91	9.43	−7.02	−141.76	6.71	−190.18
Deposit Money Banks						*Billions of Rubels: End of Period*							
Reserves	20	....	.95	2.84	† 5.69	11.89	35.69	92.00	158.12	324.84	389.80	675.58	1,132.30
Foreign Assets	21	....	3.69	3.33	† 5.11	11.37	67.89	107.82	389.51	468.96	506.52	719.35	987.98
Claims on Central Government	22a	....	.01	.64	† 2.27	6.08	21.96	53.80	176.94	302.61	550.20	849.63	1,018.86
Claims on Local Government	22b		—	—	† —	.02	.14	.36	.81	.47	81.52	194.24	83.72
Claims on Nonfin.Pub.Enterprises	22c	....	2.87	6.57	† 9.23	18.56	84.06	170.55	677.71	1,138.16	1,663.79	2,049.49	2,982.69
Claims on Private Sector	22d	....	3.13	7.36	† 12.30	30.29	113.00	279.70	802.50	1,400.76	2,320.55	4,283.53	6,885.68
Claims on Nonbank Financial Insts	22g	....	—	—	† .30	.50	.48	1.28	1.31	7.94	11.65	21.70	49.57
Demand Deposits	24	....	1.88	6.13	† 9.24	21.05	52.49	140.71	259.60	425.66	714.29	1,308.43	1,968.51
Time, Savings,& Fgn. Currency Dep	25	....	4.24	7.89	† 11.61	23.90	136.24	271.89	1,104.98	1,677.83	2,569.99	3,935.86	5,675.19
Foreign Liabilities	26c	....	1.01	1.38	† 2.21	4.90	30.62	37.07	134.60	297.18	524.80	852.90	1,336.91
Central Government Deposits	26d	....	.24	1.00	† 2.85	5.80	20.99	44.72	177.91	443.51	347.22	314.73	775.91
Credit from Monetary Authorities	26g	....	1.24	2.12	† 6.49	15.93	48.37	53.47	84.39	142.49	152.10	180.33	511.31
Capital Accounts	27a	....	1.11	4.62	† 5.28	8.92	25.55	147.11	431.90	567.36	1,160.14	2,016.22	2,924.44
Other Items (Net)	27r	....	.93	−2.40	† −2.75	−1.79	8.96	10.53	13.53	89.71	55.48	185.05	−51.47
Monetary Survey						*Billions of Rubels: End of Period*							
Foreign Assets (Net)	31n	....	2.64	3.16	† 3.82	9.01	43.01	87.38	432.49	533.79	827.80	1,162.88	1,523.41
Domestic Credit	32	....	7.08	18.23	† 28.90	62.27	247.45	601.73	1,749.98	2,888.25	4,465.35	7,623.97	10,499.86
Claims on Central Govt. (Net)	32an	....	1.07	4.17	† 6.91	12.72	49.41	147.76	260.09	328.35	370.82	1,051.49	441.75
Claims on Local Government	32b	....	—	—	† —	.02	.14	.36	.81	.47	81.52	194.24	83.72
Claims on Nonfin.Pub.Enterprises	32c	....	2.88	6.66	† 9.34	18.67	84.08	170.60	677.74	1,138.16	1,671.96	2,061.56	2,997.76
Claims on Private Sector	32d	....	3.13	7.40	† 12.34	30.36	113.34	281.74	810.03	1,413.34	2,329.40	4,294.98	6,927.06
Claims on Nonbank Financ. Insts	32g	....	—	—	† .30	.50	.48	1.28	1.31	7.94	11.65	21.70	49.57
Money	34	....	2.69	10.03	† 15.71	33.85	80.93	233.42	508.43	939.18	1,365.67	2,235.62	3,308.72
Quasi-Money	35	....	4.25	7.91	† 11.63	23.93	136.32	272.03	1,105.28	1,678.59	2,569.99	3,936.05	5,675.19
Capital Accounts	37a	....	1.41	5.26	† 6.68	12.62	31.51	172.00	561.10	753.06	1,472.01	2,491.20	3,412.55
Other Items (Net)	37r	....	1.38	−1.80	† −1.30	.89	41.69	11.66	7.66	51.22	−114.51	123.98	−373.18
Money plus Quasi-Money	35l	....	6.94	17.93	† 27.34	57.78	217.25	505.44	1,613.71	2,617.77	3,935.65	6,171.67	8,983.91
Interest Rates						*Percent Per Annum*							
Refinancing Rate (End of Per.)	60	210.0	480.0	66.0	8.3	8.9	9.6	23.4	† 80.0	48.0	38.0	28.0	17.0
Deposit Rate	60l	65.1	89.6	100.8	32.4	15.6	14.3	23.8	37.6	34.2	26.9	17.4	12.7
Lending Rate	60p	71.6	148.5	175.0	62.3	31.8	27.0	51.0	67.7	47.0	36.9	24.0	16.9
Prices and Labor						*Percent Change over Previous Period*							
Producer Prices	63.xx	1,536.3	2,170.8	499.1	34.7	87.5	72.5	355.8	185.6	71.8	40.4	37.5	24.1
Consumer Prices	64.xx	1,190.2	2,221.0	709.3	52.7	63.9	72.9	293.7	168.6	61.1	42.5	28.4	18.1
Wages	65.xx	1,106.8	1,504.4	668.9	60.5	87.3	104.2	322.4	200.9	108.8	53.8	32.5	3.2
						Number in Thousands: Period Averages							
Employment	67e	4,828	4,701	4,410	4,365	4,370	4,417	4,442	4,441	4,417	4,381	4,339	4,323
Unemployment	67c	66	101	131	183	126	106	95	96	103	131	136	83
Unemployment Rate (%)	67r	1.4	2.1	2.7	3.9	2.8	2.3	2.1	2.1	2.3	3.1	1.9	....
Intl. Transactions & Positions						*Millions of US Dollars*							
Exports	70..d	1,970	2,510	4,803	5,652	7,301	7,070	5,909	7,326	7,451	8,021	9,946	13,752
Imports, c.i.f	71..d	2,539	3,066	5,564	6,939	8,689	8,549	6,674	8,646	8,286	9,092	11,558	16,346

		1993	1994	1995	1996	1997	1998	1999	2000	2001	2002	2003	2004
Balance of Payments					*Millions of US Dollars: Minus Sign Indicates Debit*								
Current Account, n.i.e.	78ald	−435.0	−443.8	−458.3	−515.9	−859.2	−1,016.5	−193.7	−338.4	−394.4	−311.2	−423.5	−1,042.9
Goods: Exports f.o.b.	78aad	1,970.1	2,510.0	4,803.0	5,790.1	6,918.7	6,172.3	5,646.4	6,640.5	7,334.1	7,964.7	10,072.9	13,916.8
Goods: Imports f.o.b.	78abd	−2,498.0	−2,999.8	−5,468.7	−6,938.6	−8,325.7	−7,673.4	−6,216.4	−7,524.6	−8,140.8	−8,879.0	−11,328.5	−15,982.5
Trade Balance	78acd	−527.9	−489.8	−665.7	−1,148.5	−1,407.0	−1,501.1	−570.0	−884.1	−806.7	−914.3	−1,255.6	−2,065.7
Services: Credit	78add	184.9	251.4	466.1	908.0	918.8	925.1	753.2	1,000.3	1,142.3	1,340.8	1,499.9	1,749.6
Services: Debit	78aed	−136.8	−199.3	−283.7	−335.9	−364.8	−443.2	−438.8	−562.6	−841.3	−908.0	−915.0	−1,037.0
Balance on Goods & Services	78afd	−479.8	−437.7	−483.3	−576.4	−853.0	−1,019.2	−255.5	−446.4	−505.7	−481.5	−670.7	−1,353.1
Income: Credit	78agd	.1	.5	1.9	74.1	31.2	26.8	20.8	25.7	27.0	44.5	126.3	146.5
Income: Debit	78ahd	−7.5	−29.3	−52.9	−104.9	−115.8	−119.7	−62.8	−72.4	−69.8	−73.1	−101.2	−121.0
Balance on Gds, Serv. & Inc.	78aid	−487.2	−466.5	−534.3	−607.2	−937.6	−1,112.1	−297.5	−493.1	−548.5	−510.1	−645.6	−1,327.6
Current Transfers, n.i.e.: Credit	78ajd	64.6	50.9	107.2	135.5	106.1	120.9	137.0	177.1	202.6	260.4	291.7	378.7
Current Transfers: Debit	78akd	−12.4	−28.2	−31.2	−44.2	−27.7	−25.3	−33.2	−22.4	−48.5	−61.5	−69.6	−94.0
Capital Account, n.i.e.	78bcd	—	23.8	7.3	101.1	133.2	170.1	60.4	69.4	56.3	52.7	68.9	48.8
Capital Account, n.i.e.: Credit	78bad	—	23.8	7.3	257.2	248.0	261.3	131.1	125.6	132.3	119.8	133.2	128.3
Capital Account: Debit	78bbd	....	....	....	−156.1	−114.8	−91.2	−70.7	−56.2	−76.0	−67.1	−64.3	−79.5
Financial Account, n.i.e.	78bjd	294.1	144.6	204.0	378.7	738.1	354.8	399.5	140.1	265.0	482.5	231.9	872.5
Direct Investment Abroad	78bdd	....	....	....	....	−2.1	−2.3	−.8	−.2	−.3	206.2	−1.5	−1.3
Dir. Invest. in Rep. Econ., n.i.e.	78bed	17.6	10.5	14.7	104.5	351.6	203.2	444.0	118.8	95.8	247.1	171.8	169.4
Portfolio Investment Assets	78bfd	....	....	....	−17.7	−61.6	28.0	−15.4	−5.7	25.5	−2.4	.8	3.2
Equity Securities	78bkd	....	....	....	....	−.6	.3	−7.3	.5	.7	6.9	−1.1	.6
Debt Securities	78bld	....	....	....	−17.7	−61.0	27.7	−8.1	−6.2	24.8	−9.3	1.9	2.6
Portfolio Investment Liab., n.i.e.	78bgd	....	....	....	3.2	41.8	−13.4	−5.2	50.1	−45.4	−6.7	5.3	56.5
Equity Securities	78bmd	....	....	....	....	....	2.7	....	.5	2.5	.7	3.3	.5
Debt Securities	78bnd	....	....	....	3.2	41.8	−16.1	−5.2	49.6	−47.9	−7.4	2.0	56.0
Financial Derivatives Assets	78bwd	....	....	....	....	....	....	....	....	....	....	....	....
Financial Derivatives Liabilities	78bxd	....	....	....	....	....	....	....	....	....	....	....	....
Other Investment Assets	78bhd	−118.1	−232.5	−155.4	−131.5	49.9	199.4	−36.7	41.7	−139.2	−309.4	−61.0	−145.6
Monetary Authorities	78bod	....	....	....	....	1.5	−.9	1.1	−.2	−99.3	−215.1	−10.0	231.5
General Government	78bpd	....	....	14.0	....	....	....	....	....	....	....	—	—
Banks	78bqd	−60.6	−94.2	58.6	−40.2	−12.6	19.0	−16.4	8.4	17.5	19.1	−61.1	−120.5
Other Sectors	78brd	−57.5	−138.3	−228.0	−91.3	61.0	181.3	−21.4	33.5	−57.4	−113.4	10.1	−256.6
Other Investment Liab., n.i.e.	78bid	394.6	366.6	344.7	420.2	358.5	−60.1	13.6	−64.6	328.6	347.7	116.5	790.3
Monetary Authorities	78bsd	—	−.3	3.7	133.1	−86.8	6.8	.7	−21.2	20.2	20.4	−135.3	−299.5
General Government	78btd	243.9	239.4	81.7	33.4	62.4	24.7	−28.5	−37.2	44.9	9.3	−43.2	122.1
Banks	78bud	−4.8	34.9	24.1	23.1	16.6	−20.3	−24.1	1.9	81.4	90.8	118.7	219.6
Other Sectors	78bvd	155.5	92.6	235.2	230.6	366.3	−71.3	65.5	−8.1	182.1	227.2	176.3	748.1
Net Errors and Omissions	78cad	3.4	−41.6	168.6	−178.1	53.0	172.3	−246.3	254.2	−5.4	−126.9	41.4	306.7
Overall Balance	78cbd	−137.5	−317.0	−78.4	−214.2	65.1	−319.3	19.9	125.3	−78.5	97.1	−81.4	185.1
Reserves and Related Items	79dad	137.5	317.0	78.4	214.2	−65.1	319.3	−19.9	−125.3	78.5	−97.1	81.4	−185.1
Reserve Assets	79dbd	12.5	−58.6	−283.7	−78.6	75.3	54.6	34.6	−75.7	5.2	−100.9	13.8	−255.8
Use of Fund Credit and Loans	79dcd	98.2	—	177.8	—	—	−24.4	−58.1	−55.8	−29.8	−30.2	−32.3	−17.3
Exceptional Financing	79ded	26.8	375.6	184.3	292.8	−140.4	289.1	3.6	6.2	103.1	33.9	99.8	88.0
International Investment Position					*Millions of US Dollars*								
Assets	79aad	....	....	....	1,335.4	1,273.7	991.3	1,008.5	1,015.2	1,171.2	1,561.7	1,683.8	2,117.1
Direct Investment Abroad	79abd	....	....	....	—	2.1	4.4	24.3	23.8	20.1	3.7	6.2	8.2
Portfolio Investment	79acd	....	....	....	21.5	83.1	55.1	54.2	57.5	31.6	16.3	16.3	13.7
Equity Securities	79add	....	....	....	2.3	2.9	2.6	9.8	9.3	8.3	.8	1.8	1.3
Debt Securities	79aed	....	....	....	19.2	80.2	52.5	44.4	48.2	23.3	15.5	14.5	12.4
Financial Derivatives	79ald	....	....	....	....	....	....	....	....	....	....	....	....
Other Investment	79afd	....	....	....	844.8	794.9	592.8	625.4	577.1	760.1	1,066.1	1,162.2	1,325.0
Monetary Authorities	79agd	....	....	....	9.0	7.5	8.4	7.4	2.2	148.4	361.0	401.1	181.6
General Government	79ahd	....	....	....	....	....	....	....	....	....	....	....	....
Banks	79aid	....	....	....	291.7	304.3	285.4	298.2	288.9	268.6	247.8	311.9	435.8
Other Sectors	79ajd	....	....	....	544.1	483.1	299.0	319.8	286.0	343.1	457.3	449.2	707.6
Reserve Assets	79akd	....	....	....	469.1	393.6	339.0	304.6	356.8	359.4	475.6	499.1	770.2
Liabilities	79lad	....	....	....	2,064.7	2,656.7	3,086.9	3,388.3	3,436.8	3,855.3	4,523.7	4,988.4	6,085.8
Dir. Invest. in Rep. Economy	79lbd	....	....	....	154.3	505.9	709.1	1,155.7	1,305.5	1,397.2	1,645.9	1,898.6	2,062.5
Portfolio Investment	79lcd	....	....	....	34.6	76.4	63.0	23.5	78.6	36.1	20.3	24.0	80.8
Equity Securities	79ldd	....	....	....	5.5	5.5	8.2	8.2	8.8	11.4	9.8	11.7	12.3
Debt Securities	79led	....	....	....	29.1	70.9	54.8	15.3	69.8	24.7	10.5	12.3	68.5
Financial Derivatives	79lld	....	....	....	....	....	....	....	....	....	....	....	....
Other Investment	79lfd	....	....	....	1,875.8	2,074.4	2,314.8	2,209.1	2,052.7	2,422.0	2,857.5	3,065.8	3,942.5
Monetary Authorities	79lgd	....	....	....	409.9	303.4	298.6	230.1	142.4	194.8	281.8	280.6	76.9
General Government	79lhd	....	....	....	639.5	683.0	386.3	375.9	346.0	353.3	361.7	340.9	433.6
Banks	79lid	....	....	....	142.8	159.4	139.1	112.4	114.1	188.1	273.4	395.6	616.1
Other Sectors	79ljd	....	....	....	683.6	928.6	1,490.8	1,490.7	1,450.2	1,685.8	1,940.6	2,048.7	2,815.9
Government Finance					*Billions of Rubels: Year Ending December 31*								
Deficit (-) or Surplus	80	−.04	−.33	−3.22	−3.46	−5.72	−5.99	−60.22	7.30	−235.68	....	....	....
Total Revenue and Grants	81y	.38	6.01	37.10	58.99	117.87	206.59	876.23	2,646.10	4,938.20	....	....	....
Revenue	81	.38	6.01	37.10	58.99	117.87	206.59	876.23	2,646.00	4,938.20	....	....	....
Grants	81z	—	—	—	—	—	—	—	.10	....	....	....	....
Exp. & Lending Minus Repay.	82z	.42	6.34	40.33	62.46	123.59	212.58	936.45	2,638.80	5,173.88	....	....	....
Expenditure	82	.42	6.34	40.33	62.51	121.79	213.22	933.87	2,639.80	5,080.21	....	....	....
Lending Minus Repayments	83	—	—	—	−.06	1.80	−.64	2.58	−1.00	93.67	....	....	....
Total Financing	80h	.04	.33	3.22	3.46	5.72	5.99	60.22	−7.30	235.68	....	....	....
Domestic	84a	—	−.13	2.79	3.69	4.11	7.97	84.65	42.90	−19.56	....	....	....
Foreign	85a	.04	.45	.43	−.22	1.61	−1.98	−24.43	−50.20	255.24	....	....	....
Total Debt by Residence	88	.05	13.51	20.49	22.10	44.65	141.70	....	....	....	....	....	....
Domestic	88a	.05	.51	3.04	7.42	14.63	33.56	....	....	....	....	....	....
Foreign	89a	—	13.01	17.46	14.68	30.02	108.14	....	....	....	....	....	....

Belarus 913

		1993	1994	1995	1996	1997	1998	1999	2000	2001	2002	2003	2004
National Accounts							*Billions of Rubels*							
Househ.Cons.Expend.,incl.NPISHs....	96f	.6	10.6	71.7	115.1	209.3	406.2	1,774.6	5,198.1	9,895.9	15,549.9	20,889.7	27,900.0
Government Consumption Expend...	91f	.2	3.6	24.9	39.4	74.5	139.5	590.2	1,779.1	3,701.3	5,496.7	7,817.3	9,986.2
Gross Fixed Capital Formation..........	93e	.3	5.9	30.0	40.4	92.6	182.1	796.7	2,301.9	3,893.0	5,746.4	9,288.5	13,259.5
Changes in Inventories....................	93i	.1	−.1	.1	4.7	5.9	5.5	−79.3	18.0	187.5	50.2	441.0	739.6
Exports of Goods and Services.........	90c	.7	12.7	60.3	88.9	219.6	414.6	1,791.5	6,321.6	11,462.7	16,631.2	23,824.3	33,859.7
Imports of Goods and Services (-).....	98c	.8	15.0	65.6	96.7	240.8	448.7	1,865.0	6,612.7	12,072.3	17,610.6	25,267.2	36,784.5
Statistical Discrepancy.....................	99bs	....	....	....	....	5.8	3.0	17.4	127.8	105.1	274.5	−428.8	484.7
Gross Domestic Product (GDP).........	99b	1.0	17.8	121.4	191.8	366.8	702.2	3,026.1	9,133.8	17,173.2	26,138.3	36,564.8	49,445.2
Net Primary Income from Abroad.....	98.n	—	—	−.1	.2	−.5	−.4	2.8	11.2	29.3	21.7	−73.2	....
Gross National Income (GNI)............	99a	1.0	17.8	121.4	192.0	366.3	701.8	3,028.9	9,145.0	17,202.5	26,160.0	36,491.6	....
Net Current Transf.from Abroad.......	98t	—	—	.8	1.2	2.1	4.5	31.2	118.1	217.9	309.9	403.7	....
Gross Nat'l Disposable Inc.(GNDI)....	99i	1.0	17.8	122.2	193.2	368.4	706.3	3,060.1	9,263.1	17,420.4	26,469.9	36,895.3	....
Gross Saving....................................	99s	.3	3.6	25.5	38.7	84.5	160.7	695.3	2,285.9	3,823.2	5,423.3	8,188.3	....
GDP Volume 1995 Ref., Chained.....	99b.p	153.5	135.6	121.4	124.8	139.0	150.7	155.8	164.8	....	....	....	....
GDP Volume 2000 Ref., Chained.....	99b.p	....	....	....	....	....	....	....	9,133.8	9,565.4	10,048.0	10,755.7	11,943.1
GDP Volume (2000=100)................	99bvp	93.1	82.2	73.7	75.7	84.4	91.4	94.5	† 100.0	104.7	110.0	117.8	130.8
GDP Deflator (2000=100)................	99bip	—	.2	1.8	2.8	4.8	8.4	35.1	100.0	179.5	260.1	340.0	414.0
							Millions: Midyear Estimates							
Population................................	99z	10.29	10.27	10.25	10.22	10.18	10.13	10.08	10.03	9.98	9.92	9.87	9.81

Belgium 124

		1993	1994	1995	1996	1997	1998	1999	2000	2001	2002	2003	2004
Exchange Rates		*Francs per SDR through 1998, Euros per SDR Thereafter: End of Period*											
Market Rate..........aa=......	aa	49.599	46.478	43.725	46.022	49.814	48.682	1.3662	1.4002	1.4260	1.2964	1.1765	1.1402
		Francs per US Dollar through 1998, Euros per US Dollar Thereafter: End of Period (we) Period Average (wf)											
Market Rate..........ae=......	ae	36.110	31.838	29.415	32.005	36.920	34.575	.9954	1.0747	1.1347	.9536	.7918	.7342
Market Rate..........rf=......	rf	34.597	33.456	29.480	30.962	35.774	36.299	.9386	1.0854	1.1175	1.0626	.8860	.8054
		Francs per ECU: End of Period (ea) Period Average (eb)											
ECU Rate..................	ea	40.287	39.161	38.698	40.102	40.771	40.340	....	....	....	....	....	....
ECU Rate..................	eb	40.466	39.662	38.537	39.290	40.529	40.623	....	....	....	....	....	....
		Index Numbers (2000=100): Period Averages											
Market Rate (1995=100)......	ahx	85.2	88.2	100.0	95.1	82.4	81.2	....	....	....	....	....	....
Nominal Effective Exchange Rate.....	neu	106.2	108.4	114.1	111.1	105.4	105.7	104.0	100.0	100.5	101.6	105.7	106.8
Real Effective Exchange Rate..........	reu	114.5	114.2	119.4	114.4	109.5	109.5	105.5	100.0	101.5	104.6	108.6	111.3
Fund Position		*Millions of SDRs: End of Period*											
Quota..................	2f.s	3,102	3,102	3,102	3,102	3,102	3,102	4,605	4,605	4,605	4,605	4,605	4,605
SDRs..................	1b.s	125	123	331	346	363	433	197	236	376	408	434	225
Reserve Position in the Fund..........	1c.s	560	556	676	747	876	1,348	1,668	1,304	1,632	1,759	1,812	1,479
of which: Outstg.Fund Borrowing...	2c	—	—	—	—	—	140	—	—	—	—	—	—
International Liquidity		*Millions of US Dollars Unless Otherwise Indicated: End of Period*											
Total Res.Min.Gold (Eurosys.Def)......	1l.d	11,415	13,876	16,177	16,953	16,190	18,272	† 10,938	9,994	11,266	11,855	10,989	10,361
SDRs..................	1b.d	171	180	492	498	489	610	271	307	472	554	645	350
Reserve Position in the Fund..........	1c.d	769	812	1,005	1,075	1,182	1,899	2,290	1,699	2,051	2,392	2,693	2,296
Foreign Exchange..........	1d.d	10,474	12,884	14,680	15,380	14,519	15,763	† 8,377	7,988	8,743	8,909	7,651	7,715
o/w:Fin.Deriv.Rel.to Reserves.......	1ddd	....	....	....	....	....	....	—	—	—	—		119.86
Other Reserve Assets.......	1e.d	....	....	....	....	....	....	....					
Gold (Million Fine Troy Ounces)........	1ad	25.04	25.04	20.54	15.32	15.32	9.52	8.30	8.30	8.30	8.29	8.29	8.29
Gold (Eurosystem Valuation)............	1and	9,955	8,482	7,306	6,171	5,140	2,565	2,408	2,277	2,294	2,843	3,459	3,630
Memo:Euro Cl. on Non-EA Res........	1dgd	....	....	....	....	....	....	257	....	....	....	....	....
Non-Euro Cl. on EA Res.......	1dhd	....	....	....	....	....	....	139	427	704	313	405	569
Mon. Auth.: Other Foreign Assets....	3..d	140	115	113	100	91	97	† —	—	—	—		
Foreign Liabilities..................	4..d	341	477	629	144	81	382	† 7,341	1,081	1,719	1,141	1,646	1,957
Banking Insts.: Foreign Assets..........	7a.d	211,230	238,602	273,058	267,758	262,470	....	† 112,048	108,165	126,964	164,254	194,310	236,399
Foreign Liab..........	7b.d	228,782	263,337	302,856	293,657	280,033	....	† 181,820	163,882	176,325	199,014	236,307	274,681
Monetary Authorities		*Billions of Francs through 1998; Millions of Euros Beginning 1999: End of Period*											
Fgn. Assets (Cl.on Non-EA Ctys)......	11	764.7	729.1	692.6	741.4	793.7	712.1	13,303	12,737	15,024	13,675	11,321	10,531
Claims on General Government........	12a.u	....	....	....	....	....	....	3,683	3,630	3,668	2,937	2,960	3,448
o/w: Claims on Gen.Govt.in Cty....	12a	90.3	79.3	86.3	91.0	94.1	47.0	1,123	1,220	1,158	805	666	681
Claims on Banking Institutions..........	12e.u	....	....	....	....	....	....	25,795	17,312	9,699	18,118	30,707	42,768
o/w: Claims on Bank.Inst.in Cty....	12e	155.4	128.3	151.3	151.4	150.5	185.0	20,457	15,481	7,672	10,953	16,891	22,775
Claims on Other Resident Sectors.....	12d.u	....	....	....	....	....	....	92	24	59	45	18	22
o/w: Cl. on Oth.Res.Sect.in Cty....	12d	....	....	....	....	....	....	3	3	2	2	2	2
Currency Issued..................	14a	459.3	431.4	465.9	486.2	501.1	505.8	13,535	13,496	9,081	12,715	14,877	17,223
Liabilities to Banking Insts..........	14c.u	....	....	....	....	....	....	17,500	13,675	11,116	17,401	26,226	35,480
o/w: Liabs to Bank.Inst.in Cty......	14c	5.5	2.3	7.6	4.7	1.2	279.0	3,509	7,130	5,945	4,482	8,325	5,416
Demand Dep. of Other Res.Sect......	14d.u	....	....	....	....	....	....	19	12	7	6	9	6
o/w:D.Dep.of Oth.Res.Sect.in Cty...	14d	....	....	....	....	....	....	19	12	7	6	8	5
Other Dep. of Other Res.Sect.......	15..u	....	....	....	....	....	....	—	—	—	—		
o/w:O.Dep.of Oth.Res.Sect.in Cty...	15	....	....	....	....	....	....						
Bonds & Money Mkt. Instruments....	16n.u	....	....	....	....	....	....						
o/w: Bonds Held by Resid.of Cty....	16n	—	—	—	230.0	230.0	—	....	....	....	....	....	....
Foreign Liab. (to Non-EA Ctys).........	16c	12.3	15.2	18.5	4.6	3.0	13.2	7,307	1,162	1,950	1,088	1,303	1,437
Central Government Deposits..........	16d.u	....	....	....	....	....	....	64	62	118	115	152	135
o/w: Cent.Govt.Dep. in Cty..........	16d	1.3	1.0	.5	.7	.1	.4	64	62	118	115	152	135
Capital Accounts..................	17a	43.6	46.5	48.6	50.6	53.1	53.6	5,369	5,816	6,108	4,724	4,265	4,238
Other Items (Net)..................	17r	488.5	440.2	389.1	206.9	249.8	92.3	−921	−520	72	−1,272	−1,824	−1,750
Memo: Net Claims on Eurosystem....	12e.s	....	....	....	....	....	....	−8,690	−5,103	−3,736	−6,655	−5,325	−11,469
Currency Put into Circ..............	14m	....	....	....	....	....	....					7,887	3,807	126
Banking Institutions		*Billions of Francs through 1998; Millions of Euros Beginning 1999: End of Period*											
Claims on Monetary Authorities.......	20	34.3	35.1	37.9	245.8	228.6	....	3,509	7,130	5,945	4,482	8,325	5,416
Claims on Bk.Inst.in Oth.EA Ctys.......	20b.u	....	....	....	....	....	....	97,105	91,411	90,488	105,573	147,544	172,802
Fgn. Assets (Cl.on Non-EA Ctys).......	21	7,627.5	7,596.5	8,032.0	8,569.6	9,690.4	....	111,535	116,244	144,064	156,626	153,848	173,555
Claims on General Government........	22a.u	....	....	....	....	....	....	175,991	160,255	180,779	166,928	172,616	178,590
o/w: Claims on Gen.Govt.in Cty......	22a	5,528.2	6,101.4	6,215.7	6,296.0	6,236.2	....	134,534	119,713	111,147	102,045	96,484	90,556
Claims on Other Resident Sectors.....	22d.u	....	....	....	....	....	....	218,724	225,662	230,712	234,954	241,277	250,701
o/w: Cl. on Oth.Res.Sect.in Cty......	22d	5,794.3	5,979.9	6,099.0	6,402.6	6,749.2	....	192,349	196,554	197,316	198,894	203,825	207,363
Demand Deposits..................	24..u	....	....	....	....	....	....	53,554	58,499	61,397	62,067	67,348	78,158
o/w:D.Dep.of Oth.Res.Sect.in Cty...	24	1,060.6	1,111.3	1,152.7	1,200.0	1,237.0	....	50,428	53,682	56,546	57,877	62,071	72,713
Other Deposits..................	25..u	....	....	....	....	....	....	188,347	182,139	199,536	212,803	230,923	251,408
o/w:O.Dep.of Oth.Res.Sect.in Cty...	25	4,560.7	4,706.0	4,936.3	5,490.4	5,915.4	....	157,750	154,139	167,216	176,584	193,039	208,015
Money Market Fund Shares.........	26m.u	....	....	....	....	....	....	1,029	804	1,191	1,609	1,815	1,994
Bonds & Money Mkt. Instruments....	26n.u	....	....	....	....	....	....	80,682	85,516	79,747	75,651	66,741	61,256
o/w: Held by Resid.of Cty..............	26n	3,583.8	3,703.8	3,691.3	3,593.6	3,291.5	....	....	....	....	....	....	....
Foreign Liab. (to Non-EA Ctys).........	26c	8,261.3	8,384.0	8,908.5	9,398.5	10,338.8	....	180,987	176,122	200,074	189,772	187,100	201,660
Central Government Deposits..........	26d.u	....	....	....	....	....	....	1,222	763	1,109	917	2,896	1,435
o/w: Cent.Govt.Dep. in Cty..........	26d	270.3	217.0	78.8	60.6	245.6	....	863	586	868	789	2,778	878
Credit from Monetary Authorities.....	26g	139.0	123.8	106.7	121.7	75.5	....	20,457	15,481	7,672	10,953	16,891	22,775
Liab. to Bk.Inst.in Oth. EA Ctys........	26h.u	....	....	....	....	....	....	58,685	56,463	73,442	77,142	108,304	126,843
Capital Accounts..................	27a	787.6	856.8	894.7	1,621.1	2,077.7	....	29,525	32,448	34,027	36,300	35,470	35,414
Other Items (Net)..................	27r	321.3	609.7	615.3	27.9	−277.3	....	−7,627	−7,532	−6,209	1,346	6,123	122

Belgium 124

		1993	1994	1995	1996	1997	1998	1999	2000	2001	2002	2003	2004
Banking Survey (Nat'l Residency)		*Billions of Francs through 1998; Millions of Euros Beginning 1999: End of Period*											
Foreign Assets (Net)	31n	118.6	−73.6	−202.4	−92.1	142.3	....	10,450	29,696	49,596	74,985	94,445	111,777
Domestic Credit	32	11,141.2	11,942.6	12,321.7	12,728.3	12,833.8	....	327,082	316,842	308,637	300,842	298,047	297,589
Claims on General Govt. (Net)	32an	5,346.9	5,962.7	6,222.7	6,325.7	6,084.6	....	134,730	120,285	111,319	101,946	94,220	90,224
Claims on Other Resident Sectors	32d	5,794.3	5,979.9	6,099.0	6,402.6	6,749.2	....	192,352	196,557	197,318	198,896	203,827	207,365
Currency Issued	34a.n	459.3	431.4	465.9	486.2	501.1	505.8	13,535	13,496	9,081	12,715	14,877	17,223
Demand Deposits	34b.n	1,060.6	1,111.3	1,152.7	1,200.0	1,237.0	....	50,447	53,694	56,553	57,883	62,079	72,718
Other Deposits	35..n	4,560.7	4,706.0	4,936.3	5,490.4	5,915.4	....	157,750	154,139	167,216	176,584	193,039	208,015
Money Market Fund Shares	36m	....	....	....	....	....	....	1,029	804	1,191	1,609	1,815	1,994
Bonds & Money Mkt. Instruments	36n	3,583.8	3,703.8	3,691.3	3,823.6	3,521.5	....	80,682	85,516	79,747	75,651	66,741	61,256
o/w: Over Two Years	36na	....	....	....	....	....	....	66,704	66,949	64,789	62,698	55,598	50,590
Capital Accounts	37a	831.2	903.3	943.3	1,671.7	2,130.8	....	34,894	38,264	40,135	41,024	39,735	39,652
Other Items (Net)	37r	764.6	1,012.6	929.5	−36.0	−329.9	....	−808	626	4,310	10,360	14,209	8,509
Banking Survey (EA-Wide Residency)		*Millions of Euros: End of Period*											
Foreign Assets (Net)	31n.u	....	....	....	....	....	....	−63,456	−48,303	−42,936	−20,559	−23,234	−19,011
Domestic Credit	32..u	....	....	....	....	....	....	397,204	388,746	413,991	403,832	413,823	431,191
Claims on General Govt. (Net)	32anu	....	....	....	....	....	....	178,388	163,060	183,220	168,833	172,528	180,468
Claims on Other Resident Sect.	32d.u	....	....	....	....	....	....	218,816	225,686	230,771	234,999	241,295	250,723
Currency Issued	34a.u	....	....	....	....	....	....	13,535	13,496	9,081	12,715	14,877	17,223
Demand Deposits	34b.u	....	....	....	....	....	....	53,573	58,511	61,404	62,073	67,357	78,164
Other Deposits	35..u	....	....	....	....	....	....	188,347	182,139	199,536	212,803	230,923	251,408
o/w: Other Dep. Over Two Yrs.	35abu	....	....	....	....	....	....	19,642	21,591	23,859	24,343	27,347	30,242
Money Market Fund Shares	36m.u	....	....	....	....	....	....	1,029	804	1,191	1,609	1,815	1,994
Bonds & Money Mkt. Instruments	36n.u	....	....	....	....	....	....	80,682	85,516	79,747	75,651	66,741	61,256
o/w: Over Two Years	36nau	....	....	....	....	....	....	66,704	66,949	64,789	62,698	55,598	50,590
Capital Accounts	37a	....	....	....	....	....	....	34,894	38,264	40,135	41,024	39,735	39,652
Other Items (Net)	37r.u	....	....	....	....	....	....	−38,315	−38,286	−20,039	−22,603	−30,856	−37,516
Interest Rates		*Percent Per Annum*											
Discount Rate (End of Period)	60	5.25	4.50	3.00	2.50	2.75	2.75	....	....	....	....	....	....
Money Market Rate	60b	8.21	5.72	4.80	3.24	3.46	3.58	....	....	....	....	....	....
Treasury Bill Rate	60c	8.52	5.57	4.67	3.19	3.38	3.51	2.72	4.02	4.16	3.17	2.23	1.97
Deposit Rate	60l	† 7.11	4.86	4.04	2.66	2.88	3.01	2.42	3.58	3.40	2.60	1.65	....
Deposit Rate (Households)	60lhs	....	....	....	....	....	....	....	....	....	....	2.63	2.39
Deposit Rate (Corporations)	60lcs	....	....	....	....	....	....	....	....	....	....	2.36	2.12
Lending Rate	60p	11.81	9.42	8.42	7.17	7.06	7.25	6.71	7.98	8.46	7.71	6.89	6.70
Lending Rate (Households)	60phm	....	....	....	....	....	....	....	....	....	....	5.54	5.19
Lending Rate (Corporations)	60pcs	....	....	....	....	....	....	....	....	....	....	4.32	4.11
Government Bond Yield	61	7.19	7.82	7.45	6.45	5.74	4.72	4.81	5.58	5.13	4.96	4.18	4.15
Prices, Production, Labor		*Index Numbers (2000=100): Period Averages*											
Industrial Share Prices	62	93	106	100	....	....	....	....	....	....	....	....	....
Producer Prices													
Home and Import Goods	63	82.9	84.2	† 87.0	88.9	92.2	90.4	90.4	100.0	102.0	101.2	100.8	104.9
Industrial Production Prices	63b	88.1	89.3	† 91.4	91.9	93.4	92.3	91.9	100.0	100.8	102.2	102.9	107.4
Consumer Prices	64	88.7	90.8	92.1	† 94.0	95.5	96.4	97.5	100.0	102.5	104.2	105.8	108.0
Harmonized CPI	64h	....	....	92.4	94.0	95.4	96.3	97.4	100.0	102.4	104.0	105.6	107.6
Wages	65	85.4	87.5	89.3	91.1	93.0	95.3	97.9	100.0	102.8	105.4	107.4	109.8
Industrial Production	66	80.1	81.8	86.5	87.0	91.0	94.1	94.9	100.0	99.0	100.3	101.0	104.3
		Number in Thousands: Period Averages											
Labor Force	67d	....	4,160	4,185	4,196	4,214	4,241	4,382	4,401	....	4,402	4,070	....
Employment	67e	3,746	3,755	3,794	3,792	3,839	3,858	† 4,007	4,092	4,051	4,070	4,070	....
Unemployment	67c	550	589	597	588	570	541	508	474	470	....	538	577
Unemployment Rate (%)	67r	12.9	13.9	14.1	13.8	13.3	12.6	11.7	10.9	10.8	....	12.3	12.8
Intl. Transactions & Positions													
(BLEU: Country Code (126))		*Billions of Francs*											
Exports	70	4,129.0	4,579.0	4,996.1	5,133.1	5,916.2	....	....	....	....	....	....	....
Imports, c.i.f.	71	3,875.0	4,192.0	4,568.4	4,729.1	5,554.4	....	....	....	....	....	....	....
		1995=100											
Volume of Exports	72	† 83.8	92.6	100.0	102.5	109.7	....	....	....	....	....	....	....
Volume of Imports	73	† 82.6	94.8	100.0	106.2	110.5	....	....	....	....	....	....	....
Unit Value of Exports	74	† 100.6	100.0	100.0	102.0	106.4	....	....	....	....	....	....	....
Unit Value of Imports	75	† 98.5	98.0	100.0	101.9	107.3	....	....	....	....	....	....	....
(For Belgium Only)		*Billions of Francs through 1998; Billions of Euros Beginning 1999*											
Exports	70	4,349.1	4,792.7	5,177.8	5,430.2	6,142.9	6,491.3	† 168.10	203.94	212.55	228.58	225.88	246.43
Imports, c.i.f.	71	3,953.5	4,339.7	4,702.0	5,065.8	5,619.2	5,967.9	† 154.62	192.18	199.49	209.73	207.56	229.49
		2000=100											
Volume of Exports	72	64.2	69.9	74.3	75.9	81.5	86.3	90.6	100.0	102.0	110.7	112.8	120.9
Volume of Imports	73	65.9	71.0	74.6	77.5	81.0	87.7	90.5	100.0	101.5	109.2	110.7	118.3
Unit Value of Exports	74	82.3	83.3	84.8	87.0	91.6	91.5	91.0	100.0	102.2	101.3	98.3	100.3
Unit Value of Imports	75	77.4	78.9	81.3	84.3	89.5	87.8	88.9	100.0	102.4	100.0	97.8	101.1

Balance of Payments
(For Belgium-Luxembourg (126))

Millions of US Dollars: Minus Sign Indicates Debit

		1993	1994	1995	1996	1997	1998	1999	2000	2001	2002	2003	2004
Current Account, n.i.e.	78ald	11,237	12,571	14,232	13,762	13,914	12,168	14,086	11,381	9,392	....	....	....
Goods: Exports f.o.b.	78aad	106,302	122,795	155,219	154,695	149,497	153,558	161,263	164,677	163,498	....	....	....
Goods: Imports f.o.b.	78abd	-100,522	-115,895	-145,664	-146,004	-141,794	-146,577	-154,237	-162,086	-159,790	....	....	....
Trade Balance	78acd	5,780	6,901	9,555	8,690	7,703	6,981	7,027	2,591	3,707	....	....	....
Services: Credit	78add	33,366	40,440	35,466	34,702	35,503	38,081	45,291	49,789	50,314	....	....	....
Services: Debit	78aed	-29,995	-36,500	-33,134	-32,069	-31,664	-34,411	-39,167	-41,868	-43,316	....	....	....
Balance on Goods & Services	78afd	9,151	10,841	11,887	11,322	11,542	10,651	13,151	10,512	10,705	....	....	....
Income: Credit	78agd	83,011	89,403	74,798	62,884	58,237	65,251	71,892	75,673	78,906	....	....	....
Income: Debit	78ahd	-78,138	-84,166	-67,990	-55,838	-51,882	-59,315	-66,125	-70,625	-75,999	....	....	....
Balance on Gds, Serv. & Inc.	78aid	14,024	16,078	18,695	18,368	17,896	16,588	18,918	15,560	13,612	....	....	....
Current Transfers, n.i.e.: Credit	78ajd	4,198	4,501	7,822	7,474	7,142	7,006	7,041	7,014	7,316	....	....	....
Current Transfers: Debit	78akd	-6,986	-8,009	-12,285	-12,081	-11,124	-11,426	-11,872	-11,193	-11,535	....	....	....
Capital Account, n.i.e.	78bcd	—	....	378	179	403	-113	-54	-213	26	....	....	....
Capital Account, n.i.e.: Credit	78bad	—	....	734	673	783	323	449	222	480	....	....	....
Capital Account: Debit	78bbd	—	....	-356	-494	-379	-436	-503	-436	-454	....	....	....
Financial Account, n.i.e.	78bjd	-13,563	-10,182	-12,912	-12,257	-12,091	-16,043	-13,470	-9,233	-7,978	....	....	....
Direct Investment Abroad	78bdd	-4,904	-1,371	-11,603	-8,026	-7,252	-28,845	-130,012	-207,472	-86,091	....	....	....
Dir. Invest. in Rep. Econ., n.i.e.	78bed	10,750	8,514	10,689	14,064	11,998	22,690	142,703	214,941	73,635	....	....	....
Portfolio Investment Assets	78bfd	-58,431	-40,963	-29,472	-48,409	-62,657	-100,234	-161,521	-122,814	-125,068	....	....	....
Equity Securities	78bkd	-9,465	-10,649	-3,525	-3,582	-21,006	-29,087	-60,678	-103,290	-57,427	....	....	....
Debt Securities	78bld	-48,966	-30,314	-25,946	-44,827	-41,651	-71,147	-100,842	-19,524	-67,642	....	....	....
Portfolio Investment Liab., n.i.e.	78bgd	50,472	17,445	4,649	36,666	54,047	59,253	135,837	132,547	140,588	....	....	....
Equity Securities	78bmd	46,838	22,489	6,505	34,243	47,207	58,418	92,372	82,908	97,662	....	....	....
Debt Securities	78bnd	3,634	-5,043	-1,856	2,423	6,840	835	43,466	49,639	42,926	....	....	....
Financial Derivatives Assets	78bwd	—	....	1,213	-970	-330	489	884	-3,653	-5,089	....	....	....
Financial Derivatives Liabilities	78bxd	—	....	630	483	444	302	1,142	1,252	942	....	....	....
Other Investment Assets	78bhd	-51,772	11,269	-23,445	-14,977	-48,692	7,467	-58,713	-39,033	-70,053	....	....	....
Monetary Authorities	78bod	—	....	—	—	—	-147	-991	-342	13	....	....	....
General Government	78bpd	-802	-294	-72	-372	-306	371	-1,848	-236	-137	....	....	....
Banks	78bqd	-45,916	9,829	-16,926	9,164	-28,220	3,886	-12,806	-22,296	-58,086	....	....	....
Other Sectors	78brd	-5,054	1,734	-6,447	-23,769	-20,166	3,357	-43,067	-16,159	-11,843	....	....	....
Other Investment Liab., n.i.e.	78bid	40,321	-5,076	34,426	8,913	40,352	22,836	56,210	14,999	63,158	....	....	....
Monetary Authorities	78bsd	—	—	223	-458	-50	193	23,578	-1,386	-3,903	....	....	....
General Government	78btd	10,758	-5,233	322	-40	-161	203	1,405	-1,279	415	....	....	....
Banks	78bud	19,043	64	42,121	6,469	31,211	18,087	6,702	7,139	67,159	....	....	....
Other Sectors	78bvd	10,520	93	-8,240	2,941	9,352	4,352	24,525	10,524	-513	....	....	....
Net Errors and Omissions	78cad	204	-2,169	-1,456	-1,091	-1,171	1,893	-2,430	-2,894	3	....	....	....
Overall Balance	78cbd	-2,122	219	243	593	1,056	-2,095	-1,867	-959	1,442	....	....	....
Reserves and Related Items	79dad	2,122	-219	-243	-593	-1,056	2,095	1,867	959	-1,442	....	....	....
Reserve Assets	79dbd	2,122	-219	-243	-593	-1,056	2,095	1,867	959	-1,442	....	....	....
Use of Fund Credit and Loans	79dcd	—	—	—	—	—	—	—	—	—	....	....	....
Exceptional Financing	79ded	—	....	....	....	....	....	....	....	....	....	....	....

Balance of Payments
(For Belgium Only)

Millions of US Dollars: Minus Sign Indicates Debit

		1993	1994	1995	1996	1997	1998	1999	2000	2001	2002	2003	2004
Current Account, n.i.e.	78ald	....	....	....	....	....	....	....	....	....	14,025	13,780	14,011
Goods: Exports f.o.b.	78aad	....	....	....	....	....	....	....	....	....	168,194	203,851	245,468
Goods: Imports f.o.b.	78abd	....	....	....	....	....	....	....	....	....	-159,460	-193,616	-235,728
Trade Balance	78acd	....	....	....	....	....	....	....	....	....	8,733	10,234	9,740
Services: Credit	78add	....	....	....	....	....	....	....	....	....	37,858	44,970	52,303
Services: Debit	78aed	....	....	....	....	....	....	....	....	....	-35,820	-43,010	-49,001
Balance on Goods & Services	78afd	....	....	....	....	....	....	....	....	....	10,772	12,195	13,041
Income: Credit	78agd	....	....	....	....	....	....	....	....	....	37,183	38,488	43,147
Income: Debit	78ahd	....	....	....	....	....	....	....	....	....	-29,622	-30,604	-35,534
Balance on Gds, Serv. & Inc.	78aid	....	....	....	....	....	....	....	....	....	18,333	20,078	20,655
Current Transfers, n.i.e.: Credit	78ajd	....	....	....	....	....	....	....	....	....	5,297	6,483	7,585
Current Transfers: Debit	78akd	....	....	....	....	....	....	....	....	....	-9,605	-12,781	-14,229
Capital Account, n.i.e.	78bcd	....	....	....	....	....	....	....	....	....	-658	-969	-484
Capital Account, n.i.e.: Credit	78bad	....	....	....	....	....	....	....	....	....	201	254	385
Capital Account: Debit	78bbd	....	....	....	....	....	....	....	....	....	-859	-1,224	-869
Financial Account, n.i.e.	78bjd	....	....	....	....	....	....	....	....	....	-8,958	1,018	-1,613
Direct Investment Abroad	78bdd	....	....	....	....	....	....	....	....	....	-8,279	-23,186	-11,727
Dir. Invest. in Rep. Econ., n.i.e.	78bed	....	....	....	....	....	....	....	....	....	16,421	33,156	36,688
Portfolio Investment Assets	78bfd	....	....	....	....	....	....	....	....	....	-5,695	-6,039	-35,555
Equity Securities	78bkd	....	....	....	....	....	....	....	....	....	-3,539	-5,502	-8,168
Debt Securities	78bld	....	....	....	....	....	....	....	....	....	-2,156	-537	-27,386
Portfolio Investment Liab., n.i.e.	78bgd	....	....	....	....	....	....	....	....	....	19,680	5,805	1,918
Equity Securities	78bmd	....	....	....	....	....	....	....	....	....	-460	3,182	4,111
Debt Securities	78bnd	....	....	....	....	....	....	....	....	....	20,141	2,624	-2,192
Financial Derivatives Assets	78bwd	....	....	....	....	....	....	....	....	....	-3,862	-7,206	-11,138
Financial Derivatives Liabilities	78bxd	....	....	....	....	....	....	....	....	....	1,917	3,570	3,063
Other Investment Assets	78bhd	....	....	....	....	....	....	....	....	....	-44,549	-76,762	-65,670
Monetary Authorities	78bod	....	....	....	....	....	....	....	....	....	186	-107	-853
General Government	78bpd	....	....	....	....	....	....	....	....	....	—	879	-421
Banks	78bqd	....	....	....	....	....	....	....	....	....	-40,292	-69,464	-64,840
Other Sectors	78brd	....	....	....	....	....	....	....	....	....	-4,442	-8,070	1,556
Other Investment Liab., n.i.e.	78bid	....	....	....	....	....	....	....	....	....	15,409	71,679	80,807
Monetary Authorities	78bsd	....	....	....	....	....	....	....	....	....	6,695	6,663	15,366
General Government	78btd	....	....	....	....	....	....	....	....	....	-1,200	-628	-771
Banks	78bud	....	....	....	....	....	....	....	....	....	6,681	57,497	57,694
Other Sectors	78bvd	....	....	....	....	....	....	....	....	....	3,233	8,147	8,520
Net Errors and Omissions	78cad	....	....	....	....	....	....	....	....	....	-4,444	-15,554	-12,888
Overall Balance	78cbd	....	....	....	....	....	....	....	....	....	-35	-1,725	-974
Reserves and Related Items	79dad	....	....	....	....	....	....	....	....	....	35	1,725	974

Belgium 124

		1993	1994	1995	1996	1997	1998	1999	2000	2001	2002	2003	2004
Balance of Payments(Cont.)													
Reserve Assets	79dbd	....	....	....	....	....	....	....	....	....	35	1,725	974
Use of Fund Credit and Loans	79dcd	....	....	....	....	....	....	....	....	....	—	—	—
Exceptional Financing	79ded	....	....	....	....	....	....	....	....	....	....	....	....
International Investment Position							*Millions of US Dollars*						
(For Belgium Only)													
Assets	79aad	469,094	533,478	602,052	609,439	608,200	702,972	762,666	757,673	771,750	919,531	1,234,114	....
Direct Investment Abroad	79abd	62,642	69,541	80,690	87,311	94,734	134,982	151,795	179,773	181,459	223,940	325,370	....
Portfolio Investment	79acd	145,694	161,256	190,573	194,879	199,743	250,060	312,632	297,202	320,225	351,786	421,822	....
Equity Securities	79add	59,319	59,804	63,767	64,571	64,661	94,142	125,274	124,687	110,226	104,971	139,191	....
Debt Securities	79aed	86,375	101,453	126,806	130,308	135,081	155,918	187,358	172,515	209,999	246,816	282,630	....
Financial Derivatives	79ald	—	—	653	1,362	1,869	2,383	3,516	4,187	6,564	476	611	....
Other Investment	79afd	238,244	279,199	306,655	302,837	290,473	295,043	281,414	264,269	249,933	328,630	471,862	....
Monetary Authorities	79agd	775	597	1,625	1,028	141	416	1,708	1,861	1,756	1,905	2,407	....
General Government	79ahd	2,049	1,947	7,952	7,277	6,333	6,375	5,425	5,025	4,815	405	834	....
Banks	79aid	178,926	203,816	219,643	207,834	199,252	197,284	183,264	162,845	172,133	256,278	365,852	....
Other Sectors	79ajd	56,494	72,839	77,435	86,698	84,748	90,968	91,017	94,539	71,228	70,042	102,769	....
Reserve Assets	79akd	22,514	23,482	23,482	23,050	21,382	20,503	13,310	12,242	13,569	14,698	14,449	....
Liabilities	79lad	437,690	495,611	554,101	542,475	528,266	604,018	617,628	615,340	653,214	815,099	1,106,649	....
Dir. Invest. in Rep. Economy	79lbd	94,295	105,881	112,960	123,883	128,728	180,492	179,924	195,219	203,537	255,745	358,538	....
Portfolio Investment	79lcd	93,603	103,808	106,724	97,497	89,423	91,255	112,113	126,455	127,152	167,594	214,468	....
Equity Securities	79ldd	8,253	9,737	10,012	11,173	12,099	17,843	15,471	14,237	15,663	18,060	26,369	....
Debt Securities	79led	85,350	94,071	96,713	86,324	77,324	73,412	96,643	112,218	111,489	149,534	188,099	....
Financial Derivatives	79lld	—	—	568	940	1,268	1,909	3,516	4,746	4,421	—	—	....
Other Investment	79lfd	249,792	285,921	333,849	320,154	308,847	330,362	322,075	288,920	318,103	391,760	533,644	....
Monetary Authorities	79lgd	665	848	1,132	522	452	847	17,279	7,165	6,274	14,649	24,266	....
General Government	79lhd	305	942	864	694	385	411	1,808	651	888	4,394	4,784	....
Banks	79lid	219,247	251,590	310,283	296,380	284,299	297,515	272,146	245,931	276,091	343,375	457,619	....
Other Sectors	79ljd	29,576	32,540	21,571	22,559	23,711	31,589	30,841	35,173	34,850	29,342	46,975	....
Government Finance													
Central Government				*Billions of Francs through 1998; Millions of Euros Beginning 1999: Year Ending December 31*									
Deficit (-) or Surplus	80	−450.2	−324.9	−259.1	†−210.2	−165.1	−162.1	†−3,644.0	−550.4	−1,856.9	−1,778.4	−728.4	−6,174.2
Revenue	81	3,263.4	3,476.4	3,567.5	†3,685.2	3,820.1	3,986.1	†39,405.1	42,181.4	42,278.1	45,189.6	50,387.4	47,914.0
Grants Received	81z	4.6	5.7	11.1	†5.0	20.3	6.8	....	....	....	....	....	....
Expenditure	82	3,699.5	3,821.3	3,885.6	†3,909.5	4,032.3	4,152.3	†43,049.1	42,731.8	44,135.0	46,968.0	51,115.8	54,088.2
Lending Minus Repayments	83	18.7	−14.3	−47.9	†−9.1	−26.8	2.7	....	....	....	....	....	....
Financing													
Net Borrowing: National Currency	84a	112.3	360.1	380.1	†612.9	104.7	273.1	†7,990.6	2,283.1	3,763.1	4,767.8	3,556.7	7,297.1
Net borrowing: Foreign Currency	85a	454.9	−152.4	−262.0	†−334.1	−1.0	−79.6	†−4,345.7	−1,727.9	−1,911.2	−2,989.8	−2,828.4	−1,122.9
Use of Cash Balances	87	−117.0	117.2	141.0	†−68.6	61.4	−31.4	....	....	....	....	....	....
Debt: National Currency	88a	8,075.9	8,623.7	9,063.4	†9,576.7	9,702.8	9,717.7	†236,314.4	242,454.7	250,084.9	257,288.0	259,294.0	263.1
Debt: Foreign Currency	89a	1,519.9	1,349.5	1,085.3	†734.0	784.4	701.7	†10,441.3	8,606.9	7,079.8	5,464.0	3,724.0	....
General Government						*As Percent of Gross Domestic Product*							
Deficit (-) or Surplus	80g	−7.1	−4.9	−4.0	−3.7	−1.9	−.8	−.6	.1	.2	....	....	....
Debt	88g	135.2	133.2	132.2	128.3	125.3	119.3	115.0	109.3	107.5	....	....	....
National Accounts				*Billions of Francs through 1998; Billions of Euros Beginning 1999*									
Househ.Cons.Expend.,incl.NPISHs	96f	4,093	4,286	4,421	4,565	4,741	4,935	†127	134	139	142	147	153
Government Consumption Expend	91f	1,597	1,668	1,745	1,809	1,857	1,917	†50	52	55	58	61	64
Gross Fixed Capital Formation	93e	1,491	1,533	1,621	1,660	1,789	1,874	†49	53	53	51	51	52
Changes in Inventories	93i	19	64	17	−27	−13	−28	†−1	1	−1	−1	—	6
Exports of Goods and Services	90c	4,813	5,282	5,632	5,896	6,545	6,850	†178	212	218	219	220	237
Imports of Goods and Services (-)	98c	4,548	4,965	5,282	5,556	6,159	6,463	†168	204	209	207	210	229
Gross Domestic Product (GDP)	99b	7,466	7,868	8,154	8,348	8,760	9,086	†236	248	254	261	270	284
Net Primary Income from Abroad	98.n	114	182	168	166	173	194	†5	5	5	6	5	4
Gross National Income (GNI)	99a	7,580	8,050	8,322	8,514	8,933	9,280	†241	253	259	267	275	287
Net Current Transf.from Abroad	98t	−51	−61	−56	−83	−83	−95	†−2	−2	−2	−3	−2	....
Gross Nat'l Disposable Inc.(GNDI)	99i	7,529	7,989	8,268	8,434	8,852	9,185	†238	250	257	265	272	....
Gross Saving	99s	1,838	2,035	2,101	2,057	2,252	2,331	†61	64	63	65	65	....
Consumption of Fixed Capital	99cf	1,053	1,108	1,178	1,242	1,299	1,362	†36	38	40	41	43	45
GDP Volume 1995 Prices	99b.p	7,724	7,980	8,162	8,231	8,551	8,728	†222.8					
GDP Volume 2000 Prices	99b.p	....	....	....	....	....	....	†238.9	247.6	249.8	252.0	255.2	262.2
GDP Volume (2000=100)	99bvp	77.3	79.9	81.7	82.4	85.6	87.4	†96.5	100.0	100.9	101.8	103.1	105.9
GDP Deflator (2000=100)	99bip	96.5	98.5	99.8	101.3	102.3	104.0	†98.6	100.0	101.6	103.5	105.5	108.1
							Millions: Midyear Estimates						
Population	99z	10.07	10.10	10.14	10.17	10.21	10.24	10.27	10.30	10.33	10.36	10.38	10.40

		1993	1994	1995	1996	1997	1998	1999	2000	2001	2002	2003	2004
Exchange Rates		*Belize Dollars per SDR: End of Period (aa) Belize Dollars per US Dollar: End of Period (ae)*											
Official Rate...............	aa	2.7471	2.9197	2.9730	2.8759	2.6985	2.8161	2.7450	2.6058	2.5135	2.7190	2.9719	3.1060
Official Rate...............	ae	2.0000	2.0000	2.0000	2.0000	2.0000	2.0000	2.0000	2.0000	2.0000	2.0000	2.0000	2.0000
		Index Numbers (2000=100): Period Averages											
Official Rate...............	ahx	100.0	100.0	100.0	100.0	100.0	100.0	100.0	100.0	100.0	100.0	100.0	100.0
Nominal Effective Exchange Rate.....	nec	81.8	85.7	86.0	88.7	92.8	95.4	96.3	100.0	103.2	102.2	96.4	92.3
Real Effective Exchange Rate...........	rec	99.2	95.7	93.5	98.3	101.4	101.1	98.6	100.0	101.5	101.3	95.9	92.4
Fund Position		*Millions of SDRs: End of Period*											
Quota.........................	2f.s	13.50	13.50	13.50	13.50	13.50	13.50	18.80	18.80	18.80	18.80	18.80	18.80
SDRs..........................	1b.s	.29	.37	.47	.61	.71	.82	1.01	1.20	1.37	1.48	1.56	1.64
Reserve Position in the Fund...........	1c.s	2.91	2.91	2.91	2.91	2.91	2.91	4.24	4.24	4.24	4.24	4.24	4.24
Total Fund Cred.&Loans Outstg......	2tl	—	—	—	—	—	—	—	—	—	—	—	—
International Liquidity		*Millions of US Dollars Unless Otherwise Indicated: End of Period*											
Total Reserves minus Gold..............	1l.d	38.75	34.52	37.61	58.40	59.42	44.09	71.31	122.90	112.04	114.51	84.68	48.25
SDRs............................	1b.d	.39	.54	.70	.88	.96	1.16	1.39	1.56	1.72	2.01	2.32	2.55
Reserve Position in the Fund.........	1c.d	4.00	4.25	4.33	4.19	3.93	4.10	5.82	5.52	5.33	5.76	6.30	6.58
Foreign Exchange.....................	1d.d	34.35	29.72	32.58	53.34	54.53	38.82	64.10	115.82	104.99	106.74	76.07	39.12
Monetary Authorities: Other Liab.....	4..d	6.81	6.21	5.31	1.77	3.64	1.61	1.04	.84	1.47	2.99	2.90	1.40
Deposit Money Banks: Assets...........	7a.d	23.64	24.27	26.21	38.45	35.84	37.94	45.64	71.64	69.17	58.95	62.09	67.05
Liabilities..................	7b.d	49.15	51.68	39.59	41.40	43.71	50.69	43.06	59.83	71.64	71.35	101.82	99.80
Other Banking Insts.: Assets.............	7e.d	—	—	—	—	—	—	—	—	—	—	—	—
Liabilities..................	7f.d	14.11	14.20	14.33	13.64	17.88	17.97	21.11	64.25	108.18	126.07	95.90	64.97
Monetary Authorities		*Millions of Belize Dollars: End of Period*											
Foreign Assets..........................	11	77.27	68.94	75.24	116.85	118.89	88.23	142.90	245.85	224.15	229.98	169.43	96.57
Claims on Central Government.........	12a	61.47	67.54	81.72	110.78	89.86	94.89	67.38	62.49	78.03	63.59	165.37	165.13
Claims on Deposit Money Banks......	12e	8.50	7.84	7.06	6.39	4.18	2.25	1.00	84.19	84.00	15.00	15.12	32.52
Reserve Money..........................	14	104.63	102.50	116.21	119.64	125.81	135.57	165.22	202.80	257.79	198.86	207.09	232.65
of which: Currency Outside DMBs..	14a	54.19	56.74	61.42	63.61	66.45	70.38	84.15	95.96	105.17	106.80	103.27	115.31
Foreign Liabilities......................	16c	13.62	12.41	10.62	3.54	7.29	3.22	2.08	1.67	2.94	5.99	5.79	2.79
Central Government Deposits...........	16d	15.06	17.88	19.42	65.93	47.31	21.48	25.87	91.92	31.48	83.08	123.06	48.09
Capital Accounts........................	17a	17.18	17.78	18.50	19.30	20.19	20.82	21.30	21.52	21.72	22.18	22.49	19.35
Other Items (Net).......................	17r	−3.25	−6.24	−.73	25.62	12.35	4.29	−3.19	74.62	72.25	−1.54	−8.51	−8.65
Deposit Money Banks		*Millions of Belize Dollars: End of Period*											
Reserves.................................	20	49.95	45.13	53.77	54.71	58.68	64.85	59.02	101.45	103.28	84.42	100.36	114.69
Foreign Assets..........................	21	47.28	48.53	52.42	76.90	71.68	75.89	91.27	143.27	138.34	117.90	124.18	134.10
Claims on Central Government.........	22a	48.93	52.99	63.88	39.77	61.92	58.39	80.11	87.12	87.87	62.98	54.98	81.55
Claims on Local Government..........	22b	.01	.11		.05	.01	.23	1.38	1.16	2.17	2.49	3.27	5.43
Claims on Official Entities.............	22bx	.31	.27	2.73	2.81	5.18	9.36	4.99	9.03	10.72	6.90	5.31	7.45
Claims on Private Sector................	22d	385.99	405.27	436.44	478.03	540.03	610.72	641.14	679.71	771.03	884.12	1,010.75	1,124.92
Demand Deposits.......................	24	81.65	86.81	93.32	99.12	99.03	115.85	141.86	185.99	225.05	214.13	295.42	321.98
Time, Savings,& Fgn.Currency Dep...	25	288.57	316.35	388.84	421.56	486.98	504.93	552.39	612.72	631.29	665.59	638.57	690.29
Foreign Liabilities......................	26c	98.30	103.36	79.18	82.79	87.42	101.39	86.12	119.67	143.27	142.70	203.64	199.59
Central Government Deposits...........	26d	49.30	43.86	23.59	27.78	26.89	40.68	21.56	24.31	20.93	27.47	20.50	82.17
Credit from Monetary Authorities......	26g	5.32	1.66	1.48	1.28	1.09	.88	.63	.41	.16		5.12	
Capital Accounts........................	27a	31.00	31.04	39.40	43.54	49.77	51.73	69.71	71.33	89.16	112.06	154.42	192.03
Other Items (Net).......................	27r	−21.66	−30.78	−16.57	−23.81	−13.69	4.00	5.64	7.31	3.55	−3.14	−18.82	−17.92
Monetary Survey		*Millions of Belize Dollars: End of Period*											
Foreign Assets (Net).......................	31n	12.64	1.70	37.85	107.43	95.86	59.51	145.97	267.79	216.28	199.19	84.18	28.29
Domestic Credit..........................	32	432.35	464.44	541.76	537.72	622.80	711.44	747.57	723.29	897.41	909.53	1,096.12	1,254.23
Claims on Central Govt. (Net)........	32an	46.03	58.80	102.59	56.83	77.58	91.13	100.07	33.38	113.50	16.02	76.80	116.42
Claims on Local Government..........	32b	.01	.11	—	.05	.01	.23	1.38	1.16	2.17	2.49	3.27	5.43
Claims on Official Entities.............	32bx	.31	.27	2.73	2.81	5.18	9.36	4.99	9.03	10.72	6.90	5.31	7.45
Claims on Private Sector................	32d	385.99	405.27	436.44	478.03	540.03	610.72	641.14	679.71	771.03	884.12	1,010.75	1,124.92
Money.....................................	34	136.35	144.18	155.47	164.02	166.17	186.65	248.24	287.32	379.65	328.47	402.17	439.93
Quasi-Money..............................	35	288.57	316.35	388.84	421.56	486.98	504.93	552.39	612.72	631.29	665.59	638.57	690.29
Capital Accounts........................	37a	48.18	48.82	57.90	62.84	69.95	72.55	91.00	92.85	110.88	134.24	176.91	211.38
Other Items (Net).......................	37r	−28.11	−43.20	−22.59	−3.28	−4.45	6.83	1.92	−1.82	−8.12	−19.59	−37.35	−59.09
Money plus Quasi-Money...............	35l	424.92	460.53	544.31	585.58	653.15	691.58	800.62	900.04	1,010.93	994.07	1,040.74	1,130.23
Other Banking Institutions		*Millions of Belize Dollars: End of Period*											
Reserves.................................	40	1.28	1.41	2.47	.93	3.17	1.58	11.35	10.17	20.68	8.36	5.85	5.34
Foreign Assets..........................	41	—	—	—	—	—	—	—	—	—	—	—	—
Claims on Central Government........	42a	—	—	—	—	—	—	—	—	—	—	—	7.88
Claims on Official Entities.............	42bx	.17	—	—	—	—	—	—	—	—	—	—	28.04
Claims on Private Sector................	42d	40.66	45.70	47.03	53.75	60.78	65.96	61.92	199.33	266.63	216.41	224.24	295.43
Foreign Liabilities......................	46c	28.22	28.41	28.66	27.29	35.77	35.93	42.22	128.50	216.35	252.14	191.81	129.94
Central Government Deposits...........	46d	.80	1.23	1.40	1.07	1.20	2.71	27.06	6.10	3.35	8.81	85.36	222.18
Credit from Monetary Authorities.....	46g	3.08	3.35	4.07	6.30	6.02	5.77	5.36	4.45	85.27	16.57	11.10	33.64
Capital Accounts........................	47a	−.26	1.21	3.48	8.69	10.68	11.88	13.80	15.84	23.90	29.13	31.55	40.53
Other Items (Net).......................	47r	10.29	12.90	11.89	11.34	10.29	11.25	−15.17	54.61	−41.57	−81.88	−89.72	−89.61
Banking Survey		*Millions of Belize Dollars: End of Period*											
Foreign Assets (Net).......................	51n	−15.58	−26.70	9.20	80.14	60.09	23.58	103.75	139.29	−.07	−52.96	−107.63	−101.66
Domestic Credit..........................	52	472.39	508.91	587.39	590.40	682.38	774.70	782.43	916.52	1,160.69	1,117.13	1,235.00	1,363.39
Claims on Central Govt. (Net)........	52an	45.24	57.57	101.20	55.76	76.38	88.42	73.01	27.29	110.15	7.21	−8.56	−97.88
Claims on Local Government..........	52b	.01	.11		.05	.01	.23	1.38	1.16	2.17	2.49	3.27	5.43
Claims on Official Entities.............	52bx	.48	.27	2.73	2.81	5.18	9.36	4.99	9.03	10.72	6.90	5.31	35.49
Claims on Private Sector................	52d	426.66	450.97	483.47	531.79	600.81	676.69	703.06	879.03	1,037.66	1,100.53	1,234.99	1,420.35
Liquid Liabilities.........................	55l	423.64	459.12	541.85	584.65	649.98	690.00	789.27	889.87	990.25	985.71	1,034.89	1,124.89
Capital Accounts........................	57a	47.92	50.04	61.38	71.53	80.63	84.43	104.80	108.69	134.78	163.37	208.46	251.90
Other Items (Net).......................	57r	−14.74	−26.95	−6.63	14.36	11.86	23.86	−7.89	57.24	35.58	−84.90	−115.97	−115.06

		1993	1994	1995	1996	1997	1998	1999	2000	2001	2002	2003	2004
Interest Rates						*Percent Per Annum*							
Discount Rate (End of Period)...........	60	12.00	12.00	12.00	12.00	12.00	12.00	12.00	12.00	12.00	12.00	12.00	12.00
Treasury Bill Rate.............................	60c	4.59	4.27	4.10	3.78	3.51	3.83	5.91	5.91	5.91	4.59	3.22	3.22
Savings Rate..................................	60k	5.40	5.32	5.30	5.30	5.35	5.43	5.42	5.43	5.44	5.10	5.05	5.08
Deposit Rate.................................	60l	8.13	8.55	9.37	9.08	9.19	8.76	8.12	7.69	6.35	6.28	6.93	7.42
Lending Rate.................................	60p	14.37	14.78	15.69	16.30	16.29	16.50	16.27	16.01	15.45	14.83	14.35	13.94
Prices and Labor					*Index Numbers (2000=100): Period Averages*								
Consumer Prices......................	64	89.4	91.8	94.4	100.4	101.5	100.6	99.4	100.0	101.2	103.4	106.1	109.4
					Number in Thousands: Period Averages								
Labor Force..................................	67d	....	70	....	75	81	86	89	....	94	94	102	108
Employment..................................	67e	62	62	63	65	71	73	78	84	86	85	89	96
Unemployment...............................	67c	7	8	9	10	10	12	11	....	9	9	13	13
Unemployment Rate (%).................	67r	9.8	11.1	12.5	13.8	12.7	14.3	12.8	11.1	9.1	10.0	12.9	11.6
Intl. Transactions & Positions						*Millions of Belize Dollars*							
Exports..	70	272.97	301.98	323.25	335.27	352.95	344.26	372.08	436.95	337.29	337.11	409.21	426.24
Imports, c.i.f..................................	71	561.92	519.86	514.43	510.97	572.42	590.32	739.82	1,048.57	1,033.65	1,049.03	1,104.17	1,028.21
Balance of Payments					*Millions of US Dollars: Minus Sign Indicates Debit*								
Current Account, n.i.e....................	78ald	−48.5	−40.1	−17.2	−6.6	−31.9	−59.8	−77.5	−139.5	−184.9	−162.7	−180.9	....
Goods: Exports f.o.b......................	78aad	132.0	156.5	164.6	171.3	193.4	186.2	213.2	212.3	275.0	310.4	316.3	....
Goods: Imports f.o.b......................	78abd	−250.5	−231.9	−230.6	−229.5	−282.9	−290.9	−337.5	−403.7	−488.7	−500.3	−525.6	....
Trade Balance.............................	78acd	−118.5	−75.4	−66.1	−58.2	−89.5	−104.7	−124.3	−191.4	−213.7	−189.9	−209.3	....
Services: Credit.............................	78add	150.5	121.1	132.8	137.9	137.8	140.5	161.6	172.4	174.6	184.1	212.9	....
Services: Debit..............................	78aed	−92.5	−88.0	−94.9	−91.3	−91.7	−99.0	−108.2	−119.8	−121.8	−130.7	−139.3	....
Balance on Goods & Services.......	78afd	−60.5	−42.2	−28.1	−11.7	−43.3	−63.3	−70.8	−138.8	−161.0	−136.5	−135.7	....
Income: Credit...............................	78agd	5.9	2.9	2.8	6.3	7.5	7.2	2.7	4.8	11.1	7.1	4.2	....
Income: Debit...............................	78ahd	−23.4	−28.2	−25.1	−32.4	−30.8	−39.3	−46.6	−58.9	−83.2	−79.2	−94.0	....
Balance on Gds, Serv. & Inc.......	78aid	−78.0	−67.5	−50.4	−37.8	−66.7	−95.4	−114.7	−192.9	−233.1	−208.7	−225.5	....
Current Transfers, n.i.e.: Credit......	78ajd	33.8	34.4	38.3	34.2	38.2	38.4	40.6	56.6	50.0	48.0	47.0	....
Current Transfers: Debit................	78akd	−4.3	−6.9	−5.2	−3.1	−3.4	−2.8	−3.5	−3.2	−1.8	−2.1	−2.5	....
Capital Account, n.i.e....................	78bcd	—	—	—	−2.2	−3.4	−1.9	−2.0	.5	.5	7.5	−50.5	....
Capital Account, n.i.e.: Credit.......	78bad	—	—	—	—	—	—	.5	.9	2.1	9.6	2.4	....
Capital Account: Debit..................	78bbd	—	—	—	−2.2	−3.4	−1.9	−2.4	−.5	−1.7	−2.1	−52.9	....
Financial Account, n.i.e.................	78bjd	32.8	3.6	−1.0	11.0	27.6	23.5	91.5	88.4	171.5	143.7	214.5	....
Direct Investment Abroad..............	78bdd	—	—	—	−5.7	−3.9	−4.5	—	....	—	—	−.4	....
Dir. Invest. in Rep. Econ., n.i.e.......	78bed	9.2	15.4	21.1	16.6	12.0	17.7	47.4	17.7	59.9	25.0	28.8	....
Portfolio Investment Assets...........	78bfd	—	—	—	—	—	....	—	....	—	—	−.2	....
Equity Securities........................	78bkd	—	—	—	—	—	....	—	....	—	—	−.2	....
Debt Securities..........................	78bld	—	—	—	—	—	....	—	....	—	—	—	....
Portfolio Investment Liab., n.i.e......	78bgd	7.0	6.1	3.5	10.1	10.2	12.5	32.9	26.9	−14.9	110.0	75.5	....
Equity Securities........................	78bmd	—	—	—	—	—	....	—	....	—	—	—	....
Debt Securities..........................	78bnd	7.0	6.1	3.5	10.1	10.2	12.5	32.9	26.9	−14.9	110.0	75.5	....
Financial Derivatives Assets...........	78bwd	....	....	....	—	—	....	—	....	—	.8	.6	....
Financial Derivatives Liabilities......	78bxd	....	....	....	—	—	....	—	....	—	—	—	....
Other Investment Assets...............	78bhd	−11.6	−17.1	−14.1	−12.2	2.8	—	−8.9	−39.4	−2.4	−1.4	−8.5	....
Monetary Authorities..................	78bod	....	—	—	—	—	....	—	....	—	—	—	....
General Government..................	78bpd	—	—	—	—	—	....	....	−11.1	−3.1	−8.0	−3.0	....
Banks....................................	78bqd	−11.6	−3.3	−1.7	−12.2	2.8	—	−6.3	−26.3	2.5	9.3	−3.0	....
Other Sectors...........................	78brd	—	−13.8	−12.4	—	—	....	−2.7	−2.1	−1.9	−2.7	−2.6	....
Other Investment Liab., n.i.e..........	78bid	28.2	−.8	−11.5	2.2	6.5	−2.2	20.2	83.3	129.0	9.4	118.7	....
Monetary Authorities..................	78bsd	—	—	—	—	—	—	−.6	41.8	−.6	−33.0	−2.6	....
General Government..................	78btd	16.3	8.9	−2.6	19.7	11.5	8.8	14.9	46.1	122.6	11.6	72.5	....
Banks....................................	78bud	18.7	−9.3	−12.1	−6.3	4.8	7.2	−8.9	15.5	11.6	−1.4	30.2	....
Other Sectors...........................	78bvd	−6.8	−.3	3.2	−11.2	−9.8	−18.2	14.8	−20.2	−4.6	32.2	18.6	....
Net Errors and Omissions................	78cad	1.5	32.8	22.4	18.4	9.1	24.5	.9	7.3	9.4	3.8	6.1	....
Overall Balance.........................	78cbd	−14.2	−3.6	4.1	20.6	1.4	−13.7	12.9	−43.3	−3.5	−7.7	−10.8	....
Reserves and Related Items.............	79dad	14.2	3.6	−4.1	−20.6	−1.4	13.7	−12.9	43.3	3.5	7.7	10.8	....
Reserve Assets.........................	79dbd	14.2	3.6	−4.1	−20.6	−1.4	13.7	−27.5	−51.8	3.2	5.5	30.8	....
Use of Fund Credit and Loans........	79dcd	—	—	—	—	—	—	—	—	—	—	—	....
Exceptional Financing...................	79ded	—	—	—	—	....	—	14.6	95.2	.3	2.2	−20.0	....
Government Finance					*Thousands of Belize Dollars: Year Beginning April 1*								
Deficit (-) or Surplus......................	80	−82,365	−70,802	−39,698	−15,671	−32,588f	....	....	....	....	....	....	....
Revenue.......................................	81	247,864	258,978	261,658	288,256	283,357f	....	....	....	....	....	....	....
Grants Received........................	81z	6,953	13,264	1,079	4,076	41,191f	....	....	....	....	....	....	....
Expenditure.................................	82	342,935	348,953	306,090	317,781	362,261f	....	....	....	....	....	....	....
Lending Minus Repayments...........	83	−5,753	−5,909	−3,655	−9,778	−5,125f	....	....	....	....	....	....	....
Financing													
Domestic....................................	84a	42,583	45,433	41,604	−33,262	....	....	....	....	....	....	....	....
Foreign......................................	85a	39,782	25,369	−1,906	48,933	....	....	....	....	....	....	....	....
Debt: Domestic.............................	88a	136,104	145,985	167,747	168,330	....	....	....	....	....	....	....	....
Foreign..	89a	259,453	285,800	282,610	329,798	....	....	....	....	....	....	....	....

Belize 339

National Accounts		1993	1994	1995	1996	1997	1998	1999	2000	2001	2002	2003	2004
						Millions of Belize Dollars							
Househ.Cons.Expend.,incl.NPISHs....	96f	764.0	823.8	891.1	956.9	994.9	1,067.1	1,133.5	1,231.8	1,357.4	1,456.8	1,519.8	1,632.8
Government Consumption Expend...	91f	166.2	177.6	177.1	181.4	190.2	197.5	197.9	214.8	228.3	266.8	289.6	300.9
Gross Fixed Capital Formation..........	93e	317.5	238.8	269.2	260.6	261.0	259.0	360.4	477.0	438.4	421.5	374.8	373.3
Changes in Inventories....................	93i	—	—	—	.5	3.0	3.8	−.1	50.7	−6.2	23.0	31.1	36.8
Exports of Goods and Services..........	90c	522.8	578.9	594.9	641.4	690.7	724.5	806.8	881.5	887.0	980.3	1,055.4	1,002.6
Imports of Goods and Services (-).....	98c	561.9	609.2	609.1	644.8	729.0	784.5	987.1	1,226.0	1,204.9	1,233.4	1,306.0	1,239.7
Gross Domestic Product (GDP).........	99b	1,119.2	1,161.3	1,240.0	1,282.6	1,308.8	1,377.6	1,464.7	1,664.7	1,737.6	1,853.0	1,961.6	2,071.2
Net Primary Income from Abroad.....	98.n	—	−59.9	−55.6	−64.4	−59.3	−70.2	−87.1	−113.9	−150.2	−149.8	−184.8	....
Gross National Income (GNI)............	99a	1,126.9	1,107.2	1,189.6	1,219.7	1,250.7	1,305.4	1,378.1	1,537.5	1,581.9	1,713.9	1,787.5	....
Consumption of Fixed Capital..........	99cf	70.4	53.9	60.1	59.5	60.1	996.1	1,098.3	1,183.7	....	....	....	....
GDP Volume 2000 Prices.................	99b.p	1,233.0	1,235.3	1,243.5	1,261.2	1,306.5	1,354.8	1,473.2	1,664.7	1,741.5	1,823.7	1,990.9	2,082.6
GDP Volume (2000=100)................	99bvp	74.1	74.2	74.7	75.8	78.5	81.4	88.5	100.0	104.6	109.6	119.6	125.1
GDP Deflator (2000=100)...............	99bip	90.8	94.0	99.7	101.7	100.2	101.7	99.4	100.0	99.8	101.6	98.5	99.5
						Millions: Midyear Estimates							
Population................................	99z	.20	.21	.21	.22	.23	.23	.24	.24	.25	.25	.26	.26

2005, International Monetary Fund : *International Financial Statistics Yearbook*

Benin   638

		1993	1994	1995	1996	1997	1998	1999	2000	2001	2002	2003	2004
Exchange Rates					*Francs per SDR: End of Period*								
Official Rate	aa	404.89	† 780.44	728.38	753.06	807.94	791.61	† 896.19	918.49	935.39	850.37	771.76	747.90
					Francs per US Dollar: End of Period (ae) Period Average (rf)								
Official Rate	ae	294.78	† 534.60	490.00	523.70	598.81	562.21	† 652.95	704.95	744.31	625.50	519.36	481.58
Official Rate	rf	283.16	† 555.20	499.15	511.55	583.67	589.95	† 615.70	711.98	733.04	696.99	581.20	528.28
Fund Position					*Millions of SDRs: End of Period*								
Quota	2f.s	45.3	45.3	45.3	45.3	45.3	45.3	61.9	61.9	61.9	61.9	61.9	61.9
SDRs	1b.s	.1	—	.1	.2	—	—	.2	.1	.3	.1	.1	—
Reserve Position in the Fund	1c.s	2.1	2.1	2.1	2.2	2.2	2.2	2.2	2.2	2.2	2.2	2.2	2.2
Total Fund Cred.&Loans Outstg	2tl	31.3	48.8	56.6	68.9	70.3	66.4	67.1	64.4	61.1	53.9	49.2	42.0
International Liquidity					*Millions of US Dollars Unless Otherwise Indicated: End of Period*								
Total Reserves minus Gold	1l.d	244.0	† 258.2	197.9	261.8	253.1	261.5	400.1	458.1	578.1	615.7	717.9	640.0
SDRs	1b.d	.1	—	.1	.3	.1	.1	.2	.1	.4	.1	.2	—
Reserve Position in the Fund	1c.d	2.9	2.1	3.2	3.1	2.9	3.1	3.0	2.9	2.7	3.0	3.3	3.4
Foreign Exchange	1d.d	241.0	† 255.1	194.7	258.4	250.1	258.4	396.9	455.2	574.9	612.6	714.4	636.5
Gold (Million Fine Troy Ounces)	1ad	.011	.011	—	—	—	—	—	—	—	—	—	—
Gold (National Valuation)	1and	4.1	4.1	—	—	—	—	—	—	—	—	—	—
Monetary Authorities: Other Liab.	4..d	13.6	3.8	6.1	10.9	12.8	2.6	2.0	1.7	−2.5	2.8	6.3	26.6
Deposit Money Banks: Assets	7a.d	96.2	143.9	239.3	278.8	265.0	288.9	253.9	214.2	239.7	271.8	283.8	332.6
Liabilities	7b.d	50.7	30.4	50.2	102.0	53.1	89.5	107.3	88.2	99.0	100.3	151.5	172.7
Monetary Authorities					*Billions of Francs: End of Period*								
Foreign Assets	11	71.9	138.1	97.0	137.1	151.5	147.0	261.2	322.9	430.3	385.1	372.8	308.2
Claims on Central Government	12a	23.2	28.3	41.9	42.6	55.1	52.0	52.7	52.8	51.1	45.5	41.9	36.2
Claims on Deposit Money Banks	12e	50.3	—	—	2.0	1.0	—	—	—	—	—	—	—
Reserve Money	14	107.4	108.9	80.5	87.9	105.4	100.7	177.0	249.1	306.8	266.7	273.0	221.5
of which: Currency Outside DMBs	14a	25.5	77.3	50.6	68.9	80.8	70.4	160.3	211.8	222.3	167.9	190.3	129.9
Foreign Liabilities	16c	16.7	40.1	44.2	57.6	64.5	54.1	61.4	60.4	55.3	47.6	41.2	44.3
Central Government Deposits	16d	17.4	18.7	15.1	37.0	31.1	36.7	71.1	63.4	112.8	91.6	87.7	66.1
Other Items (Net)	17r	3.9	−1.4	−.9	−.8	6.6	7.5	4.4	2.9	6.5	24.8	12.7	12.5
Deposit Money Banks					*Billions of Francs: End of Period*								
Reserves	20	93.2	30.9	32.4	17.1	31.9	31.5	16.5	37.1	77.0	86.3	78.0	112.3
Foreign Assets	21	28.4	76.9	117.3	146.0	158.7	162.4	165.8	151.0	178.4	170.0	147.4	160.2
Claims on Central Government	22a	7.1	44.4	40.6	44.2	32.9	30.7	25.9	25.8	23.1	20.6	23.8	20.0
Claims on Private Sector	22d	67.7	75.0	80.4	102.4	71.7	100.1	161.7	194.0	192.8	222.2	293.8	312.1
Claims on Other Financial Insts.	22f	—	1.0	1.0	—	—	—	—	—	—	—	—	—
Demand Deposits	24	84.6	106.3	107.8	114.8	107.5	108.4	104.2	146.7	167.2	191.3	208.8	198.6
Time Deposits	25	59.3	66.1	86.0	90.5	99.6	98.3	110.2	114.6	136.8	133.3	146.9	165.4
Foreign Liabilities	26c	14.0	14.9	24.1	52.8	31.0	49.6	67.6	59.8	72.9	61.4	76.2	81.2
Long-Term Foreign Liabilities	26cl	.9	1.3	.5	.6	.8	.7	2.4	2.3	.9	1.4	2.5	2.0
Central Government Deposits	26d	25.6	35.0	34.0	35.1	39.8	56.1	74.4	79.4	84.5	95.0	81.9	97.0
Credit from Monetary Authorities	26g	50.3	—	—	4.0	1.0	—	—	—	—	—	—	—
Other Items (Net)	27r	−38.4	4.5	19.3	12.0	15.5	11.6	10.9	5.2	9.2	16.9	26.8	60.3
Treasury Claims: Private Sector	22d.i	—	—	—	—	—	—	—	—	—	—	—	—
Post Office: Checking Deposits	24..i	.6	2.0	2.8	5.3	4.4	4.7	5.1	5.8	9.6	7.3	7.4	8.1
Monetary Survey					*Billions of Francs: End of Period*								
Foreign Assets (Net)	31n	69.5	159.9	146.0	172.7	214.7	205.7	298.0	353.8	480.5	446.2	402.8	342.9
Domestic Credit	32	55.7	97.0	117.7	122.4	93.2	94.7	99.9	135.7	79.3	109.1	197.4	213.2
Claims on Central Govt. (Net)	32an	−12.1	21.0	36.3	20.0	21.5	−5.4	−61.7	−58.3	−113.5	−113.2	−96.5	−98.8
Claims on Private Sector	32d	67.7	75.0	80.4	102.4	71.7	100.1	161.7	194.0	192.8	222.2	293.8	312.1
Claims on Other Financial Insts.	32f	—	1.0	1.0	—	—	—	—	—	—	—	—	—
Money	34	111.3	186.2	161.7	189.5	193.4	184.2	270.6	365.4	401.8	367.3	407.5	337.2
Quasi-Money	35	59.3	66.1	86.0	90.5	99.6	98.3	110.2	114.6	136.8	133.3	146.9	165.4
Long-Term Foreign Liabilities	36cl	.9	1.3	.5	.6	.8	.7	2.4	2.3	.9	1.4	2.5	2.0
Other Items (Net)	37r	−46.3	3.3	15.4	14.5	14.2	17.2	14.6	7.2	20.5	53.3	43.2	51.5
Money plus Quasi-Money	35l	170.6	252.3	247.7	280.0	293.0	282.5	380.8	480.0	538.5	500.6	554.4	502.6
Interest Rates					*Percent Per Annum*								
Bank Rate (End of Period)	60	† 6.00	6.00	6.00	6.00	6.00	6.00	6.00	6.00	6.00	6.00	4.50	4.00
Money Market Rate	60b	4.95	4.95	4.95	4.95	4.95	4.95	4.95	4.95	4.95	4.95	4.95	4.95
Deposit Rate	60l	3.50	3.50	3.50	3.50	3.50	3.50	3.50	3.50	3.50	3.50	3.50	3.50
Prices and Labor					*Index Numbers (2000=100): Period Averages*								
Consumer Prices	64	52.6	72.8	83.4	87.5	† 90.5	95.7	96.0	100.0	104.0	106.6	108.2	109.1
					Number in Thousands: Period Averages								
Labor Force	67d	....	....	....	3,211	....	....	....	....	....	....	....	....
Intl. Transactions & Positions					*Billions of Francs*								
Exports	70	108.60	220.90	209.60	334.70	243.40	240.40	259.50	279.40	150.30	167.60	157.90	159.80
Imports, c.i.f.	71	161.78	239.35	372.20	334.70	397.90	434.00	464.58	433.30	456.50	502.40	514.90	450.10

		1993	1994	1995	1996	1997	1998	1999	2000	2001	2002	2003	2004
Balance of Payments		\multicolumn{12}{c}{*Millions of US Dollars: Minus Sign Indicates Debit*}										
Current Account, n.i.e.	78ald	−101.0	−23.2	−206.6	−57.4	−169.9	−151.5	−191.4	−111.0	−160.5	....	....	....
Goods: Exports f.o.b.	78aad	393.5	397.9	419.9	527.7	424.0	414.3	421.5	392.4	373.5			
Goods: Imports f.o.b.	78abd	−561.4	−451.5	−622.5	−559.7	−576.9	−572.6	−635.2	−516.1	−553.0			
Trade Balance	78acd	−167.9	−53.6	−202.5	−32.0	−152.9	−158.3	−213.7	−123.7	−179.5			
Services: Credit	78add	146.6	142.2	194.3	126.1	116.0	142.3	176.9	136.1	147.1			
Services: Debit	78aed	−175.1	−181.4	−272.2	−188.8	−172.3	−191.4	−215.3	−191.7	−191.9			
Balance on Goods & Services	78afd	−196.4	−92.8	−280.4	−94.7	−209.2	−207.4	−252.2	−179.4	−224.3			
Income: Credit	78agd	37.8	18.8	24.0	29.6	24.4	27.8	27.7	28.3	29.4			
Income: Debit	78ahd	−32.8	−21.7	−25.1	−50.6	−44.4	−41.2	−39.1	−40.3	−42.9			
Balance on Gds, Serv. & Inc.	78aid	−191.4	−95.7	−281.5	−115.6	−229.2	−220.8	−263.6	−191.6	−237.7			
Current Transfers, n.i.e.: Credit	78ajd	118.5	98.5	105.4	92.4	77.8	102.0	87.1	91.3	87.3			
Current Transfers: Debit	78akd	−28.1	−25.9	−30.5	−34.2	−18.5	−32.7	−14.9	−10.7	−10.0			
Capital Account, n.i.e.	78bcd	75.5	75.2	85.6	6.4	84.5	66.6	69.9	73.3	70.0			
Capital Account, n.i.e.: Credit	78bad	75.5	75.2	85.6	6.4	84.5	66.6	69.9	73.4	70.0			
Capital Account: Debit	78bbd	—	—	—	—	—	—	....	−.1	—			
Financial Account, n.i.e.	78bjd	−123.3	−17.6	−132.9	−104.2	−21.3	−8.9	25.4	10.8	40.5			
Direct Investment Abroad	78bdd	—	—	−.6	−15.0	−12.1	−1.9	−1.4	−8.1	−2.3			
Dir. Invest. in Rep. Econ., n.i.e.	78bed	1.4	13.6	7.4	28.6	26.0	34.7	39.3	64.3	43.9			
Portfolio Investment Assets	78bfd	−9.1	−26.4	−64.2	−7.7	−7.8	1.2	−1.4	5.7	3.1			
Equity Securities	78bkd	—	—	—	1.4	—	.1	−.9	.9	−1.1			
Debt Securities	78bld	−9.1	−26.4	−64.2	−9.1	−7.7	1.1	−.5	4.7	4.2			
Portfolio Investment Liab., n.i.e.	78bgd	—	—	.3	2.5	2.0	1.2	2.0	.1	−.4			
Equity Securities	78bmd	—	—	.3	2.5	2.0	1.2	2.0	.1	−.4			
Debt Securities	78bnd	—	—	—	—	—	—	—	—	—			
Financial Derivatives Assets	78bwd	....	....	....				−.1	—	−.2			
Financial Derivatives Liabilities	78bxd	—	—	—	—	—	—	8.6	—	—			
Other Investment Assets	78bhd	−73.9	−52.2	−62.1	−4.0	−12.4	−9.6	−58.3	25.1	−34.4			
Monetary Authorities	78bod	—	—	—	—	—	—	—	—	—			
General Government	78bpd	−2.2	11.9	−6.9	—	−.1	—	—	—	—			
Banks	78bqd	−48.9	−50.8	−44.2	11.8	−41.1	12.4	−26.7	1.8	−46.6			
Other Sectors	78brd	−22.9	−13.3	−10.9	−15.8	28.8	−22.0	−31.6	23.4	12.2			
Other Investment Liab., n.i.e.	78bid	−41.7	47.4	−13.7	−108.6	−17.0	−34.4	36.8	−76.2	30.8			
Monetary Authorities	78bsd	8.6	.6	−2.7	5.2	4.7	−5.4	.3	−1.4	.8			
General Government	78btd	−68.0	−28.1	−36.0	−129.4	−26.8	−29.7	−33.6	−49.2	−30.9			
Banks	78bud	35.0	9.8	−.5	4.5	−11.6	21.1	33.3	−21.0	13.6			
Other Sectors	78bvd	−17.2	65.1	25.4	11.1	16.7	−20.4	36.8	−4.7	47.4			
Net Errors and Omissions	78cad	−8.1	−16.3	−1.0	6.3	6.7	7.1	7.3	6.7	3.6			
Overall Balance	78cbd	−156.9	18.1	−254.9	−149.0	−100.0	−86.7	−88.7	−20.3	−46.4			
Reserves and Related Items	79dad	156.9	−18.1	254.9	149.0	100.0	86.7	88.7	20.3	46.4			
Reserve Assets	79dbd	−15.4	−117.7	81.9	−78.3	−24.5	7.0	−40.2	−87.3	−147.4			
Use of Fund Credit and Loans	79dcd	21.9	24.9	12.2	18.0	1.9	−5.3	1.1	−3.6	−4.1			
Exceptional Financing	79ded	150.4	74.6	160.7	209.3	122.6	85.0	127.8	111.2	197.9			
International Investment Position		\multicolumn{12}{c}{*Millions of US Dollars*}										
Assets	79aad	....	....	....	613.1	664.5	598.7	726.4	737.4	904.9			
Direct Investment Abroad	79abd	....	....	....	13.7	−2.3	5.3	5.6	10.5	12.6			
Portfolio Investment	79acd	....	....	....	75.9	75.2	94.4	81.4	67.6	63.2			
Equity Securities	79add	....	....	....	.2	—	2.5	1.7	3.2	3.2			
Debt Securities	79aed	....	....	....	75.8	75.2	91.9	79.7	64.4	60.0			
Financial Derivatives	79ald	....	....	....	.1	—	—	.1	—	.2			
Other Investment	79afd	....	....	....	261.6	338.4	236.9	239.2	200.5	249.2			
Monetary Authorities	79agd	....	....	....	—	—	—	—	—	—			
General Government	79ahd	....	....	....	.1	.1	.1	.1	.1	.1			
Banks	79aid	....	....	....	166.9	186.2	185.1	170.0	155.3	187.8			
Other Sectors	79ajd	....	....	....	94.6	152.2	51.7	69.2	45.1	61.3			
Reserve Assets	79akd	....	....	....	261.8	253.1	262.2	400.1	458.8	579.7			
Liabilities	79lad	....	....	....	1,802.5	1,628.9	1,776.1	1,748.1	1,842.2	1,900.9			
Dir. Invest. in Rep. Economy	79lbd	....	....	....	62.3	46.9	67.0	73.5	213.2	173.8			
Portfolio Investment	79lcd	....	....	....	81.7	62.2	91.2	95.1	16.3	11.5			
Equity Securities	79ldd	....	....	....	2.5	3.5	6.3	6.5	6.1	4.8			
Debt Securities	79led	....	....	....	79.2	58.7	84.9	88.6	10.2	6.6			
Financial Derivatives	79lld	....	....	....	.8	—	—	8.1	—	—			
Other Investment	79lfd	....	....	....	1,657.8	1,519.7	1,618.0	1,571.4	1,612.7	1,715.6			
Monetary Authorities	79lgd	....	....	....	115.1	109.1	102.1	99.6	89.3	82.2			
General Government	79lhd	....	....	....	1,368.5	1,165.8	1,288.4	1,204.2	1,291.5	1,310.0			
Banks	79lid	....	....	....	3.2	34.6	59.0	83.7	70.7	88.7			
Other Sectors	79ljd	....	....	....	171.0	210.2	168.4	183.9	161.2	234.6			
National Accounts		\multicolumn{12}{c}{*Billions of Francs*}										
Househ.Cons.Expend.,incl.NPISHs	96f	508.9	657.8	791.2	913.9	961.2	1,073.0	1,144.6	1,227.3	1,403.8	1,525.8	1,595.1	1,611.3
Government Consumption Expend	91f	69.4	90.1	100.1	108.3	174.9	190.0	199.7	211.1	224.3	241.1	261.0	272.7
Gross Fixed Capital Formation	93e	89.4	144.1	190.0	196.7	245.5	263.0	281.0	313.5	360.4	361.1	419.8	431.3
Changes in Inventories	93i	−3.9	10.0	45.8	5.6	17.5	12.7	6.3	10.7	26.7	−9.2	15.7	15.1
Exports of Goods and Services	90c	144.7	248.9	269.9	300.2	359.8	392.4	445.4	427.4	409.4	434.8	433.7	428.8
Imports of Goods and Services (-)	98c	212.0	319.9	394.0	395.1	417.5	470.7	538.3	499.6	565.9	605.8	642.2	612.7
Gross Domestic Product (GDP)	99b	596.4	831.1	1,002.9	1,129.5	1,323.9	1,448.4	1,532.4	1,679.6	1,832.1	1,956.8	2,068.1	2,163.2
Net Primary Income from Abroad	98.n	−1.8	−14.5	−22.1	....	....	....	....	....	....			
Gross National Income (GNI)	99a	594.6	816.6	980.8	....	....	....	....	....	....			
GDP Volume 1985 Prices	99b.p	552.7	576.9	603.5	636.9	701.5	729.3	768.2	805.6	855.9	893.8	928.5	953.2
GDP Volume (2000=100)	99bvp	68.6	71.6	74.9	79.1	87.1	90.5	95.4	100.0	106.2	110.9	115.3	118.3
GDP Deflator (2000=100)	99bip	51.8	69.1	79.7	85.1	90.5	95.3	95.7	100.0	102.7	105.0	106.8	108.8
		\multicolumn{12}{c}{*Millions: Midyear Estimates*}										
Population	99z	5.78	6.00	6.20	6.40	6.59	6.78	6.98	7.20	7.43	7.67	7.92	8.18

Bhutan 514

		1993	1994	1995	1996	1997	1998	1999	2000	2001	2002	2003	2004
Exchange Rates					*Ngultrum per SDR: End of Period*								
Official Rate	aa	43.102	45.810	52.295	51.666	52.999	59.813	59.690	60.911	60.549	65.298	67.768	67.688
				Ngultrum per US Dollar: End of Period (ae) Period Average (rf)									
Official Rate	ae	31.380	31.380	35.180	35.930	39.280	42.480	43.490	46.750	48.180	48.030	45.605	43.585
Official Rate	rf	30.493	31.374	32.427	35.433	36.313	41.259	43.055	44.942	47.186	48.610	46.583	45.316
Fund Position					*Millions of SDRs: End of Period*								
Quota	2f.s	4.500	4.500	4.500	4.500	4.500	4.500	6.300	6.300	6.300	6.300	6.300	6.300
SDRs	1b.s	.376	.405	.438	.471	.504	.541	.134	.174	.211	.235	.252	.270
Reserve Position in the Fund	1c.s	.570	.570	.570	.570	.570	.570	1.020	1.020	1.020	1.020	1.020	1.020
Total Fund Cred.&Loans Outstg.	2tl	—											
International Liquidity				*Millions of US Dollars Unless Otherwise Indicated: End of Period*									
Total Reserves minus Gold	1l.d	97.96	121.40	† 130.46	190.07	188.72	256.80	292.29	317.63	323.36	354.95	366.60	398.62
SDRs	1b.d	.52	.59	.65	.68	.68	.76	.18	.23	.27	.32	.37	.42
Reserve Position in the Fund	1c.d	.78	.83	.85	.82	.77	.80	1.40	1.33	1.28	1.39	1.52	1.58
Foreign Exchange	1d.d	96.66	119.98	† 128.96	188.57	187.27	255.24	290.70	316.08	321.81	353.24	364.71	396.62
of which: Convertible Currency	1dxd	94.77	116.56	† 127.17	150.95	155.27	189.55	214.66	236.69	230.94	258.16	286.30	271.65
Deposit Money Banks: Assets	7a.d	13.84	8.88	7.17	43.01	38.86	72.22	93.24	100.88	105.45	110.45	107.53	99.27
Liabilities	7b.d	18.09	—	—	—	—	—	—	—	20.20	—	—	—
Monetary Authorities					*Millions of Ngultrum End of Period*								
Foreign Assets	11	† 2,945	3,533	4,341	5,289	6,069	8,030	8,850	10,362	10,718	12,004	11,865	13,005
Claims on Central Government	12a	74	—	50	—	51	—	—	—	—	127	56	37
Claims on Deposit Money Banks	12e	108	7	3	308	3	1,193	1,188	893	293	194	303	895
Claims on Other Financial Insts	12f	† —	55	5	5	5	—	—	—	—	—	—	—
Reserve Money	14	† 1,931	1,287	2,149	2,328	2,545	3,954	4,971	6,022	6,161	6,982	8,368	9,223
of which: Currency Outside DMBs	14a	† 335	348	433	423	721	769	969	1,270	1,610	1,648	1,802	2,072
Liabs.of Central Bank:Securities	16ac	—	600	550	1,000	681	560	487	410	410	1,100	—	200
Foreign Liabilities	16c	—	617	161	250	250	250	—	—	—	—	—	—
Central Government Deposits	16d	† 25	30	29	334	28	1,207	1,234	918	338	141	357	1,088
Other Items (Net)	17r	† 1,170	1,062	1,510	1,690	2,624	3,252	3,344	3,905	4,102	4,101	3,499	3,428
of which: Valuation Adjustment	17rv	....	....	1,451	1,653	2,013	1,905	1,610	1,780	1,705	2,077	1,197	822
Deposit Money Banks					*Millions of Ngultrum End of Period*								
Reserves	20	† 1,001	829	1,850	1,490	2,338	2,475	3,215	4,375	4,519	5,385	6,342	6,410
Claims on Mon.Author.:Securities	20c	—	588	532	595	671	426	460	295	405	1,089	—	198
Foreign Assets	21	† 434	279	252	1,545	1,526	3,068	4,055	4,716	5,081	5,305	4,904	4,327
Claims on Central Government	22a	† 2	5	2	100	201	50	50	50	370	974	1,213	2,303
Claims on Nonfin.Pub.Enterprises	22c	† 796	561	535	484	449	411	372	333	315	252	252	233
Claims on Private Sector	22d	† 489	724	751	748	1,472	1,472	1,490	1,748	2,420	3,147	4,249	6,057
Demand Deposits	24	† 487	697	890	1,652	1,447	1,860	2,755	2,669	3,238	5,323	4,968	5,983
Time & Foreign Currency Deposits	25	† 1,120	1,351	1,926	1,465	3,458	3,782	4,741	5,996	5,868	6,732	7,076	8,546
Foreign Liabilities	26c	† 568	—	—	—	—	—	—	—	973	—	—	—
Central Government Deposits	26d	† 311	140	344	459	209	322	914	631	1,288	1,415	1,951	1,829
Capital Accounts	27a	† 330	324	371	371	539	561	633	756	958	1,194	1,735	1,849
Other Items (Net)	27r	† −90	473	390	1,016	1,007	1,365	599	1,463	784	1,487	1,231	1,322
Monetary Survey					*Millions of Ngultrum: End of Period*								
Foreign Assets (Net)	31n	† 2,811	3,195	4,432	6,584	7,346	10,848	12,905	15,078	14,825	17,309	16,769	17,332
Domestic Credit	32	† 1,024	1,175	969	545	1,941	404	−236	581	1,479	2,943	3,462	5,714
Claims on Central Govt. (Net)	32an	† −261	−165	−321	−692	15	−1,480	−2,098	−1,499	−1,256	−456	−1,038	−577
Claims on Nonfin.Pub.Enterprises	32c	† 796	561	535	484	449	411	372	333	315	252	252	233
Claims on Private Sector	32d	† 489	724	751	748	1,472	1,472	1,490	1,748	2,420	3,147	4,249	6,057
Claims on Other Financial Insts	32f	† —	55	5	5	5	—	—	—	—	—	—	—
Money	34	† 822	1,044	1,322	2,074	2,168	2,629	3,724	3,939	4,849	6,971	6,770	8,055
Quasi-Money	35	† 1,120	1,351	1,926	1,465	3,458	3,782	4,741	5,996	5,868	6,732	7,076	8,546
Liabs.of Central Bank:Securities	36ac	—	12	18	405	11	134	26	115	6	11	—	2
Other Items (Net)	37r	† 1,897	1,962	2,135	3,185	3,652	4,696	4,176	5,609	5,582	6,537	6,385	6,443
Money plus Quasi-Money	35l	† 1,942	2,395	3,249	3,540	5,626	6,410	8,465	9,935	10,716	13,703	13,846	16,601
Interest Rates					*Percent Per Annum*								
Deposit Rate	60l	8.0	8.0	8.0	8.3	8.3	8.3	8.3	8.3	7.5	7.0	5.0	....
Lending Rate	60p	17.0	16.0	16.0	16.0	16.0	16.0	16.0	16.0	15.8	15.3	15.0	....
Prices and Tourism				*Index Numbers (2000=100): Period Averages*									
Consumer Prices	64	60.0	64.2	70.3	76.4	81.4	90.0	96.1	† 100.0	103.4	106.0	108.2	113.2
Tourist Arrivals	66ta	39.6	52.5	63.0	67.9	71.6	81.6	94.7	100.0	84.6	74.1	82.8	122.4
Intl. Transactions & Positions				*Millions of Ngultrum: Year Ending June 30*									
Exports	70	1,991.7	2,082.7	3,350.1	3,553.8	4,274.2	4,455.6	4,988.0	4,615.8	4,994.7	5,478.6	6,190.1	....
Imports, c.i.f	71	2,745.3	2,876.4	3,641.9	4,525.2	4,977.9	5,516.4	7,834.9	7,875.0	8,990.2	9,553.9	11,598.5	....
Government Finance				*Millions of Ngultrum: Year Ending June 30*									
Deficit (-) or Surplus	80	312.2	−45.1	7.8	238.6	−300.9	143.4	−304.9	−764.6	−2,490.8	−1,756.7p	....	....
Revenue	81	1,650.9	1,666.3	1,877.4	2,127.7	2,424.2	3,133.1	3,656.9	4,585.4	4,975.7	5,140.6p	....	....
Grants Received	81z	1,230.1	1,456.2	1,773.2	2,363.6	2,232.1	1,816.3	3,262.6	3,274.1	3,711.0	2,918.4p	....	....
Expenditure	82	2,397.3	2,891.0	3,655.6	4,152.6	4,630.6	4,588.4	7,284.0	8,334.2	10,716.5	9,813.7p	....	....
Lending Minus Repayments	83	171.5	276.6	−12.8	100.1	326.6	217.6	−59.6	289.9	461.0	2.0p	....	....
Financing													
Total Financing	84	−312.2	45.1	−7.8	−238.6	300.9	−143.3	304.9	764.6	2,490.8	1,756.7p	....	....
Domestic	84a	−334.7	21.0	−1.1	−211.8	176.6	−479.5	−248.8	158.0	1,434.1	1,047.1p	....	....
Foreign	85a	22.5	24.1	−6.7	−26.8	124.3	336.2	553.7	606.6	1,056.7	709.6p	....	....
Debt: Domestic	88a	19.3	64.9	28.4	107.4	—	—	—	—	—	....	....	....
Foreign	89a	2,801.8	2,733.3	2,634.0	3,962.1	4,084.9	4,661.2	6,205.3	7,721.8	15,723.8	....	....	....

Bhutan 514

		1993	1994	1995	1996	1997	1998	1999	2000	2001	2002	2003	2004
National Accounts						*Millions of Ngultrum: Calendar Year*							
Househ.Cons.Expend.,incl.NPISHs....	96f	3,537	3,770	3,428	5,171	7,138	9,322	10,067	11,329	....	....	....	....
Government Consumption Expend...	91f	1,241	1,585	2,400	2,502	3,651	3,308	4,271	4,422	....	....	....	....
Gross Fixed Capital Formation..........	93e	3,374	3,945	4,487	5,094	5,514	6,200	8,127	9,447	....	....	....	....
Changes in Inventories....................	93i	−60	129	228	182	−632	45	108	49	....	....	....	....
Exports of Goods and Services..........	90c	2,264	2,508	3,712	3,979	4,771	5,148	5,714	6,456	....	....	....	....
Imports of Goods and Services (-).....	98c	3,163	3,349	4,190	5,120	6,128	7,686	9,164	10,004	....	....	....	....
Gross Domestic Product (GDP).........	99b	7,193	8,589	10,064	11,808	14,314	16,337	19,122	21,698	....	....	....	....
Net Primary Income from Abroad.....	98.n	−734	−634	−1,208	−1,247	−1,141	−2,323	−3,083	−3,458	....	....	....	....
Gross National Income (GNI)...........	99a	6,458	7,954	8,856	10,562	13,173	14,013	16,040	18,240	....	....	....	....
GDP at Factor Cost.......................	99ba	7,008	8,238	9,707	11,449	13,808	15,791	18,514	21,127	....	....	....	....
GDP at Fac.Cost,Vol.1980 Prices......	99bap	2,555	2,713	2,921	3,070	3,306	3,514	3,773	3,989	....	....	....	....
GDP Volume (2000=100)................	99bvp	64.1	68.0	73.2	77.0	82.9	88.1	94.6	100.0	....	....	....	....
GDP Deflator (2000=100)...............	99bip	51.8	57.3	62.7	70.4	78.9	84.8	92.6	100.0	....	....	....	....
						Millions: Midyear Estimates							
Population...............................	99z	1.69	1.71	1.73	1.76	1.80	1.85	1.89	1.94	1.98	2.03	2.07	2.12

Bolivia 218

		1993	1994	1995	1996	1997	1998	1999	2000	2001	2002	2003	2004
Exchange Rates					*Bolivianos per SDR: End of Period*								
Market Rate	aa	6.1467	6.8540	7.3358	7.4558	7.2387	7.9483	8.2213	8.3256	8.5709	10.1828	11.6351	12.5017
					Bolivianos per US Dollar: End of Period (ae) Period Average (rf)								
Market Rate	ae	4.4750	4.6950	4.9350	5.1850	5.3650	5.6450	5.9900	6.3900	6.8200	7.4900	7.8300	8.0500
Market Rate	rf	4.2651	4.6205	4.8003	5.0746	5.2543	5.5101	5.8124	6.1835	6.6069	7.1700	7.6592	7.9363
					Index Numbers (2000=100): Period Averages								
Market Rate	ahx	145.02	133.82	128.78	121.78	117.66	112.21	106.38	100.00	93.60	86.27	80.72	77.90
Nominal Effective Exchange Rate	nec	60.53	96.58	98.68	96.93	99.56	99.20	102.05	100.00	101.23	102.53	91.17	83.35
Real Effective Exchange Rate	rec	91.98	87.28	84.98	89.22	92.90	97.56	100.52	100.00	99.79	98.07	86.14	80.12
Fund Position					*Millions of SDRs: End of Period*								
Quota	2f.s	126.2	126.2	126.2	126.2	126.2	126.2	171.5	171.5	171.5	171.5	171.5	171.5
SDRs	1b.s	10.2	17.0	26.9	26.8	26.8	26.8	27.3	27.3	27.3	27.3	27.1	26.6
Reserve Position in the Fund	1c.s	8.9	8.9	8.9	8.9	8.9	8.9	8.9	8.9	8.9	8.9	8.9	8.9
Total Fund Cred.&Loans Outstg	2tl	160.5	180.5	180.1	192.0	183.9	187.6	180.0	168.8	164.8	143.7	187.5	197.7
International Liquidity					*Millions of US Dollars Unless Otherwise Indicated: End of Period*								
Total Reserves minus Gold	1l.d	223.4	451.0	660.0	955.0	1,086.6	948.5	974.9	926.4	886.4	580.5	716.8	872.4
SDRs	1b.d	14.0	24.8	40.0	38.5	36.2	37.7	37.4	35.6	34.3	37.2	40.3	41.2
Reserve Position in the Fund	1c.d	12.2	13.0	13.2	12.8	12.0	12.5	12.2	11.6	11.2	12.1	13.2	13.8
Foreign Exchange	1d.d	197.2	413.2	606.8	903.7	1,038.5	898.3	925.3	879.3	840.9	531.2	663.3	817.3
Gold (Million Fine Troy Ounces)	1ad	.894	.893	.893	.939	.939	.939	.943	.939	.939	.911	.911	.911
Gold (National Valuation)	1and	39.6	37.7	37.7	39.6	39.6	234.9	235.7	244.8	259.6	316.4	379.4	399.4
Monetary Authorities: Other Liab.	4..d	432.1	503.9	545.9	419.3	370.1	323.9	297.1	283.0	237.3	56.9	52.4	49.0
Deposit Money Banks: Assets	7a.d	72.2	84.5	103.6	124.4	137.9	409.8	471.8	552.8	693.9	604.1	550.8	527.6
Liabilities	7b.d	318.1	476.8	544.0	540.9	721.4	879.7	744.6	461.3	214.7	181.1	107.2	119.2
Other Banking Insts.: Assets	7e.d	—	—	—	3.8	6.6	46.9	55.9	63.4	74.3	35.7	78.9	78.2
Liabilities	7f.d	4.1	4.1	—	2.5	2.4	8.1	13.3	16.5	15.0	19.1	28.3	51.7
Monetary Authorities					*Millions of Bolivianos: End of Period*								
Foreign Assets	11	2,917	3,702	4,538	† 7,032	7,735	8,217	8,905	9,161	9,651	8,940	11,090	12,944
Claims on Central Government	12a	4,700	5,009	4,328	† 3,889	3,475	3,598	4,123	4,731	5,436	6,492	7,253	7,866
Claims on State and Local Govts	12b	20	18	—	† —								
Claims on Nonfin.Pub.Enterprises	12c	814	891	113	† 119					3	4	3	2
Claims on Private Sector	12d	—	—	—	† 2	2	2	2	3	3	3	4	2
Claims on Deposit Money Banks	12e	1,392	2,405	3,032	† 3,394	3,427	3,444	3,506	2,873	3,028	2,671	2,750	2,458
Claims on Other Banking Insts	12f				† 107	66	72	42	52	64			3
Claims on Nonbank Financial Insts	12g	91	108	119	† —			206	220	235	—	—	—
Reserve Money	14	2,557	2,668	3,291	† 4,194	5,036	3,989	4,441	4,905	5,497	5,582	6,338	7,471
of which: Currency Outside DMBs	14a	1,034	1,406	1,694	† 1,802	2,061	2,193	2,173	2,189	2,422	2,707	3,231	3,917
Time, Savings,& Fgn.Currency Dep.	15	568	1,682	897	† 547	452	451	994	542	624	441	581	708
of which: Fgn. Currency Deposits	15b	244	1,235	522	† 573	442	446	990	530	597	435	571	673
Foreign Liabilities	16c	2,279	2,698	2,970	† 3,606	3,317	3,320	3,259	3,214	3,031	1,889	2,592	2,865
Central Government Deposits	16d	2,524	2,589	3,565	† 4,460	3,591	3,489	3,642	3,679	3,750	3,237	3,659	4,288
Central Govt. Lending Funds	16f	2,238	2,684	1,240	† 1,081	919	989	999	972	936	728	813	20
Capital Accounts	17a	1,075	1,673	2,516	† 1,057	1,441	3,287	3,857	4,381	5,246	6,906	7,915	8,569
Other Items (Net)	17r	−1,307	−1,861	−2,347	† −403	−52	−192	−407	−653	−667	−678	−803	−647
Deposit Money Banks					*Millions of Bolivianos: End of Period*								
Reserves	20	1,539	1,133	1,450	† 2,788	3,588	1,426	1,459	1,797	1,827	1,753	1,789	1,990
Foreign Assets	21	323	397	511	† 645	740	2,313	2,826	3,532	4,732	4,525	4,313	4,247
Claims on Central Government	22a	29	103	572	† 1,522	1,590	1,322	924	1,053	1,530	1,919	1,765	2,025
Claims on State and Local Govts	22b	—	—	—	† —								
Claims on Nonfin.Pub.Enterprises	22c	—	—	—	† —	5	1	2	2	39	28	53	66
Claims on Private Sector	22d	10,740	13,452	15,152	† 17,568	21,017	26,103	27,331	26,403	24,152	23,753	23,721	22,862
Claims on Other Banking Insts	22f	—	—	—	† —		11	10	—	6	54	2	3
Claims on Nonbank Financial Insts	22g	—	—	—	† 153	131	309	291	263	407	451	482	467
Demand Deposits	24	1,466	1,826	2,219	† 867	1,036	1,124	1,031	1,150	1,353	1,271	1,385	1,427
Time, Savings,& Fgn.Currency Dep	25	7,175	7,809	8,887	† 13,542	15,916	18,237	19,203	19,424	19,130	17,651	19,779	19,172
of which: Fgn. Currency Deposits	25b	7,036	7,568	8,700	† 13,201	15,546	17,799	18,737	18,947	18,601	17,229	19,190	17,851
Money Market Instruments	26aa				† —		70	68	891	1,576	2,235	34	—
Foreign Liabilities	26c	1,424	2,239	2,685	† 2,805	3,870	4,966	4,460	2,948	1,464	1,357	840	960
Central Government Deposits	26d	49	74	179	† 935	1,319	260	97	117	139	97	72	115
Credit from Monetary Authorities	26g	1,334	2,260	2,984	† 3,830	3,721	3,499	3,920	3,914	3,802	3,767	3,661	3,671
Liabilities to Other Banking Insts.	26i	—	—	—	† —		95	93	103	103	127	163	263
Liab. to Nonbank Financial Insts	26j	—	—	—	† —	310	520	894	927	2,069	2,332	2,158	2,042
Capital Accounts	27a	1,577	1,899	2,043	† 2,352	2,821	3,822	4,626	5,252	5,732	6,608	6,978	6,713
Other Items (Net)	27r	−393	−1,023	−1,312	† −1,655	−1,921	−1,108	−1,550	−1,676	−2,676	−2,962	−2,944	−2,703
Monetary Survey					*Millions of Bolivianos: End of Period*								
Foreign Assets (Net)	31n	−462	−837	−606	† 1,266	1,288	2,244	4,012	6,532	9,888	10,219	11,971	13,366
Domestic Credit	32	13,821	16,917	16,541	† 17,964	21,377	27,669	29,192	28,931	27,984	29,366	29,548	28,892
Claims on Central Govt. (Net)	32an	2,156	2,449	1,156	† 16	155	1,171	1,308	1,988	3,078	5,076	5,287	5,488
Claims on State and Local Govts.	32b	20	18	—	† —				—	—	—	—	—
Claims on Nonfin.Pub.Enterprises	32c	814	891	113	† 119	5	1	2	2	39	28	53	66
Claims on Private Sector	32d	10,740	13,452	15,152	† 17,570	21,019	26,105	27,333	26,406	24,156	23,757	23,725	22,864
Claims on Other Banking Insts.	32f	—	—	—	† 107	66	83	52	52	70	54	2	6
Claims on Nonbank Financial Inst.	32g	91	108	119	† 153	131	309	497	483	642	451	482	467
Money	34	2,499	3,232	3,913	† 3,055	3,636	3,895	3,670	3,995	4,743	4,725	5,636	6,686
Quasi-Money	35	7,743	9,490	9,784	† 14,089	16,368	18,688	20,197	19,966	19,754	18,093	20,360	19,880
Money Market Instruments	36aa				† —		70	68	891	1,576	2,235	34	—
Central Govt. Lending Funds	36f	2,238	2,684	1,240	† 1,081	919	989	999	972	936	728	813	20
Liabilities to Other Banking Insts	36i	—	—	—	† —	—	95	93	103	103	127	163	263
Liab. to Nonbank Financial Insts.	36j	—	—	—	† —	310	520	894	927	2,069	2,332	2,158	2,042
Capital Accounts	37a	2,652	3,573	4,559	† 3,409	4,263	7,109	8,483	9,633	10,978	13,514	14,893	15,282
Other Items (Net)	37r	−1,773	−2,899	−3,560	† −2,405	−2,831	−1,452	−1,201	−1,025	−2,288	−2,169	−2,537	−1,915
Money plus Quasi-Money	35l	10,242	12,722	13,697	† 17,145	20,004	22,583	23,867	23,961	24,497	22,818	25,996	26,566

		1993	1994	1995	1996	1997	1998	1999	2000	2001	2002	2003	2004
Other Banking Institutions					*Millions of Bolivianos: End of Period*								
Reserves...........................	40	—	1	—	† 160	192	80	84	135	178	400	177	174
Foreign Assets....................	41	—	—	—	† 20	35	265	335	405	507	268	618	629
Claims on Central Government........	42a	3	3	3	† 106	91	118	14	150	529	497	785	900
Claims on State and Local Govts.....	42b				† —								
Claims on Nonfin.Pub.Enterprises.....	42c	—	—	—	† —	—	—	—	—	—	4	—	—
Claims on Private Sector..............	42d	389	349	386	† 2,226	3,249	3,885	3,703	4,087	4,552	5,007	5,784	6,491
Claims on Deposit Money Banks....	42e	—	—	—	† —	—	140	86	346	414	416	337	208
Claims on Nonbank Financial Insts...	42g	—	—	—	† 4	4	26	57	88	164	35	58	90
Demand Deposits....................	44	—	—	—	† —	1	1	1	11	4	5	6	6
Time, Savings,& Fgn.Currency Dep...	45	1	1	—	† 2,305	3,185	3,693	3,480	4,132	5,132	5,044	6,300	6,486
of which: Fgn. Currency Deposits...	45b	1	1	—	† 2,251	3,114	3,619	3,429	4,075	5,073	4,981	6,210	6,294
Money Market Instruments..............	46aa	—	—	—	† —	—	—	—	68	208	364	—	
Foreign Liabilities....................	46c	18	19	—	† 13	13	46	80	106	102	143	221	416
Central Government Deposits..........	46d	1	1	—	† 6	14	16	8	21	13	15	17	47
Credit from Monetary Authorities.....	46g	292	272	548	† 4	6	8	11	21	80	67	54	26
Credit from Deposit Money Banks....	46h	—	—	—	† 86	100	72	55	39	47	29	30	31
Liabs. to Nonbank Financial Insts.....	46j	—	—	—	† 245	303	294	301	299	325	368	384	469
Capital Accounts....................	47a	34	21	−289	† 447	579	775	819	986	1,188	1,416	1,649	1,828
Other Items (Net)....................	47r	46	40	130	† −592	−630	−391	−476	−470	−756	−823	−902	−817
Banking Survey					*Millions of Bolivianos: End of Period*								
Foreign Assets (Net)......................	51n	−480	−857	−606	† 1,273	1,310	2,463	4,267	6,831	10,292	10,344	12,367	13,579
Domestic Credit.....................	52	14,211	17,269	16,930	† 20,187	24,641	31,599	32,907	33,184	33,145	34,841	36,156	36,320
Claims on Central Govt. (Net)........	52an	2,158	2,452	1,160	† 116	232	1,273	1,314	2,117	3,593	5,559	6,055	6,341
Claims on State and Local Govts....	52b	20	18	—	† —	—	—	—	—	—	—	—	—
Claims on Nonfin.Pub.Enterprises...	52c	814	891	113	† 119	5	1	2	2	39	32	53	66
Claims on Private Sector.............	52d	11,128	13,801	15,538	† 19,796	24,268	29,991	31,037	30,493	28,708	28,764	29,508	29,356
Claims on Nonbank Financial Inst..	52g	91	108	119	† 157	135	335	554	572	806	486	540	557
Liquid Liabilities....................	55l	10,243	12,723	13,697	† 19,291	22,998	26,198	27,265	27,969	29,456	27,467	32,124	32,884
Money Market Instruments..............	56aa	—	—	—	† —	—	70	68	959	1,784	2,599	34	
Central Govt. Lending Funds.......	56f	2,238	2,684	1,240	† 1,081	919	989	999	972	936	728	813	20
Liab. to Nonbank Financial Insts.......	56j	—	—	—	† 245	613	813	1,195	1,227	2,394	2,699	2,542	2,511
Capital Accounts....................	57a	2,686	3,593	4,270	† 3,856	4,842	7,884	9,302	10,619	12,166	14,930	16,542	17,110
Other Items (Net)....................	57r	−1,435	−2,588	−2,882	† −3,014	−3,421	−1,892	−1,655	−1,730	−3,299	−3,239	−3,531	−2,625
Money (National Definitions)					*Millions of Bolivianos: End of Period*								
Base Money...........................	19ma	2,352	2,760	3,105	3,963	4,731	3,560	3,685	4,104	4,455	4,790	5,186	5,804
M1..................................	59ma	1,417	1,890	2,333	2,580	3,061	3,276	3,153	3,287	3,709	3,908	4,532	5,258
M'1..................................	59maa	2,499	3,232	3,913	4,768	5,738	6,342	5,893	6,406	7,533	8,115	9,206	9,372
M2..................................	59mb	1,499	1,997	2,425	2,791	3,355	3,589	3,480	3,617	4,151	4,291	5,051	6,392
M'2..................................	59mba	3,544	4,534	5,460	8,028	10,219	11,533	11,212	12,678	15,367	15,439	18,219	16,279
M3..................................	59mc	1,555	2,132	2,520	2,983	3,526	3,766	3,646	3,798	4,295	4,408	5,220	6,764
M'3..................................	59mca	9,675	11,767	12,880	18,430	22,039	25,118	25,777	27,264	29,160	28,473	29,912	30,194
M4..................................	59md	1,555	2,136	2,523	3,106	3,532	3,782	3,646	3,803	4,332	4,432	5,261	6,824
M'4..................................	59mda	9,675	12,036	13,330	18,948	22,408	25,552	26,162	28,013	31,341	29,971	31,832	32,785
Interest Rates					*Percent Per Annum*								
Discount Rate (End of Period)..........	60	....	....	....	16.50	13.25	14.10	12.50	10.00	8.50	12.50	7.50	6.00
Discount Rate (Fgn.Cur.)(End per)....	60..f	....	....	....	9.89	8.58	9.30	9.04	7.41	5.69	5.58	6.38	7.46
Money Market Rate...................	60b	....	....	22.42	20.27	13.97	12.57	13.49	7.40	6.99	8.41	4.07	4.05
Money Market Rate (Fgn. Cur.).......	60b.f	....	....	14.16	9.54	7.85	9.26	8.29	5.68	3.57	2.96	2.12	3.02
Treasury Bill Rate.....................	60c	....	17.89	24.51	19.93	13.65	12.33	14.07	10.99	11.48	12.41	9.92	7.41
Treasury Bill Rate (Fgn.Currency)......	60c.f	....	8.22	13.20	9.89	7.15	7.48	7.84	7.02	4.19	3.56	2.53	3.34
Savings Rate.........................	60k	20.92	17.46	16.52	16.43	14.30	12.08	10.79	9.39	6.57	6.20	5.52	4.51
Savings Rate (Fgn.Currency).............	60k.f	7.97	7.16	7.03	7.20	6.60	5.93	5.50	4.76	2.68	1.10	.73	.57
Deposit Rate.........................	60l	22.18	18.43	18.87	19.16	14.73	12.82	12.26	10.98	9.82	9.58	11.41	7.42
Deposit Rate (Fgn.Currency).............	60l.f	11.19	9.89	10.36	10.13	8.32	7.96	8.78	7.84	5.21	2.82	2.01	1.98
Lending Rate.........................	60p	53.88	55.57	51.02	55.97	50.05	39.41	35.37	34.60	20.06	20.63	17.66	14.47
Lending Rate (Fgn.Currency).............	60p.f	18.46	16.46	16.86	17.64	16.48	15.66	16.03	15.68	14.46	12.11	10.30	10.00
Prices, Production, Labor					*Index Numbers (2000=100): Period Averages*								
Consumer Prices.....................	64	62.1	67.0	73.8	83.0	86.9	93.6	95.6	100.0	101.6	102.5	106.0	110.7
Crude Petroleum Production............	66aa	70.6	81.6	90.0	92.9	95.4	119.7	103.0	100.0	113.6	115.2	125.5	147.8
					Number in Thousands: Period Averages								
Labor Force..........................	67d	....	....	1,317	1,413	3,645	....	....	3,824	....	....	....	....
Employment..........................	67e	1,091	1,195	1,257	† 1,849	1,878	....	2,017	2,091	2,156	2,118	....	....
Unemployment.......................	67c	70	39	47	† 74	71	....	157	169	200	202	....	....
Unemployment Rate (%)..............	67r	6.0	3.1	3.6	† 3.8	3.7	....	7.2	7.5	9.4	9.2	9.7	....
Intl. Transactions & Positions					*Millions of US Dollars*								
Exports..................................	70..d	727.5	1,032.4	1,100.7	1,137.1	1,166.5	1,103.9	1,051.2	1,229.5	1,284.8	1,298.7	1,597.8	2,146.0
Tin..................................	70q.d	83.3	91.1	88.6	85.5	75.1	59.9	65.3	70.5	52.6	53.2	66.0	131.7
Zinc..................................	70t.d	119.5	105.3	151.3	153.4	119.3	92.3	91.4	101.3	71.6	66.5	73.2	90.0
Imports, c.i.f..........................	71..d	1,205.9	1,209.0	1,423.8	1,635.0	1,850.9	1,983.0	1,755.1	1,829.7	1,707.7	1,770.1	1,615.9	1,844.2
Imports, f.o.b..........................	71.vd	1,111.6	1,121.7	1,263.2	1,450.5	1,698.1	1,824.4	1,539.1	1,604.5	1,497.5	1,552.3	1,497.7	1,724.9
					2000=100								
Volume of Exports.....................	72	91.0	89.4	95.6	97.6	101.6	96.2	87.7	100.0	107.3	129.1	145.3	173.4
Tin..................................	72q	114.8	120.9	102.1	100.6	103.1	81.9	92.2	100.0	78.9	101.2	110.5	126.5
Zinc..................................	72t	82.2	71.2	97.3	100.6	102.1	101.6	96.2	100.0	87.2	95.2	110.8	97.2
					2000=100: Indices of Unit Values in US Dollars								
Unit Value of Exports/Export Prices...	74..d	123.0	131.5	141.1	138.4	98.2	86.8	85.4	100.0	91.5	80.5	90.4	121.9
Tin..................................	74q.d	139.5	145.6	166.7	169.9	103.6	100.0	98.0	100.0	91.2	74.3	85.3	150.2
Zinc..................................	74t.d	143.1	146.8	154.2	150.7	116.1	89.7	93.7	100.0	81.6	68.7	65.2	91.4

Bolivia 218

		1993	1994	1995	1996	1997	1998	1999	2000	2001	2002	2003	2004
Balance of Payments						*Millions of US Dollars: Minus Sign Indicates Debit*							
Current Account, n.i.e.	78ald	−505.5	−90.2	−302.5	−404.3	−553.5	−666.1	−488.0	−446.3	−274.0	−351.9	35.6	....
Goods: Exports f.o.b.	78aad	715.5	985.1	1,041.4	1,132.0	1,166.6	1,104.0	1,051.2	1,246.1	1,284.8	1,298.7	1,573.4	....
Goods: Imports f.o.b.	78abd	−1,111.7	−1,015.3	−1,223.7	−1,368.0	−1,643.6	−1,759.5	−1,539.0	−1,610.2	−1,580.0	−1,638.7	−1,498.3	....
Trade Balance	78acd	−396.2	−30.2	−182.3	−236.0	−477.0	−655.5	−487.8	−364.1	−295.2	−340.0	75.1	....
Services: Credit	78add	181.4	196.0	192.4	180.9	247.2	251.2	259.4	224.0	235.9	256.6	298.5	....
Services: Debit	78aed	−321.7	−337.5	−350.2	−363.4	−418.7	−440.5	−449.7	−467.7	−399.4	−433.3	−477.9	....
Balance on Goods & Services	78afd	−536.5	−171.7	−340.1	−418.5	−648.5	−844.8	−678.1	−607.8	−458.7	−516.7	−104.3	....
Income: Credit	78agd	9.2	18.7	28.3	28.6	98.2	127.4	157.3	139.7	121.2	103.2	71.7	....
Income: Debit	78ahd	−215.1	−201.2	−234.9	−236.8	−294.7	−289.3	−353.3	−365.0	−332.5	−307.9	−372.8	....
Balance on Gds, Serv. & Inc	78aid	−742.4	−354.2	−546.7	−626.7	−845.0	−1,006.7	−874.1	−833.1	−670.1	−721.4	−405.5	....
Current Transfers, n.i.e.: Credit	78ajd	241.0	269.2	248.0	226.2	300.3	352.3	414.7	420.0	431.6	407.8	478.9	....
Current Transfers: Debit	78akd	−4.1	−5.2	−3.8	−3.8	−8.8	−11.7	−28.6	−33.2	−35.5	−38.4	−37.9	....
Capital Account, n.i.e.	78bcd	1.0	1.2	2.0	2.8	25.3	9.9	—	—	—	—	—	....
Capital Account, n.i.e.: Credit	78bad	1.0	1.2	2.0	2.8	25.3	9.9	—	—	—	—	—	....
Capital Account: Debit	78bbd	—	—	—	—	—	—	—	—	—	—	—	....
Financial Account, n.i.e.	78bjd	347.1	315.3	505.2	701.0	889.9	1,181.6	868.2	461.8	440.7	649.0	−64.1	....
Direct Investment Abroad	78bed	−2.0	−2.2	−2.0	−2.1	−2.4	−2.8	−2.8	−2.8	−2.5	−2.5	−2.5	....
Dir. Invest. in Rep. Econ., n.i.e.	78bed	123.8	130.2	392.7	474.1	730.6	949.3	1,010.5	736.4	705.8	676.6	166.8	....
Portfolio Investment Assets	78bfd	—	—	—	.3	−53.2	−74.5	−44.4	55.4	−23.0	−19.3	−68.2	....
Equity Securities	78bkd	—	—	—	—	—	—	—	—	—	—	—	....
Debt Securities	78bld	—	—	—	.3	−53.2	−74.5	−44.4	55.4	−23.0	−19.3	−68.2	....
Portfolio Investment Liab., n.i.e.	78bgd	—	—	—	—	—	—	−16.9	—	—	—	—	....
Equity Securities	78bmd	—	—	—	—	—	—	—	—	—	—	—	....
Debt Securities	78bnd	—	—	—	—	—	—	−16.9	—	—	—	—	....
Financial Derivatives Assets	78bwd	....	....	....	....	—	—	....	....	....	....	....	....
Financial Derivatives Liabilities	78bxd	....	....	....	....	—	—	....	....	....	....	....	....
Other Investment Assets	78bhd	17.1	−104.0	−38.4	12.2	−19.9	−13.2	−47.7	−146.1	−166.7	−193.4	−463.3	....
Monetary Authorities	78bod	....	....	....	....	—	−8.4	−9.2	−1.2				....
General Government	78bpd	−6.1	—	—	−.2	—			−7.9	−15.7	−17.1	−18.2	....
Banks	78bqd	−6.4	−104.0	−38.4	12.4	−19.9	66.1	−24.2	−94.4	−157.0	49.8	46.3	....
Other Sectors	78brd	29.6	—	—	—	—	−70.9	−14.3	−42.6	6.1	−226.1	−491.5	....
Other Investment Liab., n.i.e.	78bid	208.2	291.3	152.9	216.5	234.8	322.8	−30.5	−181.1	−72.9	187.7	303.0	....
Monetary Authorities	78bsd	42.5	40.8	78.0	11.7	1.5	−46.0	−11.6	−23.7	−20.3	−18.1	−2.7	....
General Government	78btd	−23.7	−16.9	−41.0	206.9	199.7	149.4	123.1	131.4	226.1	310.3	280.1	....
Banks	78bud	124.4	206.3	78.8	2.8	169.7	137.9	−138.1	−280.1	−247.7	−35.5	−80.6	....
Other Sectors	78bvd	65.0	61.1	37.1	−4.9	−136.1	81.5	−3.9	−8.7	−31.0	−69.0	106.2	....
Net Errors and Omissions	78cad	123.6	−315.8	−112.3	−31.6	−260.7	−400.7	−353.2	−54.8	−202.7	−639.8	−33.0	....
Overall Balance	78cbd	−33.7	−89.5	92.4	268.0	101.0	124.7	27.0	−39.4	−36.0	−342.7	−61.6	....
Reserves and Related Items	79dad	33.7	89.5	−92.4	−268.0	−101.0	−124.7	−27.0	39.4	36.0	342.7	61.6	....
Reserve Assets	79dbd	−81.7	−26.4	−147.4	−310.1	−89.6	−133.0	−31.9	38.8	32.5	303.0	−152.0	....
Use of Fund Credit and Loans	79dcd	−28.7	28.7	−1.1	17.1	−11.4	5.7	−10.9	−14.5	−5.3	−27.7	60.0	....
Exceptional Financing	79ded	144.2	87.3	56.1	25.1	—	2.6	15.8	15.1	8.8	67.3	153.5	....
International Investment Position						*Millions of US Dollars*							
Assets	79aad	....	....	....	....	2,058.0	2,520.5	2,606.6	2,647.4	2,834.7	2,953.3	3,424.3	....
Direct Investment Abroad	79abd	....	....	....	....	21.9	24.4	26.9	29.4	31.9	34.4	36.9	....
Portfolio Investment	79acd	....	....	....	....	293.7	689.2	733.6	662.9	685.9	837.0	905.4	....
Equity Securities	79add	....	....	....	....	—	—	—	—	—	—	—	....
Debt Securities	79aed	....	....	....	....	293.7	689.2	733.6	662.9	685.9	837.0	905.4	....
Financial Derivatives	79ald	....	....	....	....	—	—	—	—	—	—	—	....
Other Investment	79afd	....	....	....	....	428.1	479.4	485.7	650.2	831.9	1,033.1	1,229.1	....
Monetary Authorities	79agd	....	....	....	....	139.4	167.3	176.5	123.7	124.9	134.3	152.1	....
General Government	79ahd	....	....	....	....				61.9	88.5	104.0	121.6	....
Banks	79aid	....	....	....	....	128.7	141.1	165.2	271.7	428.7	378.9	332.6	....
Other Sectors	79ajd	....	....	....	....	160.0	171.0	144.0	192.9	189.8	415.9	622.9	....
Reserve Assets	79akd	....	....	....	....	1,314.3	1,327.5	1,360.4	1,304.9	1,285.0	1,048.8	1,252.9	....
Liabilities	79lad	....	....	....	....	7,822.9	9,277.4	10,056.1	10,400.0	11,175.3	11,706.0	12,634.5	....
Dir. Invest. in Rep. Economy	79lbd	....	....	....	....	2,414.7	3,440.8	4,451.3	5,187.7	5,893.5	6,570.0	6,732.7	....
Portfolio Investment	79lcd	....	....	....	....	15.0	36.9	20.0	20.0	—	—	—	....
Equity Securities	79ldd	....	....	....	....	—	—	—	—	—	—	—	....
Debt Securities	79led	....	....	....	....	15.0	36.9	20.0	20.0	—	—	—	....
Financial Derivatives	79lld	....	....	....	....	—	—	—	—	—	—	—	....
Other Investment	79lfd	....	....	....	....	5,393.2	5,799.7	5,584.8	5,192.3	5,281.8	5,135.9	5,901.8	....
Monetary Authorities	79lgd	....	....	....	....	733.1	707.1	667.8	597.7	342.4	335.4	424.9	....
General Government	79lhd	....	....	....	....	3,304.7	3,490.1	3,454.8	3,434.5	3,774.3	3,773.7	4,426.3	....
Banks	79lid	....	....	....	....	847.6	1,006.8	854.2	579.5	312.3	301.0	235.4	....
Other Sectors	79ljd	....	....	....	....	507.8	595.7	608.0	580.6	852.9	725.8	815.2	....
Government Finance						*Millions of Bolivianos: Year Ending December 31*							
Deficit (-) or Surplus	80	† −1,161	−902	−697	−869	−1,783	−1,917	−1,969	−2,317	−3,915	−5,484	−4,543	....
Revenue	81	† 5,273	6,532	7,687	9,014	9,884	11,699	12,131	13,048	12,906	13,524	14,717	....
Expenditure	82	† 6,434	7,434	8,384	9,883	11,667	13,615	14,100	15,365	16,821	19,008	19,259	....
Financing													
Domestic	84a	† 259	165	−327	−355	602	646	860	1,314	2,373	2,023	721	....
Foreign	85a	† 903	737	1,024	1,224	1,181	1,271	1,109	1,003	1,543	3,461	3,821	....

Bolivia   218

National Accounts		1993	1994	1995	1996	1997	1998	1999	2000	2001	2002	2003	2004
						Millions of Bolivianos							
Househ.Cons.Expend.,incl.NPISHs....	96f	19,413	21,444	24,440	28,201	31,113	35,144	37,002	39,655	40,499	41,802	43,987	47,458
Government Consumption Expend...	91f	3,270	3,750	4,375	5,003	5,790	6,658	7,126	7,550	8,458	9,051	10,227	10,551
Gross Fixed Capital Formation..........	93e	4,076	4,104	5,007	6,072	7,899	10,841	9,197	9,289	7,491	8,915	7,973	8,787
Changes in Inventories....................	93i	−25	−133	−93	23	276	212	−157	133	184	497	299	−179
Exports of Goods and Services..........	90c	4,667	5,987	7,269	8,476	8,791	9,223	8,129	9,490	10,743	12,263	15,796	21,373
Imports of Goods and Services (-).....	98c	6,943	7,516	8,764	10,238	12,226	15,256	13,141	14,188	13,585	15,710	16,322	18,364
Gross Domestic Product (GDP).........	99b	24,459	27,636	32,235	37,537	41,644	46,822	48,156	51,928	53,790	56,818	61,959	69,626
GDP Volume 1990 Prices.................	99b.p	17,230	18,034	18,877	19,701	20,677	21,717	21,809	22,356	22,733	23,286	23,934	24,792
GDP Volume (2000=100)...............	99bvp	77.1	80.7	84.4	88.1	92.5	97.1	97.6	100.0	101.7	104.2	107.1	110.9
GDP Deflator (2000=100)...............	99bip	61.1	66.0	73.5	82.0	86.7	92.8	95.1	100.0	101.9	105.0	111.5	120.9
						Millions: Midyear Estimates							
Population...............................	99z	7.15	7.32	7.48	7.65	7.81	7.98	8.15	8.32	8.49	8.66	8.84	9.01

Bosnia and Herzegovina 963

		1993	1994	1995	1996	1997	1998	1999	2000	2001	2002	2003	2004
Exchange Rates						*Convertible Marka per SDR: End of Period*							
Official Rate	aa	....	....	....	....	2.418	2.356	2.672	2.739	2.789	2.536	2.301	2.230
						Convertible Marka per US Dollar: End of Period (ae) Period Average (rf)							
Official Rate	ae	....	....	....	....	1.792	1.673	1.947	2.102	2.219	1.865	1.549	1.436
Official Rate	rf	....	....	....	....	1.734	1.760	1.836	2.123	2.186	2.078	1.733	1.575
Fund Position						*Millions of SDRs: End of Period*							
Quota	2f.s	—	—	121.2	121.2	121.2	121.2	169.1	169.1	169.1	169.1	169.1	169.1
SDRs	1b.s	—	—	5.0	1.8	—	3.7	5.6	8.2	4.9	2.3	2.3	.3
Reserve Position in the Fund	1c.s	—	—	—	—	—	—	—	—	—	—	—	—
Total Fund Cred.&Loans Outstg	2tl	—	—	32.5	31.0	30.3	54.5	68.4	80.4	88.4	102.4	90.1	70.0
International Liquidity						*Millions of US Dollars Unless Otherwise Indicated: End of Period*							
Total Reserves minus Gold	1l.d	....	....	....	....	80	175	452	497	1,221	1,321	1,796	2,408
SDRs	1b.d	—	—	8	3	—	5	8	11	6	3	3	1
Reserve Position in the Fund	1c.d	—	—	—	—	—	—	—	—	—	—	—	—
Foreign Exchange	1d.d	....	....	....	....	80	169	445	486	1,215	1,318	1,792	2,407
Monetary Authorities						*Millions of Convertible Marka End of Period*							
Foreign Assets	11	....	....	....	....	144	292	881	1,044	2,737	2,492	2,808	3,485
Reserve Money	14	....	....	....	....	170	236	807	961	2,544	2,318	2,608	3,239
of which: Currency Outside Banks	14a	....	....	....	....	113	162	515	652	1,674	1,734	1,601	1,670
Foreign Liabilities	16c	....	....	....	....	73	128	183	220	276	261	208	157
Central Government Deposits	16d	....	....	....	....	—	7	9	10	49	27	19	45
Capital Accounts	17a	....	....	....	....	1	30	34	58	121	181	215	227
Other Items (Net)	17r	....	....	....	....	−101	−109	−151	−207	−253	−295	−241	−182
Deposit Money Banks						*Millions of Convertible Marka End of Period*							
Reserves	20	....	....	....	....	71	90	275	287	872	595	1,005	1,567
Foreign Assets	21	....	....	....	....	1,299	1,172	1,134	1,246	1,364	1,469	1,562	1,906
Claims on State Government	22ab	....	....	....	....	129	106	26	24	11	29	24	21
Claims on Local Government	22b	....	....	....	....	4	7	11	9	22	23	21	25
Claims on Other Resident Sectors	22d	....	....	....	....	3,835	4,193	4,129	4,368	3,306	4,220	5,076	5,882
Demand Deposits	24	....	....	....	....	134	147	566	730	957	1,221	1,442	1,762
Time & Savings Deposits	25a	....	....	....	....	10	8	22	78	140	272	462	703
Foreign Currency Deposits	25b	....	....	....	....	907	1,219	1,039	970	1,827	1,786	1,914	2,586
Foreign Liabilities	26c	....	....	....	....	3,428	3,375	3,289	3,347	1,527	1,794	2,437	2,651
Central Government Deposits	26d	....	....	....	....	—	1	9	18	28	81	77	36
State Government Deposits	26da	....	....	....	....	331	288	183	158	318	365	471	490
Capital Accounts	27a	....	....	....	....	1,043	1,305	1,257	1,096	1,119	1,214	1,305	1,472
Other Items (Net)	27r	....	....	....	....	−514	−775	−791	−462	−341	−395	−421	−302
Monetary Survey						*Millions of Convertible Marka End of Period*							
Foreign Assets (Net)	31n	....	....	....	....	−2,058	−2,040	−1,457	−1,277	2,298	1,906	1,725	2,583
Domestic Credit	32	....	....	....	....	3,969	4,297	4,148	4,373	3,262	4,165	5,026	5,846
Claims on Central Govt. (Net)	32an	....	....	....	....	—	−8	−18	−28	−77	−107	−95	−81
Claims on State Government	32ab	....	....	....	....	129	106	26	24	11	29	24	21
Claims on Local Government	32b	....	....	....	....	4	7	11	9	22	23	21	25
Claims on Other Resident Sectors	32d	....	....	....	....	3,835	4,193	4,129	4,368	3,306	4,220	5,076	5,882
Money	34	....	....	....	....	343	384	1,149	1,471	2,790	3,154	3,289	3,788
Quasi-Money	35	....	....	....	....	1,152	1,440	1,177	1,117	2,126	2,224	2,601	3,425
Capital Accounts	37a	....	....	....	....	1,045	1,335	1,291	1,155	1,240	1,394	1,520	1,699
Other Items (Net)	37r	....	....	....	....	−629	−901	−926	−647	−596	−701	−660	−482
Money plus Quasi-Money	35l	....	....	....	....	1,495	1,824	2,326	2,588	4,916	5,378	5,891	7,212
Interest Rates						*Percent Per Annum*							
Deposit Rate	60l	....	....	....	....	....	51.88	9.07	14.67	....	† 4.53	4.03	3.72
Lending Rate	60p	....	....	....	....	....	73.50	24.29	30.50	....	† 12.70	10.87	10.28
Intl. Transactions & Positions						*Millions of Convertible Marka*							
Exports	70	....	....	....	....	....	1,043	1,376	2,265	2,256	2,089	2,363	....
Imports, f.o.b	71	....	....	....	....	....	5,120	6,048	6,583	7,331	8,048	8,223	....

Bosnia and Herzegovina   963

		1993	1994	1995	1996	1997	1998	1999	2000	2001	2002	2003	2004
Balance of Payments							*Millions of US Dollars: Minus Sign Indicates Debit*						
Current Account, n.i.e.	78ald	....	....	....	....	....	−370.8	−547.1	−462.9	−805.1	−1,253.3	−1,745.4	−1,917.0
Goods: Exports f.o.b.	78aad	....	....	....	....	....	663.8	831.8	1,129.8	1,134.2	1,109.7	1,477.5	2,086.7
Goods: Imports f.o.b.	78abd	....	....	....	....	....	−3,779.4	−4,128.7	−3,894.2	−4,092.0	−4,449.4	−5,636.8	−6,656.2
Trade Balance	78acd	....	....	....	....	....	−3,115.6	−3,296.9	−2,764.4	−2,957.8	−3,339.7	−4,159.3	−4,569.5
Services: Credit	78add	....	....	....	....	....	451.5	452.9	435.3	482.0	509.7	681.5	827.5
Services: Debit	78aed	....	....	....	....	....	−276.0	−290.4	−283.3	−284.4	−323.3	−414.6	−455.2
Balance on Goods & Services	78afd	....	....	....	....	....	−2,940.0	−3,134.5	−2,612.4	−2,760.1	−3,153.2	−3,892.4	−4,197.2
Income: Credit	78agd	....	....	....	....	....	863.0	777.9	652.9	625.2	602.8	648.4	571.7
Income: Debit	78ahd	....	....	....	....	....	−53.7	−64.9	−75.6	−86.4	−93.9	−117.4	−124.6
Balance on Gds, Serv. & Inc.	78aid	....	....	....	....	....	−2,130.7	−2,421.5	−2,035.1	−2,221.4	−2,644.3	−3,361.4	−3,750.1
Current Transfers, n.i.e.: Credit	78ajd	....	....	....	....	....	1,846.2	1,960.8	1,647.6	1,489.2	1,492.9	1,738.8	1,999.6
Current Transfers: Debit	78akd	....	....	....	....	....	−86.3	−86.4	−75.4	−72.9	−101.9	−122.8	−166.5
Capital Account, n.i.e.	78bcd	....	....	....	....	....	495.2	625.3	546.4	395.5	412.4	462.1	491.9
Capital Account, n.i.e.: Credit	78bad	....	....	....	....	....	495.2	625.3	546.4	395.5	412.4	462.1	491.9
Capital Account: Debit	78bbd	....	....	....	....	....	—	—	—	—	—	—	—
Financial Account, n.i.e.	78bjd	....	....	....	....	....	−589.9	−699.9	−460.2	770.0	222.5	855.8	932.6
Direct Investment Abroad	78bdd	....	....	....	....	....	—	—	—	—	—	—	−.7
Dir. Invest. in Rep. Econ., n.i.e.	78bed	....	....	....	....	....	66.7	176.8	146.1	118.5	267.8	381.8	498.2
Portfolio Investment Assets	78bfd	....	....	....	....	....	—	—	—	—	—	—	....
Equity Securities	78bkd	....	....	....	....	....	—	—	—	—	—	—	....
Debt Securities	78bld	....	....	....	....	....	—	—	—	—	—	—	....
Portfolio Investment Liab., n.i.e.	78bgd	....	....	....	....	....	—	—	—	—	—	—	....
Equity Securities	78bmd	....	....	....	....	....	—	—	—	—	—	—	....
Debt Securities	78bnd	....	....	....	....	....	—	—	—	—	—	—	....
Financial Derivatives Assets	78bwd	....	....	....	....	....							
Financial Derivatives Liabilities	78bxd	....	....	....	....	....							
Other Investment Assets	78bhd	....	....	....	....	....	−623.9	−792.3	−612.5	710.8	−39.5	178.2	169.8
Monetary Authorities	78bod	....	....	....	....	....	....	....	....	....	....	....	....
General Government	78bpd	....	....	....	....	....	....	....	....	....	....	....	....
Banks	78bqd	....	....	....	....	....	71.9	21.1	−52.9	−185.6	−40.5	−56.8	−192.0
Other Sectors	78brd	....	....	....	....	....	−695.8	−813.5	−559.6	896.5	1.0	235.0	361.8
Other Investment Liab., n.i.e.	78bid	....	....	....	....	....	−32.8	−84.3	6.2	−59.3	−5.7	295.9	265.3
Monetary Authorities	78bsd	....	....	....	....	....	—	—	1.3	13.6	−26.8	−.2	—
General Government	78btd	....	....	....	....	....	—	−36.9	−27.9	−24.4	−62.6	−97.5	−93.3
Banks	78bud	....	....	....	....	....	−29.8	−47.1	27.2	−22.5	130.8	382.4	285.0
Other Sectors	78bvd	....	....	....	....	....	−3.0	−.3	5.7	−26.0	−47.2	11.1	73.6
Net Errors and Omissions	78cad	....	....	....	....	....	105.7	25.3	112.8	106.5	58.6	340.8	583.1
Overall Balance	78cbd	....	....	....	....	....	−359.9	−596.4	−263.9	466.9	−559.8	−86.7	90.6
Reserves and Related Items	79dad	....	....	....	....	....	359.9	596.4	263.9	−466.9	559.8	86.7	−90.6
Reserve Assets	79dbd	....	....	....	....	....	−84.0	−319.4	−76.5	−761.6	109.6	−196.6	−426.6
Use of Fund Credit and Loans	79dcd	....	....	....	....	....	32.3	18.2	15.5	9.9	19.0	−17.1	−29.7
Exceptional Financing	79ded	....	....	....	....	....	411.5	897.6	324.8	284.8	431.3	300.4	365.7
National Accounts							*Millions of Convertible Marka*						
Gross Domestic Product (GDP)	99b	....	....	....	4,192	6,367	7,244	8,990	10,050	10,960	11,650	12,170	....
Population	99z	3.73	3.53	3.42	3.41	† 3.49	3.62	3.75	3.85	3.90	3.92	3.92	3.91

(Population: Millions: Midyear Estimates)

Botswana 616

		1993	1994	1995	1996	1997	1998	1999	2000	2001	2002	2003	2004
Exchange Rates						*Pula per SDR: End of Period*							
Official Rate	aa	3.5229	3.9670	4.1944	5.2404	5.1400	6.2774	6.3572	6.9861	8.7760	7.4331	6.6014	6.6482
						Pula per US Dollar: End of Period (ae) Period Average (rf)							
Official Rate	ae	2.5648	2.7174	2.8217	3.6443	3.8095	4.4583	4.6318	5.3619	6.9832	5.4675	4.4425	4.2808
Official Rate	rf	2.4231	2.6846	2.7722	3.3242	3.6508	4.2259	4.6244	5.1018	5.8412	6.3278	4.9499	4.6929
Fund Position						*Millions of SDRs: End of Period*							
Quota	2f.s	36.60	36.60	36.60	36.60	36.60	36.60	63.00	63.00	63.00	63.00	63.00	63.00
SDRs	1b.s	24.03	25.39	27.06	28.71	30.36	32.41	28.05	29.89	31.53	32.63	33.52	34.42
Reserve Position in the Fund	1c.s	16.60	16.34	19.28	19.91	18.13	27.61	22.59	17.74	22.28	23.80	30.32	20.50
Total Fund Cred.&Loans Outstg	2tl	—	—	—	—	—	—	—	—	—	—	—	—
International Liquidity					*Millions of US Dollars Unless Otherwise Indicated: End of Period*								
Total Reserves minus Gold	1l.d	4,097.34	4,401.47	4,695.48	5,027.66	5,675.00	5,940.67	6,298.72	6,318.21	5,897.25	5,473.92	5,339.78	5,661.43
SDRs	1b.d	33.00	37.07	40.22	41.28	40.96	45.63	38.50	38.94	39.62	44.36	49.81	53.46
Reserve Position in the Fund	1c.d	22.79	23.86	28.66	28.63	24.46	38.87	31.00	23.11	28.00	32.36	45.05	31.84
Foreign Exchange	1d.d	4,041.54	4,340.54	4,626.60	4,957.75	5,609.58	5,856.17	6,229.21	6,256.16	5,829.63	5,397.20	5,244.92	5,576.13
Monetary Authorities: Other Liab.	4..d	—	—	—	—	—	—	—	—	—	—	—	—
Deposit Money Banks: Assets	7a.d	61.17	63.42	69.60	124.51	211.33	317.73	290.52	267.62	319.47	284.37	398.85	346.85
Liabilities	7b.d	54.32	24.22	35.05	41.61	31.61	38.49	34.79	41.93	52.65	53.33	94.76	77.83
Monetary Authorities						*Millions of Pula: End of Period*							
Foreign Assets	11	10,506	10,567	12,115	18,356	21,637	26,502	28,867	33,900	41,211	29,984	23,887	24,368
Reserve Money	14	395	392	405	453	572	707	808	857	970	1,050	1,338	1,262
of which: Currency Outside DMBs	14a	180	195	223	247	276	353	404	427	481	470	533	637
Time Deposits	15	38	46	48	47	63	26	172	183	184	286	231	852
Liabs. of Central Bank: Securities	16ac	1,201	1,451	1,964	2,816	3,308	3,246	4,230	3,712	5,148	7,663	8,739	9,649
Foreign Liabilities	16c	—	—	—	—	—	—	—	—	—	—	—	—
Central Government Deposits	16d	5,586	6,689	6,469	7,221	15,362	19,072	20,086	24,026	27,719	16,433	10,514	9,272
Capital Accounts	17a	2,167	2,935	2,942	6,107	1,888	3,229	3,415	4,384	6,668	4,107	2,758	3,054
Other Items (Net)	17r	1,119	−945	288	1,713	444	223	156	737	524	445	307	278
Deposit Money Banks						*Millions of Pula: End of Period*							
Reserves	20	194	160	166	177	271	331	353	229	263	311	397	470
Claims on Mon.Author.:Securities	20c	361	493	832	1,192	1,572	1,322	1,718	1,197	1,874	1,732	2,229	2,749
Foreign Assets	21	157	172	196	454	805	1,417	1,346	1,435	2,231	1,555	1,772	1,485
Claims on Central Government	22a	—	2	—	—	2	14	15	2	1	—	—	—
Claims on Local Government	22b	3	2	3	2	2	14	15	2	1	—	—	—
Claims on Nonfin.Pub.Enterprises	22c	94	148	95	70	61	267	528	458	480	462	381	433
Claims on Private Sector	22d	1,434	1,600	1,560	1,626	1,775	2,461	3,518	4,344	4,915	6,155	6,821	8,007
Claims on Other Financial Insts	22f	32	95	122	100	61	231	130	123	64	4	—	—
Demand Deposits	24	516	579	607	704	762	1,160	1,371	1,470	1,869	2,054	2,290	2,989
Time and Savings Deposits	25	1,386	1,573	1,809	2,192	3,003	4,183	5,282	5,248	7,082	6,698	7,924	8,253
Foreign Liabilities	26c	139	66	99	152	120	172	161	225	368	292	421	333
Central Government Deposits	26d	31	16	19	40	36	29	66	107	61	58	148	433
Capital Accounts	27a	244	308	337	402	464	568	732	843	1,042	1,102	1,346	1,395
Other Items (Net)	27r	−43	131	103	131	162	−70	−4	−103	−594	16	−529	−258
Monetary Survey						*Millions of Pula: End of Period*							
Foreign Assets (Net)	31n	10,524	10,673	12,213	18,658	22,321	27,747	30,051	35,110	43,075	31,247	25,238	25,519
Domestic Credit	32	−4,054	−4,859	−4,709	−5,463	−13,499	−16,128	−15,961	−19,205	−22,320	−9,870	−3,460	−1,264
Claims on Central Govt. (Net)	32an	−5,617	−6,703	−6,488	−7,261	−15,398	−19,101	−20,152	−24,133	−27,779	−16,491	−10,662	−9,705
Claims on Local Government	32b	3	2	3	2	2	14	15	2	1	—	—	—
Claims on Nonfin.Pub.Enterprises	32c	94	148	95	70	61	267	528	458	480	462	381	433
Claims on Private Sector	32d	1,434	1,600	1,560	1,626	1,775	2,461	3,518	4,344	4,915	6,155	6,821	8,007
Claims on Other Financial Insts	32f	32	95	122	100	61	231	130	123	64	4	—	—
Money	34	696	774	829	951	1,038	1,513	1,775	1,897	2,351	2,524	2,822	3,626
Quasi-Money	35	1,424	1,619	1,856	2,239	3,066	4,209	5,454	5,432	7,266	6,984	8,155	9,105
Liabs. of Central Bank: Securities	36ac	840	958	1,132	1,623	1,736	1,924	2,513	2,515	3,274	5,931	6,510	6,900
Capital Accounts	37a	2,412	3,243	3,279	6,509	2,352	3,797	4,147	5,227	7,710	5,209	4,104	4,450
Other Items (Net)	37r	1,097	−778	407	1,873	631	177	202	835	155	730	187	175
Money plus Quasi-Money	35l	2,121	2,392	2,686	3,190	4,104	5,722	7,228	7,328	9,617	9,508	10,977	12,731
Interest Rates						*Percent Per Annum*							
Bank Rate (End of Period)	60	14.25	13.50	13.00	13.00	12.00	12.75	13.75	14.25	14.25	15.25	14.25	14.25
Savings Rate	60k	....	....	....	7.05	7.57	6.78	7.27	7.93	8.60	7.98	8.17	7.66
Deposit Rate	60l	13.49	10.59	9.79	9.68	9.51	8.43	9.10	9.42	10.09	10.45	9.95	9.85
Deposit Rate (Fgn. Currency)	60l.f	....	....	....	4.60	4.43	4.52	4.46	5.93	4.06	1.52	.96	1.36
Lending Rate	60p	14.92	13.92	14.42	14.50	13.95	13.65	14.78	15.48	15.75	16.21	16.33	15.75
Government Bond Yield	61	....	....	....	....	....	....	....	....	....	....	10.46	10.07
Prices and Labor						*Index Numbers (2000=100): Period Averages*							
Consumer Prices	64	54.8	60.6	66.9	† 73.7	80.1	85.5	92.1	100.0	106.6	115.1	125.7	134.4
						Number in Thousands: Period Averages							
Employment	67e	228	231	233	238	230	242	257	265	271	279	....	....
Intl. Transactions & Positions						*Millions of Pula*							
Exports	70	4,270.9	4,965.0	5,941.5	8,133.4	10,390.7	8,696.9	12,227.8	13,834.7	14,306.5	14,671.5	....	....
Imports, c.i.f	71	4,285.0	4,407.3	5,305.1	5,742.9	8,250.0	9,803.8	10,164.4	12,646.8	10,556.9	12,191.0	....	....

		1993	1994	1995	1996	1997	1998	1999	2000	2001	2002	2003	2004
Balance of Payments						*Millions of US Dollars: Minus Sign Indicates Debit*							
Current Account, n.i.e.	78ald	426.9	221.6	299.7	495.0	721.4	169.7	583.5	545.2	597.7	170.2	....	....
Goods: Exports f.o.b.	78aad	1,722.2	1,874.3	2,160.2	2,217.5	2,819.8	2,060.6	2,658.2	2,675.4	2,314.5	2,318.6	....	....
Goods: Imports f.o.b.	78abd	−1,455.4	−1,364.3	−1,605.4	−1,467.7	−1,924.5	−1,983.1	−1,873.5	−1,773.2	−1,604.1	−1,642.3	....	....
Trade Balance	78acd	266.8	510.0	554.8	749.8	895.4	77.5	784.7	902.1	710.4	676.3	....	....
Services: Credit	78add	191.3	186.1	260.4	163.0	210.2	254.9	331.2	324.8	340.3	489.6	....	....
Services: Debit	78aed	−325.6	−312.0	−444.2	−343.6	−440.7	−522.4	−518.0	−547.5	−513.3	−509.7	....	....
Balance on Goods & Services	78afd	132.5	384.2	370.9	569.2	664.9	−190.0	597.9	679.4	537.3	656.2	....	....
Income: Credit	78agd	554.5	230.8	483.2	501.7	622.1	622.7	429.8	378.1	358.4	268.4	....	....
Income: Debit	78ahd	−260.9	−455.1	−515.6	−754.8	−766.9	−503.1	−696.0	−729.5	−495.4	−966.6	....	....
Balance on Gds, Serv. & Inc.	78aid	426.1	159.9	338.5	316.1	520.1	−70.5	331.7	328.1	400.2	−42.1	....	....
Current Transfers, n.i.e.: Credit	78ajd	275.9	356.8	330.7	355.4	456.8	460.9	474.4	426.1	383.0	400.4	....	....
Current Transfers: Debit	78akd	−275.1	−295.1	−369.5	−176.6	−255.5	−220.8	−222.6	−209.0	−185.5	−188.1	....	....
Capital Account, n.i.e.	78bcd	84.9	19.2	14.4	6.2	16.9	31.8	20.6	38.1	5.8	15.7	....	....
Capital Account, n.i.e.: Credit	78bad	86.1	19.6	15.4	18.1	29.4	44.2	33.5	51.5	18.7	29.7	....	....
Capital Account: Debit	78bbd	−1.3	−.4	−.9	−11.9	−12.5	−12.4	−12.9	−13.3	−12.9	−14.0	....	....
Financial Account, n.i.e.	78bjd	−40.3	41.1	−33.9	42.4	5.6	−202.4	−231.0	−214.0	−509.4	−217.3	....	....
Direct Investment Abroad	78bdd	−9.5	−9.5	−40.9	1.1	−4.1	−3.5	−1.5	−2.3	−370.9	−42.9	....	....
Dir. Invest. in Rep. Econ., n.i.e.	78bed	−286.9	−14.2	70.4	71.2	100.1	95.3	36.7	57.2	22.1	403.4	....	....
Portfolio Investment Assets	78bfd	—	—	−36.2	−35.5	−28.5	−42.8	−22.8	−34.1	−68.4	−420.2	....	....
Equity Securities	78bkd	—	—	−30.8	−26.7	−33.1	−16.9	6.5	−3.4	−5.8	−325.5	....	....
Debt Securities	78bld	—	—	−5.4	−8.9	4.7	−25.9	−29.3	−30.7	−62.6	−94.8	....	....
Portfolio Investment Liab., n.i.e.	78bgd	.2	−.1	5.5	28.9	10.8	−14.1	−7.5	−5.9	6.0	7.1	....	....
Equity Securities	78bmd	—	—	5.5	28.7	10.8	−14.1	−7.5	−5.9	6.0	7.1	....	....
Debt Securities	78bnd	.2	−.1	—	.2	—	—	—	—	—	—	....	....
Financial Derivatives Assets	78bwd	....	....	−.2	—	—	—	—	—	—	—	....	....
Financial Derivatives Liabilities	78bxd	....	....	.3	2.1	−15.4	5.2	−4.6	−3.0	—	—	....	....
Other Investment Assets	78bhd	63.4	15.8	−88.7	−95.6	−166.6	−310.8	−274.7	−263.6	−152.7	−221.1	....	....
Monetary Authorities	78bod	....	....	....	....	....	....	....	....	....	....	....	....
General Government	78bpd	56.1	19.7	−46.1	−28.7	−78.0	−101.1	−86.3	−90.4	−52.6	−80.8	....	....
Banks	78bqd	14.3	.4	−8.7	−35.1	−76.9	−139.7	−154.7	−135.0	−78.5	−112.9	....	....
Other Sectors	78brd	−6.9	−4.3	−34.0	−31.8	−11.7	−70.0	−33.7	−38.3	−21.6	−27.3	....	....
Other Investment Liab., n.i.e.	78bid	192.5	49.0	55.9	70.3	109.3	68.2	43.5	37.7	54.4	56.3	....	....
Monetary Authorities	78bsd	—	—	—	—	—	—	—	—	—	—	....	....
General Government	78btd	67.0	6.5	−12.3	−19.6	51.3	22.2	−16.1	−22.5	−21.1	−23.1	....	....
Banks	78bud	23.1	−2.8	−2.5	17.8	−3.4	−3.5	1.4	1.4	7.2	7.6	....	....
Other Sectors	78bvd	102.4	45.3	70.7	72.1	61.4	49.5	58.1	58.9	68.3	71.9	....	....
Net Errors and Omissions	78cad	−74.5	−146.7	−73.6	−32.9	−108.8	45.1	21.1	−1.9	75.8	92.0	....	....
Overall Balance	78cbd	397.0	135.2	206.6	510.7	635.1	44.2	394.1	367.4	170.0	60.6	....	....
Reserves and Related Items	79dad	−397.0	−135.2	−206.6	−510.7	−635.1	−44.2	−394.1	−367.4	−170.0	−60.6	....	....
Reserve Assets	79dbd	−397.0	−135.2	−206.6	−510.7	−635.1	−44.2	−394.1	−367.4	−170.0	−60.6	....	....
Use of Fund Credit and Loans	79dcd	—	—	—	—	—	—	—	—	—	—	....	....
Exceptional Financing	79ded	....	....	....	....	....	....	....	....	....	....	....	....
International Investment Position						*Millions of US Dollars*							
Assets	79aad	....	5,084.0	5,643.9	6,001.0	6,510.5	6,855.1	7,356.3	7,391.7	7,390.1	7,633.9		
Direct Investment Abroad	79abd	....	484.5	650.1	576.7	404.5	257.5	596.9	516.6	865.8	1,023.7		
Portfolio Investment	79acd	....	26.9	61.5	139.1	132.2	214.6	148.2	226.1	296.8	755.8		
Equity Securities	79add	....	16.1	45.8	105.8	81.7	73.6	120.2	129.7	197.7	430.4		
Debt Securities	79aed	....	10.9	15.8	33.3	50.5	141.0	28.0	96.4	99.1	325.3		
Financial Derivatives	79ald	....	—	.2	—	17.1	9.7	—	—	—	—		
Other Investment	79afd	....	171.3	239.1	253.1	280.3	433.0	382.4	330.8	330.2	380.5		
Monetary Authorities	79agd	....	—	—	—	—	—	—	—	—	—		
General Government	79ahd	....	—	—	—	—	—	—	—	—	—		
Banks	79aid	....	63.3	69.5	99.9	186.2	291.5	289.9	250.9	274.3	361.9		
Other Sectors	79ajd	....	107.9	169.6	153.3	94.2	141.5	92.5	79.9	55.8	18.6		
Reserve Assets	79akd	....	4,401.3	4,693.0	5,032.1	5,676.5	5,940.3	6,228.8	6,318.2	5,897.2	5,473.9		
Liabilities	79lad	....	2,005.3	1,995.1	1,941.9	2,151.9	2,248.7	2,514.8	3,056.6	2,338.7	1,987.2		
Dir. Invest. in Rep. Economy	79lbd	....	998.5	1,126.4	1,058.1	1,172.9	1,294.8	1,387.3	1,826.6	1,388.5	854.1		
Portfolio Investment	79lcd	....	10.9	15.9	50.4	60.5	34.2	24.0	13.4	15.4	23.5		
Equity Securities	79ldd	....	10.9	15.9	50.4	60.0	33.4	22.7	12.7	14.8	23.5		
Debt Securities	79led	....	—	—	—	.5	.8	1.3	.7	.5	—		
Financial Derivatives	79lld	....	—	.2	1.9	—	—	—	—	—	—		
Other Investment	79lfd	....	996.0	852.6	831.5	918.5	919.7	1,103.5	1,216.5	934.9	1,109.7		
Monetary Authorities	79lgd	....	—	—	—	—	—	—	—	—	—		
General Government	79lhd	....	496.9	495.8	387.9	483.1	482.7	523.6	419.3	314.8	467.1		
Banks	79lid	....	38.9	35.1	27.4	23.7	16.8	15.3	25.3	25.5	31.1		
Other Sectors	79ljd	....	460.1	321.7	416.2	411.7	420.3	564.6	771.9	594.6	611.5		
Government Finance						*Millions of Pula: Year Beginning April 1*							
Deficit (-) or Surplus	80	878.30	195.60	269.90	1,302.40	875.19	−1,387.80	1,535.58	† 2,782.78	−931.23	−1,475.82	−133.89	
Total Revenue and Grants	81y	5,359.50	4,472.50	5,464.40	7,394.80	8,281.29	7,677.62	11,963.09	† 13,975.10	12,585.86	14,227.61	16,135.93	....
Revenue	81	5,172.90	4,396.80	5,427.30	7,311.80	8,169.20	7,539.93	11,837.04	† 13,920.76	12,527.87	13,999.19	16,074.57	
Grants	81z	186.60	75.70	37.10	83.00	112.09	137.69	126.05	† 54.34	57.99	228.42	61.36	
Exp. & Lending Minus Repay	82z	4,481.20	4,276.90	5,194.50	6,092.40	7,406.10	9,065.42	10,427.51	† 11,192.32	13,517.09	15,703.43	16,269.82	
Expenditure	82	4,291.90	4,389.10	5,181.60	6,283.50	7,188.10	9,199.78	10,608.94	† 11,102.91	13,404.19	15,693.45	17,191.18	
Lending Minus Repayments	83	189.30	−112.20	12.90	−191.10	218.00	−134.36	−181.43	† 89.41	112.90	9.98	−921.36	
Total Financing	80h	−878.30	−195.70	−269.80	−1,302.30	−875.14	1,387.80	−1,535.58	† −2,782.78	931.23	1,475.82	133.89	
Total Net Borrowing	84	90.90	69.50	89.80	−8,148.70	13,467.36	1,098.16	−216.47	† 899.26	−1,878.81	−6,256.77	−3,818.51	
Use of Cash Balances	87	−969.20	−265.20	−359.60	6,846.40	−14,342.50	289.64	−1,319.11	† −3,682.04	2,810.04	7,732.59	3,952.40	
Total Debt by Currency	88	1,267.80	1,377.70	1,439.90	1,791.20	1,996.90	2,422.80	2,425.30	2,426.20	2,917.50	2,194.70	2,194.50	
Domestic	88b	—	—	—	—	—	—	—	—	—	—	—	
Foreign	89b	1,267.80	1,377.70	1,439.90	1,791.20	1,996.90	2,422.80	2,425.30	2,426.20	2,917.50	2,194.70	2,194.50	....

Botswana 616

		1993	1994	1995	1996	1997	1998	1999	2000	2001	2002	2003	2004
National Accounts						*Millions of Pula: Year Ending June 30*							
Househ.Cons.Expend.,incl.NPISHs....	96f	3,282.2	3,843.0	4,258.5	4,714.7	5,314.7	6,136.1	6,936.8	7,841.1	8,438.6	9,307.6	10,336.0	11,474.6
Government Consumption Expend...	91f	2,595.2	3,049.0	3,546.7	4,006.7	4,711.0	5,452.9	6,578.8	7,524.5	8,741.8	10,552.7	12,167.5	13,692.4
Gross Fixed Capital Formation..........	93e	2,618.7	2,813.8	3,135.2	3,632.4	4,275.9	5,170.1	6,263.3	6,751.0	6,898.2	7,743.3	8,735.7	9,556.1
Changes in Inventories....................	93i	165.3	204.3	13.7	−261.4	328.2	886.0	1,653.9	−1,650.2	−1,291.2	607.6	2,001.2	2,411.0
Exports of Goods and Services..........	90c	4,082.8	5,412.0	6,071.4	7,411.6	9,881.6	11,392.8	10,051.6	15,318.5	17,555.0	15,564.3	16,132.4	15,864.3
Imports of Goods and Services (-).....	98c	3,625.0	4,260.3	4,772.5	5,300.1	6,771.1	8,875.3	9,960.6	10,422.4	10,805.9	11,737.9	12,312.7	12,857.4
Gross Domestic Product (GDP)........	99b	9,119.2	19,561.9	21,806.7	24,804.2	31,282.4	37,913.3	41,445.1	24,943.1	50,248.3	31,922.4	61,340.5	39,880.9
Consumption of Fixed Capital..........	99cf	1,245.6	1,483.1	1,720.7	1,933.6	2,210.7	2,421.3	2,647.4	3,067.1	—	....	....	....
GDP Volume 1993/94 Prices............	99b.p	10,612.0	11,041.4	11,397.6	12,029.5	12,704.2	13,728.6	14,295.6	15,238.8	16,535.3	16,879.6	18,193.1	19,236.0
GDP Volume (2000=100)...............	99bvp	69.6	72.5	74.8	78.9	83.4	90.1	93.8	100.0	108.5	110.8	119.4	126.2
GDP Deflator (2000=100)...............	99bip	52.5	108.2	116.9	126.0	150.4	168.7	177.1	100.0	185.7	115.5	206.0	126.7
						Millions: Midyear Estimates							
Population...............................	99z	1.54	1.58	1.62	1.65	1.68	1.71	1.74	1.75	1.77	1.77	1.77	1.77

		1993	1994	1995	1996	1997	1998	1999	2000	2001	2002	2003	2004
Exchange Rates						*Reais per SDR: End of Period*							
Principal Rate	aa	.163	† 1.235	1.446	1.495	1.506	1.702	2.455	2.547	2.916	4.803	4.292	4.121
						Reais per US dollar: End of Period (ae)Period Average (rf)							
Principal Rate	ae	.119	† .846	.973	1.039	1.116	1.209	1.789	1.955	2.320	3.533	2.888	2.654
Principal Rate	rf	.032	† .639	.918	1.005	1.078	1.161	1.815	1.830	2.358	2.921	3.077	2.925
Fund Position						*Millions of SDRs: End of Period*							
Quota	2f.s	2,171	2,171	2,171	2,171	2,171	2,171	3,036	3,036	3,036	3,036	3,036	3,036
SDRs	1b.s	2	—	1	1	—	1	7	—	8	202	2	3
Reserve Position in the Fund	1c.s												
Total Fund Cred.&Loans Outstg	2tl	221	128	95	47	23	3,427	6,431	1,357	6,634	15,320	19,056	16,117
International Liquidity						*Millions of US Dollars Unless Otherwise Indicated: End of Period*							
Total Reserves minus Gold	1l.d	30,604	37,070	49,708	58,323	50,827	42,580	34,796	32,488	35,739	37,683	49,111	52,740
SDRs	1b.d	2	—	1	1	1	2	10	—	11	275	2	4
Reserve Position in the Fund	1c.d												
Foreign Exchange	1d.d	30,602	37,069	49,707	58,322	50,826	42,578	34,786	32,488	35,729	37,409	49,108	52,736
Other Liquid Foreign Assets	1e.d	501	319	365	467	503	585	618	—	—	—	—	—
Gold (Million Fine Troy Ounces)	1ad	2.93	3.71	4.58	3.69	3.03	4.60	3.17	1.89	.46	.44	.45	.45
Gold (National Valuation)	1and	1,107	1,418	1,767	1,381	903	1,358	929	523	127	153	186	195
Monetary Authorities:Other Assets	3..d	2,056	1,851	4,077	5,050	4,935	5,456	5,334	6,110	—	—	—	—
Other Liab.	4..d	48,399	6,888	5,614	3,239	2,948	8,284	5,288	2,419	1,255	4,735	9,435	4,523
Deposit Money Banks: Assets	7a.d	15,196	20,855	18,682	20,345	19,550	17,622	16,754	15,876	16,525	12,697	19,237	18,851
Liabilities	7b.d	31,054	36,771	42,494	51,432	54,756	51,207	42,286	40,953	40,215	31,545	30,578	29,990
Other Banking Insts.: Assets	7e.d	702	1,504	393	177	143	87	68	207	156	230	428	202
Liabilities	7f.d	2,527	2,224	2,247	3,211	4,398	9,406	8,217	7,975	8,532	8,873	9,651	8,749
Monetary Authorities						*Thousands of Reais through 1992; Millions of Reais Beginning 1993: End of Period*							
Foreign Assets	11	3,968	35,326	55,218	69,829	61,745	55,053	69,273	76,097	82,026	133,291	150,909	145,848
Claims on Central Government	12a	7,941	26,509	31,221	27,713	41,233	136,916	121,463	130,779	189,786	284,115	290,363	311,198
Claims on State and Local Govts	12b	9	—	—	—	—	—	—	—	—	—	—	—
Claims on Nonfin.Pub.Enterprises	12c												
Claims on Private Sector	12d	—	3	5	5	5	—	—	—	—	—	—	—
Claims on Deposit Money Banks	12e	120	20,557	34,576	67,642	68,012	40,368	33,755	38,604	20,679	2,924	226	4,164
Claims on Other Banking Insts	12f	1	5	5	3	902	—	—	—	1,764	—	—	—
Claims on Nonbank Financial Insts	12g	—	—	—	6	7	1,926	2,036	1,373	1,456	1,070	606	—
Reserve Money	14	1,543	36,130	40,430	49,638	66,636	59,213	63,849	66,901	79,639	199,066	190,801	211,341
of which: Currency Outside DMBs	14a	340	8,700	12,517	15,316	18,141	21,186	25,977	28,641	32,627	42,351	43,065	52,020
Money Market Instruments	16aa	—	—	—	—	—	—	—	—	—	122	79	154
Liabs. of Central Bank: Securities	16ac	867	39,289	52,457	83,106	65,724	104,709	62,468	85,839	126,524	67,021	30,619	13,569
Restricted Deposits	16b	75	306	190	125	12	10	13	13	15	23	18	12
Foreign Liabilities	16c	5,775	5,970	5,594	3,435	3,324	15,834	25,239	8,184	22,249	90,301	109,044	78,443
Central Government Deposits	16d	1,023	12,094	22,239	25,143	41,135	50,403	75,779	88,380	82,516	89,151	120,264	158,817
Capital Accounts	17a	1,838	998	1,408	4,190	4,198	3,809	−4,496	−8,312	6,814	−12,032	8,788	13,648
Other Items (Net)	17r	918	−12,387	−1,293	−438	−9,125	285	3,674	5,847	−22,045	−12,251	−17,509	−14,774
Deposit Money Banks						*Thousands of Reais through 1992; Millions of Reais Beginning 1993: End of Period*							
Reserves	20	901	22,956	22,126	22,035	42,494	32,716	38,029	38,342	46,388	152,714	140,334	151,683
Claims on Mon.Author.:Securities	20c	320	5,192	6,578	18,932	11,603	54,196	40,140	52,257	61,525	36,467	19,021	9,223
Blocked Financial Assets	20d	—	—	—	—	—	—	—	—	—	—	—	—
Foreign Assets	21	1,802	17,602	18,159	21,130	21,810	21,285	29,959	31,032	38,331	44,850	55,565	50,039
Claims on Central Government	22a	1,027	8,963	28,869	48,056	111,023	127,933	185,809	218,079	263,553	271,926	318,731	334,285
Claims on State and Local Govts	22b	1,522	27,482	25,986	56,061	39,447	38,229	19,000	4,274	2,753	2,476	2,504	3,105
Claims on Nonfin.Pub.Enterprises	22c	1,158	10,245	12,399	18,736	5,716	12,996	15,481	3,710	1,544	2,321	2,160	3,043
Claims on Private Sector	22d	11,588	174,702	210,464	220,681	254,568	278,787	287,129	311,354	342,176	381,562	434,510	487,499
Claims on Other Banking Insts	22f	80	879	826	1,100	3,397	5,234	7,181	9,016	10,681	11,804	13,756	15,090
Claims on Nonbank Financial Insts	22g	—	—	—	—	—	5,910	985	794	3,676	484	147	156
Demand Deposits	24	497	13,979	14,034	14,320	27,912	29,064	36,258	45,057	50,388	64,680	65,879	75,207
Time and Savings Deposits	25	7,919	99,074	135,641	146,719	174,020	192,218	201,714	200,215	225,453	275,740	285,088	342,297
Money Market Instruments	26aa	283	3,320	4,744	7,029	10,283	12,684	13,377	22,880	32,739	20,140	34,560	33,104
Restricted Deposits	26b	1,791	18,868	24,707	26,237	28,952	33,331	35,564	39,059	41,835	48,564	55,088	58,491
Foreign Liabilities	26c	3,682	31,035	41,304	53,417	61,086	61,853	75,616	80,047	93,283	111,432	88,322	79,605
Central Government Deposits	26d	1,411	18,288	14,670	16,074	17,939	12,338	7,918	10,066	11,950	8,377	13,014	16,342
Credit from Monetary Authorities	26g	146	20,455	23,407	39,025	30,272	11,623	3,159	8,568	23,916	3,357	219	4,447
Liabilities to Other Banking Insts	26i	1,081	11,914	9,396	22,017	21,973	43,712	54,338	70,959	85,951	141,546	165,208	156,406
Liab. to Nonbank Financial Insts	26j	1	92	111	60	234	6,059	1,033	1,745	3,246	2,326	2,286	1,811
Capital Accounts	27a	4,069	44,094	57,704	74,127	95,976	117,477	135,963	136,846	166,080	192,483	227,739	250,025
Other Items (Net)	27r	−2,482	6,902	−311	7,707	21,411	56,928	58,772	53,416	35,784	35,961	49,324	36,387
Monetary Survey						*Thousands of Reais through 1992; Millions of Reais Beginning 1993: End of Period*							
Foreign Assets (Net)	31n	−3,688	15,923	26,479	34,107	19,145	−1,349	−1,623	18,897	4,825	−23,590	9,108	37,839
Domestic Credit	32	20,893	218,406	272,866	331,145	397,224	545,191	555,386	580,934	722,922	858,230	929,500	979,216
Claims on Central Govt. (Net)	32an	6,535	5,090	23,181	34,552	93,182	202,108	223,574	250,412	358,872	458,513	475,817	470,324
Claims on State and Local Govts	32b	1,531	27,482	25,986	56,061	39,447	38,229	19,000	4,274	2,753	2,476	2,504	3,105
Claims on Nonfin.Pub.Enterprises	32c	1,158	10,245	12,399	18,736	5,716	12,996	15,481	3,710	1,544	2,321	2,160	3,043
Claims on Private Sector	32d	11,588	174,705	210,469	220,686	254,573	278,787	287,129	311,354	342,176	381,562	434,510	487,499
Claims on Other Banking Insts	32f	80	884	831	1,103	4,299	5,234	7,181	9,016	12,445	11,804	13,756	15,090
Claims on Nonbank Financial Inst	32g	—	—	—	6	7	7,836	3,021	2,167	5,132	1,554	753	156
Money	34	1,113	25,540	32,094	41,683	50,999	54,824	62,294	74,078	83,060	107,209	111,542	131,152
Quasi-Money	35	7,919	99,074	135,641	146,719	174,020	192,218	201,714	200,215	225,453	275,740	285,088	342,297
Money Market Instruments	36aa	283	3,320	4,744	7,029	10,283	12,684	13,377	22,880	32,739	20,262	34,639	33,258
Liabs. of Central Bank: Securities	36ac	547	34,097	45,879	64,174	54,121	50,513	22,328	33,582	64,999	30,554	11,598	4,346
Restricted Deposits	36b	1,866	19,174	24,897	26,362	28,964	33,341	35,577	39,072	41,850	48,587	55,106	58,503
Liabilities to Other Banking Insts	36i	1,081	11,914	9,396	22,017	21,973	43,712	54,338	70,959	85,951	141,546	165,208	156,406
Liab. to Nonbank Financial Insts	36j	1	92	111	60	234	6,059	1,033	1,745	3,246	2,326	2,286	1,811
Capital Accounts	37a	5,908	45,092	59,112	78,317	100,174	121,286	131,467	128,534	172,894	180,450	236,528	263,672
Other Items (Net)	37r	−1,513	−3,974	−12,529	−21,109	−24,399	29,204	31,635	28,766	17,556	27,966	36,613	25,611
Money plus Quasi-Money	35l	9,032	124,614	167,735	188,402	225,019	247,043	264,008	274,293	308,513	382,948	396,630	473,448

		1993	1994	1995	1996	1997	1998	1999	2000	2001	2002	2003	2004
Other Banking Institutions		*Thousands of Reais through 1992; Millions of Reais Beginning 1993: End of Period*											
Reserves	40	53	1,526	611	768	1,174	5,427	224	547	245	393	3,066	4,461
Claims on Mon.Author.:Securities	40c	15	113	459	1,195	3,015	37,625	18,530	27,186	59,004	19,704	10,940	4,304
Blocked Financial Assets	40d	—	—	—	—	—	—	—	—	—	—	—	—
Foreign Assets	41	83	1,269	382	184	159	105	121	405	362	811	1,237	537
Claims on Central Government	42a	164	2,820	4,720	4,085	6,980	71,066	143,315	180,058	168,895	185,858	301,821	377,073
Claims on State and Local Govts	42b	156	918	1,890	1,164	2,441	7,013	4,773	3,133	2,917	3,902	4,786	5,939
Claims on Nonfin.Pub.Enterprises	42c	355	2,705	6,674	3,560	2,859	3,194	3,574	6,902	13,983	9,331	7,603	6,399
Claims on Private Sector	42d	1,981	28,158	30,305	29,298	33,356	37,441	54,610	87,037	80,607	99,298	105,748	133,437
Claims on Deposit Money Banks	42e	1,025	11,491	15,627	19,344	22,533	56,821	76,160	96,708	137,578	187,496	221,787	242,363
Claims on Nonbank Financial Insts	42g	—	—	—	—	—	—	434	179	783	592	1,945	756	138
Demand Deposits	44	—	—	—	—	—	—	—	—	—	—	—	—
Time and Savings Deposits	45	669	7,675	4,997	6,035	7,032	6,976	3,903	3,340	3,354	3,907	5,545	7,191
Money Market Instruments	46aa	9	178	138	525	485	137,513	204,315	271,162	319,921	313,565	451,461	542,887
Restricted Deposits	46b	16	190	301	304	249	529	626	820	625	575	505	509
Foreign Liabilities	46c	300	1,877	2,184	3,335	4,906	11,362	11,234	15,588	19,791	31,343	27,875	23,223
Central Government Deposits	46d	1,086	10,432	12,308	14,607	16,443	25,643	28,378	32,476	33,880	44,317	52,996	55,910
Credit from Monetary Authorities	46g	57	778	1,035	1,065	2,020	354	385	287	1,967	289	266	290
Credit from Deposit Money Banks	46h	145	958	1,162	1,152	3,804	1,667	1,362	1,144	1,856	1,818	3,379	3,504
Liab. to Nonbank Financial Insts	46j	—	—	—	—	—	74	51	28	1	262	52	69
Capital Accounts	47a	1,382	16,756	21,323	18,350	19,931	19,935	20,711	22,016	64,516	80,793	88,483	98,913
Other Items (Net)	47r	169	10,156	17,219	14,225	17,646	15,074	30,521	55,897	18,271	31,869	27,181	42,154
Banking Survey		*Thousands of Reais through 1992; Millions of Reais Beginning 1993: End of Period*											
Foreign Assets (Net)	51n	–3,904	15,315	24,677	30,956	14,398	–12,606	–12,736	3,714	–14,603	–54,122	–17,531	15,153
Domestic Credit	52	22,382	241,692	303,315	353,542	422,118	633,462	726,280	817,355	943,589	1,102,441	1,283,463	1,431,202
Claims on Central Govt. (Net)	52an	5,613	–2,522	15,593	24,031	83,719	247,532	338,512	397,994	493,887	600,053	724,642	791,487
Claims on State and Local Govts	52b	1,687	28,400	27,875	57,225	41,889	45,242	23,774	7,408	5,669	6,378	7,290	9,044
Claims on Nonfin.Pub.Enterprises	52c	1,513	12,950	19,073	22,296	8,575	16,190	19,055	10,611	15,527	11,652	9,763	9,442
Claims on Private Sector	52d	13,570	202,863	240,774	249,984	287,929	316,228	341,739	398,392	422,782	480,860	540,258	620,936
Claims on Nonbank Financial Inst	52g	—	—	—	6	7	8,270	3,200	2,950	5,724	3,498	1,510	294
Liquid Liabilities	55l	9,618	130,475	171,812	193,431	230,740	235,331	252,159	266,630	286,934	364,889	366,635	418,783
Money Market Instruments	56aa	291	3,492	4,826	7,532	10,724	148,639	213,634	288,365	345,699	323,831	475,629	564,320
Liabs. of Central Bank: Securities	56ac	532	33,984	45,420	62,979	51,106	12,888	3,799	6,396	5,995	10,849	658	43
Restricted Deposits	56b	1,882	19,364	25,198	26,666	29,213	33,870	36,203	39,892	42,475	49,162	55,611	59,012
Liab. to Nonbank Financial Insts	56j	1	92	111	60	234	6,133	1,084	1,773	3,247	2,588	2,339	1,880
Capital Accounts	57a	7,289	61,848	80,435	96,667	120,105	141,221	152,178	150,550	237,410	261,243	325,011	362,585
Other Items (Net)	57r	–1,134	7,752	190	–2,837	–5,606	42,773	54,487	67,462	7,226	35,757	40,050	39,733
Nonbank Financial Institutions		*Thousands of Reais through 1992; Millions of Reais Beginning 1993: End of Period*											
Reserves	40..n	—	3	6	31	14	3	4	4	5	98	7	11
Claims on Mon.Author.:Securities	40c.n	8	405	154	350	364	704	375	1,085	1,523	1,128	423	43
Blocked Financial Assets	40d.n	—	—	—	—	—	—	—	—	—	—	—	—
Foreign Assets	41..n	11	76	87	93	45	44	105	118	18	37	29	29
Claims on Central Government	42a.n	65	17	55	1,090	1,229	2,465	4,243	4,138	4,192	3,680	3,875	3,094
Claims on State and Local Govt	42b.n	26	360	348	408	103	617	43	38	66	133	207	399
Claims on Nonfin.Pub.Enterprises	42c.n	4	36	14	14	14	13	7	11	47	102	155	34
Claims on Private Sector	42d.n	89	11,219	15,678	10,208	11,366	11,458	12,509	16,397	15,206	14,023	13,488	17,387
Claims on Deposit Money Banks	42e.n	179	1,329	1,737	2,824	2,421	10,735	4,416	4,760	5,073	4,207	5,610	3,213
Claims on Other Banking Insts	42f.n	3	23	197	35	73	1,130	326	260	1,237	1,535	1,826	1,492
Money Market Instruments	46aan	131	1,181	3,901	5,482	8,307	9,247	7,033	7,428	6,253	6,721	9,933	12,530
Restricted Deposits	46b.n	—	—	—	—	—	—	—	—	—	—	—	—
Foreign Liabilities	46c.n	170	1,529	2,293	2,994	3,728	4,224	5,115	4,862	4,073	4,625	3,395	1,112
Central Government Deposits	46d.n	—	—	—	1	1	3	36	37	104	14	22	34
Credit from Monetary Authorities	46g.n	—	—	—	—	—	—	—	—	98	75	129	—
Cred. from Deposit Money Banks	46h.n	—	—	—	—	—	6,488	1,071	838	3,651	360	196	177
Liabilities to Other Banking Insts	46i.n	118	1,517	1,619	3,670	4,093	5,617	5,036	3,063	2,024	2,886	3,144	2,104
Capital Accounts	47a.n	444	5,767	8,783	10,848	11,187	13,324	17,061	17,659	21,280	23,908	24,933	25,753
Other Items (Net)	47r.n	–479	3,474	1,680	–7,942	–11,687	–11,735	–13,324	–7,076	–10,116	–13,648	–16,132	–16,009
Money (National Definitions)		*Thousands of Reais through 1992; Millions of Reais Beginning 1993: End of Period*											
Base Money	19ma	517	17,685	21,682	19,796	31,828	39,184	48,430	47,686	53,256	73,302	73,219	88,733
Base Money (BA)	19maa	....	80,734	122,291	184,050	280,070	352,345	447,132	538,693	646,672	788,034	886,894	979,233
Base Money (B2)	19mab	....	101,902	156,428	231,898	318,599	374,282	458,567	540,894	649,254	789,960	887,675	980,140
M1	59ma	848	22,773	28,493	29,807	47,363	50,707	62,744	74,352	83,707	107,846	109,648	127,946
M2	59mb	10,223	132,558	178,755	188,735	239,777	254,965	274,770	283,785	321,612	397,503	412,895	493,497
M2A	59mba	....	60,443	72,380	60,084	63,353	63,170	271,790	356,298	....	....	....	....
M3	59mc	11,759	154,544	225,008	285,942	340,210	376,015	468,728	556,577	625,057	688,269	838,386	988,622
M3A	59mca	....	119,882	143,410	142,159	173,436	185,294	386,382	468,390	....	....	....	....
M4	59md	13,938	176,449	261,176	336,148	405,946	459,308	551,092	652,093	756,181	807,523	960,061	1,109,519
M4A	59mda	....	174,523	259,381	342,305	422,306	480,202	575,666	677,021	....	....	....	....
Interest Rates		*Percent Per Annum*											
Discount Rate (End of Period)	60	....	....	....	25.34	45.09	39.41	21.37	† 18.52	21.43	30.42	23.92	24.55
Money Market Rate	60b	3,284.44	4,820.64	53.37	27.45	25.00	29.50	26.26	17.59	17.47	19.11	23.37	16.24
Treasury Bill Rate	60c	....	....	49.93	25.73	24.79	28.57	26.39	18.51	20.06	19.43	22.10	17.14
Treasury Bill Rate (Fgn.Currency)	60c.f	....	....	17.78	15.13	11.60	15.04	....	....	11.46	....	....	....
Savings Rate	60k	2,743.33	4,206.04	40.26	16.39	16.62	14.48	12.31	8.44	8.66	9.27	11.26	8.09
Deposit Rate	60l	3,293.50	5,175.24	52.25	26.45	24.35	28.00	26.02	17.20	17.86	19.14	21.97	15.42
Lending Rate	60p	....	....	....	....	78.19	86.36	80.44	56.83	57.62	62.88	67.08	55.08

		1993	1994	1995	1996	1997	1998	1999	2000	2001	2002	2003	2004
Prices and Labor		*Index Numbers (2000=100): Period Averages*											
Share Prices	62	.7	20.8	24.4	37.0	64.3	57.0	71.0	100.0	87.0	71.7	91.8	139.8
Wholesale Prices	63	1.6	38.8	† 61.0	64.9	70.1	72.6	84.7	100.0	112.6	132.6	170.5	188.4
Consumer Prices	64	† 1.9	42.0	69.7	80.7	86.3	89.1	93.4	100.0	106.8	115.9	132.9	141.7
		Number in Thousands: Period Averages											
Labor Force	67d	67,159	....	70,539	70,182	75,213	76,886	79,315	....	83,243	....	....	....
Employment	67e	66,570	....	69,629	67,920	69,332	69,963	71,676	76,159	75,458	78,180	79,251	....
Unemployment	67c	4,396	....	4,510	5,076	5,882	6,923	7,639	....	7,785	7,876	8,537	....
Unemployment Rate (%)	67r	† 6.2	5.1	6.1	7.0	7.8	9.0	9.6	....	9.4	11.7	12.3	11.5
Intl. Transactions & Positions		*Millions of US Dollars*											
Exports	70..d	38,555	43,545	46,506	47,747	52,994	51,140	48,011	55,086	58,223	60,362	73,084	96,475
Coffee	70e.d	1,065	2,219	1,970	1,719	2,746	2,332	2,230	1,559	1,208	1,195	1,302	1,750
Imports, c.i.f.	71..d	27,740	35,997	53,783	56,947	64,999	60,652	51,759	58,631	58,351	49,599	50,706	65,949
Imports, f.o.b.	71.vd	25,256	33,079	49,972	53,346	59,747	57,763	49,295	55,839	55,572	47,237	48,291	62,809
		2000=100											
Volume of Exports	72	74.7	79.8	82.1	81.5	85.4	94.1	93.5	100.0	111.4	120.8	131.3	156.6
Coffee	72e	99.8	90.1	74.6	80.5	89.9	103.0	131.5	100.0	129.5	160.4	141.6	145.9
Volume of Imports	73	83.8	87.6	95.3	96.6	94.2	98.2	92.2	100.0	100.0	97.5	100.4	110.8
		2000=100: Indices of Unit Values in US Dollars											
Unit Value of Exports/Export Prices	74..d	93.7	99.0	102.9	106.4	112.7	98.6	93.3	100.0	94.8	90.7	101.1	111.8
Coffee (Unit Value)	74e.d	68.5	157.9	169.3	137.0	196.0	145.2	108.8	100.0	59.8	47.8	59.0	76.9
Coffee (Wholesale Price)	76ebd	83.4	179.6	182.9	150.7	209.0	152.6	111.4	100.0	63.3	56.4	63.6	86.8
Unit Value of Imports/Import Prices	75..d	54.0	67.6	93.9	98.9	113.6	105.3	95.8	100.0	99.5	86.8	86.2	101.5
Balance of Payments		*Millions of US Dollars: Minus Sign Indicates Debit*											
Current Account, n.i.e.	78ald	20	−1,153	−18,136	−23,248	−30,491	−33,829	−25,400	−24,225	−23,215	−7,637	4,177	11,669
Goods: Exports f.o.b.	78aad	39,630	44,102	46,506	47,851	53,189	51,136	48,011	55,086	58,223	60,362	73,084	96,475
Goods: Imports f.o.b.	78abd	−25,301	−33,241	−49,663	−53,304	−59,841	−57,739	−49,272	−55,783	−55,572	−47,240	−48,290	−62,782
Trade Balance	78acd	14,329	10,861	−3,157	−5,453	−6,652	−6,603	−1,261	−698	2,650	13,121	24,794	33,693
Services: Credit	78add	3,965	4,908	6,135	4,655	5,989	7,631	7,189	9,498	9,322	9,551	10,447	12,442
Services: Debit	78aed	−9,555	−10,254	−13,630	−12,714	−15,298	−16,676	−14,172	−16,660	−17,081	−14,509	−15,378	−17,215
Balance on Goods & Services	78afd	8,739	5,515	−10,652	−13,512	−15,961	−15,648	−8,244	−7,860	−5,109	8,164	19,863	28,921
Income: Credit	78agd	1,308	2,202	3,457	5,350	5,344	4,914	3,936	3,621	3,280	3,295	3,339	3,199
Income: Debit	78ahd	−11,630	−11,293	−14,562	−17,527	−21,688	−24,531	−22,780	−21,507	−23,023	−21,486	−21,891	−23,719
Balance on Gds, Serv. & Inc.	78aid	−1,583	−3,576	−21,757	−25,689	−32,305	−35,265	−27,088	−25,746	−24,852	−10,026	1,311	8,401
Current Transfers, n.i.e.: Credit	78ajd	1,704	2,577	3,861	2,699	2,130	1,795	1,969	1,828	1,934	2,627	3,132	3,582
Current Transfers: Debit	78akd	−101	−154	−240	−258	−316	−359	−281	−307	−296	−237	−265	−314
Capital Account, n.i.e.	78bcd	81	173	352	494	482	375	339	273	−36	433	498	703
Capital Account, n.i.e.: Credit	78bad	86	175	363	507	519	488	361	300	328	464	535	764
Capital Account: Debit	78bbd	−5	−2	−11	−13	−37	−113	−22	−28	−364	−31	−37	−61
Financial Account, n.i.e.	78bjd	7,604	8,020	29,306	33,428	24,918	20,063	8,056	29,376	20,331	−3,909	−157	−3,651
Direct Investment Abroad	78bdd	−491	−1,037	−1,384	467	−1,042	−2,721	−1,690	−2,282	2,258	−2,482	−249	−9,471
Dir. Invest. in Rep. Econ., n.i.e.	78bed	1,292	3,072	4,859	11,200	19,650	31,913	28,576	32,779	22,457	16,590	10,144	18,166
Portfolio Investment Assets	78bfd	−606	−3,052	−936	−257	−335	−594	258	−1,696	−795	−321	179	−755
Equity Securities	78bkd	−607	—	−168	−49	−306	−553	−865	−1,953	−1,121	−389	−258	−121
Debt Securities	78bld	1	−3,052	−768	−208	−29	−41	1,123	258	326	67	437	−633
Portfolio Investment Liab., n.i.e.	78bgd	12,928	47,784	10,171	21,089	10,393	19,013	3,542	8,651	872	−4,797	5,129	−3,996
Equity Securities	78bmd	6,570	7,280	2,775	5,785	5,099	−1,768	2,572	3,076	2,481	1,981	2,973	2,081
Debt Securities	78bnd	6,358	40,504	7,396	15,304	5,294	20,781	970	5,575	−1,609	−6,778	2,156	−6,076
Financial Derivatives Assets	78bwd	—	—	....	....	....	....	642	386	567	933	683	467
Financial Derivatives Liabilities	78bxd	—	—	....	....	....	....	−729	−583	−1,038	−1,289	−834	−1,145
Other Investment Assets	78bhd	−2,696	−4,368	−1,783	−3,327	2,251	−5,992	−4,399	−2,989	−6,586	−3,211	−9,483	−1,462
Monetary Authorities	78bod	−34	—	....	−44	−67	−84	1,668	−18	2,430	2	—	—
General Government	78bpd	29	—	....	....	2,146	60	−880	193	−1,085	−979	−1,101	−1,591
Banks	78bqd	−2,980	−4,077	−228	−4,610	5,133	3,383	−121	1,551	−3,561	4,335	−6,999	2,209
Other Sectors	78brd	289	−291	−1,555	1,327	−4,961	−9,351	−5,066	−4,715	−4,370	−6,569	−1,383	−2,081
Other Investment Liab., n.i.e.	78bid	−2,823	−34,379	18,379	4,256	−5,999	−21,556	−18,144	−4,890	2,596	−9,331	−5,724	−5,456
Monetary Authorities	78bsd	−140	−545	−1,652	−3,773	−1,698	−1,704	−6,671	−201	−171	−156	−162	−163
General Government	78btd	−2,622	−35,609	....	—	....	....	934	1,540	−26	−493	−1,561	−2,636
Banks	78bud	−2,269	−1,439	7,071	6,450	−897	−8,570	−5,059	1,718	−741	−3,835	348	619
Other Sectors	78bvd	2,208	3,214	12,960	1,579	−3,404	−11,282	−7,348	−7,946	3,534	−4,847	−4,350	−3,276
Net Errors and Omissions	78cad	−815	−442	1,447	−1,992	−3,160	−2,911	240	2,557	−498	−154	−933	−2,122
Overall Balance	78cbd	6,890	6,598	12,969	8,682	−8,251	−16,302	−16,765	7,981	−3,418	−11,266	3,586	6,599
Reserves and Related Items	79dad	−6,890	−6,598	−12,969	−8,682	8,251	16,302	16,765	−7,981	3,418	11,266	−3,586	−6,599
Reserve Assets	79dbd	−8,709	−7,215	−12,920	−8,326	8,284	6,990	7,783	2,260	−3,311	−314	−8,479	−2,238
Use of Fund Credit and Loans	79dcd	−504	−133	−49	−70	−33	4,773	4,059	−6,795	6,729	11,580	4,893	−4,362
Exceptional Financing	79ded	2,323	750	—	−286	—	4,539	4,924	−3,446	—	—	—	—

Brazil 223

		1993	1994	1995	1996	1997	1998	1999	2000	2001	2002	2003	2004
International Investment Position						*Millions of US Dollars*							
Assets......................................	79aad	....	....	....	....	....	....	....	....	107,086	112,914	134,223	150,026
Direct Investment Abroad..............	79abd	....	....	....	....	....	....	....	....	49,689	54,423	54,892	70,692
Portfolio Investment......................	79acd	....	....	....	....	....	....	....	....	6,402	5,845	6,950	9,330
Equity Securities.........................	79add	....	....	....	....	....	....	....	....	3,001	2,388	2,596	2,335
Debt Securities...........................	79aed	....	....	....	....	....	....	....	....	3,401	3,457	4,354	6,995
Financial Derivatives.....................	79ald	....	....	....	....	....	....	....	....	42	105	81	109
Other Investment..........................	79afd	....	....	....	....	....	....	....	....	15,087	14,705	23,004	16,960
Monetary Authorities..................	79agd	....	....	....	....	....	....	....	....	1,383	1,357	1,230	1,229
General Government....................	79ahd	....	....	....	....	....	....	....	....	—	—	—	—
Banks..	79aid	....	....	....	....	....	....	....	....	5,521	4,052	10,850	6,957
Other Sectors.............................	79ajd	....	....	....	....	....	....	....	....	8,183	9,296	10,924	8,774
Reserve Assets...............................	79akd	....	....	....	....	....	....	....	....	35,866	37,837	49,296	52,935
Liabilities......................................	79lad	....	....	....	....	....	....	....	....	372,052	343,450	406,759	446,208
Dir. Invest. in Rep. Economy..........	79lbd	....	....	....	....	....	....	....	....	121,948	100,847	132,799	161,238
Portfolio Investment......................	79lcd	....	....	....	....	....	....	....	....	151,741	137,355	166,095	185,824
Equity Securities.........................	79ldd	....	....	....	....	....	....	....	....	36,910	27,249	53,138	77,261
Debt Securities...........................	79led	....	....	....	....	....	....	....	....	114,831	110,106	112,957	108,563
Financial Derivatives.....................	79lld	....	....	....	....	....	....	....	....	45	250	125	320
Other Investment..........................	79lfd	....	....	....	....	....	....	....	....	98,317	104,999	107,740	98,826
Monetary Authorities..................	79lgd	....	....	....	....	....	....	....	....	9,250	21,729	28,965	25,577
General Government....................	79lhd	....	....	....	....	....	....	....	....	—	—	—	—
Banks..	79lid	....	....	....	....	....	....	....	....	7,777	8,731	8,500	10,009
Other Sectors.............................	79ljd	....	....	....	....	....	....	....	....	81,291	74,538	70,276	63,240
Government Finance		*Thousands of Reais through 1992; Millions of Reais Beginning 1993: Year Ending December 31*											
Deficit (-) or Surplus........................	80	−1,315	−21,270	....	....	−63,664	−70,880	....	....	....	....	....	....
Revenue...	81	4,272	108,280	....	....	213,409	237,116	....	....	....	....	....	....
Grants Received.............................	81z	2	125	....	....	9	71	....	....	....	....	....	....
Expenditure....................................	82	5,250	117,906	....	....	213,484	245,032	....	....	....	....	....	....
Lending Minus Repayments...........	83	338	11,769	....	....	63,597	63,034	....	....	....	....	....	....
National Accounts						*Thousands of Reais*							
Househ.Cons.Expend.,incl.NPISHs....	96f	8,471	208,256	386,910	486,813	545,698	566,192	606,701	670,702	725,760	781,174	882,983	975,245
Government Consumption Expend...	91f	2,490	62,388	126,652	144,001	158,502	174,847	185,828	209,953	230,741	270,965	309,631	332,332
Gross Fixed Capital Formation..........	93e	2,718	72,453	132,753	150,050	172,939	179,982	184,098	212,384	233,384	246,606	276,741	346,335
Changes in Inventories....................	93i	221	4,880	11,274	12,903	14,248	13,074	12,238	24,871	20,753	19,348	30,750	30,238
Exports of Goods and Services..........	90c	1,481	33,220	49,917	54,430	65,356	67,862	100,136	117,423	158,501	208,489	254,832	318,387
Imports of Goods and Services (-).....	98c	1,282	31,993	61,314	69,311	86,000	87,769	115,154	134,079	170,403	180,554	198,754	235,917
Gross Domestic Product (GDP).........	99b	14,096	349,205	646,192	778,887	870,743	914,188	973,846	1,101,255	1,198,736	1,346,028	1,556,182	1,766,621
Net Primary Income from Abroad.....	98.n	−355	−5,913	−10,154	−12,228	−17,436	−21,241	−34,107	−32,597	−45,284	−51,944	−55,150	−58,491
Gross National Income (GNI)............	99a	13,742	343,292	636,038	766,659	853,307	892,947	939,739	1,068,658	1,153,452	1,294,084	1,501,032	1,708,130
GDP Volume 1990 Prices................	99b.p	12,176	12,888	13,432	13,789	14,240	14,259	14,374	15,001	15,198	15,491	15,790	16,095
GDP Volume (2000=100)................	99bvp	81.2	85.9	89.5	91.9	94.9	95.1	95.8	100.0	101.3	103.3	105.3	107.3
GDP Deflator (2000=100)................	99bip	1.6	36.9	65.5	76.9	83.3	87.3	92.3	100.0	107.4	118.4	134.3	149.5
						Millions: Midyear Estimates							
Population................................	99z	156.61	158.98	161.38	163.82	166.30	168.81	171.34	173.86	176.38	178.89	181.41	183.91

		1993	1994	1995	1996	1997	1998	1999	2000	2001	2002	2003	2004
Exchange Rates						*Leva per SDR: End of Period*							
Official Rate	aa	.0449	.0964	.1051	.7008	2.3969	2.3586	2.6721	2.7386	2.7891	2.5627	2.3012	2.2300
						Leva per US Dollar: End of Period (ae) Period Average (rf)							
Official Rate	ae	.0327	.0660	.0707	.4874	1.7765	1.6751	1.9469	2.1019	2.2193	1.8850	1.5486	1.4359
Official Rate	rf	.0276	.0541	.0672	.1779	1.6819	1.7604	1.8364	2.1233	2.1847	2.0770	1.7327	1.5751
						Index Numbers (2000=100): Period Averages							
Nominal Effective Exchange Rate	nec	2,671.51	1,910.87	1,647.66	941.10	92.26	90.28	99.05	100.00	105.05	109.73	118.77	123.15
Real Effective Exchange Rate	rec	77.12	69.66	80.06	68.92	82.76	94.50	98.04	100.00	104.82	109.50	115.50	121.71
Fund Position						*Millions of SDRs: End of Period*							
Quota	2f.s	464.90	464.90	464.90	464.90	464.90	464.90	640.20	640.20	640.20	640.20	640.20	640.20
SDRs	1b.s	.83	10.39	20.08	8.31	8.37	21.38	59.53	64.97	1.80	.55	45.54	8.45
Reserve Position in the Fund	1c.s	32.63	32.63	32.63	32.63	32.63	32.63	32.69	32.74	32.78	32.78	32.78	32.85
Total Fund Cred.&Loans Outstg	2tl	459.90	644.41	482.12	407.25	698.02	792.27	910.74	1,014.62	883.00	771.75	799.16	761.95
International Liquidity						*Millions of US Dollars Unless Otherwise Indicated: End of Period*							
Total Reserves minus Gold	1l.d	655.16	1,001.80	1,236.45	483.57	2,111.52	2,684.71	2,892.12	3,154.93	3,290.77	4,407.06	6,291.01	8,776.25
SDRs	1b.d	1.14	15.16	29.84	11.95	11.29	30.10	81.70	84.65	2.26	.74	67.67	13.12
Reserve Position in the Fund	1c.d	44.82	47.63	48.50	46.92	44.03	45.95	44.87	42.66	41.19	44.56	48.71	51.02
Foreign Exchange	1d.d	609.20	939.00	1,158.10	424.70	2,056.20	2,608.65	2,765.54	3,027.63	3,247.32	4,361.76	6,174.64	8,712.10
Gold (Million Fine Troy Ounces)	1ad	1.017	1.031	1.031	1.031	1.288	1.293	1.284	1.284	1.285	1.282	1.282	1.281
Gold (National Valuation)	1and	305.00	309.37	309.37	309.37	† 362.57	371.67	329.65	305.33	289.56	339.98	413.76	445.90
Monetary Authorities:Other Liab.	4..d	355.42	635.08	† 657.61	689.55	—	—	—	—	—	—	—	—
Deposit Money Banks: Assets	7a.d	1,331	1,659	† 1,063	973	1,360	1,469	1,492	1,942	2,102	2,018	1,939	3,126
Liabilities	7b.d	11,776	3,578	† 579	402	103	127	172	260	314	474	957	3,381
Monetary Authorities						*Millions of Leva: End of Period*							
Foreign Assets	11	33.9	124.6	† 154.0	618.0	4,666.1	5,243.1	6,353.5	7,379.7	7,888.2	8,795.0	10,192.8	13,079.2
Claims on Central Government	12a	34.8	54.2	† 100.7	410.9	1,632.1	1,665.9	2,203.2	2,560.9	2,314.6	1,926.4	1,838.9	1,693.5
Claims on Other Resident Sectors	12d	—	—	† .3	.5	.7	1.4	2.1	2.3	2.3	73.1	74.2	74.2
Claims on Banking Institutions	12e	32.1	54.8	† 40.7	238.8	213.9	143.5	125.9	73.1	36.1	24.2	6.8	6.8
Reserve Money	14	54.5	85.0	† 129.1	247.3	2,292.0	2,526.6	2,972.5	3,301.3	4,303.2	4,646.8	5,394.8	7,564.6
of which: Currency Outside Bls.	14a	25.2	38.5	† 61.6	126.5	1,316.2	1,743.0	1,961.6	2,374.1	3,081.0	3,334.9	3,874.1	4,627.9
Other Liabs. to Banking Insts.	14n	.4	3.8	† 25.2	82.5	—	—	—	—	—	—	—	—
Other Deposits	15	.3	—	† —	3.7	16.9	28.1	.4	973.6	712.2	855.7	1,384.7	870.4
Foreign Liabilities	16c	32.3	104.0	† 97.2	621.4	1,673.1	1,868.6	2,433.6	2,778.6	2,462.7	1,977.8	1,839.0	1,699.1
Central Government Deposits	16d	11.8	42.2	† 51.0	192.4	1,592.8	1,807.8	2,445.7	2,029.6	1,778.9	2,177.7	2,347.3	3,530.0
Capital Accounts	17a	30.5	91.3	† 102.2	307.3	961.7	916.3	1,019.5	1,190.6	1,229.8	1,371.3	1,455.7	1,487.9
Other Items (Net)	17r	−28.9	−92.7	† −109.1	−186.5	−23.8	−93.6	−187.0	−257.6	−245.6	−210.5	−308.8	−298.2
Banking Institutions						*Millions of Leva: End of Period*							
Reserves	20	24.6	43.5	† 67.6	118.6	800.2	643.8	745.3	598.1	864.4	1,071.2	1,388.2	2,428.4
Other Claims on Dep.Money Banks	20n	....	....	25.2	82.5	—	—	—	—	—	—	—	—
Foreign Assets	21	43.5	109.5	† 75.2	474.2	2,416.7	2,459.9	2,904.5	4,081.9	4,665.3	3,803.1	3,002.7	4,488.9
Claims on Central Government	22a	179.6	283.6	† 226.1	615.1	2,168.4	1,526.3	1,202.7	1,068.0	1,338.0	1,945.5	2,024.0	2,211.6
Claims on Other General Govt.	22b	2.4	2.8	† .1	—	—	17.0	30.3	30.6	39.6	12.5	27.0	28.3
Claims on Other Resident Sectors	22d	198.6	258.8	† 351.0	1,108.5	1,625.9	2,365.5	2,872.4	3,360.2	4,440.6	6,324.0	9,413.2	14,022.4
Demand Deposits	24	23.2	36.6	† 94.4	369.1	1,811.9	1,823.7	1,829.0	2,142.5	2,681.3	3,196.9	4,027.3	5,163.9
Other Deposits	25	185.5	342.9	† 432.1	818.0	2,676.7	2,912.6	3,497.1	4,085.9	5,670.0	6,395.9	7,351.2	9,620.2
Bonds	26n	....	....	−.5	−3.7	—	—	—	—	8.5	36.9	103.7	187.9
Foreign Liabilities	26c	385.2	236.2	† 41.0	196.1	183.1	212.5	334.5	547.2	696.8	893.6	1,482.2	4,854.8
Central Government Deposits	26d	5.8	13.6	† 21.2	28.4	207.0	265.7	224.6	222.3	347.6	447.5	778.7	742.5
Credit from Central Bank	26g	9.6	28.7	† 34.5	106.1	58.0	7.5	.8	1.6	.3	.3	.3	.3
Capital Accounts	27a	36.1	79.0	† 87.1	771.6	795.5	1,134.8	1,283.5	1,493.1	1,637.3	1,921.6	2,270.3	2,708.2
Other Items (Net)	27r	−196.6	−38.8	† 35.4	113.4	1,279.1	655.8	585.8	646.3	306.0	263.5	−158.7	−98.3
Banking Survey						*Millions of Leva: End of Period*							
Foreign Assets (Net)	31n	−340.1	−106.1	† 91.1	274.7	5,226.5	5,621.9	6,489.9	8,135.7	9,394.0	9,726.7	9,874.3	11,014.1
Domestic Credit	32	397.9	543.7	† 605.9	1,914.2	3,627.3	3,502.6	3,640.4	4,770.2	6,008.6	7,656.4	10,251.4	13,757.4
Claims on Central Govt. (Net)	32an	196.9	282.1	† 254.5	805.2	2,000.8	1,118.7	735.6	1,377.1	1,526.1	1,246.7	736.9	−367.5
Claims on Other General Govt.	32b	2.4	2.8	† .1	—	—	17.0	30.3	30.6	39.6	12.5	27.0	28.3
Claims on Other Resident Sectors	32d	198.6	258.8	† 351.3	1,109.1	1,626.5	2,366.8	2,874.5	3,362.5	4,442.9	6,397.2	9,487.4	14,096.6
Money	34	50.3	76.0	† 156.3	495.7	3,253.9	3,706.0	4,038.2	4,797.2	6,033.0	6,696.2	8,029.9	10,297.9
Quasi-Money	35	185.8	342.9	† 432.1	821.7	2,693.6	2,940.8	3,497.4	5,059.4	6,382.2	7,251.6	8,736.0	10,490.6
Bonds	36n	....	....	† −.5	−3.7	—	—	—	—	8.5	36.9	103.7	187.9
Capital Accounts	37a	66.7	170.3	† 189.4	1,079.0	1,757.2	2,051.1	2,303.0	2,683.7	2,867.2	3,292.8	3,726.0	4,196.1
Other Items (Net)	37r	−244.9	−151.6	† −80.3	−203.8	1,149.1	426.7	291.6	365.6	111.6	105.5	−470.0	−400.9
Money plus Quasi-Money	35l	236.0	418.9	† 588.4	1,317.4	5,947.5	6,646.7	7,535.6	9,856.6	12,415.2	13,947.8	16,765.9	20,788.4
Money (National Definitions)						*Millions of Leva: End of Period*							
M3	59mc	....	....	588.4	1,317.4	5,947.5	6,646.7	7,535.6	9,856.6	12,400.5	13,857.3	16,566.5	20,394.4
Interest Rates						*Percent Per Annum*							
Bank Rate (End of Period)	60	52.00	72.00	34.00	180.00	† 6.65	5.08	4.46	4.63	4.65	3.31	2.83	2.37
Money Market Rate	60b	48.07	66.43	53.09	119.88	66.43	2.48	2.93	3.02	3.74	2.47	1.95	1.95
Treasury Bill Yield	60c	45.45	57.72	48.27	114.31	78.35	6.02	5.43	4.21	4.57	4.29	2.81	2.64
Deposit Rate	60l	42.56	51.14	35.94	74.68	46.83	3.00	3.21	3.10	2.88	2.77	2.89	3.01
Lending Rate	60p	58.30	72.58	58.98	123.48	83.96	13.30	12.79	11.52	11.11	9.35	8.82	8.77
Government Bond Yield	61	....	56.86	49.76	....	....	10.10	7.38	6.70	6.75	....	....	....
Prices, Production, Labor						*Index Numbers (2000=100): Period Averages*							
Producer Prices	63	.1	1.8	† 2.8	6.6	70.7	82.8	85.1	100.0	103.7	105.0	110.2	116.8
Consumer Prices	64	.9	1.8	2.9	6.4	74.5	88.4	90.6	100.0	107.4	113.6	116.0	123.4
Industrial Production	66	....	....	....	....	....	....	....	100.0	102.2	106.9	123.3	145.1
						Number in Thousands: Period Averages							
Labor Force	67d	2,856	2,521	2,265	2,721	2,679	2,527	2,489	2,323	2,563	2,520	3,283	3,322
Employment	67e	2,267	2,032	1,910	2,242	2,155	2,086	1,994	1,901	1,900	1,906	2,835	2,923
Unemployment	67c	626	488	424	479	524	465	611	567	663	592	449	405
Unemployment Rate (%)	67r	16.4	12.4	11.1	12.5	13.7	12.2	16.0	16.9	19.8	17.8	13.7	12.4

		1993	1994	1995	1996	1997	1998	1999	2000	2001	2002	2003	2004
Intl. Transactions & Positions						*Millions of Leva*							
Exports.................................	70	102.9	216.2	359.7	859.8	8,281.4	7,391.1	7,302.6	10,247.1	11,176.1	11,857.9	13,041.9	15,617.1
Imports, c.i.f............................	71	131.5	227.0	380.0	892.1	8,268.5	8,709.4	10,052.8	13,856.8	15,896.6	16,450.9	18,796.6	22,725.8
Balance of Payments						*Millions of US Dollars: Minus Sign Indicates Debit*							
Current Account, n.i.e.................	78ald	−1,098.8	−31.8	−25.8	15.7	426.9	−61.9	−652.1	−703.7	−984.0	−826.7	−1,675.8	−1,805.7
Goods: Exports f.o.b....................	78aad	3,726.5	3,935.1	5,345.0	4,890.2	4,939.6	4,193.5	4,006.4	4,824.6	5,112.9	5,692.1	7,444.8	9,858.6
Goods: Imports f.o.b....................	78abd	−4,611.9	−3,951.9	−5,224.0	−4,702.6	−4,559.3	−4,574.2	−5,087.4	−6,000.2	−6,693.4	−7,286.6	−9,922.8	−13,211.5
Trade Balance............................	78acd	−885.4	−16.8	121.0	187.6	380.3	−380.7	−1,081.0	−1,175.5	−1,580.5	−1,594.4	−2,478.0	−3,352.9
Services: Credit.........................	78add	1,171.3	1,256.9	1,431.4	1,366.0	1,337.4	1,787.8	1,788.4	2,175.2	2,123.4	2,364.9	3,163.8	4,128.0
Services: Debit..........................	78aed	−1,229.3	−1,246.1	−1,277.9	−1,245.9	−1,171.0	−1,415.2	−1,474.1	−1,669.6	−1,721.3	−1,883.4	−2,564.2	−3,250.7
Balance on Goods & Services......	78afd	−943.4	−6.0	274.5	307.7	546.7	−8.0	−766.7	−670.0	−1,178.4	−1,112.9	−1,878.4	−2,475.6
Income: Credit...........................	78agd	92.6	84.6	149.7	181.0	210.8	306.3	265.4	320.8	352.0	319.7	328.0	354.0
Income: Debit...........................	78ahd	−284.9	−277.1	−581.9	−577.2	−567.4	−590.2	−450.5	−644.2	−656.0	−580.9	−817.1	−778.0
Balance on Gds, Serv. & Inc........	78aid	−1,135.7	−198.5	−157.7	−88.5	190.1	−291.9	−951.9	−993.4	−1,482.3	−1,374.1	−2,367.5	−2,899.6
Current Transfers, n.i.e.: Credit....	78ajd	285.9	357.1	256.8	231.8	275.5	261.5	328.7	354.1	598.5	653.6	862.9	1,291.1
Current Transfers: Debit..............	78akd	−249.0	−190.4	−124.9	−127.6	−38.7	−31.5	−29.0	−64.3	−100.2	−106.2	−171.2	−197.3
Capital Account, n.i.e..................	78bcd	—	763.3	—	65.9	—	—	−2.4	24.9	−.1	−.1	−.2	−.1
Capital Account, n.i.e.: Credit......	78bad	—	763.3	—	65.9	—	—	—	25.0	—	—	—	—
Capital Account: Debit.................	78bbd	—	—	—	....	—	—	−2.4	−.1	−.1	−.1	−.2	−.1
Financial Account, n.i.e...............	78bjd	759.0	−1,018.7	326.6	−715.0	462.0	266.8	720.9	781.3	662.8	1,750.2	2,058.1	3,345.5
Direct Investment Abroad.............	78bdd	—	—	8.0	28.5	1.7	−.1	−17.1	−3.3	−9.7	−28.3	−21.8	228.4
Dir. Invest. in Rep. Econ., n.i.e....	78bed	40.0	105.4	90.4	109.0	504.8	537.3	818.8	1,001.5	812.9	904.7	1,419.4	1,802.8
Portfolio Investment Assets..........	78bfd	—	−222.0	9.7	−7.1	−13.7	−129.4	−207.4	−62.2	−40.3	218.3	−72.0	17.6
Equity Securities......................	78bkd	—	—	9.7	−7.1	−8.5	−10.6	—	−8.2	−33.5	−16.8	−7.9	−26.6
Debt Securities.........................	78bld	—	−222.0	—	—	−5.2	−118.8	−207.4	−54.0	−6.8	235.1	−64.1	44.3
Portfolio Investment Liab., n.i.e.....	78bgd	—	−9.8	−75.4	−122.2	146.5	−112.0	8.0	−114.7	105.1	−302.1	−130.0	−685.7
Equity Securities......................	78bmd	—	—	—	2.0	52.0	19.3	1.9	4.9	−8.6	−22.9	−25.6	—
Debt Securities.........................	78bnd	—	−9.8	−75.4	−124.2	94.5	−131.3	6.2	−119.6	113.7	−279.1	−104.4	−685.7
Financial Derivatives Assets.........	78bwd	....	....	....	....	....	....	....	—	—	—	—	—
Financial Derivatives Liabilities.....	78bxd	....	....	....	....	....	....	....	−1.8	17.5	6.7	−1.1	−5.7
Other Investment Assets..............	78bhd	338.4	−209.2	404.2	−568.1	−53.9	222.3	−52.3	−332.1	−100.4	283.0	147.5	−407.2
Monetary Authorities..................	78bod	....							.9	−2.1	2.1	—	—
General Government..................	78bpd	285.5	90.1	292.6	293.7	106.5	−19.8	−17.5	−9.1	−20.7	10.1	−1.8	194.9
Banks....................................	78bqd	52.9	−299.3	111.6	113.7	−440.6	102.9	25.7	−495.8	−129.8	263.1	263.8	−762.6
Other Sectors..........................	78brd	—	—	—	−975.5	280.2	139.1	−60.5	171.9	52.2	7.6	−114.6	160.5
Other Investment Liab., n.i.e........	78bid	380.6	−683.1	−110.3	−155.1	−123.4	−251.2	170.9	293.8	−122.3	667.9	716.1	2,395.3
Monetary Authorities..................	78bsd	3.0											
General Government..................	78btd	−59.6	−951.0	−1.9	44.0	−82.1	−213.8	−104.9	−223.9	−310.0	−130.6	−99.9	−46.9
Banks....................................	78bud	10.2	−39.2	−94.8	−179.7	−52.3	−65.2	10.1	108.4	102.9	256.3	403.1	1,145.2
Other Sectors..........................	78bvd	427.0	307.1	−13.6	−19.4	11.0	27.8	265.8	409.3	84.8	542.2	412.8	1,296.9
Net Errors and Omissions............	78cad	18.1	71.6	143.8	−105.3	256.4	−299.2	29.9	34.5	694.7	−208.3	349.9	190.5
Overall Balance.......................	78cbd	−321.7	−215.6	444.6	−738.7	1,145.3	−94.3	96.2	137.0	373.4	715.1	732.0	1,730.2
Reserves and Related Items............	79dad	321.7	215.6	−444.6	738.7	−1,145.3	94.3	−96.2	−137.0	−373.4	−715.1	−732.0	−1,730.2
Reserve Assets..........................	79dbd	247.0	−341.6	−233.7	750.9	−1,641.3	−461.4	−527.6	−408.9	−275.4	−586.2	−932.4	−1,829.4
Use of Fund Credit and Loans.......	79dcd	42.7	262.4	−245.9	−108.7	396.9	129.4	161.9	136.0	−168.5	−142.3	36.4	−55.2
Exceptional Financing.................	79ded	32.0	294.8	35.0	96.5	99.1	426.3	269.5	136.0	70.5	13.4	164.0	154.5
International Investment Position						*Millions of US Dollars*							
Assets.....................................	79aad	....	....	....	....	....	7,869.6	8,057.0	8,825.7	9,145.5	10,029.1	11,610.8	....
Direct Investment Abroad.............	79abd	....	....	....	....	....	74.5	10.9	87.0	96.7	125.0	146.8	....
Portfolio Investment...................	79acd	....	....	....	....	....	521.9	677.6	728.2	798.7	667.5	692.7	....
Equity Securities......................	79add	....	....	....	....	....	20.6	20.6	28.7	.4	.8	1.3	....
Debt Securities.........................	79aed	....	....	....	....	....	501.4	657.0	699.5	798.2	666.7	691.4	....
Financial Derivatives..................	79ald	....	....	....	....	....							....
Other Investment......................	79afd	....	....	....	....	....	4,216.8	4,146.7	4,550.2	4,669.8	4,489.5	4,314.7	....
Monetary Authorities..................	79agd	....	....	....	....	....	3.1	.4	.4	.4	3.7	.5	....
General Government..................	79ahd	....	....	....	....	....	2,348.2	2,389.9	2,416.7	2,446.7	2,461.1	2,135.1	....
Banks....................................	79aid	....	....	....	....	....	1,524.5	1,397.4	1,806.1	1,848.7	1,633.0	1,450.4	....
Other Sectors..........................	79ajd	....	....	....	....	....	341.0	359.0	327.1	374.1	391.7	728.7	....
Reserve Assets..........................	79akd	....	....	....	....	....	3,056.4	3,221.7	3,460.3	3,580.3	4,747.0	6,456.7	....
Liabilities.................................	79lad	....	....	....	....	....	12,538.1	13,086.9	13,215.7	13,019.1	14,506.4	17,198.7	....
Dir. Invest. in Rep. Economy..........	79lbd	....	....	....	....	....	1,596.6	2,402.6	2,257.3	2,757.7	3,662.3	5,081.8	....
Portfolio Investment...................	79lcd	....	....	....	....	....	5,173.1	5,195.3	5,193.6	5,073.2	4,666.9	4,638.8	....
Equity Securities......................	79ldd	....	....	....	....	....	113.4	97.9	99.8	95.3	76.3	47.8	....
Debt Securities.........................	79led	....	....	....	....	....	5,059.7	5,097.5	5,093.8	4,977.9	4,590.6	4,591.0	....
Financial Derivatives..................	79lld	....	....	....	....	....			1.8	19.2			....
Other Investment......................	79lfd	....	....	....	....	....	5,768.5	5,488.9	5,763.0	5,169.0	6,177.1	7,478.1	....
Monetary Authorities..................	79lgd	....	....	....	....	....	1,116.3	1,250.8	1,322.9	1,110.0	1,049.3	1,187.5	....
General Government..................	79lhd	....	....	....	....	....	3,170.9	2,525.3	2,336.1	2,111.1	2,195.1	2,583.7	....
Banks....................................	79lid	....	....	....	....	....	440.8	325.3	396.2	373.8	647.6	958.1	....
Other Sectors..........................	79ljd	....	....	....	....	....	1,040.4	1,387.4	1,707.8	1,574.2	2,285.2	2,748.8	....

Bulgaria   918

		1993	1994	1995	1996	1997	1998	1999	2000	2001	2002	2003	2004
Government Finance						*Millions of Leva: Year Ending December 31*							
Deficit (-) or Surplus	80	−36.1	† −24.5	−46.2	−332.8	353.3	599.2	348.7	154.9	556.2	−9.8	255.4	1,329.0
Total Revenue and Grants	81y	100.0	† 209.3	315.5	703.3	5,662.1	7,530.6	8,219.9	9,340.1	10,268.4	10,637.4	12,057.2	14,385.0
Revenue	81	99.9	† 209.3	314.6	699.1	5,558.0	7,380.3	8,015.0	9,124.7	9,874.4	10,229.5	11,760.6	14,355.5
Grants	81z	.1	† —	.9	4.2	104.1	150.3	204.9	215.4	394.0	407.9	296.7	29.5
Exp. & Lending Minus Repay	82z	136.1	† 233.8	361.7	1,036.1	5,308.8	6,931.4	7,871.1	9,185.2	9,712.2	10,647.2	11,801.8	13,056.0
Expenditure	82	133.9	† 235.9	360.6	1,040.9	5,733.2	7,227.6	8,122.6	9,444.9	10,212.5	10,820.2	11,993.6	13,760.0
Lending Minus Repayments	83	2.2	† −2.1	1.1	−4.8	−424.4	−296.2	−251.5	−259.7	−500.3	−173.0	−191.8	−704.0
Total Financing	80h	36.1	† 24.5	46.2	332.8	−353.3	−599.2	−348.9	−154.9	−556.2	9.9	−255.4	−1,328.9
Total Net Borrowing	84	35.5	† 53.0	58.7	295.5	1,261.0	−213.3	227.3	−434.0	−276.4	633.5	275.2	−302.1
Net Domestic	84a	38.3	† 44.6	65.5	331.3	1,204.3	−65.8	49.9	−3.9	−224.3	129.8	294.8	359.8
Net Foreign	85a	−2.8	† 8.4	−6.8	−35.8	56.7	−147.5	177.4	−430.1	−52.1	503.7	−19.6	−661.9
Use of Cash Balances	87	.6	† −28.5	−12.5	37.3	−1,614.3	−386.0	−576.2	279.1	−279.8	−623.6	−530.6	−1,026.8
Total Debt by Residence	88	....	....	....	....	....	....	....	....	....	....	....	....
Domestic	88a	112.0	† 275.1	345.4	1,052.8	....	....	....	....	....	....	....	....
Foreign	89a	....	....	....	....	....	....	....	....	....	....	....	....
National Accounts						*Millions of Leva*							
Househ.Cons.Expend.,incl.NPISHs	96f	220	389	622	1,313	12,724	15,144	16,964	18,506	20,642	22,238	23,759	25,892
Government Consumption Expend	91f	56	90	134	210	2,188	3,440	3,937	4,786	5,177	5,832	6,555	7,108
Gross Fixed Capital Formation	93e	39	72	134	238	1,914	2,920	3,600	4,206	5,415	5,909	6,694	7,957
Changes in Inventories	93i	7	−23	4	−95	−191	865	662	688	726	497	816	981
Exports of Goods and Services	90c	114	237	393	976	10,155	10,553	10,601	14,902	16,510	17,180	18,500	22,210
Imports of Goods and Services (-)	98c	137	240	407	881	9,358	10,501	11,974	16,334	18,760	19,321	21,779	26,111
Gross Domestic Product (GDP)	99b	299	526	880	1,761	17,433	22,421	23,790	26,753	29,709	32,335	34,547	38,008
Statistical Discrepancy	99bs	....	—	—	—	—	—	—	—	—	—	—	−30
Net Primary Income from Abroad	98.n	−5	−11	−29	−69	−589	−510	−327	−671	−664	−489	−1,108	−678
Gross National Income (GNI)	99a	294	515	852	1,692	16,844	21,911	23,464	26,082	29,045	31,777	33,439	37,331
Net Current Transf.from Abroad	98t	—	1	1	17	399	404	552	618	1,099	1,109	1,198	1,737
Gross Nat'l Disposable Inc.(GNDI)	99i	294	516	853	1,709	17,242	22,315	24,016	26,701	30,144	32,944	34,637	39,068
Gross Saving	99s	18	37	96	186	2,330	3,731	3,115	3,409	4,325	4,712	4,322	6,067
GDP Volume (1995=100)	99bvp	† 95.5	† 97.2	† 100.0	† 89.9	83.7	....	....	....	....	....	....	....
GDP Deflator (1995=100)	99bip	35.6	61.4	100.0	222.5	2,366.0	....	....	....	....	....	....	....
						Millions: Midyear Estimates							
Population	99z	8.46	8.38	8.30	8.23	8.16	8.11	8.05	† 8.00	7.94	7.89	7.83	7.78

Burkina Faso 748

		1993	1994	1995	1996	1997	1998	1999	2000	2001	2002	2003	2004
Exchange Rates						*Francs per SDR: End of Period*							
Official Rate	aa	404.89	† 780.44	728.38	753.06	807.94	791.61	† 896.19	918.49	935.39	850.37	771.76	747.90
						Francs per US Dollar: End of Period (ae) Period Average (rf)							
Official Rate	ae	294.77	† 534.60	490.00	523.70	598.81	562.21	† 652.95	704.95	744.31	625.50	519.36	481.58
Official Rate	rf	283.16	† 555.20	499.15	511.55	583.67	589.95	† 615.70	711.98	733.04	696.99	581.20	528.28
Fund Position						*Millions of SDRs: End of Period*							
Quota	2f.s	44.2	44.2	44.2	44.2	44.2	44.2	60.2	60.2	60.2	60.2	60.2	60.2
SDRs	1b.s	5.6	5.6	5.5	1.8	1.6	.5	.5	.3	.4	.3	.2	.1
Reserve Position in the Fund	1c.s	7.2	7.2	7.2	7.2	7.2	7.2	7.2	7.2	7.2	7.3	7.3	7.3
Total Fund Cred.&Loans Outstg.	2tl	15.2	32.8	50.5	56.5	68.5	79.6	87.9	86.1	92.7	93.0	83.9	73.8
International Liquidity					*Millions of US Dollars Unless Otherwise Indicated: End of Period*								
Total Reserves minus Gold	1l.d	382.3	237.2	347.4	338.6	344.8	373.3	295.0	243.6	260.5	313.4	752.2	669.1
SDRs	1b.d	7.7	8.1	8.2	2.6	2.2	.8	.7	.4	.5	.4	.3	.2
Reserve Position in the Fund	1c.d	9.9	10.5	10.7	10.4	9.7	10.2	9.9	9.4	9.1	9.9	10.8	11.3
Foreign Exchange	1d.d	364.7	218.6	328.4	325.6	332.9	362.4	284.4	233.8	250.9	303.1	741.1	657.6
Gold (Million Fine Troy Ounces)	1ad	.011	.011	—	—	—	—	—	—	—	—	—	—
Gold (National Valuation)	1and	4.1	4.1	—	—	—	—	—	—	—	—	—	—
Monetary Authorities: Other Liab.	4..d	29.8	14.9	4.1	5.8	29.0	43.9	29.3	37.8	22.6	20.1	41.9	41.3
Deposit Money Banks: Assets	7a.d	53.1	155.5	253.5	212.8	167.5	167.5	232.9	212.6	188.8	203.0	249.1	274.0
Liabilities	7b.d	42.5	39.7	58.7	44.0	54.5	67.0	129.1	105.3	119.5	111.2	176.4	186.2
Monetary Authorities						*Billions of Francs: End of Period*							
Foreign Assets	11	112.7	126.8	170.2	177.3	206.5	209.9	192.6	171.7	193.9	196.0	390.7	322.2
Claims on Central Government	12a	26.3	44.8	55.7	59.3	80.1	92.9	103.7	104.4	110.7	112.5	103.3	92.5
Claims on Deposit Money Banks	12e	9.0	—	2.5	4.0	14.6	24.7	3.9	10.3	3.3	—	—	—
Claims on Other Financial Insts.	12f	.9	.4	.3	.4	.7	1.1	1.1	1.1	1.1	1.1	1.0	1.2
Reserve Money	14	121.4	120.4	149.3	156.3	193.1	186.2	160.0	160.2	160.5	121.7	328.5	241.8
of which: Currency Outside DMBs	14a	78.5	94.9	123.5	139.6	170.1	165.0	142.5	136.6	120.9	83.2	255.8	175.0
Foreign Liabilities	16c	14.9	33.6	38.8	45.6	72.7	87.7	97.9	105.7	103.6	91.7	86.5	75.1
Central Government Deposits	16d	8.4	19.5	37.4	37.3	29.5	48.4	45.0	22.9	41.4	79.9	65.3	83.3
Other Items (Net)	17r	4.1	−1.4	3.2	1.7	6.6	6.2	−1.6	−1.3	3.5	16.3	14.6	15.7
Deposit Money Banks						*Billions of Francs: End of Period*							
Reserves	20	41.0	20.9	17.7	9.1	15.7	14.4	19.8	18.1	35.4	30.1	61.8	65.8
Foreign Assets	21	15.7	83.1	124.2	111.5	100.3	94.2	152.1	149.9	140.5	127.0	129.4	131.9
Claims on Central Government	22a	13.5	35.3	27.3	26.1	28.1	32.7	26.1	21.4	15.0	20.6	31.3	36.0
Claims on Private Sector	22d	87.6	72.3	79.0	89.9	163.2	180.9	186.5	217.6	247.9	293.6	338.6	380.3
Claims on Other Financial Insts.	22f	.3	.3	—	—	—	—	—	—	—	—	—	—
Demand Deposits	24	42.0	69.8	81.5	80.2	90.7	89.5	107.7	126.0	135.7	152.9	183.3	193.9
Time Deposits	25	57.4	62.6	71.0	70.7	83.7	94.3	108.5	117.5	131.7	152.6	184.6	205.5
Foreign Liabilities	26c	6.9	12.2	19.7	23.1	30.5	33.0	77.2	68.4	82.5	60.7	82.3	79.9
Long-Term Foreign Liabilities	26cl	5.6	9.0	9.1	—	2.1	4.7	7.1	5.8	6.4	8.8	9.3	9.8
Central Government Deposits	26d	47.8	59.0	61.3	54.6	57.5	58.0	60.5	60.1	57.1	74.0	78.9	86.4
Credit from Monetary Authorities	26g	9.0	—	2.5	—	14.6	25.2	4.4	10.3	3.3	—	—	—
Other Items (Net)	27r	−10.5	−.7	3.1	7.9	28.3	17.6	19.2	18.8	22.1	22.2	22.8	38.5
Treasury Claims: Private Sector	22d.i	.9	1.7	1.6	1.6	1.8	1.4	1.1	.4	.5	.9	1.3	.4
Post Office: Checking Deposits	24..i	1.6	2.4	2.7	2.7	2.1	2.3	2.3	2.3	1.9	2.5	3.1	4.5
Monetary Survey						*Billions of Francs: End of Period*							
Foreign Assets (Net)	31n	106.5	164.2	236.0	220.1	203.5	183.4	169.6	147.5	148.4	170.5	351.3	299.1
Domestic Credit	32	74.1	77.0	66.3	86.5	187.3	203.5	214.2	263.7	278.0	276.4	333.1	344.8
Claims on Central Govt. (Net)	32an	−15.7	2.4	−14.6	−5.4	21.5	20.1	25.4	44.7	28.5	−19.2	−7.8	−37.2
Claims on Private Sector	32d	88.5	73.9	80.6	91.5	165.0	182.3	187.6	217.9	248.4	294.5	339.9	380.7
Claims on Other Financial Insts.	32f	1.2	.6	.3	.4	.7	1.1	1.1	1.1	1.1	1.1	1.0	1.2
Money	34	122.6	170.3	213.7	228.7	268.9	261.9	256.9	270.4	262.3	243.7	452.0	378.2
Quasi-Money	35	57.4	62.6	71.0	70.7	83.7	94.3	108.5	117.5	131.7	152.6	184.6	205.5
Long-Term Foreign Liabilities	36cl	5.6	9.0	9.1	—	2.1	4.7	7.1	5.8	6.4	8.8	9.3	9.8
Other Items (Net)	37r	−5.0	−.8	8.5	7.2	36.2	26.0	11.4	17.5	26.0	41.8	38.6	50.5
Money plus Quasi-Money	35l	180.0	232.9	284.7	299.4	352.5	356.2	365.3	387.9	394.0	396.3	636.5	583.7
Interest Rates						*Percent Per Annum*							
Bank Rate (End of Period)	60	† 6.00	6.00	6.00	6.00	6.00	6.00	6.00	6.00	6.00	6.00	4.50	4.00
Money Market Rate	60b	4.95	4.95	4.95	4.95	4.95	4.95	4.95	4.95	4.95	4.95	4.95	4.95
Deposit Rate	60l	3.50	3.50	3.50	3.50	3.50	3.50	3.50	3.50	3.50	3.50	3.50	3.50
Prices and Labor						*Index Numbers (2000=100): Period Averages*							
Consumer Prices	64	66.1	82.7	88.9	94.3	94.4	100.3	101.4	100.0	105.0	107.3	109.5	109.0
						Number in Thousands: Period Averages							
Unemployment	67c	30	27	14	13	9	9	8	7	....	....	....	....
Intl. Transactions & Positions						*Billions of Francs*							
Exports	70	19.66	59.22	138.00	119.04	133.62	190.44	132.19	168.73	190.09	202.13	218.27	271.65
Imports, c.i.f.	71	144.02	193.70	227.00	330.96	342.35	430.33	350.77	468.19	476.11	485.55	537.58	585.61
						1995=100							
Unit Value of Exports	74	64.7	84.8	100.0	97.8	....	....	....	....	....	....	....	....
Unit Value of Imports	75	56.8	93.5	100.0	103.7	....	....	....	....	....	....	....	....

		1993	1994	1995	1996	1997	1998	1999	2000	2001	2002	2003	2004
Balance of Payments		*Millions of US Dollars: Minus Sign Indicates Debit*											
Current Account, n.i.e.	78ald	−71.1	14.9	....	....	....	....	....	−392.0	−380.8	....	....	....
Goods: Exports f.o.b.	78aad	226.1	215.6	....	....	....	....	....	205.6	223.5	....	....	....
Goods: Imports f.o.b.	78abd	−469.1	−344.3	....	....	....	....	....	−517.7	−509.3	....	....	....
Trade Balance	78acd	−243.0	−128.7	....	....	....	....	....	−312.1	−285.8	....	....	....
Services: Credit	78add	64.6	56.3	....	....	....	....	....	31.4	36.5	....	....	....
Services: Debit	78aed	−209.0	−138.3	....	....	....	....	....	−139.9	−141.2	....	....	....
Balance on Goods & Services	78afd	−387.4	−210.7	....	....	....	....	....	−420.6	−390.5	....	....	....
Income: Credit	78agd	21.5	8.7	....	....	....	....	....	13.5	15.2	....	....	....
Income: Debit	78ahd	−28.6	−38.1	....	....	....	....	....	−33.6	−39.7	....	....	....
Balance on Gds, Serv. & Inc.	78aid	−394.5	−240.1	....	....	....	....	....	−440.7	−414.9	....	....	....
Current Transfers, n.i.e.: Credit	78ajd	389.6	308.0	....	....	....	....	....	87.6	72.0	....	....	....
Current Transfers: Debit	78akd	−66.3	−53.0	....	....	....	....	....	−38.9	−37.9	....	....	....
Capital Account, n.i.e.	78bcd	—	—	....	....	....	....	....	175.9	165.2	....	....	....
Capital Account, n.i.e.: Credit	78bad	—	—	....	....	....	....	....	175.9	165.2	....	....	....
Capital Account: Debit	78bbd	—	....	....	....	....	....	....	—	—	....	....	....
Financial Account, n.i.e.	78bjd	69.1	−13.9	....	....	....	....	....	19.2	25.2	....	....	....
Direct Investment Abroad	78bdd	—	....	....	....	....	....	....	−.2	−.6	....	....	....
Dir. Invest. in Rep. Econ., n.i.e.	78bed	—	—	....	....	....	....	....	23.2	8.8	....	....	....
Portfolio Investment Assets	78bfd	—	....	....	....	....	....	....	6.2	10.0	....	....	....
Equity Securities	78bkd	—	....	....	....	....	....	....	.4	−2.1	....	....	....
Debt Securities	78bld	—	....	....	....	....	....	....	5.8	12.2	....	....	....
Portfolio Investment Liab., n.i.e.	78bgd	—	....	....	....	....	....	....	−2.6	.7	....	....	....
Equity Securities	78bmd	—	....	....	....	....	....	....	−2.6	.7	....	....	....
Debt Securities	78bnd	—	....	....	....	....	....	....	—	—	....	....	....
Financial Derivatives Assets	78bwd	....	....	....	....	....	....	....	—	—	....	....	....
Financial Derivatives Liabilities	78bxd	....	....	....	....	....	....	....	—	—	....	....	....
Other Investment Assets	78bhd	24.2	−139.2	....	....	....	....	....	−9.7	5.6	....	....	....
Monetary Authorities	78bod	....	....	....	....	....	....	....	....	....	....	....	....
General Government	78bpd	—	—	....	....	....	....	....	−2.1	−.5	....	....	....
Banks	78bqd	24.2	−135.2	....	....	....	....	....	−3.0	16.4	....	....	....
Other Sectors	78brd	—	−4.0	....	....	....	....	....	−4.6	−10.3	....	....	....
Other Investment Liab., n.i.e.	78bid	44.9	125.3	....	....	....	....	....	2.2	.6	....	....	....
Monetary Authorities	78bsd	—	—	....	....	....	....	....	5.7	.7	....	....	....
General Government	78btd	84.4	29.3	....	....	....	....	....	....	....	....	....	....
Banks	78bud	−47.1	41.9	....	....	....	....	....	−13.7	−4.2	....	....	....
Other Sectors	78bvd	7.7	54.0	....	....	....	....	....	10.2	4.2	....	....	....
Net Errors and Omissions	78cad	4.6	−8.3	....	....	....	....	....	5.1	3.4	....	....	....
Overall Balance	78cbd	2.5	−7.3	....	....	....	....	....	−191.8	−187.0	....	....	....
Reserves and Related Items	79dad	−2.5	7.3	....	....	....	....	....	191.8	187.0	....	....	....
Reserve Assets	79dbd	−53.5	−17.4	....	....	....	....	....	30.6	−31.0	....	....	....
Use of Fund Credit and Loans	79dcd	12.5	25.5	....	....	....	....	....	−2.4	8.5	....	....	....
Exceptional Financing	79ded	38.5	−.7	....	....	....	....	....	163.6	209.6	....	....	....
International Investment Position		*Millions of US Dollars*											
Assets	79aad	....	....	....	....	....	....	....	457.2	428.8	....	....	....
Direct Investment Abroad	79abd	....	....	....	....	....	....	....	.4	.7	....	....	....
Portfolio Investment	79acd	....	....	....	....	....	....	....	84.0	51.8	....	....	....
Equity Securities	79add	....	....	....	....	....	....	....	1.3	3.1	....	....	....
Debt Securities	79aed	....	....	....	....	....	....	....	82.7	48.7	....	....	....
Financial Derivatives	79ald	....	....	....	....	....	....	....	....	....	....	....	....
Other Investment	79afd	....	....	....	....	....	....	....	130.1	115.8	....	....	....
Monetary Authorities	79agd	....	....	....	....	....	....	....	—	—	....	....	....
General Government	79ahd	....	....	....	....	....	....	....	3.7	7.2	....	....	....
Banks	79aid	....	....	....	....	....	....	....	125.0	102.2	....	....	....
Other Sectors	79ajd	....	....	....	....	....	....	....	1.3	6.3	....	....	....
Reserve Assets	79akd	....	....	....	....	....	....	....	242.6	260.5	....	....	....
Liabilities	79lad	....	....	....	....	....	....	....	1,815.3	1,513.9	....	....	....
Dir. Invest. in Rep. Economy	79lbd	....	....	....	....	....	....	....	27.8	15.9	....	....	....
Portfolio Investment	79lcd	....	....	....	....	....	....	....	4.3	2.9	....	....	....
Equity Securities	79ldd	....	....	....	....	....	....	....	1.5	1.6	....	....	....
Debt Securities	79led	....	....	....	....	....	....	....	2.8	1.3	....	....	....
Financial Derivatives	79lld	....	....	....	....	....	....	....	—	—	....	....	....
Other Investment	79lfd	....	....	....	....	....	....	....	1,783.2	1,495.1	....	....	....
Monetary Authorities	79lgd	....	....	....	....	....	....	....	149.5	119.3	....	....	....
General Government	79lhd	....	....	....	....	....	....	....	....	....	....	....	....
Banks	79lid	....	....	....	....	....	....	....	98.7	85.1	....	....	....
Other Sectors	79ljd	....	....	....	....	....	....	....	....	....	....	....	....
Government Finance		*Millions of Francs: Year Ending December 31*											
Deficit (-) or Surplus	80	−37,540	−46,806	−37,971	−23,579	−50,500	−50,300	−63,800	−67,500	−61,796	−55,628	−88,796	−111,332
Total Revenue and Grants	81y	139,800	189,669	225,178	223,280	279,200	303,100	377,600	363,000	313,231	335,183	434,302	467,880
Revenue	81	100,800	114,325	137,183	160,812	181,400	199,400	236,500	219,300	227,966	258,897	300,971	350,549
Grants	81z	39,000	75,344	87,995	62,468	97,800	103,700	141,100	143,700	85,265	76,286	133,331	117,331
Exp. & Lending Minus Repay	82z	181,940	225,115	244,859	229,859	323,200	347,900	432,100	431,500	387,948	422,519	508,231	587,566
Expenditure	82	183,940	227,449	247,053	231,552	325,700	348,500	431,800	428,400	389,841	422,606	484,727	592,953
Lending Minus Repayments	83	−2,000	−2,334	−2,194	−1,693	−2,500	−600	300	3,100	−1,893	−87	23,504	−5,387
Adjustment to Cash Basis	80x	4,600	−11,360	−18,290	−17,000	−6,500	−5,500	−9,300	1,000	12,921	31,708	−14,867	8,354
Total Financing	80h	37,540	46,806	37,971	23,579	50,500	50,300	63,800	67,500	61,796	55,628	88,796	111,332

National Accounts		1993	1994	1995	1996	1997	1998	1999	2000	2001	2002	2003	2004
						Billions of Francs							
Househ.Cons.Expend.,incl.NPISHs....	96f	647.0	726.6	887.4	1,041.0	1,074.0	1,300.9	1,301.6	1,306.4	1,482.4	1,616.7	1,743.8	1,928.1
Government Consumption Expend...	91f	220.2	281.1	306.9	330.9	347.6	378.1	428.4	438.5	467.1	498.5	517.9	556.4
Gross Fixed Capital Formation..........	93e	167.7	271.6	267.0	298.4	346.2	370.2	386.1	404.3	448.0	449.9	500.2	559.3
Changes in Inventories....................	93i	−8.5	15.3	17.2	31.7	45.2	29.8	−9.8	−17.4	−41.5	−29.7	15.4	−79.4
Exports of Goods and Services..........	90c	81.1	149.4	168.0	139.8	154.5	211.9	176.7	168.7	190.1	202.1	218.3	271.7
Imports of Goods and Services (-).....	98c	187.3	263.4	316.0	365.4	380.1	465.5	448.6	468.2	476.1	485.6	537.6	585.6
Gross Domestic Product (GDP).........	99b	920.2	1,180.7	1,330.4	1,476.2	1,587.8	1,825.5	1,834.3	1,832.4	2,070.1	2,252.0	2,458.0	2,650.4
Net Primary Income from Abroad.....	98.n	65.0	92.5	115.8	111.7	102.4	118.7	93.9	90.3	93.3	100.2	136.2	117.3
Gross National Income (GNI)............	99a	985.2	1,273.2	1,446.2	1,587.9	1,690.2	1,944.2	1,928.2	1,922.6	2,163.3	2,352.1	2,594.2	2,767.7
GDP Volume 1985 Prices.................	99b.p	948.8	968.6	1,031.4	1,133.2	1,210.6	1,313.2	1,362.4	1,384.0	1,477.9	1,545.3	1,668.4	1,744.6
GDP Volume (2000=100)...............	99bvp	68.6	70.0	74.5	81.9	87.5	94.9	98.4	100.0	106.8	111.7	120.5	126.1
GDP Deflator (2000=100)..............	99bip	73.3	92.1	97.4	98.4	99.1	105.0	101.7	100.0	105.8	110.1	111.3	114.7
						Millions: Midyear Estimates							
Population................................	99z	9.30	9.56	9.83	10.10	10.38	† 10.66	10.96	11.29	11.64	12.02	12.42	12.82

		1993	1994	1995	1996	1997	1998	1999	2000	2001	2002	2003	2004
Exchange Rates						*Francs per SDR: End of Period*							
Official Rate	aa	362.99	360.78	413.37	462.63	551.56	710.64	860.83	1,014.76	1,090.92	1,451.07	1,618.31	1,717.35
					Francs per US Dollar: End of Period (ae) Period Average (rf)								
Official Rate	ae	264.38	246.94	277.92	322.35	408.38	505.16	628.58	778.20	864.20	1,071.23	1,093.00	1,109.51
Official Rate	rf	242.78	252.66	249.76	302.75	352.35	447.77	563.56	720.67	830.35	930.75	1,082.62	1,100.91
					Index Numbers (2000=100): Period Averages								
Official Rate	ahx	294.3	282.6	286.5	236.6	203.2	160.5	127.2	100.0	86.2	77.5	65.9	64.8
Nominal Effective Exchange Rate	nec	173.0	193.2	196.2	170.9	161.4	133.5	114.6	100.0	90.3	80.1	61.2	56.6
Real Effective Exchange Rate	rec	88.9	92.7	102.0	107.1	127.5	114.8	96.1	100.0	94.2	80.0	65.5	63.2
Fund Position						*Millions of SDRs: End of Period*							
Quota	2f.s	57.20	57.20	57.20	57.20	57.20	57.20	77.00	77.00	77.00	77.00	77.00	77.00
SDRs	1b.s	.51	.14	.05	.08	.05	.07	.07	.03	.04	.12	.09	.23
Reserve Position in the Fund	1c.s	5.86	5.86	5.86	5.86	5.86	5.86	5.86	5.86	.36	.36	.36	.36
Total Fund Cred.&Loans Outstg	2tl	44.40	40.13	34.16	28.18	22.20	15.37	9.82	5.98	2.13	9.63	19.25	26.40
International Liquidity					*Millions of US Dollars Unless Otherwise Indicated: End of Period*								
Total Reserves minus Gold	1l.d	162.98	204.70	209.45	139.60	113.04	65.52	47.98	32.92	17.71	58.78	66.97	65.75
SDRs	1b.d	.70	.21	.07	.11	.06	.09	.10	.04	.06	.16	.14	.35
Reserve Position in the Fund	1c.d	8.05	8.56	8.71	8.43	7.91	8.25	8.04	7.64	.45	.49	.54	.56
Foreign Exchange	1d.d	154.23	195.94	200.67	131.06	105.07	57.18	39.84	25.24	17.20	58.13	66.29	64.84
Gold (Million Fine Troy Ounces)	1ad	.017	.017	.017	.017	.017	.017	.017	.017	.001	.001	.001	.001
Gold (National Valuation)	1and	6.66	6.59	6.66	6.36	4.99	4.95	5.00	4.74	.27	.34	.40	.42
Monetary Authorities: Other Liab	4..d	74.82	71.02	60.59	48.11	36.17	28.35	19.60	14.16	7.78	37.34	36.41	51.22
Deposit Money Banks: Assets	7a.d	10.00	19.00	17.00	24.00	12.00	5.00	13.00	18.00	14.00	18.00	39.33	49.59
Liabilities	7b.d	9.00	13.00	11.00	8.00	8.00	8.00	8.00	14.00	19.00	22.00	30.59	45.55
Other Banking Insts.: Assets	7e.d	—	—	—	—	—	—	—	—	—	—	—	—
Liabilities	7f.d	14.00	18.21	18.41	16.20	13.72	12.25	10.35	9.14	8.41	9.48	10.90	7.80
Monetary Authorities						*Millions of Francs: End of Period*							
Foreign Assets	11	46,912	54,230	61,439	48,407	49,620	37,711	33,642	33,702	20,573	64,415	75,336	77,622
Claims on Central Government	12a	9,170	8,698	10,504	12,443	20,702	27,498	41,685	59,106	69,082	75,991	103,781	129,673
Claims on Nonfin.Pub.Enterprises	12c	25	25	25	25	25	25	25	25	25	25	25	25
Claims on Private Sector	12d	421	420	1,486	1,563	1,181	1,220	703	827	1,191	1,414	1,578	1,817
Claims on Deposit Money Banks	12e	3,355	2,538	2,210	9,239	3,838	15,460	13,983	23,028	15,532	26,093	10,220	3,607
Claims on Other Financial Insts	12f	1,487	634	1,307	761	162	781	117	1,660	4,914	9,233	1,411	1,474
Reserve Money	14	17,617	22,292	22,114	26,346	26,854	27,566	37,387	36,398	40,431	49,820	55,246	75,771
of which: Currency Outside DMBs	14a	14,440	19,073	19,495	23,974	23,693	24,180	32,087	31,300	34,058	42,752	† 44,515	57,153
Nonfin.Pub.Ent. Deps	14e	1,118	649	577	371	749	860	710	1,044	347	449	1,158	1,218
Bonds	16ab	2,174	2,701	2,329	2,531	2,400	1,915	3,924	3,689	1,278	2,159	4,353	6,745
Restricted Deposits	16b	1,019	842	1,164	540	2,230	3,014	1,752	5,035	2,941	609	1,053	7,249
Stabilization Fund	16bb	4	4	74	16	20	—	4	47	51	19	15	22
Foreign Liabilities	16c	19,782	17,537	16,840	15,508	14,770	14,320	12,319	11,023	6,724	40,001	39,793	56,829
Central Government Deposits	16d	8,299	7,710	10,764	7,290	6,062	7,629	7,108	31,081	21,893	42,267	48,245	21,363
Capital Accounts	17a	12,490	12,744	15,926	17,531	20,418	20,262	22,482	24,206	22,068	24,087	25,568	28,714
Other Items (Net)	17r	−15	2,714	7,762	2,675	2,773	7,987	5,179	6,870	15,932	18,210	18,079	17,526
Deposit Money Banks													
Commercial Banks						*Millions of Francs: End of Period*							
Reserves	20	1,761	2,171	1,290	1,716	2,852	2,839	4,754	3,625	6,289	† 6,720	† 9,308	17,712
Foreign Assets	21	2,553	4,773	4,760	7,907	4,898	2,650	8,427	14,352	12,334	† 16,878	† 42,990	55,018
Claims on Central Government	22a	2,441	5,311	6,799	8,824	10,524	10,879	9,888	220	4,361	† 3,107	† 3,107	11,024
Claims on Nonfin.Pub.Enterprises	22c	1,591	2,749	1,322	1,673	2,213	3,515	4,538	3,230	4,634	† 5,297	† 6,930	6,849
Claims on Private Sector	22d	31,557	34,022	29,162	35,886	39,516	52,948	69,385	101,356	110,418	† 143,552	† 158,978	161,388
Claims on Other Financial Insts	22f	114	142	284	1,748	104	106	105	265	273	† 1,350	† 96	91
Demand Deposits	24	14,721	19,095	18,730	18,038	22,235	22,180	34,296	34,860	44,244	† 55,838	† 72,107	91,079
Savings Deposits	25	10,135	14,951	10,681	16,373	17,038	15,955	26,144	30,976	35,126	† 48,691	† 53,090	52,364
Foreign Liabilities	26c	1,969	3,155	3,048	2,447	3,019	3,796	4,848	11,115	16,579	† 22,887	† 33,431	50,543
Central Government Deposits	26d	526	76	192	14	—	180	150	773	476	† 340	† 13,921	15,127
Credit from Monetary Authorities	26g	4,044	2,602	806	8,020	1,128	14,518	13,199	22,338	14,663	† 24,867	† 9,743	3,775
Capital Accounts	27a	7,085	8,281	8,221	11,446	12,625	14,510	17,470	21,297	24,892	† 31,872	† 47,623	54,633
Other Items (Net)	27r	1,536	1,008	1,939	1,414	4,064	1,798	989	1,689	2,328	† −2,163	† −7,838	−15,439
Other Monetary Institutions						*Millions of Francs: End of Period*							
Reserves	20..h	169	72	....	7	342	....	....	....	....	....	....	....
Claims on Central Government	22a.h	1,052	1,355	....	1,262	1,531	1,602	2,203	1,373	1,437	1,494	† 2,114	....
Claims on Nonfin.Pub.Enterprises	22c.h	1,286	1,071	....	† 1,896	1,312	....	....	....	....	....	....	....
Claims on Private Sector	22d.h	1,404	1,675	....	2,690	2,133	....	....	....	....	....	....	....
Claims on Other Financial Insts	22f.h	6	6	....	6	6	....	....	....	....	....	....	....
Demand Deposits	24..h	1,021	1,329	....	1,259	1,527	1,595	2,200	1,369	1,431	1,487	1,857	....
Time and Savings Deposits	25..h	347	598	....	1,484	2,052	2	2	2	2	2	2	....
Foreign Liabilities	26c.h	66	43	....	29	29	....	....	....	....	....	....	....
Central Government Deposits	26d.h	1,779	1,811	....	639	500	....	....	....	....	....	....	....
Cred.from Monetary Authorities	26g.h	749	303	....	1,195	1,172	....	....	....	....	....	....	....
Other Items (Net)	27r.h	−7	115	....	1,256	69	4	1	2	3	5	5	....
Monetary Survey						*Millions of Francs: End of Period*							
Foreign Assets (Net)	31n	27,648	38,267	46,311	38,330	36,699	22,244	24,902	25,916	9,604	† 18,405	† 45,102	25,268
Domestic Credit	32	41,721	48,316	39,933	61,466	73,341	90,764	121,389	136,209	173,966	† 202,135	† 215,853	....
Claims on Central Govt. (Net)	32an	3,838	7,578	6,347	15,225	26,695	32,169	46,517	28,846	52,510	† 41,265	† 46,835	....
Claims on Nonfin.Pub.Enterprises	32c	2,902	3,844	1,347	3,593	3,550	3,540	4,563	3,255	4,659	† 5,322	† 6,955	6,874
Claims on Private Sector	32d	33,381	36,117	30,648	40,138	42,830	54,168	70,087	102,183	111,609	† 144,965	† 160,556	163,204
Claims on Other Financial Insts	32f	1,601	776	1,591	2,510	267	887	222	1,925	5,188	† 10,583	† 1,507	1,565
Money	34	31,300	40,146	38,802	43,642	48,203	48,816	69,293	68,573	80,080	† 100,527	† 119,637	....
Quasi-Money	35	10,482	15,549	10,681	17,857	19,089	15,957	26,146	30,978	35,128	† 48,693	† 53,092	....
Other Items (Net)	37r	32,883	36,348	44,703	45,033	51,035	57,943	59,304	68,639	70,689	73,904	† 88,644	....
Money plus Quasi-Money	35l	41,782	55,695	49,482	61,499	67,292	64,773	95,439	99,551	115,209	† 149,220	† 172,729	....

Burundi 618

		1993	1994	1995	1996	1997	1998	1999	2000	2001	2002	2003	2004
Other Banking Institutions					*Millions of Francs: End of Period*								
Cash	40..f	....	132	123	191	† 478	102	291	† 799	178	† 145	† 255	....
Foreign Assets	41..f	—	—	—	—	—	—	....	—	—	—	—	—
Claims on Central Government	42a.f	73	52	111	87	† 405	1,057	1,491	† 618	2,121	† 2,675	† 1,198	....
Claims on Private Sector	42d.f	....	12,577	13,319	14,304	† 15,376	16,637	18,068	† 21,256	25,902	† 29,972	† 20,466	....
Bonds	46abf	....	3,347	2,324	3,224	† 2,829	2,561	2,980	† 3,981	5,198	† 4,873	† 1,521	....
Long-Term Foreign Liabilities	46clf	....	4,496	5,117	5,222	† 6,057	6,641	6,962	† 7,717	8,091	† 10,814	12,386	....
Central Govt. Lending Funds	46f.f	....	1,151	1,185	1,045	914	1,371	1,340	1,280	1,772	2,390	2,574	2,028
Credit from Monetary Authorities	46g.f	....	228	1,043	599	—	623	118	972	3,331	6,645	† 722	837
Credit from Depos. Money Banks	46h.f	....	—	4	375	—	1	—	† —	—	† —	† —	....
Capital Accounts	47a.f	....	2,990	3,589	4,357	† 7,125	7,834	10,142	† 10,737	12,494	† 13,910	† 12,496	....
Other Items (Net)	47r.f	....	548	290	−242	† −667	−1,235	−1,692	† −2,015	−2,686	† −5,840	† −7,781	....
Banking Survey					*Millions of Francs: End of Period*								
Foreign Assets (Net)	51n	34,621	38,267	46,311	38,330	36,699	22,244	24,902	25,916	9,604	† 18,405	† 45,102	25,268
Domestic Credit	52	....	58,377	....	72,709	85,811	103,539	135,963	149,216	187,112	† 215,072	† 236,010	....
Claims on Central Govt. (Net)	52an	2,168	5,840	....	14,674	26,625	32,526	47,248	† 29,464	54,631	† 43,940	† 48,033	....
Claims on Nonfin.Pub.Enterprises	52c	2,902	3,844	1,347	3,593	3,550	3,540	4,563	3,255	4,659	† 5,322	† 6,955	6,874
Claims on Private Sector	52d	....	48,693	43,967	54,442	55,637	67,473	84,152	† 123,439	137,511	† 174,937	180,855	....
Liquid Liabilities	55l	....	55,563	....	61,308	66,815	64,671	95,148	† 98,753	115,030	† 149,075	† 172,474	....
Other Items (Net)	57r	....	41,081	54,331	49,731	55,695	61,113	65,716	† 82,444	84,013	† 84,402	† 108,638	....
Interest Rates					*Percent Per Annum*								
Discount Rate (End of Period)	60	10.00	10.00	10.00	10.00	12.00	12.00	12.00	14.00	14.00	15.50	14.50	14.50
Lending Rate	60p	13.77	14.20	15.26	....	....	....	15.24	15.77	16.82	19.47	18.23	18.25
Prices					*Index Numbers (2000=100): Period Averages*								
Consumer Prices	64	† 30.5	35.0	41.7	52.7	69.2	77.8	80.4	100.0	109.2	102.3	114.3	129.2
Intl. Transactions & Positions					*Millions of Francs*								
Exports	70	15,019	30,034	25,982	11,372	30,767	28,635	30,971	35,223	31,978	28,867	40,698	51,706
Imports, c.i.f.	71	47,435	56,511	58,186	37,332	43,250	70,274	66,308	106,059	115,249	121,028	169,742	194,054
Balance of Payments					*Millions of US Dollars: Minus Sign Indicates Debit*								
Current Account, n.i.e.	78ald	−28.1	−16.9	10.4	−40.0	−.3	−51.4	−23.0	−53.2	−39.0	−10.2	−37.3	....
Goods: Exports f.o.b.	78aad	73.9	80.7	112.9	40.4	87.5	64.0	55.0	49.1	39.2	31.0	37.5	....
Goods: Imports f.o.b.	78abd	−172.8	−172.6	−175.6	−100.0	−96.1	−123.5	−97.3	−107.9	−108.3	−104.8	−130.0	....
Trade Balance	78acd	−99.0	−91.9	−62.7	−59.6	−8.6	−59.5	−42.3	−58.8	−69.1	−73.8	−92.5	....
Services: Credit	78add	14.6	14.9	16.4	10.5	5.2	4.5	4.4	4.0	5.2	6.3	5.6	....
Services: Debit	78aed	−114.8	−93.9	−83.3	−38.4	−35.5	−41.6	−25.3	−42.8	−37.9	−43.2	−45.0	....
Balance on Goods & Services	78afd	−199.2	−170.9	−129.6	−87.4	−38.8	−96.6	−63.2	−97.6	−101.8	−110.7	−131.9	....
Income: Credit	78agd	11.2	8.1	10.4	6.4	4.3	3.6	1.9	2.4	1.9	.9	1.3	....
Income: Debit	78ahd	−22.2	−19.5	−22.9	−20.4	−16.8	−11.9	−11.3	−14.5	−15.8	−12.6	−18.6	....
Balance on Gds, Serv. & Inc.	78aid	−210.2	−182.3	−142.1	−101.4	−51.4	−104.9	−72.6	−109.7	−115.7	−122.4	−149.3	....
Current Transfers, n.i.e.: Credit	78ajd	183.8	167.0	154.7	62.5	55.6	56.8	51.4	58.3	79.6	115.5	115.5	....
Current Transfers: Debit	78akd	−1.8	−1.6	−2.1	−1.1	−4.5	−3.3	−1.8	−1.8	−2.9	−3.3	−3.5	....
Capital Account, n.i.e.	78bcd	−1.2	−.2	−.8	−.3	−.1	—	—	—	—	−.5	−.9	....
Capital Account, n.i.e.: Credit	78bad	—	—	—	—	—	—	—	—	—	—	—	....
Capital Account: Debit	78bbd	−1.2	−.2	−.8	−.3	−.1	—	—	—	—	−.5	−.9	....
Financial Account, n.i.e.	78bjd	52.5	31.1	21.1	14.1	−12.3	−7.8	−6.5	−7.5	−4.0	−40.5	−50.0	....
Direct Investment Abroad	78bdd	−.1	−.1	−.6	—	—	—	−.5	—	—	—	—	....
Dir. Invest. in Rep. Econ., n.i.e.	78bed	.5	—	2.0	—	—	—	.2	11.7	—	—	—	....
Portfolio Investment Assets	78bfd	—	—	—	—	—	—	—	—	—	—	....	....
Equity Securities	78bkd	—	—	—	—	—	—	—	—	—	—	....	....
Debt Securities	78bld	—	—	—	—	—	—	—	—	—	—	....	....
Portfolio Investment Liab., n.i.e.	78bgd	—	—	—	—	—	—	—	—	—	—	....	....
Equity Securities	78bmd	—	—	—	—	—	—	—	—	—	—	....	....
Debt Securities	78bnd	—	—	—	—	—	—	—	—	—	—	....	....
Financial Derivatives Assets	78bwd	....	....	....	....	—	—	—	—	—	—	....	....
Financial Derivatives Liabilities	78bxd	....	....	....	....	—	—	—	—	—	—	....	....
Other Investment Assets	78bhd	−1.5	−1.6	8.2	6.6	15.3	10.7	14.2	6.8	24.0	−4.3	−19.9	....
Monetary Authorities	78bod	....	....	....	....	—	—	—	—	—	—	—	....
General Government	78bpd	−.3	−.8	−.4	−.3	−.4	−.3	−.3	—	—	—	—	....
Banks	78bqd	−4.2	−8.8	.1	−10.4	8.5	5.0	−10.3	−8.2	2.4	−7.7	−22.2	....
Other Sectors	78brd	3.0	7.9	8.6	17.3	7.1	6.0	24.7	15.0	21.6	3.4	2.3	....
Other Investment Liab., n.i.e.	78bid	53.6	32.9	11.5	7.6	−27.6	−18.5	−20.4	−25.9	−28.0	−36.2	−30.1	....
Monetary Authorities	78bsd	—	—	—	—	—	—	—	—	—	—	—	....
General Government	78btd	47.2	25.2	4.9	7.3	−34.0	−21.4	−23.4	−35.8	−34.6	−42.9	−41.0	....
Banks	78bud	.4	4.7	−.4	−2.0	1.6	1.7	1.9	8.7	6.6	6.8	10.0	....
Other Sectors	78bvd	6.0	3.0	7.0	2.2	4.8	1.1	1.1	1.2	.1	−.1	.9	....
Net Errors and Omissions	78cad	−7.2	21.1	5.9	−9.2	−27.8	−18.8	−19.0	−34.2	−31.2	3.9	−12.6	....
Overall Balance	78cbd	16.0	35.2	36.7	−35.3	−40.5	−78.1	−48.6	−94.8	−74.3	−47.2	−100.9	....
Reserves and Related Items	79dad	−16.0	−35.2	−36.7	35.3	40.5	78.1	48.6	94.8	74.3	47.2	100.9	....
Reserve Assets	79dbd	−11.9	−29.0	−27.6	44.0	−2.0	28.7	8.8	1.2	16.1	−46.9	−9.6	....
Use of Fund Credit and Loans	79dcd	−4.1	−6.1	−9.0	−8.7	−8.3	−9.3	−7.6	−5.0	−4.8	9.9	13.6	....
Exceptional Financing	79ded	....	....	....	....	50.8	58.6	47.4	98.7	63.0	84.3	97.0	....

Burundi 618

		1993	1994	1995	1996	1997	1998	1999	2000	2001	2002	2003	2004
International Investment Position							*Millions of US Dollars*						
Assets...............................	79aad	....	....	....	....	....	....	88.4	75.6	....	....	....	....
Direct Investment Abroad..............	79abd	....	....	....	....	—	—	−.4	—	—	—	—	....
Portfolio Investment......................	79acd	....	....	....	....	—	—	—	—	—	—	—	....
Equity Securities......................	79add	....	....	....	....	—	—	—	—	—	—	—	....
Debt Securities...........................	79aed	....	....	....	....	—	—	—	—	—	—	—	....
Financial Derivatives.....................	79ald	....	....	....	....	....	....	—	—	....	....	....	....
Other Investment...........................	79afd	....	....	....	....	17.8	10.3	35.3	32.3	35.0	21.0	42.0	....
Monetary Authorities...................	79agd	....	....	....	....	....	....	—	—	—	—	—	....
General Government....................	79ahd	....	....	....	....	....	−.3	−.3	—	—	−.1	−.1	....
Banks..	79aid	....	....	....	....	12.0	5.2	13.4	18.4	14.3	18.2	39.8	....
Other Sectors............................	79ajd	....	....	....	....	6.2	5.3	22.2	13.9	20.7	2.9	2.3	....
Reserve Assets...............................	79akd	....	....	....	....	121.5	74.7	53.5	43.3	23.8	65.5	73.8	....
Liabilities......................................	79lad	....	....	....	....	....	....	22.5	63.9	....	....	....	....
Dir. Invest. in Rep. Economy..........	79lbd	....	....	....	....	—	—	.2	10.8	—	—	—	....
Portfolio Investment......................	79lcd	....	....	....	....	—	—	—	—	—	—	—	....
Equity Securities......................	79ldd	....	....	....	....	—	—	—	—	—	—	—	....
Debt Securities...........................	79led	....	....	....	....	—	—	—	—	—	—	—	....
Financial Derivatives.....................	79lld	....	....	....	....	....	....	—	—	....	....	....	....
Other Investment...........................	79lfd	....	....	....	....	34.6	43.6	22.3	53.0	8.0	43.3	77.0	....
Monetary Authorities...................	79lgd	....	....	....	....	....	21.6	13.4	7.8	2.7	13.0	28.5	....
General Government....................	79lhd	....	....	....	....	....	13.5	.2	29.8	−14.0	8.8	16.7	....
Banks..	79lid	....	....	....	....	7.4	7.5	7.7	14.3	19.2	21.4	30.8	....
Other Sectors............................	79ljd	....	....	....	....	....	1.0	1.0	1.2	.1	.1	1.0	....
Government Finance							*Millions of Francs: Year Ending December 31*						
Deficit (-) or Surplus........................	80	−12,476.6	−13,305.2	−6,638.4	−21,154.4	−18,271.9	−19,390.0	−26,831.3	−20,322.5	−38.2	−6,317.2	−32,871.2	−54,314.6
Total Revenue and Grants..............	81y	63,024.4	68,493.8	58,743.4	47,086.9	59,150.3	85,639.4	99,076.1	114,215.4	161,346.9	185,911.5	200,319.3	218,892.5
Revenue.....................................	81	38,679.8	40,335.6	44,074.2	37,754.0	48,879.8	75,165.1	87,721.5	98,340.6	118,188.3	122,896.1	135,035.8	147,093.7
Grants...	81z	24,344.6	28,158.2	14,669.2	9,332.9	10,270.5	10,474.3	11,354.6	15,874.8	43,158.6	63,015.4	65,283.5	71,798.8
Exp. & Lending Minus Repay.........	82z	75,501.0	81,799.0	65,381.8	68,241.3	77,422.2	105,029.4	125,907.4	134,537.9	161,385.1	192,228.7	233,190.5	273,207.1
Expenditure..................................	82	74,780.1	81,898.7	65,152.6	67,556.6	78,598.1	106,295.2	126,713.5	138,304.1	166,072.2	193,740.2	235,124.6	274,423.8
Lending Minus Repayments.........	83	720.9	−99.7	229.2	684.7	−1,175.9	−1,265.8	−806.1	−3,766.2	−4,687.1	−1,511.5	−1,934.1	−1,216.7
Total Financing...............................	80h	12,476.6	13,305.2	6,638.4	21,154.4	18,271.9	19,390.0	26,831.1	20,322.4	38.2	6,317.2	32,871.2	54,314.6
Domestic......................................	84a	224.7	4,675.6	−38.6	5,057.6	7,851.6	3,459.7	20,194.7	−30,359.2	3,254.6	−21,545.6	12,002.9	34,386.7
Foreign..	85a	12,251.9	8,629.6	6,677.0	16,096.8	10,420.3	15,930.3	6,636.4	50,681.6	−3,216.4	27,862.8	20,868.3	19,927.9
Total Debt by Residence..................	88	272,667	278,631	323,864	380,437	464,228	605,411	740,305	920,581	968,564	1,269,334	1,487,783	1,639,877
Domestic......................................	88a	13,694	13,502	17,695	27,357	39,989	49,659	64,528	68,072	80,294	95,081	117,255	163,094
Foreign..	89a	258,973	265,129	306,169	353,080	424,239	555,752	675,777	852,509	888,270	1,174,253	1,370,528	1,476,783
National Accounts							*Millions of Francs*						
House.Cons.Expend.,incl.NPISHs....	96f	217,092	256,656	228,920	216,869	283,525	359,511	395,805	465,738	487,057	518,951	561,832	638,547
Government Consumption Expend...	91f	30,280	32,459	33,600	39,911	50,299	58,630	63,547	75,577	80,479	108,750	136,151	163,470
Gross Fixed Capital Formation..........	93e	36,193	23,446	23,419	32,712	21,975	24,000	34,314	38,564	40,073	55,787	69,131	84,139
Changes in Inventories....................	93i	1,002	53	−199	−400	2,700	3,200	—	—	—	3,000	—	176
Exports of Goods and Services..........	90c	21,370	24,029	32,298	15,426	33,760	32,018	34,507	39,761	38,236	35,967	48,686	60,202
Imports of Goods and Services (-).....	98c	69,261	66,592	68,173	41,443	49,473	77,193	72,730	108,601	121,464	137,849	171,120	198,047
Gross Domestic Product (GDP).........	99b	236,676	270,051	249,865	263,075	342,786	400,166	455,443	511,039	549,981	584,605	644,680	748,486
Net Primary Income from Abroad.....	98.n	−2,674	−2,876	−3,152	−4,003	−4,416	−3,699	−5,315	−8,698	−11,545	−10,906	−18,778	−34,286
Gross National Income (GNI)...........	99a	234,002	267,175	246,713	259,072	338,370	396,467	450,128	502,341	538,436	573,699	625,902	714,200
GDP Volume 1980 Prices...............	99b.p	127,635	123,698	115,013	105,113	105,512	110,249	109,147	108,164	110,436	115,405	114,020	119,037
GDP Volume (2000=100)...............	99bvp	118.0	114.4	106.3	97.2	97.5	101.9	100.9	100.0	102.1	106.7	105.4	110.1
GDP Deflator (2000=100)...............	99bip	39.2	46.2	46.0	53.0	68.8	76.8	88.3	100.0	105.4	107.2	119.7	133.1
							Millions: Midyear Estimates						
Population...............................	99z	6.00	6.09	6.16	6.21	6.26	6.31	6.38	6.49	6.63	6.82	7.04	7.28

Cambodia 522

		1993	1994	1995	1996	1997	1998	1999	2000	2001	2002	2003	2004
Exchange Rates						*Riels per SDR: End of Period*							
Official Rate	aa	3,166.1	3,759.1	3,754.9	3,901.2	4,657.6	5,308.3	5,174.4	5,087.9	4,895.0	5,342.9	5,920.1	6,254.0
				Riels per US Dollar: End of Period (ae) Period Average (rf)									
Official Rate	ae	2,305.0	2,575.0	2,526.0	2,713.0	3,452.0	3,770.0	3,770.0	3,905.0	3,895.0	3,930.0	3,984.0	4,027.0
Official Rate	rf	2,689.0	2,545.3	2,450.8	2,624.1	2,946.3	3,744.4	3,807.8	3,840.8	3,916.3	3,912.1	3,973.3	4,016.3
Fund Position						*Millions of SDRs: End of Period*							
Quota	2f.s	25.00	65.00	65.00	65.00	65.00	65.00	87.50	87.50	87.50	87.50	87.50	87.50
SDRs	1b.s	11.42	10.89	10.21	9.51	8.77	6.95	3.78	.14	.41	.40	.14	.05
Reserve Position in the Fund	1c.s	—	—	—	—	—	—	—	—	—	—	—	—
Total Fund Cred.&Loans Outstg	2tl	6.25	20.25	48.25	48.25	48.25	47.21	53.12	56.24	63.51	70.78	69.70	62.70
International Liquidity					*Millions of US Dollars Unless Otherwise Indicated: End of Period*								
Total Reserves minus Gold	1l.d	24.18	118.50	191.98	265.78	298.63	324.38	393.19	501.68	586.81	776.15	815.53	943.21
SDRs	1b.d	15.68	15.90	15.18	13.68	11.83	9.78	5.19	.18	.51	.55	.20	.08
Reserve Position in the Fund	1c.d	—	—	—	—	—	—	—	—	—	—	—	—
Foreign Exchange	1d.d	8.50	102.60	176.80	252.10	286.80	314.60	388.00	501.50	586.30	775.60	815.33	943.13
Gold (Million Fine Troy Ounces)	1ad	—	—	—	—	—	.3998	.3998	.3998	.3998	.3998	.3998	.3998
Gold (National Valuation)	1and	—	—	—	—	—	114.85	116.27	109.21	110.75	137.54	166.40	177.90
Deposit Money Banks: Assets	7a.d	103.69	126.75	161.57	186.57	162.08	139.55	154.43	167.33	216.74	173.28	209.50	242.14
Liabilities	7b.d	68.43	63.93	65.78	59.55	58.03	59.51	56.88	44.23	50.27	41.61	79.88	72.72
Monetary Authorities						*Billions of Riels: End of Period*							
Foreign Assets	11	56.44	305.09	484.88	720.91	1,033.02	1,675.22	1,923.51	2,388.61	2,740.07	3,598.33	3,906.16	† 4,506.44
Claims on Central Government	12a	206.26	215.02	217.11	213.58	211.28	288.55	283.04	271.83	271.14	269.05	269.39	† 269.78
Claims on Private Sector	12d	3.93	2.70	—	—	—	—	—	—	—	—	—	† 2.54
Claims on Deposit Money Banks	12e	32.49	34.20	10.09	9.48	6.19	8.10	4.94	15.81	53.19	13.19	17.09	† 16.67
Reserve Money	14	228.09	285.91	314.53	449.83	545.33	802.61	929.87	1,161.01	1,359.61	1,980.66	2,149.95	† 2,664.50
of which: Currency Outside DMBs	14a	189.72	176.30	250.92	299.84	356.06	509.06	489.86	494.60	577.78	765.98	906.39	† 1,114.75
Restricted Deposits	16b	16.23	26.17	24.55	70.93	42.94	68.67	75.52	84.40	98.21	94.13	107.48	† 100.57
Foreign Liabilities	16c	19.79	76.12	181.17	188.23	224.73	250.59	274.88	286.14	310.89	378.19	412.63	† 392.12
Central Government Deposits	16d	5.59	70.12	62.36	81.86	153.49	106.11	176.26	268.08	346.16	429.09	488.04	† 525.61
Capital Accounts	17a	57.61	127.42	115.87	200.71	391.54	839.59	870.19	1,000.17	1,035.12	1,134.32	1,228.70	† 1,269.21
Other Items (Net)	17r	−28.17	−28.74	13.60	−47.61	−107.53	−95.70	−115.22	−123.55	−85.58	−135.81	−194.17	† −156.59
Deposit Money Banks						*Billions of Riels: End of Period*							
Reserves	20	11.67	88.75	88.15	178.43	199.15	346.00	503.74	737.13	866.85	1,270.85	1,329.73	† 1,569.14
Foreign Assets	21	239.01	326.39	408.14	506.15	559.51	526.10	582.19	653.43	844.19	680.99	834.64	† 975.09
Claims on Central Government	22a	.07	.01	.31	.31	.31	.31	.31	.31	.01	40.91	90.81	† 90.20
Claims on Nonfin.Pub.Enterprises	22c	6.21	6.00	5.11	5.22	5.93	5.86	10.14	2.65	6.55	2.03	.01	† —
Claims on Private Sector	22d	157.67	234.39	293.40	434.55	636.79	654.60	763.23	898.46	936.11	1,058.91	1,336.62	† 1,813.97
Demand Deposits	24	11.77	20.94	27.29	29.09	28.70	34.21	42.09	45.04	31.94	47.30	29.47	† 33.12
Time and Savings Deposits	25a	8.51	17.80	5.07	7.85	13.21	19.77	31.71	45.89	55.50	74.31	81.87	† 97.33
Foreign Currency Deposits	25b	121.13	232.57	365.55	574.84	664.90	667.03	878.84	1,244.97	1,538.65	2,000.83	2,301.09	† 3,079.09
Restricted Deposits	26b	10.30	3.22	4.04	11.45	4.23	3.97	4.04	1.87	1.48	1.41	1.43	† 1.06
Foreign Liabilities	26c	157.74	164.61	166.15	161.56	200.32	224.37	214.45	172.73	195.82	163.54	318.26	† 292.84
Central Government Deposits	26d	25.43	1.75	7.14	4.38	4.26	4.20	4.15	.71	.01	—	.07	† 43.06
Credit from Monetary Authorities	26g	3.03	2.96	4.81	3.51	6.55	5.87	7.52	6.04	8.11	8.74	67.39	† —
Capital Accounts	27a	121.81	356.49	356.11	454.98	602.77	689.78	767.43	791.25	923.56	808.64	839.90	† 922.70
Other Items (Net)	27r	−45.08	−144.79	−141.05	−123.00	−123.26	−116.42	−90.62	−16.53	−101.37	−51.09	−47.68	† −20.81
Monetary Survey						*Billions of Riels: End of Period*							
Foreign Assets (Net)	31n	117.93	390.75	545.70	877.28	1,167.48	1,726.36	2,016.37	2,583.18	3,077.55	3,737.59	4,009.90	† 4,796.56
Domestic Credit	32	343.14	386.25	446.43	567.41	696.55	839.01	876.31	904.45	867.64	941.81	1,208.72	† 1,607.81
Claims on Central Govt. (Net)	32an	175.32	143.16	147.92	127.64	53.84	178.55	102.95	3.34	−75.02	−119.13	−127.92	† −208.69
Claims on Nonfin.Pub.Enterprises	32c	6.21	6.00	5.11	5.22	5.93	5.86	10.14	2.65	6.55	2.03	.01	† —
Claims on Private Sector	32d	161.61	237.09	293.40	434.55	636.79	654.60	763.23	898.46	936.11	1,058.91	1,336.62	† 1,816.50
Money	34	203.82	201.68	278.49	328.93	384.76	543.27	531.95	539.64	609.72	813.28	935.86	† 1,152.88
Quasi-Money	35	129.65	250.37	370.62	582.69	678.11	686.80	910.55	1,290.87	1,594.15	2,075.14	2,382.96	† 3,176.42
Capital Accounts	37a	179.42	483.91	471.98	655.70	994.31	1,529.37	1,637.62	1,791.41	1,958.69	1,942.95	2,068.60	† 2,191.91
Other Items (Net)	37r	−51.82	−158.95	−128.96	−122.63	−193.15	−194.15	−187.44	−134.30	−217.37	−151.98	−168.80	† −116.83
Money plus Quasi-Money	35l	333.47	452.05	649.11	911.62	1,062.87	1,230.07	1,442.50	1,830.51	2,203.87	2,888.43	3,318.82	† 4,329.30
Interest Rates						*Percent Per Annum*							
Deposit Rate	60l	....	....	8.7	8.8	8.0	7.8	7.3	6.8	4.4	2.5	2.0	1.8
Lending Rate	60p	....	....	18.7	18.8	18.4	18.3	17.6	17.3	16.5	16.2	18.5	17.6
Prices and Labor						*Index Numbers (2000=100): Period Averages*							
Consumer Prices	64	....	73.6	74.3	81.8	84.4	96.9	100.8	100.0	† 99.4	102.6	104.0	107.8
						Number in Thousands: Period Averages							
Labor Force	67d	4,010	....	....	4,680	4,904	5,038	5,830	5,409	5,225	....	....	....
Intl. Transactions & Positions						*Millions of US Dollars*							
Exports	70..d	....	....	....	....	626	933	1,040	1,123	1,296	1,489	1,771	....
Imports, c.i.f	71..d	....	....	....	....	1,116	1,129	1,243	1,424	1,456	1,675	1,732	....

		1993	1994	1995	1996	1997	1998	1999	2000	2001	2002	2003	2004
Balance of Payments						*Millions of US Dollars: Minus Sign Indicates Debit*							
Current Account, n.i.e.	78ald	−103.9	−156.6	−185.7	−184.9	−209.9	−205.2	−243.1	−206.4	−137.9	−119.6	−155.2	....
Goods: Exports f.o.b.	78aad	283.7	489.9	855.2	643.6	736.0	800.5	1,129.3	1,401.1	1,571.2	1,750.1	2,046.2	....
Goods: Imports f.o.b.	78abd	−471.1	−744.4	−1,186.8	−1,071.8	−1,064.0	−1,165.8	−1,591.0	−1,939.3	−2,094.0	−2,313.5	−2,595.6	....
Trade Balance	78acd	−187.4	−254.5	−331.6	−428.2	−328.0	−365.3	−461.6	−538.2	−522.8	−563.5	−549.3	....
Services: Credit	78add	63.9	54.5	114.0	162.8	160.4	177.3	293.8	428.4	524.6	604.2	526.1	....
Services: Debit	78aed	−120.5	−139.6	−187.9	−214.8	−188.0	−220.5	−291.5	−327.9	−347.3	−373.8	−394.0	....
Balance on Goods & Services	78afd	−244.0	−339.6	−405.5	−480.2	−355.6	−408.5	−459.4	−437.7	−345.5	−333.1	−417.2	....
Income: Credit	78agd	.5	2.1	9.7	12.6	16.0	47.9	51.4	67.1	57.5	50.6	43.7	....
Income: Debit	78ahd	−16.6	−49.1	−66.9	−98.3	−58.5	−108.0	−150.2	−189.6	−193.4	−219.5	−226.8	....
Balance on Gds, Serv. & Inc.	78aid	−260.1	−386.6	−462.7	−565.9	−398.1	−468.6	−558.2	−560.2	−481.4	−502.0	−600.3	....
Current Transfers, n.i.e.: Credit	78ajd	156.4	230.0	277.9	383.4	188.5	269.0	322.7	361.0	351.8	391.7	455.4	....
Current Transfers: Debit	78akd	−.2	—	−.9	−2.4	−.3	−5.6	−7.6	−7.3	−8.3	−9.3	−10.3	....
Capital Account, n.i.e.	78bcd	123.4	73.2	78.0	75.8	65.2	−4.8	10.9	35.6	44.9	13.3	−6.0	....
Capital Account, n.i.e.: Credit	78bad	123.4	73.2	78.0	75.8	65.2	89.5	78.7	79.8	102.8	76.7	53.2	....
Capital Account: Debit	78bbd	....	—	—	—	—	−94.3	−67.7	−44.2	−58.0	−63.4	−59.2	....
Financial Account, n.i.e.	78bjd	.2	54.0	122.4	259.1	219.8	239.4	201.6	190.4	151.1	249.7	184.7	....
Direct Investment Abroad	78bdd	....	....	....	....	....	−19.8	−9.1	−6.6	−7.3	−6.0	−9.7	....
Dir. Invest. in Rep. Econ., n.i.e.	78bed	54.1	68.9	150.8	293.6	203.7	242.9	230.3	148.5	149.3	145.1	87.0	....
Portfolio Investment Assets	78bfd	....	....	....	....	....	−13.5	−7.8	−7.2	−7.7	−7.5	−7.7	....
Equity Securities	78bkd	....	....	....	....	....	−13.5	−7.8	−7.2	−7.7	−7.5	−7.7	....
Debt Securities	78bld	....	....	....	....	....	....	....	....	....	....	....	....
Portfolio Investment Liab., n.i.e.	78bgd	....	....	....	....	....	....	....	....	....	....	....	....
Equity Securities	78bmd	....	....	....	....	....	....	....	....	....	....	....	....
Debt Securities	78bnd	....	....	....	....	....	....	....	....	....	....	....	....
Financial Derivatives Assets	78bwd												
Financial Derivatives Liabilities	78bxd												
Other Investment Assets	78bhd	−51.1	−46.8	−103.4	−118.0	−23.6	−72.8	−60.9	−181.3	−114.8	−111.3	−184.5	....
Monetary Authorities	78bod	....	....	....	....	....	....	....	....	....	....	....	....
General Government	78bpd	−.4	....	....	....	....	....	....	....	....	....	....	....
Banks	78bqd	−25.6	—	−39.8	−23.6	23.6	20.6	−16.8	−11.2	−45.4	39.8	−78.5	....
Other Sectors	78brd	−25.1	−46.8	−63.6	−94.4	−47.2	−93.4	−44.2	−170.1	−69.4	−151.1	−106.0	....
Other Investment Liab., n.i.e.	78bid	−2.8	31.9	75.0	83.5	39.7	102.6	49.2	236.9	131.5	229.4	299.6	....
Monetary Authorities	78bsd	—	—	—	—	—	—	—	−5.5	−10.7	−10.9	—	....
General Government	78btd	3.2	51.4	73.1	89.7	41.2	54.7	55.2	87.4	90.9	137.0	161.4	....
Banks	78bud	−6.0	−19.5	1.9	−6.2	−1.5	1.5	−2.6	−6.7	.1	−8.6	34.3	....
Other Sectors	78bvd	....	....	....	....	....	46.5	−3.4	161.8	51.3	111.9	103.9	....
Net Errors and Omissions	78cad	1.1	65.6	11.5	−78.0	−41.2	−28.7	32.1	14.1	−29.3	−29.8	−10.7	....
Overall Balance	78cbd	20.8	36.2	26.2	72.0	33.9	.7	1.5	33.7	28.8	113.7	12.8	....
Reserves and Related Items	79dad	−20.8	−36.2	−26.2	−72.0	−33.9	−.7	−1.5	−33.7	−28.8	−113.7	−12.8	....
Reserve Assets	79dbd	−23.0	−71.2	−73.2	−68.9	−34.3	−29.3	−65.1	−108.7	−90.2	−187.8	−41.2	....
Use of Fund Credit and Loans	79dcd	—	19.8	42.3	—	—	−1.4	8.3	4.0	9.3	9.3	−1.7	....
Exceptional Financing	79ded	2.2	15.2	4.7	−3.1	.4	30.0	55.3	71.0	52.1	64.9	30.2	....
International Investment Position						*Millions of US Dollars*							
Assets	79aad	....	....	....	....	....	1,805.8	1,991.5	2,337.1	2,612.8	3,008.1	3,279.7	....
Direct Investment Abroad	79abd	....	....	....	....	....	159.0	176.9	193.2	211.0	228.5	241.5	....
Portfolio Investment	79acd	....	....	....	....	....	164.8	181.7	198.8	217.4	236.8	253.8	....
Equity Securities	79add	....	....	....	....	....	148.3	163.5	178.9	195.6	213.1	228.5	....
Debt Securities	79aed	....	....	....	....	....	16.5	18.2	19.9	21.7	23.7	25.4	....
Financial Derivatives	79ald	....	....	....	....	....	—	—	—	—	—	—	....
Other Investment	79afd	....	....	182.3	206.9	223.2	1,035.2	1,123.4	1,334.4	1,481.8	1,628.6	1,831.8	....
Monetary Authorities	79agd	....	....	—	—	—	—	—	—	—	—	—	....
General Government	79ahd	....	....	—	—	—	225.0	215.5	379.8	400.7	517.7	630.7	....
Banks	79aid	....	....	163.3	186.9	163.2	—	—	—	—	—	—	....
Other Sectors	79ajd	....	....	19.0	20.0	60.0	810.2	907.9	954.6	1,081.1	1,110.9	1,201.1	....
Reserve Assets	79akd	....	....	192.1	504.1	575.2	446.9	509.5	610.7	702.6	914.2	952.6	....
Liabilities	79lad	....	....	1,108.0	1,351.2	1,210.5	2,294.2	2,580.0	2,971.3	3,269.4	3,671.2	4,058.8	....
Dir. Invest. in Rep. Economy	79lbd	....	....	498.1	677.6	580.4	1,199.1	1,429.4	1,577.9	1,727.3	1,872.3	1,959.3	....
Portfolio Investment	79lcd	....	....	—	—	—	—	—	—	—	—	—	....
Equity Securities	79ldd	....	....	—	—	—	—	—	—	—	—	—	....
Debt Securities	79led	....	....	—	—	—	—	—	—	—	—	—	....
Financial Derivatives	79lld	....	....	—	—	—	—	—	—	—	—	—	....
Other Investment	79lfd	....	....	609.9	673.6	630.1	1,095.1	1,150.6	1,393.3	1,542.2	1,798.9	2,099.5	....
Monetary Authorities	79lgd	....	....	71.7	69.4	65.1	66.5	72.9	73.3	79.8	96.2	103.6	....
General Government	79lhd	....	....	472.5	544.7	506.9	—	—	—	—	—	—	....
Banks	79lid	....	....	65.7	59.6	58.1	—	—	—	—	—	—	....
Other sectors	79ljd	....	....	—	—	—	1,028.6	1,077.7	1,320.1	1,462.4	1,702.7	1,995.9	....
Government Finance						*Trillions of Riels: Year Ending December 31*							
Deficit (-) or Surplus	80	....	....	....	....	....	....	....	....	−439.86	−577.04	....	....
Revenue	81	....	....	....	....	....	....	....	....	1,521.19	1,729.37	....	....
Grants	81z	....	....	....	....	....	....	....	....	500.73	452.97	....	....
Expenditure	82	....	....	....	....	....	....	....	....	2,461.77	2,759.38	....	....
Financing													
Domestic	84a	....	....	....	....	....	....	....	....	51.22	−30.89	....	....
Foreign	85a	....	....	....	....	....	....	....	....	388.64	607.94	....	....

Cambodia 522

		1993	1994	1995	1996	1997	1998	1999	2000	2001	2002	2003	2004
National Accounts							*Billions of Riels*						
Househ.Cons.Expend.,incl.NPISHs....	96f	6,896	6,750	8,100	8,990	9,183	11,096	11,865	12,024	12,304	12,776	13,163	....
Government Consumption Expend...	91f	306	493	413	529	553	563	661	737	828	913	976	....
Gross Fixed Capital Formation.........	93e	733	760	1,174	1,166	1,361	1,463	2,031	2,576	2,787	3,549	3,551	....
Changes in Inventories...................	93i	17	73	37	164	137	−84	201	−191	229	−69	552	....
Exports of Goods and Services..........	90c	1,094	1,833	2,630	2,334	3,411	3,727	4,994	7,028	8,042	9,275	10,225	....
Imports of Goods and Services (-).....	98c	2,186	2,751	4,001	4,042	4,625	5,254	6,716	8,695	9,375	10,558	11,803	....
Statistical Discrepancy......................	99bs	−195	−171	−61	−120	−97	90	132	371	−240	−191	−213	....
Gross Domestic Product (GDP)........	99b	6,666	6,985	8,293	9,022	9,923	11,603	13,168	13,850	14,574	15,696	16,451	....
GDP Volume 2000 Prices................	99b.p	8,595	9,372	10,019	10,515	11,230	11,645	12,946	13,850	14,621	15,421	16,246	....
GDP Volume (2000=100)................	99bvp	† 62.1	67.7	72.3	75.9	81.1	84.1	93.5	100.0	105.6	111.3	117.3	....
GDP Deflator (2000=100)................	99bip	77.6	74.5	82.8	85.8	88.4	99.6	101.7	100.0	99.7	101.8	101.3	....
							Millions: Midyear Estimates						
Population................................	99z	10.74	11.06	11.37	11.66	11.94	† 12.21	12.48	12.74	13.01	13.27	13.53	13.80

Cameroon 622

		1993	1994	1995	1996	1997	1998	1999	2000	2001	2002	2003	2004
Exchange Rates						*Francs per SDR: End of Period*							
Official Rate	aa	404.89	† 780.44	728.38	753.06	807.94	791.61	† 896.19	918.49	935.39	850.37	771.76	747.90
						Francs per US Dollar: End of Period (ae) Period Average (rf)							
Official Rate	ae	294.78	† 534.60	490.00	523.70	598.81	562.21	† 652.95	704.95	744.31	625.50	519.36	481.58
Official Rate	rf	283.16	† 555.20	499.15	511.55	583.67	589.95	† 615.70	711.98	733.04	696.99	581.20	528.28
						Index Numbers (2000=100): Period Averages							
Official Rate	ahx	250.9	128.1	142.3	138.8	121.8	120.5	115.5	100.0	96.9	102.2	122.4	134.6
Nominal Effective Exchange Rate	nec	172.4	96.3	104.8	105.5	101.4	103.7	105.8	100.0	101.6	104.8	111.8	114.7
Real Effective Exchange Rate	rec	140.9	90.7	104.7	106.3	101.4	106.8	111.6	100.0	103.2	106.9	112.3	112.7
Fund Position						*Millions of SDRs: End of Period*							
Quota	2f.s	135.10	135.10	135.10	135.10	135.10	135.10	185.70	185.70	185.70	185.70	185.70	185.70
SDRs	1b.s	.06	.03	.03	.11	—	.01	1.90	5.93	.01	.87	.99	.43
Reserve Position in the Fund	1c.s	.34	.34	.36	.37	.41	.45	.50	.52	.54	.58	.64	.65
Total Fund Cred.&Loans Outstg	2tl	11.86	29.91	34.41	50.11	68.91	110.94	142.65	180.50	193.96	225.80	233.60	214.69
International Liquidity						*Millions of US Dollars Unless Otherwise Indicated: End of Period*							
Total Reserves minus Gold	1l.d	2.45	† 2.26	3.79	2.77	.86	1.29	4.43	212.00	331.83	629.66	639.64	829.31
SDRs	1b.d	.09	.05	.04	.16	—	.02	2.61	7.73	.02	1.18	1.47	.67
Reserve Position in the Fund	1c.d	.47	.49	.53	.53	.55	.63	.69	.67	.68	.79	.96	1.01
Foreign Exchange	1d.d	1.90	† 1.72	3.22	2.08	.31	.64	1.13	203.60	331.14	627.70	637.21	827.63
Gold (Million Fine Troy Ounces)	1ad	.030	.030	.030	.030	.030	.030	.030	.030	.030	.030	.030	.030
Gold (National Valuation)	1and	11.91	† 11.33	11.56	11.04	8.72	8.61	† 8.69	8.17	8.33	10.27	12.52	13.14
Monetary Authorities: Other Liab	4..d	762.34	650.63	713.03	537.11	300.24	238.09	188.63	62.45	57.36	63.77	72.18	75.20
Deposit Money Banks: Assets	7a.d	88.27	135.55	131.07	90.23	105.23	122.82	163.34	163.10	153.17	248.67	317.31	391.47
Liabilities	7b.d	125.49	50.01	81.98	71.50	62.51	85.92	84.52	70.75	67.43	96.10	114.56	151.84
Monetary Authorities						*Billions of Francs: End of Period*							
Foreign Assets	11	4.17	7.37	7.53	7.25	5.70	5.57	8.57	155.21	253.18	400.27	338.70	405.71
Claims on Central Government	12a	319.09	340.51	338.23	340.59	338.61	358.64	403.25	434.19	499.81	518.28	490.23	442.91
Claims on Deposit Money Banks	12e	52.06	27.07	21.41	4.93	4.07	13.51	2.17	1.12	.15	—	—	—
Claims on Other Banking Insts	12f	—	—	—	—	—	—	—	—	—	—	—	—
Reserve Money	14	129.79	180.77	142.77	183.17	256.74	282.83	305.91	410.67	502.29	641.32	568.66	662.67
of which: Currency Outside DMBs	14a	116.13	136.33	102.29	95.32	180.28	205.76	237.40	264.96	296.14	333.74	298.02	324.04
Foreign Liabilities	16c	229.52	371.17	374.45	319.02	235.47	221.67	251.01	209.81	224.12	231.90	217.78	196.78
Central Government Deposits	16d	14.85	44.83	63.03	59.71	49.52	63.96	57.54	171.12	213.39	208.32	193.84	134.79
Capital Accounts	17a	13.59	22.17	20.38	21.00	22.19	21.45	25.24	26.74	27.89	26.06	23.87	23.21
Other Items (Net)	17r	−12.43	−243.99	−233.45	−230.12	−215.54	−212.19	−224.75	−227.82	−214.54	−189.05	−175.21	−168.83
Deposit Money Banks						*Billions of Francs: End of Period*							
Reserves	20	12.39	42.57	37.49	82.48	70.57	68.60	62.66	141.59	201.24	301.04	260.33	324.85
Foreign Assets	21	26.02	72.46	64.22	47.25	63.01	69.05	106.65	114.98	114.01	155.54	164.80	188.52
Claims on Central Government	22a	154.08	185.76	187.67	159.72	171.59	173.66	173.85	168.57	165.04	156.99	139.34	139.28
Claims on Nonfin.Pub.Enterprises	22c	52.68	39.45	42.06	36.26	39.76	53.95	54.35	89.19	82.95	84.92	97.12	80.69
Claims on Private Sector	22d	368.81	369.54	371.39	385.89	348.14	428.82	481.46	543.95	605.78	676.26	740.15	754.99
Claims on Other Banking Insts	22f	.01	.03	.19	.05	.06	.19	.08	—	.04	.01	—	.03
Claims on Nonbank Financial Insts	22g	3.05	4.43	8.83	9.16	11.95	14.57	5.41	4.56	7.20	10.87	8.11	11.43
Demand Deposits	24	150.06	223.09	213.97	213.45	237.72	271.06	294.49	361.99	410.94	473.35	462.88	492.14
Time and Savings Deposits	25	278.67	329.79	329.30	268.89	267.45	259.81	306.43	374.62	445.75	528.07	588.18	616.76
Bonds	26ab	5.01	3.85	3.85	.90	5.30	.90	.90	—	—	—	.28	.25
Foreign Liabilities	26c	32.58	17.44	36.08	34.84	34.74	43.80	47.21	39.18	47.73	58.15	47.36	63.07
Long-Term Foreign Liabilities	26cl	4.41	9.30	4.09	2.60	2.69	4.50	7.98	10.70	2.46	1.96	12.14	10.05
Central Government Deposits	26d	77.65	97.04	94.00	109.15	55.43	85.19	101.56	117.74	113.66	159.38	122.65	137.66
Credit from Monetary Authorities	26g	52.06	27.07	21.41	4.93	4.07	13.51	2.17	1.12	.15	—	—	—
Capital Accounts	27a	75.87	84.39	62.25	102.79	112.58	129.23	150.84	154.45	175.85	195.08	206.98	219.15
Other Items (Net)	27r	−59.27	−77.72	−53.09	−16.75	−14.91	.84	−27.10	3.03	−20.28	−30.35	−30.62	−39.29
Monetary Survey						*Billions of Francs: End of Period*							
Foreign Assets (Net)	31n	−236.32	−318.07	−342.86	−301.96	−204.18	−195.36	−190.98	10.49	92.89	263.80	226.23	324.33
Domestic Credit	32	805.22	797.85	791.34	762.82	806.10	881.16	959.54	952.03	1,033.83	1,079.63	1,158.46	1,157.05
Claims on Central Govt. (Net)	32an	380.67	384.40	368.88	331.46	405.25	383.15	418.00	313.90	337.80	307.57	313.08	309.74
Claims on Nonfin.Pub.Enterprises	32c	52.68	39.45	42.06	36.26	39.76	53.95	54.35	89.19	82.95	84.92	97.12	80.69
Claims on Private Sector	32d	368.81	369.54	371.39	385.89	348.14	428.82	481.46	543.95	605.78	676.26	740.15	754.99
Claims on Other Banking Insts	32f	.01	.03	.19	.05	.06	.19	.08	—	.04	.01	—	.03
Claims on Nonbank Financial Inst	32g	3.05	4.43	8.83	9.16	12.89	15.06	5.64	4.99	7.26	10.87	8.11	11.60
Money	34	267.46	361.29	319.24	314.14	423.90	485.29	537.73	631.06	711.98	813.63	771.21	829.96
Quasi-Money	35	278.67	329.79	329.30	268.89	267.45	259.81	306.43	374.62	445.75	528.07	588.18	616.76
Bonds	36ab	5.01	3.85	3.85	.90	5.30	.90	.90	—	—	—	.28	.25
Other Items (Net)	37r	17.76	−215.15	−203.91	−123.08	−94.74	−60.19	−75.54	−43.16	−31.02	1.74	25.03	34.41
Money plus Quasi-Money	35l	546.13	691.08	648.55	583.03	691.35	745.09	844.17	1,005.69	1,157.74	1,341.70	1,359.38	1,446.72
Interest Rates						*Percent Per Annum*							
Discount Rate (End of Period)	60	11.50	† 7.75	8.60	7.75	7.50	7.00	7.30	7.00	6.50	6.30	6.00	6.00
Deposit Rate	60l	7.75	8.08	5.50	5.38	5.04	5.00	5.00	5.00	5.00	5.00	5.00	5.00
Lending Rate	60p	17.46	17.50	16.00	22.00	22.00	22.00	22.00	22.00	20.67	18.00	18.00	18.00
Prices						*Index Numbers (2000=100): Period Averages*							
Consumer Prices	64	60.7	† 82.1	89.5	93.0	97.5	100.6	102.1	100.0	104.5	107.4	....	....
Intl. Transactions & Positions						*Billions of Francs*							
Exports	70	533.24	825.20	811.02	821.61	982.81	1,084.15	939.59	1,092.20	1,540.20	1,586.50	....	....
Imports, c.i.f	71	311.96	601.50	464.73	572.62	708.17	874.61	816.83	910.68	1,157.80	1,978.90	....	....

		1993	1994	1995	1996	1997	1998	1999	2000	2001	2002	2003	2004
Balance of Payments					*Millions of US Dollars: Minus Sign Indicates Debit*								
Current Account, n.i.e.	78ald	−565.4	−56.1	89.9	....	....	....	....	....	....	....	....	....
Goods: Exports f.o.b.	78aad	1,507.7	1,454.2	1,735.9	....	....	....	....	....	....	....	....	....
Goods: Imports f.o.b.	78abd	−1,005.3	−1,052.3	−1,109.0	....	....	....	....	....	....	....	....	....
Trade Balance	78acd	502.4	401.9	626.9	....	....	....	....	....	....	....	....	....
Services: Credit	78add	390.9	330.8	304.4	....	....	....	....	....	....	....	....	....
Services: Debit	78aed	−741.1	−493.2	−498.6	....	....	....	....	....	....	....	....	....
Balance on Goods & Services	78afd	152.2	239.6	432.6	....	....	....	....	....	....	....	....	....
Income: Credit	78agd	17.0	19.9	12.4	....	....	....	....	....	....	....	....	....
Income: Debit	78ahd	−669.5	−336.4	−424.6	....	....	....	....	....	....	....	....	....
Balance on Gds, Serv. & Inc.	78aid	−500.3	−76.9	20.4	....	....	....	....	....	....	....	....	....
Current Transfers, n.i.e.: Credit	78ajd	65.2	83.8	100.7	....	....	....	....	....	....	....	....	....
Current Transfers: Debit	78akd	−130.2	−63.0	−31.2	....	....	....	....	....	....	....	....	....
Capital Account, n.i.e.	78bcd	6.3	14.1	20.4	....	....	....	....	....	....	....	....	....
Capital Account, n.i.e.: Credit	78bad	6.4	14.1	21.1	....	....	....	....	....	....	....	....	....
Capital Account: Debit	78bbd	−.1	—	−.7	....	....	....	....	....	....	....	....	....
Financial Account, n.i.e.	78bjd	−310.0	−626.4	43.3	....	....	....	....	....	....	....	....	....
Direct Investment Abroad	78bdd	−22.1	−.4	−.6	....	....	....	....	....	....	....	....	....
Dir. Invest. in Rep. Econ., n.i.e.	78bed	5.1	−9.0	7.3	....	....	....	....	....	....	....	....	....
Portfolio Investment Assets	78bfd	−106.3	−74.6	−26.2	....	....	....	....	....	....	....	....	....
Equity Securities	78bkd	8.0	6.4	—	....	....	....	....	....	....	....	....	....
Debt Securities	78bld	−114.4	−81.1	−26.2	....	....	....	....	....	....	....	....	....
Portfolio Investment Liab., n.i.e.	78bgd	—	—	—	....	....	....	....	....	....	....	....	....
Equity Securities	78bmd	—	—	—	....	....	....	....	....	....	....	....	....
Debt Securities	78bnd	—	—	—	....	....	....	....	....	....	....	....	....
Financial Derivatives Assets	78bwd	....	....	....	....	....	....	....	....	....	....	....	....
Financial Derivatives Liabilities	78bxd	....	....	....	....	....	....	....	....	....	....	....	....
Other Investment Assets	78bhd	105.5	138.4	−146.8	....	....	....	....	....	....	....	....	....
Monetary Authorities	78bod	....	....	....	....	....	....	....	....	....	....	....	....
General Government	78bpd	—	—	—	....	....	....	....	....	....	....	....	....
Banks	78bqd	42.8	−27.9	6.6	....	....	....	....	....	....	....	....	....
Other Sectors	78brd	62.6	166.3	−153.4	....	....	....	....	....	....	....	....	....
Other Investment Liab., n.i.e.	78bid	−292.2	−680.7	209.6	....	....	....	....	....	....	....	....	....
Monetary Authorities	78bsd	−5.4	−181.3	666.9	....	....	....	....	....	....	....	....	....
General Government	78btd	−22.5	−272.3	−457.0	....	....	....	....	....	....	....	....	....
Banks	78bud	−104.1	−76.2	17.0	....	....	....	....	....	....	....	....	....
Other Sectors	78bvd	−160.1	−150.9	−17.3	....	....	....	....	....	....	....	....	....
Net Errors and Omissions	78cad	−16.2	117.0	−138.1	....	....	....	....	....	....	....	....	....
Overall Balance	78cbd	−885.3	−551.3	15.4	....	....	....	....	....	....	....	....	....
Reserves and Related Items	79dad	885.3	551.3	−15.4	....	....	....	....	....	....	....	....	....
Reserve Assets	79dbd	14.9	.4	14.5	....	....	....	....	....	....	....	....	....
Use of Fund Credit and Loans	79dcd	−47.4	25.3	6.7	....	....	....	....	....	....	....	....	....
Exceptional Financing	79ded	917.8	525.6	−36.6	....	....	....	....	....	....	....	....	....
Government Finance						*Billions of Francs: Year Ending June 30*							
Deficit (-) or Surplus	80	−54.74	−99.05	† 8.25	....	....	83.71	7.16	....	....	....		
Revenue	81	448.41	385.90	† 536.54	....	....	862.31	867.46	....	....	....		
Grants Received	81z	—	—	† —	....	....	—	—	....	....	....		
Expenditure	82	501.15	483.49	† 525.27	....	....	777.60	859.80	....	....	....		
Lending Minus Repayments	83	2.00	1.46	† 3.02	....	....	1.00	.50	....	....	....		
Financing													
Domestic	84a	12.45	−13.09	† −13.17	....	....	−19.40	−14.90	....	....	....		
Foreign	85a	61.16	120.84	† 14.42	....	....	−63.10	8.50	....	....	....		
Adj. to Total Financing	84x	−18.87	−8.70	† −9.50	....	....	−1.21	−.76	....	....	....		
Debt: Domestic	88a	374.16	1,179.18	† 1,419.89	....	....	1,391.38	1,224.04	....	....	....		
Foreign	89a	1,852.61	4,084.80	† 4,343.87	....	....	4,261.53	4,432.12	....	....	....		
National Accounts						*Billions of Francs: Year Ending June 30*							
Househ.Cons.Expend.,incl.NPISHs	96f	2,233.6	2,538.9	3,018.9	3,354.8	3,537.2	....	....	....	....	....		
Government Consumption Expend	91f	343.0	257.5	299.9	305.0	332.1	....	....	....	....	....		
Gross Fixed Capital Formation	93e	492.5	533.0	597.5	729.3	850.5	....	....	....	....	....		
Changes in Inventories	93i	29.8	—	—	—	—	....	....	....	....	....		
Exports of Goods and Services	90c	531.3	768.5	1,068.3	1,116.3	1,335.8	....	....	....	....	....		
Imports of Goods and Services (-)	98c	504.7	681.8	834.5	950.4	1,038.2	....	....	....	....	....		
Gross Domestic Product (GDP)	99b	3,125.6	3,786.0	4,365.5	4,836.5	5,266.5	5,572.0	6,010.6	6,611.0	7,136.7	7,609.3		
Net Primary Income from Abroad	98.n	−198.9	−190.0	−168.5	−284.0	−299.0	....	....	....	....	....		
Gross National Income (GNI)	99a	2,926.6	3,226.0	3,981.7	4,271.0	4,718.4	....	....	....	....	....		
GDP Volume 1985 Prices	99b.p	3,058.3	2,977.6	3,075.9	3,229.7	3,391.1	....	....	....	....	....		
GDP Volume (1995=100)	99bvp	99.4	96.8	100.0	105.0	110.2	....	....	....	....	....		
GDP Deflator (1995=100)	99bip	72.0	89.6	100.0	105.5	109.4	....	....	....	....	....		
						Millions: Midyear Estimates							
Population	99z	12.65	12.98	13.30	13.62	13.94	14.25	14.55	14.86	15.16	15.45	15.75	16.04

Canada 156

		1993	1994	1995	1996	1997	1998	1999	2000	2001	2002	2003	2004
Exchange Rates						*Canadian Dollars per SDR: End of Period*							
Market Rate	aa	1.8186	2.0479	2.0294	1.9694	1.9282	2.1550	1.9809	1.9546	2.0015	2.1475	1.9205	1.8692
						Canadian Dollars per US Dollar: End of Period (ae) Period Average (rf)							
Market Rate	ae	1.3240	1.4028	1.3652	1.3696	1.4291	1.5305	1.4433	1.5002	1.5926	1.5796	1.2924	1.2036
Market Rate	rf	1.2901	1.3656	1.3724	1.3635	1.3846	1.4835	1.4857	1.4851	1.5488	1.5693	1.4011	1.3010
						Index Numbers (2000=100): Period Averages							
Market Rate	ahx	115.1	108.7	108.2	108.9	107.2	100.2	99.9	100.0	95.9	94.6	106.3	114.3
Nominal Effective Exchange Rate	neu	111.6	104.6	102.2	104.0	104.6	98.5	98.1	100.0	97.2	95.1	103.6	109.2
Real Effective Exchange Rate	reu	110.9	104.0	102.9	103.8	107.3	101.2	100.8	100.0	99.5	96.3	102.8	109.5
Fund Position						*Millions of SDRs: End of Period*							
Quota	2f.s	4,320	4,320	4,320	4,320	4,320	4,320	6,369	6,369	6,369	6,369	6,369	6,369
SDRs	1b.s	773	786	792	812	834	780	384	441	489	529	564	595
Reserve Position in the Fund	1c.s	690	629	836	853	1,167	1,633	2,308	1,926	2,278	2,633	2,589	2,150
of which: Outstg.Fund Borrowing	2c	—	—	—	—	—	204	—	—	—	—	—	—
International Liquidity						*Millions of US Dollars Unless Otherwise Indicated: End of Period*							
Total Reserves minus Gold	1l.d	12,481	12,286	15,049	20,422	17,823	23,308	28,126	31,924	33,962	36,984	36,222	34,430
SDRs	1b.d	1,062	1,148	1,177	1,168	1,126	1,098	527	574	614	719	838	924
Reserve Position in the Fund	1c.d	948	919	1,243	1,226	1,575	2,299	3,168	2,509	2,863	3,580	3,847	3,338
Foreign Exchange	1d.d	10,471	10,219	12,629	18,028	15,122	19,911	24,432	28,841	30,484	32,685	31,537	30,167
of which: US Dollars	1dxd	9,950	9,693	12,127	17,521	14,630	15,907	18,838	21,692	19,748	17,946	15,576	14,427
Gold (Million Fine Troy Ounces)	1ad	6.05	3.89	3.41	3.09	3.09	2.49	1.81	1.18	1.05	.60	.11	.11
Gold (National Valuation)	1and	292	198	178	155	146	122	524	323	291	205	45	48
Monetary Authorities: Other Liab.	4..d	276	355	349	139	99	64	187	65	67	134	85	107
Deposit Money Banks: Assets	7a.d	41,114	54,614	64,061	76,144	84,432	86,257	78,983	91,241	102,279	105,517	121,933	128,725
Liabilities	7b.d	67,151	80,507	77,143	87,951	108,978	111,723	92,325	94,728	109,353	116,856	127,172	133,561
Monetary Authorities						*Billions of Canadian Dollars: End of Period*							
Foreign Assets	11	16.91	17.51	20.79	28.18	25.68	35.86	40.72	47.97	54.16	58.47	46.82	41.45
Claims on Central Government	12a	29.63	30.41	30.09	31.03	31.81	32.41	41.68	36.98	40.08	41.89	43.22	46.82
Reserve Money	14	30.93	31.65	32.08	33.46	34.58	36.86	45.83	42.45	44.24	46.66	47.11	49.29
of which: Currency Outside DMBs	14a	25.57	27.30	27.99	28.78	30.15	32.32	38.72	36.34	38.66	41.13	42.35	44.54
Foreign Liabilities	16c	.37	.50	.48	.19	.14	.10	.27	.10	.11	.21	.11	.13
Central Government Deposits	16d	14.41	15.01	17.69	25.01	22.09	30.83	35.85	43.95	49.85	52.73	41.70	37.76
Other Items (Net)	17r	.83	.76	.64	.56	.68	.47	.45	−1.55	.05	.76	1.12	1.08
Deposit Money Banks						*Billions of Canadian Dollars: End of Period*							
Reserves	20	5.92	5.04	4.67	5.24	4.79	4.89	8.56	6.87	6.07	5.96	5.10	5.41
Foreign Assets	21	51.74	73.94	83.18	97.07	109.86	122.21	104.96	127.50	148.80	152.19	147.45	145.09
Claims on Central Government	22a	69.59	78.33	84.20	81.50	72.55	71.89	70.75	85.79	100.16	100.04	103.31	98.71
Claims on Local Government	22b	9.67	13.15	13.01	12.91	14.80	15.24	15.95	16.37	17.58	23.10	22.65	25.25
Claims on Private Sector	22d	415.63	450.77	474.89	531.94	607.32	617.22	643.28	714.84	757.23	799.50	842.02	948.18
Demand Deposits	24	91.87	97.84	109.89	126.60	139.61	147.04	160.24	188.58	214.89	227.04	241.67	267.29
Savings & Fgn Currency Deposits	25	301.19	326.97	342.32	348.69	377.66	380.37	392.79	449.05	464.64	490.02	527.38	582.68
Foreign Liabilities	26c	82.23	105.94	97.52	113.51	146.31	160.94	122.40	129.33	157.69	170.59	149.86	145.06
Central Government Deposits	26d	2.44	2.78	6.19	4.22	6.63	5.89	11.59	4.17	4.12	2.26	3.48	2.45
Other Items (Net)	27r	74.83	87.70	104.04	135.63	139.12	137.21	156.48	180.24	188.49	190.87	198.14	225.15
Monetary Survey						*Billions of Canadian Dollars: End of Period*							
Foreign Assets (Net)	31n	−13.94	−14.99	5.98	11.55	−10.91	−2.97	23.01	46.05	45.17	39.86	44.30	41.35
Domestic Credit	32	507.66	554.86	578.31	628.15	697.75	700.04	724.22	805.85	861.07	909.54	966.03	1,078.74
Claims on Central Govt. (Net)	32an	82.36	90.94	90.41	83.30	75.64	67.58	64.99	74.64	86.26	86.94	101.35	105.31
Claims on Local Government	32b	9.67	13.15	13.01	12.91	14.80	15.24	15.95	16.37	17.58	23.10	22.65	25.25
Claims on Private Sector	32d	415.63	450.77	474.89	531.94	607.32	617.22	643.28	714.84	757.23	799.50	842.02	948.18
Money	34	117.58	125.32	138.07	155.56	169.92	179.58	199.24	225.19	253.75	268.50	284.39	312.21
Quasi-Money	35	301.19	326.97	342.32	348.69	377.66	380.37	392.79	449.05	464.64	490.02	527.38	582.68
Other Items (Net)	37r	74.96	87.58	103.90	135.45	139.27	137.12	155.21	177.66	187.84	190.87	198.56	225.20
Money plus Quasi-Money	35l	418.77	452.29	480.40	504.25	547.57	559.95	592.03	674.24	718.40	758.52	811.76	894.89
Other Banking Institutions						*Billions of Canadian Dollars: End of Period*							
Reserves	40	14.95	14.94	16.77	16.57	15.45	16.93	19.56	20.98	12.55	12.72	14.32	14.30
Claims on Central Government	42a	7.55	6.74	7.41	7.58	5.18	5.47	6.49	1.35	3.30	3.12	4.15	5.01
Claims on State and Local Govts	42b	2.13	1.63	1.48	1.33	1.26	.94	.84	1.02	3.26	3.32	4.17	4.21
Claims on Private Sector	42d	148.62	141.24	140.10	144.18	132.09	133.94	135.34	103.52	113.07	121.40	133.48	146.44
Demand Deposits	44	9.47	8.96	8.37	8.69	7.87	8.07	8.11	.13	.19	.11	.11	.12
Time and Savings Deposits	45	148.27	141.95	143.53	145.42	131.64	136.34	141.39	116.16	125.00	133.21	144.81	154.98
Money Market Instruments	46aa	.80	1.01	1.29	3.07	1.63	2.06	2.57	.03	.04	.08	.11	.08
Capital Accounts	47a	10.27	9.40	9.54	9.84	9.60	9.91	10.18	9.32	10.16	10.81	12.09	13.45
Other Items (Net)	47r	4.43	3.22	3.03	2.63	3.23	.91	−.03	1.22	−3.21	−3.66	−.99	1.33
Banking Survey						*Billions of Canadian Dollars: End of Period*							
Foreign Assets (Net)	51n	−13.94	−14.99	5.98	11.55	−10.91	−2.97	23.01	46.05	45.17	39.86	44.30	41.35
Domestic Credit	52	665.97	704.47	727.30	781.23	836.28	840.38	866.88	911.74	980.70	1,037.37	1,107.83	1,234.40
Claims on Central Govt. (Net)	52an	89.91	97.68	97.83	90.88	80.82	73.05	71.48	75.99	89.56	90.06	105.50	110.32
Claims on State and Local Govts	52b	11.80	14.79	14.49	14.23	16.06	16.18	16.79	17.39	20.85	26.42	26.82	29.46
Claims on Private Sector	52d	564.25	592.01	614.99	676.11	739.40	751.15	778.62	818.35	870.30	920.89	975.51	1,094.62
Liquid Liabilities	55l	561.57	588.27	615.53	641.79	671.64	687.42	721.97	769.56	831.03	879.12	942.37	1,035.69
Money Market Instruments	56aa	.80	1.01	1.29	3.07	1.63	2.06	2.57	.03	.04	.08	.11	.08
Other Items (Net)	57r	89.66	100.21	116.47	147.92	152.11	147.94	165.35	188.21	194.79	198.02	209.65	239.98

		1993	1994	1995	1996	1997	1998	1999	2000	2001	2002	2003	2004
Nonbank Financial Institutions		*Billions of Canadian Dollars: End of Period*											
Reserves....................	40..n	2.19	2.42	3.63	3.72	3.78	3.86	† 4.57	6.00	6.89	5.96	9.42	8.99
Claims on Central Government........	42a.n	22.24	25.50	29.43	28.56	30.05	31.33	† 32.20	29.22	29.83	32.34	33.84	32.11
Claims on State & Local Govts........	42b.n	16.80	17.51	20.60	23.41	23.68	24.43	† 26.68	31.98	33.50	35.79	41.22	45.25
Claims on Private Sector.................	42d.n	123.86	126.46	131.93	137.89	154.64	164.51	† 196.09	211.66	219.16	228.52	243.36	265.38
Claims on Deposit Money Banks.....	42e.n	2.32	2.43	2.17	3.83	4.73	5.42	† 7.39	8.74	9.36	9.13	10.92	13.31
Money Market Instruments.............	46aan	6.20	8.50	8.89	10.57	16.71	18.80	† 29.01	27.13	18.78	19.77	16.46	17.19
Bonds....................	46abn	8.83	9.45	11.12	11.41	16.83	23.41	† 32.79	35.52	40.13	41.30	43.65	48.16
Cred. from Deposit Money Banks.....	46h.n	.34	.30	.28	.21	.36	.36	† 3.34	5.04	5.54	6.71	5.23	4.44
Capital Accounts....................	47a.n	165.31	173.06	183.54	190.49	201.44	212.41	† 239.75	262.42	267.33	285.68	311.06	334.55
Other Items (Net)....................	47r.n	−13.27	−16.99	−16.06	−15.27	−18.45	−25.44	† −37.96	−42.52	−33.04	−41.71	−37.65	−39.32
Money (National Definitions)		*Billions of Canadian Dollars: End of Period*											
M1....................	59ma	56.53	60.99	65.53	77.92	86.50	93.62	101.18	116.10	133.86	140.20	154.20	171.52
M1, Seasonally Adjusted...............	59mac	54.77	59.21	63.70	75.76	84.01	90.76	97.93	112.14	129.32	135.82	149.95	167.25
Gross M1....................	59maa	54.85	58.58	64.33	74.04	84.92	90.78	99.65	115.44	132.09	141.34	155.31	172.98
Gross M1, Seasonally Adjusted.......	59maf	52.90	56.63	62.31	71.85	82.50	88.32	96.98	112.23	128.41	137.42	151.07	168.39
M1+....................	59mab	151.50	156.28	160.40	179.46	197.60	205.51	221.76	249.20	279.64	297.66	315.45	344.79
M1+, Seasonally Adjusted.............	59mag	148.40	153.21	157.27	175.96	193.65	201.27	217.02	243.77	273.50	291.22	308.87	337.93
M1++....................	59mad	232.03	225.55	227.23	242.06	254.87	257.61	275.29	303.38	345.98	373.95	401.87	444.17
M1++, Seasonally Adjusted.............	59mah	228.71	222.32	223.89	238.42	250.92	253.50	270.76	298.34	340.25	368.02	395.93	438.13
M2....................	59mb	417.02	428.43	446.24	455.91	450.30	454.58	478.33	510.16	540.83	567.69	601.28	638.58
M2, Seasonally Adjusted.................	59mbc	413.87	425.14	442.75	452.13	446.15	449.80	472.78	503.84	534.16	561.07	594.94	632.38
M2+....................	59mba	582.50	593.08	619.27	643.48	634.01	641.82	675.45	713.50	778.14	812.16	848.55	890.83
M2+, Seasonally Adjusted..............	59mbf	579.46	589.94	615.88	639.70	629.72	636.73	669.41	706.58	770.78	804.91	841.77	884.38
M2++....................	59mbb	696.20	730.59	763.71	824.68	875.62	924.40	976.00	1,053.96	1,134.23	1,177.60	1,223.04	1,290.88
M2++, Seasonally Adjusted.............	59mbg	693.00	727.24	760.10	820.85	871.71	919.68	970.47	1,047.77	1,127.99	1,171.75	1,218.01	1,286.32
M3....................	59mc	486.92	512.14	537.78	567.31	597.51	617.51	636.85	697.50	731.83	769.31	821.68	907.14
M3, Seasonally Adjusted.................	59mcc	483.00	507.59	532.64	561.40	590.70	609.83	636.85	688.40	722.72	760.29	812.66	897.70
Interest Rates		*Percent Per Annum*											
Bank Rate (End of Period)................	60	4.11	7.43	5.79	3.25	4.50	5.25	5.00	6.00	2.50	3.00	3.00	2.75
Money Market Rate........................	60b	4.62	5.05	6.92	4.32	3.26	4.87	4.74	5.52	4.11	2.45	2.93	2.25
Corporate Paper Rate.....................	60bc	4.97	5.66	7.22	4.35	3.61	5.05	4.94	5.71	3.87	2.66	2.94	2.31
Treasury Bill Rate....................	60c	4.84	5.54	6.89	4.21	3.26	4.73	4.72	5.49	3.77	2.59	2.87	2.22
Savings Rate....................	60k	.77	.50	.50	.50	.50	.24	.10	.10	.10	.05	.05	.05
Deposit Rate....................	60l	3.21	3.98	5.28	3.00	1.90	3.08	2.88	3.48	2.25	.83	1.10	.78
Lending Rate....................	60p	5.94	6.88	8.65	6.06	4.96	6.60	6.44	7.27	5.81	4.21	4.69	4.00
Govt. Bond Yield: Med.-Term..........	61a	6.46	7.79	7.64	6.21	5.33	5.16	5.50	5.99	4.88	4.44	3.88	3.67
Long-Term....	61	7.85	8.63	8.28	7.50	6.42	5.47	5.69	5.89	5.78	5.66	5.28	5.08
Prices, Production, Labor		*Index Numbers (2000=100): Period Averages*											
Industrial Share Prices....................	62	40.6	44.6	46.1	54.8	67.2	70.3	73.5	100.0	80.5	73.2	74.5	90.0
Prices: Industry Selling....................	63	81.2	86.1	92.5	92.9	93.7	93.7	95.2	100.0	† 101.1	101.2	100.0	102.8
Consumer Prices....................	64	89.7	89.8	† 91.8	93.2	94.7	95.7	97.3	100.0	102.5	104.8	107.7	109.7
Wages: Hourly Earnings (Mfg)..........	65ey	88.2	89.7	90.9	93.6	94.3	96.2	97.5	100.0	101.6	104.4	107.8	110.6
Industrial Production....................	66	....	....	78.6	79.5	84.0	86.9	92.1	100.0	96.1	97.5	98.3	101.8
Manufacturing Employment.............	67ey	82.5	84.2	85.8	87.8	91.0	94.0	96.0	100.0	100.0	100.7	100.4	98.0
		Number in Thousands: Period Averages											
Labor Force....................	67d	13,946	14,832	14,928	15,145	15,354	15,632	15,721	15,999	16,246	16,690	17,047	17,183
Employment....................	67e	13,015	13,292	† 13,506	13,676	13,941	14,326	14,531	14,910	15,077	15,412	15,746	16,021
Unemployment....................	67c	1,649	1,541	† 1,422	1,469	1,414	1,305	1,216	1,103	1,170	1,278	1,301	1,249
Unemployment Rate (%)..................	67r	11.2	10.4	† 9.6	9.7	9.2	8.3	† 7.6	6.8	7.2	....	7.6	7.2
Intl. Transactions & Positions		*Millions of Canadian Dollars*											
Exports....................	70	187,346	225,908	263,697	274,884	296,928	317,903	354,108	410,994	402,172	396,020	381,655	395,897
Imports, f.o.b....................	71.v	175,049	206,626	224,977	232,672	271,422	298,076	319,008	354,728	343,311	348,198	334,331	354,859
		2000=100											
Volume of Exports....................	72	53.4	59.8	65.8	69.8	† 75.6	82.0	91.2	100.0	96.1	96.1	94.5	101.1
Volume of Imports....................	73	53.0	58.9	63.5	66.9	† 79.3	86.1	95.8	100.0	94.5	95.9	99.2	108.6
Unit Value of Exports....................	74	79.1	84.7	91.4	92.0	† 91.6	97.3	105.7	100.0	102.0	100.5	99.6	100.7
Unit Value of Imports....................	75	85.3	90.7	94.1	93.7	† 94.3	94.2	95.7	100.0	103.0	103.8	96.2	94.5

Canada 156

		1993	1994	1995	1996	1997	1998	1999	2000	2001	2002	2003	2004
Balance of Payments						*Millions of US Dollars: Minus Sign Indicates Debit*							
Current Account, n.i.e.	78ald	−21,822	−13,024	−4,328	3,378	−8,233	−7,839	1,765	19,622	16,281	13,456	13,360	22,000
Goods: Exports f.o.b.	78aad	147,418	166,990	193,373	205,443	219,063	220,539	248,494	289,022	271,849	263,919	285,912	330,112
Goods: Imports f.o.b.	78abd	−137,281	−152,155	−167,517	−174,352	−200,498	−204,617	−220,203	−243,975	−226,132	−227,431	−244,836	−279,430
Trade Balance	78acd	10,136	14,834	25,855	31,091	18,565	15,922	28,292	45,047	45,716	36,488	41,076	50,682
Services: Credit	78add	21,868	23,958	26,128	29,243	31,596	33,836	36,117	40,230	38,804	39,759	42,624	47,534
Services: Debit	78aed	−32,446	−32,530	−33,473	−35,906	−38,013	−38,156	−40,573	−44,118	−43,843	−44,653	−50,732	−57,303
Balance on Goods & Services	78afd	−442	6,262	18,510	24,428	12,148	11,602	23,836	41,159	40,678	31,594	32,968	40,913
Income: Credit	78agd	10,697	15,443	18,888	19,204	23,998	21,830	22,158	24,746	16,822	19,972	21,580	29,573
Income: Debit	78ahd	−31,499	−34,382	−41,609	−40,755	−44,878	−41,815	−44,777	−47,036	−42,238	−38,707	−41,364	−48,740
Balance on Gds, Serv. & Inc.	78aid	−21,243	−12,676	−4,211	2,877	−8,732	−8,383	1,216	18,868	15,262	12,859	13,185	21,746
Current Transfers, n.i.e.: Credit	78ajd	2,593	2,625	2,878	3,594	3,634	3,407	3,796	4,122	4,499	4,387	4,722	5,608
Current Transfers: Debit	78akd	−3,172	−2,973	−2,995	−3,092	−3,135	−2,863	−3,247	−3,368	−3,480	−3,791	−4,546	−5,355
Capital Account, n.i.e.	78bcd	8,292	7,498	4,950	5,833	5,429	3,336	3,400	3,581	3,721	3,145	2,843	3,394
Capital Account, n.i.e.: Credit	78bad	8,908	7,876	5,666	6,262	5,862	3,794	3,862	4,045	4,191	3,599	3,454	3,949
Capital Account: Debit	78bbd	−617	−378	−716	−429	−433	−457	−462	−464	−471	−454	−612	−555
Financial Account, n.i.e.	78bjd	19,505	5,159	−1,277	−9,277	3,394	4,944	−5,968	−14,500	−11,609	−11,663	−18,288	−23,578
Direct Investment Abroad	78bdd	−5,711	−9,303	−11,490	−13,107	−23,069	−34,112	−17,262	−44,487	−36,152	−26,801	−22,140	−47,013
Dir. Invest. in Rep. Econ., n.i.e.	78bed	4,749	8,224	9,319	9,635	11,523	22,742	24,789	66,144	27,711	21,404	6,059	6,284
Portfolio Investment Assets	78bfd	−13,784	−6,587	−5,328	−14,183	−8,568	−15,106	−15,579	−42,975	−24,374	−17,044	−11,429	−14,390
Equity Securities	78bkd	−9,886	−6,898	−4,570	−12,661	−3,777	−10,428	−13,910	−40,229	−23,120	−11,965	−3,459	−1,152
Debt Securities	78bld	−3,898	311	−759	−1,522	−4,792	−4,678	−1,669	−2,746	−1,254	−5,079	−7,970	−13,238
Portfolio Investment Liab., n.i.e.	78bgd	41,352	17,155	18,402	13,718	11,692	16,590	2,653	10,259	24,166	13,442	14,549	42,519
Equity Securities	78bmd	9,334	4,718	−3,077	5,900	5,461	9,645	9,722	24,239	2,713	−914	9,947	27,220
Debt Securities	78bnd	32,018	12,437	21,479	7,818	6,230	6,945	−7,069	−13,980	21,454	14,355	4,603	15,299
Financial Derivatives Assets	78bwd	....	....	....	....	....	....	....	....	....	....	....	....
Financial Derivatives Liabilities	78bxd												
Other Investment Assets	78bhd	−415	−20,378	−8,328	−21,064	−16,167	9,400	10,235	−4,195	−10,739	−8,064	−17,006	−4,972
Monetary Authorities	78bod	....	....	....	....	....	....	....	....	....	....	....	....
General Government	78bpd	−230	−436	−336	−119	−515	−579	−305	−232	−131	−19	318	−285
Banks	78bqd	5,848	−12,575	−8,314	−13,847	−5,419	969	13,368	−7,301	−2,183	2,278	−15,172	−984
Other Sectors	78brd	−6,033	−7,366	322	−7,098	−10,233	9,010	−2,828	3,338	−8,425	−10,324	−2,153	−3,703
Other Investment Liab., n.i.e.	78bid	−6,686	16,049	−3,852	15,724	27,983	5,430	−10,804	754	7,779	5,401	11,679	−6,007
Monetary Authorities	78bsd	—	—	—	—	—	—	—	—	—	—	—	—
General Government	78btd	−179	586	−484	−508	−321	−270	−318	−350	−237	−116	−527	−754
Banks	78bud	−6,649	15,233	−4,579	12,707	24,630	953	−16,273	−626	15,314	8,525	12,568	−1,017
Other Sectors	78bvd	142	230	1,211	3,525	3,673	4,747	5,788	1,730	−7,298	−3,008	−363	−4,235
Net Errors and Omissions	78cad	−5,070	−26	3,366	5,563	−2,983	4,555	6,736	−4,984	−6,220	−5,123	−1,170	−4,651
Overall Balance	78cbd	904	−392	2,711	5,498	−2,393	4,996	5,933	3,720	2,172	−185	−3,255	−2,836
Reserves and Related Items	79dad	−904	392	−2,711	−5,498	2,393	−4,996	−5,933	−3,720	−2,172	185	3,255	2,836
Reserve Assets	79dbd	−904	392	−2,711	−5,498	2,393	−4,996	−5,933	−3,720	−2,172	185	3,255	2,836
Use of Fund Credit and Loans	79dcd	—	—	—	—	—	—	—	—	—	—	—	—
Exceptional Financing	79ded	....	....	....	....	....	....	....	....	....	....	....	....
International Investment Position						*Millions of US Dollars*							
Assets	79aad	246,426	282,944	324,692	371,736	419,480	448,443	497,023	551,648	578,917	620,047	710,478	793,832
Direct Investment Abroad	79abd	92,468	104,302	118,105	132,329	152,969	171,780	201,434	237,639	250,692	274,350	312,167	369,777
Portfolio Investment	79acd	53,200	59,601	66,487	79,054	91,222	102,845	124,558	139,456	150,547	169,960	194,196	212,054
Equity Securities	79add	39,982	46,543	52,700	63,529	72,619	81,118	103,263	115,699	126,141	136,440	150,797	155,100
Debt Securities	79aed	13,218	13,057	13,787	15,525	18,603	21,728	21,294	23,757	24,407	33,520	43,400	56,954
Financial Derivatives	79ald	—	—	—	—	—	—	—	—	—	—	—	—
Other Investment	79afd	88,007	106,564	124,885	139,761	157,305	150,351	142,298	142,687	144,189	140,113	168,777	178,489
Monetary Authorities	79agd	—	—	—	—	—	—	—	—	—	—	—	—
General Government	79ahd	14,966	15,419	15,656	15,868	16,759	18,716	20,835	21,983	22,857	23,396	23,525	23,300
Banks	79aid	37,279	49,976	60,268	73,657	76,024	74,550	61,364	68,306	66,413	61,149	77,614	78,485
Other Sectors	79ajd	35,762	41,170	48,961	50,236	64,522	57,084	60,099	52,398	54,919	55,569	67,638	76,704
Reserve Assets	79akd	12,751	12,476	15,216	20,591	17,984	23,467	28,732	31,866	33,488	35,622	35,338	33,512
Liabilities	79lad	490,942	520,374	562,156	599,081	622,564	644,239	665,852	690,851	706,652	751,033	870,018	944,303
Dir. Invest. in Rep. Economy	79lbd	106,868	110,204	123,181	132,978	135,944	143,344	174,990	212,716	213,757	224,185	274,269	303,818
Portfolio Investment	79lcd	266,961	281,767	309,774	323,661	321,742	334,129	336,824	324,968	330,389	351,916	394,960	443,058
Equity Securities	79ldd	17,685	22,001	27,170	34,537	35,968	42,041	47,856	58,070	48,654	51,084	64,466	90,191
Debt Securities	79led	249,276	259,766	282,604	289,125	285,774	292,088	288,968	266,899	281,735	300,833	330,494	352,868
Financial Derivatives	79lld	—	—	—	—	—	—	—	—	—	—	—	—
Other Investment	79lfd	117,113	128,403	129,201	142,442	164,879	166,766	154,038	153,167	162,506	174,932	200,789	197,427
Monetary Authorities	79lgd	—	—	—	—	—	—	—	—	—	—	—	—
General Government	79lhd	3,889	4,568	4,059	3,334	2,790	2,648	2,530	2,011	1,609	1,638	1,299	608
Banks	79lid	68,757	83,691	79,735	92,486	115,623	118,008	100,131	98,443	113,639	123,359	141,643	146,120
Other Sectors	79ljd	44,468	40,145	45,407	46,622	46,466	46,110	51,377	52,713	47,257	49,935	57,847	50,698
Government Finance						*Billions of Canadian Dollars: Year Beginning April 1*							
Deficit (-) or Surplus	80	−42.28	−36.70	−29.22	−15.55	5.33	3.10	9.14	13.39	14.38	....	....	....
Revenue	81	148.33	157.60	164.25	174.51	188.91	195.82	209.54	228.76	226.83	....	....	....
Grants Received	81z	.54	.53	.52	.54	.52	.50	.56	.57	.61	....	....	....
Expenditure	82	191.20	196.04	199.90	190.91	186.95	193.92	201.68	213.48	212.61	....	....	....
Lending Minus Repayments	83	−.04	−1.20	−5.91	−.31	−2.85	−.70	−.72	2.46	.45	....	....	....
Financing													
Total Net Borrowing	84	43.76	35.59	40.04	19.43	−6.95	8.56	2.92	3.83	−15.55	....	....	....
Net Domestic	84a	47.55	42.91	29.10	22.10	−1.53	5.61	−12.75	−12.50	−20.44	....	....	....
Net Foreign	85a	−3.79	−7.32	10.94	−2.67	−5.42	2.95	15.67	16.33	4.89	....	....	....
Use of Cash Balances	87	−1.48	1.11	−10.81	−3.88	1.63	−11.66	−12.05	−17.22	1.17	....	....	....
Total Debt	88z	557.60	595.88	634.94	651.12	645.73	648.39	648.21	644.90	629.09	....	....	....
Domestic	88a	544.60	577.02	616.22	626.32	616.73	610.73	614.22	610.25	600.69	....	....	....
Foreign	89a	13.00	18.86	18.71	24.81	28.99	37.65	33.99	34.65	28.41	....	....	....

		1993	1994	1995	1996	1997	1998	1999	2000	2001	2002	2003	2004
National Accounts						*Billions of Canadian dollars*							
Househ.Cons.Expend.,incl.NPISHs....	**96f.c**	430.16	447.75	462.87	482.37	512.86	534.39	561.57	594.09	623.17	656.18	689.42	721.24
Government Consumption Expend...	**91f.c**	171.27	171.73	172.65	171.35	171.88	176.84	183.29	196.00	207.51	218.90	231.00	248.53
Gross Fixed Capital Formation.........	**93e.c**	131.07	144.96	143.00	149.94	174.84	181.62	193.83	209.94	219.85	227.19	237.19	258.96
Changes in Inventories....................	**93i.c**	−.95	.45	8.91	2.34	8.18	5.79	3.91	8.00	−5.24	2.87	7.56	7.22
Exports of Goods and Services..........	**90c.c**	219.66	262.13	302.48	321.25	348.60	377.35	418.54	484.33	482.07	474.30	459.56	492.58
Imports of Goods and Services (-)....	**98c.c**	219.67	253.01	276.62	287.55	331.27	360.26	386.03	428.93	418.81	423.99	409.99	438.35
Gross Domestic Product (GDP)........	**99b.c**	727.18	770.87	810.43	836.86	882.73	914.97	982.44	1,075.57	1,107.46	1,154.95	1,214.60	1,290.19
Net Primary Income from Abroad.....	**98.nc**	−25.17	−27.99	−28.55	−28.33	−27.70	−30.04	−29.51	−22.37	−29.61	−27.39	−25.06	−22.48
Gross National Income (GNI)............	**99a.c**	704.41	744.83	783.91	810.73	857.32	885.83	945.75	1,042.63	1,077.85	1,127.56	1,189.54	1,270.81
Gross Nat'l Disposable Inc.(GNDI)....	**99i.c**	703.67	744.36	783.75	811.42	858.02	886.60	946.88	1,044.10	1,079.53	1,128.92	1,190.09	1,270.04
Gross Saving.................................	**99s.c**	....	....	....	....	182.81	187.46	198.21	219.51	213.52	229.56	244.30	262.69
Consumption of Fixed Capital..........	**99cfc**	94.04	99.63	105.02	110.82	116.57	122.30	127.72	135.78	146.80	155.00	164.03	174.22
GDP Volume 1997 Ref., Chained.....	**99b.r**	773.53	810.70	833.46	846.95	882.73	918.91	969.75	1,020.79	1,040.39	1,074.52	1,092.89	1,126.63
GDP Volume (2000=100)................	**99bvr**	75.8	79.4	81.6	83.0	86.5	90.0	95.0	100.0	101.9	105.3	107.1	110.4
GDP Deflator (2000=100)................	**99bir**	89.2	90.2	92.3	93.8	94.9	94.5	96.1	100.0	101.0	102.0	105.5	108.7
						Millions: Midyear Estimates							
Population................................	**99z**	28.70	29.01	29.30	29.59	29.86	30.13	30.40	30.69	30.99	31.31	31.64	31.96

Cape Verde 624

		1993	1994	1995	1996	1997	1998	1999	2000	2001	2002	2003	2004
Exchange Rates					*Escudos per SDR: End of Period*								
Official Rate	aa	118.115	118.452	115.136	122.464	129.845	132.714	150.654	154.403	157.245	142.952	129.737	125.725
					Escudos per US Dollar: End of Period (ae) Period Average (rf)								
Official Rate	ae	85.992	81.140	77.455	85.165	96.235	94.255	109.765	118.506	125.122	105.149	87.308	80.956
Official Rate	rf	80.427	81.891	76.853	82.591	93.177	98.158	103.502	119.687	123.228	117.168	97.703	88.808
Fund Position					*Millions of SDRs: End of Period*								
Quota	2f.s	7.00	7.00	7.00	7.00	7.00	7.00	9.60	9.60	9.60	9.60	9.60	9.60
SDRs	1b.s	.02	.05	.02	.04	.02	.04	.01	.04	.01	—	—	.02
Reserve Position in the Fund	1c.s	—	—	—	—	—	—	—	—	—	—	—	—
Total Fund Cred.&Loans Outstg	2tl	—	—	—	—	—	—	—	—	—	2.46	4.92	6.15
International Liquidity					*Millions of US Dollars Unless Otherwise Indicated: End of Period*								
Total Reserves minus Gold	1l.d	57.69	42.08	36.89	27.57	19.32	8.32	42.62	28.26	45.43	79.80	93.61	139.53
SDRs	1b.d	.03	.07	.03	.06	.03	.06	.02	.05	.02	—	—	.04
Reserve Position in the Fund	1c.d	—	—	—	—	—	—	—	—	—	.01	.01	.01
Foreign Exchange	1d.d	57.66	42.01	36.86	27.50	19.29	8.26	42.59	28.21	45.40	79.79	93.60	139.49
Monetary Authorities: Other Liab	4..d	.80	.60	6.47	3.51	2.60	.94	1.09	1.35	1.36	1.42	.97	.70
Deposit Money Banks: Assets	7a.d	14.47	31.60	10.62	32.35	23.89	33.41	30.10	42.45	42.95	44.76	52.87	66.53
Liabilities	7b.d	2.47	3.38	6.32	5.73	9.95	11.16	15.21	16.41	14.08	19.09	25.75	28.37
Monetary Authorities					*Millions of Escudos: End of Period*								
Foreign Assets	11	4,999.9	3,483.1	† 5,154.8	4,838.5	4,521.9	3,584.9	8,203.7	4,221.8	6,561.2	9,135.4	8,817.8	11,526.8
Claims on Central Government	12a	5,068.2	4,446.4	† 4,964.4	4,315.8	6,001.6	5,615.2	5,865.2	9,209.4	9,024.0	9,469.0	9,977.4	9,383.5
Claims on Local Government	12b	27.6	—	† —									
Claims on Nonfin.Pub.Enterprises	12c	2,136.9	119.7	† 118.8	113.9	.1	—	86.8	82.3	82.3	72.3	72.3	60.5
Claims on Private Sector	12d	2,005.7	1,091.2	† 1,099.4	2,049.4	1,151.9	1,142.7	1,100.8	1,074.9	1,106.3	1,111.9	1,107.1	1,105.8
Claims on Deposit Money Banks	12e	612.8	592.1	† 632.7	630.3	519.8	361.6	331.4	1,098.9	438.4	274.5	409.8	44.0
Claims on Other Banking Insts	12f	—	—	† —									
Claims on Nonbank Financial Insts	12g	—	—	† —	—	—	5.5	5.5	—	—	—	32.8	29.5
Reserve Money	14	14,205.4	8,685.9	† 10,655.6	9,982.8	10,035.2	10,971.4	11,701.4	13,552.2	14,580.5	16,812.2	17,288.5	18,488.6
of which: Currency Outside DMBs	14a	3,549.4	3,929.7	† 4,635.1	4,513.0	4,853.6	5,059.8	6,026.1	6,458.2	6,702.9	6,459.3	6,515.6	6,765.0
Time & Foreign Currency Deposits	15	—	173.9	† 101.4	—								
Foreign Liabilities	16c	69.2	48.7	† 500.9	298.8	249.8	88.8	119.7	159.6	170.0	500.7	722.9	829.8
Central Government Deposits	16d	—	—	† 245.9	230.8	944.7	516.6	2,446.1	607.7	675.1	1,199.7	948.5	1,184.6
Capital Accounts	17a	2,190.4	2,069.3	† 2,338.7	2,739.2	3,114.5	3,051.5	2,376.6	2,917.5	2,999.7	2,447.4	2,483.4	2,516.5
Other Items (Net)	17r	−1,613.9	−1,245.3	† −1,872.4	−1,303.7	−2,149.0	−3,918.4	−1,050.4	−1,549.7	−1,213.1	−896.9	−1,026.2	−869.4
Deposit Money Banks					*Millions of Escudos: End of Period*								
Reserves	20	10,604.3	4,803.9	† 5,987.1	5,472.5	5,701.4	5,820.3	5,648.0	7,111.0	7,869.1	9,760.4	10,796.5	11,695.1
Foreign Assets	21	1,244.4	2,563.7	† 822.3	2,754.7	2,299.1	3,149.0	3,303.5	5,031.1	5,373.5	4,706.1	4,615.9	5,386.0
Claims on Central Government	22a	—	6,046.7	† 7,557.0	8,944.3	10,357.8	10,347.4	10,036.0	14,472.6	14,961.6	17,677.1	18,157.5	19,139.3
Claims on Local Government	22b	48.7	76.2	† 97.1	109.1	.2	10.7	238.0	289.3	260.9	266.4	239.3	208.9
Claims on Nonfin.Pub.Enterprises	22c	433.9	432.7	† 545.0	378.5	24.2	21.4	425.3	73.3	132.9	157.8	107.6	100.5
Claims on Private Sector	22d	5,495.8	6,473.9	† 9,292.1	10,159.8	13,540.5	15,308.7	17,289.2	18,252.2	21,099.2	23,778.0	27,619.1	30,324.6
Claims on Nonbank Financial Insts	22g	—	—	† —						7.0	5.5	3.9	14.2
Demand Deposits	24	7,049.3	7,542.3	† 7,232.4	8,609.7	11,106.4	10,573.4	12,216.4	13,966.4	14,247.6	16,337.9	16,574.9	17,696.4
Time, Savings,& Fgn.Currency Dep	25	9,039.4	10,394.4	† 12,974.5	14,251.9	14,386.0	15,557.7	17,494.4	20,301.7	23,826.3	28,050.8	32,342.0	37,084.8
Restricted Deposits	26b	300.9	203.8	† 257.6	491.7	398.1	710.0	242.6	502.8	210.4	187.4	192.5	236.9
Foreign Liabilities	26c	212.8	274.3	† 489.7	488.3	957.1	1,051.5	1,669.6	1,944.8	1,761.9	2,007.4	2,248.1	2,296.9
Central Government Deposits	26d	847.8	1,035.7	† 2,401.0	2,539.4	2,038.2	2,100.4	1,165.9	1,324.8	1,621.4	1,164.0	1,693.0	1,729.1
Counterpart Funds	26e	—	—	† —	—	2.0	3.4						
Credit from Monetary Authorities	26g	612.8	592.1	† 573.5	551.4	519.8	361.6	331.4	1,098.9	438.4	274.5	409.8	44.0
Liab. to Nonbank Financial Insts	26j	3.4	20.3	† 181.1	298.7	125.6	36.2	306.0	257.0	276.3	188.4	184.6	162.2
Capital Accounts	27a	1,292.9	1,638.8	† 2,833.5	3,433.6	4,426.3	5,365.6	5,954.5	7,007.2	7,903.9	8,340.4	8,871.8	9,210.2
Other Items (Net)	27r	−1,532.2	−1,304.6	† −2,642.8	−2,845.9	−2,036.3	−1,102.3	−2,440.8	−1,174.1	−582.0	−199.5	−976.9	−1,591.9
Monetary Survey					*Millions of Escudos: End of Period*								
Foreign Assets (Net)	31n	5,962.3	5,723.8	† 4,986.5	6,806.0	5,614.0	5,593.6	9,717.9	7,148.5	10,002.8	11,333.5	10,462.7	13,786.1
Domestic Credit	32	14,369.0	17,651.1	† 21,026.9	23,300.6	28,093.4	29,834.6	31,434.8	41,521.5	44,377.7	50,174.3	54,675.5	57,453.1
Claims on Central Govt. (Net)	32an	4,220.4	9,457.4	† 9,874.5	10,489.9	13,376.5	13,345.6	12,289.2	21,749.5	21,689.1	24,782.4	25,493.4	25,609.1
Claims on Local Government	32b	76.3	76.2	† 97.1	109.1	.2	10.7	238.0	289.3	260.9	266.4	239.3	208.9
Claims on Nonfin.Pub.Enterprises	32c	2,570.8	552.4	† 663.8	492.4	24.3	21.4	512.1	155.6	215.2	230.1	179.9	161.0
Claims on Private Sector	32d	7,501.5	7,565.1	† 10,391.5	12,209.2	14,692.4	16,451.4	18,390.0	19,327.1	22,205.5	24,889.9	28,726.2	31,430.4
Claims on Other Banking Insts	32f	—	—	† —	—	—	—	—	—	—	—	—	—
Claims on Nonbank Financial Inst	32g	—	—	† —	—	—	5.5	5.5	—	7.0	5.5	36.7	43.7
Money	34	10,598.7	11,472.0	† 11,867.5	13,122.7	15,960.0	15,633.2	18,332.6	20,425.3	20,951.3	22,798.3	23,090.9	24,482.8
Quasi-Money	35	9,039.4	10,568.3	† 13,075.9	14,251.9	14,386.0	15,557.7	17,494.4	20,301.7	23,826.3	28,050.8	32,342.0	37,084.8
Restricted Deposits	36b	300.9	203.8	† 257.6	491.7	398.1	710.0	242.6	502.8	210.4	187.4	192.5	236.9
Counterpart Funds	36e	—	—	† —	—	2.0	3.4						
Liab. to Nonbank Financial Insts	36j	3.4	20.3	† 181.1	298.7	125.6	36.2	306.0	257.0	276.3	188.4	184.6	162.2
Capital Accounts	37a	3,483.3	3,708.1	† 5,172.2	6,172.8	7,540.8	8,417.1	8,331.1	9,924.7	10,903.6	10,787.8	11,355.2	11,726.7
Other Items (Net)	37r	−3,094.4	−2,597.6	† −4,541.0	−4,231.2	−4,705.1	−4,929.4	−3,554.0	−2,741.5	−1,787.4	−505.0	−2,027.1	−2,454.2
Money plus Quasi-Money	35l	19,638.1	22,040.3	† 24,943.4	27,374.6	30,346.0	31,190.9	35,827.0	40,727.0	44,777.6	50,849.1	55,432.9	61,567.6
Interest Rates					*Percent Per Annum*								
Deposit Rate	60l	4.00	4.00	† 5.00	5.00	5.04	5.27	4.76	4.34	4.67	4.86	3.93	3.46
Lending Rate	60p	10.00	10.67	12.00	12.00	12.06	12.51	12.03	11.94	12.85	13.17	12.73	12.69
Prices					*Index Numbers (2000=100): Period Averages*								
Consumer Prices	64	73	76	82	87	94	98	103	100	103	105	107	105
Intl. Transactions & Positions					*Millions of Escudos*								
Exports	70	312	408	687	1,046	1,295	1,016	1,170	1,261	1,202	1,237	....	....
Imports, c.i.f	71	12,387	17,113	19,394	19,355	21,764	22,597	26,916	27,519	30,519	34,238	....	....

Cape Verde 624

		1993	1994	1995	1996	1997	1998	1999	2000	2001	2002	2003	2004
Balance of Payments		*Millions of US Dollars: Minus Sign Indicates Debit*											
Current Account, n.i.e.	78ald	−23.93	−45.73	−61.62	−35.04	−29.72	−58.51	−74.18	−58.03	−55.73	−71.52	−77.25	....
Goods: Exports f.o.b.	78aad	9.05	14.16	16.58	23.88	43.24	32.69	26.03	38.30	37.17	41.76	52.83	....
Goods: Imports f.o.b.	78abd	−151.95	−195.26	−233.63	−207.52	−215.10	−218.81	−239.03	−225.66	−231.52	−278.02	−343.95	....
Trade Balance	78acd	−142.90	−181.10	−217.05	−183.64	−171.87	−186.13	−213.00	−187.36	−194.35	−236.26	−291.11	....
Services: Credit	78add	40.09	47.01	66.90	77.52	91.31	86.45	105.06	107.58	129.68	152.83	224.08	....
Services: Debit	78aed	−29.39	−34.52	−60.50	−70.03	−71.90	−90.59	−115.82	−100.24	−119.01	−142.08	−203.25	....
Balance on Goods & Services	78afd	−132.20	−168.61	−210.65	−176.15	−152.46	−190.27	−223.76	−180.01	−183.68	−225.51	−270.29	....
Income: Credit	78agd	4.81	4.22	4.00	2.98	4.87	2.51	1.90	5.03	7.53	6.41	13.14	....
Income: Debit	78ahd	−3.85	−4.56	−6.57	−7.38	−8.46	−8.07	−10.41	−17.67	−12.66	−18.26	−29.79	....
Balance on Gds, Serv. & Inc.	78aid	−131.24	−168.95	−213.22	−180.55	−156.05	−195.83	−232.27	−192.66	−188.81	−237.36	−286.93	....
Current Transfers, n.i.e.: Credit	78ajd	110.41	125.55	155.96	148.38	129.91	142.46	167.12	146.28	155.55	181.57	228.99	....
Current Transfers: Debit	78akd	−3.11	−2.33	−4.36	−2.87	−3.58	−5.15	−9.04	−11.66	−22.47	−15.73	−19.30	....
Capital Account, n.i.e.	78bcd	19.02	20.07	20.88	12.83	6.30	19.01	4.47	10.76	24.36	8.64	21.07	....
Capital Account, n.i.e.: Credit	78bad	19.02	20.07	20.88	12.83	6.30	19.01	4.47	10.76	24.36	8.64	21.09	....
Capital Account: Debit	78bbd	—	—	—	—	—	....	....	....	....	....	−.02	....
Financial Account, n.i.e.	78bjd	17.52	39.60	44.51	46.00	44.06	36.99	127.77	31.53	38.53	80.67	5.55	....
Direct Investment Abroad	78bdd	−.66	−.42	−.57	−.26	−.05	....	−.42	−1.36	−.52	....	....	....
Dir. Invest. in Rep. Econ., n.i.e.	78bed	3.64	2.13	26.18	28.53	11.58	9.04	53.32	33.42	9.11	14.81	14.78	....
Portfolio Investment Assets	78bfd	....	....	....	....	....	....	....	−.12	1.45	....	....	....
Equity Securities	78bkd	....	....	....	....	....	....	....	....	1.56	....	....	....
Debt Securities	78bld	....	....	....	....	....	....	....	−.12	−.11	....	....	....
Portfolio Investment Liab., n.i.e.	78bgd	....	....	....	....	....	....	2.98	....	....	....	....	....
Equity Securities	78bmd	....	....	....	....	....	....	2.98	....	....	....	....	....
Debt Securities	78bnd	....	....	....	....	....	....	....	....	....	....	....	....
Financial Derivatives Assets	78bwd	....	....	....	....	....	....	....	....	....	....	....	....
Financial Derivatives Liabilities	78bxd	....	....	....	....	....	....	....	....	....	....	....	....
Other Investment Assets	78bhd	−6.75	1.61	−1.67	−2.25	−1.79	−22.44	−13.91	−22.01	−3.30	−2.02	−7.24	....
Monetary Authorities	78bod	−6.75	1.61	2.32	−2.34	−1.84	4.02	5.19	....	−.10	−.07	1.01	....
General Government	78bpd	—	—	—	....	....	−28.39	−18.54	−21.33	....	....	−4.29	....
Banks	78bqd	—	—	−3.99	.09	.05	3.02	−.05	−.68	−1.64	−1.95	−3.95	....
Other Sectors	78brd	—	—	—	....	....	−1.09	−.51	....	−1.56	....	....	....
Other Investment Liab., n.i.e.	78bid	21.29	36.28	20.57	19.99	34.33	50.39	85.79	21.60	31.79	67.89	−2.00	....
Monetary Authorities	78bsd	.88	−1.21	−.93	−.12	−.12	−.01	.17	—	.03	2.97	....	....
General Government	78btd	19.69	22.74	17.57	22.88	19.79	28.49	42.98	9.68	2.98	9.58	−21.89	....
Banks	78bud	2.65	1.11	2.38	.02	4.94	8.00	27.18	18.83	26.93	35.96	33.10	....
Other Sectors	78bvd	−1.93	13.64	1.55	−2.80	9.72	13.91	15.45	−6.91	1.85	19.37	−13.21	....
Net Errors and Omissions	78cad	2.38	8.31	−35.64	−1.34	−20.40	13.28	−8.74	−12.03	−23.91	−7.67	−5.35	....
Overall Balance	78cbd	14.99	22.24	−31.87	22.46	.24	10.76	49.31	−27.77	−16.74	10.13	−55.98	....
Reserves and Related Items	79dad	−14.99	−22.24	31.87	−22.46	−.24	−10.76	−49.31	27.77	16.74	−10.13	55.98	....
Reserve Assets	79dbd	−11.50	−20.78	30.93	−19.76	9.84	−8.50	−41.86	10.27	23.37	.17	9.92	....
Use of Fund Credit and Loans	79dcd	—	—	—	—	—	—	—	—	—	3.19	3.52	....
Exceptional Financing	79ded	−3.49	−1.46	.95	−2.70	−10.08	−2.26	−7.45	17.49	−6.63	−13.49	42.54	....
National Accounts		*Millions of Escudos*											
Gross Domestic Product (GDP)	99b	29,078	33,497	37,705	41,698	45,968	51,599	61,774	64,539	....	....	....	....
GDP Volume 1980 Prices	99b.p	10,682	11,422	12,278	13,100	14,100	15,287	17,100	18,432	....	....	....	....
GDP Volume (1995=100)	99bvp	87.0	93.0	100.0	106.7	114.8	124.5	139.3	150.1	....	....	....	....
GDP Deflator (1995=100)	99bip	88.6	95.5	100.0	103.7	106.2	109.9	117.6	114.0	....	....	....	....
		Millions: Midyear Estimates											
Population	99z	.37	.38	.39	.40	.41	.42	.43	.44	.44	.45	.46	.50

		1993	1994	1995	1996	1997	1998	1999	2000	2001	2002	2003	2004
Exchange Rates						*Francs per SDR: End of Period*							
Official Rate	aa	404.89	† 780.44	728.38	753.06	807.94	791.61	† 896.19	918.49	935.39	850.37	771.76	747.90
				Francs per US Dollar: End of Period (ae) Period Average (rf)									
Official Rate	ae	294.77	† 534.60	490.00	523.70	598.81	562.21	† 652.95	704.95	744.31	625.50	519.36	481.58
Official Rate	rf	283.16	† 555.20	499.15	511.55	583.67	589.95	† 615.70	711.98	733.04	696.99	581.20	528.28
Fund Position						*Millions of SDRs: End of Period*							
Quota	2f.s	410.10	410.10	410.10	410.10	410.10	410.10	568.90	568.90	568.90	568.90	568.90	568.90
SDRs	1b.s	1.02	1.13	1.35	.35	.08	.24	6.50	6.19	5.26	4.13	2.32	16.35
Reserve Position in the Fund	1c.s	1.23	1.23	1.28	1.35	1.39	1.43	1.52	1.59	1.65	1.70	1.80	1.81
Total Fund Cred.&Loans Outstg	2tl	101.37	176.40	181.00	236.12	259.81	281.17	299.45	360.80	381.52	403.55	387.88	387.94
International Liquidity						*Millions of US Dollars Unless Otherwise Indicated: End of Period*							
Total Reserves minus Gold	1l.d	....	....	....	....	....	....	....	1,256.72	1,079.10	1,600.67	1,812.80	3,110.41
SDRs	1b.d	1.40	1.64	2.01	.51	.11	.33	8.93	8.06	6.61	5.62	3.45	25.39
Reserve Position in the Fund	1c.d	1.69	1.80	1.91	1.94	1.87	2.01	2.09	2.07	2.07	2.31	2.68	2.81
Foreign Exchange	1d.d	....	....	....	....	....	....	....	1,246.59	1,070.41	1,592.75	1,806.67	3,082.21
Gold (Million Fine Troy Ounces)	1ad	....	....	.229	.229	.229	.229	.229	.229	.229	.229	.229	.229
Gold (National Valuation)	1and	....	....	† 87.89	83.93	66.29	65.59	† 66.23	62.21	63.61	78.40	95.59	78.32
Monetary Authorities: Other Liab.	4..d	....	....	....	....	....	....	....	.49	.49	.56	.61	.63
Deposit Money Banks: Assets	7a.d	....	....	....	....	....	....	....	.44	.30	.53	.53	.91
Liabilities	7b.d	....	....	....	....	....	....	....	.13	.15	.28	.28	.31
Monetary Authorities						*Billions of Francs: End of Period*							
Foreign Assets	11	....	....	....	....	....	....	....	929.77	849.75	1,049.72	991.10	1,535.59
Claims on Central Government	12a	....	....	....	....	....	....	....	864.55	1,070.37	1,090.21	1,037.75	1,002.31
Claims on Deposit Money Banks	12e	....	....	....	....	....	....	....	11.43	12.34	12.84	12.86	12.27
Claims on Other Banking Insts	12f	....	....	....	....	....	....	....	4.00	3.00	—	—	—
Reserve Money	14	....	....	....	....	....	....	....	1,054.43	1,113.04	1,271.89	1,288.55	1,516.18
of which: Currency Outside DMBs	14a	....	....	....	....	....	....	....	690.21	760.84	814.94	770.56	855.81
Foreign Liabilities	16c	....	....	....	....	....	....	....	342.03	365.31	353.04	315.71	302.70
Central Government Deposits	16d	....	....	....	....	....	....	....	245.77	274.38	337.84	268.43	584.89
Capital Accounts	17a	....	....	....	....	....	....	....	229.01	235.80	233.13	232.73	228.63
Other Items (Net)	17r	....	....	....	....	....	....	....	−61.49	−53.06	−43.14	−63.71	−82.24
Deposit Money Banks						*Billions of Francs: End of Period*							
Reserves	20	....	....	....	....	....	....	....	344.42	331.88	437.54	492.77	633.62
Foreign Assets	21	....	....	....	....	....	....	....	311.88	224.25	333.37	274.16	437.39
Claims on Central Government	22a	....	....	....	....	....	....	....	293.33	288.30	308.11	283.71	290.49
Claims on Nonfin.Pub.Enterprises	22c	....	....	....	....	....	....	....	144.46	141.79	135.29	150.33	133.97
Claims on Private Sector	22d	....	....	....	....	....	....	....	1,101.02	1,198.05	1,309.97	1,389.40	1,369.97
Claims on Other Banking Insts	22f	....	....	....	....	....	....	....	.82	.64	.65	.59	.62
Claims on Nonbank Financial Insts	22g	....	....	....	....	....	....	....	29.95	30.37	37.69	33.55	41.07
Demand Deposits	24	....	....	....	....	....	....	....	807.44	776.84	944.44	928.62	1,059.25
Time and Savings Deposits	25	....	....	....	....	....	....	....	633.03	729.59	849.46	948.82	1,007.06
Bonds	26ab	....	....	....	....	....	....	....	2.65	2.25	1.85	1.34	1.53
Foreign Liabilities	26c	....	....	....	....	....	....	....	86.86	107.35	166.65	124.77	136.84
Long-Term Foreign Liabilities	26cl	....	....	....	....	....	....	....	8.04	5.90	10.70	22.92	10.65
Central Government Deposits	26d	....	....	....	....	....	....	....	301.53	257.65	303.63	249.50	287.39
Credit from Monetary Authorities	26g	....	....	....	....	....	....	....	11.43	12.34	12.84	12.86	12.27
Capital Accounts	27a	....	....	....	....	....	....	....	383.06	385.38	390.82	430.38	474.74
Other Items (Net)	27r	....	....	....	....	....	....	....	−8.16	−62.01	−117.77	−94.70	−82.57
Monetary Survey						*Billions of Francs: End of Period*							
Foreign Assets (Net)	31n	....	....	....	....	....	....	....	804.72	595.44	852.70	801.85	1,522.80
Domestic Credit	32	....	....	....	....	....	....	....	1,891.26	2,200.56	2,240.44	2,377.40	1,966.33
Claims on Central Govt. (Net)	32an	....	....	....	....	....	....	....	610.57	826.64	756.84	803.53	420.52
Claims on Nonfin.Pub.Enterprises	32c	....	....	....	....	....	....	....	144.46	141.79	135.29	150.33	133.97
Claims on Private Sector	32d	....	....	....	....	....	....	....	1,101.02	1,198.05	1,309.97	1,389.40	1,369.97
Claims on Other Banking Insts	32f	....	....	....	....	....	....	....	4.82	3.64	.65	.59	.62
Claims on Nonbank Financial Inst	32g	....	....	....	....	....	....	....	30.38	30.44	37.69	33.55	41.24
Money	34	....	....	....	....	....	....	....	1,517.45	1,558.00	1,778.79	1,724.41	1,941.80
Quasi-Money	35	....	....	....	....	....	....	....	633.03	729.59	849.46	948.82	1,007.06
Bonds	36ab	....	....	....	....	....	....	....	2.65	2.25	1.85	1.34	1.53
Other Items (Net)	37r	....	....	....	....	....	....	....	542.84	506.17	463.04	504.69	538.74
Money plus Quasi-Money	35l	....	....	....	....	....	....	....	2,150.48	2,287.59	2,628.25	2,673.23	2,948.86
Interest Rates						*Percent Per Annum*							
Discount Rate (End of Period)	60	11.50	† 7.75	8.60	7.75	7.50	7.00	7.30	7.00	6.50	6.30	6.00	6.00
Deposit Rate	60l	7.75	5.50	5.50	5.00	5.00	5.00	5.00	5.00	5.00	5.00	5.00	5.00
Lending Rate	60p	17.50	16.00	16.00	22.00	22.00	22.00	22.00	22.00	18.00	18.00	18.00	18.00

Central African Republic 626

Central African Republic 626

		1993	1994	1995	1996	1997	1998	1999	2000	2001	2002	2003	2004
Exchange Rates					*Francs per SDR: End of Period*								
Official Rate	aa	404.89	† 780.44	728.38	753.06	807.94	791.61	† 896.19	918.49	935.39	850.37	771.76	747.90
					Francs per US Dollar: End of Period (ae) Period Average (rf)								
Official Rate	ae	294.77	† 534.60	490.00	523.70	598.81	562.21	† 652.95	704.95	744.31	625.50	519.36	481.58
Official Rate	rf	283.16	† 555.20	499.15	511.55	583.67	589.95	† 615.70	711.98	733.04	696.99	581.20	528.28
					Index Numbers (2000=100): Period Averages								
Official Rate	ahx	250.9	128.1	142.3	138.8	121.8	120.5	115.5	100.0	96.9	102.2	122.4	134.6
Nominal Effective Exchange Rate	nec	139.8	87.7	94.9	99.6	99.1	100.2	99.9	100.0	105.3	108.9	113.5	115.4
Real Effective Exchange Rate	rec	151.6	95.0	112.1	114.5	110.9	108.1	102.4	100.0	103.3	107.0	114.4	111.7
Fund Position					*Millions of SDRs: End of Period*								
Quota	2f.s	41.20	41.20	41.20	41.20	41.20	41.20	55.70	55.70	55.70	55.70	55.70	55.70
SDRs	1b.s	.03	.01	.02	.01	—	.01	.04	—	.01	.01	.01	1.58
Reserve Position in the Fund	1c.s	.09	.09	.09	.10	.10	.10	.10	.11	.11	.12	.16	.16
Total Fund Cred.&Loans Outstg	2tl	20.96	28.34	23.48	19.22	13.80	12.47	17.09	16.48	24.48	24.48	24.48	28.40
International Liquidity					*Millions of US Dollars Unless Otherwise Indicated: End of Period*								
Total Reserves minus Gold	1l.d	111.98	210.01	233.64	232.24	178.56	145.70	136.28	133.26	118.75	123.24	132.41	148.32
SDRs	1b.d	.04	.01	.02	.01	—	.01	.05	—	.01	.01	.01	2.46
Reserve Position in the Fund	1c.d	.13	.14	.14	.14	.13	.13	.13	.15	.14	.16	.24	.25
Foreign Exchange	1d.d	111.81	209.86	233.48	232.09	178.43	145.56	136.10	133.11	118.60	123.06	132.17	145.62
Gold (Million Fine Troy Ounces)	1ad	.011	.011	.011	.011	.011	.011	.011	.011	.011	.011	.011	.011
Gold (National Valuation)	1and	4.42	† 4.21	4.29	4.10	3.24	3.20	† 3.23	3.03	3.09	3.81	4.65	4.88
Monetary Authorities: Other Liab.	4..d	12.45	12.57	12.79	12.43	11.87	12.90	17.24	16.36	16.85	17.14	18.64	21.14
Deposit Money Banks: Assets	7a.d	6.85	11.45	6.39	4.41	4.99	5.91	10.48	7.96	4.52	5.84	6.33	12.95
Liabilities	7b.d	12.04	12.10	7.93	7.35	6.36	7.43	8.81	9.39	8.10	9.64	15.10	16.83
Monetary Authorities					*Billions of Francs: End of Period*								
Foreign Assets	11	34.29	114.56	116.59	123.77	108.86	83.71	91.10	96.08	90.69	79.47	71.19	73.78
Claims on Central Government	12a	28.34	41.99	36.97	37.69	32.76	32.28	37.86	41.62	44.43	46.54	50.50	60.86
Claims on Deposit Money Banks	12e	3.66	—	1.60	1.24	.50	5.00	4.79	3.14	2.25	3.34	1.82	4.07
Claims on Other Banking Insts.	12f												
Reserve Money	14	52.46	96.65	101.04	108.82	95.35	76.11	81.96	89.59	84.01	78.96	72.64	83.73
of which: Currency Outside DMBs	14a	52.16	88.53	98.97	104.00	92.96	75.25	81.12	88.62	82.57	77.43	70.37	81.34
Foreign Liabilities	16c	12.16	28.84	23.37	20.98	18.25	17.13	26.57	26.67	35.44	31.54	28.58	31.42
Central Government Deposits	16d	1.69	1.89	1.58	2.82	1.36	.91	3.45	2.36	6.00	.85	.87	2.17
Capital Accounts	17a	1.27	1.01	.83	.90	.65	.64	.97	1.32	1.72	1.58	1.74	1.71
Other Items (Net)	17r	−1.28	28.16	28.35	29.18	26.51	26.20	20.81	20.90	10.21	16.43	19.68	19.68
Deposit Money Banks					*Billions of Francs: End of Period*								
Reserves	20	.30	8.11	2.07	4.82	2.38	.86	.84	.96	1.44	1.53	2.27	2.39
Foreign Assets	21	2.02	6.12	3.13	2.31	2.99	3.32	6.84	5.61	3.37	3.66	3.29	6.24
Claims on Central Government	22a	5.21	5.07	4.35	3.33	4.47	3.50	3.96	10.68	11.79	8.32	8.06	5.68
Claims on Nonfin.Pub.Enterprises	22c	4.54	5.84	7.65	7.14	6.37	7.97	14.71	7.99	7.95	8.06	8.44	6.74
Claims on Private Sector	22d	15.93	18.70	23.16	23.25	24.17	27.95	27.77	30.90	34.52	41.32	40.98	49.65
Claims on Other Banking Insts.	22f	—	—	—	—	—	—	—	—	—	—	—	—
Claims on Nonbank Financial Insts.	22g	—	—	—	—	—	—	.92	.02	—	—	—	—
Demand Deposits	24	7.26	14.86	12.27	12.64	14.22	12.33	17.53	13.21	16.58	17.31	15.06	16.38
Time and Savings Deposits	25	5.16	11.89	8.98	9.42	9.14	9.97	9.69	9.08	10.54	10.19	11.08	12.51
Foreign Liabilities	26c	3.18	5.80	3.45	3.43	3.45	3.52	5.66	6.61	6.03	5.78	6.15	4.26
Long-Term Foreign Liabilities	26cl	.37	.66	.44	.42	.36	.66	.10	.01	.01	.25	1.69	3.85
Central Government Deposits	26d	1.98	3.55	7.22	7.77	7.04	4.73	6.25	10.44	5.82	6.86	4.93	5.41
Credit from Monetary Authorities	26g	3.66	—	1.60	1.24	.50	5.00	4.79	3.14	2.25	3.34	1.82	4.07
Capital Accounts	27a	8.10	8.70	9.35	7.78	7.44	8.20	13.35	15.49	18.92	22.42	22.21	23.23
Other Items (Net)	27r	−1.71	−1.62	−2.94	−1.85	−1.77	−.79	−2.31	−1.82	−1.08	−3.25	.09	.99
Monetary Survey					*Billions of Francs: End of Period*								
Foreign Assets (Net)	31n	20.60	85.38	92.47	101.25	89.79	65.73	65.62	68.40	52.58	45.55	38.05	40.48
Domestic Credit	32	50.35	66.15	63.33	60.82	59.38	66.06	75.53	78.41	86.88	96.55	102.18	115.35
Claims on Central Govt. (Net)	32an	29.88	41.61	32.52	30.44	28.84	30.14	32.13	39.51	44.41	47.16	52.76	58.96
Claims on Nonfin.Pub.Enterprises	32c	4.54	5.84	7.65	7.14	6.37	7.97	14.71	7.99	7.95	8.06	8.44	6.74
Claims on Private Sector	32d	15.93	18.70	23.16	23.25	24.17	27.95	27.77	30.90	34.52	41.32	40.98	49.65
Claims on Other Banking Insts.	32f	—	—	—	—	—	—	—	—	—	—	—	—
Claims on Nonbank Financial Inst.	32g	—	—	—	—	—	—	.92	.02	—	—	—	—
Money	34	59.42	103.40	111.24	116.64	107.19	87.58	98.64	101.83	99.15	94.74	85.44	97.72
Quasi-Money	35	5.16	11.89	8.98	9.42	9.14	9.97	9.69	9.08	10.54	10.19	11.08	12.51
Other Items (Net)	37r	6.38	36.25	35.58	36.00	32.84	34.25	32.81	35.90	29.77	37.17	43.72	45.61
Money plus Quasi-Money	35l	64.58	115.29	120.22	126.07	116.33	97.54	108.34	110.91	109.69	104.93	96.51	110.23
Interest Rates					*Percent Per Annum*								
Discount Rate (End of Period)	60	11.50	† 7.75	8.60	7.75	7.50	7.00	7.60	7.00	6.50	6.30	6.00	6.00
Deposit Rate	60l	7.75	8.08	5.50	5.46	5.00	5.00	5.00	5.00	5.00	5.00	5.00	5.00
Lending Rate	60p	17.46	17.50	16.00	22.00	22.00	22.00	22.00	22.00	20.67	18.00	18.00	18.00
Prices					*Index Numbers (2000=100): Period Averages*								
Wholesale Prices	63	60.2	....	....	....	92.9	92.9	94.0	100.0	108.9	118.3	122.8	122.1
Consumer Prices	64	64.0	79.7	95.0	98.6	100.2	98.3	96.9	100.0	103.8	106.3	110.6	108.4
Intl. Transactions & Positions					*Millions of Francs*								
Exports	70	31,079	83,900	85,300	75,100	94,850	89,309	90,136	114,414	104,299	102,292	74,493	53,038
Imports, c.i.f	71	35,559	77,300	86,900	72,300	82,039	86,375	80,689	83,290	78,464	83,795	68,352	83,574

Central African Republic 626

		1993	1994	1995	1996	1997	1998	1999	2000	2001	2002	2003	2004
Balance of Payments					*Millions of US Dollars: Minus Sign Indicates Debit*								
Current Account, n.i.e.....................	78ald	−13.0	−24.7	....	....	....	....	....	....	....	....	....	....
Goods: Exports f.o.b......................	78aad	132.5	145.9	....	....	....	....	....	....	....	....	....	....
Goods: Imports f.o.b......................	78abd	−158.1	−130.6	....	....	....	....	....	....	....	....	....	....
Trade Balance........................	78acd	−25.7	15.3	....	....	....	....	....	....	....	....	....	....
Services: Credit...........................	78add	49.3	33.1	....	....	....	....	....	....	....	....	....	....
Services: Debit...........................	78aed	−131.9	−113.8	....	....	....	....	....	....	....	....	....	....
Balance on Goods & Services.......	78afd	−108.3	−65.4	....	....	....	....	....	....	....	....	....	....
Income: Credit...........................	78agd	4.5	—	....	....	....	....	....	....	....	....	....	....
Income: Debit............................	78ahd	−23.2	−22.7	....	....	....	....	....	....	....	....	....	....
Balance on Gds, Serv. & Inc.........	78aid	−127.1	−88.1	....	....	....	....	....	....	....	....	....	....
Current Transfers, n.i.e.: Credit......	78ajd	152.4	92.6	....	....	....	....	....	....	....	....	....	....
Current Transfers: Debit...............	78akd	−38.3	−29.2	....	....	....	....	....	....	....	....	....	....
Capital Account, n.i.e.....................	78bcd	....	....	....	....	....	....	....	....	....	....	....	....
Capital Account, n.i.e.: Credit.......	78bad	....	....	....	....	....	....	....	....	....	....	....	....
Capital Account: Debit.................	78bbd	....	....	....	....	....	....	....	....	....	....	....	....
Financial Account, n.i.e..................	78bjd	−7.1	52.8	....	....	....	....	....	....	....	....	....	....
Direct Investment Abroad..............	78bdd	−5.3	−7.2	....	....	....	....	....	....	....	....	....	....
Dir. Invest. in Rep. Econ., n.i.e.......	78bed	−10.0	3.6	....	....	....	....	....	....	....	....	....	....
Portfolio Investment Assets...........	78bfd	....	....	....	....	....	....	....	....	....	....	....	....
Equity Securities.........................	78bkd	....	....	....	....	....	....	....	....	....	....	....	....
Debt Securities...........................	78bld	....	....	....	....	....	....	....	....	....	....	....	....
Portfolio Investment Liab., n.i.e......	78bgd	....	....	....	....	....	....	....	....	....	....	....	....
Equity Securities.........................	78bmd	....	....	....	....	....	....	....	....	....	....	....	....
Debt Securities...........................	78bnd	....	....	....	....	....	....	....	....	....	....	....	....
Financial Derivatives Assets...........	78bwd	....	....	....	....	....	....	....	....	....	....	....	....
Financial Derivatives Liabilities.......	78bxd	....	....	....	....	....	....	....	....	....	....	....	....
Other Investment Assets.............	78bhd	−18.2	8.1	....	....	....	....	....	....	....	....	....	....
Monetary Authorities...................	78bod	....	....	....	....	....	....	....	....	....	....	....	....
General Government....................	78bpd	....	....	....	....	....	....	....	....	....	....	....	....
Banks.......................................	78bqd	2.5	—	....	....	....	....	....	....	....	....	....	....
Other Sectors............................	78brd	−20.7	8.1	....	....	....	....	....	....	....	....	....	....
Other Investment Liab., n.i.e.........	78bid	26.4	48.3	....	....	....	....	....	....	....	....	....	....
Monetary Authorities...................	78bsd	−8.4	—	....	....	....	....	....	....	....	....	....	....
General Government....................	78btd	23.2	43.9	....	....	....	....	....	....	....	....	....	....
Banks.......................................	78bud	3.2	5.9	....	....	....	....	....	....	....	....	....	....
Other Sectors............................	78bvd	8.4	−1.6	....	....	....	....	....	....	....	....	....	....
Net Errors and Omissions................	78cad	6.3	−15.0	....	....	....	....	....	....	....	....	....	....
Overall Balance.........................	78cbd	−13.7	13.1	....	....	....	....	....	....	....	....	....	....
Reserves and Related Items.............	79dad	13.7	−13.1	....	....	....	....	....	....	....	....	....	....
Reserve Assets............................	79dbd	−20.1	−56.0	....	....	....	....	....	....	....	....	....	....
Use of Fund Credit and Loans........	79dcd	−1.6	10.3	....	....	....	....	....	....	....	....	....	....
Exceptional Financing..................	79ded	35.4	32.6	....	....	....	....	....	....	....	....	....	....
National Accounts					*Billions of Francs*								
Househ.Cons.Expend.,incl.NPISHs.....	96f	289	347	429	433	438	482	471	516	570	567	596	611
Government Consumption Expend...	91f	55	78	83	67	65	89	105	106	96	96	77	77
Gross Fixed Capital Formation.........	93e	36	56	73	35	43	72	85	78	76	72	46	52
Changes in Inventories....................	93i	3	−1	6	3	12	—	—	—	—	—	—	—
Exports of Goods and Services.........	90c	62	111	124	111	147	123	118	133	117	113	122	92
Imports of Goods and Services (-).....	98c	83	118	157	132	158	167	148	165	154	138	156	152
Gross Domestic Product (GDP).........	99b	362	473	557	516	547	598	631	668	705	709	684	681
Population..............................	99z	3.25	3.33	3.41	3.49	† 3.57	3.65	3.71	3.78	3.84	3.89	3.94	3.99

Millions: Midyear Estimates

Chad 628

		1993	1994	1995	1996	1997	1998	1999	2000	2001	2002	2003	2004
Exchange Rates		\multicolumn{12}{c}{*Francs per SDR: End of Period*}										
Official Rate............................	aa	404.89	† 780.44	728.38	753.06	807.94	791.61	† 896.19	918.49	935.39	850.37	771.76	747.90
		\multicolumn{12}{c}{*Francs per US Dollar: End of Period (ae) Period Average (rf)*}										
Official Rate............................	ae	294.78	† 534.60	490.00	523.70	598.81	562.21	† 652.95	704.95	744.31	625.50	519.36	481.58
Official Rate............................	rf	283.16	† 555.20	499.15	511.55	583.67	589.95	† 615.70	711.98	733.04	696.99	581.20	528.28
Fund Position		\multicolumn{12}{c}{*Millions of SDRs: End of Period*}										
Quota....................................	2f.s	41.30	41.30	41.30	41.30	41.30	41.30	56.00	56.00	56.00	56.00	56.00	56.00
SDRs.....................................	1b.s	.01	—	.02	.16	.01	.01	.02	—	—	.01	—	.04
Reserve Position in the Fund...........	1c.s	.28	.28	.28	.28	.28	.28	.28	.28	.28	.28	.28	.28
Total Fund Cred.&Loans Outstg.......	2tl	20.20	29.30	32.97	45.20	45.31	45.34	50.17	59.96	70.88	78.50	71.28	61.78
International Liquidity		\multicolumn{12}{c}{*Millions of US Dollars Unless Otherwise Indicated: End of Period*}										
Total Reserves minus Gold..............	1l.d	38.94	76.01	142.52	164.48	135.82	120.09	95.02	110.70	122.37	218.70	187.10	221.73
SDRs...................................	1b.d	.01	—	.03	.24	.01	.01	.03	—	—	.01	—	.07
Reserve Position in the Fund..........	1c.d	.38	.41	.42	.40	.38	.40	.39	.37	.35	.38	.42	.44
Foreign Exchange.....................	1d.d	38.54	75.60	142.07	163.84	135.44	119.68	94.60	110.33	122.02	218.31	186.68	221.23
Gold (Million Fine Troy Ounces)........	1ad	.011	.011	.011	.011	.011	.011	.011	.011	.011	.011	.011	.011
Gold (National Valuation)................	1and	4.42	† 4.21	4.29	4.10	3.24	3.20	† 3.23	3.03	3.09	3.81	4.65	4.88
Monetary Authorities: Other Liab.....	4..d	.01	.75	.44	1.10	16.61	12.47	18.56	21.07	18.28	18.42	21.03	21.41
Deposit Money Banks: Assets...........	7a.d	8.55	11.09	9.91	10.55	32.35	24.20	39.72	27.66	42.53	41.20	38.59	39.38
Liabilities................	7b.d	26.43	22.36	17.37	8.83	14.78	8.59	14.56	12.96	15.53	29.48	34.04	53.09
Monetary Authorities		\multicolumn{12}{c}{*Billions of Francs: End of Period*}										
Foreign Assets..............................	11	12.75	42.93	75.53	88.29	83.26	69.31	64.15	80.18	93.39	139.18	99.59	109.13
Claims on Central Government........	12a	33.79	48.48	49.71	61.94	65.56	64.83	73.94	89.78	101.14	106.76	93.50	105.73
Claims on Deposit Money Banks......	12e	9.69	.50	1.00	7.66	5.20	10.70	4.05	.50	4.50	1.50	10.43	7.81
Claims on Other Banking Insts.........	12f	—	—	—	—	1.50	3.85	3.30	4.00	3.00			
Reserve Money............................	14	38.25	47.24	74.73	98.29	94.13	84.51	79.22	92.11	108.15	145.39	130.48	139.99
of which: Currency Outside DMBs..	14a	35.84	39.69	61.98	89.36	78.81	73.62	68.25	81.27	94.77	116.80	110.92	110.11
Foreign Liabilities.........................	16c	8.18	23.27	24.23	34.62	46.55	42.91	57.08	69.92	79.91	78.28	65.93	56.51
Central Government Deposits...........	16d	.56	3.61	10.78	6.99	3.40	9.87	3.27	6.16	9.86	13.57	6.15	17.84
Capital Accounts...........................	17a	5.06	8.38	8.44	8.81	9.03	8.94	9.93	10.42	10.78	10.05	9.41	9.26
Other Items (Net)...........................	17r	4.12	9.41	8.06	9.18	2.40	2.46	−4.06	−4.16	−6.66	.16	−8.45	−.94
Deposit Money Banks		\multicolumn{12}{c}{*Billions of Francs: End of Period*}										
Reserves.....................................	20	1.98	6.17	10.08	7.39	12.77	10.13	10.35	9.89	12.89	28.59	19.54	29.87
Foreign Assets..............................	21	2.52	5.93	4.86	5.52	19.37	13.61	25.94	19.50	31.65	25.77	20.04	18.96
Claims on Central Government........	22a	6.37	7.98	8.19	2.22	2.49	1.88	1.60	3.08	7.40	8.81	12.49	23.71
Claims on Nonfin.Pub.Enterprises.....	22c	6.71	7.13	7.25	17.24	20.77	19.95	15.05	19.49	21.97	22.51	29.88	18.88
Claims on Private Sector..................	22d	20.86	23.75	27.79	29.95	29.16	34.03	33.89	34.31	43.29	56.48	67.08	73.10
Claims on Other Banking Insts.........	22f	—	—	—	—	—	—	—	—	—	—	—	—
Claims on Nonbank Financial Insts...	22g	—	—	—	—	—	.36	.27	.02	.16	.14	1.13	.87
Demand Deposits...........................	24	9.19	18.73	20.68	22.98	27.11	25.38	27.80	31.60	43.43	59.79	60.23	65.31
Time and Savings Deposits..............	25	2.20	2.86	7.87	5.36	5.87	5.77	6.11	7.95	9.92	11.61	11.16	13.28
Foreign Liabilities.........................	26c	7.58	11.22	8.42	4.62	8.79	4.83	7.52	6.87	9.70	16.07	13.41	20.09
Long-Term Foreign Liabilities...........	26cl	.21	.73	.09	—	.06	—	1.99	2.27	1.86	2.37	4.27	5.48
Central Government Deposits...........	26d	6.53	4.91	10.84	13.27	24.60	21.36	23.71	22.77	20.20	29.59	25.51	27.71
Credit from Monetary Authorities.....	26g	5.88	.50	1.00	7.66	5.20	10.70	4.05	.50	4.50	1.50	10.43	7.81
Capital Accounts...........................	27a	10.64	11.95	11.57	13.45	15.52	15.83	17.83	27.35	39.23	27.68	30.59	35.64
Other Items (Net)...........................	27r	−3.79	.06	−2.30	−5.01	−2.60	−3.90	−1.91	−13.03	−11.47	−6.29	−5.43	−10.58
Monetary Survey		\multicolumn{12}{c}{*Billions of Francs: End of Period*}										
Foreign Assets (Net).......................	31n	−.70	13.64	47.64	54.57	47.23	35.18	23.50	20.61	33.57	68.24	36.02	46.01
Domestic Credit............................	32	60.64	78.82	71.33	91.09	91.48	93.68	101.07	121.75	146.90	151.56	172.42	176.74
Claims on Central Govt. (Net)........	32an	33.07	47.94	36.28	43.90	40.06	35.48	48.57	63.93	78.49	72.42	74.33	83.89
Claims on Nonfin.Pub.Enterprises...	32c	6.71	7.13	7.25	17.24	20.77	19.95	15.05	19.49	21.97	22.51	29.88	18.88
Claims on Private Sector...............	32d	20.86	23.75	27.79	29.95	29.16	34.03	33.89	34.31	43.29	56.48	67.08	73.10
Claims on Other Banking Insts.......	32f	—	—	—	—	1.50	3.85	3.30	4.00	3.00	—	—	—
Claims on Nonbank Financial Inst..	32g	—	—	—	—	—	.36	.27	.02	.16	.14	1.13	.87
Money.......................................	34	45.47	59.79	85.33	113.88	108.47	99.75	96.67	113.82	138.69	176.59	171.17	175.44
Quasi-Money...............................	35	2.20	2.86	7.87	5.36	5.87	5.77	6.11	7.95	9.92	11.61	11.16	13.28
Other Items (Net)..........................	37r	12.22	29.80	25.76	26.43	24.36	23.33	21.79	20.58	31.86	31.59	26.11	33.37
Money plus Quasi-Money...............	35l	47.67	62.66	93.20	119.23	114.35	105.52	102.78	121.78	148.61	188.21	182.33	188.72
Interest Rates		\multicolumn{12}{c}{*Percent Per Annum*}										
Discount Rate (End of Period)..........	60	11.50	† 7.75	8.60	7.75	7.50	7.00	7.60	7.00	6.50	6.30	6.00	6.00
Deposit Rate.................................	60l	7.75	8.08	5.50	5.46	5.00	5.00	5.00	5.00	5.00	5.00	5.00	5.00
Lending Rate.................................	60p	17.46	17.50	16.00	22.00	22.00	22.00	22.00	22.00	20.67	18.00	18.00	18.00
Prices		\multicolumn{12}{c}{*Index Numbers (2000=100): Period Averages*}										
Consumer Prices............................	64	50.7	71.2	77.7	87.3	92.2	103.4	96.3	100.0	112.4	118.3	116.0	....
Intl. Transactions & Positions		\multicolumn{12}{c}{*Millions of Francs*}										
Exports......................................	70	37,330	82,160	121,273	121,895	138,130	154,455	149,635	130,200	138,300	128,685	....	....
Imports, c.i.f.................................	71	56,910	98,310	182,400	169,733	194,732	210,207	194,523	224,386	497,417	1,146,934	....	....

Chad 628

		1993	1994	1995	1996	1997	1998	1999	2000	2001	2002	2003	2004
Balance of Payments					*Millions of US Dollars: Minus Sign Indicates Debit*								
Current Account, n.i.e.	78ald	−116.6	−37.7	....	....	....	....	....	....	....	....	....	....
Goods: Exports f.o.b.	78aad	151.8	135.3	....	....	....	....	....	....	....	....	....	....
Goods: Imports f.o.b.	78abd	−215.2	−212.1	....	....	....	....	....	....	....	....	....	....
Trade Balance	78acd	−63.5	−76.8	....	....	....	....	....	....	....	....	....	....
Services: Credit	78add	47.1	54.8	....	....	....	....	....	....	....	....	....	....
Services: Debit	78aed	−235.1	−199.4	....	....	....	....	....	....	....	....	....	....
Balance on Goods & Services	78afd	−251.4	−221.4	....	....	....	....	....	....	....	....	....	....
Income: Credit	78agd	4.3	5.0	....	....	....	....	....	....	....	....	....	....
Income: Debit	78ahd	−15.7	−12.4	....	....	....	....	....	....	....	....	....	....
Balance on Gds, Serv. & Inc.	78aid	−262.9	−228.7	....	....	....	....	....	....	....	....	....	....
Current Transfers, n.i.e.: Credit	78ajd	192.4	209.4	....	....	....	....	....	....	....	....	....	....
Current Transfers: Debit	78akd	−46.2	−18.4	....	....	....	....	....	....	....	....	....	....
Capital Account, n.i.e.	78bcd	—	—	....	....	....	....	....	....	....	....	....	....
Capital Account, n.i.e.: Credit	78bad	—	—	....	....	....	....	....	....	....	....	....	....
Capital Account: Debit	78bbd	—	—	....	....	....	....	....	....	....	....	....	....
Financial Account, n.i.e.	78bjd	68.8	76.3	....	....	....	....	....	....	....	....	....	....
Direct Investment Abroad	78bdd	−10.9	−.6	....	....	....	....	....	....	....	....	....	....
Dir. Invest. in Rep. Econ., n.i.e.	78bed	15.2	27.1	....	....	....	....	....	....	....	....	....	....
Portfolio Investment Assets	78bfd	—	—	....	....	....	....	....	....	....	....	....	....
Equity Securities	78bkd	—	—	....	....	....	....	....	....	....	....	....	....
Debt Securities	78bld	—	—	....	....	....	....	....	....	....	....	....	....
Portfolio Investment Liab., n.i.e.	78bgd	—	—	....	....	....	....	....	....	....	....	....	....
Equity Securities	78bmd	—	—	....	....	....	....	....	....	....	....	....	....
Debt Securities	78bnd	—	—	....	....	....	....	....	....	....	....	....	....
Financial Derivatives Assets	78bwd	....	....	....	....	....	....	....	....	....	....	....	....
Financial Derivatives Liabilities	78bxd	....	....	....	....	....	....	....	....	....	....	....	....
Other Investment Assets	78bhd	42.1	.6	....	....	....	....	....	....	....	....	....	....
Monetary Authorities	78bod	....	....	....	....	....	....	....	....	....	....	....	....
General Government	78bpd	....	....	....	....	....	....	....	....	....	....	....	....
Banks	78bqd	31.0	−4.8	....	....	....	....	....	....	....	....	....	....
Other Sectors	78brd	11.0	5.4	....	....	....	....	....	....	....	....	....	....
Other Investment Liab., n.i.e.	78bid	22.5	49.2	....	....	....	....	....	....	....	....	....	....
Monetary Authorities	78bsd	−5.2	−.1	....	....	....	....	....	....	....	....	....	....
General Government	78btd	102.1	49.8	....	....	....	....	....	....	....	....	....	....
Banks	78bud	—		....	....	....	....	....	....	....	....	....	....
Other Sectors	78bvd	−74.4	−.6	....	....	....	....	....	....	....	....	....	....
Net Errors and Omissions	78cad	−.1	−33.0	....	....	....	....	....	....	....	....	....	....
Overall Balance	78cbd	−47.9	5.5	....	....	....	....	....	....	....	....	....	....
Reserves and Related Items	79dad	47.9	−5.5	....	....	....	....	....	....	....	....	....	....
Reserve Assets	79dbd	39.4	−30.7	....	....	....	....	....	....	....	....	....	....
Use of Fund Credit and Loans	79dcd	−1.7	12.7	....	....	....	....	....	....	....	....	....	....
Exceptional Financing	79ded	10.2	12.4	....	....	....	....	....	....	....	....	....	....
Government Finance					*Millions of Francs: Year Ending December 31*								
Deficit (-) or Surplus	80	−22,954	−82,198	−45,532	−97,696	−65,653	−65,161	−56,178	−47,612	3,653	....	....	....
Total Revenue and Grants	81y	79,116	87,592	98,502	110,407	128,747	115,415	107,489	136,732	145,106	....	....	....
Revenue	81	29,150	31,964	44,834	59,790	72,359	77,347	79,289	88,750	96,867	....	....	....
Grants	81z	49,966	55,628	53,668	50,617	56,388	38,068	28,200	47,982	48,239	....	....	....
Exp. & Lending Minus Repay	82z	102,070	169,790	144,034	208,103	194,400	180,576	163,667	184,344	141,453	....	....	....
Expenditure	82	104,840	148,300	130,304	151,794	159,400	153,028	163,667	184,344	141,453	....	....	....
Lending Minus Repayments	83	−2,770	21,490	13,730	56,309	35,000	27,548	—	—	—	....	....	....
Statistical Discrepancy	80xx	−4,428	−1,341	31,313	22,600	46,377	13,208	32,642	−23,310	34,390	....	....	....
Total Financing	80h	18,526	80,857	76,845	120,296	112,030	78,369	88,820	24,302	30,737	....	....	....
Domestic	84a	9,916	−460	−5,817	14,546	28,432	5,041	32,650	9,658	1,141	....	....	....
Foreign	85a	8,610	81,317	82,662	105,750	83,598	73,328	56,170	14,644	29,596	....	....	....
Total Debt by Residence	88	225,936	423,574	435,728	489,035	546,857	525,691	642,939	800,014	862,293	....	....	....
Domestic	88a	4,236	6,503	5,481	4,236	7,108	7,310	24,000	65,113	66,300	....	....	....
Foreign	89a	221,700	417,071	430,247	484,799	539,749	518,381	618,939	734,901	795,993	....	....	....
National Accounts					*Billions of Francs*								
Gross Domestic Product (GDP)	99b	412.0	655.0	717.8	822.0	911.0	1,003.0	943.0	996.0	1,235.0	1,405.0	1,548.0	....
					Millions: Midyear Estimates								
Population	99z	6.62	6.83	7.03	7.25	7.47	7.70	7.95	8.22	8.51	8.81	9.13	9.45

Chile 228

		1993	1994	1995	1996	1997	1998	1999	2000	2001	2002	2003	2004
Exchange Rates						*Pesos per SDR: End of Period*							
Market Rate	aa	592.06	589.91	605.19	611.09	593.41	667.08	727.53	746.15	824.67	968.49	890.72	869.42
						Pesos per US Dollar: End of Period (ae) Period Average (rf)							
Market Rate	ae	431.04	404.09	407.13	424.97	439.81	473.77	530.07	572.68	656.20	712.38	599.42	559.83
Market Rate	rf	404.17	420.18	396.77	412.27	419.30	460.29	508.78	539.59	634.94	688.94	691.43	609.37
						Index Numbers (2000=100): Period Averages							
Market Rate	ahx	133.3	128.2	135.9	130.6	128.4	117.0	106.0	100.0	85.3	78.3	79.2	87.8
Nominal Effective Exchange Rate	nec	85.8	101.7	107.4	107.2	113.3	107.9	100.6	100.0	90.2	85.0	78.0	82.9
Real Effective Exchange Rate	rec	87.1	89.7	95.1	97.6	106.7	105.5	100.1	100.0	91.1	85.7	78.5	83.0
Fund Position						*Millions of SDRs: End of Period*							
Quota	2f.s	621.7	621.7	621.7	621.7	621.7	621.7	856.1	856.1	856.1	856.1	856.1	856.1
SDRs	1b.s	.9	.5	2.1	1.3	1.0	5.9	13.5	18.9	23.0	26.9	30.7	33.9
Reserve Position in the Fund	1c.s	—	—	—	35.0	232.0	429.6	299.4	248.8	245.7	360.9	392.3	287.0
Total Fund Cred.&Loans Outstg	2tl	346.5	199.5	—	—	—	—	—	—	—	—	—	—
International Liquidity						*Millions of US Dollars Unless Otherwise Indicated: End of Period*							
Total Reserves minus Gold	1l.d	9,640.3	13,087.6	14,139.8	14,972.6	17,573.2	15,869.3	14,616.6	15,034.9	14,379.0	15,341.1	15,839.6	15,993.8
SDRs	1b.d	1.3	.7	3.1	1.9	1.3	8.3	18.5	24.6	28.9	36.5	45.7	52.6
Reserve Position in the Fund	1c.d	—	—	—	50.4	313.1	604.9	411.0	324.2	308.7	490.7	582.9	445.8
Foreign Exchange	1d.d	9,639.0	13,086.9	14,136.7	14,920.3	17,258.9	15,256.1	14,187.1	14,686.1	14,041.3	14,813.9	15,211.0	15,495.4
Gold (Million Fine Troy Ounces)	1ad	1.865	1.864	1.861	1.859	1.858	1.222	1.220	.074	.074	.008	.008	.008
Gold (National Valuation)	1and	612.0	652.0	642.8	637.4	533.0	321.9	316.9	318.3	18.6	2.3	2.7	3.0
Monetary Authorities: Other Liab.	4..d	2,100.5	2,573.3	1,596.2	7.9	353.6	330.6	488.6	316.9	274.1	235.3	235.3	253.2
Banking Institutions: Assets	7a.d	525.5	549.1	491.7	605.2	1,522.0	2,441.5	5,638.7	5,162.5	4,096.0	2,494.0	1,962.4	2,668.5
Liabilities	7b.d	—	—	—	—	2,151.7	2,267.5	1,505.2	1,214.0	1,991.3	3,317.2	4,841.0	5,423.4
Nonbank Financial Insts.: Assets	7e.d	89.8	199.3	51.6	148.4	351.9	1,748.5	4,572.9	3,871.8	4,684.3	5,781.5	11,697.8	16,469.2
Monetary Authorities						*Billions of Pesos: End of Period*							
Foreign Assets	11	4,749.6	5,999.0	6,439.5	7,230.9	†8,062.0	7,784.1	8,097.1	8,770.8	9,608.7	11,000.7	9,668.5	9,138.8
Claims on Central Government	12a	3,814.8	3,597.8	3,805.1	3,817.6	†3,863.8	3,890.8	4,099.6	4,546.3	5,046.6	5,067.1	4,085.6	3,321.5
Claims on Nonfin.Pub.Enterprises	12c	—	—	—	†	—	—	—	—	—	—	—	—
Claims on Private Sector	12d	167.5	188.0	200.8	224.8	†837.6	846.3	863.5	878.5	880.8	892.6	924.3	934.7
Claims on Banking Institutions	12e	2,535.3	2,440.7	2,454.6	2,257.2	†635.1	482.4	567.9	578.0	681.1	132.3	101.7	134.3
Reserve Money	14	844.8	994.5	1,206.7	1,345.4	†1,824.3	2,003.4	2,093.2	1,945.7	2,118.5	2,242.8	2,158.5	2,585.8
of which: Currency Outside DMBs	14a	582.1	667.3	784.2	859.5	†978.5	969.5	1,167.9	1,113.7	1,214.7	1,301.5	1,379.7	1,584.6
Time, Savings,& Fgn.Currency Dep	15	285.7	258.9	110.9	62.7	†3.3	1.7	4.3	.4	.2	.8	—	.1
Liabs. of Central Bank: Securities	16ac	5,814.2	7,045.3	7,951.2	9,267.6	†10,540.3	10,018.5	10,793.9	12,151.4	12,414.1	13,313.6	12,417.9	11,170.3
Foreign Liabilities	16c	1,110.6	1,157.6	649.9	3.4	†155.5	156.6	259.0	181.5	179.9	167.6	141.0	141.8
Central Government Deposits	16d	1,371.0	1,573.3	1,753.7	2,011.3	†2,131.2	1,919.9	1,326.0	966.3	621.5	430.2	87.8	158.7
Capital Accounts	17a	520.7	−113.3	374.1	268.3	†−1,319.0	−1,796.6	−1,535.9	−1,432.3	−206.9	615.6	−819.4	−1,527.7
Other Items (Net)	17r	1,320.4	1,309.0	853.5	571.8	†62.9	700.2	687.8	960.5	1,089.9	322.0	794.3	1,000.3
Banking Institutions						*Billions of Pesos: End of Period*							
Reserves	20	575.7	713.0	719.9	750.9	†664.8	911.5	916.0	880.3	948.6	931.2	1,523.0	1,962.4
Claims on Mon.Author.:Securities	20c	1,691.1	2,077.6	2,293.0	2,405.1	†3,115.3	2,714.2	3,649.1	4,163.7	4,913.2	6,135.3	5,206.3	5,491.1
Foreign Assets	21	225.7	221.0	199.4	256.5	†669.4	1,156.7	2,988.9	2,956.5	2,687.8	1,776.7	1,176.3	1,493.9
Claims on Central Government	22a	51.3	56.6	84.0	137.0	†320.2	264.8	247.2	315.0	335.3	432.3	331.7	1,289.5
Claims on Local Government	22b	.4	.4	.5	.5	†.4	.3	.3	.3	.7	.7	.6	.6
Claims on Nonfin.Pub.Enterprises	22c	170.5	124.6	95.4	88.7	†133.5	550.0	128.2	73.3	247.5	61.3	160.8	161.6
Claims on Private Sector	22d	9,324.2	10,953.1	13,871.5	16,675.1	†18,745.3	20,470.3	21,995.4	24,876.8	26,569.0	29,186.1	30,750.0	35,272.5
Claims on Nonbank Financial Insts.	22g	—	—	—	—	†697.9	617.2	760.7	407.4	829.8	240.0	434.8	895.6
Demand Deposits	24	1,040.6	1,212.7	1,515.5	1,816.9	†2,101.0	1,967.1	2,233.3	2,531.3	2,847.6	3,129.3	3,551.0	4,148.2
Time, Savings,& Fgn.Currency Dep	25	5,603.9	6,250.2	8,021.0	9,788.5	†10,676.7	12,233.3	12,947.6	13,701.5	13,680.2	13,262.8	14,189.5	14,965.7
Money Market Instruments	26aa	415.4	559.9	674.9	833.9	†5,898.9	5,280.2	6,543.8	7,475.6	8,196.2	9,644.1	9,105.5	4,126.9
Bonds	26ab	1,049.5	1,554.9	2,229.2	2,894.2	†639.0	750.7	1,057.7	1,252.5	1,338.1	1,335.5	1,200.2	1,414.4
Foreign Liabilities	26c	1,635.0	1,720.7	1,613.0	1,544.4	†946.4	1,074.3	797.9	695.2	1,306.7	2,363.1	2,901.8	3,036.2
Central Government Deposits	26d	426.0	490.2	708.7	686.2	†816.5	664.3	898.9	774.4	1,090.4	1,170.7	1,258.9	1,461.3
Credit from Monetary Authorities	26g	542.1	443.3	361.7	326.5	†228.4	176.8	119.9	140.3	561.5	262.8	699.0	1,062.5
Liabs. to Nonbank Financial Insts.	26j	287.2	437.4	425.3	323.1	†2,408.1	3,126.5	4,215.0	4,951.3	5,599.9	7,439.8	6,203.3	8,940.5
Capital Accounts	27a	1,652.7	2,334.5	3,133.0	3,743.7	†2,509.0	2,848.2	3,075.7	3,492.9	3,781.1	4,069.5	4,343.8	4,669.0
Other Items (Net)	27r	−613.6	−857.5	−1,418.6	−1,643.7	†−1,877.0	−1,436.5	−1,203.9	−1,341.8	−1,869.9	−3,914.2	−3,868.6	2,742.5
Banking Survey						*Billions of Pesos: End of Period*							
Foreign Assets (Net)	31n	2,229.7	3,341.7	4,375.9	5,939.6	†7,629.5	7,709.9	10,029.2	10,850.6	10,809.9	10,246.6	7,801.9	7,454.7
Domestic Credit	32	11,731.5	12,856.9	15,595.1	18,246.2	†21,651.1	24,055.5	25,870.2	29,356.8	32,197.9	34,279.0	35,341.1	40,255.9
Claims on Central Govt. (Net)	32an	2,069.1	1,590.8	1,426.8	1,257.1	†1,236.3	1,571.4	2,122.0	3,120.5	3,670.1	3,898.4	3,070.6	2,990.9
Claims on Local Government	32b	.4	.4	.5	.5	†.4	.3	.3	.3	.7	.7	.6	.6
Claims on Nonfin.Pub.Enterprises	32c	170.5	124.6	95.4	88.7	†133.5	550.0	128.2	73.3	247.5	61.3	160.8	161.6
Claims on Private Sector	32d	9,491.6	11,141.1	14,072.3	16,899.9	†19,582.9	21,316.6	22,859.0	25,755.3	27,449.8	30,078.7	31,674.3	36,207.2
Claims on Nonbank Financial Insts.	32g	—	—	—	—	†697.9	617.2	760.7	407.4	829.8	240.0	434.8	895.6
Money	34	1,623.1	1,880.2	2,300.0	2,677.0	†3,079.5	2,936.5	3,401.2	3,645.2	4,062.3	4,430.8	4,930.7	5,732.8
Quasi-Money	35	5,889.5	6,509.1	8,131.9	9,851.2	†10,680.0	12,235.1	12,951.9	13,701.9	13,680.4	13,263.7	14,189.5	14,965.8
Money Market Instruments	36aa	415.4	559.9	674.9	833.9	†5,898.9	5,280.2	6,543.8	7,475.6	8,196.2	9,644.1	9,105.5	4,126.9
Bonds	36ab	1,049.5	1,554.9	2,229.2	2,894.2	†639.0	750.7	1,057.7	1,252.5	1,338.1	1,335.5	1,200.2	1,414.4
Liabs. of Central Bank: Securities	36ac	4,123.0	4,967.7	5,658.2	6,862.5	†7,424.9	7,304.3	7,144.8	7,987.6	7,500.9	7,178.3	7,211.5	5,679.2
Liabs. to Nonbank Financial Insts.	36j	287.2	437.4	425.3	323.1	†2,408.1	3,126.5	4,215.0	4,951.3	5,599.9	7,439.8	6,203.3	8,940.5
Capital Accounts	37a	2,173.3	2,221.2	3,507.1	4,012.0	†1,190.0	1,051.6	1,539.8	2,060.6	3,574.2	4,685.1	3,524.4	3,141.2
Other Items (Net)	37r	−1,599.9	−1,931.8	−2,955.7	−3,268.1	†−2,039.7	−919.4	−954.7	−867.5	−944.3	−3,451.7	−3,221.2	3,709.9
Money plus Quasi-Money	35l	7,512.6	8,389.3	10,431.9	12,528.1	†13,759.5	15,171.6	16,353.1	17,347.1	17,742.7	17,694.5	19,120.3	20,698.5
Nonbank Financial Institutions						*Billions of Pesos End of Period*							
Claims on Mon.Author.:Securities	40c.p	2,656.8	3,462.9	3,883.0	4,538.6	4,937.3	5,521.9	5,670.3	6,566.5	6,958.9	6,224.2	5,646.4	4,252.2
Foreign Assets	41..p	38.7	80.5	21.0	63.1	154.8	828.4	2,423.9	2,217.3	3,073.8	4,118.6	7,011.9	9,219.9
Claims on Central Government	42a.p	32.8	108.3	195.7	384.5	428.7	505.2	655.9	790.0	1,172.1	1,428.8	1,641.1	2,073.8
Claims on Private Sector	42d.p	2,693.5	3,536.8	3,848.1	3,832.4	3,924.8	3,114.6	3,339.1	3,616.8	4,293.7	4,706.1	7,085.5	8,272.3
Claims on Banking Institutions	42e.p	1,415.5	1,807.2	2,391.5	2,872.4	4,083.6	4,715.4	6,163.9	7,333.3	7,680.9	8,944.0	8,052.5	10,008.5
Reserve Funds and Capital	47a.p	6,831.4	8,983.6	10,231.0	11,555.6	13,405.8	14,552.5	18,093.0	20,343.4	22,956.0	25,227.1	29,176.6	33,511.0
Other Items (Net)	47r.p	5.9	12.2	108.3	135.4	123.2	133.0	160.1	180.4	223.5	194.6	261.0	315.7

		1993	1994	1995	1996	1997	1998	1999	2000	2001	2002	2003	2004
Interest Rates							*Percent Per Annum*						
Discount Rate (End of Period)..........	60	7.96	13.89	7.96	11.75	7.96	9.12	7.44	8.73	6.50	3.00	2.45	2.25
Money Market Rate.......................	60b	....	....	....	....	....	....	....	10.09	6.81	4.08	2.72	1.88
Savings Rate...............................	60k	3.52	3.53	3.53	3.51	3.50	3.50	3.50	3.50	2.39	.69	.26	.22
Deposit Rate................................	60l	18.24	15.12	13.73	13.48	12.02	14.92	8.56	9.20	6.19	3.80	2.73	1.94
Deposit Rate (Foreign Currency).......	60l.f	3.96	4.05	5.45	5.24	5.02	4.41	4.39	5.48	3.51	1.59	1.39	1.63
Lending Rate...............................	60p	24.35	20.34	18.16	17.37	15.67	20.17	12.62	14.84	11.89	7.76	6.18	5.13
Lending Rate (Foreign Currency)......	60p.f	6.76	8.42	9.96	9.27	9.49	8.73	7.38	7.76	5.50	3.83	3.37	2.95
Prices, Production, Labor						*Index Numbers (2000=100): Period Averages*							
Industrial Share Prices....................	62	77.7	108.1	137.6	122.8	111.3	83.3	90.3	100.0	106.6	104.2	131.4	174.3
Prices: Home & Import Goods..........	63	66.9	72.1	77.5	82.4	83.7	85.3	89.8	100.0	107.8	115.2	122.8	125.8
Home Goods..........	63a	65.8	71.2	77.8	83.0	85.1	86.0	89.5	100.0	105.9	112.4	120.2	126.2
Consumer Prices..........................	64	64.5	71.9	77.8	83.5	88.7	93.2	96.3	100.0	103.6	106.1	109.1	110.3
Wages, Hourly...........................	65a	56.3	59.2	66.7	76.6	83.2	89.7	95.0	100.0	105.2	110.0	114.2	117.5
Manufacturing Production...............	66ey	82.4	84.5	88.6	91.9	96.4	96.5	96.5	100.0	101.9	† 102.6	108.0	116.6
Mining Production........................	66zx	48.5	51.6	57.2	70.2	76.6	81.6	94.8	100.0	101.6	98.0	104.4	114.7
Copper Production.......................	66c	45.3	47.9	53.9	67.2	73.9	79.6	95.4	100.0	102.6	99.6	105.6	116.5
Employment...............................	67	93.7	94.8	95.9	97.2	99.3	101.2	98.9	100.0	100.3	101.4	104.5	106.4
						Number in Thousands: Period Averages							
Labor Force.................................	67d	5,219	5,300	5,274	5,601	5,684	5,852	5,934	5,871	5,949	6,000	6,128	....
Employment...............................	67e	4,986	† 4,988	5,026	† 5,299	5,380	5,432	5,405	5,382	5,479	5,531	5,675	5,863
Unemployment...........................	67c	234	† 427	402	350	344	384	572	536	535	529	515	546
Unemployment Rate (%).................	67r	4.5	† 5.9	4.7	5.4	5.3	7.2	8.9	8.3	7.9	7.8	7.4	8.8
Intl. Transactions & Positions							*Millions of US Dollars*						
Exports.......................................	70..d	9,199	11,604	16,024	15,657	17,902	16,323	17,162	19,210	18,272	18,180	21,524	32,025
Imports, c.i.f................................	71..d	11,134	11,820	15,900	19,199	20,822	19,882	15,987	18,507	17,429	17,091	19,381	24,871
Imports, f.o.b..............................	71.vd	10,189	10,872	14,643	17,699	19,298	18,363	14,735	17,091	16,428	15,794	18,002	23,006
						1995=100							
Import Prices...............................	76.x	91.7	97.5	100.0	110.2	....	....	....	....	....	....	....	....
Balance of Payments						*Millions of US Dollars: Minus Sign Indicates Debit*							
Current Account, n.i.e.....................	78ald	−2,555	−1,586	−1,350	−3,083	−3,660	−3,918	99	−898	−1,100	−580	−1,102	1,390
Goods: Exports f.o.b....................	78aad	9,199	11,604	16,025	16,627	17,870	16,323	17,162	19,210	18,272	18,180	21,524	32,025
Goods: Imports f.o.b....................	78abd	−10,189	−10,872	−14,644	−17,699	−19,298	−18,363	−14,735	−17,091	−16,428	−15,794	−18,002	−23,006
Trade Balance........................	78acd	−990	732	1,381	−1,072	−1,428	−2,040	2,427	2,119	1,844	2,386	3,522	9,019
Services: Credit...........................	78add	2,513	2,840	3,333	3,588	3,892	3,952	3,869	4,083	4,138	4,386	4,950	5,956
Services: Debit............................	78aed	−2,742	−2,990	−3,657	−3,589	−4,028	−4,404	−4,606	−4,802	−4,983	−5,087	−5,567	−6,537
Balance on Goods & Services......	78afd	−1,219	582	1,057	−1,073	−1,563	−2,492	1,690	1,400	999	1,684	2,905	8,439
Income: Credit............................	78agd	502	556	869	842	1,170	1,196	912	1,598	1,458	1,114	1,435	1,510
Income: Debit.............................	78ahd	−2,158	−3,056	−3,582	−3,359	−3,787	−3,085	−3,145	−4,453	−3,985	−3,960	−6,042	−9,610
Balance on Gds, Serv. & Inc........	78aid	−2,875	−1,917	−1,657	−3,590	−4,180	−4,381	−543	−1,456	−1,527	−1,163	−1,702	338
Current Transfers, n.i.e.: Credit......	78ajd	536	449	482	665	835	810	841	765	713	954	928	1,395
Current Transfers: Debit................	78akd	−216	−118	−175	−158	−315	−348	−198	−207	−286	−372	−329	−344
Capital Account, n.i.e.	78bcd	—	—	—	—	—	—	—	—	—	83	—	5
Capital Account, n.i.e.: Credit........	78bad	—	—	—	—	—	—	—	—	—	83	—	5
Capital Account: Debit..................	78bbd	—	—	—	—	—	—	—	—	—	—	—	—
Financial Account, n.i.e.	78bjd	2,995	5,294	2,357	5,660	6,742	1,966	237	787	1,362	1,634	1,661	−524
Direct Investment Abroad..............	78bdd	−434	−911	−752	−1,133	−1,463	−1,483	−2,558	−3,987	−1,610	−343	−1,884	−943
Dir. Invest. in Rep. Econ., n.i.e.......	78bed	1,034	2,583	2,957	4,815	5,271	4,628	8,761	4,860	4,200	2,550	4,385	7,603
Portfolio Investment Assets...........	78bfd	−90	−351	−14	−135	−989	−3,311	−5,795	766	−1,386	−3,316	−4,172	−4,557
Equity Securities........................	78bkd	−90	−351	−14	−43	−743	−2,518	−3,474	821	−2,094	−3,272	−4,356	−3,821
Debt Securities..........................	78bld	—	—	—	−92	−246	−792	−2,321	−55	708	−44	184	−736
Portfolio Investment Liab., n.i.e......	78bgd	820	1,259	48	1,269	2,614	842	2,578	−127	1,525	999	2,054	1,123
Equity Securities........................	78bmd	816	1,259	−249	700	1,720	580	524	−427	−217	−320	318	8
Debt Securities..........................	78bnd	4	—	297	569	894	262	2,054	300	1,742	1,319	1,736	1,116
Financial Derivatives Assets...........	78bwd	—	—	—	—	—	—	....	....	....	....	....	....
Financial Derivatives Liabilities.......	78bxd	—	—	—	−22	165	−59	−6	2	−86	−124	118	−84
Other Investment Assets...............	78bhd	726	−152	−309	−855	−457	−1,953	−3,369	−2,065	−1,326	1,141	−384	−2,966
Monetary Authorities..................	78bod	−4	−57	10	—	—	—	—	—	—	—	−60	—
General Government....................	78bpd	—	—	—	—	—	—	—	—	—	—	1	—
Banks....................................	78bqd	7	−26	57	−87	−547	−381	−1,642	653	145	635	299	−166
Other Sectors...........................	78brd	723	−70	−376	−768	90	−1,572	−1,727	−2,717	−1,471	505	−624	−2,800
Other Investment Liab., n.i.e.........	78bid	939	2,865	427	1,721	1,600	3,303	626	1,338	44	728	1,544	−700
Monetary Authorities..................	78bsd	−240	−99	−402	−74	−24	−74	−66	36	−47	−2	−3	6
General Government....................	78btd	−119	−99	−1,323	−545	−386	−171	−101	−128	−132	−294	−117	−115
Banks....................................	78bud	61	407	−322	−444	−1,498	−36	−840	−278	771	1,302	1,606	168
Other Sectors...........................	78bvd	1,237	2,656	2,474	2,784	3,508	3,584	1,633	1,707	−548	−279	58	−759
Net Errors and Omissions.................	78cad	−12	−557	132	16	237	−239	−1,083	427	−861	−952	−916	−1,062
Overall Balance..........................	78cbd	428	3,151	1,139	2,593	3,318	−2,191	−747	317	−599	185	−357	−191
Reserves and Related Items..............	79dad	−428	−3,151	−1,139	−2,593	−3,318	2,191	747	−317	599	−185	357	191
Reserve Assets............................	79dbd	−170	−2,918	−740	−1,119	−3,318	2,191	747	−317	599	−185	357	191
Use of Fund Credit and Loans........	79dcd	−249	−210	−298	—	—	—	—	—	—	—	—	—
Exceptional Financing..................	79ded	−9	−22	−101	−1,475	—	—	—	—	—	—	—	—

Chile 228

		1993	1994	1995	1996	1997	1998	1999	2000	2001	2002	2003	2004
International Investment Position						*Millions of US Dollars*							
Assets	79aad	....	....	....	....	32,134	36,815	46,699	47,007	47,455	50,197	60,938	75,173
Direct Investment Abroad	79abd	....	....	....	—	5,110	6,735	9,000	11,154	11,720	12,239	13,852	17,278
Portfolio Investment	79acd	....	....	....	—	1,176	4,717	11,402	9,876	10,562	13,019	20,967	27,972
Equity Securities	79add	....	....	....	—	902	3,411	7,670	6,911	7,870	10,682	18,375	24,273
Debt Securities	79aed	....	....	....	—	274	1,306	3,732	2,965	2,692	2,337	2,592	3,699
Financial Derivatives	79ald	....	....	....	....	—	—	—	—	406	268	535	786
Other Investment	79afd	....	....	....	598	7,575	9,071	11,344	10,863	10,358	9,319	9,733	13,121
Monetary Authorities	79agd	....	....	....	—	—	—	—	—	—	—	62	65
General Government	79ahd	....	....	....	—	—	—	—	—	—	—	—	—
Banks	79aid	....	....	....	598	1,055	1,284	2,741	2,486	2,341	1,706	1,408	1,573
Other Sectors	79ajd	....	....	....	—	6,520	7,787	8,603	8,377	8,017	7,613	8,262	11,483
Reserve Assets	79akd	....	....	....	15,660	18,273	16,292	14,952	15,114	14,410	15,352	15,852	16,016
Liabilities	79lad	....	....	....	....	66,973	71,588	80,230	82,219	81,218	80,906	98,373	110,713
Dir. Invest. in Rep. Economy	79lbd	....	....	....	—	34,523	37,630	43,498	45,753	43,482	42,311	53,960	65,571
Portfolio Investment	79lcd	....	....	....	6,417	9,172	7,966	10,611	9,187	10,121	10,527	14,632	16,186
Equity Securities	79ldd	....	....	....	5,223	7,111	5,704	6,451	4,701	3,590	2,304	3,974	4,622
Debt Securities	79led	....	....	....	1,194	2,061	2,262	4,159	4,486	6,532	8,223	10,658	11,564
Financial Derivatives	79lld	....	....	....	....	—	—	—	—	363	102	222	448
Other Investment	79lfd	....	....	....	21,367	23,279	25,992	26,122	27,278	27,252	27,966	29,558	28,509
Monetary Authorities	79lgd	....	....	....	189	166	92	26	62	15	13	10	17
General Government	79lhd	....	....	....	2,653	2,284	2,183	2,094	1,920	1,742	1,467	1,392	1,287
Banks	79lid	....	....	....	3,599	2,106	2,185	1,438	1,158	1,927	3,229	4,834	4,999
Other Sectors	79ljd	....	....	....	14,926	18,723	21,533	22,563	24,138	23,568	23,257	23,322	22,206
Government Finance						*Billions of Pesos: Year Ending December 31*							
Deficit (-) or Surplus	80	356.6	361.9	667.7	657.8	623.3	131.8	−502.4	56.4	....	....	....	....
Total Revenue and Grants	81y	4,172.7	4,822.8	5,747.7	6,626.3	7,358.9	7,726.9	7,737.8	8,976.1	....	....	....	....
Revenue	81	4,172.7	4,822.8	5,747.7	6,626.3	7,358.9	7,726.9	7,737.8	8,976.1	....	....	....	....
Grants	81z	—	—	—	—	—	—	—	—	....	....	....	....
Exp. & Lending Minus Repay	82z	3,816.1	4,460.9	5,080.1	5,968.5	6,735.6	7,595.1	8,240.2	8,919.7	....	....	....	....
Expenditure	82	3,842.7	4,482.0	5,137.1	5,982.8	6,695.3	7,575.8	8,235.4	8,853.3	....	....	....	....
Lending Minus Repayments	83	−26.6	−21.1	−57.0	−14.3	40.3	19.3	4.8	66.4	....	....	....	....
Total Debt by Residence	88	5,686.4	5,477.7	5,056.4	4,719.1	4,588.0	4,657.6	5,159.4	5,606.9	....	....	....	....
Domestic	88a	3,431.6	3,305.6	3,432.1	3,392.0	3,476.5	3,491.6	3,684.3	4,129.2	....	....	....	....
Foreign	89a	2,254.8	2,172.1	1,624.3	1,327.1	1,111.5	1,165.9	1,475.1	1,477.7	....	....	....	....
National Accounts						*Billions of Pesos*							
Househ.Cons.Expend.,incl.NPISHs	96f	12,458.9	14,648.7	17,270.3	19,785.0	21,972.0	23,703.6	23,927.9	25,897.2	27,772.0	29,241.8	31,229.5	33,097.8
Government Consumption Expend	91f	2,017.9	2,420.1	2,938.5	3,426.1	3,860.5	4,197.1	4,603.8	5,053.9	5,480.8	5,943.9	6,313.7	6,656.3
Gross Fixed Capital Formation	93e	5,001.7	5,649.2	7,117.9	8,240.7	9,414.2	9,545.7	7,740.1	8,410.7	9,456.7	9,879.1	10,769.3	11,822.2
Changes in Inventories	93i	189.7	110.3	294.9	312.9	211.8	281.7	22.8	457.4	159.6	157.0	393.8	617.0
Exports of Goods and Services	90c	5,132.0	6,544.1	8,295.4	8,520.5	9,404.2	9,608.6	10,992.3	12,820.2	14,501.0	15,773.5	18,553.3	23,487.9
Imports of Goods and Services (-)	98c	5,516.7	6,158.5	7,672.6	9,047.9	10,140.1	10,801.9	10,148.4	12,064.1	13,833.3	14,653.5	16,528.9	18,324.2
Gross Domestic Product (GDP)	99b	19,276.5	23,714.7	28,309.2	31,237.3	34,722.6	36,534.9	37,138.5	40,575.3	43,536.8	46,341.8	50,730.7	57,357.0
Net Primary Income from Abroad	98.n	−689.7	−1,072.3	−1,106.4	−1,033.0	−1,104.5	−869.6	−1,132.6	−1,552.5	−1,588.0	−1,965.1	−3,165.2	−4,939.3
Gross National Income (GNI)	99a	17,285.2	20,322.9	24,769.3	30,204.3	33,618.1	35,665.3	36,005.9	39,022.8	41,948.8	44,376.8	47,565.5	52,417.7
Consumption of Fixed Capital	99cf	1,692.7	1,957.3	2,269.8	4,122.4	4,424.2	4,644.6	5,007.2	5,257.3	5,706.9	6,184.2	6,579.1	....
Net National Income	99e	17,414.7	20,461.7	24,892.5	30,414.1	33,837.0	35,879.9	36,410.1	39,151.9	40,860.7	....	....	....
GDP Vol.1996 Prices	99b.p	24,868.7	26,289.6	29,084.5	31,237.3	33,300.7	34,376.6	34,115.0	35,646.5	37,007.0	37,655.1	39,060.2	41,427.3
GDP Volume (2000=100)	99bvp	69.8	73.8	81.6	87.6	93.4	96.4	95.7	100.0	103.8	105.6	109.6	116.2
GDP Deflator (2000=100)	99bip	68.1	79.2	85.5	87.9	91.6	93.4	95.6	100.0	103.4	108.1	114.1	121.6
						Millions: Midyear Estimates							
Population	99z	13.92	14.16	14.39	14.62	14.83	15.03	15.22	15.41	15.60	15.78	15.95	16.12

		1993	1994	1995	1996	1997	1998	1999	2000	2001	2002	2003	2004
Exchange Rates						*Yuan per SDR: End of Period*							
Market Rate............aa=.........	wa	7.9666	12.3302	12.3637	11.9325	11.1715	11.6567	11.3637	10.7847	10.4017	11.2532	12.2989	12.8535
					Yuan per US Dollar: End of Period (we) Period Average (wf)								
Market Rate............ae=.........	we	5.8000	8.4462	8.3174	8.2982	8.2798	8.2787	8.2795	8.2774	8.2768	8.2773	8.2767	8.2765
Market Rate............rf=.........	wf	5.7620	8.6187	8.3514	8.3142	8.2898	8.2790	8.2783	8.2771	8.2770	8.2770	8.2768
					Index Numbers (2000=100): Period Averages								
Nominal Effective Exchange Rate.....	nec	95.75	86.68	85.63	89.25	95.11	99.45	97.31	100.00	104.49	103.59	96.47	92.01
Real Effective Exchange Rate...........	rec	69.81	75.90	84.57	92.76	98.84	100.81	97.51	100.00	104.32	102.64	96.67	94.95
Fund Position						*Millions of SDRs: End of Period*							
Quota..	2f.s	3,385	3,385	3,385	3,385	3,385	3,385	4,687	4,687	6,369	6,369	6,369	6,369
SDRs..	1b.s	352	369	392	427	447	480	540	613	677	734	741	803
Reserve Position in the Fund...........	1c.s	513	517	818	971	1,682	2,523	1,685	1,462	2,061	2,738	2,556	2,138
Total Fund Cred.&Loans Outstg........	2tl	—	—	—	—	—	—	—	—	—	—	—	—
International Liquidity						*Millions of US Dollars Unless Otherwise Indicated: End of Period*							
Total Reserves Minus Gold..............	1l.d	22,387	52,914	75,377	107,039	142,762	149,188	157,728	168,278	215,605	291,128	408,151	614,500
SDRs....................................	1b.d	484	539	582	614	602	676	741	798	851	998	1,102	1,247
Reserve Position in the Fund.........	1c.d	704	755	1,216	1,396	2,270	3,553	2,312	1,905	2,590	3,723	3,798	3,320
Foreign Exchange........................	1d.d	21,199	51,620	73,579	105,029	139,890	144,959	154,675	165,574	212,165	286,407	403,251	609,932
Gold (Million Fine Troy Ounces)........	1ad	12.7	12.7	12.7	12.7	12.7	12.7	12.7	12.7	16.1	19.3	19.3	19.3
Gold (National Valuation).................	1and	612	646	660	637	601	624	608	578	3,093	4,074	4,074	4,074
Banking Institutions: Liabilities.........	7b.d	† 39,230	44,890	50,370	55,990	59,035	54,685	47,057	49,536	37,477	47,317	53,221	64,588
Monetary Authorities						*Billions of Yuan: End of Period*							
Foreign Assets..............................	11	† 154.95	445.13	666.95	956.22	1,345.21	1,376.17	1,485.75	1,558.28	1,986.04	2,324.29	3,114.18	4,696.01
Claims on Central Government.........	12a	158.27	168.77	158.28	158.28	158.28	158.28	158.28	158.28	282.13	286.38	290.10	296.96
Claims on Other Sectors..................	12d	† 68.23	72.83	68.01	65.87	17.10	10.38	10.15	11.02	19.55	20.67	20.63	13.63
Claims on Deposit Money Banks......	12e	† 960.95	1,045.10	1,151.03	1,451.84	1,435.79	1,305.75	1,537.39	1,351.92	1,131.16	998.26	1,061.95	937.64
Claims on Other Banking Insts.........	12f	25.17	26.99	18.16	11.77	207.23	296.28	383.31	860.04	854.73	† 230.51	136.33	104.79
Claims on Nonbank Financial Insts...	12g						....	....	....	....	724.03	725.60	886.51
Reserve Money...............................	14	† 1,314.70	1,721.78	2,075.98	2,688.85	3,145.45	3,233.94	3,478.81	3,791.38	4,171.30	4,692.18	5,517.17	6,234.67
Of which Curr.Outside Banking Inst	14a	† 577.65	728.44	788.19	879.89	1,017.46	1,120.07	1,345.21	1,464.99	1,568.73	1,727.80	1,974.60	2,131.29
Bonds..	16ab	—	—	19.71	—	11.89	11.89	11.89			148.75	303.16	1,107.90
Foreign Liabilities...........................	16c	—	—	—	—	22.29	20.14	39.90	39.39	50.91	42.31	48.26	56.23
Central Government Deposits...........	16d	† 47.34	83.33	97.34	122.54	† 66.42	72.20	61.73	167.81	98.93	130.19	262.44	234.16
Capital Accounts.............................	17a	32.92	29.49	40.04	39.51	39.27	39.44	39.37	38.23	37.98	24.64	24.89	25.02
Other Items (Net).............................	17r	† −27.39	−75.78	−170.64	−206.92	−121.70	−230.76	−56.82	−97.26	−85.50	−453.93	−807.12	−722.45
Banking Institutions						*Billions of Yuan: End of Period*							
Reserves.......................................	20	† 594.32	768.59	1,006.41	1,387.00	1,645.68	1,511.15	1,610.78	1,619.32	1,817.14	2,041.32	2,428.93	3,739.81
Foreign Assets..............................	21	† 294.87	440.47	390.50	428.68	531.95	600.90	646.58	903.57	1,017.55	1,284.31	1,147.86	1,429.77
Claims on Central Government.........	22a	7.45	47.82	105.73	182.30	151.98	498.79	607.94	739.31	1,104.51	1,355.36	1,523.22	1,849.78
Claims on Other Sectors..................	22d	† 3,388.60	4,104.28	5,097.18	6,358.26	7,693.40	8,951.61	9,986.66	11,132.41	12,180.33	† 14,280.97	17,249.40	19,186.46
Claims on Nonbank Financial Insts...	22g	....	....	....	....	....	....	....	....	....	903.62	1,314.89	791.80
Demand Deposits...........................	24	† 969.29	1,238.99	1,520.16	1,876.49	2,381.03	2,648.57	3,235.62	3,846.88	4,414.01	5,356.21	6,431.42	7,442.32
Savings Deposits............................	25aa	† 1,458.29	2,051.60	2,804.55	3,637.34	4,363.52	5,020.57	5,580.51	5,975.44	6,785.08	7,954.16	9,463.32	11,955.54
Time Deposits................................	25ab	218.88	194.31	332.42	504.19	673.85	830.19	947.68	1,126.11	1,418.01	1,643.38	2,094.04	2,538.22
Foreign Currency Deposits...............	25b	....	....	....	....	....	....	....	....	....	1,215.91	1,188.43	1,212.86
Other Deposits...............................	25e	214.80	292.13	377.70	401.74	315.07	383.55	496.20	586.97	679.86	804.18	1,021.00	1,062.62
Bonds..	26ab	24.79	21.30	18.91	29.98	354.18	520.38	635.46	742.89	844.80	1,010.24	1,165.40	1,520.35
Foreign Liabilities...........................	26c	† 227.53	379.15	418.95	464.61	488.80	452.72	389.61	410.03	310.19	391.66	440.50	534.57
Credit from Monetary Authorities.....	26g	† 971.56	1,034.44	1,119.78	1,423.29	1,403.85	1,206.98	828.92	913.44	964.67	1,243.39	1,086.14	980.29
Liabilities to Nonbank Fin. Insts........	26j	....	....	....	....	....	....	....	....	....	856.73	995.55	951.54
Capital Accounts.............................	27a	† 283.72	343.25	351.58	411.37	428.59	658.27	626.34	739.67	765.98	877.22	1,072.93	1,179.14
Other Items (Net).............................	27r	† −83.62	−194.01	−344.23	−392.77	−385.88	−158.78	111.64	53.18	−63.07	−1,487.51	−1,294.43	−2,379.83
Banking Survey						*Billions of Yuan: End of Period*							
Foreign Assets (Net)........................	31n	† 222.29	506.45	638.50	920.29	1,366.07	1,504.20	1,702.82	2,012.43	2,642.48	3,174.63	3,773.29	5,534.99
Domestic Credit..............................	32	† 3,575.21	4,310.37	5,331.86	6,642.17	7,954.34	9,546.87	10,701.30	11,873.21	13,487.60	17,440.83	20,861.40	22,790.97
Claims on Central Govt. (Net)........	32an	† 118.38	133.26	166.67	218.04	243.84	584.88	704.49	729.79	1,287.71	1,511.55	1,550.89	1,912.58
Claims on Other Sectors...............	32d	† 3,456.83	4,177.11	5,165.19	6,424.13	7,710.50	8,961.99	9,996.82	11,143.43	12,199.89	† 14,301.64	17,270.02	19,200.09
Claims on Nonbank Financial Insts.	32g										1,627.64	2,040.49	1,678.30
Money...	34	† 1,546.94	1,967.43	2,308.35	2,756.38	3,480.65	3,869.05	4,697.64	5,454.10	6,168.85	7,266.54	8,644.89	9,930.60
Quasi-Money..................................	35	† 2,021.14	2,724.60	3,766.00	4,853.15	5,706.13	6,686.96	7,406.57	8,141.93	9,472.34	† 11,412.52	13,710.43	15,723.69
Foreign Currency Deposits..............	35b	....	....	....	....	....	....	....	....	....	1,215.91	1,188.43	1,212.86
Bonds..	36ab	24.79	21.30	38.62	29.98	356.31	526.40	642.69	742.12	844.23	1,079.66	1,173.93	1,678.71
Capital Accounts.............................	37a	† 316.64	372.74	391.62	450.88	467.86	697.71	665.70	777.90	803.96	901.86	1,097.82	1,204.15
Other Items (Net).............................	37r	† −112.01	−269.25	−534.23	−527.93	−690.53	−729.05	−1,008.46	−1,230.39	−1,159.30	† −1,261.02	−1,180.80	−1,424.06
Money plus Quasi-Money.................	35l	† 3,568.08	4,692.03	6,074.35	7,609.53	9,186.78	10,556.01	12,104.21	13,596.02	15,641.19	18,679.05	22,355.32	25,654.29
Interest Rates						*Percent per Annum*							
Bank Rate......................................	60	10.08	10.08	10.44	9.00	8.55	4.59	3.24	3.24	3.24	2.70	2.70	3.33
Deposit Rate..................................	60l	10.98	10.98	10.98	7.47	5.67	3.78	2.25	2.25	2.25	1.98	1.98	2.25
Lending Rate..................................	60p	10.98	10.98	12.06	10.08	8.64	6.39	5.85	5.85	5.85	5.31	5.31	5.58
Prices, Production, Labor						*Percent Change over Corresponding Period of Previous Year*							
Consumer Prices............................	64..x	14.6	24.2	16.9	8.3	2.8	−.8	−1.4	.3	.5	−.8	1.2	4.0
Industrial Production........................	66..x	....	21.4	16.1	15.1	13.2	9.6	9.8	11.2	9.9	....	....	....
						Number in Thousands: Period Averages							
Employment...................................	67e	663,730	674,550	680,650	689,500	698,200	706,370	713,940	720,850	730,250	737,400	....	....
Unemployment...............................	67c	4,201	4,764	5,196	5,528	5,768	5,710	5,750	5,950	6,810	7,700	....	....
Unemployment Rate (%).................	67r	2.6	2.8	2.9	3.0	3.0	3.1	3.1	3.1	3.6	4.0	....	....
Intl. Transactions & Positions						*Millions of US Dollars*							
Exports.......................................	70..d	91,744	121,006	148,780	151,048	182,792	183,712	194,931	249,203	266,098	325,591	437,899	593,439
Imports, c.i.f.................................	71..d	103,959	115,614	132,084	138,833	142,370	140,237	165,699	225,094	243,553	295,171	413,062	560,683

		1993	1994	1995	1996	1997	1998	1999	2000	2001	2002	2003	2004
Balance of Payments		*Millions of US Dollars: Minus Sign Indicates Debit*											
Current Account, n.i.e....................	78ald	−11,609	6,908	1,618	7,243	36,963	31,472	21,115	20,518	17,401	35,422	45,875	....
Goods: Exports f.o.b.....................	78aad	75,659	102,561	128,110	151,077	182,670	183,529	194,716	249,131	266,075	325,651	438,270	....
Goods: Imports f.o.b.....................	78abd	−86,313	−95,271	−110,060	−131,542	−136,448	−136,915	−158,734	−214,657	−232,058	−281,484	−393,618	....
Trade Balance.............................	78acd	−10,654	7,290	18,050	19,535	46,222	46,614	35,982	34,474	34,017	44,167	44,652	....
Services: Credit...........................	78add	11,193	16,620	19,130	20,601	24,569	23,895	26,248	30,430	33,334	39,745	46,734	
Services: Debit.............................	78aed	−12,036	−16,299	−25,223	−22,585	−27,967	−26,672	−31,589	−36,031	−39,267	−46,528	−55,306	
Balance on Goods & Services......	78afd	−11,497	7,611	11,958	17,551	42,824	43,837	30,641	28,874	28,084	37,383	36,079	
Income: Credit.............................	78agd	4,390	5,737	5,191	7,318	5,710	5,584	8,330	12,550	9,388	8,344	16,095	
Income: Debit..............................	78ahd	−5,674	−6,775	−16,965	−19,755	−16,715	−22,228	−22,800	−27,216	−28,563	−23,289	−23,933	
Balance on Gds, Serv. & Inc........	78aid	−12,781	6,573	184	5,114	31,819	27,193	16,171	14,207	8,909	22,438	28,241	
Current Transfers, n.i.e.: Credit.....	78ajd	1,290	1,269	1,827	2,368	5,477	4,661	5,368	6,861	9,125	13,795	18,482	
Current Transfers: Debit................	78akd	−118	−934	−392	−239	−333	−382	−424	−550	−633	−811	−848	
Capital Account, n.i.e...................	78bcd	—	—	—	—	−21	−47	−26	−35	−54	−50	−48	
Capital Account, n.i.e.: Credit.......	78bad	—	—	—	—								
Capital Account: Debit.................	78bbd	—	—	—	—	−21	−47	−26	−35	−54	−50	−48	
Financial Account, n.i.e.................	78bjd	23,474	32,645	38,674	39,966	21,037	−6,275	5,204	1,958	34,832	32,341	52,774	
Direct Investment Abroad.............	78bdd	−4,400	−2,000	−2,000	−2,114	−2,563	−2,634	−1,775	−916	−6,884	−2,518	152	
Dir. Invest. in Rep. Econ., n.i.e.......	78bed	27,515	33,787	35,849	40,180	44,237	43,751	38,753	38,399	44,241	49,308	47,077	
Portfolio Investment Assets...........	78bfd	−597	−380	79	−628	−899	−3,830	−10,535	−11,307	−20,654	−12,095	2,983	
Equity Securities.......................	78bkd	—	—	—	—	—	....	....	....	32			
Debt Securities.........................	78bld	−597	−380	79	−628	−899	−3,830	−10,535	−11,307	−20,686	−12,095	2,983	
Portfolio Investment Liab., n.i.e......	78bgd	3,646	3,923	710	2,372	7,842	98	−699	7,317	1,249	1,752	8,444	
Equity Securities.......................	78bmd	—	....	....	....	5,657	765	612	6,912	849	2,249	7,729	
Debt Securities.........................	78bnd	3,646	3,923	710	2,372	2,185	−667	−1,311	405	400	−497	715	
Financial Derivatives Assets...........	78bwd	....	....	....	....	....	....	....	....	....	....	....	
Financial Derivatives Liabilities.......	78bxd	....	....	....	....	....	....	....	....	....	....	....	
Other Investment Assets..............	78bhd	−2,114	−1,189	−1,081	−1,126	−39,608	−35,041	−24,394	−43,864	20,813	−3,077	−17,922	
Monetary Authorities................	78bod	....	....	....	....	−7,977	−2,417	−5,715	−7,261	−5,387			
General Government..................	78bpd	−1,741	−1,136	−367	−1,102	....	....	....		—	—	—	
Banks......................................	78bqd	—	....	....	....	−12,572	2,841	6,075	−21,430	16,800	−10,258	−15,733	
Other Sectors...........................	78brd	−373	−53	−714	−24	−19,059	−35,465	−24,754	−15,173	9,400	7,181	−2,189	
Other Investment Liab., n.i.e.........	78bid	−576	−1,496	5,116	1,282	12,028	−8,619	3,854	12,329	−3,933	−1,029	12,040	
Monetary Authorities................	78bsd	175	1,004	1,154	1,256	−2,037	−5,441	−3,936	—	—	—	—	
General Government..................	78btd	1,564	5,178	6,021	4,995			3,233	3,153	1,124	40	−2,758	
Banks......................................	78bud	−415	−5,222	−4,045	−5,959	6,968	−3,150	−5,021	−8,281	−1,305	−1,725	10,269	
Other Sectors...........................	78bvd	−1,900	−2,456	1,986	990	7,097	−28	9,578	17,457	−3,752	655	4,529	
Net Errors and Omissions................	78cad	−10,096	−9,100	−17,823	−15,504	−22,122	−18,902	−17,641	−11,748	−4,732	7,504	17,985	
Overall Balance..........................	78cbd	1,769	30,453	22,469	31,705	35,857	6,248	8,652	10,693	47,447	75,217	116,586	
Reserves and Related Items............	79dad	−1,769	−30,453	−22,469	−31,705	−35,857	−6,248	−8,652	−10,693	−47,447	−75,217	−116,586	
Reserve Assets..........................	79dbd	−1,769	−30,453	−22,469	−31,705	−35,857	−6,248	−8,652	−10,693	−47,447	−75,217	−116,586	
Use of Fund Credit and Loans........	79dcd	—	—	—	—	—	—	—	—	—	—	—	
Exceptional Financing...................	79ded	....	....	....	....	....	....	....	....	....	—	....	
Government Finance		*Billions of Yuan: Year Ending December 31*											
Deficit (-) or Surplus......................	80	−70.46	−94.07	−90.93	−86.70	−92.70	−125.57	−203.39	−277.03	−438.29f	−309.78	−291.69	
Total Revenue and Grants.............	81y	434.90	521.81	624.22	740.80	865.11	987.60	1,144.40	1,339.50	1,476.00f	1,917.35	2,191.71	
Exp. & Lending Minus Repay..........	82z	505.36	615.88	715.15	827.50	957.81	1,113.17	1,347.79	1,616.53	1,914.29	2,227.13	2,483.40	
Financing													
Domestic.................................	84a	33.36	63.64	69.96	55.35	56.44	95.25	188.26	260.49	256.90	319.33	315.69	
Foreign...................................	85a	−4.02	3.06	−3.68	6.53	−.60	.56	−9.10	−.45	3.61	−9.53	4.61	
Use of Cash Balances.....................	87	—	−9.25	−8.13	−7.93	—	−3.58	−4.80	−10.56	....	....	....	
National Accounts		*Billions of Yuan*											
Househ.Cons.Expend.,incl.NPISHs....	96f	1,568.2	2,081.0	2,694.5	3,215.2	3,485.5	3,692.1	3,933.4	4,291.1	4,592.3	4,888.2	5,267.9	....
Government Consumption Expend...	91f	450.0	598.6	669.1	785.2	872.5	948.5	1,038.8	1,170.5	1,302.9	1,391.7	1,476.4	
Gross Fixed Capital Formation.........	93e	1,298.0	1,685.6	2,030.1	2,333.6	2,515.4	2,763.1	2,947.6	3,262.4	3,681.3	4,191.8	5,124.8	
Changes in Inventories....................	93i	201.8	240.4	357.7	353.1	330.3	191.5	122.6	−12.4	64.8	38.7	13.4	....
Exports (Net)................................	90n	−67.9	63.4	99.9	145.9	285.7	305.2	244.9	224.0	220.5	279.4	268.6	....
Gross Domestic Product (GDP)........	99b	3,450.1	4,669.1	5,851.1	6,833.0	7,489.4	7,900.3	8,267.3	8,934.1	9,859.3	10,789.8	12,151.1	13,651.5
Net Primary Income from Abroad.....	98.n	−7.4	−8.9	−98.3	....	....	....	....	....	....	....	....	
Gross National Income (GNI)...........	99a	3,442.7	4,660.1	5,752.7	....	....	....	....	....	....	....	....	
GDP Volume 1995 Prices..............	99b.p	4,699.7	5,294.8	5,851.1	6,412.0	6,976.5	7,520.9	8,055.9	8,700.4	....	....	....	
GDP Volume (2000=100)...............	99bvp	54.0	60.9	67.3	73.7	80.2	86.4	92.6	100.0	....	....	....	
GDP Deflator (2000=100)...............	99bip	71.5	85.9	97.4	103.8	104.5	102.3	99.9	100.0	....	....	....	
		Millions: Midyear Estimates											
Population...............................	99z	1,195.7	1,207.6	1,219.3	1,231.0	1,242.4	1,253.5	1,264.1	1,274.0	1,283.2	1,291.8	1,300.0	1,308.0

		1993	1994	1995	1996	1997	1998	1999	2000	2001	2002	2003	2004
Exchange Rates						*Hong Kong Dollars per SDR: End of Period*							
Market Rate	aa	10.612	11.296	11.494	11.124	10.451	10.907	10.666	10.157	9.799	10.602	11.536	12.072
					Hong Kong Dollars per US Dollar: End of Period (ae) Period Average (rf)								
Market Rate	ae	7.726	7.738	7.732	7.736	7.746	7.746	7.771	7.796	7.797	7.798	7.763	7.774
Market Rate	rf	7.736	7.728	7.736	7.734	7.742	7.745	7.758	7.791	7.799	7.799	7.787	7.788
					Index Numbers (2000=100) Period Averages								
Nominal Effective Exchange Rate	nec	92.45	92.59	88.28	91.36	96.28	101.77	98.95	100.00	104.37	103.76	98.16	94.21
Fund Position						*Millions of SDRs: End of Period*							
Reserve Position in the Fund	1c.s	—	—	—	—	31.34	—	—	—	—	—	—	—
of which: Outstg.Fund Borrowing	2c	—	—	—	—	31.34	—	—	—	—	—	—	—
International Liquidity					*Billions of US Dollars Unless Otherwise Indicated: End of Period*								
Total Reserves minus Gold	1l.d	42.99	49.25	55.40	63.81	92.80	89.65	96.24	107.54	111.16	111.90	118.36	123.54
Reserve Position in the Fund	1c.d	—	—	—	—	—	.04	—	—	—	—	—	—
Foreign Exchange	1d.d	42.99	49.25	55.40	63.81	†92.80	†89.61	96.24	107.54	111.16	111.90	118.36	123.54
Gold (Million Fine Troy Ounces)	1ad	.068	.068	.067	.067	.067	.067	.067	.067	.067	.067	.067	.067
Gold (National Valuation)	1and	.026	.026	.026	.025	.019	.019	.019	.018	.019	.023	.028	.029
Banking Institutions: Assets	7a.d	518.78	614.80	655.58	608.62	600.63	501.17	475.78	450.48	405.22	394.41	440.28	508.07
Liabilities	7b.d	477.58	582.33	620.40	579.85	597.32	447.35	371.87	319.15	264.39	244.74	267.03	308.54
Monetary Authorities						*Billions of Hong Kong Dollars: End of Period*							
Foreign Assets	11	290.52	297.27	376.59	463.89	549.97	672.68	691.27	803.69	822.50	832.87	868.65	904.91
Reserve Money	14	72.79	79.88	82.96	87.12	92.71	94.77	†234.39	215.40	229.74	246.11	292.67	294.87
of which: Currency Outside Banks	14a	62.89	67.31	70.87	76.05	80.34	80.92	99.27	91.51	101.38	112.98	127.61	140.55
Foreign Liabilities	16c	.03	1.54	.03	.32	.04	.27	.04	19.82	42.08	1.67	1.01	.10
Government Deposits	16d	115.68	131.24	125.92	145.90	237.63	424.56	392.21	417.16	380.60	301.67	252.30	280.09
Capital Accounts	17a	127.54	125.77	160.13	172.86	190.21	242.22	290.86	307.10	302.59	327.17	384.88	423.59
Other Items (Net)	17r	−25.52	−41.17	7.56	57.69	29.38	−89.15	−226.22	−155.79	−132.51	−43.75	−62.21	−93.75
Banking Institutions						*Billions of Hong Kong Dollars: End of Period*							
Reserves	20	9.91	12.57	12.09	11.07	12.37	13.85	32.67	14.34	12.53	11.91	41.18	28.36
Foreign Assets	21	4,008.11	4,757.31	5,068.93	4,708.31	4,652.49	3,882.07	3,697.31	3,511.95	3,159.51	3,075.65	3,417.93	3,949.50
Claims on Government	22a	56.77	106.77	57.25	104.74	143.61	140.34	166.64	201.19	212.75	234.12	220.67	272.53
Claims on Other Sectors	22d	1,256.02	1,506.39	1,671.93	1,935.32	2,324.36	2,181.93	1,964.83	2,010.95	1,968.19	1,890.33	1,837.65	1,906.44
Demand Deposits	24	87.71	83.38	80.32	98.33	87.44	79.07	85.35	93.05	109.51	127.39	196.44	231.83
Time, Savings,& Fgn.Currency Dep	25	1,357.87	1,534.82	1,713.81	1,923.57	2,113.05	2,374.65	2,560.47	2,816.59	2,781.96	2,768.92	2,874.11	3,060.47
Money Market Instruments	26aa	46.83	71.26	82.62	107.13	118.16	116.51	110.77	103.79	107.79	143.08	170.67	190.98
Foreign Liabilities	26c	3,689.75	4,506.08	4,796.95	4,485.74	4,626.87	3,465.16	2,889.78	2,488.13	2,061.42	1,908.48	2,072.93	2,398.47
Government Deposits	26d	26.60	18.87	14.43	19.09	5.16	6.15	3.78	2.93	1.46	2.51	2.38	4.16
Capital Accounts	27a	104.85	113.03	132.61	153.91	170.34	153.67	154.03	164.10	204.27	207.72	188.87	214.60
Other Items (Net)	27r	17.20	55.58	−10.56	−28.33	11.78	22.98	57.27	69.84	86.58	53.91	12.01	56.34
Banking Survey						*Billions of Hong Kong Dollars: End of Period*							
Foreign Assets (Net)	31n	608.86	546.96	648.53	686.14	575.54	1,089.32	1,498.76	1,807.70	1,878.52	1,998.37	2,212.64	2,455.84
Domestic Credit	32	1,170.50	1,463.04	1,588.84	1,875.07	2,225.17	1,891.55	1,735.49	1,792.05	1,798.88	1,820.27	1,803.64	1,894.73
Claims on Government (net)	32an	−85.51	−43.34	−83.10	−60.25	−99.18	−290.38	−229.34	−218.90	−169.31	−70.06	−34.00	−11.71
Claims on Other Sectors	32d	1,256.02	1,506.39	1,671.93	1,935.32	2,324.36	2,181.93	1,964.83	2,010.95	1,968.19	1,890.33	1,837.65	1,906.44
Money	34	150.60	150.70	151.19	174.38	167.78	159.99	184.62	184.56	210.88	240.37	324.06	372.38
Quasi-Money	35	1,357.87	1,534.82	1,713.81	1,923.57	2,113.05	2,374.65	2,560.47	2,816.59	2,781.96	2,768.92	2,874.11	3,060.47
Money Market Instruments	36aa	46.83	71.26	82.62	107.13	118.16	116.51	110.77	103.79	107.79	143.08	170.67	190.98
Capital Accounts	37a	232.39	238.81	292.75	326.77	360.55	395.89	444.89	471.20	506.86	534.90	573.75	638.19
Other Items (Net)	37r	−8.32	14.40	−3.00	29.36	41.16	−66.17	−66.49	23.61	69.90	131.37	73.69	88.54
Money plus Quasi-Money	35l	1,508.46	1,685.52	1,865.00	2,097.95	2,280.84	2,534.64	2,745.08	3,001.15	2,992.84	3,009.29	3,198.17	3,432.85
Interest Rates						*Percent Per Annum*							
Discount Rate (End of Period)	60	4.00	5.75	6.25	6.00	7.00	6.25	7.00	8.00	3.25	2.75	2.50	3.75
Money Market Rate	60b	4.00	5.44	6.00	5.13	4.50	5.50	5.75	7.13	2.69	1.50	.07	.13
Treasury Bill Rate	60c	3.17	5.66	5.55	4.45	7.50	5.04	4.94	5.69	1.69	1.35	−.08	.07
Deposit Rate	60l	2.25	3.54	5.63	4.64	5.98	6.62	4.50	4.80	2.38	.35	.07	.03
Lending Rate	60p	6.50	8.50	8.75	8.50	9.50	9.50	9.00	8.50	5.13	5.00	5.00	5.00
Prices, Production, Labor						*Index Numbers (2000=100): Period Averages*							
Share Prices	62	46.5	59.4	56.2	71.6	83.4	58.8	79.1	100.0	78.4	65.2	64.1	80.5
Producer Prices	63	98.8	100.9	103.7	103.6	†103.3	101.4	99.8	100.0	98.4	95.7	95.4	97.6
Consumer Prices	64	78.8	85.7	93.5	99.4	105.2	108.2	103.9	100.0	98.4	95.4	92.9	92.5
Wages:Avg.Earnings(Mfg)	65	....	72.4	80.2	†86.3	93.4	99.3	98.6	100.0	102.1	100.9	97.8	97.2
Wage Rates (Manufacturing)	65a	75.5	81.6	86.2	92.7	97.6	98.4	97.8	100.0	102.7	101.1	97.3	96.3
Manufacturing Production	66ey	122.2	121.9	123.1	118.5	†117.6	107.4	100.5	100.0	95.6	86.3	78.3	80.6
						Number in Thousands: Period Averages							
Labor Force	67d	2,873	2,972	3,001	3,094	3,216	3,359	....	3,383	3,427	3,488	3,501	....
Employment	67e	2,800	2,873	2,905	†3,073	3,164	3,122	3,112	3,207	3,252	3,232	3,223	....
Unemployment	67c	56	56	96	†87	71	154	208	167	175	256	277	241
Unemployment Rate (%)	67r	2.0	1.9	3.2	†2.8	2.2	4.7	6.3	5.0	5.1	7.3	7.9	6.8
Intl. Transactions & Positions						*Billions of US Dollars*							
Exports	70..d	135.24	151.40	173.75	180.75	188.06	174.00	173.89	201.86	189.89	200.09	223.76	259.31
Imports, c.i.f	71..d	138.65	161.84	192.75	198.55	208.61	184.52	179.52	212.81	201.08	207.64	231.90	271.16
						2000=100							
Volume of Exports	72	62.6	69.1	77.4	81.1	86.1	82.4	85.4	100.0	96.7	104.9	119.6	138.0
Volume of Imports	73	62.8	71.6	81.4	84.9	91.0	84.5	84.7	100.0	98.0	105.7	119.2	135.9
Unit Value of Exports	74	104.1	105.6	109.1	108.8	107.0	103.0	100.2	100.0	97.7	95.1	93.8	94.8
Unit Value of Imports	75	102.4	105.1	110.4	109.0	106.5	101.3	99.2	100.0	96.9	93.1	92.8	95.4

		1993	1994	1995	1996	1997	1998	1999	2000	2001	2002	2003	2004
Balance of Payments						*Millions of US Dollars Minus Sign Indicates Debit*								
Current Account, n.i.e.	78ald	....	....	....	....	....	2,529	10,248	6,993	9,786	12,412	16,470	16,357
Goods: Exports f.o.b.	78aad	....	....	....	....	....	175,833	174,719	202,698	190,926	200,300	224,656	260,263
Goods: Imports f.o.b.	78abd	....	....	....	....	....	−183,666	−177,878	−210,891	−199,257	−205,353	−230,435	−269,575
Trade Balance	78acd	....	....	....	....	....	−7,833	−3,159	−8,193	−8,331	−5,053	−5,779	−9,312
Services: Credit	78add	....	....	....	....	....	33,235	34,226	38,735	39,449	43,001	45,625	53,578
Services: Debit	78aed	....	....	....	....	....	−24,991	−23,725	−24,584	−24,677	−25,603	−25,921	−29,818
Balance on Goods & Services	78afd	....	....	....	....	....	412	7,342	5,958	6,441	12,345	13,925	14,449
Income: Credit	78agd	....	....	....	....	....	46,831	47,147	53,623	49,464	43,342	44,620	50,756
Income: Debit	78ahd	....	....	....	....	....	−43,117	−42,701	−50,917	−44,340	−41,380	−40,238	−46,866
Balance on Gds, Serv. & Inc.	78aid	....	....	....	....	....	4,125	11,788	8,663	11,565	14,307	18,307	18,338
Current Transfers, n.i.e.: Credit	78ajd	....	....	....	....	....	669	570	538	605	777	529	590
Current Transfers: Debit	78akd	....	....	....	....	....	−2,265	−2,109	−2,208	−2,385	−2,673	−2,366	−2,571
Capital Account, n.i.e.	78bcd	....	....	....	....	....	−2,382	−1,780	−1,546	−1,174	−2,011	−1,065	−275
Capital Account, n.i.e.: Credit	78bad	....	....	....	....	....	377	103	57	41	31	132	1,130
Capital Account: Debit	78bbd	....	....	....	....	....	−2,759	−1,883	−1,602	−1,215	−2,042	−1,197	−1,406
Financial Account, n.i.e.	78bjd	....	....	....	....	....	−8,476	1,061	4,165	−6,626	−19,751	−20,953	−13,944
Direct Investment Abroad	78bdd	....	....	....	....	....	−16,985	−19,369	−59,352	−11,345	−17,463	−5,492	−39,753
Dir. Invest. in Rep. Econ., n.i.e.	78bed	....	....	....	....	....	14,765	24,578	61,924	23,776	9,682	13,624	34,034
Portfolio Investment Assets	78bfd	....	....	....	....	....	25,492	−25,440	−22,022	−40,133	−37,702	−35,386	−36,919
Equity Securities	78bkd	....	....	....	....	....	8,507	−30,337	−17,606	−22,682	−15,756	−9,951	−27,747
Debt Securities	78bld	....	....	....	....	....	16,985	4,897	−4,416	−17,452	−21,946	−25,435	−9,172
Portfolio Investment Liab., n.i.e.	78bgd	....	....	....	....	....	−3,407	58,525	46,508	−1,161	−1,084	1,386	4,646
Equity Securities	78bmd	....	....	....	....	....	−2,106	60,470	46,976	−855	1,391	5,771	3,041
Debt Securities	78bnd	....	....	....	....	....	−1,301	−1,944	−468	−305	−2,475	−4,385	1,605
Financial Derivatives Assets	78bwd	....	....	....	....	....	10,837	21,224	8,445	17,971	20,035	30,005	18,145
Financial Derivatives Liabilities	78bxd	....	....	....	....	....	−7,538	−11,011	−8,240	−12,888	−13,424	−19,958	−11,874
Other Investment Assets	78bhd	....	....	....	....	....	119,830	42,963	18,279	59,137	46,617	−28,671	−41,402
Monetary Authorities	78bod	....	....	....	....	....	....	....	....	....	....	....	....
General Government	78bpd	....	....	....	....	....	....	....	....	....	....	....	....
Banks	78bqd	....	....	....	....	....	101,774	34,181	23,857	61,452	46,037	−18,154	−53,279
Other Sectors	78brd	....	....	....	....	....	18,057	8,781	−5,578	−2,315	580	−10,517	11,877
Other Investment Liab., n.i.e.	78bid	....	....	....	....	....	−151,470	−90,410	−41,375	−41,985	−26,412	23,539	59,177
Monetary Authorities	78bsd	....	....	....	....	....	....	....	....	....	....	....	....
General Government	78btd	....	....	....	....	....	....	....	....	....	....	....	....
Banks	78bud	....	....	....	....	....	−148,616	−85,768	−44,259	−42,888	−20,937	20,199	56,526
Other Sectors	78bvd	....	....	....	....	....	−2,854	−4,642	2,884	903	−5,475	3,340	2,651
Net Errors and Omissions	78cad	....	....	....	....	....	1,539	499	431	2,699	6,973	6,541	1,148
Overall Balance	78cbd	....	....	....	....	....	−6,789	10,028	10,044	4,684	−2,377	994	3,286
Reserves and Related Items	79dad	....	....	....	....	....	6,789	−10,028	−10,044	−4,684	2,377	−994	−3,286
Reserve Assets	79dbd	....	....	....	....	....	6,789	−10,028	−10,044	−4,684	2,377	−994	−3,286
Use of Fund Credit and Loans	79dcd	....	....	....	....	....	....	....	....	....	....	....	....
Exceptional Financing	79ded	....	....	....	....	....	....	....	....	....	....	....	....
International Investment Position						*Millions of US Dollars*								
Assets	79aad	....	....	....	....	....	....	....	1,141,521	1,071,005	1,030,103	1,185,407	1,382,397
Direct Investment Abroad	79abd	....	....	....	....	235,763	223,811	321,635	388,380	352,602	309,430	339,649	405,615
Portfolio Investment	79acd	....	....	....	....	....	....	....	178,851	205,600	244,068	334,912	400,289
Equity Securities	79add	....	....	....	....	....	....	....	88,325	94,615	95,721	152,831	199,447
Debt Securities	79aed	....	....	....	....	....	....	....	90,526	110,984	148,347	182,081	200,842
Financial Derivatives	79ald	....	....	....	....	....	....	....	16,812	17,529	22,521	19,846	22,342
Other Investment	79afd	....	....	....	....	....	....	....	449,880	384,088	342,158	372,604	430,595
Monetary Authorities	79agd	....	....	....	....	....	....	....	....	....	....	....	....
General Government	79ahd	....	....	....	....	....	....	....	....	....	....	....	....
Banks	79aid	....	....	....	....	....	....	....	393,157	318,398	275,831	299,642	355,961
Other Sectors	79ajd	....	....	....	....	....	....	....	56,723	65,690	66,327	72,961	74,634
Reserve Assets	79akd	....	....	....	....	92,855	89,639	96,287	107,599	111,187	111,927	118,396	123,556
Liabilities	79lad	....	....	....	....	....	....	....	919,670	805,779	686,763	791,251	952,047
Dir. Invest. in Rep. Economy	79lbd	....	....	....	....	249,360	225,078	405,266	455,469	419,348	336,278	381,342	456,862
Portfolio Investment	79lcd	....	....	....	....	....	....	....	153,217	117,031	93,544	125,309	154,645
Equity Securities	79ldd	....	....	....	....	....	....	....	138,078	102,833	79,289	115,688	143,266
Debt Securities	79led	....	....	....	....	....	....	....	15,139	14,198	14,255	9,621	11,379
Financial Derivatives	79lld	....	....	....	....	....	....	....	12,517	12,059	21,198	19,598	21,191
Other Investment	79lfd	....	....	....	....	....	....	....	298,467	257,342	235,742	265,002	319,348
Monetary Authorities	79lgd	....	....	....	....	....	....	....	....	....	....	....	....
General Government	79lhd	....	....	....	....	....	....	....	....	....	....	....	....
Banks	79lid	....	....	....	....	....	....	....	279,017	231,182	213,161	236,968	291,935
Other Sectors	79ljd	....	....	....	....	....	....	....	19,451	26,160	22,581	28,034	27,414

		1993	1994	1995	1996	1997	1998	1999	2000	2001	2002	2003	2004
National Accounts						*Billions of Hong Kong Dollars*							
Househ.Cons.Expend.,incl.NPISHs....	96f	534	617	683	748	825	787	754	760	765	729	699	745
Government Consumption Expend...	91f	72	83	94	104	113	117	120	120	129	131	130	127
Gross Fixed Capital Formation..........	93e	249	306	334	378	452	389	325	347	333	286	261	279
Changes in Inventories....................	93i	2	21	46	10	12	−16	−11	14	−4	6	9	6
Exports of Goods and Services..........	90c	1,246	1,392	1,585	1,670	1,729	1,605	1,615	1,875	1,789	1,897	2,104	2,444
Imports of Goods and Services (-).....	98c	1,191	1,390	1,645	1,699	1,786	1,602	1,558	1,828	1,742	1,801	1,996	2,332
Gross Domestic Product (GDP).........	99b	913	1,030	1,096	1,211	1,345	1,280	1,246	1,288	1,270	1,248	1,208	1,269
Net Primary Income from Abroad.....	98.n	13	12	21	—	10	29	34	21	40	15	34	30
Gross National Income (GNI)............	99a	926	1,042	1,117	1,211	1,355	1,308	1,281	1,309	1,310	1,263	1,242	1,300
Net Current Transf.from Abroad.......	98t	....	....	....	....	−12	−12	−12	−13	−14	−15	−14	−15
Gross Nat'l Disposable Inc.(GNDI)....	99i	....	....	....	....	1,342	1,296	1,269	1,296	1,296	1,248	1,228	1,284
Gross Saving...................................	99s	....	....	....	....	404	393	394	416	402	388	399	412
GDP Volume 1995 Prices.................	99b.p	991	1,045	1,086	1,133	1,190	1,131	1,169	1,288	1,294	1,319	1,361	1,472
GDP Volume (2000=100)...............	99bvp	76.9	81.1	84.3	87.9	92.4	87.8	90.8	100.0	100.5	102.4	105.6	114.2
GDP Deflator (2000=100)...............	99bip	92.1	98.5	101.0	106.9	113.0	113.2	106.6	100.0	98.1	94.6	88.8	86.3
						Millions: Midyear Estimates							
Population..............................	99z	5.98	6.09	6.19	6.28	6.38	6.46	6.55	6.64	6.72	6.80	6.88	6.96

		1993	1994	1995	1996	1997	1998	1999	2000	2001	2002	2003	2004
Exchange Rates						*Patacas Per SDR: End of Period*							
Market Rate	aa	10.928	11.635	11.839	11.457	10.769	11.236	10.987	10.467	10.093	10.921	11.883	12.439
						Patacas per US Dollar: End of Period (ae) Period Average (rf)							
Market Rate	ae	7.956	7.970	7.965	7.968	7.982	7.980	8.005	8.034	8.031	8.033	7.997	8.010
Market Rate	rf	7.968	7.960	7.968	7.966	7.975	7.979	7.992	8.026	8.034	8.033	8.021	8.022
International Liquidity						*Billions of US Dollars Unless Otherwise Indicated: End of Period*							
Total Reserves minus Gold	1l.d	1.57	1.97	2.26	2.42	2.53	2.46	2.86	3.32	3.51	3.80	4.34	5.44
Foreign Exchange	1d.d	1.57	1.97	2.26	2.42	2.53	2.46	2.86	3.32	3.51	3.80	4.34	5.44
Gold (Million Fine Troy Ounces)	1ad	—	—	—	—	—	—	—	—	—	—	—	—
Gold (National Valuation)	1and	—	—	—	—	—	—	—	—	—	—	—	—
Banking Institutions: Assets	7a.d	6.61	6.08	6.77	10.83	10.75	† 12.63	7.83	8.58	9.30	10.65	11.72	12.88
Liabilities	7b.d	4.62	3.96	4.10	7.82	7.92	† 8.30	3.30	3.06	2.85	2.98	2.69	3.10
Monetary Authorities						*Millions of Patacas: End of Period*							
Foreign Assets	11	12,483.6	15,672.0	17,972.4	19,298.9	20,215.3	19,651.1	22,873.1	30,646.3	33,431.6	36,380.5	42,483.7	52,284.1
Claims on Government	12a	132.6	67.2	69.2	85.5	115.0	143.3	190.9	188.6	181.5	191.6	206.4	220.7
Claims on Deposit Money Banks	12e	45.1	59.6	42.3	55.7	53.6	37.7	515.4	6,284.9	5,013.8	3,596.8	2,685.1	2,212.2
Reserve Money	14	2,138.7	2,405.7	2,735.1	2,909.6	3,047.8	3,239.1	3,957.9	3,665.3	3,871.6	4,208.8	4,885.1	5,591.5
of which: Currency Outside Banks	14a	1,080.9	1,197.8	1,280.1	1,426.7	1,518.3	1,554.6	1,819.4	1,717.2	1,895.8	2,053.0	2,361.8	2,772.7
Liab. of Central Bank: Securities	16ac	5,876.5	8,686.3	11,242.7	11,207.2	10,942.6	11,803.9	15,086.4	17,530.0	16,927.7	15,837.5	17,076.1	18,157.0
Foreign Liabilities	16c	.1	.9	.1	103.1	.1	.2	—	—	4.9	—	.1	1.9
Government Deposits	16d	3,761.2	4,246.0	3,160.3	4,555.6	5,744.6	3,835.0	3,450.8	14,320.4	15,662.8	17,596.8	20,643.9	27,891.0
Capital Accounts	17a	1,216.7	1,071.2	1,569.6	1,693.1	1,979.1	2,437.9	2,333.9	2,878.0	3,077.5	3,286.1	3,439.1	3,836.4
Other Items (Net)	17r	−337.1	−611.2	−624.1	−1,028.6	−1,330.2	−1,483.8	−1,249.8	−1,274.0	−917.7	−760.4	−669.1	−760.7
Banking Institutions						*Millions of Patacas: End of Period*							
Reserves	20	1,057.8	1,207.9	1,455.0	1,482.9	1,529.5	1,684.5	2,138.5	1,948.1	1,975.8	2,155.8	2,523.3	2,818.8
Claims on Mon.Author.: Securities	20c	5,876.7	8,686.3	11,242.7	11,207.2	10,942.6	11,803.9	15,086.4	17,530.0	16,927.7	15,837.5	17,076.1	18,157.0
Foreign Assets	21	52,554.5	48,434.0	53,955.6	86,316.3	85,763.6	† 100,793.3	62,680.8	68,927.7	74,657.0	85,554.1	93,722.5	103,190.6
Claims on Government	22a	214.5	143.0	71.5	—	.3	2.2	—	—				
Claims on Nonfin.Pub. Enterprises	22c									1,438.7	2,008.4	1,951.8	1,947.2
Claims on Other Sectors	22d	35,997.1	39,707.3	41,694.5	44,492.5	48,890.5	† 42,808.1	42,111.3	39,127.6	34,897.7	32,321.9	31,895.7	34,768.2
Demand Deposits	24	4,679.7	4,038.6	4,337.6	4,289.2	3,790.7	† 3,954.1	3,543.7	3,228.2	4,020.9	4,297.8	6,427.8	10,668.0
Time & Savings Deposits	25	48,552.9	55,976.9	63,825.8	68,616.8	72,873.9	† 75,118.9	80,733.2	79,972.4	85,633.3	92,608.6	102,300.6	107,506.3
Foreign Liabilities	26c	36,786.8	31,533.0	32,685.2	62,316.5	63,178.3	† 66,239.9	26,433.7	24,598.4	22,861.4	23,974.1	21,488.8	24,797.9
Government Deposits	26d	1,208.3	1,161.6	1,439.4	1,677.6	2,275.6	4,244.5	2,784.9	4,447.9	3,943.1	4,468.7	4,686.0	5,477.1
Credit from Monetary Authorities	26g	45.1	59.6	42.3	55.7	53.6	37.7	515.4	6,284.9	5,013.8	3,596.8	2,685.1	2,212.2
Capital Accounts	27a	3,938.7	4,812.2	5,005.5	5,561.0	6,222.5	6,330.2	5,707.4	6,593.4	7,000.4	7,733.3	8,570.6	9,511.1
Other Items (Net)	27r	490.3	596.6	1,083.4	982.2	−1,268.1	1,166.7	2,298.8	2,408.5	1,424.0	1,198.2	1,010.7	709.1
Banking Survey						*Millions of Patacas: End of Period*							
Foreign Assets (Net)	31n	28,251.2	32,572.1	39,242.7	43,195.6	42,800.5	† 54,204.3	59,120.2	74,975.6	85,222.3	97,960.5	114,717.3	130,674.9
Domestic Credit	32	31,374.7	34,509.9	37,235.5	38,344.8	40,985.6	† 34,874.1	36,066.5	20,547.9	16,912.0	12,456.4	8,724.0	3,568.0
Claims on Government (net)	32an	−4,622.4	−5,197.4	−4,459.0	−6,147.7	−7,904.9	−7,934.0	−6,044.8	−18,579.7	−19,424.4	−21,873.9	−25,123.5	−33,147.4
Claims on Nonfin.Pub. Enterprises	32c	....	....	....	....	....	....	....	....	1,438.7	2,008.4	1,951.8	1,947.2
Claims on Other Sectors	32d	35,997.1	39,707.3	41,694.5	44,492.5	48,890.5	† 42,808.1	42,111.3	39,127.6	34,897.7	32,321.9	31,895.7	34,768.2
Money	34	5,760.6	5,236.4	5,617.7	5,715.9	5,309.0	† 5,508.7	5,363.1	4,945.4	5,916.7	6,350.8	8,789.6	13,440.7
Quasi-Money	35	48,552.9	55,976.9	63,825.8	68,616.8	72,873.9	† 75,118.9	80,733.2	79,972.4	85,633.3	92,608.6	102,300.6	107,506.3
Capital Accounts	37a	5,155.4	5,883.4	6,575.1	7,254.1	8,201.6	8,768.1	8,041.3	9,471.4	10,077.9	11,019.4	12,009.7	13,347.5
Other Items (Net)	37r	153.0	−14.6	459.3	−46.4	−2,598.3	−317.1	1,049.0	1,134.5	506.3	437.8	341.6	−51.6
Money plus Quasi-Money	35l	54,313.5	61,213.3	69,443.5	74,332.7	78,182.9	† 80,627.6	86,096.3	84,917.8	91,550.0	98,959.4	111,090.2	120,947.0
Interest Rates						*Percent Per Annum*							
Interbank Rate (End of Period)	60b	3.79	5.91	6.01	5.60	7.54	5.41	5.70	6.29	2.11	1.48	.11	.27
Deposit Rate	60l	2.75	4.21	5.93	5.23	6.22	7.00	5.30	5.33	2.59	.63	....	....
Lending Rate	60p	6.50	7.95	9.90	9.56	9.73	10.97	9.46	9.89	7.99	6.11	6.00	....
Prices and Labor						*Index Numbers (2000=100): Period Averages*							
Consumer Prices	64	....	....	....	....	....	....	105.0	101.6	100.0	98.0	95.4	93.9	94.9
						Number in Thousands: Period Averages							
Labor Force	67d	175	177	187	202	202	206	209	210	217	214	216	229
Employment	67e	171	173	180	194	196	197	196	195	203	201	203	218
Unemployment	67c	4	4	7	9	7	10	13	14	14	13	13	11
Unemployment Rate (%)	67r	2.1	2.5	3.6	4.3	3.2	4.6	6.3	6.4	6.3	6.0	6.0	4.8
Intl. Transactions & Positions						*Millions of US Dollars*							
Exports	70..d	1,786.6	1,866.0	1,997.3	1,995.8	2,147.8	2,141.1	2,199.6	2,539.0	2,299.5	2,355.8	2,580.8	2,811.8
Imports, c.i.f.	71..d	2,025.5	2,126.2	2,041.6	1,999.8	2,081.8	1,954.9	2,039.5	2,254.7	2,386.3	2,529.8	2,755.2	3,477.9

		1993	1994	1995	1996	1997	1998	1999	2000	2001	2002	2003	2004
Balance of Payments					*Millions of US Dollars Minus Sign Indicates Debit*								
Current Account, n.i.e.....................	78ald	....	....	....	....	....	....	....	....	....	2,737	3,177	....
Goods: Exports f.o.b.....................	78aad	....	....	....	....	....	....	....	....	....	2,358	2,585	....
Goods: Imports f.o.b.....................	78abd	....	....	....	....	....	....	....	....	....	−3,277	−3,678	....
Trade Balance........................	78acd	....	....	....	....	....	....	....	....	....	−920	−1,093	....
Services: Credit...........................	78add	....	....	....	....	....	....	....	....	....	4,758	5,605	....
Services: Debit............................	78aed	....	....	....	....	....	....	....	....	....	−1,073	−1,177	....
Balance on Goods & Services......	78afd	....	....	....	....	....	....	....	....	....	2,766	3,335	....
Income: Credit...........................	78agd	....	....	....	....	....	....	....	....	....	449	394	....
Income: Debit............................	78ahd	....	....	....	....	....	....	....	....	....	−469	−547	....
Balance on Gds, Serv. & Inc.........	78aid	....	....	....	....	....	....	....	....	....	2,746	3,182	....
Current Transfers, n.i.e.: Credit......	78ajd	....	....	....	....	....	....	....	....	....	90	103	....
Current Transfers: Debit................	78akd	....	....	....	....	....	....	....	....	....	−99	−108	....
Capital Account, n.i.e....................	78bcd	....	....	....	....	....	....	....	....	....	139	88	....
Capital Account, n.i.e.: Credit........	78bad	....	....	....	....	....	....	....	....	....	161	113	....
Capital Account: Debit..................	78bbd	....	....	....	....	....	....	....	....	....	−23	−25	....
Financial Account, n.i.e................	78bjd	....	....	....	....	....	....	....	....	....	−1,088	−1,684	....
Direct Investment Abroad..............	78bdd	....	....	....	....	....	....	....	....	....	−71	5	....
Dir. Invest. in Rep. Econ., n.i.e......	78bed	....	....	....	....	....	....	....	....	....	412	509	....
Portfolio Investment Assets...........	78bfd	....	....	....	....	....	....	....	....	....	−903	−1,191	....
Equity Securities....................	78bkd	....	....	....	....	....	....	....	....	....	−290	−358	....
Debt Securities......................	78bld	....	....	....	....	....	....	....	....	....	−613	−834	....
Portfolio Investment Liab., n.i.e......	78bgd	....	....	....	....	....	....	....	....	....	1	—	....
Equity Securities....................	78bmd	....	....	....	....	....	....	....	....	....	1	—	....
Debt Securities......................	78bnd	....	....	....	....	....	....	....	....	....	....	....	....
Financial Derivatives Assets...........	78bwd	....	....	....	....	....	....	....	....	....	118	−114	....
Financial Derivatives Liabilities.......	78bxd	....	....	....	....	....	....	....	....	....	....	....	....
Other Investment Assets...............	78bhd	....	....	....	....	....	....	....	....	....	−877	−816	....
Monetary Authorities..................	78bod	....	....	....	....	....	....	....	....	....	—	—	....
General Government....................	78bpd	....	....	....	....	....	....	....	....	....	−15	−12	....
Banks...........................	78bqd	....	....	....	....	....	....	....	....	....	−1,015	−760	....
Other Sectors......................	78brd	....	....	....	....	....	....	....	....	....	153	−44	....
Other Investment Liab., n.i.e..........	78bid	....	....	....	....	....	....	....	....	....	232	−78	....
Monetary Authorities..................	78bsd	....	....	....	....	....	....	....	....	....	....	....	....
General Government....................	78btd	....	....	....	....	....	....	....	....	....	—	—	....
Banks...........................	78bud	....	....	....	....	....	....	....	....	....	265	−119	....
Other Sectors......................	78bvd	....	....	....	....	....	....	....	....	....	−33	41	....
Net Errors and Omissions................	78cad	....	....	....	....	....	....	....	....	....	−1,495	−1,056	....
Overall Balance........................	78cbd	....	....	....	....	....	....	....	....	....	293	524	....
Reserves and Related Items.............	79dad	....	....	....	....	....	....	....	....	....	−293	−524	....
Reserve Assets........................	79dbd	....	....	....	....	....	....	....	....	....	−293	−524	....
Use of Fund Credit and Loans........	79dcd	....	....	....	....	....	....	....	....	....	....	....	....
Exceptional Financing...................	79ded	....	....	....	....	....	....	....	....	....	....	....	....
Government Finance					*Millions of Patacas: Year Ending December 31*								
Deficit (-) or Surplus........................	80	....	....	....	25.4	882.2	−457.3	−452.8	777.3	....	....	....	....
Total Revenue and Grants..............	81y	....	....	....	9,491.9	10,934.6	10,098.8	10,749.4	9,809.6	....	....	....	....
Revenue.................................	81	....	....	....	9,491.6	10,934.3	10,098.7	10,749.4	9,809.6	....	....	....	....
Grants..................................	81z	....	....	....	.3	.3	.1	—	—	....	....	....	....
Exp. & Lending Minus Repay.........	82z	....	....	....	9,466.5	10,052.4	10,556.1	11,202.2	9,032.3	....	....	....	....
Expenditure...........................	82	....	....	....	8,817.8	9,530.9	10,071.0	11,033.7	9,004.5	....	....	....	....
Lending Minus Repayments.........	83	....	....	....	648.7	521.5	485.1	168.5	27.8	....	....	....	....
National Accounts					*Millions of Patacas*								
Househ.Cons.Expend.,incl.NPISHs...	96f	14,585.6	16,494.8	18,202.6	19,760.0	20,537.0	20,231.9	20,102.4	19,706.9	19,797.6	20,222.5	20,670.5	22,735.0
Government Consumption Expend...	91f	3,589.1	4,159.2	4,791.5	5,335.9	5,877.4	6,182.2	6,918.8	6,045.1	6,108.2	6,322.9	6,828.3	7,095.3
Gross Fixed Capital Formation.........	93e	14,140.5	15,620.1	14,654.0	10,769.9	10,811.2	8,829.8	8,275.1	5,618.3	5,119.0	5,800.7	8,981.9	13,392.0
Changes in Inventories....................	93i	421.6	585.3	253.6	540.7	112.8	−71.8	83.3	73.7	18.8	240.2	318.0	375.0
Exports of Goods and Services..........	90c	35,711.5	38,418.4	43,232.5	44,063.2	44,552.6	41,756.6	41,119.1	49,179.5	51,038.3	57,166.0	65,691.5	87,549.9
Imports of Goods and Services (-).....	98c	26,378.0	28,562.6	28,860.5	27,664.3	28,659.5	27,568.2	29,211.2	31,651.2	32,377.4	34,933.5	38,925.8	48,461.7
Gross Domestic Product (GDP)........	99b	42,070.4	46,715.3	52,273.9	52,805.5	53,231.5	49,360.4	47,287.4	48,972.4	49,704.4	54,818.7	63,564.3	82,685.5
GDP Volume 1996 Prices................	99b.p	51,561.6	53,754.6	55,526.3	55,293.5	55,139.1	52,618.8	51,021.4	53,380.6	54,560.2	60,031.7	69,409.6	....
GDP Volume 2002 Prices................	99b.p	....	....	....	....	....	46,862.1	45,756.8	48,386.4	49,784.0	54,818.7	62,581.7	80,089.0
GDP Volume (2000=100)...............	99bvp	94.9	98.9	102.2	101.8	101.5	† 96.8	94.6	100.0	102.9	113.3	129.3	165.5
GDP Deflator (2000=100)...............	99bip	90.5	96.4	104.4	105.9	107.1	104.1	102.1	100.0	98.6	98.8	100.4	102.0
					Millions: Midyear Estimates								
Population..............................	99z	.40	.41	.41	.42	.43	.43	.44	.44	.45	.45	.45	.46

		1993	1994	1995	1996	1997	1998	1999	2000	2001	2002	2003	2004
Exchange Rates						*Pesos per SDR: End of Period*							
Principal Rate	aa	1,260.01	1,213.53	1,468.13	1,445.62	1,745.36	2,122.63	2,571.77	2,849.49	2,892.15	3,894.74	4,132.22	3,746.02
						Pesos per US Dollar: End of Period (ae) Period Average (rf)							
Principal Rate	ae	917.33	831.27	987.65	1,005.33	1,293.58	1,507.52	1,873.77	2,187.02	2,301.33	2,864.79	2,780.82	2,412.10
Principal Rate	rf	863.06	844.84	912.83	1,036.69	1,140.96	1,426.04	1,756.23	2,087.90	2,299.63	2,504.24	2,877.65	2,628.61
						Index Numbers (2000=100): Period Averages							
Principal Rate	ahx	241.6	247.0	229.0	201.0	183.8	146.6	119.6	100.0	90.6	82.4	72.4	79.3
Nominal Effective Exchange Rate	nec	177.2	198.9	180.7	168.6	165.2	136.4	113.9	100.0	94.7	86.8	71.6	74.9
Real Effective Exchange Rate	rec	91.3	102.9	104.6	111.9	124.5	118.7	107.4	100.0	100.2	95.2	82.0	88.4
Fund Position						*Millions of SDRs: End of Period*							
Quota	2f.s	561	561	561	561	561	561	774	774	774	774	774	774
SDRs	1b.s	115	116	119	123	128	139	95	103	108	113	115	117
Reserve Position in the Fund	1c.s	80	87	135	165	263	408	286	286	286	286	286	286
Total Fund Cred.&Loans Outstg.	2tl	—	—	—	—	—	—	—	—	—	—	—	—
International Liquidity						*Millions of US Dollars Unless Otherwise Indicated: End of Period*							
Total Reserves minus Gold	1l.d	7,930	7,991	8,349	9,845	9,803	8,651	8,008	8,916	10,154	10,732	10,784	13,394
SDRs	1b.d	158	170	177	177	172	196	131	135	135	154	171	181
Reserve Position in the Fund	1c.d	110	127	201	237	355	575	392	372	359	389	425	444
Foreign Exchange	1d.d	7,663	7,694	7,971	9,431	9,275	7,880	7,485	8,409	9,659	10,190	10,188	12,769
Gold (Million Fine Troy Ounces)	1ad	.302	.293	.267	.252	.358	.358	.328	.328	.327	.327	.327	.327
Gold (National Valuation)	1and	119	112	119	94	104	103	95	89	91	112	136	143
Monetary Authorities:Other Assets	3..d	378	425	420	420	419	422	418	448	412	452	464	473
Other Liab.	4..d	602	383	473	355	249	237	212	187	184	133	129	60
Deposit Money Banks: Assets	7a.d	544	506	443	484	1,031	944	552	458	357	341	516	513
Liabilities	7b.d	1,655	1,854	2,136	2,654	3,316	2,868	1,712	1,365	1,120	1,122	793	1,346
Other Banking Insts.: Assets	7e.d	149	169	134	257	199	162	211	133	164	121	132	539
Liabilities	7f.d	2,271	3,182	3,476	4,241	3,834	3,352	2,837	1,860	1,287	1,221	847	966
Monetary Authorities						*Billions of Pesos: End of Period*							
Foreign Assets	11	6,709.4	7,073.1	8,760.5	10,402.8	13,295.7	13,841.5	15,953.9	20,665.9	24,660.9	31,824.1	31,941.6	33,497.2
Claims on Central Government	12a	679.6	711.1	565.0	725.0	574.3	951.6	2,397.2	2,767.5	2,034.3	2,384.3	3,210.7	990.4
Claims on Nonfin.Pub.Enterprises	12c	9.3	—	—	—	—	—	—	—	—	—	—	—
Claims on Private Sector	12d	6.2	52.2	81.6	105.8	128.3	538.8	541.4	397.6	203.0	200.8	181.6	205.4
Claims on Deposit Money Banks	12e	75.6	66.3	239.9	62.6	416.3	905.8	2,508.5	1,536.3	919.2	1,807.4	3,206.1	1,992.4
Claims on Other Banking Insts.	12f	322.6	339.0	436.9	264.9	286.0	377.9	481.5	853.9	374.3	544.7	484.8	460.8
Claims on Nonbank Financial Insts.	12g	—	—	—	133.1	408.8	579.5	681.6	802.7	893.2	1,000.9	1,050.5	1,057.2
Reserve Money	14	4,605.8	5,902.5	6,301.1	7,415.6	8,640.7	7,165.0	10,012.5	10,922.4	12,003.0	14,441.8	16,816.9	19,402.1
of which: Currency Outside DMBs.	14a	1,804.4	2,373.3	2,994.3	3,536.0	4,453.0	4,997.3	6,505.9	7,676.6	8,653.6	10,188.5	12,196.6	13,948.7
Time, Savings,& Fgn.Currency Dep.	15	31.7	49.6	9.9	14.0	.8	120.4	101.3	7.9	2.0	1.3	1.0	.8
Money Market Instruments	16aa	1,231.7	392.2	214.7	723.0	.5	15.8	—	—	—	—	—	—
Restricted Deposits	16b	.4	.4	.4	.4	.3	.4	.3	.3	—	—	—	—
Foreign Liabilities	16c	483.5	317.8	466.3	356.1	320.6	358.5	396.5	407.8	461.0	375.3	361.0	144.4
Central Government Deposits	16d	414.3	475.6	128.4	247.3	349.0	236.8	235.5	339.6	402.6	283.3	341.2	1,182.4
Capital Accounts	17a	1,104.3	1,388.1	3,110.2	3,231.1	6,120.0	9,644.1	12,089.9	15,696.9	16,963.9	23,484.6	23,470.6	18,494.2
Other Items (Net)	17r	−69.0	−284.5	−147.1	−293.3	−322.6	−345.9	−271.8	−351.0	−747.5	−824.2	−915.2	−1,020.5
Deposit Money Banks						*Billions of Pesos: End of Period*							
Reserves	20	2,461.1	2,937.1	2,736.3	2,890.2	3,544.7	2,157.1	3,242.9	3,008.2	3,201.2	4,112.9	4,459.2	5,287.1
Foreign Assets	21	437.3	419.9	437.0	485.9	1,326.9	1,427.0	1,033.9	1,001.5	893.9	961.0	1,449.4	1,226.2
Claims on Central Government	22a	337.8	430.9	463.7	617.1	1,441.0	2,454.1	2,167.1	5,525.5	9,616.7	13,179.7	16,569.7	22,358.1
Claims on Local Government	22b	347.3	1,009.7	1,407.0	1,715.4	3,214.1	3,498.4	3,577.6	3,373.2	3,746.1	3,783.4	3,582.4	3,244.8
Claims on Nonfin.Pub.Enterprises	22c	8.1	68.7	100.0	89.1	136.4	301.4	295.5	450.3	395.3	427.6	379.0	739.9
Claims on Private Sector	22d	7,701.0	11,266.6	15,162.0	18,547.0	26,167.9	33,048.8	31,334.5	32,452.5	36,215.7	40,461.1	44,158.2	49,138.8
Claims on Other Banking Insts.	22f	560.7	1,081.2	1,581.3	2,714.1	2,970.9	3,125.2	6,597.7	7,243.4	7,015.5	6,336.9	7,169.6	8,031.0
Demand Deposits	24	2,883.8	3,626.1	4,271.9	5,272.8	6,251.6	5,673.3	6,533.1	8,825.6	9,622.9	11,256.3	12,545.1	14,769.6
Time, Savings,& Fgn.Currency Dep.	25	4,217.7	6,447.3	8,005.4	10,036.5	16,709.5	23,452.4	25,587.6	27,956.5	33,498.9	37,454.3	39,933.3	47,758.8
Money Market Instruments	26aa	221.5	294.7	247.4	185.1	122.9	103.7	56.9	45.2	48.3	40.1	27.4	34.2
Bonds	26ab	69.7	670.5	823.2	1,715.6	2,772.2	2,826.9	1,684.7	1,406.3	1,467.1	1,384.4	1,199.6	1,724.7
Restricted Deposits	26b	5.8	18.5	21.8	25.6	32.6	37.9	29.8	140.8	84.0	142.6	481.2	575.4
Foreign Liabilities	26c	1,329.9	1,537.2	2,107.6	2,664.2	4,267.7	4,333.4	3,205.0	2,984.3	2,807.6	3,156.9	2,227.4	3,217.0
Central Government Deposits	26d	816.7	1,015.3	1,319.0	1,666.7	2,333.0	2,457.4	2,243.1	2,615.1	3,526.4	3,443.9	5,393.3	4,856.1
Credit from Monetary Authorities	26g	119.6	122.9	119.4	104.0	73.3	934.0	2,471.6	1,538.5	904.9	1,908.4	3,106.7	1,992.1
Liabilities to Other Banking Insts.	26i	1,484.5	1,878.4	2,474.4	2,708.5	3,011.4	4,250.2	3,586.7	4,308.9	3,970.3	4,063.5	4,500.4	4,770.9
Capital Accounts	27a	1,719.5	2,676.0	3,558.6	4,808.3	6,159.0	5,179.0	6,120.2	6,201.0	6,477.8	7,131.9	8,231.4	10,128.0
Other Items (Net)	27r	−1,015.4	−1,072.8	−1,061.4	−2,128.5	−2,931.3	−3,236.2	−3,269.5	−2,967.8	−1,323.7	−719.6	121.8	199.1
Monetary Survey						*Billions of Pesos: End of Period*							
Foreign Assets (Net)	31n	5,333.3	5,638.0	6,623.6	7,868.4	10,034.3	10,576.6	13,386.4	18,275.3	22,286.3	29,252.8	30,802.7	31,362.0
Domestic Credit	32	8,741.6	13,468.5	18,350.1	22,997.5	32,645.6	42,181.5	45,595.6	50,911.8	56,565.0	64,592.1	71,052.2	80,188.0
Claims on Central Govt. (Net)	32an	−213.6	−348.9	−418.7	−571.9	−666.7	711.5	2,085.8	5,338.3	7,722.0	11,836.7	14,045.9	17,310.0
Claims on Local Government	32b	347.3	1,009.7	1,407.0	1,715.4	3,214.1	3,498.4	3,577.6	3,373.2	3,746.1	3,783.4	3,582.4	3,244.8
Claims on Nonfin.Pub.Enterprises	32c	17.4	68.7	100.0	89.1	136.4	301.4	295.5	450.3	395.3	427.6	379.0	739.9
Claims on Private Sector	32d	7,707.2	11,318.8	15,243.6	18,652.8	26,296.2	33,587.6	31,875.9	32,850.1	36,418.6	40,662.0	44,339.9	49,344.2
Claims on Other Banking Insts.	32f	883.3	1,420.2	2,018.2	2,979.0	3,256.9	3,503.1	7,079.3	8,097.3	7,389.8	6,881.6	7,654.5	8,491.8
Claims on Nonbank Financial Inst.	32g	—	—	—	133.1	408.8	579.5	681.6	802.7	893.2	1,000.9	1,050.5	1,057.2
Money	34	5,211.3	6,722.4	8,078.5	9,966.0	11,697.9	10,772.0	13,376.7	16,837.0	18,450.6	21,576.4	24,916.9	28,904.8
Quasi-Money	35	4,249.4	6,496.9	8,015.3	10,050.5	16,710.3	23,572.8	25,688.9	27,964.4	33,500.9	37,455.6	39,934.3	47,759.6
Money Market Instruments	36aa	1,453.2	686.9	462.1	908.1	123.4	119.5	56.9	45.2	48.3	40.1	27.4	34.2
Bonds	36ab	69.7	670.5	823.2	1,715.6	2,772.2	2,826.9	1,684.7	1,406.3	1,467.1	1,384.4	1,199.6	1,724.7
Restricted Deposits	36b	6.2	18.9	22.2	26.0	32.9	38.3	30.2	141.2	84.0	142.6	481.2	575.4
Liabilities to Other Banking Insts.	36i	1,484.5	1,878.4	2,474.4	2,708.5	3,011.4	4,250.2	3,586.7	4,308.9	3,970.3	4,063.5	4,500.4	4,770.9
Capital Accounts	37a	2,823.8	4,064.1	6,668.8	8,039.4	12,279.0	14,823.1	18,210.1	21,897.9	23,441.7	30,616.6	31,702.0	28,622.2
Other Items (Net)	37r	−1,223.2	−1,431.6	−1,570.8	−2,548.2	−3,947.3	−3,644.7	−3,652.2	−3,413.8	−2,111.6	−1,434.2	−906.9	−841.9
Money plus Quasi-Money	35l	9,460.7	13,219.3	16,093.8	20,016.5	28,408.2	34,344.8	39,065.6	44,801.4	51,951.5	59,032.0	64,851.2	76,664.4

Colombia   233

		1993	1994	1995	1996	1997	1998	1999	2000	2001	2002	2003	2004
Other Banking Institutions						*Billions of Pesos: End of Period*							
Reserves	40	548.5	702.0	988.1	1,282.4	1,103.8	334.8	641.8	481.5	269.9	131.6	188.2	199.6
Foreign Assets	41	120.0	140.2	132.0	258.5	256.7	244.9	394.2	289.8	411.0	339.6	370.7	1,288.7
Claims on Central Government	42a	202.0	273.7	131.1	155.7	265.2	1,306.3	3,607.2	3,519.3	3,519.0	3,956.9	4,801.2	5,121.4
Claims on Local Government	42b	30.8	783.2	1,294.4	1,472.6	1,256.2	870.9	649.1	630.1	465.1	398.8	521.4	418.7
Claims on Nonfin.Pub.Enterprises	42c	1,329.9	676.7	765.9	974.7	1,329.3	2,244.4	1,759.3	1,853.6	1,777.9	1,944.3	2,029.9	1,724.8
Claims on Private Sector	42d	7,623.3	10,207.6	13,978.3	17,955.1	19,457.4	18,014.6	18,975.6	13,836.5	11,240.7	10,202.0	7,947.1	9,316.5
Claims on Deposit Money Banks	42e	1,560.4	2,271.5	2,993.6	3,275.9	3,466.2	4,692.0	4,633.3	5,169.5	5,336.4	5,566.9	8,398.4	9,158.5
Demand Deposits	44	—	—	—	—	—	—	—	—	—	—	—	—
Time, Savings,& Fgn.Currency Dep	45	6,064.6	9,501.0	12,870.1	15,339.3	15,222.5	13,657.5	15,000.6	11,166.5	8,457.3	5,537.4	7,407.9	9,168.6
Money Market Instruments	46aa	15.2	89.4	35.0	15.1	13.1	16.9	1.5	1.6	1.4	1.3	—	—
Bonds	46ab	869.0	578.8	1,052.1	3,379.5	3,577.5	2,976.2	2,534.3	1,447.4	1,194.8	1,029.3	966.1	1,561.3
Restricted Deposits	46b	7.6	7.1	6.4	5.9	.7	.7	3.1	3.3	22.3	—	.4	.5
Foreign Liabilities	46c	1,824.9	2,638.9	3,430.4	4,258.3	4,934.8	5,065.1	5,310.9	4,065.4	3,227.4	3,435.9	2,378.0	2,309.2
Central Government Deposits	46d	261.5	322.8	390.7	357.4	266.1	420.8	598.8	584.0	378.3	228.7	119.3	737.8
Credit from Monetary Authorities	46g	250.2	280.5	232.4	209.5	96.6	362.7	533.7	976.5	375.5	407.5	392.6	378.3
Credit from Deposit Money Banks	46h	628.0	1,112.2	1,632.2	1,617.5	2,176.8	2,505.6	5,695.9	6,519.5	7,440.2	8,065.0	8,140.6	8,065.4
Capital Accounts	47a	1,985.7	2,874.4	4,034.8	5,214.9	6,004.5	7,076.0	7,952.5	7,991.1	7,788.8	7,953.2	6,074.7	7,140.0
Other Items (Net)	47r	−491.8	−2,350.2	−3,400.7	−5,022.6	−5,157.8	−4,373.4	−6,970.7	−6,974.7	−5,866.1	−4,118.1	−1,222.9	−2,132.9
Banking Survey						*Billions of Pesos: End of Period*							
Foreign Assets (Net)	51n	3,628.4	3,139.3	3,325.2	3,868.6	5,356.2	5,756.4	8,469.6	14,499.7	19,469.8	26,156.5	28,795.3	30,341.5
Domestic Credit	52	16,782.8	23,666.7	32,110.9	40,219.2	51,430.7	60,693.8	62,908.8	62,070.2	65,799.6	73,983.9	78,578.0	87,539.8
Claims on Central Govt. (Net)	52an	−273.1	−398.0	−678.3	−773.6	−667.6	1,597.0	5,094.2	8,273.6	10,862.6	15,564.9	18,727.8	21,693.6
Claims on Local Government	52b	378.1	1,792.9	2,701.4	3,188.0	4,470.3	4,369.3	4,226.8	4,003.3	4,211.3	4,182.2	4,103.8	3,663.5
Claims on Nonfin.Pub.Enterprises	52c	1,347.3	745.4	865.9	1,063.8	1,465.7	2,545.8	2,054.8	2,303.9	2,173.2	2,371.9	2,409.0	2,464.7
Claims on Private Sector	52d	15,330.5	21,526.4	29,221.9	36,608.0	45,753.6	51,602.2	50,851.5	46,686.7	47,659.3	50,864.0	52,286.9	58,660.8
Claims on Nonbank Financial Inst.	52g	—	—	—	133.1	408.8	579.5	681.6	802.7	893.2	1,000.9	1,050.5	1,057.2
Liquid Liabilities	55l	14,976.8	22,018.3	27,975.8	34,073.4	42,527.0	47,667.6	53,424.3	55,486.4	60,138.9	64,437.8	72,070.8	85,633.4
Money Market Instruments	56aa	1,468.4	776.3	497.1	923.2	136.5	136.4	58.4	46.8	49.7	41.3	27.5	34.2
Bonds	56ab	938.7	1,249.3	1,875.3	5,095.1	6,349.7	5,803.1	4,219.0	2,853.7	2,661.9	2,413.7	2,165.8	3,286.0
Restricted Deposits	56b	13.8	26.0	28.6	31.9	33.6	38.9	33.2	144.4	106.4	142.6	481.6	576.0
Capital Accounts	57a	4,809.5	6,938.5	10,703.6	13,254.3	18,283.5	21,899.1	26,162.6	29,889.0	31,230.5	38,569.8	37,776.8	35,762.2
Other Items (Net)	57r	−1,796.0	−4,202.4	−5,644.3	−9,290.1	−10,543.4	−9,094.8	−12,519.0	−11,850.4	−8,917.9	−5,464.8	−5,149.0	−7,410.5
Money (National Definitions)						*Billions of Pesos: End of Period*							
Reserve Money	19mb	4,419.0	5,634.4	6,267.1	6,627.6	8,287.1	6,923.1	9,739.6	10,710.4	11,647.9	14,107.4	16,441.5	19,260.2
M1	59ma	5,124.8	6,419.0	7,717.8	8,992.8	10,948.0	10,526.5	12,814.0	16,720.8	18,737.0	21,635.6	24,918.3	29,113.7
M2	59mb	15,817.3	22,569.1	28,961.3	34,815.5	43,794.6	48,558.1	53,670.5	56,178.6	62,158.4	66,672.2	74,758.4	88,342.4
M3	59mc	17,222.7	24,623.9	31,900.8	41,299.2	52,528.2	56,638.6	60,574.0	62,276.3	68,572.5	74,199.6	83,153.9	97,097.8
Interest Rates						*Percent Per Annum*							
Discount Rate (End of Period)	60	33.49	44.90	40.42	35.05	31.32	42.28	23.05	18.28	16.40	12.73	12.95	12.76
Money Market Rate	60b	....	....	22.40	28.37	23.83	35.00	18.81	10.87	10.43	6.06	6.95	7.01
Deposit Rate	60l	25.84	29.42	32.34	31.15	24.13	32.58	21.33	12.15	12.44	8.94	7.80	7.80
Lending Rate	60p	35.81	40.47	42.72	41.99	34.22	42.24	† 25.77	18.79	20.72	16.33	15.19	15.08
Prices, Production, Labor						*Index Numbers (2000=100): Period Averages*							
Share Prices	62	62.9	114.7	95.5	100.0	148.8	129.4	115.6	100.0	106.2	148.6	234.8	399.9
Producer Prices	63	37.3	43.7	51.6	† 59.4	68.6	80.4	88.3	100.0	109.4	115.2	125.7	132.2
Consumer Prices	64	32.6	40.4	48.8	† 58.7	69.6	82.6	91.6	100.0	108.0	114.8	123.0	130.3
Manufacturing Production	66ey	101.5	105.0	107.2	104.4	106.9	105.3	....	100.0	102.0	102.3	106.1	111.1
Vol.of Gold Produced(1990=100)	66kr	92.8	71.1	....	....	....	....	....	100.0	....	....	....	....
Crude Petroleum Prod	66aa	65.1	65.1	83.8	90.2	91.5	104.9	115.4	100.0	87.7	82.3	76.8	73.8
Labor Force	67d	....	5,261	....	6,153	6,452	6,653	7,056	7,436	† 19,617	19,704	20,409	....
Employment	67e	5,333	5,408	5,494	5,451	5,702	5,655	5,641	5,910	† 16,498	16,620	17,467	....
Unemployment	67c	447	442	522	735	782	998	1,415	1,526	† 2,942	3,098	2,878	2,767
Unemployment Rate (%)	67r	7.8	7.6	8.7	11.9	12.1	15.0	20.1	20.5	† 14.7	15.7	14.2	13.6
Intl. Transactions & Positions						*Millions of US Dollars*							
Exports	70..d	7,115.9	8,418.5	10,056.2	10,587.0	11,522.4	10,890.1	11,575.4	13,043.3	12,289.9	11,911.0	12,671.0	16,223.5
Coffee	70e.d	1,139.7	1,990.1	1,831.8	1,576.5	2,259.0	1,891.0	1,324.0	1,080.3	764.2	772.0	806.5	....
Imports, c.i.f	71..d	9,831.5	11,882.9	13,852.9	13,683.6	15,377.7	14,634.5	10,658.6	11,538.8	12,833.6	12,737.7	13,892.4	16,745.7
Imports, f.o.b	71.vd	9,085.7	11,039.3	12,921.2	12,793.7	14,408.9	13,726.2	9,990.1	10,783.6	12,009.8	11,911.2	13,034.9	15,629.2
Volume of Exports						*2000=100*							
Coffee	72e	146.9	127.5	105.9	114.5	119.0	121.7	108.2	100.0	118.6	126.1	125.3	....
Export Prices in Pesos	76	31.9	41.6	48.8	† 51.8	62.8	70.0	80.2	100.0	98.1	102.4	120.4	121.1
Import Prices in Pesos	76.x	42.2	45.9	53.0	† 60.8	65.2	75.3	86.1	100.0	108.2	114.8	131.0	130.5
Export Prices						*2000=100: Indices of Prices in US Dollars*							
Coffee	76e.d	70.4	129.0	158.7	128.5	196.6	142.9	116.5	100.0	69.4	63.0	64.0	....

		1993	1994	1995	1996	1997	1998	1999	2000	2001	2002	2003	2004
Balance of Payments						*Millions of US Dollars: Minus Sign Indicates Debit*							
Current Account, n.i.e.	78ald	−2,102	−3,667	−4,516	−4,627	−5,739	−4,850	679	768	−1,085	−1,332	−969	−952
Goods: Exports f.o.b.	78aad	7,429	9,059	10,593	10,966	12,065	11,480	12,037	13,722	12,848	12,316	13,825	17,246
Goods: Imports f.o.b.	78abd	−9,086	−11,288	−13,139	−13,058	−14,703	−13,930	−10,262	−11,090	−12,269	−12,077	−13,258	−15,878
Trade Balance	78acd	−1,657	−2,229	−2,546	−2,092	−2,638	−2,450	1,775	2,633	579	239	567	1,368
Services: Credit	78add	2,520	1,571	1,700	2,192	2,156	1,955	1,940	2,049	2,190	1,867	1,900	2,236
Services: Debit	78aed	−2,321	−2,620	−2,873	−3,371	−3,645	−3,409	−3,136	−3,300	−3,594	−3,294	−3,322	−4,009
Balance on Goods & Services	78afd	−1,458	−3,277	−3,719	−3,270	−4,127	−3,904	579	1,382	−825	−1,188	−855	−405
Income: Credit	78agd	561	702	678	716	920	949	923	1,051	914	711	548	663
Income: Debit	78ahd	−2,344	−2,161	−2,274	−2,778	−3,246	−2,646	−2,278	−3,337	−3,529	−3,559	−3,994	−4,857
Balance on Gds, Serv. & Inc.	78aid	−3,240	−4,736	−5,315	−5,333	−6,453	−5,601	−776	−905	−3,439	−4,037	−4,302	−4,599
Current Transfers, n.i.e.: Credit	78ajd	1,350	1,262	1,033	924	931	912	1,703	1,911	2,656	3,008	3,568	3,917
Current Transfers: Debit	78akd	−212	−193	−234	−218	−217	−162	−248	−238	−302	−304	−234	−270
Capital Account, n.i.e.	78bcd	—	—	—	—	—	—	—	—	—	—	—	—
Capital Account, n.i.e.: Credit	78bad	—	—	—	—	—	—	—	—	—	—	—	—
Capital Account: Debit	78bbd	—	—	—	—	—	—	—	—	—	—	—	—
Financial Account, n.i.e.	78bjd	2,701	3,393	4,560	6,683	6,587	3,307	−551	50	2,465	1,280	742	3,127
Direct Investment Abroad	78bdd	−240	−149	−256	−328	−809	−796	−116	−325	−16	−857	−938	−142
Dir. Invest. in Rep. Econ., n.i.e.	78bed	959	1,446	968	3,112	5,562	2,829	1,508	2,395	2,525	2,115	1,801	3,005
Portfolio Investment Assets	78bfd	—	−1,381	395	−586	−769	286	−1,345	−1,173	−3,460	2,030	−1,753	−1,565
Equity Securities	78bkd	....	—	—	—	—	—	—	—	—	—	—	—
Debt Securities	78bld	—	−1,381	395	−586	−769	286	−1,345	−1,173	−3,460	2,030	−1,753	−1,565
Portfolio Investment Liab., n.i.e.	78bgd	498	1,593	1,042	2,270	1,701	916	720	1,453	3,453	−933	130	1,136
Equity Securities	78bmd	....	478	165	292	278	47	−27	17	−42	17	−52	130
Debt Securities	78bnd	498	1,115	877	1,978	1,424	869	747	1,436	3,495	−950	181	1,006
Financial Derivatives Assets	78bwd	....	—	—	—	—	—	—	—	—	—	—	—
Financial Derivatives Liabilities	78bxd	....	—	—	—	295	−39	101	−125	−133	−111	−101	−190
Other Investment Assets	78bhd	160	55	−3	−1,015	−1,656	−801	−789	−551	231	282	1,642	432
Monetary Authorities	78bod	−40	—	—	—	—	−7	5	−8	7	—	−4	−71
General Government	78bpd	267	−31	−23	−20	−19	−15	−23	−40	−35	−30	−30	−51
Banks	78bqd	−74	−68	70	−41	−231	−177	118	145	102	57	−149	58
Other Sectors	78brd	7	155	−50	−954	−1,407	−603	−889	−648	157	254	1,825	496
Other Investment Liab., n.i.e.	78bid	1,325	1,828	2,414	3,230	2,263	912	−630	−1,623	−136	−1,246	−39	452
Monetary Authorities	78bsd	−99	−177	51	14	−18	−22	−11	−15	−12	−13	−12	−68
General Government	78btd	−329	−384	−80	−266	−54	347	910	340	226	−203	2,180	598
Banks	78bud	710	727	588	417	487	−861	−1,208	−1,149	−331	−376	−531	573
Other Sectors	78bvd	1,043	1,663	1,854	3,066	1,848	1,448	−321	−799	−18	−654	−1,676	−651
Net Errors and Omissions	78cad	−135	457	−48	−327	−570	146	−440	43	−154	191	39	295
Overall Balance	78cbd	464	182	−4	1,729	278	−1,398	−312	862	1,225	139	−188	2,470
Reserves and Related Items	79dad	−464	−182	4	−1,729	−278	1,398	312	−862	−1,225	−139	188	−2,470
Reserve Assets	79dbd	−464	−182	4	−1,729	−278	1,398	312	−862	−1,225	−139	188	−2,470
Use of Fund Credit and Loans	79dcd	—	—	—	—	—	—	—	—	—	—	—	—
Exceptional Financing	79ded	....	—	—	—	—	—	—	—	—	—	—	—
International Investment Position						*Millions of US Dollars*							
Assets	79aad	12,701	15,149	16,445	17,652	20,839	20,928	22,491	25,408	29,855	28,748	29,790	33,442
Direct Investment Abroad	79abd	592	744	1,028	1,096	1,893	2,648	2,703	2,989	2,952	3,553	4,390	4,357
Portfolio Investment	79acd	—	447	1,171	2,453	3,221	2,936	4,281	5,454	8,914	6,884	8,637	10,202
Equity Securities	79add	—	447	1,171	—	—	—	—	—	—	—	—	—
Debt Securities	79aed	—	—	—	2,453	3,221	2,936	4,281	5,454	8,914	6,884	8,637	10,202
Financial Derivatives	79ald	—	—	—	—	—	—	—	—	—	—	—	—
Other Investment	79afd	4,163	5,845	5,786	4,165	5,817	6,611	7,405	7,970	7,748	7,468	5,849	5,422
Monetary Authorities	79agd	40	40	40	477	472	473	473	501	502	503	530	607
General Government	79ahd	561	1,545	1,052	109	128	142	165	205	240	270	300	349
Banks	79aid	1,109	1,150	1,051	263	493	670	552	406	304	247	396	337
Other Sectors	79ajd	2,452	3,110	3,643	3,316	4,723	5,326	6,215	6,858	6,701	6,448	4,624	4,129
Reserve Assets	79akd	7,946	8,114	8,462	9,939	9,908	8,733	8,102	8,995	10,242	10,843	10,914	13,461
Liabilities	79lad	24,937	30,129	35,297	44,193	56,267	54,409	50,898	47,706	54,914	55,723	59,187	65,559
Dir. Invest. in Rep. Economy	79lbd	5,779	6,916	8,563	11,773	19,694	16,645	13,424	10,991	15,194	17,830	20,419	24,708
Portfolio Investment	79lcd	741	2,026	2,591	5,945	7,984	8,278	8,413	9,621	13,008	12,307	12,964	14,489
Equity Securities	79ldd	215	693	858	942	1,553	880	586	397	325	325	405	718
Debt Securities	79led	525	1,333	1,733	5,003	6,432	7,398	7,827	9,224	12,683	11,982	12,559	13,770
Financial Derivatives	79lld	—	—	—	—	295	256	357	253	139	57	12	—
Other Investment	79lfd	18,417	21,187	24,144	26,475	28,294	29,230	28,704	26,841	26,573	25,529	25,792	26,363
Monetary Authorities	79lgd	452	231	301	329	252	236	211	186	199	134	130	60
General Government	79lhd	5,202	5,102	5,144	4,723	4,516	5,000	5,864	6,580	6,878	6,876	9,357	10,027
Banks	79lid	3,741	4,518	5,169	5,547	6,004	4,950	3,886	2,714	2,335	1,962	1,377	1,950
Other Sectors	79ljd	9,023	11,336	13,530	15,876	17,523	19,045	18,743	17,362	17,160	16,556	14,927	14,325
Government Finance						*Billions of Pesos: Year Ending December 31*							
Deficit (-) or Surplus	80	−329.2	−1,027.2	−1,939.8	−3,780.2	−4,504.0	−6,940.6	−8,888.9	−11,945.5	−11,169.7	−11,134.1	−11,128.2	−9,990.7
Total Revenue and Grants	81y	5,715.3	7,656.1	9,521.2	12,007.3	15,282.6	16,880.2	20,144.0	23,285.3	28,941.6	31,459.1	35,798.3	41,593.3
Revenue	81	....	7,656.1	9,521.2	12,007.3	15,282.6	16,880.2	20,144.0	23,285.3	28,941.6	31,459.1	35,798.3	41,593.3
Grants	81z	....											
Exp. & Lending Minus Repay.	82z	6,044.6	8,683.3	11,461.0	15,787.5	19,786.6	23,820.8	29,032.9	35,230.8	40,111.3	42,593.2	46,926.4	51,584.0
Expenditure	82	....	8,553.8	11,289.5	15,610.9	19,583.6	23,492.0	28,153.8	34,444.4	38,640.9	41,334.2	46,061.6	51,312.4
Lending Minus Repayments	83	....	129.5	171.5	176.6	203.0	328.8	879.1	786.4	1,470.4	1,259.0	864.8	271.6
Total Financing	80h	329.1	1,027.2	1,939.8	3,780.2	4,504.0	6,940.6	8,888.9	11,945.5	11,169.7	11,134.1	11,128.2	9,990.7
Domestic	84a	809.8	907.7	1,717.5	2,516.5	3,140.4	4,522.0	4,569.7	7,137.8	5,242.1	7,824.7	6,358.2	5,846.3
Foreign	85a	−480.6	119.5	222.3	1,263.7	1,363.6	2,418.6	4,319.2	4,807.7	5,927.6	3,309.4	4,769.9	4,144.4

		1993	1994	1995	1996	1997	1998	1999	2000	2001	2002	2003	2004
National Accounts							*Billions of Pesos*						
Househ.Cons.Expend.,incl.NPISHs....	96f	30,513	44,510	55,462	65,966	79,194	92,501	97,631	110,217	123,745	134,534	....	....
Government Consumption Expend...	91f	5,108	9,774	12,622	18,123	24,246	28,548	33,588	37,057	38,765	41,808	....	....
Gross Fixed Capital Formation..........	93e	8,251	15,727	18,911	21,750	24,592	26,603	20,079	21,952	25,695	30,112	....	....
Changes in Inventories...................	93i	1,049	1,497	2,806	462	708	941	−725	1,793	967	1,162		
Exports of Goods and Services..........	90c	7,937	10,129	12,272	15,308	18,063	21,083	27,807	37,606	38,477	38,847	46,997	53,527
Imports of Goods and Services (-).....	98c	10,973	14,127	17,701	20,993	25,261	29,363	26,983	33,926	39,308	42,176	52,211	57,156
Gross Domestic Product (GDP).........	99b	52,272	67,533	84,439	100,711	121,708	140,483	151,565	174,896	188,559	204,530	230,467	256,862
Net Primary Income from Abroad.....	98.n	−8,128	−1,200	−1,442	−2,128	−2,706	−2,510	−2,663	−4,772	−6,013	−7,134	....	....
Gross National Income (GNI)...........	99a	44,143	66,333	82,997	98,583	119,002	137,973	148,902	170,124	182,545	197,396	....	....
Net Current Transf.from Abroad.......	98t	1,552	3,458	4,536	3,958	3,681	4,547	2,856	3,625	....	....	....	....
Gross Nat'l Disposable Inc.(GNDI)....	99i	44,143	69,791	87,534	102,541	123,147	142,128	151,758	172,107	....	....	....	....
Gross Saving................................	99s	8,582	15,506	19,450	18,453	19,707	20,556	20,540	22,136	....	....	....	....
GDP Volume 1994 Prices.................	99b.p	64,227	67,533	71,046	72,507	74,994	75,421	72,251	74,364	75,458	76,914	80,087	83,370
GDP Volume (2000=100)...............	99bvp	86.4	90.8	95.5	97.5	100.8	101.4	97.2	100.0	101.5	103.4	107.7	112.1
GDP Deflator (2000=100)...............	99bip	34.6	42.5	50.5	59.1	69.0	79.2	89.2	100.0	106.2	113.1	122.4	131.0
							Millions: Midyear Estimates						
Population...............................	99z	37.10	37.82	38.54	39.26	39.98	40.70	41.41	42.12	42.83	43.53	44.22	44.92

Comoros 632

		1993	1994	1995	1996	1997	1998	1999	2000	2001	2002	2003	2004
Exchange Rates		Francs per SDR: End of Period (aa)											
Official Rate	aa	404.89	† 585.32	546.28	564.79	605.95	593.70	672.14	688.87	701.54	637.78	578.82	560.92
		Francs per US Dollar: End of Period (ae) Period Average (rf)											
Official Rate	ae	294.77	† 400.95	367.50	392.77	449.10	421.65	489.72	528.71	558.23	469.12	389.52	361.18
Official Rate	rf	283.16	416.40	374.36	383.66	437.75	442.46	461.77	533.98	549.78	522.74	435.90	396.21
Fund Position		Millions of SDRs: End of Period											
Quota	2f.s	6.50	6.50	6.50	6.50	6.50	6.50	8.90	8.90	8.90	8.90	8.90	8.90
SDRs	1b.s	.07	.03	.07	.04	.10	—	.12	.13	.02	.03	—	—
Reserve Position in the Fund	1c.s	.50	.52	.54	.54	.54	.54	.54	.54	.54	.54	.54	.54
Total Fund Cred.&Loans Outstg	2tl	.90	2.25	2.25	2.25	2.07	1.89	1.58	1.13	.68	.41	.14	—
International Liquidity		Millions of US Dollars Unless Otherwise Indicated: End of Period											
Total Reserves minus Gold	1l.d	38.63	44.03	44.48	50.55	40.48	39.14	37.15	43.21	62.32	79.94	94.30	103.74
SDRs	1b.d	.09	.05	.11	.05	.13	.01	.16	.16	.02	.04	.01	—
Reserve Position in the Fund	1c.d	.69	.76	.80	.78	.73	.76	.74	.70	.68	.73	.81	.84
Foreign Exchange	1d.d	37.85	43.22	43.58	49.72	39.62	38.38	36.24	42.34	61.62	79.17	93.48	102.89
Gold (Million Fine Troy Ounces)	1ad	.001	.001	.001	.001	.001	.001	.001	.001	.001	.001	.001	.001
Gold (National Valuation)	1and	.22	.22	.22	.21	.18	.17	.17	.16	.15	.20	.24	.25
Deposit Money Banks: Assets	7a.d	2.73	.29	2.42	2.16	4.29	† 2.04	8.10	5.69	8.71	6.78	4.34	2.85
Liabilities	7b.d	2.66	.01	.25	.02	—	† 1.99	2.45	4.35	4.18	4.81	4.46	3.86
Monetary Authorities		Millions of Francs: End of Period											
Foreign Assets	11	11,475	17,729	16,422	19,950	18,305	† 16,582	18,294	23,017	34,879	38,796	37,860	37,571
Claims on Central Government	12a	2,648	3,483	3,589	3,569	3,646	† 3,806	3,814	3,858	3,654	3,930	3,120	3,457
Claims on Private Sector	12d	....	....	....	....	....	57	49	64	70	81	65	48
Claims on Other Banking Insts.	12f	....	....	....	....	....	50	75	75	75	75	75	80
Reserve Money	14	8,539	9,756	8,760	11,936	10,454	† 9,326	11,104	13,980	23,851	28,358	27,940	27,505
of which: Currency Outside DMBs	14a	4,402	5,100	5,672	5,639	5,433	† 5,418	6,310	7,564	12,355	12,503	11,505	11,730
Foreign Liabilities	16c	524	1,428	1,421	1,393	1,385	† 1,183	1,171	915	1,393	397	223	163
Central Government Deposits	16d	2,287	1,743	1,278	1,723	1,515	† 542	518	508	712	582	1,126	1,270
Counterpart Funds	16e	....	....	....	....	....	56	49	49	49	49	49	50
Central Govt. Lending Funds	16f	....	....	....	....	....	504	314	316	1,374	1,191	465	550
Capital Accounts	17a	2,971	8,491	8,673	8,670	8,770	† 9,241	9,277	11,120	11,056	12,056	12,567	12,146
Other Items (Net)	17r	−198	−206	−121	−203	−173	† −359	−199	126	245	250	−1,249	−526
Deposit Money Banks		Millions of Francs: End of Period											
Reserves	20	2,972	3,082	1,631	4,719	4,024	† 5,195	3,796	5,257	8,806	12,547	13,214	13,156
Foreign Assets	21	804	115	889	848	1,927	† 859	3,966	3,009	4,864	3,182	1,690	1,029
Claims on Central Government	22a	—	—	—	415	94	† 358	554	300	301	301	300	781
Claims on Private Sector	22d	8,829	8,579	9,452	6,712	8,458	† 6,948	8,600	9,480	9,223	10,278	11,379	10,354
Demand Deposits	24	3,710	3,954	4,170	4,487	4,518	† 4,250	4,386	5,626	8,955	10,655	11,075	9,704
Time and Savings Deposits	25a	5,781	5,910	5,442	6,167	7,771	† 5,737	6,974	7,237	8,363	8,874	8,952	8,480
Foreign Currency Deposits	25b	....	....	....	....	....	21	62	63	125	110	151	356
Restricted Deposits	26b	....	....	....	....	....	260	618	111	482	1,348	767	1,276
Foreign Liabilities	26c	783	3	93	8	—	† 840	1,200	2,298	2,331	2,257	1,738	1,393
Central Government Deposits	26d	377	—	167	132	209	† 362	240	378	509	501	690	798
Credit From Monetary Authorities	26g	87	122	—	—	—	† —	—	—	—	—	—	—
Capital Accounts	27a	1,586	1,850	2,194	2,022	2,235	† 2,667	3,368	3,504	3,904	3,947	4,281	4,342
Other Items (Net)	27r	281	−63	−94	−122	−230	† −777	68	−1,171	−1,475	−1,384	−1,072	−1,029
Monetary Survey		Millions of Francs: End of Period											
Foreign Assets (Net)	31n	10,972	16,413	15,797	19,397	18,847	† 15,418	19,889	22,813	36,019	39,324	37,587	37,045
Domestic Credit	32	11,465	12,497	12,450	10,213	10,474	† 10,315	12,342	12,891	12,103	13,590	13,133	12,671
Claims on Central Govt. (Net)	32an	2,566	3,822	2,925	3,422	2,016	† 3,260	3,610	3,272	2,733	3,148	1,604	2,170
Claims on Private Sector	32d	8,899	8,675	9,525	6,791	8,458	† 7,005	8,649	9,544	9,294	10,359	11,444	10,402
Claims on Other Banking Insts.	32f	....	....	....	....	....	50	83	75	76	83	86	98
Money	34	11,575	12,714	12,040	13,021	10,603	† 10,015	11,662	14,115	22,937	25,323	24,793	23,368
Quasi-Money	35	5,781	5,910	5,442	6,167	7,771	† 5,758	7,036	7,300	8,487	8,984	9,102	8,836
Restricted Deposits	36b	....	....	....	....	....	260	618	111	482	1,348	767	1,276
Counterpart Funds	36e	....	....	....	....	....	56	49	49	49	49	49	50
Central Govt. Lending Funds	36f	....	....	....	....	....	504	314	316	1,374	1,191	465	550
Other Items (Net)	37r	5,081	10,286	10,765	10,422	10,947	† 9,139	12,553	13,813	14,793	16,020	15,545	15,636
Money plus Quasi-Money	35l	17,356	18,624	17,482	19,188	18,374	† 15,773	18,698	21,415	31,424	34,307	33,896	32,204
Other Banking Institutions		Millions of Francs: End of Period											
Reserves	40	697	1,340	1,250	856	88	† 475	1,060	947	1,484	2,013	1,578	1,479
Foreign Assets	41	2	4	2	5	—	† 89	96	9	10	11	11	9
Claims on Central Government	42a	526	11	—	—	—	† —	—	—	—	—	—	—
Claims on Private Sector	42d	1,916	1,985	2,200	3,029	4,022	† 4,038	3,329	3,334	2,928	2,293	2,594	2,690
Time Deposits	45	473	387	267	694	760	† 709	768	837	963	1,070	1,223	1,806
Central Government Deposits	46d	—	—	—	—	—	† 263	153	749	146	146	633	146
Long-Term Foreign Liabilities	46cl	1,551	1,838	1,964	1,588	1,633	† 845	688	527	364	197	104	—
Central Govt. Lending Funds	46f	233	230	296	317	306	† 883	896	280	809	979	394	619
Capital Accounts	47a	887	918	1,018	1,399	1,494	† 2,090	1,971	1,988	1,978	1,950	2,292	2,313
Other Items (Net)	47r	−3	−33	−93	−108	−83	† −188	9	−91	161	−26	−463	−706
Banking Survey		Millions of Francs: End of Period											
Foreign Assets (Net)	51n	9,423	14,579	13,835	17,814	17,214	† 14,662	19,297	22,295	35,666	39,138	37,494	37,055
Domestic Credit	52	13,907	14,493	14,650	13,242	14,496	† 14,040	15,435	15,401	14,809	15,654	15,009	15,116
Claims on Central Govt. (Net)	52an	3,092	3,833	2,925	3,422	2,016	† 2,997	3,457	2,523	2,587	3,002	971	2,024
Claims on Private Sector	52d	10,815	10,660	11,725	9,820	12,480	† 11,043	11,978	12,878	12,221	12,652	14,039	13,092
Liquid Liabilities	55l	17,172	17,704	16,525	19,002	19,114	† 16,166	18,522	21,360	30,812	33,257	33,113	32,220
Money	54	10,918	11,407	10,816	12,141	10,583	† 9,699	10,718	13,223	21,362	23,202	22,788	21,578
Quasi-Money	55	6,254	6,297	5,709	6,861	8,531	† 6,467	7,804	8,137	9,450	10,054	10,325	10,642
Restricted Deposits	56b	....	....	....	....	....	260	618	111	482	1,348	767	1,276
Counterpart Funds	56e	....	....	....	....	....	56	49	49	49	49	49	50
Central Govt. Lending Funds	56f	583	230	296	317	306	† 1,387	1,210	596	2,183	2,170	859	1,170
Other Items (Net)	57r	5,575	11,138	11,664	11,737	12,290	† 10,832	14,334	15,580	16,949	17,969	17,716	17,456

Comoros 632

		1993	1994	1995	1996	1997	1998	1999	2000	2001	2002	2003	2004
Interest Rates							*Percent Per Annum*						
Discount Rate............................	60	....	....	....	....	....	....	† 6.36	5.63	5.89	4.79	3.82	3.55
Deposit Rate..............................	60l	....	....	....	....	....	....	† 11.42	3.00	3.00	3.17	3.50	3.50
Lending Rate.............................	60p	....	....	....	....	....	....	† 13.67	12.00	12.00	12.00	11.83	11.00
Balance of Payments						*Millions of US Dollars: Minus Sign Indicates Debit*							
Current Account, n.i.e..................	78ald	9.57	−7.22	−18.96	....	....	....	....	....	....	....	....	....
Goods: Exports f.o.b......................	78aad	21.58	10.79	11.32	....	....	....	....	....	....	....	....	....
Goods: Imports f.o.b......................	78abd	−49.54	−44.94	−53.50	....	....	....	....	....	....	....	....	....
Trade Balance.......................	78acd	−27.96	−34.16	−42.18	....	....	....	....	....	....	....	....	....
Services: Credit........................	78add	31.06	28.84	34.51	....	....	....	....	....	....	....	....	....
Services: Debit........................	78aed	−49.87	−45.59	−49.85	....	....	....	....	....	....	....	....	....
Balance on Goods & Services.......	78afd	−46.77	−50.91	−57.53	....	....	....	....	....	....	....	....	....
Income: Credit........................	78agd	3.30	2.62	3.40	....	....	....	....	....	....	....	....	....
Income: Debit...........................	78ahd	−1.27	−2.69	−2.39	....	....	....	....	....	....	....	....	....
Balance on Gds, Serv. & Inc.......	78aid	−44.74	−50.98	−56.52	....	....	....	....	....	....	....	....	....
Current Transfers, n.i.e.: Credit......	78ajd	59.83	49.95	41.06	....	....	....	....	....	....	....	....	....
Current Transfers: Debit..............	78akd	−5.52	−6.19	−3.50	....	....	....	....	....	....	....	....	....
Capital Account, n.i.e..................	78bcd	—	—	—	....	....	....	....	....	....	....	....	....
Capital Account, n.i.e.: Credit........	78bad	—	—	—	....	....	....	....	....	....	....	....	....
Capital Account: Debit.................	78bbd	—	—	—	....	....	....	....	....	....	....	....	....
Financial Account, n.i.e...............	78bjd	4.05	18.54	10.87	....	....	....	....	....	....	....	....	....
Direct Investment Abroad.............	78bdd	—	—	—	....	....	....	....	....	....	....	....	....
Dir. Invest. in Rep. Econ., n.i.e.......	78bed	.19	.18	.89	....	....	....	....	....	....	....	....	....
Portfolio Investment Assets...........	78bfd	—	—	—	....	....	....	....	....	....	....	....	....
Equity Securities......................	78bkd	—	—	—	....	....	....	....	....	....	....	....	....
Debt Securities........................	78bld	—	—	—	....	....	....	....	....	....	....	....	....
Portfolio Investment Liab., n.i.e......	78bgd	—	—	—	....	....	....	....	....	....	....	....	....
Equity Securities......................	78bmd	—	—	—	....	....	....	....	....	....	....	....	....
Debt Securities........................	78bnd	—	—	—	....	....	....	....	....	....	....	....	....
Financial Derivatives Assets...........	78bwd	....	....	....	....	....	....	....	....	....	....	....	....
Financial Derivatives Liabilities.......	78bxd	....	....	....	....	....	....	....	....	....	....	....	....
Other Investment Assets...............	78bhd	−1.45	1.66	−1.83	....	....	....	....	....	....	....	....	....
Monetary Authorities................	78bod	....	....	....	....	....	....	....	....	....	....	....	....
General Government..................	78bpd	—	—	—	....	....	....	....	....	....	....	....	....
Banks.................................	78bqd	−1.45	1.66	−1.83	....	....	....	....	....	....	....	....	....
Other Sectors...........................	78brd	—	—	—	....	....	....	....	....	....	....	....	....
Other Investment Liab., n.i.e.........	78bid	5.30	16.70	11.81	....	....	....	....	....	....	....	....	....
Monetary Authorities................	78bsd	2.99	7.93	2.02	....	....	....	....	....	....	....	....	....
General Government..................	78btd	2.06	10.63	8.72	....	....	....	....	....	....	....	....	....
Banks.................................	78bud	—	—	—	....	....	....	....	....	....	....	....	....
Other Sectors...........................	78bvd	.25	−1.86	1.06	....	....	....	....	....	....	....	....	....
Net Errors and Omissions...............	78cad	−5.84	−6.33	−1.77	....	....	....	....	....	....	....	....	....
Overall Balance.......................	78cbd	7.78	4.99	−9.86	....	....	....	....	....	....	....	....	....
Reserves and Related Items............	79dad	−7.78	−4.99	9.86	....	....	....	....	....	....	....	....	....
Reserve Assets..........................	79dbd	−14.00	−14.97	3.37	....	....	....	....	....	....	....	....	....
Use of Fund Credit and Loans........	79dcd	—	1.89	—	....	....	....	....	....	....	....	....	....
Exceptional Financing..................	79ded	6.22	8.09	6.49	....	....	....	....	....	....	....	....	....
National Accounts						*Billions of Francs*							
Gross Domestic Product (GDP).........	99b	75.5	80.4	84.1	....	....	....	....	....	....	....	....	....
					Millions: Midyear Estimates								
Population.............................	99z	.57	.59	.61	.62	.64	.66	.68	.70	.72	.74	.76	.78

		1993	1994	1995	1996	1997	1998	1999	2000	2001	2002	2003	2004
Exchange Rates					*Congo Francs per Thousand SDRs through 1994, per SDR Thereafter: End of Period*								
Market Rate	aa	.481	47.445	.220	1.662	1.430	† 3.450	6.176	65.146	394.111	519.527	549.200	703.638
				Congo Francs per Thousand US$ through 1994, per US$ Thereafter: End of Period (ae) Period Average (rf)									
Market Rate	ae	.350	32.500	.148	1.156	1.060	† 2.450	4.500	50.000	313.600	382.140	369.590	453.080
Market Rate	rf	.025	11.941	.070	.502	1.313	1.607	4.018	21.818	206.618	346.485	405.340	401.041
					Index Numbers (2000=100): Period Averages								
Market Rate	ahx	—	—	100.0	13.8	4.1	924.1	363.6	100.0	12.9	4.0	3.4	3.5
Nominal Effective Exchange Rate	nec												
Real Effective Exchange Rate	rec	53.9	40.9	36.0	35.8	43.9	45.6	122.4	100.0	89.6	39.3	35.1	32.0
Fund Position						*Millions of SDRs: End of Period*							
Quota	2f.s	291.00	291.00	291.00	291.00	291.00	291.00	291.00	291.00	291.00	533.00	533.00	533.00
SDRs	1b.s	—	—	—	—	—	—	—	—	—	6.12	5.35	3.54
Reserve Position in the Fund	1c.s	—	—	—	—	—	—	—	—	—	—	—	—
Total Fund Cred.&Loans Outstg	2tl	330.31	327.27	326.37	301.26	301.26	300.71	300.03	300.02	300.02	420.00	473.37	526.77
International Liquidity				*Millions of US Dollars Unless Otherwise Indicated: End of Period*									
Total Reserves minus Gold	1l.d	46.20	120.69	146.60	82.50	....	....	....	....	....	....	....	....
SDRs	1b.d	—	—	—	—	—	—	—	—	—	8.32	7.96	5.50
Reserve Position in the Fund	1c.d	—	—	—	—	—	—	—	—	—	—	—	—
Foreign Exchange	1d.d	46.20	120.69	146.60	82.50	....	....	....	....	....	....	....	....
Gold (Million Fine Troy Ounces)	1ad	.022	.028	.028	....	.054	....	....	....	....	....	....	....
Gold (National Valuation)	1and	8.59	10.71	10.83	....	15.80	....	....	....	....	....	....	....
Monetary Authorities: Other Liab	4..d	272.40	280.95	331.50	244.16	205.15	5,841.57	5,423.52	−49.34	−38.34	139.49	192.99	182.45
Deposit Money Banks: Assets	7a.d	62.37	81.18	69.18	....	....	....	....	....	93.42	95.64	181.79	238.46
Liabilities	7b.d	27.31	31.29	16.75	35.04	....	....	....	....	48.77	41.96	84.68	93.22
Monetary Authorities			*Congo Francs through 1993; Thousands of Congo Francs 1994–95; Millions Beginning 1996: End of Period*										
Foreign Assets	11	66,820	† 5,148	25,276	† 107	67	1,834	4,125	2,571	20,163	28,663	36,414	110,243
Claims on Central Government	12a	41,830	† 1,675	1,675	† 54	332	6,416	37,068	16,415	20,142	13,089	29,835	100,288
Claims on Nonfin.Pub.Enterprises	12c	20	† 5	323	† 7	6	149	272	301	1,895	—	—	—
Claims on Private Sector	12d	800	† 34	705	† 7	14	170	460	524	899	1,283	1,943	1,057
Claims on Deposit Money Banks	12e	1,270	† 163	8,234	† 17	9	150	526	132	425	2,799	3,901	7,276
Claims on Other Banking Insts	12f	70	† 10	931	† —	—	—	—	3	—	—	—	—
Reserve Money	14	69,990	† 2,355	17,668	† 110	228	6,353	33,057	20,314	43,205	52,376	67,728	111,923
of which: Currency Outside DMBs	14a	46,930	† 2,771	16,839	† 83	152	5,145	29,445	18,180	36,110	49,757	63,148	101,467
Time & Foreign Currency Deposits	15	6,880	† 707	1,522	† 8	9	195	436	470	2,524	5,333	3,964	6,071
Restricted Deposits	16b	12,620	† 1,005	4,870	† 38	29	703	1,526	1,224	6,936	3,650	3,459	4,688
Foreign Liabilities	16c	254,135	† 24,658	121,116	† 783	648	15,349	26,259	17,078	106,216	271,507	331,302	453,320
Central Government Deposits	16d	340	† 298	660	† 8	60	1,025	5,513	2,393	6,759	20,335	24,085	112,131
Counterpart Funds	16e	—	† —	—	† —	—	—	—	—	—	—	—	—
Capital Accounts	17a	45,370	† 4,124	24,842	† 128	449	4,760	6,104	4,150	17,043	−317,454	−360,408	−353,635
Other Items (Net)	17r	137,605	† −25,179	−46,070	† −891	−995	−19,667	−30,445	−24,224	−138,495	10,085	1,965	−115,632
Deposit Money Banks			*Congo Francs through 1993; Thousands of Congo Francs 1994–95; Millions Beginning 1996: End of Period*										
Reserves	20	21,220	† 265	643	....	....	....	....	....	4,359	3,072	5,912	10,855
Foreign Assets	21	21,830	† 2,638	10,260	....	....	....	....	....	29,295	36,548	67,188	108,043
Claims on Central Government	22a	230	† 180	80	....	....	....	....	....	1,253	593	14,361	15,486
Claims on Nonfin.Pub.Enterprises	22c	80	† 76	170	....	....	....	....	....	395	827	228	1,799
Claims on Private Sector	22d	2,460	† 700	3,510	....	....	....	....	....	9,644	11,842	17,704	38,646
Claims on Other Banking Insts	22f	—	† —	—	....	....	....	....	....	903	—	1	32
Demand Deposits	24	16,180	† 919	1,870	....	....	....	....	....	7,922	7,956	8,606	15,364
Time & Foreign Currency Deposits	25	10,770	† 1,407	6,304	....	....	....	....	....	18,497	30,863	48,429	91,759
Restricted Deposits	26b	1,940	† 63	208	....	....	....	....	....	1,101	1,094	2,157	2,269
Foreign Liabilities	26c	9,560	† 1,017	2,484	....	....	....	....	....	15,295	16,036	31,295	42,235
Central Government Deposits	26d	1,000	† —	—	....	....	....	....	....	2,092	3,737	8,008	12,893
Counterpart Funds	26e	—	† —	—	....	....	....	....	....	—	—	—	—
Credit from Monetary Authorities	26g	1,270	† 163	8,234	† 17	9	150	526	132	622	1,533	3,218	7,276
Capital Accounts	27a	1,140	† 201	4,125	....	....	....	....	....	9,860	12,445	16,717	19,234
Other Items (Net)	27r	5,230	† 253	−327	....	....	....	....	....	−9,541	−20,784	−13,035	−17,564
Post Office: Checking Deposits	24..i	—	† —	—	....	....	....	....	....	....	....	....	....
Monetary Survey			*Congo Francs through 1993; Thousands of Congo Francs 1994–95; Millions Beginning 1996: End of Period*										
Foreign Assets (Net)	31n	−175,045	† −17,889	−88,064	....	....	....	....	....	−72,052	−222,333	−258,995	−277,269
Domestic Credit	32	44,150	† 2,383	6,733	....	....	....	....	....	26,224	3,561	31,982	32,285
Claims on Central Govt. (Net)	32an	40,720	† 1,557	1,095	....	....	....	....	....	12,488	−10,391	12,104	−9,250
Claims on Nonfin.Pub.Enterprises	32c	100	† 81	493	....	....	....	....	....	2,290	827	228	1,799
Claims on Private Sector	32d	3,260	† 735	4,214	....	....	....	....	....	10,543	13,125	19,648	39,703
Claims on Other Banking Insts	32f	70	† 10	931	....	....	....	....	....	903	—	1	32
Money	34	64,950	† 3,725	18,895	....	....	....	....	....	41,064	57,893	72,110	117,078
Quasi-Money	35	17,650	† 2,114	7,826	....	....	....	....	....	26,134	36,196	52,393	97,830
of which: Fgn. Currency Deposits	35x	17,650	† 2,114	7,826	....	....	....	....	....	21,021	36,196	52,393	97,830
Restricted Deposits	36b	14,560	† 1,068	5,077	....	....	....	....	....	8,037	4,744	5,616	6,956
Counterpart Funds	36e	—	† —	—	....	....	....	....	....	—	—	—	—
Capital Accounts	37a	46,510	† 4,324	28,967	....	....	....	....	....	26,903	−305,008	−343,691	−334,402
Revaluation Accounts	37ar	−115,720	† −14,351	−68,579	....	....	....	....	....	−105,946	—	—	−100,014
Other Items (Net)	37r	−157,575	† −12,223	−65,283	....	....	....	....	....	−41,500	−12,597	−13,441	−33,828
Money plus Quasi-Money	35l	82,600	† 5,839	26,721	....	....	....	....	....	67,198	94,089	124,503	214,908
Interest Rates						*Percent Per Annum*							
Discount Rate (End of Period)	60	95.0	145.0	125.0	238.0	13.0	22.0	120.0	120.0	140.0	24.0	8.0	....
Deposit Rate	60l	....	60.0	60.0	60.0	....	....	....	....	....	....	....	....
Lending Rate	60p	....	398.3	293.9	247.0	134.6	29.0	124.6	165.0	167.9	66.8	....	....
Prices						*Index Numbers (2000=100): Period Averages*							
Consumer Prices	64	—	—	† .2	1.0	3.1	4.0	15.4	100.0	413.7	571.3	644.6	670.9
Intl. Transactions & Positions						*Millions of US Dollars*							
Exports	70..d	....	....	1,563	1,547	1,449	1,422	809	824	901	1,132	1,374	1,850
Imports, c.i.f	71..d	....	....	871	1,089	770	1,102	568	697	807	1,081	1,594	1,986

Congo, Democratic Republic of   636

		1993	1994	1995	1996	1997	1998	1999	2000	2001	2002	2003	2004
Government Finance		*Congo Francs through 1993; Thousands of Congo Francs 1994–95; Millions Beginning 1996: Year Ending December 31*											
Deficit (-) or Surplus.........................	80	−36,940	† −1,228	80	† −9	−63	....	....	....	....	....	....	....
Revenue...	81	12,160	† 2,084	21,200	† 157	404	....	....	....	....	....	....	....
Grants Received............................	81z	300	† 168	11,770	† 171	323	....	....	....	....	....	....	....
Expenditure..................................	82	48,310	† 3,312	32,890	† 337	790	....	....	....	....	....	....	....
Lending Minus Repayments...........	83	1,090	† 168	—	† —	—	....	....	....	....	....	....	....
Financing													
Domestic..................................	84a	35,960	† 1,060	−80	† 9	63	....	....	....	....	....	....	....
Foreign....................................	85a	990	† 168	—	† —	—	....	....	....	....	....	....	....
Debt: Domestic...............................	88a	40,722	† 1,557	1,750	† 37	304	....	....	....	....	....	....	....
Foreign.................................	89a	239,254	† 116,448	921,660	† 7,019	11,871	....	....	....	....	....	....	....
National Accounts		*Thousands of Congo Francs through 1995; Millions of Congo Francs Beginning 1996*											
Househ.Cons.Expend.,incl.NPISHs....	96f	....	† 61,700	314,200	† 2,066	6,436	8,445	42,115	242,586	1,241,371	1,588,181	1,982,429	1,955,705
Government Consumption Expend...	91f	....	† 3,000	19,600	† 179	614	1,018	4,595	22,289	69,655	99,954	148,214	215,603
Gross Fixed Capital Formation..........	93e	....	† 5,200	38,300	† 450	666	731	2,251	31,114	107,279	165,080	286,759	481,185
Changes in Inventories....................	93i	....	† −2,800	5,500	† −36	−30	−77	2,746	1,677	6,733	13,455	28,321	30,567
Exports of Goods and Services..........	90c	....	† 16,900	112,900	† 896	1,876	2,494	3,427	19,427	199,468	468,482	616,491	913,996
Imports of Goods and Services (-).....	98c	....	† 14,700	94,100	† 659	1,758	2,621	3,310	20,027	216,960	412,853	778,694	987,507
Gross Domestic Product (GDP).........	99b	....	† 69,300	396,400	† 2,896	7,804	9,989	51,824	297,065	1,407,545	1,922,300	2,283,520	2,609,549
Net Primary Income from Abroad.....	98.n	....	† −500	−56,400	† −397	−360	−400	−2,060	−8,753	−112,581	−108,743	−72,409	−150,615
Gross National Income (GNI)............	99a	....	† 68,800	340,000	† 2,499	7,444	9,589	49,764	288,312	1,294,964	1,813,557	2,211,111	2,458,935
Consumption of Fixed Capital..........	99cf	....	† −2,100	−11,900	† −87	−234	−300	−1,555	−10,048	−2,642	....	....	....
Net National Income.......................	99e	....	† 66,700	328,100	† 2,412	7,210	9,289	48,209	279,400	1,252,737	1,755,888	2,142,606	2,380,648
GDP Vol.1987 Prices.......................	99b.p	....	† 181,300	182,600	† 181	171	168	161	150	151	....	....	....
GDP Volume (2000=100)...............	99bvp	126.2	121.3	122.1	120.8	114.2	112.2	107.5	100.0	100.9	....	....	....
GDP Deflator (2000=100)...............	99bip	—	—	.1	.8	2.3	3.0	16.2	100.0	469.4	....	....	....
		Millions: Midyear Estimates											
Population..............................	99z	42.22	43.69	45.00	46.12	47.10	48.00	48.96	50.05	51.31	52.71	54.23	55.85

2005, International Monetary Fund : *International Financial Statistics Yearbook*

		1993	1994	1995	1996	1997	1998	1999	2000	2001	2002	2003	2004
Exchange Rates						*Francs per SDR: End of Period*							
Official Rate	aa	404.89	† 780.44	728.38	753.06	807.94	791.61	† 896.19	918.49	935.39	850.37	771.76	747.90
					Francs per US Dollar: End of Period (ae) Period Average (rf)								
Official Rate	ae	294.77	† 534.60	490.00	523.70	598.81	562.21	† 652.95	704.95	744.31	625.50	519.36	481.58
Official Rate	rf	283.16	† 555.20	499.15	511.55	583.67	589.95	† 615.70	711.98	733.04	696.99	581.20	528.28
Fund Position						*Millions of SDRs: End of Period*							
Quota	2f.s	57.90	57.90	57.90	57.90	57.90	57.90	84.60	84.60	84.60	84.60	84.60	84.60
SDRs	1b.s	.01	.03	.02	.01	.01	—	.08	.03	.15	2.38	.43	4.66
Reserve Position in the Fund	1c.s	.47	.47	.50	.54	.54	.54	.54	.54	.54	.54	.54	.54
Total Fund Cred.&Loans Outstg	2tl	3.50	14.00	12.50	26.40	24.83	24.26	21.14	31.71	30.81	24.41	18.91	18.71
International Liquidity					*Millions of US Dollars Unless Otherwise Indicated: End of Period*								
Total Reserves minus Gold	1l.d	1.34	50.36	59.30	90.99	59.92	.84	39.35	222.01	68.91	31.63	34.80	119.60
SDRs	1b.d	.02	.05	.03	.02	.01	.01	.11	.04	.19	3.23	.64	7.23
Reserve Position in the Fund	1c.d	.64	.68	.75	.77	.72	.75	.74	.70	.67	.73	.80	.83
Foreign Exchange	1d.d	.68	49.63	58.52	90.20	59.19	.08	38.51	221.27	68.05	27.67	33.36	111.54
Gold (Million Fine Troy Ounces)	1ad	.011	.011	.011	.011	.011	.011	.011	.011	.011	.011	.011	.011
Gold (National Valuation)	1and	4.42	† 4.21	4.29	4.10	3.24	3.20	† 3.23	3.03	3.09	3.81	4.65	4.88
Monetary Authorities: Other Liab	4..d	38.71	17.20	18.62	16.48	13.53	35.97	25.10	24.66	22.97	27.65	28.74	32.04
Deposit Money Banks: Assets	7a.d	82.84	41.43	33.16	33.17	27.79	29.01	34.07	140.68	21.84	130.81	42.62	87.53
Liabilities	7b.d	58.86	50.04	28.91	25.81	14.13	41.82	39.17	17.98	17.79	68.69	39.94	57.27
Monetary Authorities						*Billions of Francs: End of Period*							
Foreign Assets	11	1.67	29.21	31.17	49.81	37.81	2.27	27.80	158.64	53.60	22.18	20.49	59.94
Claims on Central Government	12a	72.61	77.25	80.75	92.48	110.27	123.14	120.76	128.71	173.15	171.64	195.30	194.85
Claims on Deposit Money Banks	12e	1.51	1.54	4.26	3.70	5.01	7.16	6.20	6.45	2.44	—	.61	.39
Claims on Other Banking Insts	12f	—	—	—	—	—	—	—	—	—	—	—	—
Reserve Money	14	63.50	85.97	93.09	101.08	112.80	89.44	120.07	243.82	186.79	170.80	183.09	220.39
of which: Currency Outside DMBs	14a	53.71	69.49	81.58	87.35	93.26	73.26	102.34	123.87	142.91	129.00	131.92	155.89
Foreign Liabilities	16c	12.83	20.12	18.23	28.51	28.17	39.43	35.33	46.51	45.91	38.05	29.52	29.42
Central Government Deposits	16d	4.95	22.34	15.87	24.01	19.59	11.33	12.77	21.03	12.90	7.69	13.25	17.47
Capital Accounts	17a	6.10	9.35	8.51	8.68	8.99	8.50	9.82	10.89	11.20	10.56	9.76	9.31
Other Items (Net)	17r	−11.58	−29.78	−19.53	−16.30	−16.46	−16.13	−23.24	−28.45	−27.61	−33.28	−19.21	−21.42
Deposit Money Banks						*Billions of Francs: End of Period*							
Reserves	20	9.68	12.05	7.41	8.99	15.08	13.85	12.72	105.99	30.07	29.34	37.44	52.33
Foreign Assets	21	24.42	22.15	16.25	17.37	16.64	16.31	22.25	99.17	16.25	81.82	22.13	42.15
Claims on Central Government	22a	17.84	30.76	28.91	29.45	25.74	28.74	20.12	26.43	15.07	24.86	16.81	23.08
Claims on Nonfin.Pub.Enterprises	22c	11.28	10.17	13.75	13.96	13.35	16.16	13.98	10.65	6.98	4.81	5.12	10.82
Claims on Private Sector	22d	66.02	75.62	85.68	98.09	106.53	112.01	158.00	109.59	101.03	60.62	75.06	73.02
Claims on Other Banking Insts	22f	.06	.01	.02	.01	.30	.13	.78	.08	—	—	—	—
Claims on Nonbank Financial Insts	22g	.40	.60	.84	1.05	1.16	1.33	.63	.05	.98	.98	1.57	1.20
Demand Deposits	24	41.94	60.57	49.16	61.08	68.85	68.39	76.68	171.74	81.36	129.77	89.50	110.72
Time and Savings Deposits	25	28.48	24.78	24.34	31.00	35.14	31.94	26.84	24.70	19.93	20.46	49.44	55.45
Foreign Liabilities	26c	17.18	26.75	14.04	13.51	8.45	23.51	25.57	12.67	13.24	42.97	20.74	27.08
Long-Term Foreign Liabilities	26cl	.17	—	.13	.01	.01	—	—	—	—	—	—	.51
Central Government Deposits	26d	2.61	6.10	11.03	12.65	10.95	17.44	25.53	56.16	11.83	15.48	15.14	11.28
Credit from Monetary Authorities	26g	1.51	1.54	4.26	3.70	5.01	7.16	6.20	6.45	2.44	—	.61	.39
Capital Accounts	27a	36.24	41.05	54.40	59.64	62.30	45.04	62.95	36.19	48.65	9.42	12.23	16.44
Other Items (Net)	27r	1.57	−9.42	−4.51	−12.65	−11.91	−4.96	4.70	44.04	−7.08	−15.66	−30.19	−19.88
Monetary Survey						*Billions of Francs: End of Period*							
Foreign Assets (Net)	31n	−4.09	4.49	15.02	25.15	17.82	−44.36	−10.86	198.63	10.70	22.99	−7.64	45.09
Domestic Credit	32	160.65	165.98	183.04	198.39	226.80	252.73	275.96	198.32	272.48	239.75	265.46	274.22
Claims on Central Govt. (Net)	32an	82.89	79.58	82.75	85.27	105.46	123.10	102.58	77.94	163.49	173.34	183.73	189.17
Claims on Nonfin.Pub.Enterprises	32c	11.28	10.17	13.75	13.96	13.35	16.16	13.98	10.65	6.98	4.81	5.12	10.82
Claims on Private Sector	32d	66.02	75.62	85.68	98.09	106.53	112.01	158.00	109.59	101.03	60.62	75.06	73.02
Claims on Other Banking Insts	32f	.06	.01	.02	.01	.30	.13	.78	.08	—	—	—	—
Claims on Nonbank Financial Inst	32g	.40	.60	.84	1.05	1.16	1.33	.63	.05	.98	.98	1.57	1.20
Money	34	95.76	134.49	134.85	153.18	166.56	143.98	184.03	309.58	238.08	271.24	235.15	278.79
Quasi-Money	35	28.48	24.78	24.34	31.00	35.14	31.94	26.84	24.70	19.93	20.46	49.44	55.45
Other Items (Net)	37r	32.32	11.20	38.87	39.37	42.92	32.45	54.23	62.67	25.16	−28.96	−27.42	−15.56
Money plus Quasi-Money	35l	124.24	159.27	159.19	184.17	201.70	175.92	210.87	334.28	258.01	291.69	284.59	334.24
Interest Rates						*Percent Per Annum*							
Discount Rate (End of Period)	60	11.50	† 7.75	8.60	7.75	7.50	7.00	7.60	7.00	6.50	6.30	6.00	6.00
Deposit Rate	60l	7.75	8.08	5.50	5.46	5.00	5.00	5.00	5.00	5.00	5.00	5.00	5.00
Lending Rate	60p	17.46	17.50	16.00	22.00	22.00	22.00	22.00	22.00	20.67	18.00	18.00	18.00
Prices and Production						*Index Numbers (2000=100): Period Averages*							
Wholesale Prices (1990=100)	63	101.0	....	....	....	....	....	....	....	....	....	....	....
Consumer Prices	64	49.5	70.5	77.1	84.8	....	95.7	100.9	100.0	100.1	104.7	103.8	106.3
Crude Petroleum Production	66aa	75.0	71.0	72.8	81.6	91.1	96.4	100.3	100.0	92.1	91.3	148.3	107.7
Intl. Transactions & Positions						*Billions of Francs*							
Exports	70	302.63	532.40	585.30	688.10	973.70	806.90	960.50	1,772.20	....	....	....	....
Imports, c.i.f	71	164.79	350.41	334.18	793.31	540.65	401.29	505.22	330.94	....	....	....	....
Imports, f.o.b	71.v	134.08	340.20	324.50	770.20	524.90	329.40	429.80	321.30	....	....	....	....

Congo, Republic of   634

		1993	1994	1995	1996	1997	1998	1999	2000	2001	2002	2003	2004
Balance of Payments		*Millions of US Dollars: Minus Sign Indicates Debit*											
Current Account, n.i.e.	78ald	−552.7	−793.4	−625.2	−650.9	−155.8	−240.6	−230.6	648.1	−28.4	−34.5	−2.6	....
Goods: Exports f.o.b.	78aad	1,119.1	958.9	1,286.6	1,654.9	1,661.5	1,367.8	1,560.1	2,491.8	2,055.3	2,288.8	1,461.1	....
Goods: Imports f.o.b.	78abd	−500.1	−612.7	−654.2	−587.2	−648.8	−558.4	−522.7	−455.3	−681.3	−691.1	−449.9	....
Trade Balance	78acd	619.1	346.2	632.4	1,067.7	1,012.7	809.4	1,037.4	2,036.5	1,373.9	1,597.7	1,011.2	....
Services: Credit	78add	56.2	67.0	87.4	91.9	99.7	117.6	146.0	136.5	143.8	164.8	84.7	....
Services: Debit	78aed	−845.5	−995.8	−691.7	−936.0	−748.5	−857.4	−868.6	−738.3	−852.2	−926.9	−544.9	....
Balance on Goods & Services	78afd	−170.2	−582.7	28.2	223.5	363.9	69.6	314.9	1,434.7	665.6	835.6	551.0	....
Income: Credit	78agd	11.3	2.0	8.6	9.3	5.9	4.0	29.6	14.0	15.2	6.2	4.3	....
Income: Debit	78ahd	−384.9	−291.1	−703.8	−914.7	−527.7	−311.1	−569.8	−819.3	−694.0	−866.4	−550.4	....
Balance on Gds, Serv. & Inc.	78aid	−543.9	−871.8	−667.0	−681.9	−157.9	−237.6	−225.3	629.3	−13.2	−24.7	4.9	....
Current Transfers, n.i.e.: Credit	78ajd	50.5	111.3	52.0	54.5	9.0	10.0	14.9	38.9	18.3	12.9	9.6	....
Current Transfers: Debit	78akd	−59.3	−33.0	−10.3	−23.5	−6.9	−13.0	−20.2	−20.1	−33.5	−22.7	−17.1	....
Capital Account, n.i.e.	78bcd	—	—	18.9	10.9	17.5	−.2	10.2	8.4	12.7	5.3	9.9	....
Capital Account, n.i.e.: Credit	78bad	—	—	18.9	11.6	17.5	—	10.3	8.9	13.3	5.3	9.9	....
Capital Account: Debit	78bbd	—	—	—	−.7	—	−.2	−.1	−.6	−.7	....	—	....
Financial Account, n.i.e.	78bjd	−111.2	605.4	80.6	−663.4	−604.5	−715.9	−336.2	−821.8	−653.1	−464.3	−58.5	....
Direct Investment Abroad	78bdd	—	—	−1.6	.4	−3.5	8.1	−19.3	−3.8	−5.9	−4.2	.3	....
Dir. Invest. in Rep. Econ., n.i.e.	78bed	—	—	125.0	72.6	79.2	32.8	538.2	165.9	77.2	331.2	200.7	....
Portfolio Investment Assets	78bfd	—	—	−2.0	−1.0	−5.2	−13.5	−17.5	−4.5	−11.5	−7.0	−5.1	....
Equity Securities	78bkd	—	—	−2.5	−4.4	−3.8	−14.2	.6	−3.9	−10.2	−3.8	−5.1	....
Debt Securities	78bld	—	—	.5	3.4	−1.4	.8	−18.2	−.6	−1.3	−3.2	—	....
Portfolio Investment Liab., n.i.e.	78bgd	—	—	—	.1	.1	.7	−.2	−.1	....	....	....	....
Equity Securities	78bmd	—	—	—	—	.1	....	−.2	−.1				
Debt Securities	78bnd	—	—	—	.1	—	.7	....	....	....	....	....	....
Financial Derivatives Assets	78bwd	....	....	....	....	....	....	....	....	....	....	....	....
Financial Derivatives Liabilities	78bxd	....	....	....	....	....	....	....	....	....	....	....	....
Other Investment Assets	78bhd	−22.6	35.5	115.5	33.8	−19.9	49.5	84.3	−73.8	−41.1	−25.0	—	....
Monetary Authorities	78bod	....	....	....	....	....	....	....	....	....	....		
General Government	78bpd	....	....	....	....	....	....	....	....	....	....		
Banks	78bqd	−14.8	33.9	13.1	−2.9	1.3	−5.5	−3.8	−20.4	27.1	31.9		
Other Sectors	78brd	−7.8	1.6	102.4	36.7	−21.1	55.0	88.1	−53.5	−68.2	−56.8	—	
Other Investment Liab., n.i.e.	78bid	−88.6	569.9	−156.3	−769.2	−655.2	−793.5	−921.7	−905.4	−671.8	−759.3	−254.4	....
Monetary Authorities	78bsd	—	—	1.1	−1.5	13.3	20.5	−6.2	1.4	−.4	−47.2	—	
General Government	78btd	−288.9	88.4	−457.9	−906.0	−586.4	−812.3	−459.6	−365.2	−606.8	−418.8	21.6	
Banks	78bud	—	—	−25.4	−1.3	−8.7	14.8	13.6	−12.5	1.3	14.5	—	
Other Sectors	78bvd	200.2	481.4	325.9	139.5	−73.4	−16.7	−469.5	−529.2	−65.9	−307.8	−276.0	....
Net Errors and Omissions	78cad	244.0	33.1	−54.9	−12.8	60.5	−72.0	−99.0	−77.6	−11.8	−219.7	−110.3	....
Overall Balance	78cbd	−420.0	−154.9	−580.7	−1,316.1	−682.4	−1,028.6	−655.6	−242.8	−680.6	−713.1	−161.5	....
Reserves and Related Items	79dad	420.0	154.9	580.7	1,316.1	682.4	1,028.6	655.6	242.8	680.6	713.1	161.5	....
Reserve Assets	79dbd	−1.7	−55.5	−4.3	−36.3	20.2	60.0	−40.9	−183.7	143.5	91.1	3.4	....
Use of Fund Credit and Loans	79dcd	−.7	15.0	−2.3	20.1	−2.1	−1.0	−4.2	13.6	−1.1	−8.2	−7.6	....
Exceptional Financing	79ded	422.4	195.4	587.3	1,332.2	664.3	969.6	700.7	413.0	538.3	630.3	165.7	....
Government Finance		*Billions of Francs: Year Ending December 31*											
Deficit (-) or Surplus	80	−95.9	−129.9	−86.3	−24.5	−109.6	−226.0	−81.4	26.5	117.5p	....	....	....
Total Revenue and Grants	81y	183.2	230.6	260.4	362.1	401.6	266.8	394.1	611.3	642.4p	....	....	....
Revenue	81	183.1	220.2	249.7	357.8	400.2	263.2	387.8	604.5	637.4p	....	....	....
Grants	81z	.1	10.4	10.7	4.3	1.4	3.6	6.3	6.8	5.0p	....	....	....
Exp. & Lending Minus Repay.	82z	279.1	360.5	346.6	386.6	511.2	492.8	475.5	584.8	524.9p	....	....	....
Expenditure	82	279.1	360.5	346.6	386.6	511.2	492.8	475.5	584.8	524.9p	....	....	....
Lending Minus Repayments	83	—	—	—	—	—	—	—	—	—p	....	....	....
Total Financing	80h	125.9	129.9	86.2	24.5	109.6	226.0	81.5	−26.5	....	....	....	....
Domestic	84a	91.4	12.9	15.9	−51.1	−77.3	39.7	−4.0	−71.8	....	....	....	....
Foreign	85a	34.5	117.0	70.3	75.6	186.9	186.3	85.4	45.3	....	....	....	....
Total Debt by Residence	88	....	....	....	....	....	....	4,112.3	3,681.5	....	....	....	....
Domestic	88a	....	....	....	....	....	....	390.0	433.6	....	....	....	....
Foreign	89a	1,295.7	2,875.4	2,839.4	3,318.7	3,468.4	3,770.4	3,722.4	3,247.9	....	....	....	....
National Accounts		*Billions of Francs*											
Househ.Cons.Expend.,incl.NPISHs.	96f	434.7	499.9	372.2	671.5	551.3	373.3	506.7	507.4	634.6	669.9	661.4	769.4
Government Consumption Expend.	91f	182.3	200.8	133.6	133.8	257.2	164.1	185.3	215.9	205.2	272.2	213.0	224.2
Gross Fixed Capital Formation	93e	140.7	439.6	521.8	364.9	329.3	557.6	512.3	534.5	682.9	599.2	555.7	650.0
Changes in Inventories	93i	4.2	13.8	24.0	13.9	8.6	15.0	51.0	3.0	50.0	−50.0	−10.2	12.0
Exports of Goods and Services	90c	323.5	557.6	682.9	894.8	1,024.9	875.5	1,050.5	1,881.8	1,601.1	1,593.2	1,645.6	1,732.8
Imports of Goods and Services (-)	98c	325.3	725.4	666.7	779.1	815.6	835.3	856.6	849.8	1,125.4	981.5	995.5	1,142.6
Gross Domestic Product (GDP)	99b	760.2	982.3	1,056.2	1,299.7	1,355.7	1,150.1	1,449.4	2,292.5	2,048.3	2,103.0	2,069.9	2,246.4
Net Primary Income from Abroad	98.n	−105.8	−160.5	−352.9	−463.2	−304.5	−181.2	−332.6	−573.8	−497.5	−464.0	−340.6	587.6
Gross National Income (GNI)	99a	662.6	780.9	703.3	836.5	1,051.2	968.9	1,116.8	1,718.7	1,550.8	1,639.0	1,729.3	1,658.8
GDP Volume 1978 Prices	99b.p	424.5	401.3	410.1	....	....	....	....	....	....	....	....	....
GDP Volume (2000=100)	99bvp	92.0	86.9	† 88.8	92.6	92.2	95.7	92.6	100.0	....	....	....	....
GDP Deflator (2000=100)	99bip	36.1	49.3	51.9	61.2	64.1	52.4	68.3	100.0	....	....	....	....
		Millions: Midyear Estimates											
Population	99z	2.73	2.82	2.92	3.01	3.12	3.22	3.33	3.44	3.55	3.66	3.77	3.88

2005, International Monetary Fund : *International Financial Statistics Yearbook*

Costa Rica   238

	code	1993	1994	1995	1996	1997	1998	1999	2000	2001	2002	2003	2004
Exchange Rates						*Colones per SDR: End of Period*							
Market Rate................................	aa	208.01	240.98	289.72	316.51	329.61	382.17	409.27	414.35	429.39	514.88	621.92	712.23
					Colones per US Dollar: End of Period (ae) Period Average (rf)								
Market Rate................................	ae	151.44	165.07	194.90	220.11	244.29	271.42	298.19	318.02	341.67	378.72	418.53	458.61
Market Rate................................	rf	142.17	157.07	179.73	207.69	232.60	257.23	285.68	308.19	328.87	359.82	398.66	437.91
					Index Numbers (2000=100): Period Averages								
Market Rate................................	ahx	216.9	196.3	171.8	148.6	132.6	119.9	107.9	100.0	93.7	85.7	77.3	70.4
Nominal Effective Exchange Rate.....	nec	161.2	164.4	145.0	130.3	121.9	113.8	104.4	100.0	96.8	88.7	76.6	67.6
Real Effective Exchange Rate...........	rec	92.4	91.7	93.4	94.1	96.5	98.0	96.7	100.0	104.5	102.2	94.2	91.1
Fund Position						*Millions of SDRs: End of Period*							
Quota......................................	2f.s	119.00	119.00	119.00	119.00	119.00	119.00	164.10	164.10	164.10	164.10	164.10	164.10
SDRs..	1b.s	.12	.12	.04	.01	.02	.05	.59	.33	.07	.06	.04	.09
Reserve Position in the Fund..........	1c.s	8.73	8.73	8.73	8.73	8.73	8.73	20.00	20.00	20.00	20.00	20.00	20.00
Total Fund Cred.&Loans Outstg.......	2tl	59.28	45.46	16.32	.50	—	—	—	—	—	—	—	—
International Liquidity					*Millions of US Dollars Unless Otherwise Indicated: End of Period*								
Total Reserves minus Gold...............	1l.d	1,024.03	893.20	1,046.64	1,000.23	1,261.82	1,063.39	1,460.40	1,317.76	1,329.82	1,496.54	1,836.27	1,917.91
SDRs..	1b.d	.16	.18	.06	.01	.03	.07	.81	.43	.09	.09	.05	.13
Reserve Position in the Fund..........	1c.d	11.98	12.74	12.97	12.55	11.77	12.29	27.45	26.06	25.13	27.19	29.72	31.06
Foreign Exchange.....................	1d.d	1,011.89	880.28	1,033.61	987.67	1,250.02	1,051.04	1,432.14	1,291.27	1,304.59	1,469.27	1,806.49	1,886.71
Gold (Million Fine Troy Ounces).......	1ad	.035	.034	.034	.002	.002	.002	.002	.002	.002	.002	.002	.002
Gold (National Valuation)................	1and	13.46	....	....	....	.03	.02	.02	.02	.02	.02	.02	.02
Monetary Authorities: Other Liab.....	4..d	1,452.73	1,294.60	1,217.58	1,115.12	1,047.67	1,078.46	1,013.79	917.51	811.13	671.21	574.96	283.21
Deposit Money Banks: Assets...........	7a.d	151.99	199.11	203.90	248.10	251.59	324.56	284.38	330.69	362.78	335.19	384.00	644.22
Liabilities............	7b.d	90.29	102.24	166.96	200.85	293.53	333.73	387.96	529.25	651.69	727.40	901.48	1,008.60
Other Banking Insts.: Liabilities........	7f.d	3.81	3.58	....	....	....	....	....	....	....	....	....	....
Monetary Authorities						*Billions of Colones: End of Period*							
Foreign Assets.............................	11	162.3	155.9	196.7	203.7	† 364.0	370.6	556.3	536.1	534.6	636.8	819.4	974.0
Claims on Central Government........	12a	52.0	71.5	100.2	283.4	† 359.7	416.8	312.1	234.5	82.8	83.6	90.2	100.5
Claims on Nonfin.Pub.Enterprises.....	12c	28.8	23.5	23.4	25.4	† 8.7	9.3	9.9	10.0	9.9	9.9	9.6	9.1
Claims on Deposit Money Banks.....	12e	30.9	62.7	38.3	43.4	† 22.0	20.8	22.9	18.7	17.6	16.2	16.2	15.6
Claims on Other Banking Insts.........	12f	3.5	3.3	3.1	3.3	† 1.0	.9	.8	.7	.7	.6	.5	.5
Reserve Money.............................	14	208.4	270.0	313.7	382.2	† 446.8	497.0	533.5	508.5	376.6	392.9	510.0	644.4
of which: Currency Outside DMBs..	14a	54.7	74.9	84.8	91.7	† 106.8	124.2	152.6	141.4	156.5	169.7	186.9	205.6
Time, Savings,& Fgn.Currency Dep...	15	8.9	4.8	4.7	8.2	† 4.2	4.3	3.7	3.2	3.3	1.8	—	—
Liabs. of Central Bank: Securities.....	16ac	45.5	78.9	128.5	46.8	† 196.4	184.2	379.4	406.9	496.2	696.5	906.8	930.3
Restricted Deposits........................	16b	—	—	—	—	† .3	.3	.3	.3	.3	—	—	—
Foreign Liabilities.........................	16c	232.3	224.7	242.0	245.6	† 255.9	292.7	302.3	291.8	277.1	254.2	240.6	129.9
Central Government Deposits...........	16d	14.1	9.3	28.5	111.9	† 63.2	60.8	80.4	32.1	77.4	71.5	65.4	139.0
Counterpart Funds........................	16e	—	—	—	—	† 8.6	10.8	2.5	2.3	5.0	.6	.6	.6
Capital Accounts..........................	17a	25.1	26.8	29.0	126.9	† 126.5	105.8	−221.0	−280.4	−559.8	−675.7	−811.7	−870.2
Other Items (Net).........................	17r	−256.8	−297.5	−384.8	−362.4	† −346.5	−337.5	−179.1	−164.7	−30.6	5.3	24.3	125.7
of which: Valuation Adjustment.....	17rv	−293.3	−335.0	−415.0	−401.3	† −353.0	−346.5	−196.6	−107.2	−41.9	−4.4	−2.3	−3.6
Deposit Money Banks						*Billions of Colones: End of Period*							
Reserves.....................................	20	155.7	196.2	232.3	289.9	† 248.8	282.5	294.0	282.1	275.2	288.5	325.7	420.8
Claims on Mon.Author.:Securities....	20c	1.5	7.7	36.1	30.3	† 109.4	36.7	171.9	203.6	181.6	263.9	284.0	445.2
Foreign Assets.............................	21	23.0	32.9	39.7	54.6	† 61.5	88.1	84.8	105.2	124.0	126.9	160.7	295.4
Claims on Central Government........	22a	6.6	34.6	28.4	89.7	† 130.1	133.1	134.4	162.0	228.5	356.4	453.1	788.0
Claims on Nonfin.Pub.Enterprises....	22c	2.6	2.8	2.4	2.5	† 7.3	7.0	9.8	23.4	11.1	11.5	11.1	16.7
Claims on Private Sector.................	22d	190.3	222.9	223.0	329.9	† 434.3	670.6	914.3	1,180.0	1,493.3	1,824.4	2,176.4	2,613.9
Claims on Other Banking Insts.........	22f	2.9	2.6	.1	—	† 9.6	26.4	9.5	20.5	19.4	21.8	32.3	34.3
Demand Deposits.........................	24	62.4	86.6	67.0	84.9	† 243.7	279.6	350.5	479.7	542.3	662.6	779.0	837.6
Time, Savings,& Fgn.Currency Dep...	25	301.3	355.1	389.7	620.7	† 578.1	763.8	989.1	1,164.7	1,267.6	1,567.7	1,845.2	2,720.3
Bonds......................................	26ab	—	—	—	—	† 7.0	16.3	37.2	35.5	35.3	39.6	39.0	44.4
Restricted Deposits........................	26b	—	—	—	—	† .3	.1	—	—	.1	.1	.1	.2
Foreign Liabilities.........................	26c	13.7	16.9	32.5	44.2	† 71.7	90.6	115.7	168.3	222.7	275.5	377.3	462.6
Central Government Deposits...........	26d	5.6	41.4	15.0	3.4	† —	—	—	—	—	—	—	—
Credit from Monetary Authorities.....	26g	17.4	45.8	14.5	11.0	† 9.2	7.9	7.5	4.9	7.7	4.6	2.8	1.0
Capital Accounts..........................	27a	43.0	31.8	63.7	95.5	† 185.6	229.1	306.7	370.6	486.8	589.6	738.7	852.0
Other Items (Net).........................	27r	−60.8	−78.0	−20.6	−62.7	† −94.6	−143.0	−187.8	−246.8	−229.3	−246.3	−338.8	−303.6
Monetary Survey						*Billions of Colones: End of Period*							
Foreign Assets (Net).......................	31n	−60.7	−52.8	−38.1	−31.5	† 97.8	75.4	223.2	181.2	158.8	234.1	362.2	677.0
Domestic Credit............................	32	267.0	310.5	336.9	618.9	† 887.5	1,203.4	1,310.4	1,599.0	1,768.2	2,236.7	2,707.9	3,424.1
Claims on Central Govt. (Net)........	32an	38.8	55.4	85.0	257.8	† 426.6	489.1	366.0	364.3	233.9	368.6	478.0	749.5
Claims on Nonfin.Pub.Enterprises...	32c	31.4	26.3	25.8	27.9	† 16.0	16.4	19.7	33.4	21.0	21.4	20.7	25.9
Claims on Private Sector..............	32d	190.3	222.9	223.0	329.9	† 434.3	670.6	914.3	1,180.0	1,493.3	1,824.4	2,176.4	2,613.9
Claims on Other Banking Insts........	32f	6.4	5.9	3.1	3.3	† 10.6	27.3	10.3	21.3	20.1	22.4	32.8	34.8
Money.......................................	34	117.2	161.6	151.9	177.5	† 354.6	415.4	534.1	639.7	724.2	843.1	970.1	1,046.7
Quasi-Money................................	35	310.2	359.8	394.4	628.8	† 582.3	768.1	992.7	1,167.9	1,270.9	1,569.5	1,845.3	2,720.3
Bonds.......................................	36ab	—	—	—	—	† 7.0	16.3	37.2	35.5	35.3	39.6	39.0	44.4
Liabs. of Central Bank: Securities....	36ac	44.0	71.2	92.4	16.5	† 87.0	147.5	207.5	203.3	314.6	432.6	622.8	485.0
Restricted Deposits.......................	36b					† .5	.4	.3	.3	.4	.1	.1	.2
Counterpart Funds........................	36e	—	—	—	—	† 8.6	10.8	2.5	2.3	5.0	.6	.6	.6
Capital Accounts..........................	37a	68.1	58.6	92.7	222.3	† 312.1	335.0	85.7	90.2	−73.0	−86.0	−73.0	−18.1
Other Items (Net).........................	37r	−333.2	−393.5	−432.7	−457.7	† −366.9	−414.6	−326.4	−359.1	−350.3	−328.7	−334.7	−178.1
Money plus Quasi-Money................	35l	427.4	521.4	546.3	806.3	† 936.9	1,183.5	1,526.8	1,807.6	1,995.1	2,412.6	2,815.4	3,767.0

Costa Rica   238

		1993	1994	1995	1996	1997	1998	1999	2000	2001	2002	2003	2004
Other Banking Institutions					*Billions of Colones: End of Period*								
Cash	40	.1	—	....	....	....	....	....	....	....	....	....	....
Claims on Central Government	42a	.8	.4	....	....	....	....	....	....	....	....	....	....
Claims on Official Entities	42bx	—	—	....	....	....	....	....	....	....	....	....	....
Claims on Private Sector	42d	5.0	7.3	....	....	....	....	....	....	....	....	....	....
Demand Deposits	44	—	—	....	....	....	....	....	....	....	....	....	....
Time, Savings,& Fgn.Currency Dep...	45	.4	.5	....	....	....	....	....	....	....	....	....	....
Bonds	46ab	2.0	2.1	....	....	....	....	....	....	....	....	....	....
Foreign Liabilities	46c	.6	.6	....	....	....	....	....	....	....	....	....	....
Central Government Deposits	46d	—	—	....	....	....	....	....	....	....	....	....	....
Credit from Monetary Authorities	46g	.7	2.4	....	....	....	....	....	....	....	....	....	....
Credit from Deposit Money Banks	46h	2.3	2.2	....	....	....	....	....	....	....	....	....	....
Capital Accounts	47a	.1	.2	....	....	....	....	....	....	....	....	....	....
Other Items (Net)	47r	−.3	−.1	....	....	....	....	....	....	....	....	....	....
Banking Survey					*Billions of Colones: End of Period*								
Foreign Assets (net)	51n	−61.2	−53.4	....	....	....	....	....	....	....	....	....	....
Domestic Credit	52	266.3	312.3	....	....	....	....	....	....	....	....	....	....
Claims on Central Govt. (Net)	52an	39.6	55.8	....	....	....	....	....	....	....	....	....	....
Claims on Official Entities	52bx	31.4	26.3	....	....	....	....	....	....	....	....	....	....
Claims on Private Sector	52d	195.3	230.2	....	....	....	....	....	....	....	....	....	....
Liquid Liabilities	55l	427.8	521.8	....	....	....	....	....	....	....	....	....	....
Bonds	56ab	46.0	73.3	....	....	....	....	....	....	....	....	....	....
Capital Accounts	57a	68.2	58.8	....	....	....	....	....	....	....	....	....	....
Other Items (Net)	57r	−336.9	−395.0	....	....	....	....	....	....	....	....	....	....
Interest Rates					*Percent Per Annum*								
Discount Rate (End of Period)	60	35.00	37.75	38.50	35.00	31.00	37.00	34.00	31.50	28.75	31.25	26.00	26.00
Deposit Rate	60l	16.90	17.72	23.88	17.29	13.03	12.76	14.31	13.38	11.77	11.46	10.41	9.51
Lending Rate	60p	30.02	33.03	36.70	26.27	22.48	22.47	25.74	24.89	23.83	26.42	25.58	23.43
Prices and Labor					*Index Numbers (2000=100): Period Averages*								
Producer Prices	63	† 41.4	46.9	58.1	67.4	75.2	81.8	90.1	100.0	109.3	118.0	130.5	150.7
Consumer Prices	64	39.4	† 44.7	55.1	64.8	73.3	81.9	90.1	100.0	111.2	121.4	132.9	149.3
					Number in Thousands: Period Averages								
Labor Force	67d	1,119	1,160	....	1,199	1,277	1,377	1,383	1,391	....	....	....	....
Employment	67e	1,096	1,138	1,174	1,145	1,227	1,300	1,300	1,319	1,553	1,587	1,640	1,654
Unemployment	67c	47	49	64	76	74	77	83	72	100	109	117	115
Unemployment Rate (%)	67r	4.1	4.2	5.2	6.2	5.7	5.6	6.0	5.2	6.1	6.4	6.7	6.5
Intl. Transactions & Positions					*Millions of US Dollars*								
Exports	70..d	2,625.5	2,878.2	3,475.9	3,758.4	4,334.5	5,525.6	6,662.4	5,849.7	5,021.4	5,263.5	6,102.2	6,297.0
Imports, c.i.f	71..d	3,515.1	3,788.5	4,090.0	4,326.6	4,969.6	6,238.7	6,354.6	6,388.5	6,568.6	7,187.9	7,662.6	8,268.0
Balance of Payments					*Millions of US Dollars: Minus Sign Indicates Debit*								
Current Account, n.i.e	78ald	−620.2	−244.0	−358.1	−263.7	−480.9	−520.8	−666.4	−706.8	−712.7	−916.1	−928.7	−831.5
Goods: Exports f.o.b	78aad	1,866.8	2,122.0	3,481.8	3,774.1	4,220.6	5,538.3	6,576.4	5,813.4	4,923.2	5,269.9	6,163.0	6,369.7
Goods: Imports f.o.b	78abd	−2,627.6	−2,727.8	−3,804.4	−4,023.3	−4,718.2	−5,937.4	−5,996.1	−6,023.8	−5,743.3	−6,537.1	−7,294.4	−7,832.7
Trade Balance	78acd	−760.8	−605.8	−322.6	−249.2	−497.6	−399.0	580.3	−210.5	−820.1	−1,267.2	−1,131.4	−1,463.0
Services: Credit	78add	1,039.3	1,195.0	969.1	1,053.5	1,128.6	1,343.4	1,666.1	1,936.3	1,900.6	1,869.9	2,027.0	2,240.4
Services: Debit	78aed	−816.4	−860.1	−913.0	−1,033.3	−988.4	−1,109.8	−1,195.1	−1,273.5	−1,168.9	−1,182.1	−1,188.4	−1,307.6
Balance on Goods & Services	78afd	−537.9	−270.9	−266.5	−228.9	−357.4	−165.5	1,051.2	452.3	−88.4	−579.5	−292.7	−530.2
Income: Credit	78agd	111.2	154.6	146.4	142.5	185.4	182.7	198.2	242.8	196.0	317.9	213.3	487.3
Income: Debit	78ahd	−336.6	−283.0	−371.9	−326.7	−434.4	−651.2	−2,019.8	−1,495.2	−975.6	−835.2	−1,061.9	−1,004.3
Balance on Gds, Serv. & Inc	78aid	−763.3	−399.3	−492.0	−413.2	−606.4	−634.0	−770.4	−800.1	−867.9	−1,096.8	−1,141.4	−1,047.1
Current Transfers, n.i.e.: Credit	78ajd	149.3	164.5	165.2	192.7	191.2	190.5	201.4	203.8	266.4	296.9	368.6	371.2
Current Transfers: Debit	78akd	−6.2	−9.2	−31.3	−43.2	−65.7	−77.3	−97.5	−110.5	−111.1	−116.2	−156.0	−155.5
Capital Account, n.i.e	78bcd	—	—	—	28.2	....	....	—	8.9	12.4	5.7	26.1	9.4
Capital Account, n.i.e.: Credit	78bad	—	—	—	28.2	....	....	—	8.9	12.4	5.7	26.1	9.4
Capital Account: Debit	78bbd				....	....	....					—	—
Financial Account, n.i.e	78bjd	62.8	−108.4	517.3	47.5	129.7	199.0	683.1	−38.0	320.4	844.8	594.3	707.7
Direct Investment Abroad	78bdd	−2.3	−4.7	−5.5	−5.7	−4.4	−4.8	−5.0	−8.5	−11.1	−34.1	−26.9	−60.6
Dir. Invest. in Rep. Econ., n.i.e	78bed	246.7	297.6	336.9	427.0	408.2	613.1	619.5	408.6	453.6	661.9	574.2	617.6
Portfolio Investment Assets	78bfd	—	—	−.4	....	−22.5	−33.9	−11.0	−18.5	−81.2	28.4	−91.6	53.1
Equity Securities	78bkd	—	—	−.4	....	−22.5	−33.9	−28.1	−4.0	−21.9	4.6	−1.5	−6.6
Debt Securities	78bld	—	—	—	....	....	....	17.1	−14.4	−59.2	23.8	−90.1	59.8
Portfolio Investment Liab., n.i.e	78bgd	−5.1	−1.2	−24.4	−21.5	−190.8	−296.0	−123.2	−67.5	−57.9	−125.8	−304.5	−25.4
Equity Securities	78bmd	—	—	—									
Debt Securities	78bnd	−5.1	−1.2	−24.4	−21.5	−190.8	−296.0	−123.2	−67.5	−57.9	−125.8	−304.5	−25.4
Financial Derivatives Assets	78bwd	....	....	....	....	....	....	....	....	....	....	....	....
Financial Derivatives Liabilities	78bxd	....	....	....	....	....	....	....	....	....	....	....	....
Other Investment Assets	78bhd	54.5	−76.2	16.8	−159.3	−267.4	−95.6	156.1	−344.3	106.2	217.5	162.4	−110.6
Monetary Authorities	78bod	....	....	.1	−6.3	−.1	−95.6	−.1	−.2	−.2	−.2	−27.6	−4.1
General Government	78bpd	34.9	−4.4	—	....	—	—	—	—	—	—	—	....
Banks	78bqd	—	—	−9.8	−17.8	43.3	−29.8	43.6	−76.3	54.4	.6	−35.2	−318.4
Other Sectors	78brd	19.6	−71.8	26.5	−135.2	−310.6	−65.8	112.7	−267.8	52.0	217.0	225.2	211.9
Other Investment Liab., n.i.e	78bid	−231.0	−323.9	193.9	−192.9	206.7	16.2	46.8	−7.8	−89.2	96.9	280.8	233.5
Monetary Authorities	78bsd	−256.8	−216.1	−94.4	−104.0	−118.6	−98.5	−93.7	−175.3	−135.2	−76.7	−47.4	−77.0
General Government	78btd	−25.7	−106.2	12.9	−85.2	−64.1	−60.7	−77.9	−74.6	−65.3	−57.7	−86.5	−69.9
Banks	78bud	27.7	−18.8	23.0	48.7	73.7	37.3	49.0	142.9	144.6	59.2	173.2	106.8
Other Sectors	78bvd	23.8	17.2	252.4	−52.3	315.7	138.1	169.4	99.1	−33.4	172.1	241.5	273.7
Net Errors and Omissions	78cad	299.0	249.1	57.1	118.7	157.8	−182.5	213.1	394.5	243.9	28.2	82.3	80.9
Overall Balance	78cbd	−258.4	−103.3	216.2	−69.3	−193.3	−504.3	229.7	−341.4	−136.0	−37.4	−226.1	−33.5
Reserves and Related Items	79dad	258.4	103.3	−216.2	69.3	193.3	504.3	−229.7	341.4	136.0	37.4	226.1	33.5
Reserve Assets	79dbd	59.6	65.5	−179.2	77.3	−215.7	149.6	−481.0	152.9	−13.0	−163.0	−338.9	−80.3
Use of Fund Credit and Loans	79dcd	—	−20.3	−44.4	−23.1	−.7	—	—	—	—	—	—	—
Exceptional Financing	79ded	198.8	58.1	7.4	15.0	409.7	354.7	251.3	188.4	149.0	200.4	564.9	113.8

Costa Rica   238

		1993	1994	1995	1996	1997	1998	1999	2000	2001	2002	2003	2004
International Investment Position					*Millions of US Dollars*								
Assets..	79aad	....	....	....	3,367.6	3,887.1	3,806.3	4,089.3	4,295.5	4,246.2	4,147.8	4,428.2	4,587.1
Direct Investment Abroad...............	79abd	....	....	....	60.0	65.7	71.4	77.6	86.1	97.4	128.9	153.9	212.7
Portfolio Investment.....................	79acd	....	....	....	86.2	108.7	105.8	90.1	108.5	142.5	131.1	222.7	169.5
Equity Securities............................	79add	....	....	....	19.0	41.5	38.6	40.0	44.0	7.4	2.7	4.3	10.9
Debt Securities...............................	79aed	....	....	....	67.2	67.2	67.2	50.1	64.5	135.1	128.3	218.4	158.6
Financial Derivatives......................	79ald	....	....	....	—	—	—	—	—	—	—	—	—
Other Investment...........................	79afd	....	....	....	2,212.6	2,488.9	2,554.2	2,366.1	2,699.8	2,593.1	2,309.5	2,132.0	2,203.7
Monetary Authorities..................	79agd	....	....	....	132.6	132.7	132.7	132.8	133.0	133.2	133.3	160.9	165.0
General Government....................	79ahd	....	....	....	—	—	—	—	—	—	—	—	—
Banks...	79aid	....	....	....	247.6	204.4	234.2	190.6	239.8	231.7	209.0	244.2	563.4
Other Sectors...............................	79ajd	....	....	....	1,832.3	2,151.9	2,187.3	2,042.6	2,327.0	2,228.3	1,967.2	1,727.0	1,475.2
Reserve Assets...............................	79akd	....	....	....	1,008.8	1,223.8	1,074.9	1,555.6	1,401.1	1,413.2	1,578.3	1,919.6	2,001.3
Liabilities.......................................	79lad	....	....	....	5,369.5	6,053.5	6,672.8	7,433.2	7,561.5	8,057.4	8,716.1	9,567.9	9,668.8
Dir. Invest. in Rep. Economy..........	79lbd	....	....	....	836.1	1,221.5	1,759.0	2,364.7	2,709.1	3,182.8	3,739.3	4,258.3	4,443.6
Portfolio Investment.....................	79lcd	....	....	....	674.2	773.1	699.6	794.9	744.5	844.3	921.8	863.6	632.6
Equity Securities............................	79ldd	....	....	....	—	—	—	—	—	—	—	—	—
Debt Securities...............................	79led	....	....	....	674.2	773.1	699.6	794.9	744.5	844.3	921.8	863.6	632.6
Financial Derivatives......................	79lld	....	....	....	—	—	—	—	—	—	—	—	—
Other Investment...........................	79lfd	....	....	....	3,859.2	4,058.9	4,214.2	4,273.7	4,107.8	4,030.3	4,055.1	4,446.0	4,592.6
Monetary Authorities..................	79lgd	....	....	....	659.5	548.4	559.0	493.8	419.5	318.6	262.7	335.7	259.3
General Government....................	79lhd	....	....	....	1,026.0	975.7	942.3	865.1	819.4	807.1	757.1	703.1	651.2
Banks...	79lid	....	....	....	191.6	266.1	303.2	359.7	537.6	664.8	722.9	894.7	970.3
Other Sectors...............................	79ljd	....	....	....	1,982.1	2,268.7	2,409.7	2,555.1	2,331.3	2,239.8	2,312.3	2,512.5	2,711.9
Government Finance					*Millions of Colones: Year Ending December 31*								
Deficit (-) or Surplus......................	80	−24,131	−85,361	−84,575	−95,471	−81,769	−89,435	−98,989	−140,173	−144,246	−239,767	....	....
Total Revenue and Grants..............	81y	166,065	191,247	253,699	302,497	363,540	444,486	547,435	599,101	704,131	781,797	....	....
Revenue.......................................	81	166,065	191,247	253,699	302,497	363,540	444,486	547,435	599,101	704,131	781,797	....	....
Grants..	81z	—	—	—	—	—	—	—	—	—	—	....	....
Exp. & Lending Minus Repay..........	82z	190,196	276,608	338,274	397,968	445,309	533,921	646,424	739,274	848,377	1,021,564	....	....
Expenditure.................................	82	190,196	276,608	338,274	397,968	445,309	533,921	646,424	739,274	848,377	1,021,564	....	....
Lending Minus Repayments.........	83	—	—	—	—	—	—	—	—	—	—	....	....
Total Financing..............................	80h	24,131	85,361	84,575	95,472	81,769	89,436	98,991	140,175	144,246	239,767	....	....
Domestic.....................................	84a	33,742	88,498	101,350	120,983	106,561	39,827	34,517	69,303	89,679	....	....	....
Foreign..	85a	−9,611	−3,138	−16,775	−25,511	−24,792	49,609	64,474	70,872	54,567	....	....	....
Total Debt by Residence.................	88	398,135	506,771	671,357	922,811	1,080,891	1,283,354	1,599,430	1,797,993	2,140,538	2,593,277	....	....
Domestic Debt.............................	88a	228,678	320,272	463,933	697,676	706,375	977,150	1,235,767	1,343,884	1,547,216	1,796,466	....	....
Foreign Debt................................	89a	169,457	186,499	207,424	225,135	374,516	306,204	363,663	454,109	593,322	796,811	....	....
National Accounts					*Millions of Colones*								
Househ.Cons.Expend.,incl.NPISHs....	96f	992,516	1,189,292	1,496,157	1,822,342	2,168,885	2,510,880	2,916,434	3,290,353	3,689,866	4,106,884	4,652,840	....
Government Consumption Expend...	91f	180,214	228,887	284,636	330,455	390,087	469,886	565,207	652,654	772,575	900,615	1,013,482	....
Gross Fixed Capital Formation..........	93e	280,900	324,161	399,983	421,650	538,478	740,341	811,325	873,951	987,278	1,143,140	1,332,290	....
Changes in Inventories....................	93i	5,270	8,282	−15,918	−29,099	1,161	1,626	−42,745	−42,854	106,985	221,601	96,130	....
Exports of Goods and Services..........	90c	490,201	589,686	790,800	967,130	1,215,914	1,720,723	2,335,125	2,389,590	2,236,333	2,569,619	3,260,846	....
Imports of Goods and Services (-).....	98c	578,808	682,071	849,971	1,052,522	1,330,505	1,816,627	2,072,582	2,249,196	2,398,442	2,882,965	3,384,774	....
Gross Domestic Product (GDP).........	99b	1,370,292	1,658,236	2,105,687	2,459,957	2,984,020	3,626,830	4,512,763	4,914,498	5,394,595	6,058,895	6,970,815	....
Net Primary Income from Abroad.....	98.n	−34,039	−21,837	−40,473	−38,353	−57,912	−120,500	−520,932	−385,150	−257,766	−248,837	−313,426	....
Gross National Income (GNI)............	99a	1,336,253	1,636,400	2,065,214	2,421,604	2,926,108	3,506,330	3,991,831	4,529,348	5,136,829	5,810,058	6,657,389	....
Consumption of Fixed Capital..........	99cf	78,649	92,123	115,025	138,579	168,727	201,867	256,097	284,228	319,941	368,045	418,912	....
GDP Volume 1991 Prices.................	99b.p	1,028,127	1,076,753	1,118,971	1,128,892	1,191,864	1,291,955	1,398,182	1,423,344	1,438,695	1,480,666	1,577,362	....
GDP Volume (2000=100)................	99bvp	72.2	75.6	78.6	79.3	83.7	90.8	98.2	100.0	101.1	104.0	110.8	....
GDP Deflator (2000=100)...............	99bip	38.6	44.6	54.5	63.1	72.5	81.3	93.5	100.0	108.6	118.5	128.0	....
					Millions: Midyear Estimates								
Population................................	99z	3.31	3.39	3.47	3.56	3.65	3.75	3.84	3.93	4.01	4.10	4.18	4.25

		1993	1994	1995	1996	1997	1998	1999	2000	2001	2002	2003	2004
Exchange Rates						*Francs per SDR: End of Period*							
Official Rate	aa	404.89	† 780.44	728.38	753.06	807.94	791.61	† 896.19	918.49	935.39	850.37	771.76	747.90
						Francs per US Dollar: End of Period (ae) Period Average (rf)							
Official Rate	ae	294.77	† 534.60	490.00	523.70	598.81	562.21	† 652.95	704.95	744.31	625.50	519.36	747.90
Official Rate	rf	283.16	† 555.20	499.15	511.55	583.67	589.95	† 615.70	711.98	733.04	696.99	581.20	528.28
						Index Numbers (2000=100): Period Averages							
Official Rate	ahx	250.9	128.1	142.3	138.8	121.8	120.5	115.5	100.0	96.9	102.2	122.4	134.6
Nominal Effective Exchange Rate	nec	172.1	99.5	105.9	106.6	102.7	107.3	106.1	100.0	102.0	105.0	112.1	114.8
Real Effective Exchange Rate	rec	144.8	89.2	103.1	103.6	101.9	108.7	106.5	100.0	103.5	107.6	115.8	117.6
Fund Position						*Millions of SDRs: End of Period*							
Quota	2f.s	238.2	238.2	238.2	238.2	238.2	238.2	325.2	325.2	325.2	325.2	325.2	325.2
SDRs	1b.s	.8	.1	1.2	.8	—	.1	2.5	1.0	.6	.9	.2	.1
Reserve Position in the Fund	1c.s	.1	.1	.1	.1	.2	.2	.2	.3	.3	.4	.6	.6
Total Fund Cred.&Loans Outstg	2tl	159.1	224.8	287.1	349.6	333.5	457.3	451.4	421.6	369.2	361.1	286.0	200.5
International Liquidity						*Millions of US Dollars Unless Otherwise Indicated: End of Period*							
Total Reserves minus Gold	1l.d	2.3	204.3	529.0	605.8	618.4	855.5	630.4	667.9	1,019.0	1,863.3	1,303.9	1,693.6
SDRs	1b.d	1.1	.2	1.8	1.2	—	.2	3.4	1.3	.7	1.2	.3	.2
Reserve Position in the Fund	1c.d	.1	.1	.1	.2	.2	.3	.3	.4	.4	.6	.8	.9
Foreign Exchange	1d.d	1.1	204.0	527.0	604.4	618.1	855.0	626.6	666.2	1,017.9	1,861.5	1,302.7	1,692.5
Gold (Million Fine Troy Ounces)	1ad	.045	.045	—	—	—	—	—	—	—	—	—	—
Gold (National Valuation)	1and	16.6	16.6	—	—	—	—	—	—	—	—	—	—
Monetary Authorities: Other Liab	4..d	1,382.4	1.7	9.6	7.8	10.6	14.4	8.1	.5	6.6	16.3	8.9	10.8
Deposit Money Banks: Assets	7a.d	176.5	202.1	352.6	268.5	266.8	311.3	351.9	252.5	222.3	364.6	290.1	351.2
Liabilities	7b.d	486.4	299.8	400.6	312.0	295.4	363.0	389.7	317.2	345.8	258.3	240.0	301.2
Monetary Authorities						*Billions of Francs: End of Period*							
Foreign Assets	11	.7	109.2	259.2	317.2	370.3	481.0	412.0	475.1	766.6	1,165.5	677.6	819.5
Claims on Central Government	12a	273.2	433.2	382.6	439.8	449.3	572.3	596.4	538.3	491.1	497.6	432.6	360.3
Claims on Deposit Money Banks	12e	506.6	130.0	140.8	125.8	104.7	114.6	99.8	75.3	36.8	14.7	.5	—
Claims on Other Financial Insts	12f	10.6	5.1	12.3	14.4	13.4	14.7	14.2	12.7	9.7	7.9	5.2	—
Reserve Money	14	295.8	462.4	516.0	550.8	615.7	733.1	676.7	690.1	926.9	1,297.5	752.5	907.8
of which: Currency Outside DMBs	14a	272.5	392.6	451.4	473.2	571.8	652.1	615.5	620.7	774.7	1,146.7	568.6	671.5
Foreign Liabilities	16c	471.9	176.3	213.8	267.3	275.8	370.2	409.8	387.6	350.3	317.2	225.4	155.2
Central Government Deposits	16d	13.1	45.8	43.0	49.5	27.8	51.1	56.7	39.3	40.8	44.2	97.8	75.5
Other Items (Net)	17r	10.3	−6.9	22.0	29.5	18.4	28.2	−20.8	−15.6	−13.9	26.7	40.2	41.2
Deposit Money Banks						*Billions of Francs: End of Period*							
Reserves	20	20.6	66.6	58.1	74.7	45.4	67.2	60.7	64.7	96.1	106.4	172.4	221.1
Foreign Assets	21	52.0	108.0	172.8	140.6	159.8	175.0	229.8	178.0	165.5	228.1	150.7	169.1
Claims on Central Government	22a	224.7	314.9	371.1	413.4	415.9	412.6	382.8	325.4	302.5	292.8	300.5	277.6
Claims on Private Sector	22d	878.5	828.2	997.1	1,016.0	1,147.4	1,186.7	1,084.5	1,136.2	1,192.3	1,192.3	1,073.3	1,164.1
Claims on Other Financial Insts	22f	6.2	5.8	1.7									
Demand Deposits	24	219.2	403.3	490.7	489.0	502.8	562.0	576.7	526.7	507.8	571.6	563.3	619.0
Time Deposits	25	331.0	412.1	485.3	519.6	527.7	485.1	477.7	489.3	515.3	641.1	618.6	632.2
Foreign Liabilities	26c	95.8	112.5	160.1	128.2	153.8	172.3	207.1	192.4	185.3	145.1	109.3	131.8
Long-Term Foreign Liabilities	26cl	47.6	47.8	36.2	35.2	23.1	31.7	47.4	31.3	72.1	16.4	15.3	13.3
Central Government Deposits	26d	92.5	171.1	183.1	243.3	278.9	325.7	234.4	267.3	287.6	262.3	214.6	214.3
Credit from Monetary Authorities	26g	497.3	134.4	152.2	124.3	104.7	116.0	91.0	76.8	37.0	14.7	.5	—
Other Items (Net)	27r	−101.3	42.3	93.0	105.0	177.6	148.7	123.5	120.5	151.2	168.4	175.2	221.4
Treasury Claims: Private Sector	22d.i	17.8	26.7	19.0	22.7	22.0	—	16.0	13.4	21.2	16.3	14.2	9.8
Post Office: Checking Deposits	24..i	1.7	2.1	1.5	2.4	3.6	2.0	3.0	3.9	3.6	4.7	6.1	5.6
Monetary Survey						*Billions of Francs: End of Period*							
Foreign Assets (Net)	31n	−515.0	−71.5	58.1	62.3	100.5	113.5	24.8	73.2	396.4	931.2	493.5	701.7
Domestic Credit	32	1,289.3	1,372.4	1,540.1	1,593.1	1,722.9	1,811.5	1,789.8	1,709.8	1,670.6	1,688.8	1,505.2	1,517.7
Claims on Central Govt. (Net)	32an	376.1	506.5	510.1	540.0	540.1	610.1	675.1	547.6	447.5	472.3	412.5	343.7
Claims on Private Sector	32d	896.3	854.9	1,016.0	1,038.7	1,169.4	1,186.7	1,100.5	1,149.5	1,213.5	1,208.6	1,087.5	1,174.0
Claims on Other Financial Insts	32f	16.9	10.9	13.9	14.4	13.4	14.7	14.2	12.7	9.7	7.9	5.2	—
Money	34	494.0	798.8	944.5	966.4	1,080.0	1,219.3	1,198.0	1,154.0	1,324.8	1,750.5	1,145.1	1,300.4
Quasi-Money	35	331.0	412.1	485.3	519.6	527.7	485.1	477.7	489.3	515.3	641.1	618.6	632.2
Long-Term Foreign Liabilities	36cl	47.6	47.8	36.2	35.2	23.1	31.7	47.4	31.3	72.1	16.4	15.3	13.3
Other Items (Net)	37r	−98.3	42.1	132.0	134.2	192.6	188.9	91.6	108.5	154.9	212.0	219.7	273.6
Money plus Quasi-Money	35l	825.0	1,210.9	1,429.9	1,486.0	1,607.7	1,704.4	1,675.7	1,643.3	1,840.1	2,391.6	1,763.7	1,932.6
Interest Rates						*Percent Per Annum*							
Bank Rate (End of Period)	60	† 6.00	6.00	6.00	6.00	6.00	6.00	6.00	6.00	6.00	6.00	4.50	4.00
Money Market Rate	60b	4.95	4.95	4.95	4.95	4.95	4.95	4.95	4.95	4.95	4.95	4.95	4.95
Deposit Rate	60l	3.50	3.50	3.50	3.50	3.50	3.50	3.50	3.50	3.50	3.50	3.50	3.50
Prices, Production, Labor						*Index Numbers (2000=100): Period Averages*							
Consumer Prices	64	60.2	75.9	86.8	88.9	92.5	96.8	97.6	100.0	104.3	107.5	111.1	112.7
Industrial Production	66	66.7	68.8	74.8	84.8	94.9	105.5	108.5	100.0	96.1	92.2	85.1	....
						Number in Thousands: Period Averages							
Unemployment	67c	175	186	216	238	....	....	....	....	....	....	....	....
Unemployment Rate	67r	27.7	30.0	35.6	38.8	....	....	....	....	....	....	....	....
Intl. Transactions & Positions						*Billions of Francs*							
Exports	70	713.20	1,522.50	1,899.70	2,274.40	2,598.10	2,717.60	2,870.10	2,768.20	2,892.70	3,676.60	3,396.50	....
Imports, c.i.f.	71	599.00	1,064.60	1,463.00	1,484.50	1,623.10	1,973.77	1,703.10	1,710.00	1,772.30	1,711.60	1,929.60	....

Côte d'Ivoire   662

		1993	1994	1995	1996	1997	1998	1999	2000	2001	2002	2003	2004
Balance of Payments						*Millions of US Dollars: Minus Sign Indicates Debit*							
Current Account, n.i.e.	78ald	−891.7	−13.8	−492.4	−162.3	−154.7	−290.2	−119.5	−241.3	−61.3	768.2	294.6	302.6
Goods: Exports f.o.b.	78aad	2,518.7	2,895.9	3,805.9	4,446.1	4,451.2	4,606.4	4,661.5	3,888.0	3,945.9	5,274.8	5,787.7	6,902.1
Goods: Imports f.o.b.	78abd	−1,770.4	−1,606.8	−2,430.3	−2,622.4	−2,658.4	−2,886.4	−2,766.0	−2,401.8	−2,417.7	−2,455.6	−3,230.9	−4,167.7
Trade Balance	78acd	748.3	1,289.1	1,375.5	1,823.7	1,792.8	1,720.0	1,895.5	1,486.2	1,528.2	2,819.3	2,556.8	2,734.4
Services: Credit	78add	675.9	507.7	530.9	565.7	579.6	614.5	586.5	482.4	577.8	585.3	664.3	748.3
Services: Debit	78aed	−1,331.7	−1,011.1	−1,375.7	−1,440.3	−1,478.6	−1,524.1	−1,459.0	−1,226.9	−1,271.3	−1,544.7	−1,780.1	−2,012.9
Balance on Goods & Services	78afd	92.5	785.7	530.7	949.1	893.8	810.4	1,022.9	741.7	834.8	1,859.9	1,441.0	1,469.8
Income: Credit	78agd	97.8	133.8	189.5	170.7	161.2	169.0	162.6	141.6	137.3	141.2	170.6	179.3
Income: Debit	78ahd	−887.8	−817.5	−976.1	−939.5	−829.2	−876.1	−919.2	−794.5	−723.1	−770.9	−830.1	−884.6
Balance on Gds, Serv. & Inc.	78aid	−697.5	102.0	−255.8	180.2	225.8	103.4	266.3	88.8	249.0	1,230.2	781.5	764.5
Current Transfers, n.i.e.: Credit	78ajd	270.9	246.8	277.7	204.1	137.7	148.2	136.8	79.4	88.5	131.9	196.4	202.9
Current Transfers: Debit	78akd	−465.1	−362.6	−514.3	−546.6	−518.3	−541.7	−522.6	−409.4	−398.7	−593.8	−683.3	−664.8
Capital Account, n.i.e.	78bcd	—	527.6	291.3	47.1	40.6	25.6	13.8	8.4	10.0	8.3	13.7	8.9
Capital Account, n.i.e.: Credit	78bad	—	527.6	291.3	49.8	50.5	35.9	17.4	9.9	11.5	9.1	14.1	11.5
Capital Account: Debit	78bbd	—	—	—	−2.7	−9.9	−10.3	−3.6	−1.4	−1.4	−.8	−.4	−2.7
Financial Account, n.i.e.	78bjd	−356.0	−523.1	−88.6	−717.3	−323.0	−417.1	−580.6	−365.2	−69.8	−1,034.6	−1,041.7	−1,124.4
Direct Investment Abroad	78bdd					−.4							
Dir. Invest. in Rep. Econ., n.i.e.	78bed	87.9	78.0	211.5	269.2	415.3	380.0	323.7	234.7	272.7	212.6	165.3	174.5
Portfolio Investment Assets	78bfd	7.4	−27.4	−8.4	−16.0	−26.9	−29.8	−31.9	−15.1	−15.8	−27.1	−41.7	−41.5
Equity Securities	78bkd	7.4	7.7	1.2	−1.6	.2	−1.7	−1.6	−1.3	−1.3	−2.0	−14.1	
Debt Securities	78bld	—	−35.1	−9.6	−14.5	−27.1	−28.2	−30.3	−13.8	−14.5	−25.1	−27.5	−41.5
Portfolio Investment Liab., n.i.e.	78bgd	—	−.7	10.0	25.0	19.2	19.5	13.4	4.5	4.0	51.7	66.8	−1.3
Equity Securities	78bmd	—	1.1	1.2	10.2	8.6	8.6	5.6	1.2	2.4	3.6	15.8	−1.3
Debt Securities	78bnd	—	−1.8	8.8	14.9	10.6	10.8	7.8	3.4	1.6	48.1	51.1	—
Financial Derivatives Assets	78bwd	—	—	—	—	—	−3.2	−3.1	−2.6	−3.8	−6.0	−7.9	—
Financial Derivatives Liabilities	78bxd	—	—	—	−3.3	−3.1					1.9	2.6	—
Other Investment Assets	78bhd	51.9	−39.6	−323.2	−256.5	−304.8	−317.6	−350.6	−182.4	−129.1	−439.0	−341.7	−437.5
Monetary Authorities	78bod	—	—	—	....	....	....	—	—	—	—	—	—
General Government	78bpd		−11.9	−14.2	−22.3	−9.9	−7.7	−5.2	−4.5	−5.1	−7.8	−4.0	−8.3
Banks	78bqd	72.7	−95.3	−33.1	35.2	−25.7	−16.4	−49.1	2.8	37.7	−89.8	62.6	—
Other Sectors	78brd	−20.8	67.5	−275.9	−269.4	−269.2	−293.5	−296.3	−180.7	−161.8	−341.5	−400.3	−429.1
Other Investment Liab., n.i.e.	78bid	−503.2	−533.3	21.4	−735.8	−422.7	−465.9	−532.0	−404.3	−197.8	−828.6	−885.2	−818.7
Monetary Authorities	78bsd	−44.1	−726.6	1.8	−1.2	4.3	3.1	−5.2	−.7	−14.4	10.5	−6.7	—
General Government	78btd	−444.6	249.8	−105.8	−621.6	−473.6	−597.3	−583.6	−523.3	−487.3	−737.2	−678.8	−658.4
Banks	78bud	7.8	75.1	77.1	−38.5	64.9	37.3	42.0	23.1	46.1	−136.4	−9.6	—
Other Sectors	78bvd	−22.2	−131.7	48.3	−74.5	−18.3	91.0	14.7	96.6	257.8	34.5	−190.1	−160.3
Net Errors and Omissions	78cad	11.1	−11.1	35.6	−15.4	−39.6	32.1	−21.5	−10.3	35.0	−20.3	−53.8	32.2
Overall Balance	78cbd	−1,236.6	−20.3	−254.2	−848.4	−476.6	−649.6	−707.9	−608.3	−86.1	−278.4	−787.2	−780.8
Reserves and Related Items	79dad	1,236.6	20.3	254.2	848.4	476.6	649.6	707.9	608.3	86.1	278.4	787.2	780.8
Reserve Assets	79dbd	4.4	−194.5	−302.5	−113.4	−95.4	−179.8	109.8	−89.0	−386.6	−584.1	12.0	−15.1
Use of Fund Credit and Loans	79dcd	−49.0	94.3	94.9	90.3	−22.3	168.8	−8.2	−38.8	−66.4	−13.5	−106.4	−127.1
Exceptional Financing	79ded	1,281.2	120.5	461.8	871.5	594.3	660.6	606.3	736.1	539.1	876.1	881.6	923.0
International Investment Position						*Millions of US Dollars*							
Assets	79aad	....	....	....	....	....	2,768.3	2,640.9	2,735.7	3,114.5	4,876.3	6,288.1	7,323.4
Direct Investment Abroad	79abd	....	—	—	—	—	—	—	—	—	—	—	—
Portfolio Investment	79acd	....	—	—	—	—	158.9	166.9	169.9	176.4	240.2	335.9	407.7
Equity Securities	79add	....	—	—	—	—	10.5	10.5	11.1	11.8	16.3	35.4	38.2
Debt Securities	79aed	....	—	—	—	—	148.4	156.3	158.7	164.6	223.9	300.5	369.5
Financial Derivatives	79ald	....	—	—	—	—	—	—	—	—	—	—	—
Other Investment	79afd	....	337.4	378.6	268.3	266.9	1,757.3	1,843.7	1,891.9	1,919.1	2,772.8	3,721.7	4,493.6
Monetary Authorities	79agd	....	....	....	....	....	—	—	—	—	—	—	—
General Government	79ahd	....	....	....	....	....	—	—	—	—	—	—	—
Banks	79aid	....	230.5	249.8	81.0	100.7							
Other Sectors	79ajd	....	....	....	....	....	1,757.3	1,843.7	1,891.9	1,919.1	2,772.8	3,721.7	4,493.6
Reserve Assets	79akd	....	204.4	531.0	607.0	623.0	852.1	630.4	673.9	1,019.0	1,863.3	2,230.5	2,422.1
Liabilities	79lad	....	....	....	....	....	18,731.5	16,581.2	15,907.8	12,696.6	15,390.7	17,811.6	18,691.8
Dir. Invest. in Rep. Economy	79lbd	....	—	—	—	—	1,858.2	1,905.1	2,001.6	2,164.4	2,812.4	3,572.1	4,043.9
Portfolio Investment	79lcd	....	—	—	—	—	244.4	223.1	211.2	205.8	299.3	435.2	467.9
Equity Securities	79ldd	....	—	—	—	—							
Debt Securities	79led	....	—	—	—	—	244.4	223.1	211.2	205.8	299.3	435.2	467.9
Financial Derivatives	79lld	....	....	....	....	....							
Other Investment	79lfd	....	15,272.6	17,009.2	16,101.1	14,046.3	16,628.9	14,453.0	13,695.0	10,326.5	12,279.0	13,804.2	14,180.0
Monetary Authorities	79lgd	....	329.8	436.8	510.7	461.3	644.0	619.5	549.3	464.0	490.9	425.0	311.4
General Government	79lhd	....	....	....	....	....	14,790.1	12,756.1	12,027.6	8,518.3	10,291.1	11,841.9	12,386.6
Banks	79lid	....	743.5	522.9	266.2	295.4	437.8	429.2	454.9	511.8	507.1	562.8	431.1
Other Sectors	79ljd	....	....	....	....	....	757.0	648.2	663.2	832.3	990.0	974.5	1,051.0
Government Finance						*Billions of Francs: Year Ending December 31*							
Deficit (-) or Surplus	80	....	−280.1	−147.3	−57.7	23.2	−84.0	−11.0	....	....	....	....	....
Total Revenue and Grants	81y	....	878.7	1,142.2	1,274.5	1,374.2	1,442.7	1,482.1	....	....	....	....	....
Revenue	81	....	849.0	1,107.2	1,234.0	1,330.2	1,392.2	1,442.1	....	....	....	....	....
Grants	81z	....	29.7	35.0	40.5	44.1	50.5	40.0	....	....	....	....	....
Exp. & Lending Minus Repay.	82z	....	1,158.8	1,289.5	1,332.2	1,351.0	1,526.7	1,493.1	....	....	....	....	....
Expenditure	82	....	1,166.0	1,322.6	1,385.2	1,494.5	1,557.3	1,533.1	....	....	....	....	....
Lending Minus Repayments	83	....	−7.2	−33.1	−53.0	−143.5	−30.6	−40.0	....	....	....	....	....
Total Financing	80h	....	280.1	147.3	57.7	−23.2	84.0	11.0	....	....	....	....	....
Domestic	84a	....	−153.1	−61.6	−107.5	−85.0	36.3	−104.2	....	....	....	....	....
Foreign	85a	....	433.2	208.9	165.2	61.8	47.7	115.2	....	....	....	....	....
Total Debt by Residence	88	....	9,148.6	9,392.7	9,606.0	10,056.3	7,620.7	....	....	....	....	....	....
Domestic	88a	....	1,320.4	1,230.7	1,137.8	1,070.6	1,039.5	....	....	....	....	....	....
Foreign	89a	....	7,828.2	8,162.0	8,468.2	8,985.7	6,581.2	....	....	....	....	....	....

Côte d'Ivoire   662

		1993	1994	1995	1996	1997	1998	1999	2000	2001	2002	2003	2004
National Accounts							*Billions of Francs*						
Househ.Cons.Expend.,incl.NPISHs....	96f	2,185.0	2,749.2	3,379.0	3,502.3	4,535.0	4,916.0	4,868.0	5,076.6	5,241.7	4,834.1	5,225.9	....
Government Consumption Expend...	91f	484.0	555.0	594.0	714.4	713.2	1,132.0	1,150.0	1,050.0	1,100.5	1,290.6	1,279.2	....
Gross Fixed Capital Formation..........	93e	230.9	473.0	641.2	846.5	959.8	1,167.3	1,124.1	821.8	760.8	807.6	748.8	....
Changes in Inventories....................	93i	13.3	60.8	104.6	−112.0	−37.2	−294.3	−100.1	−30.0	98.0	−79.2	32.0	....
Exports of Goods and Services..........	90c	847.0	1,827.0	2,051.0	2,533.0	2,737.8	2,835.0	3,074.0	3,010.0	3,163.0	4,084.4	3,810.8	....
Imports of Goods and Services (-).....	98c	814.0	1,409.0	394.5	1,960.7	2,074.3	2,215.0	2,382.0	2,381.9	2,494.5	2,788.3	2,933.8	....
Gross Domestic Product (GDP).........	99b	2,946.2	4,256.0	4,987.7	5,548.2	6,834.4	7,541.1	7,734.1	7,546.5	7,869.5	8,149.3	8,162.9	8,468.0
							Millions: Midyear Estimates						
Population..............................	99z	13.92	14.34	14.76	15.17	15.59	16.00	16.38	16.73	17.05	17.34	17.60	17.87

Croatia 960

		1993	1994	1995	1996	1997	1998	1999	2000	2001	2002	2003	2004
Exchange Rates						*Kuna per SDR: End of Period*							
Official Rate	aa	9.013	8.217	7.902	7.966	8.504	8.797	10.496	10.626	10.501	9.715	9.092	8.754
						Kuna per US Dollar: End of Period (ae) Period Average (rf)							
Official Rate	ae	6.562	5.629	5.316	5.540	6.303	6.248	7.648	8.155	8.356	7.146	6.119	5.637
Official Rate	rf	3.577	5.996	5.230	5.434	6.101	6.362	7.112	8.277	8.340	7.869	6.704	6.036
						Index Numbers (2000=100): Period Averages							
Nominal Effective Exchange Rate	nec	248.15	98.89	105.67	106.05	107.89	105.96	100.16	100.00	103.66	105.22	104.84	106.89
Real Effective Exchange Rate	rec	78.06	98.57	100.99	100.13	101.55	101.99	98.03	100.00	104.46	105.00	103.08	104.71
Fund Position						*Millions of SDRs: End of Period*							
Quota	2f.s	261.6	261.6	261.6	261.6	261.6	261.6	365.1	365.1	365.1	365.1	365.1	365.1
SDRs	1b.s	.8	3.1	94.4	87.3	109.0	164.2	138.1	113.0	85.5	1.1	—	—
Reserve Position in the Fund	1c.s	—	—	—	—	.1	.1	.1	.2	.2	.2	.2	.2
Total Fund Cred.&Loans Outstg	2tl	14.8	87.1	148.6	145.4	172.7	166.1	143.2	121.4	97.2			
International Liquidity						*Millions of US Dollars Unless Otherwise Indicated: End of Period*							
Total Reserves minus Gold	1l.d	616.2	1,405.0	1,895.7	2,314.0	2,539.1	2,815.7	3,025.0	3,524.4	4,703.2	5,884.9	8,190.5	8,758.2
SDRs	1b.d	1.1	4.5	140.3	125.6	147.1	231.2	189.5	147.2	107.4	1.5		.1
Reserve Position in the Fund	1c.d	—	—	—	—	.1	.2	.2	.2	.2	.2	.2	.2
Foreign Exchange	1d.d	615.1	1,400.5	1,755.4	2,188.4	2,391.9	2,584.4	2,835.3	3,376.9	4,595.6	5,883.2	8,190.2	8,757.9
Gold (Million Fine Troy Ounces)	1ad	—	—	—	—	—	—	—	—	—	—	—	—
Gold (National Valuation)	1and	—	—	—	—	—	—	—	—	—	—	—	—
Monetary Authorities: Other Liab	4..d	.1	.1	.2	.3	.5	.7	22.2	41.8	68.5	27.0	457.3	3.2
Deposit Money Banks: Assets	7a.d	946.7	1,258.3	1,748.8	2,265.4	2,567.9	2,042.9	1,621.4	2,416.9	3,926.2	3,635.4	5,782.9	7,726.1
Liabilities	7b.d	1,838.9	2,333.5	2,849.8	2,250.6	2,190.5	2,589.3	2,183.8	2,615.8	4,901.3	8,160.8	10,850.6	
Monetary Authorities						*Millions of Kuna: End of Period*							
Foreign Assets	11	4,026.5	7,908.3	10,077.7	12,818.6	16,005.6	17,592.6	23,135.7	28,743.7	39,306.1	42,057.0	50,118.5	49,373.4
Claims on Central Government	12a	535.1	250.6	390.1	218.8	—	3.8	24.1	—	—	.5	1.4	3.3
Claims on Private Sector	12d	.3	.7	.9	1.1	24.4	1.0	276.1	289.5	229.2	110.6	93.6	82.9
Claims on Deposit Money Banks	12e	191.6	223.8	220.2	213.9	33.5	1,043.7	1,139.4	329.9	18.5	17.9	972.0	408.9
Reserve Money	14	2,248.9	4,714.2	6,744.1	8,770.3	10,346.2	11,622.7	14,946.1	17,207.7	23,508.4	30,070.1	37,272.8	44,689.1
of which: Currency Outside DMBs	14a	1,367.0	2,658.2	3,365.1	4,366.2	5,319.6	5,730.1	5,958.9	6,636.7	8,507.4	9,680.9	10,573.1	10,955.6
DMBs' Fgn.Currency Deposits	14cf						1,668.4	4,636.2	5,490.5	5,705.1	7,042.3	6,686.6	10,764.7
Liabs. of Central Bank: Securities	16ac	21.2	375.1	168.3	665.7	722.0	2,242.9	2,887.2	4,207.3	6,372.3	6,212.4	4,920.2	—
Restricted Deposits	16b	1.4	40.3	212.2	243.2	101.1	119.1	380.6	315.0	325.4	49.0	12.6	12.4
Foreign Liabilities	16c	133.9	716.2	1,175.2	1,160.4	1,471.4	1,465.4	1,672.9	1,630.8	1,593.1	192.8	2,798.0	18.1
Central Government Deposits	16d	—	793.8	395.5	557.6	1,032.7	434.8	397.2	1,157.4	1,752.1	768.1	1,551.1	263.2
Capital Accounts	17a	2,366.0	2,066.0	2,019.4	1,900.1	2,361.8	2,902.1	4,535.5	5,216.6	6,425.2	5,354.7	5,039.0	5,096.5
Other Items (Net)	17r	−18.0	−322.2	−25.8	−44.7	28.4	−146.0	−244.3	−371.6	−422.6	−461.3	−408.2	−210.8
Deposit Money Banks						*Millions of Kuna: End of Period*							
Reserves	20	862.1	2,039.7	3,508.3	4,573.9	5,056.7	5,908.1	8,987.9	10,588.9	15,002.7	20,373.5	26,783.7	33,718.2
Claims on Mon. Author.:Securities	20c	23.0	378.6	163.3	669.5	673.3	2,233.9	2,793.8	4,136.7	6,221.7	5,805.9	4,951.7	—
Foreign Assets	21	6,212.1	7,082.5	9,296.6	12,549.6	16,185.8	12,763.1	12,400.0	19,710.4	32,807.7	25,977.8	35,382.9	43,551.0
Claims on Central Government	22a	† 19,971.9	17,837.0	17,188.1	16,693.4	15,238.8	14,864.2	16,264.4	19,055.5	20,059.8	21,917.7	21,543.6	21,051.3
Claims on Local Government	22b	11.4	112.9	147.1	145.4	308.8	654.0	905.6	1,174.9	1,280.0	1,422.4	1,563.1	1,787.9
Claims on Nonfin.Pub.Enterprises	22c	1,802.4	2,141.4	1,896.2	1,943.8	2,182.5	2,291.8	1,794.2	2,413.4	3,180.0	3,813.3	4,083.0	4,987.9
Claims on Private Sector	22d	† 18,447.9	25,344.4	30,674.5	31,600.7	46,100.9	56,650.9	52,699.9	56,775.7	69,823.7	90,982.7	104,728.2	118,932.1
Claims on Other Banking Insts	22f	10.2	—	—	—	—	.4	45.4	68.7	170.2	219.5	431.8	624.0
Claims on Nonbank Financial Insts	22g	15.7	62.1	100.8	140.2	246.8	193.9	154.0	161.7	281.4	915.3	761.8	893.9
Demand Deposits	24	1,758.7	3,969.7	4,870.0	7,007.5	8,423.8	7,808.9	7,891.5	11,386.0	15,180.6	21,166.2	23,315.0	23,591.3
Time, Savings,& Fgn.Currency Dep	25	6,878.3	10,828.8	16,257.4	25,204.1	36,876.9	43,654.7	42,363.6	54,552.7	82,050.0	85,055.7	94,406.1	104,222.1
Money Market Instruments	26aa	3.3	1.5	.2	.9	7.0	4.5	1.4	—	—	5.1		
Bonds	26ab	45.0	207.0	130.5	127.2	126.6	149.7	435.4	478.2	317.8	211.2	598.4	1,163.5
Restricted Deposits	26b	14,261.5	12,087.7	10,662.4	8,223.6	5,852.3	4,196.0	3,434.2	2,549.6	1,600.8	1,680.5	1,709.0	2,054.6
Foreign Liabilities	26c	12,066.4	13,134.8	15,150.0	12,467.4	13,807.1	16,176.8	17,209.2	17,809.8	21,857.8	35,023.5	49,932.0	61,163.7
Central Government Deposits	26d	1,437.8	1,675.0	2,025.6	1,720.9	6,874.7	7,298.3	5,828.6	6,730.5	5,634.7	6,094.9	5,283.3	6,821.8
Credit from Monetary Authorities	26g	275.2	224.6	182.6	267.7	33.7	1,049.2	1,138.7	328.8	16.6	17.6	968.9	408.9
Capital Accounts	27a	11,203.3	13,883.6	15,392.4	15,441.8	17,023.6	19,786.8	21,975.4	24,953.1	25,455.1	26,323.2	27,389.5	28,666.4
Other Items (Net)	27r	† −573.0	−1,013.9	−1,695.9	−2,144.4	−3,032.2	−4,564.5	−4,232.7	−4,702.9	−3,286.2	−4,149.7	−3,372.5	−2,546.3
Monetary Survey						*Millions of Kuna: End of Period*							
Foreign Assets (Net)	31n	−1,961.7	1,139.8	3,049.2	11,740.6	16,912.9	12,713.5	16,653.6	29,013.5	48,662.9	32,818.4	32,771.3	31,742.6
Domestic Credit	32	† 39,357.0	43,280.3	47,976.5	48,464.9	56,194.8	66,937.0	65,937.9	72,051.5	87,637.5	112,518.9	126,372.0	141,278.1
Claims on Central Govt. (Net)	32an	† 19,069.1	15,618.7	15,157.1	14,633.7	7,331.4	7,134.9	10,062.7	11,167.6	12,673.0	15,055.2	14,710.6	13,969.6
Claims on Local Government	32b	11.4	112.9	147.1	145.4	308.8	654.0	905.6	1,174.9	1,280.0	1,422.4	1,563.1	1,787.9
Claims on Nonfin.Pub.Enterprises	32c	1,802.4	2,141.4	1,896.2	1,943.8	2,182.5	2,291.8	1,794.2	2,413.4	3,180.0	3,813.3	4,083.0	4,987.9
Claims on Private Sector	32d	† 18,448.2	25,345.1	30,675.3	31,601.8	46,125.3	56,651.9	52,976.0	57,065.2	70,052.9	91,093.2	104,821.7	119,015.0
Claims on Other Banking Insts	32f	10.2	—	—	—	—	10.5	45.4	68.7	170.2	219.5	431.8	624.0
Claims on Nonbank Financial Inst	32g	15.7	62.1	100.8	140.2	246.8	193.9	154.0	161.7	281.4	915.3	761.8	893.9
Money	34	3,133.9	6,648.8	8,283.6	11,419.6	13,814.3	13,621.1	13,858.9	18,030.2	23,703.6	30,869.8	33,888.7	34,562.1
Quasi-Money	35	6,878.3	10,828.8	16,257.4	25,204.1	36,876.9	43,654.7	42,363.6	54,552.7	82,050.0	85,055.7	94,406.1	104,222.1
Money Market Instruments	36aa	3.3	1.5	.2	.9	7.0	4.5	1.4	—	—	5.1		
Bonds	36ab	45.0	207.0	130.5	127.2	126.6	149.7	435.4	478.2	317.8	211.2	598.4	1,163.5
Restricted Deposits	36b	14,262.9	12,128.0	10,874.6	8,466.8	5,953.4	4,315.1	3,814.8	2,864.6	1,926.2	1,729.5	1,721.6	2,067.0
Capital Accounts	37a	13,569.3	15,949.6	17,411.8	17,341.9	19,385.4	22,688.9	26,510.9	30,169.7	31,880.3	31,677.8	32,428.5	33,763.0
Other Items (Net)	37r	† −497.5	−1,343.4	−1,932.0	−2,354.7	−3,055.9	−4,783.5	−4,393.5	−5,030.4	−3,577.4	−4,211.7	−3,900.0	−2,756.9
Money plus Quasi-Money	35l	10,012.2	17,477.6	24,541.0	36,623.7	50,691.2	57,275.8	56,222.5	72,582.9	105,753.6	115,925.5	128,294.7	138,784.2
Interest Rates						*Percent Per Annum*							
Discount Rate (End of Period)	60	34.49	8.50	8.50	6.50	5.90	5.90	7.90	5.90	5.90	4.50	4.50	4.50
Money Market Rate	60b	1,370.50	26.93	21.13	17.60	9.71	11.16	10.21	6.78	3.42	1.75	3.31	5.11
Deposit Rate	60l	379.31	6.52	5.53	5.59	4.30	4.62	4.31	3.74	3.23	1.89	1.53	1.87
Lending Rate	60p	1,443.61	22.91	20.24	22.52	15.47	15.75	14.94	12.07	9.55	† 12.84	11.58	11.75

Croatia 960

Prices, Production, Labor		1993	1994	1995	1996	1997	1998	1999	2000	2001	2002	2003	2004
		Index Numbers (2000=100): Period Averages											
Producer Prices	63	47.5	84.3	84.9	86.1	88.0	87.0	89.2	100.0	101.1	103.0	102.7	106.2
Consumer Prices	64	36.9	76.4	79.4	82.8	86.3	91.8	95.0	100.0	† 104.8	106.5	106.7	110.7
Wages	65	15,825.5	37.5	54.7	61.1	71.5	80.6	91.9	100.0	106.5	111.8	118.5	125.4
Industrial Production	66	89.5	87.1	87.3	90.1	96.4	99.8	98.4	100.0	106.0	111.8	116.4	120.6
Total Employment	67	107.9	107.2	105.7	99.2	97.8	103.4	100.4	100.0	100.5	101.3	103.9	105.1
		Number in Thousands: Period Averages											
Employment	67e	1,108	1,061	1,027	1,012	996	1,071	1,058	1,050	1,056	1,060	1,055	1,085
Unemployment	67c	251	243	241	261	278	288	322	358	380	390	330	250
Unemployment Rate (%)	67r	14.8	14.5	14.5	16.4	17.5	17.2	19.1	21.1	22.0	22.3	19.5	13.8
Intl. Transactions & Positions		Millions of US Dollars											
Exports	70..d	3,903.8	4,260.4	4,632.7	4,511.8	4,170.7	4,541.1	4,302.5	4,431.6	4,665.9	4,898.7	6,186.6	8,024.2
Imports, c.i.f	71..d	4,666.4	5,229.3	7,509.9	7,787.9	9,104.0	8,383.1	7,798.6	7,886.5	9,147.1	10,713.5	14,209.0	16,589.2
Balance of Payments		Millions of US Dollars: Minus Sign Indicates Debit											
Current Account, n.i.e.	78ald	624.9	554.1	−1,591.8	−1,049.1	−2,825.4	−1,468.0	−1,408.1	−470.6	−727.4	−1,916.6	−2,066.4	−1,668.3
Goods: Exports f.o.b.	78aad	3,910.4	4,402.8	4,517.3	4,677.5	4,021.1	4,580.6	4,394.7	4,567.2	4,759.3	5,003.9	6,308.0	8,208.2
Goods: Imports f.o.b.	78abd	−4,619.6	−5,681.2	−7,744.8	−8,165.5	−9,404.1	−8,652.1	−7,693.3	−7,770.2	−8,860.0	−10,652.2	−14,216.0	−16,554.5
Trade Balance	78acd	−709.2	−1,278.4	−3,227.5	−3,488.0	−5,383.0	−4,071.5	−3,298.6	−3,203.1	−4,100.8	−5,648.3	−7,908.0	−8,346.3
Services: Credit	78add	2,215.9	2,660.6	2,223.4	3,193.2	3,984.6	3,949.1	3,724.1	4,070.9	4,883.9	5,582.4	8,634.7	9,616.1
Services: Debit	78aed	−1,089.8	−1,190.3	−1,361.1	−1,707.0	−2,273.9	−1,887.1	−2,097.8	−1,821.7	−1,949.2	−2,414.4	−2,981.8	−3,619.6
Balance on Goods & Services	78afd	416.9	191.9	−2,365.2	−2,001.8	−3,672.3	−2,009.5	−1,672.3	−953.9	−1,166.0	−2,480.3	−2,255.0	−2,349.8
Income: Credit	78agd	128.0	149.0	218.8	269.9	363.7	394.8	254.8	343.5	422.9	433.2	508.5	794.4
Income: Debit	78ahd	−247.5	−313.2	−247.7	−339.7	−386.1	−559.1	−623.3	−740.6	−967.6	−960.0	−1,726.9	−1,556.2
Balance on Gds, Serv. & Inc.	78aid	297.4	27.7	−2,394.1	−2,071.6	−3,694.7	−2,173.8	−2,040.8	−1,351.0	−1,710.8	−3,007.0	−3,473.4	−3,111.6
Current Transfers, n.i.e.: Credit	78ajd	507.5	669.2	971.2	1,173.3	963.8	919.1	967.6	1,098.2	1,192.7	1,375.0	1,741.4	1,900.8
Current Transfers: Debit	78akd	−180.0	−142.8	−168.9	−150.8	−94.5	−213.3	−335.0	−217.8	−209.3	−284.6	−334.4	−457.5
Capital Account, n.i.e.	78bcd	—	—	—	16.2	21.3	19.1	24.9	20.6	133.6	443.4	83.9	28.5
Capital Account, n.i.e.: Credit	78bad	—	—	—	18.0	23.5	24.1	28.2	24.2	138.2	450.2	95.6	37.3
Capital Account: Debit	78bbd	—	—	—	−1.8	−2.2	−5.0	−3.4	−3.6	−4.6	−6.8	−11.7	−8.9
Financial Account, n.i.e.	78bjd	−156.4	16.4	1,135.3	2,996.3	3,020.8	1,610.3	2,868.6	1,790.2	2,200.7	2,993.1	4,783.1	2,914.9
Direct Investment Abroad	78bdd	−18.5	−6.7	−5.5	−24.4	−186.1	−97.5	−56.2	−2.6	−154.5	−538.7	−107.8	−313.9
Dir. Invest. in Rep. Econ., n.i.e.	78bed	120.3	116.9	114.3	510.8	532.8	932.3	1,463.7	1,085.3	1,337.7	1,212.8	2,132.9	1,175.5
Portfolio Investment Assets	78bfd	−.4	1.0	.3	6.2	11.2	−.1	−38.3	−22.7	−129.3	−626.5	143.9	−948.7
Equity Securities	78bkd	−.4	1.0	.3	6.2	.2	−.1	−.3	−.2	.3	−69.4	−66.0	−40.5
Debt Securities	78bld	—	—	—	—	11.0	—	−38.0	−22.5	−129.6	−557.2	210.0	−908.2
Portfolio Investment Liab., n.i.e.	78bgd	.4	9.9	4.5	622.0	565.7	15.1	571.1	730.3	730.4	187.3	820.4	1,196.3
Equity Securities	78bmd	.4	9.9	4.5	−6.8	15.9	1.3	−18.3	−.2	14.0	36.4	16.2	176.7
Debt Securities	78bnd	—	—	—	628.8	549.8	13.8	589.4	730.5	716.4	150.9	804.2	1,019.6
Financial Derivatives Assets	78bwd	....	....	....	....	....	....	....	....	....	....	....	....
Financial Derivatives Liabilities	78bxd	....	....	....	....	....	....	....	....	....	....	....	....
Other Investment Assets	78bhd	−165.8	−15.9	419.5	794.5	171.2	348.8	−15.4	−966.0	360.4	357.5	−2,526.6	−508.9
Monetary Authorities	78bod	—	—	—	—	—	—	—	—	—	—	—	—
General Government	78bpd	−5.2	−.2	−15.5	−33.4	30.7	−22.3	15.1	−25.8	−19.2	−30.5	26.5	96.0
Banks	78bqd	−205.4	−189.3	−451.6	−589.2	−371.8	406.1	168.6	−899.1	−1,611.2	1,323.9	−2,304.4	−452.1
Other Sectors	78brd	44.8	173.6	886.6	1,417.1	512.3	−35.0	−199.1	−41.2	1,990.8	−936.0	−248.7	−152.8
Other Investment Liab., n.i.e.	78bid	−92.4	−88.8	602.2	1,087.2	1,926.0	411.7	943.7	965.9	55.9	2,400.7	4,320.1	2,314.6
Monetary Authorities	78bsd	—	—	—	—	—	—	21.6	18.5	25.6	−56.1	374.5	−445.5
General Government	78btd	−119.3	−131.5	−47.2	268.8	95.7	−61.3	187.0	297.7	−192.5	413.6	586.4	500.1
Banks	78bud	−20.6	52.6	492.5	226.2	670.3	135.7	38.4	−12.6	277.2	1,249.8	2,506.1	1,165.5
Other Sectors	78bvd	47.5	−9.9	156.9	592.2	1,160.0	337.3	696.7	662.4	−54.3	793.4	853.1	1,094.5
Net Errors and Omissions	78cad	−280.2	−294.0	496.9	−946.1	173.7	−.9	−1,027.5	−684.6	−209.3	−705.4	−1,399.8	−1,206.8
Overall Balance	78cbd	188.3	276.5	40.4	1,017.3	390.4	160.5	457.9	655.6	1,397.6	814.6	1,400.8	68.2
Reserves and Related Items	79dad	−188.3	−276.5	−40.4	−1,017.3	−390.4	−160.5	−457.9	−655.6	−1,397.6	−814.6	−1,400.8	−68.2
Reserve Assets	79dbd	−466.4	−742.8	−443.2	−533.4	−428.0	−151.7	−426.4	−627.0	−1,366.7	−685.7	−1,400.8	−68.2
Use of Fund Credit and Loans	79dcd	19.8	107.0	97.1	−4.5	37.5	−8.9	−31.5	−28.6	−30.8	−128.9	—	—
Exceptional Financing	79ded	258.3	359.3	305.7	−479.4								
International Investment Position		Millions of US Dollars											
Assets	79aad	....	....	....	....	....	7,020.7	7,142.9	8,353.4	11,081.9	12,267.4	17,662.0	18,696.8
Direct Investment Abroad	79abd	....	....	....	....	....	1,002.4	881.7	875.1	966.6	1,825.9	2,053.3	2,426.2
Portfolio Investment	79acd	....	....	....	....	....	29.7	26.0	14.3	22.5	40.9	50.7	59.0
Equity Securities	79add	....	....	....	....	....	29.7	26.0	14.3	22.5	40.9	50.7	59.0
Debt Securities	79aed	....	....	....	....	....							
Financial Derivatives	79ald	....	....	....	....	....	—	—	—	—	—	—	—
Other Investment	79afd	....	....	....	....	....	3,172.9	3,210.2	3,942.3	5,389.6	4,515.7	7,367.4	7,453.4
Monetary Authorities	79agd	....	....	....	....	....	—	—	—	—	—	—	—
General Government	79ahd	....	....	....	....	....	70.0	49.7	72.5	88.9	126.4	108.9	19.4
Banks	79aid	....	....	....	....	....	1,978.6	1,657.7	2,510.9	3,988.0	2,966.1	5,796.7	5,983.8
Other Sectors	79ajd	....	....	....	....	....	1,124.3	1,502.8	1,358.9	1,312.7	1,423.2	1,461.8	1,450.2
Reserve Assets	79akd	....	....	....	....	....	2,815.7	3,025.0	3,521.8	4,703.3	5,884.9	8,190.5	8,758.2
Liabilities	79lad	....	....	....	....	....	12,434.0	12,475.3	14,293.3	15,291.9	21,304.7	33,142.7	41,469.6
Dir. Invest. in Rep. Economy	79lbd	....	....	....	....	....	1,939.7	2,566.9	3,568.0	4,239.0	6,909.7	10,476.0	12,988.6
Portfolio Investment	79lcd	....	....	....	....	....	2,417.2	2,751.5	3,355.4	3,964.8	4,460.0	6,074.3	7,761.4
Equity Securities	79ldd	....	....	....	....	....	87.3	128.3	108.8	145.4	180.8	213.1	325.5
Debt Securities	79led	....	....	....	....	....	2,329.8	2,623.2	3,246.6	3,819.4	4,279.2	5,861.1	7,436.0
Financial Derivatives	79lld	....	....	....	....	....	—	—	—	—	—	—	—
Other Investment	79lfd	....	....	....	....	....	8,077.1	7,156.9	7,369.8	7,088.1	9,935.0	16,592.5	20,719.6
Monetary Authorities	79lgd	....	....	....	....	....	233.9	217.9	198.8	189.9	24.2	457.0	3.2
General Government	79lhd	....	....	....	....	....	1,589.5	1,468.5	1,708.1	1,476.7	2,033.8	2,861.6	3,539.4
Banks	79lid	....	....	....	....	....	2,569.7	2,144.2	2,045.8	2,246.6	3,946.9	7,650.1	9,809.3
Other Sectors	79ljd	....	....	....	....	....	3,684.0	3,326.4	3,417.1	3,174.9	3,930.1	5,623.7	7,367.6

Croatia 960

		1993	1994	1995	1996	1997	1998	1999	2000	2001	2002	2003	2004
Government Finance						*Millions of Kuna: Year Ending December 31*							
Deficit (-) or Surplus......................	80	....	543.9	−715.4	−133.8	−1,160.2	1,256.7	−2,522.0	−6,107.9	−3,758.5	−3,872.0	....	....
Total Revenue and Grants..............	81y	....	22,817.3	27,485.1	30,813.1	33,702.4	42,376.2	40,277.9	41,774.7	49,156.8	69,870.2	....	....
Revenue.....................................	81	....	22,817.3	27,385.1	30,813.1	33,702.4	42,376.2	40,277.9	41,774.7	49,156.8	69,870.2	....	....
Grants...	81z	....	—	100.0	—	—	—	—	—	—	—	....	....
Exp. & Lending Minus Repay..........	82z	....	22,273.4	28,200.5	30,946.9	34,862.5	41,119.6	42,799.9	47,882.6	52,915.3	73,742.2	....	....
Expenditure..................................	82	....	22,282.8	28,475.6	30,971.2	34,395.2	41,390.4	47,379.6	49,567.5	56,386.7	72,186.2	....	....
Lending Minus Repayments.........	83	....	−9.3	−275.1	−24.3	467.4	−270.8	−4,579.7	−1,684.9	−3,471.4	1,556.0	....	....
Total Financing..............................	80h	....	−543.9	715.3	134.0	1,160.2	−1,256.7	2,521.9	6,107.8	3,758.5	3,872.0	....	....
Domestic.....................................	84a	....	−591.2	29.3	−669.9	−1,825.7	−1,247.6	−2,093.1	−813.6	−353.9	1,597.7	....	....
Foreign.......................................	85a	....	47.3	686.0	804.0	2,985.9	−9.1	4,615.0	6,921.4	4,112.4	2,274.3	....	....
Total Debt by Residence..................	88	....	....	27,739.7	29,814.0	32,760.0						....	....
Domestic.....................................	88a	20,768.6	17,284.7	16,405.4	16,533.7	14,501.6	13,697.5	13,944.0	14,549.8	21,944.3	23,596.6	....	....
Foreign.......................................	89a	....	....	11,334.3	13,280.3	18,258.4	....	....	....	....	....	....	....
National Accounts							*Millions of Kuna:*						
Househ.Cons.Expend.,incl.NPISHs....	96f	....	46,575	64,042	67,045	79,010	84,194	81,545	89,637	98,054	107,427	113,396	120,312
Government Consumption Expend...	91f	....	25,738	18,437	18,533	32,183	36,642	39,341	39,816	37,956	37,741	39,789	41,188
Gross Fixed Capital Formation.........	93e	....	12,210	15,398	22,089	29,936	32,066	33,025	33,281	36,984	44,114	53,168	57,141
Changes in Inventories....................	93i	....	2,982	1,916	1,599	4,143	982	−404	−2,421	2,665	6,822	5,508	5,384
Exports of Goods and Services.........	90c	....	40,086	37,951	43,402	50,873	54,546	57,920	71,899	80,246	81,375	90,927	98,330
Imports of Goods and Services (-).....	98c	....	40,149	48,681	53,630	70,351	67,700	69,731	79,693	90,265	98,089	109,721	115,273
Gross Domestic Product (GDP)........	99b	41,833	87,441	98,382	107,981	123,811	137,604	141,579	152,519	165,640	179,390	193,067	207,082
GDP Volume 1990 Prices................	99b.p	192	193	196	205	219	....	....	....	....	....	....	....
GDP Volume 1997 Prices................	99b.p	....	....	....	....	123,811	126,936	125,843	129,438	134,318	141,339	147,356	153,947
GDP Volume (2000=100)..............	99bvp	84.0	84.5	85.9	89.6	† 95.7	98.1	97.2	100.0	103.8	109.2	113.8	118.9
GDP Deflator (2000=100)..............	99bip	32.7	67.8	75.1	79.0	84.9	92.0	95.5	100.0	104.7	107.7	111.2	114.2
						Millions: Midyear Estimates							
Population...............................	99z	4.63	4.66	4.67	4.65	4.62	4.57	4.53	4.51	4.50	4.51	4.52	4.54

Cyprus 423

		1993	1994	1995	1996	1997	1998	1999	2000	2001	2002	2003	2004
Exchange Rates					*SDRs per Pound: End of Period*								
Official Rate	ac	1.4006	1.4384	1.4735	1.4800	1.4097	1.4255	1.2680	1.2444	1.2238	1.3451	1.4465	1.5151
					US Dollars per Pound: End of Period (ag) Period Average (rh)								
Official Rate	ag	1.9238	2.0998	2.1903	2.1282	1.9021	2.0071	1.7404	1.6214	1.5380	1.8287	2.1494	2.3529
Official Rate	rh	2.0120	2.0347	2.2113	2.1446	1.9476	1.9342	1.8440	1.6107	1.5559	1.6431	1.9356	2.1366
					Index Numbers (2000=100): Period Averages								
Official Rate	ahx	124.9	126.3	137.3	133.1	120.9	120.1	114.5	100.0	96.6	102.0	120.2	132.7
Nominal Effective Exchange Rate	nec	91.0	94.3	97.9	99.8	100.6	106.0	103.7	100.0	103.8	106.5	111.1	113.3
Real Effective Exchange Rate	rec	99.6	102.8	103.9	104.0	103.9	107.3	102.9	100.0	102.2	104.6	110.5	112.8
Fund Position					*Millions of SDRs: End of Period*								
Quota	2f.s	100.0	100.0	100.0	100.0	100.0	100.0	139.6	139.6	139.6	139.6	139.6	139.6
SDRs	1b.s	.1	.1	—	—	.2	.2	.4	.8	1.1	1.5	2.0	2.5
Reserve Position in the Fund	1c.s	25.5	25.5	25.5	25.5	25.5	25.5	35.4	35.4	35.4	49.1	66.8	47.3
Total Fund Cred.&Loans Outstg.	2tl	—	—	—	—	—	—	—	—	—	—	—	—
International Liquidity					*Millions of US Dollars Unless Otherwise Indicated: End of Period*								
Total Reserves minus Gold	1l.d	1,096.7	1,464.5	1,116.9	1,541.9	1,391.6	1,379.7	1,832.9	1,741.1	2,267.8	3,022.0	3,256.7	3,910.0
SDRs	1b.d	.1	.2	—	—	.3	.3	.5	1.0	1.4	2.1	3.0	3.9
Reserve Position in the Fund	1c.d	35.0	37.2	37.8	36.6	34.3	35.8	48.5	46.1	44.4	66.8	99.3	73.4
Foreign Exchange	1d.d	1,061.6	1,427.2	1,079.0	1,505.3	1,356.9	1,343.6	1,783.8	1,694.0	2,221.9	2,953.2	3,154.5	3,832.7
Gold (Million Fine Troy Ounces)	1ad	.460	.459	.460	.440	.462	.462	.464	.464	.464	.465	.465	.465
Gold (National Valuation)	1and	14.2	15.6	16.7	170.2	133.9	132.9	142.6	127.6	127.6	149.2	196.2	204.1
Monetary Authorities: Other Liab.	4..d	53.9	55.7	89.6	56.4	73.2	57.1	49.7	24.5	40.5	15.5	15.9	15.5
Deposit Money Banks: Assets	7a.d	1,554.3	1,915.4	3,083.3	3,255.1	3,612.4	3,519.3	† 3,880.2	5,377.6	6,191.7	6,348.5	8,686.2	11,318.7
Liabilities	7b.d	2,187.8	2,697.5	3,738.3	4,302.8	4,694.4	4,790.3	† 5,273.4	6,579.1	7,683.4	8,621.3	10,328.7	12,705.9
Other Banking Insts.: Liabilities	7f.d	1,722.9	2,052.7	2,257.4	3,189.6	13,090.6	8,607.2	8,060.5	10,564.4	10,161.4	....	....	....
Monetary Authorities					*Millions of Pounds: End of Period*								
Foreign Assets	11	578.1	705.6	518.2	805.2	802.7	754.4	1,135.8	1,153.3	1,558.4	1,734.9	1,607.2	1,749.2
Claims on Central Government	12a	407.3	398.5	607.2	570.5	558.4	596.7	534.9	770.7	696.5	992.4	968.5	1,017.3
Claims on Deposit Money Banks	12e	13.4	12.4	22.4	6.5	.1	104.6	.1	3.1	—	—	8.0	
Reserve Money	14	775.6	872.4	834.6	761.5	755.5	878.0	1,008.3	1,117.0	1,201.5	1,498.8	1,571.4	1,697.2
of which: Currency Outside DMBs	14a	229.4	246.6	257.1	265.8	276.3	290.1	313.6	333.3	356.5	392.8	467.2	513.7
Foreign Liabilities	16c	28.0	26.6	40.9	26.5	38.5	28.4	28.5	15.1	26.3	8.5	7.4	6.6
Central Government Deposits	16d	154.8	175.2	227.3	342.9	339.5	325.7	316.4	451.2	559.5	598.8	755.2	858.2
Other Items (Net)	17r	40.4	42.4	45.1	251.3	227.7	223.6	317.4	343.8	467.6	621.3	249.7	204.6
Deposit Money Banks					*Millions of Pounds: End of Period*								
Reserves	20	538.0	612.4	555.1	479.7	452.9	455.4	† 681.3	761.0	941.3	1,481.3	1,128.6	1,178.6
Foreign Assets	21	807.9	912.2	1,407.7	1,529.5	1,899.1	1,753.4	† 2,229.5	3,316.6	4,025.8	3,471.6	4,041.2	4,810.6
Claims on Central Government	22a	519.9	566.5	463.7	722.1	834.5	854.0	† 983.3	902.4	1,409.2	1,415.9	1,765.4	1,716.0
Claims on Private Sector	22d	2,436.7	2,754.3	3,225.3	3,667.0	4,109.7	4,635.2	† 5,543.9	6,344.0	7,136.9	7,726.6	8,123.8	8,675.6
Demand Deposits	24	317.2	326.1	353.9	386.5	427.2	439.2	† 723.5	681.5	653.4	613.3	865.7	910.8
Time and Savings Deposits	25	2,440.9	2,785.4	3,131.2	3,487.3	3,890.0	4,243.3	† 4,971.3	5,575.0	6,462.9	7,143.6	7,159.9	7,536.0
Foreign Liabilities	26c	1,137.3	1,284.6	1,706.8	2,021.8	2,468.0	2,386.7	† 3,030.0	4,057.7	4,995.7	4,714.4	4,805.4	5,400.1
Central Government Deposits	26d	38.1	38.4	42.7	40.7	44.8	50.3	† 63.8	76.8	72.2	71.2	71.9	80.5
Credit from Monetary Authorities	26g	13.4	12.4	22.4	6.5	.1	5.6	† .1	3.1			8.0	—
Other Items (Net)	27r	355.5	398.5	394.8	455.5	466.2	573.1	† 649.4	929.9	1,329.1	1,552.9	2,148.1	2,453.3
Monetary Survey					*Millions of Pounds: End of Period*								
Foreign Assets (Net)	31n	220.8	306.6	178.3	286.4	195.4	92.7	† 306.7	397.1	562.2	483.6	835.7	1,153.1
Domestic Credit	32	3,225.9	3,579.3	4,108.1	4,670.8	5,229.1	5,847.5	† 6,840.1	7,661.3	8,794.1	9,642.4	10,208.8	10,638.8
Claims on Central Govt. (Net)	32an	734.2	751.5	800.9	908.9	1,008.6	1,074.8	† 1,137.9	1,145.1	1,474.1	1,738.3	1,906.8	1,794.6
Claims on Local Government	32b	37.5	42.9	46.8	55.6	65.4	79.3	† 90.9	92.4	127.5	132.6	142.4	133.2
Claims on Nonfin.Pub.Enterprises	32c	14.9	28.1	34.8	38.9	45.0	57.9	† 66.8	78.9	55.7	44.9	35.8	35.4
Claims on Private Sector	32d	2,439.2	2,756.8	3,225.7	3,667.4	4,110.0	4,635.6	† 5,544.6	6,344.7	7,136.9	7,726.6	8,123.8	8,675.6
Money	34	549.1	576.2	612.0	653.5	704.5	730.3	† 1,037.6	1,015.3	1,010.6	1,021.6	1,333.8	1,435.6
Quasi-Money	35	2,448.0	2,794.3	3,142.2	3,495.6	3,900.4	4,255.6	† 4,986.8	5,595.2	6,483.3	7,143.6	7,159.9	7,536.0
Other Items (Net)	37r	449.5	515.4	532.0	808.1	819.6	954.4	† 1,122.5	1,447.6	1,862.4	1,960.9	2,550.9	2,820.3
Money plus Quasi-Money	35l	2,997.1	3,370.5	3,754.4	4,149.1	4,604.9	4,985.9	† 6,024.4	6,610.5	7,493.9	8,165.2	8,493.6	8,971.6
Other Banking Institutions					*Millions of Pounds: End of Period*								
Reserves	40	18.3	27.0	25.1	20.6	32.3	39.6	35.2	76.3	90.1	....	....	....
Foreign Assets	41	894.9	977.1	1,030.2	1,498.4	6,901.6	4,290.9	4,647.4	6,527.0	6,615.8	....	....	....
Claims on Private Sector	42d	1,405.8	1,599.8	1,826.0	2,056.5	2,244.4	2,431.6	2,747.0	2,868.3	2,987.5	....	....	....
Liquid Liabilities	45l	1,475.7	1,685.0	1,897.6	2,095.8	2,327.6	2,582.7	2,754.2	3,072.8	3,428.0	....	....	....
Foreign Liabilities	46c	895.6	977.6	1,030.6	1,498.7	6,882.2	4,288.4	4,631.4	6,515.6	6,606.9	....	....	....
Capital Accounts	47a	38.3	41.9	39.9	42.9	43.8	48.6	80.0	90.3	92.5	....	....	....
Other Items (Net)	47r	−90.6	−100.6	−86.8	−62.0	−75.2	−157.6	−36.0	−207.0	−434.1	....	....	....
Banking Survey					*Millions of Pounds: End of Period*								
Foreign Assets (Net)	51n	220.1	306.1	177.8	286.0	214.8	95.2	322.7	408.5	571.0	....	....	....
Domestic Credit	52	4,635.8	5,182.2	5,940.0	6,737.5	7,482.1	8,292.5	9,578.6	10,523.7	11,710.9	....	....	....
Claims on Central Govt. (Net)	52an	740.9	757.2	807.2	919.5	1,017.5	1,088.5	1,137.9	1,145.1	1,371.3	....	....	....
Claims on Local Government	52b	37.5	42.9	46.8	55.6	65.4	79.3	86.5	90.6	122.8	....	....	....
Claims on Nonfin.Pub.Enterprises	52c	14.9	28.1	34.8	38.9	45.0	57.9	63.3	75.8	92.4	....	....	....
Claims on Private Sector	52d	3,842.5	4,354.1	5,051.3	5,723.5	6,354.1	7,066.8	8,290.9	9,212.3	10,124.4	....	....	....
Monetary Liabilities	54	539.8	560.1	601.7	644.7	685.1	708.3	1,024.7	1,038.9	1,016.0	....	....	....
Quasi-Monetary Liabilities	55	3,915.3	4,468.6	5,026.2	5,580.0	6,214.4	6,822.0	7,722.7	8,644.1	9,885.2	....	....	....
Other Items (Net)	57r	400.8	459.6	489.9	798.7	797.4	857.5	1,184.3	1,398.7	1,654.7	....	....	....
Liquid Liabilities	55l	4,454.6	5,028.4	5,626.9	6,224.4	6,900.2	7,529.1	8,743.9	9,684.9	10,902.7	....	....	....
Interest Rates					*Percent Per Annum*								
Discount Rate (End of Period)	60	6.50	6.50	6.50	† 7.50	7.00	7.00	7.00	7.00	5.50	5.00	4.50	5.50
Money Market Rate	60b	....	....	....	6.85	4.82	4.80	5.15	5.96	4.93	3.42	3.35	4.01
Treasury Bill Rate	60c	6.00	6.00	6.00	6.05	5.38	5.59	5.59	6.01			3.56	
Deposit Rate	60l	5.75	5.75	5.75	† 7.00	6.50	6.50	6.50	6.50	4.65	4.20	3.30	3.99
Lending Rate	60p	9.00	8.83	8.50	8.50	8.08	8.00	8.00	8.00	† 7.52	7.15	6.95	7.66

Cyprus 423

Prices, Production, Labor		1993	1994	1995	1996	1997	1998	1999	2000	2001	2002	2003	2004
		Index Numbers (2000=100): Period Averages											
Wholesale Prices	63	81.6	84.3	87.4	89.2	91.7	92.2	93.3	100.0	101.6	103.0	106.0	111.0
Wholesale Prices: Home Goods	63a	....	....	† 86.2	88.7	91.6	93.7	95.1	100.0	101.9	105.6	110.3	117.8
Consumer Prices	64	80.6	84.4	86.6	89.2	92.4	† 94.5	96.0	100.0	102.0	104.8	109.2	111.7
Harmonized CPI (2002=100)	64h	....	....	....	....	....	....	....	....	....	100.0	104.0	105.9
Industrial Production	66	90.0	93.1	94.6	91.8	91.5	94.1	† 95.7	† 100.0	101.8	105.8	107.8	109.6
Mining Production	66zx	74.9	81.0	74.6	76.4	76.5	90.2	† 96.3	† 100.0	95.4	105.4	108.4	111.1
		Number in Thousands: Period Averages											
Labor Force	67d	....	....	302	306	308	311	318	325	315	326	341	....
Employment	67e	267	271	284	286	286	289	279	294	310	315	327	336
Unemployment	67c	8	8	8	9	10	10	11	11	10	11	12	....
Unemployment Rate (%)	67r	2.6	2.7	2.6	3.1	3.4	3.4	3.6	3.4	3.0	....	....	....
Intl. Transactions & Positions		*Millions of Pounds*											
Exports	70	431.40	474.99	554.91	651.01	563.89	551.13	541.79	590.35	628.90	514.66	431.88	540.46
Imports, c.i.f.	71	1,288.29	1,481.66	1,670.41	1,857.53	1,899.37	1,904.84	1,970.92	2,401.96	2,526.73	2,486.63	2,302.08	2,679.31
Balance of Payments		*Millions of US Dollars: Minus Sign Indicates Debit*											
Current Account, n.i.e.	78ald	109.8	74.4	−205.1	−467.7	−418.1	291.4	−170.2	−488.1	−322.2	−457.8	−441.8	−914.8
Goods: Exports f.o.b.	78aad	867.7	967.5	1,228.7	1,392.4	1,245.8	1,064.6	1,000.3	950.9	975.2	855.1	955.4	1,175.0
Goods: Imports f.o.b.	78abd	−2,374.5	−2,703.0	−3,314.2	−3,575.7	−3,317.2	−3,490.4	−3,309.5	−3,556.6	−3,552.5	−3,702.6	−4,089.8	−5,217.8
Trade Balance	78acd	−1,506.8	−1,735.5	−2,085.5	−2,183.3	−2,071.4	−2,425.7	−2,309.2	−2,605.7	−2,577.3	−2,847.4	−3,134.4	−4,042.8
Services: Credit	78add	2,335.1	2,646.7	3,377.6	3,309.8	3,305.1	3,594.7	3,947.0	4,068.1	4,340.0	4,511.7	5,213.7	6,132.7
Services: Debit	78aed	−765.0	−862.1	−1,312.7	−1,407.2	−1,401.5	−1,497.6	−1,559.6	−1,585.3	−1,614.6	−1,764.2	−2,277.9	−2,654.9
Balance on Goods & Services	78afd	63.3	49.2	−20.6	−280.7	−167.8	−328.6	78.1	−122.9	148.1	−99.9	−198.6	−565.0
Income: Credit	78agd	131.9	121.5	443.8	417.7	440.1	470.2	493.3	572.4	558.9	390.8	491.9	649.1
Income: Debit	78ahd	−198.4	−211.1	−679.2	−643.8	−727.0	104.6	−844.7	−1,114.8	−1,083.3	−860.0	−879.0	−1,176.4
Balance on Gds, Serv. & Inc.	78aid	−3.2	−40.4	−256.0	−506.7	−454.7	246.2	−273.4	−665.3	−376.2	−569.1	−585.7	−1,092.3
Current Transfers, n.i.e.: Credit	78ajd	118.4	125.0	61.9	52.8	48.8	94.0	145.5	236.8	147.3	271.9	387.0	594.2
Current Transfers: Debit	78akd	−5.4	−10.2	−11.1	−13.7	−12.3	−48.9	−42.4	−59.6	−93.3	−160.6	−243.0	−416.7
Capital Account, n.i.e.	78bcd	....	....	—	—	—	—	—	4.8	5.7	−5.4	20.3	125.3
Capital Account, n.i.e.: Credit	78bad	....	....	—	—	—	—	—	19.3	27.1	22.2	41.4	183.1
Capital Account: Debit	78bbd	....	....	—	—	—	—	—	−14.5	−21.5	−27.6	−21.1	−57.8
Financial Account, n.i.e.	78bjd	−3.8	185.7	−80.7	445.4	541.6	−420.2	844.9	530.3	965.1	939.6	188.6	1,144.2
Direct Investment Abroad	78bdd	−12.3	−6.1	−15.7	−35.2	−27.9	−70.7	−182.6	−172.1	−249.1	−487.2	−538.5	−637.3
Dir. Invest. in Rep. Econ., n.i.e.	78bed	83.4	75.2	375.8	428.9	546.5	345.4	813.1	854.9	944.7	1,086.5	1,025.1	1,160.1
Portfolio Investment Assets	78bfd	−18.9	−244.6	−110.5	−142.8	−145.4	−160.3	−736.7	−453.4	−249.2	−1,094.3	−482.5	−1,873.3
Equity Securities	78bkd	....	....						−94.5	−52.0	−543.5	161.9	−74.5
Debt Securities	78bld	−18.9	−244.6	−110.5	−142.8	−145.4	−160.3	−736.7	−358.9	−197.3	−550.8	−644.4	−1,798.8
Portfolio Investment Liab., n.i.e.	78bgd	−33.4	84.5	−27.4	69.7	254.7	355.1	493.6	169.7	517.7	552.6	802.5	2,979.0
Equity Securities	78bmd	....	....						29.1	88.9	−3.8	−.1	−13.9
Debt Securities	78bnd	−33.4	84.5	−27.4	69.7	254.7	355.1	493.6	140.5	428.8	556.5	802.6	2,992.9
Financial Derivatives Assets	78bwd	....	....	....	....	....	....	....			−50.3	16.6	−23.6
Financial Derivatives Liabilities	78bxd	....	....	....	....	....	....	....	3.2	—	—	—	−21.1
Other Investment Assets	78bhd	−231.2	56.3	−1,162.6	−366.3	−1,529.9	−485.9	−408.1	−1,285.3	−1,478.4	1,420.5	−2,479.2	−2,999.1
Monetary Authorities	78bod	....	....	—	—	—	—	—	—	—			159.0
General Government	78bpd	10.1	1.0	—	—	—	—	—	—	—	13.1	−20.8	−17.6
Banks	78bqd	−246.1	55.3	—	—	—	—	—	—	—	1,414.3	−2,563.8	−3,067.6
Other Sectors	78brd	4.8	....	−1,162.6	−366.3	−1,529.9	−485.9	−408.1	−1,285.3	−1,478.4	−6.9	105.4	−72.8
Other Investment Liab., n.i.e.	78bid	208.5	220.4	859.8	491.1	1,443.5	−403.8	865.6	1,413.4	1,479.4	−488.2	1,844.7	2,559.5
Monetary Authorities	78bsd	−23.1	.4	—	—	—	—	—	—	—	−19.0	−2.5	−1.8
General Government	78btd	−155.0	−228.6	—	—	—	—	—	—	—	−38.1	244.6	162.9
Banks	78bud	331.3	301.5	—	—	—	—	—	—	—	−539.9	1,648.5	2,467.9
Other Sectors	78bvd	55.3	147.1	859.8	491.1	1,443.5	−403.8	865.6	1,413.4	1,479.4	108.8	−46.0	−69.5
Net Errors and Omissions	78cad	38.8	−13.1	−77.3	−37.5	−170.5	46.2	−35.6	−55.2	−37.9	−87.4	45.2	16.7
Overall Balance	78cbd	144.8	246.9	−363.1	−59.8	−47.0	−82.5	639.0	−8.2	610.6	389.0	−187.6	371.4
Reserves and Related Items	79dad	−144.8	−246.9	363.1	59.8	47.0	82.5	−639.0	8.2	−610.6	−389.0	187.6	−371.4
Reserve Assets	79dbd	−144.8	−246.9	363.1	59.8	47.0	82.5	−639.0	8.2	−610.6	−389.0	187.6	−371.4
Use of Fund Credit and Loans	79dcd	—	—	—	—	—	—	—	—	—	—	—	—
Exceptional Financing	79ded	....	....	—	—	—	—	—	—	—	—	—	—
International Investment Position		*Millions of US Dollars*											
Assets	79aad	....	....	....	....	....	....	....	....	....	23,523.8	29,143.1	....
Direct Investment Abroad	79abd	....	....	....	....	....	....	....	....	....	1,279.0	2,054.4	....
Portfolio Investment	79acd	....	....	....	....	....	....	....	1,088.3	1,590.3	5,383.4	6,554.9	....
Equity Securities	79add	....	....	....	....	....	....	....	.3	129.3	1,122.5	1,206.2	....
Debt Securities	79aed	....	....	....	....	....	....	....	1,088.0	1,460.9	4,260.9	5,348.7	....
Financial Derivatives	79ald	....	....	....	....	....	....	....	....	....	2.7	4.9	....
Other Investment	79afd	....	....	....	....	....	....	....	3,951.0	4,269.6	13,686.1	17,074.5	....
Monetary Authorities	79agd	....	....	....	....	....	....	....	....	....	....	....	....
General Government	79ahd	....	....	....	....	....	....	....	....	....	43.2	48.6	....
Banks	79aid	....	....	....	....	....	....	....	3,951.0	4,268.9	9,048.9	11,848.0	....
Other Sectors	79ajd	....	....	....	....	....	....	....	....	....	4,594.0	5,177.9	....
Reserve Assets	79akd	....	....	....	....	....	....	....	1,869.9	2,396.4	3,172.7	3,454.4	....
Liabilities	79lad	....	....	....	....	....	....	....	....	....	22,447.8	28,975.9	....
Dir. Invest. in Rep. Economy	79lbd	....	....	....	....	....	....	....	....	....	4,912.3	6,986.2	....
Portfolio Investment	79lcd	....	....	....	....	....	....	....	979.3	1,445.1	2,234.2	3,328.1	....
Equity Securities	79ldd	....	....	....	....	....	....	....	—	—	383.6	333.2	....
Debt Securities	79led	....	....	....	....	....	....	....	979.3	1,445.1	1,850.5	2,995.0	....
Financial Derivatives	79lld	....	....	....	....	....	....	....	....	....	3.0	23.3	....
Other Investment	79lfd	....	....	....	....	....	....	....	8,691.0	9,367.7	15,298.4	18,638.3	....
Monetary Authorities	79lgd	....	....	....	....	....	....	....	.2	.2	43.7	45.0	....
General Government	79lhd	....	....	....	....	....	....	....	403.9	279.9	280.0	589.4	....
Banks	79lid	....	....	....	....	....	....	....	6,723.5	7,568.0	13,319.7	16,068.6	....
Other Sectors	79ljd	....	....	....	....	....	....	....	1,563.5	1,519.5	1,655.0	1,935.3	....

Cyprus 423

		1993	1994	1995	1996	1997	1998	1999	2000	2001	2002	2003	2004
Government Finance					*Millions of Pounds: Year Ending December 31*								
Deficit (-) or Surplus	80	−77.82	−51.85	−39.90	−142.08	−231.22	−257.58	−201.27	−128.70	−129.41	−273.50	−416.20	...
Revenue	81	987.93	1,140.55	1,266.90	1,321.30	1,373.39	1,473.17	1,590.06	1,857.50	2,081.20	2,122.30	2,400.60	...
Grants Received	81z	3.75	3.97	3.90	2.35	1.64	.74	.94	2.50	2.50	2.80	5.20	...
Expenditure	82	1,053.83	1,192.36	1,306.10	1,462.72	1,603.53	1,731.70	1,787.73	1,988.70	2,213.11	2,398.60	2,822.00	...
Lending Minus Repayments	83	15.67	4.01	4.60	3.01	2.72	−.21	4.54	—	—	—	—	...
Financing													
Net Borrowing: Domestic	84a	219.76	106.87	117.40	203.91	143.13	109.31	52.57	163.50	194.41	226.60	216.10	...
Foreign	85a	−91.04	−65.02	−77.50	−61.83	88.08	148.28	148.70	−34.80	−65.00	46.90	200.10	...
Use of Cash Balances	87	−50.90	10.00	—	—	—	−.01	—	—	—	—	—	...
Debt: Domestic	88a	1,295.36	1,402.51	1,583.40	1,837.56	1,987.35	2,130.72	2,165.40	2,586.90	3,019.78	2,830.58	3,108.41	...
Foreign	89a	627.81	556.65	479.27	402.95	515.33	664.77	850.68	820.82	760.56	844.75	1,059.15	...
National Accounts						*Millions of Pounds*							
Househ.Cons.Expend.,incl.NPISHs	96f	1,934.3	2,111.0	2,686.3	2,830.2	2,964.6	3,165.6p	3,325.1p	3,712.8	3,927.3	4,083.4	4,310.0	4,676.0
Government Consumption Expend	91f	552.5	608.1	566.9	671.7	772.0	822.2	923.9	929.7	1,067.9	1,168.9	1,356.5	1,323.1
Gross Fixed Capital Formation	93e	741.2	751.5	778.6	861.2	847.1	925.2	935.4	981.7	1,041.4	1,161.6	1,182.6	1,336.6
Changes in Inventories	93i	47.6	180.0	125.7	67.6	24.7	9.9	−45.6	64.3	−33.6	34.0	36.3	158.4
Exports of Goods and Services	90c	1,555.2	1,741.1	2,084.0	2,192.7	2,338.7	2,412.8	2,686.1	3,123.9	3,426.3	3,244.3	3,210.3	3,385.6
Imports of Goods and Services (-)	98c	1,569.4	1,755.5	2,093.3	2,323.6	2,425.0	2,472.9	2,610.7	3,133.4	3,325.7	3,321.9	3,290.6	3,663.4
Gross Domestic Product (GDP)	99b	3,285.4	3,663.2	4,148.2	4,299.8	4,522.1	4,862.8	5,214.2	5,679.0	6,103.6	6,370.3	6,805.1	7,216.3
Net Primary Income from Abroad	98.n	36.6	28.8	−106.5	−105.4	−147.4	297.7	−190.8	−337.6	−338.2	−274.4	−198.1	−203.0
Gross National Income (GNI)	99a	3,322.0	3,692.0	4,041.7	4,194.4	4,374.7	5,160.5	5,023.4	5,341.4	5,765.4	6,095.9	6,607.0	7,013.3
Consumption of Fixed Capital	99cf	348.8	387.7	439.5	459.8	487.1	509.5	540.9	569.9	605.8	642.9	693.1	733.9
GDP Volume 1995 Prices	99b.p	3,563.5	3,773.7	4,148.2	4,222.9	4,320.0	4,534.7	4,752.6	4,992.2	5,197.6	5,307.2	5,408.4	5,610.4
GDP Volume (2000=100)	99bvp	71.4	75.6	83.1	84.6	86.5	90.8	95.2	100.0	104.1	106.3	108.3	112.4
GDP Deflator (2000=100)	99bip	81.0	85.3	87.9	89.5	92.0	94.3	96.4	100.0	103.2	105.5	110.6	113.1
					Millions: Midyear Estimates								
Population	99z	.71	.72	.73	.74	.75	.76	.78	.79	.80	.81	.82	.83

		1993	1994	1995	1996	1997	1998	1999	2000	2001	2002	2003	2004
Exchange Rates						*Koruny per SDR: End of Period*							
Official Rate	aa	41.145	40.947	39.544	39.302	46.733	42.037	49.382	49.267	45.568	40.977	38.121	34.733
						Koruny per US Dollar: End of Period (ae) Period Average (rf)							
Official Rate	ae	29.955	28.049	26.602	27.332	34.636	29.855	35.979	37.813	36.259	30.141	25.654	22.365
Official Rate	rf	29.153	28.785	26.541	27.145	31.698	32.281	34.569	38.598	38.035	32.739	28.209	25.700
						Index Numbers (2000=100): Period Averages							
Nominal Effective Exchange Rate	nec	97.43	99.75	99.75	101.65	98.14	98.82	98.95	100.00	104.68	115.82	117.00	119.36
Real Effective Exchange Rate	rec	80.14	84.17	87.01	92.75	93.47	101.12	99.74	100.00	105.71	116.59	114.23	115.79
Fund Position						*Millions of SDRs: End of Period*							
Quota	2f.s	589.6	589.6	589.6	589.6	589.6	589.6	819.3	819.3	819.3	819.3	819.3	819.3
SDRs	1b.s	6.0	—	.1	—	—	—	—	.2	.7	3.4	6.3	3.4
Reserve Position in the Fund	1c.s	—	—	—	—	—	—	—	2.4	120.5	173.5	314.6	264.0
Total Fund Cred.&Loans Outstg	2tl	780.7	—	—	—	—	—	—	—	—	—	—	—
International Liquidity						*Millions of US Dollars Unless Otherwise Indicated: End of Period*							
Total Reserves minus Gold	1l.d	3,789	6,145	13,843	12,352	9,734	12,542	12,806	13,019	14,341	23,556	26,771	28,259
SDRs	1b.d	8	—	—	—	—	—	—	—	1	5	9	5
Reserve Position in the Fund	1c.d	—	—	—	—	—	—	—	3	151	236	468	410
Foreign Exchange	1d.d	3,781	6,145	13,843	12,352	9,734	12,542	12,806	13,016	14,189	23,315	26,294	27,844
Gold (Million Fine Troy Ounces)	1ad	1.950	2.098	1.990	1.985	1.041	.288	.446	.446	.444	.442	.442	.438
Gold (National Valuation)	1and	129	140	141	137	57	18	23	22	23	28	32	37
Monetary Authorities:Other Assets	3..d	2,264	1,043	1,084	1,161	843	946	1,285	378	435	† 309	118	1,108
Other Liab.	4..d	2,905	1,791	1,802	658	696	381	849	366	407	† 157	120	1,053
Deposit Money Banks: Assets	7a.d	2,802	3,203	3,783	5,767	8,585	11,793	13,302	13,259	15,609	† 14,598	15,317	20,530
Liabilities	7b.d	1,459	2,464	6,428	9,048	9,124	10,799	9,678	8,419	7,714	† 7,664	10,094	10,275
Monetary Authorities						*Billions of Koruny: End of Period*							
Foreign Assets	11	185.20	205.53	400.83	373.08	368.28	403.23	507.82	507.43	536.61	† 720.12	690.65	657.63
Claims on Central Government	12a	44.98	39.73	12.63	.32	—	—	—	—	11.65	† 10.69	9.68	13.18
Claims on Other Resident Sectors	12d	2.16	1.33	1.51	5.10	† 22.14	48.50	61.11	42.43	40.77	† 38.52	36.89	31.19
Claims on Banking Institutions	12e	78.40	77.71	74.84	84.88	100.49	74.91	50.47	37.10	20.52	† .13	.11	.08
Reserve Money	14	166.12	223.23	342.77	344.40	† 344.60	422.24	459.78	491.57	515.76	† 260.14	279.08	289.06
of which: Currency Outside Bls.	14a	59.04	83.58	104.27	118.90	118.74	127.16	157.90	171.82	180.38	† 197.81	221.36	236.77
Other Liabs. to Banking Insts	14n	....	....	....	....	....	....	....	....	....	455.20	439.50	402.86
Other Deposits	15	.14	9.22	52.68	40.27	† .68	.79	.85	.70	.74	† .72	.66	.63
Foreign Liabilities	16c	119.15	50.25	47.93	17.98	24.11	11.38	30.55	13.83	14.74	† 4.73	3.09	23.55
Central Government Deposits	16d	33.41	51.86	41.15	43.09	† 68.46	63.07	62.44	57.97	84.25	† 82.26	73.28	92.15
Capital Accounts	17a	† 9.90	18.00	27.34	29.56	60.56	39.07	82.84	36.83	8.25	† −22.32	−40.40	−96.31
Other Items (Net)	17r	† −17.98	−28.26	−22.05	−11.91	−7.51	−9.92	−17.06	−13.93	−14.19	† −11.27	−17.88	−9.85
Banking Institutions						*Billions of Koruny: End of Period*							
Reserves	20	71.45	80.78	160.93	158.50	214.94	288.85	296.54	310.93	333.32	† 60.20	56.56	49.99
Other Claims on Monetary Author.	20n	....	....	....	....	....	....	....	....	....	455.20	439.50	402.86
Foreign Assets	21	83.95	89.84	100.64	157.64	297.34	352.08	478.59	501.35	565.97	† 440.00	392.95	459.16
Claims on Central Government	22a	78.18	94.64	130.94	103.86	62.05	73.66	93.76	117.90	270.78	† 433.78	520.96	437.98
Claims on Other General Govt	22b	....	....	....	....	....	....	....	....	....	21.81	24.26	27.86
Claims on Other Resident Sectors	22d	731.67	904.27	1,036.60	1,153.91	† 1,250.40	1,176.26	1,098.47	1,029.89	916.37	† 720.70	782.47	886.85
Demand Deposits	24	201.96	307.64	310.89	317.46	297.24	275.68	288.88	326.53	402.50	† 626.31	741.80	787.22
Other Deposits	25	428.21	426.43	601.90	663.78	755.75	809.54	797.54	945.94	1,022.98	† 890.51	880.24	899.92
Money Market Fund Shares	26m	....	....	....	....	....	....	....	....	....	—	—	48.19
Bonds	26n	3.78	21.21	46.68	60.88	81.58	113.38	189.74	93.39	76.74	† 48.58	51.58	26.89
Foreign Liabilities	26c	43.70	69.12	170.99	247.29	316.01	322.40	348.22	318.35	279.70	† 231.01	258.96	229.80
Central Government Deposits	26d	78.73	90.33	92.38	88.19	51.87	55.31	54.59	50.83	80.54	† 101.89	48.63	46.60
Credit from Monetary Authorities	26g	76.35	77.71	74.01	79.82	96.93	52.76	33.68	18.27	4.66	† 2.74	.12	.07
Capital Accounts	27a	160.75	185.37	195.88	204.28	† 348.20	395.15	411.80	405.39	291.53	† 291.86	282.78	291.59
Other Items (Net)	27r	−28.25	−8.29	−63.62	−87.77	−122.85	−133.39	−157.09	−198.63	−72.20	† −61.23	−47.41	−65.60
Banking Survey						*Billions of Koruny: End of Period*							
Foreign Assets (Net)	31n	106.29	176.00	282.55	265.44	325.50	421.52	607.64	676.60	808.14	† 924.38	821.56	863.45
Domestic Credit	32	744.85	897.77	1,048.15	1,131.92	† 1,214.25	1,180.04	1,136.31	1,081.43	1,074.78	† 1,041.33	1,252.35	1,258.30
Claims on Central Govt. (Net)	32an	11.03	−7.82	10.04	−27.10	† −58.28	−44.71	−23.27	9.10	117.65	† 260.31	408.72	312.40
Claims on Other General Govt	32b	....	....	....	....	....	....	....	....	....	21.81	24.26	27.86
Claims on Other Resident Sectors	32d	733.83	905.59	1,038.12	1,159.02	† 1,272.53	1,224.76	1,159.58	1,072.33	957.13	† 759.22	819.36	918.04
Money	34	268.98	403.97	431.08	451.55	† 418.39	404.00	447.81	498.96	583.55	† 827.04	964.18	1,026.29
Quasi-Money	35	428.35	435.65	654.58	704.05	† 756.44	810.33	798.39	946.64	1,023.72	† 891.23	880.90	900.55
Money Market Fund Shares	36m	....	....	....	....	....	....	....	....	....	....	—	48.19
Bonds	36n	3.78	21.21	46.68	60.88	81.58	113.38	189.74	93.39	76.74	† 48.58	51.58	26.89
Capital Accounts	37a	170.10	202.22	221.26	231.06	† 408.76	434.22	494.64	442.22	299.78	† 269.54	242.38	195.28
Other Items (Net)	37r	−20.61	9.57	−24.86	−52.94	−125.41	−160.39	−186.63	−223.18	−100.87	† −70.67	−65.14	−75.46
Money plus Quasi-Money	35l	697.33	839.62	1,085.66	1,155.59	† 1,174.83	1,214.33	1,246.20	1,445.60	1,607.27	† 1,718.27	1,845.08	1,926.84
Interest Rates						*Percent Per Annum*							
Bank Rate (End of Period)	60	8.00	8.50	11.30	12.40	14.75	9.50	5.25	5.25	4.50	2.75	2.00	2.50
Money Market Rate	60b	8.00	12.65	10.93	12.67	17.50	10.08	5.58	5.42	4.69	2.63	2.08	2.56
Treasury Bill Rate	60c	6.62	6.98	8.99	11.91	11.21	10.51	5.71	5.37	5.06	2.72	2.04	2.57
Deposit Rate	60l	7.03	7.07	6.96	6.79	7.71	8.08	4.48	3.42	2.87	2.00	1.33	1.28
Lending Rate	60p	14.07	13.12	12.80	12.54	13.20	12.81	8.68	7.16	7.20	6.72	5.95	6.03
Government Bond Yield	61	....	....	....	....	....	....	....	6.72	4.84	3.17	3.77	3.33

Czech Republic 935

		1993	1994	1995	1996	1997	1998	1999	2000	2001	2002	2003	2004
Prices, Production, Labor		*Index Numbers (2000=100): Period Averages*											
Producer Prices	63	72.3	76.1	81.8	85.8	89.9	94.4	95.3	100.0	102.8	102.3	102.0	107.7
Consumer Prices	64	† 60.1	66.1	72.1	78.5	85.2	94.2	96.2	100.0	104.7	106.6	106.7	109.7
Harmonized CPI (2002=100)	64h	....	....	....	....	....	....	....	....	....	100.0	99.9	102.5
Wages	65	43.4	51.4	61.0	72.2	79.3	86.7	94.0	100.0	108.7	116.5	124.3	132.5
Industrial Production	66	89.3	91.2	90.5	92.3	96.4	98.0	94.9	100.0	106.5	116.6	123.4	135.6
Industrial Employment	67	120.8	115.1	103.1	98.2	111.1	110.6	104.3	100.0	100.5	98.7	96.8	96.9
		Number in Thousands: Period Averages											
Labor Force	67d	....	....	....	5,199	5,215	5,233	5,236	5,181	5,171	5,139	....	....
Employment	67e	4,932	4,943	4,995	† 4,980	4,927	4,853	4,764	4,732	4,728	4,765	....	....
Unemployment	67c	200	202	181	206	248	336	454	455	418	457	523	457
Unemployment Rate (%)	67r	3.8	3.9	3.5	4.0	4.8	6.5	8.7	8.8	8.1	8.8	9.9	8.3
Intl. Transactions & Positions		*Millions of Koruny*											
Exports	70	† 421,601	466,403	574,722	594,630	722,501	850,240	908,756	1,121,099	1,269,634	1,254,394	1,370,930	1,713,694
Imports, f.o.b.	71.v	† 426,084	501,549	670,445	752,343	861,770	926,559	973,169	1,241,924	1,386,319	1,325,717	1,440,723	1,736,019
Balance of Payments		*Millions of US Dollars: Minus Sign Indicates Debit*											
Current Account, n.i.e.	78ald	466	−820	−1,374	−4,128	−3,622	−1,308	−1,466	−2,690	−3,273	−4,265	−5,785	−5,595
Goods: Exports f.o.b.	78aad	14,231	15,964	21,477	21,950	22,319	25,886	26,259	29,019	33,404	38,480	48,705	66,874
Goods: Imports f.o.b.	78abd	−14,748	−17,372	−25,162	−27,656	−27,257	−28,532	−28,161	−32,114	−36,482	−40,720	−51,224	−67,750
Trade Balance	78acd	−517	−1,408	−3,685	−5,706	−4,938	−2,647	−1,902	−3,095	−3,078	−2,240	−2,519	−876
Services: Credit	78add	4,721	5,167	6,725	8,181	7,132	7,665	7,048	6,839	7,092	7,083	7,789	9,695
Services: Debit	78aed	−3,709	−4,685	−4,882	−6,264	−5,389	−5,750	−5,850	−5,436	−5,567	−6,439	−7,320	−9,217
Balance on Goods & Services	78afd	496	−926	−1,842	−3,789	−3,196	−731	−704	−1,692	−1,554	−1,597	−2,049	−397
Income: Credit	78agd	548	791	1,197	1,170	1,405	1,713	1,859	1,952	2,233	2,052	2,681	2,740
Income: Debit	78ahd	−664	−812	−1,301	−1,892	−2,197	−2,806	−3,209	−3,323	−4,422	−5,632	−6,966	−8,173
Balance on Gds, Serv. & Inc.	78aid	379	−947	−1,945	−4,512	−3,987	−1,825	−2,053	−3,063	−3,743	−5,177	−6,334	−5,830
Current Transfers, n.i.e.: Credit	78ajd	242	298	664	617	866	1,067	1,310	948	959	1,465	1,663	1,802
Current Transfers: Debit	78akd	−154	−171	−92	−233	−501	−550	−722	−575	−489	−553	−1,114	−1,567
Capital Account, n.i.e.	78bcd	−563	—	7	1	11	2	−2	−5	−9	−4	−3	−595
Capital Account, n.i.e.: Credit	78bad	208	—	12	1	17	14	18	6	2	7	7	218
Capital Account: Debit	78bbd	−771	—	−5	—	−5	−12	−21	−11	−11	−11	−10	−813
Financial Account, n.i.e.	78bjd	3,043	4,504	8,225	4,202	1,122	2,908	3,080	3,835	4,569	10,621	5,620	7,165
Direct Investment Abroad	78bdd	−90	−116	−37	−155	−28	−125	−90	−43	−165	−211	−208	−572
Dir. Invest. in Rep. Econ., n.i.e.	78bed	654	878	2,568	1,435	1,286	3,700	6,313	4,987	5,641	8,497	2,021	4,454
Portfolio Investment Assets	78bfd	−232	−47	−325	−50	−159	−44	−1,882	−2,236	125	−2,373	−2,934	−2,448
Equity Securities	78bkd	−232	−47	−325	−50	3	119	−1,409	−1,167	247	−231	188	−1,089
Debt Securities	78bld	....	....	....	....	−162	−163	−473	−1,069	−121	−2,142	−3,122	−1,359
Portfolio Investment Liab., n.i.e.	78bgd	1,840	893	1,695	771	1,152	1,146	499	482	798	814	1,753	4,795
Equity Securities	78bmd	1,125	497	1,236	601	378	1,096	120	619	616	−265	1,104	738
Debt Securities	78bnd	715	396	460	170	774	49	380	−137	181	1,079	649	4,057
Financial Derivatives Assets	78bwd	....	....	....	....	....	....	....	−129	−254	−476	257	−591
Financial Derivatives Liabilities	78bxd	....	....	....	....	....	....	....	89	168	347	−114	515
Other Investment Assets	78bhd	−2,867	−2,437	−2,492	−2,370	−4,427	−1,552	−2,688	984	−1,199	4,015	2,279	−1,286
Monetary Authorities	78bod	—	—	—	—	—	—	—	—	—	—	—	−7
General Government	78bpd	−3,054	−2,362	−2,138	48	16	20	28	76	180	651	278	941
Banks	78bqd	36	−163	−224	−2,317	−4,161	−1,652	−2,642	1,011	−1,299	3,844	1,469	−1,272
Other Sectors	78brd	151	88	−130	−101	−281	80	−74	−102	−80	−480	533	−948
Other Investment Liab., n.i.e.	78bid	3,738	5,333	6,816	4,571	3,298	−217	927	−300	−544	9	2,565	2,298
Monetary Authorities	78bsd	106	−47	40	−2	−11	−7	−57	—	1	−1	−2	27
General Government	78btd	3,037	2,821	1,657	−295	−360	−364	−185	−49	−129	−45	372	369
Banks	78bud	4	888	3,310	2,858	1,638	387	886	−974	−1,152	−282	1,214	−453
Other Sectors	78bvd	591	1,671	1,809	2,011	2,030	−234	283	723	735	338	981	2,355
Net Errors and Omissions	78cad	95	−210	596	−901	730	288	27	−296	499	266	611	−712
Overall Balance	78cbd	3,041	3,474	7,453	−825	−1,758	1,890	1,639	844	1,787	6,618	442	263
Reserves and Related Items	79dad	−3,041	−3,474	−7,453	825	1,758	−1,890	−1,639	−844	−1,787	−6,618	−442	−263
Reserve Assets	79dbd	−3,039	−2,357	−7,453	825	1,758	−1,890	−1,639	−844	−1,787	−6,618	−442	−263
Use of Fund Credit and Loans	79dcd	−3	−1,117	—	—	—	—	—	—	—	—	—	—
Exceptional Financing	79ded	....	....	....	....	....	....	....	....	....	—	—	—
International Investment Position		*Millions of US Dollars*											
Assets	79aad	17,950	20,471	29,396	30,629	29,779	36,426	37,465	38,304	42,609	52,419	59,926	68,637
Direct Investment Abroad	79abd	181	300	345	498	548	804	698	738	1,136	1,473	2,284	3,061
Portfolio Investment	79acd	276	433	755	1,372	1,032	1,202	2,900	4,772	5,106	9,102	13,408	16,518
Equity Securities	79add	264	334	693	748	417	449	1,843	2,439	1,894	2,869	1,845	3,278
Debt Securities	79aed	12	99	62	624	615	752	1,057	2,333	3,212	6,233	11,563	13,240
Financial Derivatives	79ald	—	—	—	—	—	—	—	168	435	1,036	941	1,701
Other Investment	79afd	13,621	13,494	14,273	16,323	18,425	21,804	21,042	19,488	21,469	17,098	16,336	18,909
Monetary Authorities	79agd	820	876	984	956	754	875	—	10	10	22	22	30
General Government	79ahd	6,469	6,278	5,987	5,931	5,923	5,902	5,843	5,839	5,813	3,301	3,102	2,188
Banks	79aid	2,837	2,944	3,469	5,622	8,308	11,263	11,841	10,305	12,116	9,349	8,859	10,874
Other Sectors	79ajd	3,495	3,396	3,833	3,814	3,440	3,763	3,358	3,335	3,530	4,427	4,353	5,817
Reserve Assets	79akd	3,872	6,243	14,023	12,435	9,774	12,617	12,825	13,139	14,464	23,710	26,957	28,449
Liabilities	79lad	14,123	18,088	27,182	33,151	32,863	40,361	40,548	43,378	49,340	65,598	80,485	105,523
Dir. Invest. in Rep. Economy	79lbd	3,423	4,547	7,350	8,572	9,234	14,375	17,552	21,644	27,092	38,669	45,287	56,415
Portfolio Investment	79lcd	1,956	2,910	4,696	5,298	4,880	5,564	4,602	4,353	4,974	6,673	8,717	17,036
Equity Securities	79ldd	1,101	1,331	2,642	3,398	3,028	3,793	2,724	3,059	3,551	4,250	5,488	9,339
Debt Securities	79led	855	1,579	2,054	1,900	1,853	1,771	1,878	1,294	1,423	2,423	3,229	7,697
Financial Derivatives	79lld	—	—	—	—	—	—	—	140	317	752	758	1,422
Other Investment	79lfd	8,744	10,631	15,136	19,280	18,749	20,422	18,394	17,242	16,957	19,504	25,724	30,650
Monetary Authorities	79lgd	1,272	62	98	85	64	64	6	5	5	5	5	42
General Government	79lhd	2,748	2,910	2,031	1,619	1,098	801	580	521	261	314	875	1,434
Banks	79lid	1,283	2,402	6,007	8,964	9,009	10,640	9,682	8,219	7,286	7,954	10,392	10,623
Other Sectors	79ljd	3,442	5,257	6,999	8,612	8,577	8,916	8,126	8,497	9,405	11,230	14,452	18,551

Czech Republic 935

		1993	1994	1995	1996	1997	1998	1999	2000	2001	2002	2003	2004
Government Finance		*Billions of Koruny: Year Ending December 31*											
Deficit (-) or Surplus......................	80	1.1	10.4	7.2	−1.8	−15.9	−29.2	−29.7	−46.1	−67.9	−45.6	−109.1	−93.7
Total Revenue and Grants..............	81y	349.0	381.3	440.4	476.4	500.8	530.6	563.3	583.1	623.2	683.4	697.3	767.2
Revenue......................................	81	349.0	381.3	440.4	476.4	500.8	530.6	563.3	583.1	623.2	657.7	691.3	754.2
Grants.......................................	81z	—	—	—	—	—	—	—	—	—	25.7	6.0	13.0
Exp. & Lending Minus Repay..........	82z	347.9	370.9	433.2	478.2	516.7	559.8	593.0	629.2	691.1	729.0	806.4	860.9
Expenditure................................	82	351.9	373.1	433.9	480.6	521.2	561.6	593.8	629.5	688.2	746.2	806.1	862.5
Lending Minus Repayments..........	83	−4.0	−2.2	−.7	−2.4	−4.5	−1.8	−.8	−.3	2.9	−17.3	.3	−1.6
Total Financing.............................	80h	−1.1	−10.4	−7.2	1.7	15.9	29.3	29.6	46.1	67.8	45.6	109.1	93.7
Domestic.....................................	84a	−1.1	−10.4	−7.2	1.7	15.9	29.3	29.6	46.1	67.8	45.6	109.1	93.7
Foreign.......................................	85a	—	—	—	—	—	—	—	—	—	—	—	—
Total Debt by Residence..................	88	158.9	161.7	154.4	155.2	167.2	194.5	228.3	289.3	345.0	395.9	493.2	592.9
Domestic.....................................	88a	86.5	90.2	101.3	110.9	128.9	169.9	207.1	259.5	323.7	371.5	453.9	471.0
Foreign.......................................	89a	72.4	71.5	53.1	44.3	38.3	24.6	21.2	29.8	21.3	24.4	39.3	121.9
National Accounts		*Billions of Koruny*											
Househ.Cons.Expend.,incl.NPISHs.....	96f	515.4	607.0	† 734.6	859.0	945.6	1,011.9	1,059.6	1,122.8	1,192.3	1,234.7	1,315.1	1,378.6
Government Consumption Expend...	91f	221.6	255.5	† 318.4	352.3	389.2	412.5	456.1	475.0	513.0	555.2	604.4	623.0
Gross Fixed Capital Formation..........	93e	289.6	339.8	† 463.5	521.0	534.4	554.6	550.6	594.9	638.6	643.3	685.6	749.9
Changes in Inventories.....................	93i	−11.2	12.2	† 13.4	27.4	11.0	5.6	−.6	23.6	30.0	30.9	7.3	8.1
Exports of Goods and Services..........	90c	559.5	597.1	† 743.8	822.1	941.3	1,080.9	1,152.6	1,385.9	1,539.3	1,485.5	1,590.1	1,973.2
Imports of Goods and Services (-).....	98c	551.5	628.8	† 807.0	921.1	1,036.4	1,103.0	1,176.9	1,452.2	1,598.0	1,535.0	1,646.6	1,982.6
Gross Domestic Product (GDP)........	99b	1,020.3	1,182.8	1,466.7	1,660.6	1,785.1	1,962.5	2,041.4	2,150.1	2,315.3	2,414.7	2,555.8	2,750.3
Net Primary Income from Abroad.....	98.n	−4.3	−.8	−7.2	−24.8	−29.2	−35.1	−46.7	−53.2	−83.8	−116.2	−114.5	−135.8
Gross National Income (GNI)............	99a	1,016.0	1,181.9	1,459.5	1,635.9	1,755.9	1,927.4	1,994.7	2,096.9	2,231.5	2,298.4	2,441.3	2,614.5
Net Current Transf.from Abroad.......	98t	3.2	3.6	15.2	10.4	12.0	16.6	20.4	14.5	17.7	14.6	15.8	6.1
Gross Nat'l Disposable Inc.(GNDI)....	99i	1,003.0	1,185.6	1,474.7	1,646.3	1,767.9	1,944.0	2,015.1	2,111.3	2,249.2	2,313.0	2,457.1	2,620.6
Gross Saving..................................	99s	285.3	323.0	421.6	435.1	433.0	519.7	499.4	513.5	543.9	523.0	537.7	619.0
GDP Volume 1995 Prices.................	99b.p	1,275.3	1,303.6	1,466.7	1,527.7	1,516.6	1,499.2	1,517.3	1,576.3	1,617.9	1,642.0	1,694.7	1,769.9
GDP Volume (2000=100)...............	99bvp	80.9	82.7	93.0	96.9	96.2	95.1	96.3	100.0	102.6	104.2	107.5	112.3
GDP Deflator (2000=100)...............	99bip	58.7	66.5	73.3	79.7	86.3	96.0	98.6	100.0	104.9	107.8	110.6	113.9
		Millions: Midyear Estimates											
Population...............................	99z	10.33	10.33	10.33	10.32	10.31	10.30	10.28	10.27	10.26	10.25	10.24	10.23

		1993	1994	1995	1996	1997	1998	1999	2000	2001	2002	2003	2004
Exchange Rates							*Kroner per SDR: End of Period*						
Market Rate..................	aa	9.302	8.880	8.244	8.548	9.210	8.992	10.155	10.450	10.568	9.628	8.853	8.491
						Kroner per US Dollar: End of Period (ae) Period Average (rf)							
Market Rate..................	ae	6.773	6.083	5.546	5.945	6.826	6.387	7.399	8.021	8.410	7.082	5.958	5.468
Market Rate..................	rf	6.484	6.361	5.602	5.799	6.604	6.701	6.976	8.083	8.323	7.895	6.588	5.991
				Kroner per ECU through 1998; Kroner per Euro Beginning 1999: End of Period (ea) Period Average (eb)									
Euro Rate..................	ea	7.5508	7.4823	7.2940	7.4466	7.5312	7.4488	† 7.4432	7.4631	7.4357	7.4243	7.4450	7.4334
Euro Rate..................	ag	....	....	....	....	....	....	1.0046	.9305	.8813	1.0487	1.2630	1.3621
Euro Rate..................	eb	7.5916	7.5415	7.3271	7.3598	7.4830	7.4999	† 7.4356	7.4529	7.4521	7.4301	7.4306	7.4399
Euro Rate..................	rh	....	....	....	....	....	....	1.0668	.9240	.8956	.9444	1.1308	1.2433
					Index Numbers (2000=100): Period Averages								
Market Rate..................	ahx	124.5	127.0	144.0	139.0	122.2	120.4	115.7	100.0	96.9	102.4	122.6	134.7
Nominal Effective Exchange Rate.....	neu	105.3	105.5	110.5	108.9	105.2	106.1	104.5	100.0	101.3	102.3	106.2	107.4
Real Effective Exchange Rate...........	reu	103.4	103.1	107.4	105.9	102.8	104.9	104.4	100.0	101.9	104.2	109.6	112.0
Fund Position							*Millions of SDRs: End of Period*						
Quota..................	2f.s	1,069.9	1,069.9	1,069.9	1,069.9	1,069.9	1,069.9	1,642.8	1,642.8	1,642.8	1,642.8	1,642.8	1,642.8
SDRs..................	1b.s	62.4	124.6	106.8	116.7	248.7	246.0	249.9	50.5	223.5	75.9	54.6	28.8
Reserve Position in the Fund...........	1c.s	309.1	294.6	400.0	421.8	467.9	827.5	582.1	440.1	566.8	722.0	686.3	542.8
of which: Outstg.Fund Borrowing...	2c	—		—			34.2		—		—		—
International Liquidity					*Millions of US Dollars Unless Otherwise Indicated: End of Period*								
Total Reserves minus Gold..............	1l.d	10,301	9,056	11,016	14,140	19,124	15,264	22,287	15,108	17,110	26,986	37,105	39,084
SDRs..................	1b.d	86	182	159	168	336	346	343	66	281	103	81	45
Reserve Position in the Fund........	1c.d	425	430	595	607	631	1,165	799	573	712	982	1,020	843
Foreign Exchange..................	1d.d	9,791	8,444	10,262	13,366	18,157	13,753	21,145	14,469	16,117	25,901	36,004	38,196
Gold (Million Fine Troy Ounces)........	1ad	2	2	2	2	2	2	2	2	2	2	2	2
Gold (National Valuation)...............	1and	478	703	714	590	545	677	531	569	557	703	872	970
Monetary Authorities: Other Liab.....	4..d	117	253	397	275	124	196	297	381	421	400	481	266
Banking Institutions: Assets............	7a.d	57,272	50,945	56,593	62,392	65,675	76,754	68,432	† 71,009	60,469	72,054	102,896	128,511
Liabilities..................	7b.d	27,128	30,141	33,246	40,172	50,347	61,484	63,340	62,554	58,799	75,582	110,390	129,545
Monetary Authorities							*Billions of Kroner: End of Period*						
Foreign Assets..................	11	70.88	63.18	69.34	86.25	129.49	101.85	169.06	† 120.86	152.26	199.74	227.62	219.35
Claims on Central Government.........	12a	10.04	20.05	14.83	15.47	15.19	15.50	14.80	† 14.97	16.47	18.33	17.15	15.44
Claims on Banking Institutions........	12e	79.21	57.28	45.33	40.72	31.57	36.96	70.19	† 52.72	89.99	106.94	73.65	97.56
Claims on Other Banking Insts.......	12f	30.95	24.99	19.97	21.26	20.24	22.95	24.56	....	....	....	....	....
Claims on Other Resident Sectors.....	12d	.24	2.86	1.64	6.14	3.44	1.67	2.50	† 1.85	1.93	.23	.51	.47
Reserve Money..................	14	62.70	63.15	71.69	95.55	125.31	97.00	192.86	† 58.28	54.99	60.96	66.28	61.45
of which: Currency Outside BIs......	14a	25.72	28.93	30.59	30.94	33.25	34.49	36.86	† 37.43	39.21	38.98	40.99	43.72
Money Market Instruments.............	16m	....	....	....	....	....	....	....	51.87	113.62	160.66	157.28	160.38
Foreign Liabilities..................	16c	.79	1.54	2.20	1.63	.88	1.25	2.43	† 3.37	3.89	3.70	3.09	1.76
Central Government Deposits........	16d	89.57	56.91	35.44	31.65	30.73	34.03	36.49	† 35.32	40.56	47.06	40.89	58.08
Capital Accounts..................	17a	....	....	....	....	....	....	....	49.45	50.90	58.01	55.05	54.34
Other Items (Net)..................	17r	38.26	46.77	41.78	41.00	43.00	46.66	49.33	† -7.91	-3.32	-5.15	-3.67	-3.20
Banking Institutions							*Billions of Kroner: End of Period*						
Reserves..................	20	35.33	32.69	39.57	51.62	70.63	54.20	96.26	† 23.82	17.37	32.47	18.91	27.70
Claims on Mon.Author.:Securities.....	20c	....	....	....	....	....	....	....	50.56	113.88	151.14	156.66	157.65
Foreign Assets..................	21	387.88	309.90	313.87	370.89	448.30	490.19	506.32	† 569.52	508.52	510.30	613.02	702.65
Claims on Central Government........	22a	70.18	124.60	99.53	85.34	69.80	71.14	65.37	† 89.38	112.10	119.04	102.18	71.54
Claims on Other General Govt........	22b	....	....	....	....	....	....	....	....	57.95	61.17	66.27	75.03	83.06
Claims on Other Banking Insts........	22f	136.53	108.44	125.15	157.66	181.52	218.24	191.46	....	....	....	....	....
Claims on Other Resident Sectors.....	22d	317.67	297.74	312.89	331.06	357.73	405.37	420.62	† 1,750.73	1,904.42	1,999.09	2,122.47	2,318.41
Demand Deposits..................	24	255.44	248.31	259.86	287.09	304.47	321.44	336.34	† 346.55	373.20	391.63	427.72	492.54
Other Deposits..................	25	318.06	262.20	282.89	296.17	320.02	325.42	298.27	† 258.93	253.06	265.42	269.11	283.03
Money Market Instruments.............	26m	....	....	....	....	....	....	....	2.22	8.55	2.17	2.11	.20
Bonds..................	26n	....	....	....	....	....	....	....	1,173.61	1,268.87	1,363.06	1,417.13	1,513.98
Foreign Liabilities..................	26c	183.73	183.35	184.38	238.80	343.67	392.67	468.64	† 501.72	494.47	535.28	657.66	708.30
Central Government Deposits...........	26d	....	....	....	....	....	....	....	5.23	17.04	18.62	16.54	15.01
Credit from Monetary Authorities.....	26g	80.56	58.66	45.94	35.73	21.46	34.03	34.01	† 30.19	69.62	86.34	57.00	90.25
Capital Accounts..................	27a	72.13	79.54	75.37	77.42	82.25	87.64	91.43	† 221.46	212.55	207.06	235.80	241.96
Other Items (Net)..................	27r	37.67	41.31	42.58	61.35	56.11	77.93	51.34	† 2.28	20.12	8.69	5.16	15.37
Banking Survey							*Billions of Kroner: End of Period*						
Foreign Assets (Net)..................	31n	274.24	188.19	196.62	216.70	233.24	198.12	204.31	† 185.29	162.42	171.06	179.88	211.94
Domestic Credit..................	32	482.44	528.22	545.50	592.83	629.40	714.58	697.55	† 1,874.33	2,038.48	2,137.28	2,259.90	2,415.82
Claims on Central Govt. (Net)........	32an	-9.36	87.74	78.91	69.16	54.26	52.62	43.68	† 63.80	70.96	71.69	61.89	13.89
Claims on Other General Govt........	32b	6.40	6.44	6.93	7.56	12.22	13.73	14.74	† 57.95	61.17	66.27	75.03	83.06
Claims on Other Banking Insts.......	32f	167.48	133.43	145.13	178.91	201.75	241.19	216.02	....	....	....	....	....
Claims on Other Resident Sectors...	32d	317.91	300.61	314.53	337.19	361.17	407.04	423.12	† 1,752.58	1,906.35	1,999.32	2,122.98	2,318.88
Money..................	34	283.00	279.05	291.98	325.52	344.05	360.74	381.77	† 385.98	414.85	430.82	469.15	536.62
Quasi-Money..................	35	318.06	262.20	282.89	296.17	320.02	325.42	298.27	† 258.93	253.06	265.42	269.11	283.03
Money Market Instruments.............	36m	....	....	....	....	....	....	....	3.53	8.30	11.70	2.73	2.93
Bonds..................	36n	....	....	....	....	....	....	....	1,148.73	1,244.30	1,340.38	1,394.52	1,492.32
Capital Accounts..................	37a	....	....	....	....	....	....	....	270.91	263.45	265.08	290.85	296.31
Other Items (Net)..................	37r	155.62	175.16	167.25	187.84	198.57	226.54	221.82	† -8.24	16.96	-5.08	13.38	16.19
Money plus Quasi-Money...............	35l	601.06	541.25	574.87	621.69	664.08	686.16	680.04	† 644.91	667.91	696.24	738.27	819.65
Money (National Definitions)							*Billions of Kroner: End of Period*						
Broad Money..................	59mc	416.42	394.03	410.01	439.74	462.66	476.23	495.94	505.91	546.18	604.71	680.56	699.08
Interest Rates							*Percent Per Annum*						
Discount Rate (End of Period)...........	60	6.25	5.00	4.25	3.25	3.50	3.50	3.00	4.75	3.25	2.86	2.00	2.00
Money Market Rate..................	60b	† 11.49	6.30	6.19	3.98	3.71	4.27	3.37	4.98	....	3.56	2.38	2.16
Deposit Rate..................	60l	6.5	† 3.5	3.9	2.8	2.7	3.1	2.4	3.2	3.3	† 2.4	2.4	....
Lending Rate..................	60p	10.5	† 10.0	10.3	8.7	7.7	7.9	7.1	8.1	8.2	† 7.1	....	....
Government Bond Yield..................	61	7.08	7.41	7.58	6.04	5.08	4.59	4.30	5.54	....	4.57	3.53	3.32
Mortgage Bond Yield..................	61a	8.17	8.34	8.97	7.84	7.14	6.04	6.08	7.06	....	6.13	5.16	5.01

Denmark 128

		1993	1994	1995	1996	1997	1998	1999	2000	2001	2002	2003	2004
Prices, Production, Labor		*Index Numbers (2000=100): Period Averages*											
Share Prices: Industrial	62a	34	40	40	49	65	70	62	100	....	....	....	....
Shipping	62b	30	33	30	37	66	68	77	100	....	....	....	....
Prices: Home & Import Goods	63	† 88.1	89.1	91.7	92.7	94.5	93.9	94.4	† 100.0	102.0	102.1	102.3	104.5
Home Goods	63a	† 87.8	88.8	91.6	93.0	94.7	94.2	95.1	† 100.0	102.8	103.5	104.8	108.7
Consumer Prices	64	85.7	87.4	89.2	91.1	93.1	94.8	97.2	100.0	102.4	104.8	107.0	108.3
Harmonized CPI	64h	....	....	90.5	92.4	94.1	95.4	97.3	100.0	102.3	104.7	106.8	107.8
Wages: Hourly Earnings	65..c	....	79.3	82.3	85.4	88.8	92.6	96.5	100.0	104.2	108.3	112.3	115.7
Industrial Production	66	75.4	83.2	86.5	87.6	92.0	94.7	94.9	100.0	102.0	103.0	102.3	102.0
Agricultural Production (1995=100).	66bx	† 101.7	101.1	100.0	100.2	101.0	104.6	104.8	....	....	....	....	....
		Number in Thousands: Period Averages											
Labor Force	67d	2,893	2,777	....	2,822	2,856	2,848	....	2,853	2,862	2,849	2,850	....
Employment	67e	2,584	† 2,555	2,607	2,627	2,678	2,691	2,708	2,722	2,725	2,712	2,693	2,720
Unemployment	67c	349	343	288	246	220	183	158	151	135	138	160	166
Unemployment Rate (%)	67r	12.4	12.2	10.3	8.8	7.9	6.6	5.7	5.4	4.8	4.9	5.7	5.9
Intl. Transactions & Positions		*Millions of Kroner*											
Exports	70	247,750	273,163	288,186	298,562	324,271	326,504	351,916	408,239	424,670	442,754	429,272	453,678
Imports, c.i.f	71	203,029	231,794	256,094	260,977	293,063	309,787	310,586	358,871	367,032	384,710	369,701	398,237
		2000=100											
Volume of Exports	72	64	69	† 78	80	84	86	92	100	103	109	108	112
Volume of Imports	73	61	69	† 81	82	88	93	93	100	102	108	107	114
Unit Value of Exports	74	89	90	† 90	92	94	93	93	100	102	100	100	101
Unit Value of Imports	75	85	86	† 88	90	93	93	93	100	101	99	97	98
Import Prices	76.x	† 89	90	92	92	94	93	93	100	101	100	99	100
Balance of Payments		*Millions of US Dollars: Minus Sign Indicates Debit*											
Current Account, n.i.e	78ald	4,832	3,189	1,855	3,090	921	−2,008	3,047	2,262	4,848	3,460	6,963	....
Goods: Exports f.o.b	78aad	36,948	41,741	50,348	50,735	48,103	47,908	49,787	50,084	50,466	55,473	64,537	....
Goods: Imports f.o.b	78abd	−29,229	−34,300	−43,821	−43,203	−42,734	−44,021	−43,128	−43,443	−43,048	−47,810	−54,840	....
Trade Balance	78acd	7,719	7,441	6,528	7,532	5,369	3,886	6,658	6,641	7,418	7,662	9,697	....
Services: Credit	78add	12,564	13,661	15,307	16,502	14,044	15,212	19,982	23,721	25,134	26,667	31,672	....
Services: Debit	78aed	−10,467	−12,067	−14,040	−14,771	−13,727	−15,779	−18,402	−21,063	−22,121	−24,305	−28,254	....
Balance on Goods & Services	78afd	9,816	9,035	7,795	9,263	5,685	3,319	8,238	9,300	10,431	10,024	13,116	....
Income: Credit	78agd	23,091	22,743	28,433	37,626	18,774	10,401	9,090	11,883	10,737	9,265	11,180	....
Income: Debit	78ahd	−27,480	−27,385	−32,982	−42,235	−22,203	−14,247	−11,546	−15,907	−13,748	−12,805	−13,796	....
Balance on Gds, Serv. & Inc	78aid	5,427	4,394	3,246	4,655	2,256	−527	5,782	5,276	7,420	6,484	10,499	....
Current Transfers, n.i.e.: Credit	78ajd	2,442	2,261	2,580	2,398	3,633	3,443	4,239	3,395	3,719	3,466	4,615	....
Current Transfers: Debit	78akd	−3,037	−3,466	−3,970	−3,963	−4,968	−4,924	−6,974	−6,410	−6,291	−6,489	−8,151	....
Capital Account, n.i.e	78bcd	—	....	....	....	128	50	128	−11	14	152	−7	....
Capital Account, n.i.e.: Credit	78bad	—	....	....	....	128	81	372	320	300	411	344	....
Capital Account: Debit	78bbd	—	....	....	....	—	−31	−245	−332	−286	−258	−351	....
Financial Account, n.i.e	78bjd	−6,545	−5,647	−432	1,882	8,496	−1,489	7,414	−3,311	−5,712	3,819	−5,129	....
Direct Investment Abroad	78bdd	−1,373	−4,162	−2,969	−2,510	−4,355	−4,215	−17,819	−28,381	−13,154	−2,650	−856	....
Dir. Invest. in Rep. Econ., n.i.e	78bed	1,713	5,006	4,139	773	2,792	6,675	16,848	36,013	9,286	4,431	1,185	....
Portfolio Investment Assets	78bfd	2	−1,175	−1,171	−2,349	−6,239	−7,563	−9,721	−23,582	−14,772	−4,356	−21,930	....
Equity Securities	78bkd	—	....	....	....	....	....	−6,202	−13,944	−4,318	199	−3,467	....
Debt Securities	78bld	2	−1,175	−1,171	−2,349	....	....	−3,519	−9,638	−10,454	−4,555	−18,463	....
Portfolio Investment Liab., n.i.e	78bgd	12,659	−10,596	7,487	7,865	11,186	−2,598	7,014	5,783	10,510	4,843	6,010	....
Equity Securities	78bmd	—	....	....	....	....	....	−18	2,341	861	591	1,389	....
Debt Securities	78bnd	12,659	−10,596	7,487	7,865	....	....	7,031	3,442	9,649	4,253	4,621	....
Financial Derivatives Assets	78bwd	....	....	....	....	....	....	—	—	—	—	—	....
Financial Derivatives Liabilities	78bxd	....	....	....	....	....	....	320	326	694	390	−12	....
Other Investment Assets	78bhd	−14,812	12,136	−1,330	−9,339	−8,033	−1,797	−906	−2,025	9,054	−6,839	−9,314	....
Monetary Authorities	78bod	....	....	....	....	....	....	−32	15	−13	−41	56	....
General Government	78bpd	—	....	....	....	....	....	31	25	41	18	365	....
Banks	78bqd	−14,812	12,136	−1,330	−9,339	....	....	329	−1,713	7,232	−6,062	−12,623	....
Other Sectors	78brd	....	....	....	....	−8,033	−1,797	−1,234	−352	1,794	−755	2,888	....
Other Investment Liab., n.i.e	78bid	−4,734	−6,856	−6,589	7,442	13,145	8,009	11,677	8,554	−7,331	8,000	19,789	....
Monetary Authorities	78bsd	−4,419	122	133	−108	....	....	158	113	61	−30	−27	....
General Government	78btd	8,648	−4,058	−3,380	−1,563	....	....	−232	−329	−191	−158	−438	....
Banks	78bud	−6,497	414	15	9,343	....	....	7,659	10,466	−1,720	10,806	24,714	....
Other Sectors	78bvd	−2,467	−3,333	−3,357	−231	13,145	8,009	4,092	−1,696	−5,481	−2,619	−4,461	....
Net Errors and Omissions	78cad	1,146	606	1,075	−1,408	−3,012	−792	−1,024	−4,460	4,167	−1,887	2,846	....
Overall Balance	78cbd	−567	−1,851	2,498	3,563	6,532	−4,239	9,564	−5,521	3,317	5,546	4,674	....
Reserves and Related Items	79dad	567	1,851	−2,498	−3,563	−6,532	4,239	−9,564	5,521	−3,317	−5,546	−4,674	....
Reserve Assets	79dbd	567	1,851	−2,498	−3,563	−6,532	4,239	−9,564	5,521	−3,317	−5,546	−4,674	....
Use of Fund Credit and Loans	79dcd	—	—	—	—	....	....	....	....	....	....	....	....
Exceptional Financing	79ded	....	....	....	....	....	....	....	....	....	....	....	....

Denmark 128

		1993	1994	1995	1996	1997	1998	1999	2000	2001	2002	2003	2004
International Investment Position							*Millions of US Dollars*						
Assets...............................	79aad	111,991	109,111	123,004	145,614	156,402	187,516	219,613	249,021	241,767	....	....	....
Direct Investment Abroad..............	79abd	15,799	19,892	24,702	27,589	28,128	34,664	44,841	65,890	69,760	....	....	....
Portfolio Investment...................	79acd	17,866	17,261	22,899	29,944	37,064	51,792	70,762	84,973	82,938	....	....	....
Equity Securities....................	79add	7,973	8,877	10,819	16,149	22,414	32,623	50,132	56,480	46,845	....	....	....
Debt Securities....................	79aed	9,893	8,384	12,081	13,794	14,650	19,169	20,630	28,493	36,093	....	....	....
Financial Derivatives..................	79ald	—	—	—	—	—	2,502	9,285	14,093	11,201	....	....	....
Other Investment....................	79afd	67,183	62,798	63,469	73,513	71,931	82,423	72,054	69,009	59,784	....	....	....
Monetary Authorities................	79agd	—	—	—	—	—	—	—	—	—	....	....	....
General Government.................	79ahd	2,362	2,795	2,524	2,187	2,051	2,524	2,621	3,396	3,422	....	....	....
Banks.............................	79aid	51,384	46,359	49,766	55,177	56,255	64,534	54,775	51,786	42,099	....	....	....
Other Sectors......................	79ajd	13,437	13,645	11,179	16,149	13,624	15,365	14,658	13,827	14,262	....	....	....
Reserve Assets.......................	79akd	11,142	9,160	11,933	14,569	19,279	16,136	22,670	15,056	18,084	....	....	....
Liabilities............................	79lad	155,186	151,734	170,934	187,737	197,480	235,320	241,569	272,052	268,174	....	....	....
Dir. Invest. in Rep. Economy..........	79lbd	14,618	18,083	23,801	22,205	22,268	31,055	41,225	66,459	65,827	....	....	....
Portfolio Investment...................	79lcd	84,016	72,826	88,713	101,607	106,505	117,215	105,272	104,119	112,111	....	....	....
Equity Securities....................	79ldd	3,248	6,740	8,294	12,448	20,363	20,556	20,740	26,023	22,853	....	....	....
Debt Securities....................	79led	80,768	66,086	80,418	89,158	86,141	96,658	84,532	78,095	89,258	....	....	....
Financial Derivatives..................	79lld	—	—	—	—	—	2,159	8,453	13,363	10,828	....	....	....
Other Investment....................	79lfd	56,552	60,825	58,420	63,925	68,708	84,891	86,619	88,111	79,408	....	....	....
Monetary Authorities................	79lgd	148	329	361	336	146	204	328	420	463	....	....	....
General Government.................	79lhd	2,067	3,123	1,983	1,178	732	1,265	949	468	474	....	....	....
Banks.............................	79lid	22,444	27,289	29,210	35,159	42,631	53,475	52,813	60,547	56,584	....	....	....
Other Sectors......................	79ljd	31,894	30,084	26,866	27,252	25,198	29,948	32,530	26,675	21,887	....	....	....
Government Finance							*Millions of Kroner: Year Ending December 31*						
Deficit (-) or Surplus..................	80	−21,935	−26,398	−23,692	−3,081	12,661p	19,479p	6,296p	20,804f		....	....	....
Revenue.............................	81	358,056	385,593	391,286	417,948	434,423p	449,490p	462,510p	470,916f		....	....	....
Grants Received......................	81z	5,973	5,546	3,873	3,771	4,583p	4,826p	4,665p	5,507f		....	....	....
Expenditure..........................	82	381,805	412,967	417,654	423,596	425,124p	434,285p	443,021p	452,939f		....	....	....
Lending Minus Repayments...........	83	4,157	4,570	1,195	1,202	1,222p	554p	17,857p	2,677f		....	....	....
National Accounts							*Billions of Kroner*						
Househ.Cons.Expend.,incl.NPISHs....	96f	450.2	493.8	509.6	533.2	560.9	581.3	599.5	610.5	624.5	641.9	659.3	695.3
Government Consumption Expend...	91f	240.9	250.3	260.3	274.6	284.5	300.5	312.1	323.3	343.3	358.5	371.8	385.6
Gross Fixed Capital Formation..........	93e	154.3	167.0	187.9	196.8	218.8	238.3	238.8	256.3	266.6	271.0	272.6	285.6
Changes in Inventories....................	93i	−6.5	3.0	10.7	4.1	12.9	12.1	−.5	12.6	3.1	2.5	.7	6.0
Exports of Goods and Services..........	90c	318.6	342.6	356.9	378.9	406.3	412.8	459.1	562.9	590.9	602.2	594.3	628.7
Imports of Goods and Services (-).....	98c	257.3	291.0	315.6	326.6	367.1	389.5	401.3	486.7	505.4	525.2	508.2	554.9
Gross Domestic Product (GDP).........	99b	900.2	965.7	1,009.8	1,060.9	1,116.3	1,155.4	1,207.7	1,279.0	1,323.0	1,350.8	1,390.5	1,446.5
Net Primary Income from Abroad.....	98.n	−16.0	−16.0	−12.7	−14.0	−16.0	−12.1	−10.1	−26.8	−18.3	−20.7	−10.5	−6.6
Gross National Income (GNI)...........	99a	884.2	949.7	997.1	1,046.9	1,100.3	1,143.3	1,197.7	1,252.1	1,304.6	1,330.0	1,380.1	1,439.9
Net Current Transf.from Abroad.......	98t	−20.1	−20.8	−21.5	−22.8	−18.7	−21.4	−26.6	−30.7	−26.7	−28.6	−29.8	−31.4
Gross Nat'l Disposable Inc.(GNDI)....	99i	864.1	928.9	975.6	1,024.1	1,081.6	1,121.9	1,171.1	1,221.4	1,277.9	1,301.4	1,350.3	1,408.4
Gross Saving.........................	99s	173.0	184.8	205.8	216.3	236.2	240.1	259.5	287.6	310.1	301.1	319.2	327.5
Consumption of Fixed Capital..........	99cf	144.7	154.0	161.3	168.8	177.4	183.3	189.7	199.6	211.3	218.5	222.2	222.0
GDP Volume 1995 Prices.................	99b.p	931.8	982.7	1,009.8	1,035.2	1,065.9	1,092.2	1,121.0	1,152.8	1,167.8	1,173.7	1,181.9	1,210.2
GDP Volume (2000=100)...............	99bvp	80.8	85.2	87.6	89.8	92.5	94.7	97.2	100.0	101.3	101.8	102.5	105.0
GDP Deflator (2000=100)...............	99bip	87.1	88.6	90.1	92.4	94.4	95.3	97.1	100.0	102.1	103.7	106.0	107.7
							Millions: Midyear Estimates						
Population..............................	99z	5.19	5.21	5.23	5.25	5.27	5.30	5.32	5.34	5.36	5.38	5.40	5.41

		1993	1994	1995	1996	1997	1998	1999	2000	2001	2002	2003	2004
Exchange Rates							*Francs per SDR: End of Period (aa)*						
Official Rate	aa	244.11	259.45	264.18	255.56	239.79	250.24	243.92	231.55	223.35	241.62	264.09	276.00
						Francs per US Dollar: End of Period (ae) Period Average (rf)							
Official Rate	ae	177.72	177.72	177.72	177.72	177.72	177.72	177.72	177.72	177.72	177.72	177.72	177.72
Official Rate	rf	177.72	177.72	177.72	177.72	177.72	177.72	177.72	177.72	177.72	177.72	177.72	177.72
Fund Position							*Millions of SDRs: End of Period*						
Quota	2f.s	11.50	11.50	11.50	11.50	11.50	11.50	15.90	15.90	15.90	15.90	15.90	15.90
SDRs	1b.s	.15	.11	.06	.10	.55	.27	.06	.28	.10	.76	.09	.64
Reserve Position in the Fund	1c.s	—	—	—	—	—	—	1.10	1.10	1.10	1.10	1.10	1.10
Total Fund Cred.&Loans Outstg	2tl	—	—	—	2.88	3.98	6.30	9.28	10.29	12.32	15.06	13.75	13.63
International Liquidity						*Millions of US Dollars Unless Otherwise Indicated: End of Period*							
Total Reserves minus Gold	1l.d	75.10	73.76	72.16	76.97	66.57	66.45	70.61	67.80	70.31	73.71	100.13	93.94
SDRs	1b.d	.21	.16	.09	.15	.75	.38	.09	.36	.13	1.03	.14	.99
Reserve Position in the Fund	1c.d	—	—	—	—	—	—	1.51	1.43	1.38	1.50	1.63	1.71
Foreign Exchange	1d.d	74.89	73.60	72.07	76.82	65.82	66.07	69.01	66.01	68.80	71.18	98.36	91.24
Deposit Money Banks: Assets	7a.d	219.26	211.53	209.96	173.31	167.22	169.95	178.25	166.03	201.85	251.41	296.17	372.84
Liabilities	7b.d	84.81	88.65	91.10	89.01	83.33	88.47	45.30	50.12	38.75	43.04	36.37	41.92
Other Banking Insts.: Liabilities	7f.d	4.01	3.43	3.21	3.26	....	....	....	....	....	....	....	....
Monetary Authorities							*Millions of Francs: End of Period*						
Foreign Assets	11	13,347	13,990	12,688	13,683	12,064	11,518	12,507	12,051	12,498	13,215	17,915	16,696
Claims on Central Government	12a	307	534	534	1,275	1,487	2,176	2,928	2,832	3,234	3,177	4,331	4,620
Claims on Deposit Money Banks	12e	40	40	42	44	44	44	—	—	—	—	—	—
Reserve Money	14	11,250	11,869	10,370	9,989	9,783	9,588	10,011	9,932	10,467	11,409	14,965	14,197
of which: Currency Outside DMBs	14a	10,401	10,693	9,367	9,686	9,450	9,112	9,289	9,207	9,370	10,188	11,113	12,358
Central Government Deposits	16d	716	797	1,074	284	106	676	1,152	514	319	115	792	176
Capital Accounts	17a	1,425	1,390	1,712	1,729	1,872	2,361	2,537	2,713	2,786	2,807	2,834	2,897
Other Items (Net)	17r	303	511	108	3,000	1,889	1,125	1,735	1,724	2,161	2,062	3,656	4,046
Deposit Money Banks							*Millions of Francs: End of Period*						
Reserves	20	925	1,148	1,065	638	778	575	743	718	1,056	1,221	3,854	1,888
Foreign Assets	21	38,967	37,594	37,314	30,801	29,719	30,204	31,679	29,507	35,873	44,681	52,636	66,261
Claims on Central Government	22a	446	2,525	2,144	1,569	1,678	724	214	111	74	1,478	1,318	1,069
Claims on Nonfin.Pub.Enterprises	22c	483	419	464	599	778	2,115	2,309	1,540	1,758	1,374	1,259	1,099
Claims on Private Sector	22d	32,057	33,382	37,783	38,826	38,469	42,098	27,491	31,413	26,898	25,629	24,967	24,991
Demand Deposits	24	22,209	21,814	21,157	18,738	17,506	20,146	20,985	18,704	19,275	25,327	31,737	35,085
Time Deposits	25	22,094	23,030	26,841	23,185	23,943	24,845	21,747	24,697	27,924	29,922	34,207	40,311
Foreign Liabilities	26c	15,073	15,755	16,191	15,819	14,810	15,723	8,051	8,908	6,886	7,650	6,464	7,450
Central Government Deposits	26d	925	2,089	727	568	605	877	233	87	31	3	12	54
Credit From Monetary Authorities	26g	40	40	40	52	406	40	—	—	—	—	—	—
Capital Accounts	27a	8,082	9,854	10,051	10,053	9,609	9,814	8,730	7,550	7,646	7,676	7,643	6,412
Other Items (Net)	27r	4,456	2,485	3,763	4,021	4,544	4,271	2,690	3,342	3,896	3,804	3,970	5,995
Monetary Survey							*Millions of Francs: End of Period*						
Foreign Assets (Net)	31n	37,222	35,815	33,794	27,904	25,959	24,336	33,720	29,979	38,410	47,230	59,918	71,057
Domestic Credit	32	35,446	39,075	45,598	48,918	47,223	45,560	31,557	35,295	31,614	31,540	31,071	31,549
Claims on Central Govt. (Net)	32an	2,158	5,180	7,233	9,384	7,873	1,347	1,757	2,342	2,958	4,537	4,845	5,459
Claims on Nonfin.Pub.Enterprises	32c	483	419	464	599	778	2,115	2,309	1,540	1,758	1,374	1,259	1,099
Claims on Private Sector	32d	32,805	33,476	37,901	38,935	38,572	42,098	27,491	31,413	26,898	25,629	24,967	24,991
Money	34	36,404	37,608	36,998	35,925	32,478	29,258	30,274	27,911	28,645	35,515	42,850	47,443
Quasi-Money	35	22,094	23,030	26,841	23,185	23,943	24,845	21,747	24,697	27,924	29,922	34,207	40,311
Other Items (Net)	37r	14,171	14,254	15,553	17,715	16,817	15,805	13,256	12,665	13,455	13,333	13,932	14,851
Money plus Quasi-Money	35l	58,498	60,638	63,839	59,110	56,421	54,103	52,021	52,608	56,569	65,437	77,057	87,754
Other Banking Institutions							*Millions of Francs: End of Period*						
Reserves	40	261	167	80	30	....	....	....	....	....	....	....	....
Claims on Private Sector	42d	4,472	4,277	4,126	3,537	....	....	....	....	....	....	....	....
Long-Term Foreign Liabilities	46cl	712	610	570	580	....	....	....	....	....	....	....	....
Central Govt. Lending Funds	46f	1,788	1,542	1,533	1,180	....	....	....	....	....	....	....	....
Capital Accounts	47a	1,557	1,557	1,817	1,696	....	....	....	....	....	....	....	....
Other Items (Net)	47r	676	735	286	111	....	....	....	....	....	....	....	....
Interest Rates							*Percent Per Annum*						
Deposit Rate	60l	....	....	....	....	....	....	....	....	2.81	1.23	.82	.80
Lending Rate	60p	....	....	....	....	....	....	....	....	11.46	11.30	11.30	11.25
Intl. Transactions & Positions							*Millions of Francs*						
Exports	70	2,151	2,151	2,414	2,439	1,917	2,195	2,168	....	....	....	....	....
Imports	71	37,499	34,908	31,395	31,805	26,322	28,120	27,131	....	....	....	....	....
							1995=100						
Volume of Imports	73	115.7	107.0	100.0	90.8	75.9	88.2	99.3	....	....	....	....	....
Import Prices	76.x	101.4	100.6	100.0	110.5	102.1	103.8	95.3	....	....	....	....	....

Djibouti 611

		1993	1994	1995	1996	1997	1998	1999	2000	2001	2002	2003	2004
Balance of Payments					*Millions of US Dollars: Minus Sign Indicates Debit*								
Current Account, n.i.e.	78ald	−34.3	−46.1	−23.0	....	....	....	....	....	....	....	....	....
Goods: Exports f.o.b.	78aad	71.2	56.4	33.5	....	....	....	....	....	....	....	....	....
Goods: Imports f.o.b.	78abd	−255.1	−237.1	−205.0	....	....	....	....	....	....	....	....	....
Trade Balance	78acd	−183.9	−180.7	−171.5	....	....	....	....	....	....	....	....	....
Services: Credit	78add	156.9	152.3	151.4	....	....	....	....	....	....	....	....	....
Services: Debit	78aed	−110.8	−89.7	−87.2	....	....	....	....	....	....	....	....	....
Balance on Goods & Services	78afd	−137.8	−118.1	−107.3	....	....	....	....	....	....	....	....	....
Income: Credit	78agd	30.3	23.7	25.9	....	....	....	....	....	....	....	....	....
Income: Debit	78ahd	−7.2	−7.0	−8.7	....	....	....	....	....	....	....	....	....
Balance on Gds, Serv. & Inc.	78aid	−114.8	−101.4	−90.0	....	....	....	....	....	....	....	....	....
Current Transfers, n.i.e.: Credit	78ajd	96.6	73.7	85.4	....	....	....	....	....	....	....	....	....
Current Transfers: Debit	78akd	−16.1	−18.3	−18.4	....	....	....	....	....	....	....	....	....
Capital Account, n.i.e.	78bcd	—	—	—	....	....	....	....	....	....	....	....	....
Capital Account, n.i.e.: Credit	78bad	—	—	—	....	....	....	....	....	....	....	....	....
Capital Account: Debit	78bbd	—	—	—	....	....	....	....	....	....	....	....	....
Financial Account, n.i.e.	78bjd	16.6	39.0	−2.1	....	....	....	....	....	....	....	....	....
Direct Investment Abroad	78bdd	—	—	—	....	....	....	....	....	....	....	....	....
Dir. Invest. in Rep. Econ., n.i.e.	78bed	1.4	1.4	3.2	....	....	....	....	....	....	....	....	....
Portfolio Investment Assets	78bfd	—	—	—	....	....	....	....	....	....	....	....	....
Equity Securities	78bkd	—	—	—	....	....	....	....	....	....	....	....	....
Debt Securities	78bld	—	—	—	....	....	....	....	....	....	....	....	....
Portfolio Investment Liab., n.i.e.	78bgd	—	—	—	....	....	....	....	....	....	....	....	....
Equity Securities	78bmd	—	—	—	....	....	....	....	....	....	....	....	....
Debt Securities	78bnd	—	—	—	....	....	....	....	....	....	....	....	....
Financial Derivatives Assets	78bwd	....	....	....	....	....	....	....	....	....	....	....	....
Financial Derivatives Liabilities	78bxd	....	....	....	....	....	....	....	....	....	....	....	....
Other Investment Assets	78bhd	—	—	—	....	....	....	....	....	....	....	....	....
Monetary Authorities	78bod	....	....	....	....	....	....	....	....	....	....	....	....
General Government	78bpd	—	—	—	....	....	....	....	....	....	....	....	....
Banks	78bqd	—	—	—	....	....	....	....	....	....	....	....	....
Other Sectors	78brd	—	—	—	....	....	....	....	....	....	....	....	....
Other Investment Liab., n.i.e.	78bid	15.2	37.6	−5.4	....	....	....	....	....	....	....	....	....
Monetary Authorities	78bsd	—	—	—	....	....	....	....	....	....	....	....	....
General Government	78btd	15.9	12.0	−9.4	....	....	....	....	....	....	....	....	....
Banks	78bud	−18.8	11.6	4.0	....	....	....	....	....	....	....	....	....
Other Sectors	78bvd	18.1	14.1	.1	....	....	....	....	....	....	....	....	....
Net Errors and Omissions	78cad	6.0	7.9	.7	....	....	....	....	....	....	....	....	....
Overall Balance	78cbd	−11.7	.8	−24.5	....	....	....	....	....	....	....	....	....
Reserves and Related Items	79dad	11.7	−.8	24.5	....	....	....	....	....	....	....	....	....
Reserve Assets	79dbd	11.3	−3.4	7.3	....	....	....	....	....	....	....	....	....
Use of Fund Credit and Loans	79dcd	—	—	—	....	....	....	....	....	....	....	....	....
Exceptional Financing	79ded	.4	2.6	17.2	....	....	....	....	....	....	....	....	....
				Millions: Midyear Estimates									
Population	99z	.59	.60	.61	.63	.65	.67	.69	.71	.73	.75	.76	.78

Dominica 321

		1993	1994	1995	1996	1997	1998	1999	2000	2001	2002	2003	2004
Exchange Rates		*E.Caribbean Dollars per SDR: End of Period (aa) E.Caribbean Dollars per US Dollar: End of Period (ae)*											
Official Rate....................	aa	3.7086	3.9416	4.0135	3.8825	3.6430	3.8017	3.7058	3.5179	3.3932	3.6707	4.0121	4.1931
Official Rate....................	ae	2.7000	2.7000	2.7000	2.7000	2.7000	2.7000	2.7000	2.7000	2.7000	2.7000	2.7000	2.7000
		Index Numbers (2000=100): Period Averages											
Nominal Effective Exchange Rate.....	nec	83.09	87.09	84.46	86.93	91.96	97.54	96.64	100.00	104.62	103.36	96.72	92.08
Real Effective Exchange Rate...........	rec	96.98	93.53	88.06	89.26	94.09	98.67	97.76	100.00	103.29	100.66	93.97	89.31
Fund Position		*Millions of SDRs: End of Period*											
Quota.............................	2f.s	6.00	6.00	6.00	6.00	6.00	6.00	8.20	8.20	8.20	8.20	8.20	8.20
SDRs..............................	1b.s	—	—	—	—	—	—	.01	—	—	—	—	.03
Reserve Position in the Fund............	1c.s	.01	.01	.01	.01	.01	.01	.01	.01	.01	.01	.01	.01
Total Fund Cred.&Loans Outstg........	2tl	2.26	1.71	1.15	.59	.19	.03	—	—	—	2.05	5.33	5.95
International Liquidity		*Millions of US Dollars Unless Otherwise Indicated: End of Period*											
Total Reserves minus Gold...............	1l.d	19.92	15.41	22.12	22.89	23.89	27.67	31.57	29.37	31.22	45.50	47.74	42.32
SDRs.....................	1b.d	—	—	—	—	—	—	.01	—	—	—	—	.05
Reserve Position in the Fund..........	1c.d	.01	.01	.01	.01	.01	.01	.01	.01	.01	.01	.01	.01
Foreign Exchange...................	1d.d	19.90	15.40	22.11	22.88	23.88	27.65	31.55	29.36	31.21	45.48	47.72	42.25
Monetary Authorities: Other Liab.....	4..d	—	—	—	—	—	—	—	—	—	—	—	—
Deposit Money Banks: Assets..........	7a.d	24.13	26.62	28.14	38.81	43.08	51.84	60.28	44.68	51.24	77.01	101.93	149.15
Liabilities...................	7b.d	30.77	39.49	34.45	35.63	43.28	46.01	45.66	49.75	46.32	48.05	38.83	59.18
Monetary Authorities		*Millions of E. Caribbean Dollars: End of Period*											
Foreign Assets.....................	11	53.71	41.74	60.65	62.71	64.67	74.87	85.34	79.41	84.38	122.96	129.09	114.98
Claims on Central Government.........	12a	24.04	26.16	19.74	14.78	13.31	11.30	11.07	11.41	10.71	17.09	30.51	31.94
Claims on Deposit Money Banks......	12e	.37	2.04	.01	.01	.03	.03	.01	3.92	.01	.02	.01	—
Reserve Money.....................	14	69.74	63.21	74.20	73.69	75.76	84.55	95.02	92.46	91.69	130.64	126.16	117.77
of which: Currency Outside DMBs..	14a	27.85	24.49	29.16	28.53	28.21	29.13	34.09	35.45	34.61	35.51	34.18	37.60
Foreign Liabilities..................	16c	8.38	6.72	4.60	2.28	.68	.10	—	—	—	7.52	21.39	24.93
Central Government Deposits...........	16d	—		.79	.72	.75	.74	.57	1.46	2.56	1.08	11.24	3.39
Other Items (Net)...........................	17r	—	—	.82	.82	.82	.82	.82	.82	.86	.83	.83	.83
Deposit Money Banks		*Millions of E. Caribbean Dollars: End of Period*											
Reserves..........................	20	42.78	33.46	45.86	46.52	44.93	56.16	68.92	56.53	58.48	98.16	85.59	73.79
Foreign Assets.....................	21	65.16	71.88	75.98	104.78	116.31	139.96	162.76	120.63	138.34	207.93	275.20	402.72
Claims on Central Government.........	22a	53.46	66.56	77.86	79.34	87.40	87.73	94.14	102.78	110.22	103.78	91.55	57.68
Claims on Local Government............	22b	.05	.23	.17	.17	.12	.09	.06	.05	.02	.01	.02	.05
Claims on Nonfin.Pub.Enterprises....	22c	26.40	29.07	29.13	19.27	21.77	23.05	24.25	27.82	24.29	23.37	22.21	21.63
Claims on Private Sector...............	22d	289.57	312.48	344.63	358.48	386.35	409.97	419.77	454.09	439.58	433.34	420.62	450.66
Claims on Nonbank Financial Insts....	22g	1.29	.42	.46	1.57	1.48	1.52	1.22	3.11	2.86	2.05	2.39	2.43
Demand Deposits......................	24	51.27	50.66	60.67	63.94	66.18	70.60	94.56	67.69	70.63	96.06	97.23	108.34
Time, Savings,& Fgn.Currency Dep...	25	244.57	260.18	319.08	342.74	358.88	379.83	398.90	413.50	444.86	474.59	513.27	535.11
Foreign Liabilities..................	26c	83.08	106.61	93.02	96.20	116.85	124.23	123.29	134.32	125.06	129.72	104.85	159.79
Central Government Deposits...........	26d	43.14	57.29	56.21	48.45	61.70	70.32	65.29	57.56	38.84	69.12	82.54	81.28
Credit from Monetary Authorities.....	26g	9.68	2.00	—	—	—	2.80	.85	5.30	—	—	—	—
Capital Accounts.....................	27a	40.92	45.93	49.60	51.31	50.39	51.60	62.70	67.02	78.37	76.55	80.81	90.45
Other Items (Net).....................	27r	6.06	−8.56	−4.49	7.50	4.36	19.10	25.53	19.61	16.02	22.60	18.89	33.97
Monetary Survey		*Millions of E. Caribbean Dollars: End of Period*											
Foreign Assets (Net).....................	31n	27.42	.29	39.01	69.01	63.45	90.50	124.81	65.72	97.67	193.64	278.06	332.98
Domestic Credit.......................	32	351.67	377.63	415.00	424.45	447.99	462.60	484.64	540.23	546.28	509.44	473.52	479.70
Claims on Central Govt. (Net)........	32an	34.36	35.44	40.60	44.95	38.27	27.97	39.34	55.17	79.53	50.67	28.28	4.94
Claims on Local Government...........	32b	.05	.23	.17	.17	.12	.09	.06	.05	.02	.01	.02	.05
Claims on Nonfin.Pub.Enterprises...	32c	26.40	29.07	29.13	19.27	21.77	23.05	24.25	27.82	24.29	23.37	22.21	21.63
Claims on Private Sector...............	32d	289.57	312.48	344.63	358.48	386.35	409.97	419.77	454.09	439.58	433.34	420.62	450.66
Claims on Nonbank Financial Inst..	32g	1.29	.42	.46	1.57	1.48	1.52	1.22	3.11	2.86	2.05	2.39	2.43
Money.................................	34	79.19	75.23	89.97	92.73	94.45	99.89	128.92	103.23	105.32	131.64	131.54	146.08
Quasi-Money..........................	35	244.57	260.18	319.90	343.56	359.70	380.64	399.72	414.32	445.72	475.42	514.10	535.94
Capital Accounts......................	37a	43.10	48.26	51.97	53.61	52.55	53.86	64.89	69.11	80.38	78.72	83.19	92.94
Other Items (Net)......................	37r	12.22	−5.75	−7.83	3.57	4.74	18.71	15.92	19.30	12.52	17.31	22.75	37.72
Money plus Quasi-Money..............	35l	323.76	335.41	409.87	436.29	454.14	480.54	528.64	517.54	551.04	607.06	645.64	682.02
Money (National Definitions)		*Millions of E. Caribbean Dollars: End of Period*											
M1...............................	59ma	64.58	62.29	72.88	71.43	74.70	85.45	106.82	90.33	91.58	106.65	107.88	111.20
M2...............................	59mb	281.94	293.30	361.01	368.10	380.95	424.32	468.30	471.05	505.99	549.25	554.47	587.37
Interest Rates		*Percent Per Annum*											
Discount Rate (End of Period)...........	60	....	9.00	9.00	9.00	8.00	8.00	8.00	8.00	7.00	7.00	6.50	6.50
Money Market Rate......................	60b	5.25	5.25	5.25	5.25	5.25	5.25	5.25	5.25	† 5.64	6.32	6.07	4.67
Treasury Bill Rate......................	60c	6.40	6.40	6.40	6.40	6.40	6.40	6.40	6.40	6.40	6.40	6.40	6.40
Savings Rate...........................	60k	5.00	5.46	5.50	5.50	5.50	5.50	5.50	5.50	5.50	5.00	† 3.38	3.41
Deposit Rate...........................	60l	4.19	4.50	4.20	4.30	4.27	4.23	4.38	3.87	3.98	3.91	3.66	3.26
Lending Rate..........................	60p	11.92	11.61	11.50	11.43	11.17	11.27	11.40	11.68	11.14	10.97	11.50	8.94
Prices		*Index Numbers (2000=100): Period Averages*											
Consumer Prices........................	64	91.9	91.9	93.1	94.7	97.0	† 98.0	99.2	100.0	101.5	101.8	103.3	105.4
Intl. Transactions & Positions		*Millions of E. Caribbean Dollars*											
Exports.................................	70	131.67	127.30	121.81	138.46	143.01	167.45	150.45	144.67	118.03	115.20	105.37	108.61
Imports, c.i.f.............................	71	252.99	260.10	316.66	350.85	336.31	356.99	373.23	400.24	355.02	314.05	339.04	389.92

		1993	1994	1995	1996	1997	1998	1999	2000	2001	2002	2003	2004
Balance of Payments						*Millions of US Dollars: Minus Sign Indicates Debit*							
Current Account, n.i.e.	78ald	−27.48	−37.55	−40.73	−51.16	−42.25	−23.06	−35.77	−52.91	−49.09	−38.09	....	....
Goods: Exports f.o.b.	78aad	49.29	48.33	50.27	52.91	53.77	63.19	56.01	54.75	44.41	42.93	....	....
Goods: Imports f.o.b.	78abd	−91.96	−95.76	−103.21	−117.20	−118.71	−116.35	−121.57	−130.39	−115.71	−102.35	....	....
Trade Balance	78acd	−42.68	−47.43	−52.94	−64.29	−64.94	−53.16	−65.56	−75.64	−71.30	−59.42	....	....
Services: Credit	78add	48.54	51.59	61.36	68.94	83.39	88.41	100.79	89.74	75.41	79.70	....	....
Services: Debit	78aed	−35.66	−37.76	−43.72	−47.17	−54.14	−55.83	−59.03	−52.69	−50.04	−53.72	....	....
Balance on Goods & Services	78afd	−29.80	−33.60	−35.30	−42.53	−35.70	−20.58	−23.79	−38.59	−45.93	−33.44	....	....
Income: Credit	78agd	2.97	3.08	3.29	2.85	3.60	4.65	4.63	4.67	3.59	2.74	....	....
Income: Debit	78ahd	−9.34	−14.10	−16.59	−21.66	−20.51	−19.87	−30.17	−37.07	−24.23	−21.21	....	....
Balance on Gds, Serv. & Inc.	78aid	−36.18	−44.62	−48.59	−61.33	−52.61	−35.80	−49.33	−70.98	−66.56	−51.91	....	....
Current Transfers, n.i.e.: Credit	78ajd	12.42	14.86	16.26	17.83	17.44	19.92	20.46	25.09	24.77	20.56	....	....
Current Transfers: Debit	78akd	−3.72	−7.79	−8.39	−7.66	−7.09	−7.18	−6.90	−7.02	−7.30	−6.74	....	....
Capital Account, n.i.e.	78bcd	9.72	6.90	24.54	25.30	22.52	14.75	11.76	10.89	17.97	20.49	....	....
Capital Account, n.i.e.: Credit	78bad	11.20	9.37	24.65	25.42	22.64	14.87	12.06	12.41	18.10	20.62	....	....
Capital Account: Debit	78bbd	−1.48	−2.47	−.11	−.12	−.12	−.13	−.30	−1.52	−.13	−.13	....	....
Financial Account, n.i.e.	78bjd	19.65	30.00	42.15	6.10	25.83	−2.23	38.37	43.38	24.95	8.94	....	....
Direct Investment Abroad	78bdd	—	—	—	—	—	—	—	—	—	—	....	....
Dir. Invest. in Rep. Econ., n.i.e.	78bed	13.20	22.60	54.09	17.80	21.11	6.51	17.96	10.82	11.90	11.44	....	....
Portfolio Investment Assets	78bfd	—	.01	−7.96	—	—	—	−9.81	−.40	.01	.01	....	....
Equity Securities	78bkd	....	....	....	....	....	....	....	....	....	....	....	....
Debt Securities	78bld	....	....	....	....	....	....	....	....	....	....	....	....
Portfolio Investment Liab., n.i.e.	78bgd	—	—	—	.46	−.18	.53	39.47	11.21	−.24	12.10	....	....
Equity Securities	78bmd	....	....	....	....	....	....	....	....	....	....	....	....
Debt Securities	78bnd	....	....	....	....	....	....	....	....	....	....	....	....
Financial Derivatives Assets	78bwd	....	....	....	....	....	....	....	....	....	....	....	....
Financial Derivatives Liabilities	78bxd	....	....	....	....	....	....	....	....	....	....	....	....
Other Investment Assets	78bhd	2.10	−4.31	−3.60	−5.79	−3.01	−5.37	−3.92	−10.42	−5.03	−2.81	....	....
Monetary Authorities	78bod	....	....	....	....	....	....	....	....	....	....	....	....
General Government	78bpd	....	....	....	....	....	....	....	....	....	....	....	....
Banks	78bqd	....	....	....	....	....	....	....	....	....	....	....	....
Other Sectors	78brd	....	....	....	....	....	....	....	....	....	....	....	....
Other Investment Liab., n.i.e.	78bid	4.34	11.71	−.38	−6.37	7.90	−3.90	−5.33	32.17	18.32	−11.81	....	....
Monetary Authorities	78bsd	—	—	—	—	—	—	—	—	—	—	....	....
General Government	78btd	....	....	....	....	....	....	....	....	....	....	....	....
Banks	78bud	....	....	....	....	....	....	....	....	....	....	....	....
Other Sectors	78bvd	....	....	....	....	....	−3.90	−5.33	32.17	18.32	−11.81	....	....
Net Errors and Omissions	78cad	−.97	−2.71	−17.62	21.99	−5.46	14.09	−3.33	−.88	9.63	16.97	....	....
Overall Balance	78cbd	.92	−3.35	8.34	2.24	.64	3.54	11.02	.47	3.46	8.32	....	....
Reserves and Related Items	79dad	−.92	3.35	−8.34	−2.24	−.64	−3.54	−11.03	−.48	−3.46	−8.32	....	....
Reserve Assets	79dbd	−.19	4.15	−7.48	−1.43	−.09	−3.32	−10.99	−.48	−3.46	−11.03	....	....
Use of Fund Credit and Loans	79dcd	−.73	−.80	−.86	−.81	−.55	−.22	−.04	—	—	2.71	....	....
Exceptional Financing	79ded	....	....	....	....	....	....	....	....	....	....	....	....
National Accounts						*Millions of E. Caribbean Dollars*							
Househ.Cons.Expend.,incl.NPISHs.	96f	358.5	404.9	381.4	440.2	407.5	412.2	427.6	470.3	517.5	490.4	480.5	....
Government Consumption Expend.	91f	112.2	117.4	123.2	128.9	143.1	153.0	159.3	160.6	152.8	147.3	135.1	....
Gross Fixed Capital Formation	93e	137.8	148.4	186.4	183.6	207.4	190.9	200.3	205.4	171.8	142.4	177.3	....
Exports of Goods and Services	90c	262.8	272.2	301.4	329.0	370.3	409.3	423.4	390.1	324.0	331.1	340.3	....
Imports of Goods and Services (-)	98c	330.2	365.1	396.7	443.8	466.7	464.9	487.6	494.3	447.5	421.4	425.8	....
Gross Domestic Product (GDP)	99b	541.1	577.8	595.6	637.9	661.6	700.5	722.8	732.2	718.6	689.9	707.5	....
Net Primary Income from Abroad	98.n	−17.2	−29.8	−35.9	−50.8	−45.7	−41.1	−69.1	−87.5	−55.7	−49.9	−54.8	....
Gross National Income (GNI)	99a	523.9	548.0	559.7	587.1	616.0	659.4	653.9	644.7	662.9	640.0	652.6	....
Net Current Transf.from Abroad	98t	23.5	19.1	21.2	27.5	28.0	34.4	36.6	48.8	47.2	37.3	46.6	....
Gross Nat'l Disposable Inc.(GNDI)	99i	547.4	567.1	581.0	614.5	643.9	693.8	690.5	693.5	710.1	677.3	699.2	....
Gross Saving	99s	76.7	44.8	76.4	45.5	93.3	128.6	103.7	62.6	39.8	39.6	83.6	....
GDP Volume 1990 Prices	99b.p	468.8	475.5	484.9	501.9	514.5	530.7	534.1	537.5	517.4	496.4	506.1	....
GDP Volume (2000=100)	99bvp	87.2	88.5	90.2	93.4	95.7	98.7	99.4	100.0	96.2	92.3	94.2	....
GDP Deflator (2000=100)	99bip	84.7	89.2	90.2	93.3	94.4	96.9	99.4	100.0	102.0	102.0	102.6	....
						Millions: Midyear Estimates							
Population	99z	.07	.07	.08	.08	.08	† .08	.08	.08	.08	.08	.08	.08

Dominican Republic 243

		1993	1994	1995	1996	1997	1998	1999	2000	2001	2002	2003	2004
Exchange Rates						*Pesos per SDR: End of Period*							
Market Rate.............aa=.........	wa	17.536	19.071	20.015	20.220	19.383	22.230	22.014	21.725	21.551	28.813	55.352	48.313
						Pesos per US Dollar: End of Period (we) Period Average (wf)							
Market Rate.............ae=.........	we	12.767	13.064	13.465	14.062	14.366	15.788	16.039	16.674	17.149	21.194	37.250	31.109
Market Rate.............rf=..........	wf	12.676	13.160	13.597	13.775	14.265	15.267	16.033	16.415	16.952	18.610	30.831	42.120
						Index Numbers (2000=100): Period Averages							
Market Rate..................	ahx	129.5	124.7	120.7	119.2	115.0	107.3	102.4	100.0	96.8	88.6	55.2	40.3
Nominal Effective Exchange Rate.....	nec	106.4	114.2	109.4	109.7	108.9	105.3	99.7	100.0	100.1	92.2	56.0	39.0
Real Effective Exchange Rate...........	rec	84.0	87.8	90.4	92.3	96.7	96.1	95.2	100.0	106.3	101.1	74.8	79.3
Fund Position						*Millions of SDRs: End of Period*							
Quota........................	2f.s	158.8	158.8	158.8	158.8	158.8	158.8	218.9	218.9	218.9	218.9	218.9	218.9
SDRs........................	1b.s	10.3	2.5	.3	.3	.2	.2	.2	.3	.3	.2	.1	1.0
Reserve Position in the Fund..........	1c.s	—	—	—	—	—	—	—	—	—	—	—	—
Total Fund Cred.&Loans Outstg.......	2tl	135.5	129.9	107.5	66.5	21.1	39.7	39.7	39.7	39.7	19.9	87.6	131.3
International Liquidity						*Millions of US Dollars Unless Otherwise Indicated: End of Period*							
Total Reserves minus Gold..............	1l.d	651.2	252.1	365.6	350.3	391.0	501.9	694.0	627.2	1,099.5	468.4	253.1	798.3
SDRs........................	1b.d	14.1	3.7	.5	.4	.3	.3	.3	.4	.4	.3	.1	1.6
Reserve Position in the Fund..........	1c.d	—	—	—	—	—	—	—	—	—	—	—	—
Foreign Exchange..................	1d.d	637.1	248.4	365.0	349.8	390.7	501.6	693.7	626.8	1,099.0	468.1	253.0	796.7
Gold (Million Fine Troy Ounces).......	1ad	.018	.018	.018	.018	.018	.018	.018	.018	.018	.018	.018	.018
Gold (National Valuation)...............	1and	6.9	6.8	6.8	6.7	5.5	5.3	5.2	5.0	5.1	5.2	7.6	8.0
Monetary Authorities: Other Liab.....	4..d	1,259.3	916.0	967.7	975.1	938.2	881.2	865.5	879.3	838.7	668.0	643.6	645.0
Deposit Money Banks: Assets...........	7a.d	191.8	189.4	183.8	174.5	236.7	307.0	322.5	416.4	527.0	515.5	648.8	993.7
Liabilities.....	7b.d	184.0	183.3	55.0	97.6	188.6	401.4	458.9	739.3	684.5	924.5	517.1	260.1
Other Banking Insts.: Liabilities........	7f.d	62.7	91.2	8.4	10.9	6.3	17.2	22.7	24.3	27.2	36.5	26.9	33.7
Monetary Authorities						*Millions of Pesos: End of Period*							
Foreign Assets....................	11	9,008	4,804	6,577	6,962	7,696	10,071	13,599	13,128	22,364	13,208	15,926	30,584
Claims on Central Government........	12a	938	558	605	1,236	1,537	1,632	2,416	4,026	4,023	4,631	75	39,610
Claims on Nonfin.Pub.Enterprises.....	12c	738	2,959	1,609	1,632	1,665	1,987	2,520	2,631	2,676	2,638	3,105	4,916
Claims on Private Sector...............	12d	550	45	45	45	45	5	5	2	1	—	—	—
Claims on Deposit Money Banks......	12e	1,343	2,075	2,092	3,108	2,161	2,917	2,992	2,874	3,510	9,896	105,493	106,104
Claims on Other Banking Insts........	12f	923	292	307	320	388	384	375	345	347	231	36	30
Reserve Money....................	14	14,889	14,956	17,412	19,306	22,963	28,110	32,328	35,667	45,980	41,961	87,367	92,332
of which: Currency Outside DMBs..	14a	6,905	7,679	8,892	9,635	11,534	12,568	16,889	15,076	16,628	18,265	29,631	32,548
Liabs.of Centl.Bank: Securities.........	16ac	196	743	1,991	4,099	4,357	3,499	5,135	4,369	3,276	6,905	60,008	110,809
Foreign Liabilities..................	16c	18,453	14,443	15,180	15,056	13,887	14,794	14,755	15,523	15,238	14,729	28,820	26,411
Central Government Deposits...........	16d	2,179	151	344	400	351	424	479	414	1,838	834	4,113	1,060
Counterpart Funds.....................	16e	—	—	—	—	—	—	—	—	—	—	—	—
Capital Accounts.....................	17a	−18,805	−16,906	−18,443	−20,241	−21,519	−23,395	−25,126	−26,960	−27,817	−28,456	−56,803	−52,482
of which: Revaluation of Reserves..	17rv	−17,883	−16,415	−16,961	−17,326	−17,376	−17,872	−18,169	−18,315	−18,315	−18,632	—	—
Other Items (Net).....................	17r	−3,412	−2,653	−5,249	−5,318	−6,547	−6,435	−5,665	−6,008	−5,594	−5,369	1,130	3,114
Deposit Money Banks						*Millions of Pesos: End of Period*							
Reserves........................	20	8,992	9,214	10,654	10,761	12,964	16,947	17,331	26,692	30,404	28,653	58,047	56,548
Claims on Mon.Author.:Securities.....	20c	15	180	914	2,264	2,118	675	1,443	215	26	2,121	19,758	30,187
Foreign Assets....................	21	2,449	2,474	2,475	2,453	3,400	4,846	5,172	6,943	9,037	10,925	24,167	30,914
Claims on Central Government........	22a	371	540	505	536	1,934	1,998	4,144	4,813	11,678	14,091	17,386	25,737
Claims on Local Government.........	22b	5	6	29	4	6	4	4	14	29	32	1	142	412
Claims on Nonfin.Pub.Enterprises.....	22c	1,417	1,290	1,453	2,221	2,308	3,263	3,271	2,521	2,540	2,943	4,539	3,487
Claims on Private Sector..................	22d	19,442	22,166	27,688	34,500	44,404	52,744	66,877	82,120	101,941	123,242	165,620	162,822
Claims on Other Banking Insts.........	22f	805	799	554	778	764	957	760	593	928	1,081	2,290	1,521
Demand Deposits....................	24	8,104	8,470	10,064	13,540	16,081	16,782	18,884	20,290	24,529	25,341	41,736	43,241
Time, Savings,& Fgn.Currency Dep...	25	17,092	19,854	23,458	27,022	34,725	43,380	54,211	70,282	92,908	104,184	169,315	186,887
Bonds..........................	26ab	133	122	80	138	76	17	398	112	2	14	27	7
Foreign Liabilities..................	26c	2,349	2,394	740	1,372	2,710	6,337	7,361	12,328	11,738	19,594	19,261	8,092
Central Government Deposits..........	26d	2,568	1,746	2,533	2,594	3,076	2,500	3,578	3,192	6,566	6,076	7,268	8,142
Credit from Monetary Authorities.....	26g	902	1,334	1,310	1,220	1,532	2,222	2,449	2,931	3,226	7,971	72,091	72,122
Capital Accounts....................	27a	3,388	4,050	4,581	5,203	6,524	8,220	10,224	12,667	16,707	19,901	−9,773	−7,730
Other Items (Net).....................	27r	−1,042	−1,301	1,506	2,428	3,175	1,975	1,907	2,124	911	−26	−7,975	867
Monetary Survey						*Millions of Pesos: End of Period*							
Foreign Assets (Net)......................	31n	−9,345	−9,559	−6,868	−7,013	−5,501	−6,213	−3,345	−7,780	4,424	−10,191	−7,988	26,995
Domestic Credit.....................	32	20,442	26,759	29,919	38,278	49,624	60,051	76,324	93,474	115,762	141,948	181,813	229,333
Claims on Central Govt. (Net)........	32an	−3,438	−798	−1,766	−1,221	43	706	2,503	5,233	7,296	11,812	6,080	56,146
Claims on Local Government.........	32b	5	6	29	4	6	4	14	29	32	1	142	412
Claims on Nonfin.Pub.Enterprises...	32c	2,155	4,249	3,062	3,853	3,973	5,250	5,791	5,152	5,216	5,582	7,644	8,403
Claims on Private Sector...............	32d	19,992	22,211	27,733	34,545	44,449	52,749	66,881	82,122	101,942	123,242	165,620	162,822
Claims on Other Banking Insts.......	32f	1,728	1,091	861	1,098	1,152	1,342	1,135	938	1,275	1,313	2,326	1,551
Money..........................	34	15,065	16,198	18,996	23,225	27,703	29,416	35,840	35,445	41,258	43,765	72,013	76,153
Quasi-Money.......................	35	17,092	19,854	23,458	27,022	34,725	43,380	54,211	70,282	92,908	104,184	169,315	186,887
Bonds..........................	36ab	133	122	80	138	76	17	398	112	2	14	27	7
Liabs.of Centl.Bank: Securities..........	36ac	182	564	1,078	1,835	2,239	2,825	3,692	4,154	3,250	4,784	40,250	80,621
Capital Accounts...........................	37a	−15,416	−12,857	−13,863	−15,038	−14,996	−15,175	−14,902	−14,293	−11,111	−8,555	−66,576	−60,212
Other Items (Net)........................	37r	−5,959	−6,682	−6,698	−5,917	−5,625	−6,625	−6,259	−10,008	−6,121	−12,434	−41,205	−27,128
Money plus Quasi-Money................	35l	32,157	36,052	42,454	50,247	62,428	72,795	90,051	105,727	134,166	147,948	241,328	263,040

		1993	1994	1995	1996	1997	1998	1999	2000	2001	2002	2003	2004
Other Banking Institutions		*Millions of Pesos: End of Period*											
Reserves..........................	40	316	329	332	353	429	483	796	951	1,037	1,315	3,072	5,594
Claims on Mon.Author.:Securities....	40c	—	—	—	—	1,080	1,153	1,483	1,596	1,772	3,781	4,532	5,207
Claims on Central Government........	42a	474	522	774	569	452	837	971	971	699	872	893	742
Claims on Nonfin.Pub.Enterprises.....	42c	10	12	19	18	18	19	19	19	28	31	30	30
Claims on Private Sector.................	42d	10,365	12,263	12,513	13,797	16,324	19,797	24,375	30,407	34,552	36,922	43,819	56,390
Claims on Deposit Money Banks......	42e	3,388	2,358	3,097	3,674	3,223	4,216	4,950	6,149	10,353	6,776	8,843	6,663
Time, Savings,& Fgn.Currency Dep...	45	3,881	4,112	4,396	4,628	5,682	7,387	7,691	8,433	9,545	10,531	11,240	13,063
Bonds............................	46ab	6,589	7,290	8,474	9,418	11,295	13,120	17,634	22,433	27,956	27,359	32,854	41,462
Foreign Liabilities..............................	46c	800	1,192	113	153	90	271	364	405	467	774	1,003	1,049
Credit from Monetary Authorities.....	46g	1,641	1,623	1,464	1,434	1,360	1,298	1,112	1,118	1,092	931	921	834
Credit from Deposit Money Banks....	46h	429	424	460	478	457	539	458	513	495	569	584	553
Capital Accounts.......................	47a	2,543	2,667	2,818	2,855	3,390	4,430	5,889	7,572	9,200	12,083	17,161	21,175
Other Items (Net)...........................	47r	−1,330	−1,824	−990	−558	−748	−542	−554	−380	−315	−2,550	−2,573	−3,509
Banking Survey		*Millions of Pesos: End of Period*											
Foreign Assets (Net)......................	51n	−10,145	−10,751	−6,981	−7,166	−5,592	−6,484	−3,709	−8,185	3,957	−10,965	−8,991	25,946
Domestic Credit........................	52	29,563	38,464	42,364	51,564	65,266	79,362	100,554	123,933	149,764	178,461	224,229	284,945
Claims on Central Govt. (Net)........	52an	−2,964	−276	−992	−652	496	1,543	3,474	6,205	7,995	12,684	6,973	56,888
Claims on Local Government..........	52b	5	6	29	4	6	4	14	29	32	1	142	412
Claims on Nonfin.Pub.Enterprises...	52c	2,165	4,261	3,081	3,871	3,991	5,269	5,810	5,171	5,243	5,612	7,674	8,433
Claims on Private Sector................	52d	30,356	34,474	40,246	48,342	60,772	72,545	91,256	112,529	136,494	160,164	209,439	219,212
Liquid Liabilities.............................	55l	35,722	39,835	46,518	54,522	67,681	79,699	96,946	113,209	142,674	157,164	249,496	270,509
Bonds...............................	56ab	6,722	7,412	8,554	9,556	11,371	13,137	18,032	22,545	27,958	27,373	32,881	41,468
Liabs.of Centl.Bank: Securities.........	56ac	182	564	1,078	1,835	1,158	1,672	2,208	2,558	1,478	1,003	35,718	75,414
Capital Accounts...........................	57a	−12,873	−10,190	−11,045	−12,182	−11,606	−10,745	−9,013	−6,720	−1,911	3,528	−49,415	−39,037
Other Items (Net)...........................	57r	−10,335	−9,907	−9,721	−9,333	−8,931	−10,886	−11,327	−15,843	−16,478	−21,573	−53,442	−37,463
Interest Rates		*Percent Per Annum*											
Money Market Rate......................	60b	....	....	....	14.70	13.01	16.68	15.30	18.28	13.47	14.50	24.24	36.76
Savings Rate................................	60k	5.00	4.87	4.66	5.00	4.74	4.51	4.54	4.29	4.29	4.30	4.26	4.36
Savings Rate (Foreign Currency).......	60k.f	....	....	....	4.67	4.29	3.62	3.58	4.16	4.00	3.81	3.83	2.88
Deposit Rate................................	60l	14.04	13.70	14.94	13.91	13.40	17.65	16.07	17.65	15.61	16.54	20.50	21.12
Deposit Rate (Foreign Currency).......	60l.f				6.69	6.98	6.50	6.66	7.57	6.88	6.37	6.55	5.31
Lending Rate................................	60p	29.89	28.68	30.68	23.73	21.01	25.64	25.05	26.80	24.26	26.06	31.39	32.63
Lending Rate (Foreign Currency).......	60p.f	....	....	....	13.87	12.75	11.95	11.73	11.56	11.17	10.27	10.58	10.79
Prices and Labor		*Index Numbers (2000=100): Period Averages*											
Consumer Prices...........................	64	59.8	64.7	72.9	76.8	83.2	† 87.2	92.8	100.0	108.9	114.6	146.0	221.2
		Number in Thousands: Period Averages											
Labor Force.................................	67d	....	....	3,008	2,920	3,594	....	....	....	....	....	....	....
Employment.................................	67e	2,417	2,401	2,401	2,523	2,652	....	....	....	....	....	....	....
Unemployment.............................	67c	599	457	452	† 506	504	....	....	....	....	....	....	....
Unemployment Rate (%).................	67r	19.9	16.0	15.9	† 16.7	15.9	....	....	....	....	....	....	....
Intl. Transactions & Positions		*Millions of US Dollars*											
Exports.......................................	70..d	511.0	644.0	872.1	945.5	1,017.4	880.2	805.2	966.2	804.8	833.7	1,040.7	....
Imports, f.o.b................................	71.vd	2,118.4	2,991.7	3,164.2	3,580.7	4,192.0	4,896.6	5,206.8	6,416.1	5,936.9	6,037.3	5,265.8	....
		1995=100											
Volume of Exports.........................	72	99	96	100	106	109	103	....	....	....	....	....	....
		1995=100: Indices of Unit Values in US Dollars											
Unit Value of Exports/Export Prices...	74..d	72	89	102	95	106	85	....	....	....	....	....	....

Dominican Republic   243

		1993	1994	1995	1996	1997	1998	1999	2000	2001	2002	2003	2004
Balance of Payments		*Millions of US Dollars: Minus Sign Indicates Debit*											
Current Account, n.i.e......................	78ald	−532.9	−283.0	−182.8	−212.7	−163.0	−338.4	−429.2	−1,026.5	−740.8	−797.9	867.1	....
Goods: Exports f.o.b....................	78aad	3,211.0	3,452.5	3,779.5	4,052.8	4,613.7	4,980.5	5,136.7	5,736.7	5,276.3	5,165.0	5,439.4	....
Goods: Imports f.o.b.....................	78abd	−4,654.2	−4,903.2	−5,170.4	−5,727.0	−6,608.7	−7,597.3	−8,041.1	−9,478.5	−8,779.3	−8,837.7	−7,883.4	....
Trade Balance...........................	78acd	−1,443.2	−1,450.7	−1,390.9	−1,674.2	−1,995.0	−2,616.8	−2,904.4	−3,741.8	−3,503.0	−3,672.7	−2,444.0	....
Services: Credit...........................	78add	1,537.1	1,787.9	1,951.3	2,140.0	2,446.6	2,501.5	2,850.3	3,227.6	3,110.3	3,070.8	3,435.3	....
Services: Debit............................	78aed	−823.8	−921.1	−966.4	−1,121.4	−1,171.3	−1,319.5	−1,248.0	−1,373.3	−1,283.9	−1,313.5	−1,216.1	....
Balance on Goods & Services.......	78afd	−729.9	−583.9	−406.0	−655.6	−719.7	−1,434.8	−1,302.1	−1,887.5	−1,676.6	−1,915.4	−224.8	....
Income: Credit.............................	78agd	103.6	101.4	128.1	130.3	140.4	168.2	218.3	299.7	271.2	300.4	343.7	....
Income: Debit..............................	78ahd	−800.6	−783.3	−897.1	−855.1	−935.8	−1,058.3	−1,193.2	−1,341.0	−1,362.9	−1,452.2	−1,587.3	....
Balance on Gds, Serv. & Inc..........	78aid	−1,426.9	−1,265.8	−1,175.0	−1,380.4	−1,515.1	−2,324.9	−2,277.0	−2,928.8	−2,768.3	−3,067.2	−1,468.4	....
Current Transfers, n.i.e.: Credit......	78ajd	908.4	996.8	1,007.7	1,187.6	1,373.1	2,016.9	1,997.1	2,095.6	2,232.0	2,451.9	2,510.3	....
Current Transfers: Debit................	78akd	−14.4	−14.0	−15.5	−19.9	−21.0	−30.4	−149.3	−193.3	−204.5	−182.6	−174.8	....
Capital Account, n.i.e...................	78bcd	—	—	—	....	—	—	—	—	—	—	—	....
Capital Account, n.i.e.: Credit........	78bad	—	—	—	—	—	—	—	—	—	—	—	....
Capital Account: Debit..................	78bbd	—	—	—	....	....	—	—	—	—	—	—	....
Financial Account, n.i.e.................	78bjd	−226.6	368.0	253.6	64.1	447.6	688.1	1,061.0	1,596.6	1,707.4	383.0	−853.4	....
Direct Investment Abroad.............	78bdd	—	—	—	—	....	....	....	....	....	....	....	....
Dir. Invest. in Rep. Econ., n.i.e.......	78bed	189.3	206.8	414.3	96.5	420.6	699.8	1,337.8	952.9	1,079.1	916.8	309.9	....
Portfolio Investment Assets...........	78bfd	—	−38.9	−2.9	−7.3	−5.6	−17.5	−433.0	268.4	123.5	−14.0	−20.1	....
Equity Securities......................	78bkd	....	....	....	−4.0	−2.1	−13.7	−428.9	270.6	128.2	−2.5	−7.1	....
Debt Securities........................	78bld	....	−38.9	−2.9	−3.3	−3.5	−3.8	−4.1	−2.2	−4.7	−11.5	−13.0	....
Portfolio Investment Liab., n.i.e......	78bgd	....	—	....	....	−1.9	−3.8	−3.8	−3.9	480.2	−11.7	552.6	....
Equity Securities......................	78bmd	....	....	....	....	....	....	—	—	—	—	—	....
Debt Securities........................	78bnd	....	—	....	....	−1.9	−3.8	−3.8	−3.9	480.2	−11.7	552.6	....
Financial Derivatives Assets..........	78bwd	....	....	....	....	....	....	....	....	—	—	—	....
Financial Derivatives Liabilities.......	78bxd	....	....	....	....	....	....	....	....	—	—	—	....
Other Investment Assets..............	78bhd	−49.2	176.8	−263.1	42.3	−220.1	−66.4	−53.4	−165.0	−155.5	−1,402.2	−1,535.2	....
Monetary Authorities...............	78bod	....	−15.2	−.6	−.9	−.9	−1.0	−1.0	−1.2	−.8	−3.9	1.9	....
General Government..................	78bpd	....	....	....	....	....	....	....	....	....	....	....	....
Banks...................................	78bqd	−26.7	18.0	−39.0	17.0	−40.7	−53.2	−18.8	−64.4	−94.9	11.0	−121.2	....
Other Sectors.........................	78brd	−22.5	174.0	−223.5	26.2	−178.5	−12.2	−33.6	−99.4	−59.8	−1,409.3	−1,415.9	....
Other Investment Liab., n.i.e..........	78bid	−366.7	23.3	105.3	−67.4	254.6	76.0	213.4	544.2	180.1	894.1	−160.6	....
Monetary Authorities...............	78bsd	−465.2	31.1	27.1	−22.8	−17.3	−88.7	−24.7	72.0	−22.3	91.0	−222.9	....
General Government..................	78btd	−75.9	−59.5	−18.8	−35.3	−64.2	−38.5	124.2	119.1	119.3	252.6	672.4	....
Banks...................................	78bud	−9.5	45.4	32.1	89.7	172.3	218.5	106.9	234.2	−37.0	115.6	−172.2	....
Other Sectors.........................	78bvd	183.9	6.3	64.9	−99.0	163.8	−15.3	7.0	118.9	120.1	434.9	−437.9	....
Net Errors and Omissions..............	78cad	215.1	−596.0	75.3	108.8	−193.7	−338.6	−480.4	−618.5	−451.9	−139.3	−468.1	....
Overall Balance...........................	78cbd	−544.4	−511.0	146.1	−39.8	90.9	11.1	151.4	−48.4	514.7	−554.2	−454.4	....
Reserves and Related Items.............	79dad	544.4	511.0	−146.1	39.8	−90.9	−11.1	−151.4	48.4	−514.7	554.2	454.4	....
Reserve Assets............................	79dbd	−153.5	384.7	−131.2	15.2	−39.5	−98.2	−193.6	69.9	−518.2	526.0	351.7	....
Use of Fund Credit and Loans........	79dcd	63.9	−8.1	−34.0	−59.4	−62.4	26.8	—	—	—	−25.7	94.5	....
Exceptional Financing...................	79ded	634.0	134.4	19.1	84.1	11.0	60.3	42.2	−21.5	3.5	53.9	8.2	....
Government Finance		*Millions of Pesos: Year Ending December 31*											
Deficit (-) or Surplus......................	80	288.1	−690.6	1,720.3	540.6	2,038.0	2,109.8	−1,267.2	3,449.5	....	216.0	....	20,158.4
Total Revenue and Grants...............	81y	20,188.0	21,499.9	24,890.8	27,133.6	34,729.1	38,867.3	43,947.3	51,651.8	....	67,593.2	....	127,588.0
Revenue.......................................	81	19,776.1	21,482.3	24,890.8	26,921.3	34,729.1	38,564.8	43,483.6	51,271.3	....	67,077.5	....	126,281.9
Grants...	81z	411.9	17.6	—	212.3	—	302.5	463.7	380.5	....	515.7	....	1,306.1
Exp. & Lending Minus Repay..........	82z	19,899.9	22,190.5	23,170.5	26,593.0	32,691.1	36,757.5	45,214.5	48,202.3	....	67,377.2	....	107,429.6
Expenditure............................	82	19,899.9	22,190.5	23,170.5	26,593.0	32,691.1	36,757.5	45,164.5	48,202.3	....	67,377.2	....	107,429.6
Lending Minus Repayments.........	83	—	—	—	—	—	—	50.0	—	....	—	....	—
Total Financing............................	80h	−288.1	690.6	−1,720.3	−540.6	−2,038.4	−2,110.0	1,217.1	−3,449.7	....	−216.0	....	−20,158.5
Domestic....................................	84a	1,708.5	2,522.1	1.8	1,289.3	379.2	−8.4	1,862.4	6.4	....	3,569.5	....	−5,869.0
Foreign.......................................	85a	−1,996.6	−1,831.5	−1,722.1	−1,829.9	−2,417.6	−2,101.6	−645.4	−3,456.1	....	−3,785.5	....	−14,289.5
National Accounts		*Millions of Pesos*											
Househ.Cons.Expend.,incl.NPISHs....	96f	96,467	109,023	127,819	147,082	166,081	186,288	207,367	252,670	278,648	309,130	345,823	517,239
Government Consumption Expend...	91f	5,398	6,692	8,331	10,413	16,403	20,674	24,569	27,140	32,847	37,564	43,122	69,013
Gross Fixed Capital Formation..........	93e	28,771	29,020	31,146	34,230	41,987	56,102	66,650	76,236	82,726	90,417	116,056	186,376
Changes in Inventories...................	93i	351	396	468	528	619	697	803	935	1,056	1,160	1,451	2,240
Exports of Goods and Services.........	90c	59,703	67,847	77,150	84,621	100,513	113,793	127,887	145,616	141,165	151,880	266,656	382,885
Imports of Goods and Services (-).....	98c	68,883	75,412	82,632	93,513	110,739	135,577	148,646	178,036	170,209	187,718	269,807	380,566
Gross Domestic Product (GDP)........	99b	121,808	137,566	162,283	183,361	214,864	241,977	278,630	324,562	366,232	402,432	503,300	777,188
Net Primary Income from Abroad.....	98.n	−8,761	−8,851	−10,405	−9,966	−11,342	−13,550	−15,616	−17,144	−18,531	−21,504	−43,096	−56,304
Gross National Income (GNI)............	99a	113,047	128,715	151,878	173,395	203,521	228,427	263,013	307,418	347,702	380,928	460,204	720,883
Consumption of Fixed Capital..........	99cf	7,309	8,254	9,737	11,002	12,892	14,519	16,718	19,474	21,974	24,146	30,198	46,631
GDP Volume 1970 Prices................	99b.p	4,194	4,375	4,579	4,907	5,308	5,702	6,167	6,668	6,910	7,217	7,082	7,220
GDP Volume (2000=100)................	99bvp	62.9	65.6	68.7	73.6	79.6	85.5	92.5	100.0	103.6	108.2	106.2	108.3
GDP Deflator (2000=100)...............	99bip	59.7	64.6	72.8	76.8	83.2	87.2	92.8	100.0	108.9	114.6	146.0	221.2
		Millions: Midyear Estimates											
Population..............................	99z	7.19	7.29	7.39	7.50	7.60	7.71	7.83	7.94	8.05	8.17	8.29	8.41

		1993	1994	1995	1996	1997	1998	1999	2000	2001	2002	2003	2004
Exchange Rates		E. Caribbean Dollars per SDR: End of Period (aa) E. Caribbean Dollars per US Dollar: End of Period (ae)											
Official Rate	aa	3.7086	3.9416	4.0135	3.8825	3.6430	3.8017	3.7058	3.5179	3.3932	3.6707	4.0121	4.1931
Official Rate	ae	2.7000	2.7000	2.7000	2.7000	2.7000	2.7000	2.7000	2.7000	2.7000	2.7000	2.7000	2.7000
Fund Position		*Millions of SDRs: End of Period*											
Quota	2f.s	46.50	46.50	46.50	46.50	46.50	46.50	63.60	65.90	65.90	65.90	65.90	65.90
SDRs	1b.s	3.24	3.36	3.47	3.60	3.67	3.80	3.89	3.91	4.02	4.07	4.11	1.56
Reserve Position in the Fund	1c.s	.53	.53	.53	.53	.53	.53	.58	.59	.59	.59	.60	.60
Total Fund Cred.&Loans Outstg	2tl	2.26	1.71	1.15	.59	.19	1.65	1.63	1.63	1.63	2.86	8.26	11.80
International Liquidity		*Millions of US Dollars: End of Period*											
Total Reserves minus Gold	1l.d	269.13	261.52	312.93	291.36	307.84	360.76	367.63	386.41	448.54	508.25	543.73	634.07
SDRs	1b.d	4.46	4.91	5.16	5.17	4.95	5.36	5.34	5.10	5.05	5.54	6.11	2.42
Reserve Position in the Fund	1c.d	.72	.77	.78	.76	.71	.74	.80	.77	.75	.81	.90	.94
Foreign Exchange	1d.d	263.95	255.84	306.99	285.43	302.19	354.66	361.49	380.55	442.74	501.91	536.72	630.72
Monetary Authorities: Other Liab.	4..d	6.57	9.46	8.71	9.50	5.97	3.67	6.34	8.23	7.55	4.89	4.96	4.52
Deposit Money Banks: Assets	7a.d	246.58	270.67	304.74	312.47	321.14	402.51	495.69	478.78	618.11	746.99	956.87	1,169.35
Liabilities	7b.d	239.82	263.29	263.56	335.81	381.54	388.92	447.97	476.56	525.38	577.00	608.67	732.17
Monetary Authorities		*Millions of E. Caribbean Dollars: End of Period*											
Foreign Assets	11	726.64	706.09	844.91	786.67	831.17	974.05	992.59	1,043.32	1,211.06	1,370.68	1,466.13	1,716.56
Claims on Central Government	12a	122.69	116.46	105.54	109.13	95.34	89.32	94.20	96.60	91.07	72.75	89.36	59.31
Claims on Private Sector	12d	—	—	7.36	8.13	9.88	10.64	10.94	12.94	14.65	14.01	12.47	14.77
Claims on Deposit Money Banks	12e	2.38	7.22	1.33	1.10	1.08	1.09	.90	19.75	.61	.54	.52	.42
Claims on Nonbank Financial Insts	12g	.64	1.62	5.12	5.99	6.60	7.58	7.86	10.93	12.90	12.73	13.17	13.29
Reserve Money	14	710.46	730.35	808.81	760.96	812.36	954.70	1,016.00	1,060.05	1,207.38	1,308.01	1,448.23	1,649.17
of which: Currency Outside DMBs	14a	272.73	285.55	311.58	298.36	315.31	347.02	391.46	389.47	375.92	395.72	429.61	486.14
Foreign Liabilities	16c	26.13	32.28	28.13	27.93	16.80	16.18	23.15	27.95	25.89	23.70	46.55	61.68
Central Government Deposits	16d	47.26	46.64	46.52	64.88	59.02	73.98	66.62	65.94	56.06	70.04	57.08	100.28
Capital Accounts	17a	114.30	82.62	133.13	105.15	105.01	110.92	84.98	112.99	122.58	148.93	131.35	118.98
Other Items (Net)	17r	−45.81	−60.51	−52.33	−47.90	−49.11	−73.10	−84.25	−83.38	−81.61	−79.97	−101.56	−125.76
Deposit Money Banks		*Millions of E. Caribbean Dollars: End of Period*											
Reserves	20	462.40	448.45	475.41	454.93	503.49	625.33	652.56	670.63	845.93	919.40	981.19	1,185.64
Foreign Assets	21	665.76	730.82	822.79	843.68	867.07	1,086.77	1,338.36	1,292.71	1,668.90	2,016.87	2,583.54	3,157.26
Claims on Central Government	22a	386.36	410.53	519.58	567.50	625.09	749.90	853.94	1,063.19	1,086.18	1,195.31	1,198.57	1,327.94
Claims on Local Government	22b	10.32	9.83	11.59	9.57	9.73	16.16	21.85	46.65	57.92	69.20	84.52	122.08
Claims on Nonfin.Pub.Enterprises	22c	165.99	202.93	253.66	270.23	281.12	311.51	363.39	415.04	470.05	498.18	511.23	653.77
Claims on Private Sector	22d	3,067.80	3,187.72	3,511.33	3,940.59	4,471.39	4,839.12	5,333.95	5,892.02	6,017.45	6,251.22	6,292.24	6,730.49
Claims on Nonbank Financial Insts	22g	33.17	62.49	61.87	75.76	69.66	89.36	120.92	119.22	133.72	147.24	217.02	278.55
Demand Deposits	24	561.67	610.96	697.19	691.63	751.45	877.41	928.40	935.39	1,013.16	1,097.32	1,287.98	1,726.04
Time, Savings,& Fgn.Currency Dep	25	2,678.95	2,885.29	3,276.61	3,401.37	3,695.73	4,172.08	4,798.86	5,363.40	5,735.46	6,195.26	6,638.21	7,159.27
Foreign Liabilities	26c	647.51	710.90	711.61	906.69	1,030.16	1,050.09	1,209.51	1,286.72	1,418.52	1,557.91	1,643.42	1,976.85
Central Government Deposits	26d	528.17	593.72	678.28	763.19	849.00	1,007.02	1,078.17	1,167.22	1,231.14	1,335.81	1,402.94	1,618.60
Credit from Monetary Authorities	26g	25.72	16.66	8.12	12.88	11.71	34.07	23.63	48.95	105.35	64.78	30.80	25.28
Capital Accounts	27a	319.29	376.16	415.02	431.08	489.34	539.75	655.66	698.11	829.14	937.38	1,004.09	1,188.67
Other Items (Net)	27r	30.49	−140.92	−130.59	−44.58	.16	37.73	−9.28	−.33	−52.63	−91.05	−139.11	−238.99
Monetary Survey		*Millions of E. Caribbean Dollars: End of Period*											
Foreign Assets (Net)	31n	718.76	693.74	927.96	695.72	651.29	994.55	1,098.29	1,021.37	1,435.54	1,805.94	2,359.70	2,835.29
Domestic Credit	32	3,211.55	3,351.44	3,751.26	4,158.82	4,660.80	5,032.59	5,662.48	6,423.43	6,596.74	6,854.78	6,958.57	7,481.32
Claims on Central Govt. (Net)	32an	−66.39	−113.38	−99.68	−151.44	−187.59	−241.77	−196.66	−73.37	−109.96	−137.80	−172.08	−331.64
Claims on Local Government	32b	10.32	9.83	11.59	9.57	9.73	16.16	21.85	46.65	57.92	69.20	84.52	122.08
Claims on Nonfin.Pub.Enterprises	32c	165.99	203.17	253.66	270.23	281.12	311.51	363.62	415.04	470.05	498.18	511.23	653.77
Claims on Private Sector	32d	3,067.80	3,187.72	3,518.69	3,948.71	4,481.27	4,849.75	5,344.89	5,904.96	6,032.10	6,265.23	6,304.70	6,745.26
Claims on Nonbank Financial Inst	32g	33.81	64.11	67.00	81.75	76.26	96.94	128.78	130.15	146.63	159.98	230.19	291.85
Money	34	835.02	897.56	1,017.74	992.09	1,069.05	1,226.51	1,322.91	1,327.77	1,393.48	1,493.96	1,729.10	2,213.39
Quasi-Money	35	2,678.95	2,885.29	3,277.43	3,402.19	3,696.55	4,173.90	4,800.68	5,365.22	5,737.33	6,197.10	6,639.04	7,160.10
Capital Accounts	37a	433.60	458.79	548.16	536.23	594.35	650.66	740.64	811.09	951.71	1,086.31	1,135.44	1,307.65
Other Items (Net)	37r	−17.26	−196.45	−164.11	−75.95	−47.87	−23.93	−103.46	−59.29	−50.24	−116.65	−185.31	−364.54
Money plus Quasi-Money	35l	3,513.97	3,782.84	4,295.17	4,394.28	4,765.60	5,400.40	6,123.59	6,692.99	7,130.81	7,691.05	8,368.14	9,373.49
Money (National Definitions)		*Millions of E. Caribbean Dollars: End of Period*											
M1	59ma	747.98	793.20	912.86	882.90	963.94	1,091.06	1,193.49	1,214.24	1,248.49	1,321.66	1,508.13	1,886.82
M2	59mb	3,148.04	3,395.26	3,874.39	3,948.43	4,325.35	4,881.69	5,399.32	5,971.19	6,322.12	6,736.98	7,379.69	8,351.69
Interest Rates		*Percent Per Annum*											
Discount Rate (End of Period)	60	....	9.00	9.00	9.00	8.00	8.00	8.00	8.00	7.00	7.00	6.50	6.50
Money Market Rate	60b	5.25	5.25	5.25	5.25	5.25	5.25	5.25	5.25	† 5.64	6.32	6.07	4.67
Savings Rate	60k	8.00	8.00	8.00	8.00	8.00	8.00	8.00	8.00	8.00	8.00	† 3.90	3.80
Deposit Rate	60l	7.21	† 3.87	4.06	4.16	4.20	4.30	4.35	4.46	4.37	4.04	4.76	4.05
Deposit Rate (Fgn. Currency)	60l.f	....	....	....	....	....	....	....	....	....	....	4.06	2.90
Lending Rate	60p	11.81	11.71	11.94	11.74	11.77	11.60	11.91	11.98	11.55	11.47	13.34	13.49

Eastern Caribbean Currency Union 309

		1993	1994	1995	1996	1997	1998	1999	2000	2001	2002	2003	2004
Balance of Payments						*Millions of US Dollars: Minus Sign Indicates Debit*							
Current Account, n.i.e.	78ald	−190.6	−212.3	−215.4	−329.3	−402.7	−365.8	−450.4	−438.3	−475.8	−570.6	....	....
Goods: Exports f.o.b.	78aad	350.8	300.9	350.3	337.8	298.2	316.1	327.4	359.2	303.1	310.4	....	....
Goods: Imports f.o.b.	78abd	−1,006.0	−1,040.2	−1,106.7	−1,190.8	−1,245.8	−1,298.6	−1,383.2	−1,425.5	−1,309.9	−1,315.2	....	....
Trade Balance	78acd	−655.2	−739.3	−756.4	−853.0	−947.6	−982.5	−1,055.8	−1,066.3	−1,006.8	−1,004.8	....	....
Services: Credit	78add	939.1	1,026.4	1,010.5	1,064.0	1,156.5	1,256.5	1,306.0	1,285.5	1,209.9	1,169.4	....	....
Services: Debit	78aed	−422.7	−456.0	−508.8	−537.3	−580.4	−627.2	−663.6	−614.3	−615.2	−642.7	....	....
Balance on Goods & Services	78afd	−138.8	−168.8	−254.6	−326.3	−371.5	−353.2	−413.4	−395.0	−412.1	−478.1	....	....
Income: Credit	78agd	19.6	24.6	32.7	26.7	25.1	35.3	37.5	43.3	38.8	33.9	....	....
Income: Debit	78ahd	−122.8	−142.1	−157.7	−153.7	−156.8	−181.8	−207.5	−250.7	−215.9	−235.7	....	....
Balance on Gds, Serv. & Inc.	78aid	−242.0	−286.3	−379.6	−453.3	−503.1	−499.7	−583.4	−602.4	−589.2	−679.9	....	....
Current Transfers, n.i.e.: Credit	78ajd	107.3	127.1	219.4	175.1	157.6	193.9	185.1	227.5	189.2	192.6	....	....
Current Transfers: Debit	78akd	−55.9	−53.2	−55.2	−51.1	−57.2	−60.0	−52.1	−63.4	−75.7	−83.4	....	....
Capital Account, n.i.e.	78bcd	56.8	67.8	94.3	73.5	89.2	255.3	108.6	122.3	134.2	132.2	....	....
Capital Account, n.i.e.: Credit	78bad	62.1	77.0	100.2	91.8	98.0	264.4	118.0	133.9	142.2	140.4	....	....
Capital Account: Debit	78bbd	−5.4	−9.1	−6.0	−18.3	−8.8	−9.1	−9.4	−11.6	−8.0	−8.1	....	....
Financial Account, n.i.e.	78bjd	149.4	152.6	137.3	260.5	362.1	194.2	406.9	378.6	345.9	434.8	....	....
Direct Investment Abroad	78bdd	—								−.1		....	....
Dir. Invest. in Rep. Econ., n.i.e.	78bed	139.3	179.8	210.0	183.3	261.3	312.9	335.2	306.8	281.1	316.3	....	....
Portfolio Investment Assets	78bfd	2.5	−2.0	−5.7	−.4	—	−.4	−10.5	−1.7	−5.7	−27.4	....	....
Equity Securities	78bkd	....	....	....	....	....	....	....	....	....	....		
Debt Securities	78bld	....	....	....	....	....	....	....	....	....	....		
Portfolio Investment Liab., n.i.e.	78bgd	.6	1.1	−.4	6.1	20.2	6.0	58.9	69.7	54.4	195.1	....	....
Equity Securities	78bmd	....	....	....	....	....	....	....	....	....	....		
Debt Securities	78bnd	....	....	....	....	....	....	....	....	....	....		
Financial Derivatives Assets	78bwd	....	....	....	....	....	....	....	....	....	....		
Financial Derivatives Liabilities	78bxd	....	....	....	....	....	....	....	....	....	....		
Other Investment Assets	78bhd	−12.3	−18.3	−51.0	−31.3	−16.2	−49.2	19.3	−61.7	−54.3	−52.2	....	....
Monetary Authorities	78bod	....	....	....	....	....	....	....	....	....	....		
General Government	78bpd	....	....	....	....	....	....	....	....	....	....		
Banks	78bqd	....	....	....	....	....	....	....	....	....	....		
Other Sectors	78brd	....	....	....	....	....	....	....	....	....	....		
Other Investment Liab., n.i.e.	78bid	19.3	−8.0	−15.7	102.7	96.8	−75.1	4.0	65.5	70.6	2.9	....	....
Monetary Authorities	78bsd	—				—							
General Government	78btd	....	....	....	....	....	....	....	....	....	....		
Banks	78bud	....	....	....	....	....	....	....	....	....	....		
Other Sectors	78bvd	....	....	....	....	....	....	....	....	....	....		
Net Errors and Omissions	78cad	−18.2	−16.9	35.5	−23.7	−25.3	−32.3	−43.5	−50.3	61.6	61.4	....	....
Overall Balance	78cbd	−2.7	−8.8	51.6	−19.0	23.3	51.5	21.6	12.3	66.0	57.8	....	....
Reserves and Related Items	79dad	2.7	8.8	−51.6	19.0	−23.3	−51.5	−21.6	−12.3	−66.0	−57.8	....	....
Reserve Assets	79dbd	3.4	9.6	−50.8	19.9	−22.8	−53.5	−21.6	−12.3	−66.0	−59.5	....	....
Use of Fund Credit and Loans	79dcd	−.7	−.8	−.9	−.8	−.6	2.1			—	1.7	....	....
Exceptional Financing	79ded	....	....	....	....	....	....	....	....	....	....		
National Accounts						*Millions of E. Caribbean Dollars*							
Gross Domestic Product (GDP)	99b	4,491.8	4,795.5	4,963.1	5,199.6	5,490.4	5,854.0	6,204.5	6,461.6	6,493.1	6,569.9		
GDP Volume 1990 Prices	99b.p	4,066.7	4,188.8	4,216.2	4,328.9	4,469.2	4,647.3	4,837.6	4,973.8	4,909.0	4,918.2		
GDP Volume (2000=100)	99bvp	81.8	84.2	84.8	87.0	89.9	93.4	97.3	100.0	98.7	98.9		
GDP Deflator (2000=100)	99bip	85.0	88.1	90.6	92.5	94.6	97.0	98.7	100.0	101.8	102.8	....	....
						Millions: Midyear Estimates							
Population	99z	.556	.561	.566	.570	.573	.576	.579	.582	.585	.589	.593	.598

Ecuador 248

		1993	1994	1995	1996	1997	1998	1999	2000	2001	2002	2003	2004
Exchange Rates						*Sucres per SDR: End of Period*							
Principal Rate..............	aa	2,807.3	3,312.4	4,345.8	5,227.0	5,974.5	9,609.8	27,783.7	32,572.8	31,418.3	33,988.0	37,149.3	38,825.3
					Sucres per US Dollar: End of Period (ae) Period Average (rf)								
Principal Rate..............	ae	2,043.8	2,269.0	2,923.5	3,635.0	4,428.0	6,825.0	20,243.0	25,000.0	25,000.0	25,000.0	25,000.0	25,000.0
Principal Rate..............	rf	1,919.1	2,196.7	2,564.5	3,189.5	3,998.3	5,446.6	11,786.8	24,988.4	25,000.0	25,000.0	25,000.0	25,000.0
					Index Numbers (2000=100): Period Averages								
Principal Rate..............	ahx	1,297.5	1,139.3	977.7	796.5	624.6	468.0	228.7	100.0	100.0	100.0	100.0	100.0
Nominal Effective Exchange Rate.....	nec	849.8	911.7	789.9	656.9	555.6	426.1	216.9	100.0	104.6	106.1	99.6	94.8
Real Effective Exchange Rate...........	rec	129.2	138.3	136.2	135.2	145.1	147.1	109.8	100.0	139.9	155.7	153.4	146.4
Fund Position						*Millions of SDRs: End of Period*							
Quota..........	2f.s	219.2	219.2	219.2	219.2	219.2	219.2	302.3	302.3	302.3	302.3	302.3	302.3
SDRs..........	1b.s	3.2	3.0	2.1	1.9	.4	.2	1.7	.2	1.8	1.4	.7	36.1
Reserve Position in the Fund..........	1c.s	17.1	17.1	17.2	17.2	17.2	17.2	17.2	17.2	17.2	17.2	17.2	17.2
Total Fund Cred.&Loans Outstg.......	2tl	51.8	135.7	116.7	100.9	49.5			113.3	151.1	226.7	262.3	186.8
International Liquidity					*Millions of US Dollars Unless Otherwise Indicated: End of Period*								
Total Reserves minus Gold..............	1l.d	1,379.9	1,844.2	1,627.6	1,858.5	2,092.8	1,619.7	1,642.4	946.9	839.8	714.6	812.6	1,069.6
SDRs..........	1b.d	4.3	4.3	3.1	2.7	.5	.3	2.3	.3	2.3	1.9	1.0	56.1
Reserve Position in the Fund..........	1c.d	23.5	25.0	25.5	24.7	23.1	24.2	23.5	22.3	21.6	23.3	25.5	26.6
Foreign Exchange..........	1d.d	1,352.1	1,814.9	1,599.0	1,831.1	2,069.1	1,595.3	1,616.5	924.3	815.9	689.4	786.1	986.9
Gold (Million Fine Troy Ounces)....	1ad	.414	.414	.414	.414	.414	.414	†.845	.845	.845	.845	.845	.845
Gold (National Valuation)...............	1and	165.6	165.6	166.6	166.6	166.7	166.7	245.4	232.7	233.8	293.3	348.0	368.0
Monetary Authorities: Other Liab.....	4..d	4,079.9	4,052.7	196.1	178.3	147.5	310.6	673.6	400.6	375.5	154.4	53.5	39.8
Banking Institutions: Assets............	7a.d	180.1	355.4	398.4	561.1	938.3	972.3	748.9	819.4	1,013.1	1,367.1	1,985.6	2,453.0
Liabilities.........	7b.d	390.5	847.8	1,074.6	1,229.4	1,795.2	1,527.0	862.0	595.3	512.3	452.5	472.1	574.4
Nonbank Financial Insts.: Assets......	7e.d	....	....	....	....	....	20.1	16.8	26.7	41.5	32.6	35.8	50.4
Liabilities...............	7f.d	....	....	....	....	....	523.3	383.2	321.4	274.5	.3	.1	3.3
Monetary Authorities						*Millions of US Dollars: End of Period*							
Foreign Assets....................	11	1,489.3	1,986.6	1,746.7	1,992.2	2,254.8	†1,663.1	†1,527.7	1,538.6	1,563.0	†1,522.2	1,715.9	2,051.2
Claims on Central Government........	12a	3,924.6	4,021.3	194.7	166.1	129.0	†303.0	†1,479.2	1,425.0	1,278.8	†1,145.0	1,244.3	1,155.4
Claims on State & Local Govts......	12b	—	—	—	—	—	†—	†—	—	—	†—		
Claims on Nonfin.Pub.Enterprises.....	12c	.1	.1	—	—	—	†—	†—	—	—	†—	1.5	2.6
Claims on Private Sector................	12d	14.6	21.2	6.1	8.2	7.2	†18.4	†1.8	3.6	2.9	†16.8	15.2	161.7
Claims on Banking Institutions......	12e	77.9	15.7	185.8	267.4	44.8	†944.0	†424.4	314.4	348.5	†272.7	100.1	92.8
Claims on Nonbank Financial Insts...	12g						†—	†—	24.6	25.3	†26.7	18.3	9.1
Reserve Money....................	14	1,207.2	1,237.8	1,120.3	1,198.6	1,285.0	†1,053.3	†828.6	474.6	528.7	†426.3	468.7	534.6
of which: Currency Outside Banks..	14a	417.1	493.6	469.6	516.6	537.5	†426.6	†576.3	31.7	21.8	†39.6	49.7	58.1
Time and Savings Deposits..............	15	125.5	175.6	130.9	121.1	111.9	†—	†86.1	115.0	98.2	†97.3	125.3	170.9
Liabs. of Central Bank: Securities.....	16ac	88.5	36.0	19.8	9.4	.4	†319.8	†341.8	6.2	54.7	†8.7	43.7	31.1
Foreign Liabilities....................	16c	4,151.0	4,250.9	369.6	323.4	280.9	†380.2	†673.6	548.2	565.4	†462.7	443.3	329.8
Central Government Deposits..........	16d	627.0	816.1	634.1	699.4	600.5	†391.2	†388.7	887.9	818.0	†864.1	1,076.7	1,218.9
Capital Accounts..............	17a	303.1	344.6	331.8	533.1	448.8	†1,169.7	†1,243.2	1,542.2	1,571.6	†1,363.4	1,432.8	1,583.9
Other Items (Net)........................	17r	−995.7	−816.1	−473.2	−451.1	−291.8	†−385.7	†−128.8	−268.0	−418.1	†−239.0	−495.3	−396.5
Banking Institutions						*Millions of US Dollars: End of Period*							
Reserves........................	20	423.9	413.4	444.9	539.0	566.6	†686.5	†180.8	243.5	250.7	†326.3	258.0	340.2
Claims on Mon.Author.:Securities....	20c	37.0	36.0	19.8	9.4	.4	†.1	†117.9	2.1	8.7	†4.2	12.0	30.4
Foreign Assets....................	21	180.1	355.4	398.4	561.1	938.3	†972.3	†748.9	819.4	1,013.1	†1,367.1	1,985.6	2,453.0
Claims on Central Government........	22a	33.4	64.3	129.3	221.3	387.8	†892.9	†490.1	399.0	568.0	†527.7	349.9	276.4
Claims on State & Local Govts......	22b	—	—	—	—	—	†—	†—	—	—	†—	11.1	7.8
Claims on Nonfin.Pub.Enterprises.....	22c	21.3	—	—	—	—	†—	†—	—	—	†—	1.5	1.1
Claims on Private Sector................	22d	2,871.2	4,648.0	5,387.6	5,591.5	6,740.6	†6,126.3	†4,400.6	4,766.7	5,861.5	†5,150.0	5,398.4	6,635.5
Claims on Nonbank Financial Insts...	22g	.1	.1	—	21.2	24.4	†45.5	†—	—	—	†131.4	343.0	287.7
Demand Deposits....................	24	804.5	977.4	765.9	819.1	883.3	†951.3	†614.9	996.7	1,552.7	†1,629.1	1,793.0	2,315.0
Time, Savings,& Fgn.Currency Dep...	25	1,881.3	2,905.3	3,606.4	4,186.3	4,611.2	†3,701.0	†1,239.2	2,434.3	3,087.3	†3,073.6	3,791.3	4,648.6
Bonds........................	26ab	59.9	61.7	161.5	508.2	687.8	†661.7	†347.0	233.6	171.7	†—		
Restricted Deposits....................	26b	58.5	84.5	121.4	162.7	174.9	†—	†1,057.5	364.8	159.0	†25.8	1.0	1.6
Foreign Liabilities....................	26c	390.5	847.8	1,074.6	1,229.4	1,795.2	†1,527.0	†862.0	595.3	512.3	†452.5	472.1	574.4
Central Government Deposits..........	26d	—	—	2.6	4.1	6.5	†131.2	†48.0	128.6	1,007.0	†1,120.1	1,290.2	1,674.2
Credit from Monetary Authorities.....	26g	89.5	26.1	162.8	132.9	6.8	†652.5	†311.1	136.4	169.1	†71.2	54.4	52.6
Liab. to Nonbank Financial Insts.......	26j	72.3	165.9	237.7	18.3	13.8	†34.3	†88.7	135.1	139.4	†67.6	74.3	103.6
Capital Accounts..............	27a	895.9	1,306.8	1,614.0	1,685.5	1,937.0	†1,719.8	†−95.8	−365.0	−875.2	†−985.9	−793.9	−713.7
Other Items (Net)........................	27r	−685.4	−858.1	−1,366.8	−1,803.0	−1,458.4	†−655.1	†1,465.7	1,570.9	1,778.7	†2,052.8	1,677.0	1,375.7
Banking Survey						*Millions of US Dollars: End of Period*							
Foreign Assets (Net)......................	31n	−2,872.2	−2,756.6	700.9	1,000.5	1,117.0	†728.3	†741.1	1,214.6	1,498.4	†1,974.2	2,786.0	3,600.0
Domestic Credit............................	32	6,238.4	7,938.8	5,081.0	5,304.8	6,681.9	†6,863.7	†5,935.0	5,602.3	5,911.4	†5,013.4	5,016.2	5,644.1
Claims on Central Govt. (Net)........	32an	3,331.0	3,269.5	−312.7	−316.1	−90.3	†673.5	†1,532.6	807.5	21.7	†−311.5	−772.6	−1,461.3
Claims on State and Local Govts....	32b	—	—	—	—	—	†—	†—	—	—	†—	12.5	10.4
Claims on Nonfin.Pub.Enterprises...	32c	21.4	.1	—	—	—	†—	†—	—	—	†—	1.5	1.1
Claims on Private Sector............	32d	2,885.9	4,669.2	5,393.7	5,599.8	6,747.7	†6,144.8	†4,402.4	4,770.2	5,864.4	†5,166.8	5,413.6	6,797.1
Claims on Nonbank Financial Insts.	32g	.1	.1	—	21.2	24.4	†45.5	†—	24.6	25.3	†158.1	361.2	296.8
Money................................	34	1,438.2	1,711.2	1,379.3	1,445.1	1,551.8	†1,546.7	†1,255.9	1,245.2	1,814.1	†1,794.8	1,985.3	2,510.0
Quasi-Money............................	35	2,006.8	3,080.8	3,737.2	4,307.4	4,723.1	†3,701.0	†1,325.4	2,549.3	3,185.4	†3,170.9	3,916.6	4,819.5
Bonds................................	36ab	59.9	61.7	161.5	508.2	687.8	†661.7	†347.0	233.6	171.7	†—	—	—
Liabs. of Central Bank: Securities.....	36ac	51.4	—	—	—	—	†319.7	†223.8	4.0	45.9	†4.4	31.7	.7
Restricted Deposits........................	36b	58.8	84.7	121.6	162.8	175.0	†—	†1,057.5	364.8	159.0	†25.8	1.0	1.6
Liab. to Nonbank Financial Insts.......	36j	72.3	165.9	237.7	18.3	13.8	†34.3	†88.7	135.1	139.4	†67.6	74.3	103.6
Capital Accounts..............	37a	1,199.0	1,651.3	1,945.8	2,218.7	2,385.8	†2,889.5	†1,147.4	1,177.3	696.4	†377.5	638.9	870.2
Other Items (Net)........................	37r	−1,520.3	−1,573.5	−1,801.2	−2,355.1	−1,738.4	†−1,560.9	†1,230.4	1,107.7	1,197.8	†1,546.5	1,154.4	938.4
Money plus Quasi-Money................	35l	3,445.0	4,792.0	5,116.6	5,752.5	6,274.9	†5,247.6	†2,581.2	3,794.5	4,999.5	†4,965.7	5,901.9	7,329.5

Ecuador 248

		1993	1994	1995	1996	1997	1998	1999	2000	2001	2002	2003	2004
Nonbank Financial Institutions							*Millions of US Dollars: End of Period*							
Reserves...	40	....	....	....	....	....	2.0	† 1.3	5.0	8.3	† 1.2	3.5	3.0
Claims on Mon.Author.:Securities....	40c	....	....	....	....	....	—	† —			† .7	—	—
Foreign Assets..............................	41	....	....	....	....	....	20.1	† 16.8	26.7	41.5	† 32.6	35.8	50.4
Claims on Central Government.........	42a	....	....	....	....	....	8.1	† 257.5	227.9	151.6	† 125.1	109.0	124.9
Claims on State & Local Govts.........	42b	....	....	....	....	....	—	† —			† —	—	—
Claims on Nonfin.Pub.Enterprises.....	42c	....	....	....	....	....	—	† —			† —	—	—
Claims on Private Sector..................	42d	....	....	....	....	....	994.1	† 738.6	420.2	383.8	† 21.6	10.5	28.2
Claims on Banking Institutions.........	42e	....	....	....	....	....	8.1	† 40.7	332.9	6.7	† 303.7	261.3	301.4
Restricted Deposits........................	46b	....	....	....	....	....	17.9	† 11.1	20.6	15.3	† —		35.8
Foreign Liabilities..........................	46c	....	....	....	....	....	523.3	† 383.2	321.4	274.5	† .3	.1	3.3
Central Government Deposits...........	46d	....	....	....	....	....	92.6	† 80.0	104.1	106.8	† 98.6	98.3	135.9
Credit from Monetary Authorities.....	46g	....	....	....	....	....	232.0	† 176.8	125.0	75.9	† 32.1	20.1	10.5
Credit from Banking Institutions.......	46h	....	....	....	....	....	.7	† —	1.2	16.8	† 3.1	2.3	2.0
Capital Accounts...........................	47a	....	....	....	....	....	149.0	† 134.8	133.3	80.2	† 160.9	167.9	244.0
Other Items (Net)..........................	47r	....	....	....	....	....	17.0	† 269.0	307.0	22.5	† 190.1	131.4	76.5
Interest Rates							*Percent Per Annum*							
Discount Rate (End of Period)..........	60	33.57	44.88	59.41	46.38	37.46	61.84	64.40	† 13.16	16.44	14.55	11.19	9.86
Savings Rate.................................	60k	19.22	16.71	21.64	19.90	16.62	16.25	† 4.91	4.47	3.49	2.45	2.24	1.99
Deposit Rate.................................	60l	31.97	33.65	43.31	41.50	28.09	39.39	† 10.03	8.46	6.58	5.47	5.53	4.08
Lending Rate................................	60p	47.83	43.99	55.67	54.50	43.02	49.55	† 16.53	16.26	15.46	15.08	13.08	9.65
Prices, Production, Labor							*Index Numbers (2000=100): Period Averages*							
Producer Prices.............................	63	....	....	8.3	....	....	18.7	37.8	100.0	99.8	106.5	114.3	124.7
Consumer Prices............................	64	9.7	12.3	† 15.1	18.8	24.6	33.5	51.0	† 100.0	137.7	154.9	167.1	171.7
Crude Petroleum Production............	66aa	85.7	94.7	95.9	96.1	96.9	93.7	93.2	100.0	101.6	98.0	104.3	130.4
Prices, Production, Labor							*Number in Thousands: Period Averages*							
Labor Force.................................	67d	2,892	2,905	3,104	3,169	3,326	3,560	3,770	3,709	4,124	3,801	3,992	4,221
Employment.................................	67e	2,651	2,698	2,892	2,889	3,062	3,151	3,226	3,376	3,673	3,459	3,531	3,859
Unemployment..............................	67c	241	207	213	335	312	409	543	333	451	354	461	362
Unemployment Rate (%).................	67r	8.3	7.1	6.9	10.4	9.2	11.5	14.4	9.0	11.0	9.3	11.5	8.6
Intl. Transactions & Positions							*Millions of US Dollars*							
Exports...	70..d	2,903.7	3,819.9	4,307.2	5,198.6	5,264.4	4,203.1	4,451.1	4,926.6	4,678.4	5,041.5	6,038.4	7,655.4
Imports, c.i.f..................................	71..d	2,562.2	3,622.0	4,152.6	4,283.7	4,954.8	5,575.7	3,017.3	3,721.1	5,362.9	6,431.1	6,534.4	7,861.1
Imports, f.o.b.................................	71.vd	2,223.0	3,252.5	3,774.8	3,906.1	4,520.1	5,109.9	2,736.9	3,401.0	4,936.0	5,953.4	6,071.1	7,272.5
							2000=100							
Volume of Exports..........................	72	80.2	89.1	99.7	304.8	304.0	287.8	97.2	100.0	101.1	99.2	106.0	133.0
Volume of Imports.........................	73	49.3	74.7	100.1	273.0	375.9	466.3	95.9	100.0	119.5	148.1	161.1	167.8
Unit Value of Exports/Export Prices...	74..d	71.4	73.0	75.4	29.1	28.7	21.6	78.1	100.0	87.8	94.3	106.3	117.9
Balance of Payments							*Millions of US Dollars: Minus Sign Indicates Debit*							
Current Account, n.i.e......................	78ald	–849	–898	–1,000	–55	–457	–2,099	918	921	–695	–1,359	–455	....
Goods: Exports f.o.b......................	78aad	3,136	3,936	4,468	4,929	5,360	4,326	4,615	5,137	4,781	5,198	6,197	....
Goods: Imports f.o.b......................	78abd	–2,922	–3,787	–4,535	–4,008	–4,869	–5,458	–3,028	–3,743	–5,179	–6,196	–6,268	
Trade Balance.............................	78acd	214	149	–66	921	491	–1,132	1,588	1,395	–397	–998	–71	....
Services: Credit............................	78add	636	676	728	683	686	678	730	849	862	923	898	....
Services: Debit.............................	78aed	–1,089	–1,107	–1,173	–1,110	–1,230	–1,241	–1,181	–1,269	–1,434	–1,632	–1,590	....
Balance on Goods & Services.......	78afd	–240	–283	–512	494	–52	–1,695	1,136	975	–969	–1,707	–763	....
Income: Credit.............................	78agd	32	61	98	80	128	119	75	70	48	30	27	....
Income: Debit..............................	78ahd	–896	–999	–1,029	–1,121	–1,154	–1,290	–1,383	–1,476	–1,412	–1,335	–1,492	....
Balance on Gds, Serv. & Inc.........	78aid	–1,104	–1,221	–1,442	–547	–1,078	–2,865	–171	–431	–2,333	–3,012	–2,227	....
Current Transfers, n.i.e.: Credit......	78ajd	318	391	506	616	738	933	1,188	1,437	1,686	1,712	1,794	....
Current Transfers: Debit.................	78akd	–62	–69	–64	–124	–117	–166	–99	–85	–47	–58	–22	....
Capital Account, n.i.e.....................	78bcd	5	18	17	14	11	14	2	–1	–63	20	25	....
Capital Account, n.i.e.: Credit........	78bad	8	21	21	18	17	23	11	8	21	24	26	....
Capital Account: Debit...................	78bbd	–3	–3	–4	–4	–6	–9	–9	–10	–84	–4	–1	....
Financial Account, n.i.e..................	78bjd	–44	332	–43	103	–14	1,448	–1,344	–6,602	775	1,122	316	....
Direct Investment Abroad...............	78bdd	....	....	....	....	....	....	....	....	—	—	—	....
Dir. Invest. in Rep. Econ., n.i.e........	78bed	474	576	452	500	724	870	648	720	1,330	1,275	1,555	....
Portfolio Investment Assets............	78bfd	....	....	....	....	....	....	....	....				....
Equity Securities........................	78bkd	....	....	....	....	....	....	....	....				....
Debt Securities..........................	78bld	....	....	....	....	....	....	....	....				....
Portfolio Investment Liab., n.i.e......	78bgd	1	6	3	–4	–242	–34	–46	–5,583	–148	—	8	....
Equity Securities........................	78bmd	1	6	13	6	22	5	1	—	1	1	9	....
Debt Securities..........................	78bnd		—	–10	–10	–264	–40	–47	–5,583	–149	–1	–1	....
Financial Derivatives Assets...........	78bwd	....	....	....	....	....	....	....	....	....	....	....	....
Financial Derivatives Liabilities.......	78bxd	....	....	....	....	....	....	....	....	....	....	....	....
Other Investment Assets................	78bhd	–140	–177	–668	–302	–560	–54	–725	–1,274	–1,275	–1,394	–904	....
Monetary Authorities...................	78bod	....	....	....	....	....	....	....	....	—	—	—	....
General Government....................	78bpd	....	....	....	....	....	....	....	....	—	—	—	....
Banks.......................................	78bqd	....	....	....	....	....	....	....	....	—	—	—	....
Other Sectors.............................	78bxd	–140	–177	–668	–302	–560	–54	–725	–1,274	–1,275	–1,394	–904	....
Other Investment Liab., n.i.e.........	78bid	–380	–75	170	–91	64	666	–1,221	–465	868	1,240	–343	....
Monetary Authorities...................	78bsd	–119	83	–54	–48	–18	230	–76	–135	–144	–138	–17	....
General Government....................	78btd	–640	–727	–692	127	–190	–37	117	206	188	–22	–10	....
Banks.......................................	78bud	27	26	31	95	26	–24	–72	–37	–108	–19	–22	....
Other Sectors.............................	78bvd	351	544	885	–265	245	497	–1,190	–499	932	1,418	–295	....
Net Errors and Omissions...............	78cad	206	–226	–433	–189	–62	–147	–521	–15	–276	–4	184	....
Overall Balance...........................	78cbd	–682	–775	–1,459	–126	–521	–784	–944	–5,697	–258	–221	70	....
Reserves and Related Items.............	79dad	682	775	1,459	126	521	784	944	5,697	258	221	–70	....
Reserve Assets.............................	79dbd	–442	–578	174	–247	–253	461	489	–307	105	68	–150	....
Use of Fund Credit and Loans........	79dcd	–29	122	–29	–23	–3	–67	–68	151	48	95	48	....
Exceptional Financing...................	79ded	1,153	1,231	1,314	396	777	391	523	5,853	105	58	32	....

Ecuador 248

		1993	1994	1995	1996	1997	1998	1999	2000	2001	2002	2003	2004
International Investment Position						*Millions of US Dollars*							
Assets	**79aad**	1,641	2,442	2,388	2,650	2,942	2,387	1,319	1,904	2,451	2,709	3,709	...
Direct Investment Abroad	**79abd**	—	—	—	—	—	—	—	—	—	—	—	...
Portfolio Investment	**79acd**	—	—	—	—	—	—	—	—	—	—	—	...
Equity Securities	**79add**	—	—	—	—	—	—	—	—	—	—	—	...
Debt Securities	**79aed**	—	—	—	—	—	—	—	—	—	—	—	...
Financial Derivatives	**79ald**	—	—	—	—	—	—	—	—	—	—	—	...
Other Investment	**79afd**	317	538	658	674	715	619	445	724	1,377	1,701	2,549	...
Monetary Authorities	**79agd**	—	—	—	—	—	—	—	—	—	—	—	...
General Government	**79ahd**	—	—	—	—	—	—	—	—	—	—	—	...
Banks	**79aid**	317	538	658	674	715	619	445	724	1,377	1,701	2,549	...
Other Sectors	**79ajd**	—	—	—	—	—	—	—	—	—	—	—	...
Reserve Assets	**79akd**	1,324	1,904	1,730	1,976	2,227	1,768	874	1,180	1,074	1,008	1,161	...
Liabilities	**79lad**	16,410	18,366	18,391	19,442	20,912	23,255	23,416	21,331	24,059	26,905	28,363	...
Dir. Invest. in Rep. Economy	**79lbd**	2,590	3,166	3,619	4,118	4,842	5,712	6,361	7,081	8,410	9,686	11,240	...
Portfolio Investment	**79lcd**	1	199	6,019	6,039	6,382	6,437	6,465	4,017	4,134	4,134	4,142	...
Equity Securities	**79ldd**	1	8	20	26	48	53	54	54	55	56	66	...
Debt Securities	**79led**	—	191	5,999	6,013	6,334	6,383	6,411	3,963	4,079	4,078	4,077	...
Financial Derivatives	**79lld**	—	—	—	—	—	—	—	—	—	—	—	...
Other Investment	**79lfd**	13,819	15,001	8,753	9,284	9,688	11,106	10,590	10,234	11,515	13,085	12,981	...
Monetary Authorities	**79lgd**	511	729	669	591	549	721	665	458	356	334	398	...
General Government	**79lhd**	11,202	11,526	4,408	4,578	4,274	4,670	5,109	6,015	6,162	6,676	6,969	...
Banks	**79lid**	515	856	1,142	1,137	1,364	1,674	1,298	1,184	1,626	897	706	...
Other Sectors	**79ljd**	1,590	1,891	2,534	2,979	3,501	4,041	3,517	2,577	3,370	5,178	4,908	...
Government Finance						*Millions of US Dollars: Year Ending December 31*							
Deficit (-) or Surplus	**80**	287.0	52.4	−163.8	−88.7	−291.4	68.7	−99.0	90.0	98.9	135.1	−321.2	−126.8
Revenue	**81**	2,248.2	2,570.9	3,131.4	3,334.1	3,380.3	3,280.3	2,705.1	3,056.6	3,873.7	4,205.3	4,761.6	4,907.7
Expenditure	**82**	1,961.3	2,518.5	3,295.2	3,422.7	3,671.7	3,211.6	2,804.1	2,966.6	3,774.8	4,070.2	5,082.8	5,034.4
Financing													
Domestic	**84a**	−30.9	237.5	365.4	150.2	824.4	−68.8	32.3	−269.4	−22.3	17.4	87.6	607.7
Foreign	**85a**	−256.0	−290.0	−201.6	−61.5	−533.0	.1	66.8	179.4	−76.9	−152.7	233.5	−481.0
National Accounts						*Millions of US Dollars*							
Househ.Cons.Expend.,incl.NPISHs.	**96f.d**	10,454	12,592	13,827	14,022	15,682	16,120	11,035	10,199	14,491	16,837	18,473	19,769
Government Consumption Expend...	**91f.d**	1,767	2,237	2,525	2,567	2,902	2,857	2,088	1,564	2,134	2,550	2,583	2,740
Gross Fixed Capital Formation	**93e.d**	2,857	3,521	3,797	3,852	4,234	4,623	2,826	3,265	4,541	5,549	6,192	6,571
Changes in Inventories	**93i.d**	219	540	557	338	838	1,253	−371	−60	854	1,191	1,329	1,852
Exports of Goods and Services	**90c.d**	3,778	4,576	5,196	5,612	6,058	4,997	5,257	5,906	5,613	5,829	6,461	8,029
Imports of Goods and Services (-)	**98c.d**	4,018	4,894	5,707	5,124	6,078	6,595	4,161	4,939	6,608	7,644	7,837	8,679
Gross Domestic Product (GDP)	**99b.d**	15,057	18,573	20,196	21,268	23,636	23,255	16,675	15,934	21,024	24,311	27,201	30,282
Net Primary Income from Abroad	**98.n**	−572	−1,279	−1,262	−1,304	−1,422	−1,625	−1,741	−2,229	−1,911	...	...	...
Gross National Income (GNI)	**99a**	13,732	15,327	16,677	17,736	18,347	18,098	11,948	11,698	15,208	...	...	...
GDP Volume 2000 Prices	**99bpd**	14,270	14,941	15,203	15,568	16,199	16,541	15,499	15,934	16,749	17,321	17,781	19,016
GDP Volume (2000=100)	**99bvp**	† 89.6	93.8	95.4	97.7	101.7	103.8	† 97.3	100.0	105.1	108.7	111.6	119.3
GDP Deflator (2000=100)	**99bip**	105.5	124.3	132.8	136.6	145.9	140.6	107.6	100.0	125.5	140.4	153.0	159.2
						Millions: Midyear Estimates							
Population	**99z**	10.97	11.19	11.40	11.59	11.78	11.95	12.13	12.31	12.49	12.67	12.85	13.04

		1993	1994	1995	1996	1997	1998	1999	2000	2001	2002	2003	2004
Exchange Rates						*Pounds per SDR: End of Period*							
Market Rate..............aa=........	wa	4.6314	4.9504	5.0392	4.8718	4.5713	4.7704	4.6734	4.8077	5.6427	6.1178	9.1435	9.5221
						Pounds per US Dollar: End of Period							
Market Rate..............ae=........	we	3.3718	3.3910	3.3900	3.3880	3.3880	3.3880	3.4050	3.6900	4.4900	4.5000	6.1532	6.1314
Fund Position						*Millions of SDRs: End of Period*							
Quota.............................	2f.s	678	678	678	678	678	678	944	944	944	944	944	944
SDRs...............................	1b.s	50	59	70	86	84	114	30	37	28	67	127	106
Reserve Position in the Fund...........	1c.s	54	54	54	54	54	54	120	120	—	—	—	—
Total Fund Cred.&Loans Outstg.......	2tl	147	132	70	11	—	—	—	—	—	—	—	—
International Liquidity					*Millions of US Dollars Unless Otherwise Indicated: End of Period*								
Total Reserves minus Gold..............	1l.d	12,904	13,481	16,181	17,398	18,665	18,124	14,484	13,118	12,926	13,242	13,589	14,273
SDRs...............................	1b.d	69	86	103	123	113	160	41	48	35	91	189	165
Reserve Position in the Fund.........	1c.d	74	78	80	77	73	76	165	156	—	—	—	—
Foreign Exchange...................	1d.d	12,761	13,316	15,998	17,198	18,479	17,888	14,278	12,913	12,891	13,151	13,400	14,108
Gold (Million Fine Troy Ounces)........	1ad	2.432	2.432	2.432	2.432	2.432	2.432	2.432	2.432	2.432	2.432	2.432	2.432
Gold (National Valuation)..............	1and	616	694	704	695	609	541	475	511	488	571	631	717
Monetary Authorities:Other Assets...	3..d	1,274	1,293	1,131	1,003	938	874	811	762	715	668	629	528
Other Liab..............	4..d	11,842	12,551	13,298	12,324	11,384	11,873	11,296	11,091	10,569	11,866	13,061	13,481
Deposit Money Banks: Assets..........	7a.d	10,786.5	11,432.3	11,070.3	10,736.2	9,153.2	7,815.1	7,441.1	7,297.1	5,915.0	6,279.5	7,782.2	10,913.7
Liabilities........	7b.d	1,782.0	1,465.3	1,500.2	1,844.2	3,555.7	4,995.3	4,318.3	4,232.6	4,268.9	4,264.0	3,553.2	3,225.3
Other Banking Insts.: Assets.............	7e.d	51.2	29.5	29.8	22.0	16.9	14.8	7.3	7.0	10.3	7.7	24.8	46.6
Liabilities.........	7f.d	486.5	457.1	275.5	255.4	267.4	219.9	215.1	240.8	161.5	173.2	166.9	149.0
Monetary Authorities						*Millions of Pounds: End of Period*							
Foreign Assets................................	11	55,894	60,529	61,901	65,189	68,799	66,782	52,923	52,478	61,332	63,203	88,391	92,422
Claims on Central Government........	12a	52,849	50,978	51,615	47,015	44,368	61,209	75,447	95,715	116,392	131,068	177,255	248,614
Claims on Nonfin.Pub.Enterprises.....	12c	820	799	799	900	849	817	1,029	1,177	1,330	1,661	2,103	2,257
Claims on Deposit Money Banks......	12e	11,655	12,224	12,892	12,700	12,438	8,359	6,462	6,577	7,094	6,621	7,048	7,631
Claims on Other Banking Insts.........	12f	2,134	2,040	2,095	2,147	2,261	2,275	3,336	2,846	2,901	2,319	2,509	2,849
Reserve Money..........................	14	42,554	47,888	52,357	54,562	60,610	72,336	73,522	87,271	102,094	111,002	155,065	183,888
of which: Currency Outside DMBs..	14a	17,818	20,612	22,750	24,954	28,215	31,502	35,310	37,902	40,548	45,281	52,475	59,795
Foreign Liabilities........................	16c	40,609	43,215	45,430	41,807	38,570	40,224	38,464	40,926	47,454	53,398	80,365	82,656
Central Government Deposits...........	16d	38,481	33,617	29,661	28,476	26,738	22,296	23,298	27,676	42,862	43,420	59,364	107,643
Other Items (Net).........................	17r	1,707	1,851	1,855	3,105	2,797	4,586	3,913	2,920	−3,359	−2,948	−17,487	−20,413
Deposit Money Banks						*Millions of Pounds: End of Period*							
Reserves.......................................	20	23,097	25,402	28,094	28,146	30,241	33,262	34,636	46,432	61,180	62,156	104,221	123,935
Foreign Assets..............................	21	36,370	38,767	37,528	36,374	31,011	26,477	25,337	26,926	26,559	28,258	47,886	66,916
Claims on Central Government........	22a	41,262	42,398	41,882	47,567	54,479	47,244	40,363	47,276	54,991	80,056	91,095	102,951
Claims on Nonfin.Pub.Enterprises.....	22c	29,283	29,998	33,180	37,481	38,643	38,801	42,109	38,141	42,062	42,655	45,896	52,549
Claims on Private Sector.................	22d	36,885	48,831	66,777	83,810	105,545	133,799	159,958	176,693	197,038	207,089	225,023	233,685
Claims on Other Banking Insts........	22f	1,432	1,284	1,630	2,424	2,988	4,251	2,958	3,429	4,918	6,186	5,459	4,695
Demand Deposits.........................	24	14,940	15,919	17,282	18,026	18,920	19,335	20,506	21,747	23,515	27,021	36,627	43,230
Time, Savings,& Fgn.Currency Dep...	25	98,598	109,810	121,175	135,764	150,966	162,512	174,713	198,421	228,053	256,045	308,286	352,164
Bonds......................................	26ab	—	—	—	800	1,675	1,675	2,238	2,238	2,238	1,563	1,263	1,113
Restricted Deposits.......................	26b	8,239	9,182	10,858	12,513	14,081	15,771	18,113	17,502	19,658	20,161	22,750	22,912
Foreign Liabilities........................	26c	6,009	4,969	5,086	6,248	12,047	16,924	14,704	15,618	19,167	19,188	21,864	19,776
Central Government Deposits........	26d	6,907	7,805	11,016	13,638	14,670	18,906	23,889	28,596	34,429	40,488	51,498	57,958
Credit from Monetary Authorities.....	26g	15,598	17,571	20,842	20,648	20,938	11,244	7,256	7,464	7,547	7,475	7,675	8,110
Other Items (Net).........................	27r	18,040	21,423	22,832	28,165	29,609	37,468	43,943	47,310	52,141	54,461	69,616	79,469
Monetary Survey						*Millions of Pounds: End of Period*							
Foreign Assets (Net)........................	31n	45,646	51,111	48,914	53,508	49,194	36,111	25,092	22,860	21,270	18,875	34,049	56,907
Domestic Credit..............................	32	119,278	134,906	157,300	179,230	207,724	247,195	278,013	309,006	342,342	387,126	438,479	481,998
Claims on Central Govt. (Net)........	32an	48,724	51,953	52,820	52,467	57,439	67,252	68,623	86,720	94,091	127,216	157,489	185,964
Claims on Nonfin.Pub.Enterprises...	32c	30,103	30,797	33,979	38,381	39,492	39,618	43,138	39,318	43,393	44,316	47,999	54,806
Claims on Private Sector................	32d	36,885	48,831	66,777	83,810	105,545	133,799	159,958	176,693	197,038	207,089	225,023	233,685
Claims on Other Banking Insts.......	32f	3,566	3,324	3,724	4,571	5,248	6,526	6,294	6,275	7,820	8,505	7,968	7,544
Money...	34	34,571	38,275	41,540	44,521	48,708	58,577	59,066	62,195	67,078	75,781	93,520	108,498
of which: Foreign Currency Deps....	34a	10,918	9,892	10,980	10,260	9,332	10,225	11,148	17,493	31,330	32,734	52,864	56,810
Quasi-Money..................................	35	98,602	109,834	121,227	135,882	151,129	162,795	174,844	198,804	228,413	257,031	310,114	353,389
of which: Fgn. Currency Deposits....	35a	25,964	30,851	33,335	32,015	31,792	33,271	37,435	47,102	60,149	65,939	95,788	107,031
Bonds......................................	36ab	—	—	—	800	1,675	1,675	2,238	2,238	2,238	1,563	1,263	1,113
Restricted Deposits........................	36b	8,239	9,182	10,858	12,513	14,081	15,771	18,113	17,502	19,658	20,161	22,750	22,912
Other Items (Net)..........................	37r	23,512	28,727	32,590	39,021	41,325	44,489	48,845	51,125	46,226	51,466	44,880	52,994
Money plus Quasi-Money.................	35l	133,174	148,109	162,766	180,404	199,837	221,372	233,909	260,999	295,491	332,813	403,634	461,887
Other Banking Institutions													
Specialized Banks						*Millions of Pounds: End of Period*							
Cash...	40	184	169	262	288	300	467	382	583	912	1,338	2,725	2,288
Foreign Assets...............................	41	173	100	101	74	57	50	25	26	46	35	153	286
Claims on Nonfin.Pub.Enterprises...	42c	1,961	2,067	2,130	2,170	2,112	2,073	2,397	2,246	2,262	2,720	2,447	2,526
Claims on Private Sector.................	42d	6,361	7,425	8,785	11,355	13,814	17,607	20,657	22,884	25,728	27,614	30,261	30,856
Demand Deposits..........................	44	722	912	1,195	1,434	2,010	2,366	652	660	774	753	1,058	826
Time and Savings Deposits..............	45	1,705	2,322	2,751	3,464	4,297	5,703	8,835	9,807	11,304	13,382	16,360	18,919
Restricted Deposits........................	46b	32	20	32	36	42	59	53	43	14	13	36	76
Foreign Liabilities.........................	46c	1,640	1,550	934	865	906	745	732	889	725	779	1,027	914
Central Government Deposits..........	46d	592	713	893	1,614	1,980	1,712	1,860	2,058	2,146	2,133	2,274	2,344
Credit from Monetary Authorities.....	46g	2,067	2,043	2,112	2,155	2,279	2,299	3,375	3,372	3,435	2,856	3,042	3,378
Credit from Deposit Money Banks....	46h	1,410	1,021	1,500	2,292	2,790	3,932	2,442	2,911	4,496	5,324	4,899	4,267
Other Items (Net)..........................	47r	509	1,180	1,861	2,027	1,980	3,381	5,513	5,999	6,054	6,465	6,890	5,234
Post Office: Savings Deposits.........	45..i	1,335	1,866	2,591	3,524	4,877	6,680	8,783	11,322	14,584	18,902	24,037	30,067

		1993	1994	1995	1996	1997	1998	1999	2000	2001	2002	2003	2004
Banking Survey						*Millions of Pounds: End of Period*							
Foreign Assets (Net)........................	51n	44,178	49,661	48,081	52,717	48,346	35,416	24,384	21,997	20,591	18,130	33,175	56,280
Domestic Credit...............................	52	124,880	142,295	166,797	190,938	222,041	266,064	301,818	337,171	374,998	425,773	486,385	537,292
Claims on Central Govt. (Net)........	52an	49,570	53,175	55,127	55,223	61,079	72,968	75,668	96,030	106,577	144,035	180,655	215,419
Claims on Nonfin.Pub.Enterprises...	52c	32,064	32,864	36,108	40,551	41,603	41,691	45,535	41,564	45,655	47,035	50,446	57,332
Claims on Private Sector.................	52d	43,246	56,256	75,562	95,164	119,359	151,406	180,615	199,577	222,766	234,703	255,283	264,541
Liquid Liabilities.............................	55l	136,752	153,040	169,041	188,538	210,721	235,654	251,797	282,205	321,241	364,512	442,364	509,411
Bonds..	56ab	—	—	—	800	1,675	1,675	2,238	2,238	2,238	1,563	1,263	1,113
Restricted Deposits.........................	56b	8,271	9,202	10,890	12,550	14,123	15,830	18,166	17,546	19,672	20,174	22,786	22,988
Other Items (Net)............................	57r	24,035	29,714	34,948	41,768	43,868	48,322	54,003	57,178	52,439	57,657	53,146	60,061
Interest Rates						*Percent Per Annum*							
Discount Rate (End of Period)..........	60	16.50	14.00	13.50	13.00	12.25	12.00	12.00	12.00	11.00	10.00	10.00	10.00
Treasury Bill Rate............................	60c	....	....	....	....	8.8	8.8	9.0	9.1	7.2	5.5	6.9	9.9
Deposit Rate..................................	60l	12.0	11.8	10.9	10.5	9.8	9.4	9.2	9.5	9.5	9.3	8.2	7.7
Lending Rate..................................	60p	18.3	16.5	16.5	15.6	13.8	13.0	13.0	13.2	13.3	13.8	13.5	13.4
Prices and Labor						*Index Numbers (2000=100): Period Averages*							
Industrial Share Price......................	62	....	....	....	....	63.80	67.43	83.34	100.00	109.41	119.62	133.56	199.23
Wholesale Prices............................	63	† 76.5	80.0	85.1	92.2	96.0	97.4	98.2	100.0	101.0	107.5	122.9	143.9
Consumer Prices.............................	64	64.8	70.1	81.1	86.9	91.0	† 94.5	97.4	100.0	102.3	105.1	† 109.8	122.2
						Number in Thousands: Period Averages							
Labor Force...................................	67d	16,494	17,174	17,365	....	....	18,027	18,616	....	19,253	....	....	....
Employment...................................	67e	† 14,703	15,241	15,344	....	15,830	16,183	16,750	17,203	17,557	17,856	18,119	....
Unemployment...............................	67c	1,801	1,877	1,917	....	† 1,446	1,448	1,481	1,698	1,783	2,021	....	....
Unemployment Rate (%)..................	67r	10.9	11.0	11.3	....	† 8.4	8.2	8.1	9.0	9.2	10.2	11.0	....
Intl. Transactions & Positions						*Millions of Pounds*							
Exports..	70	7,558.8	11,767.9	11,703.8	12,004.1	13,285.9	10,605.9	12,086.1	16,273.8	16,343.3	21,183.5	36,822.9	46,665.3
Suez Canal Dues............................	70.s	6,628.4	6,998.1	6,692.9	6,381.4	6,072.5	6,108.9	6,015.3	6,223.1	7,545.6	8,978.4	15,158.6	18,988.7
Imports, c.i.f..................................	71	27,553.8	34,598.9	39,892.0	44,218.0	44,769.0	54,771.0	54,399.0	48,645.0	50,660.0	56,480.0	65,082.0	79,708.0
Balance of Payments						*Millions of US Dollars: Minus Sign Indicates Debit*							
Current Account, n.i.e.....................	78ald	2,299	31	−254	−192	−711	−2,566	−1,635	−971	−388	622	3,743	3,922
Goods: Exports f.o.b.....................	78aad	3,545	4,044	4,670	4,779	5,525	4,403	5,237	7,061	7,025	7,118	8,987	12,320
Goods: Imports f.o.b.....................	78abd	−9,923	−9,997	−12,267	−13,169	−14,157	−14,617	−15,165	−15,382	−13,960	−12,879	−13,189	−18,895
Trade Balance............................	78acd	−6,378	−5,953	−7,597	−8,390	−8,632	−10,214	−9,928	−8,321	−6,935	−5,762	−4,201	−6,576
Services: Credit............................	78add	7,895	8,070	8,590	9,271	9,380	8,141	9,494	9,803	9,042	9,320	11,073	14,197
Services: Debit.............................	78aed	−5,367	−5,645	−4,873	−5,084	−6,770	−6,492	−6,452	−7,513	−7,037	−6,629	−6,474	−8,020
Balance on Goods & Services......	78afd	−3,850	−3,528	−3,880	−4,203	−6,021	−8,565	−6,886	−6,031	−4,929	−3,071	398	−399
Income: Credit..............................	78agd	1,110	1,330	1,578	1,901	2,122	2,030	1,788	1,871	1,468	698	578	572
Income: Debit..............................	78ahd	−1,967	−2,114	−1,983	−1,556	−1,185	−1,075	−1,045	−983	−885	−965	−832	−818
Balance on Gds, Serv. & Inc........	78aid	−4,707	−4,312	−4,285	−3,858	−5,085	−7,610	−6,143	−5,143	−4,346	−3,338	145	−645
Current Transfers, n.i.e.: Credit......	78ajd	7,006	4,622	4,284	3,888	4,738	5,166	4,564	4,224	4,056	4,002	3,708	4,615
Current Transfers: Debit................	78akd	—	−279	−253	−222	−363	−122	−55	−52	−98	−42	−109	−48
Capital Account, n.i.e......................	78bcd	—	—	—	....	....	....	....	—	....	....	....	....
Capital Account, n.i.e.: Credit........	78bad	—	—	—	....	....	....	....	—	....	....	....	....
Capital Account: Debit..................	78bbd	—	—	—	....	....	....	....	—	....	....	....	....
Financial Account, n.i.e...................	78bjd	−762	−1,450	−1,845	−1,459	1,958	1,901	−1,421	−1,646	190	−3,333	−5,725	−4,461
Direct Investment Abroad..............	78bdd	—	−43	−93	−5	−129	−45	−38	−51	−12	−28	−21	−159
Dir. Invest. in Rep. Econ., n.i.e.....	78bed	493	1,256	598	636	891	1,076	1,065	1,235	510	647	237	1,253
Portfolio Investment Assets............	78bfd	—	—	....	—	....	−63	−22	−3	−2	−6	−25	324
Equity Securities.........................	78bkd	—	—	....	—	....	−63	−22	−3	−2	−6	−25	324
Debt Securities...........................	78bld	—	—	....	—	....	....	....	....	—	—	—	324
Portfolio Investment Liab., n.i.e......	78bgd	4	3	20	545	816	−537	617	269	1,463	−672	−18	−85
Equity Securities.........................	78bmd	—	—	....	—	515	−160	658	269	39	−217	37	26
Debt Securities...........................	78bnd	4	3	20	545	301	−377	−41	....	1,424	−455	−55	−111
Financial Derivatives Assets............	78bwd	....	—	....	....	....	....	....	....	....	....	....	....
Financial Derivatives Liabilities.......	78bxd	....	—	....	....	....	....	....	....	....	....	....	....
Other Investment Assets................	78bhd	319	−905	−396	−565	−170	39	−1,805	−2,991	−1,261	−2,943	−4,651	−5,888
Monetary Authorities..................	78bod	−21	−25	65	65	37	24	−14	−21	−73	29	−38	−4
General Government.....................	78bpd	−4	—	—	—	....	....	....	....	....	....	....	....
Banks...	78bqd	523	−634	371	338	1,599	1,357	372	257	1,369	−331	−1,682	−3,215
Other Sectors..............................	78brd	−179	−246	−832	−968	−1,806	−1,342	−2,163	−3,227	−2,556	−2,641	−2,931	−2,669
Other Investment Liab., n.i.e.........	78bid	−1,578	−1,761	−1,974	−2,070	551	1,431	−1,240	−105	−509	−331	−1,248	94
Monetary Authorities..................	78bsd	629	−5	−21	−4	−19	−204	−3	−5	104	5	6	−16
General Government.....................	78btd	−1,761	−1,536	−1,783	−2,578	−1,506	−946	−989	−1,109	−1,157	−1,358	−1,673	−1,740
Banks...	78bud	−202	−256	−148	324	1,715	1,393	−692	−129	−56	−9	−601	−326
Other Sectors..............................	78bvd	−244	36	−22	188	361	1,188	444	1,138	601	1,031	1,020	2,175
Net Errors and Omissions................	78cad	−1,519	255	272	−74	−1,882	−722	−1,558	587	−1,146	1,906	1,575	−45
Overall Balance............................	78cbd	18	−1,164	−1,827	−1,725	−635	−1,387	−4,614	−2,030	−1,345	−804	−407	−584
Reserves and Related Items.............	79dad	−18	1,164	1,827	1,725	635	1,387	4,614	2,030	1,345	804	407	584
Reserve Assets..............................	79dbd	−2,809	−1,193	−409	−1,010	−1,185	535	4,027	1,306	507	−57	−395	−684
Use of Fund Credit and Loans........	79dcd	—	−22	−95	−85	−15	—	....	....	....	....	—	—
Exceptional Financing....................	79ded	2,791	2,379	2,331	2,820	1,836	852	587	724	838	861	801	1,269
Government Finance						*Millions of Pounds: Year Ending June 30*							
Deficit (-) or Surplus.......................	80	2,681	589	1,828	† −4,411	−5,178	−2,591	−220	−4,161	−8,018	−9,623	....	....
Revenue...	81	59,443	67,828	73,654	† 69,233	72,782	69,091	90,163	95,900	99,480	100,329	....	....
Grants Received.............................	81z	3,269	2,811	2,056	† 1,954	1,392	1,689	1,649	1,773	1,571	3,713	....	....
Expenditure...................................	82	56,143	65,382	68,689	† 74,400	78,503	72,048	84,906	92,950	105,086	106,506	....	....
Lending Minus Repayments.............	83	3,888	4,668	5,193	† 1,198	849	1,323	7,126	8,884	3,983	7,159	....	....
Financing													
Domestic......................................	84a	−1,319	1,454	−60	† 5,844	6,785	4,397	....	....	....	....	....	....
Foreign...	85a	−1,362	−2,043	−1,768	† −1,433	−1,607	−1,806	....	....	....	....	....	....

Egypt 469

		1993	1994	1995	1996	1997	1998	1999	2000	2001	2002	2003	2004
National Accounts						*Millions of Pounds: Year Ending June 30*							
Househ.Cons.Expend.,incl.NPISHs....	96f	115,000	130,500	151,900	176,490	200,500	220,400	230,800	258,000	270,000	279,000	304,300	346,000
Government Consumption Expend...	91f	16,000	18,000	21,500	23,800	26,100	32,500	35,700	38,100	40,600	47,200	53,300	60,000
Gross Fixed Capital Formation..........	93e	25,500	29,000	33,100	36,760	47,700	61,300	64,000	64,400	63,600	67,500	68,100	79,600
Changes in Inventories....................	93i	—	—	2,000	1,340	−1,000	500	2,500	2,100	1,900	1,700	2,900	1,000
Exports of Goods and Services..........	90c	40,100	39,500	45,990	47,620	50,100	46,600	46,300	55,100	62,700	69,400	90,000	138,600
Imports of Goods and Services (-).....	98c	48,700	50,100	58,290	61,100	66,200	73,900	71,700	77,600	80,100	85,900	101,100	140,400
Gross Domestic Product (GDP)........	99b	157,300	175,000	204,000	229,400	257,200	287,400	307,600	340,100	358,700	378,900	417,500	485,000
GDP Volume 1996/97 Prices............	99b.p	....	....	....	....	257,200	276,600	293,500	309,300	320,200	330,400	....	....
GDP Volume 2001/02....................	99b.p	....	....	....	....	....	....	....	....	....	378,900	390,700	407,000
GDP Volume (2000=100)...............	99bvp	69.0	71.7	75.1	78.8	† 83.2	89.4	94.9	100.0	103.5	† 106.8	110.1	114.7
GDP Deflator (2000=100)...............	99bip	67.0	71.7	79.9	85.6	90.9	94.5	95.3	100.0	101.9	104.3	111.4	124.3
						Millions: Midyear Estimates							
Population.................................	99z	59.00	60.10	61.22	62.38	63.56	64.77	66.02	67.29	68.58	69.91	71.27	72.64

		1993	1994	1995	1996	1997	1998	1999	2000	2001	2002	2003	2004
Exchange Rates		Colones per SDR: End of Period (aa) Colones per US Dollar: End of Period (ae)											
Market Rate............................	aa	11.909	12.774	13.014	12.589	11.813	12.327	12.016	11.407	10.996	11.896	13.002	13.589
Market Rate............................	ae	8.670	8.750	8.755	8.755	8.755	8.755	8.755	8.755	8.750	8.750	8.750	8.750
Fund Position		Millions of SDRs: End of Period											
Quota...................................	2f.s	125.6	125.6	125.6	125.6	125.6	125.6	171.3	171.3	171.3	171.3	171.3	171.3
SDRs.....................................	1b.s	—	.1	25.0	25.0	25.0	25.0	25.0	25.0	25.0	25.0	25.0	25.0
Reserve Position in the Fund..........	1c.s	—	—	—	—	—	—	—	—	—	—	—	—
Total Fund Cred.&Loans Outstg........	2tl	—	—	—	—	—	—	—	—	—	—	—	—
International Liquidity		Millions of US Dollars Unless Otherwise Indicated: End of Period											
Total Reserves minus Gold..............	1l.d	536.2	649.4	758.3	936.9	1,307.9	1,613.1	2,003.8	1,922.4	1,741.0	1,622.8	1,942.9	1,927.2
SDRs..................................	1b.d	—	.1	37.1	35.9	33.7	35.2	34.3	32.6	31.4	34.0	37.1	38.8
Reserve Position in the Fund.........	1c.d												
Foreign Exchange.....................	1d.d	536.2	649.3	721.2	901.0	1,274.2	1,577.9	1,969.5	1,889.8	1,709.6	1,588.8	1,905.8	1,888.4
Gold (Million Fine Troy Ounces).......	1ad	.469	.469	.469	.469	.469	.469	.469	.469	.469	.469	.469	.419
Gold (National Valuation)...............	1and	181.1	179.8	181.5	173.2	152.5	152.5	152.4	120.7	117.8	117.8	117.8	138.9
Monetary Authorities: Other Liab.....	4..d	293.1	158.6	175.6	217.9	244.4	169.5	166.5	190.9	159.5	130.8	299.0	226.4
Banking Institutions: Assets............	7a.d	94.0	59.6	69.9	106.2	113.4	121.3	125.3	280.0	793.8	867.0	975.9	1,102.1
Liabilities..................	7b.d	48.5	142.3	361.7	404.6	534.9	514.4	549.7	671.2	949.9	1,085.1	1,573.5	1,784.4
Nonbank Financial Insts.:Assets.......	7e.d	....	....	....	....	....	....	....	2.1	27.3	43.7	86.2	170.1
Liabs.......	7f.d	....	....	....	....	....	....	....	60.0	73.1	91.1	153.7	201.0
Monetary Authorities		Millions of US Dollars: End of Period											
Foreign Assets.........................	11	736.5	854.1	937.9	1,110.3	1,452.9	1,776.8	1,971.2	† 1,992.6	1,810.7	1,689.8	2,007.5	1,989.6
Claims on Central Government........	12a	787.2	721.6	708.2	663.9	649.7	614.9	637.2	† 678.6	692.4	708.8	708.7	712.9
Claims on Local Government...........	12b	1.3	1.3	1.3	1.2	1.1	.9	.8	† .7	.6	.5	.3	.2
Claims on Nonfin.Pub.Enterprises.....	12c	—	—	—	—	—	—	—	† —	—	—	—	—
Claims on Private Sector................	12d	—	—	—	—	—	—	—	† 5.9	5.9	13.7	13.7	13.7
Claims on Banking Institutions.........	12e	227.7	262.0	340.3	401.0	421.1	476.0	518.7	† 119.8	105.5	88.0	87.1	1.9
Claims on Nonbank Financial Insts...	12g	—	—	—	—	—	—	—	† 698.2	658.2	625.8	588.8	593.9
Reserve Money.........................	14	1,006.9	1,229.9	1,382.2	1,520.6	1,722.9	1,866.3	2,056.4	† 1,318.3	932.9	723.9	1,105.4	887.4
of which: Currency Outside Banks..	14a	306.3	339.4	357.6	355.0	369.7	403.0	538.4	† 451.5	220.2	60.6	36.4	35.4
Time, Savings,& Fgn.Currency Dep...	15	98.4	96.1	101.3	37.4	8.4	6.4	2.9	† 5.2	20.1	25.5	31.7	38.7
Liabs. of Central Bank: Securities.....	16ac	386.0	324.1	210.7	294.8	427.3	478.9	596.2	† 1,155.4	1,327.6	1,287.9	1,223.2	1,314.5
Restricted Deposits....................	16b	.1	—	.1	—	—	—	—	† .8	.8	.8	.8	3.2
Foreign Liabilities......................	16c	293.1	158.6	175.6	217.9	244.4	169.5	166.5	† 190.9	159.5	130.8	299.0	226.4
Central Government Deposits...........	16d	186.2	235.7	204.0	140.3	141.1	469.6	529.3	† 634.2	613.5	691.0	467.5	531.8
Capital Accounts.......................	17a	248.7	255.5	227.2	226.0	230.8	249.4	266.3	† 249.7	172.7	185.3	188.0	222.0
Other Items (Net).......................	17r	−466.7	−461.1	−313.5	−260.6	−250.2	−371.4	−489.6	† −58.8	46.2	81.4	90.4	88.4
Banking Institutions		Millions of US Dollars: End of Period											
Reserves.................................	20	581.2	858.9	967.1	1,094.6	1,222.4	1,337.9	1,464.9	† 782.2	712.2	660.2	987.7	840.4
Claims on Mon.Author.:Securities....	20c	150.2	182.8	137.8	106.3	138.4	61.7	357.3	† 627.9	984.4	1,063.2	936.0	974.9
Foreign Assets.........................	21	94.0	59.6	69.9	106.2	113.4	121.3	125.3	† 280.0	793.8	867.0	975.9	1,102.1
Claims on Central Government........	22a	116.4	157.3	157.0	170.4	144.0	90.3	128.3	† 364.8	590.4	409.2	454.6	572.6
Claims on Local Government...........	22b	—	—	—	—	1.9	2.8	8.0	† —	—	—	—	—
Claims on Private Sector...............	22d	1,661.4	2,634.0	3,378.7	3,828.7	4,520.6	5,039.4	5,475.9	† 5,857.3	5,456.3	5,639.5	6,115.1	6,393.4
Claims on Nonbank Financial Insts...	22g	—	—	—	—	—	—	—	† 151.6	350.0	380.5	341.6	307.3
Demand Deposits.......................	24	404.4	404.4	449.3	570.6	562.1	601.7	618.7	† 630.2	977.7	1,027.1	1,085.6	1,218.8
Time, Savings,& Fgn.Currency Dep...	25	1,722.4	2,723.2	3,078.6	3,577.8	4,080.8	4,459.0	4,791.7	† 4,976.7	5,082.5	4,990.4	5,013.8	5,052.0
Money Market Instruments.............	26aa	12.9	20.6	65.0	127.4	187.6	191.6	241.3	† 327.4	322.6	339.8	415.9	462.1
Foreign Liabilities......................	26c	48.5	142.3	361.7	404.6	534.9	514.4	549.7	† 671.2	949.9	1,085.1	1,573.5	1,784.4
Central Government Deposits...........	26d	64.8	138.0	205.9	215.3	242.7	324.0	303.3	† 335.5	416.5	457.8	479.2	494.4
Credit from Monetary Authorities.....	26g	151.9	2.0	—	—	26.9	81.2	148.1	† 92.5	106.1	87.6	86.9	1.2
Liab. to Nonbank Financial Insts.......	26j	71.0	77.1	79.3	88.7	138.0	129.2	80.8	† 473.0	414.3	353.8	313.0	318.9
Capital Accounts.......................	27a	99.2	272.3	345.8	445.4	489.1	570.5	609.0	† 640.4	694.2	762.5	836.6	920.5
Other Items (Net).......................	27r	28.0	112.6	124.6	−123.6	−121.4	−218.1	217.2	† −83.0	−76.6	−84.7	6.3	−61.6
Banking Survey		Millions of US Dollars: End of Period											
Foreign Assets (Net).....................	31n	488.9	612.8	470.5	594.0	786.9	1,214.2	1,380.3	† 1,410.5	1,495.1	1,340.9	1,111.0	1,081.0
Domestic Credit........................	32	2,315.4	3,140.4	3,835.2	4,308.6	4,933.5	4,954.8	5,422.3	† 6,787.5	6,723.8	6,629.1	7,276.0	7,567.9
Claims on Central Govt. (Net).......	32an	652.6	505.1	455.3	478.7	409.9	−88.4	−67.1	† 73.7	252.8	−30.9	216.5	259.4
Claims on Local Government........	32b	1.3	1.3	1.3	1.2	3.0	3.8	8.8	† .7	.6	.5	.3	.2
Claims on Nonfin.Pub.Enterprises...	32c	—	—	—	—	—	—	4.7	† —	—	—	—	—
Claims on Private Sector...............	32d	1,661.4	2,634.0	3,378.7	3,828.7	4,520.6	5,039.4	5,475.9	† 5,863.2	5,462.2	5,653.1	6,128.8	6,407.1
Claims on Nonbank Financial Insts.	32g	—	—	—	—	—	—	—	† 849.8	1,008.2	1,006.4	930.3	901.2
Money..................................	34	718.2	746.5	812.0	927.7	933.1	1,007.7	1,160.2	† 1,093.0	1,198.1	1,090.4	1,198.6	1,255.8
Quasi-Money...........................	35	1,820.8	2,819.3	3,180.0	3,615.1	4,089.2	4,465.4	4,794.6	† 4,981.9	5,102.6	5,015.9	5,045.6	5,090.7
Money Market Instruments..............	36aa	12.9	20.6	65.0	127.4	187.6	191.6	241.3	† 327.4	322.6	339.8	415.9	462.1
Liabs. of Central Bank: Securities.....	36ac	235.8	141.4	72.9	188.5	288.9	417.2	238.8	† 527.6	343.2	224.7	287.3	339.6
Restricted Deposits....................	36b	.1	—	.1	—	—	—	—	† .8	.8	.8	.8	3.2
Liab. to Nonbank Financial Insts.......	36j	71.0	77.1	79.3	88.7	138.0	129.2	80.8	† 473.0	414.3	353.8	313.0	318.9
Capital Accounts.......................	37a	347.9	527.8	573.0	671.5	719.9	819.9	875.2	† 890.1	866.9	947.8	1,024.6	1,142.5
Other Items (Net).......................	37r	−402.4	−579.6	−476.5	−716.3	−636.3	−862.0	−588.4	† −95.8	−29.6	−3.4	101.1	36.1
Money plus Quasi-Money..............	35l	2,539.0	3,565.8	3,991.9	4,542.9	5,022.3	5,473.1	5,954.9	† 6,074.9	6,300.6	6,106.4	6,244.2	6,346.5
Nonbank Financial Institutions		Millions of US Dollars: End of Period											
Reserves.................................	40	....	....	....	....	....	....	....	8.3	—	2.6	68.5	1.3
Claims on Mon.Author.:Securities.....	40c	....	....	....	....	....	....	....	148.9	133.0	158.8	133.0	157.6
Foreign Assets.........................	41	....	....	....	....	....	....	....	2.1	27.3	43.7	86.2	170.1
Claims on Banking Institutions........	42e	....	....	....	....	....	....	....	354.6	369.1	304.3	243.2	225.3
Foreign Liabilities......................	46c	....	....	....	....	....	....	....	60.0	73.1	91.1	153.7	201.0
Credit from Monetary Authorities......	46g	....	....	....	....	....	....	....	451.5	419.4	388.3	357.5	326.2
Capital Accounts.......................	47a	....	....	....	....	....	....	....	31.3	35.9	43.8	47.8	53.2
Other Items (Net).......................	47r	....	....	....	....	....	....	....	−29.0	1.1	−13.8	−28.0	−26.1

		1993	1994	1995	1996	1997	1998	1999	2000	2001	2002	2003	2004
Interest Rates						*Percent Per Annum*							
Money Market Rate......................	60b	....	....	....	....	10.43	9.43	10.68	6.93	5.28	4.40	3.86	4.36
Deposit Rate...............................	60l	15.27	13.57	14.37	13.98	11.77	10.32	10.75	9.31	....	....	....	....
Deposit Rate (Fgn. Currency)............	60l.f	....	....	....	8.38	7.68	6.86	6.61	6.50	5.48	3.41	3.37	3.34
Lending Rate...............................	60p	19.42	19.03	19.08	18.57	16.05	14.98	15.46	13.96	....	....	....	....
Lending Rate (Fgn. Currency)..........	60p.f	....	....	....	12.53	10.82	9.93	10.38	10.74	9.60	7.14	6.56	6.30
Prices and Labor						*Index Numbers (2000=100): Period Averages*							
Producer Prices (2000=100)...........	63	....	....	....	....	....	....	93.9	100.0	101.0	98.8	101.3	108.9
Wholesale Prices........................	63a	82.9	89.4	98.7	103.5	104.5	98.3	96.8	100.0	98.4	94.3	96.6	102.0
Consumer Prices...........................	64	68.0	75.2	82.7	90.8	94.9	97.3	97.8	100.0	103.8	105.7	107.9	112.7
						Number in Thousands: Period Averages							
Labor Force................................	67d	....	2,010	2,051	2,140	2,188	2,403	2,445	....	....	....	....	....
Employment...............................	67e	....	1,951	1,973	2,056	2,076	2,228	2,275	2,323	2,451	2,413	2,520	....
Unemployment...........................	67c	† 109	162	163	171	180	176	170	174	184	160	....	....
Unemployment Rate (%)................	67r	† 9.9	7.7	7.7	7.7	8.0	7.3	7.0	7.0	7.0	6.2	6.9	....
Intl. Transactions & Positions						*Millions of US Dollars*							
Exports......................................	70..d	731.7	843.9	998.0	1,024.4	1,371.1	1,256.4	1,176.6	1,332.3	1,213.1	1,237.6	1,255.0	1,474.7
Imports, c.i.f.............................	71..d	1,912.2	2,248.7	2,853.3	2,670.9	2,980.5	3,121.4	3,140.0	3,794.9	3,866.2	3,901.9	4,375.0	4,891.0
Balance of Payments						*Millions of US Dollars: Minus Sign Indicates Debit*							
Current Account, n.i.e....................	78ald	−122.8	−18.0	−261.6	−169.0	−97.8	−90.7	−239.3	−430.5	−150.3	−405.2	−763.6	−611.5
Goods: Exports f.o.b...................	78aad	1,031.8	1,252.3	1,651.1	1,787.4	2,437.1	2,459.5	2,534.3	2,963.2	2,891.6	3,019.7	3,152.6	3,329.6
Goods: Imports f.o.b...................	78abd	−1,994.0	−2,422.3	−3,113.5	−3,029.7	−3,580.3	−3,765.2	−3,890.4	−4,702.8	−4,824.1	−4,884.7	−5,428.0	−5,948.8
Trade Balance...........................	78acd	−962.3	−1,170.0	−1,462.3	−1,242.3	−1,143.2	−1,305.7	−1,356.1	−1,739.6	−1,932.5	−1,865.0	−2,275.4	−2,619.1
Services: Credit...........................	78add	335.5	387.2	388.6	414.4	475.8	588.5	640.4	698.4	703.6	783.3	853.4	971.6
Services: Debit...........................	78aed	−386.7	−428.9	−509.8	−504.6	−628.0	−737.3	−822.9	−933.3	−954.0	−1,023.0	−1,033.4	−1,080.4
Balance on Goods & Services.......	78afd	−1,013.4	−1,211.7	−1,583.5	−1,332.5	−1,295.4	−1,454.5	−1,538.6	−1,974.5	−2,182.9	−2,104.7	−2,455.4	−2,727.9
Income: Credit............................	78agd	30.8	35.5	54.0	44.1	75.1	111.4	112.9	141.3	168.9	159.1	140.4	144.1
Income: Debit..............................	78ahd	−142.4	−130.1	−120.7	−134.4	−238.3	−274.4	−395.1	−394.4	−434.6	−482.5	−562.8	−603.5
Balance on Gds, Serv. & Inc.........	78aid	−1,125.0	−1,306.4	−1,650.2	−1,422.8	−1,458.6	−1,617.5	−1,820.8	−2,227.6	−2,448.6	−2,428.1	−2,877.8	−3,187.3
Current Transfers, n.i.e.: Credit......	78ajd	1,004.7	1,290.9	1,393.2	1,258.6	1,363.6	1,534.1	1,590.5	1,830.3	2,373.5	2,111.1	2,200.2	2,634.4
Current Transfers: Debit................	78akd	−2.5	−2.5	−4.6	−4.8	−2.7	−7.3	−9.0	−33.2	−75.2	−88.2	−85.9	−58.6
Capital Account, n.i.e....................	78bcd	—	—	—	—	11.6	28.6	78.6	109.0	198.9	208.9	112.9	99.7
Capital Account, n.i.e.: Credit........	78bad	—	—	—	—	11.6	28.9	78.8	109.4	199.3	209.4	113.4	100.5
Capital Account: Debit..................	78bbd	—	—	—	....	—	−.3	−.2	−.4	−.4	−.5	−.5	−.8
Financial Account, n.i.e.................	78bjd	73.9	115.8	438.3	358.1	653.2	1,034.3	574.5	287.5	230.3	688.0	1,239.3	426.4
Direct Investment Abroad..............	78bdd	—	—	—	−2.4	—	−1.0	−53.8	5.0	9.7	25.7	−18.6	−7.4
Dir. Invest. in Rep. Econ., n.i.e.......	78bed	16.4	—	38.0	−4.8	59.0	1,103.7	215.9	173.4	278.9	470.0	171.8	465.9
Portfolio Investment Assets...........	78bfd	—	—	—	.5	—	—	−1.7	−8.9	−126.5	−289.2	−263.7	−124.8
Equity Securities........................	78bkd	—	—	—	.5	—	—	—	—	—	—	—	—
Debt Securities..........................	78bld	—	—	—	....	—	—	−1.7	−8.9	−126.5	−289.2	−263.7	−124.8
Portfolio Investment Liab., n.i.e......	78bgd	—	—	68.5	150.0	115.9	−226.4	75.2	−16.8	155.5	554.8	452.9	424.8
Equity Securities........................	78bmd	—	—	....	....	—	—	—	—	2.4	−2.4	—	—
Debt Securities..........................	78bnd	—	—	68.5	150.0	115.9	−226.4	75.2	−16.8	153.1	557.2	452.9	424.8
Financial Derivatives Assets...........	78bwd	....	....	....	....	....	....	....	....	....	....	....	....
Financial Derivatives Liabilities.......	78bxd	....	....	....	....	....	....	....	....	....	....	....	....
Other Investment Assets................	78bhd	18.5	−8.7	24.2	4.7	−19.9	12.2	−126.9	−245.2	−629.1	−223.7	8.0	−153.0
Monetary Authorities..................	78bod	14.4	—	35.0	—	—	—	—	—	—	—	—	—
General Government...................	78bpd	—	—	—	—	—	—	—	—	—	—	—	—
Banks.......................................	78bqd	4.1	−8.7	−10.2	—	2.1	−8.0	−4.6	−146.4	−391.3	−83.1	133.7	−19.7
Other Sectors............................	78brd	—	—	−.6	4.7	−21.9	20.2	−122.3	−98.8	−237.8	−140.6	−125.7	−133.3
Other Investment Liab., n.i.e.........	78bid	39.0	124.5	307.5	210.2	498.2	145.7	465.8	380.0	541.8	150.4	888.9	−179.1
Monetary Authorities..................	78bsd	−91.1	−147.2	38.2	51.2	27.9	−72.2	−2.1	−19.5	−30.8	−27.7	76.7	−40.8
General Government...................	78btd	115.4	177.0	46.4	162.8	154.6	162.9	51.4	83.3	201.0	217.6	33.2	−144.8
Banks.......................................	78bud	14.7	94.7	219.9	−3.2	130.8	−20.4	35.0	120.0	278.3	139.2	491.5	214.0
Other Sectors............................	78bvd	—	—	3.1	−.6	184.9	75.5	381.5	196.2	93.3	−178.7	287.5	−207.5
Net Errors and Omissions................	78cad	107.6	15.4	−28.4	−24.2	−204.4	−668.9	−206.0	−11.5	−456.6	−615.2	−272.4	45.4
Overall Balance........................	78cbd	58.6	113.3	148.3	164.8	362.7	303.3	207.8	−45.5	−177.7	−123.5	316.2	−40.0
Reserves and Related Items.............	79dad	−58.6	−113.3	−148.3	−164.8	−362.7	−303.3	−207.8	45.5	177.7	123.5	−316.2	40.0
Reserve Assets...........................	79dbd	−111.9	−113.3	−148.3	−164.8	−362.7	−303.3	−207.8	45.5	177.7	123.5	−316.2	40.0
Use of Fund Credit and Loans.......	79dcd	—	—	—	—	—	—	—	—	—	—	—	—
Exceptional Financing..................	79ded	53.3	—	—	—	—	—	—	—	—	—	—	—

		1993	1994	1995	1996	1997	1998	1999	2000	2001	2002	2003	2004
International Investment Position							*Millions of US Dollars*						
Assets....................................	79aad	....	....	....	1,771.3	2,153.8	2,445.6	2,832.4	3,004.0	3,309.9	4,688.1	5,527.7	6,394.7
Direct Investment Abroad..............	79abd	—	—	—	55.7	55.7	56.7	110.5	103.9	64.3	34.0	146.4	97.0
Portfolio Investment.....................	79acd	—	—	—	—	—	—	2.1	11.0	152.5	595.8	859.7	1,057.7
Equity Securities....................	79add	....	....	....	—	—	—	—	—	17.8	260.1	260.4	257.9
Debt Securities.....................	79aed	....	....	....	—	—	—	2.1	11.0	134.7	335.7	599.3	799.8
Financial Derivatives.....................	79ald	....	....	....									
Other Investment.......................	79afd	51.4	59.9	70.1	615.9	635.8	623.5	747.5	995.8	1,381.5	1,659.3	1,556.9	1,703.1
Monetary Authorities................	79agd	....	....	....									
General Government.................	79ahd	....	....	....	22.0	22.0	22.0	22.0	22.0	—	—	—	—
Banks.................................	79aid	....	....	....	115.8	113.8	121.8	123.5	273.1	658.5	738.8	601.2	607.9
Other Sectors........................	79ajd	....	....	....	478.0	500.0	479.7	602.0	700.7	723.0	920.5	955.7	1,095.2
Reserve Assets...........................	79akd	707.3	812.9	959.6	1,099.7	1,462.3	1,765.4	1,972.3	1,893.2	1,711.6	2,399.0	2,964.7	3,536.9
Liabilities................................	79lad	....	....	....	4,335.6	4,990.5	6,025.5	6,854.7	7,358.3	8,340.2	9,743.9	11,364.5	11,983.1
Dir. Invest. in Rep. Economy..........	79lbd	—	—	—	421.2	480.3	1,583.9	1,815.2	2,000.6	2,240.9	3,133.7	3,306.6	3,772.5
Portfolio Investment.....................	79lcd	—	—	—	241.0	357.0	130.5	205.0	202.8	352.6	948.6	1,402.5	1,569.6
Equity Securities....................	79ldd	....	....	....	—	—	—	—	—	2.4	—	—	—
Debt Securities.....................	79led	....	....	....	241.0	357.0	130.5	205.0	202.8	350.2	948.6	1,402.5	1,569.6
Financial Derivatives.....................	79lld	....	....	....									
Other Investment.......................	79lfd	2,042.7	2,198.1	2,530.1	3,673.3	4,153.3	4,311.1	4,834.5	5,154.9	5,746.7	5,661.6	6,655.4	6,641.0
Monetary Authorities................	79lgd	....	....	....	220.4	237.5	165.4	202.4	181.9	153.6	126.0	202.3	176.2
General Government.................	79lhd	....	....	....	2,075.8	2,194.9	2,350.1	2,423.2	2,448.3	2,678.0	2,510.7	2,629.0	2,626.4
Banks.................................	79lid	....	....	....	406.2	531.0	516.5	548.3	673.8	950.0	1,104.0	1,596.3	1,810.7
Other Sectors........................	79ljd	....	....	....	970.9	1,189.9	1,279.1	1,660.6	1,850.9	1,965.1	1,921.0	2,227.8	2,027.7
Government Finance						*Millions of Colones: Year Ending December 31*							
Deficit (-) or Surplus....................	80	−1,284.4	† −521.8	−455.2	−1,841.3	−1,102.1	−1,920.9	−2,456.0	−2,658.6	....	....	....	....
Total Revenue and Grants..............	81y	7,215.7	† 9,529.7	11,436.9	12,248.9	12,204.7	13,202.2	12,570.2	13,857.3	....	....	....	....
Revenue.................................	81	....	....	....	....	....	13,104.2	12,471.4	13,030.6	....	....	....	....
Grants...................................	81z	....	....	....	....	....	98.0	98.8	826.7	....	....	....	....
Exp. & Lending Minus Repay.........	82z	8,500.1	† 10,051.5	11,892.1	14,090.2	13,306.8	15,123.1	15,026.2	16,515.9	....	....	....	....
Expenditure............................	82	8,314.0	† 9,970.9	11,755.7	14,070.3	13,533.6	15,227.1	15,094.3	16,628.1	....	....	....	....
Lending Minus Repayments.........	83	186.1	† 80.6	136.4	19.9	−226.8	−104.0	−68.1	−112.2	....	....	....	....
Total Financing............................	80h	....	† 521.9	455.2	1,841.3	1,102.1	1,920.1	2,456.0	2,658.7	....	....	....	....
Domestic................................	84a	....	† −844.2	−542.3	−86.2	−553.4	2,159.8	1,296.7	1,300.6	....	....	....	....
Foreign..................................	85a	1,305.0	† 1,366.1	997.5	1,927.5	1,655.5	−239.7	1,159.3	1,358.1	....	....	....	....
Use of Cash Balances.................	87	....	−527.8	−313.6						....	....	....	....
Total Debt by Residence...............	88	25,292.0	† 21,305.8	22,066.6	23,968.0	24,759.7	24,663.7	27,714.1	30,634.4	....	....	....	....
Domestic................................	88a	9,995.6	† 8,463.0	8,226.3	7,883.7	7,460.9	7,119.9	8,015.2	10,687.0	....	....	....	....
Foreign..................................	89a	15,296.4	† 12,842.8	13,840.3	16,084.3	17,298.8	17,543.8	19,698.9	19,947.4	....	....	....	....
National Accounts							*Millions of Colones*						
Househ.Cons.Expend.,incl.NPISHs....	96f	52,672	61,658	72,725	79,765	85,266	89,356	93,740	101,117	107,136	110,374	116,198	125,801
Government Consumption Expend...	91f	5,178	5,942	7,188	8,443	8,847	10,248	10,935	11,696	12,677	13,097	14,112	14,535
Gross Fixed Capital Formation..........	93e	10,700	13,067	15,566	14,275	15,672	17,527	17,532	19,471	19,857	20,596	21,794	21,538
Changes in Inventories....................	93i	476	865	1,107	−559	−936	927	394	−8	292	−324	—	—
Exports of Goods and Services..........	90c	11,643	14,126	17,997	19,034	25,243	26,062	27,213	31,508	31,220	33,014	34,882	37,715
Imports of Goods and Services (-).....	98c	20,517	24,909	31,406	30,644	36,607	38,987	40,685	48,794	50,320	51,527	56,258	61,131
Gross Domestic Product (GDP)........	99b	60,152	70,749	83,177	90,313	97,484	105,134	109,128	114,989	120,862	125,230	130,728	138,459
Net Primary Income from Abroad.....	98.n	−976	−804	−839	−1,063	−1,430	−1,427	−2,470	−2,216	−2,325	−2,830	−3,567	−4,354
Gross National Income (GNI)...........	99a	59,168	69,936	82,328	89,241	96,045	103,698	106,649	112,765	118,528	122,391	127,151	134,096
GDP Volume 1990 Prices................	99b.p	49,782	53,281	56,721	57,688	60,138	62,393	64,545	65,934	67,023	68,517	69,759	70,835
GDP Volume (2000=100)................	99bvp	75.5	80.8	86.0	87.5	91.2	94.6	97.9	100.0	101.7	103.9	105.8	107.4
GDP Deflator (2000=100)...............	99bip	69.3	76.1	84.1	89.8	92.9	96.6	96.9	100.0	103.4	104.8	107.5	112.1
						Millions: Midyear Estimates							
Population..............................	99z	5.43	5.55	5.67	5.79	5.91	6.04	6.16	6.28	6.40	6.52	6.64	6.76

		1993	1994	1995	1996	1997	1998	1999	2000	2001	2002	2003	2004
Exchange Rates						*Francs per SDR: End of Period*							
Official Rate...............	aa	404.89	† 780.44	728.38	753.06	807.94	791.61	† 896.19	918.49	935.39	850.37	771.76	747.90
						Francs per US Dollar: End of Period(ae)Period Average(rf)							
Official Rate...............	ae	294.77	† 534.60	490.00	523.70	598.81	562.21	† 652.95	704.95	744.31	625.50	519.36	481.58
Official Rate...............	rf	283.16	† 555.20	499.15	511.55	583.67	589.95	† 615.70	711.98	733.04	696.99	581.20	528.28
						Index Numbers (2000=100): Period Averages							
Nominal Effective Exchange Rate.....	nec	166.22	103.40	108.20	107.70	104.29	106.11	104.59	100.00	100.71	102.65	107.12	109.01
Real Effective Exchange Rate...........	rec	115.97	83.21	97.78	98.57	96.40	103.55	100.41	100.00	105.91	114.38	125.64	131.06
Fund Position						*Millions of SDRs: End of Period*							
Quota...................	2f.s	24.30	24.30	24.30	24.30	24.30	24.30	32.60	32.60	32.60	32.60	32.60	32.60
SDRs....................	1b.s	.28	.01	.01	.01	—	.01	—	.09	.79	.44	.03	.44
Reserve Position in the Fund...........	1c.s	—	—	—	—	—	—	—	—	—	—	—	—
Total Fund Cred.&Loans Outstg........	2tl	11.96	13.43	12.70	11.93	9.75	7.64	5.80	3.77	1.75	.83	.18	—
International Liquidity						*Millions of US Dollars Unless Otherwise Indicated: End of Period*							
Total Reserves minus Gold..............	1l.d	.48	.39	.04	.52	4.93	.80	3.35	23.01	70.85	88.54	237.69	944.98
SDRs....................	1b.d	.38	.02	.01	.01	—	.01	—	.12	.99	.60	.04	.68
Reserve Position in the Fund..........	1c.d	—	—	—	—	—	—	—	—	—	—	—	—
Foreign Exchange.........................	1d.d	.10	.37	.03	.51	4.93	.79	3.35	22.89	69.86	87.94	237.65	944.30
Monetary Authorities: Other Liab......	4..d	11.02	9.16	2.97	.12	.11	4.80	7.46	7.52	6.94	7.53	10.19	10.01
Deposit Money Banks: Assets...........	7a.d	4.07	5.78	5.08	4.92	2.38	18.07	39.45	27.51	41.56	106.01	73.28	110.02
Liabilities....................	7b.d	2.17	2.67	3.56	1.96	6.18	5.22	19.31	14.82	21.88	18.71	4.73	7.65
Monetary Authorities						*Billions of Francs: End of Period*							
Foreign Assets..............................	11	.14	.21	.02	.27	2.95	.45	2.19	16.22	52.74	55.38	123.45	455.08
Claims on Central Government........	12a	12.18	17.84	17.42	17.33	15.86	14.03	20.90	14.24	3.90	2.50	1.44	.79
Claims on Deposit Money Banks......	12e	—	—	—	—	—	—	—	—	—	—	—	—
Claims on Other Banking Insts.........	12f	—	—	—	—	—	—	—	—	—	—	—	—
Reserve Money.............................	14	2.46	4.38	8.72	9.99	10.97	8.79	17.17	25.57	47.45	49.61	120.29	150.53
of which: Currency Outside DMBs..	14a	1.21	3.77	6.78	8.50	6.59	5.79	12.06	15.20	17.63	25.95	35.12	45.73
Foreign Liabilities..........................	16c	8.09	15.38	10.70	9.05	7.94	8.74	10.07	8.77	6.80	5.42	5.43	4.82
Central Government Deposits...........	16d	.17	.06	.07	.08	.48	1.08	1.19	1.92	7.44	6.61	4.03	303.16
Capital Accounts............................	17a	2.55	4.82	4.53	4.63	4.95	4.83	5.56	5.91	6.22	5.90	5.56	5.33
Other Items (Net)...........................	17r	−.95	−6.58	−6.58	−6.15	−5.54	−8.96	−10.90	−11.71	−11.26	−9.66	−10.42	−7.97
Deposit Money Banks						*Billions of Francs: End of Period*							
Reserves.....................................	20	1.25	.62	1.95	1.49	4.38	3.00	5.11	10.37	29.02	22.86	84.37	104.71
Foreign Assets..............................	21	1.20	3.09	2.49	2.57	1.43	10.16	25.76	19.39	30.93	66.31	38.06	52.98
Claims on Central Government........	22a	.05	.23	.25	.51	1.63	.94	.46	1.89	.30	4.14	2.09	5.78
Claims on Nonfin.Pub.Enterprises.....	22c	.44	.72	.72	.96	.80	.72	.03	—	.40	1.45	.86	.76
Claims on Private Sector..................	22d	1.99	2.25	3.40	6.20	12.02	14.13	21.29	27.06	36.49	52.77	50.76	62.08
Claims on Other Banking Insts.........	22f	—	—	—	—	—	—	—	—	—	—	—	—
Claims on Nonbank Financial Insts...	22g	—	—	—	—	—	—	—	—	—	—	—	—
Demand Deposits...........................	24	1.34	2.24	2.73	5.78	7.07	9.19	16.39	23.14	29.88	46.52	78.53	124.71
Time and Savings Deposits..............	25	.69	1.76	2.05	2.23	4.38	5.86	6.72	9.58	16.42	25.81	40.79	36.65
Foreign Liabilities..........................	26c	.41	1.24	1.60	.92	3.67	2.94	12.61	9.90	15.97	11.56	2.46	3.64
Long-Term Foreign Liabilities..........	26cl	.23	.19	.14	.11	.03	—	—	.55	.31	.15	—	.05
Central Government Deposits...........	26d	.53	.46	.88	1.86	3.10	6.12	10.76	6.49	24.82	50.83	33.85	35.42
Credit from Monetary Authorities.....	26g	—	—	—	—	—	—	—	—	—	—	—	—
Capital Accounts............................	27a	1.67	1.36	2.30	1.26	3.02	5.26	6.67	7.69	13.44	16.02	21.43	29.49
Other Items (Net)...........................	27r	.07	−.33	−.91	−.43	−1.03	−.42	−.50	1.37	−3.70	−3.36	−.92	−3.64
Monetary Survey						*Billions of Francs: End of Period*							
Foreign Assets (Net).......................	31n	−7.39	−13.51	−9.94	−7.23	−7.26	−1.07	5.27	16.40	60.58	104.57	153.62	499.56
Domestic Credit............................	32	13.96	20.52	20.83	23.05	26.72	22.66	30.73	34.78	8.84	3.41	17.27	−269.17
Claims on Central Govt. (Net).........	32an	11.53	17.55	16.72	15.90	13.90	7.78	9.41	7.72	−28.05	−50.81	−34.35	−332.01
Claims on Nonfin.Pub.Enterprises...	32c	.44	.72	.72	.96	.80	.72	.03	—	.40	1.45	.86	.76
Claims on Private Sector.............	32d	1.99	2.25	3.40	6.20	12.02	14.13	21.29	27.06	36.49	52.77	50.76	62.08
Claims on Other Banking Insts.......	32f	—	—	—	—	—	—	—	—	—	—	—	—
Claims on Nonbank Financial Inst..	32g	—	—	—	—	—	.03	—	—	—	—	—	—
Money.......................................	34	2.55	6.01	9.51	14.28	13.66	14.99	28.45	38.33	48.31	73.28	114.45	170.53
Quasi-Money...............................	35	.69	1.76	2.05	2.23	4.38	5.86	6.72	9.58	16.42	25.81	40.79	36.65
Other Items (Net).........................	37r	3.34	−.73	−.66	−.68	1.59	.75	.84	3.27	4.69	8.90	15.65	23.21
Money plus Quasi-Money................	35l	3.24	7.76	11.56	16.51	18.04	20.85	35.16	47.91	64.73	99.08	155.24	207.18
Interest Rates						*Percent Per Annum*							
Discount Rate (End of Period)...........	60	11.50	† 7.75	8.60	7.75	7.50	7.00	7.60	7.00	6.50	6.30	6.00	6.00
Deposit Rate.................................	60l	7.75	8.08	5.50	5.46	5.00	5.00	5.00	5.00	5.00	5.00	5.00	5.00
Lending Rate.................................	60p	17.46	17.50	16.00	22.00	22.00	22.00	22.00	22.00	20.67	18.00	18.00	18.00
Prices						*Index Numbers (1990=100): Period Averages*							
Consumer Prices...........................	64	† 93.49	127.54	....	....	....	....	....	....	....	....	....	....
Intl. Transactions & Positions						*Millions of Francs*							
Exports.......................................	70	16,060	34,420	42,683	89,682	289,204	258,957	436,735	780,819	....	....	....	....
Imports, c.i.f.................................	71	17,000	20,514	24,897	149,384	192,800	187,167	261,784	320,800	....	....	....	....

		1993	1994	1995	1996	1997	1998	1999	2000	2001	2002	2003	2004
Balance of Payments					*Millions of US Dollars: Minus Sign Indicates Debit*								
Current Account, n.i.e.	78ald	2.84	−.38	−123.40	−344.04	....	....	....	....	....	....	....	....
Goods: Exports f.o.b.	78aad	61.06	62.00	89.93	175.31	....	....	....	....	....	....	....	....
Goods: Imports f.o.b.	78abd	−51.03	−36.95	−120.57	−292.04	....	....	....	....	....	....	....	....
Trade Balance	78acd	10.03	25.05	−30.64	−116.73	....	....	....	....	....	....	....	....
Services: Credit	78add	8.99	3.36	4.18	4.88	....	....	....	....	....	....	....	....
Services: Debit	78aed	−38.53	−23.82	−75.54	−184.58	....	....	....	....	....	....	....	....
Balance on Goods & Services	78afd	−19.51	4.59	−102.00	−296.43	....	....	....	....	....	....	....	....
Income: Credit	78agd	—	—	.10	.16	....	....	....	....	....	....	....	....
Income: Debit	78ahd	−9.30	−8.75	−25.03	−45.18	....	....	....	....	....	....	....	....
Balance on Gds, Serv. & Inc.	78aid	−28.80	−4.16	−126.93	−341.44	....	....	....	....	....	....	....	....
Current Transfers, n.i.e.: Credit	78ajd	37.76	5.67	6.83	4.03	....	....	....	....	....	....	....	....
Current Transfers: Debit	78akd	−6.11	−1.89	−3.30	−6.62	....	....	....	....	....	....	....	....
Capital Account, n.i.e.	78bcd	—	—	—	—	....	....	....	....	....	....	....	....
Capital Account, n.i.e.: Credit	78bad	—	—	—	—	....	....	....	....	....	....	....	....
Capital Account: Debit	78bbd	....	....	—	—	....	....	....	....	....	....	....	....
Financial Account, n.i.e.	78bjd	13.95	−15.04	101.56	313.75	....	....	....	....	....	....	....	....
Direct Investment Abroad	78bdd	—	—	—	—	....	....	....	....	....	....	....	....
Dir. Invest. in Rep. Econ., n.i.e.	78bed	22.30	17.00	126.92	376.18	....	....	....	....	....	....	....	....
Portfolio Investment Assets	78bfd	—	—	—	—	....	....	....	....	....	....	....	....
Equity Securities	78bkd	—	—	—	—	....	....	....	....	....	....	....	....
Debt Securities	78bld	—	—	—	—	....	....	....	....	....	....	....	....
Portfolio Investment Liab., n.i.e.	78bgd	—	—	—	—	....	....	....	....	....	....	....	....
Equity Securities	78bmd	—	—	—	—	....	....	....	....	....	....	....	....
Debt Securities	78bnd	—	—	—	—	....	....	....	....	....	....	....	....
Financial Derivatives Assets	78bwd	....	....	....	....	....	....	....	....	....	....	....	....
Financial Derivatives Liabilities	78bxd	....	....	....	....	....	....	....	....	....	....	....	....
Other Investment Assets	78bhd	—	—	—	—	....	....	....	....	....	....	....	....
Monetary Authorities	78bod	....	....	....	....	....	....	....	....	....	....	....	....
General Government	78bpd	—	—	—	—	....	....	....	....	....	....	....	....
Banks	78bqd	—	—	—	—	....	....	....	....	....	....	....	....
Other Sectors	78brd	—	—	—	—	....	....	....	....	....	....	....	....
Other Investment Liab., n.i.e.	78bid	−8.35	−32.04	−25.36	−62.43	....	....	....	....	....	....	....	....
Monetary Authorities	78bsd	—	—	—	—	....	....	....	....	....	....	....	....
General Government	78btd	−3.12	−7.32	−13.95	−3.84	....	....	....	....	....	....	....	....
Banks	78bud	1.05	−1.98	1.84	−1.57	....	....	....	....	....	....	....	....
Other Sectors	78bvd	−6.28	−22.73	−13.25	−57.02	....	....	....	....	....	....	....	....
Net Errors and Omissions	78cad	−27.17	−2.93	10.33	24.82	....	....	....	....	....	....	....	....
Overall Balance	78cbd	−10.38	−18.36	−11.52	−5.46	....	....	....	....	....	....	....	....
Reserves and Related Items	79dad	10.38	18.36	11.52	5.46	....	....	....	....	....	....	....	....
Reserve Assets	79dbd	−1.02	−.92	−8.98	−3.59	....	....	....	....	....	....	....	....
Use of Fund Credit and Loans	79dcd	3.79	2.08	−1.11	−1.11	....	....	....	....	....	....	....	....
Exceptional Financing	79ded	7.61	17.20	21.61	10.17	....	....	....	....	....	....	....	....
National Accounts					*Millions of Francs*								
Househ.Cons.Expend.,incl.NPISHs.	96f	25,150	24,300	18,646	49,826	157,939	....	....	....	....	....	....	....
Government Consumption Expend.	91f	7,996	6,938	10,791	18,274	27,811	....	....	....	....	....	....	....
Gross Fixed Capital Formation	93e	17,620	55,126	64,528	176,141	197,359	....	....	....	....	....	....	....
Changes in Inventories	93i	531	−20	−9	−11	−13	....	....	....	....	....	....	....
Exports of Goods and Services	90c	19,837	36,308	45,088	105,083	292,158	....	....	....	....	....	....	....
Imports of Goods and Services (-)	98c	25,361	42,332	59,662	211,429	358,965	....	....	....	....	....	....	....
Gross Domestic Product (GDP)	99b	49,100	66,500	83,000	140,000	307,000	260,200	445,700	865,500	1,302,300	1,523,700	1,729,500	2,757,400
GDP Volume 1985 Prices	99b.p	46,323	53,358	61,956	89,995	182,536	....	....	....	....	....	....	....
GDP Volume (1995=100)	99bvp	74.8	86.1	100.0	145.3	294.6	....	....	....	....	....	....	....
GDP Deflator (1995=100)	99bip	79.1	93.0	100.0	116.1	125.5	....	....	....	....	....	....	....
					Millions: Midyear Estimates								
Population	99z	.38	.39	.40	.41	.42	.43	.44	.45	.46	.47	.48	.49

		1993	1994	1995	1996	1997	1998	1999	2000	2001	2002	2003	2004
Exchange Rates						*Nakfa per SDR: End of Period*							
Official Rate	aa	6.8678	8.6861	9.3946	9.2403	† 9.6134	10.6967	13.1761	13.2897	17.3397	19.2117	20.4878	21.4121
					Nakfa per US Dollar: End of Period (ae) Period Average (rf)								
Official Rate	ae	5.0000	5.9500	6.3200	6.4260	† 7.1250	7.5969	9.6000	10.2000	13.7975	14.1313	13.7875	13.7875
Official Rate	rf	5.0047	5.4702	6.1642	6.3577	† 6.8373	7.3619	8.1526	9.6250	11.3095	13.9582	13.8779	13.7875
Fund Position						*Millions of SDRs: End of Period*							
Quota	2f.s	—	11.5	11.5	11.5	11.5	11.5	15.9	15.9	15.9	15.9	15.9	15.9
SDRs	1b.s	—	—	—	—	—	—	—	—	—	—	—	—
Reserve Position in the Fund	1c.s	—	—	—	—	—	—	—	—	—	—	—	—
Total Fund Cred.&Loans Outstg	2tl	—	—	—	—	—	—	—	—	—	—	—	—
International Liquidity					*Millions of US Dollars Unless Otherwise Indicated: End of Period*								
Total Reserves minus Gold	1l.d	....	....	40.5	81.3	199.4	23.1	34.2	25.5	39.8	30.3	24.7	34.7
SDRs	1b.d	—	—	—	—	—	—	—	—	—	—	—	—
Reserve Position in the Fund	1c.d	—	—	—	—	—	—	—	—	—	—	—	—
Foreign Exchange	1d.d	....	....	40.5	81.3	199.4	23.1	34.2	25.5	39.7	30.3	24.7	34.7
Gold (Million Fine Troy Ounces)	1ad	....	....	....	....	.104	.157	.085	.039	.039	—	—	—
Gold (National Valuation)	1and	....	....	20.9	27.2	42.6	44.7	19.7	10.4	10.5	—	—	—
Monetary Authorities:Other Assets	3..d	....	....	43.7	36.1	2.5	1.0	1.6	1.5	1.4	1.3	1.9	1.9
Other Liab	4..d	....	....	19.0	18.8	16.3	16.3	30.1	33.6	28.9	26.9	44.5	36.8
Banking Institutions: Assets	7a.d	....	....	317.9	309.3	50.0	72.6	88.9	89.5	153.3	187.2	227.8	237.3
Liabilities	7b.d	....	....	4.4	2.4	2.6	2.2	1.7	13.5	7.1	2.9	3.0	2.6
Monetary Authorities						*Millions of Nakfa: End of Period*							
Foreign Assets	11	....	....	664	930	1,742	522	534	383	713	452	366	505
Claims on Central Government	12a	....	....	1,013	1,820	2,009	1,788	3,794	4,155	4,043	5,450	7,232	7,676
Claims on Private Sector	12d	....	....	40	60	102	75	95	161	117	188	155	156
Claims on Banking Institutions	12e	....	....	—	100	235	381	371	448	653	887	236	249
Reserve Money	14	....	....	1,340	2,494	4,701	3,065	4,239	4,563	4,407	5,152	5,849	6,210
of which: Currency Outside Banks	14a	....	....	—	—	574	825	1,138	1,468	1,868	2,279	2,765	3,253
Foreign Currency Deposits	15	....	....	157	157	22	23	77	100	108	48	20	18
Foreign Liabilities	16c	....	....	13	15	13	11	113	139	194	193	310	189
Central Government Deposits	16d	....	....	131	203	401	369	926	604	806	912	991	1,030
Capital Accounts	17a	....	....	117	148	213	350	470	796	718	752	844	1,013
Other Items (Net)	17r	....	....	−41	−108	−1,261	−1,051	−1,030	−1,056	−707	−80	−23	127
Banking Institutions						*Millions of Nakfa: End of Period*							
Reserves	20	....	....	1,340	2,494	4,049	2,154	2,897	3,055	2,447	2,827	2,973	2,906
Foreign Assets	21	....	....	2,009	1,987	356	551	854	913	2,115	2,679	3,141	3,272
Claims on Central Government	22a	....	....	—	—	135	2,262	3,207	4,639	5,397	6,076	5,714	7,408
Claims on State and Local Govts	22b	....	....	—	—	—	—	—	—	—	—	—	—
Claims on Nonfin.Pub.Enterprises	22c	....	....	461	459	385	265	697	402	349	365	392	492
Claims on Private Sector	22d	....	....	592	1,468	1,639	2,475	1,775	1,823	2,367	2,726	3,372	4,024
Demand Deposits	24	....	....	1,135	1,474	1,355	1,456	2,133	2,425	3,081	3,667	4,036	4,491
Time, Savings,& Fgn.Currency Dep	25	....	....	1,927	2,264	2,961	3,624	4,641	5,566	7,579	9,316	10,708	11,890
Foreign Liabilities	26c	....	....	28	15	19	17	16	138	98	42	41	36
Central Government Deposits	26d	....	....	121	196	244	378	362	372	435	379	435	631
Credit from Monetary Authorities	26g	....	....	—	100	235	362	364	474	760	886	147	147
Capital Accounts	27a	....	....	159	245	169	253	297	353	413	441	844	1,361
Other Items (Net)	27r	....	....	1,032	2,114	1,581	1,619	1,614	1,504	308	−59	−618	−454
Banking Survey						*Millions of Nakfa: End of Period*							
Foreign Assets (Net)	31n	....	....	2,632	2,886	2,067	1,046	1,258	1,018	2,536	2,896	3,157	3,552
Domestic Credit	32	....	....	1,853	3,407	3,625	6,120	8,304	10,230	11,042	13,514	15,441	18,094
Claims on Central Govt. (Net)	32an	....	....	760	1,421	1,499	3,304	5,713	7,818	8,200	10,235	11,521	13,422
Claims on State and Local Govts	32b	....	....	—	—	—	—	—	—	—	—	—	—
Claims on Nonfin.Pub.Enterprises	32c	....	....	461	459	385	265	697	402	349	365	392	492
Claims on Private Sector	32d	....	....	632	1,528	1,740	2,551	1,870	1,985	2,483	2,913	3,528	4,180
Money	34	....	....	1,135	1,474	2,007	2,367	3,465	3,930	5,035	5,982	6,932	7,806
Quasi-Money	35	....	....	2,084	2,422	2,983	3,646	4,718	5,666	7,686	9,364	10,728	11,907
Capital Accounts	37a	....	....	276	392	382	604	767	1,149	1,131	1,193	1,688	2,374
Other Items (Net)	37r	....	....	991	2,006	321	549	612	502	−275	−129	−750	−440
Money plus Quasi-Money	35l	....	....	3,219	3,896	4,989	6,013	8,184	9,596	12,721	15,347	17,659	19,713
Money (National Definitions)						*Millions of Nakfa: End of Period*							
Reserve Money	19mb	....	....	1,340	2,494	4,701	3,065	4,239	4,563	4,407	5,152	5,844	6,210
M1	59ma	....	....	1,135	1,474	2,007	2,365	3,348	3,915	5,027	5,982	6,927	7,799
M2	59mb	....	....	3,013	3,622	4,693	5,636	7,437	8,712	10,941	13,146	14,841	16,535

Balance of Payments		1993	1994	1995	1996	1997	1998	1999	2000	2001	2002	2003	2004
		Millions of US Dollars: Minus Sign Indicates Debit											
Current Account, n.i.e.	78ald	107.2	123.7	−31.6	−59.8	5.1	−292.7	−208.8	−104.7	....	....	....	....
Goods: Exports f.o.b.	78aad	41.9	78.0	86.0	98.0	56.8	28.1	20.7	36.8	....	....	....	....
Goods: Imports f.o.b.	78abd	−348.9	−488.9	−453.5	−552.8	−525.3	−508.3	−510.2	−471.4	....	....	....	....
Trade Balance	78acd	−307.0	−410.9	−367.5	−454.8	−468.5	−480.2	−489.5	−434.6	....	....	....	....
Services: Credit	78add	107.7	89.9	48.6	104.9	159.2	81.8	47.6	60.9	....	....	....	....
Services: Debit	78aed	−1.0	−7.7	−44.7	−53.7	−100.3	−187.1	−104.6	−28.4	....	....	....	....
Balance on Goods & Services	78afd	−200.4	−328.7	−363.7	−403.6	−409.6	−585.5	−546.5	−402.0	....	....	....	....
Income: Credit	78agd	....	3.6	7.8	8.3	10.8	11.6	8.5	9.1	....	....	....	....
Income: Debit	78ahd	....	....	....	−15.6	−14.4	−7.3	−2.1	−10.5	....	....	....	....
Balance on Gds, Serv. & Inc.	78aid	−200.4	−325.1	−355.9	−410.9	−413.2	−581.2	−540.2	−403.4	....	....	....	....
Current Transfers, n.i.e.: Credit	78ajd	307.7	465.3	324.9	354.6	423.5	293.3	346.5	306.1	....	....	....	....
Current Transfers: Debit	78akd	−.1	−16.5	−.6	−3.5	−5.3	−4.9	−15.1	−7.3	....	....	....	....
Capital Account, n.i.e.	78bcd	....	....	....	....	....	2.7	.6	....	....	....	....	....
Capital Account, n.i.e.: Credit	78bad	....	....	....	....	....	2.7	.6	....	....	....	....	....
Capital Account: Debit	78bbd	....	....	....	....	....	....	....	....	....	....	....	....
Financial Account, n.i.e.	78bjd	−105.9	−7.9	69.2	181.4	255.4	197.0	196.3	63.2	....	....	....	....
Direct Investment Abroad	78bdd	....	....	....	....	....	....	....	....	....	....	....	....
Dir. Invest. in Rep. Econ., n.i.e.	78bed	....	....	....	36.7	41.1	148.5	83.2	27.9	....	....	....	....
Portfolio Investment Assets	78bfd	....	....	....	....	....	....	....	....	....	....	....	....
Equity Securities	78bkd	....	....	....	....	....	....	....	....	....	....	....	....
Debt Securities	78bld	....	....	....	....	....	....	....	....	....	....	....	....
Portfolio Investment Liab., n.i.e.	78bgd	....	....	....	....	....	....	....	....	....	....	....	....
Equity Securities	78bmd	....	....	....	....	....	....	....	....	....	....	....	....
Debt Securities	78bnd	....	....	....	....	....	....	....	....	....	....	....	....
Financial Derivatives Assets	78bwd	....	....	....	....	....	....	....	....	....	....	....	....
Financial Derivatives Liabilities	78bxd	....	....	....	....	....	....	....	....	....	....	....	....
Other Investment Assets	78bhd	−108.4	−39.8	60.8	137.3	184.5	−20.0	−26.2	−25.9	....	....	....	....
Monetary Authorities	78bod	....	....	....	....	....	....	....	....	....	....	....	....
General Government	78bpd	....	....	....	....	....	....	....	....	....	....	....	....
Banks	78bqd	−108.4	−39.8	60.8	137.3	184.5	−15.3	−23.9	−25.1	....	....	....	....
Other Sectors	78brd	....	....	....	....	....	−4.7	−2.4	−.8	....	....	....	....
Other Investment Liab., n.i.e.	78bid	2.5	31.9	8.4	7.4	29.9	68.5	139.3	61.2	....	....	....	....
Monetary Authorities	78bsd	—	—	—	—	—	—	—	—	....	....	....	....
General Government	78btd	2.5	32.9	8.4	7.4	29.9	59.3	128.9	52.3	....	....	....	....
Banks	78bud	....	....	....	....	....	10.1	10.4	8.8	....	....	....	....
Other Sectors	78bvd	—	−1.0	—	—	—	−.9	....	—	....	....	....	....
Net Errors and Omissions	78cad	31.7	−61.5	−40.5	−64.5	−140.4	−66.5	12.8	−22.9	....	....	....	....
Overall Balance	78cbd	33.1	54.3	−2.9	57.1	120.1	−159.5	.9	−64.3	....	....	....	....
Reserves and Related Items	79dad	−33.1	−54.3	2.9	−57.1	−120.1	159.5	−.9	64.3	....	....	....	....
Reserve Assets	79dbd	−33.1	−54.3	2.9	−57.1	−120.1	159.5	−.9	61.2	....	....	....	....
Use of Fund Credit and Loans	79dcd	—	—	—	—	—	—	—	—	....	....	....	....
Exceptional Financing	79ded	....	....	....	....	....	....	....	3.2	....	....	....	....
		Millions: Midyear Estimates											
Population	99z	3.06	3.07	3.10	3.15	3.22	3.31	3.43	3.56	3.71	3.88	4.05	4.23

Estonia 939

		1993	1994	1995	1996	1997	1998	1999	2000	2001	2002	2003	2004
Exchange Rates						*Krooni per SDR: End of Period*							
Official Rate	aa	19.062	18.088	17.038	17.888	19.343	18.882	21.359	21.915	22.234	20.306	18.440	17.815
						Krooni per US Dollar: End of Period (ae) Period Average (rf)							
Official Rate	ae	13.878	12.390	11.462	12.440	14.336	13.410	15.562	16.820	17.692	14.936	12.410	11.471
Official Rate	rf	13.223	12.991	11.465	12.038	13.882	14.075	14.678	16.969	17.478	16.612	13.856	12.596
Fund Position						*Millions of SDRs: End of Period*							
Quota	2f.s	46.50	46.50	46.50	46.50	46.50	46.50	65.20	65.20	65.20	65.20	65.20	65.20
SDRs	1b.s	41.56	1.09	.20	.12	.01	.05	.99	.01	.03	.05	.05	.05
Reserve Position in the Fund	1c.s	—	.01	.01	.01	.01	.01	.01	.01	.01	.01	.01	.01
Total Fund Cred.&Loans Outstg	2tl	41.85	41.85	61.81	54.15	40.01	21.31	18.41	14.53	10.66	—	—	—
International Liquidity						*Millions of US Dollars Unless Otherwise Indicated: End of Period*							
Total Reserves minus Gold	1l.d	386.12	443.35	579.91	636.82	757.72	810.60	853.49	920.64	820.24	1,000.42	1,373.36	1,788.23
SDRs	1b.d	57.08	1.58	.29	.17	.01	.07	1.36	.02	.03	.07	.08	.08
Reserve Position in the Fund	1c.d	—	.01	.01	.01	.01	.01	.01	.01	.01	.01	.01	.01
Foreign Exchange	1d.d	329.04	441.76	579.61	636.64	757.70	810.53	852.12	920.62	820.20	1,000.34	1,373.27	1,788.13
Gold (Million Fine Troy Ounces)	1ad	.0080	.0080	.0080	.0080	.0080	.0080	.0080	.0080	.0080	.0080	.0080	.0080
Gold (National Valuation)	1and	3.22	3.61	3.19	3.03	2.39	2.37	2.38	2.25	2.29	2.83	3.44	3.61
Monetary Authorities:Other Liab	4..d	65.89	60.88	65.84	48.52	24.75	1.02	3.29	1.04	7.03	39.11	44.25
Banks: Assets	7a.d	103.10	243.80	322.58	320.69	563.45	483.29	563.67	615.88	874.72	1,104.93	1,375.84	2,387.66
Liabilities	7b.d	14.34	55.98	140.83	337.97	913.11	884.58	879.19	976.66	989.70	1,582.58	2,808.67	5,137.62
Monetary Authorities						*Millions of Krooni: End of Period*							
Foreign Assets	11	† 5,418.0	5,540.6	6,688.0	7,954.2	10,900.8	10,908.7	13,334.3	15,539.2	14,573.2	14,995.0	17,194.7	20,625.9
Claims on Central Government	12a	† 45.2		3.0	48.5	4.1	3.0	3.1	3.4	1.3	.2	.2	—
Claims on Nonfin.Pub.Enterprises	12c	† 63.5	14.8	.8									
Claims on Private Sector	12d	† 4.6	8.2	14.5	44.2	44.1	57.2	66.5	69.5	74.8	78.8	75.4	54.7
Claims on Banks	12e	† 473.7	480.9	194.0	168.0	82.4	280.3	267.3	9.8	8.0	9.0		
Reserve Money	14	† 3,786.6	4,225.1	5,066.7	6,190.9	8,526.7	9,070.3	11,496.0	13,207.1	11,910.2	11,732.1	13,450.4	16,672.1
of which: Currency Outside Banks	14a	† 2,380.6	3,071.3	3,803.6	4,268.5	4,588.5	4,538.6	5,711.3	6,201.3	6,951.9	6,994.9	7,139.7	7,714.2
Foreign Liabilities	16c	† 1,712.2	1,511.2	1,807.7	1,572.3	1,128.8	416.1	403.0	373.8	255.4	104.9	485.3	507.6
Central Government Deposits	16d	† 5.1	.2	.1	.3	355.5	6.4	27.1	7.2	7.8	5.6	5.1	4.9
Capital Accounts	17a	† 1,342.2	1,256.1	1,223.2	1,325.9	1,881.1	2,276.5	2,141.3	2,424.1	2,889.7	3,377.5	3,512.0	3,692.8
Other Items (Net)	17r	† −841.1	−948.0	−1,197.4	−874.7	−860.7	−520.1	−396.2	−390.3	−405.8	−137.1	−182.4	−196.7
Banking Institutions						*Millions of Krooni: End of Period*							
Reserves	20	1,437.7	1,208.4	1,293.1	1,922.5	3,885.3	4,509.5	5,790.9	6,787.1	4,896.6	4,678.0	6,243.0	8,875.8
Foreign Assets	21	1,430.8	3,020.7	3,697.4	3,989.4	8,077.7	6,480.9	8,771.9	10,358.9	15,475.5	16,503.6	17,073.6	27,389.1
Claims on Central Government	22a	293.2	297.0	345.4	614.0	561.1	303.6	404.5	445.4	445.5	480.2	538.1	475.4
Claims on Local Government	22b	1.5	108.3	303.9	159.9	547.2	651.5	767.6	822.9	1,296.9	1,959.1	2,311.9	2,380.8
Claims on Nonfin.Pub.Enterprises	22c	416.7	346.0	334.5	304.6	328.6	225.8	372.5	262.7	141.8	245.0	221.4	651.5
Claims on Private Sector	22d	2,409.8	4,176.0	6,041.3	10,088.3	16,908.5	18,532.4	19,810.4	22,134.0	26,246.5	31,433.7	41,693.3	59,943.0
Claims on Nonbank Financial Insts	22g	8.7	12.2	628.9	2,036.4	5,127.7	6,336.8	6,489.2	12,370.2	16,106.6	22,644.3	27,104.3	30,004.5
Demand Deposits	24	2,847.4	3,248.6	4,399.6	7,019.6	9,357.2	8,577.3	11,600.5	14,456.8	17,967.9	20,225.5	23,603.3	28,388.2
Time, Savings,& Fgn.Currency Dep	25	1,241.0	2,088.8	2,616.6	3,560.9	6,467.6	8,208.1	9,024.3	12,292.5	15,855.1	18,099.7	19,497.4	22,073.3
Money Market Instruments	26aa	.6	220.2	11.5		44.8	85.9	266.3	296.5	508.9	999.2	280.7	276.4
Bonds	26ab	—	40.0	82.5	67.5	70.0	65.6	113.0	41.5	14.1	310.2	612.9	1,055.7
Foreign Liabilities	26c	199.0	693.5	1,614.2	4,204.4	13,090.4	11,862.2	13,682.0	16,427.2	17,509.9	23,638.1	34,854.5	58,934.1
Central Government Deposits	26d	527.8	1,180.9	1,894.8	1,735.4	2,472.6	1,881.5	1,345.4	2,342.5	2,311.4	3,268.3	3,006.8	4,457.0
Counterpart Funds	26e	114.3	112.0	102.0									
Government Lending Funds	26f	151.8	487.1	819.5	987.7	739.7	555.2	540.7	450.9	306.4	240.4	222.4	149.3
Credit from Monetary Authorities	26g	337.9	401.7	88.6	47.9	23.2	14.5	11.4	8.4	6.3	6.6	7.5	—
Capital Accounts	27a	776.8	994.4	1,834.9	2,519.4	5,372.5	7,845.3	8,459.5	8,340.0	10,432.5	11,239.7	12,195.2	13,738.4
Other Items (Net)	27r	−198.5	−298.6	−819.7	−1,027.6	−2,202.0	−2,055.1	−2,636.0	−1,475.3	−303.2	−83.8	905.0	647.7
Banking Survey						*Millions of Krooni: End of Period*							
Foreign Assets (Net)	31n	† 4,937.5	6,356.5	6,963.5	6,166.8	4,759.3	5,111.3	8,021.2	9,097.1	12,283.4	7,755.6	−1,071.5	−11,426.7
Domestic Credit	32	† 2,813.3	3,781.4	5,777.4	11,663.5	20,796.6	24,222.7	26,541.6	33,758.5	41,994.3	53,567.5	68,933.1	89,048.2
Claims on Central Govt. (Net)	32an	† −194.5	−884.1	−1,546.6	−1,073.3	−2,262.9	−1,581.4	−964.9	−1,901.0	−1,872.4	−2,793.4	−2,473.4	−3,986.4
Claims on Local Government	32b	† 1.5	108.3	303.9	159.9	547.2	651.5	767.6	822.9	1,296.9	1,959.1	2,311.9	2,380.8
Claims on Nonfin.Pub.Enterprises	32c	† 480.1	360.8	335.3	304.6	328.6	225.8	372.5	262.7	141.8	245.0	221.4	651.5
Claims on Private Sector	32d	† 2,414.5	4,184.3	6,055.8	10,132.5	16,952.7	18,589.7	19,876.9	22,203.5	26,321.2	31,512.5	41,768.7	59,997.6
Claims on Nonbank Financial Inst.	32g	† 111.7	12.2	628.9	2,139.7	5,231.0	6,337.1	6,489.5	12,370.5	16,106.7	22,644.3	27,104.5	30,004.7
Money	34	† 5,228.2	6,319.9	8,203.2	11,289.7	13,998.0	13,119.8	17,335.5	20,884.1	24,948.2	27,274.5	30,806.6	36,177.5
Quasi-Money	35	† 1,301.0	2,191.8	2,650.5	3,562.9	6,467.6	8,208.1	9,054.3	12,292.5	15,855.1	18,099.7	19,497.4	22,073.3
Money Market Instruments	36aa	† .6	220.2	11.5	—	44.8	85.9	266.3	296.5	508.9	999.2	280.7	276.4
Bonds	36ab	† —	40.0	82.5	67.5	70.0	65.6	113.0	41.5	14.1	310.2	612.9	1,055.7
Counterpart Funds	36e	† 114.3	112.0	102.0	—								
Government Lending Funds	36f	† 151.8	487.1	819.5	987.7	739.7	555.2	540.7	450.9	306.4	240.4	222.4	149.3
Capital Accounts	37a	† 2,119.1	2,250.4	3,058.1	3,845.3	7,253.6	10,121.8	10,600.8	10,764.1	13,322.2	14,617.2	15,707.2	17,431.2
Other Items (Net)	37r	† −1,164.3	−1,483.5	−2,186.4	−1,922.7	−3,017.9	−2,822.4	−3,347.7	−1,873.9	−677.1	−218.2	734.3	458.1
Money plus Quasi-Money	35l	† 6,529.2	8,511.7	10,853.7	14,852.6	20,465.6	21,327.9	26,389.9	33,176.6	40,803.2	45,374.2	50,304.0	58,250.8
Interest Rates						*Percent Per Annum*							
Money Market Rate	60b	....	5.67	4.94	3.53	6.45	11.66	5.39	† 5.68	5.31	3.88	2.92	2.50
Deposit Rate	60l		11.51	8.74	6.05	6.19	8.07	4.19	3.76	4.03	2.74	2.40	2.16
Lending Rate	60p	33.66	24.65	19.01	14.87	11.76	15.06	11.09	7.43	7.78	6.70	5.51	5.66
Prices and Labor						*Index Numbers (2000=100): Period Averages*							
Share Prices	62	....	....	....	....	200.5	118.3	75.9	100.0	91.6	122.5	171.0	242.0
Producer Prices	63	....	59.3	74.5	85.5	† 92.6	96.6	95.4	100.0	104.4	104.8	105.1	108.1
Consumer Prices	64	† 33.2	49.1	63.2	77.8	† 86.0	93.1	96.1	100.0		79.5	111.0	114.4
Harmonized CPI (2002=100)	64h	....	....	....		....	....				100.0	101.4	104.5
						Number in Thousand							
Labor Force	67d	....	....	734	....	708	71				53	661	....
Employment	67e	708	693	656	646	† 648	6			578	586	594	596
Unemployment	67c	50	56	68	68	† 66			90	83	67	66	64
Unemployment Rate (%)	67r	6.5	7.6	9.7	9.9	† 9.7	9	12.2	13.6	12.6	10.3	10.0	9.7

		1993	1994	1995	1996	1997	1998	1999	2000	2001	2002	2003	2004
Intl. Transactions & Positions					*Millions of Krooni*								
Exports...........................	70	10,642	† 16,941	21,040	25,024	40,662	43,952	43,178	53,324	57,528	56,920	62,523	73,860
Imports, c.i.f....................	71	11,848	† 21,525	29,101	38,887	61,610	64,897	60,248	72,309	75,163	79,468	89,709	106,860
Imports, f.o.b....................	71.v	10,944	† 19,883	26,881	35,920	56,909	59,945	55,651	66,792	69,428	....	....	....
Balance of Payments					*Millions of US Dollars: Minus Sign Indicates Debit*								
Current Account, n.i.e...............	78ald	21.6	−166.3	−157.8	−398.2	−561.7	−478.4	−294.6	−294.0	−338.8	−716.6	−1,116.3	−1,431.7
Goods: Exports f.o.b................	78aad	811.7	1,225.0	1,696.3	1,811.8	2,289.6	2,690.1	2,453.1	3,311.4	3,359.7	3,532.2	4,608.3	5,970.3
Goods: Imports f.o.b................	78abd	−956.6	−1,581.4	−2,362.3	−2,830.6	−3,413.7	−3,805.4	−3,330.6	−4,079.5	−4,148.4	−4,621.3	−6,162.1	−7,936.3
Trade Balance...................	78acd	−144.9	−356.5	−666.0	−1,018.8	−1,124.1	−1,115.2	−877.5	−768.1	−788.7	−1,089.2	−1,553.8	−1,966.1
Services: Credit...................	78add	334.6	515.3	876.8	1,107.9	1,318.0	1,479.6	1,489.7	1,499.0	1,649.3	1,712.7	2,234.1	2,824.1
Services: Debit....................	78aed	−259.4	−410.2	−497.7	−589.6	−726.6	−910.1	−917.6	−936.3	−1,069.2	−1,126.1	−1,380.9	−1,737.5
Balance on Goods & Services.......	78afd	−69.7	−251.3	−286.9	−500.6	−532.7	−545.7	−305.4	−205.4	−208.6	−502.5	−700.6	−879.4
Income: Credit....................	78agd	26.9	37.3	63.6	112.2	115.1	133.5	133.8	117.6	171.3	203.1	247.3	433.6
Income: Debit.....................	78ahd	−40.8	−66.9	−60.8	−110.3	−260.8	−214.5	−235.5	−321.7	−453.5	−530.2	−786.0	−1,151.3
Balance on Gds, Serv. & Inc........	78aid	−83.6	−280.9	−284.1	−498.7	−678.4	−626.7	−407.1	−409.6	−490.8	−829.6	−1,239.3	−1,597.2
Current Transfers: Credit..........	78ajd	108.4	120.3	134.5	116.7	135.3	172.9	153.7	144.7	181.4	174.3	232.6	457.3
Current Transfers: Debit...........	78akd	−3.2	−5.7	−8.2	−16.3	−18.6	−24.6	−41.3	−29.1	−29.4	−61.3	−109.5	−291.8
Capital Account, n.i.e..............	78bcd	—	−.6	−.8	−.7	−.2	1.8	1.2	16.5	5.1	19.0	47.6	83.7
Capital Account, n.i.e.: Credit.......	78bad	—	.5	1.4	.2	.7	2.1	1.4	16.8	5.5	20.1	55.7	90.5
Capital Account: Debit.............	78bbd		−1.1	−2.2	−.8	−.9	−.3	−.2	−.2	−.4	−1.0	−8.2	−6.8
Financial Account, n.i.e.............	78bjd	188.9	167.2	233.4	540.8	802.8	508.1	418.2	392.9	269.4	751.5	1,274.8	1,700.7
Direct Investment Abroad............	78bdd	−6.2	−2.4	−2.5	−40.0	−136.6	−6.3	−82.9	−63.4	−200.1	−131.9	−156.1	−268.2
Dir. Invest. in Rep. Econ., n.i.e......	78bed	162.2	214.4	201.5	150.2	266.2	580.5	305.2	387.3	542.5	284.5	919.0	1,048.6
Portfolio Investment Assets.........	78bfd	−.4	−22.5	−33.2	−52.7	−165.0	−10.9	−132.3	15.5	−118.8	−192.0	−394.3	−378.7
Equity Securities..............	78bkd	−.4	−14.5	5.1	−15.0	−87.8	35.1	12.9	3.5	14.3	.3	−75.5	−232.4
Debt Securities................	78bld		−8.0	−38.2	−37.6	−77.2	−46.0	−145.2	12.1	−133.2	−192.3	−318.8	−146.3
Portfolio Investment Liab., n.i.e......	78bgd	.2	8.4	11.1	198.0	427.5	1.1	153.3	75.6	84.7	344.9	561.2	1,114.4
Equity Securities..............	78bmd	.1	8.4	9.9	172.2	127.8	25.7	235.4	−28.5	31.9	53.3	110.6	176.2
Debt Securities................	78bnd	.1	—	1.2	25.7	299.7	−24.6	−82.1	104.1	52.8	291.6	450.6	938.3
Financial Derivatives Assets........	78bwd	....	....	....	....	....	....	....	−4.7	−.1	−2.6	−9.9	−2.9
Financial Derivatives Liabilities.......	78bxd	....	....	....	....	....	....	....	5.4	−2.1	−1.4	8.1	2.6
Other Investment Assets............	78bhd	−144.7	−146.7	−98.9	−7.2	−334.2	−168.5	−110.3	−166.7	−220.3	50.5	−154.4	−901.2
Monetary Authorities............	78bod	5.7	.1	.1	.1	—	—	−18.3	−9.6	−11.3	−2.8	.1	−.8
General Government.............	78bpd	−17.1	.4	−.4	−3.3	−24.7	−61.9	−60.8	43.1	35.9	−23.4	39.8	−12.6
Banks.........................	78bqd	−44.7	−102.8	−41.1	20.9	−195.9	61.3	−53.8	−77.0	−219.3	−28.3	−87.0	−674.6
Other Sectors..................	78brd	−88.6	−44.4	−57.5	−24.9	−113.5	−167.9	22.5	−123.3	−25.6	105.1	−107.3	−213.2
Other Investment Liab., n.i.e........	78bid	177.8	115.9	155.4	292.5	744.8	112.1	285.2	143.8	183.6	399.4	501.2	1,086.1
Monetary Authorities............	78bsd	14.9	6.2	−13.5	−6.7	−2.5	−1.1	7.3	1.7	−5.4	32.5	43.5	17.9
General Government.............	78btd	77.3	19.8	61.0	31.2	−3.3	4.4	9.8	−17.2	−7.3	−53.1	29.3	−15.4
Banks.........................	78bud	7.2	37.5	82.2	173.6	492.4	−17.3	188.3	76.8	59.4	344.1	336.3	948.0
Other Sectors..................	78bvd	78.4	52.3	25.7	94.3	258.2	126.0	79.8	82.5	136.9	75.9	92.0	135.8
Net Errors and Omissions............	78cad	−45.9	17.2	8.7	−35.6	−25.1	5.9	−5.5	12.2	22.3	15.3	−36.7	−81.5
Overall Balance..................	78cbd	164.6	17.5	83.5	106.3	215.9	37.3	119.3	127.6	−41.9	69.3	169.4	271.2
Reserves and Related Items............	79dad	−164.6	−17.5	−83.5	−106.3	−215.9	−37.3	−119.3	−127.6	41.9	−69.3	−169.4	−271.2
Reserve Assets...................	79dbd	−212.4	−17.5	−112.9	−95.2	−196.4	−11.7	−115.3	−122.4	46.9	−55.2	−169.4	−271.2
Use of Fund Credit and Loans........	79dcd	47.7	—	29.4	−11.1	−19.4	−25.6	−4.0	−5.2	−4.9	−14.0	—	—
Exceptional Financing..................	79ded	....	....	....	....	....	....	....	....	....	....	....	....
International Investment Position					*Millions of US Dollars*								
Assets.........................	79aad	....	....	....	1,344.1	2,045.5	2,300.4	2,415.1	2,614.0	2,920.5	4,078.2	6,081.7	8,694.5
Direct Investment Abroad..............	79abd	....	....	....	107.7	215.3	198.4	281.2	259.1	441.8	676.0	1,028.3	1,418.8
Portfolio Investment..................	79acd	....	....	....	121.0	249.3	211.2	305.2	271.8	262.1	824.1	1,504.5	2,154.7
Equity Securities..................	79add	....	....	....	26.1	98.5	31.5	12.4	26.4	22.5	36.8	154.3	447.7
Debt Securities..................	79aed	....	....	....	94.9	150.9	179.7	292.9	245.4	239.6	787.3	1,350.2	1,707.0
Financial Derivatives..................	79ald	....	....	....	—	—	—	—	9.1	8.7	13.0	26.9	32.1
Other Investment..................	79afd	....	....	....	475.9	820.4	1,077.4	972.4	1,151.0	1,385.3	1,561.8	2,137.4	3,292.6
Monetary Authorities..................	79agd	....	....	....	—	—	—	—	1.0	6.9	.9	.9	1.9
General Government..................	79ahd	....	....	....	4.6	26.7	97.7	129.6	87.5	98.0	52.7	37.3	54.4
Banks..................	79aid	....	....	....	246.9	392.8	360.9	374.4	411.8	601.1	782.6	1,043.4	1,857.8
Other Sectors..................	79ajd	....	....	....	224.3	400.8	618.7	468.4	650.8	679.2	725.5	1,055.8	1,378.5
Reserve Assets..................	79akd	....	....	....	639.6	760.5	813.5	856.2	922.9	822.5	1,003.2	1,384.7	1,796.2
Liabilities..................	79lad	....	....	....	1,974.9	3,757.8	4,451.9	5,199.6	5,389.5	6,017.7	8,488.0	13,366.9	20,097.8
Dir. Invest. in Rep. Economy..........	79lbd	....	....	....	824.6	1,147.9	1,821.7	2,467.3	2,644.7	3,159.9	4,226.4	7,001.1	10,067.3
Portfolio Investment..................	79lcd	....	....	....	117.4	954.2	702.9	771.8	761.4	764.3	1,378.9	2,373.4	4,500.6
Equity Securities..................	79ldd	....	....	....	76.3	572.9	301.2	500.7	431.6	403.0	634.9	949.6	1,942.0
Debt Securities..................	79led	....	....	....	41.1	381.3	401.7	271.2	329.8	361.3	744.0	1,423.9	2,558.7
Financial Derivatives..................	79lld	....	....	....					10.2	6.3	5.9	16.8	20.7
Other Investment..................	79lfd	....	....	....	1,033.0	1,655.6	1,927.4	1,960.4	1,973.1	2,087.2	2,876.7	3,975.5	5,509.1
Monetary Authorities..................	79lgd	....	....	....	151.4	55.7	30.8	25.8	22.1	14.4	17.1	39.1	44.3
General Government..................	79lhd	....	....	....	175.3	161.4	173.6	178.6	153.6	155.6	113.9	173.2	170.3
Banks..................	79lid	....	....	....	299.1	747.1	692.7	778.2	809.0	827.8	1,362.5	1,971.1	3,174.2
Other Sectors..................	79ljd	....	....	....	407.1	691.5	1,030.3	977.8	988.6	1,089.5	1,383.3	1,792.2	2,120.3
Government Finance					*Millions of Krooni: Year Ending December 31*								
Deficit (-) or Surplus..................	80	−458.5	416.8	−233.6	−433.7	1,632.4	−42.3	−120.9	137.4	2,492.0	....	....	....
Revenue..................	81	6,320.3	10,566.8	14,649.3	17,544.8	22,360.5	24,006.5	23,397.4	26,474.5	29,602.4	....	....	....
Grants Received..................	81z	243.7	—	132.0	—	25.0	124.0	302.5	258.5	624.0	....	....	....
Expenditure..................	82	6,088.5	9,590.3	14,523.5	17,713.7	20,551.8	24,103.3	26,815.5	27,373.3	29,236.5	....	....	....
Lending Minus Repayments..........	83	934.0	559.7	491.4	264.8	201.3	69.5	−2,994.7	−777.7	−1,502.1	....	....	....
Financing														
Domestic..................	84a	....	....	−150.2	49.3	−974.0	524.0	469.7	−87.4	−2,177.9	....	....	....
Foreign..................	85a	....	....	383.8	384.4	−658.4	−481.7	−348.8	−50.0	−314.1	....	....	....
Total Debt														
Domestic..................	88a	....	....	....	682.1	572.5	413.4	338.8	210.0	180.0	....	....	....
Foreign..................	89a	....	....	....	2,584.6	2,770.9	2,715.6	3,175.1	2,505.6	2,411.1	....	....	....

Estonia 939

		1993	1994	1995	1996	1997	1998	1999	2000	2001	2002	2003	2004
							Millions of Krooni						
National Accounts													
Househ.Cons.Expend.,incl.NPISHs....	96f	13,238	18,295	23,971	33,123	39,974	45,648	47,359	52,873	59,775	68,254	73,966	78,918
Government Consumption Expend...	91f	5,232	8,121	11,780	14,187	15,570	17,046	18,333	18,775	20,193	22,425	24,643	26,870
Gross Fixed Capital Formation.........	93e	5,440	8,299	11,168	14,535	18,984	23,366	20,239	23,769	28,134	33,555	36,761	40,180
Changes in Inventories....................	93i	541	181	305	564	1,882	311	132	2,060	2,336	3,610	3,991	3,985
Exports of Goods and Services.........	90c	15,200	22,500	29,476	35,220	50,297	58,707	59,062	82,112	87,725	86,830	94,667	110,965
Imports of Goods and Services (-).....	98c	16,128	25,755	32,754	41,382	57,779	66,381	62,853	85,511	91,304	95,152	104,250	121,815
Gross Domestic Product (GDP).........	99b	22,820	31,349	43,061	55,895	68,576	78,028	81,776	92,938	104,459	116,915	127,334	141,493
Net Primary Income from Abroad.....	98.n	−185	−378	28	26	−2,011	−1,164	−1,506	−3,483	−4,926	−5,423	−7,411	−8,986
Gross National Income (GNI)............	99a	22,635	30,971	43,089	55,922	66,566	76,864	80,270	89,454	99,533	111,492	119,923	132,508
Net Current Transf.from Abroad.......	98t	1,392	1,486	1,446	1,210	1,620	2,080	1,654	1,959	2,660	1,858	1,710	1,811
Gross Nat'l Disposable Inc.(GNDI)....	99i	24,163	32,482	44,553	57,203	67,937	79,258	81,787	91,193	102,072	113,304	119,370	131,983
Gross Saving................................	99s	5,558	6,041	8,784	9,822	12,642	16,250	16,232	19,766	22,226	22,672	23,024	28,531
Consumption of Fixed Capital..........	99cf	4,127	5,257	7,015	8,655	10,718	13,366	14,817	11,896	18,290	18,691	17,981	18,096
GDP Volume 2000 Prices.................	99b.p	68,977	67,844	70,916	74,036	82,253	85,906	86,170	92,938	98,945	106,111	113,208	122,049
GDP Volume (2000=100)................	99bvp	74.2	73.0	76.3	79.7	88.5	92.4	92.7	100.0	106.5	114.2	121.8	131.3
GDP Deflator (2000=100)...............	99bip	33.1	46.2	60.7	75.5	83.4	90.8	94.9	100.0	105.6	110.2	112.5	115.9
							Millions: Midyear Estimates						
Population...............................	99z	1.51	1.48	1.45	1.42	1.41	1.39	1.38	1.37	1.36	1.35	1.34	1.34

		1993	1994	1995	1996	1997	1998	1999	2000	2001	2002	2003	2004
Exchange Rates						*Birr per SDR: End of Period*							
Official Rate	aa	6.8678	8.6861	9.3946	9.2403	9.2613	10.5644	11.1640	10.8324	10.7555	11.6659	12.8100	13.4365
						Birr per US Dollar: End of Period (ae) Period Average (rf)							
Official Rate	ae	5.0000	5.9500	6.3200	6.4260	6.8640	7.5030	8.1340	8.3140	8.5583	8.5809	8.6206	8.6519
Official Rate	rf	5.0000	5.4650	6.1583	6.3517	6.7093	7.1159	7.9423	8.2173	8.4575	8.5678	8.5997	8.6362
Fund Position						*Millions of SDRs: End of Period*							
Quota	2f.s	98.3	98.3	98.3	98.3	98.3	98.3	133.7	133.7	133.7	133.7	133.7	133.7
SDRs	1b.s	.2	.3	.2	—	.1	.1		—	.1	.1	.1	.3
Reserve Position in the Fund	1c.s	7.0	7.0	7.0	7.1	7.1	7.1	7.1	7.1	7.1	7.2	7.2	7.2
Total Fund Cred.&Loans Outstg	2tl	35.3	49.4	49.4	64.2	64.2	76.1	69.0	59.1	84.0	105.4	105.8	118.0
International Liquidity						*Millions of US Dollars Unless Otherwise Indicated: End of Period*							
Total Reserves minus Gold	1l.d	455.8	544.2	771.5	732.2	501.1	511.1	458.5	306.3	433.2	881.7	955.6	1,496.8
SDRs	1b.d	.3	.4	.3		.1	.1	.1	—	.2	.1	.1	.5
Reserve Position in the Fund	1c.d	9.6	10.2	10.5	10.1	9.5	10.0	9.7	9.2	9.0	9.7	10.7	11.2
Foreign Exchange	1d.d	445.9	533.6	760.8	722.0	491.4	501.0	448.7	297.1	424.1	871.9	944.8	1,485.1
Gold (Million Fine Troy Ounces)	1ad	.113	.113	.113	.301	.301	.303	.303	.205	.205	.246	—	—
Gold (National Valuation)	1and	11.4	11.4	11.4	.4	.4	.4	.3	.3	.3	.3	—	—
Monetary Authorities: Other Liab	4..d	252.2	319.0	286.3	279.3	4.2	.3	.9	.4	.3	3.7	.1	.3
Deposit Money Banks: Assets	7a.d	236.2	533.3	454.2	435.9	680.8	652.9	542.1	597.3	624.4	698.9	862.3	333.9
Liabilities	7b.d	68.6	108.3	192.3	221.5	225.4	218.4	250.2	227.0	180.8	187.5	210.6	59.2
Other Banking Insts.: Assets	7e.d	1.0	3.5	2.5	8.6	9.3	9.2	6.8	5.7	.6	1.3	2.6	6.3
Liabilities	7f.d	58.9	52.8	45.0	39.0	36.9	27.2	28.1	29.5	28.9	29.5	29.5	32.9
Monetary Authorities						*Millions of Birr: End of Period*							
Foreign Assets	11	2,680.0	3,413.5	4,891.8	4,722.6	3,456.1	3,893.3	3,666.4	2,535.9	3,614.8	7,682.8	9,134.2	13,184.7
Claims on Central Government	12a	8,244.0	8,443.5	8,182.1	7,694.6	8,549.3	9,218.4	10,301.1	13,896.5	12,524.9	15,100.4	15,665.4	22,726.2
Claims on Other Financial Insts	12f	457.8	464.0	465.1	465.1	465.1	465.1	466.1	395.3	395.3	395.3	395.3	395.3
Reserve Money	14	6,421.1	7,084.4	7,976.6	6,664.0	7,249.7	6,362.5	6,050.6	8,394.9	7,639.8	10,301.8	11,858.5	22,472.8
of which: Currency Outside DMBs	14a	4,776.0	5,380.4	5,718.0	5,401.5	4,964.3	3,977.7	4,506.8	4,590.8	4,870.3	5,686.3	6,874.3	8,274.5
Foreign Liabilities	16c	1,503.3	2,327.4	2,273.5	2,388.0	622.9	806.4	777.6	643.6	906.1	1,261.7	1,357.0	1,587.5
Central Government Deposits	16d	2,141.6	2,082.8	2,229.8	2,294.8	2,544.4	2,630.9	3,086.5	2,812.4	4,381.9	7,165.9	6,966.0	6,496.9
Central Government Lending Funds	16f	—	—	—	—	792.3	1,041.6	1,650.7	1,381.3	460.4	584.8	436.8	736.9
Capital Accounts	17a	478.4	728.4	879.5	1,159.7	1,198.1	1,272.5	1,422.3	1,646.1	2,100.5	2,674.5	3,763.4	3,452.7
Other Items (Net)	17r	837.5	98.0	179.6	375.9	63.1	1,462.9	1,445.9	1,949.4	1,046.2	1,189.8	813.3	1,559.4
Deposit Money Banks						*Millions of Birr: End of Period*							
Reserves	20	1,634.8	1,665.7	2,197.1	1,227.7	2,173.1	2,312.2	1,314.6	3,197.1	2,213.0	3,833.2	4,913.9	14,239.6
Foreign Assets	21	1,180.9	3,173.0	2,870.6	2,801.3	4,673.0	4,899.0	4,409.5	4,965.7	5,344.1	5,997.4	7,433.3	2,888.6
Claims on Central Government	22a	2,617.1	2,617.2	2,773.0	2,612.7	2,361.0	2,629.4	5,233.7	5,556.2	7,499.5	9,242.8	10,992.2	6,060.0
Claims on Nonfin.Pub.Enterprises	22c	1,515.2	1,630.0	1,630.0	1,794.6	1,589.7	1,612.2	798.3	775.5	851.8	646.8	829.5	2,592.5
Claims on Private Sector	22d	1,349.7	1,988.1	3,706.0	6,448.6	8,007.1	8,693.6	11,216.2	11,836.2	12,187.0	12,057.4	12,946.0	14,432.6
Claims on Other Financial Insts	22f	—	—	—	279.0	248.0	217.0	486.5	435.0	389.5	369.5	407.2	570.9
Demand Deposits	24	2,788.0	3,803.5	3,711.4	3,761.7	5,967.2	6,501.2	7,143.8	8,004.3	8,484.8	10,185.4	11,659.4	13,933.1
Time, Savings,& Fgn.Currency Dep	25	2,845.0	3,637.4	4,549.7	6,069.6	7,241.7	7,554.9	8,474.9	10,001.9	11,609.8	12,976.3	14,612.6	17,292.9
Foreign Liabilities	26c	343.2	644.4	1,215.6	1,423.5	1,547.3	1,638.5	2,035.0	1,887.1	1,547.3	1,608.7	1,815.3	512.0
Central Government Deposits	26d	411.8	619.2	810.1	736.7	91.9	75.9	56.3	72.2	57.4	86.8	107.4	858.6
Central Government Lending Funds	26f	—	—	—	43.4	51.1	21.0	44.2	36.4	45.5	45.7	33.1	26.2
Capital Accounts	27a	330.2	439.2	567.4	1,270.0	1,351.4	1,808.8	1,939.5	2,235.6	2,553.8	2,528.8	2,801.7	3,087.6
Other Items (Net)	27r	1,579.4	1,930.2	2,322.4	1,859.0	2,801.2	2,763.1	3,765.1	4,528.3	4,186.3	4,715.5	6,492.7	5,073.7
Monetary Survey						*Millions of Birr: End of Period*							
Foreign Assets (Net)	31n	2,014.4	3,614.7	4,273.2	3,712.3	5,958.9	6,347.3	5,263.2	4,970.9	6,505.6	10,809.8	13,395.3	13,973.7
Domestic Credit	32	11,630.5	12,440.8	13,716.4	16,263.1	18,583.8	20,128.9	25,359.2	30,010.1	29,408.6	30,559.6	34,166.0	39,423.6
Claims on Central Govt. (Net)	32an	8,307.7	8,358.7	7,915.3	7,275.8	8,273.9	9,140.9	12,392.0	16,568.1	15,585.0	17,090.6	19,584.2	21,430.6
Claims on Nonfin.Pub.Enterprises	32c	1,515.2	1,630.0	1,630.0	1,794.6	1,589.7	1,612.2	798.3	775.5	851.8	646.8	829.5	2,592.5
Claims on Private Sector	32d	1,349.7	1,988.1	3,706.0	6,448.6	8,007.1	8,693.6	11,216.2	11,836.2	12,187.0	12,057.4	12,949.7	14,434.2
Claims on Other Financial Insts	32f	457.8	464.0	465.1	744.1	713.1	682.1	952.6	830.3	784.8	764.8	802.5	966.2
Money	34	7,564.1	9,184.0	9,429.5	9,174.0	11,024.0	10,511.0	12,067.0	13,225.7	13,865.2	16,557.9	18,595.1	22,312.0
Quasi-Money	35	2,845.0	3,637.4	4,549.7	6,069.6	7,241.7	7,554.9	8,474.9	10,001.9	11,609.8	12,976.3	14,612.6	17,292.9
Central Government Lending Funds	36f				43.4	843.4	1,062.6	1,694.9	1,417.6	505.9	630.5	469.9	763.1
Capital Accounts	37a	808.6	1,167.6	1,447.0	2,429.6	2,549.5	3,081.3	3,361.7	3,881.7	4,654.3	5,203.3	6,565.1	6,540.3
Other Items (Net)	37r	2,427.2	2,066.5	2,563.5	2,258.8	2,884.2	4,266.5	5,023.8	6,454.1	5,279.0	6,001.3	7,318.6	6,489.0
Money plus Quasi-Money	35l	10,409.1	12,821.4	13,979.2	15,243.6	18,265.6	18,065.9	20,541.9	23,227.5	25,475.0	29,534.2	33,207.6	39,604.9
Other Banking Institutions						*Millions of Birr: End of Period*							
Reserves	40	369.3	233.7	9.7	8.1	22.7	8.1	57.6	28.4	17.4	18.0	31.4	72.6
Foreign Assets	41	5.1	20.7	15.9	55.4	63.5	69.1	55.3	47.1	4.9	11.2	22.0	54.7
Claims on Central Government	42a	131.6	123.2	—	—	—	—	42.5	42.5	34.0	34.0	104.6	96.6
Claims on Nonfin.Pub.Enterprises	42c			492.4	574.8	396.7	299.7	257.9	226.0	200.8	197.4	175.7	179.5
Claims on Private Sector	42d	954.3	1,205.7	701.4	1,173.4	1,773.5	2,475.8	3,222.0	3,540.1	2,401.7	2,036.3	1,966.4	2,330.5
Claims on Deposit Money Banks	42e	—	—	—	—	—	—	170.3	110.4	83.4	118.4	146.6	156.4
Demand Deposits	44	—	—	9.5	22.2	31.3	15.8	26.0	11.4	5.6	3.4	6.3	13.5
Time and Savings Deposits	45	529.9	538.1	48.6	2.1	234.4	681.4	734.6	717.4	678.3	742.3	711.7	685.1
Foreign Liabilities	46c	294.6	314.4	284.6	250.4	253.5	204.3	228.2	245.6	247.5	253.1	254.2	284.3
Central Govt. Lending Funds	46f	100.0	54.1	13.8	13.8	13.8	13.8	13.8	13.8	13.8	83.8	72.6	72.6
Credit from Monetary Authorities	46g	457.8	464.0	465.1	465.1	465.1	465.1	387.8	387.8	387.8	387.8	381.4	381.4
Credit from Deposit Money Banks	46h	97.0	116.1	414.6	685.5	958.1	894.5	1,410.1	1,646.7	456.3	369.5	408.2	565.3
Capital Accounts	47a	−106.4	101.1	176.9	390.8	361.2	380.5	397.4	415.0	429.3	425.9	524.9	520.3
Other Items (Net)	47r	87.4	−4.5	−193.7	−18.2	−61.0	197.3	607.7	557.0	523.6	149.6	87.4	367.9

2005, International Monetary Fund : *International Financial Statistics Yearbook*

Ethiopia 644

		1993	1994	1995	1996	1997	1998	1999	2000	2001	2002	2003	2004
Banking Survey						*Millions of Birr: End of Period*							
Foreign Assets (Net)	51n	1,724.9	3,321.0	4,004.5	3,517.3	5,768.9	6,212.1	5,090.4	4,772.4	6,262.9	10,567.9	13,163.2	13,744.1
Domestic Credit	52	12,258.6	13,305.7	14,445.1	17,267.2	20,040.9	22,222.3	27,928.9	32,988.5	31,260.3	32,062.4	35,610.1	41,064.1
Claims on Central Government(Net	52an	8,439.3	8,481.9	7,915.3	7,275.8	8,273.9	9,140.9	12,434.5	16,610.6	15,619.0	17,124.6	19,688.8	21,527.3
Claims on Nonfin. Pub. Enterprises.	52c	1,515.2	1,630.0	2,122.4	2,369.4	1,986.4	1,911.9	1,056.2	1,001.6	1,052.6	844.2	1,005.2	2,772.1
Claims on Private Sector	52d	2,304.0	3,193.8	4,407.4	7,622.0	9,780.6	11,169.4	14,438.3	15,376.3	14,588.7	14,093.7	14,916.1	16,764.7
Liquid Liabilities	55l	10,569.7	13,125.8	14,027.6	15,259.8	18,508.6	18,755.0	21,245.0	23,927.9	26,141.4	30,261.9	33,894.2	40,230.9
Central Government Lending Funds..	56f	100.0	54.1	13.8	57.2	857.2	1,076.4	1,708.7	1,431.4	519.7	714.3	542.5	835.7
Capital Accounts	57a	702.2	1,268.7	1,623.9	2,820.4	2,910.7	3,461.8	3,759.2	4,296.7	5,083.6	5,629.2	7,090.0	7,060.6
Other Items (Net)	57r	2,611.6	2,178.1	2,784.4	2,647.1	3,533.3	5,141.3	6,306.5	8,104.9	5,778.4	6,025.0	7,246.5	6,681.0
Money (National Definitions)						*Millions of Birr: End of Period*							
Base Money	19ma	6,432.6	7,070.8	7,963.0	6,650.4	7,249.7	6,362.5	6,050.6	8,394.9	7,639.8	10,301.8	11,858.5	22,705.6
M1	59ma	7,588.5	9,230.2	10,050.3	10,031.2	11,017.7	10,581.8	12,157.9	13,322.7	14,000.4	16,811.9	18,858.4	18,662.9
M2	59mb	10,433.5	12,867.6	15,076.6	16,093.6	18,493.8	18,818.1	21,487.8	24,218.8	26,542.1	30,812.9	34,509.8	35,882.0
Interest Rates						*Percent Per Annum*							
Discount Rate	60	12.00	12.00	12.00	....	....	....	....	....	....	....	....	....
Treasury Bill Rate	60c	12.00	12.00	12.00	7.22	3.97	3.48	3.65	2.74	3.06	1.30	† 1.31	.56
Savings Rate	60k	....	....	....	....	....	....	....	....	3.00	3.00	3.00
Deposit Rate	60l	11.50	11.50	11.46	9.42	7.00	6.00	6.32	6.00	6.00	3.79	3.35	3.38
Lending Rate	60p	14.00	14.33	15.08	13.92	10.50	10.50	10.58	10.89	10.87	8.66	† 7.00	7.00
Government Bond Yield	61	13.00	13.00	13.00	13.00	....	....	....	....	....	....	† 3.05	4.00
Prices and Labor						*Index Numbers (2000=100): Period Averages*							
Consumer Prices	64	78.0	83.9	92.4	† 87.7	89.8	† 92.1	99.3	100.0	91.9	93.3	109.9	
						Number in Thousands: Period Averages							
Labor Force	67d	....	....	24,606	....	26,408	....	27,272	....	....	....	....	....
Employment	67e	683	....	....	....	....	....	....	....	....	....	....	....
Unemployment	67c	63	65	23	28	35	29	26	....	....	....	....	....
Unemployment Rate (%)	67r	62.9	....	....	....	....	....	....	....	....	....	....	....
Intl. Transactions & Positions						*Millions of Birr*							
Exports	70	994.2	2,062.4	2,602.9	2,650.6	3,941.3	3,967.0	3,711.0	3,991.0	3,850.0	4,115.0		
Imports, c.i.f.	71	3,936.7	5,658.0	7,052.5	8,899.2	....	10,792.0	12,274.0	10,368.0	15,347.0	14,272.0	....	....
Balance of Payments						*Millions of US Dollars: Minus Sign Indicates Debit*							
Current Account, n.i.e.	78ald	−50.0	125.4	39.4	79.6	−40.3	−332.6	−465.2	10.2	−401.4	−169.8	−199.0	....
Goods: Exports f.o.b.	78aad	198.8	372.0	423.0	417.5	588.3	560.3	467.4	486.1	455.6	480.2	504.3	
Goods: Imports f.o.b.	78abd	−706.0	−925.7	−1,092.8	−1,002.8	−1,001.6	−1,359.8	−1,387.2	−1,131.4	−1,625.8	−1,455.0	−1,922.0	
Trade Balance	78acd	−507.1	−553.7	−669.8	−585.3	−413.4	−799.4	−919.8	−645.3	−1,170.3	−974.8	−1,417.7	
Services: Credit	78add	277.2	294.6	344.5	377.2	390.7	391.5	473.6	506.2	523.1	585.4	761.0	
Services: Debit	78aed	−299.0	−310.4	−352.8	−349.8	−394.2	−455.6	−466.3	−489.6	−524.5	−580.4	−714.5	
Balance on Goods & Services	78afd	−528.9	−569.5	−678.1	−557.9	−416.9	−863.5	−912.5	−628.7	−1,171.6	−969.8	−1,371.2	
Income: Credit	78agd	25.9	42.9	68.4	41.2	24.2	21.0	16.6	16.2	16.3	14.3	18.9	
Income: Debit	78ahd	−78.4	−74.6	−87.1	−75.2	−65.5	−64.2	−50.4	−52.0	−48.3	−36.9	−43.1	
Balance on Gds, Serv. & Inc.	78aid	−581.4	−601.1	−696.9	−591.8	−458.2	−906.7	−946.3	−664.5	−1,203.7	−992.3	−1,395.4	
Current Transfers, n.i.e.: Credit	78ajd	532.6	728.5	737.3	679.0	425.5	589.8	500.7	697.9	854.3	876.4	1,266.5	
Current Transfers: Debit	78akd	−1.2	−2.0	−1.1	−7.5	−7.6	−15.7	−19.7	−23.1	−52.1	−53.8	−70.1	
Capital Account, n.i.e.	78bcd	—	3.7	2.6	.9	—	1.4	1.8	....	....	....	—	
Capital Account, n.i.e.: Credit	78bad	—	3.7	2.6	.9	—	1.4	1.8	....	....	....	—	
Capital Account: Debit	78bbd	—	—	....	....	....	....	....	....	....	....	....	
Financial Account, n.i.e.	78bjd	97.7	−199.0	−24.9	−499.6	241.2	−21.3	−180.1	34.8	−210.2	−96.8	264.8	
Direct Investment Abroad	78bdd	—	—	....	....	....	....	....	....	....	....	....	
Dir. Invest. in Rep. Econ., n.i.e.	78bed	—	—	....	....	....	....	....	....	....	....	....	
Portfolio Investment Assets	78bfd	—	—	....	....	....	....	....	....	....	....	....	
Equity Securities	78bkd	—	—	....	....	....	....	....	....	....	....	....	
Debt Securities	78bld	—	—	....	....	....	....	....	....	....	....	....	
Portfolio Investment Liab., n.i.e.	78bgd	—	—	....	....	....	....	....	....	....	....	....	
Equity Securities	78bmd	—	—	....	....	....	....	....	....	....	....	....	
Debt Securities	78bnd	—	—	....	....	....	....	....	....	....	....	....	
Financial Derivatives Assets	78bwd	....	....	....	....	....	....	....	....	....	....	....	
Financial Derivatives Liabilities	78bxd	....	....	....	....	....	....	....	....	....	....	....	
Other Investment Assets	78bhd	−31.7	−318.5	57.7	−306.8	318.5	59.8	−85.3	116.1	22.9	−4.1	68.8	
Monetary Authorities	78bod	....	....	....	....	....	....	....	....	....	....	....	
General Government	78bpd	....	....	....	....	....	....	....	....	....	—		
Banks	78bqd	−40.2	−358.5	44.7	−283.0	350.7	26.3	−69.6	23.2	29.7	75.2	95.0	....
Other Sectors	78brd	8.4	40.0	13.1	−23.8	−32.2	33.5	−15.8	92.8	−6.8	−79.4	−26.2	....
Other Investment Liab., n.i.e.	78bid	129.4	119.5	−82.6	−192.8	−77.3	−81.0	−94.7	−81.3	−233.1	−92.6	196.1	....
Monetary Authorities	78bsd	−50.9	25.4	.4	−7.8	−.1	−.4	.4	47.0	−54.6	5.7	11.0	....
General Government	78btd	209.1	82.4	−145.1	−131.5	−91.0	−79.9	−125.7	−165.5	−139.7	−106.0	147.0	....
Banks	78bud	26.5	55.3	91.2	205.6	15.0	2.4	62.2	4.1	−70.5	6.7	24.0	....
Other Sectors	78bvd	−55.2	−43.6	−29.1	−259.0	−1.2	−3.1	−31.6	33.0	31.7	.9	14.1	....
Net Errors and Omissions	78cad	−15.2	69.5	−122.4	−45.8	−629.5	−7.9	407.2	−258.6	−159.7	−821.3	−275.0	
Overall Balance	78cbd	32.4	−.4	−105.2	−464.8	−428.6	−360.4	−236.3	−213.6	771.3	1,087.9	209.1	....
Reserves and Related Items	79dad	−32.4	.4	105.2	464.8	428.6	360.4	236.3	213.6	−771.3	−1,087.9	−209.1	....
Reserve Assets	79dbd	−296.2	−124.7	−204.8	20.0	192.1	179.0	−49.7	−84.5	117.2	438.7	112.6	....
Use of Fund Credit and Loans	79dcd	29.7	20.8	—	21.2	—	16.9	−9.7	−13.0	31.8	27.1	.6	....
Exceptional Financing	79ded	234.0	104.3	310.0	423.6	236.5	164.5	295.7	311.0	622.5	622.1	95.9	....

		1993	1994	1995	1996	1997	1998	1999	2000	2001	2002	2003	2004
Government Finance						*Millions of Birr: Year Ending July 7*							
Deficit (-) or Surplus	80	−1,465.3	−2,814.8	−1,379.3	−749.2	−635.8	−1,786.5	−2,524.3	....	....	....	....	....
Total Revenue and Grants	81y	3,733.5	5,060.7	6,874.1	7,824.0	9,381.4	9,673.5	8,265.5	....	....	....	....	....
Revenue	81	3,206.6	3,842.6	5,839.2	6,817.3	7,877.4	8,400.2	7,847.0	....	....	....	....	....
Grants	81z	526.9	1,218.1	1,034.9	1,006.7	1,504.0	1,273.3	418.5	....	....	....	....	....
Exp. & Lending Minus Repay	82z	5,198.8	7,875.5	8,253.4	8,573.2	10,017.2	11,460.0	10,789.8	....	....	....	....	....
Total Financing	80h	1,465.3	2,814.8	1,379.3	749.2	635.8	1,786.5	2,524.5	....	....	....	....	....
Domestic	84a	750.8	709.6	60.0	−652.6	−92.1	1,007.0	1,175.8	....	....	....	....	....
Foreign	85a	714.5	2,105.2	1,319.3	1,401.8	727.9	779.5	1,348.7	....	....	....	....	....
Use of Cash Balances	87	714.5	2,105.2	1,319.3	1,401.8	727.9	779.5	1,348.7	....	....	....	....	....
Total Debt by Residence	88	27,645.6	37,063.1	39,599.8	38,967.1	38,748.5	41,947.3	49,485.0	....	....	....	....	....
Domestic	88a	9,474.5	11,778.3	11,654.8	11,950.8	12,359.0	13,339.0	14,700.3	....	....	....	....	....
Foreign	89a	18,171.1	25,284.8	27,945.0	27,016.3	26,389.5	28,608.3	34,784.7	....	....	....	....	....
National Accounts						*Millions of Birr: Year Ending July 7*							
Househ.Cons.Expend.,incl.NPISHs	96f	22,359	23,748	27,942	31,299	41,665	35,110	38,999	40,566	43,416	....	....	
Government Consumption Expend	91f	2,819	3,155	3,675	4,173	5,157	6,233	9,105	12,029	9,065	....	....	
Gross Capital Formation	93	3,792	4,294	5,569	7,246	7,691	7,713	7,790	7,995	8,747	....	....	
Exports of Goods and Services	90c	2,223	3,223	4,852	5,240	6,780	7,382	7,258	8,086	8,106	....	....	
Imports of Goods and Services (-)	98c	4,521	6,091	8,154	9,284	10,663	11,767	14,884	16,105	16,335	....	....	
GDP at Factor Cost	99ba	26,671	28,329	33,885	37,938	41,465	44,840	48,803	53,190	54,211	51,761	57,077	
Net Primary Income from Abroad	98.n	−414	−460	−378	−275	−224	−178	....	....	....	....	....	
Gross National Income (GNI)	99a	26,257	27,869	33,508	37,662	41,241	44,857						
GDP at Factor Cost	99ba	26,671	28,329	33,885	37,938	41,465	44,840	48,803	53,190	54,211	51,761	57,077	
GDP Fact.Cost,Vol.'80/81 Prices	99bap	12,419	12,852	13,639	15,126	15,941	15,644	16,483	17,464	19,004	19,520	18,800	....
GDP Volume (2000=100)	99bvp	71.1	73.6	78.1	86.6	91.3	89.6	94.4	100.0	108.8	111.8	107.7	
GDP Deflator (2000=100)	99bip	70.5	72.4	81.6	82.3	85.4	94.1	97.2	100.0	93.7	87.1	99.7	....
						Millions: Midyear Estimates							
Population	99z	56.40	58.22	60.01	61.75	63.45	65.13	66.82	68.53	70.26	72.01	73.79	75.60

		1993	1994	1995	1996	1997	1998	1999	2000	2001	2002	2003	2004
Exchange Rates							*Euros per SDR: End of Period*						
Market Rate	aa	....	....	....	....	....	....	1.36623	1.40023	1.42600	1.29639	1.17654	1.14016
							Euros per US Dollar: End of Period (ae) Period Average (rf)						
Market Rate	ae	....	....	....	....	....	....	.99542	1.07469	1.13469	.95356	.79177	.73416
Market Rate	rf	....	....	....	....	....	....	.93863	1.08540	1.11751	1.06255	.88603	.80537
							Index Numbers (2000=100): Period Averages						
Nominal Effective Exchange Rate	neu	124.77	122.87	129.46	129.19	116.93	117.06	111.46	100.00	101.19	104.28	116.07	119.98
Real Effective Exchange Rate	reu	126.33	124.62	132.06	133.33	120.17	117.13	112.17	100.00	101.86	105.42	116.44	119.93
International Liquidity							*Millions of US Dollars Unless Otherwise Indicated: End of Period*						
Tot.Res.minus Gold (Eurosyst.Def)	1l.d	....	....	....	....	....	....	256,780	242,325	234,965	246,995	222,716	211,293
SDRs	1b.d	3,039	3,519	5,572	5,440	5,359	6,015	4,546	4,032	4,757	4,866	5,275	5,100
Reserve Position in the Fund	1c.d	12,691	12,941	16,100	16,572	18,637	27,364	24,245	19,662	22,294	26,317	29,431	25,452
Foreign Exchange	1d.d	....	....	....	....	....	....	227,989	218,631	207,914	215,811	188,011	180,741
of which: Fin.Deriv.rel.to Res	1ddd	....	....	....	....	....	....	−209	679	346	456	865	88
Other Reserve Assets	1e.d	....	....	....	....	....	....	—	—	—	—	—	—
Gold (Million Fine Troy Ounces)	1ad	....	....	....	....	....	....	402.76	399.54	401.88	399.02	393.54	390.00
Gold (Eurosystem Valuation)	1and	....	....	....	....	....	....	116,901	109,653	111,119	136,765	164,206	170,819
Memo:Euro Cl. on Non-EA Res	1dgd	....	....	....	....	....	....	....	....	....	....	....	....
Non-Euro Cl. on EA Res	1dhd	....	....	....	....	....	....	14,691	14,685	21,797	23,451	25,674	25,950
Mon. Auth.: Other Foreign Assets	3..d	....	....	....	....	....	....	....	....	....	....	....	....
Foreign Liabilities	4..d	....	....	....	....	....	....	49,993	27,856	31,417	34,461	34,777	37,055
Banking Insts: Foreign Assets	7a.d	....	....	....	....	....	....	1,725,336	1,880,119	2,117,536	2,579,882	3,243,168	4,008,419
Foreign Liabs	7b.d	....	....	....	....	....	....	1,884,344	2,139,834	2,368,396	2,719,024	3,291,925	3,834,284
Monetary Authorities (Eurosyst.)							*Billions of Euros: End of Period*						
Foreign Assets (on Non-EA Ctys)	11	....	....	....	....	323.7	322.3	400.6	380.7	399.0	374.2	317.9	291.6
Claims on General Government	12a.u	....	....	....	....	132.9	106.6	105.8	110.7	127.5	110.2	144.1	161.5
Claims on EA Banking Sector	12e.u	....	....	....	....	216.2	205.7	426.3	429.9	390.2	399.0	458.8	537.4
Claims on Other Resident Sectors	12d.u	....	....	....	....	4.5	4.4	11.5	12.7	11.1	9.9	10.3	12.1
Currency in Circulation	14a	....	....	....	....	355.0	359.1	393.3	390.2	285.9	392.9	450.5	517.3
Liabilities to EA Banking Sector	14c.u	....	....	....	....	92.4	94.2	279.3	270.4	342.4	283.3	285.8	306.8
Deposits of Other Resident Sect	15..u	....	....	....	....	3.4	3.5	8.8	9.8	14.4	15.6	16.9	15.0
Bonds & Money Mkt. Instruments	16n.u	....	....	....	....	28.2	13.8	7.9	3.8	4.6	3.6	1.6	.5
Foreign Liabs. (to Non-EA Ctys)	16c	....	....	....	....	32.8	18.6	49.8	29.9	35.6	32.9	27.5	27.2
Central Government Deposits	16d.u	....	....	....	....	51.7	54.4	53.4	47.1	35.1	29.5	21.3	24.7
Capital Accounts	17a	....	....	....	....	106.0	97.1	174.3	197.5	209.8	165.9	143.8	138.4
Other Items (Net)	17r	....	....	....	....	7.8	−1.6	−14.6	—	−30.4	−16.2	−27.3	
Banking Institutions (Oth.MFIs)							*Billions of Euros: End of Period*						
Claims on EA Banking Sector	20..u	....	....	....	....	3,639.7	3,972.3	4,370.5	4,561.8	4,917.0	5,188.2	5,467.5	5,879.2
Foreign Assets (on Non-EA Ctys)	21	....	....	....	....	1,595.4	1,587.8	1,717.4	2,020.5	2,402.7	2,460.1	2,567.8	2,942.8
Claims on General Government	22a.u	....	....	....	....	1,874.9	1,934.0	1,952.4	1,813.9	1,899.4	1,948.0	2,060.1	2,112.3
Claims on Oth. Resident Sectors	22d.u	....	....	....	....	5,130.7	5,652.6	6,207.2	6,866.3	7,413.2	7,711.1	8,144.8	8,679.3
Demand (Overnight) Deposits	24..u	600.1	621.7	949.9	1,072.7	1,233.0	1,387.1	1,538.2	1,648.9	1,936.9	2,041.0	2,251.7	2,390.9
Deposits with Agreed Maturity	25a.u	....	....	....	....	1,901.9	1,929.1	2,043.3	2,159.6	2,257.5	2,264.7	2,295.3	2,404.9
Deposits Redeemable at Notice	25b.u	....	....	....	....	1,328.4	1,392.6	1,331.5	1,276.9	1,350.2	1,421.7	1,519.7	1,616.4
Repurchase Agreements	25f.u	....	....	....	....	205.4	176.5	144.1	174.9	218.5	226.9	208.7	229.7
Money Market Fund Shares	26m.u	....	....	....	....	252.2	241.4	293.4	323.3	436.5	533.4	648.8	677.4
Bonds & Money Mkt. Instruments	26n.u	....	....	....	....	2,063.5	2,261.5	2,531.1	2,712.9	2,882.9	2,993.5	3,161.4	3,496.9
Foreign Liabs. (to Non-EA Ctys)	26c	....	....	....	....	1,381.3	1,507.0	1,875.7	2,299.7	2,687.4	2,592.8	2,606.4	2,815.0
Central Government Deposits	26d.u	....	....	....	....	102.1	95.4	90.0	117.4	103.9	106.9	134.4	137.7
Credit fr. EA Banking Sector	26g.u	....	....	....	....	3,009.6	3,305.3	3,597.3	3,679.3	3,829.6	4,136.6	4,364.9	4,708.0
Capital Accounts	27a	....	....	....	....	684.9	750.7	845.7	936.3	1,037.5	1,103.9	1,145.0	1,199.5
Other Items (Net)	27r	....	....	....	....	78.3	100.0	−43.0	−66.6	−108.6	−114.0	−96.2	−62.7
Banking Survey							*Billions of Euros: End of Period*						
Foreign Assets (Net)	31n.u	....	....	....	....	505.0	384.6	192.5	71.7	78.7	208.7	251.8	392.3
Domestic Credit	32..u	....	....	....	....	6,989.1	7,547.7	8,133.5	8,639.2	9,312.3	9,642.8	10,203.6	10,802.8
Claims on General Govt. (Net)	32anu	....	....	....	....	1,853.9	1,890.8	1,914.8	1,760.2	1,887.9	1,921.8	2,048.5	2,111.4
Claims on Oth. Resident Sectors	32d.u	....	....	....	....	5,135.2	5,656.9	6,218.7	6,879.1	7,424.4	7,721.0	8,155.1	8,691.4
Currency in Circulation	34a.u	277.1	292.2	303.8	313.3	320.6	323.4	350.8	348.4	239.7	341.2	397.9	468.4
Demand (Overnight) Deposits	34b.u	602.9	624.5	952.6	1,075.7	1,236.4	1,390.5	1,547.0	1,658.7	1,951.0	2,056.3	2,268.4	2,405.8
Deposits with Agreed Maturity	35a.u	....	....	....	....	1,901.9	1,929.1	2,043.3	2,159.6	2,257.9	2,265.0	2,295.5	2,405.0
of which: Over 2-Yr. Maturity	35abu	....	....	....	....	1,004.1	1,033.0	1,161.0	1,168.3	1,169.1	1,189.5	1,256.5	1,365.1
Deposits Redeemable at Notice	35b.u	....	....	....	....	1,328.4	1,392.6	1,331.5	1,276.9	1,350.2	1,421.7	1,519.7	1,616.4
of which: Over 3-Mos Notice	35bbu	....	....	....	....	219.5	214.4	112.2	125.4	115.8	105.6	92.2	91.1
Repurchase Agreements	35f.u	....	....	....	....	205.4	176.5	144.1	174.9	218.5	226.9	208.7	229.7
Money Market Fund Shares	36m.u	....	....	....	....	244.3	231.1	280.0	300.0	398.0	471.0	581.5	604.9
Bonds & Money Mkt. Instruments	36n.u	....	....	....	....	1,361.0	1,456.5	1,591.8	1,662.8	1,760.8	1,819.0	1,878.5	2,061.7
of which: Over 2-Yr. Maturity	36nau	....	....	....	....	1,230.5	1,312.3	1,446.1	1,525.3	1,613.6	1,689.3	1,785.4	1,958.0
Capital Accounts	37a	....	....	....	....	696.7	677.6	804.3	889.3	990.8	1,001.6	1,004.7	1,047.0
Other Items (Net)	37r.u	....	....	....	....	199.4	354.9	233.1	240.2	224.1	248.8	300.4	356.3
Money (Eurosystem Definition)							*Billions of Euros: End of Period*						
M1	59mau	1,287.9	1,343.1	1,423.1	1,528.5	1,626.9	1,785.4	1,972.0	2,084.6	2,279.0	2,499.4	2,727.1	2,948.9
M2	59mbu	3,150.3	3,243.8	3,397.5	3,562.5	3,687.2	3,920.2	4,142.3	4,299.6	4,684.4	4,981.4	5,295.8	5,632.2
M3	59mcu	3,651.8	3,735.8	3,937.4	4,090.3	4,267.3	4,472.0	4,709.0	4,910.3	5,446.8	5,807.8	6,178.7	6,569.1
Nonmonetary Liabs. of MFIs	59mfu	2,015.9	2,123.0	2,469.6	2,772.0	3,150.9	3,237.2	3,523.6	3,708.3	3,889.3	3,986.0	4,138.7	4,461.2

		1993	1994	1995	1996	1997	1998	1999	2000	2001	2002	2003	2004
Interest Rates							*Percent Per Annum*						
Eurosyst.Marg.Lending Fac.Rate	60	….	….	….	….	….	….	4.00	5.75	4.25	3.75	3.00	3.00
Eurosyst. Refinancing Rate	60r	….	….	….	….	….	….	2.71	….	† 4.30	3.29	2.32	2.03
Eurosyst. Deposit Facility Rate	60x	….	….	….	….	….	….	1.71	3.06	3.23	2.21	1.25	1.00
Interbank Rate (Overnight)	60a	….	6.18	6.09	4.58	4.02	3.73	2.74	4.12	4.38	3.28	2.32	2.05
Interbank Rate (3-Mos Maturity)	60b		6.53	6.82	5.09	4.38	3.96	2.97	4.39	4.26	3.32	2.34	2.11
Deposit Rate	60l				4.08	3.41	3.20	2.45	3.45	3.49	2.80	….	….
Deposit Rate (Households)	60lhs	….	….	….	….	….	….	….	….	….	….	1.97	1.92
Deposit Rate (Corporations)	60lcs	….	….	….	….	….	….	….	….	….	….	2.15	2.16
Lending Rate	60p	….	….	….	8.88	7.58	6.73	5.65	6.60	6.83	6.14	….	….
Lending Rate (Households)	60phm	….	….	….	….	….	….	….	….	….	….	5.15	4.83
Lending Rate (Corporations)	60pcs	….	….	….	….	….	….	….	….	….	….	4.46	4.34
Government Bond Yield	61	….	8.18	8.73	7.23	5.96	4.70	4.65	5.44	5.03	4.92	4.16	4.14
Prices, Production, Labor						*Index Numbers (2000=100): Period Averages*							
Producer Prices	63	….	….	….	….	….	† 95.4	95.0	100.0	102.2	102.1	103.6	105.8
Harmonized CPI (hcpi)	64h	….	….	….	….	….	96.6	97.7	100.0	102.1	104.4	106.6	108.9
Wages/Labor Costs	65..c	….	….	….	….	….	95.2	97.3	100.0	103.2	107.1	….	….
Employment	67..c	….	….	….	….	….	….	97.9	100.0	101.4	101.8	….	….
						Number in Thousands: Period Averages							
Unemployment	67c.c	….	….	….	….	….	….	12,253	11,092	11,042	11,654	12,334	12,680
Unemployment Rate (%)	67r.c	….	….	….	….	….	….	9	8	8	8	9	9
Intl. Transactions & Positions							*Billions of Euros*						
Exports	70	….	….	….	….	….	791.5	† 831.8	1,003.0	1,046.4	1,065.6	1,035.0	1,134.8
Imports, c.i.f.	71	….	….	….	….	….	709.3	† 780.5	990.5	1,003.9	960.6	968.2	1,064.0
							2000=100						
Volume of Exports	72	….	….	….	….	….	† 87.0	88.9	100.0	105.1	107.8	….	….
Volume of Imports	73	….	….	….	….	….	† 89.0	94.5	100.0	99.0	98.6	….	….
Unit Value of Exports	74	….	….	….	….	….	† 90.5	92.4	100.0	101.0	100.3	97.2	96.9
Unit Value of Imports	75	….	….	….	….	….	† 79.4	82.0	100.0	100.2	97.8	95.1	96.8
Balance of Payments						*Billions of US Dollars Minus Sign Indicates Debit*							
Current Account, n.i.e	78ald	….	….	….	….	….	31.35	−23.42	−65.99	† −3.09	61.85	23.50	58.67
Goods: Exports f.o.b	78aad	….	….	….	….	….	878.06	870.37	910.54	† 925.62	1,003.30	1,176.01	1,404.35
Goods: Imports f.o.b	78abd	….	….	….	….	….	−756.11	−790.05	−881.92	† −860.34	−881.17	−1,059.22	−1,277.17
Trade Balance	78acd	….	….	….	….	….	121.95	80.33	28.62	† 65.28	122.13	116.78	127.18
Services: Credit	78add	….	….	….	….	….	258.93	260.89	261.66	† 288.30	314.37	372.69	441.59
Services: Debit	78aed	….	….	….	….	….	−265.56	−277.70	−277.20	† −288.59	−298.37	−350.20	−407.40
Balance on Goods & Services	78afd	….	….	….	….	….	115.33	63.52	13.07	† 64.99	138.13	139.27	161.36
Income: Credit	78agd	….	….	….	….	….	222.66	224.19	250.14	† 244.79	233.40	255.47	315.89
Income: Debit	78ahd	….	….	….	….	….	−253.59	−262.46	−279.51	† −267.18	−263.29	−307.30	−349.62
Balance on Gds, Serv. & Inc	78aid	….	….	….	….	….	84.40	25.25	−16.29	† 42.60	108.25	87.44	127.63
Current Transfers, n.i.e.: Credit	78ajd	….	….	….	….	….	70.06	69.68	62.26	† 70.97	79.86	90.63	99.67
Current Transfers: Debit	78akd	….	….	….	….	….	−123.10	−118.36	−111.95	† −116.66	−126.25	−154.57	−168.62
Capital Account, n.i.e	78bcd	….	….	….	….	….	13.92	13.58	9.05	† 5.78	9.56	15.19	21.75
Capital Account, n.i.e.: Credit	78bad	….	….	….	….	….	19.85	20.31	16.81	† 15.57	18.11	26.52	29.29
Capital Account: Debit	78bbd	….	….	….	….	….	−5.93	−6.73	−7.76	† −9.80	−8.56	−11.33	−7.55
Financial Account, n.i.e	78bjd	….	….	….	….	….	−86.05	4.66	47.61	† −54.53	−45.01	−41.51	−24.12
Direct Investment Abroad	78bdd	….	….	….	….	….	−195.08	−338.23	−404.90	† −284.71	−170.16	−153.45	−196.15
Dir. Invest. in Rep. Econ., n.i.e	78bed	….	….	….	….	….	101.63	209.68	404.82	† 175.71	171.16	158.18	97.14
Portfolio Investment Assets	78bfd	….	….	….	….	….	−403.37	−330.49	−385.17	† −254.61	−162.92	−313.85	−353.36
Equity Securities	78bkd	….	….	….	….	….	−129.30	−165.52	−267.56	† −91.08	−33.84	−77.90	−92.63
Debt Securities	78bld	….	….	….	….	….	−274.06	−164.97	−117.61	† −163.52	−129.07	−235.95	−260.73
Portfolio Investment Liab., n.i.e	78bgd	….	….	….	….	….	280.04	282.86	270.75	† 316.54	286.21	363.16	444.09
Equity Securities	78bmd	….	….	….	….	….	117.31	97.05	37.89	† 206.15	79.27	134.59	156.00
Debt Securities	78bnd	….	….	….	….	….	162.73	185.81	232.86	† 110.40	206.94	228.57	288.10
Financial Derivatives Assets	78bwd	….	….	….	….	….	—	….	….	….	….	….	….
Financial Derivatives Liabilities	78bxd	….	….	….	….	….	−9.74	3.53	−8.91	† −.94	−11.10	−13.82	−2.28
Other Investment Assets	78bhd	….	….	….	….	….	−86.08	−31.00	−166.16	† −244.34	−218.88	−269.81	−362.81
Monetary Authorities	78bod	….	….	….	….	….	−.84	−2.05	−.98	† .22	−.78	−.92	.22
General Government	78bpd	….	….	….	….	….	−.76	3.56	−2.43	† 2.69	.08	−.39	−1.92
Banks	78bqd	….	….	….	….	….	−21.81	17.77	−118.37	† −209.01	−164.43	−176.05	−326.90
Other Sectors	78brd	….	….	….	….	….	−63.19	−50.27	−44.38	† −38.24	−53.75	−92.45	−34.22
Other Investment Liab., n.i.e	78bid	….	….	….	….	….	226.54	208.30	337.17	† 237.81	60.68	188.08	349.25
Monetary Authorities	78bsd	….	….	….	….	….	4.02	7.23	.54	† 3.82	18.23	11.17	9.14
General Government	78btd	….	….	….	….	….	−6.82	−14.03	.01	† −.68	−7.52	−4.19	−3.68
Banks	78bud	….	….	….	….	….	211.64	174.23	272.79	† 216.23	23.59	153.46	309.60
Other Sectors	78bvd	….	….	….	….	….	16.88	40.88	63.84	† 18.43	26.39	27.63	34.18
Net Errors and Omissions	78cad	….	….	….	….	….	31.15	−6.40	−6.82	† 35.33	−23.76	−32.40	−71.70
Overall Balance	78cbd	….	….	….	….	….	−9.64	−11.58	−16.15	† −16.51	2.64	−35.23	−15.40
Reserves and Related Items	79dad	….	….	….	….	….	9.64	11.58	16.15	† 16.51	−2.64	35.23	15.40
Reserve Assets	79dbd	….	….	….	….	….	9.64	11.58	16.15	† 16.51	−2.64	35.23	15.40
Use of Fund Credit and Loans	79dcd	….	….	….	….	….	—	….	….	….	….	….	….
Exceptional Financing	79ded	….	….	….	….	….	—	….	….	….	….	….	….

		1993	1994	1995	1996	1997	1998	1999	2000	2001	2002	2003	2004
International Investment Position							*Billions of US Dollars*						
Assets	79aad	....	....	....	....	....	....	5,891.88	6,298.70	† 6,722.59	7,614.08	9,811.01	12,069.89
Direct Investment Abroad	79abd	....	....	....	....	....	....	1,237.50	1,516.39	† 1,719.72	1,968.83	2,665.44	3,067.98
Portfolio Investment	79acd	....	....	....	....	....	....	2,086.54	2,196.73	† 2,216.48	2,414.74	3,293.13	3,996.08
Equity Securities	79add	....	....	....	....	....	....	1,010.30	1,075.95	† 984.14	894.78	1,332.00	1,636.86
Debt Securities	79aed	....	....	....	....	....	....	1,076.24	1,120.78	† 1,232.34	1,519.96	1,961.13	2,359.22
Financial Derivatives	79ald	....	....	....	....	....	....	111.63	98.44	† 114.49	142.53	197.81	224.64
Other Investment	79afd	....	....	....	....	....	....	2,082.52	2,135.85	† 2,325.91	2,704.22	3,267.71	4,398.85
Monetary Authorities	79agd	....	....	....	....	....	....	2.91	3.29	† 2.71	3.64	6.06	9.29
General Government	79ahd	....	....	....	....	....	....	126.11	124.59	† 112.36	119.99	117.09	144.36
Banks	79aid	....	....	....	....	....	....	1,318.79	1,354.84	† 1,511.70	1,768.72	2,227.11	2,725.04
Other Sectors	79ajd	....	....	....	....	....	....	634.71	653.12	† 699.13	811.87	917.45	1,520.16
Reserve Assets	79akd	....	....	....	....	....	....	373.68	351.29	† 345.99	383.76	386.93	382.34
Liabilities	79lad	....	....	....	....	....	....	6,270.39	6,719.64	† 7,074.11	8,262.31	10,770.58	12,803.52
Dir. Invest. in Rep. Economy	79lbd	....	....	....	....	....	....	903.23	1,170.55	† 1,358.24	1,754.67	2,564.82	2,988.89
Portfolio Investment	79lcd	....	....	....	....	....	....	2,988.76	2,918.08	† 2,939.81	3,336.58	4,333.21	5,302.97
Equity Securities	79ldd	....	....	....	....	....	....	1,735.05	1,500.54	† 1,445.76	1,432.63	1,915.01	2,427.70
Debt Securities	79led	....	....	....	....	....	....	1,253.71	1,417.53	† 1,494.05	1,903.95	2,418.20	2,875.27
Financial Derivatives	79lld	....	....	....	....	....	....	95.54	96.55	† 112.25	155.14	207.24	244.30
Other Investment	79lfd	....	....	....	....	....	....	2,282.87	2,534.47	† 2,663.81	3,015.92	3,665.31	4,267.36
Monetary Authorities	79lgd	....	....	....	....	....	....	39.68	39.31	† 35.84	60.18	82.72	....
General Government	79lhd	....	....	....	....	....	....	51.44	48.29	† 50.51	59.14	54.94	....
Banks	79lid	....	....	....	....	....	....	1,830.41	2,013.49	† 2,127.38	2,349.74	2,863.99	....
Other Sectors	79ljd	....	....	....	....	....	....	361.35	433.38	† 450.08	546.87	663.66	....
National Accounts							*Billions of Euros:*						
Househ.Cons.Expend.,incl.NPISHs	96f.c	....	....	....	....	....	3,309.5	† 3,482.2	3,763.2	3,923.2	4,037.0	4,159.7	4,294.1
Government Consumption Expend	91f.c	....	....	....	....	....	1,168.0	† 1,229.8	1,307.2	1,371.4	1,443.6	1,500.7	1,548.4
Gross Fixed Capital Formation	93e.c	....	....	....	....	....	1,186.8	† 1,291.4	1,420.2	1,443.7	1,430.3	1,440.7	1,507.0
Changes in Inventories	93i.c	....	....	....	....	....	59.9	† 22.3	28.4	−8.8	−18.1	3.4	38.7
Exports of Goods and Services	90c.c	....	....	....	....	....	1,925.5	† 2,052.7	2,448.1	2,563.8	2,600.3	2,588.5	2,771.1
Imports of Goods and Services (-)	98c.c	....	....	....	....	....	1,778.2	† 1,951.1	2,391.0	2,450.4	2,417.2	2,437.2	2,612.7
Gross Domestic Product (GDP)	99b.c	....	....	....	....	....	5,871.4	† 6,132.8	6,425.6	6,842.9	7,075.9	7,255.9	7,546.5
Net Primary Income from Abroad	98.nc	....	....	....	....	....	−35.6	† −39.1	....	....	....	....	....
GDP Volume 1995 Prices	99b.r	....	....	....	....	....	5,647.3	† 5,819.7	6,008.7	6,227.3	6,279.4	6,317.5	6,427.7
GDP Volume (2000=100)	99bvr	....	....	....	....	....	94.5	† 96.9	100.0	103.6	104.5	105.1	107.0
GDP Deflator (2000=100)	99bir	....	....	....	....	....	94.8	† 98.5	100.0	102.8	105.4	107.4	109.8

Fiji 819

		1993	1994	1995	1996	1997	1998	1999	2000	2001	2002	2003	2004
Exchange Rates													
Official Rate	aa												

Exchange Rates

Fiji Dollars per SDR: End of Period

		1993	1994	1995	1996	1997	1998	1999	2000	2001	2002	2003	2004
Official Rate	aa	2.1164	2.0570	2.1248	1.9900	2.0902	2.7965	2.6981	2.8479	2.9017	2.8072	2.5589	2.5547

Fiji Dollars per US Dollar: End of Period (ae) Period Average (rf)

		1993	1994	1995	1996	1997	1998	1999	2000	2001	2002	2003	2004
Official Rate	ae	1.5408	1.4090	1.4294	1.3839	1.5492	1.9861	1.9658	2.1858	2.3089	2.0648	1.7221	1.6450
Official Rate	rf	1.5418	1.4641	1.4063	1.4033	1.4437	1.9868	1.9696	2.1286	2.2766	2.1869	1.8958	1.7330

Index Numbers (2000=100): Period Averages

		1993	1994	1995	1996	1997	1998	1999	2000	2001	2002	2003	2004
Official Rate	ahx	137.8	145.2	151.1	151.4	147.3	107.0	107.9	100.0	93.3	97.3	112.3	122.7
Nominal Effective Exchange Rate	nec	120.8	122.9	121.9	123.5	127.6	101.8	100.9	100.0	98.9	100.1	103.3	104.6
Real Effective Exchange Rate	rec	117.2	116.5	114.3	116.4	122.0	101.4	100.0	100.0	100.3	100.9	106.6	108.6

Fund Position — *Millions of SDRs: End of Period*

		1993	1994	1995	1996	1997	1998	1999	2000	2001	2002	2003	2004
Quota	2f.s	51.10	51.10	51.10	51.10	51.10	51.10	70.30	70.30	70.30	70.30	70.30	70.30
SDRs	1b.s	6.26	7.39	7.67	7.99	8.29	8.62	4.10	4.47	4.81	5.02	5.18	5.35
Reserve Position in the Fund	1c.s	9.95	9.99	10.00	10.05	10.08	10.12	14.94	14.98	15.00	15.07	15.19	15.26
Total Fund Cred.&Loans Outstg	2tl	—	—	—	—	—	—	—	—	—	—	—	—

International Liquidity — *Millions of US Dollars Unless Otherwise Indicated: End of Period*

		1993	1994	1995	1996	1997	1998	1999	2000	2001	2002	2003	2004
Total Reserves minus Gold	1l.d	269.46	273.14	349.03	427.24	360.29	385.67	428.69	411.79	366.39	358.82	423.62	478.10
SDRs	1b.d	8.59	10.79	11.41	11.49	11.18	12.14	5.63	5.82	6.04	6.83	7.70	8.31
Reserve Position in the Fund	1c.d	13.67	14.58	14.87	14.45	13.60	14.25	20.50	19.52	18.85	20.49	22.57	23.70
Foreign Exchange	1d.d	247.19	247.77	322.76	401.30	335.51	359.29	402.55	386.45	341.50	331.50	393.35	446.10
Gold (Million Fine Troy Ounces)	1ad	.001	.001	.001	.001	.001	.001	.001	.001	.001	.001	.001	.001
Gold (National Valuation)	1and	.33	.32	.32	.31	.24	.24	.24	.23	.23	.29	.35	.38
Monetary Authorities: Other Liab	4..d	—	—	—	—	—	—	—	—	—	—	—	—
Deposit Money Banks: Assets	7a.d	58.69	62.91	50.13	78.07	89.31	136.34	200.07	81.06	84.21	93.30	147.74	115.42
Liabilities	7b.d	64.30	65.66	73.89	124.33	123.48	108.04	159.49	114.08	120.65	148.10	181.70	135.44

Monetary Authorities — *Millions of Fiji Dollars: End of Period*

		1993	1994	1995	1996	1997	1998	1999	2000	2001	2002	2003	2004
Foreign Assets	11	414.8	384.9	498.9	591.2	558.1	765.5	842.7	900.1	846.0	741.2	729.5	786.5
Claims on Central Government	12a	6.7	—	—	—	—	—	50.7	56.1	66.2	59.0	90.4	78.8
Claims on Official Entities	12bx	2.2	.1	.1	—	—	—	—	—	—	—	—	—
Reserve Money	14	219.9	223.6	243.4	247.9	260.4	276.8	434.2	352.2	420.0	460.1	606.8	519.8
of which: Currency Outside DMBs	14a	112.4	115.6	117.8	125.4	134.0	159.8	189.9	163.3	181.7	202.6	226.2	252.3
Liabs.of Central Bank: Securities	16ac	108.9	126.6	220.5	253.3	210.7	252.9	255.8	415.7	338.6	219.9	119.1	254.6
Foreign Liabilities	16c	—	—	—	—	—	—	—	—	—	—	—	—
Central Government Deposits	16d	14.3	14.8	6.8	47.2	40.0	22.3	42.6	22.5	17.3	6.0	8.0	12.0
Capital Accounts	17a	62.7	45.8	49.3	42.3	50.5	197.1	169.0	136.5	115.3	103.1	90.6	88.9
Other Items (Net)	17r	17.9	−25.8	−21.0	.4	−3.4	16.4	−8.3	29.2	21.0	11.1	−4.7	−10.1

Deposit Money Banks — *Millions of Fiji Dollars: End of Period*

		1993	1994	1995	1996	1997	1998	1999	2000	2001	2002	2003	2004
Reserves	20	107.5	107.9	125.5	120.2	126.4	111.5	237.3	174.2	233.3	243.9	372.7	252.5
Claims on Mon.Author.:Securities	20c	44.6	44.0	104.1	106.0	60.4	44.4	54.5	43.7	17.1	29.8	54.2	97.0
Foreign Assets	21	90.4	88.6	71.7	108.0	138.4	270.8	393.3	177.2	194.4	192.7	254.4	189.9
Claims on Central Government	22a	88.9	80.7	65.4	78.8	87.0	107.0	117.8	95.3	129.9	164.2	222.8	185.3
Claims on Official Entities	22bx	141.9	144.4	137.7	145.8	164.5	154.4	137.1	138.7	120.0	97.7	100.1	127.3
Claims on Private Sector	22d	994.4	1,080.9	1,112.2	1,165.0	1,013.9	963.8	997.0	1,145.9	1,081.8	1,136.1	1,326.4	1,565.8
Demand Deposits	24	240.5	216.0	257.0	317.3	300.8	315.6	475.1	402.0	420.2	480.0	642.9	727.8
Time Deposits	25	1,013.7	1,069.7	1,089.6	1,032.1	913.2	859.9	851.6	920.1	846.2	870.6	1,080.5	1,167.7
Money Market Instruments	26aa	10.9	13.0	11.4	11.4	10.5	13.1	22.4	13.7	14.1	15.9	23.1	22.9
Foreign Liabilities	26c	99.1	92.5	105.6	172.1	191.3	214.6	313.5	249.3	278.6	305.8	312.9	222.8
Central Government Deposits	26d	21.5	40.5	40.1	21.0	37.8	78.6	122.5	54.6	56.1	59.2	68.9	74.0
Other Items (Net)	27r	81.9	114.7	112.8	170.1	136.9	170.2	151.8	135.1	161.6	133.0	202.3	202.6

Monetary Survey — *Millions of Fiji Dollars: End of Period*

		1993	1994	1995	1996	1997	1998	1999	2000	2001	2002	2003	2004
Foreign Assets (Net)	31n	406.2	381.0	464.9	527.2	505.2	821.7	922.5	827.9	761.8	628.0	671.0	753.6
Domestic Credit	32	1,198.2	1,250.7	1,268.3	1,321.3	1,187.6	1,124.3	1,137.5	1,358.8	1,324.6	1,391.7	1,662.9	1,871.2
Claims on Central Govt. (Net)	32an	59.8	25.3	18.4	10.5	9.1	6.1	3.3	74.2	122.8	158.0	236.4	178.1
Claims on Official Entities	32bx	144.1	144.5	137.8	145.8	164.5	154.4	137.1	138.7	120.0	97.7	100.1	127.3
Claims on Private Sector	32d	994.4	1,080.9	1,112.2	1,165.0	1,013.9	963.8	997.0	1,145.9	1,081.8	1,136.1	1,326.4	1,565.8
Money	34	352.9	331.6	374.8	444.9	434.8	480.9	672.0	580.0	606.9	696.1	877.5	995.1
Quasi-Money	35	1,013.7	1,069.7	1,089.6	1,032.1	913.2	859.9	851.6	920.1	846.2	870.6	1,080.5	1,167.7
Money Market Instruments	36aa	10.9	13.0	11.4	11.4	10.5	13.1	22.4	13.7	14.1	15.9	23.1	22.9
Liabs.of Central Bank: Securities	36ac	64.4	82.5	116.4	147.3	150.3	208.4	201.3	372.0	321.4	190.1	64.9	157.6
Capital Accounts	37a	62.7	45.8	49.3	42.3	50.5	197.1	169.0	136.5	115.3	103.1	90.6	88.9
Other Items (Net)	37r	99.8	89.0	91.8	170.5	133.4	186.6	143.5	164.3	182.5	144.1	197.2	192.5
Money plus Quasi-Money	35l	1,366.7	1,401.4	1,464.3	1,476.9	1,348.0	1,340.8	1,523.7	1,500.1	1,453.1	1,566.7	1,958.0	2,162.8

Nonbank Financial Institutions — *Millions of Fiji Dollars: End of Period*

		1993	1994	1995	1996	1997	1998	1999	2000	2001	2002	2003	2004
Claims on Central Government	42a.l	55.3	58.1	58.2	77.4	127.7	127.0	134.8	146.8	164.2	186.2	201.0	222.2
Claims on Local Government	42b.l	14.9	20.6	26.8	26.9	—	—	—	—	—	—	—	—
Claims on Nonfin.Pub.Enterprises	42c.l	15.2	26.7	36.2	54.4	—	—	—	—	—	—	—	—
Claims on Private Sector	42d.l	42.6	59.0	68.3	73.8	93.5	100.5	119.8	126.7	134.5	139.2	153.4	168.6
Incr.in Total Assets(Within Per.)	49z.l	22.1	23.2	27.6	15.1	−14.4	14.8	28.7	25.9	34.0	31.2	34.4	28.5

Money (National Definitions) — *Millions of Fiji Dollars: End of Period*

		1993	1994	1995	1996	1997	1998	1999	2000	2001	2002	2003	2004
M1	59ma	386.0	367.5	412.5	456.3	445.3	493.9	694.5	593.7	620.9	712.0	900.0	1,018.0
M2	59mb	1,413.5	1,455.5	1,524.4	1,488.4	1,358.5	1,353.8	1,546.1	1,513.9	1,467.1	1,582.5	1,980.5	2,185.7

Interest Rates — *Percent Per Annum*

		1993	1994	1995	1996	1997	1998	1999	2000	2001	2002	2003	2004
Bank Rate (End of Period)	60	6.00	6.00	6.00	6.00	1.88	2.50	2.50	8.00	1.75	1.75	1.75	2.25
Money Market Rate	60b	2.91	4.10	3.95	2.43	1.91	1.27	1.27	2.58	.79	.92	.86	.90
Treasury Bill Rate	60c	2.91	2.69	3.15	2.98	2.60	2.00	2.00	3.63	1.51	1.66	1.06	1.56
Deposit Rate	60l	3.69	3.15	3.18	3.38	3.08	2.17	1.24	.90	.78	.62	.51	.38
Lending Rate	60p	11.74	11.28	11.06	11.33	11.03	9.66	8.77	8.40	8.34	8.05	7.60	7.17
Government Bond Yield	61	7.26	6.49	6.69	7.41	7.08	6.49	6.17	5.57	4.79	4.28	3.27	2.56

Fiji 819

		1993	1994	1995	1996	1997	1998	1999	2000	2001	2002	2003	2004
Prices, Production, Labor		*Index Numbers (2000=100): Period Averages*											
Consumer Prices	64	† 83.6	84.3	86.2	88.8	91.8	97.0	98.9	100.0	104.3	105.1	109.5	112.5
Wage Rates	65	90.9	93.7	94.9	106.6	98.8	94.6	99.0	100.0	104.3	105.2	109.5	....
Industrial Production	66	85.3	89.5	92.0	84.6	83.7	98.1	116.7	100.0	101.9	98.2	....	....
Tourist Arrivals	66.t	97.8	108.4	108.3	115.5	122.2	126.3	139.4	100.0	118.3	135.3	146.5	....
Industrial Employment	67	85.8	86.6	88.3	100.4	102.2	101.8	100.6	100.0	104.1	106.8	108.6	....
		Number in Thousands: Period Averages											
Labor Force	67d	269	....	....	298	....	320	331	341	....	....	....	....
Employment	67e	95	96	98	111	113	113	111	111	115	118	120	....
Unemployment	67c	16	16	15	....	....	....	....	....	....	....	....	....
Unemployment Rate (%)	67r	5.9	5.7	5.4	....	....	....	....	....	....	....	....	....
Intl. Transactions & Positions		*Millions of Fiji Dollars*											
Exports	70	692.40	825.60	869.94	1,049.81	897.04	1,016.29	1,200.53	1,243.66	1,223.94	1,192.08	1,273.07	....
Imports, c.i.f	71	1,109.81	1,209.85	1,253.83	1,384.46	1,392.66	1,434.17	1,778.71	1,756.39	1,807.86	1,953.22	2,214.59	2,204.73
Imports, f.o.b	71.v	1,006.50	1,053.70	1,070.80	1,178.70	1,182.20	1,221.00	....	1,756.40	1,808.00	1,953.32	1,953.31	....
Balance of Payments		*Millions of US Dollars: Minus Sign Indicates Debit*											
Current Account, n.i.e	78ald	−138.1	−112.8	−112.7	13.5	−34.1	−59.9	12.7	....	....	....	....	....
Goods: Exports f.o.b	78aad	370.9	490.2	519.6	672.2	535.6	428.9	537.7	....	....	....	....	....
Goods: Imports f.o.b	78abd	−652.8	−719.7	−761.4	−839.9	−818.9	−614.6	−653.3	....	....	....	....	....
Trade Balance	78acd	−281.9	−229.5	−241.8	−167.7	−283.2	−185.6	−115.6	....	....	....	....	....
Services: Credit	78add	481.1	534.7	564.1	612.6	667.9	503.2	525.1	....	....	....	....	....
Services: Debit	78aed	−321.1	−366.0	−398.6	−412.9	−405.6	−352.0	−389.8	....	....	....	....	....
Balance on Goods & Services	78afd	−121.8	−60.8	−76.3	31.9	−20.9	−34.4	19.7	....	....	....	....	....
Income: Credit	78agd	52.1	49.2	55.4	63.6	61.7	54.6	47.3	....	....	....	....	....
Income: Debit	78ahd	−80.4	−105.7	−94.6	−91.6	−99.2	−110.6	−82.8	....	....	....	....	....
Balance on Gds, Serv. & Inc	78aid	−150.1	−117.3	−115.5	4.0	−58.4	−90.4	−15.8	....	....	....	....	....
Current Transfers, n.i.e.: Credit	78ajd	40.2	38.1	36.0	44.1	54.6	45.3	42.7	....	....	....	....	....
Current Transfers: Debit	78akd	−28.2	−33.5	−33.1	−34.6	−30.3	−14.7	−14.2	....	....	....	....	....
Capital Account, n.i.e	78bcd	57.1	43.4	87.0	70.8	48.5	60.6	14.0	....	....	....	....	....
Capital Account, n.i.e.: Credit	78bad	83.7	76.0	120.1	114.5	88.9	100.6	59.3	....	....	....	....	....
Capital Account: Debit	78bbd	−26.7	−32.6	−33.1	−43.8	−40.5	−40.0	−45.3	....	....	....	....	....
Financial Account, n.i.e	78bjd	45.1	61.0	88.3	3.6	−15.1	28.7	−104.0	....	....	....	....	....
Direct Investment Abroad	78bdd	−28.9	.3	2.8	−9.8	−30.0	−62.6	−53.0	....	....	....	....	....
Dir. Invest. in Rep. Econ., n.i.e	78bed	91.2	67.5	69.5	2.4	15.6	107.0	−33.2	....	....	....	....	....
Portfolio Investment Assets	78bfd	—	—	—	—	—	—	....	....	....	....	....	....
Equity Securities	78bkd	—	—	—	—	—	—	....	....	....	....	....	....
Debt Securities	78bld	—	—	—	—	—	—	....	....	....	....	....	....
Portfolio Investment Liab., n.i.e	78bgd	—	—	—	—	—	—	....	....	....	....	....	....
Equity Securities	78bmd	—	—	—	—	—	—	....	....	....	....	....	....
Debt Securities	78bnd	—	—	—	—	—	—	....	....	....	....	....	....
Financial Derivatives Assets	78bwd	—	—	—	—	—	—	....	....	....	....	....	....
Financial Derivatives Liabilities	78bxd	—	—	—	—	—	—	....	....	....	....	....	....
Other Investment Assets	78bhd	−13.5	1.2	12.0	−25.9	−21.1	−66.6	−62.2	....	....	....	....	....
Monetary Authorities	78bod	—	—	—	—	—	—	....	....	....	....	....	....
General Government	78bpd	—	—	—	—	—	—	....	....	....	....	....	....
Banks	78bqd	−13.5	1.2	12.0	−25.9	−21.1	−66.6	−62.2	....	....	....	....	....
Other Sectors	78brd	—	—	—	—	—	—	....	....	....	....	....	....
Other Investment Liab., n.i.e	78bid	−3.8	−8.1	3.9	36.8	20.4	51.0	44.4	....	....	....	....	....
Monetary Authorities	78bsd	—	—	—	—	—	—	—	....	....	....	....	....
General Government	78btd	—	—	—	—	—	—	—	....	....	....	....	....
Banks	78bud	−3.8	−8.1	3.9	36.8	20.4	51.0	44.4	....	....	....	....	....
Other Sectors	78bvd	—	—	—	—	—	—	—	....	....	....	....	....
Net Errors and Omissions	78cad	22.4	30.9	30.4	−9.7	−24.3	−24.6	32.5	....	....	....	....	....
Overall Balance	78cbd	−13.6	22.5	93.0	78.1	−25.1	4.9	−44.9	....	....	....	....	....
Reserves and Related Items	79dad	13.6	−22.5	−93.0	−78.1	25.1	−4.9	44.9	....	....	....	....	....
Reserve Assets	79dbd	45.2	10.7	−76.6	−71.1	29.7	−27.4	−30.5	....	....	....	....	....
Use of Fund Credit and Loans	79dcd	—	—	—	—	—	—	—	....	....	....	....	....
Exceptional Financing	79ded	−31.7	−33.2	−16.4	−7.0	−4.6	22.5	75.3	....	....	....	....	....
Government Finance		*Millions of Fiji Dollars: Year Ending December 31*											
Deficit (-) or Surplus	80	−158.7	−114.6	−92.7	−211.4	−281.9	−104.3	....	....	....	....	....	....
Total Revenue and Grants	81y	654.0	697.9	718.9	743.6	803.4	1,141.2	....	....	....	....	....	....
Revenue	81	649.9	693.4	712.6	736.3	798.5	1,138.6	....	....	....	....	....	....
Grants	81z	4.1	4.5	6.3	7.3	4.9	2.6	....	....	....	....	....	....
Exp. & Lending Minus Repay	82z	812.7	812.5	811.6	955.0	1,085.3	1,245.5	....	....	....	....	....	....
Expenditure	82	799.1	794.4	803.6	945.2	1,081.8	1,231.5	....	....	....	....	....	....
Lending Minus Repayments	83	13.6	18.1	8.0	9.8	3.5	14.0	....	....	....	....	....	....
Total Financing	80h	158.7	114.6	92.7	211.4	281.9	104.3	....	....	....	....	....	....
Domestic	84a	146.9	83.6	71.5	193.9	273.2	93.5	....	....	....	....	....	....
Foreign	85a	11.8	31.0	21.2	17.5	8.7	10.8	....	....	....	....	....	....
Total Debt by Residence	88	923.7	981.8	1,001.8	1,133.5	1,356.3	1,454.9	....	....	....	....	....	....
Domestic	88a	733.3	792.2	807.3	942.8	1,156.1	1,060.6	....	....	....	....	....	....
Foreign	89a	190.4	189.6	194.5	190.7	200.2	394.3	....	....	....	....	....	....

Fiji 819

		1993	1994	1995	1996	1997	1998	1999	2000	2001	2002	2003	2004
National Accounts							*Millions of Fiji Dollars*						
Househ.Cons.Expend.,incl.NPISHs....	96f	1,643.0	1,666.0	1,764.7	1,858.2	1,868.8	1,934.3	1,976.2	2,069.0	2,188.0	....	....	....
Government Consumption Expend...	91f	466.5	437.2	446.4	474.1	507.5	572.6	607.7	633.7	655.4	....	....	....
Gross Fixed Capital Formation..........	93e	364.9	320.5	350.0	296.8	312.2	482.2	507.2	403.1	516.8	....	....	....
Changes in Inventories.....................	93i	38.0	40.0	30.0	40.0	40.0	40.0	40.0	40.0	40.0	....	....	....
Exports of Goods and Services..........	90c	1,320.7	1,507.8	1,532.2	1,771.4	1,765.1	1,837.5	2,210.3	2,092.2	2,136.0	....	....	....
Imports of Goods and Services (-).....	98c	1,499.0	1,588.8	1,630.6	1,758.3	1,766.7	1,918.3	2,349.5	2,355.0	2,327.0	....	....	....
Gross Domestic Product (GDP)........	99b	2,522.5	2,673.1	2,799.9	2,962.3	3,060.9	3,283.8	3,662.3	3,504.8	3,835.8	....	....	....
Net National Income......................	99e	....	....	2,553.0	2,719.3	2,803.0	2,857.5	3,179.8	3,196.3	3,339.1	....	....	....
GDP at Factor Cost.........................	99ba	2,169.3	2,293.4	2,402.0	2,552.8	2,617.1	2,807.2	3,136.8	3,070.9	3,300.3	3,462.9	....	....
Net Primary Income from Abroad.....	98.n	75.6	54.1	81.6	70.2	67.6	152.0	100.9	76.1	202.4	....	....	....
Gross National Income (GNI)...........	99a	2,478.9	2,590.3	2,744.7	2,923.0	3,006.8	3,172.4	3,511.0	3,459.5	3,676.6	....	....	....
Consumption of Fixed Capital..........	99cf	183	183	192	204	204	315	331	263	337	....	....	....
GDP at Fact.Cost,Vol.'89 Prices........	99bap	1,707.5	1,794.4	1,838.9	1,895.6	1,879.4	1,907.3	2,089.4	2,023.1	2,084.7	2,170.1	....	....
GDP Volume (2000=100).................	99bvp	84.4	88.7	90.9	93.7	92.9	94.3	103.3	100.0	103.0	107.3	....	....
GDP Deflator (2000=100)...............	99bip	83.7	84.2	86.1	88.7	91.7	97.0	98.9	100.0	104.3	105.1	....	....
							Millions: Midyear Estimates						
Population.................................	99z	.75	.76	.77	.78	.79	.79	.80	.81	.82	.83	.83	.84

2005, International Monetary Fund : *International Financial Statistics Yearbook*

		1993	1994	1995	1996	1997	1998	1999	2000	2001	2002	2003	2004
Exchange Rates		*Markkaa per SDR through 1998, Euros per SDR Thereafter: End of Period*											
Official Rate	aa	7.9454	6.9244	6.4790	6.6777	7.3139	7.1753	1.3662	1.4002	1.4260	1.2964	1.1765	1.1402
		Markkaa per US Dollar through 1998; Euros per US Dollar Thereafter: End of Period (ae) Period Average (rf)											
Official Rate	ae	5.7845	4.7432	4.3586	4.6439	5.4207	5.0960	.9954	1.0747	1.1347	.9536	.7918	.7342
Official Rate	rf	5.7123	5.2235	4.3667	4.5936	5.1914	5.3441	.9386	1.0854	1.1175	1.0626	.8860	.8054
		Markkaa per ECU: End of Period (ea) Period Average (eb)											
ECU Rate	ea	6.4785	5.8343	5.7282	5.8188	5.9856	5.9458	....	....	....	....	....	....
ECU Rate	eb	6.6963	6.2084	5.7122	5.8245	5.8874	5.9855	....	....	....	....	....	....
		Index Numbers (2000=100): Period Averages											
Official Rate (1995=100)	ahx	76.4	83.9	100.0	95.0	84.1	81.7						
Nominal Effective Exchange Rate	neu	95.8	103.6	114.8	111.3	107.9	107.2	104.9	100.0	101.3	102.4	106.9	108.4
Real Effective Exchange Rate	reu	107.6	113.5	126.7	118.5	111.7	111.0	107.1	100.0	103.0	102.9	106.0	108.3
Fund Position		*Millions of SDRs: End of Period*											
Quota	2f.s	861.8	861.8	861.8	861.8	861.8	861.8	1,263.8	1,263.8	1,263.8	1,263.8	1,263.8	1,263.8
SDRs	1b.s	83.8	222.7	241.6	201.6	241.7	247.5	211.3	106.5	186.3	147.0	131.0	106.7
Reserve Position in the Fund	1c.s	220.4	196.1	259.5	292.8	414.2	595.0	464.3	381.8	439.0	476.8	522.1	406.0
of which: Outstg.Fund Borrowing	2c	—	—	—	—	—	31.3	—	—	—	—	—	—
Total Fund Cred.&Loans Outstg	2tl	—	—	—	—	—	—	—	—	—	—	—	—
International Liquidity		*Millions of US Dollars Unless Otherwise Indicated: End of Period*											
Total Res.Min.Gold (Eurosys.Def)	1l.d	5,410.8	10,662.0	10,038.3	6,916.3	8,416.6	9,694.5	†8,219.7	7,976.9	7,983.3	9,285.0	10,514.9	12,318.2
SDRs	1b.d	115.1	325.1	359.2	289.9	326.1	348.5	290.1	138.7	234.1	199.9	194.6	165.7
Reserve Position in the Fund	1c.d	302.7	286.3	385.8	421.1	558.8	837.8	637.3	497.5	551.7	648.3	775.8	630.5
Foreign Exchange	1d.d	4,993.0	10,050.6	9,293.4	6,205.3	7,531.7	8,508.2	7,292.4	7,340.7	7,197.6	8,436.8	9,544.5	11,522.0
o/w:Fin.Deriv.Rel.to Reserves	1ddd	....	....	....	....	....	....	—	—	—	1.05	7.58	1.36
Other Reserve Assets	1e.d	....	....	....	....	....	....						
Gold (Million Fine Troy Ounces)	1ad	2.002	2.003	1.600	1.600	1.600	2.002	1.577	1.577	1.577	1.577	1.577	1.580
Gold (Eurosystem Valuation)	1and	376.9	459.6	399.7	375.1	321.4	427.8	457.7	432.8	436.0	540.5	658.0	692.0
Memo:Euro Cl. on Non-EA Res	1dgd	....	....	....	....	....	....	2,686	—	—	30	254	311
Non-Euro Cl. on EA Res	1dhd	....	....	....	....	....	....	682	812	653	733	976	947
Mon. Auth.: Other Foreign Assets	3..d	....	....	....	....	....	....	†—	—	—	733.0	975.1	932.5
Foreign Liabilities	4..d	33.4	27.5	278.6	201.2	107.8	143.9	†437.0	458.7	97.8	4.2	314.5	1,266.8
Banking Insts.: Foreign Assets	7a.d	21,608	22,295	24,169	26,986	21,364	21,845	†15,715	19,914	35,258	41,884	51,763	66,705
Foreign Liab.	7b.d	31,854	30,679	29,269	25,884	17,916	19,991	†9,372	15,472	28,041	26,341	25,265	34,950
Monetary Authorities		*Millions of Markkaa through 1998; Millions of Euros Beginning 1999: End of Period*											
Fgn. Assets (Cl.on Non-EA Ctys)	11	33,478	52,752	48,916	36,461	51,505	51,999	10,926	8,897	9,419	9,398	9,002	9,716
Claims on General Government	12a.u	....	....	....	....	....	....	91	107	142	111	115	130
o/w: Claims on Gen.Govt.in Cty	12a	1,788	1,806	1,882	1,907	2,015	2,074						
Claims on Banking Institutions	12e.u	....	....	....	....	....	....	4,565	1,654	2,327	6,820	7,269	7,340
o/w: Claims on Bank.Inst.in Cty	12e	7,575	1,718	8,415	13,301	2,837	19	1,513	471	1,294	2,970	2,850	2,450
Claims on Other Resident Sectors	12d.u	....	....	....	....	....	....	535	429	361	385	349	346
o/w: Cl. on Oth.Res.Sect.in Cty	12d	4,404	3,951	3,302	2,462	1,877	1,541	234	171	106	34	7	7
Currency Issued	14a	14,994	14,315	15,611	16,891	17,817	17,689	3,350	3,336	2,687	6,258	7,215	8,643
Liabilities to Banking Insts	14c.u	....	....	....	....	....	....	8,238	2,646	5,007	5,923	4,918	3,677
o/w: Liabs to Bank.Inst.in Cty	14c	23,037	43,148	42,766	22,359	18,412	17,888	4,884	2,475	4,111	3,759	2,146	3,156
Demand Dep. of Other Res.Sect.	14d.u												
o/w:D.Dep.of Oth.Res.Sect.in Cty	14d	—	—	—	—	—	—	—	—	—	—	—	—
Other Dep. of Other Res.Sect.	15..u							1	—	—	—	—	—
o/w:O.Dep.of Oth.Res.Sect.in Cty	15	2,087	1,549	994	574	32	6	1	—	—	—	—	—
Bonds & Money Mkt. Instruments	16n.u												
o/w: Held by Resid.of Cty	16n	....	....	....	....	....	....	....	....	....	....	....	....
Foreign Liab. (to Non-EA Ctys)	16c	193	130	1,214	934	584	733	435	493	111	4	249	930
Central Government Deposits	16d.u	....	....	....	....	....	....	—	—	—	—	—	—
o/w: Cent.Govt.Dep. in Cty	16d	784	93	75	—	—	—	—	—	—	—	—	—
Capital Accounts	17a	6,895	6,749	6,691	6,716	6,810	6,785	4,552	5,061	5,332	5,342	4,654	4,833
Other Items (Net)	17r	−745	−5,756	−4,836	6,658	14,579	12,533	−459	−449	−890	−812	−302	−551
Memo: Currency Put into Circ	14m	....	....	....	....	....	....				3,446	3,918	4,796
Banking Institutions		*Millions of Markkaa through 1998; Millions of Euros Beginning 1999: End of Period*											
Claims on Monetary Authorities	20	27,638	46,653	45,976	25,604	21,711	20,774	4,884	2,475	4,111	3,759	2,146	3,156
Claims on Bk.Inst.in Oth.EA Ctys	20b.u	....	....	....	....	....	....	5,775	7,515	3,951	2,866	3,622	5,306
Fgn. Assets (Cl.on Non-EA Ctys)	21	124,993	105,751	105,344	125,320	115,806	111,320	15,643	21,401	40,007	39,939	40,984	48,972
Claims on General Government	22a.u	....	....	....	....	....	....	8,690	9,017	11,543	10,356	8,464	7,203
o/w: Claims on Gen.Govt.in Cty	22a	11,117	15,630	37,442	30,796	37,738	41,067	7,792	7,738	9,842	8,005	6,742	6,001
Claims on Other Resident Sectors	22d.u	....	....	....	....	....	....	65,481	70,733	78,285	84,208	94,637	104,759
o/w: Cl. on Oth.Res.Sect.in Cty	22d	398,932	360,408	350,038	347,768	337,266	358,798	64,975	70,091	77,784	83,773	93,389	102,930
Demand Deposits	24..u	....	....	....	....	....	....	38,335	37,129	39,014	40,952	44,455	46,158
o/w:D.Dep.of Oth.Res.Sect.in Cty	24	131,365	143,547	163,521	191,188	201,557	211,632	38,277	37,033	38,866	40,807	44,382	46,041
Other Deposits	25..u	....	....	....	....	....	....	22,246	23,873	25,103	27,418	26,429	28,076
o/w:O.Dep.of Oth.Res.Sect.in Cty	25	153,618	145,670	142,710	104,963	102,154	103,542	22,209	23,823	24,980	27,213	26,157	27,450
Money Market Fund Shares	26m.u	....	....	....	....	....	....	360	1,524	2,906	4,668	7,080	8,974
Bonds & Money Mkt. Instruments	26n.u	....	....	....	....	....	....	24,953	23,708	25,475	28,218	31,509	38,365
o/w: Held by Resid.of Cty	26n	....	....	....	....	....	....	....	....	....	....	....	....
Foreign Liab. (to Non-EA Ctys)	26c	184,260	145,519	127,572	120,204	97,118	101,876	9,329	16,628	31,818	25,118	20,004	25,659
Central Government Deposits	26d.u	....	....	....	....	....	....	2,553	4,368	1,697	1,424	2,824	3,091
o/w: Cent.Govt.Dep. in Cty	26d	10,174	11,250	19,057	19,881	27,569	17,951	2,552	4,368	1,696	1,423	2,823	3,090
Credit from Monetary Authorities	26g	7,576	1,718	8,415	13,301	2,837	19	1,514	455	1,293	2,970	2,850	2,450
Liab. to Bk.Inst.in Oth. EA Ctys	26h.u	....	....	....	....	....	....	3,153	1,964	2,397	2,387	2,616	5,427
Capital Accounts	27a	38,496	31,789	31,579	29,799	34,003	34,113	6,763	8,156	16,986	17,304	18,650	18,368
Other Items (Net)	27r	37,190	48,948	45,947	50,152	47,285	62,826	−8,733	−6,665	−8,790	−9,329	−6,562	−7,155

Finland 172

		1993	1994	1995	1996	1997	1998	1999	2000	2001	2002	2003	2004
Banking Survey (Nat'l Residency)		*Millions of Markkaa through 1998; Millions of Euros Beginning 1999: End of Period*											
Foreign Assets (Net)....................	31n	−25,982	12,854	25,474	40,643	69,609	60,710	20,912	21,967	21,602	29,347	35,537	39,177
Domestic Credit.............................	32	405,283	370,451	373,532	363,052	351,327	385,529	70,449	73,632	86,036	90,389	97,315	105,848
Claims on General Govt. (Net).......	32an	1,947	6,092	20,192	12,821	12,184	25,190	5,240	3,370	8,146	6,582	3,919	2,911
Claims on Other Resident Sectors.....	32d	403,335	364,359	353,340	350,231	339,143	360,339	65,209	70,262	77,890	83,807	93,396	102,937
Currency Issued..........................	34a.n	14,994	14,315	15,611	16,891	17,817	17,689	3,350	3,336	2,687	6,258	7,215	8,643
Demand Deposits..........................	34b.n	131,365	143,547	163,521	191,188	201,557	211,632	38,277	37,033	38,866	40,807	44,382	46,041
Other Deposits............................	35..n	155,705	147,218	143,704	105,537	102,186	103,548	22,210	23,823	24,980	27,213	26,157	27,450
Money Market Fund Shares.............	36m	....	....	....	....	....	....	360	1,524	2,906	4,668	7,080	8,974
Bonds & Money Mkt. Instruments....	36n	....	....	....	....	....	....	24,953	23,708	25,475	28,218	31,509	38,365
o/w: Over Two Years....................	36na	....	....	....	....	....	....	4,985	8,682	9,419	10,048	10,600	14,128
Capital Accounts............................	37a	45,391	38,538	38,270	36,514	40,813	40,897	11,315	13,217	22,318	22,646	23,304	23,201
Other Items (Net)...........................	37r	31,846	39,688	37,901	53,564	58,563	72,473	−9,104	−7,043	−9,594	−10,071	−6,794	−7,632
Banking Survey (EA-Wide Residency)		*Millions of Euros: End of Period*											
Foreign Assets (Net)......................	31n.u	....	....	....	....	....	....	16,805	13,177	17,497	24,215	29,733	32,099
Domestic Credit............................	32..u	....	....	....	....	....	....	72,244	75,918	88,634	93,636	100,741	109,347
Claims on General Govt. (Net)........	32anu	....	....	....	....	....	....	6,228	4,756	9,988	9,043	5,755	4,242
Claims on Other Resident Sect......	32d.u	....	....	....	....	....	....	66,016	71,162	78,646	84,593	94,986	105,105
Currency Issued...........................	34a.u	....	....	....	....	....	....	3,350	3,336	2,687	6,258	7,215	8,643
Demand Deposits..........................	34b.u	....	....	....	....	....	....	38,335	37,129	39,014	40,952	44,455	46,158
Other Deposits............................	35..u	....	....	....	....	....	....	22,247	23,873	25,103	27,418	26,429	28,076
o/w: Other Dep. Over Two Yrs........	35abu	....	....	....	....	....	....	2,088	2,631	2,230	3,094	2,423	2,601
Money Market Fund Shares.............	36m.u	....	....	....	....	....	....	360	1,524	2,906	4,668	7,080	8,974
Bonds & Money Mkt. Instruments....	36n.u	....	....	....	....	....	....	24,953	23,708	25,475	28,218	31,509	38,365
o/w: Over Two Years....................	36nau	....	....	....	....	....	....	4,985	8,682	9,419	10,048	10,600	14,128
Capital Accounts............................	37a	....	....	....	....	....	....	11,315	13,217	22,318	22,646	23,304	23,201
Other Items (Net)...........................	37r.u	....	....	....	....	....	....	−11,511	−13,693	−11,372	−12,306	−9,517	−11,954
Interest Rates		*Percent Per Annum*											
Discount Rate (End of Period)..........	60	5.50	5.25	4.88	4.00	4.00	3.50	....	....	....	....		
Money Market Rate.......................	60b	7.77	5.35	5.75	3.63	3.23	3.57	2.96	4.39	4.26	3.32	2.33	2.11
Deposit Rate...................................	60l	4.75	3.27	3.19	2.35	2.00	....	1.22	1.63	1.94	1.49	....	....
Deposit Rate (Households)...............	60lhs	....	....	....	....	....	....	....	....	....	....	2.11	2.08
Deposit Rate (Corporations)............	60lcs	....	....	....	....	....	....	....	....	....	....	2.00	1.98
Lending Rate...................................	60p	9.92	7.91	7.75	6.16	5.29	5.35	4.71	5.61	5.79	4.82	....	....
Lending Rate (Households)...............	60phm	....	....	....	....	....	....	....	....	....	....	3.55	3.37
Lending Rate (Corporations)............	60pcs	....	....	....	....	....	....	....	....	....	....	3.61	3.72
Government Bond Yield..................	61	8.8	9.0	8.8	....	....	....	4.7	5.5	5.0	5.0	4.1	4.1
Prices, Production, Labor		*Index Numbers (2000=100): Period Averages*											
Industrial Share Prices....................	62	10.7	16.5	18.3	16.2	21.5	30.4	52.3	100.0	57.5	44.5	38.1	41.0
Prices: Domestic Supply..................	63	† 91.4	92.6	93.2	92.3	93.8	92.5	† 92.4	† 100.0	99.7	98.5	98.4	99.9
Producer, Manufacturing..........	63ey	90.3	91.7	94.8	† 94.9	96.1	94.7	93.7	100.0	97.8	94.8	92.8	93.1
Consumer Prices.............................	64	90.7	91.7	† 92.6	93.2	94.3	95.6	96.7	† 100.0	102.6	104.2	105.1	105.3
Harmonized CPI.............................	64h	....	....	92.5	93.5	94.6	95.9	97.1	100.0	102.7	104.7	106.1	106.2
Wages: Hourly Earnings...................	65ey	79.5	81.1	84.7	88.2	90.4	93.6	96.1	† 100.0	104.8	108.9	113.6	118.2
Industrial Production.......................	66	57.5	64.0	69.1	71.3	77.3	84.3	89.0	100.0	99.8	102.0	103.2	107.6
Industrial Employment, Seas.Adj......	67eyc	85.9	86.4	92.5	93.0	93.8	96.2	98.8	100.0	100.7	99.4	95.2	92.9
		Number in Thousands: Period Averages											
Labor Force....................................	67d	2,507	....	2,481	2,490	2,484	2,507	2,557	2,609	2,626	2,630	2,600	2,594
Employment....................................	67e	† 2,099	2,080	2,128	2,158	† 2,194	2,247	2,317	2,355	2,388	2,393	2,365	2,365
Unemployment................................	67c	444	456	382	448	† 409	372	348	321	302	294	277	229
Unemployment Rate (%).................	67r	17.9	18.4	17.2	17.9	† 16.4	14.7	13.9	12.6	11.7	11.3	10.6	8.8
Intl. Transactions & Positions		*Millions of Markkaa through 1998 Millions of Euros Beginning 1999*											
Exports..	70	133,962	153,690	172,380	176,592	204,202	229,233	† 39,306	49,485	47,768	47,245	46,378	48,775
Newsprint..................................	70ul	2,955	2,915	3,187	3,342	3,169	3,205	† 593	594	....	....	....	....
Imports, c.i.f...................................	71	103,162	119,897	122,428	134,422	154,681	172,315	† 29,691	36,837	35,845	35,611	36,775	40,256
		1995=100											
Volume of Exports..........................	72	82.1	93.3	100.0	105.6	118.4	....	....	....	....	....	....	....
Newsprint..................................	72ul	113.6	115.1	100.0	92.7	107.5	109.6	111.7	....	....	....	....	....
Volume of Imports..........................	73	77.3	92.9	100.0	107.8	117.0	....	....	....	....	....	....	....
Unit Value of Exports.....................	74	92.5	94.1	100.0	100.0	101.6	....	....	....	....	....	....	....
Newsprint..................................	74ul	81.6	79.5	100.0	113.2	92.5	91.8	....	....	....	....	....	....
Unit Value of Imports.....................	75	103.8	100.6	100.0	101.9	105.1	....	....	....	....	....	....	....
Export Prices (2000=100)................	76	90.4	91.7	98.2	99.0	97.0	96.9	† 92.6	† 100.0	95.6	90.4	86.5	87.0
Import Prices (2000=100)...............	76.x	89.0	88.8	88.8	90.1	91.1	87.9	† 88.4	† 100.0	97.1	94.3	93.7	97.1

Finland 172

		1993	1994	1995	1996	1997	1998	1999	2000	2001	2002	2003	2004
Balance of Payments						*Millions of US Dollars: Minus Sign Indicates Debit*							
Current Account, n.i.e.	78ald	−1,135	1,110	5,231	5,003	6,633	7,340	8,045	8,975	8,704	10,148	6,497	7,529
Goods: Exports f.o.b.	78aad	23,587	29,881	40,558	40,725	41,148	43,393	41,983	45,703	42,980	44,856	52,736	61,083
Goods: Imports f.o.b.	78abd	−17,138	−22,158	−28,121	−29,411	−29,604	−30,903	−29,815	−32,019	−30,321	−31,974	−39,790	−48,262
Trade Balance	78acd	6,449	7,723	12,437	11,314	11,544	12,490	12,168	13,684	12,659	12,882	12,947	12,821
Services: Credit	78add	4,412	5,490	7,415	7,129	6,640	6,698	6,522	6,177	5,832	6,490	7,893	9,013
Services: Debit	78aed	−6,637	−7,335	−9,584	−8,817	−8,235	−7,767	−7,615	−8,440	−8,105	−8,009	−10,056	−11,894
Balance on Goods & Services	78afd	4,225	5,878	10,268	9,627	9,949	11,421	11,075	11,421	10,386	11,363	10,784	9,940
Income: Credit	78agd	1,154	1,789	2,879	2,868	4,136	4,237	5,664	7,265	8,568	8,657	9,079	11,131
Income: Debit	78ahd	−6,086	−6,103	−7,318	−6,503	−6,600	−7,320	−7,712	−8,989	−9,573	−9,259	−12,376	−12,501
Balance on Gds, Serv. & Inc.	78aid	−707	1,564	5,828	5,992	7,485	8,338	9,026	9,698	9,381	10,761	7,487	8,570
Current Transfers, n.i.e.: Credit	78ajd	475	410	1,536	1,253	1,210	1,523	1,658	1,611	1,562	1,732	2,020	2,263
Current Transfers: Debit	78akd	−903	−863	−2,133	−2,242	−2,062	−2,521	−2,640	−2,334	−2,239	−2,344	−3,010	−3,304
Capital Account, n.i.e.	78bcd	—	—	66	56	247	91	49	103	83	89	104	134
Capital Account, n.i.e.: Credit	78bad	—	—	114	130	247	91	85	111	93	93	108	134
Capital Account: Debit	78bbd	—	—	−48	−74	—	—	−36	−7	−10	−4	−5	....
Financial Account, n.i.e.	78bjd	374	4,093	−4,284	−7,718	−2,976	−1,722	−6,414	−8,841	−10,942	−8,603	−12,666	−6,685
Direct Investment Abroad	78bdd	−1,401	−4,354	−1,494	−3,583	−5,260	−18,698	−6,739	−23,898	−8,458	−7,801	2,583	1,106
Dir. Invest. in Rep. Econ., n.i.e.	78bed	864	1,496	1,044	1,118	2,129	12,029	4,649	9,125	3,739	8,156	3,436	4,662
Portfolio Investment Assets	78bfd	−604	775	204	−4,186	−4,600	−3,906	−15,699	−18,920	−11,594	−13,432	−10,041	−20,546
Equity Securities	78bkd	−151	−78	−209	−736	−1,694	−2,099	−5,527	−7,164	−5,153	−5,387	−5,774	−8,101
Debt Securities	78bld	−452	853	414	−3,450	−2,906	−1,807	−10,173	−11,756	−6,441	−8,045	−4,267	−12,445
Portfolio Investment Liab., n.i.e.	78bgd	6,836	6,180	−1,779	1,153	3,843	3,866	13,550	17,116	5,985	8,899	7,788	11,322
Equity Securities	78bmd	2,216	2,541	2,027	1,915	4,023	7,931	10,279	10,114	3,960	2,527	−597	101
Debt Securities	78bnd	4,620	3,640	−3,807	−761	−181	−4,065	3,271	7,002	2,025	6,372	8,385	11,221
Financial Derivatives Assets	78bwd	—	51	38	38	−72	89	—	—	—	—	—	—
Financial Derivatives Liabilities	78bxd	—	5	600	325	114	−725	−419	−630	38	−325	1,717	422
Other Investment Assets	78bhd	−1,832	−668	−2,863	−4,683	−2,201	331	−3,324	−5,636	−10,117	−1,328	−15,925	−12,150
Monetary Authorities	78bod	−29	99	146	27	94	145	−343	−129	77	−53	−55	156
General Government	78bpd	−344	−445	−366	−719	−609	−126	−224	−171	−966	−617	−3,048	−962
Banks	78bqd	−987	−511	−1,926	−3,815	−1,725	41	−1,566	−4,107	−8,197	1,204	−10,282	−11,185
Other Sectors	78brd	−472	189	−717	−175	39	270	−1,191	−1,229	−1,032	−1,863	−2,540	−158
Other Investment Liab., n.i.e.	78bid	−3,488	607	−35	2,099	3,072	5,292	1,567	14,001	9,465	−2,773	−2,225	8,499
Monetary Authorities	78bsd	−298	−107	92	−96	−173	−180	−872	1,433	282	1,127	695	−2,133
General Government	78btd	983	965	−331	764	1,478	394	−420	−1,272	467	343	2,396	−8
Banks	78bud	−4,970	−1,088	869	−626	1,876	3,607	−154	4,098	8,762	−4,665	−3,460	13,196
Other Sectors	78bvd	796	837	−666	2,056	−110	1,471	3,014	9,742	−47	422	−1,856	−2,557
Net Errors and Omissions	78cad	1,053	−489	−1,384	−375	−1,600	−5,412	−1,667	114	2,565	−1,747	5,557	−72
Overall Balance	78cbd	291	4,714	−372	−3,036	2,304	296	13	351	410	−113	−508	906
Reserves and Related Items	79dad	−291	−4,714	372	3,036	−2,304	−296	−13	−351	−410	113	508	−906
Reserve Assets	79dbd	−291	−4,714	372	3,036	−2,304	−296	−13	−351	−410	113	508	−906
Use of Fund Credit and Loans	79dcd	—	—	—	—	—	—	—	—	—	—	—	—
Exceptional Financing	79ded	—	....	....	....	....	....	—	—	—	—	—	....
International Investment Position						*Millions of US Dollars*							
Assets	79aad	40,838	51,570	57,970	65,385	71,091	85,854	109,967	148,094	161,069	202,570	292,463	366,997
Direct Investment Abroad	79abd	9,178	12,534	14,993	17,666	20,297	29,407	33,850	52,109	52,226	63,924	76,129	80,982
Portfolio Investment	79acd	4,067	3,417	3,572	7,713	11,659	16,825	33,621	51,125	55,905	76,017	107,413	145,938
Equity Securities	79add	308	418	738	1,564	3,245	5,271	13,670	20,263	20,157	22,939	36,492	52,839
Debt Securities	79aed	3,758	2,999	2,835	6,149	8,414	11,554	19,951	30,862	35,748	53,078	70,921	93,100
Financial Derivatives	79ald	77	103	41	−5	259	151	3,469	2,816	2,110	4,069	26,131	40,742
Other Investment	79afd	21,729	24,395	28,153	32,173	29,385	29,684	30,348	33,637	42,407	48,736	71,617	86,326
Monetary Authorities	79agd	874	969	911	830	617	1,078	821	887	767	997	1,260	1,195
General Government	79ahd	1,841	2,481	2,966	3,636	3,497	3,611	3,670	3,460	4,352	5,740	9,197	11,186
Banks	79aid	10,933	12,021	14,203	17,872	18,430	18,004	18,169	20,957	31,303	33,145	47,794	63,065
Other Sectors	79ajd	8,081	8,924	10,073	9,835	6,842	6,992	7,688	8,334	5,986	8,854	13,365	10,880
Reserve Assets	79akd	5,788	11,122	11,210	7,839	9,490	9,787	8,679	8,408	8,420	9,824	11,173	13,009
Liabilities	79lad	85,949	107,281	111,245	118,245	119,705	186,126	325,521	329,900	261,959	256,656	331,255	389,709
Dir. Invest. in Rep. Economy	79lbd	4,217	6,714	8,465	8,797	9,530	16,455	18,320	24,272	24,071	34,007	46,226	55,992
Portfolio Investment	79lcd	53,875	69,508	69,408	75,311	76,436	131,124	266,119	253,376	178,121	158,592	196,616	218,157
Equity Securities	79ldd	5,251	12,767	14,625	23,457	28,870	79,722	219,531	204,361	128,039	89,176	103,315	101,244
Debt Securities	79led	48,624	56,741	54,782	51,855	47,566	51,403	46,587	49,015	50,083	69,416	93,302	116,913
Financial Derivatives	79lld	−1,055	−1,092	354	723	1,153	229	2,965	1,925	1,678	3,102	26,020	39,480
Other Investment	79lfd	28,913	32,151	33,018	33,414	32,586	38,317	38,118	50,327	58,089	60,955	62,392	76,080
Monetary Authorities	79lgd	908	996	1,176	1,018	713	734	−690	614	887	2,274	3,816	1,976
General Government	79lhd	2,767	4,016	3,886	4,299	5,340	6,133	5,575	4,040	4,273	5,221	6,821	7,991
Banks	79lid	12,708	12,620	13,824	12,527	13,003	16,135	14,484	17,825	31,785	29,773	27,963	42,769
Other Sectors	79ljd	12,530	14,519	14,133	15,570	13,530	15,316	18,749	27,848	21,144	23,687	23,792	23,344

Finland 172

		1993	1994	1995	1996	1997	1998	1999	2000	2001	2002	2003	2004
Government Finance													
Central Government		*Millions of Markkaa through 1998; Millions of Euros Beginning 1999: Year Ending December 31*											
Deficit (-) or Surplus	80	−64,554	−58,781	−53,599	−36,571	−15,523	−1,904	1,583	3,920	−291	2,362	31	1,647
Total Revenue and Grants	81y	165,820	173,827	187,954	199,273	205,870	226,344	32,853	37,936	37,345	37,301	36,996	38,359
Revenue	81	160,235	168,307	178,584	192,955	199,126	221,033	32,853	37,936	37,345	37,301	36,996	38,359
Grants	81z	5,585	5,520	9,370	6,318	6,744	5,311	—	—	—	—	—	—
Exp. & Lending Minus Repay.	82z	230,374	232,608	241,553	235,844	221,394	228,250	31,270	34,016	37,637	34,939	36,965	36,712
Expenditure	82	218,612	223,119	232,883	231,425	219,527	230,509	36,353	36,646	35,574	34,352	34,613	37,324
Lending Minus Repayments	83	11,762	9,489	8,670	4,419	1,867	−2,259	−5,083	−2,630	2,063	588	2,352	−612
Total Financing	80h	64,554	58,751	53,599	36,571	15,524	1,906	−1,583	−3,920	292	−2,362	−30	−1,647
Total Net Borrowing	84	....	58,781	53,599	36,571	15,524	1,906	....	−4,141	−1,701	−2,529	3,827	400
Net Domestic	84a	15,431	26,024	53,823	36,203	34,420	9,721	....	−4,141	−1,701	−2,529	3,827	400
Net foreign	85a	....	32,727	−224	368	−18,896	−7,815	—					
Use of Cash Balances	87	....	....	....	....	....	....	....	221	1,992	167	−3,857	−2,047
Total Debt by Currency	88	272,778	314,285	362,202	396,718	419,346	421,390	68,052	63,435	61,760	59,253	63,320	63,788
Domestic	88b	....	123,434	174,874	196,836	210,088	211,413	57,008	53,844	52,678	51,456	62,079	63,745
Foreign	89b	....	190,851	187,328	199,882	209,258	209,977	11,044	9,590	9,082	7,797	1,241	43
General Government		*As Percent of Gross Domestic Product*											
Deficit (-) or Surplus	80g	−8.0	−6.4	−4.6	−3.2	−1.5	1.3	1.9	7.0	4.9	....	....	....
Debt	88g	58.0	59.6	58.1	57.1	54.1	48.8	46.8	44.0	43.6	....	....	....
National Accounts		*Billions of Markkaa through 1998; Billions of Euros Beginning in 1999*											
Househ.Cons.Expend.,incl.NPISHs.	96f	267.34	276.46	289.86	305.56	322.07	342.53	† 60.35	64.45	67.92	71.14	74.92	77.43
Government Consumption Expend.	91f	119.70	122.51	129.31	136.29	141.66	149.04	† 25.93	26.87	28.39	30.30	31.69	33.52
Gross Fixed Capital Formation	93e	82.50	82.73	95.33	101.96	118.67	133.15	† 23.49	25.75	27.73	26.58	26.32	27.90
Changes in Inventories	93i	1.05	10.47	7.38	−1.68	2.81	5.88	† −.02	1.04	.14	.55	.73	1.15
Exports of Goods and Services	90c	158.75	182.58	207.90	218.87	246.88	266.80	† 45.35	55.95	54.07	54.12	53.21	55.62
Imports of Goods and Services (-)	98c	135.35	152.19	163.38	174.55	195.73	205.86	† 35.11	43.91	42.78	42.37	43.81	47.19
Gross Domestic Product (GDP)	99b	493.99	522.57	566.40	586.45	636.37	691.55	† 119.99	130.15	135.47	140.28	143.34	149.74
Net Primary Income from Abroad	98.n	−28.08	−22.75	−20.45	−16.55	−12.36	−16.30	† −1.80	−1.63	−.85	−.22	−1.91	−.73
Gross National Income (GNI)	99a	465.91	499.82	545.95	569.90	624.02	675.25	† 118.19	128.51	134.62	140.06	141.43	149.01
Net Current Transf.from Abroad	98t	−2.45	−2.42	−.75	−3.78	−3.61	−5.43	† −1.01	−1.00	−1.07	−1.67	.35	....
Gross Nat'l Disposable Inc.(GNDI)	99i	462.08	497.13	543.18	565.18	619.22	668.89	† 117.18	127.52	133.54	138.39	141.78	....
Gross Saving	99s	73.21	96.29	122.15	121.05	152.93	171.82	† 30.90	36.20	37.23	36.95	35.21	....
Consumption of Fixed Capital	99cf	99.26	101.49	102.84	104.47	108.28	113.68	† 19.85	21.19	22.35	22.59	23.31	24.10
GDP Volume 1995 Prices	99b.p	523.16	543.85	564.57	587.20	624.15	657.45	† 114.10	....	....	....	....	....
GDP Volume 2000 Prices	99b.p	....	....	....	....	....	....	† 123.80	130.15	131.53	134.42	137.65	142.70
GDP Volume (2000=100)	99bvp	67.6	70.3	73.0	75.9	80.7	85.0	† 95.1	100.0	101.1	103.3	105.8	109.6
GDP Deflator (2000=100)	99bip	94.2	96.0	100.0	99.8	101.8	104.9	† 96.9	100.0	103.0	104.0	104.2	104.9
		Millions: Midyear Estimates											
Population	99z	5.06	5.09	5.11	5.13	5.14	5.15	5.16	5.18	5.19	5.21	5.22	5.24

France 132

		1993	1994	1995	1996	1997	1998	1999	2000	2001	2002	2003	2004
Exchange Rates		*Francs per SDR through 1998, Euros per SDR Thereafter: End of Period*											
Market Rate..................................	aa	8.0978	7.8044	7.2838	7.5306	8.0794	7.9161	1.3662	1.4002	1.4260	1.2964	1.1765	1.1402
		Francs per US Dollar through 1998, Euros per US Dollar Thereafter: End of Period (ae) Period Average (rf)											
Market Rate..................................	ae	5.8955	5.3460	4.9000	5.2370	5.9881	5.6221	.9954	1.0747	1.1347	.9536	.7918	.7342
Market Rate..................................	rf	5.6632	5.5520	4.9915	5.1155	5.8367	5.8995	.9386	1.0854	1.1175	1.0626	.8860	.8054
		Francs per ECU: End of Period (ea) Period Average (eb)											
ECU Rate.................................	ea	6.5742	6.5758	6.4458	6.5619	6.6135	6.5596	....	....	....	....	....	....
ECU Rate.................................	eb	6.6334	6.5796	6.5250	6.4928	6.6122	6.6015	....	....	....	....	....	....
		Index Numbers (2000=100): Period Averages											
Market Rate (1995=100)................	ahx	88.2	90.0	100.0	97.5	85.6	84.7						
Nominal Effective Exchange Rate.....	neu	105.1	106.3	110.3	110.0	105.5	106.4	104.4	100.0	100.4	101.7	106.2	107.6
Real Effective Exchange Rate...........	reu	116.1	115.2	117.3	113.8	108.0	107.3	105.4	100.0	97.6	98.7	102.7	103.9
Fund Position		*Millions of SDRs: End of Period*											
Quota...	2f.s	7,415	7,415	7,415	7,415	7,415	7,415	10,739	10,739	10,739	10,739	10,739	10,739
SDRs...	1b.s	241	248	643	682	720	786	253	309	392	458	512	563
Reserve Position in the Fund............	1c.s	1,682	1,627	1,854	1,875	2,119	3,162	3,950	3,471	3,894	4,250	4,242	3,453
of which: Outstg.Fund Borrowing...	2c	—	—	—	—	—	382	—	—	—	—	—	—
International Liquidity		*Millions of US Dollars Unless Otherwise Indicated: End of Period*											
Total Res.Min.Gold (Eurosys.Def).....	1l.d	22,649	26,257	26,853	26,796	30,927	44,312	† 39,701	37,039	31,749	28,365	30,186	35,314
SDRs...	1b.d	331	362	955	981	971	1,107	347	402	492	622	761	875
Reserve Position in the Fund..........	1c.d	2,310	2,375	2,756	2,695	2,859	4,452	5,421	4,522	4,894	5,778	6,303	5,363
Foreign Exchange..........................	1d.d	20,008	23,520	23,142	23,120	27,097	38,753	33,933	32,114	26,363	21,965	23,122	29,077
o/w:Fin.Deriv.Rel.to Reserves.......	1ddd	....	....	....	....	....	....	—	—	—	—	—	—
Other Reserve Assets.....................	1e.d	....	....	....	....	....	....	—	—	—	—	—	—
Gold (Million Fine Troy Ounces).......	1ad	81.85	81.85	81.85	81.85	81.89	102.37	97.25	97.25	97.25	97.25	97.25	95.98
Gold (Eurosystem Valuation)............	1and	30,729	30,730	31,658	30,368	25,002	29,871	28,225	26,689	26,888	33,331	40,576	42,039
Memo:Euro Cl. on Non-EA Res........	1dgd	....	....	....	....	....	....	—	—	—	—	—	—
Non-Euro Cl. on EA Res................	1dhd							3,330	3,870	3,562	3,861	3,035	4,171
Mon. Auth.: Other Foreign Assets....	3..d												
Foreign Liabilities.............	4..d	20,553	11,650	11,649	† 796	618	1,014	† 7,678	1,007	3,233	1,838	4,801	9,956
Banking Insts.: Foreign Assets..........	7a.d	581,393	599,906	705,082	684,056	736,795	....	† 430,976	435,489	447,009	538,479	635,130	828,745
Foreign Liab...........	7b.d	523,077	592,630	662,469	671,759	694,578	....	† 337,028	384,578	399,215	464,826	547,132	701,857
Monetary Authorities		*Billions of Francs through 1998; Millions of Euros Beginning 1999: End of Period*											
Fgn. Assets (Cl.on Non-EA Ctys).......	11	351	372	346	† 309	335	420	68,150	68,300	66,406	58,934	55,979	55,925
Claims on General Government........	12a.u	....	....	....	....	....	....	4,051	4,044	3,691	3,314	5,029	5,680
o/w: Claims on Gen.Govt.in Cty.	12a	75	72	59	58	52	51	4,051	4,044	3,691	3,314	5,029	5,680
Claims on Banking Institutions.........	12e.u	....	....	....	....	....	....	65,188	42,512	44,767	81,628	84,513	90,541
o/w: Claims on Bank.Inst.in Cty.	12e	372	200	147	143	125	167	48,448	29,013	16,413	16,107	11,084	17,315
Claims on Other Resident Sectors....	12d.u	....	....	....	....	....	....	380	361	341	323	294	258
o/w: Cl. on Oth.Res.Sect.in Cty.	12d	4	4	6	18	19	20	380	361	341	323	294	258
Currency Issued..............................	14a	267	270	275	278	283	287	49,282	49,187	34,575	74,153	84,978	97,804
Liabilities to Banking Insts................	14c.u	....	....	....	....	....	....	51,345	28,083	29,467	34,591	27,774	28,675
o/w: Liabs to Bank.Inst.in Cty.	14c	14	10	30	33	36	129	24,371	28,083	29,467	34,591	27,774	28,675
Demand Dep. of Other Res.Sect.	14d.u	....	....	....	....	....	....	1,573	801	846	811	752	363
o/w:D.Dep.of Oth.Res.Sect.in Cty...	14d	3	3	4	4	4	4	1,573	801	846	811	752	363
Other Dep. of Other Res.Sect..........	15..u							—	—	—	—	—	—
o/w:O.Dep.of Oth.Res.Sect.in Cty.	15							—	—	—	—	—	—
Bonds & Money Mkt. Instruments....	16n.u							—	—	—	—	—	—
o/w: Held by Resid.of Cty..........	16n	....	....	....	....	....	....	....	....	....	....	....	....
Foreign Liab. (to Non-EA Ctys).........	16c	121	62	57	† 4	4	6	7,643	1,082	3,669	1,753	3,801	7,309
Central Government Deposits..........	16d.u	....	....	....	....	....	....	1,057	1,982	2,455	811	280	295
o/w: Cent.Govt.Dep. in Cty.	16d	198	123	58	20	43	89	1,057	1,982	2,455	811	280	295
Capital Accounts.............................	17a	225	201	177	191	201	168	35,675	39,750	44,024	39,842	36,766	34,180
Other Items (Net)............................	17r	−26	−23	−44	−3	−39	−25	−8,807	−5,668	169	−7,762	−8,535	−16,222
Memo: Currency Put into Circ..........	14m	....	....	....	....	....	....	....	....	....	41,636	43,250	47,649
Banking Institutions		*Billions of Francs through 1998; Millions of Euros Beginning 1999: End of Period*											
Claims on Monetary Authorities.......	20	27	26	47	51	48	....	24,371	28,083	29,467	34,591	27,774	26,384
Claims on Bk.Inst.in Oth.EA Ctys....	20b.u	....	....	....	....	....	....	192,409	186,176	211,491	231,399	262,766	314,768
Fgn. Assets (Cl.on Non-EA Ctys).......	21	3,428	3,207	3,455	3,582	4,412	....	429,003	468,016	507,215	513,473	502,874	608,432
Claims on General Government........	22a.u	....	....	....	....	....	....	387,081	338,822	336,930	375,275	402,395	407,907
o/w: Claims on Gen.Govt.in Cty.	22a	798	1,074	1,275	1,566	1,729	....	312,765	268,206	269,527	279,124	299,509	295,268
Claims on Other Resident Sectors.....	22d.u	....	....	....	....	....	....	1,159,879	1,276,183	1,380,548	1,402,545	1,499,829	1,616,015
o/w: Cl. on Oth.Res.Sect.in Cty.	22d	6,712	6,589	6,745	6,653	6,785	....	1,115,273	1,225,195	1,314,276	1,325,885	1,403,834	1,496,580
Demand Deposits............................	24..u	....	....	....	....	....	....	247,576	269,174	305,546	295,536	350,139	364,054
o/w:D.Dep.of Oth.Res.Sect.in Cty...	24	1,364	1,415	1,557	1,554	1,670	....	243,048	264,944	300,271	290,917	344,061	357,103
Other Deposits................................	25..u	....	....	....	....	....	....	650,373	654,500	684,583	710,793	752,835	800,245
o/w:O.Dep.of Oth.Res.Sect.in Cty.	25	2,776	3,012	3,374	3,582	3,855	....	633,043	636,781	666,151	691,318	731,410	772,532
Money Market Fund Shares...............	26m.u							179,867	210,662	255,856	297,874	324,445	350,522
Bonds & Money Mkt. Instruments....	26n.u							478,806	502,177	554,152	561,360	593,490	664,167
o/w: Held by Resid.of Cty.	26n	2,673	2,538	2,548	2,266	2,151							
Foreign Liab. (to Non-EA Ctys).........	26c	3,084	3,168	3,246	3,518	4,159	....	335,485	413,303	452,984	443,240	433,200	515,276
Central Government Deposits..........	26d.u	....	....	....	....	....	....	11,472	5,865	4,937	12,110	39,745	46,371
o/w: Cent.Govt.Dep. in Cty............	26d	50	55	124	156	152	....	11,205	5,637	4,403	11,666	38,999	43,937
Credit from Monetary Authorities.....	26g	372	200	147	143	125	167	48,448	29,013	16,413	16,107	11,084	14,571
Liab. to Bk.Inst.in Oth. EA Ctys........	26h.u							150,040	139,026	149,425	170,842	173,576	201,540
Capital Accounts.............................	27a	1,240	1,293	1,284	1,288	1,320	....	245,638	249,326	270,482	284,117	294,879	310,242
Other Items (Net)............................	27r	−595	−785	−759	−654	−459	....	−154,962	−175,766	−228,727	−234,696	−277,755	−293,482

France 132

		1993	1994	1995	1996	1997	1998	1999	2000	2001	2002	2003	2004
Banking Survey (Nat'l Residency)		*Billions of Francs through 1998; Millions of Euros Beginning 1999: End of Period*											
Foreign Assets (Net)	31n	573	349	497	† 369	584	....	291,224	292,786	326,850	412,752	467,022	537,488
Domestic Credit	32	7,342	7,560	7,903	8,118	8,390	....	1,420,207	1,490,187	1,580,977	1,596,169	1,669,387	1,753,554
Claims on General Govt. (Net)	32an	626	968	1,152	1,447	1,586	....	304,554	264,631	266,360	269,961	265,259	256,716
Claims on Other Resident Sectors	32d	6,716	6,593	6,751	6,671	6,804	....	1,115,653	1,225,556	1,314,617	1,326,208	1,404,128	1,496,838
Currency Issued	34a.n	267	270	275	278	283	287	49,282	49,187	34,575	74,153	84,978	97,804
Demand Deposits	34b.n	1,368	1,418	1,561	1,557	1,674	....	244,621	265,745	301,117	291,728	344,813	357,466
Other Deposits	35..n	2,776	3,012	3,374	3,582	3,855	....	633,043	636,781	666,151	691,318	731,410	772,532
Money Market Fund Shares	36m	....	....	....	....	....	....	179,867	210,662	255,856	297,874	324,445	350,522
Bonds & Money Mkt. Instruments	36n	2,673	2,538	2,548	2,266	2,151	....	478,806	502,177	554,152	561,360	593,490	664,167
o/w: Over Two Years	36na	....	....	....	....	....	....	322,255	338,332	357,016	354,893	375,237	404,784
Capital Accounts	37a	1,465	1,494	1,462	1,479	1,521	....	281,313	289,076	314,506	323,959	331,645	344,422
Other Items (Net)	37r	−633	−824	−819	−675	−509	....	−155,502	−170,655	−218,530	−231,471	−274,371	−295,871
Banking Survey (EA-Wide Residency)		*Millions of Euros: End of Period*											
Foreign Assets (Net)	31n.u	....	....	....	....	....	....	154,025	121,931	116,968	127,414	121,852	141,772
Domestic Credit	32..u	....	....	....	....	....	....	1,538,862	1,611,563	1,714,118	1,768,536	1,867,522	1,983,194
Claims on General Govt. (Net)	32anu	....	....	....	....	....	....	378,603	335,019	333,229	365,668	367,399	366,921
Claims on Other Resident Sect.	32d.u	....	....	....	....	....	....	1,160,259	1,276,544	1,380,889	1,402,868	1,500,123	1,616,273
Currency Issued	34a.u	....	....	....	....	....	....	49,282	49,187	34,575	74,153	84,978	97,804
Demand Deposits	34b.u	....	....	....	....	....	....	249,149	269,975	306,392	296,347	350,891	364,417
Other Deposits	35..u	....	....	....	....	....	....	650,373	654,500	684,583	710,793	752,835	800,245
o/w: Other Dep. Over Two Yrs	35abu	....	....	....	....	....	....	299,627	281,832	279,539	285,760	303,383	310,903
Money Market Fund Shares	36m.u	....	....	....	....	....	....	179,867	210,662	255,856	297,874	324,445	350,522
Bonds & Money Mkt. Instruments	36n.u	....	....	....	....	....	....	478,806	502,177	554,152	561,360	593,490	664,167
o/w: Over Two Years	36nau	....	....	....	....	....	....	322,255	338,332	357,016	354,893	375,237	404,784
Capital Accounts	37a	....	....	....	....	....	....	281,313	289,076	314,506	323,959	331,645	344,422
Other Items (Net)	37r.u	....	....	....	....	....	....	−195,904	−242,083	−318,978	−368,536	−448,909	−496,611
Money (National Definitions)		*Billions of Francs: End of Period*											
M1	59ma	1,626	1,671	1,800	1,815	1,933	1,993	....	....	....	....	....	....
M1, Seasonally Adjusted	59mac	1,513	1,559	1,581	1,666	1,735	1,884	....	....	....	....	....	....
M2	59mb	2,854	3,003	3,246	3,363	3,624	3,781	....	....	....	....	....	....
M2, Seasonally Adjusted	59mbc	2,696	2,806	2,935	3,143	3,356	3,641	....	....	....	....	....	....
M3	59mc	5,134	5,225	5,463	5,281	5,385	5,532	....	....	....	....	....	....
M3, Seasonally Adjusted	59mcc	5,217	5,083	5,283	5,318	5,263	5,492	....	....	....	....	....	....
L	59mf	5,184	5,296	5,541	5,364	5,511	5,622	....	....	....	....	....	....
L, Seasonally Adjusted	59mfc	5,273	5,142	5,360	5,409	5,369	5,590	....	....	....	....	....	....
Interest Rates		*Percent Per Annum*											
Repurchase of Agreements	60a	7.60	5.44	4.96	3.60	3.15	3.28	....	....	....	....	....	....
Money Market Rate	60b	8.75	5.69	6.35	3.73	3.24	3.39	....	....	....	....	....	....
Treasury Bill Rate	60c	8.41	5.79	6.58	3.84	3.35	3.45	2.72	4.23	4.26	3.28	2.27	....
Deposit Rate	60l	4.50	4.50	4.50	3.67	3.50	3.21	2.69	2.63	3.00	3.00	2.69	2.25
Deposit Rate (Households)	60lhs	....	....	....	....	....	....	....	....	....	....	2.59	2.50
Deposit Rate (Corporations)	60lcs	....	....	....	....	....	....	....	....	....	....	2.54	2.42
Lending Rate	60p	8.90	7.89	8.12	6.77	6.34	6.55	6.36	6.70	6.98	6.60	6.60	6.60
Lending Rate (Households)	60phm	....	....	....	....	....	....	....	....	....	....	5.23	4.85
Lending Rate (Corporations)	60pcs	....	....	....	....	....	....	....	....	....	....	3.53	3.66
Government Bond Yield	61	6.91	7.35	7.59	6.39	5.63	4.72	4.69	5.45	5.05	4.93	4.18	4.15
Prices, Production, Labor		*Index Numbers (2000=100): Period Averages*											
Share Prices	62	32.7	32.7	29.6	33.7	44.4	59.8	74.0	100.0	80.1	60.4	....	....
Producer Prices	63	....	....	....	....	....	....	† 95.8	100.0	101.2	101.0	101.9	104.0
Intermediate Indust. Goods	63a	† 94.4	95.5	† 101.3	98.6	98.0	97.1	95.8	100.0	101.2	100.7	101.1	103.7
Imported Raw Materials	63b	67.4	81.2	88.1	78.7	88.7	75.4	76.9	100.0	91.5	85.8	81.0	95.2
Consumer Prices	64	91.0	92.5	94.1	96.0	97.2	† 97.8	98.3	100.0	101.7	103.6	105.8	108.1
Harmonized CPI	64h	....	....	93.8	95.8	97.0	97.7	98.2	100.0	101.8	103.7	106.0	108.5
Labor Costs	65	83.8	86.3	87.0	† 88.5	91.0	93.6	95.7	100.0	104.5	108.4	112.8	116.1
Industrial Production	66	† 80.6	84.0	75.1	75.0	78.1	80.9	96.6	100.0	101.2	100.2	85.4	87.4
Industrial Employment, Seas. Adj	67..c	105.5	103.3	102.2	99.4	98.7	99.0	98.7	100.0	101.3	99.3	97.1	94.9
		Number in Thousands: Period Averages											
Labor Force	67d	25,756	....	26,803	26,404	26,404	....	....	26,226	26,385	26,653	27,287	27,455
Employment	67e	† 20,705	21,875	20,233	22,311	20,413	22,479	20,864	23,262	23,759	23,942	24,485	24,720
Unemployment	67c	3,172	3,329	† 2,893	3,063	3,102	2,977	2,772	2,338	2,152	2,259	2,396	2,439
Unemployment Rate (%)	67r	11.1	12.4	11.6	12.1	12.3	11.8	9.5	11.9	11.6	12.3	....	....
Intl. Transactions & Positions		*Billions of Francs through 1998; Billions of Euros Beginning 1999*											
Exports	70	177.95	196.38	214.69	224.10	258.29	275.38	† 284.13	325.71	331.90	330.44	323.05	341.19
Imports, c.i.f.	71	1,149.13	1,298.43	1,403.80	1,441.62	1,585.34	1,708.92	† 277.03	337.67	337.20	330.72	327.71	355.90
Imports, f.o.b.	71.v	169.68	190.05	205.61	212.64	234.52	254.69	† 269.83	329.91	331.37	325.23	322.15	349.80
		2000=100											
Volume of Exports	72	51.1	53.8	59.5	64.6	75.0	82.7	88.6	100.0	63.4	88.9	65.4	48.3
Volume of Imports	73	51.3	55.1	59.0	62.8	70.6	79.4	87.4	100.0	64.2	66.5	66.1	74.1
Unit Value of Exports	74	106.6	112.1	111.2	107.8	105.3	102.1	98.6	100.0	110.9	106.7	106.7	75.6
Unit Value of Imports	75	100.1	104.3	104.5	102.5	102.0	97.8	93.9	100.0	102.4	96.9	96.9	94.7

France 132

Balance of Payments

		1993	1994	1995	1996	1997	1998	1999	2000	2001	2002	2003	2004
Balance of Payments		*Billions of US Dollars: Minus Sign Indicates Debit*											
Current Account, n.i.e.	78ald	8.99	7.42	10.84	20.56	37.80	37.70	41.51	18.58	28.76	11.00	11.80	−4.83
Goods: Exports f.o.b.	78aad	199.04	230.81	278.63	281.85	286.07	303.02	299.95	298.20	294.62	307.20	361.91	421.12
Goods: Imports f.o.b.	78abd	−191.53	−223.56	−267.63	−266.91	−259.17	−278.08	−283.01	−301.82	−291.78	−299.56	−358.49	−429.07
Trade Balance	78acd	7.52	7.25	11.00	14.94	26.90	24.94	16.94	−3.62	2.84	7.64	3.43	−7.94
Services: Credit	78add	86.38	75.52	84.09	83.53	80.79	84.96	82.09	80.92	82.30	86.13	98.76	110.31
Services: Debit	78aed	−69.54	−57.67	−66.12	−67.28	−64.16	−67.73	−63.52	−61.04	−56.86	−68.91	−82.86	−97.52
Balance on Goods & Services	78afd	24.36	25.10	28.97	31.19	43.52	42.17	35.50	16.25	28.27	24.86	19.32	4.85
Income: Credit	78agd	98.99	41.56	45.18	47.55	57.13	66.66	71.24	72.39	74.11	58.04	88.73	112.97
Income: Debit	78ahd	−108.16	−48.32	−54.15	−50.25	−50.04	−58.00	−52.21	−56.81	−59.04	−57.43	−76.80	−100.89
Balance on Gds, Serv. & Inc.	78aid	15.19	18.34	20.01	28.48	50.62	50.83	54.53	31.84	43.34	25.46	31.25	16.92
Current Transfers, n.i.e.: Credit	78ajd	16.74	18.22	22.01	22.76	19.61	19.65	18.77	17.87	17.28	19.77	24.05	26.03
Current Transfers: Debit	78akd	−22.94	−29.15	−31.17	−30.68	−32.43	−32.79	−31.79	−31.13	−31.86	−34.23	−43.49	−47.79
Capital Account, n.i.e.	78bcd	.03	−4.18	.51	1.23	1.48	1.47	1.42	1.39	−.31	−.19	−8.23	2.16
Capital Account, n.i.e.: Credit	78bad	.30	.99	1.16	1.88	2.41	2.10	1.99	1.92	1.10	.91	1.93	3.19
Capital Account: Debit	78bbd	−.28	−5.16	−.66	−.65	−.93	−.63	−.57	−.53	−1.41	−1.10	−10.16	−1.03
Financial Account, n.i.e.	78bjd	−16.67	10.18	−7.52	−22.64	−37.60	−29.29	−50.47	−32.55	−33.25	−20.34	13.54	5.45
Direct Investment Abroad	78bdd	−20.60	−24.44	−15.82	−30.36	−35.49	−45.70	−133.92	−174.32	−86.98	−50.60	−53.36	−47.71
Dir. Invest. in Rep. Econ., n.i.e.	78bed	20.75	15.80	23.74	21.97	23.05	29.52	45.98	42.37	50.36	49.54	43.07	24.50
Portfolio Investment Assets	78bfd	−31.16	−21.96	−7.42	−46.63	−60.79	−105.22	−126.89	−97.44	−85.48	−84.65	−192.72	−176.29
Equity Securities	78bkd	−2.52	−1.02	1.78	−1.08	−9.67	−24.46	−20.78	−32.54	−19.15	−16.35	−48.08	−51.08
Debt Securities	78bld	−28.64	−20.94	−9.20	−45.55	−51.12	−80.76	−106.11	−64.90	−66.34	−68.30	−144.64	−125.21
Portfolio Investment Liab., n.i.e.	78bgd	34.52	−27.90	13.08	−15.35	35.32	59.75	117.56	132.33	106.90	76.76	198.85	119.01
Equity Securities	78bmd	13.58	5.26	6.82	12.20	11.97	17.21	49.37	49.97	13.65	−4.37	20.72	12.16
Debt Securities	78bnd	20.94	−33.16	6.26	−27.56	23.36	42.54	68.19	82.36	93.25	81.13	178.13	106.86
Financial Derivatives Assets	78bwd	−.34	—	—	−6.47								
Financial Derivatives Liabilities	78bxd	....	—	1.00	7.81	4.10	−.44	−1.53	4.78	2.29	5.31	−7.05	6.32
Other Investment Assets	78bhd	−13.38	23.05	−40.16	26.31	−53.64	26.11	−27.15	.63	−59.15	−44.17	−14.88	−114.08
Monetary Authorities	78bod	—	−.24	.50	.13	−.43	−.05	−10.25	−6.00	−12.50	−4.63	—	11.42
General Government	78bpd	−3.91	3.08	−.64	1.11	1.18	.86	.16	−.08	.14	.52	−2.43	1.55
Banks	78bqd	−46.69	22.72	−43.19	28.59	−46.82	41.70	−11.77	7.08	−46.96	−35.09	−3.92	−119.92
Other Sectors	78brd	37.22	−2.50	3.18	−3.52	−7.57	−16.40	−5.29	−.37	.18	−4.98	−8.53	−7.13
Other Investment Liab., n.i.e.	78bid	−6.46	45.63	18.06	20.08	49.85	6.70	75.47	59.09	38.82	27.47	39.62	193.68
Monetary Authorities	78bsd	−1.07	.55	.25	−.78	.13	.31	28.80	−23.39	1.15	−1.28	2.11	1.81
General Government	78btd	.23	3.16	1.10	−.01	4.67	.15	2.82	2.69	1.32	.25	−.44	2.42
Banks	78bud	−5.69	32.11	13.13	15.83	39.05	2.26	43.91	55.65	42.81	29.22	39.27	170.21
Other Sectors	78bvd	.07	9.81	3.59	5.04	6.00	3.98	−.06	24.14	−6.46	−.72	−1.32	19.24
Net Errors and Omissions	78cad	2.65	−10.97	−3.12	1.09	4.26	9.94	6.09	10.14	−.77	5.57	−15.84	1.34
Overall Balance	78cbd	−5.01	2.45	.71	.24	5.94	19.82	−1.45	−2.43	−5.57	−3.97	1.27	4.11
Reserves and Related Items	79dad	5.01	−2.45	−.71	−.24	−5.94	−19.82	1.45	2.43	5.57	3.97	−1.27	−4.11
Reserve Assets	79dbd	5.01	−2.45	−.71	−.24	−5.94	−19.82	1.45	2.43	5.57	3.97	−1.27	−4.11
Use of Fund Credit and Loans	79dcd	—	—	—	—	—	—	—	—	—	—	—	—
Exceptional Financing	79ded	....	....	....	....								
International Investment Position		*Billions of US Dollars*											
Assets	79aad	927.97	1,202.25	1,383.08	1,482.34	1,698.37	2,052.67	2,319.06	2,481.26	2,455.31	2,678.91	3,513.03	....
Direct Investment Abroad	79abd	159.13	300.86	374.96	482.74	598.65	747.30	912.98	1,054.72	931.09	855.21	1,173.96	....
Portfolio Investment	79acd	130.47	184.92	203.62	248.12	340.21	489.01	590.20	663.73	710.33	880.91	1,249.23	....
Equity Securities	79add	51.97	53.74	58.36	73.52	99.13	143.05	190.67	210.01	201.73	196.84	300.22	....
Debt Securities	79aed	78.51	131.17	145.25	174.60	241.09	345.96	399.53	453.71	508.60	684.07	949.02	....
Financial Derivatives	79ald	—	24.78	31.33	34.71	42.62	76.07	110.00	95.00	109.81	108.12	125.29	....
Other Investment	79afd	583.10	633.73	714.57	659.48	661.24	670.19	637.82	604.27	645.38	773.00	893.83	....
Monetary Authorities	79agd	—	1.23	.92	.75	1.88	2.09	11.55	16.10	27.94	37.33	43.70	....
General Government	79ahd	—	31.28	34.80	33.33	29.79	31.63	28.73	27.17	26.26	29.26	36.75	....
Banks	79aid	—	469.32	530.27	484.61	498.42	487.70	457.70	429.70	453.16	541.55	620.89	....
Other Sectors	79ajd	583.10	131.89	148.59	140.79	131.15	148.77	139.84	131.29	138.01	164.86	192.48	....
Reserve Assets	79akd	55.27	57.96	58.61	57.30	55.65	70.09	68.05	63.55	58.70	61.67	70.72	....
Liabilities	79lad	989.90	1,227.25	1,418.35	1,438.55	1,543.08	1,919.90	2,254.32	2,312.01	2,302.84	2,547.50	3,380.80	....
Dir. Invest. in Rep. Economy	79lbd	135.38	301.83	341.10	359.21	399.73	548.62	648.87	598.50	529.84	534.21	748.58	....
Portfolio Investment	79lcd	366.99	366.66	456.61	460.09	518.04	671.45	865.56	949.20	976.57	1,074.39	1,512.95	....
Equity Securities	79ldd	103.82	102.21	120.76	155.32	208.58	300.44	482.21	502.10	415.97	339.15	502.17	....
Debt Securities	79led	263.17	264.45	335.86	304.77	309.46	371.01	383.36	447.11	560.59	735.24	1,010.78	....
Financial Derivatives	79lld	—	20.24	32.94	38.32	45.24	81.09	105.08	98.26	104.79	112.32	134.26	....
Other Investment	79lfd	487.53	538.52	587.69	580.93	580.07	618.74	634.81	666.05	691.64	826.59	985.01	....
Monetary Authorities	79lgd	—	1.72	2.00	2.26	2.30	2.68	28.03	2.33	3.35	2.20	4.42	....
General Government	79lhd	—	9.45	11.24	10.64	16.33	15.05	14.47	15.82	17.01	20.34	23.74	....
Banks	79lid	—	435.09	466.41	468.95	472.90	501.82	500.79	530.29	548.26	662.04	787.10	....
Other Sectors	79ljd	487.53	92.26	108.04	99.08	88.53	99.18	91.52	117.62	123.03	141.99	169.75	....

France 132

		1993	1994	1995	1996	1997	1998	1999	2000	2001	2002	2003	2004
Government Finance													
Central Government				*Billions of Francs through 1998; Millions of Euros Beginning 1999: Year Ending December 31*									
Deficit (-) or Surplus	80	−402.0	−412.0	−502.6	−413.3	−284.4	....	....	....	....	....	....	....
Revenue	81	2,871.3	2,983.5	3,116.5	3,271.2	3,438.7	....	....	....	....	....	....	....
Grants Received	81z	50.2	48.8	53.0	46.6	51.8	....	....	....	....	....	....	....
Exp. & Lending Minus Repay.	82z	3,319.0	3,429.8	3,662.0	3,740.9	3,797.3	....	....	....	....	....	....	....
Expenditure	82	3,336.9	3,458.2	3,564.7	3,687.2	3,789.2	....	....	....	....	....	....	....
Lending Minus Repayments	83	−17.9	−28.4	97.3	53.7	8.1	....	....	....	....	....	....	....
Overall Adj. to Cash Basis	80x	−4.5	−14.5	−10.1	9.8	22.4	....	....	....	....	....	....	....
Financing													
Net Borrowing	84	460.3	326.7	451.5	364.9	....	....	....	....	....	....	....	....
Domestic	84a	420.5	375.9	396.1	350.0	....	....	....	....	....	....	....	....
Foreign	85a	39.8	−49.2	55.4	14.9	....	....	....	....	....	....	....	....
Use of Cash Balances	87	−58.3	85.3	51.1	48.4	....	....	....	....	....	....	....	....
Debt: Francs	88b	2,417.1	2,859.2	3,214.2	3,506.8	3,738.2	3,977.9	....	....	....	....	....	....
Foreign Currency	89b	57.9	62.6	58.6	57.1	56.4	49.8	....	....	....	....	....	....
General Government				*As Percent of Gross Domestic Product*									
Deficit (-) or Surplus	80g	−5.8	−5.8	−4.9	−4.2	....	....	....	....	....	....	....	....
Debt	88g	45.3	48.5	52.8	57.1	59.3	59.5	....	....	....	....	....	....
National Accounts				*Billions of Francs through 1998; Billions of Euros Beginning 1999:*									
Househ.Cons.Expend.,incl.NPISHs	96f.c	4,204.5	4,321.5	† 4,436.1	4,583.1	4,642.7	4,831.5	† 758.1	803.3	838.2	866.1	890.0	924.3
Government Consumption Expend	91f.c	1,758.4	1,797.6	† 1,850.9	1,922.1	1,984.7	2,004.5	† 316.7	330.1	341.2	362.2	377.4	394.4
Gross Fixed Capital Formation	93e.c	1,366.6	1,396.7	† 1,419.6	1,440.5	1,451.4	1,555.4	† 256.7	280.7	291.6	290.6	300.3	316.0
Changes in Inventories	93i.c	−80.2	−1.9	† 41.4	−13.2	.7	75.5	† 6.2	14.3	8.9	3.2	−.2	9.5
Exports of Goods and Services	90c.c	1,537.8	1,655.0	† 1,784.7	1,866.9	2,136.8	2,278.5	† 357.6	411.7	421.0	419.9	407.7	428.1
Imports of Goods and Services (-)	98c.c	1,470.5	1,589.4	† 1,695.4	1,745.8	1,895.6	2,056.7	† 329.0	398.7	403.8	393.4	390.2	424.0
Gross Domestic Product (GDP)	99b.c	7,316.5	7,579.4	† 7,837.4	8,053.7	8,320.7	8,688.6	† 1,366.5	1,441.4	1,497.2	1,548.6	1,585.2	1,648.4
Net Primary Income from Abroad	98.nc	−6.4	−28.7	−41.0	−4.6	19.0	39.9	† 20.9	19.8	17.7	4.2	7.2	8.8
Gross National Income (GNI)	99a.c	7,387.4	7,610.3	7,850.7	8,095.5	8,375.3	8,753.9	† 1,387.4	1,461.2	1,514.9	1,552.8	1,592.4	1,657.1
Net Current Transf.from Abroad	98t.c	−26.0	−28.9	−18.2	−31.9	−34.3	−40.1	† −44.1	−56.4	−53.1	−53.4	−69.9	....
Gross Nat'l Disposable Inc.(GNDI)	99i.c	7,170.8	7,418.0	7,666.5	7,892.3	8,170.9	8,542.0	† 1,343.3	1,404.8	1,461.8	1,499.4	1,522.5	....
Gross Saving	99s.c	1,370.8	1,440.5	1,512.2	1,528.7	1,673.8	1,837.3	† 285.2	301.7	311.6	303.1	286.2	314.3
Consumption of Fixed Capital	99cfc	1,009.2	1,037.9	1,064.9	1,110.1	1,141.3	1,172.2	† 168.4	180.7	192.5	200.4	203.7	208.5
GDP Vol. 1995 Ref., Chained	99b.r	7,480.8	7,615.4	7,758.9	7,841.5	7,990.3	8,268.1	† 1,323.9	1,377.8	1,406.0	1,423.2	1,434.6	1,467.9
GDP Volume (2000=100)	99bvr	82.8	84.3	85.9	86.8	88.4	91.5	† 96.1	100.0	102.1	103.3	104.1	106.5
GDP Deflator (2000=100)	99bir	93.5	95.1	† 96.6	98.2	99.5	100.4	† 98.7	100.0	101.8	104.0	105.6	107.3
				Millions: Midyear Estimates									
Population	99z	57.65	57.94	58.20	58.44	58.66	58.86	59.06	59.28	59.51	59.76	60.01	60.26

Gabon 646

		1993	1994	1995	1996	1997	1998	1999	2000	2001	2002	2003	2004
Exchange Rates						*Francs per SDR: End of Period*							
Official Rate	aa	404.89	† 780.44	728.38	753.06	807.94	791.61	† 896.19	918.49	935.39	850.37	771.76	747.90
					Francs per US Dollar: End of Period (ae) Period Average (rf)								
Official Rate	ae	294.77	† 534.60	490.00	523.70	598.81	562.21	† 652.95	704.95	744.31	625.50	519.36	481.58
Official Rate	rf	283.16	† 555.20	499.15	511.55	583.67	589.95	† 615.70	711.98	733.04	696.99	581.20	528.28
					Index Numbers (2000=100): Period Averages								
Official Rate	ahx	250.9	128.1	142.3	138.8	121.8	120.5	115.5	100.0	96.9	102.2	122.4	134.6
Nominal Effective Exchange Rate	nec	195.3	104.7	109.1	109.6	105.9	108.5	105.8	100.0	101.4	103.7	109.0	111.1
Real Effective Exchange Rate	rec	149.7	101.0	111.5	110.2	108.6	112.3	107.4	100.0	101.4	101.9	107.8	108.2
Fund Position						*Millions of SDRs: End of Period*							
Quota	2f.s	110.30	110.30	110.30	110.30	110.30	110.30	154.30	154.30	154.30	154.30	154.30	154.30
SDRs	1b.s	.03	.17	—	.02	—	.01	—	.05	.04	—	—	4.03
Reserve Position in the Fund	1c.s	.05	.05	.05	.07	.07	.07	.11	.15	.18	.18	.18	.18
Total Fund Cred.&Loans Outstg	2tl	32.89	61.42	64.95	83.26	97.20	80.52	62.60	68.38	59.64	49.53	39.42	64.36
International Liquidity					*Millions of US Dollars Unless Otherwise Indicated: End of Period*								
Total Reserves minus Gold	1l.d	.75	175.19	148.09	248.72	282.60	15.41	17.95	190.09	9.85	139.65	196.57	443.42
SDRs	1b.d	.03	.25	—	.03	—	.01	.01	.07	.06	—	—	6.26
Reserve Position in the Fund	1c.d	.07	.08	.08	.09	.09	.09	.15	.19	.23	.24	.27	.28
Foreign Exchange	1d.d	.64	174.86	148.01	248.59	282.51	15.30	17.79	189.83	9.57	139.40	196.30	436.88
Gold (Million Fine Troy Ounces)	1ad	.013	.013	.013	.013	.013	.013	.013	.013	.013	.013	.013	.013
Gold (National Valuation)	1and	5.11	† 4.85	4.95	4.73	3.74	3.69	† 3.73	3.50	3.57	4.40	5.36	5.63
Monetary Authorities: Other Liab.	4..d	35.48	33.67	34.56	33.52	53.73	34.62	46.34	44.91	41.61	48.64	64.32	59.34
Deposit Money Banks: Assets	7a.d	53.13	82.23	75.69	159.03	64.55	71.56	74.88	239.68	132.33	115.94	166.73	402.16
Liabilities	7b.d	89.15	41.28	79.93	94.16	50.58	56.73	77.78	91.62	81.39	131.84	138.52	140.12
Monetary Authorities						*Billions of Francs: End of Period*							
Foreign Assets	11	1.70	96.30	74.99	132.74	171.45	10.74	14.15	136.47	9.99	90.10	104.88	216.26
Claims on Central Government	12a	62.47	95.83	101.92	123.60	87.49	211.13	200.78	157.33	248.21	231.47	196.78	197.18
Claims on Deposit Money Banks	12e	19.82	.16	3.74	.75	—	8.11	11.63	.22	3.00	8.00	—	—
Claims on Other Banking Insts	12f	—	—	—	—	—	—	—	—	—	—	—	—
Reserve Money	14	58.38	133.91	128.24	165.20	167.93	153.60	141.52	192.68	184.59	186.61	213.40	258.85
of which: Currency Outside DMBs	14a	50.47	76.93	100.69	110.88	121.03	124.72	105.26	116.18	128.19	132.02	124.22	138.69
Foreign Liabilities	16c	23.78	65.94	64.24	80.26	110.71	83.21	86.36	94.46	86.76	72.54	63.83	76.71
Central Government Deposits	16d	3.11	18.51	10.67	32.35	16.13	12.14	26.10	43.18	24.57	100.81	50.30	109.45
Capital Accounts	17a	7.59	12.49	11.53	11.89	12.32	11.87	13.76	14.46	15.24	14.52	13.35	14.22
Other Items (Net)	17r	−8.87	−38.56	−34.03	−32.61	−48.15	−30.85	−41.17	−50.75	−49.97	−44.90	−39.23	−45.82
Deposit Money Banks						*Billions of Francs: End of Period*							
Reserves	20	7.86	56.87	27.06	48.32	44.10	27.47	34.75	75.73	56.10	54.19	88.82	119.47
Foreign Assets	21	15.66	43.96	37.09	83.28	38.65	40.23	48.89	168.96	98.49	72.52	86.59	193.67
Claims on Central Government	22a	99.25	172.94	161.16	152.37	143.46	135.76	137.99	92.91	88.71	104.98	104.94	92.97
Claims on Nonfin.Pub.Enterprises	22c	9.88	10.17	9.49	13.60	26.91	23.20	22.32	17.11	21.39	13.53	8.92	16.08
Claims on Private Sector	22d	157.91	157.20	196.08	191.93	269.89	285.12	286.06	313.79	375.04	415.74	380.53	330.26
Claims on Other Banking Insts	22f	—	.88	.88	.91	1.39	.60	.74	.74	.60	.63	.59	.59
Claims on Nonbank Financial Insts	22g	4.22	7.07	10.22	7.99	7.66	7.55	10.53	25.30	22.05	25.70	22.74	27.57
Demand Deposits	24	86.92	117.96	117.90	159.11	174.41	156.99	161.85	203.51	203.74	214.27	220.52	248.06
Time and Savings Deposits	25	99.87	130.98	139.87	144.78	169.98	176.47	177.21	206.85	234.47	252.33	246.66	271.50
Bonds	26ab	1.20	.30	.23	.15	.08	3.09	5.55	2.65	2.25	1.85	.41	—
Foreign Liabilities	26c	19.37	13.73	36.34	46.79	28.24	22.66	38.99	56.61	58.85	74.03	57.40	58.40
Long-Term Foreign Liabilities	26cl	6.91	8.34	2.83	2.52	2.05	9.24	11.80	7.98	1.72	8.44	14.54	9.07
Central Government Deposits	26d	16.72	32.21	15.35	20.93	20.62	21.82	29.67	112.30	71.32	41.42	47.38	69.84
Credit from Monetary Authorities	26g	19.82	.16	3.74	.75	—	8.11	11.63	.22	3.00	8.00	—	—
Capital Accounts	27a	54.55	133.44	128.50	123.58	115.89	122.47	120.48	85.73	107.75	120.20	136.94	150.79
Other Items (Net)	27r	−10.58	11.97	−2.78	−.21	20.78	−.92	−15.89	18.68	−20.73	−33.25	−30.72	−27.06
Monetary Survey						*Billions of Francs: End of Period*							
Foreign Assets (Net)	31n	−32.70	52.25	8.68	86.45	69.10	−64.14	−74.10	146.38	−38.86	7.62	55.70	265.74
Domestic Credit	32	313.90	393.36	453.74	437.12	500.04	629.38	602.65	451.70	660.10	649.82	616.82	485.35
Claims on Central Govt. (Net)	32an	141.89	218.05	237.06	222.68	194.19	312.92	283.00	94.76	241.03	194.22	204.04	110.85
Claims on Nonfin.Pub.Enterprises	32c	9.88	10.17	9.49	13.60	26.91	23.20	22.32	17.11	21.39	13.53	8.92	16.08
Claims on Private Sector	32d	157.91	157.20	196.08	191.93	269.89	285.12	286.06	313.79	375.04	415.74	380.53	330.26
Claims on Other Banking Insts	32f	—	.88	.88	.91	1.39	.60	.74	.74	.60	.63	.59	.59
Claims on Nonbank Financial Inst	32g	4.22	7.07	10.22	7.99	7.66	7.55	10.53	25.30	22.05	25.70	22.74	27.57
Money	34	137.44	195.01	219.09	276.00	298.25	283.12	268.61	320.46	332.22	346.69	345.10	387.45
Quasi-Money	35	99.87	130.98	139.87	144.78	169.98	176.47	177.21	206.85	234.47	252.33	246.66	271.50
Bonds	36ab	1.20	.30	.23	.15	.08	3.09	5.55	2.65	2.25	1.85	.41	—
Other Items (Net)	37r	42.69	119.33	103.23	102.64	100.84	102.57	77.17	68.12	52.30	56.56	80.34	92.14
Money plus Quasi-Money	35l	237.31	325.98	358.96	420.78	468.22	459.59	445.82	527.31	566.69	599.03	591.76	658.95
Interest Rates						*Percent Per Annum*							
Discount Rate (End of Period)	60	11.50	† 7.75	8.60	7.75	7.50	7.00	7.60	7.00	6.50	6.30	6.00	6.00
Deposit Rate	60l	7.75	8.08	5.50	5.46	5.00	5.00	5.00	5.00	5.00	5.00	5.00	5.00
Lending Rate	60p	17.46	17.50	16.00	22.00	22.00	22.00	22.00	22.00	20.67	18.00	18.00	18.00
Prices and Production						*Index Numbers (2000=100): Period Averages*							
Consumer Prices	64	64.0	87.1	95.5	96.2	100.0	101.5	99.5	100.0	102.1	102.2	104.5	104.9
Crude Petroleum	66aa	87.4	97.8	101.1	106.7	108.8	107.6	101.3	100.0	85.2	79.1	80.5	70.0
Intl. Transactions & Positions						*Billions of Francs*							
Exports	70	649.80	1,304.90	1,354.40	1,628.70	1,765.20	1,130.20	1,473.80	1,753.00	1,942.00	....	....	....
Imports, c.i.f.	71	239.30	420.00	440.20	489.30	644.30	650.80	518.00	708.00	629.50	....	....	....
Imports, c.i.f., from DOTS	71y	259.86	392.82	464.29	459.63	719.62	645.74	963.12	993.69	1,071.32	797.63	....	....

Gabon 646

		1993	1994	1995	1996	1997	1998	1999	2000	2001	2002	2003	2004
Balance of Payments						*Millions of US Dollars: Minus Sign Indicates Debit*							
Current Account, n.i.e.	78ald	−49.1	317.4	464.7	888.6	531.4	−595.5	390.4	....	....	....	....	....
Goods: Exports f.o.b.	78aad	2,326.2	2,365.3	2,727.8	3,334.2	3,032.7	1,907.6	2,498.8	....	....	....	....	....
Goods: Imports f.o.b.	78abd	−845.1	−776.7	−880.9	−961.6	−1,030.6	−1,163.2	−910.5	....	....	....	....	....
Trade Balance	78acd	1,481.1	1,588.6	1,846.9	2,372.5	2,002.1	744.4	1,588.3	....	....	....	....	....
Services: Credit	78add	311.1	219.6	217.1	233.9	232.9	219.6	280.9	....	....	....	....	....
Services: Debit	78aed	−1,022.7	−826.7	−891.6	−917.8	−952.7	−991.0	−867.0	....	....	....	....	....
Balance on Goods & Services	78afd	769.5	981.4	1,172.4	1,688.6	1,282.3	−27.0	1,002.2	....	....	....	....	....
Income: Credit	78agd	32.1	11.9	35.0	42.8	39.0	57.5	84.2	....	....	....	....	....
Income: Debit	78ahd	−658.3	−509.9	−700.5	−805.8	−755.5	−572.5	−653.1	....	....	....	....	....
Balance on Gds, Serv. & Inc.	78aid	143.4	483.4	507.0	925.6	565.8	−542.1	433.3	....	....	....	....	....
Current Transfers, n.i.e.: Credit	78ajd	48.0	18.7	58.0	65.2	62.7	36.6	42.6	....	....	....	....	....
Current Transfers: Debit	78akd	−240.5	−184.8	−100.3	−102.1	−97.1	−90.0	−85.6	....	....	....	....	....
Capital Account, n.i.e.	78bcd	—	—	4.8	5.1	5.8	1.8	5.4	....	....	....	....	....
Capital Account, n.i.e.: Credit	78bad	—	—	5.6	9.6	7.5	3.6	5.7	....	....	....	....	....
Capital Account: Debit	78bbd	—	—	−.8	−4.5	−1.7	−1.8	−.3	....	....	....	....	....
Financial Account, n.i.e.	78bjd	−389.2	−745.0	−724.7	−1,047.6	−626.2	−165.8	−686.8	....	....	....	....	....
Direct Investment Abroad	78bdd	−2.5	—	−35.0	−2.3	−21.0	−33.2	−73.9	....	....	....	....	....
Dir. Invest. in Rep. Econ., n.i.e.	78bed	−113.7	−99.6	−314.5	−489.1	−311.3	146.6	−156.6	....	....	....	....	....
Portfolio Investment Assets	78bfd	—	....	−29.8	−21.1	260.1	19.2	22.4	....	....	....	....	....
Equity Securities	78bkd	—	....	−45.0	−16.7	311.3	19.2	44.0	....	....	....	....	....
Debt Securities	78bld	—	....	15.2	−4.4	−51.2	—	−21.6	....	....	....	....	....
Portfolio Investment Liab., n.i.e.	78bgd	—	....	80.3	4.6	−20.7	−.2	−.7	....	....	....	....	....
Equity Securities	78bmd	—	....	—	−7.5	—	−.2	—	....	....	....	....	....
Debt Securities	78bnd	—	....	80.3	12.1	−20.7	—	−.7	....	....	....	....	....
Financial Derivatives Assets	78bwd	....	....	....	....	....	....	....	....	....	....	....	....
Financial Derivatives Liabilities	78bxd	....	....	....	....	....	....	....	....	....	....	....	....
Other Investment Assets	78bhd	−7.8	−258.6	−39.9	−215.1	18.3	−220.7	−109.0	....	....	....	....	....
Monetary Authorities	78bod	....	....	−2.1	1.2	25.0	−21.5	17.5	....	....	....	....	....
General Government	78bpd	—	—	—	—	—	—	—	....	....	....	....	....
Banks	78bqd	4.6	−22.9	13.8	−90.3	76.5	−2.7	−14.0	....	....	....	....	....
Other Sectors	78brd	−12.4	−235.8	−51.5	−126.0	−83.2	−196.4	−112.5	....	....	....	....	....
Other Investment Liab., n.i.e.	78bid	−265.2	−386.7	−385.7	−324.7	−551.6	−77.5	−369.1	....	....	....	....	....
Monetary Authorities	78bsd	−6.4	−203.9	—	—	—	—	—	....	....	....	....	....
General Government	78btd	−174.1	−133.1	−280.3	−208.4	−251.7	−276.0	−268.5	....	....	....	....	....
Banks	78bud	1.8	−54.9	34.3	19.8	−32.6	2.7	30.7	....	....	....	....	....
Other Sectors	78bvd	−86.5	5.2	−139.7	−136.1	−267.3	195.8	−131.3	....	....	....	....	....
Net Errors and Omissions	78cad	−13.6	254.6	−181.1	−97.4	−108.4	92.5	−106.7	....	....	....	....	....
Overall Balance	78cbd	−451.9	−173.0	−436.3	−251.2	−197.4	−667.0	−397.8	....	....	....	....	....
Reserves and Related Items	79dad	451.9	173.0	436.3	251.2	197.4	667.0	397.8	....	....	....	....	....
Reserve Assets	79dbd	67.5	−173.8	42.2	−112.8	−66.8	272.2	−4.9	....	....	....	....	....
Use of Fund Credit and Loans	79dcd	−35.9	40.9	5.0	26.4	19.4	−22.7	−24.5	....	....	....	....	....
Exceptional Financing	79ded	420.3	306.0	389.1	337.6	244.8	417.5	427.3	....	....	....	....	....
National Accounts						*Billions of Francs*							
Househ.Cons.Expend.,incl.NPISHs	96f	729.5	959.6	1,119.3	1,169.1	1,348.2	1,408.6	....	....	....	....	....	....
Government Consumption Expend.	91f	234.3	278.9	291.0	308.8	345.0	425.7	....	....	....	....	....	....
Gross Capital Formation	93	344.7	483.2	546.0	662.4	760.6	842.1	....	....	....	....	....	....
Exports of Goods and Services	90c	750.4	1,451.7	1,455.8	1,853.5	1,920.4	1,362.3	....	....	....	....	....	....
Imports of Goods and Services (-)	98c	521.2	865.2	952.4	1,133.5	1,266.9	1,310.7	....	....	....	....	....	....
Gross Domestic Product (GDP)	99b	1,530.8	2,326.7	2,475.2	2,912.6	3,109.0	2,645.2	2,870.8	3,558.3	3,340.3	....	....	....
Net Primary Income from Abroad	98.n	−190.6	−308.2	−376.8	−400.7	−395.8	−416.7	....	....	....	....	....	....
Gross National Income (GNI)	99a	1,347.1	2,000.0	2,082.9	2,459.4	2,711.5	2,311.3	....	....	....	....	....	....
Consumption of Fixed Capital	99cf	216.6	243.7	274.2	308.5	347.1	390.5	....	....	....	....	....	....
						Millions: Midyear Estimates							
Population	99z	1.05	1.09	1.12	1.15	1.18	1.21	1.24	1.27	1.30	1.32	1.34	1.36

Gambia, The   648

		1993	1994	1995	1996	1997	1998	1999	2000	2001	2002	2003	2004
Exchange Rates						*Dalasis per SDR: End of Period*							
Market Rate	aa	13.096	13.983	14.330	14.225	14.207	15.476	15.849	19.397	21.279	31.802	46.005	46.083
					Dalasis per US Dollar: End of Period (ae) Period Average (rf)								
Market Rate	ae	9.535	9.579	9.640	9.892	10.530	10.991	11.547	14.888	16.932	23.392	30.960	29.674
Market Rate	rf	9.129	9.576	9.546	9.789	10.200	10.643	11.395	12.788	15.687	19.918	27.306	30.030
					Index Numbers (2000=100): Period Averages								
Market Rate	ahx	139.51	132.84	133.29	130.02	124.81	119.59	111.74	100.00	81.26	64.54	46.87	42.38
Nominal Effective Exchange Rate	nec	105.18	110.40	105.39	106.15	110.25	109.05	103.83	100.00	85.90	66.50	41.60	36.23
Real Effective Exchange Rate	rec	118.28	109.80	105.81	104.68	109.88	107.54	105.19	100.00	87.77	72.34	52.10	51.14
Fund Position						*Millions of SDRs: End of Period*							
Quota	2f.s	22.90	22.90	22.90	22.90	22.90	22.90	31.10	31.10	31.10	31.10	31.10	31.10
SDRs	1b.s	.23	.18	.09	.20	.09	.30	.49	.17	.01	.01	.02	.48
Reserve Position in the Fund	1c.s	1.49	1.48	1.48	1.48	1.48	1.48	1.48	1.48	1.48	1.48	1.48	1.48
Total Fund Cred.&Loans Outstg	2tl	26.68	23.94	19.84	14.71	9.58	8.91	9.26	14.42	20.61	23.50	23.50	15.94
International Liquidity					*Millions of US Dollars Unless Otherwise Indicated: End of Period*								
Total Reserves minus Gold	1l.d	105.75	98.02	106.15	102.13	96.04	106.36	111.25	109.43	106.01	106.88	59.31	83.77
SDRs	1b.d	.31	.26	.13	.29	.11	.42	.67	.23	.02	.02	.03	.75
Reserve Position in the Fund	1c.d	2.04	2.17	2.21	2.14	2.00	2.09	2.04	1.93	1.87	2.02	2.21	2.31
Foreign Exchange	1d.d	103.40	95.59	103.81	99.71	93.92	103.85	108.54	107.27	104.13	104.84	57.07	80.72
Monetary Authorities: Other Liab.	4..d	29.54	26.15	22.03	17.38	11.69	12.22	12.71	18.79	25.90	31.95	34.92	24.76
Deposit Money Banks: Assets	7a.d	2.81	3.59	5.64	3.43	10.68	6.54	10.92	9.23	.92	24.28	34.09	50.79
Liabilities	7b.d	4.05	3.03	2.52	6.28	14.52	12.93	17.01	8.88	10.38	18.20	1.35	2.71
Monetary Authorities						*Millions of Dalasis: End of Period*							
Foreign Assets	11	1,020.68	948.01	1,030.19	1,011.63	1,010.13	1,163.67	1,277.17	1,626.32	1,793.06	2,499.12	1,834.48	2,468.80
Claims on Central Government	12a	270.72	297.93	253.65	259.73	240.84	239.90	239.39	223.20	250.52	405.91	1,176.72	1,307.96
Claims on Official Entities	12bx	—	—	—	—	—	—	—	—	—	—	—	—
Claims on Private Sector	12d	15.02	17.02	20.45	21.54	21.08	20.86	21.91	22.71	24.13	23.72	24.39	28.82
Claims on Deposit Money Banks	12e	—	—	—	—	—	—	—	—	56.98	31.35	21.20	33.62
Reserve Money	14	319.64	307.08	385.02	386.85	490.42	525.60	601.65	702.68	850.40	1,140.53	1,855.88	2,060.73
of which: Currency Outside DMBs	14a	224.49	207.36	247.97	255.03	360.51	347.55	379.72	540.26	600.75	797.37	1,182.89	1,416.27
Restricted Deposits	16b	—	—	—	—	—	—	—	—	—	—	—	—
Foreign Liabilities	16c	407.04	354.07	284.26	209.19	136.05	137.85	146.82	279.79	438.56	747.34	1,081.12	734.71
Central Government Deposits	16d	553.08	597.69	559.54	669.41	718.02	782.05	808.47	984.40	767.72	750.76	404.54	1,563.16
Capital Accounts	17a	73.70	75.50	83.59	80.87	81.34	85.33	86.76	91.53	107.09	122.05	181.94	190.46
Other Items (Net)	17r	−47.04	−71.38	−8.11	−53.42	−153.78	−106.39	−105.23	−186.16	−39.09	199.43	−466.69	−709.86
of which: Valuation Adjustment	17rv	199.18	217.07	249.70	231.01	129.79	154.75	390.50	306.25	95.79	599.47	1,255.73	1,333.14
Deposit Money Banks						*Millions of Dalasis: End of Period*							
Reserves	20	98.01	97.09	117.71	128.16	129.91	178.05	221.93	162.43	249.65	367.65	586.28	670.93
Foreign Assets	21	26.80	34.41	54.36	33.94	112.47	71.90	126.06	137.47	15.51	568.05	1,055.55	1,507.23
Claims on Central Government	22a	135.74	100.50	228.00	355.70	447.25	516.62	587.86	819.73	1,078.99	913.64	653.96	1,195.55
Claims on Official Entities	22bx	3.81	.10	.18	.43	1.11	3.86	9.20	11.86	75.79	74.69	205.87	86.46
Claims on Private Sector	22d	361.90	385.44	342.35	341.89	425.26	489.76	591.41	652.18	873.21	1,203.05	1,609.04	1,425.27
Demand Deposits	24	236.89	200.17	223.50	198.46	268.90	279.02	336.32	443.27	524.66	959.40	1,690.14	1,691.34
Time and Savings Deposits	25	371.17	393.49	443.45	514.30	560.66	685.01	754.26	998.82	1,241.90	1,445.75	1,720.00	2,324.35
Restricted Deposits	26b	—	—	—	—	—	—	—	—	—	—	—	—
Foreign Liabilities	26c	38.65	28.98	24.25	62.10	152.86	142.17	196.46	132.14	175.83	425.63	41.68	80.52
Central Government Deposits	26d	3.96	3.96	3.96	3.96	3.96	3.96	3.96	3.96	3.96	3.96	—	—
Credit from Monetary Authorities	26g												
Capital Accounts	27a	68.77	72.28	77.98	88.13	113.08	126.34	188.41	246.75	315.19	491.54	604.35	652.55
Other Items (Net)	27r	−93.18	−81.34	−30.54	−6.83	16.54	23.69	57.05	−41.27	31.61	−199.20	54.53	136.68
Monetary Survey						*Millions of Dalasis: End of Period*							
Foreign Assets (Net)	31n	601.79	599.37	776.05	774.28	833.70	955.55	1,059.95	1,351.87	1,194.18	1,894.21	1,767.23	3,160.81
Domestic Credit	32	230.15	199.34	281.13	305.92	413.56	484.99	637.34	741.32	1,530.96	1,866.29	3,265.44	2,480.90
Claims on Central Govt. (Net)	32an	−150.58	−203.22	−81.85	−57.94	−33.89	−29.49	14.82	54.57	557.83	564.83	1,426.14	940.35
Claims on Official Entities	32bx	3.81	.10	.18	.43	1.11	3.86	9.20	11.86	75.79	74.69	205.87	86.46
Claims on Private Sector	32d	376.92	402.46	362.80	363.43	446.34	510.62	613.32	674.89	897.34	1,226.77	1,633.43	1,454.09
Money	34	461.38	407.53	471.47	453.49	629.41	626.57	716.04	983.53	1,125.41	1,756.77	2,873.03	3,107.61
Quasi-Money	35	371.17	393.49	443.45	514.30	560.66	685.01	754.26	998.82	1,241.90	1,445.75	1,720.00	2,324.35
Restricted Deposits	36b	—	—	—	—	—	—	—	—	—	—	—	—
Capital Accounts	37a	142.47	147.78	161.57	169.00	194.42	211.67	275.17	338.28	422.28	613.59	786.29	843.01
Other Items (Net)	37r	−143.08	−150.09	−19.31	−56.59	−137.24	−82.70	−48.18	−227.44	−64.46	−55.62	−346.65	−633.27
Money plus Quasi-Money	35l	832.55	801.02	914.92	967.79	1,190.07	1,311.58	1,470.30	1,982.35	2,367.31	3,202.52	4,593.03	5,431.96
Interest Rates						*Percent Per Annum*							
Discount Rate (End of Period)	60	13.50	13.50	14.00	14.00	14.00	12.00	10.50	10.00	13.00	18.00	29.00	28.00
Savings Rate	60k	9.92	9.50	9.50	9.50	9.50	9.50	9.33	8.17	8.00	8.00	9.29	9.67
Deposit Rate	60l	13.00	12.58	12.50	12.50	12.50	12.50	12.50	12.50	12.50	12.71	16.42	22.00
Lending Rate	60p	26.08	25.00	25.04	25.50	25.50	25.50	25.38	24.00	24.00	24.00	29.33	36.50
Prices						*Index Numbers (2000=100): Period Averages*							
Consumer Prices	64	83.5	84.9	90.9	91.8	94.4	97.7	99.8	100.0	108.1	113.4	132.7	151.6
Intl. Transactions & Positions						*Millions of Dalasis*							
Exports	70	604.73	337.80	155.23	209.15	149.82	221.51	51.45	195.00	47.76	37.94	....	299.83
Imports, c.i.f.	71	2,372.27	2,032.75	1,741.26	2,527.62	1,773.80	2,426.44	2,186.82	2,394.93	2,106.96	2,974.04	....	6,870.01
Government Finance						*Millions of Dalasis: Year Ending June 30*							
Deficit (-) or Surplus	80	120.69p	....	....	....	....	....	....	....	....	....	....	....
Revenue	81	791.77p	....	....	....	....	....	....	....	....	....	....	....
Grants Received	81z	8.14p	....	....	....	....	....	....	....	....	....	....	....
Expenditure	82	695.14p	....	....	....	....	....	....	....	....	....	....	....
Lending Minus Repayments	83	−15.92p	....	....	....	....	....	....	....	....	....	....	....
Financing													
Domestic	84a	−219.12p	....	....	....	....	....	....	....	....	....	....	....
Foreign	85a	98.43p	....	....	....	....	....	....	....	....	....	....	....

Gambia, The   648

		1993	1994	1995	1996	1997	1998	1999	2000	2001	2002	2003	2004
National Accounts					*Millions of Dalasis: Year Ending June 30*								
Gross Domestic Product (GDP)	**99b**	2,518.5	2,886.3	....	....	....	....	....	....	....	....	....	....
GDP Volume 1976 Prices	**99b.p**	604.0	626.1	600.4	....	....	....	....	....	....	....	....	....
GDP Volume (1995=100)	**99bvp**	100.6	104.3	100.0	....	....	....	....	....	....	....	....	....
GDP Deflator (1990=100)	**99bip**	94.3	104.3	....	....	....	....	....	....	....	....	....	....
					Millions: Midyear Estimates								
Population	**99z**	1.04	1.08	1.12	1.15	1.19	1.23	1.28	1.32	1.36	1.40	1.44	1.48

		1993	1994	1995	1996	1997	1998	1999	2000	2001	2002	2003	2004
Exchange Rates					*Lari per SDR: End of Period*								
Official Rate	aa	....	....	1.8284	1.8348	1.7594	2.5345	2.6489	2.5732	2.5889	2.8414	3.0834	2.8342
				Lari per US Dollar: End of Period (ae) Period Average (rf)									
Official Rate	ae	....	....	1.2300	1.2760	1.3040	1.8000	1.9300	1.9750	2.0600	2.0900	2.0750	1.8250
Official Rate	rf	....	....	....	1.2628	1.2975	1.3898	2.0245	1.9762	2.0730	2.1957	2.1457	1.9167
				Index Numbers (2000=100): Period Averages									
Nominal Effective Exchange Rate	nec	....	158.36	100.00	117.88	138.71	159.99	....	....	....	....	....	....
Real Effective Exchange Rate	rec	....	44.73	100.00	129.37	136.48	135.73	....	....	....	....	....	....
Fund Position					*Millions of SDRs: End of Period*								
Quota	2f.s	111.00	111.00	111.00	111.00	111.00	111.00	150.30	150.30	150.30	150.30	150.30	150.30
SDRs	1b.s	—	1.61	1.12	.05	.10	3.69	6.13	2.51	3.15	2.13	3.31	7.22
Reserve Position in the Fund	1c.s	.01	.01	.01	.01	.01	.01	.01	.01	.01	.01	.01	.01
Total Fund Cred.& Loans Outstg	2tl	—	27.75	77.70	133.20	188.70	215.76	233.33	213.68	228.65	228.03	194.26	171.26
International Liquidity				*Millions of US Dollars Unless Otherwise Indicated: End of Period*									
Total Reserves minus Gold	1l.d	....	....	194.01	188.91	199.80	122.99	132.39	109.41	159.37	197.55	190.72	382.90
SDRs	1b.d	—	2.35	1.66	.07	.13	5.20	8.42	3.27	3.96	2.89	4.91	11.22
Reserve Position in the Fund	1c.d	.01	.01	.01	.01	.01	.01	.01	.01	.01	.01	.01	.02
Foreign Exchange	1d.d	....	....	192.33	188.83	199.66	117.78	123.96	106.13	155.40	194.64	185.79	371.66
Gold(Millions Fine Troy Ounces)	1ad	....	....	—	—	—	—	—	—	—	—	—	—
Gold (National Valuation)	1and	....	....	—	—	—	—	—	—	—	—	—	—
Monetary Authorities:Other Assets	3..d	....	....	.11	—	—	—	—	—	—	—	—	—
Other Liab	4..d	....	....	.06	.06	27.75	36.68	41.18	38.79	40.27	46.60	55.98	62.81
Deposit Money Banks: Assets	7a.d	....	....	26.88	33.88	39.10	46.41	48.57	54.11	84.53	94.32	114.47	158.80
Liabilities	7b.d	....	....	49.26	4.80	11.95	35.99	46.94	57.64	70.58	87.89	97.43	118.40
Monetary Authorities					*Millions of Lari: End of Period*								
Foreign Assets	11	....	....	238.75	241.15	260.50	221.53	255.50	216.12	† 337.19	422.35	407.02	705.41
Claims on General Government	12a	....	....	112.45	296.72	437.52	541.78	717.82	802.49	† 767.62	776.87	816.53	841.41
Claims on Nonfin. Pub. Enterprises	12c	....	....	—	—	—	—	—	—	† 79.04	95.28	114.18	110.10
Claims on Private Sector	12d	....	....	—	—	36.67	66.67	80.86	77.88	† 1.17	1.59	2.01	2.44
Claims on Deposit Money Banks	12e	....	....	3.66	14.30	5.26	6.56	1.86	4.49	† 1.76	.25	6.81	.31
Reserve Money	14	....	....	153.28	208.96	277.07	259.72	308.47	391.66	† 431.78	516.38	590.36	884.52
of which: Currency Outside DMBs	14a	....	....	124.78	176.76	239.87	212.19	244.00	315.18	† 348.85	390.79	441.54	615.99
Time, Savings,& Fgn. Currency Dep	15	....	....	—	—	—	—	—	—	† 1.82	1.52	1.01	.60
Foreign Liabilities	16c	....	....	142.14	244.47	368.19	612.84	697.55	626.45	† 674.90	745.30	715.14	600.03
General Government Deposits	16d	....	....	57.17	87.86	52.08	41.94	21.74	20.26	† 28.60	20.95	33.62	119.69
Counterpart Funds	16e	....	....	—	—	—	4.41	.75	—	† —			
Capital Accounts	17a	....	....	14.88	18.53	94.02	−14.88	182.32	176.07	† 74.20	54.89	49.03	98.09
Other Items (Net)	17r	....	....	−12.61	−7.65	−51.41	−67.49	−154.79	−113.47	† −24.51	−42.70	−42.61	−43.26
Deposit Money Banks					*Millions of Lari: End of Period*								
Reserves	20	....	....	38.00	30.39	39.62	45.01	56.37	76.65	† 82.45	126.13	148.91	220.40
Foreign Assets	21	....	....	33.06	43.23	50.99	83.55	93.73	106.86	† 174.12	197.13	237.52	289.82
Claims on General Government	22a	....	....	1.47	1.27	4.86	1.12	1.70	5.72	† 17.02	37.35	53.17	42.73
of which: Claims on Local Govt	22ab	....	....	1.42	1.26	1.09	1.12	—	.30	† 2.04	2.87	10.61	.24
Claims on Nonfin. Pub. Enterprises	22c	....	....	—	—	—	—	—	—	† 25.00	39.62	39.33	23.47
Claims on Private Sector	22d	....	....	148.71	127.80	175.06	239.95	339.74	446.96	† 496.38	602.46	743.93	960.39
Claims on Nonbank Fin. Insts	22g	....	....	.31	.06	—	—	—	—	† —			
Demand Deposits	24	....	....	30.02	35.78	38.67	38.38	31.51	53.20	† 45.33	62.01	75.32	202.68
Time,Savings,& Fgn.Currency Dep	25	....	....	28.51	46.69	94.82	118.63	171.44	254.51	† 341.94	415.86	550.92	701.48
Money Market Instruments	26aa	....	....	—	—	—	—	—	—	† .02	.11	.02	—
Foreign Liabilities	26c	....	....	60.59	6.12	15.58	64.79	90.59	113.84	† 145.40	183.70	202.16	216.07
General Government Deposits	26d	....	....	14.27	18.30	9.08	15.61	10.71	11.15	† 26.46	74.28	66.87	23.11
of which: Local Govt. Deposits	26db	....	....	4.91	4.72	3.50	4.69	3.88	4.54	† 6.45	59.50	54.53	17.27
Counterpart Funds	26e	....	....	—	10.26	10.37	8.10	1.33	.24	† .36	.36	.36	—
Central Govt. Lending Funds	26f	....	....	—	—	—	—	3.52	6.29	† 6.29	6.94	6.69	5.50
Credit from Monetary Authorities	26g	....	....	—	—	—	—	—	—	† 1.21	.61	7.12	—
Liab. to Nonbank Financial Insts	26j	....	....	—	—	—	—	—	—	† .15	—	—	73.00
Capital Accounts	27a	....	....	61.09	90.82	145.14	200.17	280.27	376.61	† 471.60	495.13	578.09	662.08
Other Items (Net)	27r	....	....	27.08	−5.22	−43.12	−76.05	−97.82	−179.64	† −243.80	−236.30	−264.69	−347.12
Monetary Survey					*Millions of Lari: End of Period*								
Foreign Assets (Net)	31n	....	....	69.09	33.79	−72.29	−372.55	−438.90	−417.31	† −308.98	−309.52	−272.77	179.13
Domestic Credit	32	....	....	191.50	319.69	592.96	791.97	1,107.67	1,301.63	† 1,331.16	1,457.94	1,668.67	1,837.73
Claims on General Govt. (Net)	32an	....	....	42.48	191.83	381.22	485.35	687.07	776.79	† 729.58	718.98	769.21	741.34
Claims on Nonfin.Pub. Enterprises	32c	....	....	—	—	—	—	—	—	† 104.04	134.90	153.51	133.57
Claims on Private Sector	32d	....	....	148.71	127.80	211.73	306.62	420.60	524.84	† 497.55	604.06	745.95	962.82
Claims on Nonbank Fin. Insts	32g	....	....	.31	.06	—	—	—	—	† —	—	—	—
Money	34	....	....	154.80	212.54	278.54	250.58	275.50	368.37	† 394.23	452.84	516.92	819.49
Quasi-Money	35	....	....	28.51	46.69	94.82	118.63	171.44	254.51	† 343.76	417.38	551.93	702.09
Money Market Instruments	36aa	....	....	—	—	—	—	—	—	† .02	.11	.02	—
Counterpart Funds	36e	....	....	—	10.26	10.37	12.50	2.08	.24	† .36	.36	.36	—
Central Govt. Lending Funds	36f	....	....	—	—	—	—	3.52	6.29	† 6.29	6.94	6.69	5.50
Liab. to Nonbank Financial Insts	36j	....	....	—	—	—	—	—	—	† .15	—	—	73.00
Capital Accounts	37a	....	....	75.97	109.35	239.16	185.30	462.58	552.68	† 545.80	550.01	627.12	760.17
Other Items (Net)	37r	....	....	1.31	−25.36	−102.21	−147.58	−246.36	−297.77	† −268.44	−279.22	−307.15	−343.39
Money plus Quasi-Money	35l	....	....	183.31	259.23	373.36	369.20	446.94	622.88	† 737.99	870.22	1,068.85	1,521.57
Money (National Definitions)					*Millions of Lari: End of Period*								
Reserve Money	19mb	....	....	....	....	....	....	....	....	429.86	508.97	579.91	836.54
M2	59mb	....	....	....	....	....	....	....	....	403.84	462.27	527.40	846.10
M3	59mc	....	....	....	....	....	....	....	....	732.45	863.57	1,060.39	1,511.93

Georgia 915

		1993	1994	1995	1996	1997	1998	1999	2000	2001	2002	2003	2004
Interest Rates							*Percent Per Annum*						
Money Market Rate	60b	....	....	....	43.39	26.58	43.26	34.61	18.17	† 17.52	27.69	16.88	11.87
Treasury Bill Rate	60c	....	....	....						29.93	43.42	44.26	19.16
Deposit Rate	60l	....	....	....	31.05	13.73	17.00	14.58	10.17	7.75	9.82	9.28	7.24
Deposit Rate (Foreign Currency)	60l.f	....	....	....	24.55	19.11	15.75	14.58	12.00	10.42	10.23	9.19	7.66
Lending Rate	60p	....	....	....	58.24	50.64	46.00	33.42	32.75	27.25	31.83	32.27	31.23
Lending Rate (Foreign Currency)	60p.f	....	....	....	51.92	54.16	46.75	42.92	36.58	32.17	29.27	27.62	27.06
Prices and Labor						*Index Numbers (2000=100): Period Averages*							
Producer Prices	63	....	....	....	....		82.7	† 94.5	100.0	† 103.7	109.9	....	....
Consumer Prices	64	....	19.9	52.2	72.7	77.8	80.6	96.1	100.0	104.6	110.5	115.8	122.3
					Number in Thousands: Period Averages								
Labor Force	67d	....	....	....	....	1,999	2,026	2,010	2,052	2,113	2,104	2,050	....
Employment	67e	....	....	....	....	1,848	1,731	1,733	1,839	1,878	1,839	1,814	....
Unemployment	67c	....	....	....	....	152	295	277	212	236	265	236	....
Unemployment Rate (%)	67r	....	....	....	....	7.6	14.5	13.8	10.3	11.1	12.6	11.5	....
Intl. Transactions & Positions						*Millions of Lari*							
Exports	70	....	163	194	251	312	267	481	645	657	769	1,022	....
Imports, c.i.f.	71	....	288	507	868	1,224	1,229	1,184	1,423	1,560	1,743	2,448	....
Imports, f.o.b.	71.v	....	259	456	781	1,103	1,107	....	....	....	....	....	....
Balance of Payments					*Millions of US Dollars: Minus Sign Indicates Debit*								
Current Account, n.i.e.	78ald	....	....	....	....	−514.2	−275.7	−198.4	−269.0	−211.7	−221.3	−374.8	−425.6
Goods: Exports f.o.b.	78aad	....	....	....	....	376.5	299.9	329.5	459.0	496.1	601.7	830.6	1,092.5
Goods: Imports f.o.b.	78abd	....	....	....	....	−1,162.9	−994.5	−863.4	−970.5	−1,045.6	−1,084.7	−1,466.6	−2,008.6
Trade Balance	78acd	....	....	....	....	−786.4	−694.6	−533.9	−511.5	−549.5	−483.0	−636.0	−916.0
Services: Credit	78add	....	....	....	....	198.0	365.3	216.9	206.4	314.1	392.2	442.7	538.5
Services: Debit	78aed	....	....	....	....	−249.7	−345.2	−224.0	−216.3	−236.9	−356.7	−388.7	−482.4
Balance on Goods & Services	78afd	....	....	....	....	−838.1	−674.5	−541.0	−521.4	−472.3	−447.5	−582.0	−859.9
Income: Credit	78agd	....	....	....	....	186.6	243.4	211.4	178.6	97.7	160.6	177.4	251.7
Income: Debit	78ahd	....	....	....	....	−59.2	−52.7	−64.5	−61.1	−65.4	−127.4	−145.0	−155.0
Balance on Gds, Serv. & Inc.	78aid	....	....	....	....	−710.7	−483.8	−394.1	−403.9	−440.0	−414.3	−549.7	−763.2
Current Transfers, n.i.e.: Credit	78ajd	....	....	....	....	205.5	219.9	228.7	163.2	246.4	222.0	211.1	389.1
Current Transfers: Debit	78akd	....	....	....	....	−9.0	−11.8	−33.0	−28.3	−18.1	−29.0	−36.2	−51.5
Capital Account, n.i.e.	78bcd	....	....	....	....	−6.5	−6.1	−7.1	−4.8	−5.2	18.4	19.9	40.8
Capital Account, n.i.e.: Credit	78bad	....	....	....	....	—	—	—	—	....	27.1	27.9	44.2
Capital Account: Debit	78bbd	....	....	....	....	−6.5	−6.1	−7.1	−4.8	−5.2	−8.6	−8.0	−3.4
Financial Account, n.i.e.	78bjd	....	....	....	....	322.7	348.8	135.5	92.8	209.7	19.2	322.7	479.0
Direct Investment Abroad	78bdd	....	....	....	....	—	—	−1.0	.5	.1	−4.1	−3.8	−9.6
Dir. Invest. in Rep. Econ., n.i.e.	78bed	....	....	....	....	242.5	265.3	82.3	131.1	109.8	167.4	339.4	499.1
Portfolio Investment Assets	78bfd	....	....	....	....	....	....	....	2.7	−.1	—	—	−13.1
Equity Securities	78bkd	....	....	....	....	....	....	....	2.7	—	—	—	−13.1
Debt Securities	78bld	....	....	....	....	....	....	....	....	....	....	....	....
Portfolio Investment Liab., n.i.e.	78bgd	....	....	....	....	2.4	—	6.2	—	....	....	....	....
Equity Securities	78bmd	....	....	....	....	2.4	—	6.2	—	....	....	....	....
Debt Securities	78bnd	....	....	....	....	....	....	....	....	....	....	....	....
Financial Derivatives Assets	78bwd	....	....	....	....	....	....	....	....	....	....	....	....
Financial Derivatives Liabilities	78bxd	....	....	....	....	....	....	....	....	....	....	....	....
Other Investment Assets	78bhd	....	....	....	....	−24.8	−86.9	9.3	−7.7	−24.6	−72.8	−15.3	−25.7
Monetary Authorities	78bod	....	....	....	....	—	—	—	—	—	—	—	—
General Government	78bpd	....	....	....	....	—	−45.0	—	—	....	−5.0	−5.0	−4.7
Banks	78bqd	....	....	....	....	−15.0	−23.2	9.3	−7.7	−24.6	−59.3	.5	−21.1
Other Sectors	78brd	....	....	....	....	−9.8	−18.7	—	—	....	−8.5	−10.8	.1
Other Investment Liab., n.i.e.	78bid	....	....	....	....	102.6	170.4	38.7	−33.8	124.5	−71.3	2.4	28.2
Monetary Authorities	78bsd	....	....	....	....	—	—	—	—	—	—	−.5	—
General Government	78btd	....	....	....	....	90.0	141.5	17.6	−41.1	99.1	−132.6	−56.7	−47.3
Banks	78bud	....	....	....	....	7.4	37.4	26.3	7.3	25.4	16.3	4.1	27.6
Other Sectors	78bvd	....	....	....	....	5.2	−8.5	−5.2	—	—	45.1	55.4	48.0
Net Errors and Omissions	78cad	....	....	....	....	136.0	−170.5	55.7	187.4	34.9	−6.0	−16.8	14.7
Overall Balance	78cbd	....	....	....	....	−62.0	−103.5	−14.3	6.4	27.7	−189.7	−49.0	108.8
Reserves and Related Items	79dad	....	....	....	....	62.0	103.5	14.3	−6.4	−27.7	189.7	49.0	−108.8
Reserve Assets	79dbd	....	....	....	....	−14.1	67.6	−9.6	19.8	−47.0	−37.7	6.0	−191.9
Use of Fund Credit and Loans	79dcd	....	....	....	....	76.1	35.8	23.9	−26.2	19.4	−.1	−47.4	−34.2
Exceptional Financing	79ded	....	....	....	....	....	....	....	....	....	227.4	90.4	117.3
Government Finance					*Millions of Lari: Year Ending December 31*								
Deficit (-) or Surplus	80	....	....	....	....	....	−175.39	−128.46	−193.61	−103.96	−185.15	−153.85	−150.61
Total Revenue and Grants	81y	....	....	....	....	....	621.87	723.96	640.26	740.34	818.01	914.76	1,709.18
Revenue	81	....	....	....	....	....	591.43	674.62	625.93	692.26	795.41	866.35	1,585.23
Grants	81z	....	....	....	....	....	30.44	49.35	14.33	48.08	22.60	48.41	123.95
Exp.& Lending Minus Repayments	82z	....	....	....	....	....	797.25	852.42	833.87	844.30	1,003.16	1,068.60	1,859.78
Expenditure	82	....	....	....	....	....	761.51	849.12	737.78	726.57	834.12	927.88	1,692.46
Lending Minus Repayments	83	....	....	....	....	....	35.74	3.30	96.09	117.73	169.04	140.72	167.32
Total Financing	80h	....	....	....	....	....	175.39	128.46	193.61	103.96	185.13	153.85	150.61
Domestic	84a	....	....	....	....	....	145.47	109.77	149.18	2.21	53.05	63.15	16.55
Foreign	85a	....	....	....	....	....	29.91	18.69	44.44	101.75	132.08	90.70	134.06
Total Debt by Residence	88	....	....	....	....	....	2,857.83	4,077.92	4,192.54	4,449.53	4,843.33	4,608.05	4,306.62
Domestic	88a	....	....	....	....	....	556.52	1,343.49	1,497.97	1,492.41	1,520.35	1,567.90	1,575.78
Foreign	89a	....	....	....	....	....	2,301.30	2,734.43	2,694.56	2,957.12	3,322.98	3,040.15	2,730.84

Georgia 915

		1993	1994	1995	1996	1997	1998	1999	2000	2001	2002	2003	2004
National Accounts							*Millions of Lari*						
Househ.Cons.Expend.,incl.NPISHs....	96f	....	....	3,368	4,007	4,545	4,258	4,648	5,332	5,464	6,087	....	....
Government Consumption Expend...	91f	....	....	295	298	463	557	603	516	644	732	....	....
Gross Fixed Capital Formation..........	93e	....	....	714	416	519	755	1,252	1,308	1,374	1,575	....	....
Changes in Inventories....................	93i	....	....	173	46	49	81	14	73	67	73	....	....
Exports of Goods and Services..........	90c	....	....	516	516	711	827	1,080	1,390	1,633	2,045	....	....
Imports of Goods and Services (-).....	98c	....	....	1,053	1,252	1,920	1,864	2,160	2,397	2,594	2,917	....	....
Gross Domestic Product (GDP).........	99b	....	....	3,694	3,846	4,639	5,040	5,665	6,013	6,638	7,457	....	....
							Millions: Midyear Estimates						
Population................................	99z	5.23	5.13	5.03	4.95	4.89	4.83	4.77	4.72	4.67	4.61	4.56	4.52

Germany 134

		1993	1994	1995	1996	1997	1998	1999	2000	2001	2002	2003	2004
Exchange Rates		*Deutsche Mark per SDR through 1998, Euros per SDR Thereafter: End of Period*											
Market Rate	aa	2.3712	2.2610	2.1309	2.2357	2.4180	2.3556	1.3662	1.4002	1.4260	1.2964	1.1765	1.1402
		Deutsche Mark per US Dollar through 1998, Euros per US Dollar Thereafter: End of Period (ae) Period Average (rf)											
Market Rate	ae	1.7263	1.5488	1.4335	1.5548	1.7921	1.6730	.9954	1.0747	1.1347	.9536	.7918	.7342
Market Rate	rf	1.6533	1.6228	1.4331	1.5048	1.7341	1.7597	.9386	1.0854	1.1175	1.0626	.8860	.8054
		Deutsche Mark per ECU: End of Period (ea) Period Average (eb)											
ECU Rate	ea	1.9357	1.9053	1.8840	1.9465	1.9763	1.9558	....	....	....	....	....	....
ECU Rate	eb	1.9368	1.9248	1.8736	1.9096	1.9642	1.9692	....	....	....	....	....	....
		Index Numbers (2000=100): Period Averages											
Market Rate (1995=100)	ahx	86.6	88.4	100.0	95.2	82.7	81.5	....	....	....	....	....	....
Nominal Effective Exchange Rate	neu	109.7	110.2	116.7	113.4	107.2	107.7	105.2	100.0	100.5	102.0	107.2	109.0
Real Effective Exchange Rate	reu	105.4	109.0	118.2	117.0	109.5	107.2	104.7	100.0	99.8	99.2	101.7	100.1
Fund Position		*Millions of SDRs: End of Period*											
Quota	2f.s	8,242	8,242	8,242	8,242	8,242	8,242	13,008	13,008	13,008	13,008	13,008	13,008
SDRs	1b.s	700	763	1,346	1,326	1,325	1,327	1,427	1,353	1,426	1,456	1,307	1,327
Reserve Position in the Fund	1c.s	2,877	2,760	3,505	3,803	4,407	5,698	4,677	4,191	4,696	4,925	5,152	4,419
of which: Outstg.Fund Borrowing	2c	—	—	—	—	—	530	—	—	—	—	—	—
International Liquidity		*Millions of US Dollars Unless Otherwise Indicated: End of Period*											
Total Res.Min.Gold (Eurosys.Def)	1l.d	77,640	77,363	85,005	83,178	77,587	74,024	† 61,039	56,890	51,404	51,171	50,694	48,823
SDRs	1b.d	962	1,114	2,001	1,907	1,788	1,868	1,959	1,763	1,793	1,980	1,942	2,061
Reserve Position in the Fund	1c.d	3,951	4,030	5,210	5,468	5,946	8,023	6,419	5,460	5,901	6,695	7,656	6,863
Foreign Exchange	1d.d	72,727	72,219	77,794	75,803	69,853	64,133	† 52,661	49,667	43,710	42,495	41,095	39,899
o/w:Fin.Deriv.Rel.to Reserves	1ddd	....	....	....	....	....	....	—	—	—	—	—	—
Other Reserve Assets	1e.d	....	....	....	....	....	....	—	—	—	—	—	—
Gold (Million Fine Troy Ounces)	1ad	95.18	95.18	95.18	95.18	95.18	118.98	111.52	111.52	111.13	110.79	110.58	110.38
Gold (Eurosystem Valuation)	1and	7,929	8,838	9,549	8,804	7,638	10,227	32,368	30,606	30,728	37,972	46,141	48,347
Memo:Euro Cl. on Non-EA Res.	1dgd							9,191	279	264	315	379	409
Non-Euro Cl. on EA Res.	1dhd	....	....	....	....	....	....	—	—	—	—	—	—
Mon. Auth.: Other Foreign Assets	3..d	1,548	1,539	1,371	944	559	680	† 9,204	291	276	327	394	425
Foreign Liabilities	4..d	22,909	15,620	11,435	10,035	9,436	9,551	† 6,195	6,125	7,670	9,409	13,178	10,792
Banking Insts.: Foreign Assets	7a.d	461,962	484,892	578,196	606,018	650,287	828,893	† 513,967	579,527	641,339	774,425	1,018,880	1,223,062
Foreign Liab.	7b.d	286,135	378,834	482,236	490,213	561,585	760,827	† 491,336	559,069	571,750	629,904	719,203	787,909
Monetary Authorities		*Billions of Deutsche Mark through 1998; Billions of Euros Beginning 1999: End of Period*											
Fgn. Assets (Cl.on Non-EA Ctys)	11	134.5	128.7	132.9	132.2	129.7	135.1	102.2	94.1	93.5	85.3	77.0	71.7
Claims on General Government	12a.u	....	....	....	....	....	....	4.4	4.4	4.4	4.4	4.4	4.4
o/w: Claims on Gen.Govt.in Cty	12a	27.7	26.6	24.7	24.0	24.2	24.3	4.4	4.4	4.4	4.4	4.4	4.4
Claims on Banking Institutions	12e.u	....	....	....	....	....	....	135.9	151.5	135.3	145.1	181.4	212.8
o/w: Claims on Bank.Inst.in Cty	12e	257.5	217.7	213.1	226.2	235.2	216.0	90.6	139.2	123.0	127.9	164.3	192.6
Claims on Other Resident Sectors	12d.u	....	....	....	....	....	....	—	—	—	—	—	—
o/w: Cl. on Oth.Res.Sect.in Cty	12d	....	....	....	....	....	....	—	—	—	—	—	—
Currency Issued	14a	238.6	250.9	263.5	275.7	276.2	271.0	148.2	142.2	82.8	112.2	125.9	141.3
Liabilities to Banking Insts	14c.u	....	....	....	....	....	....	48.8	53.9	88.4	74.0	89.4	104.9
o/w: Liabs to Bank.Inst.in Cty	14c	73.4	56.2	49.7	51.9	48.7	57.7	41.9	47.0	57.4	44.8	44.7	41.5
Demand Dep. of Other Res.Sect.	14d.u	....	....	....	....	....	....	.5	.4	1.0	.6	.6	.4
o/w:D.Dep.of Oth.Res.Sect.in Cty	14d	.8	.7	.7	1.3	1.1	1.0	.5	.4	1.0	.6	.5	.4
Other Dep. of Other Res.Sect.	15..u	....	....	....	....	....	....	—	—	—	—	—	—
o/w:O.Dep.of Oth.Res.Sect.in Cty	15	....	....	....	....	....	....	—	—	—	—	—	—
Bonds & Money Mkt. Instruments	16n.u	....	....	....	....	....	....	—	—	—	—	—	—
Foreign Liab. (to Non-EA Ctys)	16c	23.2	19.6	16.4	15.6	16.9	16.0	6.2	6.6	8.7	9.0	10.4	7.9
Central Government Deposits	16d.u	....	....	....	....	....	....	—	—	—	—	—	—
o/w: Cent.Govt.Dep. in Cty	16d	13.4	.2	.1	.4	.3	.2	—	—	—	—	—	—
Capital Accounts	17a	21.1	23.1	22.4	23.1	24.6	21.5	41.7	46.0	48.4	40.8	35.5	34.2
Other Items (Net)	17r	49.2	22.2	17.9	14.4	21.3	8.0	−2.8	1.0	3.9	−1.6	1.1	.2
Memo: Net Claims on Eurosystem	12e.s	....	....	....	....	....	....	38.5	5.4	−18.6	−12.1	−27.9	−43.6
Currency Put into Circ	14m	....	....	....	....	....	....	:	:	:	141.3	170.5	204.7
Banking Institutions		*Billions of Deutsche Mark through 1998; Billions of Euros Beginning 1999: End of Period*											
Claims on Monetary Authorities	20	102.0	86.5	87.0	88.6	89.5	92.1	45.6	51.0	56.4	45.6	46.9	41.2
Claims on Bk.Inst.in Oth.EA Ctys	20b.u	....	....	....	....	....	....	203.1	244.4	286.3	346.8	375.5	419.7
Fgn. Assets (Cl.on Non-EA Ctys)	21	797.5	751.0	828.8	942.2	1,165.4	1,386.7	511.6	622.8	727.7	738.5	806.7	897.9
Claims on General Government	22a.u	....	....	....	....	....	....	735.7	720.4	708.8	709.4	702.3	738.4
o/w: Claims on Gen.Govt.in Cty	22a	849.3	937.4	1,078.7	1,161.4	1,223.7	1,251.8	632.1	616.9	587.8	586.4	585.6	603.8
Claims on Other Resident Sectors	22d.u	....	....	....	....	....	....	2,391.7	2,529.4	2,608.3	2,630.8	2,630.9	2,620.3
o/w: Cl. on Oth.Res.Sect.in Cty	22d	3,206.4	3,451.4	3,630.7	3,900.1	4,137.6	4,471.9	2,326.4	2,445.7	2,497.1	2,505.8	2,497.4	2,479.7
Demand Deposits	24..u	....	....	....	....	....	....	426.0	448.2	532.7	582.9	631.4	655.0
o/w:D.Dep.of Oth.Res.Sect.in Cty	24	484.8	505.3	545.4	631.8	650.0	747.7	419.5	441.4	525.0	574.8	622.1	646.2
Other Deposits	25..u	....	....	....	....	....	....	1,541.7	1,533.6	1,557.2	1,542.8	1,551.3	1,580.2
o/w:O.Dep.of Oth.Res.Sect.in Cty	25	1,500.9	1,523.6	1,572.2	1,649.6	1,692.4	1,752.4	1,435.6	1,432.3	1,457.8	1,461.6	1,474.1	1,512.5
Money Market Fund Shares	26m.u	....	....	....	....	....	....	20.8	19.3	32.6	37.2	36.7	31.5
Bonds & Money Mkt. Instruments	26n.u	....	....	....	....	....	....	1,348.1	1,455.8	1,488.3	1,517.5	1,531.1	1,594.6
o/w: Held by Resid.of Cty	26n	1,467.6	1,612.5	1,786.9	1,948.0	2,075.8	2,196.0	....	....	....	....	....	....
Foreign Liab. (to Non-EA Ctys)	26c	494.0	586.7	691.3	762.2	1,006.4	1,272.9	489.1	600.8	648.8	600.7	569.4	578.5
Central Government Deposits	26d.u	....	....	....	....	....	....	46.6	69.9	49.1	47.7	45.9	43.8
o/w: Cent.Govt.Dep. in Cty	26d	242.9	249.5	245.4	248.1	248.4	251.3	45.9	67.6	46.9	45.6	44.2	41.4
Credit from Monetary Authorities	26g	257.5	217.7	213.1	226.2	235.2	216.0	92.1	139.3	125.0	125.4	162.8	190.9
Liab. to Bk.Inst.in Oth. EA Ctys	26h.u	....	....	....	....	....	....	166.3	190.5	215.9	242.4	241.6	257.6
Capital Accounts	27a	391.6	410.1	438.1	463.9	507.0	544.9	237.0	258.5	275.7	291.7	294.4	288.1
Other Items (Net)	27r	116.1	120.7	132.8	162.7	201.0	221.4	−480.0	−547.8	−537.5	−517.3	−502.2	−502.7

		1993	1994	1995	1996	1997	1998	1999	2000	2001	2002	2003	2004
Banking Survey (Nat'l Residency)			*Billions of Deutsche Mark through 1998; Billions of Euros Beginning 1999: End of Period*										
Foreign Assets (Net)	31n	414.9	273.3	254.0	296.6	271.7	233.0	266.1	271.3	361.9	486.5	594.4	719.0
Domestic Credit	32	3,827.2	4,165.6	4,488.6	4,837.1	5,137.0	5,496.5	2,917.1	2,999.4	3,042.3	3,051.0	3,043.3	3,046.4
Claims on General Govt. (Net)	32an	620.7	714.2	857.8	937.0	999.4	1,024.6	590.6	553.8	545.3	545.2	545.9	566.7
Claims on Other Resident Sectors	32d	3,206.4	3,451.4	3,630.7	3,900.1	4,137.6	4,471.9	2,326.4	2,445.7	2,497.1	2,505.8	2,497.4	2,479.7
Currency Issued	34a.n	238.6	250.9	263.5	275.7	276.2	271.0	148.2	142.2	82.8	112.2	125.9	141.3
Demand Deposits	34b.n	485.6	506.1	546.2	633.0	651.1	748.7	420.0	441.8	526.0	575.4	622.6	646.5
Other Deposits	35..n	1,500.9	1,523.6	1,572.2	1,649.6	1,692.4	1,752.4	1,435.6	1,432.3	1,457.8	1,461.6	1,474.1	1,512.5
Money Market Fund Shares	36m	....	....	....	....	....	....	20.8	19.3	32.6	37.2	36.7	31.5
Bonds & Money Mkt. Instruments	36n	1,467.6	1,612.5	1,786.9	1,948.0	2,075.8	2,196.0	1,348.1	1,455.8	1,488.3	1,517.5	1,531.1	1,594.6
o/w: Over Two Years	36na	....	....	....	....	....	....	1,226.2	1,303.8	1,316.1	1,326.4	1,355.6	1,437.9
Capital Accounts	37a	412.6	433.2	460.5	487.0	531.6	566.4	278.7	304.5	324.1	332.5	329.9	322.3
Other Items (Net)	37r	136.7	112.7	113.3	140.3	181.5	194.9	−468.2	−525.1	−507.3	−498.8	−482.6	−483.2
Banking Survey (EA-Wide Residency)							*Billions of Euros: End of Period*						
Foreign Assets (Net)	31n.u	....	....	....	....	....	....	118.6	109.5	163.8	214.2	303.8	383.2
Domestic Credit	32..u	....	....	....	....	....	....	3,085.2	3,184.4	3,272.4	3,296.9	3,291.8	3,319.3
Claims on General Govt. (Net)	32anu	....	....	....	....	....	....	693.5	655.0	664.1	666.1	660.8	699.1
Claims on Other Resident Sect.	32d.u	....	....	....	....	....	....	2,391.7	2,529.4	2,608.3	2,630.8	2,630.9	2,620.3
Currency Issued	34a.u	....	....	....	....	....	....	148.2	142.2	82.8	112.2	125.9	141.3
Demand Deposits	34b.u	....	....	....	....	....	....	426.5	448.7	533.7	583.5	631.9	655.4
Other Deposits	35..u	....	....	....	....	....	....	1,541.7	1,533.6	1,557.2	1,542.8	1,551.3	1,580.2
o/w: Other Dep. Over Two Yrs.	35abu	....	....	....	....	....	....	664.4	674.0	672.8	670.2	683.7	708.9
Money Market Fund Shares	36m.u	....	....	....	....	....	....	20.8	19.3	32.6	37.2	36.7	31.5
Bonds & Money Mkt. Instruments	36n.u	....	....	....	....	....	....	1,348.1	1,455.8	1,488.3	1,517.5	1,531.1	1,594.6
o/w: Over Two Years	36nau	....	....	....	....	....	....	1,226.2	1,303.8	1,316.1	1,326.4	1,355.6	1,437.9
Capital Accounts	37a	....	....	....	....	....	....	278.7	304.5	324.1	332.5	329.9	322.3
Other Items (Net)	37r.u	....	....	....	....	....	....	−560.3	−610.1	−582.4	−614.6	−611.3	−622.7
Money (National Definitions)							*Billions of Deutsche Mark: End of Period*						
Central Bank Money,Seas. Adj.	19mbc	229.8	249.7	258.8	274.3	282.5	281.8	....	....	....	....	....	....
M1, Seasonally Adjusted	59mac	641.2	703.0	729.0	805.0	872.9	930.6	....	....	....	....	....	....
Money M2, Seasonally Adjusted	59mbc	1,204.4	1,279.2	1,206.5	1,224.6	1,265.7	1,322.1	....	....	....	....	....	....
Money M3, Seasonally Adjusted	59mcc	1,720.8	1,875.1	1,885.6	2,026.1	2,151.3	2,245.2	....	....	....	....	....	....
M3, Extended, Seasonally Adjusted	59mcd	1,986.0	2,179.7	2,215.8	2,341.6	2,460.5	2,569.4	....	....	....	....	....	....
Interest Rates							*Percent Per Annum*						
Discount Rate (End of Period)	60	5.75	4.50	3.00	2.50	2.50	2.50	....	....	....	....	....	....
Money Market Rate	60b	7.49	5.35	4.50	3.27	3.18	3.41	2.73	4.11	4.37	3.28	2.32	2.05
Treasury Bill Rate	60c	6.22	5.05	4.40	3.30	3.32	3.42	2.88	4.32	3.66	2.97	1.98	2.00
Deposit Rate	60l	6.27	4.47	3.85	2.83	2.69	2.88	2.43	3.40	3.56	2.65	....	....
Deposit Rate (Households)	60lhs	....	....	....	....	....	....	....	....	....	....	2.00	1.94
Deposit Rate (Corporations)	60lcs	....	....	....	....	....	....	....	....	....	....	2.05	2.07
Lending Rate	60p	12.85	11.48	10.94	10.02	9.13	9.02	8.81	9.63	10.01	9.70	....	....
Lending Rate (Households)	60phm	....	....	....	....	....	....	....	....	....	....	5.79	5.63
Lending Rate (Corporations)	60pcs	....	....	....	....	....	....	....	....	....	....	4.84	4.64
Government Bond Yield	61	6.28	6.67	6.50	5.63	5.08	4.39	4.26	5.24	4.70	4.61	3.81	3.75
Prices, Production, Labor							*Index Numbers (2000=100): Period Averages*						
Share Prices	62	35.0	39.7	38.7	44.1	60.4	77.3	80.1	100.0	76.2	57.6	45.5	55.8
Producer Prices	63	96.0	96.6	† 98.3	97.1	98.2	97.8	96.8	100.0	103.0	† 102.6	104.4	106.1
Consumer Prices	64	89.9	92.3	93.9	95.3	97.1	98.0	98.6	100.0	102.0	103.4	104.5	106.2
Harmonized CPI	64h	....	....	94.2	95.3	96.8	97.3	98.0	100.0	101.2	102.6	103.7	105.5
Industrial Production	66	84.0	86.7	† 87.4	87.6	90.3	93.6	94.7	100.0	100.2	99.2	99.6	102.6
Wages: Hrly Earn.,s.a.	65..c	81.2	83.2	86.9	91.0	92.7	94.6	97.2	100.0	103.3	106.5	108.0	110.0
							Number in Thousands: Period Averages						
Labor Force	67d	39	39	40,083	39,455	39,694	39,709	39,905	39,731	39,966	40,022	40,195	....
Employment	67e	36,380	† 36,075	36,048	35,982	35,805	35,860	36,402	36,604	36,816	36,536	36,172	38,868
Unemployment	67c	3,443	3,693	3,612	3,980	4,400	4,266	4,093	3,887	3,852	4,071	4,380	4,387
Unemployment Rate (%)	67r	9.8	10.6	10.4	11.5	12.7	12.3	11.7	10.7	10.4	10.9	11.7	11.7
Intl. Transactions & Positions							*Billions of Deutsche Mark through 1998; Billions of Euros Beginning 1999*						
Exports	70	632.22	694.69	749.54	788.94	888.64	954.67	† 510.01	597.44	638.27	651.32	664.46	733.46
Imports, c.i.f.	71	571.91	622.92	664.23	690.40	772.33	828.29	† 444.80	538.31	542.77	518.53	534.53	577.38
Imports, f.o.b.	71.v	556.41	605.96	646.14	671.59	751.29	805.72	† 432.68	523.65	527.99	504.41	519.30	....
							1995=100						
Volume of Exports	72	84.0	96.0	† 100.0	107.6	120.7	130.5	136.4	....	....	....	....	....
Volume of Imports	73	90.3	98.4	† 100.0	106.0	115.5	126.9	132.9	....	....	....	....	....
							2000=100						
Unit Value of Exports	74	98.9	98.0	† 100.2	98.1	98.4	97.9	96.4	† 100.0	101.9	99.3	96.6	95.7
Unit Value of Imports	75	89.1	90.8	† 93.3	91.5	93.9	91.7	90.1	† 100.0	100.0	95.1	90.1	89.3
Export Prices	76	93.6	94.5	95.8	95.8	97.2	97.2	96.6	100.0	101.0	100.9	† 100.9	101.5
Import Prices	76.x	88.7	89.5	89.7	90.1	93.3	90.4	89.9	100.0	100.6	98.1	† 96.3	97.4

		1993	1994	1995	1996	1997	1998	1999	2000	2001	2002	2003	2004
Balance of Payments					*Billions of US Dollars: Minus Sign Indicates Debit*								
Current Account, n.i.e.	78ald	−13.81	−29.42	−26.96	−13.73	−8.66	−11.65	−25.55	−29.60	3.07	45.64	51.45	103.43
Goods: Exports f.o.b.	78aad	382.68	430.55	523.58	522.58	510.02	542.62	541.92	549.11	569.68	616.62	752.44	909.70
Goods: Imports f.o.b.	78abd	−341.51	−379.52	−459.67	−453.20	−439.90	−465.71	−472.28	−491.90	−480.48	−488.79	−604.51	−717.92
Trade Balance	78acd	41.17	51.03	63.91	69.38	70.12	76.91	69.65	57.22	89.20	127.83	147.93	191.78
Services: Credit	78add	63.67	65.71	80.23	83.85	82.73	84.50	83.92	83.15	88.72	103.01	123.47	141.23
Services: Debit	78aed	−101.98	−112.17	−132.52	−134.35	−129.65	−135.12	−141.00	−137.25	−141.92	−144.81	−172.08	−194.65
Balance on Goods & Services	78afd	2.86	4.57	11.62	18.87	23.21	26.29	12.57	3.11	36.00	86.03	99.32	138.37
Income: Credit	78agd	79.01	70.01	82.76	81.58	80.43	83.43	92.40	106.63	91.21	97.58	109.94	132.84
Income: Debit	78ahd	−62.36	−67.09	−82.57	−80.36	−81.92	−91.03	−103.95	−113.32	−99.66	−111.44	−125.37	−132.56
Balance on Gds, Serv. & Inc.	78aid	19.51	7.49	11.81	20.09	21.72	18.69	1.01	−3.57	27.55	72.17	83.89	138.65
Current Transfers, n.i.e.: Credit	78ajd	13.18	13.63	16.44	17.50	15.95	15.96	17.07	14.98	14.84	15.38	18.43	19.36
Current Transfers: Debit	78akd	−46.50	−50.54	−55.21	−51.32	−46.33	−46.30	−43.63	−41.00	−39.32	−41.91	−50.87	−54.59
Capital Account, n.i.e.	78bcd	−1.15	−1.67	−2.73	−2.18	—	.72	−.15	6.19	−.33	−.23	.35	.51
Capital Account, n.i.e.: Credit	78bad	1.38	1.56	1.68	2.76	2.83	3.31	3.01	9.41	1.87	2.09	3.23	3.30
Capital Account: Debit	78bbd	−2.53	−3.23	−4.41	−4.94	−2.82	−2.59	−3.16	−3.22	−2.20	−2.32	−2.87	−2.79
Financial Account, n.i.e.	78bjd	12.84	34.34	44.09	16.12	1.19	17.84	−26.88	28.99	−16.13	−43.27	−53.31	−122.38
Direct Investment Abroad	78bdd	−17.14	−18.94	−39.10	−50.75	−42.73	−89.93	−108.66	−59.74	−39.25	−15.80	4.40	8.10
Dir. Invest. in Rep. Econ., n.i.e.	78bed	.40	7.29	11.99	6.43	12.80	23.64	55.91	210.09	26.17	50.54	25.57	−38.57
Portfolio Investment Assets	78bfd	−25.33	−41.48	−18.05	−30.89	−90.02	−145.49	−190.26	−191.55	−111.68	−57.60	−54.49	−139.67
Equity Securities	78bkd	−16.80	−20.97	.28	−17.52	−42.62	−78.33	−87.57	−127.50	−27.65	−10.34	2.73	−7.26
Debt Securities	78bld	−8.53	−20.51	−18.33	−13.38	−47.39	−67.17	−102.69	−64.04	−84.03	−47.26	−57.22	−132.41
Portfolio Investment Liab., n.i.e.	78bgd	145.72	10.64	53.15	93.91	91.03	150.91	177.86	40.88	138.36	117.81	127.37	166.35
Equity Securities	78bmd	7.54	3.92	−1.51	12.98	12.87	56.77	28.71	−27.96	76.89	13.81	26.64	.18
Debt Securities	78bnd	138.18	6.72	54.66	80.92	78.16	94.14	149.15	68.84	61.47	104.00	100.73	166.17
Financial Derivatives Assets	78bwd	—	—	—	—	—	—	—	—	—	—	—	—
Financial Derivatives Liabilities	78bxd	−.66	.81	−.56	−5.73	−8.70	−7.99	−2.10	−11.44	6.05	−1.16	−.19	−5.44
Other Investment Assets	78bhd	−131.42	−.71	−61.28	−39.77	−83.53	−86.02	−70.85	−80.17	−102.46	−164.69	−171.22	−159.20
Monetary Authorities	78bod	−.01	.17	.28	.35	.29	−.11	−51.70	39.37	20.70	−33.41	−.21	−4.03
General Government	78bpd	−7.07	2.46	−6.72	−.34	−2.33	−.63	8.46	−17.98	14.84	6.70	1.44	3.19
Banks	78bqd	−88.30	14.90	−55.17	−39.13	−80.40	−79.22	−46.32	−92.60	−118.47	−126.98	−135.11	−151.80
Other Sectors	78brd	−36.05	−18.24	.34	−.64	−1.09	−6.06	18.71	−8.97	−19.54	−11.00	−37.34	−6.57
Other Investment Liab., n.i.e.	78bid	41.28	76.72	97.94	42.93	122.34	172.73	111.24	120.93	66.67	27.63	15.25	46.05
Monetary Authorities	78bsd	−1.57	−2.04	−2.65	−1.17	−.39	2.16	−2.21	.37	2.35	.53	2.13	−2.98
General Government	78btd	3.73	2.12	3.84	3.45	−7.75	.10	−12.29	.29	.68	−1.37	4.03	−2.29
Banks	78bud	35.36	69.32	83.74	36.62	120.20	159.94	103.54	109.95	52.86	25.88	8.58	42.07
Other Sectors	78bvd	3.76	7.32	13.01	4.03	10.29	10.53	22.21	10.32	10.79	2.60	.50	9.25
Net Errors and Omissions	78cad	−12.08	−5.29	−7.17	−1.41	3.71	−2.90	38.47	−10.80	7.92	−4.13	.83	16.64
Overall Balance	78cbd	−14.20	−2.04	7.22	−1.20	−3.75	4.02	−14.11	−5.22	−5.47	−1.98	−.68	−1.81
Reserves and Related Items	79dad	14.20	2.04	−7.22	1.20	3.75	−4.02	14.11	5.22	5.47	1.98	.68	1.81
Reserve Assets	79dbd	14.20	2.04	−7.22	1.20	3.75	−4.02	14.11	5.22	5.47	1.98	.68	1.81
Use of Fund Credit and Loans	79dcd	—	—	—	—	—	—	—	—	—	—	—	—
Exceptional Financing	79ded	....	....	....	....	....	....	....	....	....	....	....	....
International Investment Position							*Billions of US Dollars*						
Assets	79aad	1,285.19	1,431.95	1,663.83	1,699.68	1,749.43	2,208.94	2,390.41	2,591.04	2,692.33	3,162.85	3,963.64	....
Direct Investment Abroad	79abd	156.70	188.32	234.13	250.14	296.28	365.22	412.87	486.75	550.31	615.91	718.08	....
Portfolio Investment	79acd	279.91	320.00	385.42	413.69	502.70	724.01	893.30	995.95	975.72	1,081.32	1,366.33	....
Equity Securities	79aed	115.20	145.79	165.97	187.49	241.39	370.57	507.08	573.06	490.65	437.78	577.06	....
Debt Securities	79aed	164.70	174.22	219.45	226.20	261.31	353.44	386.21	422.89	485.07	643.53	789.27	....
Financial Derivatives	79ald	—	—	—	—	—	—	—	—	—	—	—	....
Other Investment	79afd	778.99	850.27	959.66	958.95	879.65	1,039.60	990.77	1,021.04	1,084.13	1,376.48	1,782.40	....
Monetary Authorities	79agd	1.52	1.52	1.36	.93	.54	.64	49.14	6.46	−15.04	19.69	23.06	....
General Government	79ahd	48.60	52.34	62.62	59.52	55.32	61.63	44.38	61.07	44.79	45.76	53.02	....
Banks	79aid	413.31	426.96	504.96	516.49	545.60	662.82	625.10	679.87	768.93	997.42	1,292.08	....
Other Sectors	79ajd	315.56	369.45	390.72	382.01	278.19	314.50	272.15	273.63	285.46	313.61	414.23	....
Reserve Assets	79akd	69.59	73.35	84.62	76.90	70.79	80.11	93.48	87.30	82.16	89.14	96.84	....
Liabilities	79lad	1,079.71	1,236.60	1,534.68	1,610.14	1,663.59	2,200.26	2,300.10	2,534.42	2,530.22	3,033.13	3,794.05	....
Dir. Invest. in Rep. Economy	79lbd	71.17	85.72	101.48	101.73	190.74	252.41	290.45	462.53	416.83	522.84	659.55	....
Portfolio Investment	79lcd	486.93	493.72	636.90	705.19	756.01	1,023.21	1,083.63	1,043.22	1,058.61	1,273.52	1,688.84	....
Equity Securities	79ldd	93.61	99.51	110.78	140.29	186.98	289.98	375.41	300.75	294.69	212.50	364.87	....
Debt Securities	79led	393.32	394.21	526.13	564.90	569.04	733.23	708.22	742.47	763.92	1,061.02	1,323.97	....
Financial Derivatives	79lld	—	—	—	—	—	—	—	—	—	—	—	....
Other Investment	79lfd	521.62	657.16	796.29	803.22	716.84	924.65	926.02	1,028.67	1,054.78	1,236.76	1,445.66	....
Monetary Authorities	79lgd	22.01	22.13	20.88	18.88	6.91	9.55	6.21	6.13	7.71	9.44	13.19	....
General Government	79lhd	28.17	33.51	46.24	45.54	27.24	26.99	13.80	12.71	12.76	15.33	23.13	....
Banks	79lid	285.75	380.24	485.00	493.21	564.48	760.33	781.77	847.60	866.16	987.31	1,144.25	....
Other Sectors	79ljd	185.69	221.29	244.18	245.59	118.21	127.78	124.24	162.23	168.15	224.68	265.09	....

Germany 134

		1993	1994	1995	1996	1997	1998	1999	2000	2001	2002	2003	2004
Government Finance													
Central Government						*Billions of Deutsche Mark through 1998; Millions of Euros Beginning 1999: Year Ending December 31*							
Deficit (-) or Surplus	80	−78.79	−44.85	−61.83	−74.19	−48.97p	−35.12p	....	....	....	....	....	....
Revenue	81	1,017.55	1,099.41	1,124.66	1,133.06	1,160.25	1,188.14	....	....	....	....	....	....
Grants Received	81z	5.11	5.24	6.10	6.70	6.44	6.31	....	....	....	....	....	....
Expenditure	82	1,084.30	1,142.81	1,188.04	1,213.20	1,214.65	1,233.89	....	....	....	....	....	....
Lending Minus Repayments	83	12.10	15.84	3.60	3.02	−3.01	−17.98	....	....	....	....	....	....
Overall Cash Adjustment	80x	−5.05	9.15	−.95	2.27	−4.02	−13.66	....	....	....	....	....	....
Financing													
Net Borrowing	84	91.49	34.23	46.86	70.19	50.41	35.73	25.10	....	....	....	....	....
Net borrowing: Domestic	84a	−16.45	57.19	−11.61	15.91	−29.50	−44.59	2.16	....	....	....	....	....
Net borrowing: Foreign	85a	107.94	−22.96	58.47	54.28	79.91	80.32	22.94	....	....	....	....	....
Use of Cash Balances	87	−12.70	10.62	14.97	4.00	−1.44	−.61	−6.30	....	....	....	....	....
Debt	88	902.71	1,004.15	1,289.81	1,373.07	1,423.68	1,461.87	772.44	....	....	....	....	....
Debt: Domestic	88a	496.94	610.53	762.27	791.26	758.67	716.52	368.41	....	....	....	....	....
Debt: Foreign	89a	405.77	393.62	527.54	581.81	665.01	745.35	404.03	....	....	....	....	....
General Government						*As Percent of Gross Domestic Product*							
Deficit (-) or Surplus	80g	−3.2	−2.4	−3.3	−3.4	−2.7	−2.2	−1.6	1.2	−2.7	....	....	....
Debt	88g	48.0	50.2	58.3	59.8	60.9	60.9	61.3	60.3	59.8	....	....	....
National Accounts						*Billions of Deutsche Mark: through 1998; Billions of Euros Beginning 1999*							
Househ.Cons.Expend.,incl.NPISHs.	96f.c	1,929.5	2,016.7	2,087.2	2,134.8	2,182.3	2,224.8	† 1,175.0	1,214.2	1,257.5	1,266.7	1,286.3	1,304.2
Government Consumption Expend	91f.c	650.6	678.5	707.7	727.1	726.5	736.1	† 387.2	391.9	400.3	411.8	414.6	412.9
Gross Fixed Capital Formation	93e.c	745.5	785.9	792.0	782.0	787.0	810.7	† 428.4	442.4	422.9	392.9	380.7	379.5
Changes in Inventories	93i.c	−10.9	−3.2	11.4	−7.4	4.0	19.9	† 3.9	6.8	−9.3	−18.8	−3.4	1.7
Exports of Goods and Services	90c.c	738.4	804.3	866.0	913.5	1,029.3	1,101.6	† 591.5	688.4	735.3	767.3	768.8	838.6
Imports of Goods and Services (-)	98c.c	739.3	799.3	849.1	880.6	982.5	1,049.1	† 574.1	681.1	693.1	671.1	682.2	729.7
Gross Domestic Product (GDP)	99b.c	3,313.9	3,482.9	3,615.3	3,669.5	3,746.5	3,843.9	† 2,012.0	2,062.5	2,113.6	2,148.8	2,164.9	2,207.2
Net Primary Income from Abroad	98.nc	5.1	−18.7	−26.8	−19.3	−27.1	−39.8	† −21.5	−19.3	−23.0	−25.7	−14.6	−10.6
Gross National Income (GNI)	99a.c	3,319.0	3,464.2	3,588.5	3,650.1	3,719.4	3,804.1	† 1,990.5	2,043.2	2,090.6	2,123.1	2,150.3	2,196.7
Net Current Transf.from Abroad	98t.c	−37.5	−39.7	−32.7	−33.7	−36.3	−39.5	† −19.7	−21.5	−22.3	−24.8	−26.1	−25.9
Gross Nat'l Disposable Inc.(GNDI)	99i.c	3,212.3	3,341.6	3,471.8	3,537.6	3,612.6	3,719.4	† 1,970.7	2,021.7	2,068.3	2,098.3	2,124.2	2,170.8
Gross Saving	99s.c	710.5	745.1	770.2	764.8	787.1	819.1	† 408.5	415.6	410.5	419.7	423.3	453.7
Consumption of Fixed Capital	99cfc	....	....	....	....	....	....	† 297.1	308.5	316.7	321.8	322.4	328.3
GDP Volume 1995 Prices	99b.r	3,456.3	3,548.2	3,615.3	3,651.2	3,717.1	3,792.5	† 1,978.1	2,041.6	2,065.9	2,069.1	2,069.1	2,101.6
GDP Volume (2000=100)	99bvr	86.6	88.9	90.5	91.4	93.1	95.0	† 96.9	100.0	101.2	101.3	101.3	102.9
GDP Deflator (2000=100)	99bir	94.9	97.2	99.0	99.5	99.8	100.3	† 100.7	100.0	101.3	102.8	103.6	104.0
						Millions: Midyear Estimates							
Population	99z	80.88	81.31	81.66	81.92	82.09	82.19	82.27	82.34	82.43	82.51	82.58	82.65

		1993	1994	1995	1996	1997	1998	1999	2000	2001	2002	2003	2004
Exchange Rates							*Cedis per SDR: End of Period*						
Market Rate	aa	1,125.87	1,536.68	2,154.33	2,522.74	3,066.48	3,274.49	4,852.02	9,182.45	9,201.70	11,472.74	13,154.28	14,061.36
						Cedis per US Dollar: End of Period (ae) Period Average (rf)							
Market Rate	ae	819.67	1,052.63	1,449.28	1,754.39	2,272.73	2,325.58	3,535.14	7,047.65	7,321.94	8,438.82	8,852.32	9,054.26
Market Rate	rf	649.06	956.71	1,200.43	1,637.23	2,050.17	2,314.15	2,669.30	5,455.06	7,170.76	7,932.70	8,677.37	9,004.63
						Index Numbers (2000=100): Period Averages							
Nominal Effective Exchange Rate	nec	621.79	454.71	347.85	262.39	222.97	205.51	186.37	100.00	75.99	67.08	55.21	49.48
Real Effective Exchange Rate	rec	133.49	107.94	124.53	134.59	142.65	154.29	155.05	100.00	100.65	100.00	102.50	100.35
Fund Position							*Millions of SDRs: End of Period*						
Quota	2f.s	274.0	274.0	274.0	274.0	274.0	274.0	369.0	369.0	369.0	369.0	369.0	369.0
SDRs	1b.s	.4	2.9	1.6	1.6	2.5	42.4	13.3	.4	3.2	2.7	31.5	13.3
Reserve Position in the Fund	1c.s	17.4	17.4	17.4	17.4	17.4	17.4	41.1	—	—	—	—	—
Total Fund Cred.&Loans Outstg	2tl	537.3	479.7	436.2	377.3	257.0	236.9	225.8	224.5	225.7	267.3	304.9	301.6
International Liquidity						*Millions of US Dollars Unless Otherwise Indicated: End of Period*							
Total Reserves minus Gold	1l.d	409.7	583.9	697.5	828.7	537.8	377.0	453.8	232.1	298.2	539.7	1,352.8	1,626.7
SDRs	1b.d	.5	4.2	2.4	2.2	3.4	59.7	18.2	.5	4.0	3.7	46.8	20.7
Reserve Position in the Fund	1c.d	23.9	25.4	25.8	25.0	23.4	24.5	56.5	—	—	—	—	—
Foreign Exchange	1d.d	385.3	554.3	669.2	801.5	511.0	292.8	379.1	231.5	294.2	536.1	1,306.0	1,605.9
Gold (Million Fine Troy Ounces)	1ad	.275	.275	.275	.275	.275	.277	.279	.280	.281	.281	.281	.281
Gold (National Valuation)	1and	77.2	77.2	77.4	77.2	77.3	78.8	78.9	79.3	78.9	96.5	116.1	122.6
Monetary Authorities:Other Assets	3..d	33.5	36.6	52.4	55.4	47.0	47.8	48.7	48.9	37.5	37.8	38.1	38.3
Other Liab.	4..d	56.3	96.5	34.8	45.4	126.7	53.3	41.0	119.0	38.0	46.9	48.2	78.0
Banking Institutions: Assets	7a.d	313.8	405.4	327.9	396.7	392.3	242.9	194.4	168.6	181.4	207.5	331.1	411.9
Liabilities	7b.d	35.3	32.4	45.8	62.8	75.7	26.1	140.4	116.3	51.7	66.3	140.5	148.9
Monetary Authorities							*Billions of Cedis: End of Period*						
Foreign Assets	11	380.0	663.2	1,079.9	1,182.1	1,337.6	† 1,464.0	1,382.3	2,522.4	2,865.4	5,728.2	12,967.2	15,996.3
Claims on Central Government	12a	850.6	893.0	1,405.5	1,553.3	2,001.7	† 10,999.6	15,242.7	24,281.3	2,480.3	30,939.8	7,520.0	12,108.2
Claims on Nonfin.Pub.Enterprises	12c	44.8	148.8	151.9	135.8	71.9	† 37.5	54.6	23.8	4.4	283.4	3.4	471.8
Claims on Private Sector	12d	—	—	—	—	—	† 26.8	32.2	42.5	52.7	72.5	70.1	91.4
Claims on Banking Institutions	12e	6.8	6.7	8.3	9.4	33.0	† 50.3	465.9	842.8	1,398.4	1,136.1	597.1	16.2
Claims on Nonbank Financial Insts	12g	—	—	37.2	10.7	4.6	† .9	.9	.3	.3	.3	4.7	.3
Reserve Money	14	257.9	461.3	623.1	902.2	1,203.1	† 1,518.0	2,101.6	3,247.1	4,580.0	6,696.0	8,578.1	10,116.6
of which: Currency Outside Banks	14a	222.2	368.8	546.3	724.0	981.8	† 1,164.6	1,585.9	2,637.6	3,089.0	4,671.6	6,337.8	7,306.5
Other Liabs. to Banking Insts	14n	—	—	—	—	—	† 56.6	124.6	328.9	87.5	598.5	2,273.2	2,584.4
Time, Savings,& Fgn.Ccy. Deposits	15	—	—	—	—	—	† 8.8	135.7	546.8	30.2	32.8	181.1	706.3
Liabs. of Central Bank: Securities	16ac	334.5	479.5	722.4	518.2	182.6	†	—	—	—	—	1,817.3	3,545.3
Restricted Deposits	16b	.9	.9	.9	.9	—	†	—	—	—	—	—	—
Foreign Liabilities	16c	651.1	838.7	990.3	1,031.5	1,076.0	† 899.6	1,240.6	2,900.1	2,354.7	3,462.6	4,438.0	4,948.0
Central Government Deposits	16d	237.2	318.1	494.3	324.5	484.7	† 9,945.0	13,768.5	21,704.2	525.5	28,127.8	5,086.5	6,145.0
Capital Accounts	17a	88.5	127.1	296.7	351.1	626.1	† 419.8	500.3	815.7	797.5	1,163.1	1,044.7	797.2
Other Items (Net)	17r	−287.8	−514.0	−444.9	−237.2	−123.7	† −268.6	−692.6	−1,829.8	−1,574.0	−1,920.6	−2,256.4	−158.6
Banking Institutions							*Billions of Cedis: End of Period*						
Reserves	20	41.6	88.8	106.8	194.1	219.3	† 365.3	559.0	779.1	1,398.0	1,576.2	2,325.4	2,822.0
Claims on Mon.Author.:Securities	20c	293.9	410.5	614.8	512.1	182.6	†	—	—	—	—	1,033.2	1,585.9
Other Claims on Monetary Author	20n	—	—	—	—	—	† 56.6	124.6	259.8	65.6	598.5	584.1	191.3
Foreign Assets	21	257.2	426.8	475.3	695.9	891.7	† 564.9	687.2	1,188.3	1,328.4	1,751.3	2,930.9	3,729.4
Claims on Central Government	22a	.3	.3	.3	74.1	752.3	† 1,444.5	2,413.5	2,913.6	4,481.3	5,603.6	6,214.0	7,665.3
Claims on Local Government	22b	—	—	—	—	—	† —	—	—	.2	—	—	—
Claims on Nonfin.Pub.Enterprises	22c	44.1	29.5	44.5	57.4	144.0	† 263.8	373.2	1,225.6	1,805.4	949.7	2,003.1	1,708.3
Claims on Private Sector	22d	187.3	273.3	393.3	680.9	1,156.6	† 1,591.9	2,553.0	3,751.1	4,460.5	5,813.2	7,759.7	10,357.7
Claims on Nonbank Financial Insts	22g	.1	.2	1.7	—	—	† 26.7	77.7	392.5	343.6	801.1	74.6	44.0
Demand Deposits	24	235.3	320.9	371.1	485.0	788.5	† 981.8	892.1	791.7	1,930.3	3,339.5	4,342.8	6,358.0
Time, Savings,& Fgn.Ccy. Deposits	25	306.7	478.3	752.4	1,116.8	1,585.7	† 1,793.4	2,332.3	3,659.5	5,006.2	6,909.9	9,218.4	11,193.0
Money Market Instruments	26aa	—	—	—	—	—	† —	11.5	.1	93.6	137.6	—	—
Restricted Deposits	26b	—	—	—	—	—	† 120.9	141.2	727.7	1,186.3	603.6	588.1	528.6
Foreign Liabilities	26c	28.9	34.1	66.3	110.2	172.0	† 60.6	496.3	819.7	378.8	559.7	1,243.9	1,348.1
Central Government Deposits	26d	63.5	69.2	76.0	105.4	45.9	† 197.4	286.2	256.1	406.7	743.0	1,460.0	1,954.0
Credit from Monetary Authorities	26g	5.8	19.8	50.9	40.1	48.2	† 87.7	514.7	931.5	1,114.1	850.4	650.9	63.4
Liab. to Nonbank Financial Insts	26j	—	—	—	—	—	† 16.9	56.2	167.0	284.6	431.9	221.3	597.2
Capital Accounts	27a	135.5	257.2	276.2	363.7	534.2	† 608.3	879.2	1,419.3	1,923.2	2,359.0	3,077.7	4,016.0
Other Items (Net)	27r	48.8	49.9	43.7	−6.5	171.9	† 446.7	1,178.5	1,737.5	1,559.3	1,158.9	2,121.8	2,045.7
Banking Survey							*Billions of Cedis: End of Period*						
Foreign Assets (Net)	31n	−42.8	217.1	498.6	736.3	981.3	† 1,068.7	332.5	−9.1	1,460.3	3,457.1	10,216.2	13,429.6
Domestic Credit	32	826.6	957.7	1,464.1	2,082.3	3,600.4	† 4,249.3	6,693.2	10,670.3	12,696.5	15,592.7	17,103.3	24,348.1
Claims on Central Govt. (Net)	32an	550.3	506.0	835.5	1,197.5	2,223.3	† 2,301.8	3,601.5	5,234.5	6,029.4	7,672.6	7,187.5	11,674.5
Claims on Local Government	32b	—	—	—	—	—	† —	—	—	.2	—	—	—
Claims on Nonfin.Pub.Enterprises	32c	88.9	178.3	196.4	193.2	215.9	† 301.3	427.8	1,249.3	1,809.8	1,233.1	2,006.5	2,180.2
Claims on Private Sector	32d	187.3	273.3	393.3	680.9	1,156.6	† 1,618.7	2,585.3	3,793.6	4,513.2	5,885.7	7,829.9	10,449.1
Claims on Nonbank Financial Insts.	32g	.1	.2	38.9	10.7	4.6	† 27.6	78.6	392.8	343.9	801.4	79.3	44.3
Money	34	461.3	693.5	925.3	1,218.6	1,779.3	† 2,151.2	2,490.2	3,441.5	5,035.0	8,048.6	10,723.4	13,745.3
Quasi-Money	35	306.7	478.3	752.4	1,116.8	1,585.7	† 1,802.2	2,468.0	4,206.3	5,036.4	6,942.7	9,399.6	11,899.4
Money Market Instruments	36aa	—	—	—	—	—	† —	11.5	.1	93.6	137.6	—	—
Liabs. of Central Bank: Securities	36ac	40.6	69.0	107.6	6.1	—	† —	—	—	—	—	784.1	1,959.3
Restricted Deposits	36b	.9	.9	.9	.9	—	† 120.9	141.2	727.7	1,186.3	603.6	588.1	528.6
Liab. to Nonbank Financial Insts	36j	—	—	—	—	—	† 16.9	56.2	167.0	284.6	431.9	221.3	597.2
Capital Accounts	37a	223.9	384.3	572.9	714.7	1,160.3	† 1,028.1	1,379.5	2,234.9	2,720.7	3,522.1	4,122.4	4,813.2
Other Items (Net)	37r	−249.7	−451.2	−396.5	−238.5	56.5	† 198.8	479.1	−116.3	−199.8	−636.7	1,480.4	4,234.6
Money plus Quasi-Money	35l	768.0	1,171.8	1,677.7	2,335.3	3,364.9	† 3,953.4	4,958.3	7,647.8	10,071.4	14,991.3	20,123.0	25,644.7

Ghana 652

		1993	1994	1995	1996	1997	1998	1999	2000	2001	2002	2003	2004
Interest Rates							*Percent Per Annum*						
Discount Rate (End of Period)	60	35.00	33.00	45.00	45.00	45.00	37.00	27.00	27.00	27.00	24.50	21.50	18.50
Money Market Rate	60b	....	....	....	....	....	....	....	....	....	....	24.71	15.73
Treasury Bill Rate	60c	30.95	27.72	35.38	41.64	42.77	34.33	26.37	36.28	40.96	25.11	27.25	16.57
Savings Rate	60k	18.50	17.63	22.19	27.51	27.49	23.48	14.75	15.83	17.21	11.13	11.08	9.50
Deposit Rate	60l	23.63	23.15	28.73	34.50	35.76	32.05	23.56	28.60	30.85	16.21	14.32	13.63
Government Bond Yield	61	....	....	....	....	....	....	....	....	....	....	....	21.50
Prices and Labor						*Index Numbers (2000=100): Period Averages*							
Consumer Prices	64	16.6	20.7	33.1	48.5	† 62.0	71.1	79.9	100.0	132.9	152.6	193.3	217.7
					Number in Thousands: Period Averages								
Unemployment	67c	39	37	41	....	....	....	....	....	....	....	....	....
Intl. Transactions & Positions						*Billions of Cedis*							
Exports	70	632	1,359	2,070	2,733	3,353	4,151	....	....	....	....	....	....
Cocoa Beans	70r	162	266	457	791	826	1,437	1,422	2,170	....	....	....	....
Imports, c.i.f.	71	2,439	2,029	2,289	3,452	4,769	5,932	9,347	16,171	....	....	....	....
Volume of Exports							*1995=100*						
Cocoa Beans	72r	101.6	94.2	100.0	142.6	10.3	129.6	152.1	....	....	....	....	....
Export Prices													
Cocoa Beans (Unit Value)	74r	34.9	61.8	100.0	121.4	1,748.6	242.8	204.6	....	....	....	....	....
Balance of Payments						*Millions of US Dollars: Minus Sign Indicates Debit*							
Current Account, n.i.e.	78ald	−558.8	−254.6	−143.7	−306.9	−403.5	−521.7	−964.3	−386.5	−324.6	−32.0	255.2	−235.7
Goods: Exports f.o.b.	78aad	1,063.6	1,237.7	1,431.2	1,570.0	1,489.9	2,090.8	2,005.5	1,936.3	1,867.1	2,015.2	2,562.4	2,784.6
Goods: Imports f.o.b.	78abd	−1,728.0	−1,579.9	−1,687.8	−1,950.7	−2,143.7	−2,991.6	−3,279.9	−2,766.6	−2,968.5	−2,707.0	−3,276.1	−4,297.3
Trade Balance	78acd	−664.4	−342.2	−256.6	−380.7	−653.9	−900.8	−1,274.4	−830.3	−1,101.4	−691.8	−713.7	−1,512.6
Services: Credit	78add	144.7	147.5	150.6	156.8	164.9	440.9	467.8	504.2	531.7	554.9	630.0	702.3
Services: Debit	78aed	−445.3	−420.8	−431.7	−424.8	−468.7	−659.4	−646.0	−583.7	−606.1	−620.9	−903.7	−1,058.5
Balance on Goods & Services	78afd	−965.0	−615.5	−537.7	−648.7	−957.7	−1,119.3	−1,452.6	−909.8	−1,175.8	−757.8	−987.4	−1,868.8
Income: Credit	78agd	−6.2	−3.0	13.7	23.5	26.7	26.7	15.0	15.6	16.3	14.7	21.4	44.5
Income: Debit	78ahd	−105.1	−107.9	−142.9	−163.4	−32.6	−163.0	−146.8	−123.2	−124.1	−188.9	−178.0	−242.3
Balance on Gds, Serv. & Inc.	78aid	−1,076.3	−726.4	−666.9	−788.6	−963.6	−1,255.6	−1,584.4	−1,017.4	−1,283.6	−932.0	−1,144.0	−2,066.6
Current Transfers, n.i.e.: Credit	78ajd	532.0	487.3	538.9	497.9	576.5	751.0	637.9	649.3	978.4	912.2	1,408.4	1,831.0
Current Transfers: Debit	78akd	−14.5	−15.5	−15.7	−16.2	−16.4	−17.1	−17.8	−18.4	−19.4	−12.2	−9.2	—
Capital Account, n.i.e.	78bcd	−.1	−.1	—	—	—	—	—	—	—	—	—	—
Capital Account, n.i.e.: Credit	78bad	—	—	—	—	—	—	—	—	—	—	—	—
Capital Account: Debit	78bbd	−.1	−.1	—	—	—	—	—	—	—	—	—	—
Financial Account, n.i.e.	78bjd	642.6	481.7	459.1	285.5	492.8	560.9	746.0	369.3	392.2	−38.7	347.3	201.6
Direct Investment Abroad	78bdd	—	—	—	—	—	—	—	—	—	—	—	—
Dir. Invest. in Rep. Econ., n.i.e.	78bed	125.0	233.0	106.5	120.0	81.8	167.4	243.7	165.9	89.3	58.9	136.7	139.3
Portfolio Investment Assets	78bfd	—	—	—	—	—	—	—	—	—	—	—	—
Equity Securities	78bkd	—	—	—	—	—	—	—	—	—	—	—	—
Debt Securities	78bld	—	—	—	—	—	—	—	—	—	—	—	—
Portfolio Investment Liab., n.i.e.	78bgd	—	—	—	—	—	—	—	—	—	—	—	—
Equity Securities	78bmd	—	—	—	—	—	—	—	—	—	—	—	—
Debt Securities	78bnd	—	—	—	—	—	—	—	—	—	—	—	—
Financial Derivatives Assets	78bwd	....	....	—	—	—	—	—	—	—	—	—	—
Financial Derivatives Liabilities	78bxd	....	....	—	—	—	—	—	—	—	—	—	—
Other Investment Assets	78bhd	5.8	−119.6	116.6	50.0	—	45.0	47.5	70.0	65.0	94.7	68.0	−175.0
Monetary Authorities	78bod	—	—	—	—	—	—	—	—	—	—	—	—
General Government	78bpd	—	—	41.6	—	—	—	47.5	70.0	—	14.7	—	—
Banks	78bqd	−1.2	−93.3	—	—	—	—	—	—	65.0	80.0	68.0	−175.0
Other Sectors	78brd	7.0	−26.3	75.0	50.0	—	45.0	—	—	237.9	−192.3	142.6	237.3
Other Investment Liab., n.i.e.	78bid	511.8	368.3	236.0	115.5	411.0	348.5	454.8	133.4	237.9	−192.3	142.6	237.3
Monetary Authorities	78bsd	32.2	−19.4	—	—	—	—	—	—	—	—	—	—
General Government	78btd	370.2	295.3	135.5	313.9	404.5	327.2	144.8	81.7	45.6	−115.2	62.7	139.2
Banks	78bud	44.8	64.8	−54.2	−148.4	32.9	88.0	186.4	40.8	144.3	−123.8	9.7	−94.6
Other Sectors	78bvd	64.6	27.6	154.7	−50.0	−26.4	−66.7	123.6	10.9	48.0	46.7	70.2	192.7
Net Errors and Omissions	78cad	−49.9	26.1	−132.6	−3.7	−12.1	−11.5	81.9	−352.1	−189.1	57.1	−98.8	20.9
Overall Balance	78cbd	33.8	253.1	182.8	−25.0	77.2	27.6	−136.4	−369.3	−121.5	−13.6	503.6	−13.2
Reserves and Related Items	79dad	−33.8	−253.1	−182.8	25.0	−77.2	−27.6	136.4	369.3	121.5	13.6	−503.6	13.2
Reserve Assets	79dbd	−32.7	−170.2	−117.5	110.3	88.5	−1.5	89.4	344.5	−80.3	−155.8	−657.6	−177.5
Use of Fund Credit and Loans	79dcd	−1.1	−82.9	−65.2	−85.3	−165.8	−26.1	−15.0	−2.3	.8	51.4	54.6	−5.3
Exceptional Financing	79ded							62.0	27.0	201.0	118.0	99.4	196.0
Government Finance						*Billions of Cedis: Year Ending December 31*							
Deficit (-) or Surplus	80	−97.3	111.7	70.3	−335.5	−297.6	−1,048.8	....	....	....	....	....	....
Revenue	81	657.6	1,221.8	1,691.0	2,191.0	2,549.9	3,276.1	....	....	....	....	....	....
Grants Received	81z	66.6	39.5	93.8	77.5	66.6	161.9	....	....	....	....	....	....
Expenditure	82	813.5	1,141.3	1,698.7	2,515.2	2,908.9	4,513.2	....	....	....	....	....	....
Lending Minus Repayments	83	8.0	8.3	15.8	88.8	5.2	−26.4	....	....	....	....	....	....
Financing													
Domestic	84a	45.4	−26.7	−27.7	531.1	728.0	672.6	....	....	....	....	....	....
Foreign	85a	51.9	−85.0	−42.6	−195.7	−430.3	376.2	....	....	....	....	....	....

Ghana 652

		1993	1994	1995	1996	1997	1998	1999	2000	2001	2002	2003	2004
National Accounts							*Billions of Cedis: End of Period*						
Househ.Cons.Expend.,incl.NPISHs....	96f	3,048.7	3,834.9	5,909.9	8,629.0	11,267.0	....	....	....	....	....	....	....
Government Consumption Expend...	91f	568.2	714.3	935.9	1,365.6	1,743.8	....	....	....	....	....	....	....
Gross Fixed Capital Formation..........	93e	921.3	1,174.5	1,638.0	2,332.0	3,338.2	....	....	....	....	....	....	....
Changes in Inventories....................	93i	−60.7	72.2	−85.9	102.2	127.3	....	....	....	....	....	....	....
Exports of Goods and Services..........	90c	693.3	1,171.5	1,898.9	2,827.3	2,794.6	....	....	....	....	....	....	....
Imports of Goods and Services (-).....	98c	1,298.3	1,762.2	2,544.2	3,916.9	5,157.5	....	....	....	....	....	....	....
Gross Domestic Product (GDP).........	99b	3,872.5	5,205.2	7,752.6	11,339.2	14,113.4	....	....	....	....	....	....	....
Net Primary Income from Abroad.....	98.n	72.9	106.1	155.1	220.0	273.9	....	....	....	....	....	....	....
Gross National Income (GNI)............	99a	3,799.6	5,099.1	7,597.5	11,119.2	13,839.5	....	....	....	....	....	....	....
Consumption of Fixed Capital..........	99cf	329.0	411.2	514.0	800.8	996.7	....	....	....	....	....	....	....
GDP Volume 1993 Prices.................	99b.p	3,872.5	3,999.1	4,160.0	4,351.2	4,533.0	....	....	....	....	....	....	....
GDP Volume (1995=100)................	99bvp	† 93.1	96.1	100.0	104.6	109.0	....	....	....	....	....	....	....
GDP Deflator (1995=100)...............	99bip	53.7	69.8	100.0	139.8	167.1	....	....	....	....	....	....	....
							Millions: Midyear Estimates						
Population...............................	99z	16.83	17.28	17.73	18.16	18.59	19.01	19.43	19.87	20.31	20.76	21.21	21.66

Greece 174

		1993	1994	1995	1996	1997	1998	1999	2000	2001	2002	2003	2004
Exchange Rates					*Drachmas per SDR Through 2000, Euros per SDR Thereafter End of Period*								
Market Rate	aa	342.32	350.51	352.36	355.20	381.31	397.87	450.79	476.37	1.4260	1.2964	1.1765	1.1402
				Drachmas per US Dollar through 2000, Euros per US Dollar Thereafter: End of Period (ae) Period Average (rf)									
Market Rate	ae	249.22	240.10	237.04	247.02	282.61	282.57	328.44	365.62	1.1347	.9536	.7918	.7342
Market Rate	rf	229.25	242.60	231.66	240.71	273.06	295.53	305.65	365.40	1.1175	1.0626	.8860	.8054
				Drachmas per ECU through 1998; Drachmas per Euro through 2000: End of Period (ea) Period Average (eb)									
Euro Rate	ea	278.20	294.78	303.76	306.83	312.12	330.01	† 330.35	340.75	....	....	....	....
Euro Rate	eb	267.99	287.21	299.54	301.48	308.51	331.50	† 325.76	336.66	....	....	....	....
				Index Numbers (2000=100): Period Averages									
Market Rate	ahx	159.1	150.0	157.3	151.3	133.5	123.4	119.0	100.0	....	....	....	....
Nominal Effective Exchange Rate	neu	131.9	123.0	119.8	117.5	114.3	107.6	106.9	100.0	99.4	100.3	103.5	104.3
Real Effective Exchange Rate	reu	93.0	95.1	101.8	105.1	108.6	105.4	106.8	100.0	101.0	104.0	108.9	112.0
Fund Position					*Millions of SDRs: End of Period*								
Quota	2f.s	587.6	587.6	587.6	587.6	587.6	587.6	823.0	823.0	823.0	823.0	823.0	823.0
SDRs	1b.s	.1	.2	—	.4	.2	.3	3.8	9.2	7.7	11.1	14.4	17.4
Reserve Position in the Fund	1c.s	113.7	113.7	113.7	113.7	113.7	191.5	285.0	227.8	284.3	322.5	334.3	270.6
Total Fund Cred.&Loans Outstg.	2tl	—	—	—	—	—	—	—	—				
International Liquidity					*Millions of US Dollars Unless Otherwise Indicated: End of Period*								
Total Res.Min.Gold(Eurosys.Def.)	1l.d	7,790.3	14,487.9	14,780.0	17,501.4	12,594.8	17,458.4	18,122.3	13,424.3	† 5,154.2	8,082.8	4,361.4	1,191.0
SDRs	1b.d	.2	.3	—	.6	.3	.5	5.2	12.0	9.7	15.1	21.4	27.0
Reserve Position in the Fund	1c.d	156.2	166.0	169.0	163.5	153.4	269.6	391.1	296.8	357.3	438.4	496.7	420.2
Foreign Exchange	1d.d	7,634.0	14,321.6	14,611.0	17,337.3	12,441.1	17,188.3	17,726.0	13,115.5	† 4,787.2	7,629.3	3,843.3	743.7
o/w:Fin.Deriv.Rel.to Reserves	1ddd	....	....	....	....	....	....	....	....	....	....	....	....
Other Reserve Assets	1e.d	....	....	....	....	....	....	....	....	....	....	....	....
Gold (Million Fine Troy Ounces)	1ad	3.443	3.448	3.461	3.469	3.644	3.623	4.237	4.262	3.942	3.935	3.451	3.463
Gold (Eurosystem Valuation)	1and	856.3	850.9	871.7	833.2	684.5	685.3	781.8	753.2	1,090.0	1,348.7	1,439.9	1,516.8
Memo:Euro Cl. on Non-EA Res.	1dgd	....	....	....	....	....	....	....	....	61.0			
Non-Euro Cl. on EA Res.	1dhd	....	....	....	....	....	....	....	....	5,566.3	4,014.4	2,979.4	1,834.7
Mon. Auth.: Other Foreign Assets	3..d	....	....	....	....	....	....	....	....				
Foreign Liabilities	4..d	731.4	777.5	860.4	795.5	1,336.5	888.4	733.4	179.1	665.4	713.1	764.1	884.0
Banking Insts.: Foreign Assets	7a.d	5,358.7	6,051.3	8,962.9	12,656.1	15,994.8	15,550.7	13,848.5	12,627.4	† 16,386.0	21,765.8	32,368.2	39,507.7
Foreign Liab.	7b.d	18,235.5	26,410.3	34,286.1	38,540.2	42,278.6	46,854.1	41,732.5	39,645.4	† 9,636.1	18,557.8	27,716.5	44,525.7
Monetary Authorities					*Billions of Drachmas through 2000; Billions of Euros Beginning 2001: End of Period*								
Fgn. Assets (Cl.on Non-EA Ctys)	11	2,975.5	4,463.9	4,333.9	5,253.9	4,020.3	5,414.0	6,434.2	4,961.0	6.97	9.00	5.10	3.22
Claims on General Government	12a.u									18.45	19.13	19.60	22.06
o/w: Claims on Gen.Govt.in Cty.	12a	† 7,966.2	7,352.3	7,059.4	6,457.6	6,012.1	5,757.9	5,911.7	5,759.1	17.23	17.02	15.25	14.54
Claims on Banking Institutions	12e.u	....	....	....	....	....	....	....	....	5.16	5.19	6.49	2.21
o/w: Claims on Bank.Inst.in Cty.	12e	580.3	377.8	461.4	332.8	791.9	447.2	54.4	299.3	.65	3.02	4.42	.27
Claims on Other Resident Sectors	12d.u	....	....	....	....	....	....	....	....	.17	.20	.23	.25
o/w: Cl. on Oth.Res.Sect.in Cty.	12d	3.8	4.8	14.1	19.9	21.9	24.6	27.3	37.5	.17	.20	.23	.25
Currency Issued	14a	1,641.6	1,839.8	2,061.0	2,251.1	2,451.5	2,519.4	3,154.1	3,097.3	8.71	9.21	10.65	12.76
Liabilities to Banking Insts.	14c.u									15.79	19.89	18.50	12.36
o/w: Liabs to Bank.Inst.in Cty.	14c	4,236.5	5,364.8	5,084.2	5,406.7	5,189.2	6,634.0	7,033.2	5,955.8	7.70	1.71	2.41	5.39
Demand Dep. of Other Res.Sect.	14d.u									.42	.34	.31	.60
o/w:D.Dep.of Oth.Res.Sect.in Cty.	14d	63.9	27.3	47.3	29.7	5.2	4.5	165.8	60.8	.42	.34	.31	.60
Other Dep. of Other Res.Sect.	15..u	....	....	....	....	....	....	....	....	.36	.30	.19	.11
o/w:O.Dep.of Oth.Res.Sect.in Cty.	15	....	....	....	....	....	....	....	....	.36	.30	.19	.11
Bonds & Money Mkt. Instruments	16n.u	....	....	....	....	....	....	....	....	1.68	1.56	.55	.54
o/w:Bonds Held by Resid.of Cty.	16n	3,626.6	3,342.7	2,742.2	2,102.0	1,533.9	1,065.9	1,015.0	606.0	....	....	....	....
Foreign Liab. (to Non-EA Ctys)	16c	182.3	186.7	203.9	196.5	377.7	251.0	240.9	65.5	.76	.68	.61	.65
Central Government Deposits	16d.u	....	....	....	....	....	....	....	....	.44	.08	.07	.49
o/w: Cent.Govt.Dep. in Cty.	16d	259.6	237.6	621.2	672.5	443.4	345.5	128.9	194.6	.44	.08	.07	.49
Capital Accounts	17a	62.7	69.5	71.8	74.1	166.2	196.1	290.0	293.1	2.53	2.51	1.68	.99
Other Items (Net)	17r	1,452.7	1,130.5	1,037.1	1,331.6	679.1	627.4	399.7	783.8	.08	−1.04	−1.12	−.75
Memo: Net Claims on Eurosystem	12e.s	....	....	....	....	....	....	....	....	−7.06	−17.16	−15.05	−5.92
Currency Put into Circ.	14m	....	....	....	....	....	....	....	....		9.98	11.38	13.19
Banking Institutions					*Billions of Drachmas through 2000; Billions of Euros Beginning 2001: End of Period*								
Claims on Monetary Authorities	20	2,531.4	2,905.2	5,000.4	5,080.2	5,583.7	7,464.1	8,196.2	7,034.8	11.52	4.84	2.48	5.39
Claims on Bk.Inst.in Oth.EA Ctys.	20b.u									9.42	10.80	12.13	12.71
Fgn. Assets (Cl.on Non-EA Ctys)	21	1,335.5	1,452.9	2,124.6	3,126.3	4,520.3	4,394.2	4,548.4	4,616.8	18.59	20.76	25.63	29.01
Claims on General Government	22a.u									45.94	46.13	40.00	35.82
o/w: Claims on Gen.Govt.in Cty.	22a	8,957.3	9,522.7	10,448.8	11,082.1	11,565.5	11,354.2	12,447.7	14,506.2	45.87	45.24	36.96	34.47
Claims on Other Resident Sectors	22d.u									84.80	97.28	113.03	132.51
o/w: Cl. on Oth.Res.Sect.in Cty.	22d	6,644.9	7,531.6	9,142.9	10,371.1	11,902.0	13,721.5	17,734.0	21,775.7	83.13	94.47	110.44	129.71
Demand Deposits	24..u									70.39	71.37	79.14	91.10
o/w:D.Dep.of Oth.Res.Sect.in Cty.	24	1,126.5	1,619.7	1,874.6	2,340.2	2,699.4	3,104.6	4,337.2	4,287.4	70.19	71.18	78.96	90.89
Other Deposits	25..u									59.04	55.49	49.47	48.96
o/w:O.Dep.of Oth.Res.Sect.in Cty.	25	9,760.5	11,925.5	13,684.8	15,339.1	16,704.7	16,564.0	17,975.3	19,164.2	57.93	54.53	48.96	48.46
Money Market Fund Shares	26m.u	....	....	....	....	....	....	....	....	9.66	10.72	15.73	15.35
Bonds & Money Mkt. Instruments	26n.u									.29	.43	.73	.73
o/w: Held by Resid.of Cty.	26n	703.5	838.4	570.8	59.8	126.7	163.6	78.7	85.3	....	....	....	....
Foreign Liab. (to Non-EA Ctys)	26c	4,544.7	6,341.1	8,127.2	9,520.2	11,948.4	13,239.6	13,706.6	14,495.2	10.93	17.70	21.95	32.69
Central Government Deposits	26d.u									1.38	2.32	2.48	3.33
o/w: Cent.Govt.Dep. in Cty.	26d	....	....	....	....	....	....	....	....	1.38	2.32	2.48	3.33
Credit from Monetary Authorities	26g	2,166.2	486.3	551.0	409.4	826.6	1,771.1	3,342.1	3,930.6	.71	2.15	4.43	.27
Liab. to Bk.Inst.in Oth. EA Ctys.	26h.u									4.67	6.40	5.43	4.17
Capital Accounts	27a	1,510.2	1,481.2	1,740.7	1,881.7	2,217.3	2,860.2	5,157.3	5,876.1	19.49	19.88	17.49	19.53
Other Items (Net)	27r	−342.5	−1,279.8	167.7	109.4	−951.6	−769.2	−1,670.9	94.8	−6.29	−6.63	−3.58	−.69

Greece 174

		1993	1994	1995	1996	1997	1998	1999	2000	2001	2002	2003	2004
Banking Survey (Nat'l Residency)		*Billions of Drachmas through 2000; Billions of Euros Beginning 2001: End of Period*											
Foreign Assets (Net)	31n	−416.0	−611.0	−1,872.7	−1,336.5	−3,785.5	−3,682.5	−2,965.0	−4,982.8	17.17	4.90	10.62	13.82
Domestic Credit	32	† 23,312.6	24,173.8	26,044.0	27,258.3	29,058.1	30,512.8	35,991.7	41,884.0	144.58	154.54	160.33	175.15
Claims on General Govt. (Net)	32an	† 16,663.9	16,637.4	16,887.0	16,867.2	17,134.2	16,766.7	18,230.5	20,070.7	61.28	59.87	49.67	45.19
Claims on Other Resident Sectors	32d	6,648.7	7,536.5	9,157.0	10,391.0	11,924.0	13,746.1	17,761.3	21,813.3	83.30	94.67	110.67	129.96
Currency Issued	34a.n	1,641.6	1,839.8	2,061.0	2,251.1	2,451.5	2,519.4	3,154.1	3,097.3	8.71	9.21	10.65	12.76
Demand Deposits	34b.n	1,190.3	1,647.0	1,921.9	2,369.9	2,704.5	3,109.1	4,503.0	4,348.3	70.61	71.52	79.27	91.49
Other Deposits	35..n	9,760.5	11,925.5	13,684.8	15,339.1	16,704.7	16,564.0	17,975.3	19,164.2	58.29	54.83	49.15	48.56
Money Market Fund Shares	36m	....	....	....	....	....	....	....	....	9.66	10.72	15.73	15.35
Bonds & Money Mkt. Instruments	36n	4,330.1	4,181.1	3,313.0	2,161.9	1,660.6	1,229.5	1,093.7	691.4	1.96	1.98	1.28	1.26
o/w: Over Two Years	36na	....	....	....	....	....	....	....	....	1.79	1.67	.80	.78
Capital Accounts	37a	1,573.0	1,550.7	1,812.5	1,955.7	2,383.5	3,056.3	5,447.3	6,169.2	22.02	22.39	19.17	20.53
Other Items (Net)	37r	4,401.2	2,418.7	1,378.1	1,844.1	−632.1	352.0	853.5	3,431.0	−9.49	−11.21	−4.29	−.98
Banking Survey (EA-Wide Residency)		*Billions of Euros: End of Period*											
Foreign Assets (Net)	31n.u	....	....	....	....	....	....	....	....	13.87	11.38	8.18	−1.12
Domestic Credit	32..u	....	....	....	....	....	....	....	....	147.54	160.35	170.31	186.83
Claims on General Govt. (Net)	32anu	....	....	....	....	....	....	....	....	62.57	62.87	57.05	54.07
Claims on Other Resident Sect.	32d.u	....	....	....	....	....	....	....	....	84.97	97.49	113.25	132.76
Currency Issued	34a.u	....	....	....	....	....	....	....	....	8.71	9.21	10.65	12.76
Demand Deposits	34b.u	....	....	....	....	....	....	....	....	70.81	71.71	79.45	91.70
Other Deposits	35..u	....	....	....	....	....	....	....	....	59.40	55.79	49.65	49.06
o/w: Other Dep. Over Two Yrs.	35abu	....	....	....	....	....	....	....	....	2.10	2.87	3.26	3.05
Money Market Fund Shares	36m.u	....	....	....	....	....	....	....	....	9.66	10.72	15.73	15.35
Bonds & Money Mkt. Instruments	36n.u	....	....	....	....	....	....	....	....	1.96	1.98	1.28	1.26
o/w: Over Two Years	36nau	....	....	....	....	....	....	....	....	1.79	1.67	.80	.78
Capital Accounts	37a	....	....	....	....	....	....	....	....	22.02	22.39	19.17	20.53
Other Items (Net)	37r.u	....	....	....	....	....	....	....	....	−11.14	−.06	2.56	−4.94
Interest Rates		*Percent Per Annum*											
Central Bank Rate	60	21.5	20.5	18.0	16.5	14.5	....	† 11.8	8.1	....	....	....	....
Money Market Rate	60b	....	24.60	16.40	13.80	12.80	13.99	....	....	....	....	....	....
Treasury Bill Rate	60c	20.3	17.5	14.2	11.2	11.4	10.3	8.3	† 6.2	4.1	3.5	2.3	2.3
Deposit Rate	60l	19.33	18.92	15.75	13.51	10.11	10.70	8.69	6.13	3.32	2.76	2.48	2.29
Deposit Rate (Households)	60lhs	....	....	....	....	....	....	....	....	....	....	2.42	2.44
Deposit Rate (Corporations)	60lcs	....	....	....	....	....	....	....	....	....	....	2.23	2.15
Lending Rate	60p	28.56	27.44	23.05	20.96	18.92	18.56	15.00	12.32	8.59	7.41	6.79	....
Lending Rate (Households)	60phm	....	....	....	....	....	....	....	....	....	....	5.16	4.96
Lending Rate (Corporations)	60pcs	....	....	....	....	....	....	....	....	....	....	5.82	5.85
Government Bond Yield	61	....	....	....	....	....	8.48	6.30	6.10	5.30	5.12	4.27	4.26
Prices, Production, Labor		*Index Numbers (2000=100): Period Averages*											
Producer Prices	63	....	....	77.4	83.5	84.8	86.8	88.1	100.0	103.6	106.0	108.5	112.3
Consumer Prices	64	65.3	† 72.5	78.9	85.4	† 90.1	94.4	96.9	100.0	103.4	107.1	110.9	114.1
Harmonized CPI	64h	....	....	80.0	86.3	91.0	95.2	97.2	100.0	103.7	107.7	111.4	114.8
Wages: Monthly Earnings	65	....	....	....	....	....	....	96.9	100.0	101.5	105.9	124.3	130.4
Manufacturing Production	66ey	84.7	85.4	† 87.1	86.8	88.8	96.0	95.2	100.0	97.5	97.4	97.0	98.1
Labor Force		*Number in Thousands: Period Averages*											
Labor Force	67d	4,112	4,188	4,249	4,314	4,294	4,470	4,500	4,475	4,403	4,450	4,503	4,819
Employment	67e	3,720	3,790	3,824	3,872	3,854	3,978	3,968	3,979	3,941	4,006	4,084	4,313
Unemployment	67c	398	404	425	446	440	† 508	555	523	494	480	460	506
Unemployment Rate (%)	67r	9.7	9.6	10.0	10.3	10.3	† 11.2	12.1	11.4	10.8	10.3	9.7	10.5
Intl. Transactions & Positions		*Millions of US Dollars*											
Exports	70..d	9,092.7	8,807.6	10,960.8	11,948.2	11,127.7	10,731.9	10,475.1	10,747.0	9,483.3	10,315.2	13,195.2	14,995.7
Imports, c.i.f	71..d	20,200.3	21,381.3	26,795.2	29,672.4	27,898.7	29,388.1	28,719.5	29,221.4	29,927.7	31,164.4	44,375.2	51,559.4
		1995=100											
Volume of Exports	72	87.1	90.7	100.0	106.8	118.7	134.9	143.7	....	....	....	....	....
Volume of Imports	73	87.5	92.3	100.0	109.0	110.7	134.5	141.9	....	....	....	....	....
Unit Value of Exports	74	89.2	99.3	100.0	105.2	100.7	93.3	92.7	....	....	....	....	....
Unit Value of Imports	75	99.6	98.3	100.0	105.4	112.3	109.7	109.0	....	....	....	....	....
		2000=100											
Export Prices	76	65.2	70.8	† 78.1	83.9	86.6	88.5	89.0	100.0	100.7	102.6	102.6	106.2
Import Prices	76.x	72.2	78.9	† 84.4	86.6	88.6	93.4	94.0	100.0	101.9	102.3	103.4	103.9

		1993	1994	1995	1996	1997	1998	1999	2000	2001	2002	2003	2004
Balance of Payments		*Millions of US Dollars: Minus Sign Indicates Debit*											
Current Account, n.i.e.	78ald	−747	−146	−2,864	−4,554	−4,860	....	−7,295	−9,820	−9,400	−10,405	−11,225	....
Goods: Exports f.o.b.	78aad	5,112	5,338	5,918	5,890	5,576	....	8,545	10,202	10,615	9,868	12,578	....
Goods: Imports f.o.b.	78abd	−15,611	−16,611	−20,343	−21,395	−20,951	....	−26,496	−30,440	−29,702	−31,320	−38,184	....
Trade Balance	78acd	−10,499	−11,273	−14,425	−15,505	−15,375	....	−17,951	−20,239	−19,087	−21,452	−25,606	....
Services: Credit	78add	8,214	9,213	9,605	9,348	9,287	....	16,506	19,239	19,456	20,223	24,286	....
Services: Debit	78aed	−3,521	−3,774	−4,368	−4,238	−4,650	....	−9,251	−11,286	−11,589	−10,677	−11,253	....
Balance on Goods & Services	78afd	−5,806	−5,834	−9,188	−10,395	−10,738	....	−10,696	−12,286	−11,220	−11,906	−12,573	....
Income: Credit	78agd	927	1,099	1,312	1,156	1,208	....	2,577	2,807	1,885	1,530	1,769	....
Income: Debit	78ahd	−2,367	−2,347	−2,996	−3,337	−2,840	....	−3,248	−3,692	−3,652	−3,487	−4,693	....
Balance on Gds, Serv. & Inc.	78aid	−7,246	−7,082	−10,872	−12,576	−12,370	....	−11,367	−13,171	−12,987	−13,863	−15,497	....
Current Transfers, n.i.e.: Credit	78ajd	6,516	6,964	8,039	8,053	7,538	....	4,957	4,116	4,592	4,901	7,202	....
Current Transfers: Debit	78akd	−17	−28	−31	−31	−28	....	−884	−764	−1,005	−1,443	−2,930	....
Capital Account, n.i.e.	78bcd	—	—	—	—	—	....	2,211	2,112	2,153	1,522	1,411	....
Capital Account, n.i.e.: Credit	78bad	—	—	—	—	—	....	2,318	2,244	2,320	1,692	1,585	....
Capital Account: Debit	78bbd	—	—	—	—	—	....	−107	−131	−167	−170	−174	....
Financial Account, n.i.e.	78bjd	4,817	6,903	3,162	8,658	119	....	7,478	10,830	537	11,574	6,168	....
Direct Investment Abroad	78bdd	—	—	—	—	—	....	−542	−2,099	−611	−669	−9	....
Dir. Invest. in Rep. Econ., n.i.e.	78bed	977	981	1,053	1,058	984	....	567	1,083	1,585	53	717	....
Portfolio Investment Assets	78bfd	—	—	—	—	—	....	−858	−1,184	−474	−1,893	−9,807	....
Equity Securities	78bkd	—	—	—	—	—	....	−166	−846	−1,020	−314	−507	....
Debt Securities	78bld	—	—	—	—	—	....	−692	−338	546	−1,579	−9,300	....
Portfolio Investment Liab., n.i.e.	78bgd	—	—	—	—	—	....	6,754	9,262	9,012	12,315	23,456	....
Equity Securities	78bmd	—	—	—	—	—	....	−2,589	1,637	1,829	1,381	2,569	....
Debt Securities	78bnd	—	—	—	—	—	....	9,343	7,625	7,183	10,935	20,887	....
Financial Derivatives Assets	78bwd	....	....	....	....	....	....	....	....	....	....	....	....
Financial Derivatives Liabilities	78bxd	....	....	....	....	....	....	419	348	74	−176	111	....
Other Investment Assets	78bhd	—	—	—	—	980	....	−2,913	6,970	−1,539	−6,953	−4,413	....
Monetary Authorities	78bod	....	....	....	....	....	....	—	—	—	—	—	....
General Government	78bpd	—	—	—	—	980	....	−2,913	6,970	−1,539	−6,953	−4,413	....
Banks	78bqd	—	—	—	—	—	....	—	—	—	—	—	....
Other Sectors	78brd	....	....	....	....	....	....	....	....	....	....	....	....
Other Investment Liab., n.i.e.	78bid	3,840	5,922	2,109	7,600	−1,845	....	4,050	−3,551	−7,511	8,896	−3,887	....
Monetary Authorities	78bsd	2,584	−1,791	−2,385	−2,194	−2,570	....	—	—	—	—	—	....
General Government	78btd	884	4,703	3,441	3,530	7,101	....	—	—	—	—	—	....
Banks	78bud	78	89	−2,110	−598	−3,348	....	1,644	−3,425	−6,989	11,197	2,256	....
Other Sectors	78bvd	294	2,921	3,163	6,862	−3,028	....	2,406	−126	−522	−2,301	−6,143	....
Net Errors and Omissions	78cad	−631	−448	−321	111	226	....	42	−550	1,011	−828	−1,076	....
Overall Balance	78cbd	3,439	6,309	−23	4,215	−4,515	....	2,435	2,573	−5,699	1,863	−4,722	....
Reserves and Related Items	79dad	−3,439	−6,309	23	−4,215	4,515	....	−2,435	−2,573	5,699	−1,863	4,722	....
Reserve Assets	79dbd	−3,019	−6,309	23	−4,215	4,515	....	−2,435	−2,573	5,699	−1,863	4,722	....
Use of Fund Credit and Loans	79dcd	—	—	—	—	—	....	....	....	....	....	....	....
Exceptional Financing	79ded	−420	—	—	—	—	....	....	....	....	....	....	....
International Investment Position		*Millions of US Dollars*											
Assets	79aad	....	....	....	....	....	55,491	59,106	57,194	59,753	83,972	112,652	139,298
Direct Investment Abroad	79abd	....	....	....	....	....	2,792	3,809	5,852	7,020	9,001	11,271	13,057
Portfolio Investment	79acd	....	....	....	....	....	4,503	4,778	3,848	9,376	17,974	34,966	52,666
Equity Securities	79add	....	....	....	....	....	1,177	1,147	1,346	2,559	3,020	4,893	6,200
Debt Securities	79aed	....	....	....	....	....	3,326	3,631	2,502	6,817	14,953	30,073	46,465
Financial Derivatives	79ald	....	....	....	....	....	12	13	12	88	315	326	821
Other Investment	79afd	....	....	....	....	....	38,726	40,361	35,227	37,099	47,250	60,288	70,046
Monetary Authorities	79agd	....	....	....	....	....	7,239	6,134	477	3,958	2,343	2,708	3,328
General Government	79ahd	....	....	....	....	....	—	—	—	—	—	—	—
Banks	79aid	....	....	....	....	....	18,712	20,881	20,908	19,510	26,440	36,782	41,988
Other Sectors	79ajd	....	....	....	....	....	12,775	13,346	13,841	13,631	18,468	20,798	24,730
Reserve Assets	79akd	....	....	....	....	....	9,458	10,145	12,255	6,169	9,432	5,801	2,708
Liabilities	79lad	....	....	....	....	....	91,539	102,665	106,690	116,557	164,027	229,229	288,248
Dir. Invest. in Rep. Economy	79lbd	....	....	....	....	....	13,084	15,386	12,480	13,941	15,561	21,576	27,215
Portfolio Investment	79lcd	....	....	....	....	....	45,330	52,758	57,294	59,610	78,524	122,191	167,907
Equity Securities	79ldd	....	....	....	....	....	12,001	15,211	9,584	7,711	8,425	16,140	28,386
Debt Securities	79led	....	....	....	....	....	33,329	37,547	47,710	51,899	70,098	106,052	139,521
Financial Derivatives	79lld	....	....	....	....	....	—	—	—	—	—	—	—
Other Investment	79lfd	....	....	....	....	....	33,125	34,521	36,917	43,006	69,943	85,462	93,125
Monetary Authorities	79lgd	....	....	....	....	....	—	—	7,132	18,259	19,391	8,916	
General Government	79lhd	....	....	....	....	....	8,071	7,949	8,837	10,101	11,922	14,151	15,934
Banks	79lid	....	....	....	....	....	15,384	16,551	18,846	14,879	26,452	35,378	51,054
Other Sectors	79ljd	....	....	....	....	....	9,670	10,021	9,233	10,894	13,310	16,543	17,221
Government Finance		*Billions of Drachmas: Year Ending December 31*											
Budgetary Central Government													
Deficit (-) or Surplus	80	−2,431.7	−5,050.3	−3,252.2	−2,904.2	−2,505.4	−2,125.5	−1,930.0	....	....	....	....	....
Total Revenue and Grants	81y	5,281.7	6,191.7	7,113.6	7,956.4	9,185.4	10,412.5	11,603.0	....	....	....	....	....
Revenue	81	4,989.1	5,883.4	6,753.5	7,306.9	....	....	....	....	....	....	....	....
Grants Received	81z	292.6	308.3	360.1	649.5	....	....	....	....	....	....	....	....
Expenditure	82	7,713.4	11,242.0	10,365.8	10,860.6	11,690.8	12,538.0	13,533.0	....	....	....	....	....
Financing													
Net Borrowing	84	2,431.7	5,050.3	3,252.2	2,904.2	2,505.4	2,125.5	1,930.0	....	....	....	....	....
Borrowing: Domestic	84c	3,385.9	6,439.2	5,111.7	5,180.4	....	....	....	....	....	....	....	....
Borrowing: Foreign	85c	649.8	1,138.0	914.0	1,362.0	....	....	....	....	....	....	....	....
Amortization	84y	−1,604.0	−2,526.9	−2,773.5	−3,638.2	−3,589.4	−3,536.4	−3,362.3	....	....	....	....	....
General Government		*As Percent of Gross Domestic Product*											
Deficit (-) or Surplus	80g	....	....	....	....	....	−2.4	−1.7	−.8	.1	....	....	....
Debt	88g	....	....	....	....	....	105.0	103.8	102.8	99.7	....	....	....

Greece 174

		1993	1994	1995	1996	1997	1998	1999	2000	2001	2002	2003	2004
National Accounts					*Billions of Drachmas through 2000; Billions of Euros Beginning 2001*								
Househ.Cons.Expend.,incl.NPISHs....	96f	15,662.6	17,731.0	† 19,901.5	22,050.6	23,901.9	25,850.0	27,105.3	28,571.9	† 89.2	94.8	102.2	109.0
Government Consumption Expend...	91f	3,060.2	3,342.0	† 4,174.2	4,348.0	5,013.5	5,506.9	5,920.2	7,321.7	† 22.0	24.9	25.2	28.2
Gross Fixed Capital Formation.........	93e	4,339.6	4,529.2	† 5,065.9	5,828.2	6,558.8	7,615.1	8,699.0	9,785.0	† 31.3	33.8	39.3	42.2
Changes in Inventories....................	93i	−75.5	25.8	† 85.9	96.4	93.0	79.7	−48.0	128.8	† −.1	−.3	.1	—
Exports of Goods and Services.........	90c	3,677.1	4,288.3	† 4,800.1	5,245.5	6,523.7	7,150.6	8,607.0	10,610.6	† 31.2	29.5	30.5	34.6
Imports of Goods and Services (-).....	98c	5,412.8	5,801.7	† 6,792.5	7,633.8	8,958.0	10,159.8	11,886.0	14,948.7	† 42.4	41.5	44.1	48.7
Gross Domestic Product (GDP).........	99b	21,424.0	24,296.0	27,235.1	29,935.2	33,132.8	36,042.1	38,397.8	41,469.6	† 131.3	141.7	153.5	165.3
Net Primary Income from Abroad.....	98.n	137.8	212.8	861.8	835.2	897.5	976.6	510.8	356.8	† .1	.1	—	.2
Gross National Income (GNI)............	99a	21,273.5	24,195.7	† 28,096.9	30,770.4	34,061.0	37,018.7	38,908.5	41,830.8	† 131.4	141.7	153.4	165.5
Net Current Transf.from Abroad.......	98t	....	....	....	....	....	....	....	....	† 1.7	.9	1.0	1.1
Gross Nat'l Disposable Inc.(GNDI)....	99i	....	....	....	....	....	....	....	....	† 133.1	142.7	154.4	166.5
Gross Saving...............................	99s	....	....	....	....	....	....	....	....	† 21.9	22.5	26.7	29.3
Consumption of Fixed Capital.........	99cf	1,847.7	2,117.2	2,469.1	2,737.6	2,976.8	3,260.0	3,475.7	....	† 11.6	12.4	13.3	14.3
GDP Volume 1995 Prices................	99b.p	26,151.9	26,674.9	27,235.2	27,877.5	28,891.4	29,863.2	30,939.7	32,217.2	† 98.7	102.4	107.2	111.7
GDP Volume (2000=100)...............	99bvp	81.2	82.8	84.5	86.5	89.7	92.7	96.0	100.0	104.4	108.3	113.4	118.1
GDP Deflator (2000=100)...............	99bip	63.6	70.8	† 77.7	83.4	89.1	93.8	96.4	100.0	103.7	107.6	111.4	115.1
								Millions: Midyear Estimates					
Population...............................	99z	10.45	10.56	10.66	10.74	10.81	10.87	10.93	10.98	11.02	11.05	11.07	11.10

2005, International Monetary Fund : *International Financial Statistics Yearbook*

Grenada 328

		1993	1994	1995	1996	1997	1998	1999	2000	2001	2002	2003	2004
Exchange Rates		*E.Caribbean Dollars per SDR: End of Period (aa) E.Caribbean Dollars per US Dollar: End of Period (ae)*											
Official Rate	aa	3.7086	3.9416	4.0135	3.8825	3.6430	3.8017	3.7058	3.5179	3.3932	3.6707	4.0121	4.1931
Official Rate	ae	2.7000	2.7000	2.7000	2.7000	2.7000	2.7000	2.7000	2.7000	2.7000	2.7000	2.7000	2.7000
		Index Numbers (2000=100): Period Averages											
Official Rate	ahx	100.0	100.0	100.0	100.0	100.0	100.0	100.0	100.0	100.0	100.0	100.0	100.0
Nominal Effective Exchange Rate	nec	76.9	87.9	87.0	88.9	92.5	93.9	96.0	100.0	103.4	102.6	96.4	91.9
Real Effective Exchange Rate	rec	94.5	94.9	91.6	92.4	94.8	95.8	96.4	100.0	103.9	102.2	94.8	90.2
Fund Position		*Millions of SDRs: End of Period*											
Quota	2f.s	8.50	8.50	8.50	8.50	8.50	8.50	11.70	11.70	11.70	11.70	11.70	11.70
SDRs	1b.s	—	.02	.02	.04	—	.03	—	—	—	—	—	.01
Reserve Position in the Fund	1c.s	—	—	—	—	—	—	—	—	—	—	—	—
Total Fund Cred.&Loans Outstg	2tl	—	—	—	—	—	—	—	—	—	—	2.93	5.86
International Liquidity		*Millions of US Dollars Unless Otherwise Indicated: End of Period*											
Total Reserves minus Gold	1l.d	26.90	31.23	36.73	35.73	42.67	46.84	50.84	57.66	63.94	87.84	83.23	121.73
SDRs	1b.d	—	.03	.02	.06	.01	.04	—	—	—	—	—	.01
Reserve Position in the Fund	1c.d	—	—	—	—	—	—	—	—	—	—	—	—
Foreign Exchange	1d.d	26.90	31.20	36.71	35.67	42.66	46.80	50.84	57.66	63.94	87.84	83.22	121.72
Monetary Authorities: Other Liab.	4..d	—	—	—	—	—	—	—	—	—	—	—	—
Deposit Money Banks: Assets	7a.d	35.68	51.88	59.06	61.88	57.07	54.97	72.71	69.81	113.23	137.94	170.05	270.10
Liabilities	7b.d	37.26	41.15	38.98	50.55	68.25	69.12	74.01	76.85	99.94	104.39	107.89	151.59
Monetary Authorities		*Millions of E. Caribbean Dollars: End of Period*											
Foreign Assets	11	72.71	84.27	99.27	96.50	115.30	126.52	137.20	155.57	173.02	237.88	225.95	330.08
Claims on Central Government	12a	28.34	24.30	21.70	20.82	18.69	18.64	16.33	13.84	11.17	5.63	26.77	26.55
Claims on Deposit Money Banks	12e	.48	.27	.09	.01	.01	.02	.03	.02	.04	.01	.02	.02
Reserve Money	14	100.82	107.30	116.40	116.77	131.40	139.75	148.10	163.52	181.87	215.94	235.46	329.30
of which: Currency Outside DMBs	14a	46.56	52.96	53.83	53.18	58.35	64.08	64.75	71.14	70.20	75.15	84.68	102.10
Foreign Liabilities	16c	—	—	—	—	—	—	—	—	—	—	11.76	24.55
Central Government Deposits	16d	.71	1.54	4.66	.55	2.61	5.44	5.66	5.92	2.33	27.57	5.52	2.79
Other Items (Net)	17r	—	—	—	—	—	—	—	-.22	—	—	—	—
Deposit Money Banks		*Millions of E. Caribbean Dollars: End of Period*											
Reserves	20	53.14	56.10	56.87	59.35	73.43	76.10	92.36	98.26	107.62	138.17	149.50	237.62
Foreign Assets	21	96.33	140.08	159.47	167.09	154.08	148.42	196.32	188.48	305.73	372.43	459.15	729.27
Claims on Central Government	22a	38.39	42.98	46.44	55.93	74.32	80.49	64.91	84.37	101.89	115.60	143.93	124.15
Claims on Local Government	22b	—	.06	—	—	—	—	—	.79	3.51	—	—	—
Claims on Nonfin.Pub.Enterprises	22c	9.74	6.71	6.12	16.07	20.92	25.88	26.13	46.43	65.79	75.83	31.42	22.87
Claims on Private Sector	22d	413.64	414.60	437.29	495.26	587.95	684.68	767.87	878.39	886.41	896.24	932.95	996.59
Claims on Nonbank Financial Insts.	22g	4.32	4.24	6.06	10.31	10.09	15.59	23.33	31.50	39.30	55.85	29.87	17.46
Demand Deposits	24	79.58	87.26	93.77	95.43	97.51	114.34	121.25	130.47	141.41	169.92	197.21	323.26
Time, Savings,& Fgn.Currency Dep	25	364.42	409.15	455.19	504.59	564.27	627.50	722.76	846.61	949.71	1,013.31	1,059.95	1,190.91
Foreign Liabilities	26c	100.60	111.11	105.24	136.50	184.29	186.63	199.83	207.51	269.84	281.85	291.31	409.29
Central Government Deposits	26d	20.35	24.37	30.55	41.02	42.04	56.74	71.04	71.67	65.49	95.51	99.86	144.23
Credit from Monetary Authorities	26g	.58	.25	.07	.02	.02	2.72	.02	.03	.01	—	1.86	.02
Capital Accounts	27a	46.56	50.00	50.47	54.27	60.91	64.96	74.66	83.00	95.94	119.35	144.83	146.26
Other Items (Net)	27r	3.46	-17.38	-23.04	-27.81	-28.23	-21.73	-18.62	-11.05	-12.15	-25.82	-48.18	-86.02
Monetary Survey		*Millions of E. Caribbean Dollars: End of Period*											
Foreign Assets (Net)	31n	68.44	113.24	153.50	127.09	85.10	88.31	133.70	136.54	208.91	328.45	382.03	625.50
Domestic Credit	32	473.36	466.97	482.40	556.82	667.32	763.09	822.09	977.73	1,040.25	1,026.07	1,059.57	1,040.60
Claims on Central Govt. (Net)	32an	45.65	41.36	32.93	35.18	48.36	36.96	4.54	20.62	45.24	-1.86	65.32	3.67
Claims on Local Government	32b	—	.06	—	—	—	—	—	.79	3.51	—	—	—
Claims on Nonfin.Pub.Enterprises	32c	9.74	6.71	6.12	16.07	20.92	25.88	26.35	46.43	65.79	75.83	31.42	22.87
Claims on Private Sector	32d	413.64	414.60	437.29	495.26	587.95	684.68	767.87	878.39	886.41	896.24	932.95	996.59
Claims on Nonbank Financial Inst.	32g	4.32	4.24	6.06	10.31	10.09	15.59	23.33	31.50	39.30	55.85	29.87	17.46
Money	34	126.14	140.36	147.85	148.63	155.87	178.41	186.00	201.71	211.67	245.51	281.93	425.64
Quasi-Money	35	364.42	409.15	455.19	504.59	564.27	627.50	722.76	846.61	949.71	1,013.31	1,059.95	1,190.91
Capital Accounts	37a	50.01	53.67	54.20	57.88	64.30	68.50	78.10	86.27	99.09	122.76	148.56	150.16
Other Items (Net)	37r	1.23	-22.97	-21.33	-27.19	-32.02	-23.00	-31.08	-20.32	-11.32	-27.06	-48.84	-100.61
Money plus Quasi-Money	35l	490.56	549.51	603.03	653.22	720.14	805.91	908.76	1,048.32	1,161.38	1,258.82	1,341.88	1,616.55
Money (National Definitions)		*Millions of E. Caribbean Dollars: End of Period*											
M1	59ma	109.66	124.16	131.65	131.44	144.51	159.41	175.15	182.38	192.34	211.98	241.08	340.25
M2	59mb	453.99	504.52	550.69	600.74	671.52	750.44	854.56	985.84	1,090.37	1,167.38	1,260.37	1,483.35
Interest Rates		*Percent Per Annum*											
Discount Rate (End of Period)	60	....	9.00	9.00	9.00	8.00	8.00	8.00	8.00	7.00	7.00	6.50	6.50
Money Market Rate	60b	5.25	5.25	5.25	5.25	5.25	5.25	5.25	5.25	† 5.64	6.32	6.07	4.67
Treasury Bill Rate	60c	6.50	6.50	6.50	6.50	6.50	6.50	6.50	6.50	† 7.00	7.00	6.50	6.00
Savings Rate	60k	5.00	5.46	5.00	5.00	5.33	6.00	6.00	6.00	6.00	5.83	† 3.25	3.53
Deposit Rate	60l	3.88	3.61	3.67	3.74	3.93	4.16	4.30	4.24	4.23	3.59	3.39	3.32
Deposit Rate (Fgn. Currency)	60l.f	....	....	....	....	....	....	....	....	....	....	3.69	2.46
Lending Rate	60p	11.83	11.03	11.08	9.99	11.24	11.73	11.62	11.60	10.19	11.31	12.05	10.18
Prices		*Index Numbers (2000=100): Period Averages*											
Consumer Prices	64	87.9	91.2	92.9	94.8	† 96.0	97.3	97.9	100.0	101.7	102.8	....	....
Intl. Transactions & Positions		*Millions of E. Caribbean Dollars*											
Exports	70	55.10	64.30	58.70	54.00	61.50	72.50	....	....	....	....	....	....
Imports, c.i.f	71	319.60	320.60	333.80	411.10	468.20	540.40	....	....	....	....	....	....

		1993	1994	1995	1996	1997	1998	1999	2000	2001	2002	2003	2004
Balance of Payments					*Millions of US Dollars: Minus Sign Indicates Debit*								
Current Account, n.i.e.	78ald	−43.68	−26.93	−40.84	−55.54	−67.87	−81.51	−53.04	−84.33	−98.54	−116.22	....	....
Goods: Exports f.o.b.	78aad	22.74	25.24	24.57	24.96	32.80	45.95	74.30	82.96	63.60	41.99	....	....
Goods: Imports f.o.b.	78abd	−118.13	−119.45	−129.78	−147.44	−154.90	−183.01	−184.57	−220.94	−196.83	−181.42	....	....
Trade Balance	78acd	−95.38	−94.21	−105.21	−122.48	−122.10	−137.06	−110.28	−137.98	−133.23	−139.43	....	....
Services: Credit	78add	87.68	101.53	99.19	106.70	106.14	119.77	143.72	152.76	133.34	133.04	....	....
Services: Debit	78aed	−41.19	−41.26	−38.46	−45.78	−56.48	−70.16	−79.86	−87.41	−82.22	−88.16	....	....
Balance on Goods & Services	78afd	−48.89	−33.94	−44.48	−61.56	−72.44	−87.45	−46.41	−72.63	−82.10	−94.56	....	....
Income: Credit	78agd	2.68	3.61	4.91	4.71	4.70	4.13	4.33	5.08	3.73	4.13	....	....
Income: Debit	78ahd	−11.16	−12.43	−18.36	−20.10	−21.65	−27.38	−30.15	−36.89	−41.81	−48.92	....	....
Balance on Gds, Serv. & Inc.	78aid	−57.37	−42.76	−57.92	−76.94	−89.39	−110.70	−72.23	−104.43	−120.18	−139.35	....	....
Current Transfers, n.i.e.: Credit	78ajd	16.10	19.75	21.58	25.47	25.53	34.19	26.76	30.35	31.00	31.83	....	....
Current Transfers: Debit	78akd	−2.41	−3.92	−4.50	−4.07	−4.01	−5.00	−7.57	−10.25	−9.36	−8.70	....	....
Capital Account, n.i.e.	78bcd	16.89	21.67	25.84	31.42	31.78	28.58	31.18	32.13	42.36	31.83	....	....
Capital Account, n.i.e.: Credit	78bad	18.27	23.04	27.28	31.42	33.42	30.36	33.10	34.21	44.39	33.87	....	....
Capital Account: Debit	78bbd	−1.38	−1.38	−1.44	—	−1.64	−1.78	−1.92	−2.08	−2.04	−2.04	....	....
Financial Account, n.i.e.	78bjd	17.74	4.06	3.10	27.39	59.16	55.77	27.56	63.74	47.26	108.25	....	....
Direct Investment Abroad	78bdd	—	—	—	—	—	—	—	—	—	—	....	....
Dir. Invest. in Rep. Econ., n.i.e.	78bed	20.25	19.31	19.98	16.95	33.50	48.69	41.55	37.41	58.75	57.61	....	....
Portfolio Investment Assets	78bfd	.20	−.38	−.87	—	−.04	.04	−.36	−.07	−.42	−1.69	....	....
Equity Securities	78bkd	....	....	....	....	....	....	....	....	....	....	....	....
Debt Securities	78bld	....	....	....	....	....	....	....	....	....	....	....	....
Portfolio Investment Liab., n.i.e.	78bgd	—	—	—	—	−.01	.75	19.52	.17	109.42		....	....
Equity Securities	78bmd	....	....	....	....	....	....	....	....	....	....	....	....
Debt Securities	78bnd	....	....	....	....	....	....	....	....	....	....	....	....
Financial Derivatives Assets	78bwd	....	....	....	....	....	....	....	....	....	....	....	....
Financial Derivatives Liabilities	78bxd	....	....	....	....	....	....	....	....	....	....	....	....
Other Investment Assets	78bhd	−9.95	−23.59	−11.02	−3.70	−5.89	−3.80	−12.39	−11.07	−5.31	−14.21	....	....
Monetary Authorities	78bod	....	....	....	....	....	....	....	....	....	....	....	....
General Government	78bpd	....	....	....	....	....	....	....	....	....	....	....	....
Banks	78bqd	....	....	....	....	....	....	....	....	....	....	....	....
Other Sectors	78brd	....	—	....	....	....	....	....	....	....	....	....	....
Other Investment Liab., n.i.e.	78bid	7.24	8.72	−4.99	14.15	31.59	10.85	−2.00	17.96	−5.93	−42.89	....	....
Monetary Authorities	78bsd	....	....	....	....	....	....	....	....	....	....	....	....
General Government	78btd	....	....	....	....	....	....	....	....	....	....	....	....
Banks	78bud	....	....	....	....	....	....	....	....	....	....	....	....
Other Sectors	78bvd	....	....	....	....	....	....	....	....	....	....	....	....
Net Errors and Omissions	78cad	9.49	5.88	17.94	−2.83	−16.14	1.26	−1.04	−4.95	14.77	7.36	....	....
Overall Balance	78cbd	.44	4.68	6.03	.45	6.93	4.09	4.66	6.60	5.84	31.22	....	....
Reserves and Related Items	79dad	−.44	−4.68	−6.03	−.45	−6.93	−4.09	−4.66	−6.60	−5.84	−31.22	....	....
Reserve Assets	79dbd	−.44	−4.68	−6.03	−.45	−6.93	−4.09	−4.66	−6.60	−5.84	−31.22	....	....
Use of Fund Credit and Loans	79dcd	—	—	—	—	—	—	—	—	—	—	....	....
Exceptional Financing	79ded	—	—	—	....	....	....	....	....	—	—	....	....
Government Finance					*Millions of E. Caribbean Dollars: Year Ending December 31*								
Deficit (-) or Surplus	80	−1.42	−7.86	16.79	....	....	....	....	....				
Revenue	81	178.27	194.26	205.00	....	....	....	....	....				
Grants Received	81z	16.33	26.50	21.48	....	....	....	....	....				
Expenditure	82	196.02	228.62	209.69	....	....	....	....	....				
Lending Minus Repayments	83	—	—	—	....	....	....	....	....				
National Accounts					*Millions of E. Caribbean Dollars*								
Househ.Cons.Expend.,incl.NPISHs	96f	472.9	420.2	503.3	551.4	590.5	697.1	544.1	758.6	....	....	....	....
Government Consumption Expend	91f	123.7	126.6	123.7	130.3	137.5	150.8	147.5	161.4	....	....	....	....
Gross Fixed Capital Formation	93e	210.5	253.8	239.3	280.4	311.2	343.9	408.9	453.8	....	....	....	....
Exports of Goods and Services	90c	297.7	342.3	334.2	355.1	381.7	448.8	636.8	674.0	....	....	....	....
Imports of Goods and Services (-)	98c	429.7	433.9	454.5	521.6	570.7	694.0	716.2	939.2	....	....	....	....
Gross Domestic Product (GDP)	99b	675.1	708.9	746.0	795.6	850.2	946.7	1,021.1	1,108.5	....	....	....	....
Net Primary Income from Abroad	98.n	−22.6	−23.8	−36.3	−41.6	−46.8	−64.2	−80.2	−90.9	....	....	....	....
Gross National Income (GNI)	99a	652.5	685.1	709.7	754.0	803.4	882.5	940.9	1,017.7	....	....	....	....
Net Current Transf.from Abroad	98t	37.0	42.7	46.1	51.2	53.9	78.9	75.6	78.0	....	....	....	....
Gross Nat'l Disposable Inc.(GNDI)	99i	689.5	727.9	755.8	805.2	857.3	961.4	1,016.5	1,095.6	....	....	....	....
Gross Saving	99s	92.9	181.1	128.8	123.5	129.3	113.4	325.0	175.6	....	....	....	....
					Millions: Midyear Estimates								
Population	99z	.10	.10	.10	.10	.10	.10	.10	.10	.10	.10	.10	.10

Guatemala 258

Guatemala 258

		1993	1994	1995	1996	1997	1998	1999	2000	2001	2002	2003	2004
Exchange Rates						*Quetzales per SDR: End of Period*							
Market Rate.............aa=	wa	7.9876	8.2460	8.9810	8.5782	8.3342	9.6425	10.7342	10.0731	10.0544	10.6140	11.9482	12.0334
						Quetzales per US Dollar: End of Period (we) Period Average (wf)							
Market Rate.............ae=	we	5.8152	5.6485	6.0418	5.9656	6.1769	6.8482	7.8208	7.7312	8.0005	7.8072	8.0407	7.7484
Market Rate.............rf=	wf	5.6354	5.7512	5.8103	6.0495	6.0653	6.3947	7.3856	7.7632	7.8586	7.8216	7.9408	7.9465
Secondary Rate.............	xe	1.00	1.00	1.00	1.00	1.00	1.00	1.00	1.00	....	....	....	....
Secondary Rate.............	xf	1.00	1.00	1.00	1.00	1.00	1.00	1.00	1.00	....	....	....	....
Fund Position						*Millions of SDRs: End of Period*							
Quota....................	2f.s	153.8	153.8	153.8	153.8	153.8	153.8	210.2	210.2	210.2	210.2	210.2	210.2
SDRs....................	1b.s	11.4	11.4	10.6	10.2	9.4	8.7	8.4	7.5	6.7	6.1	5.5	5.1
Reserve Position in the Fund............	1c.s	—	—	—	—	—	—	—	—	—	—	—	—
of which: Outstg.Fund Borrowing...	2c	—	—	—	—	—	—	—	—	—	—	—	—
Total Fund Cred.&Loans Outstg........	2tl	—	—	—	—	—	—	—	—	—	—	—	—
International Liquidity						*Millions of US Dollars Unless Otherwise Indicated: End of Period*							
Total Reserves minus Gold............	1l.d	867.8	863.1	702.0	869.7	1,111.1	1,335.1	1,189.2	1,746.4	2,292.2	2,299.1	2,833.2	3,426.3
SDRs....................	1b.d	15.7	16.6	15.8	14.6	12.7	12.2	11.5	9.8	8.5	8.2	8.2	8.0
Reserve Position in the Fund..........	1c.d	—	—	—	—	—	—	—	—	—	—	—	—
Foreign Exchange..........	1d.d	852.1	846.5	686.2	855.1	1,098.4	1,322.9	1,177.7	1,736.6	2,283.7	2,290.9	2,825.0	3,418.3
Gold (Million Fine Troy Ounces)........	1ad	.209	.209	.210	.212	.213	.215	.215	.216	.217	.216	.220	.219
Gold (National Valuation)................	1and	8.8	8.8	8.9	8.9	9.0	9.1	9.1	9.1	9.2	9.1	9.3	9.3
Monetary Authorities: Other Liab...	4..d	89.6	66.5	55.4	48.1	184.3	152.3	126.4	102.3	90.1	79.1	69.1	.9
Deposit Money Banks: Assets..........	7a.d	8.6	17.7	66.3	81.2	72.6	65.6	84.1	123.6	203.4	245.2	293.5	314.2
Liabilities..................	7b.d	113.1	373.3	266.2	375.4	413.4	500.9	452.5	613.8	656.6	689.2	732.1	860.6
Other Banking Insts.: Assets............	7e.d	.1	4.1	4.3	4.5	1.8	12.1	4.3	3.2	6.1	22.8	30.1	27.8
Liabilities..................	7f.d	79.9	100.2	515.8	554.3	592.0	615.8	633.7	654.1	526.0	534.3	552.4	567.8
Monetary Authorities						*Millions of Quetzales: End of Period*							
Foreign Assets......................	11	1,307.4	1,292.5	1,157.7	1,341.6	† 7,566.2	10,109.3	10,521.1	15,038.3	19,265.5	18,920.6	24,029.8	27,840.5
Claims on Central Government........	12a	112.5	357.6	187.4	698.0	† 78.7	.2	.2	.2	.2	.2	.2	—
Claims on Local Government............	12b	2.6	2.0	1.3	.6	† .3	—	—	—	—	—	—	—
Claims on Nonfin.Pub.Enterprises...	12c	7.4	7.4	7.4	—	† —	—	—	—	—	—	—	—
Claims on Private Sector.............	12d	—	—	—	—	† 29.7	30.0	29.9	30.6	31.5	32.2	33.2	—
Claims on Deposit Money Banks......	12e	184.8	61.3	123.3	97.5	† 81.9	228.5	652.6	793.8	2,227.2	2,146.5	2,081.3	2,077.3
Claims on Other Banking Insts.........	12f	245.2	188.3	148.4	97.1	† 44.1	12.8	41.7	7.5	7.4	.4	.4	.4
Reserve Money......................	14	5,255.3	5,494.3	5,689.3	6,418.2	† 10,746.6	10,324.2	10,608.5	12,653.6	14,702.7	17,403.2	19,340.6	22,824.7
of which: Currency Outside DMBs..	14a	3,097.3	3,714.6	4,018.9	4,179.1	† 4,890.2	5,632.5	7,752.8	7,298.2	8,360.7	8,729.4	10,608.8	11,194.8
Time and Foreign Currency Deposits.	15	2,460.9	3,845.6	4,600.0	6,582.4	† 665.2	1,103.4	1,995.1	6,872.7	8,083.6	8,997.9	9,925.3	9,478.8
Liabs. of Central Bank: Securities.....	16ac	670.7	372.9	76.0	50.3	† 212.7	67.5	60.9	58.4	57.1	53.8	53.9	52.2
Foreign Liabilities....................	16c	323.5	338.3	352.6	359.5	† 1,138.6	1,043.2	988.6	790.8	721.2	617.7	556.0	6.8
Central Government Deposits.........	16d	1,421.5	1,566.3	1,439.6	1,872.3	† 5,293.5	7,586.1	6,405.8	5,527.8	9,162.1	6,446.5	8,700.0	11,805.1
Liabilities to Other Banking Insts......	16i	—	—	—	—	† 2.0	—	—	—	—	1.4	.5	.5
Capital Accounts....................	17a	354.1	363.5	384.6	372.1	† 330.2	366.4	396.6	3,595.0	3,958.3	2,924.3	2,824.8	2,740.3
Other Items (Net)......................	17r	−9,077.7	−10,349.5	−11,152.8	−13,622.1	† −10,587.9	−10,110.0	−9,210.0	−13,627.9	−15,153.2	−15,344.9	−15,256.2	−16,990.2
Deposit Money Banks						*Millions of Quetzales: End of Period*							
Reserves......................	20	2,815.2	2,175.5	4,019.2	4,794.7	† 5,731.3	4,823.0	3,121.7	5,132.4	6,120.3	9,051.8	7,879.7	9,474.8
Foreign Assets.............	21	50.0	100.1	400.8	484.2	† 448.4	449.5	657.4	955.4	1,627.4	1,914.5	2,360.2	2,434.4
Claims on Central Government........	22a	1,794.1	2,869.7	1,292.5	1,676.9	† 2,870.0	2,389.0	2,277.1	3,361.2	4,654.9	4,799.2	5,104.9	6,866.7
Claims on Local Government............	22b	—	—	—	—	† 81.3	14.4	14.6	38.1	30.4	67.4	—	—
Claims on Nonfin.Pub.Enterprises.....	22c	—	—	—	—	† —	—	63.1	—	—	—	—	—
Claims on Private Sector.............	22d	7,434.4	9,156.9	13,898.6	15,446.7	† 16,603.7	21,142.4	24,115.9	26,416.0	30,155.3	32,502.5	35,350.6	41,007.1
Claims on Other Banking Insts.........	22f	—	—	—	—	† 2,116.8	2,482.6	2,034.7	2,155.3	2,174.0	1,854.3	1,530.5	1,889.4
Demand Deposits........................	24	1,928.0	3,336.2	3,728.4	4,617.5	† 6,856.2	7,866.9	7,614.1	11,271.5	12,512.2	13,930.4	16,188.0	17,470.8
Time, Savings,& Fgn.Currency Dep...	25	8,893.9	7,450.0	8,900.3	8,802.5	† 10,535.8	12,976.8	13,682.8	16,506.1	20,722.1	23,935.5	27,270.2	31,924.2
Bonds................................	26ab	—	—	—	—	† 5,139.9	4,480.2	4,266.1	4,286.1	3,917.4	3,655.9	2,699.8	2,497.7
Foreign Liabilities....................	26c	657.9	2,108.7	1,608.2	2,239.3	† 2,553.6	3,430.5	3,539.0	4,745.1	5,253.0	5,380.4	5,886.7	6,668.5
Central Government Deposits.........	26d	76.7	71.0	171.5	194.4	† 410.7	677.9	1,197.0	2,675.4	3,722.9	4,739.6	3,853.0	5,861.1
Credit from Monetary Authorities.....	26g	185.9	66.0	123.5	97.6	† 7.4	162.7	804.6	755.1	2,195.8	2,102.0	2,063.8	2,063.9
Liabilities to Other Banking Insts......	26i	—	—	—	—	† 478.9	575.9	578.0	658.0	1,277.6	1,013.7	900.1	1,149.3
Capital Accounts........................	27a	1,293.0	1,586.7	1,821.9	2,019.8	† 2,315.5	2,775.7	3,810.3	4,464.9	2,834.7	3,077.5	3,315.1	4,002.3
Other Items (Net)......................	27r	−941.7	−316.4	3,257.3	4,431.4	† −446.5	−1,645.7	−3,207.4	−7,303.8	−7,673.4	−7,645.3	−9,950.9	−9,965.3
Monetary Survey						*Millions of Quetzales: End of Period*							
Foreign Assets (Net)........................	31n	376.0	−1,054.4	−402.3	−773.0	† 4,322.4	6,085.1	6,650.9	10,457.8	14,918.7	14,837.0	19,947.3	23,599.5
Domestic Credit........................	32	8,098.0	10,944.6	13,924.5	15,852.6	† 16,120.4	17,807.4	20,974.4	23,805.7	24,168.7	28,070.2	29,466.8	32,097.4
Claims on Central Govt. (Net)........	32an	408.4	1,590.0	−131.2	308.2	† −2,755.5	−5,874.8	−5,325.5	−4,841.8	−8,229.9	−6,386.7	−7,447.8	−10,799.5
Claims on Local Government........	32b	2.6	2.0	1.3	.6	† 81.6	14.4	14.6	38.1	30.4	67.4	—	—
Claims on Nonfin.Pub.Enterprises...	32c	7.4	7.4	7.4	—	† —	—	63.1	—	—	—	—	—
Claims on Private Sector...............	32d	7,434.4	9,156.9	13,898.6	15,446.7	† 16,633.4	21,172.4	24,145.8	26,446.6	30,186.8	32,534.7	35,383.7	41,007.1
Claims on Other Banking Insts.......	32f	245.2	188.3	148.4	97.1	† 2,160.9	2,495.4	2,076.4	2,162.8	2,181.4	1,854.7	1,530.9	1,889.8
Money......................	34	5,048.1	7,073.6	7,771.8	8,822.4	† 11,997.5	13,613.5	15,467.6	18,832.2	21,059.0	22,835.7	26,937.7	28,741.0
Quasi-Money........................	35	11,354.8	11,295.6	13,500.3	15,384.9	† 11,201.0	14,080.2	15,677.9	23,378.8	28,805.7	32,933.4	37,195.5	41,403.0
Bonds................................	36ab	—	—	—	—	† 5,139.9	4,480.2	4,266.1	4,286.1	3,917.4	3,655.9	2,699.8	2,497.7
Liabs. of Central Bank: Securities......	36ac	670.7	372.9	76.0	50.3	† 212.7	67.5	60.9	58.4	57.1	53.8	53.9	52.2
Liabilities to Other Banking Insts......	36i	—	—	—	—	† 480.9	575.9	578.0	658.0	1,277.6	1,015.1	900.6	1,149.8
Capital Accounts........................	37a	1,647.1	1,950.2	2,206.5	2,391.9	† 2,645.7	3,142.1	4,206.9	8,059.6	6,793.0	6,001.8	6,139.9	6,742.7
Other Items (Net)........................	37r	−10,698.3	−11,079.8	−10,268.6	−11,772.0	† −11,234.9	−12,066.9	−12,632.1	−21,009.9	−22,822.4	−23,588.5	−24,513.3	−24,889.3
Money plus Quasi-Money................	35l	16,402.9	18,369.2	21,272.1	24,207.3	† 23,198.5	27,693.7	31,145.5	42,211.0	49,864.7	55,769.1	64,133.2	70,143.9

Guatemala 258

		1993	1994	1995	1996	1997	1998	1999	2000	2001	2002	2003	2004
Other Banking Institutions						*Millions of Quetzales: End of Period*							
Reserves............................	40	66.1	31.5	48.3	69.6	† 14.9	120.8	45.8	30.2	50.6	49.5	70.0	17.7
Foreign Assets........................	41	.4	23.4	26.2	26.6	† 10.9	83.2	33.9	24.7	48.6	177.6	242.1	215.6
Claims on Central Government.......	42a	36.2	48.4	42.6	111.5	† 77.0	120.0	88.7	155.6	220.0	235.6	385.3	708.3
Claims on Nonfin.Pub.Enterprises.....	42c	—	—	—	—	† 13.2	.2	.2	.2	.2	.2	—	.2
Claims on Private Sector.................	42d	1,489.9	2,055.3	2,512.4	2,655.5	† 3,388.5	4,310.1	3,859.8	3,181.8	2,813.0	2,185.7	2,209.3	2,120.0
Claims on Deposit Money Banks......	42e	331.7	309.3	458.5	443.5	† 555.7	550.1	453.8	540.5	567.2	556.4	267.0	258.2
Time, Savings,& Fgn.Currency Dep...	45	—	—	—	—	† 3.8	201.4	4.5	3.3	5.9	4.0	4.4	1.3
Bonds............................	46ab	1,326.4	1,710.5	1,176.0	1,378.7	† 2,298.6	2,692.3	2,192.6	2,314.7	2,171.6	1,843.1	1,476.8	1,258.9
Foreign Liabilities....................	46c	26.4	99.7	146.1	157.7	† 3,656.5	4,216.9	4,956.2	5,057.0	4,208.6	4,171.5	4,441.6	4,399.2
Credit from Monetary Authorities.....	46g	259.3	195.4	144.2	102.3	† —	—	—	—	—	—	—	—
Credit from Deposit Money Banks....	46h	523.5	877.6	1,637.1	1,689.4	† 1,584.0	1,925.9	2,110.8	1,629.1	1,436.3	1,264.7	1,473.1	1,803.2
Capital Accounts....................	47a	−142.8	−107.4	−2,559.7	−2,667.4	† −2,849.0	−3,329.4	−4,019.0	−4,242.2	−3,414.7	−3,417.2	−3,641.6	−3,506.0
Other Items (Net)...................	47r	−506.5	−774.3	−425.7	−503.1	† −633.7	−522.7	−762.9	−828.9	−708.1	−661.1	−580.5	−636.4
Banking Survey						*Millions of Quetzales: End of Period*							
Foreign Assets (Net)......................	51n	350.0	−1,130.7	−522.2	−904.1	† 676.8	1,951.4	1,728.6	5,425.5	10,758.7	10,843.2	15,747.8	19,415.9
Domestic Credit.......................	52	9,378.9	12,860.0	16,331.1	18,522.5	† 17,438.2	19,743.0	22,853.3	24,980.5	25,020.5	28,640.8	30,530.6	33,036.2
Claims on Central Govt. (Net).......	52an	444.6	1,638.4	−88.6	419.7	† −2,678.5	−5,754.8	−5,236.8	−4,686.2	−8,009.9	−6,151.0	−7,062.5	−10,091.1
Claims on Local Government........	52b	2.6	2.0	1.3	.6	† 81.6	15.1	21.2	38.1	30.4	71.2	—	—
Claims on Nonfin.Pub.Enterprises...	52c	7.4	7.4	7.4	—	† 13.2	.2	63.3	.2	.2	.2	—	.2
Claims on Private Sector..............	52d	8,924.3	11,212.2	16,411.0	18,102.2	† 20,021.9	25,482.5	28,005.6	29,628.4	32,999.8	34,720.5	37,593.1	43,127.2
Liquid Liabilities.....................	55l	16,336.8	18,337.7	21,223.8	24,137.7	† 23,186.8	27,912.3	31,097.0	42,176.7	49,815.0	55,709.7	64,064.3	70,126.3
Bonds............................	56ab	1,326.4	1,710.5	1,176.0	1,378.7	† 7,438.5	7,172.5	6,458.7	6,600.8	6,089.0	5,499.0	4,176.6	3,756.5
Liabs. of Central Bank: Securities.....	56ac	670.7	372.9	76.0	50.3	† 212.7	67.5	60.9	58.4	57.1	53.8	53.9	52.2
Capital Accounts.....................	57a	1,504.3	1,842.8	−353.2	−275.5	† −203.3	−187.3	187.9	3,817.7	3,378.3	2,584.6	2,498.2	3,236.6
Other Items (Net)...................	57r	−10,998.9	−11,278.7	−9,519.9	−11,024.0	† −12,519.7	−13,270.6	−13,222.6	−22,247.6	−23,560.2	−24,363.1	−24,514.7	−24,719.4
Money (National Definitions)						*Millions of Quetzales: End of Period*							
Base Money......................	19ma	....	....	....	....	10,509.9	10,243.6	11,089.1	12,302.5	13,953.2	16,280.5	17,038.4	19,074.2
M1..............................	59ma	....	....	....	....	11,948.2	13,565.6	15,497.2	18,651.8	20,112.6	21,624.5	26,051.1	27,878.5
M2..............................	59mb	....	....	....	....	27,564.1	30,999.7	33,456.2	39,497.4	47,228.2	51,474.0	58,281.6	58,013.9
Interest Rates						*Percent Per Annum*							
Money Market Rate.....................	60b	....	....	....	....	7.77	6.62	9.23	9.33	10.58	9.11	6.65	6.16
Savings Rate.........................	60k	....	....	....	....	5.13	4.50	5.19	5.41	4.51	3.31	2.09	1.77
Deposit Rate........................	60l	12.63	9.69	7.87	7.65	† 5.83	5.44	7.96	10.17	8.75	6.92	4.78	4.19
Lending Rate.......................	60p	24.73	22.93	21.16	22.72	† 18.64	16.56	19.51	20.88	18.96	16.86	14.98	13.81
Prices and Labor						*Index Numbers (2000=100): Period Averages*							
Consumer Prices......................	64	57.7	64.0	69.3	77.0	84.1	90.0	94.4	† 100.0	107.6	116.3	122.6	131.7
						Number in Thousands: Period Averages							
Labor Force.........................	67d	....	2,326	....	....	....	....	3,982	4	....	....	....	....
Employment.........................	67e	823	830	856	852	844	887	893	908	928	953	958	....
Unemployment.......................	67c	1	1	1	....	....	....	....	2	....	2	....	....
Intl. Transactions & Positions						*Millions of US Dollars*							
Exports.............................	70..d	1,340.4	1,550.2	1,990.8	2,056.3	2,390.6	2,562.7	2,493.6	2,711.2	2,463.6	2,473.2	2,631.7	2,938.7
Imports, c.i.f........................	71..d	2,599.3	2,781.4	3,292.5	3,146.2	3,851.9	4,650.9	4,560.0	5,171.4	5,606.4	6,304.1	6,721.5	7,811.6
Imports, f.o.b.......................	71.vd	2,384.0	2,595.9	3,061.7	2,925.7	3,581.7	4,319.7	4,240.4	4,808.5	5,210.0	5,866.0	6,253.1	7,279.0

2005, International Monetary Fund : *International Financial Statistics Yearbook*

		1993	1994	1995	1996	1997	1998	1999	2000	2001	2002	2003	2004
Balance of Payments		*Millions of US Dollars: Minus Sign Indicates Debit*											
Current Account, n.i.e.	78ald	−701.7	−625.3	−572.0	−451.5	−633.5	−1,039.1	−1,025.9	−1,049.6	−1,252.9	−1,234.9	−1,039.1	−1,188.3
Goods: Exports f.o.b.	78aad	1,363.2	1,550.1	2,157.5	2,236.9	2,602.9	2,846.9	2,780.6	3,085.1	2,859.8	2,818.9	3,059.9	3,429.5
Goods: Imports f.o.b.	78abd	−2,384.0	−2,546.6	−3,032.6	−2,880.3	−3,542.7	−4,255.7	−4,225.7	−4,742.0	−5,142.0	−5,791.0	−6,175.7	−7,189.1
Trade Balance	78acd	−1,020.8	−996.5	−875.1	−643.4	−939.8	−1,408.8	−1,445.1	−1,656.9	−2,282.2	−2,972.1	−3,115.8	−3,759.6
Services: Credit	78add	660.4	697.5	665.9	559.0	588.8	639.9	699.5	777.0	1,044.8	1,145.4	1,058.8	1,178.2
Services: Debit	78aed	−586.1	−644.9	−694.9	−659.7	−650.5	−791.8	−790.7	−825.4	−927.9	−1,066.1	−1,126.1	−1,293.8
Balance on Goods & Services	78afd	−946.5	−943.9	−904.1	−744.1	−1,001.5	−1,560.7	−1,536.3	−1,705.3	−2,165.3	−2,892.8	−3,183.1	−3,875.2
Income: Credit	78agd	61.1	63.6	46.6	40.2	72.4	91.4	76.2	214.4	317.5	161.1	179.1	173.3
Income: Debit	78ahd	−179.5	−193.6	−205.7	−270.1	−311.1	−275.1	−280.7	−424.0	−401.9	−479.5	−497.0	−492.1
Balance on Gds, Serv. & Inc.	78aid	−1,064.9	−1,073.9	−1,063.2	−974.0	−1,240.2	−1,744.4	−1,740.8	−1,914.9	−2,249.7	−3,211.1	−3,501.0	−4,194.0
Current Transfers, n.i.e.: Credit	78ajd	371.4	456.4	508.2	537.1	628.8	742.9	754.4	908.2	1,024.3	2,077.7	2,558.9	3,048.6
Current Transfers: Debit	78akd	−8.2	−7.8	−17.0	−14.6	−22.1	−37.6	−39.5	−42.9	−27.5	−101.5	−97.0	−42.9
Capital Account, n.i.e.	78bcd	—	—	61.6	65.0	85.0	71.0	68.4	85.5	93.4	124.2	133.8	135.3
Capital Account, n.i.e.: Credit	78bad	—	—	61.6	65.0	85.0	71.0	68.4	85.5	93.4	124.2	133.8	135.3
Capital Account: Debit	78bbd	—	—	....	....	....	....	....	....	....	....	....	....
Financial Account, n.i.e.	78bjd	816.2	655.2	494.8	672.3	737.4	1,136.7	637.5	1,520.7	1,546.7	1,196.5	1,516.3	1,597.8
Direct Investment Abroad	78bdd	—	—	....	....	....	....	....	....	—	—	—	—
Dir. Invest. in Rep. Econ., n.i.e.	78bed	142.5	65.2	75.2	76.9	84.4	672.8	154.6	229.9	455.5	110.6	131.0	154.7
Portfolio Investment Assets	78bfd	112.4	−9.8	−22.2	−11.5	−18.1	−11.6	−26.0	−36.3	−45.0	−38.3	18.1	111.1
Equity Securities	78bkd	....	—	....	....	....	....	....	....	—	—	—	—
Debt Securities	78bld	112.4	−9.8	−22.2	−11.5	−18.1	−11.6	−26.0	−36.3	−45.0	−38.3	18.1	111.1
Portfolio Investment Liab., n.i.e.	78bgd	−27.0	7.1	5.9	−4.5	249.7	65.8	136.5	78.9	175.3	−107.8	−11.0	238.0
Equity Securities	78bmd	....	—	....	....	....	....	....	....	—	—	—	—
Debt Securities	78bnd	−27.0	7.1	5.9	−4.5	249.7	65.8	136.5	78.9	175.3	−107.8	−11.0	238.0
Financial Derivatives Assets	78bwd	....	—	....	....	....	....	....	....	—	—	—	—
Financial Derivatives Liabilities	78bxd	....	—	....	....	....	....	....	....	—	—	—	—
Other Investment Assets	78bhd	−3.0	116.8	125.1	199.2	221.2	241.7	199.9	213.2	156.7	196.4	173.5	252.0
Monetary Authorities	78bod	....	—	....	....	....	....	....	....	—	—	—	—
General Government	78bpd	−45.9	−49.2	....	....	....	....	....	....	—	—	—	—
Banks	78bqd	—	—	....	....	....	....	....	....	—	—	—	—
Other Sectors	78brd	42.9	166.0	125.1	199.2	221.2	241.7	199.9	213.2	156.7	196.4	173.5	252.0
Other Investment Liab., n.i.e.	78bid	591.3	475.9	310.8	412.2	200.2	168.0	172.5	1,035.0	804.0	1,035.6	1,204.7	842.0
Monetary Authorities	78bsd	−44.1	−63.9	−78.3	−56.3	−108.6	−54.2	−25.6	−24.0	−11.2	−11.3	−11.7	−68.3
General Government	78btd	−51.3	132.7	11.8	91.1	89.5	252.4	295.9	92.7	42.6	172.7	307.9	79.4
Banks	78bud	—	—	7.3	19.4	−4.6	3.2	23.0	−17.4	21.8	—	—	—
Other Sectors	78bvd	686.7	407.1	370.0	358.0	223.9	−33.4	−120.8	983.7	750.9	874.3	908.5	831.0
Net Errors and Omissions	78cad	85.2	−23.6	−136.2	−71.7	40.7	66.8	195.0	86.1	87.2	−64.7	−60.8	63.5
Overall Balance	78cbd	199.7	6.3	−151.8	214.1	229.6	235.4	−125.0	642.7	474.4	21.1	550.1	608.3
Reserves and Related Items	79dad	−199.7	−6.3	151.8	−214.1	−229.6	−235.4	125.0	−642.7	−474.4	−21.1	−550.1	−608.3
Reserve Assets	79dbd	−120.5	−47.3	157.3	−199.0	−257.7	−263.0	125.0	−642.7	−474.4	−21.2	−550.1	−608.3
Use of Fund Credit and Loans	79dcd	−31.3	—	—	—	—	—	—	—	—	—	—	—
Exceptional Financing	79ded	−47.9	41.0	−5.5	−15.1	28.1	27.6	....	....	—	—	—	—
Government Finance		*Millions of Quetzales: Year Ending December 31*											
Deficit (-) or Surplus	80	−1,064.5	† −938.7	−218.4	−268.0	−2,244.3	−2,708.9	−3,804.2	−2,709.8	−3,105.0	−1,351.8	−3,540.2	−2,386.1
Revenue	81	5,645.8	† 5,712.3	7,227.7	8,605.1	9,730.3	12,714.0	14,735.7	16,050.5	17,656.4	20,503.5	21,811.6	22,338.1
Grants Received	81z	....	† 74.3	39.1	53.0	55.1	94.2	188.2	348.5	565.7	377.8	278.4	309.3
Exp. & Lending Minus Repay	82z	....	† 6,725.3	7,485.2	8,926.1	12,029.7	15,517.1	18,728.1	19,108.8	21,327.1	22,233.1	25,630.2	25,033.5
Expenditure	82	6,710.3	† 6,592.2	7,512.4	8,378.5	11,408.0	15,517.1	18,728.1	19,108.8	21,327.1	22,233.1	25,630.2	25,033.5
Lending Minus Repayments	83	....	† 237.8	308.4	235.9	—	—	—	—	—	—	—	—
Adjustment to Cash Basis	82x	....	† −104.7	−335.6	311.7	621.7	—	—	—	—	—	—	—
Financing (by Residence of Lender)													
Domestic	84a	....	† −187.5	433.0	−54.7	92.9	1,306.7	1,541.9	2,058.4	−129.2	156.4	1,199.3	−1,050.2
Foreign	85a	....	† 1,126.2	−214.6	322.7	2,151.4	1,402.2	2,262.3	651.4	3,234.2	1,195.4	2,340.9	3,436.3
Debt: Domestic	88a	....	4,854.7	4,485.2	5,093.0	5,862.2	6,259.8	7,807.1	8,629.7	9,281.1	8,169.9	11,192.5	12,840.8
Foreign	89a	....	887.8	1,203.5	1,308.2	1,491.3	1,693.8	2,034.4	2,058.0	2,350.1	2,956.4	3,385.8	3,841.6
Financing (by Currency)													
Net Borrowing: Quetzales	84b	551.7	....	....	....	....	....	....	....	....	....	....	....
Foreign Currency	85b	−84.9	....	....	....	....	....	....	....	....	....	....	....
Use of Cash Balances	87	597.7	....	....	....	....	....	....	....	....	....	....	....
National Accounts		*Millions of Quetzales*											
Househ.Cons.Expend.,incl.NPISHs.	96f	54,165	63,893	72,899	83,072	93,804	105,429	114,554	125,661	139,917	156,945	171,951	191,783
Government Consumption Expend.	91f	4,151	4,468	4,692	4,851	5,391	7,041	8,552	10,486	12,420	13,005	14,313	13,157
Gross Fixed Capital Formation	93e	10,335	10,622	12,360	12,727	16,302	20,645	24,205	24,147	25,486	28,164	28,771	32,388
Changes in Inventories	93i	745	1,087	460	−614	−1,540	929	−728	2,560	3,822	6,660	6,746	5,542
Exports of Goods and Services	90c	11,613	13,170	16,400	17,005	19,370	22,537	25,711	30,241	30,999	31,153	32,920	36,412
Imports of Goods and Services (-)	98c	16,765	18,571	21,656	21,562	25,454	32,559	37,008	43,351	47,774	53,652	58,004	66,189
Gross Domestic Product (GDP)	99b	64,243	74,669	85,157	95,479	107,873	124,022	135,287	149,743	164,870	182,275	196,696	213,093
Net Primary Income from Abroad	98.n	−854	−856	−926	−1,400	−1,451	−979	−1,480	−1,751	−899	−2,603	−2,796	−2,874
Gross National Income (GNI)	99a	63,389	73,813	84,231	94,079	106,422	123,043	133,807	147,992	163,971	179,672	193,899	210,219
Consumption of Fixed Capital	99cf	1,362	1,672	1,990	2,361	2,742	3,231	3,850	4,576	5,300	6,065	6,909	7,772
GDP Volume 1958 Prices	99b.p	3,828	3,983	4,180	4,303	4,491	4,716	4,897	5,074	5,192	5,309	5,421	5,565
GDP Volume (2000=100)	99bvp	75.4	78.5	82.4	84.8	88.5	93.0	96.5	100.0	102.3	104.6	106.8	109.7
GDP Deflator (2000=100)	99bip	56.9	63.5	69.0	75.2	81.4	89.1	93.6	100.0	107.6	116.3	122.9	129.7
		Millions: Midyear Estimates											
Population	99z	9.53	9.75	9.97	10.20	10.43	10.66	10.91	11.17	11.43	11.71	12.00	12.29

Guinea 656

		1993	1994	1995	1996	1997	1998	1999	2000	2001	2002	2003	2004
Exchange Rates						*Francs per SDR: End of Period*							
Official Rate	aa	1,335.7	1,432.1	1,483.5	1,494.2	1,544.8	1,827.7	2,382.7	2,452.4	2,498.8	2,620.2	2,964.2	3,516.3
						Francs per US Dollar: End of Period (ae) Period Average (rf)							
Official Rate	ae	972.4	981.0	998.0	1,039.1	1,145.0	1,298.0	1,736.0	1,882.3	1,988.3	1,976.0	2,000.0	2,550.0
Official Rate	rf	955.5	976.6	991.4	1,004.0	1,095.3	1,236.8	1,387.4	1,746.9	1,950.6	1,975.8	1,984.9	2,225.0
Fund Position						*Millions of SDRs: End of Period*							
Quota	2f.s	78.70	78.70	78.70	78.70	78.70	78.70	107.10	107.10	107.10	107.10	107.10	107.10
SDRs	1b.s	8.49	3.79	5.01	.54	1.97	1.02	.94	.19	.63	1.22	.15	—
Reserve Position in the Fund	1c.s	.07	.07	.07	.08	.08	.08	.08	.08	.08	.08	.08	.08
Total Fund Cred.&Loans Outstg.	2tl	44.00	48.64	63.11	57.32	73.39	90.05	92.71	86.63	98.08	102.23	91.70	78.52
International Liquidity					*Millions of US Dollars Unless Otherwise Indicated: End of Period*								
Total Reserves minus Gold	1l.d	132.12	87.85	86.76	87.34	121.63	236.71	199.68	147.91	200.23	171.40	....	....
SDRs	1b.d	11.67	5.53	7.45	.77	2.66	1.43	1.29	.25	.80	1.66	.22	—
Reserve Position in the Fund	1c.d	.09	.10	.10	.11	.10	.11	.10	.10	.09	.10	.11	.12
Foreign Exchange	1d.d	120.36	82.22	79.21	86.46	118.88	235.17	198.29	147.56	199.34	169.64	....	....
Gold (Million Fine Troy Ounces)	1ad	.003	....	....	....	....	....	....	.072	.030	.268	....	....
Gold (National Valuation)	1and	58.67	70.16	98.70	106.20	100.26	12.02	8.81	10.22	6.17	90.85	....	....
Monetary Authorities: Other Liab.	4..d	5.50	6.70	5.30	44.61	10.13	10.51	....	7.78	21.94	7.62	11.09	13.04
Deposit Money Banks: Assets	7a.d	85.47	86.27	90.89	81.05	73.08	85.27	77.53	80.32	68.46	73.85	68.11	110.60
Liabilities	7b.d	46.81	52.39	79.93	70.17	53.86	58.75	62.70	40.88	27.33	38.68	34.73	38.04
Monetary Authorities						*Millions of Francs: End of Period*							
Foreign Assets	11	185,522	155,011	185,089	201,116	254,054	319,566	....	303,361	407,345	332,610	268,660	285,007
Claims on Central Government	12a	183,958	225,807	332,922	429,007	532,766	662,569	....	802,821	1,421,713	842,762	1,130,869	1,304,367
Claims on Nonfin.Pub.Enterprises	12c	2,352	3,059	3,685	4,063	4,659	31,740	....	33,048	33,236	2,670	2,688	2,660
Claims on Private Sector	12d	42	129	108	159	3,362	5,763	....	5,313	12,924	26,619	33,503	31,941
Claims on Deposit Money Banks	12e	8,211	8,587	8,632	8,196	26,227	6,701	....	8,090	3,043	4,349	1,557	2,009
Claims on Other Banking Insts.	12f	—	48	493	—	—	439	....	193	78	—	—	—
Reserve Money	14	196,468	176,724	198,442	195,681	248,968	† 262,015	....	385,183	442,501	538,658	634,343	861,418
of which: Currency Outside DMBs	14a	166,609	154,748	167,144	154,420	191,635	209,682	....	288,468	310,063	349,781	478,133	536,169
Foreign Liabilities	16c	64,127	76,223	98,912	132,011	124,978	178,215	....	227,096	288,707	282,906	293,998	309,344
Central Government Deposits	16d	129,003	151,170	249,942	313,926	444,141	590,113	....	576,045	1,170,909	407,441	574,870	613,880
Capital Accounts	17a	51,848	57,608	55,460	51,645	52,291	55,559	....	74,939	91,303	54,101	111,184	131,732
Other Items (Net)	17r	−61,361	−69,088	−71,830	−50,726	−49,316	−59,124	....	−110,436	−115,080	−74,095	−177,118	−290,390
Deposit Money Banks						*Millions of Francs: End of Period*							
Reserves	20	20,458	15,380	28,310	31,930	46,130	50,064	59,859	66,492	101,186	138,767	116,171	232,320
Foreign Assets	21	83,110	84,630	90,710	84,220	83,670	110,678	134,586	151,182	136,119	145,935	136,221	282,018
Claims on Central Government	22a	12,596	13,210	29,910	38,500	46,750	44,054	39,287	18,037	46,993	134,114	285,888	386,175
Claims on Nonfin.Pub.Enterprises	22c	124	10	270	430	260	273	54	185	60	9,964	3,891	1
Claims on Private Sector	22d	130,322	144,410	181,410	188,270	184,070	156,383	178,654	203,379	210,107	215,213	255,654	276,869
Demand Deposits	24	86,763	94,430	104,060	112,590	130,430	144,030	139,940	177,997	226,047	300,520	386,359	518,469
Time, Savings,& Fgn.Currency Dep.	25	54,794	52,180	64,950	77,710	83,430	81,176	99,528	111,339	129,777	144,302	206,281	356,870
Foreign Liabilities	26c	45,523	51,400	79,770	72,920	61,670	76,257	108,851	76,944	54,341	76,439	69,457	97,008
Central Government Deposits	26d	15,267	17,100	16,490	15,800	19,960	23,575	25,296	23,108	27,527	30,135	40,470	60,652
Credit from Monetary Authorities	26g	9,601	10,360	11,580	10,360	10,660	7,239	7,822	8,995	4,775	15,456	6,407	2,903
Capital Accounts	27a	47,601	46,400	50,870	38,980	49,600	34,986	43,293	53,695	53,017	81,611	71,187	177,045
Other Items (Net)	27r	−12,939	−14,230	2,920	14,960	5,120	−5,811	−12,290	−12,803	−1,019	−4,470	17,664	−35,565
Monetary Survey						*Millions of Francs: End of Period*							
Foreign Assets (Net)	31n	158,982	112,018	97,118	80,405	151,077	175,772	....	150,503	200,416	119,201	41,426	160,672
Domestic Credit	32	185,124	218,403	282,366	330,703	307,766	287,534	....	466,370	526,693	794,387	1,098,650	1,331,455
Claims on Central Govt. (Net)	32an	52,284	70,747	96,400	137,781	115,415	92,935	....	221,705	270,270	539,300	801,417	1,016,010
Claims on Nonfin.Pub.Enterprises	32c	2,476	3,069	3,955	4,493	4,919	32,013	....	33,233	33,296	12,634	6,579	2,661
Claims on Private Sector	32d	130,364	144,539	181,518	188,429	187,432	162,146	....	208,692	223,031	241,832	289,157	308,810
Claims on Other Banking Insts.	32f	—	48	493	—	—	439	....	193	78	—	—	—
Money	34	260,854	252,582	274,125	273,465	331,666	† 361,469	....	499,885	559,993	681,228	893,055	1,143,312
Quasi-Money	35	54,794	52,180	64,950	77,710	83,430	81,176	99,528	111,339	129,777	144,302	206,281	356,870
Capital Accounts	37a	99,449	104,008	106,330	90,625	101,891	90,545	....	128,634	144,320	135,712	182,371	308,777
Other Items (Net)	37r	−70,991	−78,353	−65,895	−30,726	−58,161	−69,885	....	−122,984	−106,980	−47,654	−141,631	−316,832
Money plus Quasi-Money	35l	315,648	304,762	339,075	351,175	415,096	† 442,645	....	611,224	689,770	825,530	1,099,336	1,500,182
Interest Rates						*Percent Per Annum*							
Refinancing Rate (End of Period)	60	17.00	17.00	18.00	18.00	15.00	....	....	11.50	16.25	16.25	16.25	16.25
Savings Rate	60k	17.00	16.00	15.50	....	....	....	....	....	....	....	....	....
Deposit Rate	60l	19.75	18.00	17.50	....	....	6.38	5.67	7.50	8.03	7.40	6.50	8.85
Lending Rate	60p	24.50	22.00	21.50	....	....	19.56	19.88	19.38	....	....	....	....

Guinea 656

		1993	1994	1995	1996	1997	1998	1999	2000	2001	2002	2003	2004
Balance of Payments					*Millions of US Dollars: Minus Sign Indicates Debit*								
Current Account, n.i.e.	78ald	−56.8	−248.0	−216.5	−177.3	−91.1	−183.6	−214.4	−155.2	−102.2	−199.8	−187.5	−174.8
Goods: Exports f.o.b.	78aad	561.1	515.7	582.8	636.5	630.1	693.0	635.7	666.3	731.1	708.6	609.3	725.6
Goods: Imports f.o.b.	78abd	−582.7	−685.4	−621.7	−525.3	−512.5	−572.0	−581.7	−587.1	−561.9	−668.5	−644.3	−688.4
Trade Balance	78acd	−21.6	−169.7	−39.0	111.2	117.6	121.0	54.0	79.3	169.2	40.1	−35.0	37.2
Services: Credit	78add	186.8	152.9	117.5	124.1	110.7	110.8	113.2	68.0	102.8	90.5	133.7	85.4
Services: Debit	78aed	−334.8	−366.0	−389.3	−422.2	−321.6	−382.7	−364.4	−284.9	−319.0	−330.6	−307.3	−275.2
Balance on Goods & Services	78afd	−169.6	−382.9	−310.8	−186.8	−93.3	−150.9	−197.2	−137.7	−47.0	−200.1	−208.6	−152.7
Income: Credit	78agd	9.3	6.5	12.9	12.8	7.8	9.0	24.7	23.5	11.3	6.1	12.6	9.8
Income: Debit	78ahd	−92.6	−79.8	−97.5	−105.7	−121.3	−133.5	−106.9	−101.1	−113.6	−51.6	−124.3	−37.1
Balance on Gds, Serv. & Inc.	78aid	−252.9	−456.1	−395.5	−279.8	−206.9	−275.5	−279.4	−215.3	−149.3	−245.6	−320.3	−180.0
Current Transfers, n.i.e.: Credit	78ajd	260.3	280.6	258.3	137.8	131.4	116.2	80.0	88.6	91.6	70.5	194.6	55.1
Current Transfers: Debit	78akd	−64.2	−72.5	−79.3	−35.3	−15.6	−24.3	−15.1	−28.5	−44.5	−24.8	−61.7	−49.9
Capital Account, n.i.e.	78bcd	5.0	—	—	—	—	—	—	—	—	91.9	57.6	−30.2
Capital Account, n.i.e.: Credit	78bad	5.0	—	—	—	—	—	—	—	—	91.9	57.6	
Capital Account: Debit	78bbd	....	—	—	—	—	....	....	—	—	—	—	−30.2
Financial Account, n.i.e.	78bjd	62.6	84.2	109.2	47.5	−89.3	8.0	117.1	8.4	−12.1	−115.1	58.6	77.7
Direct Investment Abroad	78bdd	....	....	....	−.5	—	—	—	—	—	—	—	—
Dir. Invest. in Rep. Econ., n.i.e.	78bed	2.7	.2	.8	23.8	17.3	17.8	63.5	9.9	1.7	30.0	79.0	—
Portfolio Investment Assets	78bfd	....	....	....	....	....	−82.7	−20.0	8.7	4.6	5.1	−4.6	14.8
Equity Securities	78bkd	....	....	....	....	....	—	—	—	—	—	—	—
Debt Securities	78bld	....	....	....	....	....	−82.7	−20.0	8.7	4.6	5.1	−4.6	14.8
Portfolio Investment Liab., n.i.e.	78bgd	....	....	....	....	....	—	—	—	—	—	—	—
Equity Securities	78bmd	....	....	....	....	....	—	—	—	—	—	—	—
Debt Securities	78bnd	....	....	....	....	....	—	—	—	—	—	—	—
Financial Derivatives Assets	78bwd	....	....	....	....	....	....	....	....	....	....	....	....
Financial Derivatives Liabilities	78bxd	....	....	....	....	....	....	....	....	....	....	....	....
Other Investment Assets	78bhd	−20.1	−14.5	−73.7	−19.8	−99.1	−14.6	.6	−17.0	11.7	−71.0	−4.4	49.5
Monetary Authorities	78bod	....	−6.5	9.0	6.0	2.4	1.2	−.9	−13.7	1.5	—	1.8	7.0
General Government	78bpd	2.2	....	....	....	....	....	....	....	....	....	....	
Banks	78bqd	—	−2.2	−4.6	9.0	9.3	−12.5	7.6	−1.3	9.5	−69.1	−6.1	42.5
Other Sectors	78brd	−22.3	−5.8	−78.2	−34.7	−110.8	−3.3	−6.0	−2.0	.6	−2.0	—	—
Other Investment Liab., n.i.e.	78bid	80.0	98.5	182.2	44.0	−7.5	87.5	73.0	6.8	−30.1	−79.2	−11.4	13.4
Monetary Authorities	78bsd	−.1	.1	−.5	39.1	−35.3	−3.0	.2	−.8	13.4	1.6	2.0	2.9
General Government	78btd	54.6	79.6	106.5	−14.4	48.2	37.6	84.2	61.6	26.5	−36.3	−8.9	7.2
Banks	78bud	.1	8.3	26.0	−9.8	−18.1	6.7	3.7	−23.1	−12.4	—	−4.2	3.3
Other Sectors	78bvd	25.4	10.5	50.2	29.0	−2.3	46.2	−15.0	−30.8	−57.5	−44.5	−.4	
Net Errors and Omissions	78cad	−107.5	39.7	34.8	69.9	49.8	17.8	21.4	83.9	−2.2	143.1	−157.1	68.6
Overall Balance	78cbd	−96.7	−124.1	−72.5	−59.9	−130.6	−157.8	−75.9	−62.9	−116.5	−79.8	−228.5	−58.6
Reserves and Related Items	79dad	96.7	124.1	72.5	59.9	130.6	157.8	75.9	62.9	116.5	79.8	228.5	58.6
Reserve Assets	79dbd	−49.9	32.4	−43.8	−6.5	−20.3	60.7	60.6	50.5	−3.9	75.7	131.5	11.8
Use of Fund Credit and Loans	79dcd	−3.2	7.0	22.1	−8.4	22.4	22.8	3.7	−7.9	14.8	5.7	−14.8	−19.5
Exceptional Financing	79ded	149.9	84.7	94.2	74.9	128.5	74.3	11.5	20.4	105.7	−1.6	111.8	66.3
Government Finance					*Millions of Francs: Year Ending December 31*								
Deficit (-) or Surplus	80	....	....	....	....	....	−192,650	−116,309f	....	....	....	....	....
Revenue	81	....	....	....	....	....	497,293	574,901f	....	....	....	....	....
Grants Received	81z	....	....	....	....	....	106,481	320,500f	....	....	....	....	....
Expenditure	82	....	....	....	....	....	792,554	1,010,060f	....	....	....	....	....
Lending Minus Repayments	83	....	....	....	....	....	3,870	1,650f	....	....	....	....	....
Financing													
Domestic	84a	....	....	....	....	....	−2,610	8,249f	....	....	....	....	....
Foreign	85a	....	....	....	....	....	195,260	108,060f	....	....	....	....	....
					Millions: Midyear Estimates								
Population	99z	7.01	7.28	7.52	7.74	7.93	8.09	8.26	8.43	8.62	8.81	9.00	9.20

		1993	1994	1995	1996	1997	1998	1999	2000	2001	2002	2003	2004
Exchange Rates						*Francs per SDR: End of Period*							
Official Rate	aa	242.25	345.18	501.49	772.88	807.94	791.61	896.19	918.49	935.39	850.37	771.76	747.90
						Francs per US Dollar: End of Period (ae) Period Average (rf)							
Official Rate	ae	176.37	236.45	337.37	537.48	598.81	562.21	652.95	704.95	744.31	625.50	519.36	481.58
Official Rate	rf	155.11	198.34	278.04	405.75	583.67	589.95	† 615.70	711.98	733.04	696.99	581.20	528.28
Fund Position						*Millions of SDRs: End of Period*							
Quota	2f.s	10.50	10.50	10.50	10.50	10.50	10.50	14.20	14.20	14.20	14.20	14.20	14.20
SDRs	1b.s	.01	—	.01	.01	.04	.02	.06	.03	.16	.30	.80	.44
Reserve Position in the Fund	1c.s	—	—	—	—	—	—	—	—	—	—	—	—
Total Fund Cred.&Loans Outstg	2tl	3.45	3.15	3.98	5.33	9.04	10.95	12.63	18.97	18.45	17.24	13.78	10.17
International Liquidity						*Millions of US Dollars Unless Otherwise Indicated: End of Period*							
Total Reserves minus Gold	1l.d	14.17	18.43	20.27	11.53	33.70	35.76	35.28	66.73	69.47	102.71	32.90	73.09
SDRs	1b.d	.01	—	.01	.01	.06	.03	.08	.04	.20	.40	1.18	.68
Reserve Position in the Fund	1c.d	—	—	—	—	—	—	—	—	—	—	—	—
Foreign Exchange	1d.d	14.16	18.43	20.26	11.52	33.65	35.73	35.21	66.69	69.28	102.31	31.71	72.41
Monetary Authorities: Other Liab	4..d	48.3	42.6	38.6	18.2	1.8	.7	1.4	−.6	1.0	−.1	−.7	.6
Deposit Money Banks: Assets	7a.d	10.8	12.1	18.7	16.7	19.2	19.3	16.6	2.3	3.8	8.7	11.6	13.4
Liabilities	7b.d	.7	7.2	6.9	7.5	11.7	12.9	11.1	13.7	11.5	13.5	—	1.1
Monetary Authorities						*Millions of Francs: End of Period*							
Foreign Assets	11	2,499	4,357	6,837	6,196	20,183	20,105	23,038	47,044	51,711	64,246	17,087	35,197
Claims on Central Government	12a	3,197	4,144	4,728	7,679	10,690	12,453	13,081	20,343	20,288	20,214	17,885	15,098
Claims on Other Financial Insts	12f	—	—	—	—	—	—	—	—	—	—	—	—
Reserve Money	14	4,005	5,300	6,998	9,709	21,922	19,011	25,561	47,936	55,559	72,528	23,336	37,019
of which: Currency Outside DMBs	14a	2,039	3,015	4,278	6,370	20,137	17,642	24,186	44,245	53,054	70,223	21,282	32,570
Foreign Liabilities	16c	9,360	11,157	15,012	13,878	8,359	9,055	12,251	17,006	18,019	14,565	10,271	7,902
Central Government Deposits	16d	2,642	4,915	7,722	9,080	6,110	8,148	2,994	3,567	3,742	492	1,928	4,638
Other Items (Net)	17r	−5,985	−8,542	−13,840	−18,793	−5,518	−3,655	−4,686	−1,122	−5,320	−3,049	−564	736
Deposit Money Banks						*Millions of Francs: End of Period*							
Reserves	20	2,052	2,420	3,362	2,614	4,392	2,728	2,728	6,256	2,397	1,667	2,027	4,467
Foreign Assets	21	1,912	2,856	6,295	8,989	11,479	10,827	10,827	1,621	2,850	5,470	6,032	6,464
Claims on Central Government	22a	544	576	567	77	21	21	21	—	—	—	456	1,008
Claims on Private Sector	22d	2,859	4,617	4,612	5,305	7,651	9,859	9,859	12,121	4,436	4,211	2,651	2,251
Claims on Other Financial Insts	22f	—	—	—	—	—	—	—	—	—	—	—	—
Demand Deposits	24	1,050	1,855	2,880	4,507	16,431	14,476	14,476	19,985	16,261	14,623	8,319	10,277
Time & Foreign Currency Deposits	25	2,361	3,207	4,395	6,320	1,132	1,355	1,355	1,037	794	1,282	564	577
Foreign Liabilities	26c	114	1,700	2,330	3,999	6,984	7,220	7,220	2,924	543	439	2	521
Long-Term Foreign Liabilities	26cl	4	6	8	13	14	14	14	6,744	8,001	8,001	—	—
Central Government Deposits	26d	132	47	14	561	820	1,014	1,014	1,066	1,144	1,156	1,286	1,742
Credit from Monetary Authorities	26g	4,328	4,328	4,328	97	—	—	—	—	—	—	—	—
Other Items (Net)	27r	−622	−674	881	1,489	−1,838	−644	−644	−11,758	−17,061	−14,153	995	1,073
Monetary Survey						*Millions of Francs: End of Period*							
Foreign Assets (Net)	31n	−5,064	−5,644	−4,211	−2,692	16,318	14,657	14,394	28,735	35,999	54,712	12,845	33,238
Domestic Credit	32	3,825	4,374	2,171	3,420	11,432	13,172	18,954	27,831	19,838	22,777	17,777	11,977
Claims on Central Govt. (Net)	32an	−542	−2,302	−3,959	−3,923	331	613	9,095	15,709	15,402	18,566	15,126	9,726
Claims on Private Sector	32d	4,368	6,677	6,129	7,343	11,101	12,559	9,859	12,121	4,436	4,211	2,651	2,251
Claims on Other Financial Insts	32f	—	—	—	—	—	—	—	—	—	—	—	—
Money	34	3,105	4,910	7,211	10,891	36,625	32,194	39,420	64,524	69,535	85,074	29,922	42,964
Quasi-Money	35	2,361	3,207	4,395	6,320	1,132	1,355	1,355	1,037	794	1,282	564	577
Long-Term Foriegn Liabilities	36cl	4	6	8	13	14	14	14	6,744	8,001	8,001	—	—
Other Items (Net)	37r	−8,598	−11,538	−16,195	−19,639	−10,020	−5,733	−7,440	−15,739	−22,493	−16,868	137	1,673
Money plus Quasi-Money	35l	5,466	8,116	11,606	17,212	37,757	33,548	40,774	65,561	70,329	86,356	30,486	43,541
Interest Rates						*Percent Per Annum*							
Bank Rate (End of Period)	60	† 6.00	6.00	6.00	6.00	6.00	6.00	6.00	6.00	6.00	6.00	4.50	4.00
Money Market Rate	60b	4.95	4.95	4.95	4.95	4.95	4.95	4.95	4.95	4.95	4.95	4.95	4.95
Deposit Rate	60l	3.50	3.50	3.50	3.50	3.50	3.50	3.50	3.50	3.50	3.50	3.50	3.50
Lending Rate	60p	63.58	36.33	32.92	51.75	....	....	....	....	....	....	....	....
Prices						*Index Numbers (2000=100): Period Averages*							
Consumer Prices	64	23.5	27.0	39.3	59.2	88.2	† 94.0	92.1	100.0	103.2	106.6	102.9	103.8
Intl. Transactions & Positions						*Millions of Francs*							
Exports	70	4,360	16,580	12,310	11,030	28,300	15,800	31,500	44,300	46,100	37,800	39,900	....
Imports, c.i.f.	71	9,541	32,530	36,990	35,240	51,800	37,000	31,500	35,000	45,300	40,700	40,000	....

		1993	1994	1995	1996	1997	1998	1999	2000	2001	2002	2003	2004
Balance of Payments						*Millions of US Dollars: Minus Sign Indicates Debit*							
Current Account, n.i.e.	78ald	−65.48	−47.63	−50.65	−60.43	−30.28	....	....	....	−26.89	−8.69	−5.87	....
Goods: Exports f.o.b.	78aad	15.96	33.21	23.90	21.61	48.86	....	....	....	62.89	54.38	65.01	....
Goods: Imports f.o.b.	78abd	−53.82	−53.80	−59.34	−56.80	−62.49	....	....	....	−61.72	−58.50	−65.30	....
Trade Balance	78acd	−37.86	−20.59	−35.44	−35.19	−13.63	....	....	....	1.17	−4.12	−.29	....
Services: Credit	78add	9.76	5.61	5.69	6.96	8.00	....	....	....	4.46	6.50	6.00	....
Services: Debit	78aed	−21.14	−27.11	−29.91	−29.25	−26.15	....	....	....	−30.27	−27.48	−36.21	....
Balance on Goods & Services	78afd	−49.24	−42.09	−59.66	−57.48	−31.78	....	....	....	−24.63	−25.10	−30.50	....
Income: Credit	78agd	—								.57	1.29	2.08	....
Income: Debit	78ahd	−28.98	−26.27	−21.09	−18.65	−14.30				−12.58	−10.05	−10.31	....
Balance on Gds, Serv. & Inc.	78aid	−78.22	−68.36	−80.75	−76.13	−46.08				−36.64	−33.86	−38.73	
Current Transfers, n.i.e.: Credit	78ajd	14.39	21.79	31.42	15.70	15.80				9.76	30.22	39.69	....
Current Transfers: Debit	78akd	−1.65	−1.06	−1.32	—					−.01	−5.05	−6.83	
Capital Account, n.i.e.	78bcd	36.57	44.42	49.20	40.70	32.20				25.33	38.86	42.82	
Capital Account, n.i.e.: Credit	78bad	36.57	44.42	49.20	40.70	32.20				25.05	40.36	42.82	
Capital Account: Debit	78bbd	—	—	—	—	—				.28	−1.50		
Financial Account, n.i.e.	78bjd	−15.82	−26.98	−28.25	−12.30	2.03				−17.34	−21.39	−13.06	
Direct Investment Abroad	78bdd	—	....	....	....	.....				.40	−1.00	−.52	
Dir. Invest. in Rep. Econ., n.i.e.	78bed	—	....	....	....	.....				.40	3.56	4.01	
Portfolio Investment Assets	78bfd	—	....	....	....	.....				—	1.15	.60	
Equity Securities	78bkd	—	....	....	....	.....				—	1.15	—	
Debt Securities	78bld	—	....	....	....	.....				—	—	.60	
Portfolio Investment Liab., n.i.e.	78bgd	—	....	....	....	.....				—	.65	.34	
Equity Securities	78bmd	—	....	....	....	.....				—	.65	.34	
Debt Securities	78bnd	....	....	....	....	.....				....	....	....	
Financial Derivatives Assets	78bwd	....	....	....	....	.....				....	....	....	
Financial Derivatives Liabilities	78bxd	....	....	....	....	.....				....	....	....	
Other Investment Assets	78bhd	—	....	....	....	−5.80				4.21	−6.85	−18.99	
Monetary Authorities	78bod	....	....	....	....	....				....	....	....	
General Government	78bpd	—	....	....	....	....				....	....	....	
Banks	78bqd	—	....	....	....	−5.80				4.21	−3.73	−16.33	
Other Sectors	78brd	—	....	....	....	....				—	−3.12	−2.66	
Other Investment Liab., n.i.e.	78bid	−15.82	−26.98	−28.25	−12.30	7.83				−22.34	−18.89	1.50	
Monetary Authorities	78bsd	−2.27	—	−6.88		.43				1.08	−1.27	−.45	
General Government	78btd	−13.55	−26.98	−21.37	−12.30	7.40				−20.08	−29.27	7.63	
Banks	78bud	—	....	....	....	....				−4.12	−.15	.46	
Other Sectors	78bvd	—	....	....	....	....				.78	11.80	−6.14	
Net Errors and Omissions	78cad	−15.97	−24.34	−10.90	−11.47	−19.19				5.86	−2.92	5.55	
Overall Balance	78cbd	−60.70	−54.53	−40.60	−43.50	−15.24				−13.04	5.86	29.44	
Reserves and Related Items	79dad	60.70	54.53	40.60	43.50	15.24				13.04	−5.86	−29.44	
Reserve Assets	79dbd	9.02	6.24	−3.64	−8.90	−35.15				−6.34	−18.00	−38.22	
Use of Fund Credit and Loans	79dcd	−.42	−.43	1.19	1.94	5.11				−.67	−1.60	−4.85	
Exceptional Financing	79ded	52.10	48.72	43.05	50.46	45.28	....		....	20.05	13.73	13.64	
International Investment Position						*Millions of US Dollars*							
Assets	79aad	....	....	....	....	.....	....	....	....	73.33	113.28	....	....
Direct Investment Abroad	79abd	....	....	....	....	.....				—	1.12		
Portfolio Investment	79acd	....	....	....	....	.....				—	—		
Equity Securities	79add	....	....	....	....	.....				—	—		
Debt Securities	79aed	....	....	....	....	.....				—	—		
Financial Derivatives	79ald	....	....	....	....	.....				—	—		
Other Investment	79afd	....	....	....	....	.....				3.85	9.45		
Monetary Authorities	79agd	....	....	....	....	.....				....	....		
General Government	79ahd	....	....	....	....	.....				....	....		
Banks	79aid	....	....	....	....	.....				3.85	8.75		
Other Sectors	79ajd	....	....	....	....	.....				—	.71		
Reserve Assets	79akd	.01	—	.01	....	.....				69.48	102.71		
Liabilities	79lad	....	....	....	....	.....				814.98	1,256.22		
Dir. Invest. in Rep. Economy	79lbd	....	....	....	....	.....				.39	3.02		
Portfolio Investment	79lcd	....	....	....	....	.....				—	.72		
Equity Securities	79ldd	....	....	....	....	.....				—	.72		
Debt Securities	79led	....	....	....	....	.....				—	—		
Financial Derivatives	79lld	....	....	....	....	.....				—	—		
Other Investment	79lfd	4.74	4.60	5.91	....	.....				814.59	1,252.48		
Monetary Authorities	79lgd	....	....	....	....	.....				24.25	23.29		
General Government	79lhd	....	....	....	....	.....				778.04	1,215.42		
Banks	79lid	....	....	....	....	.....				11.53	13.74		
Other Sectors	79ljd	....	....	....	....	.....				.77	.03		
National Accounts						*Millions of Francs*							
Househ.Cons.Expend.,incl.NPISHs.	96f	58,010	119,594	117,485	128,800	145,300	103,600	117,900	122,200	114,800	119,000	105,900	....
Government Consumption Expend.	91f	8,573	15,645	10,033	10,891	13,500	9,600	12,500	17,900	25,900	19,400	22,500	....
Gross Fixed Capital Formation	93e	15,255	23,302	22,373	21,248	21,278	....	....	....	....	....	....	
Changes in Inventories	93i	1,182	−7,021	154	5,624	27							
Exports of Goods and Services	90c	7,149	23,222	16,051	17,304	33,000	3,900	33,000	38,500	49,400	42,500	44,500	....
Imports of Goods and Services (-)	98c	24,490	48,871	42,122	47,932	62,500	42,600	64,700	68,700	67,400	59,900	59,000	....
Gross Domestic Product (GDP)	99b	65,600	125,800	124,100	135,900	163,100	121,800	138,200	153,400	145,900	141,900	138,700	148,000
Net Primary Income from Abroad	98.n	−131	....	....	....	.....				....	....	....	
Gross National Income (GNI)	99a	36,264	....	....	....	.....				....	....	....	
GDP Volume 1986 Prices	99b.p	98,600	103,500	107,300	112,500	117,900	....	....	....	....	....	....	
GDP Volume (1995=100)	99bvp	91.9	96.5	100.0	104.8	109.9	....	....	....	....	....	....	
GDP Deflator (1995=100)	99bip	57.5	105.1	100.0	104.4	119.6	....	....	....	....	....	....	
						Millions: Midyear Estimates							
Population	99z	1.12	1.15	1.19	1.22	1.26	1.29	1.33	1.37	1.41	1.45	1.49	1.54

		1993	1994	1995	1996	1997	1998	1999	2000	2001	2002	2003	2004
Exchange Rates							*Guyana Dollars per SDR: End of Period*						
Market Rate...............................	aa	179.6	208.0	208.9	203.1	194.3	228.5	247.7	240.7	238.2	260.7	288.6	310.2
					Guyana Dollars per US Dollar: End of Period (ae) Period Average (rf)								
Market Rate...............................	ae	130.8	142.5	140.5	141.3	144.0	162.3	180.5	184.8	189.5	191.8	194.3	199.8
Market Rate...............................	rf	126.7	138.3	142.0	140.4	142.4	150.5	178.0	182.4	187.3	190.7	193.9	198.3
						Index Numbers (2000=100): Period Averages							
Market Rate...............................	ahx	144.0	132.1	128.6	129.9	127.9	121.5	102.6	100.0	97.4	95.7	94.1	92.0
Nominal Effective Exchange Rate.....	nec	111.3	113.7	108.4	112.4	117.1	114.8	98.2	100.0	101.8	98.9	90.2	83.4
Real Effective Exchange Rate...........	rec	90.6	89.9	91.5	98.8	104.1	104.7	94.8	100.0	102.0	102.8	96.9	91.7
Fund Position							*Millions of SDRs: End of Period*						
Quota.......................................	2f.s	67.20	67.20	67.20	67.20	67.20	67.20	90.90	90.90	90.90	90.90	90.90	90.90
SDRs.......................................	1b.s	—	.05	.09	.07	.14	.17	.92	7.02	1.96	3.43	3.26	4.60
Reserve Position in the Fund............	1c.s	—	—	—	—	—	—	—	—	—	—	—	—
Total Fund Cred.&Loans Outstg........	2tl	128.60	122.25	115.60	117.11	116.44	109.50	102.15	90.12	77.67	70.73	64.18	56.71
International Liquidity					*Millions of US Dollars Unless Otherwise Indicated: End of Period*								
Total Reserves minus Gold..............	1l.d	247.45	247.13	268.94	329.68	315.51	276.60	268.28	304.96	287.26	284.47	276.39	231.84
SDRs...................................	1b.d	—	.08	.14	.11	.20	.24	1.27	9.15	2.47	4.66	4.84	7.15
Reserve Position in the Fund..........	1c.d	—	—	—	—	—	—	—	—	—	—	—	—
Foreign Exchange.........................	1d.d	247.45	247.05	268.80	329.57	315.31	276.36	267.01	295.81	284.79	279.81	271.55	224.70
Monetary Authorities: Other Liab.....	4..d	715.25	656.62	725.00	448.57	286.86	222.56	187.68	186.51	179.00	69.17	61.43	53.22
Deposit Money Banks: Assets.......	7a.d	24.40	24.88	27.03	26.55	24.29	23.91	40.13	38.77	46.36	63.06	92.70	108.91
Liabilities...............	7b.d	15.92	20.57	20.52	25.62	34.47	31.93	22.23	20.66	17.55	25.94	25.43	36.01
Other Banking Insts.: Assets............	7e.d	.94	1.21	1.28	1.38	2.38	1.98	2.59	7.32	7.67	11.73	8.39	10.49
Liabilities..................	7f.d	.04	—	7.30	1.03	1.12	.69	.46	3.42	5.38	5.06	5.00	5.14
Monetary Authorities						*Millions of Guyana Dollars: End of Period*							
Foreign Assets...........................	11	† 31,557	35,741	38,398	46,466	43,578	40,149	44,590	54,645	53,979	53,634	52,731	44,881
Claims on Central Government........	12a	† 109,080	118,849	125,918	96,232	76,959	67,904	71,686	72,208	70,613	50,267	50,956	50,523
Claims on Nonfin.Pub.Enterprises.....	12c	† 762	1,098	811	2,441	3,238	3,320	4,709	4,710	4,710	4,710	4,710	4,710
Reserve Money............................	14	† 12,523	16,453	19,603	20,760	24,314	27,179	26,128	29,794	33,043	36,359	40,112	43,760
of which: Currency Outside DMBs..	14a	† 6,480	8,167	8,967	9,959	11,210	11,334	13,394	14,495	15,138	15,410	17,888	19,546
Time, Savings,& Fgn.Currency Dep...	15	† 378	335	561	489	749	694	1,219	1,146	921	565	692	575
Restricted Deposits.......................	16b	† —											
Foreign Liabilities............................	16c	† 116,616	119,000	126,005	87,146	63,931	61,126	59,184	56,151	52,417	31,701	30,457	28,222
Central Government Deposits...........	16d	† 15,220	22,623	21,335	30,256	27,147	22,066	34,594	39,130	37,965	37,399	36,750	27,247
Capital Accounts.........................	17a	† −1,455	2,345	3,253	2,567	3,449	5,184	5,891	6,822	7,290	6,636	6,889	7,368
Other Items (Net).........................	17r	† −1,882	−5,068	−5,631	3,921	4,187	−4,875	−6,030	−1,482	−2,334	−4,049	−6,503	−7,056
Deposit Money Banks						*Millions of Guyana Dollars: End of Period*							
Reserves...................................	20	5,503	8,171	10,326	10,781	13,315	16,070	12,419	15,510	18,340	21,031	21,883	23,318
Foreign Assets............................	21	3,190	3,546	3,798	3,750	3,497	3,880	7,243	7,163	8,786	12,091	18,006	21,755
Claims on Central Government........	22a	20,064	15,651	14,847	17,251	18,028	15,851	13,346	20,264	20,766	23,959	32,249	38,136
Claims on Local Government...........	22b	36	—	36	1	4	500	48	39	1	7	62	50
Claims on Nonfin.Pub.Enterprises.....	22c	471	188	410	254	216	410	683	420	852	807	822	1,265
Claims on Private Sector..................	22d	10,254	13,900	21,107	36,309	44,863	51,838	55,823	58,341	58,943	59,200	48,594	48,386
Claims on Other Banking Insts........	22f	28	13	73	183	118	195	569	660	464	724	855	490
Demand Deposits.........................	24	4,902	4,941	6,336	7,565	8,064	7,639	9,949	11,286	10,945	12,700	14,223	17,052
Time, Savings,& Fgn.Currency Dep...	25	25,271	28,764	36,661	44,708	49,032	53,981	57,049	61,514	69,109	72,942	76,696	81,894
Restricted Deposits......................	26b	368	334	330	330	318	307	70	66	56	56	58	58
Foreign Liabilities.........................	26c	2,081	2,931	2,883	3,619	4,964	5,181	4,012	3,816	3,325	4,975	4,940	7,193
Central Government Deposits...........	26d	3,161	3,246	2,071	2,920	5,662	5,782	3,857	7,284	5,488	7,375	8,361	8,648
Liabilities to Other Banking Insts......	26i	2,895	1,356	1,827	2,757	3,778	5,898	5,796	8,455	8,009	9,222	10,934	11,921
Capital Accounts.........................	27a	3,660	3,968	5,392	13,712	15,054	19,385	21,477	22,277	22,722	22,308	14,667	15,005
Other Items (Net)..........................	27r	−2,792	−4,072	−4,903	−7,079	−6,828	−9,429	−12,081	−12,302	−11,501	−11,759	−7,407	−8,369
Monetary Survey						*Millions of Guyana Dollars: End of Period*							
Foreign Assets (Net).......................	31n	† −83,949	−82,644	−86,692	−40,549	−21,819	−22,278	−11,363	1,840	7,023	29,049	35,341	31,221
Domestic Credit............................	32	† 122,314	123,830	139,796	119,495	110,619	112,172	108,412	110,227	112,896	94,900	93,137	107,666
Claims on Central Govt. (Net)........	32an	† 110,763	108,630	117,360	80,307	62,178	55,908	46,581	46,058	47,927	29,452	38,094	52,764
Claims on Local Government..........	32b	† 36	—	36	1	4	500	48	39	1	7	62	50
Claims on Nonfin.Pub.Enterprises...	32c	† 1,232	1,286	1,220	2,695	3,455	3,730	5,392	5,129	5,562	5,518	5,532	5,976
Claims on Private Sector...............	32d	† 10,254	13,900	21,107	36,309	44,863	51,838	55,823	58,341	58,943	59,200	48,594	48,386
Claims on Other Banking Insts.......	32f	† 28	13	73	183	118	195	569	660	464	724	855	490
Money.......................................	34	† 11,881	13,115	15,310	17,531	19,281	18,980	23,350	25,788	26,089	28,116	32,117	36,604
Quasi-Money..............................	35	† 25,649	29,100	37,222	45,197	49,780	54,675	58,268	62,660	70,029	73,507	77,389	82,469
Restricted Deposits......................	36b	† 368	334	330	330	318	307	70	66	56	56	58	58
Liabilities to Other Banking Insts.....	36i	† 2,895	1,356	1,827	2,757	3,778	5,898	5,796	8,455	8,009	9,222	10,934	11,921
Capital Accounts.........................	37a	† 2,205	6,313	8,645	16,278	18,503	24,569	27,368	29,099	30,013	28,944	21,556	22,372
Other Items (Net).........................	37r	† −4,634	−9,032	−10,231	−3,146	−2,860	−14,536	−17,803	−14,000	−14,277	−15,896	−13,575	−14,536
Money plus Quasi-Money...............	35l	† 37,531	42,214	52,532	62,727	69,061	73,655	81,618	88,448	96,119	101,624	109,506	119,072
Other Banking Institutions						*Millions of Guyana Dollars: End of Period*							
Cash...	40	129	9	21	50	29	44	184	331	464	623	666	791
Foreign Assets............................	41	123	172	180	195	342	321	467	1,353	1,454	2,248	1,630	2,096
Claims on Central Government........	42a	2,611	3,444	3,410	4,339	5,055	5,226	4,725	5,227	7,020	7,872	9,668	9,897
Claims on Local Government...........	42b	18	17	17									
Claims on Private Sector................	42d	2,102	2,446	3,615	5,335	6,609	8,718	14,759	15,939	18,034	19,185	21,667	21,505
Claims on Deposit Money Banks.....	42e	530	131	555	460	233	287	255	1,168	1,790	2,594	2,757	2,814
Time, Savings,& Fgn.Currency Dep...	45	4,339	5,254	6,360	8,450	10,477	12,065	13,352	15,641	19,648	23,099	25,098	26,364
Foreign Liabilities..........................	46c	5	—	1,025	145	162	111	83	632	1,020	970	971	1,026
Capital Accounts.........................	47a	581	778	1,078	1,990	2,658	3,515	4,721	5,358	5,828	5,735	6,567	7,090
Other Items (Net).........................	47r	588	188	−665	−205	−1,027	−1,095	2,234	2,386	2,265	2,718	3,751	2,622

		1993	1994	1995	1996	1997	1998	1999	2000	2001	2002	2003	2004
Banking Survey					*Millions of Guyana Dollars: End of Period*								
Foreign Assets (Net)	51n	†−83,831	−82,472	−87,537	−40,499	−21,639	−22,068	−10,978	2,561	7,456	30,328	36,000	32,291
Domestic Credit	52	†127,017	129,724	146,764	128,986	122,165	125,921	127,328	130,733	137,487	121,232	123,615	138,577
Claims on Central Govt. (Net)	52an	†113,374	112,074	120,769	84,646	67,234	61,134	51,306	51,285	54,947	37,323	47,761	62,661
Claims on Local Government	52b	†55	17	53	1	4	500	48	39	1	7	62	50
Claims on Nonfin.Pub.Enterprises	52c	†1,232	1,286	1,220	2,695	3,455	3,730	5,392	5,129	5,562	5,518	5,532	5,976
Claims on Private Sector	52d	†12,356	16,346	24,722	41,644	51,472	60,556	70,583	74,280	76,977	78,385	70,260	69,891
Liquid Liabilities	55l	†41,741	47,459	58,871	71,128	79,509	85,676	94,786	103,758	115,303	124,100	133,938	144,645
Restricted Deposits	56b	†368	334	330	330	318	307	70	66	56	56	58	58
Capital Accounts	57a	†2,786	7,091	9,723	18,268	21,161	28,084	32,089	34,457	35,841	34,679	28,122	29,463
Other Items (Net)	57r	†−1,709	−7,633	−9,697	−1,238	−461	−10,215	−10,596	−4,987	−6,257	−7,274	−2,503	−3,297
Money (National Definitions)					*Millions of Guyana Dollars: End of Period*								
Base Money	19ma	....	....	....	....	....	11,334	13,394	14,495	15,138	15,410	17,888	19,546
Reserve Money	19mb	....	....	....	....	....	27,173	26,122	29,788	33,037	36,352	40,105	43,283
M1	59ma	....	....	....	....	....	17,821	21,548	24,827	24,807	26,365	30,793	34,606
M2	59mb	....	....	....	....	....	68,696	76,980	85,445	93,035	98,147	106,259	114,495
Interest Rates						*Percent Per Annum*							
Discount Rate (End of Period)	60	17.00	20.25	17.25	12.00	11.00	11.25	13.25	11.75	8.75	6.25	5.50	6.00
Treasury Bill Rate	60c	16.83	17.66	17.51	11.35	8.91	8.33	11.31	9.88	7.78	4.94	3.04	3.62
Savings Rate	60k	10.88	9.94	10.95	8.75	7.48	7.16	7.73	7.65	7.09	5.02	3.84	3.43
Deposit Rate	60l	12.26	11.42	12.90	10.49	8.56	8.10	9.08	8.71	7.63	4.53	3.18	2.67
Lending Rate	60p	19.36	18.36	19.22	17.79	17.04	16.77	17.11	17.30	17.01	16.33	14.99	14.54
Prices					*Index Numbers (2000=100): Period Averages*								
Consumer Prices	64	....	67.3	75.5	80.9	83.8	87.6	94.2	100.0	102.6	108.1	114.6	119.9
Intl. Transactions & Positions					*Millions of Guyana Dollars*								
Exports	70	52,506.9	63,389.8	64,581.3	72,597.9	91,808.7	73,336.3	93,138.0	90,830.4	89,593.4	93,938.0	123,048.2	117,736.7
Imports, c.i.f.	71	61,376.0	70,000.6	74,911.5	83,895.0	89,746.8	....	....	....	109,362.4	107,273.7	198,001.4	134,986.5
							2000=100						
Volume of Exports	72	80	86	104	73	101	96	104	100	33	90	98	78
Balance of Payments					*Millions of US Dollars: Minus Sign Indicates Debit*								
Current Account, n.i.e.	78ald	−140.2	−124.9	−134.8	−69.1	−111.4	−102.0	−78.2	−115.3	−133.8	−110.6	−90.6	....
Goods: Exports f.o.b.	78aad	415.5	463.4	495.7	574.8	593.4	547.0	525.0	505.2	490.3	494.9	512.8	....
Goods: Imports f.o.b.	78abd	−483.8	−504.0	−536.5	−595.0	−641.6	−601.2	−550.2	−585.4	−584.1	−563.1	−571.7	....
Trade Balance	78acd	−68.3	−40.6	−40.8	−20.2	−48.2	−54.2	−25.2	−80.2	−93.8	−68.2	−58.9	....
Services: Credit	78add	115.3	120.7	133.5	146.1	148.1	141.8	147.0	169.2	172.0	172.3	185.5	....
Services: Debit	78aed	−148.1	−160.9	−171.8	−168.6	−171.3	−173.9	−178.1	−193.2	−192.4	−195.8	−205.4	....
Balance on Goods & Services	78afd	−101.1	−80.8	−79.2	−42.7	−71.4	−86.3	−56.3	−104.2	−114.2	−91.7	−78.8	....
Income: Credit	78agd	5.1	8.7	12.2	11.6	12.5	11.9	11.3	11.7	10.1	7.8	4.6	....
Income: Debit	78ahd	−106.8	−114.8	−129.9	−79.0	−92.5	−71.6	−72.2	−69.8	−73.7	−66.7	−56.7	....
Balance on Gds, Serv. & Inc.	78aid	−202.9	−186.9	−196.8	−110.1	−151.4	−146.0	−117.2	−162.3	−177.8	−150.6	−130.9	....
Current Transfers, n.i.e.: Credit	78ajd	70.0	68.1	67.4	69.1	67.1	74.3	76.1	100.8	98.1	128.7	143.7	....
Current Transfers: Debit	78akd	−7.4	−6.2	−5.3	−28.1	−27.1	−30.3	−37.1	−53.8	−54.1	−88.7	−103.4	....
Capital Account, n.i.e.	78bcd	4.4	8.3	9.5	—	23.7	13.1	15.5	16.3	31.9	33.7	43.8	....
Capital Account, n.i.e.: Credit	78bad	6.6	11.0	12.5	—	23.7	13.1	15.5	16.3	31.9	33.7	43.8	....
Capital Account: Debit	78bbd	−2.2	−2.7	−3.0	....	....	....	....	....	....	....	....	....
Financial Account, n.i.e.	78bjd	88.7	126.9	71.1	69.5	96.9	64.0	87.3	114.6	101.9	89.5	40.0	....
Direct Investment Abroad	78bxd	....	....	....	....	....	....	....	....	....	....	....	....
Dir. Invest. in Rep. Econ., n.i.e.	78bed	69.5	106.7	74.4	59.0	52.0	44.0	46.0	67.1	56.0	43.6	26.1	....
Portfolio Investment Assets	78bfd	....	....	....	−.4	−2.3	−.8	16.6	−3.4	9.7	17.8	−22.1	....
Equity Securities	78bkd	....	....	....	....	....	....	....	....	....	....	....	....
Debt Securities	78bld	....	....	....	−.4	−2.3	−.8	16.6	−3.4	9.7	17.8	−22.1	....
Portfolio Investment Liab., n.i.e.	78bgd	3.6	15.8	3.2	4.8	9.2	−3.1	−9.2	−1.5	−3.2	8.4	4.5	....
Equity Securities	78bmd	....	....	....	....	....	....	....	....	....	....	....	....
Debt Securities	78bnd	3.6	15.8	3.2	4.8	9.2	−3.1	−9.2	−1.5	−3.2	8.4	4.5	....
Financial Derivatives Assets	78bwd	....	....	....	....	....	....	....	....	....	....	....	....
Financial Derivatives Liabilities	78bxd	....	....	....	....	....	....	....	....	....	....	....	....
Other Investment Assets	78bhd	8.8	−5.8	−8.9	40.2	67.0	59.7	47.4	66.1	65.8	45.3	43.3	....
Monetary Authorities	78bod	....	....	....	....	....	....	....	....	....	....	....	....
General Government	78bpd	1.4	1.3	−2.2	40.2	67.0	59.7	47.4	66.1	65.8	45.3	43.3	....
Banks	78bqd	3.2	4.2	−2.8	....	....	....	....	....	....	....	....	....
Other Sectors	78brd	4.2	−11.2	−3.9	....	....	....	....	....	....	....	....	....
Other Investment Liab., n.i.e.	78bid	6.7	10.2	2.3	−34.1	−29.0	−35.8	−13.5	−13.7	−26.4	−25.6	−11.8	....
Monetary Authorities	78bsd	−13.9	1.3	18.6	—	—	—	—	—	—	—	—	....
General Government	78btd	27.3	−1.0	−5.4	−34.1	−29.0	−45.8	−23.5	−23.7	−26.4	−25.6	−31.8	....
Banks	78bud	−4.9	−2.9	−.4	....	....	....	....	....	....	....	....	....
Other Sectors	78bvd	−1.8	12.9	−10.5	....	....	10.0	10.0	10.0	....	....	20.0	....
Net Errors and Omissions	78cad	11.0	−16.3	11.2	11.5	−10.8	11.9	−3.0	24.6	26.2	2.1	16.6	....
Overall Balance	78cbd	−36.1	−6.0	−43.0	11.9	−1.6	−13.0	21.6	40.2	26.2	14.7	9.8	....
Reserves and Related Items	79dad	36.1	6.0	43.0	−11.9	1.6	13.0	−21.6	−40.2	−26.2	−14.7	−9.8	....
Reserve Assets	79dbd	−57.1	−21.8	.8	−13.9	2.9	22.6	−11.4	−24.0	−10.4	−5.9	−.5	....
Use of Fund Credit and Loans	79dcd	9.1	−8.8	−9.7	2.0	−1.3	−9.6	−10.2	−16.2	−15.8	−8.9	−9.3	....
Exceptional Financing	79ded	84.2	36.6	52.0	—	....	....	....	....	....	....	....	....

		1993	1994	1995	1996	1997	1998	1999	2000	2001	2002	2003	2004
Government Finance					*Millions of Guyana Dollars: Year Ending December 31*								
Deficit (-) or Surplus.........................	80	−4,001	−5,092	−2,886	−3,115	−6,611	....	....	....	....	....	....	....
Total Revenue and Grants..............	81y	23,901	29,133	32,428	37,180	39,071	....	....	....	....	....	....	....
Revenue...	81	23,191	28,138	30,823	34,666	36,006	....	....	....	....	....	....	....
Grants...	81z	710	995	1,605	2,515	3,065	....	....	....	....	....	....	....
Exp. & Lending Minus Repay.........	82z	27,902	34,226	35,314	40,295	45,682	....	....	....	....	....	....	....
Expenditure.................................	82	27,902	34,226	35,314	40,295	45,682	....	....	....	....	....	....	....
Lending Minus Repayments.........	83	—	—	—	—	—	....	....	....	....	....	....	....
Total Financing................................	80h	4,001	5,092	2,886	3,115	6,611	....	....	....	....	....	....	....
Total Net Borrowing....................	84	−5,398	−699	2,826	−931	4,310	....	....	....	....	....	....	....
Net Domestic..............................	84a	−6,573	−4,394	1,627	−7,298	−162	....	....	....	....	....	....	....
Net Foreign.................................	85a	1,175	3,695	1,199	6,367	4,473	....	....	....	....	....	....	....
Use of Cash Balances....................	87	9,399	5,791	60	4,046	2,301	....	....	....	....	....	....	....
Total Debt......................................	88	283,213	316,419	322,444	249,167	258,325	....	....	....	....	....	....	....
Domestic.......................................	88a	27,793	31,490	33,252	37,478	35,888	....	....	....	....	....	....	....
Foreign...	89a	255,420	284,929	289,191	211,688	222,436	....	....	....	....	....	....	....
National Accounts						*Millions of Guyana Dollars*							
Househ.Cons.Expend.,incl.NPISHs....	96f	29,134	36,131	40,897	44,224	47,147	....	....	....	....	....	....	....
Government Consumption Expend...	91f	8,529	11,817	14,092	17,330	21,747	....	....	....	....	....	....	....
Gross Fixed Capital Formation.........	93e	30,745	34,348	40,077	43,436	47,099	....	....	....	....	....	....	....
Exports of Goods and Services.........	90c	52,518	59,185	70,315	82,155	84,375	....	....	....	....	....	....	....
Imports of Goods and Services (-).....	98c	64,370	64,370	74,912	83,895	91,749	....	....	....	....	....	....	....
Gross Domestic Product (GDP).........	99b	59,124	75,412	88,271	99,038	105,859	....	....	....	....	....	....	....
Net Primary Income from Abroad.....	98.n	−11,912	−11,473	−12,203	−7,319	−10,406	....	....	....	....	....	....	....
Gross National Income (GNI)...........	99a	47,212	63,939	76,068	91,719	95,399	....	....	....	....	....	....	....
Net National Income......................	99e	47,212	63,939	76,068	91,719	95,399	....	....	....	....	....	....	....
GDP Volume 1988 Prices.................	99b.p	4,104	....	....	....	....	....	....	....	....	....	....	....
GDP Volume (1990=100)...............	99bvp	123.7	....	....	....	....	....	....	....	....	....	....	....
GDP Deflator (1990=100)...............	99bip	305.2	....	....	....	....	....	....	....	....	....	....	....
					Millions: Midyear Estimates								
Population..............................	99z	.73	.73	.73	.73	.74	.74	.74	.74	.75	.75	.75	.75

Haiti 263

		1993	1994	1995	1996	1997	1998	1999	2000	2001	2002	2003	2004
Exchange Rates						*Gourdes per SDR: End of Period*							
Market Rate...................................	aa	17.588	18.900	24.022	21.703	23.357	23.239	24.658	29.347	33.101	51.130	62.537	57.821
					Gourdes per US Dollar: End of Period (ae) Period Average (rf)								
Market Rate...................................	ae	12.805	12.947	16.160	15.093	17.311	16.505	17.965	22.524	26.339	37.609	42.085	37.232
Market Rate...................................	rf	12.823	15.040	15.110	15.701	16.655	16.766	16.938	21.171	24.429	29.250	42.367	38.352
Fund Position						*Millions of SDRs: End of Period*							
Quota...	2f.s	44.1	44.1	60.7	60.7	60.7	60.7	60.7	60.7	60.7	60.7	81.9	81.9
SDRs...	1b.s	—	—	.4	—	.1	.4	.6	.1	.4	.4	.2	.1
Reserve Position in the Fund............	1c.s	—	—	—	—	—	—	—	.1	.1	.1	.1	.1
Total Fund Cred.&Loans Outstg........	2tl	23.8	3.8	18.2	31.6	31.6	40.8	32.6	30.4	30.4	19.7	9.1	6.1
International Liquidity					*Millions of US Dollars Unless Otherwise Indicated: End of Period*								
Total Reserves minus Gold...............	1l.d	32.1	51.1	191.6	216.1	207.1	258.2	264.0	182.1	141.4	81.7	62.0	114.4
SDRs..	1b.d	—	—	.5	.1	.1	.5	.9	.1	.5	.5	.3	.2
Reserve Position in the Fund..........	1c.d	.1	.1	.1	.1	.1	.1	.1	.1	.1	.1	.1	.1
Foreign Exchange......................	1d.d	32.0	51.0	191.0	216.0	206.9	257.6	263.1	182.0	140.8	81.1	61.6	114.1
Gold (Million Fine Troy Ounces)........	1ad	.019	.019	.019	.019	.020	.020	.001	.001	.001	.001	.001	.001
Monetary Authorities: Other Liab......	4..d	9.7	48.3	20.6	82.1	59.6	60.4	60.7	61.4	62.2	61.1	63.8	65.9
Deposit Money Banks: Assets..........	7a.d	78.3	96.1	98.1	114.9	133.1	124.4	150.7	199.1	177.0	137.8	237.1	243.8
Liabilities....................	7b.d		.8	4.9	6.9	17.9	8.3	16.7	21.8	18.7	20.8	26.7	38.5
Monetary Authorities						*Millions of Gourdes: End of Period*							
Foreign Assets............................	11	236.8	834.0	3,073.7	3,988.0	† 4,757.2	5,308.4	5,916.0	5,549.2	6,988.4	7,274.7	8,684.2	10,720.0
Claims on Central Government........	12a	4,394.6	5,860.7	7,074.0	7,238.8	† 7,668.1	8,273.3	10,302.3	11,802.0	13,846.8	17,920.5	22,663.1	24,618.8
Claims on Local Government...........	12b				12.9	† 8.5	5.0	1.7	.6				
Claims on Nonfin.Pub.Enterprises.....	12c	426.5	328.1	152.1	80.8	† 50.9	85.5	84.5	1,820.3	1,996.3	2,155.5	2,162.9	2,116.8
Claims on Private Sector.................	12d	—	—	—	141.2	† 163.5	233.1	304.2	358.8	452.9	543.7	721.9	1,000.8
Claims on Deposit Money Banks......	12e	754.6	415.6	65.0	70.2	† 129.2	106.2	264.6	228.5	93.1	423.7	813.5	91.2
Claims on Other Banking Insts.........	12f	—	—	28.6	—	† —	—	—	—	—	—	—	—
Claims on Nonbank Financial Insts...	12g	—	—	—	4.7	† 22.4	19.8	13.9	12.0	9.8	7.7	5.2	2.6
Reserve Money.............................	14	5,616.6	6,954.9	7,975.8	7,645.1	† 7,653.3	7,672.5	9,894.3	12,452.2	14,556.2	18,038.3	23,702.1	27,939.8
of which: Currency Outside DMBs..	14a	2,668.8	3,029.5	3,536.7	3,435.7	† 3,935.4	3,905.4	4,927.1	5,807.2	6,584.3	8,687.5	9,843.2	10,218.3
Time, Savings,& Fgn.Currency Dep...	15	—	—	—	—	† 8.4	37.3	55.9	84.0	101.8	122.0	36.7	382.1
Liabs. of Central Bank: Securities......	16ac					† 857.0	1,980.0	2,335.0	944.0	2,432.0	2,563.0	4,996.0	3,544.0
Foreign Liabilities.........................	16c	543.7	696.6	768.7	1,595.1	† 1,768.4	1,944.8	1,893.6	2,273.8	2,643.1	3,306.9	3,253.0	2,805.3
Central Government Deposits...........	16d	481.3	892.7	1,983.0	1,617.2	† 1,514.2	1,647.6	1,895.3	1,125.1	1,093.7	1,440.9	2,005.7	3,813.6
Capital Accounts...........................	17a	472.2	564.0	1,139.1	857.2	† 1,266.5	1,313.1	1,566.8	3,974.8	4,143.9	4,504.9	3,656.1	2,692.1
Other Items (Net).........................	17r	−1,301.3	−1,669.8	−1,473.3	−178.0	† −268.1	−563.6	−753.7	−1,082.6	−1,583.5	−1,650.2	−2,598.8	−2,626.7
Deposit Money Banks						*Millions of Gourdes: End of Period*							
Reserves.....................................	20	3,059.1	3,718.1	3,608.0	3,979.8	† 3,323.6	3,411.0	4,394.1	6,297.4	7,713.6	8,805.2	12,936.4	17,140.4
Claims on Mon.Author.:Securities....	20c					† 857.0	1,980.0	2,335.0	944.0	2,432.0	2,563.0	4,996.0	3,544.0
Foreign Assets.............................	21	1,002.7	1,243.6	1,584.9	1,734.2	† 2,303.9	2,053.8	2,706.8	4,484.6	4,662.5	5,183.1	9,979.6	9,076.6
Claims on Central Government........	22a	8.0	114.1	11.3	6.5	† 6.5	6.5	169.3	164.3	99.3	59.3	—	—
Claims on Private Sector.................	22d	2,516.3	3,253.2	5,072.4	5,825.0	† 8,511.2	9,156.2	10,128.9	12,074.3	12,914.0	16,785.7	20,448.6	20,859.4
Claims on Other Banking Insts.........	22f	—	—	—	—	† —	—	—	170.0	—	—	—	—
Demand Deposits..........................	24	1,429.6	1,578.0	2,372.7	2,211.1	† 2,435.2	2,544.2	3,241.3	3,251.2	3,749.2	4,394.7	6,142.5	7,145.5
Time, Savings,& Fgn.Currency Dep...	25	4,944.8	6,486.8	8,018.7	9,064.7	† 11,499.7	13,209.8	15,997.4	20,102.3	22,847.1	27,582.9	41,036.9	41,942.6
Bonds.......................................	26ab	—	—	—	—	† 46.1	44.9	21.9	113.6	148.2	385.2	481.9	685.4
Foreign Liabilities.........................	26c	.3	10.7	78.6	104.5	† 310.3	136.4	299.8	490.4	492.9	782.1	1,124.7	1,433.4
Central Government Deposits...........	26d	27.0	27.6	37.5	54.5	† 514.7	475.1	402.9	257.2	157.5	80.3	361.9	322.3
Credit from Monetary Authorities.....	26g	—	—	72.6	81.9	† 49.0	42.8	134.7	72.1	32.1	293.0	33.0	3.0
Capital Accounts...........................	27a	320.9	395.7	525.7	946.2	† 1,060.5	1,314.2	1,346.0	1,752.2	2,050.9	2,343.3	3,067.5	3,112.9
Other Items (Net).........................	27r	−136.5	−169.8	−829.1	−917.4	† −913.2	−1,159.9	−1,709.9	−1,904.3	−1,656.4	−2,465.2	−3,887.7	−4,024.7
Monetary Survey						*Millions of Gourdes: End of Period*							
Foreign Assets (Net)......................	31n	695.5	1,370.3	3,811.3	4,022.6	† 4,982.4	5,281.4	6,429.4	7,269.6	8,514.9	8,368.7	14,286.2	15,557.8
Domestic Credit............................	32	6,837.1	8,440.9	10,317.9	11,638.2	† 14,402.1	15,656.7	18,706.6	25,020.0	28,067.9	35,951.2	43,634.2	44,462.5
Claims on Central Govt. (Net)........	32an	3,894.3	4,861.4	5,064.8	5,573.6	† 5,645.7	6,157.1	8,173.4	10,584.0	12,694.9	16,458.6	20,295.6	20,482.9
Claims on Local Government..........	32b				12.9	† 8.5	5.0	1.7	.6				
Claims on Nonfin.Pub.Enterprises...	32c	426.5	326.3	152.1	80.8	† 50.9	85.5	84.5	1,820.3	1,996.3	2,155.5	2,162.9	2,116.8
Claims on Private Sector...............	32d	2,516.3	3,253.2	5,072.4	5,966.2	† 8,674.6	9,389.3	10,433.0	12,433.1	13,367.0	17,329.4	21,170.5	21,860.2
Claims on Other Banking Insts.......	32f	—	—	28.6	—	† —	—	—	170.0	—	—	—	—
Claims on Nonbank Financial Inst..	32g	—	—	—	4.7	† 22.4	19.8	13.9	12.0	9.8	7.7	5.2	2.6
Money..	34	3,866.4	5,095.5	6,703.9	5,823.9	† 6,633.5	6,650.9	8,422.8	9,220.2	10,610.2	13,501.5	16,222.1	17,975.8
Quasi-Money................................	35	4,944.8	6,486.8	8,018.7	9,064.7	† 11,508.1	13,247.1	16,053.3	20,186.3	22,948.9	27,704.8	41,073.6	42,324.6
Bonds.......................................	36ab	—	—	—	—	† 46.1	44.9	21.9	113.6	148.2	385.2	481.9	685.4
Capital Accounts...........................	37a	793.1	959.7	1,664.7	1,803.4	† 2,327.0	2,627.3	2,912.7	5,727.0	6,194.8	6,848.1	6,723.6	5,805.0
Other Items (Net).........................	37r	−2,071.7	−2,730.8	−2,258.1	−1,031.3	† −1,130.1	−1,632.1	−2,274.8	−2,957.5	−3,319.3	−4,119.7	−6,580.9	−6,770.5
Money plus Quasi-Money................	35l	8,811.2	11,582.3	14,722.5	14,888.6	† 18,141.5	19,898.0	24,476.2	29,406.4	33,559.1	41,206.3	57,295.7	60,300.4
Interest Rates						*Percent per Annum*							
Treasury Bill Rate..........................	60c	....	....	....	....	14.13	16.21	7.71	12.33	13.53	7.56	20.50	12.23
Savings Rate.................................	60k	....	....	....	....	5.36	5.50	3.51	3.57	3.35	2.52	3.01	2.24
Savings Rate (Foreign Currency).......	60k.f	....	....	....	....	....	....	....	....	1.73	1.47	1.38	1.25
Deposit Rate................................	60l	....	....	....	....	10.74	13.06	7.39	11.85	13.66	8.24	13.99	10.79
Deposit Rate (Foreign Currency).......	60l.f	....	....	....	....	....	....	....	....	4.66	2.83	3.39	2.78
Lending Rate................................	60p	....	....	....	....	21.00	23.62	22.88	25.09	28.63	25.67	30.58	34.08
Lending Rate (Foreign Currency).......	60p.f	....	....	....	....	....	....	....	....	14.76	12.23	13.92	14.13
Prices						*Index Numbers (2000=100): Period Averages*							
Consumer Prices............................	64	28.3	39.4	50.3	60.7	73.1	80.9	87.9	100.0	114.2	125.4	174.7	214.5
Intl. Transactions & Positions						*Millions of Gourdes*							
Exports.......................................	70	1,029.3	1,236.7	1,666.5	1,413.9	3,537.1	5,365.0	5,661.3	6,725.3	6,700.7	8,203.0	14,682.2	15,006.8
Imports, c.i.f.................................	71	4,555.7	3,783.6	9,866.2	10,448.2	10,792.1	13,365.6	17,366.9	21,936.2	24,745.7	33,060.7	50,323.7	50,087.8

		1993	1994	1995	1996	1997	1998	1999	2000	2001	2002	2003	2004
Balance of Payments		*Millions of US Dollars: F.Y. Ending Sept 30; Minus Sign Indicates Debit*											
Current Account, n.i.e.	78ald	−11.8	−23.4	−87.1	−137.7	−47.7	28.7	−59.8	−85.2	−94.6	−47.6	−13.1	....
Goods: Exports f.o.b.	78aad	80.3	60.3	88.3	82.5	205.4	294.8	343.3	331.7	305.2	274.4	333.2	....
Goods: Imports f.o.b.	78abd	−260.5	−171.5	−517.2	−498.6	−559.6	−822.1	−1,017.5	−1,086.7	−1,055.4	−980.4	−1,115.8	....
Trade Balance	78acd	−180.2	−111.2	−428.9	−416.1	−354.2	−527.3	−674.3	−755.0	−750.2	−706.0	−782.7	....
Services: Credit	78add	35.8	6.7	104.1	109.1	173.7	179.0	188.0	172.0	139.0	148.0	136.0	....
Services: Debit	78aed	−30.2	−63.9	−284.5	−283.3	−331.5	−218.5	−234.6	−264.0	−242.5	−251.6	−259.0	....
Balance on Goods & Services	78afd	−174.6	−168.4	−609.3	−590.3	−512.0	−566.7	−720.9	−847.0	−853.7	−809.6	−905.7	....
Income: Credit	78agd	2.0				....	....						....
Income: Debit	78ahd	−12.6	−11.2	−30.6	−9.9	−13.6	−11.1	−12.6	−9.2	−9.5	−13.7	−14.3	....
Balance on Gds, Serv. & Inc.	78aid	−185.2	−179.6	−639.9	−600.2	−525.6	−577.8	−733.5	−856.2	−863.1	−823.3	−919.9	....
Current Transfers, n.i.e.: Credit	78ajd	173.4	156.2	552.9	462.5	477.9	606.5	673.7	771.0	768.6	775.7	906.8	....
Current Transfers: Debit	78akd	—	—	—	—	—	—	—	—	—	—	—	....
Capital Account, n.i.e.	78bcd	—	—	—	....	....	—	—	—	—	—	—	....
Capital Account, n.i.e.: Credit	78bad	—	—	—	....	....	—	—	—	—	—	—	....
Capital Account: Debit	78bbd	—	—	—	....	....	—	—	—	—	—	—	....
Financial Account, n.i.e.	78bjd	−46.5	−15.8	99.2	67.9	61.5	186.8	85.3	−16.0	82.5	−17.3	−76.5	....
Direct Investment Abroad	78bdd	—	—	—	—	—	—	—	—	—	—	—	....
Dir. Invest. in Rep. Econ., n.i.e.	78bed	−2.8	—	7.4	4.1	4.0	10.8	30.0	13.3	4.4	5.7	7.8	....
Portfolio Investment Assets	78bfd	—	—	—	—	—	—	—	—	—	—	—	....
Equity Securities	78bkd	—	—	—	—	—	—	—	—	—	—	—	....
Debt Securities	78bld	—	—	—	—	—	—	—	—	—	—	—	....
Portfolio Investment Liab., n.i.e.	78bgd	—	—	—	—	—	—	—	—	—	—	—	....
Equity Securities	78bmd	—	—	—	—	—	—	—	—	—	—	—	....
Debt Securities	78bnd	—	—	—	—	—	—	—	—	—	—	—	....
Financial Derivatives Assets	78bwd	....	....	....	....	....	....	....	....	....	....	....	....
Financial Derivatives Liabilities	78bxd	....	....	....	....	....	....	....	....	....	....	....	....
Other Investment Assets	78bhd	−30.6	−5.5	−11.2	−4.6	21.6	86.8	−15.3	−43.3	−3.0	27.3	−98.0	....
Monetary Authorities	78bod	....	....	....	....	....	....	....	....	....	....	....	....
General Government	78bpd							2.0	−5.4	2.8	.1	−.6	....
Banks	78bqd	−30.6	−5.5	−11.2	−4.6	3.6	2.8	−3.4	−63.9	17.2	−.8	−50.3	....
Other Sectors	78brd	—	—	—	—	18.0	84.0	−14.0	26.0	−23.0	28.0	−47.0	....
Other Investment Liab., n.i.e.	78bid	−13.1	−10.3	103.1	68.4	35.9	89.2	70.6	14.0	81.1	−50.3	13.7	....
Monetary Authorities	78bsd	2.2	2.1										....
General Government	78btd	−15.3	−12.4	112.5	68.8	37.7	37.7	71.9	22.4	−3.0	−46.6	5.1	....
Banks	78bud	—	—	.4	−.4	12.3	−4.6	−.5	8.8	−.9	4.2	1.3	....
Other Sectors	78bvd	—	—	−9.8	.1	−14.1	56.0	−.7	−17.2	85.0	−7.8	7.3	....
Net Errors and Omissions	78cad	35.3	−10.5	125.9	19.5	16.1	−181.3	1.0	44.3	6.9	−3.1	85.0	....
Overall Balance	78cbd	−23.0	−49.7	138.1	50.4	29.9	34.2	26.5	−56.9	−5.2	−67.9	−4.6	....
Reserves and Related Items	79dad	23.0	49.7	−138.1	50.4	−29.9	−34.2	−26.5	56.9	5.2	67.9	4.6	....
Reserve Assets	79dbd	−19.1	12.8	−175.6	48.5	−50.6	−28.9	−36.5	57.3	−5.3	49.0	22.1	....
Use of Fund Credit and Loans	79dcd	—	—	−6.6	−2.6	20.6	−5.3	10.0	−5.8	—	−9.2	−14.5	....
Exceptional Financing	79ded	42.1	36.9	44.1	4.4	....			5.5	10.5	28.2	−3.0	....
International Investment Position		*Millions of US Dollars*											
Assets	79aad	....	....	....	....	....	....	....	....	....	....	....	....
Direct Investment Abroad	79abd	....	....	....	....	....	—	—	—	—	—	—	....
Portfolio Investment	79acd	....	....	....	....	....	—	—	—	—	—	—	....
Equity Securities	79add	....	....	....	....	....	—	—	—	—	—	—	....
Debt Securities	79aed	....	....	....	....	....	—	—	—	—	—	—	....
Financial Derivatives	79ald	....	....	....	....	....	....	....	....	....	....	....	....
Other Investment	79afd	....	....	....	....	....	200.6	215.9	259.2	262.2	234.9	332.9	....
Monetary Authorities	79agd	....	....	....	....	....	—	—	—	—	—	—	....
General Government	79ahd	....	....	....	....	....	—	—	—	—	—	—	....
Banks	79aid	....	....	....	....	....	121.5	124.9	188.8	171.6	172.4	222.7	....
Other Sectors	79ajd	....	....	....	....	....	79.1	91.1	70.4	90.6	62.5	110.2	....
Reserve Assets	79akd	....	....	....	....	....	292.7	329.2	271.9	277.0	228.8	206.7	....
Liabilities	79lad	....	....	....	....	....	....	....	....	....	....	....	....
Dir. Invest. in Rep. Economy	79lbd	....	....	....	....	....	51.5	81.5	94.7	99.1	104.8	112.6	....
Portfolio Investment	79lcd	....	....	....	....	....	—	—	—	—	—	—	....
Equity Securities	79ldd	....	....	....	....	....	—	—	—	—	—	—	....
Debt Securities	79led	....	....	....	....	....	—	—	—	—	—	—	....
Financial Derivatives	79lld	....	....	....	....	....	....	....	....	....	....	....	....
Other Investment	79lfd	....	....	....	....	....	1,276.3	1,346.4	1,343.3	1,437.8	1,448.7	1,521.6	....
Monetary Authorities	79lgd	....	....	....	....	....	98.0	108.6	99.8	100.9	92.5	81.3	....
General Government	79lhd	....	....	....	....	....	1,104.2	1,165.6	1,179.6	1,188.9	1,211.9	1,287.4	....
Banks	79lid	....	....	....	....	....	12.7	12.2	21.0	20.0	24.2	25.5	....
Other Sectors	79ljd	....	....	....	....	....	61.4	60.1	42.9	127.9	120.1	127.4	....
Government Finance		*Millions of Gourdes: Year Ending September 30*											
Deficit (-) or Surplus	80	−506.9	−947.1	−986.1	−329.5	−320.5	−776.5	−1,647.7	−1,774.1	−1,887.0	−2,542.3	−3,363.9	−4,674.9
Revenue	81	1,284.2	874.8	2,456.0	3,436.1	4,781.8	5,330.0	6,211.2	6,169.4	6,332.2	7,721.7	10,502.5	12,469.0
Grants Received	81z	1.1	2.2	696.7	354.3	694.6	644.7	47.0	197.2	369.8	112.7	283.3	21.0
Expenditure	82	1,792.2	1,824.1	4,138.8	4,119.9	5,796.9	6,751.2	7,905.9	8,140.7	8,589.0	10,376.7	14,149.7	17,164.9
Financing													
Net Domestic Borrowing	84a	516.9	1,109.6	885.7	650.4	223.7	431.5	1,900.1	1,529.9	2,143.8	2,874.7	3,478.4	4,565.1
Monetary Authorities	84aa	516.9	1,109.6	885.7	650.4	223.7	591.5	1,799.6	1,566.1	2,148.0	2,912.3	3,795.7	4,678.9
Other	84ac						−160.0	100.5	−36.2	−4.2	−37.6	−317.3	−113.8
Net Foreign Borrowing	85a	—	—	1,031.3	−260.7	−272.0	−421.7	−577.5	−389.5	−309.6	−277.2	−743.3	−969.9
Use of Cash Balances	87	39.1	−88.1	−975.8	−28.4	−327.3	85.5	−544.4	371.5	233.3	−20.8	19.3	−1,784.0
Adjustment to Financing	84x	−49.1	−74.4	44.9	−31.8	696.1	681.2	869.5	262.2	−180.5	−34.4	609.5	2,863.7

Haiti 263

		1993	1994	1995	1996	1997	1998	1999	2000	2001	2002	2003	2004
National Accounts					*Millions of Gourdes: Year Ending September 30*								
Househ.Cons.Expend.,incl.NPISHs....	**96f**	21,344	31,310	38,167	41,719	49,393	57,148	62,157	72,446	83,921	92,388	120,528	141,243
Gross Fixed Capital Formation..........	**93e**	1,467	1,857	4,867	13,122	13,247	16,382	19,182	21,208	22,158	23,412	36,732	38,312
Exports of Goods and Services..........	**90c**	1,912	1,942	3,845	5,284	5,646	6,237	8,482	9,849	10,594	11,403	18,945	20,194
Imports of Goods and Services (-).....	**98c**	4,849	4,173	11,634	13,479	14,280	16,770	20,568	25,923	30,973	33,363	56,589	59,755
Gross Domestic Product (GDP)........	**99b**	19,894	30,936	35,265	46,647	54,005	62,997	69,254	77,580	85,700	93,840	119,616	139,994
GDP Volume 1976 Prices................	**99b.p**	4,525	4,150	4,334	4,451	....	....	....	....	....	....	....	....
GDP Volume 1987 Prices................	**99b.p**	....	....	....	12,083	12,410	12,681	13,025	13,138	13,001	12,930	12,992	12,502
GDP Volume (2000=100)................	**99bvp**	93.5	85.8	89.6	† 92.0	94.5	96.5	99.1	100.0	99.0	98.4	98.9	95.2
GDP Deflator (2000=100)...............	**99bip**	27.4	46.5	50.8	65.4	73.7	84.1	90.0	100.0	111.6	122.9	155.9	189.6
						Millions: Midyear Estimates								
Population..............................	**99z**	7.27	7.38	7.49	7.59	7.69	7.80	7.90	8.01	8.11	8.22	8.33	....

2005, International Monetary Fund : *International Financial Statistics Yearbook*

329

		1993	1994	1995	1996	1997	1998	1999	2000	2001	2002	2003	2004
Exchange Rates						*Lempiras per SDR: End of Period*							
Market Rate	aa	9.9720	13.7227	15.3751	18.5057	17.6673	19.4415	19.9067	19.7270	20.0068	23.0076	26.3733	28.9369
					Lempiras per US Dollar: End of Period (ae) Period Average (rf)								
Market Rate	ae	7.2600	9.4001	10.3432	12.8694	13.0942	13.8076	14.5039	15.1407	15.9197	16.9233	17.7482	18.6328
Market Rate	rf	6.4716	8.4088	9.4710	11.7053	13.0035	13.3850	14.2132	14.8392	15.4737	16.4334	17.3453	18.2062
Fund Position						*Millions of SDRs: End of Period*							
Quota	2f.s	95.00	95.00	95.00	95.00	95.00	95.00	129.50	129.50	129.50	129.50	129.50	129.50
SDRs	1b.s	.11	.15	.10	.06	.06	.05	.68	.08	.25	.35	.08	.06
Reserve Position in the Fund	1c.s	—	—	—	—	—	—	8.63	8.63	8.63	8.63	8.63	8.63
Total Fund Cred.&Loans Outstg.	2tl	86.01	74.81	66.36	40.28	33.90	80.04	153.33	165.75	175.12	144.59	115.42	125.71
International Liquidity						*Millions of US Dollars Unless Otherwise Indicated: End of Period*							
Total Reserves minus Gold	1l.d	97.15	171.01	261.45	249.19	580.37	818.07	1,257.58	1,313.04	1,415.56	1,524.10	1,430.03	1,970.38
SDRs	1b.d	.15	.21	.15	.09	.07	.07	.94	.10	.32	.47	.11	.09
Reserve Position in the Fund	1c.d	—	—	—	—	—	—	11.84	11.24	10.84	11.73	12.82	13.40
Foreign Exchange	1d.d	97.00	170.80	261.30	249.10	580.30	818.00	1,244.80	1,301.70	1,404.40	1,511.90	1,417.10	1,956.90
Gold (Million Fine Troy Ounces)	1ad	.021	.021	.021	.021	.021	.021	.021	.021	.021	.021	.021	.021
Gold (National Valuation)	1and	8.47	8.30	8.41	8.03	6.43	6.25	6.28	5.99	6.05	7.11	9.26	9.93
Monetary Authorities: Other Liab.	4..d	560.88	599.86	595.09	509.27	379.96	361.89	443.44	427.88	412.08	400.10	396.09	409.23
Deposit Money Banks: Assets	7a.d	75.65	84.32	123.47	209.97	228.00	275.70	379.81	451.94	487.77	565.46	551.08	657.10
Liabilities	7b.d	28.71	68.89	103.20	154.84	271.39	344.95	297.64	272.02	228.04	230.62	221.51	400.94
Other Banking Insts.: Assets	7e.d	8.79	10.20	9.29	12.39	8.06	6.80	7.67	11.77	11.42	10.01	8.25	6.62
Liabilities	7f.d	13.93	15.80	16.49	13.01	15.80	17.19	9.84	38.26	56.86	39.01	23.75	14.44
Monetary Authorities						*Millions of Lempiras: End of Period*							
Foreign Assets	11	954	1,930	3,058	3,641	† 10,437	14,282	21,375	23,151	25,978	29,586	29,402	40,945
Claims on Central Government	12a	2,023	1,512	1,284	1,220	† 1,462	1,534	1,014	1,109	935	919	2,296	1,182
Claims on Local Government	12b	63	60	53	92	† 48	45	42	39	36	33	29	26
Claims on Private Sector	12d	59	58	64	58	† 1	1	1	1	1	—	—	—
Claims on Deposit Money Banks	12e	665	678	616	721	† 136	99	60	33	215	5	269	—
Claims on Other Banking Insts	12f	547	569	572	555	† 157	108	108	97	74	61	49	38
Reserve Money	14	1,852	2,723	3,373	4,842	† 9,045	10,501	11,720	12,813	14,071	17,762	18,935	26,262
of which: Currency Outside DMBs	14a	1,448	1,995	2,111	2,630	† 3,315	3,744	4,714	4,727	5,166	5,549	6,448	7,639
Time, Savings,& Fgn.Currency Dep	15	52	86	318	219	† 791	503	1,582	3,599	5,979	6,662	7,501	9,121
Foreign Liabilities	16c	4,794	6,479	6,654	6,672	† 4,975	5,920	7,377	7,415	7,510	7,317	7,030	7,625
Central Government Deposits	16d	1,751	1,229	1,562	2,042	† 2,878	4,766	7,409	6,112	4,834	5,081	5,222	6,674
Capital Accounts	17a	1,116	1,422	1,762	1,930	† 1,623	908	945	973	1,080	1,136	1,457	3,015
Other Items (Net)	17r	−5,255	−7,133	−8,022	−9,419	† −7,072	−6,528	−6,432	−6,483	−6,236	−7,353	−8,099	−10,508
Deposit Money Banks						*Millions of Lempiras: End of Period*							
Reserves	20	423	668	1,118	1,968	† 5,021	6,018	6,374	7,134	8,091	11,269	11,042	16,312
Foreign Assets	21	549	793	1,277	2,702	† 2,985	3,807	5,509	6,843	7,765	9,570	9,781	12,244
Claims on Central Government	22a	968	1,287	1,205	867	† 275	77	41	370	732	935	1,260	1,745
Claims on Local Government	22b	2	1	10	15	† 54	147	125	136	79	255	354	500
Claims on Private Sector	22d	5,009	6,364	7,711	10,966	† 16,744	23,247	28,014	32,021	35,524	38,001	45,208	52,558
Claims on Other Banking Insts	22f	6	37	55	29	† 26	43	473	195	280	391	3,674	3,503
Demand Deposits	24	1,313	1,761	2,368	3,074	† 4,287	4,841	5,666	6,180	6,344	7,658	9,315	9,840
Time, Savings,& Fgn.Currency Dep	25	3,432	4,287	5,626	8,721	† 13,657	18,094	22,228	27,819	32,585	37,027	42,288	51,805
Bonds	26ab	16	14	29	33	† 61	90	58	50	42	33	66	41
Foreign Liabilities	26c	208	648	1,067	1,993	† 3,554	4,763	4,317	4,119	3,630	3,903	3,931	7,471
Central Government Deposits	26d	349	300	270	331	† 1,059	2,004	2,846	2,457	2,103	2,651	2,491	2,679
Credit from Monetary Authorities	26g	704	691	619	760	† 156	90	60	33	215	11	269	—
Liabilities to Other Banking Insts	26i	—	—	—	—	833	1,453	2,575	2,897	3,421	3,205	5,266	4,948
Capital Accounts	27a	1,234	1,670	2,224	2,846	† 3,885	4,876	5,958	7,168	8,343	8,888	9,860	12,264
Other Items (Net)	27r	−302	−222	−829	−1,212	† −2,385	−2,872	−3,173	−4,024	−4,212	−2,956	−2,168	−2,185
Monetary Survey						*Millions of Lempiras: End of Period*							
Foreign Assets (Net)	31n	−3,499	−4,404	−3,386	−2,322	† 4,894	7,406	15,190	18,460	22,602	27,936	28,222	38,092
Domestic Credit	32	6,577	8,359	9,122	11,427	† 14,830	18,432	19,563	25,397	30,724	32,863	45,158	50,197
Claims on Central Govt. (Net)	32an	890	1,270	657	−287	† −2,200	−5,158	−9,200	−7,091	−5,271	−5,877	−4,157	−6,427
Claims on Local Government	32b	66	61	63	107	† 102	192	168	175	116	288	383	526
Claims on Private Sector	32d	5,068	6,422	7,775	11,024	† 16,745	23,247	28,015	32,021	35,525	38,001	45,208	52,558
Claims on Other Banking Insts	32f	553	606	627	583	† 183	151	581	292	354	452	3,723	3,541
Money	34	2,825	3,845	4,678	6,053	† 8,294	9,349	11,050	11,954	12,388	14,224	17,251	20,019
Quasi-Money	35	3,485	4,374	5,945	8,941	† 14,448	18,597	23,810	31,418	38,564	43,689	49,789	60,926
Bonds	36ab	16	14	29	33	† 61	90	58	50	42	33	66	41
Liabilities to Other Banking Insts	36i	—	—	—	—	833	1,453	2,575	2,897	3,421	3,205	5,266	4,948
Capital Accounts	37a	2,350	3,093	3,986	4,775	† 5,509	5,784	6,903	8,141	9,423	10,024	11,317	15,279
Other Items (Net)	37r	−5,599	−7,370	−8,902	−10,697	† −9,420	−9,436	−9,643	−10,602	−10,512	−10,375	−10,310	−12,923
Money plus Quasi-Money	35l	6,309	8,219	10,623	14,994	† 22,742	27,946	34,860	43,371	50,952	57,913	67,040	80,945
Other Banking Institutions						*Millions of Lempiras: End of Period*							
Reserves	40	75	139	124	121	† 661	759	654	1,057	945	1,089	1,507	2,552
Foreign Assets	41	64	96	96	160	† 106	94	111	178	182	169	146	123
Claims on Central Government	42a	79	110	137	156	† 294	79	54	46	209	304	2,090	1,600
Claims on Local Government	42b	80	86	93	95	† 136	131	112	110	99	55	51	51
Claims on Private Sector	42d	1,094	1,261	1,529	1,507	† 3,044	3,337	3,969	4,363	5,282	5,904	4,085	4,388
Claims on Deposit Money Banks	42e	20	27	38	34	† 881	1,462	2,597	2,918	3,463	3,300	5,321	4,983
Demand Deposits	44	19	21	19	20	† 26	18	40	38	41	34	49	37
Time, Savings,& Fgn.Currency Dep	45	675	744	938	1,063	† 3,387	3,154	3,504	3,531	4,121	4,435	2,805	3,017
Bonds	46ab	1	1	1	—	† 17	7	—	—	—	—	105	361
Foreign Liabilities	46c	101	149	171	167	† 207	237	143	579	905	660	422	269
Central Government Deposits	46d	217	326	425	407	† 636	1,091	1,462	1,851	1,685	1,729	1,924	1,910
Credit from Monetary Authorities	46g	579	647	586	584	† 177	110	112	102	74	61	49	38
Credit from Deposit Money Banks	46h	5	36	54	28	† 70	92	527	186	213	315	3,655	3,470
Capital Accounts	47a	301	407	449	497	† 2,058	2,087	2,866	3,479	4,378	4,783	4,977	5,541
Other Items (Net)	47r	−487	−611	−623	−693	† −1,456	−935	−1,157	−1,094	−1,237	−1,196	−787	−945

Honduras 268

		1993	1994	1995	1996	1997	1998	1999	2000	2001	2002	2003	2004
Banking Survey						*Millions of Lempiras: End of Period*							
Foreign Assets (Net)	51n	−3,537	−4,457	−3,461	−2,329	† 4,792	7,262	15,158	18,059	21,879	27,445	27,946	37,947
Domestic Credit	52	7,059	8,884	9,830	12,195	† 17,484	20,737	21,655	27,774	34,276	36,945	45,736	50,786
Claims on Central Govt. (Net)	52an	752	1,054	369	−537	† −2,542	−6,171	−10,609	−8,896	−6,746	−7,303	−3,991	−6,737
Claims on Local Government	52b	146	146	156	202	† 238	323	280	285	215	344	434	577
Claims on Private Sector	52d	6,161	7,683	9,305	12,530	† 19,788	26,584	31,983	36,384	40,807	43,905	49,293	56,946
Liquid Liabilities	55l	6,928	8,845	11,455	15,956	† 25,494	30,359	37,749	45,883	54,170	61,293	68,388	81,446
Bonds	56ab	17	14	30	33	† 78	97	58	50	42	34	171	402
Capital Accounts	57a	2,652	3,500	4,434	5,272	† 7,566	7,870	9,769	11,620	13,802	14,806	16,294	20,820
Other Items (Net)	57r	−6,074	−7,932	−9,550	−11,396	† −10,861	−10,328	−10,764	−11,721	−11,859	−11,742	−11,171	−13,936
Money (National Definitions)						*Millions of Lempiras: End of Period*							
Base Money	19ma	....	....	....	4,627	8,102	9,281	10,079	10,353	9,790	10,992	11,945	14,666
M1	59ma	2,762	3,783	4,474	5,690	7,609	8,577	10,450	10,943	11,515	13,192	15,804	17,499
M2	59mb	6,822	8,537	10,224	12,560	20,344	23,706	28,723	33,482	36,253	40,336	45,865	54,347
M3	59mc	7,517	9,834	12,173	16,727	25,716	30,395	37,155	43,924	50,115	56,733	64,752	77,251
Interest Rates						*Percent Per Annum*							
Savings Rate	60k	9.20	9.44	10.02	9.93	12.56	12.27	12.05	10.88	9.96	8.26	6.60	6.04
Savings Rate (Fgn.Currency)	60k.f	....	....	....	....	4.66	4.53	3.99	3.67	3.18	1.95	1.39	1.16
Deposit Rate	60l	11.60	11.56	11.97	16.70	21.28	18.58	19.97	15.93	14.48	13.74	11.48	11.09
Deposit Rate (Fgn.Currency)	60l.f	....	....	....	....	9.89	9.53	9.09	7.53	6.36	4.05	2.80	2.59
Lending Rate	60p	22.06	24.68	26.95	29.74	32.07	30.69	30.15	26.82	23.76	22.69	20.80	19.88
Lending Rate (Fgn.Currency)	60p.f	....	....	....	....	12.88	12.53	12.60	12.91	12.68	11.48	10.00	8.77
Government Bond Yield	61	10.40	23.11	27.24	35.55	29.59	20.34	14.79	15.28	11.97	11.26	11.67
Prices and Labor						*Index Numbers (2000=100): Period Averages*							
Consumer Prices	64	30.2	36.8	47.7	59.0	† 70.9	80.6	90.0	100.0	109.7	118.1	127.2	137.5
						Number in Thousands: Period Averages							
Labor Force	67d	....	....	1,777	1,977	2,053	2,135	2,388	....	....	....	....	....
Employment	67e	....	....	1,806	1,985	2,088	2,135	2,299	....	2,335	2,389	2,351	....
Unemployment	67c	....	....	59	89	69	88	89	....	103	....	....	....
Unemployment Rate (%)	67r	....	....	3.2	4.3	3.2	3.9	3.7	....	4.0	....	....	....
Intl. Transactions & Positions						*Millions of US Dollars*							
Exports	70..d	814.0	842.0	1,220.2	1,316.0	1,445.7	1,532.8	1,164.4	1,380.0	1,324.4	1,321.2	1,332.3	1,537.4
Imports, c.i.f.	71..d	1,130.0	1,055.9	1,642.7	1,839.9	2,148.6	2,534.8	2,676.1	2,854.7	2,941.6	2,981.2	3,275.6	3,916.2
Imports, f.o.b.	71.vd	1,022.6	955.6	1,486.6	1,665.1	1,944.4	2,293.9	2,421.8	2,583.5	2,662.1	2,697.9	2,964.4	3,534.2
						2000=100							
Volume of Exports	72	71.6	66.1	68.3	78.2	58.6	76.8	69.8	100.0	133.4	117.8	93.6	109.3
Export Prices	74..d	90.1	98.4	132.4	118.6	135.6	138.2	102.9	100.0	101.0	95.2	83.1	102.2
Balance of Payments						*Millions of US Dollars: Minus Sign Indicates Debit*							
Current Account, n.i.e.	78ald	−308.7	−343.3	−200.9	−335.4	−272.2	−394.8	−624.6	−262.2	−339.2	−264.2	−314.3	−412.9
Goods: Exports f.o.b.	78aad	999.6	1,101.5	1,377.2	1,638.4	1,856.5	2,047.9	1,756.3	2,011.6	1,935.5	1,977.1	2,094.4	2,411.2
Goods: Imports f.o.b.	78abd	−1,203.1	−1,351.1	−1,518.6	−1,925.8	−2,150.4	−2,370.5	−2,509.6	−2,669.6	−2,769.4	−2,806.1	−3,059.0	−3,678.5
Trade Balance	78acd	−203.5	−249.6	−141.4	−287.4	−293.9	−322.6	−753.3	−658.0	−833.9	−829.0	−964.5	−1,267.3
Services: Credit	78add	223.9	242.4	257.6	283.3	334.9	377.1	474.1	478.9	487.3	530.4	598.5	654.6
Services: Debit	78aed	−294.7	−311.0	−333.7	−327.8	−360.9	−446.8	−502.4	−597.4	−626.6	−620.2	−677.2	−751.8
Balance on Goods & Services	78afd	−274.3	−318.2	−217.5	−331.9	−319.9	−392.3	−781.6	−776.5	−973.2	−918.8	−1,043.3	−1,364.4
Income: Credit	78agd	16.6	24.0	32.3	61.2	70.0	59.5	80.5	118.5	92.0	58.1	48.6	49.0
Income: Debit	78ahd	−215.3	−238.1	−258.2	−292.0	−281.8	−263.6	−235.7	−251.2	−262.0	−251.1	−300.6	−327.9
Balance on Gds, Serv. & Inc.	78aid	−473.0	−532.3	−443.4	−562.7	−531.7	−596.4	−936.8	−909.7	−1,143.3	−1,111.9	−1,295.3	−1,643.3
Current Transfers, n.i.e.: Credit	78ajd	165.5	190.2	243.7	271.7	306.8	241.7	354.6	717.9	894.0	946.7	1,085.0	1,358.8
Current Transfers: Debit	78akd	−1.2	−1.2	−1.2	−44.4	−47.3	−40.1	−42.4	−70.4	−89.9	−99.0	−104.0	−128.4
Capital Account, n.i.e.	78bcd	—	—	—	28.5	14.6	29.4	110.9	30.1	36.7	23.6	22.4	21.8
Capital Account, n.i.e.: Credit	78bad	—	—	—	29.2	15.3	29.4	110.9	30.1	36.7	23.6	22.4	21.8
Capital Account: Debit	78bbd	—	—	—	−.7	−.7	—	—	—	—	—	—	—
Financial Account, n.i.e.	78bjd	22.8	157.5	114.6	70.2	243.3	113.9	203.4	−28.8	123.6	158.2	72.2	724.1
Direct Investment Abroad	78bdd	—	—	—	—	—	—	—	—	—	—	—	—
Dir. Invest. in Rep. Econ., n.i.e.	78bed	26.7	34.8	50.0	90.9	121.5	99.0	237.3	281.9	193.1	175.3	247.1	293.0
Portfolio Investment Assets	78bfd	—	—	—	16.0	—	—	−72.4	−59.4	−3.6	−3.8	−4.1	−4.3
Equity Securities	78bkd	—	....	....	16.0	—	—	—	—	—	—	—	—
Debt Securities	78bld	—	—	—	....	....	—	−72.4	−59.4	−3.6	−3.8	−4.1	−4.3
Portfolio Investment Liab., n.i.e.	78bgd	—	—	—	....	....	—	—	−1.2	—	—	—	—
Equity Securities	78bmd	—	—	—	....	....	—	—	—	—	—	—	—
Debt Securities	78bnd	—	—	—	....	....	—	—	−1.2	—	—	—	—
Financial Derivatives Assets	78bwd	....	....	....	....	....	—	—	—	—	—	—	—
Financial Derivatives Liabilities	78bxd	....	....	....	....	....	−25.8	−16.1	—	—	—	—	—
Other Investment Assets	78bhd	−139.6	8.9	−12.8	−89.4	−53.4	−61.7	−132.2	−203.8	−99.1	23.3	−55.1	36.8
Monetary Authorities	78bod	3.9	3.3	11.7	....	....	—	—	—	−.—	—	—	—
General Government	78bpd	−132.0	14.4	14.4	....	....	—	—	—	—	—	—	—
Banks	78bqd	−11.5	−8.8	−38.9	−89.4	−53.4	−61.7	−132.2	−97.9	−65.1	−83.5	12.5	−6.5
Other Sectors	78brd	—	....	....	....	....	—	—	−105.9	−34.0	106.8	−67.6	43.3
Other Investment Liab., n.i.e.	78bid	135.7	113.8	77.4	52.7	175.2	102.4	186.8	−46.3	33.2	−36.6	−115.7	398.6
Monetary Authorities	78bsd	−73.6	−60.7	−73.1	−180.1	−24.1	−27.2	−22.2	−32.5	−20.6	−23.1	−15.7	−15.8
General Government	78btd	224.8	96.2	101.7	141.9	−48.4	−30.3	168.8	10.4	127.1	−6.2	21.9	198.4
Banks	78bud	1.7	−2.2	6.3	34.5	113.8	51.1	−11.5	−39.5	−43.6	−9.6	−12.8	78.8
Other Sectors	78bvd	−17.2	80.5	42.5	56.4	133.9	108.8	51.7	15.3	−29.7	2.3	−109.0	137.2
Net Errors and Omissions	78cad	−47.5	115.5	45.0	157.9	196.5	96.1	122.0	104.3	104.8	63.7	21.9	35.3
Overall Balance	78cbd	−333.4	−70.3	−41.3	−78.8	182.2	−155.4	−188.3	−156.6	−74.1	−18.7	−197.9	368.3
Reserves and Related Items	79dad	333.4	70.3	41.3	78.8	−182.2	155.4	188.3	156.6	74.1	18.7	197.9	−368.3
Reserve Assets	79dbd	99.6	−74.1	−90.3	12.7	−307.9	−229.8	−441.9	−32.3	−85.6	−92.0	100.2	−519.8
Use of Fund Credit and Loans	79dcd	6.4	−16.1	−13.7	−38.0	−8.8	64.8	99.5	16.4	12.0	−39.7	−41.1	15.1
Exceptional Financing	79ded	227.4	160.4	145.3	104.1	134.5	320.4	530.6	172.5	147.7	150.5	138.8	136.4

		1993	1994	1995	1996	1997	1998	1999	2000	2001	2002	2003	2004
Government Finance					*Millions of Lempiras: Year Ending December 31*								
Deficit (-) or Surplus........................	80	−1,447.7	−1,458.6	−1,326.1	−1,516.1	−1,260.2	−277.5	−1,115.4	−3,847.6	....	....	−6,526.7	−4,199.3
Total Revenue and Grants..............	81y	4,453.1	4,952.1	7,296.6	8,512.4	11,091.2	14,012.5	16,395.1	17,128.1	....	....	23,562.1	27,821.1
Revenue...................................	81	4,182.2	4,809.8	7,139.5	8,256.8	10,773.8	13,641.8	15,136.2	15,872.0	....	....	22,233.9	26,526.1
Grants.....................................	81z	270.9	142.3	157.1	255.6	317.4	370.7	1,258.9	1,256.1	....	....	1,328.2	1,295.0
Exp. & Lending Minus Repay..........	82z	5,900.8	6,410.7	8,622.7	10,028.5	12,351.4	14,290.0	17,510.5	20,975.7	....	....	30,088.8	32,020.4
Expenditure...............................	82	5,888.7	6,030.7	7,780.4	9,778.8	12,727.6	14,583.9	16,312.8	20,477.8	....	....	29,417.2	31,909.2
Lending Minus Repayments..........	83	12.1	380.0	842.3	249.7	−376.2	−293.9	1,197.7	497.9	....	....	671.6	111.2
Total Financing.............................	80h	1,447.7	1,458.6	1,326.1	1,516.1	1,260.2	277.5	1,115.4	3,847.6	....	....	6,526.7	4,199.3
Domestic.....................................	84a	−322.8	505.2	−134.8	337.4	129.0	−685.8	−3,282.5	1,722.4	....	....	3,980.3	−1,508.7
Foreign.......................................	85a	1,770.5	953.4	1,460.9	1,178.7	1,131.2	963.3	4,397.9	2,125.2	....	....	2,546.4	5,708.0
Total Debt by Residence.................	88	22,597.0	30,997.1	36,435.5	44,360.1	46,672.5	50,721.6	56,112.1	58,646.1	....	....	84,696.9	93,842.5
Domestic.....................................	88a	3,460.8	3,570.3	3,711.7	3,875.5	4,424.1	3,970.4	3,280.2	3,825.0	....	....	9,006.2	7,445.9
Foreign.......................................	89a	19,136.2	27,426.8	32,723.8	40,484.6	42,248.4	46,751.2	52,831.9	54,821.1	....	....	75,690.7	86,396.6
Memorandum Item:													
Intragovernmental Debt................	88s	−67.3	−332.2	−347.8	−394.1	−304.4	−330.2	−163.4	−20.3	....	....	−8.2	....
National Accounts						*Millions of Lempiras*							
Househ.Cons.Expend.,incl.NPISHs....	96f	14,718	18,113	23,819	30,782	39,626	46,930	53,168	63,119	72,198	82,063	91,627	....
Government Consumption Expend...	91f	2,405	2,780	3,495	4,556	5,422	7,117	8,726	11,218	13,792	14,925	16,209	....
Gross Fixed Capital Formation..........	93e	6,535	8,110	8,994	11,468	15,732	19,874	23,045	23,372	23,525	23,992	28,124	....
Changes in Inventories....................	93i	1,079	2,751	2,842	3,400	3,994	1,910	3,687	4,095	5,756	3,710	4,261	....
Exports of Goods and Services..........	90c	7,869	11,498	16,390	22,378	28,322	32,699	31,627	36,959	37,481	41,203	46,684	....
Imports of Goods and Services (-).....	98c	9,916	14,391	18,033	24,821	31,775	38,092	43,157	49,362	53,720	57,770	66,440	....
Gross Domestic Product (GDP)........	99b	22,689	28,862	37,507	47,763	61,322	70,438	77,096	89,401	99,032	108,124	120,465	....
Net Primary Income from Abroad.....	98.n	−1,498	−1,843	−2,532	−3,069	−2,812	−2,845	−2,335	−2,202	−2,788	−3,344	−4,665	....
Gross National Income (GNI)............	99a	21,191	27,019	34,975	44,694	58,510	67,593	74,761	87,199	96,245	104,780	115,799	....
Consumption of Fixed Capital..........	99cf	1,372	1,707	2,258	2,845	3,528	4,086	4,645	5,269	5,908	6,507	7,180	....
GDP Volume 1978 Prices.................	99b.p	5,985	5,907	6,148	6,368	6,686	6,880	6,750	7,138	7,324	7,523	7,785	....
GDP Volume (2000=100)................	99bvp	83.8	82.8	86.1	89.2	93.7	96.4	94.6	100.0	102.6	105.4	109.1	....
GDP Deflator (2000=100)................	99bip	30.3	39.0	48.7	59.9	73.2	81.7	91.2	100.0	108.0	114.8	123.5	....
						Millions: Midyear Estimates							
Population................................	99z	5.31	5.47	5.62	5.78	5.94	6.10	6.27	6.42	6.58	6.74	6.89	7.05

		1993	1994	1995	1996	1997	1998	1999	2000	2001	2002	2003	2004
Exchange Rates						*Forint per SDR: End of Period*							
Official Rate	aa	138.317	161.591	207.321	237.163	274.572	308.401	346.586	370.978	350.665	306.110	308.963	279.992
					Forint per US Dollar: End of Period (ae) Period Average (rf)								
Official Rate	ae	100.700	110.690	139.470	164.930	203.500	219.030	252.520	284.730	279.030	225.160	207.920	180.290
Official Rate	rf	91.933	105.160	125.681	152.647	186.789	214.402	237.146	282.179	286.490	257.887	224.307	202.746
					Index Numbers (2000=100): Period Averages								
Official Rate	ahx	306.8	267.5	224.8	184.4	151.0	131.2	118.7	100.0	98.2	109.4	125.4	138.9
Nominal Effective Exchange Rate	nec	229.0	202.8	158.1	135.5	125.9	112.3	105.8	100.0	101.9	109.4	109.3	111.7
Real Effective Exchange Rate	rec	96.0	95.0	91.3	93.7	98.5	97.7	99.3	100.0	105.8	117.3	121.7	131.4
Fund Position						*Millions of SDRs: End of Period*							
Quota	2f.s	755	755	755	755	755	755	1,038	1,038	1,038	1,038	1,038	1,038
SDRs	1b.s	2	1	1	—	—	1	3	9	16	24	31	38
Reserve Position in the Fund	1c.s	56	56	56	56	56	56	177	202	322	437	455	346
Total Fund Cred.&Loans Outstg	2tl	896	782	259	119	119	—	—	—	—	—	—	—
International Liquidity					*Millions of US Dollars Unless Otherwise Indicated: End of Period*								
Total Reserves minus Gold	1l.d	6,700	6,735	11,974	9,720	8,408	9,319	10,954	11,190	10,727	10,348	12,737	15,908
SDRs	1b.d	3	2	1	—	—	1	4	12	21	33	46	58
Reserve Position in the Fund	1c.d	77	82	83	81	76	79	243	263	405	595	676	538
Foreign Exchange	1d.d	6,620	6,652	11,890	9,639	8,332	9,239	10,707	10,915	10,302	9,721	12,015	15,312
Gold (Million Fine Troy Ounces)	1ad	.114	.110	.111	.101	.101	.101	.101	.101	.101	.101	.101	.099
Gold (National Valuation)	1and	45	42	43	37	29	29	29	28	28	35	42	43
Monetary Authorities:Other Liabs	4..d	17,244	19,191	20,836	16,239	11,647	11,677	9,847	8,537	6,614	5,338	4,393	2,976
Deposit Money Banks: Assets	7a.d	1,331	1,030	921	1,679	2,495	3,306	3,594	2,745	4,439	4,359	5,939	7,200
Liabilities	7b.d	1,783	2,379	2,878	3,077	4,482	5,464	5,577	5,514	5,966	7,432	13,667	18,912
Monetary Authorities						*Billions of Forint: End of Period*							
Foreign Assets	11	689.8	784.0	1,680.7	1,614.9	1,723.3	2,054.3	2,992.4	3,463.4	3,336.2	2,469.2	2,834.2	2,887.1
Claims on Consolidated Cent.Govt	12a	2,166.9	2,558.3	3,144.7	2,902.9	2,854.0	2,930.0	2,488.2	2,202.4	1,664.6	1,216.3	910.2	614.2
Other Claims on Residents	12d	4.4	4.4	3.8	.6	.7	.8	.7	.7	.7	.8	3.3	2.6
Claims on Banking Institutions	12e	368.8	405.8	302.6	231.4	185.3	178.4	126.6	93.8	46.9	22.8	12.5	11.0
Reserve Money	14	624.2	614.1	723.5	662.0	860.3	1,037.5	1,309.7	1,535.9	1,562.6	1,648.6	1,816.0	2,028.8
of which: Currency Outside DMBs	14a	371.2	410.7	443.9	497.7	562.6	669.0	855.3	883.9	1,037.6	1,181.9	1,346.8	1,341.5
Other Liabilities to Banks	14n	387.0	533.9	748.4	920.8	835.4	820.5	1,075.0	774.8	526.9	648.0	387.5	548.4
Time & Foreign Currency Deposits	15	4.1	7.0	8.6	6.9	7.8	21.4	15.3	12.9	6.4	6.7	7.2	4.9
Money Market Instruments	16aa	—	—	—	—	68.9	152.2	—	349.7	402.7	.1	.4	.3
Bonds	16ab	7.6	6.4	5.2	3.5	2.3	—	—	—	—	—	—	—
Liabs. of Central Bank: Securities	16ac	8.0	21.0	44.2	76.2	272.5	340.7	242.7	305.8	248.6	142.4	105.5	47.5
Foreign Liabilities	16c	140.6	148.3	104.9	57.8	138.2	42.6	137.0	334.4	268.3	121.4	127.6	57.4
Long-Term Foreign Liabilities	16cl	1,719.9	2,102.3	2,854.7	2,648.7	2,264.7	2,515.1	2,349.6	2,096.3	1,577.2	1,080.5	785.7	479.1
Consolidated Centr.Govt.Deposits	16d	341.1	316.8	561.8	389.9	328.4	194.1	555.8	434.4	745.1	197.7	297.8	345.6
Capital Accounts	17a	46.1	31.6	55.2	59.3	72.7	128.2	74.0	65.0	65.0	40.9	12.7	91.1
Other Items (Net)	17r	−48.1	−28.0	26.5	−74.1	−86.3	−87.2	−149.9	−147.5	−354.2	−177.3	219.7	−88.4
Banking Institutions						*Billions of Forint: End of Period*							
Reserves	20	234.6	194.1	273.7	154.0	291.1	365.6	447.5	646.9	519.6	464.1	406.8	677.3
Claims on Mon.Author.:Securities	20c	8.0	21.0	44.2	76.2	272.5	353.5	242.7	346.2	284.2	145.3	108.3	48.0
Other Claims on Monetary Author	20n	387.0	533.9	748.4	920.8	835.4	820.5	1,075.0	774.6	526.9	648.3	430.9	547.9
Foreign Assets	21	134.1	114.0	128.5	276.9	507.7	724.0	907.5	781.5	1,238.6	981.5	1,234.7	1,298.1
Claims on Consolidated Cent.Govt	22a	601.8	649.7	742.4	934.2	979.7	1,159.9	1,112.0	1,191.3	1,501.0	1,996.4	2,119.9	2,173.5
Claims on Local Government	22b	22.6	47.6	49.9	38.5	30.3	44.4	50.3	57.6	73.1	115.9	147.8	184.5
Other Claims on Residents	22d	1,003.8	1,152.9	1,263.1	1,520.7	† 2,076.9	2,440.4	2,968.0	4,247.6	5,007.8	5,989.2	7,986.0	9,479.5
Demand Deposits	24	512.4	553.9	561.4	730.6	960.9	1,120.8	1,275.7	1,491.8	1,738.3	2,113.3	2,287.1	2,308.0
Time, Savings,& Fgn.Currency Dep	25	1,061.6	1,266.0	1,696.7	2,074.9	2,437.2	2,781.1	3,161.6	3,592.2	4,165.7	4,626.6	5,272.7	6,052.6
Bonds	26ab	41.8	26.7	15.8	30.8	36.8	29.6	51.0	70.7	114.2	405.1	980.1	1,142.3
Foreign Liabilities	26c	90.6	134.3	196.0	307.9	593.3	689.2	746.7	725.8	610.4	562.7	1,036.5	1,070.5
Long-Term Foreign Liabilities	26cl	89.0	129.1	205.4	199.7	318.8	507.5	661.7	844.2	1,054.4	1,110.7	1,805.1	2,339.0
Consolidated Centr.Govt.Deposits	26d	16.1	31.1	13.0	10.0	7.6	5.0	4.7	23.3	28.6	27.8	54.2	60.2
Credit from Monetary Authorities	26g	368.8	405.8	302.6	231.4	185.3	178.4	126.6	91.5	44.6	21.1	11.6	10.7
Money Market Fund Shares	26m	....	....	9.7	23.9	35.1	47.6	71.2	81.5	121.6	186.3	174.5	299.2
Capital Accounts	27a	174.0	230.8	316.7	382.9	559.8	596.7	662.9	817.6	953.9	1,043.8	1,243.3	1,464.3
Other Items (Net)	27r	37.6	−64.5	−67.0	−70.6	−141.3	−47.6	40.9	307.3	319.6	243.1	−430.6	−338.0
Banking Survey						*Billions of Forint End of Period*							
Foreign Assets (Net)	31n	592.7	615.4	1,508.3	1,526.2	1,499.5	2,046.6	3,016.2	3,184.6	3,696.2	2,766.6	2,904.8	3,057.2
Domestic Credit	32	3,442.3	4,064.9	4,629.1	4,997.2	† 5,605.5	6,376.3	6,058.8	7,242.0	7,473.7	9,093.1	10,815.3	12,048.5
Claims on Cons.Cent.Govt.(Net)	32an	2,411.4	2,860.1	3,312.3	3,437.3	3,497.7	3,890.8	3,039.7	2,936.0	2,392.0	2,987.2	2,678.2	2,381.8
Claims on Local Government	32b	22.6	47.6	49.9	38.5	30.3	44.4	50.3	57.6	73.1	115.9	147.8	184.5
Other Claims on Residents	32d	1,008.2	1,157.2	1,266.9	1,521.4	† 2,077.6	2,441.2	2,968.8	4,248.3	5,008.6	5,990.0	7,989.3	9,482.1
Money	34	901.9	973.9	1,011.2	1,238.6	1,530.1	1,792.7	2,137.9	2,379.7	2,779.0	3,298.0	3,638.8	3,654.1
Quasi-Money	35	1,065.7	1,273.0	1,705.3	2,081.8	2,445.1	2,802.5	3,176.9	3,605.1	4,172.0	4,633.3	5,280.0	6,057.5
Money Market Instruments	36aa	—	—	—	—	68.9	152.2	—	349.7	402.7	.1	.4	.3
Bonds	36ab	49.4	33.1	21.0	34.4	39.0	29.6	51.0	70.7	114.2	405.1	980.1	1,142.3
Long-Term Foreign Liabilities	36cl	1,808.9	2,231.3	3,060.1	2,848.4	2,583.4	3,022.6	3,011.3	2,940.5	2,631.7	2,191.3	2,590.8	2,818.1
Money Market Fund Shares	36m	....	....	9.7	23.9	35.1	47.6	71.2	81.5	121.6	186.3	174.5	299.2
Capital Accounts	37a	220.1	262.4	371.8	442.2	632.5	724.9	736.9	882.6	1,018.9	1,084.7	1,255.9	1,555.4
Other Items (Net)	37r	−10.5	−92.5	−40.5	−144.7	−227.6	−147.5	−109.0	118.4	−70.1	61.0	−200.4	−421.3
Money plus Quasi-Money	35l	1,967.6	2,246.9	2,716.5	3,320.3	3,975.1	4,595.2	5,314.8	5,984.8	6,951.0	7,931.3	8,918.7	9,711.6
Money (National Definition)						*Billions of Forint: End of Period*							
Monetary Base	19ma	599.8	621.0	749.6	859.1	994.6	1,244.0	1,465.8	1,649.1	1,608.5	1,763.9	2,091.8	2,014.7
M1	59ma	882.6	1,038.1	1,166.4	1,374.8	1,703.3	1,987.4	2,358.4	2,653.8	3,113.3	3,648.0	4,027.6	4,169.3
M2	59mb	1,879.2	2,148.6	2,590.2	3,162.5	3,787.3	4,373.4	5,063.0	5,680.6	6,634.2	7,543.2	8,575.1	9,427.3
M3	59mc	1,892.1	2,157.2	2,605.4	3,196.7	3,923.1	4,585.2	5,187.3	6,129.5	7,177.7	7,846.9	8,788.8	9,804.5
M4	59md	2,223.5	2,628.1	3,285.5	4,170.2	5,293.9	6,352.9	7,557.1	8,690.1	10,058.9	11,387.4	13,084.1	14,504.6

		1993	1994	1995	1996	1997	1998	1999	2000	2001	2002	2003	2004
Interest Rates							*Percent Per Annum*						
Discount Rate (End of Period)..........	60	22.0	25.0	28.0	23.0	20.5	17.0	14.5	11.0	9.8	8.5	12.5	9.5
Treasury Bill Rate............................	60c	17.2	26.9	32.0	24.0	20.1	17.8	14.7	11.0	10.8	8.9	8.2	11.3
Deposit Rate..................................	60l	15.7	20.3	† 24.4	18.6	16.9	14.4	11.9	9.5	8.4	7.4	11.0	9.1
Lending Rate.................................	60p	25.4	27.4	32.6	27.3	21.8	19.3	16.3	12.6	12.1	10.2	9.6	12.8
Prices, Production, Labor						*Index Numbers (2000=100): Period Averages*							
Producer Prices..............................	63	36.2	40.6	52.2	63.6	76.5	85.2	89.5	100.0	104.8	103.3	105.8	109.6
Consumer Prices.............................	64	32.5	38.6	† 49.6	61.3	72.5	82.8	91.1	100.0	109.2	115.0	120.3	128.5
Harmonized CPI (2002=100)..........	64h	....	....	....	....	....	....	....	....	....	100.0	104.7	111.8
Wages: Avg. Earnings.....................	65	31.9	40.0	46.4	54.6	67.7	79.1	88.7	100.0	113.2	130.2	146.7	159.1
Industrial Production........................	66	48.5	53.2	59.4	61.4	68.2	76.7	84.6	100.0	103.6	106.4	113.2	122.6
Industrial Employment.....................	67	116.2	108.3	102.5	97.1	96.4	97.9	98.7	100.0	99.3	97.3	95.3	93.0
						Number in Thousands: Period Averages							
Labor Force....................................	67d	....	4,144	4,095	4,048	3,995	4,011	4,096	4,112	4,102	4,109	4,167	4,153
Employment...................................	67e	3,827	3,752	3,679	3,648	3,646	3,698	3,811	3,849	3,868	3,871	3,922	3,900
Unemployment...............................	67c	519	449	417	400	349	313	285	263	234	239	245	253
Unemployment Rate (%).................	67r	11.9	10.7	10.2	9.9	8.7	7.8	7.0	6.4	5.7	5.8	5.9	6.1
Intl. Transactions & Positions							*Billions of Forint*						
Exports...	70	819.9	1,101.4	1,622.1	2,392.1	3,567.0	4,934.4	5,938.6	7,942.8	8,748.3	8,874.0	9,528.6	11,093.9
Imports, c.i.f.................................	71	1,153.5	1,505.7	1,936.1	2,764.0	3,961.0	5,511.4	6,645.6	9,064.0	9,665.0	9,704.1	10,662.8	12,063.7
Imports, f.o.b.................................	71.v	1,162.5	1,518.1	1,913.1	2,735.5	3,919.9	5,451.0	6,558.0	8,958.4	9,534.9	9,578.8	10,513.7	11,869.4
							2000=100						
Volume of Exports..........................	72	33.6	39.3	42.6	44.5	† 57.8	70.9	82.2	100.0	107.8	114.1	124.2	145.6
Volume of Imports..........................	73	39.6	45.3	43.5	45.9	† 58.0	72.4	82.8	100.0	104.0	109.3	120.4	137.0
Export Prices.................................	76	36.3	42.8	57.3	67.6	77.7	87.7	91.0	100.0	102.2	97.1	96.7	95.2
Import Prices.................................	76.x	35.7	41.8	55.0	66.4	75.3	83.9	88.6	100.0	102.5	96.9	97.0	96.2
Balance of Payments					*Millions of US Dollars: Minus Sign Indicates Debit*								
Current Account, n.i.e......................	78ald	−4,262	−4,054	−1,650	−1,766	−2,080	−3,391	−3,775	−4,004	−3,205	−4,693	−7,211	−8,819
Goods: Exports f.o.b......................	78aad	8,119	7,648	14,619	15,966	19,284	23,698	25,608	28,762	31,080	34,792	43,475	55,368
Goods: Imports f.o.b......................	78abd	−12,140	−11,364	−16,078	−17,640	−20,611	−25,583	−27,778	−31,675	−33,318	−36,911	−46,753	−58,290
Trade Balance............................	78acd	−4,021	−3,716	−1,459	−1,673	−1,328	−1,885	−2,170	−2,913	−2,237	−2,119	−3,278	−2,922
Services: Credit............................	78add	2,836	3,117	5,146	5,866	5,793	5,401	5,213	5,901	7,029	7,417	8,693	10,093
Services: Debit.............................	78aed	−2,620	−2,958	−3,839	−3,979	−4,049	−4,198	−4,360	−4,775	−5,550	−6,849	−9,116	−10,121
Balance on Goods & Services......	78afd	−3,805	−3,557	−152	213	416	−682	−1,317	−1,787	−759	−1,551	−3,701	−2,950
Income: Credit............................	78agd	465	676	983	1,321	1,546	1,252	902	1,165	1,302	1,236	1,376	1,294
Income: Debit.............................	78ahd	−1,655	−2,082	−2,684	−3,297	−4,246	−4,205	−3,794	−3,740	−4,152	−4,870	−5,552	−7,424
Balance on Gds, Serv. & Inc.......	78aid	−4,995	−4,963	−1,852	−1,764	−2,283	−3,635	−4,208	−4,361	−3,609	−5,184	−7,877	−9,079
Current Transfers, n.i.e.: Credit......	78ajd	2,694	2,871	482	270	463	510	711	674	781	1,070	1,282	1,646
Current Transfers: Debit.................	78akd	−1,961	−1,961	−279	−272	−260	−266	−278	−316	−377	−579	−616	−1,386
Capital Account, n.i.e.....................	78bcd	—	—	60	156	117	189	29	270	317	191	−27	396
Capital Account, n.i.e.: Credit..........	78bad	—	—	80	266	266	408	509	458	417	238	240	595
Capital Account: Debit..................	78bbd	—	—	−20	−110	−149	−219	−480	−188	−101	−48	−267	−199
Financial Account, n.i.e...................	78bjd	6,083	3,370	5,706	−429	2,095	4,439	6,469	4,960	2,775	2,565	7,329	10,452
Direct Investment Abroad..............	78bdd	−11	−49	−59	4	−449	−278	−248	−589	−364	−282	−1,663	−535
Dir. Invest. in Rep. Econ., n.i.e......	78bed	2,350	1,144	4,804	3,289	4,155	3,343	3,308	2,770	3,944	3,013	2,202	4,184
Portfolio Investment Assets............	78bfd	−8	6	−1	−35	−134	−93	−75	−309	−149	−43	15	−433
Equity Securities.........................	78bkd	—	−10	—	−15	−32	−45	16	−151	−55	−50	−42	−438
Debt Securities...........................	78bld	−8	16	—	−20	−102	−48	−91	−158	−95	7	57	5
Portfolio Investment Liab., n.i.e......	78bgd	3,927	2,458	2,213	−396	−939	1,925	2,065	−141	1,523	1,844	2,902	7,484
Equity Securities.........................	78bmd	46	224	−62	359	979	556	1,191	−369	134	−137	269	1,491
Debt Securities...........................	78bnd	3,881	2,234	2,275	−754	−1,918	1,369	874	229	1,389	1,982	2,633	5,993
Financial Derivatives Assets............	78bwd	....	....	157	17	12	185	852	754	582	1,796	2,320	4,205
Financial Derivatives Liabilities........	78bxd	....	....	102	−1	−4	−38	−899	−698	−471	−1,647	−2,069	−3,795
Other Investment Assets................	78bhd	881	362	−1,083	−2,013	−1,095	−591	−579	939	−2,754	−1,599	−2,374	−3,396
Monetary Authorities..................	78bod	....	....	−17	14	1	4	—	−8	4	36	−1,049	1,100
General Government....................	78bpd	811	156	27	44	189	75	30	38	−9	14	198	−66
Banks......................................	78bqd	−127	191	125	−1,129	−789	−333	−430	755	−1,463	528	−951	−350
Other Sectors...........................	78brd	198	15	−1,218	−942	−496	−337	−178	154	−1,287	−2,176	−573	−4,080
Other Investment Liab., n.i.e...........	78bid	−1,055	−551	−427	−1,294	549	−13	2,046	2,232	465	−517	5,996	2,737
Monetary Authorities..................	78bsd	54	17	−906	−1,875	−659	−15	286	613	−644	−622	588	−916
General Government....................	78btd	−1,541	−1,761	−438	−331	−106	−288	235	−225	−47	766	319	162
Banks......................................	78bud	−69	365	323	394	1,123	619	522	401	294	647	3,986	2,334
Other Sectors...........................	78bvd	501	828	595	518	190	−329	1,002	1,442	862	−1,308	1,103	1,157
Net Errors and Omissions................	78cad	724	209	1,267	802	−307	−285	−389	−174	29	145	245	−47
Overall Balance...........................	78cbd	2,545	−475	5,384	−1,237	−175	951	2,335	1,052	−84	−1,792	336	1,981
Reserves and Related Items.............	79dad	−2,545	475	−5,384	1,237	175	−951	−2,335	−1,052	84	1,792	−336	−1,981
Reserve Assets............................	79dbd	−2,574	640	−4,599	1,441	175	−791	−2,335	−1,052	84	1,792	−336	−1,981
Use of Fund Credit and Loans........	79dcd	30	−165	−785	−203	—	−160	—	—	—	—	—	—
Exceptional Financing...................	79ded	....	....	—	—	—	—	—	—	—	—	—	—

Hungary 944

		1993	1994	1995	1996	1997	1998	1999	2000	2001	2002	2003	2004
International Investment Position						*Millions of US Dollars*							
Assets	79aad	....	....	....	....	14,952	16,989	19,845	19,629	22,743	24,288	32,123	42,289
Direct Investment Abroad	79abd	....	....	....	....	647	784	924	1,280	1,556	2,166	3,537	4,484
Portfolio Investment	79acd	....	....	....	....	171	293	367	667	814	931	1,045	1,569
Equity Securities	79add	....	....	....	....	32	87	73	221	271	355	425	908
Debt Securities	79aed	....	....	....	....	139	206	294	447	543	576	620	661
Financial Derivatives	79ald	....	....	....	....	—	9	880	859	1,165	909	1,604	2,481
Other Investment	79afd	....	....	....	....	5,698	6,556	6,690	5,606	8,452	9,898	13,157	17,804
Monetary Authorities	79agd	....	....	....	....	32	23	20	75	63	30	1,107	23
General Government	79ahd	....	....	....	....	657	570	530	469	478	531	418	469
Banks	79aid	....	....	....	....	2,323	3,083	3,387	2,559	4,040	3,862	5,313	6,421
Other Sectors	79ajd	....	....	....	....	2,686	2,879	2,753	2,503	3,871	5,475	6,318	10,890
Reserve Assets	79akd	....	....	....	....	8,437	9,348	10,983	11,217	10,755	10,383	12,780	15,951
Liabilities	79lad	....	....	....	....	42,987	47,827	53,873	53,010	58,653	73,854	102,834	136,764
Dir. Invest. in Rep. Economy	79lbd	....	....	....	....	17,968	20,733	23,260	22,870	27,407	36,224	48,320	60,328
Portfolio Investment	79lcd	....	....	....	....	12,408	14,558	16,955	14,812	15,691	20,910	27,793	44,013
Equity Securities	79ldd	....	....	....	....	2,494	2,341	4,356	2,986	2,906	3,784	5,604	12,079
Debt Securities	79led	....	....	....	....	9,914	12,217	12,599	11,825	12,786	17,126	22,189	31,935
Financial Derivatives	79lld	....	....	....	....	450	11	164	276	483	624	2,000	2,605
Other Investment	79lfd	....	....	....	....	12,161	12,524	13,494	15,053	15,072	16,096	24,720	29,817
Monetary Authorities	79lgd	....	....	....	....	1,216	1,094	1,322	1,863	1,165	574	1,240	357
General Government	79lhd	....	....	....	....	1,635	1,380	1,532	1,246	1,167	2,118	2,806	3,216
Banks	79lid	....	....	....	....	4,290	5,185	5,297	5,476	5,581	6,784	11,993	15,652
Other Sectors	79ljd	....	....	....	....	5,019	4,866	5,343	6,468	7,159	6,620	8,681	10,592
Government Finance						*Billions of Forint: Year Ending December 31*							
Deficit (-) or Surplus	80	−202.9	−310.8	−355.5	−213.1	−383.6	−631.5	−420.0	−449.3	−444.8	−1,569.0	−1,062.9	−1,284.1
Total Revenue and Grants	81y	1,716.1	2,085.4	2,393.6	2,908.9	3,205.9	4,072.5	4,663.1	5,228.1	5,831.5	6,191.5	6,942.8	7,690.3
Revenue	81	1,716.1	2,085.2	2,393.4	2,908.5	3,205.3	4,065.5	4,649.9	5,193.7	5,801.1	6,152.8	6,902.4	7,375.7
Grants	81z	—	.2	.2	.4	.6	7.0	13.2	34.4	30.4	38.7	40.4	314.6
Exp. & Lending Minus Repay	82z	1,919.0	2,396.2	2,749.1	3,122.0	3,589.5	4,704.0	5,083.1	5,677.4	6,276.3	7,760.5	8,005.7	8,974.4
Expenditure	82	1,985.6	2,390.9	2,734.4	3,122.1	3,644.0	4,671.6	5,070.0	5,682.5	6,273.3	7,672.0	8,040.6	8,998.2
Lending Minus Repayments	83	−66.6	5.3	14.7	−.1	−54.5	32.4	13.1	−5.1	3.0	88.5	−34.9	−23.8
Total Financing	80h	203.0	310.8	355.5	213.2	....	....	....	....	444.8	1,569.0	1,062.9	1,284.1
Total Net Borrowing	84	221.8	203.9	204.4	380.6	....	....	....	....	635.9	1,279.1	1,062.8	1,420.6
Net Domestic	84a	216.7	202.4	198.5	373.7	....	....	....	....	408.0	1,028.2	476.2	770.7
Net Foreign	85a	5.1	1.5	5.9	6.9	....	....	....	....	227.9	250.9	586.6	649.9
Use of Cash Balances	87	−18.8	106.9	151.1	−167.4	....	....	....	....	−191.1	289.9	.1	−136.5
Total Debt by Residence	88	3,181.6	3,801.0	4,781.6	4,959.1	5,405.7	6,161.5	6,890.5	7,228.7	7,721.6	9,223.7	10,588.1	11,592.4
Domestic	88a	2,978.9	3,564.5	4,461.7	4,669.2	5,055.4	5,867.3	5,940.0	6,144.2	6,486.1	7,806.0	8,494.4	8,996.7
Foreign	89a	202.7	236.5	319.9	289.9	350.3	294.2	950.5	1,084.5	1,235.5	1,417.7	2,093.7	2,595.7
Memorandum Item:													
Privatization Receipts	83a	7.2	31.0	150.0	219.9	161.9	13.0	4.0	.9	....	....	....	....
National Accounts						*Billions of Forint*							
Househ.Cons.Expend.,incl.NPISHs	96f	2,639.9	3,151.7	3,730.3	4,400.4	5,283.0	6,297.2	7,274.2	8,334.9	9,574.7	11,077.8	12,592.5	13,850.5
Government Consumption Expend	91f	491.4	527.1	617.7	703.6	900.8	1,024.6	1,156.7	1,273.3	1,513.7	1,826.7	2,041.3	2,166.1
Gross Fixed Capital Formation	93e	670.0	878.5	1,125.4	1,475.5	1,898.9	2,384.6	2,724.5	3,099.1	3,493.0	3,916.9	4,141.3	4,598.9
Changes in Inventories	93i	38.1	90.1	143.4	282.5	370.6	526.0	548.0	971.8	487.9	307.3	462.5	324.2
Exports of Goods and Services	90c	937.0	1,262.5	2,505.2	3,341.8	4,709.2	6,247.0	7,329.0	9,820.3	10,913.0	10,843.5	11,688.3	13,238.3
Imports of Goods and Services (-)	98c	1,228.1	1,545.1	2,507.9	3,310.0	4,621.8	6,392.0	7,639.0	10,327.3	11,132.5	11,231.8	12,517.1	13,839.9
Gross Domestic Product (GDP)	99b	3,548.3	4,364.8	5,614.0	6,893.9	8,540.7	10,087.4	11,393.5	13,172.3	14,849.8	16,740.4	18,408.8	20,338.2
GDP Volume 1991 Prices	99b.p	2,407.8	2,478.8	2,515.7	....	....	....	....	....	....	....	....	....
GDP Volume 2000 Prices	99b.p	....	....	10,820.8	10,963.6	11,464.2	12,021.4	12,520.7	13,172.3	13,679.4	14,157.4	14,574.0	15,190.0
GDP Volume (2000=100)	99bvp	78.6	80.9	†82.1	83.2	87.0	91.3	95.1	100.0	103.8	107.5	110.6	115.3
GDP Deflator (2000=100)	99bip	34.3	40.9	51.9	62.9	74.5	83.9	91.0	100.0	108.6	118.2	126.3	133.9
						Millions: Midyear Estimates							
Population	99z	10.34	10.34	10.33	10.32	10.30	10.27	10.25	10.23	10.20	10.18	10.15	10.12

Iceland 176

		1993	1994	1995	1996	1997	1998	1999	2000	2001	2002	2003	2004
Exchange Rates						*Kronur per SDR: End of Period*							
Official Rate	aa	99.899	99.708	96.964	96.185	97.389	97.605	99.576	110.356	129.380	109.550	105.489	94.796
						Kronur per US Dollar: End of Period (ae) Period Average (rf)							
Official Rate	ae	72.730	68.300	65.230	66.890	72.180	69.320	72.550	84.700	102.950	80.580	70.990	61.040
Official Rate	rf	67.603	69.944	64.692	66.500	70.904	70.958	72.335	78.616	97.425	91.662	76.709	70.192
					Index Numbers (2000=100): Period Averages								
Official Rate	ahx	116.2	112.0	121.1	117.7	110.4	110.4	108.3	100.0	80.8	85.8	102.1	111.8
Nominal Effective Exchange Rate	nec	95.4	94.3	95.4	95.6	97.8	100.3	99.9	100.0	84.7	87.0	91.7	93.1
Real Effective Exchange Rate	rec	97.2	91.3	91.0	91.4	93.3	95.7	97.3	100.0	88.2	93.8	99.0	101.6
Fund Position						*Millions of SDRs: End of Period*							
Quota	2f.s	85.3	85.3	85.3	85.3	85.3	85.3	117.6	117.6	117.6	117.6	117.6	117.6
SDRs	1b.s	—	.1	—	—	—	—	—	—	.1	.1	—	.1
Reserve Position in the Fund	1c.s	10.5	10.5	10.5	10.5	10.5	10.5	18.6	18.6	18.6	18.6	18.6	18.6
Total Fund Cred.&Loans Outstg	2tl	—	—	—	—	—	—	—	—	—	—	—	—
International Liquidity					*Millions of US Dollars Unless Otherwise Indicated: End of Period*								
Total Reserves minus Gold	1l.d	426.4	292.9	308.1	453.7	383.7	426.4	478.4	388.9	338.2	440.1	792.3	1,046.2
SDRs	1b.d	.1	.1	—	—	—	—	—	—	.1	.1	—	.1
Reserve Position in the Fund	1c.d	14.4	15.3	15.6	15.1	14.2	14.8	25.5	24.2	23.3	25.3	27.6	28.9
Foreign Exchange	1d.d	412.0	277.5	292.5	438.6	369.5	411.6	452.9	364.6	314.8	414.7	764.6	1,017.3
Gold (Million Fine Troy Ounces)	1ad	.049	.049	.049	.049	.049	.056	.056	.059	.062	.063	.063	.064
Gold (National Valuation)	1and	2.4	2.5	2.6	2.7	2.6	2.8	† 17.0	16.4	17.0	21.4	26.4	28.0
Monetary Authorities: Other Liab	4..d	36.8	137.5	176.5	75.5	75.1	130.9	67.5	186.1	145.5	204.8	1.7	2.3
Deposit Money Banks: Assets	7a.d	124.0	152.6	87.0	108.6	133.0	119.0	218.1	266.0	324.0	1,491.0	1,592.5	2,743.2
Liabilities	7b.d	593.0	464.1	419.4	639.0	875.8	1,477.8	1,989.9	2,649.4	2,503.0	2,807.6	3,046.2	3,648.7
Monetary Authorities						*Millions of Kronur: End of Period*							
Foreign Assets	11	31,318	24,347	25,961	36,151	33,274	35,136	† 37,139	34,495	36,819	37,376	58,272	65,718
Claims on Central Government	12a	12,865	24,546	18,476	10,534	12,852	5,011	† 3,988	4,579	2,466	1,841	758	72
Claims on Private Sector	12d	330	408	413	487	142	113	† 86	52	28	41	44	45
Claims on Deposit Money Banks	12e	2,630	2,226	5,353	1,878	6,496	19,600	† 29,520	38,978	54,053	69,141	24,038	31,771
Claims on Other Financial Insts	12f	639	4,490	3,380	3,443	3,472	7,770	† 9,672	13,074	22,774	8,227	4,193	8,993
Reserve Money	14	20,333	20,949	17,164	21,691	24,153	24,690	† 38,442	33,921	29,942	33,961	21,732	52,249
of which: Currency Outside DMBs	14a	3,906	4,641	5,169	5,475	5,751	6,322	† 7,125	7,151	7,406	7,666	8,390	9,153
Foreign Liabilities	16c	2,678	9,389	11,513	5,049	5,418	9,073	† 4,900	15,763	14,979	16,499	124	142
Central Government Deposits	16d	7,350	7,419	6,177	6,850	6,438	13,176	† 15,550	16,594	33,488	22,667	22,901	17,833
Capital Accounts	17a	16,135	16,656	16,849	17,613	19,217	19,652	† 20,320	23,422	36,456	40,629	41,952	35,775
Other Items (Net)	17r	1,286	1,602	1,879	1,290	1,009	1,039	† 1,192	1,477	1,275	2,869	595	601
Deposit Money Banks						*Millions of Kronur: End of Period*							
Reserves	20	11,747	11,540	10,325	13,418	14,100	13,990	29,026	25,731	20,701	† 25,294	13,294	29,395
Foreign Assets	21	6,835	8,105	5,213	7,285	11,076	11,276	13,699	20,641	29,939	† 45,715	113,053	167,447
Claims on Central Government	22a	26,746	19,168	11,432	13,241	10,578	6,287	7,271	4,126	13,077	† 9,037	17,168	4,551
Claims on Private Sector	22d	193,643	196,262	208,982	236,720	348,883	376,255	461,004	663,599	772,541	† 858,886	1,097,188	1,514,887
Claims on Other Financial Insts	22f	4,265	4,485	1,750	1,167	1,680	375	934	2,486	2,167	†		
Demand Deposits	24	27,663	30,313	33,146	36,081	42,600	51,852	63,346	65,117	63,413	† 80,089	106,362	129,428
Savings Deposits	25	132,526	132,482	133,341	140,725	150,977	171,434	198,763	225,879	271,691	† 306,132	367,306	406,967
Bonds	26a	22,699	22,337	24,095	32,166	40,731	53,419	62,938	169,070	196,279	† 274,353	564,111	998,127
Restricted Deposits	26b	—	—	6	2	5	2	1	—	—	†		
Foreign Liabilities	26c	43,127	31,697	27,356	42,741	63,215	102,438	144,370	224,406	257,682	† 226,236	216,253	222,718
Credit from Monetary Authorities	26g	1,600	4,833	4,860	1,954	6,480	21,000	30,797	39,016	54,194	† 69,311	24,062	33,256
Capital Accounts	27a	22,446	23,186	23,296	27,617	28,907	35,604	42,424	66,448	95,709	† 116,685	157,014	333,820
Other Items (Net)	27r	−8,757	−7,623	−8,278	−9,330	53,400	−27,551	−30,706	−73,352	−100,540	† −133,875	−194,406	−408,035
Monetary Survey						*Millions of Kronur: End of Period*							
Foreign Assets (Net)	31n	−7,652	−8,635	−7,695	−4,354	−24,282	−65,099	† −98,432	−185,033	−205,903	† −159,644	−45,053	10,306
Domestic Credit	32	231,138	241,940	238,256	258,743	371,168	382,635	† 467,406	671,321	779,565	† 855,364	1,096,450	1,510,715
Claims on Central Govt. (Net)	32an	32,260	36,295	23,731	16,925	16,991	−1,878	† −4,291	−7,889	−17,946	† −11,789	−4,975	−13,210
Claims on Private Sector	32d	193,973	196,670	209,395	237,207	349,025	376,368	† 461,090	663,651	772,569	† 858,927	1,097,232	1,514,931
Claims on Other Financial Inst	32f	4,904	8,975	5,130	4,610	5,152	8,145	† 10,606	15,560	24,942	† 8,227	4,193	8,993
Money	34	31,569	34,954	38,315	41,556	48,351	58,174	† 70,471	72,268	70,819	† 87,755	114,751	138,581
Quasi-Money	35	132,526	132,482	133,341	140,725	150,977	171,434	198,763	225,879	271,691	† 306,132	367,306	406,967
Bonds	36a	22,699	22,337	24,095	32,166	40,731	53,419	62,938	169,070	196,279	† 274,353	564,111	998,127
Capital Accounts	37a	38,581	39,842	40,145	45,230	48,124	55,256	† 62,744	89,870	132,165	† 157,314	198,966	369,595
Other Items (Net)	37r	−3,821	1,354	−5,215	−5,163	58,700	−20,732	† −25,944	−70,798	−97,289	† −129,834	−193,739	−392,249
Money plus Quasi-Money	35l	164,095	167,436	171,656	182,281	199,328	229,608	† 269,234	298,147	342,510	† 393,888	482,058	545,548
Interest Rates						*Percent Per Annum*							
Discount Rate (End of Period)	60	....	4.70	5.93	5.70	6.55	† 8.50	10.00	12.40	12.00	8.20	7.70	10.25
Money Market Rate	60b	8.61	4.96	6.58	6.96	7.38	8.12	9.24	11.61	14.51	11.21	5.14	6.09
Treasury Bill Rate	60c	8.35	4.95	7.22	6.97	7.04	7.40	8.61	11.12	11.03	8.01	4.93	6.04
Deposit Rate	60l	6.63	3.03	3.69	4.25	4.72	4.50	4.82	7.11	6.94	4.69	4.81	4.85
Housing Bond Rate	60m	....	5.75	5.80	5.78	5.30	4.71	4.78	6.31	6.07	5.18	4.64	4.64
Lending Rate	60p	14.11	10.57	11.58	12.43	12.89	12.78	13.30	16.80	17.95	15.37	11.95	12.02
Government Bond Yield	61	6.80	5.02	7.18	5.61	5.49	4.73	4.28	5.35	5.33	5.23	4.41	3.88
Prices, Production, Labor						*Index Numbers (2000=100): Period Averages*							
Consumer Prices	64	84.3	85.6	87.0	89.0	90.6	92.1	95.1	100.0	106.4	111.9	† 114.2	117.4
Wages	65a	66.6	67.6	71.6	75.1	81.2	87.5	92.9	100.0	109.6	115.5	121.7	129.0
Total Fish Catch	66al	100.3	86.2	92.0	117.4	133.5	91.5	86.1	100.0	117.0	126.2	118.2	103.0
						Number in Thousands: Period Averages							
Labor Force	67d	144	145	149	148	148	152	157	160	163	162	162	161
Employment	67e	137	138	142	142	142	148	153	156	159	157	157	156
Unemployment	67c	6	6	7	6	5	4	3	2	2	4	5	5
Unemployment Rate (%)	67r	4.3	4.7	4.9	4.4	3.9	2.8	1.9	1.4	1.4	2.5	3.3	3.1

		1993	1994	1995	1996	1997	1998	1999	2000	2001	2002	2003	2004
Intl. Transactions & Positions							*Millions of Kronur*						
Exports................................	70	94,711	113,279	116,613	108,977	131,228	145,008	145,132	148,516	196,803	204,078	182,960	202,824
Fish......................................	70al	45,754	54,644	50,535	46,030	46,712	54,722	60,028	57,442	66,986	72,691	68,422	69,289
Fishmeal..............................	70z	5,015	4,757	4,789	8,792	9,460	9,896	7,404	9,299	12,906	18,064	13,044	6,020
Imports, c.i.f........................	71	90,775	102,499	113,388	135,165	141,355	176,521	181,321	203,847	218,296	207,632	213,590	249,063
							1995=100						
Volume of Exports................	72	91.3	102.3	100.0	109.0	111.1	107.9	....	....	....	....	....	....
Volume of Imports................	73	87.4	93.9	100.0	116.5	123.7	154.2	....	....	....	....	....	....
Unit Value of Exports...........	74	91.3	95.4	100.0	98.4	99.6	....	....	....	....	....	....	....
Unit Value of Imports...........	75	90.9	96.1	100.0	102.7	103.4	....	....	....	....	....	....	....
Balance of Payments						*Millions of US Dollars: Minus Sign Indicates Debit*							
Current Account, n.i.e...........	78ald	37	116	52	−131	−128	−555	−589	−847	−336	128	−534	−1,055
Goods: Exports f.o.b.............	78aad	1,399	1,560	1,804	1,890	1,855	1,927	2,009	1,902	2,016	2,240	2,386	2,897
Goods: Imports f.o.b.............	78abd	−1,218	−1,288	−1,598	−1,871	−1,850	−2,279	−2,316	−2,376	−2,091	−2,090	−2,596	−3,415
Trade Balance......................	78acd	181	272	206	19	5	−351	−307	−474	−75	150	−210	−519
Services: Credit....................	78add	601	619	691	768	843	953	930	1,044	1,086	1,122	1,377	1,620
Services: Debit.....................	78aed	−592	−577	−642	−741	−802	−965	−1,027	−1,164	−1,074	−1,123	−1,501	−1,835
Balance on Goods & Services......	78afd	190	314	255	46	47	−363	−404	−595	−63	149	−334	−733
Income: Credit......................	78agd	85	72	82	104	101	120	129	147	171	305	372	597
Income: Debit.......................	78ahd	−235	−262	−280	−274	−272	−298	−304	−390	−435	−341	−556	−902
Balance on Gds, Serv. & Inc.....	78aid	40	124	56	−124	−125	−541	−579	−837	−326	114	−518	−1,038
Current Transfers, n.i.e.: Credit.......	78ajd	18	12	15	10	17	4	5	6	8	36	12	10
Current Transfers: Debit........	78akd	−21	−21	−20	−17	−20	−18	−15	−16	−17	−22	−28	−27
Capital Account, n.i.e............	78bcd	−1	−6	−4	—	—	−5	−1	−3	4	−1	−5	−3
Capital Account, n.i.e.: Credit.......	78bad	11	6	12	10	11	9	17	17	15	14	15	32
Capital Account: Debit..........	78bbd	−12	−12	−17	−10	−11	−14	−18	−21	−12	−15	−20	−35
Financial Account, n.i.e.........	78bjd	−48	−291	2	318	203	683	864	846	172	38	531	2,158
Direct Investment Abroad......	78bdd	−15	−23	−25	−64	−57	−75	−125	−375	−332	−339	−374	−2,596
Dir. Invest. in Rep. Econ., n.i.e......	78bed	—	−1	−9	83	148	150	65	155	166	96	322	312
Portfolio Investment Assets...........	78bfd	−31	−72	−64	−51	−202	−303	−448	−667	−64	−337	−593	−1,094
Equity Securities...............	78bkd	−12	−24	−44	−68	−180	−253	−369	−651	−67	−287	−531	−1,031
Debt Securities.................	78bld	−19	−48	−20	17	−22	−51	−79	−16	3	−50	−62	−64
Portfolio Investment Liab., n.i.e.....	78bgd	305	242	215	175	−39	68	1,030	1,142	665	575	3,591	8,422
Equity Securities...............	78bmd	—	—	—	1	−1	14	56	−44	43	55	−72	289
Debt Securities.................	78bnd	305	242	214	174	−38	54	974	1,186	622	521	3,663	8,134
Financial Derivatives Assets...........	78bwd	—	−49	−17	—	—	—	59	15	—	—	—	—
Financial Derivatives Liabilities.......	78bxd	—	55	16	−1	−1	−1	−57	−16	—	—	—	—
Other Investment Assets........	78bhd	−28	−31	25	−30	−162	2	−173	−79	−475	−336	−2,076	−3,447
Monetary Authorities............	78bod	—	—	—	—	—	—	—	—	—	—	—	—
General Government.............	78bpd	—	—	—	—	—	—	—	—	—	—	—	—
Banks..................................	78bqd	−28	−17	49	−37	−86	28	−92	−71	−216	−380	−2,157	−3,187
Other Sectors......................	78brd	—	−15	−24	7	−76	−26	−81	−8	−259	43	81	−260
Other Investment Liab., n.i.e........	78bid	−280	−412	−139	206	517	843	511	671	213	379	−339	562
Monetary Authorities............	78bsd	22	41	21	−99	—	55	−3	142	−33	48	−206	—
General Government.............	78btd	−46	−76	60	−17	34	81	43	27	79	41	−76	−51
Banks..................................	78bud	−69	−158	−54	288	307	420	441	332	−104	296	−37	668
Other Sectors......................	78bvd	−187	−219	−166	34	176	287	31	170	271	−5	−20	−55
Net Errors and Omissions................	78cad	−47	31	−45	−33	−119	−91	−189	−70	111	−104	315	−898
Overall Balance....................	78cbd	−59	−150	4	153	−44	32	86	−74	−48	61	307	202
Reserves and Related Items...........	79dad	59	150	−4	−153	44	−32	−86	74	48	−61	−307	−202
Reserve Assets......................	79dbd	59	150	−4	−153	44	−32	−86	74	48	−61	−307	−202
Use of Fund Credit and Loans.......	79dcd	—	—	—	—	—	—	—	—	—	—	—	—
Exceptional Financing...............	79ded	—	—	—	—	—	—	—	—	—	—	....	....
International Investment Position						*Millions of US Dollars*							
Assets..................................	79aad	787	872	1,009	1,306	1,599	2,199	3,374	3,738	4,040	5,079	9,959	18,292
Direct Investment Abroad..............	79abd	114	149	180	241	272	342	456	665	843	1,256	1,709	3,896
Portfolio Investment..............	79acd	41	118	198	264	488	967	1,902	2,205	1,916	1,982	3,695	5,643
Equity Securities...............	79add	22	48	103	183	398	830	1,718	2,128	1,795	1,853	3,369	5,186
Debt Securities.................	79aed	19	71	95	81	90	137	185	78	121	129	326	457
Financial Derivatives..............	79ald	4	59	81	80	76	76	78	16	—	—	—	—
Other Investment..................	79afd	201	248	235	259	376	384	506	463	925	1,380	3,736	7,679
Monetary Authorities............	79agd	—	—	—	—	—	—	—	—	—	—	—	—
General Government.............	79ahd	—	—	—	—	—	—	—	—	—	—	—	—
Banks..................................	79aid	94	119	80	115	164	142	184	229	442	1,101	3,510	7,165
Other Sectors......................	79ajd	107	129	155	144	211	243	321	233	483	279	226	515
Reserve Assets......................	79akd	428	298	315	461	386	427	495	405	355	462	819	1,074
Liabilities.............................	79lad	4,125	4,245	4,478	4,720	5,024	6,371	7,553	9,050	9,833	12,276	17,735	29,652
Dir. Invest. in Rep. Economy.........	79lbd	117	127	129	200	336	466	482	492	688	798	1,192	1,807
Portfolio Investment..............	79lcd	1,550	1,882	2,128	2,213	2,039	2,200	3,127	4,105	4,578	6,084	10,933	21,333
Equity Securities...............	79ldd	—	—	—	1	—	14	66	15	118	445	600	1,417
Debt Securities.................	79led	1,550	1,882	2,128	2,212	2,039	2,186	3,061	4,090	4,460	5,640	10,333	19,916
Financial Derivatives..............	79lld	4	56	74	74	74	74	16	—	—	—	—	—
Other Investment..................	79lfd	2,454	2,180	2,146	2,233	2,575	3,631	3,928	4,454	4,567	5,394	5,610	6,513
Monetary Authorities............	79lgd	33	81	103	2	1	57	51	187	145	205	2	2
General Government.............	79lhd	333	287	377	334	345	446	444	456	520	631	612	576
Banks..................................	79lid	592	459	421	660	903	1,427	1,814	2,273	2,097	3,039	3,349	4,249
Other Sectors......................	79ljd	1,495	1,352	1,246	1,238	1,326	1,701	1,618	1,538	1,804	1,520	1,648	1,686

Iceland 176

		1993	1994	1995	1996	1997	1998	1999	2000	2001	2002	2003	2004
Government Finance		*Millions of Kronur: Year Ending December 31*											
Deficit (-) or Surplus	80	−16,844	−21,972	−20,270	−4,389	1,863	† 16,284	20,435	9,548	−25,714	−4,133	11,843	22,408
Total Revenue and Grants	81y	122,810	130,008	135,715	150,816	155,200	† 167,388	194,993	207,561	219,748	230,510	249,606	280,696
Revenue	81	122,285	129,409	135,715	150,816	155,200	† 166,529	194,250	206,993	219,029	229,815	248,201	280,028
Grants	81z	525	599	—	—	—	† 859	743	568	719	695	1,405	668
Exp. & Lending Minus Repay	82z	139,655	151,980	155,985	155,205	153,337	† 151,104	174,558	198,013	245,462	234,643	237,763	258,288
Expenditure	82	135,537	142,756	146,826	156,454	152,990	† 159,651	177,964	195,411	221,305	246,810	268,714	280,382
Lending Minus Repayments	83	4,117	9,224	9,159	−1,248	347	† −8,547	−3,406	2,602	24,157	−12,167	−30,951	−22,094
Financing													
Total Financing	80h	....	....	....	....	....	† −16,284	−20,435	−9,548	25,714	4,134	−11,842	−22,408
Total Net Borrowing	84	16,844	21,972	20,270	4,389	−1,863	† −10,498	−20,691	−9,246	26,539	−4,292	−13,452	−14,110
Net Domestic	84a	13,866	10,493	5,185	−2,254	4,660	† 48	−19,586	−17,443	−4,840	−492	10,308	....
Net Foreign	85a	2,979	11,479	15,085	6,643	−6,523	† −10,546	−1,105	8,197	31,379	−3,800	−23,760	....
Use of Cash Balances	87	....	....	....	....	....	† −5,786	256	−302	−825	8,426	1,610	−8,298
Total Debt by Residence	88	181,030	197,106	213,575	225,677	226,111	† 209,020	190,693	187,972	242,353	279,055	255,697	241,734
Domestic	88a	78,725	83,473	86,314	93,459	99,483	† 92,938	74,480	61,643	69,160	70,336	89,749	86,569
Foreign	89a	102,305	113,633	127,261	132,218	126,628	† 116,082	116,213	126,329	173,193	208,719	165,948	155,165
National Accounts		*Millions of Kronur*											
Househ.Cons.Expend.,incl.NPISHs	96f	237,402	247,821	258,215	278,656	290,901	325,305	359,881	391,747	407,986	420,214	451,237	496,292
Government Consumption Expend	91f	88,618	93,823	98,961	105,563	112,776	127,752	142,430	157,934	176,656	196,978	211,797	228,244
Gross Fixed Capital Formation	93e	71,776	74,398	75,386	97,867	103,667	139,220	135,333	157,917	165,564	135,475	160,678	188,742
Changes in Inventories	93i	2,307	260	3,052	25	102	906	120	2,494	−2,084	−182	−1,501	−3,383
Exports of Goods and Services	90c	135,694	157,436	161,250	176,836	190,653	204,214	212,166	229,520	299,412	305,864	288,314	316,139
Imports of Goods and Services (-)	98c	122,466	134,631	144,725	173,755	187,717	230,055	241,482	278,637	306,897	292,110	313,037	367,113
Gross Domestic Product (GDP)	99b	413,331	439,108	452,139	485,192	510,383	567,342	608,448	660,975	740,636	766,239	797,487	858,921
Net Primary Income from Abroad	98.n	−10,108	−13,659	−12,829	−11,317	−12,116	−12,647	−12,567	−19,409	−25,285	−6,245	−16,502	−17,717
Gross National Income (GNI)	99a	403,223	425,449	439,310	473,875	498,267	554,695	595,881	641,566	715,351	759,994	780,985	841,204
Consumption of Fixed Capital	99cf	61,028	63,427	64,960	67,526	60,216	62,837	69,729	77,346	91,328	97,219	98,638	106,046
GDP Volume 1990 Prices	99b.p	361,876	376,465	376,770	396,438	414,939	....	....	....	....	....	....	....
GDP Volume 1997 Prices	99b.p	....	....	....	....	424,281	427,184	446,039	471,379	483,618	473,478	493,528	519,128
GDP Volume (2000=100)	99bvp	78.5	81.7	81.7	86.0	† 90.0	90.6	94.6	100.0	102.6	100.4	104.7	110.1
GDP Deflator (2000=100)	99bip	79.7	81.4	83.7	85.4	85.8	94.7	97.3	100.0	109.2	115.4	115.2	118.0
		Millions: Midyear Estimates											
Population	99z	.26	.26	.27	.27	.27	.28	.28	.28	.28	.29	.29	.29

India   534

		1993	1994	1995	1996	1997	1998	1999	2000	2001	2002	2003	2004
Exchange Rates						*Rupees per SDR: End of Period*							
Market Rate	aa	43.102	45.810	52.295	51.666	52.999	59.813	59.690	60.911	60.549	65.298	67.768	67.688
					Rupees per US Dollar: End of Period (ae) Period Average (rf)								
Market Rate	ae	31.380	31.380	35.180	35.930	39.280	42.480	43.490	46.750	48.180	48.030	45.605	43.585
Market Rate	rf	30.493	31.374	32.427	35.433	36.313	41.259	43.055	44.942	47.186	48.610	46.583	45.316
Fund Position						*Millions of SDRs: End of Period*							
Quota	2f.s	3,056	3,056	3,056	3,056	3,056	3,056	4,158	4,158	4,158	4,158	4,158	4,158
SDRs	1b.s	73	1	93	85	57	59	3	1	4	5	2	3
Reserve Position in the Fund	1c.s	213	213	213	213	213	213	489	489	489	489	887	917
Total Fund Cred.&Loans Outstg	2tl	3,585	2,763	1,967	1,085	590	285	39	—	—	—	—	—
International Liquidity					*Millions of US Dollars Unless Otherwise Indicated: End of Period*								
Total Reserves minus Gold	1l.d	10,199	19,698	17,922	20,170	24,688	27,341	32,667	37,902	45,870	67,665	98,938	126,593
SDRs	1b.d	100	2	139	122	77	83	4	2	5	7	3	5
Reserve Position in the Fund	1c.d	292	310	316	306	287	300	671	637	614	665	1,318	1,424
Foreign Exchange	1d.d	9,807	19,386	17,467	19,742	24,324	26,958	31,992	37,264	45,251	66,994	97,617	125,164
Gold (Million Fine Troy Ounces)	1ad	11.457	11.800	12.780	12.781	12.740	11.487	11.502	11.502	11.502	11.502	11.502	11.502
Gold (National Valuation)	1and	3,325	3,355	3,669	3,614	2,880	2,492	2,403	2,252	2,329	2,712	3,323	3,808
Monetary Authorities						*Billions of Rupees: Last Friday of Period*							
Foreign Assets	11	413.0	721.3	749.0	847.8	1,058.1	1,256.4	1,525.2	1,876.8	2,326.0	3,379.6	4,612.5	5,706.7
Claims on Central Government	12a	1,155.7	1,034.9	1,128.0	1,360.6	1,373.8	1,571.3	1,631.0	1,538.5	1,553.0	1,190.3	565.4	857.3
Claims on Deposit Money Banks	12e	13.2	25.2	60.1	7.9	12.7	31.9	26.8	68.0	70.8	.7	.1	6.7
Claims on Other Financial Insts	12f	103.8	120.7	125.2	124.0	134.9	146.2	158.6	210.4	194.9	107.4	67.7	82.6
Reserve Money	14	1,268.0	1,543.8	1,737.8	1,903.2	2,116.1	2,378.7	2,649.3	2,854.2	3,145.1	3,438.3	3,911.5	4,549.6
of which: Currency Outside DMBs	14a	783.3	948.5	1,136.2	1,295.2	1,443.0	1,624.4	1,925.0	2,038.5	2,296.9	2,609.8	3,004.8	3,418.4
Foreign Liabilities	16c	154.5	126.6	102.8	56.1	31.3	17.0	2.3	—	—	—	—	—
Central Government Deposits	16d	.7	.7	.7	.6	.6	.6	1.4	1.4	1.4	1.4	1.4	752.0
Capital Accounts	17a	152.9	154.8	159.2	158.8	166.8	167.4	164.3	161.7	157.5	111.5	113.2	113.2
Other Items (Net)	17r	109.5	76.4	61.7	221.5	264.7	442.0	524.2	676.2	840.7	1,126.8	1,219.5	1,238.6
Deposit Money Banks						*Billions of Rupees: Last Friday of Period*							
Reserves	20	483.9	628.8	646.9	568.7	604.3	783.7	661.7	747.4	769.8	733.6	799.5	1,182.7
Claims on Central Government	22a	922.1	1,223.3	1,291.1	1,545.9	1,896.4	2,237.7	2,768.1	3,333.8	4,082.5	5,097.4	6,358.9	6,950.0
Claims on Private Sector	22d	2,087.7	2,429.9	2,713.9	3,264.2	3,640.0	4,196.4	5,054.7	6,064.3	6,626.1	8,052.8	8,831.7	11,531.9
Demand Deposits	24	530.6	710.8	686.2	808.5	933.1	1,039.1	1,203.4	1,435.5	1,523.9	1,689.0	1,984.2	2,602.0
Time Deposits	25	2,601.5	3,034.0	3,366.2	4,084.4	4,914.7	5,963.3	6,991.9	8,197.5	9,522.0	11,283.7	12,617.0	14,527.4
Credit from Monetary Authorities	26g	16.2	77.6	138.4	18.1	7.7	63.1	25.5	66.9	69.9	.7	.3	1.5
Other Items (Net)	27r	345.3	459.7	461.1	467.8	285.2	152.3	263.6	445.6	362.6	910.3	1,388.5	2,533.6
Monetary Survey						*Billions of Rupees: Last Friday of Period*							
Foreign Assets (Net)	31n	258.4	594.8	646.2	791.7	1,026.8	1,239.3	1,522.9	1,876.8	2,326.0	3,379.6	4,612.5	5,706.7
Domestic Credit	32	4,268.6	4,808.2	5,257.5	6,294.0	7,044.4	8,151.0	9,610.9	11,145.5	12,455.1	14,446.4	15,822.2	18,669.9
Claims on Central Govt. (Net)	32an	2,077.1	2,257.6	2,418.4	2,905.9	3,269.6	3,808.4	4,397.6	4,870.8	5,634.1	6,286.2	6,922.8	7,055.3
Claims on Private Sector	32d	2,087.7	2,429.9	2,713.9	3,264.2	3,640.0	4,196.4	5,054.7	6,064.3	6,626.1	8,052.8	8,831.7	11,531.9
Claims on Other Financial Insts	32f	103.8	120.7	125.2	124.0	134.9	146.2	158.6	210.4	194.9	107.4	67.7	82.6
Money	34	1,330.2	1,695.0	1,883.5	2,148.9	2,419.3	2,703.5	3,161.2	3,495.9	3,846.0	4,324.9	5,026.0	6,067.6
Quasi-Money	35	2,601.5	3,034.0	3,366.2	4,084.4	4,914.7	5,963.3	6,991.9	8,197.5	9,522.0	11,283.7	12,617.0	14,527.4
Other Items (Net)	37r	595.3	673.9	653.9	852.4	737.3	723.6	980.7	1,328.9	1,413.1	2,217.4	2,791.7	3,781.5
Money plus Quasi-Money	35l	3,931.8	4,729.0	5,249.7	6,233.4	7,334.0	8,666.8	10,153.0	11,693.4	13,368.0	15,608.6	17,643.0	20,595.0
Interest Rates						*Percent Per Annum*							
Bank Rate (End of Period)	60	12.00	12.00	12.00	12.00	9.00	9.00	8.00	8.00	6.50	6.25	6.00	6.00
Money Market Rate	60b	8.64	7.14	15.57	11.04	5.29	....	....	....	....	....	....	....
Lending Rate	60p	16.25	14.75	15.46	15.96	13.83	13.54	12.54	12.29	12.08	11.92	11.46	10.92
Prices, Production, Labor						*Index Numbers (2000=100): Period Averages*							
Share Prices	62	55.4	88.2	72.8	73.3	82.4	72.4	89.9	100.0	75.5	70.7	117.6	138.6
Wholesale Prices	63	64.9	71.8	† 78.5	82.0	85.7	90.7	93.9	100.0	104.8	107.5	113.3	120.7
Consumer Prices	64	57.2	63.0	69.5	75.7	81.1	91.9	96.1	100.0	103.7	108.2	112.4	116.6
Industrial Production	66	59.3	64.9	† 73.1	79.4	83.7	86.5	93.1	100.0	102.1	107.3	114.2	123.7
						Number in Thousands: Period Averages							
Employment	67e	27,177	27,375	27,987	27,941	28,245	28,166	28,113	27,960	27,789	27,206	....	....
Unemployment	67c	36,276	36,692	36,742	37,430	39,140	40,090	40,371	41,344	41,996	41,171	....	....
Intl. Transactions & Positions						*Billions of Rupees*							
Exports	70	657	785	995	1,172	1,271	1,379	1,536	1,907	2,045	2,394	2,656	3,252
Imports, c.i.f.	71	694	842	1,127	1,344	1,505	1,772	2,024	2,317	2,378	2,747	3,313	4,262
						2000=100							
Unit Value of Exports	74	76	79	78	81	94	98	97	100	99	99	....	....
Unit Value of Imports	75	67	67	72	82	83	84	92	100	101	112	....	....

		1993	1994	1995	1996	1997	1998	1999	2000	2001	2002	2003	2004
Balance of Payments						*Millions of US Dollars: Minus Sign Indicates Debit*							
Current Account, n.i.e.	78ald	−1,876	−1,676	−5,563	−5,956	−2,965	−6,903	−3,228	−4,702	1,251	6,964	6,718	....
Goods: Exports f.o.b.	78aad	22,016	25,523	31,239	33,737	35,702	34,076	36,877	43,247	44,793	51,141	59,338	....
Goods: Imports f.o.b.	78abd	−24,108	−29,673	−37,957	−43,789	−45,730	−44,828	−45,556	−53,887	−51,211	−54,700	−68,208	....
Trade Balance	78acd	−2,093	−4,150	−6,719	−10,052	−10,028	−10,752	−8,679	−10,640	−6,418	−3,559	−8,870	....
Services: Credit	78add	5,107	6,038	6,775	7,238	9,111	11,691	14,509	16,684	17,337	19,478	23,397	....
Services: Debit	78aed	−6,497	−8,200	−10,268	−11,171	−12,443	−14,540	−17,271	−19,187	−20,099	−21,041	−25,710	....
Balance on Goods & Services	78afd	−3,482	−6,312	−10,212	−13,984	−13,360	−13,601	−11,441	−13,143	−9,181	−5,122	−11,183	....
Income: Credit	78agd	375	821	1,486	1,411	1,484	1,806	1,919	2,521	3,524	3,188	3,779	....
Income: Debit	78ahd	−4,121	−4,370	−5,219	−4,667	−5,002	−5,443	−5,629	−7,414	−7,666	−7,097	−8,230	....
Balance on Gds, Serv. & Inc.	78aid	−7,228	−9,861	−13,945	−17,240	−16,878	−17,238	−15,151	−18,036	−13,323	−9,031	−15,635	....
Current Transfers, n.i.e.: Credit	78ajd	5,375	8,208	8,410	11,350	13,975	10,402	11,958	13,447	14,981	16,692	22,697	....
Current Transfers: Debit	78akd	−23	−23	−27	−66	−62	−67	−35	−114	−407	−698	−345	....
Capital Account, n.i.e.	78bcd	....	....	....	....	—	—	....	716	743	102	3,839	....
Capital Account, n.i.e.: Credit	78bad	....	....	....	....	—	—	....	2,758	2,227	1,409	5,595	....
Capital Account: Debit	78bbd	....	....	....	....	—	—	....	−2,042	−1,484	−1,307	−1,756	....
Financial Account, n.i.e.	78bjd	7,074	10,576	3,861	11,848	9,635	8,584	9,579	9,751	7,045	11,576	15,267	....
Direct Investment Abroad	78bdd	—	−83	−117	−239	−113	−48	−79	−510	−1,398	−1,678	−1,324	....
Dir. Invest. in Rep. Econ., n.i.e.	78bed	550	973	2,144	2,426	3,577	2,635	2,169	3,584	5,476	5,640	4,633	....
Portfolio Investment Assets	78bfd	....	....	....	....	—	—	....	1,017	2,853	1,022	8,216	....
Equity Securities	78bkd	....	....	....	....	—	—	....	9,645	10,674	9,071	20,001	....
Debt Securities	78bld	....	....	....	....	—	—	....	−8,628	−7,821	−8,048	−11,785	....
Portfolio Investment Liab., n.i.e.	78bgd	1,369	5,491	1,590	3,958	2,556	−601	2,317	1,328	—	—	—	....
Equity Securities	78bmd	1,369	5,491	1,590	3,958	2,556	−601	2,317	1,328	—	—	—	....
Debt Securities	78bnd	....	....	....	....	—	—	....	....	....	....	....	....
Financial Derivatives Assets	78bwd	....	....	....	....	—	—	....	....	....	....	....	....
Financial Derivatives Liabilities	78bxd	....	....	....	....	—	—	....	....	....	....	....	....
Other Investment Assets	78bhd	1,830	1,170	−1,179	−4,710	−4,743	−3,239	−450	1,712	−2,834	3,699	−3,259	....
Monetary Authorities	78bod	3	1	....	....	—	—	−498	9,069	7,365	10,163	13,057	....
General Government	78bpd	309	9	−29	−5	67	11	33	−104	646	400	−4,341	....
Banks	78bqd	−148	−1,029	−92	−1,642	−2,156	−1,355	1,140	−369	−3,012	−2,836	−4,608	....
Other Sectors	78brd	1,667	2,189	−1,058	−3,063	−2,653	−1,896	−1,126	−6,884	−7,833	−4,028	−7,366	....
Other Investment Liab., n.i.e.	78bid	3,325	3,024	1,423	10,413	8,357	9,837	5,623	2,619	2,949	2,893	7,001	....
Monetary Authorities	78bsd	81	142	−65	45	233	122	1,344	—	—	—	—	....
General Government	78btd	141	92	1,483	1,698	397	−72	237	1,467	2,949	2,893	7,001	....
Banks	78bud	2,045	1,307	266	2,989	1,098	1,739	2,458	562	—	—	—	....
Other Sectors	78bvd	1,058	1,483	−261	5,680	6,629	8,047	1,584	590	—	—	—	....
Net Errors and Omissions	78cad	−987	1,492	970	−1,934	−1,348	1,390	313	331	−715	−191	183	....
Overall Balance	78cbd	4,211	10,391	−733	3,958	5,321	3,071	6,664	6,095	8,324	18,451	26,007	....
Reserves and Related Items	79dad	−4,211	−10,391	733	−3,958	−5,321	−3,071	−6,664	−6,095	−8,324	−18,451	−26,007	....
Reserve Assets	79dbd	−4,663	−9,238	1,956	−2,676	−4,637	−2,659	−6,327	−6,017	−8,690	−18,853	−25,667	....
Use of Fund Credit and Loans	79dcd	451	−1,153	−1,223	−1,282	−684	−412	−337	−52	—	—	—	....
Exceptional Financing	79ded	....	....	....	....	—	—	....	−26	366	402	−340	....
International Investment Position						*Millions of US Dollars*							
Assets	79aad	....	....	....	....	37,782	41,636	46,826	54,692	62,474	73,699	....	....
Direct Investment Abroad	79abd	....	....	....	....	617	706	1,707	1,859	2,615	4,006	....	....
Portfolio Investment	79acd	....	....	....	....	282	275	130	121	505	670	....	....
Equity Securities	79add	....	....	....	....	172	165	25	21	270	356	....	....
Debt Securities	79aed	....	....	....	....	110	111	105	100	235	314	....	....
Financial Derivatives	79ald	....	....	....	....	—	—	—	—	—	—	....	....
Other Investment	79afd	....	....	....	....	10,097	10,906	11,832	14,043	16,456	14,256	....	....
Monetary Authorities	79agd	....	....	....	....	—	—	—	—	—	—	....	....
General Government	79ahd	....	....	....	....	1,057	1,026	1,002	1,011	1,032	1,061	....	....
Banks	79aid	....	....	....	....	7,269	7,688	7,680	10,599	12,648	10,801	....	....
Other Sectors	79ajd	....	....	....	....	1,771	2,192	3,150	2,432	2,777	2,394	....	....
Reserve Assets	79akd	....	....	....	....	26,785	29,749	33,157	38,670	42,898	54,767	....	....
Liabilities	79lad	....	....	....	....	118,246	121,938	125,615	131,538	138,626	142,469	....	....
Dir. Invest. in Rep. Economy	79lbd	....	....	....	....	10,630	14,065	15,426	17,517	20,326	25,408	....	....
Portfolio Investment	79lcd	....	....	....	....	18,744	20,410	23,105	25,009	31,295	31,540	....	....
Equity Securities	79ldd	....	....	....	....	13,631	14,109	13,080	15,734	17,414	18,614	....	....
Debt Securities	79led	....	....	....	....	5,113	6,301	10,026	9,275	13,882	12,927	....	....
Financial Derivatives	79lld	....	....	....	....	—	—	—	—	—	—	....	....
Other Investment	79lfd	....	....	....	....	88,872	87,462	87,083	89,012	87,005	85,521	....	....
Monetary Authorities	79lgd	....	....	....	....	1,319	886	584	361	282	386	....	....
General Government	79lhd	....	....	....	....	47,828	45,408	45,244	45,991	43,330	42,863	....	....
Banks	79lid	....	....	....	....	17,154	16,169	16,111	17,294	19,595	20,197	....	....
Other Sectors	79ljd	....	....	....	....	22,571	24,999	25,144	25,366	23,798	22,075	....	....
Government Finance						*Billions of Rupees: Year Beginning April 1*							
Deficit (-) or Surplus	80	−605.3	−567.5	−598.5	−668.8	−741.9	−917.2	−1,061.5	−1,087.1p	−1,079.2f	....	....	....
Revenue	81	1,011.7	1,283.2	1,488.8	1,717.1	1,864.5	2,015.3	2,349.7	2,696.9p	3,093.7f	....	....	....
Grants Received	81z	9.9	10.4	11.4	11.9	10.2	9.9	11.1	7.3p	7.0f	....	....	....
Expenditure	82	1,363.7	1,540.6	1,763.1	2,010.6	2,305.8	2,610.5	3,013.1	3,486.8p	3,953.1f	....	....	....
Lending Minus Repayments	83	263.2	320.5	335.6	387.2	310.7	331.9	409.1	304.5p	226.8f	....	....	....
Financing													
Net Borrowing: Domestic	84a	564.8	519.4	611.8	634.3	740.1	900.4	1,041.0	1,055.3p	1,060.6f	....	....	....
Foreign	85a	50.7	35.8	3.2	29.9	10.9	19.2	11.8	5.7p	18.7f	....	....	....
Use of Cash Balances	87	−10.2	12.3	−16.6	4.6	−9.1	−2.4	8.6	26.1p	—f	....	....	....
Debt: Domestic	88a	4,060.7	4,586.9	5,213.0	5,835.2	7,229.6	8,345.5	9,625.9	11,052.1p	12,563.6f	....	....	....
Foreign	89a	473.5	509.3	512.5	542.4	553.3	572.5	584.4	584.3p	595.9f	....	....	....

		1993	1994	1995	1996	1997	1998	1999	2000	2001	2002	2003	2004
National Accounts						*Billions of Rupees: Year Beginning April 1*							
Househ.Cons.Expend.,incl.NPISHs....	**96f**	5,747.7	6,641.6	7,658.0	9,036.5	9,816.7	11,394.1	12,715.6	13,600.2	14,887.8	15,851.3	17,638.5	....
Government Consumption Expend...	**91f**	977.3	1,086.4	1,288.2	1,457.3	1,721.9	2,140.3	2,511.1	2,642.4	2,827.7	2,919.5	3,121.2	....
Gross Fixed Capital Formation.........	**93e**	1,842.9	2,222.4	2,894.1	3,118.5	3,304.2	3,743.4	4,219.0	4,592.4	5,004.1	5,552.2	6,273.1	....
Changes in Inventories....................	**93i**	−16.7	145.5	257.7	−139.9	132.9	−21.3	363.6	138.3	86.5	−100.1	83.9	....
Exports of Goods and Services..........	**90c**	861.5	1,016.1	1,307.3	1,448.5	1,652.0	1,952.8	2,277.0	2,781.3	2,907.6	3,555.6	4,078.0	....
Imports of Goods and Services (-).....	**98c**	860.0	1,047.1	1,449.5	1,610.2	1,843.3	2,247.5	2,657.0	2,975.2	3,110.5	3,799.8	4,434.0	....
Gross Domestic Product (GDP).........	**99b**	8,592.2	10,127.7	11,880.1	13,682.1	15,225.5	17,409.9	19,368.3	20,895.0	22,719.8	24,633.2	27,600.3	31,085.6
Net Primary Income from Abroad.....	**98.n**	−120.8	−130.8	−134.8	−130.8	−132.1	−149.7	−154.3	−172.9	−120.9	−192.2	....	....
Gross National Income (GNI)............	**99a**	8,471.4	9,996.9	11,745.3	13,551.3	15,093.4	17,260.2	19,214.0	20,722.1	22,700.6	24,501.6	27,459.5	....
Gross Nat'l Disposable Inc.(GNDI)....	**99i**	7,803.0	9,271.1	10,787.1	12,625.9	14,011.1	16,012.5	17,851.2	19,474.4	21,270.5	....	....	....
Gross Saving.................................	**99s**	1,936.2	2,514.6	2,987.5	3,172.6	3,521.8	3,749.3	4,686.8	4,959.9	5,351.8	6,423.0	7,764.2	....
Consumption of Fixed Capital..........	**99cf**	833.5	979.9	1,179.3	1,365.0	1,520.0	1,680.7	1,823.6	1,979.0	2,177.5	2,350.4	2,336.4	....
GDP at Factor Cost........................	**99ba**	7,813.5	9,170.6	10,732.7	12,435.5	13,901.5	15,981.3	17,618.4	19,030.0	20,814.7	22,548.9	25,197.9	28,381.2
GDP Vol.,fact.cost,93/94 Prices.......	**99bap**	7,813.5	8,380.3	8,995.6	9,700.8	10,166.0	10,827.5	11,483.7	11,985.9	12,678.3	13,183.2	14,267.0	....
GDP Volume 1993/94 Prices............	**99b.p**	8,592.2	9,244.6	9,939.5	10,674.5	11,152.5	11,820.2	12,662.8	13,162.0	13,840.1	14,476.0	15,674.0	....
GDP Volume (2000=100)................	**99bvp**	65.3	70.2	75.5	81.1	84.7	89.8	96.2	100.0	105.2	110.0	119.1	....
GDP Deflator (2000=100)................	**99bip**	63.0	68.9	75.1	80.7	86.1	93.0	96.6	100.0	103.4	107.7	111.2	....
						Millions: Midyear Estimates							
Population..............................	**99z**	901.00	918.29	935.57	952.83	970.04	987.18	1,004.20	1,021.08	1,037.81	1,054.37	1,070.80	1,087.12

Indonesia 536

		1993	1994	1995	1996	1997	1998	1999	2000	2001	2002	2003	2004
Exchange Rates						*Rupiah per SDR: End of Period*							
Market Rate	aa	2,898.2	3,211.7	3,430.8	3,426.7	6,274.0	11,299.4	9,724.2	12,501.4	13,070.0	12,154.1	12,578.7	14,427.5
						Rupiah per US Dollar: End of Period (ae) Period Average (rf)							
Market Rate	ae	2,110.0	2,200.0	2,308.0	2,383.0	4,650.0	8,025.0	7,085.0	9,595.0	10,400.0	8,940.0	8,465.0	9,290.0
Market Rate	rf	2,087.1	2,160.8	2,248.6	2,342.3	2,909.4	10,013.6	7,855.2	8,421.8	10,260.9	9,311.2	8,577.1	8,938.9
Fund Position						*Millions of SDRs: End of Period*							
Quota	2f.s	1,498	1,498	1,498	1,498	1,498	1,498	2,079	2,079	2,079	2,079	2,079	2,079
SDRs	1b.s	—	—	1	2	370	222		24	13	14	2	2
Reserve Position in the Fund	1c.s	200	214	270	298	—	—	145	145	145	145	145	145
Total Fund Cred.&Loans Outstg	2tl					2,201	6,456	7,467	8,318	7,252	6,518	6,915	6,237
International Liquidity						*Millions of US Dollars Unless Otherwise Indicated: End of Period*							
Total Reserves minus Gold	1l.d	11,263	12,133	13,708	18,251	16,587	22,713	26,445	28,502	27,246	30,971	34,962	34,952
SDRs	1b.d	—	—	1	2	499	312		32	16	19	4	2
Reserve Position in the Fund	1c.d	274	312	401	429	—	—	200	190	183	198	216	226
Foreign Exchange	1d.d	10,988	11,820	13,306	17,820	16,088	22,401	26,245	28,280	27,048	30,754	34,742	34,724
Gold (Million Fine Troy Ounces)	1ad	3.101	3.101	3.101	3.101	3.101	3.101	3.101	3.101	3.101	3.101	3.101	3.101
Gold (National Valuation)	1and	1,092	1,067	1,079	1,030	809	803	812	766	772	1,077	1,291	1,351
Monetary Authorities: Other Liab	4..d	22	20	21	21	419	3,374	3,586	2,260	2,151	2,136	2,146	2,146
Deposit Money Banks: Assets	7a.d	5,374	5,852	7,407	8,737	10,067	14,412	16,967	10,649	10,555	10,084	9,136	7,341
Liabilities	7b.d	9,691	11,311	11,678	12,482	15,147	12,192	14,167	9,659	6,577	5,805	3,716	5,310
Monetary Authorities						*Billions of Rupiah: End of Period*							
Foreign Assets	11	39,949	38,405	43,642	60,607	99,716	194,054	194,325	294,112	304,982	293,802	313,585	344,121
Claims on Central Government	12a	9,013	7,510	4,672	4,269	5,470	35,700	248,095	233,669	267,464	304,058	260,629	270,905
Claims on Nonfin.Pub.Enterprises	12c	13	8	4									
Claims on Private Sector	12d	256	196	218	197	205	265	1,230	6,382	6,194	6,295	6,280	6,218
Claims on Deposit Money Banks	12e	9,950	13,333	15,722	14,438	58,624	113,543	14,437	18,790	17,907	16,861	15,065	10,693
Claims on Nonbank Financial Insts	12g	935	274	734	744	8,535	53,356	28,984	29,571	30,015	30,365	30,852	38,104
Reserve Money	14	18,414	23,053	27,160	36,895	51,013	90,690	125,848	156,420	181,508	179,896	202,870	252,236
of which: Currency Outside DMBs	14a	14,430	18,634	20,807	22,486	28,423	41,393	58,352	72,370	76,342	80,659	94,539	109,273
Foreign Currency Deposits	15	—	—	—	—	—	—	—	192	126	129	25	—
Liabs. of Central Bank: Securities	16ac	23,339	15,051	11,851	18,553	14,885	49,590	63,049	60,076	55,742	77,654	107,025	103,825
Restricted Deposits	16b	534	497	461	436	267	660	244	290	505	299	175	416
Foreign Liabilities	16c	46	43	49	50	15,761	100,025	98,018	125,676	117,149	98,319	105,147	109,921
Central Government Deposits	16d	13,016	13,536	15,558	16,856	33,472	35,438	83,990	96,820	93,138	114,581	73,070	44,509
Capital Accounts	17a	4,889	7,399	8,807	7,421	56,851	122,284	84,687	118,814	127,678	123,943	97,017	120,398
Other Items (Net)	17r	−122	147	1,106	45	301	−1,770	31,235	24,237	50,715	56,560	41,082	38,736
Deposit Money Banks						*Billions of Rupiah: End of Period*							
Reserves	20	4,591	5,051	7,371	14,896	24,172	50,229	68,479	66,537	93,357	94,633	105,650	131,517
Claims on Mon.Author.:Securities	20c	14,799	7,619	5,152	11,225	6,318	44,964	63,049	58,700	55,742	76,859	102,259	94,058
Foreign Assets	21	11,340	12,874	17,096	20,820	46,810	115,657	120,209	102,179	109,774	90,147	77,340	68,202
Claims on Central Government	22a	4,004	2,843	4,165	5,727	8,571	10,230	274,551	439,177	423,735	393,338	361,397	323,449
Claims on State and Local Govts	22b	256	113	276	290	292	319	214	376	446	310	2,718	1,260
Claims on Nonfin.Pub.Enterprises	22c	6,492	6,866	8,423	9,248	11,036	15,128	11,854	10,343	10,748	15,946	11,107	16,236
Claims on Private Sector	22d	161,273	198,311	243,067	295,195	381,741	508,558	225,236	270,301	298,901	352,378	426,685	538,305
Claims on Other Banking Insts	22f	190	236	312	370	364	277	100	101	130	194	353	768
Claims on Nonbank Financial Insts	22g	1,276	2,329	2,785	4,897	6,353	5,763	1,998	2,554	4,025	5,602	7,214	10,229
Demand Deposits	24	19,979	24,135	28,639	31,766	43,879	49,185	57,646	82,241	97,746	106,558	125,329	141,498
Time, Savings,& Fgn. Currency Dep	25	109,402	130,280	171,257	226,097	279,073	481,350	525,227	587,730	669,789	695,181	734,197	782,280
Money Market Instruments	26aa	2,435	2,437	4,162	3,353	4,306	3,223	2,986	2,253	1,847	1,962	6,273	9,042
Restricted Deposits	26b	1,699	1,541	1,779	2,099	1,419	2,417	1,659	4,783	7,966	5,075	3,096	3,053
Foreign Liabilities	26c	20,448	24,885	26,952	29,744	70,434	97,842	100,375	92,675	68,406	51,895	31,458	49,327
Central Government Deposits	26d	10,761	8,919	9,407	10,975	13,282	19,701	21,017	43,106	39,963	36,509	38,970	37,130
Central Govt. Lending Funds	26f	3,307	3,801	3,871	5,029	1,653	1,416	4,508	9,178	9,450	514	628	606
Credit from Monetary Authorities	26g	16,237	11,432	10,394	11,622	23,008	112,947	33,360	16,547	15,225	12,694	10,971	11,932
Liab. to Nonbank Financial Insts	26j	1,153	1,326	1,564	2,533	7,536	39,332	14,725	14,690	2,845	4,652	4,860	5,436
Capital Accounts	27a	21,973	26,775	36,506	42,523	53,408	−94,556	−17,346	52,327	66,988	93,823	113,081	133,066
Other Items (Net)	27r	−3,173	711	−5,884	−3,073	−12,341	38,268	21,533	44,739	16,632	20,545	25,863	10,653
Monetary Survey						*Billions of Rupiah: End of Period*							
Foreign Assets (Net)	31n	30,795	26,351	33,737	51,633	60,331	111,844	116,141	177,941	229,202	233,736	254,321	253,075
Domestic Credit	32	159,931	196,231	239,691	293,106	375,813	574,457	687,255	852,548	908,557	957,396	995,197	1,123,834
Claims on Central Govt. (Net)	32an	−10,760	−12,102	−16,128	−17,835	−32,713	−9,209	417,639	532,919	558,098	546,305	509,987	512,714
Claims on State and Local Govts	32b	256	113	276	290	292	319	214	376	446	310	2,718	1,260
Claims on Nonfin.Pub.Enterprises	32c	6,505	6,874	8,427	9,248	11,036	15,128	11,854	10,343	10,748	15,946	11,107	16,236
Claims on Private Sector	32d	161,529	198,507	243,285	295,392	381,946	508,823	226,466	276,683	305,095	358,673	432,965	544,523
Claims on Other Banking Insts	32f	190	236	312	370	364	277	100	101	130	194	353	768
Claims on Nonbank Financial Inst	32g	2,211	2,603	3,519	5,641	14,888	59,119	30,982	32,125	34,039	35,968	38,066	48,333
Money	34	34,661	42,887	49,572	54,534	72,431	90,768	116,880	160,923	175,110	188,008	220,552	251,243
Quasi-Money	35	109,402	130,280	171,257	226,097	279,073	481,350	525,227	587,922	669,916	695,310	734,223	782,280
Money Market Instruments	36aa	2,435	2,437	4,162	3,353	4,306	3,223	2,986	2,253	1,847	1,962	6,273	9,042
Liabs. of Central Bank: Securities	36ac	8,540	7,432	6,699	7,328	8,567	4,626	—	1,376	—	796	4,766	9,767
Restricted Deposits	36b	2,233	2,038	2,240	2,535	1,686	3,077	1,903	5,073	8,472	5,374	3,271	3,470
Central Govt. Lending Funds	36f	3,307	3,801	3,871	5,029	1,653	1,416	4,508	9,178	9,450	514	628	606
Liab. to Nonbank Financial Insts	36j	1,153	1,326	1,564	2,533	7,536	39,332	14,725	14,690	2,845	4,652	4,860	5,436
Capital Accounts	37a	26,862	34,174	45,313	49,944	110,259	27,728	67,341	171,141	194,666	217,766	210,098	253,464
Other Items (Net)	37r	2,133	−1,793	−11,250	−6,613	−49,367	34,780	69,826	77,934	75,454	76,750	64,847	61,602
Money plus Quasi-Money	35l	144,063	173,167	220,829	280,631	351,504	572,118	642,107	748,845	845,026	883,318	954,775	1,033,523
Money (National Definitions)						*Billions of Rupiah: End of Period*							
Base Money	19ma	....	....	25,852	34,405	46,086	75,120	101,790	125,615	127,796	138,250	166,474	206,180
M1	59ma	....	....	52,677	64,089	78,343	101,197	124,633	162,186	177,731	191,939	223,799	245,946
M2	59mb	....	....	222,638	288,632	355,643	577,381	646,205	747,028	844,053	883,908	955,692	1,033,877

Indonesia 536

		1993	1994	1995	1996	1997	1998	1999	2000	2001	2002	2003	2004
Interest Rates							*Percent Per Annum*						
Discount Rate (End of Period)	60	8.82	12.44	13.99	12.80	20.00	38.44	12.51	14.53	17.62	12.93	8.31	7.43
Money Market Rate	60b	8.66	9.74	13.64	13.96	27.82	62.79	23.58	10.32	15.03	13.54	7.76	5.38
Deposit Rate	60l	14.55	12.53	16.72	17.26	20.01	39.07	25.74	12.50	15.48	15.50	10.59	6.44
Deposit Rate (Foreign Currency)	60l.f	....	....	....	....	....	....	7.45	5.56	5.37	3.26	2.17	1.74
Lending Rate	60p	20.59	17.76	18.85	19.22	21.82	32.15	27.66	18.46	18.55	18.95	16.94	14.12
Lending Rate (Foreign Currency)	60p.f	....	....	....	....	....	....	....	....	8.95	7.38	6.52	5.70
Prices, Production, Labor						*Index Numbers (2000=100): Period Averages*							
Share Prices	62	....	....	101.0	119.2	121.5	84.8	110.0	100.0	82.1	91.6	104.3	163.1
Wholesale Prices: Incl. Petroleum	63	28.9	30.5	33.9	36.6	39.9	80.5	† 88.9	100.0	114.2	117.3	119.8	130.0
Excl. Petroleum	63a	30.9	34.1	38.9	41.3	44.5	80.2	† 94.6	100.0	117.1	124.2	126.2	132.4
Consumer Prices	64	37.1	40.3	44.0	† 47.6	50.5	80.0	96.4	100.0	111.5	124.7	† 133.0	141.3
Crude Petroleum Production	66aa	107.8	113.7	113.4	112.8	83.6	103.9	95.8	100.0	94.7	88.6	80.0	....
Manufacturing Production	66ey	† 91.6	107.7	119.8	125.7	115.9	94.7	96.5	100.0	98.9	91.9	97.3	....
					Number in Thousands: Period Averages								
Employment	67e	79,201	80,110	82,038	85,702	87,050	87,674	88,817	89,838	90,807	91,647	....	....
Unemployment	67c	2	4	....	3,625	4,197	5,063	6,030	5,813	8,005	9,132	....	....
Unemployment Rate (%)	67r	2.8	4.4	....	4.0	4.7	5.5	6.4	6.1	8.1	9.1	....	....
Intl. Transactions & Positions						*Millions of US Dollars*							
Exports	70..d	36,823	40,055	45,417	49,814	56,298	50,370	51,243	65,403	57,361	60,164	64,107	71,261
Crude Petroleum & Products	70a.d	5,009	6,006	6,441	7,243	6,822	4,264	3,855	7,761	6,916	6,544	7,167	7,316
Crude Petroleum	70aad	4,259	5,072	5,146	5,712	5,479	3,349	3,162	6,090	5,715	5,205	5,579	5,691
Imports, c.i.f.	71..d	28,328	31,983	40,630	42,929	51,304	35,280	33,321	43,595	37,534	38,310	42,243	52,076
							2000=100						
Volume of Exports	72	70.8	78.0	81.5	85.6	110.0	102.3	84.0	100.0	121.0	99.7	97.0	101.2
Crude Petroleum	72aa	98.8	149.5	139.2	130.8	133.4	125.8	218.6	100.0	112.4	99.6	89.3	80.3
Export Prices					*2000=100: Indices of Unit Values in US Dollars*								
Exports (Unit Value)	74..d	91.0	90.3	103.1	109.0	103.6	80.8	64.9	100.0	89.9	95.5	102.7	120.4
Crude Petroleum (Unit Value)	74aad	63.6	58.0	87.4	92.4	87.8	60.9	55.0	100.0	1,000.9	1,036.4	206.0	129.0
Crude Petroleum (Ofc.Price)	76aad	61.2	56.3	61.0	71.3	66.7	43.2	61.7	100.0	84.1	88.0	101.8	....
Balance of Payments					*Millions of US Dollars: Minus Sign Indicates Debit*								
Current Account, n.i.e.	78ald	−2,106	−2,792	−6,431	−7,663	−4,889	4,097	5,783	7,992	6,901	7,824	7,252	....
Goods: Exports f.o.b.	78aad	36,607	40,223	47,454	50,188	56,298	50,371	51,242	65,407	57,365	59,165	63,254	....
Goods: Imports f.o.b.	78abd	−28,376	−32,322	−40,921	−44,240	−46,223	−31,942	−30,598	−40,365	−34,668	−35,652	−39,546	....
Trade Balance	78acd	8,231	7,901	6,533	5,948	10,075	18,429	20,643	25,042	22,696	23,513	23,708	....
Services: Credit	78add	3,959	4,797	5,469	6,599	6,941	4,479	4,599	5,214	5,500	6,663	5,293	....
Services: Debit	78aed	−9,846	−11,416	−13,540	−15,139	−16,607	−12,088	−12,376	−15,637	−15,880	−17,045	−17,400	....
Balance on Goods & Services	78afd	2,344	1,282	−1,538	−2,592	409	10,820	12,866	14,619	12,316	13,131	11,600	....
Income: Credit	78agd	1,028	1,048	1,306	1,210	1,855	1,910	1,891	2,458	2,004	1,318	1,055	....
Income: Debit	78ahd	−6,015	−5,741	−7,180	−7,218	−8,187	−10,099	−10,887	−10,901	−8,940	−8,365	−7,272	....
Balance on Gds, Serv. & Inc.	78aid	−2,643	−3,411	−7,412	−8,600	−5,923	2,631	3,869	6,176	5,381	6,083	5,383	....
Current Transfers, n.i.e.: Credit	78ajd	537	619	981	937	1,034	1,466	1,914	1,816	1,520	2,210	2,053	....
Current Transfers: Debit	78akd	—	—	—	—	—	—	—	—	—	−470	−184	....
Capital Account, n.i.e.	78bcd	—	—	—	—	—	—	—	—	—	—	—	....
Capital Account, n.i.e.: Credit	78bad	—	—	—	—	—	—	—	—	—	—	—	....
Capital Account: Debit	78bbd	—	—	—	—	—	—	—	—	—	—	—	....
Financial Account, n.i.e.	78bjd	5,632	3,839	10,259	10,847	−603	−9,633	−5,944	−7,896	−7,617	−1,103	−949	....
Direct Investment Abroad	78bdd	−356	−609	−603	−600	−178	—	—	—	—	—	—	....
Dir. Invest. in Rep. Econ., n.i.e.	78bed	2,004	2,109	4,346	6,194	4,677	−241	−1,866	−4,550	−2,977	145	−597	....
Portfolio Investment Assets	78bfd	—	—	....	....	....	....	....	....	....	....	....	....
Equity Securities	78bkd	—	—	....	....	....	....	....	....	....	....	....	....
Debt Securities	78bld	—	—	....	....	....	....	....	....	....	....	....	....
Portfolio Investment Liab., n.i.e.	78bgd	1,805	3,877	4,100	5,005	−2,632	−1,878	−1,792	−1,911	−244	1,222	2,251	....
Equity Securities	78bmd	1,805	1,900	1,493	1,819	−4,987	−4,371	−782	−1,021	442	877	1,131	....
Debt Securities	78bnd	—	1,977	2,607	3,186	2,355	2,493	−1,010	−890	−686	345	1,121	....
Financial Derivatives Assets	78bwd	....	....	....	....	....	....	....	....	....	....	....	....
Financial Derivatives Liabilities	78bxd	....	....	....	....	....	....	....	....	....	....	....	....
Other Investment Assets	78bhd	....	....	....	—	—	−44	−72	−150	−125	−500	−5	....
Monetary Authorities	78bod	....	....	....	....	....	....	....	....	....	....	....	....
General Government	78bpd	—	—	....	....	....	....	....	....	....	....	....	....
Banks	78bqd	—	—	....	....	....	....	....	....	....	....	....	....
Other Sectors	78brd	—	—	....	....	....	−44	−72	−150	−125	−500	−5	....
Other Investment Liab., n.i.e.	78bid	2,179	−1,538	2,416	248	−2,470	−7,470	−2,214	−1,285	−4,271	−1,970	−2,599	....
Monetary Authorities	78bsd	—	—	—	—	—	—	—	—	—	—	—	....
General Government	78btd	552	137	6	−663	−265	4,210	3,979	2,094	635	457	−398	....
Banks	78bud	1,357	527	1,953	−758	−276	−2,305	125	−1,420	−1,867	−1,217	−69	....
Other Sectors	78bvd	270	−2,202	457	1,669	−1,929	−9,375	−6,318	−1,959	−3,039	−1,210	−2,132	....
Net Errors and Omissions	78cad	−2,932	−263	−2,255	1,319	−2,645	2,099	2,077	3,829	701	−1,763	−2,655	....
Overall Balance	78cbd	594	784	1,573	4,503	−8,137	−3,437	1,916	3,926	−15	4,958	3,647	....
Reserves and Related Items	79dad	−594	−784	−1,573	−4,503	8,137	3,437	−1,916	−3,926	15	−4,958	−3,647	....
Reserve Assets	79dbd	−594	−784	−1,573	−4,503	5,113	−2,345	−3,286	−5,051	1,371	−4,010	−4,236	....
Use of Fund Credit and Loans	79dcd	—	—	—	—	3,025	5,782	1,371	1,125	−1,356	−948	588	....
Exceptional Financing	79ded	....	....	....	....	....	....	....	....	....	....	....	....

		1993	1994	1995	1996	1997	1998	1999	2000	2001	2002	2003	2004
International Investment Position						*Millions of US Dollars*							
Assets	79aad	....	....	....	....	....	....	....	....	41,880	47,912	56,013	....
Direct Investment Abroad	79abd	....	....	....	....	....	....	....	....	−1,413	−328	−208	....
Portfolio Investment	79acd	....	....	....	....	....	....	....	....	2,894	2,473	2,877	....
Equity Securities	79add	....	....	....	....	....	....	....	....	17	23	20	....
Debt Securities	79aed	....	....	....	....	....	....	....	....	2,878	2,451	2,857	....
Financial Derivatives	79ald	....	....	....	....	....	....	....	....	40	84	33	....
Other Investment	79afd	....	....	....	....	....	....	....	....	12,344	13,641	17,014	....
Monetary Authorities	79agd	....	....	....	....	....	....	....	....	927	1,265	1,906	....
General Government	79ahd	....	....	....	....	....	....	....	....	—	44	42	....
Banks	79aid	....	....	....	....	....	....	....	....	8,022	8,260	9,175	....
Other Sectors	79ajd	....	....	....	....	....	....	....	....	3,394	4,072	5,891	....
Reserve Assets	79akd	....	....	....	....	....	....	....	....	28,014	32,042	36,297	....
Liabilities	79lad	....	....	....	....	....	....	....	....	155,091	172,498	162,447	....
Dir. Invest. in Rep. Economy	79lbd	....	....	....	....	....	....	....	....	15,203	31,020	10,329	....
Portfolio Investment	79lcd	....	....	....	....	....	....	....	....	13,315	14,332	23,297	....
Equity Securities	79ldd	....	....	....	....	....	....	....	....	4,475	6,452	14,808	....
Debt Securities	79led	....	....	....	....	....	....	....	....	8,840	7,881	8,489	....
Financial Derivatives	79lld	....	....	....	....	....	....	....	....	79	63	32	....
Other Investment	79lfd	....	....	....	....	....	....	....	....	126,494	127,082	128,790	....
Monetary Authorities	79lgd	....	....	....	....	....	....	....	....	12,386	10,769	12,191	....
General Government	79lhd	....	....	....	....	....	....	....	....	58,060	63,429	68,421	....
Banks	79lid	....	....	....	....	....	....	....	....	7,102	7,185	3,759	....
Other Sectors	79ljd	....	....	....	....	....	....	....	....	48,945	45,699	44,420	....
Government Finance						*Billions of Rupiah: Year Beginning April 1*							
Deficit (-) or Surplus	80	2,018	3,581	10,085	6,180	−4,211	−28,191	† −12,645	3,139	−40,485p	−23,574	−33,669	....
Revenue	81	56,318	69,402	80,427	90,298	113,882	157,412	† 198,673	210,443	300,600p	298,528	340,658	....
Grants Received	81z	—	67	—	—	—	—	—	—	478p	78	437	....
Expenditure	82	54,983	61,866	66,723	77,964	112,893	174,097	225,874	227,892	341,563p	322,180	374,764	....
Lending Minus Repayments	83	−683	4,022	3,619	6,154	5,200	11,506	−14,556	−20,588	—p	—	—	....
Financing													
Net Borrowing: Domestic	84a	444	−4,295	....	−3,058	5,210	9,593	−9,446	8,721	32,178p	16,946	32,115	....
Net borrowing: Foreign	85a	−451	−303	−1,677	−2,659	−4,674	49,705	15,942	16,196	10,267p	6,628	1,554	....
Use of Cash Balances	87	−2,011	1,017	....	−463	3,676	−31,106	6,149	−28,056	−1,960p	—	—	....
Debt: Domestic	88a	4,861	939	3,229	83	4,097	13,481	6,481	1,940	1,018	....	....	....
Debt: Foreign	89a	118,797	138,841	136,781	127,324	450,890	514,134	490,685	613,199	621,446	582,631	598,412	....
National Accounts						*Billions of Rupiah*							
Househ.Cons.Expend.,incl.NPISHs.	96f	† 192,958	228,119	279,876	332,094	387,171	647,824	813,183	856,798	1,039,655	1,231,965	1,372,078	1,532,388
Government Consumption Expend	91f	† 29,757	31,014	35,584	40,299	42,952	54,416	72,631	90,780	113,416	132,219	163,701	187,774
Gross Fixed Capital Formation	93e	86,667	105,381	129,218	157,653	177,686	243,043	221,472	275,881	323,875	353,967	386,219	483,441
Changes in Inventories	93i	10,546	13,326	15,900	5,800	21,615	−82,716	−96,461	20,138	71,166	30,426	−32,212	7,835
Exports of Goods and Services	90c	† 88,231	101,332	119,593	137,533	174,871	506,245	390,560	569,490	642,595	595,514	627,065	711,778
Imports of Goods and Services (-)	98c	† 78,383	96,953	125,657	140,812	176,600	413,058	301,654	423,318	506,426	480,815	470,998	620,184
Gross Domestic Product (GDP)	99b	† 329,776	382,220	454,514	532,568	627,695	955,754	1,099,732	1,389,770	1,684,281	1,863,275	2,045,854	2,303,031
Net Primary Income from Abroad	98.n	† −12,553	−10,248	−13,366	−14,272	−18,355	−53,894	−83,764	−92,162	−61,051	−54,513	−79,629	−79,049
Gross National Income (GNI)	99a	† 296,095	348,072	413,661	489,377	571,512	895,379	998,017	1,297,608	1,623,229	1,808,762	1,966,225	2,223,983
Consumption of Fixed Capital	99cf	16,489	19,111	22,725	26,629	31,385	47,788	54,987	69,489	84,214	93,164	102,293	115,152
GDP Volume 1993 Prices	99b.p	329,776	354,641	383,792	413,798	433,246	376,375	379,353	569,490	....	....	....	....
GDP Volume 2000 Prices	99b.p	....	....	....	....	....	....	....	1,389,770	1,442,985	1,506,124	1,579,559	1,660,579
GDP Volume (2000=100)	99bvp	† 57.9	62.3	67.4	72.7	76.1	66.1	66.6	† 100.0	103.8	108.4	113.7	119.5
GDP Deflator (2000=100)	99bip	† 41.0	44.2	48.5	52.7	59.4	104.1	118.8	100.0	116.7	123.7	129.5	138.7
						Millions: Midyear Estimates							
Population	99z	190.07	192.88	195.65	198.39	201.09	† 203.78	206.47	209.17	211.89	214.62	217.35	220.08

Iran, Islamic Republic of   429

		1993	1994	1995	1996	1997	1998	1999	2000	2001	2002	2003	2004
Exchange Rates							Rials per SDR: End of Period						
Official Rate	aa	2,415.49	2,534.26	2,597.64	2,515.19	2,366.94	2,465.36	2,405.04	2,948.39	2,200.47	† 10,810.87	12,292.11	13,655.62
						Rials per US Dollar: End of Period (ae) Period Average (rf)							
Official Rate	ae	1,758.56	1,735.97	1,747.50	1,749.14	1,754.26	1,750.93	1,752.29	2,262.93	1,750.95	† 7,951.98	8,272.11	8,793.00
Official Rate	rf	1,267.77	1,748.75	1,747.93	1,750.76	1,752.92	1,751.86	1,752.93	1,764.43	1,753.56	† 6,906.96	8,193.89	8,613.99
						Rials per US Dollar: End of Period							
Market Rate	aea	....	....	....	....	4,645	5,721	8,135	7,909	7,924		....	....	....
						Rials per US Dollar: Months Ending the 20th							
Weighted Average	yf	890	1,222	1,726	2,194	2,780	3,206	4,172	5,731	6,163	....	....	....
						Index Numbers (2000=100): Period Averages							
Nominal Effective Exchange Rate	nec	307.93	222.78	128.05	128.20	143.50	138.78	98.43	100.00	111.22	109.38	93.28	81.77
Real Effective Exchange Rate	rec	97.40	81.95	65.53	80.46	100.28	108.69	89.23	100.00	118.58	128.58	124.09	122.09
Fund Position							Millions of SDRs: End of Period						
Quota	2f.s	1,079	1,079	1,079	1,079	1,079	1,079	1,497	1,497	1,497	1,497	1,497	1,497
SDRs	1b.s	105	98	90	240	245	1	101	267	267	268	268	274
Reserve Position in the Fund	1c.s	—	—	—	—	—	—	—	—	—	—	—	—
Total Fund Cred.&Loans Outstg	2tl	—	—	—	—	—	—	—	—	—	—	—	—
International Liquidity						Millions of US Dollars Unless Otherwise Indicated: End of Period							
SDRs	1b.d	144	143	134	345	330	2	139	349	336	364	399	425
Reserve Position in the Fund	1c.d	—	—	—	—	—	—	—	—	—	—	—	—
Gold (Million Fine Troy Ounces)	1ad	4.765	4.740	4.842	....	....	....	....	....	....	....	....	....
Gold (National Valuation)	1and	229	242	252	....	....	....	....	....	....	....	....	....
Monetary Authorities:Other Assets	3..d	....	....	....	....	....	....	....	....	....	....	....	....
Deposit Money Banks: Assets	7a.d	1,459	3,321	3,354	4,319	4,403	4,648	2,258	3,112	6,298	7,244	8,903	....
Liabilities	7b.d	3,397	5,589	4,015	2,668	2,128	2,771	3,410	3,486	6,695	8,657	13,749	....
Other Banking Insts.: Liabilities	7f.d	71	53	118	110	66	136	250	266	403	409	522	2,151
Monetary Authorities							Billions of Rials: Months Ending the 20th						
Foreign Assets	11	7,916	9,681	14,413	19,454	15,669	9,827	11,413	24,478	28,151	154,928	188,442	263,305
Claims on Central Government	12a	16,002	28,169	32,648	42,461	42,624	55,710	61,731	60,207	64,673	101,692	111,341	107,594
Claims on Official Entities	12bx	3,792	5,549	10,704	18,826	15,618	18,842	19,794	23,189	16,287	19,200	21,897	23,417
Claims on Deposit Money Banks	12e	3,751	1,967	10,462	2,056	11,162	9,565	13,392	17,567	18,589	17,732	23,823	....
Reserve Money	14	16,511	22,165	32,805	41,708	51,298	60,533	70,911	82,726	88,015	111,487	127,554	....
of which: Currency Outside DMBs	14a	4,925	6,199	7,949	9,598	11,271	14,050	16,652	20,020	21,840	25,945	30,809	....
Nonfin.Pub.Ent. Deps	14e	862	1,604	2,020	2,639	2,642	4,662	5,304	7,859	4,552	5,401	6,800	8,611
Restricted Deposits	16b	1,158	4,004	7,085	8,764	6,789	3,810	4,066	3,351	4,133	1,182	1,415	1,216
Foreign Liabilities	16c	2,924	2,883	2,679	3,466	5,057	8,012	6,562	7,094	13,991	83,330	77,087	82,275
Central Government Deposits	16d	4,965	6,752	9,738	13,035	13,837	13,814	18,275	28,645	37,312	57,194	60,139	92,882
Capital Accounts	17a	801	903	989	1,004	1,003	1,012	1,097	1,064	1,235	3,225	3,991	4,790
Other Items (Net)	17r	5,104	8,658	14,929	14,820	7,089	6,763	5,420	2,561	−16,986	37,132	75,318	....
Deposit Money Banks							Billions of Rials: Months Ending the 20th						
Reserves	20	10,586	14,179	22,519	28,865	36,563	40,385	47,190	51,536	58,559	72,743	82,353	....
Foreign Assets	21	2,566	5,766	5,861	7,555	7,724	8,138	3,957	7,043	11,027	57,605	73,648	....
Claims on Central Government	22a	1,236	1,232	1,827	1,823	1,821	1,821	7,494	5,800	5,648	7,187	15,856	....
Claims on Private Sector	22d	22,131	27,535	32,938	41,043	52,579	63,716	85,701	112,986	155,268	206,970	291,624	....
Demand Deposits	24	12,519	18,120	24,373	33,628	41,064	48,732	59,996	74,291	99,275	123,963	147,018	....
Time and Savings Deposits	25	23,181	29,377	37,599	49,426	62,881	74,438	90,435	108,884	143,689	181,022	234,086	....
Foreign Liabilities	26c	5,973	9,703	7,016	4,667	3,734	4,851	5,975	7,890	11,723	68,837	113,736	....
Credit from Monetary Authorities	26g	3,751	1,967	10,462	2,056	11,162	9,565	13,392	17,567	18,589	17,732	23,823	....
Capital Accounts	27a	3,719	3,724	3,724	3,724	3,724	3,724	3,764	3,764	8,564	8,564	8,564	....
Other Items (Net)	27r	−12,625	−14,180	−20,030	−14,215	−23,878	−27,250	−29,220	−35,031	−51,338	−55,612	−63,745	....
Monetary Survey							Billions of Rials: Months Ending the 20th						
Foreign Assets (Net)	31n	1,585	2,860	10,578	18,876	14,603	5,102	2,833	16,538	13,465	60,366	71,268	....
Domestic Credit	32	43,385	59,484	74,426	101,566	115,511	151,740	187,227	211,234	246,942	319,626	416,605	....
Claims on Central Govt. (Net)	32an	12,211	22,556	24,674	31,026	30,370	43,463	48,057	34,512	30,557	39,216	45,566	....
Claims on Official Entities	32bx	9,043	9,393	16,814	29,498	32,562	44,561	53,469	63,736	61,117	73,440	79,415	....
Claims on Private Sector	32d	22,131	27,535	32,938	41,043	52,579	63,716	85,701	112,986	155,268	206,970	291,624	....
Money	34	18,305	25,923	34,342	45,865	54,977	67,444	81,952	102,170	125,667	155,309	184,627	....
Quasi-Money	35	23,181	29,377	37,599	49,426	62,881	74,438	90,435	108,884	143,689	181,022	234,086	....
Restricted Deposits	36b	1,158	4,004	7,085	8,764	6,789	3,810	4,066	3,351	4,133	1,182	1,415	1,216
Other Items (Net)	37r	2,327	3,040	5,977	16,387	5,467	11,150	13,608	13,367	−13,082	42,479	67,746	....
Money plus Quasi-Money	35l	41,486	55,299	71,941	95,291	117,858	141,883	172,387	211,054	269,356	336,331	418,712	....
Other Banking Institutions							Billions of Rials: Months Ending the 20th						
Cash	40	166	218	361	671	912	1,549	1,901	3,417	3,094	7,449	7,667	8,724
Claims on Central Government	42a	2	2	2	2	2	2	941	1,249	1,755	1,846	3,522	4,470
Claims on Official Entities	42bx	113	141	90	163	591	1,002	195	208	222	909	885	1,340
Claims on Private Sector	42d	6,159	7,504	9,831	13,506	18,611	25,812	36,411	51,503	66,108	88,257	105,605	131,732
Demand Deposits	44	767	870	1,287	2,129	3,325	4,002	4,001	6,023	6,948	11,435	14,789	16,093
Private Sector	44x	767	870	1,287	2,129	3,325	4,002	4,001	6,023	6,948	11,435	14,784	16,093
Official Entities	44y	—	—	—	—	—	—	—	—	—	—	5	—
Time and Savings Deposits	45	914	1,409	2,367	3,327	5,591	9,157	12,584	15,831	24,110	35,582	46,604	67,137
Foreign Liabilities	46c	125	91	207	192	116	238	438	601	705	3,253	4,319	18,912
Central Government Deposits	46d	139	114	124	175	158	106	69	87	112	557	2,986	6,646
Credit from Monetary Authorities	46g	215	795	3,437	8,126	3,518	4,635	5,895	9,358	652	2,025	4,410	4,468
Capital Accounts	47a	870	1,928	1,928	1,940	1,940	1,940	1,940	2,960	6,385	6,409	6,409	11,484
Other Items (Net)	47r	3,409	2,658	935	−1,548	5,469	8,287	14,522	21,517	32,267	39,201	38,170	21,525
Liquid Liabilities	55l	43,002	57,360	75,232	100,077	125,862	153,493	187,070	229,491	297,320	375,899	472,437	....
Interest Rates							Percent Per Annum						
Deposit Rate (End of Period)	60l	....	....	....	....	....	....	....	....	....	....	11.68	11.70
Lending Rate (End of Period)	60p	....	....	....	....	....	....	....	....	....	....	....	16.65

		1993	1994	1995	1996	1997	1998	1999	2000	2001	2002	2003	2004
Prices and Production						*Index Numbers (2000=100)*							
Share Prices................	62	16.9	18.3	36.8	76.9	73.8	65.2	70.1	100.0	133.8	178.7	307.3	510.2
Wholesale Prices...........	63	19.4	26.7	42.9	57.0	63.1	70.6	† 84.1	† 100.0	105.9	114.6	126.7	142.6
Home Goods.............	63a	19.5	26.8	41.1	53.8	60.2	70.4	† 84.4	100.0	107.3	118.0	132.1	148.7
Consumer Prices...........	64	20.7	27.3	40.8	52.6	61.7	72.8	87.4	100.0	111.3	127.2	148.2	170.1
Crude Petroleum Production...........	66aa	97.0	95.6	95.7	97.6	96.4	95.4	93.2	100.0	96.8	90.9	99.3	103.3
Intl. Transactions & Positions						*Millions of US Dollars Year Ending March 20*							
Exports.............	70..d	18,080	19,434	18,360	22,391	18,381	13,118	21,030	28,461	23,904	28,186	33,788	....
Imports, c.i.f.............	71..d	21,427	13,774	12,313	15,117	14,196	14,323	12,683	14,347	17,626	21,180	27,676	....
Volume of Exports							*2000=100*						
Petroleum.................	72a	109.5	107.5	110.2	110.5	107.4	102.2	95.4	100.0	....	....	....	....
Crude Petroleum........	72aa	112.7	110.0	111.6	111.6	107.1	105.2	95.1	100.0	....	....	....	....
Export Prices.............	76	....	....	178.7	169.5	127.2	79.9	110.6	100.0	....	....	....	....
Import Prices.............	76.x	....	....	102.5	118.8	107.3	145.0	114.1	100.0	....	....	....	....
Balance of Payments						*Millions of US$: Year Beginning March 21: Minus Sign Indicates Debit*							
Current Account, n.i.e....................	78ald	−4,215	4,956	3,358	5,232	2,213	−2,139	6,589	12,645	....	....	....	....
Goods: Exports f.o.b..............	78aad	18,080	19,434	18,360	22,391	18,381	13,118	21,030	28,345	....	....	....	....
Goods: Imports f.o.b...............	78abd	−19,287	−12,617	−12,774	−14,989	−14,123	−14,286	−13,433	−15,207	....	....	....	....
Trade Balance...........	78acd	−1,207	6,817	5,586	7,402	4,258	−1,168	7,597	13,138	....	....	....	....
Services: Credit............	78add	1,084	438	593	860	1,192	1,793	1,216	1,382	....	....	....	....
Services: Debit.............	78aed	−5,600	−3,226	−2,339	−3,083	−3,371	−2,760	−2,457	−2,296	....	....	....	....
Balance on Goods & Services......	78afd	−5,723	4,029	3,840	5,179	2,079	−2,135	6,356	12,224	....	....	....	....
Income: Credit..........	78agd	151	142	316	488	466	230	181	404	....	....	....	....
Income: Debit............	78ahd	−143	−413	−794	−898	−725	−731	−473	−604	....	....	....	....
Balance on Gds, Serv. & Inc..........	78aid	−5,715	3,758	3,362	4,769	1,820	−2,636	6,064	12,024	....	....	....	....
Current Transfers, n.i.e.: Credit....	78ajd	1,500	1,200	—	471	400	500	508	539	....	....	....	....
Current Transfers: Debit................	78akd	—	−2	−4	−8	−7	−3	17	82	....	....	....	....
Capital Account, n.i.e...................	78bcd	—	—	—	—	—	—	—	—	....	....	....	....
Capital Account, n.i.e.: Credit.......	78bad	—	—	—	—	—	—	—	—	....	....	....	....
Capital Account: Debit..................	78bbd	—	—	—	—	—	—	—	—	....	....	....	....
Financial Account, n.i.e.............	78bjd	5,563	−346	−774	−5,508	−4,822	2,270	−5,894	−10,189	....	....	....	....
Direct Investment Abroad...........	78bdd	—	—	—	—	—	—	—	—	....	....	....	....
Dir. Invest. in Rep. Econ., n.i.e......	78bed	—	2	17	26	53	24	35	39	....	....	....	....
Portfolio Investment Assets...........	78bfd	—	—	—	—	—	—	—	—	....	....	....	....
Equity Securities.............	78bkd	—	—	—	—	—	—	—	—	....	....	....	....
Debt Securities..............	78bld	—	—	—	—	—	—	—	—	....	....	....	....
Portfolio Investment Liab., n.i.e......	78bgd	—	—	—	—	—	—	—	—	....	....	....	....
Equity Securities.............	78bmd	—	—	—	—	—	—	—	—	....	....	....	....
Debt Securities..............	78bnd	—	—	—	—	—	—	—	—	....	....	....	....
Financial Derivatives Assets...........	78bwd	....	....	....	....	....							
Financial Derivatives Liabilities......	78bxd	....	....	....	....	....							
Other Investment Assets..............	78bhd	1,250	−1,258	−419	−1,305	2,293	963	−1,650	−8,257	....	....	....	....
Monetary Authorities..................	78bod	....	....	....	....	....							
General Government.................	78bpd	44	−42	235	−48	−99	−21	−6	−5,932	....	....	....	....
Banks..............	78bqd	1,206	−1,216	−654	−1,257	2,392	984	−1,638	−1,783	....	....	....	....
Other Sectors..............	78brd	—	—	—	—	—	—	−6	−542	....	....	....	....
Other Investment Liab., n.i.e........	78bid	4,313	910	−372	−4,229	−7,168	1,283	−4,279	−1,971	....	....	....	....
Monetary Authorities..................	78bsd	68	−252	−64	−283	179	93	−5,517	−1,410	....	....	....	....
General Government.................	78btd	−1,358	10,447	1,684	−4,523	−4,035	−489	104	−621	....	....	....	....
Banks.............	78bud	—	—	—	—	—	—	—	—	....	....	....	....
Other Sectors..............	78bvd	5,603	−9,285	−1,992	577	−3,312	1,679	1,134	60	....	....	....	....
Net Errors and Omissions................	78cad	−1,120	−3,702	202	2,717	−1,088	−1,122	−244	−1,373	....	....	....	....
Overall Balance............	78cbd	228	908	2,786	2,441	−3,697	−991	451	1,083	....	....	....	....
Reserves and Related Items..............	79dad	−228	−908	−2,786	−2,441	3,697	991	−451	−1,083	....	....	....	....
Reserve Assets.............	79dbd	−228	−908	−2,786	−2,441	3,697	991	−451	−1,083	....	....	....	....
Use of Fund Credit and Loans........	79dcd	—	—	—	—	—	—	—	—	....	....	....	....
Exceptional Financing...................	79ded	....	....	....	....	....	—	—	—	....	....	....	....
Government Finance						*Billions of Rials: Year Beginning March 21*							
Deficit (-) or Surplus.....................	80	−636	332	245	493	−3,060	−17,344	−927	−3,981	−2,571	−20,300	−31,371	....
Revenue........................	81	20,251	29,245	41,575	57,276	62,378	53,626	92,316	104,641	125,480	165,210	311,754	....
Grants...........................	81z	....	....	....	....	....	....	....	....	....	....	....	....
Exp. & Lending Minus Repay..........	82z	....	....	....	....	....	....	....	....	....	....	....	....
Expenditure.................	82	20,887	28,912	41,331	56,783	65,438	70,970	93,243	108,622	128,050	185,510	343,124	....
Lending Minus Repayments..........	83	....	....	....	....	....	....	....	....	....	....	....	....
Total Financing.....................	80h	636	−332	−245	−493	3,060	17,344	927	3,981	2,571	20,300	31,371	....
National Accounts						*Billions of Rials: Year Beginning March 21*							
Househ.Cons.Expend.,incl.NPISHs...	96f	43,550	60,138	87,496	113,240	140,807	181,172	225,770	276,612	323,314	417,081	500,497	....
Government Consumption Expend...	91f	15,517	21,005	29,708	35,174	38,207	47,037	55,998	80,554	94,029	118,408	138,176	....
Gross Fixed Capital Formation..........	93e	24,858	28,819	38,954	65,626	83,765	96,051	124,202	153,462	187,999	261,136	319,296	....
Changes in Inventories...............	93i	8,435	866	15,329	23,485	20,855	12,044	5,670	37,958	48,669	76,691	115,770	....
Exports of Goods and Services........	90c	27,420	39,632	40,362	51,746	51,007	44,857	93,509	131,811	137,732	245,868	309,739	....
Imports of Goods and Services (-).....	98c	19,847	17,024	24,386	37,160	44,728	51,567	64,931	101,190	126,201	210,570	282,466	....
Gross Domestic Product (GDP)........	99b	100,047	130,565	185,928	248,348	292,678	329,134	436,625	580,473	671,736	925,906	1,107,717	....
Net Primary Income from Abroad.....	98.n	−1,390	−2,267	−1,346	−1,649	−491	380	−532	278	1,455	−15,932	−22,667	....
Gross National Income (GNI)...........	99a	98,657	128,298	184,582	246,699	292,187	239,514	436,093	580,751	673,191	909,974	1,085,051	....
GDP Volume 1997 Prices...............	99b.p	....	....	....	....	292,678	300,699	306,514	322,278	334,104	359,011	383,160	....
GDP Volume (2000=100)...............	99bvp	76.9	78.2	80.8	86.2	† 90.8	93.3	95.1	100.0	103.7	111.4	118.9	....
GDP Deflator (2000=100)...............	99bip	22.4	28.8	39.6	49.6	55.5	60.8	79.1	100.0	111.6	143.2	160.5	....
						Millions: Midyear Estimates							
Population............................	99z	60.33	61.36	62.32	63.24	64.10	64.92	65.67	66.36	67.00	67.59	68.17	68.80

Iraq   433

		1993	1994	1995	1996	1997	1998	1999	2000	2001	2002	2003	2004
Exchange Rates						*SDRs per Dinar: End of Period*								
Principal Rate............................	ac	2.3420	2.2036	2.1641	2.2371	2.3842	2.2847	2.3438	2.4690	2.5597	2.3662	....	....
					US Dollars per Dinar: End of Period (ag) Period Average (rh)									
Principal Rate............................	ag	3.2169	3.2169	3.2169	3.2169	3.2169	3.2169	3.2169	3.2169	3.2169	3.2169	....	....
Principal Rate............................	rh	3.2169	3.2169	3.2169	3.2169	3.2169	3.2169	3.2169	3.2169	3.2169	3.2169	....	....
					Index Numbers (2000=100): Period Averages									
Principal Rate............................	ahx	100.0	100.0	100.0	100.0	100.0	100.0	100.0	100.0	100.0	100.0	....	....
Nominal Effective Exchange Rate.....	nec	56.1	64.5	63.9	69.0	78.8	83.8	89.5	100.0	109.8	109.5	98.7	92.0
Fund Position						*Millions of SDRs: End of Period*								
Quota..	2f.s	504.0	504.0	504.0	504.0	504.0	504.0	504.0	504.0	504.0	504.0	504.0	1,188.4
SDRs..	1b.s	—	—	—	—	—	—	—	—	—	—	—	296.1
Reserve Position in the Fund............	1c.s	—	—	—	—	—	—	—	—	—	—	—	171.1
Total Fund Cred.&Loans Outstg........	2tl	—	—	—	—	—	—	—	—	—	—	—	297.1
International Liquidity					*Millions of US Dollars Unless Otherwise Indicated: End of Period*									
SDRs..	1b.d	—	—	—	—	—	—	—	—	—	—	—	459.9
Reserve Position in the Fund..........	1c.d	—	—	—	—	—	—	—	—	—	—	—	265.7
Production						*Index Numbers (2000=100): Period Averages*								
Crude Petroleum............................	66aa	23.2	23.2	23.2	24.4	47.0	76.6	93.6	100.0	93.0	73.4	53.5	81.6
Intl. Transactions & Positions						*Millions of Dinars*								
Imports, c.i.f., from DOTS................	71y	165.6	155.0	206.9	176.7	353.2	576.0	656.0	1,064.8	1,751.4	1,810.7	....	....
National Accounts						*Millions of Dinars*								
Househ.Cons.Expend.,incl.NPISHs....	96f	81,106.0	....	....	....	....	....	....	....	....	....	....	....
Government Consumption Expend...	91f	15,576.3	....	....	....	....	....	....	....	....	....	....	....
Gross Fixed Capital Formation..........	93e	16,258.7	....	....	....	....	....	....	....	....	....	....	....
Changes in Inventories....................	93i	1,102.0	....	....	....	....	....	....	....	....	....	....	....
Exports of Goods and Services..........	90c	1,474.0	....	....	....	....	....	....	....	....	....	....	....
Imports of Goods and Services (-).....	98c	3,375.0	....	....	....	....	....	....	....	....	....	....	....
Gross Domestic Product (GDP).........	99b	112,142.0	....	....	....	....	....	....	....	....	....	....	....
						Millions: Midyear Estimates								
Population.................................	99z	20.31	20.97	21.63	22.30	22.98	23.66	24.36	25.07	25.81	26.55	27.30	28.06

Ireland 178

		1993	1994	1995	1996	1997	1998	1999	2000	2001	2002	2003	2004
Exchange Rates		*SDRs per Pound through 1998, SDRs per Euro Thereafter: End of Period*											
Market Rate	ac	1.0271	1.0598	1.0801	1.1691	1.0601	1.0563	.7319	.7142	.7013	.7714	.8499	.8771
		US Dollars per Pound through 1998, US Dollars per Euro Thereafter: End of Period (ag) Period Average (rh)											
Market Rate	ag	1.4108	1.5471	1.6055	1.6811	1.4304	1.4873	1.0046	.9305	.8813	1.0487	1.2630	1.3621
Market Rate	rh	1.4671	1.4978	1.6038	1.6006	1.5180	1.4257	1.0668	.9240	.8956	.9444	1.1308	1.2433
		ECUs per Pound: End of Period (ec) Period Average (ed)											
ECU Rate	ec	1.2630	1.2578	1.2218	1.3417	1.2960	1.2697	....	....	....	....	....	....
ECU Rate	ed	1.2514	1.2604	1.2263	1.2611	1.3380	1.2717	....	....	....	....	....	....
		Index Numbers (2000=100): Period Averages											
Market Rate (1995=100)	ahx	91.5	93.4	100.0	99.8	94.7	88.9						
Nominal Effective Exchange Rate	neu	113.02	112.50	113.64	116.15	116.76	111.12	107.11	100.00	100.54	102.59	110.25	112.52
Fund Position		*Millions of SDRs: End of Period*											
Quota	2f.s	525	525	525	525	525	525	838	838	838	838	838	838
SDRs	1b.s	97	101	107	115	123	137	29	37	43	49	53	57
Reserve Position in the Fund	1c.s	155	152	197	226	252	414	303	252	268	345	387	269
Total Fund Cred.&Loans Outstg	2tl	—	—	—	—	—	—	—	—	—	—	—	—
International Liquidity		*Millions of US Dollars Unless Otherwise Indicated: End of Period*											
Total Res.Min.Gold (Eurosys.Def)	1l.d	5,925	6,115	8,630	8,205	6,526	9,397	† 5,325	5,360	5,587	5,415	4,079	2,831
SDRs	1b.d	133	148	159	165	166	193	40	48	55	66	79	89
Reserve Position in the Fund	1c.d	213	222	294	325	340	582	416	329	336	469	575	418
Foreign Exchange	1d.d	5,579	5,745	8,178	7,715	6,020	8,622	4,869	4,983	5,196	4,879	3,425	2,324
o/w:Fin.Deriv.Rel.to Reserves	1ddd	....	....	....	....	....	....						
Other Reserve Assets	1e.d	....	....	....	....	....	....	—	—	—	—	—	—
Gold (Million Fine Troy Ounces)	1ad	.360	.360	.361	.361	.361	.451	.176	.176	.176	.176	.176	.176
Gold (Eurosystem Valuation)	1and	123	141	137	143	116	132	51	48	49	60	73	77
Memo:Euro Cl. on Non-EA Res	1dgd	....	....	....	....	....	....	43.17	19.54	185.07	372.29	1,207.43	1,472.43
Non-Euro Cl. on EA Res	1dhd	....	....	....	....	....	....	94.34	275.49	357.68	292.01	318.05	111.69
Mon. Auth.: Other Foreign Assets	3..d	....	....	....	....	....	....						
Foreign Liabilities	4..d	—	—	—	—	—	—	† 1,389	573	78	91	110	475
Banking Insts.: Foreign Assets	7a.d	21,381	30,088	46,679	70,324	101,447	142,089	† 78,106	135,339	173,199	236,529	324,806	433,634
Foreign Liab	7b.d	19,146	28,127	49,100	70,169	99,225	142,772	† 77,733	141,507	191,246	255,228	338,470	428,831
Monetary Authorities		*Millions of Pounds through 1998; Millions of Euros Beginning 1999: End of Period*											
Fgn. Assets (Cl.on Non-EA Ctys)	11	4,283	4,173	5,471	4,959	4,634	6,445	5,411	6,333	6,617	5,601	4,296	3,642
Claims on General Government	12a.u	....	....	....	....	....	....	2,109	2,183	2,029	1,650	2,958	3,495
o/w: Claims on Gen.Govt.in Cty	12a	315	254	183	132	132	132	279	229	29	—	21	—
Claims on Banking Institutions	12e.u	....	....	....	....	....	....	8,662	9,012	13,977	11,939	18,947	19,208
o/w: Claims on Bank.Inst.in Cty	12e	....	....	....	....	....	....	5,062	8,407	13,201	11,158	17,535	17,508
Claims on Other Resident Sectors	12d.u	....	....	....	....	....	....	—	—	—	—	7	6
o/w: Cl. on Oth.Res.Sect.in Cty	12d	—	—	—	—	—	—	—	—	—	—	7	6
Currency Issued	14a	1,776	1,907	2,092	2,287	2,619	3,040	4,848	5,368	4,704	4,278	4,650	6,437
Liabilities to Banking Insts	14c.u	....	....	....	....	....	....	4,228	6,426	8,619	10,405	17,702	16,077
o/w: Liabs to Bank.Inst.in Cty	14c	709	685	1,188	1,030	1,326	2,258	2,074	2,426	3,506	4,509	3,815	4,342
Demand Dep. of Other Res.Sect	14d.u	....	....	....	....	....	....	—	—	—	—	—	—
o/w:D.Dep.of Oth.Res.Sect.in Cty	14d	....	....	....	....	....	....	—	—	—	—	—	—
Other Dep. of Other Res.Sect	15..u	....	....	....	....	....	....	—	—	—	—	—	—
o/w:O.Dep.of Oth.Res.Sect.in Cty	15	....	....	....	....	....	....	—	—	—	—	—	—
Bonds & Money Mkt. Instruments	16n.u	....	....	....	....	....	....	—	—	—	—	—	—
o/w: Held by Resid.of Cty	16n	....	....	....	....	....	....	—	—	—	—	—	—
Foreign Liab. (to Non-EA Ctys)	16c	—	—	—	—	—	—	1,383	616	89	87	87	349
Central Government Deposits	16d.u	....	....	....	....	....	....	3,546	2,139	5,151	3,826	3,529	3,877
o/w: Cent.Govt.Dep. in Cty	16d	1,426	836	1,082	1,178	1,191	1,674	3,546	2,139	5,151	3,826	3,529	3,877
Capital Accounts	17a	1,366	1,416	1,264	841	1,265	1,248	2,593	2,923	3,073	2,069	1,838	1,587
Other Items (Net)	17r	−679	−417	28	−245	−1,635	−1,642	−416	58	985	−1,475	−1,596	−1,975
Memo: Currency Put into Circ	14m	....	....	....	....	....	....				6,583	8,197	11,491
Banking Institutions		*Millions of Pounds through 1998; Millions of Euros Beginning 1999: End of Period*											
Claims on Monetary Authorities	20	775	675	1,436	1,348	1,686	2,706	2,486	....	4,324	4,909	4,303	4,760
Claims on Bk.Inst.in Oth.EA Ctys	20b.u							34,495	49,609	63,850	75,392	94,066	109,995
Fgn. Assets (Cl.on Non-EA Ctys)	21	15,155	19,448	29,074	41,832	70,922	95,535	77,748	145,448	196,527	225,545	257,170	318,357
Claims on General Government	22a.u	....	....	....	....	....	....	29,909	30,698	38,230	40,400	60,322	73,682
o/w: Claims on Gen.Govt.in Cty	22a	3,196	3,581	4,637	4,049	4,220	4,676	6,335	5,465	5,363	5,017	5,279	4,751
Claims on Other Resident Sectors	22d.u	....	....	....	....	....	....	109,999	136,032	161,126	175,193	199,215	247,207
o/w: Cl. on Oth.Res.Sect.in Cty	22d	14,835	16,571	29,106	33,978	44,058	54,020	91,795	110,652	129,079	142,382	160,220	200,306
Demand Deposits	24..u	....	....	....	....	....	....	12,711	15,117	18,871	19,671	49,721	55,371
o/w:D.Dep.of Oth.Res.Sect.in Cty	24	3,103	3,539	6,808	7,552	5,199	6,802	12,649	15,032	18,768	19,624	48,828	54,260
Other Deposits	25..u	....	....	....	....	....	....	67,614	76,097	81,626	93,246	75,417	85,604
o/w:O.Dep.of Oth.Res.Sect.in Cty	25	12,693	13,848	20,494	24,324	32,890	38,108	59,223	67,035	71,694	80,225	62,017	70,603
Money Market Fund Shares	26m.u	....	....	....	....	....	....	—	7,742	9,504	15,681	17,646	25,361
Bonds & Money Mkt. Instruments	26n.u	....	....	....	....	....	....	24,237	28,224	41,322	43,636	65,518	118,023
o/w: Held by Resid.of Cty	26n	....	....	....	....	....	....						
Foreign Liab. (to Non-EA Ctys)	26c	13,571	18,180	30,582	41,740	69,369	95,994	77,377	152,076	217,004	243,376	267,989	314,831
Central Government Deposits	26d.u	....	....	....	....	....	....	1,274	1,970	1,471	790	1,747	1,525
o/w: Cent.Govt.Dep. in Cty	26d	119	360	239	248	299	332	1,274	1,970	1,454	790	747	825
Credit from Monetary Authorities	26g	737	403	37	261	1,637	1,755	5,245	....	13,316	11,290	17,738	17,641
Liab. to Bk.Inst.in Oth. EA Ctys	26h.u							44,248	44,476	50,923	63,083	86,853	102,433
Capital Accounts	27a	4,322	4,854	6,486	7,249	10,280	12,881	22,091	26,993	31,133	33,664	37,769	44,257
Other Items (Net)	27r	−584	−909	−394	−167	1,211	1,067	−158	....	−1,113	−2,996	−5,321	−11,015

Ireland 178

		1993	1994	1995	1996	1997	1998	1999	2000	2001	2002	2003	2004
Banking Survey (Nat'l Residency)		*Millions of Pounds through 1998; Millions of Euros Beginning 1999: End of Period*											
Foreign Assets (Net)	31n	5,867	5,440	3,963	5,051	6,187	5,986	31,539	....	52,094	54,300	72,185	109,477
Domestic Credit	32	16,801	19,210	32,604	36,733	46,920	56,822	93,589	112,237	127,866	142,783	161,251	200,361
Claims on General Govt. (Net)	32an	1,966	2,639	3,498	2,755	2,862	2,802	1,794	1,585	-1,213	401	1,024	49
Claims on Other Resident Sectors	32d	14,835	16,571	29,106	33,978	44,058	54,020	91,795	110,652	129,079	142,382	160,227	200,312
Currency Issued	34a.n	1,776	1,907	2,092	2,287	2,619	3,040	5,528	5,368	4,704	4,278	4,650	6,437
Demand Deposits	34b.n	3,103	3,539	6,808	7,552	5,199	6,802	12,649	15,032	18,768	19,624	48,828	54,260
Other Deposits	35..n	12,693	13,848	20,494	24,324	32,890	38,108	59,223	67,035	71,694	80,225	62,017	70,603
Money Market Fund Shares	36m	....	....	....	....	....	....	—	7,742	9,504	15,681	17,646	25,361
Bonds & Money Mkt. Instruments	36n	....	....	....	....	....	....	24,237	28,224	41,322	43,636	65,518	118,023
o/w: Over Two Years	36na	....	....	....	....	....	....	10,200	11,038	12,563	14,377	32,411	61,946
Capital Accounts	37a	5,688	6,271	7,750	8,090	11,545	14,129	24,684	29,916	34,206	35,733	39,607	45,844
Other Items (Net)	37r	-591	-914	-577	-469	853	732	-1,191	....	-240	-2,092	-4,827	-10,659
Banking Survey (EA-Wide Residency)		*Millions of Euros: End of Period*											
Foreign Assets (Net)	31n.u	....	....	....	....	....	....	4,399	-911	-13,949	-12,317	-6,610	6,819
Domestic Credit	32..u	....	....	....	....	....	....	137,197	164,804	194,763	212,627	257,226	318,988
Claims on General Govt. (Net)	32anu	....	....	....	....	....	....	27,198	28,772	33,637	37,434	58,004	71,775
Claims on Other Resident Sect.	32d.u	....	....	....	....	....	....	109,999	136,032	161,126	175,193	199,222	247,213
Currency Issued	34a.u	....	....	....	....	....	....	5,528	5,368	4,704	4,278	4,650	6,437
Demand Deposits	34b.u	....	....	....	....	....	....	12,711	15,117	18,871	19,671	49,721	55,371
Other Deposits	35..u	....	....	....	....	....	....	67,614	76,097	81,626	93,246	75,417	85,604
o/w: Other Dep. Over Two Yrs	35abu	....	....	....	....	....	....	7,633	8,496	9,904	13,499	16,643	21,378
Money Market Fund Shares	36m.u	....	....	....	....	....	....	—	7,742	9,504	15,681	17,646	25,361
Bonds & Money Mkt. Instruments	36n.u	....	....	....	....	....	....	24,237	28,224	41,322	43,636	65,518	118,023
o/w: Over Two Years	36nau	....	....	....	....	....	....	10,200	11,038	12,563	14,377	32,411	61,946
Capital Accounts	37a	....	....	....	....	....	....	24,684	29,916	34,206	35,733	39,607	45,844
Other Items (Net)	37r.u	....	....	....	....	....	....	6,824	1,431	-9,421	-11,933	-1,940	-10,802
Nonbank Financial Institutions		*Millions of Pounds: End of Period*											
Cash	40..k	1,559	1,676	† 18	6	5	5	....	....	....	....	....	....
Foreign Assets	41..k	241	704	† 2	5	8	11	....	....	....	....	....	....
Claims on Central Government	42a.k	1,801	1,777	† 717	762	786	819	....	....	....	....	....	....
Claims on Private Sector	42d.k	7,634	8,438	† 644	703	878	1,051	....	....	....	....	....	....
Quasi-Monetary Liabilities	45..k	8,682	9,274	† 917	1,039	1,154	1,237	....	....	....	....	....	....
Foreign Liabilities	46c.k	1,690	2,233	† 2	5	8	10	....	....	....	....	....	....
Cred.from Deposit Money Banks	46h.k	1,009	1,285	† 394	339	448	564	....	....	....	....	....	....
Capital Accounts	47a.k	795	928	† 35	78	53	56	....	....	....	....	....	....
Other Items (Net)	47r.k	-941	-1,125	† 33	15	15	18	....	....	....	....	....	....
Interest Rates		*Percent Per Annum*											
Discount Rate (End of Period)	60	7.00	6.25	6.50	6.25	6.75	4.06	....	....	....	....	....	....
Money Market Rate	60b	10.49	† 5.75	5.45	5.74	6.43	3.23	3.14	4.84	3.31	2.88	2.08	2.13
Treasury Bill Rate	60c	† 9.06	5.87	6.19	5.36	6.03	5.37	....	....	....	....	.04	.01
Deposit Rate	60l	2.27	.33	.44	.29	.46	.43	.10	.10	.10	.10	.04	.01
Deposit Rate (Households)	60lhs	....	....	....	....	....	....	....	....	....	....	1.97	1.98
Deposit Rate (Corporations)	60lcs	....	....	....	....	....	....	....	....	....	....	2.03	2.04
Lending Rate	60p	9.93	6.13	6.56	5.85	6.57	6.22	3.34	4.77	4.84	3.83	2.85	2.57
Lending Rate (Households)	60phm	....	....	....	....	....	....	....	....	....	....	3.65	3.46
Lending Rate (Corporations)	60pcs	....	....	....	....	....	....	....	....	....	....	5.18	4.69
Government Bond Yield	61	7.72	8.19	8.30	7.48	6.49	4.99	....	....	....	....	....	....
Prices, Production, Labor		*Index Numbers (2000=100): Period Averages*											
Share Prices	62	30.5	34.8	38.1	47.6	64.6	90.9	93.6	100.0	108.2	87.2	81.9	102.9
Wholesale Prices	63	89.1	89.9	91.8	92.3	91.8	93.2	94.2	† 100.0	102.9	103.1	97.4	....
Output Manufacturing Industry	63a	89.5	90.5	92.8	93.4	92.9	93.7	94.6	† 100.0	101.7	100.5	92.4	90.2
Consumer Prices	64	84.0	86.0	88.2	89.7	91.0	93.2	94.7	100.0	† 104.9	109.8	113.6	116.1
Harmonized CPI	64h	....	....	87.8	89.7	90.8	92.7	95.0	100.0	104.0	108.9	113.2	115.9
Wages: Weekly Earnings	65ey	75.2	77.4	79.1	81.1	85.0	88.5	93.7	† 100.0	109.1	115.2	122.6	128.7
Industrial Production	66	36.8	41.2	† 49.6	53.6	63.0	75.5	86.6	100.0	110.2	118.5	124.3	124.9
Manufacturing Employment	67ey	77.3	80.2	85.1	89.2	94.4	97.1	96.2	100.0	101.0	96.3	92.5	89.8
		Number in Thousands: Period Averages											
Labor Force	67d	1,477	1,503	1,559	1,608	1,634	1,748	1,809	1,848	1,886	1,928	1,983	2,031
Employment	67e	1,183	1,221	† 1,282	1,329	1,380	1,521	1,616	1,692	1,741	1,765	1,811	1,865
Unemployment	67c	294	282	277	279	254	227	193	155	144	162	172	166
Unemployment Rate (%)	67r	16.7	15.1	14.1	11.8	10.1	7.1	5.3	4.1	4.0	4.4	4.7	4.5
Intl. Transactions & Positions		*Millions of Pounds through 1998; Millions of Euros Beginning 1999*											
Exports	70	19,830	22,753	27,825	30,407	35,336	45,145	† 66,956	83,889	92,730	92,893	81,639	83,807
Imports, c.i.f.	71	14,885	17,283	20,619	22,429	25,882	31,278	† 44,327	55,909	57,230	54,805	47,107	49,347
		2000=100											
Volume of Exports	72	33.2	38.2	45.8	50.4	57.9	72.0	83.8	100.0	105.0	104.3	99.2	110.5
Volume of Imports	73	41.1	46.5	53.2	58.5	67.2	79.3	85.9	100.0	99.4	97.3	90.0	97.9
Unit Value of Exports	74	85.9	85.9	87.4	86.9	87.9	90.2	95.1	100.0	101.2	101.0	93.7	85.7
Unit Value of Imports	75	82.1	85.1	88.4	87.1	87.5	89.5	92.2	100.0	103.0	99.0	90.7	89.5

		1993	1994	1995	1996	1997	1998	1999	2000	2001	2002	2003	2004
Balance of Payments		\multicolumn{12}{c}{*Millions of US Dollars: Minus Sign Indicates Debit*}											
Current Account, n.i.e.	78ald	1,765	1,577	1,721	2,049	1,866	1,016	245	−516	−690	−1,399	−2,105	−748
Goods: Exports f.o.b.	78aad	28,728	33,642	44,423	49,184	55,293	78,562	67,831	73,530	77,623	84,216	89,570	98,745
Goods: Imports f.o.b.	78abd	−20,553	−24,275	−30,866	−33,430	−36,668	−53,172	−44,244	−48,520	−50,360	−50,769	−51,763	−59,183
Trade Balance	78acd	8,175	9,366	13,557	15,754	18,625	25,390	23,587	25,010	27,263	33,447	37,807	39,562
Services: Credit	78add	3,769	4,319	5,017	5,749	6,186	16,735	15,688	18,538	23,465	28,600	38,008	47,162
Services: Debit	78aed	−6,760	−8,452	−11,303	−13,448	−15,195	−29,626	−26,534	−31,272	−35,339	−41,963	−52,314	−58,495
Balance on Goods & Services	78afd	5,185	5,233	7,270	8,055	9,616	12,499	12,741	12,276	15,389	20,084	23,501	28,229
Income: Credit	78agd	2,780	3,513	5,110	5,576	7,353	25,430	24,442	27,613	28,850	27,281	32,191	38,543
Income: Debit	78ahd	−8,116	−8,919	−12,435	−13,772	−17,059	−38,800	−38,191	−41,160	−45,202	−49,464	−58,333	−67,951
Balance on Gds, Serv. & Inc.	78aid	−151	−173	−55	−141	−90	−870	−1,008	−1,271	−962	−2,099	−2,641	−1,179
Current Transfers, n.i.e.: Credit	78ajd	2,858	2,850	3,009	3,538	3,083	7,428	5,308	4,143	7,400	7,719	7,159	6,960
Current Transfers: Debit	78akd	−941	−1,100	−1,233	−1,349	−1,128	−5,543	−4,055	−3,388	−7,128	−7,018	−6,623	−6,530
Capital Account, n.i.e.	78bcd	775	387	817	785	871	1,218	593	1,074	635	512	442	471
Capital Account, n.i.e.: Credit	78bad	863	477	914	881	962	1,327	674	1,167	719	656	617	653
Capital Account: Debit	78bbd	−89	−90	−96	−96	−91	−108	−81	−93	−84	−144	−175	−181
Financial Account, n.i.e.	78bjd	−901	−3,963	−33	−2,780	−7,484	4,686	−4,185	7,912	16	1,866	951	3,472
Direct Investment Abroad	78bdd	−220	−438	−820	−727	−1,008	−4,955	−6,102	−4,641	−4,103	−8,524	−3,528	−11,271
Dir. Invest. in Rep. Econ., n.i.e.	78bed	1,121	838	1,447	2,618	2,743	11,035	18,323	25,501	9,573	29,131	26,599	13,725
Portfolio Investment Assets	78bfd	−272	−1,019	−1,056	−183	−716	−66,738	−82,813	−83,075	−111,347	−105,302	−161,319	−166,155
Equity Securities	78bkd	—	—	—	—	—	−27,624	−36,357	−28,849	−23,808	−27,179	−26,839	−44,517
Debt Securities	78bld	−272	−1,019	−1,056	−183	−716	−39,114	−46,457	−54,226	−87,539	−78,123	−134,480	−121,638
Portfolio Investment Liab., n.i.e.	78bgd	2,723	−379	771	982	−2,505	54,735	67,377	77,906	89,085	68,812	106,389	135,870
Equity Securities	78bmd	—	—	—	—	—	47,948	52,061	69,606	79,352	68,780	77,218	79,994
Debt Securities	78bnd	2,723	−379	771	982	−2,505	6,787	15,316	8,300	9,733	33	29,172	55,877
Financial Derivatives Assets	78bwd	....	....	....	....	....	....	....	416	−576	1,996	−2,297	−221
Financial Derivatives Liabilities	78bxd	....	....	....	....	....	....	....	−42	957	−19	−58	2,854
Other Investment Assets	78bhd	−10,642	−4,483	−16,572	−22,162	−48,337	−25,211	−38,545	−37,036	−21,431	−33,267	−48,864	−39,920
Monetary Authorities	78bod								−16	−121	−583	−1,576	—
General Government	78bpd	—	−76	76	—	—	....	....	−2,057	725	3,327	−148	—
Banks	78bqd	−9,486	−2,919	−14,083	−19,623	−43,421	....	....	−12,563	−5,348	−20,722	−35,545	—
Other Sectors	78brd	−1,157	−1,489	−2,565	−2,539	−4,916	....	....	−22,400	−16,687	−15,290	−11,596	—
Other Investment Liab., n.i.e.	78bid	6,389	1,519	16,197	16,691	42,340	35,820	37,576	28,882	37,859	49,038	84,028	68,591
Monetary Authorities	78bsd	−1,255	—	—	—	—	—	—	3,493	922	−1,583	7,461	—
General Government	78btd	−580	−1,585	−808	−947	−812	....	....	−160	−2	−34	−286	—
Banks	78bud	8,224	3,103	17,005	17,639	43,152	....	....	19,637	18,656	32,823	62,399	—
Other Sectors	78bvd								5,913	18,283	17,833	14,455	—
Net Errors and Omissions	78cad	1,021	1,823	−167	−106	3,639	−3,708	1,373	−8,509	434	−1,271	−1,178	−4,630
Overall Balance	78cbd	2,660	−176	2,339	−52	−1,109	3,212	−1,973	−39	395	−292	−1,890	−1,435
Reserves and Related Items	79dad	−2,660	176	−2,339	52	1,109	−3,212	1,973	39	−395	292	1,890	1,435
Reserve Assets	79dbd	−2,660	176	−2,339	52	1,109	−3,212	1,973	−121	−395	292	1,890	1,435
Use of Fund Credit and Loans	79dcd	—	—	—	—	—	—	—	—	—	—	—	—
Exceptional Financing	79ded	....	....	....	....	....	....	....	160	....	....	—	—
International Investment Position		\multicolumn{12}{c}{*Millions of US Dollars*}											
Assets	79aad	....	....	....	....	....	....	....	....	749,233	941,911	1,282,653	....
Direct Investment Abroad	79abd	....	....	....	....	....	....	....	....	40,819	54,026	64,458	....
Portfolio Investment	79acd	....	....	....	....	....	....	....	....	432,843	573,837	811,645	....
Equity Securities	79add	....	....	....	....	....	....	....	....	133,758	154,346	211,416	....
Debt Securities	79aed	....	....	....	....	....	....	....	....	299,084	419,492	600,229	....
Financial Derivatives	79ald	....	....	....	....	....	....	....	....	7,874	4,293	8,327	....
Other Investment	79afd	....	....	....	....	....	....	....	....	262,055	304,274	394,062	....
Monetary Authorities	79agd	....	....	....	....	....	....	....	....	669	1,489	3,589	....
General Government	79ahd	....	....	....	....	....	....	....	....	3,954	744	928	....
Banks	79aid	....	....	....	....	....	....	....	....	117,373	134,384	200,226	....
Other Sectors	79ajd	....	....	....	....	....	....	....	....	140,059	167,658	189,319	....
Reserve Assets	79akd	....	....	....	....	....	....	....	....	5,641	5,481	4,159	....
Liabilities	79lad	....	....	....	....	....	....	....	....	764,959	962,947	1,314,311	....
Dir. Invest. in Rep. Economy	79lbd	....	....	....	....	....	....	....	....	134,052	178,575	217,164	....
Portfolio Investment	79lcd	....	....	....	....	....	....	....	....	363,168	441,779	608,691	....
Equity Securities	79ldd	....	....	....	....	....	....	....	....	279,225	350,063	479,157	....
Debt Securities	79led	....	....	....	....	....	....	....	....	83,943	91,715	129,535	....
Financial Derivatives	79lld	....	....	....	....	....	....	....	....	2,944	3,412	7,180	....
Other Investment	79lfd	....	....	....	....	....	....	....	....	264,795	339,181	481,275	....
Monetary Authorities	79lgd	....	....	....	....	....	....	....	....	4,635	3,905	13,201	....
General Government	79lhd	....	....	....	....	....	....	....	....	501	541	318	....
Banks	79lid	....	....	....	....	....	....	....	....	153,426	207,664	312,917	....
Other Sectors	79ljd	....	....	....	....	....	....	....	....	106,234	127,071	154,839	....
Government Finance													
Central Government		\multicolumn{12}{c}{*Millions of Pounds through 1998; Millions of Euros Beginning 1999: Year Ending December 31*}											
Deficit (-) or Surplus	80	−260.4	−322.6	−259.5	102.0	289.7	1,226.2	† 1,513.0	3,171.2	649.7	94.9	....	....
Revenue	81	10,872.8	11,676.6	12,423.4	13,422.3	15,108.6	17,175.6	† 29,441.7	29,865.1	30,204.1	32,610.5	....	....
Expenditure	82	11,133.2	11,999.2	12,682.9	13,320.3	14,818.9	15,949.4	† 27,928.7	26,693.9	29,554.4	32,515.6	....	....
Financing													
Net Borrowing	84	850.2	−18.6	535.0	164.5	−109.3	−881.8	† −1,686.3	−3,177.3	−80.9	−742.6	....	....
Use of Cash Balances	87	−589.8	341.2	−275.5	−266.5	−180.4	−344.4	† 173.3	6.1	−569.0	647.7	....	....
General Government		\multicolumn{12}{c}{*As Percent of Gross Domestic Product*}											
Deficit (-) or Surplus	80g	−2.4	−1.7	−2.1	−.6	.7	2.3	2.3	4.5	1.7	....	....	....
Debt	88g	96.3	88.2	78.9	74.1	65.1	55.1	49.6	39.0	36.6	....	....	....

Ireland 178

		1993	1994	1995	1996	1997	1998	1999	2000	2001	2002	2003	2004
National Accounts					*Millions of Pounds through 1998; Millions of Euros Beginning in 1999*								
Househ.Cons.Expend.,incl.NPISHs....	96f	20,162	21,621	23,192	25,311	27,900	31,219	† 43,721	49,488	54,349	59,019	62,935	66,439
Government Consumption Expend...	91f	5,495	5,838	6,177	6,514	7,274	7,978	† 11,383	13,050	15,474	17,692	19,232	21,017
Gross Fixed Capital Formation.........	93e	5,259	6,043	7,072	8,512	10,650	13,275	† 21,712	25,321	27,056	28,983	31,816	36,509
Changes in Inventories....................	93i	−112	−135	428	427	683	886	† 391	819	377	114	498	80
Exports of Goods and Services.........	90c	22,475	25,923	31,679	35,453	42,121	52,585	† 79,096	100,719	113,642	119,701	112,759	117,363
Imports of Goods and Services (-).....	98c	18,860	22,301	26,936	30,142	35,442	45,678	† 66,816	87,110	96,301	98,508	91,981	94,616
Statistical Discrepancy.....................	99bs	−364	−365	−202	−440	−426	318	† −31	777	835	990	−473	−514
Gross Domestic Product (GDP)........	99b	34,054	36,624	41,409	45,634	52,760	60,582	† 89,457	103,065	115,432	127,992	134,786	146,279
Net Primary Income from Abroad.....	98.n	−3,671	−3,716	−4,685	−5,147	−6,332	−7,389	† −13,098	−14,910	−18,327	−23,518	−23,115	−23,727
Gross National Income (GNI)...........	99a	30,383	32,908	36,725	40,487	46,428	53,193	† 76,359	88,155	97,105	104,474	111,671	122,552
Net National Income......................	99e	27,037	29,170	32,366	35,618	40,392	46,109	† 68,540	78,130	85,575	91,999	98,011	. . .
GDP Volume 1995 Prices................	99b.p	35,682	37,736	41,409	44,719	49,564	53,830	† 76,261	83,824	88,860	94,309	97,756	102,519
GDP Volume (2000=100)................	99bvp	54.0	57.2	62.7	67.7	75.1	81.5	† 91.0	100.0	106.0	112.5	116.6	122.3
GDP Deflator (2000=100)...............	99bip	77.6	78.9	81.3	83.0	86.6	91.5	† 95.4	100.0	105.7	110.4	112.1	116.0
							Millions: Midyear Estimates							
Population...............................	99z	3.56	3.58	3.61	3.64	3.67	3.71	3.75	3.80	3.86	3.93	4.01	4.08

		1993	1994	1995	1996	1997	1998	1999	2000	2001	2002	2003	2004
Exchange Rates						*New Sheqalim per SDR: End of Period*							
Market Rate	aa	4.1015	4.4058	4.6601	4.6748	4.7709	5.8588	5.7000	5.2651	5.5497	6.4400	6.5071	6.6904
						New Sheqalim per US Dollar: End of Period (ae) Period Average (rf)							
Market Rate	ae	2.9860	3.0180	3.1350	3.2510	3.5360	4.1610	4.1530	4.0410	4.4160	4.7370	4.3790	4.3080
Market Rate	rf	2.8301	3.0111	3.0113	3.1917	3.4494	3.8001	4.1397	4.0773	4.2057	4.7378	4.5541	4.4820
						Index Numbers (2000=100): Period Averages							
Nominal Effective Exchange Rate	nec	125.27	115.79	108.70	105.82	106.06	99.26	91.63	100.00	100.67	87.07	80.95	76.89
Real Effective Exchange Rate	rec	86.42	87.35	88.05	93.21	99.72	96.78	92.38	100.00	100.36	90.33	83.18	77.24
Fund Position						*Millions of SDRs: End of Period*							
Quota	2f.s	666.2	666.2	666.2	666.2	666.2	666.2	928.2	928.2	928.2	928.2	928.2	928.2
SDRs	1b.s	.4	.2	.4	1.0	—	.2	.1	.8	1.4	3.4	6.4	9.8
Reserve Position in the Fund	1c.s	—	—	—	—	—	—	65.5	89.9	157.4	304.0	354.8	298.3
Total Fund Cred.&Loans Outstg	2tl	178.6	178.6	111.7	22.3	—	—	—	—	—	—	—	—
International Liquidity						*Millions of US Dollars Unless Otherwise Indicated: End of Period*							
Total Reserves minus Gold	1l.d	6,382.6	6,792.4	8,119.3	11,414.6	20,332.1	22,674.3	22,604.9	23,281.2	23,378.6	24,082.9	26,315.1	27,094.4
SDRs	1b.d	.5	.4	.6	1.4	—	.3	.2	1.1	1.7	4.6	9.5	15.2
Reserve Position in the Fund	1c.d	—	—	—	—	—	—	89.9	117.1	197.8	413.3	527.2	463.2
Foreign Exchange	1d.d	6,382.1	6,792.0	8,118.7	11,413.2	† 20,332.0	22,674.0	22,514.8	23,163.0	23,179.1	23,665.0	25,778.4	26,616.0
Gold (Million Fine Troy Ounces)	1ad	.009	.009	.009	.009	.009	—	—	—	—	—	—	—
Gold (National Valuation)	1and	.4	.4	.5	.4	.4	—	—	—	—	—	—	—
Monetary Authorities: Other Liab	4..d	38.5	37.8	38.6	38.1	30.0	21.9	17.8	18.1	17.0	16.0	15.5	14.9
Deposit Money Banks: Assets	7a.d	10,137.7	11,330.0	12,055.9	12,945.4	10,823.5	12,746.6	14,146.6	16,095.4	15,644.9	14,475.2	17,936.1	21,753.2
Liabilities	7b.d	12,159.1	13,098.9	14,514.4	15,113.4	16,738.3	18,334.0	20,452.0	21,872.6	22,106.4	21,821.6	21,796.1	21,432.9
Monetary Authorities						*Millions of New Sheqalim: End of Period*							
Foreign Assets	11	19,065	20,508	25,578	37,130	70,970	94,326	93,878	94,084	103,248	114,102	115,275	116,789
Claims on Central Government	12a	10,338	9,976	10,818	12,304	12,199	12,288	12,416	12,530	12,204	11,056	10,048	8,758
Claims on Deposit Money Banks	12e	16,972	15,555	4,503	1,236	1,519	838	810	787	802	3,006	2,727	2,191
Reserve Money	14	28,051	26,166	19,157	25,838	56,659	64,802	80,218	80,706	81,237	68,440	63,312	48,964
of which: Currency Outside DMBs	14a	4,852	5,467	6,731	7,772	8,767	10,051	12,178	12,347	14,580	15,580	16,184	17,758
Foreign Cur.Deps	14cf	20,203	16,413	10,119	7,982	7,633	7,931	10,741	9,100	10,773	7,066	2,624	1,591
Foreign Liabilities	16c	848	901	641	228	106	91	74	73	75	76	68	64
Central Government Deposits	16d	16,165	17,456	19,325	23,013	26,509	39,407	32,242	37,369	39,290	51,914	62,643	78,418
Other Items (Net)	17r	1,311	1,516	1,775	1,591	1,414	3,152	−5,430	−10,747	−4,348	7,734	2,027	292
Deposit Money Banks						*Millions of New Sheqalim: End of Period*							
Reserves	20	23,223	20,743	12,425	18,085	48,103	54,578	68,029	67,882	65,788	52,630	46,825	30,872
Foreign Assets	21	30,271	34,194	37,795	42,086	38,272	53,038	58,751	65,041	69,088	68,569	78,542	93,713
Claims on Central Government	22a	65,080	66,289	69,960	77,542	66,136	63,806	61,984	44,464	43,883	45,563	49,349	55,939
Claims on Private Sector	22d	121,800	154,285	185,123	219,842	254,886	303,434	347,382	390,938	439,228	480,467	462,949	482,871
Demand Deposits	24	8,526	8,946	9,870	12,227	13,502	14,937	17,933	18,536	23,053	22,619	26,483	35,012
Time and Savings Deposits	25	104,678	139,899	171,485	217,117	251,747	306,960	352,568	381,425	412,502	451,051	439,538	450,464
Restricted Deposits	26b	28,775	28,730	22,979	21,481	19,368	17,063	13,593	11,002	6,489	8,147	6,366	5,930
Foreign Liabilities	26c	36,307	39,533	45,503	49,134	59,187	76,288	84,937	88,387	97,622	103,369	95,445	92,333
Central Government Deposits	26d	19,604	23,211	26,684	27,590	28,190	24,286	24,300	21,082	22,058	25,412	23,391	32,785
Credit from Monetary Authorities	26g	16,896	15,569	4,212	1,186	1,506	835	814	787	806	3,004	2,725	2,187
Other Items (Net)	27r	25,587	19,621	24,570	28,821	33,895	34,486	42,001	47,106	55,462	33,631	43,715	44,684
Monetary Survey						*Millions of New Sheqalim: End of Period*							
Foreign Assets (Net)	31n	12,181	14,268	17,229	29,854	49,949	70,986	67,618	70,665	74,639	79,226	98,304	118,105
Domestic Credit	32	161,448	189,882	219,891	259,086	278,521	315,834	365,240	389,482	433,967	459,760	436,312	436,365
Claims on Central Govt. (Net)	32an	39,649	35,598	34,768	39,244	23,635	12,401	17,858	−1,457	−5,261	−20,707	−26,637	−46,506
Claims on Private Sector	32d	121,800	154,285	185,123	219,842	254,886	303,434	347,382	390,938	439,228	480,467	462,949	482,871
Money	34	13,486	14,523	16,716	20,131	22,401	25,145	30,263	31,030	37,796	38,364	42,838	52,931
Quasi-Money	35	121,441	153,587	187,829	235,519	271,480	326,491	376,013	407,831	442,567	475,268	470,048	478,441
Restricted Deposits	36b	28,775	28,730	22,979	21,481	19,368	17,063	13,593	11,002	6,489	8,147	6,366	5,930
Other Items (Net)	37r	9,928	7,310	9,596	11,809	15,221	18,120	12,990	10,283	21,759	17,211	15,362	17,168
Money plus Quasi-Money	35l	134,926	168,109	204,545	255,650	293,881	351,636	406,276	438,862	480,363	513,632	512,886	531,372
Interest Rates						*Percent Per Annum*							
Discount Rate	60	9.8	17.0	14.2	15.3	13.7	13.5	11.2	8.2	5.7	9.2	5.2	3.9
Treasury Bill Rate	60c	10.5	11.8	14.4	15.3	13.4	11.3	11.4	8.8	6.5	7.4	7.0	4.8
Deposit Rate	60l	10.4	12.2	14.1	14.5	13.1	11.0	11.3	8.6	6.2	6.0	6.6	3.6
Lending Rate	60p	16.4	17.4	20.2	20.7	18.7	16.2	16.4	12.9	10.0	9.9	10.7	7.4
Prices, Production, Labor						*Index Numbers (2000=100): Period Averages*							
Share Prices	62	61.6	37.3	42.6	42.9	58.4	60.0	99.5	100.0	93.1	74.3	115.7	135.8
Prices: Industrial Products	63	62.8	67.7	74.9	81.4	86.5	90.1	96.5	100.0	99.9	103.8	108.2	114.1
Consumer Prices	64	† 59.5	66.8	73.5	81.8	89.1	94.0	98.9	† 100.0	101.1	† 106.8	107.6	107.1
Wages: Daily Earnings	65	47.7	52.8	† 60.6	68.9	79.2	87.1	94.1	100.0	108.6	109.7	111.9	114.5
Industrial Employment	67	93.6	† 96.9	† 100.6	102.2	101.1	100.2	98.7	100.0	97.2	93.3	91.0	92.1
						Number in Thousands: Period Averages							
Labor Force	67d	1,946	2,030	† 2,110	2,157	2,210	† 2,266	2,345	2,435	2,499	2,547	2,610	2,679
Employment	67e	1,751	1,871	† 1,965	2,013	2,040	† 2,073	2,137	2,221	2,265	2,284	2,330	2,401
Unemployment	67c	195	158	† 145	144	170	† 193	208	214	234	262	280	278
Unemployment Rate (%)	67r	10.0	7.8	† 6.9	6.7	7.7	† 8.6	8.9	8.8	9.4	10.3	10.7	10.4
Intl. Transactions & Positions						*Millions of US Dollars*							
Exports	70..d	14,826	16,884	19,046	20,610	22,503	22,993	25,794	31,404	29,081	29,347	31,784	38,618
Imports, c.i.f.	71..d	22,624	25,237	29,579	31,620	30,781	29,342	33,166	31,404	35,449	35,517	36,303	42,864
Imports,c.i.f.,excl. Military Gds	71.md	20,518	23,776	28,287	29,951	29,084	27,470	31,090	35,750	33,303	33,106	34,212	40,969
						2000=100							
Volume of Exports	72	47.2	54.6	58.6	† 63.0	69.4	73.6	79.7	100.0	† 95.9	96.9	100.6	115.7
Volume of Imports	73	56.9	64.5	70.9	† 75.6	76.6	76.8	88.0	100.0	† 92.6	93.4	92.0	103.1
Unit Value of Exports(US$)	74..d	99.5	98.0	102.7	† 102.7	101.8	98.8	99.9	100.0	† 96.4	96.3	100.4	105.8
Unit Value of Imports(US$)	75..d	100.7	102.8	111.5	† 110.7	105.7	99.9	97.0	100.0	† 98.6	98.5	104.5	111.9

		1993	1994	1995	1996	1997	1998	1999	2000	2001	2002	2003	2004
Balance of Payments							*Millions of US Dollars: Minus Sign Indicates Debit*						
Current Account, n.i.e.	78ald	−2,480	−3,447	−4,647	−5,124	−3,289	−1,149	−1,646	−1,230	−1,580	−1,288	795	1,474
Goods: Exports f.o.b.	78aad	14,926	17,242	19,694	21,515	22,867	23,190	25,816	31,188	27,967	27,535	30,098	36,585
Goods: Imports f.o.b.	78abd	−20,533	−22,728	−26,890	−28,469	−27,875	−26,241	−30,054	−34,059	−31,014	−31,229	−32,338	−38,473
Trade Balance	78acd	−5,607	−5,486	−7,196	−6,954	−5,008	−3,051	−4,238	−2,870	−3,047	−3,694	−2,240	−1,888
Services: Credit	78add	5,967	6,579	7,788	8,027	8,734	9,490	11,699	14,703	11,992	11,271	12,667	14,861
Services: Debit	78aed	−6,397	−7,590	−8,401	−9,107	−9,299	−9,636	−10,709	−12,508	−12,481	−11,578	−12,012	−13,567
Balance on Goods & Services	78afd	−6,037	−6,497	−7,808	−8,034	−5,573	−3,197	−3,248	−675	−3,536	−4,001	−1,585	−595
Income: Credit	78agd	1,295	1,160	1,751	1,832	2,068	2,508	2,701	3,553	2,640	2,374	2,705	2,298
Income: Debit	78ahd	−3,344	−3,711	−4,263	−5,058	−5,834	−6,537	−7,411	−10,590	−7,376	−6,424	−6,696	−6,460
Balance on Gds, Serv. & Inc.	78aid	−8,087	−9,048	−10,320	−11,260	−9,339	−7,226	−7,958	−7,712	−8,271	−8,050	−5,577	−4,756
Current Transfers, n.i.e.: Credit	78ajd	5,911	5,850	5,941	6,440	6,377	6,683	7,122	7,467	7,799	8,124	7,497	7,307
Current Transfers: Debit	78akd	−304	−250	−268	−304	−328	−606	−809	−985	−1,107	−1,362	−1,125	−1,076
Capital Account, n.i.e.	78bcd	863	786	609	576	552	397	569	455	679	151	465	524
Capital Account, n.i.e.: Credit	78bad	863	786	609	576	552	397	569	455	679	151	465	524
Capital Account: Debit	78bdd	—	—	—	—	—	—	—	—	—	—	—	—
Financial Account, n.i.e.	78bjd	1,041	−959	4,206	4,537	7,207	−172	2,047	1,870	961	−1,601	−2,807	−4,143
Direct Investment Abroad	78bdd	−615	−742	−820	−815	−923	−1,125	−831	−3,337	−688	−983	−2,074	−3,180
Dir. Invest. in Rep. Econ., n.i.e.	78bed	605	442	1,351	1,398	1,635	1,737	3,130	5,064	3,626	1,765	3,863	1,664
Portfolio Investment Assets	78bfd	−812	−1,772	98	368	215	106	−686	−2,814	−1,623	−2,708	−2,838	−1,909
Equity Securities	78bkd	80	303	16	160	166	154	382	−1,544	−421	−558	−923	−699
Debt Securities	78bld	−891	−2,075	82	208	49	−47	−1,067	−1,270	−1,201	−2,149	−1,916	−1,210
Portfolio Investment Liab., n.i.e.	78bgd	276	481	978	1,438	1,712	423	1,455	4,418	576	436	419	3,701
Equity Securities	78bmd	284	469	991	1,440	1,719	476	1,496	4,418	576	436	419	3,701
Debt Securities	78bnd	−7	13	−13	−2	−7	−53	−41	—	—	—	—	—
Financial Derivatives Assets	78bwd	....	....	....	....	....	....	....	....	....	....	....	....
Financial Derivatives Liabilities	78bxd	—	—	—	—	—	—	—	—	8	−11	−4	−26
Other Investment Assets	78bhd	1,003	−1,063	−586	845	1,600	−1,595	−3,220	−2,957	−2,639	−1,038	−2,213	−4,608
Monetary Authorities	78bod	....	....	....	....	....	....						
General Government	78bpd	261	−28	−1,230	864	−19	−13	−458	−1	−561	110	−13	13
Banks	78bqd	940	−1,736	−216	−1,165	1,686	−1,808	−758	−1,189	−392	340	−1,255	−3,658
Other Sectors	78brd	−197	701	860	1,146	−66	225	−2,005	−1,768	−1,686	−1,489	−945	−964
Other Investment Liab., n.i.e.	78bid	583	1,695	3,185	1,303	2,969	282	2,201	1,496	1,700	937	40	213
Monetary Authorities	78bsd	—	—	—	—	—	—	—	—	—	—	—	—
General Government	78btd	225	−64	215	77	−272	−383	369	−67	185	17	−68	−203
Banks	78bud	280	1,000	1,219	612	2,352	1,525	2,385	1,644	1,318	117	−558	−1,121
Other Sectors	78bvd	78	760	1,751	615	889	−859	−553	−82	198	804	667	1,538
Net Errors and Omissions	78cad	249	1,510	312	1,218	2,606	769	−1,064	−830	300	1,800	1,210	573
Overall Balance	78cbd	−327	−2,111	480	1,206	7,077	−155	−94	266	360	−938	−337	−1,573
Reserves and Related Items	79dad	327	2,111	−480	−1,206	−7,077	155	94	−266	−360	938	337	1,573
Reserve Assets	79dbd	−1,533	−124	−1,123	−3,413	−9,378	−1,880	−996	−895	141	651	−1,269	−292
Use of Fund Credit and Loans	79dcd	—	—	−101	−129	−31	—	—	—	—	—	—	—
Exceptional Financing	79ded	1,861	2,235	745	2,336	2,332	2,036	1,090	629	−502	287	1,605	1,865
International Investment Position							*Millions of US Dollars*						
Assets	79aad	21,944	26,345	30,754	34,751	44,602	50,536	60,406	69,020	72,712	77,891	88,779	100,272
Direct Investment Abroad	79abd	—	—	2,867	3,283	5,223	5,376	6,283	9,091	9,249	10,319	13,064	16,135
Portfolio Investment	79acd	2,518	2,866	2,801	2,609	2,711	3,027	4,983	7,281	7,975	10,181	13,750	16,191
Equity Securities	79add	—	374	430	356	447	499	1,432	2,506	2,024	1,766	3,115	4,221
Debt Securities	79aed	2,518	2,492	2,371	2,253	2,264	2,528	3,551	4,775	5,951	8,415	10,635	11,970
Financial Derivatives	79ald												
Other Investment	79afd	12,656	16,315	16,698	17,211	16,264	19,384	26,457	29,286	32,026	33,224	35,503	40,702
Monetary Authorities	79agd	—	—	—	—	—	—	—	—	—	—	—	—
General Government	79ahd	—	—	222	104	242	387	656	515	979	774	779	850
Banks	79aid	7,776	9,789	10,262	11,223	9,155	11,070	11,571	12,613	12,887	12,900	14,710	18,716
Other Sectors	79ajd	4,880	6,526	6,214	5,884	6,867	7,927	14,229	16,158	18,160	19,550	20,014	21,136
Reserve Assets	79akd	6,770	7,164	8,387	11,648	20,404	22,749	22,684	23,362	23,462	24,168	26,462	27,244
Liabilities	79lad	40,969	47,586	58,088	64,169	74,593	77,755	106,792	117,825	107,421	104,274	123,052	134,973
Dir. Invest. in Rep. Economy	79lbd	402	474	5,741	7,096	9,315	10,507	18,658	22,562	23,896	23,691	30,265	32,168
Portfolio Investment	79lcd	7,315	12,437	14,998	19,427	25,754	27,047	45,279	51,279	38,178	33,187	43,824	53,108
Equity Securities	79ldd	—	2,893	4,706	6,806	10,789	9,912	27,147	32,637	20,169	14,701	23,626	30,811
Debt Securities	79led	7,315	9,544	10,292	12,621	14,965	17,135	18,132	18,642	18,009	18,486	20,198	22,297
Financial Derivatives	79lld	—	—	—	—	—	—	—	—	—	—	—	—
Other Investment	79lfd	33,253	34,676	37,350	37,647	39,524	40,201	42,856	43,984	45,347	47,396	48,962	49,696
Monetary Authorities	79lgd	284	317	235	98	30	21	31	38	29	54	236	122
General Government	79lhd	13,023	12,944	13,335	13,289	12,724	12,614	12,845	12,693	12,825	13,005	13,115	12,984
Banks	79lid	12,211	13,500	14,958	15,428	17,470	19,129	21,218	22,668	23,790	24,505	24,745	23,988
Other Sectors	79ljd	7,736	7,915	8,822	8,832	9,300	8,436	8,762	8,585	8,703	9,833	10,866	12,603
Government Finance						*Millions of New Sheqalim: Year Ending December 31*							
Deficit (-) or Surplus	80	−4,675	−6,882	−11,971	−13,253	1,017	−5,519	−8,698	4,019	−17,270	....	....	....
Revenue	81	73,482	88,559	108,032	123,796	145,110	159,911	173,187	194,736	195,376	....	....	....
Grants Received	81z	8,229	7,927	6,340	12,953	11,437	12,158	12,327	11,957	11,534	....	....	....
Expenditure	82	86,273	102,350	125,369	149,571	165,250	183,046	197,954	208,603	224,287	....	....	....
Lending Minus Repayments	83	113	1,018	974	431	−9,720	−5,458	−3,742	−5,929	−107	....	....	....
Financing													
Domestic	84a	−273	655	12,615	7,431	−5,091	538	11,602	−1,783	17,750	....	....	....
Foreign	85a	4,948	6,227	−644	5,822	4,074	4,981	−2,904	−2,236	−480	....	....	....
Debt: Domestic	88a	188,706	211,726	240,333	277,034	292,401	318,398	330,062	328,534	348,388	....	....	....
Foreign	89a	64,112	71,069	75,083	83,673	92,523	114,261	113,472	111,644	121,212	....	....	....

Israel   436

		1993	1994	1995	1996	1997	1998	1999	2000	2001	2002	2003	2004
National Accounts							*Millions of New Sheqalim*							
Househ.Cons.Expend.,incl.NPISHs....	96f	116,158	141,769	† 157,290	182,397	201,913	220,881	240,541	262,194	272,252	288,794	295,385	312,362
Government Consumption Expend...	91f	53,486	64,081	† 79,683	94,358	104,943	114,544	124,669	132,581	141,411	154,182	151,606	154,041
Gross Fixed Capital Formation..........	93e	44,759	55,333	† 68,596	79,270	83,894	85,763	92,225	93,032	90,739	90,914	88,485	89,740
Changes in Inventories.....................	93i	4,736	3,094	† 2,796	1,983	2,411	3,140	6,402	8,905	10,230	2,057	−3,668	3,127
Exports of Goods and Services..........	90c	61,021	73,553	† 83,071	94,462	109,236	124,176	155,163	186,731	167,357	182,796	192,762	226,017
Imports of Goods and Services (-).....	98c	89,753	106,579	† 121,717	136,975	145,745	154,368	189,082	212,710	204,191	225,035	222,586	258,435
Gross Domestic Product (GDP).........	99b	190,407	231,251	† 269,719	315,495	356,651	394,136	429,918	470,733	477,797	493,707	501,984	526,852
Net Primary Income from Abroad.....	98.n	−3,306	−3,722	† 4,387	6,799	9,899	12,416	15,584	25,749	17,251	15,269	14,903	12,469
Gross National Income (GNI)...........	99a	187,101	227,529	† 265,332	308,696	346,752	381,720	414,334	444,984	460,546	478,438	487,081	514,383
Consumption of Fixed Capital..........	99cf	26,814	31,886	† 39,305	45,086	52,128	59,257	67,373	70,043	75,003	85,906	87,952	89,629
Net National Income.......................	99e	160,287	195,643	† 226,027	263,610	294,624	322,463	346,961	374,941	385,543	392,532	399,129	424,754
GDP Volume 1990 Prices................	99b.p	122,965	131,280	140,540	....	....	....	....	....	....	....	....	....
GDP Volume 2000 Prices................	99b.p	....	....	† 376,496	396,148	409,975	425,289	435,787	470,733	466,514	463,128	469,114	489,312
GDP Volume (2000=100)................	99bvp	70.0	74.7	† 80.0	84.2	87.1	90.3	92.6	100.0	99.1	98.4	99.7	103.9
GDP Deflator (2000=100)................	99bip	57.8	65.8	† 71.6	79.6	87.0	92.7	98.7	100.0	102.4	106.6	107.0	107.7
							Millions: Midyear Estimates							
Population................................	99z	5.02	5.20	5.37	5.53	5.68	5.82	5.95	6.08	6.22	6.35	6.47	6.60

		1993	1994	1995	1996	1997	1998	1999	2000	2001	2002	2003	2004
Exchange Rates					*Lire per SDR through 1998, Euros per SDR Thereafter: End of Period*								
Market Rate	aa	2,340.5	2,379.2	2,355.7	2,200.9	2,373.6	2,327.6	1.3662	1.4002	1.4260	1.2964	1.1765	1.1402
			Lire per US Dollar through 1998, Euros per US Dollar Thereafter: End of Period (ae) Period Average (rf)										
Market Rate	ae	1,704.0	1,629.7	1,584.7	1,530.6	1,759.2	1,653.1	.9954	1.0747	1.1347	.9536	.7918	.7342
Market Rate	rf	1,573.7	1,612.4	1,628.9	1,542.9	1,703.1	1,736.2	.9386	1.0854	1.1175	1.0626	.8860	.8054
			Lire per ECU: End of Period (ea) Period Average (eb)										
ECU Rate	ea	1,908.4	1,997.5	2,082.7	1,913.7	1,940.7	1,936.3	....	....	....	....	....	....
ECU Rate	eb	1,841.6	1,913.9	2,131.3	1,958.6	1,929.7	1,943.7	....	....	....	....	....	....
			Index Numbers (2000=100): Period Averages										
Market Rate (1995=100)	ahx	103.6	101.1	100.0	105.5	95.7	93.9	....	....	....	....	....	....
Nominal Effective Exchange Rate	neu	112.2	107.6	97.8	106.6	106.6	106.5	104.2	100.0	100.4	101.6	105.8	107.2
Real Effective Exchange Rate	reu	101.7	96.6	89.9	103.4	105.4	104.2	104.1	100.0	103.5	106.2	112.9	118.4
Fund Position			*Millions of SDRs: End of Period*										
Quota	2f.s	4,591	4,591	4,591	4,591	4,591	4,591	7,056	7,056	7,056	7,056	7,056	7,056
SDRs	1b.s	175	86	—	20	50	79	122	182	236	79	105	93
Reserve Position in the Fund	1c.s	1,575	1,393	1,321	1,290	1,661	3,075	2,584	2,230	2,560	2,874	2,796	2,385
of which: Outstg.Fund Borrowing	2c	—	—	—	—	—	257	—	—	—	—	—	—
Total Fund Cred.&Loans Outstg	2tl	—	—	—	—	—	—	—	—	—	—	—	—
International Liquidity			*Millions of US Dollars Unless Otherwise Indicated: End of Period*										
Total Res.Min.Gold (Eurosys.Def)	1l.d	27,545	32,265	34,905	45,948	55,739	29,888	† 22,422	25,567	24,419	28,603	30,366	27,859
SDRs	1b.d	241	125	—	29	67	111	168	238	297	108	156	145
Reserve Position in the Fund	1c.d	2,164	2,033	1,963	1,855	2,241	4,330	3,546	2,906	3,217	3,907	4,154	3,703
Foreign Exchange	1d.d	25,140	30,107	32,942	44,064	53,431	25,447	† 18,708	22,423	20,905	24,588	26,056	24,011
o/w:Fin.Deriv.Rel.to Reserves	1ddd	....	....	....	....	....	....	—	—	—	—	—	—
Other Reserve Assets	1e.d	....	....	....	....	....	....	—	—	—	—	—	—
Gold (Million Fine Troy Ounces)	1ad	66.67	66.67	66.67	66.67	66.67	83.36	78.83	78.83	78.83	78.83	78.83	78.83
Gold (Eurosystem Valuation)	1and	23,593	26,342	25,570	25,369	21,806	24,711	22,880	21,635	21,796	27,019	32,891	34,527
Memo:Euro Cl. on Non-EA Res	1dgd	....	....	....	....	....	....	1	476	451	537	125	139
Non-Euro Cl. on EA Res	1dhd	....	....	....	....	....	....	3,620	2,812	4,814	5,556	8,145	7,621
Mon. Auth.: Other Foreign Assets	3..d	....	....	....	....	....	....	....	....	....	....	....	....
Foreign Liabilities	4..d	1,543	1,510	2,598	1,249	1,123	1,045	† 6,315	235	2,198	3,078	509	925
Banking Insts.: Foreign Assets	7a.d	134,425	123,919	145,842	193,215	177,149	193,743	† 90,837	85,886	75,040	94,258	117,858	122,615
Foreign Liab.	7b.d	217,128	230,505	216,808	237,872	223,249	236,896	† 136,369	146,783	150,863	153,427	201,524	214,467
Monetary Authorities			*Trillions of Lire through 1998; Billions of Euros Beginning 1999: End of Period*										
Fgn. Assets (Cl.on Non-EA Ctys.)	11	86.57	93.90	95.59	108.65	135.62	90.33	45.80	50.49	52.42	52.74	49.88	45.55
Claims on General Government	12a.u	....	....	....	....	....	....	60.12	63.25	65.06	44.49	53.72	60.52
o/w: Claims on Gen.Govt.in Cty.	12a	170.23	195.88	196.42	168.95	174.17	156.37	60.12	63.25	65.06	44.49	53.72	60.52
Claims on Banking Institutions	12e.u	....	....	....	....	....	....	51.35	36.49	33.51	19.96	22.48	34.87
o/w: Claims on Bank.Inst.in Cty.	12e	44.94	42.50	41.04	50.03	32.30	11.04	36.01	26.53	10.70	7.76	9.72	15.61
Claims on Other Resident Sectors	12d.u	....	....	....	....	....	....	7.36	8.29	6.75	5.28	5.75	6.94
o/w: Cl. on Oth.Res.Sect.in Cty.	12d	4.35	.56	2.64	—	—	—	7.13	8.06	6.49	5.25	5.74	6.86
Currency Issued	14a	95.23	101.86	105.22	108.16	116.27	124.88	71.96	76.42	65.89	65.49	76.09	86.79
Liabilities to Banking Insts.	14c.u	....	....	....	....	....	....	24.84	25.52	26.28	18.43	18.03	19.05
o/w: Liabs to Bank.Inst.in Cty.	14c	104.19	87.54	72.30	73.69	79.08	13.78	9.23	7.75	26.28	10.45	10.30	12.97
Demand Dep. of Other Res.Sect.	14d.u	....	....	....	....	....	....	.39	.08	.23	.01	.08	.11
o/w:D.Dep.of Oth.Res.Sect.in Cty.	14d	....	....	....	....	....	....	.39	.08	.23	.01	.08	.11
Other Dep. of Other Res.Sect.	15..u	....	....	....	....	....	....	—	—	—	—	—	—
o/w:O.Dep.of Oth.Res.Sect.in Cty.	15	....	....	....	....	....	....	—	—	—	—	—	—
Bonds & Money Mkt. Instruments	16n.u	....	....	....	....	....	....	—	—	—	—	—	—
o/w: Bonds Held by Resid.of Cty.	16n	1.22	1.47	1.99	1.66	1.20	.92	....	....	....	....	....	....
Foreign Liab. (to Non-EA Ctys)	16c	2.63	2.46	4.12	1.91	1.98	1.73	6.29	.25	2.49	2.94	.40	.68
Central Government Deposits	16d.u	....	....	....	....	....	....	29.08	19.37	23.46	21.32	13.30	15.86
o/w: Cent.Govt.Dep. in Cty.	16d	30.67	63.94	72.13	54.76	57.78	42.21	29.08	19.37	23.46	21.32	13.30	15.86
Capital Accounts	17a	84.36	90.66	94.79	99.84	98.93	75.85	35.37	40.44	41.46	25.26	25.02	27.45
Other Items (Net)	17r	−12.21	−15.09	−14.85	−12.39	−13.15	−1.61	−3.30	−3.56	−2.09	−10.98	−1.08	−2.05
Memo: Net Claims on Eurosystem	12e.s	....	....	....	....	....	....	−3.85	−10.31	18.16	−6.15	−5.95	2.37
Currency Put into Circ.	14m	....	....	....	....	....	....	....	....	....	71.23	81.78	92.87
Banking Institutions			*Trillions of Lire through 1998; Billions of Euros Beginning 1999: End of Period*										
Claims on Monetary Authorities	20	109.65	93.29	79.31	81.70	87.81	23.65	9.90	8.16	25.73	10.34	10.38	13.13
Claims on Bk.Inst.in Oth.EA Ctys	20b.u	....	....	....	....	....	....	67.89	69.20	62.36	86.55	91.52	112.15
Fgn. Assets (Cl.on Non-EA Ctys)	21	229.06	201.96	231.12	295.73	311.64	320.28	90.42	92.30	85.15	89.88	93.32	90.02
Claims on General Government	22a.u	....	....	....	....	....	....	243.13	211.34	211.95	207.66	237.56	240.83
o/w: Claims on Gen.Govt.in Cty.	22a	404.16	434.80	413.46	442.92	408.43	395.40	240.00	206.65	207.15	201.86	219.97	214.75
Claims on Other Resident Sectors	22d.u	....	....	....	....	....	....	811.05	926.19	997.04	1,063.70	1,148.35	1,215.48
o/w: Cl. on Oth.Res.Sect.in Cty.	22d	969.94	983.66	1,027.70	1,060.42	1,123.53	1,224.36	788.23	896.82	966.60	1,030.75	1,110.79	1,180.85
Demand Deposits	24..u	....	....	....	....	....	....	386.95	410.65	449.75	492.52	519.59	549.46
o/w:D.Dep.of Oth.Res.Sect.in Cty.	24	454.92	471.38	471.06	498.87	531.72	601.15	384.91	407.91	446.12	488.03	515.62	546.14
Other Deposits	25..u	....	....	....	....	....	....	194.71	194.55	192.43	205.83	181.64	189.51
o/w:D.Dep.of Oth.Res.Sect.in Cty.	25	469.88	458.91	476.50	469.39	359.51	287.75	190.61	190.26	190.54	201.04	176.34	179.61
Money Market Fund Shares	26m.u	....	....	....	....	....	....	13.06	10.04	26.10	41.69	106.70	100.66
Bonds & Money Mkt. Instruments	26n.u	....	....	....	....	....	....	271.55	302.48	334.67	367.97	399.96	442.99
o/w: Held by Resid.of Cty.	26n	289.91	303.38	341.95	399.97	510.23	544.00	....	....	....	....	....	....
Foreign Liab. (to Non-EA Ctys)	26c	369.98	375.66	343.58	364.08	392.74	391.61	135.75	157.75	171.18	146.30	159.56	157.45
Central Government Deposits	26d.u	....	....	....	....	....	....	7.96	7.00	7.51	7.12	7.75	7.24
o/w: Cent.Govt.Dep. in Cty.	26d	13.40	13.23	9.29	11.15	12.73	13.40	7.92	6.96	7.21	7.11	7.73	7.22
Credit from Monetary Authorities	26g	44.94	42.50	41.04	50.03	32.30	11.04	33.29	26.46	10.81	7.62	9.16	15.63
Liab. to Bk.Inst.in Oth. EA Ctys.	26h.u	....	....	....	....	....	....	98.65	107.61	109.57	111.65	118.93	126.29
Capital Accounts	27a	206.02	219.39	232.44	250.19	257.05	280.93	118.27	123.93	133.63	146.17	156.73	163.18
Other Items (Net)	27r	−136.25	−170.74	−164.29	−162.91	−164.86	−166.20	−37.79	−33.28	−53.44	−68.74	−78.87	−80.81
Post Office: Checking Deposits	24..i	9.48	8.16	8.49	7.28	6.67	1.66	....	....	....	....	....	....
Post Office: Savings Deposits	25..i	30.86	39.15	43.94	46.26	52.00	58.33	....	....	....	....	....	....
Savings Certif.	26abi	72.16	87.05	97.77	110.61	117.35	121.65	....	....	....	....	....	....

		1993	1994	1995	1996	1997	1998	1999	2000	2001	2002	2003	2004
Banking Survey (Nat'l Residency)		*Trillions of Lire through 1998; Billions of Euros Beginning 1999: End of Period*											
Foreign Assets (Net)	31n	−56.99	−82.27	−20.99	38.39	52.54	17.26	−11.03	−27.51	−23.60	9.43	12.70	30.23
Domestic Credit	32	1,617.11	1,672.10	1,708.99	1,770.52	1,811.64	1,902.18	1,058.49	1,148.44	1,214.62	1,253.91	1,369.21	1,439.90
Claims on General Govt. (Net)	32an	642.82	687.88	678.65	710.10	688.11	677.82	263.13	243.56	241.53	217.92	252.67	252.19
Claims on Other Resident Sectors	32d	974.29	984.22	1,030.34	1,060.42	1,123.53	1,224.36	795.36	904.89	973.09	1,036.00	1,116.53	1,187.71
Currency Issued	34a.n	104.71	110.02	113.71	115.44	122.94	126.54	71.96	76.42	65.89	65.49	76.09	86.79
Demand Deposits	34b.n	454.92	471.38	471.06	498.87	531.72	601.15	385.30	407.99	446.35	488.03	515.70	546.25
Other Deposits	35..n	500.75	498.06	520.44	515.65	411.52	346.08	190.61	190.26	190.54	201.04	176.34	179.61
Money Market Fund Shares	36m	....	....	....	....	....	....	13.06	10.04	26.10	41.69	106.70	100.66
Bonds & Money Mkt. Instruments	36n	363.30	391.90	441.72	512.24	628.77	666.57	271.55	302.48	334.67	367.97	399.96	442.99
o/w: Over Two Years	36na	....	....	....	....	....	....	259.05	289.12	322.13	353.93	388.79	433.97
Capital Accounts	37a	290.37	310.05	327.22	350.03	355.99	356.78	153.63	164.37	175.10	171.43	181.75	190.63
Other Items (Net)	37r	−153.92	−191.58	−186.14	−183.31	−186.74	−177.68	−38.66	−30.63	−47.64	−72.32	−74.61	−76.81
Banking Survey (EA-Wide Residency)		*Billions of Euros: End of Period*											
Foreign Assets (Net)	31n.u	....	....	....	....	....	....	−5.81	−15.21	−36.11	−6.62	−16.76	−22.56
Domestic Credit	32..u	....	....	....	....	....	....	1,084.62	1,182.69	1,249.82	1,292.69	1,424.35	1,500.68
Claims on General Govt. (Net)	32anu	....	....	....	....	....	....	266.21	248.22	246.04	223.71	270.24	278.26
Claims on Other Resident Sect.	32d.u	....	....	....	....	....	....	818.41	934.47	1,003.78	1,068.98	1,154.11	1,222.41
Currency Issued	34a.u	....	....	....	....	....	....	71.96	76.42	65.89	65.49	76.09	86.79
Demand Deposits	34b.u	....	....	....	....	....	....	387.33	410.74	449.98	492.53	519.67	549.57
Other Deposits	35..u	....	....	....	....	....	....	194.71	194.55	192.43	205.83	181.64	189.51
o/w: Other Dep. Over Two Yrs	35abu	....	....	....	....	....	....	17.00	11.49	6.41	4.07	4.32	3.71
Money Market Fund Shares	36m.u	....	....	....	....	....	....	13.06	10.04	26.10	41.69	106.70	100.66
Bonds & Money Mkt. Instruments	36n.u	....	....	....	....	....	....	271.55	302.48	334.67	367.97	399.96	442.99
o/w: Over Two Years	36nau	....	....	....	....	....	....	259.05	289.12	322.13	353.93	388.79	433.97
Capital Accounts	37a	....	....	....	....	....	....	153.63	164.37	175.10	171.43	181.75	190.63
Other Items (Net)	37r.u	....	....	....	....	....	....	−13.44	8.89	−30.46	−58.87	−58.21	−82.03
Money (National Definitions)		*Trillions of Lire: End of Period*											
M2	59mb	841.32	847.42	834.15	863.29	930.99	975.34	....	....	....	....	....	....
Interest Rates		*Percent Per Annum*											
Discount Rate (End of Period)	60	8.00	7.50	9.00	7.50	5.50	3.00	....	....	....	....	....	....
Money Market Rate	60b	10.20	8.51	10.46	8.82	6.88	4.99	2.95	4.39	4.26	3.32	2.33	2.10
Treasury Bill Rate	60c	10.58	9.17	10.85	8.46	6.33	4.59	3.01	4.53	4.05	3.26	2.19	2.08
Deposit Rate	60l	† 7.79	6.20	6.45	6.49	4.83	3.16	1.61	1.84	1.96	1.43	.95	1.47
Deposit Rate (Households)	60lhs	....	....	....	....	....	....	....	....	....	....	1.62	1.47
Lending Rate	60p	13.87	11.22	12.47	12.06	9.75	7.88	5.58	6.26	6.53	5.78	5.03	....
Lending Rate (Households)	60phm	....	....	....	....	....	....	....	....	....	....	4.67	4.37
Lending Rate (Corporations)	60pcs	....	....	....	....	....	....	....	....	....	....	4.98	4.91
Govt Bond Yield (Long-Term)	61	11.31	10.56	12.21	9.40	6.86	4.90	4.73	5.58	5.19	5.03	4.25	4.26
Govt Bond Yield (Medium-Term)	61b	11.21	10.57	11.98	8.93	6.47	4.55	4.04	5.29	4.64	4.48	3.36	3.34
Prices, Production, Labor		*Index Numbers (2000=100): Period Averages*											
Share Prices	62	27.4	34.2	31.4	31.5	43.2	69.1	77.0	100.0	81.1	64.3	58.1	66.8
Producer Prices	63	81.8	84.9	91.5	93.3	94.5	94.6	94.3	100.0	101.9	† 101.8	103.4	106.2
Consumer Prices	64	81.0	84.3	† 88.7	92.2	94.1	95.9	97.5	100.0	102.8	105.3	108.1	110.5
Harmonized CPI	64h	....	....	88.8	92.3	94.0	95.9	97.5	100.0	102.3	105.0	107.9	110.4
Wages: Contractual	65	81.7	84.6	87.2	90.0	93.2	95.8	98.0	100.0	101.8	104.5	107.2	110.5
Industrial Production	66	83.1	88.0	92.9	91.3	94.9	96.0	95.9	100.0	99.0	97.4	96.9	96.2
Industrial Employment	67	104.7	102.4	100.7	99.6	98.9	99.8	100.0	100.0	100.8	101.9	103.7	104.5
		Number in Thousands: Period Averages											
Labor Force	67d	....	22,680	22,734	22,849	22,889	23,363	23,361	23,720	23,900	24,086	24,229	....
Employment	67e	† 20,765	20,393	20,240	20,328	20,384	20,591	20,847	21,210	21,605	21,913	22,241	22,404
Unemployment	67c	† 2,299	2,508	2,638	2,555	2,585	2,634	2,560	2,388	2,164	2,062	2,048	1,960
Unemployment Rate (%)	67r	† 9.6	11.1	11.7	11.2	11.3	11.3	11.0	10.2	9.1	8.6	8.5	8.1
Intl. Transactions & Positions		*Billions of Lire through 1998; Millions of Euros Beginning 1999*											
Exports	70	266,213	308,045	381,175	388,885	409,128	426,182	† 221,040	260,414	272,990	269,064	264,615	284,647
Imports, c.i.f.	71	232,991	272,382	335,661	321,286	357,587	378,784	† 207,016	258,507	263,756	261,226	262,997	285,261
		2000=100											
Volume of Exports	72	74.1	82.8	93.8	† 91.7	93.5	94.2	91.7	100.0	101.5	98.6	96.0	97.6
Volume of Imports	73	64.7	72.7	79.8	† 76.0	83.2	89.6	93.0	100.0	99.5	98.8	99.5	102.1
Unit Value of Exports	74	71.5	74.1	81.0	† 84.5	87.2	90.2	92.6	100.0	103.6	105.0	105.8	110.4
Unit Value of Imports	75	72.2	75.2	84.4	† 84.5	85.9	84.6	86.0	100.0	102.7	102.2	101.9	106.8

		1993	1994	1995	1996	1997	1998	1999	2000	2001	2002	2003	2004
Balance of Payments						*Millions of US Dollars: Minus Sign Indicates Debit*							
Current Account, n.i.e.	78ald	7,802	13,209	25,076	39,999	32,403	19,998	8,111	−5,781	−652	−9,369	−19,406	−15,137
Goods: Exports f.o.b.	78aad	169,153	191,421	233,998	252,039	240,404	242,572	235,856	240,473	244,931	252,618	298,118	352,166
Goods: Imports f.o.b.	78abd	−140,264	−159,854	−195,269	−197,921	−200,527	−206,941	−212,420	−230,925	−229,392	−239,206	−286,641	−341,255
Trade Balance	78acd	28,889	31,568	38,729	54,118	39,878	35,631	23,437	9,549	15,540	13,412	11,477	10,911
Services: Credit	78add	52,284	53,681	61,619	65,660	66,991	67,549	58,788	56,556	57,676	60,439	71,767	83,706
Services: Debit	78aed	−48,939	−48,238	−55,050	−57,605	−59,227	−63,379	−57,707	−55,601	−57,753	−63,166	−74,332	−81,987
Balance on Goods & Services	78afd	32,235	37,011	45,299	62,173	47,642	39,801	24,517	10,504	15,463	10,685	8,912	12,630
Income: Credit	78agd	31,844	28,599	34,168	40,142	45,734	51,319	46,361	38,671	38,574	43,303	48,780	53,219
Income: Debit	78ahd	−49,062	−45,289	−49,812	−55,101	−56,936	−63,636	−57,411	−50,680	−48,911	−57,854	−69,003	−71,424
Balance on Gds, Serv. & Inc.	78aid	15,017	20,321	29,655	47,213	36,440	27,483	13,467	−1,506	5,127	−3,865	−11,312	−5,574
Current Transfers, n.i.e.: Credit	78ajd	12,925	12,254	14,287	14,320	15,552	14,402	16,776	15,797	16,136	20,871	20,650	21,854
Current Transfers: Debit	78akd	−20,140	−19,366	−18,866	−21,535	−19,588	−21,887	−22,132	−20,073	−21,915	−26,375	−28,744	−31,417
Capital Account, n.i.e.	78bcd	1,659	1,026	1,671	66	3,434	2,358	2,964	2,879	846	−80	2,941	2,645
Capital Account, n.i.e.: Credit	78bad	2,807	2,213	2,797	1,414	4,582	3,359	4,572	4,172	2,098	2,060	4,950	4,113
Capital Account: Debit	78bbd	−1,149	−1,187	−1,125	−1,348	−1,148	−1,001	−1,608	−1,293	−1,252	−2,140	−2,009	−1,468
Financial Account, n.i.e.	78bjd	5,260	−14,207	−2,889	−7,982	−6,878	−18,074	−17,415	7,504	−3,570	11,224	20,437	8,165
Direct Investment Abroad	78bdd	−7,329	−5,239	−7,024	−8,697	−10,414	−12,407	−6,723	−12,077	−21,758	−17,247	−8,986	−19,144
Dir. Invest. in Rep. Econ., n.i.e.	78bed	3,749	2,199	4,842	3,546	3,700	2,635	6,943	13,176	14,874	14,699	16,538	16,772
Portfolio Investment Assets	78bfd	12,187	−37,718	−4,938	−25,598	−61,857	−109,064	−129,624	−80,263	−36,167	−15,265	−57,408	−26,394
Equity Securities	78bkd	385	−3,360	1,014	−1,036	−15,116	−26,570	−63,277	−77,036	−9,988	−5,198	−15,999	−16,178
Debt Securities	78bld	11,802	−34,358	−5,952	−24,562	−46,741	−82,493	−66,347	−3,227	−26,179	−10,067	−41,409	−10,216
Portfolio Investment Liab., n.i.e.	78bgd	62,107	29,895	45,583	74,655	73,375	111,987	104,607	57,020	29,329	32,924	60,150	58,551
Equity Securities	78bmd	4,133	−1,395	5,358	9,331	9,414	14,423	−4,537	−2,426	−245	−6,268	−2,010	17,183
Debt Securities	78bnd	57,974	31,290	40,225	65,324	63,962	97,563	109,144	59,446	29,573	39,193	62,160	41,368
Financial Derivatives Assets	78bwd	−8	87	−852	−1,009	−1,118	−850	161	744	−2,277	−6,137	−10,284	−6,657
Financial Derivatives Liabilities	78bxd	−221	628	1,079	1,272	1,273	1,041	1,709	1,588	1,839	3,431	4,814	8,941
Other Investment Assets	78bhd	−44,197	2,092	−28,947	−68,358	−25,541	−21,232	−33,573	242	2,032	6,229	−20,584	−47,563
Monetary Authorities	78bod	....	....	....	....	....	....	5,396	3,034	−27,626	13,536	−65	−8,703
General Government	78bpd	−1,539	−2,023	−2,148	−1,112	−62	−1,101	−163	−649	−355	1,372	1,405	−537
Banks	78bqd	−33,300	22,599	−18,689	−45,046	−1,602	−7,052	−9,643	2,388	12,091	−34,000	429	−28,323
Other Sectors	78brd	−9,358	−18,483	−8,110	−22,199	−23,877	−13,078	−29,163	−4,532	17,921	25,320	−22,353	−9,999
Other Investment Liab., n.i.e.	78bid	−21,027	−6,152	−12,632	16,206	13,703	9,816	39,085	27,074	8,560	−7,412	36,199	23,659
Monetary Authorities	78bsd	−4,602	−95	1,062	−1,269	−48	−128	916	−690	1,928	869	−2,548	388
General Government	78btd	765	−1,812	4,893	−2,583	−1,798	−5,739	−3,255	−3,549	−759	−537	−1,015	−655
Banks	78bud	−16,752	−1,527	−22,716	26,613	6,861	12,780	1,109	24,875	12,783	−6,123	43,746	14,719
Other Sectors	78bvd	−439	−2,719	4,129	−6,555	8,688	2,903	40,315	6,438	−5,392	−1,621	−3,984	9,207
Net Errors and Omissions	78cad	−17,856	1,547	−21,054	−20,176	−15,810	−25,754	−1,711	−1,355	2,787	1,395	−2,858	1,484
Overall Balance	78cbd	−3,135	1,575	2,804	11,907	13,150	−21,472	−8,051	3,247	−588	3,169	1,115	−2,844
Reserves and Related Items	79dad	3,135	−1,575	−2,804	−11,907	−13,150	21,472	8,051	−3,247	588	−3,169	−1,115	2,844
Reserve Assets	79dbd	3,135	−1,575	−2,804	−11,907	−13,150	21,472	8,051	−3,247	588	−3,169	−1,115	2,844
Use of Fund Credit and Loans	79dcd	—	—	—	—	—	—	—	—	—	—	—	—
Exceptional Financing	79ded	....	....	....	....	....	....	....	....	....	....	....	....
International Investment Position							*Millions of US Dollars*						
Assets	79aad	450,985	516,329	597,810	727,498	809,597	1,002,865	1,081,092	1,119,394	1,078,391	1,201,342	1,559,848	....
Direct Investment Abroad	79abd	81,892	91,097	109,176	113,251	130,668	165,412	181,852	180,275	182,375	194,496	238,885	....
Portfolio Investment	79acd	130,670	150,426	171,793	192,351	257,494	394,501	546,903	590,753	552,028	595,922	791,147	....
Equity Securities	79add	11,723	14,015	13,982	16,915	26,600	37,690	210,929	285,553	239,473	247,462	331,049	....
Debt Securities	79aed	118,947	136,411	157,811	175,436	230,894	356,811	335,974	305,200	312,555	348,460	460,098	....
Financial Derivatives	79ald	—	—	—	—	—	—	2,951	3,533	4,315	11,050	22,704	....
Other Investment	79afd	187,620	217,192	256,520	350,907	344,344	388,310	304,085	297,775	293,458	344,253	443,850	....
Monetary Authorities	79agd							−4,190	−6,715	20,629	8,944	12,244	....
General Government	79ahd	13,641	16,459	19,542	21,777	20,180	22,567	20,417	23,316	23,057	25,403	28,924	....
Banks	79aid	116,107	121,726	146,945	214,524	198,520	225,089	138,717	140,447	119,177	181,173	225,428	....
Other Sectors	79ajd	57,872	79,006	90,034	114,606	125,644	140,653	149,141	140,727	130,595	128,732	177,254	....
Reserve Assets	79akd	50,803	57,615	60,321	70,989	77,091	54,642	45,302	47,058	46,215	55,622	63,262	....
Liabilities	79lad	535,352	587,612	650,102	761,656	807,436	1,022,711	1,027,672	1,072,544	1,051,312	1,272,221	1,643,720	....
Dir. Invest. in Rep. Economy	79lbd	54,538	60,955	65,980	74,640	83,158	105,397	108,638	113,047	108,007	126,481	173,598	....
Portfolio Investment	79lcd	160,403	188,595	237,861	333,422	385,388	544,602	549,251	570,236	561,024	704,422	913,328	....
Equity Securities	79ldd	11,123	11,118	16,434	27,245	35,500	65,833	53,380	53,182	35,743	29,505	31,090	....
Debt Securities	79led	149,280	177,477	221,427	306,177	349,888	478,769	495,871	517,054	525,281	674,917	882,238	....
Financial Derivatives	79lld	—	—	—	—	—	—	3,244	2,641	4,522	8,919	15,896	....
Other Investment	79lfd	320,411	338,063	346,261	353,593	338,891	372,772	366,538	386,620	377,760	432,399	540,897	....
Monetary Authorities	79lgd	578	485	1,554	239	175	56	950	235	2,197	3,078	633	....
General Government	79lhd	21,506	21,551	26,328	22,187	21,470	15,595	8,881	7,272	6,062	6,341	6,511	....
Banks	79lid	213,524	229,119	228,859	247,732	239,171	268,935	241,669	265,040	260,561	296,676	386,976	....
Other Sectors	79ljd	84,803	86,907	89,521	83,436	78,075	88,186	115,039	114,073	108,939	126,303	146,778	....
Government Finance													
Central Government					*Trillions of Lire through 1998; Billions of Euros Beginning 1999: Year Ending December 31*								
Deficit (-) or Surplus	80	† −157.8	−152.9	−122.6	−136.1	−31.0	−47.9	.3	−14.6	−40.8	....	....	....
Revenue	81	† 470.1	477.1	524.8	549.7	621.3	594.7	353.1	350.6	351.7	....	....	....
Expenditure	82	† 610.3	601.8	619.3	652.8	602.6	611.3	327.5	341.3	372.8	....	....	....
Lending Minus Repayments	83	† 17.6	28.2	28.0	32.9	49.7	31.3	25.3	24.0	19.7	....	....	....
Financing	80h	164.8	153.0	122.7	136.1	31.3	48.0	−.4	14.7	40.9	....	....	....
Domestic	84a	....	109.5	61.6	34.4	−72.3	−91.9	−92.9	−34.4	28.8	....	....	....
Foreign	85a	....	43.5	61.1	101.7	103.6	139.9	92.5	49.1	12.1	....	....	....
Total Debt by Residence	88	1,765.5	† 1,931.8	2,073.7	2,206.1	2,250.8	2,290.5	1,188.0	1,212.8	1,255.1	....	....	....
Debt: Domestic	88a	....	1,621.8	1,720.3	1,769.8	1,719.1	1,630.0	756.0	742.5	775.8	....	....	....
Foreign	89a	....	310.0	353.4	436.3	531.7	660.5	432.0	470.3	479.3	....	....	....
Net Borrowing: Lire	84b	150.3	147.5	100.9	129.9	....	....	....	....	....	....	....	....
Net Borrowing: Foreign Currency	85b	14.4	9.2	25.8	12.9	....	....	....	....	....	....	....	....
Monetary Operations	86c	.1	.1	.1	.1	....	....	....	....	....	....	....	....
General Government						*As Percent of Gross Domestic Product*							
Deficit (-) or Surplus	80g	−9.5	−9.2	−7.7	−7.1	−2.7	−2.8	−1.8	−.5	−1.4	....	....	....
Debt	88g	119.1	124.9	125.3	122.1	120.1	116.4	114.5	110.6	109.4	....	....	....

Italy   136

National Accounts		1993	1994	1995	1996	1997	1998	1999	2000	2001	2002	2003	2004
		Trillions of Lire through 1998; Billions of Euros Beginning 1999											
Househ.Cons.Expend.,incl.NPISHs....	96f.c	913.7	973.7	1,049.7	1,109.4	1,170.9	1,234.1	† 667.9	706.2	731.3	757.0	787.0	812.6
Government Consumption Expend...	91f.c	311.7	316.3	319.1	343.8	361.0	372.2	† 199.5	213.3	229.5	238.9	253.0	260.1
Gross Fixed Capital Formation..........	93e.c	288.2	297.6	327.9	348.8	362.8	384.0	† 210.6	230.9	240.6	249.3	249.6	262.9
Changes in Inventories....................	93i.c	−1.1	8.1	17.8	6.4	12.0	16.7	† 7.1	4.7	−.4	2.4	3.6	4.8
Exports of Goods and Services..........	90c.c	347.9	394.4	483.2	491.1	524.1	547.5	† 283.0	330.0	345.9	340.3	336.1	360.0
Imports of Goods and Services (-).....	98c.c	297.2	336.8	410.5	397.3	443.6	476.7	† 260.3	318.6	328.4	327.4	328.4	349.0
Gross Domestic Product (GDP)........	99b.c	1,563.3	1,653.4	1,787.3	1,902.3	1,987.2	2,077.7	† 1,108.0	1,166.5	1,218.5	1,260.6	1,300.9	1,351.3
Net Primary Income from Abroad.....	98.n	−26.7	−26.6	−25.5	−22.7	−18.2	−19.7	† −7.3	−9.5	−8.8	−9.8	−14.0	....
Gross National Income (GNI)............	99a	1,536.6	1,626.8	1,761.7	1,879.5	1,968.9	2,057.6	† 1,100.7	1,157.0	1,209.7	1,250.8	1,286.9	....
Net Current Transf.from Abroad......	98t	−8.5	−5.7	−2.4	−6.6	−7.1	−9.4	† −4.4	−3.9	−5.3	−6.6	−8.4	....
Gross Nat'l Disposable Inc.(GNDI)....	99i	1,525.2	1,615.7	1,754.5	1,869.5	1,961.8	2,044.8	† 1,096.3	1,153.1	1,204.5	1,244.3	1,278.5	....
Gross Saving.................................	99s	299.7	325.7	385.7	416.3	429.9	439.1	† 228.8	233.6	243.6	248.0	238.9	....
Consumption of Fixed Capital..........	99cfc	208.4	219.5	234.2	246.4	257.2	268.6	† 144.1	152.4	160.5	168.9	176.1	186.2
GDP Volume 1995 Prices.................	99b.r	1,699.0	1,736.5	1,787.3	1,806.8	1,843.4	1,876.8	† 985.3	1,015.1	1,033.0	1,036.9	1,039.6	1,052.3
GDP Volume (2000=100)...............	99bvr	86.4	88.4	90.9	91.9	93.8	95.5	† 97.1	100.0	101.8	102.2	102.4	103.7
GDP Deflator (2000=100)...............	99bir	80.1	82.9	87.0	91.6	93.8	96.3	† 97.9	100.0	102.6	105.8	108.9	111.7
		Millions: Midyear Estimates											
Population...............................	99z	57.05	57.18	57.30	57.40	57.49	57.56	57.64	57.71	57.80	57.88	57.96	58.03

		1993	1994	1995	1996	1997	1998	1999	2000	2001	2002	2003	2004
Exchange Rates					*Jamaica Dollars per SDR: End of Period*								
Market Rate..................aa=........	wa	44.606	48.469	58.889	50.135	49.033	52.174	56.672	59.172	59.426	69.012	89.927	95.432
				Jamaica Dollars per US Dollar: End of Period (we) Period Average (wf)									
Market Rate..................ae=........	we	32.475	33.202	39.616	34.865	36.341	37.055	41.291	45.415	47.286	50.762	60.517	61.450
Market Rate..................rf=..........	wf	24.949	33.086	35.142	37.120	35.404	36.550	39.044	42.986	45.996	48.416	57.741	61.197
Fund Position					*Millions of SDRs: End of Period*								
Quota..	2f.s	200.9	200.9	200.9	200.9	200.9	200.9	273.5	273.5	273.5	273.5	273.5	273.5
SDRs..	1b.s	9.1	—	.3	—	.2	.5	.5	.1	1.2	.7	—	.1
Reserve Position in the Fund............	1c.s												
Total Fund Cred.&Loans Outstg........	2tl	244.2	217.6	161.7	112.2	87.1	74.7	60.8	46.3	31.9	17.4	6.0	.6
International Liquidity					*Millions of US Dollars Unless Otherwise Indicated: End of Period*								
Total Reserves minus Gold...............	1l.d	417.0	735.9	681.3	880.0	682.1	709.5	554.5	1,053.7	1,900.5	1,645.1	1,194.9	1,846.5
SDRs....................................	1b.d	12.4	—	.5	.1	.2	.7	.7	.1	1.5	.9	.1	.1
Reserve Position in the Fund..........	1c.d												
Foreign Exchange.......................	1d.d	404.6	735.9	680.8	879.9	681.9	708.8	553.8	1,053.6	1,899.0	1,644.2	1,194.8	1,846.4
Other Official Insts.: Assets............	3b.d	17.5	8.3	7.7	8.0	1.1	1.0	3.2	3.1	6.6	2.9	4.3	5.2
Monetary Authorities: Other Liab.....	4..d	65.1	58.2	....	....	....	....	....	....	....	....	....	....
Deposit Money Banks: Assets..........	7a.d	292.6	449.5	489.0	464.6	542.0	457.9	571.8	593.8	811.8	898.8	941.6	1,160.2
Liabilities...........	7b.d	238.3	393.2	336.2	370.2	371.6	328.0	267.2	219.7	368.7	360.2	432.9	591.8
Other Banking Insts.: Assets.............	7e.d	1.8	34.1	7.0	9.1	16.7	23.8	33.7	37.8	133.7	348.8	378.5	523.6
Liabilities..................	7f.d	3.9	53.8	47.0	43.5	11.7	6.4	5.4	12.9	53.5	215.9	270.9	390.5
Monetary Authorities					*Millions of Jamaica Dollars: End of Period*								
Foreign Assets..............................	11	12,618	24,486	27,084	30,663	24,739	26,280	22,850	47,664	89,818	83,151	72,171	113,769
Claims on Central Government........	12a	7,055	7,466	15,702	20,751	39,777	51,219	57,268	54,930	56,038	57,270	78,188	85,171
Claims on Deposit Money Banks......	12e	—	—	—	—	—	—	—	—	—	—	—	—
Reserve Money.............................	14	18,588	24,969	32,381	33,668	38,770	47,324	45,343	48,887	45,735	44,292	55,127	61,625
of which: Currency Outside DMBs..	14a	5,228	7,118	9,516	10,760	12,449	13,504	17,821	17,607	18,783	20,399	23,186	26,683
Foreign Liabilities........................	16c	13,007	12,480	8,077	2,136	1,588	1,345	906	685	448	441	469	424
Central Government Deposits...........	16d	17,255	26,512	28,948	37,755	41,571	45,837	48,058	64,072	110,622	98,225	86,452	136,390
Capital Accounts..........................	17a	1,815	1,972	2,396	2,060	2,015	2,143	2,326	2,427	2,437	2,827	3,656	3,900
Other Items (Net).........................	17r	−30,993	−33,981	−29,015	−24,205	−19,427	−19,150	−16,515	−13,477	−13,386	−5,363	4,654	−3,399
Deposit Money Banks					*Millions of Jamaica Dollars: End of Period*								
Reserves.......................................	20	13,681	18,794	25,623	23,568	29,167	30,812	26,972	32,236	40,378	44,099	46,530	37,668
Foreign Assets..............................	21	9,501	14,924	19,373	16,197	19,697	16,966	23,608	26,967	38,388	45,624	56,983	71,293
Claims on Central Government........	22a	7,580	16,967	13,716	22,281	23,898	23,280	30,373	34,886	93,576	80,134	87,205	94,649
Claims on Local Government...........	22b	—	6	6	2	3	1	—	—	—	—	3	4
Claims on Nonfin.Pub.Enterprises.....	22c	730	1,016	2,081	1,902	3,326	3,462	3,236	4,269	6,094	15,869	17,967	19,761
Claims on Private Sector..................	22d	23,326	32,164	44,408	52,006	57,482	74,777	84,593	102,602	42,312	56,047	76,845	91,428
Claims on Other Banking Insts.........	22f	281	686	803	380	512	342	579	1,059	42	284	132	72
Demand Deposits..........................	24	11,675	14,134	19,804	22,788	22,022	23,160	27,221	30,289	35,359	39,020	39,871	48,010
Time and Savings Deposits..............	25	29,725	44,300	57,075	62,243	74,017	80,138	86,054	100,215	106,772	120,730	136,079	152,372
Foreign Liabilities........................	26c	7,740	13,055	13,319	12,905	13,504	12,153	11,031	9,978	17,436	18,284	26,201	36,365
Central Government Deposits...........	26d	2,304	6,529	6,945	6,690	8,086	5,736	8,075	15,816	11,261	12,286	10,863	14,306
Credit from Monetary Authorities.....	26g	38	283	3,721	8,120	5,239	101	1,527	3,044	83	135	168	230
Capital Accounts..........................	27a	4,564	7,580	8,911	12,042	12,070	24,868	28,002	25,499	26,772	27,890	31,557	39,011
Other Items (Net).........................	27r	−947	−1,322	−3,766	−8,454	−852	3,483	7,452	17,177	23,107	23,713	40,927	24,580
Monetary Survey					*Millions of Jamaica Dollars: End of Period*								
Foreign Assets (Net)......................	31n	1,372	13,876	25,061	31,818	29,345	29,748	34,521	63,967	110,322	110,051	102,484	148,273
Domestic Credit............................	32	19,442	25,492	41,074	53,129	75,593	101,760	120,167	118,003	76,315	99,217	163,137	140,472
Claims on Central Govt. (Net)........	32an	−4,924	−8,608	−6,475	−1,413	14,019	22,926	31,508	9,928	27,732	26,893	68,078	29,124
Claims on Local Government..........	32b	—	6	6	2	3	1	—	—	—	—	3	4
Claims on Nonfin.Pub.Enterprises...	32c	730	1,016	2,081	1,902	3,326	3,462	3,236	4,269	6,094	15,869	17,967	19,761
Claims on Private Sector.................	32d	23,355	32,391	44,660	52,258	57,734	75,029	84,845	102,747	42,447	56,171	76,957	91,511
Claims on Other Banking Insts.......	32f	281	686	803	380	512	342	579	1,059	42	284	132	72
Money..	34	16,903	21,252	29,320	33,548	34,470	36,664	45,042	47,897	54,142	59,419	63,057	74,693
Quasi-Money.................................	35	29,725	44,300	57,075	62,243	74,017	80,138	86,054	100,215	106,772	120,730	136,079	152,372
Capital Accounts...........................	37a	6,379	9,553	11,307	14,102	14,086	27,011	30,328	27,927	29,210	30,716	35,214	42,911
Other Items (Net).........................	37r	−32,193	−35,736	−31,567	−24,946	−17,635	−12,305	−6,735	5,932	−3,487	−1,597	31,271	18,768
Money plus Quasi-Money...............	35l	46,628	65,552	86,396	95,791	108,487	116,803	131,095	148,112	160,914	180,149	199,136	227,065
Other Banking Institutions					*Millions of Jamaica Dollars: End of Period*								
Reserves.......................................	40	1,396	1,276	1,287	1,390	1,233	1,279	765	454	828	744	495	820
Foreign Assets..............................	41	59	1,133	277	318	608	882	1,393	1,718	6,322	17,706	22,904	32,174
Claims on Central Government........	42a	312	1,681	2,818	4,404	4,281	1,894	1,500	2,004	4,167	2,612	9,333	6,858
Claims on Private Sector..................	42d	7,468	7,627	9,890	10,662	7,069	5,781	4,354	2,855	3,372	3,572	5,954	6,860
Claims on Deposit Money Banks......	42e	686	1,148	932	865	1,442	379	299	143	251	370	85	172
Demand Deposits..........................	44												
Time and Savings Deposits..............	45	7,306	6,998	7,077	6,996	6,862	5,759	4,938	3,966	7,290	8,368	9,330	11,436
Foreign Liabilities........................	46c	127	1,786	1,863	1,516	425	237	224	586	2,531	10,959	16,395	23,998
Credit from Deposit Money Banks.....	46h	949	1,312	1,096	5,463	4,098	1,120	—	170	160	196	50	24
Capital Accounts..........................	47a	1,738	2,521	2,924	3,013	1,688	2,946	4,259	2,820	4,117	4,760	4,943	6,141
Other Items (Net).........................	47r	−200	249	2,244	649	1,559	153	−1,111	−367	844	720	8,052	5,284
Banking Survey					*Millions of Jamaica Dollars: End of Period*								
Foreign Assets (Net)......................	51n	1,304	13,223	23,476	30,620	29,527	30,393	35,690	65,100	114,113	116,798	108,993	156,449
Domestic Credit............................	52	26,940	34,114	52,979	67,815	86,431	109,094	125,442	121,804	83,813	105,117	178,292	154,117
Claims on Central Govt. (Net)........	52an	−4,612	−6,927	−3,658	2,991	18,299	24,821	33,008	11,932	31,899	29,505	77,411	35,981
Claims on Local Government..........	52b	—	6	6	2	3	1	—	—	—	—	3	4
Claims on Nonfin.Pub.Enterprises...	52c	730	1,016	2,081	1,902	3,326	3,462	3,236	4,269	6,094	15,869	17,967	19,761
Claims on Private Sector...............	52d	30,823	40,018	54,550	62,920	64,803	80,810	89,198	105,603	45,819	59,743	82,912	98,371
Liquid Liabilities..........................	55l	52,538	71,273	92,186	101,398	114,116	121,282	135,267	151,624	167,375	187,772	207,972	237,682
Capital Accounts..........................	57a	8,117	12,074	14,231	17,116	15,773	29,957	34,587	30,747	33,327	35,476	40,157	49,052
Other Items (Net).........................	57r	−32,411	−36,010	−29,961	−20,078	−13,931	−11,753	−8,723	4,533	−2,776	−1,334	39,157	23,833

		1993	1994	1995	1996	1997	1998	1999	2000	2001	2002	2003	2004
Interest Rates							*Percent Per Annum*						
Treasury Bill Rate	60c	28.85	42.98	27.65	37.95	21.14	25.65	20.75	18.24	16.71	15.54	25.94	15.47
Savings Rate	60k	15.00	15.00	15.00	15.00	10.96	9.69	8.75	8.50	7.75	7.50	5.21	1.25
Deposit Rate	60l	27.59	36.41	23.21	25.16	13.95	15.61	13.48	11.62	9.64	8.58	8.46	7.98
Lending Rate	60p	43.71	49.46	43.58	39.83	32.86	31.59	27.01	23.35	20.61	18.50	18.89	18.14
Government Bond Yield	61	24.82	26.82	26.85	26.87	26.85	....	....	....	....	....	....	....
Prices and Labor						*Index Numbers (2000=100): Period Averages*							
Industrial Share Prices	62	73.7	50.2	60.2	48.9	58.6	73.8	69.3	100.0	110.6	134.1	184.7	334.1
Consumer Prices	64	35.8	48.3	57.9	73.2	80.3	87.3	92.4	100.0	107.0	114.6	126.4	143.6
						Number in Thousands: Period Averages							
Labor Force	67d	1,083	1,140	1,150	1,143	1,134	1,129	1,119	1,105	1,105	1,125	1,098	....
Employment	67e	906	923	963	960	956	954	937	936	942	942	....	....
Unemployment	67c	177	167	187	183	187	175	176	171	166	170	144	....
Unemployment Rate (%)	67r	16.3	15.4	16.2	16.0	16.5	15.5	15.7	15.5	15.0	15.1	13.1	....
Intl. Transactions & Positions						*Millions of Jamaica Dollars*							
Exports	70	26,421	40,121	49,916	51,513	48,971	47,940	48,425	55,621	56,061	53,897	67,931	85,017
Imports, c.i.f.	71	53,737	73,631	99,418	109,687	110,932	110,926	113,472	141,987	154,526	171,201	209,852	230,964
						2000=100							
Volume of Exports	72	91.0	96.8	90.9	100.1	101.4	104.7	103.2	100.0	104.1	106.7	108.3	111.1
Balance of Payments					*Millions of US Dollars: Minus Sign Indicates Debit*								
Current Account, n.i.e.	78ald	−184.0	81.6	−98.9	−142.6	−332.2	−333.8	−216.3	−367.4	−758.8	−1,074.2	−761.4	....
Goods: Exports f.o.b.	78aad	1,105.4	1,548.0	1,796.0	1,721.0	1,700.3	1,613.4	1,499.1	1,562.8	1,454.4	1,309.1	1,385.6	....
Goods: Imports f.o.b.	78abd	−1,920.5	−2,099.2	−2,625.3	−2,715.2	−2,832.6	−2,743.9	−2,685.6	−3,004.3	−3,072.6	−3,179.6	−3,329.4	....
Trade Balance	78acd	−815.1	−551.2	−829.3	−994.2	−1,132.3	−1,130.5	−1,186.5	−1,441.5	−1,618.2	−1,870.5	−1,943.8	....
Services: Credit	78add	1,260.7	1,480.2	1,597.9	1,601.9	1,698.9	1,770.4	1,978.4	2,025.7	1,897.0	1,912.2	2,131.6	....
Services: Debit	78aed	−823.5	−955.3	−1,103.8	−1,149.2	−1,231.7	−1,293.6	−1,323.0	−1,422.5	−1,513.9	−1,597.5	−1,566.9	....
Balance on Goods & Services	78afd	−377.9	−26.3	−335.2	−541.5	−665.1	−653.7	−531.1	−838.3	−1,235.1	−1,555.8	−1,379.1	....
Income: Credit	78agd	117.0	104.6	146.6	141.8	147.3	156.3	165.8	193.1	218.2	221.0	217.6	....
Income: Debit	78ahd	−312.9	−456.6	−517.3	−366.5	−439.2	−464.4	−498.3	−543.0	−656.0	−826.3	−789.0	....
Balance on Gds, Serv. & Inc.	78aid	−573.8	−378.3	−705.9	−766.2	−957.0	−961.8	−863.6	−1,188.2	−1,672.9	−2,161.1	−1,950.5	....
Current Transfers, n.i.e.: Credit	78ajd	415.9	504.2	669.6	709.3	705.7	727.6	757.9	969.4	1,090.7	1,337.9	1,523.5	....
Current Transfers: Debit	78akd	−26.1	−44.3	−62.6	−85.7	−80.9	−99.6	−110.6	−148.6	−176.6	−251.0	−334.4	....
Capital Account, n.i.e.	78bcd	−12.9	10.4	10.5	16.6	−11.6	−8.7	−10.9	2.2	−22.3	−16.9	.1	....
Capital Account, n.i.e.: Credit	78bad	—	33.2	34.5	42.5	21.7	20.3	19.1	29.6	15.2	18.9	19.3	....
Capital Account: Debit	78bbd	−12.9	−22.8	−24.0	−25.9	−33.3	−29.0	−30.0	−27.4	−37.5	−35.8	−19.2	....
Financial Account, n.i.e.	78bjd	257.1	256.1	108.3	388.6	163.5	337.3	94.8	853.9	1,660.5	906.4	312.1	....
Direct Investment Abroad	78bdd	—	−52.7	−66.3	−93.3	−56.6	−82.0	−94.9	−74.3	−89.0	−73.9	−116.3	....
Dir. Invest. in Rep. Econ., n.i.e.	78bed	77.9	129.7	147.4	183.7	203.3	369.1	523.7	468.3	613.9	481.1	720.7	....
Portfolio Investment Assets	78bfd	—	....	....	....	....	−3.9	−3.7	−70.0	−39.3	−351.3	−1,105.2	....
Equity Securities	78bkd	—	....	....	....	....							
Debt Securities	78bld	—	—	—	—	—	−3.9	−3.7	−70.0	−39.3	−351.3	−1,105.2	....
Portfolio Investment Liab., n.i.e.	78bgd	—	—	—	—	5.7	10.9	8.6	5.9	69.7	155.8	819.6	....
Equity Securities	78bmd	—	....	....	....	....							
Debt Securities	78bnd	—	—	—	—	5.7	10.9	8.6	5.9	69.7	155.8	819.6	....
Financial Derivatives Assets	78bwd	....	....	....	....	....	—	—	—	—	—	—	....
Financial Derivatives Liabilities	78bxd	....	....	....	....	....	—	—	—	—	—	—	....
Other Investment Assets	78bhd	1.1	−141.3	−148.8	−13.8	−113.2	−59.1	−122.7	−95.5	−215.5	−164.9	−308.8	....
Monetary Authorities	78bod	....	—	—	—	—	—	—	—	—	—	—	....
General Government	78bpd	−1.4	—	—	—	—	—	—	—	—	—	—	....
Banks	78bqd	2.5	−177.9	−199.2	−88.1	−186.9	−142.3	−215.1	−181.5	−282.9	−227.0	−362.8	....
Other Sectors	78brd	—	36.6	50.4	74.3	73.7	83.2	92.4	86.0	67.4	62.1	54.0	....
Other Investment Liab., n.i.e.	78bid	178.1	320.4	176.0	312.0	124.3	102.3	−216.2	619.5	1,320.7	859.6	302.1	....
Monetary Authorities	78bsd	−35.9	—	—	—	—	—	—	—	—	—	—	....
General Government	78btd	37.8	−127.4	−97.0	−144.7	43.1	−41.3	−331.4	383.6	653.4	77.1	−363.7	....
Banks	78bud	−6.0	142.2	74.7	130.7	156.7	205.5	122.2	167.9	250.5	158.0	395.5	....
Other Sectors	78bvd	182.2	305.6	198.3	326.0	−75.5	−61.9	−7.0	68.0	416.8	624.5	270.3	....
Net Errors and Omissions	78cad	49.7	9.6	7.1	8.8	9.9	49.1	−4.0	29.7	−14.4	−55.1	14.1	....
Overall Balance	78cbd	109.9	357.7	27.0	271.4	−170.4	43.9	−136.4	518.4	865.0	−239.8	−435.1	....
Reserves and Related Items	79dad	−109.9	−357.7	−27.0	−271.4	170.4	−43.9	136.4	−518.4	−865.0	239.8	435.1	....
Reserve Assets	79dbd	−92.9	−321.0	55.8	−201.7	205.0	−26.9	155.3	−499.4	−846.6	258.6	451.2	....
Use of Fund Credit and Loans	79dcd	−21.3	−38.2	−84.6	−71.9	−34.6	−17.0	−18.9	−19.0	−18.3	−18.9	−16.1	....
Exceptional Financing	79ded	4.4	1.5	1.9	2.2	—	—	—	—	—	—	—	....
National Accounts						*Millions of Jamaica Dollars*							
Househ.Cons.Expend.,incl.NPISHs.	96f	82,125	111,242	143,438	166,989	180,041	191,055	205,999	233,586	266,035	293,869	345,412	....
Government Consumption Expend.	91f	13,876	16,469	22,635	32,476	40,235	47,156	46,926	53,647	59,146	66,734	71,015	....
Gross Fixed Capital Formation	93e	33,781	43,499	57,901	70,022	76,494	72,660	73,531	90,338	108,323	129,497	140,427	....
Changes in Inventories	93i	828	333	688	460	614	393	319	611	408	664	769	....
Exports of Goods and Services	90c	57,835	83,815	103,214	106,090	103,466	114,038	124,754	146,163	144,614	147,948	191,473	....
Imports of Goods and Services (-)	98c	67,882	93,908	124,175	133,943	137,264	142,266	149,721	184,815	205,484	229,947	278,656	....
Gross Domestic Product (GDP)	99b	120,562	161,450	203,701	242,094	263,586	283,036	301,808	339,528	373,043	408,765	470,440	....
Net Primary Income from Abroad	98.n	−4,689	−7,952	−8,575	−4,852	−4,655	−9,847	−12,543	−14,058	−20,277	−28,872	−35,881	....
Gross National Income (GNI)	99a	115,873	153,498	195,126	237,242	258,931	273,189	289,264	325,471	352,816	379,893	434,559	....
GDP Volume 1996 Prices	99b.p	217,050	219,187	224,565	225,129	222,707	220,172	222,083	223,770	227,070	229,536	234,730	....
GDP Volume (2000=100)	99bvp	97.0	98.0	100.4	100.6	99.5	98.4	99.2	100.0	101.5	102.6	104.9	....
GDP Deflator (2000=100)	99bip	36.6	48.5	59.8	70.9	78.0	84.7	89.6	100.0	108.3	117.4	132.1	....
						Millions: Midyear Estimates							
Population	99z	2.44	2.46	2.48	2.51	2.53	2.55	2.57	2.58	2.60	2.61	2.63	2.64

Japan   158

		1993	1994	1995	1996	1997	1998	1999	2000	2001	2002	2003	2004
Exchange Rates		\multicolumn 13 *Yen per SDR: End of Period*											
Market Rate	aa	153.63	145.61	152.86	166.80	175.34	162.77	140.27	149.70	165.64	163.01	159.15	161.70
		\multicolumn 13 *Yen per US Dollar: End of Period (ae) Period Average (rf)*											
Market Rate	ae	111.85	99.74	102.83	116.00	129.95	115.60	102.20	114.90	131.80	119.90	107.10	104.12
Market Rate	rf	111.20	102.21	94.06	108.78	120.99	130.91	113.91	107.77	121.53	125.39	115.93	108.19
		\multicolumn 13 *Index Numbers (2000=100): Period Averages*											
Market Rate	ahx	97.2	105.6	115.2	99.1	89.2	82.7	94.6	100.0	88.7	86.1	93.1	99.6
Nominal Effective Exchange Rate	neu	87.9	94.8	99.4	86.2	81.3	76.5	89.4	100.0	90.5	85.7	85.4	87.1
Real Effective Exchange Rate	reu	99.4	105.6	110.7	94.3	89.8	83.7	94.6	100.0	89.3	80.0	76.6	76.2
Fund Position		\multicolumn 13 *Millions of SDRs: End of Period*											
Quota	2f.s	8,242	8,242	8,242	8,242	8,242	8,242	13,313	13,313	13,313	13,313	13,313	13,313
SDRs	1b.s	1,123	1,427	1,821	1,837	1,955	1,891	1,935	1,870	1,892	1,857	1,861	1,828
Reserve Position in the Fund	1c.s	6,015	5,912	5,449	4,639	6,777	6,813	4,774	4,032	4,019	5,298	5,204	4,371
of which: Outstg.Fund Borrowing	2c	2,985	2,913	1,137	—	—	508	—	—	—	—	—	—
International Liquidity		\multicolumn 13 *Millions of US Dollars Unless Otherwise Indicated: End of Period*											
Total Reserves minus Gold	1l.d	98,524	125,860	183,250	216,648	219,648	215,471	286,916	354,902	395,155	461,186	663,289	833,891
SDRs	1b.d	1,543	2,083	2,707	2,642	2,638	2,663	2,656	2,437	2,377	2,524	2,766	2,839
Reserve Position in the Fund	1c.d	8,261	8,631	8,100	6,671	9,144	9,593	6,552	5,253	5,051	7,203	7,733	6,789
Foreign Exchange	1d.d	88,720	115,146	172,443	207,335	207,866	203,215	277,708	347,212	387,727	451,458	652,790	824,264
Gold (Million Fine Troy Ounces)	1ad	24.23	24.23	24.23	24.23	24.23	24.23	24.23	24.55	24.60	24.60	24.60	24.60
Gold (National Valuation)	1and	1,165	1,238	1,260	1,219	1,144	1,194	1,164	1,119	1,082	1,171	1,280	1,337
Deposit Money Banks: Assets	7a.d	914,502	991,478	1,069,795	900,940	990,635	943,546	760,709	738,876	708,522	757,364	746,081	826,331
Liabilities	7b.d	690,577	717,676	734,542	690,224	709,950	693,631	533,627	533,424	521,465	561,288	546,627	598,806
Monetary Authorities		\multicolumn 13 *Trillions of Yen: End of Period*											
Foreign Assets	11	6.73	7.25	11.54	17.49	16.86	† 3.86	4.19	4.14	4.03	4.72	4.79	4.89
Claims on Central Government	12a	21.40	21.98	25.08	31.30	32.87	† 67.92	62.98	54.18	79.88	87.49	97.93	99.52
Claims on Private Sector	12d	—	—	—	—	—	—	—	—	—	.15	1.95	2.10
Claims on Deposit Money Banks	12e	14.13	12.92	11.62	9.91	13.80	† 20.81	46.13	51.26	36.38	36.06	30.06	41.61
Reserve Money	14	48.03	49.44	53.32	57.84	62.09	64.36	92.98	74.45	88.91	99.40	111.36	115.63
of which: Currency Outside DMBs	14a	40.85	42.35	46.23	49.08	52.73	54.31	59.40	61.95	66.69	71.33	72.46	73.31
Foreign Liabilities	16c	—	—	—	—	—	† .06	.04	.02	.93	1.38	2.01	2.16
Central Government Deposits	16d	1.97	5.03	5.85	7.64	3.79	† 12.32	17.04	27.42	25.42	20.77	16.07	24.54
Other Items (Net)	17r	−7.73	−12.31	−10.93	−6.77	−2.35	† 15.85	3.24	7.69	5.03	6.87	5.28	5.79
Deposit Money Banks		\multicolumn 13 *Trillions of Yen: End of Period*											
Reserves	20	7.18	7.09	7.09	8.75	9.36	10.03	30.22	11.33	19.27	26.59	34.29	37.56
Foreign Assets	21	102.29	98.89	110.01	104.51	128.73	109.07	77.74	84.90	93.38	90.81	79.91	86.04
Claims on Central Government	22a	42.89	40.14	38.50	37.04	37.68	52.66	74.32	120.25	115.51	118.59	152.21	159.80
Claims on Local Government	22b	14.95	17.38	19.78	20.72	21.39	23.75	24.79	24.33	25.27	25.67	26.13	27.25
Claims on Nonfin.Pub.Enterprises	22c	13.47	12.55	11.57	10.06	9.01	8.34	8.06	8.99	10.58	11.56	13.81	15.38
Claims on Private Sector	22d	558.67	559.81	569.20	575.88	578.79	601.64	586.93	576.65	561.80	532.54	508.52	495.37
Demand Deposits	24	104.77	109.31	125.31	139.06	151.55	160.09	180.13	185.91	215.11	276.65	291.04	304.67
Time, Savings,& Fgn.Currency Dep	25	372.57	382.44	377.04	373.00	374.11	387.86	383.27	381.76	361.53	317.22	313.36	309.69
Certificates of Deposit	26aa	8.65	7.32	10.22	14.16	19.10	19.23	15.21	20.24	27.95	18.39	17.86	19.89
Bonds	26ab	64.39	63.90	62.22	62.10	53.56	57.13	57.12	50.12	44.94	37.20	30.99	27.59
Foreign Liabilities	26c	77.24	71.58	75.53	80.07	92.26	80.18	54.54	61.29	68.73	67.30	58.54	62.35
Credit from Monetary Authorities	26g	14.13	12.92	11.62	9.91	13.80	† 20.81	46.13	51.26	36.38	36.06	30.06	41.61
Other Items (Net)	27r	97.69	88.38	94.19	78.67	80.58	80.19	65.67	75.85	71.19	52.92	73.01	55.61
Monetary Survey		\multicolumn 13 *Trillions of Yen: End of Period*											
Foreign Assets (Net)	31n	31.78	34.56	46.01	41.94	53.33	† 32.75	27.36	27.73	27.76	26.85	24.14	26.42
Domestic Credit	32	649.41	646.82	658.28	667.36	675.96	† 742.00	740.04	756.98	767.62	755.22	784.48	774.88
Claims on Central Govt. (Net)	32an	62.32	57.09	57.73	60.70	66.76	† 108.27	120.26	147.00	169.97	185.30	234.07	234.78
Claims on Local Government	32b	14.95	17.38	19.78	20.72	21.39	23.75	24.79	24.33	25.27	25.67	26.13	27.25
Claims on Nonfin.Pub.Enterprises	32c	13.47	12.55	11.57	10.06	9.01	8.34	8.06	8.99	10.58	11.56	13.81	15.38
Claims on Private Sector	32d	558.67	559.81	569.20	575.88	578.79	601.64	586.93	576.65	561.80	532.69	510.47	497.47
Money	34	145.61	151.67	171.54	188.15	204.28	214.40	239.54	247.86	281.80	347.98	363.49	377.98
Quasi-Money	35	372.57	382.44	377.04	373.00	374.11	387.86	383.27	381.76	361.53	317.22	313.36	309.69
Certificates of Deposit	36aa	8.65	7.32	10.22	14.16	19.10	19.23	15.21	20.24	27.95	18.39	17.86	19.89
Bonds	36ab	64.39	63.90	62.22	62.10	53.56	57.13	57.12	50.12	44.94	37.20	30.99	27.59
Other Items (Net)	37r	89.96	76.07	83.27	71.90	78.23	† 96.07	72.27	84.72	79.17	61.27	82.92	66.16
Money plus Quasi-Money	35l	518.19	534.10	548.59	561.14	578.39	602.26	622.80	629.62	643.33	665.20	676.85	687.67
Other Banking Institutions		\multicolumn 13 *Trillions of Yen: End of Period*											
Cash	40	82.85	76.56	82.47	87.21	84.43	....	....	....	....	....	....	....
Claims on Central Government	42a	117.65	126.45	142.11	151.55	170.24	....	....	....	....	....	....	....
Claims on Local Government	42b	74.34	82.91	89.40	100.50	110.58	....	....	....	....	....	....	....
Claims on Nonfin.Pub.Enterprises	42c	43.44	47.27	50.76	54.46	57.78	....	....	....	....	....	....	....
Claims on Private Sector	42d	307.76	324.62	327.79	339.87	332.09	....	....	....	....	....	....	....
Demand and Time Deposits	45a	430.84	456.40	479.69	502.71	531.44	....	....	....	....	....	....	....
Deposits with Trust Fund Bureau	46b	147.58	153.18	150.65	155.69	153.94	....	....	....	....	....	....	....
Insurance Reserves	47d	71.34	79.86	88.88	88.16	95.68	....	....	....	....	....	....	....
Other Items (Net)	47r	−23.73	−31.64	−26.70	−12.97	−25.93	....	....	....	....	....	....	....
Nonbank Financial Institutions		\multicolumn 13 *Trillions of Yen: End of Period*											
Cash	40..s	27.30	30.88	33.05	27.86	33.77	....	....	....	....	....	....	....
Claims on Central Government	42a.s	14.86	20.86	29.58	29.72	31.36	....	....	....	....	....	....	....
Claims on Local Government	42b.s	2.98	4.44	6.78	7.90	8.79	....	....	....	....	....	....	....
Claims on Nonfin.Pub.Enterprises	42c.s	3.62	4.42	4.44	4.83	5.20	....	....	....	....	....	....	....
Claims on Private Sector	42d.s	111.33	114.86	112.66	120.58	108.74	....	....	....	....	....	....	....
Insurance and Pension Reserves	47d.s	186.38	199.49	210.48	226.01	230.02	....	....	....	....	....	....	....
Other Items (Net)	47r.s	−26.30	−24.04	−23.99	−35.12	−42.17	....	....	....	....	....	....	....

		1993	1994	1995	1996	1997	1998	1999	2000	2001	2002	2003	2004
Financial Survey						*Trillions of Yen: End of Period*							
Foreign Assets (Net)	51n	31.78	34.56	46.01	41.94	† 90.22	109.48	103.15	110.55	123.25	116.68	....	....
Domestic Credit	52	1,325.38	1,372.64	1,421.79	1,476.78	† 1,524.71	1,551.73	1,632.01	1,622.45	1,604.30	1,564.85	....	....
Claims on Central Govt. (Net)	52an	194.82	204.40	229.42	241.97	† 287.42	317.87	363.67	392.86	408.45	433.89	....	....
Claims on Local Government	52b	92.27	104.72	115.95	129.13	† 127.42	135.38	144.48	150.40	154.06	159.81	....	....
Claims on Nonfin.Pub.Enterprises	52c	60.53	64.24	66.77	69.35	† 111.30	92.31	92.85	93.94	95.44	93.13	....	....
Claims on Private Sector	52d	977.75	999.29	1,009.65	1,036.33	† 998.58	1,006.17	1,031.01	985.26	946.35	878.01	....	....
Liquid Liabilities	55l	900.42	945.09	976.19	1,019.37	† 920.87	955.29	983.02	989.24	1,002.50	1,009.00	....	....
Bonds	56ab	64.39	63.90	62.22	62.10	† 121.12	116.88	121.41	117.09	111.78	85.94	....	....
Deposits with Fiscal Loan Fund	56b	147.58	153.18	150.65	155.69	† 147.35	152.85	156.60	159.19	147.35	129.52	....	....
Insurance and Pension Reserves	57d	257.73	279.35	299.37	314.17	† 360.26	373.34	384.24	396.87	400.74	401.63	....	....
Other Items (Net)	57r	−12.96	−34.33	−20.64	−32.62	† 65.34	62.85	89.88	70.61	65.18	55.45	....	....
Interest Rates						*Percent Per Annum*							
Discount Rate (End of Period)	60	1.750	1.750	.500	.500	.500	.500	.500	.500	.100	.100	.100	.100
Money Market Rate	60b	† 3.060	2.196	1.213	.470	.484	.371	.059	.108	.058	.011	.001	.001
Private Bill Rate	60bs	2.966	2.242	1.218	.594	.620	.717	.155	.227	....	....	....	....
Deposit Rate	60l	2.144	1.698	.902	.301	.301	.266	.117	.070	.057	.036	.043	.080
Lending Rate	60p	† 4.410	4.133	3.506	2.658	2.449	2.321	2.161	2.067	1.969	1.865	1.822	1.767
Government Bond Yield	61	3.693	3.714	2.532	2.225	1.688	1.097	† 1.771	1.748	1.334	1.251	1.013	1.501
Prices, Production, Labor						*Index Numbers (2000=100): Period Averages*							
Share Prices	62	98.5	103.4	89.3	103.8	90.2	76.2	89.6	100.0	77.3	62.7	59.4	72.3
Wholesale Prices	63	106.7	104.9	104.1	102.4	103.0	101.5	100.0	100.0	97.7	95.7	95.0	96.1
Consumer Prices	64	97.9	98.6	98.5	98.6	100.4	101.0	100.7	100.0	99.3	98.4	98.1	98.1
Wages: Monthly Earnings	65	92.4	94.6	96.5	98.3	99.8	99.5	99.8	100.0	99.5	97.9	97.9	97.9
Industrial Production	66	90.8	92.0	95.5	97.7	101.2	94.5	94.8	100.0	93.7	92.6	95.4	100.5
Mfg. Employment, Seas. Adj.	67eyc	116.1	113.5	111.4	109.0	107.8	105.9	102.8	100.0	97.0	92.4	89.4	88.2
						Number in Thousands: Period Averages							
Labor Force	67d	66,150	66,450	66,660	67,110	67,870	67,930	67,790	67,660	67,520	66,890	66,670	....
Employment	67e	64,500	64,530	64,570	64,860	65,570	65,140	64,623	64,464	64,121	63,303	63,189	63,286
Unemployment	67c	1,656	1,920	2,098	2,250	2,303	2,787	3,171	3,198	3,395	3,588	3,504	3,134
Unemployment Rate (%)	67r	2.5	2.9	3.2	3.4	3.4	4.1	4.7	4.7	5.0	5.4	5.3	4.7
Intl. Transactions & Positions						*Billions of Yen*							
Exports	70	40,200	40,470	41,532	44,729	50,938	50,644	47,549	51,649	49,010	52,109	54,549	61,170
Imports, c.i.f.	71	26,824	28,051	31,534	37,992	40,956	36,653	35,270	40,915	42,402	42,177	44,319	49,147
						2000=100							
Volume of Exports	72	76.6	78.0	† 80.5	81.1	90.7	89.5	91.5	100.0	89.9	† 97.4	102.2	113.0
Volume of Imports	73	63.7	72.4	† 81.4	85.4	86.9	82.3	90.2	100.0	98.7	† 100.2	107.4	114.9
Unit Value of Exports	74	101.6	100.6	† 100.0	106.8	108.8	109.6	100.9	100.0	105.6	† 103.7	103.5	104.8
Unit Value of Imports	75	103.2	95.0	† 94.8	108.7	115.3	109.0	95.7	† 100.0	98.2	100.0	98.2	101.7
Export Prices	76	113.4	110.3	† 107.9	113.0	115.1	116.6	104.9	100.0	103.0	101.9	97.8	96.4
Import Prices	76.x	99.5	94.0	† 93.9	103.0	110.7	105.3	95.5	100.0	102.5	101.0	100.1	104.3
Balance of Payments						*Billions of US Dollars: Minus Sign Indicates Debit*							
Current Account, n.i.e.	78ald	131.64	130.26	111.04	65.79	96.81	118.75	114.60	119.66	87.80	112.45	136.22	172.06
Goods: Exports f.o.b.	78aad	352.66	385.70	428.72	400.29	409.24	374.04	403.69	459.51	383.59	395.58	449.12	539.00
Goods: Imports f.o.b.	78abd	−213.24	−241.51	−296.93	−316.70	−307.64	−251.66	−280.37	−342.80	−313.38	−301.75	−342.72	−406.87
Trade Balance	78acd	139.42	144.19	131.79	83.58	101.60	122.39	123.32	116.72	70.21	93.83	106.40	132.13
Services: Credit	78add	53.22	58.30	65.27	67.71	69.30	62.41	61.00	69.24	64.52	65.71	77.62	97.61
Services: Debit	78aed	−96.30	−106.36	−122.63	−129.99	−123.45	−111.83	−115.16	−116.86	−108.25	−107.94	−111.53	−135.51
Balance on Goods & Services	78afd	96.33	96.13	74.43	21.31	47.45	72.97	69.16	69.09	26.48	51.60	72.49	94.23
Income: Credit	78agd	147.83	155.19	192.45	112.44	111.83	100.33	92.05	97.20	103.09	91.48	95.21	113.33
Income: Debit	78ahd	−107.42	−114.96	−148.16	−58.95	−53.63	−45.71	−34.47	−36.80	−33.87	−25.71	−23.97	−27.63
Balance on Gds, Serv. & Inc.	78aid	136.74	136.36	118.72	74.80	105.65	127.59	126.74	129.49	95.70	117.37	143.73	179.93
Current Transfers, n.i.e.: Credit	78ajd	1.58	1.83	1.98	6.02	6.01	5.53	6.21	7.38	6.15	10.04	6.51	6.91
Current Transfers: Debit	78akd	−6.68	−7.94	−9.66	−15.03	−14.84	−14.37	−18.35	−17.21	−14.06	−14.96	−14.02	−14.78
Capital Account, n.i.e.	78bcd	−1.46	−1.85	−2.23	−3.29	−4.05	−14.45	−16.47	−9.26	−2.87	−3.32	−4.00	−4.79
Capital Account, n.i.e.: Credit	78bad	—	—	.01	1.22	1.52	1.57	.75	.78	.99	.91	.39	.44
Capital Account: Debit	78bbd	−1.46	−1.85	−2.24	−4.51	−5.57	−16.02	−17.21	−10.04	−3.86	−4.24	−4.39	−5.23
Financial Account, n.i.e.	78bjd	−102.21	−85.11	−63.98	−28.02	−120.51	−114.82	−38.85	−78.31	−48.16	−63.38	71.92	22.49
Direct Investment Abroad	78bdd	−13.83	−18.09	−22.51	−23.45	−26.06	−24.62	−22.27	−31.53	−38.50	−32.02	−28.77	−30.96
Dir. Invest. in Rep. Econ., n.i.e.	78bed	.12	.91	.04	.21	3.20	3.27	12.31	8.23	6.19	9.09	6.24	7.80
Portfolio Investment Assets	78bfd	−63.74	−91.97	−86.05	−100.61	−47.06	−95.24	−154.41	−83.36	−106.79	−85.93	−176.29	−173.77
Equity Securities	78bkd	−15.28	−14.00	.07	−8.17	−13.73	−14.00	−32.40	−19.72	−11.28	−37.28	−4.47	−31.47
Debt Securities	78bld	−48.46	−77.97	−86.11	−92.43	−33.34	−81.24	−122.01	−63.64	−95.51	−48.65	−171.82	−142.30
Portfolio Investment Liab., n.i.e.	78bgd	−6.11	64.53	59.79	66.79	79.19	56.06	126.93	47.39	60.50	−20.04	81.18	196.72
Equity Securities	78bmd	19.86	48.95	50.60	49.45	27.00	16.11	103.89	−1.29	39.10	−16.69	87.78	98.28
Debt Securities	78bnd	−25.97	15.58	9.19	17.34	52.19	39.95	23.04	48.67	21.40	−3.35	−6.59	98.44
Financial Derivatives Assets	78bwd	−.49	.43	−1.20	98.70	86.17	90.75	83.80	106.74	102.79	77.25	64.96	56.44
Financial Derivatives Liabilities	78bxd	−.54	−.20	−9.12	−105.95	−92.02	−89.65	−86.43	−111.41	−101.40	−74.77	−59.38	−54.04
Other Investment Assets	78bhd	15.07	−35.12	−102.24	5.21	−191.96	37.94	266.34	−4.15	46.59	36.41	149.89	−48.01
Monetary Authorities	78bod	....	....	....	....	....	....	....	....	....	....	....	....
General Government	78bpd	−7.80	−8.76	−8.66	−5.28	−9.12	−15.50	−11.56	−1.89	−3.95	.92	4.49	3.87
Banks	78bqd	27.73	−10.67	−85.62	75.57	−140.18	54.14	239.40	36.51	15.59	1.59	140.78	3.24
Other Sectors	78brd	−4.85	−15.69	−7.96	−65.08	−42.66	−.70	38.50	−38.77	34.95	33.90	4.62	−55.12
Other Investment Liab., n.i.e.	78bid	−32.70	−5.60	97.30	31.08	68.03	−93.33	−265.12	−10.21	−17.55	26.63	34.10	68.30
Monetary Authorities	78bsd	—	—	—	—	—	—	—	—	—	—	—	—
General Government	78btd	−.10	−2.00	1.18	−2.12	−.11	−1.30	.55	−.93	7.01	.06	5.14	.98
Banks	78bud	−37.90	4.87	17.27	−9.06	43.34	−23.75	−189.16	28.22	4.99	22.46	−26.22	42.73
Other Sectors	78bvd	5.30	−8.47	78.86	42.27	24.80	−68.28	−76.50	−37.49	−29.54	4.11	55.17	24.59
Net Errors and Omissions	78cad	−.50	−18.03	13.78	.65	34.31	4.36	16.97	16.87	3.72	.39	−16.99	−28.90
Overall Balance	78cbd	27.47	25.27	58.61	35.14	6.57	−6.16	76.26	48.95	40.49	46.13	187.15	160.85
Reserves and Related Items	79dad	−27.47	−25.27	−58.61	−35.14	−6.57	6.16	−76.26	−48.95	−40.49	−46.13	−187.15	−160.85
Reserve Assets	79dbd	−27.47	−25.27	−58.61	−35.14	−6.57	6.16	−76.26	−48.95	−40.49	−46.13	−187.15	−160.85
Use of Fund Credit and Loans	79dcd	—	—	—	—	—	—	—	—	—	—	—	—
Exceptional Financing	79ded	....	....	....	....	....	....	....	....	....	....	....	....

Japan 158

		1993	1994	1995	1996	1997	1998	1999	2000	2001	2002	2003	2004
International Investment Position							*Billions of US Dollars*						
Assets......................	79aad	2,180.88	2,424.24	2,632.86	2,652.61	2,737.45	2,986.33	3,013.60	2,969.59	2,881.51	3,052.08	3,599.80	....
Direct Investment Abroad.............	79abd	259.80	275.57	238.45	258.61	271.90	270.04	248.78	278.44	300.11	304.23	335.50	....
Portfolio Investment....................	79acd	771.11	858.69	855.07	933.20	902.26	1,056.49	1,242.37	1,306.48	1,289.75	1,394.52	1,721.32	....
Equity Securities..........................	79add	....	....	146.26	154.90	158.77	209.38	285.34	262.25	227.35	210.82	274.46	....
Debt Securities...........................	79aed	....	....	708.81	778.30	743.49	847.11	957.04	1,044.23	1,062.40	1,183.70	1,446.86	....
Financial Derivatives....................	79ald	....	....	3.21	3.97	4.41	5.09	4.46	3.31	3.00	3.37	4.90	....
Other Investment.........................	79afd	1,050.29	1,162.87	1,351.31	1,239.23	1,338.08	1,438.88	1,230.34	1,020.36	888.23	882.34	865.03	....
Monetary Authorities...................	79agd	—	—	—	—	—	—	—	—	—	—	—	....
General Government....................	79ahd	142.22	165.01	184.05	170.47	162.32	196.16	230.91	210.17	191.93	206.97	228.79	....
Banks..	79aid	701.47	752.12	911.23	773.14	861.44	876.07	630.02	529.23	467.46	486.66	447.35	....
Other Sectors............................	79ajd	206.60	245.74	256.02	295.63	314.32	366.65	369.41	280.96	228.84	188.71	188.88	....
Reserve Assets..........................	79akd	99.68	127.10	184.82	217.61	220.81	215.83	287.66	360.99	400.41	467.62	673.06	....
Liabilities..................................	79lad	1,568.84	1,733.92	1,815.26	1,761.59	1,778.72	1,832.69	2,184.48	1,811.65	1,521.42	1,589.92	1,986.18	....
Dir. Invest. in Rep. Economy..........	79lbd	16.89	19.17	33.51	29.94	27.08	26.07	46.12	50.32	50.32	78.14	89.73	....
Portfolio Investment....................	79lcd	545.32	630.67	545.42	556.25	582.48	632.76	1,165.44	884.32	665.79	610.42	867.17	....
Equity Securities........................	79ldd	171.17	250.88	306.28	315.65	279.53	304.33	833.43	550.23	376.05	339.93	561.02	....
Debt Securities..........................	79led	374.15	379.79	239.14	240.60	302.95	328.43	332.01	334.09	289.75	270.49	306.14	....
Financial Derivatives....................	79lld	—	—	2.85	2.72	4.10	4.54	3.10	3.19	3.54	3.71	6.79	....
Other Investment.........................	79lfd	1,006.63	1,084.08	1,233.48	1,172.69	1,165.06	1,169.32	969.83	873.82	801.77	897.65	1,022.50	....
Monetary Authorities...................	79lgd	65.52	99.85	—	—	—	—	—	—	—	—	—	....
General Government....................	79lhd	—	—	14.96	11.35	10.12	9.65	11.62	9.68	8.15	5.26	5.14	....
Banks.......................................	79lid	673.58	694.94	745.42	701.56	714.28	751.47	570.71	603.99	568.40	631.12	660.40	....
Other Sectors............................	79ljd	267.53	289.29	473.10	459.78	440.66	408.20	387.50	260.15	225.21	261.27	356.96	....
Government Finance						*Billions of Yen: Year Beginning April 1*							
Deficit (-) or Surplus........................	80	−7,318p	....	....	....	....	....	....	....	....	....	....	....
Revenue......................................	81	99,866p	....	....	....	....	....	....	....	....	....	....	....
Grants Received............................	81z	3,498p	....	....	....	....	....	....	....	....	....	....	....
Expenditure.................................	82	112,655p	....	....	....	....	....	....	....	....	....	....	....
Lending Minus Repayments...........	83	−1,973p	....	....	....	....	....	....	....	....	....	....	....
Financing													
Domestic...................................	84a	7,318p	....	....	....	....	....	....	....	....	....	....	....
Debt: Domestic............................	88a	212,474p	....	....	....	....	....	....	....	....	....	....	....
Foreign...................................	89a	....	....	....	....	....	....	....	....	....	....	....	....
National Accounts						*Billions of Yen*							
Househ.Cons.Expend.,incl.NPISHs....	96f.c	264,149	272,646	276,844	283,433	288,788	288,406	286,784	285,940	286,172	284,356	282,902	285,544
Government Consumption Expend...	91f.c	67,014	69,510	72,789	75,491	77,094	78,582	80,843	84,019	86,419	88,003	87,957	89,176
Gross Fixed Capital Formation..........	93e.c	142,008	138,676	138,099	145,022	146,161	138,422	133,694	134,850	130,423	120,577	119,222	120,356
Changes in Inventories..................	93i.c	298	−710	2,233	3,499	3,137	28	−1,717	−365	−22	−1,139	−258	484
Exports of Goods and Services..........	90.c.c	44,109	44,270	45,230	49,561	56,074	55,051	51,144	55,256	52,567	55,829	58,882	66,286
Imports of Goods and Services (-).....	98.c.c	33,344	34,387	38,272	47,022	50,316	45,607	43,251	47,940	49,393	49,417	50,907	56,660
Gross Domestic Product (GDP)........	99b.c	484,234	490,005	496,922	509,984	520,937	514,882	507,496	511,760	506,165	498,208	497,798	505,185
Net Primary Income from Abroad.....	98.nc	4,163	3,812	3,836	5,471	6,758	6,653	6,112	6,421	8,321	8,193	8,524	9,620
Gross National Income (GNI)............	99a.c	488,397	493,818	500,758	515,455	527,695	521,535	513,608	518,181	514,486	506,402	506,322	514,805
Net Current Transf.from Abroad.......	98t.c	−11,841	−13,570	−14,672	−10,509	−15,397	−19,818	−19,913	−18,762	—	—	—	4,463
Gross Nat'l Disposable Inc.(GNDI)...	99i.c	478,840	482,076	486,901	505,762	513,220	502,955	499,001	499,494	....	....	....	....
Gross Saving................................	99s.c	155,365	150,179	148,959	157,999	157,300	147,390	139,993	140,110	....	....	....	....
Consumption of Fixed Capital..........	99cf	84,602	86,676	88,950	92,051	94,234	96,149	95,681	97,841	99,095	....	....	....
GDP Volume 1995 Prices................	99b.r	482,049	487,482	496,668	514,641	524,031	517,941	518,950	533,872	536,016	533,411	547,112	567,177
GDP Volume (2000=100)...............	99bvr	90.3	91.3	93.0	96.4	98.2	97.0	97.2	100.0	100.4	99.9	102.5	106.2
GDP Deflator (2000=100)...............	99bir	104.8	104.9	104.4	103.4	103.7	103.7	102.0	100.0	98.5	97.4	94.9	92.9
						Millions: Midyear Estimates							
Population................................	99z	124.76	125.12	125.47	125.81	126.14	126.46	126.76	127.03	127.29	127.52	127.74	127.92

Jordan 439

		1993	1994	1995	1996	1997	1998	1999	2000	2001	2002	2003	2004
Exchange Rates						*SDRs per Dinar: End of Period*							
Official Rate....................	ac	1.0341	.9772	.9488	.9809	1.0454	1.0017	1.0276	1.0825	1.1223	1.0375	.9492	.9082
						US Dollars per Dinar: End of Period (ag) Period Average (rh)							
Official Rate....................	ag	1.4205	1.4265	1.4104	1.4104	1.4104	1.4104	1.4104	1.4104	1.4104	1.4104	1.4104	1.4104
Official Rate....................	rh	1.4434	1.4312	1.4276	1.4104	1.4104	1.4104	1.4104	1.4104	1.4105	1.4104	1.4104	1.4104
Fund Position						*Millions of SDRs: End of Period*							
Quota........................	2f.s	121.7	121.7	121.7	121.7	121.7	121.7	170.5	170.5	170.5	170.5	170.5	170.5
SDRs........................	1b.s	4.0	.5	.8	.6	.1	.6	.2	.5	.9	.6	.7	1.1
Reserve Position in the Fund...........	1c.s	—	—	—	—	—	—	—	.1	.1	.1	.1	.1
Total Fund Cred.&Loans Outstg.......	2tl	59.2	98.9	169.2	236.1	316.6	333.4	362.9	354.3	344.5	355.0	283.6	217.5
International Liquidity						*Millions of US Dollars Unless Otherwise Indicated: End of Period*							
Total Reserves minus Gold..............	1l.d	† 1,637.4	1,692.6	1,972.9	1,759.3	2,200.3	1,750.4	2,629.1	3,331.3	3,062.2	3,975.9	5,194.3	5,266.6
SDRs........................	1b.d	5.5	.7	1.2	.8	.2	.8	.3	.6	1.2	.9	1.1	1.7
Reserve Position in the Fund.........	1c.d	—	—	—	—	—	—	—	.1	.1	.1	.1	.1
Foreign Exchange..................	1d.d	† 1,631.9	1,691.9	1,971.7	1,758.5	2,200.1	1,749.6	2,628.8	3,330.6	3,061.0	3,975.0	5,193.1	5,264.8
Gold (Million Fine Troy Ounces).......	1ad	.791	.794	.793	.800	.812	.827	.486	.401	.405	.410	.411	.411
Gold (National Valuation)..............	1and	99.8	198.5	195.9	197.7	200.7	204.3	120.0	99.1	112.2	141.2	171.3	179.6
Monetary Authorities: Other Liab.....	4..d	125.6	117.5	82.3	71.3	43.8	32.8	230.6	177.6	181.3	180.3	176.1	158.3
Deposit Money Banks: Assets.......	7a.d	2,216.3	2,399.3	2,655.3	2,845.0	3,077.5	3,607.1	4,101.5	5,235.3	6,104.4	6,336.8	6,180.4	7,055.0
Liabilities.......	7b.d	2,166.6	2,518.5	2,926.5	3,100.7	3,084.7	3,079.7	3,285.2	3,819.0	4,213.5	4,718.1	4,379.0	4,892.5
Other Banking Insts.: Liabilities........	7f.d	112.3	120.6	130.3	117.0	126.0	124.7	120.9	114.9	....	....	....	....
Monetary Authorities						*Millions of Dinars: End of Period*							
Foreign Assets......................	11	† 1,688.7	1,904.3	2,185.2	2,253.9	2,557.1	2,297.7	2,889.6	3,267.4	3,064.2	3,694.0	4,571.1	4,628.2
Claims on Central Government........	12a	772.5	905.3	867.1	930.9	989.4	1,033.4	1,015.8	1,125.7	1,097.0	1,007.1	938.8	891.0
Reserve Money....................	14	† 2,236.0	2,349.5	2,498.9	2,164.4	2,104.0	2,005.0	2,246.9	2,264.8	2,135.7	2,218.9	2,593.6	2,676.6
of which: Currency Outside DMBs..	14a	1,047.9	1,072.6	1,050.9	952.1	987.6	952.8	1,106.6	1,239.9	1,202.4	1,252.7	1,443.7	1,414.4
Foreign Liabilities..................	16c	† 145.7	183.6	236.7	291.3	333.9	356.1	516.6	453.2	435.5	470.0	423.6	351.7
Central Government Deposits........	16d	101.3	225.1	163.5	323.7	321.0	137.7	145.9	420.7	401.6	401.9	190.8	218.2
Other Items (Net)...................	17r	† −21.8	51.4	153.1	405.4	787.6	832.3	995.9	1,254.4	1,188.4	1,610.2	2,301.9	2,272.7
Deposit Money Banks						*Millions of Dinars: End of Period*							
Reserves............................	20	1,477.1	1,576.9	1,799.6	1,854.9	2,163.8	2,015.9	2,389.2	2,518.2	2,383.3	2,826.5	3,586.8	3,784.1
Foreign Assets......................	21	1,560.3	1,681.9	1,882.6	2,017.1	2,182.0	2,557.5	2,907.9	3,711.8	4,328.0	4,492.8	4,381.9	5,002.0
Claims on Central Government........	22a	358.7	307.0	240.0	238.1	163.0	412.5	618.5	733.1	902.5	1,087.9	887.8	1,101.8
Claims on Private Sector..............	22d	2,310.5	2,763.4	3,192.5	3,354.9	3,526.5	3,803.2	4,050.2	4,230.8	4,709.9	4,833.4	5,000.5	5,866.6
Demand Deposits...................	24	† 669.6	666.0	664.7	578.1	636.1	648.5	658.0	774.2	888.3	1,019.2	1,385.0	1,721.1
Time and Savings Deposits..........	25	† 2,510.0	2,782.4	3,040.5	3,209.8	3,469.3	3,734.4	4,212.9	4,651.8	4,963.3	5,430.2	6,082.8	6,922.7
Foreign Liabilities..................	26c	1,525.3	1,765.5	2,074.9	2,198.4	2,187.1	2,183.5	2,329.2	2,707.7	2,987.4	3,345.1	3,104.7	3,468.8
Central Government Deposits........	26d	† 424.8	499.8	550.9	634.6	736.3	848.3	1,011.0	1,062.8	1,071.4	914.8	692.5	757.3
Capital Accounts....................	27a	492.6	582.8	701.7	771.0	1,047.7	1,181.3	1,316.6	1,378.0	1,436.2	1,545.1	1,623.2	1,874.4
Other Items (Net)...................	27r	† 84.3	32.9	82.0	73.2	−41.1	193.2	484.3	619.4	977.1	986.2	968.8	1,010.2
Monetary Survey						*Millions of Dinars: End of Period*							
Foreign Assets (Net).................	31n	† 1,578.0	1,637.2	1,756.2	1,781.3	2,218.1	2,315.6	2,951.7	3,818.3	3,969.3	4,371.7	5,424.7	5,809.8
Domestic Credit....................	32	† 3,324.8	3,723.1	4,089.0	4,114.2	4,184.4	4,780.0	4,925.6	5,016.2	5,613.0	5,961.8	6,310.3	7,469.4
Claims on Central Govt. (Net).......	32an	† 605.1	487.4	392.7	210.8	95.1	459.9	477.3	375.3	526.5	778.3	943.3	1,017.3
Claims on Nonfin.Pub.Enterprises...	32c	† 296.8	341.9	362.2	408.9	425.3	381.2	307.9	316.9	284.3	261.3	278.0	472.6
Claims on Private Sector.............	32d	2,316.1	2,769.9	3,200.1	3,363.0	3,535.2	3,812.7	4,062.1	4,244.0	4,723.6	4,847.9	5,015.6	5,884.9
Money............................	34	† 1,719.4	1,741.6	1,738.7	1,532.8	1,626.1	1,612.6	1,766.1	2,017.4	2,094.6	2,273.1	2,829.9	3,138.5
Quasi-Money.......................	35	† 2,664.7	2,788.6	3,051.0	3,213.3	3,482.7	3,818.8	4,507.2	4,734.2	5,204.0	5,652.5	6,412.6	7,070.9
Other Items (Net)...................	37r	† 518.8	830.1	1,055.6	1,149.4	1,293.7	1,664.1	1,604.0	2,082.9	2,283.7	2,407.9	2,492.5	3,069.8
Money plus Quasi-Money.............	35l	† 4,384.1	4,530.2	4,789.7	4,746.1	5,108.8	5,431.4	6,273.3	6,751.6	7,298.6	7,925.6	9,242.5	10,209.4
Other Banking Institutions						*Millions of Dinars: End of Period*							
Cash..............................	40	† 70.6	59.9	63.3	54.3	53.0	41.2	22.5	71.2	....	....	....	....
Claims on Private Sector..............	42d	† 294.9	284.8	306.2	315.0	334.9	349.3	362.2	343.0	....	....	....	....
Deposits..........................	45	† 66.5	47.4	32.7	24.5	17.0	11.8	8.8	9.5	....	....	....	....
Foreign Liabilities..................	46c	† 79.0	84.6	92.4	83.0	89.3	88.4	85.7	81.5	....	....	....	....
Central Govt. Lending Funds..........	46f	† 17.1	16.2	16.2	15.0	14.3	13.7	13.1	50.3	....	....	....	....
Capital Accounts....................	47a	† 90.9	91.6	111.5	132.0	153.2	164.5	177.4	186.4	....	....	....	....
Other Items (Net)...................	47r	† 111.9	104.9	116.8	114.9	114.2	112.0	99.7	86.4	....	....	....	....
Liquid Liabilities....................	55l	† 4,380.0	4,517.8	4,759.1	4,716.3	5,072.7	5,402.0	6,259.6	6,689.9	....	....	....	....
Interest Rates						*Percent Per Annum*							
Discount Rate (End of Period)..........	60	8.50	8.50	8.50	8.50	7.75	9.00	8.00	6.50	5.00	4.50	2.50	3.75
Money Market Rate..................	60b	....	....	....	....	....	....	5.19	5.28	4.63	3.49	2.58	2.18
Savings Rate.......................	60k	....	....	....	....	....	....	4.49	4.04	3.52	2.49	1.28	.76
Deposit Rate (Period Average).........	60l	6.88	7.09	7.68	8.50	9.10	8.21	8.30	6.97	5.81	4.43	3.14	2.49
Lending Rate (Period Average).........	60p	10.23	10.45	10.66	11.25	12.25	12.61	12.33	11.80	10.94	10.18	9.30	8.26
Prices and Production						*Index Numbers (2000=100): Period Averages*							
Producer Prices (2002=100)...........	63	....	....	....	....	....	....	....	....	....	100.0	102.6	108.7
Wholesale Prices....................	63a	99.6	104.4	101.9	103.9	105.6	† 106.3	103.7	100.0	98.5	96.9	98.1	106.3
Consumer Prices....................	64	82.4	85.3	87.3	93.0	† 95.8	98.7	99.3	† 100.0	101.8	103.6	105.3	108.9
Industrial Production.................	66	79.0	† 83.4	93.8	89.0	92.1	94.0	96.2	† 100.0	106.6	118.5	108.5	121.5
Intl. Transactions & Positions						*Millions of Dinars*							
Exports............................	70	864.7	995.2	1,241.1	1,288.2	1,301.4	1,277.9	1,298.8	1,346.6	1,626.4	1,963.9	2,184.9	2,800.3
Imports, c.i.f.......................	71	2,453.6	2,362.6	2,590.3	3,043.6	2,908.1	2,714.4	2,635.2	3,259.4	3,453.7	3,599.2	4,072.0	5,762.9
						2000=100							
Volume of Exports...................	72	72.6	† 77.7	84.5	82.2	87.8	90.3	92.9	100.0	123.3	141.8	152.4	189.7
Volume of Imports...................	73	89.2	† 86.9	84.2	90.7	88.6	83.8	82.8	100.0	103.2	104.1	108.6	135.5
Unit Value of Exports................	74	90.2	† 94.5	110.0	117.0	113.6	107.3	104.6	100.0	101.4	101.7	101.9	113.7
Unit Value of Imports................	75	85.9	† 83.5	94.6	103.2	100.9	100.1	97.7	100.0	102.3	105.1	115.3	130.2

		1993	1994	1995	1996	1997	1998	1999	2000	2001	2002	2003	2004
Balance of Payments					*Millions of US Dollars: Minus Sign Indicates Debit*								
Current Account, n.i.e.	78ald	−629.1	−398.0	−258.6	−221.9	29.3	14.1	404.9	59.4	−4.1	537.2	1,178.6	−17.9
Goods: Exports f.o.b.	78aad	1,246.3	1,424.5	1,769.6	1,816.9	1,835.5	1,802.4	1,831.9	1,899.3	2,294.4	2,770.0	3,081.6	3,882.9
Goods: Imports f.o.b.	78abd	−3,145.2	−3,003.8	−3,287.8	−3,818.1	−3,648.5	−3,403.9	−3,292.0	−4,073.7	−4,301.5	−4,500.9	−5,077.9	−7,261.1
Trade Balance	78acd	−1,898.8	−1,579.4	−1,518.2	−2,001.1	−1,813.0	−1,601.6	−1,460.1	−2,174.4	−2,007.0	−1,730.9	−1,996.3	−3,378.1
Services: Credit	78add	1,573.7	1,562.0	1,709.2	1,846.3	1,736.8	1,825.1	1,701.7	1,637.0	1,482.5	1,775.0	1,739.9	2,100.1
Services: Debit	78aed	−1,347.2	−1,392.7	−1,614.9	−1,597.7	−1,537.2	−1,783.8	−1,698.0	−1,722.1	−1,725.9	−1,882.9	−1,889.2	−2,145.8
Balance on Goods & Services	78afd	−1,672.3	−1,410.1	−1,424.0	−1,752.6	−1,613.4	−1,560.2	−1,456.4	−2,259.5	−2,250.4	−1,838.8	−2,145.6	−3,423.8
Income: Credit	78agd	99.0	72.7	115.7	111.7	248.2	306.9	467.6	670.3	648.7	484.1	492.7	515.2
Income: Debit	78ahd	−409.4	−387.5	−394.5	−412.7	−457.0	−445.0	−479.7	−535.4	−461.2	−372.3	−374.3	−325.5
Balance on Gds, Serv. & Inc.	78aid	−1,982.8	−1,724.9	−1,702.8	−2,053.6	−1,822.1	−1,698.3	−1,468.5	−2,124.5	−2,062.9	−1,727.0	−2,027.3	−3,234.1
Current Transfers, n.i.e.: Credit	78ajd	1,441.1	1,447.4	1,591.8	1,970.2	2,096.1	1,984.3	2,154.9	2,611.3	2,365.8	2,524.3	3,501.0	3,562.5
Current Transfers: Debit	78akd	−87.4	−120.5	−147.6	−138.5	−244.6	−271.9	−281.4	−427.4	−306.9	−260.1	−295.1	−346.3
Capital Account, n.i.e.	78bcd	—	—	197.2	157.7	163.8	81.1	87.6	64.9	21.6	68.8	93.5	2.0
Capital Account, n.i.e.: Credit	78bad	—	—	197.2	157.7	163.8	81.1	87.6	64.9	21.6	68.8	93.5	2.0
Capital Account: Debit	78bbd	—	—	—	—	—	—	—	—	—	—	—	—
Financial Account, n.i.e.	78bjd	−530.0	188.9	230.0	233.9	242.3	−177.3	230.9	270.9	−319.0	474.8	−199.4	−307.2
Direct Investment Abroad	78bdd	53.0	23.1	27.3	43.3	....	....	−4.5	−1.8	−5.6	....	....	....
Dir. Invest. in Rep. Econ., n.i.e.	78bed	−33.5	2.9	13.3	15.5	360.9	310.0	158.0	800.8	120.2	64.0	424.1	620.3
Portfolio Investment Assets	78bfd	—	—	....	....	....	....	37.8	−45.1	−227.1	−191.8	−118.9	−217.2
Equity Securities	78bkd	—	—	....	....	....	....	37.8	−45.1	−227.1	−191.8	−118.9	−217.2
Debt Securities	78bld	—	—	....	....	....	....						
Portfolio Investment Liab., n.i.e.	78bgd	—	—	—	—	—	—	−28.1	−140.9	−171.7	−52.2	−349.1	−119.9
Equity Securities	78bmd	—	—	—	—	—	—	21.9	−16.8	−145.1	−52.2	−57.8	−119.9
Debt Securities	78bnd	—	—	—	—	—	—	−49.9	−124.1	−26.5	—	−291.3	—
Financial Derivatives Assets	78bwd	....	....	....	....	....	....	....	....	....	....	....	....
Financial Derivatives Liabilities	78bxd	....	....	....	....	....	....	....	....	....	....	....	....
Other Investment Assets	78bhd	384.8	62.5	−313.4	−5.9	16.4	−80.3	−541.7	−942.2	−615.1	11.4	283.1	−659.9
Monetary Authorities	78bod	−94.9	−163.5	−313.4	−5.9	16.4	−80.3	−41.9	148.5	30.6	54.7	11.3	—
General Government	78bpd	−.3	—	....	....	....	....						
Banks	78bqd			....	....	....	....	−499.9	−1,090.7	−645.7	−43.3	271.8	−659.9
Other Sectors	78brd	480.0	225.9	....	....	....	....						
Other Investment Liab., n.i.e.	78bid	−934.3	100.4	502.8	181.0	−135.0	−407.1	609.4	600.1	580.3	643.3	−438.6	69.5
Monetary Authorities	78bsd	.7	−8.7	−34.4	−11.0	−27.6	−11.0	183.5	−69.8	4.7	−15.0	−13.4	−29.3
General Government	78btd	−675.8	−235.4	96.8	17.8	−91.4	−391.0	285.8	154.3	231.7	106.5	−327.2	−195.1
Banks	78bud	−257.5	344.5	440.5	174.2	−15.9	−5.1	197.0	395.2	309.6	466.0	−99.4	329.3
Other Sectors	78bvd	−1.7	—	—	—	—	—	−56.8	120.5	34.3	85.8	1.4	−35.4
Net Errors and Omissions	78cad	298.0	−55.8	−339.9	−357.9	−160.8	−454.0	28.7	297.7	57.7	−150.5	275.5	501.7
Overall Balance	78cbd	−861.1	−264.9	−171.3	−188.2	274.6	−536.1	752.1	692.9	−243.9	930.3	1,348.2	178.6
Reserves and Related Items	79dad	861.1	264.9	171.3	188.2	−274.6	536.1	−752.1	−692.9	243.9	−930.3	−1,348.2	−178.6
Reserve Assets	79dcd	402.9	−216.8	−371.5	−280.7	−677.1	−83.4	−794.5	−681.7	256.0	−942.8	−1,248.2	−80.5
Use of Fund Credit and Loans	79dcd	−31.0	57.6	106.5	97.6	110.3	22.4	39.7	−11.2	−12.1	12.5	−100.0	−98.1
Exceptional Financing	79ded	489.1	424.1	436.3	371.4	292.2	597.0	2.7	—	—	—	—	—
International Investment Position					*Millions of US Dollars*								
Assets	79aad	....	....	....	....	....	....	....	....	....	....	....	....
Direct Investment Abroad	79abd	....	....	....	....	....	....	....	....	....	....	....	....
Portfolio Investment	79acd	....	....	....	74.3	143.9	145.1	139.5	184.6	411.7	603.7	722.6	939.9
Equity Securities	79add	....	....	....	44.6	65.9	64.9	48.0	56.7	89.8	107.6	103.0	126.4
Debt Securities	79aed	....	....	....	29.8	78.0	80.3	91.5	127.9	321.9	496.1	619.6	813.5
Financial Derivatives	79ald	....	....	....	....	....	....	....	....	....	....	....	....
Other Investment	79afd	....	....	....	4,037.2	4,184.1	4,793.0	5,333.6	6,274.1	6,886.3	6,882.9	6,596.2	7,253.9
Monetary Authorities	79agd	....	....	....	1,266.6	1,250.4	1,330.9	1,371.7	1,223.4	1,193.7	1,149.8	1,138.5	1,138.6
General Government	79ahd	....	....	....									
Banks	79aid	....	....	....	2,770.7	2,933.7	3,462.1	3,961.9	5,050.6	5,692.7	5,733.2	5,457.7	6,115.2
Other Sectors	79ajd	....	....	....									
Reserve Assets	79akd	....	....	....	1,957.0	2,401.0	1,954.7	2,749.1	3,430.5	3,174.3	4,117.1	5,365.7	5,446.3
Liabilities	79lad	....	....	....	....	....	....	....	....	....	....	....	....
Dir. Invest. in Rep. Economy	79lbd	....	....	....	....	....	....	....	....	....	....	....	....
Portfolio Investment	79lcd	....	....	....	622.6	588.9	456.8	456.8	350.9	320.2	320.2	—	—
Equity Securities	79ldd	....	....	....	—	—	—	—	—	—	—	—	—
Debt Securities	79led	....	....	....	622.6	588.9	456.8	456.8	350.9	320.2	320.2	—	—
Financial Derivatives	79lld	....	....	....	....	....	....	....	....	....	....	....	....
Other Investment	79lfd	....	....	....	10,017.2	9,867.8	10,474.0	11,092.4	11,056.0	11,400.0	12,518.5	12,554.4	12,953.4
Monetary Authorities	79lgd	....	....	....	450.9	535.6	579.0	789.3	680.1	654.8	690.8	618.3	505.9
General Government	79lhd	....	....	....	6,282.2	5,991.4	6,520.2	6,755.7	6,259.0	6,215.7	6,718.1	7,161.9	7,197.2
Banks	79lid	....	....	....	3,100.8	3,084.8	3,079.6	3,285.2	3,819.0	4,213.5	4,718.1	4,379.0	4,892.5
Other Sectors	79ljd	....	....	....	183.2	256.0	295.2	262.2	297.9	315.9	391.5	395.2	357.8
Government Finance					*Millions of Dinars: Year Ending December 31*								
Deficit (-) or Surplus	80	141.7	45.2	49.3	−66.3	−163.4	−327.1	−140.4	−119.8	−155.5	....	....	....
Revenue	81	1,191.6	1,162.4	1,332.6	1,366.9	1,312.6	1,422.4	1,530.5	1,506.6	1,578.7	....	....	....
Grants Received	81z	163.3	175.6	182.8	219.9	205.0	172.2	198.5	240.2	249.4	....	....	....
Expenditure	82	1,235.1	1,312.8	1,471.5	1,666.9	1,681.9	1,876.8	1,804.1	1,868.6	2,027.7	....	....	....
Lending Minus Repayments	83	−21.9	−20.0	−5.4	−13.8	−.9	44.9	65.3	−2.0	−44.1	....	....	....
Financing													
Net Borrowing: Dinars	84b	−47.7	−15.5	−18.3	−15.2	−11.6	−7.3	−2.8	−33.2	−110.7	....	....	....
Foreign Currency	85b	−133.2	75.4	287.8	302.1	84.3	−12.3	55.7	−103.3	−5.8	....	....	....
Use of Cash Balances	87	39.2	−105.1	−318.8	−220.6	90.7	346.7	87.5			....	....	....
Debt: Domestic	88a	1,106.50	1,098.70	838.60	831.50	822.70	1,006.90	889.00	1,119.80	1,260.30	....	....	....
Foreign	89a	3,772.70	3,975.20	4,114.80	4,386.30	4,334.40	4,668.70	4,883.90	4,501.60	4,491.10	....	....	....

National Accounts		1993	1994	1995	1996	1997	1998	1999	2000	2001	2002	2003	2004
							Millions of Dinars						
Househ.Cons.Expend.,incl.NPISHs....	**96f**	2,793.0	2,935.6	3,045.9	3,451.5	3,647.4	4,111.9	4,167.9	4,842.7	5,158.1	5,198.4	....	....
Government Consumption Expend...	**91f**	857.9	985.6	1,111.3	1,204.1	1,312.5	1,367.0	1,386.7	1,421.6	1,458.4	1,541.6	....	....
Gross Fixed Capital Formation..........	**93e**	1,303.6	1,391.2	1,395.0	1,444.8	1,325.0	1,187.5	1,351.7	1,263.2	1,238.8	1,294.4	....	....
Changes in Inventories.....................	**93i**	119.2	60.0	159.1	54.5	−3.2	36.5	−106.4	64.1	79.2	52.3	....	....
Exports of Goods and Services..........	**90c**	1,962.1	2,093.4	2,438.5	2,597.2	2,532.5	2,515.7	2,505.4	2,507.0	2,677.2	3,036.3	....	....
Imports of Goods and Services (-).....	**98c**	3,151.7	3,107.6	3,435.2	3,839.9	3,676.7	3,608.7	3,537.9	4,109.5	4,272.7	4,424.2	....	....
Gross Domestic Product (GDP)........	**99b**	3,884.2	4,358.1	4,714.7	4,912.2	5,137.4	5,609.9	5,767.3	5,989.0	6,339.0	6,698.8	7,056.2	....
Net Primary Income from Abroad.....	**98.n**	−149.1	−151.4	−116.8	−112.3	−47.4	−5.8	−8.7	95.5	132.7	79.0	....	....
Gross National Income (GNI)...........	**99a**	3,735.1	4,206.7	4,597.9	4,799.9	5,090.1	5,604.0	5,758.7	6,084.5	6,471.7	6,777.8	....	....
Net National Income.......................	**99e**	3,382.7	3,816.6	4,164.5	4,305.5	4,525.5	4,987.9	5,083.4	5,413.6	5,780.6	6,056.5	....	....
GDP Volume 1994 Prices.................	**99b.p**	4,151.1	4,358.2	4,627.6	4,723.5	4,880.5	5,027.5	5,181.4	5,393.7	5,658.1	5,930.6	6,123.5	....
GDP Volume (2000=100)................	**99bvp**	77.0	80.8	85.8	87.6	90.5	93.2	96.1	100.0	104.9	110.0	113.5	....
GDP Deflator (2000=100)................	**99bip**	84.3	90.1	91.8	93.7	94.8	100.5	100.2	100.0	100.9	101.7	103.8	....
							Millions: Midyear Estimates						
Population...............................	**99z**	3.88	4.09	4.29	4.45	4.59	4.72	4.84	4.97	5.11	5.26	5.41	5.56

Kazakhstan 916

		1993	1994	1995	1996	1997	1998	1999	2000	2001	2002	2003	2004
Exchange Rates						*Tenge per SDR: End of Period*							
Official Rate	aa	8.67	79.21	95.06	105.40	101.94	117.99	189.68	188.27	188.76	210.18	214.31	201.89
					Tenge per US Dollar: End of Period (ae) Period Average (rf)								
Official Rate	ae	6.31	54.26	63.95	73.30	75.55	83.80	138.20	144.50	150.20	154.60	144.22	130.00
Official Rate	rf	....	35.54	60.95	67.30	75.44	78.30	119.52	142.13	146.74	153.28	149.58	136.04
Fund Position						*Millions of SDRs: End of Period*							
Quota	2f.s	247.50	247.50	247.50	247.50	247.50	247.50	365.70	365.70	365.70	365.70	365.70	365.70
SDRs	1b.s	13.98	69.54	154.87	240.19	327.15	275.08	164.24	.01	—	.76	.78	.79
Reserve Position in the Fund	1c.s	.01	.01	.01	.01	.01	.01	.01	.01	.01	.01	.01	.01
Total Fund Cred.&Loans Outstg	2tl	61.88	198.00	290.82	383.60	378.96	463.66	335.15	—	—	—	—	—
International Liquidity					*Millions of US Dollars Unless Otherwise Indicated: End of Period*								
Total Reserves minus Gold	1l.d	455.7	837.5	1,135.5	1,294.1	1,697.1	1,461.2	1,479.2	1,594.1	1,997.2	2,555.3	4,236.2	8,473.1
SDRs	1b.d	19.2	101.5	230.2	345.4	441.4	387.3	225.4	—	—	1.0	1.2	1.2
Reserve Position in the Fund	1c.d	.01	.01	.01	.01	.01	.01	.01	.01	.01	.01	.01	.01
Foreign Exchange	1d.d	436.5	736.0	905.3	948.7	1,255.7	1,073.9	1,253.8	1,594.1	1,997.2	2,554.2	4,235.0	8,471.9
Gold (Million Fine Troy Ounces)	1ad	.65	.99	1.36	1.80	1.81	1.75	1.80	1.84	1.84	1.71	1.74	1.83
Gold (National Valuation)	1and	255.5	378.0	524.3	666.6	523.9	503.6	522.8	501.5	510.7	585.6	725.9	803.6
Monetary Authorities:Other Assets	3..d	825.2	1,117.5	1,432.0	1,425.4	† 1,848.1	1,577.6	1,776.8	2,096.5	3,767.1	5,096.5	8,607.4	14,407.5
Other liab	4..d	336.6	15.9	59.4	76.0	† 50.0	19.6	18.3	2.0	2.3	2.5	45.4	3.3
Deposit Money Banks: Assets	7a.d	345.6	271.9	440.9	330.1	273.8	344.6	570.6	383.5	556.0	1,331.9	2,049.8	3,861.5
Liabilities	7b.d	563.5	1,195.8	414.2	138.1	207.5	390.5	232.2	379.6	982.2	1,802.5	3,952.5	7,485.0
Monetary Authorities						*Millions of Tenge: End of Period*							
Foreign Assets	11	5,328	66,143	106,300	129,801	† 172,971	164,663	276,713	302,950	565,816	788,081	1,241,532	1,873,130
Claims on Central Government	12a	1,696	20,236	39,467	39,265	† 77,078	87,931	109,304	41,568	19,134	19,230	2,946	4,997
Claims on Rest of the Economy	12d	197	760	332	16,906	† 620	7,277	12,657	2,146	3,587	4,060	6,349	8,443
Claims on Deposit Money Banks	12e	6,095	13,355	10,487	9,059	† 8,248	2,084	4,634	2,774	1,810	3,758	3,150	26,126
Reserve Money	14	4,309	31,171	66,550	84,354	† 115,389	81,427	126,749	134,416	175,551	208,171	316,872	577,847
of which: Currency Outside Banks	14a	2,273	20,255	47,998	62,811	† 92,796	68,720	103,486	106,428	131,175	161,701	238,545	379,273
Other Deposits	15	127	738	445	3,068	† 18	47	1,107	702	750	138	82	112,465
Liabs. of Central Bank:Securities	16ac	....	....	....	....	6,855	12,046	6,206	49,180	17,796	65,166	205,681	407,667
Foreign Liabilities	16c	2,660	16,548	31,444	46,001	† 42,409	56,354	66,097	286	345	390	6,543	429
Central Government Deposits	16d	2,016	8,337	14,641	13,908	† 53,647	59,766	93,898	57,507	256,768	356,425	570,924	744,222
Capital Accounts	17a	2,744	47,653	62,822	64,993	† 52,611	63,480	121,957	118,963	134,375	179,834	167,299	84,257
Other Items (Net)	17r	1,460	−3,953	−19,317	−17,293	† −12,012	−11,167	−12,707	−11,615	4,762	5,005	−13,424	−14,191
Deposit Money Banks						*Millions of Tenge: End of Period*							
Reserves	20	1,914	8,638	14,771	16,891	† 22,361	12,144	21,793	24,359	42,343	45,362	76,222	195,805
Claims on Central Bank: Securities	20c	....	....	....	....	....	2,018	4,235	41,591	7,182	25,119	85,282	192,162
Other Claims on Central Bank	20n	....	....	....	....	—	—	6,390	3,700	16,748	1	3,608	4,332
Foreign Assets	21	2,181	14,755	28,197	24,196	† 20,685	28,874	78,863	55,410	83,512	205,913	295,626	501,993
Claims on Central Government	22a	514	426	5,104	8,691	† 25,303	21,184	34,752	59,512	† 75,847	107,424	106,226	125,696
Claims on Local Government	22b	....	....	....	....	....	....	....	....	5,205	1,792	2,993	3,360
Claims on Nonfin.Pub.Enterprises	22c	....	....	....	....	....	....	....	....	14,564	12,795	30,158	18,502
Claims on Rest of the Economy	22d	14,310	111,747	71,988	72,448	† 85,866	102,887	153,534	288,856	† 515,735	699,030	1,010,888	1,560,721
Claims on Nonbank Financial Insts	22g	....	....	....	....	....	....	2,195	2,904	3,703	16,079	22,795	31,886	59,633
Demand Deposits	24	5,593	32,894	63,930	71,938	† 57,998	49,511	101,050	126,124	137,014	219,423	238,890	373,288
Other Deposits	25	....	....	....	....	† 22,073	29,767	66,844	160,150	† 285,867	341,811	458,713	720,295
Bonds	26ab	—	92	1,902	119	† 30	—	32	1,173	1,613	6,675	12,729	31,097
Restricted Deposits	26b	....	....	....	....	....	....	....	....	19,397	41,011	33,841	62,059
Foreign Liabilities	26c	3,556	64,883	26,485	10,120	† 15,674	32,727	32,087	54,857	147,524	278,665	570,024	973,055
Central Government Deposits	26d	111	1,494	5,416	11,494	† 26,484	10,986	15,178	17,242	† 14,699	17,708	5,887	3,954
Liabilities to Local Government	26db	....	....	....	....	....	....	....	....	2,627	3,457	3,116	2,681
Credit from Central Bank	26g	6,049	14,204	5,883	11,482	† 8,208	5,092	4,699	2,915	1,888	5,347	9,139	39,592
Capital Accounts	27a	1,091	14,662	29,259	39,289	† 40,183	59,735	89,539	107,159	159,897	179,516	258,048	405,326
Other Items (Net)	27r	2,521	7,338	−12,815	−22,216	† −16,436	−18,517	−6,957	7,509	6,690	26,616	50,954	50,855
Monetary Survey						*Millions of Tenge: End of Period*							
Foreign Assets (Net)	31n	1,293	−533	76,568	97,876	† 135,572	104,455	257,392	303,217	501,460	714,938	960,591	1,401,638
Domestic Credit	32	14,590	123,338	96,834	111,908	† 108,737	150,721	204,074	321,036	376,057	489,536	611,520	1,030,495
Claims on Central Govt. (Net)	32an	83	10,831	24,514	22,554	† 22,250	38,363	34,979	26,331	† −176,487	−247,478	−467,639	−617,482
Claims on Local Government	32b	....	....	....	....	....	....	....	....	2,578	−1,666	−123	678
Claims on Nonfin.Pub.Enterprises	32c	....	....	....	....	....	....	....	....	14,564	12,795	30,158	18,502
Claims on Rest of the Economy	32d	14,507	112,507	72,320	89,354	† 86,487	110,163	166,191	291,002	† 519,321	703,090	1,017,237	1,569,164
Claims on Nonbank Fin. Insts	32g	....	....	....	....	....	....	2,195	2,904	3,703	16,079	22,795	31,886	59,633
Money	34	8,198	55,417	115,384	139,452	† 150,908	118,735	205,929	236,163	270,009	381,975	479,023	755,296
Quasi-Money	35	....	....	....	....	† 22,091	29,815	67,951	160,852	† 286,617	341,949	458,795	832,760
Bonds	36ab	—	92	1,902	119	† 30	—	32	1,173	1,613	6,675	12,729	31,097
Liabs. of Central Bank: Securities	36ac	—	92	1,902	119	6,855	† 10,028	1,971	7,589	10,614	40,047	120,399	215,505
Restricted Deposits	36b	....	....	....	....	....	....	....	....	19,397	41,011	33,841	62,059
Capital Accounts	37a	3,835	62,315	92,081	104,282	† 92,794	123,215	211,495	226,122	294,271	359,350	425,347	489,583
Other Items (Net)	37r	3,852	4,982	−35,966	−34,069	† −28,369	−26,617	−25,912	−7,647	−5,006	33,466	40,428	45,833
Money plus Quasi-Money	35l	8,198	55,417	115,384	139,452	† 172,999	148,549	273,880	397,015	† 556,626	723,925	937,819	1,588,056
Interest Rates						*Percent Per Annum*							
Refinancing Rate (End of Per.)	60	170.00	230.00	† 52.50	35.00	18.50	25.00	18.00	14.00	9.00	7.50	7.00	7.00
Treasury Bill Rate	60c	....	214.34	48.98	28.91	15.15	23.59	15.63	6.59	5.28	5.20	5.86	3.28
Prices and Labor						*Index Numbers (2000=100): Period Averages*							
Producer Prices	63	....	....	42.2	† 52.3	60.4	61.0	72.5	100.0	100.3	100.5	109.9	128.3
Consumer Prices	64	.9	16.9	46.6	† 64.9	76.1	81.6	88.4	100.0	108.4	114.7	122.1	130.5
Wages: Monthly Earnings	65	.9	12.0	33.3	47.6	59.4	67.4	82.5	100.0	120.4	141.4	160.9	196.7
Total Employment	67	227.4	212.7	185.5	178.7	148.3	124.9	111.1	100.0	102.3	105.9	109.3	113.5
						Number in Thousands: Period Averages							
Employment	67e	6,963	6,582	6,552	6,519	6,472	6,127	6,105	6,201	6,697	6,709	6,985	7,185
Unemployment	67c		536	808	971	967	925	950	906	780	691	672	658
Unemployment Rate (%)	67r	....	7.5	11.0	13.0	13.0	13.1	13.5	12.8	10.4	9.3	8.8	8.4

		1993	1994	1995	1996	1997	1998	1999	2000	2001	2002	2003	2004
Intl. Transactions & Positions						*Millions of US Dollars*							
Exports	70..d	3,277.0	3,230.8	5,250.2	5,911.0	6,497.0	5,334.1	5,871.6	8,812.2	8,639.1	9,670.3	12,926.7	20,093.1
Imports, c.i.f.	71..d	3,887.4	3,561.2	3,806.7	4,241.1	4,300.8	4,313.9	3,655.1	5,040.0	6,446.0	6,584.0	8,408.7	12,781.2
Balance of Payments						*Millions of US Dollars: Minus Sign Indicates Debit*							
Current Account, n.i.e.	78ald	....	....	−213.1	−751.0	−799.3	−1,224.9	−171.0	366.3	−1,389.5	−1,024.3	−270.1	532.9
Goods: Exports f.o.b.	78aad	....	....	5,440.0	6,291.6	6,899.3	5,870.5	5,988.7	9,288.1	8,927.8	10,026.9	13,232.6	20,603.1
Goods: Imports f.o.b.	78abd	....	....	−5,325.9	−6,626.7	−7,175.7	−6,671.7	−5,645.0	−7,119.7	−7,944.4	−8,039.8	−9,553.6	−13,817.6
Trade Balance	78acd	....	....	114.1	−335.1	−276.4	−801.2	343.7	2,168.4	983.4	1,987.1	3,679.0	6,785.6
Services: Credit	78add	....	....	535.1	674.4	841.9	904.3	932.5	1,053.0	1,260.2	1,540.4	1,712.3	2,001.1
Services: Debit	78aed	....	....	−775.8	−928.3	−1,124.4	−1,154.1	−1,104.2	−1,850.0	−2,634.6	−3,538.3	−3,752.7	−4,987.0
Balance on Goods & Services	78afd	....	....	−126.6	−589.0	−558.9	−1,051.0	172.0	1,371.4	−391.0	−10.7	1,638.6	3,799.6
Income: Credit	78agd	....	....	44.6	56.7	73.8	95.5	108.6	138.6	224.8	233.8	256.4	422.5
Income: Debit	78ahd	....	....	−190.1	−277.1	−388.8	−391.8	−608.3	−1,392.7	−1,461.7	−1,361.1	−2,000.4	−3,201.1
Balance on Gds, Serv. & Inc.	78aid	....	....	−272.1	−809.4	−873.9	−1,347.3	−327.7	117.3	−1,628.0	−1,138.1	−105.4	1,021.0
Current Transfers, n.i.e.: Credit	78ajd	....	....	79.9	83.4	104.7	141.4	174.7	352.2	394.4	425.9	278.6	352.9
Current Transfers: Debit	78akd	....	....	−20.9	−25.0	−30.1	−19.0	−18.0	−103.2	−156.0	−312.1	−443.3	−841.1
Capital Account, n.i.e.	78bcd	....	....	−380.6	−315.5	−439.8	−369.1	−234.0	−290.5	−185.0	−119.8	−27.8	−20.3
Capital Account, n.i.e.: Credit	78bad	....	....	116.1	87.9	58.3	65.9	61.1	66.4	99.2	109.8	123.1	114.4
Capital Account: Debit	78bbd	....	....	−496.7	−403.4	−498.1	−435.0	−295.1	−356.9	−284.2	−229.7	−150.9	−134.6
Financial Account, n.i.e.	78bjd	....	....	1,162.5	2,005.1	2,901.6	2,229.1	1,299.2	1,307.0	2,613.7	1,359.1	2,783.9	4,612.7
Direct Investment Abroad	78bdd	....	....	−.3	....	−1.4	−8.1	−3.6	−4.4	25.6	−426.4	121.3	1,279.2
Dir. Invest. in Rep. Econ., n.i.e.	78bed	....	....	964.2	1,137.0	1,321.4	1,151.4	1,587.0	1,282.5	2,835.0	2,590.2	2,088.4	4,269.2
Portfolio Investment Assets	78bfd	....	....	—	....	−1.2	−5.3	−5.6	−85.5	−1,348.9	−1,063.9	−2,073.1	−1,092.1
Equity Securities	78bkd	....	....	....	....	−1.2	−.4	−1.8	.7	−10.4	−374.4	−311.8	−362.8
Debt Securities	78bld	....	....	—	....	....	−4.9	−3.8	−86.2	−1,338.5	−689.5	−1,761.2	−729.3
Portfolio Investment Liab., n.i.e.	78bgd	....	....	7.2	223.5	405.4	66.2	−39.9	30.4	31.4	−182.9	182.1	670.3
Equity Securities	78bmd	....	....	....	....	....	....	....	19.3	55.4	39.3	63.8	−14.3
Debt Securities	78bnd	....	....	7.2	223.5	405.4	66.2	−39.9	11.1	−23.9	−222.1	118.3	684.6
Financial Derivatives Assets	78bwd	....	....	....	....	....	....	....	....	....	....	....	−44.6
Financial Derivatives Liabilities	78bxd	....	....	....	....	....	....	....	....	....	....	15.9	−1.8
Other Investment Assets	78bhd	....	....	−657.4	243.8	−139.5	−220.5	−778.4	42.9	464.8	−1,116.8	−949.7	−4,527.1
Monetary Authorities	78bod	....	....	21.3	2.1	....	....	−.3	−.4	.3	−14.8	−128.9	−9.3
General Government	78bpd	....	....	—	27.8	.3	−41.1	16.3	−.4	209.7	321.2	275.0	—
Banks	78bqd	....	....	−152.3	174.4	−66.0	−67.9	−205.8	154.4	−63.6	−624.7	−314.3	−1,776.9
Other Sectors	78brd	....	....	−526.4	39.5	−73.8	−111.5	−588.6	−110.7	318.5	−798.6	−781.5	−2,741.0
Other Investment Liab., n.i.e.	78bid	....	....	848.8	400.8	1,316.9	1,245.4	539.7	41.0	605.7	1,558.8	3,398.9	4,059.7
Monetary Authorities	78bsd	....	....	−4.9	12.1	−5.0	−37.7	....	−2.6	.4	.2	85.5	−67.4
General Government	78btd	....	....	331.3	323.4	317.2	673.3	291.5	88.1	51.3	1.7	57.4	−69.0
Banks	78bud	....	....	−251.5	−125.7	161.4	60.2	−20.2	165.0	432.8	937.0	2,142.5	2,956.7
Other Sectors	78bvd	....	....	773.9	191.0	843.3	549.6	268.4	−209.5	121.2	619.9	1,113.6	1,239.3
Net Errors and Omissions	78cad	....	....	−270.1	−780.0	−1,114.1	−1,078.4	−641.6	−812.7	−654.5	320.2	−952.5	−1,126.4
Overall Balance	78cbd	....	....	298.7	158.6	548.4	−443.3	252.6	570.1	384.7	535.1	1,533.5	3,999.0
Reserves and Related Items	79dad	....	....	−298.7	−158.6	−548.4	443.3	−252.6	−570.1	−384.7	−535.1	−1,533.5	−3,999.0
Reserve Assets	79dbd	....	....	−440.1	−293.7	−542.0	321.7	−77.1	−129.1	−384.7	−535.1	−1,533.5	−3,999.0
Use of Fund Credit and Loans	79dcd	....	....	141.4	135.1	−6.4	121.6	−175.5	−441.0	—	—	—	—
Exceptional Financing	79ded	....	....	....	....	....	....	....	....	—	—	—	—
International Investment Position						*Millions of US Dollars*							
Assets	79aad	....	....	....	....	2,629.1	2,391.8	2,598.4	4,612.9	6,117.0	9,321.5	14,254.2	23,206.0
Direct Investment Abroad	79abd	....	....	....	....	2.6	3.1	3.1	15.5	−9.7	417.2	300.4	−971.7
Portfolio Investment	79acd	....	....	....	....	2.0	4.2	1.0	69.7	1,430.8	2,396.1	4,563.6	5,903.3
Equity Securities	79add	....	....	....	....	—	—	—	3.4	15.2	308.9	641.5	1,075.2
Debt Securities	79aed	....	....	....	....	2.0	4.2	1.0	66.3	1,415.6	2,087.2	3,922.0	4,828.1
Financial Derivatives	79ald	....	....	....	....	—	2.0	—	—	—	—	—	48.4
Other Investment	79afd	....	....	....	....	335.3	417.7	592.2	2,432.1	2,187.8	3,367.4	4,428.1	8,945.5
Monetary Authorities	79agd	....	....	....	....	.3	.1	.3	.7	.3	54.3	183.3	192.6
General Government	79ahd	....	....	....	....	46.8	46.8	46.8	852.3	636.1	314.9	39.9	39.9
Banks	79aid	....	....	....	....	288.2	370.8	545.1	359.8	423.0	1,048.3	1,340.0	3,060.2
Other Sectors	79ajd	....	....	....	....	....	....	....	1,219.3	1,128.4	1,949.9	2,864.9	5,652.8
Reserve Assets	79akd	....	....	....	....	2,289.2	1,964.8	2,002.1	2,095.7	2,508.2	3,140.8	4,962.1	9,280.5
Liabilities	79lad	....	....	....	....	2,595.3	3,594.3	3,678.4	15,726.9	19,192.4	23,056.5	29,041.7	38,760.4
Dir. Invest. in Rep. Economy	79lbd	....	....	....	....	50.1	122.3	115.9	10,077.7	12,916.6	15,464.3	17,586.4	22,399.1
Portfolio Investment	79lcd	....	....	....	....	623.9	663.4	617.2	695.9	725.0	337.8	572.5	1,299.4
Equity Securities	79ldd	....	....	....	....	53.9	49.9	37.7	101.6	146.9	142.0	221.6	280.6
Debt Securities	79led	....	....	....	....	570.0	613.5	579.5	594.3	578.1	195.7	350.9	1,018.8
Financial Derivatives	79lld	....	....	....	....	—	—	—	—	—	25.0	40.9	38.8
Other Investment	79lfd	....	....	....	....	1,921.3	2,808.6	2,945.3	4,953.3	5,550.8	7,229.4	10,842.0	15,023.1
Monetary Authorities	79lgd	....	....	....	....	553.0	655.4	462.6	1.9	2.3	2.5	88.0	20.7
General Government	79lhd	....	....	....	....	1,175.3	1,896.4	2,231.3	2,277.0	2,249.0	2,294.1	2,423.2	2,382.7
Banks	79lid	....	....	....	....	193.0	256.8	251.4	392.2	859.3	1,791.8	3,994.1	6,972.6
Other Sectors	79ljd	....	....	....	....	—	—	—	2,282.3	2,440.2	3,141.0	4,336.7	5,647.1
Government Finance						*Millions of Tenge: Year Ending December 31*							
Deficit (-) or Surplus	80	....	−30,382	−25,181	−59,564	−63,998	−72,073	−69,830	−3,279	−12,998	−13,004	−46,182	−18,697
Total Revenue and Grants	81y	....	79,474	178,347	306,943	405,624	379,521	395,580	590,236	733,893	807,853	1,004,565	1,286,734
Revenue	81	....	79,413	178,347	306,943	405,342	379,311	392,951	587,039	733,659	807,853	1,004,565	1,286,734
Grants Received	81z	....	61	—	—	282	210	2,629	3,197	234	—	—	—
Exp. & Lending Minus Repay.	82z	....	109,856	203,528	366,507	469,622	451,594	465,410	593,515	746,891	820,857	1,050,747	1,305,431
Expenditure	82	....	109,672	210,603	381,602	439,476	426,142	447,426	576,182	726,015	801,071	1,026,991	1,287,938
Lending Minus Repayments	83	....	184	−7,075	−15,095	30,146	25,452	17,984	17,333	20,876	19,786	23,756	17,492
Total Financing													
Domestic	84a	....	....	....	....	17,170	20,504	20,671	−28,515	2,591	64,929	38,908	68,064
Foreign	85a	....	....	....	....	46,828	51,569	49,159	31,794	10,407	−51,925	7,274	−49,368

		1993	1994	1995	1996	1997	1998	1999	2000	2001	2002	2003	2004
National Accounts						*Billions of Tenge*							
Househ.Cons.Expend.,incl.NPISHs....	96f	20.85	328.85	721.13	952.79	1,179.14	1,270.02	1,460.12	1,599.73	1,882.49	2,205.94	2,516.69	3,159.05
Government Consumption Expend...	91f	4.09	45.23	137.75	182.79	207.02	186.87	232.71	313.99	436.04	435.00	510.44	682.13
Gross Fixed Capital Formation..........	93e	8.21	110.65	233.81	243.88	271.77	272.44	326.26	450.26	771.39	907.13	1,062.24	1,256.78
Changes in Inventories.....................	93i	−2.32	10.90	2.69	−15.28	−10.94	1.49	32.19	21.34	102.26	123.33	122.01	74.58
Exports of Goods and Services..........	90c	11.15	156.96	395.27	499.32	583.86	525.95	856.23	1,481.10	1,501.29	1,781.69	2,242.20	3,056.30
Imports of Goods and Services (-).....	98c	13.75	199.53	441.67	509.74	626.10	604.22	808.94	1,258.20	1,531.33	1,747.96	1,964.74	2,546.83
Gross Domestic Product (GDP).........	99b	28.23	453.07	1,048.99	1,353.75	1,604.76	1,652.55	2,098.57	2,608.21	3,162.14	3,705.13	4,488.83	5,582.00
Net Primary Income from Abroad.....	98.n	−.07	−2.17	−9.11	−12.28	−23.38	−23.33	−62.78	−162.36	−167.26	−158.30	−261.73	....
Gross National Income (GNI)............	99a	29.35	421.30	1,005.08	1,403.47	1,648.76	1,709.93	1,953.68	2,437.54	3,083.33	3,617.98	4,188.07	....
Net Current Transf.from Abroad.......	98t	.34	7.36	7.88	9.81	5.63	6.11	18.38	35.45	33.96	17.33	−24.51	....
Gross Nat'l Disposable Inc.(GNDI)....	99i	29.69	428.66	1,012.96	1,413.29	1,654.40	1,716.05	1,972.06	2,472.99	3,117.29	3,635.31	4,163.56	....
Gross Saving...................................	99s	4.75	54.58	154.09	277.71	268.23	259.16	279.23	559.27	798.76	994.37	1,136.44	....
Consumption of Fixed Capital..........	99cf	5.29	84.31	154.42	228.04	253.96	238.76	286.95	420.52	498.16	576.88	....	....
GDP, Production Based....................	99bp	29.42	423.47	1,014.19	1,415.75	1,672.14	1,733.26	2,016.46	2,599.90	3,250.59	3,776.28	4,449.80	5,842.42
Statistical Discrepancy.....................	99bs	1.19	−29.60	−34.80	61.99	67.39	80.71	−82.11	−8.30	88.46	71.15	−39.03	....
GDP Volume (2000=100)................	99bvp	....	† 96.3	88.4	88.9	90.4	88.7	91.1	100.0	113.5	124.7	136.2	....
GDP Deflator (2000=100)...............	99bip	....	† 18.0	45.5	58.4	68.1	71.4	88.3	100.0	106.8	113.9	126.4	....
						Millions: Midyear Estimates							
Population................................	99z	16.22	16.05	15.87	15.68	15.50	15.32	15.16	15.03	14.94	14.89	14.86	14.84

		1993	1994	1995	1996	1997	1998	1999	2000	2001	2002	2003	2004
Exchange Rates						*Shillings per SDR: End of Period*							
Principal Rate	aa	93.626	65.458	83.153	79.118	84.568	87.165	100.098	101.674	98.779	104.781	113.140	120.117
						Shillings per US Dollar: End of Period (ae) Period Average (rf)							
Principal Rate	ae	68.163	44.839	55.939	55.021	62.678	61.906	72.931	78.036	78.600	77.072	76.139	77.344
Principal Rate	rf	58.001	56.051	51.430	57.115	58.732	60.367	70.326	76.176	78.563	78.749	75.936	79.174
Fund Position						*Millions of SDRs: End of Period*							
Quota	2f.s	199.4	199.4	199.4	199.4	199.4	199.4	271.4	271.4	271.4	271.4	271.4	271.4
SDRs	1b.s	.8	.5	.2	.5	.5	.4	1.7	.2	.8	.6	1.4	.4
Reserve Position in the Fund	1c.s	12.2	12.3	12.3	12.3	12.4	12.4	12.4	12.5	12.5	12.6	12.7	12.7
Total Fund Cred.&Loans Outstg	2tl	264.3	277.3	251.5	234.5	185.6	139.5	95.8	97.2	78.6	64.6	75.6	66.1
International Liquidity						*Millions of US Dollars Unless Otherwise Indicated: End of Period*							
Total Reserves minus Gold	1l.d	405.6	557.6	353.4	746.5	787.9	783.1	791.6	897.7	1,064.9	1,068.0	1,481.9	1,519.3
SDRs	1b.d	1.1	.7	.3	.8	.7	.6	2.4	.3	1.0	.8	2.0	.6
Reserve Position in the Fund	1c.d	16.8	18.0	18.3	17.7	16.7	17.5	17.1	16.2	15.8	17.1	18.8	19.7
Foreign Exchange	1d.d	387.7	538.9	334.8	728.0	770.6	765.0	772.2	881.2	1,048.1	1,050.0	1,461.0	1,499.0
Gold (Million Fine Troy Ounces)	1ad	.080	.080	.080	.080	.080	—	—	.001	.001	.001	.001	.001
Gold (National Valuation)	1and	14.3	15.2	15.4	14.8	23.1	—	—	.1	.1	.2	.2	.2
Monetary Authorities: Other Liab	4..d	232.0	278.1	265.7	261.6	205.8	174.8	126.5	127.9	99.2	88.1	125.4	123.2
Deposit Money Banks: Assets	7a.d	348.9	425.4	439.6	444.2	594.2	501.6	313.6	500.7	395.0	546.6	408.6	616.8
Liabilities	7b.d	49.8	293.1	103.8	103.3	165.2	195.8	218.2	173.0	162.3	142.1	107.4	151.9
Other Banking Insts.: Assets	7e.d	—	—	.1	.2	.1	.9		1.8	.1	.1	.8	.8
Liabilities	7f.d	10.2	11.0	8.7	7.0	18.9	1.2	.8	.5	.4	.2	—	.8
Monetary Authorities						*Millions of Shillings: End of Period*							
Foreign Assets	11	34,527	28,227	25,683	47,266	44,499	47,103	57,816	71,245	83,499	82,304	112,771	117,710
Claims on Central Government	12a	49,275	53,857	98,401	57,287	47,905	43,585	39,028	36,742	37,421	40,947	40,836	47,657
Claims on Private Sector	12d	—	—	839	1,151	1,053	1,291	1,380	1,386	1,496	1,670	1,820	1,984
Claims on Deposit Money Banks	12e	11,484	10,072	9,766	9,056	9,124	1,140	904	4,884	1,362	7,484	674	67
Reserve Money	14	47,628	58,472	76,610	82,903	84,621	84,269	89,341	88,758	87,859	98,311	97,205	111,433
of which: Currency Outside DMBs	14a	21,355	24,817	28,887	30,390	36,178	38,713	42,963	43,466	45,349	53,895	55,550	62,728
Foreign Liabilities	16c	24,854	18,277	20,944	18,604	15,720	12,246	9,655	9,982	7,796	6,790	9,549	9,528
Central Government Deposits	16d	38,289	32,920	55,239	27,349	11,698	17,172	18,922	26,526	28,537	25,886	42,237	28,868
Counterpart Funds	16e	73	127	6	—	—	—	—	—	—	—	—	—
Capital Accounts	17a	4,184	3,235	4,155	4,819	5,612	7,281	8,800	9,322	9,622	13,548	14,805	15,696
Other Items (Net)	17r	−19,742	−20,875	−22,265	−18,915	−15,070	−27,850	−27,589	−20,331	−10,036	−12,129	−7,696	1,893
Deposit Money Banks						*Millions of Shillings: End of Period*							
Reserves	20	20,870	31,790	35,316	42,460	39,736	34,970	36,081	31,762	37,062	34,165	31,588	39,959
Foreign Assets	21	23,783	19,073	24,594	24,440	37,240	31,051	22,871	39,072	31,049	42,126	31,113	47,704
Claims on Central Government	22a	21,136	38,088	26,417	42,576	46,121	70,550	68,415	71,206	89,091	98,549	137,614	109,869
Claims on Local Government	22b	219	249	304	358	582	595	895	1,143	659	687	658	338
Claims on Nonfin.Pub.Enterprises	22c	3,885	5,174	4,987	5,290	7,572	6,922	6,479	7,013	6,839	7,846	6,403	11,291
Claims on Private Sector	22d	61,705	79,467	119,261	148,018	186,558	202,592	239,586	247,913	239,340	248,536	261,261	324,604
Claims on Other Banking Insts	22f	3,523	2,671	4,897	5,852	3,176	2,283	1,294	752	561	982	513	569
Claims on Nonbank Financial Insts	22g	270	3,506	4,539	6,676	8,774	10,608	12,095	14,720	15,533	21,090	24,536	27,505
Demand Deposits	24	33,664	34,909	36,186	40,337	44,708	46,670	56,411	64,911	75,559	86,070	128,297	136,729
Time & Foreign Currency Deposits	25	64,332	89,908	129,961	170,009	206,488	211,161	215,348	221,665	224,238	241,727	244,327	288,010
Money Market Instruments	26aa	3,187	4,458	3,932	2,965	5,651	5,899	3,963	4,817	3,851	6,142	4,881	7,658
Foreign Liabilities	26c	3,392	13,144	5,807	5,681	10,356	12,122	15,914	13,501	12,756	10,954	8,176	11,747
Central Government Deposits	26d	4,790	4,950	5,531	3,822	4,226	9,592	8,754	5,310	4,333	7,922	10,341
Credit from Monetary Authorities	26g	252	—	—	—	448	4,335	1,614	3,635	2,974	2,673	740	57
Credit from Other Banking Insts	26i	—	10,697	6,403	8,165	6,005	5,082	3,879	2,683	1,676	1,827	2,026	3,098
Liab. to Nonbank Financial Insts	26j	—	12	2	—	49	3	4	2	3	2	230	196
Capital Accounts	27a	17,010	23,024	33,200	42,210	53,168	54,349	46,063	53,097	54,343	53,905	60,959	66,934
Other Items (Net)	27r	8,765	−1,083	−707	2,482	−1,340	10,355	35,766	40,885	39,424	46,350	36,129	37,067
Monetary Survey						*Millions of Shillings: End of Period*							
Foreign Assets (Net)	31n	30,063	15,878	23,525	47,420	55,664	53,785	55,119	86,833	93,996	106,687	126,160	144,138
Domestic Credit	32	96,935	145,142	198,876	236,037	285,817	311,661	341,495	345,964	357,093	390,088	423,482	484,608
Claims on Central Govt. (Net)	32an	27,332	54,075	64,048	68,693	78,101	87,370	79,767	73,037	92,665	109,277	128,290	118,317
Claims on Local Government	32b	219	249	304	358	582	595	895	1,143	659	687	658	338
Claims on Nonfin.Pub.Enterprises	32c	3,885	5,174	4,987	5,290	7,572	6,922	6,479	7,013	6,839	7,846	6,403	11,291
Claims on Private Sector	32d	61,705	79,467	120,100	149,169	187,611	203,883	240,966	249,299	240,836	250,206	263,081	326,587
Claims on Other Banking Insts	32f	3,523	2,671	4,897	5,852	3,176	2,283	1,294	752	561	982	513	569
Claims on Nonbank Financial Insts	32g	270	3,506	4,539	6,676	8,774	10,608	12,095	14,720	15,533	21,090	24,536	27,505
Money	34	59,322	62,407	66,525	76,238	89,487	93,489	109,067	118,672	125,670	149,130	193,130	209,368
Quasi-Money	35	64,332	89,908	129,961	170,009	206,488	211,161	215,348	221,665	224,238	241,727	244,327	288,010
Money Market Instruments	36aa	3,187	4,458	3,932	2,965	5,651	5,899	3,963	4,817	3,851	6,142	4,881	7,658
Counterpart Funds	36e	73	127	6	—	—	—	—	—	—	—	—	—
Liab. to Other Banking Insts	36i	—	10,697	6,403	8,165	6,005	5,082	3,879	2,683	1,676	1,827	2,026	3,098
Liab. to Nonbank Financial Insts	36j	—	12	2	—	49	3	4	2	3	2	230	196
Capital Accounts	37a	21,194	26,258	37,355	47,029	58,780	61,630	54,863	62,419	63,965	67,453	75,764	82,630
Other Items (Net)	37r	−21,110	−32,845	−21,783	−20,947	−24,980	−11,819	9,490	22,539	31,686	30,495	29,284	37,785
Money plus Quasi-Money	35l	123,654	152,314	196,486	246,246	295,975	304,650	324,415	340,337	349,909	390,857	437,457	497,379

Kenya 664

		1993	1994	1995	1996	1997	1998	1999	2000	2001	2002	2003	2004
Other Banking Institutions					*Millions of Shillings: End of Period*								
Reserves..........................	40	161	92	7,478	4,708	1,413	1,097	822	572	225	231	181	184
Foreign Assets....................	41	1	1	8	10	9	58	1	138	11	11	63	63
Claims on Central Government........	42a	20,933	24,065	10,748	7,193	8,826	7,163	8,122	9,323	10,454	11,268	4,577	4,689
Claims on Local Government..........	42b	39	35	35	16	7	8	8	—	—	—	—	—
Claims on Nonfin.Pub.Enterprises.....	42c	348	1,031	48	34	10	6	6	6	—	—	—	—
Claims on Private Sector..................	42d	35,734	37,808	40,629	36,398	27,632	28,723	24,378	25,860	16,460	17,575	15,340	14,825
Claims on Deposit Money Banks......	42e	5,770	9,115	5,537	7,653	3,735	5,802	4,103	4,129	2,107	1,509	2,427	1,416
Claims on Nonbank Financial Insts....	42g	125	591	503	146	119	103	96	114	97	24	58	57
Demand Deposits..................	44	7,746	12,718	5,506	2,844	2,126	2,241	1,898	1,594	1,605	1,499	1,694	1,847
Time and Savings Deposits..............	45	37,448	42,832	42,335	36,397	22,364	24,752	23,335	23,586	20,349	20,450	13,996	12,300
Money Market Instruments..............	46aa	—	—	90	—	—	—	—	—	—	—	—	—
Foreign Liabilities.................	46c	697	494	487	384	1,185	75	58	41	33	17	—	—
Central Government Deposits..........	46d	403	908	572	459	667	661	775	775	486	308	51	63
Credit from Monetary Authorities.....	46g	—	—	9	—	—	—	—	—	—	—	—	—
Credit from Deposit Money Banks....	46h	661	674	2,843	2,847	1,630	1,442	232	581	160	—	—	105
Liab. to Nonbank Financial Insts.......	46j	17	2	1	—	—	—	550	—	—	—	—	—
Capital Accounts............................	47a	6,315	7,773	7,148	6,366	4,257	4,279	4,410	3,545	2,343	2,339	2,318	2,364
Other Items (Net)..................	47r	9,823	7,337	5,994	6,859	9,522	9,511	6,278	10,019	4,378	6,005	4,588	4,553
Banking Survey					*Millions of Shillings: End of Period*								
Foreign Assets (Net)......................	51n	29,367	15,386	23,046	47,046	54,488	53,769	55,062	86,929	93,973	106,682	126,222	144,201
Domestic Credit...........................	52	150,188	205,092	245,370	273,513	318,568	344,721	372,036	379,740	383,058	417,665	442,894	503,547
Claims on Central Govt. (Net)........	52an	47,862	77,232	74,224	75,427	86,260	93,872	87,114	81,585	102,633	120,237	132,817	122,943
Claims on Local Government.........	52b	258	284	339	374	589	603	903	1,143	659	687	658	338
Claims on Nonfin.Pub.Enterprises...	52c	4,233	6,204	5,035	5,324	7,582	6,928	6,485	7,019	6,839	7,846	6,403	11,291
Claims on Private Sector...............	52d	97,440	117,275	160,729	185,567	215,243	232,606	265,344	275,159	257,296	267,781	278,421	341,412
Claims on Nonbank Financial Insts.	52g	395	4,096	5,043	6,821	8,893	10,711	12,191	14,834	15,631	21,113	24,594	27,563
Liquid Liabilities........................	55l	168,687	207,772	236,849	280,780	319,052	330,547	348,826	364,945	371,638	412,575	452,966	511,343
Money Market Instruments..............	56aa	3,187	4,458	4,023	2,965	5,651	5,899	3,963	4,817	3,851	6,142	4,881	7,658
Counterpart Funds..........................	56e	73	127	6	—	—	—	—	—	—	—	—	—
Liab. to Nonbank Financial Insts.......	56j	17	14	3	—	49	3	554	2	3	2	230	196
Capital Accounts............................	57a	27,509	34,031	44,503	53,395	63,037	65,909	59,273	65,964	66,308	69,792	78,082	84,994
Other Items (Net)..................	57r	−19,918	−25,924	−16,968	−16,580	−14,733	−3,869	14,482	30,942	35,232	35,835	32,958	43,557
Interest Rates					*Percent Per Annum*								
Discount Rate (End of Period)..........	60	45.50	21.50	24.50	26.88	32.27	17.07	26.46	....	....	....	....	....
Treasury Bill Rate........................	60c	49.80	23.32	18.29	22.25	22.87	22.83	13.87	12.05	12.60	8.95	3.51	3.17
Savings Rate............................	60k	17.78	20.80	12.77	13.45	11.87	10.29	5.45	4.95	4.52	3.84	2.41	1.17
Savings Rate (Fgn. Currency)...........	60k.f	....	....										.91
Deposit Rate............................	60l	....	....	13.60	17.59	16.72	18.40	9.55	8.10	6.64	5.49	4.13	† 2.43
Deposit Rate (Fgn. Currency)...........	60l.f	....	....	....	....	....	....	....	....	....			1.62
Lending Rate..............................	60p	29.99	36.24	28.80	33.79	30.25	29.49	22.38	22.34	19.67	18.45	16.57	† 12.53
Lending Rate (Fgn. Currency)...........	60p.f	....	....	....	....	....	....	....	....	....	....	....	5.83
Prices, Production, Labor					*Index Numbers (2000=100): Period Averages*								
Consumer Prices........................	64	50.8	65.4	66.5	72.4	† 80.6	86.0	90.9	100.0	105.7	107.8	118.4	132.2
Industrial Production (1995=100)....	66	73.8	83.2	100.0	90.7	....	....	....	....	....	....	....	....
					Number in Thousands: Period Averages								
Employment...........................	67e	1,475	1,506	1,557	1,607	1,647	1,665	1,673	1,677	....	....	....	....
Intl. Transactions & Positions					*Millions of Shillings*								
Exports................................	70	77,919	87,142	97,284	118,226	119,960	121,252	122,067	132,183	152,712	166,635	183,121	212,602
Imports, c.i.f.................................	71	101,128	115,080	155,168	168,486	190,674	193,032	198,313	236,613	250,782	255,569	282,616	360,812
					2000=100								
Volume of Exports (1995=100)........	72	73	83	100	....	....	....	....	....	....	....	....	....
Volume of Imports.........................	73	62	77	90	89	95	96	87	100	....	....	....	....
Export Prices..............................	74	71	73	79	84	98	99	93	100	....	....	....	....
Unit Value of Imports......................	75	66	60	69	76	81	83	90	100	....	....	....	....

Kenya 664

		1993	1994	1995	1996	1997	1998	1999	2000	2001	2002	2003	2004
Balance of Payments		*Millions of US Dollars: Minus Sign Indicates Debit*											
Current Account, n.i.e.	78ald	71.2	97.9	−400.4	−73.5	−456.8	−475.3	−89.6	−199.4	−341.4	−136.9	67.7	....
Goods: Exports f.o.b.	78aad	1,262.6	1,537.0	1,923.7	2,083.3	2,062.6	2,017.0	1,756.7	1,782.2	1,891.4	2,162.5	2,412.2	....
Goods: Imports f.o.b.	78abd	−1,509.6	−1,775.3	−2,673.9	−2,598.2	−2,948.4	−3,028.7	−2,731.8	−3,043.9	−3,238.2	−3,159.0	−3,554.8	....
Trade Balance	78acd	−247.0	−238.4	−750.1	−514.8	−885.9	−1,011.7	−975.1	−1,261.7	−1,346.9	−996.5	−1,142.6	....
Services: Credit	78add	1,063.5	1,117.3	1,024.5	936.2	914.5	830.4	934.5	993.4	1,089.4	1,018.1	1,153.2	....
Services: Debit	78aed	−569.4	−686.8	−868.1	−854.0	−826.0	−694.7	−570.4	−718.7	−765.8	−645.9	−670.9	....
Balance on Goods & Services	78afd	247.0	192.2	−593.7	−432.6	−797.4	−876.0	−611.0	−987.0	−1,023.3	−624.2	−660.4	....
Income: Credit	78agd	3.3	20.9	25.6	21.4	23.0	41.2	31.7	45.0	46.1	35.4	59.6	....
Income: Debit	78ahd	−392.2	−385.7	−350.5	−242.2	−254.9	−214.7	−190.9	−178.1	−167.3	−178.2	−147.8	....
Balance on Gds, Serv. & Inc.	78aid	−141.8	−172.6	−918.6	−653.4	−1,029.4	−1,049.4	−770.2	−1,120.2	−1,144.5	−767.1	−748.5	....
Current Transfers, n.i.e.: Credit	78ajd	276.0	333.7	563.6	585.4	572.5	578.6	685.3	926.6	804.8	632.1	818.6	....
Current Transfers: Debit	78akd	−63.0	−63.2	−45.5	−5.4	....	−4.5	−4.7	−5.8	−1.6	−1.9	−2.3	....
Capital Account, n.i.e.	78bcd	28.1	−.4	−.4	−.4	76.8	84.3	55.4	49.6	51.5	81.2	163.0	....
Capital Account, n.i.e.: Credit	78bad	28.5	—	....	....	76.8	84.3	55.4	49.6	51.5	82.1	163.0	....
Capital Account: Debit	78bbd	−.4	−.4	−.4	−.4	....	....	....	—	—	−.9	—	....
Financial Account, n.i.e.	78bjd	55.1	−41.7	247.9	589.1	362.6	562.1	165.7	269.8	148.1	−173.9	406.3	....
Direct Investment Abroad	78bdd	—	—	—	.5	−2.1	....	....	—	—	−7.4	−2.1	....
Dir. Invest. in Rep. Econ., n.i.e.	78bed	1.6	3.7	32.5	12.7	19.7	11.4	13.8	110.9	5.3	27.6	81.7	....
Portfolio Investment Assets	78bfd	....	....	....	....	....	....	....	−10.9	−6.9	−10.0	−38.6	....
Equity Securities	78bkd	....	....	....	....	....	....	....	−.5	−.9	−2.0	−12.2	....
Debt Securities	78bld	....	....	....	....	....	....	....	−10.4	−6.0	−8.1	−26.4	....
Portfolio Investment Liab., n.i.e.	78bgd	—	—	6.0	7.5	34.2	1.3	−8.0	−3.5	5.5	5.3	.9	....
Equity Securities	78bmd	—	—	6.0	7.5	26.9	1.3	−8.0	−6.0	2.4	3.0	.6	....
Debt Securities	78bnd	—	—	....	....	7.3	....	....	2.5	3.1	2.3	.3	....
Financial Derivatives Assets	78bwd	....	....	....	....	....	....	....	....	....	....	....	....
Financial Derivatives Liabilities	78bxd	....	....	....	....	....	....	....	....	....	....	....	....
Other Investment Assets	78bhd	−31.4	171.1	277.1	628.2	−53.6	−58.6	−89.8	−55.7	−86.4	−132.6	−67.4	....
Monetary Authorities	78bod	....	....	....	....	....	....	....	....	....	....	....	....
General Government	78bpd	....	....	....	....	−4.7	....	....	....	....	....	....	....
Banks	78bqd	−310.7	−61.2	—	—	−44.2	−44.4	−74.3	−5.3	−6.6	−7.8	−11.0	....
Other Sectors	78brd	279.3	232.3	277.1	628.2	−4.7	−14.3	−15.5	−50.4	−79.8	−124.9	−56.4	....
Other Investment Liab., n.i.e.	78bid	85.0	−216.5	−67.7	−59.9	364.6	608.0	249.7	228.9	230.6	−56.7	431.7	....
Monetary Authorities	78bsd	—	—	—	—	—	—	—	—	—	—	—	....
General Government	78btd	152.7	−113.3	−5.7	5.0	−110.9	−109.4	−257.4	243.8	−158.4	−133.7	−81.3	....
Banks	78bud	25.4	32.1	....	....	....	22.6	31.0	....	....	....	....	....
Other Sectors	78bvd	−93.0	−135.3	−61.9	−64.9	475.5	694.8	476.1	−14.9	389.0	77.0	513.0	....
Net Errors and Omissions	78cad	257.5	5.8	11.4	−128.2	32.8	−88.6	−165.5	−127.1	151.7	213.2	−211.9	....
Overall Balance	78cbd	411.8	61.6	−141.6	387.0	15.5	82.6	−34.0	−7.2	10.0	−16.4	425.2	....
Reserves and Related Items	79dad	−411.8	−61.6	141.6	−387.0	−15.5	−82.6	34.0	7.2	−10.0	16.4	−425.2	....
Reserve Assets	79dbd	−477.3	−95.3	174.2	−378.1	70.8	5.4	−9.2	−107.1	−167.8	−1.7	−412.6	....
Use of Fund Credit and Loans	79dcd	−30.6	19.3	−39.1	−24.6	−67.3	−62.8	−59.5	1.3	−23.6	−18.4	16.7	....
Exceptional Financing	79ded	96.2	14.4	6.5	15.8	−19.0	−25.2	102.7	113.0	181.4	36.5	−29.3	....
Government Finance		*Millions of Shillings: Year Ending June 30*											
Deficit (-) or Surplus	80	−14,931	−23,415	−6,172	6,228	† −13,605	−5,304	−2,271	7,461	−13,105	−26,990	−35,769	−4,830
Total Revenue and Grants	81y	78,469	112,413	138,181	156,804	† 156,167	179,055	201,177	188,350	216,393	205,546	225,692	270,905
Revenue	81	69,661	103,250	125,312	145,558	† 150,384	173,783	196,257	184,103	192,313	198,723	210,750	254,681
Grants	81z	8,808	9,163	12,869	11,246	5,783	5,272	4,920	4,247	24,080	6,823	14,942	16,224
Expenditure	82	93,400	135,828	144,353	150,576	† 169,772	184,359	203,448	180,889	229,498	232,536	261,461	275,735
Statistical Discrepancy	80xx	....	....	....	—	† −1,048	64	−178	1	—	535	989	4,882
Total Financing	80h	14,931	23,415	6,172	−6,228	† 14,653	5,240	2,449	−7,462	13,105	26,455	34,780	−51
Domestic	84a	8,571	21,962	16,977	−5,437	† 21,287	12,441	11,194	11,876	616	39,766	46,923	8,809
Foreign	85a	6,360	1,453	−10,805	−791	−6,634	−7,201	−8,745	−19,338	12,489	−13,311	−12,143	−8,860
Total Debt	88	....	....	....	....	463,507	441,561	455,050	550,185	† 605,791	613,739	689,013	747,416
Domestic	88a	....	....	....	....	145,810	145,541	150,499	163,405	† 211,813	235,991	289,377	306,235
Foreign	89a	....	....	....	....	317,697	296,020	304,551	386,780	393,978	377,748	399,636	441,182
National Accounts		*Millions of Shillings*											
Househ.Cons.Expend.,incl.NPISHs.	96f	210,596	250,098	322,622	359,442	453,173	513,249	540,400	757,727	812,269	814,919	868,547	954,649
Government Consumption Expend.	91f	48,307	60,719	69,057	84,523	100,712	113,568	125,943	145,701	159,536	173,297	202,927	216,563
Gross Fixed Capital Formation	93e	56,505	75,616	99,497	104,470	109,873	113,879	112,961	161,714	185,186	177,781	179,248	208,248
Changes in Inventories	93i	2,245	1,683	2,020	3,000	5,400	6,210	7,142	6,826	11,596	−8,404	19,519	24,596
Exports of Goods and Services	90c	134,918	148,225	152,596	172,459	174,846	171,895	189,265	214,831	228,054	252,207	281,394	357,243
Imports of Goods and Services (-)	98c	118,958	135,641	180,139	195,155	220,769	224,772	232,233	292,493	345,899	326,340	360,960	473,982
Gross Domestic Product (GDP)	99b	333,616	400,700	465,654	528,740	623,235	694,029	743,479	967,838	1,025,918	1,038,764	1,141,780	1,273,716
Net Primary Income from Abroad	98.n	−24,380	−23,074	−19,832	−15,837	−13,623	−10,468	−11,196	−10,140	−9,523	−11,249	−6,696	−7,342
Gross National Income (GNI)	99a	309,233	377,626	445,821	512,130	609,730	681,652	732,283	957,698	1,016,395	1,027,515	1,135,084	1,266,374
GDP Volume 1982 Prices	99b.p	100,411	103,054	107,595	112,058	115,418	115,736	111,573	119,454	....	....	....	....
GDP Volume 2001 Prices	99b.p	....	....	....	....	....	....	....	982,855	1,025,918	1,029,978	1,058,470	1,104,356
GDP Volume (2000=100)	99bvp	84.1	86.3	90.1	93.8	96.6	96.9	93.4	† 100.0	104.4	104.8	107.7	112.4
GDP Deflator (2000=100)	99bip	41.0	48.0	53.4	58.2	66.6	74.0	82.2	100.0	101.6	102.4	109.5	117.1
Population		*Millions: Midyear Estimates*											
Population	99z	† 25.74	26.49	27.23	27.94	† 28.64	29.33	30.01	30.69	31.36	32.04	32.73	33.47

Korea, Republic of 542

		1993	1994	1995	1996	1997	1998	1999	2000	2001	2002	2003	2004
Exchange Rates					*Won per SDR: End of Period*								
Market Rate	aa	1,109.97	1,151.38	1,151.58	1,213.93	2,286.98	1,695.27	1,561.92	1,647.53	1,650.71	1,612.66	1,772.17	1,607.52
				Won per US Dollar: End of Period (ae) Period Average (rf)									
Market Rate	ae	808.10	788.70	774.70	844.20	1,695.00	1,204.00	1,138.00	1,264.50	1,313.50	1,186.20	1,192.60	1,035.10
Market Rate	rf	802.67	803.45	771.27	804.45	951.29	1,401.44	1,188.82	1,130.96	1,290.99	1,251.09	1,191.61	1,145.32
Fund Position					*Millions of SDRs: End of Period*								
Quota	2f.s	799.6	799.6	799.6	799.6	799.6	799.6	1,633.6	1,633.6	1,633.6	1,633.6	1,633.6	1,633.6
SDRs	1b.s	42.3	52.3	65.7	82.3	43.6	8.1	.5	2.7	2.7	8.7	14.2	21.1
Reserve Position in the Fund	1c.s	339.2	363.6	438.5	474.3	443.7	.1	208.6	208.6	208.8	384.0	507.7	507.7
Total Fund Cred.&Loans Outstg	2tl	—	—	—	—	8,200.0	12,000.0	4,462.5	4,462.5	—	—	—	—
International Liquidity					*Millions of US Dollars Unless Otherwise Indicated: End of Period*								
Total Reserves minus Gold	1l.d	20,228.2	25,639.3	32,677.7	34,037.1	20,367.9	51,974.5	73,987.3	96,130.5	102,753.3	121,345.2	155,284.2	198,996.6
SDRs	1b.d	58.1	76.3	97.7	118.4	58.8	11.4	.7	3.5	3.3	11.8	21.1	32.8
Reserve Position in the Fund	1c.d	465.9	530.8	651.8	682.0	598.7	.1	286.3	271.8	262.4	522.0	754.4	788.4
Foreign Exchange	1d.d	19,704.2	25,032.1	31,928.2	33,236.7	19,710.4	51,963.0	73,700.3	95,855.1	102,487.5	120,811.4	154,508.8	198,175.3
Gold (Million Fine Troy Ounces)	1ad	.324	.325	.327	.327	.335	.435	.437	.439	.442	.444	.449	.454
Gold (National Valuation)	1and	33.3	33.6	34.4	36.0	36.9	66.3	67.1	67.6	68.3	69.2	70.9	72.3
Monetary Authorities: Other Liab	4..d	95.4	442.4	158.6	381.1	140.1	160.9	307.6	286.1	4,877.1	8,371.9	6,952.5	19,906.1
Deposit Money Banks: Assets	7a.d	16,211.0	20,937.9	27,806.5	33,909.6	32,748.7	34,309.6	34,748.2	34,562.3	28,086.2	25,851.3	30,923.2	39,510.6
Liabilities	7b.d	14,795.8	21,170.3	31,446.0	43,181.5	27,975.3	29,455.3	27,546.5	24,804.8	21,289.5	36,680.7	43,689.0	50,731.1
Other Banking Insts.: Assets	7e.d	5,365.0	7,897.0	4,136.0	7,144.0	10,761.0	10,027.0	8,975.0	11,926.0	13,058.0	17,371.0	....	....
Liabilities	7f.d	15,834.0	21,692.0	21,816.0	26,857.0	29,661.0	22,466.0	18,033.0	15,222.0	13,387.0	16,521.0	....	....
Monetary Authorities					*Billions of Won: End of Period*								
Foreign Assets	11	16,672	20,880	25,390	28,173	29,227	64,832	85,342	121,558	142,589	155,362	194,033	228,060
Claims on Central Government	12a	2,659	2,628	1,951	2,235	5,562	5,961	6,382	4,958	5,570	5,091	6,110	4,514
Claims on Official Entities	12bx	570	570	570	370	2,370	8,640	2,370	2,370	2,370	2,370	1,370	—
Claims on Deposit Money Banks	12e	29,169	28,971	28,076	24,378	62,442	37,830	26,003	15,563	11,637	6,849	8,117	8,298
Reserve Money	14	23,080	25,204	29,306	25,723	22,519	20,703	28,487	28,238	32,827	37,987	40,749	38,792
of which: Currency Outside DMBs	14a	12,109	13,127	15,061	15,453	15,448	13,670	19,475	17,636	18,702	19,863	20,111	20,772
Liabs.of the Central Bank:Securities	16ac	27,148	29,114	29,598	29,068	26,701	53,580	61,389	79,142	93,120	104,929	133,938	170,192
Foreign Liabilities	16c	77	349	123	322	18,991	20,537	7,320	7,714	6,406	9,931	8,292	20,605
Central Government Deposits	16d	5,059	6,477	6,917	6,684	5,410	5,917	9,126	10,608	7,347	11,178	5,482	1,196
Other Items (Net)	17r	−6,293	−8,095	−9,956	−6,640	25,980	16,526	13,775	18,747	22,466	5,647	21,170	10,087
Deposit Money Banks					*Billions of Won: End of Period*								
Reserves	20	10,836	11,947	14,092	10,181	6,798	6,610	8,958	10,434	14,063	17,904	20,427	17,793
Claims on Mon.Author.:Securities	20c	8,865	12,700	15,775	18,419	20,996	29,559	27,375	33,073	36,238	43,515	51,019	53,923
Foreign Assets	21	13,100	16,514	21,542	28,627	55,509	41,309	39,543	43,704	36,891	30,665	36,879	40,897
Claims on Central Government	22a	4,912	5,196	5,373	4,897	6,341	13,564	21,372	23,677	22,959	24,369	29,538	37,369
Claims on Private Sector	22d	144,828	173,903	200,769	240,936	293,812	318,667	383,884	457,258	520,733	628,230	684,192	693,139
Demand Deposits	24	17,344	19,593	23,672	24,221	19,331	21,569	25,139	29,193	34,918	43,265	45,226	47,424
Time, Savings,& Fgn.Currency Dep	25	83,178	100,668	115,072	138,769	168,482	222,926	284,916	366,041	414,031	455,741	488,084	481,575
Bonds	26ab	2,270	2,923	4,782	6,167	5,954	17,072	11,287	14,699	19,920	45,236	54,005	66,560
Restricted Deposits	26b	635	792	904	988	1,214	772	803	1,030	908	974	1,159	1,068
Foreign Liabilities	26c	11,957	16,697	24,361	36,454	47,418	35,464	31,348	31,366	27,964	43,511	52,104	52,512
Central Government Deposits	26d	424	286	948	1,632	3,290	4,499	5,493	9,442	10,446	12,743	18,968	20,133
Central Govt. Lending Funds	26f	9,234	11,032	13,493	14,828	23,193	26,703	29,946	29,182	29,340	25,461	25,323	22,947
Credit from Monetary Authorities	26g	29,420	29,256	28,429	24,460	63,076	38,738	26,242	17,191	13,515	10,591	12,682	9,060
Capital Accounts	27a	17,110	20,406	22,523	24,877	22,673	21,891	28,152	29,883	34,792	38,696	41,158	46,056
Other Items (Net)	27r	10,970	18,605	23,366	30,663	28,825	20,075	37,807	40,120	45,051	68,465	83,347	95,787
Monetary Survey					*Billions of Won: End of Period*								
Foreign Assets (Net)	31n	17,739	20,347	22,448	20,024	18,327	50,140	86,217	126,182	145,110	132,585	170,517	195,841
Domestic Credit	32	157,358	186,520	213,688	255,240	314,581	351,179	412,126	479,780	546,056	645,391	705,594	722,700
Claims on Central Govt. (Net)	32an	2,089	1,061	−541	−1,183	3,204	9,108	13,135	8,585	10,736	5,539	11,198	20,555
Claims on Official Entities	32bx	570	570	570	370	2,370	8,640	2,370	2,370	2,370	2,370	1,370	—
Claims on Private Sector	32d	154,699	184,888	213,658	256,054	309,008	333,431	396,621	468,825	532,951	637,482	693,025	702,145
Money	34	29,041	32,511	38,873	39,542	35,036	35,583	44,375	46,997	53,506	63,151	65,481	68,423
Quasi-Money	35	83,178	100,668	115,073	138,770	168,495	222,956	284,943	366,052	414,072	455,754	488,102	481,604
Bonds	36ab	20,553	19,338	18,606	16,817	11,659	41,092	45,301	60,767	76,802	106,650	136,924	182,829
Restricted Deposits	36b	635	792	904	988	1,214	772	803	1,030	908	974	1,159	1,068
Central Govt. Lending Funds	36f	9,234	11,032	13,493	14,828	23,193	26,703	29,946	29,182	29,340	25,461	25,323	22,947
Other Items (Net)	37r	32,455	42,526	49,187	64,320	93,311	74,214	92,975	101,934	116,539	125,986	159,121	161,670
Money plus Quasi-Money	35l	112,219	133,179	153,946	178,312	203,532	258,538	329,317	413,049	467,577	518,904	553,583	550,027
Other Banking Institutions													
Development Institutions					*Billions of Won: End of Period*								
Claims on Private Sector	42d	23,874	26,771	30,616	35,600	48,097	55,361	55,283	58,351	55,843	51,933	56,062	62,354
Bonds	46ab	13,921	16,617	19,639	23,764	34,782	36,096	34,666	35,251	34,317	32,620	35,584	39,032
Counterpart Funds	46e	1	1	1	1	1	1	1	—	—	—	—	—
Central Govt. Lending Funds	46f	3,045	2,967	3,018	3,336	3,822	14,549	15,380	16,889	14,533	13,644	10,199	9,518
Credit from Deposit Money Banks	46h	5,110	5,450	5,710	5,564	2,130	2,397	1,358	704	1,594	560	662	688
Capital Accounts	47a	1,382	1,615	1,614	1,814	2,909	4,486	6,247	3,773	6,931	6,926	7,688	10,129
Other Items (Net)	47r	414	121	634	1,122	4,454	−2,168	−2,367	1,734	−1,532	−1,817	1,929	2,988
Trust Accounts of Coml. Banks					*Billions of Won: End of Period*								
Claims on Private Sector	42d.g	112,416	143,539	182,319	216,569	253,305	307,920	273,872	178,537	181,683	197,589	152,187	146,529
Claims on Deposit Money Banks	42e.g	1,000	1,118	1,475	1,982	2,797	8,570	9,366	6,787	10,967	5,972	10,671	6,522
Quasi-Monetary Liabilities	45..g	71,319	93,415	124,891	151,093	171,456	138,941	115,360	77,594	81,330	73,713	58,135	47,899
Other Items (Net)	47r.g	42,096	51,242	58,903	67,458	84,646	177,549	167,878	107,730	111,319	129,848	104,723	105,152
Postal Savings Deposits	45..h	4,078	5,948	5,321	6,421	7,280	11,491	14,980	22,150	26,111	29,400	35,985	32,808

2005, International Monetary Fund : *International Financial Statistics Yearbook*

373

		1993	1994	1995	1996	1997	1998	1999	2000	2001	2002	2003	2004
Nonbank Financial Institutions							*Billions of Won: End of Period*						
Cash.................................	40..s	3,186	3,633	5,984	8,310	12,071	7,906	5,836	6,638	6,602	3,686	3,511	3,797
Claims on Central Government........	42a.s	452	269	107	123	163	510	1,677	2,571	4,536	12,202	18,850	27,894
Claims on Private Sector.................	42d.s	33,091	38,931	43,207	51,210	55,510	43,442	42,937	53,578	58,010	65,418	70,299	71,893
Real Estate..............................	42h.s	3,842	4,504	5,124	6,173	7,333	8,703	9,752	10,113	9,757	9,435	9,313	9,774
Incr.in Total Assets(Within Per.).......	49z.s	5,607	7,230	10,951	13,101	12,461	357	15,997	13,896	16,280	25,095	20,435	26,662
Liquid Liabilities....................	55l	184,430	228,909	278,174	327,515	370,197	401,064	453,822	506,155	568,417	618,332	644,192	626,937
Interest Rates							*Percent Per Annum*						
Discount Rate (End of Period)..........	60	5.0	5.0	5.0	5.0	5.0	3.0	3.0	3.0	2.5	2.5	2.5	2.0
Money Market Rate.....................	60b	12.1	12.5	12.6	12.4	13.2	15.0	5.0	5.2	4.7	4.2	4.0	3.6
Corporate Bond Rate....................	60bc	12.6	12.9	13.8	11.8	13.4	15.1	8.9	9.4	7.1	6.6	5.4	4.7
Deposit Rate...........................	60l	8.6	8.5	8.8	7.5	† 10.8	13.3	7.9	7.9	5.8	4.9	4.3	3.9
Lending Rate...........................	60p	8.6	8.5	9.0	8.8	† 11.9	15.3	9.4	8.5	7.7	6.8	6.2	5.9
Government Bond Yield..................	61	12.1	12.3	12.4	10.9	11.7	12.8	8.7	8.5	6.7	6.5	4.9	4.5
Prices, Production, Labor							*Index Numbers (2000=100): Period Averages*						
Share Prices...........................	62	100.2	132.2	125.8	113.6	89.2	55.8	109.5	100.0	78.3	103.5	92.9	113.9
Producer Prices........................	63	77.4	79.5	83.2	85.9	89.2	100.1	98.0	100.0	99.5	99.2	101.4	107.6
Consumer Prices........................	64	74.2	78.8	82.3	86.4	90.2	97.0	97.8	100.0	104.1	106.9	110.7	114.7
Wages: Monthly Earnings...............	65ey	62.2	70.1	78.0	87.2	93.4	91.0	92.1	100.0	105.8	118.5	128.7	140.9
Industrial Production..................	66	52.2	58.0	64.9	70.4	73.7	69.0	85.6	100.0	100.7	108.8	114.2	126.1
Manufacturing Employment.............	67ey	109.9	110.8	112.2	110.1	105.7	91.2	93.8	100.0	99.4	98.8	97.9	99.9
							Number in Thousands: Period Averages						
Labor Force............................	67d	19,806	20,353	20,845	21,288	21,782	21,428	21,666	22,069	22,417	22,877	22,916	....
Employment............................	67e	19,253	19,837	20,379	20,764	21,048	19,926	20,281	21,061	21,362	22,169	....	....
Unemployment.........................	67c	550	489	419	425	557	1,463	1,353	913	845	710	777	813
Unemployment Rate (%)................	67r	2.8	2.4	2.0	2.0	2.6	6.8	6.3	4.1	3.8	3.1	3.4	3.5
Intl. Transactions & Positions							*Millions of US Dollars*						
Exports..................................	70..d	82,236	96,013	125,058	129,715	136,164	132,313	143,686	172,268	150,439	162,471	193,817	253,845
Imports, c.i.f...........................	71..d	83,800	102,348	135,119	150,339	144,616	93,282	119,725	160,481	141,098	152,126	178,827	224,463
							2000=100						
Volume of Exports.....................	72	33.2	37.7	46.1	54.1	62.1	74.0	82.9	100.0	100.7	114.1	133.4	163.4
Volume of Imports.....................	73	48.5	59.4	73.7	85.2	86.9	65.1	84.0	100.0	97.7	109.7	117.7	131.8
Unit Value of Exports..................	74	104.2	107.0	110.3	99.9	107.6	126.4	104.7	100.0	99.2	91.9	89.7	92.7
Unit Value of Imports..................	75	78.8	78.2	79.7	79.7	88.1	108.3	91.8	100.0	103.9	96.8	100.7	108.7
Export Prices...........................	76	89.1	91.6	92.9	89.0	94.8	124.5	101.0	100.0	96.2	89.5	87.5	92.9
Import Prices...........................	76.x	68.0	70.7	74.8	75.3	82.4	105.7	92.9	100.0	103.5	97.1	98.9	108.9
Balance of Payments							*Millions of US Dollars: Minus Sign Indicates Debit*						
Current Account, n.i.e...................	78ald	821	−4,024	−8,665	−23,210	−8,384	40,371	24,522	12,251	8,033	5,394	12,321	27,613
Goods: Exports f.o.b...................	78aad	82,098	94,983	124,934	130,038	138,731	132,251	145,375	176,221	151,478	163,414	197,637	257,745
Goods: Imports f.o.b..................	78abd	−79,948	−98,000	−129,298	−145,115	−141,986	−90,586	−116,912	−159,267	−137,990	−148,637	−175,476	−219,584
Trade Balance.......................	78acd	2,150	−3,017	−4,365	−15,077	−3,256	41,665	28,463	16,954	13,488	14,777	22,161	38,161
Services: Credit........................	78add	12,950	16,805	22,827	23,412	26,301	25,565	26,529	30,534	29,055	28,388	32,702	41,429
Services: Debit.........................	78aed	−15,076	−18,606	−25,806	−29,592	−29,502	−24,541	−27,180	−33,381	−32,927	−36,585	−40,313	−50,198
Balance on Goods & Services.......	78afd	24	−4,818	−7,343	−21,257	−6,456	42,689	27,812	14,106	9,616	6,580	14,550	29,392
Income: Credit........................	78agd	2,509	2,835	3,486	3,576	3,788	2,675	3,245	6,375	6,650	6,900	7,111	8,722
Income: Debit.........................	78ahd	−2,900	−3,322	−4,788	−5,480	−6,338	−8,313	−8,404	−8,797	−7,848	−6,467	−6,515	−7,997
Balance on Gds, Serv. & Inc.......	78aid	−367	−5,305	−8,646	−23,161	−9,007	37,051	22,653	11,685	8,418	7,012	15,146	30,117
Current Transfers, n.i.e.: Credit......	78ajd	3,382	3,672	4,104	4,279	5,288	6,737	6,421	6,500	6,687	7,314	7,879	9,179
Current Transfers: Debit...............	78akd	−2,194	−2,392	−4,123	−4,328	−4,665	−3,416	−4,552	−5,934	−7,072	−8,932	−10,703	−11,683
Capital Account, n.i.e..................	78bcd	−475	−437	−488	−598	−608	171	−389	−615	−731	−1,087	−1,402	−1,773
Capital Account, n.i.e.: Credit.......	78bad	2	8	15	19	17	464	95	98	42	47	53	72
Capital Account: Debit................	78bbd	−477	−445	−502	−617	−624	−293	−484	−713	−773	−1,133	−1,455	−1,845
Financial Account, n.i.e................	78bjd	3,216	10,732	17,273	24,009	−9,150	−8,381	12,709	12,725	3,025	7,338	14,530	10,092
Direct Investment Abroad..............	78bdd	−1,340	−2,461	−3,552	−4,585	−4,404	−4,740	−4,198	−4,999	−2,420	−2,617	−3,429	−4,792
Dir. Invest. in Rep. Econ., n.i.e.......	78bed	588	809	1,776	2,325	2,844	5,412	9,333	9,283	3,528	2,392	3,222	8,189
Portfolio Investment Assets...........	78bfd	−986	−2,481	−2,907	−6,413	1,076	−1,999	1,282	−520	−5,521	−5,032	−4,333	−9,801
Equity Securities......................	78bkd	−204	−382	−238	−653	−320	42	−271	−480	−492	−1,460	−1,993	−3,664
Debt Securities........................	78bld	−781	−2,098	−2,669	−5,760	1,395	−2,041	1,553	−40	−5,029	−3,571	−2,340	−6,137
Portfolio Investment Liab., n.i.e.......	78bgd	11,088	8,713	14,619	21,514	13,308	775	7,908	12,697	12,227	5,378	22,653	19,007
Equity Securities......................	78bmd	6,615	3,614	4,219	5,954	2,525	3,856	12,072	13,094	10,266	395	14,213	9,483
Debt Securities........................	78bnd	4,473	5,099	10,400	15,561	10,783	−3,081	−4,164	−397	1,962	4,983	8,439	9,524
Financial Derivatives Assets...........	78bwd	448	452	623	414	932	412	401	532	463	1,288	888	2,291
Financial Derivatives Liabilities.......	78bxd	−535	−565	−744	−331	−1,021	−1,066	−915	−711	−586	−926	−1,248	−2,228
Other Investment Assets...............	78bhd	−4,592	−7,369	−13,991	−13,487	−13,568	6,693	−2,606	−2,289	7,085	2,557	−3,496	−7,001
Monetary Authorities................	78bod	−42	−72	−36	—	−86	−36	−164	−44	−38	−40	−48	−3
General Government.................	78bpd	−625	−296	−156	−543	−149	−46	−169	−155	−509	−311	−27	−1,382
Banks.................................	78bqd	−3,993	−5,061	−9,199	−8,173	−8,336	6,970	−203	−1,219	8,755	3,087	−3,918	−5,051
Other Sectors........................	78brd	68	−1,940	−4,600	−4,770	−4,996	−194	−2,071	−871	−1,124	−179	496	−566
Other Investment Liab., n.i.e...........	78bid	−1,455	13,632	21,450	24,571	−8,317	−13,868	1,502	−1,268	−11,751	4,297	274	4,427
Monetary Authorities................	78bsd	15	−2	−10	−29	23	148	25	28	63	−52	−35	−9
General Government.................	78btd	−1,842	−335	−593	−493	4,671	4,628	3,309	110	−397	−1,436	−5,239	−2,359
Banks.................................	78bud	720	7,368	11,389	9,952	−9,785	−6,233	1,418	−4,538	−4,147	6,257	2,561	2,120
Other Sectors........................	78bvd	−348	6,600	10,664	15,142	−3,226	−12,288	−3,372	3,132	−7,271	−473	2,988	4,675
Net Errors and Omissions................	78cad	−553	−1,657	−1,081	1,214	−4,839	−6,231	−3,581	−571	2,951	124	342	2,743
Overall Balance.....................	78cbd	3,009	4,614	7,039	1,416	−22,979	25,930	33,260	23,790	13,278	11,769	25,791	38,675
Reserves and Related Items.............	79dad	−3,009	−4,614	−7,039	−1,416	22,979	−25,930	−33,260	−23,790	−13,278	−11,769	−25,791	−38,675
Reserve Assets........................	79dbd	−3,009	−4,614	−7,039	−1,416	11,875	−30,968	−22,989	−23,790	−7,586	−11,769	−25,791	−38,675
Use of Fund Credit and Loans........	79dcd	—	—	—	—	11,104	5,038	−10,271	—	−5,692	—	—	—
Exceptional Financing.................	79ded	....	....	....	....	....	....	....	....	....	....	....	....

Korea, Republic of 542

		1993	1994	1995	1996	1997	1998	1999	2000	2001	2002	2003	2004
International Investment Position						*Millions of US Dollars*							
Assets...	79aad	46,762	60,612	....	....	....	....	....	....	186,577	208,527	256,643	....
Direct Investment Abroad..............	79abd	5,555	7,630	....	....	....	....	....	....	19,967	20,735	24,986	....
Portfolio Investment......................	79acd	522	992	....	....	....	....	....	....	7,813	11,492	17,343	....
Equity Securities.......................	79add	—	—	....	....	....	....	....	....	1,301	1,794	3,416	....
Debt Securities.........................	79aed	522	992	....	....	....	....	....	....	6,513	9,698	13,927	....
Financial Derivatives.....................	79ald	—	—	....	....	....	....	....	....	414	917	777	....
Other Investment..........................	79afd	20,423	26,317	....	....	....	....	....	....	55,561	53,970	58,182	....
Monetary Authorities.................	79agd	—	—	....	....	....	....	....	....	2,446	2,878	2,942	....
General Government..................	79ahd	—	—	....	....	....	....	....	....	973	1,111	1,211	....
Banks...	79aid	15,389	19,944	....	....	....	....	....	....	40,059	40,084	45,629	....
Other Sectors............................	79ajd	5,034	6,373	....	....	....	....	....	....	12,083	9,898	8,401	....
Reserve Assets...............................	79akd	20,262	25,673	....	....	....	....	....	....	102,822	121,414	155,355	....
Liabilities......................................	79lad	53,706	69,830	....	....	....	....	....	....	249,964	279,463	342,840	....
Dir. Invest. in Rep. Economy..........	79lbd	6,984	7,715	....	....	....	....	....	....	53,208	62,658	66,070	....
Portfolio Investment......................	79lcd	22,438	29,714	....	....	....	....	....	....	105,593	116,636	168,250	....
Equity Securities.......................	79ldd	9,316	11,796	....	....	....	....	....	....	69,968	77,017	120,071	....
Debt Securities.........................	79led	13,122	17,918	....	....	....	....	....	....	35,624	39,619	48,179	....
Financial Derivatives.....................	79lld	—	—	....	....	....	....	....	....	417	936	899	....
Other Investment..........................	79lfd	24,284	32,401	....	....	....	....	....	....	90,747	99,233	107,622	....
Monetary Authorities.................	79lgd	208	207	....	....	....	....	....	....	1,515	1,458	1,226	....
General Government..................	79lhd	—	—	....	....	....	....	....	....	17,891	16,662	11,506	....
Banks...	79lid	24,076	32,194	....	....	....	....	....	....	38,661	47,035	53,524	....
Other Sectors............................	79ljd	—	—	....	....	....	....	....	....	32,680	34,078	41,367	....
Government Finance					*Billions of Won: Year Ending December 31*								
Deficit (-) or Surplus......................	80	1,704	984	1,035	431	−5,747	....	....	....	....	....	....	....
Revenue...	81	50,750	61,109	72,087	84,272	91,979	....	....	....	....	....	....	....
Grants Received.............................	81z	—	—	—	—	—	....	....	....	....	....	....	....
Expenditure...................................	82	45,010	53,887	62,320	72,600	79,004	....	....	....	....	....	....	....
Lending Minus Repayments...........	83	4,036	6,238	8,732	11,241	18,722	....	....	....	....	....	....	....
Financing													
Domestic.......................................	84a	−1,257	−589	−678	−136	−1,214	....	....	....	....	....	....	....
Foreign..	85a	−447	−395	−357	−295	6,961	....	....	....	....	....	....	....
Debt...	88	28,998	30,466	31,537	33,687	47,045	....	....	....	....	....	....	....
Domestic.......................................	88a	23,504	24,800	26,296	28,636	31,724	....	....	....	....	....	....	....
Foreign..	89a	5,494	5,666	5,241	5,051	15,321	....	....	....	....	....	....	....
National Accounts						*Billions of Won*							
Househ.Cons.Expend.,incl.NPISHs....	96f	149,686	177,904	208,462	236,194	258,636	238,811	274,934	312,301	343,417	381,063	389,177	400,696
Government Consumption Expend...	91f	34,413	38,942	44,687	52,138	56,749	61,981	65,174	70,098	80,298	88,512	96,203	104,961
Gross Fixed Capital Formation.........	93e	105,623	123,899	148,820	168,157	174,961	146,914	157,407	179,908	183,792	199,047	216,807	229,691
Changes in Inventories...................	93i	−1,760	1,825	1,410	6,225	1,706	−25,903	−3,199	−494	−1,315	−41	292	5,544
Exports of Goods and Services.........	90c	77,112	90,624	114,978	124,988	159,091	223,481	206,842	236,210	235,187	241,209	274,995	343,229
Imports of Goods and Services (-).....	98c	75,975	93,149	119,336	140,574	162,056	161,180	171,437	217,979	220,914	231,765	257,728	309,366
Statistical Discrepancy....................	99bs	1,576	164	−183	1,468	2,049	−1	−221	−1,377	1,657	6,238	4,928	3,690
Gross Domestic Product (GDP)........	99b	290,676	340,208	398,838	448,596	491,135	484,103	529,500	578,665	622,123	684,263	724,675	778,445
Net Primary Income from Abroad.....	98.n	−588	−865	−1,379	−1,740	−2,677	−7,857	−6,144	−2,505	−1,095	806	745	1,023
Gross National Income (GNI)...........	99a	290,088	339,343	397,459	446,856	488,457	476,245	523,355	576,160	621,028	685,069	725,420	779,468
Consumption of Fixed Capital..........	99cf	31,855	36,221	48,131	56,784	66,147	74,349	79,006	83,416	88,113	91,113	98,851	104,013
GDP Volume 2000 Prices.................	99b.p	394,216	427,868	467,099	499,790	523,035	487,184	533,399	578,665	600,866	642,748	662,655	693,424
GDP Volume (2000=100)...............	99bvp	† 68.1	73.9	80.7	86.4	90.4	84.2	92.2	100.0	103.8	111.1	114.5	119.8
GDP Deflator (2000=100)...............	99bip	73.7	79.5	85.4	89.8	93.9	99.4	99.3	100.0	103.5	106.5	109.4	112.3
					Millions: Midyear Estimates								
Population...............................	99z	44.16	44.59	45.01	45.41	45.79	46.15	46.48	46.78	47.04	47.27	47.46	47.64

		1993	1994	1995	1996	1997	1998	1999	2000	2001	2002	2003	2004
Exchange Rates						*SDRs per Dinar: End of Period*							
Official Rate	ac	2.4396	2.2824	2.2504	2.3190	2.4308	2.3551	2.3953	2.5130	2.5846	2.4554	2.2835	2.1850
						US Dollars per Dinar: End of Period (ag) Period Average (rh)							
Official Rate	ag	3.3510	3.3320	3.3453	3.3346	3.2798	3.3161	3.2875	3.2742	3.2481	3.3382	3.3933	3.3933
Official Rate	rh	3.3147	3.3600	3.3509	3.3399	3.2966	3.2814	3.2850	3.2600	3.2607	3.2906	3.3557	3.3933
Fund Position						*Millions of SDRs: End of Period*							
Quota	2f.s	995.2	995.2	995.2	995.2	995.2	995.2	1,381.1	1,381.1	1,381.1	1,381.1	1,381.1	1,381.1
SDRs	1b.s	49.1	55.0	61.3	68.2	74.1	82.5	53.7	69.8	85.9	97.7	107.5	117.1
Reserve Position in the Fund	1c.s	167.8	142.6	139.0	136.5	167.5	244.8	368.3	373.8	476.1	528.3	522.7	458.9
of which: Outstg.Fund Borrowing	2c	—	—	—	—	—	31.8	—	—	—	—	—	—
International Liquidity						*Millions of US Dollars Unless Otherwise Indicated: End of Period*							
Total Reserves minus Gold	1l.d	4,214.1	3,500.7	3,560.8	3,515.1	3,451.8	3,947.1	4,823.7	7,082.4	9,897.3	9,208.1	7,577.0	8,241.9
SDRs	1b.d	67.4	80.3	91.1	98.0	100.0	116.2	73.8	90.9	108.0	132.9	159.8	181.8
Reserve Position in the Fund	1c.d	230.5	208.2	206.6	196.3	226.1	344.6	505.5	487.0	598.3	718.2	776.8	712.7
Foreign Exchange	1d.d	3,916.3	3,212.2	3,263.2	3,220.8	3,125.7	3,486.3	4,244.4	6,504.4	9,191.1	8,357.0	6,640.5	7,347.4
Gold (Million Fine Troy Ounces)	1ad	2.539	2.539	2.539	2.539	2.539	2.539	2.539	2.539	2.539	2.539	2.539	2.539
Gold (National Valuation)	1and	106.2	105.6	106.0	105.7	104.0	105.1	104.2	103.9	103.1	105.9	107.7	107.7
Deposit Money Banks: Assets	7a.d	5,946.6	6,419.1	7,127.7	7,230.3	6,945.2	5,928.5	5,873.8	6,444.9	6,582.6	8,148.5	8,229.9	10,831.5
Liabilities	7b.d	1,803.2	2,377.0	2,239.0	2,536.6	4,009.2	3,595.3	3,971.0	3,913.3	5,101.3	6,782.3	6,531.6	6,183.4
Other Financial Insts.: Assets	7e.d	3,772.2	3,706.5	3,666.7	3,556.0	4,339.1	5,498.4	6,013.2	7,184.2	6,795.5	7,001.5	8,235.1	8,901.0
Liab	7f.d	1,790.8	1,533.7	1,584.6	1,592.9	2,330.6	3,504.4	3,693.2	4,582.2	4,628.6	4,637.1	5,182.7	5,354.0
Monetary Authorities						*Millions of Dinars: End of Period*							
Foreign Assets	11	1,151.4	1,168.2	1,124.1	1,112.0	1,108.7	1,186.3	1,476.1	2,157.3	3,037.7	2,748.0	2,216.5	2,405.8
Claims on Central Government	12a	87.1	59.2	2.3	41.2	39.3	.1	45.1	—	—	—	—	—
Claims on Deposit Money Banks	12e	142.4	90.8	—	—	6.0	—	—	14.0	—	—	—	—
Reserve Money	14	503.4	504.0	470.9	474.7	426.9	448.4	582.9	534.6	521.4	590.2	690.1	782.3
of which: Currency Outside DMBs	14a	355.2	351.3	311.5	350.1	345.3	348.7	442.9	416.6	401.2	442.2	494.1	531.0
Central Government Deposits	16d	497.2	368.8	163.9	265.7	298.7	229.0	450.8	547.8	602.3	381.9	440.7	681.2
Capital Accounts	17a	210.3	209.7	193.7	188.5	189.6	186.1	186.5	188.0	187.5	195.9	218.5	234.9
Other Items (Net)	17r	170.0	236.1	298.0	224.2	238.9	322.9	301.0	900.9	1,726.5	1,580.0	867.2	707.4
Deposit Money Banks						*Millions of Dinars: End of Period*							
Reserves	20	146.0	151.8	158.1	123.0	79.0	98.0	141.2	119.3	119.5	143.7	199.4	251.2
Foreign Assets	21	1,774.6	1,926.5	2,130.7	2,168.3	2,117.6	1,787.8	1,786.7	1,968.4	2,026.6	2,441.0	2,425.3	3,192.0
Claims on Central Government	22a	5,989.9	5,881.7	5,760.3	4,901.3	4,782.8	4,641.5	4,619.6	4,246.8	4,127.4	4,118.2	4,009.7	3,768.7
Claims on Private Sector	22d	1,240.9	1,703.2	2,436.3	3,173.1	4,324.2	4,801.6	5,015.1	5,251.7	6,125.3	6,953.4	8,419.4	9,867.0
Demand Deposits	24	758.8	774.7	873.5	892.5	902.2	794.7	928.5	1,051.1	1,240.2	1,624.6	2,117.4	2,643.3
Time and Savings Deposits	25	5,282.5	5,616.9	6,189.8	6,088.3	6,368.5	6,413.1	6,306.6	6,695.5	7,567.1	7,579.6	7,789.7	8,481.0
Foreign Liabilities	26c	538.1	713.4	669.3	760.7	1,222.4	1,084.2	1,207.9	1,195.2	1,570.5	2,031.7	1,924.9	1,822.2
Central Government Deposits	26d	555.9	421.3	459.4	374.1	343.6	256.8	195.0	185.1	230.9	299.4	315.2	842.0
Credit from Monetary Authorities	26g	196.4	112.0	6.0	—	6.0	.7	—	14.0	—	—	—	—
Capital Accounts	27a	1,059.8	1,090.1	1,201.5	1,259.0	1,407.8	1,469.9	1,511.9	1,776.3	1,681.9	1,763.4	2,008.7	2,311.3
Other Items (Net)	27r	760.0	935.0	1,086.2	991.2	1,053.1	1,309.7	1,412.4	669.0	108.1	357.6	898.0	979.2
Monetary Survey						*Millions of Dinars: End of Period*							
Foreign Assets (Net)	31n	2,387.9	2,381.3	2,585.5	2,519.6	2,003.9	1,889.9	2,054.9	2,930.5	3,493.8	3,157.2	2,717.0	3,775.6
Domestic Credit	32	6,264.8	6,854.0	7,575.6	7,475.8	8,504.0	8,957.4	9,034.0	8,765.6	9,419.5	10,390.3	11,673.3	12,112.5
Claims on Central Govt. (Net)	32an	5,023.9	5,150.8	5,139.3	4,302.7	4,179.8	4,155.8	4,018.9	3,513.9	3,294.2	3,437.0	3,253.9	2,245.5
Claims on Private Sector	32d	1,240.9	1,703.2	2,436.3	3,173.1	4,324.2	4,801.6	5,015.1	5,251.7	6,125.3	6,953.4	8,419.4	9,867.0
Money	34	1,114.0	1,126.0	1,185.0	1,242.6	1,247.5	1,143.4	1,371.4	1,467.7	1,641.4	2,066.7	2,611.5	3,174.2
Quasi-Money	35	5,282.5	5,616.9	6,189.8	6,088.3	6,368.5	6,413.1	6,306.6	6,695.5	7,567.1	7,579.6	7,789.7	8,481.0
Other Items (Net)	37r	2,256.3	2,493.0	2,786.7	2,664.5	2,892.0	3,291.0	3,410.6	3,532.9	3,704.8	3,901.3	3,989.0	4,232.9
Money plus Quasi-Money	35l	6,396.5	6,742.9	7,374.8	7,330.9	7,616.0	7,556.5	7,678.0	8,163.2	9,208.5	9,646.3	10,401.2	11,655.2
Other Financial Institutions						*Millions of Dinars: End of Period*							
Cash	40	132.6	120.5	95.7	125.8	153.9	258.7	207.8	154.1	167.7	133.6	135.9	172.5
Foreign Assets	41	1,125.7	1,112.4	1,096.1	1,066.4	1,323.0	1,658.1	1,829.1	2,194.2	2,092.1	2,097.4	2,426.9	2,623.1
Claims on Private Sector	42d	713.1	596.6	632.9	707.6	904.0	1,244.9	931.7	766.0	852.1	970.3	1,514.4	1,892.1
Foreign Liabilities	46c	534.4	460.3	473.7	477.7	710.6	1,056.8	1,123.4	1,399.5	1,425.0	1,389.1	1,527.3	1,577.8
Central Government Deposits	46d	181.0	119.9	101.1	142.7	94.5	84.8	7.5	7.0	7.5	.3	63.8	73.1
Credit from Deposit Money Banks	46h	186.5	134.7	185.5	158.5	206.9	296.1	207.7	239.8	392.6	416.9	572.0	556.8
Capital Accounts	47a	609.7	686.0	769.1	861.6	1,018.5	1,325.5	1,255.0	1,294.7	1,005.4	1,029.5	1,285.1	1,476.1
Other Items (Net)	47r	460.0	428.5	295.3	259.4	350.8	398.6	374.9	173.8	281.4	365.5	629.0	1,003.9
Interest Rates						*Percent Per Annum*							
Discount Rate (End of Period)	60	5.75	7.00	7.25	7.25	7.50	7.00	6.75	7.25	4.25	3.25	3.25	4.75
Money Market Rate	60b	7.43	6.31	7.43	6.98	7.05	7.24	6.32	6.82	4.62	2.99	2.47	2.14
Treasury Bill Rate	60c	....	6.32	7.35	6.93	6.98	....	....	....	....	....	....	....
Deposit Rate	60l	7.07	5.70	6.53	6.05	5.93	6.32	5.76	5.89	4.47	3.15	2.42	2.65
Lending Rate	60p	7.95	7.61	8.37	8.77	8.80	8.93	8.56	8.87	7.88	6.48	5.42	5.64
Prices, Production, Labor						*Index Numbers (2000=100): Period Averages*							
Wholesale Prices	63	97.6	97.4	98.7	103.8	102.5	100.8	99.6	100.0	102.0	105.3	107.4	107.8
Consumer Prices	64	86.8	89.0	91.4	94.6	95.2	95.4	98.2	100.0	101.7	103.1	† 104.1	105.3
Crude Petroleum Production	66aa	103.4	112.3	112.7	114.2	115.2	115.3	104.5	100.0	93.4	88.3	88.5	111.4
						Number in Thousands: Period Averages							
Labor Force	67d	....	....	748	1,140	1,217	....	86	....	....	....	....	....
Intl. Transactions & Positions						*Millions of Dinars*							
Exports	70	3,091.2	3,342.3	3,814.5	4,458.0	4,314.3	2,911.6	3,702.8	5,962.7	4,969.7	4,666.2	6,162.1	8,466.5
Oil Exports	70a	2,929.6	3,112.7	3,597.1	4,231.3	4,085.4	2,581.8	3,356.4	5,578.3	4,590.8	4,272.8	5,663.5	7,861.1
Imports, c.i.f	71	2,123.8	1,988.2	2,323.1	2,507.2	2,501.6	2,626.2	2,318.3	2,195.4	2,413.3	2,735.6	3,274.1	3,538.0

		1993	1994	1995	1996	1997	1998	1999	2000	2001	2002	2003	2004
Balance of Payments		*Millions of US Dollars: Minus Sign Indicates Debit*											
Current Account, n.i.e.	78ald	2,499	3,243	5,016	7,107	7,935	2,215	5,010	14,672	8,324	4,251	9,416	18,884
Goods: Exports f.o.b.	78aad	10,264	11,284	12,833	14,946	14,281	9,618	12,223	19,478	16,238	15,366	21,794	30,221
Goods: Imports f.o.b.	78abd	−6,940	−6,600	−7,254	−7,949	−7,747	−7,714	−6,708	−6,451	−7,046	−8,124	−9,882	−10,920
Trade Balance	78acd	3,324	4,685	5,579	6,997	6,534	1,903	5,516	13,027	9,192	7,242	11,912	19,301
Services: Credit	78add	1,242	1,415	1,401	1,520	1,760	1,762	1,560	1,822	1,663	1,648	3,144	3,322
Services: Debit	78aed	−4,589	−4,531	−5,381	−5,100	−5,129	−5,542	−5,171	−4,920	−5,354	−5,837	−6,617	−7,591
Balance on Goods & Services	78afd	−23	1,569	1,598	3,417	3,165	−1,877	1,905	9,929	5,500	3,053	8,439	15,032
Income: Credit	78agd	4,489	4,174	6,125	6,409	7,744	7,163	6,094	7,315	5,426	3,708	3,725	6,844
Income: Debit	78ahd	−663	−1,004	−1,243	−1,229	−1,467	−1,296	−985	−616	−525	−365	−369	−445
Balance on Gds, Serv. & Inc.	78aid	3,804	4,739	6,480	8,597	9,441	3,990	7,013	16,628	10,401	6,397	11,795	21,432
Current Transfers, n.i.e.: Credit	78ajd	109	94	54	53	79	98	99	85	52	49	67	88
Current Transfers: Debit	78akd	−1,415	−1,590	−1,518	−1,543	−1,586	−1,874	−2,102	−2,041	−2,129	−2,195	−2,446	−2,637
Capital Account, n.i.e.	78bcd	−205	−205	−194	−204	−96	79	703	2,217	2,931	1,672	1,429	434
Capital Account, n.i.e.: Credit	78bad	—	—	—	3	115	289	716	2,236	2,951	1,708	1,463	475
Capital Account: Debit	78bbd	−205	−205	−194	−207	−211	−210	−13	−20	−20	−36	−34	−41
Financial Account, n.i.e.	78bjd	421	3,304	157	−7,632	−6,211	−2,920	−5,706	−13,773	−6,313	−5,163	−11,942	−20,048
Direct Investment Abroad	78bdd	−653	1,519	1,022	−1,740	969	1,867	−23	303	−365	155	4,983	−1,873
Dir. Invest. in Rep. Econ., n.i.e.	78bed	13	—	7	347	20	59	72	16	−147	7	−67	−20
Portfolio Investment Assets	78bfd	−931	394	−2,064	−788	−6,926	−4,768	−2,638	−12,923	−7,366	−3,425	−13,580	−13,784
Equity Securities	78bkd												....
Debt Securities	78bld	−931	394	−2,064	−788	−6,926	−4,768	−2,638	−12,923	−7,366	−3,425	−13,580	−13,784
Portfolio Investment Liab., n.i.e.	78bgd	—	—	−50	27	—	—	79	254	−78	161	336	288
Equity Securities	78bmd	—	—	—	—	—	—	—	—	—	—	—	....
Debt Securities	78bnd	—	—	−50	27	—	—	79	254	−78	161	336	288
Financial Derivatives Assets	78bwd	—	—	—	—	—	—	—	—	—	—	—	....
Financial Derivatives Liabilities	78bxd	—	—	—	—	—	—	—	—	—	—	—	....
Other Investment Assets	78bhd	−669	529	−221	−745	3,356	646	−3,512	−1,108	505	−3,754	−3,329	−5,036
Monetary Authorities	78bod	—	—	—	—	—	—	—	—	—	—	—	....
General Government	78bpd	−523	825	724	−1,122	2,993	−10	−3,288	−284	900	−3,879	−3,319	−1,863
Banks	78bqd	−301	−401	−734	−23	260	929	−161	−1,004	241	−599	81	−3,247
Other Sectors	78brd	156	104	−211	401	102	−272	−62	179	−636	724	−91	75
Other Investment Liab., n.i.e.	78bid	2,660	862	1,464	−4,733	−3,629	−725	315	−316	1,138	1,695	−285	377
Monetary Authorities	78bsd	7	−3	−54	−17	3	−10	—	7	—	26	30	31
General Government	78btd	3,429	525	1,541	−5,371	−6,290	−1,316	−115	−838	−33	401	−181	−27
Banks	78bud	−159	589	−97	304	1,523	−456	302	−297	1,301	1,356	−550	268
Other Sectors	78bvd	−616	−249	74	351	1,134	1,057	128	812	−130	−89	416	105
Net Errors and Omissions	78cad	−4,192	−6,292	−5,120	704	−1,623	885	912	−847	−2,038	−1,733	−727	1,355
Overall Balance	78cbd	−1,478	50	−141	−25	6	258	918	2,268	2,905	−973	−1,824	626
Reserves and Related Items	79dad	1,478	−50	141	25	−6	−258	−918	−2,268	−2,905	973	1,824	−626
Reserve Assets	79dbd	1,478	−50	141	25	−6	−258	−918	−2,268	−2,905	973	1,824	−626
Use of Fund Credit and Loans	79dcd	—	—	—	—	—	—	—	—	—	—	—	—
Exceptional Financing	79ded	—	—	—	—	—	—	—	—	—	—	—	—
Government Finance		*Millions of Dinars: Year Ending December 31*											
Deficit (-) or Surplus	80	....	−977	−656	1,031	1,050	−456	385	3,055	1,855	1,534	2,521	3,340
Total Revenue and Grants	81y	....	2,787	3,076	4,198	4,179	2,859	3,710	6,434	5,632	5,632	6,801	8,402
Revenue	81	....	2,787	3,076	4,198	4,179	2,859	3,710	6,434	5,632	5,632	6,801	8,402
Grants	81z	....											
Exp. & Lending Minus Repay.	82z	....	3,763	3,732	3,167	3,129	3,315	3,325	3,379	3,778	4,098	4,279	5,063
Expenditure	82	....	3,763	3,732	3,167	3,129	3,315	3,325	3,379	3,778	4,098	4,279	5,063
Lending Minus Repayments	83	....	—	—	—	—	—	—	—	—	—	—	—
National Accounts		*Millions of Dinars*											
Househ.Cons.Expend.,incl.NPISHs	96f	3,143	3,029	3,461	4,199	4,279	4,608	4,776	4,958	5,320	5,855	6,169	....
Government Consumption Expend.	91f	2,593	2,503	2,612	2,571	2,452	2,412	2,463	2,485	2,529	2,929	3,224	....
Gross Capital Formation	93	1,243	1,192	1,198	1,424	1,256	1,459	1,335	868	910	979	1,076	....
Gross Fixed Capital Formation	93e	1,094	982	1,100	1,319	1,240	1,448	1,300	868	910	979	1,076	....
Changes in Inventories	93i	149	210	97	106	15	11	35	....	....	....	....	....
Exports of Goods and Services	90c	3,454	3,753	4,248	4,930	4,866	3,468	4,212	6,534	5,490	5,171	6,817	....
Imports of Goods and Services (-)	98c	3,202	3,098	3,405	3,695	3,645	4,040	3,616	3,488	3,803	4,243	4,844	....
Gross Domestic Product (GDP)	99b	7,231	7,380	8,114	9,429	9,207	7,907	9,170	11,357	10,446	10,691	12,441	....
Net Primary Income from Abroad	98.n	1,155	941	1,457	1,551	1,904	1,788	1,555	2,055	1,503	1,016	991	....
Gross National Income (GNI)	99a	8,386	8,321	9,571	10,980	11,111	9,695	10,725	13,412	11,949	11,707	13,432	....
Consumption of Fixed Capital	99cf	571	639	711	671	701	768	614	399	419	450	479	....
GDP Volume 1984 Prices	99b.p	8,702	9,453	9,583	....	....	....	....	....	....	....	....	....
GDP Volume 1995 Prices	99b.p	....	....	8,114	8,162	8,366	8,672	8,517	8,680	8,742	8,697	9,541	....
GDP Volume (2000=100)	99bvp	84.9	92.2	† 93.5	94.0	96.4	99.9	98.1	100.0	100.7	100.2	109.9	....
GDP Deflator (2000=100)	99bip	75.0	70.5	76.4	88.3	84.1	69.7	82.3	100.0	91.3	94.0	99.7	....
		Millions: Midyear Estimates											
Population	99z	1.85	1.74	1.70	1.73	1.82	1.95	2.10	2.23	† 2.34	2.44	2.52	2.61

		1993	1994	1995	1996	1997	1998	1999	2000	2001	2002	2003	2004
Exchange Rates						*Soms per SDR: End of Period*							
Official Rate	aa	11.030	15.547	16.649	24.014	23.443	41.362	62.352	62.936	59.969	62.667	65.665	64.643
						Soms per US Dollar: End of Period (ae) Period Average (rf)							
Official Rate	ae	8.030	10.650	11.200	16.700	17.375	29.376	45.429	48.304	47.719	46.095	44.190	41.625
Official Rate	rf	....	10.842	10.822	12.810	17.362	20.838	39.008	47.704	48.378	46.937	43.648	42.650
Fund Position						*Millions of SDRs: End of Period*							
Quota	2f.s	64.5	64.5	64.5	64.5	64.5	64.5	88.8	88.8	88.8	88.8	88.8	88.8
SDRs	1b.s	9.4	.7	9.6	5.1	.7	.2	3.7	.5	1.1	.5	6.9	12.8
Reserve Position in the Fund	1c.s	—	—	—	—	—	—	—	—	—	—	—	—
Total Fund Cred.&Loans Outstg	2tl	43.9	53.3	83.6	97.1	122.2	124.4	138.7	144.3	142.7	136.3	135.9	133.2
International Liquidity						*Millions of US Dollars Unless Otherwise Indicated: End of Period*							
Total Reserves minus Gold	1l.d	48.2	26.2	81.0	94.6	170.2	163.8	229.7	239.0	263.5	288.8	364.6	548.7
SDRs	1b.d	12.9	1.0	14.3	7.4	.9	.3	5.1	.7	1.3	.6	10.3	19.9
Reserve Position in the Fund	1c.d	—	—	—	—	—	—	—	—	—	—	—	—
Foreign Exchange	1d.d	35.4	25.2	66.7	87.2	169.3	163.4	224.6	238.3	262.2	288.2	354.3	528.8
Gold (Million Fine Troy Ounces)	1ad	....	....	.1362	.1235	.0830	.0831	.0831	.0831	.0831	.0831	.0831	.0831
Gold (National Valuation)	1and	....	....	43.22	28.13	29.08	23.88	24.17	22.80	22.97	28.48	34.67	36.39
Monetary Authorities: Other Liab.	4..d	....	....	73.5	65.8	59.2	39.7	44.1	55.5	57.4	58.1	57.5	58.1
Banking Institutions: Assets	7a.d	....	....	19.6	13.1	34.3	17.1	15.8	18.0	32.8	72.6	124.0	193.5
Liabilities	7b.d	....	....	2.8	1.8	13.1	8.3	1.8	3.0	3.4	36.4	71.9	101.4
Monetary Authorities						*Millions of Soms: End of Period*							
Foreign Assets	11	....	....	1,393	2,035	3,368	5,517	11,338	12,687	13,632	14,620	17,197	23,540
Claims on General Government	12a	....	....	2,049	3,911	4,473	4,940	5,787	6,144	6,186	7,090	6,752	6,672
Claims on Banking Institutions	12e	....	....	1,153	124	92	333	543	609	506	490	421	412
Reserve Money	14	....	....	2,044	2,533	3,069	3,303	4,317	4,821	5,375	7,670	10,171	12,392
of which: Currency Outside Banks	14a	....	....	1,938	2,416	2,678	2,829	3,578	4,102	5,016	6,866	9,302	11,109
Other Liabilities to DMBs	14n	....	....	—	—	200	36	243	189	—	—	147	—
Foreign Liabilities	16c	....	....	2,216	3,430	3,893	6,314	10,652	11,763	11,296	11,218	11,461	11,034
General Government Deposits	16d	....	....	15	147	253	250	1,152	1,059	2,035	1,980	1,585	6,150
Capital Accounts	17a	....	....	136	243	506	949	1,118	989	1,096	1,518	1,105	1,227
Other Items (Net)	17r	....	....	171	−311	−40	−133	98	493	323	−378	−350	−439
Banking Institutions						*Millions of Soms: End of Period*							
Reserves	20	....	....	113	110	381	449	739	700	343	792	773	1,270
Other Claims on Monetary Author.	20n	....	....	—	—	162	107	172	172	3	8	180	49
Foreign Assets	21	....	....	219	219	596	503	719	870	1,563	3,344	5,478	8,055
Claims on General Government	22a	....	....	83	93	323	378	150	202	487	597	746	938
Claims on Rest of the Economy	22d	....	....	2,024	2,026	1,047	1,804	2,448	2,679	2,780	3,098	3,963	6,633
Demand Deposits	24	....	....	545	478	442	379	624	504	542	811	1,314	1,935
Time & Foreign Currency Deposits	25	....	....	295	295	1,095	1,745	2,418	2,791	2,676	3,346	4,085	6,372
Foreign Liabilities	26c	....	....	31	31	228	245	84	143	164	1,680	3,179	4,222
General Government Deposits	26d	....	....	—	—	30	45	64	49	71	107	188	225
Credit from Monetary Authorities	26g	....	....	1,188	1,188	118	318	605	619	597	575	543	572
Capital Accounts	27a	....	....	120	149	735	980	1,125	1,229	1,802	2,134	2,365	2,963
Other Items (Net)	27r	....	....	261	307	−138	−471	−694	−712	−676	−813	−535	656
Banking Survey						*Millions of Soms: End of Period*							
Foreign Assets (Net)	31n	....	....	−635	−1,207	−157	−539	1,321	1,651	3,736	5,067	8,034	16,340
Domestic Credit	32	....	....	4,142	5,882	5,579	6,852	7,208	7,957	7,396	8,750	9,738	7,910
Claims on General Govt. (Net)	32an	....	....	2,117	3,856	4,513	5,023	4,721	5,238	4,567	5,601	5,726	1,234
Claims on Rest of the Economy	32d	....	....	2,024	2,026	1,066	1,828	2,487	2,720	2,829	3,149	4,012	6,677
Money	34	....	....	2,482	2,893	3,119	3,208	4,203	4,606	5,558	7,677	10,616	13,045
Quasi-Money	35	....	....	295	295	1,095	1,745	2,418	2,791	2,676	3,346	4,085	6,372
Capital Accounts	37a	....	....	256	392	1,242	1,929	2,243	2,218	2,898	3,651	3,470	4,190
Other Items (Net)	37r	....	....	461	1,069	−85	−641	−423	−131	−200	−1,051	−650	384
Money plus Quasi-Money	35l	....	....	2,777	3,188	4,214	4,953	6,621	7,397	8,234	11,024	14,701	19,416
Interest Rates						*Percent per Annum*							
Lombard Rate	60.a	265.5	94.1	64.1	43.1	43.2	54.0	51.6	32.8	10.7	6.8	4.0	4.6
Money Market Rate	60b	....	....	....	....	....	44.0	43.7	24.3	11.9	....	....	....
Treasury Bill Rate	60c	....	143.1	34.9	40.1	35.8	43.7	47.2	32.3	19.1	10.2	7.2	4.9
Deposit Rate	60l	....	....	....	36.7	39.6	35.8	35.6	18.4	12.5	5.9	5.0	6.7
Lending Rate	60p	....	....	....	65.0	49.4	73.4	60.9	51.9	37.3	24.8	19.1	29.3
Prices and Labor						*Index Numbers (2000=100): Period Averages*							
Producer Prices	63	7.7	24.4	29.7	36.5	46.1	49.8	76.5	100.0	112.0	117.4	122.8	† 130.2
Consumer Prices	64	....	....	34.5	45.5	56.1	62.0	84.3	100.0	106.9	109.2	113.0	† 122.7
Wages: Average Earnings	65	7.1	19.8	31.2	41.7	57.6	71.2	82.1	100.0	118.2	136.9	161.6	186.6
						Number in Thousands: Period Averages							
Employment	67e	....	....	....	....	....	....	576	557	537	518	506	499
Unemployment	67c	....	....	50	77	55	56	56	59	61	60	59	58
Unemployment Rate	67r	.2	.8	3.0	4.5	3.1	3.2	3.0	3.1	3.2	....	....	....
Intl. Transactions & Positions						*Millions of US Dollars*							
Exports	70..d	339.7	340.0	408.9	505.4	603.8	513.6	453.8	504.5	476.1	485.5	581.7	718.8
Imports, c.i.f.	71..d	429.5	315.9	522.3	837.7	709.3	841.5	599.7	554.1	467.2	586.7	717.0	941.0

		1993	1994	1995	1996	1997	1998	1999	2000	2001	2002	2003	2004
Balance of Payments		*Millions of US Dollars: Minus Sign Indicates Debit*											
Current Account, n.i.e.	78ald	−87.6	−84.0	−234.7	−424.8	−138.5	−412.5	−252.2	−124.3	−56.7	−80.0	−99.0	−100.7
Goods: Exports f.o.b.	78aad	339.6	340.0	408.9	531.2	630.8	535.1	462.6	510.9	480.3	498.1	590.3	733.2
Goods: Imports f.o.b.	78abd	−446.7	−426.1	−531.0	−782.9	−646.1	−755.7	−551.1	−506.9	−449.5	−572.1	−723.8	−904.5
Trade Balance	78acd	−107.1	−86.1	−122.0	−251.7	−15.3	−220.7	−88.6	4.0	30.8	−74.0	−133.5	−171.3
Services: Credit	78add	8.7	32.7	39.2	31.5	45.0	62.8	64.9	61.8	80.3	142.0	154.7	208.9
Services: Debit	78aed	−50.7	−71.1	−195.1	−249.0	−171.2	−175.7	−154.6	−148.8	−126.1	−148.4	−151.2	−231.0
Balance on Goods & Services	78afd	−149.1	−124.6	−278.0	−469.2	−141.4	−333.5	−178.2	−82.9	−15.0	−80.5	−130.0	−193.4
Income: Credit	78agd	....	....	3.7	4.4	6.8	12.6	10.9	17.0	11.8	6.3	5.2	11.2
Income: Debit	78ahd	−5.7	−22.0	−39.2	−43.9	−71.4	−91.7	−84.9	−98.9	−71.8	−63.7	−67.6	−101.4
Balance on Gds, Serv. & Inc.	78aid	−154.8	−146.6	−313.4	−508.7	−206.1	−412.6	−252.2	−164.9	−75.0	−137.8	−192.3	−283.6
Current Transfers, n.i.e.: Credit	78ajd	68.0	63.4	80.4	85.9	69.8	2.2	1.1	42.9	22.8	60.7	100.4	200.6
Current Transfers: Debit	78akd	−.8	−.8	−1.7	−1.9	−2.2	−2.0	−1.2	−2.4	−4.5	−2.9	−7.0	−17.6
Capital Account, n.i.e.	78bcd	−107.1	−62.4	−29.0	−15.9	−8.4	−8.1	−15.2	−11.4	−32.0	−7.9	−.9	−19.9
Capital Account, n.i.e.: Credit	78bad	....	.3	2.2	9.0	6.2	26.4	24.0	22.8	9.2	35.1	36.0	33.7
Capital Account: Debit	78bbd	−107.1	−62.7	−31.3	−25.0	−14.6	−34.5	−39.2	−34.2	−41.2	−43.0	−36.9	−53.6
Financial Account, n.i.e.	78bjd	199.1	85.7	260.1	362.5	250.4	299.8	244.2	99.8	54.5	108.7	24.9	185.7
Direct Investment Abroad	78bdd	....	....	....	....	....	−22.6	−6.1	−4.5	−6.1	...	...	−43.9
Dir. Invest. in Rep. Econ., n.i.e.	78bed	10.0	38.2	96.1	47.2	83.8	109.2	44.4	−2.4	5.0	4.7	45.5	175.4
Portfolio Investment Assets	78bfd	....	....	−.1	.1	.6	−.2	—	−1.6	1.2	−2.5	1.1	−2.5
Equity Securities	78bkd	....	....	....	....	....	—	—	—	—	—	—	—
Debt Securities	78bld	....	....	−.1	.1	.6	−.2	—	−1.6	1.2	−2.5	1.1	−2.5
Portfolio Investment Liab., n.i.e.	78bgd	....	....	1.8	−1.8	5.0	−4.1	−.1	.3	—	−9.5	5.0	—
Equity Securities	78bmd	....	....	....	....	....	—	—	—	—	—	—	—
Debt Securities	78bnd	....	....	1.8	−1.8	5.0	−4.1	−.1	.3	—	−9.5	5.0	—
Financial Derivatives Assets	78bwd	....	....	....	....	19.0	30.6	26.4	25.8	17.6	−5.1	−20.0	−20.5
Financial Derivatives Liabilities	78bxd	....	....	....	....	....	....	....	....	....	....	....	....
Other Investment Assets	78bhd	−53.0	−43.2	11.9	1.9	−43.1	−84.1	−.7	−27.3	−4.0	21.5	−78.7	−29.6
Monetary Authorities	78bod	....	....	−1.0	....	−3.0	−2.0	—	8.6	—	23.9	−2.1	—
General Government	78bpd	....	−1.7	−2.1	13.3	—	−.3	−.3	−.1	−.1	—	−.2	—
Banks	78bqd	−13.4	1.3	−1.2	1.6	−18.7	9.6	−1.4	−1.6	−16.5	−42.3	−50.2	−49.4
Other Sectors	78brd	−39.6	−42.9	16.2	−13.0	−21.5	−91.4	.9	−34.3	12.6	39.9	−26.3	19.8
Other Investment Liab., n.i.e.	78bid	242.1	90.8	150.4	315.1	185.1	271.1	180.3	109.5	40.8	99.6	72.1	106.8
Monetary Authorities	78bsd	35.8	−35.4	.5	.2	—	−.1						
General Government	78btd	179.5	110.9	102.0	104.7	137.2	137.8	199.2	121.4	82.4	66.9	73.4	93.6
Banks	78bud	5.7	3.6	−3.3	−2.1	14.0	1.0	−2.8	−.3	3.9	32.7	36.6	25.8
Other Sectors	78bvd	21.1	11.7	51.2	212.2	33.9	132.4	−16.1	−11.5	−45.6	—	−38.0	−12.5
Net Errors and Omissions	78cad	−34.1	65.7	−77.1	58.4	−57.4	63.5	−2.9	3.1	21.3	−.3	121.7	79.5
Overall Balance	78cbd	−29.6	5.0	−80.7	−19.8	46.2	−57.2	−26.1	−32.9	−12.9	20.4	46.8	144.5
Reserves and Related Items	79dad	29.6	−5.0	80.7	19.8	−46.2	57.2	26.1	32.9	12.9	−20.4	−46.8	−144.5
Reserve Assets	79dbd	−35.5	−31.9	.1	−18.6	−82.8	5.9	−61.3	−21.3	−17.7	−43.0	−64.2	−166.2
Use of Fund Credit and Loans	79dcd	62.1	13.8	46.3	19.6	34.1	2.8	19.4	7.4	−2.1	−8.0	−.9	−3.9
Exceptional Financing	79ded	3.0	13.1	34.4	18.8	2.6	48.6	68.0	46.8	32.7	30.6	18.3	25.6
International Investment Position		*Millions of US Dollars*											
Assets	79aad	118.5	190.1	202.4	203.9	341.3	366.2	394.2	489.3	488.8	551.3	711.6	1,048.1
Direct Investment Abroad	79abd	—	—	—	—	—	22.6	28.7	33.2	39.3	39.3	39.3	83.2
Portfolio Investment	79acd	—	—	.1	.6	—	.2	.2	3.1	3.7	6.2	7.6	10.7
Equity Securities	79add	—	—	—	—	—	—	—	—	—	—	—	—
Debt Securities	79aed	—	—	.1	.6	—	.2	.2	3.1	3.7	6.2	7.6	10.7
Financial Derivatives	79ald	—	—	—	—	31.7	7.8	7.3	19.5	17.2	—	—	—
Other Investment	79afd	55.1	92.2	88.6	75.8	113.7	146.9	174.9	229.5	192.8	216.1	305.5	410.2
Monetary Authorities	79agd	—	—	—	—	—	—	—	2.4	2.3	1.5	1.2	.9
General Government	79ahd	33.9	72.4	67.7	56.3	42.7	69.1	65.6	57.1	49.3	27.0	29.8	21.4
Banks	79aid	21.2	19.9	20.9	19.5	38.1	29.2	30.8	70.7	35.8	94.1	156.8	311.0
Other Sectors	79ajd	—	—	—	—	32.9	48.7	78.5	99.3	105.4	93.6	117.8	76.9
Reserve Assets	79akd	63.5	97.9	113.7	127.5	195.9	188.6	183.2	204.0	235.9	289.7	359.3	543.9
Liabilities	79lad	350.9	528.4	913.8	1,301.3	1,711.7	1,962.5	2,128.9	2,195.2	2,241.2	2,350.6	2,584.2	2,822.4
Dir. Invest. in Rep. Economy	79lbd	10.0	48.2	144.3	191.0	274.1	383.3	431.6	446.6	440.8	479.1	491.5	677.0
Portfolio Investment	79lcd	—	—	1.8	—	5.0	.9	—	9.6	112.6	103.4	102.6	97.3
Equity Securities	79ldd	—	—	—	—	—	—	—	—	—	—	—	—
Debt Securities	79led	—	—	1.8	—	5.0	.9	—	9.6	112.6	103.4	102.6	97.3
Financial Derivatives	79lld	—	—	—	—	—	—	—	—	—	29.7	24.6	—
Other Investment	79lfd	340.9	480.2	767.8	1,110.3	1,432.6	1,578.3	1,697.3	1,739.0	1,687.8	1,738.3	1,965.6	2,048.1
Monetary Authorities	79lgd	60.2	77.8	124.3	139.6	164.9	175.2	190.3	188.0	179.3	185.2	201.9	206.9
General Government	79lhd	274.9	393.1	547.8	673.7	839.9	979.4	1,122.2	1,207.5	1,158.1	1,298.0	1,477.9	1,656.9
Banks	79lid	5.7	9.3	6.0	4.0	17.9	18.9	16.1	3.7	5.6	38.5	79.8	115.9
Other Sectors	79ljd	—	—	89.7	293.0	409.9	404.8	368.7	339.8	344.7	216.5	206.0	68.4
Government Finance		*Millions of Soms: Year Ending December 31*											
Deficit (-) or Surplus	80	−377.9	−921.6	−1,864.6	−1,269.3	−1,605.4	−1,035.8	−1,213.5	−1,244.8	286.8	−798.1	−681.0	−505.8
Total Revenue and Grants	81y	847.9	1,891.2	2,745.9	3,933.1	5,090.3	6,262.6	7,828.7	10,039.6	12,543.7	14,392.1	16,214.9	18,335.9
Exp. & Lending Minus Repay.	82z	1,225.8	2,812.8	4,610.5	5,202.4	6,695.7	7,298.4	9,042.2	11,284.4	12,256.9	15,190.2	16,895.9	18,841.7
Financing													
Domestic	84a	297.8	406.5	995.5	604.8	287.9	68.7	−379.6	−334.1	−101.8	−52.5	−96.7	209.8
Foreign	85a	80.0	515.1	851.1	664.5	1,317.5	966.8	1,593.1	1,579.0	−185.1	850.6	777.8	296.0

National Accounts		1993	1994	1995	1996	1997	1998	1999	2000	2001	2002	2003	2004
							Millions of Soms						
Househ.Cons.Expend.,incl.NPISHs....	96f	† 4,053	9,422	12,111	19,212	21,151	30,163	37,848	42,930	47,893	50,897	65,344	74,714
Government Consumption Expend...	91f	† 1,086	2,272	3,155	4,333	5,307	6,103	9,320	13,099	12,912	14,033	14,116	15,577
Gross Fixed Capital Formation..........	93e	† 715	1,493	3,338	5,296	3,802	4,404	7,663	11,782	10,721	12,418	11,600	11,723
Changes in Inventories...................	93i	† −90	−409	−377	600	2,781	780	993	1,136	724	852	−1,678	−2,330
Exports of Goods and Services..........	90c	† 1,796	4,058	4,758	7,193	11,749	12,471	20,571	27,351	27,133	29,831	32,442	40,289
Imports of Goods and Services (-).....	98c	† 2,205	4,816	6,839	13,234	14,174	19,834	27,782	31,099	27,353	32,664	37,953	49,482
Statistical Discrepancy.....................	99bs	....	....	....	....	....	....	....	—	—	−504	−273	3,588
Gross Domestic Product (GDP)........	99b	† 5,355	12,019	16,145	23,399	30,686	34,181	48,744	65,358	73,883	75,367	83,872	94,078
Net Primary Income from Abroad.....	98.n	† −68	−190	−200	−485	−1,004	−1,748	−2,940	−3,848	−3,139	−2,825	−2,617	....
Gross National Income (GNI)...........	99a	† 5,286	11,830	15,945	22,914	29,682	32,433	45,804	61,510	70,744	72,542	81,255	....
Net Current Transf.from Abroad......	98t	521	665	820	1,438	1,161	1,043	1,969	3,911	2,507	5,487	4,598	....
Gross Nat'l Disposable Inc.(GNDI)....	99i	5,808	12,495	16,765	24,352	30,843	33,476	47,773	65,421	73,251	78,028	85,853	....
Gross Saving.................................	99s	668	801	1,500	807	4,385	−2,790	605	9,393	12,446	13,099	6,392	....
Consumption of Fixed Capital..........	99cf	545	1,220	1,644	2,963	3,731	4,902	6,332	8,623	8,920	9,259	9,145	....
GDP Volume 1995 Prices.................	99b.p	† 21,360	17,067	16,145	17,289	19,003	19,406	20,101	21,215	....	....	....	....
GDP Volume 2000 Prices.................	99b.p	....	....	....	....	....	....	....	65,358	68,836	68,836	73,651	78,854
GDP Volume (2000=100)................	99bvp	† 100.7	80.4	76.1	81.5	89.6	91.5	94.7	† 100.0	105.3	105.3	112.7	120.6
GDP Deflator (2000=100)...............	99bip	† 8.1	22.9	32.5	43.9	52.4	57.2	78.7	100.0	107.3	109.5	113.9	119.3
							Millions: Midyear Estimates						
Population.................................	99z	4.51	4.54	4.59	4.65	4.72	4.80	4.88	4.95	5.02	5.08	5.14	5.20

Lao People's Democratic Republic 544

		1993	1994	1995	1996	1997	1998	1999	2000	2001	2002	2003	2004
Exchange Rates						*Kip per SDR: End of Period*							
Official Rate....................	aa	986.22	1,049.63	†1,372.03	1,344.49	3,554.60	6,017.92	10,431.08	10,707.31	11,926.37	14,519.67	15,553.65	16,114.81
						Kip per US Dollar: End of Period (ae) Period Average (rf)							
Official Rate....................	ae	718.00	719.00	†923.00	935.00	2,634.50	4,274.00	7,600.00	8,218.00	9,490.00	10,680.00	10,467.00	10,376.50
Official Rate....................	rf	716.25	717.67	†804.69	921.02	1,259.98	3,298.33	7,102.03	7,887.64	8,954.58	10,056.33	10,569.04	10,585.54
Fund Position						*Millions of SDRs: End of Period*							
Quota.............................	2f.s	39.10	39.10	39.10	39.10	39.10	39.10	39.10	39.10	52.90	52.90	52.90	52.90
SDRs..............................	1b.s	1.90	7.46	9.49	7.17	9.31	4.32	.05	.07	2.72	4.47	12.87	9.90
Reserve Position in the Fund...........	1c.s	—	—	—	—	—	—	—	—	—	—	—	—
Total Fund Cred.&Loans Outstg.......	2tl	26.38	32.24	42.80	46.61	48.96	44.27	38.41	32.55	29.75	31.77	29.85	24.57
International Liquidity						*Millions of US Dollars Unless Otherwise Indicated: End of Period*							
Total Reserves minus Gold..............	1l.d	62.96e	60.93e	92.11	169.50	112.18	112.21	101.19	138.97	130.93	191.59	208.59	223.25
SDRs..............................	1b.d	2.61	10.89	14.10	10.31	12.56	6.09	.07	.10	3.42	6.07	19.13	15.37
Reserve Position in the Fund...........	1c.d	—	—	—	—	—	—	—	—	—	—	—	—
Foreign Exchange....................	1d.d	60.34e	50.03e	78.01	159.19	99.62	106.13	101.12	138.87	127.51	185.51	189.46	207.87
Gold (Million Fine Troy Ounces)........	1ad	.0171	.0171	.0171	.0171	.0171	.0171	.1171	.0169	.0723	.0723	.1171	.1171
Gold (National Valuation)..............	1and	.60	.60	.60	.60	.60	.60	4.10	.59	2.53	2.53	4.10	4.10
Deposit Money Banks: Assets...........	7a.d	.09	.10	.10	.11	.07	.11	.15	.13	.09	.15	.16	.22
Liabilities..................	7b.d	.01	.03	.04	.05	.03	.04	.04	.04	.04	.08	.07	.10
Monetary Authorities						*Billions of Kip: End of Period*							
Foreign Assets...................	11	45.36	43.96	85.18	158.64	295.70	479.76	799.78	1,146.86	1,265.54	2,069.17	2,226.69	2,359.91
Claims on Central Government........	12a	8.96	12.16	4.25	4.25	4.70	91.27	198.83	158.51	184.98	239.27	234.17	185.86
Claims on Nonfin.Pub.Enterprises.....	12c	.86	1.86	6.98	10.87	59.54	112.80	223.71	346.10	488.49	566.64	523.51	575.14
Claims on Private Sector..................	12d	3.01	6.83	10.40	13.90	38.22	72.05	143.25	143.23	150.82	175.88	153.24	153.59
Claims on Deposit Money Banks.....	12e	34.62	37.05	46.59	52.37	57.94	80.35	301.90	445.60	347.66	218.07	137.63	131.04
Reserve Money.....................	14	60.70	74.23	84.17	104.37	150.09	281.75	481.75	766.65	822.49	1,079.11	1,329.94	1,545.29
of which: Currency Outside DMBs..	14a	33.24	38.61	41.95	42.97	53.31	63.16	77.79	67.83	113.08	228.81	399.10	666.42
Foreign Liabilities....................	16c	26.01	33.84	58.72	62.67	174.04	266.43	400.67	348.51	354.80	461.31	464.28	395.97
Central Government Deposits...........	16d	8.59	13.52	7.45	64.82	52.74	77.51	235.23	505.77	281.32	650.15	608.53	636.86
Government Lending Funds..............	16f	18.34	12.07	16.17	18.04	31.09	54.37	87.33	211.05	346.68	428.12	323.82	303.63
Capital Accounts...........................	17a	13.85	15.23	26.44	25.21	91.25	172.61	456.94	463.05	706.21	838.10	896.94	954.06
Other Items (Net).........................	17r	−34.68	−47.02	−39.56	−35.08	−43.10	−16.43	5.86	−54.42	−73.99	−187.77	−348.27	−430.27
Deposit Money Banks						*Billions of Kip: End of Period*							
Reserves..........................	20	30.66	36.45	44.16	59.24	77.70	212.42	402.96	688.77	714.46	939.28	1,109.01	982.05
Foreign Assets...........................	21	62.82	69.79	91.20	107.47	180.35	452.00	1,142.98	1,075.88	865.78	1,577.12	1,713.16	2,271.14
Claims on Central Government........	22a	—	26.81	19.38	39.18	40.78	37.86	11.35	7.64	29.74	69.16	324.36	355.84
Claims on Nonfin.Pub.Enterprises.....	22c	17.47	15.57	20.69	26.06	60.88	110.75	221.69	296.54	528.24	566.40	402.59	423.46
Claims on Private Sector..................	22d	62.90	92.02	118.46	141.79	247.35	460.77	728.69	1,074.91	1,354.49	1,329.22	1,318.96	1,528.05
Demand Deposits.....................	24	18.99	22.73	25.22	32.59	32.26	105.82	141.19	272.23	256.88	358.15	437.29	537.54
Time, Savings,& Fgn.Currency Dep...	25	73.61	104.69	126.09	169.37	326.07	696.95	1,325.52	1,911.25	2,193.15	2,942.40	3,401.38	3,947.56
Foreign Liabilities....................	26c	9.28	21.51	39.76	46.87	77.24	169.34	281.96	349.38	376.08	863.70	752.28	988.65
Central Government Deposits...........	26d	9.79	12.69	15.41	21.60	36.34	103.46	247.16	79.93	51.42	37.20	80.71	114.94
Credit from Monetary Authorities.....	26g	29.57	35.04	41.93	49.12	51.46	81.67	314.49	489.84	383.78	252.38	165.62	98.39
Capital Accounts...........................	27a	33.83	47.45	56.55	66.51	126.78	215.97	457.31	519.89	574.10	487.44	201.02	60.18
Other Items (Net).........................	27r	−1.23	−3.47	−11.05	−12.31	−37.46	−99.42	−259.97	−478.79	−342.73	−460.11	−170.23	−186.74
Monetary Survey						*Billions of Kip: End of Period*							
Foreign Assets (Net).........................	31n	72.89	58.40	77.90	156.57	224.77	496.00	1,260.13	1,524.85	1,400.44	2,321.28	2,723.29	3,246.44
Domestic Credit............................	32	74.82	129.04	157.30	149.62	362.39	704.53	1,045.12	1,441.22	2,404.02	2,259.22	2,267.59	2,470.14
Claims on Central Govt. (Net)........	32an	−9.42	12.77	.78	−43.00	−43.61	−51.84	−272.21	−419.56	−118.02	−378.92	−130.71	−210.10
Claims on Nonfin.Pub.Enterprises...	32c	18.33	17.43	27.67	36.93	120.42	223.55	445.39	642.63	1,016.73	1,133.04	926.10	998.60
Claims on Private Sector................	32d	65.91	98.85	128.86	155.69	285.58	532.82	871.94	1,218.14	1,505.31	1,505.10	1,472.20	1,681.64
Money...............................	34	52.24	61.34	67.18	75.56	79.94	168.98	218.98	344.35	371.84	587.00	836.54	1,207.29
Quasi-Money........................	35	73.61	104.69	126.09	169.37	326.07	696.95	1,325.52	1,911.25	2,193.15	2,942.40	3,401.38	3,947.56
Other Items (Net)........................	37r	21.87	21.41	41.93	61.27	181.15	334.60	761.06	710.77	1,239.46	1,051.07	752.95	561.71
Money plus Quasi-Money.................	35l	125.85	166.03	193.27	244.93	406.00	865.93	1,544.50	2,255.60	2,564.99	3,529.40	4,237.92	5,154.85
Interest Rates						*Percent Per Annum*							
Bank Rate (End of Period)...............	60	25.00	30.00	32.08	35.00	....	35.00	34.89	35.17	35.00	20.00	20.00	20.00
Treasury Bill Rate..........................	60c	....	....	20.46	....	....	23.66	30.00	29.94	22.70	21.41	24.87	20.37
Deposit Rate..............................	60l	13.33	12.00	14.00	16.00	....	17.79	13.42	12.00	6.50	6.00	6.58	7.85
Lending Rate................................	60p	†25.33	24.00	†25.67	27.00	....	29.28	32.00	32.00	26.17	29.33	30.50	29.25
Prices						*Index Numbers (2000=100): Period Averages*							
Consumer Prices............................	64	10.0	10.6	12.7	†14.4	18.3	35.0	†79.9	100.0	107.8	119.3	137.7	152.2
Intl. Transactions & Positions						*Millions of US Dollars*							
Exports.......................................	70..d	241.0	300.5	311.0	322.8	359.0	369.5	310.8	330.3	331.3	297.7	378.1	361.1
Imports, c.i.f.................................	71..d	432.0	564.1	588.8	689.6	706.0	552.8	524.8	535.3	527.9	431.1	524.2	505.8

Lao People's Democratic Republic 544

Balance of Payments		1993	1994	1995	1996	1997	1998	1999	2000	2001	2002	2003	2004
		Millions of US Dollars: Minus Sign Indicates Debit											
Current Account, n.i.e.	78ald	−139.2	−284.0	−346.2	−346.8	−305.5	−150.1	−121.1	−8.5	−82.4	....	....	....
Goods: Exports f.o.b.	78aad	247.9	305.5	310.9	322.8	318.3	342.1	338.2	330.3	311.1	....	....	....
Goods: Imports f.o.b.	78abd	−397.4	−519.2	−626.8	−643.7	−601.3	−506.8	−527.7	−535.3	−527.9	....	....	....
Trade Balance	78acd	−149.5	−213.7	−315.9	−320.9	−283.0	−164.7	−189.5	−205.0	−216.8	....	....	....
Services: Credit	78add	85.2	87.0	96.8	104.4	105.8	145.0	130.0	175.7	166.1	....	....	....
Services: Debit	78aed	−75.9	−152.1	−121.6	−126.0	−110.5	−95.5	−51.8	−43.1	−31.6	....	....	....
Balance on Goods & Services	78afd	−140.2	−278.8	−340.7	−342.5	−287.7	−115.2	−111.3	−72.4	−82.3	....	....	....
Income: Credit	78agd	8.6	7.2	7.4	9.2	11.1	6.9	10.5	7.3	5.8	....	....	....
Income: Debit	78ahd	−5.6	−9.2	−12.9	−13.5	−28.9	−41.8	−49.9	−59.7	−39.6	....	....	....
Balance on Gds, Serv. & Inc.	78aid	−137.2	−280.8	−346.2	−346.8	−305.5	−150.1	−150.7	−124.7	−116.1	....	....	....
Current Transfers, n.i.e.: Credit.	78ajd	—	—	—	—	—	—	80.2	116.3	33.7	....	....	....
Current Transfers: Debit	78akd	−2.0	−3.2	—	—	—	—	−50.6	....	....	....	....	....
Capital Account, n.i.e.	78bcd	9.5	9.5	13.2	35.0	33.4	43.1		....	....	....	....	....
Capital Account, n.i.e.: Credit.	78bad	9.5	9.5	21.7	44.9	40.3	49.4	—	....	....	....	....	....
Capital Account: Debit	78bbd	—	—	−8.5	−9.9	−6.9	−6.3	—	....	....	....	....	....
Financial Account, n.i.e.	78bjd	−21.0	24.3	90.0	135.7	3.5	−43.4	−46.9	126.1	135.7	....	....	....
Direct Investment Abroad	78bdd	—	—	—	....	—	—	—	....	....	....	....	....
Dir. Invest. in Rep. Econ., n.i.e.	78bed	29.9	59.2	95.1	159.8	—	—	—	33.9	23.9	....	....	....
Portfolio Investment Assets	78bfd	—	—	—	....	—	—	—	....	....	....	....	....
Equity Securities	78bkd	—	—	—	....	—	—	—	....	....	....	....	....
Debt Securities	78bld	—	—	—	....	—	—	—	....	....	....	....	....
Portfolio Investment Liab., n.i.e.	78bgd	—	—	—	....	—	—	—	....	....	....	....	....
Equity Securities	78bmd	—	—	—	....	—	—	—	....	....	....	....	....
Debt Securities	78bnd	—	—	—	....	—	—	—	....	....	....	....	....
Financial Derivatives Assets	78bwd	....	....	....	....	....	....	....	....	....	....	....	....
Financial Derivatives Liabilities	78bxd	....	....	....	....	....	....	....	....	....	....	....	....
Other Investment Assets	78bhd	−43.2	−9.6	−1.5	−14.1	39.5	−22.8	−43.2	18.8	25.2	....	....	....
Monetary Authorities	78bod	....	....	....	....	....	....	....	....	....	....	....	....
General Government	78bpd	—	—	—	....	....	....	....	....	....	....	....	....
Banks	78bqd	−43.2	−9.6	−1.5	−14.1	39.5	−22.8	−43.2	18.8	25.2	....	....	....
Other Sectors	78brd	—	—	—	....	....	....	....	....	....	....	....	....
Other Investment Liab., n.i.e.	78bid	−7.7	−25.3	−3.6	−10.0	−36.0	−20.6	−3.7	73.3	86.6	....	....	....
Monetary Authorities	78bsd	—	—	−15.4	−17.5	−18.2	−25.3	—	—	—	....	....	....
General Government	78btd	−9.3	−8.3	—	—	—	—	—	67.2	79.0	....	....	....
Banks	78bud	−7.4	−17.0	11.8	7.5	−17.8	4.7	−3.7	6.2	7.6	....	....	....
Other Sectors	78bvd	9.0	—	—	—	—	—		....	....	....	....	....
Net Errors and Omissions	78cad	13.2	71.8	92.4	17.7	−100.5	−103.8	−165.1	−74.2	−57.2	....	....	....
Overall Balance	78cbd	−137.5	−178.4	−150.6	−158.4	−369.1	−254.2	−333.1	43.4	−3.9	....	....	....
Reserves and Related Items	79dad	137.5	178.4	150.6	158.4	369.1	254.2	333.1	−43.4	3.9	....	....	....
Reserve Assets	79dbd	−24.1	−5.6	−73.0	−70.7	25.4	28.1	12.4	−35.7	7.4	....	....	....
Use of Fund Credit and Loans	79dcd	8.3	8.1	15.6	5.5	3.3	−6.4	−8.0	−7.7	−3.6	....	....	....
Exceptional Financing	79ded	153.3	175.9	208.0	223.6	340.4	232.5	328.7	....	....	....	....	....
National Accounts		*Billions of Kip*											
Gross Domestic Product (GDP)	99b	951.0	1,107.8	1,430.4	1,725.7	2,201.0	4,240.0	10,329.0	13,669.0	15,702.0	18,390.0	20,307.0	24,621.0
GDP Volume 1990 Prices	99b.p	712.8	780.7	835.7	893.3	955.0	993.1	1,065.4	1,127.0	1,192.0	1,262.0	1,336.0	1,403.0
GDP Volume (2000=100)	99bvp	63.3	69.3	74.2	79.3	84.7	88.1	94.5	100.0	105.8	112.0	118.5	124.5
GDP Deflator (2000=100)	99bip	11.0	11.7	14.1	15.9	19.0	35.2	79.9	100.0	108.6	120.1	125.3	144.7
		Millions: Midyear Estimates											
Population	99z	4.46	4.57	4.69	4.80	4.92	5.04	5.16	5.28	5.40	5.53	5.66	5.79

Latvia 941

		1993	1994	1995	1996	1997	1998	1999	2000	2001	2002	2003	2004
Exchange Rates													
		Lats per SDR: End of Period											
Official Rate	aa	.817	.800	.798	.800	.796	.801	.800	.799	.802	.808	.804	.801
		Lats per US Dollar: End of Period (ae) Period Average (rf)											
Official Rate	ae	.595	.548	.537	.556	.590	.569	.583	.613	.638	.594	.541	.516
Official Rate	rf	.675	.560	.528	.551	.581	.590	.585	.607	.628	.618	.571	.540
Fund Position		*Millions of SDRs: End of Period*											
Quota	2f.s	91.50	91.50	91.50	91.50	91.50	91.50	126.80	126.80	126.80	126.80	126.80	126.80
SDRs	1b.s	71.10	.21	1.49	1.56	1.50	.21	2.24	—	.07	.05	.09	.10
Reserve Position in the Fund	1c.s	.01	.01	.01	.01	.01	.01	.01	.06	.06	.06	.06	.06
Total Fund Cred.&Loans Outstg	2tl	77.78	109.80	107.89	90.36	63.67	45.37	34.31	26.69	19.06	11.44	3.81	—
International Liquidity		*Millions of US Dollars Unless Otherwise Indicated: End of Period*											
Total Reserves minus Gold	1l.d	431.55	545.18	505.70	654.07	760.20	801.23	872.00	850.91	1,148.74	1,241.42	1,432.44	1,911.98
SDRs	1b.d	97.66	.31	2.22	2.25	2.03	.29	3.07	.01	.09	.07	.14	.15
Reserve Position in the Fund	1c.d	.01	.01	.01	.01	.01	.01	.01	.07	.07	.08	.08	.09
Foreign Exchange	1d.d	333.88	544.86	503.47	651.81	758.17	800.93	868.92	850.83	1,148.59	1,241.27	1,432.22	1,911.74
Gold (Million Fine Troy Ounces)	1ad	.2428	.2492	.2492	.2493	.2491	.2493	.2493	.2487	.2486	.2486	.2486	.2486
Gold (National Valuation)	1and	72.80	74.80	74.77	74.78	73.13	71.44	72.41	68.38	69.66	85.90	102.67	110.27
Monetary Authorities:Other Assets	3..d	.01	—	—	—	—	.01	.01	.01	—	.01	.01	.05
Other Liab	4..d	.01	—	—	—	—	—	—	—	—	.01	.02	.01
Deposit Money Banks: Assets	7a.d	229.93	664.25	599.56	1,021.16	1,546.56	1,258.96	1,489.19	2,112.97	2,271.57	3,019.08	4,071.00	5,816.06
Liabilities	7b.d	92.26	448.07	452.38	852.57	1,297.97	1,342.03	1,767.48	2,141.32	2,649.83	3,735.76	5,454.74	8,277.84
Monetary Authorities		*Millions of Lats: End of Period*											
Foreign Assets	11	307.13	341.98	313.52	407.63	461.47	461.23	535.64	568.45	780.39	793.51	836.43	1,067.63
Claims on Central Government	12a	—	6.59	39.38	22.33	72.88	81.00	57.70	73.47	43.33	76.13	65.29	93.21
Claims on Banks	12e	13.31	21.40	22.04	20.22	7.55	52.04	63.32	47.23	30.69	59.32	12.88	12.88
Reserve Money	14	225.56	269.43	273.62	336.66	441.74	471.45	526.28	566.72	641.88	759.87	807.63	957.53
of which: Currency Outside Banks	14a	152.75	213.06	209.54	264.00	332.65	340.19	377.41	427.66	485.19	543.13	601.05	645.41
Foreign Liabilities	16c	67.11	88.46	86.56	72.55	51.17	36.66	31.54	28.35	21.58	15.63	12.19	29.42
Central Government Deposits	16d	3.08	10.78	3.62	35.40	24.91	42.03	79.03	45.93	119.59	62.08	80.25	105.67
Capital Accounts	17a	14.70	8.02	11.00	20.89	36.60	47.22	47.23	52.02	61.64	82.76	83.17	92.23
Other Items (Net)	17r	10.00	−6.71	.15	−15.32	−12.52	−3.09	−27.40	−8.56	−2.13	−19.99	−22.20	−11.13
Banking Institutions		*Millions of Lats: End of Period*											
Reserves	20	69.31	57.29	64.15	71.69	107.23	129.93	144.46	135.11	153.25	213.73	204.90	310.82
Foreign Assets	21	136.81	364.01	321.96	567.77	912.47	716.35	868.20	1,295.25	1,449.26	1,793.33	2,202.41	3,001.09
Claims on Central Government	22a	520.53	† 97.14	120.81	140.09	113.01	71.41	114.01	138.36	170.10	180.33	273.65	246.07
Claims on Local Government	22b		6.66	11.51	15.52	2.66	4.41	15.77	36.22	51.71	42.70	67.84	67.74
Claims on Nonfin.Pub.Enterprises	22c	16.94	39.59	24.99	17.71	28.15	23.82	30.61	52.53	81.21	112.50	87.42	87.69
Claims on Private Sector	22d	253.97	335.67	184.13	202.99	344.28	533.10	612.18	804.74	1,100.54	1,506.83	2,189.49	3,283.84
Claims on Nonbank Financial Insts	22g	—	—	—	—	19.24	25.34	25.90	56.69	190.68	254.59	294.93	403.16
Demand Deposits	24	115.03	138.08	144.24	156.36	232.76	259.75	257.52	332.97	374.97	501.36	630.02	860.97
Time, Savings,& Fgn.Currency Dep	25	196.49	346.82	195.06	230.50	331.56	357.60	398.73	554.19	716.43	847.19	1,081.23	1,423.30
Money Market Instruments	26aa	—	—	—	—	—	—	—	—	—	.61	—	—
Foreign Liabilities	26c	54.90	245.54	242.93	474.03	765.80	763.61	1,030.44	1,312.63	1,690.59	2,219.04	2,951.02	4,271.37
Central Government Deposits	26d	520.57	† 13.92	36.98	6.31	50.33	32.83	18.10	10.14	31.37	55.07	22.80	64.61
Government Lending Funds	26f	16.94	61.43	39.68	22.00	19.66	16.73	22.48	22.55	21.26	9.94	6.80	5.39
Credit from Central Bank	26g	—	1.44	3.52	4.32	6.94	54.94	63.18	42.53	18.83	30.69	59.32	12.88
Capital Accounts	27a	73.52	96.79	77.58	118.67	117.56	62.05	40.07	230.18	314.26	389.68	493.07	647.10
Other Items (Net)	27r	20.12	−3.64	−12.44	3.58	2.43	−43.16	−19.39	13.70	29.04	50.45	76.39	114.80
Banking Survey		*Millions of Lats: End of Period*											
Foreign Assets (Net)	31n	321.94	371.98	306.00	428.82	556.97	377.31	341.86	522.72	517.48	352.18	75.64	−232.07
Domestic Credit	32	267.79	† 460.96	340.22	356.93	504.98	664.22	759.05	1,105.94	1,486.61	2,055.94	2,875.56	4,011.45
Claims on Central Govt. (Net)	32an	−3.12	† 79.04	119.59	120.71	110.66	77.55	74.60	155.77	62.46	139.31	235.88	169.01
Claims on Local Government	32b		6.66	11.51	15.52	2.66	4.41	15.77	36.22	51.71	42.70	67.84	67.74
Claims on Nonfin.Pub.Enterprises	32c	16.94	39.59	24.99	17.71	28.15	23.82	30.61	52.53	81.21	112.50	87.42	87.69
Claims on Private Sector	32d	253.97	335.67	184.13	202.99	344.28	533.10	612.18	804.74	1,100.54	1,506.83	2,189.49	3,283.84
Claims on Nonbank Fin. Insts	32g	—	—	—	—	19.24	25.34	25.90	56.69	190.68	254.59	294.93	403.16
Money	34	267.78	351.13	353.78	425.65	567.27	601.27	639.34	764.57	863.59	1,047.50	1,232.74	1,507.68
Quasi-Money	35	196.49	346.82	195.06	230.50	331.56	357.60	398.73	554.19	716.43	847.19	1,081.23	1,423.30
Money Market Instruments	36aa										.61		
Government Lending Funds	36f	16.94	61.43	39.68	22.00	19.66	16.73	22.48	22.55	21.26	9.94	6.80	5.39
Capital Accounts	37a	88.23	104.81	88.58	139.56	154.16	109.27	87.30	282.19	375.89	472.43	576.24	739.33
Other Items (Net)	37r	20.30	−31.24	−30.88	−31.97	−10.69	−43.34	−46.94	5.14	26.91	30.46	54.19	103.68
Money plus Quasi-Money	35l	464.27	697.95	548.84	656.15	898.83	958.87	1,038.01	1,318.77	1,580.02	1,894.69	2,313.97	2,930.98
Interest Rates		*Percent Per Annum*											
Discount Rate (End of Period)	60	27.00	25.00	24.00	9.50	4.00	4.00	4.00	3.50	3.50	3.00	3.00	4.00
Money Market Rate	60b	....	37.18	22.39	13.08	3.76	4.42	4.72	2.97	5.23	3.01	2.86	3.25
Treasury Bill Rate	60c	....	....	28.24	16.27	4.73	5.27	6.23	† 4.85	5.63	3.52	3.24	....
Deposit Rate	60l	34.78	31.68	14.79	11.71	5.90	5.33	5.04	4.38	5.24	3.23	3.02	3.27
Lending Rate	60p	86.36	55.86	34.56	25.78	15.25	14.29	14.20	11.87	11.17	7.97	5.38	7.45
Prices and Labor		*Index Numbers (2000=100): Period Averages*											
Share Prices	62	....	....	....	....	345.8	181.4	72.4	100.0	136.1	149.1	172.2	....
Producer Prices	63	65.7	76.7	85.9	97.6	101.6	103.5	99.4	† 100.0	101.7	102.7	105.9	115.0
Consumer Prices	64	42.0	57.1	71.3	83.9	90.9	95.2	97.4	100.0	† 102.5	104.5	107.5	114.2
Harmonized CPI (2002=100)	64h	....	....	....	....	....	....	....	....	....	100.0	102.9	109.3
Wages: Average Earnings	65	31.7	50.5	62.9	72.5	87.5	93.3	97.0	100.0	104.9	111.5	121.6	133.5
Industrial Employment	67	128.2	110.6	104.9	104.7	102.0	107.5	99.9	100.0	97.2	96.5	99.3	99.6
		Number in Thousands: Period Averages											
Labor Force	67d	1,320	1,300	....	1,182	1,186	1,168	1,157	1,132	1,106	1,124	1,126	....
Employment	67e	1,205	1,083	1,046	1,018	1,037	1,043	1,038	1,038	1,037	989	1,007	1,018
Unemployment	67c	77	84	83	91	85	111	110	93	92	....	119	118
Unemployment Rate (%)	67r	5.8	6.5	6.6	7.2	7.0	9.2	9.1	7.8	7.7	....	10.6	10.4

		1993	1994	1995	1996	1997	1998	1999	2000	2001	2002	2003	2004
Intl. Transactions & Positions							*Millions of Lats*						
Exports	70	676	553	688	795	972	1,069	1,008	1,131	1,256	1,409	1,651	2,115
Imports, c.i.f.	71	....	....	960	1,278	1,582	1,881	1,724	1,934	2,202	2,497	2,989	3,744
Imports, f.o.b.	71.v	639	695	923	1,223	1,513	1,796	1,652	....	....	....	....	....
						(2000=100) Period Averages							
Volume of Exports	72	76.7	52.0	59.1	63.9	84.7	85.7	87.3	100.0	102.5	112.2	121.5	....
Unit Value of Exports	74	72.9	84.0	97.5	103.6	105.2	105.1	101.2	†100.0	102.6	105.4	113.8	129.1
Balance of Payments						*Millions of US Dollars: Minus Sign Indicates Debit*							
Current Account, n.i.e.	78ald	417	201	−16	−280	−345	−650	−654	−355	−626	−621	−917	−1,673
Goods: Exports f.o.b.	78aad	1,054	1,022	1,368	1,488	1,838	2,011	1,889	2,080	2,243	2,545	3,171	4,185
Goods: Imports f.o.b.	78abd	−1,051	−1,322	−1,947	−2,286	−2,686	−3,141	−2,916	−3,123	−3,578	−4,024	−5,174	−6,935
Trade Balance	78acd	3	−301	−580	−798	−848	−1,130	−1,027	−1,044	−1,335	−1,479	−2,003	−2,749
Services: Credit	78add	533	657	720	1,126	1,033	1,108	1,024	1,173	1,182	1,244	1,514	1,783
Services: Debit	78aed	−205	−297	−246	−742	−662	−806	−689	−696	−672	−707	−938	−1,179
Balance on Goods & Services	78afd	332	60	−106	−414	−477	−827	−691	−567	−826	−942	−1,427	−2,145
Income: Credit	78agd	17	51	71	140	177	207	158	215	278	289	369	500
Income: Debit	78ahd	−10	−42	−53	−99	−122	−154	−214	−198	−221	−235	−390	−717
Balance on Gds, Serv. & Inc.	78aid	339	68	−87	−373	−422	−774	−747	−550	−769	−888	−1,448	−2,363
Current Transfers, n.i.e.: Credit	78ajd	81	136	75	98	91	137	114	406	372	538	924	1,289
Current Transfers: Debit	78akd	−3	−3	−5	−5	−14	−13	−21	−211	−229	−271	−393	−600
Capital Account, n.i.e.	78bcd	....	....	....	....	14	14	13	35	41	21	76	144
Capital Account, n.i.e.: Credit	78bad	....	....	....	....	14	14	13	40	50	26	80	150
Capital Account: Debit	78bbd	....	....	....	....	—	—	—	−5	−9	−6	−4	−7
Financial Account, n.i.e.	78bjd	67	363	636	537	347	601	768	412	897	687	897	1,968
Direct Investment Abroad	78bdd	5	65	65	−3	−6	−54	−17	−12	−19	−4	−36	−109
Dir. Invest. in Rep. Econ., n.i.e.	78bed	45	214	180	382	521	357	348	413	132	254	300	647
Portfolio Investment Assets	78bfd	—	−22	−37	−165	−539	−33	58	−351	−57	−220	−286	7
Equity Securities	78bkd	—	−12	−7	12	−113	7	77	−34	6	−2	6	−13
Debt Securities	78bld	—	−10	−30	−177	−426	−40	−19	−317	−64	−218	−292	20
Portfolio Investment Liab., n.i.e.	78bgd	....	....	—	24	−32	27	215	26	187	20	70	268
Equity Securities	78bmd	....	....	....	−2	6	30	7	−7	1	23	39	31
Debt Securities	78bnd	....	....	....	26	−39	−3	209	33	186	−3	31	237
Financial Derivatives Assets	78bwd	....	....	....	....	—	—	—	2	3	−7	−5	−35
Financial Derivatives Liabilities	78bxd	....	....	....	....	—	—	....	—	−3	20	11	−13
Other Investment Assets	78bhd	−129	−387	−31	−214	−326	75	−214	−389	−81	−472	−685	−1,692
Monetary Authorities	78bod	39	5	1	−1	—	—	36	—	—	—	—	−2
General Government	78bpd	....	....	....	....	—	—	—	—	−7	6	—	1
Banks	78bqd	−119	−400	99	−261	−253	67	−275	−370	−107	−469	−635	−1,601
Other Sectors	78brd	−50	8	−130	48	−73	9	25	−18	32	−8	−51	−91
Other Investment Liab., n.i.e.	78bid	146	493	458	513	730	229	379	724	734	1,095	1,528	2,894
Monetary Authorities	78bsd	−4	−5	—	—	—	—	6	—	1	−1	—	44
General Government	78btd	99	54	55	45	20	45	14	−8	7	−3	−65	−3
Banks	78bud	76	272	88	385	558	69	354	719	529	984	1,479	2,533
Other Sectors	78bvd	−25	172	315	84	152	115	4	12	197	115	113	320
Net Errors and Omissions	78cad	−186	−508	−653	−46	87	97	38	−90	2	−74	23	−35
Overall Balance	78cbd	298	57	−33	211	102	63	165	3	314	12	80	403
Reserves and Related Items	79dad	−298	−57	33	−211	−102	−63	−165	−3	−314	−12	−80	−403
Reserve Assets	79dbd	−371	−103	36	−186	−65	−38	−150	7	−305	−2	−69	−397
Use of Fund Credit and Loans	79dcd	74	47	−3	−25	−37	−25	−15	−10	−10	−10	−11	−6
Exceptional Financing	79ded	....	....	....	....	....	....	....	—	—	—	—	—
International Investment Position							*Millions of US Dollars*						
Assets	79aad	....	....	1,851	2,366	3,262	3,051	3,278	3,962	4,117	5,124	6,645	9,209
Direct Investment Abroad	79abd	....	....	231	209	222	281	244	241	44	64	106	226
Portfolio Investment	79acd	....	....	62	227	755	590	518	858	672	914	1,256	1,293
Equity Securities	79add	....	....	21	9	123	113	22	58	51	55	50	65
Debt Securities	79aed	....	....	41	218	633	477	495	800	621	859	1,207	1,229
Financial Derivatives	79ald	....	....	—	—	4	6	4	1	4	12	18	55
Other Investment	79afd	....	....	972	1,158	1,447	1,301	1,568	1,942	2,179	2,807	3,730	5,612
Monetary Authorities	79agd	....	....	2	3	7	4	2	1	1	1	1	2
General Government	79ahd	....	....	—	—	—	—	—	3	7	1	2	—
Banks	79aid	....	....	542	800	1,047	872	1,135	1,516	1,615	2,120	2,843	4,546
Other Sectors	79ajd	....	....	429	356	393	425	431	423	555	685	885	1,064
Reserve Assets	79akd	....	....	586	772	833	873	944	919	1,218	1,327	1,535	2,022
Liabilities	79lad	....	....	1,932	2,717	3,710	4,252	5,110	6,061	7,167	9,105	11,785	16,623
Dir. Invest. in Rep. Economy	79lbd	....	....	616	936	1,272	1,558	1,794	2,084	2,328	2,751	3,282	4,493
Portfolio Investment	79lcd	....	....	23	46	13	42	248	255	428	511	687	1,036
Equity Securities	79ldd	....	....	7	5	9	41	51	40	42	70	121	152
Debt Securities	79led	....	....	16	41	4	1	197	215	386	442	566	885
Financial Derivatives	79lld	....	....	—	—	4	2	9	—	7	29	43	32
Other Investment	79lfd	....	....	1,294	1,735	2,422	2,650	3,059	3,723	4,404	5,813	7,773	11,062
Monetary Authorities	79lgd	....	....	161	130	87	65	49	36	27	17	8	49
General Government	79lhd	....	....	242	279	284	343	345	327	324	337	297	311
Banks	79lid	....	....	399	782	1,332	1,278	1,619	2,328	2,615	3,688	5,380	8,159
Other Sectors	79ljd	....	....	492	544	719	965	1,047	1,031	1,438	1,771	2,088	2,544
Government Finance						*Millions of Lats: Year Ending December 31*							
Deficit (-) or Surplus	80	....	....	....	†−44.13	†23.34	†5.32	−140.15	−118.96	−67.96	−98.27	−90.79	−81.63
Total Revenue and Grants	81y	....	....	357.10	†874.92	1,174.54	†1,289.69	1,291.17	1,305.64	1,383.04	1,545.13	1,726.54	2,062.77
Revenue	81	....	....	....	....	....	....	....	....	....	....	....	....
Grants	81z	....	....	....	....	....	....	....	....	....	....	....	....
Exp. & Lending Minus Repay	82z	....	....	....	†919.05	†1,151.20	†1,284.37	1,431.32	1,424.60	1,451.00	1,643.40	1,817.33	2,144.40
Expenditure	82	....	....	445.60	†907.14	†1,116.81	†1,283.65	1,419.29	1,412.14	1,442.07	1,648.65	1,830.97	2,164.47
Lending Minus Repayments	83	....	....	....	†11.91	34.39	†.72	12.03	12.46	8.93	−5.25	−13.64	−20.07
Total Financing	80h	....	....	....	†44.13	−23.34	†−5.32	140.15	118.96	67.96	98.27	90.79	81.63
Domestic	84a	....	....	....	†31.81	−41.06	†−18.38	13.28	130.97	−37.57	86.96	135.84	−45.73
Foreign	85a	....	....	....	†12.32	17.72	†13.06	126.87	−12.01	105.53	11.31	−45.05	127.36

National Accounts		1993	1994	1995	1996	1997	1998	1999	2000	2001	2002	2003	2004
						Millions of Lats							
Househ.Cons.Expend.,incl.NPISHs....	96f	779.0	1,206.1	1,637.3	2,106.1	2,402.5	2,531.3	2,683.9	2,953.5	3,251.4	3,566.7	3,985.5	4,599.7
Government Consumption Expend...	91f	294.6	410.6	630.4	731.1	742.7	917.3	961.2	1,009.6	1,065.2	1,150.2	1,317.1	1,540.0
Gross Fixed Capital Formation..........	93e	201.8	303.9	354.9	512.8	613.7	979.5	980.0	1,151.5	1,297.5	1,370.6	1,527.8	1,908.3
Changes in Inventories.....................	93i	−67.2	86.9	14.2	−45.2	82.3	−39.7	.9	−52.7	91.9	154.5	295.9	471.1
Exports of Goods and Services..........	90c	1,074.4	948.8	1,101.0	1,440.1	1,669.1	1,841.4	1,708.1	1,983.8	2,138.3	2,361.6	2,680.5	3,222.3
Imports of Goods and Services (-).....	98c	835.9	906.8	1,157.8	1,668.8	1,947.3	2,326.8	2,109.8	2,360.0	2,676.0	2,912.6	3,484.2	4,381.9
Gross Domestic Product (GDP)........	99b	1,467.0	2,042.6	2,580.1	3,076.1	3,562.9	3,902.9	4,224.2	4,685.7	5,168.3	5,691.1	6,322.5	7,359.4
Net Primary Income from Abroad.....	98.n	156.6	215.8	11.5	22.9	32.1	31.9	−32.1	15.8	27.8	−4.8	−33.9	−119.0
Gross National Income (GNI)...........	99a	1,623.6	2,258.3	2,591.6	3,099.1	3,594.9	3,934.8	4,192.1	4,701.5	5,196.1	5,686.3	6,288.6	7,240.4
Net Current Transf.from Abroad......	98t	51.8	74.3	−214.9	−217.3	−248.4	−237.6	−280.3	−278.0	−306.4	....	....	....
Gross Nat'l Disposable Inc.(GNDI)....	99i	1,517.5	2,112.9	2,376.7	2,881.8	3,346.5	3,697.2	3,911.9	4,423.5	4,889.7	....	....	....
Gross Saving..................................	99s	601.8	716.0	359.6	379.7	494.8	559.4	604.6	877.5	977.7	1,116.2	1,251.8	1,471.5
Consumption of Fixed Capital..........	99cf	143.4	254.7	676.1	713.5	799.6	971.0	1,016.2	1,034.1	1,070.0	1,114.2	1,201.3	1,254.8
GDP Volume 2000 Prices.................	99b.p	4,780.3	4,893.0	3,606.0	3,742.7	4,052.7	4,244.1	4,383.6	4,685.7	5,061.0	5,387.3	5,348.9	6,282.8
GDP Volume (2000=100)...............	99bvp	102.0	104.4	77.0	79.9	86.5	90.6	93.6	100.0	108.0	115.0	114.2	134.1
GDP Deflator (2000=100)...............	99bip	30.7	41.7	71.6	82.2	87.9	92.0	96.4	100.0	102.1	105.6	118.2	117.1
						Millions: Midyear Estimates							
Population................................	99z	2.60	2.54	2.50	2.46	2.43	2.41	2.39	2.37	2.36	2.34	2.33	2.32

Lebanon 446

		1993	1994	1995	1996	1997	1998	1999	2000	2001	2002	2003	2004
Exchange Rates						*Pounds per SDR: End of Period*							
Market Rate	aa	2,350.2	2,404.4	2,372.4	2,231.7	2,060.3	2,123.3	2,069.1	1,964.1	1,894.5	2,049.5	2,240.1	2,341.2
					Pounds per US Dollar: End of Period (ae) Period Average (rf)								
Market Rate	ae	1,711.0	1,647.0	1,596.0	1,552.0	1,527.0	1,508.0	1,507.5	1,507.5	1,507.5	1,507.5	1,507.5	1,507.5
Market Rate	rf	1,741.4	1,680.1	1,621.4	1,571.4	1,539.5	1,516.1	1,507.8	1,507.5	1,507.5	1,507.5	1,507.5	1,507.5
					Index Numbers (2000=100): Period Averages								
Market Rate	ahx	86.62	89.76	92.98	95.94	97.95	99.42	99.97	100.00	100.07	100.13	100.13	100.13
Nominal Effective Exchange Rate	nec	63.56	70.00	69.38	74.00	83.53	88.51	91.43	100.00	105.22	102.62	91.12	84.81
Fund Position						*Millions of SDRs: End of Period*							
Quota	2f.s	78.7	146.0	146.0	146.0	146.0	146.0	203.0	203.0	203.0	203.0	203.0	203.0
SDRs	1b.s	10.5	11.4	12.3	13.3	14.3	15.4	16.4	18.2	19.4	20.1	20.6	21.2
Reserve Position in the Fund	1c.s	18.8	18.8	18.8	18.8	18.8	18.8	18.8	18.8	18.8	18.8	18.8	18.8
Total Fund Cred.&Loans Outstg	2tl	—	—	—	—	—	—	—	—	—	—	—	—
International Liquidity					*Millions of US Dollars Unless Otherwise Indicated: End of Period*								
Total Reserves minus Gold	1l.d	2,260.3	3,884.2	4,533.3	5,931.9	5,976.4	6,556.3	7,775.6	5,943.7	5,013.8	7,243.8	12,519.4	11,734.6
SDRs	1b.d	14.4	16.6	18.3	19.2	19.3	21.7	22.5	23.7	24.3	27.3	30.7	32.9
Reserve Position in the Fund	1c.d	25.9	27.5	28.0	27.1	25.4	26.5	25.8	24.5	23.7	25.6	28.0	29.2
Foreign Exchange	1d.d	2,220.0	3,840.1	4,487.0	5,885.6	5,931.6	6,508.0	7,727.3	5,895.4	4,965.8	7,190.9	12,460.8	11,672.4
Gold (Million Fine Troy Ounces)	1ad	9.222	9.222	9.222	9.222	9.222	9.222	9.222	9.222	9.222	9.222	9.222	9.222
Gold (National Valuation)	1and	3,603.6	3,534.5	3,571.8	3,410.0	2,670.3	2,651.0	2,678.0	2,524.6	2,561.1	3,216.3	3,833.5	4,006.0
Monetary Authorities: Other Liab	4..d	5.6	29.5	71.3	54.4	72.9	174.0	156.3	138.4	152.0	158.0	134.7	128.4
Deposit Money Banks: Assets	7a.d	4,114.9	3,806.5	3,970.7	4,329.2	6,014.4	6,620.8	5,910.8	8,159.3	8,615.7	9,503.8	9,908.3	13,552.9
Liabilities	7b.d	1,198.6	1,579.7	2,063.4	2,989.5	4,189.3	5,908.2	6,392.5	7,190.2	7,347.2	7,360.2	9,327.6	12,096.3
Monetary Authorities						*Billions of Pounds: End of Period*							
Foreign Assets	11	10,025.9	12,208.7	12,923.9	14,486.2	13,191.4	13,851.8	15,725.0	12,730.1	10,531.7	12,566.0	21,216.7	20,423.6
Claims on Central Government	12a	427.8	31.6	57.2	63.6	354.8	113.0	147.5	2,060.8	6,835.9	3,829.0	12,064.4	13,641.6
Claims on Private Sector	12d	44.4	73.1	120.0	338.7	587.7	640.3	578.7	628.8	696.1	914.4	973.4	900.4
Claims on Deposit Money Banks	12e	187.1	166.8	289.9	105.1	96.8	346.1	405.9	734.8	781.0	1,719.6	1,826.8	1,859.2
Reserve Money	14	2,159.8	3,816.7	4,624.5	5,604.4	8,404.0	7,944.3	8,378.2	8,927.4	12,246.5	13,487.7	29,908.7	30,906.2
of which: Currency Outside DMBs	14a	714.7	938.8	1,046.2	1,160.7	1,210.1	1,241.3	1,369.3	1,423.4	1,381.7	1,375.3	1,530.6	1,586.5
Foreign Liabilities	16c	9.6	48.6	113.8	84.4	111.3	262.3	235.6	208.7	229.1	238.3	203.1	193.6
Long-Term Foreign Liabilities	16cl	....	....	....	....	....	1,068.1	1,068.1	1,068.1	1,386.2	1,418.9	1,342.6	961.0
Central Government Deposits	16d	1,237.3	2,383.5	2,440.5	3,585.5	1,189.3	1,795.8	3,304.4	1,910.2	1,401.9	2,373.2	1,693.3	2,507.1
Capital Accounts	17a	95.7	88.5	134.1	312.7	328.1	796.7	883.1	911.9	1,049.2	1,255.5	1,913.9	1,899.8
Other Items (Net)	17r	13,813.1	12,236.7	11,990.3	10,629.3	7,814.0	6,130.6	5,906.1	5,649.8	5,273.9	358.0	1,665.7	357.0
of which: Valuation Adjustment	17rv	6,630.3	6,094.0	5,912.1	5,222.7	3,616.3	3,046.4	2,918.3	2,521.6	2,742.2	102.5	645.9	372.4
Deposit Money Banks						*Billions of Pounds: End of Period*							
Reserves	20	1,434.9	2,786.4	3,541.5	4,377.9	6,224.6	6,513.4	6,826.7	7,330.8	10,655.9	11,959.8	28,332.5	29,878.7
Foreign Assets	21	7,040.6	6,269.3	6,337.3	6,718.9	9,184.0	9,984.2	8,910.5	12,300.2	12,988.2	14,327.0	14,936.8	20,430.9
Claims on Central Government	22a	4,013.3	6,908.6	7,948.9	12,060.3	13,234.2	17,942.1	21,840.8	23,271.3	23,066.8	26,577.4	21,005.8	24,155.4
Claims on Private Sector	22d	5,897.9	7,799.8	10,320.0	12,687.0	15,451.3	18,681.5	20,994.3	22,243.2	22,192.0	22,926.5	22,835.7	24,020.4
Demand Deposits	24	422.4	492.7	508.0	568.7	685.5	758.3	845.8	862.2	889.6	1,094.3	1,277.3	1,389.3
Time & Foreign Currency Deposits	25	13,986.8	18,193.7	21,297.8	26,935.9	32,621.4	38,067.1	42,458.0	46,720.0	50,344.6	54,356.3	60,514.1	66,879.0
Foreign Liabilities	26c	2,050.9	2,601.7	3,293.1	4,639.8	6,397.1	8,909.6	9,636.7	10,839.2	11,075.9	11,095.5	14,061.4	18,235.2
Central Government Deposits	26d	151.7	255.4	261.0	285.1	216.6	346.1	701.7	720.9	525.5	591.0	1,325.3	1,480.0
Credit from Monetary Authorities	26g	187.1	166.8	289.9	105.1	96.8	346.1	405.9	734.8	781.0	1,719.6	1,826.8	1,859.2
Capital Accounts	27a	444.1	675.8	1,145.9	1,943.5	2,990.1	3,619.9	4,019.3	4,376.3	4,463.2	5,023.5	5,498.6	5,808.5
Other Items (Net)	27r	1,143.6	1,378.0	1,351.9	1,366.1	1,086.5	1,074.0	504.8	892.1	823.1	1,910.6	2,607.3	2,834.3
Monetary Survey						*Billions of Pounds: End of Period*							
Foreign Assets (Net)	31n	15,006.0	15,827.6	15,854.3	16,481.0	15,866.9	13,596.1	13,695.1	12,914.3	10,828.7	14,140.4	20,546.4	21,464.6
Domestic Credit	32	8,994.3	12,174.1	15,744.6	21,279.0	28,222.0	35,235.0	39,555.2	45,573.0	50,863.4	51,283.1	53,860.7	58,730.8
Claims on Central Govt. (Net)	32an	3,052.0	4,301.3	5,304.6	8,253.3	12,183.0	15,913.2	17,982.2	22,701.0	27,975.3	27,442.2	30,051.6	33,809.9
Claims on Private Sector	32d	5,942.3	7,872.9	10,440.0	13,025.7	16,039.0	19,321.8	21,573.0	22,872.0	22,888.1	23,840.9	23,809.1	24,920.9
Money	34	1,143.2	1,436.8	1,560.6	1,753.4	1,929.4	2,051.5	2,260.8	2,389.3	2,365.3	2,566.4	2,847.0	3,030.6
Quasi-Money	35	14,535.2	18,214.5	21,322.7	27,161.6	32,640.2	38,087.2	42,564.3	46,845.5	50,545.1	54,611.1	61,788.7	68,129.2
Other Items (Net)	37r	8,321.8	8,350.4	8,715.5	8,844.9	9,519.2	8,692.3	8,425.2	9,252.5	8,781.6	8,246.1	9,771.5	8,663.2
Money plus Quasi-Money	35l	15,678.5	19,651.3	22,883.3	28,915.1	34,569.6	40,138.8	44,825.1	49,234.8	52,910.4	57,177.5	64,635.7	71,159.8
Interest Rates						*Percent Per Annum*							
Discount Rate (End of Period)	60	20.22	16.49	19.01	25.00	30.00	30.00	25.00	20.00	20.00	20.00	20.00	20.00
Treasury Bill Rate	60c	18.27	15.09	19.40	15.19	13.42	12.70	11.57	11.18	11.18	10.90	....	5.25
Deposit Rate	60l	15.56	14.80	16.30	15.54	13.37	13.61	12.50	11.21	10.85	11.03	8.69	7.37
Lending Rate	60p	28.53	23.88	24.69	25.21	20.29	....	19.48	18.15	17.19	16.58	13.43	10.81
Intl. Transactions & Positions						*Millions of US Dollars*							
Exports	70..d	452	470	656	736	643	662	677	715	870	1,046	1,524	1,748
Imports, c.i.f	71..d	† 2,215	2,598	5,480	7,540	7,467	7,070	6,207	6,230	7,293	6,447	7,171	9,354
Government Finance						*Billions of Pounds: Year Ending December 31*							
Deficit (-) or Surplus	80	−1,017.0	−2,631.0	−3,309.3	−4,198.3	−5,902.8	−3,936.1	−4,029.8	−4,788.1	−4,003.3	−3,670.4	....	....
Revenue	81	1,855.0	2,241.0	3,032.7	3,533.7	3,753.2	4,449.4	4,868.2	4,171.7	4,259.6	5,385.3	....	....
Grants Received	81z	197.0	507.0	—	—	72.0	—	12.0	—	.2	.1	....	....
Expenditure	82	3,069.0	5,379.0	6,342.0	7,732.0	9,728.0	8,385.5	8,910.0	8,959.8	8,263.1	9,055.8	....	....
Lending Minus Repayments	83	—	—	—	—	—	—	—	—	—	—	....	....
Financing													
Domestic	84a	868.0	1,946.0	2,452.3	3,334.3	5,158.3	1,468.8	2,008.3	2,361.2	435.0	−3,785.8	....	....
Foreign	85a	149.0	685.0	857.0	864.0	744.5	2,467.3	2,021.5	2,426.9	3,568.3	7,456.2	....	....
Debt: Domestic	88a	6,089.4	9,347.5	11,997.2	17,228.8	19,797.1	21,685.7	25,382.8	27,161.2	28,213.8	26,302.3	....	....
Debt: Foreign	89a	563.6	1,286.0	2,157.8	2,958.5	3,713.3	6,282.5	8,350.8	10,494.7	14,423.5	21,972.4	....	....
						Millions: Midyear Estimates							
Population	99z	2.99	3.09	3.18	3.24	3.29	3.33	3.36	3.40	3.43	3.47	3.50	3.54

Lesotho 666

		1993	1994	1995	1996	1997	1998	1999	2000	2001	2002	2003	2004
Exchange Rates		\multicolumn{12}{c}{*Loti per SDR: End of Period*}											
Principal Rate	aa	4.66667	5.17298	5.42197	6.73325	6.56747	8.25106	8.44711	9.86107	15.23974	11.74625	9.86684	8.74345
		\multicolumn{12}{c}{*Loti per US Dollar: End of Period (ae) Period Average (rf)*}											
Principal Rate	ae	3.39750	3.54350	3.64750	4.68250	4.86750	5.86000	6.15450	7.56850	12.12650	8.64000	6.64000	5.63000
Principal Rate	rf	3.26774	3.55080	3.62709	4.29935	4.60796	5.52828	6.10948	6.93983	8.60918	10.54075	7.56475	6.45969
		\multicolumn{12}{c}{*Index Numbers (2000=100): Period Averages*}											
Principal Rate	ahx	211.6	194.6	190.4	161.7	150.0	126.0	113.0	100.0	81.3	66.7	91.6	107.2
Nominal Effective Exchange Rate	nec	186.6	171.5	162.1	140.1	136.5	117.3	107.6	100.0	83.1	66.2	88.5	101.8
Real Effective Exchange Rate	rec	131.2	124.9	124.9	113.7	117.1	106.4	104.2	100.0	86.7	75.9	102.5	88.7
Fund Position		\multicolumn{12}{c}{*Millions of SDRs: End of Period*}											
Quota	2f.s	23.90	23.90	23.90	23.90	23.90	23.90	34.90	34.90	34.90	34.90	34.90	34.90
SDRs	1b.s	.41	.33	.24	.92	.89	.86	.85	.51	.46	.44	.42	.40
Reserve Position in the Fund	1c.s	3.51	3.51	3.51	3.51	3.52	3.53	3.53	3.54	3.54	3.54	3.54	3.56
Total Fund Cred.&Loans Outstg	2tl	24.92	27.63	25.82	23.48	20.39	16.76	12.46	8.53	12.13	16.19	17.88	24.50
International Liquidity		\multicolumn{12}{c}{*Millions of US Dollars Unless Otherwise Indicated: End of Period*}											
Total Reserves minus Gold	1l.d	252.69	372.62	456.74	460.51	571.74	575.08	499.56	417.89	386.49	406.37	460.33	502.82
SDRs	1b.d	.56	.47	.35	1.33	1.20	1.22	1.17	.66	.58	.60	.63	.62
Reserve Position in the Fund	1c.d	4.82	5.13	5.22	5.05	4.75	4.98	4.85	4.61	4.45	4.82	5.26	5.53
Foreign Exchange	1d.d	247.30	367.02	451.17	454.13	565.78	568.89	493.54	412.62	381.46	400.95	454.44	496.67
Monetary Authorities: Other Liab.	4..d	1.63	1.85	33.39	28.73	26.79	24.79	42.72	37.78	27.16	52.98	47.33	55.69
Deposit Money Banks: Assets	7a.d	65.84	48.52	65.04	58.36	41.80	72.97	80.37	80.48	65.11	76.28	126.11	222.70
Liabilities	7b.d	9.64	10.29	16.51	12.83	11.69	8.05	6.48	18.50	8.48	11.53	34.58	24.14
Monetary Authorities		\multicolumn{12}{c}{*Millions of Maloti: End of Period*}											
Foreign Assets	11	869.28	1,337.58	1,802.01	2,310.26	2,929.82	3,549.85	3,349.33	3,486.14	5,138.38	3,858.43	3,341.55	3,351.63
Claims on Central Government	12a	375.85	381.63	287.92	318.78	166.39	145.88	110.39	105.04	250.96	192.44	176.44	214.25
Claims on Private Sector	12d	—	—	8.91	8.69	10.52	11.54	12.20	13.90	13.56	13.53	14.99	16.30
Claims on Deposit Money Banks	12e	.39	.44	—	—	—	—	—	—	—	—	—	—
Reserve Money	14	233.68	249.15	329.83	346.37	388.95	540.13	717.32	669.79	499.36	500.91	533.95	566.78
of which: Currency Outside DMBs	14a	43.75	52.57	74.11	84.09	92.51	134.50	122.66	139.34	147.14	179.68	183.52	204.54
Foreign Liabilities	16c	121.82	149.49	261.78	292.62	264.26	283.56	368.13	370.06	514.22	647.88	490.68	527.75
Central Government Deposits	16d	790.87	1,134.25	1,350.19	1,659.50	2,062.82	2,125.51	1,602.59	1,356.38	1,502.35	1,257.31	1,263.91	1,411.84
Capital Accounts	17a	77.86	82.34	185.68	368.79	409.22	735.54	805.41	1,208.99	2,858.28	1,772.05	1,393.50	1,204.24
Other Items (Net)	17r	21.30	104.42	−28.64	−29.55	−18.54	22.52	−21.54	−.14	28.69	−113.75	−149.06	−128.43
Deposit Money Banks		\multicolumn{12}{c}{*Millions of Maloti: End of Period*}											
Reserves	20	179.47	180.45	165.68	245.58	245.22	490.59	573.72	506.81	127.06	159.15	181.10	172.46
Foreign Assets	21	223.69	171.94	237.24	273.27	203.46	427.59	494.65	609.09	789.61	659.10	837.34	1,253.79
Claims on Central Government	22a	99.72	103.95	74.91	74.35	74.23	51.53	586.38	586.20	691.32	812.38	991.45	543.43
Claims on Nonfin.Pub.Enterprises	22c	29.31	30.92	80.53	141.33	127.62	225.53	105.28	79.22	46.39	42.75	38.94	52.16
Claims on Private Sector	22d	502.61	699.24	665.46	667.27	979.29	829.70	845.29	869.11	927.44	1,062.83	493.73	540.26
Claims on Other Banking Insts	22f	10.00	10.39	—	—	—	—	—	—	—	—	—	—
Demand Deposits	24	389.43	434.02	445.91	548.00	686.57	836.92	821.27	873.73	939.04	1,099.15	1,185.21	1,197.50
Time and Savings Deposits	25	501.99	550.42	601.05	692.40	743.97	785.67	720.52	664.94	700.44	727.24	760.10	783.63
Money Market Instruments	26aa	11.18	12.22	7.48	2.68	9.10	1.97	4.82	10.12	34.05	8.25	17.43	16.90
Foreign Liabilities	26c	32.74	36.47	60.23	60.06	56.89	47.20	39.89	140.01	102.82	99.63	229.64	135.90
Central Government Deposits	26d	48.30	39.59	37.53	43.66	46.04	76.77	77.12	68.38	63.31	63.89	68.35	57.76
Capital Accounts	27a	189.51	233.51	119.12	56.11	−74.15	−38.31	209.92	318.90	279.18	286.81	301.92	346.86
Other Items (Net)	27r	−128.35	−109.33	−47.50	−1.12	161.40	314.73	731.78	574.35	462.99	451.24	−20.09	23.57
Monetary Survey		\multicolumn{12}{c}{*Millions of Maloti: End of Period*}											
Foreign Assets (Net)	31n	938.41	1,323.56	1,717.24	2,230.85	2,812.12	3,646.68	3,435.95	3,585.17	5,310.96	3,770.03	3,458.57	3,941.78
Domestic Credit	32	178.33	52.29	−270.00	−492.76	−750.82	−938.11	−20.17	228.70	364.01	802.72	383.30	−103.20
Claims on Central Govt. (Net)	32an	−363.59	−688.26	−1,024.89	−1,310.03	−1,868.24	−2,004.88	−982.95	−733.52	−623.38	−316.38	−164.36	−711.92
Claims on Nonfin.Pub.Enterprises	32c	29.31	30.92	80.53	141.33	127.62	225.53	105.28	79.22	46.39	42.75	38.94	52.16
Claims on Private Sector	32d	502.61	699.24	674.37	675.95	989.81	841.24	857.49	883.00	941.00	1,076.35	508.72	556.56
Claims on Other Banking Insts	32f	10.00	10.39	—	—	—	—	—	—	—	—	—	—
Money	34	433.18	486.59	537.70	641.62	787.03	983.17	957.32	1,035.96	1,292.27	1,440.94	1,537.75	1,589.42
Quasi-Money	35	501.99	550.42	601.05	692.40	743.97	785.67	720.52	664.94	700.44	727.24	760.10	783.63
Money Market Instruments	36aa	11.18	12.22	7.48	2.68	9.10	1.97	4.82	10.12	34.05	8.25	17.43	16.90
Capital Accounts	37a	267.37	315.85	304.80	424.89	335.07	697.22	1,015.34	1,527.89	3,137.46	2,058.86	1,695.42	1,551.10
Other Items (Net)	37r	−96.98	10.78	−3.77	−23.51	186.13	240.54	717.78	574.95	510.75	337.46	−168.84	−102.46
Money plus Quasi-Money	35l	935.17	1,037.01	1,138.74	1,334.02	1,531.00	1,768.83	1,677.84	1,700.90	1,992.71	2,168.18	2,297.85	2,373.05
Interest Rates		\multicolumn{12}{c}{*Percent Per Annum*}											
Discount Rate (End of Period)	60	13.50	13.50	15.50	17.00	15.60	19.50	19.00	15.00	13.00	16.19	15.00	13.00
Treasury Bill Rate	60c	† 10.01	9.44	12.40	13.89	14.83	15.47	12.45	9.06	9.49	11.34	11.96	8.55
Savings Rate	60k	7.84	6.75	9.53	10.67	10.08	9.47	5.95	3.50	4.00	4.00	3.39	1.89
Deposit Rate	60l	8.06	8.43	13.34	12.73	11.81	10.73	7.45	4.92	4.83	5.19	5.16	4.24
Lending Rate	60p	15.83	14.25	16.38	17.71	18.03	20.06	19.06	17.11	16.55	17.11	16.02	12.38
Prices		\multicolumn{12}{c}{*Index Numbers (2000=100): Period Averages*}											
Consumer Prices	64	58.9	63.8	69.7	76.2	....	....	94.2	100.0	90.4	120.9	129.0	....
Intl. Transactions & Positions		\multicolumn{12}{c}{*Millions of Maloti*}											
Exports	70	438.0	509.0	581.0	812.0	904.0	1,071.0	1,053.3	1,528.0	2,426.2	3,852.0	3,604.9	4,218.4
Imports, c.i.f.	71	2,839.0	3,000.0	3,576.0	4,303.0	4,722.0	4,699.0	4,773.2	5,048.0	5,823.8	8,120.0	7,693.3	....

Lesotho 666

		1993	1994	1995	1996	1997	1998	1999	2000	2001	2002	2003	2004
Balance of Payments		*Millions of US Dollars: Minus Sign Indicates Debit*											
Current Account, n.i.e.	78ald	29.3	108.1	−323.0	−302.5	−269.2	−280.2	−220.8	−151.4	−95.1	−126.7	−134.7	−76.0
Goods: Exports f.o.b.	78aad	134.0	143.5	160.0	186.9	196.1	193.4	172.5	211.1	278.6	357.3	475.0	707.3
Goods: Imports f.o.b.	78abd	−868.1	−810.2	−985.2	−998.6	−1,024.4	−866.0	−779.2	−727.6	−678.6	−762.7	−994.4	−1,302.0
Trade Balance	78acd	−734.1	−666.7	−825.2	−811.8	−828.3	−672.5	−606.7	−516.5	−400.0	−405.5	−519.4	−594.7
Services: Credit	78add	37.0	37.8	39.0	42.6	86.9	53.6	43.7	42.7	40.5	34.9	50.0	63.9
Services: Debit	78aed	−70.5	−64.2	−61.1	−55.9	−67.6	−52.2	−50.1	−42.5	−49.0	−56.0	−85.0	−96.1
Balance on Goods & Services	78afd	−767.6	−693.2	−847.3	−825.1	−809.0	−671.2	−613.1	−516.4	−408.5	−426.5	−554.4	−626.9
Income: Credit	78agd	444.5	369.6	471.6	453.0	447.4	357.7	325.0	288.8	235.3	206.8	304.1	379.1
Income: Debit	78ahd	−22.8	−39.4	−157.4	−119.5	−110.0	−123.6	−80.6	−62.6	−56.7	−28.6	−54.3	−76.3
Balance on Gds, Serv. & Inc	78aid	−345.9	−363.0	−533.2	−491.6	−471.6	−437.1	−368.6	−290.2	−229.9	−248.3	−304.7	−324.1
Current Transfers, n.i.e.: Credit	78ajd	376.5	472.1	211.3	190.2	202.9	158.0	149.4	139.8	137.2	123.3	171.8	250.7
Current Transfers: Debit	78akd	−1.3	−.9	−1.2	−1.1	−.5	−1.2	−1.6	−1.0	−2.5	−1.7	−1.9	−2.5
Capital Account, n.i.e.	78bcd	—	—	43.7	45.5	44.5	22.9	15.2	22.0	16.8	23.5	27.5	33.4
Capital Account, n.i.e.: Credit	78bad	—	—	43.7	45.5	44.5	22.9	15.2	22.0	16.8	23.5	27.5	33.4
Capital Account: Debit	78bbd	—	—	—	—	—	—	—	—	—	—	—	....
Financial Account, n.i.e.	78bjd	55.2	33.0	349.1	350.6	323.7	316.1	135.8	85.2	88.6	92.0	98.2	63.3
Direct Investment Abroad	78bdd	—	—	....	....	....	....	....	....	....	—	....	−.1
Dir. Invest. in Rep. Econ., n.i.e.	78bed	15.0	18.7	275.3	287.5	268.1	264.8	163.3	117.8	117.0	84.1	115.7	123.5
Portfolio Investment Assets	78bfd	—	—	....	....	....	....	....	....	....	....	....	....
Equity Securities	78bkd	—	—	....	....	....	....	....	....	....	—	....	....
Debt Securities	78bld	—	—	....	....	....	....	....	....	....	—	....	....
Portfolio Investment Liab., n.i.e.	78bgd	—	—	....	....	....	....	....	....	....	....	....	....
Equity Securities	78bmd	—	—	....	....	....	....	....	....	....	....	....	....
Debt Securities	78bnd	—	—	....	....	....	....	....	....	....	....	....	....
Financial Derivatives Assets	78bwd	....	....	....	....	....	....	....	....	....	....	....	....
Financial Derivatives Liabilities	78bxd	....	....	....	....	....	....	....	....	....	....	....	....
Other Investment Assets	78bhd	8.9	−13.4	18.8	−7.0	−5.0	−1.7	−11.0	−19.1	−20.2	1.5	−8.8	−48.9
Monetary Authorities	78bod	....	....	....	....	....	....	....	....	....	....	....	....
General Government	78bpd	....	....	....	....	....	....	....	....	....	....	....	....
Banks	78bqd	8.9	−13.4	18.8	−7.0	−5.0	−1.7	−11.0	−19.1	−20.2	1.5	−8.8	−48.9
Other Sectors	78brd	—	—	....	....	....	....	....	....	....	....	....	....
Other Investment Liab., n.i.e.	78bid	31.3	27.6	55.0	70.1	60.5	53.0	−16.6	−13.5	−8.2	6.4	−8.7	−11.2
Monetary Authorities	78bsd	—	.3	6.3	−.2	—	.1	−5.4	−3.5	16.0	3.9	−17.8	.9
General Government	78btd	27.7	26.0	49.2	71.8	68.6	59.8	−9.3	−15.1	−19.0	2.9	−10.0	1.6
Banks	78bud	1.5	1.9	....	....	−7.2	−6.7	−1.2	5.2	−4.8	—	19.2	−13.7
Other Sectors	78bvd	2.1	−.5	−.5	−1.4	−.9	−.1	−.6	−.1	−.5	−.4	−.1	—
Net Errors and Omissions	78cad	17.8	−20.3	28.1	23.3	42.1	56.8	29.0	62.1	155.4	−166.4	−56.6	−15.8
Overall Balance	78cbd	102.3	120.9	97.8	116.9	141.0	115.6	−40.8	17.8	165.7	−177.6	−65.7	4.9
Reserves and Related Items	79dad	−102.3	−120.9	−97.8	−116.9	−141.0	−115.6	40.8	−17.8	−165.7	177.6	65.7	−4.9
Reserve Assets	79dbd	−111.7	−124.6	−95.1	−113.5	−136.8	−110.7	46.7	−12.6	−170.2	172.4	63.2	−14.7
Use of Fund Credit and Loans	79dcd	9.5	3.8	−2.7	−3.4	−4.3	−4.9	−5.9	−5.2	4.5	5.2	2.5	9.8
Exceptional Financing	79ded	....	....	....	....	....	....	....	....	....	....	....	....
International Investment Position		*Millions of US Dollars*											
Assets	79aad	....	....	....	....	....	....	....	....	....	....	....	....
Direct Investment Abroad	79abd	....	....	—	—	—	—	—	—	—	—	—	—
Portfolio Investment	79acd	....	....	—	—	—	—	—	—	—	—	—	—
Equity Securities	79add	....	....	—	—	—	—	—	—	—	—	—	—
Debt Securities	79aed	....	....	—	—	—	—	—	—	—	—	—	—
Financial Derivatives	79ald	....	....	....	....	....	....	....	....	....	....	....	....
Other Investment	79afd	....	....	71.8	61.9	114.5	83.8	79.6	80.5	65.1	89.4	126.6	222.7
Monetary Authorities	79agd	....	....	—	—	—	—	—	—	—	—	—	—
General Government	79ahd	....	....	—	—	—	—	—	—	—	—	—	—
Banks	79aid	....	....	71.8	61.9	114.5	83.8	79.6	80.5	65.1	89.4	126.6	222.7
Other Sectors	79ajd	....	....	—	—	—	—	—	—	—	—	—	—
Reserve Assets	79akd	....	....	456.7	460.5	571.7	575.1	499.8	419.8	423.7	446.6	503.2	593.9
Liabilities	79lad	....	....	....	....	....	....	....	....	....	....	....	....
Dir. Invest. in Rep. Economy	79lbd	....	....	—	—	—	—	—	—	—	—	—	—
Portfolio Investment	79lcd	....	....	—	—	—	—	—	—	—	—	—	—
Equity Securities	79ldd	....	....	—	—	—	—	—	—	—	—	—	—
Debt Securities	79led	....	....	—	—	—	—	—	—	—	—	—	—
Financial Derivatives	79lld	....	....	....	....	....	....	....	....	....	....	....	....
Other Investment	79lfd	....	....	566.8	535.6	512.6	590.7	559.5	600.9	580.9	702.2	802.1	886.4
Monetary Authorities	79lgd	....	....	39.9	35.1	28.8	24.7	18.2	11.7	57.3	96.9	100.1	131.8
General Government	79lhd	....	....	510.3	487.7	475.3	543.5	534.8	570.7	515.1	593.8	667.5	730.5
Banks	79lid	....	....	16.5	12.8	8.5	22.4	6.5	18.5	8.5	11.5	34.6	24.1
Other Sectors	79ljd	....	....	—	—	—	—	—	—	—	—	—	—
Government Finance		*Millions of Maloti: Year Beginning April 1*											
Deficit (-) or Surplus	80	147.2	149.3	108.6	137.4	88.8	−188.8	−286.8	−204.8	−42.6	−342.9	−247.3	....
Revenue	81	1,269.4	1,438.5	1,681.6	2,034.6	2,353.4	2,158.7	2,275.7	2,626.6	2,787.5	3,035.0	3,368.1	....
Grants Received	81z	137.4	143.6	163.2	203.4	178.7	120.0	130.0	125.6	188.8	286.7	276.8	....
Exp. & Lending Minus Repay	82z	1,259.6	1,432.8	1,736.2	2,100.6	2,443.3	2,467.5	2,692.5	2,957.0	3,018.9	3,664.6	3,892.2	....
Expenditure	82	1,169.4	994.1	1,118.1	1,179.0	1,537.6	1,971.7	2,311.5	2,457.9	2,393.3	2,935.0	3,151.3	....
Lending Minus Repayments	83	90.2	438.7	618.1	921.6	905.7	495.8	381.0	499.1	625.6	729.6	740.9	....
Financing													
Domestic	84a	−298.9	−252.5	−319.5	−537.3	−559.8	155.1	386.3	426.5	10.7	328.5	273.2	....
Foreign	85a	151.7	103.2	210.9	399.9	471.0	33.7	−99.8	−221.7	31.9	14.4	−25.9	....
Debt: Domestic	88a	....	....	....	....	190.2	160.1	730.1	788.5	763.3	929.0	1,159.7	....
Debt: Foreign	89a	....	1,704.4	1,861.5	2,255.1	2,313.4	3,185.1	3,121.9	4,319.6	6,246.2	6,059.5	4,432.0	....

Lesotho   666

		1993	1994	1995	1996	1997	1998	1999	2000	2001	2002	2003	2004
National Accounts						*Millions of Maloti: Year Beginning April 1*							
Househ.Cons.Expend.,incl.NPISHs....	96f	3,472.3	3,544.9	4,075.3	4,834.8	5,399.5	5,543.7	5,730.1	6,041.3	6,468.4	7,345.2	....	....
Government Consumption Expend...	91f	403.6	486.5	607.2	658.6	800.0	1,023.4	1,080.8	1,139.8	1,188.2	1,323.0	....	....
Gross Fixed Capital Formation.........	93e	1,476.5	1,693.1	2,071.2	2,360.2	2,593.5	2,411.0	2,651.0	2,657.1	2,810.0	3,254.6	3,287.1	....
Changes in Inventories....................	93i	−16.1	−44.6	−24.3	7.8	−47.1	−93.4	−56.2	−178.2	−171.1	−135.4	—	....
Exports of Goods and Services.........	90c	559.6	642.8	720.4	965.6	1,261.3	1,320.7	1,322.4	1,775.6	2,771.7	4,112.9	4,195.3	....
Imports of Goods and Services (-).....	98c	3,231.9	3,357.4	4,066.1	4,801.8	5,287.7	5,284.6	5,275.6	5,511.9	6,458.3	8,039.7	8,284.6	....
Gross Domestic Product (GDP)........	99b	2,664.1	2,965.3	3,383.7	4,053.7	4,719.5	4,920.7	5,564.9	5,964.0	6,608.8	7,773.1	8,617.8	....
Net Primary Income from Abroad.....	98.n	1,325.2	1,348.5	1,410.9	1,421.5	1,538.9	1,384.7	1,492.5	1,522.3	1,509.9	1,700.5	1,823.2	....
Gross National Income (GNI)............	99a	3,989.3	4,310.8	4,794.6	5,475.1	6,258.5	6,305.4	7,057.4	7,485.8	8,117.6	9,473.6	10,441.0	....
Net National Income........................	99e	4,664.4	5,103.1	5,713.2	6,473.4	7,396.3	7,272.9	8,055.5	8,529.8	9,402.4	10,751.3	11,714.7	....
GDP Volume 1995 Prices.................	99b.p	3,134.8	3,241.5	3,383.7	3,720.6	4,023.8	3,837.0	3,846.4	3,897.1	4,022.2	4,175.2	....	....
GDP Volume (2000=100)................	99bvp	80.4	83.2	86.8	95.5	103.3	98.5	98.7	100.0	103.2	107.1	....	....
GDP Deflator (2000=100)...............	99bip	55.5	59.8	65.3	71.2	76.6	83.8	94.5	100.0	107.4	121.7	....	....
						Millions: Midyear Estimates							
Population...............................	99z	1.65	1.67	1.69	1.71	1.74	1.76	1.77	1.79	1.80	1.80	1.80	1.80

		1993	1994	1995	1996	1997	1998	1999	2000	2001	2002	2003	2004
Exchange Rates					*Liberian Dollars per SDR: End of Period*								
Market Rate	aa	1.3736	1.4599	1.4865	1.4380	1.3493	†60.8973	54.2141	55.6994	62.2081	88.3688	75.0415	84.6390
					Liberian Dollars per US Dollar: End of Period (ae) Period Average (rf)								
Market Rate	ae	1.0000	1.0000	1.0000	1.0000	1.0000	†43.2500	39.5000	42.7500	49.5000	65.0000	50.5000	54.5000
Market Rate	rf	1.0000	1.0000	1.0000	1.0000	1.0000	†41.5075	41.9025	40.9525	48.5833	61.7542	59.3788	54.9058
Fund Position					*Millions of SDRs: End of Period*								
Quota	2f.s	71.30	71.30	71.30	71.30	71.30	71.30	71.30	71.30	71.30	71.30	71.30	71.30
SDRs	1b.s	—	—	—	—	—	—	—	—	—	—	—	—
Reserve Position in the Fund	1c.s	.03	.03	.03	.03	.03	.03	.03	.03	.03	.03	.03	.03
Total Fund Cred.&Loans Outstg	2tl	226.52	225.83	225.74	225.74	225.70	225.26	224.82	224.36	223.91	223.67	223.67	223.67
International Liquidity					*Millions of US Dollars: End of Period*								
Total Reserves minus Gold	1l.d	2.36	5.07	28.09	.38	.42	.62	.43	.27	.48	3.30	7.38	18.74
SDRs	1b.d	—	—	—	—	—	—	—	—	—	—	—	—
Reserve Position in the Fund	1c.d	.04	.04	.04	.04	.04	.04	.04	.04	.04	.04	.04	.05
Foreign Exchange	1d.d	2.32	5.03	28.05	.34	.38	.58	.39	.23	.44	3.26	7.33	18.69
Monetary Authorities: Other Liab	4..d	9.45	9.08	9.68	12.40	12.56	10.87	10.48	9.78	6.38	7.16	7.16	7.09
Banking Institutions: Assets	7a.d	49.05	9.46	12.04	9.49	15.59	10.36	16.80	12.39	11.04	10.36	15.21	35.73
Liabilities	7b.d	17.86	46.33	15.35	5.12	8.44	2.47	3.01	10.01	11.87	9.65	10.55	22.54
Monetary Authorities					*Millions of Liberian Dollars: End of Period*								
Foreign Assets	11	2.4	5.1	28.1	.4	.4	26.7	17.0	†11.4	23.8	214.4	372.5	1,021.7
Claims on Central Government	12a	1,264.1	1,284.9	1,513.0	1,803.1	1,916.2	35,687.0	32,605.1	†36,643.0	41,690.6	59,640.5	50,482.3	56,911.6
Claims on Nonfin.Pub.Enterprises	12c	4.8	4.8	4.8	5.6	5.6	5.8	5.5	†—		.8	.6	.5
Claims on Private Sector	12d	17.8	15.5	15.4	20.5	20.2	25.5	24.6	†48.9	16.5	50.5	64.5	100.0
Claims on Banking Institutions	12e	23.4	51.4	61.5	2.5	2.3	4.3	1.7	†77.3	134.9	163.0	65.7	81.1
Claims on Nonbank Financial Insts	12g	.7	.7		.2	.2	1.5	1.5	†				
Reserve Money	14	522.9	551.1	723.4	852.6	920.5	938.4	979.9	†1,384.7	1,548.2	1,645.9	1,793.0	2,910.3
of which: Currency Outside Banks	14a	274.1	302.9	485.8	568.4	576.6	565.5	556.9	†698.3	845.1	1,045.0	1,303.7	1,754.9
Other Liabs. to Banking Insts	14n	—	—	—	—	—	—	—	†6.3	5.5	865.5	715.6	710.1
Time Deposits	15	2.2	2.1	2.7	3.9	4.8	3.0	1.7	†533.2	716.9	83.8	65.8	70.2
Restricted Deposits	16b	—	—	—	—	—	—	—	†14.0	14.0	18.8	138.4	18.8
Foreign Liabilities	16c	571.5	622.4	651.1	646.9	622.4	28,629.2	25,893.0	†27,242.9	30,922.3	44,487.4	38,133.7	43,466.2
Central Government Deposits	16d	71.6	74.2	15.1	18.6	20.0	137.4	71.0	†8.9	42.2	70.8	193.4	63.2
Capital Accounts	17a	69.6	60.8	12.7	42.3	61.8	9,259.2	7,735.2	†7,619.1	8,815.5	14,414.3	11,330.8	12,176.6
Other Items (Net)	17r	75.4	51.8	217.7	267.8	315.3	−3,216.4	−2,025.2	†−14.4	−184.8	−1,498.7	−1,246.7	−1,281.6
Banking Institutions					*Millions of Liberian Dollars: End of Period*								
Reserves	20	217.3	215.4	201.8	188.4	240.0	768.5	815.2	†1,168.2	1,397.3	782.4	692.5	1,537.0
Other Claims on Monetary Author	20n	—	—	—	—	—	—	—	†6.3	5.5	865.5	715.6	710.1
Foreign Assets	21	49.1	9.5	12.0	9.5	15.6	447.9	660.2	†529.8	546.7	673.2	768.2	1,947.2
Claims on Central Government	22a	8.8	5.4	5.1	3.5	—	306.2	358.1	†425.3	580.9	921.3	661.4	738.7
Claims on Nonfin.Pub.Enterprises	22c	82.7	63.1	21.0	5.7	7.9	12.2	44.5	†39.5	64.6	85.1	58.4	105.8
Claims on Private Sector	22d	127.2	222.7	176.0	55.4	82.7	1,148.1	900.9	†663.2	877.0	1,125.9	1,071.7	1,550.9
Claims on Nonbank Financial Insts	22g	.3	—	2.1	5.3	—	—	—	†123.6	181.2	104.7	85.9	186.7
Demand Deposits	24	151.6	155.3	167.0	127.4	110.0	1,005.5	1,247.9	†898.8	851.6	1,318.2	1,391.3	1,971.9
Time and Savings Deposits	25	274.5	324.4	360.9	195.5	235.5	335.8	324.7	†391.5	422.4	535.2	443.8	960.3
Restricted Deposits	26b	—	—	—	—	—	—	—	†152.1	152.1	201.4	419.8	432.6
Foreign Liabilities	26c	17.9	46.3	15.3	5.1	8.4	106.9	119.0	†427.9	587.4	627.2	532.6	1,228.3
Central Government Deposits	26d	30.5	35.3	30.3	10.6	51.1	112.0	165.4	†134.1	122.8	202.1	160.2	161.9
Credit from Monetary Authorities	26g	20.0	23.7	16.9		—	1.9	2.0	†104.3	115.8	37.0	34.2	29.9
Capital Accounts	27a	22.7	33.5	3.8	3.4	−5.5	36.3	685.6	†785.0	1,097.0	1,057.3	661.1	885.4
Other Items (Net)	27r	−31.7	−102.4	−176.3	−74.1	−53.4	1,084.5	234.3	†62.1	304.1	579.6	410.8	1,106.1
Banking Survey					*Millions of Liberian Dollars: End of Period*								
Foreign Assets (Net)	31n	−538.0	−654.2	−626.3	−642.2	−614.9	−28,261.6	−25,334.9	†−27,129.6	−30,939.3	−44,227.0	−37,525.6	−41,725.6
Domestic Credit	32	1,404.4	1,487.6	1,692.0	1,870.1	1,961.7	36,936.9	33,703.9	†37,800.5	43,245.7	61,655.8	52,071.1	59,369.1
Claims on Central Govt. (Net)	32an	1,170.8	1,180.7	1,472.6	1,777.4	1,845.0	35,743.8	32,726.8	†36,925.4	42,106.4	60,288.8	50,790.0	57,425.2
Claims on Nonfin.Pub.Enterprises	32c	87.5	68.0	25.8	11.3	13.5	18.0	50.1	†39.5	64.6	85.9	59.0	106.3
Claims on Private Sector	32d	145.1	238.2	191.5	75.8	102.9	1,173.6	925.5	†712.1	893.5	1,176.4	1,136.2	1,650.9
Claims on Nonbank Fin. Insts	32g	1.0	.7	2.1	5.5	.2	1.5	1.5	†123.6	181.2	104.7	85.9	186.7
Money	34	425.8	458.3	652.8	696.2	686.8	1,571.0	1,804.8	†1,597.0	1,703.4	2,363.5	2,755.6	3,727.5
Quasi-Money	35	276.7	326.5	363.6	199.4	240.3	338.8	326.4	†924.7	1,139.3	619.1	509.6	1,030.4
Restricted Deposits	36b	—	—	—	—	—	—	—	†166.1	166.1	220.2	558.2	451.4
Capital Accounts	37a	92.2	94.3	16.6	45.7	56.3	9,295.6	8,420.7	†8,404.1	9,912.5	15,471.6	11,991.9	13,062.1
Other Items (Net)	37r	71.7	−45.7	32.7	286.6	363.5	−2,530.0	−2,182.9	†−421.1	−614.8	−1,245.5	−1,269.7	−627.9
Money plus Quasi-Money	35l	702.5	784.8	1,016.4	895.6	927.0	1,909.8	2,131.2	†2,521.8	2,842.7	2,982.6	3,265.3	4,757.9
Interest Rates					*Percent Per Annum*								
Savings Rate	60k	....	6.16	6.12	....	6.08	6.00	6.02	5.83	5.63	5.43	4.50	4.60
Deposit Rate	60l	....	6.34	6.37	....	6.43	6.22	6.25	6.18	5.94	6.25	5.29	3.84
Lending Rate	60p	....	14.53	15.57	....	16.83	†21.74	16.72	20.53	22.14	20.21	17.06	18.10
Population					*Millions: Midyear Estimates*								
Population	99z	2.05	2.07	2.14	2.28	2.48	†2.70	2.91	3.07	3.16	3.21	3.22	3.24

Libya 672

		1993	1994	1995	1996	1997	1998	1999	2000	2001	2002	2003	2004
Exchange Rates		*SDRs per Dinar: End of Period (ac) US Dollars per Dinar: End of Period (ag)*											
Official Rate	ac	2.2400	1.5770	1.5770	1.5770	1.5770	1.5770	1.5770	1.4204	1.2240	.6080	.5175	.5175
Official Rate	ag	3.0768	2.3022	2.3442	2.2677	2.1278	2.2205	2.1645	1.8507	1.5382	.8266	.7690	.8037
Fund Position		*Millions of SDRs: End of Period*											
Quota	2f.s	818	818	818	818	818	818	1,124	1,124	1,124	1,124	1,124	1,124
SDRs	1b.s	303	325	350	374	398	426	373	413	441	449	462	475
Reserve Position in the Fund	1c.s	319	319	319	319	319	319	396	396	396	396	396	396
Total Fund Cred.&Loans Outstg.	2tl	—	—	—	—	—	—	—	—	—	—	—	—
International Liquidity		*Millions of US Dollars Unless Otherwise Indicated: End of Period*											
Total Reserves minus Gold	1l.d	....	....	....	....	....	7,270	7,280	12,461	14,800	14,307	19,584	25,689
SDRs	1b.d	417	474	520	538	538	600	511	538	554	610	686	738
Reserve Position in the Fund	1c.d	438	466	474	459	430	449	543	515	497	538	588	614
Foreign Exchange	1d.d	....	....	....	....	....	6,221	6,226	11,408	13,749	13,159	18,310	24,336
Gold (Million Fine Troy Ounces)	1ad	....	....	....	....	....	4.616	4.624	4.624	4.624	4.624	4.624	4.624
Gold (National Valuation)	1and	....	....	....	....	....	194	194	194	194	194	194	194
Deposit Money Banks: Assets	7a.d	401	319	380	483	979	619	735	937	928	637	606	1,053
Liabilities	7b.d	171	169	109	207	2,965	2,165	1,834	1,461	2,484	1,476	1,224	836
Monetary Authorities		*Millions of Dinars: End of Period*											
Foreign Assets	11	1,435.5	1,745.0	2,487.4	2,815.9	3,658.5	3,658.5	3,813.4	7,295.9	9,489.2	19,192.3	27,757.4	33,072.7
Claims on Central Government	12a	4,740.0	4,815.0	5,064.6	5,107.4	5,406.7	5,927.2	5,320.1	6,832.6	6,789.0	6,789.5	7,012.3	828.2
Claims on Nonfin.Pub.Enterprises	12c	1,230.0	1,890.1	2,208.3	2,336.3	1,671.4	1,559.2	1,704.0	2,567.9	2,694.2	4,063.2	5,475.5	7,280.8
Claims on Private Sector	12d	6.3	6.7	6.6	6.4	6.4	6.4	7.1	8.0	9.5	11.1	12.8	14.7
Claims on Deposit Money Banks	12e	298.8	283.5	283.5	200.0	144.4	144.4	144.4	115.5	86.6	57.8	28.9	1.0
Reserve Money	14	3,992.6	4,627.4	4,985.7	5,434.8	†5,821.2	5,760.4	5,455.4	5,404.8	5,946.9	6,100.7	6,782.3	9,920.7
of which: Currency Outside DMBs	14a	2,216.8	1,989.8	2,035.4	2,419.8	2,534.2	2,698.6	2,657.5	2,711.0	2,577.4	2,630.5	2,780.1	2,612.7
Nonfin.Pub.Enterp.Dep.	14e	264.3	478.8	603.9	414.5	536.2	176.3	133.7	200.8	297.8	349.3	240.8	246.3
Time & Foreign Currency Deposits	15	529.5	615.0	701.4	522.8	†62.6	65.3	19.4	38.9	245.2	204.3	108.3	44.9
Restricted Deposits	16b	248.6	988.1	344.8	414.2	414.2	332.0	428.1	561.9	738.2	1,185.0	1,702.2	1,351.6
Foreign Liabilities	16c	—	—	—	—	618.3	476.9	623.8	1,501.5	1,673.2	3,297.8	4,920.5	5,335.0
Central Government Deposits	16d	676.6	678.2	708.3	741.2	†3,368.6	3,696.4	4,450.6	6,941.0	7,439.1	7,936.3	12,199.9	18,755.0
Capital Accounts	17a	356.2	367.3	367.3	367.3	†1,214.3	1,250.0	1,076.6	1,520.0	2,634.6	9,919.5	13,991.0	4,314.5
Other Items (Net)	17r	1,907.1	1,464.3	2,942.9	2,985.8	−611.4	−285.3	−1,064.9	851.9	391.3	1,470.3	585.6	1,475.8
Deposit Money Banks		*Millions of Dinars: End of Period*											
Reserves	20	1,506.6	2,204.6	2,336.6	2,606.1	2,705.8	2,776.1	2,428.4	2,357.2	2,346.1	2,458.7	3,192.1	6,341.6
Foreign Assets	21	130.3	138.6	162.2	212.8	460.3	278.6	339.7	506.4	603.1	770.1	787.5	1,309.9
Claims on Central Government	22a	1,444.1	1,451.1	1,451.1	1,436.5	1,387.5	1,387.5	1,387.5	1,392.5	1,810.5	1,810.5	1,810.5	373.0
Claims on Nonfin. Pub. Enterprises	22c	127.1	146.2	153.2	328.8	†1,440.7	1,491.9	1,866.4	1,776.5	3,163.7	3,649.9	3,257.1	3,672.3
Claims on Private Sector	22d	3,001.2	3,223.6	3,468.1	2,878.4	3,109.1	3,123.4	3,989.1	4,004.0	4,039.0	4,004.9	4,450.2	4,437.6
Claims on Other Banking Insts.	22f	....	....	....	....	....	....	40.3	49.7	27.3	29.1	27.6	27.9
Claims on Nonbank Financial Insts.	22g	....	....	....	....	....	....	124.2	506.7	75.6	69.8	123.0	214.7
Demand Deposits	24	2,728.2	3,417.3	3,612.1	3,489.4	3,556.5	3,753.4	4,162.8	4,363.1	4,370.1	4,753.6	5,209.9	6,801.6
Time & Foreign Currency Deposits	25	1,069.4	1,260.5	1,550.4	1,744.0	1,555.2	1,838.0	†2,202.1	2,156.7	2,271.6	1,983.7	2,369.5	2,554.0
Restricted Deposits	26b	208.7	173.9	271.7	277.3	368.1	331.0	266.5	341.0	709.1	633.9	768.2	856.5
Foreign Liabilities	26c	55.7	60.8	38.5	75.7	†1,393.3	975.0	847.4	789.5	1,614.8	1,785.2	1,592.0	1,040.7
Central Government Deposits	26d	175.5	171.5	114.3	340.0	385.0	354.9	284.6	267.9	259.0	609.3	566.0	1,146.7
Credit from Monetary Authorities	26g	299.9	283.5	283.5	203.6	147.9	147.9	147.9	119.1	90.2	61.3	32.4	1.0
Capital Accounts	27a	391.2	405.2	411.8	491.5	601.3	659.7	728.5	793.9	962.4	1,202.1	1,362.5	1,566.4
Other Items (Net)	27r	1,280.6	1,391.7	1,289.9	841.1	1,096.3	997.9	1,535.8	1,761.8	1,787.8	1,763.9	1,747.5	2,410.1
Monetary Survey		*Millions of Dinars: End of Period*											
Foreign Assets (Net)	31n	1,510.1	1,822.8	2,611.1	2,953.0	2,107.2	2,485.2	2,681.9	5,511.3	6,804.3	14,879.4	22,032.4	28,006.9
Domestic Credit	32	9,696.7	10,683.0	11,529.3	11,012.6	†9,268.2	9,444.3	9,703.5	9,929.0	10,910.7	11,882.4	9,403.1	−3,052.5
Claims on Central Govt. (Net)	32an	5,332.1	5,416.4	5,693.1	5,462.7	†3,040.6	3,263.4	1,972.4	1,016.2	901.4	54.4	−3,943.1	−18,700.5
Claims on Nonfin.Pub.Enterprises	32c	1,357.1	2,036.3	2,361.5	2,665.1	†3,112.1	3,051.1	3,570.4	4,344.4	5,857.9	7,713.1	8,732.6	10,953.1
Claims on Private Sector	32d	3,007.5	3,230.3	3,474.7	2,884.8	3,115.5	3,129.8	3,996.2	4,012.0	4,048.5	4,016.0	4,463.0	4,452.3
Claims on Other Banking Insts.	32f	....	....	....	....	—	—	40.3	49.7	27.3	29.1	27.6	27.9
Claims on Nonbank Fin. Insts.	32g	....	....	....	....	....	....	124.2	506.7	75.6	69.8	123.0	214.7
Money	34	5,209.3	5,885.9	6,251.4	6,323.7	6,654.5	6,683.8	7,001.2	7,313.5	7,402.7	7,843.4	8,340.9	10,154.0
Quasi-Money	35	1,598.9	1,875.5	2,251.8	2,266.8	1,617.8	1,903.3	2,221.5	2,195.6	2,516.8	2,188.0	2,477.8	2,598.9
Restricted Deposits	36b	457.3	1,162.0	616.5	691.5	782.3	663.0	694.6	902.9	1,447.3	1,818.9	2,470.4	2,208.1
Capital Accounts	37a	747.4	766.1	772.7	852.4	1,815.6	1,909.7	1,805.1	2,313.9	3,597.0	11,121.6	15,353.5	5,880.9
Other Items (Net)	37r	3,193.7	2,810.1	4,242.6	3,824.9	505.8	770.0	663.0	2,714.5	2,750.9	3,789.9	2,795.8	4,112.6
Money plus Quasi-Money	35l	6,808.2	7,761.4	8,503.2	8,590.5	8,272.3	8,587.1	9,222.7	9,509.1	9,919.5	10,031.4	10,818.7	12,752.9
Other Banking Institutions		*Millions of Dinars: End of Period*											
Cash	40	73.10	53.60	41.40	40.80	54.40	29.40	85.50	96.40	269.20	187.60	....	....
Claims on Private Sector	42d	40.30	38.80	48.90	51.00	63.90	63.50	97.40	118.70	201.60	350.60	....	....
Capital Accounts	47a	82.80	84.70	85.50	86.40	89.60	90.70	84.40	88.40	89.10	92.20	....	....
Other Items (Net)	47r	30.60	7.60	4.80	5.40	28.70	2.20	98.50	126.70	381.70	445.90	....	....
Interest Rates		*Percent Per Annum*											
Discount Rate (End of Period)	60	5.0	....	....	....	....	3.0	5.0	5.0	5.0	5.0	5.0	4.0
Money Market Rate	60b	4.0	....	....	....	....	4.0	4.0	4.0	4.0	4.0	4.0	4.0
Deposit Rate	60l	5.5	....	....	....	....	....	3.2	3.0	3.0	3.0	3.0	2.1
Lending Rate	60p	7.0	....	....	....	....	....	7.0	7.0	7.0	7.0	7.0	6.1
Prices		*Index Numbers (2000=100): Period Averages*											
Consumer Prices	64	79.7	83.7	89.8	93.4	96.7	100.3	†103.0	100.0	91.2	82.2	80.5	78.7
Intl. Transactions & Positions		*Millions of Dinars*											
Exports	70	2,477.6	3,177.2	3,222.1	3,578.7	3,455.6	2,374.1	3,682.2	5,221.5	5,394.0	10,177.0	14,806.0	....
Imports, c.i.f.	71	1,711.3	1,487.9	1,728.5	1,914.8	2,138.6	2,203.8	1,928.6	1,911.4	2,660.4	5,585.7	5,597.9	....
		2000=100											
Volume of Exports	72	126.6	133.3	†132.5	122.6	129.0	94.2	107.9	100.0	110.5	94.6	....	....
Volume of Imports	73	188.6	162.9	†170.9	184.8	208.4	156.1	146.8	100.0	173.2	213.8	....	....
Unit Value of Exports	74	41.2	49.4	†52.1	63.6	57.4	48.3	65.3	100.0	102.6	216.9	....	....
Unit Value of Imports	75	67.3	71.5	†79.7	82.1	83.3	87.5	103.1	100.0	98.1	116.7	....	....

Libya 672

		1993	1994	1995	1996	1997	1998	1999	2000	2001	2002	2003	2004
Balance of Payments							*Millions of US Dollars: Minus Sign Indicates Debit*						
Current Account, n.i.e......................	78ald	–1,366	26	1,650	1,220	1,550	–351	2,136	7,740	3,417	117	3,642	....
Goods: Exports f.o.b......................	78aad	8,544	7,704	7,483	7,930	8,177	5,326	7,276	13,508	10,985	9,851	14,664	....
Goods: Imports f.o.b......................	78abd	–8,431	–6,760	–5,181	–5,845	–5,928	–4,930	–4,302	–4,129	–4,825	–7,408	–7,200	....
Trade Balance..........................	78acd	113	945	2,302	2,085	2,249	396	2,974	9,379	6,160	2,443	7,464	
Services: Credit...........................	78add	55	37	31	26	28	40	59	172	184	401	442	
Services: Debit...........................	78aed	–1,174	–718	–597	–790	–765	–877	–989	–895	–1,034	–1,544	–1,597	
Balance on Goods & Services.......	78afd	–1,006	263	1,736	1,321	1,512	–441	2,044	8,656	5,310	1,300	6,309	
Income: Credit...........................	78agd	571	448	435	474	530	533	546	723	684	1,249	1,587	
Income: Debit...........................	78ahd	–602	–403	–302	–295	–293	–218	–235	–1,152	–1,849	–1,653	–2,581	
Balance on Gds, Serv. & Inc........	78aid	–1,037	308	1,870	1,500	1,748	–127	2,355	8,227	4,145	896	5,315	
Current Transfers, n.i.e.: Credit.....	78ajd	8	5	4	3	3	4	7	16	20	13	255	
Current Transfers: Debit...............	78akd	–337	–286	–224	–283	–202	–229	–226	–503	–748	–792	–1,928	
Capital Account, n.i.e....................	78bcd	—	—	—	—	—	—	—	—	—	—	—	
Capital Account, n.i.e.: Credit........	78bad	—	—	....	....	....	....	....	—	—	—	—	
Capital Account: Debit.................	78bbd	—	—	....	....	....	....	....	—	—	—	—	
Financial Account, n.i.e.................	78bjd	–202	147	–207	186	–732	–467	–1,045	–149	–711	89	–167	
Direct Investment Abroad..............	78bdd	479	–26	–69	–52	–233	–256	–226	–98	–175	136	–63	
Dir. Invest. in Rep. Econ., n.i.e.......	78bed	58	–73	–88	–112	–68	–128	–128	141	133	145	142	
Portfolio Investment Assets...........	78bfd	–62	–126	–106	—	–641	–178	–3	–706	–1,359	72	–607	
Equity Securities.....................	78bkd	–62	–126	–106	—	–641	–178	–3	–13	–985	21	–18	
Debt Securities......................	78bld	—	—	....	....	....	....	....	–693	–374	51	–589	
Portfolio Investment Liab., n.i.e.....	78bgd	—	—	....	....	....	....	....	—	—	—	—	
Equity Securities.....................	78bmd	—	—	....	....	....	....	....	—	—	—	—	
Debt Securities......................	78bnd	—	—	....	....	....	....	....	—	—	—	—	
Financial Derivatives Assets...........	78bwd	....	....	....	....	....	....	....	....	....	....	....	
Financial Derivatives Liabilities.......	78bxd	....	....	....	....	....	....	....	....	....	....	....	
Other Investment Assets...............	78bhd	–487	–1,754	–1,363	–1,435	–861	–138	–315	–333	–97	62	–163	
Monetary Authorities.................	78bod	241	–9	38	–27	38	–6	–650	—	—	—	—	
General Government..................	78bpd	–731	–1,728	–1,372	–1,275	–561	–497	496	—	—	—	6	
Banks.................................	78bqd	3	–17	–29	–133	–338	365	–161	–294	–121	102	–152	
Other Sectors........................	78brd	....	....	....	....	....	....	....	–39	24	–40	–17	
Other Investment Liab., n.i.e..........	78bid	–191	2,126	1,419	1,785	1,071	233	–373	847	787	–326	524	
Monetary Authorities.................	78bsd	96	169	171	367	–181	–5	–78	—	309	–197	–7	
General Government..................	78btd	213	1,942	1,301	1,392	1,305	221	–230	—	—	—	—	
Banks.................................	78bud	–499	14	–53	27	–52	17	–65	847	488	–149	548	
Other Sectors........................	78bvd	....	....	....	....	....	....	....	—	–10	20	–17	
Net Errors and Omissions................	78cad	–149	100	258	–185	735	392	–403	–1,133	–1,413	72	–459	
Overall Balance....................	78cbd	–1,716	274	1,701	1,221	1,553	–426	688	6,458	1,293	278	3,016	
Reserves and Related Items..............	79dad	1,716	–274	–1,701	–1,221	–1,553	426	–688	–6,458	–1,293	–278	–3,016	
Reserve Assets...........................	79dbd	1,716	–274	–1,701	–1,221	–1,553	426	–688	–6,458	–1,293	–278	–3,016	
Use of Fund Credit and Loans........	79dcd	—	—	—	—	—	—	—	—	—	—	—	
Exceptional Financing..................	79ded	....	....	....	....	....	....	....	—	—	—	—	
National Accounts							*Millions of Dinars*						
Househ.Cons.Expend.,incl.NPISHs....	96f	5,989	5,993	6,276	6,809	8,368	8,072	8,514	8,150	8,994	13,939	....	....
Government Consumption Expend...	91f	2,132	2,254	2,383	2,903	3,333	3,339	3,102	3,616	3,925	4,077	....	....
Gross Fixed Capital Formation..........	93e	1,504	1,622	1,245	1,640	1,685	1,397	1,536	2,214	2,158	3,366	....	....
Changes in Inventories.................	93i	15	6	54	248	64	127	46	74	74	150	....	....
Exports of Goods and Services..........	90c	2,636	2,695	3,116	3,490	3,790	2,468	3,374	6,186	5,478	11,645	....	....
Imports of Goods and Services (-)....	98c	2,944	2,603	2,394	2,910	3,091	2,661	2,433	2,690	3,433	8,868	....	....
Gross Domestic Product (GDP).........	99b	9,332	9,967	10,680	12,180	14,149	12,742	14,139	17,550	17,196	24,309	....	....
Net Primary Income from Abroad.....	98.n	–91	–114	–146	–202	–201	–248	–243	–341	–445	–672	....	....
Gross National Income (GNI)...........	99a	9,241	9,853	10,534	11,978	13,948	12,494	13,896	17,209	16,751	23,637	....	....
Population							*Millions: Midyear Estimates*						
Population...............................	99z	4.62	4.71	† 4.81	4.90	5.00	5.10	5.20	5.31	5.41	5.52	5.63	5.74

		1993	1994	1995	1996	1997	1998	1999	2000	2001	2002	2003	2004
Exchange Rates					*Litai per SDR: End of Period*								
Official Rate	aa	5.357	5.839	5.946	5.752	5.397	5.632	5.490	5.212	5.027	4.502	4.104	3.936
					Litai per US Dollar: End of Period (ae) Period Average (rf)								
Official Rate	ae	3.900	4.000	4.000	4.000	4.000	4.000	4.000	4.000	4.000	3.311	2.762	2.535
Official Rate	rf	4.344	3.978	4.000	4.000	4.000	4.000	4.000	4.000	4.000	3.677	3.061	2.781
Fund Position					*Millions of SDRs: End of Period*								
Quota	2f.s	103.50	103.50	103.50	103.50	103.50	103.50	144.20	144.20	144.20	144.20	144.20	144.20
SDRs	1b.s	54.71	10.38	12.22	7.09	7.95	11.50	3.19	1.01	14.67	39.31	.04	.06
Reserve Position in the Fund	1c.s	.01	.01	.01	.01	.01	.02	.02	.02	.02	.02	.02	.02
Total Fund Cred.&Loans Outstg	2tl	87.98	134.55	175.95	190.11	200.46	179.83	167.76	147.06	120.32	89.27	30.19	16.82
International Liquidity					*Millions of US Dollars Unless Otherwise Indicated: End of Period*								
Total Reserves minus Gold	1l.d	350.32	525.48	757.05	772.25	1,009.95	1,409.13	1,195.01	1,311.55	1,617.72	2,349.32	3,371.98	3,512.58
SDRs	1b.d	75.14	15.15	18.16	10.20	10.73	16.19	4.38	1.32	18.43	53.44	.06	.09
Reserve Position in the Fund	1c.d	.01	.01	.01	.01	.01	.02	.02	.02	.02	.02	.02	.02
Foreign Exchange	1d.d	275.17	510.33	738.88	762.04	999.21	1,392.92	1,190.61	1,310.21	1,599.27	2,295.86	3,371.89	3,512.47
Gold (Million Fine Troy Ounces)	1ad	.1859	.1858	.1860	.1863	.1864	.1861	.1863	.1863	.1861	.1862	.1862	.1858
Gold (National Valuation)	1and	61.90	61.86	61.95	62.04	52.74	50.87	47.10	47.10	51.47	63.82	77.69	81.40
Monetary Authorities: Other Liab	4..d	28.05	26.38	.28	1.30	.35	.33	.25	.18	51.85	58.65	67.27	4.02
Banking Institutions: Assets	7a.d	77.77	96.68	123.35	293.60	370.63	302.15	423.30	693.30	751.85	723.77	926.83	1,848.92
Liabilities	7b.d	9.54	82.70	88.45	195.83	292.48	438.15	522.70	503.05	599.83	827.32	1,816.55	2,725.23
Monetary Authorities					*Millions of Litai: End of Period*								
Foreign Assets	11	1,904.6	2,618.1	3,284.7	3,345.3	4,258.6	5,847.7	4,976.2	5,375.7	6,629.3	7,933.5	9,448.3	9,028.5
Claims on Central Government	12a	—	—	19.2	—	—	—	6.8	6.8	6.8	6.8	5.4	4.1
Claims on Private Sector	12d	1.4	5.9	12.1	9.9	7.6	6.9	6.1	5.5	6.4	7.8	9.6	10.8
Claims on Banking Institutions	12e	292.1	157.0	168.1	142.4	70.4	52.3	30.1	23.7	15.3	15.9	10.0	10.0
Claims on Nonbank Financial Insts	12g			.3	3.1	19.4	6.9	20.0	—	—	—	—	—
Reserve Money	14	1,256.8	1,812.4	2,446.2	2,499.3	3,308.8	4,260.4	4,088.3	3,952.4	4,279.6	5,168.0	6,540.2	7,001.6
of which: Currency Outside Banks	14a	791.3	1,334.3	1,907.0	1,899.3	2,535.5	2,800.4	2,738.7	2,658.3	2,919.9	3,756.4	4,632.0	5,121.2
Foreign Currency Deposits	15		1.9	43.8	19.8	8.2	6.5	1.5	.1	.1	.1	.1	.1
Foreign Liabilities	16c	580.7	891.2	1,047.3	1,098.7	1,083.3	1,014.1	922.0	767.1	812.2	596.1	309.7	76.4
Central Government Deposits	16d	93.1	45.0	111.0	66.0	268.7	904.4	302.1	781.8	1,488.2	1,950.3	2,213.7	1,470.9
Counterpart Funds	16e		14.7	37.5	41.9	38.1	40.8	30.8	29.2	28.2	28.5	29.0	29.4
Central Government Lending Funds	16f	—	.6	.7	—	.6	1.5						
Capital Accounts	17a	1,029.6	54.8	−77.8	−48.4	−247.3	−111.8	−90.4	117.2	270.4	453.2	612.6	730.2
Other Items (Net)	17r	−762.1	−39.6	−124.3	−176.6	−104.3	−202.1	−215.1	−236.1	−220.9	−232.2	−232.0	−255.3
Banking Institutions					*Millions of Litai: End of Period*								
Reserves	20	469.0	464.1	522.7	583.6	742.1	1,447.5	1,342.3	1,282.4	1,343.1	1,391.8	1,897.1	1,864.1
Foreign Assets	21	303.3	386.7	493.4	1,174.4	1,482.5	1,208.6	1,693.2	2,773.2	3,007.4	2,396.7	2,560.0	4,686.1
Claims on Central Government	22a	—	240.8	505.2	860.7	1,890.0	1,965.5	1,665.9	2,151.1	2,637.3	2,950.8	2,691.3	2,787.4
Claims on State and Local Govts	22b		2.0	7.7	37.1	51.9	123.8	212.3	273.5	279.6	302.5	397.1	411.8
Claims on Nonfin.Pub.Enterprises	22c	409.3	398.6	237.5	134.4	109.4	272.7	276.9	304.5	253.1	197.8	148.0	88.5
Claims on Private Sector	22d	1,603.5	† 2,974.6	3,654.8	3,496.2	4,161.9	4,866.7	5,538.7	5,203.2	5,531.7	7,213.5	11,460.2	16,019.3
Claims on Nonbank Financial Insts	22g	5.0	20.6	49.5	44.7	150.2	462.8	448.3	513.5	791.3	980.5	1,358.0	1,895.6
Demand Deposits	24	954.4	1,134.8	1,566.5	1,694.3	2,543.1	2,757.9	2,528.9	3,002.6	3,808.0	4,553.0	5,891.9	7,334.5
Time, Savings,& Fgn.Currency Dep	25	926.8	1,879.5	2,086.2	1,793.3	2,153.8	2,750.0	3,695.5	4,782.6	5,946.2	6,505.4	7,001.5	9,293.4
Foreign Liabilities	26c	37.2	330.8	353.8	783.3	1,169.9	1,752.6	2,090.8	2,012.2	2,399.3	2,739.6	5,017.5	6,907.1
Central Government Deposits	26d	122.5	357.6	683.7	779.3	1,008.1	792.0	778.4	740.7	438.9	439.4	652.4	1,143.4
Counterpart Funds	26e	16.4	28.2	52.6	59.3	50.7	22.8	19.5	23.3	2.0	10.0	1.4	2.0
Central Government Lending Funds	26f	174.5	337.7	480.3	473.3	615.4	754.1	555.5	287.3	19.6	23.8	37.9	39.1
Credit from Monetary Authorities	26g	285.5	157.0	168.1	142.0	70.3	52.3	30.2	23.8	15.4	15.8	9.9	9.9
Capital Accounts	27a	467.7	936.1	996.7	1,448.1	2,021.4	2,690.4	2,849.7	2,928.6	1,992.6	2,226.6	2,484.5	2,979.0
Other Items (Net)	27r	−194.9	† −674.3	−917.1	−841.8	−1,044.7	−1,224.5	−1,370.9	−1,299.9	−778.5	−1,080.0	−585.3	44.5
Banking Survey					*Millions of Litai: End of Period*								
Foreign Assets (Net)	31n	1,590.0	1,782.8	2,377.0	2,637.7	3,488.0	4,289.6	3,656.6	5,369.6	6,425.2	6,994.5	6,681.1	6,731.1
Domestic Credit	32	1,803.6	† 3,239.9	3,691.6	3,740.8	5,113.6	6,008.9	7,094.5	6,935.6	7,579.1	9,270.0	13,203.5	18,603.2
Claims on Central Govt. (Net)	32an	−215.6	−161.8	−270.3	15.4	613.2	269.1	592.2	635.4	717.0	567.9	−169.4	177.2
Claims on State and Local Govts	32b	—	2.0	7.7	37.1	51.9	123.8	212.3	273.5	279.6	302.5	397.1	411.8
Claims on Nonfin.Pub.Enterprises	32c	409.3	398.6	237.5	134.4	109.4	272.7	276.9	304.5	253.1	197.8	148.0	88.5
Claims on Private Sector	32d	1,604.9	† 2,980.5	3,666.9	3,506.1	4,169.6	4,873.6	5,544.8	5,208.7	5,538.1	7,221.3	11,469.8	16,030.1
Claims on Nonbank Fin. Insts	32g	5.0	20.6	49.5	47.8	169.6	469.7	468.3	513.5	791.3	980.5	1,358.0	1,895.6
Money	34	1,746.4	2,475.7	3,488.4	3,610.9	5,109.9	5,570.8	5,275.0	5,672.6	6,744.5	8,329.2	10,535.1	12,472.0
Quasi-Money	35	926.8	1,881.4	2,130.0	1,813.1	2,162.0	2,756.5	3,697.0	4,782.9	5,946.3	6,505.5	7,001.6	9,293.5
of which: Fgn. Currency Deposits	35b	681.4	1,169.6	1,462.9	1,325.4	1,539.0	2,006.8	2,724.6	3,554.5	4,181.5	3,613.8	3,427.0	4,319.7
Counterpart Funds	36e	16.4	42.9	90.1	101.2	88.8	63.6	50.3	52.5	30.2	38.5	30.4	31.4
Central Government Lending Funds	36f	174.5	338.3	481.0	473.3	616.0	755.6	555.5	287.3	19.6	23.8	37.9	39.1
Capital Accounts	37a	1,497.3	990.9	918.9	1,399.7	1,774.1	2,578.6	2,759.3	3,045.8	2,263.0	2,679.8	3,097.1	3,709.2
Other Items (Net)	37r	−967.8	† −706.5	−1,039.8	−1,019.7	−1,149.2	−1,426.6	−1,586.0	−1,535.9	−999.3	−1,312.3	−817.5	−210.9
Money plus Quasi-Money	35l	2,673.2	4,357.1	5,618.4	5,424.0	7,271.9	8,327.3	8,972.0	10,455.5	12,690.8	14,834.7	17,536.7	21,765.5
Money (National Definitions)					*Millions of Litai: End of Period*								
Monetary Base	19ma	....	....	....	2,482.0	3,277.5	4,247.9	3,852.0	3,940.8	4,263.0	5,148.2	6,521.5	6,978.9
M1	59ma	....	....	....	3,610.9	5,109.9	5,570.7	5,274.9	5,672.6	6,744.3	8,329.2	10,535.2	12,472.0
M2	59mb	....	....	....	5,424.1	7,271.8	8,327.1	8,971.9	10,455.4	12,690.6	14,834.6	17,536.8	21,765.5
Interest Rates					*Percent Per Annum*								
Money Market Rate	60b	....	69.48	26.73	20.26	9.55	† 6.12	6.26	3.60	3.37	2.21	1.79	1.53
Money Market Rate (Fgn. Currency)	60b.f	....	....	....	....	....	5.52	5.05	6.10	4.03	1.92	1.72	1.73
Treasury Bill Rate	60c	....	....	26.82	20.95	8.64	10.69	11.14	† 9.27	5.68	3.72	2.61	....
Savings Rate	60k	....	....	....	....	....	....	6.46	6.43	6.32	3.36	2.14	2.03
Savings Rate (Fgn. Currency)	60k.f	....	....	....	....	....	....	4.06	4.18	3.61	1.81	1.43	1.45
Deposit Rate	60l	88.29	48.43	20.05	13.95	7.89	5.98	4.94	3.86	3.00	1.70	1.27	1.22
Deposit Rate (Fgn. Currency)	60l.f	23.58	24.91	15.97	9.36	5.49	4.24	4.38	4.39	3.11	1.80	1.52	1.44
Lending Rate	60p	91.84	62.30	27.08	21.56	14.39	12.21	13.09	12.14	9.63	6.84	5.84	5.74
Lending Rate (Fgn. Currency)	60p.f	68.70	51.98	26.93	21.63	12.39	10.28	11.46	10.62	8.01	5.74	4.29	3.95

Lithuania 946

		1993	1994	1995	1996	1997	1998	1999	2000	2001	2002	2003	2004
Prices, Production, Labor		\multicolumn{12}{c}{*Index Numbers (2000=100): Period Averages*}											
Producer Prices	63	39.9	57.8	74.1	† 86.9	90.6	83.9	85.1	100.0	96.3	92.8	92.5	99.6
Consumer Prices	64	† 28.7	49.4	68.9	85.9	93.5	98.3	† 99.0	100.0	101.3	101.6	100.4	101.6
Harmonized CPI (2002=100)	64h	....	....	....	....	....	....	....	....	....	100.0	98.9	100.1
Wages: Average Earnings	65	21.5	35.4	50.7	68.5	84.5	95.2	100.7	100.0	100.9	102.9	106.5	114.2
Industrial Production	66	....	....	84.2	87.1	† 94.1	107.3	94.9	100.0	116.1	119.3	135.9	151.5
Manufacturing Employment	67	159.4	127.2	† 109.1	104.5	104.7	103.6	102.1	100.0	97.1	....	....	....
		\multicolumn{12}{c}{*Number in Thousands: Period Averages*}											
Labor Force	67d	1,859	1,741	1,753	1,784	1,820	1,843	1,862	1,820	1,760	1,630	1,642	....
Employment	67e	1,778	1,656	1,632	1,620	1,571	1,489	1,457	1,398	1,352	1,406	1,438	1,463
Unemployment	67c	66	78	128	109	120	123	177	226	224	....	168	142
Unemployment Rate (%)	67r	3.5	4.5	7.3	6.2	6.7	6.5	10.0	12.6	12.9	....	11.3	6.8
Intl. Transactions & Positions		\multicolumn{12}{c}{*Millions of Litai*}											
Exports	70	8,707	8,077	8,157	10,622	12,801	12,941	11,015	14,193	17,117	19,117	21,263	25,728
Imports, c.i.f	71	9,798	9,355	12,052	15,532	20,098	21,456	18,508	20,877	24,241	27,479	29,438	34,096
Balance of Payments		\multicolumn{12}{c}{*Millions of US Dollars: Minus Sign Indicates Debit*}											
Current Account, n.i.e	78ald	−85.7	−94.0	−614.4	−722.6	−981.3	−1,298.2	−1,194.0	−674.9	−573.6	−720.7	−1,278.4	−1,589.7
Goods: Exports f.o.b	78aad	2,025.8	2,029.2	2,706.1	3,413.2	4,192.4	3,961.6	3,146.7	4,050.4	4,889.0	6,028.4	7,657.8	9,273.8
Goods: Imports f.o.b	78abd	−2,180.5	−2,234.1	−3,404.0	−4,309.3	−5,339.9	−5,479.8	−4,551.2	−5,154.1	−5,997.0	−7,343.3	−9,362.0	−11,590.4
Trade Balance	78acd	−154.7	−204.9	−697.9	−896.2	−1,147.5	−1,518.3	−1,404.6	−1,103.8	−1,108.0	−1,314.9	−1,704.2	−2,316.6
Services: Credit	78add	197.8	321.9	485.2	797.5	1,031.8	1,109.0	1,091.5	1,058.8	1,157.0	1,463.7	1,878.0	2,483.8
Services: Debit	78aed	−252.9	−376.5	−498.1	−676.7	−897.4	−868.5	−786.1	−678.7	−700.3	−915.0	−1,263.6	−1,566.1
Balance on Goods & Services	78afd	−209.8	−259.4	−710.8	−775.4	−1,013.0	−1,277.8	−1,099.1	−723.7	−651.4	−766.1	−1,089.8	−1,398.9
Income: Credit	78agd	12.5	21.4	50.9	52.0	80.4	124.6	114.8	185.5	205.7	191.6	235.2	438.4
Income: Debit	78ahd	−4.3	−12.8	−63.7	−143.0	−278.8	−380.0	−372.6	−379.3	−385.5	−375.0	−717.4	−967.2
Balance on Gds, Serv. & Inc	78aid	−201.5	−250.8	−723.7	−866.4	−1,211.4	−1,533.2	−1,356.8	−917.5	−831.1	−949.5	−1,572.0	−1,927.7
Current Transfers, n.i.e.: Credit	78ajd	115.9	161.6	112.3	149.4	237.0	240.4	167.4	246.8	262.0	231.7	301.5	492.1
Current Transfers: Debit	78akd	—	−4.8	−3.0	−5.6	−7.0	−5.4	−4.6	−4.3	−4.5	−2.9	−7.8	−154.2
Capital Account, n.i.e	78bcd	—	12.9	−39.0	5.5	4.1	−1.7	−3.3	2.1	1.4	56.5	67.5	287.2
Capital Account, n.i.e.: Credit	78bad	—	12.9	3.3	5.5	4.5	.9	2.7	2.6	1.5	56.8	68.3	288.1
Capital Account: Debit	78bbd	—	—	−42.3	—	−.4	−2.6	−6.0	−.4	−.1	−.4	−.8	−1.0
Financial Account, n.i.e	78bjd	301.5	240.9	534.5	645.6	1,005.6	1,443.9	1,060.7	702.4	777.6	1,048.4	1,642.3	1,014.6
Direct Investment Abroad	78bdd	....	....	−1.0	−.1	−26.9	−4.2	−8.6	−3.7	−7.1	−17.7	−37.2	−262.6
Dir. Invest. in Rep. Econ., n.i.e	78bed	30.2	31.3	72.6	152.4	354.5	925.5	486.5	378.9	445.8	712.5	179.2	773.1
Portfolio Investment Assets	78bfd	−.9	−.2	−10.5	−26.9	7.7	−10.1	−1.9	−141.4	26.2	−124.5	29.8	−219.9
Equity Securities	78bkd	−.9	−.2	−3.0	.8	.1	−.3	−3.0	−1.4	1.1	−3.7	−1.8	−18.8
Debt Securities	78bld	....	—	−7.5	−27.7	7.6	−9.8	1.1	−140.0	25.1	−120.9	31.6	−201.0
Portfolio Investment Liab., n.i.e	78bgd	.6	4.6	26.6	89.6	180.5	−42.7	507.5	405.9	238.0	148.8	222.3	431.1
Equity Securities	78bmd	.6	4.6	6.2	15.9	30.5	11.4	8.9	121.5	−16.3	5.6	4.2	7.9
Debt Securities	78bnd	....	—	20.4	73.7	150.1	−54.1	498.6	284.4	254.3	143.2	218.0	423.1
Financial Derivatives Assets	78bwd	....	....	....	....	....	—	—	—	18.3	19.6	28.1	60.0
Financial Derivatives Liabilities	78bxd	....	....	....	....	....	—	—	—	−19.6	−22.7	−56.2	−57.4
Other Investment Assets	78bhd	95.3	−26.4	−36.1	−170.4	−219.3	−24.0	−182.5	39.9	−225.0	154.7	−100.9	−709.8
Monetary Authorities	78bod	....	....	67.0	.2	.1	—	—	—	—	—	—	—
General Government	78bpd	....	....	....	....	....	—	—	—	−2.6	—	—	−7.3
Banks	78bqd	108.9	−17.3	−18.0	−139.5	−88.1	57.2	−125.7	−142.2	−158.2	212.7	−161.0	−671.1
Other Sectors	78brd	−13.6	−9.2	−85.0	−31.1	−131.3	−81.2	−56.7	182.1	−64.2	−58.0	60.1	−31.3
Other Investment Liab., n.i.e	78bid	176.5	231.6	482.8	601.0	709.1	599.3	259.7	22.8	300.9	177.7	1,377.2	1,000.1
Monetary Authorities	78bsd	—	−.9	−25.1	1.0	−1.0	—	—	−.1	−102.0	51.7	−3.6	−66.7
General Government	78btd	255.7	85.5	178.5	228.5	42.9	129.3	212.0	—	−53.7	−70.6	−9.4	−306.7
Banks	78bud	−62.9	75.8	10.8	108.5	104.3	177.9	99.9	53.1	169.4	111.8	737.6	870.4
Other Sectors	78bvd	−16.3	71.2	318.5	263.1	562.8	292.1	−52.1	71.7	133.5	140.0	657.0	503.2
Net Errors and Omissions	78cad	−7.4	−46.9	287.2	66.7	195.8	282.9	−42.2	128.3	153.6	78.5	181.2	183.6
Overall Balance	78cbd	208.5	112.8	168.3	−4.8	224.2	426.8	−178.7	158.0	359.0	462.7	612.7	−104.3
Reserves and Related Items	79dad	−208.5	−112.8	−168.3	4.8	−224.2	−426.8	178.7	−158.0	−359.0	−462.7	−612.7	104.3
Reserve Assets	79dbd	−308.0	−179.7	−231.3	−15.9	−238.2	−398.8	195.3	−130.7	−325.0	−422.5	−531.2	124.1
Use of Fund Credit and Loans	79dcd	99.5	66.9	63.0	20.7	14.1	−28.0	−16.6	−27.3	−34.0	−40.2	−81.4	−19.8
Exceptional Financing	79ded	....	—	—	—	—	—	—	—	—	—	—	—
International Investment Position		\multicolumn{12}{c}{*Millions of US Dollars*}											
Assets	79aad	....	997.6	1,274.6	1,692.7	2,148.6	2,472.2	2,452.7	2,677.7	3,126.3	4,225.5	5,717.0	7,408.3
Direct Investment Abroad	79abd	....	.2	1.2	2.8	26.0	16.5	25.9	29.3	47.9	59.5	119.7	422.8
Portfolio Investment	79acd	....	.6	11.1	38.1	29.7	38.0	32.5	172.3	138.2	286.3	268.8	516.7
Equity Securities	79add	....	.2	3.1	2.6	2.9	2.9	5.9	6.0	4.9	10.5	11.8	36.2
Debt Securities	79aed	....	.5	7.9	35.5	26.8	35.1	26.7	166.4	133.2	275.8	257.0	480.5
Financial Derivatives	79ald	....	—	—	—	—	—	—	—	—	—	.2	—
Other Investment	79afd	....	409.4	443.4	817.5	1,030.2	957.7	1,152.1	1,117.4	1,271.1	1,459.7	1,878.7	2,874.8
Monetary Authorities	79agd	....	67.2	.2	.1	—	—	—	—	—	—	—	—
General Government	79ahd	....	....	....	....	....	—	—	—	—	—	—	—
Banks	79aid	....	103.3	119.2	243.3	331.3	273.7	390.5	539.7	636.5	504.0	736.3	1,479.1
Other Sectors	79ajd	....	238.9	323.9	574.1	699.0	684.0	761.7	577.7	634.5	955.6	1,142.4	1,395.7
Reserve Assets	79akd	....	587.4	819.0	834.3	1,062.7	1,460.0	1,242.1	1,358.7	1,669.2	2,420.0	3,449.7	3,594.0
Liabilities	79lad	....	1,115.8	1,795.8	2,813.2	3,964.8	4,928.8	6,114.1	6,693.3	7,331.4	9,373.3	12,575.8	15,950.7
Dir. Invest. in Rep. Economy	79lbd	....	262.2	353.9	700.3	1,040.6	1,625.3	2,063.0	2,334.3	2,665.5	3,981.3	4,959.8	6,388.9
Portfolio Investment	79lcd	....	12.9	40.5	306.8	416.1	368.2	833.6	1,140.4	1,312.6	1,511.2	2,077.3	2,812.0
Equity Securities	79ldd	....	5.8	12.4	31.5	61.3	67.1	62.0	128.1	95.6	111.0	144.0	172.5
Debt Securities	79led	....	7.2	28.1	275.3	354.7	301.1	771.6	1,012.3	1,217.1	1,400.3	1,933.3	2,639.5
Financial Derivatives	79lld	....	....	....	....	....	—	—	—	—	10.1	10.2	2.9
Other Investment	79lfd	....	840.7	1,401.4	1,806.1	2,508.1	2,935.3	3,217.5	3,218.6	3,353.3	3,870.5	5,528.6	6,747.0
Monetary Authorities	79lgd	....	221.6	261.6	275.1	270.8	253.5	230.5	191.8	203.1	180.0	112.1	30.1
General Government	79lhd	....	235.2	424.0	447.4	549.2	694.2	881.3	767.0	694.1	669.2	717.7	472.0
Banks	79lid	....	86.1	99.2	182.3	282.8	463.3	539.8	568.2	691.1	933.4	1,910.2	2,839.0
Other Sectors	79ljd	....	297.8	616.7	901.3	1,405.4	1,524.3	1,566.0	1,691.6	1,765.0	2,087.9	2,788.5	3,405.8

Lithuania 946

		1993	1994	1995	1996	1997	1998	1999	2000	2001	2002	2003	2004
Government Finance					*Millions of Litai: Year Ending December 31*								
Deficit (-) or Surplus	80	−694.2	−797.0	−1,151.5	−1,145.1	† −735.8	−183.6	−3,006.6	−584.7	−171.8	−593.3	....	....
Total Revenue and Grants	81y	2,693.6	4,034.1	5,661.1	7,157.3	† 10,198.6	11,474.9	11,051.0	11,135.3	11,999.1	14,180.0	....	....
Revenue	81	2,688.1	4,031.9	5,661.1	7,128.8	† 10,198.3	11,474.9	11,051.0	11,135.3	11,759.2	13,846.8	....	....
Grants	81z	5.5	2.2	—	28.5	.3	—	—	—	239.9	333.2	....	....
Exp.& Lending Minus Repayments	82z	3,387.8	4,831.1	6,812.6	8,302.4	† 10,934.4	11,658.5	14,057.6	11,720.0	12,170.9	14,773.3	....	....
Expenditure	82	2,475.3	4,292.1	6,079.1	7,894.1	† 10,515.0	13,037.6	13,260.8	12,447.3	12,616.8	15,098.8	....	....
Lending Minus Repayments	83	912.5	539.0	733.5	408.3	419.4	−1,379.1	796.8	−727.3	−445.9	−325.5	....	....
Total Financing													
Domestic	84a	71.4	518.2	417.9	138.7	† 451.6	−574.1	129.1	−334.2	−307.2	178.8	....	....
Foreign	85a	622.8	278.8	733.6	1,006.4	† 284.2	757.7	2,877.5	918.9	479.0	414.5	....	....
Total Debt by Currency	88z	1,749.4	2,639.1	4,470.6	4,749.9	8,077.4	9,613.6	12,069.3	12,729.9	12,903.6	13,161.5	13,137.3	....
National	88b	514.6	654.3	1,111.4	2,024.0	2,470.1	2,876.1	2,354.1	2,827.4	3,047.4	3,983.7	4,267.0	....
Foreign	89b	1,234.8	1,984.8	3,359.2	2,725.9	5,607.3	6,737.5	9,715.2	9,902.5	9,856.2	9,177.8	8,870.3	....
National Accounts						*Millions of Litai*							
Househ.Cons.Expend.,incl.NPISHs	96f	8,474	11,489	17,076	21,499	24,789	27,380	28,387	29,663	31,485	33,308	36,478	40,422
Government Consumption Expend	91f	1,800	3,319	5,602	7,201	8,967	10,767	9,634	9,854	9,598	9,990	10,371	11,030
Gross Fixed Capital Formation	93e	2,677	3,905	5,460	6,902	9,049	10,723	9,614	8,565	9,785	10,549	12,024	13,585
Changes in Inventories	93i	−455	−792	273	−210	625	618	121	339	131	676	560	755
Exports of Goods and Services	90c	9,567	9,361	12,765	16,843	20,897	20,282	16,953	20,437	24,182	27,411	29,121	32,634
Imports of Goods and Services (-)	98c	10,472	10,378	15,609	19,944	24,949	25,393	21,350	23,331	26,789	30,291	32,374	36,529
Gross Domestic Product (GDP)	99b	11,590	16,904	25,568	32,290	39,378	44,377	43,359	45,526	48,379	51,643	56,179	61,898
Net Primary Income from Abroad	98.n	34	34	−51	−364	−794	−1,022	−1,031	−775	−719	−642	−1,491	−1,488
Gross National Income (GNI)	99a	11,624	16,938	25,516	31,926	38,584	43,356	42,328	44,751	47,660	51,001	54,688	60,410
Net Current Transf.from Abroad	98t	508	624	437	575	920	940	651	970	1,030	852	890	728
Gross Nat'l Disposable Inc.(GNDI)	99i	12,132	17,562	25,954	32,501	39,504	44,296	42,980	45,721	48,690	51,852	55,578	61,138
Gross Saving	99s	1,859	2,754	3,276	3,801	5,748	6,148	4,959	6,204	7,621	8,555	8,730	9,686
Consumption of Fixed Capital	99cf	1,040	1,496	2,861	4,219	5,067	5,649	6,020	6,301	6,667	6,849	7,145	7,616
GDP Volume 2000 Prices	99b.p	39,791	35,905	37,086	38,821	41,541	44,565	43,810	45,526	48,429	51,704	56,716	60,511
GDP Volume (2000=100)	99bvp	87.4	78.9	81.5	85.3	91.2	97.9	96.2	100.0	106.4	113.6	124.6	132.9
GDP Deflator (2000=100)	99bip	29.1	47.1	68.9	83.2	94.8	99.6	99.0	100.0	99.9	99.9	99.1	102.3
						Millions: Midyear Estimates							
Population	99z	3.68	3.65	3.63	3.60	3.57	3.55	3.52	3.50	3.48	3.47	3.45	3.44

		1993	1994	1995	1996	1997	1998	1999	2000	2001	2002	2003	2004
Exchange Rates						*Francs per SDR through 1998, Euros per SDR Thereafter: End of Period*							
Market Rate	aa	49.599	46.478	43.725	46.022	49.814	48.682	1.3662	1.4002	1.4260	1.2964	1.1765	1.1402
						Francs per US Dollar through 1998, Euros per US Dollar Thereafter: End of Period (ae) Period Average (rf)							
Market Rate	ae	36.110	31.838	29.415	32.005	36.920	34.575	.9954	1.0747	1.1347	.9536	.7918	.7342
Market Rate	rf	34.597	33.456	29.480	30.962	35.774	36.299	.9386	1.0854	1.1175	1.0626	.8860	.8054
						Francs per ECU: End of Period (ea) Period Average (eb)							
ECU Rate	ea	40.266	39.161	38.697	40.102	40.781	40.340	....	....	....	....	....	....
ECU Rate	eb	40.468	39.661	38.548	39.295	40.529	40.621	....	....	....	....	....	....
						Index Numbers (2000=100): Period Averages							
Market Rate (1995=100)	ahx	85.2	88.2	100.0	95.1	82.4	81.2	....	....	....	....	....	....
Nominal Effective Exchange Rate	nec	101.6	102.8	104.7	103.5	101.5	101.3	101.0	100.0	99.9	100.1	101.4	101.8
Real Effective Exchange Rate	rec	101.9	102.8	104.8	102.9	100.6	100.3	100.0	100.0	100.3	100.9	102.6	103.2
Fund Position						*Millions of SDRs: End of Period*							
Quota	2f.s	135.50	135.50	135.50	135.50	135.50	135.50	279.10	279.10	279.10	279.10	279.10	279.10
SDRs	1b.s	6.98	7.22	7.46	7.75	8.04	8.72	1.78	3.22	5.00	6.72	8.29	9.83
Reserve Position in the Fund	1c.s	23.58	23.61	22.94	23.56	21.75	59.37	54.37	55.47	78.95	104.75	120.26	89.66
of which: Outstg.Fund Borrowing	2c	—	—	—	—	—	31.34	—	—	—	—	—	—
International Liquidity						*Millions of US Dollars Unless Otherwise Indicated: End of Period*							
Total Res.Min.Gold (Eurosys.Def)	1l.d	67.38	75.73	74.98	73.68	64.07	....	† 77.40	76.61	105.62	151.72	279.91	298.37
SDRs	1b.d	9.59	10.54	11.09	11.14	10.85	12.28	2.45	4.19	6.28	9.14	12.32	15.26
Reserve Position in the Fund	1c.d	32.38	34.46	34.10	33.87	29.35	83.60	74.62	72.27	99.21	142.41	178.70	139.25
Foreign Exchange	1d.d	25.40	30.73	29.79	28.67	23.87	....	.33	.15	.13	.18	88.89	143.87
o/w:Fin.Deriv.Rel.to Reserves	1ddd	....	....	....	....	....	....	....	....	....	....	....	....
Other Reserve Assets	1e.d	....	....	....	....	....	....	—	—	—	—	—	—
Gold (Million Fine Troy Ounces)	1ad	.305	.305	.305	.305	.305	....	.076	.076	.076	.076	.075	.074
Gold (Eurosystem Valuation)	1and	14.90	16.90	18.28	16.81	14.44	....	22.16	20.96	21.11	26.05	31.29	32.41
Memo:Euro Cl. on Non-EA Res.	1dgd	....	....	....	....	....	....	....	....	....	....	....	....
Non-Euro Cl. on EA Res.	1dhd	....	....	....	....	....	....	....	....	....	....	....	....
Mon. Auth.: Other Foreign Assets	3..d	....	....	....	....	....	....	—	—	—	—	—	—
Foreign Liabilities	4..d	25.48	30.78	29.58	28.43	24.11	....	† 2,171.54	47.73	56.03	56.59	90.59	150.08
Banking Insts.: Foreign Assets	7a.d	....	451,135	504,838	496,510	471,904	....	† 178,653	174,954	207,513	237,001	301,437	332,047
Foreign Liab.	7b.d	....	386,770	434,105	415,569	389,816	....	† 164,243	159,292	163,497	173,268	198,972	221,673
Monetary Authorities						*Billions of Francs through 1998; Millions of Euros Beginning 1999: End of Period*							
Fgn. Assets (Cl.on Non-EA Ctys)	11	8.3	8.5	8.3	7.5	6.2	....	952	156	333	436	762	957
Claims on General Government	12a.u	....	....	....	....	....	....	97	45	20	46	113	83
o/w: Claims on Gen.Govt in Cty	12a	5.5	5.5	4.9	4.8	4.7	....	—	—	—	—	—	—
Claims on Banking Institutions	12e.u	....	....	....	....	....	....	13,038	19,495	16,751	23,568	26,306	32,695
o/w: Claims on Bank.Inst.in Cty	12e	.1	.1	.2	1.0	2.6	....	9,000	19,282	16,511	23,371	23,423	28,406
Claims on Other Resident Sectors	12d.u	....	....	....	....	....	....	163	242	217	342	502	853
o/w: Cl. on Oth.Res.Sect.in Cty	12d	....	....	....	....	....	....	—	—	—	—	93	23
Currency Issued	14a	5.5	5.5	4.9	5.7	5.7	....	585	661	647	677	821	1,117
Liabilities to Banking Insts.	14c.u	....	....	....	....	....	....	11,509	19,272	16,555	23,197	25,845	32,405
o/w: Liabs to Bank.Inst.in Cty	14c	....	....	....	....	....	....	4,183	4,912	5,981	4,638	6,766	5,063
Demand Dep. of Other Res.Sect.	14d.u	....	....	....	....	....	....	18	16	15	—	—	—
o/w:D.Dep.of Oth.Res.Sect.in Cty	14d	....	....	....	....	....	....	3	—	—	—	—	—
Other Dep. of Other Res.Sect.	15..u	....	....	....	....	....	....	—	—	—	—	—	—
o/w:O.Dep.of Oth.Res.Sect.in Cty	15	....	....	....	....	....	....	—	—	—	—	—	—
Bonds & Money Mkt. Instruments	16n.u	....	....	....	....	....	....	—	—	—	—	—	—
o/w: Held by Resid.of Cty	16n	....	....	....	....	....	....	—	—	—	—	—	—
Foreign Liab. (to Non-EA Ctys)	16c	.9	1.0	.9	.9	.9	....	2,162	51	64	54	72	110
Central Government Deposits	16d.u	....	....	....	....	....	....	485	569	581	526	592	555
o/w: Cent.Govt.Dep. in Cty	16d	3.2	3.4	3.4	3.3	3.4	....	485	569	581	526	592	555
Capital Accounts	17a	4.1	4.2	4.2	4.3	4.5	....	199	203	188	205	192	546
Other Items (Net)	17r	.2	.1	—	−.9	−1.1	....	−709	−833	−730	−268	161	−145
Memo: Net Claims on Eurosystem	12e.s	....	....	....	....	....	....	−3,376	−14,211	−10,425	−18,408	−16,583	−23,766
Currency Put into Circ	14m	....	....	....	....	....	....	....	....	....	9,932	19,900	28,459
Banking Institutions						*Billions of Francs through 1998; Millions of Euros Beginning 1999: End of Period*							
Claims on Monetary Authorities	20	....	3.0	3.7	19.1	13.6	....	4,183	4,912	5,981	4,638	6,766	5,063
Claims on Bk.Inst.in Oth.EA Ctys	20b.u	....	....	....	....	....	....	228,490	254,464	283,512	291,098	307,198	322,883
Fgn. Assets (Cl.on Non-EA Ctys)	21	....	14,363.0	14,849.8	15,890.8	17,422.7	....	177,835	188,021	235,462	225,995	238,667	243,776
Claims on General Government	22a.u	....	....	....	....	....	....	53,469	46,551	49,303	48,921	60,573	66,277
o/w: Claims on Gen.Govt in Cty	22a	....	12.2	54.3	22.1	19.9	....	733	1,078	1,050	1,027	1,291	1,189
Claims on Other Resident Sectors	22d.u	....	....	....	....	....	....	82,554	98,232	107,910	105,621	108,296	109,911
o/w: Cl. on Oth.Res.Sect.in Cty	22d	....	489.7	525.4	552.9	616.0	....	19,778	22,495	29,128	24,879	26,536	29,115
Demand Deposits	24..u	....	....	....	....	....	....	42,610	50,376	50,708	48,161	50,377	56,020
o/w:D.Dep.of Oth.Res.Sect.in Cty	24	....	78.5	72.7	79.5	81.5	....	26,687	34,188	31,842	31,519	33,777	40,613
Other Deposits	25..u	....	....	....	....	....	....	89,947	99,507	104,401	102,256	104,507	113,466
o/w:O.Dep.of Oth.Res.Sect.in Cty	25	....	1,674.0	1,677.1	1,933.2	2,155.8	....	32,027	34,711	38,855	39,367	41,854	46,048
Money Market Fund Shares	26m.u	....	....	....	....	....	....	65,940	76,337	119,162	138,406	161,713	157,449
Bonds & Money Mkt. Instruments	26n.u	....	....	....	....	....	....	38,771	44,774	52,322	54,359	74,347	76,923
o/w: Held by Resid.of Cty	26n	....	293.8	453.3	599.1	797.7	....						
Foreign Liab. (to Non-EA Ctys)	26c	....	12,313.8	12,769.2	13,300.3	14,392.0	....	163,491	171,190	185,518	165,222	157,539	162,744
Central Government Deposits	26d.u	....	....	....	....	....	....	4,595	12,745	8,819	3,178	5,686	4,443
o/w: Cent.Govt.Dep. in Cty	26d	....	53.8	59.8	72.1	79.6	....	3,377	3,213	2,118	1,915	2,965	2,841
Credit from Monetary Authorities	26g	....	3.8	35.5	3.8	4.6	....	9,000	19,282	16,511	23,371	23,423	28,406
Liab. to Bk.Inst.in Oth. EA Ctys	26h.u	....	....	....	....	....	....	105,620	93,339	119,350	116,015	116,903	119,246
Capital Accounts	27a	....	486.3	526.5	549.0	562.0	....	16,551	34,090	37,432	39,962	39,712	41,124
Other Items (Net)	27r	....	† −36.2	−161.0	−51.9	−1.0	....	10,005	−9,459	−12,056	−14,657	−12,605	−11,911
Central Govt. Monetary Liabilities	25.iu	....	....	....	....	12,008	12,778	327	344	438	502	694	608

		1993	1994	1995	1996	1997	1998	1999	2000	2001	2002	2003	2004
Banking Survey (Nat'l Residency)					*Billions of Francs through 1998; Millions of Euros Beginning 1999: End of Period*								
Foreign Assets (Net)	31n	....	2,056.7	2,088.0	2,597.1	3,036.0	....	164,333	185,959	209,704	237,495	256,087	282,175
Domestic Credit	32	....	† 450.2	521.4	504.4	557.6	....	16,649	19,791	27,479	23,465	24,363	26,931
Claims on General Govt. (Net)	32an	....	† −39.5	−4.0	−48.5	−58.4	....	−3,129	−2,704	−1,649	−1,414	−2,266	−2,207
Claims on Other Resident Sectors	32d	....	489.7	525.4	552.9	616.0	....	19,778	22,495	29,128	24,879	26,629	29,138
Currency Issued	34a.n	5.5	5.5	4.9	5.7	5.7	....	585	661	647	677	821	1,117
Demand Deposits	34b.n	....	78.5	72.7	79.5	81.5	....	26,690	34,188	31,842	31,519	33,777	40,613
Other Deposits	35..n	....	1,674.0	1,677.1	1,933.2	2,155.8	....	32,027	34,711	38,855	39,367	41,854	46,048
Money Market Fund Shares	36m	....	....	....	....	....	....	35,981	40,002	55,128	274,685	79,973	84,270
Bonds & Money Mkt. Instruments	36n	....	293.8	453.3	599.1	797.7	....	55,678	66,598	79,848	78,841	74,399	76,901
o/w: Over Two Years	36na	....	....	....	....	....	....	31,161	34,014	37,960	40,999	45,217	54,463
Capital Accounts	37a	....	490.5	530.7	553.3	566.5	....	16,750	34,292	37,620	40,168	39,904	41,670
Other Items (Net)	37r	....	† −35.4	−129.4	−69.0	−13.7	....	13,271	−4,703	−6,707	90	9,720	18,445
Banking Survey (EA-Wide Residency)						*Millions of Euros: End of Period*							
Foreign Assets (Net)	31n.u	....	....	....	....	....	....	13,134	16,937	50,213	61,155	81,819	81,878
Domestic Credit	32..u	....	....	....	....	....	....	131,203	131,756	148,048	151,226	163,206	172,126
Claims on General Govt. (Net)	32anu	....	....	....	....	....	....	48,486	33,281	39,922	45,264	54,408	61,361
Claims on Other Resident Sect.	32d.u	....	....	....	....	....	....	82,717	98,474	108,127	105,962	108,798	110,765
Currency Issued	34a.u	....	....	....	....	....	....	585	661	647	677	821	1,117
Demand Deposits	34b.u	....	....	....	....	....	....	42,628	50,391	50,723	48,161	50,277	56,020
Other Deposits	35..u	....	....	....	....	....	....	89,947	99,507	104,401	102,256	104,507	113,466
o/w: Other Dep. Over Two Yrs.	35abu	....	....	....	....	....	....	6,926	3,823	5,371	5,038	7,839	12,504
Money Market Fund Shares	36m.u	....	....	....	....	....	....	65,940	76,337	119,162	138,406	161,713	157,449
Bonds & Money Mkt. Instruments	36n.u	....	....	....	....	....	....	38,771	44,774	52,322	54,359	74,347	76,923
o/w: Over Two Years	36nau	....	....	....	....	....	....	31,161	34,014	38,011	41,048	45,127	54,479
Capital Accounts	37a	....	....	....	....	....	....	16,750	34,292	37,620	40,168	39,904	41,670
Other Items (Net)	37r.u	....	....	....	....	....	....	−110,285	−157,271	−166,615	−171,646	−186,544	−192,640
Money (National Definitions)						*Billions of Francs: End of Period*							
Money	59ma	....	104.5	....	111.4	115.0	....	....	....	....	....	....	....
Quasi-Money	59maa	....	399.6	....	423.5	396.0	....	....	....	....	....	....	....
Broad Money	59mb	....	504.1	....	534.9	511.0	....	....	....	....	....	....	....
Interest Rates						*Percent Per Annum*							
Money Market Rate	60b	8.09	5.16	4.26	3.29	3.36	3.48	....	....	....	....	....	....
Deposit Rate	60l	5.33	5.00	5.00	3.54	3.46	3.31	....	....	....	....	....	....
Deposit Rate (Households)	60lhs	....	....	....	....	....	....	....	....	....	....	1.77	1.80
Deposit Rate (Corporations)	60lcs	....	....	....	....	....	....	....	....	....	....	2.01	2.13
Lending Rate	60p	7.65	6.58	6.50	5.50	5.50	5.27	....	....	....	....	....	....
Lending Rate (Households)	60phm	....	....	....	....	....	....	....	....	....	....	3.64	3.48
Lending Rate (Corporations)	60pcs	....	....	....	....	....	....	....	....	....	....	3.32	3.20
Government Bond Yield	61	6.93	6.38	6.05	5.21	5.39	5.29	....	....	....	....	....	....
Prices, Production, Labor						*Index Numbers (2000=100): Period Averages*							
Share Prices (1995=100)	62	78.3	110.4	100.0	117.5	152.5	194.2	....	....	....	....	....	....
Producer Prices in Industry	63a	92.7	† 94.1	97.8	94.7	96.1	98.5	† 95.4	100.0	99.8	99.0	100.2	109.3
Consumer Prices	64	88.8	90.8	92.5	† 93.8	95.1	96.0	96.9	100.0	102.7	104.8	106.9	109.3
Harmonized CPI	64h	....	....	92.1	93.2	94.5	95.4	96.4	100.0	102.4	104.5	107.2	110.6
Industrial Production	66	75.2	79.7	† 81.3	81.4	86.1	86.0	95.9	100.0	103.1	105.2	110.7	117.8
Employment	67	....	....	....	....	....	....	94.7	100.0	† 105.6	109.0	111.0	113.9
						Number in Thousands: Period Averages							
Employment	67e	....	....	214	220	227	237	248	265	280	288	294	....
Unemployment	67c	4	5	5	6	6	6	5	5	5	6	8	9
Unemployment Rate (%)	67r	2.1	2.8	3.0	3.3	3.6	3.1	2.9	2.7	2.6	2.9	3.8	4.2
Intl. Transactions & Positions						*Billions of Francs through 1998; Millions of Euros Beginning 1999*							
Exports	70	203.60	219.10	228.40	223.20	250.10	287.30	† 7.42	8.62	9.21	9.01	8.81	9.80
Imports, c.i.f.	71	265.90	280.00	287.30	299.20	335.70	370.60	† 10.38	11.65	12.47	12.28	12.10	13.44

		1993	1994	1995	1996	1997	1998	1999	2000	2001	2002	2003	2004
Balance of Payments					*Millions of US Dollars: Minus Sign Indicates Debit*								
Current Account, n.i.e.	78ald	....	....	2,426	2,219	1,834	1,626	1,650	2,562	1,674	2,436	2,230	2,710
Goods: Exports f.o.b.	78aad	....	....	8,578	7,944	7,745	8,557	8,565	8,635	8,996	9,605	11,312	13,706
Goods: Imports f.o.b.	78abd	....	....	−10,269	−9,872	−9,770	−10,881	−11,151	−11,056	−11,395	−11,704	−13,964	−16,989
Trade Balance	78acd	....	....	−1,690	−1,928	−2,025	−2,324	−2,586	−2,420	−2,399	−2,099	−2,652	−3,283
Services: Credit	78add	....	....	10,619	11,930	12,583	14,084	17,134	20,301	19,945	20,182	24,890	33,278
Services: Debit	78aed	....	....	−7,519	−8,483	−8,683	−9,947	−11,840	−13,581	−13,708	−13,168	−16,476	−22,301
Balance on Goods & Services	78afd	....	....	1,410	1,519	1,874	1,813	2,708	4,300	3,838	4,915	5,762	7,693
Income: Credit	78agd	....	....	48,798	40,476	38,439	46,814	47,931	50,400	52,302	49,374	52,092	61,081
Income: Debit	78ahd	....	....	−47,209	−39,220	−37,971	−46,578	−48,413	−51,678	−53,941	−51,624	−55,090	−64,832
Balance on Gds, Serv. & Inc.	78aid	....	....	2,999	2,774	2,342	2,049	2,227	3,022	2,199	2,666	2,764	3,942
Current Transfers, n.i.e.: Credit	78ajd	....	....	1,791	2,186	1,985	2,185	2,282	2,750	2,269	3,476	3,905	4,258
Current Transfers: Debit	78akd	....	....	−2,364	−2,741	−2,493	−2,608	−2,859	−3,211	−2,793	−3,706	−4,439	−5,489
Capital Account, n.i.e.	78bcd	....	....	....	....	....	....	....	....	....	−168	−178	−303
Capital Account, n.i.e.: Credit	78bad	....	....	....	....	....	....	....	....	....	54	55	32
Capital Account: Debit	78bbd	....	....	....	....	....	....	....	....	....	−222	−233	−335
Financial Account, n.i.e.	78bjd	....	....	....	....	....	....	....	....	....	−1,585	−1,717	−3,424
Direct Investment Abroad	78bdd	....	....	....	....	....	....	....	....	....	−129,237	−101,741	−78,065
Dir. Invest. in Rep. Econ., n.i.e.	78bed	....	....	....	....	....	....	....	....	....	120,374	92,898	76,311
Portfolio Investment Assets	78bfd	....	....	....	....	....	....	....	....	....	6,254	−78,422	−87,546
Equity Securities	78bkd	....	....	....	....	....	....	....	....	....	4,301	−35,857	−45,835
Debt Securities	78bld	....	....	....	....	....	....	....	....	....	1,953	−42,565	−41,711
Portfolio Investment Liab., n.i.e.	78bgd	....	....	....	....	....	....	....	....	....	64,211	99,493	140,330
Equity Securities	78bmd	....	....	....	....	....	....	....	....	....	36,081	70,450	121,615
Debt Securities	78bnd	....	....	....	....	....	....	....	....	....	28,129	29,043	18,715
Financial Derivatives Assets	78bwd	....	....	....	....	....	....	....	....	....	....	....	−2,685
Financial Derivatives Liabilities	78bxd	....	....	....	....	....	....	....	....	....	−38	6,843	−87
Other Investment Assets	78bhd	....	....	....	....	....	....	....	....	....	−42,807	−30,022	−119,766
Monetary Authorities	78bod	....	....	....	....	....	....	....	....	....	—	—	−7,210
General Government	78bpd	....	....	....	....	....	....	....	....	....	−50	−11	7
Banks	78bqd	....	....	....	....	....	....	....	....	....	19,337	−3,623	−43,871
Other Sectors	78brd	....	....	....	....	....	....	....	....	....	−62,095	−26,388	−68,691
Other Investment Liab., n.i.e.	78bid	....	....	....	....	....	....	....	....	....	−20,342	9,236	68,084
Monetary Authorities	78bsd	....	....	....	....	....	....	....	....	....	−887	−13,465	6,208
General Government	78btd	....	....	....	....	....	....	....	....	....	3	−1	−16
Banks	78bud	....	....	....	....	....	....	....	....	....	−27,719	17,866	31,295
Other Sectors	78bvd	....	....	....	....	....	....	....	....	....	8,261	4,836	30,598
Net Errors and Omissions	78cad	....	....	....	....	....	....	....	....	....	−648	−227	1,025
Overall Balance	78cbd	....	....	....	....	....	....	....	....	....	35	108	8
Reserves and Related Items	79dad	....	....	....	....	....	....	....	....	....	−35	−108	−8
Reserve Assets	79dbd	....	....	—	....	—	....	....	....	....	−35	−108	−8
Use of Fund Credit and Loans	79dcd	....	....	....	....	....	....	....	....	....	—	—	—
Exceptional Financing	79ded	....	....	....	....	....	....	....	....	....	—	....	....
Government Finance													
Central Government					*Millions of Francs through 1998; Millions of Euros Beginning 1999: Year Ending December 31*								
Deficit (-) or Surplus	80	....	2,656	12,573	25,846	12,609	....	....	....	....	....	....	....
Revenue	81	202,183	217,830	220,074	239,082	261,696	....	....	....	....	....	....	....
Grants Received	81z	944	596	797	507	7,037	....	....	....	....	....	....	....
Expenditure	82	192,807	205,656	211,557	222,710	240,847	....	....	....	....	....	....	....
Lending Minus Repayments	83	603	700	613	641	−5,563	....	....	....	....	....	....	....
Adjustment for Complem. Period	80x	....	−9,414	3,872	9,608	−20,840	....	....	....	....	....	....	....
Financing													
Total Financing	84	....	−2,656	−11,810	−25,846	−12,609	....	....	....	....	....	....	....
Domestic	84a	....	−2,300	−11,776	−25,598	−12,455	....	....	....	....	....	....	....
Foreign	85a	....	−356	−34	−248	−154	....	....	....	....	....	....	....
Debt: Domestic	88a	15,473	....	....	....	24,616	....	....	....	....	....	....	....
Foreign	89a	512	....	....	....	6,311	....	....	....	....	....	....	....
General Government					*As Percent of Gross Domestic Product*								
Deficit (-) or Surplus	80g	1.7	2.8	1.8	2.7	3.6	3.2	3.8	5.8	5.0	....	....	....
Debt	88g	6.1	5.7	5.8	6.2	6.0	6.3	6.0	5.6	5.5	....	....	....
National Accounts					*Billions of Francs through 1998; Billions of Euros Beginning 1999*								
Househ.Cons.Expend.,incl.NPISHs.	96f	230.2	245.7	† 255.3	270.2	284.7	306.6	† 7.9	8.5	9.2	9.6	10.0	10.4
Government Consumption Expend.	91f	87.5	91.3	† 98.2	106.2	112.0	115.0	† 3.1	3.3	3.7	4.0	4.4	4.7
Gross Fixed Capital Formation	93e	113.4	115.1	† 115.0	120.0	139.1	155.3	† 4.5	4.4	5.0	5.0	4.7	5.0
Changes in Inventories	93i	2.5	2.8	† −.8	1.5	4.9	7.4	† .1	.6	.2	−.2	.3	—
Exports of Goods and Services	90c	493.1	547.6	† 581.5	624.5	745.5	873.5	† 25.5	32.3	33.7	32.8	32.9	37.5
Imports of Goods and Services (-)	98c	448.9	489.0	† 516.2	560.6	661.3	771.6	† 22.4	27.9	29.9	28.5	28.4	32.0
Gross Domestic Product (GDP)	99b	477.8	513.6	† 533.1	561.9	624.9	686.1	† 18.7	21.3	22.0	22.8	24.0	25.7
Net Primary Income from Abroad	98.n	....	48.2	† 32.2	30.1	14.0	−11.5	† −.6	−2.0	....	....	....	....
Gross National Income (GNI)	99a	511.2	529.4	† 566.6	597.6	632.9	684.9	† 18.3	19.3	20.5	20.9	21.2	22.6
Net Current Transf.from Abroad	98t	....	....	....	....	....		† −.5	−.8	−2.4	....	....	....
Gross Nat'l Disposable Inc.(GNDI)	99i	....	....	....	....	....		† 17.8	18.4	18.1	....	....	....
Consumption of Fixed Capital	99cf	74.8	79.2	82.7	86.9	87.9	92.6	† 2.4	2.6	2.9	3.1	3.1	....
GDP Volume 1995 Prices	99b.p	....	....	533.1	552.4	602.6	638.4	† 17.0	18.6	18.9	19.3	19.9	20.8
GDP Volume (2000=100)	99bvp	....	....	71.1	73.7	80.4	85.2	† 91.7	100.0	101.5	104.1	107.1	112.0
GDP Deflator (2000=100)	99bip	....	....	† 87.3	88.8	90.6	93.9	† 96.0	100.0	101.9	103.0	105.1	107.7
						Millions: Midyear Estimates							
Population	99z	.39	.40	.41	.41	.42	.42	.43	.44	.44	.45	.45	.46

Macedonia, FYR 962

		1993	1994	1995	1996	1997	1998	1999	2000	2001	2002	2003	2004
Exchange Rates						*Denar per SDR: End of Period*							
Market Rate....................	aa	61.062	59.264	56.456	59.547	74.776	72.987	82.816	86.420	86.930	79.665	72.887	69.990
						Denar per US Dollar: End of Period (ae) Period Average (rf)							
Market Rate....................	ae	44.456	40.596	37.980	41.411	55.421	51.836	60.339	66.328	69.172	58.598	49.050	45.068
Market Rate....................	rf	....	43.263	37.882	39.981	50.004	54.462	56.902	65.904	68.037	64.350	54.322	49.410
						Index Numbers (2000=100): Period Averages							
Nominal Effective Exchange Rate.....	nec	70.63	44.44	54.39	64.19	89.03	88.11	99.67	100.00	102.70	105.65	109.37	110.65
Real Effective Exchange Rate...........	rec	123.96	127.92	139.10	134.41	115.13	101.39	101.54	100.00	100.32	99.54	100.00	98.46
Fund Position						*Millions of SDRs: End of Period*							
Quota.................................	2f.s	49.6	49.6	49.6	49.6	49.6	49.6	68.9	68.9	68.9	68.9	68.9	68.9
SDRs...................................	1b.s	—	—	.2	—	.3	.8	.9	.5	1.8	4.5	.2	.5
Reserve Position in the Fund...........	1c.s	—	—	—	—	—	—	—	—	—	—	—	—
Total Fund Cred.&Loans Outstg.......	2tl	2.8	14.0	38.1	47.4	65.3	72.7	74.1	62.3	56.3	49.6	46.0	40.3
International Liquidity					*Millions of US Dollars Unless Otherwise Indicated: End of Period*								
Total Reserves minus Gold..............	1l.d	104.59	149.05	257.49	239.55	257.00	306.11	429.92	429.38	745.17	722.03	897.67	904.97
SDRs...................................	1b.d	—	—	.2	—	.4	1.1	1.2	.7	2.2	6.1	.3	.8
Reserve Position in the Fund.........	1c.d	—	—	—	—	—	—	—	—	—	—	—	—
Foreign Exchange...........................	1d.d	104.57	149.04	257.26	239.51	256.61	305.04	428.73	428.73	742.94	715.91	897.39	904.21
Gold (Million Fine Troy Ounces)........	1ad	.041	.045	.046	.076	.081	.100	.102	.112	.194	.198	.089	.197
Gold (National Valuation).................	1and	14.66	16.36	17.61	27.98	23.45	28.50	29.69	30.66	53.68	67.81	37.08	86.47
Other Liab....................	4..d								14.01				
Deposit Money Banks: Assets...........	7a.d	158.20	232.98	254.61	229.70	286.84	337.78	404.22	430.92	643.02	560.34	674.80	823.90
Liabilities....................	7b.d	579.43	528.30	84.62	138.39	185.76	250.00	262.28	233.08	195.31	205.59	199.65	223.31
Monetary Authorities						*Millions of Denar: End of Period*							
Foreign Assets..............................	11	5,303	6,715	10,732	11,453	15,894	18,977	30,072	47,910	70,945	45,560	45,835	44,412
Claims on Central Government........	12a	749	2,400	2,395	3,049	8,706	8,675	8,116	5,869	8,796	8,275	3,878	3,467
Claims on Deposit Money Banks......	12e	1,830	2,333	4,673	5,642	3,672	3,538	1,918	1,259	394	410	240	199
Reserve Money..............................	14	3,705	6,360	† 8,306	8,044	9,872	10,421	13,508	19,804	21,402	22,209	23,944	23,865
of which: Currency Outside DMBs...	14a	2,703	4,786	5,965	6,401	6,846	6,964	8,271	9,522	14,134	14,136	14,177	14,162
Restricted Deposits.........................	16b	—	—	114	136	9	56	271	135	588	560	648	223
Foreign Liabilities.........................	16c	172	831	2,150	2,822	4,882	5,308	6,137	6,314	4,897	3,949	3,353	2,819
Central Government Deposits..........	16d	14	31	2,633	3,695	5,070	6,152	9,465	16,759	24,926	17,318	11,667	12,554
Capital Accounts............................	17a	4,754	4,682	5,059	5,771	8,398	8,130	9,547	11,076	12,348	9,984	7,729	7,154
Other Items (Net)...........................	17r	−911	−360	−462	−325	41	1,123	1,178	950	15,974	225	2,612	1,463
Deposit Money Banks						*Millions of Denar: End of Period*							
Reserves.....................................	20	678	1,470	1,836	1,125	2,158	2,379	3,861	6,192	6,195	6,364	8,098	8,110
Foreign Assets..............................	21	7,033	9,458	9,670	9,512	15,897	17,509	24,390	28,582	44,479	32,835	33,099	37,131
Claims on Central Government........	22a	52,503	48,954	5,624	6,311	1,782	1,288	1,289	7,337	7,744	8,257	6,745	7,164
Claims on Local Government...........	22b	—	—	2	12	27	20	14	44	7	11	2	20
Claims on Nonfin.Pub.Enterprises.....	22c	—	—	528	121	208	293	237	515	755	814	458	677
Claims on Private Sector.................	22d	35,107	66,392	39,181	46,826	50,711	34,531	43,611	42,157	41,151	43,104	49,937	61,470
Demand Deposits...........................	24	2,853	5,080	5,567	4,854	6,281	7,336	10,458	11,896	11,168	12,255	12,800	13,154
Time, Savings,& Fgn.Currency Dep...	25	38,138	9,726	8,417	8,652	11,537	13,573	17,846	23,294	49,200	42,096	52,584	65,009
Restricted Deposits.........................	26b	9,613	38,938	1,039	1,111	1,006	1,099	1,185	1,373	1,708	692	567	680
Foreign Liabilities...........................	26c	25,759	21,447	3,214	5,731	10,295	12,959	15,826	15,460	13,510	12,047	9,793	10,064
Central Government Deposits..........	26d	445	2,411	1,481	1,345	1,678	2,181	2,904	5,214	4,150	2,692	2,034	1,660
Credit from Monetary Authorities.....	26g	1,310	1,961	4,016	4,395	2,388	2,303	1,287	805	427	398	374	779
Capital Accounts............................	27a	10,520	15,567	17,483	23,799	23,157	23,651	29,046	33,120	30,105	30,102	31,723	34,664
Other Items (Net)...........................	27r	6,687	31,132	15,624	14,021	14,441	−7,082	−5,150	−6,335	−9,937	−8,897	−11,536	−11,438
Monetary Survey						*Millions of Denar: End of Period*							
Foreign Assets (Net).......................	31n	−13,595	−6,106	15,038	12,412	16,614	18,219	32,499	54,718	30,969	66,617	65,789	68,660
Domestic Credit.............................	32	87,900	115,304	43,635	51,406	54,797	36,637	41,075	34,027	45,516	38,805	47,321	58,584
Claims on Central Govt. (Net).......	32an	52,793	48,912	3,905	4,320	3,740	1,630	−2,964	−8,767	3,594	−5,124	−3,078	−3,583
Claims on Local Government.........	32b	—	—	2	12	27	20	14	44	7	11	2	20
Claims on Nonfin.Pub.Enterprises...	32c	—	—	528	121	208	293	237	515	755	814	458	677
Claims on Private Sector...............	32d	35,107	66,392	39,181	46,826	50,711	34,531	43,611	42,157	41,151	43,104	49,937	61,470
Money...	34	5,590	9,965	† 12,223	11,788	13,702	14,952	19,795	22,392	11,168	27,722	28,291	28,884
Quasi-Money.................................	35	37,510	8,507	† 8,417	8,652	11,537	13,573	17,846	23,294	49,200	42,096	52,584	65,009
Restricted Deposits.........................	36b	9,613	38,938	1,153	1,247	1,015	1,155	1,456	1,508	1,708	1,381	1,215	903
Capital Accounts............................	37a	15,274	20,249	22,542	29,570	31,555	31,781	38,593	44,196	30,105	40,994	39,452	41,818
Other Items (Net)...........................	37r	6,174	31,624	14,338	12,561	13,602	−6,605	−4,116	−2,645	−15,696	−6,771	−8,433	−9,370
Money plus Quasi-Money.................	35l	43,100	18,472	† 20,640	20,440	25,239	28,525	37,641	45,686	60,368	69,818	80,875	93,893
Interest Rates						*Percent Per Annum*							
Bank Rate (End of Period)................	60	295.00	33.00	15.00	9.20	8.90	8.90	8.90	7.90	10.70	10.70	6.50	6.50
Deposit Rate.................................	60l	....	117.56	24.07	12.75	11.64	11.68	11.40	11.18	9.97	9.56	7.97	6.54
Lending Rate.................................	60p	....	159.82	45.95	21.58	21.42	21.03	20.45	18.93	19.35	18.36	16.00	12.44
Prices, Production, Labor						*Index Numbers (2000=100): Period Averages*							
Producer Prices..............................	63	41.5	78.6	82.3	82.3	85.7	89.3	90.2	100.0	102.7	102.0	102.0	103.1
Consumer Prices.............................	64	34.5	78.2	91.0	93.3	94.5	95.0	† 93.8	100.0	105.2	107.6	108.8	108.4
Wages: Average Monthly.................	65	....	76.2	84.2	86.5	88.9	92.1	94.7	100.0	103.6	110.7	116.0	120.5
Industrial Production.......................	66	115.0	103.7	93.3	97.5	93.4	97.2	96.6	100.0	89.9	86.0	90.1	78.3
						Number in Thousands: Period Averages							
Employment...................................	67e	421	396	357	340	319	310	316	312	292	280	268	259
Unemployment...............................	67c	175	186	216	238	253	....	....	....	263	263	316	....
Intl. Transactions & Positions						*Millions of US Dollars*							
Exports...	70..d	1,055.3	1,086.3	1,204.0	1,147.4	1,236.8	1,310.7	1,191.3	1,322.6	1,157.5	1,115.5	1,363.3	1,661.1
Imports, c.i.f...................................	71..d	1,199.3	1,484.1	1,718.9	1,626.9	1,778.5	1,914.7	1,776.2	2,093.9	1,693.6	1,995.2	2,299.9	2,875.3

		1993	1994	1995	1996	1997	1998	1999	2000	2001	2002	2003	2004
Balance of Payments					*Millions of US Dollars: Minus Sign Indicates Debit*								
Current Account, n.i.e.	78ald	....	....	....	−288.1	−275.5	−269.7	−32.4	−72.4	−243.6	−357.9	−278.5	....
Goods: Exports f.o.b.	78aad	....	....	....	1,147.4	1,201.4	1,291.5	1,190.0	1,320.7	1,155.4	1,112.1	1,359.0	....
Goods: Imports f.o.b.	78abd	....	....	....	−1,464.0	−1,589.1	−1,806.6	−1,685.8	−2,011.1	−1,681.8	−1,916.5	−2,210.5	....
Trade Balance	78acd	....	....	....	−316.5	−387.6	−515.1	−495.8	−690.4	−526.4	−804.3	−851.5	....
Services: Credit	78add	....	....	....	154.3	128.3	149.3	272.8	316.7	244.6	253.0	326.0	....
Services: Debit	78aed	....	....	....	−309.3	−272.9	−209.1	−230.9	−268.0	−263.8	−275.3	−328.6	....
Balance on Goods & Services	78afd	....	....	....	−471.5	−532.2	−574.9	−453.8	−641.7	−545.6	−826.6	−854.1	....
Income: Credit	78agd	....	....	....	45.3	39.0	23.5	24.2	41.6	52.6	51.0	60.3	....
Income: Debit	78ahd	....	....	....	−75.0	−72.6	−68.5	−66.5	−87.3	−93.3	−80.8	−92.7	....
Balance on Gds, Serv. & Inc.	78aid	....	....	....	−501.2	−565.8	−619.9	−496.1	−687.3	−586.3	−856.4	−886.4	....
Current Transfers, n.i.e.: Credit	78ajd	....	....	....	475.4	535.0	542.7	618.5	788.2	725.7	535.7	646.1	....
Current Transfers: Debit	78akd	....	....	....	−262.3	−244.8	−192.5	−154.8	−173.3	−383.0	−37.2	−38.2	....
Capital Account, n.i.e.	78bcd	....	....	....			−1.8	—	.3	1.3	8.3	−6.7	....
Capital Account, n.i.e.: Credit	78bad	....	....	....	....	....		—	.3	3.6	9.9	—	....
Capital Account: Debit	78bbd	....	....	....			−1.8	—	—	−2.3	−1.7	−6.7	....
Financial Account, n.i.e.	78bjd	....	....	....	174.3	186.8	329.9	14.2	290.3	325.7	257.2	248.4	....
Direct Investment Abroad	78bdd	....	....	....				−.3	.6	−.9	−.1	−.3	....
Dir. Invest. in Rep. Econ., n.i.e.	78bed	....	....	....	11.2	15.7	127.7	32.7	174.5	441.5	77.8	94.6	....
Portfolio Investment Assets	78bfd	....	....	....	−.5	−2.5	.2	.1	−.8	3.2	1.2	.3	....
Equity Securities	78bkd	....	....	....	−.5	−2.5	—	—	—	—	.3	.1	....
Debt Securities	78bld	....	....	....	....		.2	.1	−.8	3.2	.9	.3	....
Portfolio Investment Liab., n.i.e.	78bgd	....	....	....	.8	4.6	.1	—	−.1	.4	.1	3.3	....
Equity Securities	78bmd	....	....	....	.8	4.6	—	—	—	—	—	.7	....
Debt Securities	78bnd	....	....	....			.1	—	−.1	.4	—	2.6	....
Financial Derivatives Assets	78bwd	....	....	....	....	....				....	....	....	....
Financial Derivatives Liabilities	78bxd	....	....	....			—	—	—	....	....		....
Other Investment Assets	78bhd	....	....	....	−133.2	−73.0	−58.9	−184.1	−77.7	−98.1	246.2	12.2	....
Monetary Authorities	78bod	....	....	....			−15.2	−6.2	14.1	−236.8	223.0	17.8	....
General Government	78bpd	....	....	....									....
Banks	78bqd	....	....	....	25.3	−57.5	−31.3	−114.9	−62.1	−237.6	159.4	−27.3	....
Other Sectors	78brd	....	....	....	−158.5	−15.6	−12.3	−62.9	−29.6	376.2	−136.3	21.7	....
Other Investment Liab., n.i.e.	78bid	....	....	....	295.9	242.0	260.9	165.8	193.7	−20.4	−67.9	138.3	....
Monetary Authorities	78bsd	....	....	....	—	—	—	—	14.7	140.1	−154.2	—	....
General Government	78btd	....	....	....	59.9	−71.6	109.2	89.4	77.3	−65.4	11.0	28.3	....
Banks	78bud	....	....	....	−1.2	29.8	105.1	68.1	−44.0	−38.3	−4.6	−38.9	....
Other Sectors	78bvd	....	....	....	237.3	283.8	46.5	8.2	145.7	−56.8	79.9	148.9	....
Net Errors and Omissions	78cad	....	....	....	18.8	−29.9	−15.1	159.9	61.0	2.3	−29.7	90.4	....
Overall Balance	78cbd	....	....	....	−95.1	−118.6	43.3	141.7	279.2	85.6	−122.1	53.5	....
Reserves and Related Items	79dad	....	....	....	95.1	118.6	−43.3	−141.7	−279.2	−85.6	122.1	−53.5	....
Reserve Assets	79dbd	....	....	....	7.6	−35.1	−53.2	−143.5	−263.6	−78.0	130.9	−48.9	....
Use of Fund Credit and Loans	79dcd	....	....	....	13.5	24.6	9.9	1.8	−15.6	−7.6	−8.8	−4.7	....
Exceptional Financing	79ded	....	....	....	73.9	129.2	—	—	—	—	—	—	....
International Investment Position					*Millions of US Dollars*								
Assets	79aad	....	....	....	....	....	....	....	....	....	....	....	....
Direct Investment Abroad	79abd	....	....	....	—	—	—	—	—	—	—	—	....
Portfolio Investment	79acd	....	....	....	—	—	—	—	—	—	3.5	4.0	....
Equity Securities	79add	....	....	....	—	—	—	—	—	—	—	—	....
Debt Securities	79aed	....	....	....	—	—	—	—	—	—	3.5	4.0	....
Financial Derivatives	79ald	....	....	....	....	....	....	....	....	....	....	....	....
Other Investment	79afd	....	....	....	229.3	286.8	337.8	425.4	458.8	895.7	601.4	701.0	....
Monetary Authorities	79agd	....	....	....	—	—	—	21.2	21.4	252.7	49.2	31.4	....
General Government	79ahd	....	....	....									....
Banks	79aid	....	....	....	229.3	286.8	337.8	404.2	437.4	643.0	552.2	669.6	....
Other Sectors	79ajd	....	....	....									....
Reserve Assets	79akd	....	....	....	267.5	280.4	367.2	478.3	712.6	775.2	734.4	903.3	....
Liabilities	79lad	....	....	....	....	....	....	....	....	....	....	....	....
Dir. Invest. in Rep. Economy	79lbd	....	....	....	—	—	—	—	—	—	—	—	....
Portfolio Investment	79lcd	....	....	....	—	—	—	—	—	—	—	—	....
Equity Securities	79ldd	....	....	....	—	—	—	—	—	—	—	—	....
Debt Securities	79led	....	....	....	—	—	—	—	—	—	—	—	....
Financial Derivatives	79lld	....	....	....									....
Other Investment	79lfd	....	....	....	1,243.1	1,259.7	1,545.0	1,603.7	1,603.0	1,654.3	1,642.8	1,838.5	....
Monetary Authorities	79lgd	....	....	....	68.2	88.1	102.4	101.7	95.4	225.0	67.4	68.4	....
General Government	79lhd	....	....	....	1,041.2	999.3	1,126.2	1,156.3	1,216.3	1,147.8	1,131.6	1,256.5	....
Banks	79lid	....	....	....	121.3	156.3	289.7	321.2	217.4	177.3	188.4	171.3	....
Other Sectors	79ljd	....	....	....	12.4	16.0	26.8	24.5	73.9	104.2	255.4	342.3	....
Government Finance					*Millions of Denar: Year Ending December 31*								
Deficit (-) or Surplus	80	....	....	2,267.6	175.3		....	....	....	....	....	....	....
Total Revenue and Grants	81y	....	....	40,437.0	39,865.2	....	....	....	....	....	....	....	....
Revenue	81	....	....	39,775.8	39,766.1	....	....	....	....	....	....	....	....
Grants	81z	....	....	661.2	99.1	....	....	....	....	....	....	....	....
Exp. & Lending Minus Repay	82z	....	....	38,169.4	39,689.9	....	....	....	....	....	....	....	....
Expenditure	82	....	....	36,511.0	37,423.3	....	....	....	....	....	....	....	....
Lending Minus Repayments	83	....	....	1,658.4	2,266.6	....	....	....	....	....	....	....	....
Total Financing	80h	....	....	−2,267.6	−175.3	....	....	....	....	....	....	....	....
Total Net Borrowing	84	....	....	−3,445.2	−175.5	....	....	....	....	....	....	....	....
Net Domestic	84a	....	....	−3,334.1	−1,200.0	....	....	....	....	....	....	....	....
Net Foreign	85a	....	....	−111.1	1,024.5	....	....	....	....	....	....	....	....
Use of Cash Balances	87	....	....	1,177.6	.2	....	....	....	....	....	....	....	....

		1993	1994	1995	1996	1997	1998	1999	2000	2001	2002	2003	2004
National Accounts							*Millions of Denar*						
Househ.Cons.Expend.,incl.NPISHs....	96f	47,182	110,847	119,381	127,253	135,487	141,078	145,693	175,965	163,788	188,179	193,874	....
Government Consumption Expend...	91f	12,472	27,875	31,491	31,985	36,700	39,504	43,009	43,021	57,983	54,616	51,980	....
Gross Fixed Capital Formation.........	93e	10,994	22,461	28,027	30,654	32,236	33,982	34,710	38,332	34,716	40,448	42,110	....
Changes in Inventories....................	93i	−416	182	7,162	4,790	6,778	9,426	6,461	14,274	9,902	9,991	8,117	....
Exports of Goods and Services.........	90c	27,660	55,920	55,961	49,722	69,408	80,343	88,143	114,958	99,833	92,791	95,254	....
Imports of Goods and Services (-).....	98c	32,360	70,876	72,501	67,961	94,590	109,355	109,007	150,161	132,381	142,055	137,882	....
GDP, Production Based...................	99bp	59,165	146,409	169,521	176,444	186,019	194,979	209,010	236,389	233,841	243,970	253,454	....
Statistical Discrepancy.....................	99bs	−6,368	—	—	—	—	—	—	—	—	—	—	....
						Millions: Midyear Estimates							
Population................................	99z	2	2	2	2	2	2	2	2	2	2	2	2

		1993	1994	1995	1996	1997	1998	1999	2000	2001	2002	2003	2004
Exchange Rates						*Ariary per SDR: End of Period*							
Official Rate	aa	539.2	1,130.2	1,017.6	1,244.8	1,426.1	1,521.3	1,796.1	1,706.9	1,666.7	1,749.6	1,812.3	2,903.2
					Ariary per US Dollar: End of Period (ae) Period Average (rf)								
Official Rate	ae	392.5	774.2	684.6	865.7	1,056.9	1,080.4	1,308.6	1,310.1	1,326.2	1,287.0	1,219.6	1,869.4
Official Rate	rf	382.8	613.5	853.1	812.3	1,018.2	1,088.3	1,256.8	1,353.5	1,317.7	1,366.4	1,238.3	1,868.9
Fund Position						*Millions of SDRs: End of Period*							
Quota	2f.s	90.4	90.4	90.4	90.4	90.4	90.4	122.2	122.2	122.2	122.2	122.2	122.2
SDRs	1b.s	.1	—	—	—	—	—	—	.1	—	.1	—	—	.1
Reserve Position in the Fund	1c.s	—	—	—	—	—	—	—	—	—	—	—	—
Total Fund Cred.&Loans Outstg	2tl	67.0	58.6	48.9	50.8	51.5	41.2	45.8	80.0	101.4	110.0	115.9	145.4
International Liquidity					*Millions of US Dollars Unless Otherwise Indicated: End of Period*								
Total Reserves minus Gold	1l.d	80.6	71.6	109.0	240.9	281.6	171.4	227.2	285.2	398.3	363.3	414.3	503.5
SDRs	1b.d	.1	—	—	.1	.1	—	—	.1	—	.1	—	.2
Reserve Position in the Fund	1c.d	—	—	—	—	—	—	—	—	—	—	—	—
Foreign Exchange	1d.d	80.5	71.6	108.9	240.8	281.5	171.3	227.0	285.1	398.2	363.2	414.2	503.3
Deposit Money Banks: Assets	7a.d	126.7	157.7	176.6	137.9	151.7	142.0	140.5	180.4	158.4	188.5	230.4	260.8
Liabilities	7b.d	22.2	38.6	33.5	37.3	32.0	40.0	50.9	62.2	57.7	50.8	57.3	61.4
Monetary Authorities						*Billions of Ariary: End of Period*							
Foreign Assets	11	31.36	47.61	74.91	208.72	298.58	185.35	297.44	390.76	526.46	458.61	508.08	932.06
Claims on Central Government	12a	250.59	282.47	289.16	287.40	272.03	350.45	376.20	405.68	419.26	427.42	474.41	379.45
Claims on Nonfin.Pub.Enterprises	12c	1.62	1.39	2.52	2.83	3.01	3.17	3.16	22.21	55.28	72.82	3.54	3.86
Claims on Deposit Money Banks	12e	9.90	26.93	35.01	25.49	21.45	20.54	15.03	11.90	8.07	5.44	3.45	−7.67
Reserve Money	14	103.98	178.78	231.79	344.62	348.36	370.99	467.79	522.84	677.01	707.13	705.46	839.79
of which: Currency Outside DMBs	14a	75.75	122.91	151.74	165.87	204.05	233.97	286.97	357.82	431.92	466.02	514.00	591.38
Time, Savings,& Fgn. Currency Dep	15	....	....	1.5	.3	.6	.7	1.0	—	.1	.1	.2
Foreign Liabilities	16c	75.75	143.91	113.60	128.49	133.87	116.42	129.56	174.21	202.06	209.78	224.24	438.01
Central Government Deposits	16d	77.95	56.68	110.56	121.88	174.29	131.64	127.34	172.05	177.74	110.42	134.98	114.72
Counterpart Funds	16e	—	—	—	—	—	—	—	—	—	—	—	—
Capital Accounts	17a	8.44	8.76	24.52	6.70	18.78	18.83	21.45	18.59	24.30	48.00	48.95	19.98
Other Items (Net)	17r	27.35	−29.73	−80.25	−77.55	−80.81	−79.00	−55.36	−57.16	−72.08	−111.10	−124.25	−105.04
Deposit Money Banks						*Billions of Ariary: End of Period*							
Reserves	20	28.23	55.87	80.05	178.74	144.31	135.74	177.42	164.68	245.05	240.99	190.92	248.35
Foreign Assets	21	49.73	122.07	120.88	119.40	160.31	153.39	183.83	236.36	210.10	242.57	280.98	487.58
Claims on Central Government	22a	44.03	50.12	34.81	41.25	71.30	87.29	96.19	121.30	236.48	305.32	359.75	271.10
Claims on Private Sector	22d	212.32	267.71	310.08	314.73	359.53	362.35	387.50	460.65	500.15	486.90	594.89	814.70
Demand Deposits	24	129.13	197.79	217.86	267.66	328.73	356.62	423.09	445.77	614.82	659.56	658.46	808.05
Time Deposits	25	91.37	131.23	154.11	175.16	202.41	190.04	220.12	287.34	304.12	332.75	414.38	587.55
Bonds	26ab	7.93	8.53	11.69	19.10	14.07	25.96	30.36	33.86	34.55	35.47	35.44	28.35
Foreign Liabilities	26c	7.48	25.62	18.98	27.34	27.15	38.19	52.58	69.19	53.41	52.62	52.62	94.85
Long-Term Foreign Liabilities	26cl	1.26	4.24	3.98	4.98	6.66	5.02	14.04	12.35	23.05	12.73	17.29	19.91
Central Government Deposits	26d	31.10	28.27	24.78	32.08	31.51	28.24	26.97	40.10	67.03	78.82	80.64	127.33
Central Govt. Lending Funds	26f	.21	.28	.17	.58	.48	.17	1.22	1.07	1.45	2.18	2.90	2.82
Credit from Monetary Authorities	26g	9.90	26.93	34.88	25.49	21.45	20.54	15.03	11.90	8.07	5.44	3.45	−7.67
Capital Accounts	27a	21.31	19.51	41.40	107.13	129.18	79.90	89.15	103.58	124.13	145.25	158.29	173.68
Other Items (Net)	27r	34.61	53.37	37.96	−5.41	−26.19	−5.92	−27.61	−22.17	−38.84	−49.05	3.08	−13.13
Treasury Claims: Private Sector	22d.i	1.99	2.05	2.80	2.65	.27	.11	.42	.11	.23	.61	.25	.11
Post Office: Checking Deposits	24..i	1.05	.90	1.15	2.31	2.99	2.38	2.45	15.21	39.28	26.94	4.36	3.09
Treasury: Checking Deposits	24..r	1.95	1.95	1.95	1.95	1.95	1.95	1.95	1.95	1.95	1.95	1.95	1.95
Monetary Survey						*Billions of Ariary: End of Period*							
Foreign Assets (Net)	31n	−2.14	.15	63.22	172.29	297.87	184.12	299.12	383.72	481.09	438.77	512.20	886.79
Domestic Credit	32	399.50	516.74	501.24	492.26	500.09	643.38	708.73	797.69	966.41	1,103.22	1,216.97	1,227.07
Claims on Central Govt. (Net)	32an	185.56	247.64	188.63	174.71	137.55	277.85	318.08	314.82	410.97	543.50	618.54	408.50
Claims on Private Sector	32d	213.94	269.10	312.60	317.55	362.54	365.53	390.66	482.87	555.44	559.73	598.43	818.56
Money	34	204.88	320.70	369.60	433.54	532.79	590.63	710.06	803.59	1,046.74	1,125.58	1,172.46	1,399.43
Quasi-Money	35	91.37	131.23	155.61	175.47	203.00	190.72	221.15	287.36	304.16	332.81	414.48	587.79
Bonds	36ab	7.93	8.53	11.69	19.10	14.07	25.96	30.36	33.86	34.55	35.47	35.44	28.35
Long-Term Foreign Liabilities	36cl	1.26	4.24	3.98	4.98	6.66	5.02	14.04	12.35	23.05	12.73	17.29	19.91
Other Items (Net)	37r	91.92	52.20	23.67	31.46	41.44	15.22	32.24	44.25	39.00	35.40	89.51	78.37
Money plus Quasi-Money	35l	296.25	451.93	525.21	609.01	735.79	781.35	931.22	1,090.95	1,350.90	1,458.39	1,586.94	1,987.22
Liquid Liabilities	55l	327.27	494.63	580.28	721.59	900.23	1,014.17	1,217.93	1,405.47	....	....	....	....
Interest Rates						*Percent Per Annum*							
Discount Rate (End of Period)	60	....	....	....	....	....	....	15.00	....	....	....	....	....
Base Rate (End of Period)	60a	12.0	15.6	31.3	26.4	12.8	9.3	....	....	11.0	9.0	7.0	11.7
Money Market Rate	60b	....	....	29.0	10.0	....	11.2	....	16.0	....	....	10.5	16.5
Treasury Bill Rate	60c	....	....	....	....	....	....	....	....	10.3	....	11.9	12.9
Deposit Rate	60l	19.5	19.5	18.5	19.0	14.4	8.0	15.3	15.0	12.0	12.0	11.5	....
Lending Rate	60p	26.0	30.5	37.5	32.8	30.0	27.0	28.0	26.5	25.3	25.3	24.3	....
Prices and Labor						*Index Numbers (2000=100): Period Averages*							
Consumer Prices	64	29.5	41.0	61.1	73.2	76.5	81.2	89.3	† 100.0	106.9	124.0	122.5	139.4
						Number in Thousands: Period Averages							
Employment	67e	315	322	337	....	....	....	....	....	....	....	....	....
Intl. Transactions & Positions						*Billions of Ariary*							
Exports	70	99.80	249.34	313.88	370.02	421.93	601.45	753.94	1,115.62	912.63	684.64	1,050.28	....
Imports, c.i.f.	71	179.14	281.72	466.78	422.96	506.95	590.64	739.26	990.68	978.80	691.60	1,501.49	....

Madagascar 674

		1993	1994	1995	1996	1997	1998	1999	2000	2001	2002	2003	2004
Balance of Payments		*Millions of US Dollars: Minus Sign Indicates Debit*											
Current Account, n.i.e.	78ald	−258	−277	−276	−291	−266	−301	−252	−283	−170	−298	−439	....
Goods: Exports f.o.b.	78aad	335	450	507	509	516	538	584	824	928	486	856	....
Goods: Imports f.o.b.	78abd	−514	−546	−628	−629	−694	−693	−742	−997	−955	−603	−1,109	....
Trade Balance	78acd	−180	−96	−122	−120	−178	−154	−158	−174	−27	−117	−254	....
Services: Credit	78add	187	206	242	293	272	291	326	364	351	224	270	....
Services: Debit	78aed	−302	−328	−359	−373	−386	−436	−456	−522	−511	−398	−545	....
Balance on Goods & Services	78afd	−295	−218	−238	−200	−292	−299	−289	−332	−187	−291	−529	....
Income: Credit	78agd	3	2	7	6	20	25	21	22	24	26	16	....
Income: Debit	78ahd	−154	−158	−174	−169	−115	−103	−63	−64	−106	−101	−95	....
Balance on Gds, Serv. & Inc.	78aid	−446	−374	−405	−363	−387	−377	−331	−373	−270	−366	−607	....
Current Transfers, n.i.e.: Credit	78ajd	202	114	141	94	156	109	111	122	114	88	349	....
Current Transfers: Debit	78akd	−14	−17	−12	−23	−35	−33	−32	−31	−15	−21	−180	....
Capital Account, n.i.e.	78bcd	78	62	45	5	115	103	129	115	113	58	140	....
Capital Account, n.i.e.: Credit	78bad	78	62	45	5	115	103	129	115	113	58	140	....
Capital Account: Debit	78bbd	—	—	—	....	....	....	....	....	—	—	—	....
Financial Account, n.i.e.	78bjd	−158	−122	−198	133	110	−76	−14	−31	−139	−54	−118	....
Direct Investment Abroad	78bdd	—	—	—	....	....	....	....	....	—	—	—	....
Dir. Invest. in Rep. Econ., n.i.e.	78bed	15	6	10	10	14	17	58	83	93	8	13	....
Portfolio Investment Assets	78bfd	—								—	—	—	....
Equity Securities	78bkd	....	....	....	....	....	....	....	....	—	—	—	....
Debt Securities	78bld	....	....	....	....	....	....	....	....	—	—	—	....
Portfolio Investment Liab., n.i.e.	78bgd	....	....	....	....	....	....	....	....	—	—	—	....
Equity Securities	78bmd	....	....	....	....	....	....	....	....	—	—	—	....
Debt Securities	78bnd	....	....	....	....	....	....	....	....	—	—	—	....
Financial Derivatives Assets	78bwd	....	....	....	....	....	....	....	....	....	....	....	....
Financial Derivatives Liabilities	78bxd	....	....	....	....	....	....	....	....	....	....	....	....
Other Investment Assets	78bhd	−47	19	−62	37	135	−68	−73	−87	−128	42	−27	....
Monetary Authorities	78bod	−19	38	−45	....	157	−84	−71	−40	−144	58	5	....
General Government	78bpd	....	....	....	....	....	....	....	....	—	—	—	....
Banks	78bqd	−28	−18	−12	37	−22	16	−2	−48	15	−16	−32	....
Other Sectors	78brd	....	−1	−5	....	....	....	....	....	—	—	—	....
Other Investment Liab., n.i.e.	78bid	−126	−147	−145	86	−39	−25	1	−26	−103	−104	−104	....
Monetary Authorities	78bsd	−254	−235	−230	—	—	—	—	−1	—	2	−1	....
General Government	78btd	123	79	91	−167	−28	−26	−3	−28	−84	−93	−95	....
Banks	78bud	5	6	−8	....	−4	9	6	15	−11	−3	3	....
Other Sectors	78bvd	—	3	3	253	−8	−7	−2	−12	−8	−10	−11	....
Net Errors and Omissions	78cad	4	61	98	59	25	−25	32	39	−57	11	52	....
Overall Balance	78cbd	−334	−276	−330	−94	−16	−299	−104	−160	−253	−283	−365	....
Reserves and Related Items	79dad	334	276	330	94	16	299	104	160	253	283	365	....
Reserve Assets	79dbd	23	−14	−2	−137	−214	205	11	−30	18	8	−28	....
Use of Fund Credit and Loans	79dcd	−14	−12	−15	3	1	−14	6	45	27	12	8	....
Exceptional Financing	79ded	326	303	347	228	229	108	88	145	208	264	384	....
Government Finance		*Billions of Ariary: Year Ending December 31*											
Deficit (-) or Surplus	80	−61.5	−73.5	−42.6	−43.5	−85.7	−129.4	−124.9	−125.1	−240.6	....	....	....
Revenue	81	126.7	152.4	229.9	281.4	349.4	415.4	533.4	613.6	605.8	....	....	....
Grants Received	81z	45.1	54.8	78.4	136.7	147.1	141.6	154.0	189.3	200.7	....	....	....
Expenditure	82	253.5	346.9	468.8	563.4	575.9	695.5	813.8	910.2	1,036.4	....	....	....
Lending Minus Repayments	83	11.0	8.9	5.9	13.2	1.8	−7.8	10.2	5.3	5.4	....	....	....
Adjustment to Cash Basis	80x	31.3	75.0	123.9	115.1	−4.5	1.4	11.7	−12.6	−5.4	....	....	....
Financing													
Domestic	84a	24.4	42.7	−7.6	−3.0	−29.1	152.2	25.2	24.3	116.2	....	....	....
Foreign	85a	37.1	30.9	50.2	46.5	114.8	−22.8	89.4	91.5	103.6	....	....	....
Adjustment to Total Financing	84x	....	....	....	—	—	—	10.4	9.3	20.8	....	....	....
Debt: Domestic	88a	187.0	224.8	215.3	179.1	....	....	....	....	....	....	....	....
Debt: Foreign	89a	1,433.8	3,129.3	3,014.5	....	....	....	....	....	....	....	....	....
National Accounts		*Billions of Ariary*											
Househ.Cons.Expend.,incl.NPISHs	96f	1,150.2	1,620.6	2,424.2	2,892.6	3,258.9	3,545.2	4,006.4	4,496.6	4,800.2	5,244.2	5,873.6	6,830.4
Government Consumption Expend	91f	112.2	144.8	180.8	146.4	219.5	324.2	348.2	412.8	527.8	502.0	710.2	745.2
Gross Fixed Capital Formation	93e	147.7	199.1	295.0	377.6	427.9	535.6	674.8	850.0	1,068.0	803.8	1,097.8	2,038.6
Exports of Goods and Services	90c	197.6	402.4	683.6	665.2	787.7	871.6	1,173.4	1,596.8	1,725.4	958.6	1,351.6	2,479.0
Imports of Goods and Services (-)	98c	317.6	540.6	854.9	836.9	1,083.9	1,206.9	1,525.9	2,107.8	2,149.2	1,500.4	2,254.6	3,937.6
Gross Domestic Product (GDP)	99b	1,290.2	1,826.3	2,695.7	3,244.9	3,610.2	4,069.9	4,676.8	5,248.4	5,968.6	6,008.4	6,778.6	8,155.6
GDP Volume 1984 Prices	99b.p	380.0	379.8	386.3	394.5	409.1	425.2	445.1	466.2	494.2	431.6	473.8	498.8
GDP Volume (2000=100)	99bvp	81.5	81.5	82.9	84.6	87.8	91.2	95.5	100.0	106.0	92.6	101.6	107.0
GDP Deflator (2000=100)	99bip	30.2	42.7	62.0	73.1	78.4	85.0	93.3	100.0	107.3	123.7	127.1	145.2
		Millions: Midyear Estimates											
Population	99z	13.14	13.54	13.95	14.37	14.81	15.27	15.73	16.20	16.67	17.14	17.63	18.11

		1993	1994	1995	1996	1997	1998	1999	2000	2001	2002	2003	2004
Exchange Rates						*Kwacha per SDR: End of Period*							
Official Rate	aa	6.1733	22.3337	22.7479	22.0340	28.6416	61.7894	63.7362	104.3318	84.5705	118.4665	161.3258	169.1899
					Kwacha per US Dollar: End of Period (ae) Period Average (rf)								
Official Rate	ae	4.4944	15.2986	15.3031	15.3231	21.2278	43.8836	46.4377	80.0760	67.2941	87.1385	108.5660	108.9432
Official Rate	rf	4.4028	8.7364	15.2837	15.3085	16.4442	31.0727	44.0881	59.5438	72.1973	76.6866	97.4325	108.8975
					Index Numbers (2000=100): Period Averages								
Official Rate	ahx	1,292.9	743.2	373.0	372.3	348.8	195.9	129.3	100.0	79.7	74.7	58.9	52.3
Nominal Effective Exchange Rate	nec	906.0	575.5	277.8	288.9	290.8	173.0	121.0	100.0	84.4	77.8	63.7	59.9
Real Effective Exchange Rate	rec	143.4	101.8	88.8	122.3	136.6	99.3	99.7	100.0	103.4	102.2	79.6	74.7
Fund Position						*Millions of SDRs: End of Period*							
Quota	2f.s	50.90	50.90	50.90	50.90	50.90	50.90	69.40	69.40	69.40	69.40	69.40	69.40
SDRs	1b.s	.17	4.25	.59	.94	.07	4.84	.29	.36	.67	.07	.32	.77
Reserve Position in the Fund	1c.s	2.22	2.22	2.22	2.22	2.22	2.24	2.24	2.24	2.27	2.28	2.29	2.29
Total Fund Cred.&Loans Outstg.	2tl	62.62	76.90	78.02	83.06	78.42	72.57	63.79	63.35	57.90	69.55	68.77	59.55
International Liquidity					*Millions of US Dollars Unless Otherwise Indicated: End of Period*								
Total Reserves minus Gold	1l.d	56.88	42.80	110.01	225.72	162.25	269.73	250.62	246.91	206.74	165.17	126.46	133.35
SDRs	1b.d	.23	6.20	.88	1.36	.09	6.82	.39	.47	.84	.09	.47	1.20
Reserve Position in the Fund	1c.d	3.05	3.25	3.31	3.20	3.00	3.15	3.07	2.91	2.85	3.11	3.40	3.56
Foreign Exchange	1d.d	53.59	33.35	105.82	221.16	159.16	259.76	247.15	243.52	203.05	161.98	122.58	128.59
Gold (Million Fine Troy Ounces)	1ad	.013	.013	.013	.013	.013	.013	.013	.013	.013	.013	.013	.013
Gold (National Valuation)	1and	.54	.55	.54	.54	.54	.54	.54	.54	.54	.51	.54	.54
Monetary Authorities: Other Liab.	4..d	36.81	21.92	.02	.02	.09	.06	.59	19.86	.06	50.00	7.55	.02
Deposit Money Banks: Assets	7a.d	17.34	25.61	29.39	36.17	41.63	61.64	49.74	58.27	76.10	49.31	51.71	52.61
Liabilities	7b.d	24.47	27.22	9.80	10.37	10.67	13.75	16.03	16.86	15.09	12.83	14.76	15.60
Other Banking Institutions: Assets	7e.d	—	—	—	—	—	—	9.84	4.06	5.59	7.09	11.05	14.67
Liabilities	7f.d	—	—	—	—	.06	—	8.87	10.64	10.87	18.38	12.88	8.43
Monetary Authorities						*Millions of Kwacha: End of Period*							
Foreign Assets	11	255.6	613.6	1,670.0	3,387.7	3,342.4	11,327.9	11,468.6	19,500.3	13,663.9	14,115.5	14,127.8	14,009.0
Claims on Central Government	12a	958.7	1,309.5	1,266.2	710.8	877.0	3,727.9	2,559.3	445.8	5,846.3	13,407.4	14,707.0	18,990.0
Claims on Nonfin.Pub.Enterprises	12c	117.5	115.5	127.0	159.3	187.5	191.4	274.6	313.7	313.7	—	—	—
Claims on Deposit Money Banks	12e	—	—	—	140.0								
Claims on Other Banking Insts.	12f	36.6	28.2	13.4	10.5	9.8	9.4	8.2	112.2	3.5	3.3	2.9	1.7
Reserve Money	14	880.7	1,244.8	2,360.6	3,269.7	3,277.0	4,542.6	6,001.4	6,349.2	8,497.7	10,767.2	13,742.9	17,967.5
of which: Currency Outside DMBs	14a	414.2	624.7	987.5	1,223.8	1,375.3	1,986.5	2,959.3	4,023.7	4,066.3	5,964.0	7,838.1	10,992.8
Liabs. of Central Bank: Securities	16ac	—	—	—	—	—	—	—	1,713.3	8,519.2	6,425.0	2,914.0	4,555.9
Restricted Deposits	16b	—	—	—	—	—	—	—	—	—	—	—	—
Foreign Liabilities	16c	552.0	2,052.7	1,775.2	1,830.5	2,247.9	4,486.2	4,093.5	8,200.3	4,900.3	12,596.9	11,914.2	10,076.8
Central Government Deposits	16d	351.7	349.5	591.8	883.3	291.3	4,564.6	3,035.3	1,513.5	2,182.9	3,655.9	6,461.6	6,944.4
Capital Accounts	17a	153.0	330.3	280.7	476.8	653.9	1,072.0	1,101.6	1,547.2	1,269.9	1,641.9	2,076.6	2,162.9
Other Items (Net)	17r	−569.0	−1,910.6	−1,931.6	−2,052.0	−2,053.3	591.2	78.9	1,048.6	−5,542.5	−7,560.8	−8,271.6	−8,706.7
Deposit Money Banks						*Millions of Kwacha: End of Period*							
Reserves	20	380.2	591.4	1,311.7	1,814.5	1,803.6	2,273.6	2,877.1	2,290.1	4,158.7	4,837.7	5,350.5	7,033.9
Claims on Mon.Author.:Securities	20c	—	—	—	—	—	—	—	250.0	1,419.6	1,342.1	340.0	210.0
Foreign Assets	21	77.9	391.7	449.8	554.2	883.7	2,705.0	2,310.0	4,666.1	5,121.3	4,296.4	5,613.5	5,731.3
Claims on Central Government	22a	335.3	387.9	867.3	1,746.3	1,206.7	1,388.0	1,412.7	2,418.9	2,731.4	6,748.3	10,967.5	10,711.0
Claims on Nonfin.Pub.Enterprises	22c	154.3	47.6	183.0	398.0	413.6	185.8	1,442.9	1,218.2	575.1	676.5	277.4	299.5
Claims on Private Sector	22d	764.9	1,178.1	1,252.6	1,406.8	1,603.3	3,478.8	3,717.1	5,817.5	6,454.0	7,363.5	9,808.7	13,926.3
Demand Deposits	24	560.2	895.9	1,218.1	1,518.0	1,824.4	2,996.3	3,976.2	5,594.0	6,649.4	7,929.3	9,925.2	14,730.2
Time, Savings,& Fgn. Currency Dep.	25	924.4	1,119.5	1,936.4	3,048.1	2,712.4	4,692.1	5,715.7	8,779.5	11,860.7	14,114.1	18,048.4	20,725.3
Foreign Liabilities	26c	110.0	416.5	150.0	158.8	226.4	603.5	744.4	1,349.7	1,015.7	1,118.0	1,602.9	1,699.2
Central Government Deposits	26d	1.2	2.7	471.8	469.7	557.2	1,016.1	1,349.9	783.9	565.8	788.6	518.9	434.5
Credit from Monetary Authorities	26g	6.0	6.8	9.5	7.7	3.9	3.0	—	—	—	—	—	—
Capital Accounts	27a	214.2	410.5	598.2	845.2	1,113.4	1,497.8	2,284.9	3,238.9	3,730.4	4,902.6	6,563.9	7,317.1
Other Items (Net)	27r	−103.4	−255.2	−319.6	−127.7	−526.9	−777.6	−2,311.4	−3,085.2	−3,361.9	−3,588.1	−4,301.8	−6,994.4
Monetary Survey						*Millions of Kwacha: End of Period*							
Foreign Assets (Net)	31n	−328.4	−1,463.8	194.6	1,952.6	1,751.8	8,943.1	8,940.7	14,616.5	12,869.2	4,697.0	6,224.2	7,964.3
Domestic Credit	32	2,014.4	2,714.5	2,645.9	3,078.7	3,449.4	3,400.7	5,029.5	8,029.0	13,175.5	23,754.5	28,782.9	36,549.6
Claims on Central Govt. (Net)	32an	941.0	1,345.1	1,069.8	1,104.1	1,235.2	−464.8	−413.2	567.3	5,829.0	15,711.2	18,693.9	22,322.1
Claims on Nonfin.Pub.Enterprises	32c	271.9	163.1	310.0	557.3	601.0	377.2	1,717.5	1,532.0	888.9	676.5	277.4	299.5
Claims on Private Sector	32d	764.9	1,178.1	1,252.6	1,406.8	1,603.3	3,478.8	3,717.1	5,817.5	6,454.0	7,363.5	9,808.7	13,926.3
Claims on Other Banking Insts.	32f	36.6	28.2	13.4	10.5	9.8	9.4	8.2	112.2	3.5	3.3	2.9	1.7
Money	34	1,019.9	1,535.4	2,211.2	2,756.8	3,213.0	5,248.4	7,007.3	9,736.5	11,048.7	13,979.0	17,763.4	25,723.0
Quasi-Money	35	924.4	1,119.5	1,936.4	3,048.1	2,712.4	4,692.1	5,715.7	8,779.5	11,860.7	14,114.1	18,048.4	20,725.3
Liabs. of Central Bank: Securities	36ac	—	—	—	—	—	—	—	1,463.3	7,099.6	5,082.9	2,574.0	4,345.9
Restricted Deposits	36b	—	—	—	—	—	—	—	—	—	—	—	—
Capital Accounts	37a	367.2	740.8	878.9	1,322.0	1,767.2	2,569.9	3,386.6	4,786.1	5,000.4	6,544.5	8,640.5	9,480.0
Other Items (Net)	37r	−625.6	−2,145.0	−2,186.0	−2,095.7	−2,491.4	−166.6	−2,139.2	−2,119.9	−8,964.7	−11,269.1	−12,019.1	−15,760.4
Money plus Quasi-Money	35l	1,944.3	2,654.9	4,147.6	5,805.0	5,925.4	9,940.6	12,722.9	18,516.0	22,909.4	28,093.1	35,811.8	46,448.4
Other Banking Institutions						*Millions of Kwacha: End of Period*							
Reserves	40	10.7	7.9	45.3	3.1	23.4	19.6	45.1	152.7	278.6	334.9	746.2	939.7
Claims on Mon.Author.:Securities	40c	—	—	—	—	—	—	—	—	706.6	457.7	654.2	386.3
Foreign Assets	41	—	—	—	—	—	—	457.1	324.9	376.4	617.4	1,199.2	1,598.3
Claims on Central Government	42a	262.3	284.7	351.3	414.3	648.9	1,086.5	752.7	1,415.2	2,369.2	3,225.0	5,910.5	5,964.7
Claims on Nonfin.Pub.Enterprises	42c	5.3	5.7	9.8	11.2	—	—	75.2	29.9	48.2	31.8	40.0	5.7
Claims on Private Sector	42d	91.5	118.8	134.8	167.9	275.3	388.1	2,515.8	3,604.6	3,981.4	4,494.9	3,091.7	3,346.1
Claims on Deposit Money Banks	42e	19.6	8.4	4.8	18.8	19.8	31.4	563.6	887.1	648.6	482.4	536.7	817.8
Demand Deposits	44	17.6	19.5	22.0	29.8	39.5	504.7	—	157.1	822.6	364.4	1,196.7	1,336.7
Time, Savings,& Fgn. Currency Dep.	45	263.0	319.8	404.3	580.1	612.5	663.9	3,271.6	4,083.3	5,329.6	5,580.7	7,015.6	9,400.8
Foreign Liabilities	46c	—	—	—	—	1.3	—	412.1	852.3	731.4	1,602.0	1,398.1	918.0
Credit from Monetary Authorities	46g	—	—	—	—	—	—	10.7	102.0	.9	—	—	—
Credit from Deposit Money Banks	46h	—	—	—	—	—	—	84.0	250.5	195.0	281.5	834.6	174.5
Capital Accounts	47a	103.9	124.0	152.3	216.6	308.2	429.9	569.5	905.7	1,121.3	1,607.5	2,074.4	2,127.8
Other Items (Net)	47r	4.8	−37.9	−32.6	−211.3	6.0	−73.0	61.6	63.5	208.2	208.1	−340.8	−899.2

		1993	1994	1995	1996	1997	1998	1999	2000	2001	2002	2003	2004
Banking Survey						*Millions of Kwacha: End of Period*							
Foreign Assets (Net)...................	51n	−328.4	−1,463.8	194.6	1,952.6	1,750.5	8,943.1	8,985.7	14,089.1	12,514.2	3,712.4	6,025.3	8,644.6
Domestic Credit..........................	52	2,336.8	3,095.4	3,128.4	3,661.6	4,363.7	4,865.8	8,365.1	12,966.5	19,570.8	31,502.9	37,822.2	45,864.4
Claims on Central Govt. (Net).......	52an	1,203.3	1,629.8	1,421.1	1,518.4	1,884.1	621.7	339.5	1,982.5	8,198.3	18,936.2	24,604.4	28,286.8
Claims on Nonfin.Pub.Enterprises...	52c	277.2	168.8	319.8	568.5	601.0	377.2	1,792.6	1,561.9	937.1	708.3	317.4	305.2
Claims on Private Sector...............	52d	856.4	1,296.8	1,387.5	1,574.7	1,878.6	3,866.9	6,232.9	9,422.1	10,435.4	11,858.4	12,900.4	17,272.4
Liquid Liabilities...........................	55l	2,214.3	2,986.3	4,528.6	6,411.8	6,554.0	11,089.6	15,949.4	22,603.6	28,783.0	33,703.3	43,277.8	56,246.1
Liabs.of Central Bank: Securities......	56ac	—	—	—	—	—	—	—	1,463.3	6,393.0	4,625.1	1,919.8	3,959.5
Restricted Deposits......................	56b	—	—	—	—	—	—	—					
Capital Accounts..........................	57a	471.0	864.8	1,031.2	1,538.7	2,075.4	2,999.8	3,956.1	5,691.9	6,121.6	8,152.0	10,714.9	11,607.8
Other Items (Net)..........................	57r	−676.9	−2,219.5	−2,236.8	−2,336.3	−2,515.1	−280.5	−2,554.8	−2,703.2	−9,212.7	−11,265.2	−12,064.9	−17,304.5
Nonbank Financial Institutions						*Millions of Kwacha: End of Period*							
Claims on Central Government........	42a.s	71.06	93.51	172.57	216.19	232.89	437.70	575.90	202.47	393.05	463.81	547.24	826.83
Claims on Private Sector.................	42d.s	208.70	269.01	377.83	584.02	230.34	332.00	352.89	176.86	301.35	125.74	430.28	2,301.06
of which: Policy Loans........	42dxs	11.05	12.48	15.25	16.38	22.30	33.31	23.59	31.50	133.28	24.26	24.65	61.77
Incr.in Total Assets(Within Per.)........	49z.s	70.20	103.28	242.14	296.06	−247.43	416.41	168.14	−120.83	876.12	−56.81	136.69	8,589.81
Interest Rates						*Percent Per Annum*							
Discount Rate (End of Period)...........	60	25.00	40.00	50.00	27.00	23.00	43.00	47.00	50.23	46.80	40.00	35.00	25.00
Treasury Bill Rate........................	60c	23.54	27.68	46.30	30.83	18.31	32.98	42.85	39.52	42.41	41.75	39.32	28.58
Deposit Rate............................	60l	21.75	25.00	37.27	26.33	10.21	19.06	33.21	33.25	34.96	28.08	25.13	13.73
Lending Rate............................	60p	29.50	31.00	47.33	45.33	28.25	37.67	53.58	53.13	56.17	50.54	48.92	36.83
Government Bond Yield..................	61	....	23.50	38.58	42.67	39.25	....	....	....	....	....	....	....
Prices, Production, Labor						*Index Numbers (2000=100): Period Averages*							
Consumer Prices..........................	64	11.1	14.9	27.4	37.6	41.1	53.3	77.2	† 100.0	122.7	140.8	154.3	171.6
Industrial Production......................	66	115.4	109.8	111.2	115.2	113.5	110.3	98.0	100.0	91.0	91.3	88.6	....
						Number in Thousands: Period Averages							
Employment................................	67e	583	653	701	....	....	....	....	....	....	....	....	....
Intl. Transactions & Positions						*Millions of Kwacha*							
Exports......................................	70	1,411	2,954	6,193	7,359	8,827	13,861	19,907	23,625	31,817	31,417	51,672	52,628
Imports, c.i.f...............................	71	2,405	4,214	7,255	9,545	12,848	16,431	29,696	32,283	39,480	53,658	76,650	101,555
Imports, f.o.b...............................	71.v	1,440	2,793	4,353	5,727	7,709	10,799	18,455	28,389	....	....	....	....
Balance of Payments						*Millions of US Dollars: Minus Sign Indicates Debit*							
Current Account, n.i.e....................	78ald	−165.6	−180.7	−78.0	−147.4	−276.2	−4.4	−157.5	−73.5	−60.0	−200.7	....	....
Goods: Exports f.o.b....................	78aad	317.5	323.1	445.5	509.6	540.2	539.6	448.4	403.1	427.9	422.4	....	....
Goods: Imports f.o.b....................	78abd	−340.2	−483.1	−508.8	−587.5	−698.7	−500.6	−575.0	−462.0	−472.2	−573.2	....	....
Trade Balance........................	78acd	−22.8	−160.1	−63.3	−77.9	−158.4	39.0	−126.6	−58.8	−44.3	−150.8	....	....
Services: Credit..........................	78add	30.0	26.1	24.2	36.6	38.8	31.5	49.2	34.3	43.6	49.4	....	....
Services: Debit..........................	78aed	−260.1	−147.7	−151.4	−185.7	−219.2	−161.5	−184.7	−167.1	−171.4	−221.9	....	....
Balance on Goods & Services......	78afd	−252.9	−281.7	−190.6	−227.0	−338.8	−91.1	−262.1	−191.7	−172.1	−323.3	....	....
Income: Credit..........................	78agd	2.2	4.9	3.7	9.5	12.2	11.5	25.5	33.3	12.2	6.0	....	....
Income: Debit..........................	78ahd	−70.9	−47.2	−48.0	−44.8	−40.9	−48.1	−50.5	−50.5	−42.6	−44.5	....	....
Balance on Gds, Serv. & Inc........	78aid	−321.6	−324.1	−234.9	−262.3	−367.6	−127.7	−287.0	−209.0	−202.5	−361.8	....	....
Current Transfers, n.i.e.: Credit......	78ajd	167.9	154.0	171.0	138.0	116.2	134.1	137.7	143.1	148.8	170.0	....	....
Current Transfers: Debit...............	78akd	−11.9	−10.6	−14.2	−23.0	−24.9	−10.8	−8.2	−7.6	−6.2	−8.9	....	....
Capital Account, n.i.e...................	78bcd	—	....	....	....	....	....	....	....	....	....	....	....
Capital Account, n.i.e.: Credit.......	78bad	—	....	....	....	....	....	....	....	....	....	....	....
Capital Account: Debit................	78bbd	—	....	....	....	....	....	....	....	....	....	....	....
Financial Account, n.i.e.................	78bjd	188.9	200.5	87.6	170.5	146.5	237.8	219.6	188.8	213.4	134.0	....	....
Direct Investment Abroad..............	78bdd	—	....	....	....	....	....	....	....	....	....	....	....
Dir. Invest. in Rep. Econ., n.i.e........	78bed	—	25.0	5.6	15.8	14.9	12.1	58.5	26.0	19.3	5.9	....	....
Portfolio Investment Assets............	78bfd	—	....	....	....	....	....	....	....	....	....	....	....
Equity Securities..........................	78bkd	—	....	....	....	....	....	....	....	....	....	....	....
Debt Securities..........................	78bld	—	....	....	....	....	....	....	....	....	....	....	....
Portfolio Investment Liab., n.i.e......	78bgd	—	....	....	....	....	....	....	....	....	....	....	....
Equity Securities..........................	78bmd	—	....	....	....	....	....	....	....	....	....	....	....
Debt Securities..........................	78bnd	—	....	....	....	....	....	....	....	....	....	....	....
Financial Derivatives Assets............	78bwd	....	....	....	....	....	....	....	....	....	....	....	....
Financial Derivatives Liabilities........	78bxd	....	....	....	....	....	....	....	....	....	....	....	....
Other Investment Assets...............	78bhd	−11.8	....	....	....	....	....	....	....	....	....	....	....
Monetary Authorities..................	78bod	—	....	....	....	....	....	....	....	....	....	....	....
General Government..................	78bpd	—	....	....	....	....	....	....	....	....	....	....	....
Banks....................................	78bqd	−11.8	....	....	....	....	....	....	....	....	....	....	....
Other Sectors..........................	78brd	—	....	....	....	....	....	....	....	....	....	....	....
Other Investment Liab., n.i.e.........	78bid	200.6	175.6	81.9	154.7	131.7	225.7	161.1	162.8	194.1	128.1	....	....
Monetary Authorities..................	78bsd	—	—	—	—	—	—	—	—	—	—	....	....
General Government..................	78btd	150.9	130.1	49.9	131.5	128.1	169.4	106.2	107.9	139.2	73.3	....	....
Banks....................................	78bud	—	—	—	—	—	—	—	—	—	—	....	....
Other Sectors..........................	78bvd	49.7	45.4	32.0	23.2	3.6	56.3	54.8	54.8	54.8	54.8	....	....
Net Errors and Omissions................	78cad	.7	−6.0	−84.3	−144.6	145.2	−407.6	−28.8	−23.9	−221.5	156.7	....	....
Overall Balance..........................	78cbd	24.0	13.9	−74.8	−121.6	15.5	−174.1	33.3	91.4	−68.0	90.0	....	....
Reserves and Related Items.............	79dad	−24.0	−13.9	74.8	121.6	−15.5	174.1	−33.3	−91.4	68.0	−90.0	....	....
Reserve Assets..........................	79dbd	−18.1	−34.7	73.1	114.5	−9.1	181.4	−21.4	−90.6	75.0	−105.5	....	....
Use of Fund Credit and Loans........	79dcd	−5.9	20.8	1.6	7.1	−6.5	−7.3	−11.9	−.8	−7.0	15.5	....	....
Exceptional Financing....................	79ded	—	....	....	....	....	....	....	....	....	....	....	....

Malawi   676

Malawi 676

		1993	1994	1995	1996	1997	1998	1999	2000	2001	2002	2003	2004
National Accounts							*Millions of Kwacha*						
Househ.Cons.Expend.,incl.NPISHs....	96f	7,677.6	5,869.4	16,204.8	29,391.0	36,539.0	43,058.4	68,121.1	84,230.3	97,136.5	135,724.6	161,408.1	....
Government Consumption Expend...	91f	1,423.5	4,073.1	4,474.6	4,882.0	7,673.0	7,987.2	10,527.8	15,134.0	19,591.4	21,858.1	28,025.3	....
Gross Fixed Capital Formation..........	93e	1,098.0	2,764.3	3,164.7	3,404.5	4,079.7	6,035.8	9,870.5	12,792.2	15,740.8	14,110.2	17,742.3	....
Changes in Inventories....................	93i	200.0	240.0	500.8	757.9	881.7	1,179.2	1,734.9	2,261.1	2,768.8	3,238.1	3,687.4	....
Exports of Goods and Services..........	90c	1,470.7	3,050.1	7,177.7	8,362.7	9,522.1	17,744.4	21,940.9	26,045.3	33,980.6	35,528.2	46,151.0	....
Imports of Goods and Services (-).....	98c	2,900.9	5,514.3	10,164.3	11,879.0	14,900.7	20,728.6	33,898.3	36,647.9	45,291.2	62,103.3	85,096.4	....
Gross Domestic Product (GDP)........	99b	8,968.9	10,482.6	21,358.3	34,919.2	43,794.8	55,276.3	78,297.0	103,815.0	123,926.9	148,356.0	171,917.8	....
Net Primary Income from Abroad.....	98.n	−184.0	−375.3	−725.1	−596.7	−589.7	−1,230.4	−1,185.5	−1,110.3	−2,302.7	−3,265.8	−4,503.4	....
Gross National Income (GNI).............	99a	8,784.9	10,107.3	20,633.2	34,322.5	43,205.1	54,045.9	77,111.5	102,704.7	121,624.2	145,090.2	167,414.4	....
GDP Volume 1978 Prices.................	99b.p	1,077.1	952.1	....	....	....	....	....	....	....	....	....	....
GDP Volume 1994 Prices.................	99b.p	....	10,483.0	12,056.5	13,039.7	13,868.0	14,193.6	14,371.4	14,597.9	13,897.8	14,268.3	15,134.5	....
GDP Volume (2000=100)................	99bvp	81.2	† 71.8	82.6	89.3	95.0	97.2	98.4	100.0	95.2	97.7	103.7	....
GDP Deflator (2000=100)................	99bip	10.6	14.1	24.9	37.7	44.4	54.8	76.6	100.0	125.4	146.2	159.7	....
							Millions: Midyear Estimates						
Population................................	99z	9.89	9.97	10.11	10.32	10.59	10.90	11.21	11.51	11.80	12.07	12.34	12.61

		1993	1994	1995	1996	1997	1998	1999	2000	2001	2002	2003	2004
Exchange Rates					*Ringgit per SDR: End of Period*								
Official Rate............................	aa	3.7107	3.7372	3.7787	3.6366	5.2511	5.3505	5.2155	4.9511	4.7756	5.1662	5.6467	5.9014
				Ringgit per US Dollar: End of Period (ae) Period Average (rf)									
Official Rate............................	ae	2.7015	2.5600	2.5420	2.5290	3.8919	3.8000	3.8000	3.8000	3.8000	3.8000	3.8000	3.8000
Official Rate............................	rf	2.5741	2.6243	2.5044	2.5159	2.8132	3.9244	3.8000	3.8000	3.8000	3.8000	3.8000	3.8000
				Index Numbers (2000=100): Period Averages									
Official Rate............................	ahx	147.6	144.9	151.5	151.0	137.8	97.1	100.0	100.0	100.0	100.0	100.0	100.0
Nominal Effective Exchange Rate.....	nec	125.9	125.0	124.9	128.9	125.3	96.4	97.4	100.0	105.8	105.0	98.0	93.3
Real Effective Exchange Rate...........	rec	120.5	115.8	115.7	121.1	119.4	94.9	97.6	100.0	105.5	105.6	97.1	91.9
Fund Position					*Millions of SDRs: End of Period*								
Quota....................................	2f.s	833	833	833	833	833	833	1,487	1,487	1,487	1,487	1,487	1,487
SDRs.....................................	1b.s	88	93	102	115	130	146	61	81	100	111	120	128
Reserve Position in the Fund............	1c.s	229	274	456	478	445	445	608	608	608	581	586	500
of which: Outstg.Fund Borrowing...	2c	—	—	—	—	—	—	—	—	—	—	—	—
Total Fund Cred.&Loans Outstg......	2tl	—	—	—	—	—	—	—	—	—	—	—	—
International Liquidity				*Millions of US Dollars Unless Otherwise Indicated: End of Period*									
Total Reserves minus Gold...............	1l.d	27,249	25,423	23,774	27,009	20,788	25,559	30,588	29,523	30,474	34,222	44,515	66,384
SDRs..................................	1b.d	121	135	151	166	175	205	83	105	125	151	178	199
Reserve Position in the Fund..........	1c.d	315	400	678	688	600	626	835	792	764	790	871	776
Foreign Exchange....................	1d.d	26,814	24,888	22,945	26,156	20,013	24,728	29,670	28,625	29,585	33,280	43,466	65,409
Gold (Million Fine Troy Ounces).......	1ad	2.390	2.390	2.390	2.390	2.350	2.350	1.180	1.170	1.170	1.170	1.170	1.170
Gold (National Valuation)................	1and	115	122	124	120	111	116	57	53	51	56	61	64
Monetary Authorities: Other Liab.....	4..d	14.5	11.7	10.5	6.3	.7	.8	.5	1.3	.7	.9	.8	.7
Deposit Money Banks: Assets...........	7a.d	3,893.0	4,168.0	4,178.0	4,357.3	6,003.2	5,517.3	6,519.0	7,470.4	7,161.5	7,460.5	6,213.2	11,203.7
Liabilities.................	7b.d	13,956.0	8,161.0	8,242.0	11,240.9	12,339.4	9,160.5	7,296.3	6,772.2	6,079.6	8,343.4	9,367.7	14,285.7
Other Banking Insts.: Assets........	7e.d	50.8	65.4	82.1	147.0	274.6	266.9	245.4	382.6	278.6	393.0	458.6	609.7
Liabilities..................	7f.d	—	11.9	24.3	346.0	445.7	348.6	244.6	201.0	136.9	308.9	243.9	334.1
Monetary Authorities					*Millions of Ringgit: End of Period*								
Foreign Assets..........................	11	76,485	68,200	63,790	† 70,737	60,369	99,427	117,255	113,247	116,922	131,093	170,127	253,410
Claims on Central Government........	12a	454	980	2,155	† 7,113	7,153	3,926	2,377	1,838	1,422	600	99	221
Claims on Private Sector.................	12d	1,296	601	566	† 8,270	9,843	16,018	22,517	29,476	27,403	25,029	25,118	26,254
Claims on Deposit Money Banks......	12e	3,597	3,443	3,250	† 3,676	27,451	2,512	2,135	1,616	1,193	2,902	2,894	2,888
Claims on Nonbank Financial Insts...	12g	1,104	2,718	3,505	† 634	508	2,114	2,282	2,157	2,219	1,983	1,968	1,850
Reserve Money..........................	14	28,253	38,482	47,970	† 64,559	82,896	36,178	45,675	41,372	40,022	42,582	45,534	50,087
of which: Currency Outside DMBs..	14a	13,506	15,884	17,433	† 18,979	21,360	18,162	24,757	22,263	22,148	23,897	26,101	28,617
Other Liabilities to DMBs............	14n	—	—	—	† 6,036	7,030	19,014	46,152	43,509	38,688	53,280	82,410	106,976
Time and Savings Deposits...............	15	25	16	5	† 5,790	2,320	9,079	2,043	9,171	10,637	5,601	5,379	3,622
Liabs. of Central Bank: Securities...	16ac	—	—	—	† 4,968	909	4	379	7,085	7,477	12,281	13,385	16,877
Foreign Liabilities.....................	16c	39	30	27	† 16	3	3	2	5	3	3	3	3
Central Government Deposits..........	16d	2,912	8,469	8,379	† 11,401	10,545	25,281	18,514	17,845	25,237	13,827	4,905	25,705
Capital Accounts.......................	17a	4,172	3,507	3,513	† 3,633	4,085	4,099	31,413	27,384	24,092	30,960	43,192	51,190
Other Items (Net).......................	17r	47,535	25,438	13,374	† −5,974	−2,466	30,339	2,389	1,962	3,003	3,073	5,397	30,163
Deposit Money Banks					*Millions of Ringgit: End of Period*								
Reserves..................................	20	51,493	35,670	32,421	† 30,729	42,266	13,679	16,918	14,902	13,978	14,664	15,169	18,950
Claims on Mon.Author.:Securities.....	20c	—	—	—	† 3,096	—	—	9	4,822	5,112	7,464	7,661	3,504
Other Claims on Monetary Author.....	20n	—	—	—	† 2,183	2,931	17,135	41,231	38,366	29,137	39,094	62,631	84,852
Foreign Assets..........................	21	10,482	10,542	10,320	† 11,020	23,364	20,966	24,772	28,387	27,214	28,350	23,610	42,574
Claims on Central Government........	22a	10,683	11,127	10,182	† 11,133	14,032	18,871	15,968	19,728	21,518	21,515	27,478	30,509
Claims on State & Local Govts.........	22b	—	—	—	† 556	744	721	552	639	786	518	544	782
Claims on Nonfin.Pub.Enterprises.....	22c	—	—	—	† —	2,581	3,264	4,162	4,331	2,221	2,876	3,276	4,531
Claims on Private Sector.................	22d	122,344	141,965	185,472	† 234,484	289,853	298,162	303,657	322,206	336,825	359,802	380,799	468,524
Claims on Other Banking Insts........	22f	8,770	14,463	18,631	† 29,358	43,220	25,383	12,887	15,393	18,330	18,099	29,210	10,104
Claims on Nonbank Financial Insts...	22g	—	—	—	† 8,921	16,051	23,672	21,227	22,519	22,490	20,565	20,283	20,556
Demand Deposits.......................	24	29,128	31,724	36,191	† 39,439	40,976	35,115	45,739	53,455	56,414	62,124	73,387	81,515
Time, Savings,& Fgn.Currency Dep...	25	90,184	99,776	124,935	† 145,622	181,438	194,868	227,720	250,696	254,599	264,914	286,029	355,224
Money Market Instruments..............	26aa	23,196	35,731	48,266	† 39,026	50,121	50,465	28,565	30,487	32,760	38,189	45,430	66,382
Bonds....................................	26ab	—	—	—	† 561	1,878	1,267	1,704	1,594	2,083	667	667	1,237
Foreign Liabilities......................	26c	31,488	17,000	15,873	† 28,428	48,024	34,810	27,726	25,734	23,103	31,705	35,597	54,286
Central Government Deposits..........	26d	1,903	2,795	4,149	† 15,570	16,617	19,582	24,828	20,712	20,057	17,571	16,866	18,470
Credit from Monetary Authorities.....	26g	2,171	1,781	1,772	† 1,710	18,055	12	4	82	55	12	4	981
Liabilities to Other Banking Insts......	26i	742	2,116	2,813	† 6,723	15,148	8,474	9,386	8,218	7,167	7,115	13,221	8,744
Capital Accounts.......................	27a	16,884	23,813	29,478	† 35,933	52,930	63,061	64,329	65,172	69,998	73,116	77,142	88,127
Other Items (Net).......................	27r	8,076	−970	−6,452	† 18,467	9,856	14,198	11,384	15,144	11,374	17,534	22,319	9,921
Monetary Survey					*Millions of Ringgit: End of Period*								
Foreign Assets (Net)........................	31n	55,440	61,712	58,210	† 53,313	35,706	85,579	114,299	115,895	121,030	127,734	158,137	241,695
Domestic Credit..........................	32	139,837	160,591	207,985	† 264,577	356,822	347,269	342,288	379,730	387,919	419,589	467,005	519,156
Claims on Central Govt. (Net)........	32an	6,323	844	−190	† −8,726	−5,977	−22,066	−24,996	−16,992	−22,355	−9,283	5,805	−13,444
Claims on State & Local Govts........	32b	—	—	—	† 556	744	721	552	639	786	518	544	782
Claims on Nonfin.Pub.Enterprises...	32c	—	—	—	† —	2,581	3,264	4,162	4,331	2,221	2,876	3,276	4,531
Claims on Private Sector...............	32d	123,640	142,566	186,038	† 242,754	299,695	314,181	326,174	351,682	364,228	384,831	405,918	494,778
Claims on Other Banking Insts.......	32f	8,770	14,463	18,631	† 29,358	43,220	25,383	12,887	15,393	18,330	18,099	29,210	10,104
Claims on Nonbank Financial Inst..	32g	1,104	2,718	3,505	† 634	16,559	25,786	23,509	24,676	24,710	22,548	22,251	22,405
Money....................................	34	48,077	56,175	63,594	† 73,214	81,845	57,605	74,500	79,591	82,506	90,163	103,907	112,690
Quasi-Money.............................	35	90,209	99,791	124,940	† 151,412	183,758	203,948	229,762	259,867	265,236	270,515	291,408	358,846
Money Market Instruments..............	36aa	23,196	35,731	48,266	† 39,026	50,121	50,465	28,565	30,487	32,760	38,189	45,430	66,382
Bonds....................................	36ab	—	—	—	† 561	1,878	1,267	1,704	1,594	2,083	667	667	1,237
Liabs. of Central Bank: Securities...	36ac	—	—	—	† 1,872	909	4	370	2,263	2,365	4,817	5,724	13,373
Liabilities to Other Banking Insts......	36i	742	2,116	2,813	† 6,723	15,148	8,474	9,386	8,218	7,167	7,115	13,221	8,744
Capital Accounts.......................	37a	21,056	27,321	32,991	† 39,565	57,016	67,160	95,741	92,556	94,090	104,076	120,334	139,317
Other Items (Net).......................	37r	11,996	1,168	−6,409	† 14,436	1,854	43,925	16,559	21,049	22,742	31,781	44,450	60,263
Money plus Quasi-Money..........	35l	138,286	155,966	188,533	† 224,626	265,604	261,552	304,262	339,458	347,741	360,678	395,314	471,536

		1993	1994	1995	1996	1997	1998	1999	2000	2001	2002	2003	2004
Other Banking Institutions						*Millions of Ringgit: End of Period*							
Reserves.................................	40	8,421	10,394	12,259	† 14,865	19,711	4,516	4,795	4,116	4,136	4,335	4,582	2,656
Claims on Mon.Author.:Securities....	40c	—	—	—	† 539	—	—	—	1,503	2,086	2,403	2,167	82
Other Claims on Monetary Author....	40n	—	—	—	† 113	2	1,887	4,921	5,093	9,584	13,757	18,681	19,871
Foreign Assets.............................	41	137	167	209	† 372	1,069	1,014	933	1,454	1,059	1,493	1,743	2,317
Claims on Central Government.........	42a	3,703	3,010	2,997	† 4,317	3,074	5,911	6,525	5,910	7,733	7,239	5,273	6,390
Claims on State & Local Govts.........	42b	—	—	—	† 36	55	42	17	9	55	7	9	4
Claims on Nonfin.Pub.Enterprises.....	42c	—	—	—	† —	523	663	573	239	351	281	673	659
Claims on Private Sector................	42d	59,678	70,911	90,750	† 116,616	146,626	134,775	122,425	129,459	134,845	142,128	151,012	90,021
Claims on Deposit Money Banks.....	42e	7,020	9,136	9,149	† 5,599	10,740	9,681	10,231	8,351	6,176	6,951	13,950	6,627
Claims on Nonbank Financial Insts....	42g	—	—	—	† 3,820	3,698	3,102	2,024	1,647	1,174	1,049	817	695
Time, Savings,& Fgn.Currency Dep...	45	56,353	61,072	68,712	† 80,329	88,259	93,111	93,890	98,052	100,070	108,579	111,539	77,930
Money Market Instruments..............	46aa	7,343	10,883	16,166	† 2,625	5,548	5,890	226	—	531	340	6,048	4,282
Bonds......................................	46ab	—	—	—	† 212	1,022	892	820	787	787	120	120	120
Foreign Liabilities......................	46c	—	31	62	† 875	1,735	1,325	929	764	520	1,174	927	1,270
Central Government Deposits..........	46d	722	707	1,213	† 7,554	7,254	7,165	9,500	8,442	8,982	8,224	9,046	5,889
Credit from Monetary Authorities.....	46g	—	—	—	† 510	11,788	989	553	—	132	20	21	26
Credit from Deposit Money Banks....	46h	6,981	13,267	19,094	† 31,981	43,720	22,470	19,126	15,347	18,510	17,778	29,288	10,281
Capital Accounts.........................	47a	6,834	8,588	10,746	† 14,721	19,572	20,446	20,523	21,638	24,108	25,281	26,200	17,638
Other Items (Net)........................	47r	726	–930	–630	† 7,469	6,600	9,303	6,876	12,752	13,557	18,126	15,716	11,887
Banking Survey						*Millions of Ringgit: End of Period*							
Foreign Assets (Net).....................	51n	55,577	61,849	58,357	† 52,809	35,040	85,269	114,303	116,585	121,569	128,054	158,952	242,743
Domestic Credit...........................	52	193,725	219,341	281,887	† 348,635	460,325	459,214	451,464	493,160	504,765	543,969	586,532	600,931
Claims on Central Govt. (Net).......	52an	9,304	3,146	1,594	† –11,962	–10,156	–23,321	–27,972	–19,523	–23,603	–10,268	2,032	–12,943
Claims on State & Local Govts.......	52b	—	—	—	† 593	799	763	569	649	841	525	553	785
Claims on Nonfin.Pub.Enterprises...	52c	—	—	—	† —	3,104	3,928	4,736	4,570	2,571	3,157	3,950	5,189
Claims on Private Sector.............	52d	183,317	213,477	276,788	† 359,370	446,321	448,955	448,598	481,141	499,073	526,959	556,929	584,799
Claims on Nonbank Financial Inst..	52g	1,104	2,718	3,505	† 634	20,257	28,889	25,533	26,323	25,883	23,596	23,068	23,101
Liquid Liabilities.........................	55l	186,218	206,644	244,986	† 290,090	334,151	350,147	393,357	433,394	443,675	464,922	502,272	546,810
Money Market Instruments..............	56aa	30,539	46,614	64,432	† 41,651	55,669	56,356	28,792	30,487	33,292	38,529	51,478	70,663
Bonds......................................	56ab	—	—	—	† 773	2,900	2,159	2,523	2,380	2,870	787	787	1,357
Liabs. of Central Bank: Securities.....	56ac	—	—	—	† 1,334	909	4	370	760	279	2,414	3,557	13,291
Capital Accounts.........................	57a	27,890	35,908	43,737	† 54,287	76,587	87,607	116,264	114,194	118,198	129,358	146,534	156,954
Other Items (Net)........................	57r	4,655	–7,976	–12,911	† 26,049	25,148	48,210	24,461	28,529	28,019	36,013	40,855	54,599
Money (National Definitions)						*Millions of Ringgit: End of Period*							
Reserve Money............................	19mb	27,564	39,445	47,331	64,559	82,896	36,178	45,675	41,372	40,023	42,582	45,534	50,087
M1...	59ma	41,792	46,471	51,924	60,585	63,365	54,135	73,447	78,216	80,728	89,072	102,104	114,269
M2...	59mb	139,800	160,366	198,873	238,209	292,217	296,472	337,138	354,702	362,512	383,542	426,061	534,163
M3...	59mc	196,611	222,330	271,948	329,708	390,809	401,459	434,590	456,496	469,519	501,125	549,649	617,639
Nonbank Financial Institutions						*Millions of Ringgit: End of Period*							
Claims on Central Government........	42a.s	4,546.6	6,050.1	....	....	....	....	....	....	....	....	....	....
Claims on Private Sector................	42d.s	4,108.5	6,555.5	....	....	....	....	....	....	....	....	....	....
Real Estate................................	42h.s	382.4	834.7	....	....	....	....	....	....	....	....	....	....
Interest Rates						*Percent Per Annum*							
Discount Rate (End of Period)..........	60	5.24	4.51	6.47	7.28	....	....	....	....	....	....	....	....
Money Market Rate......................	60b	7.10	4.20	5.60	6.92	7.61	8.46	3.38	2.66	2.79	2.73	2.74	2.70
Treasury Bill Rate........................	60c	6.48	3.68	5.50	6.41	6.41	6.86	3.53	2.86	2.79	2.73	2.79	2.40
Savings Rate..............................	60k	4.21	3.67	3.61	3.87	4.18	4.26	3.10	2.73	2.55	2.25	1.95	1.71
Deposit Rate..............................	60l	7.03	4.89	5.93	7.09	7.78	8.51	4.12	3.36	3.37	3.21	3.07	3.00
Lending Rate..............................	60p	10.03	8.76	8.73	9.94	10.63	12.13	8.56	7.67	7.13	6.53	6.30	6.05
Government Bond Yield.................	61	6.35	5.11	6.51	6.39	6.87	7.66	5.63	5.11	3.54	3.47	3.60	4.09
Prices, Production, Labor						*Index Numbers (2000=100): Period Averages*							
Share Prices..............................	62	93.0	125.7	117.1	134.9	116.3	61.6	82.4	100.0	76.0	84.5	83.8	101.2
Producer Prices..........................	63	77.9	81.7	† 86.2	88.2	90.5	100.3	97.0	100.0	95.0	99.2	104.8	114.4
Consumer Prices.........................	64	79.9	† 82.8	85.7	88.7	91.1	95.9	98.5	† 100.0	101.4	103.3	104.3	105.9
Industrial Production....................	66	53.3	† 59.7	67.5	74.9	82.9	77.0	83.9	100.0	95.9	100.3	109.6	122.0
Total Employment.......................	67	79.5	82.0	82.3	90.4	92.2	92.6	95.0	100.0	102.4	102.9	106.9	108.0
						Number in Thousands: Period Averages							
Labor Force...............................	67d	7,700	7,846	7,893	8,616	8,784	8,890	9,145	9,591	9,877	9,910	10,304	10,403
Employment...............................	67e	7,383	7,618	7,645	8,400	8,569	8,603	8,831	9,291	9,517	9,564	9,935	10,033
Unemployment...........................	67c	317	228	248	217	215	287	314	299	360	346	369	370
Unemployment Rate (%)................	67r	3.0	2.9	2.8	2.5	2.5	3.2	3.5	3.1	3.7	3.5	3.6	3.6
Intl. Transactions & Positions						*Millions of Ringgit*							
Exports.....................................	70	121,238	153,921	184,987	197,026	220,890	286,563	321,560	373,270	334,420	354,407	377,602	477,829
Rubber...................................	70l	2,132	2,927	4,038	3,510	2,971	2,829	2,344	2,571	1,886	2,492	3,583	5,197
Palm Oil.................................	70dg	5,799	8,365	10,395	9,435	10,817	17,779	14,475	9,948	9,876	14,861	20,286	20,029
Tin..	70q	489	507	545	533	477	485	491	435	461	426	284	947
Imports, c.i.f..............................	71	117,405	155,921	194,345	197,280	220,936	228,124	248,478	311,459	280,691	303,502	311,402	400,133
Volume of Exports						*2000=100*							
Rubber...................................	72l	95.8	104.0	103.6	100.2	104.1	101.1	98.5	100.0	84.0	93.0	96.7	117.1
Palm Oil.................................	72dg	66.4	74.3	75.1	83.1	85.6	84.8	101.1	100.0	118.1	122.7	141.5	134.8
Tin..	72q	172.4	176.2	170.8	166.6	154.2	108.6	116.5	100.0	132.3	131.3	73.5	145.4
Export Prices													
Rubber (Wholesale Price).............	76l	86.5	109.5	151.6	136.2	111.0	108.8	90.6	100.0	87.3	103.8	143.9	179.3
Palm Oil (Unit Value)..................	74dg	87.9	113.2	139.2	114.2	127.0	210.8	143.9	100.0	84.1	121.7	144.2	149.4
Tin (Unit Value)........................	76q	65.2	65.3	73.4	73.6	71.5	102.7	96.9	100.0	80.1	74.9	87.0	147.1

Malaysia 548

		1993	1994	1995	1996	1997	1998	1999	2000	2001	2002	2003	2004
Balance of Payments		*Millions of US Dollars: Minus Sign Indicates Debit*											
Current Account, n.i.e.	78ald	−2,991	−4,520	−8,644	−4,462	−5,935	9,529	12,604	8,488	7,287	7,190	13,381	....
Goods: Exports f.o.b.	78aad	46,238	56,897	71,767	76,985	77,538	71,883	84,097	98,429	87,981	93,383	104,999	....
Goods: Imports f.o.b.	78abd	−43,201	−55,320	−71,871	−73,137	−74,029	−54,378	−61,453	−77,602	−69,597	−75,248	−79,289	....
Trade Balance	78acd	3,037	1,577	−103	3,848	3,510	17,505	22,644	20,827	18,383	18,135	25,711	....
Services: Credit	78add	6,412	9,320	11,602	15,135	15,727	11,517	11,919	13,941	14,455	14,878	13,577	
Services: Debit	78aed	−9,516	−12,052	−14,981	−17,573	−18,297	−13,127	−14,735	−16,747	−16,657	−16,448	−17,532	
Balance on Goods & Services	78afd	−68	−1,155	−3,483	1,411	940	15,895	19,828	18,020	16,182	16,565	21,757	
Income: Credit	78agd	2,007	2,308	2,623	2,693	2,485	1,542	2,003	1,986	1,847	2,139	3,448	
Income: Debit	78ahd	−5,218	−5,903	−6,767	−7,383	−7,851	−5,446	−7,499	−9,594	−8,590	−8,734	−9,376	
Balance on Gds, Serv. & Inc.	78aid	−3,278	−4,750	−7,626	−3,279	−4,426	11,991	14,332	10,412	9,439	9,970	15,829	
Current Transfers, n.i.e.: Credit	78ajd	469	411	700	766	944	728	801	756	537	661	508	
Current Transfers: Debit	78akd	−181	−182	−1,717	−1,948	−2,453	−3,190	−2,529	−2,680	−2,689	−3,442	−2,955	
Capital Account, n.i.e.	78bcd	−88	−82	—	—	—	—	....	....	....	—	—	
Capital Account, n.i.e.: Credit	78bad	—	—	—	—	—	—	—	....	....	—	—	
Capital Account: Debit	78bbd	−88	−82	—	—	—	—	....	....	....	—	—	
Financial Account, n.i.e.	78bjd	10,805	1,288	7,643	9,477	2,198	−2,550	−6,619	−6,276	−3,892	−3,142	−3,196	
Direct Investment Abroad	78bdd	—	—	—	—	—	—	−1,422	−2,026	−267	−1,905	−1,369	
Dir. Invest. in Rep. Econ., n.i.e.	78bed	5,006	4,342	4,178	5,078	5,137	2,163	3,895	3,788	554	3,203	2,473	
Portfolio Investment Assets	78bfd	—	—	—	—	—	—	−133	−387	254	−563	−196	
Equity Securities	78bkd	—	—	—	—	—	—	....	....	....	−43	−18	
Debt Securities	78bld	—	—	—	—	—	—	....	....	....	−520	−178	
Portfolio Investment Liab., n.i.e.	78bgd	−709	−1,649	−436	−268	−248	283	−892	−2,145	−666	−836	1,174	
Equity Securities	78bmd										−55	1,339	
Debt Securities	78bnd	−709	−1,649	−436	−268	−248	283	....	....	....	−781	−165	
Financial Derivatives Assets	78bwd	....	....	....	....	....	....	160	279	−234	−174	−24	
Financial Derivatives Liabilities	78bxd	....	....	....	....	....	....	−291	−220	−3	−139	142	
Other Investment Assets	78bhd	−934	504	1,015	4,134	−4,604	−5,269	−7,936	−5,565	−2,702	−4,597	−4,502	
Monetary Authorities	78bod							....	....	....	—	—	
General Government	78bpd	−64	−52	5	33	−14	−11	....	....	....	−3	5	
Banks	78bqd	−2,057	−1,281	28	3,339	−979	−2,677	....	....	....	−96	904	
Other Sectors	78brd	1,187	1,837	982	762	−3,611	−2,581	....	....	....	−4,497	−5,411	
Other Investment Liab., n.i.e.	78bid	7,441	−1,909	2,885	533	1,912	272	—	—	−829	1,868	−895	
Monetary Authorities	78bsd	7	−3	—	—	—	—	—	—	—	—	−62	
General Government	78btd	−509	−163	−216	−597	−350	180	....	....	....	1,245	−2,891	
Banks	78bud	6,282	−3,789	—	—	—	—	....	....	....	862	1,715	
Other Sectors	78bvd	1,662	2,047	3,102	1,130	2,263	92	....	....	....	−239	343	
Net Errors and Omissions	78cad	3,624	154	−762	−2,502	−137	3,039	−1,273	−3,221	−2,394	−391	−4	
Overall Balance	78cbd	11,350	−3,160	−1,763	2,513	−3,875	10,018	4,712	−1,009	1,000	3,657	10,181	
Reserves and Related Items	79dad	−11,350	3,160	1,763	−2,513	3,875	−10,018	−4,712	1,009	−1,000	−3,657	−10,181	
Reserve Assets	79dbd	−11,350	3,160	1,763	−2,513	3,875	−10,018	−4,712	1,009	−1,000	−3,657	−10,181	
Use of Fund Credit and Loans	79dcd	—	—	—	—	—	—	—	—	—	—	—	
Exceptional Financing	79ded	....	....	....	....	....	....	....	....	....	—	—	
International Investment Position		*Millions of US Dollars*											
Assets	79aad	34,063	34,122	....	....	....	....	....	....	61,428	72,290	....	....
Direct Investment Abroad	79abd	1,437	2,635	....	....	....	....	....	....	9,014	10,760	....	....
Portfolio Investment	79acd	391	650	....	....	....	....	....	....	1,792	2,299	....	....
Equity Securities	79add	391	650	....	....	....	....	....	....	1,261	1,307	....	....
Debt Securities	79aed	—	—	....	....	....	....	....	....	531	992	....	....
Financial Derivatives	79ald	—	—	....	....	....	....	....	....	617	825	....	....
Other Investment	79afd	3,892	4,164	....	....	....	....	....	....	19,236	23,908	....	....
Monetary Authorities	79agd	—	—	....	....	....	....	....	....	....	....	....	....
General Government	79ahd	—	—	....	....	....	....	....	....	....	....	....	....
Banks	79aid	3,892	4,164	....	....	....	....	....	....	....	....	....	....
Other Sectors	79ajd	—	—	....	....	....	....	....	....	....	....	....	....
Reserve Assets	79akd	28,343	26,673	....	....	....	....	....	....	30,769	34,498	....	....
Liabilities	79lad	42,898	39,757	....	....	....	....	....	....	77,146	81,442	....	....
Dir. Invest. in Rep. Economy	79lbd	20,591	22,916	....	....	....	....	....	....	20,821	23,823	....	....
Portfolio Investment	79lcd	7,777	7,238	....	....	....	....	....	....	12,873	11,284	....	....
Equity Securities	79ldd	3,485	4,300	....	....	....	....	....	....	10,785	10,038	....	....
Debt Securities	79led	4,292	2,938	....	....	....	....	....	....	2,088	1,246	....	....
Financial Derivatives	79lld	—	—	....	....	....	....	....	....	568	472	....	....
Other Investment	79lfd	14,530	9,604	....	....	....	....	....	....	42,884	45,864	....	....
Monetary Authorities	79lgd	—	—	....	....	....	....	....	....	....	....	....	....
General Government	79lhd	2,875	2,956	....	....	....	....	....	....	....	....	....	....
Banks	79lid	11,656	6,647	....	....	....	....	....	....	....	....	....	....
Other Sectors	79ljd	—	—	....	....	....	....	....	....	....	....	....	....
Government Finance		*Millions of Ringgit: Year Ending December 31*											
Deficit (-) or Surplus	80	354	4,408	1,861	1,815	6,627	−5,002	−9,488	....	....	....	....	....
Revenue	81	41,691	49,446	50,954	58,279	65,736	56,710	58,675	....	....	....	....	....
Expenditure	82	41,337	45,038	49,093	56,464	59,109	60,371	68,210	....	....	....	....	....
Lending Minus Repayments	83	....	....	....	....	....	1,341	−47	....	....	....	....	....
Financing													
Net Borrowing: Domestic	84a	375	1,751	—	1,291	−2,048	11,040	5,423	....	....	....	....	....
Net borrowing: Foreign	85a	−3,134	−4,757	−1,635	−2,177	−1,682	1,819	2,923	....	....	....	....	....
Special Receipts	86	126	519	166	475	....	....	....	....	....	....	....	....
Use of Cash Balances	87	2,279	−1,921	−392	−1,404	† −2,897	−7,857	1,142	....	....	....	....	....
Debt: Domestic	88b	76,536	78,260	78,038	79,211	76,968	88,197	93,750	....	....	....	....	....
Debt: Foreign	89b	19,362	14,818	13,331	10,471	12,951	14,924	18,369	....	....	....	....	....

		1993	1994	1995	1996	1997	1998	1999	2000	2001	2002	2003	2004
National Accounts								*Millions of Ringgit*					
Househ.Cons.Expend.,incl.NPISHs....	96f	83,144	94,088	106,613	116,794	127,783	117,718	125,056	145,355	150,644	159,506	172,366	191,970
Government Consumption Expend...	91f	21,750	23,973	27,527	28,178	30,341	27,670	33,044	35,676	42,265	50,015	54,913	59,402
Gross Fixed Capital Formation..........	93e	66,937	78,664	96,967	107,825	121,494	75,982	65,841	87,729	83,345	83,764	87,089	91,819
Changes in Inventories....................	93i	535	1,870	120	−2,579	−398	−427	1,476	5,982	−3,339	2,217	−2,842	8,665
Exports of Goods and Services..........	90c	135,896	174,255	209,323	232,358	262,885	327,836	364,861	427,004	389,255	415,040	450,593	544,956
Imports of Goods and Services (-).....	98c	136,068	177,389	218,077	228,843	260,310	265,536	289,514	358,530	327,767	348,919	367,918	449,263
Gross Domestic Product (GDP).........	99b	172,194	195,461	222,473	253,732	281,795	283,243	300,764	343,215	334,404	361,624	394,200	447,547
Net Primary Income from Abroad.....	98.n	−8,265	−9,412	−10,377	−11,801	−15,095	−15,321	−20,886	−28,909	−25,623	−25,061	−22,527	....
Gross National Income (GNI)...........	99a	163,928	186,049	212,095	241,931	266,699	267,923	279,878	314,306	308,781	336,563	371,673	....
GDP Volume 1987 Prices................	99b.p	138,916	151,713	166,625	183,292	196,714	182,237	193,422	210,557	211,227	219,988	231,674	248,040
GDP Volume (2000=100)...............	99bvp	66.0	72.1	79.1	87.1	93.4	86.5	91.9	100.0	100.3	104.5	110.0	117.8
GDP Deflator (2000=100)...............	99bip	76.0	79.0	81.9	84.9	87.9	95.4	95.4	100.0	97.1	100.8	104.4	110.7
						Millions: Midyear Estimates							
Population...............................	99z	19.32	19.84	20.36	20.89	21.43	21.96	22.49	23.00	23.49	23.97	24.44	24.89

		1993	1994	1995	1996	1997	1998	1999	2000	2001	2002	2003	2004
Exchange Rates						*Rufiyaa per SDR: End of Period*							
Market Rate	aa	15.253	17.182	17.496	16.925	15.881	16.573	16.154	15.335	16.086	17.402	19.020	19.879
						Rufiyaa per US Dollar: End of Period (ae) Period Average (rf)							
Market Rate	ae	11.105	11.770	11.770	11.770	11.770	11.770	11.770	11.770	12.800	12.800	12.800	12.800
Market Rate	rf	10.957	11.586	11.770	11.770	11.770	11.770	11.770	11.770	12.242	12.800	12.800	12.800
Fund Position						*Millions of SDRs: End of Period*							
Quota	2f.s	5.5	5.5	5.5	5.5	5.5	5.5	8.2	8.2	8.2	8.2	8.2	8.2
SDRs	1b.s	—	—	—	.1	.1	.1	.1	.2	.2	.3	.3	.3
Reserve Position in the Fund	1c.s	.9	.9	.9	.9	.9	.9	1.6	1.6	1.6	1.6	1.6	1.6
Total Fund Cred.&Loans Outstg	2tl	—	—	—	—	—	—	—	—	—	—	—	—
International Liquidity					*Millions of US Dollars Unless Otherwise Indicated: End of Period*								
Total Reserves minus Gold	1l.d	26.15	31.22	47.95	76.17	98.31	118.54	127.12	122.80	93.07	133.14	159.49	203.58
SDRs	1b.d	.03	.05	.07	.09	.11	.14	.19	.26	.31	.38	.45	.50
Reserve Position in the Fund	1c.d	1.21	1.28	1.31	1.26	1.19	1.24	2.13	2.02	1.95	2.11	2.31	2.41
Foreign Exchange	1d.d	24.92	29.89	46.57	74.81	97.01	117.15	124.80	120.52	90.80	130.65	156.73	200.66
Gold (Million Fine Troy Ounces)	1ad	.001	.001	.001	.002	.002	.002	.002	.002	.002	.002	.002	.002
Gold (National Valuation)	1and	.042	.042	....	....	....	....	....	....	....	.587	.705	.739
Monetary Authorities: Other Liab	4..d	15.39	16.13	16.21	16.20	.86	.86	.86	.86	.79	.79	.79	.86
Deposit Money Banks: Assets	7a.d	10.30	10.23	14.02	22.35	13.40	23.65	19.09	22.12	26.88	33.73	63.90	80.35
Liabilities	7b.d	18.37	13.61	19.03	12.83	12.20	15.06	26.90	32.42	27.58	35.02	16.61	20.20
Monetary Authorities						*Millions of Rufiyaa: End of Period*							
Foreign Assets	11	293.92	376.86	580.10	912.94	1,173.55	1,411.67	1,512.69	1,460.53	1,207.23	1,722.66	2,060.46	2,626.01
Claims on Central Government	12a	910.65	999.33	1,076.06	987.57	920.12	1,024.38	1,156.15	1,409.01	1,584.47	1,704.26	1,517.24	1,291.42
Claims on Nonfin.Pub.Enterprises	12c	9.75	6.16	8.42	7.86	—	3.20	2.48	1.57	1.48	1.48	1.48	1.48
Claims on Deposit Money Banks	12e	7.91	6.57	5.62	1.37	1.41	1.42	1.43	—	—	—	—	—
Reserve Money	14	869.86	993.09	1,008.87	1,187.93	1,371.25	1,520.08	1,624.79	1,696.13	1,861.31	2,209.09	2,171.67	2,739.12
of which: Currency Outside DMBs	14a	330.38	382.27	405.83	425.85	489.68	524.92	593.34	618.14	566.52	569.88	624.90	762.54
Foreign Currency Deposits	15	.63	5.50	17.00	26.64	32.70	20.69	26.51	37.35	10.16	14.88	10.00	47.41
Liabs. of Central Bank: Securities	16ac	—	—	121.00	199.00	330.00	480.00	568.99	666.91	323.01	554.40	684.11	376.38
Foreign Liabilities	16c	170.90	189.90	190.76	190.65	10.10	10.13	10.15	10.16	10.15	10.15	10.16	10.96
Central Government Deposits	16d	70.28	66.47	180.22	148.50	163.00	225.18	235.02	231.83	283.81	310.58	338.72	388.34
Capital Accounts	17a	74.45	90.55	62.72	105.60	130.39	105.39	118.28	179.30	185.61	89.11	183.52	194.24
Other Items (Net)	17r	36.11	43.41	89.63	51.42	57.63	79.19	89.01	49.43	119.12	240.19	181.00	162.46
Deposit Money Banks						*Millions of Rufiyaa: End of Period*							
Reserves	20	454.02	498.55	491.78	660.80	821.61	870.72	984.48	1,025.38	1,237.95	1,587.94	1,528.52	1,895.39
Claims on Mon.Author.:Securities	20c	—	—	121.00	199.00	330.00	473.44	568.99	666.91	299.87	479.47	484.83	171.71
Foreign Assets	21	114.43	120.46	165.04	263.03	157.70	278.39	224.66	260.40	344.09	431.71	817.91	1,028.49
Claims on Central Government	22a	4.21	—	—	—	—	—	—	—	—	—	25.60	21.33
Claims on Nonfin.Pub.Enterprises	22c	177.04	137.24	160.98	147.32	103.78	161.89	193.80	183.15	182.55	209.55	88.88	248.51
Claims on Private Sector	22d	398.53	507.38	655.09	717.40	996.79	1,253.18	1,302.81	1,407.08	1,827.24	2,107.21	2,250.84	3,547.77
Demand Deposits	24	281.13	356.06	393.70	552.92	619.23	725.45	935.95	1,074.43	1,022.15	1,252.96	1,398.76	1,662.46
Time, Savings,& Fgn. Currency Dep	25	340.13	429.26	569.91	785.77	1,075.30	1,423.72	1,318.10	1,252.06	1,658.63	2,064.84	2,428.39	3,459.38
Foreign Liabilities	26c	203.95	160.22	224.00	150.98	143.65	177.25	316.60	381.62	353.07	448.23	212.59	258.56
Central Government Deposits	26d	60.40	31.52	58.43	90.24	93.48	126.08	160.95	182.16	222.09	259.80	292.26	424.93
Credit from Monetary Authorities	26g	7.64	6.63	5.15	1.34	.89	.89	.14	—	—	—	—	—
Capital Accounts	27a	122.32	143.77	157.69	281.00	358.92	486.96	496.18	610.86	572.11	646.51	685.56	875.49
Other Items (Net)	27r	132.66	136.17	185.01	125.30	118.41	97.27	46.82	41.80	63.65	143.55	179.01	232.36
Monetary Survey						*Millions of Rufiyaa: End of Period*							
Foreign Assets (Net)	31n	33.50	147.20	330.38	834.34	1,177.50	1,502.68	1,410.60	1,329.15	1,188.10	1,696.00	2,655.62	3,384.98
Domestic Credit	32	1,369.50	1,552.12	1,661.90	1,621.41	1,764.21	2,091.39	2,259.27	2,586.82	3,089.84	3,452.12	3,253.06	4,297.24
Claims on Central Govt. (Net)	32an	784.18	901.34	837.41	748.83	663.64	673.12	760.18	995.02	1,078.57	1,133.88	911.85	499.47
Claims on Nonfin.Pub.Enterprises	32c	186.79	143.40	169.40	155.18	103.78	165.09	196.28	184.72	184.03	211.03	90.37	250.00
Claims on Private Sector	32d	398.53	507.38	655.09	717.40	996.79	1,253.18	1,302.81	1,407.08	1,827.24	2,107.21	2,250.84	3,547.77
Money	34	694.54	850.87	899.06	1,059.35	1,195.60	1,384.24	1,585.18	1,760.44	1,655.91	1,886.71	2,105.35	2,520.12
Quasi-Money	35	340.76	434.76	586.91	812.41	1,108.00	1,444.41	1,344.61	1,289.41	1,668.79	2,079.71	2,438.39	3,506.79
Liabs. of Central Bank: Securities	36ac	—	—	—	—	—	6.56	.01	—	23.14	74.93	199.28	204.67
Capital Accounts	37a	196.77	234.32	220.41	386.60	489.31	592.35	614.46	790.16	757.72	735.62	869.08	1,069.74
Other Items (Net)	37r	170.93	179.37	285.90	197.39	148.79	166.50	125.61	75.96	172.37	371.14	296.57	380.90
Money plus Quasi-Money	35l	1,035.30	1,285.63	1,485.97	1,871.76	2,303.60	2,828.65	2,929.79	3,049.85	3,324.70	3,966.42	4,543.75	6,026.91
Interest Rates						*Percent Per Annum*							
Money Market Rate	60b	5.00	5.00	6.80	6.80	6.80	6.80	6.80	6.80	....	....	....	....
Savings Rate	60k	....	....	....	6.00	6.00	6.00	6.00	6.00	6.00	5.50	5.25	3.17
Deposit Rate	60l	....	....	....	6.80	6.80	6.80	6.93	6.88	6.97	7.50	7.50	6.50
Lending Rate	60p	....	....	....	15.00	15.00	15.00	12.50	13.00	13.00	13.54	14.00	13.17
Prices, Production, Labor						*Index Numbers (2000=100): Period Averages*							
Consumer Prices	64	80.0	82.7	87.2	92.7	99.7	98.3	101.2	100.0	100.7	101.6	98.7	105.0
Total Fish Catch	66al	77.9	90.1	90.5	91.3	88.2	99.7	106.8	100.0	108.3	138.8	131.9	135.2
Tourist Bed Night Index	66.t	53.1	59.7	69.2	77.2	83.1	88.1	94.4	100.0	99.9	103.3	119.5	129.8
						Number in Thousands: Period Averages							
Labor Force	67d	....	....	67	....	....	....	....	86	....	....	....	....
Intl. Transactions & Positions						*Millions of US Dollars*							
Exports	70..d	34.6	47.9	49.6	59.2	69.9	74.3	63.7	75.9	76.2	90.4	112.5	122.4
Imports, c.i.f	71..d	191.3	221.7	267.9	301.7	348.8	354.0	402.2	388.6	393.5	391.7	470.8	644.7
Imports, f.o.b	71.vd	168.3	195.1	235.8	265.5	307.0	311.5	353.9	342.0	346.3	344.7	414.3	567.3

		1993	1994	1995	1996	1997	1998	1999	2000	2001	2002	2003	2004
Balance of Payments						*Millions of US Dollars: Minus Sign Indicates Debit*							
Current Account, n.i.e......................	78ald	−53.8	−11.1	−18.2	−7.4	−34.7	−21.9	−78.9	−51.5	−58.7	−35.7	−30.4	....
Goods: Exports f.o.b....................	78aad	52.7	75.4	85.0	79.9	89.7	95.6	91.5	108.7	110.2	132.3	152.0	....
Goods: Imports f.o.b....................	78abd	−177.7	−195.1	−235.8	−265.5	−307.0	−311.5	−353.9	−342.0	−346.3	−344.7	−414.3	....
Trade Balance............................	78acd	−125.0	−119.6	−150.8	−185.6	−217.3	−215.9	−262.4	−233.3	−236.0	−212.4	−262.3	....
Services: Credit............................	78add	160.7	197.4	232.8	289.0	312.2	331.3	342.8	348.5	354.1	362.9	432.1	....
Services: Debit............................	78aed	−57.2	−62.8	−76.7	−87.9	−94.2	−98.9	−108.1	−109.7	−109.8	−111.1	−121.0	....
Balance on Goods & Services......	78afd	−21.6	15.0	5.4	15.5	.6	16.6	−27.8	5.5	8.2	39.3	48.8	....
Income: Credit............................	78agd	3.0	3.8	4.5	6.0	7.5	8.6	9.0	10.3	8.2	5.6	7.6	....
Income: Debit............................	78ahd	−22.0	−24.0	−24.5	−27.8	−34.9	−36.8	−40.1	−40.3	−45.4	−41.1	−44.6	....
Balance on Gds, Serv. & Inc.......	78aid	−40.6	−5.2	−14.6	−6.4	−26.8	−11.6	−58.8	−24.5	−29.1	3.9	11.8	....
Current Transfers, n.i.e.: Credit.....	78ajd	13.3	16.3	23.0	26.2	20.0	20.3	20.4	19.3	19.9	10.6	12.7	....
Current Transfers: Debit...............	78akd	−26.5	−22.2	−26.6	−27.3	−27.9	−30.6	−40.5	−46.2	−49.6	−50.2	−54.9	....
Capital Account, n.i.e.	78bcd	—	—	—	—	—	—	—	—	—	—	—	....
Capital Account, n.i.e.: Credit.......	78bad	—	—	—	—	—	—	—	—	—	—	—	....
Capital Account: Debit..............	78bbd	—	—	—	—	—	—	—	—	—	—	—	....
Financial Account, n.i.e.	78bjd	46.3	27.5	67.6	52.2	71.0	60.2	76.2	40.2	35.5	73.5	56.3	....
Direct Investment Abroad..........	78bdd												....
Dir. Invest. in Rep. Econ., n.i.e......	78bed	6.9	8.7	7.2	9.3	11.4	11.5	12.3	13.0	11.7	12.4	13.5	....
Portfolio Investment Assets...........	78bfd	—	—	—	—	—	—	—	—	—	—	—	....
Equity Securities.....................	78bkd	—	—	—	—	—	—	—	—	—	—	—	....
Debt Securities........................	78bld	—	—	—	—	—	—	—	—	—	—	—	....
Portfolio Investment Liab., n.i.e......	78bgd	—	—	—	—	—	—	—	—	—	—	—	....
Equity Securities.....................	78bmd	—	—	—	—	—	—	—	—	—	—	—	....
Debt Securities........................	78bnd	....	....	....	....	....	....	....	....	....	....	....	....
Financial Derivatives Assets...........	78bwd	....	....	....	....	....	....	....	....	....	....	....	....
Financial Derivatives Liabilities......	78bxd	....	....	....	....	....	....	....	....	....	....	....	....
Other Investment Assets............	78bhd	25.0	13.2	29.8	32.6	53.8	30.8	47.5	22.8	21.3	26.7	28.3	....
Monetary Authorities..................	78bod	....	....	....	....	....	....	....	....	....	....	....	....
General Government..................	78bpd												....
Banks....................................	78bqd	4.3	.1	−3.8	−8.3	10.8	−12.2	4.6	−2.8	−3.0	−7.2	−28.5	....
Other Sectors.........................	78brd	20.7	13.1	33.6	41.0	42.9	42.9	42.9	25.6	24.3	33.9	56.8	....
Other Investment Liab., n.i.e........	78bid	14.4	5.5	30.5	10.2	5.8	17.9	16.4	4.4	2.4	34.4	14.4	....
Monetary Authorities..................	78bsd	15.2	.7	.1	—	−15.3	—	—	—	−.1	—	—	....
General Government..................	78btd	3.8	8.2	24.8	17.3	21.9	14.6	5.2	−1.9	7.8	26.8	33.8	....
Banks....................................	78bud	−4.6	−3.4	5.7	−7.1	−.8	3.3	11.2	6.3	−5.3	7.6	−19.3	....
Other Sectors.........................	78bvd	—	—	—	—	—	—	—	—	....	....	....	....
Net Errors and Omissions.................	78cad	6.1	−10.9	−32.2	−16.4	−14.0	−18.2	11.4	6.9	−6.5	2.3	.3	....
Overall Balance..........................	78cbd	−1.3	5.5	17.2	28.3	22.2	20.2	8.6	−4.3	−29.7	40.1	26.2	....
Reserves and Related Items.............	79dad	1.3	−5.5	−17.2	−28.3	−22.2	−20.2	−8.6	4.3	29.7	−40.1	−26.2	....
Reserve Assets.......................	79dbd	1.3	−5.5	−17.2	−28.3	−22.2	−20.2	−8.6	4.3	29.7	−40.1	−26.2	....
Use of Fund Credit and Loans........	79dcd	—	—	—	—	—	—	—	—	—	—	—	....
Exceptional Financing...................	79ded	—	—	—	—	—	—	—	—	—	—	—	....
International Investment Position						*Millions of US Dollars*							
Assets...................................	79aad	....	....	....	....	....	....	....	....	....	....	....	....
Direct Investment Abroad..............	79abd	—	—	—	—	—	—	—	—	—	—	—	....
Portfolio Investment...................	79acd	—	—	—	—	—	—	—	—	—	—	—	....
Equity Securities......................	79add	—	—	—	—	—	—	—	—	—	—	—	....
Debt Securities........................	79aed	—	—	—	—	—	—	—	—	—	—	—	....
Financial Derivatives....................	79ald	....	....	....	....	....	....	....	....	....	....	....	....
Other Investment......................	79afd	10.3	10.2	14.0	22.3	11.5	23.7	19.1	21.9	24.9	32.1	60.6	....
Monetary Authorities..................	79agd	—	—	—	—	—	—	—	—	—	—	—	....
General Government..................	79ahd	—	—	—	—	—	—	—	—	—	—	—	....
Banks....................................	79aid	10.3	10.2	14.0	22.3	11.5	23.7	19.1	21.9	24.9	32.1	60.6	....
Other Sectors.........................	79ajd	—	—	—	—	—	—	—	—	—	—	—	....
Reserve Assets.......................	79akd	26.5	32.0	49.3	77.6	99.7	119.9	128.5	124.1	94.3	134.6	161.0	....
Liabilities.................................	79lad	....	....	....	....	....	....	....	....	....	....	....	....
Dir. Invest. in Rep. Economy...........	79lbd	—	—	—	—	—	—	—	—	—	—	—	....
Portfolio Investment...................	79lcd	—	—	—	—	—	—	—	—	—	—	—	....
Equity Securities......................	79ldd	—	—	—	—	—	—	—	—	—	—	—	....
Debt Securities........................	79led	—	—	—	—	—	—	—	—	—	—	—	....
Financial Derivatives....................	79lld	....	....	....	....	....	....	....	....	....	....	....	....
Other Investment......................	79lfd	130.4	141.9	173.1	178.1	178.9	201.6	213.8	212.4	210.6	259.8	281.6	....
Monetary Authorities..................	79lgd	15.4	16.1	16.2	16.2	.9	.9	.9	.9	.8	.8	.8	....
General Government..................	79lhd	96.7	110.8	136.2	148.4	165.3	184.7	185.6	178.0	181.5	223.1	264.2	....
Banks....................................	79lid	18.4	15.0	20.6	13.5	12.8	16.1	27.3	33.6	28.3	35.9	16.6	....
Other Sectors.........................	79ljd	—	—	—	—	—	—	—	—	—	—	—	....
Government Finance						*Millions of Rufiyaa: Year Ending December 31*							
Deficit (-) or Surplus....................	80	−412.6	−206.6	−300.1	−133.8	−81.3	−123.1	−281.1	−321.5	−363.3	−402.4	−300.3	....
Revenue.................................	81	765.2	981.7	1,209.5	1,324.9	1,656.5	1,765.7	2,062.6	2,206.8	2,310.9	2,582.4	2,964.3	....
Grants Received........................	81z	153.3	162.6	199.2	242.9	168.2	164.5	162.7	165.9	211.7	132.5	123.6	....
Expenditure.............................	82	1,317.4	1,357.5	1,717.8	1,692.6	1,936.9	2,113.9	2,494.9	2,739.9	2,912.1	3,135.5	3,551.9	....
Lending Minus Repayments...........	83	13.7	−6.6	−9.0	9.0	−30.9	−60.6	11.5	−45.7	−26.2	−18.2	−163.7	....
Financing													
Domestic................................	84a	377.0	106.4	2.1	−29.2	−90.9	−6.2	224.4	317.9	217.5	30.0	−118.9	....
Foreign.................................	85a	35.6	100.2	298.0	163.0	172.2	129.3	56.7	3.6	145.8	372.4	419.2	....
Debt: Domestic........................	88a	846.5	960.9	1,063.0	957.6	877.1	980.3	1,101.0	1,317.4	1,495.1	1,653.2	1,464.7	....
Debt: Foreign...........................	89a	762.5	862.7	1,160.7	1,323.7	1,495.9	1,625.2	1,681.9	1,685.5	1,831.3	2,203.7	2,622.9	....

Maldives 556

		1993	1994	1995	1996	1997	1998	1999	2000	2001	2002	2003	2004
National Accounts							*Millions of Rufiyaa*						
Government Consumption Expend...	91f	....	....	788	859	1,060	1,184	1,386	1,599	1,619	....	....	....
Gross Fixed Capital Formation..........	93e	....	....	1,479	1,053	2,087	2,042	2,400	1,727	2,079	....	....	....
Exports of Goods and Services.........	90c	377	555	4,961	4,954	5,476	5,859	6,107	6,796	6,817	....	....	....
Imports of Goods and Services (-)......	98c	2,097	2,571	3,153	3,361	4,774	4,961	5,604	5,809	6,022	....	....	....
Gross Domestic Product (GDP)........	99b	3,533	4,125	4,696	5,301	5,982	6,357	6,935	7,348	7,651	8,201	8,842	9,639
GDP Volume 1995 Prices.................	99b.p	3,700	3,978	4,272	4,660	5,145	5,648	6,057	6,345	6,564	6,993	7,581	8,249
GDP Volume (2000=100).................	99bvp	58.3	62.7	67.3	73.4	81.1	89.0	95.4	100.0	103.5	110.2	119.5	130.0
GDP Deflator (2000=100)................	99bip	81	88	93	97	99	97	99	100	102	....	....	....
						Millions: Midyear Estimates							
Population.................................	99z	.24	.24	.25	.26	.27	.27	.28	.29	.30	.31	.31	.32

Mali 678

		1993	1994	1995	1996	1997	1998	1999	2000	2001	2002	2003	2004
Exchange Rates						*Francs per SDR: End of Period*							
Official Rate	aa	404.89	† 780.44	728.38	753.06	807.94	791.61	† 896.19	918.49	935.39	850.37	771.76	747.90
					Francs per US Dollar: End of Period (ae) Period Average (rf)								
Official Rate	ae	294.77	† 534.60	490.00	523.70	598.81	562.21	† 652.95	704.95	744.31	625.50	519.36	481.58
Official Rate	rf	283.16	† 555.20	499.15	511.55	583.67	589.95	† 615.70	711.98	733.04	696.99	581.20	528.28
Fund Position						*Millions of SDRs: End of Period*							
Quota	2f.s	68.9	68.9	68.9	68.9	68.9	68.9	93.3	93.3	93.3	93.3	93.3	93.3
SDRs	1b.s	.1	.1	.3	.2	—	.1	.4	.1	.3	—	.6	.4
Reserve Position in the Fund	1c.s	8.7	8.7	8.7	8.8	8.8	8.8	8.8	8.8	8.8	8.8	8.9	9.0
Total Fund Cred.&Loans Outstg	2tl	51.4	74.1	99.0	114.6	130.2	132.4	140.9	134.7	136.0	121.8	113.6	93.2
International Liquidity					*Millions of US Dollars Unless Otherwise Indicated: End of Period*								
Total Reserves minus Gold	1l.d	332.4	† 221.4	323.0	431.5	414.9	402.9	349.7	381.3	348.9	594.5	952.5	860.7
SDRs	1b.d	.1	.2	.5	.3	.1	.1	.6	.1	.4	—	.9	.6
Reserve Position in the Fund	1c.d	12.0	12.7	13.0	12.6	11.8	12.4	12.1	11.4	11.1	12.0	13.2	13.9
Foreign Exchange	1d.d	320.3	† 208.5	309.5	418.6	403.0	390.4	337.1	369.7	337.4	582.4	938.4	846.2
Gold (Million Fine Troy Ounces)	1ad	.019	.019	—	—	—	—	—	—	—	—	—	—
Gold (National Valuation)	1and	7.0	7.0	—	—	—	—	—	—	—	—	—	—
Monetary Authorities: Other Liab	4..d	6.0	9.7	1.9	−6.9	3.7	1.8	3.1	2.0	2.7	5.7	6.9	8.6
Deposit Money Banks: Assets	7a.d	26.3	118.7	163.6	136.7	117.6	125.2	116.6	140.1	195.0	189.9	218.8	278.9
Liabilities	7b.d	42.2	34.3	102.1	70.0	28.2	49.1	87.9	79.6	83.9	115.2	146.8	178.8
Monetary Authorities						*Billions of Francs: End of Period*							
Foreign Assets	11	98.0	118.4	158.2	226.0	248.4	226.5	228.3	268.8	259.7	371.8	494.7	414.5
Claims on Central Government	12a	41.0	58.7	65.1	77.0	99.8	105.9	112.9	108.9	135.9	125.3	117.6	99.1
Claims on Deposit Money Banks	12e	23.9	—	—	—	—	—	—	—	—	—	—	—
Claims on Other Financial Insts	12f	—	—	—	—	—	—	—	—	—	—	—	—
Reserve Money	14	143.8	115.9	127.7	151.1	162.8	153.7	173.1	219.0	245.2	359.3	474.2	402.7
of which: Currency Outside DMBs	14a	65.1	91.1	107.5	120.3	129.5	135.3	123.4	146.9	179.0	247.5	340.9	275.4
Foreign Liabilities	16c	22.6	63.0	73.1	82.7	107.5	105.9	128.4	125.2	129.2	107.1	91.3	73.9
Central Government Deposits	16d	5.5	12.8	27.1	63.0	70.6	63.7	41.5	34.7	17.2	17.8	25.8	15.7
Other Items (Net)	17r	−9.1	−14.6	−4.6	6.2	7.4	9.2	−1.8	−1.2	4.1	12.9	21.0	21.3
Deposit Money Banks						*Billions of Francs: End of Period*							
Reserves	20	79.4	25.3	17.1	29.5	32.1	16.5	47.7	70.7	59.2	99.7	132.4	125.0
Foreign Assets	21	7.8	63.4	80.2	71.6	70.4	70.4	76.2	98.8	145.2	118.8	113.6	134.3
Claims on Central Government	22a	3.4	28.0	19.4	24.0	21.1	13.6	14.0	17.8	27.7	23.3	14.3	15.7
Claims on Private Sector	22d	93.8	84.9	130.3	171.2	195.9	251.0	286.5	283.6	342.2	412.2	482.3	515.4
Claims on Other Financial Insts	22f	—	—	—	—	—	—	—	—	—	—	—	—
Demand Deposits	24	52.7	83.0	90.5	119.5	126.2	131.8	142.3	143.6	197.8	238.2	272.8	294.1
Time Deposits	25	52.6	63.1	56.4	76.4	89.0	91.9	97.0	116.1	110.0	137.0	173.4	197.1
Foreign Liabilities	26c	8.8	11.5	45.3	30.5	5.9	19.5	50.3	45.2	52.4	59.7	60.2	69.1
Long-Term Foreign Liabilities	26cl	3.6	6.9	4.7	6.1	10.9	8.1	7.1	10.9	10.1	12.4	16.0	17.0
Central Government Deposits	26d	33.0	39.3	50.8	71.5	68.2	78.0	102.3	129.8	159.2	158.5	178.7	158.6
Credit from Monetary Authorities	26g	23.9	—	—	.1	—	—	—	—	—	—	—	—
Other Items (Net)	27r	9.8	−2.1	−.7	−8.0	19.3	22.2	25.3	25.3	44.8	48.3	41.6	54.6
Treasury Claims: Private Sector	22d.i	1.5	2.1	1.5	2.0	4.5	3.9	5.2	2.7	1.3	—	.6	.1
Post Office: Checking Deposits	24..i	—	—	—	—	—	—	—	—	—	—	—	—
Monetary Survey						*Billions of Francs: End of Period*							
Foreign Assets (Net)	31n	74.3	107.3	120.0	184.3	205.5	171.5	125.9	197.2	223.2	323.8	456.8	405.8
Domestic Credit	32	99.7	119.5	136.9	137.6	178.0	228.8	269.5	245.8	329.4	384.4	409.8	455.8
Claims on Central Govt. (Net)	32an	4.4	32.6	5.1	−35.6	−22.4	−26.1	−22.2	−40.5	−14.0	−27.8	−73.1	−59.7
Claims on Private Sector	32d	95.3	86.9	131.8	173.2	200.4	254.9	291.7	286.3	343.5	412.2	482.9	515.5
Claims on Other Financial Insts	32f	—	—	—	—	—	—	—	—	—	—	—	—
Money	34	117.8	174.2	198.2	240.4	256.0	267.6	266.0	291.2	377.2	486.1	614.2	569.7
Quasi-Money	35	52.6	63.1	56.4	76.4	89.0	91.9	97.0	116.1	110.0	137.0	173.4	197.1
Long-Term Foreign Liabilities	36cl	3.6	6.9	4.7	6.1	10.9	8.1	7.1	10.9	10.1	12.4	16.0	17.0
Other Items (Net)	37r	—	−17.3	−2.4	−1.0	27.5	32.8	25.2	24.9	55.4	72.8	63.1	77.9
Money plus Quasi-Money	35l	170.4	237.2	254.6	316.8	345.0	359.5	363.1	407.2	487.2	623.1	787.5	766.8
Interest Rates						*Percent Per Annum*							
Bank Rate (End of Period)	60	† 6.00	6.00	6.00	6.00	6.00	6.00	6.00	6.00	6.00	6.00	4.50	4.00
Money Market Rate	60b	4.95	4.95	4.95	4.95	4.95	4.95	4.95	4.95	4.95	4.95	4.95	4.95
Deposit Rate	60l	3.50	3.50	3.50	3.50	3.50	3.50	3.50	3.50	3.50	3.50	3.50	3.50
Prices						*Index Numbers (2000=100): Period Averages*							
Consumer Prices	64	65.9	81.1	92.0	98.3	† 98.0	101.9	100.7	100.0	105.2	110.5	109.0	105.6
Intl. Transactions & Positions						*Billions of Francs*							
Exports	70	135.30	185.95	220.50	221.41	327.70	331.10	351.57	388.13	531.60	609.94	577.50	....
Imports, c.i.f	71	179.43	327.22	385.40	395.17	431.20	448.80	372.80	421.50	536.72	492.70	567.82	....

		1993	1994	1995	1996	1997	1998	1999	2000	2001	2002	2003	2004
Balance of Payments						*Millions of US Dollars: Minus Sign Indicates Debit*							
Current Account, n.i.e.	78ald	−188.6	−162.6	−283.8	−260.8	−178.4	−208.2	−253.0	−254.5	−310.0	−148.8	−271.0	....
Goods: Exports f.o.b.	78aad	371.9	334.9	441.8	432.8	561.5	556.2	571.0	545.1	725.2	875.1	927.8	....
Goods: Imports f.o.b.	78abd	−492.4	−449.2	−556.8	−551.5	−545.7	−558.2	−605.5	−592.1	−734.7	−712.5	−988.3	....
Trade Balance	78acd	−120.4	−114.3	−115.0	−118.6	15.7	−2.0	−34.5	−46.9	−9.6	162.7	−60.5	....
Services: Credit	78add	74.8	69.0	87.6	91.9	81.2	83.4	110.0	99.0	151.2	169.4	224.3	....
Services: Debit	78aed	−360.8	−317.0	−434.5	−383.4	−350.0	−353.3	−372.0	−334.9	−421.4	−387.0	−482.2	....
Balance on Goods & Services	78afd	−406.4	−362.3	−461.9	−410.2	−253.1	−272.0	−296.5	−282.8	−279.7	−54.9	−318.5	....
Income: Credit	78agd	30.2	9.3	8.3	26.5	19.0	29.3	31.3	20.6	22.1	36.1	21.3	....
Income: Debit	78ahd	−43.2	−49.7	−48.9	−69.5	−70.7	−80.1	−101.4	−118.7	−188.2	−276.3	−181.2	....
Balance on Gds, Serv. & Inc	78aid	−419.4	−402.7	−502.6	−453.2	−304.8	−322.8	−366.6	−380.9	−445.8	−295.1	−478.4	....
Current Transfers, n.i.e.: Credit	78ajd	294.6	281.3	266.8	218.3	151.9	151.6	145.8	157.2	160.7	182.1	265.5	....
Current Transfers: Debit	78akd	−63.7	−41.2	−48.0	−25.9	−25.5	−37.1	−32.2	−30.8	−25.0	−35.7	−58.1	....
Capital Account, n.i.e.	78bcd	111.9	99.1	126.2	138.0	111.4	124.0	113.3	101.6	107.4	104.2	113.7	....
Capital Account, n.i.e.: Credit	78bad	111.9	99.1	126.2	138.1	112.5	124.0	113.4	101.6	107.5	104.4	113.7	....
Capital Account: Debit	78bbd	—	....	....	—	−1.1	—	−.1	—	−.1	−.2	—	....
Financial Account, n.i.e.	78bjd	−14.5	−7.0	118.6	138.0	53.1	48.0	116.9	220.4	146.2	188.6	290.1	....
Direct Investment Abroad	78bdd	—	—	—	−1.6	6.8	—	−.8	−4.0	−17.3	−1.6	−1.4	....
Dir. Invest. in Rep. Econ., n.i.e.	78bed	4.1	17.4	111.4	44.8	63.0	8.9	2.2	82.4	121.7	243.8	132.3	....
Portfolio Investment Assets	78bfd	—	—	—	−1.1	−4.2	−4.5	−21.1	15.5	−.8	−.5	−27.1	....
Equity Securities	78bkd	—	—	....	−.1	−.1	3.9	—	−.1	−.1	−.6	.2	....
Debt Securities	78bld	—	—	....	−1.0	−4.1	−8.4	−21.1	15.6	−.7	.1	−27.2	....
Portfolio Investment Liab., n.i.e.	78bgd	—	—	....	1.6	−3.6	−.4	22.0	1.0	12.4	54.1	27.6	....
Equity Securities	78bmd	—	—	....	—	.2	−.1	22.9	.4	13.5	−2.1	.9	....
Debt Securities	78bnd	—	—	....	1.6	−3.8	−.3	−1.0	.6	−1.1	56.2	26.7	....
Financial Derivatives Assets	78bwd	....	....	....	—	—	—	—	—	—	—	—	....
Financial Derivatives Liabilities	78bxd	....	....	....	.1	.1	—	—	—	—	—	—	....
Other Investment Assets	78bhd	−21.4	−104.0	−52.3	22.3	−85.4	−33.8	−45.4	−87.0	−87.7	−248.4	3.7	....
Monetary Authorities	78bod	....	....	....	—	—	—	—	—	—	—	—	....
General Government	78bpd	....	....	....	—	—	—	—	−1.4	—	—	—	....
Banks	78bqd	11.9	−100.3	−33.2	32.3	1.8	1.4	3.9	−42.5	−64.2	30.4	15.6	....
Other Sectors	78brd	−33.3	−3.7	−19.2	−10.0	−87.2	−35.2	−49.3	−43.1	−23.5	−278.7	−11.9	....
Other Investment Liab., n.i.e.	78bid	2.8	79.6	59.6	71.9	76.4	77.9	160.1	212.5	117.8	141.1	155.1	....
Monetary Authorities	78bsd	—	—	—	−9.3	10.2	−2.2	1.7	−.6	.7	2.6	1.7	....
General Government	78btd	−18.0	33.1	89.8	80.5	57.7	98.3	97.9	88.3	111.5	87.5	104.4	....
Banks	78bud	.4	11.9	−1.4	−40.5	7.0	18.9	48.1	−1.9	8.4	25.9	11.1	....
Other Sectors	78bvd	20.4	34.5	−28.7	41.2	1.5	−37.2	12.5	126.6	−2.7	25.1	37.9	....
Net Errors and Omissions	78cad	−6.0	5.6	−13.0	14.2	4.0	−9.7	9.5	−4.8	9.4	−6.1	4.6	....
Overall Balance	78cbd	−97.2	−65.0	−52.0	29.4	−9.9	−45.9	−13.4	62.6	−47.0	137.8	137.4	....
Reserves and Related Items	79dad	97.2	65.0	52.0	−29.4	9.9	45.9	13.4	−62.6	47.0	−137.8	−137.4	....
Reserve Assets	79dbd	−45.8	−37.6	−80.2	−132.0	−37.6	33.7	1.6	−57.9	14.0	−159.0	−177.4	....
Use of Fund Credit and Loans	79dcd	5.6	32.7	38.4	22.4	21.3	2.7	11.7	−8.3	1.5	−18.3	−11.8	....
Exceptional Financing	79ded	137.4	69.9	93.8	80.1	26.2	9.4	—	3.7	31.5	39.5	51.9	....
International Investment Position							*Millions of US Dollars*						
Assets	79aad	....	....	....	673.4	598.1	628.6	673.9	596.7	671.1	1,223.5	1,314.4	....
Direct Investment Abroad	79abd	....	....	....	1.8	−6.9	−.1	.7	.6	15.9	2.1	6.6	....
Portfolio Investment	79acd	....	....	....	60.1	4.5	7.4	49.3	28.4	35.0	41.1	98.3	....
Equity Securities	79add	....	....	....	.9	.5	.3	.2	1.7	.4	1.5	1.1	....
Debt Securities	79aed	....	....	....	59.2	4.0	7.1	49.1	26.6	34.6	39.7	97.2	....
Financial Derivatives	79ald	....	....	....	—	—	.1	—	—	.1	.1	.1	....
Other Investment	79afd	....	....	....	179.9	185.5	214.9	274.2	185.0	271.5	589.5	300.8	....
Monetary Authorities	79agd	....	....	....	—	—	—	—	—	—	—	—	....
General Government	79ahd	....	....	....	—	—	—	—	1.4	—	—	—	....
Banks	79aid	....	....	....	136.7	117.6	123.9	103.0	100.7	187.3	182.7	193.3	....
Other Sectors	79ajd	....	....	....	43.2	67.9	91.0	171.3	82.9	84.2	406.8	107.5	....
Reserve Assets	79akd	....	....	....	431.5	414.9	406.2	349.7	382.7	348.7	590.8	908.7	....
Liabilities	79lad	....	....	....	2,717.7	3,299.8	3,411.3	3,265.5	3,053.3	3,021.8	3,766.9	4,460.6	....
Dir. Invest. in Rep. Economy	79lbd	....	....	....	64.1	454.8	309.9	228.1	132.4	210.4	524.2	682.6	....
Portfolio Investment	79lcd	....	....	....	5.3	4.5	10.4	41.0	4.7	16.7	76.4	46.9	....
Equity Securities	79ldd	....	....	....	.9	.9	.5	37.0	.8	14.0	13.8	17.1	....
Debt Securities	79led	....	....	....	4.4	3.7	9.9	4.0	4.0	2.7	62.6	29.8	....
Financial Derivatives	79lld	....	....	....	.1	.2	—	—	—	—	—	—	....
Other Investment	79lfd	....	....	....	2,648.2	2,840.1	3,091.1	2,996.4	2,916.2	2,794.6	3,166.3	3,731.1	....
Monetary Authorities	79lgd	....	....	....	158.5	179.6	188.3	196.6	177.8	173.6	171.6	178.0	....
General Government	79lhd	....	....	....	2,391.6	2,569.2	2,804.9	2,509.2	2,295.1	2,238.5	2,576.0	3,170.3	....
Banks	79lid	....	....	....	25.6	28.2	49.9	88.2	79.9	89.5	154.3	207.3	....
Other Sectors	79ljd	....	....	....	72.5	63.2	48.0	202.3	363.4	293.1	264.3	175.5	....
Government Finance						*Billions of Francs; Year Ending December 31*							
Deficit (-) or Surplus	80	−30.6	−43.4	−36.7	−11.1	−29.9	† −38.6	−61.4	−69.1	−112.2	−84.8	−89.6p	....
Total Revenue and Grants	81y	146.7	236.7	269.7	314.0	320.5	† 344.8	356.1	371.1p	420.4	474.2	542.7	....
Revenue	81	104.7	138.9	177.3	217.5	236.3	† 254.9	272.7	269.9	320.1	388.4	434.4p	....
Grants	81z	42.0	97.8	92.4	96.5	84.2	† 89.9	83.4	101.2	100.3	85.8	108.3p	....
Exp.& Lending Minus Repay	82z	....	....	....	....	....	† 383.4	417.5	440.2	532.6	559.0	632.3p	....
Expenditure	82	177.3	280.1	306.4	325.1	350.4	† 387.0	419.7	442.7	543.2	563.9	634.6p	....
Lending Minus Repay	83	....	....	....	....	....	† −3.6	−2.2	−2.5	−10.6	−4.9	−2.3p	....
Statistical Discrepancy	80xx	8.1	−29.7	−14.0	−18.9	−8.5	−10.0	2.4	1.6	—	—	—p	....
Total Financing	80h	22.5	73.1	50.7	30.0	38.4	48.5	59.1	67.4	112.2	85.1	89.5p	....
Domestic	84a	−3.0	−3.6	−40.1	−52.1	−10.6	−9.5	−1.2	3.0	6.1	−3.4	−36.4p	....
Foreign	85a	25.5	76.7	90.8	82.1	49.0	58.0	60.3	64.4	106.1	88.5	125.9p	....
Debt													
Total Debt	88	....	....	....	....	....	....	....	....	....	....	....	....
Domestic	88a	....	....	....	....	....	....	....	....	....	....	....	....
Foreign	89a	773.9	1,576.6	1,395.2	1,498.4	1,614.8	1,684.3	1,618.0	1,701.6	1,731.7	1,776.1	1,825.7p	....

		1993	1994	1995	1996	1997	1998	1999	2000	2001	2002	2003	2004
National Accounts						*Billions of Francs*							
Househ.Cons.Expend.,incl.NPISHs....	96f	560.5	749.0	983.3	1,100.9	1,083.5	1,228.3	1,355.7	1,417.6	1,541.5	1,548.1	1,654.9	....
Government Consumption Expend...	91f	123.4	187.9	262.0	271.9	290.6	322.9	308.5	310.8	346.3	368.1	383.9	....
Gross Fixed Capital Formation..........	93e	144.7	249.3	300.2	317.1	348.1	305.4	313.0	356.4	420.6	439.5	446.8	....
Changes in Inventories.....................	93i	−21.1	−10.8	43.2	−49.6	8.7	35.8	24.2	17.4	119.6	−14.5	167.3	....
Exports of Goods and Services..........	90c	129.9	224.7	264.2	268.4	375.7	377.3	419.4	458.6	642.3	727.9	674.8	....
Imports of Goods and Services (-).....	98c	226.6	421.2	494.8	478.2	523.8	537.8	601.9	659.9	847.4	766.2	833.6	....
Gross Domestic Product (GDP)........	99b	712.1	978.7	1,358.1	1,430.5	1,582.8	1,731.9	1,818.9	1,900.9	2,222.9	2,302.9	2,494.1	2,552.0
GDP Volume 1987 Prices.................	99b.p	690.6	708.9	755.9	783.0	....	....	....	....	....	....	....	....
GDP Volume (1995=100)...............	99bvp	91.4	93.8	100.0	103.6	....	....	....	....	....	....	....	....
GDP Deflator (1995=100)...............	99bip	57.4	76.8	100.0	101.7	....	....	....	....	....	....	....	....
						Millions: Midyear Estimates							
Population................................	99z	9.62	9.88	10.15	10.42	10.71	11.01	11.32	11.65	11.99	12.36	12.74	13.12

Malta 181

		1993	1994	1995	1996	1997	1998	1999	2000	2001	2002	2003	2004
Exchange Rates						*SDRs per Lira: End of Period*							
Official Rate	ac	1.8426	1.8609	1.9090	1.9338	1.8969	1.8818	1.7681	1.7532	1.7602	1.8443	1.9648	2.0214
					US Dollars per Lira: End of Period (ag) Period Average (rh)								
Official Rate	ag	2.5309	2.7166	2.8377	2.7807	2.5594	2.6496	2.4268	2.2843	2.2121	2.5074	2.9197	3.1392
Official Rate	rh	2.6171	2.6486	2.8333	2.7745	2.5924	2.5743	2.5039	2.2855	2.2226	2.3100	2.6543	2.9061
					Index Numbers (2000=100): Period Averages								
Official Rate	ahx	114.5	115.9	124.0	121.4	113.4	112.6	109.6	100.0	97.2	101.1	116.1	127.2
Nominal Effective Exchange Rate	nec	95.5	95.9	97.1	95.9	97.4	98.4	98.4	100.0	100.9	100.4	100.1	100.6
Real Effective Exchange Rate	rec	92.1	93.6	94.6	93.4	96.1	98.6	98.4	100.0	102.4	102.6	100.8	102.1
Fund Position						*Millions of SDRs: End of Period*							
Quota	2f.s	67.5	67.5	67.5	67.5	67.5	67.5	102.0	102.0	102.0	102.0	102.0	102.0
SDRs	1b.s	35.3	35.6	37.6	39.7	41.9	44.4	22.5	24.5	26.4	28.9	29.8	30.8
Reserve Position in the Fund	1c.s	25.3	25.4	27.3	30.7	31.6	31.6	40.3	40.3	40.3	40.3	40.3	40.3
International Liquidity					*Millions of US Dollars Unless Otherwise Indicated: End of Period*								
Total Reserves minus Gold	1l.d	1,362.4	1,849.6	1,604.5	1,619.8	1,487.6	1,662.7	1,788.0	1,470.2	1,666.2	2,209.3	2,728.7	2,699.7
SDRs	1b.d	48.4	52.0	56.0	57.2	56.6	62.5	30.9	31.9	33.2	39.3	44.3	47.8
Reserve Position in the Fund	1c.d	34.7	37.1	40.5	44.1	42.7	44.5	55.3	52.5	50.6	54.7	59.8	62.5
Foreign Exchange	1d.d	1,279.3	1,760.5	1,508.0	1,518.6	1,388.3	1,555.7	1,701.9	1,385.8	1,582.4	2,115.2	2,624.5	2,589.4
Gold (Million Fine Troy Ounces)	1ad	.100	.105	.041	.044	.011	.006	.006	.004	.005	.004	.004	.004
Gold (National Valuation)	1and	38.5	40.0	15.9	7.2	3.3	1.8	1.8	1.0	1.4	1.2	1.5	1.6
Monetary Authorities:Other Assets	3..d	26.8	27.2	.1	.1	—	.1	....	....	....	....	....	....
Deposit Money Banks: Assets	7a.d	1,233.9	1,129.8	† 2,235.5	2,875.5	3,415.0	5,850.0	6,815.0	8,595.6	6,890.9	9,416.4	....	....
Liabilities	7b.d	758.9	621.5	† 1,576.0	2,333.9	2,972.8	5,242.4	6,339.0	7,905.0	6,164.1	8,361.4	....	....
Other Banking Insts.: Assets	7e.d	294.0	13.7	11.0	9.1	18.0	18.6	15.9	15.6	....	....	....	....
Liabilities	7f.d	496.3	366.3	—	—	—	—	.5	—	....	....	....	....
Monetary Authorities						*Millions of Liri: End of Period*							
Foreign Assets	11	559.11	698.01	593.74	568.12	575.53	639.77	740.30	644.17	753.93	880.86	....	....
Claims on Central Government	12a	18.08	39.22	67.73	74.28	59.16	24.32	6.15	9.18	5.80	4.29	....	....
Reserve Money	14	443.58	584.20	512.98	491.66	498.99	514.05	549.32	568.41	589.40	614.28	....	....
of which: Currency Outside DMBs	14a	353.26	365.91	352.47	362.97	364.42	368.97	385.57	397.36	419.14	436.83	....	....
Central Government Deposits	16d	21.04	22.25	42.01	33.53	35.70	47.61	96.21	56.18	69.08	146.96	....	....
Other Items (Net)	17r	112.56	130.78	106.48	117.22	100.01	102.44	100.92	28.76	101.25	123.90	....	....
Banking Institutions						*Millions of Liri: End of Period*							
Reserves	20	83.26	194.50	† 101.31	97.78	126.14	141.73	172.17	153.63	173.57	295.92	....	....
Foreign Assets	21	487.52	415.89	† 787.78	1,034.11	1,334.30	2,207.90	2,808.27	3,762.92	3,115.08	3,755.44	....	....
Claims on Central Government	22a	142.65	135.88	† 149.80	196.50	297.01	391.72	463.02	466.15	550.96	550.82	....	....
Claims on Private Sector	22d	879.53	985.51	† 1,097.10	1,261.33	1,350.46	1,492.26	1,658.93	1,822.57	1,976.37	2,015.43	....	....
Demand Deposits	24	59.42	72.15	† 80.93	87.31	111.39	146.77	190.52	194.40	215.70	241.81	....	....
Time and Savings Deposits	25	940.86	1,105.35	† 1,254.60	1,414.07	1,567.09	1,698.96	1,860.65	1,944.22	2,117.15	2,357.95	....	....
Foreign Liabilities	26c	299.86	228.78	† 555.36	839.34	1,161.54	1,978.55	2,612.12	3,460.58	2,786.53	3,334.70	....	....
Capital Accounts	27a	39.09	40.98	† 128.61	147.62	198.02	299.97	336.14	372.76	447.91	430.77	....	....
Other Items (Net)	27r	253.73	284.51	† 116.48	101.40	69.86	109.36	102.95	233.31	248.67	252.37	....	....
Banking Survey						*Millions of Liri: End of Period*							
Foreign Assets (Net)	31n	746.77	885.12	† 826.16	762.89	748.29	869.13	936.44	946.51	1,082.47	1,294.62	....	....
Domestic Credit	32	1,016.85	1,136.14	† 1,265.87	1,489.64	1,660.93	1,848.85	2,017.02	2,228.28	2,451.52	2,409.38	....	....
Claims on Central Govt. (Net)	32an	137.33	150.63	† 168.77	228.31	310.47	356.59	358.09	405.71	475.16	393.95	....	....
Claims on Private Sector	32d	879.53	985.51	† 1,097.10	1,261.33	1,350.46	1,492.26	1,658.93	1,822.57	1,976.37	2,015.43	....	....
Money	34	425.07	463.55	† 498.91	489.66	489.63	525.09	580.70	595.72	635.61	680.12	....	....
Quasi-Money	35	940.86	1,105.35	† 1,254.60	1,414.07	1,567.09	1,698.96	1,860.65	1,944.22	2,117.15	2,357.95	....	....
Other Items (Net)	37r	397.70	452.35	† 338.52	348.80	352.50	493.93	512.11	634.85	781.24	665.93	....	....
Money plus Quasi-Money	35l	1,365.93	1,568.90	† 1,753.51	1,903.73	2,056.72	2,224.05	2,441.35	2,539.94	2,752.76	3,038.07	....	....
Interest Rates						*Percent Per Annum*							
Discount Rate (End of Period)	60	5.50	5.50	5.50	5.50	5.50	5.50	4.75	4.75	4.25	3.75	....	....
Treasury Bill Rate	60c	4.60	4.29	4.65	4.99	5.08	5.41	5.15	4.89	4.93	4.03	....	....
Deposit Rate	60l	4.50	4.50	4.50	4.50	4.56	4.64	4.66	4.86	4.84	4.30	....	....
Lending Rate	60p	8.50	8.50	† 7.38	7.77	7.99	8.09	7.70	7.28	6.90	6.04		
Prices, Production, Labor						*Index Numbers (2000=100): Period Averages*							
Consumer Prices	64	81.6	85.0	88.8	90.6	93.4	95.6	97.7	100.0	102.9	† 105.2	106.0	108.9
Harmonized CPI (2002=100)	64h	....	....	....	83.7	87.0	90.2	92.3	95.1	97.5	100.0	101.9	104.7
Industrial Production	66	56.9	† 64.1	64.5	65.1	64.8	71.2	76.6	100.0	85.2	85.3	88.5	87.4
						Number in Thousands: Period Averages							
Labor Force	67d	—	135	138	140	142	143	146	152	156	159	† 160	....
Employment	67e	132	134	149	140	137	137	138	145	146	148	† 147	148
Unemployment	67c	6	6	5	6	7	7	8	7	7	7	† 8	11
Unemployment Rate (%)	67r	4.5	4.1	3.7	4.4	5.0	5.1	5.3	4.5	4.7	4.7	† 5.7	7.2
Intl. Transactions & Positions						*Millions of Liri*							
Exports	70	518.33	592.42	674.94	624.15	628.93	711.99	791.14	1,072.44	880.68	961.15	928.49	909.32
Imports, c.i.f.	71	830.92	918.77	1,037.65	1,007.80	984.23	1,034.92	1,136.23	1,492.37	1,226.42	1,227.53	1,279.83	1,316.93

		1993	1994	1995	1996	1997	1998	1999	2000	2001	2002	2003	2004
Balance of Payments		*Millions of US Dollars: Minus Sign Indicates Debit*											
Current Account, n.i.e.	78ald	−84.3	−131.5	−360.9	−406.1	−202.0	−221.4	−121.8	−469.6	−165.1	11.5	−274.6	−550.0
Goods: Exports f.o.b.	78aad	1,408.1	1,618.5	1,949.4	1,772.8	1,663.4	1,824.5	2,017.3	2,479.0	2,002.3	2,311.4	2,502.2	2,688.3
Goods: Imports f.o.b.	78abd	−1,976.4	−2,221.0	−2,759.3	−2,611.1	−2,384.6	−2,497.5	−2,680.2	−3,232.6	−2,568.4	−2,667.9	−3,199.6	−3,559.6
Trade Balance	78acd	−568.3	−602.5	−810.0	−838.4	−721.2	−673.0	−662.9	−753.6	−566.1	−356.5	−697.4	−871.3
Services: Credit	78add	912.4	994.6	1,048.0	1,069.7	1,111.3	1,181.2	1,219.8	1,105.3	1,105.9	1,144.5	1,269.3	1,402.4
Services: Debit	78aed	−604.2	−686.5	−664.5	−679.9	−656.4	−720.3	−755.0	−733.3	−738.2	−740.5	−829.4	−956.8
Balance on Goods & Services	78afd	−260.2	−294.5	−426.4	−448.5	−266.4	−212.1	−198.0	−381.7	−198.4	47.4	−257.5	−425.7
Income: Credit	78agd	241.8	219.4	287.4	309.8	360.7	511.0	1,234.9	895.4	824.1	834.2	880.1	947.5
Income: Debit	78ahd	−126.8	−150.6	−247.6	−298.0	−351.6	−578.1	−1,201.2	−1,008.8	−799.1	−832.1	−842.9	−997.4
Balance on Gds, Serv. & Inc.	78aid	−145.2	−225.7	−386.7	−436.8	−257.2	−279.2	−164.3	−495.1	−173.4	49.5	−220.3	−475.6
Current Transfers, n.i.e.: Credit	78ajd	64.9	101.2	80.3	86.7	122.4	115.0	120.4	101.8	190.5	249.3	190.6	219.9
Current Transfers: Debit	78akd	−4.1	−7.1	−54.6	−56.0	−67.2	−57.2	−77.9	−76.4	−182.3	−287.2	−244.9	−294.3
Capital Account, n.i.e.	78bcd	13.1	—	12.9	58.4	8.4	28.6	25.7	18.6	1.5	6.6	6.3	84.2
Capital Account, n.i.e.: Credit	78bad	13.1	—	16.8	64.4	32.9	33.3	31.1	24.1	4.4	8.5	7.7	87.5
Capital Account: Debit	78bbd	—	—	−3.9	−6.0	−24.4	−4.7	−5.4	−5.5	−2.9	−1.9	−1.4	−3.3
Financial Account, n.i.e.	78bjd	188.7	480.9	25.3	206.1	106.6	293.5	427.4	208.2	143.5	195.5	164.8	34.9
Direct Investment Abroad	78bdd	−.9	1.0	−2.7	−76.0	−41.3	−24.5	−62.2	−25.7	−22.0	10.7	−19.9	−8.8
Dir. Invest. in Rep. Econ., n.i.e.	78bed	56.4	151.7	129.5	293.2	82.3	285.9	859.7	604.9	248.3	−415.7	305.7	419.9
Portfolio Investment Assets	78bfd	−266.6	304.4	−459.9	−120.2	107.6	−141.5	−470.7	−781.7	−282.7	−385.2	−1,545.7	−1,668.9
Equity Securities	78bkd	13.2	247.2	−.1	−1.1	−10.1	6.2	−11.8	2.8	46.7	48.4	−12.3	−32.9
Debt Securities	78bld	−279.8	57.2	−459.8	−119.1	117.7	−147.7	−458.9	−784.6	−329.4	−433.6	−1,533.4	−1,636.0
Portfolio Investment Liab., n.i.e.	78bgd	—	—	1.9	3.0	.4	115.3	−33.6	71.0	−212.6	2.3	−10.5	−6.4
Equity Securities	78bmd	—	—	−4.1	2.8	.5	42.3	−34.7	68.1	−209.9	13.0	−3.3	−3.4
Debt Securities	78bnd	—	—	6.0	.2	—	73.0	1.1	2.9	−2.7	−10.7	−7.1	−3.0
Financial Derivatives Assets	78bwd	—	—	—	—	—	—	—	—	—	—	−5.0	−117.8
Financial Derivatives Liabilities	78bxd	—	—	—	—	—	—	—	—	—	—	30.0	121.0
Other Investment Assets	78bhd	131.1	103.4	−285.6	−565.4	−980.0	−2,055.3	−1,596.3	−226.6	1,102.4	−590.6	−38.9	−1,117.4
Monetary Authorities	78bod	—	—	—	—	—	—	—	—	—	—	—	—
General Government	78bpd	—	−.5	−5.2	5.7	−1.1	—	−.1	.4	−1.1	−.5	—	—
Banks	78bqd	146.4	79.6	−280.5	−581.2	−934.5	−2,077.1	−1,605.1	−264.6	1,104.8	−635.1	−87.3	−985.3
Other Sectors	78brd	−15.3	24.4	.1	10.2	−44.4	21.8	8.9	37.7	−1.4	45.0	48.5	−132.1
Other Investment Liab., n.i.e.	78bid	268.7	−79.7	642.0	671.5	937.6	2,113.5	1,730.4	566.3	−690.0	1,574.1	1,448.9	2,413.4
Monetary Authorities	78bsd	—	—	—	—	—	—	—	—	—	—	—	—
General Government	78btd	35.3	6.0	−7.7	−8.5	.6	−8.3	−7.0	−16.1	5.4	13.4	75.2	−22.3
Banks	78bud	111.2	−274.6	680.9	597.7	903.5	2,183.7	1,807.8	573.3	−726.8	1,597.3	1,292.1	2,442.1
Other Sectors	78bvd	122.2	188.8	−31.2	82.3	33.5	−61.8	−70.4	9.1	31.5	−36.6	81.7	−6.4
Net Errors and Omissions	78cad	17.4	33.4	15.9	56.3	93.6	90.2	−93.0	21.0	275.2	74.3	247.4	223.5
Overall Balance	78cbd	134.8	382.8	−306.8	−85.4	6.7	190.9	238.3	−221.9	255.0	287.9	144.0	−207.3
Reserves and Related Items	79dad	−134.8	−382.8	306.8	85.4	−6.7	−190.9	−238.3	221.9	−255.0	−287.9	−144.0	207.3
Reserve Assets	79dbd	−134.8	−382.8	306.8	85.4	−6.7	−190.9	−238.3	221.9	−255.0	−287.9	−144.0	207.3
Use of Fund Credit and Loans	79dcd	—	—	—	—	—	—	—	—	—	—	—	—
Exceptional Financing	79ded	—	—	—	—	—	—	—	—	—	—	—	—
International Investment Position		*Millions of US Dollars*											
Assets	79aad	....	3,479.5	4,101.6	4,755.2	5,297.2	8,017.8	9,931.7	10,224.1	9,469.7	12,884.4	17,306.5	....
Direct Investment Abroad	79abd	....	28.3	32.3	107.8	139.9	170.4	185.2	203.1	261.2	278.9	352.7	....
Portfolio Investment	79acd	....	886.4	1,394.0	1,505.3	1,286.5	1,495.8	2,113.7	2,820.5	3,025.6	4,352.4	6,986.9	....
Equity Securities	79add	....	2.4	3.8	4.8	15.3	6.5	184.9	170.9	119.7	297.7	472.6	....
Debt Securities	79aed	....	884.0	1,390.2	1,500.4	1,271.2	1,489.3	1,928.8	2,649.6	2,905.9	4,054.7	6,514.3	....
Financial Derivatives	79ald	....	—	—	—	—	—	—	—	—	—	5.2	....
Other Investment	79afd	....	689.2	1,027.4	1,601.3	2,433.5	4,656.0	5,836.3	5,729.1	4,500.7	6,044.5	7,230.1	....
Monetary Authorities	79agd	....	—	—	—	—	—	—	—	—	—	—	....
General Government	79ahd	....	2.7	7.9	2.6	3.6	3.7	3.6	3.0	2.8	3.8	4.5	....
Banks	79aid	....	396.1	693.8	1,262.5	2,073.0	4,299.2	5,481.9	5,446.4	4,210.3	5,474.1	6,461.0	....
Other Sectors	79ajd	....	290.4	325.8	336.2	356.9	353.1	350.7	279.6	287.6	566.6	764.6	....
Reserve Assets	79akd	....	1,875.6	1,647.8	1,540.8	1,437.2	1,695.6	1,796.5	1,471.4	1,682.2	2,208.7	2,731.5	....
Liabilities	79lad	....	2,126.0	2,947.3	3,877.7	4,569.1	7,231.7	9,249.8	9,983.8	8,956.6	11,276.7	15,042.3	....
Dir. Invest. in Rep. Economy	79lbd	....	415.9	562.2	844.3	858.1	1,174.3	1,872.6	2,385.5	2,560.9	2,440.6	3,136.2	....
Portfolio Investment	79lcd	....	17.4	229.1	228.9	282.1	390.3	516.5	569.4	342.4	369.3	419.1	....
Equity Securities	79ldd	....	—	—	—	—	7.1	194.0	262.4	39.3	52.7	57.7	....
Debt Securities	79led	....	17.4	229.1	228.9	282.1	383.2	322.5	307.0	303.1	316.6	361.4	....
Financial Derivatives	79lld	....	—	—	—	—	—	—	—	—	—	31.6	....
Other Investment	79lfd	....	1,692.7	2,156.0	2,804.5	3,428.9	5,667.1	6,860.8	7,029.0	6,053.3	8,466.9	11,455.4	....
Monetary Authorities	79lgd	....	—	—	—	—	—	—	—	—	—	—	....
General Government	79lhd	....	152.9	151.7	144.7	135.2	163.3	155.7	162.4	150.6	179.9	260.3	....
Banks	79lid	....	702.0	1,376.2	1,947.9	2,621.2	4,925.2	6,230.6	6,447.7	5,468.0	7,861.2	10,576.2	....
Other Sectors	79ljd	....	837.8	628.1	711.9	672.5	578.6	474.6	418.8	434.6	425.8	618.9	....
Government Finance		*Millions of Liri: Year Ending December 31*											
Deficit (-) or Surplus	80	−27.56	−37.57	−30.87	−92.92	−125.99	−76.49	....	....	....	....	....	....
Total Revenue and Grants	81y	335.53	358.31	406.84	407.43	450.75	460.30	....	....	....	....	....	....
Revenue	81	327.10	345.46	402.32	386.63	440.94	450.26	....	....	....	....	....	....
Grants	81z	8.43	12.85	4.52	20.80	9.81	10.04	....	....	....	....	....	....
Exp. & Lending Minus Repay.	82z	363.09	395.88	437.71	500.35	576.74	536.79	....	....	....	....	....	....
Expenditure	82	367.78	402.47	447.46	500.00	535.42	576.32	....	....	....	....	....	....
Lending Minus Repayments	83	−4.69	−6.59	−9.75	.35	41.32	−39.53	....	....	....	....	....	....
Total Financing	80h	27.56	37.57	30.87	92.92	125.99	76.49	....	....	....	....	....	....
Total Net Borrowing	84	28.17	35.61	32.89	104.04	145.16	95.87	....	....	....	....	....	....
Net Domestic	84b	28.66	28.70	35.44	105.44	146.70	100.01	....	....	....	....	....	....
Net Foreign	85b	−.49	6.91	−2.55	−1.40	−1.54	−4.14	....	....	....	....	....	....
Use of Cash Balances	87	−.61	1.96	−2.02	−11.12	−19.17	−19.38	....	....	....	....	....	....
Total Debt by Residence	88	296.30	339.59	410.79	514.47	661.35	761.59	....	....	....	....	....	....
Domestic	88a	245.82	283.33	357.36	462.68	610.90	715.08	....	....	....	....	....	....
Foreign	89a	50.48	56.26	53.43	51.79	50.45	46.51	....	....	....	....	....	....

		1993	1994	1995	1996	1997	1998	1999	2000	2001	2002	2003	2004
National Accounts							*Millions of Liri*						
Househ.Cons.Expend.,incl.NPISHs....	96f	561.5	608.3	700.4	764.9	803.5	846.0	915.0	1,073.4	1,093.1	1,100.3	1,130.7	1,177.1
Government Consumption Expend....	91f	188.9	209.5	235.2	259.8	264.1	269.0	272.6	323.8	354.2	373.5	393.0	408.1
Gross Fixed Capital Formation..........	93e	276.8	305.4	365.2	345.3	326.4	333.6	340.0	374.3	326.1	259.2	357.1	383.5
Changes in Inventories....................	93i	3.7	10.0	1.2	−1.4	3.0	−10.7	9.4	61.6	−16.7	11.9	10.9	22.8
Exports of Goods and Services..........	90c	896.3	994.4	1,074.7	1,045.6	1,095.8	1,194.7	1,321.3	1,572.8	1,419.8	1,492.6	1,419.6	1,408.8
Imports of Goods and Services (-).....	98c	987.2	1,099.0	1,231.2	1,212.8	1,204.6	1,270.3	1,402.2	1,740.1	1,487.6	1,473.6	1,517.9	1,553.2
Gross Domestic Product (GDP).........	99b	940.0	1,028.5	1,145.5	1,201.3	1,288.2	1,362.3	1,456.1	1,665.8	1,689.0	1,740.1	1,793.3	1,847.2
Net Primary Income from Abroad.....	98.n	35.5	19.3	12.0	3.2	4.1	−27.4	12.4	−53.1	11.1	2.6	15.4	−22.4
Gross National Income (GNI)...........	99a	975.5	1,047.9	1,157.5	1,204.5	1,292.3	1,334.9	1,468.5	1,612.7	1,700.1	1,742.6	1,808.7	1,824.8
Consumption of Fixed Capital..........	99cf	53.4	60.0	77.2	86.9	95.7	98.7	104.2	234.1	249.7	250.8	258.3	262.0
GDP Volume 1995 Prices.................	99b.p	1,017.2	1,047.8	1,145.5	1,191.2	1,249.0	1,291.8	1,344.2	1,428.9	....	....	....	....
GDP Volume 2000 Prices.................	99b.p	....	....	....	....	....	....	....	1,665.8	1,658.9	1,675.9	1,644.3	1,661.0
GDP Volume (2000=100)................	99bvp	71.2	73.3	80.2	83.4	87.4	90.4	94.1	† 100.0	99.6	100.6	98.7	99.7
GDP Deflator (2000=100)................	99bip	79.3	84.2	85.8	86.5	88.5	90.5	92.9	100.0	101.8	103.8	109.1	111.2
							Millions: Midyear Estimates						
Population...............................	99z	.37	.37	.38	.38	.38	.39	.39	.39	.39	.40	.40	.40

		1993	1994	1995	1996	1997	1998	1999	2000	2001	2002	2003	2004
Exchange Rates						*Ouguiyas per SDR: End of Period*							
Official Rate	aa	170.541	187.401	203.813	204.837	227.146	289.744	308.815	328.724	331.928	365.317	394.674	....
						Ouguiyas per US Dollar End of Period (ae) Period Average (rf)							
Official Rate	ae	124.160	128.370	137.110	142.450	168.350	205.780	225.000	252.300	264.120	268.710	265.600	....
Official Rate	rf	120.806	123.575	129.768	137.222	151.853	188.476	209.514	238.923	255.629	271.739	263.030	....
Fund Position						*Millions of SDRs: End of Period*							
Quota	2f.s	47.5	47.5	47.5	47.5	47.5	47.5	64.4	64.4	64.4	64.4	64.4	64.4
SDRs	1b.s	.1	—	—	1.0	.3	—	—	.3	.2	.2	.1	—
Reserve Position in the Fund	1c.s	—	—	—	—	—	—	—	—	—	—	—	
Total Fund Cred.&Loans Outstg	2tl	46.1	58.8	67.1	74.6	83.4	78.3	77.6	75.4	83.2	82.9	70.2	58.2
International Liquidity						*Millions of US Dollars Unless Otherwise Indicated: End of Period*							
Total Reserves minus Gold	1l.d	44.6	39.7	85.5	141.2	200.8	202.9	224.3	279.9	284.5	396.2	415.3	....
SDRs	1b.d	.1	—	.1	1.4	.4	—	—	.4	.2	.2	.1	—
Reserve Position in the Fund	1c.d	—	—	—	—	—	—	—	—	—	—	—	
Foreign Exchange	1d.d	44.4	39.7	85.4	139.8	200.4	202.8	224.3	279.5	284.3	396.0	415.2	....
Gold (Million Fine Troy Ounces)	1ad	.012	.012	.012	.012	.012	.012	.012	.012	.012	.012	.012	
Gold (National Valuation)	1and	4.5	4.3	4.4	4.2	3.3	3.3	3.3	3.1	3.1	3.1	4.0	....
Monetary Authorities: Other Liab	4..d	187.1	199.2	212.0	205.3	209.7	209.6	202.0	195.0	195.2	197.2	184.1	....
Deposit Money Banks: Assets	7a.d	25.8	27.7	25.9	27.0	24.7	24.1	22.1	21.6	19.0	19.4	18.5	....
Liabilities	7b.d	106.4	105.8	67.4	35.5	26.4	15.0	13.6	12.5	12.1	12.1	17.5	
Monetary Authorities						*Millions of Ouguiyas: End of Period*							
Foreign Assets	11	6,218	5,746	12,425	21,030	34,425	42,546	51,335	71,429	76,028	107,383	111,024	....
Claims on Central Government	12a	18,979	17,949	17,109	17,109	17,102	17,012	16,912	16,912	16,912	16,912	22,130	
Claims on Nonfin.Pub.Enterprises	12c	60	60	60	60	60	60	60	60	60	60	60	
Claims on Private Sector	12d	516	581	695	755	1,023	1,003	1,065	1,185	869	889	1,090	
Claims on Deposit Money Banks	12e	2,353	2,571	1,872	2,334	2,793	2,789	2,232	1,539	1,539	1,539	21,400	
Claims on Nonbank Financial Insts	12g	49	49	49	49	49	49	49	49	49	49	49	
Reserve Money	14	22,810	21,966	20,724	10,462	9,089	8,406	8,788	9,222	9,723	10,038	10,009	
of which: Currency Outside DMBs	14a	9,097	8,598	7,383	5,093	5,854	5,801	5,963	6,402	6,688	6,282	6,412	....
Restricted Deposits	16b	29	91	147	91	82	55	154	225	49	49	49	
Foreign Liabilities	16c	10,813	12,093	14,649	15,543	19,232	23,096	23,968	24,848	27,905	30,301	27,845	
Long-Term Foreign Liabilities	16cl	15,663	16,342	16,702	15,160	17,069	20,923	22,108	24,794	23,873	22,684	21,041	
Central Government Deposits	16d	7,573	8,024	13,342	30,844	42,765	51,300	55,512	68,516	68,413	96,974	128,029	
Capital Accounts	17a	4,946	4,888	4,415	4,059	4,821	5,161	5,594	6,339	6,912	7,181	7,126	
Other Items (Net)	17r	−33,659	−36,448	−37,769	−34,822	−37,606	−46,075	−44,471	−42,770	−41,418	−40,395	−38,353	....
Deposit Money Banks						*Millions of Ouguiyas: End of Period*							
Reserves	20	10,799	12,775	12,486	5,355	3,083	2,390	2,984	2,887	3,105	3,884	3,521	....
Foreign Assets	21	3,201	3,561	3,556	3,853	4,165	4,962	4,964	5,450	5,022	5,224	4,901	
Claims on Central Government	22a	1,083	916	782	2,742	4,302	4,202	4,637	3,882	6,152	8,602	5,479	
Claims on Nonfin.Pub.Enterprises	22c	—	—	—	—	—	—	—	—	—	—	—	
Claims on Private Sector	22d	41,191	42,500	30,722	34,634	37,279	39,835	46,942	58,486	68,939	82,534	90,197	
Claims on Nonbank Financial Insts	22g	—	—	—	—	—	—	—	—	—	—	—	
Demand Deposits	24	11,508	11,145	10,674	11,015	11,629	12,467	13,697	17,749	21,033	22,628	25,790	
Time Deposits	25	6,635	7,612	7,817	8,476	9,101	9,282	8,708	8,800	10,929	13,192	14,313	
Foreign Liabilities	26c	13,216	13,583	9,246	5,054	4,451	3,078	3,058	3,164	3,195	3,255	4,646	
Long-Term Foreign Liabilities	26cl	—	—	—	—	—	—	—	—	—	—	—	
Central Government Deposits	26d	1,330	1,552	3,198	3,428	4,058	6,487	13,596	18,085	23,365	34,050	11,757	
Central Govt. Lending Funds	26f	1,208	1,208	—	—	—	—	—	—	—	—	—	
Credit from Monetary Authorities	26g	3,351	3,358	7	7	7	7	7	7	7	7	20,477	
Capital Accounts	27a	20,802	21,972	20,709	22,359	23,260	24,203	25,169	28,636	29,923	32,358	33,243	
Other Items (Net)	27r	−1,776	−678	−4,105	−3,755	−3,677	−4,135	−4,708	−5,736	−5,233	−5,246	−6,126	
Monetary Survey						*Millions of Ouguiyas: End of Period*							
Foreign Assets (Net)	31n	−30,273	−32,711	−24,616	−10,874	−2,162	411	7,165	24,073	26,077	56,367	62,393	....
Domestic Credit	32	52,975	52,479	32,877	21,077	12,992	4,374	557	−6,027	1,203	−21,978	−20,781	
Claims on Central Govt. (Net)	32an	11,159	9,289	1,351	−14,421	−25,419	−36,573	−47,559	−65,807	−68,714	−105,510	−112,177	
Claims on Nonfin.Pub.Enterprises	32c	60	60	60	60	60	60	60	60	60	60	60	
Claims on Private Sector	32d	41,707	43,081	31,417	35,389	38,302	40,838	48,007	59,671	69,808	83,423	91,287	
Claims on Nonbank Financial Inst	32g	49	49	49	49	49	49	49	49	49	49	49	
Money	34	20,938	19,816	18,202	16,227	17,579	18,504	19,675	24,151	27,721	28,910	32,202	
Quasi-Money	35	6,635	7,612	7,817	8,476	9,101	9,282	8,708	8,800	10,929	13,192	14,313	
Restricted Deposits	36b	29	91	147	91	82	55	154	225	49	49	49	
Central Govt. Lending Funds	36f	1,208	1,208	—	—	—	—	—	—	—	—	—	
Other Items (Net)	37r	−6,108	−8,959	−17,905	−14,591	−15,932	−23,649	−20,815	−15,130	−11,418	−7,762	−4,957	
Money plus Quasi-Money	35l	27,573	27,428	26,019	24,703	26,680	27,786	28,383	32,951	38,650	42,102	46,515	....
Interest Rates						*Percent Per Annum*							
Discount Rate (End of Period)	60	....	....	....	....	....	....	....	....	....	....	11.00	....
Deposit Rate	60l	....	....	....	....	....	....	....	....	....	....	8.00	....
Lending Rate	60p	....	....	....	....	....	....	....	....	....	....	21.00	....
Prices						*Index Numbers (2000=100): Period Averages*							
Consumer Prices	64	70.9	73.8	78.6	82.3	86.1	93.1	96.8	100.0	104.7	108.8	114.4	126.3

		1993	1994	1995	1996	1997	1998	1999	2000	2001	2002	2003	2004
Intl. Transactions & Positions													
Balance of Payments					*Millions of US Dollars: Minus Sign Indicates Debit*								
Current Account, n.i.e...................	**78ald**	−174.0	−69.9	22.1	91.3	47.8	77.2	....	....	....	....	....	....
Goods: Exports f.o.b....................	**78aad**	403.0	399.7	476.4	480.0	423.6	358.6	....	....	....	....	....	....
Goods: Imports f.o.b....................	**78abd**	−400.4	−352.3	−292.6	−346.1	−316.5	−318.7	....	....	....	....	....	....
Trade Balance............................	**78acd**	2.6	47.4	183.8	133.9	107.2	40.0	....	....	....	....	....	....
Services: Credit...........................	**78add**	21.4	26.0	27.9	31.6	34.9	34.0	....	....	....	....	....	....
Services: Debit............................	**78aed**	−184.9	−181.1	−217.0	−231.3	−200.0	−152.5	....	....	....	....	....	....
Balance on Goods & Services......	**78afd**	−160.9	−107.7	−5.3	−65.8	−57.9	−78.6	....	....	....	....	....	....
Income: Credit............................	**78agd**	.8	1.1	1.3	.9	1.4	2.5	....	....	....	....	....	....
Income: Debit.............................	**78ahd**	−97.6	−47.7	−49.5	−45.9	−40.3	−34.0	....	....	....	....	....	....
Balance on Gds, Serv. & Inc.........	**78aid**	−257.8	−154.3	−53.5	−110.8	−96.8	−110.2	....	....	....	....	....	....
Current Transfers, n.i.e.: Credit......	**78ajd**	110.3	113.3	94.7	217.5	157.9	198.3	....	....	....	....	....	....
Current Transfers: Debit..............	**78akd**	−26.5	−28.9	−19.2	−15.5	−13.3	−10.8	....	....	....	....	....	....
Capital Account, n.i.e....................	**78bcd**	—	—	—	—	—	—	....	....	....	....	....	....
Capital Account, n.i.e.: Credit........	**78bad**	—	—	—	—	—	—	....	....	....	....	....	....
Capital Account: Debit..................	**78bbd**	—	—	—	—	—	—	....	....	....	....	....	....
Financial Account, n.i.e.................	**78bjd**	−134.8	−11.4	−10.2	−86.1	−17.3	−25.9	....	....	....	....	....	....
Direct Investment Abroad..............	**78bdd**	—	—	—	—	—	—	....	....	....	....	....	....
Dir. Invest. in Rep. Econ., n.i.e.......	**78bed**	16.1	2.1	7.0	—	—	.1	....	....	....	....	....	....
Portfolio Investment Assets...........	**78bfd**	—	—	—	—	—	—	....	....	....	....	....	....
Equity Securities........................	**78bkd**	—	—	—	—	—	—	....	....	....	....	....	....
Debt Securities..........................	**78bld**	—	—	—	—	—	—	....	....	....	....	....	....
Portfolio Investment Liab., n.i.e......	**78bgd**	−.1	−.2	−.5	−.4	—	−.4	....	....	....	....	....	....
Equity Securities........................	**78bmd**	—	—	—	—	—	—	....	....	....	....	....	....
Debt Securities..........................	**78bnd**	−.1	−.2	−.5	−.4	—	−.4	....	....	....	....	....	....
Financial Derivatives Assets...........	**78bwd**	....	....	....	....	....	....	....	....	....	....	....	....
Financial Derivatives Liabilities.......	**78bxd**	....	....	....	....	....	....	....	....	....	....	....	....
Other Investment Assets...............	**78bhd**	170.5	169.3	211.5	236.0	191.1	190.1	....	....	....	....	....	....
Monetary Authorities..................	**78bod**	....	....	....	....	....	....	....	....	....	....	....	....
General Government..................	**78bpd**	−.8	−2.2	−.4	−.2	—	—	....	....	....	....	....	....
Banks......................................	**78bqd**	—	—	—	—	—	—	....	....	....	....	....	....
Other Sectors...........................	**78brd**	171.3	171.5	211.9	236.2	191.1	190.1	....	....	....	....	....	....
Other Investment Liab., n.i.e.........	**78bid**	−321.3	−182.6	−228.2	−321.6	−208.4	−215.7	....	....	....	....	....	....
Monetary Authorities..................	**78bsd**	—	—	—	—	—	—	....	....	....	....	....	....
General Government..................	**78btd**	−137.6	−7.0	.2	−.2	5.3	.7	....	....	....	....	....	....
Banks......................................	**78bud**	−18.8	—	—	—	—	—	....	....	....	....	....	....
Other Sectors...........................	**78bvd**	−164.9	−175.5	−228.4	−321.4	−213.7	−216.4	....	....	....	....	....	....
Net Errors and Omissions................	**78cad**	26.7	−23.5	−18.1	−1.0	−3.0	−8.1	....	....	....	....	....	....
Overall Balance.........................	**78cbd**	−282.1	−104.7	−6.2	4.2	27.6	43.2	....	....	....	....	....	....
Reserves and Related Items.............	**79dad**	282.1	104.7	6.2	−4.2	−27.6	−43.2	....	....	....	....	....	....
Reserve Assets...........................	**79dbd**	69.0	46.9	−42.9	−58.3	−58.8	−46.3	....	....	....	....	....	....
Use of Fund Credit and Loans........	**79dcd**	5.6	17.9	12.2	10.9	12.0	−6.9	....	....	....	....	....	....
Exceptional Financing...................	**79ded**	207.5	40.0	36.9	43.3	19.3	10.0	....	....	....	....	....	....
Government Finance					*Billions of Ouguiyas: Year Ending December 31*								
Deficit (-) or Surplus........................	**80**	−8.86	−3.19	1.58	11.26	....	....	....	....	....	....	....	....
Revenue.....................................	**81**	29.32	29.46	33.21	44.72	....	....	....	....	....	....	....	....
Grants Received..........................	**81z**	3.72	2.55	2.75	3.28	....	....	....	....	....	....	....	....
Exp. & Lending Minus Repay..........	**82z**	41.90	35.20	34.38	36.74	....	....	....	....	....	....	....	....
Financing													
Domestic..................................	**84a**	3.24	−1.47	−7.52	−15.81	....	....	....	....	....	....	....	....
Foreign.....................................	**85a**	5.62	4.66	5.94	4.55	....	....	....	....	....	....	....	....
National Accounts					*Millions of Ouguiyas*								
Househ.Cons.Expend.,incl.NPISHs....	**96f**	87,887	87,863	79,984	99,913	111,297	113,422	....	....	....	....	....	....
Government Consumption Expend...	**91f**	24,814	25,883	30,072	31,111	32,456	23,525	....	....	....	....	....	....
Gross Fixed Capital Formation.........	**93e**	17,314	20,147	23,684	17,326	25,094		....	....	....	....	....	....
Changes in Inventories....................	**93i**	3,963	3,590	4,308	9,015	2,626	....	....	....	....	....	....	....
Exports of Goods and Services..........	**90c**	51,167	52,479	65,306	70,066	67,477	52,795	....	....	....	....	....	....
Imports of Goods and Services (-).....	**98c**	70,601	65,800	66,015	79,113	78,332	46,562	....	....	....	....	....	....
Gross Domestic Product (GDP).........	**99b**	114,544	124,162	137,339	148,318	160,618		....	....	....	....	....	....
					Millions: Midyear Estimates								
Population................................	**99z**	2.18	2.24	2.30	2.36	2.43	2.50	2.57	2.64	2.72	2.81	2.89	2.98

		1993	1994	1995	1996	1997	1998	1999	2000	2001	2002	2003	2004
Exchange Rates							*Rupees per SDR: End of Period*							
Market Rate	aa	25.625	26.077	26.258	25.842	30.041	34.896	34.955	36.327	38.197	39.694	38.766	43.802
						Rupees per US Dollar: End of Period (ae) Period Average (rf)								
Market Rate	ae	18.656	17.863	17.664	17.972	22.265	24.784	25.468	27.882	30.394	29.197	26.088	28.204
Market Rate	rf	17.648	17.960	17.386	17.948	21.057	23.993	25.186	26.250	29.129	29.962	27.901	27.499
Fund Position							*Millions of SDRs: End of Period*							
Quota	2f.s	73.3	73.3	73.3	73.3	73.3	73.3	101.6	101.6	101.6	101.6	101.6	101.6
SDRs	1b.s	21.0	21.3	21.7	22.2	22.5	22.8	16.1	16.5	16.8	17.0	17.2	17.5
Reserve Position in the Fund	1c.s	7.3	7.3	7.3	7.4	7.4	7.4	14.5	14.5	14.5	14.5	21.9	21.9
Total Fund Cred.&Loans Outstg	2tl	—	—	—	—	—	—	—	—	—	—	—	—
International Liquidity						*Millions of US Dollars Unless Otherwise Indicated: End of Period*								
Total Reserves minus Gold	1l.d	757.0	747.6	863.3	896.1	693.3	559.0	731.0	897.4	835.6	1,227.4	1,577.3	1,605.9
SDRs	1b.d	28.9	31.2	32.2	31.9	30.3	32.2	22.1	21.4	21.1	23.2	25.6	27.2
Reserve Position in the Fund	1c.d	10.1	10.7	10.9	10.6	9.9	10.4	19.9	18.9	18.2	19.7	32.5	34.0
Foreign Exchange	1d.d	718.1	705.7	820.2	853.7	653.0	516.5	689.1	857.1	796.3	1,184.5	1,519.2	1,544.7
Gold (Million Fine Troy Ounces)	1ad	.062	.062	.062	.062	.062	.062	.062	.062	.062	.062	.062	.062
Gold (National Valuation)	1and	3.9	4.0	4.1	4.0	6.1	11.9	12.3	12.3	12.3	12.3	21.1	23.9
Government Assets	3bad	.1	.1	....	....	....	....	....	....	....	....	....	....
Monetary Authorities: Other Liab	4..d	.6	1.9	.7	1.1	.9	.6	.2	.7	.3	.6	2.8	3.7
Deposit Money Banks: Assets	7a.d	160.4	178.3	264.2	263.6	327.4	361.0	383.8	400.2	427.0	465.5	503.1	512.5
Liabilities	7b.d	28.2	39.8	67.5	59.5	38.4	127.9	104.3	106.6	98.3	196.7	225.3	267.1
Monetary Authorities							*Millions of Rupees: End of Period*							
Foreign Assets	11	14,194.9	13,425.7	15,322.0	16,176.8	15,571.8	14,150.3	18,930.9	25,366.1	25,772.9	36,195.4	41,698.1	45,968.6
Claims on Central Government	12a	1,021.4	1,741.9	654.7	914.5	1,662.5	4,994.9	2,223.5	2,196.1	2,210.7	1,743.9	551.8	1,591.0
Claims on Deposit Money Banks	12e	523.5	291.0	672.8	446.2	410.8	707.8	375.1	328.3	726.6	2,222.7	2,188.6	2,022.6
Reserve Money	14	7,992.6	8,403.1	9,628.3	9,123.0	8,923.4	9,759.6	10,522.3	11,763.5	12,989.7	14,920.7	16,314.1	18,996.5
of which: Currency Outside DMBs	14a	4,230.9	4,412.2	4,847.2	5,050.7	5,410.4	5,832.9	6,126.7	6,647.6	7,329.0	8,286.0	9,347.0	10,731.2
Liabs. of Central Bank: Securities	16ac	1,579.0	434.0	649.9	2,955.1	430.2	—	—	—	—	8,499.0	9,529.2	
Foreign Liabilities	16c	11.1	33.2	12.1	19.9	20.7	14.8	5.7	19.2	10.4	17.9	72.1	103.5
Central Government Deposits	16d	12.0	6.2	452.7	251.2	3.1	13.6	3.4	3,421.0	757.7	9,394.2	5,734.0	1,903.9
Capital Accounts	17a	436.3	443.6	446.4	439.9	506.0	582.4	583.3	604.9	634.4	657.9	643.3	722.6
Other Items (Net)	17r	5,708.8	6,138.6	5,460.1	4,748.5	7,761.8	9,482.6	10,414.7	12,081.9	14,318.1	15,171.3	13,176.0	18,326.5
Deposit Money Banks							*Millions of Rupees: End of Period*							
Reserves	20	3,757.8	3,982.4	4,740.9	4,067.2	3,506.9	3,899.8	4,365.3	5,030.0	5,512.9	6,523.1	6,853.5	8,062.7
Claims on Mon.Author.: Securities	20c	1,517.7	434.0	490.9	2,237.4	190.2	—	—	—	—	—	5,595.3	5,700.2
Foreign Assets	21	2,991.6	3,185.7	4,667.7	4,736.9	7,289.0	8,947.3	9,775.5	11,159.4	12,978.1	13,591.6	13,124.9	14,454.4
Claims on Central Government	22a	8,329.5	10,344.5	14,623.7	14,219.6	17,025.7	13,318.5	15,759.0	15,001.3	18,286.5	28,648.0	32,361.7	39,070.6
Claims on Private Sector	22d	23,923.9	28,714.4	32,878.6	34,467.6	43,360.3	56,653.0	62,520.7	70,569.6	77,891.5	83,976.7	88,424.2	98,358.0
Claims on Other Banking Insts	22f	238.0	146.5	132.3	163.1	160.5	424.6	1,766.2	1,817.2	1,283.0	894.0	1,918.7	2,968.2
Demand Deposits	24	3,188.3	4,443.3	4,685.4	4,774.0	5,194.5	5,730.2	5,844.8	6,563.6	7,974.9	9,759.0	10,940.5	12,682.7
Time, Savings,& Fgn.Currency Dep	25	33,198.5	36,754.5	44,574.4	48,406.8	57,201.3	63,819.9	74,851.6	81,573.9	89,789.2	100,200.4	110,821.6	124,975.4
Money Market Instruments	26aa	98.8	93.9	90.9	196.3	167.9	197.3	104.0	126.4	185.2	148.0	193.9	131.5
Restricted Deposits	26b	10.9	30.4	27.7	24.9	15.7	17.4	43.1	14.3	26.5	25.9	74.9	39.0
Foreign Liabilities	26c	525.7	710.7	1,192.9	1,068.8	855.5	3,169.0	2,655.5	2,971.7	2,986.4	5,741.7	5,877.6	7,533.2
Central Government Deposits	26d	277.9	84.2	1,468.0	319.6	277.0	132.0	264.4	190.9	225.0	234.1	207.7	165.0
Credit from Monetary Authorities	26g	329.0	156.2	550.0	—	250.0	475.0	250.0	250.0	660.3	2,171.0	2,157.0	1,936.4
Capital Accounts	27a	4,758.6	5,144.4	5,447.8	6,620.4	7,842.4	9,092.1	10,848.6	11,953.6	12,037.2	14,477.0	15,602.8	19,214.2
Other Items (Net)	27r	−1,629.2	−610.1	−503.0	−1,519.0	−271.7	610.3	−675.3	−66.9	2,067.3	876.3	2,402.3	1,936.7
Monetary Survey							*Millions of Rupees: End of Period*							
Foreign Assets (Net)	31n	16,649.7	15,867.5	18,784.7	19,825.0	21,984.6	19,913.8	26,045.2	33,534.6	35,754.2	44,027.4	48,873.3	52,786.3
Domestic Credit	32	33,222.9	40,856.9	46,368.6	49,194.0	61,928.9	75,245.4	82,001.6	85,972.5	98,689.0	105,634.3	117,314.7	139,918.9
Claims on Central Govt. (Net)	32an	9,061.0	11,996.0	13,357.7	14,563.3	18,408.1	18,167.8	17,714.7	13,585.5	19,514.5	20,763.6	26,971.8	38,592.7
Claims on Private Sector	32d	23,923.9	28,714.4	32,878.6	34,467.6	43,360.3	56,653.0	62,520.7	70,569.6	77,891.5	83,976.7	88,424.2	98,358.0
Claims on Other Banking Insts	32f	238.0	146.5	132.3	163.1	160.5	424.6	1,766.2	1,817.2	1,283.0	894.0	1,918.7	2,968.2
Money	34	7,423.2	8,864.0	9,572.8	9,829.8	10,611.0	11,590.0	12,001.8	13,297.1	15,451.7	18,156.6	20,401.1	23,616.5
Quasi-Money	35	33,198.5	36,754.5	44,574.4	48,406.8	57,201.3	63,819.9	74,851.6	81,573.9	89,789.2	100,200.4	110,821.6	124,975.4
Money Market Instruments	36aa	98.8	93.9	90.9	196.3	167.9	197.3	104.0	126.4	185.2	148.0	193.9	131.5
Liabs. of Central Bank: Securities	36ac	61.3		159.0	717.7	240.0	—	—	—	—	—	2,903.7	3,829.0
Restricted Deposits	36b	10.9	30.4	27.7	24.9	15.7	17.4	43.1	14.3	26.5	25.9	74.9	39.0
Capital Accounts	37a	5,194.9	5,588.0	5,894.2	7,060.3	8,348.4	9,674.5	11,431.9	12,558.5	12,671.6	15,134.9	16,246.1	19,936.8
Other Items (Net)	37r	3,885.0	5,393.7	4,834.3	2,783.3	7,329.3	9,860.1	9,614.3	11,936.7	16,319.1	15,995.9	15,546.7	20,177.0
Money plus Quasi-Money	35l	40,621.7	45,618.5	54,147.2	58,236.6	67,812.3	75,409.9	86,853.4	94,871.0	105,240.9	118,357.0	131,222.7	148,591.9
Other Banking Institutions							*Millions of Rupees: End of Period*							
Deposits	45	373.8	397.0	420.4	448.2	494.8	557.3	611.0	670.9	762.6	1,105.5	....	....
Liquid Liabilities	55l	40,995.5	46,015.5	54,567.6	58,684.8	68,307.1	75,967.2	87,464.4	95,541.9	106,003.5	119,462.5	....	....
Interest Rates							*Percent Per Annum*							
Discount Rate (End of Period)	60	8.30	13.80	11.40	11.82	10.46	17.19	....	....	....	....	....	....
Money Market Rate	60b	7.73	10.23	10.35	9.96	9.43	8.99	10.01	7.66	7.25	6.20	3.22	1.33
Savings Rate	60k	7.50	8.50	8.08	8.00	8.00	8.08	9.00	7.46	7.08	6.44	5.25	3.88
Deposit Rate	60l	8.40	11.04	12.23	10.77	9.08	9.28	10.92	9.61	9.78	9.88	9.53	8.15
Lending Rate	60p	16.58	18.92	20.81	20.81	18.92	19.92	21.63	20.77	21.10	21.00	21.00	21.00
Prices and Labor							*Index Numbers (2000=100): Period Averages*							
Share Prices	62	63.2	96.2	92.5	81.6	92.6	110.4	101.5	100.0	91.3	90.0	115.6	156.1
Consumer Prices	64	64.9	69.6	73.8	78.7	† 84.0	89.8	96.0	100.0	† 105.4	112.1	116.5	122.0
							Number in Thousands: Period Averages							
Labor Force	67d	485	499	484	482	491	499	507	514	522	524	531	533
Employment	67e	290	292	290	287	288	295	297	298	301	296	296	488
Unemployment	67c	....	....	....	28	32	34	39	45	48	51	54	45
Unemployment Rate	67r	....	....	....	5.8	6.6	6.9	7.7	8.8	9.1	9.7	10.2	8.5

Mauritius 684

		1993	1994	1995	1996	1997	1998	1999	2000	2001	2002	2003	2004
Intl. Transactions & Positions							*Millions of Rupees*						
Exports............................	70	22,992	24,097	26,756	32,312	33,694	39,634	40,025	40,882	47,511	53,893	53,022	55,223
Imports, c.i.f.............................	71	30,319	34,548	34,363	41,082	46,093	49,811	56,629	54,928	57,940	64,608	65,942	76,577
Imports, f.o.b.................................	71.v	27,507	31,601	31,508	38,073	42,570	46,015	....	....	....	....	....	....
							2000=100						
Volume of Exports.........................	72	80.2	80.4	84.1	88.6	92.0	† 95.4	97.7	100.0	115.6	120.7	112.3	106.4
Volume of Imports.........................	73	75.6	80.3	75.5	84.1	92.5	99.3	106.5	100.0	97.7	103.4	100.6	97.1
Unit Value of Exports......................	74	70.0	73.2	77.7	86.4	† 89.3	101.8	101.1	100.0	101.8	110.7	116.7	128.6
Unit Value of Imports......................	75	68.7	73.7	78.0	83.5	† 85.5	90.6	96.2	100.0	107.7	112.8	120.3	144.9
Balance of Payments							*Millions of US Dollars: Minus Sign Indicates Debit*						
Current Account, n.i.e...................	78ald	−92.0	−232.1	−21.9	34.0	−88.9	3.3	−124.2	−36.9	276.1	249.4	93.2	−107.5
Goods: Exports f.o.b...................	78aad	1,334.4	1,376.9	1,571.7	1,810.6	1,600.1	1,669.3	1,589.2	1,552.2	1,628.2	1,801.3	1,898.1	2,004.3
Goods: Imports f.o.b...................	78abd	−1,576.0	−1,773.9	−1,812.2	−2,136.3	−2,036.1	−1,933.3	−2,107.9	−1,944.4	−1,846.0	−2,012.6	−2,201.1	−2,579.4
Trade Balance......................	78acd	−241.6	−397.0	−240.5	−325.7	−436.0	−264.0	−518.7	−392.1	−217.7	−211.3	−303.0	−575.0
Services: Credit.....................	78add	566.2	632.7	777.7	960.8	893.7	916.9	1,035.6	1,070.2	1,222.0	1,148.7	1,280.1	1,455.6
Services: Debit......................	78aed	−521.7	−546.4	−641.3	−672.9	−656.3	−718.0	−728.2	−762.5	−810.1	−792.7	−906.3	−1,023.5
Balance on Goods & Services......	78afd	−197.1	−310.6	−104.2	−37.9	−198.6	−65.1	−211.3	−84.5	194.1	144.7	70.8	−142.9
Income: Credit.......................	78agd	70.0	31.7	52.2	31.1	47.0	47.8	43.0	48.7	75.2	79.9	47.0	51.8
Income: Debit........................	78ahd	−66.5	−56.4	−71.3	−75.1	−64.6	−74.4	−59.5	−64.9	−60.9	−66.7	−77.1	−65.7
Balance on Gds, Serv. & Inc.........	78aid	−193.6	−335.3	−123.3	−81.8	−216.3	−91.7	−227.8	−100.7	208.4	157.9	40.8	−156.8
Current Transfers, n.i.e.: Credit.....	78ajd	115.9	129.6	146.8	182.8	206.4	186.8	196.4	167.6	193.1	195.3	163.0	168.1
Current Transfers: Debit...............	78akd	−14.4	−26.3	−45.4	−67.0	−79.0	−91.8	−92.8	−103.8	−125.4	−103.8	−110.6	−118.7
Capital Account, n.i.e...................	78bcd	−1.5	−1.3	−1.1	−.8	−.5	−.8	−.5	−.6	−1.4	−1.9	−.9	−1.6
Capital Account, n.i.e.: Credit.......	78bad	—	—	—	—	—	—	—	—	.4	—	—	—
Capital Account: Debit..................	78bbd	−1.5	−1.3	−1.1	−.8	−.5	−.8	−.5	−.6	−1.8	−1.9	−.9	−1.6
Financial Account, n.i.e.................	78bjd	19.3	41.4	25.1	91.9	−18.6	−26.0	180.5	258.0	−240.2	84.2	89.7	−72.7
Direct Investment Abroad............	78bdd	−33.2	−1.1	−3.6	−2.7	−3.2	−13.7	−6.4	−13.0	−2.9	−8.7	6.0	−31.8
Dir. Invest. in Rep. Econ., n.i.e......	78bed	14.7	20.0	18.7	36.7	55.3	12.2	49.4	265.6	−27.7	32.1	62.6	13.9
Portfolio Investment Assets...........	78bfd	−2.2	−.3	—	−2.0	−96.8	43.6	59.5	−18.8	−17.7	−18.3	−27.1	−52.4
Equity Securities....................	78bkd	—	—	—	—	—	—	−3.3	59.5	−18.8	−17.7	−18.3	−27.1	−52.4
Debt Securities......................	78bld	−2.2	−.3	—	−2.0	−96.8	46.9	—	—	—	—	—	—
Portfolio Investment Liab., n.i.e......	78bgd	—	2.1	175.9	36.8	30.6	−28.7	−15.3	−120.4	−1.6	.9	8.9	15.3
Equity Securities....................	78bmd	—	2.1	22.0	36.8	30.6	5.0	−15.3	−3.5	−8.7	−.7	8.1	19.3
Debt Securities......................	78bnd	—	—	154.0	—	—	−33.7	—	−116.8	7.1	1.6	.8	−3.9
Financial Derivatives Assets...........	78bwd	....	....	—	—	—	—	—	—	....	....	....	....
Financial Derivatives Liabilities.......	78bxd	....	....	—	—	—	—	—	—	....	....	....	....
Other Investment Assets..............	78bhd	−26.7	−64.6	−136.4	17.9	−115.7	−66.7	−245.9	−307.6	−253.0	−106.7	−22.8	−49.4
Monetary Authorities..................	78bod	—	—	....	....	....	....	....	....	....	....	—	—
General Government..................	78bpd	—	—	—	—	—	—	—	—	—	—	—	—
Banks.................................	78bqd	−49.0	−11.5	−85.2	−3.9	−121.2	−69.1	−32.9	−51.5	−61.7	−20.4	14.1	−44.2
Other Sectors.........................	78brd	22.3	−53.1	−51.2	21.8	5.5	2.4	−213.0	−256.1	−191.3	−86.2	−36.9	−5.2
Other Investment Liab., n.i.e..........	78bid	66.6	85.2	−29.5	5.1	111.2	27.3	339.4	452.1	62.7	184.9	62.0	31.6
Monetary Authorities..................	78bsd	—	—	—	—	—	—	—	—	—	—	—	—
General Government..................	78btd	1.4	−14.1	−18.8	−20.4	9.0	−14.2	−11.4	91.6	−118.7	34.5	−8.2	−7.3
Banks.................................	78bud	26.6	9.2	27.7	−6.9	−10.1	96.4	−20.4	13.7	.4	93.1	6.1	56.7
Other Sectors.........................	78bvd	38.6	90.1	−38.5	32.5	112.3	−54.9	371.2	346.8	181.0	57.3	64.1	−17.7
Net Errors and Omissions.................	78cad	81.2	148.5	106.7	−76.8	73.4	−41.9	133.9	10.1	−86.3	9.4	40.4	154.3
Overall Balance..........................	78cbd	7.0	−43.5	108.8	48.3	−34.6	−65.4	189.7	230.6	−51.8	341.1	222.4	−27.5
Reserves and Related Items.............	79dad	−7.0	43.5	−108.8	−48.3	34.6	65.4	−189.7	−230.6	51.8	−341.1	−222.4	27.5
Reserve Assets........................	79dbd	−7.0	43.5	−108.8	−48.3	34.6	65.4	−189.7	−230.6	51.8	−341.1	−222.4	27.5
Use of Fund Credit and Loans........	79dcd	—	—	—	—	—	—	—	—	—	—	—	—
Exceptional Financing...................	79ded	—	—	—	—	—	—	—	—	—	—	—	....
International Investment Position							*Millions of US Dollars*						
Assets.................................	79aad	....	....	....	....	....	....	....	....	....	....	....	....
Direct Investment Abroad..............	79abd	—	—	—	—	—	—	—	—	—	—	—	—
Portfolio Investment......................	79acd	—	—	—	—	—	—	—	—	—	—	—	—
Equity Securities........................	79add	....	....	—	—	—	—	—	—	—	—	—	—
Debt Securities.........................	79aed	....	....	—	—	—	—	—	—	—	—	—	—
Financial Derivatives....................	79ald	....	....	....	....	....	....	....	....	....	....	....	....
Other Investment.........................	79afd	187.0	243.0	364.8	342.9	386.1	394.7	652.3	887.2	1,055.2	1,208.1	1,375.9	1,328.0
Monetary Authorities..................	79agd	—	—	—	—	—	—	—	—	—	—	—	—
General Government..................	79ahd	—	—	—	—	—	—	—	—	—	—	—	—
Banks.................................	79aid	126.4	142.5	227.9	228.4	298.8	335.1	383.8	400.2	427.0	465.5	503.1	512.5
Other Sectors.........................	79ajd	60.6	100.5	136.9	114.6	87.3	59.6	268.5	487.0	628.2	742.6	872.7	815.5
Reserve Assets..........................	79akd	760.9	751.8	867.5	900.2	699.5	571.0	743.3	909.8	848.0	1,239.8	1,598.4	1,629.9
Liabilities..............................	79lad	....	....	....	....	....	....	....	....	....	....	....	....
Dir. Invest. in Rep. Economy..........	79lbd	....	....	....	....	....	....	....	....	....	....	....	....
Portfolio Investment......................	79lcd	—	—	156.3	167.2	150.9	117.7	168.1	40.0	35.0	37.3	51.6	62.5
Equity Securities........................	79ldd	....	....	—	—	—	—	40.2	33.4	22.2	22.5	33.8	49.9
Debt Securities.........................	79led	....	....	156.3	167.2	150.9	117.7	127.9	6.6	12.9	14.9	17.8	12.7
Financial Derivatives....................	79lld	....	....	....	....	....	....	....	....	....	....	....	....
Other Investment.........................	79lfd	937.5	1,128.3	1,189.2	1,259.9	1,167.2	1,202.3	1,483.6	1,831.0	1,810.6	2,128.8	2,470.7	2,403.3
Monetary Authorities..................	79lgd	—	—	—	—	—	—	—	—	—	—	—	—
General Government..................	79lhd	316.6	324.8	328.3	352.6	300.1	294.1	273.4	358.3	230.2	285.6	300.4	294.4
Banks.................................	79lid	28.2	39.8	67.5	59.5	38.4	127.9	104.3	106.6	98.3	196.7	225.3	267.3
Other Sectors.........................	79ljd	592.7	763.7	793.4	847.9	828.7	780.3	1,105.9	1,366.1	1,482.1	1,646.5	1,945.0	1,841.7

		1993	1994	1995	1996	1997	1998	1999	2000	2001	2002	2003	2004
Government Finance						*Millions of Rupees: Year Ending June 30*							
Deficit (-) or Surplus	80	† 19	† −167	−812	−3,083	−3,427	858	† −1,559	−1,458	† 1,170	−5,608	−6,012	....
Revenue	81	12,364	14,076	14,398	14,469	18,277	20,327	† 23,082	25,587	† 25,374	27,418	32,447	....
Grants Received	81z	78	130	262	221	63	216	† 135	161	† 199	317	363	....
Expenditure	82	12,148	14,271	15,502	17,280	20,260	21,446	† 25,479	27,032	† 30,592	32,843	37,863	....
Lending Minus Repayments	83	275	102	−31	493	1,506	−1,761	† −703	174	† −6,189	500	959	....
Financing													
Net Borrowing: Domestic	84a	† 725	† 1,737	2,059	1,544	3,228	3,010	† 1,191	3,560	† 2,241	9,419	12,822	....
Net borrowing: Foreign	85a	† −313	† −113	−371	2,374	198	−274	† −1,170	−510	† −3,584	1,030	87	....
Use of Cash Balances	87	† −431	† −1,458	−874	−834	2	−3,594	† 1,538	−1,592	† 172	−4,841	−6,897	....
Debt: Domestic	88a	11,696	14,149	17,311	19,215	21,921	22,857	† 24,326	29,424	† 33,764	48,973	63,531	....
Debt: Foreign	89a	5,712	5,766	5,778	9,159	9,666	10,752	† 10,037	9,891	† 6,816	8,785	9,074	....
National Accounts							*Millions of Rupees*							
Househ.Cons.Expend.,incl.NPISHs	96f	35,996	40,524	44,768	49,759	55,056	62,436	68,710	73,939	80,219	86,736	96,153	110,847
Government Consumption Expend	91f	7,486	8,658	9,212	10,565	11,508	12,648	14,193	15,582	16,749	19,855	22,272	25,022
Gross Fixed Capital Formation	93e	16,101	19,400	16,798	20,181	23,481	23,082	29,676	28,069	29,798	31,074	35,554	37,729
Changes in Inventories	93i	1,532	1,050	1,208	−874	2,358	2,230	−1,373	2,576	−2,375	801	902	4,908
Exports of Goods and Services	90c	33,543	36,249	41,205	50,465	54,194	65,711	69,099	73,841	90,463	88,301	88,716	95,177
Imports of Goods and Services (-)	98c	37,021	41,833	42,908	51,010	58,498	66,543	72,861	74,513	82,636	83,964	86,694	99,215
Gross Domestic Product (GDP)	99b	57,637	64,048	70,283	79,086	88,099	99,564	107,444	119,494	132,218	142,802	156,903	174,468
Net Primary Income from Abroad	98.n	63	−443	−332	−789	−372	−637	−594	−783	393	396	−833	−388
Gross National Income (GNI)	99a	57,700	63,605	69,951	78,297	87,727	98,927	106,850	118,711	132,611	143,198	156,070	174,080
GDP Volume 1992 Prices	99b.p	52,779	55,016	57,446	60,638	64,133	67,996	69,970	76,378	80,410	79,765	82,834	86,770
GDP Volume (2000=100)	99bvp	69.1	72.0	75.2	79.4	84.0	89.0	91.6	100.0	105.3	104.4	108.5	113.6
GDP Deflator (2000=100)	99bip	69.8	74.4	78.2	83.4	87.8	93.6	98.2	100.0	105.1	114.4	121.1	128.5
						Millions: Midyear Estimates								
Population	99z	1.10	1.11	1.12	1.14	1.15	1.16	1.17	1.19	1.20	1.21	1.22	1.23

		1993	1994	1995	1996	1997	1998	1999	2000	2001	2002	2003	2004
Exchange Rates						*Pesos per SDR: End of Period*							
Market Rate..............aa=.........	wa	4.2661	7.7737	11.3605	11.2893	10.9064	13.8902	13.0585	12.4717	11.4894	14.0201	16.6964	17.4943
						Pesos per US Dollar: End of Period (we) Period Average (wf)							
Market Rate..............ae=.........	we	3.1059	5.3250	7.6425	7.8509	8.0833	9.8650	9.5143	9.5722	9.1423	10.3125	11.2360	11.2648
Market Rate..............rf=..........	wf	3.1156	3.3751	6.4194	7.5994	7.9185	9.1360	9.5604	9.4556	9.3423	9.6560	10.7890	11.2860
Fund Position						*Millions of SDRs: End of Period*							
Quota...............................	2f.s	1,753	1,753	1,753	1,753	1,753	1,753	2,586	2,586	2,586	2,586	2,586	2,586
SDRs...............................	1b.s	163	121	1,074	179	490	240	575	281	283	288	292	299
Reserve Position in the Fund...........	1c.s	—	—	—	—	—	—	—	—	—	226	527	578
Total Fund Cred.&Loans Outstg.......	2tl	3,485	2,644	10,648	9,234	6,735	5,952	3,259	—	—	—	—	—
International Liquidity						*Millions of US Dollars Unless Otherwise Indicated: End of Period*							
Total Reserves minus Gold.............	1l.d	25,110	6,278	16,847	19,433	28,797	31,799	31,782	35,509	44,741	50,594	58,956	64,141
SDRs............................	1b.d	223	177	1,597	257	661	337	790	366	356	392	433	465
Reserve Position in the Fund.........	1c.d	—	—	—	—	—	—	—	—	—	308	782	898
Foreign Exchange..................	1d.d	24,886	6,101	15,250	19,176	28,136	31,461	30,992	35,142	44,384	49,895	57,740	62,778
Gold (Million Fine Troy Ounces)........	1ad	.484	.426	.514	.255	.190	.223	.159	.249	.231	.225	.170	.139
Monetary Authorities: Other Liab.....	4..d	75	66	91	84	560	552	377	226	214	170	153	147
Banking Institutions: Assets........	7a.d	1,721	2,829	4,089	4,825	12,612	14,954	20,292	35,890	46,342	50,913	86,537	94,622
Liabilities............	7b.d	36,580	43,800	44,355	38,029	41,380	39,852	40,010	50,627	51,847	59,493	107,348	123,563
Nonbank Financial Insts.: Assets......	7e.d	....	....	....	....								
Liabilities..................	7f.d	....	....	....	....	—	—	—	—	—	—	—	—
Monetary Authorities						*Millions of Pesos: End of Period*							
Foreign Assets.....................	11	79,710	34,490	122,814	140,217	† 239,470	323,604	310,238	349,523	418,139	537,194	672,107	724,431
Claims on Central Government........	12a	9,864	2,000	13,211	10,488	† —							
Claims on Nonbank Pub.Fin.Insts....	12cg	21,227	38,043	78,001	70,327	† 43,023	55,753	63,827	69,722	73,290	69,642	67,006	59,353
Claims on Banking Institutions.........	12e	3,641	102,100	45,021	11,883	† 2,430	699	96,326	95,120	83,533	110,132	89,564	105,243
Claims on Nonbank Financial Insts.....	12g	—	—	—	—	† 38,043	38,043	36,099	33,033	30,527	27,558	25,053	22,548
Reserve Money......................	14	50,274	60,923	81,274	100,069	† 150,907	206,943	286,280	267,505	329,252	416,947	487,103	573,017
of which: Currency Outside Banks..	14a	43,351	52,035	60,839	74,338	† 94,185	115,917	164,158	181,938	198,849	232,082	263,387	300,977
Time & Foreign Currency Deposits....	15	592	10	6	12	† 4,795	3,736	7,756	13,151	4,567	14,034	16,707	19,455
Liabs. of Central Bank: Securities......	16ac					† —			21,834	156,725	225,051	231,806	232,996
Foreign Liabilities...................	16c	15,101	20,906	121,665	104,910	† 77,835	88,390	46,072	2,169	1,964	1,772	1,716	1,638
Central Government Deposits.........	16d	18,678	71,270	26,195	16,124	† 82,330	95,005	185,941	274,351	180,545	102,723	112,492	121,975
Liab. to Nonbank Pub.Fin.Insts.....	16dg	5,801	8,884	23,420	18,732	† 21,159	12,936	5,387	5	6	6		
Capital Accounts...................	17a	1,309	2,327	3,367	3,346	† 30,030	49,767	35,949	30,163	−4,447	24,470	24,712	−14,609
Other Items (Net)..................	17r	22,686	12,313	3,120	−10,279	† −44,090	−38,676	−60,893	−61,781	−63,123	−40,475	−20,806	−22,896
Banking Institutions						*Millions of Pesos: End of Period*							
Reserves...........................	20	7,679	10,879	117,373	241,398	† 55,773	72,038	115,255	72,543	116,266	183,561	223,982	271,152
Claims on Mon.Author.:Securities....	20c	—	—	—	—	† —	—	—	845	108,791	165,523	179,937	149,423
Foreign Assets.....................	21	5,344	15,065	31,250	37,877	† 102,614	147,522	193,066	344,894	424,932	531,501	972,431	1,054,985
Claims on Central Government........	22a	56,659	106,267	185,036	176,293	† 545,296	601,093	759,777	901,439	817,342	830,290	856,485	870,194
Claims on State and Local Govts....	22b	14,620	23,773	16,574	13,032	† 20,902	24,641	25,908	31,249	36,075	42,485	55,455	100,315
Claims on Nonfin.Pub.Enterprises....	22c	4,650	8,083	8,868	7,629	† 12,454	15,137	12,860	19,645	18,461	21,048	34,992	49,033
Claims on Nonbank Pub.Fin.Insts.....	22cg	1,841	3,388	69,246	210,476	† 289,200	399,857	556,972	559,866	685,400	749,380	704,830	635,224
Claims on Private Sector..............	22d	398,519	550,204	537,611	474,757	† 801,971	866,844	883,086	943,328	850,201	1,059,796	1,024,288	1,098,670
Claims on Nonbank Financial Insts.....	22g	33,413	45,092	47,955	25,187	† 39,385	63,719	85,691	47,044	114,423	62,907	112,503	119,061
Demand Deposits..................	24	100,549	93,080	87,695	131,732	† 173,026	193,564	233,478	273,265	324,282	364,664	415,909	435,392
Time, Savings,& Fgn.Currency Dep...	25	212,074	283,140	416,152	511,140	† 852,953	993,605	1,153,602	1,019,917	1,153,339	1,213,735	1,257,697	1,407,705
Money Market Instruments..............	26aa	24,283	30,693	50,762	52,031	† 241,844	255,835	324,367	320,638	501,203	514,256	494,021	541,336
Foreign Liabilities...................	26c	113,614	233,235	338,986	298,561	† 336,668	393,141	380,662	486,519	475,412	621,068	1,206,292	1,377,660
Central Government Deposits.........	26d	5,653	8,510	18,349	27,075	† 22,031	29,454	21,358	19,915	25,877	50,156	33,882	31,806
Liab. to Nonbank Pub.Fin.Insts.....	26dg	27,322	39,508	76,040	119,675	† 126,365	211,436	200,383	186,809	230,096	285,062	286,478	38,987
Credit from Monetary Authorities.....	26g	5,873	46,223	48,184	16,769	† 7,021	6,361	101,918	102,149	85,208	110,949	98,889	120,719
Liab. to Nonbank Financial Insts.......	26j				—	† 117,448	137,863	165,720	142,822	153,105	136,988	142,698	140,735
Capital Accounts...................	27a	34,919	44,014	21,911	20,970	† 26,784	41,678	42,913	38,862	9,833	43,560	41,888	299,701
Other Items (Net)..................	27r	−1,562	−15,652	−44,166	8,696	† −36,546	−72,087	8,213	329,958	213,536	306,054	187,149	−45,984
Banking Survey						*Millions of Pesos: End of Period*							
Foreign Assets (Net)...............	31n	−43,661	−204,586	−306,587	−225,377	† −72,419	−10,405	76,571	205,729	365,695	445,855	436,530	400,119
Domestic Credit....................	32	493,844	655,639	764,711	664,187	† 1,353,690	1,485,018	1,596,122	1,681,473	1,660,607	1,891,206	1,962,402	2,106,040
Claims on Central Govt. (Net).......	32an	42,192	28,487	153,703	143,582	† 440,935	476,633	552,478	607,173	610,919	677,411	710,111	716,413
Claims on State and Local Govts......	32b	14,620	23,773	16,574	13,032	† 20,902	24,641	25,908	31,249	36,075	42,485	55,455	100,315
Claims on Nonfin.Pub.Enterprises.....	32c	4,650	8,083	8,868	7,629	† 12,454	15,137	12,860	19,645	18,461	21,048	34,992	49,033
Claims on Private Sector...............	32d	398,969	550,204	537,611	474,757	† 801,971	866,844	883,086	943,328	850,201	1,059,796	1,024,288	1,098,670
Claims on Nonbank Financial Inst...	32g	33,413	45,092	47,955	25,187	† 77,428	101,762	121,790	80,077	144,951	90,466	137,556	141,609
Money.............................	34	143,900	145,115	148,534	206,070	† 267,211	323,912	407,601	465,485	527,513	596,746	679,296	736,369
Quasi-Money.......................	35	212,666	283,150	416,158	511,152	† 857,749	997,340	1,161,358	1,033,068	1,157,906	1,227,769	1,274,404	1,427,160
Money Market Instruments..............	36aa	24,283	30,693	50,762	52,031	† 241,844	255,835	324,367	320,638	501,203	514,256	494,021	541,336
Liabs. of Central Bank: Securities......	36ac	—	—	—	—	† —	—	—	20,989	47,934	59,528	51,869	83,573
Liab. to Nonbank Financial Insts.......	36j				—	† 117,448	137,863	165,720	142,822	153,105	136,988	142,698	140,735
Capital Accounts...................	37a	36,228	46,341	25,278	24,316	† 56,813	91,445	78,862	69,025	5,386	68,030	66,600	285,092
Other Items (Net)...................	37r	33,105	−54,246	−182,608	−354,760	† −259,795	−331,783	−465,217	−164,827	−366,746	−266,254	−309,955	−708,106
Money plus Quasi-Money............	35l	356,566	428,265	564,692	717,222	† 1,124,959	1,321,252	1,568,960	1,498,554	1,685,419	1,824,515	1,953,700	2,163,529

		1993	1994	1995	1996	1997	1998	1999	2000	2001	2002	2003	2004
Nonbank Financial Institutions		*Millions of Pesos End of Period*											
Reserves............	40	....	....	....	....	86	14,568	10,418	10,648	4,035	—	220	522
Claims on Mon.Author.:Securities....	40c	....	....	....	....	—	—	—	680	4,546	10,721	14,843	46,697
Foreign Assets............	41	....	....	....	....	—	—	—	—	—	—	—	—
Claims on Central Government........	42a	....	....	....	....	25,866	77,863	145,919	209,235	309,187	390,111	476,465	530,790
Claims on State and Local Govts......	42b	....	....	....	....	793	901	979	1,002	992	972	405	340
Claims on Nonfin.Pub.Enterprises.....	42c	....	....	....	....	—	—	—	—	—	—	—	—
Claims on Nonbank Pub.Fin.Insts.....	42cg	....	....	....	....	—	—	—	1,070	7,526	10,051	14,632	33,826
Claims on Private Sector..............	42d	....	....	....	....	39,982	46,419	54,664	63,399	82,886	118,860	146,328	165,559
Claims on Banking Institutions........	42e	....	....	....	....	149,809	159,688	183,637	150,659	143,735	135,919	134,225	133,187
Foreign Liabilities...........	46c	....	....	....	....	—	—	—	—	—	—	—	—
Central Government Deposits..........	46d	....	....	....	....	4,139	7,072	7,324	361	308	193	162	119
Credit from Monetary Authorities.....	46g	....	....	....	....	86,892	104,060	116,901	118,479	118,316	113,413	106,962	100,637
Credit from Banking Institutions.......	46h	....	....	....	....	6,662	6,912	5,779	6,577	9,298	7,199	7,528	7,009
Capital Accounts............	47a	....	....	....	....	117,831	200,830	299,582	361,997	475,557	585,509	701,529	822,775
Other Items (Net)...........	47r	....	....	....	....	1,012	−19,435	−33,969	−50,721	−50,572	−39,680	−29,063	−19,619
Financial Survey		*Millions of Pesos: End of Period*											
Foreign Assets (Net)............	51n	....	....	....	....	−72,419	−10,405	76,571	205,729	365,695	445,855	436,530	400,119
Domestic Credit..............	52	....	....	....	....	1,338,763	1,501,367	1,668,570	1,874,670	1,908,414	2,310,491	2,447,882	2,661,001
Claims on Central Govt. (Net).......	52an	....	....	....	....	462,662	547,424	691,073	816,047	919,798	1,067,329	1,186,414	1,247,084
Claims on State and Local Govts...	52b	....	....	....	....	21,695	25,542	26,887	32,251	37,067	43,457	55,860	100,655
Claims on Nonfin.Pub.Enterprises...	52c	....	....	....	....	12,454	15,137	12,860	19,645	18,461	21,048	34,992	49,033
Claims on Private Sector...............	52d	....	....	....	....	841,953	913,263	937,750	1,006,727	933,087	1,178,656	1,170,616	1,264,229
Liquid Liabilities...............	55l	....	....	....	....	1,124,873	1,306,684	1,558,542	1,487,906	1,681,384	1,824,515	1,953,480	2,163,007
Money Market Instruments..........	56aa	....	....	....	....	241,844	255,835	324,367	320,638	501,203	514,256	494,021	541,336
Liabs. of Central Bank: Securities.....	56ac	....	....	....	....	—	—	—	20,309	43,388	48,807	37,026	36,876
Capital Accounts............	57a	....	....	....	....	174,644	292,275	378,444	431,022	480,943	653,539	768,129	1,107,867
Other Items (Net)............	57r	....	....	....	....	−275,018	−363,833	−516,213	−179,475	−432,810	−284,770	−368,243	−787,966
Money (National Definitions)		*Millions of Pesos: End of Period*											
Base Money...................	19ma	47,193	56,935	66,809	83,991	108,891	131,528	188,718	208,943	225,580	263,937	303,614	340,178
M1...................	59ma	157,044	163,828	171,638	245,260	325,760	388,240	489,943	565,014	680,706	766,486	857,692	946,566
M2...................	59mb	469,738	554,930	754,407	995,166	1,290,063	1,663,220	2,030,685	2,284,030	2,731,762	3,027,890	3,420,526	3,777,231
M3...................	59mc	540,845	657,102	784,495	1,025,835	1,320,540	1,689,755	2,047,566	2,312,408	2,760,176	3,053,144	3,454,361	3,866,386
M4...................	59md	580,326	724,203	869,209	1,116,079	1,400,372	1,775,644	2,121,261	2,368,789	2,809,004	3,096,919	3,487,026	3,905,357
M4a...................	59mda	590,378	737,608	898,115	1,183,256	1,521,907	1,903,797	2,278,628	2,571,000	2,982,719	3,304,619	3,750,715	4,222,005
M4 National Currency........	59mdb	527,218	530,328	754,710	985,566	1,278,477	1,633,640	1,977,057	2,231,984	2,653,662	2,949,614	3,361,912	3,746,012
M4 Foreign Currency..................	59mdd	53,108	193,876	114,498	130,512	121,895	142,004	144,204	136,805	155,342	147,305	125,114	159,345
Interest Rates		*Percent Per Annum*											
Money Market Rate...................	60b	17.39	16.47	† 60.92	33.61	21.91	26.89	24.10	16.96	12.89	8.17	6.83	7.15
Treasury Bill Rate...................	60c	14.99	14.10	48.44	31.39	19.80	24.76	21.41	15.24	11.31	7.09	6.23	6.82
Savings Rate...................	60k	8.41	5.38	6.67	6.58	7.57	6.38	5.85	4.86	3.26	2.00	1.72	1.42
Deposit Rate...................	60l	16.69	15.03	39.82	26.40	16.36	15.45	11.60	8.26	6.23	3.76	3.09	2.70
Average Cost of Funds..................	60n	18.56	15.50	45.12	† 31.57	20.04	22.39	20.89	14.59	10.95	6.17	5.15	5.41
Lending Rate..................	60p	17.73	19.30	59.43	36.39	22.14	26.36	23.74	16.93	12.80	8.20	6.91	7.22
Government Bond Yield..........	61	....	....	51.74	32.81	21.44	....	20.11	† 15.81	† 10.28	10.13	8.98	9.54
Prices, Production, Labor		*Index Numbers (2000=100): Period Averages*											
Share Prices...................	62	28.5	38.7	34.1	48.5	68.2	65.1	81.8	100.0	93.9	100.0	110.3	163.9
Wholesale Prices..................	63	30.2	32.1	44.5	59.5	70.0	81.2	92.7	100.0	105.0	110.4	† 118.6	129.7
Consumer Prices..................	64	28.9	30.9	41.7	56.0	67.6	78.3	91.3	100.0	† 106.4	111.7	116.8	122.3
Wages, Monthly..................	65	† 110.8	115.4	100.9	90.9	90.4	93.0	94.4	100.0	106.7	108.7	110.2	110.2
Industrial Production..................	66	72.9	76.4	70.4	77.5	84.7	90.0	94.3	100.0	96.5	96.4	96.3	100.0
Manufacturing Production.............	66ey	† 69.4	72.2	68.7	76.2	83.6	89.8	93.5	100.0	96.2	95.6	94.3	97.9
Mining Production..................	66zx	† 85.0	87.1	84.8	91.8	95.8	98.4	96.3	100.0	101.5	101.9	105.6	108.3
Crude Petroleum..................	66aa	86.9	87.3	85.9	94.2	99.3	101.6	97.1	100.0	102.4	103.3	108.8	109.9
		Number in Thousands: Period Averages											
Labor Force...................	67d	....	....	34,309	35,444	37,217	39,507	39,751	39,634	39,683	41,086	....	....
Employment...................	67e	32,833	....	33,881	35,226	37,360	38,659	38,953	39,502	39,386	40,302	40,633	....
Unemployment...................	67c	819	....	1,677	1,355	985	904	695	659	637	784	883	....
Unemployment Rate (%).................	67r	2.4	....	4.7	3.7	2.6	2.3	1.7	1.6	1.7	1.9	2.1	....
Intl. Transactions & Positions		*Millions of US Dollars*											
Excluding Maquiladoras													
Exports...................	70n.d	30,003	34,318	46,864	59,084	65,266	64,376	72,954	86,987	81,562	82,641	87,561	101,252
Imports, f.o.b...................	71nvd	49,054	58,362	44,893	58,961	73,475	82,816	91,655	112,749	110,798	109,383	111,933	128,723
Including Maquiladoras													
Exports...................	70..d	51,886	60,882	79,542	96,000	110,431	117,460	136,391	166,368	158,547	160,682	165,396	189,084
Imports, f.o.b...................	71.vd	65,367	79,346	72,453	89,469	109,808	125,373	141,975	174,501	168,276	168,679	170,490	197,347

		1993	1994	1995	1996	1997	1998	1999	2000	2001	2002	2003	2004
Balance of Payments		*Millions of US Dollars: Minus Sign Indicates Debit*											
Current Account, n.i.e.	78ald	−23,400	−29,662	−1,576	−2,537	−7,695	−16,017	−13,931	−18,620	−17,342	−13,008	−6,479	−7,409
Goods: Exports f.o.b.	78aad	51,885	60,882	79,542	96,000	110,431	117,539	136,362	166,121	158,780	161,046	164,766	187,999
Goods: Imports f.o.b.	78abd	−65,366	−79,346	−72,453	−89,469	−109,808	−125,373	−141,975	−174,458	−168,397	−168,679	−170,546	−196,810
Trade Balance	78acd	−13,481	−18,464	7,089	6,531	623	−7,834	−5,613	−8,337	−9,617	−7,633	−5,780	−8,811
Services: Credit	78add	9,517	10,321	9,780	10,723	11,183	11,661	11,734	13,756	12,701	12,740	12,617	14,004
Services: Debit	78aed	−12,046	−13,043	−9,715	−10,818	−12,614	−13,008	−14,471	−17,360	−17,194	−17,660	−18,141	−19,779
Balance on Goods & Services	78afd	−16,010	−21,185	7,153	6,436	−807	−9,181	−8,350	−11,942	−14,110	−12,553	−11,304	−14,586
Income: Credit	78agd	2,694	3,347	3,713	4,032	4,431	4,909	4,475	5,977	5,587	4,405	5,847	5,049
Income: Debit	78ahd	−13,724	−15,605	−16,402	−17,507	−16,536	−17,733	−16,342	−19,625	−18,133	−15,112	−14,865	−14,901
Balance on Gds, Serv. & Inc.	78aid	−27,040	−33,444	−5,536	−7,039	−12,913	−22,005	−20,218	−25,590	−26,656	−23,261	−20,322	−24,437
Current Transfers, n.i.e.: Credit	78ajd	3,656	3,822	3,995	4,533	5,243	6,015	6,313	6,999	9,336	10,287	13,880	17,108
Current Transfers: Debit	78akd	−16	−40	−35	−30	−25	−27	−27	−30	−22	−35	−37	−80
Capital Account, n.i.e.	78bcd	—	....	....	—	—	—	—	—	—	—	—	—
Capital Account, n.i.e.: Credit	78bad	—	....	....	—	—	—	—	—	—	—	—	—
Capital Account: Debit	78bbd	—	....	....	—	—	—	—	—	—	—	—	—
Financial Account, n.i.e.	78bjd	33,760	15,787	−10,487	13,298	24,445	18,686	17,848	22,981	26,234	22,963	18,042	12,310
Direct Investment Abroad	78bdd	—	—	—	—	—	—	—	—	−4,404	−930	−1,784	−3,490
Dir. Invest. in Rep. Econ., n.i.e.	78bed	4,389	10,973	9,526	9,186	12,830	11,223	13,427	16,910	27,721	15,325	11,664	16,602
Portfolio Investment Assets	78bfd	−564	−767	−662	544	−708	−769	−836	1,290	3,857	1,134	91	1,718
Equity Securities	78bkd												
Debt Securities	78bld	−564	−767	−662	544	−708	−769	−836	1,290	3,857	1,134	91	1,718
Portfolio Investment Liab., n.i.e.	78bgd	28,919	8,182	−9,715	12,585	4,704	1,027	12,005	−1,134	3,882	−632	3,864	6,126
Equity Securities	78bmd	10,716	4,084	519	2,801	3,215	−666	3,769	447	151	−104	−123	−2,522
Debt Securities	78bnd	18,203	4,099	−10,234	9,785	1,488	1,693	8,236	−1,581	3,731	−528	3,987	8,649
Financial Derivatives Assets	78bwd	....	....	....	....	....	....	....	....	....	....	....	....
Financial Derivatives Liabilities	78bxd	....	—	—	—	—	....	....	....	....	....	....	....
Other Investment Assets	78bhd	−3,038	−4,903	−6,694	−6,885	7,423	1,200	−3,169	5,809	−3,287	11,601	8,627	−4,066
Monetary Authorities	78bod	....	....	....	—	—	—	—	—	—	—	—	—
General Government	78bpd	—	−1,400	−3,619	−22	56	25	—	—	—	—	—	—
Banks	78bqd	−1,683	−885	−1,510	−1,017	5,111	−1,208	−1,894	45	−5,423	7,401	4,456	−376
Other Sectors	78brd	−1,355	−2,618	−1,565	−5,846	2,256	2,384	−1,275	5,764	2,136	4,199	4,171	−3,689
Other Investment Liab., n.i.e.	78bid	4,054	2,302	−2,942	−2,132	196	6,004	−3,580	107	−1,534	−3,535	−4,419	−4,581
Monetary Authorities	78bsd			−788	−1,459	—	—	—	—	—	—	—	—
General Government	78btd	−1,136	−986	210	−659	206	1,355	−4,294	−2,896	−603	316	832	752
Banks	78bud	3,622	2,799	−5,297	—	—	97	−2,312	−883	−4,222	−2,861	−1,145	−2,686
Other Sectors	78bvd	1,568	488	2,933	−14	−10	4,552	3,026	3,886	3,291	−990	−4,106	−2,647
Net Errors and Omissions	78cad	−3,128	−3,323	−4,248	236	2,412	501	333	2,765	−1,578	−2,595	−1,745	−796
Overall Balance	78cbd	7,232	−17,199	−16,312	10,997	19,162	3,170	4,250	7,126	7,314	7,359	9,817	4,104
Reserves and Related Items	79dad	−7,232	17,199	16,312	−10,997	−19,162	−3,170	−4,250	−7,126	−7,314	−7,359	−9,817	−4,104
Reserve Assets	79dbd	−6,057	18,398	−9,648	−1,805	−10,512	−2,120	−596	−2,862	−7,338	−7,376	−9,833	−4,120
Use of Fund Credit and Loans	79dcd	−1,175	−1,199	11,950	−2,057	−3,485	−1,075	−3,681	−4,288	—	—	—	—
Exceptional Financing	79ded	—	—	14,010	−7,135	−5,165	24	27	24	24	16	16	16
International Investment Position		*Millions of US Dollars*											
Assets	79aad	....	....	....	....	....	....	....	....	111,278	105,770	108,476	118,379
Direct Investment Abroad	79abd	....	....	....	....	....	....	....	....	11,944	12,067	14,039	17,529
Portfolio Investment	79acd	....	....	....	....	....	....	....	....	5,747	3,806	3,321	1,545
Equity Securities	79add	....	....	....	....	....	....	....	....				
Debt Securities	79aed	....	....	....	....	....	....	....	....	5,747	3,806	3,321	1,545
Financial Derivatives	79ald	....	....	....	....	....	....	....	....				
Other Investment	79afd	....	....	....	....	....	....	....	....	52,707	41,914	33,681	37,805
Monetary Authorities	79agd	....	....	....	....	....	....	....	....	....	....	....	....
General Government	79ahd	....	....	....	....	....	....	....	....	....	....	....	....
Banks	79aid	....	....	....	....	....	....	....	....	....	....	....	....
Other Sectors	79ajd	....	....	....	....	....	....	....	....	....	....	....	....
Reserve Assets	79akd	....	....	....	....	....	....	....	....	40,880	47,984	57,435	61,501
Liabilities	79lad	....	....	....	....	....	....	....	....	359,553	361,570	386,208	428,685
Dir. Invest. in Rep. Economy	79lbd	....	....	....	....	....	....	....	....	140,376	155,701	167,365	183,967
Portfolio Investment	79lcd	....	....	....	....	....	....	....	....	132,643	122,709	139,431	166,200
Equity Securities	79ldd	....	....	....	....	....	....	....	....	54,940	44,564	56,516	73,967
Debt Securities	79led	....	....	....	....	....	....	....	....	77,703	78,145	82,915	92,233
Financial Derivatives	79lld	....	....	....	....	....	....	....	....				
Other Investment	79lfd	....	....	....	....	....	....	....	....	86,534	83,160	79,412	78,519
Monetary Authorities	79lgd	....	....	....	....	....	....	....	....	....	....	....	....
General Government	79lhd	....	....	....	....	....	....	....	....	....	....	....	....
Banks	79lid	....	....	....	....	....	....	....	....	....	....	....	....
Other Sectors	79ljd	....	....	....	....	....	....	....	....	....	....	....	....
Government Finance		*Millions of Pesos: Year Ending December 31*											
Deficit (-) or Surplus	80	6,451	−386	−9,784	−5,546	−34,161	−55,591	−71,289	−69,256	−42,377	−111,592	−75,772	−78,008
Total Revenue and Grants	81y	186,644	211,434	278,626	379,573	459,047	488,959	620,135	791,040	859,998	875,710	1,049,198	1,170,956
Revenue	81	186,644	211,434	278,626	379,573	459,047	488,959	620,135	791,040	859,998	875,710	1,049,198	1,170,956
Grants	81z	—	—	—	—	—	—	—	—	—	—	—	—
Exp.& Lending Minus Repayments	82z	180,193	211,820	288,410	385,119	493,208	544,550	691,424	860,296	902,375	987,302	1,124,970	1,248,964
Expenditure	82	183,876	217,249	285,147	382,499	505,902	556,079	689,921	848,502	897,049	1,009,733	1,118,033	1,248,109
Lending Minus Repayments	83	−3,683	−5,429	3,263	2,620	−12,694	−11,529	1,503	11,794	5,326	−22,431	6,937	855
Total Financing	80h	−6,451	386	9,784	5,546	34,161	55,591	71,289	69,256	42,377	111,592	75,772	78,008
Domestic	84a	−1,397	4,934	−90,101	24,233	56,387	35,073	64,994	117,589	46,922	125,971	80,538	65,763
Foreign	85a	−5,054	−4,548	99,885	−18,687	−22,226	20,518	6,295	−48,333	−4,545	−14,379	−4,766	12,245
Total Debt by Residence	88	317,977	417,115	751,601	787,822	821,777	1,073,220	1,175,528	1,276,451	1,306,415	1,504,286	1,667,603	1,776,043
Domestic	88a	134,769	178,960	155,360	192,162	273,656	378,256	506,389	675,107	763,559	907,408	1,011,889	1,099,206
Foreign	89a	183,208	238,155	596,241	595,660	548,121	694,964	669,139	601,344	542,856	596,878	655,714	676,837

		1993	1994	1995	1996	1997	1998	1999	2000	2001	2002	2003	2004
National Accounts							*Billions of Pesos*						
Househ.Cons.Expend.,incl.NPISHs....	**96f.c**	† 903.17	1,016.13	1,232.00	1,646.26	2,042.08	2,593.35	3,084.14	3,682.55	4,044.88	4,326.51	4,731.20	5,227.00
Government Consumption Expend...	**91f.c**	† 138.56	164.16	191.98	243.71	314.62	399.96	506.46	612.62	683.38	759.87	855.75	890.46
Gross Fixed Capital Formation..........	**93e.c**	† 233.18	274.86	296.71	451.08	619.49	804.00	973.80	1,174.30	1,161.95	1,205.94	1,304.89	1,541.00
Changes in Inventories....................	**93i.c**	† 30.60	33.54	67.39	132.48	201.46	131.41	104.55	128.74	51.35	87.39	111.39	119.56
Exports of Goods and Services.........	**90c.c**	† 191.54	238.96	558.80	811.51	962.22	1,180.39	1,414.34	1,704.08	1,598.52	1,678.38	1,919.36	2,295.73
Imports of Goods and Services (-).....	**98c.c**	† 240.86	307.49	509.86	759.45	965.61	1,262.76	1,488.56	1,810.58	1,730.39	1,794.95	2,031.15	2,438.82
Gross Domestic Product (GDP)........	**99b.c**	† 1,256.20	1,420.16	1,837.02	2,525.58	3,174.28	3,846.35	4,594.72	5,491.71	5,809.69	6,263.14	6,891.43	7,634.93
Net Primary Income from Abroad.....	**98.nc**	−36	−42	−84	−104	−99	−121	−120	−132	−126	−117	−133	....
Gross National Income (GNI)...........	**99a.c**	1,220	1,378	1,753	2,421	3,075	3,726	4,475	5,360	5,684	6,146	6,758	....
GDP Volume 1993 Prices................	**99b.r**	1,256.20	1,311.66	1,230.77	1,294.20	1,381.84	1,451.35	1,505.88	1,605.13	1,604.60	1,616.99	1,640.26	1,709.78
GDP Volume (2000=100)...............	**99bvr**	78.3	81.7	76.7	80.6	86.1	90.4	93.8	100.0	100.0	100.7	102.2	106.5
GDP Deflator (2000=100)...............	**99bir**	† 29.2	31.6	43.6	57.0	67.1	77.5	89.2	100.0	105.8	113.2	122.8	130.5
						Millions: Midyear Estimates							
Population.................................	**99z**	89.28	90.92	92.52	94.10	95.64	97.14	98.63	100.09	101.53	102.95	104.34	105.70

Micronesia, Federated States of   868

		1993	1994	1995	1996	1997	1998	1999	2000	2001	2002	2003	2004
Exchange Rates						*US Dollars per SDR: End of Period*							
Market Rate	aa	1.3736	1.4599	1.4865	1.4380	1.3493	1.4080	1.3725	1.3029	1.2567	1.3595	1.4860	1.5530
Fund Position						*Millions of SDRs: End of Period*							
Quota	2f.s	3.5	3.5	3.5	3.5	3.5	3.5	5.1	5.1	5.1	5.1	5.1	5.1
SDRs	1b.s	.8	.9	.9	.9	1.0	1.0	1.1	1.1	1.1	1.2	1.2	1.2
Reserve Position in the Fund	1c.s	—	—	—	—	—	—	—	—	—	—	—	—
Total Fund Cred.&Loans Outstg.	2tl	—	—	—	—	—	—	—	—	—	—	—	—
International Liquidity						*Millions of US Dollars Unless Otherwise Indicated: End of Period*							
Total Reserves minus Gold	1l.d	....	....	69.500	89.600	85.801	101.602	92.669	113.047	98.330	117.391	89.607	54.839
SDRs	1b.d	1.141	1.264	1.349	1.357	1.325	1.442	1.455	1.442	1.445	1.598	1.777	1.890
Reserve Position in the Fund	1c.d	—	.001	.001	.001	.001	.001	.001	.001	.001	.001	.001	.001
Foreign Exchange	1d.d	....	....	68.150	88.242	84.475	100.159	91.213	111.605	96.885	115.792	87.829	52.948
Gold (Million Fine Troy Ounces)	1ad	....	....	—	—	—	—	—	—	—	—	—	—
Gold (National Valuation)	1and	....	....	—	—	—	—	—	—	—	—	—	—
Monetary Authorities:Other Assets	3..d	....	....	60.749	54.035	51.537	55.579	55.283	47.408	36.989	33.503	41.792	43.751
Other Liab.	4..d	....	....	—	—	—	—	—	—	—	—	—	—
Banking Institutions: Assets	7a.d	....	....	82.200	97.210	96.273	93.042	93.472	91.259	97.967	112.961	117.521	115.506
Liabilities	7b.d	....	....	1.962	1.332	.948	.131	.107	—	—	5.226	1.604	1.663
Monetary Authorities						*Millions of US Dollars: End of Period*							
Foreign Assets	11	....	....	130.249	143.635	137.338	157.181	147.952	160.455	135.319	150.894	131.399	98.590
Foreign Liabilities	16c	....	....	—	—	—	—	—	—	—	—	—	—
Central Government Deposits	16d	....	....	130.249	143.635	137.338	157.181	147.952	160.456	135.319	150.893	131.399	98.589
Other Items (Net)	17r	....	....	—	—	—	—	—	−.001	—	.001	—	.001
Banking Institutions						*Millions of US Dollars: End of Period*							
Foreign Assets	21	....	....	82.200	97.210	96.273	93.042	93.472	91.259	97.967	112.961	117.521	115.506
Claims on Central Government	22a	....	....	—	—	—	—	—	—	.173	—	—	—
Claims on State & Local Govts	22b	....	....	—	—	—	—	.787	.442	—	.117	—	—
Claims on Nonfin.Pub.Enterprises	22c	....	....	.699	.106	—	—	.001	—	—	—	—	—
Claims on Private Sector	22d	....	....	65.572	60.141	58.129	65.618	70.749	71.595	69.907	50.558	40.048	43.176
Demand Deposits	24	....	....	19.863	19.528	21.514	21.284	19.891	18.802	21.245	19.697	22.476	23.578
Time, Savings,& Fgn. Currency Dep.	25	....	....	87.971	82.067	83.947	84.933	89.926	89.965	94.015	81.766	75.187	74.030
Foreign Liabilities	26c	....	....	1.962	1.332	.948	.131	.107	—	—	5.226	1.604	1.663
Central Government Deposits	26d	....	....	4.949	14.976	11.745	11.736	11.351	10.336	7.727	12.754	12.659	16.660
Liab. to Nonbank Financial Insts	26j	....	....	.365	2.836	1.446	.587	2.007	.958	1.827	3.268	3.643	2.353
Capital Accounts	27a	....	....	39.137	43.175	44.506	46.739	46.152	47.017	49.433	48.543	50.472	52.805
Other Items (Net)	27r	....	....	−5.776	−6.457	−9.704	−6.750	−4.425	−3.782	−6.200	−7.618	−8.472	−12.407
Banking Survey						*Millions of US Dollars: End of Period*							
Foreign Assets (Net)	31n	....	....	210.487	239.513	232.663	250.092	241.317	251.714	233.286	258.629	247.316	212.433
Domestic Credit	32	....	....	−68.927	−98.364	−90.954	−103.299	−87.766	−98.755	−72.966	−112.972	−104.010	−72.073
Claims on Central Govt. (Net)	32an	....	....	−135.198	−158.611	−149.083	−168.917	−159.303	−170.792	−142.873	−163.647	−144.058	−115.249
Claims on Local Government	32b	....	....	—	—	—	—	.787	.442	—	.117	—	—
Claims on Nonfin.Pub.Enterprises	32c	....	....	.699	.106	—	—	.001	—	—	—	—	—
Claims on Private Sector	32d	....	....	65.572	60.141	58.129	65.618	70.749	71.595	69.907	50.558	40.048	43.176
Money	34	....	....	19.863	19.528	21.514	21.284	19.891	18.802	21.245	19.697	22.476	23.578
Quasi-Money	35	....	....	87.971	82.067	83.947	84.933	89.926	89.965	94.015	81.766	75.187	74.030
Liab. to Nonbank Financial Insts	36j	....	....	.365	2.836	1.446	.587	2.007	.958	1.827	3.268	3.643	2.353
Capital Accounts	37a	....	....	39.137	43.175	44.506	46.739	46.152	47.017	49.433	48.543	50.472	52.805
Other Items (Net)	37r	....	....	−5.776	−6.457	−9.704	−6.750	−4.425	−3.783	−6.200	−7.617	−8.472	−12.406
Money plus Quasi-Money	35l	....	....	107.834	101.595	105.461	106.217	109.817	108.767	115.260	101.463	97.663	97.608
Interest Rates						*Percent Per Annum*							
Savings Rate	60k	....	....	3.17	3.01	3.00	2.90	2.72	2.67	2.47	1.33	.95	.88
Deposit Rate	60l	....	....	5.33	4.58	4.21	3.98	3.72	4.59	3.17	1.47	1.02	1.02
Lending Rate	60p	....	....	15.00	15.00	15.00	15.00	15.17	15.33	15.33	15.28	15.00	15.38
						Millions: Midyear Estimates							
Population	99z	.10	† .11	.11	.11	.11	.11	.11	.11	.11	.11	.11	.11

		1993	1994	1995	1996	1997	1998	1999	2000	2001	2002	2003	2004
Exchange Rates						*Lei per SDR: End of Period*							
Official Rate	aa	4.9998	6.2336	6.6877	6.7215	6.2882	11.7185	15.9077	16.1343	16.4517	18.7913	19.6445	19.3522
						Lei per US Dollar: End of Period (ae) Period Average (rf)							
Official Rate	ae	3.6400	4.2700	4.4990	4.6743	4.6605	8.3226	11.5902	12.3833	13.0909	13.8220	13.2200	12.4611
Official Rate	rf	....	....	4.4958	4.6045	4.6236	5.3707	10.5158	12.4342	12.8651	13.5705	13.9449	12.3297
						Index Numbers (2000=100): Period Averages							
Nominal Effective Exchange Rate	nec	....	27.67	48.97	57.48	75.90	89.88	94.52	100.00	106.71	107.30	102.18	110.97
Real Effective Exchange Rate	rec	....	105.38	91.15	89.18	96.34	97.59	91.43	100.00	97.52	91.57	87.66	97.39
Fund Position						*Millions of SDRs: End of Period*							
Quota	2f.s	90.00	90.00	90.00	90.00	90.00	90.00	123.20	123.20	123.20	123.20	123.20	123.20
SDRs	1b.s	25.05	14.62	8.81	5.45	.89	.50	.23	.26	.59	.20	.03	.05
Reserve Position in the Fund	1c.s	.01	.01	.01	.01	.01	.01	.01	.01	.01	—	.01	.01
Total Fund Cred.&Loans Outstg	2tl	63.00	112.45	154.85	172.29	172.73	125.56	127.69	118.30	116.29	111.78	95.95	81.37
International Liquidity						*Millions of US Dollars Unless Otherwise Indicated: End of Period*							
Total Reserves minus Gold	1l.d	76.34	179.92	257.01	311.96	365.99	143.56	185.70	222.49	228.53	268.86	302.27	470.26
SDRs	1b.d	34.41	21.34	13.10	7.84	1.21	.70	.32	.34	.74	.27	.04	.07
Reserve Position in the Fund	1c.d	.01	.01	.01	.01	.01	.01	.01	.01	.01	.01	.01	.01
Foreign Exchange	1d.d	41.92	158.57	243.90	304.11	364.77	142.85	185.37	222.15	227.78	268.58	302.22	470.18
Gold (Million Fine Troy Ounces)	1ad	—	—	—	—	—	—	—	—	—	—	—	—
Gold (National Valuation)	1and	—	—	—	—	—	—	—	—	—	—	—	—
Monetary Authorities: Other Liab	4..d	12.02	10.10	7.42	4.94	4.00	2.77	10.06	9.66	1.30	.83	1.53	1.54
Dep.Money Banks: Assets Conv	7axd	14.92	18.86	32.77	37.41	23.78	32.33	53.42	67.22	59.77	70.05	103.79	95.72
Assets Nonconv	7ayd	2.14	7.79	5.24	5.55	9.25	3.44	2.23	5.16	4.92	7.15	8.06	3.27
Dep.Money Banks: Liab. Conv	7bxd	.51	1.42	10.60	50.70	58.10	67.27	41.78	44.42	41.70	44.51	54.58	60.05
Liab. Nonconv	7byd	1.51	.41	3.10	1.55	4.91	7.62	3.33	5.80	5.45	9.00	5.20	8.93
Monetary Authorities						*Millions of Lei: End of Period*							
Foreign Assets	11	345.41	825.14	1,198.42	† 1,486.91	1,716.60	1,199.82	2,207.49	2,876.49	3,008.38	3,727.14	4,010.31	6,111.68
Claims on Central Government	12a	236.21	284.01	452.92	† 496.12	524.83	1,409.21	1,737.46	1,730.79	1,899.28	2,158.18	2,175.41	2,740.99
Claims on Private Sector	12d	—	—	1.79	† 2.88	3.92	5.10	6.03	7.28	7.10	6.37	6.11	5.78
Claims on Deposit Money Banks	12e	98.68	274.67	366.55	† 362.63	286.02	233.02	130.27	105.44	91.15	81.40	72.29	62.28
Reserve Money	14	241.14	551.94	779.85	† 854.28	1,135.64	1,059.95	1,486.63	1,945.86	2,488.94	3,262.81	3,804.18	5,319.06
of which: Currency Outside DMB	14a	119.45	345.55	640.15	† 731.06	972.10	† 855.45	1,122.07	1,469.26	1,834.20	2,288.56	2,740.52	3,699.91
Other Liabilities to DMBs	14n	—	—	—	† —	3.00	3.50	20.00	43.00	15.50	23.00	92.59	1,227.86
Restricted Deposits	16b	—	—	—	† —	—	—	—	—	—	—	14.99	3.97
Foreign Liabilities	16c	358.73	744.09	1,068.96	† 1,181.13	1,104.75	1,494.36	2,147.89	2,028.31	1,930.21	2,112.02	1,905.15	1,593.65
Central Government Deposits	16d	90.12	17.45	21.38	† 126.37	9.99	60.00	85.72	277.93	100.52	71.91	3.81	44.85
Capital Accounts	17a	1.72	24.72	79.11	† 95.26	91.92	93.42	146.03	231.02	357.04	334.38	439.69	555.83
Other Items (Net)	17r	−11.40	45.63	70.37	† 91.49	186.07	135.91	194.99	193.90	113.70	168.96	3.72	175.52
Deposit Money Banks						*Millions of Lei: End of Period*							
Reserves	20	48.87	52.44	54.38	36.54	52.05	† 200.66	360.92	465.22	652.38	979.20	1,063.38	1,614.23
Other Claims on Monetary Author	20n	—	—	—	—	—	† —	—	—	—	—	92.59	1,227.86
Foreign Assets	21	62.11	113.76	171.03	200.79	153.90	† 297.69	644.99	896.23	846.80	1,067.07	1,478.66	1,233.37
Claims on Central Government	22a	122.13	31.56	10.31	13.68	67.58	† 184.46	267.81	335.33	571.44	668.42	598.05	788.23
Claims on Local Government	22b	10.21	22.82	2.59	13.19	23.68	† 33.01	14.98	17.24	25.45	105.86	70.48	79.33
Claims on Nonfin.Pub.Enterprises	22c	243.28	493.91	692.37	852.27	1,120.82	† 144.17	146.32	230.71	293.61	315.16	449.14	552.56
Claims on Private Sector	22d	91.06	174.79	433.62	600.88	617.05	† 1,265.65	1,453.15	2,025.31	2,804.49	3,867.39	5,605.06	6,794.87
Claims on Nonbank Financial Insts	22g						† 23.06	37.30	28.36	5.65	9.47	1.01	51.24
Demand Deposits	24	121.24	173.69	244.57	263.13	326.49	† 210.00	357.76	553.75	665.76	1,271.14	1,674.28	2,401.62
Time, Savings,& Fgn.Currency Dep	25	106.02	228.68	358.18	435.57	624.02	† 698.48	1,040.18	1,548.25	2,350.96	3,165.91	4,357.36	6,155.22
Money Market Instruments	26aa	—	—	—	—	—	† 1.21	2.10	.20	.29	.28	.86	.46
Restricted Deposits	26b	—	—	—	—	—	† —	—	—	—	—	32.41	29.90
Foreign Liabilities	26c	7.36	7.80	61.64	244.21	293.67	† 623.24	522.87	621.93	617.29	739.57	790.40	859.55
Central Government Deposits	26d	149.65	56.54	35.81	27.84	33.55	† 13.51	44.72	57.11	270.93	502.38	753.60	716.78
Credit from Monetary Authorities	26g	104.70	292.23	389.12	368.12	285.91	† 229.83	130.27	106.44	93.15	85.31	72.31	63.29
Liabs. to Nonbank Financial Insts	26j						† .77	1.55	2.22	2.45	26.48	13.71	49.92
Capital Accounts	27a	136.65	333.05	569.03	731.41	839.27	† 756.20	1,242.83	1,692.04	1,896.54	2,099.43	2,506.26	3,020.63
Other Items (Net)	27r	−47.96	−202.72	−294.04	−352.93	−367.84	† −384.56	−416.81	−583.56	−697.56	−877.92	−842.81	−955.69
Monetary Survey						*Millions of Lei: End of Period*							
Foreign Assets (Net)	31n	41.44	187.01	238.85	† 262.37	472.08	† −620.10	181.71	1,122.48	1,307.68	1,942.62	2,793.42	4,891.85
Domestic Credit	32	463.12	933.10	1,536.40	† 1,824.80	2,314.34	† 2,991.14	3,532.62	4,039.97	5,235.57	6,556.57	8,147.84	10,251.37
Claims on Central Govt. (Net)	32an	118.57	241.58	406.04	† 355.59	548.88	† 1,520.16	1,874.84	1,731.07	2,099.27	2,252.32	2,016.06	2,767.60
Claims on Local Government	32b	10.21	22.82	2.59	† 13.19	23.68	† 33.01	14.98	17.24	25.45	105.86	70.48	79.33
Claims on Nonfin.Pub.Enterprises	32c	243.28	493.91	692.37	† 852.27	1,120.82	† 144.17	146.32	230.71	293.61	315.16	449.14	552.56
Claims on Private Sector	32d	91.06	174.79	435.41	† 603.76	620.97	† 1,270.75	1,459.19	2,032.59	2,811.59	3,873.76	5,611.17	6,800.65
Claims on Nonbank Financial Inst	32g	—	—	—	† —	—	† 23.06	37.30	28.36	5.65	9.47	1.01	51.24
Money	34	242.07	524.20	885.04	† 994.51	1,298.83	† 1,065.46	1,479.84	2,023.22	2,500.00	3,559.80	4,415.07	6,106.45
Quasi-Money	35	107.17	229.01	360.18	† 435.57	624.02	† 698.48	1,040.18	1,548.25	2,350.96	3,165.91	4,357.36	6,155.22
Money Market Instruments	36aa	—	—	—	† —	—	† 1.21	2.10	.20	.29	.28	.86	.46
Restricted Deposits	36b	—	—	—	† —	—	† —	—	—	—	—	47.40	33.86
Liabs. to Nonbank Financial Insts	36j	—	—	—	† —	—	† .77	1.55	2.22	2.45	26.48	13.71	49.92
Capital Accounts	37a	138.37	357.77	648.15	† 826.67	931.20	† 849.62	1,388.86	1,923.05	2,253.58	2,433.81	2,945.95	3,576.46
Other Items (Net)	37r	16.94	9.13	−118.10	† −169.58	−67.63	† −244.50	−198.19	−334.50	−564.03	−687.09	−839.07	−779.15
Money plus Quasi-Money	35l	349.24	753.21	1,245.22	† 1,430.08	1,922.86	† 1,763.94	2,520.02	3,571.47	4,850.95	6,725.71	8,772.43	12,261.67
Interest Rates						*Percent Per Annum*							
Refinancing Rate	60a	....	143.94	28.25	20.15	19.03	....	....	....	....	....	....	....
Money Market Rate	60b	....	....	....	....	28.10	30.91	32.60	20.77	11.04	5.13	11.51	13.19
Money Market Rate (Fgn. Cur.)	60b.f	....	....	....	....	....	....	11.88	6.86	9.06	4.80	2.51	.78
Treasury Bill Rate	60c	....	....	52.90	39.01	23.63	30.54	28.49	22.20	14.24	5.89	15.08	11.89
Deposit Rate	60l	....	....	25.43	23.47	21.68	27.54	24.87	20.93	14.20	12.55	15.12
Deposit Rate (Foreign Currency)	60l.f	....	....	....	....	9.86	5.27	5.12	4.09	3.22	3.13	4.97
Lending Rate	60p	....	....	....	36.67	33.33	30.83	35.54	33.78	28.69	23.52	19.29	20.94
Lending Rate (Foreign Currency)	60p.f	....	....	....	....	....	22.03	20.37	17.12	14.22	12.32	10.98	11.40

Moldova 921

		1993	1994	1995	1996	1997	1998	1999	2000	2001	2002	2003	2004
Prices and Labor					*Index Numbers (2000=100): Period Averages*								
Consumer Prices	64	....	33.4	37.5	45.3	48.9	52.2	76.2	100.0	109.8	115.6	129.2	145.3
					Number in Thousands: Period Averages								
Labor Force	67d	....	....	....	1,686	....	1,659	1,682	1,655	1,617	1,615	1,474	....
Employment	67e	1,688	1,681	1,673	1,660	1,646	1,642	1,494	1,515	1,499	1,501	1,357	....
Unemployment	67c	14	21	25	23	28	32	187	140	118	110	117	....
Unemployment Rate (%)	67r	.7	1.1	1.0	1.5	1.5	1.9	11.2	8.5	7.3	6.8	7.4	....
Intl. Transactions & Positions							*Millions of US Dollars*						
Exports	70..d	483	558	739	823	890	644	474	472	568	644	789	980
Imports, c.i.f	71..d	628	703	841	1,072	1,171	1,024	586	776	893	1,039	1,403	1,773
Imports, f.o.b	71.vd	....	672	809	1,083	1,083	1,238	1,032	611	770	880	1,038	1,429
Balance of Payments						*Millions of US Dollars: Minus Sign Indicates Debit*							
Current Account, n.i.e	78ald	....	−82.0	−87.8	−194.8	−274.9	−334.7	−78.6	−108.1	−34.3	−71.8	−130.5	−113.9
Goods: Exports f.o.b	78aad	....	618.5	739.0	822.9	889.6	643.6	474.3	476.8	567.3	659.8	805.2	995.2
Goods: Imports f.o.b	78abd	....	−672.4	−809.2	−1,082.5	−1,237.6	−1,031.7	−611.5	−770.3	−880.1	−1,038.0	−1,428.5	−1,753.5
Trade Balance	78acd	....	−53.9	−70.2	−259.7	−348.0	−388.1	−137.2	−293.6	−312.8	−378.2	−623.4	−758.3
Services: Credit	78add	....	32.8	144.5	106.0	167.7	152.0	135.7	164.9	171.4	217.5	254.4	322.3
Services: Debit	78aed	....	−79.0	−196.3	−166.4	−196.1	−198.6	−177.9	−201.6	−208.8	−257.0	−299.8	−377.1
Balance on Goods & Services	78afd	....	−100.0	−122.0	−320.0	−376.4	−434.6	−179.4	−330.3	−350.2	−417.7	−668.8	−813.1
Income: Credit	78agd	....	10.8	14.2	99.3	132.7	136.8	120.5	139.1	173.9	229.4	340.7	490.0
Income: Debit	78ahd	....	−26.1	−32.4	−44.2	−85.3	−102.3	−95.8	−117.5	−78.1	−119.7	−106.6	−153.5
Balance on Gds, Serv. & Inc	78aid	....	−115.4	−140.2	−264.9	−329.0	−400.1	−154.7	−308.7	−254.4	−308.0	−434.7	−476.5
Current Transfers, n.i.e.: Credit	78ajd	....	36.9	66.6	72.9	104.1	110.9	111.5	213.6	236.0	255.5	331.7	397.9
Current Transfers: Debit	78akd	....	−3.6	−14.1	−2.8	−50.0	−45.5	−35.4	−13.1	−15.9	−19.3	−27.5	−35.2
Capital Account, n.i.e	78bcd	....	−1.0	−.4	−.1	−.2	−.4	1.1	−14.3	−20.7	−15.3	−12.8	−10.9
Capital Account, n.i.e.: Credit	78bad	....	—	—	.1	.1	2.1	1.5	2.8	1.1	.8	3.5	5.3
Capital Account: Debit	78bbd	....	−1.0	−.4	−.1	−.3	−2.5	−.4	−17.1	−21.8	−16.1	−16.3	−16.1
Financial Account, n.i.e	78bjd	....	211.1	−68.8	76.6	95.2	5.2	−34.6	127.0	15.9	60.3	51.4	146.8
Direct Investment Abroad	78bdd	....	....	−.5	−.6	−.5	.7	−.1	−.1	−.1	−.5	−.1	−3.3
Dir. Invest. in Rep. Econ., n.i.e	78bed	....	11.6	25.9	23.7	78.7	75.5	37.9	126.8	53.1	132.4	71.1	87.9
Portfolio Investment Assets	78bfd	....	−.4	—	—	—	—	—	—	−3.2	−1.5	.4	−1.5
Equity Securities	78bkd	....	−.4	....	....	....	....	—	—	—	—	−.1	−.2
Debt Securities	78bld	....	....	....	....	....	....	—	—	−3.2	−1.5	.5	−1.3
Portfolio Investment Liab., n.i.e	78bgd	....	.6	−.5	30.8	18.6	−59.1	−7.3	−4.0	−3.9	−25.9	−24.2	−9.0
Equity Securities	78bmd	....	.6	−.5	.8	3.7	6.5	5.2	2.9	2.8	2.3	.7	−1.5
Debt Securities	78bnd	....	....	—	30.0	14.9	−65.6	−12.5	−6.9	−6.8	−28.2	−24.9	−7.5
Financial Derivatives Assets	78bwd	....	....	....	....	....	....	....	....	....	....	.1	−.5
Financial Derivatives Liabilities	78bxd	....	....	....	....	....	....	....	....	....	....	.1	1.0
Other Investment Assets	78bhd	....	−81.7	−116.4	−51.4	1.8	−86.8	−107.4	−35.9	−22.2	−43.9	−17.0	−52.8
Monetary Authorities	78bod	....	−1.3	2.9	.3	3.7	2.9	—	.1	—	—	—	—
General Government	78bpd	....	−4.1	11.9	12.2	1.6	−.6	−4.3	—	8.3	.5	−.2	.3
Banks	78bqd	....	−10.1	−13.5	−6.5	10.6	−10.9	−15.4	−16.5	1.2	−15.7	−19.6	5.8
Other Sectors	78brd	....	−66.2	−117.7	−57.4	−14.2	−78.2	−87.8	−19.6	−31.7	−28.7	2.9	−58.9
Other Investment Liab., n.i.e	78bid	....	281.0	22.7	74.0	−3.4	74.8	42.3	40.3	−7.7	−.4	21.2	124.8
Monetary Authorities	78bsd	....	3.1	1.8	−1.9	−2.7	5.2	−2.4	1.6	−1.0	.1	.5	2.5
General Government	78btd	....	147.0	−19.7	43.2	−59.2	9.7	−22.4	−11.1	−14.3	−12.6	−25.1	−19.1
Banks	78bud	....	−.8	11.4	21.9	11.8	6.9	−21.2	2.4	−1.3	10.8	13.5	14.3
Other Sectors	78bvd	....	131.6	29.2	10.7	46.6	53.1	88.3	47.4	8.8	1.3	32.2	127.2
Net Errors and Omissions	78cad	....	−115.2	−18.4	15.5	−7.9	−22.8	−3.8	−10.0	14.0	−20.2	69.7	116.9
Overall Balance	78cbd	....	12.9	−175.4	−102.7	−187.8	−352.8	−115.9	−5.4	−25.1	−47.0	−22.1	138.9
Reserves and Related Items	79dad	....	−12.9	175.4	102.7	187.8	352.8	115.9	5.4	25.1	47.0	22.1	−138.9
Reserve Assets	79dbd	....	−103.1	−76.7	−56.9	−50.2	225.7	−48.8	−47.4	−9.5	−27.0	−14.1	−148.0
Use of Fund Credit and Loans	79dcd	....	71.5	64.8	25.2	.8	−64.4	4.0	−12.7	−2.3	−5.6	−22.2	−21.6
Exceptional Financing	79ded	....	18.7	187.3	134.4	237.2	191.4	160.6	65.5	37.0	79.5	58.4	30.7
International Investment Position							*Millions of US Dollars*						
Assets	79aad	....	303.2	499.7	616.8	643.1	474.1	586.2	656.9	680.1	765.1	833.1	1,067.3
Direct Investment Abroad	79abd	....	17.8	18.3	23.1	23.5	22.8	22.9	23.0	23.1	23.5	23.6	26.9
Portfolio Investment	79acd	....	.4	.4	.4	.4	.4	.4	.4	3.6	5.1	4.7	6.1
Equity Securities	79add	....	.4	.4	.4	.4	.4	.4	.4	.4	.4	.5	.7
Debt Securities	79aed	....	—	—	—	—	—	—	—	3.2	4.7	4.2	5.5
Financial Derivatives	79ald	....											.4
Other Investment	79afd	....	105.3	224.0	279.8	257.0	314.1	382.6	410.9	425.0	467.6	502.6	563.6
Monetary Authorities	79agd	....	9.9	7.1	6.8	3.1	.1	.1	—	—	—	—	—
General Government	79ahd	....	31.7	19.9	7.9	6.2	6.8	10.1	9.9	1.6	1.1	1.4	1.1
Banks	79aid	....	27.4	40.8	47.3	36.7	44.9	58.1	74.4	72.7	89.6	115.2	112.5
Other Sectors	79ajd	....	36.3	156.3	217.9	211.1	262.4	314.4	326.6	350.7	376.9	386.0	450.0
Reserve Assets	79akd	....	179.8	257.0	313.5	362.2	136.9	180.4	222.6	228.5	268.9	302.3	470.3
Liabilities	79lad	....	723.1	1,029.8	1,282.9	1,588.4	1,815.4	1,932.6	2,105.0	2,131.2	2,353.7	2,523.7	2,705.3
Dir. Invest. in Rep. Economy	79lbd	....	28.6	94.2	116.9	186.4	244.3	310.3	438.7	536.3	675.1	748.7	902.5
Portfolio Investment	79lcd	....	.7	.4	60.7	296.3	232.3	86.6	201.3	161.5	133.7	110.9	51.1
Equity Securities	79ldd	....	.7	.4	.8	6.0	10.4	11.5	11.9	14.1	14.5	16.5	19.3
Debt Securities	79led	....	—	.1	59.9	290.3	221.9	75.1	189.5	147.4	119.2	94.3	31.8
Financial Derivatives	79lld	....	—	—	—	—	—	—	—	—	—	—	1.1
Other Investment	79lfd	....	693.9	935.2	1,105.3	1,105.7	1,338.8	1,535.7	1,465.0	1,433.5	1,544.9	1,664.1	1,750.6
Monetary Authorities	79lgd	....	170.6	238.5	254.1	236.7	181.2	176.4	156.7	147.7	153.5	144.7	131.0
General Government	79lhd	....	345.5	425.8	479.0	463.4	573.1	631.1	625.8	603.1	655.7	714.2	667.4
Banks	79lid	....	1.1	12.4	32.7	42.1	51.4	29.3	32.3	30.8	41.7	55.5	70.1
Other Sectors	79ljd	....	176.6	258.5	339.5	363.5	533.1	698.9	650.2	652.0	694.2	749.8	882.2

Moldova 921

		1993	1994	1995	1996	1997	1998	1999	2000	2001	2002	2003	2004
Government Finance						*Millions of Lei: Year Ending December 31*							
Deficit(-) or Surplus..........................	80	....	....	−412	−443	−679	−288	−420	−206	208	−320	....	....
Total Revenue and Grants.............	81y	....	....	1,903	2,022	3,150	2,946	3,300	4,500	4,519	5,422	....	....
Revenue....................................	81	....	....	1,858	1,976	2,844	2,809	3,064	4,034	4,078	4,978	....	....
Grants......................................	81z	....	....	45	46	306	137	236	466	441	445	....	....
Exp. & Lending Minus Repayments.	82z	....	....	2,315	2,465	3,828	3,234	3,721	4,706	4,311	5,742	....	....
Expenditure..............................	82	....	....	2,315	2,217	3,710	3,272	3,660	4,739	4,336	5,757	....	....
Lending Minus Repayments..........	83	....	....	—	248	119	−38	60	−33	−25	−14	....	....
Financing: Domestic........................	84a	....	....	....	236	302	591	224	238	313	884	....	....
Financing: Foreign.........................	85a	....	....	....	208	376	−302	196	−32	−520	−564	....	....
National Accounts							*Millions of Lei*						
Househ.Cons.Expend.,incl.NPISHs....	96f	728	2,486	3,616	5,243	6,017	6,876	9,137	14,031	17,037	....	....	....
Government Consumption Expend...	91f	290	1,087	1,755	2,113	2,663	2,327	1,954	2,472	2,812	....	....	....
Gross Fixed Capital Formation..........	93e	283	914	1,034	1,540	1,774	2,012	2,272	2,473	2,575	....	....	....
Changes in Inventories...................	93i	734	451	578	351	349	349	548	1,364	1,241	....	....	....
Exports (Net)...............................	90n	−213	−202	−503	−1,449	−1,887	−2,441	−1,588	−4,319	−4,646	....	....	....
Gross Domestic Product (GDP)........	99b	1,821	4,737	6,480	7,798	8,917	9,122	12,322	16,020	19,019	....	....	....
Net Primary Income from Abroad.....	98.n	−12	−24	....	−114	−209	−365	....	....	....	....	....	....
Gross National Income (GNI)...........	99a	1,809	4,713	6,480	8,070	9,207	9,279	12,678	16,814	....	....	....	....
Net Current Transf.from Abroad......	98t	26	125	97	317	403	438	798	1,795	....	....	....	....
Gross Nat'l Disposable Inc.(GNDI)....	99i	1,836	4,838	6,577	8,387	9,610	9,717	13,476	18,609	....	....	....	....
Gross Saving.................................	99s	818	1,265	1,206	1,031	930	513	2,385	2,106	....	....	....	....
						Millions: Midyear Estimates							
Population............................	99z	4.36	4.35	4.34	4.33	† 4.31	4.30	4.29	4.27	4.26	4.25	4.23	4.22

Mongolia 948

		1993	1994	1995	1996	1997	1998	1999	2000	2001	2002	2003	2004
Exchange Rates						*Togrogs per SDR: End of Period*							
Market Rate	aa	† 544.63	604.51	704.03	997.24	1,097.16	1,270.04	1,471.84	1,429.29	1,384.92	1,529.46	1,735.61	1,877.59
						Togrogs per US Dollar: End of Period (ae) Period Average (rf)							
Market Rate	ae	† 396.51	414.09	473.62	693.51	813.16	902.00	1,072.37	1,097.00	1,102.00	1,125.00	1,168.00	1,209.00
Market Rate	rf	† 295.01	412.72	448.61	548.40	789.99	840.83	1,021.87	1,076.67	1,097.70	1,110.31	1,146.54	1,185.28
Fund Position						*Millions of SDRs: End of Period*							
Quota	2f.s	37.10	37.10	37.10	37.10	37.10	37.10	51.10	51.10	51.10	51.10	51.10	51.10
SDRs	1b.s	.02	1.98	1.70	.30	.52	.34	.12	.01	.01	.03	.03	.03
Reserve Position in the Fund	1c.s	.01	—	—	—	—	—	.02	.04	.06	.08	.10	.12
Total Fund Cred.&Loans Outstg	2tl	23.03	37.87	31.62	30.31	35.25	34.32	37.47	38.58	37.27	31.34	33.36	28.50
International Liquidity						*Millions of US Dollars Unless Otherwise Indicated: End of Period*							
Total Reserves Minus Gold	1l.d	59.74	81.39	117.03	107.44	175.71	94.09	136.49	178.77	205.70	349.65	236.08	236.34
SDRs	1b.d	.03	2.89	2.52	.43	.70	.48	.16	.01	.02	.04	.04	.04
Reserve Position in the Fund	1c.d	.01	.01	.01	.01	.01	.01	.03	.05	.08	.12	.14	.19
Foreign Exchange	1d.d	59.70	78.49	114.50	107.00	175.00	93.60	136.30	178.70	205.60	349.50	235.90	236.10
Gold (Million Fine Troy Ounces)	1ad	.02	.03	.10	.15	.08	.03	—	.08	.18	.14	.02	.03
Gold (National Valuation)	1and	5.31	11.00	34.50	53.60	24.60	9.10	.40	23.31	50.91	49.79	6.65	14.06
Monetary Authorities: Other Liab	4..d	26.13	28.77	30.17	16.04	4.50	—	5.30	—	—	—	25.03	18.52
Deposit Money Banks: Assets	7a.d	41.17	41.71	53.66	60.86	81.68	28.95	38.90	48.85	47.50	62.87	113.27	169.48
Liabilities	7b.d	11.67	11.90	14.06	12.38	15.06	22.14	9.13	10.20	11.58	14.65	44.03	76.83
Monetary Authorities						*Millions of Togrogs: End of Period*							
Foreign Assets	11	25,630	40,380	60,836	67,814	113,878	114,319	174,385	210,591	227,812	302,920	252,482	252,328
Claims on Central Government	12a	7,477	13,661	4,520	38,953	23,980	26,111	24,136	21,443	13,570	—	164,482	105,300
Claims on Deposit Money Banks	12e	6,637	10,375	7,740	1,712	3,093	5,631	6,651	4,777	7,348	8,038	12,689	22,332
Reserve Money	14	14,266	29,081	37,508	51,167	62,967	74,491	112,062	134,689	143,780	175,292	200,789	234,858
of which: Currency Outside DMBs	14a	8,751	18,946	25,591	40,136	49,768	56,446	87,281	100,910	109,131	120,755	131,482	143,513
Liabs. of Central Bank: Securities	16ac	1,500	2,106	830	—	19,296	11,715	21,200	21,080	50,000	61,000	76,000	68,551
Foreign Liabilities	16c	22,899	34,804	36,548	41,343	42,328	43,585	60,832	55,148	51,622	47,931	87,126	75,899
Central Government Deposits	16d	580	2,465	9,500	8,388	14,417	3,673	4,833	19,289	16,930	33,517	91,714	53,026
Capital Accounts	17a	2,980	4,998	7,998	24,004	37,082	41,049	37,921	44,431	41,992	33,160	41,084	31,985
Other Items (Net)	17r	−2,481	−9,039	−19,289	−16,422	−35,140	−28,452	−31,676	−37,826	−55,594	−39,941	−67,060	−84,359
Deposit Money Banks						*Millions of Togrogs: End of Period*							
Reserves	20	5,690	10,319	12,531	17,848	13,457	17,921	24,171	33,858	34,637	54,530	73,480	88,487
Claims on Mon.Author.:Securities	20c	1,500	2,106	830	—	19,055	11,697	21,200	21,080	49,651	60,768	75,487	68,551
Foreign Assets	21	16,325	17,272	25,412	42,207	66,416	26,116	41,711	53,591	52,341	70,730	132,295	204,906
Claims on Central Government	22a	513	737	643	10,472	35,451	38,328	39,269	43,371	32,458	30,743	46,905	31,226
Claims on Nonfin.Pub.Enterprises	22c	16,938	12,193	10,883	8,660	7,963	10,151	4,661	5,929	9,823	11,492	16,022	12,769
Claims on Private Sector	22d	14,675	40,763	51,838	59,763	44,256	77,293	75,821	83,959	139,989	232,768	441,515	612,025
Demand Deposits	24	9,756	14,104	17,045	20,702	26,341	26,136	27,544	29,842	46,995	66,944	81,337	78,572
Time, Savings,& Fgn.Currency Dep	25	24,216	43,906	59,408	58,757	93,957	84,668	105,341	128,068	174,909	282,398	490,463	625,120
Money Market Instruments	26aa	—	—	—	287	29	26	24	—	—	173	4,036	645
Restricted Deposits	26b	—	—	—	15,821	6,430	6,938	3,604	5,814	7,699	11,580	13,193	11,034
Foreign Liabilities	26c	4,629	4,926	6,660	8,585	12,246	19,973	9,794	11,193	12,758	16,477	51,429	92,887
Central Government Deposits	26d	7,498	8,451	16,655	21,768	33,258	20,081	24,126	26,732	35,927	29,665	22,720	42,994
Credit from Monetary Authorities	26g	5,391	10,152	7,402	18,574	763	4,459	1,900	1,647	4,094	4,327	12,839	23,838
Capital Accounts	27a	11,460	15,892	18,725	4,789	28,518	34,167	41,568	50,527	62,730	79,596	131,959	196,808
Other Items (Net)	27r	−7,307	−14,041	−23,758	−10,334	−14,944	−14,943	−7,070	−12,034	−26,214	−30,131	−22,270	−53,935
Monetary Survey						*Millions of Togrogs: End of Period*							
Foreign Assets (Net)	31n	14,427	17,920	43,040	60,093	125,718	76,876	145,470	197,841	215,773	309,242	246,222	288,448
Domestic Credit	32	31,535	56,446	41,730	93,206	67,882	137,089	119,493	109,584	144,015	212,851	555,047	665,301
Claims on Central Govt. (Net)	32an	−87	3,483	−20,992	19,270	11,755	40,685	34,446	18,793	−6,829	−32,439	96,953	40,506
Claims on Nonfin.Pub.Enterprises	32c	16,938	12,193	10,883	8,660	7,963	10,151	4,661	5,929	9,823	11,492	16,022	12,769
Claims on Private Sector	32d	14,684	40,770	51,839	65,277	48,164	86,253	80,386	84,862	141,021	233,799	442,072	612,025
Money	34	18,547	33,050	42,637	60,838	76,109	82,582	114,826	130,751	156,126	187,699	212,819	222,085
Quasi-Money	35	24,216	43,906	59,408	58,757	93,957	84,668	105,341	128,068	174,909	282,398	490,463	625,120
Money Market Instruments	36aa	—	—	—	287	29	26	24	—	—	173	4,036	645
Liabs. of Central Bank: Securities	36ac	—	—	—	—	241	18	—	—	349	232	513	—
Restricted Deposits	36b	—	—	—	15,821	6,430	6,938	3,604	5,814	7,699	11,580	13,193	11,034
Capital Accounts	37a	14,440	20,891	26,723	28,794	65,599	75,216	79,489	94,958	104,722	112,756	173,043	228,793
Other Items (Net)	37r	−11,241	−23,480	−43,998	−11,198	−48,764	−35,483	−38,322	−52,165	−84,017	−72,745	−92,796	−133,928
Money plus Quasi-Money	35l	42,763	76,956	102,045	119,595	170,066	167,250	220,167	258,819	331,035	470,097	703,282	847,205
Interest Rates						*Percent per Annum*							
Bank Rate (End of Period)	60	628.80	180.00	150.00	109.00	45.50	23.30	11.40	8.65	8.60	9.90	11.50	15.75
Deposit Rate (End of Period)	60l	280.20	115.71	74.62	44.75	36.37	27.51	23.42	16.80	14.30	13.22	14.00	14.15
Lending Rate (End of Period)	60p	300.00	279.22	134.37	87.91	82.05	46.77	39.29	32.75	30.24	28.38	26.31	25.38
Prices and Production						*Index Numbers (2000=100): Period Averages*							
Consumer Prices	64	12.9	24.2	† 38.0	55.8	76.2	83.3	89.6	100.0	106.3	107.3	112.8	122.0
Industrial Production ('90=100)	66	63.0	65.3	....	....	....	....	....	....	....	....	....	....
Intl. Transactions & Positions						*Millions of US Dollars*							
Exports	70..d	360.9	353.2	473.3	423.0	568.5	345.2	454.2	535.8	521.4	524.0	615.9	853.3
Imports, c.i.f	71..d	386.4	229.1	415.3	438.5	468.3	503.3	512.8	614.5	637.7	690.7	801.0	1,011.3

		1993	1994	1995	1996	1997	1998	1999	2000	2001	2002	2003	2004
Balance of Payments		*Millions of US Dollars: Minus Sign Indicates Debit*											
Current Account, n.i.e.	78ald	31.1	46.4	38.9	−100.5	55.2	−128.5	−112.2	−156.1	−154.2	−158.0	....	....
Goods: Exports f.o.b.	78aad	365.8	367.0	451.0	423.4	568.5	462.4	454.3	535.8	523.2	524.0	....	....
Goods: Imports f.o.b.	78abd	−344.5	−333.3	−425.7	−459.7	−453.1	−524.2	−510.7	−608.4	−623.8	−680.2	....	....
Trade Balance	78acd	21.3	33.7	25.3	−36.3	115.4	−61.8	−56.4	−72.6	−100.6	−156.2	....	....
Services: Credit	78add	26.0	45.4	57.3	55.7	52.7	77.8	75.8	77.7	113.5	183.9	....	....
Services: Debit	78aed	−66.9	−91.2	−95.4	−112.8	−105.1	−146.8	−145.7	−162.8	−205.4	−265.8	....	....
Balance on Goods & Services	78afd	−19.6	−12.1	−12.8	−93.4	63.0	−130.8	−126.3	−157.7	−192.5	−238.1	....	....
Income: Credit	78agd	.8	3.2	3.0	13.4	6.1	10.1	6.7	13.0	14.8	14.1	....	....
Income: Debit	78ahd	−21.0	−22.5	−28.4	−26.7	−18.1	−9.7	−6.6	−19.5	−16.8	−18.6	....	....
Balance on Gds, Serv. & Inc	78aid	−39.8	−31.4	−38.2	−106.7	51.0	−130.4	−126.2	−164.2	−194.5	−242.6	....	....
Current Transfers, n.i.e.: Credit	78ajd	66.7	77.8	77.1	6.2	4.2	5.5	17.6	25.0	40.3	126.9	....	....
Current Transfers: Debit	78akd	4.2	—	—	—	—	−3.6	−3.6	−16.9	—	−42.3	....	....
Capital Account, n.i.e.	78bcd	—	—	—	—	—	—	—	....	—	—	....	....
Capital Account, n.i.e.: Credit	78bad	—	—	—	—	—	—	—	....	—	—	....	....
Capital Account: Debit	78bbd	—	—	—	—	—	—	—	....	—	—	....	....
Financial Account, n.i.e.	78bjd	−11.8	−39.0	−15.9	41.3	27.0	126.2	69.6	89.9	107.0	157.4	....	....
Direct Investment Abroad	78bdd	—	—	—	—	—	—	—	....	—	—	....	....
Dir. Invest. in Rep. Econ., n.i.e.	78bed	7.7	6.9	9.8	15.9	25.0	18.9	30.4	53.7	43.0	77.8	....	....
Portfolio Investment Assets	78bfd	—	—	—	—	—	—	—	....	—	—	....	....
Equity Securities	78bkd	—	—	—	—	—	—	—	....	—	—	....	....
Debt Securities	78bld	—	—	—	—	—	—	....	....	—	—	....	....
Portfolio Investment Liab., n.i.e.	78bgd	—	—	1.0	—	—	—	—	....	....	....	....	....
Equity Securities	78bmd	—	—	—	—	—	—	—	....	....	....	....	....
Debt Securities	78bnd	—	—	1.0	—	—	—	....	....	....	....	....	....
Financial Derivatives Assets	78bwd	....	....	....	....	....	....	....	....	....	....	....	....
Financial Derivatives Liabilities	78bxd	—	—	....	....	....	....	....	....	....	....	....	....
Other Investment Assets	78bhd	−35.4	−51.0	−49.2	−76.4	−108.1	−54.8	−51.8	−44.3	−5.2	−32.1	....	....
Monetary Authorities	78bod	—	—	—	—	—	—	....	....	—	—	....	....
General Government	78bpd	—	—	—	—	—	—	....	....	—	—	....	....
Banks	78bqd	−24.9	−15.3	−15.3	−9.3	−18.1	—	−14.8	−10.7	1.1	−24.4	....	....
Other Sectors	78brd	−10.5	−35.7	−33.9	−67.1	−90.0	−54.8	−37.0	−33.6	−6.3	−7.8	....	....
Other Investment Liab., n.i.e.	78bid	15.9	5.1	22.5	101.8	110.1	162.1	91.0	80.5	69.2	111.7	....	....
Monetary Authorities	78bsd	−11.2	—	—	—	—	−5.2	—	—	—	—	....	....
General Government	78btd	32.5	7.9	22.5	56.1	79.3	80.8	91.4	60.5	66.2	72.5	....	....
Banks	78bud	3.6	—	—	—	—	40.0	−4.8	−2.3	.6	6.9	....	....
Other Sectors	78bvd	−9.0	−2.8	—	45.7	30.8	46.5	4.4	22.3	2.4	32.3	....	....
Net Errors and Omissions	78cad	−4.8	−1.0	9.1	−28.1	−75.6	−50.2	23.6	−19.3	−32.2	14.1	....	....
Overall Balance	78cbd	14.5	6.4	32.1	−87.3	6.6	−52.5	−19.0	−85.5	−79.4	13.4	....	....
Reserves and Related Items	79dad	−14.5	−6.4	−32.1	87.3	−6.6	52.5	19.0	85.5	79.4	−13.4	....	....
Reserve Assets	79dbd	−23.5	−27.4	−22.6	19.6	−61.2	−6.3	−40.6	−2.5	−15.8	−58.1	....	....
Use of Fund Credit and Loans	79dcd	13.1	21.1	−9.5	−1.8	−61.2	0.1	4.2	1.8	−1.6	−7.7	....	....
Exceptional Financing	79ded	−4.1	—	—	69.5	47.9	60.2	55.5	86.2	96.9	52.3	....	....
Government Finance		*Millions of Togrogs: Year Ending December 31*											
Deficit (-) or Surplus	80	−27,706	−23,647	−29,185	−49,679	† −65,909	−94,913	−99,816	−63,227	−45,824	....	....	
Total Revenue and Grants	81y	48,637	65,267	113,568	126,725	† 176,152	192,103	203,452	308,283	367,420	....	....	
Revenue	81	45,610	62,002	108,483	122,316	† 171,744	183,552	196,561	303,215	358,244	....	....	
Grants	81z	3,027	3,265	5,085	4,409	† 4,408	8,551	6,891	5,068	9,176	....	....	
Exp. & Lending Minus Repay	82z	76,343	88,914	142,753	176,404	† 242,061	287,016	303,268	371,510	413,244	....	....	
Expenditure	82	42,468	63,824	97,656	121,233	† 176,436	201,279	232,795	306,037	353,580	....	....	
Lending Minus Repayments	83	33,875	25,090	45,097	55,171	† 65,625	85,737	70,473	65,473	59,664	....	....	
Total Financing	80h	27,707	23,648	29,185	49,679	† 65,909	94,913	99,816	63,227	45,824	....	....	
Domestic	84a	−4,650	5,010	5,271	14,804	† −24,989	26,319	−6,020	−3,346	−26,166	....	....	
Foreign	85a	32,357	18,638	23,914	34,875	† 90,898	68,594	105,836	66,573	71,990	....	....	
Total Debt by Residence	88	94,353	196,533	241,503	365,158	† 509,635	676,717	906,723	959,889	961,785	....	....	
Domestic	88a	233	5,281	233	41,206	† 69,151	82,158	90,039	104,192	82,865	....	....	
Foreign	89a	94,120	191,252	241,270	323,952	† 440,484	594,559	816,684	855,697	878,920	....	....	
National Accounts		*Millions of Togrogs*											
Gross Domestic Product (GDP)	99b	166,219	283,263	550,254	646,559	832,636	817,393	925,300	1,018,900	1,115,600	1,225,300	1,362,200	....
GDP Volume 1995 Prices	99b.p	394,646	403,723	550,254	563,201	585,720	606,410	625,910	632,976	639,013	664,253	697,465	....
GDP Volume (2000=100)	99bvp	62.3	63.8	86.9	89.0	92.5	95.8	98.9	100.0	101.0	104.9	110.2	....
GDP Deflator (2000=100)	99bip	26.2	43.6	62.1	71.3	88.3	83.7	91.8	100.0	108.5	114.6	121.3	....
		Millions: Midyear Estimates											
Population	99z	2.33	2.36	2.39	2.41	2.43	2.45	2.47	2.50	2.52	2.55	2.58	2.61

Montserrat 351

		1993	1994	1995	1996	1997	1998	1999	2000	2001	2002	2003	2004
Exchange Rates		*E. Caribbean Dollars per SDR: End of Period (aa) E. Caribbean Dollars per US Dollar: End of Period (ae)*											
Official Rate..................	aa	3.7086	3.9416	4.0135	3.8825	3.6430	3.8017	3.7058	3.5179	3.3932	3.6707	4.0121	4.1931
Official Rate..................	ae	2.7000	2.7000	2.7000	2.7000	2.7000	2.7000	2.7000	2.7000	2.7000	2.7000	2.7000	2.7000
International Liquidity		*Millions of US Dollars: End of Period*											
Total Reserves minus Gold..............	1l.d	6.16	7.62	8.81	8.66	11.30	24.78	14.02	10.40	12.50	14.40	15.23	14.10
Foreign Exchange......................	1d.d	6.16	7.62	8.81	8.66	11.30	24.78	14.02	10.40	12.50	14.40	15.23	14.10
Monetary Authorities: Other Liab.....	4..d	—	—	—	—	—	—	—	—	—	—	—	—
Deposit Money Banks: Assets..........	7a.d	12.63	15.45	19.09	23.50	32.75	33.01	44.27	44.99	44.94	45.93	55.71	61.75
Liabilities..................	7b.d	9.64	6.80	10.06	9.04	7.29	9.20	8.86	11.29	9.23	9.85	10.35	11.73
Monetary Authorities		*Millions of E. Caribbean Dollars: End of Period*											
Foreign Assets..........................	11	16.65	20.18	23.87	23.52	30.69	67.35	38.39	28.63	33.99	38.89	41.11	38.07
Claims on Central Government........	12a	1.83	1.83	1.83	1.83	1.89	1.83	1.93	1.71	.88	.86	.87	.93
Claims on Deposit Money Banks......	12e	.01	.02	.01	.01	.02	.02	.03	.02	.01	.01	.01	.02
Reserve Money..........................	14	18.37	21.95	23.92	24.65	31.08	66.90	37.47	28.15	32.33	36.65	38.89	35.66
of which: Currency Outside DMBs..	14a	6.63	7.44	7.72	9.03	17.55	13.27	13.36	9.66	11.83	10.81	12.55	12.96
Foreign Liabilities......................	16c	—	—	—	—	—	—	—	—	—	—	—	—
Central Government Deposits...........	16d	.12	.08	1.79	.71	1.52	2.29	2.87	2.21	2.55	3.10	3.10	3.35
Other Items (Net).........................	17r	—	—	—	—	—	—	—	—	—	—	—	—
Deposit Money Banks		*Millions of E. Caribbean Dollars: End of Period*											
Reserves..................................	20	10.97	13.28	17.85	13.73	20.03	67.15	23.99	18.61	21.60	26.33	29.24	34.87
Foreign Assets..........................	21	34.09	41.71	51.55	63.45	88.42	89.14	119.52	121.47	121.34	124.02	150.41	166.73
Claims on Central Government........	22a	.62	.50	.25	.50	.50	.25	2.17	2.33	.87	2.27	1.18	.97
Claims on Local Government............	22b	—	—	.52	—	—	—	—	—	.10	—	—	—
Claims on Nonfin.Pub.Enterprises.....	22c	.06	.09	2.80	3.12	2.68	—	—	—	—	—	—	—
Claims on Private Sector..................	22d	78.81	74.97	70.24	65.39	57.41	32.78	22.72	23.12	23.88	22.24	22.94	23.71
Claims on Nonbank Financial Insts....	22g	.34	.31	.62	.50	.40	.36	.33	.25	1.79	.12	.39	.81
Demand Deposits.......................	24	16.16	20.02	19.64	16.47	23.75	29.55	23.32	20.41	20.51	22.09	29.66	31.51
Time, Savings,& Fgn.Currency Dep...	25	65.89	79.27	78.58	71.48	71.51	82.33	83.05	79.19	81.02	79.57	83.36	92.18
Foreign Liabilities......................	26c	26.02	18.36	27.17	24.41	19.68	24.84	23.92	30.49	24.93	26.60	27.96	31.67
Central Government Deposits..........	26d	6.35	1.97	5.17	11.72	28.97	22.12	18.08	14.94	19.15	29.04	39.44	45.97
Credit from Monetary Authorities.....	26g	.01	.01	—	.01	—	.01	1.03	—	.01	.01	.12	.37
Capital Accounts........................	27a	5.62	5.07	4.69	2.14	4.59	5.44	6.89	8.20	9.80	11.32	13.75	18.44
Other Items (Net)..........................	27r	4.83	6.16	8.59	20.47	20.92	25.39	12.44	12.56	14.17	6.35	9.86	6.95
Monetary Survey		*Millions of E. Caribbean Dollars: End of Period*											
Foreign Assets (Net)......................	31n	24.72	43.53	48.26	62.56	99.43	131.65	133.99	119.62	130.41	136.31	163.57	173.13
Domestic Credit..........................	32	75.18	75.64	69.29	58.91	32.38	10.80	6.18	10.26	5.81	−6.65	−17.17	−22.91
Claims on Central Govt. (Net)........	32an	−4.02	.28	−4.88	−10.10	−28.10	−22.34	−16.86	−13.11	−19.96	−29.02	−40.50	−47.42
Claims on Local Government..........	32b	—	—	.52	—	—	—	—	—	.10	—	—	—
Claims on Nonfin.Pub.Enterprises...	32c	.06	.09	2.80	3.12	2.68	—	—	—	—	—	—	—
Claims on Private Sector...............	32d	78.81	74.97	70.24	65.39	57.41	32.78	22.72	23.12	23.88	22.24	22.94	23.71
Claims on Nonbank Financial Inst..	32g	.34	.31	.62	.50	.40	.36	.33	.25	1.79	.12	.39	.81
Money......................................	34	22.80	27.45	27.36	25.51	41.30	42.82	36.68	31.07	32.34	32.90	42.22	44.47
Quasi-Money...............................	35	65.89	79.27	78.58	71.48	71.51	82.33	83.05	79.19	81.02	79.57	83.36	92.18
Capital Accounts.........................	37a	5.62	5.07	4.69	2.14	4.59	5.44	6.89	8.20	9.80	11.32	13.75	18.44
Other Items (Net).........................	37r	5.59	7.37	6.92	22.35	14.41	11.87	13.56	11.42	13.06	5.87	7.07	−4.87
Money plus Quasi-Money..............	35l	88.69	106.72	105.94	96.98	112.81	125.14	119.73	110.26	113.36	112.46	125.57	136.65
Money (National Definitions)		*Millions of E. Caribbean Dollars: End of Period*											
M1..	59ma	17.03	20.34	20.88	22.94	34.29	37.41	31.44	26.11	25.45	26.33	32.73	36.05
M2..	59mb	73.14	85.49	81.42	84.08	98.84	117.44	111.30	101.05	102.03	99.80	108.26	119.51
Interest Rates		*Percent Per Annum*											
Discount Rate (End of Period)..........	60	....	9.00	9.00	9.00	8.00	8.00	8.00	8.00	7.00	7.00	6.50	6.50
Money Market Rate.....................	60b	5.25	5.25	5.25	5.25	5.25	5.25	5.25	5.25	† 5.64	6.32	6.07	4.67
Savings Rate.............................	60k	4.54	4.00	4.00	4.00	4.00	4.00	4.21	4.50	4.50	4.50	† 4.20	3.38
Deposit Rate.............................	60l	3.44	3.25	3.24	3.29	3.02	2.74	3.14	3.35	3.35	3.08	3.06	2.29
Deposit Rate (Fgn. Currency)............	60l.f	....	....	....	....	....	....	....	....	....	....	5.70	4.34
Lending Rate..............................	60p	13.12	13.06	12.63	12.37	12.37	12.15	11.52	11.52	11.52	11.34	12.10	10.95

Montserrat 351

Balance of Payments		1993	1994	1995	1996	1997	1998	1999	2000	2001	2002	2003	2004
		Millions of US Dollars: Minus Sign Indicates Debit											
Current Account, n.i.e.	78ald	−7.89	−12.24	−1.96	15.71	−1.97	3.41	−1.41	−6.51	−5.62	−8.16	....	....
Goods: Exports f.o.b.	78aad	2.27	2.92	12.14	41.34	8.20	1.20	1.26	1.12	.73	1.47	....	....
Goods: Imports f.o.b.	78abd	−24.23	−30.04	−33.90	−35.97	−28.11	−19.35	−19.27	−19.02	−17.05	−22.38	....	....
Trade Balance	78acd	−21.96	−27.12	−21.76	5.38	−19.91	−18.15	−18.00	−17.90	−16.33	−20.91	....	....
Services: Credit	78add	23.34	27.16	24.61	15.54	13.88	13.00	20.26	15.83	14.21	14.13	....	....
Services: Debit	78aed	−11.34	−14.32	−14.77	−17.39	−12.92	−20.71	−21.53	−18.73	−24.03	−23.22	....	....
Balance on Goods & Services	78afd	−9.96	−14.28	−11.92	3.53	−18.95	−25.87	−19.28	−20.81	−26.15	−30.01	....	....
Income: Credit	78agd	.42	−.01	.66	.54	.97	.77	1.19	1.48	1.28	1.45	....	....
Income: Debit	78ahd	−3.90	−4.44	−2.93	−2.00	−3.29	−2.55	−7.13	−4.17	−1.94	−4.54	....	....
Balance on Gds, Serv. & Inc.	78aid	−13.44	−18.73	−14.19	2.08	−21.27	−27.64	−25.22	−23.50	−26.81	−33.10	....	....
Current Transfers, n.i.e.: Credit	78ajd	9.71	10.61	13.55	14.90	20.38	33.24	26.49	18.90	23.66	28.13	....	....
Current Transfers: Debit	78akd	−4.16	−4.12	−1.33	−1.26	−1.08	−2.19	−2.69	−1.91	−2.47	−3.19	....	....
Capital Account, n.i.e.	78bcd	5.41	10.10	5.16	−12.50	3.56	3.59	1.33	4.43	7.70	12.55	....	....
Capital Account, n.i.e.: Credit	78bad	5.41	10.10	6.67	2.32	7.19	7.22	4.96	7.32	9.66	14.64	....	....
Capital Account: Debit	78bbd	—	—	−1.51	−14.81	−3.63	−3.63	−3.63	−2.89	−1.96	−2.09	....	....
Financial Account, n.i.e.	78bjd	1.40	.73	1.93	−6.00	−9.07	3.92	−5.90	3.59	−3.16	−.14	....	....
Direct Investment Abroad	78bdd	—	—									....	....
Dir. Invest. in Rep. Econ., n.i.e.	78bed	4.86	7.16	3.03	−.32	2.57	2.57	8.21	3.46	.96	2.09	....	....
Portfolio Investment Assets	78bfd	—	−.03	−.03				—				....	....
Equity Securities	78bkd	....	....	....	....	....	....	....	....	....	....	....	....
Debt Securities	78bld	....	....	....	....	....	....	....	....	....	....	....	....
Portfolio Investment Liab., n.i.e.	78bgd	.10	—	.06	—	.06	.09	−.03	.55	−.60	−.22	....	....
Equity Securities	78bmd	....	....	....	....	....	....	....	....	....	....	....	....
Debt Securities	78bnd	....	....	....	....	....	....	....	....	....	....	....	....
Financial Derivatives Assets	78bwd	....	....	....	....	....	....	....	....	....	....	....	....
Financial Derivatives Liabilities	78bxd	....	....	....	....	....	....	....	....	....	....	....	....
Other Investment Assets	78bhd	−8.23	−3.60	−4.20	−.84	−1.23	−1.09	−.93	−4.61	−.83	−.25	....	....
Monetary Authorities	78bod	....	....	....	....	....	....	....	....	....	....	....	....
General Government	78bpd	....	....	....	....	....	....	....	....	....	....	....	....
Banks	78bqd	....	....	....	....	....	....	....	....	....	....	....	....
Other Sectors	78brd	....	....	....	....	....	....	....	....	....	....	....	....
Other Investment Liab., n.i.e.	78bid	4.67	−2.81	3.06	−4.84	−10.47	2.35	−13.16	4.19	−2.69	−1.77	....	....
Monetary Authorities	78bsd	....	....	....	....	....	....	....	....	....	....	....	....
General Government	78btd	....	....	....	....	....	....	....	....	....	....	....	....
Banks	78bud	....	....	....	....	....	....	....	....	....	....	....	....
Other Sectors	78bvd	....	....	....	....	....	....	....	....	....	....	....	....
Net Errors and Omissions	78cad	.73	2.97	−3.94	2.63	10.11	2.61	−4.71	−5.06	3.20	−2.57	....	....
Overall Balance	78cbd	−.35	1.57	1.19	−.15	2.63	13.53	−10.69	−3.55	2.12	1.67	....	....
Reserves and Related Items	79dad	.36	−1.57	−1.19	.15	−2.63	−13.53	10.69	3.55	−2.12	−1.67	....	....
Reserve Assets	79dbd	.36	−1.57	−1.19	.15	−2.63	−13.53	10.69	3.55	−2.12	−1.67	....	....
Use of Fund Credit and Loans	79dcd	....	....	....	....	....	....	....	....	....	....	....	....
Exceptional Financing	79ded	....	....	....	....	....	....	....	....	....	....	....	....
National Accounts		*Millions of E. Caribbean Dollars*											
Gross Domestic Product (GDP)	99b	140.0	147.3	139.2	113.1	95.8	88.6	80.3	79.3	82.6	88.0	....	....
GDP Volume 1990 Prices	99b.p	131.0	132.1	122.1	95.9	76.7	69.0	60.3	58.5	56.9	59.5	....	....
GDP Volume (2000=100)	99bvp	223.8	225.8	208.6	163.9	131.2	117.9	103.1	100.0	97.2	101.6	....	....
GDP Deflator (2000=100)	99bip	78.8	82.2	84.1	87.0	92.0	94.7	98.2	100.0	107.1	109.1	....	....
		Millions: Midyear Estimates											
Population	99z	.0110	.0108	.0102	.0092	.0078	.0062	.0048	.0039	.0035	.0035	.0038	.0042

Morocco 686

		1993	1994	1995	1996	1997	1998	1999	2000	2001	2002	2003	2004
Exchange Rates						*Dirhams per SDR: End of Period*							
Official Rate	aa	13.257	13.080	12.589	12.653	13.107	13.031	13.845	13.836	14.528	13.822	13.002	12.762
						Dirhams per US Dollar: End of Period (ae) Period Average (rf)							
Official Rate	ae	9.651	8.960	8.469	8.800	9.714	9.255	10.087	10.619	11.560	10.167	8.750	8.218
Official Rate	rf	9.299	9.203	8.540	8.716	9.527	9.604	9.804	10.626	11.303	11.021	9.574	8.868
						Index Numbers (2000=100): Period Averages							
Official Rate	ahx	114.2	115.5	124.4	121.8	111.5	110.6	108.3	100.0	94.0	96.5	111.0	119.8
Nominal Effective Exchange Rate	nec	84.9	90.5	91.8	92.5	94.2	95.3	96.9	100.0	97.7	96.7	96.2	95.7
Real Effective Exchange Rate	rec	86.8	89.5	92.4	93.2	94.0	96.3	97.3	100.0	95.9	95.6	94.3	93.6
Fund Position						*Millions of SDRs: End of Period*							
Quota	2f.s	428	428	428	428	428	428	588	588	588	588	588	588
SDRs	1b.s	25	18	17	5	1	2	62	92	98	90	76	77
Reserve Position in the Fund	1c.s	30	30	30	30	30	30	70	70	70	70	70	70
Total Fund Cred.&Loans Outstg	2tl	207	101	35	2	—	—	—	—	—	—	—	—
International Liquidity						*Millions of US Dollars Unless Otherwise Indicated: End of Period*							
Total Reserves minus Gold	1l.d	3,655	4,352	3,601	3,794	3,993	4,435	5,689	4,823	8,474	10,133	13,851	16,337
SDRs	1b.d	34	26	26	7	1	3	85	119	123	122	112	120
Reserve Position in the Fund	1c.d	42	44	45	44	41	43	97	92	89	96	105	109
Foreign Exchange	1d.d	3,579	4,281	3,530	3,743	3,951	4,389	5,507	4,612	8,262	9,915	13,634	16,107
Gold (Million Fine Troy Ounces)	1ad	.704	.704	.704	.704	.704	.704	.704	.706	.707	.708	.708	.708
Gold (National Valuation)	1and	202	218	230	222	201	211	193	184	169	193	224	239
Monetary Authorities: Other Liab	4..d	53	47	41	62	84	78	82	84	80	80	135	217
Deposit Money Banks: Assets	7a.d	518	755	653	665	† 381	496	477	599	568	888	996	1,508
Liabilities	7b.d	386	672	442	520	† 351	462	457	407	336	269	412	408
Other Banking Insts.: Liabilities	7f.d	1,450	1,534	1,589	1,452	....	....	....	....	....	....	....	....
Monetary Authorities						*Millions of Dirhams: End of Period*							
Foreign Assets	11	37,243	41,001	32,509	35,402	40,808	43,070	59,392	53,224	99,920	104,979	123,156	136,793
Claims on Central Government	12a	8,752	8,305	18,389	19,179	† 27,860	27,459	21,129	24,310	15,993	16,485	18,093	18,532
Claims on Private Sector	12d	8,803	8,416	9,129	9,075	† 40	114	47	82	64	65	73	86
Claims on Deposit Money Banks	12e	599	512	500	1,250	† 1,210	3,381	1,346	7,161	7	1	—	3
Reserve Money	14	47,796	50,746	53,384	57,467	† 62,557	66,999	75,912	78,356	95,151	98,581	114,594	129,054
of which: Currency Outside DMBs	14a	37,202	41,107	43,261	46,581	48,662	50,644	56,713	58,169	66,025	69,565	74,893	79,715
Foreign Liabilities	16c	3,256	1,745	787	577	† 817	725	826	893	927	809	1,183	1,787
Central Government Deposits	16d	523	605	633	816	† 786	826	532	806	10,806	11,322	13,801	15,207
Capital Accounts	17a	....	....	....	....	4,799	4,877	4,977	5,107	5,252	5,410	5,455	5,411
Other Items (Net)	17r	3,822	5,139	5,722	6,046	† 959	597	−332	−384	3,848	5,408	6,289	3,955
Deposit Money Banks						*Millions of Dirhams: End of Period*							
Reserves	20	8,671	8,293	9,018	9,419	† 11,936	13,380	17,100	18,980	27,466	27,535	39,446	48,812
Foreign Assets	21	5,002	6,765	5,533	5,855	† 3,703	4,592	4,812	6,356	6,566	9,030	8,713	12,392
Claims on Central Government	22a	44,652	50,746	49,633	50,048	58,616	58,614	54,917	61,729	73,161	76,923	77,123	72,033
Claims on Private Sector	22d	62,351	70,408	81,777	90,545	† 151,203	167,602	183,531	199,576	208,026	214,949	232,159	248,420
Claims on Other Financial Insts	22f	355	1,409	1,637	627	† 25,580	29,834	32,884	34,309	35,883	39,075	40,004	42,483
Demand Deposits	24	70,033	79,099	84,606	87,323	† 116,054	126,767	140,895	156,545	181,099	199,374	222,896	247,310
Time Deposits	25	42,687	45,958	50,552	54,962	† 64,121	65,114	69,389	76,281	84,294	83,337	87,360	87,741
Foreign Liabilities	26c	3,729	6,020	3,745	4,579	† 3,409	4,276	4,605	4,322	3,881	2,740	3,603	3,352
Credit from Monetary Authorities	26g	965	1,108	1,232	2,508	† 1,209	3,381	1,346	7,161	7	1	—	3
Capital Accounts	27a	....	....	....	....	38,174	44,973	47,759	48,890	57,568	59,850	66,685	75,025
Other Items (Net)	27r	3,617	5,436	7,463	7,122	† 27,502	29,511	29,383	27,751	24,253	22,210	16,901	10,709
Post Office: Checking Deposits	24..i	1,625	1,833	1,701	1,721	1,871	....	....	....	....	....	....	....
Treasury: Checking Deposits	24..r	4,906	4,950	5,088	6,311	6,202	....	....	....	....	....	....	....
Monetary Survey						*Millions of Dirhams: End of Period*							
Foreign Assets (Net)	31n	35,260	40,002	33,509	36,101	† 40,285	42,661	58,773	54,365	101,678	110,460	127,083	144,046
Domestic Credit	32	130,921	145,462	166,721	176,690	† 262,513	282,797	291,976	319,200	322,321	336,175	353,651	366,347
Claims on Central Govt. (Net)	32an	59,412	65,229	74,178	76,443	† 85,690	85,247	75,514	85,233	78,348	82,086	81,415	75,358
Claims on Private Sector	32d	71,154	78,824	90,906	99,620	† 152,069	168,609	185,819	200,635	208,711	216,539	234,604	251,527
Claims on Other Financial Insts	32f	355	1,409	1,637	627	† 24,754	28,941	30,643	33,332	35,262	37,550	37,632	39,462
Money	34	115,458	128,284	135,964	143,818	† 166,843	179,795	200,597	216,503	249,693	272,184	298,983	328,689
Quasi-Money	35	42,687	45,958	50,552	54,962	† 64,121	65,114	69,389	76,281	84,294	83,337	87,360	87,741
Other Items (Net)	37r	8,036	11,222	13,714	14,011	† 71,834	80,549	80,896	80,781	90,012	91,114	94,391	93,963
Money plus Quasi-Money	35l	158,145	174,242	186,516	198,780	† 230,964	244,909	269,986	292,784	333,987	355,521	386,343	416,430
Other Banking Institutions						*Millions of Dirhams: End of Period*							
Reserves	40	1,938	1,383	1,301	1,469	....	....	....	....	....	....	....	....
Claims on Central Government	42a	7,980	10,966	13,063	16,164	....	....	....	....	....	....	....	....
Claims on Official Entities	42bx	—	—	—	—	....	....	....	....	....	....	....	....
Claims on Private Sector	42d	39,365	41,311	44,167	47,249	....	....	....	....	....	....	....	....
Time Deposits	45	21,836	24,606	28,574	32,745	....	....	....	....	....	....	....	....
Bonds	46ab	10,134	10,628	10,987	11,848	....	....	....	....	....	....	....	....
Long-Term Foreign Liabilities	46cl	13,997	13,744	13,461	12,776	....	....	....	....	....	....	....	....
Central Govt. Lending Funds	46f	547	393	277	271	....	....	....	....	....	....	....	....
Credit from Monetary Authorities	46g	5	8	—	....	....	....	....	....	....	....	....	....
Credit from Deposit Money Banks	46h	508	604	623	683	....	....	....	....	....	....	....	....
Capital Accounts	47a	6,911	8,093	9,122	10,068	....	....	....	....	....	....	....	....
Other Items (Net)	47r	−4,655	−4,416	−4,513	−3,509	....	....	....	....	....	....	....	....
Liquid Liabilities	55l	179,981	198,848	215,090	231,525	....	....	....	....	....	....	....	....
Interest Rates						*Percent Per Annum*							
Discount Rate (End of Period)	60	....	7.17	....	....	....	6.04	5.42	5.00	4.71	3.79	3.25	3.25
Money Market Rate	60b	....	12.29	10.06	8.42	7.89	6.30	5.64	5.41	4.44	2.99	3.22	2.39
Treasury Bill Rate	60c	....	....	....	....	....	....	....	....	....	....	....	....
Deposit Rate	60l	....	....	....	....	....	7.3	6.4	5.2	5.0	4.5	3.8	3.6
Lending Rate	60p	....	10.0	....	....	....	13.5	13.5	13.3	13.3	13.1	12.6	11.5
Govt.Bond Yield: Long-Term	61	....	....	....	....	....	....	....	....	....	....	....	5.7
Med.-Term	61a	....	....	....	....	....	....	....	....	....	5.6	....	4.3

		1993	1994	1995	1996	1997	1998	1999	2000	2001	2002	2003	2004
Prices, Production, Labor		*Index Numbers (2000=100): Period Averages*											
Wholesale Prices	63	84.8	86.8	92.5	96.5	† 95.0	97.6	96.0	100.0	99.6	101.8	97.2	....
Producer Prices: Manufacturing	63ey	....	....	....	....	93.4	90.9	91.5	100.0	98.2	97.0	98.2	102.9
Consumer Prices	64	81.7	85.9	91.2	93.9	94.9	97.5	98.1	100.0	100.6	103.4	104.6	....
Manufacturing Production	66ey	† 81.5	86.2	85.8	89.3	92.2	94.5	96.7	100.0	103.3	106.3	....	....
Mining Production	66zx	† 88.7	95.6	96.4	98.7	107.5	107.0	103.6	100.0	102.4	105.0	....	....
Energy Production	66ze	† 85.0	92.8	91.8	91.8	97.7	97.1	103.4	100.0	107.3	106.9	....	....
		Number in Thousands: Period Averages											
Labor Force	67d	....	....	4,863	4,875	5,068	5,138	† 10,793	....	† 10,605	† 10,379	† 10,902	....
Employment	67e	3,660	....	3,870	4,034	4,224	4,168	4,175	4,199	4,372	4,541	....	....
Unemployment	67c	681	....	1,112	871	845	969	1,162	1,146	1,061	1,017	1,307	....
Unemployment Rate (%)	67r	15.9	....	22.9	18.1	16.9	19.1	22.0	21.5	19.5	18.3	12.1	....
Intl. Transactions & Positions		*Millions of Dirhams*											
Exports	70	28,446	50,965	58,673	60,013	67,057	68,608	72,283	73,869	80,667	86,389	....	....
Imports, c.i.f	71	62,606	76,059	85,493	84,612	90,712	98,676	97,454	122,527	124,718	130,410	....	....
Imports, f.o.b	71.v	60,579	60,168	78,654	77,843	83,455	90,782	97,457	122,527	114,744	....	....	....
		2000=100											
Volume of Exports	72	72.7	† 79.5	78.9	76.7	82.0	† 84.0	91.8	100.0	101.9	105.6	....	....
Volume of Imports	73	72.7	† 58.4	65.7	61.3	66.1	† 81.7	89.2	100.0	98.3	103.8	....	....
Unit Value of Exports	74	91.6	† 89.9	99.7	105.4	106.2	† 103.5	101.7	100.0	100.4	102.8	....	....
Unit Value of Imports	75	105.9	† 119.8	117.5	124.3	120.1	† 104.9	104.8	100.0	96.9	101.0	....	....
Balance of Payments		*Millions of US Dollars: Minus Sign Indicates Debit*											
Current Account, n.i.e	78ald	−521	−723	−1,296	−58	−169	−146	−171	−501	1,606	1,472	1,552	1,063
Goods: Exports f.o.b	78aad	4,936	5,541	6,871	6,886	7,039	7,144	7,509	7,419	7,142	7,839	8,771	9,744
Goods: Imports f.o.b	78abd	−7,001	−7,648	−9,353	−9,080	−8,903	−9,463	−9,957	−10,654	−10,164	−10,900	−13,117	−16,238
Trade Balance	78acd	−2,065	−2,107	−2,482	−2,193	−1,864	−2,319	−2,448	−3,235	−3,022	−3,061	−4,345	−6,494
Services: Credit	78add	2,050	2,014	2,173	2,743	2,471	2,827	3,115	3,034	4,029	4,360	5,478	6,830
Services: Debit	78aed	−1,593	−1,730	−1,890	−1,782	−1,724	−1,963	−2,003	−1,892	−2,118	−2,413	−2,861	−3,446
Balance on Goods & Services	78afd	−1,608	−1,822	−2,199	−1,233	−1,117	−1,455	−1,335	−2,093	−1,111	−1,115	−1,728	−3,109
Income: Credit	78agd	224	224	251	189	172	194	187	276	326	377	370	505
Income: Debit	78ahd	−1,431	−1,394	−1,569	−1,498	−1,348	−1,227	−1,172	−1,140	−1,159	−1,115	−1,162	−1,150
Balance on Gds, Serv. & Inc	78aid	−2,816	−2,992	−3,516	−2,541	−2,292	−2,489	−2,321	−2,958	−1,944	−1,853	−2,520	−3,754
Current Transfers, n.i.e.: Credit	78ajd	2,361	2,355	2,298	2,565	2,204	2,438	2,246	2,574	3,670	3,441	4,214	4,971
Current Transfers: Debit	78akd	−66	−86	−78	−82	−81	−95	−96	−118	−120	−115	−141	−154
Capital Account, n.i.e	78bcd	−3	−3	−6	73	−5	−10	−9	−6	−9	−6	−10	−8
Capital Account, n.i.e.: Credit	78bad	—	—	—	78	1	—	—	—	—	—	—	....
Capital Account: Debit	78bbd	−3	−4	−6	−5	−5	−10	−9	−6	−9	−6	−10	−8
Financial Account, n.i.e	78bjd	966	1,248	−984	−897	−990	−644	−13	−774	−966	−1,336	−1,091	−159
Direct Investment Abroad	78bdd	−23	−24	−15	−30	−9	−20	−18	−59	−97	−28	−13	−31
Dir. Invest. in Rep. Econ., n.i.e	78bed	491	551	92	76	4	12	3	221	144	79	2,313	745
Portfolio Investment Assets	78bfd	—	—	—	—	—	—	—	—	—	—	—	....
Equity Securities	78bkd	—	—	—	—	—	—	—	—	—	—	—	....
Debt Securities	78bld	—	—	—	—	—	—	—	—	—	—	—	....
Portfolio Investment Liab., n.i.e	78bgd	24	238	20	142	38	24	6	18	−7	−8	8	547
Equity Securities	78bmd	24	238	20	142	38	24	6	18	−7	−8	8	547
Debt Securities	78bnd	1	—	—	—	—	—	—	—	—	—	—	—
Financial Derivatives Assets	78bwd	....	....	....	....	....	....	....	....	....	....	....	....
Financial Derivatives Liabilities	78bxd	....	....	....	....	....	....	....	....	....	....	....	....
Other Investment Assets	78bhd	—	344	—	—	—	—	....	—	—	—	−869	−286
Monetary Authorities	78bod	....	—	....	—	—	—	....	—	—	—	—	....
General Government	78bpd	—	—	—	—	—	....	—	—	—	—	—	....
Banks	78bqd	—	—	....	—	—	—	....	—	—	—	−529	—
Other Sectors	78brd	—	344	—	—	—	....	—	—	—	—	−340	−286
Other Investment Liab., n.i.e	78bid	473	139	−1,083	−1,085	−1,022	−660	−4	−953	−1,006	−1,380	−2,529	−1,134
Monetary Authorities	78bsd	−7	19	—	—	—	—	—	—	—	—	—	—
General Government	78btd	59	−421	−967	−867	−1,232	−954	−1,293	−1,208	−1,215	−1,465	−1,830	−1,321
Banks	78bud	—	−48	−132	−167	−123	−197	−152	−80	−93	−128	−214	−213
Other Sectors	78bvd	422	588	16	−50	333	492	1,441	335	302	214	−486	400
Net Errors and Omissions	78cad	−5	−39	391	209	175	160	123	114	230	−182	−297	−243
Overall Balance	78cbd	436	483	−1,895	−673	−988	−640	−69	−1,166	861	−52	154	653
Reserves and Related Items	79dad	−436	−483	1,895	673	988	640	69	1,166	−861	52	−154	−653
Reserve Assets	79dbd	−280	−362	984	−274	−553	−248	−1,636	416	−3,842	−644	−1,649	−1,841
Use of Fund Credit and Loans	79dcd	−156	−152	−101	−47	−3	—	—	—	—	—	—	—
Exceptional Financing	79ded	—	31	1,013	995	1,544	887	1,705	751	2,982	696	1,495	1,188

Morocco 686

		1993	1994	1995	1996	1997	1998	1999	2000	2001	2002	2003	2004
International Investment Position								*Millions of US Dollars*					
Assets..	79aad	....	....	....	....	....	....	....	....	....	12,239	16,812	....
Direct Investment Abroad...............	79abd	....	....	....	....	....	....	....	....	....	454	548	....
Portfolio Investment......................	79acd	....	....	....	....	....	....	....	....	....	169	148	....
Equity Securities.......................	79add	....	....	....	....	....	....	....	....	....	169	148	....
Debt Securities.........................	79aed	....	....	....	....	....	....	....	....	....	—	—	....
Financial Derivatives.....................	79ald	....	....	....	....	....	....	....	....	....			....
Other Investment.........................	79afd	....	....	....	....	....	....	....	....	....	431	1,076	....
Monetary Authorities..................	79agd	....	....	....	....	....	....	....	....	....	—	—	....
General Government...................	79ahd	....	....	....	....	....	....	....	....	....	28	31	....
Banks......................................	79aid	....	....	....	....	....	....	....	....	....	23	610	....
Other Sectors............................	79ajd	....	....	....	....	....	....	....	....	....	380	435	....
Reserve Assets.............................	79akd	....	....	....	....	....	....	....	....	....	11,186	15,040	....
Liabilities.......................................	79lad	....	....	....	....	....	....	....	....	....	29,078	36,050	....
Dir. Invest. in Rep. Economy..........	79lbd	....	....	....	....	....	....	....	....	....	12,481	17,914	....
Portfolio Investment......................	79lcd	....	....	....	....	....	....	....	....	....	636	840	....
Equity Securities.......................	79ldd	....	....	....	....	....	....	....	....	....	613	799	....
Debt Securities.........................	79led	....	....	....	....	....	....	....	....	....	22	41	....
Financial Derivatives.....................	79lld	....	....	....	....	....	....	....	....	....	—	—	....
Other Investment.........................	79lfd	....	....	....	....	....	....	....	....	....	15,961	17,296	....
Monetary Authorities..................	79lgd	....	....	....	....	....	....	....	....	....	80	135	....
General Government...................	79lhd	....	....	....	....	....	....	....	....	....	9,104	9,020	....
Banks......................................	79lid	....	....	....	....	....	....	....	....	....	299	449	....
Other Sectors............................	79ljd	....	....	....	....	....	....	....	....	....	6,479	7,692	....
Government Finance						*Millions of Dirhams: Year Ending December 31*							
Deficit (-) or Surplus......................	80	−6,509	−8,915	† −12,365	−9,485	−4,778	−13,197	3,046	−20,778	−10,042	−17,251	−15,332	....
Revenue...	81	78,653	81,442	† 82,018	79,180	88,845	91,189	111,406	100,902	127,444	104,723	117,550	....
Expenditure....................................	82	84,832	90,072	† 93,889	88,667	96,461	105,539	109,424	122,019	137,887	122,242	132,637	....
Lending Minus Repayments...........	83	330	285	† 494	−2	−2,838	−1,153	−1,064	−339	−401	−268	245	....
Financing													
Net Borrowing: Domestic..............	84a	5,682	13,949	† 14,843	12,914	18,069	10,722	12,973	15,038	28,699	28,680	26,176	....
Net borrowing: Foreign.................	85a	−958	−4,428	† −2,111	−2,666	−8,398	−4,738	−4,394	−6,320	−9,861	−11,199	−8,746	....
Use of Cash Balances....................	87	1,785	−606	† −367	−763	−4,893	7,213	−11,625	12,062	−8,796	−231	−2,098	....
Debt: Domestic.............................	88a	76,847	93,843	† 93,843	110,461	121,526	131,034	136,668	149,388	175,899	191,554	211,590	....
Debt: Foreign................................	89a	141,345	134,952	† 129,766	131,038	130,377	125,864	123,955	118,646	110,597	92,800	78,800	....
National Accounts							*Billions of Dirhams*						
Househ.Cons.Expend.,incl.NPISHs....	96f	172.08	196.76	201.42	227.44	218.61	234.26	229.09	242.97	257.97	264.87	273.82	....
Government Consumption Expend...	91f	44.45	48.53	50.06	53.82	56.61	62.00	66.15	67.69	75.82	79.96	88.12	....
Gross Fixed Capital Formation.........	93e	56.72	57.90	60.39	61.94	65.79	75.74	81.90	85.42	85.37	91.14	98.38	....
Changes in Inventories....................	93i	−.74	1.72	−1.99	.60	.11	.48	−1.98	−1.48	2.35	−.83	1.14	....
Exports of Goods and Services........	90c	56.76	59.43	64.48	69.60	73.56	77.72	84.66	92.96	106.95	115.15	116.86	....
Imports of Goods and Services (-).....	98c	69.69	76.20	83.39	82.02	85.55	93.50	99.54	116.20	120.48	128.25	134.07	....
Gross Domestic Product (GDP).........	99b	250.02	279.58	282.47	319.39	318.34	344.01	345.59	354.21	383.18	397.78	418.66	....
Net Primary Income from Abroad.....	98.n	9.06	10.12	8.79	12.73	11.17	14.40	13.24	18.20	31.74	29.38	32.74	....
Gross National Income (GNI)...........	99a	258.29	289.44	290.44	332.02	329.51	358.41	358.84	372.41	414.93	427.16	451.40	....
GDP Volume 1980 Prices................	99b.p	109.91	121.60	113.62	127.03	124.20	133.73	133.62	134.90	143.39	147.97	155.73	161.06
GDP Volume (2000=100)................	99bvp	81.5	90.1	84.2	94.2	92.1	99.1	99.1	100.0	106.3	109.7	115.4	119.4
GDP Deflator (2000=100)...............	99bip	86.6	87.6	94.7	95.8	97.6	98.0	98.5	100.0	101.8	102.4	102.4	....
						Millions: Midyear Estimates							
**Population...............................	99z	26.10	26.55	27.00	27.45	27.90	28.34	28.79	29.23	29.67	30.12	30.57	31.02

Mozambique 688

		1993	1994	1995	1996	1997	1998	1999	2000	2001	2002	2003	2004
Exchange Rates						*Meticais per SDR: End of Period*							
Market Rate	aa	7,339.2	9,709.5	16,187.9	16,359.7	15,574.4	17,411.7	18,254.4	† 22,332.5	29,307.5	32,430.4	35,450.3	29,350.8
					Meticais per US Dollar: End of Period (ae) Period Average (rf)								
Market Rate	ae	5,343.2	6,651.0	10,890.0	11,377.0	11,543.0	12,366.0	13,300.0	† 17,140.5	23,320.4	23,854.3	23,856.7	18,899.3
Market Rate	rf	3,874.2	6,038.6	9,024.3	11,293.7	11,543.6	11,874.6	12,775.1	15,227.2	20,703.6	23,678.0	23,782.3	22,581.3
Fund Position						*Millions of SDRs: End of Period*							
Quota	2f.s	84.00	84.00	84.00	84.00	84.00	84.00	113.60	113.60	113.60	113.60	113.60	113.60
SDRs	1b.s	.03	.03	.03	.04	.04	.04	.05	.05	.05	.05	.05	.05
Reserve Position in the Fund	1c.s	.01	.01	.01	.01	.01	.01	.01	.01	.01	.01	.01	.01
Total Fund Cred.&Loans Outstg	2tl	137.86	145.24	135.79	125.89	140.11	147.24	145.42	168.47	155.89	147.16	140.75	127.04
International Liquidity					*Millions of US Dollars Unless Otherwise Indicated: End of Period*								
Total Reserves minus Gold	1l.d	187.24	177.51	195.32	344.06	517.35	608.50	651.60	725.11	715.57	819.19	998.45	1,130.35
SDRs	1b.d	.04	.05	.05	.05	.05	.06	.06	.06	.06	.07	.08	.08
Reserve Position in the Fund	1c.d	.01	.01	.01	.01	.01	.01	.01	.01	.01	.01	.01	.01
Foreign Exchange	1d.d	187.19	177.45	195.26	344.00	517.29	608.43	651.53	725.04	715.50	819.11	998.36	1,130.26
Monetary Authorities: Other Liab	4..d	1,185.63	645.60	551.40	537.91	591.66	593.36	587.88	545.92	470.15	480.28	494.89	5.18
Banking Institutions: Assets	7a.d	148.34	220.79	274.47	250.19	242.10	204.66	192.08	315.88	341.14	382.98	364.05	331.63
Liabilities	7b.d	55.75	56.24	76.77	60.68	95.78	80.14	41.92	72.64	83.70	42.03	57.71	72.36
Monetary Authorities						*Billions of Meticais: End of Period*							
Foreign Assets	11	1,175.2	1,367.2	2,424.4	4,359.3	6,359.0	7,928.0	9,089.9	13,018.5	17,297.2	20,164.1	23,900.1	25,328.9
Claims on Central Government	12a	545.5	578.4	663.2	496.9	369.8	82.7	6.9	6.8	6.8	10.0	.7	.4
Claims on Local Government	12b	.3	.3	.2	1.5	.2	.2	.2	.2	.2	.2	.2	.2
Claims on Nonfin.Pub.Enterprises	12c	—	.5	50.5	34.0	.5	.5	.5	.5	.5	.5	.5	.5
Claims on Private Sector	12d	.9	2.2	.9	14.3	54.7	74.7	73.9					
Claims on Banking Institutions	12e	478.1	781.5	734.9	768.6	566.7	589.5	552.8	682.8	491.3	598.8	399.6	266.3
Reserve Money	14	890.1	1,481.4	1,951.1	2,469.5	2,866.6	2,760.2	3,244.5	4,078.8	6,239.4	7,317.3	8,917.4	10,732.9
of which: Currency Outside Banks	14a	469.5	762.4	1,130.2	1,394.4	1,544.1	1,649.7	2,174.2	2,425.3	2,970.4	3,485.8	4,258.8	5,224.7
Time & Foreign Currency Deposits	15	30.7	27.9	84.3	14.8	52.0	72.2	66.0	31.5	46.2			
Liabs. of Central Bank: Securities	16ac						135.0	145.0	200.0	5.0	2,821.3	3,607.1	4,125.1
Foreign Liabilities	16c	7,346.8	5,704.1	8,202.9	8,179.2	9,011.7	9,901.2	10,473.4	13,119.6	15,532.9	16,229.1	16,796.0	3,826.7
Central Government Deposits	16d	1,105.4	1,295.4	1,711.8	3,006.9	4,145.1	4,909.8	5,051.4	5,301.0	4,405.0	4,314.3	5,726.3	10,946.6
o/w: Cent.Govt.Earmarked Funds	16df	907.9	960.6	1,125.3	2,151.5	2,900.6	3,735.6	4,118.1	3,319.7	1,807.9	1,937.2	1,280.5	1,769.9
Capital Accounts	17a	579.0	896.8	969.7	1,201.4	1,294.0	1,363.9	1,581.6	1,679.9	4,741.0	4,685.2	5,002.4	542.1
Other Items (Net)	17r	−7,752.0	−6,675.5	−9,045.6	−9,197.3	−10,018.5	−10,466.7	−10,837.7	−10,702.0	−13,173.6	−14,593.5	−15,748.1	−4,577.1
of which: Valuation Adjustment	17rv	−3,257.9	−5,663.9	−8,339.7	−8,683.2	−8,762.3	−9,192.1	−9,675.9	−10,916.7	−13,841.8	−15,036.7	−15,616.8	−4,333.5
Banking Institutions						*Billions of Meticais: End of Period*							
Reserves	20	433.1	744.6	838.6	1,111.4	1,389.9	1,310.0	1,013.1	1,545.2	3,306.8	3,773.6	4,862.1	5,295.3
Claims on Mon.Author.:Securities	20c						135.0	145.0		2,684.0	3,607.1	4,125.1	
Foreign Assets	21	792.6	1,468.5	2,989.0	2,846.4	2,794.5	2,530.8	2,554.7	5,414.3	7,955.6	9,135.8	8,685.1	6,267.5
Claims on Central Government	22a	6.6	—	.1	65.2	.1	8.3	232.7	1,610.6	2,274.1	2,834.7	4,880.0	8,747.9
Claims on Local Government	22b	—	.6	1.1	1.2	103.9	1.9	149.7	1.5	—	—	—	—
Claims on Nonfin.Pub.Enterprises	22c	121.2	170.4	111.0	65.0	223.0	181.1	46.2	85.9	12,050.1	12,756.5	12,012.8	10,665.0
Claims on Private Sector	22d	971.3	1,538.2	2,373.3	3,440.3	5,114.8	6,467.0	8,552.7	10,987.7	1,893.1	1,768.9	2,306.8	2,847.1
Claims on Nonbank Financial Insts	22g			.7	11.4	12.5	1.3	46.4	269.7				
Demand Deposits	24	1,132.2	1,653.2	2,130.4	2,486.7	3,283.0	3,894.7	4,693.0	5,992.9	6,912.7	7,850.1	9,768.8	11,054.9
Time & Foreign Currency Deposits	25	906.9	1,380.7	2,303.3	2,800.9	3,388.4	4,144.1	5,893.5	9,328.8	12,860.0	16,287.4	18,631.0	18,210.8
Foreign Liabilities	26c	297.9	374.1	836.1	690.4	1,105.6	991.1	557.5	1,245.1	1,952.0	1,002.6	1,376.9	1,367.5
Central Government Deposits	26d	238.7	228.7	375.0	430.9	350.0	313.1	356.4	588.0	1,780.4	1,638.9	2,137.1	3,945.7
o/w: Cent.Govt.Earmarked Funds	26df	23.0	22.5	141.3	204.1	95.9	92.7	91.4	37.8	513.3	273.2	434.5	1,220.8
Credit from Central Bank	26g	.8	581.2	671.0	691.1	560.6	477.4	458.3	965.5	637.5	560.8	134.8	116.0
Capital Accounts	27a	555.2	770.4	1,415.7	1,934.5	2,723.9	3,146.1	3,809.9	5,367.7	7,175.9	8,914.3	7,888.6	7,025.7
Other Items (Net)	27r	−806.9	−1,066.0	−1,417.7	−1,493.5	−1,772.2	−2,331.2	−3,028.0	−3,573.2	−3,838.8	−3,300.6	−3,583.3	−3,772.8
Banking Survey						*Billions of Meticais: End of Period*							
Foreign Assets (Net)	31n	−5,676.9	−3,242.5	−3,625.5	−1,663.9	−963.8	−433.4	613.7	4,068.1	7,767.9	12,068.2	14,412.3	26,402.2
Domestic Credit	32	302.3	766.5	1,114.2	691.9	1,384.6	1,594.7	3,701.5	7,073.8	10,039.4	11,417.6	11,337.7	7,368.8
Claims on Central Govt.(Net)	32an	−792.0	−945.7	−1,423.5	−2,875.8	−4,125.2	−5,132.0	−5,168.1	−4,271.6	−3,904.6	−3,108.5	−2,982.7	−6,144.0
Claims on Local Government	32b	.3	.9	1.3	2.7	104.1	2.1	149.9	1.7	.2	.2	.2	.2
Claims on Nonfin.Pub.Enterprises	32c	121.2	170.9	161.5	99.0	223.6	181.6	46.8	86.4	12,050.6	12,757.0	12,013.3	10,665.5
Claims on Private Sector	32d	972.2	1,540.4	2,374.2	3,454.6	5,169.5	6,541.6	8,626.6	10,987.7	1,893.1	1,768.9	2,306.8	2,847.1
Claims on Nonbank Financial Inst	32g	.6	—	.7	11.4	12.5	1.3	46.4	269.7	—	—	—	—
Money	34	1,606.1	2,417.9	3,264.0	3,917.2	4,901.7	5,613.0	6,994.4	8,557.2	10,066.0	11,520.8	14,263.4	16,579.1
Quasi-Money	35	937.6	1,408.6	2,387.6	2,815.6	3,440.4	4,216.3	5,959.5	9,360.3	12,906.2	16,287.4	18,631.0	18,210.8
Liabs. of Central Bank: Securities	36ac	—	—	—	—	—	—	—	200.0	5.0	137.3		
Capital Accounts	37a	1,134.2	1,667.2	2,385.4	3,135.9	4,017.9	4,510.0	5,391.4	7,047.7	11,916.9	13,599.5	12,891.0	7,567.8
Other Items (Net)	37r	−9,052.5	−7,969.7	−10,548.3	−10,840.7	−11,939.2	−13,178.0	−14,030.1	−14,023.2	−17,086.8	−18,059.1	−20,035.5	−8,586.7
Money plus Quasi-Money	35l	2,543.7	3,826.5	5,651.6	6,732.9	8,342.0	9,829.2	12,953.9	17,917.5	22,972.2	27,808.2	32,894.4	34,789.9
Money (National Definitions)						*Billions of Meticais: End of Period*							
Base Money	19ma	....	....	....	....	2,792.1	2,691.7	3,117.3	3,939.8	6,056.5	7,133.7	8,681.5	10,433.4
M1	59ma	....	....	....	....	6,123.1	7,019.2	9,410.7	13,199.8	17,002.7	19,852.7	23,155.8	24,479.8
M2	59mb	....	....	....	....	7,413.5	8,720.0	11,721.6	16,778.7	21,814.1	26,145.0	32,256.9	34,236.8
Interest Rates						*Percent Per Annum*							
Discount Rate (End of Period)	60		69.70	57.75	32.00	12.95	9.95	9.95	9.95	9.95	9.95	9.95	9.95
Money Market Rate	60b	....	....	....	....	....	....	9.92	16.12	† 25.00	20.40	13.34	9.87
Treasury Bill Rate	60c	....	....	....	....	....	....	....	16.97	24.77	29.55	15.31	12.37
Deposit Rate	60l	....	33.38	38.84	18.14	25.43	8.22	7.86	9.70	† 15.01	17.99	12.15	9.91
Lending Rate	60p	....	....	....	....	....	24.35	19.63	19.04	† 22.73	26.71	24.69	22.08
Prices						*Index Numbers (2000=100): Period Averages*							
Consumer Prices	64	21.2	34.5	† 53.3	79.2	85.0	86.2	88.7	100.0	109.0	127.4	144.4	160.5
Intl. Transactions & Positions						*Billions of Meticais*							
Exports	70	....	979.3	1,573.2	2,509.2	2,614.4	2,783.1	3,429.0	....	....	....	....	....
Imports, c.i.f.	71	....	3,279.0	6,527.1	8,733.7	8,704.7	9,575.9	14,859.3	....	....	....	....	....

Mozambique   688

		1993	1994	1995	1996	1997	1998	1999	2000	2001	2002	2003	2004
Balance of Payments		*Millions of US Dollars: Minus Sign Indicates Debit*											
Current Account, n.i.e.	78ald	−446.3	−467.2	−444.7	−420.5	−295.6	−429.3	−912.0	−763.6	−657.2	−869.1	−816.5	−607.4
Goods: Exports f.o.b.	78aad	131.8	149.5	168.9	226.1	230.0	244.6	283.8	364.0	726.0	809.8	1,043.9	1,503.9
Goods: Imports f.o.b.	78abd	−859.2	−916.7	−705.2	−704.4	−684.0	−735.6	−1,090.0	−1,046.0	−997.3	−1,476.5	−1,648.1	−1,849.7
Trade Balance	78acd	−727.4	−767.2	−536.3	−478.3	−454.0	−491.0	−806.2	−682.0	−271.3	−666.6	−604.2	−345.8
Services: Credit	78add	180.2	191.1	242.4	253.2	278.7	286.2	295.2	325.4	249.7	339.4	303.9	255.6
Services: Debit	78aed	−270.6	−323.3	−350.0	−319.0	−328.6	−396.2	−405.7	−445.8	−618.4	−577.0	−573.9	−531.4
Balance on Goods & Services	78afd	−817.8	−899.4	−643.9	−544.1	−503.9	−601.0	−916.7	−802.4	−640.0	−904.2	−874.1	−621.7
Income: Credit	78agd	59.6	54.8	59.1	61.0	63.6	46.3	57.8	79.3	56.0	52.1	55.9	74.5
Income: Debit	78ahd	−191.4	−187.2	−199.1	−162.1	−168.2	−187.8	−214.8	−271.4	−290.7	−655.3	−221.4	−374.0
Balance on Gds, Serv. & Inc.	78aid	−949.6	−1,031.8	−783.9	−645.2	−608.5	−742.5	−1,073.7	−994.5	−874.7	−1,507.4	−1,039.6	−921.2
Current Transfers, n.i.e.: Credit	78ajd	503.3	564.6	339.2	224.7	312.9	313.2	256.3	337.3	254.6	827.0	293.2	370.5
Current Transfers: Debit	78akd	—	—	—	—	—	—	−94.6	−106.4	−37.1	−188.7	−70.0	−56.7
Capital Account, n.i.e.	78bcd	—	—	—	—	—	—	180.3	226.8	256.7	222.0	270.7	578.1
Capital Account, n.i.e.: Credit	78bad	—	—	—	—	—	—	180.3	226.8	256.7	222.5	271.2	581.2
Capital Account: Debit	78bbd	—	—	—	—	—	—	—	—	—	−.4	−.5	−3.1
Financial Account, n.i.e.	78bjd	246.9	344.4	366.7	235.0	182.2	300.4	403.9	83.2	−24.8	−731.7	372.8	−46.5
Direct Investment Abroad	78bdd	—	—	—	—	—	—	—	—	—	—	—	—
Dir. Invest. in Rep. Econ., n.i.e.	78bed	32.0	35.0	45.0	72.5	64.4	212.7	381.7	139.2	255.4	347.6	336.7	244.7
Portfolio Investment Assets	78bfd	—	—	—	—	—	—	—	—	—	32.2	5.0	−25.4
Equity Securities	78bkd	—	—	—	—	—	—	—	—	—	32.2	5.0	−25.4
Debt Securities	78bld	—	—	—	—	—	—	—	—	—	—	—	—
Portfolio Investment Liab., n.i.e.	78bgd	—	—	—	—	—	—	—	—	—	—	—	—
Equity Securities	78bmd	—	—	—	—	—	—	—	—	—	—	—	—
Debt Securities	78bnd	—	—	—	—	—	—	—	—	—	—	—	—
Financial Derivatives Assets	78bwd	....	....	....	....	....	....	....	....	....	....	....	....
Financial Derivatives Liabilities	78bxd	....	....	....	....	....	....	....	....	....	....	....	....
Other Investment Assets	78bhd	—	—	—	—	—	19.0	2.6	−145.0	−33.8	−207.7	−77.1	−88.7
Monetary Authorities	78bod	—	—	—	—	—	—	1.3	1.7	—	−.8	−5.6	−186.4
General Government	78bpd	—	—	—	—	—	—	—	—	—	—	6.9	—
Banks	78bqd	—	—	—	—	—	17.7	13.9	−124.0	−23.9	−74.6	13.1	57.8
Other Sectors	78brd	—	—	—	—	—	—	−13.0	−21.0	−9.1	−127.5	−97.1	39.9
Other Investment Liab., n.i.e.	78bid	214.9	309.4	321.7	162.5	117.8	68.7	19.6	89.0	−246.4	−903.8	108.2	−177.1
Monetary Authorities	78bsd	—	—	—	—	—	—	−5.8	−40.8	—	10.1	22.3	−48.4
General Government	78btd	214.9	309.4	321.7	86.2	48.8	−.8	−261.7	−171.4	−263.1	−1,302.9	53.0	−47.6
Banks	78bud	—	—	—	—	—	20.3	−33.6	16.6	35.1	−43.0	15.7	9.6
Other Sectors	78bvd	—	—	—	76.3	69.0	49.2	320.7	284.6	−18.4	432.0	17.3	−90.8
Net Errors and Omissions	78cad	−447.4	−443.2	−308.6	−238.3	−364.8	−263.8	1.5	37.5	−59.6	−60.0	208.2	216.4
Overall Balance	78cbd	−646.8	−566.0	−386.6	−423.8	−478.2	−392.7	−326.3	−416.1	−484.9	−1,438.8	35.3	140.7
Reserves and Related Items	79dad	646.8	566.0	386.6	423.8	478.2	392.7	326.3	416.1	484.9	1,438.8	−35.3	−140.7
Reserve Assets	79dbd	63.6	−12.0	16.4	161.0	162.3	91.5	−44.0	−76.8	18.8	−97.8	−181.5	−169.1
Use of Fund Credit and Loans	79dcd	15.4	10.4	−14.4	−14.4	19.9	9.6	−2.9	31.1	−15.8	−11.5	−9.1	−20.4
Exceptional Financing	79ded	567.8	567.6	384.6	277.1	296.0	291.6	373.2	461.8	481.9	1,548.2	155.3	48.8
National Accounts		*Billions of Meticais*											
Househ.Cons.Expend.,incl.NPISHs	96f	8,012	12,295	20,564	30,692	35,735	38,822	40,857	46,722	53,093	60,227	69,908	....
Government Consumption Expend.	91f	1,203	2,588	2,009	2,625	3,655	4,892	6,367	6,682	10,300	13,461	18,143	....
Gross Fixed Capital Formation	93e	1,637	2,976	5,578	6,617	8,197	8,602	10,378	18,061	15,287	17,317	17,842	....
Changes in Inventories	93i	267	330	755	524	−3	2,758	8,663	1,514	4,531	8,506	13,392	....
Exports of Goods and Services	90c	757	1,547	2,601	3,982	4,510	4,923	5,256	7,436	16,203	23,175	29,250	....
Imports of Goods and Services (-)	98c	3,867	6,416	10,830	11,722	12,276	13,085	19,607	22,060	22,869	26,341	30,845	....
Gross Domestic Product (GDP)	99b	8,012	13,319	20,678	32,719	39,819	46,912	51,913	58,355	76,545	96,345	117,690	....
Gross National Income (GNI)	99a	7,136	11,665	16,128	....	....	....	....	....	....	....	....	....
GDP Volume 1996 Prices	99b.p	27,729	29,665	30,646	32,719	36,341	40,932	44,018	44,873	50,751	55,170	59,549	....
GDP Volume (2000=100)	99bvp	61.8	66.1	68.3	72.9	81.0	91.2	98.1	100.0	113.1	122.9	132.7	....
GDP Deflator (2000=100)	99bip	22.2	34.5	51.9	76.9	84.3	88.1	90.7	100.0	116.0	134.3	152.0	....
		Millions: Midyear Estimates											
Population	99z	14.77	15.33	15.85	16.32	16.75	17.14	17.53	17.91	18.30	18.68	19.05	19.42

Myanmar 518

		1993	1994	1995	1996	1997	1998	1999	2000	2001	2002	2003	2004
Exchange Rates							*Kyats per SDR: End of Period*							
Official Rate	aa	8.5085	8.5085	8.5085	8.5085	8.5085	8.5085	8.5085	8.5085	8.5085	8.5085	8.5085	8.5085
					Kyats per US Dollar: End of Period (ae) Period Average (rf)									
Official Rate	ae	6.1945	5.8283	5.7239	5.9171	6.3061	6.0428	6.1992	6.5303	6.7704	6.2584	5.7259	5.4787
Official Rate	rf	6.0938	5.9446	5.6106	5.8609	6.1838	6.2738	6.2233	6.4257	6.6841	6.5734	6.0764	5.7459
Fund Position							*Millions of SDRs: End of Period*							
Quota	2f.s	184.9	184.9	184.9	184.9	184.9	184.9	258.4	258.4	258.4	258.4	258.4	258.4
SDRs	1b.s	.2	.1	.1	.1	.1	.2	.1	.1	.4	.1	.1	—
Reserve Position in the Fund	1c.s	—	—	—	—	—	—	—	—	—	—	—	—
Total Fund Cred.&Loans Outstg.	2tl	—	—	—	—	—	—	—	—	—	—	—	—
International Liquidity						*Millions of US Dollars Unless Otherwise Indicated: End of Period*								
Total Reserves minus Gold	1l.d	302.9	422.0	561.1	229.2	249.8	314.9	265.5	223.0	400.5	470.0	550.2	672.1
SDRs	1b.d	.3	.1	.1	.1	.1	.3	.2	.1	.6	.1	.1	—
Reserve Position in the Fund	1c.d	—	—	—	—	—	—	—	—	—	—	—	—
Foreign Exchange	1d.d	302.6	421.9	561.1	229.1	249.7	314.6	265.3	222.8	399.9	469.9	550.1	672.1
Gold (Million Fine Troy Ounces)	1ad	.251	.251	.231	.231	.231	.231	.231	.231	.231	.231	.231	.231
Gold (National Valuation)	1and	12.1	12.8	12.0	11.6	10.9	11.4	11.1	10.6	10.2	11.0	12.0	12.6
Monetary Authorities: Other Liab.	4..d	336.4	346.0	328.6	335.3	343.0	337.5	338.8	336.3	531.3	542.1	555.3	569.4
Deposit Money Banks: Assets	7a.d	132.1	161.7	195.4	122.0	144.6	232.3	223.5	184.8	173.3	236.0	285.3	305.3
Liabilities	7b.d	1,765.7	1,972.9	2,119.6	1,961.2	1,706.0	1,640.1	1,705.2	1,698.9	1,645.1	1,606.6	1,858.0	1,992.6
Monetary Authorities							*Millions of Kyats: End of Period*							
Foreign Assets	11	2,030	2,656	3,587	2,119	1,690	3,663	2,494	2,933	4,149	5,136	4,410	3,798
Claims on Central Government	12a	91,399	116,131	142,023	182,431	214,392	281,383	331,425	447,581	675,040	892,581	1,262,588	1,686,341
Claims on Deposit Money Banks	12e	10,375	3,639	5,191	5,923	23,785	15,553	19,602	15,918	21,576	38,732	93,952	55,280
Reserve Money	14	79,275	97,584	124,675	164,513	213,025	270,104	320,579	431,085	653,723	882,043	1,289,016	1,666,058
of which: Currency Outside DMBs	14a	67,611	89,084	114,524	152,789	194,129	237,098	272,769	344,728	494,521	718,633	1,102,937	1,347,598
Other Liabilities to DMBs	14n	22,662	23,320	24,284	22,904	22,624	24,435	23,402	23,847	23,850	24,916	24,285	23,902
Foreign Liabilities	16c	2,050	2,056	1,843	1,965	2,121	2,117	2,108	2,170	3,551	3,562	3,379	3,270
Capital Accounts	17a	787	788	1,086	1,082	1,681	2,882	4,874	5,282	8,952	10,083	18,911	19,683
Other Items (Net)	17r	−969	−1,317	−1,086	9	414	1,062	2,559	4,048	10,690	15,846	25,360	32,507
Deposit Money Banks							*Millions of Kyats: End of Period*							
Reserves	20	5,300	−11,374	−17,511	−12,258	14,570	44,356	57,339	70,591	99,973	113,696	104,837	175,028
Other Claims on Monetary Author.	20n	22,662	23,320	24,284	22,904	22,624	24,435	23,402	23,847	23,850	24,916	24,285	23,902
Foreign Assets	21	—	1	3	8	20	1	369	3	13	9	—	—
Claims on Central Govt. (Net)	22an	2,751	−727	−305	−2,402	2,312	−30,179	12,460	36,159	40,985	43,248	35,546	89,217
Claims on Local Government	22b	449	511	310	184	61	61	—	—	—	—	—	—
Claims on Nonfin.Pub.Enterprises	22c	6,459	11,343	8,351	10,631	11,419	46,688	53,960	69,158	72,338	69,162	68,107	50,959
Claims on Private Sector	22d	23,076	28,262	45,956	75,346	115,505	155,761	188,149	266,466	416,176	608,401	341,547	428,931
Demand Deposits	24	5,827	9,183	11,241	14,961	25,600	44,782	72,707	119,746	206,349	290,520	82,948	139,880
Time, Savings,& Fgn.Currency Dep.	25	24,024	33,942	54,572	82,786	102,944	151,363	216,459	335,574	450,560	541,307	386,298	594,169
Restricted Deposits	26b	1,039	1,179	1,814	2,349	1,739	1,549	1,635	1,703	1,760	2,661	2,812	2,298
Foreign Liabilities	26c	10,759	11,725	11,889	11,494	10,549	10,287	10,611	10,961	10,995	10,557	11,306	11,443
Credit from Monetary Authorities	26g	1,823	1,777	5,038	3,835	10,119	5,762	5,030	7,439	15,601	44,251	96,692	48,210
Capital Accounts	27a	2,402	3,228	4,128	7,790	10,733	12,546	17,908	24,094	32,285	47,881	62,272	74,061
Other Items (Net)	27r	14,803	−9,696	−27,593	−28,802	4,827	14,829	11,329	−33,294	−64,216	−77,742	−67,995	−102,024
Monetary Survey							*Millions of Kyats: End of Period*							
Foreign Assets (Net)	31n	−10,779	−11,124	−10,143	−11,332	−10,960	−8,740	−9,856	−10,195	−10,384	−8,974	−10,275	−10,915
Domestic Credit	32	124,134	155,520	196,335	266,191	343,689	453,714	585,994	819,364	1,204,539	1,613,392	1,707,788	2,255,448
Claims on Central Govt. (Net)	32an	94,150	115,404	141,718	180,029	216,704	251,204	343,885	483,740	716,025	935,829	1,298,134	1,775,558
Claims on Local Government	32b	449	511	310	184	61	61	—	—	—	—	—	—
Claims on Nonfin.Pub.Enterprises	32c	6,459	11,343	8,351	10,631	11,419	46,688	53,960	69,158	72,338	69,162	68,107	50,959
Claims on Private Sector	32d	23,076	28,262	45,956	75,346	115,505	155,761	188,149	266,466	416,176	608,401	341,547	428,931
Money	34	73,457	98,289	125,956	167,971	219,983	282,087	345,765	464,968	701,153	1,009,471	1,186,104	1,487,655
Quasi-Money	35	24,024	33,942	54,572	82,786	102,944	151,363	216,459	335,574	450,560	541,307	386,298	594,169
Restricted Deposits	36b	1,039	1,179	1,814	2,349	1,739	1,549	1,635	1,703	1,760	2,661	2,812	2,298
Capital Accounts	37a	3,189	4,016	5,213	8,871	12,413	15,428	22,782	29,376	41,237	57,964	81,183	93,744
Other Items (Net)	37r	11,627	6,977	−1,361	−7,120	−4,354	−5,457	−10,502	−22,453	−555	−6,981	41,128	66,668
Money plus Quasi-Money	35l	97,480	132,231	180,528	250,758	322,927	433,451	562,224	800,542	1,151,713	1,550,778	1,572,402	2,081,824
Interest Rates							*Percent Per Annum*							
Central Bank Rate (End of Per.)	60	11.00	11.00	12.50	15.00	15.00	15.00	12.00	10.00	10.00	10.00	10.00	10.00
Deposit Rate	60l	9.00	9.00	9.75	12.50	12.50	12.50	11.00	9.75	9.50	9.50	9.50	9.50
Lending Rate	60p	....	16.50	16.50	16.50	16.50	16.50	16.13	15.25	15.00	15.00	15.00	15.00
Government Bond Yield	61	....	10.50	10.50	13.13	14.00	14.00	† 11.00	9.00	9.00	9.00	9.00	9.00
Prices and Labor							*Index Numbers (2000=100): Period Averages*							
Consumer Prices	64	23.8	29.6	37.0	43.0	55.8	84.6	† 100.1	100.0	121.1	190.2	259.8	....
						Number in Thousands: Period Averages								
Employment	67e	16,469	16,817	....	....	17,964	18,359	....	....	....	....	....	....
Unemployment	67c	518	541	....	....	535	452	425	382	398	436	327	....
Intl. Transactions & Positions							*Millions of Kyats*							
Exports	70	3,609.4	4,776.7	4,825.8	4,419.5	5,415.8	6,737.2	7,073.5	10,600.5	15,929.4	19,980.3	15,123.0	....
Imports, c.i.f.	71	5,007.0	5,285.9	7,564.2	8,032.0	12,735.9	16,920.7	14,463.9	15,426.3	19,248.3	15,373.2	12,720.7	....

Myanmar 518

		1993	1994	1995	1996	1997	1998	1999	2000	2001	2002	2003	2004
Balance of Payments						*Millions of US Dollars: Minus Sign Indicates Debit*							
Current Account, n.i.e.	78ald	−230.2	−130.3	−261.0	−282.6	−415.9	−499.1	−284.7	−211.7	−169.5	10.0	49.6	....
Goods: Exports f.o.b.	78aad	637.4	861.6	942.6	946.9	983.7	1,077.3	1,293.9	1,661.6	2,432.4	2,544.1	2,510.1	....
Goods: Imports f.o.b.	78abd	−1,273.9	−1,474.2	−1,773.9	−1,887.2	−2,126.4	−2,478.2	−2,181.3	−2,165.4	−2,376.3	−2,161.6	−1,932.4	....
Trade Balance	78acd	−636.5	−612.6	−831.3	−940.2	−1,142.7	−1,400.9	−887.3	−503.8	56.1	382.4	577.7	....
Services: Credit	78add	249.1	272.2	364.6	431.9	526.6	633.2	512.2	477.9	407.7	379.1	300.3	....
Services: Debit	78aed	−131.6	−129.5	−246.2	−304.9	−447.5	−368.8	−291.1	−328.1	−362.7	−321.5	−355.3	....
Balance on Goods & Services	78afd	−518.9	−470.0	−712.9	−813.2	−1,063.6	−1,136.5	−666.3	−354.0	101.2	440.0	522.6	....
Income: Credit	78agd	4.8	7.2	15.5	9.1	6.6	11.0	51.6	35.5	35.9	31.7	30.0	....
Income: Debit	78ahd	−63.7	−74.5	−125.4	−53.6	−20.4	−11.4	−54.6	−168.8	−510.0	−623.5	−631.8	....
Balance on Gds, Serv. & Inc.	78aid	−577.8	−537.3	−822.8	−857.7	−1,077.5	−1,137.0	−669.2	−487.3	−372.9	−151.8	−79.2	....
Current Transfers, n.i.e.: Credit	78ajd	348.2	407.6	569.9	604.1	691.6	638.1	384.8	289.7	217.7	185.8	151.1	....
Current Transfers: Debit	78akd	−.5	−.6	−8.1	−29.1	−30.0	−.3	−.3	−14.1	−14.3	−23.9	−22.3	....
Capital Account, n.i.e.	78bcd	—	—	—	—	....	....	....	....	....	....	....	....
Capital Account, n.i.e.: Credit	78bad	—	—	—	—	....	....	....	....	....	....	....	....
Capital Account: Debit	78bbd	—	—	—	—	....	....	....	....	....	....	....	....
Financial Account, n.i.e.	78bjd	162.4	186.4	245.2	269.4	473.5	540.9	251.2	212.8	303.3	97.2	28.8	....
Direct Investment Abroad	78bdd												
Dir. Invest. in Rep. Econ., n.i.e.	78bed	105.7	126.9	279.9	313.4	390.8	317.8	255.6	258.3	210.3	191.1	133.5	....
Portfolio Investment Assets	78bfd	....	....	....	....	....	....	....	....	....	....	....	....
Equity Securities	78bkd	....	....	....	....	....	....	....	....	....	....	....	....
Debt Securities	78bld	....	....	....	....	....	....	....	....	....	....	....	....
Portfolio Investment Liab., n.i.e.	78bgd	....	....	....	....	....	....	....	....	....	....	....	....
Equity Securities	78bmd	....	....	....	....	....	....	....	....	....	....	....	....
Debt Securities	78bnd	....	....	....	....	....	....	....	....	....	....	....	....
Financial Derivatives Assets	78bwd	....	....	....	....	....	....	....	....	....	....	....	....
Financial Derivatives Liabilities	78bxd	....	....	....	....	....	....	....	....	....	....	....	....
Other Investment Assets	78bhd	....	....	....	....	....	....	....	....	....	....	....	....
Monetary Authorities	78bod	....	....	....	....	....	....	....	....	....	....	....	....
General Government	78bpd	....	....	....	....	....	....	....	....	....	....	....	....
Banks	78bqd	....	....	....	....	....	....	....	....	....	....	....	....
Other Sectors	78brd	....	....	....	....	....	....	....	....	....	....	....	....
Other Investment Liab., n.i.e.	78bid	56.7	59.5	−34.7	−44.0	82.7	223.0	−4.4	−45.4	93.0	−93.9	−104.7	....
Monetary Authorities	78bsd	—	2.6	2.4	−3.1	−5.6	−2.7	1.1	7.2	200.8	−11.6	−21.2	
General Government	78btd	56.7	56.8	−37.1	−40.9	88.3	229.3	−4.1	−56.8	−101.4	−86.4	−81.7	
Banks	78bud	....	....	....	....	....	....	−3.6	−1.3	4.1	−.8	12.0	5.3
Other Sectors	78bvd	....	....	....	....	....	....	....	....	−5.6	−7.9	−7.2	
Net Errors and Omissions	78cad	−10.1	−10.4	−16.3	−11.8	−26.3	18.7	−12.4	−24.5	46.1	−61.8	−39.5	
Overall Balance	78cbd	−77.8	45.8	−32.2	−25.0	31.3	60.4	−45.9	−23.4	179.8	45.4	38.9	
Reserves and Related Items	79dad	77.8	−45.8	32.2	25.0	−31.3	−60.4	45.9	23.4	−179.8	−45.4	−38.9	
Reserve Assets	79dbd	77.8	−45.8	32.2	25.0	−31.3	−60.4	45.9	23.4	−179.8	−45.4	−38.9	
Use of Fund Credit and Loans	79dcd	—	—	—	—	—	—	—	—	—	—	—	
Exceptional Financing	79ded	....	....	....	....	....	....	....	....	....	....	....	
International Investment Position						*Millions of US Dollars*							
Assets	79aad	....	....	....	....	....	....	—	—	....	....	—	
Direct Investment Abroad	79abd	....	....	....	....	....	....	—	—	—	—	—	
Portfolio Investment	79acd	....	....	....	....	....	....	—	—	—	—	—	
Equity Securities	79add	....	....	....	....	....	....	—	—	—	—	—	
Debt Securities	79aed	....	....	....	....	....	....	—	—	—	—	—	
Financial Derivatives	79ald	....	....	....	....	....	....	—	....	....	....	—	
Other Investment	79afd	....	....	....	....	....	....	—	—	—	—	—	
Monetary Authorities	79agd	....	....	....	....	....	....	....	....	....	....	....	
General Government	79ahd	....	....	....	....	....	....	....	....	....	....	....	
Banks	79aid	....	....	....	....	....	....	....	....	....	....	....	
Other Sectors	79ajd	....	....	....	....	....	....	....	....	....	....	....	
Reserve Assets	79akd	....	....	....	....	....	....	331.7	290.4	460.4	560.5	665.6	
Liabilities	79lad	....	....	....	....	....	....	....	....	....	....	....	
Dir. Invest. in Rep. Economy	79lbd	....	....	....	....	....	....	3,130.7	3,211.0	3,304.8	3,775.2	4,268.1	
Portfolio Investment	79lcd	....	....	....	....	....	....	—	—	—	—	—	
Equity Securities	79ldd	....	....	....	....	....	....	—	—	—	—	—	
Debt Securities	79led	....	....	....	....	....	....	—	—	—	—	—	
Financial Derivatives	79lld	....	....	....	....	....	....	....	....	....	....	....	
Other Investment	79lfd	....	....	....	....	....	....	5,430.3	5,109.9	5,020.9	5,333.4	5,718.8	
Monetary Authorities	79lgd	....	....	....	....	....	....	....	....	....	....	....	
General Government	79lhd	....	....	....	....	....	....	....	....	....	....	....	
Banks	79lid	....	....	....	....	....	....	....	....	....	....	....	
Other Sectors	79ljd	....	....	....	....	....	....	....	....	....	....	....	
Government Finance						*Millions of Kyats: Year Beginning April 1*							
Deficit (-) or Surplus	80	−7,761	−15,757	−24,924	−25,052	−10,343	−6,946	−30,444	−86,578	−105,899	−72,676	....	....
Revenue	81	27,329	32,029	39,429	54,726	86,690	116,066	122,895	134,308	164,488	279,651	....	....
Grants Received	81z	456	429	744	421	1,548	524	221	242	288	358	....	....
Expenditure	82	35,696	48,021	64,884	80,120	98,426	124,064	153,497	221,255	271,371	353,389	....	....
Lending Minus Repayments	83	−150	194	213	79	155	−528	63	−127	−696	−704	....	....
Financing													
Domestic	84a	7,738	15,749	25,201	25,230	9,833	5,680	30,311	86,661	106,029	72,764	....	....
Foreign	85a	23	8	−277	−178	510	1,266	133	−83	−130	−88	....	....

		1993	1994	1995	1996	1997	1998	1999	2000	2001	2002	2003	2004
National Accounts							*Millions of Kyats: Year Beginning April 1*						
Househ.Cons.Expend.,incl.NPISHs....	96f	319,191	417,230	523,876	701,220	987,513	1,420,612	1,903,431	2,237,477	3,139,927	5,049,366	6,869,916	....
Gross Fixed Capital Formation..........	93e	37,466	54,596	82,582	118,313	150,240	206,912	255,408	300,981	413,182	551,749	845,502	....
Changes in Inventories.....................	93i	7,360	3,875	3,540	−21,262	−10,276	−7,604	38,859	16,709	−2,610	19,095	418	....
Exports of Goods and Services.........	90c	4,228	5,405	5,033	5,488	6,290	6,728	8,887	12,639	16,350	19,955	14,118	....
Imports of Goods and Services (-).....	98c	7,923	8,332	10,302	11,779	14,258	16,872	16,265	15,073	18,377	14,910	13,338	....
Gross Domestic Product (GDP)........	99b	360,321	472,774	604,729	791,980	1,119,509	1,609,776	2,190,320	2,552,733	3,548,472	5,625,255	7,716,616	....
Net Primary Income from Abroad.....	98.n	−429	−396	−689	−116	−69	34	−36	−118	−204	−20	−174	....
Gross National Income (GNI)............	99a	359,892	472,378	604,040	791,864	1,119,440	1,609,810	2,190,284	2,552,615	3,548,268	5,625,235	7,716,616	....
GDP Volume 1985/86 Prices............	99b.p	58,064	62,406	66,742	71,042	75,123	79,460	88,134	93,629	....	....	....	....
GDP Volume 2000/01 Prices............	99b.p	....	....	....	....	....	....	....	2,552,733	2,842,314	3,184,117	3,624,816	....
GDP Volume (2000=100)...............	99bvp	62.0	66.7	71.3	75.9	80.2	84.9	94.1	† 100.0	111.3	124.7	142.0	....
GDP Deflator (2000=100)...............	99bip	22.8	27.8	33.2	40.9	54.7	74.3	91.2	100.0	124.8	176.7	212.9	....
							Millions: Midyear Estimates						
Population..............................	99z	43.02	43.78	44.50	45.19	45.86	46.50	47.12	47.72	48.32	48.90	49.46	50.00

		1993	1994	1995	1996	1997	1998	1999	2000	2001	2002	2003	2004
Exchange Rates					*Namibia Dollars per SDR: End of Period*								
Market Rate	aa	4.66667	5.17298	5.42197	6.73325	6.56747	8.25106	8.44711	9.86107	15.23974	11.74625	9.86684	8.74345
					Namibia Dollars per US Dollar: End of Period (ae) Period Average (rf)								
Market Rate	ae	3.39750	3.54350	3.64750	4.68250	4.86750	5.86000	6.15450	7.56850	12.12650	8.64000	6.64000	5.63000
Market Rate	rf	3.26774	3.55080	3.62709	4.29935	4.60796	5.52828	6.10948	6.93983	8.60918	10.54075	7.56475	6.45969
Fund Position					*Millions of SDRs: End of Period*								
Quota	2f.s	100	100	100	100	100	100	137	137	137	137	137	137
SDRs	1b.s	—	—	—	—	—	—	—	—	—	—	—	—
Reserve Position in the Fund	1c.s	—	—	—	—	—	—	—	—	—	—	—	—
Total Fund Cred.&Loans Outstg	2tl	—	—	—	—	—	—	—	—	—	—	—	—
International Liquidity					*Millions of US Dollars Unless Otherwise Indicated: End of Period*								
Total Reserves minus Gold	1l.d	133.70	202.62	220.98	193.87	250.53	260.25	305.49	260.01	234.25	323.13	325.22	345.06
SDRs	1b.d	.02	.02	.02	.02	.02	.02	.02	.02	.02	.02	.03	.03
Reserve Position in the Fund	1c.d	.01	.01	.03	.04	.04	.05	.05	.05	.05	.06	.08	.09
Foreign Exchange	1d.d	133.67	202.59	220.94	193.81	250.47	260.18	305.42	259.94	234.18	323.05	325.11	344.94
Gold (Million Fine Troy Ounces)	1ad	—	—	—	—	—	—	—	—	—	—	—	—
Gold (National Valuation)	1and	—	—	—	—	—	—	—	—	—	—	—	—
Monetary Authorities: Other Liab.	4..d	179.93	200.87	212.20	181.89	4.96	6.63	7.70	8.48	5.87	6.66	23.75	....
Deposit Money Banks: Assets	7a.d	57.38	54.87	38.58	74.70	110.33	93.58	142.63	231.65	121.40	130.62	165.56	....
Liabilities	7b.d	47.35	110.49	137.26	63.00	172.31	116.20	67.99	129.63	129.09	255.33	382.21	....
Other Banking Insts.: Liabilities	7f.d	3.01	5.15	2.80	2.11	3.07	4.01	4.17	11.04	12.47	23.26	21.58	....
Monetary Authorities					*Millions of Namibia Dollars: End of Period*								
Foreign Assets	11	465.9	725.8	818.1	918.0	1,236.0	1,550.1	1,885.6	2,032.0	2,715.9	2,904.7	2,132.4	
Claims on Central Government	12a	619.6	720.0	783.7	856.9	—	—	—	—	—	—	—	
Reserve Money	14	233.3	373.6	415.6	508.3	609.3	631.4	906.7	849.6	919.7	991.7	1,187.5	
Foreign Liabilities	16c	611.3	711.8	774.0	851.7	24.1	38.8	47.4	64.2	71.2	57.5	157.7	
Central Government Deposits	16d	221.7	291.2	280.8	162.4	374.4	416.1	471.8	446.3	360.5	1,044.6	251.7	
Capital Accounts	17a	40.6	71.2	119.5	303.8	316.5	513.4	562.9	783.9	1,587.9	1,076.3	725.8	
Other Items (Net)	17r	−21.4	−2.0	11.9	−51.3	−88.4	−49.8	−103.2	−112.0	−223.3	−265.3	−190.3	
Deposit Money Banks					*Millions of Namibia Dollars: End of Period*								
Reserves	20	99.5	156.2	175.4	226.4	275.7	265.7	510.5	368.5	412.3	425.8	603.5	
Foreign Assets	21	195.0	194.4	140.7	349.8	537.0	548.4	877.8	1,753.3	1,472.2	1,128.5	1,099.3	
Claims on Central Government	22a	279.2	238.8	256.2	460.9	659.8	701.7	1,020.0	949.1	904.2	1,183.0	1,696.9	
Claims on Local Government	22b	15.0	17.2	19.2	18.6	17.4	18.8	16.3	12.4	32.8	5.7	14.6	
Claims on Nonfin.Pub.Enterprises	22c	42.2	42.1	72.1	72.2	148.8	142.7	136.6	234.0	119.1	158.1	144.3	
Claims on Private Sector	22d	2,705.5	3,542.6	4,742.8	5,663.2	6,553.5	7,129.3	7,434.2	8,699.8	10,115.5	12,161.2	15,405.8	
Claims on Other Banking Insts	22f	10.1	95.1	74.6	7.0	23.6	14.6	.6	.4	19.7	—	—	
Claims on Nonbank Financial Insts	22g	—	—	—	10.1	—	—	10.1	45.6	2.3	1.3	—	
Demand Deposits	24	1,333.1	1,465.3	1,581.9	2,516.7	2,562.5	3,315.9	4,073.6	5,284.8	5,805.2	6,152.4	7,266.8	
Time, Savings,& Fgn.Currency Dep	25	1,521.9	2,081.0	2,851.6	3,229.9	3,535.8	3,479.6	3,979.9	3,808.7	3,691.0	3,999.9	5,062.0	
Money Market Instruments	26aa	—	—	—	—	—	—	—	—	103.3	258.9	158.2	
Bonds	26ab	3.9	4.1	4.1	8.9	7.0	5.5	—	—	—	—	—	
Foreign Liabilities	26c	160.9	391.5	500.6	295.0	838.7	680.9	418.4	981.1	1,565.4	2,206.1	2,537.9	
Central Government Deposits	26d	113.3	83.1	73.5	77.9	217.6	173.2	89.2	227.5	258.6	380.6	671.2	
Credit from Monetary Authorities	26g	—	—	—	—	—	7.7	120.3	18.5	124.2	19.5	14.4	
Liabilities to Other Banking Insts	26i	7.6	5.1	74.0	20.9	67.2	45.2	56.8	50.0	—	—	20.4	
Capital Accounts	27a	273.2	293.8	432.5	644.0	782.7	919.0	1,080.7	1,291.0	1,537.1	1,604.0	2,536.3	
Other Items (Net)	27r	−67.4	−37.6	−37.2	14.8	204.4	194.0	187.3	401.5	−6.9	442.2	697.2	
Monetary Survey					*Millions of Namibia Dollars: End of Period*								
Foreign Assets (Net)	31n	−111.3	−183.0	−315.8	121.1	910.1	1,378.7	2,297.7	2,740.0	2,551.5	1,769.6	536.1	....
Domestic Credit	32	3,336.9	4,282.1	5,595.0	6,849.1	6,811.9	7,418.2	8,057.5	9,268.2	10,575.6	12,085.5	16,340.2	....
Claims on Central Govt. (Net)	32an	563.8	584.5	685.6	1,077.4	67.8	112.3	459.0	275.3	285.1	−242.1	774.0	
Claims on Local Government	32b	15.0	17.2	19.2	18.6	17.5	18.8	16.3	12.4	32.8	5.7	14.6	
Claims on Nonfin.Pub.Enterprises	32c	42.2	42.1	72.1	72.2	148.8	142.7	136.6	234.0	119.1	158.1	144.3	
Claims on Private Sector	32d	2,705.5	3,542.6	4,742.8	5,663.2	6,553.5	7,129.3	7,434.2	8,699.8	10,115.5	12,161.2	15,405.8	
Claims on Other Banking Insts	32f	10.5	95.6	75.3	7.7	24.3	15.1	1.3	1.0	20.8	1.3	1.5	
Claims on Nonbank Financial Inst	32g	—	—	—	10.1	—	—	10.1	45.6	2.3	1.3	—	
Money	34	1,466.8	1,682.8	1,822.2	2,799.5	2,898.1	3,680.9	4,496.3	5,766.0	6,312.7	6,698.2	7,851.4	
Quasi-Money	35	1,521.9	2,081.0	2,851.6	3,229.9	3,535.8	3,479.6	3,979.9	3,808.7	3,691.0	3,999.9	5,062.0	
Money Market Instruments	36aa	—	—	—	—	—	—	—	—	103.3	258.9	158.2	
Bonds	36ab	3.9	4.1	4.1	8.9	7.0	5.5	—	—	—	—	—	
Liabilities to Other Banking Insts	36i	7.6	5.1	74.0	20.9	67.2	45.2	56.8	50.0	—	—	20.4	
Capital Accounts	37a	313.8	365.0	552.0	947.8	1,099.3	1,432.4	1,643.6	2,074.9	3,125.0	2,680.3	3,262.1	
Other Items (Net)	37r	−88.4	−39.0	−24.5	−36.7	114.6	153.3	178.6	308.6	−104.9	217.9	522.2	
Money plus Quasi-Money	35l	2,988.8	3,763.8	4,673.7	6,029.4	6,433.9	7,160.5	8,476.2	9,574.7	10,003.7	10,698.1	12,913.3	
Other Banking Institutions					*Millions of Namibia Dollars: End of Period*								
Reserves	40	43.1	.6	6.9	1.1	1.2	1.4	1.9	2.0	2.2	2.1	—	....
Claims on Central Government	42a	6.0	31.0	5.1	140.0	166.4	151.9	209.5	34.3	138.5	164.0	—	
Claims on Local Government	42b	6.1	5.5	5.3	5.3	5.2	5.1	5.0	4.9	4.6	4.6	4.7	
Claims on Nonfin.Pub.Enterprises	42c	7.7	16.7	7.8	4.6	4.7	7.5	8.6	211.6	63.4	66.9	—	
Claims on Private Sector	42d	1,148.7	1,374.3	1,519.6	1,352.9	1,402.5	1,623.6	1,799.5	2,091.8	2,498.7	2,656.5	1,659.6	
Claims on Deposit Money Banks	42e	95.8	116.8	164.1	91.3	160.6	118.8	167.6	121.5	151.6	90.9	125.3	
Claims on Nonbank Financial Insts	42g	16.6	8.7	9.7	8.0	17.7	18.1	14.6	12.9	12.9	12.7	16.2	
Time, Savings,& Fgn.Currency Dep	45	499.4	701.7	795.1	718.1	845.4	868.8	1,123.3	1,284.2	1,531.5	1,613.3	524.6	
Money Market Instruments	46aa	223.8	190.9	180.3	234.6	197.8	182.5	45.8	45.4	44.4	34.9	189.0	
Foreign Liabilities	46c	10.2	18.3	10.2	9.9	15.0	23.5	25.7	83.6	151.2	201.0	143.3	
Central Government Deposits	46d	21.8	16.4	18.0	7.1	3.4	3.7	3.6	27.5	3.4	2.5	—	
Credit from Deposit Money Banks	46h	20.0	24.0	68.5	35.6	36.3	41.0	38.0	74.4	82.4	72.8	60.2	
Capital Accounts	47a	634.2	763.1	821.2	792.2	894.7	960.2	1,099.9	1,237.3	1,325.0	1,349.3	1,118.7	
Other Items (Net)	47r	−85.6	−160.8	−174.9	−194.4	−234.3	−153.3	−129.5	−273.4	−266.0	−276.1	−230.0	....

		1993	1994	1995	1996	1997	1998	1999	2000	2001	2002	2003	2004
Banking Survey					*Millions of Namibia Dollars: End of Period*								
Foreign Assets (Net)........................	51n	−120.8	−200.7	−325.5	111.2	895.2	1,355.2	2,272.0	2,656.4	2,400.4	1,568.6	392.8	....
Domestic Credit.............................	52	4,489.6	5,606.2	7,049.1	8,345.1	8,380.8	9,205.5	10,089.8	11,595.1	13,269.5	14,986.4	18,019.2	....
Claims on Central Govt. (Net)........	52an	548.0	599.1	672.7	1,210.3	230.8	260.5	664.8	282.1	420.2	−80.6	774.0	....
Claims on Local Government..........	52b	21.1	22.7	24.5	23.9	22.6	23.9	21.3	17.2	37.4	10.3	19.3	....
Claims on Nonfin.Pub.Enterprises...	52c	49.8	58.8	79.9	76.7	153.6	150.2	145.2	445.7	182.4	225.0	144.3	....
Claims on Private Sector................	52d	3,854.2	4,917.0	6,262.4	7,016.1	7,956.1	8,752.8	9,233.8	10,791.7	12,614.2	14,817.7	17,065.4	....
Claims on Nonbank Financial Inst...	52g	16.6	8.7	9.7	18.1	17.7	18.1	24.7	58.4	15.2	14.0	16.2	....
Liquid Liabilities...........................	55l	3,445.1	4,464.9	5,461.9	6,746.4	7,278.2	8,027.9	9,597.6	10,856.9	11,533.0	12,309.3	13,437.9	....
Money Market Instruments..............	56aa	223.8	190.9	180.3	234.6	197.8	182.5	45.8	45.4	147.7	293.7	347.2	....
Bonds..	56ab	3.9	4.1	4.1	8.9	7.0	5.5	—	—	—			....
Capital Accounts............................	57a	948.0	1,128.1	1,373.2	1,740.0	1,994.0	2,392.6	2,743.5	3,312.2	4,450.1	4,029.6	4,380.8	....
Other Items (Net)...........................	57r	−252.0	−382.5	−295.9	−273.5	−201.0	−47.7	−25.1	37.0	−460.9	−77.5	246.1	....
Interest Rates						*Percent Per Annum*							
BoN Overdraft Rate........................	60	14.50	15.50	17.50	17.75	16.00	18.75	11.50	11.25	9.25	12.75	7.75	7.50
Money Market Rate.........................	60b	10.83	10.25	13.08	15.00	15.41	17.14	13.17	9.19	9.53	10.46	10.03	6.93
Treasury Bill Rate..........................	60c	12.16	11.35	13.91	15.25	15.69	17.24	13.28	10.26	9.29	11.00	10.51	7.78
Deposit Rate.................................	60l	9.61	9.18	10.84	12.56	12.70	12.94	10.82	7.39	6.79	7.81	8.76	6.35
Lending Rate.................................	60p	18.02	17.05	18.51	19.16	20.18	20.72	18.48	15.28	14.53	13.84	14.70	11.39
Government Bond Yield....................	61	13.94	14.63	16.11	15.48	14.70	15.10	14.90	13.81	11.39	12.86	12.72	11.88
Prices				*Index Numbers (2000=100): Period Averages*									
Consumer Prices............................	64	55.6	61.5	67.7	73.1	79.5	84.5	91.7	100.0	109.5	122.0	130.7	135.8
Intl. Transactions & Positions					*Millions of Namibia Dollars*								
Exports...	70	4,052	4,646	5,112	6,095	6,167	6,812	7,539	9,164	10,148	....	....	....
Imports, c.i.f.................................	71	4,332	5,015	5,860	7,182	8,077	9,112	9,834	10,755	13,319	....	....	....
Imports, f.o.b................................	71.v	4,002	4,555	5,311	6,589	7,399	8,374	8,992	9,851	12,281	....	....	....
Balance of Payments				*Millions of US Dollars: Minus Sign Indicates Debit*									
Current Account, n.i.e....................	78ald	110.2	85.3	175.9	115.8	90.4	161.8	159.0	254.8	16.7	79.1	270.6	....
Goods: Exports f.o.b.....................	78aad	1,293.1	1,320.4	1,418.4	1,403.7	1,343.3	1,278.3	1,196.8	1,309.5	1,147.0	1,071.6	1,260.2	....
Goods: Imports f.o.b......................	78abd	−1,335.0	−1,406.3	−1,548.2	−1,530.9	−1,615.0	−1,450.9	−1,401.3	−1,310.0	−1,349.0	−1,282.5	−1,726.0	....
Trade Balance............................	78acd	−41.8	−85.8	−129.7	−127.1	−271.7	−172.6	−204.5	−.5	−202.0	−210.9	−465.9	....
Services: Credit............................	78add	228.1	259.0	315.3	337.4	380.1	327.0	323.5	184.4	257.0	236.6	360.4	....
Services: Debit..............................	78aed	−485.4	−468.3	−551.5	−580.9	−533.7	−456.9	−445.7	−332.6	−275.6	−223.8	−249.3	....
Balance on Goods & Services........	78afd	−299.0	−295.1	−365.9	−370.7	−425.2	−302.4	−326.7	−148.7	−220.7	−198.0	−354.7	....
Income: Credit..............................	78agd	212.7	213.8	374.0	319.2	252.0	226.7	271.6	247.1	195.5	170.6	280.3	....
Income: Debit...............................	78ahd	−154.7	−159.8	−235.1	−249.0	−180.6	−165.9	−108.4	−226.3	−269.2	−133.9	−54.0	....
Balance on Gds, Serv. & Inc........	78aid	−241.1	−241.1	−227.1	−300.5	−353.8	−241.6	−163.5	−127.9	−294.3	−161.4	−128.4	....
Current Transfers, n.i.e.: Credit......	78ajd	373.2	349.2	426.9	437.3	462.2	418.2	380.9	419.6	346.7	270.4	426.2	....
Current Transfers: Debit.................	78akd	−21.9	−22.7	−23.9	−21.0	−18.0	−14.7	−58.4	−37.0	−35.6	−29.9	−27.2	....
Capital Account, n.i.e.....................	78bcd	27.0	43.2	40.1	42.1	33.5	23.8	22.9	112.6	95.8	111.4	57.0	....
Capital Account, n.i.e.: Credit........	78bad	27.6	43.8	40.7	42.5	33.9	24.2	23.2	112.9	96.0	111.6	57.3	....
Capital Account: Debit...................	78bbd	−.6	−.6	−.6	−.5	−.4	−.4	−.3	−.3	−.2	−.2	−.4	....
Financial Account, n.i.e..................	78bjd	−62.1	−102.1	−205.3	−174.0	−71.4	−145.6	−342.6	−498.8	−533.9	−369.0	−653.3	....
Direct Investment Abroad...............	78bdd	−8.7	6.1	3.5	21.7	−.7	2.2	.7	−1.7	12.5	4.7	10.8	....
Dir. Invest. in Rep. Econ., n.i.e.......	78bed	55.3	98.0	153.0	128.7	91.0	96.2	1.6	118.9	36.1	51.2	33.3	....
Portfolio Investment Assets............	78bfd	15.5	−17.0	−5.1	−8.1	−14.6	−11.1	−26.8	−118.4	−180.2	−144.1	−217.4	....
Equity Securities..........................	78bkd	−4.9	−5.0	−3.8	−7.9	−14.6	−7.4	−18.6	−104.7	−173.2	−138.1	−208.9	....
Debt Securities............................	78bld	20.4	−12.0	−1.3	−.3	—	−3.6	−8.2	−13.7	−7.0	−6.0	−8.4	....
Portfolio Investment Liab., n.i.e......	78bgd	60.0	64.2	82.2	31.2	26.0	−4.4	40.7	34.7	25.9	8.2	3.9	....
Equity Securities..........................	78bmd	1.1	37.5	45.7	51.2	28.8	18.1	40.7	34.7	25.9	8.2	3.9	....
Debt Securities............................	78bnd	58.9	26.7	36.5	−20.0	−2.8	−22.4	—					....
Financial Derivatives Assets...........	78bwd	....	....	....	....	....	....	....	....	....	....	....	....
Financial Derivatives Liabilities.......	78bxd												....
Other Investment Assets................	78bhd	−180.9	−301.0	−428.0	−411.2	−289.9	−175.5	−304.7	−502.3	−378.4	−247.2	−451.1	....
Monetary Authorities....................	78bod	....	....	....	....	....	....	....	....	....	....	....	....
General Government......................	78bpd	−9.4	9.5	−1.4	−1.2	−1.1	−.9	−.8	−3.4	−2.8	−2.3	−3.9	....
Banks...	78bqd	56.5	.1	14.8	−48.6	−40.6	−2.1	−54.2	−118.7	34.4	47.7	28.5	....
Other Sectors..............................	78brd	−228.0	−310.7	−441.5	−361.4	−248.2	−172.6	−249.7	−380.2	−410.0	−292.6	−475.7	....
Other Investment Liab., n.i.e..........	78bid	−3.3	47.6	−10.9	63.8	116.7	−53.1	−54.1	−30.1	−49.8	−41.8	−32.7	....
Monetary Authorities....................	78bsd	—											....
General Government......................	78btd	18.5	4.9	21.8	27.7	17.4	16.9	−.4	−2.1	−2.0	−2.4	−6.9	....
Banks...	78bud	18.4	66.8	4.9	−49.0	116.5	−28.5	−46.5	−6.3	−33.9	−13.9	—	....
Other Sectors..............................	78bvd	−40.2	−24.1	−37.7	85.0	−17.1	−41.4	−7.3	−21.7	−13.9	−25.5	−25.9	....
Net Errors and Omissions...............	78cad	16.2	48.5	13.4	39.1	15.3	15.7	−42.4	−62.8	28.6	−54.0	.2	....
Overall Balance............................	78cbd	91.3	75.0	24.2	22.9	67.8	55.8	−203.0	−194.3	−392.8	−232.5	−325.5	....
Reserves and Related Items.............	79dad	−91.3	−75.0	−24.2	−22.9	−67.8	−55.8	203.0	194.3	392.8	232.5	325.5	....
Reserve Assets.............................	79dbd	−91.3	−75.0	−24.2	−22.9	−67.8	−55.8	−57.1	−10.6	−70.7	−17.9	95.1	....
Use of Fund Credit and Loans........	79dcd	—	—	—	—	—	—	—	—	—	—	—	....
Exceptional Financing....................	79ded	....	....	....	....	....	....	260.1	204.9	463.4	250.4	230.4	....

		1993	1994	1995	1996	1997	1998	1999	2000	2001	2002	2003	2004
International Investment Position						*Millions of US Dollars*							
Assets...	79aad	2,579.9	2,788.0	2,692.6	2,095.9	....	....	....	1,213.5	996.9	1,427.3	....	....
Direct Investment Abroad..............	79abd	79.2	15.8	14.8	13.0	....	....	....	44.9	10.1	19.6	....	....
Portfolio Investment......................	79acd	117.4	165.1	164.8	128.8	....	....	....	610.5	624.5	675.3	....	....
Equity Securities.........................	79add	45.6	85.2	90.2	72.8	....	....	....	603.7	....	....		
Debt Securities...........................	79aed	71.8	79.9	74.6	56.0	....	....	....	6.8	....	....		
Financial Derivatives.....................	79ald					....	....	....					
Other Investment...........................	79afd	2,249.6	2,404.1	2,291.4	1,760.6	....	....	....	295.1	139.3	408.2		
Monetary Authorities...................	79agd	—	—	—	—	....	....	....	—	—	—		
General Government.....................	79ahd	17.7	7.3	8.5	7.7	....	....	....	—	—	—		
Banks...	79aid	46.8	38.1	29.9	67.5	....	....	....	51.7	63.1	259.3		
Other Sectors..............................	79ajd	2,185.1	2,358.7	2,253.1	1,685.4	....	....	....	243.4	76.3	148.9		
Reserve Assets...............................	79akd	133.7	202.9	221.6	193.5	....	....	....	262.9	222.9	324.1		
Liabilities...	79lad	2,201.0	2,420.2	2,685.1	2,355.2	....	....	....	1,807.3	1,310.8	2,556.6		
Dir. Invest. in Rep. Economy...........	79lbd	1,490.8	1,601.2	1,707.7	1,492.2	....	....	....	1,276.3	715.0	1,822.5		
Portfolio Investment......................	79lcd	221.3	289.8	390.4	334.9	....	....	....	75.0	27.2	41.7		
Equity Securities.........................	79ldd	19.1	69.1	119.0	141.8	....	....	....	1.7	4.6	6.8		
Debt Securities...........................	79led	202.2	220.7	271.4	193.1	....	....	....	73.3	22.6	34.9		
Financial Derivatives.....................	79lld	—	—	—	—	....	....	....	—	—	—		
Other Investment...........................	79lfd	488.9	529.1	587.0	528.1	....	....	....	455.9	568.6	692.4		
Monetary Authorities...................	79lgd	181.9	203.2	214.9	183.0	....	....	....	—	—	—		
General Government.....................	79lhd	25.3	29.9	51.5	46.8	....	....	....	129.2	155.8	218.0		
Banks...	79lid	82.7	143.9	134.1	136.0	....	....	....	70.1	79.3	187.8		
Other Sectors..............................	79ljd	199.0	152.1	186.4	162.3	....	....	....	256.6	333.5	286.6		
Government Finance						*Millions of Namibia Dollars: Year Beginning April 1*							
Deficit (-) or Surplus........................	80	−333.1	−195.3	−476.1	−891.1	−439.4	−749.2	−679.3	−849.7p	....	....		
Revenue...	81	3,039.8	3,610.8	4,028.7	4,611.5	5,591.7	6,094.7	7,184.9	7,765.3p	....	....		
Grants Received.............................	81z	54.9	38.4	44.9	50.3	54.0	37.4	68.4	128.7p	....	....		
Expenditure...................................	82	3,410.0	3,812.7	4,502.3	5,461.6	6,041.5	6,839.7	7,831.3	8,610.0p	....	....		
Lending Minus Repayments...........	83	17.8	31.8	47.4	91.3	43.6	41.6	101.3	133.7p	....	....		
National Accounts						*Millions of Namibia Dollars*							
Househ.Cons.Expend.,incl.NPISHs....	96f	5,493	6,355	7,189	8,653	10,160	11,185	12,239	14,120	15,829	....		
Government Consumption Expend...	91f	2,938	3,267	3,839	4,551	5,064	5,556	6,265	6,819	7,562	....		
Gross Fixed Capital Formation..........	93e	1,967	2,255	2,817	3,535	3,288	4,321	4,760	4,464	5,932	....		
Changes in Inventories....................	93i	−436	252	−60	−65	92	518	57	171	418	....		
Exports of Goods and Services..........	90c	4,828	5,599	6,288	7,593	7,961	8,637	9,548	10,680	11,462	....		
Imports of Goods and Services (-)....	98c	5,273	5,926	7,073	8,796	9,638	10,900	11,773	12,354	14,243	....		
Gross Domestic Product (GDP).........	99b	9,302	11,549	12,706	15,011	16,754	18,790	20,693	23,264	26,689	....		
Statistical Discrepancy.....................	99bs	−213	−253	−294	−459	−174	−528	−402	−634	−271	....		
Net Primary Income from Abroad.....	98.n	184	182	569	310	305	484	−105	−356	2	....		
Gross National Income (GNI)............	99a	9,486	11,731	13,275	15,321	17,059	19,274	20,588	22,908	26,691	....		
Net Current Transf.from Abroad.......	98t	1,104	1,099	1,393	1,750	1,929	2,243	2,543	3,006	3,026	....		
Gross Nat'l Disposable Inc.(GNDI)....	99i	10,590	12,830	14,669	17,071	18,988	21,516	23,130	25,914	29,718	....		
Gross Saving....................................	99s	2,159	3,208	3,641	3,867	3,764	4,775	4,626	4,975	6,327	....		
Consumption of Fixed Capital..........	99cf	....	....	1,721	1,945	2,191	2,482	2,851	3,104	3,558	....		
GDP Volume 1995 Prices.................	99b.p	11,372	12,204	12,706	13,111	13,665	14,114	14,597	15,074	....	....		
GDP Volume (2000=100)...............	99bvp	† 75.4	81.0	84.3	87.0	90.7	93.6	96.8	100.0	....	....		
GDP Deflator (2000=100)...............	99bip	53.0	61.3	64.8	74.2	79.4	86.3	91.9	100.0	....	....		
						Millions: Midyear Estimates							
Population................................	99z	1.55	1.60	1.65	1.70	1.76	1.81	1.85	1.89	1.93	1.96	1.99	2.01

		1993	1994	1995	1996	1997	1998	1999	2000	2001	2002	2003	2004
Exchange Rates						*Rupees per SDR: End of Period*							
Market Rate	aa	67.634	72.817	83.243	82.007	85.408	95.288	94.326	96.806	96.108	106.450	110.021	111.506
					Rupees per US Dollar: End of Period (ae) Period Average (rf)								
Market Rate	ae	49.240	49.880	56.000	57.030	63.300	67.675	68.725	74.300	76.475	78.300	74.040	71.800
Market Rate	rf	48.607	49.398	51.890	56.692	58.010	65.976	68.239	71.094	74.949	77.877	76.141	73.674
Fund Position						*Millions of SDRs: End of Period*							
Quota	2f.s	52.0	52.0	52.0	52.0	52.0	52.0	71.3	71.3	71.3	71.3	71.3	71.3
SDRs	1b.s	—	.1	—		.1	—	.2	—	.1	—	.5	6.2
Reserve Position in the Fund	1c.s	5.7	5.7	5.7	5.7	5.7	5.7	5.7	5.7	5.7	5.7	5.8	—
Total Fund Cred.&Loans Outstg	2tl	35.8	37.7	32.5	27.2	22.0	17.2	12.9	9.5	6.2	2.8	7.7	14.3
International Liquidity				*Millions of US Dollars Unless Otherwise Indicated: Data as of Middle of Month*									
Total Reserves minus Gold	1l.d	640.2	693.6	586.4	571.4	626.2	756.3	845.1	945.4	1,037.7	1,017.6	1,222.5	1,462.2
SDRs	1b.d	—	.1	—		.1	—	.3	—	.1	—	.8	9.7
Reserve Position in the Fund	1c.d	7.9	8.4	8.5	8.2	7.7	8.1	7.9	7.5	7.2	7.8	8.6	—
Foreign Exchange	1d.d	632.3	685.1	577.9	563.1	618.4	748.2	836.9	937.9	1,030.4	1,009.8	1,213.1	1,452.5
Gold (Million Fine Troy Ounces)	1ad	.153	.153	.153	.153	.153	.153	.153	.153	.153	.153	.153	.153
Gold (National Valuation)	1and	6.5	6.5	6.5	6.5	6.5	6.5	6.5	6.5	6.5	6.5	6.5	6.5
Monetary Authorities: Other Liab	4..d	55.3	62.1	54.0	45.0	20.1	27.8	18.5	16.8	8.8	7.4	14.8	26.5
Deposit Money Banks: Assets	7a.d	129.9	161.6	208.9	218.1	246.1	299.0	345.3	459.9	335.8	324.8	284.5	332.5
Liabilities	7b.d	68.6	66.1	67.4	87.7	111.3	149.7	174.9	206.8	224.9	242.8	248.5	296.4
Monetary Authorities						*Millions of Rupees: Data as of Middle of Month*							
Foreign Assets	11	32,721	35,627	33,960	33,883	59,104	52,331	59,155	71,427	80,535	80,842	91,702	106,180
Claims on Central Government	12a	19,032	19,439	24,001	24,714	30,590	29,805	30,539	34,366	32,612	37,834	30,028	40,508
Claims on Private Sector	12d	544	503	547	895	1,460	1,356	1,460	1,478	1,856	2,569	1,751	1,769
Claims on Deposit Money Banks	12e	39	21	12	646	5	6	5	5	6	928	25	250
Claims on Other Financial Insts	12f	499	484	844	1,122	1,613	1,631	1,613	1,560	1,666	1,512	1,488	1,387
Reserve Money	14	25,783	28,792	31,266	34,368	55,371	50,203	55,371	66,062	74,012	73,924	76,063	87,723
of which: Currency Outside DMBs	14a	17,390	21,005	23,230	25,428	37,829	32,244	36,929	44,526	51,699	56,022	58,076	65,767
Private Sector Deposits	14d	1,307	1,097	1,396	1,358	4,346	2,287	4,346	3,160	3,570	2,350	2,557	3,315
Foreign Liabilities	16c	5,145	5,840	5,725	4,798	3,154	3,516	2,488	2,167	1,267	879	1,944	3,492
Central Government Deposits	16d	7,870	7,782	7,459	7,447	11,473	10,474	11,473	13,081	13,247	15,646	18,595	28,757
Capital Accounts	17a	10,633	12,077	15,982	16,128	22,881	21,545	22,953	25,752	27,982	31,650	31,331	28,990
Other Items (Net)	17r	3,403	1,584	−1,069	−1,481	−122	−610	472	1,759	167	1,587	−2,939	1,131
Deposit Money Banks						*Millions of Rupees: Data as of Middle of Month*							
Reserves	20	5,837	7,321	8,488	7,583	9,972	15,673	14,096	18,376	18,742	15,552	15,430	18,640
Foreign Assets	21	6,397	8,060	11,698	12,438	15,577	20,238	23,729	34,174	25,679	25,429	21,063	23,873
Claims on Central Government	22a	10,734	8,776	6,497	7,610	8,621	8,957	13,330	15,471	28,318	36,045	44,678	47,147
Claims on Nonfin.Pub.Enterprises	22c	1,954	1,621	1,721	1,713	1,459	993	1,438	1,909	1,911	3,573	2,704	4,050
Claims on Private Sector	22d	25,059	36,462	49,494	56,848	65,541	84,875	97,306	114,913	....	....	....	....
Claims on Other Financial Insts	22f	29	29	211	4,023	4,668	530	5,915	7,419	8,144	8,673	9,667	11,396
Demand Deposits	24	6,622	8,422	8,927	8,758	9,090	10,979	13,832	15,343				
Time and Savings Deposits	25	36,218	42,172	50,490	58,744	70,555	89,850	109,521	132,550	145,946	152,019	171,641	193,304
Foreign Liabilities	26c	3,380	3,297	3,776	5,003	7,048	10,134	12,020	15,367	17,202	19,015	18,398	21,280
Credit from Monetary Authorities	26g	39	21	12	646	6	6	6	45	6	928	25	250
Other Items (Net)	27r	3,749	8,356	14,906	17,063	19,138	20,297	20,435	28,958	....	....	....	....
Monetary Survey						*Millions of Rupees: Data as of Middle of Month*							
Foreign Assets (Net)	31n	30,592	34,550	36,158	36,519	64,479	58,918	68,376	88,067	87,745	86,377	92,423	105,281
Domestic Credit	32	49,986	59,539	75,863	89,486	102,486	117,680	140,135	164,043	....	....	....	....
Claims on Central Govt. (Net)	32an	21,895	20,433	23,039	24,877	27,738	28,287	32,396	36,757	47,682	58,234	56,111	58,898
Claims on Nonfin.Pub.Enterprises	32c	1,961	1,628	1,721	1,720	1,466	1,000	1,446	1,917	1,918	3,581	2,712	4,058
Claims on Private Sector	32d	25,602	36,965	50,041	57,742	67,001	86,231	98,766	116,391				
Claims on Other Financial Insts	32f	527	513	1,054	5,145	6,281	2,161	7,528	8,978	9,810	10,185	11,155	12,783
Money	34	25,320	30,524	33,553	35,544	51,265	45,509	55,107	63,028	....	....	....	....
Quasi-Money	35	36,218	42,172	50,490	58,744	70,555	89,850	109,521	132,550	145,946	152,019	171,641	193,304
Other Items (Net)	37r	19,041	21,393	27,979	31,717	45,130	41,239	43,868	56,517	....	....	....	....
Money plus Quasi-Money	35l	61,538	72,696	84,043	94,288	121,820	135,359	164,628	195,578	....	....	....	....
Interest Rates						*Percent Per Annum: Data as of Middle of Month*							
Discount Rate	60	11.00	11.00	11.00	11.00	9.00	9.00	9.00	7.50	6.50	5.50	5.50	5.50
Treasury Bill Rate	60c	4.50	6.50	9.90	11.51	2.52	3.70	4.30	5.30	5.00	3.80	3.85	2.40
Deposit Rate	60l	....	8.75	....	9.63	9.79	8.92	7.31	5.96	4.75	....	....	2.71
Lending Rate	60p	....	....	....	12.88	14.54	14.00	11.33	9.46	7.67	....	....	8.50
Government Bond Yield	61	....	9.00	3.00	9.00	9.00	9.00	8.75	8.50	8.50	8.25	7.50	6.63
Prices						*Index Numbers (2000=100): Period Averages*							
Consumer Prices	64	61.6	66.8	71.9	78.5	† 81.6	90.8	97.6	100.0	102.7	105.8	111.8	115.0
Intl. Transactions & Positions						*Millions of Rupees*							
Exports	70	18,676	17,896	17,895	21,830	23,555	31,288	41,088	57,231	55,221	44,184	50,450	55,669
Imports, c.i.f	71	43,267	57,072	69,028	79,247	97,974	81,901	97,057	111,800	110,362	110,552	133,539	137,670

Nepal 558

		1993	1994	1995	1996	1997	1998	1999	2000	2001	2002	2003	2004
Balance of Payments						*Millions of US Dollars: Minus Sign Indicates Debit*							
Current Account, n.i.e.	78ald	−222.5	−351.9	−356.4	−326.6	−388.1	−67.2	−256.5	−298.7	−339.3	55.6	110.3	....
Goods: Exports f.o.b.	78aad	397.0	368.7	349.9	388.7	413.8	482.0	612.3	776.1	720.5	632.0	694.1	....
Goods: Imports f.o.b.	78abd	−858.6	−1,158.9	−1,310.8	−1,494.7	−1,691.9	−1,239.1	−1,494.2	−1,590.1	−1,485.7	−1,425.4	−1,681.9	....
Trade Balance	78acd	−461.6	−790.3	−961.0	−1,105.9	−1,278.1	−757.1	−881.9	−814.0	−765.2	−793.4	−987.8	....
Services: Credit	78add	333.2	579.2	679.0	757.5	865.7	565.1	655.1	505.9	413.3	305.2	371.5	....
Services: Debit	78aed	−251.8	−296.6	−313.3	−242.8	−224.5	−196.2	−212.5	−199.9	−214.7	−236.8	−264.9	....
Balance on Goods & Services	78afd	−380.2	−507.6	−595.2	−591.3	−637.0	−388.1	−439.2	−508.0	−566.6	−724.9	−881.2	....
Income: Credit	78agd	28.9	34.6	43.6	33.1	31.9	45.4	55.8	72.2	70.3	56.9	48.8	....
Income: Debit	78ahd	−23.7	−30.8	−34.9	−32.0	−28.6	−26.5	−28.4	−35.2	−58.8	−71.2	−69.0	....
Balance on Gds, Serv. & Inc.	78aid	−375.0	−503.9	−586.5	−590.2	−633.7	−369.2	−411.9	−471.0	−555.2	−739.2	−901.4	....
Current Transfers, n.i.e.: Credit	78ajd	155.5	160.7	239.2	281.6	267.4	326.0	182.3	189.0	240.2	828.1	1,036.3	....
Current Transfers: Debit	78akd	−3.0	−8.7	−9.1	−18.0	−21.8	−24.1	−26.9	−16.7	−24.3	−33.2	−24.6	....
Capital Account, n.i.e.	78bcd	—	—	—	—	—	—	—	—	—	102.4	24.8	....
Capital Account, n.i.e.: Credit	78bad	—	—	—	—	—	—	—	—	—	102.4	24.8	....
Capital Account: Debit	78bbd	—	—	—	—	—	—	—	—	—	....	....	....
Financial Account, n.i.e.	78bjd	283.5	407.3	368.5	275.2	340.3	212.9	−24.5	76.1	−216.9	−404.8	−413.3	....
Direct Investment Abroad	78bdd	—	—	—	—	—	—	—	—	—	....	....	....
Dir. Invest. in Rep. Econ., n.i.e.	78bed	—	—	—	19.2	23.1	12.0	—	—	—	−6.0	14.8	....
Portfolio Investment Assets	78bfd	—	—	—	—	—	—	—	—	....	....	....	....
Equity Securities	78bkd	—	—	—	—	—	—	—	—	....	....	....	....
Debt Securities	78bld	—	—	—	—	—	—	—	—	....	....	....	....
Portfolio Investment Liab., n.i.e.	78bgd	—	—	—	—	—	—	—	—	....	....	....	....
Equity Securities	78bmd	—	—	—	—	—	—	—	—	....	....	....	....
Debt Securities	78bnd	—	—	—	—	—	—	—	—	—	....	....	....
Financial Derivatives Assets	78bwd	....	....	....	....	....	....	....	....	....	....	....	....
Financial Derivatives Liabilities	78bxd	....	....	....	....	....	....	....	....	....	....	....	....
Other Investment Assets	78bhd	149.6	159.2	264.4	91.6	89.4	90.8	48.2	128.6	11.2	−470.4	−507.1	....
Monetary Authorities	78bod	....	....	....	....	....	....	—	—	....	....	....	....
General Government	78bpd	—	—	—	—	—	—	—	—	—	....	....	....
Banks	78bqd	—	—	—	—	—	—	—	—	—	....	....	....
Other Sectors	78brd	149.6	159.2	264.4	91.6	89.4	90.8	48.2	128.6	11.2	−470.4	−507.1	....
Other Investment Liab., n.i.e.	78bid	133.9	248.0	104.1	164.5	227.8	110.0	−72.8	−52.6	−228.0	71.5	79.0	....
Monetary Authorities	78bsd	−4.0	.1	−3.3	1.0	.1	.4	−2.0	4.5	−3.5	1.8	.2	....
General Government	78btd	125.7	237.5	106.8	128.4	165.9	151.8	−56.2	−61.0	−63.5	−71.3	−67.6	....
Banks	78bud	11.7	5.4	−4.5	38.2	68.8	17.0	13.2	67.4	3.2	33.3	11.2	....
Other Sectors	78bvd	.4	.8	1.7	1.2	−7.8	−59.1	−27.8	−63.5	−164.3	107.8	135.2	....
Net Errors and Omissions	78cad	4.6	7.1	2.8	82.3	216.6	134.0	58.3	145.7	256.5	−66.6	370.8	....
Overall Balance	78cbd	65.6	62.5	15.0	30.9	168.8	279.7	−222.7	−77.0	−299.6	−313.4	92.7	....
Reserves and Related Items	79dad	−65.6	−62.5	−15.0	−30.9	−168.8	−279.7	222.7	77.0	299.6	313.4	−92.7	....
Reserve Assets	79dbd	−71.4	−65.0	−7.0	−23.4	−161.7	−273.0	−144.4	−291.0	−5.2	65.5	−210.2	....
Use of Fund Credit and Loans	79dcd	5.8	2.5	−8.0	−7.5	−7.2	−6.6	−5.9	−4.4	−4.3	−4.3	7.1	....
Exceptional Financing	79ded	—	—	....	....	....	....	....	373.0	372.4	309.1	252.3	110.4	....
Government Finance						*Millions of Rupees: Year Ending July 15*							
Deficit (-) or Surplus	80	−10,359	−7,463	−7,894	−10,976	−10,908	−13,846	−13,349	−12,454	−18,498	−16,506	−11,391	....
Revenue	81	14,316	18,862	23,206	26,643	29,346	31,494	34,814	40,491	46,607	48,326	53,657	....
Grants Received	81z	3,793	2,394	3,937	4,825	5,988	5,403	4,337	5,712	6,753	6,686	8,372	
Expenditure	82	29,180	29,309	36,242	43,520	47,073	51,963	54,720	60,794	73,905	73,394	74,715	
Lending Minus Repayments	83	−712	−590	−1,205	−1,076	−831	−1,220	−2,220	−2,137	−2,047	−1,876	−1,295	
Financing													
Net Borrowing: Domestic	84a	4,691	−233	2,410	3,500	3,967	5,572	4,693	4,323	10,954	10,558	7,937	
Foreign	85a	5,668	7,696	5,484	7,476	6,941	8,274	8,656	8,131	7,544	2,948	3,454	....
Use of Cash Balances	87	—	—	—	—	—	—	—	—	—	—	—	
Debt: Domestic	88a	24,456	30,631	32,058	34,242	35,891	38,407	49,670	54,357	60,044	73,621	81,703	....
Foreign	89a	87,421	101,967	113,000	128,044	132,087	161,208	173,861	190,691	201,551	220,126	221,992	....
National Accounts						*Millions of Rupees: Year Ending July 15*							
Househ.Cons.Expend.,incl.NPISHs.	96f	133,314	154,009	166,443	191,469	216,364	231,392	264,944	287,947	309,107	329,199	355,535	383,978
Government Consumption Expend.	91f	14,900	15,987	20,267	23,018	24,987	28,015	30,529	33,964	40,150	42,327	46,653	50,412
Gross Fixed Capital Formation	93e	37,278	42,032	48,370	56,081	60,794	65,375	65,269	73,324	78,013	81,613	86,963	92,619
Changes in Inventories	93i	2,375	2,612	6,861	11,936	10,290	9,353	4,792	18,948	20,784	20,056	30,542	39,488
Exports of Goods and Services	90c	30,948	47,548	53,084	55,405	73,853	68,659	78,150	88,360	91,821	77,068	75,764	85,409
Imports of Goods and Services (-)	98c	47,429	62,972	75,850	88,996	105,775	101,949	101,648	123,055	129,104	127,961	140,522	157,023
Gross Domestic Product (GDP)	99b	171,386	199,216	219,175	248,913	280,513	300,845	342,036	379,488	410,789	422,301	454,934	494,882
GDP Volume 1994/95 Prices	99b.p	188,780	204,397	209,976	221,930	233,040	240,816	251,758	267,096	279,750	278,848	286,480	296,459
GDP Volume (2000=100)	99bvp	70.7	76.5	78.6	83.1	87.2	90.2	94.3	100.0	104.7	104.4	107.3	111.0
GDP Deflator (2000=100)	99bip	63.9	68.6	73.5	78.9	84.7	87.9	95.6	100.0	103.4	106.6	111.8	117.5
						Millions: Midyear Estimates							
Population	99z	20.61	21.14	21.68	22.23	22.78	23.33	23.88	24.43	24.98	25.52	26.05	26.59

		1993	1994	1995	1996	1997	1998	1999	2000	2001	2002	2003	2004
Exchange Rates		\multicolumn{12}{c}{*Guilders per SDR through 1998, Euros per SDR Thereafter: End of Period*}											
Market Rate....................................	aa	2.6659	2.5330	2.3849	2.5072	2.7217	2.6595	1.3662	1.4002	1.4260	1.2964	1.1765	1.1402
		\multicolumn{12}{c}{*Guilders per US Dollar through 1998, Euros per US Dollar Thereafter: End of Period (ae) Period Average (rf)*}											
Market Rate....................................	ae	1.9409	1.7351	1.6044	1.7436	2.0172	1.8888	.9954	1.0747	1.1347	.9536	.7918	.7342
Market Rate....................................	rf	1.8573	1.8200	1.6057	1.6859	1.9513	1.9837	.9386	1.0854	1.1175	1.0626	.8860	.8054
		\multicolumn{12}{c}{*Guilders per ECU: End of Period (ea) Period Average (eb)*}											
ECU Rate....................................	ea	2.1670	2.1280	2.0554	2.1665	2.2280	2.2037	....	....	....	....	....	....
ECU Rate....................................	eb	2.1723	2.1528	2.0774	2.1113	2.2048	2.2227	....	....	....	....	....	....
		\multicolumn{12}{c}{*Index Numbers (2000=100): Period Averages*}											
Market Rate (1995=100).................	ahx	86.4	88.3	100.0	95.2	82.3	81.0	....	....	....	....	....	....
Nominal Effective Exchange Rate.....	neu	109.0	109.7	115.3	112.5	106.2	106.4	104.5	100.0	100.7	101.9	106.3	107.6
Real Effective Exchange Rate...........	reu	106.2	107.7	111.8	108.4	102.7	104.5	103.6	100.0	103.1	106.1	111.3	113.2
Fund Position		\multicolumn{12}{c}{*Millions of SDRs: End of Period*}											
Quota...	2f.s	3,444	3,444	3,444	3,444	3,444	3,444	5,162	5,162	5,162	5,162	5,162	5,162
SDRs..	1b.s	424	442	616	566	586	644	742	501	598	513	523	501
Reserve Position in the Fund...........	1c.s	795	802	1,169	1,275	1,625	2,113	1,880	1,524	1,872	2,095	2,055	1,718
of which: Outstg.Fund Borrowing...	2c	—	—	—	—	—	193	—	—	—	—	—	—
International Liquidity		\multicolumn{12}{c}{*Millions of US Dollars Unless Otherwise Indicated: End of Period*}											
Total Res.Min.Gold (Eurosys.Def).....	1l.d	31,344	34,532	33,714	26,767	24,865	21,418	† 9,886	9,643	9,034	9,563	11,012	10,102
SDRs..	1b.d	583	645	916	814	791	907	1,019	653	752	697	778	778
Reserve Position in the Fund........	1c.d	1,092	1,171	1,738	1,834	2,193	2,975	2,580	1,986	2,352	2,849	3,054	2,667
Foreign Exchange......................	1d.d	29,669	32,716	31,060	24,119	21,881	17,536	6,287	7,004	5,930	6,017	7,180	6,657
o/w:Fin.Deriv.Rel.to Reserves......	1ddd	....	....	....	....	....	....	−319.46	10.24	79.32	−45.09	−174.29	−84.45
Other Reserve Assets..................	1e.d	....	....	....	....	....	....	—	—	—	—	—	—
Gold (Million Fine Troy Ounces).......	1ad	35.05	34.77	34.77	34.77	27.07	33.83	31.57	29.32	28.44	27.38	25.00	25.00
Gold (Eurosystem Valuation)............	1and	7,639	8,477	9,168	8,622	5,801	7,299	9,164	8,046	7,863	9,385	10,430	10,948
Memo:Euro Cl. on Non-EA Res.......	1dgd	....	....	....	....	....	....	817	135	170	500	346	392
Non-Euro Cl. on EA Res...........	1dhd	....	....	....	....	....	....	1,195	491	1,355	1,516	1,465	1,855
Mon. Auth.: Other Foreign Assets....	3..d	....	....	....	....	....	....	—	—	—	—	—	—
Foreign Liabilities.................	4..d	152	263	141	79	64	725	† 542	115	45	737	1,221	133
Banking Insts.: Foreign Assets.........	7a.d	195,752	200,374	234,141	238,726	263,592	....	† 155,624	163,895	211,400	256,244	308,245	376,874
Foreign Liab....................	7b.d	169,204	186,977	220,964	245,746	290,784	....	† 194,072	206,125	250,057	305,752	328,222	392,490
Monetary Authorities		\multicolumn{12}{c}{*Billions of Guilders through 1998; Billions of Euros Beginning 1999: End of Period*}											
Fgn. Assets (Cl.on Non-EA Ctys).......	11	76.24	75.69	69.77	62.72	62.96	55.75	20.63	19.64	20.18	19.46	17.94	16.26
Claims on General Government........	12a.u	....	....	....	....	....	....	7.58	8.63	7.71	7.41	7.97	6.61
o/w: Claims on Gen.Govt.in Cty.....	12a	4.14	4.12	4.20	4.47	4.74	4.90	1.73	1.53	1.90	.72	.41	.83
Claims on Banking Institutions........	12e.u	....	....	....	....	....	....	22.76	11.98	7.96	16.18	20.71	28.76
o/w: Claims on Bank.Inst.in Cty.....	12e	4.46	8.26	9.97	16.05	11.37	18.68	9.88	9.20	3.71	10.07	15.80	20.30
Claims on Other Resident Sectors.....	12d.u	....	....	....	....	....	....	.31	.40	.49	.52	.46	.48
o/w: Cl. on Oth.Res.Sect.in Cty......	12d	.60	.35	.35	.28	.22	.22	.12	.09	.10	.07	.04	.04
Currency Issued...........................	14a	40.41	40.93	41.30	41.67	42.10	40.90	18.98	18.73	11.39	19.36	21.90	26.45
Liabilities to Banking Insts.............	14c.u	....	....	....	....	....	....	20.70	9.40	12.05	12.43	13.69	15.18
o/w: Liabs to Bank.Inst.in Cty.......	14c	15.82	18.74	11.09	8.39	13.06	17.16	7.52	9.38	10.21	8.47	12.67	11.57
Demand Dep. of Other Res.Sect.......	14d.u	....	....	....	....	....	....	—	—	.01	.01	—	—
o/w:D.Dep.of Oth.Res.Sect.in Cty...	14d	.13	.10	.02	.06	.06	.14	—	—	.01	.01	—	—
Other Dep. of Other Res.Sect...........	15..u	....	....	....	....	....	....	—	—	—	—	—	—
o/w:O.Dep.of Oth.Res.Sect.in Cty...	15	....	....	....	....	....	....	—	—	—	—	—	—
Bonds & Money Mkt. Instruments....	16n.u	....	....	....	....	....	....	—	—	—	—	—	—
o/w: Held by Resid.of Cty..............	16n	....	....	....	....	....	....	....	....	....	....	....	....
Foreign Liab. (to Non-EA Ctys)........	16c	.30	.46	.23	.14	.13	1.37	.54	.12	.05	.70	.97	.10
Central Government Deposits...........	16d.u	....	....	....	....	....	....	.01	.04	.02	—	.04	.04
o/w: Cent.Govt.Dep. in Cty...........	16d	7.99	9.61	14.84	14.44	.09	5.10	.01	.04	.02	—	.04	.04
Capital Accounts...........................	17a	21.79	20.06	17.21	19.65	24.96	17.09	12.99	14.53	15.02	13.22	12.48	13.03
Other Items (Net)...........................	17r	−1.00	−1.47	−.39	−.83	−1.10	−2.21	−1.95	−2.18	−2.20	−2.14	−1.28	−1.97
Memo: Net Claims on Eurosystem....	12e.s	....	....	....	....	....	....	−1.25	2.16	.32	.14	2.03	1.94
Currency Put into Circ................	14m	....	....	....	....	....	....	....	....	....	17.47	21.04	23.14
Banking Institutions		\multicolumn{12}{c}{*Billions of Guilders through 1998; Billions of Euros Beginning 1999: End of Period*}											
Claims on Monetary Authorities.......	20	2.81	2.80	3.09	3.38	3.36	....	7.14	9.24	9.68	8.37	12.54	11.22
Claims on Bk.Inst.in Oth.EA Ctys.....	20b.u	....	....	....	....	....	....	64.46	65.38	76.53	75.42	96.04	102.85
Fgn. Assets (Cl.on Non-EA Ctys).......	21	379.94	347.67	375.66	416.24	531.72	....	154.91	176.14	239.87	244.34	244.06	276.69
Claims on General Government........	22a.u	....	....	....	....	....	....	110.03	106.62	105.40	119.55	127.46	135.17
o/w: Claims on Gen.Govt.in Cty.....	22a	124.93	129.20	133.64	136.46	140.36	....	65.24	56.43	53.75	55.91	58.90	58.85
Claims on Other Resident Sectors.....	22d.u	....	....	....	....	....	....	496.17	577.35	627.59	679.84	737.66	816.00
o/w: Cl. on Oth.Res.Sect.in Cty......	22d	518.79	559.34	626.83	698.86	788.56	....	484.02	560.82	605.67	656.64	705.80	775.21
Demand Deposits..........................	24..u	....	....	....	....	....	....	118.42	131.89	150.97	152.52	156.07	162.25
o/w:D.Dep.of Oth.Res.Sect.in Cty...	24	111.92	114.04	134.71	155.58	170.49	....	115.67	128.40	147.78	148.89	151.96	158.48
Other Deposits..............................	25..u	....	....	....	....	....	....	242.68	270.83	295.28	307.65	342.31	363.00
o/w:O.Dep.of Oth.Res.Sect.in Cty...	25	355.15	353.92	363.23	372.14	395.16	....	228.50	257.67	278.65	292.82	327.29	341.62
Money Market Fund Shares.............	26m.u	....	....	....	....	....	....	—	—	—	—	—	—
Bonds & Money Mkt. Instruments....	26n.u	....	....	....	....	....	....	154.93	172.70	207.03	225.67	250.25	293.02
o/w: Held by Resid.of Cty..............	26n	154.41	169.53	187.19	193.55	196.41	....						
Foreign Liab. (to Non-EA Ctys)........	26c	328.41	324.42	354.51	428.48	586.57	....	193.18	221.52	283.74	291.55	259.88	288.15
Central Government Deposits...........	26d.u	....	....	....	....	....	....	1.93	.96	1.30	1.18	2.06	1.36
o/w: Cent.Govt.Dep. in Cty...........	26d	1.32	.79	1.02	1.51	1.82	....	1.92	.94	1.23	1.18	1.04	1.16
Credit from Monetary Authorities.....	26g	4.06	7.92	10.15	13.10	14.69	....	10.21	9.97	4.19	10.60	16.66	21.95
Liab. to Bk.Inst.in Oth. EA Ctys........	26h.u	....	....	....	....	....	....	54.32	50.71	55.98	74.46	112.08	127.75
Capital Accounts...........................	27a	54.30	57.52	61.65	78.17	86.89	....	47.70	58.33	60.75	63.73	63.28	64.75
Other Items (Net)...........................	27r	16.90	10.88	26.74	12.40	11.97	....	9.34	17.81	−.16	.17	15.17	19.69

		1993	1994	1995	1996	1997	1998	1999	2000	2001	2002	2003	2004
Banking Survey (Nat'l Residency)				*Billions of Guilders through 1998; Billions of Euros Beginning 1999: End of Period*									
Foreign Assets (Net).........................	31n	127.48	98.48	90.68	50.34	7.98	....	43.19	54.60	64.91	57.26	85.42	90.38
Domestic Credit................................	32	639.15	682.62	749.16	824.11	931.97	....	549.19	617.88	660.17	712.16	764.08	833.73
Claims on General Govt. (Net).......	32an	119.75	122.92	121.98	124.98	143.19	....	65.05	56.97	54.40	55.45	58.23	58.49
Claims on Other Resident Sectors.....	32d	519.40	559.69	627.18	699.13	788.78	....	484.14	560.91	605.77	656.71	705.84	775.24
Currency Issued................................	34a.n	40.41	40.93	41.30	41.67	42.10	40.90	18.98	18.73	11.39	19.36	21.90	26.45
Demand Deposits.............................	34b.n	112.05	114.14	134.74	155.65	170.55	....	115.67	128.40	147.78	148.90	151.96	158.48
Other Deposits................................	35..n	355.15	353.92	363.23	372.14	395.16	....	228.50	257.67	278.65	292.82	327.29	341.62
Money Market Fund Shares.............	36m	....	....	....	....	....	....	—	—	—	—	—	—
Bonds & Money Mkt. Instruments....	36n	154.41	169.53	187.19	193.55	196.41	....	154.93	172.70	207.03	225.67	250.25	293.02
o/w: Over Two Years..................	36na							134.74	152.76	175.59	188.59	216.71	254.82
Capital Accounts..............................	37a	76.09	77.58	78.86	97.82	111.85	17.09	60.69	72.86	75.77	76.94	75.75	77.79
Other Items (Net)............................	37r	28.51	25.01	34.52	13.62	23.88	....	13.59	22.10	4.45	5.74	23.04	27.48
Banking Survey (EA-Wide Residency)						*Billions of Euros: End of Period*							
Foreign Assets (Net).........................	31n.u	....	....	....	....	....	....	−18.19	−25.87	−23.74	−28.45	1.15	4.70
Domestic Credit................................	32..u	....	....	....	....	....	....	612.15	692.00	739.87	806.14	871.45	956.86
Claims on General Govt. (Net).......	32anu	....	....	....	....	....	....	115.67	114.25	111.79	125.78	133.33	140.39
Claims on Other Resident Sect.......	32d.u	....	....	....	....	....	....	496.48	577.75	628.09	680.36	738.12	816.47
Currency Issued................................	34a.u	....	....	....	....	....	....	18.98	18.73	11.39	19.36	21.90	26.45
Demand Deposits.............................	34b.u	....	....	....	....	....	....	118.42	131.89	150.98	152.53	156.08	162.25
Other Deposits................................	35..u	....	....	....	....	....	....	242.68	270.83	295.28	307.65	342.31	363.00
o/w: Other Dep. Over Two Yrs.......	35abu	....	....	....	....	....	....	57.62	66.15	62.84	62.99	63.58	70.89
Money Market Fund Shares.............	36m.u							—	—	—	—	—	—
Bonds & Money Mkt. Instruments....	36n.u							154.93	172.70	207.03	225.67	250.25	293.02
o/w: Over Two Years..................	36nau							134.74	152.76	175.59	188.59	216.71	254.82
Capital Accounts..............................	37a							60.69	72.86	75.77	76.94	75.75	77.79
Other Items (Net)............................	37r.u	....	....	....	....	....	....	−1.74	−.89	−24.31	−4.45	27.01	39.78
Money (National Definitions)						*Billions of Guilders: End of Period*							
M2: National Definition................	59mb	465.08	466.02	486.57	514.99	553.24	....	....	....	....	....	....	....
M2: Seasonally Adjusted...............	59mbc	474.64	469.75	489.45	515.51	553.72	....	....	....	....	....	....	....
Nonbank Financial Institutions						*Billions of Guilders: End of Period*							
Cash..	40.l	13.77	10.87	10.99	11.58	11.90	11.81	....	....	....	....	....	....
Foreign Assets................................	41..l	108.54	115.34	145.81	188.36	271.83	380.97	....	....	....	....	....	....
Claims on Central Government........	42a.l	153.09	161.40	175.66	190.88	192.82	181.40	....	....	....	....	....	....
Claims on Local Government...........	42b.l	30.88	31.81	· 31.55	30.19	27.52	25.53	....	....	....	....	....	....
Claims on Private Sector.................	42d.l	326.30	346.67	369.32	411.29	457.37	501.60	....	....	....	....	....	....
Real Estate....................................	42h.l	59.45	59.78	60.40	63.96	64.18	66.41	....	....	....	....	....	....
Capital Accounts..............................	47a.l	673.25	702.32	767.87	871.78	994.43	1,138.09	....	....	....	....	....	....
Other Items (Net)...........................	47r.l	18.79	23.56	25.85	24.49	31.19	29.64	....	....	....	....	....	....
Interest Rates							*Percent Per Annum*						
Rate on Advances..........................	60a	5.52	4.50	2.98	2.00	2.75	2.75	....	....	....	....	....	....
Money Market Rate........................	60b	7.10	5.14	4.22	2.89	3.07	3.21	....	....	....	....	....	....
Deposit Rate..................................	60l	3.11	† 4.70	4.40	3.54	3.18	3.10	2.74	2.89	3.10	2.77	2.49	2.31
Deposit Rate (Households)..............	60lhs	....	....	....	....	....	....	....	....	....	....	2.86	2.60
Deposit Rate (Corporations)............	60lcs	....	....	....	....	....	....	....	....	....	....	2.42	2.37
Lending Rate..................................	60p	10.40	8.29	7.21	5.90	6.13	6.50	† 3.46	4.79	5.00	3.96	3.00	2.75
Lending Rate (Households)..............	60phm	....	....	....	....	....	....	....	....	....	....	5.28	4.97
Lending Rate (Corporations)............	60pcs	....	....	....	....	....	....	....	....	....	....	4.39	4.25
Government Bond Yield..................	61	6.51	7.20	7.20	6.49	5.81	4.87	4.92	5.51	5.17	5.00	4.18	4.10
Prices, Production, Labor						*Index Numbers (2000=100): Period Averages*							
Share Prices: General......................	62	22.9	28.1	29.9	38.0	56.7	74.5	84.7	100.0	81.9	63.1	45.7	51.0
Manufacturing..............	62a	24.2	29.4	31.3	39.4	60.1	75.9	82.7	100.0	82.3	63.2	....	....
Prices: Final Products......................	63	89.3	† 89.7	91.1	92.9	94.6	94.4	† 95.4	100.0	103.0	103.8	105.3	109.5
Consumer Prices.............................	64	85.1	87.5	† 89.3	91.1	93.1	95.0	97.1	† 100.0	104.2	107.6	109.9	111.2
Harmonized CPI..............................	64h	....	....	91.1	92.4	94.1	95.8	97.8	100.0	105.2	109.2	111.7	113.2
Wages: Hourly Rates.......................	65	84.2	† 85.7	86.6	88.1	90.8	93.7	96.4	† 100.0	103.9	107.7	110.6	112.3
Industrial Production.......................	66	86.3	90.5	90.9	93.1	93.3	95.3	96.6	100.0	100.4	100.1	97.7	100.2
						*Number in Thousands: Period Averages*							
Labor Force....................................	67d	6,406	6,466	6,596	6,686	6,832	6,941	7,069	7,187	7,314	7,427	7,510	7,516
Employment...................................	67e	5,567	5,591	6,288	6,441	6,638	6,881	7,113	7,286	7,559	7,607	7,478	7,445
Unemployment...............................	67c	415	486	464	440	375	286	221	188	146	174	251	320
Unemployment Rate (%).................	67r	6.5	7.6	† 7.0	6.6	5.5	4.1	3.1	3.8	3.4	4.1	3.9	5.5
Intl. Transactions & Positions						*Millions of Guilders through 1998; Millions of Euros Beginning 1999*							
Exports...	70	258,343	282,209	314,693	332,920	380,018	398,686	† 188,046	231,855	241,342	234,284	228,745	255,530
Imports, c.i.f..................................	71	231,637	256,442	283,538	304,559	347,286	371,760	† 176,115	216,058	218,332	205,019	206,025	228,009
							*2000=100*						
Volume of Exports..........................	72	61.1	† 66.2	71.9	† 75.1	81.8	87.8	91.8	100.0	101.7	102.6	105.6	116.6
Volume of Imports..........................	73	58.2	† 64.1	71.7	† 75.2	80.1	87.7	94.2	100.0	97.2	94.9	98.5	107.0
Unit Value of Exports......................	74	86.8	† 87.0	88.6	† 88.8	94.3	91.3	88.9	100.0	102.6	97.3	94.3	93.7
Unit Value of Imports......................	75	85.6	† 85.6	85.8	† 86.6	91.8	89.5	89.4	100.0	104.2	99.0	95.6	96.2

		1993	1994	1995	1996	1997	1998	1999	2000	2001	2002	2003	2004
Balance of Payments		*Millions of US Dollars: Minus Sign Indicates Debit*											
Current Account, n.i.e.	78ald	13,203	17,294	25,773	21,502	25,077	13,031	12,996	6,817	7,836	10,117	16,403	23,172
Goods: Exports f.o.b.	78aad	127,876	141,810	195,600	195,079	188,988	196,041	195,691	204,410	204,507	206,887	252,380	304,306
Goods: Imports f.o.b.	78abd	−110,972	−123,124	−171,788	−172,312	−168,051	−175,611	−179,657	−186,983	−183,667	−186,943	−225,733	−273,264
Trade Balance	78acd	16,904	18,686	23,812	22,767	20,937	20,430	16,034	17,427	20,840	19,944	26,648	31,041
Services: Credit	78aed	37,923	41,523	45,917	47,237	48,975	49,760	49,210	49,318	51,214	56,011	65,033	73,472
Services: Debit	78aed	−38,004	−41,303	−44,770	−45,278	−45,699	−47,285	−49,471	−51,337	−53,713	−57,188	−66,221	−71,163
Balance on Goods & Services	78afd	16,823	18,905	24,959	24,726	24,213	22,906	15,772	15,408	18,341	18,766	25,460	33,350
Income: Credit	78agd	28,117	29,466	35,755	36,297	39,176	35,287	43,584	45,497	39,901	40,054	48,211	65,585
Income: Debit	78ahd	−27,236	−25,799	−28,508	−32,750	−32,193	−37,980	−40,008	−47,869	−43,667	−42,495	−49,455	−66,750
Balance on Gds, Serv. & Inc.	78aid	17,704	22,571	32,206	28,272	31,196	20,213	19,348	13,035	14,575	16,326	24,216	32,185
Current Transfers, n.i.e.: Credit	78ajd	4,359	4,197	4,725	4,319	4,346	3,799	4,566	4,399	4,475	5,540	6,322	7,125
Current Transfers: Debit	78akd	−8,860	−9,474	−11,159	−11,089	−10,465	−10,981	−10,918	−10,618	−11,214	−11,749	−14,135	−16,138
Capital Account, n.i.e.	78bcd	−715	−1,006	−1,099	−2,024	−1,297	−420	−214	−97	−3,200	−545	−2,028	377
Capital Account, n.i.e.: Credit	78bad	579	564	856	1,267	1,099	1,037	1,688	2,216	1,118	857	449	709
Capital Account: Debit	78bbd	−1,294	−1,569	−1,955	−3,291	−2,396	−1,457	−1,902	−2,314	−4,317	−1,402	−2,477	−332
Financial Account, n.i.e.	78bjd	−11,136	−9,969	−18,839	−5,474	−14,304	−14,398	−9,905	−7,484	504	−12,550	−23,088	−13,675
Direct Investment Abroad	78bdd	−9,954	−17,581	−20,188	−31,937	−24,499	−36,938	−57,166	−74,489	−47,137	−33,951	−35,204	−2,494
Dir. Invest. in Rep. Econ., n.i.e.	78bed	6,380	7,127	12,206	16,604	11,033	37,619	41,148	63,229	51,716	28,534	15,695	−816
Portfolio Investment Assets	78bfd	−10,702	−9,570	−16,498	−25,013	−38,942	−69,294	−94,489	−65,634	−60,994	−64,293	−57,001	−78,091
Equity Securities	78bkd	−4,235	−6,595	−8,730	−2,895	−12,140	−19,890	−52,668	−23,447	−29,565	−7,917	−12,373	−20,148
Debt Securities	78bld	−6,467	−2,975	−7,768	−22,119	−26,802	−49,404	−41,821	−42,187	−31,429	−56,375	−44,628	−57,943
Portfolio Investment Liab., n.i.e.	78bgd	12,344	−834	6,123	13,432	17,752	30,074	100,103	55,242	74,193	49,954	82,000	61,629
Equity Securities	78bmd	3,503	−1,385	−743	3,280	774	3,825	30,491	16,970	12,947	−193	4,553	4,823
Debt Securities	78bnd	8,841	551	6,865	10,152	16,979	26,248	69,611	38,272	61,246	50,147	77,448	56,806
Financial Derivatives Assets	78bwd	7,271	11,888	18,454	23,385	31,899	53,364	63,425	82,999	87,517	70,419	126,732	165,621
Financial Derivatives Liabilities	78bxd	−7,361	−12,256	−20,198	−24,134	−32,346	−52,388	−59,240	−86,979	−93,354	−77,263	−127,200	−167,116
Other Investment Assets	78bhd	−12,803	7,270	−8,127	1,582	−37,217	−56,475	354	−28,390	−69,787	−40,263	−63,605	−66,669
Monetary Authorities	78bod	—	—	—	—	—	−235	107	675	−1,175	360	277	−335
General Government	78bpd	−189	−44	7	−270	146	181	−1,442	534	−837	−1,621	−1,730	84
Banks	78bqd	−7,884	9,437	−3,474	2,926	−31,241	−49,373	9,488	−18,042	−60,706	−20,574	−55,675	−57,560
Other Sectors	78brd	−4,730	−2,124	−4,660	−1,075	−6,122	−7,047	−7,800	−11,557	−7,069	−18,428	−6,477	−8,858
Other Investment Liab., n.i.e.	78bid	3,688	3,988	9,389	20,607	58,015	79,641	−4,039	46,538	58,349	54,313	35,494	74,260
Monetary Authorities	78bsd	99	91	−137	−42	41	930	−410	−3,542	1,977	2,279	−3,554	2,085
General Government	78btd	166	1,151	24	−131	−536	284	640	329	2,828	4	−133	−1,845
Banks	78bud	3,122	−493	4,174	15,697	52,519	60,697	−1,541	18,367	57,759	52,159	41,207	77,337
Other Sectors	78bvd	301	3,239	5,327	5,083	5,990	17,730	−2,728	31,384	−4,214	−129	−2,027	−3,318
Net Errors and Omissions	78cad	5,288	−5,819	−7,745	−19,700	−12,185	−553	−7,488	984	−5,491	2,846	7,793	−10,871
Overall Balance	78cbd	6,641	500	−1,911	−5,695	−2,709	−2,339	−4,611	219	−351	−132	−920	−998
Reserves and Related Items	79dad	−6,641	−500	1,911	5,695	2,709	2,339	4,611	−219	351	132	920	998
Reserve Assets	79dbd	−6,641	−500	1,911	5,695	2,709	2,339	4,611	−219	351	132	920	998
Use of Fund Credit and Loans	79dcd	—	—	—	—	—	—	—	—	—	—	—	—
Exceptional Financing	79ded	....	....	....	....	....	....	....	....	....	....	....	....
International Investment Position		*Millions of US Dollars*											
Assets	79aad	498,632	458,187	549,583	597,917	637,987	819,882	1,072,804	1,135,519	1,238,991	1,491,841	1,960,537	2,342,560
Direct Investment Abroad	79abd	120,123	142,953	172,672	194,025	198,555	229,000	263,756	305,461	332,156	398,628	544,350	604,240
Portfolio Investment	79acd	106,470	119,467	164,012	204,757	242,157	363,140	453,076	478,298	485,696	570,003	782,593	993,780
Equity Securities	79add	59,663	67,258	91,747	107,708	124,066	173,149	249,426	253,589	235,023	217,387	327,136	410,196
Debt Securities	79aed	46,807	52,209	72,265	97,049	118,091	189,991	203,649	224,709	250,673	352,616	455,457	583,584
Financial Derivatives	79ald	—	—	—	—	—	—	39,731	29,220	44,606	71,812	86,762	85,887
Other Investment	79afd	227,612	147,863	165,718	159,487	164,556	198,202	297,172	304,903	359,604	432,450	525,390	637,603
Monetary Authorities	79agd	—	—	—	—	—	252	3,230	2,528	3,245	3,545	4,054	4,662
General Government	79ahd	20,492	21,945	23,421	22,364	20,426	21,763	22,292	20,918	19,908	23,438	6,259	7,003
Banks	79aid	158,773	84,664	96,228	93,238	101,561	126,298	197,320	203,784	255,845	302,647	403,484	485,574
Other Sectors	79ajd	48,348	41,254	46,068	43,885	42,569	49,889	74,330	77,673	80,606	102,820	111,592	140,364
Reserve Assets	79akd	44,427	47,903	47,181	39,648	32,720	29,540	19,070	17,636	16,929	18,948	21,442	21,050
Liabilities	79lad	435,686	484,362	586,112	658,739	721,135	973,052	1,098,446	1,194,747	1,291,960	1,608,297	1,978,625	2,369,837
Dir. Invest. in Rep. Economy	79lbd	74,478	93,409	116,049	126,543	122,193	164,473	192,588	243,732	282,882	349,969	433,409	488,674
Portfolio Investment	79lcd	164,632	176,410	225,266	276,532	318,336	445,573	536,599	567,014	547,592	647,363	822,843	1,031,171
Equity Securities	79ldd	92,380	105,239	129,955	179,628	224,692	308,671	363,796	350,571	283,978	262,251	263,173	341,345
Debt Securities	79led	72,252	71,171	95,311	96,903	93,645	136,902	172,803	216,443	263,614	385,112	559,671	689,826
Financial Derivatives	79lld	—	—	—	—	—	—	30,543	24,440	49,469	86,573	94,842	98,660
Other Investment	79lfd	196,576	214,543	244,797	255,665	280,606	363,005	338,716	359,561	411,964	524,392	627,530	751,333
Monetary Authorities	79lgd	152	263	141	80	64	725	3,271	115	1,666	4,889	2,595	5,094
General Government	79lhd	9,504	10,864	11,536	10,971	9,891	10,232	13,090	12,785	14,629	17,838	4,366	2,736
Banks	79lid	149,117	158,290	184,237	195,974	223,451	297,011	265,713	268,848	316,907	403,206	508,729	618,294
Other Sectors	79ljd	37,802	45,126	48,882	48,641	47,200	55,038	56,642	77,812	78,763	98,458	111,840	125,208
Government Finance													
Central Government		*Millions of Guilders through 1998; Millions of Euros Beginning 1999: Year Ending December 31*											
Deficit (-) or Surplus	80	−8,343	2,763	−23,018	−9,626	−10,921	−3,177	† −5,815	−372	−3,500	−6,902	−10,718	−7,147
Total Revenue and Grants	81y	204,088	199,517	204,769	189,159	197,347	210,688	† 105,280	108,309	115,142	120,325	122,592	135,725
Revenue	81	204,066	199,508	204,611	188,965	196,930	210,397	† 105,177	108,111	115,044	120,315	122,440	135,455
Grants	81z	22	9	158	194	417	291	† 103	198	98	10	152	270
Exp. & Lending Minus Repay	82z	212,431	196,754	227,787	198,785	208,268	213,865	† 111,095	108,681	118,642	127,227	133,310	142,872
Total Financing	80h	8,343	−2,763	23,018	9,626	10,921	3,177	† 5,815	372	3,500	6,902	10,718	7,365
Total Net Borrowing	84	13,220	−1,685	28,816	9,885	−4,072	13,348	† 2,254	−1,032	3,521	9,183	12,289	4,665
Net Domestic	84a	13,220	−1,685	28,816	9,885	−4,072	13,348	† 2,254	−1,032	3,521	9,183	12,289	4,665
Net Foreign	85a	—	—	—	—	—	—	† —	—	—	—	—	—
Use of Cash Balances	87	−4,877	−1,078	−5,798	−259	14,993	−10,171	† 3,561	1,404	−21	−2,281	−1,571	2,700
Total Debt by Currency	88z	371,209	374,645	399,825	410,989	417,467	431,383	† 200,984	204,476	211,675	226,756	256,388	231,027
National	88b	371,209	374,645	399,825	410,989	417,467	431,383	† 200,984	204,476	211,675	226,756	256,388	231,027
Foreign	89b	—	—	—	—	—	—	† —	—	—	—	—	—
General Government		*As Percent of Gross Domestic Product*											
Deficit (-) or Surplus	80g	−3.2	−3.8	−4.0	−1.8	−1.1	−.8	.4	2.2	.2	....	....	....
Debt	88g	81.1	77.9	79.0	75.3	70.0	66.8	63.1	56.0	53.2	....	....	....

		1993	1994	1995	1996	1997	1998	1999	2000	2001	2002	2003	2004
National Accounts							*Billions of Guilders through 1998; Billions of Euros Beginning 1999:*						
Househ.Cons.Expend.,incl.NPISHs....	96f.c	299.9	313.0	326.7	346.1	363.6	387.8	† 187.6	200.6	212.8	221.3	224.3	227.7
Government Consumption Expend...	91f.c	148.6	153.3	160.0	160.6	168.4	177.3	† 85.5	91.3	100.9	109.4	115.3	118.0
Gross Fixed Capital Formation..........	93e.c	124.7	128.4	135.2	146.3	158.0	168.0	† 84.2	89.0	92.9	92.6	91.6	95.4
Changes in Inventories.....................	93i.c	−4.6	.1	4.6	1.5	1.8	5.2	† .5	.4	.3	−.8	.1	—
Exports of Goods and Services..........	90c.c	316.3	348.4	382.6	402.1	449.2	475.7	† 225.4	271.4	280.0	279.5	279.4	305.2
Imports of Goods and Services (-).....	98c.c	282.8	309.7	343.1	362.2	405.6	433.5	† 209.1	250.4	257.3	256.8	256.6	280.0
Gross Domestic Product (GDP).........	99b.c	602.1	633.6	666.0	694.3	735.4	780.5	† 374.1	402.3	429.3	445.2	454.3	466.3
Net Primary Income from Abroad.....	98.n	−.6	1.7	8.0	3.5	13.1	8.6	† .7	1.7	−3.1	−6.3	−6.6	−6.3
Gross National Income (GNI)............	99a	580.9	616.0	674.0	697.8	748.0	784.8	† 374.8	404.0	426.3	438.9	447.7	460.0
Net Current Transf.from Abroad.......	98t.c	....	....	....	....	....	....	† −2.2	−3.3	−3.7	−4.3	....	....
Gross Nat'l Disposable Inc.(GNDI)....	99i.c	....	....	....	....	....	....	† 373.6	400.8	422.6	434.5	443.3	....
Gross Saving..................................	99s.c	....	....	....	....	....	....	† 43.1	47.8	42.5	31.1	26.2	....
Consumption of Fixed Capital..........	99cfc	94.8	98.1	100.7	104.9	109.8	116.7	† 56.5	61.2	65.5	69.0	71.4	....
GDP Volume 1995 Ref., Chained.....	99b.r	605.8	646.4	666.0	686.3	712.6	734.6	† 350.9	363.1	368.3	370.4	367.1	372.4
GDP Volume (2000=100)...............	99bvr	75.7	80.8	83.2	85.8	89.1	91.8	† 96.6	100.0	101.4	102.0	101.1	102.6
GDP Deflator (2000=100)...............	99bir	90.2	89.3	90.3	91.3	93.1	95.4	† 96.2	100.0	105.2	108.5	111.7	113.0
						Millions: Midyear Estimates								
Population...............................	99z	15.26	15.36	15.46	15.55	15.64	15.73	15.81	15.90	15.98	16.07	16.15	16.23

Netherlands Antilles 353

		1993	1994	1995	1996	1997	1998	1999	2000	2001	2002	2003	2004
Exchange Rates				*Guilders per SDR: End of Period (aa) Guilders per US Dollar: End of Period (ae)*									
Official Rate	aa	2.459	2.613	2.661	2.574	2.415	2.520	2.457	2.332	2.250	2.434	2.660	2.780
Official Rate	ae	1.790	1.790	1.790	1.790	1.790	1.790	1.790	1.790	1.790	1.790	1.790	1.790
				Index Numbers (2000=100): Period Averages									
Official Rate	ahx	100.0	100.0	100.0	100.0	100.0	100.0	100.0	100.0	100.0	100.0	100.0	100.0
Nominal Effective Exchange Rate	nec	76.8	81.3	80.2	84.6	90.1	92.6	94.4	100.0	103.0	103.1	97.6	93.9
Real Effective Exchange Rate	rec	96.3	94.6	90.6	93.7	98.9	99.6	97.6	100.0	100.0	97.5	89.4	83.6
International Liquidity				*Millions of US Dollars Unless Otherwise Indicated: End of Period*									
Total Reserves minus Gold	1l.d	234	179	203	189	214	248	265	261	301	406	373	415
Foreign Exchange	1d.d	234	179	203	189	214	248	265	261	301	406	373	415
Gold (Million Fine Troy Ounces)	1ad	.548	.548	.548	.548	.548	.421	.421	.421	.421	.421	.421	.421
Gold (National Valuation)	1and	38	38	117	106	106	100	100	78	78	78	132	152
Monetary Authorities: Other Liab.	4..d	2	26	32	10	8	1	1	2	—	1	—	—
Deposit Money Banks: Assets	7a.d	825	748	442	400	396	471	473	552	862	653	710	760
Liabilities	7b.d	780	720	391	402	392	421	455	568	664	496	477	510
OBU: Assets	7k.d	29,155	29,152	26,085	28,106	31,393	36,430	32,792	34,466	38,254	42,584	39,961	42,134
Liabilities	7m.d	27,619	28,315	15,256	26,263	29,437	33,772	30,029	31,423	34,567	38,954	36,472	38,275
Monetary Authorities				*Millions of Guilders End of Period*									
Foreign Assets	11	490.1	435.2	683.3	546.5	591.5	625.9	655.1	608.7	678.7	867.9	905.3	1,015.7
Claims on Central Government	12a	66.2	59.9	69.2	68.6	82.0	79.1	117.5	94.8	150.5	124.4	119.9	185.6
Reserve Money	14	401.0	375.0	449.6	385.2	445.2	489.1	460.0	497.9	678.6	847.8	796.8	954.2
of which: Currency Outside DMBs	14a	184.5	198.2	209.6	195.6	188.0	186.6	197.0	188.9	218.2	235.2	232.9	231.3
Time Deposits	15	11.0	13.2	30.3	—	—	—	—	—	—	—	—	—
Foreign Liabilities	16c	3.1	47.0	58.0	18.7	15.1	2.5	.9	3.1	.8	1.7	.8	.4
Central Government Deposits	16d	71.2	13.0	46.0	38.7	45.1	55.5	164.7	170.7	168.1	123.0	94.9	107.3
Capital Accounts	17a	65.8	65.8	201.6	185.4	185.4	182.4	182.4	141.5	141.6	141.4	240.2	274.7
Other Items (Net)	17r	4.2	−18.9	−33.0	−12.9	−17.3	−24.5	−35.4	−109.7	−159.9	−121.6	−107.5	−135.3
Deposit Money Banks				*Millions of Guilders: End of Period*									
Reserves	20	176.9	128.5	209.7	164.4	232.1	263.0	251.3	304.7	432.1	596.3	557.7	644.5
Foreign Assets	21	1,476.6	1,339.5	791.7	715.9	709.7	843.6	846.0	987.5	1,542.1	1,168.3	1,270.1	1,359.6
Claims on Local Government	22b	125.1	126.5	103.1	158.5	142.8	121.5	126.9	101.1	122.7	181.8	207.2	288.7
Claims on Private Sector	22d	1,796.9	2,034.4	2,130.2	2,275.8	2,262.8	2,299.8	2,529.3	2,677.4	2,686.9	2,782.5	2,834.4	3,059.7
Demand Deposits	24	501.8	560.7	653.6	702.9	710.7	721.7	770.3	806.8	896.4	1,064.9	1,007.7	1,096.8
Time and Savings Deposits	25a	1,136.5	1,201.7	1,231.4	1,266.4	1,325.7	1,417.1	1,484.6	1,552.9	1,743.7	1,921.2	2,195.4	2,434.6
Foreign Currency Deposits	25b	375.5	399.7	470.4	413.5	409.4	399.5	456.7	449.2	558.4	603.4	677.9	753.1
Foreign Liabilities	26c	1,396.8	1,289.6	699.0	719.1	701.5	752.9	813.6	1,017.5	1,188.7	888.2	854.2	913.3
Central Government Deposits	26d	39.0	36.0	22.6	36.5	45.7	46.2	30.0	34.5	41.8	39.3	34.9	45.8
Capital Accounts	27a	249.9	274.4	245.7	301.5	301.0	318.4	332.5	332.2	390.1	421.7	394.3	481.8
Other Items (Net)	27r	−124.0	−133.2	−88.0	−125.3	−146.6	−127.9	−134.2	−122.4	−35.3	−209.8	−295.0	−372.9
Girosystem Curacao													
Private Sector Deposits	24..i	60.1	87.1	71.4	—	....	....	....	....	....	....	....	....
Central Government Deposits	26d.i	34.3	34.9	1.5	—	....	....	....	....	....	....	....	....
Monetary Survey				*Millions of Guilders End of Period*									
Foreign Assets (Net)	31n	566.8	438.1	718.0	524.6	584.6	714.1	686.6	575.6	1,031.3	1,146.3	1,320.4	1,461.6
Domestic Credit	32	2,055.9	2,377.5	2,423.3	2,510.7	2,485.9	2,503.4	2,664.6	2,812.9	2,906.7	3,198.3	3,331.7	3,765.3
Claims on Central Govt. (Net)	32an	39.0	86.1	87.0	76.4	80.1	67.1	-6.6	−36.4	8.1	189.5	272.4	363.9
Claims on Local Government	32b	219.5	256.5	206.0	158.5	142.8	136.5	141.9	171.9	211.7	226.3	224.9	341.7
Claims on Private Sector	32d	1,797.4	2,034.9	2,130.3	2,275.8	2,263.0	2,299.8	2,529.3	2,677.4	2,686.9	2,782.5	2,834.4	3,059.7
Money	34	786.0	894.3	964.9	923.7	923.8	947.8	979.0	1,000.0	1,142.9	1,316.4	1,246.8	1,406.5
Quasi-Money	35	1,523.0	1,614.6	1,732.1	1,679.9	1,735.1	1,816.6	1,941.3	2,002.1	2,302.1	2,524.6	2,873.3	3,187.7
Other Items (Net)	37r	313.7	306.7	444.3	431.7	411.6	453.1	430.9	386.4	493.0	503.6	532.0	632.7
Money plus Quasi-Money	35l	2,309.0	2,508.9	2,697.0	2,603.6	2,658.9	2,764.4	2,920.3	3,002.1	3,445.0	3,841.0	4,120.1	4,594.2
Interest Rates				*Percent Per Annum*									
Discount Rate (End of Period)	60	5.00	5.00	6.00	6.00	6.00	6.00	6.00	6.00	6.00	6.00	....	....
Treasury Bill Rate	60c	4.83	4.48	5.46	5.66	5.77	5.82	6.15	6.15	6.15	4.96	2.80	3.86
Deposit Rate	60l	4.33	4.05	3.75	3.67	3.66	3.58	3.59	3.63	3.65	3.62	3.48	2.92
Lending Rate	60p	12.59	12.73	12.93	13.21	13.29	13.58	13.60	9.98	10.44	10.14	11.26	10.56
Government Bond Yield	61	8.14	7.48	8.02	8.25	8.67	8.60	8.75	8.77	9.00	8.20	6.72	7.09
Prices and Labor				*Index Numbers (2000=100): Period Averages*									
Consumer Prices	64	83.2	84.7	87.0	† 90.2	93.1	94.2	94.5	100.0	101.8	102.2	104.3	105.7
				Number in Thousands: Period Averages									
Labor Force	67d	....	....	62	66	66	65	61	61	....	....	....	....
Employment	67e	52	55	54	57	56	54		52	....	....	....	....
Unemployment	67c	8	8	8	9	10	11	....	9	....	....	....	....
Unemployment Rate (%)	67r	13.6	12.8	13.1	14.2	15.2	16.2	14.1	12.9	14.5	14.2	....	....
Intl. Transactions & Positions				*Millions of Guilders*									
Exports	70	2,297	2,462	....	....	....	....	....	3,554	4,292	2,881	2,078	....
Imports, c.i.f.	71	3,485	3,146	....	....	....	....	....	5,108	5,059	4,060	4,666	....
Imports, f.o.b.	71.v	3,112	2,809	....	....	....	....	....	....	....	....	....	....

Netherlands Antilles 353

		1993	1994	1995	1996	1997	1998	1999	2000	2001	2002	2003	2004
Balance of Payments		*Millions of US Dollars: Minus Sign Indicates Debit*											
Current Account, n.i.e.	78ald	1.2	−97.9	127.6	−253.8	−65.1	−136.9	−277.1	−50.7	−210.9	−58.7	6.8	....
Goods: Exports f.o.b.	78aad	306.0	351.1	586.5	614.6	501.4	465.6	467.0	676.1	638.2	575.5	681.5	....
Goods: Imports f.o.b.	78abd	−1,143.8	−1,271.6	−1,621.5	−1,743.7	−1,476.6	−1,513.2	−1,584.2	−1,661.7	−1,752.4	−1,602.4	−1,684.4	....
Trade Balance	78acd	−837.8	−920.5	−1,034.9	−1,129.1	−975.3	−1,047.7	−1,117.2	−985.6	−1,114.3	−1,026.9	−1,002.9	....
Services: Credit	78add	1,346.0	1,414.2	1,491.6	1,405.9	1,425.0	1,508.9	1,518.7	1,613.4	1,649.5	1,628.2	1,705.7	....
Services: Debit	78aed	−596.0	−670.5	−563.3	−624.0	−574.7	−611.3	−661.9	−733.5	−766.9	−769.6	−811.6	....
Balance on Goods & Services	78afd	−87.8	−176.8	−106.6	−347.3	−125.0	−150.0	−260.4	−105.8	−231.7	−168.4	−108.8	....
Income: Credit	78agd	122.7	133.7	117.4	135.4	100.8	146.2	101.0	126.0	103.7	90.9	89.8	....
Income: Debit	78ahd	−140.3	−99.4	−99.4	−71.7	−54.1	−109.3	−121.4	−103.2	−83.8	−90.1	−97.1	....
Balance on Gds, Serv. & Inc.	78aid	−105.4	−142.5	−88.5	−283.5	−78.3	−113.1	−280.8	−83.0	−211.7	−167.6	−116.0	....
Current Transfers, n.i.e.: Credit	78ajd	250.3	217.9	365.8	174.7	165.3	137.2	179.6	246.6	217.0	365.5	399.1	....
Current Transfers: Debit	78akd	−143.7	−173.3	−149.6	−145.0	−152.1	−160.9	−175.8	−214.3	−216.2	−256.6	−276.3	....
Capital Account, n.i.e.	78bcd	−.8	−.7	61.9	71.3	75.1	86.9	108.4	29.8	37.2	27.7	26.2	....
Capital Account, n.i.e.: Credit	78bad	.8	1.0	66.8	71.9	76.9	91.3	109.8	31.3	37.9	29.3	32.8	....
Capital Account: Debit	78bbd	−1.7	−1.7	−4.9	−.6	−1.7	−4.4	−1.5	−1.4	−.6	−1.6	−6.6	....
Financial Account, n.i.e.	78bjd	32.2	−2.3	−142.5	95.8	−31.2	58.0	69.5	−122.2	351.6	32.3	−52.1	....
Direct Investment Abroad	78bdd	2.2	−1.0	−1.3	.8	6.5	2.0	1.2	2.3	−.5	−1.1	.9	....
Dir. Invest. in Rep. Econ., n.i.e.	78bed	11.0	21.5	−150.0	−59.8	−88.5	−52.6	−21.8	−62.6	−4.7	7.8	−80.6	....
Portfolio Investment Assets	78bfd	−13.9	−69.1	−18.0	−22.3	9.2	−21.2	−7.1	−38.0	−31.6	−38.4	−.8	....
Equity Securities	78bkd	—	—	−15.7	−19.2	−5.4	−3.9	−3.0	−33.9	−7.2	−8.5	−42.6	....
Debt Securities	78bld	−13.9	−69.1	−2.3	−3.1	14.6	−17.3	−4.1	−4.1	−24.4	−29.9	41.8	....
Portfolio Investment Liab., n.i.e.	78bgd	1.5	10.9	1.1	−8.2	−.2	−.2	−3.1	.1	−.2	.9	5.0	....
Equity Securities	78bmd	—	—	—	....	....	....	....	—	—	—	—	....
Debt Securities	78bnd	1.5	10.9	1.1	−8.2	−.2	−.2	−3.1	.1	−.2	.9	5.0	....
Financial Derivatives Assets	78bwd	....	....	....	....	....	....	....	—	.1	—	—	....
Financial Derivatives Liabilities	78bxd	....	....	....	....	....	....	....	—	—	—	—	....
Other Investment Assets	78bhd	−38.4	15.3	67.1	84.6	46.1	111.7	34.1	−40.8	75.9	23.9	−119.5	....
Monetary Authorities	78bod	....	....	−.8	5.1	2.8	3.9	2.6	−.1	−1.2	.4	.1	....
General Government	78bpd	—	—	2.2	7.2	2.0	4.4	—	−.9	−.8	—	−5.7	....
Banks	78bqd	−46.9	−55.8	−3.4	42.8	19.3	21.7	57.2	5.2	1.5	30.9	1.2	....
Other Sectors	78brd	8.5	71.1	69.1	29.4	21.9	81.7	−25.7	−45.0	76.5	−7.5	−115.1	....
Other Investment Liab., n.i.e.	78bid	69.8	20.1	−41.3	100.7	−4.4	18.4	66.2	16.8	312.6	39.2	143.0	....
Monetary Authorities	78bsd	—	—	—	....	....	....	—	1.3	—	—	—	....
General Government	78btd	−9.5	−38.3	−19.9	−19.9	−38.2	−51.2	−67.8	−33.3	−12.9	−20.7	−37.1	....
Banks	78bud	59.7	59.7	−5.8	45.8	−5.7	−.1	3.0	40.0	91.8	−2.7	−6.1	....
Other Sectors	78bvd	19.6	−1.3	−15.6	74.8	39.5	69.7	131.1	8.8	233.7	62.5	186.2	....
Net Errors and Omissions	78cad	11.5	24.9	13.4	14.8	14.9	17.4	24.5	13.4	39.8	51.0	46.3	....
Overall Balance	78cbd	44.0	−75.9	60.4	−71.9	−6.3	25.5	−74.7	−129.6	217.7	52.3	27.1	....
Reserves and Related Items	79dad	−44.0	75.9	−60.4	71.9	6.3	−25.5	74.7	129.6	−217.7	−52.3	−27.1	....
Reserve Assets	79dbd	−44.0	75.9	−60.4	53.8	−27.8	−75.6	8.3	47.8	−231.9	−68.2	−49.7	....
Use of Fund Credit and Loans	79dcd	—	—	....	....	....	....	....	....	....	....	....	....
Exceptional Financing	79ded	—	—	....	18.1	34.1	50.2	66.5	81.8	14.2	15.9	22.6	....
Government Finance		*Millions of Guilders: Year Ending December 31*											
Deficit (-) or Surplus	80	−25.2	−40.6p	† −100.2	....	....	....	....	....	....	....	....	....
Revenue	81	587.8	663.3p	† 462.2	....	....	....	....	....	....	....	....	....
Grants Received	81z	105.0	91.9p	† 92.8	....	....	....	....	....	....	....	....	....
Expenditure	82	719.4	795.4p	† 655.1	....	....	....	....	....	....	....	....	....
Lending Minus Repayments	83	−1.4	.4p	† .1	....	....	....	....	....	....	....	....	....
Financing													
Domestic	84a	25.2	40.6p	† 100.2	....	....	....	....	....	....	....	....	....
Foreign	85a	—	—p	† —	....	....	....	....	....	....	....	....	....
Debt: Domestic	88a	616.3	618.5p	† 704.6	....	....	....	....	....	....	....	....	....
Foreign	89a	170.9	—p	† —	....	....	....	....	....	....	....	....	....
		Millions: Midyear Estimates											
Population	99z	.19	.19	.19	.18	.18	.18	.18	.18	.18	.18	.18	.18

New Zealand 196

		1993	1994	1995	1996	1997	1998	1999	2000	2001	2002	2003	2004
Exchange Rates					*SDRs per New Zealand Dollar: End of Period*								
Market Rate	ac	.4068	.4401	.4395	.4910	.4311	.3742	.3793	.3379	.3306	.3873	.4374	.4626
				US Dollars per New Zealand Dollar: End of Period (ag) Period Average (rh)									
Market Rate	ag	.5588	.6425	.6533	.7060	.5817	.5269	.5206	.4402	.4155	.5265	.6500	.7184
Market Rate	rh	.5407	.5937	.6564	.6876	.6630	.5367	.5295	.4574	.4206	.4642	.5823	.6640
				Index Numbers (2000=100): Period Averages									
Market Rate	ahx	118.2	129.8	143.5	150.3	145.0	117.3	115.8	100.0	92.0	101.5	127.3	145.2
Nominal Effective Exchange Rate	nec	105.6	112.8	118.5	127.3	131.4	112.6	109.7	100.0	97.5	105.1	118.3	125.6
Real Effective Exchange Rate	rec	106.3	113.6	120.2	129.1	132.5	113.4	109.2	100.0	98.1	107.0	120.5	128.5
Fund Position					*Millions of SDRs: End of Period*								
Quota	2f.s	650	650	650	650	650	650	895	895	895	895	895	895
SDRs	1b.s	—	—	1	—	—	1	5	10	13	16	19	22
Reserve Position in the Fund	1c.s	104	101	110	127	132	253	309	246	308	338	433	305
Total Fund Cred.&Loans Outstg	2tl	—	—	—	—	—	—	—	—	—	—	—	—
International Liquidity				*Millions of US Dollars Unless Otherwise Indicated: End of Period*									
Total Reserves minus Gold	1l.d	3,337	3,709	4,410	5,953	4,451	4,204	4,455	3,330	3,009	3,739	4,907	5,294
SDRs	1b.d	—	—	1	—	—	2	7	13	16	22	28	34
Reserve Position in the Fund	1c.d	142	147	164	182	178	356	424	320	387	459	644	474
Foreign Exchange	1d.d	3,195	3,561	4,245	5,771	4,273	3,846	4,025	2,997	2,605	3,258	4,235	4,786
Monetary Authorities	1dad	2,378	2,351	2,575	2,714	2,751	2,461	2,804	1,690	1,523	1,734	2,366	1,770
Government	1dbd	817	1,210	1,670	3,057	1,522	1,385	1,221	1,306	1,082	1,524	1,869	3,016
Gold (Million Fine Troy Ounces)	1ad	—	—	—	—	—	—	—	—	—	—	—	—
Gold (National Valuation)	1and	—	—	—	—	—	—	—	—	—	—	—	—
Monetary Authorities: Other Liab	4..d	96	—	178	299	461	383	379	605	302	501	473	975
Banking Institutions: Assets	7a.d	1,159	1,559	1,955	3,552	1,915	2,829	4,786	6,953	9,788	12,991	14,664	16,101
Liabilities	7b.d	9,249	12,319	14,439	17,197	17,024	20,031	25,261	25,554	27,632	33,990	41,785	53,906
Monetary Authorities					*Millions of New Zealand Dollars: End of Period*								
Foreign Assets	11	5,974	5,772	7,024	8,856	8,544	8,799	9,077	10,330	9,310	10,410	10,155	11,106
Claims on Central Government	12a	2,271	2,918	3,065	3,118	3,097	3,119	1,892	2,489	2,373	2,676	2,677	4,006
Claims on Banking Institutions	12e	796	301	476	1,305	1,079	451	2,178	1,802	2,247	2,931	2,829	748
Reserve Money	14	1,695	1,891	2,026	1,972	2,068	2,198	3,870	2,925	3,196	3,472	3,546	3,767
of which: Currency Outside DMBs	14a	1,199	1,367	1,489	1,497	1,633	1,724	2,077	2,069	2,241	2,451	2,597	2,737
Liabs.of Central Bank: Securities	16ac	1,149	1,185	1,218	1,242	1,250	1,076	—	—	—	—	—	—
Foreign Liabilities	16c	172	—	273	424	793	726	728	1,374	727	952	728	1,357
Central Government Deposits	16d	5,342	5,219	6,319	8,959	7,871	7,574	7,751	9,463	9,129	10,756	10,578	8,914
Capital Accounts	17a	734	748	769	745	801	853	843	893	914	868	838	1,857
Other Items (Net)	17r	−52	−53	−39	−62	−63	−58	−45	−34	−36	−31	−30	−34
Banking Institutions					*Millions of New Zealand Dollars: End of Period*								
Reserves	20	491	467	606	532	409	448	1,592	818	908	944	909	933
Claims on Mon.Author.:Securities	20c	1,149	1,185	1,218	1,242	1,250	1,076	—	—	—	—	—	—
Foreign Assets	21	2,074	2,427	2,993	5,031	3,292	5,369	9,194	15,794	23,558	24,675	22,560	22,413
Claims on Central Government	22a	7,079	5,932	4,249	3,302	3,572	4,384	6,921	7,149	5,818	8,183	7,920	5,601
Claims on Private Sector	22d	67,549	74,588	85,150	94,647	105,190	112,124	121,884	129,301	137,818	147,781	162,631	180,764
Demand Deposits	24	7,781	8,155	8,865	9,094	9,728	10,633	12,528	13,593	16,506	17,487	19,068	19,578
Time, Savings,Fgn.Currency Dep	25	53,223	57,423	62,850	74,458	78,117	78,762	81,043	82,164	85,727	92,559	102,782	109,088
of which: Fgn Currency Deposits	25b	2,535	1,849	2,030	3,764	2,806	4,198	2,521	3,296	3,194	2,638	4,667	5,620
Foreign Liabilities	26c	16,552	19,174	22,101	24,359	29,267	38,016	48,523	58,051	66,504	64,559	64,285	75,037
Central Government Deposits	26d	—	9	19	25	33	29	61	52	53	48	57	68
Capital Accounts	27a	5,255	5,158	5,798	5,547	7,262	8,224	9,348	9,685	11,790	14,022	17,803	18,396
Other Items (Net)	27r	−4,470	−5,320	−5,418	−8,727	−10,693	−12,263	−11,911	−10,483	−12,477	−7,093	−9,973	−12,455
Banking Survey					*Millions of New Zealand Dollars: End of Period*								
Foreign Assets (Net)	31n	−8,676	−10,976	−12,357	−10,896	−18,224	−24,575	−30,980	−33,300	−34,363	−30,427	−32,298	−42,874
Domestic Credit	32	71,557	78,210	86,126	92,084	103,955	112,023	122,884	129,423	136,826	147,836	162,593	181,390
Claims on Central Govt. (Net)	32an	4,007	3,622	976	−2,564	−1,234	−101	1,001	122	−992	55	−38	626
Claims on Private Sector	32d	67,549	74,588	85,150	94,647	105,190	112,124	121,884	129,301	137,818	147,781	162,631	180,764
Money	34	9,044	9,594	10,398	10,619	11,386	12,378	14,649	15,700	18,795	20,018	21,705	22,415
Quasi-Money	35	53,223	57,423	62,850	74,458	78,117	78,762	81,043	82,164	85,727	92,559	102,782	109,088
Capital Accounts	37a	5,990	5,906	6,567	6,292	8,062	9,077	10,190	10,578	12,704	14,890	18,641	20,254
Other Items (Net)	37r	−5,376	−5,688	−6,045	−10,180	−11,834	−12,767	−13,977	−12,319	−14,762	−10,058	−12,833	−13,240
Money plus Quasi-Money	35l	62,267	67,017	73,247	85,076	89,503	91,140	95,692	97,865	104,522	112,577	124,487	131,502
Money (National Definitions)					*Millions of New Zealand Dollars: End of Period*								
M1	59ma	....	10,948	10,334	10,565	11,327	12,888	14,880	15,932	19,094	20,312	22,135	22,834
M2	59mb	....	27,840	31,990	32,836	33,336	37,873	40,964	41,319	47,412	51,193	53,293	54,708
M3R	59mca	....	58,385	65,515	73,469	78,652	78,786	84,669	86,644	92,732	103,352	113,171	117,055
M3 Broad Money	59mcb	65,873	67,948	77,854	87,719	91,411	92,383	98,748	105,179	117,213	131,820	139,575	148,283
Nonbank Financial Institutions					*Millions of New Zealand Dollars: End of Period*								
Claims on Central Government	42a.s	2,328.6	2,435.4	....	....	....	....	....	....	....	....	....	....
Claims on Local Government	42b.s	782.3	546.4	526.9	624.7	551.3	....	....	....	....	....	....	....
Claims on Private Sector	42d.s	5,369.7	4,507.9	986.8	934.2	636.5	....	....	....	....	....	....	....
Real Estate	42h.s	1,488.7	1,590.9	....	....	....	....	....	....	....	....	....	....
Incr.in Total Assets(Within Per.)	49z.s	2,178.4	−618.4	....	....	....	....	....	....	....	....	....	....
Interest Rates					*Percent Per Annum*								
Discount Rate (End of Period)	60	5.70	9.75	9.80	8.80	9.70	5.60	5.00	6.50	4.75	5.75	5.00	6.50
Money Market Rate	60b	6.25	6.13	8.91	9.38	7.38	6.86	4.33	6.12	5.76	5.40	5.33	5.77
Treasury Bill Rate	60c	6.21	6.69	8.82	9.09	7.53	7.10	4.58	6.39	5.56	5.52	5.21	5.85
Deposit Rate	60l	6.24	6.38	8.49	8.49	7.26	6.78	4.56	6.36	5.35	5.33	5.10	5.77
Lending Rate	60p	10.34	9.69	12.09	12.27	11.35	11.22	8.49	10.22	9.88	9.83	9.81	10.38
Government Bond Yield	61	6.69	7.48	7.94	8.04	7.21	6.47	6.13	6.85	6.12	6.28	5.51	5.98

		1993	1994	1995	1996	1997	1998	1999	2000	2001	2002	2003	2004
Prices, Production, Labor					*Index Numbers (2000=100): Period Averages*								
Share Prices	62	53.7	68.0	71.7	80.5	93.7	109.9	97.7	100.0	105.3	115.8	128.6	163.9
Input Prices: All Industry	63	88.7	89.8	90.5	91.1	91.4	92.0	93.0	100.0	106.0	106.2	105.3	107.1
Consumer Prices	64	87.6	† 89.7	93.1	95.2	96.3	97.6	97.4	100.0	102.6	105.4	107.2	109.7
Labor Cost Index	65a	89.0	90.0	91.3	93.1	95.2	97.0	98.5	100.0	101.9	104.1	106.5	108.9
Manufacturing Prod	66ey	71.1	75.4	94.6	96.6	97.0	93.9	95.7	100.0	99.9	104.3	104.9	109.3
Manufacturing Employment	67ey	89.4	100.8	104.7	103.6	100.6	102.8	99.2	100.0	103.1	103.2	99.1	102.5
					Number in Thousands: Period Averages								
Labor Force	67d	1,653	1,766	1,809	1,866	† 1,886	1,891	1,907	1,923	1,958	2,012	2,046	2,099
Employment	67e	1,496	1,559	1,633	1,688	† 1,693	1,725	1,750	1,779	1,823	1,876	1,951	2,017
Unemployment	67c	157	185	158	154	† 165	191	217	230	194	171	145	109
Unemployment Rate (%)	67r	9.5	8.2	6.3	6.1	† 6.6	7.5	6.8	6.0	5.3	5.1	4.7	3.9
Intl. Transactions & Positions					*Millions of New Zealand Dollars*								
Exports	70	19,492.0	20,519.0	20,787.0	20,876.0	21,458.0	22,416.0	23,583.0	29,257.0	32,670.0	31,028.0	28,360.0	30,755.0
Butter	70fl	828.4	790.5	777.9	907.7	919.3	985.8	885.7	1,052.3	1,039.8	1,052.3	933.4	959.7
Imports, c.i.f	71	17,781.0	19,981.0	21,251.0	21,399.0	21,964.0	23,348.0	27,114.0	30,736.0	31,682.0	32,339.0	31,792.0	34,925.0
Imports, f.o.b	71.v	16,373.0	18,491.0	19,715.0	19,847.0	20,440.0	21,682.0	25,436.0	28,851.0	29,612.0	30,330.0	29,824.0	32,722.0
					2000=100								
Volume of Exports	72	73.9	† 81.3	83.7	87.8	92.9	92.4	94.8	100.0	103.2	108.9	111.8	119.4
Butter	72fl	73.4	222.9	206.5	80.9	97.2	87.8	91.0	100.0	86.4	114.1	107.5	97.3
Volume of Imports	73	66.6	† 77.5	82.6	85.4	88.5	90.6	102.7	100.0	101.8	111.2	123.8	142.1
Butter (Unit Value)	74fl	117.6	105.9	108.0	108.8	92.4	106.2	93.8	100.0	114.8	90.2	83.9	90.8
Export Price Index	76	90.4	86.8	85.4	82.3	80.0	83.6	84.8	100.0	108.9	97.6	87.0	88.0
Import Price Index	76.x	87.1	84.2	84.1	81.9	81.0	84.0	85.9	100.0	101.5	95.2	84.1	80.1
Butter (Wholesale Price)	76fl	112.0	101.8	107.7	....	95.9	116.0	107.5	100.0	....	....	....	....
Balance of Payments					*Millions of US Dollars: Minus Sign Indicates Debit*								
Current Account, n.i.e.	78ald	−746	−2,384	−3,003	−3,891	−4,304	−2,157	−3,515	−2,462	−1,253	−2,235	−3,357	−6,199
Goods: Exports f.o.b	78aad	10,468	12,176	13,554	14,338	14,282	12,246	12,657	13,530	13,920	14,517	16,835	20,458
Goods: Imports f.o.b	78abd	−8,749	−10,769	−12,584	−13,815	−13,380	−11,333	−13,028	−12,850	−12,448	−14,351	−17,291	−21,889
Trade Balance	78acd	1,719	1,408	971	523	903	912	−371	680	1,471	166	−456	−1,431
Services: Credit	78add	2,854	3,667	4,481	4,653	4,254	3,763	4,386	4,415	4,373	5,161	6,443	7,847
Services: Debit	78aed	−3,505	−4,101	−4,694	−4,897	−4,903	−4,499	−4,581	−4,544	−4,287	−4,718	−5,587	−6,902
Balance on Goods & Services	78afd	1,068	973	757	279	254	176	−567	551	1,557	608	399	−486
Income: Credit	78agd	394	358	940	372	393	880	919	710	596	1,077	1,380	1,527
Income: Debit	78ahd	−2,340	−4,045	−4,895	−5,085	−5,249	−3,493	−4,036	−3,959	−3,594	−4,041	−5,281	−7,320
Balance on Gds, Serv. & Inc.	78aid	−877	−2,713	−3,198	−4,434	−4,601	−2,437	−3,684	−2,698	−1,441	−2,355	−3,502	−6,279
Current Transfers, n.i.e.: Credit	78ajd	310	638	558	897	680	681	609	634	578	616	793	828
Current Transfers: Debit	78akd	−178	−309	−363	−354	−383	−401	−440	−398	−390	−496	−647	−748
Capital Account, n.i.e.	78bcd	542	617	1,224	1,336	242	−181	−217	−180	443	765	508	302
Capital Account, n.i.e.: Credit	78bad	833	995	1,652	1,838	783	263	260	238	821	1,122	966	888
Capital Account: Debit	78bbd	−291	−379	−427	−502	−541	−444	−477	−418	−378	−357	−458	−586
Financial Account, n.i.e.	78bjd	2,825	2,220	4,665	3,571	4,045	1,580	1,974	1,243	1,758	1,040	3,355	8,859
Direct Investment Abroad	78bdd	−1,276	−1,725	337	1,533	45	−928	−803	−1,300	1,144	−185	−299	825
Dir. Invest. in Rep. Econ., n.i.e.	78bed	2,350	2,543	3,659	2,231	2,624	1,191	1,412	3,370	775	738	2,438	2,271
Portfolio Investment Assets	78bfd	−283	−72	−284	−430	−1,612	−467	−666	−2,318	−1,219	−935	−856	−2,044
Equity Securities	78bkd	−187	−152	−216	−339	−925	114	−893	−1,763	−941	−944	−920	−1,786
Debt Securities	78bld	−97	81	−68	−90	−687	−581	227	−555	−278	10	65	−258
Portfolio Investment Liab., n.i.e.	78bgd	1,940	614	96	−104	403	425	−2,285	1,536	1,527	2,400	2,184	7,297
Equity Securities	78bmd	116	23	−100	175	88	22	172	−551	24	771	722	99
Debt Securities	78bnd	1,823	591	197	−279	315	402	−2,458	2,087	1,502	1,629	1,461	7,198
Financial Derivatives Assets	78bwd	....	....	....	....	....	....	....	....	....	....	....	....
Financial Derivatives Liabilities	78bxd	....	....	....	....	....	....	....	....	....	....	....	....
Other Investment Assets	78bhd	−739	−78	−392	−920	991	−305	−1,282	−476	−3,537	−1,086	317	−919
Monetary Authorities	78bod	—	—	—	—	....	....	....	....	....	....	....	....
General Government	78bpd	−62	−82	−57	−94	238	55	212	....	....	....	....	....
Banks	78bqd	−747	66	−346	−932	819	−285	−1,591	....	....	....	....	....
Other Sectors	78brd	71	−61	11	106	−65	−75	97	....	....	....	....	....
Other Investment Liab., n.i.e.	78bid	833	937	1,249	1,262	1,595	1,665	5,597	431	3,068	107	−430	1,428
Monetary Authorities	78bsd	—	—	—	—	—	—	—	....	....	....	....	....
General Government	78btd	−117	−290	−144	−135	−73	68	13	....	....	....	....	....
Banks	78bud	573	767	1,096	964	1,131	1,559	5,446	....	....	....	....	....
Other Sectors	78bvd	377	460	297	432	537	38	138	....	....	....	....	....
Net Errors and Omissions	78cad	−2,695	281	−2,502	756	−1,426	271	1,947	1,255	−1,135	1,516	277	−2,334
Overall Balance	78cbd	−74	733	384	1,772	−1,442	−486	188	−143	−187	1,086	783	629
Reserves and Related Items	79dad	74	−733	−384	−1,772	1,442	486	−188	143	187	−1,086	−783	−629
Reserve Assets	79dbd	74	−733	−384	−1,772	1,442	486	−188	143	187	−1,086	−783	−629
Use of Fund Credit and Loans	79dcd	—	—	—	—	—	—	—	....	....	....	....	....
Exceptional Financing	79ded	....	....	....	....	....	....	....	....	....	....	....	....

New Zealand 196

		1993	1994	1995	1996	1997	1998	1999	2000	2001	2002	2003	2004
IIP:End-March Stocks Through 1999							*Millions of US Dollars*						
Assets	79aad	10,118	13,206	16,201	23,573	23,023	19,348	21,320	31,689	31,806	41,152	53,274	60,905
Direct Investment Abroad	79abd	4,234	5,163	7,630	8,928	6,749	5,775	7,155	7,229	5,862	7,353	8,752	9,266
Portfolio Investment	79acd	952	1,362	1,707	5,815	6,434	6,476	6,760	11,264	11,766	13,644	19,832	24,907
Equity Securities	79add	602	834	1,226	4,407	4,895	4,620	4,447	6,721	7,114	7,652	13,433	17,596
Debt Securities	79aed	350	529	481	1,408	1,539	1,855	2,313	4,543	4,652	5,992	6,398	7,310
Financial Derivatives	79ald	—	—	—	—	—	—	—	4,289	2,462	3,484	4,678	3,719
Other Investment	79afd	1,644	2,793	2,898	4,245	5,313	2,804	3,555	4,955	8,151	11,709	13,965	16,066
Monetary Authorities	79agd	....	....	....	....	....	....	—	....	....	....	....	....
General Government	79ahd	....	....	....	....	....	....	198	....	....	....	....	....
Banks	79aid	....	....	....	....	....	....	2,100	....	....	....	....	....
Other Sectors	79ajd	....	....	....	....	....	....	1,257	....	....	....	....	....
Reserve Assets	79akd	3,288	3,888	3,967	4,584	4,528	4,293	3,850	3,952	3,566	4,963	6,048	6,946
Liabilities	79lad	44,240	51,100	62,339	71,631	78,547	68,752	67,651	72,412	70,118	93,899	122,225	150,131
Dir. Invest. in Rep. Economy	79lbd	14,849	19,315	25,574	33,381	37,491	34,889	33,555	23,098	19,564	28,255	41,773	49,813
Portfolio Investment	79lcd	15,290	17,595	19,809	19,361	20,166	17,581	17,710	25,591	25,859	33,942	43,576	57,427
Equity Securities	79ldd	1,320	816	1,483	288	1,045	208	241	4,582	4,170	5,670	8,994	12,046
Debt Securities	79led	13,970	16,779	18,327	19,072	19,121	17,373	17,469	21,009	21,689	28,272	34,582	45,381
Financial Derivatives	79lld	—	—	—	—	—	—	—	3,256	2,640	4,139	5,475	5,575
Other Investment	79lfd	14,101	14,189	16,955	18,889	20,890	16,282	16,387	20,467	22,054	27,563	31,401	37,316
Monetary Authorities	79lgd	....	....	....	....	....	....	—	....	....	....	....	....
General Government	79lhd	....	....	....	....	....	....	428	....	....	....	....	....
Banks	79lid	....	....	....	....	....	....	10,924	....	....	....	....	....
Other Sectors	79ljd	....	....	....	....	....	....	5,034	....	....	....	....	....
Government Finance						*Millions of New Zealand Dollars: Fiscal Year (see note)*							
Deficit (-) or Surplus	80	84	679	396	4,932	3,913	484	2,049	−385	....	....	....	....
Revenue	81	26,742	30,236	32,861	33,975	33,285	33,827	33,359	34,440	....	....	....	....
Expenditure	82	28,440	29,662	29,954	30,593	31,465	33,005	33,869	34,386	....	....	....	....
Lending Minus Repayments	83	−1,782	−105	2,511	−1,550	−2,093	338	−2,559	439	....	....	....	....
Financing													
Debt: Domestic	88a	24,206	20,194	21,060	19,866	15,688	18,307	19,440	20,041	....	....	....	....
Foreign	89a	23,523	26,289	23,418	21,896	20,649	19,969	17,384	16,368	....	....	....	....
National Accounts					*Millions of New Zealand Dollars; Year Beginning April 1*								
Housen.Cons.Expend.,incl.NPISHs	96f.c	47,434	51,177	54,521	58,048	60,520	63,394	65,904	68,590	72,314	76,888	81,534	87,123
Government Consumption Expend	91f.c	15,109	15,337	16,378	16,983	18,440	18,749	20,161	20,295	21,794	22,769	24,275	26,483
Gross Fixed Capital Formation	93e.c	15,035	17,747	19,890	20,877	20,610	19,719	21,835	22,449	24,673	26,418	29,917	33,364
Changes in Inventories	93i.c	1,432	1,166	1,182	809	817	270	1,537	1,419	1,888	770	1,136	1,708
Exports of Goods and Services	90c.c	25,085	26,951	27,125	27,528	28,531	30,468	33,595	41,284	43,611	41,973	40,098	42,885
Imports of Goods and Services (-)	98c.c	22,708	25,326	26,417	27,006	28,179	30,135	34,462	39,303	40,749	39,935	39,811	44,112
Gross Domestic Product (GDP)	99b.c	81,387	87,052	92,679	97,239	100,739	102,465	108,571	114,733	123,531	128,882	137,150	147,450
Net Primary Income from Abroad	98.nc	−5,638	−5,686	−5,999	−7,263	−6,399	−4,979	−6,606	−7,173	−6,635	−5,663	−6,147	....
Gross National Income (GNI)	99a.c	75,749	81,366	86,680	89,976	94,340	97,486	101,965	107,560	116,896	123,219	131,003	146,854
Consumption of Fixed Capital	99cfc	11,527	11,932	12,407	13,094	13,425	14,044	14,578	15,520	16,243	16,942	17,619	....
GDP Volume 1995/96 Prices	99b.r	84,969	89,335	92,679	95,674	98,300	99,287	104,412	106,333	110,330	115,510	119,642	123,985
GDP Volume (2000=100)	99bvr	79.9	84.0	87.2	90.0	92.4	93.4	98.2	100.0	103.8	108.6	112.5	116.6
GDP Deflator (2000=100)	99bir	88.8	90.3	92.7	94.2	95.0	95.6	96.4	100.0	103.8	103.4	106.2	110.2
						Millions: Midyear Estimates							
Population	99z	3.56	3.61	3.66	3.70	3.73	3.75	3.78	3.82	3.86	3.90	3.95	3.99

Nicaragua 278

		1993	1994	1995	1996	1997	1998	1999	2000	2001	2002	2003	2004
Exchange Rates					*Córdobas per SDR: End of Period*								
Principal Rate.................................	aa	8.72	10.38	11.84	12.83	13.49	15.76	16.91	17.01	17.39	19.95	23.11	25.36
					Córdobas per US Dollar: End of Period (ae) Period Average (rf)								
Principal Rate.................................	ae	6.35	7.11	7.97	8.92	10.00	11.19	12.32	13.06	13.84	14.67	15.55	16.33
Principal Rate.................................	rf	5.62	6.72	7.55	8.44	9.45	10.58	11.81	12.68	13.37	14.25	15.10	15.94
					Index Numbers (2000=100): Period Averages								
Principal Rate.................................	ahx	240.16	188.78	169.05	150.47	133.96	120.10	107.34	100.00	94.85	88.99	83.99	79.57
Nominal Effective Exchange Rate.....	nec	138.26	145.97	130.29	120.45	115.55	107.93	99.91	100.00	98.89	93.63	81.38	72.96
Real Effective Exchange Rate...........	rec	102.87	96.42	88.56	87.01	89.14	91.63	92.28	100.00	103.00	98.80	87.11	82.59
Fund Position					*Millions of SDRs: End of Period*								
Quota..	2f.s	96.10	96.10	96.10	96.10	96.10	96.10	130.00	130.00	130.00	130.00	130.00	130.00
SDRs..	1b.s	.03	.01	—	.02	.03	.15	.16	.05	.26	.02	.04	.32
Reserve Position in the Fund...........	1c.s	—	—	—	—	—	—	—	—	—	—	—	—
Total Fund Cred.&Loans Outstg.......	2tl	17.03	34.92	26.41	20.02	20.02	36.84	113.15	129.33	125.33	128.29	143.50	159.51
International Liquidity					*Millions of US Dollars Unless Otherwise Indicated: End of Period*								
Total Reserves minus Gold...............	1l.d	55.04	141.01	136.20	197.32	377.94	350.41	509.71	488.46	379.93	448.13	502.06	668.20
SDRs..	1b.d	.04	.01	—	.02	.04	.21	.21	.06	.33	.03	.06	.50
Reserve Position in the Fund..........	1c.d	—	—	—	—	—	—	—	—	—	—	—	—
Foreign Exchange...........................	1d.d	55.00	141.00	136.20	197.30	377.90	350.20	509.50	488.40	379.60	448.10	502.00	667.70
Gold (Million Fine Troy Ounces)........	1ad	.010	.013	.015	.015	.015	.015	.015	.015	.015	.015	.015	—
Gold (National Valuation).................	1and	.42	.55	.63	.63	.63	.63	.63	.62	.62	.62	.62	—
Monetary Authorities: Other Liab.....	4..d	3,586.21	3,470.70	2,936.22	2,113.12	2,086.84	2,046.56	1,993.95	2,134.78	1,949.79	1,979.26	2,014.99	1,913.73
Deposit Money Banks: Assets..........	7a.d	47.36	53.56	45.00	146.65	211.27	162.15	143.98	65.66	88.39	92.50	97.14	118.22
Liabilities.......	7b.d	18.74	31.62	31.34	44.61	54.65	55.09	109.86	90.42	102.58	107.00	108.99	110.93
Nonbank Financial Insts.: Assets......	7e.d	3.12	5.64	1.90	.18	.16	—	—	—	—	—	—	—
Liabilities......	7f.d	—	—	—	33.90	36.76	.06	8.97	9.32	21.56	3.31	8.51	10.65
Monetary Authorities					*Millions of Córdobas: End of Period*								
Foreign Assets...............................	11	557.9	1,226.6	1,283.5	† 2,197.5	4,034.7	4,199.5	6,466.0	6,620.8	† 7,729.4	9,438.3	11,073.2	14,383.6
Claims on Central Government........	12a	21,646.0	23,256.5	22,469.2	† 18,132.0	21,451.1	23,769.1	26,884.0	28,400.1	† 43,286.6	44,767.5	46,585.0	46,366.5
Claims on Nonfin.Pub.Enterprises....	12c	168.6	380.9	468.4	† 98.3	101.0	113.1	124.4	77.4	† 124.6	134.7	50.4	260.0
Claims on Private Sector.................	12d	—	—	12.7	† 206.0	260.4	314.7	303.4	307.3	† 42.7	45.1	39.1	68.3
Claims on Deposit Money Banks......	12e	797.8	824.4	743.4	† 152.3	806.5	99.1	326.8	2,012.8	† 434.5	10.6	1.2	.3
Claims on Nonbank Financial Insts...	12g	1,704.6	1,206.1	1,151.2	† 3,168.2	3,003.9	4,028.3	4,203.4	4,453.3	† .9	.9	1.0	.9
Reserve Money..............................	14	1,005.7	1,533.3	1,894.5	† 2,545.9	3,372.6	4,038.1	4,267.6	4,468.1	† 6,071.7	6,724.5	8,015.9	9,271.8
of which: Currency Outside DMBs..	14a	508.9	688.3	771.0	† 864.1	1,096.1	1,339.6	1,734.8	1,760.5	† 1,949.4	2,085.8	2,506.6	3,103.3
Time, Savings,& Fgn.Currency Dep...	15	18.3	17.6	11.6	† 46.2	48.3	60.1	66.6	468.6	† .4	.4	.4	—
Liabs. of Central Bank: Securities.....	16ac	—	—	—	† 436.4	3,643.5	2,250.3	2,302.9	3,658.1	† 8,732.8	9,640.6	7,953.3	6,419.7
Foreign Liabilities..........................	16c	22,919.9	25,045.1	23,699.6	† 19,114.4	21,128.0	23,489.4	26,475.1	30,074.8	† 29,166.7	31,597.0	34,652.3	35,148.9
Central Government Deposits...........	16d	396.6	329.6	198.5	† 276.3	190.0	745.4	1,695.4	1,997.8	† 742.4	2,087.3	3,468.1	6,254.6
Liab. to Nonbank Financial Insts.......	16j	44.3	184.3	122.0	† 118.6	13.4	.1	—	—	† —	—	—	—
Capital Accounts............................	17a	188.0	212.8	299.3	† 1,494.2	1,838.3	2,498.0	4,303.8	3,315.9	† 370.6	420.3	481.9	523.7
Other Items (Net)...........................	17r	302.1	−428.2	−97.1	† −77.6	−576.4	−557.5	−803.3	−2,111.5	† 6,534.0	3,927.0	3,177.8	3,460.8
of which: Valuation Adjustment.....	17rv	—	—	—	† —	—	—	—	−1,280.3	† —	—	—	—
Deposit Money Banks					*Millions of Córdobas: End of Period*								
Reserves.......................................	20	490.9	773.6	1,112.0	† 1,680.9	2,324.5	2,752.8	2,627.3	2,728.5	† 4,114.0	4,643.9	5,502.9	6,162.9
Claims on Mon.Author.:Securities....	20c	—	—	—	† 158.2	1,365.2	1,367.0	1,506.2	2,885.4	† 7,407.8	8,690.9	7,486.0	6,412.9
Foreign Assets...............................	21	300.7	380.9	358.4	† 1,308.7	2,111.7	1,815.1	1,773.5	857.3	† 1,223.4	1,357.0	1,510.7	1,922.4
Claims on Central Government........	22a	—	—	—	† 513.7	372.5	356.8	1,107.1	1,400.3	† 1,659.4	2,326.0	3,194.5	4,654.6
Claims on Local Government...........	22b	7.6	5.2	—	† 34.5	6.7	6.7	210.3	243.0	† 6.0	23.1	57.5	—
Claims on Nonfin.Pub.Enterprises.....	22c	11.8	41.4	10.0	† 24.0	5.5	5.5	26.1	23.7	† 111.0	110.5	439.3	599.2
Claims on Private Sector.................	22d	3,049.5	4,075.5	5,159.0	† 4,675.7	6,707.4	9,715.5	13,270.5	15,240.8	† 9,783.2	11,228.2	14,173.9	18,075.7
Claims on Nonbank Financial Insts...	22g	—	—	—	—	—	—	—	—	† 115.7	67.3	149.6	198.7
Demand Deposits...........................	24	295.1	407.6	471.4	† 787.4	958.7	1,195.6	1,406.0	1,565.5	† 1,316.2	1,280.5	1,696.0	1,702.3
Time, Savings,& Fgn.Currency Dep...	25	1,355.5	2,500.7	3,629.5	† 5,747.6	9,249.8	12,404.3	14,622.3	15,632.1	† 17,046.0	19,647.4	21,717.0	25,581.6
Money Market Instruments..............	26aa	—	—	—	† 365.1	508.9	360.3	320.1	270.2	† —	—	—	—
Foreign Liabilities..........................	26c	119.0	224.9	249.6	† 398.1	546.2	616.7	1,353.3	1,180.7	† 1,419.8	1,569.9	1,695.0	1,803.9
Central Government Deposits...........	26d	421.2	539.9	654.9	† 755.7	1,098.8	798.2	1,662.2	1,381.8	† 2,270.9	2,363.1	3,193.7	3,526.2
Credit from Monetary Authorities.....	26g	759.4	779.0	752.1	† 35.5	743.4	34.7	27.5	2,340.9	† 476.2	8.0	214.1	290.3
Liab. to Nonbank Financial Insts.......	26j	714.4	1,198.1	1,389.6	† 273.8	483.6	676.2	879.2	970.6	† 1,175.6	1,311.7	1,274.8	1,812.6
Capital Accounts............................	27a	502.9	648.8	406.0	† 825.0	222.4	1,201.4	1,998.5	2,696.9	† 1,654.6	2,135.1	2,593.8	3,555.0
Other Items (Net)...........................	27r	−307.0	−1,022.4	−913.7	† −792.5	−918.4	−1,267.9	−1,748.2	−2,659.7	† −939.0	131.3	130.1	−245.4
Monetary Survey					*Millions of Córdobas: End of Period*								
Foreign Assets (Net).......................	31n	−22,180.3	−23,662.5	−22,307.3	† −16,006.2	−15,527.8	−18,091.5	−19,588.9	−23,777.3	† −21,633.7	−22,371.6	−23,763.4	−20,646.8
Domestic Credit.............................	32	25,770.3	28,096.1	28,417.1	† 25,820.5	30,619.7	36,766.2	42,771.5	46,766.3	† 52,116.7	54,253.0	58,028.5	60,443.2
Claims on Central Govt. (Net)........	32an	20,828.2	22,387.0	21,615.8	† 17,613.8	20,534.7	22,582.4	24,633.4	26,420.8	† 41,932.7	42,643.1	43,117.7	41,240.3
Claims on Local Government.........	32b	7.6	5.2	—	† 34.5	6.7	6.7	210.3	243.0	† 6.0	23.1	57.5	—
Claims on Nonfin.Pub.Enterprises....	32c	180.4	422.3	478.4	† 122.3	106.5	118.5	150.5	101.1	† 235.6	245.2	489.6	859.2
Claims on Private Sector.................	32d	3,049.5	4,075.5	5,171.7	† 4,881.7	6,967.9	10,030.2	13,573.9	15,548.1	† 9,825.9	11,273.3	14,213.0	18,144.0
Claims on Nonbank Financial Inst..	32g	1,704.6	1,206.1	1,151.2	† 3,168.2	3,003.9	4,028.3	4,203.4	4,453.3	† 116.6	68.2	150.6	199.6
Money..	34	805.5	1,097.2	1,242.4	† 1,654.9	2,064.4	2,551.2	3,151.0	3,411.7	† 3,267.1	3,368.1	4,208.3	4,806.7
Quasi-Money..................................	35	1,373.8	2,518.3	3,641.1	† 5,793.8	9,298.1	12,464.3	14,688.9	16,100.7	† 17,046.4	19,647.8	21,717.4	25,581.6
Money Market Instruments.............	36aa	—	—	—	† 365.1	508.9	360.3	320.1	270.2	† —	—	—	—
Liabs. of Central Bank: Securities.....	36ac	—	—	—	† 278.2	2,278.3	883.3	796.6	772.7	† 1,325.0	949.8	467.2	6.8
Liab. to Nonbank Financial Insts......	36j	758.7	1,382.4	1,511.6	† 392.4	497.1	676.3	879.3	970.6	† 1,175.7	1,311.8	1,274.9	1,812.7
Capital Accounts............................	37a	690.9	861.6	705.3	† 2,319.2	2,060.7	3,699.4	6,302.3	6,012.8	† 2,025.2	2,555.4	3,075.8	4,078.8
Other Items (Net)...........................	37r	−38.9	−1,425.9	−990.6	† −989.4	−1,615.5	−1,960.1	−2,955.6	−4,549.7	† 5,643.6	4,048.6	3,521.6	3,509.9
Money plus Quasi-Money................	35l	2,179.3	3,615.5	4,883.5	† 7,448.6	11,362.5	15,015.5	17,839.9	19,512.4	† 20,313.5	23,015.9	25,925.7	30,388.3

		1993	1994	1995	1996	1997	1998	1999	2000	2001	2002	2003	2004
Nonbank Financial Institutions						*Millions of Córdobas: End of Period*							
Reserves...............................	40	39.1	181.5	122.0	† 122.4	4.5	.2	.1	—	.1	.7	.9	.1
Foreign Assets........................	41	19.8	40.1	15.1	† 1.6	1.6	—	—	—	—	—	—	—
Claims on Central Government.........	42a	—	—	—	† 319.3	367.0	—	—	—	—	—	—	—
Claims on Private Sector...............	42d	1,285.2	—	—	† 441.6	503.7	689.8	906.2	1,028.3	1,290.6	1,046.2	1,174.8	1,332.2
Claims on Deposit Money Banks......	42e	742.1	1,198.8	1,391.2	† 3.6	113.3	13.5	31.7	14.0	75.3	176.1	159.1	57.2
Foreign Liabilities......................	46c	—	—	—	† 302.5	367.4	.6	110.5	121.7	298.4	48.6	132.3	173.1
Central Government Deposits..........	46d	—	—	—	† —	—	19.1	125.0	226.1	315.5	333.6	285.1	245.6
Credit from Monetary Authorities.....	46g	1,704.6	1,206.1	1,151.2	† 89.7	99.8	79.8	47.6	26.2	—	—	—	—
Capital Accounts......................	47a	22.9	133.8	159.8	† 517.3	563.1	578.7	667.7	753.6	800.0	857.2	937.5	992.6
Other Items (Net)......................	47r	358.7	80.5	217.3	† −21.1	−40.2	25.3	−12.8	−85.3	−48.0	−16.4	−20.0	−21.7
Financial Survey						*Millions of Córdobas: End of Period*							
Foreign Assets (Net)......................	51n	−22,160.5	−23,622.4	−22,292.2	† −16,307.1	−15,893.6	−18,092.1	−19,699.4	−23,899.0	† −21,932.1	−22,420.2	−23,895.7	−20,819.9
Domestic Credit..........................	52	25,350.9	26,890.0	27,265.9	† 23,413.1	28,486.5	33,408.6	39,349.3	43,115.2	† 52,975.2	54,897.3	58,767.6	61,330.3
Claims on Central Govt. (Net).......	52an	20,828.2	22,387.0	21,615.8	† 17,933.1	20,901.7	22,563.3	24,508.4	26,194.7	† 41,617.1	42,309.5	42,832.6	40,994.8
Claims on Local Government.......	52b	7.6	5.2	—	† 34.5	6.7	6.7	210.3	243.0	† 6.0	23.1	57.5	—
Claims on Nonfin.Pub.Enterprises...	52c	180.4	422.3	478.4	† 122.3	106.5	118.5	150.5	101.1	† 235.6	245.2	489.6	859.2
Claims on Private Sector...............	52d	4,334.7	4,075.5	5,171.7	† 5,323.2	7,471.6	10,720.1	14,480.1	16,576.4	† 11,116.5	12,319.5	15,387.9	19,476.2
Liquid Liabilities........................	55l	2,140.2	3,434.0	4,761.5	† 7,326.3	11,358.0	15,015.3	17,839.8	19,512.4	† 20,313.4	23,015.1	25,924.7	30,388.3
Money Market Instruments..............	56aa	—	—	—	† 365.1	508.9	360.3	320.1	270.2	† —	—	—	—
Liabs. of Central Bank: Securities.....	56ac	—	—	—	† 278.2	2,278.3	883.3	796.6	772.7	† 1,325.0	949.8	467.2	6.8
Capital Accounts........................	57a	713.8	995.4	865.1	† 2,836.6	2,623.8	4,278.1	6,970.0	6,766.4	† 2,825.2	3,412.5	4,013.2	5,071.4
Other Items (Net)........................	57r	336.4	−1,161.8	−652.9	† −3,700.1	−4,176.0	−5,220.5	−6,276.6	−8,105.4	† 6,579.4	5,099.7	4,466.7	5,044.0
Interest Rates						*Percent Per Annum*							
Discount Rate (End of period)...........	60	11.75	10.50	....	....	....	....	....	....	....	....	....	....
Savings Rate...............................	60k	8.53	8.81	8.87	9.04	8.87	8.59	† 8.39	8.71	8.55	6.23	4.23	3.43
Savings Rate (Foreign Currency).......	60k.f	4.30	4.64	5.07	5.51	5.28	5.19	† 5.81	5.37	5.49	4.11	3.19	2.65
Deposit Rate...............................	60l	11.61	11.70	11.15	12.35	12.41	10.77	† 11.83	10.80	11.56	7.79	5.55	4.72
Deposit Rate (Foreign Currency).......	60l.f	5.26	5.67	6.03	7.25	7.55	7.22	† 7.95	8.86	9.01	6.94	5.08	3.91
Lending Rate...............................	60p	20.23	20.14	19.89	20.72	21.02	21.63	† 17.57	18.14	18.55	18.30	15.55	13.49
Lending Rate (Foreign Currency).......	60p.f	....	....	15.50	16.89	17.63	17.90	† 15.50	15.39	15.87	14.28	12.05	10.94
Prices and Labor						*Index Numbers (2000=100): Period Averages*							
Consumer Prices.............................	64.c	49.4	52.7	58.5	65.3	71.3	80.6	89.6	100.0	107.4	111.6	117.4	127.3
						Number in Thousands: Period Averages							
Labor Force.................................	67d	1,365	1,419	1,478	1,537	1,598	1,661	1,729	1,815	1,900	....	....	....
Employment..................................	67e	1,122	1,177	1,228	1,292	1,370	1,442	1,544	1,637	1,702	....	....	....
Unemployment..............................	67c	244	243	250	245	228	220	185	178	203	215	....	....
Unemployment Rate (%).................	67r	17.8	17.1	16.9	16.0	14.3	13.2	10.7	9.8	10.7	....	....	....
Intl. Transactions & Positions						*Millions of US Dollars*							
Exports..	70..d	269.7	334.6	466.0	466.4	576.7	573.2	546.1	642.8	589.4	561.0	604.5	755.6
Imports, c.i.f.................................	71..d	753.4	866.6	975.2	1,153.8	1,449.8	1,491.7	1,861.1	1,805.5	1,775.3	1,753.7	1,879.4	2,212.3
Imports, f.o.b.................................	71.vd	678.9	780.5	881.4	1,043.4	1,370.6	1,397.0	1,698.1	1,653.2	1,617.3	1,598.8	1,720.2	2,022.0

		1993	1994	1995	1996	1997	1998	1999	2000	2001	2002	2003	2004
Balance of Payments		*Millions of US Dollars: Minus Sign Indicates Debit*											
Current Account, n.i.e.	78ald	−644.3	−910.9	−722.5	−824.8	−840.8	−686.6	−928.4	−791.9	−796.4	−767.3	−749.3	−795.3
Goods: Exports f.o.b.	78aad	267.0	375.9	545.0	595.2	744.8	761.0	748.6	880.6	894.7	916.8	1,049.6	1,256.9
Goods: Imports f.o.b.	78abd	−659.4	−804.4	−929.5	−1,121.7	−1,473.1	−1,509.6	−1,819.8	−1,801.5	−1,804.3	−1,834.4	−2,021.3	−2,369.1
Trade Balance	78acd	−392.4	−428.5	−384.5	−526.5	−728.3	−748.6	−1,071.2	−920.9	−909.6	−917.6	−971.7	−1,112.2
Services: Credit	78add	100.2	112.7	116.6	128.8	156.8	183.7	214.2	221.3	223.1	225.5	257.6	289.7
Services: Debit	78aed	−156.6	−172.9	−220.5	−252.8	−239.4	−267.8	−334.7	−343.4	−352.1	−337.2	−363.4	−399.3
Balance on Goods & Services	78afd	−448.8	−488.7	−488.4	−650.5	−810.9	−832.7	−1,191.7	−1,043.0	−1,038.6	−1,029.3	−1,077.5	−1,221.8
Income: Credit	78agd	5.4	6.7	7.1	10.5	14.7	26.0	30.7	30.7	14.7	9.2	6.7	9.3
Income: Debit	78ahd	−434.5	−478.9	−379.2	−334.8	−279.4	−211.2	−227.5	−232.5	−255.0	−209.6	−197.4	−201.6
Balance on Gds, Serv. & Inc.	78aid	−877.9	−960.9	−860.5	−974.8	−1,075.6	−1,017.9	−1,388.5	−1,244.8	−1,278.9	−1,229.7	−1,268.2	−1,414.1
Current Transfers, n.i.e.: Credit	78ajd	233.6	50.0	138.0	150.0	234.8	331.3	460.1	452.9	482.5	462.4	518.9	618.8
Current Transfers: Debit	78akd	—	—	—	—	—	—	—	—	—	—	—	—
Capital Account, n.i.e.	78bcd	—	244.6	227.0	262.1	194.1	194.4	307.2	308.9	294.7	248.2	286.0	283.5
Capital Account, n.i.e.: Credit	78bad	—	244.6	227.0	262.1	194.1	194.4	307.2	308.9	294.7	248.2	286.0	283.5
Capital Account: Debit	78bbd	—	—	—	—	—	—	—	—	—	—	—	—
Financial Account, n.i.e.	78bjd	−502.8	−895.2	−611.5	−332.0	33.5	231.6	525.5	49.1	12.9	188.8	83.1	61.0
Direct Investment Abroad	78bdd	—	—	—	—	—	—	—	—	—	—	—	—
Dir. Invest. in Rep. Econ., n.i.e.	78bed	38.8	46.7	88.9	120.0	203.4	218.2	337.3	266.9	150.2	203.9	201.3	250.0
Portfolio Investment Assets	78bfd	—	—	—	—	—	—	—	—	—	—	—	—
Equity Securities	78bkd	—	—	—	—	—	—	—	—	—	—	—	—
Debt Securities	78bld	—	—	—	—	—	—	—	—	—	—	—	—
Portfolio Investment Liab., n.i.e.	78bgd	—	—	—	—	—	—	—	—	—	—	—	—
Equity Securities	78bmd	—	—	—	—	—	—	—	—	—	—	—	—
Debt Securities	78bnd	—	—	—	—	—	—	—	—	—	—	—	—
Financial Derivatives Assets	78bwd	....	—	—	—	—	—	—	—	—	—	—	—
Financial Derivatives Liabilities	78bxd	....	—	—	—	—	—	—	—	—	—	—	—
Other Investment Assets	78bhd	−10.1	−1.3	−32.0	−54.3	−70.8	55.2	22.2	79.9	−22.6	2.9	−16.0	−10.5
Monetary Authorities	78bod	....	—	—	—	—	—	—	—	—	—	—	—
General Government	78bpd	—	—	—	—	—	—	—	—	—	—	—	—
Banks	78bqd	−10.1	−1.3	−32.0	−54.3	−70.8	55.2	22.2	79.9	−22.6	2.9	−16.0	−10.5
Other Sectors	78brd	—	—	—	—	—	—	—	—	—	—	—	—
Other Investment Liab., n.i.e.	78bid	−531.5	−940.6	−668.4	−397.7	−99.1	−41.8	166.0	−297.7	−114.7	−18.0	−102.2	−178.5
Monetary Authorities	78bsd	−94.9	−544.3	−221.7	−126.1	−106.0	−18.1	62.4	−61.2	−14.1	−28.7	−19.8	−18.4
General Government	78btd	−390.7	−418.7	−381.2	−295.4	−103.1	−154.8	−63.9	−73.6	−81.9	−184.4	−186.1	−154.9
Banks	78bud	−16.6	14.3	5.8	6.0	25.1	.3	63.6	−19.2	38.4	−35.9	−10.7	−4.0
Other Sectors	78bvd	−29.3	8.1	−71.3	17.8	84.9	130.8	103.9	−143.7	−57.1	231.0	114.4	−1.2
Net Errors and Omissions	78cad	128.1	42.7	142.7	146.5	320.1	−141.3	−299.5	−21.9	−3.7	−70.7	−89.3	53.2
Overall Balance	78cbd	−1,019.0	−1,518.4	−964.3	−748.2	−293.1	−401.9	−395.2	−455.8	−492.5	−401.0	−469.5	−397.6
Reserves and Related Items	79dad	1,019.0	1,518.8	964.3	748.2	293.1	401.9	395.2	455.8	492.5	401.0	469.5	397.6
Reserve Assets	79dbd	79.4	−84.6	11.5	−53.1	−173.2	30.3	−156.5	16.8	113.9	−84.9	−68.7	−168.7
Use of Fund Credit and Loans	79dcd	—	26.1	−12.9	−9.3	—	22.6	105.3	20.9	−5.0	4.0	21.6	23.9
Exceptional Financing	79ded	939.6	1,577.3	965.7	810.6	466.3	349.0	446.4	418.1	383.6	481.8	516.7	542.5
Government Finance		*Millions of Córdobas: Year Ending December 31*											
Deficit (-) or Surplus	80	−4	−4	−68	−254	−243	−415	−1,282	−2,357	−3,900	−767	−1,241	....
Revenue	81	2,222	2,222	3,134	3,654	4,660	5,906	6,739	7,541	7,654	8,589	10,157	....
Grants Received	81z	806	806	1,191	1,149	822	675	1,935	1,874	1,712	2,579	3,002	....
Expenditure	82	3,009	3,009	4,246	5,055	5,719	6,995	9,774	11,755	13,136	11,935	14,423	....
Lending Minus Repayments	83	23	23	147	2	6		182	17	130	—	−23	....
Financing													
Domestic	84a	—	—	100	−598	−22	−1,266	−1,304	619	2,375	−516	−1,315	....
Foreign	85a	4	4	−32	852	265	1,680	2,586	1,738	1,525	1,283	2,556	....
National Accounts		*Millions of Córdobas*											
Househ.Cons.Expend.,incl.NPISHs	96f	9,715.0	16,162.8	18,707.7	21,844.0	25,135.6	29,202.8	34,422.2	39,460.9	43,920.5	47,535.7	51,858.2	59,154.5
Government Consumption Expend	91f	1,891.0	3,085.6	3,772.3	4,333.9	4,798.5	5,859.0	7,226.6	8,613.1	9,823.6	9,973.1	11,157.9	12,764.5
Gross Fixed Capital Formation	93e	2,134.0	4,062.4	4,855.2	6,093.1	7,762.5	9,574.4	14,698.9	14,349.1	14,757.6	14,261.8	15,334.3	18,870.4
Changes in Inventories	93i	−41.0	14.0	430.8	1,125.4	2,199.4	2,158.1	2,252.5	1,124.1	822.6	695.8	1,008.7	1,752.6
Exports of Goods and Services	90c	2,196.0	3,123.2	4,594.5	5,605.7	7,374.7	8,683.2	9,729.4	11,932.4	12,476.7	12,846.4	15,202.3	19,120.9
Imports of Goods and Services (-)	98c	5,145.0	6,439.7	8,331.1	10,993.4	15,303.7	17,673.0	24,131.8	25,527.7	26,645.7	27,936.4	31,887.5	39,059.6
Gross Domestic Product (GDP)	99b	10,750.0	20,008.4	24,029.3	28,008.7	31,967.1	37,804.5	44,197.8	49,952.0	55,155.3	57,376.3	62,673.8	72,603.3
Net Primary Income from Abroad	98.n	−2,593.2	−3,174.5	−2,801.0	−2,735.6	−2,500.9	−1,960.8	−2,324.0	−2,559.7	−3,230.8	−2,856.0	−2,880.8	−3,064.7
Gross National Income (GNI)	99a	8,156.8	16,833.8	21,228.3	25,273.1	29,466.1	35,843.7	41,873.7	47,392.2	51,924.6	54,520.4	59,793.0	69,538.6
GDP Volume 1980 Prices	99b.p	18,107.0	18,711.0	....	....	....	....	....	....	....	....	....	....
GDP Volume 1994 Prices	99b.p	....	20,008.4	21,191.3	22,535.7	23,429.6	24,299.2	26,008.9	27,075.7	27,877.4	28,087.5	28,721.2	30,199.9
GDP Volume (2000=100)	99bvp	71.5	† 73.9	78.3	83.2	86.5	89.7	96.1	100.0	103.0	103.7	106.1	111.5
GDP Deflator (2000=100)	99bip	30.1	54.2	61.5	67.4	74.0	84.3	92.1	100.0	107.2	110.7	118.3	130.3
		Millions: Midyear Estimates											
Population	99z	4.27	4.37	4.48	4.58	4.67	4.77	4.86	4.96	5.06	5.16	5.27	5.38

Niger 692

		1993	1994	1995	1996	1997	1998	1999	2000	2001	2002	2003	2004
Exchange Rates						*Francs per SDR: End of Period*							
Official Rate	aa	404.89	† 780.44	728.38	753.06	807.94	791.61	† 896.19	918.49	935.39	850.37	771.76	747.90
						Francs per US Dollar: End of Period (ae) Period Average (rf)							
Official Rate	ae	294.77	† 534.60	490.00	523.70	598.81	562.21	† 652.95	704.95	744.31	625.50	519.36	481.58
Official Rate	rf	283.16	† 555.20	499.15	511.55	583.67	589.95	† 615.70	711.98	733.04	696.99	581.20	528.28
Fund Position						*Millions of SDRs: End of Period*							
Quota	2f.s	48.3	48.3	48.3	48.3	48.3	48.3	65.8	65.8	65.8	65.8	65.8	65.8
SDRs	1b.s	.4	.3	.2	1.3	.1	.1	1.0	—	.3	.5	1.8	.6
Reserve Position in the Fund	1c.s	8.6	8.6	8.6	8.6	8.6	8.6	8.6	8.6	8.6	8.6	8.6	8.6
Total Fund Cred.&Loans Outstg	2tl	37.7	41.8	35.0	36.6	45.0	54.1	49.6	56.8	64.3	78.3	88.4	87.2
International Liquidity						*Millions of US Dollars Unless Otherwise Indicated: End of Period*							
Total Reserves minus Gold	1l.d	192.0	110.3	94.7	78.5	53.3	53.1	39.2	80.4	107.0	133.9	260.1	258.0
SDRs	1b.d	.6	.4	.3	1.9	.2	.2	1.3	—	.3	.7	2.7	.9
Reserve Position in the Fund	1c.d	11.8	12.5	12.7	12.3	11.6	12.1	11.7	11.2	10.8	11.6	12.7	13.3
Foreign Exchange	1d.d	179.7	97.4	81.7	64.3	41.5	40.8	26.1	69.2	95.9	121.6	244.7	243.7
Gold (Million Fine Troy Ounces)	1ad	.011	.011	—	—	—	—	—	—	—	—	—	—
Gold (National Valuation)	1and	4.1	4.1	—	—	—	—	—	—	—	—	-3.4	4.7
Monetary Authorities: Other Liab	4..d	49.8	2.9	1.5	2.2	.4	1.1	2.2	1.6	1.3	3.2	4.9	.9
Deposit Money Banks: Assets	7a.d	23.8	40.6	41.5	35.1	40.9	37.9	44.2	41.3	53.7	48.4	65.4	80.9
Liabilities	7b.d	55.5	49.9	44.9	41.7	32.9	30.5	39.5	42.0	35.7	26.2	50.5	41.6
Monetary Authorities						*Billions of Francs: End of Period*							
Foreign Assets	11	56.6	58.9	46.4	41.1	31.9	29.8	25.6	56.7	79.6	83.8	135.1	124.2
Claims on Central Government	12a	33.0	47.3	52.5	57.2	67.7	74.3	69.5	79.9	85.6	99.7	109.2	107.6
Claims on Deposit Money Banks	12e	27.0	1.1	4.9	4.6	3.2	3.9	1.2	1.2	1.2	1.2	1.2	1.2
Claims on Other Financial Insts	12f	—	—	—	—	—	—	—	—	—	—	—	—
Reserve Money	14	79.6	60.5	68.4	64.4	50.7	32.5	43.0	44.6	66.3	63.2	116.1	128.9
of which: Currency Outside DMBs	14a	48.3	48.7	59.6	57.7	41.7	24.5	34.1	32.2	49.3	39.3	84.9	96.8
Foreign Liabilities	16c	30.0	34.2	26.3	28.7	36.6	43.4	45.9	53.3	61.0	68.6	66.5	67.5
Central Government Deposits	16d	3.3	15.6	8.3	8.1	8.5	16.4	4.1	30.4	38.0	45.2	46.4	22.9
Other Items (Net)	17r	3.6	-3.0	.9	1.7	7.1	15.7	3.3	9.5	1.1	7.7	16.5	13.7
Deposit Money Banks						*Billions of Francs: End of Period*							
Reserves	20	29.9	9.7	8.3	5.9	8.1	7.7	8.8	10.5	15.2	22.1	30.1	31.0
Foreign Assets	21	7.0	21.7	20.3	18.4	24.5	21.3	28.9	29.1	39.9	30.3	34.0	39.0
Claims on Central Government	22a	2.9	13.4	12.4	14.1	16.7	12.9	12.1	15.3	10.7	10.4	10.9	10.3
Claims on Private Sector	22d	64.9	71.4	42.0	43.3	35.5	49.4	47.7	61.4	66.0	75.8	83.0	101.1
Claims on Other Financial Insts	22f	—	—	—	—	—	—	—	—	—	—	—	—
Demand Deposits	24	28.8	40.3	38.4	30.2	28.8	32.0	33.9	43.3	52.4	54.2	61.6	81.8
Time Deposits	25	41.4	37.2	33.6	34.3	25.3	20.6	23.8	27.2	32.7	40.5	44.4	50.3
Foreign Liabilities	26c	10.0	23.3	18.4	18.5	19.7	17.2	25.8	29.6	26.6	16.1	26.0	17.4
Long-Term Foreign Liabilities	26cl	6.4	3.3	3.6	3.3	—	—	—	—	—	.3	.3	2.6
Central Government Deposits	26d	21.5	21.0	19.3	19.8	3.9	9.8	8.8	10.2	12.0	13.5	12.8	13.8
Credit from Monetary Authorities	26g	27.0	27.8	4.9	4.6	2.0	3.9	1.2	1.2	1.2	1.2	1.2	1.2
Other Items (Net)	27r	-30.3	-36.8	-35.1	-29.0	5.2	7.7	4.0	4.9	7.0	12.7	11.6	14.2
Treasury Claims: Private Sector	22d.i	.1	—	—	—	—	—	—	—	—	—	—	.4
Post Office: Checking Deposits	24..i	1.9	2.1	1.8	2.6	2.5	2.7	.3	1.2	1.9	1.7	2.4	3.2
Monetary Survey						*Billions of Francs: End of Period*							
Foreign Assets (Net)	31n	23.7	23.2	22.1	12.2	—	-9.4	-17.2	2.9	31.9	29.4	76.6	78.3
Domestic Credit	32	77.9	97.6	81.2	89.3	110.1	113.1	116.6	117.3	114.3	128.9	146.3	185.5
Claims on Central Govt. (Net)	32an	12.9	26.1	39.2	46.0	74.5	63.7	68.9	55.8	48.3	53.1	63.3	84.0
Claims on Private Sector	32d	64.9	71.4	42.0	43.3	35.6	49.4	47.7	61.4	66.0	75.8	83.0	101.4
Claims on Other Financial Insts	32f	—	—	—	—	—	—	—	—	—	—	—	—
Money	34	79.5	91.8	100.2	90.7	73.1	59.6	68.8	76.9	104.0	95.6	149.5	181.9
Quasi-Money	35	41.4	37.2	33.6	34.3	25.3	20.6	23.8	27.2	32.7	40.5	44.4	50.3
Long-Term Foreign Liabilities	36cl	6.4	3.3	3.6	3.3	—	—	—	—	—	.3	.3	2.6
Other Items (Net)	37r	-25.7	-11.6	-34.1	-26.8	11.7	23.4	6.9	16.1	9.5	21.8	28.8	29.0
Money plus Quasi-Money	35l	120.9	129.0	133.8	125.0	98.4	80.2	92.6	104.1	136.8	136.1	193.9	232.2
Interest Rates						*Percent Per Annum*							
Bank Rate (End of Period)	60	† 6.00	6.00	6.00	6.00	6.00	6.00	6.00	6.00	6.00	6.00	4.50	4.00
Money Market Rate	60b	4.95	4.95	4.95	4.95	4.95	4.95	4.95	4.95	4.95	4.95	4.95	4.95
Deposit Rate	60l	3.50	3.50	3.50	3.50	3.50	3.50	3.50	3.50	3.50	3.50	3.50	3.50
Prices						*Index Numbers (2000=100): Period Averages*							
Consumer Prices	64	58.4	79.4	87.8	92.4	† 95.1	99.5	97.2	100.0	104.0	106.7	105.0	105.3
Intl. Transactions & Positions						*Millions of Francs*							
Exports	70	81,200	125,100	143,800	166,300	158,500	197,000	176,600	201,500	199,700	194,800	118,989	108,967
Imports, c.i.f.	71	106,123	182,097	186,501	229,271	218,067	277,886	206,500	230,400	242,800	258,700	238,085	275,425

Niger 692

		1993	1994	1995	1996	1997	1998	1999	2000	2001	2002	2003	2004
Balance of Payments					*Millions of US Dollars: Minus Sign Indicates Debit*								
Current Account, n.i.e.	78ald	−97.2	−126.1	−151.7	....	....	....	....	....	....	....	....	....
Goods: Exports f.o.b.	78aad	300.4	226.8	288.1	....	....	....	....	....	....	....	....	....
Goods: Imports f.o.b.	78abd	−312.1	−271.3	−305.6	....	....	....	....	....	....	....	....	....
Trade Balance	78acd	−11.7	−44.5	−17.6	....	....	....	....	....	....	....	....	....
Services: Credit	78add	36.5	30.4	33.3	....	....	....	....	....	....	....	....	....
Services: Debit	78aed	−185.6	−149.1	−151.8	....	....	....	....	....	....	....	....	....
Balance on Goods & Services	78afd	−160.9	−163.2	−136.0	....	....	....	....	....	....	....	....	....
Income: Credit	78agd	19.3	15.6	5.8	....	....	....	....	....	....	....	....	....
Income: Debit	78ahd	−30.2	−45.2	−52.9	....	....	....	....	....	....	....	....	....
Balance on Gds, Serv. & Inc.	78aid	−171.7	−192.8	−183.2	....	....	....	....	....	....	....	....	....
Current Transfers, n.i.e.: Credit	78ajd	139.5	115.1	60.6	....	....	....	....	....	....	....	....	....
Current Transfers: Debit	78akd	−65.0	−48.5	−29.1	....	....	....	....	....	....	....	....	....
Capital Account, n.i.e.	78bcd	109.3	88.2	65.3	....	....	....	....	....	....	....	....	....
Capital Account, n.i.e.: Credit	78bad	109.3	88.2	65.3	....	....	....	....	....	....	....	....	....
Capital Account: Debit	78bbd	....	....	....	....	....	....	....	....	....	....	....	....
Financial Account, n.i.e.	78bjd	−123.3	29.9	−46.1	....	....	....	....	....	....	....	....	....
Direct Investment Abroad	78bdd	−5.8	1.8	−7.1	....	....	....	....	....	....	....	....	....
Dir. Invest. in Rep. Econ., n.i.e.	78bed	−34.4	−11.3	7.2	....	....	....	....	....	....	....	....	....
Portfolio Investment Assets	78bfd	....	....	....	....	....	....	....	....	....	....	....	....
Equity Securities	78bkd	....	....	....	....	....	....	....	....	....	....	....	....
Debt Securities	78bld	....	....	....	....	....	....	....	....	....	....	....	....
Portfolio Investment Liab., n.i.e.	78bgd	....	....	....	....	....	....	....	....	....	....	....	....
Equity Securities	78bmd	....	....	....	....	....	....	....	....	....	....	....	....
Debt Securities	78bnd	....	....	....	....	....	....	....	....	....	....	....	....
Financial Derivatives Assets	78bwd	....	....	....	....	....	....	....	....	....	....	....	....
Financial Derivatives Liabilities	78bxd	....	....	....	....	....	....	....	....	....	....	....	....
Other Investment Assets	78bhd	11.2	22.3	−18.4	....	....	....	....	....	....	....	....	....
Monetary Authorities	78bod	....	....	....	....	....	....	....	....	....	....	....	....
General Government	78bpd	.1	.3	—	....	....	....	....	....	....	....	....	....
Banks	78bqd	....	....	....	....	....	....	....	....	....	....	....	....
Other Sectors	78brd	11.1	22.0	−18.4	....	....	....	....	....	....	....	....	....
Other Investment Liab., n.i.e.	78bid	−94.4	17.1	−27.8	....	....	....	....	....	....	....	....	....
Monetary Authorities	78bsd	7.7	−22.3	−2.3	....	....	....	....	....	....	....	....	....
General Government	78btd	−10.8	6.7	−14.8	....	....	....	....	....	....	....	....	....
Banks	78bud	−65.0	19.4	−10.8	....	....	....	....	....	....	....	....	....
Other Sectors	78bvd	−26.3	13.3	.1	....	....	....	....	....	....	....	....	....
Net Errors and Omissions	78cad	87.2	−67.8	114.4	....	....	....	....	....	....	....	....	....
Overall Balance	78cbd	−23.9	−75.8	−18.1	....	....	....	....	....	....	....	....	....
Reserves and Related Items	79dad	23.9	75.8	18.1	....	....	....	....	....	....	....	....	....
Reserve Assets	79dbd	−19.9	28.7	−25.8	....	....	....	....	....	....	....	....	....
Use of Fund Credit and Loans	79dcd	−9.6	5.4	−10.2	....	....	....	....	....	....	....	....	....
Exceptional Financing	79ded	53.3	41.7	54.1	....	....	....	....	....	....	....	....	....
National Accounts							*Billions of Francs*						
Househ.Cons.Expend.,incl.NPISHs	96f	520.1	604.5	761.8	808.1	853.7	997.1	1,011.1	874.0	1,080.1	1,029.1	1,058.0	....
Government Consumption Expend	91f	111.6	127.4	131.9	137.5	138.8	139.8	199.3	172.3	159.2	254.2	239.7	....
Gross Fixed Capital Formation	93e	75.3	102.3	98.4	122.3	129.3	181.2	124.0	146.4	153.1	170.5	167.3	....
Changes in Inventories	93i	−22.6	32.0	20.9	38.6	42.7	17.2	3.0	78.2	2.8	99.6	94.1	....
Exports of Goods and Services	90c	94.3	141.4	167.1	188.2	181.0	217.9	197.6	228.2	241.2	230.0	230.5	....
Imports of Goods and Services (-)	98c	131.3	220.6	232.6	261.5	262.5	328.2	292.4	324.3	350.6	364.8	387.8	....
Gross Domestic Product (GDP)	99b	647.3	787.1	947.5	1,033.2	1,083.0	1,225.0	1,242.6	1,176.4	1,295.2	1,418.7	1,401.9	1,601.0
GDP Volume 1987 Prices	99b.p	700.5	718.1	731.9	760.6	778.6	906.1	915.1	891.5	948.1	1,003.6	1,034.1	....
GDP Volume (2000=100)	99bvp	78.6	80.5	82.1	85.3	87.3	101.6	102.6	100.0	106.3	112.6	116.0	....
GDP Deflator (2000=100)	99bip	70.0	83.1	98.1	102.9	105.4	102.5	102.9	100.0	103.5	107.1	102.7	....
							Millions: Midyear Estimates						
Population	99z	9.31	9.61	9.93	10.27	10.62	11.00	11.38	11.78	12.19	12.62	13.05	13.50

Nigeria 694

		1993	1994	1995	1996	1997	1998	1999	2000	2001	2002	2003	2004
Exchange Rates							Naira per SDR: End of Period						
Principal Rate	aa	30.056	32.113	32.534	31.471	29.530	†30.816	134.437	142.734	141.948	171.843	202.835	205.541
						Naira per US Dollar: End of Period (ae) Period Average (rf)							
Principal Rate	ae	21.882	21.997	21.887	21.886	21.886	†21.886	97.950	109.550	112.950	126.400	136.500	132.350
Principal Rate	rf	22.065	21.996	21.895	21.884	21.886	†21.886	92.338	101.697	111.231	120.578	129.222	132.888
						Index Numbers (2000=100): Period Averages							
Principal Rate	ahx	461.1	462.5	464.3	464.5	464.5	464.5	112.0	100.0	91.4	84.5	78.7	76.5
Nominal Effective Exchange Rate	nec	293.4	386.3	200.2	193.1	208.8	212.4	102.1	100.0	95.5	85.8	72.3	65.5
Real Effective Exchange Rate	rec	78.5	145.8	123.6	152.9	175.5	192.5	97.6	100.0	111.0	111.6	104.6	107.2
Fund Position						Millions of SDRs: End of Period							
Quota	2f.s	1,282	1,282	1,282	1,282	1,282	1,282	1,753	1,753	1,753	1,753	1,753	1,753
SDRs	1b.s	—	—	—	—	—	1	—	—	1	—	—	—
Reserve Position in the Fund	1c.s	—	—	—	—	—	—	—	—	—	—	—	—
of which: Outstg.Fund Borrowing	2c	—	—	—	—	—	—	—	—	—	—	—	—
Total Fund Cred.&Loans Outstg	2tl	—	—	—	—	—	—	—	—	—	—	—	—
International Liquidity						Millions of US Dollars Unless Otherwise Indicated: End of Period							
Total Reserves minus Gold	1l.d	1,372	1,386	1,443	4,076	7,582	7,101	5,450	9,911	10,457	7,331	7,128	16,956
SDRs	1b.d	—	—	1	1	1	1	—	—	1	—	—	—
Reserve Position in the Fund	1c.d	—	—	—	—	—	—	—	—	—	—	—	—
Foreign Exchange	1d.d	1,372	1,386	1,443	4,075	7,581	7,100	5,450	9,910	10,456	7,331	7,128	16,955
Gold (Million Fine Troy Ounces)	1ad	.687	.687	.687	.687	.687	.687	.687	.687	.687	.687	.687	.687
Gold (National Valuation)	1and	1	1	1	1	1	1	1	—	—	—	—	—
Monetary Authorities: Other Liab	4..d	2,539	2,747	2,450	2,162	2,313	1,630	172	1,224	1,080	875	685	2,239
Deposit Money Banks: Assets	7a.d	1,539	1,157	3,490	2,899	3,180	4,395	1,651	2,035	2,701	3,150	3,206	3,637
Liabilities	7b.d	64	130	137	148	137	299	56	138	152	150	154	143
Monetary Authorities						Millions of Naira: End of Period							
Foreign Assets	11	31,869	33,467	41,426	180,799	173,565	149,268	506,794	1,091,108	1,156,578	1,013,516	1,065,099	2,478,626
Claims on Central Government	12a	211,409	308,858	438,481	313,849	406,053	456,985	532,292	513,003	716,769	532,453	552,859	441,590
Claims on State & Local Govts	12b	12	124	25	2	7	7	7	7	7	—	—	—
Claims on Nonfin.Pub.Enterprises	12c	2,747	3,655	3,480	1,525	1,453	926	692	951	1,080	164	212	1,931
Claims on Private Sector	12d	850	763	604	967	778	517	884	2,163	3,103	1,646	1,705	1,931
Claims on Deposit Money Banks	12e	7,802	12,987	24,222	27,697	21,282	21,818	22,070	36,176	20,604	5,554	15,572	91,982
Claims on Nonbank Financial Insts	12g	3,100	2,941	3,160	3,267	5,916	4,580	4,568	4,881	6,330	5,488	6,878	11,344
Reserve Money	14	115,542	151,737	182,795	193,953	202,667	236,470	287,893	426,610	571,928	646,876	924,393	875,830
of which: Currency Outside DMBs	14a	57,845	90,601	106,843	116,121	130,668	156,716	186,457	274,011	338,671	386,942	412,155	458,587
Foreign Liabilities	16c	55,556	60,418	53,618	47,322	50,632	35,685	16,871	134,065	121,940	110,557	93,437	296,349
Central Government Deposits	16d	63,478	66,740	194,599	253,754	394,740	362,429	516,967	856,007	896,015	574,918	362,083	1,205,811
Capital Accounts	17a	45,423	47,539	39,647	35,062	37,055	43,683	219,944	307,976	276,033	97,559	314,657	544,588
Other Items (Net)	17r	−22,211	36,362	40,738	−1,987	−75,940	−44,167	25,633	−76,369	38,548	128,911	−52,246	104,826
Deposit Money Banks						Millions of Naira: End of Period							
Reserves	20	44,488	53,441	60,281	64,343	64,903	65,895	120,585	170,099	318,986	321,495	362,400	364,193
Foreign Assets	21	33,680	25,449	76,390	63,440	69,590	96,184	161,754	222,988	305,029	398,210	437,659	481,296
Claims on Central Government	22a	39,292	47,829	22,894	56,469	46,187	58,881	202,253	292,975	182,116	467,522	378,205	609,075
Claims on State & Local Govts	22b	1,532	2,117	2,909	3,528	1,475	935	2,095	7,558	26,796	17,327	20,235	24,632
Claims on Private Sector	22d	87,249	141,400	201,181	251,325	309,883	365,609	446,959	580,442	817,690	931,138	1,182,964	1,494,611
Demand Deposits	24	55,592	74,398	85,564	104,017	131,887	150,977	209,899	356,954	448,021	503,870	577,664	728,552
Time, Savings,& Fgn.Currency Dep	25	74,058	88,505	111,255	134,756	154,633	198,337	298,908	386,396	499,162	653,241	759,633	932,930
Money Market Instruments	26aa	653	329	283	692	130	285	74	572	627	877	1,138	1,044
Bonds	26ab	302	3,030	9,002	9,899	14,488	10,929	18,100	18,212	25,610	24,533	30,657	38,396
Foreign Liabilities	26c	1,409	2,860	2,988	3,229	3,009	6,540	5,474	15,099	17,185	18,951	21,081	18,894
Central Government Deposits	26d	2,055	1,834	3,773	6,098	11,143	13,521	40,773	73,961	28,342	52,636	79,764	117,231
Credit from Monetary Authorities	26g	825	10,526	15,172	17,377	8,434	7,762	6,554	5,360	14,547	22,159	44,303	62,080
Capital Accounts	27a	36,141	38,284	45,000	60,985	89,814	108,733	139,748	146,330	226,060	294,921	291,500	348,388
Other Items (Net)	27r	35,207	50,472	90,619	102,051	78,501	90,422	214,116	271,178	391,063	564,502	575,723	726,293
Monetary Survey						Millions of Naira: End of Period							
Foreign Assets (Net)	31n	8,584	−4,362	61,210	193,687	189,613	203,226	646,203	1,164,931	1,322,480	1,282,217	1,388,239	2,644,679
Domestic Credit	32	280,658	439,114	474,361	371,079	365,871	512,490	632,010	472,012	829,528	1,328,183	1,701,210	1,262,071
Claims on Central Govt. (Net)	32an	185,168	288,114	263,003	110,466	46,358	139,916	176,805	−123,990	−25,472	372,421	489,217	−272,377
Claims on State & Local Govts	32b	1,544	2,241	2,934	3,530	1,482	941	2,102	7,564	26,796	17,327	20,235	24,632
Claims on Nonfin.Pub.Enterprises	32c	2,747	3,655	3,480	1,525	1,453	926	692	951	1,080	164	212	1,931
Claims on Private Sector	32d	88,099	142,163	201,785	252,292	310,661	366,127	447,843	582,606	820,793	932,783	1,184,669	1,496,542
Claims on Nonbank Fin. Insts	32g	3,100	2,941	3,160	3,267	5,916	4,580	4,568	4,881	6,330	5,488	6,878	11,344
Money	34	124,422	178,440	207,509	235,577	275,098	327,300	400,826	649,684	816,708	946,253	1,225,559	1,330,658
Quasi-Money	35	74,058	88,505	111,255	134,756	154,633	198,337	298,908	386,396	499,162	653,241	759,633	932,930
Money Market Instruments	36aa	653	329	283	692	130	285	74	572	627	877	1,138	1,044
Bonds	36ab	302	3,030	9,002	9,899	14,488	10,929	18,100	18,212	25,610	24,533	30,657	38,396
Capital Accounts	37a	81,564	85,823	84,647	96,047	126,868	152,416	359,692	454,306	502,093	392,480	606,157	892,975
Other Items (Net)	37r	8,244	78,625	122,876	87,794	−15,734	26,450	200,612	127,774	307,809	593,015	466,305	710,747
Money plus Quasi-Money	35l	198,479	266,945	318,763	370,334	429,731	525,638	699,735	1,036,080	1,315,869	1,599,495	1,985,192	2,263,588
Interest Rates						Percent Per Annum							
Discount Rate (End of Period)	60	26.00	13.50	13.50	13.50	13.50	13.50	18.00	14.00	20.50	16.50	15.00	15.00
Treasury Bill Rate	60c	24.50	12.87	12.50	12.25	12.00	12.26	17.82	15.50	17.50	19.03	14.79	14.34
Deposit Rate	60l	23.24	13.09	13.53	13.06	7.17	10.11	12.81	11.69	15.26	16.67	14.22	13.70
Lending Rate	60p	31.65	20.48	20.23	19.84	17.80	18.18	20.29	21.27	23.44	24.77	20.71	19.18
Prices and Production						Index Numbers (2000=100): Period Averages							
Consumer Prices	64	19.9	31.2	54.0	69.8	75.6	83.3	87.3	100.0	113.0	127.5	†145.4	167.2
Industrial Production	66	92.7	90.9	90.6	93.2	93.9	94.0	91.3	100.0	101.4	102.6	102.6	....
Crude Petroleum Production	66aa	83.3	83.9	86.2	89.2	91.6	93.5	93.9	100.0	100.0	85.1	96.7	109.1
Manufacturing Production	66ey	105.3	104.3	98.6	100.4	100.1	96.3	99.6	100.0	102.9	105.8	105.6	....

Nigeria 694

		1993	1994	1995	1996	1997	1998	1999	2000	2001	2002	2003	2004
Intl. Transactions & Positions						*Millions of US Dollars*							
Exports..............................	70..d	9,908	9,415	† 12,342	16,154	15,207	9,855	13,856	20,975	17,261	15,107	19,887	31,148
Crude Petroleum (Naira)...............	70aa	213,779	9,171	† 11,449	15,866	14,850	8,565	12,665	18,897	17,769	14,855	19,596	28,428
Imports, c.i.f........................	71..d	5,537	6,613	† 8,222	6,438	9,501	9,211	8,588	8,721	11,586	7,547	10,853	14,164
Volume of Exports							*2000=100*						
Crude Petroleum.......................	72aa	92	92	91	103	106	122	101	100	106	85	98	118
Balance of Payments						*Millions of US Dollars: Minus Sign Indicates Debit*							
Current Account, n.i.e................	78ald	−780	−2,128	−2,578	3,507	552	−4,244	506	....	....	....	....	....
Goods: Exports f.o.b.................	78aad	9,910	9,459	11,734	16,117	15,207	8,971	12,876	....	....	....	....	....
Goods: Imports f.o.b.................	78abd	−6,662	−6,511	−8,222	−6,438	−9,501	−9,211	−8,588	....	....	....	....	....
Trade Balance......................	78acd	3,248	2,948	3,513	9,679	5,706	−240	4,288	....	....	....	....	....
Services: Credit.....................	78add	1,163	371	608	733	786	884	980	....	....	....	....	....
Services: Debit......................	78aed	−2,726	−3,007	−4,619	−4,827	−4,712	−4,166	−3,476	....	....	....	....	....
Balance on Goods & Services.......	78afd	1,685	312	−499	5,584	1,781	−3,522	1,792	....	....	....	....	....
Income: Credit.......................	78agd	58	49	101	115	258	333	240	....	....	....	....	....
Income: Debit........................	78ahd	−3,335	−2,986	−2,979	−3,137	−3,404	−2,624	−2,818	....	....	....	....	....
Balance on Gds, Serv. & Inc......	78aid	−1,593	−2,626	−3,377	2,562	−1,365	−5,813	−786	....	....	....	....	....
Current Transfers, n.i.e.: Credit...	78ajd	857	550	804	947	1,920	1,574	1,301	....	....	....	....	....
Current Transfers: Debit.............	78akd	−44	−52	−5	−2	−4	−5	−9	....	....	....	....	....
Capital Account, n.i.e...............	78bcd	—	—	−66	−68	−49	−54	−48	....	....	....	....	....
Capital Account, n.i.e.: Credit.....	78bad	—	—	—	—	—	—	—	....	....	....	....	....
Capital Account: Debit...............	78bbd	—	—	−66	−68	−49	−54	−48	....	....	....	....	....
Financial Account, n.i.e.............	78bjd	−1,043	329	−46	−4,155	−425	1,502	−4,002	....	....	....	....	....
Direct Investment Abroad.............	78bdd	—	—	—	—	....	....	....	....	....	....	....	....
Dir. Invest. in Rep. Econ., n.i.e...	78bed	1,345	1,959	1,079	1,593	1,539	1,051	1,005	....	....	....	....	....
Portfolio Investment Assets..........	78bfd	—	—	—	9	51	50	....	....	....	....	....	....
Equity Securities....................	78bkd	—	—	—	....	....	....	....	....	....	....	....	....
Debt Securities......................	78bld	—	—	—	9	51	50	....	....	....	....	....	....
Portfolio Investment Liab., n.i.e....	78bgd	−18	−27	−82	−173	−76	−59	−39	....	....	....	....	....
Equity Securities....................	78bmd	—	—	—	....	....	....	....	....	....	....	....	....
Debt Securities......................	78bnd	−18	−27	−82	−173	−76	−59	−39	....	....	....	....	....
Financial Derivatives Assets.........	78bwd	....	....	....	....	....	....	....	....	....	....	....	....
Financial Derivatives Liabilities....	78bxd	....	....	....	....	....	....	....	....	....	....	....	....
Other Investment Assets..............	78bhd	−1,345	−1,286	−3,295	−4,320	−2,183	−332	−3,319	....	....	....	....	....
Monetary Authorities.................	78bod	....	....	....	....	....	....	....	....	....	....	....	....
General Government...................	78bpd	−1,087	−969	−1,030	—	....	....	....	....	....	....	....	....
Banks................................	78bqd	−249	320	−560	138	−80	−284	−651	....	....	....	....	....
Other Sectors........................	78brd	−8	−637	−1,705	−4,458	−2,103	−48	−2,668	....	....	....	....	....
Other Investment Liab., n.i.e.......	78bid	−1,026	−317	2,251	−1,256	286	792	−1,699	....	....	....	....	....
Monetary Authorities.................	78bsd	....	....	....	....	....	....	....	....	....	....	....	....
General Government...................	78btd	−1,736	−1,885	−1,535	−3,039	−2,883	−1,637	−1,659	....	....	....	....	....
Banks................................	78bud	−28	−1	—	−4	1	21	34	....	....	....	....	....
Other Sectors........................	78bvd	738	1,570	3,787	1,787	3,167	2,407	−74	....	....	....	....	....
Net Errors and Omissions.............	78cad	−88	−139	−83	−45	−62	−77	7	....	....	....	....	....
Overall Balance......................	78cbd	−1,911	−1,938	−2,774	−761	15	−2,873	−3,538	....	....	....	....	....
Reserves and Related Items..........	79dad	1,911	1,938	2,774	761	−15	2,873	3,538	....	....	....	....	....
Reserve Assets.......................	79dbd	−611	−327	217	−2,634	−3,507	481	1,650	....	....	....	....	....
Use of Fund Credit and Loans........	79dcd	—	—	—	—	—	—	—	....	....	....	....	....
Exceptional Financing................	79ded	2,522	2,265	2,557	3,395	3,491	2,392	1,887	....	....	....	....	....
Government Finance						*Millions of Naira: Year Ending December 31*							
Deficit (-) or Surplus...............	80	−107,735	−70,270	1,000	37,049	−5,000	−133,389	−285,105	−103,777	−221,049	−301,402	−202,800	−142,700
Revenue..............................	81	83,494	90,623	249,768	325,144	351,262	310,174	662,585	597,282	796,977	716,754	1,023,200	1,234,600
Grants Received......................	81z	—	—	—	—	—	—	—	—	—	—	—	—
Expenditure..........................	82	191,229	160,893	248,768	288,095	356,262	443,563	947,690	701,059	1,018,026	1,018,156	1,226,000	1,377,300
Lending Minus Repayments.............	83	—	—	—	—	—	—	—	—	—	—	—	—
Financing													
Net Borrowing: Domestic..............	84a	91,136	60,248	7,102	−143,190	−60,637	103,886	264,064	103,777	194,053	149,027	163,700	40,700
Foreign..........................	85a	16,964	8,391	22,455	7,825	13,383	16,605	21,041	....	....	....	....	....
Use of Cash Balances.................	87	−364	1,632	−30,558	98,315	52,254	12,898	....	....	....	....	....	....
Debt: Domestic.......................	88a	261,093	299,361	248,774	343,674	359,028	537,489	....	....	....	149,027	163,600	40,700
Central Bank.........................	88aa	189,773	199,662	187,509	247,461	264,229	435,131	....	....	....	−206,132	94,000	−210,300
Commercial Banks.....................	88ab	38,798	47,829	20,113	45,107	41,450	54,114	....	....	....	260,968	11,500	168,700
Other................................	88ac	32,522	51,870	41,152	51,106	53,349	48,244	−18,561	103,777	95,271	94,191	58,100	82,300
Debt: Foreign........................	89a	633,144	648,813	716,775	617,320	595,932	633,017	28,040	28,279	28,347	30,992	32,917	35,945
National Accounts						*Billions of Naira*							
Househ.Cons.Expend.,incl.NPISHs.....	96f	537	694	† 1,543	2,368	2,435	2,757	1,969	2,447	3,643	4,015	5,493	6,470
Government Consumption Expend...	91f	28	89	† 123	143	171	204	253	260	403	478	450	493
Gross Fixed Capital Formation.........	93e	81	85	† 114	172	206	193	176	269	372	500	866	1,382
Changes in Inventories...............	93i	—	—	† —	—	—	1	1	1	1	1	1	1
Exports of Goods and Services.........	90c	229	217	† 679	853	1,148	754	1,650	2,932	2,231	2,564	3,479	4,358
Imports of Goods and Services (-).....	98c	174	170	† 482	712	1,020	1,027	728	927	1,785	1,954	3,098	4,150
Gross Domestic Product (GDP)........	99b	701	915	† 1,978	2,824	2,940	2,881	3,321	4,981	4,864	5,603	7,191	8,553
Net Primary Income from Abroad.....	98.n	−74	−66	† −204	−211	−226	−176	−238	−362	−347	−386	−427	−461
Gross National Income (GNI).........	99a	628	849	† 1,774	2,613	2,714	2,705	3,082	4,619	4,517	5,217	6,764	8,092
Consumption of Fixed Capital.........	99cf	17	19	† 20	22	24	26	29	32	36	39	43	47
GDP at Fact.Cost,Vol.'84 Prices.......	99bap	100	101	† 104	108	111	114	117	121	126	131	136	....
GDP Volume (2000=100)...............	99bvp	82.6	83.7	85.5	88.8	91.7	93.8	96.4	100.0	104.2	108.5	112.6	....
GDP Deflator (2000=100)...............	99bip	17.0	22.0	† 46.4	63.9	64.4	61.7	69.1	100.0	93.7	103.7	128.2	....
						Millions: Midyear Estimates							
Population.........................	99z	98.49	101.20	103.91	106.64	109.37	112.11	114.85	117.61	120.37	123.13	125.91	128.71

		1993	1994	1995	1996	1997	1998	1999	2000	2001	2002	2003	2004
Exchange Rates						*Kroner per SDR: End of Period*							
Official Rate	aa	10.3264	9.8715	9.3931	9.2641	9.8707	10.7010	11.0343	11.5288	11.3251	9.4700	9.9263	9.3802
					Kroner per US Dollar: End of Period (ae) Period Average (rf)								
Official Rate	ae	7.5180	6.7620	6.3190	6.4425	7.3157	7.6000	8.0395	8.8485	9.0116	6.9657	6.6800	6.0400
Official Rate	rf	7.0941	7.0576	6.3352	6.4498	7.0734	7.5451	7.7992	8.8018	8.9917	7.9838	7.0802	6.7408
					Kroner per ECU through 1998; Kroner per Euro Beginning 1999; End of Period (ea) Period Average (eb)								
Euro Rate	ea	8.3878	8.3175	8.3067	8.0615	8.0867	8.8708	† 8.0765	8.2335	7.9735	7.2900	8.4200	8.2400
Euro Rate	ag	....	....	....	....	....	....	1.0046	.9305	.8813	1.0487	1.2630	1.3621
Euro Rate	eb	8.3505	8.3760	8.2859	8.1971	8.0131	8.4541	† 8.3140	8.1133	8.0493	7.5099	7.9992	8.3708
Euro Rate	rh	....	....	....	....	....	....	1.0668	.9240	.8956	.9444	1.1308	1.2433
					Index Numbers (2000=100): Period Averages								
Official Rate	ahx	123.6	124.6	138.7	136.2	124.4	116.4	112.6	100.0	97.7	110.7	123.5	130.4
Nominal Effective Exchange Rate	neu	106.3	105.0	108.1	108.0	108.1	103.6	102.4	100.0	102.8	111.6	108.9	105.2
Real Effective Exchange Rate	reu	83.7	83.8	89.0	91.3	94.8	95.8	99.6	100.0	107.1	120.5	119.8	116.0
Fund Position						*Millions of SDRs: End of Period*							
Quota	2f.s	1,104.6	1,104.6	1,104.6	1,104.6	1,104.6	1,104.6	1,671.7	1,671.7	1,671.7	1,671.7	1,671.7	1,671.7
SDRs	1b.s	288.4	266.7	311.5	247.2	257.9	294.1	298.0	235.4	282.1	232.1	225.4	232.3
Reserve Position in the Fund	1c.s	425.5	440.9	636.2	643.8	725.5	899.1	621.2	448.1	577.3	729.8	669.5	559.2
of which: Outstg.Fund Borrowing	2c	—	—	—	—	—	35.3	—	—	—	—	—	—
International Liquidity						*Millions of US Dollars Unless Otherwise Indicated: End of Period*							
Total Reserves minus Gold	1l.d	19,622.4	19,025.5	22,517.8	26,516.7	23,400.3	19,048.1	23,807.3	27,597.4	23,277.5	31,999.8	37,220.0	44,307.5
SDRs	1b.d	396.2	389.4	463.0	355.5	347.9	414.1	409.0	306.6	354.5	315.5	335.0	360.8
Reserve Position in the Fund	1c.d	584.4	643.7	945.6	925.8	978.9	1,266.0	852.6	583.8	725.6	992.2	994.9	868.5
Foreign Exchange	1d.d	18,641.8	17,992.4	21,109.2	25,235.5	22,073.5	17,368.0	22,545.7	26,706.9	22,197.5	30,692.1	35,890.2	43,078.2
Gold (Million Fine Troy Ounces)	1ad	1.184	1.184	1.184	1.184	1.184	1.184	1.184	1.183	1.183	1.182	1.180	—
Gold (National Valuation)	1and	37.9	42.1	45.1	44.2	38.8	37.5	35.3	256.5	260.3	402.8	490.6	—
Deposit Money Banks: Assets	7a.d	6,597.1	7,267.4	7,473.0	9,087.8	9,781.4	12,324.9	12,418.4	15,280.1	15,092.7	17,642.0	28,587.7	25,182.4
Liabilities	7b.d	9,637.4	9,241.3	9,617.3	19,885.4	25,617.0	29,849.7	31,818.9	37,022.4	39,759.2	52,761.4	69,457.7	76,024.7
Other Banking Insts.: Liabilities	7f.d	5,731.3	6,040.1	6,434.6	6,198.7	7,081.2	8,179.1	8,774.8	10,659.0	13,445.0	19,430.1	25,815.8	33,134.5
Monetary Authorities						*Billions of Kroner: End of Period*							
Foreign Assets	11	151.43	143.58	142.78	225.37	284.17	312.96	† 187.33	241.34	207.72	221.55	249.16	....
Claims on Central Government	12a	29.25	13.69	18.06	12.41	10.65	9.43	10.79	12.73	11.53	12.84	22.91	....
Claims on Deposit Money Banks	12e	17.48	5.86	10.09	.23	7.50	16.47	25.63	22.14	15.21	1.07	12.92	....
Reserve Money	14	42.66	44.09	46.39	70.96	62.79	55.89	83.95	70.29	69.75	104.09	74.40	....
of which: Currency Outside DMBs	14a	35.74	37.95	39.08	39.87	42.22	42.14	43.51	42.43	42.10	40.41	41.69	....
Central Government Deposits	16d	106.76	87.24	98.39	131.24	201.16	222.73	† 57.22	85.68	83.55	52.76	108.59	....
Other Items (Net)	17r	48.75	31.80	26.15	35.81	38.37	60.24	82.58	120.25	81.16	78.61	102.00	....
Deposit Money Banks						*Billions of Kroner: End of Period*							
Reserves	20	2.88	4.32	5.15	28.06	17.28	14.07	38.36	27.82	29.75	65.87	39.49	47.70
Foreign Assets	21	49.60	49.14	47.22	58.55	71.56	93.67	99.84	135.21	136.01	122.89	190.97	152.10
Claims on Central Government	22a	87.32	73.87	70.56	78.49	60.79	87.04	45.42	38.58	9.60	8.11	13.02	13.94
Claims on Local Government	22b	11.62	11.31	12.78	15.16	15.71	26.89	17.38	11.93	10.39	6.53	6.28	6.45
Claims on Nonfin.Pub.Enterprises	22c	9.05	9.24	5.80	8.04	9.19	12.03	11.21	14.05	13.96	17.07	16.02	24.40
Claims on Private Sector	22d	457.14	479.68	527.46	599.82	708.01	801.58	849.70	969.64	1,075.45	1,144.61	1,232.53	1,354.10
Claims on Other Financial Insts	22f	34.92	37.11	34.04	40.46	50.13	75.74	72.54	82.55	92.65	108.23	119.24	103.59
Demand Deposits	24	300.43	314.80	316.29	349.70	371.96	453.20	479.34	521.01	616.02	671.85	706.25	700.07
Time, Savings,& Fgn.Currency Dep	25	139.95	149.24	164.57	166.71	150.52	157.80	141.03	159.08	128.06	133.64	127.91	198.55
Foreign Liabilities	26c	72.45	62.49	60.77	128.11	187.41	226.86	255.81	327.59	358.29	367.52	463.98	459.19
Central Government Deposits	26d	36.55	33.02	34.00	37.62	32.09	57.40	25.90	24.64	6.71	7.63	11.29	7.36
Credit from Bank of Norway	26g	17.03	5.30	10.47	.45	7.88	18.79	25.94	24.70	16.72	8.81	19.99	5.27
Other Items (Net)	27r	86.13	99.57	115.92	145.98	182.80	196.97	206.44	222.75	242.00	283.86	288.13	331.84
Monetary Survey						*Billions of Kroner: End of Period*							
Foreign Assets (Net)	31n	123.14	123.81	125.01	142.13	159.34	169.03	† 3.79	−12.31	−58.28	−77.03	−75.41	....
Domestic Credit	32	486.63	505.25	536.90	586.05	621.74	735.92	† 924.49	1,019.76	1,123.97	1,237.79	1,290.67	....
Claims on Central Govt. (Net)	32an	−26.74	−32.71	−43.77	−77.96	−161.81	−183.66	† −26.91	−59.01	−69.13	−39.44	−83.95	....
Claims on Local Government	32b	11.62	11.31	12.78	15.16	15.71	26.89	17.38	11.93	10.39	6.53	6.28	....
Claims on Nonfin.Pub.Enterprises	32c	9.05	9.24	5.80	8.04	9.19	12.03	11.21	14.05	13.96	17.16	16.02	....
Claims on Private Sector	32d	457.77	480.30	528.05	600.35	708.52	802.11	850.26	970.24	1,076.09	1,145.30	1,233.09	....
Claims on Other Financial Insts	32f	34.92	37.11	34.04	40.46	50.13	78.55	72.54	82.55	92.65	108.23	119.24	....
Money	34	340.12	354.96	358.71	392.72	416.99	497.51	525.43	565.12	659.62	713.76	747.99	....
Quasi-Money	35	139.99	149.27	164.59	166.73	150.53	157.81	141.04	159.08	128.06	133.64	128.08	....
Other Items (Net)	37r	129.66	124.58	137.62	168.72	213.56	249.62	261.81	283.25	278.00	313.35	339.19	....
Money plus Quasi-Money	35l	480.11	504.23	523.30	559.45	567.52	655.32	666.47	724.20	787.68	847.41	876.07	....
Money (National Definitions)						*Billions of Kroner: End of Period*							
Broad Money (M2), Unadjusted	59mb	469.0	491.1	530.3	564.4	578.8	605.6	670.1	731.8	795.4	855.3	873.1	....
Broad Money (M2), Seasonally Adj.	59mbc	465.3	488.5	528.9	563.4	577.8	603.9	670.1	731.7	794.9	854.5	872.0	....

		1993	1994	1995	1996	1997	1998	1999	2000	2001	2002	2003	2004
Other Banking Institutions													
State Lending Institutions						*Billions of Kroner: End of Period*							
Claims on State and Local Govts......	42b	34.53	35.40	36.68	37.90	41.84	42.36	46.17	18.28	18.74	20.82	20.95	19.65
Claims on Private Sector.................	42d	145.34	139.53	138.56	135.69	131.73	140.96	146.46	152.02	161.47	166.59	167.91	167.20
Bonds (Net)...................................	46ab	21.39	16.68	10.39	11.81	16.01	20.16	28.65	.06	.05	.03	.02	.02
Foreign Liabilities...........................	46c	3.69	1.81	1.14	1.17	.33	1.39	—	—	—	—	—	—
Central Govt. Lending Funds............	46f	160.22	155.32	154.28	153.78	152.38	158.75	162.43	168.96	177.87	187.59	189.79	187.92
Capital Accounts.............................	47a	12.23	10.30	10.39	8.61	8.45	8.25	6.74	5.46	6.88	4.50	3.52	3.70
Other Items (Net)............................	47r	−17.67	−9.18	−.95	−1.79	−3.61	−5.23	−5.19	−4.17	−4.57	−4.72	−4.47	−4.79
Mortgage Institutions						*Billions of Kroner: End of Period*							
Foreign Assets................................	41..l	19.67	23.95	24.02	22.11	19.36	29.99	33.39	30.32	39.59	56.61	60.68	59.86
Claims on Central Government........	42a.l	2.85	1.48	1.94	1.55	1.22	1.53	1.09	1.16	1.26	.68	.91	.46
Claims on State and Local Govt.......	42b.l	2.00	1.91	2.64	4.33	5.60	5.55	8.08	49.83	60.37	65.25	79.40	99.72
Claims on Nonfin.Pub.Enterprises.....	42c.l	1.65	1.32	1.34	1.70	1.37	1.90	4.68	2.78	5.69	5.98	7.70	9.60
Claims on Private Sector.................	42d.l	72.15	62.34	60.05	55.55	66.33	88.87	82.04	93.61	103.07	112.08	124.20	129.75
Credit Market Instruments...............	46aal	5.45	6.97	7.40	5.49	3.70	3.13	8.21	4.81	5.57	1.75	5.81	3.25
Bonds (net)...................................	46abl	42.16	35.01	36.46	37.21	33.14	36.46	36.63	58.57	58.89	62.41	51.39	50.83
Foreign Liabilities...........................	46c.l	39.40	39.04	39.52	38.76	51.47	60.77	70.55	94.32	121.16	135.34	172.45	200.13
Capital Accounts.............................	47a.l	8.00	7.76	7.59	6.64	6.51	8.31	8.73	11.04	11.23	11.57	12.23	12.14
Other Items (Net)............................	47r.l	3.30	2.23	−.99	−2.87	−.93	19.17	5.16	8.97	13.13	29.52	30.99	33.04
Nonbank Financial Institutions						*Billions of Kroner: End of Period*							
Claims on Central Government........	42a.s	32.36	40.47	42.34	42.83	49.16	35.95	34.07	31.34	43.74	46.25	67.33	....
Claims on Local Government...........	42b.s	31.29	32.27	30.85	29.55	27.42	28.61	35.07	38.14	43.52	39.08	48.29	....
Claims on Private Sector.................	42d.s	75.78	65.71	73.90	77.07	71.55	75.08	80.43	92.75	103.63	105.19	132.10	....
Claims on Other Financial Insts.......	42f.s	24.30	28.05	32.58	38.85	42.54	48.10	46.36	36.98	50.38	58.03	59.07	....
Incr.in Total Assets(Within Per.).......	49z.s	14.67	7.94	10.92	6.91	3.02	−.86	5.77	5.74	45.69	−28.21	100.19	....
Interest Rates						*Percent Per Annum*							
Discount Rate (End of Period)...........	60	7.00	6.75	6.75	6.00	5.50	10.00	7.50	9.00	8.50	8.50	4.25	3.75
Avg.Cost for Centr.Bank Funding.....	60.a	5.70	6.46	5.40	4.96	4.80	6.18	6.86	7.31	7.45	8.22	5.60	2.22
Deposit Rate...................................	60l	5.51	5.21	4.95	4.15	3.63	7.24	5.38	6.73	† 6.43	6.46	2.12	1.48
Lending Rate..................................	60p	9.17	8.38	7.60	6.68	6.00	9.80	7.61	8.93	8.69	8.71	4.73	4.04
Three Month Interbank Rate...........	60zb	7.27	5.85	5.48	4.90	3.73	5.79	6.54	6.75	7.23	6.91	4.10	2.01
Government Bond Yield..................	61	6.52	7.13	6.82	5.94	5.13	5.35	5.38	6.38	6.31	6.33	4.50	3.60
Prices, Production, Labor						*Index Numbers (2000=100): Period Averages*							
Industrial Share Prices.....................	62	34.5	44.1	47.0	56.4	79.9	78.7	80.3	100.0	....	....	....	....
Producer Prices..............................	63	83.8	84.9	87.1	89.0	90.2	90.7	93.5	† 100.0	95.3	90.0	93.2	104.2
Consumer Prices............................	64	85.9	87.1	89.2	90.4	92.7	† 94.8	97.0	100.0	103.0	104.3	106.9	107.4
Wages: Monthly Earnings................	65	....	....	....	....	....	91.3	96.1	100.0	104.5	110.0	115.2	120.0
Industrial Production........................	66	79.6	85.2	90.4	95.0	98.4	97.4	97.1	100.0	98.7	99.6	95.5	97.4
Crude Petroleum Production..........	66aa	72.0	81.0	87.3	98.7	100.2	95.7	96.1	100.0	101.4	96.9	92.7	....
						Number in Thousands: Period Averages							
Labor Force....................................	67d	2,131	2,151	2,186	2,240	2,287	2,323	2,333	2,350	2,362	2,379	2,375	2,382
Employment...................................	67e	2,004	2,035	2,079	2,132	2,195	2,248	2,258	2,269	2,278	2,286	2,269	2,276
Unemployment..............................	67c	127	117	107	108	93	74	75	81	84	93	107	107
Unemployment Rate (%).................	67r	6.0	5.4	4.9	4.8	4.1	3.2	3.2	3.3	2.7	3.2	3.9	4.4
Intl. Transactions & Positions						*Millions of Kroner*							
Exports..	70	225,714	243,809	265,883	320,130	342,421	304,653	355,172	529,814	532,042	473,265	476,981	549,672
Imports, c.i.f...................................	71	170,069	192,073	208,627	229,720	252,232	282,638	266,677	302,852	296,135	276,563	279,240	323,081
						2000=100							
Volume of Exports..........................	72	66.0	73.8	78.0	88.0	92.8	93.0	95.1	100.0	104.6	107.1	107.4	108.4
Volume of Imports..........................	73	54.9	63.5	69.0	75.9	82.8	93.5	93.9	100.0	101.3	102.6	105.7	117.7
Unit Value of Exports......................	74	63.0	61.0	62.9	67.9	68.8	61.0	69.1	100.0	95.2	84.6	83.9	97.1
Unit Value of Imports......................	75	102.8	103.7	104.3	103.5	101.7	100.8	96.6	100.0	100.3	93.3	93.4	96.8

Norway 142

		1993	1994	1995	1996	1997	1998	1999	2000	2001	2002	2003	2004
Balance of Payments		*Millions of US Dollars: Minus Sign Indicates Debit*											
Current Account, n.i.e.	78ald	3,522	3,760	5,233	10,969	10,036	6	8,378	25,851	26,171	24,473	28,326	34,445
Goods: Exports f.o.b.	78aad	32,278	35,016	42,385	50,081	49,375	40,888	46,224	60,463	59,527	59,616	69,073	82,993
Goods: Imports f.o.b.	78abd	−25,312	−27,520	−33,701	−37,109	−37,727	−38,827	−35,501	−34,488	−33,055	−35,277	−40,803	−49,418
Trade Balance	78acd	6,966	7,496	8,685	12,972	11,648	2,061	10,723	25,975	26,472	24,340	28,269	33,576
Services: Credit	78add	12,159	12,247	13,672	14,819	15,708	15,542	15,878	17,263	17,603	18,689	21,666	26,111
Services: Debit	78aed	−11,472	−12,065	−13,147	−13,435	−14,233	−14,820	−14,882	−14,465	−15,104	−16,910	−19,938	−24,139
Balance on Goods & Services	78afd	7,653	7,678	9,210	14,356	13,123	2,783	11,719	28,773	28,971	26,119	29,998	35,547
Income: Credit	78agd	2,380	3,415	4,590	5,164	5,590	6,809	6,100	6,641	7,556	9,322	10,548	12,352
Income: Debit	78ahd	−5,167	−5,589	−6,509	−7,046	−7,284	−8,053	−7,998	−8,278	−8,737	−8,690	−9,260	−10,809
Balance on Gds, Serv. & Inc.	78aid	4,866	5,504	7,291	12,475	11,429	1,539	9,821	27,136	27,790	26,752	31,286	37,090
Current Transfers, n.i.e.: Credit	78ajd	1,533	1,291	1,280	1,329	1,468	1,500	1,681	1,605	1,760	1,810	2,008	2,408
Current Transfers: Debit	78akd	−2,877	−3,035	−3,339	−2,835	−2,861	−3,034	−3,124	−2,890	−3,379	−4,089	−4,968	−5,054
Capital Account, n.i.e.	78bcd	−31	−157	−170	−127	−184	−116	−116	−91	−4	−191	678	−154
Capital Account, n.i.e.: Credit	78bad	306	93	86	65	30	44	40	135	113	44	964	105
Capital Account: Debit	78bbd	−337	−250	−255	−192	−214	−160	−156	−225	−118	−235	−286	−260
Financial Account, n.i.e.	78bjd	6,568	−1,363	−542	−1,462	−6,607	61	431	−13,395	−27,393	−9,238	−19,373	−20,745
Direct Investment Abroad	78bdd	−718	−2,166	−2,859	−5,886	−5,003	−3,200	−6,018	−8,511	859	−3,850	−2,310	−1,948
Dir. Invest. in Rep. Econ., n.i.e.	78bed	992	2,736	2,393	3,179	3,886	4,354	8,056	5,806	2,109	502	2,055	502
Portfolio Investment Assets	78bfd	2,088	992	−3,531	−9,833	−12,618	−9,348	−7,228	−25,143	−29,674	−22,987	−19,287	−38,134
Equity Securities	78bkd	−124	213	−379	−1,177	−2,644	−9,066	−2,378	−11,034	−12,342	−6,829	−8,502	−7,255
Debt Securities	78bld	2,212	780	−3,151	−8,657	−9,974	−282	−4,850	−14,109	−17,333	−16,158	−10,785	−30,879
Portfolio Investment Liab., n.i.e.	78bgd	−1,175	−518	655	100	2,500	7,289	4,238	9,843	2,590	4,675	13,123	9,435
Equity Securities	78bmd	385	654	636	−237	−1,190	—	−1,033	1,630	2,698	352	2,040	4,442
Debt Securities	78bnd	−1,560	−1,172	19	337	3,691	7,289	5,271	8,213	−108	4,322	11,083	4,993
Financial Derivatives Assets	78bwd	....	....	....	−43	17	−162	152	−329	−1,228	−4,270	35	−636
Financial Derivatives Liabilities	78bxd	....	....	....	101	125	74	92	−131	91	−556	−161	501
Other Investment Assets	78bhd	6,198	154	961	−67	−1,403	−3,632	−7,663	−14,100	−3,931	−12,474	−25,185	−17,027
General Government	78bpd	−65	−13	−156	71	91	−1,167	−1,099	−2,072	1,379	457	−1,199	1,552
Banks	78bqd	3,997	−638	435	−1,216	−1,465	−1,062	−969	−1,806	505	674	−4,291	963
Other Sectors	78brd	2,266	804	682	1,077	−29	−1,403	−5,595	−10,223	−5,816	−13,605	−19,695	−19,542
Other Investment Liab., n.i.e.	78bid	−816	−2,562	1,840	10,987	5,888	4,685	8,802	19,171	1,791	29,723	12,358	26,562
Monetary Authorities	78bsd	217	139	−624	1,505	−803	19	−19	3	44	410	−322	117
General Government	78btd	−7	−164	3	—	94	1,346	3,460	9,657	−96	15,678	9,893	20,434
Banks	78bud	−302	−604	247	8,677	4,126	−856	1,789	1,321	2,320	8,549	377	4,265
Other Sectors	78bvd	−724	−1,933	2,214	806	2,472	4,176	3,573	8,190	−477	5,086	2,410	1,746
Net Errors and Omissions	78cad	−1,806	−1,987	−3,947	−2,910	−4,443	−6,335	−2,710	−8,680	−1,120	−9,320	−9,286	−8,318
Overall Balance	78cbd	8,253	253	575	6,470	−1,198	−6,384	5,984	3,686	−2,346	5,723	346	5,227
Reserves and Related Items	79dad	−8,253	−253	−575	−6,470	1,198	6,384	−5,984	−3,686	2,346	−5,723	−346	−5,227
Reserve Assets	79dbd	−8,253	−253	−575	−6,470	1,198	6,384	−5,984	−3,686	2,346	−5,723	−346	−5,227
Use of Fund Credit and Loans	79dcd	—	—	—	—	—	—	—	—	—	—	—	—
Exceptional Financing	79ded	....	....	....	....	....	....	....	....	....	....	....	....
International Investment Position		*Millions of US Dollars*											
Assets	79aad	46,433	....	....	....	....	....	....	....	....	....	....	....
Direct Investment Abroad	79abd	5,080	....	....	....	....	....	....	....	....	....	....	....
Portfolio Investment	79acd	5,762	....	....	....	....	....	....	....	....	....	....	....
Equity Securities	79add	—	....	....	....	....	....	....	....	....	....	....	....
Debt Securities	79aed	5,762	....	....	....	....	....	....	....	....	....	....	....
Financial Derivatives	79ald	—	....	....	....	....	....	....	....	....	....	....	....
Other Investment	79afd	19,910	....	....	....	....	....	....	....	....	....	....	....
Monetary Authorities	79agd		....	....	....	....	....	....	....	....	....	....	....
General Government	79ahd	1,868	....	....	....	....	....	....	....	....	....	....	....
Banks	79aid	5,813	....	....	....	....	....	....	....	....	....	....	....
Other Sectors	79ajd	12,228	....	....	....	....	....	....	....	....	....	....	....
Reserve Assets	79akd	15,680	....	....	....	....	....	....	....	....	....	....	....
Liabilities	79lad	57,536	....	....	....	....	....	....	....	....	....	....	....
Dir. Invest. in Rep. Economy	79lbd	3,880	....	....	....	....	....	....	....	....	....	....	....
Portfolio Investment	79lcd	22,449	....	....	....	....	....	....	....	....	....	....	....
Equity Securities	79ldd	—	....	....	....	....	....	....	....	....	....	....	....
Debt Securities	79led	22,449	....	....	....	....	....	....	....	....	....	....	....
Financial Derivatives	79lld	—	....	....	....	....	....	....	....	....	....	....	....
Other Investment	79lfd	31,207	....	....	....	....	....	....	....	....	....	....	....
Monetary Authorities	79lgd	101	....	....	....	....	....	....	....	....	....	....	....
General Government	79lhd	2,238	....	....	....	....	....	....	....	....	....	....	....
Banks	79lid	6,179	....	....	....	....	....	....	....	....	....	....	....
Other Sectors	79ljd	22,688	....	....	....	....	....	....	....	....	....	....	....
Government Finance		*Millions of Kroner: Year Ending December 31*											
Deficit (-) or Surplus	80	−45,556	−14,774	14,487	6,519	8,816	−32,427	−47,230	101,351	96,615	38,244	43,518	....
Revenue	81	326,507	348,841	383,106	425,506	469,040	464,460	495,055	642,546	710,627	698,626	721,551	....
Grants Received	81z	1,490	1,423	1,345	1,299	1,322	1,087	938	1,273	1,329	1,243	1,532	....
Expenditure	82	347,962	357,877	361,579	375,265	387,218	412,173	436,850	465,218	490,627	569,873	583,758	....
Lending Minus Repayments	83	25,591	7,161	8,385	45,021	74,328	85,801	106,373	77,250	124,714	91,752	95,807	....
Financing													
Domestic	84a	25,189	20,459	−18,296	11,276	14,516	38,579	1,692	−198,292	−82,176	−124,112	−132,148	....
Foreign	85a	20,368	−5,684	3,809	−17,795	−23,332	−6,152	45,538	105,500	−13,750	86,900	89,500	....
Debt: Domestic	88a	189,953	201,763	198,384	186,071	195,983	184,220	149,470	149,553	142,977	171,500	208,761	....
Foreign	89a	80,018	74,157	77,901	62,527	42,400	37,180	92,881	197,401	182,483	264,630	356,808	....

		1993	1994	1995	1996	1997	1998	1999	2000	2001	2002	2003	2004
National Accounts							*Billions of Kroner*						
Househ.Cons.Expend.,incl.NPISHs....	96f	416.23	435.35	462.26	498.97	527.14	554.54	584.27	625.50	651.34	680.68	718.99	755.15
Government Consumption Expend...	91f	187.47	193.83	202.14	214.68	227.49	247.44	263.73	281.12	314.80	338.47	356.17	370.89
Gross Fixed Capital Formation..........	93e	164.13	174.38	186.55	208.60	245.70	284.91	271.83	272.77	278.94	274.68	271.00	303.92
Changes in Inventories...................	93i	8.30	15.84	28.04	12.08	18.87	23.79	20.73	35.04	20.68	17.78	3.95	16.65
Exports of Goods and Services..........	90c	315.96	333.20	355.95	419.40	460.86	427.08	486.23	685.95	697.30	624.39	645.06	736.84
Imports of Goods and Services (-).....	98c	261.67	279.18	297.50	326.80	368.70	405.62	393.76	431.30	436.81	416.85	433.25	497.89
Gross Domestic Product (GDP).........	99b	830.42	873.41	937.44	1,026.93	1,111.35	1,132.13	1,233.04	1,469.08	1,526.23	1,519.13	1,561.91	1,685.55
Net Primary Income from Abroad......	98.n	−19.77	−15.42	−12.18	−12.18	−11.83	−9.37	−14.82	−14.42	−10.77	4.13	9.38	9.93
Gross National Income (GNI)...........	99a	810.64	857.99	925.27	1,014.74	1,099.52	1,122.77	1,218.22	1,454.66	1,515.46	1,523.27	1,571.29	1,695.49
Net Current Transf.from Abroad......	98t	−9.53	−12.23	−13.03	−9.71	−9.87	−11.55	−11.28	−11.36	−14.55	−17.78	−20.85	−17.67
Gross Nat'l Disposable Inc.(GNDI)....	99i	801.11	845.76	912.24	1,005.03	1,089.65	1,111.21	1,206.94	1,443.30	1,500.91	1,505.49	1,550.44	1,677.81
Gross Saving..................................	99s	197.41	216.58	247.84	291.39	335.03	309.24	358.94	536.68	534.78	486.34	475.29	551.78
Consumption of Fixed Capital..........	99cf	139.84	143.16	149.05	154.78	164.11	175.62	188.55	204.86	215.86	219.57	225.40	232.13
GDP Volume 2002 Prices.................	99b.p	1,115.75	1,174.40	1,225.57	1,289.96	1,356.90	1,392.58	1,422.28	1,462.63	1,502.51	1,519.13	1,524.82	1,569.27
GDP Volume (2000=100)...............	99bvp	76.3	80.3	83.8	88.2	92.8	95.2	97.2	100.0	102.7	103.9	104.3	107.3
GDP Deflator (2000=100)...............	99bip	74.1	74.0	76.2	79.3	81.5	80.9	86.3	100.0	101.1	99.6	102.0	106.9
						Millions: Midyear Estimates							
Population...............................	99z	4.31	4.33	4.36	4.39	4.42	4.45	4.47	4.50	4.53	4.55	4.58	4.60

Oman 449

		1993	1994	1995	1996	1997	1998	1999	2000	2001	2002	2003	2004
Exchange Rates			*Rials Omani per SDR: End of Period (aa) Rials Omani per US Dollar: End of Period (ae)*										
Official Rate	aa	.5281	.5613	.5716	.5529	.5188	.5414	.5277	.5010	.4832	.5227	.5714	.5971
Official Rate	ae	.3845	.3845	.3845	.3845	.3845	.3845	.3845	.3845	.3845	.3845	.3845	.3845
					Index Numbers (2000=100): Period Averages								
Official Rate	ahx	100.0	100.0	100.0	100.0	100.0	100.0	100.0	100.0	100.0	100.0	100.0	100.0
Nominal Effective Exchange Rate	nec	92.7	90.1	85.1	89.0	93.5	96.2	95.1	100.0	105.4	103.2	93.8	86.8
Fund Position					*Millions of SDRs: End of Period*								
Quota	2f.s	119.4	119.4	119.4	119.4	119.4	119.4	194.0	194.0	194.0	194.0	194.0	194.0
SDRs	1b.s	5.0	6.2	7.5	8.8	10.1	11.5	1.3	3.1	5.0	6.5	7.8	9.0
Reserve Position in the Fund	1c.s	37.8	36.0	34.5	34.0	31.1	31.1	49.8	49.8	65.0	73.4	77.6	63.7
of which: Outstg.Fund Borrowing	2c	—	—	—	—	—	—	—	—	—	—	—	—
International Liquidity					*Millions of US Dollars Unless Otherwise Indicated: End of Period*								
Total Reserves minus Gold	1l.d	1,803.9	1,646.2	1,830.7	1,961.6	2,069.6	1,937.7	2,767.5	2,379.9	2,364.9	3,173.5	3,593.5	3,597.3
SDRs	1b.d	6.8	9.0	11.1	12.7	13.6	16.2	1.8	4.1	6.3	8.9	11.6	13.9
Reserve Position in the Fund	1c.d	52.0	52.5	51.2	48.8	42.0	43.9	68.3	64.9	81.6	99.8	115.3	98.9
Foreign Exchange	1d.d	1,745.1	1,584.7	1,768.3	1,900.1	2,014.0	1,877.7	2,697.3	2,310.9	2,277.0	3,064.8	3,466.6	3,484.5
Gold (Million Fine Troy Ounces)	1ad	.289	.289	.291	.291	.291	.291	.291	.291	.291	.001	.001	.001
Gold (National Valuation)	1and	68.3	68.3	68.3	68.3	68.3	68.3	68.3	68.3	80.5	.2	.3	.3
Monetary Authorities:Other Assets	3..d	162.2	38.4	....	80.6	120.3	147.8	555.9	39.7	50.4	41.7	42.1	50.0
Other Liab.	4..d	1.0	1.2	1.7	1.0	1.7	1.2	1.1	1.0	1.0	1.1	1.1	2.4
Deposit Money Banks: Assets	7a.d	780.1	863.5	999.1	944.1	1,776.8	1,222.7	992.3	1,215.5	997.9	1,241.9	1,290.3	1,877.0
Liabilities	7b.d	167.1	239.5	441.4	652.4	1,326.5	1,522.2	1,662.4	1,641.8	1,532.5	1,401.8	1,176.1	953.6
Monetary Authorities					*Millions of Rials Omani: End of Period*								
Foreign Assets	11	720.1	635.0	730.4	780.8	822.4	771.6	1,090.4	941.4	940.3	1,220.3	1,382.2	1,383.7
Claims on Central Government	12a	49.3	97.0	89.4	47.0	32.7	159.6	4.1	5.0	79.5	25.7	4.3	3.6
Reserve Money	14	284.7	296.3	306.9	326.5	354.3	379.5	375.3	408.3	444.3	578.7	612.5	562.1
of which: Currency Outside DMBs	14a	232.9	245.5	235.9	231.2	242.2	244.2	273.5	276.8	275.9	289.6	303.8	329.0
Foreign Liabilities	16c	.4	.5	.6	.4	.6	.5	.4	.4	.4	.4	.4	.9
Central Government Deposits	16d	62.4	14.8	41.0	31.1	46.6	57.0	242.6	26.0	19.4	16.1	68.5	85.9
Capital Accounts	17a	219.9	235.2	251.9	268.3	283.1	297.9	312.4	342.8	373.5	406.8	403.4	412.3
Other Items (Net)	17r	201.9	185.3	219.5	201.5	170.4	196.3	163.8	168.8	182.2	243.9	301.7	326.0
Deposit Money Banks					*Millions of Rials Omani: End of Period*								
Reserves	20	49.4	51.6	67.8	86.9	116.0	132.2	99.2	129.7	136.2	164.2	129.0	165.1
Foreign Assets	21	299.9	332.0	384.2	363.0	683.2	470.1	381.5	467.4	383.7	477.5	496.1	721.7
Claims on Central Government	22a	154.1	97.9	91.9	175.8	157.4	198.0	334.7	323.0	427.0	357.2	417.7	439.9
Claims on Nonfin.Pub.Enterprises	22c	16.8	3.0	3.1	4.8	.6	—	4.1	16.3	28.1	46.0	69.0	87.3
Claims on Private Sector	22d	1,088.0	1,227.3	1,357.5	1,564.9	2,170.9	2,563.1	2,783.9	2,809.7	3,001.4	3,012.7	3,060.1	3,258.8
Demand Deposits	24	218.7	227.4	235.4	272.1	307.5	261.6	237.7	272.5	425.7	482.0	504.2	582.7
Quasi-Monetary Deposits	25	863.9	931.1	1,040.5	1,130.5	1,484.5	1,625.4	1,756.2	1,854.7	1,924.0	1,991.3	2,024.3	2,032.6
Foreign Liabilities	26c	64.2	92.1	169.7	250.9	510.0	585.3	639.2	631.3	589.3	539.0	452.2	366.7
Central Government Deposits	26d	153.4	148.9	140.7	211.3	289.8	292.4	316.1	306.0	285.5	276.4	300.0	441.4
Capital Accounts	27a	165.8	167.6	174.9	193.8	304.2	425.6	454.2	433.3	425.8	432.8	509.3	587.3
Other Items (Net)	27r	142.3	144.7	143.3	136.9	232.0	173.1	200.0	248.3	326.2	336.2	381.9	662.2
Monetary Survey					*Millions of Rials Omani: End of Period*								
Foreign Assets (Net)	31n	955.4	874.5	944.2	892.6	994.9	656.0	832.3	777.1	734.4	1,158.4	1,425.7	1,737.9
Domestic Credit	32	1,092.3	1,261.5	1,360.3	1,550.2	2,025.2	2,571.2	2,568.1	2,822.0	3,231.1	3,149.1	3,182.6	3,262.2
Claims on Central Govt. (Net)	32an	−12.5	31.2	−.4	−19.6	−146.3	8.1	−219.9	−4.1	201.6	90.4	53.5	−83.9
Claims on Nonfin.Pub.Enterprises	32c	16.8	3.0	3.1	4.8	.6	—	4.1	16.3	28.1	46.0	69.0	87.3
Claims on Private Sector	32d	1,088.0	1,227.3	1,357.5	1,564.9	2,170.9	2,563.1	2,783.9	2,809.7	3,001.4	3,012.7	3,060.1	3,258.8
Money	34	451.5	472.9	471.3	503.4	549.7	505.8	511.2	549.3	701.6	771.7	808.0	911.7
Quasi-Money	35	863.9	931.1	1,040.5	1,130.5	1,484.5	1,625.4	1,756.2	1,854.7	1,924.0	1,991.3	2,024.3	2,032.6
Other Items (Net)	37r	732.3	731.9	792.7	808.9	985.9	1,096.0	1,132.9	1,195.0	1,339.9	1,544.6	1,776.0	2,055.9
Money plus Quasi-Money	35l	1,315.5	1,404.1	1,511.8	1,633.9	2,034.2	2,131.2	2,267.5	2,404.1	2,625.6	2,762.9	2,832.3	2,944.3
Interest Rates					*Percent Per Annum*								
Deposit Rate	60l	4.17	4.34	6.53	6.85	7.30	8.46	8.12	7.63	4.50	2.89	2.37	2.32
Lending Rate	60p	8.49	8.57	9.38	9.23	9.30	10.09	10.32	10.06	9.23	8.55	8.23	7.57
Prices and Production					*Index Numbers (2000=100): Period Averages*								
Consumer Prices	64	98.4	98.8	101.2	102.1	101.6	100.7	101.2	100.0	98.9	98.3	†97.9	98.2
Crude Petroleum	66aa	81.4	84.6	89.3	93.1	93.9	92.8	93.9	100.0	99.7	93.7	85.6	81.7
Intl. Transactions & Positions					*Millions of Rials Omani*								
Exports	70	2,064.9	2,132.0	2,333.2	2,824.5	2,933.8	2,118.0	2,783.0	4,352.0	4,258.0	4,295.5	4,486.6	5,129.8
Crude Petroleum	70aa	1,602.9	1,577.8	1,796.1	2,211.0	2,171.3	1,374.3	2,059.8	3,356.7	2,934.4	2,859.3	2,981.4	3,489.5
Imports, c.i.f.	71	1,581.8	1,505.3	1,633.2	1,760.1	1,932.5	2,184.6	1,797.1	1,937.7	2,229.3	2,309.1	2,527.0	3,408.7
Volume of Exports					*2000=100*								
Crude Petroleum	72aa	81.8	82.8	87.1	90.1	93.6	91.9	94.4	100.0	101.4	93.7	85.2	80.7
Unit Value of Imports	75	98.7	108.7	119.0	102.2	101.9	121.8	106.2	100.0	99.8	93.4	88.8	....
Export Prices					*2000=100: Index of Prices in US Dollars*								
Crude Petroleum	76aad	58.4	56.9	61.3	72.7	69.7	44.6	64.9	100.0	86.1	90.9	104.2	128.8

		1993	1994	1995	1996	1997	1998	1999	2000	2001	2002	2003	2004
Balance of Payments		*Millions of US Dollars: Minus Sign Indicates Debit*											
Current Account, n.i.e.	78ald	−1,190	−805	−801	243	−166	−3,164	−460	3,263	2,008	1,770	1,446	....
Goods: Exports f.o.b.	78aad	5,365	5,542	6,065	7,373	7,657	5,520	7,237	11,318	11,073	11,172	11,670	....
Goods: Imports f.o.b.	78abd	−4,030	−3,693	−4,050	−4,231	−4,645	−5,213	−4,299	−4,593	−5,310	−5,636	−6,086	....
Trade Balance	78acd	1,336	1,849	2,015	3,142	3,012	307	2,938	6,725	5,763	5,536	5,584	....
Services: Credit	78add	13	13	13	237	269	388	413	438	351	418	457	....
Services: Debit	78aed	−906	−900	−985	−1,328	−1,556	−1,891	−1,714	−1,756	−1,896	−1,834	−2,059	....
Balance on Goods & Services	78afd	442	962	1,043	2,051	1,725	−1,196	1,638	5,407	4,219	4,119	3,981	....
Income: Credit	78agd	421	257	325	255	385	339	187	291	324	250	247	....
Income: Debit	78ahd	−688	−724	−699	−693	−776	−840	−846	−985	−1,002	−997	−1,110	....
Balance on Gds, Serv. & Inc.	78aid	175	495	669	1,613	1,335	−1,697	979	4,714	3,540	3,372	3,118	
Current Transfers, n.i.e.: Credit	78ajd	57	65	68									
Current Transfers: Debit	78akd	−1,423	−1,365	−1,537	−1,371	−1,501	−1,467	−1,438	−1,451	−1,532	−1,602	−1,672	
Capital Account, n.i.e.	78bcd	—	—	—	10	31	−6	−3	8	−10	6	10	
Capital Account, n.i.e.: Credit	78bad	—	—	—	29	55	20	16	34	8	37	26	
Capital Account: Debit	78bbd	—	—	—	−18	−23	−27	−18	−26	−18	−31	−16	
Financial Account, n.i.e.	78bjd	−79	230	−19	261	51	1,489	128	−647	−695	−1,148	−583	....
Direct Investment Abroad	78bdd	—	—	—	—	—	—	—	—	—	—	—	
Dir. Invest. in Rep. Econ., n.i.e.	78bed	142	76	46	61	65	102	40	16	83	24	138	
Portfolio Investment Assets	78bfd	—	—	—	—	—	—	—	—	—	—	—	
Equity Securities	78bkd	—	....	....	....	....	....	....	....	....	....	....	
Debt Securities	78bld	—	....	....	....	....	....	....	....	....	....	....	
Portfolio Investment Liab., n.i.e.	78bgd	—	....	....	8	18	185	25	−37	12	−18	57	
Equity Securities	78bmd	—	....	....	10	85	240	12	−11	−3	34	96	
Debt Securities	78bnd	—	....	....	−3	−68	−55	13	−26	16	−52	−39	
Financial Derivatives Assets	78bwd	....	....	....	....	....	....	....	....	....	....	....	
Financial Derivatives Liabilities	78bxd	....	....	....	....	....	....	....	....	....	....	....	
Other Investment Assets	78bhd	−187	−174	−52	−237	−715	642	−307	−497	39	−460	−78	
Monetary Authorities	78bod	....	....	....	....	....	....	....	....	....	....	....	
General Government	78bpd	−31	−104	−88	−291	117	88	−538	−273	−179	−216	−31	
Banks	78bqd	−187	−10	62	55	−832	554	232	−224	219	−245	−47	....
Other Sectors	78brd	31	−60	−26	—								
Other Investment Liab., n.i.e.	78bid	−34	328	−13	429	684	559	369	−130	−830	−693	−700	
Monetary Authorities	78bsd	—	—	—	—	—	—	—	—	—	—	—	
General Government	78btd	−91	325	−18	140	−112	−26	101	−114	−448	−599	−421	
Banks	78bud	57	3	5	289	676	315	138	−21	−231	−164	−247	
Other Sectors	78bvd	—	....	....	—	120	271	130	5	−151	70	−31	
Net Errors and Omissions	78cad	211	−86	388	−327	617	910	539	−360	−288	−320	−218	
Overall Balance	78cbd	−1,058	−661	−432	187	533	−771	205	2,263	1,015	309	656	
Reserves and Related Items	79dad	1,058	661	432	−187	−533	771	−205	−2,263	−1,015	−309	−656	....
Reserve Assets	79dbd	1,058	661	432	−187	−533	771	−205	−2,263	−1,015	−309	−656	
Use of Fund Credit and Loans	79dcd	—	—	—	—	—	—	—	—	—	—	—	
Exceptional Financing	79ded	....	....	....	....	....	....	....	....	....	....	....	
Government Finance		*Millions of Rials Omani: Year Ending December 31*											
Deficit (-) or Surplus	80	−511.1	−485.9	−468.1	−259.7	−28.3	−376.9	−474.1	−363.2	−324.1	....	....	....
Revenue	81	1,357.7	1,386.7	1,487.9	1,602.8	1,867.4	1,426.6	1,401.8	1,831.2	2,077.2	....	....	....
Grants Received	81z	19.2	29.9	13.2	10.8	20.7	8.8	5.6	13.2	2.9	....	....	....
Expenditure	82	1,871.4	1,912.7	1,971.2	1,879.4	1,848.0	1,820.1	1,859.4	2,179.5	2,295.1	....	....	....
Lending Minus Repayments	83	16.6	−10.2	−2.0	−6.1	68.4	−7.8	22.1	28.1	109.1	....	....	....
Financing													
Domestic	84a	211.2	141.8	46.4	−250.6	35.5	9.1	105.7	76.6	86.4	....	....	....
Foreign	85a	299.9	344.1	421.7	510.3	−7.2	367.8	368.4	286.6	237.7	....	....	....
Debt: Domestic	88a	291.0	313.9	306.7	325.2	314.1	471.0	493.1	392.1	623.4	....	....	....
Foreign	89a	1,020.8	1,148.8	1,148.0	1,201.1	1,132.5	1,086.1	1,118.4	1,064.8	900.5	....	....	....
National Accounts		*Millions of Rials Omani*											
Househ.Cons.Expend.,incl.NPISHs.	96f	2,389	2,349	2,600	2,799	2,901	3,120	3,001	3,000	3,174	3,365	3,652	....
Government Consumption Expend.	91f	1,333	1,429	1,462	1,446	1,415	1,402	1,440	1,580	1,823	1,800	1,853	....
Gross Capital Formation	93	842	782	795	805	1,075	1,299	897	912	967	997	1,307	....
Exports of Goods and Services	90c	2,068	2,136	2,337	2,926	3,047	2,229	2,937	4,515	4,392	4,455	4,663	....
Imports of Goods and Services (-)	98c	1,828	1,728	1,887	2,101	2,348	2,633	2,234	2,368	2,687	2,808	3,132	....
Gross Domestic Product (GDP)	99b	4,804	4,967	5,307	5,874	6,090	5,416	6,041	7,639	7,668	7,809	8,343	....
Net Primary Income from Abroad	98.n	−634	−683	−713	−695	−727	−747	−815	−282	−275	−302	−347	....
Gross National Income (GNI)	99a	4,154	4,121	4,594	5,179	5,363	4,669	5,226	7,357	7,393	7,507	7,996	....
GDP Volume 1988 Prices	99b.p	4,395	4,564	4,784	4,923	5,227	5,368	5,356	5,650	6,175	6,177	6,330	....
GDP Volume (2000=100)	99bvp	77.8	80.8	84.7	87.1	92.5	95.0	94.8	100.0	109.3	109.3	112.0	....
GDP Deflator (2000=100)	99bip	† 80.8	80.5	82.0	88.2	86.2	74.6	83.4	100.0	91.8	93.5	97.5	....
		Millions: Midyear Estimates											
Population	99z	2.05	2.11	2.18	2.24	2.30	2.35	2.40	2.44	2.47	2.49	2.51	2.53

Pakistan 564

		1993	1994	1995	1996	1997	1998	1999	2000	2001	2002	2003	2004
Exchange Rates					*Rupees per SDR: End of Period (aa)*								
Market Rate	aa	41.372	44.963	50.912	57.691	59.434	64.608	† 71.075	75.607	76.489	79.578	85.020	91.820
					Rupees per US Dollar: End of Period (ae) Period Average (rf)								
Market Rate	ae	30.120	30.800	34.250	40.120	44.050	45.885	† 51.785	58.029	60.864	58.534	57.215	59.124
Market Rate	rf	28.107	30.567	31.643	36.079	41.112	45.047	† 49.501	53.648	61.927	59.724	57.752	58.258
					Index Numbers (2000=100): Period Averages								
Nominal Effective Exchange Rate	nec	161.54	151.64	139.37	127.03	119.93	110.96	100.95	100.00	91.76	93.48	87.67	81.55
Real Effective Exchange Rate	rec	111.42	108.91	108.20	106.07	109.34	104.83	98.84	100.00	93.05	96.73	92.56	91.29
Fund Position					*Millions of SDRs: End of Period*								
Quota	2f.s	758	758	758	758	758	758	1,034	1,034	1,034	1,034	1,034	1,034
SDRs	1b.s	1	—	10	9	8	1	—	11	3	2	167	158
Reserve Position in the Fund	1c.s	—	—	—	—	—	—	—	—	—	—	—	—
Total Fund Cred.&Loans Outstg	2tl	817	1,097	1,115	1,001	980	996	1,271	1,198	1,456	1,506	1,425	1,208
International Liquidity					*Millions of US Dollars Unless Otherwise Indicated: Last Thursday of Period*								
Total Reserves minus Gold	1l.d	1,197	2,929	1,733	548	1,195	1,028	1,511	1,513	3,640	8,078	10,941	9,799
SDRs	1b.d	1	—	15	13	11	1	—	14	4	2	248	245
Reserve Position in the Fund	1c.d	—	—	—	—	—	—	—	—	—	—	—	—
Foreign Exchange	1d.d	1,196	2,929	1,718	535	1,184	1,027	1,511	1,499	3,636	8,076	10,693	9,554
Gold (Million Fine Troy Ounces)	1ad	2.044	2.052	2.055	2.056	2.066	2.077	2.088	2.091	2.091	2.093	2.096	2.099
Gold (National Valuation)	1and	692	792	721	689	635	618	543	543	595	684	733	817
Monetary Authorities: Other Liab	4..d	552	271	226	689	615	856	890	973	950	705	713	708
Deposit Money Banks: Assets	7a.d	1,405	1,582	1,605	1,546	1,406	1,281	1,365	1,440	1,771	1,574	1,582	3,175
Liabilities	7b.d	2,490	2,380	3,007	3,373	2,330	2,091	1,614	1,331	898	585	478	646
Monetary Authorities					*Millions of Rupees: Last Thursday of Period*								
Foreign Assets	11	56,923	115,577	86,701	61,805	93,159	77,768	104,870	115,554	249,986	511,539	676,336	632,633
Claims on General Government	12a	210,037	202,251	254,327	303,324	274,745	347,900	502,118	551,497	403,433	193,576	32,541	283,342
of which: Provincial Government	12ax	5,524	2,258	5,184	15,931	12,700	12,657	8,050	3,388	874	874	37,067	7,242
Claims on Deposit Money Banks	12e	78,137	89,110	98,220	67,864	119,962	171,286	192,862	195,646	184,842	160,603	194,671	207,726
Reserve Money	14	244,175	282,541	333,207	321,058	367,082	414,627	468,491	458,843	588,677	640,534	746,510	895,970
of which: Currency Outside DMBs	14a	177,856	195,827	234,011	252,069	272,052	301,146	341,024	410,469	429,360	487,745	567,519	655,287
Restricted Deposits	16b	—	—	—	—	—	—	8,115	11,124	13,187	18,049	19,315	22,862
Foreign Liabilities	16c	50,415	48,580	54,219	73,717	66,552	75,892	103,921	95,481	133,768	106,954	81,064	56,963
General Government Deposits	16d	37,304	37,682	34,365	28,502	30,603	63,742	138,006	199,021	43,203	96,550	71,757	70,976
Counterpart Funds	16e	671	614	644	686	644	585	660	532	589	562	607	648
Other Items (Net)	17r	12,533	37,524	16,813	9,030	22,985	42,110	80,659	77,694	58,836	3,068	−15,706	76,281
Deposit Money Banks					*Millions of Rupees: Last Thursday of Period*								
Reserves	20	68,030	93,268	109,689	80,122	100,518	119,696	145,480	81,205	169,195	150,861	172,747	233,785
Foreign Assets	21	42,306	48,721	54,958	62,022	61,940	58,800	70,682	83,534	107,789	92,157	90,535	187,711
Claims on General Government	22a	208,114	251,172	263,013	333,162	396,083	395,218	321,548	355,499	325,670	601,005	689,873	548,460
of which: Provincial Government	22ax	10,870	11,488	13,387	11,657	13,081	16,355	19,846	44,262	43,617	35,485	22,854	21,707
Claims on Private Sector	22d	337,082	385,463	464,913	538,370	613,944	686,932	761,793	868,069	929,064	978,492	1,215,181	1,636,664
Demand Deposits	24	191,613	235,265	253,189	269,947	420,823	423,091	447,919	457,173	524,429	628,531	816,587	1,026,569
Time Deposits	25	230,515	278,960	322,037	448,144	470,719	530,230	521,619	600,662	685,205	809,592	878,563	1,043,698
Foreign Liabilities	26c	74,987	73,295	102,995	135,309	102,617	95,936	83,579	77,248	54,662	34,230	27,330	38,223
General Government Deposits	26d	19,224	41,168	47,719	47,800	47,799	66,536	96,763	84,259	102,692	131,705	165,510	196,745
Counterpart Funds	26e	−196	−181	−8	—	—	—	—	—	—	—	—	—
Central Government Lending Funds	26f	13,074	12,235	11,853	11,788	11,634	11,676	11,493	11,244	11,148	11,071	16,154	7
Credit from Monetary Authorities	26g	66,564	77,758	86,766	57,795	108,583	126,448	148,604	144,839	120,372	136,900	155,270	176,354
Other Items (Net)	27r	59,751	60,123	68,023	42,896	10,310	6,729	−10,474	12,282	33,210	70,487	108,922	125,024
Monetary Survey					*Millions of Rupees: Last Thursday of Period*								
Foreign Assets (Net)	31n	−26,173	42,424	−15,555	−85,199	−14,070	−35,260	−11,948	6,358	169,345	462,512	658,478	725,158
Domestic Credit	32	731,780	797,149	941,758	1,140,771	1,246,571	1,349,909	1,411,041	1,560,180	1,553,264	1,577,662	1,726,304	2,219,519
Claims on General Govt. (Net)	32an	361,623	374,573	435,256	560,184	592,426	612,840	588,897	623,716	583,208	566,326	485,147	564,081
Claims on Private Sector	32d	370,157	422,576	506,502	580,587	654,345	737,069	822,144	936,464	970,056	1,011,336	1,241,157	1,655,438
Money	34	378,111	435,388	490,961	528,011	699,806	732,291	795,370	876,014	964,921	1,118,403	1,387,601	1,687,355
Quasi-Money	35	230,515	278,960	322,037	448,144	470,719	530,230	521,619	600,662	685,205	809,592	878,563	1,043,698
Restricted Deposits	36b	—	—	—	—	—	—	8,115	11,124	13,187	18,049	19,315	22,862
Counterpart Funds	36e	475	433	636	686	644	585	660	532	589	562	607	648
Central Government Lending Funds	36f	13,074	12,235	11,853	11,788	11,634	11,676	11,493	11,244	11,148	11,071	16,154	7
Other Items (Net)	37r	83,433	112,558	100,717	66,946	49,898	39,869	61,838	66,961	47,558	82,497	82,540	190,106
Money plus Quasi-Money	35l	608,626	714,348	812,998	976,155	1,170,525	1,262,521	1,316,989	1,476,676	1,650,126	1,927,995	2,266,163	2,731,053
Other Banking Institutions					*Millions of Rupees: Last Thursday of Period*								
Post Office: Savings Deposits	45..i	8,586	9,891	12,370	14,189	18,622	22,473	27,603	36,022	39,638	59,445	76,193	53,336
Liquid Liabilities	55l	617,212	724,239	825,368	990,344	1,189,147	1,284,994	1,344,592	1,512,698	1,689,764	1,987,440	2,342,356	2,784,389
Interest Rates					*Percent Per Annum*								
Discount Rate (End of Period)	60	10.00	† 15.00	17.00	20.00	18.00	16.50	13.00	13.00	10.00	7.50	7.50	7.50
Money Market Rate	60b	11.00	8.36	11.52	11.40	12.10	10.76	9.04	8.57	8.49	5.53	2.14	2.70
Treasury Bill Rate	60c	13.03	11.26	12.49	13.61	† 15.74	....	....	8.38	10.71	6.08	1.93	2.48
Government Bond Yield	61	7.40	7.07	6.63	6.06	5.43	4.79	4.16	....	....	....	....	....
Prices, Production, Labor					*Index Numbers (2000=100): Period Averages*								
Share Prices	62	125.5	204.1	145.2	119.2	111.2	80.2	79.2	100.0	75.6	82.2	141.7	219.7
Wholesale Prices	63	52.5	62.9	70.9	78.7	87.6	89.6	96.2	100.0	104.6	† 107.7	114.6	124.3
Consumer Prices	64	55.8	62.7	70.5	77.8	86.6	92.0	95.8	100.0	† 103.1	106.5	109.6	117.8
Manufacturing Production	66ey	84.7	87.0	90.5	89.9	89.5	95.8	102.9	100.0	† 110.3	114.3	130.3	153.4
					Number in Thousands: Period Averages								
Labor Force	67d	34,726	33,324	33,191	34,342	36,407	38,174	39,400	38,005	40,662	42,388	....	....
Employment	67e	30,534	31,288	31,407	32,491	34,597	36,419	37,296	36,847	37,481	38,882	....	....
Unemployment	67c	1,516	1,591	1,783	1,845	2,254	2,279	2,334	3,127	3,181	3,506	....	....
Unemployment Rate (%)	67r	4.7	4.8	5.4	5.4	6.1	5.9	5.9	7.8	7.8	8.3	....	....

		1993	1994	1995	1996	1997	1998	1999	2000	2001	2002	2003	2004
Intl. Transactions & Positions							*Millions of Rupees*						
Exports	70	187,787	225,200	252,714	335,313	359,046	382,477	417,322	484,476	572,471	591,714	688,882	779,286
Imports, c.i.f.	71	265,142	271,744	362,686	437,769	476,346	419,311	505,451	582,681	631,005	670,575	752,788	1,045,981
							2000=100						
Volume of Exports	72	75.0	92.6	73.4	87.0	†81.9	79.5	89.3	100.0	102.1	109.3	109.9	103.1
Volume of Imports	73	89.5	86.4	93.6	91.6	†94.3	89.5	101.3	100.0	112.1	123.0	122.7	141.6
Unit Value of Exports	74	47.0	55.1	69.4	76.8	†88.1	98.4	101.0	100.0	108.4	100.0	103.6	111.9
Unit Value of Imports	75	43.9	51.4	58.1	64.2	†74.2	72.1	85.5	100.0	108.5	105.5	116.8	132.3
Balance of Payments						*Millions of US Dollars: Minus Sign Indicates Debit*							
Current Account, n.i.e.	78ald	−2,901	−1,812	−3,349	−4,436	−1,712	−2,248	−920	−85	1,878	3,854	3,573	−808
Goods: Exports f.o.b.	78aad	6,793	7,117	8,356	8,507	8,351	7,850	7,673	8,739	9,131	9,832	11,869	13,352
Goods: Imports f.o.b.	78abd	−9,380	−9,355	−11,248	−12,164	−10,750	−9,834	−9,520	−9,896	−9,741	−10,428	−11,978	−16,735
Trade Balance	78acd	−2,586	−2,239	−2,891	−3,656	−2,399	−1,984	−1,847	−1,157	−610	−596	−109	−3,382
Services: Credit	78add	1,573	1,753	1,857	2,016	1,625	1,404	1,373	1,380	1,459	2,429	2,968	2,726
Services: Debit	78aed	−2,639	−2,529	−2,938	−3,459	−2,658	−2,261	−2,146	−2,252	−2,330	−2,241	−3,294	−5,322
Balance on Goods & Services	78afd	−3,652	−3,015	−3,972	−5,099	−3,433	−2,841	−2,620	−2,029	−1,481	−408	−435	−5,978
Income: Credit	78agd	63	149	187	175	147	83	119	118	113	128	180	221
Income: Debit	78ahd	−1,610	−1,830	−2,125	−2,198	−2,366	−2,263	−1,959	−2,336	−2,189	−2,414	−2,404	−2,582
Balance on Gds, Serv. & Inc.	78aid	−5,199	−4,695	−5,910	−7,121	−5,652	−5,021	−4,460	−4,247	−3,557	−2,694	−2,659	−8,340
Current Transfers, n.i.e.: Credit	78ajd	2,337	2,919	2,611	2,739	3,981	2,801	3,582	4,200	5,496	6,593	6,300	7,672
Current Transfers: Debit	78akd	−38	−35	−49	−54	−40	−28	−42	−38	−61	−45	−68	−140
Capital Account, n.i.e.	78bcd	—	—	—	—	—	....	....	....	....	40	1,138	597
Capital Account, n.i.e.: Credit	78bad	—	—	—	—	—	....	....	....	....	40	1,140	602
Capital Account: Debit	78bbd	—	—	—	—	—	....	....	....	—	—	−2	−5
Financial Account, n.i.e.	78bjd	3,334	2,977	2,449	3,496	2,321	−1,873	−2,364	−3,099	−389	−784	−1,751	−1,729
Direct Investment Abroad	78bdd	2	−1	—	−7	24	−50	−21	−11	−31	−28	−19	−56
Dir. Invest. in Rep. Econ., n.i.e.	78bed	349	421	723	922	716	506	532	308	383	823	534	1,118
Portfolio Investment Assets	78bfd	—	—	—	—	—	....	....	....	....	....	−2	9
Equity Securities	78bkd	—	—	—	—	—	....	....	....	....	....	−2	9
Debt Securities	78bld	—	—	—	—	—	....	....	....	....	....		
Portfolio Investment Liab., n.i.e.	78bgd	293	1,471	4	261	279	−57	46	−451	−192	−567	−119	393
Equity Securities	78bmd	225	1,254	10	285	330	−22	66	35	−130	79	−26	50
Debt Securities	78bnd	68	217	−6	−24	−51	−35	−20	−486	−62	−646	−93	343
Financial Derivatives Assets	78bwd	....	....	....	....	....	....	....	....	....	....	....	....
Financial Derivatives Liabilities	78bxd	....	....	....	....	....	....	....	....	....	....	....	....
Other Investment Assets	78bhd	−286	−283	−196	−164	−21	44	−523	−437	53	−64	−542	−1,338
Monetary Authorities	78bod	....	....	....	....	....	....	....	....	....	—	—	—
General Government	78bpd	46	−19	6	116	96	247	−358	−15	44	−5	19	−1
Banks	78bqd	−86	−108	−116	8	−40	172	−25	−18	−17	−6	−247	−985
Other Sectors	78brd	−246	−157	−85	−288	−77	−375	−140	−404	26	−53	−314	−353
Other Investment Liab., n.i.e.	78bid	2,976	1,369	1,919	2,484	1,323	−2,316	−2,398	−2,508	−602	−948	−1,603	−1,855
Monetary Authorities	78bsd	−140	−282	−50	474	−71	91	−262	−168	−13	−254	—	1
General Government	78btd	1,260	1,132	1,034	700	1,878	−795	2	−729	−37	−162	−1,571	−1,294
Banks	78bud	613	313	613	310	−1,044	−663	−1,292	−1,160	−14	−81	29	14
Other Sectors	78bvd	1,244	205	321	1,000	559	−949	−846	−451	−538	−451	−61	−575
Net Errors and Omissions	78cad	−6	178	−304	160	−72	1,011	768	557	708	974	−52	589
Overall Balance	78cbd	428	1,343	−1,204	−780	538	−3,110	−2,516	−2,627	2,197	4,084	2,908	−1,351
Reserves and Related Items	79dad	−428	−1,343	1,204	780	−538	3,110	2,516	2,627	−2,197	−4,084	−2,908	1,351
Reserve Assets	79dbd	−426	−1,744	1,180	946	−511	222	−842	7	−2,716	−4,525	−3,003	1,728
Use of Fund Credit and Loans	79dcd	−4	401	23	−166	−27	20	391	−101	328	68	−112	−323
Exceptional Financing	79ded	2	—	—	—	—	2,868	2,966	2,721	192	373	207	−55
Government Finance						*Millions of Rupees: Year Ending June 30*							
Deficit (-) or Surplus	80	−118,999	−113,462	−123,742	−169,477	−189,788	−171,925	−202,024	−172,117	−160,994	−176,274p	−140,442	−153,717
Revenue	81	242,812	273,238	321,323	370,510	384,263	433,636	464,372	531,300	535,091	619,069p	701,576	760,983
Grants Received	81z	—	5,665	5,513	4,804	—	—	—	37,991	46,779	91,136p	57,450	34,483
Expenditure	82	330,509	362,891	425,418	515,219	547,768	584,624	627,147	725,642	739,662	837,396p	899,611	905,549
Lending Minus Repayments	83	31,302	29,474	25,160	29,572	26,283	20,937	39,249	15,766	3,202	49,083p	−143	43,634
Financing													
Domestic	84a	86,815	78,040	82,235	128,717	142,159	129,295	91,750	143,408	85,878	142,272p	93,029	173,539
Foreign	85a	32,184	35,422	41,507	40,760	47,629	42,630	110,274	28,709	75,116	34,002p	47,413	−19,822
Debt	88	1,058,682	....	....	....	....	2,117,616	....	2,832,571	....	....	2,887,134	....
Domestic	88a	612,642	....	....	....	....	1,183,232	....	1,659,121	....	....	1,858,406	....
Foreign	89a	446,040	....	....	....	....	934,384	....	1,173,450	....	....	1,028,728	....
National Accounts						*Billions of Rupees: Year Ending June 30*							
Househ.Cons.Expend.,incl.NPISHs	96f	962.40	1,109.90	1,351.40	1,545.20	1,818.20	1,929.70	2,224.00	2,851.35	3,163.87	3,278.91	3,547.45	3,987.49
Government Consumption Expend	91f	174.68	189.10	219.12	268.10	288.81	301.61	304.40	330.69	327.56	388.45	438.06	493.98
Gross Fixed Capital Formation	93e	256.40	280.50	317.80	368.10	396.90	402.80	409.40	607.41	659.33	680.37	713.86	892.51
Changes in Inventories	93i	21.10	24.60	28.20	34.34	38.28	71.40	48.00	51.70	56.20	58.00	93.00	94.40
Exports of Goods and Services	90c	217.37	254.18	311.80	358.37	390.52	441.41	451.10	514.28	617.15	677.86	815.16	874.63
Imports of Goods and Services (-)	98c	299.15	297.30	362.41	454.29	504.37	469.31	498.50	561.99	661.46	681.88	786.22	884.94
Gross Domestic Product (GDP)	99b	1,332.80	1,561.10	1,865.90	2,120.20	2,428.30	2,677.70	2,938.40	3,793.44	4,162.65	4,401.70	4,821.30	5,458.06
Net Primary Income from Abroad	98.n	9.96	4.00	14.04	−7.14	−19.35	−24.36	−25.55	−47.96	−54.48	23.67	151.81	118.24
Gross National Income (GNI)	99a	1,342.80	1,565.10	1,880.00	2,113.00	2,409.00	2,653.30	2,912.80	3,745.48	4,108.17	4,425.36	4,973.12	5,576.31
Consumption of Fixed Capital	99cf	86.30	100.10	119.40	136.20	159.20	180.70	188.50	317.25	342.91	366.76	391.00	446.02
GDP Volume 1981 Prices	99b.p	549.45	570.86	600.19	630.15	629.55	645.61	669.24	697.75	....	....	....	....
GDP Volume 2000 Prices	99b.p	....	....	....	....	....	....	....	3,793.44	3,863.99	3,988.38	4,193.76	4,445.81
GDP Volume (2000=100)	99bvp	78.7	81.8	86.0	90.3	90.2	92.5	95.9	†100.0	101.9	105.1	110.6	117.2
GDP Deflator (2000=100)	99bip	44.6	50.3	57.2	61.9	70.9	76.3	80.8	100.0	107.7	110.4	115.0	122.8
							Millions: Midyear Estimates						
Population	99z	120.29	123.10	126.08	129.25	132.58	†136.00	139.38	142.65	145.77	148.79	151.77	154.79

Panama   283

		1993	1994	1995	1996	1997	1998	1999	2000	2001	2002	2003	2004
Exchange Rates						*Balboas per SDR: End of Period*							
Official Rate	aa	1.3736	1.4599	1.4865	1.4380	1.3493	1.4080	1.3725	1.3029	1.2567	1.3595	1.4860	1.5530
						Balboas per US Dollar: End of Period							
Official Rate	ae	1.0000	1.0000	1.0000	1.0000	1.0000	1.0000	1.0000	1.0000	1.0000	1.0000	1.0000	1.0000
Fund Position						*Millions of SDRs: End of Period*							
Quota	2f.s	149.6	149.6	149.6	149.6	149.6	149.6	206.6	206.6	206.6	206.6	206.6	206.6
SDRs	1b.s	.1	—	.6	—	.4	.1	1.2	.3	1.1	.8	.6	.6
Reserve Position in the Fund	1c.s	11.9	11.9	11.9	11.9	11.9	11.9	11.9	11.9	11.9	11.9	11.9	11.9
Total Fund Cred.&Loans Outstg	2tl	82.3	91.3	74.4	91.0	105.4	125.5	108.3	69.1	42.9	36.7	30.0	23.3
International Liquidity						*Millions of US Dollars Unless Otherwise Indicated: End of Period*							
Total Reserves minus Gold	1l.d	597.4	704.3	781.4	866.5	1,147.8	954.5	822.9	722.6	1,091.8	1,182.8	1,011.0	630.6
SDRs	1b.d	.1	—	.8	—	.5	.1	1.6	.3	1.4	1.1	.8	.9
Reserve Position in the Fund	1c.d	16.3	17.3	17.6	17.1	16.0	16.7	16.3	15.5	14.9	16.1	17.6	18.4
Foreign Exchange	1d.d	581.0	686.9	762.9	849.4	1,131.3	937.7	805.0	706.8	1,075.5	1,165.6	992.5	611.4
Gold (National Valuation)	1and	—	—	—	—	—	—	—	—	—	—	—	—
Monetary Authorities: Other Liab.	4..d	334	292	343	158	149	123	118	108	104	90	74	70
Deposit Money Banks: Assets	7a.d	12,735	16,617	15,664	15,484	16,595	13,209	12,362	12,620	12,521	10,061	9,870	11,805
Liabilities	7b.d	11,336	14,846	13,930	13,954	14,825	11,745	11,845	11,776	12,081	9,568	8,415	9,761
Monetary Authorities						*Millions of Balboas: End of Period*							
Foreign Assets	11	597.4	704.3	781.4	866.5	1,147.8	954.5	822.9	722.6	1,091.8	1,182.8	1,011.0	630.6
Claims on Central Government	12a	1,050.1	1,014.0	945.6	1,280.9	1,080.7	1,099.7	1,047.3	839.2	791.9	806.6	759.3	1,087.0
Claims on Official Entities	12bx												
Claims on Private Sector	12d	322.8	300.6	318.8	301.0	292.7	403.2	583.8	747.8	976.0	1,118.9	1,228.3	1,304.7
Claims on Deposit Money Banks	12e	633.0	732.8	948.8	615.4	765.2	949.4	999.8	908.6	607.1	264.2	103.6	72.2
Bankers Deposits	14c	184.4	167.4	172.7	266.0	252.7	272.6	284.1	301.8	280.0	276.6	278.2	285.4
Demand Deposits	14d	63.0	75.4	77.0	83.0	105.8	97.8	80.6	80.7	104.0	99.5	96.7	106.0
Time, Savings,& Fgn.Currency Dep.	15	187.3	192.5	205.0	227.2	240.8	283.4	296.5	367.4	474.0	594.0	619.1	612.9
Foreign Liabilities	16c	447.0	425.0	453.7	289.0	291.7	299.6	266.5	198.4	157.5	140.3	118.2	106.4
Central Government Deposits	16d	1,550.6	1,716.2	1,857.8	1,871.5	2,025.2	2,039.7	2,094.5	1,883.8	2,061.0	1,918.7	1,664.0	1,512.6
Capital Accounts	17a	196.0	228.3	297.7	424.9	471.5	543.9	536.1	534.3	533.1	535.8	539.1	540.9
Other Items (Net)	17r	−24.9	−53.2	−69.4	−97.8	−101.4	−130.1	−104.5	−148.2	−142.8	−192.3	−213.1	−69.7
Deposit Money Banks						*Millions of Balboas: End of Period*							
Foreign Assets	21	12,735.2	16,616.6	15,663.9	15,483.8	16,595.2	13,208.7	12,362.1	12,620.5	12,521.1	10,061.4	9,870.0	11,804.7
Claims on Central Government	22a	104.8	74.3	62.3	79.4	73.2	86.2	143.0	160.9	135.9	269.1	371.0	367.0
Claims on Private Sector	22d	4,332.5	5,118.6	5,852.4	6,347.6	7,294.0	9,010.2	10,507.1	11,092.3	11,842.8	10,881.9	10,645.0	11,220.0
Demand Deposits	24	645.2	728.6	737.7	758.3	889.7	1,027.5	1,062.2	1,095.0	1,193.0	1,224.0	1,360.0	1,508.0
Time and Savings Deposits	25	3,296.0	3,845.5	4,204.2	4,476.5	5,138.6	5,795.3	6,376.7	7,054.9	7,653.6	7,478.0	7,769.0	8,448.9
Foreign Liabilities	26c	11,336.5	14,845.9	13,929.8	13,954.3	14,825.0	11,744.7	11,844.5	11,775.8	12,081.2	9,568.0	8,415.0	9,760.6
Capital Accounts	27a	1,008.0	1,321.3	1,431.8	1,660.8	1,945.1	2,171.5	2,257.8	2,551.9	2,561.3	2,356.0	2,745.0	3,319.0
Other Items (Net)	27r	886.9	1,068.2	1,275.1	1,060.9	1,164.1	1,566.1	1,471.0	1,396.1	1,010.7	586.4	597.0	355.2
Monetary Survey						*Millions of Balboas: End of Period*							
Foreign Assets (Net)	31n	1,549.2	2,050.0	2,061.7	2,107.0	2,626.3	2,118.9	1,074.0	1,368.9	1,374.1	1,535.9	2,347.8	2,568.3
Domestic Credit	32	4,259.6	4,791.3	5,321.3	6,137.3	6,715.5	8,559.6	10,186.7	10,956.4	11,685.6	11,157.9	11,339.6	12,466.1
Claims on Central Govt. (Net)	32an	−395.7	−627.9	−849.9	−511.3	−871.2	−853.8	−904.2	−883.6	−1,133.2	−842.9	−533.7	−58.6
Claims on Private Sector	32d	4,655.3	5,419.2	6,171.2	6,648.6	7,586.7	9,413.4	11,090.9	11,840.1	12,818.8	12,000.8	11,873.3	12,524.7
Deposit Money	34	708.2	804.1	814.7	841.3	995.5	1,125.2	1,142.7	1,175.8	1,296.9	1,323.5	1,456.7	1,614.0
Quasi-Money	35	3,483.3	4,038.0	4,409.2	4,703.7	5,379.4	6,078.7	6,673.2	7,422.3	8,127.6	8,072.0	8,388.1	9,061.8
Capital Accounts	37a	1,203.9	1,549.6	1,729.6	2,085.7	2,416.6	2,715.4	2,794.0	3,086.2	3,094.4	2,891.8	3,284.1	3,859.9
Other Items (Net)	37r	413.4	449.6	429.6	613.7	550.3	759.1	650.8	641.1	540.7	406.5	558.4	498.7
Money plus Quasi-Money	35l	4,191.5	4,842.1	5,223.9	5,544.9	6,374.9	7,203.9	7,815.9	8,598.0	9,424.6	9,395.6	9,844.9	10,675.8
Interest Rates						*Percent Per Annum*							
Money Market Rate	60b	....	....	....	....	....	....	....	....	....	2.22	1.50	1.90
Savings Rate	60k	....	....	....	....	....	....	....	....	2.83	2.23	1.55	1.36
Deposit Rate	60l	5.90	6.11	7.18	7.20	7.03	6.76	6.92	7.07	6.83	4.97	3.98	2.23
Lending Rate	60p	10.06	10.15	11.10	10.62	10.63	10.82	10.05	† 10.48	10.97	10.58	9.93	8.82
Prices, Production and Labor						*Index Numbers (2000=100): Period Averages*							
Wholesale Prices	63	88.8	90.7	93.4	95.3	93.2	89.6	92.0	100.0	96.8	93.9	95.5	99.7
Consumer Prices	64	92.2	93.4	94.3	95.5	96.8	97.3	98.5	100.0	100.3	101.3	† 102.7	103.0
Manufacturing Production (1995)	66ey	96.1	99.3	100.0	99.9	105.6	109.8	105.3	....	....	....	....	....
						Number in Thousands: Period Averages							
Labor Force	67d	940	967	1,008	....	1,049	1,049	1,089	....	....	....	....	....
Employment	67e	816	832	867	867	909	937	961	940	984	1,050	1,081	....
Unemployment	67c	125	135	141	145	140	147	128	147	170	172	170	....
Unemployment Rate (%)	67r	13.3	14.0	14.0	14.3	13.4	13.6	11.8	13.5	14.7	14.1	13.6	....
Intl. Transactions & Positions						*Millions of Balboas*							
Exports	70	553.2	583.3	625.2	....	722.8	784.1	822.1	859.5	910.5	846.4	864.2	943.7
Imports, c.i.f.	71	2,187.8	2,404.1	2,510.7	2,779.9	3,002.0	3,398.3	3,515.8	3,378.7	2,963.5	2,982.0	3,086.1	3,594.2
Imports, f.o.b.	71.v	1,979.6	2,177.5	2,280.2	2,548.1	2,738.5	2,806.4	3,214.7	3,097.7	2,714.5	....	....	....
						2000=100							
Volume of Exports	72	100.2	....	....	....	....	133.6	107.1	100.0	....	81.0	84.5	83.3

Panama 283

		1993	1994	1995	1996	1997	1998	1999	2000	2001	2002	2003	2004
Balance of Payments		*Millions of US Dollars: Minus Sign Indicates Debit*											
Current Account, n.i.e.	78ald	−95.7	15.9	−470.6	−200.6	−506.7	−1,016.0	−1,158.8	−672.5	−170.3	−95.5	−437.2	−1,104.3
Goods: Exports f.o.b.	78aad	5,416.9	6,044.8	6,090.9	5,822.9	6,669.7	6,331.8	5,288.1	5,838.5	5,992.4	5,314.7	5,048.9	5,885.6
Goods: Imports f.o.b.	78abd	−5,751.1	−6,294.9	−6,679.8	−6,467.0	−7,354.9	−7,627.3	−6,628.1	−6,981.4	−6,688.6	−6,349.8	−6,161.6	−7,470.9
Trade Balance	78acd	−334.2	−250.1	−588.9	−644.1	−685.2	−1,295.5	−1,340.0	−1,142.9	−696.2	−1,035.1	−1,112.7	−1,585.3
Services: Credit	78add	1,297.4	1,403.7	1,519.4	1,592.0	1,720.7	1,891.5	1,847.5	1,994.4	1,992.8	2,277.9	2,556.6	2,725.8
Services: Debit	78aed	−976.4	−1,064.3	−1,087.8	−1,034.0	−1,293.2	−1,253.3	−1,146.3	−1,140.8	−1,102.9	−1,309.8	−1,302.5	−1,430.4
Balance on Goods & Services	78afd	−13.2	89.3	−157.3	−86.1	−257.7	−657.3	−638.8	−289.3	193.7	−67.0	141.4	−289.9
Income: Credit	78agd	1,054.7	1,202.9	1,644.1	1,422.1	1,436.0	1,679.3	1,500.5	1,575.3	1,384.0	953.2	769.5	786.0
Income: Debit	78ahd	−1,340.3	−1,425.2	−2,110.0	−1,671.3	−1,835.6	−2,196.6	−2,191.6	−2,135.5	−1,974.1	−1,225.5	−1,589.4	−1,828.4
Balance on Gds, Serv. & Inc.	78aid	−298.8	−133.0	−623.2	−335.3	−657.3	−1,174.6	−1,329.9	−849.5	−396.4	−339.3	−678.5	−1,332.3
Current Transfers, n.i.e.: Credit	78ajd	236.5	185.5	184.1	167.7	185.2	195.2	202.7	208.7	277.9	298.8	301.8	323.3
Current Transfers: Debit	78akd	−33.4	−36.6	−31.5	−33.0	−34.6	−36.6	−31.6	−31.7	−51.8	−55.0	−60.5	−95.3
Capital Account, n.i.e.	78bcd	....	....	8.5	2.5	72.7	50.9	3.0	1.7	1.6	—	—	—
Capital Account, n.i.e.: Credit	78bad	....	....	8.5	2.5	72.7	50.9	3.0	1.7	1.6	—	—	—
Capital Account: Debit	78bbd	....	....	....	....	....	....	—	—	—	—	—	—
Financial Account, n.i.e.	78bjd	−521.4	−288.2	115.6	561.2	972.3	1,249.2	1,836.9	331.8	1,301.0	194.3	25.4	1,007.5
Direct Investment Abroad	78bdd	....	....	....	....	....	—	—	—	—	—	—	—
Dir. Invest. in Rep. Econ., n.i.e.	78bed	169.6	401.5	223.0	415.5	1,299.3	1,203.1	755.6	623.9	467.1	98.6	791.5	1,012.3
Portfolio Investment Assets	78bfd	−754.6	−48.4	318.5	487.8	−1,036.5	431.7	−550.2	−93.0	−752.7	−11.9	−59.3	−605.2
Equity Securities	78bkd	....	....	.2	−10.2	−.8	−5.1	−28.7	2.0	−1.2	3.0	3.0	−1.7
Debt Securities	78bld	−754.6	−48.4	318.3	498.0	−1,035.7	436.8	−521.5	−95.0	−751.5	−14.9	−62.3	−603.5
Portfolio Investment Liab., n.i.e.	78bgd	−54.7	−.4	−.3	−67.1	−80.3	209.2	239.5	163.7	727.1	102.2	139.6	775.9
Equity Securities	78bmd	−.1	.4	.2	−.1	−.1	—	—	—	—	—	—	—
Debt Securities	78bnd	−54.6	−.8	−.5	−67.0	−80.2	209.2	239.5	163.7	727.1	102.2	139.6	775.9
Financial Derivatives Assets	78bwd	....	....	....	....	....	—	—	—	—	—	—	—
Financial Derivatives Liabilities	78bxd	....	....	....	....	....	—	—	—	—	—	—	—
Other Investment Assets	78bhd	−1,281.4	−5,277.7	−371.3	406.2	−478.7	772.8	1,991.8	489.3	818.4	3,270.4	464.1	−889.3
Monetary Authorities	78bod	....	....	....	....	....	....	−5.2	5.2	—	—	—	—
General Government	78bpd	−.9	....	−1.0	−38.2	−2.3	−263.3	266.6	−4.0	−2.1	−.9	10.4	1.5
Banks	78bqd	−1,186.6	−5,254.4	−176.3	533.1	−276.1	1,284.6	1,968.7	185.4	1,016.2	3,294.5	588.2	−652.7
Other Sectors	78brd	−93.9	−23.3	−194.0	−88.7	−200.3	−248.5	−238.3	302.7	−195.7	−23.2	−134.5	−238.1
Other Investment Liab., n.i.e.	78bid	1,399.7	4,636.8	−54.3	−681.2	1,268.5	−1,367.6	−599.8	−852.1	41.1	−3,265.0	−1,310.5	713.8
Monetary Authorities	78bsd	.8	−1.3	54.6	−1.7	6.8	−1.0	−.7	−6.4	3.7	−.9	1.6	—
General Government	78btd	−117.5	−198.8	−36.1	−50.5	130.4	85.6	33.7	−2.6	3.5	46.1	10.2	−37.0
Banks	78bud	1,606.7	4,915.5	−122.8	−793.7	1,033.2	−1,446.8	−550.8	−425.5	−3.3	−3,311.7	−1,325.0	701.9
Other Sectors	78bvd	−90.3	−78.6	50.0	164.7	98.1	−5.4	−82.0	−417.6	37.2	1.5	2.7	48.9
Net Errors and Omissions	78cad	309.0	−89.5	15.2	−96.3	−195.0	−389.1	−490.1	262.5	−498.6	45.2	257.3	−299.4
Overall Balance	78cbd	−308.1	−361.8	−331.3	266.8	343.3	−105.0	191.0	−76.5	633.7	144.0	−154.5	−396.1
Reserves and Related Items	79dad	308.1	361.8	331.3	−266.8	−343.3	105.0	−191.0	76.5	−633.7	−144.0	154.5	396.1
Reserve Assets	79dbd	−93.0	−105.7	−77.7	−297.7	−611.1	19.8	−184.5	108.1	−623.3	−135.9	164.1	397.0
Use of Fund Credit and Loans	79dcd	3.4	12.5	−25.9	24.2	19.6	27.3	−23.5	−51.7	−33.3	−8.1	−9.5	−10.0
Exceptional Financing	79ded	397.7	454.9	434.9	6.8	248.2	57.9	17.0	20.1	22.9	—	—	9.1
International Investment Position		*Millions of US Dollars*											
Assets	79aad	....	....	25,275.7	24,677.0	26,871.0	25,636.9	24,379.8	23,880.9	24,395.3	21,273.9	20,706.6	21,804.9
Direct Investment Abroad	79abd	....	....										
Portfolio Investment	79acd	....	....	1,889.4	1,401.6	2,438.1	2,006.4	2,556.6	2,649.6	3,373.0	3,384.8	3,444.1	4,049.3
Equity Securities	79add	....	....	7.6	17.8	18.6	23.7	52.4	50.4	51.6	48.6	45.6	47.3
Debt Securities	79aed	....	....	1,881.8	1,383.8	2,419.5	1,982.7	2,504.2	2,599.2	3,321.4	3,336.2	3,398.5	4,002.0
Financial Derivatives	79ald	....	....										
Other Investment	79afd	....	....	22,605.0	22,196.8	22,675.5	21,892.3	19,901.0	19,418.2	18,586.4	15,316.0	14,851.9	15,741.2
Monetary Authorities	79agd	....	....					5.2					
General Government	79ahd	....	....	27.7	63.9	66.2	329.5	62.9	66.9	69.0	69.9	59.5	58.0
Banks	79aid	....	....	20,768.8	20,235.7	20,511.8	19,227.2	17,258.5	17,073.1	16,043.5	12,749.0	12,160.8	12,813.5
Other Sectors	79ajd	....	....	1,808.5	1,897.2	2,097.5	2,335.6	2,574.4	2,278.2	2,473.9	2,497.1	2,631.6	2,869.7
Reserve Assets	79akd	....	....	781.3	1,078.6	1,757.4	1,738.2	1,922.2	1,813.1	2,435.9	2,573.2	2,410.6	2,014.4
Liabilities	79lad	....	....	31,056.1	30,081.7	32,548.8	32,658.1	33,000.6	32,300.8	33,502.2	30,382.1	29,804.7	32,289.6
Dir. Invest. in Rep. Economy	79lbd	....	....	3,244.6	3,660.1	4,959.4	6,260.1	7,015.6	6,774.9	7,314.3	7,412.9	8,204.4	9,216.7
Portfolio Investement	79lcd	....	....	432.7	3,593.9	3,528.5	3,733.8	3,948.2	4,097.6	4,821.4	4,833.7	4,956.8	5,702.8
Equity Securities	79ldd	....	....	.1	—	—	—	—	—	—	—	—	—
Debt Securities	79led	....	....	432.6	3,593.9	3,528.5	3,733.8	3,948.2	4,097.6	4,821.4	4,833.7	4,956.8	5,702.8
Financial Derivatives	79lld	....	....										
Other Investment	79lfd	....	....	27,378.8	22,827.7	24,060.9	22,664.2	22,036.8	21,428.3	21,366.5	18,135.5	16,643.5	17,370.1
Monetary Authorities	79lgd	....	....	271.5	290.1	309.9	343.5	314.7	246.3	213.9	208.9	205.3	196.9
General Government	79lhd	....	....	4,637.4	1,086.8	1,178.0	1,339.3	1,398.1	1,353.6	1,335.1	1,417.2	1,435.3	1,417.7
Banks	79lid	....	....	20,710.4	19,916.7	20,949.9	19,456.3	18,939.8	18,520.3	18,470.0	15,158.3	13,648.3	14,350.2
Other Sectors	79ljd	....	....	1,759.5	1,534.1	1,623.1	1,525.1	1,384.2	1,308.1	1,347.5	1,351.1	1,354.7	1,405.3
Government Finance		*Millions of Balboas: Year Ending December 31*											
Deficit (-) or Surplus	80	284.7	146.0	230.5	−60.9	17.9	−64.2	34.4	30.2	....	....	....	....
Revenue	81	1,950.8	2,010.5	2,065.1	2,140.3	2,202.8	2,331.2	2,664.5	2,688.4	....	....	....	....
Grants Received	81z	27.8	15.5	8.5	4.6	63.5	72.3	6.8	17.8	....	....	....	....
Expenditure	82	1,768.6	1,958.7	1,953.3	2,255.3	2,341.3	2,606.8	2,650.9	2,803.9	....	....	....	....
Lending Minus Repayments	83	−74.7	−78.7	−110.2	−49.5	−92.9	−139.1	−14.0	−127.9	....	....	....	....
Financing													
Total Financing	84	−284.7	−146.0	−230.5	60.9	−17.9	64.2	−34.4	−30.2	....	....	....	....
Domestic	84a	−226.2	−135.2	−253.2	3.7	−133.6	−297.9	−237.2	−200.7	....	....	....	....
Foreign	85a	−58.5	−10.8	22.7	57.2	115.7	362.1	202.8	170.5	....	....	....	....
Debt: Domestic	88a	1,810.1	1,805.6	1,681.4	1,794.2	1,737.5	1,737.6	2,108.8	2,090.4	2,089.0	2,122.1	2,094.3	....
Debt: Foreign	89a	2,600.2	2,812.9	3,001.5	4,542.2	4,659.6	5,042.5	5,457.6	5,552.3	6,243.3	6,298.0	6,420.8	....

		1993	1994	1995	1996	1997	1998	1999	2000	2001	2002	2003	2004
National Accounts							*Millions of Balboas*						
Househ.Cons.Expend.,incl.NPISHs....	96f	4,063.4	4,150.7	4,090.0	5,456.1	5,790.3	6,781.3	7,146.0	6,962.2	7,276.3	7,885.2	7,784.6	....
Government Consumption Expend....	91f	1,098.3	1,144.8	1,194.1	1,256.8	1,260.8	1,386.9	1,492.4	1,532.9	1,646.1	1,819.3	1,845.3	....
Gross Fixed Capital Formation..........	93e	1,681.3	1,828.8	2,057.9	1,878.4	2,021.3	2,441.4	2,556.5	2,461.9	1,794.2	1,664.8	2,207.3	....
Changes in Inventories.....................	93i	111.9	244.8	336.3	613.9	567.9	533.7	398.6	343.2	288.3	268.1	249.4	....
Exports of Goods and Services..........	90c	7,014.6	7,711.6	7,979.4	7,777.6	9,086.2	8,656.1	7,623.0	8,433.6	8,586.5	8,278.9	8,231.4	....
Imports of Goods and Services (-).....	98c	6,716.8	7,346.8	7,751.6	7,666.7	8,642.5	8,866.9	7,760.2	8,113.3	7,783.9	7,643.9	7,455.6	....
Gross Domestic Product (GDP).........	99b	7,942.3	8,469.2	8,657.8	9,322.1	10,084.0	10,932.5	11,456.3	11,620.5	11,807.5	12,272.4	12,862.4	....
Net Primary Income from Abroad.....	98.n	−338.6	−272.3	−421.5	−319.6	−451.4	−608.8	−790.7	−700.5	....	....	....	....
Gross National Income (GNI)............	99a	6,914.1	7,461.6	7,484.6	8,744.0	9,354.5	10,113.6	10,565.6	10,781.9	10,897.4	11,706.7	11,814.9	....
Consumption of Fixed Capital..........	99cf	497.0	533.3	558.9	639.3	790.4	814.4	915.4	747.2	958.2	981.7	1,004.2	....
GDP Volume 1996 Prices.................	99b.p	8,296.2	8,532.6	8,682.1	9,322.1	9,924.4	10,653.0	11,070.3	11,370.9	11,436.2	11,691.1	12,196.2	12,957.4
GDP Volume (2000=100)...............	99bvp	73.0	75.0	76.4	82.0	87.3	93.7	97.4	100.0	100.6	102.8	107.3	114.0
GDP Deflator (2000=100)...............	99bip	93.7	97.1	97.6	97.9	99.4	100.4	101.3	100.0	101.0	102.7	103.2	....
						Millions: Midyear Estimates							
Population.................................	99z	2.56	2.62	2.67	2.73	2.78	2.84	2.89	2.95	3.01	3.06	3.12	3.18

		1993	1994	1995	1996	1997	1998	1999	2000	2001	2002	2003	2004
Exchange Rates		*SDRs per Kina: End of Period*											
Official Rate	ac	.7419	.5812	.5039	.5164	.4232	.3388	.2703	.2498	.2115	.1830	.2019	.2061
		US Dollars per Kina: End of Period (ag) Period Average (rh)											
Official Rate	ag	1.0190	.8485	.7490	.7425	.5710	.4770	.3710	.3255	.2658	.2488	.3000	.3200
Official Rate	rh	1.0221	.9950	.7835	.7588	.6975	.4859	.3939	.3617	.2964	.2573	.2814	.3104
		Index Numbers (2000=100): Period Averages											
Official Rate	ahx	282.6	275.1	216.6	209.8	192.8	134.3	108.9	100.0	81.9	71.2	77.8	85.8
Nominal Effective Exchange Rate	nec	217.9	224.9	171.3	168.9	166.3	128.2	103.0	100.0	88.0	75.2	73.8	75.4
Real Effective Exchange Rate	rec	134.8	127.5	108.3	116.5	116.7	99.6	91.0	100.0	93.6	87.6	97.1	99.2
Fund Position		*Millions of SDRs: End of Period*											
Quota	2f.s	95.30	95.30	95.30	95.30	95.30	95.30	131.60	131.60	131.60	131.60	131.60	131.60
SDRs	1b.s	.03	.07	.47	.04	.06	.04	.53	9.34	6.93	4.46	2.48	.47
Reserve Position in the Fund	1c.s	.05	.05	.05	.05	.05	.05	.05	.18	.30	.36	.40	.43
Total Fund Cred.&Loans Outstg.	2tl	32.13	10.71	33.34	35.34	35.34	32.35	15.68	29.89	85.54	85.54	81.79	41.38
International Liquidity		*Millions of US Dollars Unless Otherwise Indicated: Approximately End of Period*											
Total Reserves minus Gold	1l.d	141.45	96.06	261.35	583.89	362.68	192.88	205.14	286.87	422.65	321.51	494.18	632.56
SDRs	1b.d	.05	.11	.69	.06	.08	.05	.72	12.17	8.71	6.06	3.68	.73
Reserve Position in the Fund	1c.d	.07	.08	.08	.08	.07	.07	.07	.23	.38	.49	.59	.66
Foreign Exchange	1d.d	141.34	95.88	260.58	583.75	362.53	192.76	204.35	274.46	413.56	314.96	489.90	631.17
Gold (Million Fine Troy Ounces)	1ad	.063	.063	.014	.063	.063	.063	.063	.063	.063	.063	.063	.063
Gold (National Valuation)	1and	11.30	2.39	2.11	21.02	16.17	13.31	10.35	9.08	7.42	21.89	25.83	27.55
Monetary Authorities: Other Liab.	4..d	3.64	84.39	62.28	3.39	2.79	.66	.73	.76	1.53	.67	3.96	.18
Deposit Money Banks: Assets	7a.d	160.59	175.61	100.11	119.12	117.38	136.34	103.23	95.83	112.18	153.11	106.67	116.61
Liabilities	7b.d	88.07	120.46	41.39	23.07	7.99	54.53	37.44	18.13	24.24	25.99	16.88	21.94
Monetary Authorities		*Millions of Kina: Last Wednesday of Period*											
Foreign Assets	11	138.61	112.51	357.55	789.20	666.07	391.06	552.92	909.24	1,617.94	1,380.18	1,733.33	2,062.90
Claims on Central Government	12a	421.02	776.65	592.62	587.28	880.81	1,284.96	599.66	163.60	160.19	790.21	705.98	728.25
Claims on Nonfin.Pub.Enterprises	12c	—	—	—	—	—	—	—	—	—	—	—	—
Claims on Private Sector	12d	.68	.55	.64	.67	.75	.64	3.35	5.75	3.54	3.74	4.45	4.92
Claims on Deposit Money Banks	12e	239.43	282.50	233.80	228.94	216.27	121.10	53.63	53.27	52.15	52.09	50.06	23.68
Claims on Nonbank Financial Insts.	12g	—	—	—	—	—	—	—	—	—	—	4.53	—
Reserve Money	14	199.20	221.65	255.66	488.98	321.12	387.47	671.55	561.51	592.26	699.02	785.22	868.10
of which: Currency Outside DMBs	14a	160.70	179.00	194.21	216.40	234.85	278.09	357.49	306.93	308.98	379.94	417.93	445.33
Time Deposits	15	.50	.50	.50	.50	.50	.50	.50	.50	.50	.42	1.08	5.70
Liabs. of Central Bank:Securities	16ac	—	—	—	—	—	—	—	—	—	—	—	264.43
Foreign Liabilities	16c	46.89	117.88	149.33	73.01	88.39	96.88	59.97	121.95	410.19	470.11	418.33	201.40
Central Government Deposits	16d	369.66	663.01	623.10	840.32	977.77	916.71	100.24	30.76	274.50	242.49	506.23	727.90
Capital Accounts	17a	208.07	140.20	122.57	122.13	245.05	254.78	261.74	329.89	506.68	589.51	781.66	721.94
Other Items (Net)	17r	−24.57	28.95	33.45	81.15	131.08	141.41	115.55	87.23	49.68	224.69	5.82	30.28
Deposit Money Banks		*Millions of Kina: Last Wednesday of Period*											
Reserves	20	36.68	40.67	56.20	116.43	67.21	106.03	310.37	250.67	279.48	310.49	385.81	443.75
Foreign Assets	21	157.59	206.97	133.66	160.44	205.57	285.83	278.26	294.40	422.06	615.40	355.55	364.40
Claims on Central Government	22a	502.65	446.27	727.57	1,105.13	1,107.80	888.60	791.57	1,065.24	1,121.02	991.41	1,163.57	1,769.14
Claims on Local Governments	22b	6.22	5.95	1.58	1.91	1.29	5.05	5.46	1.05	.94	2.38	6.04	3.67
Claims on Nonfin.Pub.Enterprises	22c	294.69	374.70	329.25	315.00	297.71	202.94	153.06	123.02	113.64	125.69	95.04	44.32
Claims on Private Sector	22d	820.27	897.99	900.78	908.93	1,223.08	1,577.98	1,554.88	1,668.15	1,601.47	1,503.57	1,448.75	1,381.06
Claims on Nonbank Financial Insts.	22g	6.84	—	—	—	—	—	—	—	—	—	12.92	24.71
Demand Deposits	24	431.77	433.46	501.18	692.31	752.74	829.35	982.38	1,061.86	1,104.17	1,241.13	1,474.95	1,880.69
Time, Savings,& Fgn. Currency Dep.	25	1,091.68	1,049.85	1,192.55	1,410.43	1,659.12	1,620.62	1,638.32	1,758.57	1,765.73	1,681.63	1,401.10	1,372.65
Foreign Liabilities	26c	86.43	141.79	55.26	31.07	14.00	114.33	100.91	55.70	91.19	104.48	56.27	68.56
Central Government Deposits	26d	51.45	73.13	122.48	167.22	170.65	287.49	211.71	255.06	309.80	282.60	240.36	274.67
Credit from Monetary Authorities	26g	239.43	282.50	233.80	228.94	216.28	121.10	53.63	53.39	52.15	52.09	50.06	23.68
Capital Accounts	27a	60.63	78.36	92.65	114.78	139.25	212.80	332.05	284.09	374.62	426.13	537.28	581.43
Other Items (Net)	27r	−136.45	−86.72	−48.88	−36.92	−49.39	−119.26	−225.40	−66.14	−159.07	−239.12	−292.33	−170.62
Monetary Survey		*Millions of Kina: Last Wednesday of Period*											
Foreign Assets (Net)	31n	162.88	59.63	286.63	845.56	769.26	465.68	670.29	1,025.98	1,538.61	1,420.99	1,614.28	2,157.33
Domestic Credit	32	1,631.25	1,765.96	1,806.86	1,911.38	2,363.02	2,755.96	2,796.02	2,740.98	2,416.48	2,891.92	2,694.69	2,953.51
Claims on Central Govt. (Net)	32an	502.55	486.77	574.60	684.87	840.19	969.35	1,079.27	943.01	696.90	1,256.53	1,122.96	1,494.83
Claims on Local Government	32b	6.22	5.95	1.58	1.91	1.29	5.05	5.46	1.05	.94	2.38	6.04	3.67
Claims on Nonfin.Pub.Enterprises	32c	294.69	374.70	329.25	315.00	297.71	202.94	153.06	123.02	113.64	125.69	95.04	44.32
Claims on Private Sector	32d	820.95	898.54	901.42	909.60	1,223.83	1,578.62	1,558.23	1,673.90	1,605.00	1,507.32	1,453.20	1,385.99
Claims on Nonbank Financial Insts.	32g	6.84	—	—	—	—	—	—	—	—	—	17.46	24.71
Money	34	594.29	614.48	700.64	1,064.87	1,006.66	1,110.79	1,343.56	1,372.69	1,416.95	1,629.66	1,897.48	2,330.79
Quasi-Money	35	1,092.18	1,050.35	1,193.05	1,410.93	1,659.62	1,621.12	1,638.82	1,759.07	1,766.23	1,682.05	1,402.18	1,378.35
Capital Accounts	37a	268.70	218.56	215.22	236.91	384.30	467.58	593.78	613.99	881.31	1,015.64	1,318.94	1,303.37
Other Items (Net)	37r	−161.03	−57.81	−15.42	44.23	81.69	22.15	−109.85	21.22	−109.39	−14.43	−309.64	98.34
Money plus Quasi-Money	35l	1,686.46	1,664.83	1,893.69	2,475.80	2,666.29	2,731.91	2,982.37	3,131.76	3,183.18	3,311.71	3,299.67	3,709.14
Money (National Definitions)		*Millions of Kina: Last Wednesday of Period*											
Reserve Money	19mb	....	219.62	250.40	332.83	302.10	384.20	667.86	557.61	588.40	690.40	785.20	863.30
M1*	59maa	527.54	571.31	645.86	864.89	919.50	1,021.30	1,233.70	1,271.71	1,321.20	1,535.30	1,708.30	2,214.70
M3*	59mca	1,625.35	1,664.71	1,842.24	2,431.56	2,598.20	2,645.80	2,880.00	3,034.68	3,091.30	3,226.00	3,109.80	3,597.80
Interest Rates		*Percent Per Annum*											
Discount Rate (End of Period)	60	† 6.30	6.55	† 18.00	14.86	9.49	17.07	16.66	9.79	11.73	11.71	† 15.50	12.67
Treasury Bill Rate	60c	6.25	6.85	† 17.40	14.44	9.94	21.18	22.70	17.00	12.36	10.93	18.69	8.85
Savings Rate	60k	....	....	4.00	4.00	3.83	3.94	4.13	4.06	3.88	2.44	2.40	1.63
Deposit Rate	60l	5.03	5.09	† 7.30	7.13	4.13	8.36	8.13	8.46	5.46	3.18	4.38	1.73
Lending Rate	60p	11.29	9.16	13.14	13.30	10.45	17.70	18.90	17.54	16.21	13.89	13.36	13.25
Prices and Labor		*Index Numbers (2000=100): Period Averages*											
Consumer Prices	64	47.3	48.7	57.1	63.7	66.3	75.3	86.5	100.0	109.3	122.2	140.2	143.1
Total Employment	67	89.6	96.2	91.7	98.5	98.3	96.1	98.5	† 100.0	98.2	99.7	107.3	108.4

Papua New Guinea 853

		1993	1994	1995	1996	1997	1998	1999	2000	2001	2002	2003	2004
Intl. Transactions & Positions							*Millions of Kina*						
Exports	70	2,435.5	2,670.4	3,388.3	3,313.6	3,048.8	3,707.7	4,879.4	5,812.7	6,076.6	6,386.7	7,842.3	8,233.3
Imports, c.i.f.	71	1,264.2	1,530.8	1,862.4	2,296.6	2,429.0	2,549.6	3,059.0	3,195.7	3,633.0	4,826.3	4,825.8	5,408.6
Imports, f.o.b.	71.v	1,104.9	1,333.1	1,619.6	1,996.5	2,112.1	2,217.0	2,660.0	2,778.9	3,160.0	4,196.8	4,196.4	4,703.1
							2000=100						
Volume of Exports	72	108.5	† 108.3	101.1	95.8	85.4	94.9	102.7	100.0	† 94.4	88.1	104.8	97.9
Unit Value of Exports	74	27.2	† 31.7	45.5	47.1	50.3	60.5	74.2	100.0	† 108.9	119.7	129.4	146.4
Balance of Payments						*Millions of US Dollars: Minus Sign Indicates Debit*							
Current Account, n.i.e.	78ald	474.1	402.1	491.9	188.9	−192.2	−28.9	94.7	345.4	282.1	....	....	....
Goods: Exports f.o.b.	78aad	2,604.4	2,651.0	2,670.4	2,529.8	2,160.1	1,773.3	1,927.4	2,094.1	1,812.9	....	....	....
Goods: Imports f.o.b.	78abd	−1,134.7	−1,324.9	−1,262.4	−1,513.3	−1,483.3	−1,078.3	−1,071.4	−998.8	−932.4	....	....	....
Trade Balance	78acd	1,469.7	1,326.1	1,408.0	1,016.6	676.8	695.0	856.0	1,095.3	880.5	....	....	....
Services: Credit	78add	306.7	235.4	321.3	432.2	396.9	318.0	247.5	242.7	285.1	....	....	....
Services: Debit	78aed	−804.6	−608.0	−642.1	−778.5	−923.6	−793.8	−727.9	−772.3	−662.0	....	....	....
Balance on Goods & Services	78afd	971.8	953.5	1,087.2	670.2	150.1	219.2	375.6	565.7	503.7	....	....	....
Income: Credit	78agd	31.3	22.4	22.5	32.1	35.1	20.9	18.6	32.0	20.0	....	....	....
Income: Debit	78ahd	−400.2	−423.4	−510.7	−461.2	−344.8	−279.7	−291.1	−242.1	−250.2	....	....	....
Balance on Gds, Serv. & Inc.	78aid	603.0	552.5	599.1	241.1	−159.5	−39.6	103.1	355.6	273.4	....	....	....
Current Transfers, n.i.e.: Credit	78ajd	49.0	58.8	66.7	252.1	69.9	82.4	60.3	62.4	75.9	....	....	....
Current Transfers: Debit	78akd	−178.0	−209.3	−173.9	−304.2	−102.6	−71.6	−68.7	−72.7	−67.3	....	....	....
Capital Account, n.i.e.	78bcd	—	—	—	—	—	—	—	—	—	....	....	....
Capital Account, n.i.e.: Credit	78bad	20.4	19.9	15.7	15.2	13.9	9.7	7.8	7.2	5.9	....	....	....
Capital Account: Debit	78bbd	−20.4	−19.9	−15.7	−15.2	−13.9	−9.7	−7.8	−7.2	−5.9	....	....	....
Financial Account, n.i.e.	78bjd	−716.2	−609.2	−444.7	46.6	8.0	−179.7	16.0	−254.1	−151.9	....	....	....
Direct Investment Abroad	78bdd	....	....	....	....	....	....	....	....	....	....	....	....
Dir. Invest. in Rep. Econ., n.i.e.	78bed	62.0	57.0	454.6	111.3	28.6	109.6	296.5	95.9	62.5	....	....	....
Portfolio Investment Assets	78bfd	−50.9	−2.1	−48.7	69.9	−25.5	87.0	89.0	−123.8	−72.7	....	....	....
Equity Securities	78bkd	—	—	....	....	....	....	....	....	....	....	....	....
Debt Securities	78bld	−50.9	−2.1	−48.7	69.9	−25.5	87.0	89.0	−123.8	−72.7	....	....	....
Portfolio Investment Liab., n.i.e.	78bgd	....	....	—	—	—	—	—	—	—	....	....	....
Equity Securities	78bmd	....	....	....	....	....	....	....	....	....	....	....	....
Debt Securities	78bnd	....	....	....	....	....	....	....	....	....	....	....	....
Financial Derivatives Assets	78bwd	....	....	....	....	....	....	....	....	....	....	....	....
Financial Derivatives Liabilities	78bxd	....	....	....	....	....	....	....	....	....	....	....	....
Other Investment Assets	78bhd	17.3	58.8	−283.8	180.0	29.6	−55.0	10.7	−41.0	−66.9	....	....	....
Monetary Authorities	78bod	....	....	....	....	....	....	....	....	....	....	....	....
General Government	78bpd	—	—	....	....	....	....	....	....	....	....	....	....
Banks	78bqd	....	....	....	....	....	....	−2.1	−21.2	−26.7	....	....	....
Other Sectors	78brd	17.3	58.8	−283.8	180.0	29.6	−55.0	12.8	−19.8	−40.2	....	....	....
Other Investment Liab., n.i.e.	78bid	−744.5	−722.9	−566.8	−314.6	−24.7	−321.2	−380.2	−185.2	−74.7	....	....	....
Monetary Authorities	78bsd	—	—	—	−68.2	—	—	—	—	—	....	....	....
General Government	78btd	66.5	−102.1	−23.5	10.0	−62.7	−44.2	39.4	.2	49.0	....	....	....
Banks	78bud	−110.3	−26.9	27.4	−34.0	−42.3	16.4	—	—	—	....	....	....
Other Sectors	78bvd	−700.8	−593.9	−570.7	−222.4	80.3	−293.4	−419.6	−185.4	−123.7	....	....	....
Net Errors and Omissions	78cad	−11.3	37.1	−86.6	−33.1	7.3	−12.5	14.3	13.1	−1.6	....	....	....
Overall Balance	78cbd	−253.4	−170.1	−39.5	202.5	−177.0	−221.0	125.0	104.5	128.6	....	....	....
Reserves and Related Items	79dad	253.4	170.1	39.5	−202.5	177.0	221.0	−125.0	−104.5	−128.6	....	....	....
Reserve Assets	79dbd	96.6	33.8	−177.4	−329.7	83.7	149.1	−49.7	−127.9	−203.6	....	....	....
Use of Fund Credit and Loans	79dcd	−15.0	−30.6	35.0	2.9	—	−4.2	−22.8	18.1	70.9	....	....	....
Exceptional Financing	79ded	171.8	166.8	181.9	124.4	93.2	76.1	−52.5	5.3	4.1	....	....	....
Government Finance					*Millions of Kina: Year Ending December 31*								
Deficit (-) or Surplus	80	−283.55	† −136.78	−31.77	35.39	15.41	−137.40	−241.79	−181.40	−132.51	−263.81	....	....
Total Revenue and Grants	81y	1,310.65	† 1,443.43	1,692.95	1,896.12	2,024.01	1,991.20	2,216.11	2,865.41	2,836.06	2,666.47	....	....
Revenue	81	1,128.95	† 1,278.62	1,499.84	1,730.67	1,711.98	1,686.46	1,750.59	2,459.72	2,724.83	2,618.91	....	....
Grants	81z	181.70	† 164.81	193.11	165.45	312.03	304.74	465.52	405.69	111.23	47.56	....	....
Exp. & Lending Minus Repay	82z	1,594.20	† 1,580.21	1,724.72	1,860.73	2,008.60	2,128.60	2,457.90	3,046.81	2,968.57	2,930.28	....	....
Expenditure	82	1,588.71	† 1,580.99	1,721.93	1,857.29	2,003.70	2,127.26	2,457.83	3,048.41	2,968.57	2,930.28	....	....
Lending Minus Repayments	83	5.49	† −.78	2.79	3.44	4.90	1.34	.07	−1.60	—	—	....	....
Total Financing	80h	283.55	† 136.78	31.77	−35.39	−15.40	137.40	241.80	181.40	132.51	263.81	....	....
Domestic	84a	237.83	† 255.22	75.30	−45.49	57.90	253.72	304.29	1.50	−177.05	519.16	....	....
Foreign	85a	45.72	† −118.44	−43.53	10.10	−73.30	−116.32	−62.49	179.90	309.56	−255.35	....	....
Total Debt by Residence	88	2,157.40	† 2,961.20	3,324.20	3,780.80	4,418.00	5,177.70	5,609.20	5,621.60	7,097.30	8,127.90	....	....
Domestic	88a	1,036.60	† 1,424.30	1,605.70	1,969.50	2,251.70	2,473.00	2,021.40	1,783.30	2,115.10	2,530.50	....	....
Foreign	89a	1,120.80	† 1,536.90	1,718.50	1,811.30	2,166.30	2,704.70	3,587.80	3,838.30	4,982.20	5,597.40	....	....
National Accounts							*Millions of Kina*						
Househ.Cons.Expend.,incl.NPISHs.	96f	2,046	2,240	2,454	3,375	4,119	4,620	6,123	6,462	8,451	9,882	....	....
Government Consumption Expend.	91f	1,199	1,001	1,006	1,370	1,361	1,407	1,488	1,741	1,822	1,929	....	....
Gross Fixed Capital Formation	93e	901	1,012	1,150	1,186	1,079	1,089	1,063	2,145	2,374	2,443	....	....
Changes in Inventories	93i	−43	142	149	375	409	307	377	144	186	206	....	....
Exports of Goods and Services	90c	2,562	3,031	3,675	3,575	3,312	3,942	4,153	4,720	4,975	5,189	....	....
Imports of Goods and Services (-)	98c	1,798	2,044	2,545	3,000	3,217	3,575	4,423	4,462	6,050	6,274	....	....
Gross Domestic Product (GDP)	99b	4,867	5,381	5,888	6,881	7,064	7,789	8,781	10,750	11,758	13,375	....	....
Net Primary Income from Abroad	98.n	−330	−246	−208	−307	−310	−343	−360	−391	−408	−406	....	....
Gross National Income (GNI)	99a	4,537	5,136	5,681	6,574	6,754	7,445	8,421	9,734	10,550	12,064	....	....
Consumption of Fixed Capital	99cf	433	502	571	589	535	540	527	2,145	2,374	2,443	....	....
GDP Volume 1990 Prices	99b.p	4,625	4,900	4,738	5,104	4,905	5,120	5,077	5,014	4,845	4,818	....	....
GDP Volume (2000=100)	99bvp	† 92.2	97.7	94.5	101.8	97.8	102.1	101.3	100.0	96.6	96.1	....	....
GDP Deflator (2000=100)	99bip	49.1	51.2	58.0	62.9	67.2	71.0	80.7	100.0	113.2	129.5	....	....
							Millions: Midyear Estimates						
Population	99z	4.45	4.57	4.69	4.81	† 4.93	5.05	5.18	5.30	5.42	5.54	5.66	5.77

		1993	1994	1995	1996	1997	1998	1999	2000	2001	2002	2003	2004
Exchange Rates					*Guaranies per SDR: End of Period*								
Market Rate...................aa=.........	wa	2,582.3	2,809.8	2,942.7	3,033.6	3,184.2	3,999.1	4,568.9	4,595.2	5,884.0	9,657.5	9,086.6	9,706.3
				Guaranies per US Dollar: End of Period (we) Period Average (wf)									
Market Rate...................ae=.........	we	1,880.0	1,924.7	1,979.7	2,109.7	2,360.0	2,840.2	3,328.9	3,526.9	4,682.0	7,103.6	6,115.0	6,250.0
Market Rate...................rf=.........	wf	1,744.3	1,904.8	1,963.0	2,056.8	2,177.9	2,726.5	3,119.1	3,486.4	4,105.9	5,716.3	6,424.3	5,974.6
				Index Numbers (2000=100): Period Averages									
Market Rate........................	ahx	200.1	183.0	177.6	169.5	160.1	128.1	112.2	100.0	85.6	62.1	54.5	58.4
Nominal Effective Exchange Rate.....	nec	91.6	133.8	136.0	135.6	137.5	115.7	107.1	100.0	91.9	70.0	57.7	58.7
Real Effective Exchange Rate...........	rec	96.8	101.2	102.7	107.0	112.8	103.5	100.7	100.0	95.6	78.1	71.1	73.8
Fund Position					*Millions of SDRs: End of Period*								
Quota..	2f.s	72.10	72.10	72.10	72.10	72.10	72.10	99.90	99.90	99.90	99.90	99.90	99.90
SDRs...	1b.s	65.08	67.63	70.58	73.30	76.08	79.14	74.81	78.49	81.33	83.25	84.63	86.04
Reserve Position in the Fund...........	1c.s	16.48	14.53	14.53	14.53	14.53	14.53	21.48	21.48	21.48	21.48	21.48	21.48
Total Fund Cred.&Loans Outstg.......	2tl	—	—	—	—	—	—	—	—	—	—	—	—
International Liquidity				*Millions of US Dollars Unless Otherwise Indicated: End of Period*									
Total Reserves minus Gold..............	1l.d	631.18	1,030.73	1,092.91	1,049.29	835.68	864.74	978.05	762.83	713.51	629.19	968.86	1,168.05
SDRs...................................	1b.d	89.39	98.73	104.92	105.40	102.65	111.44	102.68	102.26	102.21	113.18	125.75	133.62
Reserve Position in the Fund..........	1c.d	22.63	21.20	21.59	20.89	19.60	20.45	29.48	27.98	26.99	29.20	31.91	33.35
Foreign Exchange.........................	1d.d	519.16	910.80	966.40	923.00	713.42	732.85	845.89	632.58	584.32	486.82	811.19	1,001.07
of which: US Dollars..................	1dxd	416.00	583.80	602.40	415.53	521.25	561.87	736.13	525.20	467.98	353.95	674.97	749.50
Gold (Million Fine Troy Ounces)........	1ad	.035	.035	.035	.035	.035	.035	.035	.035	.035	.035	.035	—
Gold (National Valuation)...............	1and	13.70	13.40	13.50	12.90	10.10	10.03	10.15	9.60	9.66	12.14	14.51	—
Monetary Authorities:Other Assets...	3..d	39.40	3.98	3.44	3.44	3.44	7.07	9.84	14.06	12.41	3.25	9.03	7.43
Other Liab.................	4..d	84.60	86.57	85.11	76.47	67.87	60.76	53.37	44.88	93.88	115.11	63.96	80.16
Deposit Money Banks: Assets...........	7a.d	300.39	298.21	502.97	474.74	378.52	416.19	402.43	498.84	447.92	288.26	389.83	383.75
Liabilities..................	7b.d	147.37	124.57	453.01	256.93	304.67	232.03	119.86	105.33	96.63	69.12	46.44	50.41
Other Banking Insts.: Assets.............	7e.d	—	—	.34	.67	12.91	11.01	9.63	15.76	18.88	4.30	3.64	2.09
Liabilities..................	7f.d	36.40	32.78	—	—	8.54	2.12	.60	2.01	1.79	.72	4.32	3.92
Monetary Authorities					*Billions of Guaranies: End of Period*								
Foreign Assets..............................	11	1,289.15	2,016.58	† 2,239.16	2,263.63	1,993.00	2,521.04	3,341.31	2,804.01	3,420.08	4,528.71	6,038.97	7,362.96
Claims on Central Government..........	12a	916.73	1,047.15	† 1,038.99	1,088.06	695.48	928.81	1,113.16	1,063.78	1,477.66	2,240.39	2,159.88	2,256.35
Claims on Local Government...........	12b	.82	.82	† .67	.62	1.06	1.11	1.16	1.21	1.26	1.31	1.36	1.41
Claims on Nonfin.Pub.Enterprises.....	12c	266.79	222.35	† 239.15	268.00	303.76	329.42	358.39	381.19	216.23	283.50	291.82	364.87
Claims on Private Sector..................	12d	6.29	6.58	† 7.24	11.90	14.73	18.41	22.28	25.61	28.05	32.57	34.23	34.07
Claims on Deposit Money Banks......	12e	102.77	98.07	† 580.74	840.71	528.45	45.40	4.57	7.19	6.64	4.26	1.66	1.60
Claims on Other Banking Insts........	12f	16.21	15.65	† 21.31	104.20	20.03	33.85	26.94	35.98	44.16	58.07	27.00	—
Claims on Nonbank Financial Insts....	12g	—	—	† 23.14	21.34	86.65	96.05	103.46	113.11	123.08	133.01	142.87	152.21
Reserve Money..............................	14	1,083.20	1,378.91	† 1,738.50	1,704.98	1,829.88	1,949.68	2,127.14	2,105.35	2,234.23	2,293.74	3,461.11	4,063.10
of which: Currency Outside DMBs..	14a	635.77	800.46	† 956.00	961.77	1,122.90	1,264.08	1,398.68	1,327.19	1,377.21	1,451.20	1,814.57	2,116.69
Time & Foreign Currency Deposits.....	15	406.51	455.51	† 448.56	648.47	635.95	833.43	1,040.74	1,090.23	1,366.33	1,577.06	1,599.30	1,777.26
Liabs. of Central Bank: Securities.....	16ac	8.53	35.50	† 201.90	250.79	319.05	381.75	75.88	45.93	284.47	578.50	1,070.96	1,551.75
Restricted Deposits.........................	16b	17.11	26.47	† 26.01	51.75	54.55	58.21	72.21	80.31	87.29	124.18	131.52	110.90
Foreign Liabilities..........................	16c	159.04	166.62	† 168.94	161.28	158.14	172.57	176.91	159.11	435.14	805.79	388.26	500.19
Central Government Deposits...........	16d	134.37	414.23	† 580.16	572.39	469.51	553.16	1,327.51	813.38	723.61	730.01	1,120.48	1,188.92
Capital Accounts...........................	17a	303.95	332.20	† 519.10	611.14	2,381.56	1,619.77	2,138.81	2,151.12	2,589.63	4,076.37	2,708.77	2,935.68
Other Items (Net)..........................	17r	486.04	597.76	† 467.22	597.65	−2,205.47	−1,594.49	−1,987.93	−2,013.36	−2,403.53	−2,903.84	−1,782.57	−1,954.33
Deposit Money Banks					*Billions of Guaranies: End of Period*								
Reserves......................................	20	743.99	913.28	† 1,032.56	1,173.75	1,189.09	1,421.92	1,636.09	1,740.62	2,106.19	2,250.36	3,085.37	3,508.21
Claims on Mon.Author.:Securities.....	20c	8.53	35.50	† 173.67	238.76	287.18	209.91	60.79	39.94	172.61	324.57	642.36	1,210.28
Foreign Assets..............................	21	549.71	573.75	† 998.40	1,001.22	881.95	1,181.98	1,334.07	1,768.39	2,076.09	2,017.85	2,366.29	2,394.57
Claims on Central Government........	22a	.18	—	† 46.59	98.35	187.73	286.85	454.60	356.87	294.61	534.58	656.78	562.24
Claims on Local Government...........	22b	.55	.01	† 22.00	1.57	7.07	36.64	5.55	8.98	4.35	.95	1.78	5.85
Claims on Nonfin.Pub.Enterprises.....	22c	1.45	1.46	† —	—	—	.79	1.27	—	.02	—	—	—
Claims on Private Sector.................	22d	2,315.36	3,164.92	† 3,795.04	4,660.78	5,217.41	5,093.49	5,654.33	5,937.32	6,757.09	6,777.93	5,054.30	5,832.53
Claims on Other Banking Insts........	22f	11.08	11.58	† 15.57	8.99	29.18	20.03	16.63	37.90	29.44	26.52	28.72	44.93
Claims on Nonbank Financial Insts....	22g	—	—	† 39.39	25.98	33.45	25.52	40.35	45.80	63.21	3.21	.09	1.23
Demand Deposits...........................	24	367.48	499.43	† 594.44	681.90	698.08	678.97	730.19	1,192.53	1,326.51	1,273.39	1,918.52	2,610.19
Time, Savings,& Fgn.Currency Dep.....	25	2,170.28	2,663.58	† 3,286.94	3,844.68	4,156.49	4,522.84	5,470.17	5,444.15	6,477.35	6,582.20	6,362.06	6,851.85
Money Market Instruments..............	26aa	—	—	† 50.16	36.98	49.11	13.11	9.42	39.32	12.13	17.09	9.17	124.55
Bonds...	26ab	4.00	3.76	† 1.94	4.13	5.85	15.72	12.97	14.17	37.05	144.60	30.35	—
Restricted Deposits.........................	26b	—	—	† 3.29	15.01	3.03	18.71	23.10	60.16	51.18	92.43	98.49	101.38
Foreign Liabilities..........................	26c	269.68	239.68	† 899.23	541.86	709.87	658.96	397.35	373.41	447.87	483.82	281.87	314.55
Central Government Deposits...........	26d	209.98	432.74	† 324.39	886.07	758.05	721.32	728.42	777.54	895.15	919.28	901.47	1,080.59
Credit from Monetary Authorities......	26g	102.45	94.01	† 156.36	346.59	321.61	33.27	68.68	86.49	89.30	131.15	78.52	37.98
Liabilities to Other Banking Insts......	26i	.86	.01	† 19.24	31.45	31.02	50.11	68.47	102.10	235.49	215.34	396.44	414.78
Capital Accounts...........................	27a	483.01	719.50	† 1,020.67	1,347.22	1,627.12	1,609.57	1,715.53	1,890.09	2,132.39	2,372.02	2,147.99	2,270.17
Other Items (Net)..........................	27r	23.11	47.82	† −233.45	−526.49	−527.15	−45.45	−20.59	−44.14	−200.81	−295.34	−389.19	−246.19

		1993	1994	1995	1996	1997	1998	1999	2000	2001	2002	2003	2004
Monetary Survey					*Billions of Guaranies: End of Period*								
Foreign Assets (Net)	31n	1,410.13	2,184.04	† 2,169.39	2,561.72	2,006.94	2,871.50	4,101.12	4,039.88	4,613.16	5,256.96	7,735.13	8,942.79
Domestic Credit	32	3,191.11	3,623.54	† 4,344.52	4,831.32	5,369.00	5,596.47	5,742.22	6,416.82	7,420.40	8,442.74	6,376.91	6,986.19
Claims on Central Govt. (Net)	32an	572.56	200.17	† 181.02	−272.06	−344.34	−58.82	−488.16	−170.27	153.51	1,125.66	794.70	549.08
Claims on Local Government	32b	1.37	.83	† 22.67	2.18	8.13	37.75	6.71	10.19	5.61	2.26	3.14	7.26
Claims on Nonfin.Pub.Enterprises	32c	268.23	223.81	† 239.15	268.00	303.76	330.20	359.66	381.19	216.25	283.50	291.82	364.87
Claims on Private Sector	32d	2,321.65	3,171.50	† 3,802.28	4,672.68	5,232.14	5,111.89	5,676.61	5,962.93	6,785.14	6,810.51	5,088.53	5,866.61
Claims on Other Banking Insts	32f	27.29	27.23	† 36.87	113.19	49.21	53.88	43.58	73.88	73.60	84.59	55.76	44.93
Claims on Nonbank Fin. Insts	32g	—	—	† 62.53	47.32	120.10	121.57	143.81	158.91	186.29	136.22	142.95	153.44
Money	34	1,054.01	1,370.31	† 1,699.93	1,708.85	1,886.18	1,984.45	2,166.89	2,562.25	2,743.15	2,759.53	3,788.14	4,784.12
Quasi-Money	35	2,576.79	3,119.08	† 3,735.50	4,493.15	4,792.44	5,356.27	6,510.91	6,534.39	7,843.68	8,159.26	7,961.37	8,629.11
Money Market Instruments	36aa	—	—	† 50.16	36.98	49.11	13.11	9.42	39.32	12.13	17.09	9.17	124.55
Bonds	36ab	4.00	3.76	† 1.94	4.13	5.85	15.72	12.97	14.17	37.05	144.60	30.35	—
Liabs. of Central Bank: Securities	36ac	—	—	† 28.23	12.03	31.87	171.84	15.09	5.99	111.85	253.93	428.59	341.47
Restricted Deposits	36b	17.11	26.47	† 29.30	66.76	57.58	76.92	95.31	140.47	138.48	216.61	230.01	212.28
Liabilities to Other Banking Insts	36i	.86	.01	† 19.24	31.45	31.02	50.11	68.47	102.10	235.49	215.34	396.44	414.78
Capital Accounts	37a	786.96	1,051.70	† 1,539.78	1,958.36	4,008.68	3,229.34	3,854.34	4,041.20	4,722.02	6,448.39	4,856.76	5,205.85
Other Items (Net)	37r	161.52	236.25	† −590.17	−918.67	−3,486.79	−2,429.78	−2,890.06	−2,983.19	−3,810.29	−4,515.04	−3,588.79	−3,783.18
Money plus Quasi-Money	35l	3,630.80	4,489.40	† 5,435.43	6,202.01	6,678.62	7,340.72	8,677.80	9,096.64	10,586.83	10,918.78	11,749.51	13,413.23
Other Banking Institutions					*Billions of Guaranies: End of Period*								
Reserves	40	30.25	51.64	† 47.07	52.55	69.01	73.66	72.99	92.44	105.47	100.84	117.62	101.53
Claims on Mon.Author.: Securities	40c	—	—	† 1.29	.46	.02	3.36	5.08	5.99	2.17	6.26		.22
Foreign Assets	41	—	—	† .68	1.41	30.08	31.26	31.92	55.87	87.53	30.13	22.07	13.05
Claims on Central Government	42a	—	—	† 2.11	3.65	4.30	3.58	5.79	6.52	5.28	36.86	34.92	37.55
Claims on Local Government	42b	—	—	† —	—	.01	.03	.04	.12	.03	.09	—	—
Claims on Nonfin.Pub.Enterprises	42c	—	—	† —	—	—	—	.08					
Claims on Private Sector	42d	600.11	858.31	† 447.38	505.38	655.57	662.12	626.43	773.75	888.45	820.28	932.02	916.41
Claims on Deposit Money Banks	42e	68.59	122.40	† 30.14	38.50	39.56	57.90	87.07	74.99	92.86	95.22	148.65	100.26
Claims on Nonbank Financial Insts	42g	—	—	† 4.24	6.59	7.46	.12	1.80	4.17	18.63	4.74	2.21	1.50
Time, Savings,& Fgn.Currency Dep	45	201.09	270.97	† 352.02	401.87	501.74	491.48	475.48	615.14	766.92	747.24	931.67	905.84
Bonds	46ab	119.50	222.27	† 6.76	6.76	8.36	7.25	6.42	7.81	7.77	5.02	4.62	1.30
Foreign Liabilities	46c	66.62	63.06	† —	—	19.91	6.03	1.98	7.14	8.28	5.03	26.21	24.45
Credit from Monetary Authorities	46g	11.57	11.89	† 12.15	11.84	19.81	32.52	26.77	36.27	52.80	64.76	32.96	3.57
Credit from Deposit Money Banks	46h	2.31	1.77	† 15.86	17.52	36.28	41.58	42.75	69.00	43.87	13.96	18.78	4.66
Capital Accounts	47a	273.00	422.30	† 193.46	227.94	274.99	307.21	324.11	349.50	382.56	337.58	311.64	270.80
Other Items (Net)	47r	24.87	40.09	† −47.34	−57.40	−55.07	−54.05	−46.33	−71.07	−61.78	−79.17	−68.38	−39.88
Banking Survey					*Billions of Guaranies: End of Period*								
Foreign Assets (Net)	51n	1,343.51	2,120.97	† 2,170.07	2,563.13	2,017.11	2,896.73	4,131.06	4,088.61	4,692.41	5,282.06	7,730.99	8,931.40
Domestic Credit	52	3,763.93	4,454.62	† 4,759.09	5,233.74	5,987.13	6,208.44	6,332.78	7,127.51	8,259.19	9,220.12	7,290.30	7,896.73
Claims on Central Govt. (Net)	52an	572.56	200.17	† 180.85	−268.41	−340.05	−55.25	−482.37	−163.75	158.80	1,162.52	829.62	586.64
Claims on Local Government	52b	1.37	.83	† 22.67	2.18	8.14	37.78	6.75	10.31	5.64	2.35	3.14	7.26
Claims on Nonfin.Pub.Enterprises	52c	268.23	223.81	† 239.15	268.00	303.76	330.20	359.74	381.19	216.25	283.50	291.82	364.87
Claims on Private Sector	52d	2,921.76	4,029.80	† 4,249.65	5,178.06	5,887.71	5,774.01	6,303.04	6,736.68	7,673.59	7,630.78	6,020.56	6,783.02
Claims on Nonbank Fin. Insts	52g	—	—	† 66.77	53.91	127.56	121.69	145.62	163.08	204.92	140.96	145.16	154.94
Liquid Liabilities	55l	3,801.63	4,708.73	† 5,740.38	6,551.33	7,111.35	7,758.54	9,080.29	9,619.33	11,248.29	11,565.22	12,563.58	14,217.34
Money Market Instruments	56aa	—	—	† 50.16	36.98	49.11	13.11	9.42	39.32	12.13	17.09	9.17	124.55
Bonds	56ab	123.49	226.03	† 8.70	10.89	14.21	22.97	19.39	21.97	44.82	149.62	34.97	1.30
Liabs. of Central Bank: Securities	56ac	—	—	† 26.94	11.56	31.84	168.48	10.01	—	109.69	247.68	428.59	341.25
Restricted Deposits	56b	17.11	26.47	† 29.40	66.76	57.58	76.92	95.31	140.47	138.48	216.61	230.01	212.28
Capital Accounts	57a	1,059.96	1,474.00	† 1,733.23	2,186.30	4,283.67	3,536.55	4,178.45	4,390.71	5,104.58	6,785.96	5,168.40	5,476.65
Other Items (Net)	57r	105.24	140.37	† −659.65	−1,066.95	−3,543.53	−2,471.40	−2,929.04	−2,995.69	−3,706.39	−4,480.00	−3,413.44	−3,545.25
Money (National Definitions)					*Billions of Guaranies: End of Period*								
Base Money	19ma	1,053.31	1,342.25	1,650.91	1,703.49	1,831.80	1,987.33	2,138.55	2,106.94	2,227.57	2,193.18	3,461.74	4,060.38
M1	59ma	958.33	1,272.60	1,539.36	1,570.67	1,789.14	1,922.22	2,103.85	2,478.22	2,700.36	2,728.70	3,788.88	4,705.78
M2	59mb	1,563.47	2,166.15	2,827.35	3,204.72	3,437.43	3,341.82	3,706.11	3,824.42	4,068.44	3,914.07	5,079.18	6,299.83
M3	59mc	2,720.04	3,499.99	4,201.08	5,121.65	5,848.77	6,383.03	7,532.20	7,833.10	9,332.98	9,275.38	10,362.82	11,733.89
M4	59md	2,725.30	3,503.75	4,204.77	5,122.88	5,848.77	6,385.00	7,541.01	7,850.33	9,363.84	9,411.11	10,402.64	11,742.09
M5	59me	2,970.03	3,693.60	4,381.96	5,262.52	5,849.76	6,385.00	7,541.01	7,850.33	9,363.84	9,411.11	10,402.64	11,742.09
Interest Rates					*Percent Per Annum*								
Discount Rate (End of Period)	60	27.17	19.15	20.50	15.00	20.00	20.00	20.00	20.00	20.00	20.00	20.00	20.00
Money Market Rate	60b	22.55	18.64	20.18	16.35	12.48	20.74	17.26	10.70	13.45	13.19	13.02	1.33
Savings Rate	60k	10.60	† 12.00	11.53	9.92	6.93	5.12	6.06	6.43	5.67	9.42	6.90	1.33
Savings Rate (Fgn.Currency)	60k.f	....	4.27	4.68	4.08	3.22	2.74	2.40	2.35	2.07	1.40	.59	.15
Deposit Rate	60l	22.10	23.12	21.16	17.16	13.00	15.95	† 19.75	15.72	16.22	22.86	15.83	5.11
Deposit Rate (Fgn.Currency)	60l.f	....	....	....	....	....	5.44	5.02	4.56	3.46	1.66	1.27	.68
Lending Rate	60p	30.78	† 35.47	33.94	31.88	27.79	30.49	30.21	26.78	28.25	38.66	49.99	33.54
Lending Rate (Fgn.Currency)	60p.f	....	12.68	14.03	14.35	13.53	13.03	12.17	11.87	11.16	9.31	10.35	8.08
Prices and Labor					*Index Numbers (2000=100): Period Averages*								
Producer Prices	63	....	....	....	71.2	72.1	82.8	87.2	100.0	105.8	126.9	160.4	169.7
Consumer Prices	64	48.0	57.8	65.6	72.0	77.1	86.0	91.8	100.0	107.3	118.5	135.4	141.3
					Number in Thousands: Period Averages								
Labor Force	67d	587	† 1,053									....	....
Employment	67e	570	† 1,050	† 1,160	1,190	1,771	2,151	2,196	2,558	2,373	2,260	2,351	....
Unemployment	67c	30	† 48		106								
Unemployment Rate (%)	67r	5.1	† 4.4	....	8.2	....	....	9.4	10.3	....	14.7	11.1	....
Intl. Transactions & Positions					*Millions of U.S. Dollars*								
Exports	70..d	725.2	816.8	919.2	1,043.5	1,088.6	1,014.0	740.9	869.4	990.2	950.6	1,241.5	1,625.7
Imports, c.i.f.	71..d	1,688.8	2,140.4	2,782.2	2,850.5	3,099.2	2,470.8	1,725.1	2,050.0	1,989.0	....	....	....
Imports, f.o.b.	71.vd	1,477.5	2,140.4	2,782.2	2,850.5	3,403.0	2,470.8	1,725.1	2,050.4	1,988.8	1,510.3	1,865.3	2,651.7
					1990=100								
Volume of Exports	72	74.7	66.3	....	....	....	....	....	....	....	....	....	....

Paraguay 288

		1993	1994	1995	1996	1997	1998	1999	2000	2001	2002	2003	2004
Balance of Payments		*Millions of US Dollars: Minus Sign Indicates Debit*											
Current Account, n.i.e.	78ald	59.1	−274.1	−92.3	−352.9	−650.4	−160.0	−165.4	−162.8	−266.4	92.6	132.5	20.4
Goods: Exports f.o.b.	78aad	2,859.0	3,360.1	4,218.6	3,796.9	3,327.5	3,548.6	2,312.4	2,329.0	1,889.7	1,858.0	2,175.3	2,811.7
Goods: Imports f.o.b.	78abd	−2,779.6	−3,603.5	−4,489.0	−4,383.4	−4,192.4	−3,941.5	−2,752.9	−2,866.1	−2,503.6	−2,137.9	−2,450.5	−3,203.0
Trade Balance	78acd	79.4	−243.4	−270.4	−586.5	−864.9	−392.9	−440.5	−537.2	−613.9	−279.9	−275.2	−391.3
Services: Credit	78add	438.6	426.2	583.8	600.5	655.0	625.5	575.4	595.3	555.2	568.4	582.7	585.8
Services: Debit	78aed	−592.8	−593.4	−710.7	−658.8	−654.6	−575.9	−493.0	−420.2	−390.0	−354.6	−333.1	−336.9
Balance on Goods & Services	78afd	−74.8	−410.6	−397.3	−644.8	−864.5	−343.3	−358.1	−362.0	−448.7	−66.1	−25.5	−142.4
Income: Credit	78agd	198.3	247.9	272.6	280.9	278.1	266.3	212.5	260.5	255.9	195.7	166.3	185.9
Income: Debit	78ahd	−142.6	−134.1	−162.9	−171.2	−244.9	−260.3	−195.0	−238.1	−240.1	−152.9	−172.8	−217.2
Balance on Gds, Serv. & Inc.	78aid	−19.1	−296.8	−287.6	−535.1	−831.3	−337.3	−340.6	−339.6	−432.9	−23.3	−32.0	−173.8
Current Transfers, n.i.e.: Credit	78ajd	78.6	25.6	199.7	183.0	182.2	178.3	176.7	178.3	168.0	117.5	166.0	195.7
Current Transfers: Debit	78akd	−.4	−2.9	−4.4	−.8	−1.3	−1.0	−1.5	−1.5	−1.5	−1.6	−1.5	−1.5
Capital Account, n.i.e.	78bcd	22.1	8.8	10.6	14.2	7.5	5.4	19.6	3.0	15.0	4.0	15.0	16.0
Capital Account, n.i.e.: Credit	78bad	22.1	8.8	10.6	14.2	7.5	5.4	19.6	3.0	15.0	4.0	15.0	16.0
Capital Account: Debit	78bbd	....	....	—	—	—	—	—	—	—	—	—	—
Financial Account, n.i.e.	78bjd	8.5	212.9	232.5	152.4	421.3	312.9	89.2	63.9	148.2	40.5	173.2	113.0
Direct Investment Abroad	78bdd	....	....	−5.1	−5.2	−5.7	−5.6	−5.6	−5.7	−5.8	−5.5	−5.5	−6.0
Dir. Invest. in Rep. Econ., n.i.e.	78bed	75.0	137.1	103.2	149.4	235.8	341.9	94.5	104.1	84.2	10.0	32.8	92.5
Portfolio Investment Assets	78bfd	....	....	−.8	−3.6	−4.3	9.0	−9.0	2.0	.7	—	—	—
Equity Securities	78bkd	....	....				−.7	−6.8	1.4	.2	—	—	—
Debt Securities	78bld	....	....	−.8	−3.6	−4.3	9.7	−2.2	.6	.5	—	—	—
Portfolio Investment Liab., n.i.e.	78bgd	....	....	—	−.1	—	—	—	.5	−.1	−.1	−.4	−.1
Equity Securities	78bmd	....	....	—	—	—	—	—	....	—	—	—	—
Debt Securities	78bnd	....	....	—	−.1	—	—	—	.5	−.1	−.1	−.4	−.1
Financial Derivatives Assets	78bwd	....	....										
Financial Derivatives Liabilities	78bxd	....	....										
Other Investment Assets	78bhd	−65.4	−89.8	−58.5	−31.9	72.9	−5.0	−117.7	−212.4	64.4	−16.1	212.5	−8.5
Monetary Authorities	78bod	....	.1										
General Government	78bpd	1.6	23.1	−43.1	−59.0	−45.8	60.7	−63.6	−81.2	78.8	−77.7	−38.0	−20.1
Banks	78bqd	−75.2	−1.5	−169.7	3.5	100.5	−42.7	−1.9	−69.3	68.2	122.5	−108.7	7.4
Other Sectors	78brd	8.2	−111.5	154.3	23.6	18.2	−23.0	−52.2	−61.9	−82.6	−60.9	359.2	4.2
Other Investment Liab., n.i.e.	78bid	−1.1	165.6	193.7	43.8	122.6	−27.4	127.0	175.4	4.8	52.2	−66.3	35.2
Monetary Authorities	78bsd	2.1	−1.6	−8.7	−3.5	−5.0	−4.3	−3.8	−3.3	−3.2	−4.4	−4.4	−4.3
General Government	78btd	−2.6	29.8	101.6	122.5	137.1	112.3	97.6	90.4	41.9	23.0	53.1	5.4
Banks	78bud	−94.2	97.3	118.6	−188.4	71.6	−50.7	−101.5	−8.9	−30.5	6.3	−23.9	18.9
Other Sectors	78bvd	93.6	40.1	−17.8	113.2	−81.1	−84.7	134.7	97.2	−3.4	27.3	−91.1	15.2
Net Errors and Omissions	78cad	−46.4	353.0	−106.0	139.8	5.8	−141.6	−244.3	−243.4	52.9	−262.8	−87.8	120.5
Overall Balance	78cbd	43.3	300.6	44.8	−46.5	−215.8	16.7	−300.9	−339.3	−50.2	−125.7	232.8	270.0
Reserves and Related Items	79dad	−43.3	−300.6	−44.8	46.5	215.8	−16.7	300.9	339.3	50.2	125.7	−232.8	−270.0
Reserve Assets	79dbd	−87.2	−339.3	−60.2	39.4	205.8	−23.4	−116.7	210.1	45.4	85.6	−303.2	−181.2
Use of Fund Credit and Loans	79dcd	—	—	—	—	—	—	—	—	—	—	—	—
Exceptional Financing	79ded	43.9	38.7	15.4	7.1	10.0	6.7	417.6	129.2	4.8	40.1	70.4	−88.8
International Investment Position		*Millions of US Dollars*											
Assets	79aad	....	....	2,569.4	2,566.7	2,284.6	2,311.9	2,576.7	2,602.6	3,216.3	3,125.7	2,455.2	2,659.2
Direct Investment Abroad	79abd	....	....	178.6	186.0	194.1	201.3	208.2	213.9	139.7	137.7	143.2	149.2
Portfolio Investment	79acd	....	....	6.3	9.9	14.2	8.9	20.1	11.9	15.0	13.3	4.7	4.7
Equity Securities	79add	....	....	3.4	3.4	3.4	7.8	16.8	10.3	14.3	12.6	4.0	4.0
Debt Securities	79aed	....	....	2.9	6.5	10.8	1.1	3.3	1.6	.7	.7	.7	.7
Financial Derivatives	79aid	....	....										
Other Investment	79afd	....	....	1,278.1	1,308.5	1,230.5	1,226.9	1,360.2	1,605.0	2,338.5	2,324.5	1,314.2	1,317.3
Monetary Authorities	79agd	....	....	—	—	—	—	—	—	—	—	—	—
General Government	79ahd	....	....	188.3	247.3	293.1	232.6	296.2	377.4	332.7	410.4	448.4	468.6
Banks	79aid	....	....	511.6	507.6	404.2	442.5	443.4	512.8	444.6	280.5	389.2	381.8
Other Sectors	79ajd	....	....	578.2	553.6	533.2	551.8	620.6	714.8	1,561.2	1,633.6	476.6	466.9
Reserve Assets	79akd	....	....	1,106.4	1,062.3	845.8	874.8	988.2	771.9	723.1	650.2	993.1	1,187.9
Liabilities	79lad	....	....	2,877.1	2,954.2	3,132.1	3,385.5	3,982.3	4,377.8	4,057.4	3,939.8	4,226.0	4,343.4
Dir. Invest. in Rep. Economy	79lbd	....	....	705.2	829.3	977.7	1,196.1	1,215.7	1,324.5	1,135.4	901.5	1,084.5	1,244.1
Portfolio Investment	79lcd	....	....	.1	—	—	—	—	.5	.4	.3	—	—
Equity Securities	79ldd	....	....	—	—	—	—	—	—	—	—	—	—
Debt Securities	79led	....	....	.1	—	—	—	—	.5	.4	.3	—	—
Financial Derivatives	79lld	....	....										
Other Investment	79lfd	....	....	2,171.8	2,124.9	2,154.4	2,189.4	2,766.6	3,052.8	2,921.6	3,038.0	3,141.5	3,099.3
Monetary Authorities	79lgd	....	....	50.8	47.3	42.3	38.0	34.3	32.7	31.2	28.6	22.3	17.9
General Government	79lhd	....	....	1,004.6	1,054.8	1,146.0	1,318.1	1,854.3	2,001.7	1,963.6	2,090.4	2,302.8	2,250.8
Banks	79lid	....	....	406.5	218.1	289.5	238.4	136.6	127.6	97.0	66.4	42.7	63.2
Other Sectors	79ljd	....	....	709.9	804.7	676.6	594.9	741.4	890.8	829.8	852.7	773.8	767.5
Government Finance		*Billions of Guaranies: Year Ending December 31*											
Deficit (-) or Surplus	80	138.7	294.8	−10.2	−183.3	−251.6	−81.3	−806.2	−1,080.5	−229.7	....	....	....
Revenue	81	1,688.0	2,196.7	2,724.1	2,919.5	3,192.9	3,715.7	4,004.0	4,201.7	4,838.7	....	....	....
Grants	81z	4.0	25.8	28.8	35.4	68.4	44.7	49.7	46.1	135.9	....	....	....
Expenditure	82	1,559.4	1,953.7	2,726.9	3,116.6	3,469.6	3,811.7	4,687.3	5,216.3	5,201.4	....	....	....
Lending Minus Repayments	83	−6.0	−25.9	36.1	21.5	43.2	30.0	172.6	112.0	2.8	....	....	....
Exch.Rate Adj.to Overall Def./Sur.	80x	....	....	....	....	....	....	....	....	....	....	....	....
Total Financing	80h	−138.7	−294.8	10.2	183.3	251.6	81.3	806.2	1,080.5	229.7	....	....	....
Domestic Financing	84a	−2.0	....	....	....	....	....	....	....	....	....	....	....
Foreign Financing	85a	−96.2	....	....	....	....	....	....	....	....	....	....	....
Use of Cash Balances	87	−40.5	....	....	....	....	....	....	....	....	....	....	....
Total Debt	88	1,530.1	....	....	....	....	....	....	....	....	....	....	....
Domestic	88a	100.0	....	....	....	....	....	....	....	....	....	....	....
Foreign	89a	1,430.1	....	....	....	....	....	....	....	....	....	....	....

		1993	1994	1995	1996	1997	1998	1999	2000	2001	2002	2003	2004
National Accounts							*Billions of Guaranies*						
Househ.Cons.Expend.,incl.NPISHs....	96f	9,749.8	13,231.8	15,089.2	16,853.3	17,704.3	20,101.4	19,762.5	22,406.8	24,604.3	27,526.7	34,044.8	....
Government Consumption Expend...	91f	801.9	1,012.5	1,275.9	1,528.5	1,693.0	1,928.3	2,135.4	2,601.6	2,479.9	2,470.2	2,679.3	....
Gross Fixed Capital Formation..........	93e	2,642.1	3,366.5	4,082.8	4,478.4	4,749.1	5,168.2	5,342.1	5,638.6	5,295.0	5,812.5	7,373.6	....
Changes in Inventories....................	93i	109.6	127.7	151.8	156.7	181.0	205.6	221.7	242.5	265.5	292.3	315.7	....
Exports of Goods and Services..........	90c	4,428.6	5,120.9	6,163.8	5,707.7	5,696.2	6,613.4	5,548.6	5,260.1	6,170.1	9,822.8	12,524.1	....
Imports of Goods and Services (-).....	98c	5,740.2	7,899.3	9,064.9	8,919.8	9,089.3	10,580.0	8,866.1	9,228.7	10,696.0	13,947.6	18,131.9	....
Gross Domestic Product (GDP)........	99b	11,991.7	14,960.1	17,698.6	19,804.8	20,934.3	23,436.9	24,144.3	26,921.0	28,118.8	31,976.9	38,805.5	....
Net Primary Income from Abroad.....	98.n	42.9	78.8	158.8	145.1	221.7	304.5	132.2	380.7	164.2	629.4	725.4	....
Gross National Income (GNI)............	99a	12,034.7	15,039.0	17,857.4	19,949.9	21,156.0	23,741.4	24,276.5	27,301.7	28,283.0	32,606.3	39,530.9	....
Consumption of Fixed Capital..........	99cf	930.7	1,161.0	1,378.1	1,549.9	1,639.2	1,835.0	1,889.6	2,051.6	2,142.8	2,407.0	3,104.4	....
GDP Volume 1982 Prices.................	99b.p	1,007.4	1,038.5	1,087.4	1,101.2	1,129.7	1,125.0	1,130.4	1,126.4	1,157.0	1,130.2	1,159.0	....
GDP Volume (2000=100)...............	99bvp	89.4	92.2	96.5	97.8	100.3	99.9	100.4	100.0	102.7	100.3	102.9	....
GDP Deflator (2000=100)...............	99bip	49.8	60.3	68.1	75.3	77.5	87.2	89.4	100.0	101.7	118.4	140.1	....
							Millions: Midyear Estimates						
Population..............................	99z	4.58	4.71	4.83	4.95	5.08	5.21	5.34	5.47	5.60	5.74	5.88	6.02

		1993	1994	1995	1996	1997	1998	1999	2000	2001	2002	2003	2004
Exchange Rates						*Nuevos Soles per SDRs: End of Period*							
Market Rate..............	aa	2.9669	3.1825	3.4338	3.7387	3.6835	4.4494	4.8175	4.5954	4.3282	4.7774	5.1459	5.0962
						Nuevos Soles per US$: End of Period(ae) Period Avg.(rf)							
Market Rate..............	ae	2.1600	2.1800	2.3100	2.6000	2.7300	3.1600	3.5100	3.5270	3.4440	3.5140	3.4630	3.2815
Market Rate..............	rf	1.9883	2.1950	2.2533	2.4533	2.6642	2.9300	3.3833	3.4900	3.5068	3.5165	3.4785	3.4132
Fund Position						*Millions of SDRs: End of Period*							
Quota..............	2f.s	466.1	466.1	466.1	466.1	466.1	466.1	638.4	638.4	638.4	638.4	638.4	638.4
SDRs..............	1b.s	.7	.3	.5	.2	.2	1.5	.3	1.1	1.4	.5	.3	.2
Reserve Position in the Fund...........	1c.s	—	—	—	—	—	—	—	—	—	—	—	—
Total Fund Cred.&Loans Outstg....	2tl	642.7	642.7	642.7	642.7	749.6	642.5	535.4	428.3	307.8	173.9	93.6	66.9
International Liquidity					*Millions of US Dollars Unless Otherwise Indicated: End of Period*								
Total Reserves minus Gold..............	1l.d	3,407.9	6,992.4	8,221.7	10,578.3	10,982.2	9,565.5	8,730.5	8,374.0	8,671.8	9,339.0	9,776.8	12,176.4
SDRs..............	1b.d	.9	.4	.7	.3	.2	2.1	.4	1.5	1.7	.7	.4	.4
Reserve Position in the Fund..........	1c.d	—	—	—	—	—	—	—	—	—	—	—	—
Foreign Exchange..............	1d.d	3,407.0	6,992.0	8,221.0	10,578.0	10,982.0	9,563.4	8,730.1	8,372.5	8,670.1	9,338.3	9,776.4	12,176.1
Gold (Million Fine Troy Ounces)........	1ad	1.305	1.116	1.116	1.115	1.115	1.100	1.100	1.100	1.115	1.115	1.115	1.115
Gold (National Valuation)..............	1and	434.0	362.9	366.6	349.7	272.0	268.8	270.9	254.1	261.6	386.7	462.7	488.7
Monetary Authorities: Other Liab.....	4..d	517.7	540.6	573.4	494.2	497.8	446.6	693.8	831.6	842.0	791.0	884.1	984.2
Deposit Money Banks: Assets...........	7a.d	871.8	1,183.8	1,544.9	2,047.2	1,215.7	1,245.8	1,388.6	1,298.7	1,365.7	1,218.1	1,290.6	1,094.6
Liabilities..............	7b.d	415.3	765.8	1,566.1	1,812.4	3,473.6	3,291.0	2,286.3	2,029.9	1,562.9	1,002.1	913.7	970.4
Other Banking Insts.: Assets.............	7e.d	11.1	12.7	12.7	12.7	12.7	1.0	—	—	—	—	—	—
Liabilities..............	7f.d	107.3	71.0	71.0	71.1	71.0	10.3	—	—	—	—	—	—
Monetary Authorities						*Millions of Nuevos Soles: End of Period*							
Foreign Assets..............	11	9,335	16,001	19,093	25,933	31,208	32,399	33,548	33,200	33,344	36,836	38,410	44,751
Claims on Central Government........	12a	55	614	614	614	614	614	538	425	396	350	237	39
Claims on Deposit Money Banks.....	12e	149	64	4	107	—	203	263	97	—	170	—	—
Claims on Other Banking Insts........	12f	209	—	—	—	—	—	—	—	—	—	—	—
Reserve Money..............	14	5,715	7,487	9,823	13,536	18,773	19,847	22,952	23,405	24,474	26,510	24,865	26,166
of which: Currency Outside DMBs..	14a	1,591	2,385	3,043	3,245	3,827	3,950	4,609	4,537	4,945	5,615	6,370	8,036
Time, Savings,& Fgn.Currency Dep...	15	194	202	78	118	77	83	75	78	114	148	179	192
Restricted Deposits..............	16b	1	1	1	1	1	—	1	—	—	—	—	—
Foreign Liabilities..............	16c	3,011	3,224	3,531	3,688	4,105	4,257	5,015	4,905	4,232	3,611	3,540	3,569
Central Government Deposits...........	16d	96	3,684	5,384	8,498	7,989	7,558	4,057	2,454	1,447	2,430	3,188	4,835
Capital Accounts..............	17a	254	377	457	592	735	867	871	854	962	1,146	1,272	1,058
Other Items (Net)..............	17r	477	1,705	437	221	141	604	1,379	2,025	2,511	3,511	5,603	8,970
Deposit Money Banks						*Millions of Nuevos Soles: End of Period*							
Reserves..............	20	3,519	5,326	6,846	10,240	12,135	11,126	11,897	12,382	13,252	14,353	14,573	17,533
Foreign Assets..............	21	1,874	2,581	3,569	5,323	3,307	3,924	4,874	4,584	4,704	4,280	4,466	3,590
Claims on Central Government........	22a	1,913	1,607	1,028	924	2,437	3,764	4,954	4,778	6,506	6,908	6,631	5,988
Claims on Local Government..........	22b	35	50	31	170	244	94	380	433	337	205	340	313
Claims on Official Entities..............	22bx	369	270	204	264	376	968	398	464	419	493	294	332
Claims on Private Sector..............	22d	7,694	13,095	19,090	28,512	37,812	45,835	49,221	47,569	45,464	45,229	43,123	42,974
Claims on Other Banking Insts........	22f	7	3	3	3	—	—	—	—	—	—	—	—
Demand Deposits..............	24	2,142	3,193	4,357	5,633	7,950	10,174	11,018	9,110	8,977	8,359	8,193	9,942
Time, Savings,& Fgn.Currency Dep...	25	9,528	13,501	17,362	25,136	29,510	33,269	37,779	38,737	39,589	42,065	41,187	40,717
Bonds..............	26ab	55	102	251	539	806	933	969	871	783	952	457	468
Foreign Liabilities..............	26c	893	1,670	3,618	4,712	9,448	10,367	8,025	7,166	5,382	3,521	3,161	3,183
Central Government Deposits...........	26d	1,248	2,367	1,561	4,808	3,710	3,849	3,718	3,635	3,510	4,065	4,350	4,873
Credit from Monetary Authorities.....	26g	149	64	4	107	—	203	263	97	—	170	—	—
Capital Accounts..............	27a	3,181	4,792	6,261	8,514	11,045	14,309	18,857	20,518	22,616	23,701	21,540	21,422
Other Items (Net)..............	27r	−1,785	−2,757	−2,643	−4,013	−6,157	−7,392	−8,904	−9,925	−10,177	−11,366	−9,462	−9,877
Monetary Survey						*Millions of Nuevos Soles: End of Period*							
Foreign Assets (Net)..............	31n	7,305	13,688	15,513	22,856	20,962	21,700	25,382	25,713	28,433	33,984	36,174	41,590
Domestic Credit..............	32	8,947	9,588	14,025	17,181	29,784	39,869	47,717	47,579	48,165	46,690	43,088	39,937
Claims on Central Govt. (Net)..........	32an	625	−3,830	−5,303	−11,768	−8,648	−7,028	−2,282	−887	1,945	763	−669	−3,682
Claims on Local Government..........	32b	35	50	31	170	244	94	380	433	337	205	340	313
Claims on Official Entities..............	32bx	369	270	204	264	376	968	398	464	419	493	294	332
Claims on Private Sector..............	32d	7,702	13,095	19,090	28,512	37,812	45,835	49,221	47,569	45,464	45,229	43,123	42,974
Claims on Other Banking Insts.......	32f	216	3	3	3	—	—	—	—	—	—	—	—
Money..............	34	4,337	5,589	7,498	8,972	15,175	19,165	22,273	21,072	21,445	22,049	21,351	23,728
Quasi-Money..............	35	9,722	13,703	17,440	25,254	29,587	33,352	37,854	38,815	39,703	42,213	41,366	40,909
Bonds..............	36ab	55	102	251	539	806	933	969	871	783	952	457	468
Restricted Deposits..............	36b	1	1	1	1	1	—	1	—	—	—	—	—
Capital Accounts..............	37a	3,435	5,169	6,718	9,106	11,780	15,176	19,728	21,373	23,578	24,846	22,812	22,480
Other Items (Net)..............	37r	−1,299	−1,288	−2,370	−3,835	−6,603	−7,058	−7,726	−8,839	−8,913	−9,387	−6,724	−6,059
Money plus Quasi-Money..............	35l	14,060	19,292	24,938	34,226	44,762	52,518	60,127	59,887	61,148	64,262	62,717	64,637
Other Banking Institutions						*Millions of Nuevos Soles: End of Period*							
Reserves..............	40	4	—	—	—	—	—	—	—	—	—	—	—
Foreign Assets..............	41	24	28	29	33	35	3	—	—	—	—	—	—
Claims on Central Government........	42a	54	55	58	65	69	—	—	—	—	—	8	—
Claims on Official Entities..............	42bx	20	20	21	24	25	—	—	—	—	—	—	—
Claims on Private Sector..............	42d	743	718	744	803	828	910	809	761	644	657	686	709
Claims on Deposit Money Banks......	42e	1	2	2	2	2	—	—	—	—	90	35	18
Demand Deposits..............	44	9	9	9	9	9	21	21	20	20	20	—	—
Time, Savings,& Fgn.Currency Dep...	45	44	42	43	46	47	37	10	9	8	8	28	27
Bonds..............	46ab	11	6	6	6	6	—	—	—	—	—	—	—
Foreign Liabilities..............	46c	231	155	164	185	193	33	—	—	—	—	—	—
Central Government Deposits...........	46d	5	5	6	6	6	—	—	—	—	—	—	—
Credit from Monetary Authorities......	46g	209	—	—	—	—	—	—	—	—	—	—	—
Credit from Deposit Money Banks....	46h	13	4	4	5	5	—	—	—	—	—	—	—
Capital Accounts..............	47a	709	671	698	757	782	865	939	975	1,023	1,132	1,111	1,101
Other Items (Net)..............	47r	−385	−70	−76	−87	−92	−42	−160	−244	−406	−413	−410	−401

		1993	1994	1995	1996	1997	1998	1999	2000	2001	2002	2003	2004
Banking Survey						*Millions of Nuevos Soles: End of Period*							
Foreign Assets (Net).........................	51n	7,099	13,561	15,378	22,704	20,803	21,671	25,382	25,713	28,433	33,984	36,174	41,590
Domestic Credit.............................	52	9,543	10,373	14,840	18,063	30,698	40,778	48,526	48,340	48,809	47,346	43,782	40,646
Claims on Central Govt. (Net)........	52an	674	−3,780	−5,250	−11,708	−8,586	−7,028	−2,282	−887	1,945	763	−661	−3,682
Claims on Local Government..........	52b	35	50	31	170	244	94	380	433	337	205	340	313
Claims on Official Entities..............	52bx	389	290	225	287	400	968	398	464	419	493	294	332
Claims on Private Sector..............	52d	8,445	13,812	19,834	29,314	38,640	46,745	50,030	48,330	46,108	45,886	43,810	43,683
Liquid Liabilities.............................	55l	14,108	19,343	24,990	34,281	44,818	52,575	60,158	59,917	61,176	64,290	62,745	64,665
Bonds..	56ab	66	108	257	545	812	933	969	871	783	952	457	468
Restricted Deposits.........................	56b	1	1	1	1	1	—	1	—	—	—	—	—
Capital Accounts.............................	57a	4,144	5,840	7,416	9,863	12,562	16,041	20,667	22,348	24,601	25,978	23,923	23,580
Other Items (Net)...........................	57r	−1,679	−1,358	−2,446	−3,922	−6,691	−7,100	−7,886	−9,082	−9,319	−9,890	−7,169	−6,479
Money (National Definitions)						*Millions of Nuevos Soles: End of Period*							
Monetary Base..............................	19ma	1,803	2,672	3,658	3,996	4,761	5,023	5,876	5,642	6,087	6,759	7,441	9,327
Money.......................................	59ma	2,338	3,723	4,595	5,409	6,464	6,482	7,311	7,087	7,509	8,197	9,312	12,420
Quasi-Money in National Currency...	59mba	1,394	2,412	3,299	4,200	5,552	5,217	5,342	5,732	6,643	7,102	7,477	9,657
Quasi-Money in Foreign Currency.....	59mbb	8,335	11,518	14,410	21,200	24,471	28,162	31,674	32,508	32,121	33,626	34,018	33,762
Interest Rates						*Percent Per Annum*							
Discount Rate (End of Period)..........	60	28.63	16.08	18.44	18.16	15.94	18.72	17.80	14.00	14.00	4.75	4.25	4.25
Savings Rate.................................	60k	34.83	17.99	11.80	10.99	10.70	10.12	9.54	7.75	5.88	1.78	1.48	1.28
Deposit Rate.................................	60l	44.14	22.35	15.70	14.90	15.01	15.11	16.27	13.29	9.92	4.19	3.83	2.98
Lending Rate.................................	60p	97.37	53.56	27.16	26.07	29.96	30.80	30.79	27.91	20.43	14.73	14.21	14.49
Prices, Production, Labor						*Index Numbers (2000=100): Period Averages*							
Share Prices.................................	62	45.6	83.6	87.9	92.8	126.3	105.3	111.9	100.0	85.2	84.8	126.9	209.0
Wholesale Prices............................	63	55.6	65.6	72.5	79.3	85.2	91.4	† 95.8	100.0	101.4	100.3	102.0	107.4
Consumer Prices.............................	64	† 52.2	64.5	71.7	80.0	86.9	93.1	96.4	100.0	† 102.0	102.2	104.5	108.3
Manufacturing Production................	66ey	75.0	87.5	92.3	93.7	98.6	95.2	94.5	100.0	100.5	104.7	107.1	114.5
Industrial Employment....................	67	113.7	112.2	109.4	† 106.9	108.7	106.2	100.5	100.0	100.5	100.6	102.5	107.3
						Number in Thousands: Period Averages							
Labor Force..................................	67d	....	2,930	3,103	6,501	7,220	7,440	7,736	7,616	8,182	† 3,747	3,738	3,761
Employment.................................	67e	2,610	2,682	2,901	6,131	6,745	6,929	7,211	7,128	7,620	† 3,334	3,361	3,367
Unemployment..............................	67c	286	263	221	† 462	565	582	625	566	651	† 359	386	394
Unemployment Rate (%).................	67r	9.9	8.9	7.1	† 7.0	7.7	7.8	8.0	7.4	7.9	† 9.7	10.3	10.5
Intl. Transactions & Positions						*Millions of US Dollars*							
Exports......................................	70..d	3,384.5	4,424.1	5,491.4	5,877.6	6,824.6	5,756.8	6,087.5	6,954.9	7,025.7	7,713.9	9,090.7	12,616.9
Imports, c.i.f.................................	71..d	4,947.3	6,701.1	9,299.8	9,442.2	10,280.6	9,914.7	8,152.0	8,887.9	....	....	....	....
Imports, f.o.b.................................	71.vd	4,122.8	5,584.2	7,749.8	7,868.5	8,567.2	8,262.2	6,793.3	7,406.6	7,273.4	7,439.9	8,244.4	9,812.4
						2000=100							
Volume of Exports..........................	72	73.0	82.0	82.1	85.9	94.1	81.7	88.8	100.0	113.6	125.9	122.0	135.6
						2000=100: Indexes of Unit Values in US Dollars							
Unit Value of Exports/Export Prices...	74..d	75.0	88.5	107.2	106.8	103.6	83.9	82.7	100.0	84.8	88.0	98.5	125.6
Balance of Payments						*Millions of US Dollars: Minus Sign Indicates Debit*							
Current Account, n.i.e.....................	78ald	−2,464	−2,701	−4,625	−3,646	−3,367	−3,321	−1,464	−1,526	−1,144	−1,063	−935	−11
Goods: Exports f.o.b...................	78aad	3,385	4,424	5,491	5,878	6,825	5,757	6,088	6,955	7,026	7,714	9,091	12,616
Goods: Imports f.o.b...................	78abd	−4,160	−5,499	−7,733.	−7,869	−8,503	−8,194	−6,743	−7,366	−7,221	−7,422	−8,255	−9,824
Trade Balance.........................	78acd	−776	−1,075	−2,241	−1,991	−1,678	−2,437	−655	−411	−195	292	836	2,792
Services: Credit.......................	78add	837	1,064	1,131	1,414	1,553	1,775	1,594	1,529	1,455	1,530	1,695	1,914
Services: Debit........................	78aed	−1,387	−1,534	−1,864	−2,085	−2,339	−2,432	−2,256	−2,234	−2,345	−2,471	−2,549	−2,756
Balance on Goods & Services...	78afd	−1,326	−1,545	−2,975	−2,662	−2,465	−3,094	−1,318	−1,115	−1,085	−649	−18	1,949
Income: Credit.........................	78agd	205	338	574	610	720	786	655	737	670	370	322	332
Income: Debit.........................	78ahd	−1,876	−2,282	−3,056	−2,508	−2,542	−1,990	−1,767	−2,146	−1,771	−1,827	−2,466	−3,753
Balance on Gds, Serv. & Inc...	78aid	−2,996	−3,489	−5,457	−4,560	−4,287	−4,298	−2,430	−2,525	−2,186	−2,106	−2,162	−1,472
Current Transfers, n.i.e.: Credit...	78ajd	538	795	837	922	928	989	992	1,008	1,050	1,052	1,234	1,467
Current Transfers: Debit................	78akd	−6	−7	−5	−8	−8	−12	−27	−9	−8	−8	−6	−6
Capital Account, n.i.e.....................	78bcd	−45	−58	32	22	−50	−57	−54	−251	−143	−107	−107	−86
Capital Account, n.i.e.: Credit.	78bad	48	31	65	51	24	21	25	24	32	14	14	37
Capital Account: Debit................	78bbd	−92	−89	−34	−29	−74	−78	−79	−275	−175	−121	−121	−123
Financial Account, n.i.e.................	78bjd	919	3,870	3,718	3,797	5,696	1,773	545	1,015	1,534	1,983	820	2,375
Direct Investment Abroad............	78bdd	—	—	−8	17	−85	−62	−128	—	−74	—	−60	—
Dir. Invest. in Rep. Econ., n.i.e...	78bed	761	3,289	2,557	3,471	2,139	1,644	1,940	810	1,144	2,156	1,335	1,816
Portfolio Investment Assets............	78bfd	−26	−56	−9	−119	−257	−194	−227	−481	−318	−316	−1,287	−425
Equity Securities.....................	78bkd	−6	−32	−4	−113	−119	−188	−223	−478	−341	−388	−1,287	−426
Debt Securities.......................	78bld	−20	−24	−5	−6	−138	−6	−4	−3	23	72	—	1
Portfolio Investment Liab., n.i.e......	78bgd	228	548	163	286	406	−224	−125	75	−54	1,724	1,211	1,244
Equity Securities.....................	78bmd	222	465	171	294	156	−346	−107	123	43	−9	1	−47
Debt Securities.......................	78bnd	6	83	−8	−8	250	122	−18	−48	−97	1,733	1,210	1,291
Financial Derivatives Assets...........	78bwd	....	....	....	....	....	....	....	....	....	....	....	....
Financial Derivatives Liabilities.......	78bxd	....	....	....	....	....	....	....	....	....	....	....	....
Other Investment Assets...............	78bhd	375	−564	−270	−499	391	64	126	191	664	—	127	13
Monetary Authorities..................	78bod	84	−2	−2	−33	−104	20	−5	−31	−16	152	119	85
General Government..................	78bpd	—	—	—	—	—	—	—	−60	−5	−4	−203	−64
Banks..................................	78bqd	121	−272	−425	−464	869	25	−102	233	48	35	186	71
Other Sectors........................	78brd	170	−290	157	−2	−374	19	233	49	638	−183	25	−79
Other Investment Liab., n.i.e...........	78bid	−418	653	1,285	640	3,102	545	−1,041	421	171	−1,581	−506	−273
Monetary Authorities..................	78bsd	−943	37	−23	−87	−8	−38	−33	24	−11	−4	−8	6
General Government..................	78btd	325	98	−213	−438	713	−22	−69	666	599	−781	−294	−130
Banks..................................	78bud	146	−247	704	224	1,667	−225	−1,001	−168	−499	−513	−84	53
Other Sectors........................	78bvd	54	765	817	941	730	830	62	−101	82	−284	−119	−202
Net Errors and Omissions.................	78cad	1,231	443	285	708	−225	365	112	631	185	197	783	178
Overall Balance.........................	78cbd	−359	1,553	−590	880	2,055	−1,241	−862	−130	432	1,010	561	2,456
Reserves and Related Items............	79dad	359	−1,553	590	−880	−2,055	1,241	862	130	−432	−1,010	−561	−2,456
Reserve Assets.........................	79dbd	−663	−3,059	−921	−1,784	−1,493	1,142	985	329	−276	−851	−515	−2,442
Use of Fund Credit and Loans........	79dcd	254	—	—	—	149	−145	−147	−141	−154	−172	−110	−40
Exceptional Financing....................	79ded	768	1,506	1,512	904	−711	244	24	−58	−1	14	64	26

		1993	1994	1995	1996	1997	1998	1999	2000	2001	2002	2003	2004
International Investment Position							*Millions of US Dollars*						
Assets..	79aad	7,074	10,712	12,400	14,771	16,140	15,105	14,434	14,369	14,405	15,706	18,029	21,204
Direct Investment Abroad..............	79abd	109	109	567	543	602	438	651	505	649	666	814	874
Portfolio Investment.....................	79acd	283	313	356	501	828	1,142	1,373	2,070	2,372	2,702	4,573	5,238
Equity Securities........................	79add	283	313	294	416	582	867	1,070	1,661	1,948	2,293	3,896	4,346
Debt Securities.........................	79aed	—	—	62	85	246	275	303	409	424	409	677	892
Financial Derivatives....................	79ald	—	—	—	—	—	—	—	—	—			
Other Investment........................	79afd	2,928	3,477	3,742	4,208	3,699	3,656	3,526	3,240	2,555	2,656	2,445	2,453
Monetary Authorities.................	79agd	77	64	62	62	48	49	50	46	47	—	—	—
General Government.................	79ahd	—	—	—	—	—	—	—	—	—			
Banks.....................................	79aid	791	1,062	1,487	1,951	1,082	1,057	1,159	926	878	843	657	586
Other Sectors...........................	79ajd	2,060	2,350	2,193	2,195	2,569	2,550	2,317	2,268	1,630	1,813	1,788	1,867
Reserve Assets............................	79akd	3,754	6,813	7,735	9,518	11,011	9,869	8,883	8,553	8,829	9,682	10,197	12,639
Liabilities..	79lad	29,707	36,200	40,390	43,533	40,228	41,099	41,162	41,321	41,456	43,411	45,461	47,379
Dir. Invest. in Rep. Economy..........	79lbd	1,642	4,451	5,510	6,720	7,753	8,297	9,791	11,062	11,835	12,549	12,876	13,310
Portfolio Investment.....................	79lcd	695	1,636	1,681	3,185	8,138	7,312	7,013	6,384	6,436	7,544	8,723	9,987
Equity Securities........................	79ldd	689	1,547	1,599	3,111	3,685	2,737	2,859	2,278	2,427	2,990	2,999	2,952
Debt Securities.........................	79led	6	89	81	73	4,453	4,575	4,154	4,106	4,010	4,554	5,724	7,035
Financial Derivatives....................	79lld	—	—	—	—	—	—	—	—	—			
Other Investment........................	79lfd	27,370	30,113	33,199	33,629	24,336	25,490	24,357	23,874	23,185	23,318	23,863	24,082
Monetary Authorities.................	79lgd	1,045	1,137	1,131	1,013	1,092	947	745	592	410	256	151	122
General Government.................	79lhd	22,765	24,978	26,612	25,661	13,969	14,663	14,743	14,758	14,681	15,754	16,593	16,977
Banks.....................................	79lid	1,036	797	1,501	1,728	3,398	3,174	2,173	2,005	1,506	993	909	961
Other Sectors...........................	79ljd	2,524	3,200	3,954	5,226	5,876	6,705	6,696	6,520	6,589	6,315	6,210	6,022
Government Finance						*Millions of Nuevos Soles: Year Ending December 31*							
Deficit (-) or Surplus......................	80	−2,528	−3,123	−4,099	−1,980	−1,260	−1,877	−5,485	−5,197	−5,290	−4,263	−3,713	−2,977
Revenue.......................................	81	† 9,421	14,808	18,729	22,260	25,325	26,726	26,020	28,240	27,350	28,930	31,929	35,570
Grants Received...........................	81z	62	201	111	325	325	405	445	635	702	.....	.....	.....
Expenditure................................	82	11,605	16,985	21,903	23,183	25,406	28,056	31,415	33,202	32,413	33,062	35,510	38,415
Lending Minus Repayments...........	83	344	946	925	1,058	1,179	547	90	235	227	132	132	132
Financing													
Domestic.....................................	84a	395	664	1,222	891	1,248	1,316	5,815	3,093	3,225	267	327	−862
Foreign..	85a	2,132	2,460	2,877	1,090	12	561	−330	2,104	2,065	3,997	3,386	3,838
National Accounts							*Millions of Nuevos Soles*						
Househ.Cons.Expend.,incl.NPISHs....	96f	52,996	71,306	85,933	98,598	110,782	118,279	122,286	131,745	135,876	142,534	149,611	160,387
Government Consumption Expend...	91f	5,568	8,672	11,786	13,827	15,487	17,296	18,854	19,717	20,214	20,386	21,359	22,982
Gross Fixed Capital Formation..........	93e	12,697	20,901	29,095	30,747	37,472	39,163	37,867	37,610	35,132	35,128	39,839	43,301
Changes in Inventories.................	93i	679	1,030	918	537	479	93	−1,074	−79	275	2,177	2,091	990
Exports of Goods and Services..........	90c	8,627	12,590	15,118	17,975	22,272	22,076	25,855	29,867	30,128	32,811	37,270	49,170
Imports of Goods and Services (-).....	98c	11,304	15,922	21,991	24,754	29,219	31,014	29,907	33,434	33,312	34,379	37,146	42,382
Gross Domestic Product (GDP)........	99b	69,262	98,577	120,858	136,929	157,274	165,893	173,881	185,426	188,313	198,657	210,933	233,458
Net Primary Income from Abroad.....	98.n	−1,930	....	....	....	....	....	....	....	....	....	....	....
Gross National Income (GNI)............	99a	78,598											
GDP Volume 1994 Prices.................	99b.p	87,375	98,577	107,039	109,709	117,214	116,413	117,446	120,881	121,104	126,980	131,757	138,430
GDP Volume (2000=100)................	99bvp	72.3	81.5	88.5	90.8	97.0	96.3	97.2	100.0	100.2	105.0	109.0	114.5
GDP Deflator (2000=100)...............	99bip	51.7	65.2	73.6	81.4	87.5	92.9	96.5	100.0	101.4	102.0	104.4	109.9
							Millions: Midyear Estimates						
Population..............................	99z	23.01	23.42	23.84	24.26	24.68	25.11	25.54	25.95	26.36	26.76	27.16	27.56

		1993	1994	1995	1996	1997	1998	1999	2000	2001	2002	2003	2004
Exchange Rates						*Pesos per SDR: End of Period*							
Market Rate..................	aa	38.046	35.647	38.967	37.801	53.936	54.996	55.330	65.143	64.601	72.185	82.574	87.383
				Pesos per US Dollar: End of Period (ae) Period Average (rf)									
Market Rate..................	ae	27.699	24.418	26.214	26.288	39.975	39.059	40.313	49.998	51.404	53.096	55.569	56.267
Market Rate..................	rf	27.120	26.417	25.714	26.216	29.471	40.893	39.089	44.192	50.993	51.604	54.203	56.040
				Index Numbers (2000=100): Period Averages									
Market Rate..................	ahx	162.4	166.7	170.8	167.6	151.6	107.7	112.5	100.0	86.2	85.2	81.1	78.4
Nominal Effective Exchange Rate.....	nec	135.4	144.9	143.3	146.2	141.0	107.1	109.9	100.0	91.1	89.6	79.5	73.1
Real Effective Exchange Rate...........	rec	103.2	108.6	111.4	121.3	120.6	98.6	107.2	100.0	95.1	95.5	83.2	79.6
Fund Position						*Millions of SDRs: End of Period*							
Quota................	2f.s	633	633	633	633	633	633	880	880	880	880	880	880
SDRs................	1b.s	7	17	5	2	1	1	5	1	11	7	1	1
Reserve Position in the Fund............	1c.s	87	87	87	87	87	87	87	87	87	87	87	87
Total Fund Cred.&Loans Outstg........	2tl	881	729	489	282	634	1,114	1,328	1,559	1,553	1,240	806	487
International Liquidity				*Millions of US Dollars Unless Otherwise Indicated: End of Period*									
Total Reserves minus Gold...............	1l.d	4,676	6,038	6,396	10,058	7,297	9,274	13,270	13,090	13,476	13,329	13,655	13,116
SDRs................	1b.d	10	24	8	2	2	2	7	2	14	10	2	1
Reserve Position in the Fund.........	1c.d	120	127	129	125	118	123	120	113	110	119	130	136
Foreign Exchange..................	1d.d	4,546	5,887	6,259	9,931	7,178	9,150	13,143	12,975	13,353	13,200	13,523	12,980
Gold (Million Fine Troy Ounces)...	1ad	3.221	2.892	3.580	4.651	4.988	5.432	6.199	7.228	7.980	8.729	8.217	7.119
Gold (National Valuation)................	1and	1,245	1,104	1,403	1,715	1,472	1,555	1,782	1,973	2,216	3,036	3,408	3,112
Monetary Authorities: Other Liab.....	4..d	2,653	2,295	2,523	2,489	2,578	3,272	4,423	4,826	6,029	5,555	6,011	4,725
Deposit Money Banks: Assets........	7a.d	4,778	6,036	6,402	8,185	8,878	9,153	10,114	8,181	7,468	8,074	8,239	9,637
Liabilities........	7b.d	2,913	4,640	6,420	14,364	15,406	12,751	11,978	10,302	8,730	8,009	7,582	8,987
Other Banking Insts.: Liabilities.......	7f.d	911	963	1,080	49	62	64	46	45	47	312	44	48
OBU: Foreign Assets..................	7k.d	508	485	283	174	203	123	121	137	304	313	291	294
Foreign Liabilities..................	7m.d	1,055	1,674	1,545	1,647	1,826	1,296	1,167	928	987	807	819	820
Monetary Authorities						*Billions of Pesos: End of Period*							
Foreign Assets....................	11	† 164.01	173.78	203.60	308.76	349.29	422.13	605.18	751.29	804.92	861.63	937.49	903.08
Claims on Central Government........	12a	† 293.48	233.87	227.85	240.26	226.57	194.18	237.91	165.80	132.96	149.43	125.10	76.71
Claims on Local Government............	12b	† —	—	—	—	—	—	—	—	—	—	—	—
Claims on Nonfin.Pub.Enterprises.....	12c	† 2.31	1.97	1.93	1.82	2.98	4.26	17.76	38.33	30.12	56.04	83.45	80.73
Claims on Deposit Money Banks......	12e	† 7.27	6.17	7.31	7.68	26.43	18.20	12.69	48.98	40.94	17.46	27.83	18.09
Claims on Other Financial Insts.......	12f	† 5.91	4.60	6.26	6.48	8.02	13.51	14.18	15.10	10.87	9.85	9.14	10.56
Claims on Nonbank Financial Insts....	12g	† —	—	—	—	—	—	—	—	—	—	—	—
Reserve Money....................	14	† 210.25	226.93	255.17	338.17	317.63	323.83	442.74	395.88	351.91	409.34	447.56	466.39
of which: Currency Outside DMBs..	14a	† 84.08	95.68	110.89	122.95	143.64	146.06	218.47	192.30	194.67	220.04	238.61	259.57
Time Deposits....................	15	† 8.12	24.69	28.37	39.89	13.61	15.47	31.12	52.36	26.65	49.80	33.30	24.06
Liabs. of Central Bank: Securities.....	16ac	† 24.79	4.57	.63	.25	.03	.03	.03	.03	—	—	—	—
Restricted Deposits....................	16b	† 6.51	4.92	2.12	1.68	1.68	1.69	.39	.04	.04	.32	.22	.68
Foreign Liabilities....................	16c	† 107.00	82.01	85.22	76.10	137.26	189.08	251.76	342.86	410.25	384.47	400.54	308.42
Central Government Deposits..........	16d	† 113.80	84.54	73.43	106.54	78.35	59.49	90.74	95.42	86.52	78.89	104.23	60.29
Capital Accounts....................	17a	† 21.06	26.49	30.15	30.08	71.98	88.15	100.23	159.45	188.96	197.81	222.77	240.90
Other Items (Net)....................	17r	† –18.56	–33.76	–28.15	–27.71	–7.24	–25.44	–29.28	–26.54	–44.50	–26.23	–25.61	–11.55
Deposit Money Banks						*Billions of Pesos: End of Period*							
Reserves....................	20	114.55	123.30	123.93	142.84	161.06	168.17	190.99	178.09	181.18	216.57	206.93	202.31
Claims on Mon.Author.:Securities....	20c	2.31	.94	.08	.08	.03	.03	.03	.03	—	—	—	—
Foreign Assets....................	21	132.35	147.38	167.83	215.16	354.90	357.52	407.73	409.03	383.90	428.72	457.81	542.22
Claims on Central Government........	22a	98.89	147.56	177.21	237.53	304.31	300.34	332.42	432.55	534.56	563.11	635.41	797.43
Claims on Local Government............	22b	.80	2.37	4.68	6.95	9.07	10.34	12.20	15.52	17.15	18.41	20.27	24.42
Claims on Nonfin.Pub.Enterprises.....	22c	22.84	17.07	14.87	16.37	25.65	40.56	47.68	59.18	82.78	99.18	168.77	170.41
Claims on Private Sector....................	22d	388.87	491.98	715.32	1,063.80	1,370.07	1,279.19	1,249.58	1,316.59	1,293.29	1,303.35	1,317.66	1,439.68
Claims on Other Financial Insts........	22f	11.50	24.61	27.09	60.26	76.61	117.98	130.68	175.13	157.71	166.94	179.86	126.43
Demand Deposits....................	24	49.10	55.08	72.04	96.41	111.92	134.09	172.87	192.98	191.94	252.77	274.92	300.96
Time, Savings,& Fgn.Currency Dep...	25	477.63	613.16	765.20	949.71	1,225.32	1,332.79	1,483.42	1,622.30	1,720.15	1,833.30	1,893.55	2,097.57
Money Market Instruments.............	26aa	4.61	4.61	6.24	6.64	12.07	6.11	7.19	4.21	3.98	3.37	3.46	1.08
Restricted Deposits....................	26b	4.25	3.42	3.55	2.99	3.28	7.05	4.03	5.16	4.76	3.86	3.68	5.46
Foreign Liabilities....................	26c	80.70	113.29	168.29	377.59	615.86	498.05	482.86	515.10	448.75	425.22	421.30	505.46
Central Government Deposits..........	26d	41.76	26.62	39.41	51.73	38.90	32.43	39.86	33.97	42.39	39.87	33.91	51.28
Credit from Monetary Authorities.....	26g	22.17	17.06	16.67	15.26	15.02	10.38	8.47	38.09	26.73	16.31	19.63	10.32
Capital Accounts....................	27a	107.10	132.36	184.71	243.17	327.28	376.53	440.89	467.48	479.22	511.74	539.22	557.16
Other Items (Net)....................	27r	–15.21	–10.40	–25.10	–.51	–47.95	–123.31	–268.28	–293.17	–267.36	–290.14	–202.97	–226.60
Monetary Survey						*Billions of Pesos: End of Period*							
Foreign Assets (Net)........................	31n	† 108.66	125.86	117.92	70.23	–48.93	92.51	278.29	302.37	329.81	480.66	573.46	631.23
Domestic Credit....................	32	† 669.63	813.42	1,062.38	1,475.20	1,906.05	1,868.45	1,911.82	2,088.82	2,130.52	2,247.55	2,401.52	2,614.80
Claims on Central Govt. (Net)........	32an	† 236.81	270.27	292.21	319.53	413.64	402.61	439.74	468.97	538.61	593.77	622.37	762.57
Claims on Local Government........	32b	† .80	2.37	4.68	6.95	9.07	10.34	12.20	15.52	17.15	18.41	20.27	24.42
Claims on Nonfin.Pub.Enterprises...	32c	† 25.14	19.04	16.80	18.19	28.63	44.82	65.44	97.51	112.90	155.23	252.22	251.14
Claims on Private Sector....................	32d	† 389.47	492.53	715.34	1,063.80	1,370.08	1,279.19	1,249.59	1,316.59	1,293.29	1,303.35	1,317.66	1,439.68
Claims on Other Financial Insts.....	32f	† 17.41	29.21	33.35	66.73	84.63	131.49	144.86	190.22	168.58	176.79	188.99	136.99
Claims on Nonbank Financial Insts.	32g	† —	—	—	—	—	—	—	—	—	—	—	—
Money....................	34	† 143.71	159.90	194.63	233.12	266.33	285.95	395.56	390.55	392.25	478.48	519.84	567.74
Quasi-Money....................	35	† 485.75	637.85	793.58	989.60	1,238.93	1,348.25	1,514.53	1,674.66	1,746.80	1,883.10	1,926.86	2,121.63
Money Market Instruments.............	36aa	† 4.61	4.61	6.24	6.64	12.07	6.11	7.19	4.21	3.98	3.37	3.46	1.08
Liabs. of Central Bank: Securities.....	36ac	† 22.48	3.63	.55	.17	—	—	—	—	—	—	—	—
Restricted Deposits....................	36b	† 10.76	8.34	5.67	4.67	4.96	8.73	4.42	5.20	4.80	4.17	3.90	6.14
Capital Accounts....................	37a	† 128.16	158.84	214.86	273.25	399.26	464.68	541.12	626.94	668.17	709.55	761.99	798.05
Other Items (Net)....................	37r	† –17.18	–33.90	–35.22	37.98	–64.42	–152.77	–272.71	–310.36	–355.66	–350.46	–241.08	–248.61
Money plus Quasi-Money.................	35l	† 629.46	797.75	988.20	1,222.72	1,505.26	1,634.20	1,910.09	2,065.21	2,139.05	2,361.58	2,446.70	2,689.36

		1993	1994	1995	1996	1997	1998	1999	2000	2001	2002	2003	2004
Other Banking Institutions						*Billions of Pesos: End of Period*							
Reserves...............................	40	20.33	15.51	18.57	18.50	19.78	15.34	14.92	23.56	18.68	20.87	21.65	24.81
Claims on Central Government........	42a	10.82	12.93	19.09	3.38	3.95	2.35	1.74	3.46	1.91	24.35	4.60	6.22
Claims on Private Sector................	42d	82.32	115.93	143.41	127.55	139.92	144.74	145.55	152.43	166.17	161.22	189.60	211.22
Time and Savings Deposits..............	45	63.19	69.09	93.73	106.89	120.70	119.08	120.58	131.77	151.64	171.99	187.29	213.87
Bonds...	46ab	.15	2.28	3.65	4.22	5.39	6.38	6.29	6.38	5.49	5.14	2.76	3.38
Foreign Liabilities...........................	46c	25.23	23.51	28.31	1.29	2.49	2.49	1.87	2.23	2.44	16.56	2.44	2.67
Credit from Monetary Authorities......	46g	3.53	3.56	3.65	3.67	5.08	10.59	10.74	11.95	8.40	7.34	7.54	9.05
Capital Accounts...........................	47a	18.97	27.08	32.99	27.33	35.93	40.73	48.63	49.27	48.26	49.40	46.22	44.26
Other Items (Net)...........................	47r	2.41	18.85	18.74	6.04	−5.95	−16.84	−25.89	−22.15	−29.48	−43.98	−30.41	−30.99
Interest Rates						*Percent Per Annum*							
Discount Rate (End of Period)...........	60	9.400	8.300	10.830	11.700	14.640	12.400	7.894	13.806	8.298	4.193	5.532	8.357
Money Market Rate.........................	60b	13.765	13.989	11.925	12.770	16.155	13.900	10.165	10.835	9.751	7.149	6.969	7.047
Treasury Bill Rate...........................	60c	12.448	12.714	11.761	12.338	12.893	15.004	9.996	9.913	9.734	5.494	5.872	7.320
Savings Rate.................................	60k	8.279	8.068	8.044	7.945	8.951	10.952	7.640	7.308	7.655	4.240	4.214	4.265
Savings Rate (Foreign Currency).......	60k.f	2.213	2.268	2.275	2.200	2.200	2.200	2.200	2.200	2.004	1.288	.885	.837
Deposit Rate.................................	60l	9.606	10.539	8.392	9.683	10.194	12.106	8.167	8.305	8.744	4.608	5.221	6.178
Deposit Rate (Foreign Currency).......	60l.f	3.212	4.203	5.295	5.097	5.322	5.441	5.037	5.207	3.804	2.322	1.908	1.916
Lending Rate.................................	60p	14.683	15.057	14.682	14.840	16.276	16.777	11.776	10.907	12.402	9.139	9.472	10.079
Government Bond Yield..................	61	....	13.250	14.250	13.990	13.008	† 17.985	12.332	11.767	13.399	8.688	8.715	10.270
Prices, Production, Labor						*Index Numbers (2000=100): Period Averages*							
Share Prices.................................	62	109.7	137.3	122.4	119.3	103.9	69.1	106.7	100.0	64.4	48.4	40.8	57.9
Producer Prices.............................	63	64.1	66.7	69.6	72.4	74.9	† 83.1	88.9	100.0	117.0	120.4	130.2	140.0
Consumer Prices............................	64	63.3	† 68.6	73.2	78.7	83.1	90.8	96.2	100.0	106.8	110.0	113.8	120.6
Manufacturing Production..............	66ey	† 169.8	192.3	227.3	246.8	268.5	80.1	86.7	100.0	108.3	106.5	115.1	125.1
Manufacturing Empl. (1990=100)....	67ey	87.0	85.8	....	....	....	....	....	....	....	....	....	....
						Number in Thousands: Period Averages							
Labor Force.................................	67d	26,879	27,654	28,380	29,732	30,355	31,055	30,759	30,912	32,809	33,936	34,571	35,860
Employment.................................	67e	24,382	25,032	25,676	27,186	27,715	27,912	27,742	27,453	29,156	30,062	30,635	31,611
Unemployment.............................	67c	2,497	2,622	2,704	2,546	2,640	3,143	3,017	3,459	3,653	3,874	3,936	4,249
Unemployment Rate (%).................	67r	9.3	9.5	9.5	8.6	8.7	10.1	9.8	11.2	11.1	11.4	11.4	11.8
Intl. Transactions & Positions						*Millions of Pesos*							
Exports..	70	302,998	350,078	450,487	535,054	738,415	1,206,197	1,432,594	1,773,137	1,665,023	1,884,323	2,008,842	2,224,742
Sugar..	70i	2,740	1,629	1,713	3,544	2,864	3,200	2,597	2,227	1,124	1,830	3,122	3,733
Coconut Oil................................	70ai	9,698	12,552	21,242	14,960	19,846	28,857	13,379	20,450	21,292	18,196	27,365	32,379
Imports, c.i.f................................	71	509,035	596,611	729,960	894,665	1,139,830	1,290,274	1,273,001	1,636,810	1,780,531	1,919,156	2,141,226	2,373,188
Imports, f.o.b................................	71.v	479,296	562,163	679,701	835,863	1,060,815	1,213,859	1,201,519	1,526,636	1,684,742	1,827,806	2,030,102	2,258,633
Volume of Exports.........................	72	73.1	86.2	56.1	62.2	73.6	79.7	86.9	100.0	88.6	104.9	....	....
Sugar..	72i	229.0	128.6	108.2	224.4	139.7	130.5	100.7	100.0	40.0	62.6	97.2	162.7
Coconut Oil................................	72ai	82.8	81.8	129.2	76.4	104.1	113.6	46.1	100.0	136.6	91.0	114.3	92.4
Volume of Imports.........................	73	119.5	143.3	83.4	97.9	106.4	84.9	94.8	100.0	113.6	115.6	....	....
Export Prices.................................	76	80.3	80.7	81.3	86.2	89.4	96.7	106.3	100.0	95.5	88.6	....	....
Sugar (Wholesale Price).................	76i	49.3	53.3	65.3	65.1	67.0	98.0	118.6	100.0	116.2	120.9	132.5	94.6
Coconut Oil (W'sale price)..............	76ai	53.5	68.7	76.1	92.1	89.5	111.2	138.2	100.0	73.0	95.6	110.3	162.1
Import Prices.................................	76.x	102.9	104.0	101.0	106.1	108.1	111.1	103.8	100.0	92.2	97.3	....	....

Volume of Exports (72) through Import Prices (76.x): 2000=100

		1993	1994	1995	1996	1997	1998	1999	2000	2001	2002	2003	2004
Balance of Payments						*Millions of US Dollars: Minus Sign Indicates Debit*							
Current Account, n.i.e.	78ald	−3,016	−2,950	−1,980	−3,953	−4,351	1,546	7,219	6,258	1,323	4,383	1,396	2,080
Goods: Exports f.o.b.	78aad	11,375	13,483	17,447	20,543	25,228	29,496	34,211	37,295	31,243	34,377	35,342	38,728
Goods: Imports f.o.b.	78abd	−17,597	−21,333	−26,391	−31,885	−36,355	−29,524	−29,252	−33,481	−31,986	−33,970	−40,797	−45,109
Trade Balance	78acd	−6,222	−7,850	−8,944	−11,342	−11,127	−28	4,959	3,814	−743	407	−5,455	−6,381
Services: Credit	78add	4,673	6,768	9,348	12,947	15,137	7,477	4,803	3,972	3,148	3,055	3,299	4,101
Services: Debit	78aed	−3,090	−4,654	−6,926	−9,429	−14,122	−10,107	−7,515	−6,402	−5,198	−4,072	−5,024	−5,383
Balance on Goods & Services	78afd	−4,639	−5,736	−6,522	−7,824	−10,112	−2,658	2,247	1,384	−2,793	−610	−7,180	−7,663
Income: Credit	78agd	2,824	3,782	6,067	6,059	7,698	6,440	8,082	7,804	7,152	7,946	3,340	3,549
Income: Debit	78ahd	−1,900	−1,932	−2,405	−2,777	−3,017	−2,671	−3,622	−3,367	−3,483	−3,456	−3,566	−3,402
Balance on Gds, Serv. & Inc.	78aid	−3,715	−3,886	−2,860	−4,542	−5,431	1,111	6,707	5,821	876	3,880	−7,406	−7,516
Current Transfers, n.i.e.: Credit	78ajd	746	1,041	1,147	1,185	1,670	758	607	552	517	594	9,009	9,858
Current Transfers: Debit	78akd	−47	−105	−267	−596	−590	−323	−95	−115	−70	−91	−207	−262
Capital Account, n.i.e.	78bcd	—	—	—	—	—	—	−8	38	−12	−19	23	−23
Capital Account, n.i.e.: Credit	78bad	—	—	—	—	—	—	44	74	12	2	41	5
Capital Account: Debit	78bbd	—	—	—	—	—	—	−52	−36	−24	−21	−18	−28
Financial Account, n.i.e.	78bjd	3,267	5,120	5,309	11,277	6,498	483	−2,250	−4,042	−745	−2,399	−1,716	−2,977
Direct Investment Abroad	78bdd	−374	−302	−399	−182	−136	−160	29	108	160	−59	−197	−412
Dir. Invest. in Rep. Econ., n.i.e.	78bed	1,238	1,591	1,478	1,517	1,222	2,287	1,725	1,345	989	1,792	347	469
Portfolio Investment Assets	78bfd	−949	−632	−1,429	191	−9	−603	−807	−812	−457	−449	−1,458	−1,951
Equity Securities	78bkd	....	....	....	21	30	−184	−55	−42	−4	−26	−45	−115
Debt Securities	78bld	−949	−632	−1,429	170	−39	−419	−752	−770	−453	−423	−1,413	−1,836
Portfolio Investment Liab., n.i.e.	78bgd	897	901	2,619	5,126	600	−325	7,681	1,019	997	1,571	153	324
Equity Securities	78bmd	....	....	....	2,101	−406	264	1,410	−183	383	404	460	418
Debt Securities	78bnd	897	901	2,619	3,025	1,006	−589	6,271	1,202	614	1,167	−307	−94
Financial Derivatives Assets	78bwd	....	....	....	....	....	....	....	....	....	....	54	58
Financial Derivatives Liabilities	78bxd	....	....	....	....	....	....	....	....	....	....	−118	−85
Other Investment Assets	78bhd	—	—	—	−1,745	425	809	−18,639	−15,313	−14,034	−13,165	737	−1,581
Monetary Authorities	78bod	....	....	....	....	....	....	—	....	....	....	....	....
General Government	78bpd	....	....	....	....	....	....	—	....	....	....	....	....
Banks	78bqd	....	....	....	−1,745	425	809	−941	2,265	465	374	364	−316
Other Sectors	78brd	....	....	....	—	—	—	−17,698	−17,578	−14,499	−13,539	373	−1,265
Other Investment Liab., n.i.e.	78bid	2,455	3,562	3,040	6,370	4,396	−1,525	7,761	9,611	11,600	7,911	−1,234	201
Monetary Authorities	78bsd	—	—	—	199	−98	5	75	166	621	−814	3	−1,118
General Government	78btd	1,065	−1,121	−408	−808	−218	−207	340	−125	16	−131	−19	−487
Banks	78bud	−229	1,694	1,648	5,036	1,668	−1,118	−2,221	−1,368	−723	50	−392	1,726
Other Sectors	78bvd	1,619	2,989	1,800	1,943	3,044	−205	9,567	10,938	11,686	8,806	−826	80
Net Errors and Omissions	78cad	85	157	−2,094	−2,986	−5,241	−750	−1,311	−2,630	−270	−2,076	218	−667
Overall Balance	78cbd	336	2,327	1,235	4,338	−3,094	1,279	3,650	−376	296	−111	−79	−1,587
Reserves and Related Items	79dad	−336	−2,327	−1,235	−4,338	3,094	−1,279	−3,650	376	−296	111	79	1,587
Reserve Assets	79dbd	−447	−2,107	−873	−4,037	2,610	−1,938	−3,938	73	−465	399	356	1,637
Use of Fund Credit and Loans	79dcd	111	−220	−362	−301	485	659	288	303	−8	−407	−607	−472
Exceptional Financing	79ded	—	—	—	—	—	—	—	—	177	118	330	422
International Investment Position							*Millions of US Dollars*						
Assets	79aad	....	....	....	....	....	....	....	....	29,578	31,038	31,940	....
Direct Investment Abroad	79abd	....	....	....	....	....	....	....	....	729	815	1,194	....
Portfolio Investment	79acd	....	....	....	....	....	....	....	....	2,526	3,228	4,075	....
Equity Securities	79add	....	....	....	....	....	....	....	....	111	119	167	....
Debt Securities	79aed	....	....	....	....	....	....	....	....	2,415	3,109	3,908	....
Financial Derivatives	79ald	....	....	....	....	....	....	....	....	—	—	—	....
Other Investment	79afd	....	....	....	....	....	....	....	....	10,677	10,823	9,805	....
Monetary Authorities	79agd	....	....	....	....	....	....	....	....	—	—	—	....
General Government	79ahd	....	....	....	....	....	....	....	....	33	35	35	....
Banks	79aid	....	....	....	....	....	....	....	....	6,379	6,191	5,410	....
Other Sectors	79ajd	....	....	....	....	....	....	....	....	4,265	4,597	4,360	....
Reserve Assets	79akd	....	....	....	....	....	....	....	....	15,646	16,172	16,866	....
Liabilities	79lad	....	....	....	....	....	....	....	....	66,322	69,297	73,640	....
Dir. Invest. in Rep. Economy	79lbd	....	....	....	....	....	....	....	....	11,273	11,888	12,216	....
Portfolio Investment	79lcd	....	....	....	....	....	....	....	....	16,161	18,217	20,742	....
Equity Securities	79ldd	....	....	....	....	....	....	....	....	1,922	2,318	2,709	....
Debt Securities	79led	....	....	....	....	....	....	....	....	14,239	15,899	18,033	....
Financial Derivatives	79lld	....	....	....	....	....	....	....	....	—	—	—	....
Other Investment	79lfd	....	....	....	....	....	....	....	....	38,888	39,192	40,682	....
Monetary Authorities	79lgd	....	....	....	....	....	....	....	....	4,663	3,738	3,648	....
General Government	79lhd	....	....	....	....	....	....	....	....	13,120	14,054	15,619	....
Banks	79lid	....	....	....	....	....	....	....	....	5,271	5,915	6,291	....
Other Sectors	79ljd	....	....	....	....	....	....	....	....	15,834	15,485	15,124	....
Government Finance						*Millions of Pesos: Year Ending December 31*							
Deficit (-) or Surplus	80	−21,891	18,114	11,074	6,256	1,564	−49,981	−111,658	−136,110	−147,023	−210,741	−199,868	−187,057
Revenue	81	258,855	334,488	360,232	409,880	470,087	462,119	478,210	504,349	561,857	566,089	625,432	699,699
Grants Received	81z	1,550	739	988	569	1,756	396	292	1,376	1,991	1,052	1,198	74
Expenditure	82	272,391	309,942	341,726	401,017	466,690	511,078	585,425	638,665	706,443	775,256	818,422	881,110
Lending Minus Repayments	83	9,905	7,171	8,420	3,176	3,589	1,418	4,735	3,170	4,428	2,626	8,076	5,720
Financing													
Domestic	84a	8,979	−4,408	2,272	−348	5,254	37,635	28,858	90,927	124,108	101,628	56,006	105,890
Foreign	85a	12,912	−13,706	−13,346	−5,908	−6,818	12,346	82,800	45,183	22,915	109,113	143,862	81,167
Debt: Domestic	88a	640,867	638,025	....	....	....	....	....	....	....	....	....	....
Foreign	89a	348,955	317,068	....	....	....	....	....	....	....	....	....	....

Philippines 566

		1993	1994	1995	1996	1997	1998	1999	2000	2001	2002	2003	2004
National Accounts						*Billions of Pesos*							
Househ.Cons.Expend.,incl.NPISHs....	96f	1,122.5	1,258.8	1,411.9	1,595.3	1,762.0	1,980.1	2,161.6	2,335.5	2,565.0	2,751.0	2,988.2	3,344.2
Government Consumption Expend...	91f	149.1	182.8	217.0	259.5	319.9	354.4	389.2	438.9	444.8	456.9	477.4	494.6
Gross Fixed Capital Formation.........	93e	350.5	400.1	423.2	508.7	592.6	563.6	568.2	710.5	651.3	698.1	715.5	797.9
Changes in Inventories....................	93i	3.1	7.2	4.7	12.9	8.7	−21.5	−10.0	−.4	37.8	2.1	−.3	27.5
Exports of Goods and Services.........	90c	462.4	572.6	693.0	879.8	1,188.0	1,389.9	1,532.2	1,858.6	1,785.2	1,991.3	2,125.4	2,441.0
Imports of Goods and Services (-).....	98c	586.9	679.4	842.1	1,070.6	1,438.9	1,566.6	1,527.4	1,794.7	1,899.4	2,010.5	2,212.7	2,413.5
Gross Domestic Product (GDP).........	99b	1,474.5	1,692.9	1,906.0	2,171.9	2,426.7	2,665.1	2,976.9	3,354.7	3,631.5	3,883.2	4,210.5	4,739.1
Net Primary Income from Abroad.....	98.n	35.1	43.5	52.6	89.4	101.6	137.1	159.3	211.3	245.1	255.0	298.4	341.2
Gross National Income (GNI)............	99a	1,509.5	1,736.4	1,958.6	2,261.3	2,528.3	2,802.1	3,136.2	3,566.1	3,876.6	4,138.2	4,508.9	5,080.4
Consumption of Fixed Capital..........	99cf	131.6	151.5	172.0	190.5	....	....	....	....	....	....	....	....
GDP Volume 1985 Prices.................	99b.p	734.2	766.4	802.2	849.1	893.2	888.0	918.2	955.0	987.4	1,042.1	1,093.3	1,148.0
GDP Volume (2000=100)...............	99bvp	76.9	80.3	84.0	88.9	93.5	93.0	96.1	100.0	103.4	109.1	114.5	120.2
GDP Deflator (2000=100)...............	99bip	57.2	62.9	67.6	72.8	77.3	85.4	92.3	100.0	104.7	106.1	109.6	117.5
						Millions: Midyear Estimates							
Population...............................	99z	65.45	66.92	68.40	69.87	71.35	72.82	74.29	75.77	77.24	78.71	80.17	81.62

		1993	1994	1995	1996	1997	1998	1999	2000	2001	2002	2003	2004
Exchange Rates						*Zlotys per SDR: End of Period*							
Market Rate	aa	2.9317	3.5579	3.6687	4.1349	4.7467	4.9337	5.6936	5.3982	5.0097	5.2189	5.5587	4.6441
						Zlotys per US Dollar: End of Period (ae) Period Average (rf)							
Market Rate	ae	2.1344	2.4372	2.4680	2.8755	3.5180	3.5040	4.1483	4.1432	3.9863	3.8388	3.7408	2.9904
Market Rate	rf	1.8115	2.2723	2.4250	2.6961	3.2793	3.4754	3.9671	4.3461	4.0939	4.0800	3.8891	3.6576
						Index Numbers (2000=100): Period Averages							
Market Rate	ahx	241.8	191.2	179.0	161.2	132.8	125.0	109.6	100.0	106.0	106.4	111.6	119.3
Nominal Effective Exchange Rate	nec	187.6	149.4	130.5	122.3	113.0	108.5	98.9	100.0	110.9	107.4	97.9	97.0
Real Effective Exchange Rate	rec	75.6	76.2	81.2	88.2	91.7	96.2	92.3	100.0	111.8	108.2	98.9	99.7
Fund Position						*Millions of SDRs: End of Period*							
Quota	2f.s	989	989	989	989	989	989	1,369	1,369	1,369	1,369	1,369	1,369
SDRs	1b.s	1	1	2	3	4	5	8	14	21	29	37	45
Reserve Position in the Fund	1c.s	. 77	77	77	77	77	77	172	172	367	479	538	451
Total Fund Cred.&Loans Outstg.	2tl	498	919	—	—	—	—	—	—	—	—	—	—
International Liquidity					*Millions of US Dollars Unless Otherwise Indicated: End of Period*								
Total Reserves minus Gold	1l.d	4,091.9	5,841.8	14,774.1	17,844.0	20,407.2	27,325.2	26,354.7	26,562.0	25,648.4	28,649.7	32,579.1	35,323.9
SDRs	1b.d	.7	1.5	2.2	4.4	5.4	7.1	11.2	17.7	25.8	39.5	54.8	70.1
Reserve Position in the Fund	1c.d	105.9	112.6	114.6	110.9	104.1	108.6	236.4	224.4	461.0	651.0	799.4	700.9
Foreign Exchange	1d.d	3,985.3	5,727.7	14,657.2	17,728.7	20,297.7	27,209.5	26,107.1	26,319.9	25,161.6	27,959.2	31,724.9	34,552.8
Gold (Million Fine Troy Ounces)	1ad	.473	.473	.473	.473	.904	3.305	3.306	3.306	3.308	3.309	3.307	3.308
Gold (National Valuation)	1and	189.0	189.0	189.0	189.0	262.4	950.0	959.4	901.5	914.7	1,134.0	1,380.5	1,448.8
Monetary Authorities: Other Liab.	4..d	446.2	355.6	363.5	246.4	914.3	1,028.2	1,939.3	498.6	588.2	145.6	233.4	142.1
Deposit Money Banks: Assets	7a.d	5,925.5	7,742.2	7,154.4	6,132.1	7,275.5	5,405.3	7,874.7	11,323.1	15,307.2	13,707.8	14,920.9	28,111.2
Liabilities	7b.d	1,469.8	1,543.2	2,070.1	2,746.5	4,284.0	5,213.8	6,745.7	6,608.9	7,766.1	9,069.2	12,638.8	17,008.2
Monetary Authorities						*Millions of Zlotys: End of Period*							
Foreign Assets	11	10,113	15,475	37,532	52,498	75,500	99,213	113,910	114,258	106,183	114,772	128,207	110,456
Claims on General Government	12a	15,729	19,530	11,534	12,761	16,792	17,765	18,803	16,745	18,426	6,579	384	—
Claims on Other Resident Sectors	12d	27	23	22	59	66	60	71	68	23	23	24	108
Claims on Deposit Money Banks	12e	6,362	7,450	8,244	11,246	9,710	8,044	7,394	7,121	6,033	5,421	4,833	4,348
Reserve Money	14	15,993	19,615	28,441	34,262	45,919	53,656	52,957	48,818	63,704	62,066	66,337	69,583
of which: Currency Outside DMBs	14a	9,982	12,274	19,530	23,563	27,256	30,225	38,083	34,113	38,213	42,193	49,417	50,776
Nonreserve Liabilities to Banks	16b	1,406	3,462	9,465	14,660	15,662	28,576	24,694	33,738	24,167	20,953	14,202	13,940
Foreign Liabilities	16c	2,411	4,135	897	708	3,216	3,603	8,045	2,066	2,345	559	873	425
General Government Deposits	16d	2,272	2,773	3,440	6,127	4,285	4,010	7,040	9,774	7,689	7,414	11,429	14,595
Capital Accounts	17a	210	300	400	400	400	1,548	1,548	1,594	1,694	1,748	1,845	2,059
Other Items (Net)	17r	9,939	12,193	14,689	20,406	32,586	33,688	45,894	42,202	31,064	34,055	38,761	14,311
Deposit Money Banks						*Millions of Zlotys: End of Period*							
Reserves	20	6,045	7,343	8,806	10,633	15,049	23,336	14,867	14,661	21,485	19,857	16,903	18,396
Claims on Mon.Author.:Securities	20c	732	1,879	4,585	11,018	13,927	28,321	24,539	33,507	24,133	20,735	14,225	13,912
Other Claims on Monetary Author.	20n	674	998	3,528	2,739	1,288	—	—	—	4,000	8	12	54
Foreign Assets	21	12,647	18,869	17,657	17,633	25,595	18,940	32,666	46,914	61,019	52,622	55,816	84,064
Claims on General Government	22a	19,201	27,204	38,920	48,638	50,980	57,431	63,792	54,591	65,668	78,040	96,008	100,193
Claims on Other Resident Sectors	22d	33,274	41,908	56,946	81,194	107,294	135,498	169,828	197,759	212,575	221,809	236,650	245,176
Demand Deposits	24	9,654	15,175	17,817	28,702	34,425	41,438	49,970	48,420	51,941	70,683	84,142	95,278
Time, Savings,& Fgn.Currency Dep.	25	36,268	49,844	66,913	84,186	111,084	149,104	175,302	211,926	244,644	216,524	214,605	219,938
Foreign Liabilities	26c	3,137	3,761	5,109	7,898	15,071	18,269	27,983	27,382	30,958	34,815	47,279	50,861
General Government Deposits	26d	2,706	3,688	5,506	7,942	9,857	12,515	14,113	16,152	16,966	19,991	20,125	24,993
of which: Local Govt. Dep.	26db	1,149	1,503	2,523	3,401	4,395	5,551	7,146	7,472	7,313	8,434	8,818	11,335
Credit from Monetary Authorities	26g	6,338	7,020	7,788	10,685	9,180	7,565	7,010	6,800	5,763	4,023	3,636	3,407
Capital Accounts	27a	7,129	9,990	12,999	18,534	24,715	30,049	34,294	39,562	46,441	45,695	47,181	55,776
Other Items (Net)	27r	7,342	8,724	14,310	13,907	9,801	4,586	−2,980	−2,809	−7,832	1,339	2,648	11,542
Monetary Survey						*Millions of Zlotys: End of Period*							
Foreign Assets (Net)	31n	17,212	26,448	49,183	61,524	82,808	96,281	110,548	131,725	133,899	132,020	135,871	143,234
Domestic Credit	32	63,253	82,205	98,476	128,583	160,990	194,228	231,341	243,237	272,037	279,045	301,512	305,889
Claims on General Govt. (Net)	32an	29,952	40,274	41,508	47,330	53,630	58,671	61,442	45,409	59,439	57,214	64,838	60,605
Claims on Other Resident Sectors	32d	33,300	41,932	56,968	81,253	107,360	135,558	169,899	197,827	212,598	221,831	236,674	245,284
Money	34	19,646	27,450	37,439	52,331	61,686	71,670	88,201	82,574	94,158	112,889	133,576	146,098
Quasi-Money	35	36,278	49,852	66,913	84,331	114,705	149,110	175,307	211,930	244,647	216,527	214,608	226,134
Capital Accounts	37a	7,339	10,290	13,399	18,934	25,115	31,598	35,842	41,156	48,135	47,443	49,026	57,834
Other Items (Net)	37r	17,201	21,062	29,908	34,511	42,291	38,132	42,539	39,301	18,996	34,206	40,174	19,056
Money plus Quasi-Money	35l	55,924	77,302	104,352	136,662	176,392	220,780	263,508	294,505	338,805	329,416	348,183	372,232
Interest Rates						*Percent Per Annum*							
Discount Rate (End of Period)	60	29.0	28.0	25.0	22.0	24.5	18.3	19.0	21.5	14.0	7.8	5.8	7.0
Money Market Rate	60b	24.5	23.3	25.8	20.6	22.4	20.6	13.6	18.2	16.2	9.4	5.8	6.0
Treasury Bill Rate	60c	33.2	28.8	25.6	20.3	21.6	19.1	13.1	16.6	....	....	....	....
Deposit Rate	60l	34.0	† 33.4	26.8	20.0	19.4	18.2	11.2	14.2	11.8	6.2	3.7	3.8
Lending Rate	60p	35.3	32.8	† 33.5	26.1	25.0	24.5	16.9	20.0	18.4	12.0	7.3	7.6
Prices, Production, Labor						*Index Numbers (2000=100): Period Averages*							
Share Prices (1995=100)	62	....	....	100.0	168.9	....	....	....	....	....	....	....	....
Producer Prices: Industry	63	39.6	51.4	64.6	† 73.1	82.0	88.0	92.8	100.0	101.7	102.8	105.6	113.0
Consumer Prices	64	32.2	42.9	55.0	65.9	75.8	† 84.7	90.9	100.0	105.5	107.5	108.3	112.2
Harmonized CPI (2002=100)	64h	....	....	....	....	....	....	....	....	....	100.0	100.7	104.3
Wages: Average Earnings	65	25.6	33.7	47.7	60.3	72.3	83.1	90.6	100.0	106.9	111.0	114.2	119.8
Industrial Production	66	56.0	63.3	† 69.7	76.2	84.8	88.8	93.0	100.0	100.4	101.8	110.7	124.8
Industrial Employment	67	115.5	113.5	114.5	113.0	112.4	111.2	106.2	100.0	94.9	89.6	87.1	86.7
						Number in Thousands: Period Averages							
Labor Force	67d	17,367	17,122	17,004	17,076	17,100	17,162		17,311	17,376	17,213	16,945	....
Employment	67e	† 14,894	14,658	14,791	14,969	15,177	15,354	14,747	14,526	14,207	13,782	13,617	13,795
Unemployment	67c	† 2,890	2,838	2,629	2,360	1,826	1,831	2,350	2,703	2,912	3,162	3,238	3,200
Unemployment Rate (%)	67r	† 16.4	16.0	15.2	13.2	10.5	10.4	13.0	13.9	16.2	17.8	19.9	19.4

Poland 964

Intl. Transactions & Positions		1993	1994	1995	1996	1997	1998	1999	2000	2001	2002	2003	2004
							Millions of Zlotys						
Exports	70	25,757	39,246	55,515	65,819	84,480	95,015	108,706	137,909	148,115	167,338	208,944	272,106
Imports, c.i.f.	71	34,018	49,072	70,502	100,231	138,898	162,458	182,362	213,072	206,253	224,816	265,134	324,663
Imports, f.o.b.	71.v	29,581	42,287	61,306	87,157	120,781	141,268	....	....	....	....	....	....
							2000=100						
Volume of Exports	72	41.5	49.1	57.4	62.9	71.5	76.4	80.9	100.0	111.8	121.1	143.7	169.8
Volume of Imports	73	35.4	40.1	48.3	61.8	75.4	90.0	93.5	100.0	103.2	110.7	119.8	140.6
Export Prices	76	44.9	57.8	70.1	75.7	85.6	92.0	98.5	100.0	96.0	100.2	105.5	116.2
Import Prices	76.x	45.2	57.5	65.0	76.1	86.5	91.0	97.0	100.0	93.8	95.3	103.9	108.8
Balance of Payments							*Millions of US Dollars: Minus Sign Indicates Debit*						
Current Account, n.i.e.	78ald	−5,788	954	854	−3,264	−5,744	−6,901	−12,487	−9,981	−5,375	−5,009	−4,599	−3,594
Goods: Exports f.o.b.	78aad	13,582	18,355	25,041	27,557	30,731	32,467	30,060	35,902	41,663	46,742	61,007	81,596
Goods: Imports f.o.b.	78abd	−17,087	−18,930	−26,687	−34,844	−40,553	−45,303	−45,132	−48,209	−49,324	−53,991	−66,732	−87,180
Trade Balance	78acd	−3,505	−575	−1,646	−7,287	−9,822	−12,836	−15,072	−12,307	−7,661	−7,249	−5,725	−5,584
Services: Credit	78add	4,201	6,699	10,675	9,747	8,915	10,840	8,363	10,398	9,753	10,037	11,174	13,386
Services: Debit	78aed	−3,631	−3,859	−7,138	−6,343	−5,743	−6,624	−6,982	−8,993	−8,966	−9,186	−10,647	−12,464
Balance on Goods & Services	78afd	−2,935	2,265	1,891	−3,883	−6,650	−8,620	−13,691	−10,902	−6,874	−6,398	−5,198	−4,662
Income: Credit	78agd	579	546	1,089	1,527	1,467	2,226	1,837	2,250	2,625	1,948	2,108	2,113
Income: Debit	78ahd	−4,192	−3,109	−3,084	−2,602	−2,596	−3,404	−2,847	−3,709	−4,015	−3,837	−5,745	−6,704
Balance on Gds, Serv. & Inc.	78aid	−6,548	−298	−104	−4,958	−7,779	−9,798	−14,701	−12,361	−8,264	−8,287	−8,835	−9,253
Current Transfers, n.i.e.: Credit	78ajd	5,840	2,174	2,459	2,825	2,700	3,520	2,898	3,008	3,737	4,181	5,316	8,276
Current Transfers: Debit	78akd	−5,080	−922	−1,501	−1,131	−665	−623	−684	−628	−848	−903	−1,080	−2,617
Capital Account, n.i.e.	78bcd	—	9,215	285	94	66	63	55	34	76	−7	−46	998
Capital Account, n.i.e.: Credit	78bad	—	9,215	285	5,833	91	117	95	110	113	46	60	1,144
Capital Account: Debit	78bbd	—	—	—	−5,739	−25	−54	−40	−76	−37	−53	−106	−146
Financial Account, n.i.e.	78bjd	2,341	−9,065	9,260	6,673	7,410	13,282	10,462	10,221	3,173	7,180	3,550	436
Direct Investment Abroad	78bdd	−18	−29	−42	−53	−45	−316	−31	−16	90	−230	−196	−909
Dir. Invest. in Rep. Econ., n.i.e.	78bed	1,715	1,875	3,659	4,498	4,908	6,365	7,270	9,343	5,714	4,131	4,123	6,288
Portfolio Investment Assets	78bfd	—	−624	1	282	815	−130	−548	−84	48	−1,157	−1,296	−1,317
Equity Securities	78bkd	—	—	127	−17	56	1	−172	−20	−67	−268	183	−90
Debt Securities	78bld	—	−624	−126	299	759	−131	−376	−64	115	−889	−1,479	−1,227
Portfolio Investment Liab., n.i.e.	78bgd	—	—	1,176	22	1,295	1,827	691	3,423	1,067	3,051	3,740	10,815
Equity Securities	78bmd	—	—	219	749	599	1,734	14	447	−307	−545	−837	1,877
Debt Securities	78bnd	—	—	957	−727	696	93	677	2,976	1,374	3,596	4,577	8,938
Financial Derivatives Assets	78bwd	....	—	—	—	—	—	579	—	—	—	—	....
Financial Derivatives Liabilities	78bxd	....	—	—	−3	−12	—	−10	269	−336	−898	−870	209
Other Investment Assets	78bhd	848	−1,841	3,356	6,191	−754	2,107	−3,339	−3,870	−4,072	1,887	−1,249	−12,106
Monetary Authorities	78bod	....	194	65	37	—	1	1	2	3	—	—	−27
General Government	78bpd	16	34	46	5,767	41	53	−6	−48	−38	−37	−47	−39
Banks	78bqd	649	−1,718	1,057	453	−1,076	2,207	−2,694	−3,015	−3,398	3,107	351	−10,816
Other Sectors	78brd	183	−351	2,188	−66	281	−154	−640	−809	−639	−1,183	−1,553	−1,224
Other Investment Liab., n.i.e.	78bid	−204	−8,446	1,110	−4,264	1,203	3,429	5,850	1,156	662	396	−702	−2,544
Monetary Authorities	78bsd	—	15	14	102	−561	199	380	−1,393	118	−473	−68	−107
General Government	78btd	−570	−8,709	−3	−6,033	−52	−370	−224	−290	−3,047	−503	−1,236	−2,515
Banks	78bud	114	170	575	314	719	1,483	2,013	−474	283	−550	2,063	325
Other Sectors	78bvd	252	78	524	1,353	1,097	2,117	3,681	3,313	3,308	1,922	−1,461	−247
Net Errors and Omissions	78cad	219	−98	−564	321	1,309	−520	2,126	350	1,699	−1,516	2,301	2,961
Overall Balance	78cbd	−3,228	1,006	9,835	3,824	3,041	5,924	156	624	−427	648	1,206	801
Reserves and Related Items	79dad	3,228	−1,006	−9,835	−3,824	−3,041	−5,924	−156	−624	427	−648	−1,206	−801
Reserve Assets	79dbd	−100	−1,514	−8,431	−3,828	−3,044	−5,926	−156	−624	427	−648	−1,206	−801
Use of Fund Credit and Loans	79dcd	−138	603	−1,408	—	—	—	—	—	—	—	—	—
Exceptional Financing	79ded	3,466	−96	4	4	3	2	—	—	—	—	—	—
International Investment Position							*Millions of US Dollars*						
Assets	79aad	....	23,506	31,966	28,746	31,908	38,399	40,101	44,672	49,296	51,698	61,303	....
Direct Investment Abroad	79abd	....	461	539	735	678	1,165	1,024	1,018	1,156	1,457	1,855	....
Portfolio Investment	79acd	....	1,287	1,937	1,338	839	1,093	1,143	1,575	1,311	2,729	4,041	....
Equity Securities	79add	....	—	—	—	2	9	28	47	108	189	186	....
Debt Securities	79aed	....	—	—	—	837	1,084	1,115	1,528	1,203	2,540	3,855	....
Financial Derivatives	79ald	....	—	—	—	—	—	—	—	—	—	—	....
Other Investment	79afd	....	15,727	14,527	8,454	8,988	7,866	10,619	14,615	20,275	17,728	21,253	....
Monetary Authorities	79agd	....	252	187	150	5	4	2	1	—	—	—	....
General Government	79ahd	....	6,970	6,720	881	829	801	1,031	1,076	1,173	1,232	1,331	....
Banks	79aid	....	6,672	5,678	4,997	6,161	4,419	6,697	9,758	14,507	10,588	11,480	....
Other Sectors	79ajd	....	1,833	1,942	2,426	1,993	2,642	2,889	3,780	4,595	5,908	8,442	....
Reserve Assets	79akd	....	6,031	14,963	18,219	21,403	28,275	27,315	27,464	26,554	29,784	34,154	....
Liabilities	79lad	....	53,075	59,304	58,515	62,439	80,187	89,258	99,999	107,128	125,128	153,548	....
Dir. Invest. in Rep. Economy	79lbd	....	3,789	7,843	11,463	14,587	22,461	26,075	34,227	41,247	48,320	55,268	....
Portfolio Investment	79lcd	....	8,431	9,375	10,148	11,325	13,658	14,618	18,057	18,895	24,042	32,770	....
Equity Securities	79ldd	....	443	663	2,279	2,672	4,969	4,981	5,350	4,301	4,399	6,133	....
Debt Securities	79led	....	7,988	8,712	7,869	8,653	8,689	9,637	12,707	14,594	19,643	26,637	....
Financial Derivatives	79lld	....	—	—	—	—	—	—	—	—	—	—	....
Other Investment	79lfd	....	40,855	42,086	36,904	36,527	44,068	48,565	47,715	46,986	52,766	65,510	....
Monetary Authorities	79lgd	....	1,493	174	265	791	925	1,844	436	428	110	199	....
General Government	79lhd	....	34,507	35,955	28,709	26,584	27,061	25,199	23,749	19,006	20,775	22,473	....
Banks	79lid	....	1,394	1,834	2,231	3,054	4,735	6,404	5,812	6,437	6,882	10,850	....
Other Sectors	79ljd	....	3,461	4,123	5,699	6,098	11,347	15,118	17,718	21,115	24,999	31,988	....

		1993	1994	1995	1996	1997	1998	1999	2000	2001	2002	2003	2004
Government Finance					*Millions of Zlotys: Year Ending December 31*								
Deficit (-) or Surplus........................	80	....	−4,812	−5,762	−7,826	−8,304	−5,382	−5,021	1,935	−32,025	....	....	....
Total Revenue and Grants.............	81y	....	88,153	117,946	144,462	172,519	196,964	201,250	214,345	224,184	....	....	....
Revenue.................................	81	....	88,153	117,946	144,454	172,507	196,952	201,131	213,865	223,758	....	....	....
Grants.................................	81z	....	—	—	8	12	12	119	480	426	....	....	....
Exp. & Lending Minus Repay..........	82z	....	92,965	123,708	152,288	180,823	202,346	206,271	212,410	256,209	....	....	....
Expenditure.............................	82	....	93,039	124,322	153,047	185,431	207,370	216,912	236,865	263,580	....	....	....
Lending Minus Repayments.........	83	....	−74	−614	−759	−4,608	−5,024	−10,641	−24,455	−7,371	....	....	....
Total Financing................................	80h	....	4,812	5,762	7,826	8,304	5,382	5,021	−1,935	32,025	....	....	....
Domestic.................................	84a	....	5,855	2,604	8,695	8,393	4,379	4,445	−2,200	42,976	....	....	....
Foreign...................................	85a	....	−1,043	3,158	−869	−89	1,003	576	265	−10,951	....	....	....
Total Debt by Residence..................	88	....	152,238	167,267	185,603	221,650	237,400	266,750	270,980	291,524	....	....	....
Domestic.................................	88a	....	55,611	63,083	76,919	97,635	109,647	123,519	134,477	174,705	....	....	....
Foreign...................................	89a	....	96,627	104,184	108,684	124,015	127,753	143,231	136,503	116,819	....	....	....
National Accounts						*Millions of Zlotys*							
Househ.Cons.Expend.,incl.NPISHs....	96f	99,627	142,746	199,102	258,125	315,950	368,201	412,405	462,338	493,725	518,745	538,149	573,544
Government Consumption Expend...	91f	30,407	37,853	62,524	77,513	92,554	105,160	116,944	130,306	137,126	141,227	143,164	149,659
Gross Fixed Capital Formation.........	93e	24,749	40,385	57,405	80,390	110,853	139,205	156,690	170,430	157,209	148,338	149,962	160,835
Changes in Inventories....................	93i	−520	−715	3,300	4,428	5,150	5,801	5,595	8,132	512	−1,070	3,886	15,608
Exports of Goods and Services..........	90c	35,733	53,218	78,172	94,192	120,408	155,874	160,787	201,548	210,585	231,409	280,731	345,612
Imports of Goods and Services (-).....	98c	34,215	48,389	70,935	100,224	140,782	184,879	199,904	248,867	238,562	257,535	300,970	361,602
Gross Domestic Product (GDP)........	99b	155,780	225,098	329,567	414,425	504,133	589,361	652,517	723,886	760,595	781,112	814,922	883,656
GDP Volume 1995 Prices.................	99b.p	273,653	287,883	329,567	349,341	373,096	391,005	407,036	423,118	427,419	433,275	449,950	473,988
GDP Volume (2000=100)................	99bvp	64.7	68.0	77.9	82.6	88.2	92.4	96.2	100.0	101.0	102.4	106.3	112.0
GDP Deflator (2000=100)................	99bip	33.3	45.7	58.5	69.3	79.0	88.1	93.7	100.0	104.0	105.4	105.9	109.0
						Millions: Midyear Estimates							
Population.................................	99z	38.45	38.53	38.59	38.63	38.66	38.66	38.66	38.65	38.63	38.61	38.59	38.56

Portugal 182

		1993	1994	1995	1996	1997	1998	1999	2000	2001	2002	2003	2004
Exchange Rates		*Escudos per SDR through 1998, Euros per SDR Thereafter: End of Period*											
Market Rate	aa	242.8619	232.2519	222.1009	224.8754	247.3526	241.9404	1.3662	1.4002	1.4260	1.2964	1.1765	1.1402
		Escudos per US Dollar through 1998, Euros per US Dollar Thereafter: End of Period (ae) Period Average (rf)											
Market Rate	ae	176.8120	159.0930	149.4130	156.3850	183.3260	171.8290	.9954	1.0747	1.1347	.9536	.7918	.7342
Market Rate	rf	160.8002	165.9928	151.1055	154.2437	175.3124	180.1045	.9386	1.0854	1.1175	1.0626	.8860	.8054
		Escudos per ECU: End of Period (ea) Period Average (eb)											
ECU Rate	ea	197.20	195.17	191.58	194.27	202.13	201.22	....	....	....	....	....	....
ECU Rate	eb	187.80	196.37	194.12	193.18	197.96	201.99	....	....	....	....	....	....
		Index Numbers (2000=100): Period Averages											
Market Rate (1995=100)	ahx	94.3	91.2	100.0	97.9	86.3	84.0	....	....	....	....	....	....
Nominal Effective Exchange Rate	nec	109.7	105.9	107.7	107.9	105.7	104.5	103.0	100.0	100.6	101.4	104.2	104.8
Real Effective Exchange Rate	rec	101.4	100.2	103.1	104.1	102.2	102.6	102.5	100.0	102.5	105.0	109.1	109.9
Fund Position		*Millions of SDRs: End of Period*											
Quota	2f.s	558	558	558	558	558	558	867	867	867	867	867	867
SDRs	1b.s	42	48	57	68	79	96	32	41	49	56	61	66
Reserve Position in the Fund	1c.s	219	231	303	320	313	442	275	242	299	329	361	283
Total Fund Cred.&Loans Outstg.	2tl	—	—	—	—	—	—						
International Liquidity		*Millions of US Dollars Unless Otherwise Indicated: End of Period*											
Total Res.Min.Gold (Eurosys.Def)	1l.d	15,840	15,513	15,850	15,918	15,660	15,825	† 8,427	8,909	9,667	11,179	5,876	5,174
SDRs	1b.d	58	71	85	98	107	135	44	54	62	76	91	103
Reserve Position in the Fund	1c.d	301	337	450	461	423	623	377	316	376	447	536	440
Foreign Exchange	1d.d	15,481	15,106	15,315	15,359	15,130	15,067	† 8,006	8,539	9,228	10,656	5,249	4,631
o/w:Fin.Deriv.Rel.to Reserves	1ddd	....	....	....	....	....	....	111.51	271.71	322.42	99.63	29.77	31.15
Other Reserve Assets	1e.d	....	....	....	....	....	....						
Gold (Million Fine Troy Ounces)	1ad	16.06	16.07	16.07	16.07	16.07	20.09	19.51	19.51	19.51	19.03	16.63	14.86
Gold (Eurosystem Valuation)	1and	5,189	5,185	5,189	4,993	3,265	3,389	5,661	5,353	5,394	6,522	6,938	6,510
Memo:Euro Cl. on Non-EA Res.	1dgd	....	....	....	....	....	....	2,795	....	....	....	....	....
Non-Euro Cl. on EA Res.	1dhd	....	....	....	....	....	....	871	978	594	380	424	1,021
Mon. Auth.: Other Foreign Assets	3..d	....	....	....	....	....	....	3,666					
Foreign Liabilities	4..d	18	122	48	44	144	6	† 3,737	3,035	2,885	2,959	2,237	962
Banking Insts.: Foreign Assets	7a.d	20,042	28,500	35,922	37,500	47,451	54,669	† 25,168	29,902	26,870	28,932	34,875	37,669
Foreign Liab.	7b.d	13,875	21,527	32,432	36,975	48,282	60,976	† 31,352	47,626	50,007	62,151	84,365	93,120
Monetary Authorities		*Billions of Escudos through 1998; Billions of Euros Beginning 1999: End of Period*											
Fgn. Assets (Cl.on Non-EA Ctys)	11	3,706.7	3,294.8	3,142.8	3,250.5	3,469.8	3,324.6	16.70	15.71	19.77	17.85	11.29	9.30
Claims on General Government	12a.u	....	....	....	....	....	....	3.48	5.22	2.96	4.83	9.62	9.71
o/w: Claims on Gen.Govt.in Cty.	12a	313.0	289.9	267.6	248.2	217.6	94.6	.39	—	—	—	—	—
Claims on Banking Institutions	12e.u	....	....	....	....	....	....	11.92	4.98	3.58	4.93	7.99	10.99
o/w: Claims on Bank.Inst.in Cty.	12e	266.3	560.1	631.9	261.8	112.5	246.4	2.58	3.30	2.24	1.03	2.54	3.14
Claims on Other Resident Sectors	12d.u	....	....	....	....	....	....	.30	.58	.43	.23	.24	.24
o/w: Cl. on Oth.Res.Sect.in Cty.	12d	36.3	45.7	38.2	39.8	41.0	42.6	.22	.22	.23	.23	.24	.24
Currency Issued	14a	752.9	795.8	841.0	880.9	776.1	923.6	7.25	6.53	5.92	8.46	9.87	11.80
Liabilities to Banking Insts.	14c.u	....	....	....	....	....	....	10.92	8.65	9.80	10.41	12.54	14.10
o/w: Liabs to Bank.Inst.in Cty.	14c	2,277.0	432.3	376.8	473.5	558.8	421.1	4.02	3.88	4.81	4.62	11.71	6.25
Demand Dep. of Other Res.Sect.	14d.u	....	....	....	....	....	....	—	.02	—	—	—	—
o/w:D.Dep.of Oth.Res.Sect.in Cty.	14d	1.1	21.6	.6	.2	1.9	.4	—	.02	—	—	—	—
Other Dep. of Other Res.Sect.	15..u	....	....	....	....	....	....	—	—	—	—	—	—
o/w:O.Dep.of Oth.Res.Sect.in Cty.	15	....	....	....	....	....	....						
Bonds & Money Mkt. Instruments	16n.u	....	....	....	....	....	....	4.57	3.78	2.94	2.03	1.05	....
o/w: Held by Resid.of Cty.	16n	....	....	....	....	....	....						
Foreign Liab. (to Non-EA Ctys)	16c	3.1	19.4	7.2	6.9	26.4	1.1	3.72	3.26	3.27	2.82	1.77	.71
Central Government Deposits	16d.u	....	....	....	....	....	....	2.24	.01	.01	—	—	—
o/w: Cent.Govt.Dep. in Cty.	16d	539.8	510.6	693.0	524.0	486.7	465.1	2.24	.01	.01	—	—	—
Capital Accounts	17a	493.9	446.7	303.7	310.3	693.0	588.3	3.85	4.64	5.29	4.78	4.33	4.17
Other Items (Net)	17r	254.5	1,964.1	1,858.4	1,604.5	1,299.0	1,308.6	−.16	−.40	−.49	−.66	−.43	−.54
Memo: Net Claims on Eurosystem	12e.s	....	....	....	....	....	....	2.45	−3.35	−3.44	−1.65	4.68	−.34
Currency Put into Circ	14m	....	....	....	....	....	....	....	....	....	5.97	5.71	5.42
Banking Institutions		*Billions of Escudos through 1998; Billions of Euros Beginning 1999: End of Period*											
Claims on Monetary Authorities	20	2,188.6	2,158.1	2,090.4	1,891.3	1,648.1	1,617.9	8.26	7.33	7.57	6.51	.96	—
Claims on Bk.Inst.in Oth.EA Ctys	20b.u	....	....	....	....	....	....	18.39	17.30	24.44	25.33	32.03	31.00
Fgn. Assets (Cl.on Non-EA Ctys)	21	3,543.7	4,534.1	5,367.2	5,864.5	8,698.9	9,393.7	25.05	32.14	30.49	27.59	27.61	27.66
Claims on General Government	22a.u	....	....	....	....	....	....	9.53	8.90	10.13	9.54	9.65	10.53
o/w: Claims on Gen.Govt.in Cty.	22a	3,548.4	4,126.9	4,194.3	3,983.1	3,139.5	2,383.9	8.37	8.50	9.08	8.07	7.92	8.49
Claims on Other Resident Sectors	22d.u	....	....	....	....	....	....	133.68	168.25	184.23	195.86	202.82	216.33
o/w: Cl. on Oth.Res.Sect.in Cty.	22d	8,465.2	9,369.0	11,137.5	13,084.8	15,771.6	19,705.1	129.36	160.56	179.18	190.81	193.99	202.73
Demand Deposits	24..u	....	....	....	....	....	....	40.03	42.50	46.93	46.12	49.00	49.74
o/w:D.Dep.of Oth.Res.Sect.in Cty.	24	2,861.6	3,038.7	3,435.0	3,914.6	4,637.9	5,411.6	39.68	42.12	46.59	45.70	48.44	49.14
Other Deposits	25..u	....	....	....	....	....	....	71.25	75.32	78.58	77.80	79.03	86.37
o/w:O.Dep.of Oth.Res.Sect.in Cty.	25	9,414.9	10,360.4	11,116.5	11,465.1	11,956.0	12,064.7	67.51	71.56	72.37	71.57	71.40	75.19
Money Market Fund Shares	26m.u	....	....	....	....	....	....	—	.12	.17	.66	1.06	1.07
Bonds & Money Mkt. Instruments	26n.u	....	....	....	....	....	....	16.91	21.97	25.76	26.48	29.43	28.81
o/w: Held by Resid.of Cty.	26n	197.1	169.0	125.7	257.7	331.5	599.5	....	....	....	....	....	....
Foreign Liab. (to Non-EA Ctys)	26c	2,453.2	3,424.8	4,845.8	5,782.4	8,851.3	10,477.5	31.21	51.18	56.74	59.27	66.80	68.37
Central Government Deposits	26d.u	....	....	....	....	....	....	5.08	6.42	4.29	5.41	4.07	3.59
o/w: Cent.Govt.Dep. in Cty.	26d	454.4	541.2	701.2	800.3	906.7	1,017.4	5.07	6.42	4.27	5.39	4.05	3.57
Credit from Monetary Authorities	26g	296.0	560.3	631.9	261.8	112.5	246.4	2.58	3.30	2.24	1.03	2.54	3.10
Liab. to Bk.Inst.in Oth. EA Ctys	26h.u	....	....	....	....	....	....	22.51	23.30	32.35	36.07	41.17	37.90
Capital Accounts	27a	2,251.7	2,430.8	2,500.8	2,782.6	2,978.4	4,117.9	20.21	22.91	24.57	25.73	30.78	29.46
Other Items (Net)	27r	−183.6	−338.0	−573.1	−443.1	−515.9	−834.3	−14.87	−13.12	−14.77	−13.74	−30.82	−22.90

		1993	1994	1995	1996	1997	1998	1999	2000	2001	2002	2003	2004
Banking Survey (Nat'l Residency)				*Billions of Escudos through 1998; Billions of Euros Beginning 1999: End of Period*									
Foreign Assets (Net)	31n	4,794.2	4,384.7	3,657.0	3,325.6	3,291.0	2,239.7	10.67	−5.59	−17.74	−23.47	−21.03	−24.25
Domestic Credit	32	11,368.7	12,779.7	14,243.5	16,031.6	17,776.3	20,743.7	131.03	162.85	184.20	193.72	198.11	207.89
Claims on General Govt. (Net)	32an	2,867.2	3,365.0	3,067.8	2,907.0	1,963.7	996.0	1.45	2.07	4.80	2.68	3.88	4.92
Claims on Other Resident Sectors	32d	8,501.5	9,414.7	11,175.7	13,124.6	15,812.6	19,747.7	129.58	160.78	179.40	191.04	194.23	202.97
Currency Issued	34a.n	752.9	795.8	841.0	880.9	776.1	923.6	7.25	6.53	5.92	8.46	9.87	11.80
Demand Deposits	34b.n	2,862.7	3,060.2	3,435.5	3,914.7	4,639.7	5,412.0	39.69	42.14	46.59	45.70	48.44	49.14
Other Deposits	35..n	9,414.9	10,360.4	11,116.5	11,465.1	11,956.0	12,064.7	67.51	71.56	72.37	71.57	71.40	75.19
Money Market Fund Shares	36m							—	.12	.17	.66	1.06	1.07
Bonds & Money Mkt. Instruments	36n	197.1	169.0	125.7	257.7	331.5	599.5	21.49	25.76	28.69	28.51	30.49	28.81
o/w: Over Two Years	36na	....	....	....	....	....	....	19.87	23.24	25.79	27.06	28.92	27.21
Capital Accounts	37a	2,745.6	2,877.5	2,804.5	3,093.0	3,671.4	4,706.2	24.06	27.55	29.86	30.51	35.12	33.63
Other Items (Net)	37r	189.1	−99.4	−428.4	−256.4	−306.3	−722.4	−18.29	−16.39	−17.13	−15.16	−19.30	−16.01
Banking Survey (EA-Wide Residency)				*Billions of Euros: End of Period*									
Foreign Assets (Net)	31n.u	....	....	....	....	....	....	6.83	−6.60	−9.75	−16.65	−29.67	−32.11
Domestic Credit	32..u	....	....	....	....	....	....	139.67	176.51	193.44	205.05	218.26	233.22
Claims on General Govt. (Net)	32anu	....	....	....	....	....	....	5.70	7.69	8.78	8.96	15.20	16.65
Claims on Other Resident Sect.	32d.u	....	....	....	....	....	....	133.97	168.82	184.66	196.09	203.05	216.57
Currency Issued	34a.u	....	....	....	....	....	....	7.25	6.53	5.92	8.46	9.87	11.80
Demand Deposits	34b.u	....	....	....	....	....	....	40.03	42.52	46.93	46.13	49.00	49.74
Other Deposits	35..u	....	....	....	....	....	....	71.25	75.32	78.58	77.80	79.03	86.37
o/w: Other Dep. Over Two Yrs.	35abu	....	....	....	....	....	....	4.03	3.84	3.57	4.43	4.44	6.68
Money Market Fund Shares	36m.u	....	....	....	....	....	....	—	.12	.17	.66	1.06	1.07
Bonds & Money Mkt. Instruments	36n.u	....	....	....	....	....	....	21.49	25.76	28.69	28.51	30.49	28.81
o/w: Over Two Years	36nau	....	....	....	....	....	....	19.87	23.24	25.79	27.06	28.92	27.21
Capital Accounts	37a	....	....	....	....	....	....	24.06	27.55	29.86	30.51	35.12	33.63
Other Items (Net)	37r.u	....	....	....	....	....	....	−17.58	−7.87	−6.46	−3.66	−15.98	−10.32
Money (National Definitions)						*Billions of Escudos: End of Period*							
M1	59ma	3,354.5	3,589.4	3,901.2	4,302.2	4,882.1	5,757.4	....	....	....	....	....	....
M2	59mb	9,701.9	10,586.2	11,434.5	12,468.2	13,316.2	14,401.3	....	....	....	....	....	....
Broad Money	59mc	9,376.2	10,020.3	11,102.1	11,907.3	12,825.5	13,667.5	....	....	....	....	....	....
Interest Rates						*Percent Per Annum*							
Banco de Portugal Rate(End of Per)	60	11.00	8.88	8.50	6.70	5.31	3.00	....	....	....	....	....	....
Money Market Rate	60b	13.25	10.62	8.91	7.38	5.78	4.34	2.71	....	....	....	....	....
Treasury Bill Rate	60c	....	....	7.75	5.75	4.43	....	....	....	....	....	....	....
Deposit Rate	60l	11.06	8.37	8.38	6.32	4.56	3.37	2.40	....	....	....	....	....
Deposit Rate (Households)	60lhs	....	....	....	....	....	....	....	....	....	....	1.99	1.98
Deposit Rate (Corporations)	60lcs	....	....	....	....	....	....	....	....	....	....	2.30	2.29
Lending Rate	60p	16.48	15.01	13.80	11.73	9.15	7.24	5.19	....	....	....	....	....
Lending Rate (Households)	60phm	....	....	....	....	....	....	....	....	....	....	3.82	3.75
Lending Rate (Corporations)	60pcs	....	....	....	....	....	....	....	....	....	....	4.61	4.53
Government Bond Yield	61	12.45	10.83	10.34	7.25	5.48	4.09	....	....	....	....	....	....
Prices, Production, Labor						*Index Numbers (2000=100): Period Averages*							
Share Prices (1995=100)	62	79.3	104.1	100.0	117.3	183.4	287.7	....	....	....	....	....	....
Producer Prices	63	....	....	....	....	....	....	....	100.0	102.8	103.2	104.0	106.8
Consumer Prices	64	80.2	84.4	87.8	90.6	† 92.5	95.0	97.2	100.0	104.4	† 108.1	111.6	114.3
Harmonized CPI	64h	....	....	....	....	....	....	95.2	97.3	100.0	104.4	108.3	111.8	114.6
Industrial Production	66	77.8	77.7	84.7	89.1	91.4	96.6	99.5	100.0	103.1	102.7	102.6	94.6
						*Number in Thousands: Period Averages*							
Labor Force	67d	4,708	4,799	4,777	4,809	4,645	5,117	5,155	5,235	5,314	5,379	5,460	5,488
Employment	67e	4,493	4,482	4,442	4,467	4,307	† 4,863	4,929	5,024	5,098	5,107	5,079	5,123
Unemployment	67c	248	396	430	468	443	254	227	206	216	272	342	365
Unemployment Rate (%)	67r	5.6	6.9	7.2	7.3	6.8	5.0	4.4	3.9	4.1	5.1	6.3	6.7
Intl. Transactions & Positions						*Billions of Escudos through 1998; Millions of Euros Beginning 1999*							
Exports	70	2,474.4	2,975.6	3,501.8	3,795.9	4,195.1	4,461.0	† 23,715.6	25,241.2	27,322.8	27,089.8	27,101.9	26,586.3
Imports, c.i.f.	71	3,883.8	4,514.3	5,028.7	5,427.1	6,139.7	6,914.8	† 37,505.6	41,425.2	44,054.0	40,655.9	36,146.2	39,597.0
Imports, f.o.b.	71.v	3,521.1	4,092.7	4,559.1	4,920.3	....	....	....	....	....	....	....	....
						*2000=100*							
Volume of Exports	72	88.3	101.2	97.9	101.6	100.5	94.4	92.8	100.0	94.6	95.3	97.1	....
Volume of Imports	73	87.6	101.6	97.6	101.5	105.7	103.9	100.5	100.0	96.5	93.6	94.5	....
Export Prices	76	99.7	101.3	100.1	93.3	96.0	96.2	94.6	100.0	95.7	94.3	91.5	....
Import Prices	76.x	94.7	95.1	95.6	92.2	92.7	90.5	91.7	100.0	91.5	89.1	90.0	....

		1993	1994	1995	1996	1997	1998	1999	2000	2001	2002	2003	2004
Balance of Payments		*Millions of US Dollars: Minus Sign Indicates Debit*											
Current Account, n.i.e.	78ald	233	−2,196	−132	−5,216	−6,465	−7,833	−9,733	−11,080	−11,083	−9,115	−7,937	−12,682
Goods: Exports f.o.b.	78aad	15,931	18,645	24,024	25,623	25,379	25,618	25,474	25,154	24,666	26,500	32,448	37,278
Goods: Imports f.o.b.	78abd	−23,981	−26,966	−32,934	−35,345	−35,721	−37,829	−39,187	−39,024	−38,304	−39,177	−45,879	−55,427
Trade Balance	78acd	−8,050	−8,321	−8,910	−9,722	−10,342	−12,211	−13,714	−13,870	−13,638	−12,677	−13,431	−18,149
Services: Credit	78add	6,846	6,755	8,236	8,040	8,002	8,829	8,680	9,016	9,381	10,321	12,276	14,738
Services: Debit	78aed	−5,481	−5,486	−6,611	−6,636	−6,572	−6,903	−6,814	−7,048	−6,824	−7,143	−8,282	−9,626
Balance on Goods & Services	78afd	−6,685	−7,052	−7,285	−8,317	−8,912	−10,285	−11,848	−11,901	−11,081	−9,498	−9,437	−13,037
Income: Credit	78agd	2,455	2,232	4,095	4,250	4,238	4,496	4,261	4,570	5,435	4,901	6,243	6,608
Income: Debit	78ahd	−2,236	−2,797	−4,074	−5,420	−5,744	−6,135	−6,029	−7,101	−8,787	−7,322	−7,995	−9,703
Balance on Gds, Serv. & Inc.	78aid	−6,466	−7,616	−7,264	−9,488	−10,418	−11,924	−13,616	−14,432	−14,432	−11,920	−11,190	−16,131
Current Transfers, n.i.e.: Credit	78ajd	8,395	7,410	9,046	6,515	5,985	6,170	6,048	5,415	5,582	5,445	6,443	7,161
Current Transfers: Debit	78akd	−1,696	−1,989	−1,914	−2,243	−2,031	−2,080	−2,164	−2,063	−2,233	−2,641	−3,190	−3,711
Capital Account, n.i.e.	78bcd	—	—	—	2,695	2,704	2,546	2,459	1,512	1,069	1,906	3,010	2,805
Capital Account, n.i.e.: Credit	78bad	—	—	—	2,836	2,893	2,724	2,642	1,681	1,278	2,111	3,246	3,127
Capital Account: Debit	78bbd	—	—	—	−141	−189	−179	−183	−169	−209	−205	−236	−322
Financial Account, n.i.e.	78bjd	−3,032	1,052	3,025	3,835	6,662	5,980	9,107	10,772	11,001	7,672	−1,269	9,820
Direct Investment Abroad	78bdd	−147	−287	−688	−972	−2,187	−3,851	−3,019	−8,183	−6,209	−76	−7,355	−6,121
Dir. Invest. in Rep. Econ., n.i.e.	78bed	1,534	1,270	685	1,703	2,542	3,151	1,235	6,682	6,242	1,713	6,610	825
Portfolio Investment Assets	78bfd	−2,382	−3,456	−3,148	−5,549	−8,697	−5,997	−6,737	−4,582	−7,851	−7,034	−21,246	−11,466
Equity Securities	78bkd	−168	−66	−159	−602	−568	−975	−2,110	−1,044	−959	−813	−622	−1,099
Debt Securities	78bld	−2,214	−3,390	−2,989	−4,947	−8,129	−5,022	−4,626	−3,538	−6,892	−6,221	−20,623	−10,367
Portfolio Investment Liab., n.i.e.	78bgd	4,214	3,934	2,066	2,383	8,790	5,385	9,945	2,792	9,738	10,249	15,795	13,246
Equity Securities	78bmd	579	562	−179	1,669	3,821	2,165	691	415	2,371	3,287	9,863	6,468
Debt Securities	78bnd	3,634	3,372	2,244	714	4,970	3,221	9,254	2,376	7,367	6,962	5,932	6,778
Financial Derivatives Assets	78bwd	−5	—	—	93	341	1,116	2,682	3,673	3,226	3,796	4,590	3,998
Financial Derivatives Liabilities	78bxd	—	—	—	−130	−360	−985	−2,485	−3,351	−2,875	−3,802	−4,518	−4,069
Other Investment Assets	78bhd	−8,424	−7,098	−7,568	−3,368	−5,346	−7,100	429	−10,865	−6,209	−6,269	−9,142	−356
Monetary Authorities	78bod	9	—	−26	−3	1	−94	−1,005	10	22	−304	345	−954
General Government	78bpd	....	....	....	1	11	—	−12	−12	−49	3	−6	244
Banks	78bqd	−7,024	−4,741	−6,679	−2,945	−3,116	−3,813	973	−7,201	−1,033	−29	−8,260	−969
Other Sectors	78brd	−1,409	−2,358	−863	−422	−2,241	−3,192	473	−3,661	−5,149	−5,939	−1,221	1,323
Other Investment Liab., n.i.e.	78bid	2,178	6,689	11,678	9,675	11,579	14,260	7,055	24,606	14,939	9,094	13,997	13,764
Monetary Authorities	78bsd	−32	299	−99	731	1,343	837	−3	4,861	87	699	−6,725	7,229
General Government	78btd	−146	−139	144	−312	−40	−73	−43	−179	−190	179	−20	423
Banks	78bud	1,327	7,069	11,189	8,595	8,936	12,245	6,999	18,231	14,480	8,456	19,476	3,321
Other Sectors	78bvd	1,028	−540	444	661	1,339	1,250	102	1,693	562	−241	1,266	2,791
Net Errors and Omissions	78cad	−48	−287	−3,193	−767	−1,928	−184	−1,616	−833	−134	555	−258	−1,806
Overall Balance	78cbd	−2,848	−1,430	−300	547	974	508	216	371	852	1,017	−6,455	−1,863
Reserves and Related Items	79dad	2,848	1,430	300	−547	−974	−508	−216	−371	−852	−1,017	6,455	1,863
Reserve Assets	79dbd	2,848	1,430	300	−547	−974	−508	−216	−371	−852	−1,017	6,455	1,863
Use of Fund Credit and Loans	79dcd	—	—	—	—	—	—	—	—	—	—	—	—
Exceptional Financing	79ded	....	....	....	—	—	—	—	—	—	—	—	—
International Investment Position		*Millions of US Dollars*											
Assets	79aad	....	....	....	86,425	99,344	128,461	122,687	141,990	155,995	192,915	261,445	300,935
Direct Investment Abroad	79abd	—	—	—	4,726	5,932	9,622	10,685	17,256	21,643	22,174	35,615	45,555
Portfolio Investment	79acd	—	—	—	17,502	20,368	28,489	36,459	40,662	45,917	62,248	97,485	120,377
Equity Securities	79add	....	....	....	4,997	4,765	6,008	7,226	7,624	7,556	8,471	11,106	13,955
Debt Securities	79aed	....	....	....	12,505	15,602	22,480	29,233	33,038	38,361	53,777	86,379	106,422
Financial Derivatives	79ald	....	....	....	422	381	355	2,055	2,758	1,929	2,165	2,671	1,968
Other Investment	79afd	24,170	32,543	37,810	42,030	52,341	68,409	59,309	67,088	71,424	88,627	112,860	121,351
Monetary Authorities	79agd	—	—	—	47	28	127	1,479	1,367	1,280	1,806	1,717	2,996
General Government	79ahd	15	15	28	80	78	47	66	74	1,481	1,497	1,530	1,291
Banks	79aid	18,016	25,149	30,288	29,900	38,718	44,389	39,680	45,076	44,488	51,019	67,721	72,374
Other Sectors	79ajd	6,139	7,379	7,494	12,003	13,516	23,846	18,163	20,571	24,175	34,305	41,891	44,690
Reserve Assets	79akd	21,819	21,669	21,954	21,745	20,321	21,586	14,100	14,227	15,082	17,701	12,813	11,684
Liabilities	79lad	....	....	....	93,951	113,075	154,894	158,443	184,490	203,387	258,168	349,687	410,907
Dir. Invest. in Rep. Economy	79lbd	—	—	—	18,947	18,605	24,465	23,922	28,696	34,062	42,406	58,924	65,213
Portfolio Investment	79lcd	8,907	13,656	16,430	21,327	36,207	46,933	51,718	52,413	56,564	74,934	109,248	135,700
Equity Securities	79ldd	2,929	3,597	3,651	6,573	12,663	18,806	19,487	18,873	15,605	17,492	34,661	46,827
Debt Securities	79led	5,978	10,059	12,779	14,755	23,544	28,127	32,230	33,541	40,958	57,442	74,587	88,873
Financial Derivatives	79lld	....	....	....	—	—	63	1,412	2,223	1,185	1,662	2,706	2,840
Other Investment	79lfd	29,166	37,266	49,532	53,677	58,263	83,432	81,391	101,159	111,576	139,166	178,809	207,154
Monetary Authorities	79lgd	48	362	278	440	2,084	3,049	2,732	7,470	7,282	9,025	3,286	11,650
General Government	79lhd	2,099	1,973	2,229	1,676	1,614	2,057	2,114	1,926	1,650	1,908	2,117	2,932
Banks	79lid	13,875	21,527	32,432	36,320	42,261	56,578	57,923	73,009	84,163	106,818	146,600	160,687
Other Sectors	79ljd	13,144	13,403	14,592	15,241	12,305	21,748	18,622	18,753	18,483	21,415	26,805	31,884
Government Finance													
Central Government		*Billions of Escudos through 1998; Millions of Euros Beginning 1999: Year Ending December 31*											
Deficit (-) or Surplus	80	−932.7	−708.1	−795.8	−379.9	−372.2	−247.6	....	....	....	....	....	....
Revenue	81	4,624.9	5,016.5	5,456.7	5,759.9	6,391.8	6,984.7	....	....	....	....	....	....
Grants Received	81z	446.6	411.6	525.6	662.2	649.9	649.1	....	....	....	....	....	....
Expenditure	82	6,012.0	6,137.9	6,613.6	6,974.5	7,242.2	7,795.1	....	....	....	....	....	....
Lending Minus Repayments	83	−7.8	−1.7	164.5	−172.5	171.7	86.3	....	....	....	....	....	....
Financing													
Domestic	84a	656.5	659.0	218.2	2.7	−12.1	669.1	....	....	....	....	....	....
Foreign	85a	276.2	49.1	577.6	377.2	384.3	−421.5	....	....	....	....	....	....
General Government		*As Percent of Gross Domestic Product*											
Deficit (-) or Surplus	80g	−6.1	−6.0	−5.7	−3.8	−2.7	−2.3	−2.2	−1.5	−2.2	....	....	....
Debt	88g	63.1	63.8	65.9	63.6	59.1	54.8	54.2	53.2	55.6	....	....	....

Portugal 182

National Accounts		1993	1994	1995	1996	1997	1998	1999	2000	2001	2002	2003	2004
		Billions of Escudos through 1998; Millions of Euros Beginning 1999											
Househ.Cons.Expend.,incl.NPISHs....	96f	9,133	9,870	10,456	11,052	11,639	12,646	† 67,394	71,116	74,968	78,125	80,433	84,763
Government Consumption Expend...	91f	2,596	2,781	3,019	3,298	3,546	3,896	† 21,254	23,697	25,569	27,450	27,649	28,827
Gross Fixed Capital Formation..........	93e	3,142	3,439	3,743	4,005	4,498	4,992	† 30,585	33,703	34,552	33,407	29,791	31,676
Changes in Inventories....................	93i	−18	56	115	95	101	108	† 1,123	1,047	1,082	1,139	167	....
Exports of Goods and Services..........	90c	3,050	3,583	4,168	4,482	4,891	5,301	† 32,089	36,536	38,097	38,957	40,076	41,700
Imports of Goods and Services (-).....	98c	4,458	5,111	5,698	6,123	6,798	7,698	† 43,293	49,505	50,136	48,704	47,502	51,931
Gross Domestic Product (GDP)........	99b	13,445	14,617	15,802	16,809	17,876	19,246	† 108,030	115,546	123,054	129,280	130,448	135,035
Net Primary Income from Abroad.....	98.n	141	178	412	568	624	....	....	....	....	....	....	....
Gross National Income (GNI)..........	99a	13,436	14,541	15,660	16,513	17,558							
GDP Volume 1995 Prices................	99b.p	14,983	15,353	15,802	16,306	16,871	17,460	† 94,450	97,933	99,540	99,973	98,577	99,569
GDP Volume (2000=100)...............	99bvp	76.3	78.2	80.5	83.0	85.9	88.9	† 96.4	100.0	101.6	102.1	100.7	101.7
GDP Deflator (2000=100)...............	99bip	76.1	80.7	84.8	87.4	89.8	93.4	† 96.9	100.0	104.8	109.6	112.2	114.9
		Millions: Midyear Estimates											
Population...............................	99z	9.99	10.01	10.03	10.06	10.09	10.13	10.18	10.23	10.28	10.33	10.39	10.44

		1993	1994	1995	1996	1997	1998	1999	2000	2001	2002	2003	2004
Exchange Rates						*Riyals per SDR: End of Period*							
Official Rate	aa	4.9998	5.3139	5.4108	5.2342	4.9113	5.1252	4.9959	4.7426	4.5745	4.9487	5.4089	5.6530
					Riyals per US Dollar: End of Period (ae) Period Average (rf)								
Official Rate	ae	3.6400	3.6400	3.6400	3.6400	3.6400	3.6400	3.6400	3.6400	3.6400	3.6400	3.6400	3.6400
Official Rate	rf	3.6400	3.6400	3.6400	3.6400	3.6400	3.6400	3.6400	3.6400	3.6400	3.6400	3.6400	3.6400
					Index Numbers (2000=100): Period Averages								
Official Rate	ahx	100.0	100.0	100.0	100.0	100.0	100.0	100.0	100.0	100.0	100.0	100.0	100.0
Nominal Effective Exchange Rate	nec	82.8	85.4	81.6	84.7	91.1	95.1	94.8	100.0	105.1	103.2	93.9	88.0
Fund Position						*Millions of SDRs: End of Period*							
Quota	2f.s	190.5	190.5	190.5	190.5	190.5	190.5	263.8	263.8	263.8	263.8	263.8	263.8
SDRs	1b.s	18.7	19.9	21.2	22.5	23.8	25.1	10.7	15.8	17.9	20.0	21.7	23.4
Reserve Position in the Fund	1c.s	33.8	30.7	29.7	29.2	26.4	26.4	44.7	44.7	79.1	99.6	103.5	86.4
International Liquidity					*Millions of US Dollars Unless Otherwise Indicated: End of Period*								
Total Reserves minus Gold	1l.d	693.7	657.7	743.8	686.2	820.6	1,043.3	1,304.2	1,158.0	1,312.7	1,566.8	2,944.2	3,395.9
SDRs	1b.d	25.6	29.0	31.5	32.4	32.1	35.3	14.6	20.6	22.5	27.2	32.3	36.4
Reserve Position in the Fund	1c.d	46.4	44.7	44.2	42.0	35.6	37.2	61.4	58.3	99.4	135.4	153.7	134.1
Foreign Exchange	1d.d	621.7	584.0	668.1	611.8	752.9	970.8	1,228.2	1,079.1	1,190.8	1,404.2	2,758.1	3,225.4
Gold (Million Fine Troy Ounces)	1ad	.862	.814	.268	.268	.054	.054	.019	.019	.019	.019	.019	.042
Gold (National Valuation)	1and	41.5	41.6	41.6	41.6	15.7	15.5	5.5	5.2	5.3	6.7	7.9	18.3
Deposit Money Banks: Assets	7a.d	† 2,264.3	2,648.0	3,093.7	2,396.3	2,643.4	2,324.3	2,455.5	3,193.1	3,163.5	4,102.9	5,347.5	7,625.4
Liabilities	7b.d	† 1,370.4	1,381.3	1,768.2	1,026.6	1,274.4	1,497.6	1,605.5	611.3	586.9	655.0	1,050.9	2,097.2
Monetary Authorities						*Millions of Riyals: End of Period*							
Foreign Assets	11	† 2,686	2,546	2,859	2,649	3,044	3,854	4,767	4,234	4,798	5,727	10,746	12,428
Claims on Central Government	12a	....	....	437	546	437	—	1,467	—	124	135	16	—
Claims on Deposit Money Banks	12e	† 150	260	205	212	194	1,589	82	124	97	28	3	287
Reserve Money	14	2,181	2,030	2,131	2,261	2,481	2,557	2,868	3,061	3,416	3,995	4,590	6,019
of which: Currency Outside DMBs	14a	1,350	1,350	1,407	1,404	1,555	1,499	1,714	1,673	1,741	1,921	2,148	2,594
Central Government Deposits	16d	† 33	42	381	116	120	145	30	41	26	38	51	232
Capital Accounts	17a	† 576	705	1,178	1,242	1,339	1,466	1,536	1,456	1,402	1,848	6,112	6,428
Other Items (Net)	17r	† 46	30	−188	−212	−265	1,275	1,881	−202	174	8	11	35
Deposit Money Banks						*Millions of Riyals: End of Period*							
Reserves	20	830	680	739	852	919	1,064	1,169	1,368	1,678	2,068	2,435	3,397
Foreign Assets	21	† 8,242	9,639	11,261	8,723	9,622	8,460	8,938	11,623	11,515	14,934	19,465	27,756
Claims on Central Government	22a	9,031	10,050	10,028	11,873	12,863	16,151	19,064	17,225	23,882	22,319	23,518	21,316
Claims on Nonfin.Pub.Enterprises	22c	232	228	384	728	878	609	537	621	790	1,789	3,343	5,826
Claims on Private Sector	22d	† 10,948	9,544	10,267	10,251	12,548	14,451	15,664	17,338	17,614	19,374	23,865	29,995
Demand Deposits	24	† 2,904	2,561	2,313	2,481	2,575	2,717	2,465	2,776	3,479	4,368	9,130	12,004
Time, Savings,& Fgn.Currency Dep	25	† 12,635	14,509	14,901	15,772	17,466	19,117	21,804	24,307	23,535	25,858	25,945	30,267
Foreign Liabilities	26c	† 4,988	5,028	6,436	3,737	4,639	5,451	5,844	2,225	2,136	2,384	3,825	7,634
Central Government Deposits	26d	† 3,394	1,903	2,671	3,795	4,601	5,248	6,540	9,262	15,504	15,544	17,610	17,993
Credit from Monetary Authorities	26g	18	91	69	60	140	72	94	140	115	22	98	339
Capital Accounts	27a	† 4,659	5,049	5,473	5,702	6,249	6,821	7,467	8,070	8,925	10,189	10,618	13,476
Other Items (Net)	27r	† 685	1,001	815	880	1,160	1,309	1,157	1,394	1,785	2,120	5,399	6,578
Monetary Survey						*Millions of Riyals: End of Period*							
Foreign Assets (Net)	31n	† 5,940	7,156	7,682	7,635	8,026	6,862	7,861	13,631	14,174	18,274	26,378	32,546
Domestic Credit	32	† 16,785	17,879	18,064	19,488	22,007	25,819	30,162	25,881	26,883	28,038	33,083	38,915
Claims on Central Govt. (Net)	32an	† 5,604	8,105	7,413	8,508	8,579	10,757	13,960	7,922	8,475	6,872	5,872	3,091
Claims on Nonfin.Pub.Enterprises	32c	232	228	384	728	878	609	537	621	790	1,789	3,343	5,826
Claims on Private Sector	32d	† 10,949	9,545	10,268	10,252	12,550	14,453	15,665	17,338	17,617	19,377	23,868	29,998
Money	34	† 4,254	3,910	3,720	3,885	4,131	4,216	4,179	4,449	5,219	6,289	11,278	14,599
Quasi-Money	35	† 12,635	14,509	14,901	15,772	17,466	19,117	21,804	24,307	23,535	25,858	25,945	30,267
Other Items (Net)	37r	† 5,836	6,616	7,125	7,467	8,437	9,348	12,041	10,755	12,303	14,165	22,238	26,595
Money plus Quasi-Money	35l	† 16,889	18,419	18,622	19,657	21,596	23,333	25,982	28,756	28,755	32,147	37,223	44,865
Interest Rates						*Percent Per Annum*							
Deposit Rate	60l	4.1	4.8	6.2	6.5	6.6	6.6	6.5	....	....	....	....	....
Lending Rate	60p	7.2	8.9	....	....	....	....	....	....	....	....	....	....
Prices and Production						*Index Numbers (2000=100): Period Averages*							
Consumer Prices	64	81.5	82.6	85.0	91.3	93.8	96.3	98.3	100.0	† 101.4	101.7	104.0	111.1
Crude Petroleum	66aa	58.6	57.6	63.6	67.6	87.4	94.9	93.3	100.0	95.4	90.9	108.2	112.0
Intl. Transactions & Positions						*Millions of Riyals*							
Exports	70	....	11,453	12,672	13,659	13,801	17,763	26,258	42,202	38,969	39,207	48,021	....
Imports, c.i.f	71	6,882	7,016	12,369	10,441	12,091	12,407	9,098	11,838	13,678	14,749	17,826	21,856
National Accounts						*Millions of Riyals*							
Housuh.Cons.Expend.,incl.NPISHs	96f	8,557	8,030	9,497	8,996	9,335	9,450	9,525	9,843	10,176	....	....	....
Government Consumption Expend	91f	9,370	9,250	9,436	10,886	12,236	11,789	11,573	12,715	12,910	....	....	....
Gross Fixed Capital Formation	93e	4,849	6,575	8,895	11,532	14,226	11,540	8,273	12,584	14,100	....	....	....
Changes in Inventories	93i	300	8	1,495	262	345	395	245	443	550	....	....	....
Exports of Goods and Services	90c	12,011	12,046	13,134	14,419	19,855	19,074	27,085	43,496	40,884	....	....	....
Imports of Goods and Services (-)	98c	9,037	9,066	12,835	13,119	14,873	14,918	11,590	14,435	16,279	....	....	....
Gross Domestic Product (GDP)	99b	26,050	26,843	29,622	32,976	41,124	37,330	45,111	64,646	64,579	71,733	74,351	....
						Millions: Midyear Estimates							
Population	99z	.50	.52	† .53	.54	.55	.56	.58	.61	.64	.69	.73	.78

		1993	1994	1995	1996	1997	1998	1999	2000	2001	2002	2003	2004
Exchange Rates					*Lei per SDR: End of Period*								
Market Rate	aa	1,752.7	2,579.6	3,832.2	5,802.2	10,825.0	15,419.3	25,055.2	33,779.2	39,708.9	45,543.9	48,435.2	45,141.3
					Lei per US Dollar: End of Period (ae) Period Average (rf)								
Market Rate	ae	1,276.0	1,767.0	2,578.0	4,035.0	8,023.0	10,951.0	18,255.0	25,926.0	31,597.0	33,500.0	32,595.0	29,067.0
Market Rate	rf	760.1	1,655.1	2,033.3	3,084.2	7,167.9	8,875.6	15,332.8	21,708.7	29,060.8	33,055.4	33,200.1	32,636.6
					Index Numbers (2000=100): Period Averages								
Nominal Effective Exchange Rate	nec	2,240.54	992.97	781.08	538.38	258.38	215.68	129.73	100.00	77.84	67.03	58.92	57.84
Real Effective Exchange Rate	rec	75.29	80.78	78.90	71.21	82.82	107.58	91.46	100.00	101.48	104.20	105.29	109.92
Fund Position					*Millions of SDRs: End of Period*								
Quota	2f.s	754	754	754	754	754	754	1,030	1,030	1,030	1,030	1,030	1,030
SDRs	1b.s	1	38	38	3	77	1	7	1	5	2	—	—
Reserve Position in the Fund	1c.s	—	—	—	—	—	—	—	—	—	—	—	—
Total Fund Cred.&Loans Outstg.	2tl	751	906	698	453	475	383	334	348	308	315	401	285
International Liquidity					*Millions of US Dollars Unless Otherwise Indicated: End of Period*								
Total Reserves minus Gold	1l.d	995	2,086	1,579	2,103	3,803	2,867	1,526	2,470	3,923	6,125	8,040	14,616
SDRs	1b.d	2	56	56	4	104	1	10	1	7	2	—	1
Reserve Position in the Fund	1c.d	—	—	—	—	—	—	—	—	—	—	—	—
Foreign Exchange	1d.d	994	2,031	1,523	2,099	3,700	2,866	1,516	2,469	3,916	6,123	8,040	14,616
Gold (Million Fine Troy Ounces)	1ad	2.370	2.625	2.703	2.818	3.019	3.224	3.323	3.374	3.382	3.386	3.378	3.377
Gold (National Valuation)	1and	924	965	780	520	458	358	967	920	939	1,180	1,410	1,480
Deposit Money Banks: Assets	7a.d	223	129	73	72	79	87	91	95	94	105	126	152
Liabilities	7b.d	560	687	823	1,238	1,148	933	611	508	661	1,004	2,214	4,981
Monetary Authorities					*Billions of Lei: End of Period*								
Foreign Assets	11	† 1,234	2,796	2,942	6,432	24,849	25,182	45,581	88,067	153,654	244,776	308,037	467,876
Claims on Government	12a	† 336	1,771	3,562	—	3,271	9,142	21,412	16,176	8,415	2,484	5	—
Claims on Private Sector	12d	....	....	....	....	....	....	....	....	....	....	....	....
Claims on Deposit Money Banks	12e	† 1,880	2,395	4,724	8,822	3,367	3,618	2,433	2,296	1,148			
Reserve Money	14	† 2,031	3,809	5,952	9,008	21,305	25,738	49,520	76,598	122,483	189,463	227,272	392,250
of which: Currency Outside DMBs	14a	1,049	2,201	3,764	5,383	9,200	11,525	17,372	25,742	35,635	45,577	57,978	74,646
Transit Accounts	14x	27	21	14	—	—	27	264	294	—	15	—	1
Foreign Liabilities	16c	† 1,317	2,444	3,502	7,810	15,167	17,639	15,885	22,028	12,235	14,348	19,410	12,886
Central Government Deposits	16d	† 496	1,354	2,660	−275	701	163	5,947	3,360	8,899	10,672	12,722	52,135
Other Items (Net)	17r	† −421	−666	−899	−1,290	−5,686	−5,624	−2,190	4,261	19,600	32,763	48,639	10,604
Deposit Money Banks					*Billions of Lei: End of Period*								
Reserves	20	† 1,462	2,416	3,293	3,632	5,347	13,050	35,014	51,038	87,125	143,956	169,128	315,531
Foreign Assets	21	† 1,312	2,746	3,723	6,554	13,551	17,301	22,904	40,131	50,967	39,898	35,360	52,478
Claims on Central Government	22a	398	584	1,839	5,469	11,099	18,833	29,850	31,718	37,994	42,896	26,234	22,242
Claims on Nonfin.Pub.Enterprises	22c	4,902	9,485	16,099	13,202	12,749	11,734	9,223	10,854	16,633	24,169	30,924	30,724
Claims on Private Sector	22d	† —	—	—	12,516	21,146	43,180	44,031	57,624	90,242	126,250	179,964	238,982
Claims on Nonbank Financial Insts.	22g	—	—	—	1,124	1,986	4,172	4,511	6,529	11,380	29,208	94,594	147,918
Demand Deposits	24	1,018	2,094	3,007	5,366	8,742	9,590	11,059	18,579	25,968	38,329	49,620	69,739
Transit Accounts	24x	159	212	354	615	110	328	364	682	1,421	671	1,127	575
Savings Deposits	25	890	3,605	6,939	11,901	25,625	40,219	53,973	63,873	90,419	138,599	176,323	257,101
Other Term Deposits	25a	219	390	444	580	898	994	1,238	2,011	2,706	4,397	5,662	8,496
Foreign Currency Deposits	25b	1,296	2,358	3,953	7,086	17,681	30,202	50,473	74,856	115,784	146,812	171,169	234,636
Foreign Liabilities	26c	715	1,213	2,121	4,996	9,213	10,213	11,158	13,181	20,897	33,642	72,160	144,795
Government Deposits	26d	1,094	1,614	1,846	1,136	2,168	5,749	5,638	7,024	13,030	14,691	18,755	23,351
Credit from Monetary Authorities	26g	1,568	2,316	3,179	8,024	632	556	1,930	2,296	1,148	—	—	—
Capital Accounts	27a	565	896	2,505	5,064	9,681	10,888	17,549	24,731	49,502	64,511	80,573	109,400
Other Items (Net)	27r	† 758	843	643	−2,270	−8,869	−477	−7,849	−9,338	−26,534	−35,272	−39,183	−40,218
Monetary Survey					*Billions of Lei: End of Period*								
Foreign Assets (Net)	31n	† 514	1,884	1,043	181	14,020	14,632	41,442	92,989	171,489	236,685	251,828	362,673
Domestic Credit	32	4,046	8,872	16,994	31,450	47,383	81,150	97,442	112,517	142,734	199,644	300,245	364,380
Claims on Central Govt. (Net)	32an	† −856	−612	895	4,608	11,502	22,063	39,677	37,510	24,479	20,018	−5,237	−53,244
Claims on Nonfin.Pub.Enterprises	32c	4,902	9,485	16,099	13,202	12,749	11,734	9,223	10,854	16,633	24,169	30,924	30,724
Claims on Private Sector	32d	—	—	—	12,516	21,146	43,180	44,031	57,624	90,242	126,250	179,964	238,982
Claims on Nonbank Financial Inst.	32g	—	—	—	1,124	1,986	4,172	4,511	6,529	11,380	29,208	94,594	147,918
Money	34	2,067	4,294	6,771	10,749	17,942	21,115	28,431	44,320	61,603	83,907	107,598	144,385
Transit Accounts	34x	185	233	368	615	110	355	628	975	1,421	685	1,127	576
Quasi-Money	35	2,405	6,353	11,336	19,567	44,203	71,415	105,684	140,740	208,909	289,808	353,153	500,232
Other Items (Net)	37r	† 111	187	−403	700	−852	2,888	4,141	19,471	42,290	61,932	90,195	81,859
Money plus Quasi-Money	35l	4,472	10,648	18,107	30,316	62,145	92,530	134,114	185,060	270,512	373,714	460,751	644,617
Interest Rates					*Percent Per Annum*								
Bank Rate (End of Period)	60a	....	66.9	41.3	35.1	45.0	37.9	35.0	35.0	35.0	29.0	18.8	20.3
Treasury Bill Rate	60c	....	....	....	51.1	85.7	64.0	74.2	51.9	42.2	27.0	....	....
Prices, Production, Labor					*Index Numbers (2000=100): Period Averages*								
Producer Prices	63	2.7	6.5	8.8	13.2	† 33.9	† 45.1	65.2	† 100.0	138.1	169.9	203.1	241.8
Consumer Prices	64	2.7	6.3	8.4	11.6	29.6	47.1	68.6	100.0	134.5	164.8	189.9	† 212.5
Wages: Avg. Earnings	65	2.8	6.4	9.9	14.8	29.1	48.0	71.5	100.0	138.9	178.6	224.0	274.5
Industrial Production	66	† 102.4	105.6	115.6	† 127.0	118.7	† 98.4	93.3	100.0	108.5	† 115.0	118.8	124.0
					Number in Thousands: Period Averages								
Employment	67e	10,062	† 10,914	11,152	10,936	11,050	10,845	10,776	10,764	10,697	9,673	9,223	....
Unemployment	67c	1,165	† 1,230	1,111	814	749	917	1,119	1,067	867	955	704	523
Unemployment Rate (%)	67r	10.4	† 11.0	10.0	7.8	7.5	9.3	11.3	11.2	9.0	10.0	7.6	6.7
Intl. Transactions & Positions					*Millions of US Dollars*								
Exports	70..d	4,892.2	6,151.3	7,910.0	8,084.5	8,431.1	8,299.6	8,504.7	10,366.5	11,390.7	13,875.7	17,618.5	23,485.2
Imports, c.i.f.	71..d	6,521.7	7,109.0	10,277.9	11,435.3	11,279.7	11,821.0	10,392.1	13,054.5	15,560.9	17,861.7	24,002.7	32,663.7
Imports, f.o.b.	71.vd	6,020.1	6,562.4	9,486.7	10,555.0	10,411.4	10,911.0	9,592.1	12,049.6	14,362.9	16,486.7	22,155.1	30,149.3

		1993	1994	1995	1996	1997	1998	1999	2000	2001	2002	2003	2004
Balance of Payments							*Millions of US Dollars: Minus Sign Indicates Debit*						
Current Account, n.i.e.	78ald	−1,231	−455	−1,780	−2,579	−2,104	−2,917	−1,297	−1,355	−2,229	−1,525	−3,311	−5,589
Goods: Exports f.o.b.	78aad	4,892	6,151	7,910	8,085	8,431	8,302	8,503	10,366	11,385	13,876	17,618	23,485
Goods: Imports f.o.b.	78abd	−6,020	−6,562	−9,487	−10,555	−10,411	−10,927	−9,595	−12,050	−14,354	−16,487	−22,155	−30,150
Trade Balance	78acd	−1,128	−411	−1,577	−2,470	−1,980	−2,625	−1,092	−1,684	−2,969	−2,611	−4,537	−6,665
Services: Credit	78add	799	1,044	1,494	1,563	1,523	1,226	1,365	1,747	2,032	2,347	3,028	3,614
Services: Debit	78aed	−914	−1,215	−1,819	−1,948	−1,904	−1,829	−1,785	−1,993	−2,153	−2,338	−2,958	−3,879
Balance on Goods & Services	78afd	−1,243	−582	−1,902	−2,855	−2,361	−3,228	−1,512	−1,930	−3,090	−2,602	−4,467	−6,930
Income: Credit	78agd	63	116	81	78	204	263	152	325	455	413	372	405
Income: Debit	78ahd	−208	−245	−322	−387	−526	−705	−563	−610	−737	−872	−1,077	−2,171
Balance on Gds, Serv. & Inc.	78aid	−1,388	−711	−2,143	−3,164	−2,683	−3,670	−1,923	−2,215	−3,372	−3,061	−5,172	−8,696
Current Transfers, n.i.e.: Credit	78ajd	174	317	473	667	731	886	804	1,079	1,417	1,808	2,200	3,598
Current Transfers: Debit	78akd	−17	−61	−110	−82	−152	−133	−178	−219	−274	−272	−339	−491
Capital Account, n.i.e.	78bcd	—	—	32	152	43	39	45	36	95	93	213	643
Capital Account, n.i.e.: Credit	78bad	—	—	32	152	43	39	46	37	108	100	223	669
Capital Account: Debit	78bbd	—	—	—	—	—	—	−1	−1	−13	−7	−10	−26
Financial Account, n.i.e.	78bjd	640	535	812	1,486	2,458	2,042	697	2,102	2,938	4,079	4,400	9,687
Direct Investment Abroad	78bdd	−7	—	−2	—	9	9	−16	11	17	−16	−39	−70
Dir. Invest. in Rep. Econ., n.i.e.	78bed	94	341	419	263	1,215	2,031	1,041	1,037	1,157	1,144	1,844	5,316
Portfolio Investment Assets	78bfd	−73	75	−22	—	−6	1	9	28	−8	—	9	27
Equity Securities	78bkd	—	—	−4	—	−6	1	9	31	−7	—	14	27
Debt Securities	78bld	−73	75	−18	—	—	—	—	−3	−1	—	−5	—
Portfolio Investment Liab., n.i.e.	78bgd	—	—	54	193	540	129	−724	73	583	382	569	28
Equity Securities	78bmd	—	—	—	—	195	95	68	58	8	21	69	111
Debt Securities	78bnd	—	—	54	193	345	34	−792	15	575	361	500	−83
Financial Derivatives Assets	78bwd	....	....	—	—	—	—	....	....	....	....	....	....
Financial Derivatives Liabilities	78bxd	....	....	—	—	—	—	....	....	....	....	....	....
Other Investment Assets	78bhd	−45	−671	186	−271	−6	208	246	−407	−44	692	72	−682
Monetary Authorities	78bod	—	—	—	—	—	—	—	....	—	—	−1	—
General Government	78bpd	−49	−24	−62	−9	10	−10	9	−82	−44	−41	−36	−22
Banks	78bqd	−168	−621	254	−315	−140	179	236	−354	−102	536	229	−588
Other Sectors	78brd	172	−26	−6	53	124	39	1	29	102	197	−120	−72
Other Investment Liab., n.i.e.	78bid	671	790	177	1,301	706	−336	141	1,360	1,233	1,877	1,945	5,068
Monetary Authorities	78bsd	—	—	—	−150	—	—	73	−14	—	−100	—	99
General Government	78btd	68	75	−27	209	547	−7	40	681	320	465	889	1,058
Banks	78bud	19	190	−57	536	−132	−260	−54	−107	159	309	918	2,426
Other Sectors	78bvd	584	525	261	706	291	−69	82	800	754	1,203	138	1,485
Net Errors and Omissions	78cad	152	91	456	359	1,062	193	794	125	731	−856	−289	1,270
Overall Balance	78cbd	−439	171	−480	−582	1,459	−643	239	908	1,535	1,791	1,013	6,011
Reserves and Related Items	79dad	439	−171	480	582	−1,459	643	−239	−908	−1,535	−1,791	−1,013	−6,011
Reserve Assets	79dbd	54	−616	259	−218	−1,664	844	−173	−928	−1,484	−1,802	−1,134	−5,840
Use of Fund Credit and Loans	79dcd	—	217	−316	−356	29	−126	−66	20	−51	11	120	−171
Exceptional Financing	79ded	385	228	536	1,157	176	−75	....	—	....	....	....	....
International Investment Position							*Millions of US Dollars*						
Assets	79aad	7,483	8,847	8,492	7,832	9,046	8,365	8,216	9,494	11,418	13,303	15,164	23,336
Direct Investment Abroad	79abd	104	107	121	120	114	123	103	136	117	144	208	301
Portfolio Investment	79acd	1,208	1,179	1,224	13	11	23	34	6	11	22	14	580
Equity Securities	79add	1,124	1,176	1,211	—	—	—	30	5	10	18	10	3
Debt Securities	79aed	84	3	13	13	11	23	4	—	—	4	4	577
Financial Derivatives	79ald	—	—	—	—	—	—	—	—	—	—	—	—
Other Investment	79afd	5,215	5,964	5,768	6,107	5,860	5,921	5,587	5,963	6,430	5,831	5,892	6,172
Monetary Authorities	79agd	—	—	—	10	10	10	10	10	10	10	10	10
General Government	79ahd	2,990	3,004	3,006	3,109	2,926	3,058	3,727	3,807	3,873	3,921	3,970	4,004
Banks	79aid	871	1,491	1,244	1,556	1,637	1,472	1,178	1,487	1,552	1,099	978	1,080
Other Sectors	79ajd	1,355	1,468	1,517	1,432	1,288	1,382	672	659	995	801	933	1,078
Reserve Assets	79akd	956	1,598	1,380	1,592	3,061	2,299	2,493	3,390	4,861	7,306	9,450	16,283
Liabilities	79lad	6,196	7,500	7,976	10,318	12,846	15,097	15,360	17,957	20,878	22,952	33,062	46,033
Dir. Invest. in Rep. Economy	79lbd	216	402	421	1,097	2,352	4,418	5,469	6,480	7,638	7,799	12,815	18,484
Portfolio Investment	79lcd	858	719	785	1,229	2,023	2,249	1,605	1,654	2,187	3,234	4,503	4,833
Equity Securities	79ldd	858	719	732	—	266	361	429	487	495	516	700	877
Debt Securities	79led	—	—	54	1,229	1,757	1,888	1,176	1,167	1,692	2,718	3,802	3,955
Financial Derivatives	79lld	—	—	—	—	—	—	—	—	—	—	—	—
Other Investment	79lfd	5,123	6,379	6,770	7,991	8,471	8,430	8,286	9,823	11,053	11,919	15,744	22,716
Monetary Authorities	79lgd	1,031	1,383	1,358	941	958	580	572	553	487	428	595	543
General Government	79lhd	2,388	2,298	2,335	2,512	2,916	3,000	3,111	3,748	4,281	4,999	6,466	7,846
Banks	79lid	504	682	743	1,268	832	679	567	506	654	999	2,093	4,801
Other Sectors	79ljd	1,200	2,016	2,334	3,270	3,765	4,170	4,036	5,016	5,631	5,493	6,590	9,526
Government Finance							*Billions of Lei: Year Ending December 31*						
Deficit (-) or Surplus	80	−94	−1,248	−2,133	−4,377	−9,755	−11,033	−9,230	−31,769	−35,410	....	....	....
Revenue	81	6,389	14,884	21,327	30,194	68,394	107,051	171,135	237,161	311,320	....	....	....
Grants	81z	—	—	—	—	—	695	4,235	880	1,345	....	....	....
Expenditure	82	6,312	15,913	22,927	34,033	79,734	124,595	191,341	273,990	354,837	....	....	....
Lending Minus Repayments	83	171	220	533	538	−1,585	−5,816	−6,741	−4,180	−6,762	....	....	....
Financing													
Domestic	84a	94	1,248	....	....	7,524	....	....	23,976	25,670	....	....	....
Foreign	85a	—	—	....	....	2,232	....	....	7,794	9,740	....	....	....

		1993	1994	1995	1996	1997	1998	1999	2000	2001	2002	2003	2004
National Accounts							*Billions of Lei*						
Househ.Cons.Expend.,incl.NPISHs....	96f	12,763	31,601	48,785	75,665	187,620	283,142	405,322	563,182	817,809	1,044,715	1,310,628	1,681,603
Government Consumption Expend...	91f	2,473	6,852	9,877	14,274	31,000	54,327	79,040	129,351	176,928	227,977	304,394	379,108
Gross Fixed Capital Formation..........	93e	3,584	10,096	15,425	24,999	53,540	67,920	96,630	151,947	241,154	322,836	422,535	532,549
Changes in Inventories....................	93i	2,212	2,253	2,085	3,161	−1,369	−1,586	−8,890	4,544	22,295	5,561	14,151	17,979
Exports of Goods and Services..........	90c	4,612	12,394	19,921	30,651	73,796	84,559	152,903	264,187	389,147	536,771	685,838	885,605
Imports of Goods and Services (-).....	98c	5,608	13,422	23,958	39,831	91,661	114,563	179,275	309,437	479,646	623,110	834,192	1,108,931
Gross Domestic Product (GDP).........	99b	20,036	49,773	72,136	108,920	252,926	373,798	545,730	803,773	1,167,687	1,514,751	1,903,354	2,387,914
GDP Volume 1995 Prices.................	99b.p	64,780	67,329	72,136	74,984	70,445	67,051	66,280	67,704	71,594	75,260	79,146	85,709
GDP Volume (2000=100)...............	99bvp	95.7	99.4	106.5	110.8	104.0	99.0	97.9	100.0	105.7	111.2	116.9	126.6
GDP Deflator (2000=100)...............	99bip	2.6	6.2	8.4	12.2	30.2	47.0	69.4	100.0	137.4	169.5	202.6	234.7
							Millions: Midyear Estimates						
Population.................................	99z	22.96	22.82	22.68	22.55	22.44	22.32	22.22	22.12	22.03	21.94	21.87	21.79

Russia 922

		1993	1994	1995	1996	1997	1998	1999	2000	2001	2002	2003	2004
Exchange Rates						*Rubles per SDR: End of Period*							
Official Rate	aa	1.7128	5.1825	6.8973	7.9951	8.0415	† 29.0758	37.0578	36.6899	37.8778	43.2115	43.7685	43.0940
						Rubles per US Dollar: End of Period (ae) Period Average (rf)							
Official Rate	ae	1.2470	3.5500	4.6400	5.5600	5.9600	† 20.6500	27.0000	28.1600	30.1400	31.7844	29.4545	27.7487
Official Rate	rf	.9917	2.1908	4.5592	5.1208	5.7848	† 9.7051	24.6199	28.1292	29.1685	31.3485	30.6920	28.8137
						Index Numbers (2000=100): Period Averages							
Nominal Effective Exchange Rate	nec	....	472.81	290.15	281.62	286.92	233.02	94.33	100.00	105.73	99.64	94.87	96.01
Real Effective Exchange Rate	rec	....	102.96	112.86	137.62	145.18	128.47	90.53	100.00	118.72	122.66	126.98	136.51
Fund Position						*Millions of SDRs: End of Period*							
Quota	2f.s	4,313.1	4,313.1	4,313.1	4,313.1	4,313.1	4,313.1	5,945.4	5,945.4	5,945.4	5,945.4	5,945.4	5,945.4
SDRs	1b.s	3.7	2.1	78.5	3.1	90.7	.1	.4	.4	2.3	.9	.5	.6
Reserve Position in the Fund	1c.s	1.0	.8	.8	.9	.9	.9	.9	.9	1.1	1.2	1.4	1.8
Total Fund Cred.&Loans Outstg.	2tl	1,797.3	2,875.6	6,469.8	8,698.2	9,805.9	13,732.0	11,102.3	8,912.8	5,914.8	4,767.3	3,411.2	2,293.8
International Liquidity						*Millions of US Dollars Unless Otherwise Indicated: End of Period*							
Total Reserves minus Gold	1l.d	5,835.0	3,980.4	14,382.8	11,276.4	12,894.7	7,801.4	8,457.2	24,264.3	32,542.4	44,053.6	73,174.9	120,808.8
SDRs	1b.d	5.0	3.1	116.7	4.5	122.4	.1	.6	.5	2.9	1.2	.7	.9
Reserve Position in the Fund	1c.d	1.4	1.2	1.2	1.1	1.3	1.2	1.3	1.3	1.4	1.6	2.1	2.8
Foreign Exchange	1d.d	5,828.6	3,976.1	14,264.9	11,270.6	12,771.1	7,800.0	8,455.4	24,262.6	32,538.1	44,050.8	73,172.1	120,805.1
Gold (Million Fine Troy Ounces)	1ad	10.195	8.417	9.414	13.490	16.297	14.738	13.326	12.359	13.599	12.464	12.545	12.441
Gold (National Valuation)	1and	3,058.5	2,525.1	2,824.1	4,047.1	4,889.2	4,421.6	3,998.3	3,707.8	4,079.8	3,739.3	3,763.4	3,732.4
Monetary Authorities:Other Assets	3..d	9,074.6	5,768.2	3,458.8	3,176.8	2,911.2	1,937.8	2,010.8	2,177.2	2,385.5	3,039.5	4,241.0	5,572.3
Other Liab.	4..d	943.1	477.3	303.0	311.2	149.2	110.5	473.1	143.7	2,102.6	850.4	2,421.9	3,966.7
Deposit Money Banks: Assets	7a.d	12,669.3	13,891.6	9,946.1	13,107.0	12,513.8	11,251.1	14,281.9	17,435.3	18,146.2	19,033.0	20,660.0	25,480.5
Liabilities	7b.d	3,773.4	4,076.8	6,459.1	10,592.3	18,030.0	10,727.0	9,408.3	10,113.9	11,355.2	12,892.6	23,158.9	32,168.9
Monetary Authorities						*Millions of Rubles: End of Period*							
Foreign Assets	11	21,737	41,082	95,890	102,861	123,344	292,420	390,590	849,009	1,175,689	1,615,677	2,391,096	3,610,481
Claims on General Government	12a	16,802	84,498	138,578	187,365	226,049	525,374	572,030	504,702	488,102	551,547	477,640	426,555
Claims on Nonfin.Pub.Enterprises	12c	123	251	85	67	46	150	114	103	80	58	55	39
Claims on Private Sector	12d	21	72	237	813	281	412	316	264	168	2,181	2,264	2,282
Claims on Deposit Money Banks	12e	8,889	16,177	17,450	11,377	11,119	76,438	202,944	206,501	250,187	223,991	198,742	178,230
Reserve Money	14	20,544	62,357	129,601	164,929	210,450	269,665	446,432	746,252	963,137	1,263,728	1,947,711	2,423,889
of which: Currency Outside DMBs	14a	10,730	34,493	80,815	103,795	130,474	187,679	266,146	418,871	583,839	763,245	1,147,039	1,534,755
Time & Foreign Currency Deposits	15	1	4	17	23	240	1,828	1,575	7	2	29	5	17
Foreign Liabilities	16c	4,254	16,538	46,030	71,272	79,744	401,551	424,201	331,056	287,413	233,030	220,638	208,919
General Government Deposits	16d	7,003	17,096	24,898	15,062	21,313	41,863	75,871	240,488	294,914	357,878	446,001	1,047,907
of which: Local Govt. Deposits	16db	847	3,273	2,117	2,068	3,564	2,863	10,515	29,511	27,729	33,993	43,804	85,580
Capital Accounts	17a	638	17,014	27,530	54,179	69,552	118,113	151,844	166,048	242,312	364,731	298,234	297,706
Other Items (Net)	17r	15,132	29,071	24,164	−2,982	−20,460	61,775	66,072	76,728	126,448	174,058	157,208	239,149
Deposit Money Banks						*Millions of Rubles: End of Period*							
Reserves	20	7,914	24,151	36,712	48,301	74,981	77,728	168,180	310,781	356,771	471,563	768,914	847,419
Foreign Assets	21	15,798	49,316	46,150	72,875	74,582	232,336	385,611	490,977	546,926	604,953	608,529	707,052
Claims on General Government	22a	776	10,639	62,639	150,945	194,899	263,695	445,321	532,569	588,703	696,007	742,776	757,190
of which: Claims on Local Govts	22ab	—	—	722	2,796	18,699	26,174	22,080	20,538	27,612	52,314	98,844	133,748
Claims on Nonfin.Pub.Enterprises	22c	15,639	48,173	62,460	80,211	51,687	38,099	52,131	78,963	83,238	122,938	142,968	166,550
Claims on Private Sector	22d	20,208	74,017	133,786	166,517	250,134	410,691	631,137	969,413	1,473,097	1,915,108	2,772,461	4,118,941
Claims on Other Financial Insts	22f	—	—	525	242	8,077	7,526	13,738	15,378	23,232	32,948	55,561	73,747
Demand Deposits	24	12,519	32,589	69,332	87,303	163,658	150,931	250,927	444,625	586,721	706,693	1,003,198	1,277,488
Time, Savings,& Fgn.Currency Dep	25	17,101	61,183	124,497	164,899	160,771	287,686	463,999	688,453	944,814	1,361,495	1,780,146	2,450,337
of which: Fgn. Currency Deposits	25b	12,086	37,309	55,256	69,448	80,822	191,412	292,023	422,874	523,929	726,443	748,240	935,077
Money Market Instruments	26aa	211	3,516	11,858	26,653	31,485	42,062	113,089	199,080	263,885	399,866	545,464	543,638
Restricted Deposits	26b	—	—	—	9,929	17,423	65,596	100,849	90,509	77,582	43,759	30,360	36,112
Foreign Liabilities	26c	4,705	14,473	29,970	58,893	107,459	221,512	254,025	284,808	342,246	409,783	682,134	892,645
General Government Deposits	26d	2,117	6,914	9,741	12,142	19,105	22,723	31,272	58,923	73,538	67,892	85,484	141,762
of which: Local Govt. Deposits	26db	919	2,246	4,252	4,493	9,598	10,638	16,440	37,277	44,875	36,787	56,057	112,465
Credit from Monetary Authorities	26g	8,464	17,181	8,006	12,769	15,430	79,872	206,887	208,109	250,918	226,103	200,868	179,826
Capital Accounts	27a	12,031	26,211	56,810	106,684	124,005	102,678	166,259	234,223	352,141	491,277	686,650	898,313
Other Items (Net)	27r	3,187	44,229	32,058	39,819	15,024	57,015	108,811	189,351	180,122	136,649	76,905	250,778
Monetary Survey						*Millions of Rubles: End of Period*							
Foreign Assets (Net)	31n	28,576	59,387	66,040	45,571	10,723	−98,306	97,976	724,122	1,092,956	1,577,817	2,096,853	3,215,969
Domestic Credit	32	44,449	193,640	363,671	558,956	690,755	1,181,361	1,607,644	1,801,981	2,288,168	2,895,017	3,662,240	4,355,635
Claims on General Govt. (Net)	32an	8,458	71,127	166,578	311,106	380,530	724,483	910,208	737,860	708,353	821,784	688,931	−5,924
Claims on Nonfin.Pub.Enterprises	32c	15,762	48,424	62,545	80,278	51,733	38,249	52,245	79,066	83,318	122,996	143,023	166,589
Claims on Private Sector	32d	20,229	74,089	134,023	167,330	250,415	411,103	631,453	969,677	1,473,265	1,917,289	2,774,725	4,121,223
Claims on Other Financial Insts	32f	—	—	525	242	8,077	7,526	13,738	15,378	23,232	32,948	55,561	73,747
Money	34	23,881	68,544	151,267	192,373	299,349	344,113	527,627	880,524	1,193,395	1,498,463	2,181,933	2,848,345
Quasi-Money	35	17,102	61,187	124,514	164,922	161,011	289,514	465,574	688,460	944,816	1,361,524	1,780,151	2,450,354
Money Market Instruments	36aa	211	3,516	11,858	26,653	31,485	42,062	113,089	199,080	263,885	399,866	545,464	543,638
Restricted Deposits	36b	—	—	—	9,929	17,423	65,596	100,849	90,509	77,582	43,759	30,360	36,112
Capital Accounts	37a	12,669	43,225	84,340	160,863	193,557	220,791	318,103	400,271	594,453	856,006	984,884	1,196,019
Other Items (Net)	37r	19,162	76,555	57,732	49,787	−1,347	120,979	180,378	267,259	306,993	313,214	236,301	497,136
Money plus Quasi-Money	35l	40,983	129,731	275,781	357,295	460,360	633,627	993,201	1,568,984	2,138,211	2,859,987	3,962,084	5,298,699
Interest Rates						*Percent Per Annum*							
Refinancing Rate (End of Period)	60	....	....	160.00	48.00	28.00	60.00	55.00	25.00	25.00	21.00	16.00	13.00
Money Market Rate	60b	....	....	190.43	47.65	20.97	50.56	14.79	7.14	10.10	8.19	3.77	3.33
Treasury Bill Rate	60c	....	....	168.04	86.07	23.43	....	....	12.12	12.45	12.72	5.35	....
Deposit Rate	60l	....	....	101.96	55.05	† 16.77	17.05	13.68	6.51	4.85	4.96	4.48	3.79
Lending Rate	60p	....	....	320.31	146.81	† 32.04	41.79	39.72	24.43	17.91	15.71	12.98	11.40

		1993	1994	1995	1996	1997	1998	1999	2000	2001	2002	2003	2004
Prices and Labor		*Percent Change over Previous Period Unless Otherwise indicated*											
Producer Prices...................	63.xx	943.76	337.00	236.46	50.81	15.00	7.03	58.95	46.53	19.17	10.44	16.38	23.36
Consumer Prices (2000=100).........	64	1.7	6.9	† 20.6	30.4	34.9	44.6	82.8	100.0	† 121.5	140.6	159.8	177.2
Wages...........................	65.xx	822.1	255.9	142.2	64.8	23.7	15.3	55.4	51.9	43.2	27.3	26.1	22.5
		Index Numbers (2000=100): Period Averages											
Industrial Employment...................	67	151.8	134.4	125.6	115.3	105.4	101.4	98.2	100.0	99.2	95.7	89.8	85.0
		Number in Thousands: Period Averages											
Labor Force...................	67d	....	....	69,469	68,264	....	66,736	69,731	....	....	71,919	72,212	....
Employment...................	67e	68,642	64,785	64,149	62,928	60,021	63,575	64,400	62,675	64,412	66,071	65,766	66,496
Unemployment...................	67c	† 836	1,637	2,327	2,506	1,990	1,875	1,675	1,244	1,050	1,331	1,554	....
Unemployment Rate (%)...........	67r	5.7	† 7.5	8.9	9.9	11.3	13.3	12.7	10.6	9.0	....	....	....
Intl. Transactions & Positions		*Millions of US Dollars*											
Exports...........................	70..d	44,297	† 67,826	82,913	90,563	89,008	74,884	75,665	105,565	101,884	107,301	135,929	183,452
Imports, c.i.f........................	71..d	36,086	† 55,497	68,863	74,879	79,076	63,817	43,588	49,125	59,140	67,063	83,677	105,938
Imports, f.o.b........................	71.vd	....	....	....	....	....	....	....	....	53,764	60,966	76,070	96,307
Balance of Payments		*Millions of US Dollars: Minus Sign Indicates Debit*											
Current Account, n.i.e...................	78ald	....	7,844	6,965	10,847	−80	216	24,611	46,840	33,795	29,116	35,410	60,109
Goods: Exports f.o.b................	78aad	....	67,379	82,419	89,684	86,895	74,443	75,549	105,034	101,884	107,301	135,929	183,452
Goods: Imports f.o.b................	78abd	....	−50,451	−62,603	−68,093	−71,982	−58,014	−39,537	−44,862	−53,764	−60,966	−76,070	−96,307
Trade Balance...................	78acd	....	16,928	19,816	21,591	14,913	16,429	36,012	60,172	48,121	46,335	59,860	87,145
Services: Credit...................	78add	....	8,425	10,568	13,283	14,079	12,375	9,071	9,565	11,441	13,611	16,229	20,290
Services: Debit...................	78aed	....	−15,435	−20,206	−18,665	−20,025	−16,456	−13,352	−16,229	−20,712	−23,497	−27,122	−33,700
Balance on Goods & Services......	78afd	....	9,918	10,178	16,209	8,967	12,348	31,731	53,508	38,850	36,449	48,966	73,735
Income: Credit...................	78agd	....	3,499	4,281	4,336	4,367	4,299	3,878	4,752	6,800	5,677	11,057	9,635
Income: Debit...................	78ahd	....	−5,342	−7,650	−9,768	−13,058	−16,094	−11,599	−11,491	−11,038	−12,260	−24,228	−22,462
Balance on Gds, Serv. & Inc......	78aid	....	8,075	6,809	10,777	276	553	24,010	46,769	34,612	29,866	35,795	60,908
Current Transfers: Credit.........	78ajd	....	311	894	771	410	308	1,183	808	744	1,352	2,537	3,540
Current Transfers: Debit...........	78akd	....	−542	−738	−701	−766	−645	−582	−737	−1,561	−2,103	−2,922	−4,339
Capital Account, n.i.e...................	78bcd	....	2,408	−348	−463	−796	−382	−326	10,675	−9,378	−12,396	−995	−1,626
Capital Account, n.i.e.: Credit......	78bad	....	5,882	3,122	3,066	2,138	1,705	887	11,543	2,125	7,528	614	860
Capital Account: Debit............	78bbd	....	−3,474	−3,470	−3,529	−2,934	−2,087	−1,213	−868	−11,503	−19,924	−1,609	−2,486
Financial Account, n.i.e...........	78bjd	....	−29,340	−5,828	−19,890	3,164	−11,404	−17,434	−34,435	−3,802	1,346	1,575	−5,448
Direct Investment Abroad............	78bdd	....	−281	−605	−922	−3,186	−1,268	−2,206	−3,177	−2,533	−3,533	−9,727	−9,601
Dir. Invest. in Rep. Econ., n.i.e...	78bed	....	690	2,065	2,579	4,864	2,764	3,309	2,713	2,748	3,461	7,958	11,672
Portfolio Investment Assets.........	78bfd	....	114	−1,704	−173	−157	−258	254	−411	77	−796	−2,543	−4,101
Equity Securities............	78bkd	....	−19	−42	−117	32	−11	5	−39	−60	85	−13	3
Debt Securities............	78bld	....	133	−1,662	−56	−189	−247	249	−372	137	−880	−2,529	−4,104
Portfolio Investment Liab., n.i.e......	78bgd	....	−93	−739	4,584	17,796	6,293	−1,881	−12,809	−730	3,756	−2,338	4,698
Equity Securities............	78bmd	....	44	46	2,154	1,266	714	−287	150	542	2,626	413	672
Debt Securities............	78bnd	....	−137	−785	2,430	16,530	5,579	−1,594	−12,959	−1,272	1,130	−2,750	4,026
Financial Derivatives Assets.........	78bwd	....	....	....	....	....	....	....	....	—	80	1,017	758
Financial Derivatives Liabilities....	78bxd	....	....	....	....	....	....	....	....	—	−67	−377	−857
Other Investment Assets...............	78bhd	....	−19,557	−150	−27,666	−20,637	−14,462	−13,218	−17,662	80	2,120	−16,472	−24,835
Monetary Authorities............	78bod	....								−266	971	467	298
General Government...............	78bpd	....	−3,119	−1,040	−319	7,156	−1,149	−1,349	−1,618	10,099	16,990	−299	323
Banks...........................	78bqd	....	−3,117	4,318	−1,972	−1,084	502	−3,623	−3,332	−1,652	−675	−837	−1,964
Other Sectors............	78brd	....	−13,321	−3,428	−25,375	−26,709	−13,815	−8,246	−12,712	−8,102	−15,167	−15,802	−23,492
Other Investment Liab., n.i.e.......	78bid	....	−10,213	−4,695	1,708	4,484	−4,473	−3,692	−3,089	−3,444	−3,676	24,056	16,819
Monetary Authorities............	78bsd	....	−325	391	−230	−38	66	3	155	1,908	−1,273	1,636	1,694
General Government...............	78btd	....	−11,744	−8,716	−6,034	−10,762	−3,175	−1,975	−2,876	−7,480	−13,341	−4,197	−5,733
Banks...........................	78bud	....	1,305	2,448	4,258	8,647	−6,361	−1,272	568	1,839	2,584	11,546	6,709
Other Sectors............	78bvd	....	551	1,182	3,714	6,637	4,997	−448	−936	289	8,354	15,070	14,149
Net Errors and Omissions............	78cad	....	−25	−9,115	−7,712	−8,808	−9,808	−8,555	−9,158	−9,350	−6,502	−8,228	−6,395
Overall Balance...............	78cbd	....	−19,113	−8,326	−17,218	−6,520	−21,378	−1,704	13,922	11,266	11,563	27,762	46,640
Reserves and Related Items............	79dad	....	19,113	8,326	17,218	6,520	21,378	1,704	−13,922	−11,266	−11,563	−27,762	−46,640
Reserve Assets...................	79dbd	....	1,935	−10,382	2,840	−1,930	5,306	−1,772	−16,009	−8,210	−11,375	−26,365	−45,236
Use of Fund Credit and Loans......	79dcd	....	1,514	5,473	3,237	1,526	5,206	−3,603	−2,899	−3,829	−1,493	−1,897	−1,655
Exceptional Financing...................	79ded	....	15,663	13,235	11,141	6,924	10,866	7,079	4,986	773	1,305	500	250
International Investment Position		*Millions of US Dollars*											
Assets...........................	79aad	23,408	22,245	28,645	29,041	33,440	25,557	28,392	239,247	241,419	274,591	315,130	....
Direct Investment Abroad............	79abd	2,277	2,272	2,420	2,685	2,789	2,703	1,076	20,141	32,437	54,608	72,273	....
Portfolio Investment...........	79acd	590	486	764	1,230	1,383	1,308	861	1,268	1,342	2,539	4,778	....
Equity Securities............	79add	—	7	27	43	12	18	6	46	132	82	125	....
Debt Securities............	79aed	590	479	737	1,187	1,371	1,290	855	1,222	1,210	2,456	4,653	....
Financial Derivatives...........	79ald	—	—	—	—	—	—	—	—	—	—	55	....
Other Investment...................	79afd	11,647	12,982	8,254	9,802	11,484	9,323	14,000	189,866	171,018	169,652	161,086	....
Monetary Authorities............	79agd	—	—	—	—	—	—	—	1,436	1,677	1,518	1,095	....
General Government...............	79ahd	—	—	—	—	—	—	—	122,275	100,210	94,953	84,790	....
Banks...........................	79aid	11,647	12,982	8,254	9,802	11,484	9,323	14,000	15,585	16,946	17,796	18,961	....
Other Sectors............	79ajd	—	—	—	—	—	—	—	50,570	52,184	55,385	56,240	....
Reserve Assets...................	79akd	8,894	6,505	17,207	15,324	17,784	12,223	12,455	27,972	36,622	47,793	76,938	....
Liabilities........................	79lad	5,519	7,380	15,492	22,162	32,829	29,925	24,087	183,679	211,479	248,049	323,247	....
Dir. Invest. in Rep. Economy...........	79lbd	183	332	345	426	970	373	731	32,204	55,445	72,424	86,772	....
Portfolio Investment...........	79lcd	380	369	437	567	1,032	495	346	32,132	46,500	62,387	93,912	....
Equity Securities............	79ldd	90	79	132	122	241	36	40	11,109	21,537	31,238	58,536	....
Debt Securities............	79led	290	290	305	445	791	459	306	21,023	24,964	31,149	35,376	....
Financial Derivatives...................	79lld	—	—	—	—	—	—	—	—	—	—	31	....
Other Investment...................	79lfd	4,956	6,679	14,710	21,169	30,827	29,057	23,010	119,344	109,534	113,238	142,532	....
Monetary Authorities............	79lgd	2,469	4,198	9,617	12,508	13,231	19,335	15,238	11,939	9,741	7,531	7,807	....
General Government...............	79lhd	—	—	—	—	—	—	—	81,864	72,577	67,114	69,385	....
Banks...........................	79lid	2,487	2,481	5,093	8,661	17,596	9,722	7,772	7,990	9,702	12,326	23,525	....
Other Sectors............	79ljd	—	—	—	—	—	—	—	17,552	17,515	26,267	41,815	....

Russia 922

		1993	1994	1995	1996	1997	1998	1999	2000	2001	2002	2003	2004
Government Finance				*Millions of Rubles: Year Ending December 31*									
Deficit (-) or Surplus	80	....	....	−69,508	−147,607	−150,415	−126,958	−56,641	173,468	275,321	179,220	314,251	825,937
Total Revenue and Grants	81y	....	....	226,071	281,770	322,690	299,403	608,033	1,127,571	1,598,482	2,219,266	2,577,933	3,456,733
Revenue	81	....	....	....	....	....	....	....	....	....	2,218,389	2,577,031	3,420,810
Grants	81z	....	....	....	....	....	....	....	....	....	877	902	35,923
Exp. & Lending Minus Repay	82z	....	....	295,579	429,377	473,105	426,361	664,674	954,103	1,323,161	2,040,046	2,263,682	2,630,796
Expenditure	82	....	....	277,744	409,792	454,768	416,872	655,391	1,004,265	1,376,552	2,042,943	2,351,111	2,692,245
Lending Minus Repayments	83	....	....	17,835	19,585	18,337	9,489	9,283	−50,162	−53,391	−2,897	−87,429	−61,449
Total Financing	80h	....	....	69,508	147,607	150,415	126,958	56,641	−173,468	−275,321	−179,220	−314,251	−825,937
Total Net Borrowing	84	....	....	72,248	137,224	159,722	154,733	101,063	−173,468	−275,321	−179,220	−314,251	−825,937
Net Domestic	84a	....	....	48,814	103,968	106,253	64,545	53,644	−40,331	−50,068	−9,210	−81,435	−652,106
Net Foreign	85a	....	....	23,434	33,256	53,469	90,188	47,419	−133,137	−225,253	−170,010	−232,816	−173,831
Use of Cash Balances	87	....	....	−2,740	10,383	−9,307	−27,775	−44,422	—	—	—	—	—
Total Debt by Currency	88z	....	....	787,689	1,122,323	1,302,052	3,786,106	....	....	....	4,550,774	4,004,304	....
Debt: Domestic	88b	....	....	226,505	427,323	565,992	750,556	....	801,530	755,896	886,249	830,798	98,848
Debt: Foreign	89b	....	....	561,184	695,000	736,060	3,035,550	....	....	....	3,664,525	3,173,506	....
National Accounts				*Billions of Rubles*									
Househ.Cons.Expend.,incl.NPISHs	96f	77	285	744	1,044	1,283	1,511	2,582	3,374	4,417	5,536	6,689	8,162
Government Consumption Expend	91f	30	137	273	391	494	493	703	1,102	1,470	1,913	2,318	2,718
Gross Fixed Capital Formation	93e	35	133	301	402	429	425	694	1,232	1,689	1,939	2,408	3,002
Changes in Inventories	93i	11	23	62	74	86	−31	134	21	274	232	300	534
Exports of Goods and Services	90c	66	170	418	523	579	821	2,085	3,219	3,300	3,814	4,656	5,814
Imports of Goods and Services (-)	98c	52	142	370	439	528	646	1,262	1,756	2,166	2,646	3,154	3,710
GDP, Production Based	99bp	172	611	1,429	2,008	2,343	2,630	4,823	7,306	8,944	10,831	13,243	16,752
Statistical Discrepancy	99bs	5	5	—	12	—	57	—	—	−40	44	27	232
				Millions: Midyear Estimates									
Population	99z	148.67	148.44	148.19	147.95	147.69	147.40	147.03	146.56	145.99	145.33	144.62	143.90

Rwanda 714

		1993	1994	1995	1996	1997	1998	1999	2000	2001	2002	2003	2004
Exchange Rates						*Francs per SDR: End of Period*							
Official Rate	aa	201.39	201.39	445.67	437.37	411.31	450.75	479.24	560.67	572.84	695.88	849.07	878.35
					Francs per US Dollar: End of Period (ae) Period Average (rf)								
Official Rate	ae	146.62	137.95	299.81	304.16	304.84	320.13	349.17	430.32	455.82	511.85	571.39	565.58
Official Rate	rf	144.24	140.70	262.18	306.10	301.32	313.72	337.83	393.43	442.80	476.33	537.66	574.62
Fund Position						*Millions of SDRs: End of Period*							
Quota	2f.s	59.50	59.50	59.50	59.50	59.50	59.50	80.10	80.10	80.10	80.10	80.10	80.10
SDRs	1b.s	2.11	1.75	13.65	12.71	19.64	17.36	10.54	.87	9.82	7.48	20.03	19.45
Reserve Position in the Fund	1c.s	9.79	9.79	—	—	—	—	—	—	—	—	—	—
Total Fund Cred.&Loans Outstg	2tl	8.76	8.76	17.69	16.81	29.93	40.08	55.29	65.88	67.09	62.45	61.84	59.41
International Liquidity					*Millions of US Dollars Unless Otherwise Indicated: End of Period*								
Total Reserves minus Gold	1l.d	47.46	51.25	99.10	106.74	153.34	168.75	174.18	190.64	212.11	243.73	214.70	314.64
SDRs	1b.d	2.90	2.55	20.29	18.28	26.50	24.44	14.46	1.14	12.34	10.17	29.77	30.20
Reserve Position in the Fund	1c.d	13.45	14.29	—	—	—	—	—	—	—	—	—	—
Foreign Exchange	1d.d	31.11	34.40	78.80	88.47	126.84	144.31	159.72	189.50	199.77	233.55	184.93	284.44
Monetary Authorities: Other Liab	4..d	28.52	40.45	28.36	20.62	21.89	50.05	21.13	17.89	15.69	17.82	8.29	2.56
Deposit Money Banks: Assets	7a.d	31.68	26.63	51.92	66.27	73.17	75.22	56.23	76.54	74.87	76.17	85.77	....
Liabilities	7b.d	6.07	5.61	4.09	4.53	12.63	11.91	5.31	8.24	10.37	15.41	22.26	....
Other Banking Insts.: Liabilities	7f.d	14.73	8.67	7.96	7.41	4.70	2.99	2.92	2.39	8.09	8.09	13.39	....
Monetary Authorities						*Millions of Francs: End of Period*							
Foreign Assets	11	6,946	7,089	29,710	32,469	46,720	54,058	60,882	82,068	97,124	124,753	124,585	178,311
Claims on Central Government	12a	34,915	32,834	34,359	35,125	42,125	44,447	50,716	43,469	43,469	43,050	43,917	42,126
Claims on Official Entities	12bx	—	680	762	730	729	729	219	149	129	129	128	116
Claims on Private Sector	12d	123	151	157	253	220	342	561	1,112	1,682	2,091	2,306	2,756
Claims on Deposit Money Banks	12e	1,321	846	1,725	153	301	908	1,793	2,646	1,522	2,236	1,369	1,578
Claims on Other Financial Insts	12f	20	11	9	9	9	426	431	314	207	121	72	551
Reserve Money	14	18,024	19,708	27,340	33,507	37,314	34,016	39,051	35,803	43,767	43,358	48,331	63,973
of which: Currency Outside DMBs	14a	11,522	11,924	17,257	19,908	20,635	22,865	21,510	24,609	24,380	23,953	29,246	36,512
Time Deposits	15	346	291	207	201	181	142	855	434	1,630	1,648	1,374	1,595
Foreign Liabilities	16c	5,935	7,365	16,383	13,624	18,974	34,112	33,907	44,654	45,789	52,580	58,128	53,747
Central Government Deposits	16d	4,492	4,430	19,156	15,753	15,032	16,276	20,929	24,681	29,115	49,599	32,257	76,596
Counterpart Funds	16e	4,157	4,596	2,304	3,231	4,174	3,408	1,620	1,311	770	569	658	864
Capital Accounts	17a	12,310	13,981	20,238	13,149	11,680	12,589	15,613	15,373	18,080	23,169	29,061	27,917
Other Items (Net)	17r	−1,939	−8,758	−18,904	−10,726	2,749	367	2,627	7,500	4,984	1,458	2,568	748
Deposit Money Banks						*Millions of Francs: End of Period*							
Reserves	20	5,778	6,618	8,590	13,816	16,035	11,835	15,845	10,823	15,496	13,511	13,055	....
Foreign Assets	21	4,637	3,683	15,566	20,157	22,293	24,095	19,652	32,949	34,281	38,990	49,769	....
Claims on Central Government	22a	4,495	4,311	4,528	4,968	5,573	6,995	7,747	7,265	7,345	14,408	14,862	....
Claims on Official Entities	22bx	679	581	354	205	15	421	587	678	1,010	3,533	4,952	....
Claims on Private Sector	22d	17,875	16,234	28,381	28,615	44,948	54,079	59,686	69,289	75,264	82,906	94,658	....
Demand Deposits	24	12,876	16,165	22,586	24,979	34,523	31,509	36,936	37,575	38,522	45,346	52,220	....
Time and Savings Deposits	25	13,356	8,084	22,181	22,851	32,445	36,051	38,680	50,588	61,622	70,974	81,352	....
Foreign Liabilities	26c	889	776	1,226	1,378	3,847	3,816	1,856	3,546	4,749	7,887	12,919	....
Central Government Deposits	26d	2,854	3,370	5,482	10,944	9,072	12,322	9,705	9,442	5,401	5,235	6,298	....
Credit from Monetary Authorities	26g	719	287	1,624	63	63	61	1,550	2,358	1,352	2,080	1,216	....
Capital Accounts	27a	3,778	3,745	6,908	7,683	11,832	16,749	20,059	23,749	26,097	23,427	27,937	....
Other Items (Net)	27r	−1,008	−998	−2,589	−136	−2,919	−3,083	−5,269	−6,252	−4,542	−1,599	−4,648	....
Monetary Survey						*Millions of Francs: End of Period*							
Foreign Assets (Net)	31n	4,760	2,632	27,666	37,624	46,191	40,225	44,771	66,817	80,867	103,276	103,307	....
Domestic Credit	32	50,926	47,175	44,016	43,307	69,621	78,951	89,482	88,263	94,857	91,816	122,615	....
Claims on Central Govt. (Net)	32an	32,064	29,346	14,249	13,396	23,594	22,844	27,829	16,611	16,298	2,623	20,224	....
Claims on Official Entities	32bx	679	1,261	1,116	935	744	1,150	806	827	1,139	3,662	5,080	....
Claims on Private Sector	32d	17,998	16,385	28,538	28,868	45,168	54,421	60,248	70,401	76,946	84,997	96,963	....
Claims on Other Financial Insts	32f	185	184	113	108	115	536	599	424	474	534	348	....
Money	34	24,919	28,810	40,658	45,423	55,746	55,291	59,172	63,110	63,718	70,373	82,305	....
Quasi-Money	35	13,701	8,375	22,388	23,052	32,626	36,193	39,535	51,022	63,252	72,621	82,726	....
Other Items (Net)	37r	17,069	12,625	8,637	12,457	27,440	27,692	35,547	40,948	48,562	52,102	60,891	....
Money plus Quasi-Money	35l	38,621	37,185	63,046	68,475	88,372	91,484	98,707	114,132	126,970	142,994	165,032	....
Other Banking Institutions						*Millions of Francs: End of Period*							
Cash	40..k	1,332	1,340	1,363	1,559	1,495	862	1,445	1,090	1,638	1,261	427	....
Claims on Official Entities	42bxk	83	—	52	491	21	316	298	—	—	—	—	....
Claims on Private Sector	42d.k	2,732	3,024	3,835	3,126	4,152	5,161	5,807	6,224	6,371	7,078	9,748	....
Long Term Foreign Liabilities	46clk	2,155	1,199	2,386	2,253	1,433	957	1,021	1,027	3,706	4,140	7,772	....
Credit from Monetary Authorities	46g.k	9	9	9	9	9	9	431	314	207	121	—	....
Cred.from Deposit Money Banks	46h.k	—	—	—	—	—	—	—	—	—	—	768	....
Capital Accounts	47a.k	2,310	3,996	3,736	4,228	4,067	4,986	6,074	6,319	6,380	6,135	6,779	....
Other Items (Net)	47r.k	−327	−763	−881	−1,314	159	386	24	−345	−2,367	−2,378	−5,144	....
Interest Rates						*Percent Per Annum*							
Discount Rate (End of Period)	60	11.00	11.00	16.00	16.00	10.75	11.38	11.19	11.69	13.00	13.00	14.50	14.50
Deposit Rate	60l	5.00	....	....	10.92	9.46	8.50	7.95	8.94	9.22	8.00	8.14	....
Lending Rate	60p	15.00	....	....	....	....	....	....	....	....	....	....	....
Prices						*Index Numbers (2000=100): Period Averages*							
Consumer Prices	64	38.6	....	76.9	82.6	92.5	98.2	95.9	100.0	103.0	105.3	† 112.8	126.3
Intl. Transactions & Positions						*Millions of Francs*							
Exports	70	9,427	4,056	14,731	18,569	26,190	18,696	20,388	20,521	37,314	26,339	30,916	56,457
Imports, c.i.f	71	47,907	17,270	62,193	78,837	89,694	89,218	84,508	82,586	110,488	96,460	132,134	163,373
						1995=100							
Volume of Exports	72	363	160	100	144	200	215	....	....	....	....	....	....
Export Prices	74	86	32	100	106	118	61	....	....	....	....	....	....

		1993	1994	1995	1996	1997	1998	1999	2000	2001	2002	2003	2004
Balance of Payments						*Millions of US Dollars: Minus Sign Indicates Debit*							
Current Account, n.i.e.	78ald	−129.1	−72.2	57.5	−8.5	−62.3	−82.7	−141.4	−94.4	−102.5	−126.2	....	....
Goods: Exports f.o.b.	78aad	67.7	50.4	56.7	61.8	93.2	64.2	61.5	68.4	93.3	67.2	....	....
Goods: Imports f.o.b.	78abd	−267.9	−574.5	−219.1	−219.0	−278.4	−233.0	−246.9	−223.2	−245.2	−233.3	....	....
Trade Balance	78acd	−200.2	−524.1	−162.5	−157.2	−185.1	−168.7	−185.3	−154.7	−151.9	−166.1	....	....
Services: Credit	78add	34.3	—	17.9	21.6	51.2	48.2	50.7	59.3	65.9	65.2	....	....
Services: Debit	78aed	−136.5	−171.4	−154.7	−150.0	−198.5	−189.7	−193.3	−200.1	−189.2	−201.5	....	....
Balance on Goods & Services	78afd	−302.4	−695.5	−299.3	−285.6	−332.4	−310.2	−327.9	−295.6	−275.1	−302.4	....	....
Income: Credit	78agd	3.0	—	24.3	5.5	8.0	8.7	7.8	13.7	14.1	8.4	....	....
Income: Debit	78ahd	−18.2	—	−17.5	−18.9	−24.8	−15.9	−18.5	−28.4	−34.0	−27.2	....	....
Balance on Gds, Serv. & Inc.	78aid	−317.6	−695.5	−292.5	−299.0	−349.2	−317.3	−338.6	−310.2	−295.1	−321.1	....	....
Current Transfers, n.i.e.: Credit	78ajd	208.6	623.2	355.0	294.6	311.9	251.4	209.9	232.9	210.5	215.3	....	....
Current Transfers: Debit	78akd	−20.1	—	−4.9	−4.1	−25.0	−16.8	−12.7	−17.0	−17.9	−20.4	....	....
Capital Account, n.i.e.	78bcd	−1.3	—	—	—	—	—	70.2	62.1	50.2	65.9	....	....
Capital Account, n.i.e.: Credit	78bad	1.0	—	—	—	—	—	70.2	62.1	50.2	66.2	....	....
Capital Account: Debit	78bbd	−2.4	—	—	—	—	—	—	—	—	−.3	....	....
Financial Account, n.i.e.	78bjd	88.6	−19.6	−10.7	24.8	46.8	−16.7	−33.2	10.7	−44.1	75.5	....	....
Direct Investment Abroad	78bdd	—	—	—	—	—	—	—	—	—	—	....	....
Dir. Invest. in Rep. Econ., n.i.e.	78bed	5.9	—	2.2	2.2	2.6	7.1	1.7	8.3	4.6	2.6	....	....
Portfolio Investment Assets	78bfd	—	—	—	−.1	—	−.1	.8	.1	—	—	....	....
Equity Securities	78bkd	—	—	—	−.1	—	−.1	.8	.1	—	—	....	....
Debt Securities	78bld	—	—	—	—	—	—	—	—	—	—	....	....
Portfolio Investment Liab., n.i.e.	78bgd	—	—	—	—	—	—	—	—	—	—	....	....
Equity Securities	78bmd	—	—	—	—	—	—	—	—	—	—	....	....
Debt Securities	78bnd	—	—	—	—	—	—	—	—	—	—	....	....
Financial Derivatives Assets	78bwd	....	....	....	....	....	....	....	....	....	....	....	....
Financial Derivatives Liabilities	78bxd	....	....	....	....	....	....	....	....	....	....	....	....
Other Investment Assets	78bhd	—	—	−52.0	−13.6	1.2	−.8	−10.2	23.1	−.5	8.0	....	....
Monetary Authorities	78bod	....	—	—	—	—	—	—	—	—	—	....	....
General Government	78bpd	—	—	—	—	—	—	—	—	—	—	....	....
Banks	78bqd	—	—	−38.6	−13.6	1.2	−.8	−10.2	17.1	−4.9	−1.4	....	....
Other Sectors	78brd	—	—	−13.4	—	—	—	—	6.0	4.4	9.4	....	....
Other Investment Liab., n.i.e.	78bid	82.8	−19.6	39.1	36.4	43.1	−22.9	−25.4	−20.8	−48.2	64.9	....	....
Monetary Authorities	78bsd	3.9	—	—	—	—	—	—	—	—	—	....	....
General Government	78btd	61.9	−19.6	39.1	37.3	43.1	−22.4	−23.8	−22.8	−50.3	62.3	....	....
Banks	78bud	7.4	—	—	—	—	—	—	—	—	—	....	....
Other Sectors	78bvd	9.6	—	—	−.9	—	−.5	−1.6	2.0	2.1	2.6	....	....
Net Errors and Omissions	78cad	−8.1	97.9	5.8	4.1	46.0	92.3	32.3	−109.6	26.0	−36.0	....	....
Overall Balance	78cbd	−50.0	6.0	52.6	20.4	30.6	−7.1	−72.1	−131.1	−70.3	−20.8	....	....
Reserves and Related Items	79dad	50.0	−6.0	−52.6	−20.4	−30.6	7.1	72.1	131.1	70.3	20.8	....	....
Reserve Assets	79dbd	25.4	−6.0	−66.0	−19.1	−48.5	−21.0	37.8	78.2	10.9	19.7	....	....
Use of Fund Credit and Loans	79dcd	—	—	13.3	−1.3	17.9	13.5	20.8	13.6	1.6	−5.9	....	....
Exceptional Financing	79ded	24.5	—	—	—	—	14.7	13.5	39.2	57.8	7.0	....	....
International Investment Position							*Millions of US Dollars*						
Assets	79aad	....	....	....	....	....	244.2	231.5	267.9	287.7	320.1	....	....
Direct Investment Abroad	79abd	....	....	....	....	....	—	—	—	—	—	....	....
Portfolio Investment	79acd	....	....	....	....	....	.1	.8	.7	.6	—	....	....
Equity Securities	79add	....	....	....	....	....	.1	.8	.7	.6	—	....	....
Debt Securities	79aed	....	....	....	....	....	—	—	—	—	—	....	....
Financial Derivatives	79ald	....	....	....	....	....	—	—	—	—	—	....	....
Other Investment	79afd	....	....	....	....	....	75.3	56.4	76.6	74.1	76.4	....	....
Monetary Authorities	79agd	....	....	....	....	....	....	....	....	....	....	....	....
General Government	79ahd	....	....	....	....	....	....	....	....	....	....	....	....
Banks	79aid	....	....	....	....	....	....	....	....	....	....	....	....
Other Sectors	79ajd	....	....	....	....	....	....	....	....	....	....	....	....
Reserve Assets	79akd	....	....	....	....	....	168.8	174.3	190.7	213.0	243.7	....	....
Liabilities	79lad	....	....	....	....	....	1,373.9	1,374.4	1,355.3	1,353.4	1,584.0	....	....
Dir. Invest. in Rep. Economy	79lbd	....	....	....	....	....	62.6	59.0	55.2	56.6	52.9	....	....
Portfolio Investment	79lcd	....	....	....	....	....	.1	.1	.1	.1	.1	....	....
Equity Securities	79ldd	....	....	....	....	....	.1	.1	.1	.1	.1	....	....
Debt Securities	79led	....	....	....	....	....	—	—	—	—	—	....	....
Financial Derivatives	79lld	....	....	....	....	....	—	—	—	—	—	....	....
Other Investment	79lfd	....	....	....	....	....	1,311.2	1,315.3	1,300.0	1,296.7	1,531.1	....	....
Monetary Authorities	79lgd	....	....	....	....	....	....	....	....	....	....	....	....
General Government	79lhd	....	....	....	....	....	....	....	....	....	....	....	....
Banks	79lid	....	....	....	....	....	....	....	....	....	....	....	....
Other Sectors	79ljd	....	....	....	....	....	....	....	....	....	....	....	....
Government Finance						*Millions of Francs: Year Ending December 31*							
Deficit (-) or Surplus	80	−13,192	−3,194	5,300	−15,101	−12,275	−41,473	−41,161	−10,285	−41,307	−17,741	−30,660	....
Total Revenue and Grants	81y	44,005	7,547	61,528	70,828	95,768	99,019	103,803	132,809	150,370	172,000	175,653	....
Revenue	81	25,865	6,032	23,128	39,428	58,037	66,019	65,996	68,664	86,206	101,200	122,342	....
Grants	81z	18,140	1,515	38,400	31,400	37,731	33,000	37,807	64,145	64,164	70,800	53,311	....
Exp. & Lending Minus Repay	82z	67,186	26,550	69,528	95,335	109,608	117,471	140,458	136,772	160,978	191,573	188,434	....
Expenditure	82	65,152	26,550	69,528	95,335	110,157	117,632	138,858	136,298	160,350	191,000	186,181	....
Lending Minus Repayments	83	2,034	—	—	—	−549	−161	1,600	474	628	573	2,253	....
Statistical Discrepancy	80xx	9,989	15,809	13,300	9,406	1,565	−23,021	−4,506	−6,322	−30,699	1,832	−17,879	....
Total Financing	80h	13,192	3,194	−5,300	15,101	12,275	41,473	41,161	10,285	41,307	17,741	30,660	....
Total Net Borrowing	84	13,192	3,194	−5,300	15,101	12,275	41,473	41,161	10,285	41,307	17,741	30,660	....
Net Domestic	84a	4,643	5,636	−12,742	4,464	645	−173	7,461	−8,650	−4,602	−17,937	15,300	....
Net Foreign	85a	8,549	−2,442	7,442	10,637	11,630	41,646	33,700	18,935	45,909	35,678	15,360	....
Total Debt by Residence	88	163,882	171,065	353,894	370,697	403,971	469,522	537,278	630,670	607,500	756,100	964,399	....
Domestic	88a	52,485	56,138	55,296	58,360	81,533	85,338	87,294	82,477	80,200	87,300	81,665	....
Foreign	89a	111,397	114,927	298,598	312,337	322,438	384,184	449,984	548,193	527,300	668,800	882,734	....

		1993	1994	1995	1996	1997	1998	1999	2000	2001	2002	2003	2004
National Accounts							*Billions of Francs*						
Househ.Cons.Expend.,incl.NPISHs....	96f	241.2	229.7	338.6	408.6	536.0	577.7	571.1	641.9	696.3	781.2	868.6	....
Government Consumption Expend...	91f	32.9	13.6	30.9	44.1	49.9	54.5	61.2	60.9	69.6	75.8	82.6	....
Gross Fixed Capital Formation..........	93e	51.4	19.4	45.5	60.9	77.0	92.0	111.1	122.7	127.8	146.2	173.7	....
Changes in Inventories...................	93i	—	—	—	—	—	—	—	—	—	—	—	....
Exports of Goods and Services..........	90c	14.7	10.5	19.5	25.5	43.4	34.7	37.8	42.9	39.1	31.5	33.5	57.2
Imports of Goods and Services (-).....	98c	58.3	107.4	98.0	113.0	142.9	131.5	147.9	159.6	126.9	116.6	134.8	163.5
Gross Domestic Product (GDP).........	99b	281.9	165.8	336.5	426.2	563.4	627.3	633.3	708.9	766.3	838.5	950.1	....
Net Primary Income from Abroad.....	98.n	−1.7	−.9	1.6	−4.5	−4.3	−2.1	−3.8	−6.7				....
Gross National Income (GNI)............	99a	280.2	164.9	338.1	421.7	559.1	625.2	629.5	702.2	756.5	828.3	936.9	....
Net Current Transf.from Abroad.......	98t	99.5	391.7	223.0	200.1	171.7	163.0	200.3	204.6	....	....	....	....
Gross Saving................................	99s	9.3	−68.7	−26.9	−22.7	−19.3	−1.2	1.8	18.3	....	....	....	....
GDP Volume 1995 Prices.................	99b.p	498.1	250.7	336.5	386.6	442.0	482.7	513.9	548.1	580.2	635.6	650.8	667.0
GDP Volume (2000=100)...............	99bvp	90.9	45.7	61.4	70.5	80.6	88.1	93.8	100.0	105.9	116.0	118.7	121.7
GDP Deflator (2000=100)...............	99bip	43.8	51.1	77.3	85.2	98.6	100.5	95.3	100.0	102.1	102.0	112.9	
							Millions: Midyear Estimates						
Population.............................	99z	5.89	5.53	5.44	5.67	6.18	6.84	7.50	8.02	8.38	8.61	8.76	8.88

		1993	1994	1995	1996	1997	1998	1999	2000	2001	2002	2003	2004
Exchange Rates		E. Caribbean Dollars per SDR: End of Period (aa) E. Caribbean Dollars per US Dollar: End of Period (ae)											
Official Rate	aa	3.7086	3.9416	4.0135	3.8825	3.6430	3.8017	3.7058	3.5179	3.3932	3.6707	4.0121	4.1931
Official Rate	ae	2.7000	2.7000	2.7000	2.7000	2.7000	2.7000	2.7000	2.7000	2.7000	2.7000	2.7000	2.7000
		Index Numbers (2000=100): Period Averages											
Nominal Effective Exchange Rate	nec	94.82	94.74	92.54	93.78	96.00	96.91	97.17	100.00	101.97	100.88	95.92	92.44
Real Effective Exchange Rate	rec	87.86	86.95	85.03	85.71	93.16	95.65	97.77	100.00	101.08	100.61	94.76	88.80
Fund Position		Millions of SDRs: End of Period											
Quota	2f.s	6.50	6.50	6.50	6.50	6.50	6.50	8.90	8.90	8.90	8.90	8.90	8.90
SDRs	1b.s	—	—	—	—	—	—	—	—	.01	—	—	—
Reserve Position in the Fund	1c.s	.02	.01	.01	.01	.01	.01	.07	.08	.08	.08	.08	.08
Total Fund Cred.&Loans Outstg	2tl	—	—	—	—	—	1.63	1.63	1.63	1.63	.81	—	—
International Liquidity		Millions of US Dollars Unless Otherwise Indicated: End of Period											
Total Reserves minus Gold	1l.d	29.42	31.82	33.47	32.73	36.07	46.80	49.58	45.20	56.43	65.75	64.80	78.47
SDRs	1b.d	—	—	—	—	—	—	—	—	.02	—	—	—
Reserve Position in the Fund	1c.d	.02	.02	.02	.02	.02	.02	.10	.11	.10	.11	.12	.13
Foreign Exchange	1d.d	29.40	31.80	33.45	32.71	36.05	46.78	49.48	45.09	56.31	65.64	64.68	78.34
Monetary Authorities: Other Liab	4..d	—	—	—	—	—	—	—	—	—	—	—	—
Deposit Money Banks: Assets	7a.d	59.65	73.44	76.69	88.78	121.88	123.28	112.59	148.52	165.58	222.11	288.85	279.05
Liabilities	7b.d	58.96	73.35	77.53	90.28	106.08	105.06	125.20	137.15	133.73	171.05	194.52	254.67
Monetary Authorities		Millions of E. Caribbean Dollars: End of Period											
Foreign Assets	11	79.66	85.89	90.55	88.42	97.45	126.44	134.09	122.18	153.84	178.15	175.93	213.14
Claims on Central Government	12a	8.34	4.95	4.42	4.01	3.20	8.73	8.56	10.65	11.29	9.74	3.88	6.90
Claims on Deposit Money Banks	12e	.01	3.52	.01	—	.01	—	—	15.09	—	.02	.07	.06
Reserve Money	14	88.01	94.35	92.97	89.90	95.82	114.73	129.56	139.86	154.44	179.84	174.91	213.22
of which: Currency Outside DMBs	14a	28.08	28.28	30.29	32.38	31.85	35.84	41.45	40.59	36.10	37.69	39.93	44.61
Foreign Liabilities	16c	—	—	—	—	—	6.18	6.02	5.72	5.51	2.98	—	—
Central Government Deposits	16d	—	—	2.00	2.52	4.84	13.26	6.07	1.34	4.17	4.08	4.97	6.88
Other Items (Net)	17r	—	—	—	—	—	1.00	.99	1.00	1.02	1.00	—	—
Deposit Money Banks		Millions of E. Caribbean Dollars: End of Period											
Reserves	20	63.95	65.79	65.14	58.01	65.65	78.64	89.69	98.90	113.29	139.89	123.00	164.92
Foreign Assets	21	161.06	198.28	207.07	239.71	329.07	332.85	303.98	401.01	447.07	599.70	779.88	753.44
Claims on Central Government	22a	57.69	52.69	84.07	118.44	89.62	128.11	154.16	249.73	257.75	234.84	176.46	277.32
Claims on Local Government	22b	7.52	6.97	8.50	7.34	6.41	12.29	18.18	30.90	37.40	44.67	56.95	52.22
Claims on Nonfin.Pub.Enterprises	22c	32.46	52.51	87.13	105.75	117.67	135.32	160.45	158.26	191.67	225.42	252.13	359.65
Claims on Private Sector	22d	375.78	416.36	440.86	464.92	521.06	563.67	610.17	680.54	675.62	659.25	687.40	747.99
Claims on Nonbank Financial Insts	22g	1.18	.03	.50	1.10	1.69	3.34	5.77	5.95	6.39	6.44	41.99	74.02
Demand Deposits	24	46.81	44.09	52.21	56.26	53.11	70.57	69.08	70.38	66.86	87.42	98.37	162.41
Time, Savings,& Fgn.Currency Dep	25	332.09	339.43	390.56	395.15	465.57	506.96	524.01	694.68	711.30	758.65	857.75	979.69
Foreign Liabilities	26c	159.18	198.05	209.32	243.75	286.42	283.67	338.05	370.30	361.07	461.84	525.22	687.62
Central Government Deposits	26d	112.65	141.79	169.22	194.81	202.28	225.67	256.83	292.30	338.94	345.50	339.58	419.78
Credit from Monetary Authorities	26g	3.50	3.50	4.87	11.71	4.65	10.60	7.67	20.53	7.43	9.61	15.96	11.12
Capital Accounts	27a	46.87	49.79	60.03	70.40	81.09	84.98	96.50	103.25	123.29	175.76	206.65	224.59
Other Items (Net)	27r	−1.46	15.98	7.06	23.20	38.04	71.78	50.28	73.84	120.31	71.43	74.30	−55.65
Monetary Survey		Millions of E. Caribbean Dollars: End of Period											
Foreign Assets (Net)	31n	81.54	86.12	88.29	84.38	140.11	169.44	94.00	147.17	234.32	313.03	430.60	278.96
Domestic Credit	32	370.31	391.72	454.26	504.23	532.52	612.53	694.41	842.37	837.03	830.77	874.26	1,091.43
Claims on Central Govt. (Net)	32an	−46.62	−84.15	−82.74	−74.88	−114.30	−102.09	−100.17	−33.26	−74.06	−105.00	−164.21	−142.44
Claims on Local Government	32b	7.52	6.97	8.50	7.34	6.41	12.29	18.18	30.90	37.40	44.67	56.95	52.22
Claims on Nonfin.Pub.Enterprises	32c	32.46	52.51	87.13	105.75	117.67	135.32	160.46	158.26	191.67	225.42	252.13	359.65
Claims on Private Sector	32d	375.78	416.36	440.86	464.92	521.06	563.67	610.17	680.54	675.62	659.25	687.40	747.99
Claims on Nonbank Financial Inst	32g	1.18	.03	.50	1.10	1.69	3.34	5.77	5.95	6.39	6.44	41.99	74.02
Money	34	74.90	72.38	82.52	88.67	85.20	106.42	110.63	111.06	103.49	125.14	149.29	207.21
Quasi-Money	35	332.09	339.43	390.56	395.15	465.57	507.96	525.01	695.68	712.31	759.65	857.75	979.69
Capital Accounts	37a	46.87	49.79	60.03	70.40	81.09	84.98	96.50	103.25	123.29	175.76	206.65	224.59
Other Items (Net)	37r	−2.01	16.23	9.44	34.39	40.78	82.62	56.26	79.56	132.26	83.25	91.17	−41.10
Money plus Quasi-Money	35l	406.99	411.81	473.07	483.83	550.77	614.38	635.65	806.74	815.80	884.79	1,007.04	1,186.90
Money (National Definitions)		Millions of E. Caribbean Dollars: End of Period											
M1	59ma	69.78	68.47	75.30	83.93	82.17	91.40	106.09	110.10	106.17	119.91	133.13	166.38
M2	59mb	374.93	390.12	438.38	462.66	525.05	545.92	607.38	776.67	794.23	844.80	903.05	1,098.69
Interest Rates		Percent Per Annum											
Discount Rate (End of Period)	60	....	9.00	9.00	9.00	8.00	8.00	8.00	8.00	7.00	7.00	6.50	6.50
Money Market Rate	60b	5.25	5.25	5.25	5.25	5.25	5.25	5.25	5.25	† 5.64	6.32	6.07	4.67
Treasury Bill Rate	60c	6.50	6.50	6.50	6.50	6.50	6.50	6.50	6.50	7.50	7.50	7.17	7.00
Savings Rate	60k	5.00	5.00	5.00	5.00	5.00	6.00	6.00	6.00	6.00	5.83	† 3.59	3.58
Deposit Rate	60l	4.39	3.99	4.52	4.27	4.27	4.22	4.31	4.32	4.23	4.01	4.49	4.54
Deposit Rate (Fgn. Currency)	60l.f	....	....	....	....	....	....	....	....	....	....	3.05	1.25
Lending Rate	60p	10.28	10.94	10.89	10.92	11.16	11.42	11.21	11.10	11.08	10.89	12.22	10.25
Prices		Index Numbers (2000=100): Period Averages											
Consumer Prices	64	78.9	80.1	† 82.4	84.1	91.6	94.8	98.1	100.0	102.1	104.2	106.6	....
Intl. Transactions & Positions		Millions of E. Caribbean Dollars											
Exports	70	73	61	51	103	120	113	120	133	142	150	....	....
Imports, c.i.f.	71	319	345	359	356	353	353	365	466	450	479	....	....

		1993	1994	1995	1996	1997	1998	1999	2000	2001	2002	2003	2004
Balance of Payments							*Millions of US Dollars: Minus Sign Indicates Debit*						
Current Account, n.i.e.	78ald	−29.29	−24.30	−45.46	−65.07	−61.66	−46.31	−82.47	−66.16	−105.94	−124.02	....	....
Goods: Exports f.o.b.	78aad	31.99	28.57	36.56	39.08	45.49	44.40	44.96	51.46	55.02	64.42	....	....
Goods: Imports f.o.b.	78abd	−94.57	−98.27	−117.12	−131.93	−130.96	−130.99	−135.19	−172.67	−166.58	−177.59	....	....
Trade Balance	78acd	−62.58	−69.70	−80.56	−92.84	−85.47	−86.59	−90.23	−121.21	−111.56	−113.17	....	....
Services: Credit	78add	83.43	92.38	81.95	88.54	94.75	100.58	101.06	98.53	99.00	90.56	....	....
Services: Debit	78aed	−46.21	−44.86	−55.07	−61.31	−65.20	−62.03	−85.34	−76.01	−74.91	−79.65	....	....
Balance on Goods & Services	78afd	−25.37	−22.18	−53.68	−65.61	−55.92	−48.03	−74.51	−98.70	−87.47	−102.26	....	....
Income: Credit	78agd	2.04	2.91	6.77	3.14	2.89	4.84	6.45	5.53	4.67	5.51	....	....
Income: Debit	78ahd	−13.94	−15.91	−17.73	−18.76	−23.71	−30.19	−34.90	−35.64	−39.19	−43.68	....	....
Balance on Gds, Serv. & Inc.	78aid	−37.27	−35.19	−64.64	−81.24	−76.74	−73.39	−102.97	−128.81	−122.00	−140.43	....	....
Current Transfers, n.i.e.: Credit	78ajd	14.16	16.56	23.26	20.80	21.76	33.66	24.05	69.90	26.61	28.30	....	....
Current Transfers: Debit	78akd	−6.18	−5.67	−4.08	−4.63	−6.67	−6.58	−3.56	−7.25	−10.55	−11.89	....	....
Capital Account, n.i.e.	78bcd	3.33	1.73	7.26	5.45	4.17	8.25	5.81	5.99	10.31	14.59	....	....
Capital Account, n.i.e.: Credit	78bad	3.53	2.61	7.41	5.63	4.36	8.43	5.99	6.17	10.50	14.77	....	....
Capital Account: Debit	78bbd	−.20	−.88	−.16	−.19	−.19	−.19	−.19	−.19	−.19	−.19	....	....
Financial Account, n.i.e.	78bjd	25.53	23.74	24.79	49.10	48.19	45.67	95.48	70.20	103.95	106.92	....	....
Direct Investment Abroad	78bdd	—	—	—	—	—	—	—	—	−.13	—	....	....
Dir. Invest. in Rep. Econ., n.i.e.	78bed	13.76	15.35	20.47	35.17	19.67	31.93	57.74	96.21	88.23	80.41	....	....
Portfolio Investment Assets	78bfd	2.22	—	2.59	.88	.01	.01	.02	−.03	−1.09		....	....
Equity Securities	78bkd	....	....	....	....	....	....	....	....	....	....	....	....
Debt Securities	78bld	....	....	....	....	....	....	....	....	....	....	....	....
Portfolio Investment Liab., n.i.e.	78bgd	—	.23	.15	7.09	15.44	2.22	14.14	5.06	35.64	31.47	....	....
Equity Securities	78bmd	....	....	....	....	....	....	....	....	....	....	....	....
Debt Securities	78bnd	....	....	....	....	....	....	....	....	....	....	....	....
Financial Derivatives Assets	78bwd	....	....	....	....	....	....	....	....	....	....	....	....
Financial Derivatives Liabilities	78bxd	....	....	....	....	....	....	....	....	....	....	....	....
Other Investment Assets	78bhd	−13.50	−10.04	−3.70	−1.01	−3.30	−3.59	−9.22	−10.74	−7.71	.64	....	....
Monetary Authorities	78bod	....	....	....	....	....	....	....	....	....	....	....	....
General Government	78bpd	....	....	....	....	....	....	....	....	....	....	....	....
Banks	78bqd	....	....	....	....	....	....	....	....	....	....	....	....
Other Sectors	78brd	....	....	....	....	....	....	....	....	....	....	....	....
Other Investment Liab., n.i.e.	78bid	23.04	18.20	5.28	6.97	16.37	15.10	32.80	−20.30	−11.00	−5.60	....	....
Monetary Authorities	78bsd	—										....	....
General Government	78btd	....	....	....	....	....	....	....	....	....	....	....	....
Banks	78bud	....	....	....	....	....	....	....	....	....	....	....	....
Other Sectors	78bvd	....	....	....	....	....	....	....	....	....	....	....	....
Net Errors and Omissions	78cad	3.36	−1.77	15.71	9.63	12.96	3.38	−16.02	−14.40	3.28	12.19	....	....
Overall Balance	78cbd	2.93	−.61	2.29	−.89	3.66	10.99	2.79	−4.37	11.61	9.68	....	....
Reserves and Related Items	79dad	−2.93	.61	−2.29	.89	−3.66	−10.99	−2.79	4.37	−11.61	−9.68	....	....
Reserve Assets	79dbd	−2.93	.61	−2.29	.89	−3.66	−13.27	−2.79	4.37	−11.61	−8.62	....	....
Use of Fund Credit and Loans	79dcd	—	—	—	—	—	2.28	—	—	—	−1.06	....	....
Exceptional Financing	79ded	....	....	....	....	....	....	....	....	....	....	....	....
Government Finance						*Millions of E. Caribbean Dollars: Year Ending December 31*							
Deficit (-) or Surplus	80	9.90	6.77p	....	....	....	....	....	....	....	....	....	....
Revenue	81	165.33	181.84p	....	....	....	....	....	....	....	....	....	....
Grants Received	81z	.59	1.64p	....	....	....	....	....	....	....	....	....	....
Expenditure	82	155.98	176.49p	....	....	....	....	....	....	....	....	....	....
Lending Minus Repayments	83	.04	.22p	....	....	....	....	....	....	....	....	....	....
Financing													
Domestic	84a	−14.20	−10.88p	....	....	....	....	....	....	....	....	....	....
Foreign	85a	4.30	4.11p	....	....	....	....	....	....	....	....	....	....
National Accounts						*Millions of E. Caribbean Dollars*							
Househ.Cons.Expend.,incl.NPISHs	96f	248.0	295.3	351.7	402.1	425.0	423.7	556.5	526.7	468.2	570.7	497.6	....
Government Consumption Expend.	91f	92.2	111.1	126.5	132.1	143.2	148.3	174.6	187.8	191.5	187.2	176.2	....
Gross Fixed Capital Formation	93e	242.8	227.9	288.4	304.1	326.7	333.0	293.3	440.9	500.5	457.3	469.7	....
Exports of Goods and Services	90c	312.3	327.2	317.9	344.6	378.7	391.5	394.3	405.0	415.9	425.8	428.3	....
Imports of Goods and Services (-)	98c	380.8	386.4	464.9	521.7	529.6	521.1	595.4	671.5	652.0	694.5	587.5	....
Gross Domestic Product (GDP)	99b	514.6	575.1	619.5	661.0	743.9	775.4	823.2	888.9	924.0	946.4	984.4	....
Net Primary Income from Abroad	98.n	−32.2	−35.3	−29.6	−42.1	−56.2	−68.5	−76.8	−80.3	−93.2	−103.1	−117.9	....
Gross National Income (GNI)	99a	503.3	563.5	590.0	618.9	687.7	707.0	746.4	807.6	830.8	843.3	866.5	....
Net Current Transf.from Abroad	98t	21.5	29.4	53.9	43.7	40.7	73.1	55.3	169.2	43.4	44.3	44.7	....
Gross Nat'l Disposable Inc.(GNDI)	99i	524.9	592.9	643.9	662.6	728.4	780.1	801.7	976.7	874.1	887.6	911.1	....
Gross Saving	99s	163.7	162.8	165.7	128.4	160.2	208.0	70.7	262.2	214.5	129.8	237.3	....
GDP Volume 1990 Prices	99b.p	475.5	499.8	515.5	549.9	590.7	596.2	617.9	644.6	657.5	663.7	678.3	....
GDP Volume (2000=100)	99bvp	73.8	77.5	80.0	85.3	91.6	92.5	95.9	100.0	102.0	103.0	105.2	....
GDP Deflator (2000=100)	99bip	78.5	83.4	87.2	87.2	91.3	94.3	96.6	100.0	101.9	103.4	105.2	....
						Millions: Midyear Estimates							
Population	99z	.04	.04	.04	.04	.04	.04	.04	.04	.04	.04	.04	.04

		1993	1994	1995	1996	1997	1998	1999	2000	2001	2002	2003	2004
Exchange Rates		*E.Caribbean Dollars per SDR: End of Period (aa) E.Caribbean Dollars per US Dollar: End of Period (ae)*											
Official Rate	aa	3.7086	3.9416	4.0135	3.8825	3.6430	3.8017	3.7058	3.5179	3.3932	3.6707	4.0121	4.1931
Official Rate	ae	2.7000	2.7000	2.7000	2.7000	2.7000	2.7000	2.7000	2.7000	2.7000	2.7000	2.7000	2.7000
		Index Numbers (2000=100): Period Averages											
Official Rate	ahx	100.0	100.0	100.0	100.0	100.0	100.0	100.0	100.0	100.0	100.0	100.0	100.0
Nominal Effective Exchange Rate	nec	84.9	88.8	86.0	87.8	92.0	93.8	95.0	100.0	103.3	101.6	93.7	88.6
Real Effective Exchange Rate	rec	87.4	86.5	85.4	86.5	88.5	91.3	94.2	100.0	100.8	98.9	89.3	87.0
Fund Position		*Millions of SDRs: End of Period*											
Quota	2f.s	11.00	11.00	11.00	11.00	11.00	11.00	15.30	15.30	15.30	15.30	15.30	15.30
SDRs	1b.s	1.34	1.36	1.39	1.42	1.45	1.48	1.50	1.43	1.46	1.48	1.49	1.50
Reserve Position in the Fund	1c.s	—	—	—	—	—	—	—	—	—	—	.01	.01
Total Fund Cred.&Loans Outstg	2tl	—	—	—	—	—	—	—	—	—	—	—	—
International Liquidity		*Millions of US Dollars Unless Otherwise Indicated: End of Period*											
Total Reserves minus Gold	1l.d	60.04	57.79	63.09	56.14	60.98	70.61	74.52	78.83	88.94	93.89	106.90	132.54
SDRs	1b.d	1.84	1.99	2.07	2.04	1.95	2.08	2.06	1.87	1.84	2.01	2.22	2.34
Reserve Position in the Fund	1c.d	—	—	—	—	—	—	—	—	—	—	.01	.01
Foreign Exchange	1d.d	58.20	55.80	61.02	54.10	59.03	68.54	72.45	76.96	87.10	91.88	104.68	130.19
Monetary Authorities: Other Liab	4..d	—	—	—	—	—	—	—	—	—	—	—	—
Deposit Money Banks: Assets	7a.d	34.94	25.22	30.03	30.28	32.55	53.05	54.27	50.37	65.21	86.16	158.82	164.58
Liabilities	7b.d	50.57	53.33	56.32	80.02	95.28	88.39	97.68	85.24	109.92	138.48	139.36	176.80
Monetary Authorities		*Millions of E. Caribbean Dollars: End of Period*											
Foreign Assets	11	162.22	156.60	170.50	151.87	165.08	191.27	201.81	213.57	241.07	254.50	289.76	359.29
Claims on Central Government	12a	11.85	9.70	12.94	23.74	13.78	12.77	12.83	11.83	6.08	5.44	3.35	2.97
Claims on Deposit Money Banks	12e	.02	.02	.02	.02	.03	.09	.08	.02	.06	.05	.04	.05
Reserve Money	14	168.12	160.39	178.76	170.95	173.81	197.97	204.43	212.27	247.18	252.34	283.31	339.37
of which: Currency Outside DMBs	14a	67.15	66.85	75.13	70.30	69.61	77.52	84.06	84.60	82.09	83.59	91.30	99.16
Foreign Liabilities	16c	—	—	—	—	—	—	—	—	—	—	—	—
Central Government Deposits	16d	5.97	6.06	4.70	4.67	5.08	6.15	10.29	13.15	.04	7.65	9.83	22.93
Other Items (Net)	17r		−.13										
Deposit Money Banks		*Millions of E. Caribbean Dollars: End of Period*											
Reserves	20	106.58	103.66	97.02	101.94	105.33	108.52	129.00	121.03	152.42	173.87	194.13	240.56
Foreign Assets	21	94.34	68.09	81.07	81.77	87.89	143.24	146.52	135.99	176.07	232.64	428.81	444.37
Claims on Central Government	22a	52.12	47.49	43.65	48.13	63.06	109.65	119.95	128.28	129.64	142.29	129.75	177.86
Claims on Local Government	22b	1.88	2.09	1.57	1.47	2.31	2.19	1.76	2.39	.25	.38	1.27	.25
Claims on Nonfin.Pub.Enterprises	22c	49.25	57.48	72.67	67.82	64.61	46.72	47.09	65.51	64.56	65.30	96.04	99.88
Claims on Private Sector	22d	806.47	860.41	946.42	1,071.26	1,171.82	1,258.19	1,394.19	1,481.69	1,541.82	1,553.47	1,498.20	1,650.07
Claims on Nonbank Financial Insts	22g	1.78	8.72	8.28	13.60	14.50	14.11	30.47	30.66	25.91	28.27	31.66	30.83
Demand Deposits	24	164.42	164.03	173.43	166.21	185.02	196.45	216.22	213.36	220.68	230.83	296.48	407.56
Time, Savings,& Fgn.Currency Dep	25	568.10	618.95	673.13	731.81	756.03	848.10	912.16	978.34	1,046.25	1,070.30	1,113.29	1,119.30
Foreign Liabilities	26c	136.53	143.99	152.07	216.05	257.26	238.64	263.73	230.14	296.78	373.90	376.28	477.35
Central Government Deposits	26d	174.24	170.92	195.35	213.77	235.09	318.57	354.53	400.96	432.67	413.57	460.62	533.00
Credit from Monetary Authorities	26g	9.03	9.60	2.00	.09	2.10	—	.45	.93	63.23	48.53	4.07	—
Capital Accounts	27a	60.25	62.76	74.05	67.37	66.25	76.86	119.14	132.32	167.30	159.56	159.62	225.71
Other Items (Net)	27r	−.15	−22.32	−19.35	−9.31	7.76	4.01	2.74	9.49	−136.25	−100.47	−30.50	−119.09
Monetary Survey		*Millions of E. Caribbean Dollars: End of Period*											
Foreign Assets (Net)	31n	120.03	80.70	99.51	17.58	−4.29	95.87	84.61	119.42	120.35	113.24	342.28	326.31
Domestic Credit	32	743.14	809.04	885.49	1,007.58	1,089.91	1,118.90	1,241.45	1,306.24	1,335.56	1,373.93	1,289.81	1,405.92
Claims on Central Govt. (Net)	32an	−116.24	−119.78	−143.45	−146.57	−163.33	−202.30	−232.05	−274.00	−296.98	−273.49	−337.36	−375.10
Claims on Local Government	32b	1.88	2.09	1.57	1.47	2.31	2.19	1.76	2.39	.25	.38	1.27	.25
Claims on Nonfin.Pub.Enterprises	32c	49.25	57.61	72.67	67.82	64.61	46.72	47.09	65.51	64.56	65.30	96.04	99.88
Claims on Private Sector	32d	806.47	860.41	946.42	1,071.26	1,171.82	1,258.19	1,394.19	1,481.69	1,541.82	1,553.47	1,498.20	1,650.07
Claims on Nonbank Financial Inst	32g	1.78	8.72	8.28	13.60	14.50	14.11	30.47	30.66	25.91	28.27	31.66	30.83
Money	34	231.92	231.51	249.48	237.03	255.01	275.27	302.29	299.20	302.77	314.42	387.78	506.72
Quasi-Money	35	568.10	618.95	673.13	731.81	756.03	848.10	912.16	978.34	1,046.25	1,070.30	1,113.29	1,119.30
Capital Accounts	37a	62.99	65.69	77.02	70.24	68.95	79.68	121.89	134.93	169.82	162.28	162.59	228.82
Other Items (Net)	37r	.16	−26.40	−14.64	−13.92	5.62	11.72	−10.28	13.19	−62.92	−59.84	−31.56	−122.61
Money plus Quasi-Money	35l	800.02	850.46	922.62	968.83	1,011.04	1,123.37	1,214.45	1,277.54	1,349.02	1,384.72	1,501.07	1,626.02
Money (National Definitions)		*Millions of E. Caribbean Dollars: End of Period*											
M1	59ma	214.35	211.86	239.75	225.68	239.26	247.90	267.62	286.05	283.83	287.62	343.13	481.19
M2	59mb	707.31	748.78	818.41	832.50	888.56	996.44	1,093.27	1,179.39	1,234.33	1,273.32	1,370.41	1,509.04
Interest Rates		*Percent Per Annum*											
Discount Rate (End of Period)	60	....	9.00	9.00	9.00	8.00	8.00	8.00	8.00	7.00	7.00	6.50	6.50
Money Market Rate	60b	5.25	5.25	5.25	5.25	5.25	5.25	5.25	5.25	† 5.64	6.32	6.07	4.67
Treasury Bill Rate	60c	7.00	7.00	7.00	7.00	7.00	7.00	7.00	7.00	6.80	6.80	6.33	6.40
Savings Rate	60k	5.04	6.00	6.00	6.00	6.00	6.00	6.00	6.00	5.96	5.83	† 4.09	3.51
Deposit Rate	60l	4.04	3.83	4.43	4.50	4.65	4.80	4.76	4.80	4.88	4.27	5.47	3.05
Deposit Rate (Fgn. Currency)	60l.f	....	....	....	....	....	....	....	....	....	....	4.74	1.81
Lending Rate	60p	11.81	11.06	12.68	12.82	12.68	11.40	12.79	13.06	12.97	12.59	15.00	11.07
Prices and Labor		*Index Numbers (2000=100): Period Averages*											
Consumer Prices	64	82.6	84.7	89.4	90.3	90.3	93.2	96.3	100.0	100.1	101.7	102.7	107.4
		Number in Thousands: Period Averages											
Labor Force	67d	....	....	....	....	70.2	71.9	73.1	76.0	75.1	75.5	82.1	....
Employment	67e	....	....	....	....	55.9	56.4	59.9	63.5	62.1	62.8	63.9	....
Unemployment	67c	....	....	....	....	14.4	15.5	13.2	12.5	13.0	12.8	18.2	....
Unemployment Rate (%)	67r	....	....	....	....	20.5	21.6	18.1	16.5	17.3	16.9	22.3	....
Intl. Transactions & Positions		*Millions of E. Caribbean Dollars*											
Exports	70	323.00	254.80	294.30	214.70	165.38	167.92	150.33	117.09	119.75	120.03	168.25	....
Imports, c.i.f	71	810.50	817.10	827.30	846.10	897.36	905.10	957.29	958.66	958.66	834.24	1,089.41	....
		2002=100											
Export Prices	76	....	....	....	....	....	....	....	....	....	100.0	103.0	....
Import Prices	76.x	....	....	....	....	....	....	....	....	....	100.0	102.0	....

St. Lucia   362

Balance of Payments		1993	1994	1995	1996	1997	1998	1999	2000	2001	2002	2003	2004
		Millions of US Dollars: Minus Sign Indicates Debit											
Current Account, n.i.e.	78ald	−50.17	−48.38	−33.09	−57.84	−78.32	−60.16	−96.85	−78.80	−74.99	−103.89	....	....
Goods: Exports f.o.b.	78aad	124.97	99.92	114.65	86.33	70.25	70.37	60.93	63.06	54.37	69.97	....	....
Goods: Imports f.o.b.	78abd	−264.00	−265.62	−269.38	−267.40	−292.37	−295.06	−312.01	−312.46	−272.07	−277.00	....	....
Trade Balance	78acd	−139.03	−165.70	−154.73	−181.08	−222.12	−224.69	−251.08	−249.40	−217.71	−207.03	....	....
Services: Credit	78add	203.00	237.69	265.03	266.79	288.42	319.50	306.26	321.11	283.41	258.12	....	....
Services: Debit	78aed	−89.91	−104.16	−123.55	−122.44	−121.92	−132.18	−136.33	−124.20	−113.36	−124.51	....	....
Balance on Goods & Services	78afd	−25.95	−32.18	−13.24	−36.72	−55.62	−37.36	−81.15	−52.48	−47.66	−73.42	....	....
Income: Credit	78agd	4.33	4.97	5.75	3.36	3.29	3.39	2.38	3.90	2.62	2.56	....	....
Income: Debit	78ahd	−38.11	−38.33	−44.53	−37.66	−38.97	−45.68	−40.50	−47.77	−44.02	−46.06	....	....
Balance on Gds, Serv. & Inc.	78aid	−59.73	−65.54	−52.02	−71.02	−91.30	−79.66	−119.27	−96.35	−89.06	−116.91	....	....
Current Transfers, n.i.e.: Credit	78ajd	22.20	25.46	28.42	28.53	24.60	29.56	32.06	28.93	27.51	28.58	....	....
Current Transfers: Debit	78akd	−12.63	−8.30	−9.50	−15.35	−11.61	−10.06	−9.63	−11.38	−13.44	−15.56	....	....
Capital Account, n.i.e.	78bcd	2.63	10.71	13.21	10.40	9.59	24.65	25.11	14.18	26.40	21.44	....	....
Capital Account, n.i.e.: Credit	78bad	2.97	11.83	13.58	11.14	10.34	25.43	25.85	16.51	27.51	22.55	....	....
Capital Account: Debit	78bbd	−.34	−1.12	−.37	−.74	−.76	−.78	−.74	−2.33	−1.11	−1.11	....	....
Financial Account, n.i.e.	78bjd	62.29	41.71	27.62	49.21	85.12	58.51	66.25	70.88	43.73	68.40	....	....
Direct Investment Abroad	78bdd	—	—	—	—	—	—	—	—	—	—	....	....
Dir. Invest. in Rep. Econ., n.i.e.	78bed	34.16	32.52	32.75	18.41	47.83	83.40	82.81	54.90	23.57	48.05	....	....
Portfolio Investment Assets	78bfd	—	−.47	−.47	−.06	−.06	−.11	—	−.64	−4.29	−16.54	....	....
Equity Securities	78bkd	....	....	....	....	....	....	....	....	....	....	....	....
Debt Securities	78bld	....	....	....	....	....	....	....	....	....	....	....	....
Portfolio Investment Liab., n.i.e.	78bgd	−.19	.77	.71	1.74	3.00	3.44	1.66	29.03	17.40	35.19	....	....
Equity Securities	78bmd	....	....	....	....	....	....	....	....	....	....	....	....
Debt Securities	78bnd	....	....	....	....	....	....	....	....	....	....	....	....
Financial Derivatives Assets	78bwd	....	....	....	....	....	....	....	....	....	....	....	....
Financial Derivatives Liabilities	78bxd	....	....	....	....	....	....	....	....	....	....	....	....
Other Investment Assets	78bhd	6.83	1.47	−15.34	−9.06	3.26	−11.46	−19.33	−15.00	−17.46	−16.43	....	....
Monetary Authorities	78bod	....	....	....	....	....	....	....	....	....	....	....	....
General Government	78bpd	....	....	....	....	....	....	....	....	....	....	....	....
Banks	78bqd	....	....	....	....	....	....	....	....	....	....	....	....
Other Sectors	78brd	....	....	....	....	....	....	....	....	....	....	....	....
Other Investment Liab., n.i.e.	78bid	21.49	7.41	9.97	38.17	31.09	−16.75	1.11	2.60	24.51	18.13	....	....
Monetary Authorities	78bsd	—	—	—	—	—	—	—	—	—	—	....	....
General Government	78btd	....	....	....	....	....	....	....	....	....	....	....	....
Banks	78bud	....	....	....	....	....	....	....	....	....	....	....	....
Other Sectors	78bvd	....	....	....	....	....	....	....	....	....	....	....	....
Net Errors and Omissions	78cad	−10.13	−7.49	−2.01	−8.04	−11.42	−13.16	9.47	−1.45	16.92	19.22	....	....
Overall Balance	78cbd	4.62	−3.45	5.72	−6.28	4.97	9.84	3.97	4.81	12.06	5.17	....	....
Reserves and Related Items	79dad	−4.62	3.45	−5.72	6.28	−4.97	−9.84	−3.97	−4.81	−12.06	−5.17	....	....
Reserve Assets	79dbd	−4.62	3.45	−5.72	6.28	−4.97	−9.84	−3.97	−4.81	−12.06	−5.17	....	....
Use of Fund Credit and Loans	79dcd	—	—	—	—	—	—	—	—	—	—	....	....
Exceptional Financing	79ded	....	....	....	....	....	....	....	....	....	....	....	....
National Accounts		*Millions of E. Caribbean Dollars*											
Househ.Cons.Expend.,incl.NPISHs.	96f	840.0	872.1	901.5	991.9	1,009.7	979.7	1,116.4	1,086.7	950.2	1,119.0	1,246.5	....
Government Consumption Expend.	91f	195.4	217.1	259.7	261.2	284.1	390.8	408.7	430.1	489.5	492.1	458.0	....
Gross Fixed Capital Formation	93e	376.9	389.9	367.2	381.5	417.7	433.1	500.5	490.7	459.4	415.9	408.4	....
Exports of Goods and Services	90c	909.1	918.2	1,025.1	953.4	968.4	1,052.7	991.4	1,020.2	911.3	873.6	1,096.1	....
Imports of Goods and Services (-)	98c	977.4	997.4	1,060.9	1,052.6	1,118.6	1,153.5	1,210.5	1,179.0	1,040.7	1,084.1	1,296.4	....
Gross Domestic Product (GDP)	99b	1,343.7	1,399.9	1,492.6	1,535.6	1,561.3	1,702.7	1,806.4	1,848.8	1,769.7	1,816.6	1,912.6	....
Net Primary Income from Abroad	98.n	−91.1	−90.1	−104.7	−92.6	−97.3	−114.2	−102.9	−118.5	−111.8	−117.4	−127.5	....
Gross National Income (GNI)	99a	1,252.6	1,310.1	1,387.9	1,442.9	1,463.9	1,588.5	1,703.5	1,730.4	1,658.0	1,699.2	1,785.1	....
Net Current Transf.from Abroad	98t	25.0	48.2	51.1	35.6	35.1	52.7	60.6	47.4	38.0	35.2	35.6	....
Gross Nat'l Disposable Inc.(GNDI)	99i	1,277.5	1,358.3	1,439.0	1,478.5	1,499.0	1,641.2	1,764.0	1,777.8	1,695.9	1,734.3	1,820.7	....
Gross Saving	99s	243.7	258.8	277.8	225.4	205.2	270.7	239.0	260.9	256.2	123.2	116.3	....
GDP Volume 1990 Prices	99b.p	1,220.6	1,236.7	1,257.2	1,293.3	1,287.8	1,367.3	1,398.5	1,387.9	1,310.4	1,335.2	1,392.9	....
GDP Volume (2000=100)	99bvp	87.9	89.1	90.6	93.2	92.8	98.5	100.8	100.0	94.4	96.2	100.4	....
GDP Deflator (2000=100)	99bip	82.6	85.0	89.1	89.1	91.0	93.5	97.0	100.0	101.4	102.1	103.1	....
		Millions: Midyear Estimates											
Population	99z	.14	.15	.15	.15	.15	.15	.15	.15	.16	.16	.16	.16

		1993	1994	1995	1996	1997	1998	1999	2000	2001	2002	2003	2004
Exchange Rates		*E. Caribbean Dollars per SDR: End of Period (aa) E.Caribbean Dollars per US Dollar: End of Period (ae)*											
Official Rate.............................	aa	3.7086	3.9416	4.0135	3.8825	3.6430	3.8017	3.7058	3.5179	3.3932	3.6707	4.0121	4.1931
Official Rate.............................	ae	2.7000	2.7000	2.7000	2.7000	2.7000	2.7000	2.7000	2.7000	2.7000	2.7000	2.7000	2.7000
		*Index Numbers (2000=100): Period Averages*											
Official Rate.............................	ahx	100.0	100.0	100.0	100.0	100.0	100.0	100.0	100.0	100.0	100.0	100.0	100.0
Nominal Effective Exchange Rate.....	nec	82.1	86.6	83.7	86.0	91.0	94.1	95.1	100.0	103.8	102.2	94.4	89.4
Real Effective Exchange Rate...........	rec	94.5	92.0	87.5	91.3	94.4	97.8	97.9	100.0	102.4	99.1	90.4	86.2
Fund Position		*Millions of SDRs: End of Period*											
Quota..................................	2f.s	6.00	6.00	6.00	6.00	6.00	6.00	6.00	8.30	8.30	8.30	8.30	8.30
SDRs....................................	1b.s	.09	.09	.08	.07	.07	.07	.06	.06	.03	.02	—	—
Reserve Position in the Fund...........	1c.s	.50	.50	.50	.50	.50	.50	.50	.50	.50	.50	.50	.50
Total Fund Cred.&Loans Outstg........	2tl	—	—	—	—	—	—	—	—	—	—	—	—
International Liquidity		*Millions of US Dollars Unless Otherwise Indicated: End of Period*											
Total Reserves minus Gold..............	1l.d	31.51	31.25	29.83	30.19	31.19	38.77	42.58	55.18	61.44	53.20	51.19	74.98
SDRs....................................	1b.d	.12	.12	.12	.11	.09	.09	.09	.08	.04	.02	.01	—
Reserve Position in the Fund..........	1c.d	.69	.73	.74	.72	.67	.70	.69	.65	.63	.68	.74	.78
Foreign Exchange....................	1d.d	30.70	30.40	28.97	29.36	30.42	37.97	41.81	54.45	60.77	52.49	50.44	74.20
Monetary Authorities: Other Liab.....	4..d	—	—	—	—	—	—	—	—	—	—	—	—
Deposit Money Banks: Assets..........	7a.d	42.62	49.54	45.76	45.09	47.82	53.50	89.92	106.04	105.22	116.15	144.24	162.39
Liabilities....................	7b.d	27.95	26.77	32.13	35.35	29.73	24.98	51.95	56.70	71.93	67.59	78.61	77.66
Monetary Authorities		*Millions of E. Caribbean Dollars: End of Period*											
Foreign Assets.........................	11	85.10	84.41	80.64	81.54	84.27	104.78	114.95	148.93	165.79	143.65	138.25	202.49
Claims on Central Government........	12a	9.94	9.25	8.68	8.94	9.05	7.61	16.22	9.05	9.39	9.97	22.08	8.28
Claims on Deposit Money Banks......	12e	.01	.01	.01	—	.01	.01	.01	.03	.01	.02	—	.01
Reserve Money..........................	14	94.73	91.59	86.68	84.45	92.10	111.29	129.94	156.75	171.71	153.57	160.21	169.89
of which: Currency Outside DMBs..	14a	28.22	32.02	28.59	27.01	33.49	36.43	57.49	52.11	51.51	54.02	56.65	64.39
Foreign Liabilities.....................	16c	—	—	—	—	—	—	—	—	—	—	—	—
Central Government Deposits...........	16d	.32	2.19	2.65	6.03	1.23	1.12	1.20	1.27	3.48	.07	.13	40.88
Other Items (Net)......................	17r		−.11										
Deposit Money Banks		*Millions of E. Caribbean Dollars: End of Period*											
Reserves...............................	20	73.06	60.14	54.30	50.67	60.73	87.28	73.08	111.03	140.46	107.60	102.41	106.08
Foreign Assets.........................	21	115.09	133.75	123.56	121.75	129.13	144.44	242.78	286.30	284.10	313.60	389.45	438.45
Claims on Central Government........	22a	42.34	44.25	75.60	74.22	79.23	84.23	95.93	115.31	119.82	162.99	140.60	126.54
Claims on Local Government..........	22b		.26	.11	.06	.18	.16			.05	1.89	2.41	15.83
Claims on Nonfin.Pub.Enterprises....	22c	38.39	47.55	22.03	24.94	21.04	18.71	19.98	22.06	34.10	24.50	28.73	64.95
Claims on Private Sector...............	22d	265.98	285.12	347.02	398.83	447.16	486.42	545.63	592.09	605.45	633.38	637.47	626.17
Claims on Nonbank Financial Insts...	22g	2.65	5.85	6.12	13.50	14.45	14.80	14.69	10.71	9.41	8.14	10.28	35.74
Demand Deposits........................	24	64.85	78.50	76.57	86.07	111.55	125.99	142.23	177.18	199.42	201.34	224.99	259.89
Time, Savings,& Fgn.Currency Dep...	25	279.28	282.14	303.39	321.29	344.21	397.65	453.14	459.71	491.56	523.17	531.71	574.35
Foreign Liabilities.....................	26c	75.46	72.28	86.75	95.43	80.28	67.44	140.26	153.10	194.22	182.50	212.26	209.69
Central Government Deposits...........	26d	101.95	110.64	124.38	141.22	165.25	196.62	203.79	214.38	212.01	230.42	246.26	202.57
Credit from Monetary Authorities.....	26g	—	—	.01	—	.63	.50	.01	7.68	3.15	3.47	1.86	1.71
Capital Accounts.......................	27a	27.01	41.56	43.25	41.29	57.16	61.07	76.41	83.90	91.81	95.85	94.02	120.09
Other Items (Net)......................	27r	−11.04	−8.23	−5.62	−1.35	−7.17	−13.24	−23.75	41.56	1.21	15.34	.24	45.45
Monetary Survey		*Millions of E. Caribbean Dollars: End of Period*											
Foreign Assets (Net)...................	31n	124.72	145.87	117.45	107.85	133.11	181.78	217.46	282.13	255.67	274.75	315.44	431.25
Domestic Credit.........................	32	257.04	279.55	332.52	373.23	404.63	414.18	487.47	533.57	562.73	610.37	595.18	634.05
Claims on Central Govt. (Net)........	32an	−49.98	−59.34	−42.75	−64.09	−78.20	−105.90	−92.83	−91.28	−86.29	−57.53	−83.71	−108.63
Claims on Local Government..........	32b		.26	.11	.06	.18	.16			.05	1.89	2.41	15.83
Claims on Nonfin.Pub.Enterprises....	32c	38.39	47.66	22.03	24.94	21.04	18.71	19.98	22.06	34.10	24.50	28.73	64.95
Claims on Private Sector...............	32d	265.98	285.12	347.02	398.83	447.16	486.42	545.63	592.09	605.45	633.38	637.47	626.17
Claims on Nonbank Financial Inst..	32g	2.65	5.85	6.12	13.50	14.45	14.80	14.69	10.71	9.41	8.14	10.28	35.74
Money..................................	34	93.09	110.53	105.43	113.68	145.54	162.50	199.75	229.42	250.94	255.37	281.65	324.29
Quasi-Money............................	35	279.28	282.14	303.39	321.29	344.21	397.65	453.14	459.71	491.56	523.17	531.71	574.35
Capital Accounts.......................	37a	28.31	42.95	44.67	42.66	58.45	62.42	77.72	85.14	93.01	97.15	95.44	121.57
Other Items (Net)......................	37r	−18.91	−10.21	−3.52	3.45	−10.46	−26.60	−25.67	41.44	−17.12	9.44	1.81	45.08
Money plus Quasi-Money...............	35l	372.36	392.68	408.82	434.97	489.75	560.14	652.89	689.12	742.50	778.53	813.36	898.64
Money (National Definitions)		*Millions of E. Caribbean Dollars: End of Period*											
M1.....................................	59ma	84.93	96.19	95.21	96.25	129.25	150.75	182.73	212.25	219.16	239.16	253.70	279.02
M2.....................................	59mb	326.34	346.28	373.68	390.05	444.59	516.06	580.48	635.54	654.87	709.26	722.43	812.26
Interest Rates		*Percent Per Annum*											
Discount Rate (End of Period)..........	60	....	9.00	9.00	9.00	8.00	8.00	8.00	8.00	7.00	7.00	6.50	6.50
Money Market Rate.....................	60b	5.25	5.25	5.25	5.25	5.25	5.25	5.25	5.25	† 5.64	6.32	6.07	4.67
Treasury Bill Rate......................	60c	6.50	6.50	6.50	6.50	6.50	6.50	6.50	6.50	7.00	7.00	....	....
Savings Rate...........................	60k	5.71	6.00	6.00	5.50	5.08	5.00	5.00	5.00	4.96	5.00	† 4.24	3.40
Deposit Rate...........................	60l	3.90	3.89	4.34	4.14	4.21	4.27	4.46	4.54	4.56	4.35	4.56	3.30
Deposit Rate (Fgn. Currency)..........	60l.f	....	....	....	....	....	....	....	....	....	....	3.72	2.99
Lending Rate...........................	60p	11.92	11.73	11.07	11.23	11.29	11.31	11.55	11.46	11.63	11.56	11.83	9.66
Prices		*Index Numbers (2000=100): Period Averages*											
Consumer Prices.......................	64	89.7	90.6	92.2	96.3	96.7	98.8	99.8	100.0	† 100.8	101.6	101.9	104.9
Intl. Transactions & Positions		*Millions of E. Caribbean Dollars*											
Exports................................	70	156.1	136.1	115.2	125.2	125.0	134.0	131.4	128.0	112.0	103.0	103.0	101.0
Imports, c.i.f...........................	71	362.7	351.0	367.0	356.0	491.0	520.0	543.0	440.0	502.0	471.0	541.0	615.0

St. Vincent and the Grenadines 364

		1993	1994	1995	1996	1997	1998	1999	2000	2001	2002	2003	2004
Balance of Payments		*Millions of US Dollars: Minus Sign Indicates Debit*											
Current Account, n.i.e.	78ald	−43.87	−57.43	−40.68	−35.52	−84.18	−92.29	−72.52	−29.38	−41.29	−42.27	....	....
Goods: Exports f.o.b.	78aad	57.13	48.86	61.94	52.59	47.30	50.10	49.61	51.75	42.76	40.45	....	....
Goods: Imports f.o.b.	78abd	−118.11	−115.43	−119.37	−128.07	−152.63	−169.96	−177.05	−144.36	−151.97	−157.22	....	....
Trade Balance	78acd	−60.99	−66.57	−57.43	−75.48	−105.33	−119.86	−127.44	−92.60	−109.21	−116.77	....	....
Services: Credit	78add	62.36	63.40	74.37	96.67	99.44	107.32	125.92	126.23	131.38	136.52	....	....
Services: Debit	78aed	−44.81	−54.64	−55.14	−58.19	−76.37	−79.06	−65.96	−60.04	−59.58	−60.14	....	....
Balance on Goods & Services	78afd	−43.44	−57.81	−38.20	−37.00	−82.26	−91.60	−67.47	−26.41	−37.41	−40.39	....	....
Income: Credit	78agd	2.89	3.46	4.01	4.04	2.67	3.04	3.16	3.14	2.37	3.37	....	....
Income: Debit	78ahd	−11.11	−15.27	−15.67	−13.04	−15.33	−16.76	−22.62	−22.43	−18.85	−17.40	....	....
Balance on Gds, Serv. & Inc.	78aid	−51.66	−69.63	−49.86	−46.00	−94.92	−105.31	−86.93	−45.70	−53.90	−54.41	....	....
Current Transfers, n.i.e.: Credit	78ajd	16.37	19.42	16.81	19.74	20.81	21.60	23.40	24.70	23.24	23.74	....	....
Current Transfers: Debit	78akd	−8.59	−7.23	−7.63	−9.26	−10.07	−8.57	−8.99	−8.38	−10.63	−11.60	....	....
Capital Account, n.i.e.	78bcd	6.31	4.01	5.87	3.83	5.91	13.56	7.86	5.60	8.76	10.61	....	....
Capital Account, n.i.e.: Credit	78bad	7.00	5.37	6.92	4.94	7.02	14.82	9.13	6.86	10.03	11.87	....	....
Capital Account: Debit	78bbd	−.69	−1.36	−1.05	−1.11	−1.11	−1.27	−1.27	−1.27	−1.27	−1.27	....	....
Financial Account, n.i.e.	78bjd	32.24	39.90	35.11	41.82	81.46	92.08	54.38	24.57	49.74	12.74	....	....
Direct Investment Abroad	78bdd	....	....	....	....	....	....	....	....	....	....	....	....
Dir. Invest. in Rep. Econ., n.i.e.	78bed	31.40	46.91	30.64	42.67	92.48	88.95	56.80	37.75	21.04	32.49	....	....
Portfolio Investment Assets	78bfd	.03	.24	—	−.37	.07	−.37	−.22	−.52	.17	−5.40	....	....
Equity Securities	78bkd	....	....	....	....	....	....	....	....	....	....	....	....
Debt Securities	78bld	....	....	....	....	....	....	....	....	....	....	....	....
Portfolio Investment Liab., n.i.e.	78bgd	.66	.06	—	−2.37	1.61	.26	.11	1.96	3.32	6.41	....	....
Equity Securities	78bmd	....	....	....	....	....	....	....	....	....	....	....	....
Debt Securities	78bnd	....	....	....	....	....	....	....	....	....	....	....	....
Financial Derivatives Assets	78bwd	....	....	....	....	....	....	....	....	....	....	....	....
Financial Derivatives Liabilities	78bxd	....	....	....	....	....	....	....	....	....	....	....	....
Other Investment Assets	78bhd	−4.79	−8.92	2.06	−3.00	−3.04	−2.87	−8.42	−8.84	−10.71	−7.74	....	....
Monetary Authorities	78bod	....	....	....	....	....	....	....	....	....	....	....	....
General Government	78bpd	....	....	....	....	....	....	....	....	....	....	....	....
Banks	78bqd	....	....	....	....	....	....	....	....	....	....	....	....
Other Sectors	78brd	....	....	....	....	....	....	....	....	....	....	....	....
Other Investment Liab., n.i.e.	78bid	4.94	1.60	2.41	4.89	−9.67	6.11	6.11	−5.78	35.93	−13.02	....	....
Monetary Authorities	78bsd	—	—	—	—	—	—	—	—	—	—	....	....
General Government	78btd	....	....	....	....	....	....	....	....	....	....	....	....
Banks	78bud	....	....	....	....	....	....	....	....	....	....	....	....
Other Sectors	78bvd	....	....	....	....	....	....	....	....	....	....	....	....
Net Errors and Omissions	78cad	4.03	13.71	−1.68	−9.76	−2.12	−5.34	14.69	13.24	−8.14	12.98	....	....
Overall Balance	78cbd	−1.29	.18	−1.38	.36	1.07	8.00	4.40	14.02	9.07	−5.96	....	....
Reserves and Related Items	79dad	1.29	−.18	1.38	−.36	−1.07	−8.00	−4.40	−14.02	−9.07	5.96	....	....
Reserve Assets	79dbd	1.29	−.18	1.38	−.36	−1.07	−8.00	−4.40	−14.02	−9.07	5.96	....	....
Use of Fund Credit and Loans	79dcd	—	—	—	—	—	—	—	—	—	—	....	....
Exceptional Financing	79ded	....	....	....	....	....	....	....	....	....	....	....	....
Government Finance		*Millions of E. Caribbean Dollars: Year Ending December 31*											
Deficit (-) or Surplus	80	−22.3	−6.7	−2.2	−15.4	−83.7	−28.0	−26.4	−20.4	−8.7	....	....	....
Revenue	81	185.1	195.6	204.1	220.1	240.5	260.3	276.1	278.9	294.0	....	....	....
Grants Received	81z	.9	2.1	1.5	1.4	12.8	32.6	12.6	9.7	50.5	....	....	....
Expenditure	82	208.3	204.4	207.8	236.9	337.0	320.9	315.1	309.0	353.2	....	....	....
Lending Minus Repayments	83	—	—	—	—	—	—	—	—	—	....	....	....
Debt: Domestic	88a	117.4	124.5	133.7	139.4	144.0	147.1	167.4	195.0	212.6	....	....	....
Debt: Foreign	89a	197.3	213.6	236.2	233.0	225.8	256.8	380.6	378.6	376.1	....	....	....
National Accounts		*Millions of E. Caribbean Dollars*											
Househ.Cons.Expend.,incl.NPISHs	96f	465.2	484.1	460.5	490.6	619.3	639.8	601.7	557.5	572.8	606.0	609.0	....
Government Consumption Expend	91f	129.3	138.8	144.2	152.4	150.2	156.8	166.6	175.8	184.6	200.0	199.0	....
Gross Fixed Capital Formation	93e	165.3	185.4	215.4	212.8	243.8	306.2	308.4	247.1	277.8	292.8	344.0	....
Exports of Goods and Services	90c	322.4	303.9	368.0	402.9	396.1	424.7	473.5	480.6	469.7	475.0	456.0	....
Imports of Goods and Services (-)	98c	437.4	461.8	471.2	503.0	618.2	672.3	656.0	552.0	571.0	589.0	646.0	....
Gross Domestic Product (GDP)	99b	644.7	650.4	716.9	755.7	791.3	855.1	892.6	905.7	935.2	975.0	1,016.0	....
Net Primary Income from Abroad	98.n	−22.2	−31.3	−31.5	−24.3	−34.1	−37.1	−52.5	−52.1	−50.5	−48.0	−66.0	....
Gross National Income (GNI)	99a	622.5	627.0	682.0	738.0	759.0	820.0	839.0	852.0	888.0	926.0	950.0	....
Net Current Transf.from Abroad	98t	18.9	32.9	25.4	38.4	34.1	35.2	38.9	44.1	34.1	32.8	33.7	....
Gross Nat'l Disposable Inc.(GNDI)	99i	641.4	660.2	707.2	762.9	783.2	854.8	877.5	896.5	922.2	959.2	983.3	....
Gross Saving	99s	47.0	31.9	106.9	122.9	21.9	57.1	112.6	166.9	166.9	167.3	120.0	....
GDP Volume 1990 Prices	99b.p	588.6	576.8	620.5	629.5	652.5	686.0	714.5	727.7	735.4	755.4	785.7	....
GDP Volume (2000=100)	99bvp	80.9	79.3	85.3	86.5	89.7	94.3	98.2	100.0	101.1	103.8	108.0	....
GDP Deflator (2000=100)	99bip	88.0	90.6	92.8	96.5	97.4	100.2	100.4	100.0	102.2	103.7	103.9	....
		Millions: Midyear Estimates											
Population	99z	.11	.11	.11	.11	.11	.11	.12	.12	.12	.12	.12	.12

Samoa 862

		1993	1994	1995	1996	1997	1998	1999	2000	2001	2002	2003	2004
Exchange Rates						*SDRs per Tala: End of Period*							
Official Rate	ac	.2792	.2794	.2662	.2857	.2679	.2359	.2414	.2297	.2241	.2287	.2423	.2409
					US Dollars per Tala: End of Period (ag) Period Average (rh)								
Official Rate	ag	.3835	.4079	.3957	.4108	.3615	.3322	.3313	.2993	.2816	.3109	.3600	.3741
Official Rate	rh	.3894	.3945	.4045	.4062	.3912	.3398	.3320	.3057	.2880	.2963	.3336	.3598
					Index Numbers (2000=100): Period Averages								
Official Rate	ahx	127.4	129.1	132.3	132.9	128.0	111.2	108.6	100.0	94.2	96.9	109.1	117.7
Nominal Effective Exchange Rate	nec	104.4	107.0	104.4	106.7	109.0	104.4	101.5	100.0	100.2	100.1	99.9	99.7
Real Effective Exchange Rate	rec	101.6	108.1	98.4	103.3	110.6	106.5	102.7	100.0	101.7	107.9	105.7	120.1
Fund Position						*Millions of SDRs: End of Period*							
Quota	2f.s	8.50	8.50	8.50	8.50	8.50	8.50	11.60	11.60	11.60	11.60	11.60	11.60
SDRs	1b.s	1.95	1.99	2.04	2.10	2.14	2.19	2.24	2.29	2.34	2.38	2.40	2.43
Reserve Position in the Fund	1c.s	.66	.66	.67	.67	.68	.68	.68	.68	.68	.69	.69	.69
Total Fund Cred.&Loans Outstg	2tl	—	—	—	—	—	—	—	—	—	—	—	—
International Liquidity					*Millions of US Dollars Unless Otherwise Indicated: End of Period*								
Total Reserves minus Gold	1l.d	50.71	50.80	55.31	60.80	64.21	61.42	68.20	63.66	56.64	62.49	83.91	95.51
SDRs	1b.d	2.68	2.91	3.03	3.02	2.89	3.09	3.07	2.99	2.95	3.23	3.57	3.77
Reserve Position in the Fund	1c.d	.91	.97	1.00	.97	.92	.96	.94	.89	.86	.94	1.03	1.08
Foreign Exchange	1d.d	47.11	46.92	51.28	56.82	60.39	57.37	64.19	59.78	52.83	58.32	79.31	90.67
Monetary Authorities: Other Liab	4..d	—	—	—	—	.01	.05	.03	.50	.05	.23	.09	.09
Deposit Money Banks: Assets	7a.d	3.11	6.26	4.66	5.38	6.98	8.00	11.41	14.61	12.29	7.45	13.74	14.55
Liabilities	7b.d	.50	2.86	.30	.94	2.36	1.40	6.80	6.62	6.77	5.04	9.30	12.13
Monetary Authorities						*Millions of Tala: End of Period*							
Foreign Assets	11	112.38	109.39	119.13	134.91	158.30	166.00	171.41	163.89	157.48	174.81	194.92	217.29
Claims on Central Government	12a	1.69	.07	.07	—	—	—	—	—	—	—	—	—
Claims on Private Sector	12d	—	—	—	1.39	1.68	1.67	1.69	1.80	2.16	2.34	2.38	2.52
Claims on Deposit Money Banks	12e	6.00	6.23	.06	.03	.06	.09	.06	.83	.33	.38	.72	.88
Reserve Money	14	58.25	60.11	62.73	75.57	90.03	48.86	59.31	64.52	61.40	73.85	81.76	94.71
of which: Currency Outside DMBs	14a	13.95	16.82	21.60	20.96	30.39	24.82	29.09	28.87	29.97	32.57	35.73	38.94
Liabs. of Central Bank: Securities	16ac	—	—	—	—	—	25.51	27.39	15.66	7.74	15.96	33.54	41.19
Foreign Liabilities	16c	—	—	—	—	.03	.14	.10	1.66	.18	.73	.24	.23
Central Government Deposits	16d	64.54	49.07	48.36	56.78	69.60	90.21	83.37	78.12	85.59	79.89	74.92	73.63
Capital Accounts	17a	26.58	28.30	27.61	27.52	28.47	30.30	30.30	30.26	31.29	31.33	32.59	33.85
Other Items (Net)	17r	−29.31	−21.78	−19.44	−23.54	−28.10	−27.26	−27.31	−23.70	−26.22	−24.23	−25.04	−22.92
Deposit Money Banks						*Millions of Tala: End of Period*							
Reserves	20	44.30	43.29	41.13	54.41	59.64	24.04	30.22	35.65	31.43	41.28	46.03	55.77
Claims on Mon.Author.:Securities	20c	—	—	—	—	—	25.51	27.39	15.66	7.74	15.96	33.54	41.19
Foreign Assets	21	8.10	15.34	11.78	13.09	19.30	24.09	34.45	48.83	43.66	23.96	38.17	38.90
Claims on Central Government	22a	3.62	3.67	1.30	.66	—	—	9.41	1.59	9.68	—	8.52	3.25
Claims on Nonfin.Pub.Enterprises	22c	.56	3.16	3.70	4.08	3.24	3.26	13.61	18.79	16.77	18.59	15.05	10.61
Claims on Private Sector	22d	81.29	75.49	97.38	115.15	137.69	163.84	192.91	231.17	264.43	292.36	316.09	356.22
Demand Deposits	24	29.70	30.38	39.34	39.86	44.14	41.71	51.23	64.41	56.87	63.04	82.48	85.99
Time, Savings,& Fgn.Currency Dep	25	77.63	90.88	110.77	121.68	135.62	148.84	168.92	196.65	220.78	243.43	268.16	293.59
Foreign Liabilities	26c	1.30	7.00	.76	2.30	6.52	4.20	20.53	22.13	24.05	16.22	25.82	32.42
Central Government Deposits	26d	3.01	2.32	3.36	8.31	16.56	14.09	23.79	19.10	17.76	12.35	11.14	17.34
Credit from Monetary Authorities	26g	5.99	6.23	.06	.03	.10	.09	.05	.77	.30	.53	2.74	2.99
Capital Accounts	27a	26.05	20.56	21.23	33.18	29.87	33.31	50.56	45.98	50.29	50.72	45.00	50.29
Other Items (Net)	27r	−5.81	−16.42	−20.23	−17.97	−12.94	−1.50	−7.09	2.65	3.66	5.86	22.06	23.32
Monetary Survey						*Millions of Tala: End of Period*							
Foreign Assets (Net)	31n	119.18	117.73	130.15	145.70	171.05	185.75	185.23	188.93	176.91	181.82	207.03	223.54
Domestic Credit	32	19.61	31.00	50.73	56.19	56.45	64.47	110.46	156.13	189.69	221.05	255.98	281.63
Claims on Central Govt. (Net)	32an	−62.24	−47.65	−50.35	−64.43	−86.16	−104.30	−97.75	−95.63	−93.67	−92.24	−77.54	−87.72
Claims on Nonfin.Pub.Enterprises	32c	.56	3.16	3.70	4.08	3.24	3.26	13.61	18.79	16.77	18.59	15.05	10.61
Claims on Private Sector	32d	81.29	75.49	97.38	116.54	139.37	165.51	194.60	232.97	266.59	294.70	318.47	358.74
Money	34	43.65	47.20	60.94	60.82	74.53	66.53	80.32	93.28	86.84	95.61	118.21	124.93
Quasi-Money	35	77.63	90.88	110.77	121.68	135.62	148.84	168.92	196.65	220.78	243.43	268.16	293.59
Capital Accounts	37a	52.63	48.86	48.84	60.70	58.34	63.61	80.86	76.24	81.58	82.05	77.59	84.14
Other Items (Net)	37r	−35.13	−38.20	−39.67	−41.31	−41.00	−28.76	−34.41	−21.11	−22.59	−18.22	−.96	2.51
Money plus Quasi-Money	35l	121.28	138.08	171.71	182.50	210.15	215.37	249.24	289.93	307.62	339.04	386.37	418.52
Other Banking Institutions						*Millions of Tala: End of Period*							
Deposits	45	2.56	2.63	....	....	....	....	....	....	....	....	....	....
Liquid Liabilities	55l	123.84	140.71	....	....	....	....	....	....	....	....	....	....
Interest Rates						*Percent Per Annum*							
Deposit Rate	60l	5.50	5.50	5.50	5.50	5.50	6.50	6.50	6.46	5.53	5.10	5.10	5.10
Lending Rate	60p	12.00	12.00	12.00	12.00	12.00	11.50	11.50	11.00	9.93	9.75	9.75	9.75
Government Bond Yield	61	13.50	13.50	13.50	13.50	13.50	13.50	13.50	13.50	13.50	13.50	13.50	13.50
Prices and Production						*Index Numbers (2000=100): Period Averages*							
Consumer Prices	64	78.9	88.4	85.8	90.4	† 96.6	98.8	99.0	100.0	† 103.8	112.2	112.3	130.7
Manufacturing Prod.(1995=100)	66ey	....	80.4	100.0	111.5	101.8	98.1	....	....	....	....	....	....
Intl. Transactions & Positions						*Thousands of Tala*							
Exports	70	16,522	9,121	21,859	24,868	38,531	43,243	61,695	46,833	54,049	46,201	44,261	29,870
Imports, c.i.f	71	269,079	206,347	235,353	247,126	247,377	285,652	346,765	† 297,504	416,167	430,375	381,754	431,628

Samoa 862

		1993	1994	1995	1996	1997	1998	1999	2000	2001	2002	2003	2004
Balance of Payments					*Millions of US Dollars: Minus Sign Indicates Debit*								
Current Account, n.i.e.	78ald	−38.69	5.76	9.33	12.28	9.13	20.09	−18.79	....	....	....	....	....
Goods: Exports f.o.b.	78aad	6.44	3.52	8.76	10.08	14.63	20.40	18.15	....	....	....	....	....
Goods: Imports f.o.b.	78abd	−87.41	−68.81	−80.29	−90.76	−100.11	−96.91	−115.66	....	....	....	....	....
Trade Balance	78acd	−80.98	−65.29	−71.53	−80.67	−85.48	−76.51	−97.51	....	....	....	....	....
Services: Credit	78add	35.80	43.00	55.70	65.15	65.24	62.56	61.31	....	....	....	....	....
Services: Debit	78aed	−38.24	−28.17	−35.19	−34.33	−40.08	−29.09	−24.55	....	....	....	....	....
Balance on Goods & Services	78afd	−83.42	−50.46	−51.02	−49.85	−60.32	−43.04	−60.74	....	....	....	....	....
Income: Credit	78agd	4.33	4.03	4.66	5.45	5.52	5.97	2.75	....	....	....	....	....
Income: Debit	78ahd	−4.42	−4.45	−4.42	−2.43	−4.14	−2.39	−2.36	....	....	....	....	....
Balance on Gds, Serv. & Inc.	78aid	−83.51	−50.88	−50.79	−46.84	−58.94	−39.47	−60.34	....	....	....	....	....
Current Transfers, n.i.e.: Credit	78ajd	49.93	62.75	66.74	66.89	73.71	64.12	44.67	....	....	....	....	....
Current Transfers: Debit	78akd	−5.11	−6.11	−6.62	−7.77	−5.65	−4.56	−3.12	....	....	....	....	....
Capital Account, n.i.e.	78bcd	—	—	—	—	—	—	24.46	....	....	....	....	....
Capital Account, n.i.e.: Credit	78bad	—	—	—	—	—	—	27.11	....	....	....	....	....
Capital Account: Debit	78bbd	—	—	—	—	—	—	−2.66	....	....	....	....	....
Financial Account, n.i.e.	78bjd	15.55	−5.46	−5.60	−3.60	−5.93	−4.99	−.73	....	....	....	....	....
Direct Investment Abroad	78bdd	—	—	—	—	—	—	—	....	....	....	....	....
Dir. Invest. in Rep. Econ., n.i.e.	78bed	—	—	—	—	—	—	—	....	....	....	....	....
Portfolio Investment Assets	78bfd	—	—	—	—	—	—	—	....	....	....	....	....
Equity Securities	78bkd	—	—	—	—	—	—	—	....	....	....	....	....
Debt Securities	78bld	—	—	—	—	—	—	—	....	....	....	....	....
Portfolio Investment Liab., n.i.e.	78bgd	—	....	....	....	....	....	....	....	....	....	....	....
Equity Securities	78bmd	—	....	....	....	....	....	....	....	....	....	....	....
Debt Securities	78bnd	—	....	....	....	....	....	....	....	....	....	....	....
Financial Derivatives Assets	78bwd	....	....	....	....	....	....	....	....	....	....	....	....
Financial Derivatives Liabilities	78bxd	....	....	....	....	....	....	....	....	....	....	....	....
Other Investment Assets	78bhd	—	—	—	—	—	—	—	....	....	....	....	....
Monetary Authorities	78bod	....	....	....	....	....	....	....	....	....	....	....	....
General Government	78bpd	—	—	—	—	—	—	—	....	....	....	....	....
Banks	78bqd	—	—	—	—	—	—	—	....	....	....	....	....
Other Sectors	78brd	—	—	—	—	—	—	—	....	....	....	....	....
Other Investment Liab., n.i.e.	78bid	15.55	−5.46	−5.60	−3.60	−5.93	−4.99	−.73	....	....	....	....	....
Monetary Authorities	78bsd	—	−.13	.01	−.01	−.01	.16	—	....	....	....	....	....
General Government	78btd	15.26	6.82	3.80	.20	−1.48	−1.04	−2.79	....	....	....	....	....
Banks	78bud	.56	.03	−1.12	1.65	1.05	−.54	5.42	....	....	....	....	....
Other Sectors	78bvd	−.27	−12.18	−8.29	−5.44	−5.49	−3.57	−3.36	....	....	....	....	....
Net Errors and Omissions	78cad	13.83	−4.17	−1.70	−1.30	7.89	−9.59	2.10	....	....	....	....	....
Overall Balance	78cbd	−9.31	−3.86	2.04	7.38	11.09	5.51	7.04	....	....	....	....	....
Reserves and Related Items	79dad	9.31	3.86	−2.04	−7.38	−11.09	−5.51	−7.04	....	....	....	....	....
Reserve Assets	79dbd	8.30	3.86	−2.04	−7.38	−11.09	−5.51	−7.04	....	....	....	....	....
Use of Fund Credit and Loans	79dcd	—	—	—	—	—	....	—	....	....	....	....	....
Exceptional Financing	79ded	1.01	—	—	—	—	....	—	....	....	....	....	....
National Accounts					*Millions of Tala*								
GDP Volume 1984 Prices	99b.p	131.7	126.8	....	....	....	....	....	....	....	....	....	....
GDP Volume 1994 prices	99b.p	....	468.8	500.7	531.4	539.9	....	....	....	....	....	....	....
GDP Volume (1995=100)	99bvp	97.2	† 93.6	100.0	106.1	107.8	....	....	....	....	....	....	....
GDP Deflator (1995=100)	99bip	....	105.5	100.0	103.9	116.2	....	....	....	....	....	....	....
					Millions: Midyear Estimates								
Population	99z	.17	.17	.17	.17	.17	.17	.18	.18	.18	.18	.18	.18

San Marino 135

		1993	1994	1995	1996	1997	1998	1999	2000	2001	2002	2003	2004
Exchange Rates			*Lire per SDR through 1998, Euros per SDR Thereafter: End of Period*										
Market Rate	aa	2,340.5	2,379.2	2,355.7	2,200.9	2,373.6	2,327.6	1.3662	1.4002	1.4260	1.2964	1.1765	1.1402
		Lire per US Dollar through 1998, Euros per US Dollar Thereafter: End of Period (ae) Period Average (rf)											
Market Rate	ae	1,704.0	1,629.7	1,584.7	1,530.6	1,759.2	1,653.1	.9954	1.0747	1.1347	.9536	.7918	.7342
Market Rate	rf	1,573.7	1,612.4	1,628.9	1,542.9	1,703.1	1,736.2	.9386	1.0854	1.1175	1.0626	.8860	.8054
Fund Position		*Millions of SDRs: End of Period*											
Quota	2f.s	10.00	10.00	10.00	10.00	10.00	10.00	17.00	17.00	17.00	17.00	17.00	17.00
SDRs	1b.s	.04	.11	.18	.25	.33	.42	.08	.20	.34	.43	.49	.56
Reserve Position in the Fund	1c.s	2.35	2.35	2.35	2.35	2.35	2.35	4.10	4.10	4.10	4.10	4.10	4.10
Total Fund Cred.&Loans Outstg	2tl	—	—	—	—	—	—	—	—	—	—	—	—
International Liquidity		*Millions of US Dollars Unless Otherwise Indicated: End of Period*											
Total Reserves Minus Gold	1l.d	119.86	176.31	198.55	215.02	182.94	170.67	144.13	135.16	133.51	183.41	252.69	355.58
SDRs	1b.d	.06	.16	.27	.36	.45	.59	.11	.26	.42	.58	.73	.87
Reserve Position in the Fund	1c.d	3.23	3.43	3.50	3.38	3.17	3.31	5.63	5.34	5.15	5.58	6.09	6.37
Foreign Exchange	1d.d	116.57	172.72	194.78	211.27	179.32	166.77	138.39	129.56	127.93	177.25	245.87	348.34
Deposit Money Banks: Assets	7a.d	2,886.10	3,013.69	4,001.98	4,703.92	4,408.36	4,382.88	4,465.55	4,289.46	4,452.91	4,793.09	5,530.87	6,037.44
Liabilities	7b.d	2,094.00	2,248.21	3,156.34	4,048.64	3,793.34	3,817.43	3,870.92	3,839.12	3,968.26	3,428.61	4,259.72	5,153.35
Monetary Authorities		*Millions of Lire through 1998; Thousands of Euros Beginning 1999: End of Period*											
Foreign Assets	11	204,242	287,334	314,640	329,096	321,834	282,139	143,466	145,257	151,490	174,889	200,071	261,051
Claims on General Government	12a	877	4,242	1,233	1,855	16,966	28,514	14,559	14,851	14,259	15,310	15,427	13,958
Claims on Other Resident Sectors	12d	—	3,300	—	—	—	—	1,222	336	417	633	298	2,807
Claims on Deposit Money Banks	12e	85,905	30,273	34,373	40,896	18,542	1,855	745	4,012	9,845	3,093	7,343	—
Bankers Deposits	14c	—	—	—	—	—	3,255	294	2,288	12,867	1,911	6,764	22,556
Demand Deposits	14d	25,143	14,363	20,123	21,274	21,458	23,144	11,877	26,735	26,770	21,717	19,676	56,223
Time, Savings,& Fgn.Currency Dep	15	63	18,496	25,382	26,593	16,889	16,225	9,872	271	171	18,144	29,184	65
Foreign Liabilities	16c	1,131	—	—	—	2	191	1	1	12,867	14,732	800	554
General Government Deposits	16d	231,436	256,504	263,412	269,709	267,432	215,854	108,059	100,494	88,707	99,587	122,925	145,000
Capital Accounts	17a	33,494	36,014	41,630	54,185	62,912	67,261	36,544	38,912	40,624	41,169	46,829	49,667
Other Items (Net)	17r	−246	−230	−301	85	−11,352	−13,452	−6,655	−4,247	−5,995	−3,335	−3,040	3,750
Deposit Money Banks		*Millions of Lire through 1998; Thousands of Euros Beginning 1999: End of Period*											
Claims on Monetary Authorities	20	—	—	—	—	—	3,255	294	2,288	12,867	1,911	6,681	22,534
Foreign Assets	21	4,917,835	4,911,532	6,342,022	7,199,683	7,755,149	7,245,343	4,445,099	4,609,849	5,052,656	4,570,506	4,379,154	4,432,450
Claims on Other Resident Sectors	22d	922,700	1,118,058	1,225,826	1,303,523	1,593,667	1,865,082	1,038,224	1,289,841	1,450,709	1,641,906	1,961,168	2,596,875
Claims on Nonbank Fin. Insts	22g	126,524	143,263	167,394	172,262	189,366	236,356	131,490	165,072	199,835	327,016	380,835	522,739
Demand Deposits	24	692,456	795,744	565,206	415,528	420,685	464,148	274,054	272,388	317,164	618,910	634,108	693,647
Time, Savings,& Fgn.Currency Dep	25	1,151,241	1,092,784	1,473,536	1,264,306	1,537,896	1,486,230	884,782	984,725	1,222,172	1,845,299	1,891,256	2,157,768
Foreign Liabilities	26c	3,568,115	3,663,998	5,001,919	6,196,728	6,673,202	6,310,594	3,853,200	4,125,871	4,502,736	3,269,389	3,372,699	3,783,388
Credit from Monetary Authorities	26g	85,629	30,273	34,373	40,896	18,325	1,854	743	4,012	9,845	3,093	7,343	—
Capital Accounts	27a	482,060	575,336	701,667	814,326	857,474	1,033,915	583,206	670,996	790,635	807,930	878,385	909,090
Other Items (Net)	27r	−12,442	14,718	−41,459	−56,316	30,600	53,294	19,121	9,057	−126,485	−3,282	−55,954	30,705
Monetary Survey		*Millions of Lire through 1998; Thousands of Euros Beginning 1999: End of Period*											
Foreign Assets (Net)	31n	1,552,831	1,534,868	1,654,743	1,332,051	1,403,779	1,216,697	735,364	629,234	688,543	1,461,274	1,205,725	909,559
Domestic Credit	32	818,665	1,012,359	1,131,041	1,207,931	1,532,567	1,914,098	1,077,436	1,369,605	1,576,513	1,885,278	2,234,802	2,991,379
Claims on General Govt. (Net)	32an	−230,559	−252,262	−262,179	−267,854	−250,466	−187,340	−93,500	−85,643	−74,448	−84,277	−107,498	−131,042
Claims on Other Resident Sectors	32d	922,700	1,121,358	1,225,826	1,303,523	1,593,667	1,865,082	1,039,446	1,290,176	1,451,126	1,642,539	1,961,466	2,599,682
Claims on Nonbank Fin. Insts	32g	126,524	143,263	167,394	172,262	189,366	236,356	131,490	165,072	199,835	327,016	380,835	522,739
Deposit Money	34	717,599	810,107	585,329	436,802	442,143	487,292	285,930	299,124	343,934	640,627	653,785	749,870
Quasi-Money	35	1,151,304	1,111,280	1,498,918	1,290,899	1,554,785	1,502,485	894,653	984,996	1,222,343	1,863,443	1,920,440	2,157,833
Capital Accounts	37a	515,554	611,350	743,297	868,511	920,386	1,101,176	619,751	709,908	831,260	849,099	925,213	958,757
Other Items (Net)	37r	−12,964	14,488	−41,760	−56,231	19,031	39,841	12,464	4,810	−132,480	−6,616	−58,912	34,477
Interest Rates		*Percent Per Annum*											
Deposit Rate	60l	9.00	7.50	7.35	6.18	4.65	3.70	2.45	2.63	2.88	2.68	1.64	1.44
Lending Rate	60p	16.00	15.00	15.23	14.45	11.43	9.53	7.93	9.20	8.80	7.95	7.49	7.14
Prices and Tourism		*Index Numbers (2000=100): Period Averages*											
Consumer Prices (2003=100)	64	....	....	....	....	....	....	....	....	....	....	100.0	....
Tourist Arrivals	66ta	100.0	101.1	109.7	108.9	107.7	106.3	102.5	100.0	98.8	101.0	93.9	....
National Accounts		*Billions of Lire through 1998; Millions of Euros Beginning 1999*											
Househ.Cons.Expend.,incl.NPISHs	96f	....	....	....	....	795.41	834.22	† 447.82	465.30	475.09	479.96	....	....
Government Consumption Expend	91f	....	....	....	....	219.79	227.51	† 132.99	135.44	124.50	127.75	....	....
Changes in Inventories	93i	....	....	....	....	40.74	69.00	† 42.64	62.59	22.56	−11.56	....	....
Exports of Goods and Services	90c	....	....	....	....	3,002.40	2,834.65	† 1,581.15	1,627.05	1,682.77	1,660.20	....	....
Imports of Goods and Services (-)	98c	....	....	....	....	3,049.92	2,854.78	† 1,602.18	1,675.01	1,744.28	1,756.40	....	....
Gross Domestic Product (GDP)	99b	....	....	....	....	1,279.9	1,400.8	† 801.03	839.65	929.02	934.94	....	....
Net Primary Income from Abroad	98.n	....	....	....	....	−234.38	−267.59	† −158.52	−178.31	−229.13	−206.28	....	....
Gross National Income (GNI)	99a	....	....	....	....	1,045.48	1,133.25	† 642.51	661.34	699.89	728.66	....	....
Net Current Transf.from Abroad	98t	....	....	....	....	9.37	7.51	† 3.20	3.47	3.65	3.76	....	....
Gross Nat'l Disposable Inc.(GNDI)	99i	....	....	....	....	964.99	1,026.75	† 584.02	613.16	649.79	697.73	....	....
Gross Saving	99s	....	....	....	....	183.68	209.00	† 133.09	141.97	189.82	215.24	....	....
GDP Volume 1995 Prices	99b.p	....	....	....	....	1,210.84	1,301.90	† 732.87	749.01	806.44	793.00	....	....
GDP Volume (2000=100)	99bvp	....	....	....	....	83.5	89.8	† 97.8	100.0	107.7	105.9	....	....
GDP Deflator (2000=100)	99bip	....	....	....	....	94.3	96.0	† 97.5	100.0	102.8	105.2	....	....
		Millions: Midyear Estimates											
Population	99z	.025	.025	.026	.026	.026	.026	.027	.027	.027	.027	.028	.028

São Tomé and Príncipe   716

		1993	1994	1995	1996	1997	1998	1999	2000	2001	2002	2003	2004
Exchange Rates						*Dobras per SDR: End of Period*							
Market Rate........................	aa	709.7	1,730.4	2,611.6	4,074.0	9,403.9	9,694.3	10,019.3	11,218.9	11,335.3	12,496.5	14,051.2	15,485.1
						Dobras per US Dollar: End of Period (ae) Period Average (rf)							
Market Rate........................	ae	516.7	1,185.3	1,756.9	2,833.2	6,969.7	6,885.0	7,300.0	8,610.7	9,019.7	9,191.8	9,455.9	9,971.0
Market Rate........................	rf	429.9	732.6	1,420.3	2,203.2	4,552.5	6,883.2	7,119.0	7,978.2	8,842.1	9,088.3	9,347.6	....
Fund Position						*Millions of SDRs: End of Period*							
Quota..............................	2f.s	5.50	5.50	5.50	5.50	5.50	5.50	7.40	7.40	7.40	7.40	7.40	7.40
SDRs...............................	1b.s	.01	.01	.03	.01	—	—	—	—	—	.01	.02	—
Reserve Position in the Fund...........	1c.s	—	—	—	—	—	—	—	—	—	—	—	—
Total Fund Cred.&Loans Outstg........	2tl	.80	.72	.56	.40	.24	.08	—	1.90	1.90	1.90	1.90	1.90
International Liquidity						*Millions of US Dollars Unless Otherwise Indicated: End of Period*							
Total Reserves minus Gold..............	1l.d	....	....	5.14	5.03	12.43	9.68	10.88	11.64	15.48	17.35	25.47	19.76
SDRs..............................	1b.d	.01	.01	.04	.02	—	—	—	—	—	.01	.02	—
Reserve Position in the Fund..........	1c.d	—	—	—	—	—	—	—	—	—	—	—	—
Foreign Exchange..................	1d.d	....	....	5.09	5.01	12.43	9.68	10.88	11.64	15.48	17.34	25.45	19.76
Monetary Authorities: Other Liab......	4..d	....	....	4.22	4.36	4.98	—	—	—	—	—	—	1.00
Banking Institutions: Assets...........	7a.d	....	....	7.11	8.08	8.03	6.85	6.14	5.45	6.09	7.98	8.04	9.27
Liabilities..................	7b.d	....	....	1.49	.77	.37	1.34	.34	.43	.30	.32	.37	.28
Monetary Authorities						*Millions of Dobras: End of Period*							
Foreign Assets.....................	11	....	....	9,026	14,252	86,611	101,965	114,071	147,576	192,855	217,780	287,299	246,515
Claims on Central Government........	12a	....	....	10,290	28,743	28,939	28,831	34,535	32,653	56,425	57,432	61,309	81,777
Claims on Nonfin.Pub.Enterprises.....	12c	....	....	7,837	—	—	—	—	—	—	—	—	—
Claims on Private Sector..............	12d	....	....	80	204	50	44	38	36	—	—	4,571	7,043
Claims on Banking Institutions.........	12e	....	....	2,375	1,757	1,839	1,839	—	—	762	1,672	1,137	5,152
Reserve Money.....................	14	....	....	10,462	18,945	46,401	51,085	43,332	56,046	97,885	111,903	184,470	137,326
of which: Currency Outside Banks..	14a	....	....	4,794	6,845	14,818	18,652	20,945	25,048	35,763	39,424	55,854	60,003
Foreign Liabilities..................	16c	....	....	8,869	13,985	37,001	795	—	21,338	21,560	23,768	26,725	39,424
Central Government Deposits...........	16d	....	....	—	6,868	41,985	30,994	41,716	47,805	44,046	53,905	27,716	24,765
Counterpart Funds...................	16e	....	....	10,333	9,091	11,197	24,271	26,178	21,338	22,335	12,387	11,504	16,218
Capital Accounts....................	17a	....	....	1,887	−2,356	−13,966	46,025	54,327	57,154	64,493	76,544	100,236	119,689
of which: Valuation Adjustment.....	17rv	....	....	−2,018	−5,432	−21,841	29,394	34,783	—	—	—	28,465	46,504
Other Items (Net).....................	17r	....	....	−1,942	−1,577	−5,179	−20,491	−16,909	−23,415	−277	−1,623	3,666	3,066
Banking Institutions						*Millions of Dobras: End of Period*							
Reserves...........................	20	....	....	5,488	12,730	30,646	30,485	26,620	35,474	62,633	75,299	129,769	62,968
Foreign Assets.....................	21	....	....	12,491	22,880	55,935	47,139	44,819	46,923	54,919	73,357	76,016	92,458
Claims on Private Sector..................	22d	....	....	6,614	8,599	11,897	22,429	24,969	26,569	29,346	45,155	109,543	201,907
Demand Deposits..........................	24	....	....	9,431	16,837	34,384	27,731	29,178	36,756	57,388	69,112	106,821	112,687
Time, Savings,& Fgn.Currency Dep...	25	....	....	6,110	13,830	31,992	35,892	39,793	50,401	61,815	88,046	138,138	136,869
of which: Fgn. Currency Deposits....	25b	....	....	6,011	13,086	30,803	32,763	35,266	43,260	52,932	75,839	122,818	120,363
Foreign Liabilities..................	26c	....	....	2,626	2,173	2,562	9,205	2,485	3,679	2,721	2,901	3,510	2,802
Central Government Deposits...........	26d	....	....	2,462	3,313	1,516	2,447	1,251	2,295	529	1,295	999	4,713
Counterpart Funds.......................	26e	....	....	609	105	105	105	2,134	2,134	2,134	2,134	2,134	2,134
Credit from Monetary Authorities.....	26g	....	....	250	1,150	3,700	1,200	—	—	—	—	—	3,991
Capital Accounts..........................	27a	....	....	3,687	11,828	30,722	36,555	36,038	33,934	34,964	41,841	72,895	127,061
Other Items (Net)........................	27r	....	....	−582	−5,028	−6,503	−13,082	−14,470	−20,233	−12,651	−11,517	−9,168	−32,923
Banking Survey						*Millions of Dobras: End of Period*							
Foreign Assets (Net)........................	31n	....	....	10,021	20,974	102,983	139,104	156,406	169,482	223,494	264,468	333,080	296,748
Domestic Credit..........................	32	....	....	22,359	27,365	−2,615	17,863	16,574	9,159	41,196	47,387	146,707	261,250
Claims on Central Govt.(Net).........	32an	....	....	7,829	18,562	−14,561	−4,610	−8,432	−17,446	11,850	2,232	32,594	52,300
Claims on Nonfin.Pub.Enterprises...	32c	....	....	7,837	—	—	—	—	—	—	—	—	—
Claims on Private Sector..............	32d	....	....	6,694	8,803	11,947	22,473	25,007	26,605	29,346	45,155	114,113	208,950
Money...................................	34	....	....	14,225	23,683	49,202	47,584	50,123	61,885	95,483	108,597	162,775	172,817
Quasi-Money.............................	35	....	....	6,110	13,830	31,992	35,892	39,793	50,401	61,815	88,046	138,138	136,869
Counterpart Funds........................	36e	....	....	10,942	9,196	11,302	24,375	28,311	23,472	24,469	14,521	13,637	18,352
Capital Accounts..........................	37a	....	....	5,574	9,473	16,757	82,580	90,365	91,089	99,456	118,385	173,130	246,750
Other Items (Net)........................	37r	....	....	−4,470	−7,843	−8,885	−33,464	−35,613	−48,204	−16,534	−17,694	−7,892	−16,790
Money plus Quasi-Money..............	35l	....	....	20,335	37,513	81,195	83,476	89,916	112,286	157,298	196,643	300,913	309,686
Interest Rates						*Percent Per Annum*							
Discount Rate (End of Period)...........	60	30.00	32.00	50.00	35.00	55.00	29.50	17.00	17.00	15.50	15.50	14.50	14.50
Deposit Rate..........................	60l	35.00	35.00	35.00	31.00	36.75	38.29	27.00	† 21.00	15.00	15.00	12.29	10.55
Lending Rate..........................	60p	37.00	30.00	52.00	38.00	51.50	55.58	40.33	† 39.67	37.00	37.08	33.79	30.00

Balance of Payments		1993	1994	1995	1996	1997	1998	1999	2000	2001	2002	2003	2004
						Millions of US Dollars: Minus Sign Indicates Debit							
Current Account, n.i.e.	78ald	...	...	...	...	...	−10.47	−16.28	−19.13	−21.01	−22.77	...	...
Goods: Exports f.o.b.	78aad	...	...	...	...	...	4.74	3.90	2.69	3.28	5.12	...	...
Goods: Imports f.o.b.	78abd	...	...	...	...	...	−16.88	−21.94	−25.13	−24.43	−28.00	...	...
Trade Balance	78acd	...	...	...	...	...	−12.14	−18.04	−22.44	−21.14	−22.88	...	...
Services: Credit	78add	...	...	...	...	...	6.56	12.48	13.56	12.78	13.41	...	...
Services: Debit	78aed	...	...	...	...	...	−10.35	−11.83	−10.99	−12.07	−13.44	...	...
Balance on Goods & Services	78afd	...	...	...	...	...	−15.92	−17.40	−19.87	−20.43	−22.91	...	...
Income: Credit	78agd	...	...	...	...	...	...	...	...	...	...	...	...
Income: Debit	78ahd	...	...	...	...	...	−5.21	−5.32	−3.62	−4.62	−4.71	...	...
Balance on Gds, Serv. & Inc.	78aid	...	...	...	...	...	−21.13	−22.71	−23.49	−25.05	−27.62	...	...
Current Transfers, n.i.e.: Credit	78ajd	...	...	...	...	...	10.66	6.44	4.36	4.05	4.85	...	...
Current Transfers: Debit	78akd	...	...	...	...	...	...	...	...	...	...	...	...
Capital Account, n.i.e.	78bcd	...	...	...	...	...	3.90	9.27	12.00	15.20	12.14	...	...
Capital Account, n.i.e.: Credit	78bad	...	...	...	...	...	3.90	9.27	12.00	15.20	12.14	...	...
Capital Account: Debit	78bbd	...	...	...	...	...	...	...	...	—		...	...
Financial Account, n.i.e.	78bjd	...	...	...	...	...	.27	4.36	3.32	1.67	3.69	...	...
Direct Investment Abroad	78bdd	...	...	...	...	...	...	...	...	...	...	...	...
Dir. Invest. in Rep. Econ., n.i.e.	78bed	...	...	...	...	...	4.20	3.04	3.80	3.47	3.04	...	...
Portfolio Investment Assets	78bfd	...	...	...	...	...	...	...	...	—		...	...
Equity Securities	78bkd	...	...	...	...	...	...	...	...	—		...	...
Debt Securities	78bld	...	...	...	...	...	...	...	...	—		...	...
Portfolio Investment Liab., n.i.e.	78bgd	...	...	...	...	...	...	...	...	—		...	...
Equity Securities	78bmd	...	...	...	...	...	...	...	...	—		...	...
Debt Securities	78bnd	...	...	...	...	...	...	...	...	—		...	...
Financial Derivatives Assets	78bwd	...	...	...	...	...	...	...	...	...	...	...	...
Financial Derivatives Liabilities	78bxd	...	...	...	...	...	...	...	...	...	...	...	...
Other Investment Assets	78bhd	...	...	...	...	...	−5.23	−5.18	−4.81	−4.82	−.25	...	...
Monetary Authorities	78bod	...	...	...	...	...	...	...	...	—		...	...
General Government	78bpd	...	...	...	...	...	...	...	...	...	...	...	...
Banks	78bqd	...	...	...	...	...	−5.23	−5.18	−4.81	−4.82	−.25	...	...
Other Sectors	78brd	...	...	...	...	...	...	...	...	—		...	...
Other Investment Liab., n.i.e.	78bid	...	...	...	...	...	1.30	6.50	4.33	3.01	.90	...	...
Monetary Authorities	78bsd	...	...	...	...	...	—	—	—	—	—	...	...
General Government	78btd	...	...	...	...	...	1.30	6.50	4.33	3.01	.90	...	...
Banks	78bud	...	...	...	...	...	...	...	...	—		...	...
Other Sectors	78bvd	...	...	...	...	...	...	...	...	—		...	...
Net Errors and Omissions	78cad	...	...	...	...	...	.26	.09	−1.66	2.66	−.04	...	...
Overall Balance	78cbd	...	...	...	...	...	−6.04	−2.56	−5.46	−1.48	−6.97	...	...
Reserves and Related Items	79dad	...	...	...	...	...	6.04	2.56	5.46	1.48	6.97	...	...
Reserve Assets	79dbd	...	...	...	...	...	2.70	−1.19	−1.50	−4.33	−2.37	...	...
Use of Fund Credit and Loans	79dcd	...	...	...	...	...	−.22	−.11	2.48	—	—	...	...
Exceptional Financing	79ded	...	...	...	...	...	3.56	3.86	4.49	5.80	9.34	...	...
							Millions: Midyear Estimates						
Population	99z	.12	.13	.13	.13	.13	.13	.14	.14	.14	.15	.15	.15

Saudi Arabia 456

		1993	1994	1995	1996	1997	1998	1999	2000	2001	2002	2003	2004
Exchange Rates					*Riyals per SDR: End of Period*								
Official Rate	aa	5.1509	5.4744	5.5743	5.3924	5.0597	5.2801	5.1469	4.8859	4.7127	5.0982	5.5724	5.8238
					Riyals per US Dollar: End of Period (ae) Period Average (rf)								
Official Rate	ae	3.7500	3.7500	3.7500	3.7500	3.7500	3.7500	3.7500	3.7500	3.7500	3.7500	3.7500	3.7500
Official Rate	rf	3.7500	3.7500	3.7500	3.7500	3.7500	3.7500	3.7500	3.7500	3.7500	3.7500	3.7500	3.7500
					Index Numbers (2000=100): Period Averages								
Official Rate	ahx	100.0	100.0	100.0	100.0	100.0	100.0	100.0	100.0	100.0	100.0	100.0	100.0
Nominal Effective Exchange Rate	nec	88.3	86.6	82.2	85.1	91.2	97.0	95.3	100.0	105.3	103.0	93.9	88.1
Real Effective Exchange Rate	rec	99.4	95.3	92.2	94.5	99.1	102.6	98.3	100.0	102.3	99.0	89.1	82.2
Fund Position					*Millions of SDRs: End of Period*								
Quota	2f.s	5,131	5,131	5,131	5,131	5,131	5,131	6,986	6,986	6,986	6,986	6,986	6,986
SDRs	1b.s	403	416	448	481	512	546	110	147	192	244	290	334
Reserve Position in the Fund	1c.s	869	604	575	561	532	524	987	1,043	2,036	2,621	3,047	2,253
of which: Outstg.Fund Borrowing	2c	175	—	—	—	—	—	—	—	—	—	—	—
International Liquidity					*Millions of US Dollars Unless Otherwise Indicated: Approximately End of Period*								
Total Reserves minus Gold	1l.d	7,428	7,378	8,622	† 14,321	14,876	14,220	16,997	19,585	17,596	20,610	22,620	27,291
SDRs	1b.d	553	607	666	692	691	769	152	191	242	332	431	519
Reserve Position in the Fund	1c.d	1,193	882	854	807	718	737	1,355	1,359	2,558	3,564	4,527	3,499
Foreign Exchange	1d.d	5,682	5,888	7,101	† 12,822	13,467	12,714	15,490	18,036	14,796	16,715	17,662	23,273
Gold (Million Fine Troy Ounces)	1ad	4.596	4.596	4.596	4.596	4.596	4.596	4.596	4.596	4.596	4.596	4.596	4.596
Gold (National Valuation)	1and	221	235	239	231	217	226	221	210	202	219	239	250
Deposit Money Banks: Assets	7a.d	29,756	26,173	26,126	28,312	26,537	22,918	24,397	26,988	26,491	25,464	21,622	24,746
Liabilities	7b.d	9,945	10,440	10,581	10,308	12,278	11,495	13,641	17,185	15,897	11,466	10,684	12,199
Other Banking Insts.: Assets	7e.d	1,151	1,149	1,015	1,023	1,041	1,041	1,041	997	1,001	1,005	1,015	1,045
Monetary Authorities					*Billions of Riyals: Approximately End of Period*								
Foreign Assets	11	193.08	185.56	174.04	196.07	219.03	175.60	147.39	183.54	181.80	157.46	223.77	329.14
Reserve Money	14	53.79	56.23	54.93	54.15	58.24	57.53	71.04	68.20	65.42	71.50	75.17	83.71
of which: Currency Outside DMBs	14a	42.62	44.97	43.89	43.04	45.82	45.02	55.06	51.02	49.25	52.33	55.44	60.13
Central Government Deposits	16d	42.48	35.53	34.63	44.52	48.51	48.74	30.99	51.47	51.60	51.72	56.55	98.20
Other Items (Net)	17r	96.81	93.80	84.48	96.40	112.28	69.33	45.35	63.87	64.79	34.23	92.05	147.24
Deposit Money Banks					*Billions of Riyals: Approximately End of Period*								
Reserves	20	11.53	11.65	11.18	11.21	12.55	12.57	16.55	18.88	19.15	43.86	26.66	32.04
Foreign Assets	21	111.59	98.15	97.97	106.17	99.52	85.94	91.49	101.20	99.34	95.49	81.08	92.80
Claims on Central Government	22a	43.46	50.03	52.28	65.27	83.21	89.37	102.27	112.27	123.83	123.43	150.72	146.66
Claims on Public Enterprises	22c	22.60	26.93	24.45	16.70	20.86	23.60	14.35	12.44	10.82	11.96	25.84	29.14
Claims on Private Sector	22d	101.93	113.19	121.15	123.55	133.68	160.66	162.19	172.24	187.06	205.83	228.49	313.93
Demand Deposits	24	78.89	80.73	81.52	90.08	95.47	95.39	101.76	114.69	130.45	150.24	167.78	203.81
Quasi-Monetary Deposits	25a	56.89	60.60	69.70	81.73	86.27	91.31	95.09	100.09	100.85	118.49	125.06	153.73
Foreign Currency Deposits	25b	48.41	47.29	46.32	44.10	44.88	50.61	49.72	49.29	50.57	60.39	65.56	67.57
Foreign Liabilities	26c	37.29	39.15	39.68	38.65	46.04	43.11	51.15	64.44	59.61	43.00	40.06	45.75
Credit from Monetary Authorities	26g	19.80	21.42	18.63	13.57	18.33	29.44	20.58	10.95	7.46	6.44	8.69	7.41
Capital Accounts	27a	34.48	36.96	39.25	42.65	44.87	47.60	48.69	52.38	53.85	57.85	59.18	68.81
Other Items (Net)	27r	15.34	13.80	11.94	12.11	13.96	14.68	19.84	25.20	37.41	44.16	46.46	67.48
Monetary Survey					*Billions of Riyals: Approximately End of Period*								
Foreign Assets (Net)	31n	267.37	244.55	232.33	263.59	272.50	218.44	187.72	220.30	221.53	209.95	264.79	376.20
Domestic Credit	32	125.52	154.62	163.26	160.00	189.24	224.88	247.81	245.48	270.12	289.50	348.50	391.52
Claims on Central Govt. (Net)	32an	.98	14.50	17.66	19.75	34.69	40.63	71.27	60.80	72.24	71.71	94.17	48.46
Claims on Public Enterprises	32c	22.60	26.93	24.45	16.70	20.86	23.60	14.35	12.44	10.82	11.96	25.84	29.14
Claims on Private Sector	32d	101.93	113.19	121.15	123.55	133.68	160.66	162.19	172.24	187.06	205.83	228.49	313.93
Money	34	121.51	125.69	125.41	133.11	141.29	140.41	156.82	165.71	179.70	202.57	223.22	263.94
Quasi-Money	35	105.30	107.89	116.02	125.83	131.15	141.92	144.81	149.38	151.42	178.88	190.62	221.30
Other Items (Net)	37r	166.08	165.59	154.17	164.64	189.30	160.99	133.90	150.69	160.52	118.00	199.45	282.48
Money plus Quasi-Money	35l	226.81	233.58	241.43	258.95	272.44	282.33	301.62	315.09	331.12	381.45	413.84	485.24
Other Banking Institutions					*Billions of Riyals: Approximately End of Period*								
Cash	40	21.88	17.21	14.34	21.92	28.20	21.62	13.00	15.42	20.95	15.07	18.49	23.15
Foreign Assets	41	4.32	4.31	3.81	3.84	3.90	3.90	3.90	3.74	3.75	3.77	3.81	3.92
Claims on Private Sector	42d	168.81	172.90	178.07	181.43	178.96	188.18	199.56	198.54	196.77	204.98	216.71	211.45
Capital Accounts	47a	190.66	190.46	190.46	190.46	190.46	190.46	191.33	191.19	191.19	191.19	201.89	202.45
Other Items (Net)	47r	4.35	3.95	5.76	16.73	20.61	23.25	25.13	26.50	30.28	32.64	37.12	36.07
Interest Rates					*Percent per Annum*								
Deposit Rate	60l	3.521	5.100	6.178	5.469	5.790	6.211	6.137	6.667	3.922	2.234	1.631	1.734
Prices, Production, Labor					*Index Numbers (2000=100): Period Averages*								
Share Prices	62	79.4	56.8	60.6	67.8	86.7	62.6	89.8	100.0	107.6	111.5	196.5	363.4
Wholesale Prices	63	92.8	94.5	101.4	101.1	101.1	99.2	99.6	100.0	99.9	99.9	100.7	103.8
Consumer Prices	64	96.3	96.9	101.6	102.8	102.9	102.5	† 101.1	100.0	98.9	99.1	99.7	100.2
Crude Petroleum	66aa	98.7	98.7	98.4	99.6	98.2	100.6	93.2	100.0	94.8	89.5	102.6	107.9
					Number in Thousands: Period Averages								
Employment	67e	2,495	2,496	2,495	....	....	....	† 5,593	† 5,713	† 5,809	† 5,913	....	....
Intl. Transactions & Positions					*Billions of Riyals*								
Exports	70	158.77	159.59	187.40	227.43	227.44	145.39	190.10	290.55	254.90	271.70	349.67	471.48
Petroleum	70a	144.83	143.02	163.30	203.52	200.04	122.14	168.52	266.10	219.42	239.30	308.52	....
Crude Petroleum	70aa	120.07	117.36	133.17	163.50	163.23	98.97	138.53	232.52	190.81	206.49	264.90	....
Refined Petroleum	70ab	24.76	25.66	30.13	40.02	36.81	23.16	30.00	33.58	28.61	32.81	43.61	....
Imports, c.i.f.	71	105.60	87.40	105.20	103.90	107.60	112.40	104.90	113.24	116.93	121.01	138.43	166.94
Volume of Exports					*2000=100*								
Petroleum	72a	103.3	101.8	101.9	102.4	101.6	103.9	93.8	100.0	95.0	83.8	102.0	....
Crude Petroleum	72aa	100.6	99.7	100.6	98.0	98.9	102.2	91.5	100.0	96.5	84.5	104.3	....
Refined Petroleum	72ab	115.1	111.2	107.6	121.8	113.4	111.5	104.2	100.0	88.2	80.9	91.9	....
Export Prices					*2000=100: Index of Prices in US Dollars*								
Crude Petroleum	76aad	57.7	58.0	64.2	75.8	71.7	46.3	67.1	100.0	97.5	....	....	....

Saudi Arabia   456

		1993	1994	1995	1996	1997	1998	1999	2000	2001	2002	2003	2004
Balance of Payments		\multicolumn{12}{c}{*Millions of US Dollars: Minus Sign Indicates Debit*}											
Current Account, n.i.e..................	78ald	−17,245	−10,473	−5,318	679	305	−13,132	411	14,317	9,353	11,873	28,048	51,488
Goods: Exports f.o.b..............	78aad	42,339	42,557	49,974	60,648	60,651	38,770	50,689	77,481	67,973	72,464	93,244	126,063
Goods: Imports f.o.b.............	78abd	−25,839	−21,297	−25,616	−25,325	−26,335	−27,498	−25,683	−27,704	−28,607	−29,624	−33,868	−40,841
Trade Balance......................	78acd	16,500	21,261	24,358	35,323	34,317	11,272	25,006	49,777	39,366	42,840	59,376	85,222
Services: Credit....................	78add	3,279	3,342	3,475	2,769	4,251	4,723	5,373	4,779	5,008	5,177	5,713	5,858
Services: Debit.....................	78aed	−24,432	−17,869	−19,257	−24,263	−25,929	−16,858	−18,830	−25,228	−19,281	−19,980	−20,857	−25,677
Balance on Goods & Services.......	78afd	−4,653	6,734	8,576	13,829	12,639	−863	11,549	29,327	25,093	28,037	44,232	65,403
Income: Credit......................	78agd	6,200	4,027	4,981	5,120	5,748	5,802	5,804	3,345	4,125	3,714	2,977	3,863
Income: Debit.......................	78ahd	−2,297	−2,557	−2,181	−2,677	−2,967	−3,037	−2,883	−2,865	−4,644	−3,925	−4,277	−4,123
Balance on Gds, Serv. & Inc........	78aid	−750	8,204	11,376	16,272	15,419	1,902	14,469	29,807	24,573	27,827	42,931	65,143
Current Transfers, n.i.e.: Credit......	78ajd	—	—	—	—	—	—	—	—	—	—	—	—
Current Transfers: Debit.............	78akd	−16,495	−18,677	−16,694	−15,592	−15,114	−15,034	−14,058	−15,490	−15,220	−15,954	−14,883	−13,655
Capital Account, n.i.e..................	78bcd	—	—	—	—	—	—	—	—	—	—	—	—
Capital Account, n.i.e.: Credit........	78bad	—	—	—	—	—	—	—	—	—	—	—	—
Capital Account: Debit................	78bbd	—	—	—	—	—	—	—	—	—	—	—	—
Financial Account, n.i.e...............	78bjd	18,738	10,327	6,533	5,062	342	12,414	2,404	−11,652	−11,262	−9,137	−26,440	−46,990
Direct Investment Abroad..............	78bdd	—	—	—	—	—	—	—	—	—	—	—	—
Dir. Invest. in Rep. Econ., n.i.e.......	78bed	1,367	349	−1,875	−1,127	3,039	4,283	−779	−1,881	20	−614	−587	−1,933
Portfolio Investment Assets...........	78bfd	8,202	−2,524	4,051	−2,638	−7,352	6,932	11,700	−9,378	−2,797	7,552	−18,738	−26,654
Equity Securities.........................	78bkd	—	—	—	—	—	—	—	—	—	—	—	—
Debt Securities........................	78bld	8,202	−2,524	4,051	−2,638	−7,352	6,932	11,700	−9,378	−2,797	7,552	−18,738	−26,654
Portfolio Investment Liab., n.i.e......	78bgd	—	—	—	—	—	—	—	—	—	—	—	—
Equity Securities.....................	78bmd	—	—	—	—	—	—	—	—	—	—	—	—
Debt Securities.......................	78bnd	—	—	—	—	—	—	—	—	—	—	—	—
Financial Derivatives Assets...........	78bwd	....	....	....	....	....	....	....	....	....	....	....	....
Financial Derivatives Liabilities.......	78bxd	....	....	....	....	....	....	....	....	....	....	....	....
Other Investment Assets.............	78bhd	6,875	12,006	4,216	9,101	2,684	1,982	−10,663	−3,937	−7,197	−11,644	−6,333	−19,919
Monetary Authorities..................	78bod	—	—	—	—	—	—	—	—	—	—	—	—
General Government...................	78bpd	—	—	—	—	—	—	—	—	—	—	—	—
Banks.................................	78bqd	−2,657	3,583	47	−2,187	1,775	3,619	−1,478	−2,591	490	1,033	3,842	−3,124
Other Sectors.........................	78brd	9,533	8,422	4,169	11,288	909	−1,637	−9,185	−1,346	−7,687	−12,677	−10,175	−16,795
Other Investment Liab., n.i.e.........	78bid	2,293	496	141	−273	1,971	−784	2,146	3,544	−1,288	−4,431	−783	1,516
Monetary Authorities..................	78bsd	—	—	—	—	—	—	—	—	—	—	—	—
General Government...................	78btd	—	—	—	—	—	—	—	—	—	—	—	—
Banks.................................	78bud	2,293	496	141	−273	1,971	−784	2,146	3,544	−1,288	−4,431	−783	1,516
Other Sectors.........................	78bvd	—	—	—	—	—	—	—	—	—	—	—	—
Net Errors and Omissions................	78cad												
Overall Balance........................	78cbd	1,494	−146	1,215	5,741	647	−718	2,815	2,665	−1,909	2,736	1,608	4,498
Reserves and Related Items.............	79dad	−1,494	146	−1,215	−5,741	−647	718	−2,815	−2,665	1,909	−2,736	−1,608	−4,498
Reserve Assets........................	79dbd	−1,494	146	−1,215	−5,741	−647	718	−2,815	−2,665	1,909	−2,736	−1,608	−4,498
Use of Fund Credit and Loans........	79dcd	—	—	—	—	—	—	—	—	—	—	—	—
Exceptional Financing...................	79ded	....	....	....	....	....	....	....	....	....	....	....	....
Government Finance		\multicolumn{12}{c}{*Billions of Riyals*}											
Deficit (-) or Surplus.....................	80	....	....	....	−18.5	−17.0	−18.0	−44.0	−28.0	....	....	....	....
Total Revenue and Grants.............	81y	....	....	....	131.5	164.0	178.0	121.0	157.0	....	....	....	....
Revenue..............................	81	....	....	....	131.5	164.0	178.0	121.0	157.0	....	....	....	....
Grants................................	81z	....	....	....	—	—	—	—	—	....	....	....	....
Exp. & Lending Minus Repay..........	82z	....	....	....	150.0	181.0	196.0	165.0	185.0	....	....	....	....
Expenditure..........................	82	....	....	....	150.0	181.0	196.0	165.0	185.0	....	....	....	....
Lending Minus Repayments..........	83	....	....	....	—	—	—	—	—	....	....	....	....
National Accounts		\multicolumn{12}{c}{*Billions of Riyals*}											
Househ.Cons.Expend.,incl.NPISHs....	96f	237.75	240.48	250.28	259.49	261.43	251.42	252.22	258.13	259.55	260.40	269.98	282.45
Government Consumption Expend...	91f	130.98	122.55	125.92	144.78	161.80	155.19	154.09	183.80	188.70	184.52	198.15	218.37
Gross Fixed Capital Formation..........	93e	108.82	93.00	103.32	102.85	109.24	112.96	118.20	123.32	126.10	128.07	148.10	163.02
Changes in Inventories....................	93i	12.88	6.88	2.27	4.06	3.84	9.60	9.42	8.90	3.50	11.04	11.37	14.86
Exports of Goods and Services.........	90c	171.07	172.12	200.44	237.81	243.38	163.10	210.23	308.47	273.68	291.16	371.09	494.70
Imports of Goods and Services (-).....	98c	166.59	131.98	148.72	158.24	161.78	145.62	140.57	175.97	165.22	168.11	194.04	233.81
Gross Domestic Product (GDP).........	99b	494.91	503.05	533.50	590.75	617.90	546.65	603.59	706.66	686.30	707.07	804.65	939.59
Net Primary Income from Abroad....	98.n	9.76	2.82	8.21	.11	−.23	4.87	7.97	3.35	6.65	4.88	—	....
Gross National Income (GNI)............	99a	504.67	505.87	541.71	590.86	617.67	551.52	611.56	710.00	692.95	711.95	804.65	939.59
GDP Volume 1999 Prices...............	99b.p	552.77	556.45	557.57	576.43	591.38	608.14	603.59	632.95	636.42	637.23	686.04	721.94
GDP Volume (2000=100)...............	99bvp	87.3	87.9	88.1	91.1	93.4	96.1	95.4	100.0	100.5	100.7	108.4	114.1
GDP Deflator (2000=100).............	99bip	80.2	81.0	85.7	91.8	93.6	80.5	89.6	100.0	96.6	99.4	105.1	116.6
		\multicolumn{12}{c}{*Millions: Midyear Estimates*}											
Population..............................	99z	17.80	18.22	18.68	19.19	19.73	20.30	20.89	21.48	22.09	22.70	23.33	23.95

		1993	1994	1995	1996	1997	1998	1999	2000	2001	2002	2003	2004
Exchange Rates					*Francs per SDR: End of Period*								
Official Rate	aa	404.89	† 780.44	728.38	753.06	807.94	791.61	† 896.19	918.49	935.39	850.37	771.76	747.90
					Francs per US Dollar: End of Period (ae) Period Average (rf)								
Official Rate	ae	294.77	† 534.60	490.00	523.70	598.81	562.21	† 652.95	704.95	744.31	625.50	519.36	481.58
Official Rate	rf	283.16	† 555.20	499.15	511.55	583.67	589.95	† 615.70	711.98	733.04	696.99	581.20	528.28
Fund Position					*Millions of SDRs: End of Period*								
Quota	2f.s	118.9	118.9	118.9	118.9	118.9	118.9	161.8	161.8	161.8	161.8	161.8	161.8
SDRs	1b.s	.3	.7	2.6	1.2	.3	.4	1.8	.7	6.0	6.7	7.1	4.7
Reserve Position in the Fund	1c.s	1.1	1.1	1.2	1.3	1.3	1.4	1.4	1.4	1.4	1.5	1.5	1.5
Total Fund Cred.&Loans Outstg	2tl	177.8	205.4	233.3	226.5	216.5	207.8	198.2	195.4	197.6	185.8	161.3	131.5
International Liquidity					*Millions of US Dollars Unless Otherwise Indicated: End of Period*								
Total Reserves minus Gold	1l.d	3.4	179.6	271.8	288.3	386.2	430.8	403.0	384.0	447.3	637.4	1,110.9	1,386.4
SDRs	1b.d	.4	1.1	3.8	1.7	.5	.5	2.5	.9	7.5	9.1	10.6	7.3
Reserve Position in the Fund	1c.d	1.5	1.7	1.8	1.8	1.8	1.9	1.9	1.8	1.8	2.0	2.2	2.4
Foreign Exchange	1d.d	1.5	176.9	266.2	284.8	383.9	428.4	398.6	381.2	438.0	626.3	1,098.2	1,376.7
Gold (Million Fine Troy Ounces)	1ad	.029	.029	—	—	—	—	—	—	—	—	—	—
Gold (National Valuation)	1and	10.8	10.8	—	—	—	—	—	—	—	—	—	—
Monetary Authorities: Other Liab	4..d	408.2	144.4	122.8	116.9	101.6	109.2	96.6	97.2	86.3	107.4	143.0	138.2
Deposit Money Banks: Assets	7a.d	68.6	131.4	159.9	146.7	151.3	220.4	258.2	220.8	239.9	361.6	490.6	595.4
Liabilities	7b.d	154.7	134.0	131.7	105.0	94.0	117.5	119.9	86.9	101.6	107.2	107.0	184.1
Monetary Authorities					*Billions of Francs: End of Period*								
Foreign Assets	11	1.0	96.0	133.2	151.0	231.3	242.2	263.1	270.7	332.9	398.7	577.0	667.7
Claims on Central Government	12a	158.4	265.5	271.4	229.7	293.7	296.4	279.1	256.6	301.0	292.0	262.2	226.0
Claims on Deposit Money Banks	12e	172.3	11.5	—	2.6	31.7	26.9	12.6	2.0	—	—	—	—
Claims on Other Financial Insts	12f	.6	.6	.7	.5	.5	.4	—	—	—	—	—	—
Reserve Money	14	126.6	188.9	196.6	168.7	174.2	186.0	215.7	228.1	306.4	343.9	524.5	578.5
of which: Currency Outside DMBs	14a	93.0	145.6	152.1	141.9	142.3	158.5	179.4	171.5	211.7	191.9	337.5	342.3
Foreign Liabilities	16c	192.3	237.5	230.1	231.7	235.7	225.9	240.6	248.0	249.1	225.2	198.7	164.9
Central Government Deposits	16d	5.7	13.8	19.2	26.8	142.1	137.4	105.0	55.9	80.2	104.1	86.6	118.1
Other Items (Net)	17r	7.6	−66.5	−40.7	−43.5	5.0	16.6	−6.6	−2.7	−1.8	17.5	29.3	32.3
Deposit Money Banks					*Billions of Francs: End of Period*								
Reserves	20	34.1	31.8	31.1	24.9	32.4	27.1	35.7	55.9	93.4	153.8	185.5	235.8
Foreign Assets	21	20.2	70.2	78.4	76.8	90.6	123.9	168.6	155.6	178.5	226.2	254.8	286.7
Claims on Central Government	22a	28.6	57.9	61.5	120.0	109.6	122.4	110.6	94.0	101.8	60.6	69.1	71.7
Claims on Private Sector	22d	424.3	349.9	355.6	411.0	428.3	437.1	483.0	619.5	651.8	682.0	782.1	851.7
Claims on Other Financial Insts	22f	1.6	1.3	.2	—	—	—	—	—	—	—	—	—
Demand Deposits	24	101.4	155.3	160.2	198.5	196.3	234.0	255.9	287.7	315.3	366.1	484.7	532.5
Time Deposits	25	138.8	161.4	184.6	216.4	237.7	233.2	273.2	325.3	363.8	406.4	444.1	544.4
Foreign Liabilities	26c	36.4	58.3	51.4	42.4	50.0	62.5	72.5	56.4	65.2	54.3	36.1	64.2
Long-Term Foreign Liabilities	26cl	9.2	13.4	13.2	12.6	6.3	3.5	5.8	4.9	10.4	12.8	19.5	24.5
Central Government Deposits	26d	118.1	136.4	136.3	161.7	109.5	101.5	97.6	136.5	143.8	143.5	186.3	164.4
Credit from Monetary Authorities	26g	176.8	11.5	—	3.6	31.7	26.9	12.6	2.0	—	—	—	—
Other Items (Net)	27r	−71.9	−25.1	−18.9	−2.5	29.4	48.9	80.5	112.3	127.0	139.5	120.8	116.0
Treasury Claims: Private Sector	22d.i	2.3	2.3	2.2	3.0	2.8	2.9	3.2	2.6	4.5	5.6	2.5	3.0
Post Office: Checking Deposits	24..i	3.0	3.9	4.3	2.8	4.0	4.1	3.9	4.1	4.7	5.3	8.5	12.8
Monetary Survey					*Billions of Francs: End of Period*								
Foreign Assets (Net)	31n	−207.4	−129.5	−69.9	−46.3	36.1	77.7	118.7	121.9	197.1	345.4	597.0	725.3
Domestic Credit	32	492.7	529.0	538.1	575.5	584.5	621.5	674.1	781.9	835.3	792.2	848.8	879.7
Claims on Central Govt. (Net)	32an	63.9	174.9	179.5	161.0	152.9	181.1	187.8	159.7	179.0	104.7	64.2	25.1
Claims on Private Sector	32d	426.6	352.2	357.8	414.1	431.1	439.9	486.2	622.2	656.3	687.6	784.6	854.7
Claims on Other Financial Insts	32f	2.2	1.9	.8	.5	.5	.4	—	—	—	—	—	—
Money	34	197.7	305.3	316.8	343.6	343.2	397.0	439.8	464.0	533.0	563.9	832.2	887.9
Quasi-Money	35	138.8	161.4	184.6	216.4	237.7	233.2	273.2	325.3	363.8	406.4	444.1	544.4
Long-Term Foreign Liabilities	36cl	9.2	13.4	13.2	12.6	6.3	3.5	5.8	4.9	10.4	12.8	19.5	24.5
Other Items (Net)	37r	−60.5	−80.7	−46.4	−43.4	33.4	65.5	73.9	109.6	125.3	154.5	150.0	148.2
Money plus Quasi-Money	35l	336.5	466.7	501.4	560.0	580.9	630.2	713.0	789.3	896.8	970.3	1,276.2	1,432.3
Interest Rates					*Percent Per Annum*								
Bank Rate (End of Period)	60	† 6.00	6.00	6.00	6.00	6.00	6.00	6.00	6.00	6.00	6.00	4.50	4.00
Money Market Rate	60b	4.95	4.95	4.95	4.95	4.95	4.95	4.95	4.95	4.95	4.95	4.95	4.95
Deposit Rate	60l	3.50	3.50	3.50	3.50	3.50	3.50	3.50	3.50	3.50	3.50	3.50	3.50
Prices, Production, Labor					*Index Numbers (2000=100): Period Averages*								
Consumer Prices	64	65.4	86.5	93.3	† 95.8	97.3	98.5	99.3	100.0	103.1	105.4	105.3	105.9
Industrial Production	66	83.6	91.7	98.3	94.9	96.5	116.2	103.6	100.0	100.3	105.8	106.7	....
					Number in Thousands: Period Averages								
Unemployment	67c	10	....	....	....	....	....	....	....	....	....	....	....
Intl. Transactions & Positions					*Billions of Francs*								
Exports	70	200.20	439.10	495.80	505.40	528.00	570.90	632.40	654.90	735.30	743.40	656.90	671.20
Imports, c.i.f	71	307.70	567.40	704.90	734.60	779.00	858.50	845.30	951.60	1,047.10	1,117.90	1,370.03	1,498.20

		1993	1994	1995	1996	1997	1998	1999	2000	2001	2002	2003	2004
Balance of Payments					*Millions of US Dollars: Minus Sign Indicates Debit*								
Current Account, n.i.e.	78ald	−433.0	−187.5	−244.5	−199.4	−184.8	−247.5	−320.2	−332.4	−245.5	−317.0	....	....
Goods: Exports f.o.b.	78aad	736.8	818.8	993.3	988.0	904.6	967.7	1,027.1	919.8	1,003.1	1,066.5	....	....
Goods: Imports f.o.b.	78abd	−1,086.7	−1,022.0	−1,242.9	−1,264.0	−1,176.0	−1,280.6	−1,372.8	−1,336.6	−1,428.4	−1,603.9	....	....
Trade Balance	78acd	−349.9	−203.2	−249.6	−275.9	−271.5	−312.9	−345.8	−416.7	−425.3	−537.4		
Services: Credit	78add	413.9	412.3	512.5	378.7	371.7	425.1	416.1	386.9	398.1	456.2		
Services: Debit	78aed	−581.3	−492.7	−578.2	−395.8	−391.7	−442.9	−430.4	−405.0	−413.6	−474.4		
Balance on Goods & Services	78afd	−517.3	−283.6	−315.3	−293.0	−291.5	−330.7	−360.0	−434.8	−440.8	−555.6		
Income: Credit	78agd	82.8	63.3	87.2	81.3	67.9	76.6	83.3	85.2	67.1	67.4		
Income: Debit	78ahd	−162.3	−164.5	−211.5	−154.1	−139.8	−164.6	−202.5	−196.7	−171.9	−197.3		
Balance on Gds, Serv. & Inc.	78aid	−596.8	−384.7	−439.6	−365.9	−363.4	−418.6	−479.2	−546.3	−545.6	−685.6		
Current Transfers, n.i.e.: Credit	78ajd	267.0	267.0	284.7	244.3	258.8	254.7	225.4	274.9	353.6	414.4		
Current Transfers: Debit	78akd	−103.2	−69.7	−89.6	−77.8	−80.3	−83.6	−66.3	−61.0	−53.4	−45.8		
Capital Account, n.i.e.	78bcd	153.7	190.6	187.0	169.2	96.0	98.3	98.6	83.4	146.1	126.8		
Capital Account, n.i.e.: Credit	78bad	165.9	200.5	201.2	169.3	96.3	98.8	99.0	83.6	146.1	127.1		
Capital Account: Debit	78bbd	−12.2	−9.9	−14.2	−.1	−.3	−.4	−.5	−.3	−.1	−.2		
Financial Account, n.i.e.	78bjd	129.4	48.5	44.2	−179.0	3.5	−109.7	−54.8	27.1	−102.6	−88.2		
Direct Investment Abroad	78bdd	−.3	−17.4	3.3	−3.0	.5	−10.5	−14.5	−9.6	1.5	−36.2		
Dir. Invest. in Rep. Econ., n.i.e.	78bed	−.8	66.9	31.7	8.4	176.4	70.8	156.6	71.9	37.5	80.3		
Portfolio Investment Assets	78bfd		−1.5	−.4	−25.8	−18.9	−21.9	−31.3	11.0	15.9	−25.0		
Equity Securities	78bkd	—	−1.5	−.4	−2.4	.9	−9.8	−6.2	−.2	7.0	.5		
Debt Securities	78bld	—	—	—	−23.4	−19.9	−12.1	−25.1	11.3	8.9	−25.5		
Portfolio Investment Liab., n.i.e.	78bgd	5.8	.5	4.0	−4.8	−8.1	−3.9	—	11.9	−8.3	−13.1		
Equity Securities	78bmd	6.1	.5	4.1	—	8.4	2.6	3.4	−2.2	−5.2	3.2		
Debt Securities	78bnd	−.3	—	−.1	−4.8	−16.4	−6.5	−3.4	14.1	−3.2	−16.4		
Financial Derivatives Assets	78bwd	—	—	—	—	−.7	—	−.7	—	−.4	−1.9		
Financial Derivatives Liabilities	78bxd	—	—	—	—	—	.1	—	—	.4	−.4		
Other Investment Assets	78bhd	4.1	−92.5	−6.2	−70.7	−22.1	−58.8	−62.3	−4.4	−3.9	11.9		
Monetary Authorities	78bod	....	....										
General Government	78bpd	−.6	—	—	−3.1	−.9	−.4	—	—	—	−1.5		
Banks	78bqd	−2.6	−108.8	10.9	31.0	−24.5	−42.4	−54.8	17.2	−33.0	−16.4		
Other Sectors	78brd	7.4	16.3	−17.1	−98.5	3.3	−15.9	−7.6	−21.6	29.2	29.8		
Other Investment Liab., n.i.e.	78bid	120.7	92.6	11.8	−83.1	−123.7	−85.5	−102.6	−53.8	−145.3	−103.8		
Monetary Authorities	78bsd	135.3	−76.2	−35.7	1.6	.3	.7	2.5	8.9	−6.7	10.7		
General Government	78btd	69.0	90.7	83.9	−140.0	−132.6	−112.9	−114.8	−132.7	−136.1	−161.6		
Banks	78bud	−6.6	9.8	−27.1	−4.6	23.6	23.5	5.9	−6.1	7.8	−6.5		
Other Sectors	78bvd	−77.0	68.3	−9.3	60.0	−14.9	3.3	3.7	76.0	−10.4	53.7		
Net Errors and Omissions	78cad	8.4	−28.9	−19.6	7.7	−9.3	10.7	8.2	−9.0	7.9	30.9		
Overall Balance	78cbd	−141.5	22.8	−32.9	−201.4	−94.7	−248.1	−268.2	−231.0	−194.1	−247.3		
Reserves and Related Items	79dad	141.5	−22.8	32.9	201.4	94.7	248.1	268.2	231.0	194.1	247.3		
Reserve Assets	79dbd	8.5	−170.1	−74.8	−34.8	−137.4	−20.7	−31.6	−14.1	−90.3	−92.5		
Use of Fund Credit and Loans	79dcd	−27.4	38.9	42.9	−9.8	−12.8	−11.6	−13.4	−3.3	3.4	−15.9		
Exceptional Financing	79ded	160.3	108.4	64.9	246.0	244.8	280.4	313.2	248.4	281.0	355.8		
International Investment Position						*Millions of US Dollars*							
Assets	79aad	....	....	561.4	640.7	711.7	860.1	889.8	830.1	906.2	1,360.0		
Direct Investment Abroad	79abd	—	—	9.9	10.2	2.6	8.9	18.3	21.9	−5.2	55.1		
Portfolio Investment	79acd	—	—	8.6	33.2	52.2	78.2	93.7	95.0	90.2	133.5		
Equity Securities	79add	....	....	.9	3.2	.7	20.8	14.2	18.9	13.3	14.9		
Debt Securities	79aed	....	....	7.6	30.0	51.5	57.4	79.5	76.1	76.8	118.6		
Financial Derivatives	79ald	....	....	.1	.1	.8	—	.7	.7	1.1			
Other Investment	79afd	152.3	197.0	271.0	308.9	269.8	339.9	374.1	324.9	364.2	527.0		
Monetary Authorities	79agd	—	—	—	—	—	—	—	—	—	—		
General Government	79ahd	....	....	....	....								
Banks	79aid	152.3	197.0	144.4	104.9	115.6	167.5	195.9	164.0	187.9	241.9		
Other Sectors	79ajd	....	....	....	....								
Reserve Assets	79akd	3.4	179.6	271.8	288.3	386.2	433.1	403.0	387.6	455.9	644.4		
Liabilities	79lad	....	....	4,261.8	4,100.6	4,072.1	4,721.1	4,223.1	4,617.4	4,523.8	5,287.8		
Dir. Invest. in Rep. Economy	79lbd	—	—	78.6	76.4	256.2	372.1	329.4	294.6	194.3	241.6		
Portfolio Investment	79lcd	—	—	83.3	73.0	56.8	96.2	92.9	127.9	113.8	140.3		
Equity Securities	79ldd	....	....	10.3	9.4	17.2	66.8	63.5	93.7	83.2	107.8		
Debt Securities	79led	....	....	73.0	63.6	39.6	29.4	29.4	34.2	30.6	32.6		
Financial Derivatives	79lld	....	....				.1	—	—	.4	.1		
Other Investment	79lfd	3,643.7	3,443.6	4,099.9	3,951.2	3,759.1	4,252.7	3,800.8	4,194.9	4,215.3	4,905.8		
Monetary Authorities	79lgd	652.9	446.1	470.1	442.5	394.6	402.4	369.0	353.6	341.8	368.4		
General Government	79lhd	2,801.1	2,882.7	3,323.6	3,035.5	2,864.5	3,232.7	2,852.3	3,150.0	3,189.8	3,691.5		
Banks	79lid	189.7	114.8	184.9	171.3	176.4	210.1	218.3	197.8	242.4	256.8		
Other Sectors	79ljd	—	—	121.3	302.0	323.7	407.4	361.2	493.4	441.2	589.1		
National Accounts						*Billions of Francs*							
Househ.Cons.Expend.,incl.NPISHs	96f	1,191.5	1,450.6	1,763.9	1,769.3	1,871.5	2,029.7	2,224.3	2,314.1	2,566.3	2,775.9	2,996.7	
Government Consumption Expend.	91f	227.7	258.4	276.1	286.0	303.0	324.2	308.6	365.7	493.7	....	....	
Gross Fixed Capital Formation	93e	207.1	295.1	327.7	362.9	381.4	455.0	567.0	539.1	762.1	811.7	851.9	
Changes in Inventories	93i	3.0	49.0	45.7	52.5	—	—	14.8	134.4	−148.8	−171.5	−124.7	
Exports of Goods and Services	90c	341.2	652.0	718.2	728.0	868.4	924.4	888.6	949.5	1,011.3	....		
Imports of Goods and Services (-)	98c	432.9	683.1	897.6	849.1	915.0	1,016.8	1,110.3	1,240.0	1,350.3	1,448.6	1,548.3	
Gross Domestic Product (GDP)	99b	1,521.9	1,864.9	2,222.7	2,349.5	2,509.3	2,716.5	2,893.1	3,114.0	3,380.0	3,472.7	3,725.4	4,023.7
Net Primary Income from Abroad	98.n	79.3	179.2	86.2	217.0	209.0	192.0	164.0	161.0	338.0	....		
Gross National Income (GNI)	99a	1,617.1	2,201.4	2,320.3	2,669.0	2,785.0	2,989.0	3,164.0	3,353.0	3,681.0	....		
GDP Volume 1987 Prices	99b.p	1,481.0	1,523.5	1,602.2	1,684.7	....	....	....	....	....			
GDP Volume 1999 Prices	99b.p	....	....	....	2,619.0	2,705.0	2,825.0	2,893.1	3,089.0	3,235.0			
GDP Volume (2000=100)	99bvp	74.5	76.7	80.6	†84.8	87.6	91.5	93.7	100.0	104.7	....		
GDP Deflator (2000=100)	99bip	65.6	78.1	88.5	89.0	92.0	95.4	99.2	100.0	103.6	....		
						Millions: Midyear Estimates							
Population	99z	8.66	8.89	9.12	9.36	9.60	9.84	10.09	10.34	10.60	10.86	11.12	11.39

Seychelles 718

		1993	1994	1995	1996	1997	1998	1999	2000	2001	2002	2003	2004
Exchange Rates						*Rupees per SDR: End of Period*							
Official Rate	aa	7.2345	7.2345	7.2345	7.2345	6.9218	7.6699	7.3671	8.1642	7.2226	6.8474	8.1434	8.5131
					Rupees per US Dollar: End of Period (ae) Period Average (rf)								
Official Rate	ae	5.2579	4.9695	4.8639	4.9946	5.1249	5.4521	5.3676	6.2689	5.7522	5.0550	5.5000	5.5000
Official Rate	rf	5.1815	5.0559	4.7620	4.9700	5.0263	5.2622	5.3426	5.7138	5.8575	5.4800	5.4007	5.5000
Fund Position						*Millions of SDRs: End of Period*							
Quota	2f.s	6.00	6.00	6.00	6.00	6.00	6.00	8.80	8.80	8.80	8.80	8.80	8.80
SDRs	1b.s	.01	.02	.02	.02	.03	.03	.03	.01	.02	.01	—	—
Reserve Position in the Fund	1c.s	.80	.80	.80	.80	.80	—	—	—	—	—	—	—
Total Fund Cred.&Loans Outstg	2tl	—	—	—	—	—	—	—	—	—	—	—	—
International Liquidity					*Millions of US Dollars Unless Otherwise Indicated: End of Period*								
Total Reserves minus Gold	1l.d	35.65	30.15	27.10	21.76	26.32	21.59	30.35	43.75	37.13	69.79	67.39	34.59
SDRs	1b.d	.02	.02	.03	.03	.04	.04	.04	.01	.02	.01	—	—
Reserve Position in the Fund	1c.d	1.10	1.17	1.20	1.16	1.09	—	—	—	—	—	—	.01
Foreign Exchange	1d.d	34.53	28.96	25.87	20.57	25.20	21.55	30.31	43.74	37.11	69.78	67.38	34.58
Monetary Authorities: Other Liab.	4..d	—	—	—	2.50	12.64	31.75	39.35	64.35	64.88	158.77	126.06	89.82
Banking Institutions: Assets	7a.d	7.66	5.03	9.91	19.87	31.36	29.86	44.03	49.03	49.46	53.79	46.11	58.19
Liabilities	7b.d	7.32	6.42	10.36	17.97	33.40	34.71	47.05	100.74	91.90	106.54	80.17	77.05
Nonbank Financial Insts: Assets	7e.d	—	—	—	—	—	—	—	—	—	—	—	—
Liabilities	7f.d	18.11	19.17	19.72	18.55	17.49	18.45	17.96	16.59	19.64	23.92	23.04	24.61
Monetary Authorities						*Millions of Rupees: End of Period*							
Foreign Assets	11	180.5	142.8	126.8	99.2	127.1	115.2	160.2	271.1	210.6	352.3	369.2	187.8
Claims on Central Government	12a	302.0	529.2	663.3	790.5	926.8	575.0	640.1	698.8	774.0	1,293.2	1,011.7	1,400.6
Claims on Banking Institutions	12e	21.5	7.0	1.8	—	—	10.0	—	22.0	—	—	19.0	120.0
Reserve Money	14	383.8	566.7	684.8	778.6	924.0	468.7	512.8	528.7	566.8	717.9	578.7	1,056.1
of which: Currency Outside Banks	14a	133.0	139.4	146.8	163.9	192.2	206.4	247.9	264.4	279.9	301.0	305.9	295.8
Foreign Liabilities	16c	—	—	—	12.5	64.8	173.1	211.2	403.4	373.2	802.6	693.3	494.0
Central Government Deposits	16d	58.8	30.9	21.4	79.5	57.1	55.5	70.1	33.1	42.0	75.4	32.8	122.1
Capital Accounts	17a	14.0	13.9	13.9	13.9	13.8	14.1	25.9	43.2	51.4	56.7	109.7	56.1
Other Items (Net)	17r	47.4	67.4	71.7	5.1	−5.7	−11.2	−19.7	−16.6	−48.8	−7.0	−14.7	−19.9
Banking Institutions						*Millions of Rupees: End of Period*							
Reserves	20	252.2	426.9	539.6	614.2	731.1	261.6	264.1	263.6	286.1	416.0	271.9	759.3
Foreign Assets	21	40.3	25.0	48.2	99.3	160.7	162.8	236.4	307.4	284.5	271.9	253.6	320.1
Claims on Central Government	22a	900.9	813.6	841.0	958.9	1,086.9	2,106.7	2,526.6	2,805.7	3,101.6	3,182.4	3,335.5	2,746.6
Claims on Nonfin.Pub.Enterprises	22c	80.9	143.9	99.6	75.9	71.8	56.0	42.6	20.2	10.8	5.4	102.8	183.3
Claims on Private Sector	22d	184.6	227.7	275.1	314.6	387.6	459.9	503.4	581.6	655.5	773.9	993.8	1,164.1
Claims on Nonbank Financial Insts.	22g	1.0	1.0	1.0	1.0	1.0	1.0	1.0	1.0	1.0	1.0	1.0	1.0
Demand Deposits	24	200.7	184.4	186.2	284.0	456.5	567.4	823.3	794.9	913.0	1,105.5	1,265.0	931.1
Time, Savings, Fgn. Ccy. Deposits	25	906.7	1,149.7	1,352.6	1,478.9	1,590.8	1,819.5	2,009.7	2,164.8	2,416.4	2,604.0	2,677.5	3,061.7
Money Market Instruments	26aa	—	—	—	3.2	4.6	6.8	2.4	6.6	3.4	4.4	8.1	14.3
Foreign Liabilities	26c	38.5	31.9	50.4	89.7	171.2	189.2	252.6	631.6	528.6	538.5	440.9	423.8
Central Government Deposits	26d	107.7	118.8	112.8	88.6	163.2	187.4	203.5	207.6	228.8	247.1	244.4	234.2
Credit from Monetary Authorities	26g	21.5	7.0	1.8	—	—	10.0	—	22.0	—	—	19.0	120.0
Capital Accounts	27a	84.3	85.4	80.2	174.6	207.2	241.1	270.8	300.8	329.4	343.1	376.3	364.8
Other Items (Net)	27r	100.5	60.9	20.6	−55.1	−154.5	26.6	11.9	−148.9	−80.2	−192.0	−72.8	24.7
Banking Survey						*Millions of Rupees: End of Period*							
Foreign Assets (Net)	31n	182.3	135.9	124.6	96.2	51.9	−84.4	−67.2	−456.5	−406.8	−716.9	−511.5	−409.9
Domestic Credit	32	1,302.9	1,565.7	1,745.8	1,972.8	2,253.8	2,955.7	3,440.2	3,866.6	4,272.1	4,933.4	5,167.5	5,139.4
Claims on Central Govt. (Net)	32an	1,036.4	1,193.1	1,370.1	1,581.3	1,793.4	2,438.9	2,893.2	3,263.8	3,604.9	4,153.2	4,070.0	3,791.0
Claims on Nonfin.Pub.Enterprises	32c	80.9	143.9	99.6	75.9	71.8	56.0	42.6	20.2	10.8	5.4	102.8	183.3
Claims on Private Sector	32d	184.6	227.7	275.1	314.6	387.6	459.9	503.4	581.6	655.5	773.9	993.8	1,164.1
Claims on Nonbank Financial Insts.	32g	1.0	1.0	1.0	1.0	1.0	1.0	1.0	1.0	1.0	1.0	1.0	1.0
Money	34	334.3	324.4	333.7	448.6	649.4	774.5	1,072.0	1,060.1	1,193.7	1,407.4	1,571.8	1,227.8
Quasi-Money	35	906.7	1,149.7	1,352.6	1,478.9	1,590.8	1,819.5	2,009.7	2,164.8	2,416.4	2,604.0	2,677.5	3,061.7
Money Market Instruments	36aa	—	—	—	3.2	4.6	6.8	2.4	6.6	3.4	4.4	8.1	14.3
Capital Accounts	37a	98.3	99.3	94.2	188.6	221.0	255.2	296.7	344.1	380.8	399.8	486.0	421.0
Other Items (Net)	37r	145.9	128.1	89.9	−50.2	−160.1	15.3	−7.8	−165.4	−128.9	−199.0	−87.5	4.8
Money plus Quasi-Money	35l	1,241.0	1,474.1	1,686.3	1,927.4	2,240.2	2,594.0	3,081.7	3,224.9	3,610.1	4,011.4	4,249.3	4,289.5
Nonbank Financial Institutions						*Millions of Rupees: End of Period*							
Reserves	40	—	—	—	.2	—	—	—	.2	.2	—	—	—
Foreign Assets	41	—	—	—	—	—	—	—	—	—	—	—	—
Claims on Central Government	42a	—	—	7.5	8.1	6.4	14.0	8.5	5.8	7.9	1.2	1.7	2.4
Claims on Nonfin.Pub.Enterprises	42c	65.1	53.1	51.4	45.4	36.5	30.0	22.7	15.6	9.9	6.1	2.8	2.0
Claims on Private Sector	42d	87.5	106.2	122.4	141.6	163.8	176.2	184.7	202.1	217.9	252.3	267.4	286.4
Claims on Banking Institutions	42e	4.3	4.1	12.1	10.0	9.9	17.8	24.5	31.3	30.6	25.2	36.6	17.4
Money Market Instruments	46aa	—	—	3.1	2.3	6.7	4.0	.8	3.6	2.6	2.4	2.2	2.8
Foreign Liabilities	46c	95.2	95.2	95.9	92.6	89.7	100.6	96.4	104.0	113.0	120.9	126.7	135.3
Capital Accounts	47a	76.0	83.5	76.0	78.6	96.1	112.0	132.6	135.9	143.6	158.8	170.2	156.0
Other Items (Net)	47r	−14.3	−15.3	18.5	31.7	24.2	21.5	10.6	11.4	7.4	2.8	9.4	14.1
Money (National Definitions)						*Millions of Rupees: End of Period*							
M1	59ma	345.4	326.0	334.3	449.6	648.7	773.8	1,071.2	1,137.5	1,290.6	1,576.9	1,570.9	1,226.9
M2	59mb	1,183.0	1,094.7	1,209.3	1,388.6	1,987.8	2,383.5	2,908.9	3,174.2	3,554.8	4,062.1	4,128.0	3,680.4
M2(p)	59mba	1,183.0	1,292.8	1,510.8	1,705.7	2,205.9	2,561.8	3,056.9	3,306.5	3,682.5	4,165.4	4,230.2	4,269.9
Interest Rates						*Percent Per Annum*							
Discount Rate (End of Period)	60	13.08	12.50	12.83	11.00	11.00	5.50	5.50	5.50	5.50	5.50	4.67	3.51
Treasury Bill Rate	60c	13.25	12.50	12.28	11.55	10.50	8.13	5.00	5.00	5.00	5.00	4.61	3.17
Savings Rate	60k	8.61	8.00	8.00	8.00	8.00	5.75	3.00	3.02	3.03	3.03	2.85	2.88
Deposit Rate	60l	9.37	8.85	9.22	9.90	9.20	7.53	5.13	4.77	4.92	4.93	3.99	3.55
Lending Rate	60p	15.71	15.72	15.76	16.22	14.88	14.39	12.01	11.45	11.14	11.09	11.08	10.13
Government Bond Yield	61	14.40	14.38	13.25	13.25	11.63	8.96	8.58	8.22	8.13	8.25	5.96	6.58

Seychelles 718

		1993	1994	1995	1996	1997	1998	1999	2000	2001	2002	2003	2004
Prices and Labor		*Index Numbers (2000=100): Period Averages*											
Consumer Prices.........................	64	85.4	86.9	86.7	85.7	86.3	88.5	94.1	100.0	106.0	106.2	109.7	113.9
Employment.............................	67	78.3	78.7	79.9	81.5	87.8	91.2	96.5	100.0	103.1	105.6	102.7	101.7
		Number in Thousands: Period Averages											
Employment.............................	67e	25	25	26	26	28	29	31	32	33	34	....	....
Intl. Transactions & Positions		*Millions of Rupees*											
Exports....................................	70	265.02	262.15	253.50	693.43	569.23	643.67	775.12	1,108.48	1,263.20	1,249.04	1,141.68	1,008.97
Imports, c.i.f..............................	71	1,234.86	1,042.38	1,109.20	1,881.88	1,711.22	2,015.52	2,317.17	1,949.86	2,776.04	2,294.92	2,230.65	2,738.96
Balance of Payments		*Millions of US Dollars: Minus Sign Indicates Debit*											
Current Account, n.i.e.....................	78ald	−7.33	23.83	−2.95	−59.25	−72.78	−118.03	−127.33	−51.33	−123.24	−130.64	....	....
Goods: Exports f.o.b.............	78aad	50.33	52.99	53.51	96.66	113.56	122.84	145.66	194.77	216.44	236.70		
Goods: Imports f.o.b.............	78abd	−215.73	−188.06	−214.26	−266.98	−303.50	−334.63	−369.75	−311.60	−421.93	−376.26		
Trade Balance........................	78acd	−165.40	−135.07	−160.75	−170.32	−189.94	−211.79	−224.09	−116.82	−205.50	−139.57		
Services: Credit.......................	78add	261.72	250.34	278.69	237.06	255.86	247.48	277.30	294.23	296.38	306.52		
Services: Debit........................	78aed	−87.27	−80.19	−103.48	−114.07	−127.61	−132.17	−155.98	−174.66	−169.20	−201.28		
Balance on Goods & Services.......	78afd	9.05	35.08	14.46	−47.33	−61.70	−96.49	−102.78	2.75	−78.31	−34.33		
Income: Credit........................	78agd	1.99	8.09	12.56	10.48	9.65	5.43	8.46	9.24	8.25	7.44		
Income: Debit.........................	78ahd	−19.09	−19.84	−32.21	−25.52	−21.92	−25.31	−32.29	−57.66	−52.19	−99.98		
Balance on Gds, Serv. & Inc........	78aid	−8.05	23.34	−5.20	−62.37	−73.97	−116.36	−126.61	−45.67	−122.25	−126.87		
Current Transfers, n.i.e.: Credit......	78ajd	15.84	13.85	13.52	15.20	14.24	9.77	10.09	4.34	7.90	7.82		
Current Transfers: Debit................	78akd	−15.13	−13.35	−11.28	−12.07	−13.05	−11.44	−10.81	−9.99	−8.90	−11.59		
Capital Account, n.i.e...................	78bcd	1.74	4.27	1.05	5.65	6.76	21.66	16.47	.89	9.44	5.03		
Capital Account, n.i.e.: Credit........	78bad	1.74	4.27	1.05	5.65	6.76	21.66	16.47	.89	9.44	5.03		
Capital Account: Debit.................	78bbd	—	—	—	—	—	—	—	—	—	—		
Financial Account, n.i.e.................	78bjd	5.53	−.20	−1.18	−15.95	9.52	27.08	13.91	−32.07	52.33	−63.97		
Direct Investment Abroad..............	78bdd	−1.00	−13.33	−16.97	−12.47	−9.89	−3.00	−8.98	−6.86	−8.54	−8.90		
Dir. Invest. in Rep. Econ., n.i.e.......	78bed	18.84	30.74	45.88	28.81	53.40	53.21	55.22	24.33	59.43	61.43		
Portfolio Investment Assets...........	78bfd	−.35	−.93	−5.76	6.65	.09	−.78	−.02	−.09	.07	.07		
Equity Securities.....................	78bkd	....	....	....	....	....	....	....	....	....	....		
Debt Securities.......................	78bld	−.35	−.93	−5.76	6.65	.09	−.78	−.02	−.09	.07	.07		
Portfolio Investment Liab., n.i.e......	78bgd	.04	.16	−.17	—	2.94	2.83	.56	1.05	1.09	1.11		
Equity Securities.....................	78bmd	....	....	....	....	....	....	....	....	....	....		
Debt Securities.......................	78bnd	.04	.16	−.17	—	2.94	2.83	.56	1.05	1.09	1.11		
Financial Derivatives Assets...........	78bwd	....	....	....	....	....	....	....	....	....	....		
Financial Derivatives Liabilities.......	78bxd	....	....	....	....	....	....	....	....	....	....		
Other Investment Assets...............	78bhd	2.05	1.60	−2.56	−11.79	−12.73	−5.66	−12.97	−14.86	−8.76	−9.84		
Monetary Authorities................	78bod	....	....	....	....	....	....	....	....	....	....		
General Government.................	78bpd	....	....	....	....	....	....	....	....	....	....		
Banks.................................	78bqd	....	....	....	....	....	....	....	....	....	....		
Other Sectors........................	78brd	2.05	1.60	−2.56	−11.79	−12.73	−5.66	−12.97	−14.86	−8.76	−9.84		
Other Investment Liab., n.i.e..........	78bid	−14.04	−18.44	−21.61	−27.14	−24.29	−19.52	−19.90	−35.64	9.03	−107.84		
Monetary Authorities................	78bsd	—	−2.06	−2.86	−3.14	−10.19	—	—	−3.39	−15.94	−68.09		
General Government.................	78btd	−12.85	−14.22	−16.23	−21.33	−12.83	−16.02	−18.27	−13.56	−31.94	−7.03		
Banks.................................	78bud									−4.30	−5.70		
Other Sectors........................	78bvd	−1.20	−2.16	−2.52	−2.68	−1.27	−3.50	−1.63	−18.68	61.21	−27.03		
Net Errors and Omissions................	78cad	−30.41	−55.41	−28.70	7.04	11.65	−4.35	−2.14	−20.79	14.42	.51		
Overall Balance.....................	78cbd	−30.48	−27.51	−31.78	−62.50	−44.84	−73.64	−99.09	−103.30	−47.06	−189.07		
Reserves and Related Items.............	79dad	30.48	27.51	31.78	62.50	44.84	73.64	99.09	103.30	47.06	189.07		
Reserve Assets........................	79dbd	−4.47	7.43	3.42	4.86	−5.12	3.26	−8.42	−19.39	.10.32	−25.84		
Use of Fund Credit and Loans........	79dcd												
Exceptional Financing..............	79ded	34.95	20.09	28.36	57.63	49.96	70.38	107.51	122.69	36.74	214.92		—
Government Finance		*Millions of Rupees: Year Ending December 31*											
Deficit (-) or Surplus....................	80	−769.2	−54.0	−200.5	−365.4	107.6	38.6	−385.5	−496.5	....	....	270.4	142.3
Total Revenue and Grants..............	81y	1,323.4	1,288.9	1,172.2	1,164.1	1,288.8	1,400.7	1,533.6	1,426.7	....	....	1,867.6	1,885.0
Revenue................................	81	1,260.4	1,271.1	1,158.4	1,151.1	1,273.5	1,372.9	1,491.9	1,377.1	....	....	1,856.8	1,881.5
Grants.................................	81z	63.0	17.8	13.8	13.0	15.3	27.8	41.7	49.6	....	....	10.8	3.5
Exp. & Lending Minus Repay..........	82z	2,092.6	1,342.9	1,372.7	1,529.5	1,181.2	1,362.1	1,919.1	1,923.2	....	....	1,597.2	1,742.7
Expenditure..............................	82	1,443.0	1,325.9	1,276.5	1,495.2	1,680.9	1,879.7	1,905.0	1,969.8	....	....	1,596.1	1,741.6
Lending Minus Repayments..........	83	649.6	17.0	96.2	34.3	−499.7	−517.6	14.1	−46.6	....	....	1.2	1.0
Total Financing............................	80h	769.2	54.0	200.5	365.4	−107.6	−38.6	385.5	496.5	....	....	−270.4	−142.7
Domestic..................................	84a	749.6	63.8	246.0	324.1	−128.6	−4.3	433.6	−19.3	....	....	−283.0	−131.0
Foreign....................................	85a	19.6	−9.8	−45.5	41.3	21.0	−34.3	−48.1	515.8	....	....	12.6	−11.6
National Accounts		*Millions of Rupees*											
Househ.Cons.Expend.,incl.NPISHs....	96f	1,241.6	1,129.8	1,179.4	1,191.0	1,465.8	1,603.9	....	....	....	....	....	....
Government Consumption Expend...	91f	714.7	722.2	669.1	736.0	733.0	847.0	....	....	....	....	....	....
Gross Fixed Capital Formation..........	93e	651.2	648.5	733.9	822.6	863.1	1,100.0	....	....	....	....	....	....
Changes in Inventories...................	93i	46.0	17.4	.2	−19.0	109.1	56.0	....	....	....	....	....	....
Exports of Goods and Services..........	90c	1,319.2	1,250.5	1,292.0	1,592.9	1,896.9	2,045.5	....	....	....	....	....	....
Imports of Goods and Services (-)....	98c	1,544.2	1,326.0	1,454.8	1,841.4	2,159.7	2,525.8	....	....	....	....	....	....
Gross Domestic Product (GDP)........	99b	2,431.5	2,459.4	2,419.8	2,500.3	2,829.5	3,201.3	3,323.2	3,531.7	3,617.8	3,829.9	....	....
Net Primary Income from Abroad....	98.n	−31.6	9.6	−91.9	−73.6	−62.1	−110.1	−128.2	−151.5	....	....	....	....
Gross National Income (GNI)..........	99a	2,399.9	2,469.0	2,328.0	2,426.7	2,767.5	3,091.2	3,195.1	3,380.2	3,617.8	3,829.9	....	....
Consumption of Fixed Capital.........	99cf	202.3	211.5	210.2	240.5	276.9	291.3	318.5	....	....	....	....	....
GDP Volume 1986 Prices................	99b.p	1,965.9	1,950.0	1,933.9	2,029.0	2,121.1	2,238.8	2,303.7	2,336.0	2,358.2	....	....	....
GDP Volume (2000=100).............	99bvp	84.2	83.5	82.8	86.9	90.8	95.8	98.6	100.0	101.0	....	....	....
GDP Deflator (2000=100)..............	99bip	81.8	83.4	82.8	81.5	88.2	94.6	95.4	100.0	101.5	....	....	....
		Millions: Midyear Estimates											
Population.............................	99z	.07	.07	.08	.08	.08	.08	.08	.08	.08	.08	.08	.08

Sierra Leone 724

		1993	1994	1995	1996	1997	1998	1999	2000	2001	2002	2003	2004
Exchange Rates						*Leones per SDR: End of Period*							
Market Rate	aa	793.41	894.90	1,402.35	1,307.24	1,799.00	2,239.84	3,123.90	2,171.52	2,716.13	2,979.70	3,807.32	4,442.37
					Leones per US Dollar: End of Period (ae) Period Average (rf)								
Market Rate	ae	577.63	613.01	943.40	909.09	1,333.33	1,590.76	2,276.05	1,666.67	2,161.27	2,191.73	2,562.18	2,860.49
Market Rate	rf	567.46	586.74	755.22	920.73	981.48	1,563.62	1,804.20	2,092.13	1,986.15	2,099.03	2,347.94	2,701.30
					Index Numbers (2000=100): Period Averages								
Market Rate	ahx	366.3	354.3	282.8	226.2	217.8	132.9	116.5	100.0	105.4	99.0	88.7	77.0
Nominal Effective Exchange Rate	nec	278.7	293.7	223.7	184.9	192.6	121.8	107.5	100.0	111.0	102.1	81.7	66.0
Real Effective Exchange Rate	rec	92.6	106.7	96.4	97.2	111.5	95.0	110.9	100.0	110.7	90.1	82.4	74.4
Fund Position						*Millions of SDRs: End of Period*							
Quota	2f.s	57.9	77.2	77.2	77.2	77.2	77.2	103.7	103.7	103.7	103.7	103.7	103.7
SDRs	1b.s	2.8	6.2	11.5	5.3	8.3	7.4	15.2	4.0	.3	17.7	23.2	32.8
Reserve Position in the Fund	1c.s	—	—	—	—	—	—	—	—	—	—	—	—
Total Fund Cred.&Loans Outstg	2tl	61.0	100.2	110.9	118.8	123.9	135.4	142.0	133.2	120.8	124.5	113.8	126.0
International Liquidity					*Millions of US Dollars Unless Otherwise Indicated: End of Period*								
Total Reserves minus Gold	1l.d	29.0	40.6	34.6	26.6	38.5	43.9	39.5	49.2	51.3	84.7	66.6	125.1
SDRs	1b.d	3.8	9.0	17.1	7.6	11.2	10.4	20.8	5.2	.4	24.0	34.5	51.0
Reserve Position in the Fund	1c.d	—	—	—	—	—	—	—	—	—	—	—	—
Foreign Exchange	1d.d	25.1	31.6	17.5	18.9	27.3	33.5	18.6	43.9	50.9	60.6	32.1	74.1
Monetary Authorities: Other Liab	4..d	322.2	470.2	326.2	74.9	31.4	38.8	27.4	30.2	37.2	28.3	24.0	11.7
Deposit Money Banks: Assets	7a.d	22.5	16.9	22.5	19.9	15.6	19.2	17.9	24.4	21.9	26.6	30.8	35.0
Liabilities	7b.d	2.7	2.9	3.1	—	—	—	—	—	—	—	—	—
Monetary Authorities						*Millions of Leones: End of Period*							
Foreign Assets	11	18,943	30,443	48,695	† 27,262	53,008	83,128	98,035	86,385	115,454	191,477	168,696	365,530
Claims on Central Government	12a	25,328	462,872	408,928	† 415,564	470,930	475,265	524,834	633,405	650,358	655,133	685,472	626,112
Claims on Nonfin.Pub.Enterprises	12c	....	....	....	203	203	13	66	13	13	13	13	13
Claims on Private Sector	12d	126	160	324	† 1,031	2,577	1,749	788	1,008	1,969	6,161	1,911	2,125
Claims on Deposit Money Banks	12e	—	—	—	† 1,173	495	1,049	1,736	606	969	278	59	3,163
Claims on Other Banking Insts	12f	....	....	....	33	34	—	4	—	—	—	—	—
Claims on Nonbank Financial Insts	12g	....	....	....	302	85	6	26	853	520	102	334	263
Reserve Money	14	24,995	31,352	35,148	† 43,548	91,008	72,415	100,627	109,843	142,103	177,441	217,217	244,622
of which: Currency Outside DMBs	14a	21,882	23,604	30,023	† 36,186	57,260	61,492	82,815	88,854	116,153	148,015	188,448	204,733
Time, Savings,& Fgn.Currency Dep	15	....	....	....	812	5,397	259	1,394	4,975	3,363	4,526	4,628	2,909
Restricted Deposits	16b	....	....	....	3	213	24	34	54	31	103	94	182
Foreign Liabilities	16c	234,495	377,912	463,327	† 223,385	264,752	365,182	505,898	339,520	408,560	433,041	494,654	593,480
Central Government Deposits	16d	6,598	5,936	10,955	† 2,042	4,528	4,615	5,472	8,415	13,195	42,510	14,849	36,920
Capital Accounts	17a	149	24,151	24,156	† 190,151	227,926	153,376	156,239	222,527	261,467	261,538	226,182	198,223
of which: Valuation Adjustment	17rv	−90,274	−108,690	−111,158	† 832	−40,714	−57,997	−135,494	8,177	−9,614	−54,187	−116,625	−177,722
Other Items (Net)	17r	−221,840	54,124	−75,639	† −14,373	−66,491	−34,661	−144,178	36,937	−59,436	−65,996	−101,140	−79,131
Deposit Money Banks						*Millions of Leones: End of Period*							
Reserves	20	2,855	7,523	4,701	† 5,926	26,240	8,088	23,229	20,543	17,047	21,696	20,099	27,999
Foreign Assets	21	12,986	10,378	21,232	† 18,079	20,852	30,555	40,852	40,611	47,295	58,383	78,839	100,055
Claims on Central Government	22a	8,589	9,921	12,763	† 18,470	10,311	41,161	72,209	71,752	100,748	130,035	121,829	151,374
Claims on Nonfin.Pub.Enterprises	22c	26	81	21	† 30	335	63	68	622	486	950	3,647	3,440
Claims on Private Sector	22d	14,847	16,576	17,276	† 20,705	24,506	26,895	24,234	27,035	32,974	50,559	91,406	133,362
Claims on Nonbank Financial Insts	22g	....	....	....	598	594	2,094	2,165	10,803	11,649	16,732	14,397	15,547
Demand Deposits	24	12,753	14,719	19,462	† 15,616	24,494	25,875	47,800	48,447	67,452	90,808	94,415	127,416
Time, Savings,& Fgn.Currency Dep	25	15,951	16,955	16,481	† 32,044	37,625	50,896	58,686	72,674	98,064	124,834	161,754	204,148
Foreign Liabilities	26c	1,551	1,761	2,896	† —	—	—	—	—	—	—	—	—
Central Government Deposits	26d	1,356	1,916	2,172	† 2,102	3,190	5,059	14,107	13,266	10,894	21,244	23,196	19,547
Credit from Monetary Authorities	26g	—	—	—	† 74	74	42	21	—	—	—	—	—
Capital Accounts	27a	1,292	5,483	8,961	† 20,564	18,607	22,994	34,664	48,899	60,975	76,176	84,301	112,428
Other Items (Net)	27r	6,399	3,645	6,021	† −6,591	−1,153	3,990	7,480	−11,920	−27,186	−34,706	−33,450	−31,760
Monetary Survey						*Millions of Leones: End of Period*							
Foreign Assets (Net)	31n	−204,117	−338,852	−396,296	† −178,045	−190,891	−251,499	−367,011	−212,524	−245,811	−183,182	−247,119	−127,895
Domestic Credit	32	40,961	481,758	426,184	† 452,793	501,856	537,572	604,813	723,811	774,627	795,931	880,963	875,770
Claims on Central Govt. (Net)	32an	25,963	464,940	408,563	† 429,891	473,523	506,752	577,463	683,477	727,016	721,414	769,255	721,021
Claims on Nonfin.Pub.Enterprises	32c	26	81	21	† 233	538	76	134	635	499	963	3,661	3,453
Claims on Private Sector	32d	14,973	16,736	17,600	† 21,736	27,083	28,644	25,022	28,043	34,943	56,719	93,317	135,486
Claims on Other Banking Insts	32f	....	....	....	33	34	—	4	—	—	—	—	—
Claims on Nonbank Financial Inst	32g	....	....	....	900	679	2,100	2,190	11,656	12,169	16,834	14,730	15,810
Money	34	35,053	38,542	49,902	† 53,208	83,611	89,744	134,078	139,957	189,437	247,478	292,950	344,524
Quasi-Money	35	15,951	16,955	16,481	† 32,856	43,022	51,155	60,080	77,649	101,427	129,360	166,383	207,057
Restricted Deposits	36b	....	....	....	3	213	24	34	54	31	103	94	182
Capital Accounts	37a	1,441	29,633	33,116	† 210,715	246,533	176,370	190,903	271,426	322,443	337,714	310,483	310,651
Other Items (Net)	37r	−215,601	57,775	−69,611	† −22,033	−62,414	−31,221	−147,294	22,201	−84,521	−101,905	−136,066	−114,538
Money plus Quasi-Money	35l	51,004	55,497	66,383	† 86,064	126,633	140,899	194,159	217,605	290,864	376,838	459,333	551,581
Interest Rates						*Percent Per Annum*							
Treasury Bill Rate	60c	28.64	12.19	14.73	29.25	12.71	22.10	32.42	26.22	13.74	15.15	15.68	26.14
Deposit Rate	60l	27.00	11.63	7.03	13.96	9.91	7.12	9.50	9.25	7.67	8.23	8.42	10.14
Lending Rate	60p	50.46	27.33	28.83	32.12	23.87	23.83	26.83	26.25	24.27	22.17	20.00	22.08
Prices						*Index Numbers (2000=100): Period Averages*							
Consumer Prices	64	† 25.1	31.1	39.2	48.3	55.5	75.2	100.8	100.0	102.1	98.7	106.2	121.3
Intl. Transactions & Positions						*Millions of Leones*							
Exports	70	67,094	68,010	30,148	43,004	15,412	10,482	11,347	26,771	57,897	102,010	217,742	374,086
Imports, c.i.f.	71	83,460	88,492	102,488	193,628	80,010	148,226	153,856	314,639	368,323	554,838	707,909	775,045

Sierra Leone   724

		1993	1994	1995	1996	1997	1998	1999	2000	2001	2002	2003	2004
Balance of Payments					*Millions of US Dollars: Minus Sign Indicates Debit*								
Current Account, n.i.e.	78ald	−57.8	−89.1	−118.1	−150.5	−54.9	−33.2	−99.3	−112.3	−97.9	−73.2	−80.0	....
Goods: Exports f.o.b.	78aad	118.3	116.0	41.5	46.8	15.7	31.6	6.3	12.8	29.2	59.8	110.8	....
Goods: Imports f.o.b.	78abd	−187.1	−188.7	−168.1	−226.5	−71.9	−88.8	−86.8	−136.9	−165.1	−254.9	−310.7	....
Trade Balance	78acd	−68.8	−72.7	−126.7	−179.7	−56.2	−57.2	−80.5	−124.1	−136.0	−195.1	−199.9	....
Services: Credit	78add	58.5	100.2	86.8	62.9	31.9	19.1	22.3	42.2	52.0	38.3	66.1	....
Services: Debit	78aed	−61.5	−107.6	−91.8	−107.7	−47.8	−39.2	−100.9	−112.8	−110.9	−80.8	−93.8	....
Balance on Goods & Services	78afd	−71.9	−80.1	−131.7	−224.5	−72.1	−77.4	−159.1	−194.7	−194.9	−237.5	−227.6	....
Income: Credit	78agd	2.3	1.5	.7	.8	1.5	6.8	6.2	7.4	4.3	18.3	1.7	....
Income: Debit	78ahd	−5.6	−57.0	−30.3	−12.4	−9.4	−27.3	−14.1	−12.6	−14.8	−21.1	−16.7	....
Balance on Gds, Serv. & Inc.	78aid	−75.2	−135.7	−161.3	−236.1	−80.0	−97.8	−167.0	−199.9	−205.4	−240.4	−242.6	....
Current Transfers, n.i.e.: Credit	78ajd	19.1	47.5	44.0	87.2	25.9	65.2	68.6	92.3	120.7	170.8	167.6	....
Current Transfers: Debit	78akd	−1.7	−.9	−.8	−1.6	−.8	−.6	−1.0	−4.7	−13.2	−3.6	−5.0	....
Capital Account, n.i.e.	78bcd	.1	.1	—	.1	.1	—	—	—	.2	50.6	71.0	....
Capital Account, n.i.e.: Credit	78bad	.1	.1	—	.1	.1	—	—	—	.4	50.6	71.0	....
Capital Account: Debit	78bbd	—	—	—	—	—	—	—	—	−.1	—	—	....
Financial Account, n.i.e.	78bjd	49.1	−25.5	97.9	31.2	15.4	10.6	−27.3	124.6	30.1	10.0	28.1	....
Direct Investment Abroad	78bdd	—	—	—	....	....	—	—	—	....	—	—	....
Dir. Invest. in Rep. Econ., n.i.e.	78bed	−7.5	−2.9	7.3	.7	1.8	.1	.5	39.0	9.8	1.6	3.1	....
Portfolio Investment Assets	78bfd	—	—	—	....	....	—	—	—	....	.1	—	....
Equity Securities	78bkd	—	—	—	....	....	—	—	—	....	.1	—	....
Debt Securities	78bld	—	—	—	....	....	—	—	—	....	—	—	....
Portfolio Investment Liab., n.i.e.	78bgd	—	—	—	....	....	—	—	—	....	—	—	....
Equity Securities	78bmd	—	—	—	....	....	—	—	—	....	—	—	....
Debt Securities	78bnd	—	—	—	....	....	—	—	—	....	—	—	....
Financial Derivatives Assets	78bwd	....	....	....	....	....	....	....	....	....	....	....	....
Financial Derivatives Liabilities	78bxd	....	....	....	....	....	....	....	....	....	....	....	....
Other Investment Assets	78bhd	−14.6	−.8	15.6	1.8	−.9	−50.8	−31.3	44.2	−3.5	8.1	.5	....
Monetary Authorities	78bod	....	....	....	....	....	....	....	....	....	.8	.5	....
General Government	78bpd	—	—	—	—	—	—	—	—	—	—	—	....
Banks	78bqd	−10.0	4.4	15.9	3.5	−.9	−6.3	−5.7	.1	−3.4	1.9	—	....
Other Sectors	78brd	−4.6	−5.2	−.4	−1.6	—	−44.4	−25.6	44.1	−.1	5.4	—	....
Other Investment Liab., n.i.e.	78bid	71.2	−21.8	75.1	28.7	14.5	61.3	3.4	41.3	23.7	.2	24.4	....
Monetary Authorities	78bsd	44.5	—	—	—	—	—	—	—	—	—	—	....
General Government	78btd	31.1	−15.2	69.2	30.7	14.6	62.4	30.3	43.4	45.7	.2	24.4	....
Banks	78bud	−2.6	2.8	−1.5	—	—	—	—	—	—	—	—	....
Other Sectors	78bvd	−1.8	−9.5	7.4	−1.9	−.1	−1.1	−26.9	−2.1	−22.1	—	—	....
Net Errors and Omissions	78cad	16.1	55.1	21.5	97.1	59.1	24.7	110.5	−2.5	97.2	−7.4	−47.6	....
Overall Balance	78cbd	7.5	−59.5	1.3	−22.2	19.7	2.1	−16.1	9.8	29.6	−20.1	−28.6	....
Reserves and Related Items	79dad	−7.5	59.5	−1.3	22.2	−19.7	−2.1	16.1	−9.8	−29.6	20.1	28.6	....
Reserve Assets	79dbd	−13.6	−18.6	−17.2	10.9	−26.7	−18.2	7.2	2.0	−13.9	−32.3	24.3	....
Use of Fund Credit and Loans	79dcd	−8.4	55.1	15.9	11.3	7.0	16.1	8.9	−11.8	−15.8	5.0	−14.8	....
Exceptional Financing	79ded	14.4	22.9	—	....	....	....	....	....	....	47.4	19.2	....
International Investment Position						*Millions of US Dollars*							
Assets	79aad	....	....	....	....	....	....	....	....	....	....	....	....
Direct Investment Abroad	79abd	....	....	....	....	....	....	....	....	—	—	—	....
Portfolio Investment	79acd	....	....	....	....	....	....	....	....	.2	.9	26.3	....
Equity Securities	79add	....	....	....	....	....	....	....	....	—	—	—	....
Debt Securities	79aed	....	....	....	....	....	....	....	....	.2	.9	26.3	....
Financial Derivatives	79ald	....	....	....	....	....	....	....	....	....	....	....	....
Other Investment	79afd	....	....	....	....	....	....	....	....	9.4	8.6	8.1	....
Monetary Authorities	79agd	....	....	....	....	....	....	....	....	9.4	8.6	8.1	....
General Government	79ahd	....	....	....	....	....	....	....	....	—	—	—	....
Banks	79aid	....	....	....	....	....	....	....	....	—	—	—	....
Other Sectors	79ajd	....	....	....	....	....	....	....	....	—	—	—	....
Reserve Assets	79akd	....	....	....	....	....	....	....	....	41.2	76.3	57.0	....
Liabilities	79lad	....	....	....	....	....	....	....	....	....	....	....	....
Dir. Invest. in Rep. Economy	79lbd	....	....	....	....	....	....	....	....	—	—	—	....
Portfolio Investment	79lcd	....	....	....	....	....	....	....	....	—	—	—	....
Equity Securities	79ldd	....	....	....	....	....	....	....	....	—	—	—	....
Debt Securities	79led	....	....	....	....	....	....	....	....	—	—	—	....
Financial Derivatives	79lld	....	....	....	....	....	....	....	....	—	—	—	....
Other Investment	79lfd	....	....	....	....	....	....	....	....	1,265.9	1,383.9	1,511.0	....
Monetary Authorities	79lgd	....	....	....	....	....	....	....	....	151.8	169.3	169.1	....
General Government	79lhd	....	....	....	....	....	....	....	....	1,114.1	1,214.6	1,341.9	....
Banks	79lid	....	....	....	....	....	....	....	....	—	—	—	....
Other Sectors	79ljd	....	....	....	....	....	....	....	....	—	—	—	....
Government Finance					*Millions of Leones: Year Ending December 31*								
Deficit (-) or Surplus	80	−17,099	−26,123	−39,835	−49,925	−48,300	† −47,724	−102,373	−124,064	−165,349	−163,447	−130,816	−70,273
Revenue	81	54,294	67,414	61,743	69,713	85,498	† 77,199	85,819	152,174	207,879	238,689	287,657	356,966
Grants Received	81z	7,302	11,117	5,734	8,529	9,495	† 22,456	65,391	106,107	86,143	161,355	179,343	259,376
Expenditure	82	78,695	104,654	107,312	128,167	143,293	† 147,052	252,884	370,697	455,922	562,267	597,999	688,092
Lending Minus Repayments	83	—	—	—	—	—	† 327	699	11,648	3,449	1,224	−183	−1,477
Financing													
Domestic	84a	61	−1,681	2,431	25,270	7,488	† 47,784	88,807	11,679	53,135	22,095	88,405	−1,949
Foreign	85a	17,037	27,804	37,404	24,655	40,812	† −60	13,566	112,385	106,204	157,768	56,133	122,171
Other Financing	84d	....	....	....	....	....	....	....	....	6,010	−16,416	−13,722	−49,949
Debt: Domestic	88a	18,164	24,311	26,007	41,613	52,368	† 133,201	231,666	232,663	288,477	347,178	413,683	435,935
Debt: Foreign	89a	408,626	444,894	656,205	966,326	941,853	† 1,840,991	2,755,965	2,153,630	3,120,009	3,268,965	4,196,338	4,900,305

Sierra Leone   724

		1993	1994	1995	1996	1997	1998	1999	2000	2001	2002	2003	2004
National Accounts						*Millions of Leones: Year Ending December 31*							
Househ.Cons.Expend.,incl.NPISHs....	96f	372,262	436,876	566,824	709,799	734,139	887,613	1,040,868	1,142,681	1,398,461	1,528,299	1,713,929	....
Government Consumption Expend...	91f	44,067	54,247	57,869	84,873	85,954	107,236	119,746	134,374	255,265	325,223	353,541	....
Gross Fixed Capital Formation..........	93e	21,475	43,901	37,011	78,163	41,765	59,204	52,885	84,761	90,091	114,690	322,945	....
Changes in Inventories....................	93i	−3,687	2,507	−914	8,689	−5,460	−1,427	−10,856	1,143	—	—	—	....
Exports of Goods and Services..........	90c	93,754	106,848	129,878	171,391	165,415	203,345	225,868	230,179	228,694	293,879	323,534	....
Imports of Goods and Services (-).....	98c	95,254	109,853	133,973	177,254	192,770	206,062	229,815	261,561	484,986	618,709	850,982	....
Gross Domestic Product (GDP)........	99b	436,304	535,019	657,604	867,072	834,502	1,051,335	1,207,721	1,330,319	1,600,169	1,964,627	2,323,668	2,894,326
Net Primary Income from Abroad.....	98.n	−61,324	−70,868	−78,196	−81,853	−92,289	−110,746	−144,985	−165,955	−129,157	−187,167	−194,998	....
Gross National Income (GNI)...........	99a	400,273	473,474	626,173	773,754	725,680	817,068	1,128,867	....	....	....	....	....
Consumption of Fixed Capital..........	99cf	27,206	34,212	37,470	39,424	71,392	59,226	69,422	49,047	....	....	....	....
GDP Volume 1989/90 Prices...........	99b.p	82,677	81,066	74,583	79,128	65,205	64,658	59,407	61,669	72,874	92,886	101,513	108,986
GDP Volume (2000=100)...............	99bvp	134.1	131.5	120.9	128.3	105.7	104.8	96.3	100.0	118.2	150.6	164.6	176.7
GDP Deflator (2000=100)...............	99bip	24.5	30.6	40.9	50.8	59.3	75.4	94.2	100.0	101.8	98.0	106.1	123.1
						Millions: Midyear Estimates							
Population...............................	99z	4.12	4.12	4.14	4.17	4.21	4.28	4.38	4.51	4.68	4.89	5.12	5.34

		1993	1994	1995	1996	1997	1998	1999	2000	2001	2002	2003	2004
Exchange Rates						*Singapore Dollars per SDR: End of Period*							
Market Rate	aa	2.2087	2.1324	2.1023	2.0129	2.2607	2.3380	2.2866	2.2560	2.3262	2.3608	2.5273	2.5373
						Singapore Dollars per US Dollar: End of Period (ae) Period Average (rf)							
Market Rate	ae	1.6080	1.4607	1.4143	1.3998	1.6755	1.6605	1.6660	1.7315	1.8510	1.7365	1.7008	1.6338
Market Rate	rf	1.6158	1.5274	1.4174	1.4100	1.4848	1.6736	1.6950	1.7240	1.7917	1.7906	1.7422	1.6902
						Index Numbers (2000=100): Period Averages							
Market Rate	ahx	106.7	113.0	121.6	122.2	116.4	103.1	101.7	100.0	96.2	96.3	98.9	102.0
Nominal Effective Exchange Rate	nec	92.0	95.6	98.5	103.1	105.7	105.0	99.7	100.0	101.4	100.5	96.8	95.5
Real Effective Exchange Rate	rec	99.4	103.2	104.9	108.5	110.6	106.5	99.7	100.0	100.8	98.0	93.9	92.8
Fund Position						*Millions of SDRs: End of Period*							
Quota	2f.s	357.6	357.6	357.6	357.6	357.6	357.6	862.5	862.5	862.5	862.5	862.5	862.5
SDRs	1b.s	56.9	24.1	33.1	42.5	52.2	64.9	89.2	105.3	119.6	130.2	139.6	188.9
Reserve Position in the Fund	1c.s	157.4	172.8	199.8	204.7	248.4	297.6	303.4	237.7	297.5	351.3	379.3	283.4
of which: Outstg.Fund Borrowing..	2c	—	—	—	—	—	31.3	—	—	—	—	—	—
Total Fund Cred.&Loans Outstg	2tl	—	—	—	—	—	—	—	—	—	—	—	—
International Liquidity						*Millions of US Dollars Unless Otherwise Indicated: End of Period*							
Total Reserves (see notes)	1l.d	48,361	58,177	68,695	76,847	71,289	74,928	76,843	80,132	75,375	82,021	95,746	112,232
SDRs	1b.d	78	35	49	61	70	91	122	137	150	177	207	293
Reserve Position in the Fund	1c.d	216	252	297	294	335	419	416	310	374	478	564	440
Foreign Exchange	1d.d	48,066	57,890	68,349	76,491	70,883	74,418	76,304	79,685	74,851	81,367	94,975	111,498
Monetary Authorities: Other Liab..	4..d	299	298	262	247	164	150	792	834	731	714	741	917
Deposit Money Banks: Assets	7a.d	31,345	38,992	39,115	43,079	46,963	44,434	52,703	47,567	52,976	53,501	52,827	61,848
Liabilities	7b.d	32,085	40,976	46,753	55,327	62,784	49,747	50,414	54,193	56,062	58,287	59,840	67,696
Other Banking Insts.: Assets	7e.d	124	163	168	154	124	107	80	75	51	43	16	17
Liabilities	7f.d	10	27	19	12	11	5	8	4	2	2	1	1
ACU: Foreign Assets	7k.d	306,703	326,698	373,774	396,655	425,242	394,550	364,733	360,440	339,255	346,865	359,009	403,436
Foreign Liabilities	7m.d	321,390	340,295	391,907	419,343	447,032	417,127	384,962	386,812	375,951	387,285	404,383	464,025
Monetary Authorities						*Millions of Singapore Dollars: End of Period*							
Foreign Assets	11	77,867	85,166	97,337	107,751	119,617	124,584	128,457	139,260	139,942	142,721	163,190	183,844
Claims on Central Government	12a	—	—	—	—	—	—	—	5,250	6,251	5,808	6,395	7,039
Reserve Money	14	14,669	15,577	17,040	18,189	19,200	16,641	21,395	18,471	20,032	19,964	20,653	21,835
of which: Currency Outside DMBs..	14a	8,942	9,420	9,907	10,293	10,704	10,146	11,315	11,289	11,868	12,360	12,838	13,694
Foreign Liabilities	16c	481	435	371	346	274	249	1,319	1,444	1,353	1,240	1,261	1,498
Central Government Deposits	16d	30,080	35,669	44,471	51,554	57,520	57,484	58,994	69,958	85,106	94,404	94,391	98,497
Other Items (Net)	17r	32,637	33,485	35,455	37,662	42,623	50,210	46,749	54,637	39,702	32,921	53,280	69,053
Deposit Money Banks						*Millions of Singapore Dollars: End of Period*							
Reserves	20	5,770	6,150	7,152	7,900	8,498	6,423	10,076	7,174	8,199	7,633	7,798	8,173
Foreign Assets	21	50,402	56,956	55,321	60,302	78,687	73,782	87,803	82,363	98,058	92,905	89,848	101,048
Claims on Central Government	22a	12,758	13,568	15,754	17,538	18,883	26,477	30,949	33,719	40,512	42,621	45,556	45,058
Claims on Private Sector	22d	79,282	91,375	109,885	127,272	143,409	154,844	150,199	159,083	185,048	169,048	178,253	186,128
Demand Deposits	24	13,940	13,991	15,443	16,747	16,807	17,093	19,794	21,973	24,215	23,468	25,884	30,468
Time and Savings Deposits	25	59,248	70,569	76,618	84,911	95,933	133,545	143,365	137,636	144,826	144,480	156,106	162,816
Foreign Liabilities	26c	51,592	59,854	66,123	77,447	105,194	82,605	83,990	93,836	103,771	101,215	101,776	110,602
Central Government Deposits	26d	6,385	6,584	7,538	6,896	1,529	1,766	1,632	1,465	2,089	1,768	1,813	1,847
Other Items (Net)	27r	17,047	17,051	22,390	27,011	30,014	26,517	30,246	27,429	56,916	41,276	35,876	34,674
Monetary Survey						*Millions of Singapore Dollars: End of Period*							
Foreign Assets (Net)	31n	76,196	81,833	86,164	90,260	92,836	115,512	130,951	126,343	132,876	133,172	150,001	172,792
Domestic Credit	32	55,583	62,699	73,638	86,368	103,251	122,081	120,535	126,640	144,625	121,310	134,001	137,881
Claims on Central Govt. (Net)	32an	−23,707	−28,685	−36,255	−40,912	−40,166	−32,773	−29,677	−32,454	−40,432	−47,743	−44,253	−48,247
Claims on Private Sector	32d	79,290	91,384	109,893	127,280	143,417	154,854	150,212	159,094	185,057	169,052	178,254	186,129
Money	34	22,882	23,411	25,350	27,040	27,511	27,239	31,109	33,262	36,083	35,828	38,722	44,162
Quasi-Money	35	59,248	70,569	76,618	84,911	95,933	133,545	143,365	137,636	144,826	144,480	156,106	162,816
Other Items (Net)	37r	49,649	50,552	57,834	64,677	72,643	76,809	77,012	82,085	96,592	74,173	89,173	103,696
Money plus Quasi-Money	35l	82,130	93,980	101,968	111,951	123,444	160,784	174,474	170,898	180,909	180,308	194,828	206,978
Other Banking Institutions													
Finance Companies						*Millions of Singapore Dollars: End of Period*							
Cash	40	1,788	2,574	2,848	2,561	2,513	2,822	3,046	2,017	1,514	1,608	475	622
Foreign Assets	41	200	238	237	215	208	179	133	130	95	75	27	28
Claims on Private Sector	42d	12,047	15,110	16,717	17,073	18,034	16,891	15,751	15,880	11,919	10,752	6,632	6,854
Time and Savings Deposits	45	10,558	13,753	15,435	15,058	15,734	15,421	14,387	13,653	10,638	9,853	5,528	5,666
Foreign Liabilities	46c	17	39	26	16	18	9	14	6	4	3	2	2
Capital Accounts	47a	1,850	2,203	2,621	3,015	3,269	3,371	3,408	3,165	2,426	2,111	1,406	1,444
Other Items (Net)	47r	1,611	1,927	1,720	1,760	1,734	1,091	1,121	1,203	461	468	198	392
Post Office: Savings Deposits	45..i	20,085	20,127	22,188	24,734	25,130	....	....	....	....	....	....	....
Nonbank Financial Institutions						*Millions of Singapore Dollars: End of Period*							
Cash	40..s	1,160	1,772	2,269	2,657	3,041	3,809	4,036	3,796	4,057	4,081	4,049	4,375
Foreign Assets	41..s	1,160	1,090	1,546	2,082	2,055	2,696	3,574	7,254	10,926	12,880	16,809	17,779
Claims on Central Government	42a.s	1,190	918	901	746	815	933	2,417	3,169	6,100	8,280	10,247	13,068
Claims on Private Sector	42d.s	4,270	5,488	6,715	8,261	10,095	10,392	16,333	18,555	24,525	25,592	29,354	33,888
Fixed Assets	42h.s	313	335	657	1,173	1,377	1,861	1,874	1,868	1,891	2,342	2,344	2,172
Incr.in Total Assets(Within Per.)	49z.s	1,944	1,682	2,481	2,996	2,379	2,564	8,170	6,244	13,148	6,098	9,595	8,217
Money (National Definitions)						*Millions of Singapore Dollars: End of Period*							
M1	59ma	22,882	23,412	25,349	27,040	27,511	27,239	31,109	33,262	36,083	35,828	38,723	44,162
M2	59mb	82,130	93,981	101,967	111,951	123,443	160,784	174,474	170,898	180,909	180,308	194,829	206,978
M3	59mc	111,369	125,835	136,737	148,495	160,766	173,581	186,184	182,913	190,317	188,815	200,044	212,183
Interest Rates						*Percent Per Annum*							
Money Market Rate	60b	2.50	3.68	2.56	2.93	4.35	5.00	2.04	2.57	1.99	.96	.74	1.04
Treasury Bill Rate	60c	.92	1.94	1.05	1.38	2.32	2.12	1.12	2.18	1.69	.81	.64	.96
Eurodollar Rate in Singapore	60d	3.33	4.86	6.04	5.52	5.75	5.53	5.42	6.55	3.66	1.80	1.22	1.67
Savings Rate	60k	1.62	2.31	2.81	2.72	2.75	3.11	1.37	1.33	1.16	.61	.28	.23
Deposit Rate	60l	2.30	3.00	3.50	3.41	3.47	4.60	1.68	1.71	1.54	.91	.51	.41
Lending Rate	60p	5.39	5.88	6.37	6.26	6.32	7.44	5.80	5.83	5.66	5.37	5.31	5.30

Singapore 576

		1993	1994	1995	1996	1997	1998	1999	2000	2001	2002	2003	2004
Prices, Production, Labor						*Index Numbers (2000=100): Period Averages*							
Share Prices	62	74.7	92.3	87.2	96.5	89.1	59.6	95.2	100.0	80.7	76.6	73.0	93.5
Wholesale Prices	63	93.1	92.7	92.7	92.8	91.8	†89.0	90.8	100.0	98.4	†97.0	98.9	104.0
Consumer Prices	64	91.2	94.0	95.6	97.0	98.9	98.6	98.7	100.0	101.0	100.6	101.1	†102.8
Manufacturing Production	66ey	56.7	64.1	†70.7	73.0	76.4	†76.1	86.7	100.0	88.4	95.9	†98.6	112.2
						Number in Thousands: Period Averages							
Labor Force	67d	1,636	1,693	1,748	1,801	1,876	1,932	1,976	2,193	2,120	2,129	2,152	....
Employment	67e	1,592	1,649	1,702	1,748	1,831	1,870	1,886	2,095	2,047	2,017	2,034	....
Unemployment	67c	1	1	1	2	3	4	6	4	6	12	16	....
Unemployment Rate (%)	67r	2.7	2.6	2.7	3.0	2.4	3.2	4.6	4.4	3.4	5.2	5.4	....
Intl. Transactions & Positions						*Millions of Singapore Dollars*							
Exports	70	119,475	147,327	167,515	176,271	185,613	183,763	194,290	237,826	218,029	223,901	251,096	303,476
Imports, c.i.f.	71	137,602	156,397	176,317	185,183	196,606	174,867	188,143	232,176	207,694	208,312	222,811	276,894
						2000=100							
Volume of Exports	72	48.0	61.7	71.4	75.9	81.1	†81.9	86.4	100.0	95.3	†100.1	116.5	140.5
Volume of Imports	73	62.0	71.2	80.4	85.4	92.0	†83.5	88.3	100.0	89.2	....	....	....
Export Prices (Survey)	76	104.6	100.3	98.6	97.7	96.2	†94.4	94.6	100.0	96.2	†94.0	90.6	90.8
Import Prices (Survey)	76.x	95.5	94.5	94.5	93.4	92.0	†90.3	91.8	100.0	100.3	†99.6	100.0	101.6
Balance of Payments						*Millions of US Dollars: Minus Sign Indicates Debit*							
Current Account, n.i.e.	78ald	4,211	11,400	14,708	13,898	14,962	18,578	15,291	13,257	16,086	18,909	28,183	....
Goods: Exports f.o.b.	78aad	77,858	97,919	129,557	137,495	138,716	117,717	124,468	149,228	133,744	137,429	157,853	....
Goods: Imports f.o.b.	78abd	-80,582	-96,565	-123,105	-130,310	-132,207	-104,306	-112,026	-136,505	-118,035	-117,526	-128,530	....
Trade Balance	78acd	-2,724	1,354	6,452	7,186	6,509	13,411	12,442	12,723	15,709	19,903	29,323	....
Services: Credit	78add	18,597	23,044	27,832	29,195	28,080	23,570	26,372	29,404	29,105	29,993	30,715	....
Services: Debit	78aed	-11,321	-13,898	-20,819	-22,305	-22,298	-19,681	-24,282	-27,432	-28,382	-29,750	-29,579	....
Balance on Goods & Services	78afd	4,552	10,500	13,465	14,076	12,291	17,299	14,532	14,695	16,433	20,146	30,458	....
Income: Credit	78agd	8,075	9,783	12,512	11,997	13,257	12,248	16,232	16,028	14,276	13,796	13,415	....
Income: Debit	78ahd	-7,880	-8,222	-10,380	-11,116	-9,427	-9,869	-14,461	-16,346	-13,504	-13,946	-14,545	....
Balance on Gds, Serv. & Inc.	78aid	4,747	12,061	15,598	14,957	16,122	19,679	16,302	14,377	17,205	19,996	29,328	....
Current Transfers, n.i.e.: Credit	78ajd	140	145	160	161	153	131	135	128	122	126	129	....
Current Transfers: Debit	78akd	-676	-806	-1,050	-1,220	-1,312	-1,231	-1,146	-1,248	-1,241	-1,213	-1,273	....
Capital Account, n.i.e.	78bcd	-71	-84	-73	-139	-190	-226	-191	-163	-161	-160	-168	....
Capital Account, n.i.e.: Credit	78bad	—	—	—	—	—	—	—	—	—	—	—	....
Capital Account: Debit	78bbd	-71	-84	-73	-139	-190	-226	-191	-163	-161	-160	-168	....
Financial Account, n.i.e.	78bjd	-1,212	-8,841	-1,071	-7,926	-11,512	-17,785	-14,186	-5,751	-14,381	-13,558	-25,089	....
Direct Investment Abroad	78bdd	-2,152	-4,557	-4,463	-7,650	-12,427	-3,015	-7,517	-5,296	-17,137	-3,711	-5,537	....
Dir. Invest. in Rep. Econ., n.i.e.	78bed	4,686	8,550	11,619	9,137	13,547	7,628	16,058	17,220	15,003	5,653	11,431	....
Portfolio Investment Assets	78bfd	-7,833	-7,840	-6,927	-13,149	-14,881	-10,023	-12,376	-13,165	-10,422	-10,369	-11,265	....
Equity Securities	78bkd	-7,555	-7,414	-7,546	-10,337	-12,387	-5,631	-12,863	-8,128	-6,926	-6,010	-5,783	....
Debt Securities	78bld	-278	-426	620	-2,812	-2,493	-4,392	487	-5,037	-3,496	-4,360	-5,482	....
Portfolio Investment Liab., n.i.e.	78bgd	2,867	114	-239	1,027	-458	788	3,522	-1,832	471	-762	363	....
Equity Securities	78bmd	2,759	169	-187	1,039	-466	783	3,536	-1,836	446	-815	303	....
Debt Securities	78bnd	108	-55	-52	-12	8	5	-14	4	25	53	59	....
Financial Derivatives Assets	78bwd	....	....	....	....	....	....	....	....	....	....	....	....
Financial Derivatives Liabilities	78bxd	....	....	....	....	....	....	....	....	....	....	....	....
Other Investment Assets	78bhd	-7,104	-10,999	-11,266	-12,003	-38,283	-3,126	-20,059	-15,768	-6,709	-7,934	-18,792	....
Monetary Authorities	78bod	—	—	—	—	—	—	—	—	—	—	—	....
General Government	78bpd	—	—	—	—	—	—	—	—	—	—	—	....
Banks	78bqd	769	-4,291	1,163	-3,359	-12,289	2,200	-9,859	1,969	-9,822	1,074	10,760	....
Other Sectors	78brd	-7,872	-6,708	-12,428	-8,645	-25,994	-5,326	-10,200	-17,737	3,113	-9,007	-29,551	....
Other Investment Liab., n.i.e.	78bid	8,324	5,911	10,204	14,712	40,990	-10,038	6,186	13,092	4,413	3,565	-1,289	....
Monetary Authorities	78bsd	—	—	—	—	—	—	—	—	—	—	—	....
General Government	78btd	-9	-4	—	—	—	—	—	—	—	—	—	....
Banks	78bud	1,949	5,409	3,970	8,102	18,878	-11,082	3,155	7,702	8,219	-340	-10,775	....
Other Sectors	78bvd	6,384	506	6,235	6,611	22,112	1,044	3,031	5,390	-3,806	3,906	9,486	....
Net Errors and Omissions	78cad	4,650	2,261	-4,923	1,565	4,853	2,422	3,275	-593	-2,411	-3,863	3,747	....
Overall Balance	78cbd	7,578	4,736	8,641	7,399	8,114	2,989	4,188	6,751	-867	1,327	6,675	....
Reserves and Related Items	79dad	-7,578	-4,736	-8,641	-7,399	-8,114	-2,989	-4,188	-6,751	867	-1,327	-6,675	....
Reserve Assets	79dbd	-7,578	-4,736	-8,641	-7,399	-8,114	-2,989	-4,188	-6,751	867	-1,327	-6,675	....
Use of Fund Credit and Loans	79dcd	—	—	—	—	—	—	—	—	—	—	—	....
Exceptional Financing	79ded	....	....	—	—	—	—	—	—	—	—	—	....
International Investment Position						*Millions of US Dollars*							
Assets	79aad	....	....	....	....	....	....	....	....	372,949	412,051	450,587	....
Direct Investment Abroad	79abd	....	....	....	....	....	....	....	....	83,084	92,531	100,028	....
Portfolio Investment	79acd	....	....	....	....	....	....	....	....	57,788	65,953	76,584	....
Equity Securities	79add	....	....	....	....	....	....	....	....	30,662	32,643	36,485	....
Debt Securities	79aed	....	....	....	....	....	....	....	....	27,126	33,310	40,098	....
Financial Derivatives	79ald	....	....	....	....	....	....	....	....	—	—	—	....
Other Investment	79afd	32,963	....	....	....	....	....	....	....	156,474	171,378	178,026	....
Monetary Authorities	79agd	....	....	....	....	....	....	....	....	....	....	....	....
General Government	79ahd	....	....	....	....	....	....	....	....	....	....	....	....
Banks	79aid	....	....	....	....	....	....	....	....	....	....	....	....
Other Sectors	79ajd	....	....	....	....	....	....	....	....	....	....	....	....
Reserve Assets	79akd	48,361	....	....	....	....	....	....	....	75,604	82,189	95,949	....
Liabilities	79lad	....	....	....	....	....	....	....	....	318,300	344,151	374,545	....
Dir. Invest. in Rep. Economy	79lbd	....	....	....	....	....	....	....	....	140,278	155,231	170,818	....
Portfolio Investment	79lcd	....	....	....	....	....	....	....	....	46,198	44,771	60,119	....
Equity Securities	79ldd	....	....	....	....	....	....	....	....	36,252	33,868	45,752	....
Debt Securities	79led	....	....	....	....	....	....	....	....	9,946	10,904	14,367	....
Financial Derivatives	79ljd	....	....	....	....	....	....	....	....	—	—	—	....
Other Investment	79lfd	32,203	....	....	....	....	....	....	....	131,824	144,149	143,608	....
Monetary Authorities	79lgd	1	....	....	....	....	....	....	....	....	....	....	....
General Government	79lhd	....	....	....	....	....	....	....	....	....	....	....	....
Banks	79lid	32,145	....	....	....	....	....	....	....	....	....	....	....
Other Sectors	79ljd	....	....	....	....	....	....	....	....	....	....	....	....

Singapore 576

		1993	1994	1995	1996	1997	1998	1999	2000	2001	2002	2003	2004
Government Finance		*Millions of Singapore Dollars: Year Ending December 31*											
Deficit (-) or Surplus........................	80	12,998	13,086	15,870	18,868	13,612	23,163	14,577	18,094	−467	−2,595	10,422	10,128
Total Revenue and Grants..............	81y	29,488	33,094	40,026	47,617	57,048	59,724	49,950	52,255	35,393	27,703	33,108	35,269
Revenue......................................	81	29,488	33,094	40,026	47,617	57,048	59,724	49,950	52,255	35,393	27,703	33,108	35,269
Grants...	81z	—	—	—	—	—	—	—	—	—	—	—	—
Exp. & Lending Minus Repay..........	82z	16,490	20,008	24,156	28,749	43,436	36,561	35,373	34,161	35,860	30,298	22,686	25,141
Expenditure................................	82	14,339	15,670	17,419	20,681	29,222	25,586	26,665	30,068	34,957	30,985	28,635	30,479
Lending Minus Repayments.........	83	2,151	4,338	6,737	8,068	14,214	10,975	8,708	4,093	903	−687	−5,948	−5,337
Total Financing...............................	80h	−12,998	−13,086	−15,870	−18,868	−13,612	−23,163	−14,577	−18,093	467	2,595	−10,422	−10,128
Total Net Borrowing......................	84	5,309	12,552	16,402	10,159	12,215	22,540	17,148	16,487	8,084	137	13,170	16,119
Use of Cash Balances....................	87	−18,307	−25,638	−32,272	−29,027	−25,827	−45,703	−31,725	−34,580	−7,617	2,458	−23,592	−26,246
Total Debt by Currency...................	88z	69,944	75,467	86,630	94,831	102,372	115,183	125,777	134,370	146,996	156,751	169,332	186,598
National..	88b	....	....	....	94,831	102,372	115,183	125,777	134,370	146,996	156,751	169,332	186,598
Foreign...	89b	....	....	....	—	—	—	—	—	—	—	—	—
National Accounts		*Millions of Singapore Dollars*											
Househ.Cons.Expend.,incl.NPISHs....	96f	42,232	47,183	49,085	52,377	56,119	52,906	57,215	65,214	67,478	69,431	69,713	76,276
Government Consumption Expend...	91f	8,723	9,008	10,124	12,207	13,179	13,882	14,007	17,414	18,677	19,532	18,979	19,193
Gross Fixed Capital Formation..........	93e	32,753	36,202	39,782	49,378	54,826	51,535	47,092	47,538	45,577	40,187	39,012	43,322
Changes in Inventories...................	93i	2,505	−500	865	−2,850	760	−7,219	−2,352	4,261	−5,561	−4,152	−15,124	−10,284
Exports (Net).................................	90n	7,356	16,039	19,107	19,808	18,149	28,490	23,788	23,837	27,878	33,920	51,438	53,584
Gross Domestic Product (GDP)........	99b	94,289	107,851	118,963	129,932	141,626	137,329	139,897	159,596	153,771	158,388	160,924	180,554
Net Primary Income from Abroad.....	98.n	315	2,384	3,027	1,238	5,674	3,971	2,978	−1,280	27	−3,778	−2,500	−4,528
Gross National Income (GNI)............	99a	94,604	110,235	121,990	131,170	147,300	141,299	142,875	158,316	153,798	154,610	158,423	176,026
GDP Volume 1995 Prices................	99b.p	98,838	110,109	118,963	128,679	139,696	138,637	148,108	162,379	159,212	164,255	166,492	180,496
GDP Volume (2000=100)................	99bvp	60.9	67.8	73.3	79.2	86.0	85.4	91.2	100.0	98.0	101.2	102.5	111.2
GDP Deflator (2000=100)...............	99bip	97.1	99.7	101.7	102.7	103.1	100.8	96.1	100.0	98.3	98.1	98.3	101.8
		Millions: Midyear Estimates											
Population...............................	99z	3.27	3.37	3.48	3.59	3.70	3.82	3.92	4.02	4.10	4.16	4.22	4.27

Slovak Republic   936

		1993	1994	1995	1996	1997	1998	1999	2000	2001	2002	2003	2004
Exchange Rates						*Koruny per SDR: End of Period*							
Official Rate	aa	45.605	45.660	43.954	45.864	46.930	51.975	58.011	61.744	60.910	54.430	49.000	44.255
						Koruny per US Dollar: End of Period (ae) Period Average (rf)							
Official Rate	ae	33.202	31.277	29.569	31.895	34.782	36.913	42.266	47.389	48.467	40.036	32.975	28.496
Official Rate	rf	30.770	32.045	29.713	30.654	33.616	35.233	41.363	46.035	48.355	45.327	36.773	32.257
						Index Numbers (2000=100): Period Averages							
Nominal Effective Exchange Rate	nec	109.64	105.19	105.90	106.60	111.99	109.66	98.86	100.00	95.54	92.26	86.81	82.22
Real Effective Exchange Rate	rec	88.24	89.14	91.66	91.38	95.90	93.80	91.61	100.00	99.00	96.97	98.03	97.39
Fund Position						*Millions of SDRs: End of Period*							
Quota	2f.s	257.4	257.4	257.4	257.4	257.4	257.4	357.5	357.5	357.5	357.5	357.5	357.5
SDRs	1b.s	.3	58.9	39.0	11.2	19.6	1.2	.6	.4	.5	.8	.9	.9
Reserve Position in the Fund	1c.s	—	—	—	—	—	—	—	—	—	—	—	—
Total Fund Cred.&Loans Outstg.	2tl	405.2	439.8	307.5	222.0	184.4	134.6	96.5	—	—	—	—	—
International Liquidity					*Millions of US Dollars Unless Otherwise Indicated: End of Period*								
Total Reserves minus Gold	1l.d	416	1,691	3,364	3,419	3,230	2,869	3,371	4,022	4,141	8,809	11,678	14,417
SDRs	1b.d	—	86	58	16	26	2	1	—	1	1	1	1
Reserve Position in the Fund	1c.d	—	—	—	—	—	—	—	—	—	—	—	—
Foreign Exchange	1d.d	415	1,605	3,306	3,403	3,204	2,867	3,370	4,022	4,140	8,808	11,677	14,416
Gold (Million Fine Troy Ounces)	1ad	1.290	1.290	1.290	1.290	1.290	1.290	1.290	1.290	1.129	1.129	1.129	1.129
Gold (National Valuation)	1and	76	80	85	79	72	68	59	53	45	55	67	77
Monetary Authorities:Other Assets	3..d	98	153	171	129	202	609	564	203	762	657	367	3,397
Other Liab.	4..d	1,040	1,355	1,428	1,351	659	1,578	760	355	463	299	† 1,100	3,102
Deposit Money Banks: Assets	7a.d	987	1,427	1,823	2,514	3,618	3,794	1,618	2,346	2,390	2,053	† 2,324	2,871
Liabilities	7b.d	425	499	979	2,160	2,851	2,628	643	644	845	1,498	† 3,141	5,822
Monetary Authorities						*Millions of Koruny: End of Period*							
Foreign Assets	11	19,557	60,184	107,032	115,665	121,904	130,881	168,820	202,763	239,806	381,180	† 399,377	509,823
Claims on Central Government	12a	46,476	46,456	25,743	30,068	5,495	9,067	1,778	—	—	—	† 7,700	—
Claims on Other Resident Sectors	12d	355	305	189	327	416	509	481	382	346	286	† 10,617	7,673
Claims on Banking Institutions	12e	40,654	36,143	36,485	36,585	41,340	55,242	40,225	36,236	37,802	15,073	† 8,067	4,768
Reserve Money	14	39,006	48,319	63,208	81,339	96,134	90,768	108,925	113,310	138,902	141,201	† 130,898	131,960
of which: Currency Outside Bls.	14a	25,122	28,101	34,536	43,505	48,740	49,759	57,472	67,048	80,963	84,211	† 91,826	100,450
Other Liabilities to Banking Insts.	14n	488	225	13,324	1,833	2,682	3,369	15,191	118,534	56,572	126,826	† 105,683	218,895
Other Deposits	15	9	25	60	131	117	86	364	545	739	1,636	† 1,465	1,016
Foreign Liabilities	16c	52,997	62,454	55,736	53,259	31,559	65,244	37,727	16,813	22,427	11,979	† 36,277	88,388
Central Government Deposits	16d	6,458	11,726	16,152	18,060	16,558	11,650	25,526	27,725	31,162	115,434	† 116,378	83,783
Bonds	16n	....	....	....	....	....	....	....	....	....	....	55,760	59,725
Capital Accounts	17a	4,151	7,977	8,239	9,244	9,316	10,322	10,580	10,573	14,787	10,802	† −16,105	−53,828
Other Items (Net)	17r	3,933	12,362	12,730	18,779	12,791	14,261	12,991	−48,119	13,365	−11,340	† −4,596	−7,674
Banking Institutions						*Millions of Koruny: End of Period*							
Reserves	20	† 3,401	3,445	7,607	10,830	12,541	10,335	12,222	51,141	45,042	48,677	† 37,378	30,295
Other Claims on Monetary Author.	20n	10,560	16,211	21,433	28,798	37,564	32,406	41,428	† 26,320	51,366	84,719	† 161,470	274,495
Foreign Assets	21	† 32,773	44,634	53,916	80,189	125,842	140,045	68,402	111,169	115,818	82,200	† 76,619	81,812
Claims on Central Government	22a	28,798	50,693	74,653	89,709	112,716	93,002	76,936	113,360	301,964	289,192	† 258,052	283,139
Claims on Other General Govt.	22b	....	....	....	....	....	....	....	....	....	....	† 7,577	12,043
Claims on Other Resident Sectors	22d	234,292	201,643	211,839	280,307	† 399,242	420,986	460,428	479,203	379,653	435,123	† 379,002	406,270
Demand Deposits	24	† 90,742	94,931	113,179	129,528	116,651	96,863	95,586	118,916	144,603	160,560	† 261,072	303,057
Other Deposits	25	137,344	174,427	203,328	236,632	† 279,996	320,891	368,800	414,933	446,841	454,399	† 413,032	414,839
Bonds	26n	—	—	5,228	5,906	5,217	3,968	7,045	8,196	6,172	11,212	† 12,239	12,178
Foreign Liabilities	26c	† 13,762	14,909	28,342	68,212	98,410	95,367	25,815	28,616	39,167	54,736	† 103,566	165,916
Central Government Deposits	26d	9,458	12,151	25,436	33,197	31,917	28,018	23,248	34,230	41,446	42,246	† 12,117	41,610
Credit from Monetary Authorities	26g	† 41,204	37,705	38,406	40,224	51,606	61,528	40,741	37,402	30,661	13,016	† 7,913	4,737
Money Market Fund Shares	26m	....	....	....	....	....	....	....	....	....	....	....	32,872
Capital Accounts	27a	† 48,722	63,813	66,953	76,526	82,642	95,243	93,704	103,940	115,301	100,459	† 136,024	137,284
Other Items (Net)	27r	−32,313	−82,948	−116,453	−113,127	† 7,453	−18,724	−5,567	25,943	62,414	98,066	† −25,865	−24,441
Banking Survey						*Millions of Koruny: End of Period*							
Foreign Assets (Net)	31n	† −14,429	27,455	76,870	74,383	117,778	110,315	173,679	268,503	294,030	396,665	† 336,153	337,330
Domestic Credit	32	294,005	275,220	270,836	349,154	† 469,394	483,896	490,849	530,990	609,355	566,921	† 534,452	583,732
Claims on Central Govt. (Net)	32an	59,358	73,272	58,808	68,520	69,736	62,401	29,940	51,405	229,356	131,512	† 137,256	157,747
Claims on Other General Govt.	32b	....	....	....	....	....	....	....	....	....	....	† 7,577	12,043
Claims on Other Resident Sectors	32d	234,647	201,948	212,028	280,634	† 399,658	421,495	460,909	479,585	379,999	435,409	† 389,619	413,942
Money	34	† 116,615	123,820	149,657	173,350	165,658	146,833	153,058	185,964	225,566	244,771	† 353,971	404,722
Quasi-Money	35	137,353	174,452	203,388	236,763	† 280,113	320,977	369,164	415,478	447,580	456,035	† 414,497	415,855
Money Market Fund Shares	36m	....	....	....	....	....	....	....	....	....	....	....	32,872
Bonds	36n	564	952	9,642	17,952	18,474	15,939	15,709	15,319	11,645	11,212	† 67,999	71,902
Capital Accounts	37a	† 52,873	71,790	75,192	85,770	91,958	105,565	104,284	114,513	130,088	111,261	† 119,919	83,457
Other Items (Net)	37r	−28,170	−69,025	−90,788	−90,987	† 30,214	3,249	20,934	66,325	86,741	135,089	† −85,780	−87,745
Money plus Quasi-Money	35l	253,968	298,272	353,045	410,113	† 445,771	467,810	522,222	601,442	673,146	700,806	† 768,468	820,577
Interest Rates						*Percent Per Annum*							
Bank Rate (End of Period)	60	12.00	12.00	9.75	8.80	8.80	8.80	8.80	8.80	† 7.75	6.50	6.00	4.00
Money Market Rate	60b	....	....	....	....	....	....	....	8.08	7.76	6.33	6.08	3.82
Deposit Rate	60l	8.02	9.32	9.01	9.30	13.44	16.25	14.37	8.45	6.46	6.65	5.33	4.14
Lending Rate	60p	14.41	14.56	16.85	13.92	18.65	21.17	21.07	14.89	11.24	10.25	8.46	9.07
Government Bond Yield	61	....	....	....	....	....	....	....	8.34	8.06	6.91	4.99	5.02

		1993	1994	1995	1996	1997	1998	1999	2000	2001	2002	2003	2004
Prices, Production, Labor						*Index Numbers (2000=100): Period Averages*							
Producer Prices	63	65.1	71.6	78.1	† 81.3	85.0	87.7	91.1	100.0	† 106.6	108.8	117.9	121.9
Consumer Prices	64	54.1	61.3	67.4	† 71.3	75.7	80.7	89.3	100.0	† 107.3	110.9	120.4	129.5
Harmonized CPI (2002=100)	64h	....	....	....	....	....	....	....	....	....	100.0	108.5	116.4
Wages	65	47.1	55.1	62.9	71.3	80.7	87.5	93.9	100.0	108.2	118.2	125.7	138.4
Industrial Production	66	74.3	78.0	86.1	88.2	89.4	94.2	92.2	100.0	106.8	113.5	119.5	124.4
Employment	67	101.6	100.0	102.2	103.0	102.6	102.8	100.6	100.0	107.4	107.6	109.5	109.8
						Number in Thousands: Period Averages							
Labor Force	67d	2,509	2,511	2,481	....	2,473	....	2,558	2,594	2,634	2,623	2,629	....
Employment	67e	2	2,110	2,147	2,225	2,206	2,199	2,132	2,102	2,124	2,127	2,165	2,170
Unemployment	67c	—	334	325	278	297	317	417	485	508	487	459	481
Unemployment Rate (%)	67r	....	13.7	13.1	11.3	11.8	12.5	16.2	18.6	19.2	18.5	17.5	18.1
Intl. Transactions & Positions							*Millions of Koruny*						
Exports	70	168,114	214,375	255,096	270,643	277,434	377,807	423,648	548,527	611,325	652,018	803,238	889,703
Imports, c.i.f.	71	204,786	218,638	273,831	350,847	361,833	483,773	492,337	619,789	749,775	785,374	868,982	981,075
Imports, f.o.b.	71.v	195,034	211,811	260,791	340,903	345,006	460,736	468,892	590,275	714,071	747,975	827,602	934,357
Balance of Payments						*Millions of US Dollars: Minus Sign Indicates Debit*							
Current Account, n.i.e.	78ald	−580	671	390	−2,090	−1,961	−2,126	−1,155	−694	....	−1,955	−282	....
Goods: Exports f.o.b.	78aad	5,452	6,706	8,591	8,824	9,641	10,720	10,201	11,896	....	14,460	21,944	....
Goods: Imports f.o.b.	78abd	−6,365	−6,645	−8,820	−11,106	−11,725	−13,071	−11,310	−12,791	....	−16,626	−22,593	....
Trade Balance	78acd	−912	61	−229	−2,283	−2,084	−2,351	−1,109	−895	....	−2,166	−649	....
Services: Credit	78add	1,939	2,261	2,378	2,066	2,167	2,292	1,899	2,241	....	2,812	3,297	....
Services: Debit	78aed	−1,666	−1,600	−1,838	−2,028	−2,094	−2,276	−1,844	−1,805	....	−2,351	−3,056	....
Balance on Goods & Services	78afd	−640	722	311	−2,245	−2,011	−2,334	−1,054	−459	....	−1,705	−408	....
Income: Credit	78agd	185	155	250	224	315	437	268	268	....	342	907	....
Income: Debit	78ahd	−224	−275	−263	−270	−438	−595	−568	−623	....	−791	−1,026	....
Balance on Gds, Serv. & Inc.	78aid	−678	602	297	−2,291	−2,135	−2,492	−1,353	−814	....	−2,154	−527	....
Current Transfers, n.i.e.: Credit	78ajd	216	166	243	483	540	645	466	344	....	480	537	....
Current Transfers: Debit	78akd	−118	−98	−150	−282	−367	−279	−268	−224	....	−282	−292	....
Capital Account, n.i.e.	78bcd	564	84	46	30	—	70	158	91	....	110	102	....
Capital Account, n.i.e.: Credit	78bad	771	84	46	30	—	83	171	106	....	130	195	....
Capital Account: Debit	78bbd	−208	—	—	—	—	−12	−13	−15	....	−20	−93	....
Financial Account, n.i.e.	78bjd	−153	71	1,211	2,268	1,780	1,912	1,789	1,472	....	5,230	1,661	....
Direct Investment Abroad	78bdd	−61	−14	−10	−48	−95	−145	376	−22	....	−3	−24	....
Dir. Invest. in Rep. Econ., n.i.e.	78bed	199	270	236	351	174	562	354	2,052	....	4,104	559	....
Portfolio Investment Assets	78bfd	−774	−26	157	−12	−81	−57	247	−195	....	265	−742	....
Equity Securities	78bkd	−774	−26	174	69	86	33	2	11	....	1	−347	....
Debt Securities	78bld	....	—	−17	−81	−167	−91	246	−206	....	263	−395	....
Portfolio Investment Liab., n.i.e.	78bgd	465	304	53	29	93	841	405	1,016	....	289	168	....
Equity Securities	78bmd	465	111	−16	28	102	−35	47	−53	....	10	59	....
Debt Securities	78bnd	....	193	69	1	−10	876	358	1,069	....	279	109	....
Financial Derivatives Assets	78bwd	....	—	—	—	—	—	....	1	....	—	−43	....
Financial Derivatives Liabilities	78bxd	....	—	—	—	—	—	....	1	....	3	60	....
Other Investment Assets	78bhd	−412	−548	−116	−334	−1,028	190	1,713	−973	....	738	−20	....
Monetary Authorities	78bod	....	....	....	....	....	—	....	....	....	....	—	....
General Government	78bpd	232	−211	140	337	61	117	9	1	....	299	58	....
Banks	78bqd	−530	−344	−248	−662	−1,122	110	1,878	−748	....	569	114	....
Other Sectors	78brd	−114	7	−8	−10	33	−37	−174	−226	....	−130	−192	....
Other Investment Liab., n.i.e.	78bid	430	84	891	2,282	2,718	520	−1,307	−407	....	−165	1,703	....
Monetary Authorities	78bsd	—	38	42	52	153	55	14	−26	....	−198	618	....
General Government	78btd	145	−52	−173	−124	184	−321	55	149	....	−333	−30	....
Banks	78bud	99	38	463	1,440	1,084	−138	−1,882	30	....	390	1,260	....
Other Sectors	78bvd	186	60	559	914	1,298	924	506	−561	....	−23	−146	....
Net Errors and Omissions	78cad	183	380	144	162	280	−333	−14	51	....	298	27	....
Overall Balance	78cbd	14	1,205	1,791	370	99	−478	777	920	....	3,684	1,508	....
Reserves and Related Items	79dad	−14	−1,205	−1,791	−370	−99	478	−777	−920	....	−3,684	−1,508	....
Reserve Assets	79dbd	−104	−1,256	−1,590	−245	−47	545	−725	−794	....	−3,684	−1,508	....
Use of Fund Credit and Loans	79dcd	89	51	−201	−125	−52	−67	−52	−125	....	—	—	....
Exceptional Financing	79ded	....	....	....	....	....	....	....	....	....	—	—	....
International Investment Position							*Millions of US Dollars*						
Assets	79aad	....	8,421	10,156	10,311	10,648	10,322	8,652	10,089	10,535	14,680	19,479	....
Direct Investment Abroad	79abd	....	166	139	182	234	404	342	364	448	486	627	....
Portfolio Investment	79acd	....	429	259	282	330	406	146	336	858	686	1,786	....
Equity Securities	79add	....	424	234	171	71	35	28	15	19	42	447	....
Debt Securities	79aed	....	5	25	111	259	371	118	321	838	644	1,340	....
Financial Derivatives	79ald	....	—	—	—	—	—	—	—	—	—	59	....
Other Investment	79afd	....	5,633	5,896	5,948	6,461	6,267	4,419	5,006	4,769	4,313	4,878	....
Monetary Authorities	79agd	....	....	....	....	....	....	....	....	....	....	....	....
General Government	79ahd	....	2,947	2,928	2,393	2,136	1,897	1,657	1,484	1,465	1,101	1,248	....
Banks	79aid	....	1,451	1,676	2,276	3,141	3,203	1,526	2,186	2,002	1,660	1,538	....
Other Sectors	79ajd	....	1,234	1,291	1,280	1,185	1,167	1,236	1,335	1,301	1,552	2,092	....
Reserve Assets	79akd	....	2,192	3,862	3,898	3,623	3,244	3,745	4,384	4,461	9,196	12,129	....
Liabilities	79lad	....	6,137	7,316	9,769	11,848	14,656	13,200	14,368	15,956	20,513	28,183	....
Dir. Invest. in Rep. Economy	79lbd	....	897	1,297	2,046	2,083	2,890	3,188	4,504	5,582	8,530	11,864	....
Portfolio Investment	79lcd	....	583	608	563	595	1,549	2,039	2,830	2,878	3,323	4,166	....
Equity Securities	79ldd	....	56	43	62	157	102	341	260	401	509	493	....
Debt Securities	79led	....	527	565	500	438	1,447	1,698	2,570	2,477	2,814	3,673	....
Financial Derivatives	79lld	....	—	—	—	—	—	—	—	3	17	108	....
Other Investment	79lfd	....	4,657	5,411	7,161	9,170	10,217	7,974	7,034	7,493	8,644	12,046	....
Monetary Authorities	79lgd	....	682	537	442	507	536	522	324	266	435	1,144	....
General Government	79lhd	....	1,101	958	786	912	621	671	788	1,059	944	1,049	....
Banks	79lid	....	537	901	2,290	3,109	2,950	680	687	876	1,534	3,152	....
Other Sectors	79ljd	....	2,338	3,015	3,642	4,642	6,109	6,100	5,235	5,291	5,732	6,700	....

Slovak Republic   936

		1993	1994	1995	1996	1997	1998	1999	2000	2001	2002	2003	2004
Government Finance					*Millions of Koruny: Year Ending December 31*								
Deficit (-) or Surplus......................	80	....	....	....	−8,540	−28,430	−28,663	−26,637	−27,464	−32,012	110,172	−33,537	....
Total Revenue and Grants..............	81y	....	....	....	254,769	265,402	274,888	315,683	325,614	331,821	366,636	387,288	....
Revenue..	81	....	....	....	254,510	265,146	274,677	315,436	325,402	331,649	366,552	387,242	....
Grants...	81z	....	....	....	259	256	211	247	212	172	84	46	....
Exp. & Lending Minus Repay..........	82z	....	....	....	263,309	293,832	303,551	342,320	353,078	363,833	256,464	420,825	....
Expenditure.................................	82	....	....	....	266,814	290,026	303,952	317,447	368,407	366,901	434,127	438,960	....
Lending Minus Repayments..........	83	....	....	....	−3,505	3,806	−401	24,873	−15,329	−3,068	−177,663	−18,135	....
Total Financing..............................	80h	....	....	....	8,540	28,430	28,663	26,637	27,464	32,012	−110,172	33,537	....
Domestic.....................................	84a	....	....	....	12,761	21,518	−6,057	−2,112	−681	24,080	−104,078	36,489	....
Foreign..	85a	....	....	....	−4,221	6,912	34,720	28,749	28,145	7,932	....	−2,952	....
Total Debt by Residence..................	88	....	....	....	153,910	194,125	215,605	238,061	274,870	417,450	399,947	439,097	....
Domestic.....................................	88a	....	....	....	120,741	144,581	141,813	133,625	137,849	293,003	289,132	335,130	....
Foreign..	89a	....	....	....	33,169	49,544	73,792	104,436	137,021	124,447	110,815	103,967	....
National Accounts							*Millions of Koruny*						
Househ.Cons.Expend.,incl.NPISHs....	96f	227,835	260,998	300,439	340,419	380,935	429,243	480,727	524,196	582,522	633,563	678,075	750,606
Government Consumption Expend...	91f	99,877	102,846	118,427	143,290	153,250	169,808	167,358	184,796	203,416	219,855	239,588	257,379
Gross Fixed Capital Formation..........	93e	123,374	131,819	144,248	205,846	243,539	281,774	249,792	242,277	291,027	303,481	308,404	327,226
Changes in Inventories...................	93i	−21,970	−27,884	−1,064	15,989	2,628	−16,120	−17,094	1,864	11,952	18,882	−2,879	21,869
Exports of Goods and Services..........	90c	233,214	296,372	336,007	345,557	405,319	466,740	518,078	661,511	741,008	788,245	933,235	1,018,011
Imports of Goods and Services (-)....	98c	250,964	268,502	321,590	412,667	472,995	550,048	554,821	684,402	823,451	866,301	951,121	1,053,626
Gross Domestic Product (GDP).........	99b	411,366	495,649	576,502	638,449	712,679	781,437	844,108	934,079	1,009,839	1,098,658	1,201,196	1,325,486
GDP Volume 1995 Prices.................	99b.p	512,849	544,674	576,502	611,935	640,151	667,107	676,919	690,697	716,845	749,937	783,406	826,493
GDP Volume (2000=100)...............	99bvp	74.3	78.9	83.5	88.6	92.7	96.6	98.0	100.0	103.8	108.6	113.4	119.7
GDP Deflator (2000=100)...............	99bip	59.3	67.3	73.9	77.1	82.3	86.6	92.2	100.0	104.2	108.3	113.4	118.6
					Millions: Midyear Estimates								
Population...............................	99z	5.33	5.35	5.36	5.38	5.39	5.39	5.40	5.40	5.40	5.40	5.40	5.40

Slovenia   961

		1993	1994	1995	1996	1997	1998	1999	2000	2001	2002	2003	2004
Exchange Rates						*Tolars per SDR: End of Period*							
Official Rate	aa	181.09	184.61	187.28	203.44	228.27	226.97	270.07	296.25	315.37	300.55	281.39	273.71
						Tolars per US Dollar: End of Period (ae) Period Average (rf)							
Official Rate	ae	131.84	126.46	125.99	141.48	169.18	161.20	196.77	227.38	250.95	221.07	189.37	176.24
Official Rate	rf	113.24	128.81	118.52	135.36	159.69	166.13	181.77	222.66	242.75	240.25	207.11	192.38
Fund Position						*Millions of SDRs: End of Period*							
Quota	2f.s	150.50	150.50	150.50	150.50	150.50	150.50	231.70	231.70	231.70	231.70	231.70	231.70
SDRs	1b.s	.03	.04	.04	.09	.05	.17	1.17	2.83	4.00	5.13	6.18	7.18
Reserve Position in the Fund	1c.s	12.88	12.87	12.88	12.88	12.88	46.46	78.40	63.19	64.16	88.77	97.34	77.26
Total Fund Cred.&Loans Outstg	2tl	8.53	4.94	2.69	.90	—	—	—	—	—	—	—	—
International Liquidity						*Millions of US Dollars Unless Otherwise Indicated: End of Period*							
Total Reserves minus Gold	1l.d	787.80	1,498.98	1,820.79	2,297.36	3,314.67	3,638.52	3,168.00	3,196.01	4,329.99	6,980.23	8,496.91	8,793.39
SDRs	1b.d	.05	.06	.06	.13	.07	.24	1.60	3.69	5.03	6.98	9.18	11.15
Reserve Position in the Fund	1c.d	17.68	18.80	19.14	18.51	17.37	65.41	107.61	82.33	80.63	120.69	144.65	119.98
Foreign Exchange	1d.d	770.07	1,480.12	1,801.59	2,278.71	3,297.22	3,572.87	3,058.79	3,110.00	4,244.33	6,852.57	8,343.09	8,662.27
Gold (Million Fine Troy Ounces)	1ad	.0003	.0003	.0003	.0003	.0003	.0003	.0003	.0003	.2431	.2429	.2429	.2428
Gold (National Valuation)	1and	.13	.12	.13	.12	.09	.09	.09	.09	67.22	83.25	101.09	105.80
Monetary Authorities:Other Assets	3..d	1.08	103.28	170.14	33.70	41.27	46.83	51.95	58.05	76.11	84.72	87.22	100.90
Other Liab	4..d	.06	.09	.14	.42	.34	1.05	.63	.48	1.11	.19	.13	9.54
Deposit Money Banks: Assets	7a.d	1,431.92	2,301.70	2,395.17	2,581.52	1,869.71	2,003.17	1,807.96	2,006.24	3,266.75	2,258.44	2,578.94	3,074.14
Liabilities	7b.d	1,058.95	1,258.55	1,483.20	1,458.57	1,219.38	1,333.58	1,440.06	1,570.22	1,760.66	2,794.88	4,586.06	6,740.61
Monetary Authorities						*Billions of Tolars: End of Period*							
Foreign Assets	11	104.02	190.06	250.85	329.81	559.27	594.10	629.76	739.91	1,122.54	1,580.26	1,644.70	1,586.20
Claims on Central Government	12a	18.78	15.65	15.28	15.52	15.67	16.01	16.61	17.75	9.81	9.22	26.98	29.72
Claims on Private Sector	12d	.08	.10	.11	.15	.19	.21	.22	.25	.26	.28	.27	.28
Claims on Deposit Money Banks	12e	16.00	29.90	43.06	15.72	18.08	3.91	25.82	6.78	.47	1.29	.09	.08
Reserve Money	14	51.29	80.49	100.79	116.55	143.36	171.63	208.23	212.18	287.44	282.27	297.48	309.02
of which: Currency Outside DMBs	14a	32.72	47.28	59.96	66.84	78.12	93.65	125.01	119.82	142.11	143.05	156.04	167.92
Liabs.of Central Bank: Securities	16ac	50.39	99.77	126.67	178.45	364.97	362.48	337.76	365.27	584.69	926.77	1,027.59	924.08
Restricted Deposits	16b	.37	1.82	1.91	.86	2.29	4.30	4.30	4.58	4.91	4.76	8.22	.15
Foreign Liabilities	16c	1.55	.92	.52	.24	.06	.17	.12	.11	.28	.04	.02	1.68
Central Government Deposits	16d	5.99	27.41	47.51	22.30	23.12	18.50	26.25	39.08	60.01	164.77	146.72	188.72
Capital Accounts	17a	28.11	25.69	30.26	41.73	57.15	53.78	94.73	133.21	180.67	189.35	151.36	164.24
Other Items (Net)	17r	−.03	−1.88	.08	−.51	.77	3.36	1.03	10.28	15.09	23.08	40.64	28.39
Deposit Money Banks						*Billions of Tolars: End of Period*							
Reserves	20	12.67	31.07	38.13	48.11	63.09	74.44	79.37	87.42	138.59	130.57	130.65	128.83
Claims on Mon.Author.:Securities	20c	42.74	† 82.42	106.96	160.92	345.08	344.49	327.91	365.32	584.16	919.96	1,027.18	923.08
Foreign Assets	21	188.79	291.07	301.77	365.23	316.32	322.91	355.75	456.17	819.78	499.28	488.37	541.79
Claims on General Government	22a	208.08	257.88	315.96	319.59	372.50	407.79	428.33	479.56	548.89	606.08	638.58	745.12
Claims on Private Sector	22d	316.45	427.04	609.72	736.01	829.98	1,066.35	1,313.36	1,538.76	1,828.26	2,067.20	2,385.56	2,865.95
Claims on Other Financial Insts	22f	2.03	5.53	12.75	9.38	12.36	20.36	37.82	51.56	59.05	81.10	106.70	128.00
Demand Deposits	24	64.36	84.15	104.10	127.42	151.36	191.99	237.01	263.47	317.30	533.30	608.48	808.11
Time, Savings,& Fgn.Currency Dep	25	334.95	494.13	647.77	807.04	1,005.28	1,188.44	1,334.29	1,618.56	2,152.14	2,255.13	2,348.74	2,369.98
Money Market Instruments	26aa	16.44	12.51	26.97	13.24	18.47	21.37	13.56	24.64	52.56	92.46	115.59	72.94
Bonds	26ab	2.57	8.27	18.09	23.84	33.95	36.28	40.80	53.96	66.30	92.64	114.68	168.15
Restricted Deposits	26b	9.51	10.28	10.98	17.04	17.63	14.93	10.80	15.09	23.08	19.80	18.78	20.26
Foreign Liabilities	26c	139.61	159.15	186.87	206.36	206.29	214.97	283.36	357.03	441.83	617.87	868.45	1,187.98
General Government Deposits	26d	57.93	87.22	94.87	140.69	167.98	191.06	190.17	147.10	124.77	173.63	144.60	128.78
of which: Local Govt. Deposits	26db	7.59	8.04	11.43	6.53	6.53	6.91	10.88	11.21	5.46	9.13	10.55	13.53
Central Govt. Lending Funds	26f	2.43	4.87	8.29	12.34	14.04	24.35	27.88	34.35	36.75	46.03	22.93	18.77
Credit from Monetary Authorities	26g	15.48	29.64	41.66	15.28	17.83	3.53	25.47	22.08	260.98	1.17	.01	—
Liabilities to Other Financ. Insts	26i	9.92	5.53	10.39	15.43	23.33	33.20	41.84	57.15	71.15	87.67	120.80	142.50
Capital Accounts	27a	151.07	209.53	248.29	273.20	303.74	335.79	372.56	418.82	452.19	499.86	539.31	594.94
Other Items (Net)	27r	−33.54	−10.29	−13.00	−12.64	−20.58	−19.57	−35.19	−33.47	−20.34	−115.38	−125.33	−179.64
Monetary Survey						*Billions of Tolars: End of Period*							
Foreign Assets (Net)	31n	151.64	321.05	365.23	488.45	669.24	701.86	702.03	838.94	1,500.21	1,461.62	1,264.59	938.34
Domestic Credit	32	481.50	591.57	811.45	917.66	1,039.61	1,301.17	1,579.92	1,901.71	2,261.48	2,425.47	2,866.71	3,451.57
Claims on General Govt. (Net)	32an	162.93	158.89	188.87	172.13	197.08	214.24	228.52	311.14	373.91	276.89	374.23	457.34
Claims on Private Sector	32d	316.53	427.14	609.83	736.16	830.17	1,066.56	1,313.58	1,539.01	1,828.52	2,067.48	2,385.84	2,866.23
Claims on Other Financial Insts	32f	2.03	5.53	12.75	9.38	12.36	20.36	37.82	51.56	59.05	81.10	106.70	128.00
Money	34	97.28	131.44	164.06	194.29	229.48	287.26	363.70	385.88	462.53	680.49	767.70	982.24
Quasi-Money	35	334.95	494.13	647.77	807.04	1,005.28	1,188.44	1,334.29	1,618.56	2,152.15	2,255.17	2,348.75	2,370.34
Money Market Instruments	36aa	16.44	12.51	26.97	13.24	18.47	21.37	13.56	24.64	52.56	92.46	115.59	72.94
Bonds	36ab	2.57	8.27	18.09	23.84	33.95	36.28	40.80	53.96	66.30	92.64	114.68	168.15
Liabs.of Central Bank: Securities	36ac	7.65	† 17.35	19.71	17.53	19.89	18.00	9.85	−.05	.52	6.81	.41	.99
Restricted Deposits	36b	9.88	12.10	12.90	17.90	19.92	19.23	15.10	19.68	27.99	24.56	27.00	20.41
Central Govt. Lending Funds	36f	2.43	4.87	8.29	12.34	14.04	24.35	27.88	34.35	36.75	46.03	22.93	18.77
Liabilities to Other Financ. Insts	36i	9.92	5.53	10.39	15.43	23.33	33.20	41.84	57.15	71.15	87.67	120.80	142.50
Capital Accounts	37a	179.19	235.23	278.56	314.93	360.89	389.57	467.29	552.03	632.87	689.22	690.66	759.17
Other Items (Net)	37r	−28.39	−10.29	−11.62	−12.02	−17.90	−14.67	−32.35	−5.55	258.87	−87.94	−77.17	−145.62
Money plus Quasi-Money	35l	432.23	625.56	811.83	1,001.33	1,234.76	1,475.70	1,697.99	2,004.44	2,614.68	2,935.66	3,116.46	3,352.59
Interest Rates						*Percent Per Annum*							
Central Bank Rate (End of Per.)	60	19.00	17.00	11.00	11.00	11.00	11.00		11.00	12.00	10.50	7.25	5.00
Money Market Rate	60b	39.15	29.08	12.18	13.98	9.71	7.45	6.87	6.95	6.90	4.93	5.59	4.40
Treasury Bill Rate	60c	....	....	....	....	....	....	8.63	10.94	10.88	8.73	6.53	4.17
Deposit Rate	60l	33.04	28.10	15.38	15.08	13.19	10.54	7.24	10.05	9.81	8.24	5.95	3.82
Lending Rate	60p	48.61	38.87	23.36	22.60	20.02	16.09	12.38	15.77	15.05	13.17	10.75	8.65
Government Bond Yield	61	40.63	15.93	....	....	....	....	....	....	....	....	6.40	4.68

		1993	1994	1995	1996	1997	1998	1999	2000	2001	2002	2003	2004
Prices and Labor						*Index Numbers (2000=100): Period Averages*							
Producer Prices	63	57.1	67.2	75.8	80.9	85.8	91.0	92.9	100.0	109.0	114.6	117.5	122.5
Consumer Prices	64	49.1	59.4	† 67.4	74.0	80.2	86.6	91.9	100.0	108.5	116.6	123.1	127.5
Harmonized CPI (2002=100)	64h	....	....	....	....	....	....	....	....	93.1	100.0	105.7	109.6
Wages	65	39.4	49.4	58.4	67.4	75.3	82.5	90.4	100.0	111.9	122.9	132.1	139.6
Employment	67	94.4	93.2	93.1	92.7	92.9	91.5	94.7	100.0	100.7	101.0	100.1	100.9
					Number in Thousands: Period Averages								
Labor Force	67d	885	873	867	862	869	871	877	907	908	911	899	900
Employment	67e	756	746	745	742	743	733	758	801	806	809	801	807
Unemployment	67c	† 129	127	121	120	125	126	119	107	102	103	98	93
Unemployment Rate (%)	67r	† 14.6	14.5	14.0	13.9	14.4	14.5	13.6	11.8	11.2	11.3	10.9	10.3
Intl. Transactions & Positions						*Millions of US Dollars*							
Exports	70..d	6,083	6,828	8,316	8,310	8,369	9,051	8,546	8,732	9,252	10,357	12,767	15,879
Imports, c.i.f	71..d	6,501	7,304	9,492	9,421	9,366	10,111	10,116	10,148	10,932	13,854	17,571	
Balance of Payments						*Millions of US Dollars: Minus Sign Indicates Debit*							
Current Account, n.i.e	78ald	191.0	574.8	−74.8	55.4	50.4	−118.0	−698.3	−547.7	30.9	325.2	−98.9	−274.8
Goods: Exports f.o.b	78aad	6,082.9	6,831.7	8,350.2	8,352.6	8,405.9	9,090.9	8,623.2	8,807.9	9,342.8	10,471.1	12,913.0	15,817.8
Goods: Imports f.o.b	78abd	−6,237.1	−7,168.2	−9,304.2	−9,178.7	−9,180.7	−9,882.9	−9,858.3	−9,946.9	−9,962.3	−10,723.2	−13,538.4	−16,862.1
Trade Balance	78acd	−154.2	−336.5	−953.9	−826.1	−774.8	−792.0	−1,235.1	−1,138.9	−619.5	−252.1	−625.4	−1,044.3
Services: Credit	78add	1,392.1	1,808.1	2,026.9	2,134.7	2,040.5	2,024.6	1,875.3	1,887.6	1,959.6	2,315.8	2,795.5	3,467.2
Services: Debit	78aed	−1,017.4	−1,164.7	−1,444.2	−1,494.2	−1,404.8	−1,523.8	−1,521.8	−1,437.9	−1,457.5	−1,735.6	−2,188.9	−2,634.7
Balance on Goods & Services	78afd	220.5	306.9	−371.3	−185.6	−139.2	−291.2	−881.6	−689.2	−117.4	328.1	−18.8	−211.8
Income: Credit	78agd	114.5	324.7	405.6	413.1	391.8	412.9	426.9	434.0	462.6	458.7	597.1	689.5
Income: Debit	78ahd	−166.0	−153.3	−204.3	−259.9	−316.4	−357.0	−363.2	−407.8	−443.4	−595.9	−784.9	−792.7
Balance on Gds, Serv. & Inc	78aid	169.0	478.2	−170.0	−32.4	−63.8	−235.4	−817.9	−663.0	−98.2	191.0	−206.7	−315.0
Current Transfers, n.i.e.: Credit	78ajd	154.9	237.2	247.7	250.9	259.5	299.8	334.9	340.8	390.0	452.1	508.6	677.5
Current Transfers: Debit	78akd	−132.9	−140.6	−152.4	−163.1	−145.3	−182.4	−215.3	−225.4	−260.8	−317.9	−400.8	−637.3
Capital Account, n.i.e	78bcd	4.1	−3.2	−7.0	−1.9	1.1	−1.5	−.7	3.5	−3.6	−158.3	−190.9	−225.7
Capital Account, n.i.e.: Credit	78bad	6.7	2.7	3.1	5.5	5.0	3.5	3.3	6.8	3.3	72.0	92.8	122.7
Capital Account: Debit	78bbd	−2.6	−5.8	−10.1	−7.4	−3.9	−5.0	−4.0	−3.3	−6.9	−230.3	−283.7	−348.3
Financial Account, n.i.e	78bjd	−80.9	138.6	516.3	534.5	1,162.9	215.8	576.1	680.4	1,204.3	1,850.8	545.2	382.8
Direct Investment Abroad	78bdd	−1.3	12.7	10.0	−7.0	−31.0	5.5	−47.6	−65.3	−132.8	−153.2	−466.0	−497.9
Dir. Invest. in Rep. Econ., n.i.e	78bed	112.6	116.7	150.5	173.5	334.3	215.5	106.5	135.9	503.3	1,686.1	337.0	516.1
Portfolio Investment Assets	78bfd	−1.5	−32.5	−28.9	6.4	−.2	−30.2	−7.8	−58.4	−107.5	−93.9	−220.0	−752.5
Equity Securities	78bkd	—	....	....	....	....	....	−.5	−14.5	−23.3	−72.9	−101.3	−348.7
Debt Securities	78bld	−1.5	−32.5	−28.9	6.4	−.2	−30.2	−7.3	−43.9	−84.2	−21.0	−118.7	−403.8
Portfolio Investment Liab., n.i.e	78bgd	4.5	....	15.5	630.5	236.1	119.8	361.6	246.0	188.9	26.7	−30.3	.7
Equity Securities	78bmd	—	....	....	....	52.2	7.2	−3.2	25.4	−2.3	10.7	16.1	53.4
Debt Securities	78bnd	4.5	....	15.5	630.5	184.0	112.6	364.8	220.6	191.2	16.0	−46.4	−52.7
Financial Derivatives Assets	78bwd	....	....	....	....	....	....	....	....	....	—	—	−1.1
Financial Derivatives Liabilities	78bxd	....	....	....	....	....	....	....	....	....	—	—	—
Other Investment Assets	78bhd	−313.5	−211.5	−242.8	−442.0	262.3	−464.6	−568.5	−519.2	206.6	−659.7	−922.6	−1,683.3
Monetary Authorities	78bod	—	−98.3	−66.8	131.4	−7.6	−5.4	−5.6	−5.9	−6.2	−5.4	−.2	−1.8
General Government	78bpd	−.3	−.4	−2.2	−1.4	−1.3	−1.8	−1.6	−1.1	−.5	—	−.8	−13.1
Banks	78bqd	−473.6	−353.1	−302.3	−321.8	479.2	−51.8	−7.8	−253.7	−303.1	139.3	15.7	−314.6
Other Sectors	78brd	160.4	240.3	128.4	−250.2	−208.0	−405.6	−553.5	−258.5	516.4	−793.7	−937.3	−1,353.7
Other Investment Liab., n.i.e	78bid	118.3	253.1	612.1	173.1	361.4	369.8	732.0	941.3	545.7	1,044.8	1,847.0	2,800.8
Monetary Authorities	78bsd	—	.1	.1	.2	—	.1	−.4	.1	—	—	—	124.9
General Government	78btd	80.2	92.2	137.6	−67.6	−25.7	−18.3	−3.2	79.6	−27.8	−79.5	−77.4	8.9
Banks	78bud	−41.9	40.6	267.3	−19.8	4.7	90.6	260.5	290.8	230.6	483.2	1,205.1	1,491.8
Other Sectors	78bvd	80.0	120.3	207.1	260.4	382.5	297.3	474.9	570.9	343.0	641.0	719.3	1,175.2
Net Errors and Omissions	78cad	10.7	−63.7	−194.6	2.0	74.0	61.4	41.5	42.1	53.0	−201.0	54.8	−178.9
Overall Balance	78cbd	124.9	646.5	240.0	590.0	1,288.4	157.8	−81.4	178.3	1,284.6	1,816.7	310.2	−296.5
Reserves and Related Items	79dad	−124.9	−646.5	−240.0	−590.0	−1,288.4	−157.8	81.4	−178.3	−1,284.6	−1,816.7	−310.2	296.5
Reserve Assets	79dbd	−111.0	−641.3	−236.5	−587.4	−1,287.2	−157.8	81.4	−178.3	−1,284.6	−1,816.7	−310.2	296.5
Use of Fund Credit and Loans	79dcd	−13.8	−5.2	−3.4	−2.6	−1.2	—	—	—	—	—	—	—
Exceptional Financing	79ded	....	....	....	....		....	....	....	....	—	—	—
International Investment Position						*Millions of US Dollars*							
Assets	79aad	....	5,925.6	6,841.5	7,155.4	7,668.1	8,450.3	7,856.1	8,300.2	9,939.0	13,627.9	....	....
Direct Investment Abroad	79abd	....	354.0	489.9	459.5	459.4	636.2	626.5	767.6	1,005.1	1,475.9	....	....
Portfolio Investment	79acd	....	62.1	106.4	93.9	55.9	39.7	130.4	175.4	251.4	323.5	....	....
Equity Securities	79add	....	15.0	17.1	15.8	15.4	16.7	32.4	36.8	21.8	35.9	....	....
Debt Securities	79aed	....	47.0	89.3	78.1	40.4	22.9	98.0	138.6	229.6	287.6	....	....
Financial Derivatives	79ald	....										....	....
Other Investment	79afd	....	4,010.4	4,424.3	4,304.6	3,838.1	4,135.9	3,931.1	4,161.1	4,285.3	4,765.0	....	....
Monetary Authorities	79agd	....	103.3	170.1	33.3	40.7	46.3	51.8	57.9	76.0	84.7	....	....
General Government	79ahd	....	—	—	—	—	—	—	—	—	—	....	....
Banks	79aid	....	1,709.2	1,909.3	2,066.3	1,397.6	1,510.8	1,342.3	1,516.7	1,770.1	1,778.4	....	....
Other Sectors	79ajd	....	2,197.9	2,344.9	2,205.0	2,399.7	2,578.8	2,537.0	2,586.5	2,439.2	2,901.9	....	....
Reserve Assets	79akd	....	1,499.1	1,820.9	2,297.5	3,314.8	3,638.6	3,168.1	3,196.1	4,397.2	7,063.5	....	....
Liabilities	79lad	....	5,189.2	6,379.7	7,674.7	8,067.0	9,437.4	9,832.1	10,668.0	11,223.1	15,098.3	....	....
Dir. Invest. in Rep. Economy	79lbd	....	1,325.9	1,763.4	1,998.1	2,207.4	2,777.0	2,682.4	2,892.7	2,604.9	4,081.1	....	....
Portfolio Investment	79lcd	....	88.9	104.1	1,138.2	1,276.6	1,421.5	1,661.0	1,793.4	1,893.3	2,197.1	....	....
Equity Securities	79ldd	....	45.9	62.7	133.8	156.7	139.4	163.0	167.8	170.5	108.6	....	....
Debt Securities	79led	....	43.0	41.4	1,004.4	1,119.9	1,282.1	1,497.9	1,625.6	1,722.8	2,088.5	....	....
Financial Derivatives	79lld	....	—	—	—	—	—	—	—	—	—	....	....
Other Investment	79lfd	....	3,774.4	4,512.2	4,538.5	4,583.0	5,238.9	5,488.7	5,981.9	6,724.9	8,820.2	....	....
Monetary Authorities	79lgd	....	7.3	4.2	1.6	.2	.4	.3				....	....
General Government	79lhd	....	577.5	786.9	734.0	686.8	823.4	702.1	752.9	528.6	493.7	....	....
Banks	79lid	....	561.4	686.1	1,045.9	980.7	1,017.8	1,178.4	1,298.3	1,762.8	2,549.4	....	....
Other Sectors	79ljd	....	2,628.3	3,035.1	2,757.0	2,915.3	3,397.4	3,608.0	3,930.7	4,433.5	5,777.0	....	....

Slovenia 961

		1993	1994	1995	1996	1997	1998	1999	2000	2001	2002	2003	2004
Government Finance						*Billions of Tolars: Year Ending December 31*							
Deficit (-) or Surplus........................	80	5.37	−5.06	−6.45	1.62	−43.20	−25.04	−29.63	−50.74	−49.74	−44.72	−77.33	−93.25p
Revenue..	81	611.44	768.50	926.42	1,041.64	1,163.38	1,332.10	1,445.54	1,559.91	1,848.64	1,950.33	2,234.66	2,432.29p
Grants Received............................	81z	—	—	.49	.96	1.76	2.45	3.18	6.44	10.06	13.23	12.16	.99p
Expenditure..................................	82	606.07	773.56	933.36	1,040.98	1,208.34	1,366.47	1,477.07	1,621.84	1,920.38	2,110.64	2,322.60	2,517.03p
Lending Minus Repayments............	83	—	—	—	—	—	−6.88	1.28	−4.75	−11.94	−102.35	1.56	9.50p
Financing													
Net Borrowing: Domestic..............	84a	−3.10	−5.41	−10.53	−11.65	12.32	22.95	−19.80	−18.82	52.61	163.81	46.35	134.93p
Foreign..............................	85a	6.83	3.82	6.27	23.08	20.10	13.30	61.04	69.87	19.82	−21.30	−11.69	−50.63p
Use of Cash Balances....................	87	−9.10	6.65	10.70	−13.05	10.78	−11.21	−11.61	−.32	−22.68	−97.79	42.67	8.95p
National Accounts						*Billions of Tolars*							
Househ.Cons.Expend.,incl.NPISHs....	96f	839.2	1,050.2	1,414.9	1,605.5	1,793.8	1,986.7	2,231.4	2,426.0	2,682.0	2,900.0	3,128.0	3,341.8
Government Consumption Expend...	91f	302.6	374.3	467.7	537.7	602.5	671.0	748.3	843.5	974.7	1,073.0	1,166.0	1,227.3
Gross Fixed Capital Formation.........	93e	270.2	372.7	489.5	591.6	709.7	823.2	1,019.5	1,066.8	1,164.4	1,239.2	1,373.3	1,529.1
Changes in Inventories....................	93i	7.4	15.3	45.1	19.1	26.9	32.9	37.0	66.9	−27.3	23.7	81.7	130.7
Exports of Goods and Services.........	90c	843.1	1,111.3	1,226.0	1,424.6	1,668.8	1,842.5	1,912.2	2,387.3	2,744.5	3,060.3	3,245.4	3,710.8
Imports of Goods and Services (-)....	98c	827.5	1,070.8	1,270.6	1,450.3	1,691.5	1,891.3	2,073.6	2,538.1	2,776.5	2,981.7	3,247.3	3,748.5
Gross Domestic Product (GDP).........	99b	1,435.1	1,853.0	2,372.7	2,728.2	3,110.1	3,464.9	3,874.7	4,252.3	4,761.8	5,314.5	5,747.2	6,191.2
Net Primary Income from Abroad.....	98.n	4.1	13.9	23.7	20.5	11.9	9.2	11.2	6.0	9.3	−34.4	−41.2	−27.3
Gross National Income (GNI)............	99a	1,439.2	1,866.9	2,396.4	2,748.7	3,121.9	3,474.0	3,885.9	4,258.3	4,771.1	5,280.1	5,706.0	6,163.9
Net Current Transf.from Abroad.......	98t	11.3	17.1	11.2	11.2	18.9	20.1	22.2	25.7	31.2	32.2	22.1	−34.7
Gross Nat'l Disposable Inc.(GNDI)....	99i	1,450.5	1,884.0	2,407.6	2,759.9	3,140.8	3,494.1	3,908.1	4,284.1	4,802.3	5,312.2	5,728.1	6,175.9
Gross Saving..................................	99s	308.6	459.6	525.0	616.7	744.5	836.5	928.5	1,014.6	1,145.6	1,339.2	1,434.1	1,560.1
GDP Volume 1995 Prices.................	99b.p	2,163.8	2,279.1	2,372.7	2,459.1	2,576.2	2,668.0	2,816.2	2,925.8	3,004.1	3,104.0	3,182.4	3,328.0
GDP Volume (2000=100)...............	99bvp	74.0	77.9	81.1	84.0	88.1	91.2	96.3	100.0	102.7	106.1	108.8	113.7
GDP Deflator (2000=100)...............	99bip	45.6	55.9	68.8	76.3	83.1	89.4	94.7	100.0	109.1	117.8	124.3	128.0
						Millions: Midyear Estimates							
Population...............................	99z	1.95	1.96	1.96	1.97	1.97	1.97	1.97	1.97	1.97	1.97	1.97	1.97

Solomon Islands 813

		1993	1994	1995	1996	1997	1998	1999	2000	2001	2002	2003	2004
Exchange Rates						*Solomon Islands Dollars per SDR: End of Period*							
Official Rate	aa	4.4611	4.8597	5.1668	5.2081	6.4067	6.8417	6.9671	6.6441	6.9935	10.1381	11.1309	11.6592
					Solomon Islands Dollars per US Dollar: End of Period (ae) Period Average (rf)								
Official Rate	ae	3.2478	3.3289	3.4758	3.6219	4.7483	4.8591	5.0761	5.0994	5.5648	7.4571	7.4906	7.5075
Official Rate	rf	3.1877	3.2914	3.4059	3.5664	3.7169	4.8156	4.8381	5.0889	5.2780	6.7488	7.5059	7.4847
					Index Numbers (2000=100): Period Averages								
Official Rate	ahx	159.7	154.6	149.5	142.8	136.3	105.7	103.2	100.0	93.9	76.1	67.8	68.0
Nominal Effective Exchange Rate	nec	134.3	131.0	121.0	118.3	121.1	102.3	98.2	100.0	103.2	80.1	64.0	59.6
Real Effective Exchange Rate	rec	83.7	86.6	84.7	90.4	98.0	91.7	94.3	100.0	109.2	90.8	78.5	77.4
Fund Position						*Millions of SDRs: End of Period*							
Quota	2f.s	7.50	7.50	7.50	7.50	7.50	7.50	10.40	10.40	10.40	10.40	10.40	10.40
SDRs	1b.s	.03	.01	—	.01	—	—	.01	—	.01	—	—	—
Reserve Position in the Fund	1c.s	.54	.54	.54	.54	.54	.54	.54	.54	.54	.55	.55	.55
Total Fund Cred.&Loans Outstg	2tl	—	—	—	—	—	—	—	—	—	—	—	—
International Liquidity						*Millions of US Dollars Unless Otherwise Indicated: End of Period*							
Total Reserves minus Gold	1l.d	20.07	17.42	15.91	32.58	36.34	49.03	51.14	32.04	19.34	18.25	37.20	80.58
SDRs	1b.d	.04	.01	.01	.01	—	—	.01	—	.01	.01	—	—
Reserve Position in the Fund	1c.d	.74	.79	.80	.77	.73	.76	.74	.71	.68	.75	.82	.85
Foreign Exchange	1d.d	19.29	16.62	15.10	31.80	35.61	48.27	50.39	31.34	18.66	17.49	36.39	79.72
Monetary Authorities: Other Liab	4..d	1.75	.42	.36	.63	.12	.44	.32	.25	—	—	1.05	1.10
Deposit Money Banks: Assets	7a.d	2.13	3.57	1.30	3.27	3.94	1.29	6.06	2.43	5.51	5.36	7.36	9.58
Liabilities	7b.d	1.75	4.82	1.82	4.00	2.56	2.58	5.56	3.13	4.35	3.97	5.16	8.82
Monetary Authorities						*Millions of Solomon Islands Dollars: End of Period*							
Foreign Assets	11	65.07	58.21	55.39	117.71	153.90	237.13	261.57	163.40	106.81	136.03	277.21	604.31
Claims on Central Government	12a	45.39	64.47	77.98	73.06	76.36	76.15	46.56	44.47	174.96	173.47	173.01	172.84
Claims on Nonfin.Pub.Enterprises	12c	4.22	4.20	4.20	4.20	4.20	4.20	4.01	4.20	3.28	2.02	1.35	.67
Claims on Deposit Money Banks	12e	—	—	—	—	—	—	—	—	—	—	—	—
Reserve Money	14	46.97	61.48	75.63	98.60	92.47	134.96	134.61	154.30	149.22	173.85	221.28	382.57
of which: Currency Outside DMBs	14a	42.11	50.23	54.93	59.67	70.79	81.28	100.07	88.15	84.57	91.39	101.43	123.24
Restricted Deposits	16b	1.02	.83	1.10	1.71	1.28	3.51	1.46	.66	5.70	6.01	.23	1.19
Foreign Liabilities	16c	5.70	1.39	1.24	2.28	.59	2.13	1.64	1.29	—	.01	7.86	8.23
Central Government Deposits	16d	5.98	11.11	4.28	3.84	6.55	59.75	56.00	3.61	6.82	6.99	61.13	178.25
Capital Accounts	17a	52.31	57.39	59.41	68.82	103.81	108.23	109.93	104.45	108.91	−45.85	−20.36	28.91
Other Items (Net)	17r	2.70	−5.32	−4.10	19.71	29.77	8.89	8.51	−52.24	14.39	170.50	181.42	178.68
Deposit Money Banks						*Millions of Solomon Islands Dollars: End of Period*							
Reserves	20	4.86	12.50	22.04	39.90	21.64	51.50	52.34	60.95	64.59	81.33	115.34	260.39
Foreign Assets	21	6.91	11.88	4.51	11.85	18.69	6.29	30.78	12.41	30.65	39.95	55.17	71.86
Claims on Central Government	22a	130.86	152.14	159.00	160.33	162.70	165.53	180.30	185.25	149.84	149.84	164.21	145.88
Claims on Local Government	22b	.41	1.24	.22	.60	.31	.21	.22	.16	.16	.78	.72	.24
Claims on Nonfin.Pub.Enterprises	22c	2.71	.91	1.22	2.71	.75	.78	2.58	3.59	2.00	1.97	1.36	—
Claims on Private Sector	22d	84.22	107.06	121.96	128.20	141.27	176.99	191.74	195.22	152.73	171.32	215.99	238.59
Claims on Other Banking Insts	22f	—	—	—	—	—	—	—	—	—	—	—	—
Demand Deposits	24	81.82	112.65	116.02	138.08	141.66	130.82	166.48	162.85	162.63	164.51	230.09	251.11
Time and Savings Deposits	25	125.88	149.70	170.41	195.89	207.49	218.50	194.08	212.21	152.95	168.09	200.15	250.28
Money Market Instruments	26aa	.49	.54	—	—	.31	—	.61	.56	.48	3.78	3.17	3.64
Foreign Liabilities	26c	5.67	16.05	6.33	14.49	12.16	12.54	28.21	15.94	24.23	29.59	38.69	66.18
Central Government Deposits	26d	5.17	5.24	9.32	7.83	8.22	4.35	12.88	2.35	1.10	2.89	3.93	43.52
Credit from Monetary Authorities	26g	—	—	—	—	—	—	—	—	—	—	—	—
Capital Accounts	27a	32.30	30.87	28.80	32.54	38.35	62.39	72.19	76.35	87.88	95.84	99.57	121.05
Other Items (Net)	27r	−21.36	−29.31	−21.93	−45.25	−62.82	−27.31	−16.49	−12.68	−29.29	−19.53	−22.83	−18.81
Monetary Survey						*Millions of Solomon Islands Dollars: End of Period*							
Foreign Assets (Net)	31n	60.61	52.64	52.33	112.79	159.84	228.74	262.49	158.58	113.23	146.36	285.83	601.76
Domestic Credit	32	256.67	313.68	350.97	357.41	370.82	359.75	356.53	426.93	475.05	489.51	491.56	336.46
Claims on Central Govt. (Net)	32an	165.10	200.27	223.37	221.72	224.29	177.57	157.98	223.76	316.88	313.44	272.16	96.96
Claims on Local Government	32b	.41	1.24	.22	.60	.31	.21	.22	.16	.16	.78	.72	.24
Claims on Nonfin.Pub.Enterprises	32c	6.94	5.11	5.42	6.90	4.95	4.98	6.60	7.78	5.28	3.98	2.70	.67
Claims on Private Sector	32d	84.22	107.06	121.96	128.20	141.27	176.99	191.74	195.22	152.73	171.32	215.99	238.59
Claims on Other Banking Insts	32f	—	—	—	—	—	—	—	—	—	—	—	—
Money	34	123.93	162.88	170.96	197.75	212.45	212.10	266.54	251.00	247.20	255.90	331.52	374.35
Quasi-Money	35	125.88	149.70	170.41	195.89	207.49	218.50	194.08	212.21	152.95	168.09	200.15	250.28
Money Market Instruments	36aa	.49	.54	—	—	.31	—	.61	.56	.48	3.78	3.17	3.64
Restricted Deposits	36b	1.02	.83	1.10	1.71	1.28	3.51	1.46	.66	5.70	6.01	.23	1.19
Capital Accounts	37a	84.61	88.26	88.21	101.36	142.16	170.63	182.11	180.79	196.79	49.99	79.21	149.96
Other Items (Net)	37r	−18.65	−35.88	−27.37	−26.51	−33.02	−16.25	−25.78	−59.72	−14.83	152.09	163.11	158.80
Money plus Quasi-Money	35l	249.81	312.58	341.37	393.64	419.93	430.60	460.62	463.21	400.15	424.00	531.67	624.64
Other Banking Institutions						*Millions of Solomon Islands Dollars: End of Period*							
Reserves	40	11.35	....	....	68.17	71.50	18.56	14.56	12.56	12.16	15.28	15.25	24.38
Claims on Private Sector	42d	65.65	....	....	113.32	125.99	139.13	140.53	142.24	143.89	144.60	141.01	134.47
Quasi-Monetary Liabilities	45	9.12	10.00	11.76	13.90	16.48	17.18	19.31	19.32	25.64	25.92	25.92	26.42
Central Govt. Lending Funds	46f	12.22	7.44	2.43	1.88	1.35	1.32	1.32	7.15	7.15	7.15	7.15	—
Credit from Monetary Authorities	46g	6.81	—	—	11.77	11.35	6.13	6.44	6.13	6.13	6.13	6.32	6.13
Credit from Deposit Money Banks	46h	.04	....	....	—	—	—	—	—	—	—	—	—
Liabs. to Nonbank Financial Insts	46j	8.31	....	....	3.47	1.67	7.40	7.33	7.27	7.24	7.24	7.24	8.48
Capital Accounts	47a	16.58	....	....	18.03	26.77	34.82	29.98	12.22	12.35	12.59	27.65	9.95
Other Items (Net)	47r	23.93	....	....	132.44	139.88	90.84	90.70	102.71	97.54	100.84	81.97	107.87

		1993	1994	1995	1996	1997	1998	1999	2000	2001	2002	2003	2004
Banking Survey		*Millions of Solomon Islands Dollars: End of Period*											
Foreign Assets (Net)	51n	60.61	52.64	52.33	112.79	159.84	228.74	262.49	158.58	113.23	146.36	285.83	601.76
Domestic Credit	52	322.32	....	....	470.73	496.81	498.88	497.06	569.17	618.94	634.11	632.57	470.94
Claims on Central Govt. (Net)	52an	165.10	200.27	223.37	221.72	224.29	177.57	157.98	223.76	316.88	313.44	272.16	96.96
Claims on Local Government	52b	.41	1.24	.22	.60	.31	.21	.22	.16	.16	.78	.72	.24
Claims on Nonfin.Pub.Enterprises	52c	6.94	5.11	5.42	6.90	4.95	4.98	6.60	7.78	5.28	3.98	2.70	.67
Claims on Private Sector	52d	149.88	....	....	241.52	267.26	316.12	332.26	337.46	296.61	315.91	356.99	373.07
Liquid Liabilities	55l	247.58	....	....	339.37	364.91	429.22	465.37	469.97	413.63	434.64	542.35	626.68
Money Market Instruments	56aa	.49	.54	—	—	.31	—	.61	.56	.48	3.78	3.17	3.64
Restricted Deposits	56b	1.02	.83	1.10	1.71	1.28	3.51	1.46	.66	5.70	6.01	.23	1.19
Central Govt. Lending Funds	56f	12.22	7.44	2.43	1.88	1.35	1.32	1.32	7.15	7.15	7.15	7.15	—
Liabs. to Nonbank Financial Insts.	56j	8.31	....	....	3.47	1.67	7.40	7.33	7.27	7.24	7.24	7.24	8.48
Capital Accounts	57a	101.19	....	....	119.39	168.92	205.45	212.10	193.02	209.14	62.58	106.86	159.91
Other Items (Net)	57r	12.13	....	....	117.70	118.21	80.72	71.36	49.12	88.83	259.06	251.40	272.80
Nonbank Financial Institutions		*Millions of Solomon Islands Dollars: End of Period*											
Reserves	40..m	21.61	26.98	....	....	38.85	47.24	45.73	59.08	13.99	31.99	48.40	75.40
Claims on Central Government	42a.m	68.00	73.98	....	....	83.78	125.30	118.73	104.86	112.67	94.27	94.27	126.09
Claims on Nonfin.Pub.Enterprises	42c.m	23.72	39.95	....	....	44.44	49.24	44.70	46.68	53.02	58.31	62.96	24.59
Claims on Private Sector	42d.m	24.69	31.83	....	....	53.47	59.76	61.66	59.01	55.56	54.89	51.52	78.15
Claims on Other Banking Insts.	42f.m	8.43	7.37	....	....	25.10	7.62	3.09	3.17	3.64	4.11	4.48	4.11
Capital Accounts	47a.m	187.03	223.57	....	....	317.28	359.00	384.31	380.05	356.73	369.87	402.34	474.66
Other Items (Net)	47r.m	−40.58	−43.46	....	....	−71.64	−69.84	−110.39	−107.26	−117.85	−126.30	−140.70	−166.31
Interest Rates		*Percent Per Annum*											
Treasury Bill Rate	60c	12.15	11.25	12.50	12.75	12.88	6.00	6.00	7.05	8.23	6.87	5.85	6.00
Deposit Rate	60l	9.77	9.00	8.38	6.46	2.42	2.33	2.88	2.54	1.35	.75	.75	.92
Lending Rate	60p	17.80	15.72	16.59	17.78	15.71	14.84	14.50	15.49	15.72	16.42	16.33	16.07
Government Bond Yield	61	13.00	13.00	13.00	11.50	11.75	12.50	12.88	13.00	13.00	13.00	13.00	13.00
Prices, Production, Labor		*Index Numbers (2000=100): Period Averages*											
Consumer Prices	64	51.3	58.1	63.7	71.2	76.9	86.5	93.4	100.0	106.9	117.7	129.5	138.7
Copra Production	66ag	152.6	110.5	136.8	142.1	152.6	142.1	121.1	100.0	157.9	157.9	....	....
Fish Catch	66al	173.4	189.1	250.0	205.6	258.1	247.2	235.5	100.0	121.4	....	....	....
		Number in Thousands: Period Averages											
Labor Force	67d	....	....	....	....	....	....	85	....	....	....	....	....
Employment	67e	30	33	33	34	....	....	57	....	....	....	....	....
Unemployment	67c	....	....	....	....	....	....	28	....	....	....	....	....
Unemployment Rate	67r	....	....	....	....	....	....	21.6	....	....	....	....	....
Intl. Transactions & Positions		*Millions of Solomon Islands Dollars*											
Exports	70	411.44	467.87	573.15	576.60	581.53	568.75	607.37	....	124.63	200.97	576.00	551.90
Imports, c.i.f.	71	436.26	468.11	525.66	421.00	548.70	722.18	538.41	....	472.97	452.90	617.12	749.68
Balance of Payments		*Millions of US Dollars: Minus Sign Indicates Debit*											
Current Account, n.i.e.	78ald	−7.65	−3.43	8.34	14.58	−37.91	8.12	21.48	....	....	....	....	....
Goods: Exports f.o.b.	78aad	129.06	142.16	168.30	161.51	156.45	141.83	164.57	....	....	....	....	....
Goods: Imports f.o.b.	78abd	−136.87	−142.22	−154.53	−150.55	−184.53	−159.90	−110.04	....	....	....	....	....
Trade Balance	78acd	−7.81	−.06	13.77	10.96	−28.09	−18.07	54.53	....	....	....	....	....
Services: Credit	78add	42.44	49.95	41.81	53.14	70.35	55.07	56.30	....	....	....	....	....
Services: Debit	78aed	−80.68	−105.94	−76.93	−85.47	−107.18	−54.53	−87.49	....	....	....	....	....
Balance on Goods & Services	78afd	−46.05	−56.06	−21.35	−21.37	−64.92	−17.53	23.34	....	....	....	....	....
Income: Credit	78agd	.69	1.52	1.20	2.36	2.69	2.12	5.46	....	....	....	....	....
Income: Debit	78ahd	−4.61	−4.44	−7.96	−9.42	−11.17	−10.01	−22.38	....	....	....	....	....
Balance on Gds, Serv. & Inc.	78aid	−49.97	−58.97	−28.10	−28.43	−73.39	−25.42	6.41	....	....	....	....	....
Current Transfers, n.i.e.: Credit	78ajd	47.84	66.60	53.17	57.48	52.57	56.44	41.54	....	....	....	....	....
Current Transfers: Debit	78akd	−5.52	−11.06	−16.74	−14.47	−17.08	−22.90	−26.48	....	....	....	....	....
Capital Account, n.i.e.	78bcd	.85	2.70	.65	−2.19	−1.00	6.65	9.16	....	....	....	....	....
Capital Account, n.i.e.: Credit	78bad	.94	2.86	1.50	.50	.30	6.91	9.16	....	....	....	....	....
Capital Account: Debit	78bbd	−.09	−.15	−.85	−2.69	−1.29	−.27	—	....	....	....	....	....
Financial Account, n.i.e.	78bjd	8.22	1.49	−8.31	−1.37	45.68	16.88	−33.77	....	....	....	....	....
Direct Investment Abroad	78bdd	—	—	—	—	—	—	—	....	....	....	....	....
Dir. Invest. in Rep. Econ., n.i.e.	78bed	23.37	2.10	2.03	5.94	33.85	8.80	9.90	....	....	....	....	....
Portfolio Investment Assets	78bfd								....	....	....	....	....
Equity Securities	78bkd	—	—	—	—	—	—	—	....	....	....	....	....
Debt Securities	78bld	—	—	—	—	—	—	—	....	....	....	....	....
Portfolio Investment Liab., n.i.e.	78bgd	—	—	—	—	—	—	—	....	....	....	....	....
Equity Securities	78bmd	—	—	—	—	—	—	—	....	....	....	....	....
Debt Securities	78bnd	—	—	—	—	—	—	—	....	....	....	....	....
Financial Derivatives Assets	78bwd							....	....	....	....	....	....
Financial Derivatives Liabilities	78bxd								....	....	....	....	....
Other Investment Assets	78bhd	—	—	—	—	—	—	.04	....	....	....	....	....
Monetary Authorities	78bod	—	—	—	—	—	—	—	....	....	....	....	....
General Government	78bpd	—	—	—	—	—	—	—	....	....	....	....	....
Banks	78bqd	—	—	—	—	—	—	—	....	....	....	....	....
Other Sectors	78brd	—	—	—	—	—	—	.04	....	....	....	....	....
Other Investment Liab., n.i.e.	78bid	−15.15	−.61	−10.34	−7.32	11.84	8.08	−43.72	....	....	....	....	....
Monetary Authorities	78bsd	1.32	−1.25	.03	.08	−.62	−.37	—	....	....	....	....	....
General Government	78btd	.94	−1.34	6.20	5.72	5.17	8.60	−11.02	....	....	....	....	....
Banks	78bud	.03	3.31	−2.85	2.30	−.62	−1.23	−.27	....	....	....	....	....
Other Sectors	78bvd	−17.44	−1.34	−13.71	−15.42	7.91	1.08	−32.43	....	....	....	....	....
Net Errors and Omissions	78cad	−3.16	−2.80	−1.45	6.96	2.31	−14.41	−1.58	....	....	....	....	....
Overall Balance	78cbd	−1.74	−2.04	−.77	17.98	9.09	17.24	−4.72	....	....	....	....	....
Reserves and Related Items	79dad	1.74	2.04	.77	−17.98	−9.09	−17.24	4.72	....	....	....	....	....
Reserve Assets	79dbd	1.74	2.04	.77	−17.98	−9.09	−17.24	4.72	....	....	....	....	....
Use of Fund Credit and Loans	79dcd	—	—	—	—	—	—	—	....	....	....	....	....
Exceptional Financing	79ded	—	—	—	—	—	—	....	....	....	....	....	....

Solomon Islands   813

		1993	1994	1995	1996	1997	1998	1999	2000	2001	2002	2003	2004
Government Finance					*Millions of Solomon Islands Dollars: Year Ending December 31*								
Deficit (-) or Surplus......................	80	−44.10	−30.91	−4.56	−2.32	−54.71	−171.55	−66.02	....	....	....	....	....
Revenue...............................	81	206.00	272.89	309.54	336.58	314.69	347.35	397.58	277.77	....	....	....	....
Grants Received......................	81z	43.90	35.20	45.90	52.10	—	38.30	60.00	1.00	....	....	....	....
Expenditure..............................	82	294.00	339.00	360.00	391.00	365.00	490.00	479.00	....	....	....	....	....
Lending Minus Repayments............	83	—	—	—	—	4.40	67.20	44.60	....	....	....	....	....
Total Debt..................................	88	....	....	....	....	....	....	913.00	978.70	....	....	....	....
Domestic..............................	88a	....	....	....	....	....	....	316.10	385.00	....	....	....	....
Foreign................................	89a	....	....	....	358.30	463.70	622.00	596.90	593.70	....	....	....	....
National Accounts						*Millions of Solomon Islands Dollars*							
Househ.Cons.Expend.,incl.NPISHs....	96f	442.0	501.0	607.0	697.0	734.0	838.0	892.0	834.0	857.0	896.0	....	....
Government Consumption Expend...	91f	338.0	292.0	409.0	467.0	475.0	556.0	589.0	548.0	565.0	589.0	....	....
Gross Fixed Capital Formation..........	93e	148.0	212.0	219.0	261.0	282.0	313.0	336.0	315.0	322.0	363.0	....	....
Changes in Inventories...................	93i	10.0	12.0	19.0	18.0	20.0	24.0	24.0	23.0	24.0	—	....	....
Exports of Goods and Services..........	90c	545.0	639.0	717.0	855.0	900.0	1,016.0	1,089.0	1,017.0	1,043.0	1,092.0	....	....
Imports of Goods and Services.........	98c	580.0	604.0	730.0	861.0	893.0	1,021.0	1,090.0	1,017.0	1,045.0	1,092.0	....	....
Gross Domestic Product (GDP)........	99b	901.0	1,052.0	1,242.0	1,438.0	1,518.0	1,726.0	1,839.0	1,721.0	1,766.0	1,848.0	....	....
GDP Volume 1990 Prices.................	99b.p	654.0	714.0	762.0	788.0	770.0	779.0	769.0	661.0	628.0	603.0	....	....
GDP Volume (2000=100)...............	99bvp	98.9	108.0	115.3	119.2	116.5	117.9	116.3	100.0	95.0	91.2	....	....
						Millions: Midyear Estimates							
Population................................	99z	.34	.35	.36	.37	.38	.40	.41	.42	.43	.44	.45	.47

		1993	1994	1995	1996	1997	1998	1999	2000	2001	2002	2003	2004
Exchange Rates						*Rand per SDR: End of Period*							
Principal Rate.................aa=........	wa	4.66667	5.17298	5.42197	6.73325	6.56747	8.25106	8.44711	9.86107	15.23974	11.74625	9.86684	8.74345
					Rand per US Dollar: End of Period (we) Period Average (wf)								
Principal Rate.................ae=........	we	3.39750	3.54350	3.64750	4.68250	4.86750	5.86000	6.15450	7.56850	12.12650	8.64000	6.64000	5.63000
Principal Rate.................rf=........	wf	3.26774	3.55080	3.62709	4.29935	4.60796	5.52828	6.10948	6.93983	8.60918	10.54075	7.56475	6.45969
					Index Numbers (2000=100): Period Averages								
Principal Rate........................	ahx	211.6	194.6	190.4	161.7	150.0	126.0	113.0	100.0	81.3	65.9	91.9	107.2
Nominal Effective Exchange Rate.....	nec	173.9	165.0	152.7	134.3	135.0	116.4	105.4	100.0	85.2	67.5	83.8	91.8
Real Effective Exchange Rate...........	rec	131.3	125.7	122.2	112.7	120.6	107.9	102.1	100.0	88.3	75.5	98.0	107.8
Fund Position						*Millions of SDRs: End of Period*							
Quota..................................	2f.s	1,365	1,365	1,365	1,365	1,365	1,365	1,869	1,869	1,869	1,869	1,869	1,869
SDRs..................................	1b.s	9	1	3	1	7	132	210	222	223	223	223	223
Reserve Position in the Fund...........	1c.s	—	—	—	—	—	—	—	—	—	—	1	1
Total Fund Cred.&Loans Outstg........	2tl	614	614	614	614	307	—	—	—	—	—	—	—
International Liquidity						*Millions of US Dollars Unless Otherwise Indicated: End of Period*							
Total Reserves minus Gold...............	1l.d	1,020	1,685	2,820	942	4,799	4,357	6,353	6,083	6,045	5,904	6,496	13,141
SDRs..................................	1b.d	12	1	5	1	9	185	288	290	280	303	331	346
Reserve Position in the Fund..........	1c.d	—	—	—	—	—	—	—	—	—	1	1	1
Foreign Exchange..........................	1d.d	1,008	1,684	2,815	940	4,790	4,171	6,065	5,793	5,765	5,601	6,164	12,794
Gold (Million Fine Troy Ounces)........	1ad	4.76	4.20	4.25	3.79	3.99	4.00	3.94	5.90	5.72	5.58	3.98	3.98
Gold (National Valuation)...............	1and	1,658	1,445	1,481	1,261	1,048	1,034	1,020	1,451	1,427	1,735	1,476	1,578
Monetary Authorities:Other Assets...	3..d	453	392	306	227	24	19	12	10	6	8	9	6
Other Liab...	4..d	1,812	1,633	225	93	2,161	3,177	3,254	2,683	4,028	2,647	3,136	3,818
Banking Institutions: Assets.............	7a.d	811	1,042	799	1,412	1,603	2,874	5,122	5,432	7,341	10,267	21,435	24,678
Liabilities..........	7b.d	6,135	7,854	9,184	9,489	9,676	10,483	8,878	8,885	8,148	6,691	10,082	11,833
Monetary Authorities						*Millions of Rand: End of Period*							
Foreign Assets...............................	11	10,637	12,479	16,801	11,375	28,579	31,701	45,450	57,094	90,685	66,072	52,991	82,903
Claims on Central Government........	12a	8,844	13,531	10,274	16,254	13,067	12,578	10,943	10,378	9,007	16,995	18,635	16,945
Claims on Private Sector.................	12d	2,978	4,296	3,003	2,055	2,502	704	603	598	574	12	14	14
Claims on Banking Institutions.........	12e	6,219	5,995	6,513	11,975	10,939	6,362	6,572	10,356	13,347	12,415	13,146	13,047
Reserve Money..............................	14	16,409	19,331	25,083	28,497	31,766	33,499	41,306	43,254	49,557	56,154	62,387	76,721
of which: Currency Outside Banks..	14a	10,490	12,237	14,332	15,954	17,327	18,510	22,663	23,724	25,286	29,219	33,718	39,084
Other Liabs. to Banking Insts...........	14n	19	16	8	20	5	—	6,040	18,629	26,871	45,530	7,442	7,701
Foreign Liabilities..........................	16c	9,023	8,966	4,151	4,572	12,535	18,617	20,029	20,307	48,840	22,873	20,821	21,495
Central Government Deposits...........	16d	12,180	10,962	10,963	9,770	8,334	6,623	5,084	4,009	2,611	2,884	8,238	8,671
Capital Accounts............................	17a	1,148	1,270	1,339	1,637	1,646	2,059	2,157	2,476	2,242	2,917	2,524	2,285
Other Items (Net)............................	17r	−10,101	−4,245	−4,953	−2,837	802	−9,451	−11,048	−10,249	−16,508	−34,864	−16,625	−3,964
Banking Institutions						*Millions of Rand: End of Period*							
Reserves..................................	20	4,773	6,586	10,356	11,702	13,514	14,726	17,969	19,761	23,757	26,304	28,507	32,018
Foreign Assets..........................	21	2,757	3,693	2,913	6,610	7,805	16,844	31,522	41,115	89,019	88,709	142,327	138,938
Claims on Central Government........	22a	20,788	21,501	24,813	27,437	37,011	46,206	50,100	53,546	58,386	68,369	85,979	99,519
Claims on Private Sector.................	22d	235,544	278,079	324,111	380,493	434,884	506,140	553,159	637,212	779,931	819,137	1,035,926	1,146,153
Demand Deposits.........................	24	63,902	81,736	97,050	130,858	155,065	194,873	237,083	242,244	286,776	328,047	352,627	379,842
Time and Savings Deposits..............	25	124,142	141,757	162,301	165,626	195,762	205,958	205,309	232,628	269,562	351,692	417,158	489,341
Money Market Instruments..............	26aa	4,858	3,922	4,920	5,531	3,374	2,657	7,576	5,869	8,395	16,652	15,467	13,500
Foreign Liabilities..........................	26c	20,843	27,829	33,497	44,431	47,097	61,431	54,642	67,243	98,810	57,810	66,945	66,618
Central Government Deposits...........	26d	9,937	8,173	17,748	22,387	21,137	21,158	27,027	30,158	42,993	22,807	49,188	62,017
Capital Accounts............................	27a	20,065	23,998	29,302	34,470	41,664	51,920	63,470	75,581	96,032	104,453	112,846	125,527
Other Items (Net)............................	27r	20,114	22,444	17,375	22,939	29,115	45,919	57,643	97,911	148,525	121,059	278,509	279,783
Banking Survey						*Millions of Rand: End of Period*							
Foreign Assets (Net)........................	31n	−16,472	−20,624	−17,934	−31,018	−23,247	−31,502	2,301	10,658	32,054	74,099	107,553	133,728
Domestic Credit.............................	32	246,036	298,272	333,490	394,082	457,993	537,847	582,694	667,567	802,294	878,822	1,083,128	1,191,943
Claims on Central Govt. (Net)........	32an	7,514	15,897	6,376	11,534	20,607	31,004	28,932	29,757	21,789	59,673	47,188	45,776
Claims on Private Sector...............	32d	238,522	282,375	327,114	382,548	437,386	506,844	553,762	637,810	780,505	819,149	1,035,940	1,146,167
Money..................................	34	75,550	94,511	111,844	147,664	173,335	213,532	259,935	266,184	312,364	357,470	386,681	424,288
Quasi-Money..............................	35	124,142	141,757	162,301	165,626	195,762	205,958	205,309	232,628	269,562	351,692	417,158	489,341
Money Market Instruments..............	36aa	4,858	3,922	4,920	5,531	3,374	2,657	7,576	5,869	8,395	16,652	15,467	13,500
Capital Accounts............................	37a	21,213	25,268	30,641	36,107	43,310	53,979	65,627	78,057	98,274	107,370	115,370	127,812
Other Items (Net)............................	37r	3,801	12,190	5,850	8,136	18,965	30,220	46,547	95,487	145,752	119,737	256,005	270,730
Money plus Quasi-Money................	35l	199,692	236,268	274,145	313,290	369,097	419,490	465,244	498,812	581,926	709,162	803,839	913,629
Nonbank Financial Institutions						*Millions of Rand: End of Period*							
Cash..................................	40..s	35,931	43,655	60,144	58,805	68,998	80,453	98,868	92,396	106,932	116,047	126,285	157,456
Claims on Central Government........	42a.s	59,428	66,880	84,992	93,588	106,149	103,428	103,059	122,381	132,408	140,650	142,505	158,297
Claims on Official Entities...............	42b.s	24,813	22,889	22,765	20,969	24,130	21,204	21,553	20,541	25,255	24,751	31,694	23,020
Claims on Private Sector.................	42d.s	222,407	268,488	326,976	358,163	359,677	370,342	540,167	595,366	667,385	627,435	680,244	801,953
Real Estate..................................	42h.s	35,735	38,868	44,064	47,459	53,403	52,261	63,514	57,507	53,761	50,131	51,941	49,330
Incr.in Total Assets(Within Per.).......	49z.s	87,351	62,466	98,161	40,043	33,373	15,331	199,473	61,030	97,550	−26,727	73,655	157,387
Financial Survey						*Millions of Rand: End of Period*							
Foreign Assets (Net)........................	51n	−16,472	−20,624	−17,934	−31,018	−23,247	−31,502	2,301	10,658	32,054	74,099	107,553	133,728
Domestic Credit..........................	52	552,684	656,529	768,223	866,802	947,949	1,032,821	1,247,473	1,405,855	1,627,342	1,671,658	1,937,571	2,175,213
Claims on Central Govt. (Net)........	52an	66,942	82,777	91,368	105,122	126,756	134,432	131,991	152,138	154,197	200,323	189,693	204,073
Claims on Official Entities..............	52b	24,813	22,889	22,765	20,969	24,130	21,204	21,553	20,541	25,255	24,751	31,694	23,020
Claims on Private Sector...............	52d	460,929	550,863	654,090	740,711	797,063	877,186	1,093,929	1,233,176	1,447,890	1,446,584	1,716,184	1,948,120
Liquid Liabilities..........................	55l	163,761	192,613	214,001	254,485	300,099	339,037	366,376	406,416	474,994	593,115	677,554	756,173
Money Market Instruments..............	56aa	4,858	3,922	4,920	5,531	3,374	2,657	7,576	5,869	8,395	16,652	15,467	13,500
Other Items (Net)............................	57r	367,593	439,370	531,368	575,768	621,229	659,626	875,822	1,004,229	1,176,006	1,135,990	1,352,103	1,539,268

		1993	1994	1995	1996	1997	1998	1999	2000	2001	2002	2003	2004
Money (National Definitions)							*Millions of Rand: End of Period*						
M0	19mc	15,270	18,810	24,629	27,665	30,828	33,210	40,784	43,036	48,904	55,952	62,053	71,437
M1	59ma	76,398	94,538	112,745	147,580	173,092	213,921	258,282	266,924	313,211	358,251	387,788	421,494
M1A	59maa	46,332	57,810	67,503	82,270	101,174	114,813	145,146	147,583	175,326	196,980	218,955	244,458
M2	59mb	178,947	215,823	245,722	284,423	337,547	383,366	435,526	462,509	535,085	632,621	733,453	818,740
M3	59mc	210,978	244,150	281,156	319,428	374,218	428,672	472,177	507,591	595,473	715,817	808,047	914,150
M3 Seasonally Adjusted	59mcc	211,342	243,770	280,377	317,097	370,584	428,663	472,508	502,804	583,354	701,635	800,032	910,584
Interest Rates							*Percent Per Annum*						
Discount Rate (End of Period)	60	12.00	13.00	15.00	17.00	16.00	† 19.32	12.00	12.00	9.50	13.50	8.00	7.50
Money Market Rate	60b	10.83	10.24	13.07	15.54	15.59	17.11	13.06	9.54	† 8.49	11.11	10.93	7.15
Treasury Bill Rate	60c	11.31	10.93	13.53	15.04	15.26	16.53	12.85	10.11	9.68	11.16	10.67	7.53
Savings Rate	60k	….	….	….	….	….	….	….	1.27	3.44	4.76	4.30	3.32
Deposit Rate	60l	11.50	11.11	13.54	14.91	15.38	16.50	12.24	9.20	† 9.37	10.77	9.76	6.55
Lending Rate	60p	16.16	15.58	17.90	19.52	20.00	21.79	18.00	14.50	13.77	15.75	14.96	11.29
Government Bond Yield	61	13.97	14.83	16.11	15.48	14.70	15.12	14.90	13.79	11.41	11.50	9.62	9.53
Prices, Production, Labor							*Index Numbers (2000=100): Period Averages*						
Share Prices: All Shares	62	48.2	67.7	69.5	83.9	86.8	82.1	86.7	100.0	108.4	123.9	108.2	132.2
Industrial	62a	53.8	73.0	80.1	95.4	99.4	89.9	87.6	100.0	85.4	85.5	79.3	111.7
Gold Mining	62b	130.7	187.7	136.9	164.1	117.3	95.5	99.5	100.0	118.3	277.0	253.2	216.2
Producer Prices	63	61.6	66.7	73.1	78.1	83.7	86.6	91.6	100.0	108.5	123.8	125.9	126.8
Consumer Prices	64	61.2	66.6	72.4	77.8	84.4	90.3	94.9	100.0	105.7	115.4	122.1	123.8
Manufacturing Prod, Seas Adj	66eyc	84.1	87.2	94.3	97.7	100.3	96.9	96.4	100.0	102.8	107.5	105.4	109.9
Mining Production, Seas Adj	66zxc	106.7	105.2	104.4	102.6	104.7	103.6	101.5	100.0	101.4	102.2	106.4	110.2
Gold Production, Seas Adj	66krc	† 143.8	134.4	121.6	115.6	114.9	108.0	104.8	100.0	91.7	92.5	86.7	78.8
Mfg. Employment, Seas. Adj.	67eyc	115.1	116.0	116.7	112.4	107.7	104.2	101.5	100.0	97.4	96.8	96.5	97.7
Mining Employment, Seas Adj.	67zxc	148.1	146.0	142.8	136.1	131.5	110.4	103.9	100.0	97.7	99.0	102.2	109.6
							Number in Thousands: Period Averages						
Labor Force	67d					5,455		8,025	8,942	9,041	10,364	16,192	….
Employment	67e	5,352	5,328	5,271	5,236	5,145	4,966	4,867	4,734	4,658	5,576	6,397	6,525
Unemployment	67c	313	271	273	296	310	….	† 3,158	4,208	4,383	4,788	4,910	4,373
Unemployment Rate (%)	67r	….	4.4	4.5	5.1	5.4	….	† 23.3	25.8	29.7	30.7	29.7	27.0
Intl. Transactions & Positions							*Millions of Rand*						
Exports	70	79,279	89,907	101,051	126,101	142,937	† 145,518	163,182	208,476	249,348	311,679	274,505	295,333
Gold Output (Net)	70kr	22,449	23,671	22,537	26,300	25,818	25,907	23,289	27,159	30,909	42,344	34,749	….
Imports, c.i.f.	71	65,411	83,042	110,826	129,522	151,779	† 161,802	163,092	206,620	241,311	307,312	307,611	311,608
Imports, f.o.b.	71.v	58,779	76,154	98,039	115,524	129,735	143,326	147,091	186,382	213,763	272,682	256,833	304,616
							2000=100						
Volume of Exports	72	69.6	73.4	† 76.1	83.2	87.7	89.7	90.9	100.0	101.3	99.9	….	….
Volume of Imports	73	68.9	80.0	† 86.8	94.3	99.4	100.6	93.3	100.0	100.3	103.5	….	….
Unit Value of Exports	74	48.8	55.0	† 64.3	70.9	74.6	82.6	88.0	100.0	115.9	145.2	….	….
Unit Value of Imports	75	48.4	53.5	† 60.9	66.2	70.5	78.7	86.4	100.0	115.8	141.5	….	….
Balance of Payments							*Millions of US Dollars: Minus Sign Indicates Debit*						
Current Account, n.i.e.	78ald	2,803	30	−2,493	−1,678	−2,227	−2,199	−675	−191	153	731	−2,605	−6,982
Goods: Exports f.o.b.	78aad	26,017	26,251	29,783	30,426	31,167	29,199	28,534	31,950	31,064	31,772	38,581	48,430
Goods: Imports f.o.b.	78abd	−18,485	−21,852	−27,404	−27,568	−28,848	−27,208	−24,526	−27,252	−25,809	−27,016	−35,296	−48,545
Trade Balance	78acd	7,532	4,398	2,379	2,859	2,319	1,991	4,008	4,698	5,255	4,756	3,285	−115
Services: Credit	78add	3,278	3,751	4,619	5,069	5,394	5,396	5,210	5,046	4,650	4,671	7,516	8,304
Services: Debit	78aed	−4,707	−5,088	−5,971	−5,735	−6,003	−5,657	−5,759	−5,823	−5,227	−5,344	−8,009	−9,344
Balance on Goods & Services	78afd	6,102	3,061	1,027	2,192	1,710	1,730	3,460	3,920	4,678	4,084	2,791	−1,154
Income: Credit	78agd	696	972	1,136	1,077	1,399	1,474	1,791	2,511	2,480	2,179	2,857	3,204
Income: Debit	78ahd	−3,352	−3,394	−4,011	−4,194	−4,612	−4,659	−5,000	−5,696	−6,267	−4,975	−7,434	−7,547
Balance on Gds, Serv. & Inc.	78aid	3,445	639	−1,848	−925	−1,503	−1,455	251	736	891	1,287	−1,786	−5,497
Current Transfers, n.i.e.: Credit	78ajd	127	143	196	54	138	60	66	106	126	139	252	257
Current Transfers: Debit	78akd	−769	−752	−841	−807	−862	−804	−993	−1,033	−865	−695	−1,070	−1,742
Capital Account, n.i.e.	78bcd	−57	−67	−40	−47	−193	−56	−62	−52	−31	−15	44	53
Capital Account, n.i.e.: Credit	78bad	18	20	23	27	30	24	20	19	16	20	44	53
Capital Account: Debit	78bbd	−75	−87	−63	−74	−223	−80	−82	−71	−47	−35	—	—
Financial Account, n.i.e.	78bjd	−344	1,087	4,003	3,018	8,131	4,852	5,305	99	1,172	597	6,103	10,477
Direct Investment Abroad	78bdd	−292	−1,261	−2,494	−1,048	−2,324	−1,634	−1,584	−277	3,515	402	−565	−1,583
Dir. Invest. in Rep. Econ., n.i.e.	78bed	11	374	1,248	816	3,811	550	1,503	969	7,270	735	770	475
Portfolio Investment Assets	78bfd	−3	−82	−447	−2,000	−4,587	−5,575	−5,113	−3,672	−5,331	−875	−132	−950
Equity Securities	78bkd	−15	−29	−387	−1,698	−3,891	−4,768	−4,050	−3,019	−4,864	−572	−43	−794
Debt Securities	78bld	11	−53	−61	−302	−696	−807	−1,064	−652	−467	−303	−89	−156
Portfolio Investment Liab., n.i.e.	78bgd	751	2,918	2,937	4,446	11,274	9,869	13,799	1,807	−2,971	457	893	7,096
Equity Securities	78bmd	895	88	2,914	2,318	5,473	8,632	9,001	4,169	−962	−388	685	6,661
Debt Securities	78bnd	−145	2,830	23	2,127	5,802	1,237	4,798	−2,361	−2,009	845	207	435
Financial Derivatives Assets	78bwd	….	….	….	….			−46	−144				
Financial Derivatives Liabilities	78bxd	….	….	….	….	53	97	−76	2	—	—	—	—
Other Investment Assets	78bhd	−269	−298	−525	−599	−1,983	−694	−1,644	59	−1,561	1,761	3,592	2,918
Monetary Authorities	78bod	−24	44	75	12	206		6	—	—	—	1	4
General Government	78bpd	—	−1	1	—	2	1	—	—	−407	−424	−376	−103
Banks	78bqd	15	−85	62	−127	−122	−135	−61	−244	−334	−406	−57	391
Other Sectors	78brd	−259	−255	−663	−484	−2,069	−560	−1,589	303	−819	2,591	4,024	2,627
Other Investment Liab., n.i.e.	78bid	−542	−565	3,285	1,403	1,887	2,237	−1,535	1,354	249	−1,884	1,545	2,521
Monetary Authorities	78bsd	1,495	−105	−1,414	−89	2,186	1,172	105	−410	1,582	−1,688	169	510
General Government	78btd	−617	−467	118	469	−120	−73	−270	6	134	1,944	−277	−285
Banks	78bud	−359	360	2,945	1,044	−283	784	−945	1,196	−787	−1,568	−18	1,746
Other Sectors	78bvd	−1,061	−353	1,636	−21	105	355	−425	563	−680	−572	1,671	550
Net Errors and Omissions	78cad	−2,443	−449	−851	−2,401	−1,120	−1,742	−500	649	1,171	342	4,015	4,968
Overall Balance	78cbd	−41	601	619	−1,108	4,591	855	4,068	505	2,464	1,655	7,557	8,516
Reserves and Related Items	79dad	41	−601	−619	1,108	−4,591	−855	−4,068	−505	−2,464	−1,655	−7,557	−8,516
Reserve Assets	79dbd	−809	−601	−619	1,108	−4,170	−437	−4,068	−505	−2,464	−1,655	−7,557	−8,516
Use of Fund Credit and Loans	79dcd	850	—	—	—	−421	−418	—	—	—	—	—	—
Exceptional Financing	79ded	—	—	—	—	—	—	—	—	—	—	—	—

		1993	1994	1995	1996	1997	1998	1999	2000	2001	2002	2003	2004
International Investment Position								*Millions of US Dollars*					
Assets...	79aad	25,743	27,559	33,893	35,056	47,869	56,855	92,532	93,162	64,273	74,038	100,719	....
Direct Investment Abroad..............	79abd	17,960	19,105	23,301	24,349	23,250	26,858	32,990	32,325	17,580	21,980	27,185	....
Portfolio Investment.....................	79acd	145	98	632	2,605	12,060	18,231	41,961	45,433	30,341	30,068	40,752	....
Equity Securities..........................	79add	109	61	569	2,237	10,895	15,833	38,349	41,675	28,500	27,470	38,621	....
Debt Securities............................	79aed	36	38	63	368	1,164	2,398	3,612	3,758	1,841	2,598	2,131	....
Financial Derivatives.....................	79ald	—	—	—	—	—	—	—	—	—	—	—	....
Other Investment.........................	79afd	4,171	4,349	4,985	4,657	5,297	4,565	6,308	7,871	8,881	14,351	24,813	....
Monetary Authorities..................	79agd	453	392	306	227	24	19	12	10	6	8	9	....
General Government....................	79ahd	1,838	2,040	2,371	2,148	1,839	1,596	2,512	269	703	1,186	1,712	....
Banks...	79aid	19	104	39	150	258	300	338	4,081	5,554	9,263	17,976	....
Other Sectors.............................	79ajd	1,862	1,813	2,269	2,132	3,176	2,650	3,447	3,511	2,618	3,895	5,115	....
Reserve Assets..............................	79akd	3,467	4,008	3,445	3,445	7,262	7,201	11,273	7,532	7,471	7,638	7,970	....
Liabilities......................................	79lad	44,022	52,197	62,610	60,449	68,546	69,835	116,962	99,797	75,105	82,654	110,661	....
Dir. Invest. in Rep. Economy..........	79lbd	10,694	12,615	15,014	13,236	16,736	15,676	51,772	43,451	30,569	29,611	45,698	....
Portfolio Investment.....................	79lcd	13,470	18,998	23,446	23,804	28,143	30,547	42,249	36,564	26,402	35,677	46,257	....
Equity Securities..........................	79ldd	6,027	9,246	12,492	13,366	13,144	17,519	26,461	22,599	16,577	23,308	32,795	....
Debt Securities............................	79led	7,443	9,752	10,953	10,439	14,999	13,028	15,789	13,965	9,825	12,369	13,462	....
Financial Derivatives.....................	79lld	2	4	10	14	66	119	43	—	—	—	—	....
Other Investment.........................	79lfd	19,855	20,580	24,140	23,395	23,601	23,492	22,898	19,782	18,134	17,366	18,705	....
Monetary Authorities..................	79lgd	2,660	2,534	1,142	979	2,578	3,181	3,261	2,681	4,026	2,646	3,145	....
General Government....................	79lhd	3,512	3,108	3,072	3,244	2,776	2,537	3,125	589	717	2,805	2,747	....
Banks...	79lid	4,968	5,944	9,038	9,310	8,861	9,154	7,997	8,627	6,911	5,675	5,237	....
Other Sectors.............................	79ljd	8,715	8,993	10,889	9,861	9,386	8,620	8,515	7,885	6,480	6,240	7,576	....
Government Finance							*Millions of Rand: Year Ending December 31*						
Deficit (-) or Surplus......................	80	−28,342	−38,690	−23,465	−28,563	−28,129	−19,464	−14,775	−16,428	−9,975	−6,031	−26,071	−35,018
Total Revenue and Grants..............	81y	95,710	111,916	125,470	147,738	162,983	181,749	199,367	211,984	245,952	279,922	295,661	328,250
Expenditure.................................	82	124,052	150,606	148,935	176,301	191,112	201,213	217,100	228,412	255,927	285,953	321,732	363,268
Total Financing.............................	80h	28,342	38,690	23,465	28,563	28,129	19,465	14,775	16,428	9,975	6,031	26,071	35,023
Total Net Borrowing....................	84	31,469	37,928	25,504	24,224	26,507	21,647	13,269	17,790	19,348	7,777	45,916	43,705
Net Domestic..............................	84a	31,632	35,317	24,323	21,596	23,553	21,591	7,651	10,299	6,489	−26,476	42,987	44,094
Net Foreign.................................	85a	−163	2,611	1,181	2,628	2,954	56	5,618	7,491	12,859	34,253	2,929	−389
Use of Cash Balances...................	87	−3,127	762	−2,039	4,339	1,622	−2,182	1,509	−1,362	−9,373	−1,746	−19,845	−8,682
Total Debt by Currency..................	88z	185,538	† 239,714	275,489	302,608	† 336,133	361,401	391,420	409,363	462,446	454,365	499,813	520,428
National.....................................	88b	180,542	† 231,656	265,879	288,349	† 320,981	345,559	371,395	378,245	395,827	374,488	427,196	456,221
Foreign......................................	89b	4,996	8,058	9,610	14,259	15,152	15,842	20,025	31,118	66,619	79,877	72,617	64,207
National Accounts							*Millions of Rand*						
Househ.Cons.Expend.,incl.NPISHs....	96f.c	† 263,427	298,173	343,037	384,624	431,403	470,165	514,271	580,802	639,800	722,091	786,316	869,738
Government Consumption Expend...	91f.c	† 85,551	96,503	100,424	118,013	131,903	139,371	149,952	167,348	186,280	212,628	239,053	268,936
Gross Fixed Capital Formation.........	93e.c	† 62,601	73,045	87,042	100,632	113,221	126,913	125,754	139,647	153,525	175,592	200,290	226,118
Changes in Inventories...................	93i.c	† 2,603	8,013	12,571	6,240	875	−686	7,534	7,096	2,455	12,050	14,591	16,789
Exports of Goods and Services..........	90c.c	† 91,578	106,842	124,816	152,816	168,659	190,453	206,144	257,011	305,584	382,269	346,975	365,188
Imports of Goods and Services (-)....	98c.c	† 75,919	95,747	121,093	143,340	160,718	181,972	185,037	229,757	265,927	339,016	324,900	372,029
Gross Domestic Product (GDP)........	99b.c	† 426,133	482,120	548,100	617,954	685,730	742,424	813,683	922,148	1,020,007	1,164,945	1,251,468	1,374,476
Net Primary Income from Abroad.....	98.nc	† −8,700	−8,599	−10,427	−13,380	−14,844	−17,488	−19,601	−22,024	−32,176	−29,400	−34,768	−27,970
Gross National Income (GNI)...........	99a.c	† 417,433	473,521	537,673	604,574	670,886	724,936	794,082	900,124	987,831	1,135,545	1,216,700	1,346,506
Consumption of Fixed Capital..........	99cf	† 58,575	64,500	71,827	78,817	87,188	96,582	107,858	118,573	129,455	147,913	159,847	....
GDP Volume 2000 Prices.................	99b.r	....	....	803,713	838,327	860,516	864,968	885,365	922,148	947,373	981,102	1,008,649	1,046,087
GDP Volume (2000=100)...............	99bvr	† 81.9	84.5	† 87.2	90.9	93.3	93.8	96.0	100.0	102.7	106.4	109.4	113.4
GDP Deflator (2000=100)...............	99bir	† 56.4	61.9	68.2	73.7	79.7	85.8	91.9	100.0	107.7	118.7	124.1	131.4
							Millions: Midyear Estimates						
Population...............................	99z	39.89	40.92	41.89	42.79	43.61	44.35	45.02	45.61	46.13	46.56	46.92	47.21

		1993	1994	1995	1996	1997	1998	1999	2000	2001	2002	2003	2004
Exchange Rates		*Pesetas per SDR through 1998, Euros per SDR Thereafter: End of Period*											
Market Rate	aa	195.34	192.32	180.47	188.77	204.68	200.79	1.3662	1.4002	1.4260	1.2964	1.1765	1.1402
		Pesetas per US Dollar through 1998, Euros per US Dollar Thereafter: End of Period (ae) Period Average (rf)											
Market Rate	ae	142.21	131.74	121.41	131.28	151.70	142.61	.9954	1.0747	1.1347	.9536	.7918	.7342
Market Rate	rf	127.26	133.96	124.69	126.66	146.41	149.40	.9386	1.0854	1.1175	1.0626	.8860	.8054
		Pesetas per ECU: End of Period (ea) Period Average (eb)											
ECU Rate	ea	159.2800	161.5520	155.5610	162.6500	167.3270	166.3860	....	....	....	....	....	....
ECU Rate	eb	148.6617	158.4871	161.1758	158.6182	165.3915	167.4876	....	....	....	....	....	....
		Index Numbers (2000=100): Period Averages											
Market Rate (1995=100)	ahx	98.4	93.1	100.0	98.4	85.2	83.5						
Nominal Effective Exchange Rate	neu	117.9	110.1	109.4	110.0	105.1	104.8	103.2	100.0	100.5	101.4	104.5	105.3
Real Effective Exchange Rate	reu	108.8	102.2	101.4	104.2	101.2	103.0	102.6	100.0	103.2	107.4	114.1	117.2
Fund Position		*Millions of SDRs: End of Period*											
Quota	2f.s	1,935	1,935	1,935	1,935	1,935	1,935	3,049	3,049	3,049	3,049	3,049	3,049
SDRs	1b.s	157	174	277	314	351	408	190	223	279	260	278	214
Reserve Position in the Fund	1c.s	751	760	1,065	1,110	1,409	1,558	1,111	908	1,055	1,171	1,253	1,014
of which: Outstg.Fund Borrowing	2c	—	—	—	—	—	62	—	—	—	—	—	—
Total Fund Cred.&Loans Outstg	2tl	—	—	—	—	—	—	—	—	—	—	—	—
International Liquidity		*Millions of US Dollars Unless Otherwise Indicated: End of Period*											
Total Res.Min.Gold (Eurosys.Def)	1l.d	41,045	41,546	34,485	57,927	68,398	55,258	† 33,115	30,989	29,582	34,536	19,788	12,389
SDRs	1b.d	216	255	411	451	474	575	260	290	351	354	413	332
Reserve Position in the Fund	1c.d	1,031	1,109	1,583	1,597	1,902	2,193	1,525	1,182	1,326	1,592	1,862	1,575
Foreign Exchange	1d.d	39,798	40,182	32,491	55,879	66,023	52,490	31,329	29,516	27,905	32,590	17,513	10,481
o/w:Fin.Deriv.Rel.to Reserves	1ddd	....	....	....	....	....	....	−1.01	162.84	−55.52	400.60	1,001.56	20.43
Other Reserve Assets	1e.d	....	....	....	....	....	....						
Gold (Million Fine Troy Ounces)	1ad	15.62	15.62	15.63	15.63	15.63	19.54	16.83	16.83	16.83	16.83	16.83	16.83
Gold (Eurosystem Valuation)	1and	4,217	4,217	4,221	4,221	4,139	5,617	4,885	4,619	4,653	5,768	7,021	7,370
Memo:Euro Cl. on Non-EA Res	1dgd							4,134	36	—	—	—	
Non-Euro Cl. on EA Res	1dhd	....	....	....	....	....	....						601
Mon. Auth.: Other Foreign Assets	3..d	....	....	....	....	....	....	....	....	....	....	....	....
Foreign Liabilities	4..d	462	515	551	983	454	480	† 1,004	445	317	1,488	143	63
Banking Insts.: Foreign Assets	7a.d	117,311	110,693	146,061	129,727	111,176	126,792	† 61,250	77,370	81,999	95,103	101,125	153,239
Foreign Liab.	7b.d	87,093	100,658	109,245	123,359	135,020	179,175	† 125,663	147,328	157,560	176,270	231,737	244,313
Monetary Authorities		*Billions of Pesetas through 1998; Billions of Euros Beginning 1999: End of Period*											
Fgn. Assets (Cl.on Non-EA Ctys)	11	6,152	5,796	4,566	7,960	10,708	8,751	41.49	37.54	38.60	38.26	21.84	15.59
Claims on General Government	12a.u	....	....	....	....	....	....	15.17	14.45	13.95	14.17	30.28	36.59
o/w: Claims on Gen.Govt.in Cty	12a	−219	2,981	3,074	3,056	2,984	3,023	15.17	14.45	13.95	14.17	16.32	17.49
Claims on Banking Institutions	12e.u	....	....	....	....	....	....	60.01	61.42	39.71	40.86	51.46	55.76
o/w: Claims on Bank.Inst.in Cty	12e	6,525	5,949	6,641	4,439	2,267	4,471	24.18	16.14	10.55	18.20	33.19	23.45
Claims on Other Resident Sectors	12d.u	....	....	....	....	....	....	—	—	—	—	.06	.05
o/w: Cl. on Oth.Res.Sect.in Cty	12d	22	21	20	21	21	22	—	—	—	—	.06	.05
Currency Issued	14a	6,509	7,165	7,535	7,942	8,378	8,437	61.35	59.79	48.75	40.50	46.38	52.70
Liabilities to Banking Insts	14c.u	....	....	....	....	....	....	15.94	8.39	14.73	27.88	33.82	34.65
o/w: Liabs to Bank.Inst.in Cty	14c	1,283	1,430	1,394	1,310	1,484	1,788	12.49	8.39	14.73	9.29	14.41	13.09
Demand Dep. of Other Res.Sect	14d.u	....	....	....	....	....	....	5.22	7.34	10.52	12.43	13.92	12.43
o/w:D.Dep.of Oth.Res.Sect.in Cty	14d	131	132	193	175	207	190	5.22	7.34	10.52	12.43	13.92	12.43
Other Dep. of Other Res.Sect	15..u	....	....	....	....	....	....	—	—	—	—	—	—
o/w:O.Dep.of Oth.Res.Sect.in Cty	15	....	....	....	....	....	....	—	—	—	—	—	—
Bonds & Money Mkt. Instruments	16n.u	....	....	....	....	....	....	3.30	—	—	—	—	—
o/w: Held by Resid.of Cty	16n	3,067	2,860	2,334	1,947	1,613	1,219	....	....	....	....	....	....
Foreign Liab. (to Non-EA Ctys)	16c	66	68	67	129	69	69	1.00	.48	.36	1.42	.11	.05
Central Government Deposits	16d.u	....	....	....	....	....	....	16.87	22.91	2.79	2.80	3.32	3.48
o/w: Cent.Govt.Dep. in Cty	16d	193	2,058	1,752	2,742	1,890	2,120	16.87	22.91	2.79	2.80	3.32	3.48
Capital Accounts	17a	2,207	1,166	1,267	1,594	2,752	2,870	16.01	17.25	17.51	12.26	8.67	7.42
Other Items (Net)	17r	−975	−132	−243	−363	−412	−426	−3.01	−2.73	−2.39	−3.99	−2.59	−2.74
Memo: Net Claims on Eurosystem	12e.s	....	....	....	....	....	....	32.38	45.28	29.16	4.06	−1.14	10.35
Currency Put into Circ	14m	....	....	....	....	....	....	....	....	....	59.09	65.79	74.26
Banking Institutions		*Billions of Pesetas through 1998; Billions of Euros Beginning 1999: End of Period*											
Claims on Monetary Authorities	20	4,348	4,328	3,725	3,262	3,093	2,992	15.79	8.39	14.73	9.29	14.41	13.09
Claims on Bk.Inst.in Oth.EA Ctys	20b.u	....	....	....	....	....	....	50.08	53.56	53.52	67.72	78.66	82.51
Fgn. Assets (Cl.on Non-EA Ctys)	21	16,690	14,565	17,737	17,057	16,909	18,155	60.97	83.15	93.04	90.69	80.07	112.50
Claims on General Government	22a.u	....	....	....	....	....	....	146.00	129.59	151.68	164.17	189.34	161.83
o/w: Claims on Gen.Govt.in Cty	22a	16,114	20,853	22,358	24,083	22,400	21,258	136.21	124.10	133.84	138.22	147.75	130.64
Claims on Other Resident Sectors	22d.u	....	....	....	....	....	....	529.64	631.12	712.26	794.56	915.35	1,082.22
o/w: Cl. on Oth.Res.Sect.in Cty	22d	49,600	50,345	53,764	57,682	65,592	76,417	519.57	615.88	688.45	770.91	886.18	1,050.39
Demand Deposits	24..u	....	....	....	....	....	....	127.47	140.23	159.67	175.19	191.06	214.72
o/w:D.Dep.of Oth.Res.Sect.in Cty	24	9,657	10,159	10,291	11,144	13,391	16,768	125.54	137.52	157.23	173.08	187.93	211.56
Other Deposits	25..u	....	....	....	....	....	....	319.89	368.97	408.74	440.18	490.00	561.03
o/w:O.Dep.of Oth.Res.Sect.in Cty	25	32,208	34,492	37,397	37,579	35,679	36,346	310.68	359.38	396.10	424.87	460.72	533.04
Money Market Fund Shares	26m.u	....	....	....	....	....	....	42.34	33.11	43.44	52.92	57.65	57.71
Bonds & Money Mkt. Instruments	26n.u	....	....	....	....	....	....	53.63	51.91	65.19	77.65	118.49	178.40
o/w: Held by Resid.of Cty	26n	1,906	2,214	2,316	2,394	2,693	3,025	....	....	....	....	....	....
Foreign Liab. (to Non-EA Ctys)	26c	12,459	13,303	13,316	16,436	20,741	25,889	125.09	158.33	178.78	168.08	183.48	179.37
Central Government Deposits	26d.u	....	....	....	....	....	....	5.65	5.54	19.06	21.41	16.40	17.36
o/w: Cent.Govt.Dep. in Cty	26d	2,866	2,706	2,954	3,063	3,352	3,882	5.62	5.52	19.06	21.40	16.27	17.24
Credit from Monetary Authorities	26g	6,525	6,063	6,643	4,447	2,265	4,450	24.18	16.14	10.55	18.20	33.19	23.45
Liab. to Bk.Inst.in Oth. EA Ctys	26h.u	....	....	....	....	....	....	54.22	64.81	63.22	86.99	101.55	115.69
Capital Accounts	27a	10,234	10,709	10,807	11,261	12,026	12,668	76.53	94.41	104.07	114.42	121.89	146.63
Other Items (Net)	27r	10,897	10,445	13,860	15,761	17,847	15,794	−26.52	−27.62	−27.49	−28.62	−35.87	−42.19

		1993	1994	1995	1996	1997	1998	1999	2000	2001	2002	2003	2004
Banking Survey (Nat'l Residency)		*Billions of Pesetas through 1998; Billions of Euros Beginning 1999: End of Period*											
Foreign Assets (Net)	31n	10,317	6,990	8,921	8,452	6,808	949	16.83	8.88	3.12	−17.55	−48.44	−20.09
Domestic Credit	32	62,460	69,435	74,510	79,037	85,755	94,718	648.46	726.00	814.39	899.10	1,030.71	1,177.85
Claims on General Govt. (Net)	32an	12,837	19,069	20,726	21,334	20,142	18,279	128.89	110.12	125.94	128.19	144.48	127.41
Claims on Other Resident Sectors	32d	49,622	50,366	53,784	57,703	65,613	76,439	519.57	615.88	688.45	770.91	886.24	1,050.44
Currency Issued	34a.n	6,509	7,165	7,535	7,942	8,378	8,437	61.35	59.79	48.75	40.50	46.38	52.70
Demand Deposits	34b.n	9,788	10,291	10,484	11,319	13,598	16,959	130.76	144.86	167.74	185.51	201.85	223.99
Other Deposits	35..n	32,208	34,492	37,397	37,579	35,679	36,346	310.68	359.38	396.10	424.87	460.72	533.04
Money Market Fund Shares	36m	....	....	....	....	....	....	42.34	33.11	43.44	52.92	57.65	57.71
Bonds & Money Mkt. Instruments	36n	4,973	5,075	4,651	4,341	4,306	4,244	56.93	51.91	65.19	77.65	118.49	178.40
o/w: Over Two Years	36na	....	....	....	....	....	....	40.79	39.77	49.28	61.63	87.40	123.14
Capital Accounts	37a	12,441	11,875	12,074	12,855	14,778	15,538	92.54	111.65	121.58	126.68	130.56	154.05
Other Items (Net)	37r	6,857	7,529	11,289	13,454	15,824	14,143	−29.30	−25.82	−25.29	−26.57	−33.36	−42.13
Banking Survey (EA-Wide Residency)		*Billions of Euros: End of Period*											
Foreign Assets (Net)	31n.u	....	....	....	....	....	....	−23.63	−38.12	−47.49	−40.56	−81.69	−51.31
Domestic Credit	32..u	....	....	....	....	....	....	668.28	746.72	856.03	948.69	1,115.31	1,259.85
Claims on General Govt. (Net)	32anu	....	....	....	....	....	....	138.64	115.60	143.78	154.13	199.90	177.58
Claims on Other Resident Sect.	32d.u	....	....	....	....	....	....	529.64	631.12	712.26	794.56	915.41	1,082.27
Currency Issued	34a.u	....	....	....	....	....	....	61.35	59.79	48.75	40.50	46.38	52.70
Demand Deposits	34b.u	....	....	....	....	....	....	132.68	147.56	170.19	187.61	204.98	227.15
Other Deposits	35..u	....	....	....	....	....	....	319.89	368.97	408.74	440.18	490.00	561.03
o/w: Other Dep. Over Two Yrs.	35abu	....	....	....	....	....	....	32.17	44.32	49.80	64.14	88.74	142.43
Money Market Fund Shares	36m.u	....	....	....	....	....	....	42.34	33.11	43.44	52.92	57.65	57.71
Bonds & Money Mkt. Instruments	36n.u	....	....	....	....	....	....	56.93	51.91	65.19	77.65	118.49	178.40
o/w: Over Two Years	36nau	....	....	....	....	....	....	40.79	39.77	49.28	61.63	87.40	123.14
Capital Accounts	37a	....	....	....	....	....	....	92.54	111.65	121.58	126.68	130.56	154.05
Other Items (Net)	37r.u	....	....	....	....	....	....	−61.07	−64.39	−49.35	−17.40	−14.44	−22.51
Money (National Definitions)		*Billions of Pesetas: End of Period*											
M1	59ma	16,180.5	17,337.6	17,887.8	19,116.1	21,834.9	25,270.6	....	....	....	....	....	....
M2	59mb	26,966.7	28,753.4	29,637.5	31,717.5	35,483.7	40,616.5	....	....	....	....	....	....
M3	59mc	59,260.7	63,675.8	70,439.4	73,819.5	77,136.6	78,665.1	....	....	....	....	....	....
ALP (Broad Money)	59md	65,429.1	70,045.8	76,479.0	82,118.8	85,674.3	86,588.1	....	....	....	....	....	....
Interest Rates		*Percent Per Annum*											
Bank of Spain Rate(End of Period)	60	9.00	7.38	9.00	6.25	4.75	3.00	....	....	....	....	....	....
Money Market Rate	60b	12.33	7.81	8.98	7.65	5.49	4.34	2.72	4.11	4.36	3.28	2.31	2.04
Treasury Bill Rate	60c	10.53	8.11	9.79	7.23	5.02	3.79	3.01	4.61	3.92	3.34	2.21	2.17
Deposit Rate	60l	9.63	6.70	7.68	6.12	3.96	2.92	1.85	2.95	3.08	2.50	....	....
Deposit Rate (Households)	60lhs	....	....	....	....	....	....	....	....	....	....	2.25	1.84
Deposit Rate (Corporations)	60lcs	....	....	....	....	....	....	....	....	....	....	2.25	2.00
Lending Rate	60p	12.78	8.95	10.05	8.50	6.08	5.01	3.95	5.18	5.16	4.31	....	....
Lending Rate (Households)	60phm	....	....	....	....	....	....	....	....	....	....	4.28	3.56
Lending Rate (Corporations)	60pcs	....	....	....	....	....	....	....	....	....	....	3.61	3.49
Government Bond Yield	61	10.16	9.69	11.04	8.18	5.84	4.55	4.30	5.36	4.87	4.62	3.52	3.59
Prices, Production, Labor		*Index Numbers (2000=100): Period Averages*											
Share Prices	62	27.2	31.6	29.8	36.9	55.9	82.2	89.9	100.0	85.8	72.7	71.0	86.8
Industrial Prices	63	† 83.2	86.8	92.3	93.9	94.8	94.2	94.8	100.0	101.7	102.4	103.9	107.4
Consumer Prices	64	80.2	84.0	87.9	91.0	92.8	94.5	96.7	100.0	103.6	106.8	110.0	113.3
Harmonized CPI	64h	....	....	88.0	91.2	92.9	94.5	96.6	100.0	102.8	106.5	109.8	113.2
Wages	65	77.3	80.7	84.6	89.1	92.7	95.3	97.7	100.0	103.8	108.1	112.7	118.8
Industrial Production	66	74.3	80.0	83.9	82.7	88.5	93.4	95.8	100.0	98.5	98.7	100.0	101.6
Employment	67	81.8	81.0	83.2	85.6	88.2	91.2	95.5	100.0	102.0	112.3	115.3	118.3
		Number in Thousands: Period Averages											
Labor Force	67d	15,319.0	....	15,625.0	15,936.0	16,121.0	16,265.2	16,422.9	16,844.0	17,814.6	18,340.4	18,815.0	....
Employment	67e	11,837.4	12,207.0	12,512.0	12,835.0	13,259.5	13,807.6	14,568.0	15,369.7	15,945.6	16,257.5	16,694.6	17,116.6
Unemployment	67c	3,481	3,738	3,584	3,540	3,356	3,060	2,606	2,370	2,213	1,621	1,658	1,671
Unemployment Rate (%)	67r	22.7	24.2	22.9	22.2	20.8	18.8	15.9	14.1	13.1	11.4	8.8	10.3
Intl. Transactions & Positions		*Billions of Pesetas through 1998; Millions of Euros Beginning 1999*											
Exports	70	7,754.6	9,746.6	11,339.6	12,931.2	15,266.9	16,290.8	† 103,343.2	123,099.5	128,671.8	130,814.1	137,814.8	146,452.1
Imports, c.i.f.	71	10,131.0	12,306.3	14,106.7	15,435.7	17,966.0	19,837.9	† 135,866.3	166,138.4	171,690.8	172,788.6	184,094.8	207,125.5
		2000=100											
Volume of Exports	72	45.8	55.7	61.4	68.2	77.6	83.2	88.6	100.0	104.2	107.1	114.0	120.2
Volume of Imports	73	46.8	53.9	60.1	64.2	71.5	81.5	91.9	100.0	104.5	108.7	117.2	128.6
Unit Value of Exports	74	82.0	85.5	91.1	92.0	95.0	95.1	94.2	100.0	100.5	99.5	98.0	99.0
Unit Value of Imports	75	79.0	83.6	87.3	87.6	90.7	88.7	88.6	100.0	99.0	95.9	94.6	96.9

		1993	1994	1995	1996	1997	1998	1999	2000	2001	2002	2003	2004
Balance of Payments						*Millions of US Dollars: Minus Sign Indicates Debit*							
Current Account, n.i.e.	78ald	−5,804	−6,389	792	407	2,512	−3,135	−13,761	−19,237	−16,404	−16,044	−23,676	−49,225
Goods: Exports f.o.b.	78aad	62,021	73,925	93,439	102,735	106,926	111,986	112,664	116,205	117,935	127,949	159,545	184,255
Goods: Imports f.o.b.	78abd	−77,020	−88,817	−111,854	−119,017	−120,333	−132,744	−143,002	−151,025	−150,474	−160,790	−202,468	−248,779
Trade Balance	78acd	−14,999	−14,892	−18,415	−16,283	−13,407	−20,758	−30,339	−34,820	−32,539	−32,841	−42,923	−64,524
Services: Credit	78add	30,446	33,859	40,209	44,387	44,161	49,308	53,418	53,540	58,201	62,682	76,881	85,236
Services: Debit	78aed	−18,902	−18,865	−21,509	−23,979	−24,315	−27,421	−30,532	−31,283	−33,988	−37,365	−45,959	−54,038
Balance on Goods & Services	78afd	−3,454	102	284	4,126	6,439	1,129	−7,452	−12,564	−8,325	−7,524	−12,001	−33,326
Income: Credit	78agd	11,845	8,687	13,689	14,095	13,162	14,621	12,636	15,017	19,829	20,234	24,654	29,002
Income: Debit	78ahd	−15,456	−16,457	−17,817	−20,207	−19,911	−22,134	−22,087	−23,268	−29,576	−30,922	−36,573	−44,903
Balance on Gds, Serv. & Inc.	78aid	−7,066	−7,668	−3,843	−1,986	−310	−6,385	−16,903	−20,815	−18,073	−18,212	−23,920	−49,228
Current Transfers, n.i.e.: Credit	78ajd	8,821	9,171	12,055	11,112	11,738	12,690	13,435	11,629	12,569	14,074	17,506	19,847
Current Transfers: Debit	78akd	−7,558	−7,893	−7,420	−8,718	−8,916	−9,441	−10,292	−10,050	−10,900	−11,905	−17,262	−19,844
Capital Account, n.i.e.	78bcd	2,872	2,305	6,004	6,589	6,437	6,330	6,967	4,792	4,970	7,309	9,982	10,583
Capital Account, n.i.e.: Credit	78bad	3,997	3,571	7,374	7,713	7,275	7,160	8,060	5,806	5,864	8,192	11,040	11,624
Capital Account: Debit	78bbd	−1,125	−1,266	−1,370	−1,124	−837	−830	−1,094	−1,014	−895	−884	−1,058	−1,040
Financial Account, n.i.e.	78bjd	−434	4,491	−7,951	20,138	8,547	−14,156	−10,097	16,942	16,602	17,483	4,444	38,991
Direct Investment Abroad	78bdd	−3,188	−4,051	−4,206	−5,577	−12,423	−19,065	−41,754	−53,865	−32,875	−32,410	−23,350	−42,836
Dir. Invest. in Rep. Econ., n.i.e.	78bed	9,681	9,216	6,297	6,796	6,384	11,905	15,541	36,931	27,741	36,727	25,513	9,898
Portfolio Investment Assets	78bfd	−6,567	−1,492	−490	−3,653	−16,450	−44,193	−47,397	−59,320	−45,042	−28,983	−91,061	−37,540
Equity Securities	78bkd	−728	−1,039	−534	−776	−5,272	−10,120	−17,279	−36,136	−260	283	−12,239	−15,716
Debt Securities	78bld	−5,839	−453	44	−2,877	−11,178	−34,073	−30,118	−23,185	−44,783	−29,267	−78,822	−21,824
Portfolio Investment Liab., n.i.e.	78bgd	55,314	−20,856	21,653	3,128	11,772	16,736	45,549	58,146	27,246	34,849	40,908	134,352
Equity Securities	78bmd	6,600	1,154	4,215	147	−294	10,072	9,975	19,692	7,233	3,550	−8,558	8,020
Debt Securities	78bnd	48,714	−22,010	17,438	2,981	12,066	6,664	35,574	38,455	20,013	31,299	49,466	126,332
Financial Derivatives Assets	78bwd	—	—	—	—	—	—	....	....	....	....	....	....
Financial Derivatives Liabilities	78bxd	−2,791	158	−557	−875	41	−2,776	260	2,025	−274	−4,712	−3,699	2,278
Other Investment Assets	78bhd	−71,940	9,152	−36,816	2,469	−1,415	−21,604	−24,624	−18,640	10,362	−22,610	−14,437	−50,305
Monetary Authorities	78bod	−3	3	−71	−4	8	−422	−39,311	−7,837	14,992	6,115	5,211	−18,079
General Government	78bpd	−663	−620	−402	−502	−377	−427	−209	−253	−283	−332	−384	−1,420
Banks	78bqd	−63,178	14,437	−26,899	9,969	13,175	−1,960	5,298	−7,588	−3,873	−17,417	−12,051	−17,244
Other Sectors	78brd	−8,097	−4,668	−9,446	−6,993	−14,220	−18,795	9,599	−2,962	−474	−10,976	−7,212	−13,561
Other Investment Liab., n.i.e.	78bid	19,058	12,363	6,168	17,849	20,638	44,841	41,427	51,666	29,445	34,623	70,570	23,144
Monetary Authorities	78bsd	−121	27	23	461	−466	−2	−11	−141	−185	1,119	−1,331	−89
General Government	78btd	938	3,007	1,493	−226	4	1,043	−296	902	575	437	−1,669	6,192
Banks	78bud	13,242	10,572	4,049	18,646	20,490	38,957	26,039	36,510	15,501	26,183	62,628	14,444
Other Sectors	78bvd	4,999	−1,242	604	−1,032	611	4,843	15,695	14,395	13,553	6,883	10,942	2,598
Net Errors and Omissions	78cad	−1,838	−371	−5,260	−2,856	−5,741	−3,395	−5,059	−5,379	−6,507	−5,058	−6,237	−6,762
Overall Balance	78cbd	−5,203	36	−6,414	24,279	11,756	−14,355	−22,850	−2,881	−1,340	3,690	−15,487	−6,412
Reserves and Related Items	79dad	5,203	−36	6,414	−24,279	−11,756	14,355	22,850	2,881	1,340	−3,690	15,487	6,412
Reserve Assets	79dbd	5,203	−36	6,414	−24,279	−11,756	14,355	22,850	2,881	1,340	−3,690	15,487	6,412
Use of Fund Credit and Loans	79dcd	—	—	—	—	—	—	—	—	—	—	—	—
Exceptional Financing	79ded	—	—	—	—	—	....	....	....	....	....	....	....
International Investment Position						*Millions of US Dollars*							
Assets	79aad	213,491	221,860	268,762	289,787	311,244	397,987	464,207	566,745	594,340	755,440	997,725	....
Direct Investment Abroad	79abd	24,027	30,052	36,225	40,548	50,322	70,130	112,802	159,959	184,462	224,364	279,818	....
Portfolio Investment	79acd	14,802	17,284	18,244	21,108	34,858	81,237	127,994	180,256	205,136	272,397	432,696	....
Equity Securities	79add	2,285	3,454	3,764	4,441	9,235	19,978	42,482	78,094	65,765	53,180	83,402	....
Debt Securities	79aed	12,516	13,830	14,480	16,667	25,623	61,259	85,513	102,161	139,371	219,217	349,294	....
Financial Derivatives	79ald	—	—	—	—	—	—	—	—	—	—	—	....
Other Investment	79afd	131,562	130,690	176,931	167,717	155,680	185,832	185,401	190,953	170,488	218,376	258,402	....
Monetary Authorities	79agd	148	159	247	229	198	582	36,652	42,557	26,059	24,206	23,648	....
General Government	79ahd	4,662	5,465	6,029	6,323	6,328	6,872	6,706	6,781	6,882	7,723	8,720	....
Banks	79aid	105,292	97,086	130,872	116,763	94,956	100,738	84,840	87,836	86,771	117,944	143,128	....
Other Sectors	79ajd	21,461	27,980	39,783	44,403	54,198	77,640	57,203	53,779	50,776	68,503	82,906	....
Reserve Assets	79akd	43,100	43,834	37,362	60,414	70,384	60,788	38,010	35,576	34,254	40,304	26,809	....
Liabilities	79lad	305,835	322,228	383,415	400,206	410,687	528,172	630,123	718,800	762,749	997,006	1,360,919	....
Dir. Invest. in Rep. Economy	79lbd	80,287	96,312	109,185	107,880	100,025	118,115	116,314	144,850	165,291	236,606	313,267	....
Portfolio Investment	79lcd	103,393	83,764	118,426	126,696	137,322	183,995	269,359	288,813	293,324	375,309	520,592	....
Equity Securities	79ldd	22,818	24,146	32,461	39,162	46,974	75,775	146,619	137,268	127,040	122,687	186,788	....
Debt Securities	79led	80,576	59,618	85,966	87,534	90,348	108,221	122,740	151,545	166,284	252,621	333,805	....
Financial Derivatives	79lld	—	—	—	—	—	—	—	—	—	—	—	....
Other Investment	79lfd	122,154	142,152	155,804	165,629	173,340	226,062	244,534	285,137	304,134	385,092	527,060	....
Monetary Authorities	79lgd	49	76	107	556	53	63	34	422	263	1,438	116	....
General Government	79lhd	6,546	9,989	12,355	11,503	10,158	11,725	9,939	10,343	10,125	11,972	12,888	....
Banks	79lid	89,991	104,912	114,506	127,770	138,350	183,084	191,090	219,207	225,809	286,551	400,933	....
Other Sectors	79ljd	25,567	27,175	28,836	25,801	24,779	31,191	43,471	55,165	67,937	85,131	113,123	....
Government Finance													
Central Government					*Billions of Pesetas through 1998; Millions of Euros Beginning 1999: Year Ending December 31*								
Deficit (-) or Surplus	80	−3,738.0	−4,147.6	−3,606.3	−4,003.5	−1,909.4	−800.0	† −6,054	−833	−2,255	−3,681	−6,683	−1,549
Total Revenue and Grants	81y	12,683.7	12,960.3	14,077.2	14,629.7	16,636.5	17,519.0	† 110,370	118,693	125,193	108,456	109,655	115,270
Revenue	81	12,683.7	12,960.3	14,077.2	14,629.7	16,636.5	17,519.0	† 110,370	118,693	125,193	108,456	109,655	115,270
Grants	81z	—	—	—	—	—	—	† —					
Exp. & Lending Minus Repay	82z	16,421.7	17,107.9	17,683.5	18,633.2	18,545.9	18,319.0	† 116,424	119,527	127,449	112,137	116,338	116,819
Expenditure	82	16,465.8	16,438.3	17,241.5	18,322.2	18,694.0	18,633.4	† 116,724	121,124	128,077	111,082	113,787	114,743
Lending Minus Repayments	83	−44.1	669.6	442.0	311.0	−148.1	−314.4	† −299	−1,598	−629	1,055	2,551	2,076
Total Financing	80h	3,737.5	4,147.2	3,605.7	4,003.0	1,908.8	800.2	† 6,054	833	2,255	3,681	6,683	1,548
Total Net Borrowing	84	6,238.6	2,317.7	3,324.5	5,039.2	973.4	910.7	† 11,187	6,834	−2,646	6,107	140	2,763
Use of Cash Balances	87	2,501.1	−1,829.5	−281.2	1,036.2	−935.4	110.5	† 5,092	6,001	−4,901	2,426	−6,543	1,214
Total Debt by Residence	88	31,236.7	34,266.0	38,678.1	43,922.0	45,616.6	47,243.4	† 298,378	308,212	307,434	308,792	302,968	305,529
Domestic	88a	21,751.8	27,389.8	29,951.8	34,934.4	35,121.6	35,756.1	† 207,308	187,787	177,644	171,913	182,940	165,829
Foreign	89a	9,484.9	6,876.2	8,726.3	8,987.6	10,495.0	11,487.3	† 91,070	120,424	129,791	136,880	120,029	139,700
General Government						*As Percent of Gross Domestic Product*							
Deficit (-) or Surplus	80g	−7.0	−6.3	−7.1	−5.0	−3.2	−2.6	−1.1	−.3	—	....	....	....
Debt	88g	60.0	62.6	64.2	68.0	66.7	64.6	63.1	60.4	57.2	....	....	....

		1993	1994	1995	1996	1997	1998	1999	2000	2001	2002	2003	2004
National Accounts						***Billions of Pesetas: through 1998; Billions of Euros Beginning 1999:***								
Househ.Cons.Expend.,incl.NPISHs....	96f.c	38,538	40,848	43,554	46,063	48,771	52,012	† 335	376	401	424	448	483
Government Consumption Expend...	91f.c	11,951	12,307	13,159	13,864	14,415	15,332	† 99	108	116	125	135	148
Gross Fixed Capital Formation..........	93e.c	13,503	14,259	16,015	16,703	17,983	20,086	† 136	163	177	191	211	233
Changes in Inventories....................	93i.c	15	244	249	216	212	359	† 3	3	3	3	5	4
Exports of Goods and Services.........	90c.c	11,649	14,209	16,465	18,454	21,991	23,935	† 156	183	194	199	206	215
Imports of Goods and Services (-).....	98c.c	12,138	14,313	16,601	18,055	21,155	23,876	† 163	203	211	214	223	246
Gross Domestic Product (GDP).........	99b.c	63,517	67,554	72,842	77,245	82,218	87,848	† 565	630	680	729	781	838
Net Primary Income from Abroad.....	98.n	−526	−1,182	−607	−890	−1,135	−1,013	† −6	−27	−36	−41	−45	....
Gross National Income (GNI)............	99a	60,426	63,630	72,660	76,766	81,409	86,780	† 560	603	644	688	735	....
Net Current Transf.from Abroad......	98t	....	....	295	197	209	192	† 1	—	—	—	....	....
Gross Nat'l Disposable Inc.(GNDI)....	99i	....	....	72,954	76,963	81,618	86,972	† 561	604	644	688	625	....
Gross Saving..............................	99s	....	....	16,241	17,036	18,576	19,816	† 127	137	148	159	62	....
Consumption of Fixed Capital..........	99cf	6,980	7,428	7,951	8,363	8,851	11,430	† 74	83	90	98	—	....
GDP Volume 1995 Prices.................	99b.r	69,237	70,887	72,841	74,617	77,621	80,468	† 507.3	529.7	548.5	563.2	579.6	597.5
GDP Volume (2000=100)...............	99bvr	78.6	80.4	82.6	84.7	88.1	91.3	† 95.8	100.0	103.5	106.3	109.4	112.8
GDP Deflator (2000=100)...............	99bir	77.1	80.1	84.0	87.0	89.0	91.8	† 93.7	100.0	104.2	108.8	113.2	117.8
						Millions: Midyear Estimates								
Population.................................	99z	39.69	39.81	39.92	40.02	40.12	40.24	40.43	40.72	41.12	41.61	42.14	42.65

Sri Lanka 524

		1993	1994	1995	1996	1997	1998	1999	2000	2001	2002	2003	2004
Exchange Rates						*Rupees per SDR: End of Period*							
Market Rate............................	aa	68.076	72.963	80.341	81.540	82.689	96.164	99.054	107.594	117.075	131.500	143.750	162.453
						Rupees per US Dollar: End of Period (ae) Period Average (rf)							
Market Rate............................	ae	49.562	49.980	54.048	56.705	61.285	68.297	72.170	82.580	93.159	96.725	96.738	104.605
Market Rate............................	rf	48.322	49.415	51.252	55.271	58.995	64.450	70.635	77.005	89.383	95.662	96.521	101.194
Fund Position						*Millions of SDRs: End of Period*							
Quota..................................	2f.s	304	304	304	304	304	304	413	413	413	413	413	413
SDRs...................................	1b.s	—	—	1	1	—	1	1	—	1	2	—	—
Reserve Position in the Fund..........	1c.s	20	20	20	20	20	20	48	48	48	48	48	48
Total Fund Cred.&Loans Outstg........	2tl	376	423	400	369	321	261	188	123	171	228	265	189
International Liquidity						*Millions of US Dollars Unless Otherwise Indicated: End of Period*							
Total Reserves minus Gold.............	1l.d	1,629	2,046	2,088	1,962	2,024	1,980	1,636	1,039	1,287	1,631	2,265	2,132
SDRs..............................	1b.d	—	—	1	2	—	1	1	—	1	2	1	—
Reserve Position in the Fund..........	1c.d	28	30	30	29	27	29	65	62	60	65	71	74
Foreign Exchange..................	1d.d	1,601	2,016	2,057	1,931	1,996	1,950	1,569	976	1,226	1,564	2,193	2,058
Gold (Million Fine Troy Ounces).......	1ad	.063	.063	.063	.063	.063	.063	.063	† .336	.255	.216	.165	.167
Gold (National Valuation)...............	1and	6	6	6	5	5	4	4	† 108	71	75	69	73
Monetary Authorities: Other Liab....	4..d	416	505	575	859	820	728	833	707	636	671	....	....
Deposit Money Banks: Assets..........	7a.d	516	639	839	780	1,103	916	941	1,050	900	795	889	1,243
Liabilities	7b.d	547	615	1,004	964	1,094	859	764	909	1,009	865	863	1,066
FCBU: Assets.........................	7k.d	456	540	574	504	682	479	439	429	422	330	424	520
Liabilities.....................	7m.d	601	665	682	615	702	438	306	429	519	330	276	382
Monetary Authorities						*Millions of Rupees: End of Period*							
Foreign Assets.........................	11	76,694	95,672	105,898	† 104,899	120,675	133,128	116,796	82,334	117,507	160,499	225,879	225,225
Claims on Central Government........	12a	26,563	29,335	37,224	37,799	26,776	29,018	49,179	94,708	88,969	83,893	64,387	117,630
Claims on Deposit Money Banks......	12e	4,900	3,376	2,812	2,259	1,692	1,122	748	520	150	2,657	2,627	2,547
Reserve Money.........................	14	56,469	68,055	78,587	85,509	83,736	92,866	100,444	105,163	112,522	126,410	141,446	170,967
of which: Currency Outside DMBs..	14a	32,134	38,907	42,199	42,565	45,680	51,767	58,481	62,647	65,536	75,292	85,601	99,669
Other Liabilities to DMBs................	14n	....	....	....	—	—	—	—	—	—	11,156	20,974	7,213
Foreign Liabilities.....................	16c	30,969	35,658	40,748	† 34,787	33,170	31,355	27,710	24,716	30,190	43,316	61,302	73,535
Central Government Deposits...........	16d	1,801	2,813	3,040	3,510	6,476	3,108	2,463	3,152	4,301	201	569	523
Capital Accounts......................	17a	22,737	25,358	30,829	28,343	35,547	47,532	49,043	59,866	71,449	72,920	74,331	100,409
Other Items (Net).....................	17r	−3,817	−3,500	−7,269	† −7,191	−9,786	−11,594	−12,939	−15,335	−11,838	−6,953	−5,730	−7,245
Deposit Money Banks						*Millions of Rupees: End of Period*							
Reserves...............................	20	20,562	25,389	35,449	41,188	36,500	39,667	40,110	39,542	49,760	53,234	51,083	70,904
Other Claims on Monetary Author....	20n	....	....	....	—	—	—	—	—	—	11,156	20,974	7,213
Foreign Assets.........................	21	25,567	31,918	† 45,338	44,212	67,596	62,560	67,946	86,682	83,814	76,921	86,011	129,987
Claims on Central Government........	22a	18,782	21,039	† 23,808	29,579	42,469	53,514	60,618	69,336	143,109	125,439	129,523	124,877
Claims on Nonfin.Pub.Enterprises...	22ca	3,966	3,118	13,305	15,491	14,658	10,836	13,715	38,254	40,811	43,031	36,192	41,171
Claims on Cooperatives..................	22cb	1,903	2,541	3,939	1,465	1,661	1,812	1,608	1,668	1,577	1,349	1,365	1,148
Claims on Private Sector.................	22d	49,052	62,676	206,783	228,992	261,359	291,969	323,374	362,435	395,216	452,054	527,079	640,162
Demand Deposits......................	24	27,169	31,415	32,970	35,516	40,108	44,470	50,059	55,788	56,665	64,052	76,014	88,777
Time and Savings Deposits..............	25	100,780	121,210	† 184,224	210,454	247,817	281,473	319,765	364,944	426,927	483,135	556,220	670,191
Foreign Liabilities.....................	26c	27,119	30,746	54,256	54,678	67,030	58,656	55,141	75,101	94,030	83,655	83,513	111,464
Central Government Deposits...........	26d	6,304	9,290	† 9,483	12,947	13,765	11,646	13,122	13,292	26,333	14,535	16,436	19,802
Credit from Monetary Authorities.....	26g	5,843	4,054	3,625	4,050	4,775	4,813	5,171	5,886	4,811	4,858	6,577	6,502
Capital Accounts......................	27a	21,851	28,278	33,460	39,238	44,368	50,220	51,571	51,808	44,520	51,770	75,197	77,220
Other Items (Net).....................	27r	−932	1,877	10,603	4,045	6,380	9,081	12,543	31,098	61,001	61,180	38,269	41,506
Monetary Survey						*Millions of Rupees: End of Period*							
Foreign Assets (Net)......................	31n	44,174	61,186	56,232	† 59,646	88,070	105,677	101,890	69,198	77,100	110,450	167,074	170,213
Domestic Credit.........................	32	161,686	188,564	273,209	297,517	327,436	372,817	433,115	550,156	639,415	691,082	741,577	904,722
Claims on Central Govt. (Net)........	32an	37,240	38,271	† 48,509	50,922	49,004	67,778	94,212	147,600	201,444	194,596	176,905	222,183
Claims on Nonfin.Pub.Enterprises...	32ca	7,775	5,163	13,305	15,491	14,658	10,836	13,715	38,254	40,811	43,031	36,192	41,171
Claims on Cooperatives................	32cb	1,903	2,541	3,939	1,465	1,661	1,812	1,608	1,668	1,577	1,349	1,365	1,148
Claims on Private Sector................	32d	49,124	63,453	207,456	229,640	262,113	292,392	323,580	362,634	395,583	452,106	527,116	640,220
Money..................................	34	59,356	70,463	75,218	78,829	85,851	96,269	108,554	118,478	122,211	139,361	161,635	188,454
Quasi-Money............................	35	100,256	120,539	† 184,224	210,454	247,817	281,473	319,765	364,944	426,927	483,135	556,220	670,191
Other Items (Net).....................	37r	43,722	56,278	68,364	† 68,507	81,838	100,753	106,685	135,933	167,378	179,037	190,796	216,291
Money plus Quasi-Money..............	35l	159,611	191,002	259,442	288,656	333,668	377,741	428,319	483,421	549,138	622,496	717,855	858,644
Interest Rates						*Percent Per Annum*							
Bank Rate (End of Period).............	60	17.00	17.00	17.00	17.00	17.00	17.00	16.00	25.00	....	18.00	15.00	15.00
Money Market Rate....................	60b	25.65	18.54	41.87	24.33	18.42	15.74	16.69	17.30	21.24	12.33	9.68	8.87
Treasury Bill Rate.....................	60c	16.52	12.68	16.81	† 17.40	....	12.59	12.51	14.02	17.57	12.47	8.09	7.71
Deposit Rate..........................	60l	13.77	13.10	12.13	12.36	11.25	9.56	9.12	9.17	11.01	9.22	6.00	5.07
Lending Rate..........................	60p	20.20	18.13	18.04	18.26	14.69	15.03	14.72	16.16	19.39	13.17	10.34	9.47
Government Bond Yield.................	61	16.25	....	....	....	....	....	....	....	....	....	....	....
Prices and Labor						*Index Numbers (2000=100): Period Averages*							
Share Prices............................	62	139.9	....	148.8	124.4	135.9	123.7	111.4	100.0	91.6	143.2	203.1	275.5
Wholesale Prices.......................	63	63.1	66.3	72.1	86.9	92.9	98.7	98.3	100.0	111.7	123.7	127.4	143.4
Consumer Prices........................	64	55.5	60.1	64.8	75.1	82.3	90.0	94.2	100.0	114.2	125.1	133.0	143.0
Wages: Agr. Minimum Rates...........	65	40.8	41.7	42.1	46.1	49.3	55.7	56.6	100.0	59.7	64.4	70.1	70.9
						Number in Thousands: Period Averages							
Labor Force............................	67d	6,032	6,079	6,106	6,242	6,266	6,661	6,673	6,827	6,773	7,145	7,654	....
Employment...........................	67e	5,201	5,281	5,357	5,537	5,608	6,049	6,083	6,310	6,236	6,519	6,906	....
Unemployment.........................	67c	831	798	749	705	658	611	591	517	537	626	641	....
Unemployment Rate (%).................	67r	13.8	13.1	12.3	11.3	10.5	9.2	8.9	7.6	7.9	8.8	8.1	....

Sri Lanka   524

		1993	1994	1995	1996	1997	1998	1999	2000	2001	2002	2003	2004
Intl. Transactions & Positions							*Millions of Rupees*						
Exports...............................	70	138,175	158,554	195,117	226,801	274,193	310,398	325,171	420,114	430,372	449,850	494,648	583,968
Tea................................	70s	19,911	20,964	24,638	34,068	42,533	50,280	43,727	53,133	61,602	63,105	68,063	74,898
Imports, c.i.f.......................	71	192,899	236,030	265,996	299,663	344,533	381,943	415,487	485,084	532,963	584,491	643,749	808,364
							2000=100						
Volume of Exports..................	72	60.5	66.2	† 70.9	73.9	81.7	80.5	83.7	100.0	91.9	92.7	98.3	105.8
Tea................................	72s	75.8	79.7	83.6	84.7	93.2	94.4	93.4	100.0	102.3	101.2	102.8	104.2
Volume of Imports..................	73	63.2	71.1	† 73.1	73.4	82.5	89.5	89.8	100.0	90.8	100.6	111.3	....
Unit Value of Exports..............	74	54.5	57.2	† 65.7	73.3	80.1	92.0	92.3	100.0	111.7	112.7	120.6	133.5
Tea................................	74s	49.4	49.5	55.5	75.7	85.9	100.3	88.1	100.0	113.3	117.4	124.6	135.2
Unit Value of Imports..............	75	57.6	60.9	70.4	77.0	† 80.8	81.8	85.9	100.0	113.5	111.6	....	....
Balance of Payments						*Millions of US Dollars: Minus Sign Indicates Debit*							
Current Account, n.i.e...............	78ald	−382.2	−757.4	−769.9	−682.7	−394.7	−227.7	−561.3	−1,043.6	−237.1	−267.5	−159.8	....
Goods: Exports f.o.b..............	78aad	2,785.7	3,208.3	3,797.9	4,095.2	4,638.7	4,808.0	4,596.2	5,439.6	4,816.9	4,699.2	5,133.2	....
Goods: Imports f.o.b.............	78abd	−3,527.8	−4,293.4	−4,782.6	−4,895.0	−5,278.3	−5,313.4	−5,365.5	−6,483.6	−5,376.9	−5,495.0	−6,004.8	....
Trade Balance..................	78acd	−742.1	−1,085.0	−984.7	−799.7	−639.6	−505.4	−769.3	−1,044.0	−560.0	−795.9	−871.6	....
Services: Credit................	78add	634.4	753.9	819.2	765.5	875.3	916.6	964.3	938.7	1,355.5	1,268.3	1,407.9	....
Services: Debit.................	78aed	−874.3	−1,052.3	−1,199.1	−1,204.3	−1,302.6	−1,361.6	−1,413.7	−1,621.4	−1,749.5	−1,584.3	−1,709.1	....
Balance on Goods & Services......	78afd	−982.1	−1,383.4	−1,364.6	−1,238.6	−1,066.9	−950.5	−1,218.6	−1,726.7	−954.1	−1,111.9	−1,172.8	....
Income: Credit..................	78agd	111.4	143.9	223.3	175.1	233.3	214.2	166.7	149.0	107.9	75.3	144.0	....
Income: Debit...................	78ahd	−234.3	−312.0	−360.6	−378.2	−392.9	−394.5	−419.3	−448.9	−374.6	−327.8	−336.3	....
Balance on Gds, Serv. & Inc......	78aid	−1,105.0	−1,551.6	−1,501.9	−1,441.6	−1,226.5	−1,130.8	−1,471.2	−2,026.6	−1,220.7	−1,364.4	−1,365.1	....
Current Transfers, n.i.e.: Credit......	78ajd	795.4	882.3	846.7	881.4	966.5	1,054.5	1,078.1	1,165.7	1,155.4	1,287.1	1,413.9	....
Current Transfers: Debit............	78akd	−72.6	−88.1	−114.7	−122.4	−134.7	−151.3	−168.2	−182.7	−171.7	−190.2	−208.6	....
Capital Account, n.i.e..............	78bcd	—	—	120.6	95.9	87.1	79.9	80.0	49.4	49.9	65.0	61.4	....
Capital Account, n.i.e.: Credit.......	78bad	—	—	124.2	99.7	91.3	84.6	85.2	55.0	55.2	70.9	67.9	....
Capital Account: Debit............	78bbd	—	—	−3.5	−3.8	−4.2	−4.7	−5.2	−5.7	−5.3	−5.9	−6.5	....
Financial Account, n.i.e............	78bjd	1,022.1	958.8	730.1	452.2	466.7	345.1	413.4	447.2	331.5	405.5	679.2	....
Direct Investment Abroad..........	78bdd	−6.9	−8.3	—	—	—	—	—	—	—	−11.5	−27.3	....
Dir. Invest. in Rep. Econ., n.i.e.....	78bed	194.5	166.4	56.0	119.9	430.1	193.4	176.4	173.0	171.8	196.5	228.7	....
Portfolio Investment Assets...........	78bfd	200.1	292.9	105.3	76.8	139.9	88.9	71.8	19.1	23.6	78.0	15.5	....
Equity Securities..................	78bkd	....	....	....	....	....	....	....	....	23.6	78.0	15.5	....
Debt Securities..................	78bld	200.1	292.9	105.3	76.8	139.9	88.9	71.8	19.1				....
Portfolio Investment Liab., n.i.e......	78bgd	−132.9	−265.9	−107.3	−70.2	−126.8	−112.9	−84.6	−63.4	−34.7	−52.6	−13.9	....
Equity Securities..................	78bmd	....	....	....	....	....	....	....	....	−34.7	−52.6	−13.9	....
Debt Securities..................	78bnd	−132.9	−265.9	−107.3	−70.2	−126.8	−112.9	−84.6	−63.4	—	—	....	....
Financial Derivatives Assets..........	78bwd	....	....	....	—	....	....	....	....	....	....	....	....
Financial Derivatives Liabilities.......	78bxd	....	....	....	....	....	....	....	....	....	....	....	....
Other Investment Assets..............	78bhd	16.4	−134.0	41.7	−27.9	−392.9	75.9	23.2	−243.7	183.0	104.4	−93.8	....
Monetary Authorities..................	78bod	—	—	—	....	—	....	....	....	—	—	—	....
General Government..................	78bpd	−2.4	9.4	3.6	−6.4	1.7	−2.9	−1.1	−4.4	—	—	—	....
Banks..............................	78bqd	18.8	−143.4	38.1	−21.5	−394.6	78.8	24.3	−239.4	183.0	104.4	−93.8	....
Other Sectors......................	78brd	—	—	—	....	—	—	....	....	....	....	....	....
Other Investment Liab., n.i.e........	78bid	750.9	907.6	634.4	353.6	416.5	99.7	226.6	562.3	−12.3	90.7	570.0	....
Monetary Authorities..................	78bsd	25.9	9.6	14.4	11.6	30.3	17.5	65.8	75.8	−32.9	26.8	40.3	....
General Government................	78btd	262.6	246.9	448.4	218.0	144.5	203.6	62.5	46.6	248.9	161.9	548.5	....
Banks..............................	78bud	128.2	73.4	86.7	95.8	209.4	−130.7	−88.4	258.3	71.0	−144.5	−1.6	....
Other Sectors......................	78bvd	334.3	577.7	85.0	28.2	32.3	9.3	186.8	181.5	−299.2	46.5	−17.2	....
Net Errors and Omissions................	78cad	128.0	106.3	157.9	143.6	148.0	26.3	−27.3	186.2	15.0	136.2	−32.3	....
Overall Balance...................	78cbd	767.9	307.7	238.7	9.0	307.2	223.6	−95.2	−360.8	159.4	339.2	548.5	....
Reserves and Related Items.............	79dad	−767.9	−307.7	−238.7	−9.0	−307.2	−223.6	95.2	360.8	−159.4	−339.2	−548.5	....
Reserve Assets....................	79dbd	−820.7	−373.5	−204.7	36.3	−241.4	−141.0	194.8	446.5	−240.7	−444.4	−627.1	....
Use of Fund Credit and Loans........	79dcd	52.8	65.9	−34.1	−45.2	−65.7	−82.6	−99.7	−85.7	59.8	74.0	49.7	....
Exceptional Financing...................	79ded	—	—	—	....	....	....	....	....	21.6	31.2	28.9	....
Government Finance						*Millions of Rupees: Year Ending December 31*							
Deficit (-) or Surplus.................	80	−32,084	−49,474	−55,196	−59,913	−40,234	−81,559	−76,359	−118,995	−138,133p	....	....	....
Revenue.........................	81	98,495	110,038	136,257	146,280	165,036	175,032	195,905	211,282	231,463p	....	....	....
Grants Received...................	81z	8,025	8,257	9,028	7,739	7,329	7,200	6,761	5,145	5,500p	....	....	....
Expenditure.......................	82	134,728	157,476	195,880	212,787	228,732	253,808	267,611	322,048	367,966p	....	....	....
Lending Minus Repayments...........	83	3,876	10,293	4,601	1,145	−16,133	9,983	11,414	13,374	7,130p	....	....	....
Financing (by Residence of Lender)													
Domestic.........................	84a	22,229	37,696	33,972	49,753	30,276	71,363	74,875	118,500	123,595p	....	....	....
Foreign..........................	85a	9,855	11,778	21,224	10,160	9,958	10,196	1,484	495	14,538p	....	....	....
Debt: Domestic....................	88a	213,685	249,118	285,759	349,007	387,740	463,426	543,465	676,660p	1,450,587	948,386	1,019,969	1,084,978
Foreign..........................	89a	269,883	300,174	346,286	360,313	376,331	461,273	507,866	542,040p	634,622	721,956	843,882	920,593
Debt (by Currency)													
Debt: Rupees.....................	88b	213,685	249,118	285,759	349,007	382,962	446,547	543,465	676,660	815,965p	....	....	....
Intragovernmental Debt..............	88s	—	—	—	—	—	—	—	—	—p	....	....	....
Debt: Foreign Currency.............	89b	269,883	300,174	346,286	360,313	383,615	461,454	508,396	542,207	634,622p	....	....	....

Sri Lanka 524

National Accounts		1993	1994	1995	1996	1997	1998	1999	2000	2001	2002	2003	2004
							Millions of Rupees						
Househ.Cons.Expend.,incl.NPISHs....	96f	373,785	434,933	489,057	569,416	643,839	723,506	790,379	906,188	1,041,041	1,214,117	1,341,896	1,542,107
Government Consumption Expend...	91f	45,791	56,002	76,604	81,021	92,196	99,145	99,851	132,189	144,441	139,311	139,268	164,716
Gross Fixed Capital Formation..........	93e	125,875	154,260	170,875	183,509	216,873	255,714	301,728	352,644	309,684	337,782	388,757	507,189
Changes in Inventories...................	93i	1,800	2,250	950	2,755	230	175	95	40	40	4,261	2,135	268
Exports of Goods and Services..........	90c	168,858	195,805	237,711	268,640	325,289	368,957	392,437	490,676	525,398	570,995	632,907	738,687
Imports of Goods and Services (-).....	98c	216,544	264,166	307,425	337,213	388,154	430,111	478,526	624,048	613,167	679,550	741,667	923,258
Gross Domestic Product (GDP).........	99b	499,565	579,084	667,772	768,133	890,272	1,017,986	1,105,985	1,257,682	1,407,398	1,582,655	1,761,161	2,029,441
Net Primary Income from Abroad.....	98.n	−5,979	−8,310	−6,958	−11,258	−9,409	−11,556	−17,831	−23,083	−23,830	−25,159	−16,535	−20,688
GDP at Factor Cost........................	99ba	453,092	523,300	598,327	695,934	803,698	912,839	994,730	1,125,259	1,245,598	1,403,310	1,562,737	1,797,941
Gross National Income (GNI)............	99a	493,586	570,774	660,814	756,875	880,828	1,006,373	1,088,154	1,234,599	1,383,568	1,557,479	1,744,154	2,008,496
GDP at Fact.Cost,Vol.'82 Prices.......	99bap	150,783	159,269	167,953	174,261	....	....	....	....	....	....	....	....
GDP at Fact.Cost,Vol.'96 Prices.......	99bap	....	....	....	695,934	739,763	774,796	808,340	857,035	843,794	877,248	930,057	979,925
GDP Volume (2000=100)...............	99bvp	70.3	74.2	78.3	† 81.2	86.3	90.4	94.3	100.0	98.5	102.4	108.5	114.3
GDP Deflator (2000=100)...............	99bip	57.3	62.7	67.9	76.2	82.7	89.7	93.7	100.0	112.4	121.8	128.0	139.7
							Millions: Midyear Estimates						
Population................................	99z	18.46	18.67	18.87	19.07	19.27	19.47	19.66	19.85	20.03	20.21	20.39	20.57

Sudan 732

		1993	1994	1995	1996	1997	1998	1999	2000	2001	2002	2003	2004
Exchange Rates						*Dinars per SDR: End of Period*							
Market Rate	aa	29.86	58.39	78.24	208.40	232.35	334.83	353.70	335.30	328.55	355.76	386.59	389.23
						Dinars per US Dollar: End of Period (ae) Period Average (rf)							
Market Rate	ae	21.74	40.00	52.63	144.93	172.21	237.80	257.70	257.35	261.43	261.68	260.16	250.63
Market Rate	rf	15.93	28.96	58.09	125.08	157.57	200.80	252.55	257.12	258.70	263.31	260.98	257.91
Fund Position						*Millions of SDRs: End of Period*							
Quota	2f.s	169.7	169.7	169.7	169.7	169.7	169.7	169.7	169.7	169.7	169.7	169.7	169.7
SDRs	1b.s	—	—	—	—	—	—	—	—	—	.1	.2	—
Reserve Position in the Fund	1c.s	—	—	—	—	—	—	—	—	—	—	—	—
Total Fund Cred.&Loans Outstg	2tl	671.6	671.6	645.7	621.2	590.5	548.4	520.8	479.7	438.6	421.6	402.9	381.7
International Liquidity						*Millions of US Dollars Unless Otherwise Indicated: End of Period*							
Total Reserves minus Gold	1l.d	37.4	78.2	163.4	106.8	81.6	90.6	188.7	† 247.3	117.8	440.9	847.5	1,626.1
SDRs	1b.d	—	—	—	—	—	—	—	—	—	.2	.3	—
Reserve Position in the Fund	1c.d	—	—	—	—	—	—	—	—	—	—	—	—
Foreign Exchange	1d.d	37.4	78.1	163.3	106.8	81.6	90.6	188.7	† 247.3	117.8	440.7	847.2	1,626.1
Monetary Authorities: Other Liab	4..d	2,288.0	2,471.8	3,407.1	2,549.9	2,464.4	2,538.9	2,618.8	2,640.2	2,654.1	2,793.2	3,005.8	3,068.9
Deposit Money Banks: Assets	7a.d	44.8	27.0	32.1	20.7	25.8	26.9	266.1	286.2	343.2	488.8	500.7	563.3
Liabilities	7b.d	6.9	3.8	5.3	3.0	2.6	2.0	13.4	14.8	34.8	52.4	56.9	72.3
Monetary Authorities						*Billions of Dinars: End of Period*							
Foreign Assets	11	.82	3.13	8.61	15.50	14.07	21.58	48.64	† 73.11	41.25	119.85	229.81	420.36
Claims on Central Government	12a	16.52	22.03	32.90	76.03	84.76	101.77	134.79	† 168.95	195.46	230.35	277.93	288.26
of which:Accum. Interest Arrears	12ag	....	....	....	....	....	....	....	52.69	64.09	76.09	88.68	100.01
Claims on Nonfin.Pub.Enterprises	12c	.22	.22	.22	.22	.22	.22	3.45	† 17.14	14.81	5.74	17.34	15.48
Claims on Deposit Money Banks	12e	.52	.36	.36	.35	2.39	6.14	7.21	† 8.82	12.58	17.15	33.49	29.98
Reserve Money	14	14.45	20.21	35.72	64.94	87.18	112.81	152.42	† 223.58	233.59	283.30	360.59	462.17
of which: Currency Outside DMBs	14a	9.45	14.79	24.86	44.44	58.49	82.14	108.11	† 142.08	153.84	193.58	240.21	304.90
Quasi-Monetary Deposits	15	.63	2.08	3.21	3.24	3.06	3.34	3.21	—	—	—	—	—
Cent. Bk. Liab.: Musharaka Certif	16ac	....	....	....	....	....	4.85	4.20	† 1.11	.64	.76	2.75	—
Foreign Liabilities	16c	67.78	134.16	224.80	485.58	547.81	767.53	838.10	† 820.43	818.50	859.84	914.84	894.68
Central Government Deposits	16d	.91	.86	1.24	10.77	9.18	3.74	5.11	† 8.44	9.62	27.27	64.78	151.55
Capital Accounts	17a	.13	.24	.43	1.24	1.16	2.05	2.61	† 4.24	4.32	9.11	13.16	22.34
Valuation Adjustment	17rv	−63.09	−124.94	−206.55	−444.81	−514.97	−724.21	−772.02	† −776.69	−781.52	−783.05	−774.95	−758.65
Other Items (Net)	17r	−2.73	−6.88	−16.78	−28.85	−31.99	−40.39	−39.53	† −13.09	−21.04	−24.15	−22.62	−18.01
Deposit Money Banks						*Billions of Dinars: End of Period*							
Reserves	20	4.62	5.58	8.01	14.27	28.07	30.62	37.91	57.15	57.41	67.68	91.01	118.43
Claims on Mon.Author.:Securities	20c	....	....	....	....	....	4.85	4.20	1.11	.64	.76	2.75	—
Foreign Assets	21	9.73	10.80	16.87	29.98	44.50	63.92	68.57	73.66	89.73	127.92	130.27	141.19
Claims on Central Government	22a	.45	.21	.16	.12	.03	.13	.16	4.22	7.33	20.88	35.04	46.64
Claims on State and Local Govt	22b	.07	.03	.13	.16	.17	.05	.07	.01	.53	1.33	1.28	1.28
Claims on Nonfin.Pub.Enterprises	22c	.70	1.22	1.19	1.67	1.68	2.57	4.72	5.65	9.06	11.56	11.30	13.37
Claims on Private Sector	22d	4.51	8.82	13.07	31.90	39.35	44.34	43.58	71.48	101.14	178.43	279.63	421.16
Claims on Nonbank Financial Insts	22f	.08	.09	.12	.22	.36	.43	.35	2.09	.62	1.89	2.46	.58
Demand Deposits	24	6.25	9.49	15.60	30.92	41.35	46.94	56.90	84.13	109.14	147.46	194.63	279.46
Time and Savings Deposits	25	10.13	13.65	25.41	35.82	55.13	73.62	85.35	107.26	158.54	210.53	271.88	355.91
Foreign Liabilities	26c	1.50	1.51	2.81	4.30	4.41	4.72	3.44	3.81	9.11	13.72	14.79	18.13
Central Government Deposits	26d	.26	.23	.31	.77	.40	.42	3.53	6.35	7.08	5.09	6.44	11.29
Credit from Monetary Authorities	26g	.07	.10	.75	.08	.11	.32	3.01	2.51	2.51	7.26	14.91	10.65
Capital Accounts	27a	1.69	3.86	5.47	11.14	14.77	20.34	24.47	32.20	47.64	73.69	110.31	143.71
Valuation Adjustment	27rv	1.07	.70	1.08	1.39	2.81	2.36	−.39	−.78	−.17	−.69	−.40	−3.02
Other Items (Net)	27r	−1.58	−4.07	−13.51	−8.21	−6.53	−.93	−16.47	−19.62	−66.83	−46.63	−58.72	−73.47
Monetary Survey						*Billions of Dinars: End of Period*							
Foreign Assets (Net)	31n	−58.73	−121.73	−202.14	−444.40	−493.66	−686.75	−724.34	† −677.49	−696.62	−625.80	−569.55	−351.25
Domestic Credit	32	21.36	31.52	46.24	98.78	116.99	145.34	178.50	† 254.74	312.25	417.81	553.76	623.93
Claims on Central Govt. (Net)	32an	15.79	21.14	31.51	64.61	75.22	97.74	126.32	† 158.38	186.10	218.87	241.74	172.06
Claims on State and Local Govt	32b	.07	.03	.13	.16	.17	.05	.07	.01	.53	1.33	1.28	1.28
Claims on Nonfin.Pub.Enterprises	32c	.92	1.44	1.41	1.88	1.89	2.78	8.18	† 22.79	23.87	17.30	28.64	28.85
Claims on Private Sector	32d	4.51	8.82	13.07	31.90	39.35	44.34	43.58	71.48	101.14	178.43	279.63	421.16
Claims on Nonbank Financial Inst	32f	.08	.09	.12	.22	.36	.43	.35	2.09	.62	1.89	2.46	.58
Money	34	15.70	24.28	40.46	75.36	99.85	129.08	165.01	† 234.59	271.39	352.26	458.48	604.37
Quasi-Money	35	10.76	15.73	28.62	39.06	58.20	76.95	88.56	† 112.60	161.39	211.00	275.61	356.08
Valuation Adjustment	37rv	−62.02	−124.24	−205.47	−443.42	−512.15	−721.85	−772.41	† −777.47	−781.68	−783.73	−775.35	−761.66
Other Items (Net)	37r	−1.81	−6.00	−19.82	−16.90	−22.41	−24.72	−26.73	† 8.06	−34.90	12.48	25.56	73.90
Money plus Quasi-Money	35l	26.47	40.04	69.39	114.70	157.90	205.16	253.31	347.19	432.77	563.27	734.09	960.45
Prices and Labor						*Index Numbers (2000=100): Period Averages*							
Consumer Prices	64	5.6	12.1	20.4	47.5	69.7	81.6	† 94.6	100.0	107.2	116.2	125.2	135.8
						Number in Thousands: Period Averages							
Labor Force	67d	5,841	....	....	7,415	....	....	....	....	....	....	....	....
Intl. Transactions & Positions						*Millions of US Dollars: Year Ending June 30 through 1994, Year Ending December 31 Thereafter*							
Exports	70..d	417.3	502.6	555.6	620.3	594.2	595.8	780.0	1,806.7	1,698.7	1,949.1	2,542.2	3,777.8
Imports, c.i.f	71..d	944.9	1,227.4	† 1,218.8	1,547.5	1,579.6	1,914.7	1,415.0	1,552.7	1,585.5	2,446.4	2,736.2	....

Sudan 732

		1993	1994	1995	1996	1997	1998	1999	2000	2001	2002	2003	2004
Balance of Payments		*Millions of US Dollars: Minus Sign Indicates Debit*											
Current Account, n.i.e.	78ald	−202.2	−601.7	−499.9	−826.8	−828.1	−956.5	−464.8	−556.8	−618.3	−1,008.1	−955.4	−870.9
Goods: Exports f.o.b.	78aad	306.3	523.9	555.7	620.3	594.2	595.7	780.1	1,806.7	1,698.7	1,949.1	2,542.2	3,777.8
Goods: Imports f.o.b.	78abd	−532.8	−1,045.4	−1,066.0	−1,339.5	−1,421.9	−1,732.2	−1,256.0	−1,366.3	−1,395.1	−2,293.8	−2,536.1	−3,586.2
Trade Balance	78acd	−226.5	−521.5	−510.3	−719.2	−827.7	−1,136.5	−475.9	440.4	303.6	−344.7	6.1	191.6
Services: Credit	78add	69.4	76.2	125.3	50.7	31.5	15.8	81.6	27.4	14.6	132.2	36.5	44.1
Services: Debit	78aed	−109.8	−223.7	−172.3	−200.8	−172.8	−204.0	−274.9	−647.6	−660.3	−818.2	−830.3	−1,064.5
Balance on Goods & Services	78afd	−266.9	−669.0	−557.3	−869.3	−969.0	−1,324.7	−669.2	−179.8	−342.1	−1,030.7	−787.7	−828.8
Income: Credit	78agd	.7	1.6	1.9	6.3	16.9	13.7	19.1	4.6	17.8	29.2	10.0	21.8
Income: Debit	78ahd	−20.9	−15.9	−4.9	−.7	−5.3	−10.6	−123.2	−579.6	−571.9	−638.0	−879.2	−1,134.5
Balance on Gds, Serv. & Inc.	78aid	−287.1	−683.3	−560.3	−863.7	−957.4	−1,321.6	−773.3	−754.8	−896.2	−1,639.5	−1,657.0	−1,941.5
Current Transfers, n.i.e.: Credit	78ajd	84.9	120.1	346.2	236.3	439.1	731.8	702.2	651.3	730.4	1,085.9	1,218.4	1,580.2
Current Transfers: Debit	78akd	—	−38.5	−285.8	−199.4	−309.8	−366.7	−393.7	−453.3	−452.5	−454.5	−516.8	−509.6
Capital Account, n.i.e.	78bcd	....	....	....	....	....	−54.2	−22.9	−119.3	−93.3	† —	—	—
Capital Account, n.i.e.: Credit	78bad	....	....	....	....	....	13.0	45.8	16.5	11.9	† —	—	—
Capital Account: Debit	78bbd	....	....	....	....	....	−67.2	−68.7	−135.8	−105.2	† —	—	—
Financial Account, n.i.e.	78bjd	326.6	276.0	473.7	136.8	195.0	333.4	435.3	431.6	561.2	761.2	1,284.4	1,427.8
Direct Investment Abroad	78bdd						....	—	—	....	....	—	—
Dir. Invest. in Rep. Econ., n.i.e.	78bed	....	....	....	.4	97.9	370.7	370.8	392.2	574.0	713.2	1,349.2	1,511.1
Portfolio Investment Assets	78bfd	....	....	....	....	....	....	—	—	.7	14.8	35.3	19.9
Equity Securities	78bkd	....	—	—	....	....	....	—	—	....	....	—	—
Debt Securities	78bld	....	—	—	....	....	....	—	—	.7	14.8	35.3	19.9
Portfolio Investment Liab., n.i.e.	78bgd	—	—	—	....	....	....	—	—	—	—	—	—
Equity Securities	78bmd	—	—	—	....	....	....	—	—	—	—	—	—
Debt Securities	78bnd	—	—	—	....	....	....	—	—	—	—	—	—
Financial Derivatives Assets	78bwd	....	....	....	....	....	....	....	....	....	....	....	....
Financial Derivatives Liabilities	78bxd	....	....	....	....	....	....	....	....	....	....	....	....
Other Investment Assets	78bhd	....	....	....	....	....	−78.5	−38.4	−53.4	−55.1	−148.0	381.4	598.8
Monetary Authorities	78bod	....	....	....	....	....	....	—	—	....	—	−.2	−10.2
General Government	78bpd	....	....	....	....	....	....	—	—	....	—	141.7	373.8
Banks	78bqd	....	....	....	....	....	−78.5	−38.4	−53.4	−55.1	−145.6	−9.0	−42.0
Other Sectors	78brd	....	....	....	....	....	....	—	—	....	−2.4	248.9	277.2
Other Investment Liab., n.i.e.	78bid	326.6	276.0	473.7	136.4	97.1	41.2	102.9	92.8	41.6	181.2	−481.5	−702.0
Monetary Authorities	78bsd	163.3	28.3	73.6	62.4	20.1	8.0	−3.7	14.0	40.6	64.2	—	—
General Government	78btd	200.8	−3.1	9.8	−22.5	−45.1	−1.0	—	—	—	† −87.8	−262.2	−384.5
Banks	78bud	−37.5	250.8	390.3	96.2	119.3	34.2	106.6	78.8	1.0	204.8	4.1	13.0
Other Sectors	78bvd	....	....	....	.3	2.8	—	—	—	—	....	−223.4	−330.6
Net Errors and Omissions	78cad	−82.6	344.8	89.3	727.5	651.2	750.5	167.2	368.4	−.5	492.2	−2.4	225.5
Overall Balance	78cbd	41.8	19.1	63.1	37.5	18.1	73.2	114.8	123.9	−150.9	245.3	326.6	782.4
Reserves and Related Items	79dad	−41.8	−19.1	−63.1	−37.5	−18.1	−73.2	−114.8	−123.9	150.9	−245.3	−326.6	−782.4
Reserve Assets	79dbd	−41.8	−19.1	−23.6	−2.0	24.0	−16.0	−110.0	−108.0	127.6	−300.2	−422.7	−729.8
Use of Fund Credit and Loans	79dcd	—	—	−39.5	−35.5	−42.1	−57.2	−37.8	−54.0	−52.3	−22.3	−26.3	−31.3
Exceptional Financing	79ded	—	—	....	....	....	33.0	38.1	75.6	77.2	122.4	−21.2	
Government Finance		*Millions of Dinars: Year Ending December 31*											
Deficit (-) or Surplus	80	−7	−9	† −13,500	−34,600	−13,400	....	....	....	....	....	....	....
Revenue	81	8	13	† 36,500	62,900	107,300	....	....	....	....	....	....	....
Grants Received	81z	—	—	† —	—	—	....	....	....	....	....	....	....
Expenditure	82	15	22	† 50,000	97,500	120,700	....	....	....	....	....	....	....
Lending Minus Repayments	83	—	—	† —	—	—	....	....	....	....	....	....	....
Financing													
Domestic	84a	4	7	† 9,300	32,400	10,800	....	....	....	....	....	....	....
Foreign	85a	3	2	† 4,200	2,200	2,600	....	....	....	....	....	....	....
National Accounts		*Billions of Dinars: Yr.End.June 30 through '94, December 31 Thereafter*											
Gross Domestic Product (GDP)	99b	84	168	† 483	1,022	1,601	....	....	....	....	....	....	....
		Millions: Midyear Estimates											
Population	99z	27.97	28.66	† 29.35	30.06	30.78	31.50	32.21	32.90	33.57	34.21	34.86	35.52

Suriname 366

		1993	1994	1995	1996	1997	1998	1999	2000	2001	2002	2003	2004
Exchange Rates						*Surinamese Dollars per SDR: End of Period*							
Market Rate	aa	.0025	† .5978	.6050	.5766	.5410	.5646	1.3554	2.8384	2.7378	3.4192	† 3.9007	† 4.2164
						Surinamese Dollars per US Dollar: End of Period (ae) Period Average (rf)							
Market Rate	ae	.0018	† .4095	.4070	.4010	.4010	.4010	.9875	2.1785	2.1785	2.5150	† 2.6250	† 2.7150
Market Rate	rf	.0018	† .1341	.4422	.4013	.4010	.4010	.8594	1.3225	2.1785	2.3468	† 2.6013	† 2.7336
Fund Position						*Millions of SDRs: End of Period*							
Quota	2f.s	67.60	67.60	67.60	67.60	67.60	67.60	92.10	92.10	92.10	92.10	92.10	92.10
SDRs	1b.s	—	—	7.75	8.22	8.23	8.25	2.00	1.77	1.56	1.42	1.32	1.21
Reserve Position in the Fund	1c.s	—	—	—	—	—	—	6.13	6.13	6.13	6.13	6.12	6.12
Total Fund Cred.&Loans Outstg	2tl	—	—	—	—	—	—						
International Liquidity					*Millions of US Dollars Unless Otherwise Indicated: End of Period*								
Total Reserves minus Gold	1l.d	17.70	39.70	132.92	96.32	109.11	106.14	38.46	62.99	119.25	106.16	105.76	129.40
SDRs	1b.d	—	—	11.52	11.82	11.11	11.62	2.75	2.31	1.95	1.93	1.96	1.89
Reserve Position in the Fund	1c.d	—	—	—	—	—	—	8.41	7.98	7.70	8.33	9.10	9.51
Foreign Exchange	1d.d	17.70	39.70	121.40	84.50	98.00	94.52	27.30	52.70	109.60	95.90	94.70	118.00
Gold (Million Fine Troy Ounces)	1ad	.054	.054	.093	.134	.193	.128	.246	.256	.265	.021	.021	.021
Gold (National Valuation)	1and	841.67	14.32	41.34	58.18	54.53	177.34	70.29	64.39	68.48	6.13	7.20	† 7.52
Monetary Authorities: Other Liab.	4..d	1,316.25	18.08	3.25	3.03	74.81	229.66	111.10	103.74	77.92	1.05	.84	3.20
Deposit Money Banks: Assets	7a.d	1,093.52	49.67	68.84	116.40	128.94	122.43	180.59	131.02	188.33	142.10	194.35	243.67
Liabilities	7b.d	374.71	28.62	45.71	75.09	86.00	96.29	160.52	128.08	181.12	5.36	8.62	8.07
Monetary Authorities					*Thousands of Surinamese Dollars: End of Period*								
Foreign Assets	11	3,277	23,546	65,538	56,984	60,615	† 127,893	123,498	253,498	386,507	257,282	266,374	368,258
Claims on Central Government	12a	5,224	5,307	4,909	6,768	6,376	† 38,602	101,982	287,462	57,158	263,098	281,471	353,069
Claims on Nonfin.Pub.Enterprises	12c	—	—	—	—	—	† 4,052	3,783	6,564	1,293	1,523	1,450	1,426
Claims on Private Sector	12d	2	9	31	69	246	† 1,669	4,018	5,677	12,886	8,573	7,318	5,511
Claims on Deposit Money Banks	12e	4	13	—	26	13,414	† 19,077	38,249	43,064	44,884	21,721	22,838	22,838
Claims on Other Banking Insts.	12f	—	—	—	—	—	† 218	511	623	719	783	671	671
Reserve Money	14	5,640	17,361	56,775	50,953	50,740	† 83,301	122,806	313,164	358,470	471,690	432,727	522,249
of which: Currency Outside DMBs	14a	2,638	10,486	25,199	27,404	32,256	† 50,478	81,686	150,657	182,476	† 203,804	209,008	246,826
Time & Fgn. Currency Deposits	15	—	—	—	—	—	† 192	232	1,442	1,082	1,380	1,436	1,556
Foreign Liabilities	16c	2,349	7,403	1,321	1,214	29,997	† 92,093	109,711	225,998	169,753	2,647	2,193	8,701
Central Government Deposits	16d	29	844	9,900	9,076	3,021	† 8,317	22,493	60,746	45,963	55,730	83,121	125,518
Capital Accounts	17a	54	4,668	4,723	4,589	4,420	† 11,398	28,757	20,218	−45,757	40,594	87,149	123,839
Other Items (Net)	17r	434	−1,401	−2,240	−1,985	−7,529	† −3,789	−11,958	−24,680	−26,063	−19,061	−26,503	−30,089
Deposit Money Banks					*Thousands of Surinamese Dollars: End of Period*								
Reserves	20	2,873	6,242	29,584	19,142	18,531	31,462	32,392	122,759	124,630	† 220,338	228,082	246,917
Foreign Assets	21	1,952	20,341	28,016	46,675	51,705	49,095	178,333	285,419	410,276	† 357,389	510,166	661,553
Claims on Central Government	22a	266	392	567	913	8,639	20,814	23,594	64,030	95,884	† 98,779	99,032	162,650
Claims on Nonfin.Pub.Enterprises	22c	—	—	—	—	—	—	—	—	—	† 1,944	10,821	8,628
Claims on Private Sector	22d	3,133	6,645	20,120	45,486	63,383	79,103	106,703	93,296	147,134	† 401,942	566,365	755,405
Claims on Nonbank Financial Insts.	22g	—	—	—	—	—	—	—	—	—	† 794	5,952	11,395
Demand Deposits	24	3,276	9,763	30,912	25,156	35,476	39,929	51,367	111,010	175,972	† 279,407	324,681	414,364
Quasi-Monetary Liabilities	25	3,179	7,218	20,995	52,609	61,973	87,578	108,151	160,966	178,435	† 696,805	921,143	1,250,933
Bonds	26ab	104	153	357	256	226	28	21	13	5	† —	—	—
Foreign Liabilities	26c	669	11,721	18,603	30,113	34,486	38,612	158,517	279,029	394,561	† 13,475	22,635	21,905
Central Government Deposits	26d	103	956	1,273	371	885	167	542	525	840	† 720	1,230	1,441
Credit from Monetary Authorities	26g	4	13	—	26	14,197	15,726	34,170	38,124	39,510	† 16,508	54,110	19,388
Capital Accounts	27a	611	2,852	5,263	8,732	11,681	12,516	20,933	29,669	73,054	† 75,037	82,159	139,898
Other Items (Net)	27r	279	945	885	−5,048	−16,666	−14,082	−32,678	−53,833	−84,453	† −766	14,459	−1,381
Monetary Survey					*Thousands of Surinamese Dollars: End of Period*								
Foreign Assets (Net)	31n	2,210	24,763	73,630	72,332	47,837	† 46,283	33,603	33,889	232,469	† 598,549	751,712	999,205
Domestic Credit	32	8,493	10,554	14,456	43,789	74,737	† 135,975	217,555	396,382	268,272	† 720,987	888,729	1,171,796
Claims on Central Govt. (Net)	32an	5,358	3,900	−5,696	−1,767	11,109	† 50,932	102,541	290,222	106,240	† 305,427	296,151	388,759
Claims on Nonfin.Pub.Enterprises	32c	—	—	—	—	—	† 4,052	3,783	6,564	1,293	† 3,467	12,271	10,054
Claims on Private Sector	32d	3,135	6,654	20,152	45,556	63,628	† 80,773	110,720	98,973	160,020	† 410,515	573,683	760,916
Claims on Other Banking Insts.	32f	—	—	—	—	—	† 218	511	623	719	† 783	671	671
Claims on Nonbank Financial Insts.	32g	—	—	—	—	—	† —			—	† 794	5,952	11,395
Money	34	6,043	20,883	58,103	56,967	68,468	† 92,249	139,779	285,596	394,617	† 546,199	569,069	701,316
Quasi-Money	35	3,179	7,218	20,995	52,609	61,973	† 87,770	108,383	162,409	179,517	† 698,185	922,580	1,252,489
Bonds	36ab	104	153	357	256	226	† 28	21	13	5	† —	—	—
Capital Accounts	37a	664	7,520	9,986	13,321	16,101	† 23,914	49,690	49,887	27,297	† 115,631	169,308	263,737
Other Items (Net)	37r	712	−456	−1,355	−7,033	−24,194	† −21,704	−46,714	−67,634	−100,694	† −40,479	−20,516	−46,540
Money plus Quasi-Money	35l	9,222	28,101	79,098	109,576	130,442	† 180,019	248,162	448,004	574,134	† 1,244,384	1,491,648	1,953,805
Money (National Definitions)					*Thousands of Surinamese Dollars: End of Period*								
M1	59ma	....	....	....	....	....	....	135,548	267,357	384,688	538,388	547,094	699,500
M2	59mb	....	....	....	....	....	....	159,755	306,019	426,711	596,375	621,610	795,700
M3	59mc	....	....	....	....	....	....	246,765	439,331	572,391	768,440	795,829	1,011,900
Interest Rates						*Percent per Annum*							
Deposit Rate	60l	4.75	7.45	21.00	17.83	17.25	16.00	15.60	15.48	11.86	9.00	8.28	8.34
Lending Rate	60p	9.35	15.38	40.18	35.78	33.13	27.50	27.33	28.95	25.73	22.18	21.04	20.44
Prices and Labor					*Index Numbers (2000=100): Period Averages*								
Consumer Prices	64	1.6	7.4	24.9	24.7	26.5	31.5	† 62.7	100.0	138.6	160.1	196.9	....
					Number in Thousands: Period Averages								
Labor Force	67d	92	90	90	....	....	....	86	....	....	....	....	....
Employment	67e	83	78	82	87	83	88	73	....	....	....	....	....
Unemployment	67c	14	11	8	11	10	10	12	....	....	....	....	....
Unemployment Rate (%)	67r	14.7	12.7	8.4	11.0	....	....	....	....	....	....	....	....
Intl. Transactions & Positions						*Millions of Surinamese Dollars*							
Exports	70	2.1	60.2	211.0	215.2	226.4	204.0	398.7	668.2	877.8	1,101.7	1,658.8	....
Imports, c.i.f.	71	1.8	56.7	258.9	200.8	227.2	221.4	485.1	685.1	1,003.2	1,154.6	1,830.4	....

Suriname 366

		1993	1994	1995	1996	1997	1998	1999	2000	2001	2002	2003	2004
Balance of Payments		*Millions of US Dollars: Minus Sign Indicates Debit*											
Current Account, n.i.e.	78ald	44.0	58.6	73.4	−63.5	−67.7	−154.9	−29.1	32.3	−83.6	−131.0	−159.0	−86.7
Goods: Exports f.o.b.	78aad	298.3	293.6	415.6	397.2	401.6	349.7	342.0	399.1	437.0	369.3	487.8	833.2
Goods: Imports f.o.b.	78abd	−213.9	−194.3	−292.6	−398.8	−365.5	−376.9	−297.9	−246.1	−297.2	−321.9	−458.0	−740.0
Trade Balance	78acd	84.4	99.3	123.0	−1.6	36.1	−27.2	44.1	153.0	139.8	47.4	29.8	93.2
Services: Credit	78add	46.5	72.6	104.1	103.8	91.6	72.0	79.1	90.9	59.4	38.5	59.0	141.2
Services: Debit	78aed	−101.6	−113.5	−161.4	−169.5	−193.8	−196.9	−151.1	−215.5	−174.3	−166.1	−194.6	−271.0
Balance on Goods & Services	78afd	29.3	58.4	65.7	−67.3	−66.1	−152.1	−27.9	28.4	24.9	−80.2	−105.8	−36.6
Income: Credit	78agd	.2	.9	2.7	7.0	7.4	6.5	7.9	13.2	5.4	8.4	11.7	15.6
Income: Debit	78ahd	−6.4	−4.7	−5.3	−4.3	−10.0	−7.0	−7.6	−7.2	−113.0	−50.7	−60.2	−78.5
Balance on Gds, Serv. & Inc.	78aid	23.1	54.6	63.1	−64.6	−68.7	−152.6	−27.6	34.4	−82.7	−122.5	−154.3	−99.5
Current Transfers, n.i.e.: Credit	78ajd	26.7	6.2	12.6	3.6	4.0	1.3	1.8	1.2	2.1	12.9	24.8	75.8
Current Transfers: Debit	78akd	−5.8	−2.2	−2.3	−2.5	−3.0	−3.6	−3.3	−3.3	−3.0	−21.4	−29.5	−63.0
Capital Account, n.i.e.	78bcd	.5	−.2	22.1	41.6	14.6	6.6	3.5	2.3	1.5	5.9	9.0	7.5
Capital Account, n.i.e.: Credit	78bad	3.5	.2	22.1	41.6	14.6	6.6	3.5	2.3	1.5	5.9	9.2	7.5
Capital Account: Debit	78bbd	−3.0	−.4	—	—	—	—	—	....	....	—	−.2	—
Financial Account, n.i.e.	78bjd	−73.1	−84.1	−29.5	27.7	26.9	30.5	−21.6	−139.1	104.1	−38.1	−36.5	−39.3
Direct Investment Abroad	78bdd	—	—	—	—	—	—	....	....	....	—	—	—
Dir. Invest. in Rep. Econ., n.i.e.	78bed	−46.6	−30.2	−20.6	19.1	−9.2	9.1	−61.5	−148.0	−26.8	−73.6	−76.1	−37.3
Portfolio Investment Assets	78bfd	—	—	—	—	—	—	....	....	....	—	—	—
Equity Securities	78bkd	—	—	—	—	—	—	....	....	....	—	—	—
Debt Securities	78bld	—	—	—	—	—	—	....	....	....	—	—	—
Portfolio Investment Liab., n.i.e.	78bgd	—	—	—	—	—	—	....	....	....	—	—	—
Equity Securities	78bmd	—	—	—	—	—	—	....	....	....	—	—	—
Debt Securities	78bnd	—	—	—	—	—	—	....	....	....	—	—	—
Financial Derivatives Assets	78bwd	....	....	....	....	....	....	....	....	....	....	....	....
Financial Derivatives Liabilities	78bxd	....	....	....	....	....	....	....	....	....	....	....	....
Other Investment Assets	78bhd	−4.4	−19.1	3.2	25.5	15.2	18.6	27.1	24.6	40.7	23.9	46.9	−2.3
Monetary Authorities	78bod	....	....	....	....	....	....	....	....	....	....	....	....
General Government	78bpd							....	....	....			
Banks	78bqd	−14.5	−31.3	−10.0	—	—	—	—	—	—	—	—	—
Other Sectors	78brd	10.1	12.2	13.2	25.5	15.2	18.6	27.1	24.6	40.7	23.9	46.9	−2.3
Other Investment Liab., n.i.e.	78bid	−22.1	−34.8	−12.1	−16.9	20.9	2.8	12.8	−15.7	90.2	11.6	−7.3	.3
Monetary Authorities	78bsd	—	—	—	—	—	—	—	—	1.6	−.9	4.3	—
General Government	78btd	2.0	2.1	4.2	−15.0	1.3	19.3	16.1	−21.4	50.7	−30.8	−23.0	−18.5
Banks	78bud	−23.7	−29.6	−10.1	—	—	—	—	—	−.8	6.4	−9.1	−6.4
Other Sectors	78bvd	−.4	−7.3	−6.2	−1.9	19.6	−16.5	−3.3	5.7	38.7	36.9	20.5	25.2
Net Errors and Omissions	78cad	41.3	60.0	56.6	−7.5	45.3	125.9	42.8	114.3	56.1	144.1	193.7	194.6
Overall Balance	78cbd	12.7	34.3	122.6	−1.7	19.1	8.1	−4.4	9.8	78.1	−19.1	7.2	76.1
Reserves and Related Items	79dad	−12.7	−34.3	−122.6	1.7	−19.1	−8.1	4.4	−9.8	−78.1	19.1	−7.2	−76.1
Reserve Assets	79dbd	−12.7	−34.3	−122.6	1.7	−19.1	−8.1	4.4	−9.8	−78.1	19.1	−7.2	−76.1
Use of Fund Credit and Loans	79dcd	—	—	—	—	—	—	—	—	—	—	—	—
Exceptional Financing	79ded	....	....	....	....	....	....	....	....	....	—	—	—
National Accounts		*Millions of Surinamese Dollars*											
Househ.Cons.Expend.,incl.NPISHs	96f	3	18	37	162	213	....	....	....	....	....	....	....
Government Consumption Expend	91f	2	7	45	45	60	86	201	257	413	606	929	....
Gross Capital Formation	93	3	28	91	232	224	318	435	609	963	1,443	1,778	....
Exports of Goods and Services	90c	15	76	229	193	195	167	364	641	1,074	941	1,437	....
Imports of Goods and Services (-)	98c	12	64	201	226	222	227	413	578	1,033	1,138	1,715	....
Gross Domestic Product (GDP)	99b	11	64	253	289	311	378	650	1,017	1,475	1,946	2,570	....
Net Primary Income from Abroad	98.n	—	—	−1	−3	−11	−12	−32	−63	−232	−102	−128	....
Gross National Income (GNI)	99a	11	64	252	287	301	366	619	954	1,243	1,845	2,443	....
Net National Income	99e	9	57	206	272	328	....	....	....	....	....	....	....
GDP Volume 1990 Prices	99b.p	2	2	3	3	3	3	3	3	4	4	4	....
GDP Volume	99bvp	45.5	45.5	93.9	97.0	97.0	100.0	100.0	100.0	109.1	112.1	115.2	....
GDP Deflator	99bip	2.4	13.9	26.5	29.3	31.5	37.1	63.9	100.0	132.9	170.7	219.4	....
		Millions: Midyear Estimates											
Population	99z	.41	.41	.41	.42	.42	.43	.43	.43	.44	.44	.44	.45

Swaziland 734

		1993	1994	1995	1996	1997	1998	1999	2000	2001	2002	2003	2004
Exchange Rates						*Lilangeni per SDR: End of Period*							
Official Rate....................	aa	4.66667	5.17298	5.42197	6.73325	6.56747	8.25106	8.44711	9.86107	15.23974	11.74625	9.86684	8.74345
						Lilangeni per US Dollar: End of Period (ae) Period Average (rf)							
Official Rate....................	ae	3.39750	3.54350	3.64750	4.68250	4.86750	5.86000	6.15450	7.56850	12.12650	8.64000	6.64000	5.63000
Official Rate....................	rf	3.26774	3.55080	3.62709	4.29935	4.60796	5.52828	6.10948	6.93983	8.60918	10.54075	7.56475	6.45969
Fund Position						*Millions of SDRs: End of Period*							
Quota............................	2f.s	36.50	36.50	36.50	36.50	36.50	36.50	50.70	50.70	50.70	50.70	50.70	50.70
SDRs.............................	1b.s	5.88	5.89	5.90	5.93	5.94	5.96	2.42	2.44	2.45	2.46	2.47	2.47
Reserve Position in the Fund............	1c.s	3.00	3.00	3.00	3.00	3.00	3.00	6.55	6.55	6.55	6.55	6.55	6.56
Total Fund Cred.&Loans Outstg........	2tl	—	—	—	—	—	—	—	—	—	—	—	—
International Liquidity						*Millions of US Dollars Unless Otherwise Indicated: End of Period*							
Total Reserves minus Gold...............	1l.d	264.29	296.97	298.20	254.00	294.84	358.61	375.93	351.79	271.78	275.84	277.51	323.56
SDRs............................	1b.d	8.08	8.60	8.77	8.52	8.02	8.39	3.33	3.18	3.08	3.35	3.67	3.84
Reserve Position in the Fund..........	1c.d	4.12	4.38	4.46	4.32	4.05	4.23	8.99	8.54	8.23	8.91	9.74	10.19
Foreign Exchange...................	1d.d	252.09	283.99	284.96	241.16	282.77	345.99	363.61	340.08	260.46	263.59	264.11	309.53
Monetary Authorities: Other Liab.....	4..d	1.48	32.02	21.34	20.14	1.24	21.98	49.16	45.66	38.90	42.70	53.26	4.22
Deposit Money Banks: Assets...........	7a.d	52.43	43.59	47.52	107.45	91.79	99.16	135.46	84.13	71.89	89.29	76.46	91.20
Liabilities....................	7b.d	19.69	17.83	17.61	50.70	20.92	6.13	9.43	13.84	1.85	8.42	7.70	7.06
Monetary Authorities						*Millions of Emalangeni: End of Period*							
Foreign Assets......................	11	875.03	872.21	1,023.66	1,335.33	1,427.69	2,083.56	2,304.34	2,643.72	3,362.53	2,339.37	1,836.58	1,549.32
Claims on Central Government........	12a	—	40.00	20.63	.06	—	—	—	—	—	57.32	82.64	251.80
Claims on Private Sector...............	12d	8.87	10.63	12.52	14.02	13.06	12.30	15.23	16.34	15.50	12.98	12.02	10.03
Claims on Deposit Money Banks......	12e	6.82	5.65	30.00	36.76	43.19	42.55	44.31	41.95	41.95	—	—	—
Reserve Money......................	14	255.34	300.24	307.81	284.95	300.47	275.33	307.27	293.36	274.53	349.36	443.90	495.07
of which: Currency Outside DMBs..	14a	75.19	69.59	80.33	90.85	109.00	107.23	136.95	148.06	134.93	155.44	213.45	235.85
Time Deposits......................	15	43.92	36.90	52.57	53.45	77.68	48.33	50.14	68.30	79.54	90.05	91.81	96.23
Foreign Liabilities....................	16c	5.02	113.47	77.82	94.32	6.04	128.81	302.53	345.57	471.70	368.96	353.67	23.74
Central Government Deposits...........	16d	508.49	386.14	555.97	771.74	995.41	1,471.42	1,552.66	1,765.98	2,113.64	1,358.69	1,114.71	1,186.23
Capital Accounts.....................	17a	36.80	40.14	41.95	50.52	50.80	62.46	86.23	96.66	134.10	114.41	102.44	95.12
Other Items (Net).....................	17r	41.15	51.60	50.69	131.19	53.53	152.05	65.05	132.14	346.45	128.20	−175.30	−85.24
Deposit Money Banks						*Millions of Emalangeni: End of Period*							
Reserves............................	20	185.65	227.46	232.42	199.22	193.84	151.48	176.57	145.07	130.86	196.02	207.23	229.69
Foreign Assets......................	21	178.14	154.45	173.32	503.13	446.80	581.07	833.68	636.74	871.83	771.46	507.70	513.48
Claims on Central Government......	22a	30.00	38.00	49.79	68.35	52.17	52.73	50.21	59.49	60.00	215.43	286.68	332.49
Claims on Private Sector................	22d	739.14	902.68	915.60	971.81	1,095.03	1,159.43	1,223.39	1,308.23	1,383.56	1,770.13	2,327.69	3,013.21
Demand Deposits....................	24	215.06	241.75	282.57	331.99	382.76	393.64	525.72	512.53	619.15	670.09	834.39	843.08
Time and Savings Deposits............	25	731.45	833.28	811.70	951.43	1,135.61	1,375.32	1,512.47	1,349.40	1,467.33	1,686.86	1,829.35	2,101.58
Foreign Liabilities....................	26c	66.89	63.17	64.22	237.41	101.82	35.92	58.04	104.72	22.45	72.75	51.13	39.76
Central Government Deposits...........	26d	73.71	90.88	114.57	101.22	10.17	14.25	14.70	.22	.23	.23	.28	1.50
Liab. to Nonbank Financial Insts.......	26j	3.12	3.74	3.44	3.68	6.68	5.28	12.19	10.27	15.97	15.57	14.50	30.84
Capital Accounts.....................	27a	96.20	92.33	97.61	75.09	127.53	114.39	139.44	157.73	292.70	378.31	487.94	1,007.35
Other Items (Net).....................	27r	−53.50	−2.57	−2.96	41.69	23.28	5.91	21.29	14.67	28.44	129.22	111.71	64.76
Monetary Survey						*Millions of Emalangeni: End of Period*							
Foreign Assets (Net)......................	31n	981.26	850.02	1,054.94	1,506.73	1,766.63	2,499.89	2,777.46	2,830.18	3,740.21	2,669.12	1,939.47	1,999.30
Domestic Credit.......................	32	195.81	514.28	328.00	181.28	154.69	−261.20	−278.54	−382.14	−654.82	696.94	1,594.04	2,419.80
Claims on Central Govt. (Net)........	32an	−552.19	−399.02	−600.12	−804.55	−953.40	−1,432.94	−1,517.16	−1,706.71	−2,053.88	−1,086.18	−745.67	−603.45
Claims on Private Sector..............	32d	748.00	913.30	928.12	985.83	1,108.09	1,171.74	1,238.62	1,324.58	1,399.06	1,783.11	2,339.71	3,023.25
Money............................	34	290.50	311.59	363.16	423.03	491.75	500.87	662.69	660.58	754.08	825.53	1,047.84	1,078.93
Quasi-Money.......................	35	775.37	870.18	864.27	1,004.88	1,213.29	1,423.66	1,562.61	1,417.69	1,546.87	1,776.91	1,921.16	2,197.80
Liab. to Nonbank Financial Insts.......	36j	3.12	3.74	3.44	3.68	6.68	5.28	12.19	10.27	15.97	15.57	14.50	30.84
Capital Accounts.....................	37a	132.99	132.47	139.56	125.61	178.33	176.85	225.67	254.40	426.80	492.72	590.38	1,102.47
Other Items (Net).....................	37r	−24.90	46.33	12.52	130.81	31.26	132.04	35.76	105.10	341.68	255.32	−40.37	9.05
Money plus Quasi-Money...........	35l	1,065.87	1,181.76	1,227.43	1,427.91	1,705.04	1,924.52	2,225.30	2,078.28	2,300.95	2,602.44	2,969.00	3,276.73
Money (National Definitions)						*Millions of Emalangeni: End of Period*							
M1....................	59ma	290.50	311.59	363.16	422.96	491.75	500.87	662.69	660.58	754.08	825.53	1,047.84	1,078.93
M2....................	59mb	1,065.86	1,181.76	1,227.43	1,427.91	1,705.04	1,924.52	2,225.30	2,078.27	2,300.95	2,602.44	2,969.00	3,276.73
Interest Rates						*Percent Per Annum*							
Discount Rate (End of Period)...........	60	11.00	12.00	15.00	16.75	15.75	18.00	12.00	11.00	9.50	13.50	8.00	7.50
Money Market Rate.....................	60b	9.73	7.01	8.52	9.77	10.35	10.63	8.86	5.54	5.06	7.31	6.98	4.12
Treasury Bill Rate.....................	60c	8.25	8.35	10.87	13.68	14.37	13.09	11.19	8.30	7.16	8.59	10.61	7.94
Savings Rate......................	60k	9.06	8.04	8.99	10.21	10.72	10.25	7.73	4.00	4.43	6.20	6.68	3.71
Deposit Rate.....................	60l	7.89	7.54	9.44	11.08	12.00	11.92	9.86	6.53	6.15	8.02	7.59	4.63
Lending Rate.......................	60p	14.35	14.25	17.05	18.67	19.50	19.50	17.42	14.00	13.25	15.25	14.63	11.29
Prices and Labor						*Index Numbers (2000=100): Period Averages*							
Consumer Prices.....................	64	53.4	60.7	68.2	72.5	77.7	84.0	89.1	100.0	105.9	118.7	127.3	....
						Number in Thousands: Period Averages							
Employment.....................	67e	93	87	87	90	....	....	....	....	....	....	....	....
Intl. Transactions & Positions						*Millions of Emalangeni*							
Exports...........................	70	2,237.3	2,808.5	3,147.6	3,656.7	4,429.7	5,330.5	5,722.6	6,280.7	8,950.6	9,827.4	....	....
Imports, c.i.f......................	71	2,576.8	2,986.3	3,660.7	4,533.4	4,908.8	5,936.4	6,525.8	7,225.2	9,586.6	10,302.3	....	....

Swaziland 734

		1993	1994	1995	1996	1997	1998	1999	2000	2001	2002	2003	2004
Balance of Payments					*Millions of US Dollars: Minus Sign Indicates Debit*								
Current Account, n.i.e.	78ald	−63.7	1.8	−29.7	−52.0	−2.7	−93.3	−35.1	−65.2	−53.0	−46.3	....	....
Goods: Exports f.o.b.	78aad	684.7	790.9	867.8	850.5	961.3	967.8	936.7	905.0	1,039.7	955.2	....	....
Goods: Imports f.o.b.	78abd	−788.6	−841.0	−1,064.4	−1,054.4	−1,065.5	−1,073.8	−1,068.1	−1,041.1	−1,116.4	−1,034.6	....	....
Trade Balance	78acd	−103.9	−50.1	−196.6	−203.9	−104.2	−106.0	−131.5	−136.1	−76.7	−79.4	....	....
Services: Credit	78add	92.8	112.9	151.8	100.8	91.9	91.4	69.4	213.6	120.7	116.6	....	....
Services: Debit	78aed	−256.4	−201.9	−209.5	−240.7	−244.8	−267.7	−192.0	−290.7	−185.9	−142.2	....	....
Balance on Goods & Services	78afd	−267.5	−139.1	−254.2	−343.9	−257.1	−282.2	−254.0	−213.2	−141.8	−104.9	....	....
Income: Credit	78agd	155.2	138.5	162.6	200.8	182.7	167.8	164.0	153.5	160.1	141.4	....	....
Income: Debit	78ahd	−107.3	−155.0	−82.0	−68.7	−44.6	−111.4	−76.3	−112.6	−105.6	−93.1	....	....
Balance on Gds, Serv. & Inc.	78aid	−219.5	−155.7	−173.7	−211.8	−119.0	−225.8	−166.3	−172.2	−87.4	−56.6	....	....
Current Transfers, n.i.e.: Credit	78ajd	248.1	252.6	257.2	268.7	226.8	242.7	241.4	234.1	229.7	218.9	....	....
Current Transfers: Debit	78akd	−92.3	−95.1	−113.3	−108.9	−110.5	−110.3	−110.2	−127.0	−195.3	−208.6	....	....
Capital Account, n.i.e.	78bcd	—	−.2	—	.1	.1	—	—	.1	−.2	.5	....	....
Capital Account, n.i.e.: Credit	78bad	.3	.1	.3	.1	.1	—	—	.1	.2	.5	....	....
Capital Account: Debit	78bbd	−.3	−.3	−.3	—	—	—	—	—	−.4	−.1	....	....
Financial Account, n.i.e.	78bjd	−7.3	−54.1	−25.4	6.8	47.0	130.5	25.1	−9.6	−31.5	26.8	....	....
Direct Investment Abroad	78bdd	−27.8	−64.7	−20.6	6.4	12.0	−23.9	−13.2	−17.2	17.8	9.2	....	....
Dir. Invest. in Rep. Econ., n.i.e.	78bed	71.9	63.3	51.8	21.7	−15.3	152.7	100.4	90.2	49.8	45.0	....	....
Portfolio Investment Assets	78bfd	−.1	−3.9	−9.6	−2.0	−2.0	−2.8	3.2	−4.0	−3.9	.5	....	....
Equity Securities	78bkd	—	—	−1.9	−.2	−1.9	−1.3	1.5	−.1	−.1	—	....	....
Debt Securities	78bld	−.1	−3.9	−7.6	−1.7	—	−1.5	1.7	−3.9	−3.8	.5	....	....
Portfolio Investment Liab., n.i.e.	78bgd	−1.0	.1	.8	.4	−.1	3.4	2.7	1.4	−2.5	−.1	....	....
Equity Securities	78bmd	−1.0	.1	.8	.4	−.1	3.4	2.7	1.4	−2.5	−.1	....	....
Debt Securities	78bnd	....	....	....	....	....	....	....	....	....	....	....	....
Financial Derivatives Assets	78bwd	....	....	....	....	....	....	....	....	....	....	....	....
Financial Derivatives Liabilities	78bxd	....	....	....	....	....	....	....	....	....	....	....	....
Other Investment Assets	78bhd	−78.2	−80.5	−31.0	−120.0	−12.3	1.6	−122.4	−98.5	−155.7	−50.4	....	....
Monetary Authorities	78bod	....	....	....	....	....	....	....	....	....	....	....	....
General Government	78bpd	−25.3	−18.0	−6.7	−2.7	13.4	−4.8	16.3	8.1	−31.7	−47.1	....	....
Banks	78bqd	−6.9	5.7	−5.3	−77.0	11.1	−22.9	−41.7	27.7	−27.7	9.6	....	....
Other Sectors	78brd	−46.1	−68.3	−19.0	−40.3	−36.8	29.2	−97.0	−134.4	−96.3	−12.9	....	....
Other Investment Liab., n.i.e.	78bid	27.9	31.6	−16.7	100.2	64.7	−.4	54.4	18.5	63.0	22.6	....	....
Monetary Authorities	78bsd	.1	30.5	−9.8	3.8	−19.2	22.2	28.5	6.2	14.7	−9.8	....	....
General Government	78btd	—	—	—	—	—	—	—	—	—	—	....	....
Banks	78bud	−.3	.7	.4	41.5	−25.9	−13.8	.3	6.4	−9.5	4.7	....	....
Other Sectors	78bvd	28.1	.4	−7.3	54.9	109.8	−8.8	25.6	5.8	57.8	27.6	....	....
Net Errors and Omissions	78cad	2.4	48.9	78.9	37.0	−16.8	4.1	13.4	46.7	41.6	18.9	....	....
Overall Balance	78cbd	−68.5	−3.6	23.8	−8.1	27.5	41.3	3.3	−28.0	−43.0	−.2	....	....
Reserves and Related Items	79dad	68.5	3.6	−23.8	8.1	−27.5	−41.3	−3.3	28.0	43.0	.2	....	....
Reserve Assets	79dbd	63.7	12.6	−29.8	−15.4	−25.3	−50.5	−26.3	6.5	56.5	29.1	....	....
Use of Fund Credit and Loans	79dcd	—	—	—	—	—	—	—	—	—	—	....	....
Exceptional Financing	79ded	4.8	−8.9	6.0	23.4	−2.2	9.2	23.0	21.6	−13.5	−28.9	....	....
International Investment Position						*Millions of US Dollars*								
Assets	79aad	721.2	838.2	982.9	965.1	977.2	958.5	1,151.8	1,151.9	894.5	1,286.9	....	....
Direct Investment Abroad	79abd	52.6	108.8	135.5	95.4	82.3	90.1	98.1	94.9	46.2	53.6	....	....
Portfolio Investment	79acd	3.6	7.3	16.6	14.8	16.1	16.0	12.0	13.4	11.2	15.0	....	....
Equity Securities	79add	.8	.8	2.7	2.3	4.0	4.6	2.8	2.4	1.6	2.2	....	....
Debt Securities	79aed	2.8	6.6	14.0	12.5	12.0	11.4	9.2	11.1	9.6	12.9	....	....
Financial Derivatives	79ald												
Other Investment	79afd	425.8	479.2	553.4	572.5	589.3	497.2	669.0	696.5	561.5	949.8	....	....
Monetary Authorities	79agd	—	—	—	—	—	—	—	—	—	—	....	....
General Government	79ahd	142.3	144.6	124.6	98.8	86.5	77.0	56.2	34.3	10.7	114.8	....	....
Banks	79aid	54.8	46.9	50.8	110.3	116.1	101.0	137.5	86.4	73.6	91.6	....	....
Other Sectors	79ajd	228.7	287.7	377.9	363.5	386.6	319.2	475.4	575.8	477.2	743.4	....	....
Reserve Assets	79akd	239.2	242.9	277.4	282.4	289.5	355.3	372.6	347.1	275.6	268.4	....	....
Liabilities	79lad	820.2	848.7	981.3	894.5	846.3	929.3	1,053.8	975.3	638.7	....	....	....
Dir. Invest. in Rep. Economy	79lbd	462.5	506.8	535.6	437.2	406.4	481.6	558.2	536.7	370.3	574.7	....	....
Portfolio Investment	79lcd	.6	.7	1.4	1.5	1.4	4.3	6.8	6.8	2.4	3.3	....	....
Equity Securities	79ldd	.6	.7	1.4	1.5	1.4	4.3	6.8	6.8	2.4	3.3	....	....
Debt Securities	79led	—	—	—	—	—	—	—	—	—	—	....	....
Financial Derivatives	79lld	—	—	—	—	—	—	—	—	—	—	....	....
Other Investment	79lfd	357.1	341.2	444.2	455.7	438.5	443.4	488.8	431.8	265.9	....	....	....
Monetary Authorities	79lgd	−.3	−.3	77.3	19.9	1.0	21.8	48.9	45.5	38.8	....	....	....
General Government	79lhd	192.1	175.3	194.5	194.4	177.4	243.3	262.5	210.0	136.7	....	....	....
Banks	79lid	21.9	21.7	21.5	54.9	28.2	10.4	10.3	14.3	2.2	....	....	....
Other Sectors	79ljd	143.5	144.5	150.9	186.5	231.8	167.9	167.1	162.1	88.3	56.7	....	....
Government Finance					*Millions of Emalangeni: Year Beginning April 1*								
Deficit (-) or Surplus	80	−171.1	−197.5	68.3	−56.2	184.1	−7.1	−138.7	−141.4	−255.3	−593.1	−444.9	....
Revenue	81	953.0	1,168.7	1,447.7	1,684.0	2,020.5	2,230.3	2,536.1	2,713.2	2,922.7	3,262.8	3,681.6	....
Grants Received	81z	28.7	31.4	7.5	20.2	18.3	44.7	31.8	112.1	157.4	162.3	265.1	....
Expenditure	82	1,138.4	1,398.7	1,382.1	1,758.4	1,826.6	2,214.8	2,676.0	2,967.9	3,332.5	4,018.2	4,391.6	....
Lending Minus Repayments	83	14.4	−1.1	4.8	2.0	28.1	67.3	30.6	−1.2	2.9	—	—	....
Financing													
Domestic	84a	196.4	235.5	−80.6	41.4	−226.1	−191.2	133.1	122.5	−52.2	480.5	318.5	....
Foreign	85a	−25.3	−38.0	12.3	14.8	42.0	198.3	5.6	18.9	307.5	112.6	126.4	....
Debt: Domestic	88a	25.5	53.7	62.9	102.9	97.6	85.6	78.0	78.0	78.0	300.0	300.0	....
Foreign	89a	630.2	791.9	914.5	1,150.5	820.0	1,060.6	1,467.9	2,069.8	2,690.0	3,351.0	2,755.8	....

Swaziland 734

		1993	1994	1995	1996	1997	1998	1999	2000	2001	2002	2003	2004
National Accounts						*Millions of Emalangeni: Year Ending June 30*							
Househ.Cons.Expend.,incl.NPISHs....	96f	2,649.0	3,052.1	3,932.6	4,801.5	4,752.6	5,403.2	6,214.1	7,273.1	8,425.9	9,252.5	10,011.3	....
Government Consumption Expend...	91f	781.0	874.0	951.0	1,185.8	1,639.2	1,800.9	1,864.3	1,929.1	1,996.2	2,065.5	2,555.7	....
Gross Fixed Capital Formation.........	93e	771.8	840.7	950.0	1,125.4	1,308.1	1,665.4	1,577.1	1,916.7	1,984.5	2,225.0	1,793.0	....
Changes in Inventories....................	93i	29.0	33.9	37.4	51.2	53.9	—	—	—	—	61.6	66.0	....
Exports of Goods and Services..........	90c	2,540.6	2,970.6	3,698.4	4,090.0	5,003.2	5,917.4	6,116.1	6,141.0	7,699.4	12,676.0	13,731.2	....
Imports of Goods and Services (-).....	98c	3,414.6	3,703.2	4,620.5	5,568.4	6,144.5	7,337.5	7,363.9	7,621.0	9,135.0	13,289.4	13,662.0	....
Gross Domestic Product (GDP)........	99b	3,356.8	4,068.1	4,948.9	5,685.5	6,612.5	7,449.4	8,407.7	9,638.9	10,971.0	12,436.8	14,765.8	....
Net Primary Income from Abroad.....	98.n	156.6	−58.9	292.2	567.9	636.3	311.8	535.9	574.7	291.5	47.9	−83.9	....
Gross National Income (GNI)............	99a	3,513.4	4,009.2	5,244.1	6,253.4	7,248.8	7,761.2	8,943.6	10,213.6	11,262.5	12,484.7	14,681.9	....
Consumption of Fixed Capital..........	99cf	189.6	214.2	235.8	258.4	297.2	334.6	377.4	434.0	499.1	935.5	1,232.5	....
Net National Income.......................	99e	3,323.8	3,795.0	5,005.3	5,995.0	6,951.6	7,426.6	8,566.3	9,779.6	10,763.4	11,549.2	13,449.4	....
GDP Volume 1985 Prices...............	99b.p	1,403.1	1,450.3	1,505.2	1,563.7	1,623.6	1,676.5	1,735.6	1,770.9	1,802.3	....	....	....
GDP Volume (2000=100)...............	99bvp	79.2	81.9	85.0	88.3	91.7	94.7	98.0	100.0	101.8	....	....	....
GDP Deflator (2000=100)...............	99bip	44.0	51.5	60.4	66.8	74.8	81.6	89.0	100.0	111.8	....	....	....
						Millions: Midyear Estimates							
Population...............................	99z	.92	.94	.95	.97	† .99	1.00	1.01	1.02	1.03	1.03	1.03	1.03

		1993	1994	1995	1996	1997	1998	1999	2000	2001	2002	2003	2004
Exchange Rates							*Kronor per SDR: End of Period*							
Official Rate	aa	11.4054	10.8927	9.8973	9.8802	10.6280	11.3501	11.7006	12.4232	13.4062	11.9978	10.6829	10.2725
					Kronor per US Dollar: End of Period (ae) Period Average (rf)									
Official Rate	ae	8.3035	7.4615	6.6582	6.8710	7.8770	8.0610	8.5250	9.5350	10.6675	8.8250	7.1892	6.6146
Official Rate	rf	7.7834	7.7160	7.1333	6.7060	7.6349	7.9499	8.2624	9.1622	10.3291	9.7371	8.0863	7.3489
			Kronor per ECU through 1998; Kronor per Euro Beginning 1999: End of Period (ea) Period Average (eb)											
Euro Rate	ea	9.2963	9.1779	8.6973	8.6280	8.7323	9.4880	† 8.5625	8.8313	9.4200	9.1925	9.0800	9.0206
Euro Rate	ag	....	....	....	....	....	....	1.0046	.9305	.8813	1.0487	1.2630	1.3621
Euro Rate	eb	9.1146	9.1579	9.3337	8.5156	8.6551	8.9085	† 8.8102	8.4459	9.2553	9.1603	9.1243	9.1250
Euro Rate	rh	....	....	....	....	....	....	1.0668	.9240	.8956	.9444	1.1308	1.2433
						Index Numbers (2000=100): Period Averages								
Official Rate	ahx	117.6	118.5	128.2	136.2	119.7	114.9	110.5	100.0	88.6	94.1	113.2	124.4
Nominal Effective Exchange Rate	neu	100.2	99.1	98.9	108.2	103.8	101.9	100.2	100.0	91.7	93.4	98.2	99.7
Real Effective Exchange Rate	reu	96.6	96.1	97.5	110.0	107.0	105.5	101.8	100.0	92.3	91.8	94.3	95.7
Fund Position							*Millions of SDRs: End of Period*							
Quota	2f.s	1,614	1,614	1,614	1,614	1,614	1,614	2,396	2,396	2,396	2,396	2,396	2,396
SDRs	1b.s	42	46	297	199	277	292	228	165	157	132	133	135
Reserve Position in the Fund	1c.s	451	451	451	451	589	900	863	683	827	1,050	988	842
of which: Outstg.Fund Borrowing	2c	—	—	—	—	—	112	—	—	—	—	—	—
International Liquidity						*Millions of US Dollars Unless Otherwise Indicated: End of Period*								
Total Reserves minus Gold	1l.d	19,050	23,254	24,051	19,107	10,825	14,098	15,019	14,863	13,977	17,127	19,681	22,129
SDRs	1b.d	58	68	441	286	373	412	313	215	197	179	198	209
Reserve Position in the Fund	1c.d	620	659	671	649	795	1,267	1,184	890	1,039	1,428	1,468	1,308
Foreign Exchange	1d.d	18,372	22,527	22,939	18,172	9,657	12,420	13,522	13,757	12,740	15,520	18,015	20,611
Gold (Million Fine Troy Ounces)	1ad	6.069	6.069	4.702	4.702	4.722	4.722	5.961	5.961	5.961	5.961	5.961	5.961
Gold (National Valuation)	1and	292	310	245	237	223	233	286	272	262	284	310	324
Deposit Money Banks: Assets	7a.d	26,261	24,727	36,158	44,707	44,943	50,853	53,087	67,355	† 62,015	72,534	101,906	156,605
Liabilities	7b.d	50,253	50,925	55,100	56,670	60,376	86,846	76,769	102,345	† 78,869	91,640	108,859	157,117
Other Banking Insts.: Assets	7e.d	3,743	4,661	5,734	8,834	11,116	12,171	13,226	....	....	....	....	....
Liabilities	7f.d	20,605	22,196	16,597	14,535	13,686	29,960	34,387	....	....	....	....	....
Monetary Authorities							*Billions of Kronor: End of Period*							
Foreign Assets	11	175.69	177.95	171.96	140.21	93.41	136.22	152.55	167.92	† 176.08	176.77	165.88	168.13
Claims on Central Government	12a	98.99	87.52	71.03	59.05	53.09	32.84	† 27.69	20.23	† —	—	—	—
Claims on Banking Institutions	12e	1.26	.01	2.61	9.64	40.33	43.85	† 45.63	43.20	† 58.24	22.90	18.99	13.60
Reserve Money	14	163.84	200.59	170.74	114.30	84.76	87.95	102.91	97.77	† 108.32	107.53	108.09	109.51
of which: Currency Outside Bls	14a	67.05	68.81	68.55	70.71	72.97	74.63	78.64	89.16	† 97.89	96.28	97.13	98.19
Foreign Liabilities	16c	.08	.22	3.48	4.14	3.98	4.10	† 5.26	4.11	† 2.86	.21	1.12	5.22
Central Government Deposits	16d	21.79	—	—	—	—	—	† 2.17	1.59	† 2.20	—	—	—
Capital Accounts	17a	59.59	76.62	74.46	75.71	82.25	100.07	114.42	108.24	† 119.92	92.40	75.85	66.03
Other Items (Net)	17r	30.65	−11.95	−3.10	14.75	15.83	20.79	2.43	20.14	† 1.01	−.46	−.19	.97
Banking Institutions							*Billions of Kronor: End of Period*							
Reserves	20	21.25	8.75	9.42	11.13	10.17	13.52	30.67	9.80	† 16.01	12.09	20.52	15.82
Other Claims on Monetary Author.	20n												
Foreign Assets	21	329.24	281.57	408.71	† 572.15	682.15	698.05	741.63	961.14	† 661.54	640.11	732.63	1,035.88
Claims on Central Government	22a	149.50	162.35	143.46	122.00	109.15	167.93	86.99	115.77	† 117.82	89.28	7.49	7.62
Claims on Other General Govt	22b	14.58	17.54	24.99	31.05	36.85	37.58	42.74	39.61	† 94.05	94.80	170.17	182.05
Claims on Other Resident Sectors	22d	631.41	605.08	596.72	† 623.21	711.06	771.67	848.41	958.69	† 2,298.02	2,421.69	2,537.93	2,697.16
Demand Deposits	24	....	....	....	....	....	....	....	....	619.27	635.68	677.45	839.32
Other Deposits	25	....	....	....	....	....	....	....	....	383.72	409.48	414.01	279.40
Demand,Time,Savings,Fgn.Cur.Dep.	25l	643.01	644.16	664.37	746.37	753.29	748.02	814.05	820.67	1,002.98	1,045.16	1,091.46	1,118.72
Bonds	26n	27.77	27.00	22.83	11.25	25.12	30.81	31.96	25.81	† 1,023.27	1,055.54	1,181.10	1,336.35
Foreign Liabilities	26c	532.70	504.20	568.22	† 639.64	788.10	985.59	924.94	1,256.78	† 841.34	808.72	782.61	1,039.27
Central Government Deposits	26d	.34	.43	1.61	2.38	.86	12.24	31.02	31.51	† 11.72	9.58	14.97	7.46
Credit from Monetary Authorities	26g	.74	.02	.01	10.53	31.65	29.26	34.44	45.78	† 60.26	23.43	21.42	14.07
Capital Accounts	27a	78.31	83.63	100.76	61.74	74.37	82.99	88.53	95.95	† 281.68	274.40	294.09	338.08
Other Items (Net)	27r	−136.90	−184.16	−174.49	† −112.36	−124.00	−200.16	−174.50	−191.49	† −33.27	41.13	83.73	84.60
Banking Survey							*Billions of Kronor: End of Period*							
Foreign Assets (Net)	31n	−27.85	−44.90	8.97	† 68.58	−16.52	−155.42	† −36.02	−131.83	† −6.57	7.95	114.77	159.53
Domestic Credit	32	872.35	872.05	834.59	† 832.93	909.29	997.79	† 972.64	1,101.21	† 2,496.31	2,596.46	2,700.68	2,879.37
Claims on Central Govt. (Net)	32an	226.37	249.43	212.88	178.67	161.37	188.54	† 81.49	102.91	† 103.91	79.71	−7.48	.15
Claims on Other General Govt	32b	14.58	17.54	24.99	31.05	36.85	37.58	42.74	39.61	....	....	....	182.05
Claims on Other Resident Sectors	32d	631.41	605.08	596.72	† 623.21	711.06	771.67	848.41	958.69	† 2,298.36	2,421.96	2,537.99	2,697.16
Money	34	....	....	....	....	....	....	....	....	717.16	731.96	774.58	937.51
Quasi-Money	35	....	....	....	....	....	....	....	....	383.72	409.49	414.01	279.40
Money plus Quasi-Money	35l	723.03	728.05	750.56	817.08	826.26	822.65	892.69	909.84	1,100.88	1,141.45	1,188.59	1,216.91
Bonds	36n	27.77	27.00	22.83	11.25	25.12	30.81	31.96	25.81	1,023.27	1,055.54	1,181.10	1,336.35
Capital Accounts	37a	137.90	160.25	175.22	137.45	156.62	183.06	202.95	204.20	† 401.60	366.81	369.94	404.11
Other Items (Net)	37r	−44.20	−88.15	−105.05	† −64.27	−115.23	−194.15	† −190.97	−170.46	† −35.48	40.62	76.46	81.53
Money + Quasi-Money,Seas.Adj	35l.b	700.88	709.30	734.24	802.65	815.14	814.82	887.17	905.89	† 1,089.51	1,129.66	1,176.32	1,204.34
Money (National Definitions)							*Billions of Kronor: End of Period*							
Money	59ma	710.06	712.33	749.25	833.60	843.27	863.92	947.81	974.09	1,038.97	1,086.06	1,119.29	1,171.10

Sweden 144

		1993	1994	1995	1996	1997	1998	1999	2000	2001	2002	2003	2004
Other Banking Institutions						*Billions of Kronor: End of Period*							
Cash.................................	40	.03	.64	.02	—	—	—	—	....	....	....	....	....
Foreign Assets......................	41	37.45	46.15	38.26	† 60.70	87.56	98.11	112.75	....	....	....	....	....
Claims on Central Government........	42a	17.40	28.84	23.98	16.02	16.26	18.53	18.67	....	....	....	....	....
Claims on Local Government............	42b	—	.02	.01	† 35.70	39.04	40.72	42.16	....	....	....	....	....
Claims on Private Sector................	42d	1,124.98	1,133.60	1,162.92	† 1,154.15	1,161.62	1,200.06	1,249.53	....	....	....	....	....
Claims on Deposit Money Banks......	42e	31.36	25.92	† 28.69	39.90	46.18	59.23	54.60	....	....	....	....	....
Time, Savings,& Fgn. Currency Dep..	45	66.01	92.34	134.44	167.26	173.49	2.43	.52	....	....	....	....	....
Bonds.................................	46ab	960.64	915.53	856.98	804.90	736.65	720.90	648.43	....	....	....	....	....
Foreign Liabilities....................	46c	26.57	41.49	24.08	† 99.87	107.80	241.51	293.15	....	....	....	....	....
Central Govt. Lending Funds...........	46f	278.12	247.18	230.97	† 189.15	184.74	211.22	155.66	....	....	....	....	....
Credit from Deposit Money Banks....	46h	51.38	66.74	81.61	96.58	170.02	222.74	250.19	....	....	....	....	....
Capital Accounts.....................	47a	66.72	73.35	82.26	60.74	65.24	68.36	73.71	....	....	....	....	....
Other Items (Net)......................	47r	−238.24	−201.50	−156.47	−112.04	−87.29	−50.51	56.06	....	....	....	....	....
Nonbank Financial Institutions						*Billions of Kronor: End of Period*							
Claims on Central Bank..................	40..l	9.08	8.63	7.21	† 6.76	—	—	—	—	—	—	—	....
Foreign Assets........................	41..l	100.48	102.79	131.88	† 51.82	77.41	119.68	154.47	264.15	259.66	250.17	259.73	....
Claims on Central Government........	42a.l	130.95	161.20	254.55	† 247.21	259.93	290.98	341.92	285.64	306.40	370.19	390.28	....
Claims on State & Local Govts........	42b.l	....	....	....	† 1.69	5.09	.96	1.98	1.56	1.72	2.23	2.28	....
Claims on Nonfin.Pub.Enterprises....	42c.l	....	....	....	† 35.83	47.13	43.35	49.91	61.12	91.90	94.13	90.06	....
Claims on Other Resident Sectors.....	42d.l	201.46	215.18	239.53	† 6.14	4.91	1.43	1.24	.90	3.24	2.49	2.33	....
Claims on Banking Institutions........	42e.l	....	....	....	211.54	230.24	239.02	217.46	226.92	242.72	313.38	341.54	....
Foreign Liabilities....................	46c.l	....	....	....	† .40	.77	.71	.02	.10	.52	.25	.65	....
Credit from Banking Institutions.......	46h.l	....	....	....	† 12.86	19.26	24.36	3.98	28.73	19.68	37.75	37.61	....
Capital..............................	47a.l	....	....	....	† 419.89	469.87	552.98	685.92	665.36	612.90	477.80	565.95	....
Insurance and Technical Reserves.....	47d.l	....	....	....	550.22	673.70	770.96	968.65	1,071.41	1,188.29	1,150.28	1,247.68	....
Other Items (Net)......................	47r.l	....	....	....	† −422.39	−538.89	−653.60	−891.61	−925.31	−915.76	−633.51	−765.67	....
Interest Rates						*Percent Per Annum*							
Bank Rate (End of Period)................	60	5.00	7.00	7.00	3.50	2.50	2.00	1.50	2.00	2.00	† 4.50	3.00	2.00
Repurchase Rate (End of Period)......	60a	8.83	† 7.51	8.91	4.27	4.19	3.50	3.25	3.89	3.75	3.75	2.75	2.00
Money Market Rate....................	60b	9.08	7.36	8.54	6.28	4.21	4.24	3.14	3.81	4.09	4.19	3.29	....
Treasury Bill Rate......................	60c	8.35	7.40	8.75	5.79	4.11	4.19	3.12	3.95	....	4.07	3.04	....
Deposit Rate (End of Period)...........	60l	5.10	4.91	6.16	2.47	2.50	1.91	1.65	2.15	2.10	2.26	1.51	1.00
Lending Rate (End of Period)...........	60p	11.40	10.64	11.11	7.38	7.01	5.94	5.53	5.83	5.55	5.64	4.79	4.00
Government Bond Yield................	61	8.54	9.52	10.24	8.06	6.61	4.99	4.98	5.37	5.11	5.30	4.63	....
Prices, Production, Labor						*Index Numbers (2000=100): Period Averages*							
Share Prices.........................	62	20	26	29	....	50	59	69	100	71	54	....	....
Forest Industries.....................	62a	59	72	76	....	97	94	101	100	127	154	....	....
Industrials...........................	62b	37	48	† 55	63	87	86	93	100	93	87	....	....
Prices: Domestic Supply.................	63	83.8	87.8	94.6	92.9	94.0	93.5	94.5	100.0	103.2	103.8	102.9	105.3
Consumer Prices......................	64	93.4	95.4	97.7	98.3	98.9	98.7	99.1	100.0	102.4	104.6	106.6	107.0
Harmonized CPI........................	64h	....	....	94.7	95.4	97.2	98.2	98.7	100.0	102.7	104.7	107.1	108.2
Wages: Hourly Earnings................	65	75.0	78.2	82.4	87.8	91.7	95.0	96.7	100.0	102.9	106.4	109.4	112.3
Industrial Production.....................	66	....	....	82.3	83.0	87.1	91.2	94.2	100.0	98.9	99.9	102.2	106.8
Industrial Employment................	67	96.9	95.6	100.7	101.7	100.4	100.8	100.1	100.0	97.6	93.8	90.7	89.3
						Number in Thousands: Period Averages							
Labor Force...........................	67d	4,320	4,266	4,319	4,310	4,264	4,255	4,308	4,360	4,414	4,418	4,449	4,459
Employment..........................	67e	† 3,964	3,928	3,986	3,963	3,922	3,979	4,068	4,156	4,239	4,242	4,232	4,213
Unemployment.......................	67c	† 356	340	332	346	342	276	241	203	175	176	184	246
Unemployment Rate (%)................	67r	† 8.2	8.0	7.7	8.0	8.0	6.5	5.6	4.7	4.0	4.0	4.9	5.5
Intl. Transactions & Positions						*Millions of Kronor*							
Exports..............................	70	388,300	471,600	567,700	569,200	632,800	675,300	700,800	796,900	781,900	790,300	825,800	903,900
Imports, c.i.f.........................	71	332,490	397,410	460,500	448,700	501,100	545,300	568,100	669,200	654,000	644,500	679,500	736,300
						2000=100							
Volume of Exports....................	72	50.1	58.9	65.9	69.6	77.0	84.0	89.1	100.0	98.5	101.2	106.1	116.8
Volume of Imports....................	73	55.8	64.0	69.3	71.1	78.7	86.3	89.3	100.0	94.9	94.4	100.4	108.1
Export Prices........................	76	86.8	91.2	101.6	96.6	97.5	97.0	96.1	100.0	101.6	99.7	97.4	97.2
Import Prices........................	76.x	83.2	87.1	92.8	89.5	91.3	90.4	92.6	100.0	104.5	104.8	102.6	105.2

Sweden 144

		1993	1994	1995	1996	1997	1998	1999	2000	2001	2002	2003	2004
Balance of Payments					*Millions of US Dollars: Minus Sign Indicates Debit*								
Current Account, n.i.e.	78ald	−4,159	743	4,940	5,892	7,406	4,639	5,982	6,617	6,696	12,784	22,844	....
Goods: Exports f.o.b.	78aad	49,348	60,199	79,903	84,690	83,194	85,179	87,568	87,431	76,200	84,172	102,080	....
Goods: Imports f.o.b.	78abd	−41,801	−50,641	−63,926	−66,053	−65,195	−67,547	−71,854	−72,216	−62,368	−67,541	−83,147	....
Trade Balance	78acd	7,548	9,558	15,978	18,636	17,999	17,632	15,714	15,215	13,832	16,631	18,933	....
Services: Credit	78add	12,589	13,674	15,622	16,930	17,769	17,952	19,904	20,252	21,997	24,009	30,654	....
Services: Debit	78aed	−13,355	−14,690	−17,216	−18,755	−19,524	−21,721	−22,617	−23,440	−23,020	−23,958	−28,771	....
Balance on Goods & Services	78afd	6,782	8,542	14,384	16,811	16,245	13,862	13,001	12,027	12,809	16,682	20,816	....
Income: Credit	78agd	7,127	9,611	14,906	14,338	14,404	16,564	19,871	20,074	17,934	18,018	22,934	....
Income: Debit	78ahd	−16,261	−15,530	−21,379	−22,641	−20,513	−22,349	−23,291	−22,137	−20,786	−19,044	−22,637	....
Balance on Gds, Serv. & Inc.	78aid	−2,352	2,623	7,910	8,508	10,135	8,077	9,581	9,964	9,957	15,657	21,113	....
Current Transfers, n.i.e.: Credit	78ajd	456	544	1,555	2,524	2,319	2,266	2,341	2,602	2,578	3,345	3,577	....
Current Transfers: Debit	78akd	−2,263	−2,424	−4,525	−5,140	−5,048	−5,704	−5,940	−5,950	−5,839	−6,218	−1,845	....
Capital Account, n.i.e.	78bcd	23	23	14	9	−228	868	−2,143	384	509	−79	−46	....
Capital Account, n.i.e.: Credit	78bad	37	37	32	31	211	1,502	1,289	1,226	1,111	529	552	....
Capital Account: Debit	78bbd	−15	−14	−18	−22	−439	−634	−3,432	−841	−601	−609	−599	....
Financial Account, n.i.e.	78bjd	11,518	6,078	−5,052	−10,046	−10,121	5,961	−1,413	−3,297	1,824	−10,704	−20,163	....
Direct Investment Abroad	78bdd	−1,471	−6,685	−11,399	−5,112	−12,119	−22,671	−19,554	−39,962	−6,959	−10,673	−17,341	....
Dir. Invest. in Rep. Econ., n.i.e.	78bed	3,705	6,269	14,939	5,492	10,271	19,413	59,386	22,125	13,085	11,709	3,268	....
Portfolio Investment Assets	78bfd	−94	−2,459	−10,765	−13,136	−13,818	−17,615	−36,749	−12,772	−23,041	−4,038	−13,701	....
Equity Securities	78bkd	−76	−2,509	−9,378	−7,518	−10,179	−7,427	−29,766	758	−22,642	−124	−4,618	....
Debt Securities	78bld	−18	51	−1,386	−5,618	−3,640	−10,188	−6,983	−13,530	−400	−3,914	−9,083	....
Portfolio Investment Liab., n.i.e.	78bgd	1,472	721	8,201	1,661	−2,384	2,023	1,882	9,017	10,338	−6,691	4,134	....
Equity Securities	78bmd	4,212	6,795	1,853	4,047	−1,687	−328	−3,895	17,997	−2,336	2,536	452	....
Debt Securities	78bnd	−2,741	−6,074	6,348	−2,386	−697	2,351	5,777	−8,980	12,674	−9,227	3,682	....
Financial Derivatives Assets	78bwd	....	....	20,264	24,800	31,244	30,125	22,982	31,481	33,678	37,720	40,045	....
Financial Derivatives Liabilities	78bxd	....	....	−21,096	−23,243	−29,280	−31,428	−22,923	−31,795	−38,894	−37,888	−38,964	....
Other Investment Assets	78bhd	1,159	−3,400	−12,197	−10,828	−9,670	−5,901	−10,333	−16,000	929	−998	−8,349	....
Monetary Authorities	78bod	....	....										....
General Government	78bpd	−144	−290	−483	−303	−322	−244	−642	−150	37	−1,589	442	....
Banks	78bqd	4,682	2,902	−8,037	−10,239	−4,971	−1,135	−5,296	−13,279	1,672	697	−8,688	....
Other Sectors	78brd	−3,379	−6,012	−3,677	−287	−4,377	−4,522	−4,396	−2,571	−779	−106	−103	....
Other Investment Liab., n.i.e.	78bid	6,748	11,633	6,999	10,320	15,635	32,015	3,897	34,609	12,689	155	10,744	....
Monetary Authorities	78bsd	—	—	—	—	−39	88	−243	−556	−812	993	2,605	....
General Government	78btd	11,723	5,075	8,842	1,817	−1,583	578	1,047	129	−32	683	−941	....
Banks	78bud	−10,851	−1,957	−1,055	2,935	9,269	20,205	−3,846	29,682	10,077	−1,299	1,905	....
Other Sectors	78bvd	5,876	8,515	−788	5,569	7,988	11,144	6,938	5,354	3,455	−222	7,175	....
Net Errors and Omissions	78cad	−4,852	−4,462	−1,566	−2,241	−3,769	−8,214	−545	−3,534	−10,078	−1,336	−558	....
Overall Balance	78cbd	2,530	2,381	−1,664	−6,386	−6,712	3,254	1,881	170	−1,048	665	2,076	....
Reserves and Related Items	79dad	−2,530	−2,381	1,664	6,386	6,712	−3,254	−1,881	−170	1,048	−665	−2,076	....
Reserve Assets	79dbd	−2,530	−2,381	1,664	6,386	6,712	−3,254	−1,881	−170	1,048	−665	−2,076	....
Use of Fund Credit and Loans	79dcd	—	—	—	—	—	—	—	—	....	....	....	....
Exceptional Financing	79ded	—	—	—	—	—	—	—	—	....	....	....	....
International Investment Position						*Millions of US Dollars*							
Assets	79aad	135,124	165,515	227,989	248,580	241,838	295,255	353,559	365,450	368,231	412,424	556,611	....
Direct Investment Abroad	79abd	44,560	59,237	69,088	71,751	79,099	94,674	104,948	115,582	123,275	144,127	181,307	....
Portfolio Investment	79acd	17,583	22,114	36,947	50,357	69,478	100,589	142,802	133,506	144,072	139,935	210,128	....
Equity Securities	79add	15,054	18,227	29,738	38,859	51,248	71,207	108,387	89,546	103,990	92,376	141,731	....
Debt Securities	79aed	2,529	3,887	7,209	11,498	18,230	29,382	34,415	43,960	40,082	47,559	68,397	....
Financial Derivatives	79ald	—	—	15,920	16,446	16,450	15,579	14,990	18,679	15,663	24,563	29,938	....
Other Investment	79afd	51,785	60,310	80,352	89,652	65,265	67,529	72,855	81,368	70,405	84,687	112,868	....
Monetary Authorities	79agd	—	—	—	—	—	—	—	—	—	—	—	....
General Government	79ahd	4,456	5,227	6,158	6,258	6,174	6,517	6,508	5,984	5,856	8,124	9,314	....
Banks	79aid	26,254	24,660	36,346	44,681	46,599	46,143	48,128	56,018	47,948	57,671	78,700	....
Other Sectors	79ajd	21,075	30,423	37,848	38,713	12,492	14,869	18,219	19,365	16,601	18,892	24,854	....
Reserve Assets	79akd	21,196	23,855	25,682	20,375	11,546	16,884	17,964	16,316	14,816	19,112	22,369	....
Liabilities	79lad	215,813	261,074	324,863	352,787	339,476	389,867	430,625	424,279	421,706	476,006	629,115	....
Dir. Invest. in Rep. Economy	79lbd	12,886	23,454	33,042	34,056	42,399	53,792	68,053	77,009	91,567	117,781	151,915	....
Portfolio Investment	79lcd	47,089	57,897	77,348	99,549	207,565	225,711	259,909	225,025	207,798	207,123	286,014	....
Equity Securities	79ldd	21,798	35,918	48,061	70,295	79,472	94,033	129,384	106,660	76,522	54,043	89,738	....
Debt Securities	79led	25,291	21,979	29,287	29,253	128,093	131,678	130,575	118,365	131,276	153,080	196,277	....
Financial Derivatives	79lld	—	—	16,821	17,610	16,420	15,936	14,095	15,276	14,225	25,453	30,545	....
Other Investment	79lfd	155,838	179,723	197,651	201,572	73,091	94,427	88,518	106,969	108,116	125,649	160,640	....
Monetary Authorities	79lgd	—	—	—	146	—	—	—	—	—	—	—	....
General Government	79lhd	47,089	57,227	65,934	64,328	1,836	2,238	2,857	1,922	1,579	2,739	2,814	....
Banks	79lid	50,340	50,928	55,270	56,615	51,247	68,238	59,978	80,756	81,747	97,609	116,128	....
Other Sectors	79ljd	58,409	71,567	76,447	80,483	20,009	23,951	25,683	24,291	24,790	25,301	41,699	....
Government Finance					*Billions of Kronor: Year Ending December 31*								
Deficit (-) or Surplus	80	−231.41	† −133.63	−153.18	−58.02	† −16.66	6.84	64.01	125.82	....	† 1.11	−46.35	−53.35
Revenue	81	544.63	† 419.06	459.93	590.08	640.06	696.46	715.81	790.96	....	† 730.45	661.74	694.66
Grants Received	81z	—	—	5.66	10.40	8.88	9.87	9.28	9.02	....	....	....	....
Expenditure	82	747.15	† 552.69	618.77	658.50	† 665.60	699.49	661.08	674.16	....	† 729.34	708.09	748.01
Lending Minus Repayments	83	28.89	....	....	....	....	....	....	....	....	....	....	....
Financing													
Domestic	84a	66.36	† 129.85	135.42	27.07	−11.34	−20.25	47.13	8.78	....	† 28.99	98.65	58.03
Foreign	85a	165.05	† 3.78	17.76	30.95	28.01	13.43	−111.15	−135.30	....	−25.50	−42.42	−29.42
Total Debt	88	828.02	† 1,098.92	1,169.48	1,189.53	1,208.36	1,217.64	1,142.23	1,008.30	† 1,156.83	1,160.32	† 1,228.74	1,257.70
Debt: Domestic	88a	518.61	† 585.96	638.76	627.85	618.69	614.53	650.28	598.86	† 933.50	962.48	† 898.31	956.70
Debt: Foreign	89a	309.41	† 512.96	530.72	561.68	589.67	603.11	491.95	409.44	223.33	197.84	330.43	301.00

National Accounts		1993	1994	1995	1996	1997	1998	1999	2000	2001	2002	2003	2004
							Billions of Kronor						
Househ.Cons.Expend.,incl.NPISHs....	96f	796.01	† 832.96	865.24	890.59	931.69	967.19	1,015.74	1,078.36	1,108.42	1,144.42	1,188.15	1,224.48
Government Consumption Expend...	91f	453.55	† 466.08	481.35	504.33	513.55	540.93	569.37	583.44	613.33	657.29	690.67	706.18
Gross Fixed Capital Formation..........	93e	241.85	† 255.00	282.85	293.47	296.63	324.50	358.33	389.01	395.62	392.00	384.57	407.21
Changes in Inventories....................	93i	−4.95	† 17.15	21.48	7.14	9.37	15.31	5.35	16.47	5.90	1.66	10.63	3.56
Exports of Goods and Services..........	90c	492.99	† 582.93	695.38	688.32	781.87	838.23	885.30	1,012.09	1,042.17	1,038.34	1,068.04	1,178.07
Imports of Goods and Services (-)....	98c	435.42	508.33	† 576.06	568.70	644.88	714.29	757.56	884.40	896.29	880.83	903.61	973.74
Gross Domestic Product (GDP).........	99b	1,544.04	† 1,645.79	1,770.25	1,815.14	1,888.23	1,971.87	2,076.53	2,194.97	2,269.15	2,352.94	2,438.45	2,545.75
Net Primary Income from Abroad.....	98.n	−68.13	−45.88	−45.90	−46.72	−43.08	−28.71	−19.69	−16.45	−20.58	−6.71	−.38	29.34
Gross National Income (GNI)............	99a	1,475.91	1,599.91	1,724.35	1,768.42	1,845.15	1,943.16	2,056.84	2,178.52	2,248.57	2,346.23	2,438.07	2,575.09
Net Current Transf.from Abroad......	98t	−9.79	−9.54	−10.79	−6.70	−12.06	−15.95	−20.27	−20.10	−21.06	−24.18	−21.32	−35.57
Gross Nat'l Disposable Inc.(GNDI)....	99i	1,466.13	1,590.37	1,713.56	1,761.73	1,833.09	1,927.21	2,036.57	2,158.42	2,227.51	2,322.05	2,416.74	2,539.52
Gross Saving..............................	99s	216.56	291.33	366.96	366.81	387.85	419.09	451.45	496.62	505.76	520.35	537.91	608.86
Consumption of Fixed Capital..........	99cf	197.6	192.9	199.5	207.8	218.4	232.3	251.5	274.1	292.4	302.3	304.1	311.2
Net National Income......................	99e	1,278.28	1,407.05	1,524.84	1,560.60	1,626.70	1,710.89	1,805.38	1,904.42	1,956.15	2,043.95	2,133.97	2,263.93
GDP Volume 2000 Prices................	99b.p	1,725.97	1,797.85	1,870.72	1,894.87	1,941.06	2,011.82	2,103.93	2,194.97	2,217.95	2,261.77	2,294.94	2,377.50
GDP Volume (2000=100)...............	99bvp	78.6	81.9	85.2	86.3	88.4	91.7	95.9	100.0	101.0	103.0	104.6	108.3
GDP Deflator (2000=100)...............	99bip	89.5	† 91.5	94.6	95.8	97.3	98.0	98.7	100.0	102.3	104.0	106.3	107.1
							Millions: Midyear Estimates						
Population...............................	99z	8.74	8.79	8.83	8.85	8.86	8.86	8.86	8.88	8.90	8.93	8.97	9.01

		1993	1994	1995	1996	1997	1998	1999	2000	2001	2002	2003	2004
Exchange Rates						*Francs per SDR: End of Period*							
Market Rate	aa	2.0322	1.9146	1.7102	1.9361	1.9636	1.9382	2.1955	2.1322	2.1079	1.8854	1.8380	1.7574
					Francs per US Dollar: End of Period (ae) Period Average (rf)								
Market Rate	ae	1.4795	1.3115	1.1505	1.3464	1.4553	1.3765	1.5996	1.6365	1.6773	1.3868	1.2369	1.1316
Market Rate	rf	1.4776	1.3677	1.1825	1.2360	1.4513	1.4498	1.5022	1.6888	1.6876	1.5586	1.3467	1.2435
					Index Numbers (2000=100): Period Averages								
Market Rate	ahx	114.2	123.7	142.9	136.6	116.3	116.6	112.4	100.0	100.1	108.6	125.4	135.8
Nominal Effective Exchange Rate	neu	95.7	102.1	109.5	107.5	100.6	102.7	101.4	100.0	103.7	108.2	108.6	108.4
Real Effective Exchange Rate	reu	86.7	94.2	100.9	101.1	97.4	102.9	102.1	100.0	105.6	111.2	112.0	113.3
Fund Position						*Millions of SDRs: End of Period*							
Quota	2f.s	2,470	2,470	2,470	2,470	2,470	2,470	3,459	3,459	3,459	3,459	3,459	3,459
SDRs	1b.s	113	162	181	88	170	192	345	125	225	54	25	46
Reserve Position in the Fund	1c.s	605	643	981	1,065	1,407	1,828	1,218	964	1,259	1,410	1,383	1,154
of which: Outstg.Fund Borrowing	2c	—	—	—	—	—	230	—	—	—	—	—	—
International Liquidity					*Millions of US Dollars Unless Otherwise Indicated: End of Period*								
Total Reserves minus Gold	1l.d	32,635	34,729	36,413	38,433	39,028	41,191	36,321	32,272	32,006	40,155	47,652	55,497
SDRs	1b.d	155	236	269	126	230	271	473	162	283	74	37	71
Reserve Position in the Fund	1c.d	830	939	1,459	1,531	1,899	2,574	1,672	1,256	1,582	1,917	2,056	1,792
Foreign Exchange	1d.d	31,650	33,554	34,685	36,775	36,899	38,346	34,176	30,854	30,141	38,164	45,560	53,634
Gold (Million Fine Troy Ounces)	1ad	83.28	83.28	83.28	83.28	83.28	83.28	83.28	77.79	70.68	61.62	52.51	43.54
Gold (National Valuation)	1and	8,046	9,077	10,347	8,841	8,182	8,667	7,464	21,219	19,664	21,156	21,932	19,123
Monetary Authorities: Other Liab.	4..d	—	—	—	—	33	119	134	124	375	401	393	291
Deposit Money Banks: Assets	7a.d	154,224	187,875	212,374	† 263,362	314,438	369,712	463,670	465,833	446,488	557,850	616,287	680,718
Liabilities	7b.d	129,333	171,093	184,869	† 223,836	268,969	300,777	395,023	440,005	415,253	498,607	546,820	608,308
Trustee Accounts: Assets	7k.d	235,558	271,584	288,831	† 294,323	293,492	311,232	292,460	325,518	323,209	328,419	327,835	363,438
Liabilities	7m.d	182,470	213,280	232,765	† 239,280	241,593	255,032	243,663	264,004	265,599	273,602	276,692	306,107
Monetary Authorities						*Billions of Francs: End of Period*							
Foreign Assets	11	60.94	59.98	56.30	63.13	69.04	69.34	71.05	88.14	87.52	85.45	86.42	84.83
Claims on Central Government	12a	5.02	5.13	5.19	5.26	7.12	7.22	7.14	7.71	8.32	9.36	10.04	9.81
Claims on Deposit Money Banks	12e	1.36	1.30	1.87	2.86	1.09	17.73	28.53	24.46	25.99	28.01	27.14	24.52
Reserve Money	14	39.10	39.33	38.40	40.35	39.43	42.47	49.67	44.41	49.96	46.56	50.24	48.68
of which: Currency Outside DMBs	14a	31.38	32.64	33.02	34.61	34.33	35.43	39.44	37.78	42.17	41.94	42.93	42.14
Central Government Deposits	16d	.49	.75	1.12	1.08	† 2.69	15.36	17.16	10.21	2.59	7.29	3.01	2.32
Other Items (Net)	17r	27.73	26.33	23.84	29.83	35.15	36.46	39.87	65.68	69.29	68.96	70.35	68.17
Deposit Money Banks						*Billions of Francs: End of Period*							
Reserves	20	8.01	7.64	8.27	† 9.61	9.83	10.95	17.17	12.51	12.74	13.62	14.33	13.17
Foreign Assets	21	228.17	246.40	244.34	† 354.59	457.60	508.91	741.69	762.34	748.90	773.63	762.29	770.30
Claims on Central Government	22a	47.40	49.57	† 50.70	† 52.66	52.44	51.68	53.46	59.29	56.88	61.84	59.05	58.71
Claims on Private Sector	22d	574.31	594.37	611.70	† 608.17	625.65	635.67	676.49	668.94	660.94	662.90	686.97	716.75
Demand Deposits	24	59.86	62.22	67.63	† 93.57	105.45	113.88	124.00	122.25	131.40	149.32	194.49	181.92
Time and Savings Deposits	25	329.73	343.60	358.01	† 374.36	396.05	413.84	474.49	369.90	377.10	390.97	393.48	424.82
Bonds	26ab	173.22	164.72	161.13	† 149.66	137.25	127.55	123.04	128.19	129.07	129.91	120.29	116.22
Foreign Liabilities	26c	191.35	224.39	212.69	† 301.37	391.43	414.02	631.88	720.07	696.50	691.47	676.36	688.36
Other Items (Net)	27r	103.74	103.04	115.54	† 106.06	115.34	137.93	135.39	162.68	145.39	150.31	138.02	147.61
Monetary Survey						*Billions of Francs: End of Period*							
Foreign Assets (Net)	31n	97.76	81.99	87.94	† 116.35	135.17	164.06	180.64	130.21	139.28	167.05	171.86	166.44
Domestic Credit	32	626.24	648.31	† 666.47	† 665.01	† 682.53	679.22	719.93	725.73	723.56	726.80	753.06	782.96
Claims on Central Govt. (Net)	32an	51.93	53.94	† 54.77	† 56.84	† 56.88	43.54	43.44	56.78	62.61	63.91	66.09	66.20
Claims on Private Sector	32d	574.31	594.37	611.70	† 608.17	625.65	635.67	676.49	668.94	660.94	662.90	686.97	716.75
Money	34	91.24	94.86	100.65	† 128.18	139.78	149.31	163.44	160.03	173.57	191.26	237.41	224.06
Quasi-Money	35	329.73	343.60	358.01	† 374.36	396.05	413.84	474.49	369.90	377.10	390.97	393.48	424.82
Bonds	36ab	173.22	164.72	161.13	† 149.66	137.25	127.55	123.04	128.19	129.07	129.91	120.29	116.22
Other Items (Net)	37r	129.82	127.11	134.62	† 129.16	144.62	152.58	139.59	197.82	183.11	181.71	173.73	184.30
Money plus Quasi-Money	35l	420.97	438.46	458.66	† 502.54	535.83	563.15	637.93	529.93	550.66	582.23	630.90	648.88
Other Banking Institutions						*Billions of Francs: End of Period*							
Foreign Assets	41..x	348.51	356.18	332.30	† 396.28	427.12	428.41	467.82	532.71	542.12	455.45	405.50	411.27
Domestic Liabilities	45..x	78.54	76.47	64.50	† 74.11	75.53	77.36	78.06	100.67	96.63	76.02	63.26	64.88
Foreign Liabilities	46c.x	269.96	279.72	267.80	† 322.17	351.59	351.05	389.76	432.04	445.49	379.43	342.24	346.39
Nonbank Financial Institutions						*Billions of Francs: End of Period*							
Claims on Central Government	42a.s	....	....	....	....	....	....	....	....	....	....	....	....
Claims on Priv.Sec.& Local Govt	42d.s	139.24	152.91	163.99	180.80	200.00	227.30	250.10	254.80	264.20	263.50	269.10	....
Real Estate	42h.s	20.82	21.79	22.50	22.30	24.30	25.00	25.60	25.80	27.00	28.70	28.50	....
Incr.in Total Assets(Within Per.)	49z.s	13.09	14.64	11.79	24.11	20.50	28.10	24.60	7.30	8.50	1.50	10.00	....
Liquid Liabilities	55l	499.51	514.93	523.16	† 576.65	611.36	640.51	715.99	630.59	647.29	658.25	694.16	713.75
Interest Rates						*Percent Per Annum*							
Bank Rate (End of Period)	60	4.00	3.50	1.50	1.00	1.00	1.00	.50	† 3.20	1.59	.50	.11	.54
Money Market Rate	60b	4.94	3.85	2.89	1.78	1.35	1.22	.93	† 3.50	1.65	.44	.09	.55
Treasury Bill Rate	60c	4.75	3.97	2.78	1.72	1.45	1.32	1.17	2.93	2.68	.94	.16	.37
Deposit Rate	60l	3.50	3.63	1.28	1.34	1.00	.69	1.24	† 3.00	1.68	.43	.17	.39
Lending Rate	60p	6.40	5.51	5.48	4.97	4.47	4.07	3.90	4.29	4.30	3.93	3.27	3.20
Government Bond Yield	61	4.05	5.23	3.73	3.63	3.08	† 2.71	3.62	3.55	3.56	2.40	2.78	2.38

		1993	1994	1995	1996	1997	1998	1999	2000	2001	2002	2003	2004
Prices, Production, Labor					*Index Numbers (2000=100): Period Averages*								
Share Prices	62	31.0	35.7	37.3	46.6	66.1	88.0	89.6	100.0	88.7	72.2	61.7	72.6
Producer Prices	63	104.5	104.0	103.9	102.0	101.3	100.1	99.1	100.0	100.5	100.0	100.0	101.2
Prices: Home & Imported Goods	63s	102.9	102.6	102.6	100.2	100.3	98.7	97.4	100.0	99.9	98.7	98.4	99.4
Consumer Prices	64	93.9	94.7	96.4	97.2	97.7	97.7	98.5	100.0	101.0	101.6	102.3	103.1
Wages: Hourly Earn	65	93.5	94.9	96.2	97.4	97.8	98.5	98.8	100.0	102.5	104.3	105.8	106.7
Industrial Production	66	77.3	80.6	82.2	82.2	86.0	89.1	92.2	100.0	99.3	94.2	94.6	98.4
Manufacturing Employment	67ey	112.0	107.1	105.7	103.0	100.4	99.9	99.0	100.0	101.4	98.7	95.5	93.8
					Number in Thousands: Period Averages								
Labor Force	67d	3,873	....	3,871	3,925	3,928	3,975	3,984	3,985	4,039	4,079	4,120	4,137
Employment	67e	3,746	3,719	3,747	3,781	3,766	3,833	3,862	3,870	3,938	3,959	3,951	3,959
Unemployment	67c	163	171	153	169	188	140	99	72	67	101	144	153
Unemployment Rate (%)	67r	4.5	4.7	4.2	4.7	5.2	3.9	2.7	2.0	1.9	2.8	3.8	4.3
Intl. Transactions & Positions					*Millions of Francs*								
Exports	70	86,659	90,213	92,012	94,174	105,133	109,113	114,446	126,549	131,717	130,381	130,661	141,735
Imports, c.i.f	71	83,767	87,279	90,775	91,967	103,088	106,866	113,416	128,615	130,052	123,125	123,778	132,423
					2000=100								
Volume of Exports	72.a	73.0	76.5	79.8	80.8	†87.0	90.1	93.0	100.0	102.8	104.7	104.8	111.5
Volume of Imports	73.a	64.1	70.1	74.6	75.7	†80.5	85.7	93.1	100.0	101.1	98.6	99.5	104.1
Unit Value of Exports	74.a	93.8	93.1	91.2	92.1	†95.4	95.7	97.3	100.0	101.2	98.4	98.6	100.5
Unit Value of Imports	75.a	101.6	96.8	94.5	94.5	†99.6	96.9	94.8	100.0	100.0	97.1	96.7	98.9
Import Prices	76.x	99.6	99.5	99.7	96.0	97.9	95.8	93.7	100.0	98.4	95.6	94.7	95.5
Balance of Payments					*Millions of US Dollars: Minus Sign Indicates Debit*								
Current Account, n.i.e	78ald	16,875	16,729	20,703	19,916	25,317	25,194	27,879	32,493	21,897	24,721	43,618	50,568
Goods: Exports f.o.b	78aad	75,424	82,625	97,139	95,544	95,039	93,782	91,787	94,810	95,897	100,786	115,443	138,164
Goods: Imports f.o.b	78abd	−73,832	−79,279	−93,880	−93,675	−92,302	−92,849	−90,937	−92,739	−94,258	−94,138	−108,482	−122,617
Trade Balance	78acd	1,592	3,346	3,260	1,869	2,738	933	850	2,071	1,640	6,648	6,961	15,547
Services: Credit	78add	21,602	22,752	26,180	26,407	25,424	26,850	28,582	29,004	27,799	30,266	34,948	38,765
Services: Debit	78aed	−11,548	−12,768	−15,037	−15,691	−14,100	−15,085	−15,859	−15,561	−16,460	−17,213	−19,275	−21,257
Balance on Goods & Services	78afd	11,646	13,329	14,403	12,584	14,061	12,698	13,573	15,514	12,979	19,701	22,634	33,056
Income: Credit	78agd	25,152	26,747	31,575	32,997	35,066	45,926	50,081	61,496	52,919	41,805	63,219	68,557
Income: Debit	78ahd	−16,912	−19,886	−20,867	−21,395	−19,761	−28,855	−30,620	−40,308	−38,762	−31,084	−37,068	−45,052
Balance on Gds, Serv. & Inc	78aid	19,886	20,190	25,111	24,186	29,366	29,769	33,034	36,702	27,136	30,422	48,784	56,560
Current Transfers, n.i.e.: Credit	78ajd	2,638	2,831	3,339	3,253	2,717	2,647	7,539	6,540	9,699	10,693	13,366	14,035
Current Transfers: Debit	78akd	−5,649	−6,292	−7,748	−7,523	−6,767	−7,222	−12,694	−10,749	−14,938	−16,394	−18,532	−20,028
Capital Account, n.i.e	78bcd	−134	−350	−462	−214	−167	139	−515	−3,541	1,523	−1,159	−763	−1,282
Capital Account, n.i.e.: Credit	78bad	—	31	10	19	36	755	53	490	2,314	274	323	364
Capital Account: Debit	78bbd	−134	−380	−472	−233	−203	−616	−568	−4,031	−791	−1,433	−1,086	−1,646
Financial Account, n.i.e	78bjd	−17,528	−16,756	−11,231	−27,314	−24,712	−31,162	−33,040	−30,137	−36,869	−22,832	−24,609	−58,184
Direct Investment Abroad	78bdd	−8,148	−10,749	−11,289	−16,152	−17,732	−18,767	−33,256	−43,989	−18,326	−8,240	−15,343	−25,033
Dir. Invest. in Rep. Econ., n.i.e	78bed	1,707	3,683	4,158	4,373	7,306	9,649	12,426	19,778	9,480	6,783	17,547	5,382
Portfolio Investment Assets	78bfd	−30,121	−19,112	−8,884	−22,731	−19,739	−14,882	−47,042	−23,169	−43,088	−29,159	−32,902	−42,412
Equity Securities	78bkd	−16,650	−8,073	−4,064	−14,686	−9,159	−2,529	−17,490	−20,424	−15,134	−7,454	−2,086	−11,303
Debt Securities	78bld	−13,470	−11,040	−4,820	−8,045	−10,580	−12,353	−29,552	−2,744	−27,954	−21,705	−30,816	−31,109
Portfolio Investment Liab., n.i.e	78bgd	12,501	911	4,960	12,895	9,033	10,247	5,916	10,247	1,894	7,482	−1,662	2,858
Equity Securities	78bmd	7,923	−1,573	5,851	11,677	6,945	8,632	5,562	8,777	1,840	5,678	−4,428	−2,788
Debt Securities	78bnd	4,578	2,484	−891	1,218	2,088	1,615	354	1,470	54	1,804	2,765	5,646
Financial Derivatives Assets	78bwd	....	....	....	....	....	....	....	....	....	....	....	....
Financial Derivatives Liabilities	78bxd	....	....	....	....	....	....	....	....	....	....	....	....
Other Investment Assets	78bhd	7,221	−30,778	−368	−70,353	−55,265	−60,089	−80,244	−101,376	21,392	−38,290	−4,631	−27,186
Monetary Authorities	78bod	—	—	—	—	—	—	—	—	—	—	....	....
General Government	78bpd	−100	−51	−15	42	197	204	200	35	50	62	113	116
Banks	78bqd	−2,666	−19,166	−9,423	−59,915	−52,384	−45,489	−76,859	−83,538	25,742	−53,922	−11,657	−14,742
Other Sectors	78brd	9,987	−11,562	9,070	−10,480	−3,078	−14,804	−3,585	−17,873	−4,400	15,571	6,913	−12,561
Other Investment Liab., n.i.e	78bid	−687	39,290	191	64,654	51,683	42,681	109,160	108,372	−8,220	38,591	12,383	28,207
Monetary Authorities	78bsd	91	−104	−3	−9	11	80	32	33	840	−860	−24	222
General Government	78btd	79	40	267	31	121	−4	−53	−59	−26	154	−208	65
Banks	78bud	4,074	30,261	1,608	49,121	51,563	34,000	95,815	90,490	−14,861	35,979	6,296	27,903
Other Sectors	78bvd	−4,932	9,093	−1,680	15,511	−11	8,606	13,365	17,908	5,827	3,319	6,319	17
Net Errors and Omissions	78cad	1,271	1,386	−8,980	10,134	1,717	7,008	2,992	−3,029	14,071	1,819	−14,842	10,517
Overall Balance	78cbd	486	1,009	29	2,521	2,154	1,179	−2,685	−4,214	622	2,549	3,405	1,618
Reserves and Related Items	79dad	−486	−1,009	−29	−2,521	−2,154	−1,179	2,685	4,214	−622	−2,549	−3,405	−1,618
Reserve Assets	79dbd	−486	−1,009	−29	−2,521	−2,154	−1,179	2,685	4,214	−622	−2,549	−3,405	−1,618
Use of Fund Credit and Loans	79dcd	—	—	—	—	—	—	—	—	—	—	—	—
Exceptional Financing	79ded	—	—	—	—	—	—	—	—	—	—	....	....

		1993	1994	1995	1996	1997	1998	1999	2000	2001	2002	2003	2004
International Investment Position							*Millions of US Dollars*						
Assets	79aad	647,184	745,816	860,214	924,274	1,009,487	1,196,819	1,239,264	1,363,496	1,319,719	1,510,128	1,764,377	1,976,701
Direct Investment Abroad	79abd	91,571	112,586	142,479	141,591	165,364	184,232	194,585	233,370	253,550	293,340	342,555	393,019
Portfolio Investment	79acd	271,003	293,846	347,040	359,820	382,782	469,522	504,666	501,479	488,989	520,667	657,540	758,011
Equity Securities	79add	88,919	100,797	120,543	138,922	165,438	209,617	259,679	265,897	247,409	218,319	293,656	339,468
Debt Securities	79aed	182,084	193,049	226,497	220,898	217,344	259,905	244,987	235,582	241,580	302,347	363,884	418,543
Financial Derivatives	79ald	—	—	—	—	—	—	—	—	—	—	—	—
Other Investment	79afd	243,643	293,976	322,125	375,575	414,208	492,632	496,075	575,166	525,483	634,784	694,712	751,019
Monetary Authorities	79agd	—	—	—	—	—	—	—	—	—	—	—	—
General Government	79ahd	884	1,037	1,250	1,051	946	943	759	755	584	696	776	846
Banks	79aid	133,539	163,590	183,006	231,511	276,736	332,647	342,082	413,332	375,251	465,885	508,314	542,352
Other Sectors	79ajd	109,220	129,349	137,870	143,012	136,526	159,043	153,234	161,079	149,648	168,203	185,622	207,821
Reserve Assets	79akd	40,967	45,409	48,569	47,288	47,132	50,432	43,939	53,480	51,697	61,337	69,569	74,653
Liabilities	79lad	404,168	472,874	556,487	587,559	700,953	838,861	881,807	1,045,662	964,656	1,087,772	1,289,848	1,448,048
Dir. Invest. in Rep. Economy	79lbd	49,532	61,691	73,324	69,001	74,142	88,201	90,510	101,706	103,922	143,911	184,135	206,401
Portfolio Investment	79lcd	162,151	162,400	208,583	203,380	272,805	353,572	339,491	411,446	349,732	350,564	450,150	520,953
Equity Securities	79ldd	139,056	134,721	179,290	176,566	246,515	323,809	309,597	382,038	321,678	315,134	402,623	456,669
Debt Securities	79led	23,095	27,679	29,293	26,814	26,289	29,763	29,894	29,408	28,054	35,431	47,526	64,283
Financial Derivatives	79lld	—	—	—	—	—	—	—	—	—	—	—	—
Other Investment	79lfd	192,485	248,783	274,580	315,178	354,006	397,088	451,807	532,510	511,003	593,297	655,563	720,695
Monetary Authorities	79lgd	128	36	37	24	33	119	355	393	1,252	507	518	291
General Government	79lhd	192	258	568	514	596	626	484	413	380	616	465	580
Banks	79lid	128,116	170,567	180,873	218,606	258,708	290,465	342,709	422,205	397,644	467,174	516,834	567,552
Other Sectors	79ljd	64,049	77,923	93,102	96,034	94,669	105,879	108,259	109,500	111,727	125,000	137,745	152,271
Government Finance							*Millions of Francs: Year Ending December 31*						
Deficit (-) or Surplus	80	−8,351	−4,443	−5,141	−4,404	−4,917	363	−2,399	3,820	1,367	−3,989	−2,950	−2,724
Revenue	81	29,559	33,752	32,202	35,279	34,695	39,359	37,742	44,031	43,018	35,537	40,259	42,290
Expenditure	82	35,443	36,759	37,474	39,417	38,151	41,634	40,839	40,832	42,147	39,526	43,645	44,992
Lending Minus Repayments	83	2,467	1,436	−131	266	1,461	−2,638	−698	−621	−496	—	−436	22
Financing													
Net Domestic Borrowing	84a	14,923	7,399	6,472	5,706	8,486	13,860	−6,817	3,244	−2,419	14,277	1,886	3,466
Other Financing	86c	−1,131	−1,598	−1,050	1,202	−596	−4,245	−10,960	−9,000	−5,401	−3,223	−2,204	1,995
Use of Cash Balances	87	−5,441	−1,358	−281	−2,504	−2,973	−9,978	20,176	1,936	6,453	−7,065	3,268	−2,737
Total Debt	88	67,513	75,714	82,152	88,418	97,050	109,620	102,254	108,108	106,813	122,366	123,711	126,685
National Accounts							*Billions of Francs*						
Househ.Cons.Expend.,incl.NPISHs	96f.c	214.5	217.7	222.6	226.3	231.3	235.8	242.0	249.2	255.2	260.1	262.9	268.9
Government Consumption Expend	91f.c	42.4	43.0	43.5	44.3	44.0	44.0	44.3	46.2	49.0	51.0	52.1	53.2
Gross Fixed Capital Formation	93e.c	83.4	86.9	86.8	82.9	82.5	87.2	88.9	94.9	93.8	92.9	90.9	93.8
Changes in Inventories	93i.c	−2.5	−.1	.7	1.1	—	—	—	.1	1.0	−3.1	−4.4	−5.9
Exports of Goods and Services	90c.c	122.2	125.6	127.7	131.1	146.3	152.0	159.6	180.4	184.0	184.0	186.4	198.3
Imports of Goods and Services (-)	98c.c	101.6	105.5	109.1	111.7	123.5	128.8	136.8	155.3	160.5	153.7	154.6	163.9
Gross Domestic Product (GDP)	99b.c	358.3	367.7	372.3	374.0	380.6	390.2	397.9	415.5	422.5	431.1	433.4	444.4
Net Primary Income from Abroad	98.n	15.6	12.7	15.6	....	....	....	....	....	....	....	....	....
Gross National Income (GNI)	99a	358.4	365.6	377.6	....	....	....	....	....	....	....	....	....
Net National Income	99e	322.2	328.8	339.8	....	....	....	....	....	....	....	....	....
GDP Volume 2000 Ref., Chained	99b.r	370.5	374.5	375.9	377.9	385.1	395.8	401.0	415.5	419.9	421.2	419.7	426.8
GDP Volume (2000=100)	99bvr	89.2	90.1	90.5	90.9	92.7	95.3	96.5	100.0	101.0	101.4	101.0	102.7
GDP Deflator (2000=100)	99bir	96.7	98.2	99.0	99.0	98.8	98.6	99.2	100.0	100.6	102.3	103.2	104.1
							Millions: Midyear Estimates						
Population	99z	6.94	6.97	7.00	7.04	7.07	7.11	7.14	7.17	7.19	7.21	7.23	7.24

Syrian Arab Republic   463

		1993	1994	1995	1996	1997	1998	1999	2000	2001	2002	2003	2004
Exchange Rates		*Pounds per SDR: End of Period (aa) Pounds per US Dollar: End of Period (ae)*											
Principal Rate....................	aa	15.418	16.387	16.686	16.141	15.145	15.805	15.406	14.625	14.107	15.261	16.680	17.433
Principal Rate....................	ae	11.225	11.225	11.225	11.225	11.225	11.225	11.225	11.225	11.225	11.225	11.225	11.225
Fund Position		*Millions of SDRs: End of Period*											
Quota.........................	2f.s	210	210	210	210	210	210	294	294	294	294	294	294
SDRs...........................	1b.s	—	—	—	—	—	—	—	—	—	—	—	37
Reserve Position in the Fund...........	1c.s	—	—	—	—	—	—	—	—	—	—	—	—
Total Fund Cred.&Loans Outstg........	2tl	—	—	—	—	—	—	—	—	—	—	—	—
International Liquidity		*Millions of US Dollars Unless Otherwise Indicated: End of Period*											
SDRs...........................	1b.d	—	—	—	—	—	—	—	—	—	—	—	57
Reserve Position in the Fund.........	1c.d	—	—	—	—	—	—	—	—	—	—	—	—
Gold (Million Fine Troy Ounces).......	1ad	.833	.833	.833	.833	.833	.833	.833	.833	.833	.833	.833	....
Gold (National Valuation)...............	1and	29	29	29	29	29	29	29	29	29	29	29	....
Other Liab.................	4..d	1,037	1,041	1,124	1,041	1,084	1,137	1,150	805	730	692	581	....
Monetary Authorities		*Millions of Pounds: End of Period*											
Foreign Assets.....................	11	24,368	28,568	37,206	49,156	52,376	55,216	67,512	88,391	101,503	115,018	130,666	....
Claims on Central Government........	12a	153,089	178,802	203,998	241,730	265,783	270,370	270,369	274,877	301,278	321,202	304,929	....
Claims on Official Entities...............	12bx	106	106	106	106	106	106	106	106	106	106	106	....
Claims on Deposit Money Banks.......	12e	71,006	90,674	104,602	112,460	126,599	135,455	164,991	161,558	157,174	156,554	174,811	....
Reserve Money.................	14	151,867	164,996	172,711	185,864	194,799	204,513	219,475	252,814	295,442	342,625	377,685	....
of which: Currency Outside DMBs..	14a	126,116	135,021	143,800	153,715	159,808	178,191	182,184	203,863	229,266	258,359	285,015	....
Foreign Liabilities.....................	16c	11,640	11,683	12,614	11,686	12,168	12,768	12,911	9,040	8,196	7,773	6,520	....
Central Government Deposits...........	16d	93,898	126,027	156,479	213,995	256,253	272,085	314,414	355,693	374,313	391,594	391,924	....
Capital Accounts.....................	17a	14,242	18,755	23,902	23,902	33,839	38,195	43,909	51,426	55,814	55,815	59,195	....
Other Items (Net).....................	17r	−23,077	−23,311	−19,794	−31,995	−52,193	−66,415	−87,732	−144,041	−173,704	−204,927	−224,813	....
Deposit Money Banks		*Millions of Pounds: End of Period*											
Reserves...........................	20	24,854	31,556	29,366	38,771	25,946	21,403	23,716	31,419	42,242	71,788	85,910	....
Foreign Assets.....................	21	111,872	126,639	150,020	180,547	222,465	255,655	285,762	398,681	502,229	581,672	591,826	....
Claims on Central Government........	22a	21,992	26,252	30,931	35,560	41,573	48,639	58,275	69,385	100,656	127,428	154,462	....
Claims on Official Entities...............	22bx	160,109	120,667	140,439	147,202	164,580	160,381	179,711	187,356	191,020	157,802	173,976	....
Claims on Private Sector...............	22d	44,457	52,343	63,667	66,633	73,351	72,617	75,345	76,611	78,737	83,676	108,658	....
Demand Deposits.................	24	60,761	68,885	78,028	84,685	93,665	97,683	121,471	151,753	176,845	222,391	329,809	....
Time and Savings Deposits...............	25	67,156	83,113	91,775	104,624	116,939	135,636	160,346	194,800	276,181	330,155	261,080	....
Restricted Deposits.................	26b	30,119	24,411	26,708	27,182	33,235	22,776	20,327	28,394	40,542	50,451	73,208	....
Foreign Liabilities.....................	26c	16,584	10,347	5,574	5,551	2,782	3,653	4,915	4,583	3,891	11,116	13,576	....
Central Government Deposits...........	26d	6,302	6,327	7,780	8,643	12,863	13,686	14,960	18,078	19,310	20,154	26,536	....
Credit from Monetary Authorities.....	26g	71,068	90,741	104,712	119,897	136,811	135,199	149,810	160,744	150,193	168,217	178,531	....
Capital Accounts.....................	27a	13,529	17,546	23,065	29,908	34,666	40,576	48,878	47,799	50,598	52,098	44,622	....
Other Items (Net).....................	27r	97,765	56,087	76,780	88,224	96,955	109,485	102,102	157,300	197,322	167,784	187,469	....
Monetary Survey		*Millions of Pounds: End of Period*											
Foreign Assets (Net).....................	31n	108,016	133,177	169,038	212,466	259,891	294,450	335,448	473,449	591,645	677,801	702,396	....
Domestic Credit.........................	32	279,553	245,816	274,882	268,593	276,278	266,342	254,432	234,564	278,174	278,466	323,671	....
Claims on Central Govt. (Net).......	32an	74,881	72,700	70,670	54,652	38,241	33,238	−730	−29,509	8,311	36,882	40,931	....
Claims on Official Entities...............	32bx	160,215	120,773	140,545	147,308	164,686	160,487	179,817	187,462	191,126	157,908	174,082	....
Claims on Private Sector...............	32d	44,457	52,343	63,667	66,633	73,351	72,617	75,345	76,611	78,737	83,676	108,658	....
Money................................	34	191,432	207,106	225,038	244,495	260,927	281,926	313,318	368,670	419,911	494,681	628,279	....
Quasi-Money...........................	35	67,156	83,113	91,775	104,624	116,939	135,636	160,346	194,800	276,181	330,155	261,080	....
Restricted Deposits.................	36b	30,119	24,411	26,708	27,182	33,235	22,776	20,327	28,394	40,542	50,451	73,208	....
Other Items (Net).....................	37r	98,863	64,364	100,397	104,759	125,069	120,452	95,889	116,148	133,183	80,980	63,498	....
Money plus Quasi-Money................	35l	258,588	290,219	316,813	349,119	377,866	417,562	473,663	563,470	696,092	824,836	889,359	....
Interest Rates		*Percent Per Annum*											
Discount Rate (End of Period)...........	60	5.00	5.00	5.00	5.00	5.00	5.00	5.00	5.00	5.00	5.00	....	....
Deposit Rate...........................	60l	4.0	4.0	4.0	4.0	4.0	4.0	4.0	4.0	4.0	4.0	....	....
Lending Rate...........................	60p	9.0	9.0	9.0	9.0	9.0	9.0	9.0	9.0	9.0	9.0	....	....
Prices, Production, Labor		*Index Numbers (2000=100): Period Averages*											
Wholesale Prices.....................	63	84.1	96.1	102.7	106.0	108.7	108.0	† 106.0	100.0	95.0	102.0	....	....
Consumer Prices.....................	64	79.3	91.4	98.7	106.9	108.9	† 108.0	104.0	100.0	103.0	104.0	....	....
Industrial Production.....................	66	80.9	87.2	89.9	90.8	96.2	† 98.0	100.0	100.0	103.0	109.0	....	....
		Number in Thousands: Period Averages											
Labor Force...........................	67d	....	....	....	....	....	4,411	4,527	4,937	5,457	5,460	....	....
Employment...........................	67e	....	....	....	....	....	....	....	....	4,844	4,822	....	....
Unemployment.....................	67c	....	....	....	....	....	....	....	....	613	638	....	....
Unemployment Rate (%)...................	67r	....	....	....	....	....	....	....	....	11.2	11.7	....	....
Intl. Transactions & Positions		*Millions of Pounds*											
Exports...............................	70	35,319	34,200	40,000	44,890	43,960	32,440	38,880	† 216,190	243,000	315,920	265,038	249,014
Imports, c.i.f...........................	71	46,468	61,370	52,860	60,390	45,210	43,720	43,010	† 187,530	220,000	235,720	236,800	327,000
		1995=100											
Volume of Exports.....................	72	94.6	102.4	100.0	98.2	109.6	....	....	....	....	....	....	....
Volume of Imports.....................	73	90.7	111.3	100.0	100.8	87.9	....	....	....	....	....	....	....
Unit Value of Exports.....................	74	74.4	80.0	100.0	105.6	83.3	....	....	....	....	....	....	....
Unit Value of Imports.....................	75	78.8	89.0	100.0	105.9	90.7	....	....	....	....	....	....	....

		1993	1994	1995	1996	1997	1998	1999	2000	2001	2002	2003	2004
Balance of Payments						*Millions of US Dollars: Minus Sign Indicates Debit*							
Current Account, n.i.e.	78ald	−203	−791	263	40	461	58	201	1,061	1,221	1,440	728	360
Goods: Exports f.o.b.	78aad	3,253	3,329	3,858	4,178	4,057	3,142	3,806	5,146	5,706	6,668	5,762	5,685
Goods: Imports f.o.b.	78abd	−3,512	−4,604	−4,004	−4,516	−3,603	−3,320	−3,590	−3,723	−4,282	−4,458	−4,430	−5,800
Trade Balance	78acd	−259	−1,275	−146	−338	454	−178	216	1,423	1,424	2,210	1,332	−115
Services: Credit	78add	1,595	1,863	1,899	1,792	1,582	1,666	1,651	1,699	1,781	1,559	1,331	2,544
Services: Debit	78aed	−1,442	−1,611	−1,537	−1,555	−1,489	−1,491	−1,612	−1,667	−1,694	−1,883	−1,806	−1,962
Balance on Goods & Services	78afd	−106	−1,023	216	−101	547	−3	255	1,455	1,511	1,886	857	467
Income: Credit	78agd	432	638	444	534	421	369	356	345	379	250	282	375
Income: Debit	78ahd	−1,064	−997	−1,004	−1,017	−1,006	−839	−899	−1,224	−1,162	−1,175	−1,139	−1,114
Balance on Gds, Serv. & Inc.	78aid	−738	−1,382	−344	−584	−38	−473	−288	576	728	961	—	−272
Current Transfers, n.i.e.: Credit	78ajd	543	597	610	630	504	533	491	495	512	499	743	648
Current Transfers: Debit	78akd	−8	−6	−3	−6	−5	−2	−2	−10	−19	−20	−15	−16
Capital Account, n.i.e.	78bcd	28	102	20	26	18	27	80	63	17	20	20	18
Capital Account, n.i.e.: Credit	78bad	28	102	20	26	18	27	80	63	17	20	20	20
Capital Account: Debit	78bbd	—	—	—	—	—	—	....	....	....	....	....	−2
Financial Account, n.i.e.	78bjd	598	1,159	521	782	65	196	173	−139	−244	−250	786	871
Direct Investment Abroad	78bdd	—	—	—	—	—	—	—	—	—	—	—	—
Dir. Invest. in Rep. Econ., n.i.e.	78bed	109	251	100	89	80	82	263	270	110	115	1,084	1,206
Portfolio Investment Assets	78bfd	—	—	—	—	—	—	—	—	—	—	—	—
Equity Securities	78bkd	—	—	—	—	—	—	—	—	—	—	—	—
Debt Securities	78bld	—	—	—	—	—	—	—	—	—	—	—	—
Portfolio Investment Liab., n.i.e.	78bgd	—	—	—	—	—	—	—	—	—	—	—	—
Equity Securities	78bmd	—	—	—	—	—	—	—	—	—	—	—	—
Debt Securities	78bnd	—	—	—	—	—	—	—	—	—	—	—	—
Financial Derivatives Assets	78bwd	....	....	....	....	....	....	....	....	....	....	....	....
Financial Derivatives Liabilities	78bxd	....	....	....	....	....	....	....	....	....	....	....	....
Other Investment Assets	78bhd	−815	−718	1,510	1,660	1,496	1,422	1,332	1,206	1,136	1,180	—	—
Monetary Authorities	78bod	—	—	—	—	—	—	—	—	—	—	—	—
General Government	78bpd	—	—	—	—	—	—	—	—	—	—	—	—
Banks	78bqd	—	—	1,510	1,660	1,496	1,422	1,332	1,206	1,136	1,180	—	—
Other Sectors	78brd	−815	−718	—	—	—	—	—	—	—	—	—	—
Other Investment Liab., n.i.e.	78bid	1,304	1,626	−1,089	−967	−1,511	−1,308	−1,422	−1,615	−1,490	−1,545	−298	−335
Monetary Authorities	78bsd	11	20	—	—	—	—	—	—	—	—	—	—
General Government	78btd	−121	339	—	—	—	—	—	—	—	—	2	−187
Banks	78bud	−128	−147	−1,089	−967	−1,511	−1,308	−1,422	−1,615	−1,490	−1,545	—	....
Other Sectors	78bvd	1,542	1,414	—	—	—	—	—	—	—	—	−300	−148
Net Errors and Omissions	78cad	−119	96	35	139	−95	153	−195	−171	26	−160	−839	−832
Overall Balance	78cbd	304	566	839	987	449	434	259	814	1,020	1,050	695	417
Reserves and Related Items	79dad	−304	−566	−839	−987	−449	−434	−259	−814	−1,020	−1,050	−695	−417
Reserve Assets	79dbd	−304	−566	−839	−987	−449	−434	−259	−814	−1,020	−1,050	−719	−422
Use of Fund Credit and Loans	79dcd	—	—	—	—	—	—	—	—	—	—	—	—
Exceptional Financing	79ded	—	—	—	—	—	—	....	....	....	....	24	5
Government Finance						*Millions of Pounds: Year Ending December 31*							
Deficit (-) or Surplus	80	115	−18,860	−10,059	−1,577	−1,723	−5,534	5,827	....	....	....	....	....
Revenue	81	92,619	111,892	131,002	152,231	179,202	180,437	196,127	....	....	....	....	....
Grants Received	81z	2,864	1,264	896	1,788	798	2	—	....	....	....	....	....
Expenditure	82	95,368	132,016	141,957	155,596	181,723	185,973	190,300	....	....	....	....	....
National Accounts						*Millions of Pounds*							
Househ.Cons.Expend.,incl.NPISHs	96f	303,988	348,865	378,143	489,728	515,411	542,374	575,866	572,761	570,781	594,487	....	....
Government Consumption Expend	91f	56,239	68,019	76,709	81,316	84,994	88,521	86,857	112,244	121,723	125,007	....	....
Exports of Goods and Services	90c	115,294	167,327	177,229	219,872	241,719	241,316	264,704	326,715	359,278	404,102	....	....
Gross Capital Formation	93	107,466	151,622	155,504	163,076	155,464	162,446	153,706	156,092	199,162	200,031	....	....
Imports of Goods and Services (-)	98c	169,242	229,732	216,610	263,135	252,019	244,213	262,041	263,868	296,893	324,176	....	....
Gross Domestic Product (GDP)	99b	413,755	506,101	570,975	690,857	745,569	790,444	819,092	903,944	954,051	999,451	....	....
Consumption of Fixed Capital	99cf	14,492	17,674	20,344	26,257	30,151	31,668	34,282	38,551	38,499	40,313	....	....
GDP Volume 1995 Prices	99b.p	501,546	539,929	570,975	612,896	628,148	675,888	662,396	666,567	....	....	....	....
GDP Volume 2000 Prices	99b.p	....	....	....	....	....	....	....	903,944	934,409	964,574	....	....
GDP Volume (2000=100)	99bvp	75.2	81.0	85.7	91.9	94.2	101.4	99.4	† 100.0	103.4	106.7	....	....
GDP Deflator (2000=100)	99bip	60.8	69.1	73.7	83.1	87.5	86.2	91.2	100.0	102.1	103.6	....	....
						Millions: Midyear Estimates							
Population	99z	13.99	14.37	14.75	15.15	15.56	15.97	16.39	16.81	17.24	17.68	18.13	18.58

		1993	1994	1995	1996	1997	1998	1999	2000	2001	2002	2003	2004
Exchange Rates						*Somoni per SDR: End of Period*							
Official Rate	aa	.019	.058	.436	.472	1.008	1.377	1.971	† 2.866	3.205	4.079	4.393	4.716
						Somoni per US Dollar: End of Period (ae) Period Average (rf)							
Official Rate	ae	.014	.039	.294	.328	.747	.978	1.436	† 2.200	2.550	3.000	2.957	3.037
Official Rate	rf	.010	.024	.123	.296	.562	.777	1.238	2.076	2.372	2.764	3.061	2.971
Fund Position						*Millions of SDRs: End of Period*							
Quota	2f.s	60.00	60.00	60.00	60.00	60.00	60.00	87.00	87.00	87.00	87.00	87.00	87.00
SDRs	1b.s	—	—	—	2.21	9.06	2.05	.04	6.02	3.86	1.34	.57	.85
Reserve Position in the Fund	1c.s	—	—	—	—	—	—	—	—	—	—	—	—
Total Fund Cred.&Loans Outstg	2tl	—	—	—	15.00	22.50	70.30	73.21	85.03	87.66	69.17	67.16	78.70
International Liquidity						*Millions of US Dollars Unless Otherwise Indicated: End of Period*							
Total Reserves minus Gold	1l.d	....	....	....	....	36.5	53.6	55.2	92.9	92.6	89.5	111.9	157.5
SDRs	1b.d	—	—	—	3.2	12.2	2.9	—	7.8	4.9	1.8	.9	1.3
Reserve Position in the Fund	1c.d	—	—	—	—	—	—	—	—	—	—	—	—
Foreign Exchange	1d.d	....	....	....	....	24.3	50.7	55.1	85.0	87.7	87.7	111.0	156.2
Gold (Million Fine Troy Ounces)	1ad	....	....	....	....	.01	.01	.01	.01	.01	—	.01	.03
Gold (National Valuation)	1and	....	....	....	....	2.4	2.3	2.3	1.4	1.7	—	5.7	14.6
Monetary Authorities:Other Liab	4..d	....	....	....	....	....	2.22	.14	.09	.24	.31	.39	.56
Deposit Money Banks: Assets	7a.d	....	....	....	....	....	1.04	1.10	1.44	2.44	2.82	9.67	13.65
Liabilities	7b.d	....	....	....	....	....	74.64	42.62	65.06	86.22	92.15	106.34	222.79
Monetary Authorities						*Millions of Somoni: End of Period*							
Foreign Assets	11	....	....	....	....	67.2	83.6	209.1	256.4	294.0	402.9	578.8	
Claims on General Government	12a	....	....	....	....	102.4	64.9	131.9	92.8	156.8	153.8	153.8	
Claims on Other Resident Sectors	12d	....	....	....	....	16.7	96.5	1.1	215.9	171.4	142.1	128.7	
Claims on Deposit Money Banks	12e	....	....	....	....	26.3	49.0	150.0	37.6	34.1	42.1	88.8	
Reserve Money	14	....	....	....	....	60.4	76.5	117.0	146.2	179.8	237.7	247.5	
of which: Currency Outside Banks	14a	....	....	....	....	46.6	62.0	86.8	103.6	135.8	158.1	175.4	
Foreign Liabilities	16c	....	....	....	....	99.0	144.5	243.9	281.5	283.0	296.2	372.9	
General Government Deposits	16d	....	....	....	....	9.4	21.2	48.2	38.1	65.3	137.0	186.4	
Counterpart Funds	16e	....	....	....	....	3.0	15.0	38.8	85.8	101.0	94.6	166.0	
Capital Accounts	17a	....	....	....	....	36.3	41.5	11.5	64.8	47.4	18.4	4.8	
Other Items (Net)	17r	....	....	....	....	4.5	-4.7	32.6	-13.8	-20.2	-42.9	-23.6	
Deposit Money Banks						*Millions of Somoni: End of Period*							
Reserves	20	....	....	....	....	12.0	13.5	34.6	49.8	51.4	86.7	106.6	
Foreign Assets	21	....	....	....	....	1.0	1.6	3.2	6.2	8.5	28.6	41.5	
Claims on General Government	22a	....	....	....	....	1.1	1.1	1.3	3.1	.7	.3	.3	
Claims on Other Resident Sectors	22d	....	....	....	....	115.7	142.1	245.0	359.5	456.1	523.7	942.5	
Demand Deposits	24	....	....	....	....	12.7	7.8	15.7	23.8	36.3	61.8	64.4	
Other Deposits	25	....	....	....	....	10.2	18.9	42.7	61.9	99.7	158.3	191.7	
Foreign Liabilities	26c	....	....	....	....	73.0	61.2	143.1	219.9	276.5	314.4	676.6	
General Government Deposits	26d	....	....	....	....	—	3.8	10.9	9.0	7.9	17.1	26.0	
Credit from Monetary Authorities	26g	....	....	....	....	16.8	44.2	44.2	34.1	29.2	43.8	51.6	
Capital Accounts	27a	....	....	....	....	22.0	29.4	39.9	50.4	85.5	133.5	166.2	
Other Items (Net)	27r	....	....	....	....	-4.9	-7.1	-12.4	19.7	-18.4	-89.5	-85.5	
Monetary Survey						*Millions of Somoni: End of Period*							
Foreign Assets (Net)	31n	....	....	....	....	-103.8	-120.5	-174.8	-238.8	-257.0	-179.1	-429.3	
Domestic Credit	32	....	....	....	....	226.5	279.6	320.2	624.2	711.8	665.9	1,016.8	
Claims on General Govt. (Net)	32an	....	....	....	....	94.1	41.0	74.1	48.8	84.3	.1	-54.4	
Claims on Other Resident Sectors	32d	....	....	....	....	132.4	238.6	246.0	575.4	627.5	665.8	1,071.2	
Money	34	....	....	....	....	59.4	69.9	102.7	128.8	173.2	222.2	241.1	
Quasi-Money	35	....	....	....	....	13.2	20.5	44.9	70.5	106.8	172.3	192.2	
Counterpart Funds	36e	....	....	....	....	3.0	15.0	38.8	85.8	101.0	94.6	166.0	
Capital Accounts	37a	....	....	....	....	58.2	70.9	51.4	115.2	132.9	151.9	171.0	
Other Items (Net)	37r	....	....	....	....	-11.0	-17.3	-92.4	-14.9	-59.1	-154.1	-182.6	
Money plus Quasi-Money	35l	....	....	....	....	72.6	90.4	147.6	199.4	280.0	394.5	433.3	
Interest Rates						*Percent Per Annum*							
Refinancing Rate	60	....	....	....	....	76.00	36.40	20.10	20.60	20.00	† 24.75	† 15.00	10.00
Deposit Rate	60l	....	....	....	....	23.93	9.82	5.24	1.26	5.19	† 9.21	9.67	9.75
Lending Rate	60p	....	....	....	....	75.52	50.89	26.24	25.59	21.05	† 14.20	16.57	20.32

Balance of Payments		1993	1994	1995	1996	1997	1998	1999	2000	2001	2002	2003	2004
							Millions of US Dollars: Minus Sign Indicates Debit						
Current Account, n.i.e.	78ald	....	....	....	....	....	....	....	....	....	−15.13	−4.82	−57.04
Goods: Exports f.o.b.	78aad	....	....	....	....	....	....	....	....	....	699.15	906.20	1,096.93
Goods: Imports f.o.b.	78abd	....	....	....	....	....	....	....	....	....	−822.90	−1,025.73	−1,232.43
Trade Balance	78acd	....	....	....	....	....	....	....	....	....	−123.75	−119.53	−135.50
Services: Credit	78add	....	....	....	....	....	....	....	....	....	68.99	88.51	122.90
Services: Debit	78aed	....	....	....	....	....	....	....	....	....	−104.88	−121.53	−212.53
Balance on Goods & Services	78afd	....	....	....	....	....	....	....	....	....	−159.64	−152.56	−225.12
Income: Credit	78agd	....	....	....	....	....	....	....	....	....	1.23	.88	1.70
Income: Debit	78ahd	....	....	....	....	....	....	....	....	....	−42.36	−71.22	−59.24
Balance on Gds, Serv. & Inc.	78aid	....	....	....	....	....	....	....	....	....	−200.77	−222.90	−282.66
Current Transfers, n.i.e.: Credit	78ajd	....	....	....	....	....	....	....	....	....	201.72	285.11	348.41
Current Transfers: Debit	78akd	....	....	....	....	....	....	....	....	....	−16.08	−67.03	−122.80
Capital Account, n.i.e.	78bcd	....	....	....	....	....	....	....	....	....	—	—	—
Capital Account, n.i.e.: Credit	78bad	....	....	....	....	....	....	....	....	....	—	—	—
Capital Account: Debit	78bbd	....	....	....	....	....	....	....	....	....	—	—	—
Financial Account, n.i.e.	78bjd	....	....	....	....	....	....	....	....	....	72.39	62.69	93.41
Direct Investment Abroad	78bdd	....	....	....	....	....	....	....	....	....	—	—	—
Dir. Invest. in Rep. Econ., n.i.e.	78bed	....	....	....	....	....	....	....	....	....	36.07	31.65	272.03
Portfolio Investment Assets	78bfd	....	....	....	....	....	....	....	....	....	—	—	—
Equity Securities	78bkd	....	....	....	....	....	....	....	....	....	—	—	—
Debt Securities	78bld	....	....	....	....	....	....	....	....	....	—	—	—
Portfolio Investment Liab., n.i.e.	78bgd	....	....	....	....	....	....	....	....	....	1.51	.34	5.30
Equity Securities	78bmd	....	....	....	....	....	....	....	....	....	1.51	.34	—
Debt Securities	78bnd	....	....	....	....	....	....	....	....	....	—	—	5.30
Financial Derivatives Assets	78bwd	....	....	....	....	....	....	....	....	....	....	....	....
Financial Derivatives Liabilities	78bxd	....	....	....	....	....	....	....	....	....	....	....	....
Other Investment Assets	78bhd	....	....	....	....	....	....	....	....	....	−23.44	−15.63	−28.44
Monetary Authorities	78bod	....	....	....	....	....	....	....	....	....	—	—	—
General Government	78bpd	....	....	....	....	....	....	....	....	....	.17	−.41	−.45
Banks	78bqd	....	....	....	....	....	....	....	....	....	−6.59	−14.39	−7.35
Other Sectors	78brd	....	....	....	....	....	....	....	....	....	−17.03	−.83	−20.64
Other Investment Liab., n.i.e.	78bid	....	....	....	....	....	....	....	....	....	58.25	46.33	−155.47
Monetary Authorities	78bsd	....	....	....	....	....	....	....	....	....	—	—	—
General Government	78btd	....	....	....	....	....	....	....	....	....	−9.28	−2.12	−151.41
Banks	78bud	....	....	....	....	....	....	....	....	....	1.19	3.72	1.01
Other Sectors	78bvd	....	....	....	....	....	....	....	....	....	66.34	44.74	−5.07
Net Errors and Omissions	78cad	....	....	....	....	....	....	....	....	....	−55.60	−29.92	−32.50
Overall Balance	78cbd	....	....	....	....	....	....	....	....	....	1.65	27.95	3.86
Reserves and Related Items	79dad	....	....	....	....	....	....	....	....	....	−1.65	−27.95	−3.86
Reserve Assets	79dbd	....	....	....	....	....	....	....	....	....	.11	−40.46	−46.36
Use of Fund Credit and Loans	79dcd	....	....	....	....	....	....	....	....	....	−23.95	−2.72	16.99
Exceptional Financing	79ded	....	....	....	....	....	....	....	....	....	22.19	15.24	25.50
Government Finance							*Millions of Somoni Year Ending December 31*						
Deficit (-) or Surplus	80	....	....	....	....	....	−25.78	−10.42	−3.75	1.42	....	....	....
Total Revenue and Grants	81y	....	....	....	....	....	97.20	140.57	189.88	288.66	....	....	....
Revenue	81	....	....	....	....	....	95.04	136.99	189.88	288.66	....	....	....
Grants Received	81z	....	....	....	....	....	2.16	3.58	—	—	....	....	....
Exp. & Lending Minus Repay.	82z	....	....	....	....	....	122.98	150.99	193.63	287.24	....	....	....
Expenditure	82	....	....	....	....	....	130.56	166.97	204.30	292.54	....	....	....
Lending Minus Repayments	83	....	....	....	....	....	−7.58	−15.98	−10.67	−5.30	....	....	....
Total Financing	80h	....	....	....	....	....	25.78	10.42	3.75	−1.42	....	....	....
Domestic	84a	....	....	....	....	....	23.10	32.68	8.81	4.26	....	....	....
Foreign	85a	....	....	....	....	....	2.68	−22.26	−5.06	−5.68	....	....	....
Total Debt by Residence	88	....	....	....	....	....	1,014.60	....	2,038.20	2,046.02	....	....	....
Domestic	88a	....	....	....	....	....	44.67	....	131.92	155.32	....	....	....
Foreign	89a	....	....	....	....	....	969.93	....	1,906.28	1,890.70	....	....	....
Population	99z	5.61	5.69	5.77	5.85	5.93	6.01	6.09	6.16	6.23	6.29	6.36	6.43

Tanzania 738

		1993	1994	1995	1996	1997	1998	1999	2000	2001	2002	2003	2004
Exchange Rates					*Shillings per SDR: End of Period*								
Official Rate	aa	659.13	764.16	818.10	856.51	842.70	958.87	1,094.34	1,046.58	1,151.54	1,327.30	1,580.51	1,619.73
					Shillings per US Dollar: End of Period (ae) Period Average (rf)								
Official Rate	ae	479.87	523.45	550.36	595.64	624.57	681.00	797.33	803.26	916.30	976.30	1,063.62	1,042.96
Official Rate	rf	405.27	509.63	574.76	579.98	612.12	664.67	744.76	800.41	876.41	966.58	1,038.42	1,089.33
Fund Position					*Millions of SDRs: End of Period*								
Quota	2f.s	146.9	146.9	146.9	146.9	146.9	146.9	198.9	198.9	198.9	198.9	198.9	198.9
SDRs	1b.s	—	—	.1	.1	.1	.3	.2	.1	.4	.1	.3	—
Reserve Position in the Fund	1c.s	10.0	10.0	10.0	10.0	10.0	10.0	10.0	10.0	10.0	10.0	10.0	10.0
Total Fund Cred.&Loans Outstg	2tl	156.2	145.5	132.7	143.4	182.4	190.2	227.6	248.3	271.2	293.9	294.3	272.3
International Liquidity					*Millions of US Dollars Unless Otherwise Indicated: End of Period*								
Total Reserves minus Gold	1l.d	203.3	332.1	270.2	440.1	622.1	599.2	775.5	974.2	1,156.6	1,528.8	2,038.4	2,295.7
SDRs	1b.d	—	—	.1	.1	.1	.4	.3	.1	.5	.1	.5	.1
Reserve Position in the Fund	1c.d	13.7	14.6	14.8	14.3	13.5	14.0	13.7	13.0	12.5	13.6	14.9	15.5
Foreign Exchange	1d.d	189.6	317.5	255.3	425.6	608.5	584.8	761.5	961.1	1,143.6	1,515.2	2,023.0	2,280.1
Monetary Authorities: Other Liab	4..d	957.8	900.7	836.9	808.7	574.9	574.5	678.5	755.2	747.7	881.5	1,061.5	1,074.4
Deposit Money Banks: Assets	7a.d	145.4	146.6	309.2	304.8	373.9	392.4	377.6	511.7	588.3	585.4	644.5	655.5
Liabilities	7b.d	93.6	20.9	51.4	8.1	7.8	3.6	2.2	5.2	17.6	36.0	6.5	18.3
Monetary Authorities					*Billions of Shillings: End of Period*								
Foreign Assets	11	† 97.56	173.82	150.65	264.72	390.09	407.27	618.47	782.42	1,059.85	1,492.78	2,167.75	2,394.81
Claims on Central Government	12a	† 262.10	270.60	326.37	299.38	269.69	234.08	302.79	296.67	296.67	201.46	202.20	199.21
Claims on Deposit Money Banks	12e	† 2.07	—	5.46	5.46	4.61	5.36	4.16	—	—	—	—	—
Reserve Money	14	† 152.32	226.44	314.89	335.77	364.94	418.73	508.67	556.43	584.37	695.70	783.31	967.78
of which: Currency Outside DMBs	14a	† 122.17	176.31	244.31	257.66	287.88	307.80	384.86	392.40	411.64	495.45	553.05	664.15
Foreign Liabilities	16c	† 506.18	517.26	499.09	509.17	373.50	397.37	543.32	606.65	685.16	860.56	1,129.02	1,120.60
Central Government Deposits	16d	† 25.35	29.56	39.67	82.66	87.32	83.03	84.01	137.32	161.98	198.65	357.82	377.99
Capital Accounts	17a	† −278.34	−242.89	−266.81	−238.07	−16.35	−2.23	45.81	25.67	102.44	99.71	149.85	141.33
Other Items (Net)	17r	† −43.78	−85.94	−104.36	−119.97	−145.02	−250.20	−256.39	−246.98	−177.42	−160.39	−50.05	−13.68
Deposit Money Banks					*Billions of Shillings: End of Period*								
Reserves	20	† 30.13	49.91	66.03	72.80	59.71	113.20	123.20	172.10	177.33	195.15	226.87	310.42
Foreign Assets	21	† 69.78	76.74	170.16	181.55	233.56	267.26	301.08	410.99	539.06	571.57	685.49	683.67
Claims on Central Government	22a	† 93.39	124.41	181.09	261.94	247.39	312.75	331.26	403.76	295.70	364.64	322.41	338.54
Claims on Official Entities	22bx	† 49.26	57.18	46.83	17.34	16.22	3.06	4.72	2.98	1.02	—	—	—
Claims on Private Sector	22d	† 186.31	222.98	201.02	116.56	166.75	239.86	302.17	333.26	403.49	570.67	817.13	1,059.69
Demand Deposits	24	† 125.16	153.32	183.97	191.55	205.99	237.72	247.72	302.60	354.38	463.34	560.33	651.45
Time, Savings,& Fgn.Currency Dep	25	† 173.62	240.12	329.52	372.28	433.20	481.47	584.95	702.68	870.71	1,088.90	1,274.94	1,532.39
Foreign Liabilities	26c	† 44.94	10.92	28.26	4.83	4.88	2.46	1.77	4.16	16.17	35.19	6.88	19.04
Central Government Deposits	26d	† 4.82	22.52	21.75	20.96	28.43	25.33	21.56	26.09	29.32	30.82	81.83	135.46
Credit from Monetary Authorities	26g	† 147.40	1.34	7.59	.16	12.76	—	5.43	—	—	.08	.05	—
Capital Accounts	27a	† 48.62	139.91	−29.91	75.62	43.11	61.64	27.26	113.33	133.74	142.09	207.97	243.14
Other Items (Net)	27r	† −115.69	−36.90	123.95	−15.21	−4.74	127.52	173.73	174.23	12.28	−58.39	−80.11	−189.17
Monetary Survey					*Billions of Shillings: End of Period*								
Foreign Assets (Net)	31n	† −383.77	−277.62	−206.54	−67.72	245.27	274.70	374.46	582.60	897.58	1,168.60	1,717.35	1,938.83
Domestic Credit	32	† 560.89	623.10	693.88	591.60	584.31	681.39	835.36	873.27	805.59	907.29	902.08	1,083.98
Claims on Central Govt. (Net)	32an	† 325.32	342.94	446.03	457.70	401.34	438.47	528.48	537.03	401.08	336.62	84.95	24.30
Claims on Official Entities	32bx	† 49.26	57.18	46.83	17.34	16.22	3.06	4.72	2.98	1.02	—	—	—
Claims on Private Sector	32d	† 186.31	222.98	201.02	116.56	166.75	239.86	302.17	333.26	403.49	570.67	817.13	1,059.69
Money	34	† 247.33	329.63	428.28	449.21	493.87	545.52	632.58	695.01	766.02	958.79	1,113.38	1,315.61
Quasi-Money	35	† 173.62	240.12	329.52	372.28	433.20	481.47	584.95	702.68	870.71	1,088.90	1,274.94	1,532.39
Capital Accounts	37a	† −229.73	−102.98	−296.72	−162.45	26.76	59.41	73.07	139.00	236.18	241.80	357.83	384.47
Other Items (Net)	37r	† −14.11	−121.29	26.26	−135.17	−124.25	−130.30	−80.78	−80.82	−169.74	−213.59	−126.72	−209.65
Money plus Quasi-Money	35l	† 420.95	569.74	757.81	821.50	927.07	1,026.98	1,217.53	1,397.69	1,636.73	2,047.68	2,388.32	2,848.00
Other Banking Institutions					*Billions of Shillings: End of Period*								
Deposits	45	† 1.12	1.67	16.82	16.60	17.56	17.88	24.38	28.44	34.15	37.42	34.73	35.00
Liquid Liabilities	55l	† 422.07	571.42	774.63	838.09	944.63	1,044.87	1,241.91	1,426.13	1,670.88	2,085.11	2,423.05	2,882.99
Money (National Definitions)					*Billions of Shillings: End of Period*								
M0	19mc	152.32	226.44	314.89	335.77	364.94	418.73	508.67	556.43	584.37	695.70	783.31	967.78
M1	59ma	247.09	329.62	428.29	449.21	493.87	545.52	632.57	695.01	766.02	958.86	1,113.56	1,315.61
M2	59mb	367.09	486.49	613.70	684.99	760.35	844.93	972.09	1,093.61	1,233.67	1,507.58	1,721.30	2,050.76
M3	59mc	420.64	569.74	752.91	818.06	927.07	1,026.98	1,217.63	1,397.69	1,636.73	2,047.88	2,388.51	2,848.00
Interest Rates					*Percent Per Annum*								
Discount Rate (End of Period)	60	14.50	67.50	47.90	19.00	16.20	17.60	20.20	10.70	8.70	9.18	12.34	14.42
Treasury Bill Rate	60c	34.00	35.09	40.33	15.30	9.59	11.83	10.05	9.78	4.14	3.55	6.26	8.35
Savings Rate	60k	24.00	23.98	22.70	14.25	8.79	8.29	8.27	† 6.55	4.15	3.36	2.58	2.45
Deposit Rate	60l	. . . .	. . . .	24.63	13.59	7.83	7.75	7.75	† 7.39	4.81	3.29	3.05	4.20
Lending Rate	60p	31.00	39.00	42.83	† 33.97	26.27	22.89	21.89	† 21.58	20.26	16.43	14.48	13.92
Prices and Production					*Index Numbers (2000=100): Period Averages*								
Consumer Prices	64	32.3	43.0	55.2	66.8	77.6	87.5	94.4	100.0	† 105.1	106.2	109.9	110.0
Manufacturing Production	66ey	77.5	70.4	73.2	73.9	78.2	84.5	87.3	100.0	104.2	119.0	. . . .	. . . .
Intl. Transactions & Positions					*Millions of Shillings*								
Exports	70	181,147	265,177	390,378	455,519	459,549	391,805	412,204	531,058	681,186	873,819	1,174,785	1,448,589
Imports, c.i.f	71	615,990	765,757	968,910	804,949	818,703	967,080	1,161,841	1,219,385	1,504,415	1,604,945	2,210,265	2,732,323

Tanzania 738

		1993	1994	1995	1996	1997	1998	1999	2000	2001	2002	2003	2004
Balance of Payments						*Millions of US Dollars: Minus Sign Indicates Debit*							
Current Account, n.i.e.	78ald	−1,048.0	−710.9	−646.3	−510.9	−629.8	−919.7	−835.3	−498.6	−479.6	−251.3	....	....
Goods: Exports f.o.b.	78aad	446.9	519.4	682.5	764.1	715.3	589.5	543.3	663.3	776.4	902.5	....	....
Goods: Imports f.o.b.	78abd	−1,304.0	−1,309.3	−1,340.0	−1,213.1	−1,164.4	−1,365.3	−1,415.4	−1,367.6	−1,560.3	−1,511.3	....	....
Trade Balance	78acd	−857.1	−789.9	−657.5	−449.0	−449.1	−775.9	−872.1	−704.3	−783.9	−608.8	....	....
Services: Credit	78add	317.9	418.2	582.6	608.1	494.1	555.0	600.3	627.4	679.3	665.8	....	....
Services: Debit	78aed	−717.0	−503.3	−799.4	−953.4	−797.3	−988.1	−795.0	−682.4	−689.3	−712.6	....	....
Balance on Goods & Services	78afd	−1,256.2	−875.0	−874.2	−794.3	−752.4	−1,209.0	−1,066.8	−759.3	−793.9	−655.6	....	....
Income: Credit	78agd	21.9	30.9	31.8	50.3	44.9	35.0	43.1	50.3	55.4	74.5	....	....
Income: Debit	78ahd	−172.9	−153.4	−142.0	−105.4	−168.2	−136.8	−148.2	−180.4	−140.6	−90.7	....	....
Balance on Gds, Serv. & Inc.	78aid	−1,407.2	−997.5	−984.5	−849.4	−875.7	−1,310.8	−1,171.9	−889.4	−879.1	−671.8	....	....
Current Transfers, n.i.e.: Credit	78ajd	389.8	311.5	370.5	370.9	313.6	426.6	445.6	463.7	469.5	472.9	....	....
Current Transfers: Debit	78akd	−30.7	−25.0	−32.3	−32.3	−67.7	−35.5	−109.0	−72.9	−70.0	−52.4	....	....
Capital Account, n.i.e.	78bcd	205.2	262.6	190.9	191.0	360.6	422.9	347.8	420.4	1,078.6	1,168.0	....	....
Capital Account, n.i.e.: Credit	78bad	205.2	262.6	190.9	191.0	360.6	422.9	347.8	420.4	1,078.6	1,168.0	....	....
Capital Account: Debit	78bbd	—	—	—	—	—	—	—	—	—	—	....	....
Financial Account, n.i.e.	78bjd	130.5	−91.7	66.7	−92.8	3.6	77.6	565.2	492.6	−483.7	−507.0	....	....
Direct Investment Abroad	78bdd	—	—	—	—	—	—	—	—	—	—	....	....
Dir. Invest. in Rep. Econ., n.i.e.	78bed	20.5	50.0	119.9	150.1	157.9	172.3	516.7	463.4	327.2	240.4	....	....
Portfolio Investment Assets	78bfd	—	—	—	—	—	—	—	—	—	—	....	....
Equity Securities	78bkd	—	—	—	—	—	—	—	—	—	—	....	....
Debt Securities	78bld	—	—	—	—	—	—	—	—	—	—	....	....
Portfolio Investment Liab., n.i.e.	78bgd	—	—	—	—	—	—	—	—	—	—	....	....
Equity Securities	78bmd	—	—	—	—	—	—	—	—	—	—	....	....
Debt Securities	78bnd	—	—	—	—	—	—	—	—	—	—	....	....
Financial Derivatives Assets	78bwd	—	—	—	—	—	—	....	....	....	....	....	....
Financial Derivatives Liabilities	78bxd	—	—	—	—	—	—	....	....	....	....	....	....
Other Investment Assets	78bhd	56.7	11.9	−75.1	20.1	−85.0	−50.7	14.8	−134.0	−76.7	2.9	....	....
Monetary Authorities	78bod	—	—	—	—	—	—	—	—	—	—	....	....
General Government	78bpd	—	—	—	—	—	—	—	—	—	—	....	....
Banks	78bqd	−68.6	−75.6	−162.5	−19.6	−85.0	−50.7	14.8	−134.0	−76.7	2.9	....	....
Other Sectors	78brd	125.3	87.5	87.4	39.7	—	—	—	—	—	—	....	....
Other Investment Liab., n.i.e.	78bid	53.3	−153.6	21.8	−262.9	−69.3	−44.0	33.7	163.2	−734.2	−750.3	....	....
Monetary Authorities	78bsd	.2	11.9	5.9	14.9	24.6	−48.7	9.8	49.7	−52.9	14.2	....	....
General Government	78btd	−56.5	−202.0	−71.2	−225.9	−32.4	—	52.0	145.4	−820.7	−750.5	....	....
Banks	78bud	−1.4	6.7	22.9	−23.5	−67.6	−17.6	−1.4	3.0	12.5	18.4	....	....
Other Sectors	78bvd	111.0	29.8	64.2	−28.5	6.2	22.4	−26.7	−34.9	126.9	−32.4	....	....
Net Errors and Omissions	78cad	137.3	121.4	30.0	158.6	−31.9	−90.3	−156.7	−415.7	16.1	−83.8	....	....
Overall Balance	78cbd	−575.1	−418.6	−358.7	−254.0	−297.5	−509.4	−79.0	−1.3	131.4	325.9	....	....
Reserves and Related Items	79dad	575.1	418.6	358.7	254.0	297.5	509.4	79.0	1.3	−131.4	−325.9	....	....
Reserve Assets	79dbd	60.5	−122.8	43.3	−195.4	−206.9	22.3	−176.4	−199.2	−183.0	−371.2	....	....
Use of Fund Credit and Loans	79dcd	−6.0	−15.4	−19.6	15.7	53.2	9.6	51.5	27.6	29.5	29.1	....	....
Exceptional Financing	79ded	520.7	556.8	335.1	433.8	451.2	477.5	204.0	172.9	22.1	16.3	....	....
International Investment Position						*Millions of US Dollars*							
Assets	79aad	....	....	....	....	....	....	....	....	....	....		
Direct Investment Abroad	79abd	—	—	—	—	—	—	—	—	—	—		
Portfolio Investment	79acd	—	—	—	—	—	—	—	—	—	—		
Equity Securities	79add	—	—	—	—	—	—	—	—	—	—		
Debt Securities	79aed	—	—	—	—	—	—	—	—	—	—		
Financial Derivatives	79ald	....	....	....	....	....	....	....	....	....	....		
Other Investment	79afd	145.4	146.6	309.2	304.8	373.9	392.4	377.6	511.6	588.3	585.4		
Monetary Authorities	79agd	....	....	....	....	....	....	....	....	....	....		
General Government	79ahd	....	....	....	....	....	....	....	....	....	....		
Banks	79aid	....	....	....	304.8	373.9	392.4	377.6	511.6	588.3	585.4		
Other Sectors	79ajd	....	....	....	—	—	—	—	—	—	—		
Reserve Assets	79akd	224.8	330.4	269.6	439.6	621.7	599.0	775.4	974.0	1,156.6	1,529.1		
Liabilities	79lad	8,679.4	9,037.5	9,645.7	9,965.9	7,271.3	7,229.0	7,648.1	9,540.3	9,208.3	9,922.3		
Dir. Invest. in Rep. Economy	79lbd	24.3	71.0	224.2	351.7	490.2	619.0	700.0	1,310.1	1,637.3	1,877.7	....	....
Portfolio Investment	79lcd	—	—	—	—	—	—	—	—	—	—	....	....
Equity Securities	79ldd	—	—	—	—	—	—	—	—	—	—	....	....
Debt Securities	79led	—	—	—	—	—	—	—	—	—	—	....	....
Financial Derivatives	79lld	—	—	—	—	—	—	—	—	—	—	....	....
Other Investment	79lfd	8,655.1	8,966.5	9,421.5	9,614.2	6,781.1	6,610.0	6,948.1	8,230.2	7,571.0	8,044.6	....	....
Monetary Authorities	79lgd	214.6	212.4	197.2	206.2	246.0	315.9	370.3	431.3	395.7	468.5	....	....
General Government	79lhd	7,494.4	8,129.9	8,510.0	8,614.9	6,337.2	6,200.6	6,050.4	6,723.1	5,890.0	6,348.9	....	....
Banks	79lid							19.4	.9	5.2	17.6	36.0	
Other Sectors	79ljd	946.1	624.2	714.3	793.0	197.8	74.1	526.4	1,070.6	1,267.7	1,191.2		
Government Finance						*Millions of Shillings: Year Ending June 30*							
Deficit (-) or Surplus	80	−72,141	−104,515	−64,559	−21,269	77,143	−68,138	24,422	−114,472	−87,860	−38,191	....	....
Total Revenue and Grants	81y	222,422	349,234	389,743	495,255	653,446	738,443	859,268	1,057,952	1,215,930	1,401,774	....	....
Revenue	81	164,109	242,444	331,238	448,373	572,030	619,084	689,324	777,645	929,624	1,042,956	....	....
Grants	81z	58,313	106,790	58,505	46,882	81,416	119,359	169,944	280,307	286,306	358,818	....	....
Exp. & Lending Minus Repay.	82z	263,413	374,962	398,024	420,522	515,390	730,338	816,706	1,168,779	1,311,928	1,441,669	....	....
Expenditure	82	263,413	374,962	398,024	420,522	515,390	730,338	816,706	1,168,779	1,305,035	1,441,669	....	....
Lending Minus Repayments	83	—	—	—	—	—	—	—	—	6,893	—	....	....
Financing													
Overall Adjustment	80x	−31,150	−78,787	−56,278	−96,002	−60,913	−76,243	−18,140	−3,644	8,139	1,704	....	....
Total Financing	80h	72,141	104,515	64,559	21,269	−77,142	68,139	−24,424	114,472	87,860	38,191	....	....
Domestic	84a	44,144	40,557	61,603	56,169	−28,074	3,670	−5,740	9,055	−2,494	−83,087	....	....
Foreign	85a	27,997	63,958	2,956	−34,900	−49,068	64,468	−18,684	105,417	90,354	121,278	....	....

Tanzania 738

		1993	1994	1995	1996	1997	1998	1999	2000	2001	2002	2003	2004
National Accounts							*Billions of Shillings*						
Househ.Cons.Expend.,incl.NPISHs....	96f	1,445.37	1,931.98	2,532.84	3,130.07	3,968.07	4,909.25	5,667.44	6,069.58	6,917.58	7,499.65	8,765.51	....
Government Consumption Expend...	91f	334.52	393.50	462.32	435.33	413.56	433.79	451.14	482.72	516.33	598.94	697.76	....
Gross Fixed Capital Formation.........	93e	429.55	561.82	591.94	620.60	692.40	892.70	989.34	1,266.68	1,390.64	1,789.90	1,974.05	....
Changes in Inventories....................	93i	4.00	4.84	5.86	6.64	8.40	9.91	10.31	14.37	15.66	17.85	17.50	....
Exports of Goods and Services.........	90c	310.31	473.89	727.18	751.16	762.81	748.97	885.94	1,064.77	1,284.71	1,561.06	1,899.95	....
Imports of Goods and Services (-).....	98c	823.21	1,002.88	1,253.74	1,203.52	1,208.30	1,565.32	1,703.75	1,676.34	1,962.79	2,104.38	2,857.39	....
GDP, Production Based...................	99bp	1,725.54	2,298.87	3,020.50	3,767.64	4,703.46	5,571.26	6,432.91	7,268.38	8,274.61	9,363.67	10,692.42	....
Statistical Discrepancy.....................	99bs	25.01	−64.28	−45.89	27.36	93.04	142.34	132.50	46.61	112.47	.66	195.03	....
Net Primary Income from Abroad.....	98.n	−61.19	−62.43	−63.38	−36.92	−75.78	−52.39	−55.19	−66.70	−74.93	−87.48	−45.09	....
Gross National Income (GNI)............	99a	1,664.35	2,236.44	2,957.12	3,730.72	4,654.22	5,519.25	6,377.72	7,201.68	8,199.67	9,276.19	10,647.33	....
Net National Income.......................	99e	1,619.70	2,175.83	2,876.16	3,640.05	4,541.78	5,385.99	6,216.13	7,007.78	7,963.11	8,985.21	10,303.98	....
GDP, Prod. Based, 1992 Prices........	99bpp	1,281.01	1,298.94	1,345.25	1,401.71	1,448.21	1,505.83	1,577.29	1,654.32	1,749.36	1,857.16	1,962.04	....
GDP Volume (2000=100)................	99bvp	77.4	78.5	81.3	84.7	87.5	91.0	95.3	100.0	105.7	112.3	118.6	....
GDP Deflator (2000=100)................	99bip	30.7	40.3	51.1	61.2	73.9	84.2	92.8	100.0	107.7	114.8	124.0	....
							Millions: Midyear Estimates						
Population...............................	99z	29.08	30.03	30.93	31.77	32.56	† 33.31	34.04	34.76	35.49	36.20	36.92	37.63

Thailand 578

		1993	1994	1995	1996	1997	1998	1999	2000	2001	2002	2003	2004
Exchange Rates						*Baht per SDR: End of Period*							
Official Rate..............................	aa	35.081	36.628	37.445	36.826	† 63.748	51.662	51.428	56.374	55.575	58.665	58.831	60.662
						Baht per US Dollar: End of Period (ae) Period Average (rf)							
Official Rate..............................	ae	25.540	25.090	25.190	25.610	† 47.247	36.691	37.470	43.268	44.222	43.152	39.591	39.061
Official Rate..............................	rf	25.320	25.150	24.915	25.343	† 31.364	41.359	37.814	40.112	44.432	42.960	41.485	40.222
Fund Position						*Millions of SDRs: End of Period*							
Quota..............................	2f.s	574	574	574	574	574	574	1,082	1,082	1,082	1,082	1,082	1,082
SDRs..............................	1b.s	16	22	30	41	358	278	188	63	4	3	—	1
Reserve Position in the Fund............	1c.s	272	285	319	333	—	—	—	—	—	—	75	107
of which: Outstg.Fund Borrowing...	2c	—	—	—	—	—	—	—	—	—	—	—	—
Total Fund Cred.&Loans Outstg........	2tl	—	—	—	—	1,800	2,300	2,500	2,350	1,338	288	—	—
International Liquidity						*Millions of US Dollars Unless Otherwise Indicated: End of Period*							
Total Reserves minus Gold..............	1l.d	24,473	29,332	35,982	37,731	26,179	28,825	34,063	32,016	32,355	38,046	41,077	48,664
SDRs..............................	1b.d	22	32	45	60	482	391	258	83	5	4	—	1
Reserve Position in the Fund..........	1c.d	373	416	474	480	—	—	—	—	—	—	111	165
Foreign Exchange..........................	1d.d	24,078	28,884	35,463	37,192	25,697	28,434	33,805	31,933	32,350	38,042	40,965	48,498
Gold (Million Fine Troy Ounces)........	1ad	2.474	2.474	2.474	2.474	2.474	2.474	2.474	2.367	2.480	2.500	2.600	2.700
Gold (National Valuation)................	1and	967	947	963	914	713	711	718	645	686	869	1,071	1,167
Monetary Authorities: Other Liab.....	4..d	6	6	5	4	4,733	7,967	9,390	8,960	6,651	4,516	3	5
Deposit Money Banks: Assets..........	7a.d	6,165	6,739	9,365	7,028	8,665	12,605	15,158	16,642	16,923	14,683	15,604	14,702
Liabilities..................	7b.d	13,799	31,086	46,214	48,781	40,307	29,058	19,165	13,070	10,439	9,575	8,498	10,111
Other Banking Insts.: Assets.............	7e.d	—	27	34	72	100	407	403	403	332	413	336	363
Liabilities..................	7f.d	3,323	4,035	5,939	8,748	6,973	5,550	4,437	3,683	2,805	1,682	1,419	848
Monetary Authorities						*Billions of Baht: End of Period*							
Foreign Assets..............................	11	649.1	759.0	929.7	988.8	1,270.7	1,083.4	1,303.3	1,413.2	1,478.9	1,695.5	1,690.1	1,980.1
Claims on Central Government........	12a	50.7	32.5	29.7	33.5	31.8	170.7	139.7	109.0	146.6	131.7	135.9	136.5
Claims on Nonfin.Pub.Enterprises...	12c	—	—	8.4	17.9	71.5	75.0	64.0	48.3	33.4	23.0	14.8	5.4
Claims on Deposit Money Banks.....	12e	21.2	26.4	37.8	55.9	309.4	158.6	85.9	59.2	19.2	58.8	47.0	83.8
Claims on Other Financial Insts.......	12f	25.2	39.9	47.5	76.6	438.7	511.3	393.9	439.8	338.9	414.6	489.4	464.2
Reserve Money..............................	14	288.1	329.9	404.3	458.9	531.4	507.6	785.8	684.5	727.3	744.7	941.7	1,112.9
of which: Currency Outside DMBs..	14a	208.6	241.9	284.1	304.3	334.0	318.3	472.4	406.8	440.9	496.0	546.9	613.8
Other Liabilities to DMBs...............	14n	—	5.5	5.4	17.4	254.2	356.4	94.8	155.0	129.7	106.0	265.7	221.2
Money Market Instruments..............	16aa	—	12.6	11.5	11.1	76.3	185.3	78.1	62.9	90.8	88.0	110.5	126.7
Foreign Liabilities.........................	16c	.2	.1	.1	.1	338.4	411.1	480.4	537.6	439.6	227.9	25.8	35.1
Central Government Deposits..........	16d	213.7	235.8	328.5	341.7	283.3	96.6	81.5	45.8	38.3	76.0	60.9	51.3
Capital Accounts...........................	17a	263.1	306.8	337.8	377.8	803.2	814.0	1,013.2	1,159.7	1,092.4	1,627.4	1,676.1	1,920.7
Other Items (Net)...........................	17r	−18.9	−33.0	−34.4	−34.4	−164.6	−371.9	−547.1	−576.0	−501.3	−546.5	−703.5	−797.8
Deposit Money Banks						*Billions of Baht: End of Period*							
Reserves..............................	20	73.5	79.7	117.8	165.8	203.6	145.7	143.0	112.8	186.0	201.6	293.7	404.3
Other Claims on Monetary Author....	20n	—	5.5	5.9	17.5	262.2	356.4	94.8	155.0	129.7	106.0	266.8	221.2
Foreign Assets..............................	21	157.5	169.1	235.9	180.0	409.4	462.5	568.0	720.1	748.4	633.6	617.8	574.3
Claims on Central Government........	22a	50.3	41.8	40.7	20.2	15.6	154.7	249.2	306.3	318.0	398.7	294.4	314.8
Claims on State and Local Govts......	22b	—	—	—	—	—	—	—	—	—	—	.1	.8
Claims on Nonfin.Pub.Enterprises.....	22c	76.5	94.2	108.4	112.7	99.9	108.5	135.1	123.9	150.0	150.0	149.3	169.9
Claims on Private Sector.................	22d	2,536.5	3,304.1	4,089.2	4,688.3	5,729.6	5,299.6	5,014.5	4,211.6	3,774.7	4,404.7	4,705.3	4,958.4
Claims on Other Financial Insts........	22f	126.6	158.0	213.4	213.9	331.3	173.1	233.8	512.2	673.2	375.3	249.0	325.9
Demand Deposits..........................	24	82.4	96.4	94.3	106.1	86.6	93.9	94.9	114.0	134.4	157.8	215.5	232.2
Time, Savings,& Fgn.Currency Dep...	25	2,210.9	2,482.9	2,922.3	3,303.0	3,910.6	4,311.6	4,279.1	4,505.8	4,662.6	4,714.6	4,873.3	5,087.1
Foreign Liabilities.........................	26c	352.4	780.0	1,164.1	1,249.3	1,904.4	1,066.2	718.1	565.5	461.6	413.2	336.4	394.9
Central Government Deposits..........	26d	92.7	122.5	135.5	178.1	190.5	229.8	242.3	239.6	252.6	278.0	286.1	291.3
Credit from Monetary Authorities.....	26g	21.2	24.9	36.2	53.8	313.1	154.5	48.3	25.5	17.1	18.9	19.6	62.6
Liabilities to Other Banking Insts......	26i	20.0	55.9	86.3	85.7	118.2	56.9	152.8	142.9	126.4	100.8	200.0	188.0
Capital Accounts...........................	27a	220.6	306.4	395.0	506.4	442.9	380.2	403.1	328.8	392.2	421.2	532.6	612.4
Other Items (Net)...........................	27r	20.6	−16.8	−22.3	−83.8	85.3	407.4	499.7	219.6	−66.9	165.4	112.8	101.1
Monetary Survey						*Billions of Baht: End of Period*							
Foreign Assets (Net)........................	31n	454.0	148.0	1.4	−80.7	−562.6	68.6	672.7	1,030.1	1,326.0	1,688.0	1,945.7	2,124.4
Domestic Credit..............................	32	2,559.3	3,312.2	4,073.4	4,643.5	6,244.6	6,166.5	5,906.3	5,465.6	5,143.8	5,544.0	5,691.3	6,033.3
Claims on Central Govt. (Net)........	32an	−205.5	−284.1	−393.6	−466.1	−426.4	−1.0	65.1	130.0	173.7	176.4	83.3	108.8
Claims on State and Local Govts....	32b	—	—	—	—	—	—	—	—	—	—	.1	.8
Claims on Nonfin.Pub.Enterprises....	32c	76.5	94.2	116.8	130.7	171.3	183.5	199.1	172.1	183.4	172.9	164.1	175.3
Claims on Private Sector.................	32d	2,536.5	3,304.1	4,089.2	4,688.3	5,729.6	5,299.6	5,014.5	4,211.6	3,774.7	4,404.7	4,705.3	4,958.4
Claims on Other Financial Insts......	32f	151.8	197.9	261.0	290.5	770.1	684.4	627.6	951.9	1,012.1	789.9	738.4	790.1
Money..............................	34	296.2	346.4	388.3	423.7	430.1	451.0	739.7	684.3	650.6	674.9	869.2	950.0
Quasi-Money..............................	35	2,210.9	2,482.9	2,922.3	3,303.0	3,910.6	4,311.6	4,279.1	4,505.8	4,662.6	4,714.6	4,873.3	5,087.1
Money Market Instruments.............	36aa	—	12.6	11.5	11.1	76.3	185.3	78.1	62.9	90.8	88.0	110.5	126.7
Liabilities to Other Banking Insts......	36i	20.0	55.9	86.3	85.7	118.2	56.9	152.8	142.9	126.4	100.8	200.0	188.0
Capital Accounts..........................	37a	483.7	613.2	732.8	884.2	1,246.1	1,194.3	1,416.3	1,488.5	1,484.5	2,048.6	2,208.7	2,533.1
Other Items (Net)..........................	37r	2.4	−51.0	−66.4	−144.9	−99.3	36.1	−86.9	−388.6	−545.1	−394.9	−624.8	−727.1
Money plus Quasi-Money................	35l	2,507.1	2,829.4	3,310.6	3,726.7	4,340.7	4,762.6	5,018.8	5,190.1	5,313.2	5,389.5	5,742.5	6,037.0

		1993	1994	1995	1996	1997	1998	1999	2000	2001	2002	2003	2004
Other Banking Institutions													
Development Institutions						*Billions of Baht: End of Period*							
Reserves	40	.7	1.0	1.1	1.4	2.6	14.2	7.2	3.5	3.8	7.6	5.1	22.2
Other Claims on Monetary Author....	40n	—	—	—	—	17.4	43.0	17.3	38.4	47.5	55.7	72.3	75.5
Foreign Assets	41	—	—	—	1.0	4.0	14.4	15.0	16.1	14.5	17.7	13.2	13.6
Claims on Central Government	42a	—	—	.3	.2	—	30.4	23.7	16.0	15.0	11.6	13.6	1.8
Claims on Nonfin.Pub.Enterprises....	42c	—	—	—	.6	.1	.5	.4	1.2	8.2	9.3	3.4	4.7
Claims on Private Sector	42d	209.1	270.5	365.7	498.2	674.6	678.6	686.1	734.7	758.0	801.0	865.1	805.0
Claims on Deposit Money Banks	42e	11.9	18.9	17.2	38.4	48.4	32.7	16.1	20.5	16.9	7.3	11.3	1.4
Demand Deposits	44	46.4	60.9	54.3	40.8	52.3	69.3	80.1	63.7	80.5	90.0	107.7	129.8
Time and Savings Deposits	45	44.9	56.1	100.7	88.3	189.8	233.7	190.9	261.3	281.4	313.0	338.3	375.1
Bonds	46ab	65.7	94.6	144.7	151.3	167.0	183.7	188.8	189.3	193.2	201.4	202.5	59.5
Foreign Liabilities	46c	26.0	29.9	33.1	91.4	206.1	160.6	139.6	130.5	98.0	71.8	55.7	32.5
Central Government Deposits	46d	3.0	1.7	4.2	100.9	56.4	89.6	88.0	97.1	110.6	136.1	171.4	189.1
Credit from Monetary Authorities	46g	9.2	9.0	8.5	32.2	32.0	19.8	18.3	20.4	22.6	12.5	17.0	15.4
Credit from Deposit Money Banks....	46h	7.6	11.6	7.1	5.2	6.2	4.8	2.0	2.9	3.3	3.6	1.6	2.5
Capital Accounts	47a	25.7	35.3	41.7	49.9	60.6	79.0	110.3	119.0	135.6	150.4	166.9	170.3
Other Items (Net)	47r	−6.8	−8.8	−9.9	−20.2	−23.4	−26.7	−52.3	−53.7	−61.2	−68.7	−76.8	−50.0
Finance and Securities Companies						*Billions of Baht: End of Period*							
Reserves	40..f	3.7	5.4	11.0	11.6	14.9	18.3	166.2	159.1	60.9	1.3	5.0	1.9
Other Claims on Mon. Author.	40n.f	—	2.9	3.2	7.6	35.0	65.2	39.3	8.5	11.6	4.2	4.6	13.9
Foreign Assets	41..f	—	.7	.9	.8	.8	.5	.1	1.3	.2	.1	.1	.6
Claims on Central Government	42a.f	40.0	9.7	5.6	4.0	1.6	29.7	23.2	23.3	21.4	23.8	17.3	11.6
Claims on State & Local Govts.	42b.f	—	—	—	—	—	—	—	—	—	—	—	—
Claims on Nonfin.Pub.Enterprises.	42c.f	10.6	36.3	32.8	45.0	26.5	8.0	2.7	3.2	1.0	5.3	7.5	5.5
Claims on Private Sector	42d.f	761.1	1,035.1	1,363.1	1,554.7	1,373.8	1,165.5	347.6	301.3	330.0	213.2	285.7	300.7
Claims on Deposit Money Banks	42e.f	27.5	34.8	40.8	39.9	22.6	61.2	28.9	51.1	41.4	17.2	12.1	11.8
Bonds	46abf	559.0	763.2	931.8	1,081.1	549.8	499.8	388.0	343.7	360.8	182.6	220.9	231.4
Foreign Liabilities	46c.f	58.8	71.3	116.5	132.6	123.3	43.1	26.6	28.9	26.0	.7	.5	.6
Credit from Monetary Authorities	46g.f	3.5	8.5	9.1	30.1	449.3	561.9	439.8	364.3	363.9	—	3.5	.1
Cred. from Deposit Money Banks	46h.f	68.5	98.6	146.6	148.1	144.2	103.7	98.4	191.3	78.2	1.9	3.1	17.9
Capital Accounts	47a.f	101.0	145.6	196.7	226.2	197.4	158.6	−353.2	−418.7	−405.8	82.0	95.4	97.4
Other Items (Net)	47r.f	52.2	37.6	56.6	45.5	11.0	−18.5	8.4	38.3	43.3	−2.3	8.9	−1.5
Government Savings Bank						*Billions of Baht: End of Period*							
Reserves	40..g	1.1	1.8	1.3	4.3	2.5	8.7	4.1	4.5	3.3	4.2	12.5	5.7
Other Claims on Mon. Author.	40n.g	—	9.4	8.1	2.1	31.5	71.7	18.4	22.6	35.7	27.6	30.0	31.8
Foreign Assets	41..g	—	—	—	—	—	—	—	—	—	—	—	—
Claims on Central Government	42a.g	60.4	40.7	30.3	26.2	18.0	43.9	137.8	139.1	179.8	203.1	184.1	164.0
Claims on Nonfin.Pub.Enterprises.	42c.g	31.5	26.8	29.6	47.2	67.4	87.6	121.1	167.8	176.1	157.5	149.8	147.7
Claims on Private Sector	42d.g	18.1	26.8	35.4	45.5	64.9	68.8	69.2	81.9	112.3	170.1	245.3	268.9
Claims on Deposit Money Banks	42e.g	28.5	51.2	76.5	78.1	60.1	53.7	47.2	37.9	20.2	14.5	5.9	21.0
Demand Deposits	44..g	41.4	47.1	49.7	54.5	55.0	54.3	51.0	65.5	100.5	106.2	123.7	140.0
Time and Savings Deposits	45..g	100.7	109.8	131.3	153.0	188.4	276.4	310.2	339.3	360.4	393.4	406.4	396.5
Bonds	46abg	—	—	—	—	—	—	—	—	—	—	—	20.0
Foreign Liabilities	46c.g	—	—	—	—	—	—	—	—	—	—	—	—
Central Government Deposits	46d.g	1.5	1.2	1.1	1.2	3.5	3.3	16.3	17.5	22.3	22.9	23.9	24.0
Credit from Monetary Authorities	46g.g	—	—	—	—	—	—	—	—	—	—	—	—
Credit from Deposit Money Banks..	46h.g	—	—	—	—	—	.1	.1	.1	.1	.1	.1	.1
Capital Accounts	47a.g	13.1	15.9	18.6	21.4	19.7	25.0	38.5	41.4	49.5	64.2	69.6	75.5
Other Items (Net)	47r.g	−16.9	−17.3	−19.4	−26.8	−22.1	−24.5	−18.5	−10.0	−5.2	−9.8	3.9	−17.2
Banking Survey						*Billions of Baht: End of Period*							
Foreign Assets (Net)	51n	369.1	47.4	−147.4	−302.8	−887.4	−120.1	521.6	888.2	1,216.6	1,633.2	1,902.8	2,105.4
Domestic Credit	52	3,534.0	4,557.2	5,670.0	6,472.4	7,641.4	7,502.2	6,586.1	5,867.5	5,600.8	6,190.0	6,529.4	6,739.8
Claims on Central Govt. (Net)	52an	−109.4	−236.6	−362.8	−537.9	−466.8	10.1	145.4	193.7	257.0	255.9	103.0	72.9
Claims on State and Local Govts....	52b	—	—	—	—	—	—	—	—	—	—	.1	.8
Claims on Nonfin.Pub.Enterprises....	52c	118.6	157.3	179.2	223.4	265.4	279.6	323.3	344.3	368.7	345.1	324.9	333.2
Claims on Private Sector	52d	3,524.8	4,636.4	5,853.5	6,786.8	7,842.8	7,212.5	6,117.4	5,329.5	4,975.1	5,589.0	6,101.4	6,332.9
Liquid Liabilities	55l	2,735.0	3,095.1	3,633.0	4,046.0	4,806.0	5,355.0	5,473.5	5,752.7	6,067.9	6,279.0	6,696.0	7,048.7
Money Market Instruments	56aa	—	.2	—	.8	3.5	.9	1.4	.5	—	—	.4	.4
Bonds	56ab	624.7	857.8	1,076.5	1,232.4	716.8	683.5	576.8	533.1	554.1	384.0	423.4	310.9
Capital Accounts	57a	623.5	810.1	989.8	1,181.7	1,523.8	1,456.8	1,212.0	1,230.2	1,263.8	2,345.2	2,540.6	2,876.2
Other Items (Net)	57r	−80.0	−158.6	−176.8	−291.2	−296.1	−114.1	−156.1	−760.7	−1,068.2	−1,185.0	−1,228.2	−1,391.1
Money (National Definitions)						*Billions of Baht: End of Period*							
M0	19mc	288.1	329.9	404.3	452.9	474.1	475.2	621.8	527.2	556.3	632.7	699.7	800.5
M1	59ma	296.2	346.4	388.3	423.7	428.8	441.7	575.0	525.7	579.4	663.5	766.8	859.0
M2	59mb	2,507.1	2,829.4	3,310.6	3,726.7	4,339.3	4,753.4	4,854.7	5,032.7	5,243.7	5,378.9	5,641.8	5,948.4
M2a	59mba	....	3,557.5	4,193.4	4,725.2	4,779.2	5,118.1	5,182.5	5,296.9	5,538.4	5,530.2	5,813.2	6,180.4
M3	59mc	3,187.1	3,731.0	4,463.5	5,008.0	5,169.7	5,629.8	5,718.7	5,973.5	6,311.2	6,395.5	6,730.6	7,143.1
Interest Rates						*Percent Per Annum*							
Discount Rate (End of Period)	60	9.00	9.50	10.50	10.50	12.50	12.50	4.00	4.00	3.75	3.25	2.75	3.50
Money Market Rate	60b	6.54	7.25	10.96	9.23	14.59	13.02	1.77	1.95	2.00	1.76	1.31	1.23
Deposit Rate	60l	8.63	8.46	11.58	10.33	10.52	10.65	4.73	3.29	2.54	1.98	1.33	1.00
Lending Rate	60p	11.17	10.90	13.25	13.40	13.65	14.42	8.98	7.83	7.25	6.88	5.94	5.50
Government Bond Yield	61	10.75	10.75	10.75	10.75	10.75	10.25	6.69	6.95	5.82	5.07	3.76	5.09
Prices and Labor						*Index Numbers (2000=100): Period Averages*							
Share Prices	62	....	....	....	....	173.4	103.3	123.0	100.0	88.6	107.0	140.9	193.8
Producer Prices	63	74.8	77.8	† 84.1	85.7	90.0	101.0	96.2	100.0	102.5	104.2	108.4	115.7
Consumer Prices	64	† 73.1	76.8	81.3	86.0	90.8	98.2	98.5	100.0	101.6	102.3	104.1	107.0
						Number in Thousands: Period Averages							
Labor Force	67d	32,644	32,515	32,887	32,543	33,339	33,352	33,209	33,799	33,815	34,228	34,881	35,716
Employment	67e	32,150	32,093	32,512	32,232	33,162	32,138	32,087	33,001	32,110	33,026	33,818	34,717
Unemployment	67c	494	423	375	354	293	1,138	986	813	1,119	826	761	741
Unemployment Rate (%)	67r	1.5	1.3	1.1	1.1	.9	3.4	3.0	2.4	3.3	2.4	2.2	2.1

		1993	1994	1995	1996	1997	1998	1999	2000	2001	2002	2003	2004
Intl. Transactions & Positions							**Billions of Baht**						
Exports	70	935.9	1,137.6	1,406.3	1,412.1	1,806.7	2,247.5	2,214.0	2,777.7	2,886.8	2,923.9	3,326.0	3,922.4
Rice	70n	32.6	59.3	48.6	50.7	65.1	86.9	68.3	65.5	70.1	70.0	75.8	108.4
Rubber	70l	30.4	41.8	61.3	63.4	57.5	55.4	40.3	60.7	58.7	74.6	115.8	137.6
Maize	70j	.7	.6	.5	.4	.5	.9	.4	.4	2.5	1.2	1.6	6.0
Tin	70q	.5	.4	.4	.8	1.4	2.6	2.5	2.8	3.7	2.2	2.0	4.7
Imports, c.i.f.	71	1,166.6	1,369.0	1,763.6	1,832.8	1,924.3	1,774.1	1,907.1	2,494.2	2,752.4	2,774.8	3,137.9	3,839.8
							2000=100						
Volume of Exports	72	43.2	51.1	† 70.1	63.2	68.0	73.3	82.1	100.0	94.5	107.3	116.9	123.6
Rice	72n	81.6	79.1	100.9	88.9	155.8	106.5	111.4	100.0	124.8	119.3	119.6	162.7
Rubber	72l	61.1	67.3	68.8	75.6	75.5	78.6	79.9	100.0	100.3	109.6	122.2	129.3
Maize	72j	633.2	460.5	348.6	182.3	195.1	438.1	258.1	100.0	1,612.2	509.8	669.8	3,252.5
Tin	72q	26.8	21.0	20.4	37.6	61.7	86.5	95.8	100.0	146.0	98.1	76.3	105.3
Volume of Imports	73	86.5	100.5	† 112.8	102.2	91.4	66.6	82.2	100.0	89.3	99.0	108.2	121.3
Unit Value of Exports	74	65.0	66.8	† 72.3	80.1	95.4	109.5	96.2	100.0	109.2	97.9	101.9	114.6
Rice (Unit Value)	74n	61.0	114.3	73.5	87.1	63.8	124.5	93.6	100.0	85.7	89.6	96.7	101.7
Rice (Wholesale Price)	76n	73.5	82.9	97.8	104.9	116.1	154.6	115.2	100.0	93.9	100.9	101.3	121.1
Rubber (Unit Value)	74l	81.9	102.3	146.7	138.1	125.3	116.0	83.0	100.0	96.4	112.1	155.9	175.2
Rubber (Wholesale Price)	76l	78.6	105.7	147.0	132.6	119.1	111.4	89.7	100.0	95.4	122.7	167.7	195.8
Maize (Unit Value)	74j	27.0	32.5	40.1	60.0	69.9	50.9	43.3	100.0	39.6	62.0	60.9	46.7
Tin (Unit Value)	74q	60.6	64.4	70.9	72.7	82.5	105.7	92.9	100.0	89.2	81.6	93.1	158.9
Unit Value of Imports	75	54.1	55.4	† 62.0	70.0	83.0	100.7	89.6	100.0	120.2	109.5	113.3	124.7
Balance of Payments						**Millions of US Dollars: Minus Sign Indicates Debit**							
Current Account, n.i.e.	78ald	−6,364	−8,085	−13,554	−14,691	−3,021	14,243	12,428	9,313	6,192	7,014	7,953	7,080
Goods: Exports f.o.b.	78aad	36,398	44,478	55,447	54,408	56,656	52,753	56,775	67,894	63,082	66,089	78,083	96,107
Goods: Imports f.o.b.	78abd	−40,694	−48,204	−63,415	−63,897	−55,084	−36,515	−42,762	−56,193	−54,539	−57,008	−66,909	−84,983
Trade Balance	78acd	−4,297	−3,726	−7,968	−9,488	1,572	16,238	14,013	11,701	8,543	9,081	11,175	11,124
Services: Credit	78add	11,059	11,640	14,845	17,007	15,763	13,156	14,635	13,868	13,024	15,391	15,798	19,040
Services: Debit	78aed	−12,469	−15,396	−18,804	−19,585	−17,355	−11,998	−13,583	−15,460	−14,610	−16,720	−18,169	−23,211
Balance on Goods & Services	78afd	−5,707	−7,482	−11,927	−12,066	−20	17,395	15,066	10,109	6,957	7,751	8,804	6,954
Income: Credit	78agd	2,140	2,562	3,801	3,969	3,742	3,324	3,092	4,235	3,833	3,356	3,015	3,119
Income: Debit	78ahd	−3,546	−4,292	−5,915	−7,354	−7,223	−6,891	−6,083	−5,616	−5,200	−4,696	−4,807	−5,142
Balance on Gds, Serv. & Inc.	78aid	−7,113	−9,213	−14,040	−15,451	−3,500	13,828	12,075	8,727	5,591	6,411	7,012	4,931
Current Transfers, n.i.e.: Credit	78ajd	1,222	1,901	1,190	1,651	1,392	820	806	952	990	978	1,326	2,479
Current Transfers: Debit	78akd	−473	−774	−704	−891	−913	−405	−452	−366	−389	−375	−385	−331
Capital Account, n.i.e.	78bcd	—	—	....	....	....	....	....	....	....	....	....	....
Capital Account, n.i.e.: Credit	78bad	—	—	....	....	....	....	....	....	....	....	....	....
Capital Account: Debit	78bbd	—	—	....	....	....	....	....	....	....	....	....	....
Financial Account, n.i.e.	78bjd	10,500	12,167	21,909	19,486	−12,056	−14,110	−11,073	−10,434	−3,658	−2,887	−7,626	727
Direct Investment Abroad	78bdd	−233	−493	−886	−931	−580	−130	−346	23	−344	−106	−488	−361
Dir. Invest. in Rep. Econ., n.i.e.	78bed	1,804	1,366	2,068	2,336	3,895	7,315	6,103	3,366	3,892	953	1,949	1,412
Portfolio Investment Assets	78bfd		−5	−2	−41	−70	18	−2	−160	−360	−913	−939	1,195
Equity Securities	78bkd	....	−5	−2	−41	—	—	—	—	—	−9	−149	—
Debt Securities	78bld					−70	18	−2	−160	−360	−905	−790	1,195
Portfolio Investment Liab., n.i.e.	78bgd	5,455	2,486	4,083	3,585	4,598	338	−109	−546	−525	−694	851	61
Equity Securities	78bmd	2,679	−389	2,123	1,164	3,868	289	945	900	352	539	1,786	−475
Debt Securities	78bnd	2,776	2,875	1,960	2,421	730	48	−1,054	−1,446	−877	−1,233	−935	537
Financial Derivatives Assets	78bwd	....	....	....	....	....	....	....	....	—	—	—	....
Financial Derivatives Liabilities	78bxd	....	....	....	....	....	....	....	....	—	—	—	....
Other Investment Assets	78bhd	−3,265	−1,027	−2,738	2,661	−2,555	−3,407	−1,755	−2,203	577	4,135	−410	−441
Monetary Authorities	78bod	—	—	....	....	....	....	....	....	—	—	—	—
General Government	78bpd	—	—	....	....	....	....	....	....	−31	−5	−3	33
Banks	78bqd	−3,265	−1,027	−2,737	2,741	−2,608	−3,460	−1,708	−2,189	743	4,235	−405	−486
Other Sectors	78brd			−1	−80	53	53	−47	−14	−135	−94	−2	13
Other Investment Liab., n.i.e.	78bid	6,739	9,839	19,383	11,876	−17,343	−18,243	−14,964	−10,914	−6,897	−6,263	−8,590	−1,139
Monetary Authorities	78bsd	—	—	—	—	−5,262	658	2,731	43	894	5,352	3,031	3,022
General Government	78btd	−464	−705	46	−58	737	100	−70	93	80	−1,361	−609	−1,882
Banks	78bud	6,589	14,295	13,218	2,909	−3,045	−11,783	−11,566	−4,799	−2,534	−1,761	−1,636	−598
Other Sectors	78bvd	614	−3,751	6,118	9,025	−9,774	−7,218	−6,060	−6,251	−5,338	−8,493	−9,375	−1,681
Net Errors and Omissions	78cad	−230	87	−1,196	−2,627	−3,173	−2,828	33	−685	−258	1,410	191	−2,096
Overall Balance	78cbd	3,907	4,169	7,159	2,167	−18,250	−2,696	1,388	−1,806	2,276	5,537	518	5,710
Reserves and Related Items	79dad	−3,907	−4,169	−7,159	−2,167	18,250	2,696	−1,388	1,806	−2,276	−5,537	−518	−5,710
Reserve Assets	79dbd	−3,907	−4,169	−7,159	−2,167	9,900	−1,433	−4,556	1,608	−1,307	−4,197	−122	−5,713
Use of Fund Credit and Loans	79dcd	—	—	—	—	2,437	679	269	−192	−1,288	−1,360	−398	—
Exceptional Financing	79ded	....	....	....	....	5,913	3,450	2,898	391	320	19	3	4

Thailand 578

		1993	1994	1995	1996	1997	1998	1999	2000	2001	2002	2003	2004
International Investment Position						*Millions of US Dollars*							
Assets...............................	79aad	....	....	46,982	46,005	35,007	41,368	48,360	53,797	54,317	58,458	63,726	....
Direct Investment Abroad..............	79abd	....	....	365	481	401	410	418	2,203	2,626	2,594	3,031	....
Portfolio Investment......................	79acd	....	....	—	—	43	28	29	488	825	1,689	2,748	....
Equity Securities.....................	79add	....	....	....	....	....	....	....	53	82	84	248	....
Debt Securities........................	79aed	....	....	....	....	....	....	....	435	743	1,605	2,500	....
Financial Derivatives..................	79ald	....	....	—	—	—	—	—	517	141	282	612	....
Other Investment......................	79afd	....	....	9,672	6,879	7,671	11,394	13,132	17,928	17,684	14,968	15,186	....
Monetary Authorities................	79agd	....	....	—	—	—	—	—	—	—	—	—	....
General Government..................	79ahd	....	....	—	—	—	—	—	127	158	166	164	....
Banks.................................	79aid	....	....	9,672	6,879	7,671	11,394	13,132	16,342	15,612	11,450	12,020	....
Other Sectors........................	79ajd	....	....	—	—	—	—	—	1,459	1,914	3,352	3,002	....
Reserve Assets...........................	79akd	....	....	36,945	38,645	26,892	29,536	34,781	32,661	33,041	38,925	42,149	....
Liabilities...................................	79lad	....	....	100,832	108,742	109,276	105,061	95,051	114,241	106,169	104,200	118,499	....
Dir. Invest. in Rep. Economy...........	79lbd	....	....	4,919	4,745	4,738	6,481	6,837	29,915	33,268	38,180	47,534	....
Portfolio Investment......................	79lcd	....	....	6,684	9,472	9,774	10,552	9,921	16,360	17,123	17,811	29,111	....
Equity Securities.....................	79ldd	....	....	—	—	—	—	—	8,153	10,240	12,260	24,343	....
Debt Securities........................	79led	....	....	6,684	9,472	9,774	10,552	9,921	8,207	6,883	5,551	4,768	....
Financial Derivatives..................	79lld	....	....	—	—	—	—	—	684	507	541	768	....
Other Investment......................	79lfd	....	....	89,229	94,525	94,764	88,028	78,293	67,281	55,270	47,667	41,085	....
Monetary Authorities................	79lgd	....	....	—	—	7,157	11,203	12,817	12,019	8,327	4,904	—	....
General Government..................	79lhd	....	....	3,126	2,994	3,672	4,768	7,102	7,347	7,296	6,315	6,036	....
Banks.................................	79lid	....	....	41,346	41,410	38,898	28,083	17,450	13,656	10,434	9,298	8,282	....
Other Sectors........................	79ljd	....	....	44,757	50,121	45,037	43,974	40,924	34,259	29,213	27,150	26,767	....
Government Finance						*Millions of Baht: Year Ending December 31*							
Deficit (-) or Surplus......................	80	55,618	101,239	134,965	† 43,303	−15,061	−128,951	−154,193	−108,065	−122,993	−76,815	23,998	....
Total Revenue and Grants..............	81y	....	....	....	....	....	....	....	....	....	....	....	....
Revenue................................	81	575,100	680,455	777,286	853,201	847,689	717,779	713,066	746,817	776,362	876,901	1,012,588	....
Grants..................................	81z	....	....	....	....	....	....	....	....	....	....	....	....
Exp. & Lending Minus Repay..........	82z	....	....	....	....	....	....	....	....	....	....	....	....
Expenditure...........................	82	519,482	579,216	642,321	819,083	875,714	842,581	833,042	853,067	908,613	955,492	996,198	....
Lending Minus Repayments.........	83	....	....	....	....	....	....	....	....	....	....	....	....
Extrabudgetary Deficits/Surpluses...	80xz	....	....	....	† 9,185	12,964	−4,149	−34,217	−1,815	9,258	1,776	7,608	....
Total Financing.............................	80h	−55,618	−101,239	−134,965	† −43,303	15,061	128,951	154,192	108,065	122,993	76,815	−23,998	....
Total Net Borrowing...................	84	−44,605	−80,051	−44,147	† −28,788	−76,109	−7,764	135,204	65,101	113,520	113,439	−35,268	....
Net Domestic..........................	84a	....	....	....	−25,123	−72,348	−3,361	84,566	48,967	112,595	145,487	3,579	....
Net Foreign............................	85a	....	....	....	−3,665	−3,761	−4,403	50,638	16,134	925	−32,048	−38,847	....
Use of Cash Balances....................	87	−11,013	−21,188	−90,818	−14,515	91,170	136,715	18,988	42,964	9,473	−36,624	11,270	....
Total Debt by Currency..................	88z	271,406	219,829	193,630	175,594	299,547	674,032	991,104	1,104,586	1,263,856	1,691,215	1,631,125	....
National....................................	88b	161,071	103,200	72,696	44,254	31,755	426,928	642,371	688,937	836,689	1,293,881	1,279,282	....
Foreign....................................	89b	110,335	116,629	120,934	131,340	267,792	247,104	348,733	415,649	427,167	397,334	351,843	....
National Accounts						*Billions of Baht*							
Househ.Cons.Expend.,incl.NPISHs....	96f	1,730.5	1,958.7	2,225.7	2,479.8	2,587.0	2,505.3	2,595.1	2,762.9	2,941.0	3,113.5	3,360.6	3,662.3
Government Consumption Expend...	91f	316.0	354.4	414.4	469.5	476.7	511.7	533.0	557.8	581.1	603.7	630.4	716.2
Gross Fixed Capital Formation..........	93e	1,252.9	1,450.2	1,719.1	1,892.9	1,598.6	1,035.4	965.9	1,081.4	1,181.3	1,243.1	1,425.3	1,697.1
Changes in Inventories..................	93i	13.5	10.7	43.0	35.2	−5.5	−89.5	−15.3	42.7	55.8	56.6	57.9	86.7
Exports of Goods and Services..........	90c	1,201.5	1,410.8	1,751.7	1,809.9	2,272.1	2,724.0	2,703.3	3,287.3	3,380.8	3,499.0	3,886.6	4,603.5
Imports of Goods and Services (-).....	98c	1,335.7	1,586.6	2,033.9	2,099.2	2,205.1	1,988.9	2,120.3	2,862.3	3,047.6	3,134.3	3,485.3	4,269.9
Statistical Discrepancy....................	99bs	−13.5	31.1	66.1	22.9	8.8	−71.6	−24.6	52.9	41.1	64.4	54.9	80.3
Gross Domestic Product (GDP).........	99b	3,165.2	3,629.3	4,186.2	4,611.0	4,732.6	4,626.4	4,637.1	4,922.7	5,133.5	5,446.0	5,930.4	6,576.0
Net Primary Income from Abroad.....	98.n	−45.9	−55.8	−68.2	−102.1	−123.4	−160.0	−126.4	−76.9	−85.1	−88.6	−111.0	−128.3
Gross National Income (GNI)...........	99a	3,119.3	3,573.6	4,118.0	4,509.0	4,609.2	4,466.4	4,510.6	4,845.9	5,048.4	5,357.4	5,819.3	6,447.7
Consumption of Fixed Capital..........	99cf	335.9	397.0	471.6	556.7	599.1	....	....	....	....	....	....	....
GDP Volume 1988 Prices................	99b.p	2,470.9	2,693.0	2,941.7	3,115.3	3,072.6	2,749.7	2,872.0	3,008.4	3,073.6	3,237.6	3,460.0	3,669.4
GDP Volume (2000=100)...............	99bvp	82.1	89.5	97.8	103.6	102.1	91.4	95.5	100.0	102.2	107.6	115.0	122.0
GDP Deflator (2000=100)...............	99bip	78.3	82.4	87.0	90.5	94.1	102.8	98.7	100.0	102.1	102.8	104.7	109.5
						Millions: Midyear Estimates							
Population...............................	99z	56.92	57.64	58.34	59.00	59.64	60.25	60.85	61.44	62.02	62.59	63.14	63.69

Togo 742

		1993	1994	1995	1996	1997	1998	1999	2000	2001	2002	2003	2004
Exchange Rates					*Francs per SDR: End of Period*								
Official Rate	aa	404.89	780.44	728.38	753.06	807.94	791.61	† 896.19	918.49	935.39	850.37	771.76	747.90
					Francs per US Dollar: End of Period (ae) Period Average (rf)								
Official Rate	ae	294.77	534.60	490.00	523.70	598.81	562.21	† 652.95	704.95	744.31	625.50	519.36	481.58
Official Rate	rf	283.16	† 555.20	499.15	511.55	583.67	589.95	† 615.70	711.98	733.04	696.99	581.20	528.28
					Index Numbers (2000=100): Period Averages								
Official Rate	ahx	250.9	128.1	142.3	138.8	121.8	120.5	115.5	100.0	96.9	102.2	122.4	134.6
Nominal Effective Exchange Rate	nec	191.9	103.9	108.7	109.4	105.6	109.3	106.3	100.0	101.7	104.1	110.5	112.9
Real Effective Exchange Rate	rec	131.5	87.6	101.6	104.0	106.4	110.7	106.5	100.0	103.3	107.1	110.3	112.8
Fund Position					*Millions of SDRs: End of Period*								
Quota	2f.s	54.3	54.3	54.3	54.3	54.3	54.3	73.4	73.4	73.4	73.4	73.4	73.4
SDRs	1b.s	.1	—	.3	.2	—	.1	.2	—	.2	.2	.1	—
Reserve Position in the Fund	1c.s	.2	.3	.3	.3	.3	.3	.3	.3	.3	.3	.3	.3
Total Fund Cred.&Loans Outstg	2tl	49.9	56.0	70.4	62.5	64.9	67.4	60.4	53.3	45.3	38.0	28.2	17.4
International Liquidity					*Millions of US Dollars Unless Otherwise Indicated: End of Period*								
Total Reserves minus Gold	1l.d	156.3	94.4	130.4	88.5	118.6	117.7	122.1	152.3	126.4	205.1	204.9	359.7
SDRs	1b.d	.1	.1	.4	.4	—	.1	.2	—	.2	.3	.2	—
Reserve Position in the Fund	1c.d	.3	.4	.4	.4	.3	.4	.3	.4	.4	.4	.5	.5
Foreign Exchange	1d.d	155.9	94.0	129.6	87.8	118.3	117.3	121.5	151.9	125.8	204.4	204.2	359.2
Gold (Million Fine Troy Ounces)	1ad	.013	.013	—	—	—	—	—	—	—	—	—	—
Gold (National Valuation)	1and	4.7	4.7	—	—	—	—	—	—	—	—	—	—
Monetary Authorities: Other Liab.	4..d	10.3	5.5	1.1	2.8	2.7	8.9	3.1	6.5	6.8	40.5	31.5	91.7
Deposit Money Banks: Assets	7a.d	58.4	109.7	111.1	100.6	66.3	69.1	60.0	81.4	87.2	103.6	118.7	172.2
Liabilities	7b.d	64.8	40.6	76.1	77.8	71.8	71.5	64.1	64.9	62.1	73.3	91.9	92.6
Monetary Authorities					*Billions of Francs: End of Period*								
Foreign Assets	11	46.1	50.5	63.9	46.3	71.0	66.2	79.7	107.4	94.1	128.3	106.4	173.2
Claims on Central Government	12a	40.4	49.8	71.1	70.2	66.0	76.5	67.8	66.9	65.9	53.6	46.2	35.4
Claims on Deposit Money Banks	12e	6.4	7.2	2.0	7.5	4.2	8.5	5.0	2.6	1.8	—	—	—
Claims on Other Financial Insts	12f	1.5	1.3	.3	.2	.3	.3	.3	.3	.3	.3	—	—
Reserve Money	14	61.3	62.8	80.9	70.7	71.2	79.0	90.3	109.4	102.3	108.4	85.7	112.3
of which: Currency Outside DMBs	14a	10.3	44.8	73.5	59.7	60.3	65.3	79.5	95.7	85.7	64.0	48.6	73.3
Foreign Liabilities	16c	23.2	46.7	51.8	48.6	54.1	58.3	56.2	53.6	47.5	57.6	38.1	57.1
Central Government Deposits	16d	6.6	9.6	8.1	8.4	9.9	5.8	3.8	3.7	8.6	7.6	18.1	28.3
Other Items (Net)	17r	3.3	−10.3	−3.6	−3.4	6.3	8.3	2.6	10.5	3.7	8.6	10.7	10.8
Deposit Money Banks					*Billions of Francs: End of Period*								
Reserves	20	54.1	15.1	12.5	14.9	17.7	7.9	9.0	13.4	12.8	33.7	38.0	33.9
Foreign Assets	21	17.2	58.6	54.4	52.7	39.7	38.8	39.2	57.4	64.9	64.8	61.6	82.9
Claims on Central Government	22a	1.9	12.4	12.3	16.5	17.4	16.7	14.1	10.8	7.9	6.6	6.4	22.9
Claims on Private Sector	22d	101.9	101.8	130.4	140.2	154.8	161.9	146.6	147.6	137.3	127.7	166.7	173.9
Claims on Other Financial Insts	22f	.6	.5	—	—	—	—	—	—	—	—	—	—
Demand Deposits	24	35.1	49.3	56.4	59.9	60.6	63.5	61.1	78.4	73.0	82.4	103.3	116.9
Time Deposits	25	66.7	68.2	68.7	66.2	73.8	65.4	68.9	69.4	78.2	86.1	105.3	114.1
Foreign Liabilities	26c	17.2	19.9	33.7	37.3	42.5	39.1	40.1	44.4	45.2	45.2	47.3	44.4
Long-Term Foreign Liabilities	26cl	1.9	1.7	3.5	3.4	.5	1.2	1.7	1.4	1.0	.7	.5	.2
Central Government Deposits	26d	43.1	39.1	37.4	32.8	29.8	28.9	20.6	17.2	15.1	18.1	18.7	23.5
Credit from Monetary Authorities	26g	7.1	7.4	2.0	7.6	4.7	8.5	5.0	2.6	2.1	—	—	2.3
Other Items (Net)	27r	4.5	2.7	7.9	16.9	17.7	18.8	11.4	16.0	8.3	.3	−2.3	12.2
Treasury Claims: Private Sector	22d.i	1.4	.6	.9	.7	.7	.5	.3	.3	.3	.3	.3	.3
Post Office: Checking Deposits	24..i	1.0	1.0	1.3	1.2	1.7	1.2	1.9	1.5	1.2	1.5	1.3	1.1
Monetary Survey					*Billions of Francs: End of Period*								
Foreign Assets (Net)	31n	22.8	42.5	32.7	13.2	14.0	7.7	22.6	66.8	66.3	90.3	82.6	154.6
Domestic Credit	32	97.6	118.1	169.8	187.1	200.4	221.8	206.2	206.3	189.0	164.0	183.9	181.4
Claims on Central Govt. (Net)	32an	−7.8	13.8	38.3	46.0	44.7	59.1	59.1	58.1	51.1	35.7	16.8	7.2
Claims on Private Sector	32d	103.3	102.5	131.2	140.9	155.5	162.4	146.8	147.8	137.6	127.9	167.0	174.2
Claims on Other Financial Insts	32f	2.1	1.8	.3	.2	.3	.3	.3	.3	.3	.3	—	—
Money	34	46.6	95.3	131.2	121.0	123.3	131.8	144.8	176.9	161.5	148.4	154.7	192.9
Quasi-Money	35	66.7	68.2	68.7	66.2	73.8	65.4	68.9	69.4	78.2	86.1	105.3	114.1
Long-Term Foreign Liabilities	36cl	1.9	1.7	3.5	3.4	.5	1.2	1.7	1.4	1.0	.7	.5	.2
Other Items (Net)	37r	5.3	−4.6	−.9	9.6	16.9	31.1	13.4	25.5	14.5	19.0	6.0	28.7
Money plus Quasi-Money	35l	113.3	163.5	199.9	187.2	197.0	197.2	213.7	246.3	239.7	234.6	260.0	307.1
Interest Rates					*Percent Per Annum*								
Bank Rate (End of Period)	60	† 6.00	6.00	6.00	6.00	6.00	6.00	6.00	6.00	6.00	6.00	4.50	4.00
Money Market Rate	60b	4.95	4.95	4.95	4.95	4.95	4.95	4.95	4.95	4.95	4.95	4.95	4.95
Deposit Rate	60l	3.50	3.50	3.50	3.50	3.50	3.50	3.50	3.50	3.50	3.50	3.50	3.50
Prices and Labor					*Index Numbers (2000=100): Period Averages*								
Consumer Prices	64	† 53.0	73.7	85.8	89.9	† 97.3	98.2	98.1	100.0	103.9	107.1	106.1	106.5
					Number in Thousands: Period Averages								
Employment	67e	60	56	54	50	49	....	....	....	....	....	....	....
Intl. Transactions & Positions					*Millions of Francs*								
Exports	70	38,512	182,300	188,400	225,400	246,600	247,900	241,000	257,400	261,900	295,700	357,000	193,957
Imports, c.i.f.	71	50,810	123,265	295,700	339,900	376,400	346,700	301,300	345,100	378,300	401,200	490,200	293,823
					2000=100								
Export Prices	74	....	....	....	122.5	128.9	120.0	100.5	100.0	59.7	57.1	51.7	61.6
Unit Value of Imports	75	....	....	....	62.2	77.5	83.6	104.0	100.0	158.4	187.5	212.4	208.8

Togo 742

		1993	1994	1995	1996	1997	1998	1999	2000	2001	2002	2003	2004
Balance of Payments		*Millions of US Dollars: Minus Sign Indicates Debit*											
Current Account, n.i.e.	78ald	−82.4	−56.3	−122.0	−153.9	−116.9	−140.1	−127.1	−139.6	−169.1	−139.9	−161.9	....
Goods: Exports f.o.b.	78aad	264.0	328.4	377.4	440.6	422.5	420.3	391.5	361.8	357.2	424.2	597.7	....
Goods: Imports f.o.b.	78abd	−375.3	−365.5	−506.5	−567.8	−530.6	−553.5	−489.4	−484.6	−516.1	−575.6	−754.5	....
Trade Balance	78acd	−111.3	−37.1	−129.1	−127.2	−108.1	−133.2	−98.0	−122.8	−158.9	−151.4	−156.8	....
Services: Credit	78add	84.6	70.9	87.3	116.2	88.5	76.0	68.4	61.8	71.8	90.0	94.8	....
Services: Debit	78aed	−128.2	−125.3	−164.3	−201.4	−167.8	−149.2	−130.6	−117.5	−129.9	−148.1	−204.2	....
Balance on Goods & Services	78afd	−154.9	−91.6	−206.0	−212.3	−187.4	−206.4	−160.1	−178.5	−217.0	−209.5	−266.3	....
Income: Credit	78agd	26.8	9.1	8.8	45.6	35.0	44.4	40.2	32.9	25.9	26.2	26.8	....
Income: Debit	78ahd	−17.7	−54.0	−42.4	−72.0	−63.9	−67.7	−78.6	−62.0	−55.2	−47.8	−50.2	....
Balance on Gds, Serv. & Inc.	78aid	−145.7	−136.5	−239.6	−238.8	−216.3	−229.7	−198.5	−207.6	−246.3	−231.1	−289.6	....
Current Transfers, n.i.e.: Credit	78ajd	82.6	91.3	129.7	106.8	120.2	101.8	73.6	73.3	88.3	113.0	161.4	....
Current Transfers: Debit	78akd	−19.3	−11.2	−12.1	−21.9	−20.8	−12.2	−2.2	−5.4	−11.1	−21.8	−33.8	....
Capital Account, n.i.e.	78bcd	—	—	—	5.6	5.8	6.1	6.9	8.7	21.4	13.6	20.6	....
Capital Account, n.i.e.: Credit	78bad	—	—	—	5.6	5.8	6.1	6.9	8.7	21.4	13.6	20.6	....
Capital Account: Debit	78bbd	—	—	....	....	....	....	—	—	—	—	—	....
Financial Account, n.i.e.	78bjd	−105.1	−40.5	−52.8	151.3	126.9	114.1	155.5	162.8	151.2	150.8	142.9	....
Direct Investment Abroad	78bdd	—	—	5.8	−2.8	−2.5	−10.6	−2.9	−.4	7.3	−2.7	6.3	....
Dir. Invest. in Rep. Econ., n.i.e.	78bed	−11.9	15.4	26.2	17.3	21.0	30.2	42.6	41.9	63.6	53.7	33.7	....
Portfolio Investment Assets	78bfd	−.7	.7	5.0	−16.1	6.7	−5.2	−1.3	.8	5.3	−1.1	−4.7	....
Equity Securities	78bkd	.3	1.1	5.0	−.3	7.0	−4.4	−2.8	.6	—	−2.0	−.2	....
Debt Securities	78bld	−.9	−.4	—	−15.8	−.3	−.7	1.6	.2	5.3	.9	−4.5	....
Portfolio Investment Liab., n.i.e.	78bgd	.1	—	....	20.1	9.4	11.4	8.6	6.1	5.8	13.0	18.6	....
Equity Securities	78bmd	—	—	....	18.8	10.6	11.6	8.5	6.1	1.5	6.1	9.8	....
Debt Securities	78bnd	.1	—	....	1.3	−1.2	−.2	.1	—	4.3	6.8	8.8	....
Financial Derivatives Assets	78bwd	....	....	20.6	.3	2.1	−.1	—	—	—	—	—	....
Financial Derivatives Liabilities	78bxd	....	....	....	1.6	−7.0	−.2	−.3	−.1	—	—	—	....
Other Investment Assets	78bhd	−3.2	−1.5	12.1	−19.2	−1.6	16.2	13.0	8.8	8.2	−3.8	−28.7	....
Monetary Authorities	78bod	....	....	....	....	....	....	—	—	—	—	—	....
General Government	78bpd	—	—	....	−3.7	12.2	5.3	7.8	7.5	4.8	−.3	3.1	....
Banks	78bqd	—	—	....	4.6	....	−.7	.5	−16.8	−8.8	5.5	6.9	....
Other Sectors	78brd	−3.2	−1.5	12.1	−20.1	−13.8	11.6	4.7	18.1	12.3	−9.0	−38.6	....
Other Investment Liab., n.i.e.	78bid	−89.5	−55.2	−122.4	150.1	98.9	72.3	95.8	105.7	61.0	91.7	117.7	....
Monetary Authorities	78bsd	—	—	—	3.8	4.8	5.8	−5.0	2.5	1.7	10.4	6.7	....
General Government	78btd	−44.8	−19.3	−133.5	67.8	62.0	45.0	33.2	41.6	28.6	19.6	25.8	....
Banks	78bud	−.7	−66.2	....	13.1	....	−6.4	1.6	1.4	.4	−5.7	2.6	....
Other Sectors	78bvd	−44.0	30.3	11.0	65.4	32.0	28.0	65.9	60.1	30.3	67.5	82.6	....
Net Errors and Omissions	78cad	−2.1	−.2	−19.3	−27.9	−2.7	2.7	−3.7	5.0	−5.4	5.0	−10.2	....
Overall Balance	78cbd	−189.6	−97.1	−194.0	−24.9	13.1	−17.2	31.6	36.8	−2.0	29.6	−8.6	....
Reserves and Related Items	79dad	189.6	97.1	194.0	24.9	−13.1	17.2	−31.6	−36.8	2.0	−29.6	8.6	....
Reserve Assets	79dbd	102.2	−7.7	−26.9	34.3	−26.2	8.8	−22.2	−27.5	7.4	−20.1	22.4	....
Use of Fund Credit and Loans	79dcd	−8.3	9.3	22.0	−11.4	3.4	3.0	−9.4	−9.3	−10.2	−9.5	−13.8	....
Exceptional Financing	79ded	95.7	95.5	199.0	2.0	9.7	5.4	—	—	4.8	—	—	....
International Investment Position		*Millions of US Dollars*											
Assets	79aad	....	....	....	....	....	....	394.9	367.7	306.2	399.9	510.5	....
Direct Investment Abroad	79abd	....	....	....	....	....	....	20.8	17.4	−12.7	−12.1	2.8	....
Portfolio Investment	79acd	....	....	....	....	....	....	14.3	13.8	48.4	59.5	61.5	....
Equity Securities	79add	....	....	....	....	....	....	6.6	7.3	6.6	8.7	5.1	....
Debt Securities	79aed	....	....	....	....	....	....	7.7	6.5	41.8	50.8	56.5	....
Financial Derivatives	79ald	....	....	....	....	....	....	.1	.1	—	—	.6	....
Other Investment	79afd	....	....	....	....	....	....	237.7	195.5	144.3	180.2	263.1	....
Monetary Authorities	79agd	....	....	....	....	....	....	—	—	—	—	—	....
General Government	79ahd	....	....	....	....	....	....	35.8	21.3	—	5.8	3.5	....
Banks	79aid	....	....	....	....	....	....	67.1	83.2	87.5	98.0	107.4	....
Other Sectors	79ajd	....	....	....	....	....	....	134.8	91.0	56.8	76.4	152.2	....
Reserve Assets	79akd	....	....	....	....	....	....	122.1	140.9	126.2	172.4	182.5	....
Liabilities	79lad	....	....	....	....	....	....	1,728.8	1,745.3	1,735.4	2,149.4	2,546.2	....
Dir. Invest. in Rep. Economy	79lbd	....	....	....	....	....	....	47.5	86.8	141.1	223.6	132.4	....
Portfolio Investment	79lcd	....	....	....	....	....	....	24.2	30.1	33.2	53.7	29.1	....
Equity Securities	79ldd	....	....	....	....	....	....	24.2	30.1	29.0	41.2	16.7	....
Debt Securities	79led	....	....	....	....	....	....	.1	—	4.2	12.6	12.4	....
Financial Derivatives	79lld	....	....	....	....	....	....	.7					....
Other Investment	79lfd	....	....	....	....	....	....	1,656.5	1,628.4	1,561.2	1,872.1	2,384.7	....
Monetary Authorities	79lgd	....	....	....	....	....	....	86.9	81.6	70.9	83.4	74.3	....
General Government	79lhd	....	....	....	....	....	....	1,322.3	1,274.6	1,232.5	1,423.4	1,993.3	....
Banks	79lid	....	....	....	....	....	....	56.0	76.7	51.2	49.2	70.7	....
Other Sectors	79ljd	....	....	....	....	....	....	191.3	195.6	206.5	316.1	246.4	....
Government Finance		*Billions of Francs: Year Ending December 31*											
Deficit (-) or Surplus	80	−53	−59	−35	−24	−17	−48	−27	−43	....	....	....	....
Total Revenue and Grants	81y	39	77	109	127	140	141	142	121	....	....	....	....
Revenue	81	38	67	97	110	129	127	127	117	....	....	....	....
Grants	81z	1	10	12	16	12	14	15	4	....	....	....	....
Exp. & Lending Minus Repay.	82z	92	136	144	151	157	188	169	164	....	....	....	....
Expenditure	82	92	136	144	151	157	188	168	168	....	....	....	....
Lending Minus Repayments	83	—	—	—	—	—	1	1	−3	....	....	....	....
Statistical Discrepancy	80xx	35	21	−4	−5	−30	−1	4	28	....	....	....	....
Total Financing													
Domestic	84a	16	19	19	7	13	10	1	−4	....	....	....	....
Foreign	85a	2	19	20	22	34	39	23	20	....	....	....	....

		1993	1994	1995	1996	1997	1998	1999	2000	2001	2002	2003	2004
National Accounts							*Billions of Francs*						
Househ.Cons.Expend.,incl.NPISHs....	96f	323.5	438.1	502.4	576.2	690.0	597.7	681.1	667.1	849.2	884.8	909.3	....
Government Consumption Expend...	91f	57.8	77.1	256.9	266.7	297.5	308.2	273.3	260.2	106.4	102.4	109.1	....
Gross Fixed Capital Formation..........	93e	25.4	63.1	97.2	96.7	98.9	152.6	115.4	139.1	147.9	158.1	198.7	....
Changes in Inventories....................	93i	−10.4	18.2	15.0	10.6	9.3	−.6	−.8	6.6	10.7	6.8	4.5	....
Exports of Goods and Services.........	90c	98.7	221.7	232.0	284.9	298.2	292.7	283.1	301.7	314.5	358.4	441.7	....
Imports of Goods and Services (-).....	98c	142.6	272.5	334.8	393.5	407.6	414.4	381.7	428.8	473.5	504.4	618.9	....
Gross Domestic Product (GDP)........	99b	352.3	545.6	768.6	841.6	986.2	936.3	970.3	946.0	955.3	1,006.0	1,044.5	1,071.6
Net National Income....................	99e	321.5	468.3	574.8	664.3	775.3	742.2	764.2	829.7	....	....	....	....
GDP Volume 1978 Prices................	99b.p	179.0	209.0	223.5	245.2	255.7	250.1	257.5	255.2	256.8	264.2	....	....
GDP Volume (2000=100)...............	99bvp	70.1	81.9	87.6	96.1	100.2	98.0	100.9	100.0	100.6	103.5	....	....
GDP Deflator (2000=100)...............	99bip	53.1	70.4	92.8	92.6	104.0	101.0	101.7	100.0	100.4	102.7	....	....
							Millions: Midyear Estimates						
Population...............................	99z	4.27	4.38	4.51	4.66	4.83	5.01	5.19	5.36	5.53	5.68	5.84	5.99

Tonga 866

		1993	1994	1995	1996	1997	1998	1999	2000	2001	2002	2003	2004
Exchange Rates						*Pa'anga per SDR: End of Period*							
Official Rate	aa	1.8946	1.8371	1.8883	1.7438	1.8377	2.2749	2.2066	2.5754	2.7736	3.0299	3.0020	2.9689
						Pa'anga per US Dollar: End of Period (ae) Period Average (rf)							
Official Rate	ae	1.3793	1.2584	1.2703	1.2127	1.3620	1.6156	1.6077	1.9767	2.2070	2.2287	2.0202	1.9117
Official Rate	rf	1.3840	1.3202	1.2709	1.2319	1.2635	1.4920	1.5991	1.7585	2.1236	2.1952	2.1420	1.9716
Fund Position						*Millions of SDRs: End of Period*							
Quota	2f.s	5.00	5.00	5.00	5.00	5.00	5.00	6.90	6.90	6.90	6.90	6.90	6.90
SDRs	1b.s	.44	.49	.04	.08	.11	.15	.03	.10	.15	.19	.22	.24
Reserve Position in the Fund	1c.s	1.19	1.20	1.21	1.21	1.21	1.22	1.70	1.71	1.71	1.71	1.71	1.71
Total Fund Cred.&Loans Outstg.	2tl												
International Liquidity						*Millions of US Dollars Unless Otherwise Indicated: End of Period*							
Total Reserves minus Gold	1l.d	37.06	35.54	28.71	30.62	27.49	28.66	26.78	26.99	26.10	27.70	42.63	58.29
SDRs	1b.d	.60	.71	.06	.11	.14	.21	.05	.12	.19	.26	.32	.38
Reserve Position in the Fund	1c.d	1.64	1.76	1.80	1.74	1.63	1.72	2.33	2.23	2.15	2.33	2.54	2.66
Foreign Exchange	1d.d	34.82	33.07	26.85	28.77	25.72	26.73	24.40	24.64	23.76	25.11	39.76	55.25
Monetary Authorities: Other Liab.	4..d	.58	.36	.24	.10	.11	.39	.18	.26	.16	.18	.34	1.11
Deposit Money Banks: Assets	7a.d	1.54	1.84	1.96	1.39	1.61	4.27	2.89	11.50	10.30	5.07	11.68	6.42
Liabilities	7b.d	.64	.94	1.22	.63	4.34	4.86	4.36	6.92	5.06	5.76	10.55	5.12
Other Banking Insts.: Liabilities	7f.d	3.65	4.33	3.83	3.51	2.94	2.46	2.32	1.49	1.34	1.19	.90	.55
Monetary Authorities						*Thousands of Pa'anga: End of Period*							
Foreign Assets	11	49,994	41,812	31,493	33,157	32,798	36,311	34,569	25,977	29,709	44,696	56,743	93,377
Claims on Central Government	12a	11,236	9,516	5,493	5,439	5,439	5,456	5,404	6,380	14,095	17,446	18,162	9,924
Claims on Deposit Money Banks	12e	—	—	—	—	—	—	—	9,078	5,447	1,816		
Claims on Other Banking Insts.	12f												
Reserve Money	14	19,226	18,368	15,125	21,629	24,300	26,805	28,804	32,437	42,087	50,818	46,047	73,509
of which: Currency Outside DMBs	14a	7,894	7,346	7,321	6,850	6,471	8,076	9,443	9,966	11,355	12,168	14,322	17,292
Liabs. of Central Bank: Securities	16ac	42,590	39,200	29,367	24,893	21,818	15,963	13,471	100	—	—	—	—
Foreign Liabilities	16c	803	455	306	122	155	623	295	517	356	412	687	2,129
Central Government Deposits	16d	3,432	2,142	1,814	1,577	1,366	6,358	7,126	5,777	6,715	15,149	31,168	29,654
Capital Accounts	17a	2,789	2,922	3,000	2,459	1,676	1,146	1,039	1,331	2,147	4,071	5,995	5,628
Other Items (Net)	17r	−7,610	−11,759	−12,626	−12,084	−11,078	−9,128	−10,764	1,273	−2,054	−6,492	−8,992	−7,619
Deposit Money Banks						*Thousands of Pa'anga: End of Period*							
Reserves	20	48,582	46,688	35,000	39,252	38,006	33,857	33,572	22,483	29,814	38,137	31,025	54,925
Foreign Assets	21	2,125	2,314	2,491	1,682	2,189	6,893	4,644	22,733	22,729	11,289	23,602	12,267
Claims on Central Government	22a	6,816	6,262	9,057	8,970	10,616	10,039	9,632	9,094	9,361	8,215	8,949	9,203
Claims on Nonfin.Pub.Enterprises	22c	55	152	103	497	164	1,551	1,392	3,068	6,111	8,571	12,071	6,899
Claims on Private Sector	22d	31,351	47,273	57,191	59,114	68,094	79,720	87,420	102,774	112,835	137,506	154,151	154,902
Claims on Other Banking Insts.	22f	350	3,850	2,450	1,550	2,375	2,000	3,000	3,000	2,000	2,000	—	—
Demand Deposits	24	18,969	16,637	14,674	15,701	16,941	16,429	20,472	23,106	30,389	42,935	47,764	54,554
Time, Savings,& Fgn.Currency Dep.	25	38,730	44,553	48,567	51,483	56,684	67,350	72,854	89,042	98,505	96,094	110,814	123,870
Foreign Liabilities	26c	879	1,181	1,545	760	5,909	7,850	7,007	13,679	11,171	12,841	21,306	9,796
Central Government Deposits	26d	7,565	12,394	11,534	10,037	8,009	6,929	6,974	7,086	4,530	7,927	10,276	10,106
Credit from Monetary Authorities	26g	—	—	—	—	—	—	—	9,078	5,447	1,816		
Liabilities to Other Banking Insts.	26i	744	5,225	2,764	4,741	4,399	4,216	5,003	2,604	1,378	4,591	875	1,192
Capital Accounts	27a	27,622	30,646	30,746	31,565	30,274	31,312	27,336	29,254	31,194	32,290	36,441	30,799
Other Items (Net)	27r	−5,230	−4,097	−3,538	−3,222	−772	−26	14	−10,697	236	7,224	2,322	7,879
Monetary Survey						*Thousands of Pa'anga: End of Period*							
Foreign Assets (Net)	31n	50,437	42,490	32,133	33,957	28,923	34,731	31,910	34,514	40,912	42,732	58,352	93,719
Domestic Credit	32	38,811	52,517	60,946	63,956	77,313	85,479	92,748	111,453	133,157	150,662	151,889	141,168
Claims on Central Govt. (Net)	32an	7,055	1,242	1,202	2,795	6,680	2,208	936	2,611	12,211	2,585	−14,333	−20,633
Claims on Nonfin.Pub.Enterprises	32c	55	152	103	497	164	1,551	1,392	3,068	6,111	8,571	12,071	6,899
Claims on Private Sector	32d	31,351	47,273	57,191	59,114	68,094	79,720	87,420	102,774	112,835	137,506	154,151	154,902
Claims on Other Banking Insts.	32f	350	3,850	2,450	1,550	2,375	2,000	3,000	3,000	2,000	2,000	—	—
Money	34	27,016	25,535	21,995	22,826	23,412	24,505	29,915	33,072	41,744	55,103	62,086	71,846
Quasi-Money	35	38,730	44,553	48,567	51,483	56,684	67,350	72,854	89,042	98,505	96,094	110,814	123,870
Liabs.of Central Bank: Securities	36ac	42,590	39,200	29,367	24,893	21,818	15,963	13,471	100	—	—	—	—
Liabilities to Other Banking Insts.	36i	744	5,225	2,764	4,741	4,399	4,216	5,003	2,604	1,378	4,591	875	1,192
Capital Accounts	37a	30,411	33,568	33,746	34,024	31,950	32,458	28,375	30,585	33,341	36,361	42,436	36,427
Other Items (Net)	37r	−50,243	−53,074	−43,360	−40,054	−32,027	−24,282	−24,960	−9,436	−900	1,245	−5,970	1,552
Money plus Quasi-Money	35l	65,746	70,088	70,562	74,309	80,096	91,855	102,769	122,114	140,249	151,197	172,900	195,716
Other Banking Institutions						*Thousands of Pa'anga: End of Period*							
Reserves	40	4,277	6,695	4,290	834	475	1,247	1,734	1,607	1,815	1,818	1,824	1,571
Claims on Central Government	42a	1,651	2,000	2,000	1,700	1,700	1,700	2,000	1,500	200	200	1,200	8,434
Claims on Nonfin.Pub.Enterprises	42c	926	3,647	2,937	2,940	1,452	987	834	1,045	885	388	2,383	2,395
Claims on Private Sector	42d	29,380	31,176	37,063	38,270	41,669	41,055	31,939	33,247	35,412	40,175	43,870	36,488
Claims on Deposit Money Banks	42e	—	3,200	100	3,578	3,600	2,800	4,100	1,500	250	3,600	200	6,900
Savings Deposits	45	—	—	8	70	273	430	630	601	744	1,042	1,342	2,583
Bonds	46ab	2,476	9,189	1,823	2,005	3,908	4,604	5,022	5,696	9,133	13,915	17,516	19,730
Foreign Liabilities	46c	5,040	5,444	4,863	4,256	4,008	3,976	3,728	2,950	2,950	2,654	1,824	1,047
Central Government Deposits	46d	—	—	3,600	3,600	3,600	3,600	2,000	2,400	1,800	3,573	2,944	6,781
Central Govt. Lending Funds	46f	14,597	15,761	16,155	17,411	16,743	15,950	14,552	13,036	11,395	9,347	8,469	7,549
Credit from Monetary Authorities	46g	—	—	—	—	—	—	—	—	—	—	—	—
Credit from Deposit Money Banks	46h	—	—	2,100	1,200	2,200	2,000	2,000	3,000	2,000	2,000	—	—
Capital Accounts	47a	11,974	12,622	13,813	14,806	14,738	10,259	10,525	10,546	11,598	14,170	16,445	18,862
Other Items (Net)	47r	2,147	3,702	4,028	3,974	3,426	6,970	2,150	670	−1,058	−520	937	−764

Tonga 866

		1993	1994	1995	1996	1997	1998	1999	2000	2001	2002	2003	2004
Banking Survey		\multicolumn{12}{c}{*Thousands of Pa'anga: End of Period*}
Foreign Assets (Net)	51n	45,397	37,046	27,270	29,701	24,915	30,755	28,182	31,564	37,962	40,078	56,528	92,672
Domestic Credit	52	70,418	85,490	96,896	101,716	116,159	123,621	122,521	141,845	165,854	185,852	196,398	181,704
Claims on Central Govt. (Net)	52an	8,706	3,242	−398	895	4,780	308	936	1,711	10,611	−788	−16,077	−18,980
Claims on Nonfin.Pub.Enterprises	52c	981	3,799	3,040	3,437	1,616	2,538	2,226	4,113	6,996	8,959	14,454	9,294
Claims on Private Sector	52d	60,731	78,449	94,254	97,384	109,763	120,775	119,359	136,021	148,247	177,681	198,021	191,390
Liquid Liabilities	55l	61,469	63,393	66,280	73,545	79,894	91,038	101,665	121,108	139,178	150,421	172,418	196,728
Bonds	56ab	2,476	9,189	1,823	2,005	3,908	4,604	5,022	5,696	9,133	13,915	17,516	19,730
Liabs.of Central Bank: Securities	56ac	42,590	39,200	29,367	24,893	21,818	15,963	13,471	100	—	—	—	—
Central Govt. Lending Funds	56f	14,597	15,761	16,155	17,411	16,743	15,950	14,552	13,036	11,395	9,347	8,469	7,549
Capital Accounts	57a	42,385	46,190	47,559	48,830	46,688	42,717	38,900	41,131	44,939	50,531	58,881	55,289
Other Items (Net)	57r	−47,702	−51,197	−37,018	−35,267	−27,977	−15,896	−22,907	−7,662	−830	1,716	−4,358	−4,920
Interest Rates		\multicolumn{12}{c}{*Percent Per Annum*}
Deposit Rate	60l	4.25	4.64	4.72	5.53	5.57	5.63	5.42	5.36	5.47	5.47	5.47	5.85
Lending Rate	60p	† 9.94	9.48	9.82	10.16	10.02	10.40	10.32	10.35	11.43	11.43	10.15	12.51
Prices and Labor		\multicolumn{12}{c}{*Index Numbers (2000=100): Period Averages*}
Consumer Prices	64	80.9	81.7	82.9	85.4	87.2	90.0	94.1	100.0	108.3	119.5	133.4	148.1
		\multicolumn{12}{c}{*Number in Thousands: Period Averages*}
Labor Force	67d	35	35	....	34	....	....	....	....	....	....	....	....
Intl. Transactions & Positions		\multicolumn{12}{c}{*Thousands of Pa'anga Thousands of Pa'anga*}
Exports	70	23,430	18,367	18,443	16,263	12,800	11,600	20,000	16,000	14,600	32,300	37,200	....
Imports, c.i.f.	71	84,933	91,210	98,034	91,807	92,100	102,400	116,400	123,100	155,100	195,000	199,900	....
Balance of Payments		\multicolumn{12}{c}{*Thousands of US Dollars: Minus Sign Indicates Debit*}
Current Account, n.i.e.	78ald	−5,928	....	....	....	....	....	....	....	−10,803	−3,319	....	....
Goods: Exports f.o.b.	78aad	16,083	....	....	....	....	....	....	....	6,657	18,126	....	....
Goods: Imports f.o.b.	78abd	−56,608	....	....	....	....	....	....	....	−63,688	−73,373	....	....
Trade Balance	78acd	−40,525	....	....	....	....	....	....	....	−57,031	−55,247	....	....
Services: Credit	78add	15,953	....	....	....	....	....	....	....	19,584	22,628	....	....
Services: Debit	78aed	−21,146	....	....	....	....	....	....	....	−27,556	−31,937	....	....
Balance on Goods & Services	78afd	−45,718	....	....	....	....	....	....	....	−65,004	−64,556	....	....
Income: Credit	78agd	5,557	....	....	....	....	....	....	....	5,675	6,611	....	....
Income: Debit	78ahd	−2,383	....	....	....	....	....	....	....	−2,266	−3,791	....	....
Balance on Gds, Serv. & Inc.	78aid	−42,543	....	....	....	....	....	....	....	−61,595	−61,736	....	....
Current Transfers, n.i.e.: Credit	78ajd	49,741	....	....	....	....	....	....	....	62,507	74,536	....	....
Current Transfers: Debit	78akd	−13,126	....	....	....	....	....	....	....	−11,716	−16,120	....	....
Capital Account, n.i.e.	78bcd	605	....	....	....	....	....	....	....	9,606	13,412	....	....
Capital Account, n.i.e.: Credit	78bad	1,340	....	....	....	....	....	....	....	11,727	14,075	....	....
Capital Account: Debit	78bbd	−735	....	....	....	....	....	....	....	−2,120	−663	....	....
Financial Account, n.i.e.	78bjd	3,189	....	....	....	....	....	....	....	822	−3,174	....	....
Direct Investment Abroad	78bdd	−1	....	....	....	....	....	....	....	....	....	....	....
Dir. Invest. in Rep. Econ., n.i.e.	78bed	2,178	....	....	....	....	....	....	....	....	....	....	....
Portfolio Investment Assets	78bfd	—	....	....	....	....	....	....	....	....	....	....	....
Equity Securities	78bkd	—	....	....	....	....	....	....	....	....	....	....	....
Debt Securities	78bld	—	....	....	....	....	....	....	....	....	....	....	....
Portfolio Investment Liab., n.i.e.	78bgd	−64	....	....	....	....	....	....	....	....	....	....	....
Equity Securities	78bmd	—	....	....	....	....	....	....	....	....	....	....	....
Debt Securities	78bnd	−64	....	....	....	....	....	....	....	....	....	....	....
Financial Derivatives Assets	78bwd	....	....	....	....	....	....	....	....	....	....	....	....
Financial Derivatives Liabilities	78bxd	....	....	....	....	....	....	....	....	....	....	....	....
Other Investment Assets	78bhd	—	....	....	....	....	....	....	....	....	....	....	....
Monetary Authorities	78bod	....	....	....	....	....	....	....	....	....	....	....	....
General Government	78bpd	—	....	....	....	....	....	....	....	....	....	....	....
Banks	78bqd	—	....	....	....	....	....	....	....	....	....	....	....
Other Sectors	78brd	—	....	....	....	....	....	....	....	....	....	....	....
Other Investment Liab., n.i.e.	78bid	1,076	....	....	....	....	....	....	....	822	−3,174	....	....
Monetary Authorities	78bsd	−14	....	....	....	....	....	....	....	—	—	....	....
General Government	78btd	1,095	....	....	....	....	....	....	....	....	....	....	....
Banks	78bud	—	....	....	....	....	....	....	....	....	....	....	....
Other Sectors	78bvd	−4	....	....	....	....	....	....	....	....	....	....	....
Net Errors and Omissions	78cad	−260	....	....	....	....	....	....	....	2,093	−47	....	....
Overall Balance	78cbd	−2,394	....	....	....	....	....	....	....	1,718	6,872	....	....
Reserves and Related Items	79dad	2,394	....	....	....	....	....	....	....	−1,718	−6,872	....	....
Reserve Assets	79dbd	2,394	....	....	....	....	....	....	....	−1,718	−6,872	....	....
Use of Fund Credit and Loans	79dcd	—	....	....	....	....	....	....	....	....	....	....	....
Exceptional Financing	79ded	....	....	....	....	....	....	....	....	....	....	....	....
National Accounts		\multicolumn{12}{c}{*Millions of Pa'anga: Year Ending June 30*}
Gross Domestic Product (GDP)	99b	201.0	214.8	....	....	....	....	....	....	....	....	....	....
GDP Volume (1990=100)	99bvp	101.8	106.7	....	....	....	....	....	....	....	....	....	....
GDP Deflator (1990=100)	99bip	124.6	127.1	....	....	....	....	....	....	....	....	....	....
		\multicolumn{12}{c}{*Millions: Midyear Estimates*}
Population	99z	.10	.10	.10	.10	.10	.10	.10	.10	.10	.10	.10	.10

		1993	1994	1995	1996	1997	1998	1999	2000	2001	2002	2003	2004
Exchange Rates		*TT Dollars per SDR: End of Period*											
Market Rate	aa	7.9860	8.6616	8.9146	8.9074	8.5001	9.2881	8.6467	8.2078	7.9051	8.5648	9.3615	9.7838
		TT Dollars per US Dollar: End of Period (ae) Period Average (rf)											
Market Rate	ae	5.8141	5.9332	5.9971	6.1945	6.2999	6.5965	6.2999	6.2996	6.2902	6.2999	6.2999	6.2999
Market Rate	rf	5.3511	5.9249	5.9478	6.0051	6.2517	6.2983	6.2989	6.2998	6.2332	6.2487	6.2951	6.2990
		Index Numbers (2000=100): Period Averages											
Nominal Effective Exchange Rate	nec	92.74	90.16	88.71	92.10	92.58	94.42	95.87	100.00	104.84	105.16	99.56	95.79
Real Effective Exchange Rate	rec	95.30	88.80	86.69	88.32	88.68	93.06	95.56	100.00	107.58	110.06	104.90	101.50
Fund Position		*Millions of SDRs: End of Period*											
Quota	2f.s	246.8	246.8	246.8	246.8	246.8	246.8	335.6	335.6	335.6	335.6	335.6	335.6
SDRs	1b.s	.2	.1	.1	—	.1	.1	—	.1	.2	.3	.7	1.7
Reserve Position in the Fund	1c.s	—	—	—	—	—	—	—	—	24.6	76.4	129.3	111.1
of which: Outstg.Fund Borrowing	2c	—	—	—	—	—	—	—	—	—	—	—	—
Total Fund Cred.&Loans Outstg	2tl	112.8	62.4	33.8	16.5	3.1	—	—	—	—	—	—	—
International Liquidity		*Millions of US Dollars Unless Otherwise Indicated: End of Period*											
Total Reserves minus Gold	1l.d	206.3	352.4	358.2	543.9	706.4	783.1	945.4	1,386.3	1,907.1	2,027.7	2,451.1	3,168.2
SDRs	1b.d	.3	.1	.2	—	.1	.1	—	.1	.2	.4	1.1	2.7
Reserve Position in the Fund	1c.d	—	—	—	—	—	—	—	—	30.9	103.8	192.2	172.5
Foreign Exchange	1d.d	206.0	352.3	358.0	543.8	706.2	783.0	945.4	1,386.2	1,876.0	1,923.5	2,257.8	2,993.0
Gold (Million Fine Troy Ounces)	1ad	.056	.054	.054	.054	.058	.059	.060	.060	.061	.061	.061	.061
Gold (National Valuation)	1and	1.4	1.4	1.4	1.3	16.8	16.1	17.4	16.4	16.8	20.9	25.5	26.8
Monetary Authorities: Other Liab	4..d	99.8	55.0	33.7	32.2	29.3	31.8	37.7	32.3	38.5	37.9	38.2	43.5
Deposit Money Banks: Assets	7a.d	208.4	294.1	216.4	287.3	265.2	298.4	381.5	456.2	538.3	602.5	753.6	838.9
Liabilities	7b.d	66.5	50.5	98.7	137.6	154.1	182.2	239.8	256.0	549.9	596.3	962.9	673.8
Other Banking Insts.: Assets	7e.d	3.0	8.5	11.7	29.2	76.7	73.4	79.8	133.9	243.6	382.6	525.8	....
Liabilities	7f.d	53.2	62.4	62.2	58.2	30.2	41.2	37.6	58.2	115.5	221.8	268.8	....
Monetary Authorities		*Millions of TT Dollars: End of Period*											
Foreign Assets	11	3,610.2	4,602.3	4,577.1	†4,764.4	5,641.3	6,210.7	7,457.7	10,196.3	13,303.6	14,025.3	16,523.0	20,917.3
Claims on Central Government	12a	2,122.3	1,514.0	724.1	†93.6	752.4	709.8	899.8	765.4	961.3	1,104.7	1,129.9	925.7
Claims on Nonfin.Pub.Enterprises	12c	28.5	28.5	361.3	†346.6	345.0	336.0	334.0	328.7	310.3	300.1	280.0	245.4
Claims on Private Sector	12d	—	—	—	†52.7	48.4	44.9	41.0	36.5	27.8	23.9	21.0	18.0
Claims on Deposit Money Banks	12e	250.0	507.2	384.7	†807.2	802.6	807.2	803.4	789.0	775.7	759.3	731.8	723.6
Claims on Other Banking Insts	12f	21.7	18.7	18.7	†.5	.5	2.7	.6	.6	.6	.6	.1	—
Claims on Nonbank Financial Insts	12g	—	—	—	†56.9	48.1	36.7	31.8	23.4	15.1	6.4	6.1	6.6
Reserve Money	14	2,083.4	3,269.7	3,247.8	†3,538.0	4,106.4	4,963.7	5,146.5	5,305.4	5,872.7	5,788.6	6,156.4	5,959.5
of which: Currency Outside DMBs	14a	707.4	744.6	832.8	†909.8	1,063.0	1,046.8	1,292.4	1,271.0	1,373.5	1,501.8	1,708.6	1,957.4
Foreign Liabilities	16c	1,480.8	867.3	503.1	†346.3	211.2	209.9	237.6	203.2	242.1	238.5	240.6	274.2
Central Government Deposits	16d	526.8	780.1	579.3	†1,377.1	2,516.0	1,484.6	2,491.6	4,885.9	7,190.2	7,669.8	9,359.8	13,873.2
Capital Accounts	17a	402.2	433.4	469.7	†548.2	638.9	754.2	752.5	832.9	838.7	734.1	699.7	690.9
Other Items (Net)	17r	1,539.5	1,320.3	1,266.0	†312.3	165.8	735.6	940.0	912.0	1,250.7	1,789.4	2,235.3	2,039.0
Deposit Money Banks		*Millions of TT Dollars: End of Period*											
Reserves	20	1,221.2	2,320.3	2,245.4	†2,370.0	2,772.7	3,058.6	3,021.7	3,214.3	3,935.6	3,534.6	3,541.4	3,352.9
Foreign Assets	21	1,211.6	1,745.0	1,297.7	†1,779.4	1,671.0	1,968.2	2,404.5	2,874.0	3,386.3	3,795.9	4,747.9	5,285.2
Claims on Central Government	22a	774.9	899.4	1,729.1	†2,084.6	3,823.1	2,293.1	2,728.1	2,411.9	3,411.6	3,566.4	3,616.4	4,067.8
Claims on Local Government	22b	.7	1.9	1.9	†—	54.4	2.1	16.4	83.0	65.7	19.2	1.4	5.8
Claims on Nonfin.Pub.Enterprises	22c	747.7	377.9	801.3	†779.5	773.8	904.0	562.1	265.7	802.7	1,149.5	1,030.7	797.5
Claims on Private Sector	22d	7,995.1	7,625.6	8,739.4	†9,741.0	11,835.3	13,433.3	14,498.6	16,353.1	16,922.7	17,645.6	18,073.5	21,920.0
Claims on Other Banking Insts	22f	—	—	—	†252.1	238.0	231.0	207.7	273.0	571.7	202.8	841.0	771.5
Claims on Nonbank Financial Insts	22g	—	—	—	†1,711.1	616.6	111.2	128.0	220.7	565.0	1,255.1	1,427.2	1,275.4
Demand Deposits	24	2,274.3	2,798.8	2,921.0	†2,524.6	3,130.4	2,819.7	3,182.0	3,722.4	4,829.4	5,620.0	5,108.0	5,795.3
Time, Savings,& Fgn.Currency Dep	25	7,492.1	8,651.1	8,966.8	†12,194.9	13,215.0	15,516.0	15,790.9	17,905.9	18,432.8	18,792.7	18,712.4	21,785.1
Foreign Liabilities	26c	386.6	299.8	591.7	†852.3	970.5	1,201.9	1,510.5	1,612.4	3,459.1	3,756.8	6,066.1	4,244.9
Central Government Deposits	26d	143.2	102.1	267.8	†364.6	204.9	203.2	281.9	231.4	1,011.3	452.6	568.7	1,268.3
Credit from Monetary Authorities	26g	288.7	507.1	384.9	†395.3	388.4	386.9	385.1	383.3	381.6	379.8	382.2	380.7
Liabilities to Other Banking Insts	26i	—	—	—	†455.7	312.8	681.7	410.6	333.5	431.8	447.3	520.8	1,113.5
Capital Accounts	27a	1,122.6	1,291.0	1,389.4	†1,754.6	2,278.3	2,529.1	2,990.9	3,813.4	4,293.2	4,775.2	5,454.2	6,680.3
Other Items (Net)	27r	243.7	−679.8	293.2	†175.7	1,284.5	−1,337.0	−984.8	−2,306.6	−3,177.9	−3,055.4	−3,532.9	−3,792.1
Monetary Survey		*Millions of TT Dollars: End of Period*											
Foreign Assets (Net)	31n	2,954.4	5,180.3	4,780.0	†5,345.2	6,130.6	6,767.1	8,114.0	11,254.1	12,988.7	13,825.9	14,964.2	21,683.5
Domestic Credit	32	11,020.9	9,583.8	11,528.7	†13,376.9	15,814.6	16,417.0	16,674.6	15,644.8	15,452.9	17,151.8	16,498.6	14,892.2
Claims on Central Govt. (Net)	32an	2,227.2	1,531.2	1,606.1	†436.5	1,854.5	1,315.1	854.3	−1,940.0	−3,828.6	−3,451.3	−5,182.3	−10,148.1
Claims on Local Government	32b	.7	1.9	1.9	†—	54.4	2.1	16.4	83.0	65.7	19.2	1.4	5.8
Claims on Nonfin.Pub.Enterprises	32c	776.2	406.4	1,162.6	†1,126.1	1,118.9	1,240.0	896.1	594.5	1,113.0	1,449.6	1,310.6	1,043.0
Claims on Private Sector	32d	7,995.1	7,625.6	8,739.4	†9,793.7	11,883.6	13,478.2	14,539.6	16,389.6	16,950.5	17,669.5	18,094.5	21,938.0
Claims on Other Banking Insts	32f	21.7	18.7	18.7	†252.6	238.5	233.7	208.4	273.6	572.3	203.4	841.1	771.5
Claims on Nonbank Financial Inst	32g	—	—	—	†1,768.0	664.8	147.9	159.8	244.2	580.0	1,261.5	1,433.3	1,282.0
Money	34	3,136.5	3,748.2	3,923.4	†3,685.0	4,464.1	4,724.8	5,306.8	5,658.0	6,766.6	7,834.2	7,723.0	8,375.4
Quasi-Money	35	7,492.1	8,651.1	8,966.8	†12,194.9	13,215.0	15,516.0	15,790.9	17,905.9	18,432.8	18,792.7	18,712.4	21,785.1
Liabilities to Other Banking Insts	36i	—	—	—	†455.7	312.8	681.7	410.6	333.5	431.8	447.3	520.8	1,113.5
Capital Accounts	37a	1,524.8	1,724.4	1,859.1	†2,302.8	2,917.2	3,283.3	3,743.4	4,646.3	5,131.9	5,509.3	6,153.9	7,371.2
Other Items (Net)	37r	1,821.9	640.4	1,559.4	†83.7	1,036.1	−1,021.8	−463.1	−1,644.8	−2,321.4	−1,605.8	−1,647.2	−2,069.6
Money plus Quasi-Money	35l	10,628.6	12,399.3	12,890.2	†15,880.0	17,679.0	20,240.8	21,097.8	23,563.9	25,199.3	26,626.9	26,435.3	30,160.5

		1993	1994	1995	1996	1997	1998	1999	2000	2001	2002	2003	2004
Other Banking Institutions													
Other Banklike Institutions						*Millions of TT Dollars: End of Period*							
Reserves	40	143.7	148.0	171.5	† 241.5	272.7	409.8	485.3	534.1	513.2	510.2	661.5	....
Foreign Assets	41	17.5	50.3	70.4	† 181.1	483.1	484.4	502.7	843.5	1,532.1	2,410.4	3,312.5	....
Claims on Central Government	42a	505.7	588.7	965.4	† 1,190.0	1,437.1	1,075.4	1,098.9	1,471.6	672.5	925.5	1,513.7	....
Claims on Local Government	42b	—	—	—	† —	4.1	4.7	5.1	—	—	—	15.0	....
Claims on Nonfin.Pub.Enterprises	42c	9.2	65.5	33.0	† 147.5	137.0	80.3	196.2	291.2	562.1	418.9	550.8	....
Claims on Private Sector	42d	2,852.1	3,341.6	3,982.3	† 2,770.0	3,141.9	3,358.5	3,903.7	4,697.0	4,878.9	5,524.5	6,174.9	....
Claims on Deposit Money Banks	42e	381.8	325.2	335.6	† 786.2	645.4	1,195.6	1,418.3	1,824.6	1,787.6	2,046.1	2,148.8	....
Claims on Nonbank Financial Insts	42g				† 47.4	37.8	201.3	526.1	627.8	571.1	479.4	469.6	....
Time, Savings,& Fgn.Currency Dep	45	2,805.5	2,894.1	3,138.9	† 2,993.9	3,180.3	4,017.2	4,792.5	4,746.5	5,704.3	4,858.3	5,176.4	....
Foreign Liabilities	46c	.3	1.4	.3	† 169.5	152.5	238.0	207.3	341.5	705.6	1,380.4	1,681.0	....
Central Government Deposits	46d	—	—	—	† 47.8	100.7	33.6	34.8	87.8	20.3	79.0	131.1	....
Credit from Monetary Authorities	46g	—	—	—	† 25.3	44.6	52.7	49.9	42.6	34.7	23.6	17.0	....
Credit from Deposit Money Banks	46h	138.9	30.3	48.5	† 92.1	249.0	70.0	670.2	530.1	840.8	633.8	453.0	....
Capital Accounts	47a	470.6	512.2	690.3	† 666.3	764.7	1,049.2	1,294.1	1,658.2	2,015.6	2,482.6	3,144.7	....
Other Items (Net)	47r	494.7	1,081.3	1,680.2	† 1,368.9	1,667.1	1,349.1	1,087.5	2,883.1	1,196.1	2,857.2	4,243.8	....
Development Banks						*Millions of TT Dollars: End of Period*							
Reserves	40..n	—	—	—	—	—	—	—	—	3.6	—	18.7	....
Claims on Central Government	42a.n	—	27.8	33.7	—	—	—	—	—	—	—	—	....
Claims on Private Sector	42d.n	1,165.7	1,011.9	1,031.3	845.5	852.8	927.5	975.6	1,097.8	1,063.2	1,125.5	1,524.0	....
Claims on Deposit Money Banks	42e.n	99.4	110.6	88.6	48.0	78.2	101.3	60.1	163.8	172.0	122.3	223.9	....
Foreign Liabilities	46c.n	309.1	368.9	373.0	190.9	37.9	33.6	29.4	25.3	21.0	16.8	12.6	....
Central Government Deposits	46d.n	401.6	517.4	500.8	446.8	440.3	430.7	418.1	405.2	532.7	514.8	505.4	....
Credit from Dep. Money Banks	46h.n	27.3	28.0	40.2	16.0	30.0	17.3	34.7	34.9	20.0	24.5	23.1	....
Capital Accounts	47a.n	389.2	282.4	275.0	204.4	356.0	377.7	409.3	443.1	304.4	321.8	358.0	....
Other Items (Net)	47r.n	137.9	−46.4	−35.4	35.4	66.8	169.5	144.2	353.2	360.7	369.9	867.5	....
Banking Survey						*Millions of TT Dollars: End of Period*							
Foreign Assets (Net)	51n	2,662.5	4,860.3	4,477.1	† 5,165.9	6,423.3	6,979.9	8,380.0	11,730.9	13,794.2	14,839.1	16,583.1	....
Domestic Credit	52	15,130.3	14,083.2	17,054.9	† 17,630.1	20,645.8	21,366.6	22,718.9	23,063.5	22,075.3	24,828.5	25,269.1	....
Claims on Central Govt. (Net)	52an	2,331.3	1,630.3	2,104.4	† 1,131.9	2,750.6	1,926.2	1,500.3	−961.4	−3,709.1	−3,119.6	−4,305.1	....
Claims on Local Government	52b	.7	1.9	1.9	† —	58.6	6.8	21.5	83.0	65.7	19.2	16.4	....
Claims on Nonfin.Pub.Enterprises	52c	785.4	471.9	1,195.6	† 1,273.7	1,255.8	1,320.3	1,092.3	885.7	1,675.1	1,868.5	1,861.4	....
Claims on Private Sector	52d	12,012.9	11,979.1	13,753.0	† 13,409.1	15,878.3	17,764.2	19,418.9	22,184.4	22,892.6	24,319.5	25,793.4	....
Claims on Nonbank Financial Inst	52g	—	—	—	† 1,815.4	702.6	349.2	685.9	871.9	1,151.1	1,740.9	1,902.9	....
Liquid Liabilities	55l	13,290.4	15,145.4	15,857.6	† 18,632.3	20,586.7	23,848.2	25,404.9	27,776.3	30,386.8	30,975.1	30,931.5	....
Capital Accounts	57a	2,384.6	2,519.0	2,824.4	† 3,173.5	4,038.0	4,710.3	5,446.7	6,747.6	7,452.0	8,313.7	9,656.6	....
Other Items (Net)	57r	2,117.8	1,279.1	2,850.0	† 990.2	2,444.5	−212.0	247.3	270.6	−1,969.3	378.8	1,264.1	....
Interest Rates						*Percent Per Annum*							
Bank Rate (End of Period)	60	13.00	13.00	13.00	13.00	13.00	13.00	13.00	13.00	13.00	7.25	7.00	7.00
Treasury Bill Rate	60c	9.45	10.00	8.41	10.44	9.83	11.93	10.40	10.56	8.55	4.83	4.71	4.77
Savings Rate	60k	2.75	2.69	2.50	2.52	2.50	2.83	2.81	2.96	3.40	2.30	1.97	1.67
Deposit Rate	60l	7.06	6.91	....	....	6.91	7.95	8.51	8.15	7.66	4.76	2.91	2.79
Deposit Rate (Foreign Currency)	60l.f	....	....	....	....	6.35	6.69	6.41	6.74	7.07	4.13	2.62	2.15
Lending Rate	60p	15.50	15.98	15.17	15.79	15.33	17.33	17.04	16.50	15.67	12.48	11.17	9.31
Prices, Production, Labor						*Index Numbers (2000=100): Period Averages*							
Share Prices	62	....	18.8	26.2	35.0	53.0	91.7	87.4	100.0	93.2	105.0	128.8	198.6
Producer Prices	63	83.6	88.1	91.2	93.9	95.7	97.1	98.7	100.0	100.9	101.5	....	....
Consumer Prices	64	72.1	78.4	82.5	85.3	88.4	93.4	96.6	100.0	† 105.5	109.9	114.1	118.3
Wages: Avg Weekly Earn.('90=100)	65	104.6	109.9	....	....	....	....	....	....	....	....	....	....
Industrial Production	66	55.7	† 63.6	68.3	72.2	76.9	85.6	94.9	100.0	111.5	128.3	140.4	....
Crude Petroleum Production	66aa	103.5	109.5	109.2	108.0	103.5	102.8	104.6	100.0	95.1	109.2	112.1	....
Total Employment	67	87.9	91.8	† 85.7	88.3	91.4	95.2	97.2	100.0	102.1	104.3	106.1	....
						Number in Thousands: Period Averages							
Labor Force	67d	504	....	521	530	541	559	563	573	576	586	597	....
Employment	67e	405	416	432	444	460	479	489	503	514	525	534	562
Unemployment	67c	100	94	89	86	81	79	74	70	62	61	62	51
Unemployment Rate (%)	67r	19.8	18.4	17.2	16.3	15.0	14.2	13.2	12.2	10.8	10.4	10.5	8.4
Intl. Transactions & Positions						*Millions of TT Dollars*							
Exports	70	8,800.9	11,055.2	14,608.6	15,014.4	15,887.6	14,220.5	17,661.2	26,923.5	26,709.0	24,232.4	32,600.3	....
Imports, c.i.f	71	7,495.3	6,700.9	10,191.1	12,866.8	18,705.9	18,886.8	17,263.0	20,841.9	22,199.6	22,762.0	24,501.4	....

Trinidad and Tobago   369

		1993	1994	1995	1996	1997	1998	1999	2000	2001	2002	2003	2004
Balance of Payments		*Millions of US Dollars: Minus Sign Indicates Debit*											
Current Account, n.i.e.	78ald	113.1	217.8	293.8	105.1	−613.6	−643.5	30.6	544.3	416.0	76.4	....	....
Goods: Exports f.o.b.	78aad	1,500.1	1,777.6	2,456.1	2,354.1	2,448.0	2,258.0	2,815.8	4,290.3	4,304.2	3,920.0	....	....
Goods: Imports f.o.b.	78abd	−952.9	−1,036.6	−1,868.5	−1,971.6	−2,976.6	−2,998.9	−2,752.2	−3,321.5	−3,586.1	−3,682.3	....	....
Trade Balance	78acd	547.2	741.1	587.7	382.4	−528.6	−740.8	63.6	968.8	718.1	237.7	....	....
Services: Credit	78add	353.4	326.6	342.6	461.2	546.5	671.7	603.2	553.8	573.8	637.0	....	....
Services: Debit	78aed	−466.4	−438.1	−241.9	−217.5	−254.1	−255.4	−274.0	−387.7	−370.0	−373.0	....	....
Balance on Goods & Services	78afd	434.2	629.5	688.4	626.2	−236.2	−324.5	392.8	1,134.9	921.9	501.7	....	....
Income: Credit	78agd	40.2	56.7	76.6	39.1	63.8	64.0	68.3	80.9	108.7	63.7	....	....
Income: Debit	78ahd	−366.0	−468.7	−466.7	−553.1	−445.0	−405.3	−468.2	−709.4	−648.0	−543.5	....	....
Balance on Gds, Serv. & Inc.	78aid	108.4	217.5	298.3	112.2	−617.4	−665.8	−7.1	506.4	382.6	21.9	....	....
Current Transfers, n.i.e.: Credit	78ajd	23.7	28.3	34.0	34.2	37.0	58.4	68.9	63.9	64.0	96.2	....	....
Current Transfers: Debit	78akd	−19.0	−27.9	−38.5	−41.3	−33.2	−36.2	−31.2	−26.0	−30.6	−41.7	....	....
Capital Account, n.i.e.	78bcd	−11.5	−6.4	−11.9	....	....	....	....	....	....	....	....	....
Capital Account, n.i.e.: Credit	78bad	1.3	1.1	1.1	....	....	....	....	....	....	....	....	....
Capital Account: Debit	78bbd	−12.8	−7.5	−13.0	....	....	....	....	....	....	....	....	....
Financial Account, n.i.e.	78bjd	98.8	−32.2	−214.7	43.0	697.2	471.5	38.3	173.7	321.5	397.3	....	....
Direct Investment Abroad	78bdd	—	—	—				−264.1	−25.2	−150.0	−106.4	....	....
Dir. Invest. in Rep. Econ., n.i.e.	78bed	379.2	516.2	298.9	355.4	999.3	729.8	643.3	679.5	834.9	790.7	....	....
Portfolio Investment Assets	78bfd	—	—	−7.9	—	—	−.4	....	....	....	....	....	....
Equity Securities	78bkd	—	—	−7.9			−.4	....	....	....	....	....	....
Debt Securities	78bld	—	—		....	....		....	....	....	....	....	....
Portfolio Investment Liab., n.i.e.	78bgd	—	—	16.7	....	....		−177.5	−30.0	−206.2	−70.1	....	....
Equity Securities	78bmd	—	—	16.7								....	....
Debt Securities	78bnd	—	—		....	....		−177.5	−30.0	−206.2	−70.1	....	....
Financial Derivatives Assets	78bwd	....	....	....	....	....	....	....	....	....	....	....	....
Financial Derivatives Liabilities	78bxd	....	....	....	....	....	....	....	....	....	....	....	....
Other Investment Assets	78bhd	−76.2	−233.5	−57.3	3.0	32.6	1.0	512.3	397.7	285.0	275.2	....	....
Monetary Authorities	78bod	....	....	—				295.2	383.6	26.5	17.8	....	....
General Government	78bpd		−56.1	32.4	3.0	32.6	1.0	—	2.8	—	1.3	....	....
Banks	78bqd	−105.6	−109.3	−23.7	....	....		73.7	—	257.1	256.1	....	....
Other Sectors	78brd	29.3	−68.2	−66.0				143.4	11.3	1.4	—	....	....
Other Investment Liab., n.i.e.	78bid	−204.2	−314.9	−465.1	−315.4	−334.7	−258.8	−675.7	−848.3	−442.2	−492.1	....	....
Monetary Authorities	78bsd	—	—	—	—	—	−1.4	−170.8	−268.7	−61.2	—	....	....
General Government	78btd	19.9	−7.2	−116.8	47.3	−245.4	−104.7	−4.9	−63.8	−14.7	—	....	....
Banks	78bud	20.4	−10.2	−51.3	−27.3	−21.9	−49.6	—	−86.1	—	−335.4	....	....
Other Sectors	78bvd	−244.4	−297.4	−297.0	−335.4	−67.4	−103.2	−500.0	−429.7	−366.3	−156.7	....	....
Net Errors and Omissions	78cad	−41.8	6.3	16.5	90.0	110.0	252.2	93.2	−276.9	−235.3	−358.0	....	....
Overall Balance	78cbd	158.6	185.5	83.7	238.1	193.6	80.2	162.1	441.1	502.2	115.7	....	....
Reserves and Related Items	79dad	−158.6	−185.5	−83.7	−238.1	−193.6	−80.2	−162.1	−441.1	−502.2	−115.7	....	....
Reserve Assets	79dbd	−29.4	−113.6	−40.1	−213.0	−175.3	−76.0	−162.1	−441.1	−502.2	−115.7	....	....
Use of Fund Credit and Loans	79dcd	−129.2	−71.9	−43.6	−25.1	−18.4	−4.2	—	—	—	—	....	....
Exceptional Financing	79ded	—	—	....	....	....	....	....	....	....	....	....	....
Government Finance		*Millions of TT Dollars: Year Ending December 31*											
Deficit (-) or Surplus	80	15.9	117.5	62.5	....	....	....	....	....	....	....	....	....
Revenue	81	7,116.1	7,905.1	8,847.3	....	....	....	....	....	....	....	....	....
Grants Received	81z	17.8	36.0	51.6	....	....	....	....	....	....	....	....	....
Expenditure	82	7,193.6	7,826.9	8,917.9	....	....	....	....	....	....	....	....	....
Lending Minus Repayments	83	−75.6	−3.3	−81.5	....	....	....	....	....	....	....	....	....
Financing													
Domestic	84a	582.8	218.1	−878.7	....	....	....	....	....	....	....	....	....
Foreign	85a	−598.7	−335.6	816.2	....	....	....	....	....	....	....	....	....
National Accounts		*Millions of TT Dollars*											
Househ.Cons.Expend.,incl.NPISHs	96f	15,607	15,196	15,479	17,131	20,702	21,911	25,106	29,350	30,572	36,136	34,709	....
Government Consumption Expend	91f	4,174	4,432	5,029	5,473	5,519	5,472	6,301	6,141	7,925	9,526	10,954	....
Gross Fixed Capital Formation	93e	3,407	5,799	5,932	7,984	10,494	11,945	8,833	8,575	10,525	....	....	....
Changes in Inventories	93i	108	123	655	412	308	762	178	171	171	....	....	....
Exports of Goods and Services	90c	10,765	13,504	17,042	17,778	19,306	18,453	21,437	30,421	30,731	28,468	36,703	....
Imports of Goods and Services (-)	98c	9,569	9,742	12,440	14,191	20,457	20,478	18,966	23,286	24,916	25,468	26,582	....
Gross Domestic Product (GDP)	99b	24,491	29,312	31,697	34,587	35,871	38,065	42,889	51,371	55,009	59,487	67,692	....
Net Primary Income from Abroad	98.n	−1,852	−2,595	−2,916	−3,136	−2,490	−2,527	−2,516	−3,955	−3,405	−3,030	−2,289	....
Gross National Income (GNI)	99a	22,639	26,717	28,781	31,451	33,381	35,898	40,373	47,416	51,604	56,457	65,403	....
Consumption of Fixed Capital	99cf	2,643	3,046	2,839	3,761	3,885	4,310	5,237	5,511	5,823	....	....	....
GDP Volume 1985 Prices	99b.p	16,058	16,630	17,288	....	....	....	....	....	....	....	....	....
GDP Volume 2000 Prices	99b.p	....	....	34,558	36,339	38,835	41,817	46,268	51,485	52,822	....	....	....
GDP Volume (2000=100)	99bvp	62.3	64.6	† 67.1	70.6	75.4	81.2	89.9	100.0	102.6	....	....	....
GDP Deflator (2000=100)	99bip	76.5	88.4	91.9	95.4	92.6	91.2	92.9	100.0	104.4	....	....	....
		Millions: Midyear Estimates											
Population	99z	1.24	1.25	1.26	1.27	1.27	1.28	1.28	1.28	1.29	1.29	1.30	1.30

		1993	1994	1995	1996	1997	1998	1999	2000	2001	2002	2003	2004
Exchange Rates						*Dinars per SDR: End of Period*							
Market Rate	aa	1.4376	1.4470	1.4134	1.4358	1.5483	1.5502	1.7191	1.8049	1.8453	1.8137	1.7955	1.8627
					Dinars per US Dollar: End of Period (ae) Period Average (rf)								
Market Rate	ae	1.0466	.9912	.9508	.9985	1.1475	1.1010	1.2525	1.3853	1.4683	1.3341	1.2083	1.1994
Market Rate	rf	1.0037	1.0116	.9458	.9734	1.1059	1.1387	1.1862	1.3707	1.4387	1.4217	1.2885	1.2455
					Index Numbers (2000=100): Period Averages								
Nominal Effective Exchange Rate	nec	101.38	101.91	102.25	102.94	102.16	101.45	101.79	100.00	98.62	97.23	92.76	88.43
Real Effective Exchange Rate	rec	98.43	99.17	101.38	102.03	101.94	101.29	101.75	100.00	97.57	96.71	93.25	90.33
Fund Position						*Millions of SDRs: End of Period*							
Quota	2f.s	206.0	206.0	206.0	206.0	206.0	206.0	286.5	286.5	286.5	286.5	286.5	286.5
SDRs	1b.s	1.3	1.8	4.7	11.1	12.1	2.1	19.3	3.0	1.3	2.0	1.7	6.0
Reserve Position in the Fund	1c.s	—	—	—	—	—	—	20.2	20.2	20.2	20.2	20.2	20.2
Total Fund Cred.&Loans Outstg.	2tl	207.3	207.3	197.1	165.0	128.4	91.8	55.2	24.7	—	—	—	—
International Liquidity					*Millions of US Dollars Unless Otherwise Indicated: End of Period*								
Total Reserves minus Gold	1l.d	853.8	1,461.5	1,605.3	1,897.6	1,978.1	1,850.1	2,261.5	1,811.0	1,989.2	2,290.3	2,945.4	3,935.7
SDRs	1b.d	1.8	2.7	7.0	15.9	16.3	2.9	26.5	3.9	1.7	2.7	2.5	9.3
Reserve Position in the Fund	1c.d	—	.1	.1	.1	.1	.1	27.7	26.3	25.3	27.4	30.0	31.4
Foreign Exchange	1d.d	852.0	1,458.8	1,598.2	1,881.7	1,961.7	1,847.1	2,207.3	1,780.9	1,962.2	2,260.2	2,912.9	3,895.0
Gold (Million Fine Troy Ounces)	1ad	.215	.216	.217	.217	.217	.217	.217	.220	.218	.218	.218	.218
Gold (National Valuation)	1and	4.2	4.4	4.8	4.4	3.8	4.0	3.5	3.2	3.0	3.3	3.6	3.7
Deposit Money Banks: Assets	7a.d	545.2	536.9	451.6	569.5	607.8	643.6	621.1	669.9	550.0	641.0	706.2	755.3
Liabilities	7b.d	1,374.3	1,729.3	1,740.8	1,938.4	1,845.2	1,979.9	2,091.4	2,618.5	2,608.8	3,198.6	3,453.9	3,942.0
Other Banking Insts.: Liabilities	7f.d	—	—	—	—	—	—	—	—	—	—	—	—
Monetary Authorities						*Millions of Dinars: End of Period*							
Foreign Assets	11	930	1,462	1,536	1,913	2,277	2,053	2,868	2,527	2,899	3,097	3,594	4,814
Claims on Central Government	12a	122	93	85	103	58	78	79	132	147	129	51	71
Claims on Private Sector	12d	....	....	....	....	....	21	23	25	26	25	25	25
Claims on Deposit Money Banks	12e	1,177	835	829	178	115	†93	93	449	854	503	435	91
Reserve Money	14	1,420	1,523	1,667	2,264	2,448	2,159	2,818	2,497	2,943	2,851	3,064	3,577
of which: Currency Outside DMBs	14a	1,179	1,196	1,315	1,473	1,594	1,695	1,994	2,229	2,378	2,518	2,664	2,968
Foreign Liabilities	16c	324	326	304	251	244	173	166	249	186	72	75	55
Central Government Deposits	16d	128	198	137	254	231	241	244	206	390	418	555	668
Capital Accounts	17a	109	119	128	134	143	151	103	116	125	150	146	161
Other Items (Net)	17r	248	224	214	−709	−616	−478	−268	66	281	263	265	551
Deposit Money Banks						*Millions of Dinars: End of Period*							
Reserves	20	181	294	275	760	816	356	853	468	749	700	697	902
Foreign Assets	21	571	532	429	569	697	709	778	928	808	855	853	906
Claims on Central Government	22a	536	544	341	291	682	556	942	1,561	1,487	1,543	1,664	2,145
Claims on Private Sector	22d	7,907	8,510	9,274	9,373	10,540	11,542	12,652	15,717	17,423	18,306	19,493	21,467
Demand Deposits	24	1,676	1,957	2,092	2,371	2,847	3,091	3,435	3,779	4,169	3,918	4,178	4,589
Quasi-Monetary Liabilities	25	3,777	4,003	4,166	4,736	5,660	5,871	7,122	8,372	9,304	10,149	10,868	12,151
Foreign Liabilities	26c	614	780	817	1,076	1,214	1,260	1,684	1,839	1,827	1,913	2,054	2,471
Long-Term Foreign Liabilities	26cl	824	934	839	859	904	919	936	1,788	2,004	2,355	2,119	2,257
Counterpart Funds	26e	—	—	—	—	—	—	—	—	—	—	—	—
Central Govt. Lending Funds	26f	—	—	—	—	—	—	—	—	—	—	—	—
Credit from Monetary Authorities	26g	1,494	1,175	1,119	206	153	127	113	470	870	514	444	93
Capital Accounts	27a	1,053	1,246	1,672	1,914	2,150	2,361	2,577	2,935	2,881	3,077	3,431	3,937
Other Items (Net)	27r	−244	−214	−384	−171	−192	−467	−641	−510	−587	−522	−387	−78
Post Office: Checking Deposits	24..i	110	122	184	230	162	164	321	328	430	416	402	438
Monetary Survey						*Millions of Dinars: End of Period*							
Foreign Assets (Net)	31n	562	888	846	1,154	1,516	1,328	1,796	1,367	1,694	1,968	2,318	3,194
Domestic Credit	32	8,546	9,072	9,746	9,743	11,212	†12,121	13,774	17,558	19,122	20,001	21,079	23,478
Claims on Central Govt. (Net)	32an	639	562	473	371	672	557	1,099	1,816	1,673	1,670	1,562	1,985
Claims on Private Sector	32d	7,907	8,510	9,274	9,373	10,540	†11,564	12,675	15,742	17,449	18,332	19,517	21,493
Money	34	2,998	3,319	3,637	4,109	4,645	4,994	5,794	6,369	7,014	6,892	7,265	8,036
Quasi-Money	35	3,777	4,003	4,166	4,736	5,660	5,871	7,122	8,372	9,304	10,149	10,868	12,151
Long-Term Foreign Liabilities	36cl	824	934	839	859	904	919	936	1,788	2,004	2,355	2,119	2,257
Counterpart Funds	36e	78	49	39	47	67	80	81	174	201	176	226	270
Central Govt. Lending Funds	36f	—	—	—	—	—	—	—	—	—	—	—	—
Other Items (Net)	37r	1,430	1,655	1,912	1,146	1,453	†1,584	1,637	2,221	2,293	2,396	2,920	3,970
Money plus Quasi-Money	35l	6,775	7,322	7,803	8,845	10,304	10,865	12,916	14,742	16,318	17,042	18,133	20,186
Other Banking Institutions						*Millions of Dinars: End of Period*							
Foreign Assets (Net)	41n	25	29	18	7	37	28	41	36	−38	−29	−28	−44
Claims on Central Govt. (Net)	42an	—	1	—	9	7	7	37	62	59	83	82	35
Claims on Private Sector	42d	1,943	2,171	2,395	2,684	2,984	3,311	3,510	1,915	2,079	2,167	1,971	1,403
Monetary Deposits	44	8	7	11	8	7	11	11	14	31	33	39	35
Time and Savings Deposits	45	393	418	443	489	507	674	791	657	763	874	898	636
Long-Term Foreign Liabilities	46cl	—	—	—	—	—	—	—	—	—	—	—	—
Central Govt. Lending Funds	46f	688	843	918	985	1,061	1,012	1,005	215	172	181	256	202
Capital Accounts	47a	906	952	1,049	1,115	1,192	1,246	1,296	1,086	1,039	1,078	827	526
Other Items (Net)	47r	−27	−18	−7	104	260	402	486	41	95	55	6	−4
Banking Survey						*Millions of Dinars: End of Period*							
Foreign Assets (Net)	51n	587	917	864	1,161	1,553	1,356	1,837	1,403	1,655	1,938	2,290	3,150
Domestic Credit	52	10,490	11,244	12,142	12,437	14,203	†15,439	17,321	19,535	21,260	22,251	23,133	24,916
Claims on Government (Net)	52an	639	563	473	380	679	564	1,136	1,878	1,732	1,753	1,644	2,020
Claims on Private Sector	52d	9,851	10,681	11,669	12,057	13,524	†14,875	16,185	17,657	19,528	20,499	21,489	22,896
Liquid Liabilities	55l	7,176	7,746	8,256	9,341	10,819	11,551	13,717	15,412	17,111	17,949	19,070	20,857
Long Term Foreign Liabilities	56cl	824	934	839	859	904	919	936	1,788	2,004	2,355	2,119	2,257
Other Items (Net)	57r	3,076	3,482	3,911	3,397	4,033	†4,325	4,505	3,737	3,800	3,886	4,235	4,963
Interest Rates						*Percent Per Annum*							
Discount Rate (End of Period)	60	8.88	8.88	8.88	7.88	....	....	....	....	....	....	....	....
Money Market Rate	60b	10.48	8.81	8.81	8.64	6.88	6.89	5.99	5.88	6.04	5.93	5.14	5.00

Tunisia 744

		1993	1994	1995	1996	1997	1998	1999	2000	2001	2002	2003	2004
Prices, Production, Labor		*Index Numbers (2000=100): Period Averages*											
Producer Prices	63	80.5	83.2	88.0	91.2	93.4	96.4	96.8	100.0	101.8	104.3	106.8	110.8
Consumer Prices	64	76.7	80.3	85.3	88.5	91.7	94.6	97.2	† 100.0	102.0	104.8	107.6	111.5
Industrial Production	66	72.1	75.6	78.0	80.1	83.6	89.3	94.1	100.0	105.3	105.9	105.7	110.8
Mining Production	66x	60.2	64.8	81.9	86.4	76.3	93.2	99.6	100.0	96.6	93.5	98.2	97.5
Crude Petroleum Production	66aa	127.0	119.6	115.7	114.5	104.1	106.5	107.6	100.0	91.4	95.0	86.6	91.4
		Number in Thousands: Period Averages											
Labor Force	67d	....	2,772	....	....	2,978	....	3,144	3,216	3,293	3,376	3,461	3,329
Employment	67e	....	2,321	....	....	2,504	....	2,635	2,705	2,789	2,852	2,951	2,855
Unemployment	67c	142	160	190	181	225	278	278	305	288	294	311	474
Unemployment Rate	67r	....	15.6	....	....	15.7	....	15.8	15.6	15.0	14.9	14.3	13.9
Intl. Transactions & Positions		*Millions of Dinars*											
Exports	70	3,759.5	4,696.6	5,172.9	5,372.0	6,148.1	6,518.3	6,966.9	8,004.8	9,536.2	9,748.6	10,342.6	12,054.9
Imports, c.i.f.	71	6,172.1	6,647.3	7,464.1	7,498.8	8,793.5	9,489.5	10,070.7	11,738.0	13,697.3	13,510.9	14,038.9	15,864.2
		1990=100											
Volume of Exports	72	120.8	137.1	....	....	....	....	....	....	....	....	....	....
Volume of Imports	73	115.5	119.8	....	....	....	....	....	....	....	....	....	....
Unit Value of Exports	74	96.2	100.8	....	....	....	....	....	....	....	....	....	....
Balance of Payments		*Millions of US Dollars: Minus Sign Indicates Debit*											
Current Account, n.i.e.	78ald	−1,323	−537	−774	−478	−595	−675	−442	−821	−840	−746	−730	−555
Goods: Exports f.o.b.	78aad	3,746	4,643	5,470	5,519	5,559	5,724	5,873	5,840	6,628	6,857	8,027	9,679
Goods: Imports f.o.b.	78abd	−5,810	−6,210	−7,459	−7,280	−7,514	−7,875	−8,014	−8,093	−8,997	−8,981	−10,297	−12,114
Trade Balance	78acd	−2,064	−1,567	−1,989	−1,761	−1,955	−2,152	−2,141	−2,253	−2,369	−2,123	−2,269	−2,434
Services: Credit	78add	2,040	2,267	2,509	2,632	2,613	2,757	2,920	2,767	2,912	2,681	2,937	3,629
Services: Debit	78aed	−1,356	−1,361	−1,352	−1,244	−1,182	−1,257	−1,234	−1,218	−1,425	−1,450	−1,612	−1,986
Balance on Goods & Services	78afd	−1,380	−661	−832	−373	−524	−651	−455	−705	−882	−893	−945	−791
Income: Credit	78agd	73	71	119	66	77	90	89	94	95	72	81	114
Income: Debit	78ahd	−629	−745	−835	−1,030	−939	−947	−978	−1,036	−1,036	−1,056	−1,173	−1,412
Balance on Gds, Serv. & Inc.	78aid	−1,936	−1,336	−1,548	−1,338	−1,386	−1,507	−1,344	−1,647	−1,822	−1,877	−2,037	−2,088
Current Transfers, n.i.e.: Credit	78ajd	629	816	805	879	821	852	920	854	1,016	1,156	1,343	1,564
Current Transfers: Debit	78akd	−16	−17	−31	−20	−30	−20	−18	−29	−34	−25	−36	−31
Capital Account, n.i.e.	78bcd	−2	−3	32	37	77	61	59	3	53	75	59	108
Capital Account, n.i.e.: Credit	78bad	5	5	47	46	95	83	72	9	56	83	66	113
Capital Account: Debit	78bbd	−7	−8	−15	−9	−18	−22	−13	−6	−3	−8	−7	−6
Financial Account, n.i.e.	78bjd	1,272	1,144	958	816	699	489	1,083	646	1,063	857	1,110	1,456
Direct Investment Abroad	78bdd	—	−6	5	−1	−6	1	−3	−1	−1	−4	−2	−2
Dir. Invest. in Rep. Econ., n.i.e.	78bed	562	432	264	238	339	650	350	752	457	795	541	593
Portfolio Investment Assets	78bfd	−6	−1	2	−5	−1	—	—	—	—	—	—	—
Equity Securities	78bkd	—	1	—	—	−1	—	—	—	—	—	—	—
Debt Securities	78bld	−6	−2	2	−5	—	—	—	—	—	—	—	—
Portfolio Investment Liab., n.i.e.	78bgd	24	16	23	67	109	33	10	−20	−15	6	14	24
Equity Securities	78bmd	20	6	12	29	55	58	−3	−18	−15	6	14	24
Debt Securities	78bnd	4	10	12	38	54	−25	13	−3	—	—	....	....
Financial Derivatives Assets	78bwd	—	—	—	—	—	—	—	—	—	—	—	—
Financial Derivatives Liabilities	78bxd	—	—	—	—	—	—	—	—	—	—	—	—
Other Investment Assets	78bhd	−143	−326	−327	−705	−729	−508	−228	−624	−439	−882	−428	−283
Monetary Authorities	78bod	15	86	88	95	14	—	—	—	—	—	....	....
General Government	78bpd	—	—	—	—	—	—	—	—	—	—	....	....
Banks	78bqd	−12	67	150	−305	−250	10	8	—	—	—	....	....
Other Sectors	78brd	−146	−479	−565	−494	−493	−517	−236	−624	−439	−882	−428	−283
Other Investment Liab., n.i.e.	78bid	836	1,029	990	1,221	987	313	954	540	1,059	942	985	1,123
Monetary Authorities	78bsd	5	—	−1	−11	28	—	—	—	—	—	....	....
General Government	78btd	234	411	546	517	324	−49	314	128	752	392	649	176
Banks	78bud	75	168	44	189	90	—	—	—	—	—	....	....
Other Sectors	78bvd	522	450	401	527	544	362	640	412	307	549	336	947
Net Errors and Omissions	78cad	119	−78	−119	67	206	−12	38	−33	13	−46	−56	−32
Overall Balance	78cbd	67	527	97	442	386	−138	738	−205	288	140	383	977
Reserves and Related Items	79dad	−67	−527	−97	−442	−386	138	−738	205	−288	−140	−383	−977
Reserve Assets	79dbd	−61	−527	−82	−395	−336	187	−688	245	−257	−140	−383	−977
Use of Fund Credit and Loans	79dcd	−5	—	−15	−47	−51	−50	−50	−40	−31	—	—	—
Exceptional Financing	79ded	....	....	....	....	....	....	....	....	....	....	....	....
International Investment Position		*Millions of US Dollars*											
Assets	79aad	....	....	2,953	3,112	3,175	3,313	3,359	3,276	2,975	4,357	5,671	7,029
Direct Investment Abroad	79abd	....	....	28	29	32	35	34	32	32	37	43	47
Portfolio Investment	79acd	....	....	48	53	50	54	49	45	44	50	56	59
Equity Securities	79add	....	....	48	53	50	54	49	45	44	50	56	59
Debt Securities	79aed	....	....	—	—	—	—	—	—	—	—	—	—
Financial Derivatives	79ald	....	....	—	—	—	—	—	—	—	—	—	—
Other Investment	79afd	....	....	1,195	1,043	1,039	1,278	911	1,300	924	1,949	2,598	2,911
Monetary Authorities	79agd	....	....	—	—	—	—	—	—	—	—	—	—
General Government	79ahd	....	....	—	—	—	—	—	—	—	—	—	—
Banks	79aid	....	....	447	562	621	665	646	696	547	711	701	719
Other Sectors	79ajd	....	....	748	481	417	613	265	604	377	1,238	1,897	2,192
Reserve Assets	79akd	....	....	1,681	1,987	2,054	1,947	2,366	1,898	1,974	2,322	2,974	4,013
Liabilities	79lad	....	....	23,341	23,399	21,212	23,731	21,983	24,043	24,876	29,520	34,763	38,108
Dir. Invest. in Rep. Economy	79lbd	....	....	11,534	11,218	9,263	11,114	9,152	11,545	11,519	13,861	16,229	17,625
Portfolio Investment	79lcd	....	....	947	1,012	1,035	1,161	1,065	993	475	498	618	659
Equity Securities	79ldd	....	....	947	1,012	1,035	1,161	1,065	993	475	498	618	659
Debt Securities	79led	....	....	—	—	—	—	—	—	—	—	—	—
Financial Derivatives	79lld	....	....	—	—	—	—	—	—	—	—	—	—
Other Investment	79lfd	....	....	10,860	11,170	10,914	11,456	11,766	11,506	12,881	15,161	17,916	19,824
Monetary Authorities	79lgd	....	....	—	—	—	—	—	32	—	—	—	—
General Government	79lhd	....	....	6,896	6,979	7,014	7,381	7,646	7,334	7,671	8,761	10,369	11,003
Banks	79lid	....	....	934	1,157	1,157	1,240	1,457	1,452	1,374	1,633	1,846	2,171
Other Sectors	79ljd	....	....	3,030	3,034	2,742	2,835	2,663	2,687	3,835	4,767	5,701	6,650

Tunisia 744

		1993	1994	1995	1996	1997	1998	1999	2000	2001	2002	2003	2004
Government Finance						*Millions of Dinars: Year Ending December 31*							
Deficit (-) or Surplus......................	80	−475.4	−219.2	−543.6	−599.0	−855.2	−200.2	−646.2	....	....	....	....	....
Revenue..................................	81	4,442.1	4,958.7	5,121.9	5,670.1	6,012.8	7,058.2	7,180.2	....	....	....	....	....
Grants Received........................	81z	53.3	63.4	44.6	42.3				....	....	....	....	....
Expenditure.............................	82	4,850.6	5,101.2	5,584.2	6,208.3	6,677.4	7,160.2	7,864.8	....	....	....	....	....
Lending Minus Repayments...........	83	120.2	140.1	125.9	103.1	190.6	98.2	−38.4	....	....	....	....	....
Financing													
Domestic.................................	84a	300.3	1.2	53.8	72.6	216.8	81.5	213.5	....	....	....	....	....
Foreign...................................	85a	175.1	218.0	489.8	526.4	542.4	10.0	349.6	....	....	....	....	....
Debt: Domestic...........................	88a	2,986.3	3,165.7	3,251.4	3,574.0	4,946.4	5,240.4	5,570.3	....	....	....	....	....
Foreign...............................	89a	5,710.3	6,169.9	6,556.5	6,969.0	8,116.5	8,236.4	9,572.2	....	....	....	....	....
National Accounts						*Millions of Dinars*							
Househ.Cons.Expend.,incl.NPISHs....	96f	9,093	9,799	10,728	11,618	12,591	13,717	14,900	16,190	17,560	18,730	20,230	22,070
Government Consumption Expend...	91f	2,385	2,582	2,778	2,965	3,296	3,530	3,840	4,150	4,490	4,790	5,170	5,560
Gross Fixed Capital Formation..........	93e	4,122	4,279	4,121	4,422	5,153	5,610	6,278	6,920	7,540	7,610	7,530	7,830
Changes in Inventories...................	93i	165	−382	91	347	372	459	210	360	490	80	530	700
Exports of Goods and Services..........	90c	5,931	7,106	7,657	8,029	9,147	9,712	10,500	11,870	13,710	13,540	14,090	16,420
Imports of Goods and Services (-).....	98c	7,033	7,570	8,323	8,315	9,660	10,467	11,050	12,840	15,030	14,820	15,340	17,440
Gross Domestic Product (GDP)........	99b	14,663	15,814	17,052	19,066	20,898	22,561	24,672	26,650	28,760	29,930	32,210	35,140
Net Primary Income from Abroad.....	98.n	−874	−918	−811	−1,004	−998	−988	−1,070	−1,300	−1,310	−1,350	−1,330	−1,580
Gross National Income (GNI)...........	99a	13,789	14,896	16,241	18,062	19,900	21,574	23,602	25,350	27,450	28,580	30,880	33,560
Net Current Transf.from Abroad.......	98t	594	673	712	801	834	942	1,080	1,122	1,380	1,550	1,620	1,910
Gross Nat'l Disposable Inc.(GNDI)....	99i	14,383	15,570	16,953	18,862	20,734	22,515	24,682	26,472	28,830	30,130	32,500	35,470
GDP Volume 1990 Prices.................	99b.p	12,380	12,774	13,074	14,009	14,771	15,477	16,415	17,190	18,030	18,330	19,350	20,520
GDP Volume (2000=100)...............	99bvp	72.0	74.3	76.1	81.5	85.9	90.0	95.5	100.0	104.9	106.6	112.6	119.4
GDP Deflator (2000=100)...............	99bip	76.4	79.9	84.1	87.8	91.3	94.0	97.0	100.0	102.9	105.3	107.4	110.5
						Millions: Midyear Estimates							
Population...............................	99z	8.69	8.84	8.98	9.11	9.23	9.34	9.45	9.56	9.67	9.78	9.89	10.00

Turkey 186

		1993	1994	1995	1996	1997	1998	1999	2000	2001	2002	2003	2004
Exchange Rates		*New Liras per SDR: End of Period*											
Market Rate	aa	.0199	.0565	.0887	.1550	.2774	.4428	.7431	.8774	1.8224	2.2346	2.0754	2.0803
		New Liras per US Dollar: End of Period (ae) Period Average (rf)											
Market Rate	ae	.0145	.0387	.0597	.1078	.2056	.3145	.5414	.6734	1.4501	1.6437	1.3966	1.3395
Market Rate	rf	.0110	.0296	.0458	.0814	.1519	.2607	.4188	.6252	1.2256	1.5072	1.5009	1.4255
Fund Position		*Millions of SDRs: End of Period*											
Quota	2f.s	642	642	642	642	642	642	964	964	964	964	964	964
SDRs	1b.s	—	1	2	1	1	1	—	22	4	23	20	9
Reserve Position in the Fund	1c.s	32	32	32	32	32	32	113	113	113	113	113	113
Total Fund Cred.&Loans Outstg	2tl	—	236	461	461	440	276	649	3,205	11,233	16,246	16,213	13,848
International Liquidity		*Millions of US Dollars Unless Otherwise Indicated: End of Period*											
Total Reserves minus Gold	1l.d	6,272	7,169	12,442	16,436	18,658	19,489	23,346	22,488	18,879	27,069	33,991	35,669
SDRs	1b.d	—	1	3	1	1	1	—	29	4	31	30	14
Reserve Position in the Fund	1c.d	44	47	48	46	44	45	155	147	142	153	168	175
Foreign Exchange	1d.d	6,227	7,121	12,391	16,388	18,614	19,442	23,191	22,313	18,733	26,884	33,793	35,480
Gold (Million Fine Troy Ounces)	1ad	4.031	3.820	3.747	3.747	3.748	3.748	3.744	3.739	3.733	3.733	3.733	3.733
Gold (National Valuation)	1and	1,488	1,410	1,383	1,383	1,384	1,125	1,011	1,010	992	1,032	1,558	1,583
Monetary Authorities: Other Liab	4..d	7,490	9,650	11,797	12,054	11,502	12,809	10,816	10,634	10,940	14,271	17,495	18,824
Deposit Money Banks: Assets	7a.d	10,708	8,655	9,951	9,400	10,474	11,616	14,896	17,072	12,218	12,559	13,554	20,189
Liabilities	7b.d	9,369	3,245	5,293	8,089	11,394	14,647	18,078	22,968	9,919	9,602	13,642	19,523
Other Banking Insts.: Assets	7e.d	612	478	1,015	942	1,062	1,084	1,146	1,082	1,090	901	868	666
Liabilities	7f.d	937	799	816	839	765	864	† 2,026	2,202	1,821	1,707	2,028	2,138
Monetary Authorities		*Millions of New Liras: End of Period*											
Foreign Assets	11	125	373	889	2,029	4,260	6,896	13,864	16,627	30,790	48,273	51,101	52,402
Claims on Central Government	12a	110	216	532	846	983	878	1,135	1,727	34,692	53,910	51,620	48,282
Claims on Nonfin.Pub.Enterprises	12c	13	26	1	2	2	2	3	2	4	5	3	1
Claims on Deposit Money Banks	12e	17	21	29	73	823	2,072	3,088	6,543	9,665	2,703	1,765	1,152
Claims on Other Banking Insts	12f	2	—	—	—	—	9	—	—	—	—	—	—
Claims on Nonbank Financial Insts	12g	—	—	—	—	—	—	—	500	750	250	—	302
Reserve Money	14	129	283	508	972	1,943	3,506	6,923	10,118	18,064	21,250	25,193	33,625
of which: Currency Outside DMBs	14a	51	101	189	316	599	1,031	1,887	3,197	4,463	6,899	9,775	12,444
Other Liabilities to DMBs	14n	15	9	21	47	—	—	—	—	7,200	9,574	8,259	3,622
Time and Savings Deposits	15	3	7	12	33	56	112	232	286	419	653	837	1,094
Foreign Currency Deposits	15.a	4	3	12	39	111	135	23	142	530	33	28	77
Restricted Deposits	16b	—	—	—	—	—	—	—	1	1	—	—	—
Foreign Liabilities	16c	108	387	745	1,370	2,487	4,150	6,338	9,973	36,335	59,760	58,082	54,023
Central Government Deposits	16d	17	22	103	225	875	833	1,812	1,478	3,473	5,800	7,425	6,901
Capital Accounts	17a	9	14	19	114	204	436	1,327	2,233	9,410	5,017	3,192	2,874
Other Items (Net)	17r	−18	−102	30	149	391	685	1,435	1,168	470	3,054	1,472	−76
Deposit Money Banks		*Millions of New Liras: End of Period*											
Reserves	20	75	172	314	641	1,298	2,433	4,544	5,766	10,713	12,679	13,971	19,629
Other Claims on Monetary Auth	20n	15	9	20	47	—	—	5	59	1,126	2,079	439	141
Foreign Assets	21	155	335	594	† 1,016	2,161	3,662	8,078	11,514	17,746	20,667	19,042	27,178
Claims on Central Government	22a	100	225	412	1,423	3,593	9,849	23,148	35,251	62,070	80,303	99,960	114,060
Claims on Local Government	22b	—	3	5	6	8	20	22	48	112	83	172	298
Claims on Nonfin.Pub.Enterprises	22c	24	45	40	49	217	290	625	541	390	51	193	353
Claims on Private Sector	22d	337	572	1,357	3,203	7,252	11,493	16,565	28,515	34,995	38,548	55,736	85,145
Claims on Other Banking Insts	22f	5	18	28	58	129	204	585	719	1,054	1,070	869	828
Claims on Nonbank Financial Insts	22g	2	2	5	13	58	119	499	1,338	944	1,948	2,654	3,359
Demand Deposits	24	73	126	193	562	887	1,387	2,802	4,187	6,339	7,860	11,357	14,168
Time and Savings Deposits	25	184	435	959	2,098	4,237	9,138	17,651	24,519	35,910	50,706	67,863	89,558
Foreign Currency Deposits	25.a	187	562	1,146	2,410	4,894	8,654	18,398	25,278	59,597	72,287	68,817	76,330
Money Market Instruments	26aa	3	5	7	11	—	—	—	—	—	—	—	—
Bonds	26ab	25	16	37	6	81	123	† —	—	—	—	—	—
Foreign Liabilities	26c	136	126	316	872	2,343	4,606	9,787	15,466	14,383	15,783	19,053	26,151
Central Government Deposits	26d	66	92	144	393	838	1,495	2,961	5,053	6,163	9,478	14,094	16,199
Credit from Monetary Authorities	26g	18	13	11	33	764	1,725	2,335	5,600	5,823	191	85	76
Capital Accounts	27a	100	182	384	869	1,864	3,944	6,645	9,628	21,348	31,953	42,099	50,049
Other Items (Net)	27r	−79	−175	−423	† −796	−1,192	−3,003	−6,509	−5,980	−20,415	−30,832	−30,331	−21,547
Monetary Survey		*Millions of New Liras: End of Period*											
Foreign Assets (Net)	31n	36	195	422	† 803	1,591	1,802	5,816	2,702	−2,182	−6,603	−6,991	−593
Domestic Credit	32	509	992	2,132	4,984	10,529	20,534	37,807	62,110	125,375	160,889	189,688	229,528
Claims on Central Govt. (Net)	32an	127	327	696	1,652	2,863	8,398	19,509	30,447	87,126	118,935	130,061	139,243
Claims on Local Government	32b	—	3	5	6	8	20	22	48	112	83	172	298
Claims on Nonfin.Pub.Enterprises	32c	37	71	41	51	219	291	627	543	394	56	196	354
Claims on Private Sector	32d	337	572	1,357	3,203	7,252	11,493	16,565	28,515	34,995	38,548	55,736	85,145
Claims on Other Banking Insts	32f	7	18	28	58	129	214	585	719	1,054	1,070	869	828
Claims on Nonbank Financial Inst	32g	2	2	5	13	58	119	499	1,838	1,694	2,198	2,654	3,661
Money	34	126	228	384	882	1,492	2,433	4,710	7,407	10,840	14,814	21,194	26,782
Quasi-Money	35	377	1,006	2,130	4,580	9,298	18,040	36,303	50,226	96,457	123,680	137,545	167,059
Money Market Instruments	36aa	3	5	7	11	—	—	—	—	—	—	—	—
Bonds	36ab	25	16	37	6	81	123	† —	—	—	—	—	—
Restricted Deposits	36b	—	—	—	—	—	—	—	1	1	—	—	—
Other Items (Net)	37r	14	−81	−4	† 307	1,248	1,740	2,610	7,179	15,896	15,792	23,959	35,095
Money plus Quasi-Money	35l	503	1,235	2,514	5,462	10,790	20,473	41,013	57,633	107,296	138,494	158,738	193,841

		1993	1994	1995	1996	1997	1998	1999	2000	2001	2002	2003	2004
Other Banking Institutions						*Millions of New Liras: End of Period*							
Reserves...	40	20	52	84	147	257	457	894	1,124	1,543	1,472	1,786	2,951
Foreign Assets.................................	41	9	19	61	† 101	218	341	620	728	1,580	1,480	1,212	893
Claims on Central Government.........	42a	3	5	8	17	43	86	334	395	434	848	1,099	1,273
Claims on Local Government...........	42b	6	6	10	24	45	93	387	715	920	1,205	1,644	2,140
Claims on Nonfin.Pub.Enterprises.....	42c	2	1	9	7	17	11	42	25	29	44	68	97
Claims on Private Sector.................	42d	23	45	78	170	332	573	825	1,070	1,883	2,516	2,749	3,056
Claims on Nonbank Financial Insts....	42g	1	—	—	1	5	7	35	36	56	86	116	186
Time and Savings Deposits..............	45	2	2	3	2	3	3	—	—	—	750	653	1,100
Bonds..	46ab	17	39	51	70	130	104	—	—	—	—	—	—
Foreign Liabilities...........................	46c	14	31	49	90	157	272	† 1,097	1,483	2,640	2,805	2,832	2,864
Central Government Deposits...........	46d	13	24	44	67	142	214	181	245	519	590	580	518
Credit from Monetary Authorities........	46g	1	—	—	15	30	47	82	100	225	197	119	72
Credit from Deposit Money Banks....	46h	11	43	88	160	284	502	690	878	891	1,145	937	902
Capital Accounts.............................	47a	12	13	33	86	194	384	763	1,298	2,204	3,397	4,807	5,509
Other Items (Net)...........................	47r	−8	−24	−18	† −23	−23	42	−6	−269	−1,103	−1,233	−1,254	−370
Banking Survey						*Millions of New Liras: End of Period*							
Foreign Assets (Net).......................	51n	31	183	434	† 814	1,652	1,871	† 5,340	1,947	−3,242	−7,928	−8,612	−2,564
Domestic Credit..............................	52	523	1,008	2,166	5,077	10,700	20,877	38,664	63,388	127,124	163,928	193,915	234,935
Claims on Central Govt. (Net)......	52an	117	308	660	1,602	2,764	8,270	19,662	30,597	87,042	119,193	130,580	139,998
Claims on Local Government.........	52b	6	9	15	30	54	113	409	763	1,032	1,287	1,817	2,438
Claims on Nonfin.Pub.Enterprises...	52c	38	72	51	58	236	303	670	567	423	100	264	451
Claims on Private Sector...............	52d	359	617	1,435	3,372	7,584	12,066	17,389	29,585	36,878	41,063	58,485	88,200
Claims on Nonbank Financial Inst...	52g	3	2	5	14	62	126	534	1,875	1,750	2,284	2,770	3,848
Liquid Liabilities.............................	55l	488	1,190	2,440	5,330	10,541	20,026	40,130	56,531	105,904	137,799	157,645	192,022
Bonds..	56ab	41	55	87	76	212	227	† —	—	—	—	—	—
Other Items (Net)...........................	57r	24	−67	71	† 485	1,600	2,495	3,544	8,445	16,908	18,201	27,659	40,348
Interest Rates						*Percent Per Annum*							
Discount Rate (End of Period)..........	60	48.00	55.00	50.00	50.00	67.00	67.00	60.00	60.00	60.00	55.00	43.00	38.00
Interbank Money Market Rate..........	60b	62.83	136.47	72.30	76.24	70.32	74.60	73.53	56.72	91.95	49.51	36.16	21.57
Treasury Bill Rate............................	60c	....	....	....	....	....	....	....	25.18	85.33	59.50	34.90	21.95
Deposit Rate...................................	60l	64.58	87.79	76.02	80.74	79.49	80.11	78.43	47.16	74.70	50.49	37.68	24.26
Prices, Production, Labor						*Index Numbers (2000=100): Period Averages*							
Producer Prices (2003=100)............	63	....	....	....	....	....	....	....	....	....	....	100.0	114.6
Wholesale Prices.............................	63a	1.9	† 4.2	7.8	13.8	25.1	43.1	66.0	100.0	161.6	242.6	304.6	338.4
Consumer Prices.............................	64	1.6	† 3.4	6.3	11.4	21.2	39.2	64.6	100.0	154.4	223.8	† 280.4	304.6
Industrial Production.......................	66	81.0	76.0	82.5	87.3	96.7	97.9	94.3	100.0	91.3	99.9	108.7	119.3
						Number in Thousands: Period Averages							
Labor Force....................................	67d	20,384	....	22,078	22,259	21,818	23,415	23,779	20,579	23,491	23,818	23,787	24,188
Employment...................................	67e	19,905	20,396	21,378	21,698	20,815	21,958	22,049	22,031	21,524	21,354	21,291	21,709
Unemployment................................	67c	1,722	1,740	1,522	1,332	1,545	1,547	1,730	1,452	1,958	2,464	2,497	2,479
Unemployment Rate (%).................	67r	8.0	7.6	6.6	5.8	6.9	6.2	7.3	6.6	8.4	10.3	10.5	10.3
Intl. Transactions & Positions						*Millions of US Dollars*							
Exports..	70..d	15,345	18,106	21,637	23,225	26,261	26,974	26,587	27,775	31,334	34,561	46,576	61,682
Imports, c.i.f..................................	71..d	29,428	23,270	35,709	43,627	48,559	45,921	40,671	54,503	41,399	49,663	65,637	96,368
						2000=100							
Volume of Exports..........................	72..d	52.3	† 60.0	63.8	70.0	79.4	87.1	89.9	100.0	122.2	141.5	172.5	† 198.6
Volume of Imports..........................	73..d	51.0	† 37.8	48.9	63.3	78.2	76.3	75.4	100.0	75.2	90.8	121.0	† 153.2
Unit Value of Exports/Export Prices...	74..d	117.4	† 113.9	128.3	122.6	116.8	112.1	104.5	100.0	97.4	95.7	105.3	† 122.0
Unit Value of Imports/Import Prices..	75..d	98.4	† 105.3	123.0	115.6	105.6	101.2	95.7	100.0	99.7	98.5	106.3	† 119.6

Turkey 186

		1993	1994	1995	1996	1997	1998	1999	2000	2001	2002	2003	2004
Balance of Payments						*Millions of US Dollars: Minus Sign Indicates Debit*							
Current Account, n.i.e.	78ald	−6,433	2,631	−2,338	−2,437	−2,638	1,984	−1,344	−9,819	3,390	−1,521	−7,905	−15,543
Goods: Exports f.o.b.	78aad	15,611	18,390	21,975	32,067	32,110	30,662	28,842	30,721	34,373	40,124	51,206	67,000
Goods: Imports f.o.b.	78abd	−29,655	−22,524	−35,089	−42,331	−47,158	−44,714	−39,027	−52,680	−38,106	−47,407	−65,216	−90,925
Trade Balance	78acd	−14,044	−4,134	−13,114	−10,264	−15,048	−14,052	−10,185	−21,959	−3,733	−7,283	−14,010	−23,925
Services: Credit	78add	10,652	10,801	14,606	13,430	19,910	23,879	16,881	20,429	16,059	14,785	19,086	24,048
Services: Debit	78aed	−3,948	−3,782	−5,024	−6,773	−8,998	−10,373	−9,394	−9,061	−6,929	−6,905	−8,581	−11,274
Balance on Goods & Services	78afd	−7,340	2,885	−3,532	−3,607	−4,136	−546	−2,698	−10,591	5,397	597	−3,505	−11,151
Income: Credit	78agd	1,135	890	1,489	1,577	1,900	2,481	2,350	2,836	2,753	2,486	2,246	2,651
Income: Debit	78ahd	−3,880	−4,154	−4,693	−4,504	−4,913	−5,466	−5,887	−6,838	−7,753	−7,040	−7,673	−8,170
Balance on Gds, Serv. & Inc.	78aid	−10,085	−379	−6,736	−6,534	−7,149	−3,531	−6,235	−14,593	397	−3,957	−8,932	−16,670
Current Transfers, n.i.e.: Credit	78ajd	3,684	3,031	4,414	4,116	4,554	5,649	5,011	4,866	3,051	2,482	1,088	1,165
Current Transfers: Debit	78akd	−32	−21	−16	−19	−43	−134	−120	−92	−58	−46	−61	−38
Capital Account, n.i.e.	78bcd						....	....		....	....		
Capital Account, n.i.e.: Credit	78bad	—	—	—	—	—	—	....	—	....	—	—	—
Capital Account: Debit	78bbd	—	—	—	—	—	—	—	—	—	—	—	—
Financial Account, n.i.e.	78bjd	8,963	−4,194	4,643	5,483	6,969	−840	4,979	8,584	−14,644	1,328	6,959	17,037
Direct Investment Abroad	78bdd	−14	−49	−113	−110	−251	−367	−645	−870	−498	−176	−499	−859
Dir. Invest. in Rep. Econ., n.i.e.	78bed	636	608	885	722	805	940	783	982	3,266	1,038	1,562	2,733
Portfolio Investment Assets	78bfd	−563	35	−466	−1,380	−710	−1,622	−759	−593	−788	−2,096	−1,386	−1,388
Equity Securities	78bkd	−139	5	−75	7	−50	−21	−46	−33	−36	−42	−33	−25
Debt Securities	78bld	−424	30	−391	−1,387	−660	−1,601	−713	−560	−752	−2,054	−1,353	−1,363
Portfolio Investment Liab., n.i.e.	78bgd	4,480	1,123	703	1,950	2,344	−5,089	4,188	1,615	−3,727	1,503	3,955	9,411
Equity Securities	78bmd	570	989	195	191	8	−518	428	489	−79	−16	1,009	1,427
Debt Securities	78bnd	3,910	134	508	1,759	2,336	−4,571	3,760	1,126	−3,648	1,519	2,946	7,984
Financial Derivatives Assets	78bwd	....	....	....	....	....	—	—	....	—	—	—	—
Financial Derivatives Liabilities	78bxd	....	....	....	....	....	—	—	—	—	—	—	—
Other Investment Assets	78bhd	−3,291	2,423	−383	331	−1,750	−1,464	−2,304	−1,939	−601	−777	−986	−7,290
Monetary Authorities	78bod	−61	−18	−102	−117	−98	−95	−98	1	−39	−30	−28	−24
General Government	78bpd	....	....	....									
Banks	78bqd	−3,230	2,441	−281	1,448	−976	−942	−1,839	−1,574	233	643	348	−5,269
Other Sectors	78brd	....	....	....	−1,000	−676	−427	−367	−366	−795	−1,390	−1,306	−1,997
Other Investment Liab., n.i.e.	78bid	7,715	−8,334	4,017	3,970	6,531	6,762	3,716	9,389	−12,296	1,836	4,313	14,430
Monetary Authorities	78bsd	1,085	1,415	1,734	1,380	1,245	760	−160	706	817	1,433	605	−51
General Government	78btd	−1,953	−2,516	−1,991	−2,108	−1,456	−1,655	−1,932	−883	−1,977	−669	−2,194	−1,163
Banks	78bud	4,495	−7,053	1,973	3,046	2,232	3,195	2,655	3,736	−9,644	−2,016	2,846	6,434
Other Sectors	78bvd	4,088	−180	2,301	1,652	4,510	4,462	3,153	5,830	−1,492	3,088	3,056	9,210
Net Errors and Omissions	78cad	−2,222	1,766	2,355	1,498	−988	−703	1,719	−2,699	−1,634	−21	5,033	2,814
Overall Balance	78cbd	308	203	4,660	4,544	3,343	441	5,354	−3,934	−12,888	−214	4,087	4,308
Reserves and Related Items	79dad	−308	−203	−4,660	−4,544	−3,343	−441	−5,354	3,934	12,888	214	−4,087	−4,308
Reserve Assets	79dbd	−308	−547	−5,007	−4,544	−3,316	−217	−5,724	−383	2,718	−6,177	−4,030	−788
Use of Fund Credit and Loans	79dcd	—	344	347	—	−27	−224	519	3,316	10,169	6,390	−57	−3,520
Exceptional Financing	79ded	—	—	—	—	—	−150	—	1,000	—	—	—	—
International Investment Position						*Millions of US Dollars*							
Assets	79aad	....	....	....	....	....	....	....	53,221	52,783	62,787	74,493	86,983
Direct Investment Abroad	79abd	—	—	—	—	—	—	—	3,668	4,581	5,847	6,138	7,060
Portfolio Investment	79acd	—	—	—	5	5	5	4	4	550	809	1,963	933
Equity Securities	79add	....	....	....	5	5	5	4	4	53	45	68	122
Debt Securities	79aed	....	....	....	—	—	—	—	—	497	764	1,895	811
Financial Derivatives	79ald	....	....	....	....	....	....	....	—	—	—	—	—
Other Investment	79afd	13,545	11,624	13,571	9,909	10,448	13,708	25,039	26,196	27,687	28,014	31,188	41,333
Monetary Authorities	79agd	1,034	1,061	1,103	1,160	1,211	1,265	1,320	1,392	1,418	1,411	1,391	1,372
General Government	79ahd	—	—	—	—	—	—	—	598	584	643	762	737
Banks	79aid	12,511	10,563	12,468	8,749	9,237	10,446	11,564	12,862	13,159	12,196	12,492	18,251
Other Sectors	79ajd	—	—	—	—	—	1,997	12,155	11,344	12,526	13,764	16,543	20,973
Reserve Assets	79akd	7,746	8,570	13,825	17,704	19,587	20,780	24,343	23,353	19,965	28,117	35,204	37,657
Liabilities	79lad	....	....	....	....	....	....	....	152,290	137,489	162,536	199,545	230,635
Dir. Invest. in Rep. Economy	79lbd								19,209	19,677	18,912	32,335	30,155
Portfolio Investment	79lcd	12,623	13,788	14,186	16,166	19,749	17,734	38,409	35,882	24,740	23,935	33,228	51,617
Equity Securities	79ldd	—	—	—	3,085	6,018	3,700	15,358	7,404	5,635	3,450	8,954	16,141
Debt Securities	79led	12,623	13,788	14,186	13,081	13,731	14,034	23,051	28,478	19,105	20,485	24,274	35,476
Financial Derivatives	79lld												
Other Investment	79lfd	54,829	52,239	59,829	66,256	70,465	82,356	86,751	97,199	93,072	119,689	133,982	148,863
Monetary Authorities	79lgd	7,208	9,658	12,216	12,374	11,758	12,982	11,501	14,561	24,825	36,021	41,193	39,922
General Government	79lhd	19,733	21,660	21,428	23,895	22,113	22,405	21,742	22,559	21,094	36,020	38,671	40,559
Banks	79lid	12,461	5,814	8,025	11,210	12,568	15,988	18,726	22,222	11,789	9,836	13,221	19,533
Other Sectors	79ljd	15,427	15,107	18,160	18,777	24,026	30,981	34,782	37,857	35,364	37,812	40,897	48,849
Government Finance						*Millions of New Liras: Year Ending December 31*							
Revenue	81	356	751	1,402	2,726	6,327	12,657	19,798	35,426	54,433	....	....	....
Grants Received	81z	2	1	7	2	2	—	8	—	—	....	....	....
Expenditure	82	490	902	1,726	3,966	8,617	16,762	29,467	49,134	88,403	....	....	....
Lending Minus Repayments	83	—	—	—	—	156	282	414	554	993	....	....	....
Financing													
Domestic	84a	113	219	396	1,373	2,828	5,158	9,180	10,769	38,295	....	....	....
Foreign	85a	20	−69	−80	−134	−384	−771	896	3,494	−3,332	....	....	....
Total Debt	88	668	1,703	2,782	5,602	12,656	21,629	41,452	63,416	178,193	....	....	....
Domestic	88a	357	799	1,361	3,149	6,283	11,613	22,920	36,421	122,157	....	....	....
Foreign	89a	311	903	1,421	2,453	6,373	10,016	18,532	26,996	56,036	....	....	....

		1993	1994	1995	1996	1997	1998	1999	2000	2001	2002	2003	2004
National Accounts								*Millions of New Liras*					
Househ.Cons.Expend.,incl.NPISHs....	96f	1,369	2,706	5,458	9,938	19,619	36,123	55,928	89,098	128,513	184,036	239,087	291,468
Government Consumption Expend...	91f	258	451	837	1,709	3,535	6,633	11,748	17,539	25,405	38,722	49,005	53,245
Gross Fixed Capital Formation..........	93e	526	952	1,850	3,706	7,618	12,839	16,931	27,848	32,409	46,043	55,618	80,495
Changes in Inventories....................	93i	22	−121	127	−80	−377	−212	1,149	2,685	−2,475	13,134	26,329	28,985
Exports of Goods and Services.........	90c	271	826	1,544	3,182	7,088	12,713	17,972	29,959	60,151	81,134	98,496	124,044
Imports of Goods and Services (-).....	98c	383	789	1,890	4,111	8,763	14,573	20,801	39,285	55,862	85,232	110,334	148,452
Gross Domestic Product (GDP)........	99b	1,982	3,868	7,762	14,772	28,836	52,225	77,415	124,583	178,412	277,574	359,763	426,305
Statistical Discrepancy....................	99bs	−80	−157	−164	427	115	−1,090	−5,510	−2,442	−9,729	−969	1,063	3,360
GDP Vol. 1995 Prices......................	99b.p	7,660	7,242	7,762	8,306	8,932	9,208	8,774	9,420	8,714	9,406	9,951	10,715
GDP Volume (2000=100)................	99bvp	81.5	77.0	82.6	88.3	95.0	97.9	93.3	100.0	92.7	99.9	105.8	115.3
GDP Deflator (2000=100)...............	99bip	2.0	4.0	7.5	13.4	24.4	42.8	66.6	100.0	154.5	223.0	272.8	296.8
							Millions: Midyear Estimates						
Population.............................	99z	60.44	61.52	62.62	63.74	64.88	66.03	67.15	68.23	69.28	70.28	71.25	72.22

Uganda 746

		1993	1994	1995	1996	1997	1998	1999	2000	2001	2002	2003	2004
Exchange Rates						*Shillings per SDR: End of Period*							
Principal Rate	aa	1,552.3	1,352.9	1,500.5	1,480.5	1,538.3	1,918.7	2,067.1	2,301.8	2,170.9	2,518.6	2,875.8	2,700.0
					Shillings per US Dollar: End of Period (ae) Period Average (rf)								
Principal Rate	ae	1,130.2	926.8	1,009.5	1,029.6	1,140.1	1,362.7	1,506.0	1,766.7	1,727.4	1,852.6	1,935.3	1,738.6
Principal Rate	rf	1,195.0	979.4	968.9	1,046.1	1,083.0	1,240.3	1,454.8	1,644.5	1,755.7	1,797.6	1,963.7	1,810.3
					Index Numbers (2000=100): Period Averages								
Principal Rate	ahx	136.90	167.65	169.08	156.31	151.25	132.31	112.55	100.00	93.17	91.00	83.32	90.52
Nominal Effective Exchange Rate	nec	95.90	130.83	127.18	123.57	127.86	116.23	104.10	100.00	98.23	94.48	78.91	81.04
Real Effective Exchange Rate	rec	97.89	121.74	119.07	118.74	127.30	112.56	104.54	100.00	97.18	91.34	80.29	82.17
Fund Position						*Millions of SDRs: End of Period*							
Quota	2f.s	133.9	133.9	133.9	133.9	133.9	133.9	180.5	180.5	180.5	180.5	180.5	180.5
SDRs	1b.s	—	2.1	.3	.7	4.0	3.5	1.7	2.7	1.5	2.2	3.2	.4
Reserve Position in the Fund	1c.s	—	—	—	—	—	—	—	—	—	—	—	—
Total Fund Cred.&Loans Outstg	2tl	243.0	262.6	280.6	290.1	291.7	282.7	270.8	242.6	219.1	188.9	158.8	123.3
International Liquidity					*Millions of US Dollars Unless Otherwise Indicated: End of Period*								
Total Reserves minus Gold	1l.d	146.4	321.4	458.9	528.4	633.5	725.4	763.1	808.0	983.4	934.0	1,080.3	1,308.1
SDRs	1b.d	.1	3.1	.5	1.1	5.4	5.0	2.3	3.5	1.9	3.0	4.8	.7
Reserve Position in the Fund	1c.d	—	—	—	—	—	—	—	—	—	—	—	—
Foreign Exchange	1d.d	146.3	318.3	458.4	527.3	628.1	720.4	760.8	804.5	981.5	931.1	1,075.5	1,307.4
Monetary Authorities: Other Liab	4..d	1.8	7.7	2.7	3.0	1.4	7.5	2.0	2.3	2.4	2.8	2.6	2.4
Deposit Money Banks: Assets	7a.d	91.4	145.2	132.5	142.6	160.8	190.2	199.8	265.6	248.6	240.1	362.2	411.2
Liabilities	7b.d	.7	8.0	.1	—	2.0	2.1	25.5	41.7	32.1	38.7	25.8	28.2
Monetary Authorities						*Billions of Shillings: End of Period*							
Foreign Assets	11	172.28	299.21	466.80	538.08	660.96	951.07	1,090.38	1,363.64	1,624.55	1,660.49	2,141.52	2,289.79
Claims on Central Government	12a	791.08	963.06	1,152.68	1,227.76	1,348.13	1,591.13	1,801.56	1,911.39	1,678.33	2,022.48	1,900.14	1,969.96
Claims on Nonfin.Pub.Enterprises	12c	20.75	23.19	24.18	24.47	25.13	25.56	3.50	4.15	4.17	3.86	4.24	1.54
Claims on Private Sector	12d	4.36	1.47	.54	.54	.54	.45	27.35	52.43	85.64	82.98	60.03	66.45
Claims on Deposit Money Banks	12e	6.27	3.86	1.88	7.72	13.06	31.82	61.84	61.76	58.04	77.50	104.71	84.51
Reserve Money	14	170.97	253.14	287.89	321.37	350.61	420.77	484.14	589.68	668.44	739.76	820.95	989.18
of which: Currency Outside DMBs	14a	132.64	176.52	204.52	221.09	240.46	285.88	330.76	362.25	393.43	466.61	546.23	588.61
Liabs. of Central Bank: Securities	16ac	—	—	—	—	7.00	6.70	52.42	.02	20.02	38.71	38.21	16.00
Restricted Deposits	16b	10.55	9.33	10.45	9.96	13.43	26.58	123.49	125.60	133.22	151.19	169.04	155.92
Foreign Liabilities	16c	379.31	362.37	423.84	432.55	450.43	552.70	562.73	562.54	479.82	480.94	461.66	337.09
Central Government Deposits	16d	550.28	830.12	1,247.93	1,319.14	1,457.69	1,688.73	1,925.47	1,727.99	1,824.37	2,022.31	2,102.12	2,446.19
Capital Accounts	17a	61.50	20.49	56.71	140.81	215.89	408.85	492.39	433.31	305.79	494.48	556.95	477.28
Other Items (Net)	17r	−177.86	−184.65	−380.74	−425.26	−447.22	−504.29	−656.00	−45.76	19.05	−80.09	61.71	−9.43
Deposit Money Banks						*Billions of Shillings: End of Period*							
Reserves	20	37.06	75.12	79.60	109.62	104.22	129.41	121.02	188.93	233.79	205.80	207.26	375.63
Claims on Mon.Author.:Securities	20c	—	—	—	—	7.00	6.70	52.42	—	20.00	26.50	38.20	16.00
Foreign Assets	21	103.30	134.55	133.77	146.80	183.34	259.23	300.95	469.23	429.43	444.76	701.05	714.91
Claims on Central Government	22a	14.27	34.74	41.75	65.67	182.64	199.24	286.12	404.25	586.78	868.01	890.35	938.52
Claims on State and Local Govts	22b	—	—	—	—	—	—	1.41	1.04	.78	.88	.87	.58
Claims on Nonfin.Pub.Enterprises	22c	32.53	51.21	56.63	65.85	65.83	63.59	70.66	115.36	141.41	192.47	212.51	264.86
Claims on Private Sector	22d	166.95	190.69	245.82	323.18	319.96	424.82	491.90	531.35	503.51	596.50	757.27	836.45
Demand Deposits	24	126.76	177.50	204.18	229.74	272.08	326.56	358.60	443.24	515.36	632.83	688.68	752.63
Time, Savings,& Fgn. Currency Dep	25	155.49	209.41	233.30	315.37	402.46	512.42	588.01	703.62	739.40	961.11	1,193.75	1,356.47
Foreign Liabilities	26c	.75	7.44	.08	—	2.23	2.92	38.43	73.69	55.46	71.68	49.90	48.99
Central Government Deposits	26d	11.19	28.00	38.68	73.01	49.03	46.29	99.81	149.24	159.62	175.29	245.08	179.41
Central Government Lending Funds	26f	14.52	18.81	15.39	7.99	11.17	10.98	17.03	54.62	52.97	40.23	101.77	128.91
Credit from Monetary Authorities	26g	10.47	6.71	8.45	.15	7.24	23.40	27.22	22.22	20.30	21.48	20.30	60.12
Capital Accounts	27a	37.65	36.00	50.07	73.33	145.90	169.82	172.64	264.46	308.30	338.59	416.99	455.82
Other Items (Net)	27r	−2.72	2.44	7.42	11.52	−27.12	−9.40	22.74	−.94	64.29	93.72	91.05	164.60
Monetary Survey						*Billions of Shillings: End of Period*							
Foreign Assets (Net)	31n	−104.47	63.95	176.66	252.33	391.64	654.68	790.18	1,196.64	1,518.70	1,552.64	2,331.02	2,618.62
Domestic Credit	32	468.47	406.25	234.99	315.32	435.51	569.77	657.22	1,142.75	1,016.62	1,569.57	1,478.20	1,452.76
Claims on Central Govt. (Net)	32an	243.88	139.69	−92.18	−98.72	24.05	55.35	62.40	438.41	281.12	692.89	443.29	282.88
Claims on State and Local Govts	32b	—	—	—	—	—	—	1.41	1.04	.78	.88	.87	.58
Claims on Nonfin.Pub. Enterprises	32c	53.29	74.40	80.81	90.32	90.96	89.15	74.16	119.52	145.57	196.32	216.75	266.40
Claims on Private Sector	32d	171.30	192.16	246.36	323.72	320.51	425.28	519.25	583.79	589.15	679.48	817.30	902.91
Money	34	259.40	354.02	408.70	450.84	512.53	612.44	689.36	805.49	908.80	1,099.44	1,234.91	1,341.24
Quasi-Money	35	155.49	209.41	233.30	315.37	402.46	512.42	588.01	703.62	739.40	961.11	1,193.75	1,356.47
Liabs. of Central Bank: Securities	36ac	—	—	—	—	—	—	—	.02	.02	12.21	.01	—
Restricted Deposits	36b	10.55	9.33	10.45	9.96	13.43	26.58	123.49	125.60	133.22	151.19	169.04	155.92
Central Government Lending Funds	36f	14.52	18.81	15.39	7.99	11.17	10.98	17.03	54.62	52.97	40.23	101.77	128.91
Capital Accounts	37a	99.16	56.48	106.77	214.14	361.79	578.66	665.03	697.77	614.10	833.07	973.94	933.11
Other Items (Net)	37r	−175.11	−177.86	−362.97	−430.65	−474.22	−516.63	−635.52	−47.73	86.82	24.96	135.80	155.73
Money plus Quasi-Money	35l	414.89	563.43	642.00	766.21	914.99	1,124.86	1,277.37	1,509.11	1,648.20	2,060.55	2,428.66	2,697.71
Interest Rates						*Percent Per Annum*							
Bank Rate (End of Period)	60	24.00	15.00	13.30	15.85	14.08	9.10	15.75	18.86	8.88	13.08	25.62	16.15
Treasury Bill Rate	60c	† 21.30	12.52	8.75	11.71	10.59	7.77	7.43	13.19	11.00	5.85	16.87	9.02
Savings Rate	60k	12.28	5.95	2.76	3.18	3.76	4.14	3.95	3.99	3.72	1.81	2.38	2.03
Deposit Rate	60l	16.26	9.99	7.61	10.62	11.84	11.36	8.73	9.84	8.47	5.56	9.85	7.74
Lending Rate	60p	....	....	20.16	20.29	21.37	20.86	21.55	22.92	22.66	19.10	18.94	20.60
Prices						*Index Numbers (2000=100): Period Averages*							
Consumer Prices	64	66.9	73.5	79.8	85.5	91.5	91.4	† 97.3	100.0	102.0	101.7	109.6	113.3
Intl. Transactions & Positions						*Millions of Shillings*							
Exports	70	213,846	393,960	446,086	613,598	594,804	624,509	748,862	759,273	802,296	795,511	1,102,401	1,604,597
Imports, c.i.f. (Cash Basis)	71	732,340	850,411	1,024,317	1,247,379	1,425,904	1,753,335	1,955,849	2,486,275	2,798,212	1,998,152	2,456,629	3,646,108

		1993	1994	1995	1996	1997	1998	1999	2000	2001	2002	2003	2004
Balance of Payments		*Millions of US Dollars: Minus Sign Indicates Debit*											
Current Account, n.i.e.	78ald	−224.3	−207.5	−338.9	−252.3	−366.8	−502.6	−710.7	−825.4	−367.6	−410.9	−388.8	−253.9
Goods: Exports f.o.b.	78aad	200.0	463.0	560.3	639.3	592.6	510.2	483.5	449.9	475.6	480.7	563.0	705.3
Goods: Imports f.o.b.	78abd	−478.3	−714.2	−926.8	−986.9	−1,042.6	−1,166.3	−989.1	−949.7	−975.4	−1,053.3	−1,241.6	−1,460.3
Trade Balance	78acd	−278.3	−251.2	−366.5	−347.6	−449.9	−656.1	−505.6	−499.8	−499.9	−572.6	−678.6	−755.0
Services: Credit	78add	93.6	64.1	104.0	144.7	164.6	176.3	196.0	213.2	222.6	232.8	294.4	447.1
Services: Debit	78aed	−293.1	−436.3	−562.7	−674.6	−668.9	−728.1	−419.2	−458.8	−503.7	−540.3	−525.3	−699.0
Balance on Goods & Services	78afd	−477.8	−623.4	−825.2	−877.5	−954.2	−1,208.0	−728.8	−745.4	−781.0	−880.1	−909.5	−1,006.9
Income: Credit	78agd	6.4	13.8	17.7	29.7	40.5	50.7	35.1	53.1	37.5	24.2	27.6	35.7
Income: Debit	78ahd	−65.3	−71.0	−113.3	−79.2	−55.7	−59.9	−162.5	−165.5	−202.7	−186.9	−200.6	−225.1
Balance on Gds, Serv. & Inc.	78aid	−536.7	−680.6	−920.8	−927.0	−969.4	−1,217.2	−856.2	−857.8	−946.2	−1,042.8	−1,082.5	−1,196.4
Current Transfers, n.i.e.: Credit	78ajd	312.4	473.1	581.9	674.7	602.6	714.6	329.7	340.0	882.8	955.8	910.1	1,124.4
Current Transfers: Debit	78akd	—	—	—	—	—	—	−184.2	−307.6	−304.2	−323.9	−216.3	−181.9
Capital Account, n.i.e.	78bcd	42.4	36.1	48.3	61.4	31.9	49.5	—	—	—	—	—	—
Capital Account, n.i.e.: Credit	78bad	42.4	36.1	48.3	61.4	31.9	49.5	—	—	—	—	—	—
Capital Account: Debit	78bbd	—	—	—	—	—	—	—	—	—	—	—	—
Financial Account, n.i.e.	78bjd	56.6	76.8	210.7	140.5	298.8	372.8	253.3	320.5	441.7	234.4	432.8	380.2
Direct Investment Abroad	78bdd	—	—	—	—	—	—	—	—	—	—	—	—
Dir. Invest. in Rep. Econ., n.i.e.	78bed	54.6	88.2	121.2	121.0	175.0	210.0	140.2	160.7	151.5	202.9	210.5	237.2
Portfolio Investment Assets	78bfd	—	—	—	—	—	—	—	—	—	—	—	—
Equity Securities	78bkd	—	—	—	—	—	—	—	—	—	—	—	—
Debt Securities	78bld	—	—	—	—	—	—	—	—	—	—	—	—
Portfolio Investment Liab., n.i.e.	78bgd	—	—	—	—	—	—	—	—	.4	.4	20.8	−16.9
Equity Securities	78bmd	—	—	—	—	—	—	—	—	.4	.4	.5	.6
Debt Securities	78bnd	—	—	—	—	—	—	—	—	—	—	20.3	−17.5
Financial Derivatives Assets	78bwd	....	....	....	....	....	....	....	....	....	....	....	....
Financial Derivatives Liabilities	78bxd	....	....	....	....	....	....	....	....	....	....	....	....
Other Investment Assets	78bhd	−5.0	−40.3	−9.9	−37.2	−14.0	5.3	−8.2	−.9	29.4	−17.9	−68.1	12.7
Monetary Authorities	78bod	....	....	....	....	....	....	....	....	—	—	22.9	11.8
General Government	78bpd	—	—	—	—	—	—	—	—	—	5.3	−12.0	−12.3
Banks	78bqd	−8.7	−53.0	12.7	−10.1	−18.2	−29.4	−9.6	−65.8	17.0	8.5	−109.7	−3.8
Other Sectors	78brd	3.7	12.7	−22.6	−27.1	4.2	34.7	1.4	64.9	12.4	−31.8	30.7	17.0
Other Investment Liab., n.i.e.	78bid	7.0	28.9	99.4	56.7	137.9	157.5	121.3	160.7	260.4	49.0	269.5	147.2
Monetary Authorities	78bsd	2.2	.9	1.7	1.1	.2	—	—	—	—	—	—	—
General Government	78btd	56.3	50.8	111.7	114.4	158.2	178.2	131.1	154.9	284.0	55.7	268.5	158.9
Banks	78bud	—	—	—	—	—	—	—	—	−6.7	9.0	2.2	−17.1
Other Sectors	78bvd	−51.5	−22.8	−14.0	−58.8	−20.5	−20.7	−9.8	5.8	−16.9	−15.7	−1.1	5.5
Net Errors and Omissions	78cad	−.1	32.5	28.8	41.3	−4.8	39.7	2.0	40.6	17.0	22.7	−9.8	−3.7
Overall Balance	78cbd	−125.4	−62.1	−51.2	−9.1	−40.9	−40.6	−455.4	−464.3	91.0	−153.8	34.2	122.5
Reserves and Related Items	79dad	125.4	62.1	51.2	9.1	40.9	40.6	455.4	464.3	−91.0	153.8	−34.2	−122.5
Reserve Assets	79dbd	−49.4	−166.9	−140.7	−68.9	−105.2	−91.7	−37.8	−45.1	−160.0	100.4	−77.1	−162.0
Use of Fund Credit and Loans	79dcd	−9.8	27.1	27.5	13.3	2.5	−12.2	−16.0	−37.4	−29.6	−39.4	−42.6	−52.7
Exceptional Financing	79ded	184.7	201.9	164.3	64.8	143.6	144.4	509.2	546.8	98.7	92.8	85.5	92.2
International Investment Position		*Millions of US Dollars*											
Assets	79aad	....	....	....	....	....	....	—	—	—	....	1,443.0	....
Direct Investment Abroad	79abd	....	....	....	....	....	....	—	—	—	—	—	....
Portfolio Investment	79acd	....	....	....	....	....	....	—	—	—	—	—	....
Equity Securities	79add	....	....	....	....	....	....	—	—	—	—	—	....
Debt Securities	79aed	....	....	....	....	....	....	—	—	—	—	—	....
Financial Derivatives	79ald	....	....	....	....	....	....	—	—	—	—	—	....
Other Investment	79afd	....	....	....	....	....	....	199.8	265.6	248.6	240.1	362.7	....
Monetary Authorities	79agd	....	....	....	....	....	....	—	—	—	—	—	....
General Government	79ahd	....	....	....	....	....	....	—	—	—	—	—	....
Banks	79aid	....	....	....	....	....	....	199.8	265.6	248.6	240.1	362.7	....
Other Sectors	79ajd	....	....	....	....	....	....	—	—	—	—	—	....
Reserve Assets	79akd	....	....	....	....	....	....	763.1	808.1	983.3	934.0	1,080.3	....
Liabilities	79lad	....	....	....	....	....	....	....	....	....	....	6,063.1	....
Dir. Invest. in Rep. Economy	79lbd	....	....	....	....	....	....	666.9	807.1	962.3	1,148.9	1,343.1	....
Portfolio Investment	79lcd	....	....	....	....	....	....	—	—	—	—	22.4	....
Equity Securities	79ldd	....	....	....	....	....	....	—	—	—	—	—	....
Debt Securities	79led	....	....	....	....	....	....	—	—	—	—	22.4	....
Financial Derivatives	79lld	....	....	....	....	....	....	....	....	....	....	....	....
Other Investment	79lfd	....	....	....	....	....	....	4,106.6	3,587.5	3,821.2	4,126.1	4,697.5	....
Monetary Authorities	79lgd	....	....	....	....	....	....	371.7	316.1	275.4	256.8	236.0	....
General Government	79lhd	....	....	....	....	....	....	3,580.0	3,088.7	3,378.9	3,686.5	4,250.5	....
Banks	79lid	....	....	....	....	....	....	37.3	58.5	51.7	60.7	79.0	....
Other Sectors	79ljd	....	....	....	....	....	....	117.7	124.2	115.2	122.0	132.2	....
Government Finance		*Millions of Shillings: Year Ending June 30*											
Deficit (-) or Surplus	80	−113,513	−169,806	−131,554	−112,872	−120,191f	−49,043	−109,033	−640,250	−218,703	−473,266	−462,636	....
Revenue	81	291,075	399,152	531,194	622,790	744,344f	794,052	961,993	1,074,065	1,083,486	1,253,748	1,433,928	....
Grants Received	81z	313,754	282,487	253,876	325,023	351,091f	397,552	406,936	586,045	798,917	761,046	819,145	....
Expenditure	82	717,142	848,645	905,277	1,057,885	1,213,626f	1,237,646	1,475,643	1,817,223	2,127,236	2,483,210	2,728,226	....
Lending Minus Repayments	83	1,200	2,800	11,347	2,800	2,000f	3,000	2,319	483,137	−26,131	4,850	−12,518	....
Financing													
Total Financing	84	113,513	169,806	131,554	112,872	120,191f	49,043	109,034	640,250	218,703	473,266	462,636	....
Net Borrowing: Domestic	84a	−23,826	−26,962	−86,701	−60,262	−51,990f	−87,500	−16,749	539,885	65,920	24,946	8,658	....
Net borrowing: Foreign	85a	200,816	243,227	211,719	209,432	231,400f	254,936	218,739	193,407	323,437	484,721	545,978	....
Use of Cash Balances	87	−72,868	−51,017	−22,182	−34,200	−30,001f	−67,117	−146,123	−67,593	−186,878	−164,915	−90,848	....
Adj. to Total Financing	84x	9,391	4,558	28,718	−2,098	−29,218f	−51,276	53,167	−25,449	16,225	128,514	−1,153	....
Debt													
Domestic	88a	....	....	....	....	....	143,248	214,480	325,442	503,462	857,474	1,148,222	....
Debt: Foreign	89a	3,162,800	2,908,300	3,271,300	3,721,500	3,907,200	4,469,957	3,494,400	3,592,340	5,994,951	6,803,726	8,415,346	....

Uganda 746

National Accounts		1993	1994	1995	1996	1997	1998	1999	2000	2001	2002	2003	2004
						Billions of Shillings							
Househ.Cons.Expend.,incl.NPISHs....	96f	3,521.4	4,416.9	5,204.6	5,881.5	5,724.2	6,169.0	6,932.9	7,603.2	8,172.2	8,644.5	10,040.3	....
Government Consumption Expend...	91f	424.9	476.6	577.2	742.3	935.0	1,033.2	1,164.3	1,289.2	1,447.9	1,614.1	1,716.5	....
Gross Fixed Capital Formation..........	93e	639.3	762.4	1,008.8	1,101.3	1,177.4	1,434.0	1,728.7	1,745.2	1,960.4	2,183.0	2,734.7	....
Changes in Inventories....................	93i	3.1	−27.1	−5.2	−7.5	21.3	30.9	15.8	40.9	38.1	40.9	51.6	....
Exports of Goods and Services..........	90c	310.3	554.6	659.8	893.4	804.0	875.6	1,005.1	1,009.8	1,210.4	1,259.5	1,645.9	....
Imports of Goods and Services (-).....	98c	797.1	1,143.8	1,349.6	1,808.4	1,379.1	1,783.8	2,004.5	2,224.7	2,596.7	2,863.6	3,464.8	....
Gross Domestic Product (GDP)........	99b	3,875.6	5,059.5	5,855.5	6,406.1	7,146.3	7,861.2	8,754.2	9,428.8	10,154.5	10,812.4	12,637.5	....
GDP Volume 1997/1998 Prices........	99b.p	5,354.9	5,922.9	6,475.7	6,875.7	7,246.7	7,951.1	8,470.5	8,840.5	9,410.5	9,855.9	10,472.4	....
GDP Volume (2000=100)................	99bvp	60.6	67.0	73.3	77.8	82.0	89.9	95.8	100.0	106.4	111.5	118.5	....
GDP Deflator (2000=100)................	99bip	67.9	80.1	84.8	87.4	92.5	92.7	96.9	100.0	101.2	102.9	113.1	....
						Millions: Midyear Estimates							
Population................................	99z	19.63	20.26	20.89	21.53	22.18	22.85	23.56	24.31	25.11	25.96	26.87	27.82

		1993	1994	1995	1996	1997	1998	1999	2000	2001	2002	2003	2004
Exchange Rates							*Hryvnias per SDR: End of Period*						
Official Rate	aa	.1732	1.5212	2.6668	† 2.7163	2.5622	4.8253	7.1594	7.0807	6.6588	7.2495	7.9224	8.2393
						Hryvnias per US Dollar: End of Period (ae) Period Average (rf)							
Official Rate	ae	.1261	1.0420	1.7940	† 1.8890	1.8990	3.4270	5.2163	5.4345	5.2985	5.3324	5.3315	5.3054
Official Rate	rf	.0453	.3275	1.4731	† 1.8295	1.8617	2.4495	4.1304	5.4402	5.3722	5.3266	5.3327	5.3192
					Index Numbers (2000=100): Period Averages								
Nominal Effective Exchange Rate	nec	957.55	161.41	85.81	75.68	86.35	92.07	117.15	100.00	105.07	110.83	106.20	99.97
Real Effective Exchange Rate	rec	49.78	70.54	84.36	99.36	112.48	109.74	106.77	100.00	100.39	95.15	86.65	81.70
Fund Position							*Millions of SDRs: End of Period*						
Quota	2f.s	997.30	997.30	997.30	997.30	997.30	997.30	1,372.00	1,372.00	1,372.00	1,372.00	1,372.00	1,372.00
SDRs	1b.s	—	123.73	97.06	46.72	52.70	129.53	47.86	191.19	199.80	20.81	14.27	.75
Reserve Position in the Fund	1c.s	.01	.01	—	—	.01	.01	—	—	—	—	—	—
Total Fund Cred.&Loans Outstg.	2tl	—	249.33	1,037.30	1,573.30	1,780.56	1,985.05	2,044.62	1,591.19	1,520.74	1,379.99	1,235.48	1,033.68
International Liquidity					*Millions of US Dollars Unless Otherwise Indicated: End of Period*								
Total Reserves minus Gold	1l.d	161.6	650.7	1,050.6	1,960.0	2,341.1	761.3	1,046.4	1,352.7	2,955.3	4,241.4	6,730.7	9,302.4
SDRs	1b.d	—	180.6	144.3	67.2	71.1	182.4	65.7	249.1	251.1	28.3	21.2	1.2
Reserve Position in the Fund	1c.d	—	—	—	—	—	—	—	—	—	—	—	—
Foreign Exchange	1d.d	161.6	470.1	906.3	1,892.8	2,270.0	578.9	980.7	1,103.6	2,704.3	4,213.1	6,709.5	9,301.3
Gold (Million Fine Troy Ounces)	1ad	.0115	.0360	.0470	.0316	.0613	.1100	.1624	.4536	.4831	.5037	.4969	.5109
Gold (National Valuation)	1and	4.4	13.7	18.3	11.6	17.7	31.6	47.2	123.7	134.1	175.4	206.5	222.3
Monetary Authorities:Other Assets	3..d	88.1	4.3	2.5	2.3	—	235.9	104.9	177.4	90.3	109.2	137.5	433.2
Other Liab.	4..d	279.9	7.3	22.1	36.6	67.6	175.6	172.4	122.4	92.2	78.9	93.0	99.4
Deposit Money Banks: Assets	7a.d	1,264.5	1,406.3	1,044.3	942.1	963.1	906.8	849.2	921.5	774.7	851.6	1,357.9	2,302.2
Liabilities	7b.d	570.4	724.8	302.0	334.4	949.9	507.2	338.7	462.6	650.9	807.8	1,718.8	2,589.9
Monetary Authorities							*Millions of Hryvnias: End of Period*						
Foreign Assets	11	32.0	696.8	2,027.1	3,729.0	4,479.4	† 3,525.4	6,251.8	8,987.5	16,847.8	24,134.4	37,718.8	52,831.0
Claims on General Government	12a	131.2	1,410.7	4,393.1	6,211.3	7,430.1	† 15,075.2	19,712.8	20,854.0	19,898.4	19,634.2	18,548.2	16,720.4
Claims on Nonfin.Pub.Enterprises	12c	.5	4.8	—	—	—	† —	—	—	—	—	—	—
Claims on Private Sector	12d	.2	.3	.1	1.2	35.0	† 104.8	154.0	178.7	178.9	186.7	190.0	200.9
Claims on Banks	12e	147.7	336.3	665.2	859.6	1,555.0	† 1,365.1	1,687.8	1,600.7	1,552.7	1,755.7	2,497.3	4,185.7
Reserve Money	14	301.2	1,528.2	3,557.1	4,974.9	7,410.5	† 8,639.6	12,209.2	17,561.4	25,033.7	30,990.3	40,303.7	55,337.7
of which: Currency Outside Banks	14a	127.7	793.1	2,623.3	4,040.6	6,132.3	† 7,157.3	9,583.3	12,799.0	19,464.8	26,433.8	33,119.3	42,344.9
Time, Savings,& Fgn.Currency Dep.	15	2.5	2.1	3.1	158.4	21.8	† 31.1	23.1	57.1	110.3	205.6	76.9	102.9
Foreign Liabilities	16c	35.3	386.9	2,805.9	4,342.8	4,690.6	† 10,180.1	15,537.6	11,932.1	10,614.6	10,425.1	10,283.9	9,044.4
General Government Deposits	16d	18.6	166.7	97.7	216.0	334.0	† 455.1	592.1	915.0	1,380.3	2,185.6	4,973.2	5,262.5
Capital Accounts	17a	12.2	75.8	231.3	420.8	914.5	† 2,230.7	1,185.4	2,691.9	3,238.8	3,640.8	5,665.5	8,123.6
Other Items (Net)	17r	−58.1	289.2	390.3	688.1	128.0	† −1,466.1	−1,741.0	−1,536.6	−1,900.1	−1,736.3	−2,348.9	−3,933.1
Banking Institutions							*Millions of Hryvnias: End of Period*						
Reserves	20	182.4	762.9	960.3	848.6	925.5	† 1,454.6	2,613.3	4,749.6	5,538.9	4,515.8	7,125.8	11,771.1
Foreign Assets	21	159.5	1,465.3	1,873.4	1,779.7	1,829.0	† 3,107.6	4,429.7	5,007.8	4,104.5	4,540.9	7,239.4	12,214.3
Claims on General Government	22a	17.1	—	207.6	774.5	1,815.4	† 1,530.5	1,133.3	804.5	1,412.7	2,577.2	2,620.2	2,763.2
Claims on Nonfin.Pub.Enterprises	22c	389.5	1,426.7	3,662.8	4,932.0	5,549.0	† 1,440.9	1,782.4	1,916.1	2,876.7	3,688.9	5,654.7	6,287.1
Claims on Private Sector	22d	20.9	556.5	804.2	1,128.2	2,259.1	† 7,922.1	11,046.0	18,816.3	26,430.0	39,614.8	64,894.3	86,046.8
Claims on Nonbank Financial Insts.	22g	—	—	4.1	5.5	—	† 129.4	153.5	219.0	198.4	222.0	686.2	1,148.6
Demand Deposits	24	213.6	1,061.9	2,041.9	2,253.9	2,887.3	† 3,205.0	4,568.9	8,013.5	10,301.5	13,806.8	19,968.3	25,765.4
Time, Savings,& Fgn.Currency Dep.	25	137.1	1,353.7	2,244.9	2,890.6	3,468.6	† 5,139.1	7,683.9	10,725.0	15,279.8	23,834.8	41,256.5	57,193.9
of which: Fgn. Currency Deposits	25b	87.6	1,019.5	1,576.8	1,562.0	1,641.6	† 3,265.4	5,357.6	7,187.9	8,281.2	12,078.6	19,571.0	30,200.3
Bonds	26ab	—	—	—	—	—	† 220.2	305.0	642.0	569.4	548.4	580.4	221.6
Foreign Liabilities	26c	71.9	755.2	541.8	631.6	1,803.8	† 1,738.2	1,766.6	2,514.0	3,448.9	4,307.8	9,163.6	13,740.6
General Government Deposits	26d	87.0	323.7	514.4	795.5	805.0	† 544.2	487.7	1,358.8	1,541.1	1,752.5	1,115.3	1,638.0
Credit from Monetary Authorities	26g	158.2	169.4	632.0	699.7	979.8	† 1,237.2	1,569.4	1,604.9	1,125.8	1,305.5	2,377.3	4,067.2
Capital Accounts	27a	66.1	396.9	1,406.2	3,018.1	4,261.4	† 5,462.2	7,497.7	9,182.9	11,044.4	13,859.2	18,169.2	25,547.5
Other Items (Net)	27r	35.3	150.7	131.1	−820.9	−1,827.9	† −1,961.1	−2,721.1	−2,527.8	−2,749.6	−4,255.4	−4,409.9	−7,943.1
Banking Survey							*Millions of Hryvnias: End of Period*						
Foreign Assets (Net)	31n	84.3	1,020.0	552.8	534.3	−186.0	† −5,285.3	−6,622.6	−450.7	6,888.8	13,942.4	25,510.7	42,260.4
Domestic Credit	32	453.7	2,908.6	8,459.8	12,041.1	15,949.6	† 25,203.5	32,902.1	40,514.8	48,073.7	61,985.7	86,505.2	106,266.4
Claims on General Govt. (Net)	32an	42.6	920.3	3,988.6	5,974.2	8,106.5	† 15,606.3	19,766.2	19,384.7	18,389.7	18,273.3	15,079.9	12,583.1
Claims on Nonfin.Pub.Enterprises	32c	390.0	1,431.5	3,662.8	4,932.0	5,549.0	† 1,440.9	1,782.4	1,916.1	2,876.7	3,688.9	5,654.7	6,287.1
Claims on Private Sector	32d	21.1	556.7	804.3	1,129.4	2,294.1	† 8,026.8	11,200.0	18,995.0	26,608.9	39,801.6	65,084.3	86,247.7
Claims on Nonbank Financial Inst.	32g	—	—	4.1	5.5	—	† 129.4	153.5	219.0	198.4	222.0	686.2	1,148.6
Money	34	341.9	1,860.0	4,681.9	6,315.5	9,050.4	† 10,386.0	14,161.8	20,825.3	29,795.6	40,281.1	53,129.4	68,186.6
Quasi-Money	35	139.5	1,355.7	2,248.1	3,048.9	3,490.4	† 5,170.2	7,707.0	10,782.1	15,390.2	24,040.4	41,333.4	57,296.7
Bonds	36ab	—	—	—	—	—	† 220.2	305.0	642.0	569.4	548.4	580.4	221.6
Capital Accounts	37a	78.4	472.7	1,637.5	3,438.9	5,176.0	† 7,692.8	8,683.1	11,874.8	14,283.2	17,500.0	23,834.8	33,671.1
Other Items (Net)	37r	−21.9	240.1	445.1	−228.0	−1,953.1	† −3,551.1	−4,577.4	−4,060.2	−5,075.9	−6,441.8	−6,862.1	−10,849.1
Money plus Quasi-Money	35l	481.5	3,215.7	6,930.0	9,364.4	12,540.8	† 15,556.2	21,868.8	31,607.4	45,185.8	64,321.5	94,462.9	125,483.3
Money (National Definitions)							*Millions of Hryvnias: End of Period*						
Reserve Money	19mb	....	....	....	....	....	8,625.0	11,987.8	16,777.3	23,055.0	30,808.0	40,089.4	53,763.2
M0	19mc	128.0	793.0	2,623.0	4,041.0	6,132.0	7,158.0	9,583.0	12,799.0	19,465.0	26,434.0	33,119.0	42,344.9
M1	59ma	334.0	1,860.0	4,682.0	6,315.0	9,050.0	10,331.0	14,094.0	20,762.0	29,796.0	40,281.0	53,129.0	67,090.3
M2	59mb	482.0	3,216.0	6,846.0	9,024.0	12,448.0	15,432.0	21,714.0	31,544.0	45,186.0	64,321.0	94,855.0	125,483.3
M3	59mc	....	....	6,930.0	9,364.0	12,541.0	15,718.0	22,070.0	32,252.0	45,755.0	64,870.0	95,043.0	125,704.9
Interest Rates							*Percent Per Annum*						
Refinancing Rate (End of Period)	60	240.00	252.00	110.00	40.00	35.00	60.00	45.00	27.00	12.50	7.00	7.00	9.00
Money Market Rate	60b	....	....	....	....	22.05	40.41	44.98	18.34	16.57	5.50	7.90	6.34
Money Market Rate (Fgn. Cur.)	60b.f	....	....	....	....	....	10.61	5.44	6.27	5.87	3.14	3.61	2.15
Deposit Rate	60l	148.63	208.63	70.29	33.63	18.21	22.25	20.70	13.72	10.99	7.93	6.98	7.80
Deposit Rate (Foreign Currency)	60l.f	....	....	....	....	....	10.70	9.68	6.10	5.60	6.09	5.94	6.27
Lending Rate	60p	184.25	250.28	122.70	79.88	49.12	54.50	54.95	41.53	32.28	25.35	17.89	17.40
Lending Rate (Foreign Currency)	60p.f	....	....	....	....	....	19.98	20.62	17.42	13.51	11.98	11.95	12.29

		1993	1994	1995	1996	1997	1998	1999	2000	2001	2002	2003	2004
Prices and Labor					*Percent Change over Previous Period*								
Wholesale Prices	63.xx	4,619.3	1,143.8	487.9	51.9	7.7	13.2	31.1	20.9	8.6	3.1	7.8	20.4
Consumer Prices	64.xx	4,734.9	891.2	376.7	80.3	15.9	10.6	22.7	28.2	12.0	.8	5.2	9.0
Wages: Average Earnings	65.xx	2,331.9	786.6	† 434.2						....	....	....	....
				Index Numbers (2000=100): Period Averages									
Industrial Employment	67	174.5	159.0	146.2	134.7	124.0	120.2	114.1	100.0	94.2	103.9	99.2	98.7
				Number in Thousands: Period Averages									
Labor Force	67d	....	....	25,562			25,936	22,747	23,127	22,755	22,702	22,614	....
Employment	67e	....	....	24,125	24,114	23,756	22,998	20,048	20,420	20,238	20,401	20,555	....
Unemployment	67c	....	....	1,437	1,998	2,330	2,937	2,699	2,708	2,517	2,301	2,008	....
Unemployment Rate (%)	67r	....	....	5.6	7.6	8.9	11.3	11.9	11.7	11.1	10.2	9.1	....
Intl. Transactions & Positions					*Millions of US Dollars*								
Exports	70..d	7,817	10,305	13,128	14,401	14,232	12,637	11,582	14,573	16,265	17,957	23,080	32,672
Imports, c.i.f	71..d	9,533	10,748	15,484	17,603	17,128	14,676	11,846	13,956	15,775	16,977	23,021	28,996
Imports, f.o.b	71.vd	9,533	10,589	....	....	....	....	....	....	....	....	....	....
Balance of Payments					*Millions of US Dollars: Minus Sign Indicates Debit*								
Current Account, n.i.e	78ald	....	−1,163	−1,152	−1,184	−1,335	−1,296	1,658	1,481	1,402	3,174	2,891	6,804
Goods: Exports f.o.b	78aad		13,894	14,244	15,547	15,418	13,699	13,189	15,722	17,091	18,669	23,739	33,432
Goods: Imports f.o.b	78abd	....	−16,469	−16,946	−19,843	−19,623	−16,283	−12,945	−14,943	−16,893	−17,959	−23,221	−29,691
Trade Balance	78acd	....	−2,575	−2,702	−4,296	−4,205	−2,584	244	779	198	710	518	3,741
Services: Credit	78add	....	2,747	2,846	4,799	4,937	3,922	3,869	3,800	3,995	4,682	5,214	6,287
Services: Debit	78aed	....	−1,538	−1,334	−1,625	−2,268	−2,545	−2,292	−3,004	−3,580	−3,535	−4,444	−5,155
Balance on Goods & Services	78afd	....	−1,366	−1,190	−1,122	−1,536	−1,207	1,821	1,575	613	1,857	1,288	4,873
Income: Credit	78agd	....	56	247	102	158	122	98	143	167	165	254	389
Income: Debit	78ahd	....	−400	−681	−673	−802	−993	−967	−1,085	−834	−769	−835	−1,034
Balance on Gds, Serv. & Inc	78aid	....	−1,710	−1,624	−1,693	−2,180	−2,078	952	633	−54	1,253	707	4,228
Current Transfers, n.i.e.: Credit	78ajd	....	583	557	619	942	868	754	967	1,516	1,967	2,270	2,671
Current Transfers: Debit	78akd	....	−36	−85	−110	−97	−86	−48	−119	−60	−46	−86	−95
Capital Account, n.i.e	78bcd	....	97	6	5	—	−3	−10	−8	3	17	−17	7
Capital Account, n.i.e.: Credit	78bad	....	106	6	5	—	—	—	—	8	28	11	21
Capital Account: Debit	78bbd	....	−9	—	—	—	−3	−10	−8	−5	−11	−28	−14
Financial Account, n.i.e	78bjd	....	−557	−726	317	1,413	−1,340	−879	−752	−191	−1,065	264	−4,234
Direct Investment Abroad	78bdd	....	−8	−10	5	−42	4	−7	−1	−23	5	−13	−4
Dir. Invest. in Rep. Econ., n.i.e	78bed	....	159	267	521	623	743	496	595	792	693	1,424	1,715
Portfolio Investment Assets	78bfd	....	—	−12	−1	−2	−2	−11	−4	1	2	1	−6
Equity Securities	78bkd	....	....	....	−11	−14	−3	−5	−2	−1	....	−4	−6
Debt Securities	78bld	....	....	−12	10	12	1	−6	−2	2	2	5	—
Portfolio Investment Liab., n.i.e	78bgd	....	—	16	199	1,605	−1,379	−75	−197	−867	−1,718	−923	−70
Equity Securities	78bmd	....	....	....	46	248	227	129	−193	−734	−1,958	−1,705	−2,204
Debt Securities	78bnd	....	—	16	153	1,357	−1,606	−204	−4	−133	240	782	2,134
Financial Derivatives Assets	78bwd	....	....	....	....	....	....	....	....	....	....	....	....
Financial Derivatives Liabilities	78bxd	....	....	....	....	....	....	....	....	....	....	....	....
Other Investment Assets	78bhd	....	−3,026	−1,574	−821	−1,583	−1,321	−2,264	−449	−1,015	−781	−940	−10,065
Monetary Authorities	78bod	....	....	....	....	....	....	....	−15	1	−23	−30	−266
General Government	78bpd	....	....	....	....	....	....	....	1,002	....	—	—	—
Banks	78bqd	....	−779	−328	83	−536	−46	51	−64	137	−86	−455	−906
Other Sectors	78brd	....	−2,247	−1,246	−904	−1,047	−1,275	−2,315	−1,372	−1,153	−672	−455	−8,893
Other Investment Liab., n.i.e	78bid	....	2,318	587	414	812	615	982	−696	921	734	715	4,196
Monetary Authorities	78bsd	....	—	—	—	—	—	—	—	—	−4	16	7
General Government	78btd	....	−1,097	−783	−477	−267	−857	−231	−1,457	−537	−384	−379	922
Banks	78bud	....	577	724	565	−51	−264	−16	113	180	76	779	579
Other Sectors	78bvd	....	2,838	646	326	1,130	1,736	1,229	648	1,278	1,046	299	2,688
Net Errors and Omissions	78cad	....	423	248	259	−781	−818	−953	−148	−221	−895	−965	−54
Overall Balance	78cbd	....	−1,200	−1,624	−603	−703	−3,457	−184	573	993	1,231	2,173	2,523
Reserves and Related Items	79dad	....	1,200	1,624	603	703	3,457	184	−573	−993	−1,231	−2,173	−2,523
Reserve Assets	79dbd	....	−549	−469	−894	−385	1,328	−281	−401	−1,609	−1,047	−2,045	−2,226
Use of Fund Credit and Loans	79dcd	....	368	1,221	776	283	279	75	−603	−86	−181	−203	−298
Exceptional Financing	79ded	....	1,380	871	721	805	1,850	390	431	702	−2	75	—
International Investment Position					*Millions of US Dollars*								
Assets	79aad	....	....	....	....	....	....	....	....	6,220	7,676	11,037	15,779
Direct Investment Abroad	79abd	....	....	....	....	....	....	....	....	156	144	166	198
Portfolio Investment	79acd	....	....	....	....	....	....	....	....	30	28	26	31
Equity Securities	79add	....	....	....	....	....	....	....	....	20	19	23	28
Debt Securities	79aed	....	....	....	....	....	....	....	....	10	9	3	3
Financial Derivatives	79ald	....	....	....	....	....	....	....	....	—	—	—	—
Other Investment	79afd	....	....	....	....	....	....	....	....	2,945	3,087	3,908	6,025
Monetary Authorities	79agd	....	....	....	....	....	....	....	....	157	197	261	538
General Government	79ahd	....	....	....	....	....	....	....	....	—	—	—	—
Banks	79aid	....	....	....	....	....	....	....	....	731	840	1,355	2,303
Other Sectors	79ajd	....	....	....	....	....	....	....	....	2,057	2,050	2,292	3,184
Reserve Assets	79akd	....	....	....	....	....	....	....	....	3,089	4,417	6,937	9,525
Liabilities	79lad	....	....	....	....	....	....	....	....	25,968	28,003	31,427	40,156
Dir. Invest. in Rep. Economy	79lbd	....	....	....	....	....	....	....	....	4,801	5,924	7,566	9,517
Portfolio Investment	79lcd	....	....	....	....	....	....	....	....	2,980	3,293	4,065	6,354
Equity Securities	79ldd	....	....	....	....	....	....	....	....	763	668	464	549
Debt Securities	79led	....	....	....	....	....	....	....	....	2,217	2,625	3,601	5,805
Financial Derivatives	79lld	....	....	....	....	....	....	....	....	—	—	—	—
Other Investment	79lfd	....	....	....	....	....	....	....	....	18,187	18,786	19,796	24,285
Monetary Authorities	79lgd	....	....	....	....	....	....	....	....	1,972	1,933	1,909	1,685
General Government	79lhd	....	....	....	....	....	....	....	....	5,986	5,762	5,649	6,656
Banks	79lid	....	....	....	....	....	....	....	....	539	859	1,632	2,296
Other Sectors	79ljd	....	....	....	....	....	....	....	....	9,690	10,232	10,606	13,648

		1993	1994	1995	1996	1997	1998	1999	2000	2001	2002	2003	2004
Government Finance							*Millions of Hryvnias: Year Ending December 31*							
Deficit (-) or Surplus........................	80	....	....	....	....	....	....	−2,747	−1,061	−1,800	....	....	....
Total Revenue and Grants..............	81y	....	....	....	....	....	....	31,172	47,062	57,354	....	....	....
Revenue....................................	81	....	....	....	....	....	....	30,858	45,591	54,569	....	....	....
Grants.......................................	81z	....	....	....	....	....	....	314	1,470	2,785	....	....	....
Exp. & Lending Minus Repayments.	82z	....	....	....	....	....	....	33,919	48,123	59,154	....	....	....
Expenditure...............................	82	....	....	....	....	....	....	33,900	48,074	58,974	....	....	....
Lending Minus Repayments..........	83	....	....	....	....	....	....	19	49	181	....	....	....
Financing: Domestic........................	84a	....	....	....	....	....	....	2,829	1,645	1,333	....	....	....
Financing: Foreign..........................	85a	....	....	....	....	....	....	−82	−584	467	....	....	....
National Accounts							*Billions of Hryvnias*							
Househ.Cons.Expend.,incl.NPISHs....	96f	.7	5.8	30.1	58.0	67.1	74.8	91.1	115.9	140.0	151.0	182.6	229.1
Government Consumption Expend...	91f	.2	2.3	11.6	7.1	9.1	8.8	9.4	12.1	16.4	17.9	20.8	23.6
Gross Fixed Capital Formation..........	93e	.4	2.9	12.8	17.0	18.7	20.2	25.3	33.6	40.3	44.8	52.4	68.4
Changes in Inventories...................	93i	.2	1.4	1.8	1.5	1.3	1.1	−2.5	—	4.2	−2.7	.4	−3.6
Exports of Goods and Services..........	90c	.4	4.3	25.7	37.2	37.9	43.0	70.9	106.2	113.2	124.4	154.5	209.9
Imports of Goods and Services (-)....	98c	.4	4.6	27.3	39.3	40.8	45.3	63.7	97.6	109.9	114.5	147.5	76.8
Gross Domestic Product (GDP)........	99b	1.5	12.0	54.5	81.5	93.4	102.6	130.4	170.1	204.2	220.9	263.4	344.4
Net Primary Income from Abroad.....	98.n	—	−.1	−.9	−1.0	−1.2	−2.1	−3.5	−5.1	−3.6	....	....	....
Gross National Income (GNI)............	99a	1.4	12.0	53.6	80.5	92.2	100.5	126.9	164.9	200.6	....	....	....
Net Current Transf.from Abroad.......	98t	—	.1	.7	.9	1.5	2.7	2.9	4.9	8.0	....	....	....
Gross Nat'l Disposable Inc.(GNDI)....	99i	1.4	12.0	54.3	81.4	93.7	103.2	129.8	169.9	208.6	....	....	....
Gross Saving....................................	99s	.5	3.9	12.7	16.3	17.5	19.6	29.4	41.9	52.2	....	....	....
							Millions: Midyear Estimates							
Population................................	99z	51.92	51.78	51.53	51.18	50.73	50.22	49.67	49.12	48.57	48.04	47.51	46.99

United Arab Emirates 466

		1993	1994	1995	1996	1997	1998	1999	2000	2001	2002	2003	2004
Exchange Rates						*Dirhams per SDR: End of Period*							
Official Rate	aa	5.0423	5.3591	5.4569	5.2788	4.9551	5.1710	5.0405	4.7849	4.6153	4.9928	5.4572	5.7034
					Dirhams per US Dollar: End of Period (ae) Period Average (rf)								
Official Rate	ae	3.6710	3.6710	3.6710	3.6710	3.6725	3.6725	3.6725	3.6725	3.6725	3.6725	3.6725	3.6725
Official Rate	rf	3.6710	3.6710	3.6710	3.6710	3.6711	3.6725	3.6725	3.6725	3.6725	3.6725	3.6725	3.6725
					Index Numbers (2000=100): Period Averages								
Official Rate	ahx	100.0	100.0	100.0	100.0	100.0	100.0	100.0	100.0	100.0	100.0	100.0	100.0
Nominal Effective Exchange Rate	nec	85.8	84.3	80.0	83.1	89.9	96.9	95.2	100.0	105.7	103.6	94.4	88.8
Fund Position						*Millions of SDRs: End of Period*							
Quota	2f.s	392.1	392.1	392.1	392.1	392.1	392.1	611.7	611.7	611.7	611.7	611.7	611.7
SDRs	1b.s	54.1	55.0	55.9	57.6	58.4	59.2	4.5	3.1	1.8	1.1	.5	3.5
Reserve Position in the Fund	1c.s	162.8	149.1	185.8	204.4	197.4	233.9	212.6	164.8	179.8	235.8	239.3	203.2
of which: Outstg.Fund Borrowing	2c	—	—	—	—	—	—	—	—	—	—	—	—
International Liquidity					*Millions of US Dollars Unless Otherwise Indicated: End of Period*								
Total Reserves minus Gold	1l.d	6,103.7	6,658.8	7,470.9	8,055.5	8,372.3	9,077.1	10,675.1	13,522.7	14,146.4	15,219.4	15,087.8	18,529.9
SDRs	1b.d	74.4	80.3	83.1	82.8	78.7	83.3	6.2	4.0	2.2	1.5	.7	5.4
Reserve Position in the Fund	1c.d	223.6	217.7	276.2	293.9	266.3	329.3	291.7	214.7	225.9	320.6	355.6	315.5
Foreign Exchange	1d.d	5,805.7	6,360.8	7,111.6	7,678.8	8,027.3	8,664.4	10,377.1	13,303.9	13,918.2	14,897.2	14,731.5	18,209.0
Gold (Million Fine Troy Ounces)	1ad	.798	.795	.795	.798	.795	.795	.397	.397	.397	.397	—	—
Gold (National Valuation)	1and	182.5	181.7	181.7	182.8	181.3	181.3	90.7	90.7	90.7	90.7	—	—
Deposit Money Banks: Assets	7a.d	17,997.8	17,737.4	17,377.8	19,086.9	20,735.7	22,108.9	22,010.3	24,454.7	26,822.6	30,595.0	30,422.6	34,412.8
Liabilities	7b.d	7,221.7	8,997.8	7,653.5	10,053.4	12,351.5	14,446.6	14,577.8	14,133.4	8,137.0	8,136.7	8,248.9	11,542.8
RLB: Foreign Assets	7k.d	118.8	106.0	134.0	134.6	154.7	200.7	265.5	147.9	245.6	15.2	—	—
Foreign Liabilities	7m.d	60.2	35.4	59.1	112.8	101.3	75.4	281.0	138.6	216.5	13.6	—	—
Monetary Authorities						*Millions of Dirhams: End of Period*							
Foreign Assets	11	23,357	25,812	28,408	30,567	31,692	34,512	40,185	50,781	52,479	56,259	55,530	68,568
Claims on Central Government	12a	—	—	—	—	—	—	—	—	—	—	—	—
Claims on Official Entities	12bx	—	—	—	—	—	—	—	—	—	—	—	—
Claims on Deposit Money Banks	12e	50	50	50	50	50	50	50	50	50	50	50	—
Claims on Other Financial Insts	12f	—	—	—	—	—	—	—	—	—	—	—	—
Reserve Money	14	13,124	16,501	18,667	20,188	20,294	20,326	26,530	36,201	38,387	37,652	42,301	54,766
of which: Currency Outside DMBs	14a	5,667	6,031	6,404	6,767	7,366	8,195	10,272	10,017	10,537	11,938	13,785	15,778
Quasi-Monetary Deposits	15	—	—	—	—	—	—	—	—	—	—	—	—
Foreign Liabilities	16c	313	380	175	75	52	11	403	587	516	284	349	548
Central Government Deposits	16d	6,788	7,178	7,930	8,591	9,692	10,692	11,518	12,164	11,722	11,101	11,283	11,578
Capital Accounts	17a	1,695	1,708	1,711	1,704	1,692	1,700	1,755	1,745	1,739	1,753	1,771	1,781
Other Items (Net)	17r	1,486	96	−25	54	12	1,832	29	134	165	5,519	−125	−104
Deposit Money Banks						*Millions of Dirhams: End of Period*							
Reserves	20	7,452	10,465	12,258	13,416	12,923	12,127	16,256	25,893	27,849	25,711	28,515	38,988
Foreign Assets	21	66,070	65,114	63,794	70,068	76,152	81,195	80,833	89,810	98,506	112,360	111,727	126,381
Claims on Central Government	22a	12,334	12,558	12,787	10,394	9,105	12,719	15,725	12,581	11,035	15,650	21,407	31,776
Claims on Official Entities	22bx	2,791	5,869	5,840	5,064	5,511	5,236	5,581	5,780	5,258	7,122	12,990	13,884
Claims on Private Sector	22d	57,691	63,836	71,759	78,927	89,925	102,416	110,276	119,828	130,549	145,592	165,143	204,727
Claims on Other Financial Insts	22f	3,014	2,656	2,526	2,330	2,689	3,443	3,075	3,317	3,415	3,692	4,251	6,612
Demand Deposits	24	12,507	13,152	14,420	15,499	18,002	19,589	19,980	24,050	28,927	35,116	44,477	65,040
Time and Savings Deposits	25	50,241	54,635	60,537	64,676	69,437	71,000	79,847	92,902	116,981	126,592	142,338	167,588
Foreign Liabilities	26c	26,511	33,031	28,096	36,906	45,361	53,055	53,537	51,905	29,883	29,882	30,294	42,391
Central Government Deposits	26d	14,830	12,550	15,156	9,962	6,948	10,920	11,671	18,441	27,382	36,972	40,133	51,786
Central Govt. Lending Funds	26f	243	184	113	95	92	77	62	41	37	28	23	18
Credit from Monetary Authorities	26g	50	51	54	55	50	51	54	52	55	61	101	25
Capital Accounts	27a	17,516	19,563	21,616	23,273	25,435	29,883	31,910	34,226	36,769	40,975	44,455	52,463
Other Items (Net)	27r	27,455	27,331	28,971	29,733	30,980	32,560	34,685	35,592	36,578	40,501	42,212	43,057
Monetary Survey						*Millions of Dirhams: End of Period*							
Foreign Assets (Net)	31n	62,603	57,515	63,931	63,654	62,431	62,641	67,078	88,099	120,586	138,453	136,614	152,010
Domestic Credit	32	54,229	65,207	69,841	78,178	90,607	102,221	111,489	110,925	111,182	124,045	152,450	193,703
Claims on Central Govt. (Net)	32an	−9,284	−7,170	−10,299	−8,159	−7,535	−8,893	−7,464	−18,024	−28,069	−32,423	−30,009	−31,588
Claims on Official Entities	32bx	2,791	5,869	5,840	5,064	5,511	5,236	5,581	5,780	5,258	7,122	12,990	13,884
Claims on Private Sector	32d	57,708	63,852	71,774	78,943	89,942	102,435	110,297	119,852	130,578	145,654	165,218	204,795
Claims on Other Financial Insts	32f	3,014	2,656	2,526	2,330	2,689	3,443	3,075	3,317	3,415	3,692	4,251	6,612
Money	34	18,174	19,183	20,824	22,266	25,368	27,784	30,252	34,067	39,464	47,054	58,262	80,818
Quasi-Money	35	50,241	54,635	60,537	64,676	69,437	71,000	79,847	92,902	116,981	126,592	142,338	167,588
Other Items (Net)	37r	48,417	48,904	52,410	54,885	58,233	66,076	68,468	72,055	75,323	88,852	88,463	97,308
Money plus Quasi-Money	35l	68,415	73,818	81,361	86,942	94,805	98,784	110,099	126,969	156,445	173,646	200,600	248,406
Production						*Index Numbers (2000=100): Period Averages*							
Crude Petroleum	66aa	95.3	94.8	95.5	95.8	97.8	96.3	98.9	100.0	94.4	86.9	87.5	101.9
Intl. Transactions & Positions						*Millions of US Dollars*							
Imports, c.i.f	71..d	19,520	21,024	20,984	22,638	29,952	24,728	33,231	35,009	37,293	42,652	51,955	....
Government Finance						*Millions of Dirhams: Year Ending December 31*							
Deficit (-) or Surplus	80	−323	74	−1,249	620	897	−532	57	....	....	....	....	....
Revenue	81	2,975	3,316	3,876	5,017	5,609	5,938	6,863	....	....	....	....	....
Grants Received	81z	12,273	12,731	12,708	12,555	13,403	13,318	13,371	....	....	....	....	....
Expenditure	82	15,571	15,973	17,833	16,952	18,050	19,170	20,050	....	....	....	....	....
Lending Minus Repayments	83	—	—	—	—	65	618	127	....	....	....	....	....
Financing													
Domestic	84a	323	−73	1,249	−620	−897	532	−57	....	....	....	....	....
Foreign	85a	—	—	—	—	—	—	—	....	....	....	....	....

United Arab Emirates 466

		1993	1994	1995	1996	1997	1998	1999	2000	2001	2002	2003	2004
National Accounts							*Billions of Dirhams*						
Househ.Cons.Expend.,incl.NPISHs....	**96f**	57.7	60.7	69.3	74.4	86.2	90.7	....	....	....	....	....	....
Government Consumption Expend...	**91f**	23.4	24.2	25.4	26.2	28.1	28.6	....	....	....	....	....	....
Gross Fixed Capital Formation..........	**93e**	36.4	37.5	39.8	40.9	48.8	49.2	....	....	....	....	....	....
Changes in Inventories.....................	**93i**	1.9	2.0	2.1	2.3	2.2	2.2	....	....	....	....	....	....
Exports of Goods and Services..........	**90c**	98.4	104.8	109.4	125.8	128.6	115.0	....	....	....	....	....	....
Imports of Goods and Services (-).....	**98c**	87.3	94.6	99.0	105.9	112.7	115.0	....	....	....	....	....	....
Gross Domestic Product (GDP).........	**99b**	130.4	134.6	147.0	163.8	181.2	170.7	....	....	....	....	....	....
							Millions: Midyear Estimates						
Population.................................	**99z**	2.19	2.31	2.43	2.57	2.71	2.86	3.04	3.25	3.49	3.76	4.03	4.28

2005, International Monetary Fund : *International Financial Statistics Yearbook*

		1993	1994	1995	1996	1997	1998	1999	2000	2001	2002	2003	2004
Exchange Rates						*SDRs per Pound: End of Period*							
Market Rate..................................	ac	1.0784	1.0703	1.0427	1.1808	1.2257	1.1814	1.1777	1.1453	1.1541	1.1856	1.2010	1.2436
				US Dollars per Pound: End of Period (ag) Period Average (rh)									
Market Rate..................................	ag	1.4812	1.5625	1.5500	1.6980	1.6538	1.6635	1.6164	1.4922	1.4504	1.6118	1.7847	1.9314
Market Rate..................................	rh	1.5020	1.5316	1.5785	1.5617	1.6377	1.6564	1.6182	1.5161	1.4400	1.5013	1.6344	1.8318
		ECUs per Pound through 1998; Euros per Pound Beginning 1999: End of Period (ec) Period Average (ed)											
Euro Rate....................................	ec	1.3225	1.2705	1.1832	1.3564	1.5011	1.4175	† 1.6090	1.6037	1.6458	1.5370	1.4131	1.4180
Euro Rate....................................	ed	1.2822	1.2897	1.2070	1.2304	1.4452	1.4796	1.6456	1.6092	1.5952	1.4481	1.4753	
						Index Numbers (2000=100): Period Averages							
Market Rate..................................	ahx	99.1	101.0	104.1	103.0	108.0	109.3	106.7	100.0	95.0	99.0	107.8	120.8
Nominal Effective Exchange Rate.....	neu	83.0	83.5	79.9	81.0	93.7	97.1	96.9	100.0	98.3	98.7	93.8	97.6
Real Effective Exchange Rate...........	reu	72.9	74.8	72.8	75.5	89.4	95.0	96.2	100.0	99.5	99.7	94.2	98.7
Fund Position						*Millions of SDRs: End of Period*							
Quota..	2f.s	7,415	7,415	7,415	7,415	7,415	7,415	10,739	10,739	10,739	10,739	10,739	10,739
SDRs...	1b.s	210	335	279	239	350	332	374	250	234	267	255	211
Reserve Position in the Fund...........	1c.s	1,354	1,366	1,630	1,689	2,198	3,111	3,847	3,288	4,020	4,565	4,256	3,562
of which: Outstg.Fund Borrowing...	2c	—	—	—	—	—	382	—	—	—	—	—	—
Total Fund Cred.&Loans Outstg.......	2tl												
International Liquidity					*Billions of US Dollars Unless Otherwise Indicated: End of Period*								
Total Reserves minus Gold...............	1l.d	36.78	41.01	42.02	39.90	32.32	32.21	† 35.87	43.89	37.28	39.36	41.85	45.34
SDRs.......................................	1b.d	.29	.49	.41	.34	.47	.47	.51	.33	.29	.36	.38	.33
Reserve Position in the Fund........	1c.d	1.86	1.99	2.42	2.43	2.97	4.38	5.28	4.28	5.05	6.21	6.32	5.53
Foreign Exchange......................	1d.d	34.63	38.53	39.18	37.12	28.88	27.36	† 30.08	39.28	31.94	32.79	35.15	39.48
Other Liquid Foreign Assets............	1e.d	....	....	....	....	....	....	7.80	8.68	10.52	14.72	16.37	16.09
Gold (Million Fine Troy Ounces).....	1ad	18.45	18.44	18.43	18.43	18.42	23.00	20.55	15.67	11.42	10.09	10.07	10.04
Gold (National Valuation)................	1and	4.56	5.31	5.24	5.48	4.81	5.08	† 5.96	4.27	3.16	3.46	4.20	4.40
Banking Insts: Foreign Assets..........	7a.d	1,053.63	1,200.67	1,350.86	1,460.35	1,685.14	1,868.89	1,802.87	2,060.13	2,168.36	2,477.20	3,023.88	3,643.07
Foreign Liabs...........	7b.d	1,129.07	1,274.82	1,429.20	1,533.44	1,748.76	1,893.68	1,871.05	2,159.79	2,306.08	2,684.27	3,276.02	4,058.53
Monetary Authorities						*Billions of Pounds: End of Period*							
Foreign Assets.............................	11	30.22	28.33	31.89	27.40	22.92	† 6.52	7.98	4.34	6.24	7.92	9.15	9.83
Claims on Central Govt. (Net)..........	12an	14.97	28.53	25.07	29.86	27.63	† 14.45	20.56	14.30	16.07	16.27	15.87	17.30
Claims on Private Sector.................	12d	—	—	—	—	—	—	6.91	5.86	8.41	5.48	8.20	6.40	5.97
Reserve Money.............................	14	25.19	26.53	28.37	29.36	31.45	† 27.37	32.46	32.37	32.58	34.00	36.68	41.80
of which: Currency Outside DMBs..	14a	18.87	19.94	21.21	22.10	23.44	† 19.20	21.20	23.59	25.42	26.72	28.54	30.80
Foreign Liabilities........................	16c	25.99	31.86	31.16	28.36	23.60	† 2.28	9.62	6.28	4.75	7.92	7.49	9.00
Other Items (Net).........................	17r	−5.80	−1.52	−2.57	−.46	−4.49	† −1.77	−7.68	−11.60	−9.54	−9.53	−12.75	−17.71
Banking Institutions						*Billions of Pounds: End of Period*							
Reserves....................................	20	6.78	7.04	7.56	7.71	8.26	8.39	11.54	9.75	8.56	8.92	9.73	13.00
Foreign Assets.............................	21	686.90	741.28	845.36	835.98	1,033.98	1,143.91	1,133.76	1,417.84	1,528.23	1,563.39	1,725.58	1,969.02
Claims on Central Govt. (Net)..........	22an	2.66	11.80	19.72	14.92	10.59	10.74	† 8.17	−8.05	−1.94	8.52	1.18	8.43
Claims on Official Entities................	22bx	5.68	6.11	5.74	4.81	4.34	3.75	2.70	2.52	2.38	3.61	4.77	6.31
Claims on Private Sector.................	22d	706.86	745.43	829.14	911.89	972.88	1,016.75	† 1,094.16	1,254.50	1,368.03	1,479.65	1,624.69	1,808.27
Demand,Time,Savings,Fgn.Cur.Dep..	25l	378.48	407.82	493.35	567.10	716.32	764.84	912.81	1,014.28	1,101.68	1,157.24	1,271.74	1,403.32
Foreign Liabilities........................	26c	711.50	763.74	866.18	843.63	1,050.25	1,120.59	1,128.39	1,411.50	1,547.90	1,621.13	1,783.56	2,049.33
Other Items (Net).........................	27r	113.14	123.87	133.50	146.52	172.05	188.04	209.12	250.78	255.67	285.71	310.65	352.38
Banking Survey						*Billions of Pounds: End of Period*							
Foreign Assets (Net)......................	31n	−20.38	−25.98	−20.09	−8.62	−16.94	† 27.55	3.72	4.40	−18.18	−57.74	−56.32	−79.48
Domestic Credit...........................	32	730.18	791.87	879.67	961.48	1,015.44	† 1,052.60	† 1,131.45	1,271.68	1,390.01	1,516.25	1,652.92	1,846.27
Claims on Central Govt. (Net)........	32an	17.64	40.34	44.79	44.78	38.22	† 25.19	† 28.73	6.26	14.13	24.79	17.05	25.73
Claims on Official Entities............	32bx	5.68	6.11	5.74	4.81	4.34	3.75	2.70	2.52	2.38	3.61	4.77	6.31
Claims on Private Sector..............	32d	706.86	745.43	829.14	911.89	972.88	1,023.66	† 1,100.02	1,262.91	1,373.51	1,487.85	1,631.09	1,814.23
Money Plus Quasi-Money..............	35l	397.34	427.76	514.56	589.20	739.76	† 784.04	934.01	1,037.87	1,127.10	1,183.97	1,300.28	1,434.12
Other Items (Net).........................	37r	106.70	121.90	130.53	145.60	167.31	† 296.10	† 201.17	238.21	244.73	274.54	296.32	332.67
Money (National Definitions)						*Billions of Pounds: End of Period*							
M0..	19mc	21.73	23.32	24.54	26.15	27.80	29.35	32.77	34.57	37.32	39.54	42.32	44.47
M4..	59md	544.06	567.16	623.39	682.79	721.98	783.24	816.55	884.84	942.43	1,008.68	1,081.12	1,178.96
						Millions of Pounds: Period Change							
M0, Seasonally Adjusted................	19mcc	1,163	1,278	1,232	1,554	1,564	1,578	3,259	1,384	2,607	2,132	2,702	2,317
M4, Seasonally Adjusted...........	59mdc	24,001	25,860	55,741	59,909	79,983	60,429	33,640	67,219	58,204	68,009	68,163	....
Interest Rates						*Percent Per Annum*							
Money Market Rate.......................	60b	5.91	4.88	6.08	5.96	6.61	7.21	5.20	5.77	5.08	3.89	3.59	4.29
Treasury Bill Rate.........................	60c	5.21	5.15	6.33	5.78	6.48	6.82	5.04	5.80	4.77	3.86	3.55	4.43
Treas. Bill Rate(Bond Equivalent).....	60cs	5.35	5.18	6.40	5.89	6.62	7.23	5.14	5.83	4.79	3.96	3.55	4.44
Eurodollar Rate in London.............	60d	3.24	4.68	5.97	5.44	5.66	5.50	5.36	6.48	3.73	1.76	1.17	1.58
Deposit Rate..............................	60l	3.97	3.66	4.11	3.05	3.63	4.48	....	....	....	....	....	....
Lending Rate..............................	60p	5.92	5.48	6.69	5.96	6.58	7.21	5.33	5.98	5.08	4.00	3.69	4.40
Govt. Bond Yield: Short-Term.........	61a	6.65	7.83	7.93	7.28	6.98	5.77	5.38	5.79	5.03	4.82	4.24	4.81
Long-Term.......	61	7.87	8.05	8.26	8.10	7.09	5.45	4.70	4.68	4.78	4.83	4.64	4.77
Prices, Production, Labor						*Index Numbers (2000=100): Period Averages*							
Industrial Share Prices (1995=100)..	62	89.4	96.1	100.0	113.3	128.3	150.5	....	....	....	....	....	....
Prices: Manufacturing Output..........	63	88.8	91.1	94.8	97.2	98.1	98.1	98.5	100.0	99.7	99.8	101.3	103.8
Consumer Prices...........................	64	82.6	84.7	87.6	89.7	92.5	95.7	97.2	100.0	101.8	103.5	106.5	109.7
Harmonized CPI..........................	64h	88.3	90.0	92.4	94.7	96.4	97.9	99.2	100.0	101.2	102.5	103.9	105.3
Wages: Avg. Monthly Earnings.........	65..c	75.2	77.9	80.4	83.2	86.8	91.3	95.7	100.0	104.4	108.1	111.8	116.7
Industrial Production.....................	66	87.2	91.8	† 93.4	94.7	96.0	97.0	98.1	100.0	98.4	96.0	95.5	96.2
Employment, Seas. Adj..................	67..c	89.6	90.2	91.3	92.8	94.9	96.7	98.3	100.0	101.1	101.5	101.9	102.6
						Number in Thousands: Period Averages							
Labor Force..............................	67d	28,271	....	....	28,552	28,716	28,713	29,194	29,412	29,638	29,934	29,235	29,369
Employment..............................	67e	25,511	25,717	26,026	26,323	26,814	27,116	27,442	27,793	28,225	28,415	27,821	28,438
Unemployment...........................	67c	2,919	2,637	2,442	2,300	1,986	1,786	1,724	1,584	1,486	1,520	1,479	866
Unemployment Rate (%)..............	67r	9.9	9.0	7.7	7.2	5.4	4.6	4.2	3.6	3.2	3.1	3.1	2.8

		1993	1994	1995	1996	1997	1998	1999	2000	2001	2002	2003	2004
Intl. Transactions & Positions							*Millions of Pounds*						
Exports	70	120,936	133,030	153,353	167,764	171,595	164,066	165,739	186,171	185,673	184,161	186,175	186,418
Imports, c.i.f.	71	137,404	147,564	168,055	184,113	187,135	189,532	196,504	221,027	222,944	223,433	232,868	246,625
Imports, f.o.b. (on a BOP basis)	71.v	134,858	145,793	164,659	179,578	183,124	....	....	....	....	....	....	....
							2000=100						
Volume of Exports	72..c	60.7	66.7	73.3	78.9	85.4	86.4	89.1	100.0	102.6	100.9	100.7	102.4
Volume of Imports	73..c	59.3	61.9	65.7	71.9	79.0	85.7	91.4	100.0	105.4	110.0	112.1	119.0
Export Prices	76	105.4	107.6	111.3	112.0	106.2	101.0	98.9	100.0	98.4	98.3	100.1	99.9
Import Prices	76.x	101.0	104.4	111.1	110.9	103.5	97.3	96.9	100.0	99.1	96.6	95.9	95.2
Balance of Payments							*Billions of US Dollars: Minus Sign Indicates Debit*						
Current Account, n.i.e.	78ald	−17.97	−10.23	−14.29	−11.28	−2.95	−6.63	−39.29	−36.68	−31.85	−24.57	−27.50	−41.88
Goods: Exports f.o.b.	78aad	183.31	207.19	242.32	261.25	281.54	271.72	268.88	284.38	273.66	279.85	308.27	349.62
Goods: Imports f.o.b.	78abd	−202.96	−224.14	−261.32	−282.48	−301.74	−307.85	−315.90	−334.23	−332.14	−350.69	−386.51	−456.92
Trade Balance	78acd	−19.65	−16.95	−19.01	−21.23	−20.20	−36.13	−47.01	−49.85	−58.48	−70.84	−78.24	−107.30
Services: Credit	78add	62.14	69.54	78.78	89.04	99.79	110.94	118.61	120.06	119.56	132.99	152.91	181.44
Services: Debit	78aed	−52.31	−59.77	−65.41	−72.77	−78.17	−87.97	−96.53	−99.19	−99.81	−109.67	−125.31	−144.43
Balance on Goods & Services	78afd	−9.82	−7.18	−5.64	−4.96	1.41	−13.16	−24.93	−28.98	−38.73	−47.52	−50.64	−70.29
Income: Credit	78agd	109.38	113.97	138.87	144.06	157.40	172.05	162.16	203.75	202.41	187.50	205.95	255.86
Income: Debit	78ahd	−109.67	−108.86	−135.59	−142.94	−152.09	−151.64	−164.57	−196.74	−186.02	−151.68	−166.59	−207.83
Balance on Gds, Serv. & Inc.	78aid	−10.11	−2.08	−2.35	−3.85	6.72	7.25	−27.34	−21.97	−22.33	−11.70	−11.28	−22.26
Current Transfers, n.i.e.: Credit	78ajd	18.59	17.71	19.70	31.20	21.40	20.47	21.66	16.42	21.01	19.12	20.22	23.48
Current Transfers: Debit	78akd	−26.45	−25.86	−31.64	−38.63	−31.08	−34.35	−33.61	−31.14	−30.52	−31.99	−36.44	−43.10
Capital Account, n.i.e.	78bcd	.46	.05	.84	1.97	1.61	.86	1.25	2.31	1.73	1.32	2.15	3.63
Capital Account, n.i.e.: Credit	78bad	1.67	1.93	1.84	3.01	3.06	2.51	2.63	3.94	4.79	3.51	4.59	6.56
Capital Account: Debit	78bbd	−1.21	−1.88	−.99	−1.04	−1.45	−1.65	−1.38	−1.63	−3.06	−2.18	−2.45	−2.94
Financial Account, n.i.e.	78bjd	22.68	4.71	7.47	5.85	−20.10	16.93	34.86	26.05	23.23	13.29	34.88	22.23
Direct Investment Abroad	78bdd	−27.25	−34.90	−45.31	−34.82	−62.44	−122.06	−201.57	−245.38	−59.66	−49.46	−64.09	−80.24
Dir. Invest. in Rep. Econ., n.i.e.	78bed	16.52	10.73	21.73	27.39	37.51	74.65	89.34	122.16	53.84	25.53	20.70	72.56
Portfolio Investment Assets	78bfd	−133.55	31.47	−61.69	−93.37	−85.00	−53.23	−34.32	−97.19	−124.73	1.22	−58.42	−261.99
Equity Securities	78bkd	−11.92	−1.47	−13.15	−16.42	7.01	−4.95	−23.87	−28.46	−63.63	7.41	−29.79	−102.37
Debt Securities	78bld	−121.63	32.95	−48.55	−76.95	−92.01	−48.28	−10.45	−68.73	−61.10	−6.19	−28.63	−159.61
Portfolio Investment Liab., n.i.e.	78bgd	43.63	47.01	58.79	67.99	43.66	35.14	183.82	255.78	69.56	76.24	156.82	170.96
Equity Securities	78bmd	26.12	7.35	8.07	9.40	7.85	63.17	116.04	179.17	33.11	4.22	15.56	−15.22
Debt Securities	78bnd	17.52	39.66	50.72	58.60	35.81	−28.03	67.78	76.61	36.45	72.02	141.26	186.18
Financial Derivatives Assets	78bwd	....	....	....	....	....	....	....	....	....	....	....	....
Financial Derivatives Liabilities	78bxd	.37	3.67	2.63	1.52	1.90	−5.07	4.41	2.24	12.16	1.35	−8.49	−14.27
Other Investment Assets	78bhd	−68.46	−42.45	−74.90	−214.68	−277.94	−22.99	−96.81	−426.19	−255.00	−150.65	−421.25	−585.32
Monetary Authorities	78bod	....	....	....	....	....	....	....	....	....	....	....	....
General Government	78bpd	−.71	−.69	−.74	−2.97	−.20	.12	−.51	−.40	.01	−1.05	−.58	−.70
Banks	78bqd	6.48	−72.66	−34.91	−102.10	−241.01	−31.23	19.86	−289.04	−124.85	−111.14	−258.62	−399.79
Other Sectors	78brd	−74.23	30.90	−39.25	−109.61	−36.73	8.12	−116.16	−136.75	−130.16	−38.46	−162.06	−184.84
Other Investment Liab., n.i.e.	78bid	191.42	−10.81	106.22	251.82	322.22	110.48	89.99	414.60	327.05	109.07	409.62	720.52
Monetary Authorities	78bsd	—	—	—	—	—	—	—	—	—	—	—	—
General Government	78btd	.34	.86	.59	−1.06	−1.74	.42	.54	—	.40	−1.01	.83	−.81
Banks	78bud	59.49	76.62	41.95	111.45	243.12	84.79	20.33	308.95	182.41	141.42	279.18	554.92
Other Sectors	78bvd	131.58	−88.29	63.68	141.43	80.83	25.28	69.13	105.65	144.24	−31.35	129.62	166.41
Net Errors and Omissions	78cad	.27	6.98	5.13	2.80	17.54	−11.42	2.15	13.62	2.43	9.32	−12.11	16.44
Overall Balance	78cbd	5.44	1.50	−.85	−.65	−3.90	−.26	−1.04	5.30	−4.46	−.63	−2.59	.41
Reserves and Related Items	79dad	−5.44	−1.50	.85	.65	3.90	.26	1.04	−5.30	4.46	.63	2.59	−.41
Reserve Assets	79dbd	−1.26	−1.48	.90	.65	3.90	.26	1.04	−5.30	4.46	.63	2.59	−.41
Use of Fund Credit and Loans	79dcd	—	—	—	—	—	—	—	—	—	—	—	—
Exceptional Financing	79ded	−4.17	−.02	−.04	—	—	—	—	—	—	—	—	—
International Investment Position							*Billions of US Dollars*						
Assets	79aad	2,009.26	2,101.90	2,391.34	2,765.83	3,249.81	3,546.86	3,908.79	4,431.72	4,553.50	5,044.32	6,329.70	7,670.08
Direct Investment Abroad	79abd	255.64	275.23	315.74	342.31	369.24	498.36	691.91	906.40	875.03	1,001.64	1,242.41	1,393.56
Portfolio Investment	79acd	695.83	671.53	773.94	930.99	1,076.56	1,170.85	1,355.01	1,352.04	1,359.63	1,360.51	1,670.39	2,066.41
Equity Securities	79add	287.40	291.92	336.30	404.67	466.94	505.15	678.65	640.63	586.88	493.17	664.06	874.33
Debt Securities	79aed	408.43	379.62	437.63	526.32	609.62	665.70	676.35	711.41	772.75	867.35	1,006.33	1,192.08
Financial Derivatives	79ald	—	—	—	—	—	—	—	—	—	—	—	—
Other Investment	79afd	1,013.74	1,107.20	1,252.52	1,446.14	1,766.22	1,838.80	1,826.01	2,130.30	2,281.60	2,641.07	3,374.42	4,165.21
Monetary Authorities	79agd	—	—	—	—	—	—	—	—	—	—	—	—
General Government	79ahd	12.69	14.09	14.71	19.33	19.02	19.00	5.74	5.80	5.66	7.26	8.64	10.03
Banks	79aid	768.47	877.15	979.78	1,063.88	1,367.32	1,457.48	1,364.00	1,579.68	1,641.21	1,891.53	2,359.23	2,907.23
Other Sectors	79ajd	232.57	215.96	258.04	362.92	379.88	362.33	456.27	544.82	634.72	742.28	1,006.56	1,247.95
Reserve Assets	79akd	44.04	47.93	49.15	46.39	37.79	38.84	35.86	42.97	37.24	41.10	42.48	44.90
Liabilities	79lad	1,962.79	2,073.93	2,426.47	2,876.76	3,359.17	3,761.70	4,012.73	4,483.80	4,658.06	5,122.14	6,400.33	7,942.58
Dir. Invest. in Rep. Economy	79lbd	201.29	203.05	226.63	259.17	287.31	355.40	404.51	463.13	527.39	547.63	636.60	767.80
Portfolio Investment	79lcd	454.58	499.95	629.75	814.74	964.37	1,152.22	1,338.96	1,489.27	1,390.04	1,438.28	1,867.22	2,292.79
Equity Securities	79ldd	198.06	197.10	267.66	383.89	499.23	668.90	824.10	901.93	767.90	660.48	874.08	1,020.67
Debt Securities	79led	256.52	302.85	362.09	430.85	465.14	483.32	514.87	587.34	622.14	777.80	993.15	1,272.13
Financial Derivatives	79lld	—	—	—	—	—	—	—	—	—	—	—	—
Other Investment	79lfd	1,306.92	1,370.94	1,570.09	1,802.85	2,107.49	2,254.08	2,269.26	2,531.40	2,740.63	3,136.23	3,896.51	4,881.99
Monetary Authorities	79lgd	—	—	—	—	—	—	—	—	—	—	—	—
General Government	79lhd	5.60	6.70	7.31	6.68	4.78	5.39	5.81	5.90	6.13	5.57	7.00	6.69
Banks	79lid	982.44	1,114.40	1,242.42	1,327.38	1,577.98	1,729.58	1,669.18	1,888.52	1,992.89	2,321.90	2,866.57	3,611.75
Other Sectors	79ljd	318.88	249.84	320.36	468.79	524.73	519.11	594.27	636.99	741.62	808.76	1,022.93	1,263.55

		1993	1994	1995	1996	1997	1998	1999	2000	2001	2002	2003	2004
Government Finance							*Millions of Pounds: Year Ending December 31*						
Deficit (-) or Surplus.........................	80	−46,447	−39,868	−38,922	−27,440	−16,136	4,853	295	....	....	....	....	....
Revenue..	81	217,062	236,083	253,918	270,360	288,223	317,543	325,102	....	....	....	....	....
Grants Received............................	81z	2,558	1,752	1,233	2,424	1,739	1,384	3,176	....	....	....	....	....
Expenditure..................................	82	272,600	284,051	295,172	307,310	306,579	313,836	324,393	....	....	....	....	....
Lending Minus Repayments............	83	−6,533	−6,348	−1,099	−7,086	−481	238	3,590	....	....	....	....	....
Financing													
Domestic Borrowing.....................	84a	32,798	34,931	38,275	20,446	18,064	−2,908	2,984	....	....	....	....	....
Foreign Borrowing.......................	85a	13,649	4,937	647	6,994	−1,928	−1,945	−3,279	....	....	....	....	....
							Millions of Pounds Year Beginning April 1						
Debt: Domestic...............................	88a	201,928	243,394	277,476	314,021	341,171	....	....	....	....	....	....	....
Foreign................................	89a	47,998	58,262	56,234	58,691	60,213	....	....	....	....	....	....	....
National Accounts							*Billions of Pounds*						
Househ.Cons.Expend.,incl.NPISHs....	96f.c	415.95	437.68	459.85	492.47	523.03	557.82	592.58	626.70	660.43	693.36	725.01	760.68
Government Consumption Expend...	91f.c	130.90	135.37	140.24	146.56	148.54	154.25	166.51	179.05	191.02	210.97	231.78	246.81
Gross Fixed Capital Formation.........	93e.c	101.00	108.43	117.33	126.13	133.75	150.97	154.88	161.21	167.09	170.19	179.50	195.83
Changes in Inventories....................	93i.c	.30	3.82	4.39	1.61	4.59	5.46	6.29	5.27	6.59	3.12	4.17	4.73
Exports of Goods and Services........	90c.c	163.64	180.51	203.51	224.17	232.89	231.03	239.49	267.35	273.12	274.95	282.23	289.96
Imports of Goods and Services (-)....	98c.c	170.13	185.26	207.05	227.52	232.03	238.98	254.91	286.60	300.06	306.50	313.21	328.38
Gross Domestic Product (GDP).........	99b.c	641.69	680.44	718.38	763.56	810.60	860.52	905.44	953.58	996.76	1,048.46	1,105.92	1,164.44
Net Primary Income from Abroad.....	98.nc	−4.70	.29	−2.83	−2.07	.57	8.89	−4.41	1.08	8.18	21.77	22.35	25.18
Gross National Income (GNI)...........	99a.c	636.99	680.73	715.56	761.49	811.17	869.41	901.03	954.66	1,004.94	1,070.23	1,128.27	1,189.62
Net Current Transf.from Abroad.......	98t.c	−.73	−2.31	−2.65	−1.90	−3.21	−4.97	−4.44	−6.25	−3.43	−6.71	−8.14	−9.75
Gross Nat'l Disposable Inc.(GNDI)....	99i.c	636.26	678.42	712.91	759.59	807.96	864.45	896.59	948.40	1,001.51	1,063.52	1,120.14	1,179.87
Gross Saving..................................	99s.c	89.41	105.37	112.82	120.56	136.40	152.38	137.52	142.67	150.07	159.19	163.36	172.40
Consumption of Fixed Capital..........	99cfc	83.67	85.44	87.31	86.57	88.30	91.24	96.94	101.77	105.84	111.96	115.32	121.58
GDP Volume 2000 Ref., Chained.....	99b.r	773.81	808.05	831.10	854.52	882.52	909.82	935.82	971.94	994.31	1,011.89	1,034.20	1,066.04
GDP Volume (2000=100)................	99bvr	79.6	83.1	85.5	87.9	90.8	93.6	96.3	100.0	102.3	104.1	106.4	109.7
GDP Deflator (2000=100)...............	99bir	84.5	85.8	88.1	91.1	93.6	96.4	98.6	100.0	102.2	105.6	109.0	111.3
							Millions: Midyear Estimates						
Population................................	99z	57.29	57.48	57.67	57.87	58.06	58.26	58.47	58.67	58.87	59.08	59.28	59.48

		1993	1994	1995	1996	1997	1998	1999	2000	2001	2002	2003	2004
Exchange Rates					*End of Period (sa and sc) Period Averages (sb and sd)*								
US Dollar/SDR Rate...............aa=.....	sa	1.3736	1.4599	1.4865	1.4380	1.3493	1.4080	1.3725	1.3029	1.2567	1.3595	1.4860	1.5530
US Dollar/SDR Rate.........................	sb	1.3963	1.4317	1.5170	1.4518	1.3760	1.3565	1.3673	1.3188	1.2730	1.2948	1.3988	1.4820
SDR/US Dollar Rate...............ac=.....	sc	.7280	.6850	.6727	.6954	.7412	.7102	.7286	.7675	.7957	.7356	.6730	.6439
SDR/US Dollar Rate.........................	sd	.7162	.6985	.6592	.6888	.7267	.7372	.7314	.7583	.7855	.7723	.7152	.6749
		Dollars per ECU through 1998; Dollars per Euro Beginning 1999: End of Period (ea) Period Average (eb)											
Euro Rate......................................	ag	1.1200	1.2300	1.3142	1.2530	1.1042	1.1668	1.0046	.9305	.8813	1.0487	1.2630	1.3621
Euro Rate......................................	rh	1.1723	1.1886	1.3081	1.2680	1.1200	1.1341	1.0668	.9240	.8956	.9444	1.1308	1.2433
		Index Numbers (2000=100): Period Averages											
Nominal Effective Exchange Rate.....	neu	87.7	86.6	81.5	84.9	91.7	96.1	94.9	100.0	105.9	104.3	91.5	84.0
Real Effective Exchange Rate...........	reu	88.7	87.1	80.3	82.1	86.6	91.8	90.8	100.0	103.6	104.6	95.3	88.0
Fund Position		*Billions of SDRs: End of Period*											
Quota..	2f.s	26.53	26.53	26.53	26.53	26.53	26.53	37.15	37.15	37.15	37.15	37.15	37.15
SDRs..	1b.s	6.57	6.88	7.42	7.17	7.43	7.53	7.54	8.09	8.58	8.95	8.50	8.77
Reserve Position in the Fund...........	1c.s	8.59	8.24	9.85	10.73	13.39	17.12	13.09	11.38	14.22	16.17	15.16	12.58
of which: Outstg.Fund Borrowing...	2c	—	—	—	—	—	.98	—	—	—	—	—	—
International Liquidity		*Billions of US Dollars Unless Otherwise Indicated: End of Period*											
Total Reserves minus Gold...............	1l.d	62.35	63.28	74.78	64.04	58.91	70.71	60.50	56.60	57.63	67.96	74.89	75.89
SDRs..	1b.d	9.02	10.04	11.04	10.31	10.03	10.60	10.35	10.54	10.78	12.17	12.64	13.63
Reserve Position in the Fund..........	1c.d	11.80	12.03	14.65	15.43	18.07	24.11	17.97	14.82	17.87	21.98	22.53	19.54
Foreign Exchange..........................	1d.d	41.53	41.22	49.10	38.29	30.81	36.00	32.18	31.24	28.98	33.82	39.72	42.72
Gold (Million Fine Troy Ounces)........	1ad	261.79	261.73	261.70	261.66	261.64	261.61	261.67	261.61	262.00	262.00	261.55	261.59
Gold (National Valuation).................	1and	11.05	11.05	11.05	11.05	11.05	11.05	11.05	11.05	11.05	11.04	11.04	11.04
Monetary Authorities: Other Liab.....	4..d	.39	.25	.39	.17	.46	.17	.07	.22	.06	21.23	25.81	30.86
Deposit Money Banks: Assets...........	7a.d	552.33	546.14	606.46	665.94	791.26	813.16	860.50	961.55	1,126.71	1,257.17	1,404.03	1,792.00
Liabilities..................	7b.d	828.19	941.32	1,011.91	1,028.68	1,207.31	1,265.47	1,311.60	1,411.34	1,523.67	1,829.34	2,123.67	2,578.41
Nonbank Financial Insts.: Assets......	7e.d	—	—	—	—	—	—	—	—	—	—	—	—
Liabilities..................	7f.d	107.88	125.08	146.22	175.13	209.37	227.82	300.17	441.43	534.69	650.18	666.74	796.32
Monetary Authorities		*Billions of US Dollars: End of Period*											
Foreign Assets.................................	11	73.4	74.3	85.8	75.1	70.0	81.8	71.5	67.6	68.7	79.0	85.9	86.9
Claims on Central Government........	12a	350.3	383.5	397.7	410.2	447.5	463.5	494.2	530.7	569.0	648.3	681.8	736.9
Claims on Banking Institutions.........	12e	.1	.2	.1	.1	2.0	—	.2	.1	—	—	.1	—
Claims on Nonbank Financial Insts...	12g	4.6	3.6	2.6	2.2	.7	.3	.2	.1	—	—	—	—
Federal Reserve Float......................	13a	.9	−.7	.1	4.3	.7	1.6	−.2	.9	—	.4	−.3	.9
Reserve Money................................	14	400.2	434.6	453.8	475.2	513.2	543.8	652.4	612.7	660.8	710.1	747.3	778.9
of which: Currency Outside Banks..	14a	327.5	363.5	381.9	406.1	437.6	473.2	567.7	578.5	599.4	644.2	680.1	707.6
Foreign Liabilities............................	16c	.4	.3	.4	.2	.5	.2	.1	.2	.1	21.2	25.8	30.9
Central Government Deposits...........	16d	36.3	29.2	37.7	30.0	22.6	26.0	48.1	24.9	25.7	26.8	30.9	33.3
Other Items (Net).............................	17r	−7.5	−3.1	−5.5	−13.5	−15.4	−22.7	−134.6	−38.3	−48.8	−30.3	−36.5	−18.3
Banking Institutions													
Commercial Banks		*Billions of US Dollars: End of Period*											
Reserves...	20	64.2	67.3	67.6	67.5	74.1	66.5	89.2	61.8	62.6	67.5	68.2	62.3
Foreign Assets.................................	21	78.9	38.9	34.1	102.0	151.0	237.1	295.9	374.2	481.9	497.5	593.8	767.2
Claims on Central Government........	22a	322.2	290.4	278.7	261.8	270.1	214.1	228.9	184.5	162.7	205.8	132.9	110.1
Claims on State and Local Govts......	22b	99.2	97.6	93.4	94.2	96.7	104.8	110.8	114.1	120.2	121.7	132.5	140.8
Claims on Private Sector...................	22d	2,331.1	2,512.2	2,755.6	2,926.9	3,179.2	3,462.4	3,704.3	4,127.4	4,297.1	4,506.9	4,884.2	5,372.5
Claims on Nonbank Financial Insts...	22g	423.2	428.7	467.5	495.7	571.2	663.2	699.6	721.8	777.4	917.9	999.5	1,096.4
Demand Deposits.............................	24	788.4	756.7	710.8	676.3	656.4	622.9	626.4	540.9	628.8	571.5	602.4	647.0
Time and Savings Deposits..............	25	1,377.2	1,376.2	1,490.1	1,613.2	1,761.5	1,945.2	2,017.1	2,228.7	2,478.1	2,747.6	2,977.9	3,259.7
Money Market Instruments..............	26aa	308.9	331.7	390.9	488.2	585.8	601.0	729.8	840.3	852.8	816.0	849.6	940.9
Bonds...	26ab	134.9	142.6	161.1	168.9	192.6	220.2	240.6	273.2	310.2	332.2	379.1	437.4
Foreign Liabilities............................	26c	256.3	311.3	305.3	327.5	381.2	490.3	537.6	614.3	685.9	731.0	821.0	1,059.2
Central Government Deposits...........	26d	42.6	23.8	19.0	28.7	27.8	13.2	49.6	16.4	47.5	31.1	30.2	26.9
Credit from Monetary Authorities.....	26g	1.9	—	.3	8.7	3.5	3.3	—	1.9	—	.9	—	1.9
Liab. to Nonbank Financial Insts.......	26j	21.2	30.5	36.7	39.0	58.1	104.9	145.6	172.4	196.6	226.8	235.3	244.1
Other Items (Net).............................	27r	387.4	462.3	582.5	597.6	675.2	747.2	782.2	895.8	702.5	860.4	915.6	932.1
Credit Unions and Savings Insts		*Billions of US Dollars: End of Period*											
Reserves...	20..t	54.0	41.2	43.8	41.7	43.0	54.2	66.5	64.4	85.2	93.1	98.7	94.9
Claims on Central Government........	22a.t	50.8	49.2	36.7	34.8	30.2	23.3	19.8	17.0	18.8	17.0	21.2	18.1
Claims on State and Local Govts......	22b.t	2.1	2.0	2.0	2.1	2.1	2.5	3.0	3.2	4.5	5.5	6.3	7.1
Claims on Private Sector...................	22d.t	908.9	926.0	941.6	995.8	1,018.4	1,086.3	1,177.0	1,271.2	1,317.2	1,364.1	1,496.7	1,733.5
Claims on Nonbank Financial Insts...	22g.t	183.6	200.8	210.3	206.7	206.3	202.0	208.4	201.4	242.0	273.5	314.2	340.8
Demand Deposits.............................	24..t	115.1	111.8	128.0	154.9	186.1	228.6	267.7	317.0	371.2	430.6	495.7	563.3
Time and Savings Deposits..............	25..t	845.9	807.0	789.7	763.8	712.7	681.4	654.5	631.6	649.5	650.9	650.0	617.6
Money Market Instruments..............	26aat	106.1	122.8	133.6	141.5	154.2	183.5	216.5	233.8	275.5	313.4	376.6	467.4
Bonds...	26abt	3.9	3.1	3.1	2.7	2.8	2.6	2.7	6.3	3.6	3.4	5.1	7.6
Central Government Deposits...........	26d.t	87.3	100.0	97.4	121.9	138.0	180.1	243.7	260.0	259.1	231.7	249.3	309.3
Other Items (Net).............................	27r.t	41.1	74.5	82.6	96.4	106.3	92.1	89.6	108.4	108.8	123.0	160.3	229.2
Money Market Funds		*Billions of US Dollars: End of Period*											
Foreign Assets.................................	21..m	10.0	15.7	19.7	23.1	23.2	30.6	42.9	91.1	124.2	114.1	74.2	75.4
Claims on Central Government........	22a.m	79.4	66.1	70.0	90.2	86.2	103.6	103.8	90.4	135.7	140.2	130.2	96.4
Claims on State and Local Govts......	22b.m	105.6	113.4	127.7	144.5	167.0	193.0	210.4	244.7	281.0	282.8	297.3	318.8
Claims on Private Sector...................	22d.m	176.2	202.3	257.0	297.8	372.4	495.4	642.7	770.5	801.9	764.6	644.7	583.5
Claims on Banking Institutions.........	22e.m	30.7	28.9	48.9	81.6	112.8	126.0	158.1	144.6	224.0	203.4	155.0	174.7
Claims on Nonbank Financial Insts...	22g.m	67.8	77.2	90.8	101.8	96.3	173.8	190.9	185.2	318.4	324.1	326.2	262.2
Time Deposits..................................	25..m	559.6	600.1	741.3	886.7	1,042.5	1,329.7	1,578.8	1,812.1	2,240.7	2,223.9	2,016.0	1,879.9
Other Items (Net).............................	27r.m	−90.1	−96.6	−127.2	−147.6	−184.7	−207.2	−230.0	−285.5	−355.6	−394.8	−388.4	−368.9

		1993	1994	1995	1996	1997	1998	1999	2000	2001	2002	2003	2004
Banking Survey						*Billions of US Dollars: End of Period*							
Foreign Assets (Net)........................	31n	−94.4	−182.6	−166.1	−127.5	−137.6	−141.0	−127.4	−81.5	−11.2	−61.6	−92.9	−160.5
Domestic Credit...............................	32	4,938.7	5,200.0	5,577.3	5,884.2	6,355.7	6,969.1	7,452.7	8,161.1	8,714.2	9,282.7	9,757.2	10,447.5
Claims on Central Govt. (Net).......	32an	636.5	636.3	628.9	616.4	645.5	585.2	505.4	521.4	554.0	721.7	655.6	592.0
Claims on State and Local Govts....	32b	206.9	213.0	223.1	240.8	265.7	300.3	324.2	362.0	405.6	410.0	436.1	466.7
Claims on Private Sector...............	32d	3,416.1	3,640.5	3,954.2	4,220.5	4,570.0	5,044.1	5,524.0	6,169.1	6,416.8	6,635.6	7,025.6	7,689.6
Claims on Nonbank Financial Insts.	32g	679.2	710.3	771.2	806.4	874.5	1,039.4	1,099.1	1,108.5	1,337.8	1,515.4	1,639.9	1,699.3
Money..	34	1,231.0	1,232.0	1,220.7	1,237.3	1,280.2	1,324.7	1,461.8	1,436.4	1,599.4	1,646.3	1,778.2	1,917.9
Quasi-Money..................................	35	2,782.8	2,783.3	3,021.1	3,263.7	3,516.7	3,956.3	4,250.4	4,672.5	5,368.3	5,622.4	5,644.0	5,757.2
Money Market Instruments..............	36aa	414.9	454.5	524.5	629.7	740.1	784.5	946.2	1,074.1	1,128.3	1,129.4	1,226.2	1,408.3
Bonds...	36ab	138.8	145.7	164.2	171.6	195.5	222.8	243.3	279.4	313.8	335.6	384.2	445.1
Liab. to Nonbank Financial Insts.......	36j	21.2	30.5	36.7	39.0	58.1	104.9	145.6	172.4	196.6	226.8	235.3	244.1
Other Items (Net)...........................	37r	255.6	371.3	444.1	415.4	427.6	434.9	277.9	444.7	96.5	260.6	396.4	514.5
Money plus Quasi-Money.................	35l	4,013.8	4,015.3	4,241.8	4,501.0	4,796.9	5,281.0	5,712.2	6,108.9	6,967.8	7,268.7	7,422.2	7,675.1
Nonbank Financial Institutions													
Other Financial Institutions						*Billions of US Dollars: End of Period*							
Foreign Assets...............................	41	—	—	—	—	—	—	—	—	—	—	—	—
Claims on Central Government........	42a	203.5	182.5	258.7	168.7	187.1	208.0	130.5	156.6	156.8	171.7	211.5	136.4
Claims on State and Local Govts.	42b	392.3	395.2	397.2	399.4	395.7	425.1	444.1	437.8	478.1	524.6	547.0	568.5
Claims on Private Sector...............	42d	3,714.6	4,017.2	4,699.1	5,538.7	6,574.9	7,769.4	9,389.0	9,837.8	9,998.8	9,849.8	12,022.9	13,830.0
Claims on Banking Institutions.........	42e	151.5	181.6	186.1	223.7	244.5	336.9	422.7	457.9	591.5	616.4	587.5	592.2
Credit Market Instruments..............	46aa	1,401.3	1,584.4	1,816.9	2,320.1	2,958.3	3,630.0	4,475.2	4,513.5	4,275.0	3,744.9	4,601.9	5,224.6
Bonds...	46ab	812.9	924.4	1,089.7	1,227.1	1,315.9	1,542.4	1,671.8	1,810.6	2,028.7	2,342.6	2,763.7	3,233.9
Foreign Liabilities..........................	46c	107.9	125.1	146.2	175.1	209.4	227.8	300.2	441.4	534.7	650.2	666.7	796.3
Credit from Monetary Authorities.....	46g	4.6	3.6	2.6	2.2	.7	.3	.2	.1				
Credit from Banking Institutions.......	46h	1,428.1	1,450.2	1,613.5	1,729.2	1,884.7	2,128.9	2,317.5	2,291.0	2,404.7	2,457.8	2,680.4	2,775.4
Liabs. to Insur. Cos. & Pen. Funds.....	46j	637.8	762.2	929.4	1,023.2	1,223.7	1,330.3	1,659.5	1,738.0	1,668.0	1,650.4	1,942.1	2,183.4
Other Items (Net)...........................	47r	69.2	−73.5	−57.4	−146.5	−190.5	−120.5	−38.0	95.5	314.1	316.7	714.2	913.5
Insurance Companies & Pension Funds						*Billions of US Dollars: End of Period*							
Claims on Central Government........	42a.s	571.5	595.5	592.3	566.8	539.7	467.5	440.7	401.4	378.8	418.5	424.7	444.9
Claims on State and Local Govts......	42b.s	162.2	167.7	174.8	189.3	209.8	229.7	222.1	204.8	193.9	203.3	251.0	281.0
Claims on Private Sector.................	42d.s	3,551.5	3,666.7	4,354.8	4,912.4	5,726.5	6,499.6	7,264.9	6,909.8	6,447.1	5,789.4	6,866.8	7,591.7
Claims on Banking Institutions.........	42e.s	179.5	173.8	190.4	245.5	300.4	348.5	353.1	383.6	467.2	470.4	486.2	449.9
Claims on Nonbank Financial Insts....	42g.s	637.8	762.2	929.4	1,023.2	1,223.7	1,330.3	1,659.5	1,738.0	1,668.0	1,650.4	1,942.1	2,183.4
Insurance and Pension Reserves.......	47a.s	5,073.3	5,375.3	6,212.5	6,896.4	7,888.5	8,804.3	9,862.3	9,614.0	9,172.5	8,493.3	9,809.4	10,670.6
Other Items (Net)...........................	47r.s	29.3	−9.4	29.3	40.8	111.5	71.3	78.0	23.5	−17.5	38.8	161.5	280.3
Financial Survey						*Billions of US Dollars: End of Period*							
Foreign Assets (Net)........................	51n	−202.3	−307.7	−312.3	−302.6	−347.0	−368.8	−427.5	−523.0	−545.9	−711.8	−759.6	−956.9
Domestic Credit...............................	52	12,850.3	13,514.6	15,283.0	16,852.9	19,114.8	21,528.9	24,244.8	25,000.7	25,029.9	24,724.6	28,441.3	31,600.8
Claims on Central Govt. (Net).......	52an	1,406.8	1,414.3	1,479.9	1,351.9	1,372.2	1,260.7	1,076.5	1,079.4	1,089.5	1,311.9	1,291.9	1,173.3
Claims on State and Local Govts....	52b	761.3	775.9	795.0	829.5	871.2	955.1	990.4	1,004.7	1,077.6	1,137.9	1,234.1	1,316.2
Claims on Private Sector...............	52d	10,682.2	11,324.4	13,008.1	14,671.5	16,871.4	19,313.1	22,177.9	22,916.7	22,862.7	22,274.8	25,915.3	29,111.3
Liquid Liabilities.............................	55l	4,013.8	4,015.3	4,241.8	4,501.0	4,796.9	5,281.0	5,712.2	6,108.9	6,967.8	7,268.7	7,422.2	7,675.1
Credit Market Instruments..............	56aa	1,816.3	2,038.9	2,341.5	2,949.8	3,698.3	4,414.4	5,421.4	5,587.6	5,403.4	4,874.2	5,828.1	6,632.9
Bonds...	56ab	951.7	1,070.1	1,253.9	1,398.7	1,511.4	1,765.2	1,915.1	2,090.0	2,342.5	2,678.2	3,147.9	3,679.0
Other Items (Net)...........................	57r	5,866.3	6,082.5	7,133.6	7,700.8	8,761.3	9,699.4	10,768.6	10,691.2	9,770.3	9,191.7	11,283.6	12,657.0
Money (National Definitions)						*Billions of US Dollars: End of Period*							
Monetary Base...............................	19ma	390.6	422.5	439.0	456.6	485.0	518.3	600.7	590.1	639.9	686.2	725.2	764.6
Monetary Base, Season. Adjusted..	19mac	386.6	418.3	434.6	452.1	479.9	514.1	593.7	584.8	635.4	681.3	719.9	758.6
M1...	59ma	1,153.3	1,174.2	1,152.1	1,104.5	1,096.9	1,120.2	1,148.0	1,111.6	1,204.1	1,241.2	1,323.9	1,393.1
M1, Seasonally Adjusted...............	59mac	1,129.9	1,150.7	1,126.9	1,079.8	1,072.2	1,094.8	1,122.6	1,087.1	1,178.0	1,215.4	1,297.2	1,365.6
M2...	59mb	3,504.5	3,518.8	3,664.0	3,835.4	4,051.7	4,405.0	4,674.0	4,962.4	5,479.8	5,827.9	6,103.0	6,445.5
M2, Seasonally Adjusted...............	59mbc	3,484.4	3,497.8	3,640.3	3,814.8	4,030.1	4,382.3	4,647.4	4,930.2	5,446.1	5,798.8	6,076.6	6,422.1
M3...	59mc	4,304.5	4,389.0	4,658.8	5,007.8	5,489.0	6,087.5	6,596.6	7,174.1	8,100.4	8,629.4	8,929.0	9,480.2
M3, Seasonally Adjusted...............	59mcc	4,285.6	4,369.9	4,636.0	4,985.4	5,460.6	6,052.0	6,551.7	7,118.6	8,032.9	8,570.7	8,885.1	9,449.8
L..	59mf	5,201.9	5,344.6	5,732.8	6,111.6	6,636.7	....	....	....	....	....	....	....
L, Seasonally Adjusted...................	59mfc	5,173.3	5,315.8	5,702.3	6,083.6	6,611.3	....	....	....	....	....	....	....
Debt..	59mg	12,409.8	12,990.0	13,694.5	14,430.5	15,221.5	16,264.9	17,352.9	18,270.1	19,363.8	....	....	....
Debt, Seasonally Adjusted..............	59mgc	12,407.6	12,988.5	13,694.9	14,433.5	15,227.3	16,277.3	17,360.8	18,278.3	19,375.5	....	....	....
Treasury Securities by Holders						*Billions of US Dollars: End of Period*							
Total...	59t	3,309.9	3,465.6	3,608.5	3,755.1	3,778.3	3,723.7	3,652.7	3,357.8	3,352.7	3,609.8	4,008.2	4,370.7
Nonresidents..............................	59ta	594.6	632.6	816.9	1,040.3	1,153.2	1,166.2	1,058.4	1,021.4	1,063.1	1,254.1	1,499.2	1,856.4
Residents...................................	59tb	2,715.3	2,833.0	2,791.6	2,714.7	2,625.1	2,557.4	2,594.3	2,336.3	2,289.6	2,355.6	2,509.0	2,514.3
Monetary Authorities..................	59tba	332.0	364.5	378.2	390.9	430.7	452.1	478.0	511.7	551.7	629.4	666.7	717.8
Commercial Banks......................	59tbb	322.2	290.4	278.7	261.8	270.1	214.1	228.9	184.5	162.7	205.8	132.9	110.1
Govt. Sponsored Enterprises........	59tbc	51.6	51.9	58.0	18.8	25.9	25.2	30.9	13.3	13.6	25.7	13.5	12.9
Other Financial Institutions..........	59tbd	902.5	892.2	956.8	888.8	844.0	800.9	683.1	670.2	693.3	754.9	808.9	723.0
Nonfinancial Sectors...................	59tbe	1,107.0	1,233.9	1,119.9	1,154.5	1,054.3	1,065.2	1,173.3	956.6	868.4	739.8	887.1	950.5
Interest Rates						*Percent Per Annum*							
Discount Rate (End of Period).........	60	3.00	4.75	5.25	5.00	5.00	4.50	5.00	6.00	1.25	.75	† 2.00	3.15
Federal Funds Rate.........................	60b	3.02	4.20	5.84	5.30	5.46	5.35	4.97	6.24	3.89	1.67	1.13	1.35
Commercial Paper Rate...................	60bc	3.22	4.66	5.93	5.41	5.57	5.34	5.18	6.31	3.61	1.69	1.11	1.49
Treasury Bill Rate..........................	60c	3.02	4.27	5.51	5.02	5.07	4.82	4.66	5.84	3.45	1.61	1.01	1.38
Treas. Bill Rate(Bond Equivalent)......	60cs	3.06	4.35	5.65	5.14	5.20	4.90	4.77	6.00	3.48	1.63	1.02	1.39
Certificates of Deposit Rate.............	60lc	3.17	4.63	5.92	5.39	5.62	5.47	5.33	6.46	3.69	1.73	1.15	1.56
Lending Rate (Prime Rate)..............	60p	6.00	7.14	8.83	8.27	8.44	8.35	7.99	9.23	6.92	4.68	4.12	4.34
Govt. Bond Yield: Med.-Term.........	61a	4.44	6.26	6.26	5.99	6.10	5.14	5.49	6.22	4.08	3.10	2.11	2.78
Long-Term.......	61	5.87	7.08	6.58	6.44	6.35	5.26	5.64	6.03	5.02	4.61	4.02	4.27

		1993	1994	1995	1996	1997	1998	1999	2000	2001	2002	2003	2004
Prices, Production, Labor		\multicolumn{12}{c}{*Index Numbers (2000=100): Period Averages*}											
Industrial Share Prices.....................	62	29.5	30.8	36.7	45.3	58.4	72.8	92.1	100.0	78.9	65.3	62.9	73.7
Producer Prices...............................	63	89.6	90.8	94.0	96.2	96.1	93.8	94.5	100.0	101.1	98.8	104.1	110.5
Industrial Goods.........................	63a	88.3	89.5	93.1	94.5	94.8	92.6	93.9	100.0	100.7	98.3	103.2	109.5
Finished Goods...........................	63b	90.4	91.0	92.7	95.1	95.5	94.7	96.4	100.0	102.0	100.6	103.8	107.6
Consumer Goods.....................	63ba	89.0	89.2	90.9	93.7	94.2	93.3	95.5	100.0	102.4	100.8	105.1	109.7
Capital Equipment....................	63bb	94.6	96.6	98.5	99.6	99.6	99.1	99.1	100.0	100.6	100.2	100.5	101.9
Consumer Prices............................	64	83.9	86.1	88.5	91.1	93.2	94.7	96.7	100.0	102.8	104.5	106.8	109.7
Wages: Hourly Earnings(Mfg)..........	65ey	81.7	84.0	86.2	89.0	91.7	93.9	96.7	100.0	103.1	106.8	109.9	112.7
Industrial Production.......................	66	70.0	73.8	77.5	80.8	86.7	91.7	95.9	100.0	96.4	96.2	96.1	100.1
Crude Petroleum Production...........	66aa	117.6	114.4	112.7	111.1	110.8	107.4	101.0	100.0	99.6	98.7	97.9	93.1
Nonagr.Employment, Seas.Adj........	67..c	84.1	86.7	89.0	90.8	93.2	95.5	97.9	100.0	100.0	98.9	98.6	99.8
		\multicolumn{12}{c}{*Number in Thousands: Period Averages*}											
Labor Force...................................	67d	129,200	†131,057	132,304	133,945	†136,297	137,673	139,368	142,583	143,734	144,863	146,510	147,401
Employment..................................	67e	120,259	†123,060	124,900	126,709	†129,558	131,464	133,488	136,891	136,933	136,485	137,736	139,252
Unemployment..............................	67c	8,940	†7,997	7,404	7,236	†6,739	6,210	5,880	5,692	6,801	8,378	8,774	8,149
Unemployment Rate (%).................	67r	6.9	†6.1	5.6	5.4	†5.0	4.5	4.2	4.0	4.7	5.8	6.0	5.5
Intl. Transactions & Positions		\multicolumn{12}{c}{*Billions of US Dollars*}											
Exports, f.a.s.................................	70	464.77	512.63	584.74	625.07	689.18	682.14	695.80	781.92	729.10	693.10	724.77	818.52
Imports, c.i.f.................................	71	603.44	689.22	770.85	822.02	899.02	944.35	1,059.44	1,259.30	1,179.18	1,200.23	1,303.05	1,525.68
Imports, f.o.b................................	71.v	580.51	663.83	743.54	795.29	870.57	911.90	1,024.62	1,218.02	1,141.00	1,163.56	1,257.12	1,469.86
		\multicolumn{12}{c}{*2000=100*}											
Volume of Exports..........................	72	61.4	66.3	72.0	76.5	85.5	87.5	90.4	100.0	94.0	90.3	92.9	101.1
Volume of Imports.........................	73	50.6	56.9	60.9	64.3	72.1	80.5	89.6	100.0	97.1	101.3	106.8	118.4
Export Prices.................................	76	96.9	98.9	103.9	104.5	103.1	99.7	98.4	100.0	99.2	98.2	99.7	103.6
Import Prices.................................	76.x	94.6	96.2	100.6	101.6	99.1	93.1	93.9	100.0	96.5	94.1	96.9	102.3
Balance of Payments		\multicolumn{12}{c}{*Billions of US Dollars: Minus Sign Indicates Debit*}											
Current Account, n.i.e....................	78ald	−81.96	−118.06	−109.47	−120.17	−135.98	−209.53	−296.85	−413.44	−385.70	−473.94	−530.66	−665.94
Goods: Exports f.o.b.....................	78aad	458.84	504.91	577.04	614.01	680.33	672.38	686.27	774.63	721.84	685.34	716.41	811.08
Goods: Imports f.o.b.....................	78abd	−589.39	−668.69	−749.37	−803.11	−876.49	−917.11	−1,029.99	−1,224.42	−1,145.93	−1,164.75	−1,260.71	−1,473.12
Trade Balance...........................	78acd	−130.55	−163.78	−172.33	−189.10	−196.16	−244.74	−343.72	−449.78	−424.09	−479.41	−544.30	−662.04
Services: Credit...........................	78add	184.01	198.35	217.35	237.62	254.32	261.13	280.17	296.35	284.81	290.60	304.09	336.10
Services: Debit............................	78aed	−123.66	−132.96	−141.29	−152.43	−166.35	−181.25	−199.73	−224.91	−223.42	−232.93	−256.30	−291.14
Balance on Goods & Services.......	78afd	−70.20	−98.40	−96.27	−103.91	−108.19	−164.86	−263.28	−378.34	−362.69	−421.74	−496.51	−617.07
Income: Credit............................	78agd	136.08	166.52	210.26	226.13	256.82	261.32	293.22	350.45	286.69	266.80	294.39	368.99
Income: Debit.............................	78ahd	−110.74	−149.38	−189.36	−203.81	−244.20	−257.55	−280.04	−329.86	−263.12	−259.63	−261.10	−344.92
Balance on Gds, Serv. & Inc........	78aid	−44.86	−81.26	−75.37	−81.59	−95.57	−161.09	−250.09	−357.76	−339.12	−414.56	−463.23	−593.01
Current Transfers, n.i.e.: Credit......	78ajd	6.67	7.99	8.63	10.40	9.89	9.64	8.85	10.78	8.51	11.83	14.80	16.44
Current Transfers: Debit.................	78akd	−43.77	−44.78	−42.73	−48.98	−50.30	−58.08	−55.61	−66.46	−55.09	−71.21	−82.24	−89.37
Capital Account, n.i.e....................	78bcd	−1.30	−1.72	−.93	−.65	−1.04	−.74	−4.84	−.81	−1.08	−1.26	−3.08	−1.48
Capital Account, n.i.e.: Credit........	78bad	.81	.82	1.03	.89	.83	.93	1.08	1.07	1.03	1.13	1.12	1.17
Capital Account: Debit..................	78bbd	−2.11	−2.55	−1.96	−1.55	−1.87	−1.67	−5.92	−1.87	−2.11	−2.39	−4.20	−2.64
Financial Account, n.i.e.................	78bjd	82.91	121.72	96.02	131.05	222.30	82.51	227.82	477.39	421.00	573.91	544.24	612.69
Direct Investment Abroad..............	78bdd	−83.95	−80.18	−98.78	−91.88	−104.82	−142.64	−224.93	−159.21	−142.35	−134.84	−173.80	−248.51
Dir. Invest. in Rep. Econ., n.i.e.......	78bed	51.38	46.13	57.80	86.52	105.59	179.03	289.44	321.27	167.02	72.41	39.89	115.53
Portfolio Investment Assets............	78bfd	−146.25	−63.19	−122.39	−149.32	−116.85	−124.20	−116.24	−121.91	−84.64	15.89	−72.34	−90.84
Equity Securities.......................	78bkd	−63.37	−48.29	−65.51	−82.71	−57.29	−101.36	−114.31	−106.71	−109.12	−17.61	−100.43	−92.99
Debt Securities.........................	78bld	−82.88	−14.90	−56.89	−66.61	−59.57	−22.84	−1.93	−15.19	24.48	33.50	28.09	2.15
Portfolio Investment Liab., n.i.e......	78bgd	111.00	139.41	210.35	332.78	333.11	187.56	285.60	436.57	428.34	427.88	544.49	794.38
Equity Securities.......................	78bmd	20.94	.89	16.52	11.06	67.03	41.96	112.29	193.60	121.46	54.22	36.89	57.57
Debt Securities.........................	78bnd	90.06	138.52	193.83	321.72	266.08	145.61	173.31	242.97	306.88	373.66	507.60	736.81
Financial Derivatives Assets...........	78bwd	....	....	....	....	....	....	....	—	....	....	....	....
Financial Derivatives Liabilities........	78bxd	....	....	....	....	....	....	....	—	....	....	....	....
Other Investment Assets................	78bhd	31.02	−40.92	−121.38	−178.87	−262.82	−74.20	−171.22	−288.39	−134.86	−75.39	−38.80	−481.13
Monetary Authorities.................	78bod	—	—	—	—	—	—	—	—	—	—	—	—
General Government...................	78bpd	−.35	−.39	−.98	−.99	.07	−.42	2.75	−.94	−.49	.35	.54	1.27
Banks.....................................	78bqd	30.62	−4.20	−75.11	−91.56	−141.12	−35.57	−76.26	−148.66	−125.86	−30.31	−10.41	−353.81
Other Sectors...........................	78brd	.76	−36.33	−45.29	−86.33	−121.77	−38.20	−97.70	−138.79	−8.52	−45.43	−28.93	−128.59
Other Investment Liab., n.i.e..........	78bid	119.71	120.47	170.43	131.82	268.09	56.96	165.17	289.05	187.50	267.95	244.80	523.26
Monetary Authorities.................	78bsd	68.00	9.59	46.72	56.88	−18.85	6.88	24.59	−2.52	35.29	72.19	36.28	42.79
General Government...................	78btd	.56	2.77	.90	.73	−2.70	−3.25	−.98	−.39	−4.78	2.66	1.95	1.21
Banks.....................................	78bud	39.90	108.00	64.18	22.18	171.31	30.27	67.20	122.72	88.40	117.63	125.06	393.67
Other Sectors...........................	78bvd	11.24	.10	58.63	52.03	118.33	23.07	74.37	169.24	68.58	75.47	81.50	85.59
Net Errors and Omissions................	78cad	1.72	−7.28	24.12	−16.89	−84.27	134.49	65.14	−62.84	−29.29	−95.02	−12.02	51.92
Overall Balance..............................	78cbd	1.38	−5.35	9.75	−6.67	1.01	6.73	−8.73	.29	4.93	3.69	−1.53	−2.80
Reserves and Related Items.............	79dad	−1.38	5.35	−9.75	6.67	−1.01	−6.73	8.73	−.29	−4.93	−3.69	1.53	2.80
Reserve Assets.............................	79dbd	−1.38	5.35	−9.75	6.67	−1.01	−6.73	8.73	−.29	−4.93	−3.69	1.53	2.80
Use of Fund Credit and Loans........	79dcd	—	—	—	—	—	—	—	—	—	—	—	—
Exceptional Financing...................	79ded	—	—	—	—	—	—	—	—	—	—	—	—

		1993	1994	1995	1996	1997	1998	1999	2000	2001	2002	2003	2004
International Investment Position						*Billions of US Dollars*							
Assets	79aad	3,091.40	3,315.13	3,964.56	4,650.84	5,379.13	6,174.52	7,390.46	7,393.64	6,898.71	6,613.32	7,863.97	....
Direct Investment Abroad	79abd	1,061.30	1,114.58	1,363.79	1,608.34	1,879.29	2,279.60	2,839.64	2,694.01	2,314.93	2,039.78	2,730.29	....
Portfolio Investment	79acd	853.53	937.15	1,203.93	1,487.55	1,751.18	2,053.00	2,525.34	2,385.35	2,114.73	1,846.88	2,474.37	....
Equity Securities	79add	543.86	626.76	790.62	1,006.14	1,207.79	1,474.98	2,003.72	1,852.84	1,612.67	1,345.12	1,972.24	....
Debt Securities	79aed	309.67	310.39	413.31	481.41	543.40	578.01	521.63	532.51	502.06	501.76	502.13	....
Financial Derivatives	79ald	—	—	—	—	—	—	—	—	—	—	—	....
Other Investment	79afd	1,011.66	1,100.01	1,220.78	1,394.21	1,613.82	1,695.92	1,889.03	2,185.88	2,339.08	2,568.06	2,475.73	....
Monetary Authorities	79agd	—	—	—	—	—	—	—	—	—	—	—	....
General Government	79ahd	83.38	83.91	85.06	86.12	86.20	86.77	84.23	85.17	85.65	85.31	84.77	....
Banks	79aid	686.25	693.12	768.15	857.51	982.10	1,020.83	1,100.29	1,264.15	1,414.12	1,574.73	1,776.28	....
Other Sectors	79ajd	242.03	322.98	367.57	450.58	545.52	588.32	704.52	836.56	839.30	908.02	614.67	....
Reserve Assets	79akd	164.91	163.39	176.06	160.74	134.84	146.01	136.45	128.40	129.96	158.60	183.58	....
Liabilities	79lad	3,235.71	3,450.39	4,270.39	5,010.86	6,201.86	7,249.90	8,437.12	8,982.20	9,206.87	9,166.73	10,514.96	....
Dir. Invest. in Rep. Economy	79lbd	768.42	757.85	1,005.73	1,229.12	1,637.41	2,179.04	2,798.19	2,783.24	2,560.29	2,025.35	2,435.54	....
Portfolio Investment	79lcd	1,335.54	1,413.54	1,848.75	2,284.15	2,767.48	3,198.67	3,583.08	3,862.63	4,121.72	4,295.25	5,200.57	....
Equity Securities	79ldd	373.52	397.72	549.51	672.40	952.89	1,250.34	1,611.53	1,643.21	1,572.68	1,260.84	1,632.03	....
Debt Securities	79led	962.02	1,015.82	1,299.24	1,611.75	1,814.59	1,948.33	1,971.54	2,219.43	2,549.04	3,034.41	3,568.55	....
Financial Derivatives	79lld	—	—	—	—	—	—	—	—	—	—	—	....
Other Investment	79lfd	1,131.75	1,278.99	1,415.92	1,497.59	1,796.97	1,872.19	2,055.85	2,336.33	2,524.86	2,846.13	2,878.85	....
Monetary Authorities	79lgd	133.73	157.19	169.48	186.85	211.63	228.25	250.66	255.97	279.76	301.27	317.91	....
General Government	79lhd	22.11	23.68	23.57	22.59	21.71	18.39	21.14	19.32	17.01	17.14	16.58	....
Banks	79lid	746.87	858.31	922.44	941.35	1,104.22	1,139.88	1,206.00	1,322.14	1,429.78	1,663.09	2,077.82	....
Other Sectors	79ljd	229.04	239.82	300.42	346.81	459.41	485.68	578.05	738.90	798.31	864.63	466.54	....
Government Finance						*Billions of US Dollars: Year Ending December 31*							
Deficit (-) or Surplus	80	−226.5	−184.6	−146.2	−110.8	−2.4	54.4	156.7	254.6	92.4	−230.5	−396.3	−400.2
Total Revenue and Grants	81y	1,175.2	1,277.5	1,367.2	1,474.7	1,619.3	1,747.7	1,858.3	2,042.7	1,995.3	1,814.4	1,795.7	1,926.2
Revenue	81	....	1,277.5	1,367.2	1,474.7	1,619.3	1,747.7	1,858.3	2,042.7	1,995.3	1,814.4	1,795.7	1,926.2
Grants	81z	....	—	—	—	—	—	—	—	—	—	—	—
Exp. & Lending Minus Repay	82z	1,401.8	1,462.1	1,513.4	1,585.4	1,621.8	1,693.3	1,701.6	1,788.1	1,902.8	2,044.9	2,191.9	2,326.4
Expenditure	82	....	....	....	....	....	....	....	....	....	....	....	....
Lending Minus Repayments	83	....	....	....	....	....	....	....	....	....	....	....	....
Total Financing	80h	226.5	184.6	146.2	110.8	2.4	−54.4	−156.7	−254.6	−92.4	230.5	396.3	400.2
Total Net Borrowing	84	248.2	161.3	151.1	119.9	4.3	−62.2	−92.2	−316.7	−43.1	235.8	381.2	368.0
Net Domestic	84a	....	....	....	....	....	....	....	....	....	....	....	....
Net Foreign	85a	....	....	....	....	....	....	....	....	....	....	....	....
Use of Cash Balances	87	−21.7	23.3	−4.9	−9.1	−1.9	7.9	−64.4	62.1	−49.3	−5.2	15.0	32.2
Total Debt by Residence	88	3,403.8	3,551.7	3,698.7	3,842.1	3,866.5	3,805.7	3,711.6	3,413.2	3,394.4	3,647.9	4,042.9	4,382.6
Domestic	88a	2,753.5	2,884.4	2,863.5	2,740.0	2,624.9	2,527.0	2,442.9	2,379.0	2,343.2	2,401.1	2,505.3	2,438.4
Foreign	89a	650.3	667.3	835.2	1,102.1	1,241.6	1,278.7	1,268.7	1,034.2	1,051.2	1,246.8	1,537.6	1,944.2
National Accounts						*Billions of US Dollars*							
Househ.Cons.Expend.,incl.NPISHs	96f.c	4,477.9	4,743.3	4,975.8	5,256.8	5,547.4	5,879.5	6,282.5	6,739.4	7,055.1	7,350.8	7,709.9	8,214.3
Government Consumption Expend	91f.c	1,072.2	1,104.1	1,136.5	1,171.1	1,216.6	1,256.0	1,334.0	1,417.1	1,501.7	1,616.9	1,736.7	1,843.4
Gross Fixed Capital Formation	93e.c	1,151.6	1,254.6	1,345.6	1,454.4	1,570.0	1,700.7	1,845.6	1,983.5	1,970.1	1,914.5	2,010.2	2,245.2
Changes in Inventories	93i.c	20.8	63.8	31.1	30.8	72.0	70.8	66.9	56.5	−31.7	11.9	15.5	55.5
Exports of Goods and Services	90c.c	655.8	720.9	812.2	868.6	955.4	955.9	991.3	1,096.3	1,032.8	1,005.9	1,045.7	1,173.8
Imports of Goods and Services (-)	98c.c	720.9	814.5	903.6	964.8	1,056.9	1,115.9	1,251.8	1,475.8	1,399.9	1,430.3	1,546.5	1,797.8
Gross Domestic Product (GDP)	99b.c	6,657.4	7,072.2	7,397.7	7,816.8	8,304.3	8,747.0	9,268.4	9,817.0	10,128.0	10,469.6	10,971.3	11,734.3
Net Primary Income from Abroad	98.nc	32.0	26.2	35.8	35.0	33.0	21.4	33.8	39.0	43.7	30.6	68.1	53.8
Gross National Income (GNI)	99a.c	6,549.8	6,955.9	7,332.3	7,758.2	8,266.6	8,783.0	9,337.9	9,983.1	10,261.3	10,521.2	10,992.3	11,711.2
Net Current Transf. from Abroad	98t.c	37.3	37.8	35.4	39.1	41.6	48.8	47.2	56.1	47.0	64.5	71.7	81.5
Gross Saving	99s.c	962.5	1,070.7	1,184.6	1,291.2	1,461.1	1,598.7	1,674.3	1,770.5	1,657.6	1,489.1	1,474.1	1,572.1
Consumption of Fixed Capital	99cfc	776.4	833.7	878.4	918.1	974.5	1,030.2	1,101.3	1,187.8	1,281.5	1,292.0	1,331.3	1,435.3
GDP Volume 2000 Ref., Chained	99b.r	7,532.7	7,835.5	8,031.7	8,328.9	8,703.5	9,066.9	9,470.4	9,817.0	9,890.7	10,048.9	10,320.6	10,755.7
GDP Volume (2000=100)	99bvr	76.7	79.8	81.8	84.8	88.7	92.4	96.5	100.0	100.8	102.4	105.1	109.6
GDP Deflator (2000=100)	99bir	88.4	90.3	92.1	93.9	95.4	96.5	97.9	100.0	102.4	104.2	106.3	109.1
						Millions: Midyear Estimates							
Population	99z	263.84	266.71	269.60	272.51	275.43	278.36	281.27	284.15	287.00	289.82	292.62	295.41

Uruguay   298

		1993	1994	1995	1996	1997	1998	1999	2000	2001	2002	2003	2004
Exchange Rates						*Pesos per SDR: End of Period*							
Market Rate....................	aa	† 6.0656	8.1766	10.5704	12.5289	13.5465	15.2307	15.9417	16.3059	18.5594	36.9789	43.5389	40.9218
					Pesos per US Dollar: End of Period (ae) Period Average (rf)								
Market Rate....................	ae	† 4.4160	5.6010	7.1110	8.7130	10.0400	10.8170	11.6150	12.5150	14.7680	27.2000	29.3000	26.3500
Market Rate....................	rf	† 3.9411	5.0439	6.3490	7.9718	9.4418	10.4719	11.3393	12.0996	13.3191	21.2570	28.2087	28.7037
					Index Numbers (2000=100): Period Averages								
Market Rate....................	ahx	308.3	241.3	191.3	152.2	128.3	115.5	106.7	100.0	90.9	61.1	42.9	42.2
Nominal Effective Exchange Rate.....	nec	134.3	175.1	146.3	120.9	109.0	102.1	101.5	100.0	97.4	71.3	47.3	44.0
Real Effective Exchange Rate...........	rec	79.9	86.3	89.2	90.4	95.0	96.8	99.7	100.0	98.8	78.3	60.3	59.6
Fund Position						*Millions of SDRs: End of Period*							
Quota...........................	2f.s	225	225	225	225	225	225	307	307	307	307	307	307
SDRs............................	1b.s	—	—	2	3	—	1	1	—	1	4	3	1
Reserve Position in the Fund...........	1c.s	15	15	15	15	15	15	36	36	36	—	—	—
Total Fund Cred.&Loans Outstg........	2tl	28	20	14	6	—	114	114	114	114	1,319	1,626	1,728
International Liquidity					*Millions of US Dollars Unless Otherwise Indicated: End of Period*								
Total Reserves minus Gold..............	1l.d	758	969	1,150	1,251	1,556	2,073	2,081	2,479	3,097	769	2,083	2,508
SDRs...........................	1b.d	—	—	4	4	—	1	1	—	2	6	4	1
Reserve Position in the Fund.........	1c.d	21	22	23	22	21	22	49	46	45	—	—	—
Foreign Exchange........................	1d.d	737	946	1,124	1,225	1,536	2,051	2,031	2,432	3,050	763	2,079	2,507
Gold (Million Fine Troy Ounces)........	1ad	1.700	1.704	1.715	1.736	1.760	1.783	1.800	1.081	.008	.008	.008	.008
Gold (National Valuation)................	1and	454	497	525	672	651	517	518	295	2	3	3	4
Monetary Authorities: Other Assets..	3..d	217	234	238	255	266	270	251	253	257	780	463	320
Other Liab.............	4..d	1,062	1,030	976	941	911	884	730	673	489	476	217	220
Banking Institutions: Assets.............	7a.d	3,790	3,499	3,479	4,179	4,758	5,015	5,803	6,252	7,271	4,138	3,725	3,813
Liabilities.................	7b.d	3,393	3,335	3,364	3,966	4,697	5,315	6,076	6,815	7,969	3,586	2,512	1,926
Nonbank Financial Insts.:Assets......	7e.d	....	91	207	242	200	191	86	1,160	1,294	461	773	1,322
Liabilities..............	7f.d	....	77	185	219	180	162	63	868	993	304	706	1,239
Monetary Authorities						*Millions of Pesos: End of Period*							
Foreign Assets........................	11	6,452.5	9,847.2	14,662.8	18,854.9	23,437.0	† 30,926.9	33,135.3	37,944.3	49,565.5	42,221.0	74,714.4	74,621.6
Claims on Central Government........	12a	6,080.3	8,305.9	11,543.8	13,985.3	16,586.3	† 22,043.9	25,926.4	33,860.7	8,160.5	72,765.2	75,217.1	93,483.7
Claims on Local Government...........	12b	.1	.2	.2	.3	.3	† .3	.3	.3	.3	.7	.8	.8
Claims on Nonfin.Pub.Enterprises.....	12c	2,567.7	3,226.9	3,984.7	4,694.5	5,334.5	† 5,253.2	4,998.1	4,701.6	4,677.3	7,439.7	5,656.2	4,117.4
Claims on Private Sector.................	12d	145.0	130.2	150.5	114.9	163.0	† 433.6	458.2	484.3	284.3	2,163.3	2,066.7	1,642.5
Claims on Banking Institutions.........	12e	3,272.0	4,070.7	5,385.7	6,769.6	8,927.5	† 10,258.1	10,803.3	10,447.5	11,928.4	33,030.2	6,187.5	3,954.9
Reserve Money........................	14	8,542.6	11,314.0	14,760.9	19,563.8	24,455.0	† 27,602.3	33,455.0	36,591.5	46,166.3	46,478.7	74,668.0	61,211.1
of which: Currency Outside Banks..	14a	2,312.8	3,313.8	4,327.1	5,269.3	6,498.2	† 7,084.0	7,639.0	7,284.0	7,095.1	7,673.4	9,440.5	10,803.7
Time, Savings,& Fgn.Currency Dep...	15	716.3	997.0	2,083.1	3,926.9	4,872.6	† 6,298.9	7,247.2	5,131.6	5,844.2	7,727.1	7,866.5	9,074.7
Liabs. of Central Bank: Securities.....	16ac	—	—	1,341.9	533.3	803.2	† 1,367.8	1,882.5	519.8	531.9	914.0	7,116.4	14,830.3
Foreign Liabilities.........................	16c	4,858.4	5,936.0	7,089.4	8,275.1	9,147.0	† 11,305.1	10,303.5	10,289.0	9,342.1	61,702.3	77,141.3	76,530.7
Central Government Deposits...........	16d	5,691.3	8,342.1	11,089.0	14,208.1	18,471.3	† 26,237.6	26,300.6	38,629.3	16,040.6	38,167.3	8,263.0	28,100.9
Capital Accounts...........................	17a	−2,149.5	−2,490.5	682.8	363.4	−779.7	† 508.4	596.1	−865.1	−334.2	2,100.1	−8,176.5	−11,361.3
Other Items (Net).........................	17r	858.5	1,482.5	−1,319.3	−2,451.2	−2,520.7	† −4,404.1	−4,463.3	−2,857.4	−2,974.6	530.4	−3,036.2	−565.7
Banking Institutions						*Millions of Pesos: End of Period*							
Reserves....................................	20	6,439.4	7,651.2	9,419.5	12,931.7	15,780.5	† 17,771.7	21,389.5	23,776.6	37,789.7	39,548.8	63,422.8	47,853.9
Claims on Mon.Author.:Securities....	20c	—	—	593.2	524.5	397.3	† 911.4	1,735.1	477.7	531.9	806.4	172.3	1,328.6
Foreign Assets............................	21	16,737.6	19,599.6	24,741.8	36,409.7	47,774.0	† 54,248.8	67,402.9	78,243.2	107,379.3	112,543.6	109,142.7	100,472.6
Claims on Central Government........	22a	2,055.2	3,917.9	3,944.5	4,980.3	7,368.4	† 9,239.7	6,207.5	7,677.1	11,414.2	29,319.8	27,677.1	26,975.5
Claims on Local Government...........	22b	71.2	115.9	194.0	248.9	302.6	† 3,706.8	3,994.3	1,871.6	2,088.1	2,097.4	2,495.7	2,725.1
Claims on Nonfin.Pub.Enterprises.....	22c	161.4	284.7	535.1	712.6	820.2	† 949.2	1,238.3	1,548.5	2,275.2	5,250.4	4,413.8	3,736.6
Claims on Private Sector.................	22d	14,555.5	20,896.4	32,241.8	43,728.0	58,466.5	† 107,287.7	118,105.4	124,044.4	133,635.6	171,868.8	138,471.2	113,489.5
Demand Deposits.........................	24	1,466.1	2,012.5	2,658.7	3,474.1	3,738.0	† 7,314.2	7,216.6	7,053.7	6,641.0	6,556.6	9,706.8	10,928.0
Time, Savings,& Fgn.Currency Dep...	25	18,885.7	26,920.9	37,093.6	50,401.5	65,891.6	† 82,057.8	94,100.1	105,053.1	128,569.9	167,909.3	186,530.5	178,603.7
Money Market Instruments..............	26aa						† 3,531.2	4,640.4	4,905.9	5,890.4	10,211.1	11,540.9	2,084.4
Foreign Liabilities.........................	26c	14,985.6	18,677.1	23,918.8	34,553.9	47,156.4	† 57,489.0	70,576.9	85,293.2	117,692.2	97,548.7	73,595.2	50,760.8
Central Government Deposits...........	26d	1,093.2	1,570.0	1,844.5	2,655.0	4,522.6	† 7,537.6	4,803.5	3,860.6	4,600.4	9,249.9	23,660.5	16,237.0
Credit from Monetary Authorities.....	26g	995.7	818.2	1,042.4	1,475.9	2,072.7	† 10,135.3	10,162.5	10,602.5	11,941.2	35,542.2	5,669.6	2,397.5
Liab. to Nonbank Financial Insts......	26j					85.7	† 215.4	183.1	227.6	144.9	—		
Capital Accounts..........................	27a	2,414.0	3,249.6	5,630.9	8,053.5	10,033.8	† 32,788.5	36,132.5	31,353.1	26,216.6	−7,089.4	10,176.7	26,424.3
Other Items (Net).........................	27r	180.0	−782.6	−518.9	−1,078.1	−2,591.3	† −6,953.9	−7,742.6	−10,710.5	−6,582.7	41,506.7	24,915.3	9,145.9
Banking Survey						*Millions of Pesos: End of Period*							
Foreign Assets (Net).......................	31n	3,346.1	4,833.6	8,396.3	12,435.6	14,907.5	† 16,381.6	19,657.8	20,605.4	29,910.5	−4,486.4	33,120.6	47,802.7
Domestic Credit............................	32	18,851.9	26,966.0	39,661.2	51,601.6	66,048.1	† 115,139.1	129,824.4	131,898.5	141,896.5	243,488.0	224,074.9	201,833.0
Claims on Central Govt. (Net)........	32an	1,351.0	2,311.7	2,554.8	2,102.4	960.9	† −2,491.7	1,029.9	−952.2	−1,066.3	54,667.8	70,970.6	76,121.3
Claims on Local Government.........	32b	71.3	116.1	194.2	249.2	302.9	† 3,707.1	3,994.6	1,871.9	2,088.4	2,098.1	2,496.5	2,725.9
Claims on Nonfin.Pub.Enterprises...	32c	2,729.1	3,511.7	4,519.8	5,407.1	6,154.8	† 6,202.4	6,236.4	6,250.1	6,952.4	12,690.1	10,069.9	7,853.9
Claims on Private Sector...............	32d	14,700.5	21,026.6	32,392.3	43,842.9	58,629.5	† 107,721.3	118,563.5	124,528.7	133,919.9	174,032.0	140,537.9	115,132.0
Money.......................................	34	3,804.6	5,341.1	7,066.3	8,819.1	10,294.6	† 14,420.3	14,873.9	14,355.8	13,755.2	14,278.4	19,177.4	22,225.4
Quasi-Money................................	35	19,602.1	27,918.0	39,176.7	54,328.4	70,764.3	† 88,356.7	101,347.2	110,184.6	134,414.2	175,636.4	194,397.0	187,678.4
Money Market Instruments..............	36aa						† 3,531.2	4,640.4	4,905.9	5,890.4	10,211.1	11,540.9	2,084.4
Liabs. of Central Bank: Securities......	36ac	—	—	748.7	8.8	405.9	† 456.4	147.4	42.0	—	107.7	6,944.2	13,501.7
Liabs. to Nonbank Financial Insts.....	36j					85.7	† 215.4	183.1	227.6	144.9	—		
Capital Accounts..........................	37a	264.5	759.1	6,313.7	8,416.9	9,254.1	† 33,296.9	36,728.6	30,488.0	25,882.5	−4,989.3	2,000.3	15,063.0
Other Items (Net)........................	37r	−1,473.2	−2,218.5	−5,247.7	−7,535.9	−9,848.9	† −8,756.2	−8,438.4	−7,900.1	−8,280.1	43,757.3	23,135.8	9,082.7
Money plus Quasi-Money.................	35l	23,406.6	33,259.1	46,243.0	63,147.4	81,058.8	† 102,777.1	116,221.1	124,540.4	148,169.3	189,914.8	213,574.4	209,903.8

Uruguay 298

		1993	1994	1995	1996	1997	1998	1999	2000	2001	2002	2003	2004
Nonbank Financial Institutions							*Millions of Pesos: End of Period*						
Reserves	40	....	3.1	5.6	7.0	4.5	5.2	9.3	72.7	101.4	99.7	80.6	66.8
Claims on Mon.Author.:Securities	40c	....	2.5	2.1	2.7	2.7	2.4	2.1	22.6	22.7	4.4	3.6	—
Foreign Assets	41	....	510.0	1,469.4	2,109.7	2,011.3	2,066.0	994.3	14,513.2	19,110.9	12,531.9	22,635.1	34,834.8
Claims on Central Government	42a	....	2.6	3.7	4.3	4.3	4.2	2.1	20.4	15.8	13.7	23.1	151.4
Claims on Private Sector	42d	....	.2	1.3	1.8	2.0	.4	.1	3.4	7.0	25.8	18.0	15.9
Claims on Banking Institutions	42e	....	2.5	5.2	3.0	3.4	2.8	2.4	17.1	34.8	9.9	25.4	54.9
Foreign Currency Deposits	45	....	.1	.2	.4	.2	.2	.1	1.7	1.6	1.1	.8	1.0
Foreign Liabilities	46c	....	431.8	1,315.2	1,910.2	1,807.3	1,753.5	736.6	10,864.5	14,657.8	8,264.9	20,674.0	32,654.3
Central Government Deposits	46d	....	.5	.6	.8	.4	.5	.3	3.8	5.1	14.1	9.6	6.4
Capital Accounts	47a	....	101.3	189.2	272.2	336.0	389.9	288.1	4,296.5	5,090.3	4,973.8	3,331.2	3,287.5
Other Items (Net)	47r	....	−12.9	−17.8	−55.1	−115.7	−63.0	−14.7	−517.1	−462.2	−568.3	−1,229.7	−825.3
Money (National Definitions)							*Millions of Pesos: End of Period*						
Base Money	19ma	2,892.2	4,593.9	5,927.9	7,649.8	9,570.5	12,910.0	9,879.3	9,503.6	8,288.0	11,969.4	14,308.1	15,827.5
M1	59ma	4,399.1	6,226.1	8,273.3	10,712.5	12,577.3	14,500.8	15,000.7	14,237.2	13,729.4	14,206.0	19,444.6	22,281.4
M2	59mb	7,598.3	10,031.1	14,351.6	17,990.9	21,392.5	24,763.1	26,094.9	26,832.6	27,217.0	24,410.2	30,294.5	34,699.9
Interest Rates							*Percent Per Annum*						
Discount Rate (End of Period)	60	164.30	182.30	178.70	160.30	95.50	73.70	66.39	57.26	71.66	316.01	....	....
Discount Rate (Fgn.Cur.)(End Per)	60..f	14.30	17.40	17.60	17.50	17.30	15.30	15.68	16.73	14.06	16.96	....	....
Money Market Rate	60b	....	39.82	36.81	28.47	23.43	20.48	13.96	14.82	22.10	89.37	....	....
Treasury Bill Rate	60c	....	44.60	39.40	29.20	23.18	....	....	....	....	....	....	....
Treasury Bill Rate (Fgn.Currency)	60c.f	....	4.91	6.11	5.36	5.18	....	....	....	....	....	....	....
Savings Rate	60k	20.50	19.23	19.07	17.90	13.72	8.53	6.44	5.07	4.77	† 3.89	3.55	1.78
Savings Rate (Fgn.Currency)	60k.f	1.68	1.57	1.83	1.76	1.73	1.53	1.15	1.13	.77	† .57	.57	.27
Deposit Rate	60l	40.38	37.92	39.21	28.84	20.10	15.47	14.61	12.41	14.68	† 42.54	19.75	3.19
Deposit Rate (Fgn.Currency)	60l.f	2.24	2.50	3.30	3.51	3.51	3.56	3.61	3.76	3.09	† 2.34	1.64	.75
Lending Rate	60p	90.55	88.46	92.20	85.14	66.57	53.89	49.57	45.63	48.11	† 117.29	79.89	29.58
Lending Rate (Fgn.Currency)	60p.f	10.67	11.16	13.21	12.56	12.10	11.86	12.06	12.89	11.92	† 12.00	12.51	10.67
Prices, Production, Labor							*Index Numbers (2000=100): Period Averages*						
Wholesale Prices	63	† 32.1	43.1	59.4	74.3	86.4	94.4	93.6	100.0	† 106.6	140.6	195.3	224.0
Consumer Prices	64	25.8	37.3	53.0	68.0	81.5	90.3	95.5	100.0	104.4	118.9	142.0	155.0
Manufacturing Production	66ey	98.2	102.1	99.3	103.3	109.3	111.9	104.5	100.0	94.1	....	....	....
							Number in Thousands: Period Averages						
Labor Force	67d	1,261	1,307	1,343	....	....	1,239	1,239	1,235	1,270	....	1,241	....
Employment	67e	1,156	1,188	1,206	....	....	1,104	1,082	1,068	1,076	1,038	1,032	1,092
Unemployment	67c	105	120	138	....	....	124	138	168	193	212	212	164
Unemployment Rate (%)	67r	8.3	9.2	10.2	....	....	10.1	11.3	13.6	15.3	17.0	16.9	13.1
Intl. Transactions & Positions							*Millions of US Dollars*						
Exports	70..d	1,645.3	1,913.4	2,106.0	2,397.2	2,725.7	2,770.7	2,237.1	2,294.7	2,060.4	1,861.0	2,198.0	2,949.7
Imports, c.i.f.	71..d	2,325.7	2,786.1	2,866.9	3,322.8	3,726.8	3,810.5	3,356.8	3,465.8	3,060.8	1,964.3	2,205.9	2,918.2
Balance of Payments							*Millions of US Dollars: Minus Sign Indicates Debit*						
Current Account, n.i.e.	78ald	−243.8	−438.3	−212.5	−233.4	−287.4	−475.5	−507.6	−566.2	−487.7	322.2	52.1	....
Goods: Exports f.o.b.	78aad	1,731.6	1,917.6	2,147.6	2,448.5	2,793.1	2,829.3	2,290.6	2,383.8	2,139.4	1,922.1	2,273.3	....
Goods: Imports f.o.b.	78abd	−2,118.3	−2,623.6	−2,710.6	−3,135.4	−3,497.5	−3,601.4	−3,187.2	−3,311.1	−2,914.7	−1,873.8	−2,091.5	....
Trade Balance	78acd	−386.7	−706.0	−563.0	−686.9	−704.4	−772.1	−896.6	−927.3	−775.3	48.3	181.8	....
Services: Credit	78add	1,028.4	1,330.7	1,359.2	1,398.7	1,424.1	1,319.1	1,261.6	1,275.7	1,122.5	753.7	777.9	....
Services: Debit	78aed	−746.5	−861.6	−857.7	−839.0	−888.6	−883.5	−802.3	−881.8	−801.4	−600.3	−615.3	....
Balance on Goods & Services	78afd	−104.8	−236.9	−61.5	−127.2	−168.9	−336.6	−437.3	−533.4	−454.2	201.7	344.4	....
Income: Credit	78agd	250.1	282.5	404.3	460.5	547.3	608.0	735.5	781.5	832.0	453.4	237.8	....
Income: Debit	78ahd	−442.5	−525.1	−631.3	−649.2	−740.0	−805.9	−879.3	−841.8	−895.2	−405.1	−601.7	....
Balance on Gds, Serv. & Inc.	78aid	−297.2	−479.5	−288.5	−315.9	−361.6	−534.5	−581.1	−593.7	−517.4	250.0	−19.5	....
Current Transfers, n.i.e.: Credit	78ajd	61.2	49.2	84.0	90.7	83.0	75.0	78.4	48.0	48.0	83.7	79.8	....
Current Transfers: Debit	78akd	−7.8	−8.0	−8.0	−8.2	−8.8	−16.0	−4.9	−20.5	−18.3	−11.5	−8.2	....
Capital Account, n.i.e.	78bcd	—	—	—	—	—	—	—	—	—	—	—	....
Capital Account, n.i.e.: Credit	78bad	—	—	—	—	—	—	—	—	—	—	—	....
Capital Account: Debit	78bbd	—	—	—	—	—	—	—	—	—	—	—	....
Financial Account, n.i.e.	78bjd	228.0	537.2	421.7	233.6	608.7	545.1	147.1	779.3	457.3	−1,927.5	−342.6	....
Direct Investment Abroad	78bdd	—	—	—	—	—	−13.2	−9.3	.6	−6.2	−53.8	−3.7	....
Dir. Invest. in Rep. Econ., n.i.e.	78bed	101.5	154.5	156.6	136.8	126.4	164.1	235.3	273.5	271.0	174.6	274.6	....
Portfolio Investment Assets	78bfd	—	—	—	—	—	—	−44.3	−98.1	236.7	95.2	−521.7	....
Equity Securities	78bkd	—	—	—	—	—	—	—	—	10.2	—	—	....
Debt Securities	78bld	—	—	—	—	—	—	−44.3	−98.1	226.5	95.2	−521.7	....
Portfolio Investment Liab., n.i.e.	78bgd	29.3	158.1	288.8	179.9	209.6	419.4	128.2	289.5	264.4	204.5	22.9	....
Equity Securities	78bmd	—	—	—	—	—	—	—	—	28.1	—	—	....
Debt Securities	78bnd	29.3	158.1	288.8	179.9	209.6	419.4	128.2	289.5	236.3	204.5	22.9	....
Financial Derivatives Assets	78bwd	....	....							....	....	....	....
Financial Derivatives Liabilities	78bxd												
Other Investment Assets	78bhd	−19.3	−71.8	−961.9	−1,238.5	−626.6	−428.0	−119.3	−690.4	−2,275.2	1,825.5	−1,252.8	....
Monetary Authorities	78bod	....	−10.1	—	—	—	—	—	—	.9	−5.3	−522.6	272.4	....
General Government	78bpd	—	—	—	—	—	—	—	—	10.0	2.0	—	....
Banks	78bqd	−18.6	−44.0	−961.3	−1,232.4	−636.4	−428.0	65.4	−549.3	−2,210.5	3,014.5	−1,400.8	....
Other Sectors	78brd	−.7	−17.7	−.6	−6.1	9.8	—	−184.7	−142.0	−69.4	−668.4	−124.4	....
Other Investment Liab., n.i.e.	78bid	116.5	296.4	938.2	1,155.4	912.5	398.9	−52.8	1,004.2	1,966.6	−4,173.5	1,138.1	....
Monetary Authorities	78bsd	−23.7	5.7	−62.5	−10.3	−31.3	−37.2	−135.7	−38.8	−52.4	−13.1	−84.0	....
General Government	78btd	120.3	134.0	18.6	20.3	96.8	169.1	260.5	200.7	144.4	666.6	328.4	....
Banks	78bud	16.0	99.8	1,017.9	1,112.9	778.9	272.9	−161.3	862.5	1,780.5	−4,693.7	964.4	....
Other Sectors	78bvd	3.9	56.9	−35.8	32.5	68.1	−5.9	−16.3	−20.2	94.1	−133.3	−70.7	....
Net Errors and Omissions	78cad	208.7	10.2	18.6	152.2	78.8	285.5	250.9	−46.6	334.4	−2,291.8	1,248.5	....
Overall Balance	78cbd	192.9	109.1	227.8	152.4	400.1	355.1	−109.6	166.5	304.0	−3,897.1	957.9	....
Reserves and Related Items	79dad	−192.9	−109.1	−227.8	−152.4	−400.1	−355.1	109.6	−166.5	−304.0	3,897.1	−957.9	....
Reserve Assets	79dbd	−178.6	−98.5	−218.0	−140.8	−391.7	−515.2	109.6	−166.5	−304.0	2,331.2	−1,380.4	....
Use of Fund Credit and Loans	79dcd	−14.4	−10.6	−9.8	−11.6	−8.3	160.1	—	—	—	1,565.9	422.5	....
Exceptional Financing	79ded	—	—	—	—	....	—	—	—	—	—	—	....

		1993	1994	1995	1996	1997	1998	1999	2000	2001	2002	2003	2004
International Investment Position							*Millions of US Dollars*						
Assets.........................	79aad	....	....	....	....	....	....	12,747.3	13,789.1	16,986.1	10,271.8	13,324.8	....
Direct Investment Abroad............	79abd	—	—	—	—	—	—	47.2	54.0	132.0	108.0	111.6	....
Portfolio Investment..................	79acd	48.1	50.4	52.4	56.9	61.7	66.9	842.3	799.0	1,203.4	999.3	1,479.9	....
Equity Securities..................	79add												....
Debt Securities...................	79aed	48.1	50.4	52.4	56.9	61.7	66.9	842.3	799.0	1,203.4	999.3	1,479.9	....
Financial Derivatives.................	79ald	....	....	....	....	....	....						
Other Investment....................	79afd	3,270.3	3,892.6	4,805.5	6,060.9	6,718.3	7,276.9	8,691.9	10,158.3	12,550.7	8,392.1	9,646.6	....
Monetary Authorities.................	79agd	72.6	80.2	83.3	49.1	111.8	113.1	—	103.4	177.0	600.4	329.9	
General Government.................	79ahd	—	—	—	—	—	—	—					
Banks.............................	79aid	3,161.4	3,758.3	4,667.5	5,951.0	6,555.5	7,108.0	5,457.5	6,607.2	8,804.8	3,197.6	4,598.2	
Other Sectors.....................	79ajd	36.3	54.1	54.7	60.8	51.0	55.8	3,234.4	3,447.7	3,568.8	4,594.1	4,718.5	
Reserve Assets.....................	79akd	2,201.2	2,292.9	2,490.6	2,600.2	2,776.8	3,320.6	3,165.9	2,777.8	3,100.0	772.4	2,086.7	
Liabilities.........................	79lad	....	....	....	....	....	....	14,511.7	15,583.1	18,800.6	12,034.9	14,232.1	
Dir. Invest. in Rep. Economy..........	79lbd	—	—	—	—	—	—	1,790.3	2,088.0	2,406.2	1,402.5	1,677.1	
Portfolio Investment..................	79lcd	1,512.6	1,668.6	1,954.9	2,136.7	2,187.3	2,606.7	2,340.2	2,721.1	3,053.0	2,433.9	2,561.2	
Equity Securities..................	79ldd							—	—	—	—	—	
Debt Securities...................	79led	1,512.6	1,668.6	1,954.9	2,136.7	2,187.3	2,606.7	2,340.2	2,721.1	3,053.0	2,433.9	2,561.2	
Financial Derivatives.................	79lld												
Other Investment....................	79lfd	6,440.5	7,501.7	8,436.9	9,467.3	10,297.2	11,055.7	10,381.2	10,774.0	13,341.4	8,198.5	9,993.8	
Monetary Authorities.................	79lgd	165.6	150.2	68.0	50.3	77.4	232.0	218.9	518.5	550.8	2,093.1	2,632.2	
General Government.................	79lhd	1,268.3	1,416.9	1,537.6	1,507.2	1,594.8	1,738.3	1,976.2	1,904.1	2,077.6	2,493.8	2,848.4	
Banks.............................	79lid	3,644.8	4,150.3	5,182.4	6,275.2	7,152.8	7,628.9	6,911.5	7,753.9	9,679.6	2,999.5	3,963.8	
Other Sectors.....................	79ljd	1,361.8	1,784.3	1,648.9	1,634.6	1,472.2	1,456.5	1,274.6	597.5	1,033.4	612.1	549.4	
Government Finance						*Millions of Pesos: Year Ending December 31*							
Deficit (-) or Surplus..................	80	−304	−2,308	−1,467	−2,379	−2,435	−1,817	† −8,882	−8,322	−11,554	....	....	
Revenue............................	81	17,799	26,409	33,923	45,535	60,165	70,664	† 67,197	68,167	65,933	....	....	
Expenditure........................	82	18,103	28,717	35,390	47,914	62,363	72,673	† 76,079	76,489	77,487	....	....	
Lending Minus Repayments...........	83	—	—	—	—	237	−192	† —	—	—	....	....	
Financing													
Net Borrowing......................	84	304	2,308	....	....	....	....	....	....	....	....	....	
Domestic...................	84a	322	1,378	....	....	....	....	....	....	....	....	....	
Foreign.....................	85a	−18	930	....	....	....	....	....	....	....	....	....	
Use of Cash Balances..................	87	—	—	....	....	....	....	....	....	....	....	....	
Debt: Domestic......................	88a	3,608	7,728	....	....	....	....	....	....	....	....	....	
Foreign......................	89a	9,328	13,893	....	....	....	....	....	....	....	....	....	
National Accounts							*Millions of Pesos*						
Househ.Cons.Expend.,incl.NPISHs....	96f	42,934	64,230	89,265	117,978	148,387	169,442	173,360	181,114	183,519	192,167	235,348	281,324
Government Consumption Expend...	91f	7,199	10,464	14,505	20,952	25,324	29,357	30,871	32,070	33,837	33,622	35,833	41,137
Gross Fixed Capital Formation.........	93e	8,724	12,820	16,573	22,835	29,609	35,522	34,377	32,029	30,943	26,360	29,785	43,222
Changes in Inventories..................	93i	524	1,169	2,304	2,089	1,585	1,657	1,536	1,891	3,106	3,707	9,947	7,173
Exports of Goods and Services........	90c	11,308	17,423	23,275	32,169	42,109	46,511	42,758	46,915	45,353	57,325	82,301	112,461
Imports of Goods and Services (-).....	98c	11,564	17,965	23,403	32,478	42,088	48,222	45,758	50,993	49,546	52,214	77,535	105,999
Gross Domestic Product (GDP)........	99b	59,125	88,140	122,521	163,546	204,926	234,267	237,143	243,027	247,211	260,967	315,681	379,317
Net Primary Income from Abroad.....	98.n	−958	−1,617	−1,929	−2,265	−2,910	−3,168	−3,249	−3,386	−5,077	−2,595	−13,860	−15,513
Gross National Income (GNI)...........	99a	58,167	86,523	120,592	161,281	202,016	231,099	233,894	239,641	242,134	258,371	301,821	363,804
GDP Vol. 1983 Prices (Millions)........	99b.p	244	262	258	273	286	299	291	287	277	246	252	283
GDP Volume (2000=100)............	99bvp	85.2	91.4	90.1	95.1	99.9	104.4	101.5	100.0	96.6	86.0	87.8	98.6
GDP Deflator (2000=100)..............	99bip	28.6	39.7	56.0	70.8	84.4	92.3	96.2	100.0	105.3	124.9	147.9	158.3
							Millions: Midyear Estimates						
Population..............................	99z	3.17	3.19	3.22	3.24	3.27	3.29	3.32	3.34	3.37	3.39	3.42	3.44

		1993	1994	1995	1996	1997	1998	1999	2000	2001	2002	2003	2004
Exchange Rates		*Vatu per SDR: Unless Otherwise Indicated: End of Period*											
Official Rate	aa	165.93	163.62	169.07	159.28	167.73	182.73	176.90	186.07	184.41	181.05	166.15	165.44
		Vatu per US Dollar: End of Period (ae) Period Average (rf)											
Official Rate	ae	120.80	112.08	113.74	110.77	124.31	129.78	128.89	142.81	146.74	133.17	111.81	106.53
Official Rate	rf	121.58	116.41	112.11	111.72	115.87	127.52	129.08	137.64	145.31	139.20	122.19	111.79
Fund Position		*Millions of SDRs: Unless Otherwise Indicated: End of Period*											
Quota	2f.s	12.50	12.50	12.50	12.50	12.50	12.50	17.00	17.00	17.00	17.00	17.00	17.00
SDRs	1b.s	.15	.22	.29	.36	.44	.53	.60	.70	.79	.84	.89	.93
Reserve Position in the Fund	1c.s	2.49	2.49	2.49	2.49	2.50	2.50	2.50	2.50	2.50	2.50	2.50	2.50
Total Fund Cred.&Loans Outstg	2tl	—	—	—	—	—	—	—	—	—	—	—	—
International Liquidity		*Millions of US Dollars Unless Otherwise Indicated: End of Period*											
Total Reserves minus Gold	1l.d	45.59	43.58	48.29	43.92	37.30	44.67	41.35	38.92	37.66	36.52	43.82	61.81
SDRs	1b.d	.21	.31	.43	.52	.60	.74	.83	.91	.99	1.15	1.32	1.44
Reserve Position in the Fund	1c.d	3.42	3.63	3.70	3.58	3.37	3.51	3.43	3.25	3.14	3.39	3.71	3.88
Foreign Exchange	1d.d	41.96	39.63	44.16	39.82	33.34	40.41	37.10	34.76	33.53	31.98	38.79	56.49
Monetary Authorities	1dad	41.95	39.62	44.16	39.82	33.34	40.41	37.10	34.76	33.53	31.98	38.79	56.49
Government	1dbd	.01	.01	—	—	—	.13	.18	.23	.52	.40	.18	.06
Monetary Authorities: Other Liab	4..d	.17	.22	.04	.04	.04	.13	.18	.23	.52	.40	.18	.06
Deposit Money Banks: Assets	7a.d	157.83	158.73	183.94	205.28	204.83	189.99	164.26	160.63	192.62	215.72	243.35	263.41
Liabilities	7b.d	29.48	26.54	32.05	28.42	47.97	25.01	33.92	26.15	28.47	65.22	65.00	64.76
Other Banking Insts.: Assets	7e.d	—	—	—	—	—	....	....	....	....	....	....	....
Liabilities	7f.d	2	6	4	4	4	....	....	....	....	....	....	....
Monetary Authorities		*Millions of Vatu: End of Period*											
Foreign Assets	11	5,519	4,883	5,491	4,865	4,638	5,796	5,331	5,728	5,642	4,960	4,826	6,566
Claims on Central Government	12a	—	307	420	408	898	1,221	1,401	1,442	1,151	1,241	1,471	1,418
Claims on Nonfin.Pub.Enterprises	12c	—	310	327	353	260	36	32	58	294	320		
Claims on Private Sector	12d	73	76	95	108	124	130	148	143	155	172	180	150
Claims on Deposit Money Banks	12e	4	1	3	98	257	—	316	2	—	2	100	19
of which: Fgn.Currency Claims	12ex	4	1	3	2	1	—	—	2	—	2	—	19
Reserve Money	14	3,005	2,801	3,654	3,500	3,493	3,674	4,493	4,579	4,563	4,561	4,924	5,431
of which: Currency Outside DMBs	14a	1,224	1,351	1,566	1,571	1,662	2,042	1,936	1,834	1,941	1,916	2,108	2,490
Liabs. of Central Bank: Securities	16ac	—	—	—	—	—	—	1,233	297	99	446	324	99	1,069
Foreign Liabilities	16c	21	25	5	18	4	17	23	33	77	53	20	6
Central Government Deposits	16d	2,315	2,102	1,962	1,739	2,104	1,679	1,902	1,898	1,377	965	833	1,091
Capital Accounts	17a	748	740	641	654	672	686	698	709	724	729	792	673
Valuation Adjustment	17rv	248	134	236	87	64	61	49	32	10	39	—	—
Other Items (Net)	17r	−741	† −224	−162	−166	−161	−169	−233	23	45	22	−91	−117
Deposit Money Banks		*Millions of Vatu: End of Period*											
Reserves	20	1,821	1,397	2,033	1,829	1,742	1,238	2,215	2,547	2,496	2,563	2,720	2,805
Claims on Mon.Author.:Securities	20c	—	—	—	—	—	1,001	297	99	446	324	99	1,069
Foreign Assets	21	19,065	17,790	20,921	22,738	25,462	24,657	21,171	22,940	28,265	28,727	27,209	28,061
Claims on Central Government	22a	937	527	506	492	496	1,131	930	1,417	1,108	1,191	773	813
Claims on Local Government	22b	—	—	2	2	4	—	4	3	5	2	5	6
Claims on Nonfin.Pub.Enterprises	22c	6	105	62	30	134	108	53	100	28	15	16	29
Claims on Private Sector	22d	7,944	8,540	9,075	9,796	9,580	10,605	12,158	11,556	12,295	13,265	14,558	15,953
Claims on Other Financial Insts	22f	100	38	21	—	2	—	—	—	—	—	—	—
Demand Deposits	24	4,448	4,339	4,690	4,880	4,941	5,368	5,296	6,051	5,974	9,608	10,067	10,243
Time, Savings,& Fgn.Currency Dep	25	18,778	19,443	22,225	24,879	24,645	27,626	24,377	25,686	27,643	23,485	22,553	25,415
of which: Nonreporting Bks' Deps	25e	80	—	—	—	—	—	—	—	—	—	—	—
Foreign Liabilities	26c	3,561	2,975	3,645	3,148	5,963	3,246	4,372	3,735	4,177	8,685	7,268	6,899
Central Government Deposits	26d	709	296	161	10	52	140	141	157	292	244	282	185
Credit from Monetary Authorities	26g	3	1	3	1	3	—	—	316	—	—	—	—
Capital Accounts	27a	2,297	1,726	1,698	2,142	1,350	2,468	2,734	3,550	4,266	4,129	5,222	6,279
Other Items (Net)	27r	76	−381	199	−174	464	−108	−409	−515	2,290	−64	−11	−284
Monetary Survey		*Millions of Vatu: End of Period*											
Foreign Assets (Net)	31n	21,003	19,674	22,763	24,438	24,132	27,189	22,107	24,901	29,653	24,948	24,748	27,722
Domestic Credit	32	6,036	† 7,514	8,385	9,439	9,341	11,412	12,683	12,664	13,366	14,996	15,888	17,094
Claims on Central Govt. (Net)	32an	−2,087	−1,564	−1,197	−849	−762	533	288	804	589	1,223	1,129	954
Claims on Local Government	32b	—	—	2	2	4	—	4	3	5	2	5	6
Claims on Nonfin.Pub.Enterprises	32c	6	† 416	389	382	394	144	85	158	322	334	16	29
Claims on Private Sector	32d	8,017	8,616	9,170	9,904	9,703	10,735	12,306	11,699	12,451	13,437	14,738	16,103
Claims on Other Financial Insts	32f	100	† 46	21	—	2	—	—	—	—	—	—	—
Money	34	5,679	5,728	6,306	6,528	6,642	7,600	7,616	8,082	8,041	11,606	12,271	12,869
Quasi-Money	35	18,778	19,443	22,225	24,879	24,645	27,626	24,377	25,686	27,643	23,485	22,553	25,415
Capital Accounts	37a	3,045	2,466	2,339	2,797	2,022	3,155	3,432	4,259	4,990	4,858	6,014	6,952
Other Items (Net)	37r	−463	† −449	277	−327	163	221	−636	−462	2,344	−5	−202	−420
Money plus Quasi-Money	35l	24,457	25,171	28,531	31,407	31,287	35,226	31,994	33,769	35,684	35,091	34,824	38,284
Other Banking Institutions		*Millions of Vatu: End of Period*											
Cash	40	43	15	5	572	36	....	....	....	....	....	....	....
Foreign Assets	41	42	45	51	—	—	....	....	....	....	....	....	....
Claims on Central Government	42a	60	10	10	10	10	....	....	....	....	....	....	....
Claims on Private Sector	42d	608	598	691	40	548	....	....	....	....	....	....	....
Claims on Deposit Money Banks	42e	—	—	—	—	—	....	....	....	....	....	....	....
Time and Savings Deposits	45	—	—	—	—	—	....	....	....	....	....	....	....
Foreign Liabilities	46c	183	625	495	492	491	....	....	....	....	....	....	....
Capital Accounts	47a	450	450	535	535	535	....	....	....	....	....	....	....
Other Items (Net)	47r	120	−407	−273	−405	−432	....	....	....	....	....	....	....

Vanuatu 846

		1993	1994	1995	1996	1997	1998	1999	2000	2001	2002	2003	2004
Banking Survey							*Millions of Vatu: End of Period*						
Foreign Assets (Net)	51n	20,862	19,094	22,318	23,946	23,641	....	....	....	....	....	....	....
Domestic Credit	52	6,604	8,076	9,065	9,488	9,897	....	....	....	....	....	....	....
Claims on Central Govt. (Net)	52an	−2,027	−1,554	−1,187	−839	−752	....	....	....	....	....	....	....
Claims on Nonfin.Pub.Enterprises	52c	6	† 416	389	382	394	....	....	....	....	....	....	....
Claims on Private Sector	52d	8,625	9,214	9,861	9,944	10,251	....	....	....	....	....	....	....
Liquid Liabilities	55l	24,414	25,156	28,526	30,835	31,251	....	....	....	....	....	....	....
Other Items (Net)	57r	3,052	† 2,014	2,857	2,599	2,287	....	....	....	....	....	....	....
Interest Rates							*Percent Per Annum*						
Discount Rate (End of Period)	60	....	....	....	....	....	7.00	7.00	7.00	6.50	6.50	6.50	6.50
Money Market Rate	60b	6.00	6.00	6.00	6.00	6.00	8.65	6.99	5.58	5.50	5.50	5.50	5.50
Deposit Rate	60l	5.00	5.06	3.00	4.50	3.73	3.29	1.60	1.27	1.25	1.00	1.21	1.71
Lending Rate	60p	16.00	16.00	10.50	10.50	10.50	10.96	10.29	9.85	8.81	7.41	5.90	7.61
Government Bond Yield	61	8.00	8.00	8.00	8.00	8.00	8.00	8.50	8.50	8.50	8.50	8.50	8.50
Prices							*Index Numbers (2000=100): Period Averages*						
Consumer Prices	64	85.4	87.3	† 89.3	90.1	92.6	95.7	97.6	100.0	103.7	105.7	108.9	110.4
Intl. Transactions & Positions							*Millions of Vatu*						
Exports	70	2,758	2,911	3,173	3,368	4,087	4,323	3,327	3,622	2,895	2,590	3,252	4,168
Imports, c.i.f.	71	9,581	10,404	10,659	10,888	10,888	11,957	12,608	11,957	13,118	12,433	12,703	14,306
Balance of Payments							*Millions of US Dollars: Minus Sign Indicates Debit*						
Current Account, n.i.e.	78ald	−14.93	−19.78	−18.25	−26.94	−19.34	−9.41	−33.22	−13.65	−14.53	−31.19	−41.25	....
Goods: Exports f.o.b.	78aad	17.43	25.11	28.28	30.20	35.32	33.78	25.66	27.19	19.89	20.20	26.84	....
Goods: Imports f.o.b.	78abd	−64.71	−74.68	−79.44	−81.11	−78.99	−76.23	−84.46	−76.94	−77.96	−78.44	−91.80	....
Trade Balance	78acd	−47.28	−49.58	−51.16	−50.91	−43.67	−42.44	−58.80	−49.74	−58.07	−58.24	−64.96	....
Services: Credit	78add	68.88	78.14	81.65	92.75	87.79	113.95	114.80	129.81	119.26	81.37	94.78	....
Services: Debit	78aed	−29.97	−33.44	−35.27	−36.50	−35.95	−56.97	−72.09	−70.15	−72.99	−45.31	−54.23	....
Balance on Goods & Services	78afd	−8.36	−4.88	−4.78	5.34	8.16	14.55	−16.09	9.91	−11.80	−22.18	−24.41	....
Income: Credit	78agd	14.95	9.94	13.07	15.82	15.41	20.98	21.00	18.74	17.23	22.46	24.21	....
Income: Debit	78ahd	−43.48	−47.36	−49.79	−47.55	−45.68	−29.26	−26.09	−31.71	−21.23	−28.62	−35.96	....
Balance on Gds, Serv. & Inc.	78aid	−36.89	−42.30	−41.49	−26.39	−22.11	6.26	−21.18	−3.06	−15.80	−28.34	−36.17	....
Current Transfers, n.i.e.: Credit	78ajd	22.54	23.24	23.81	22.39	21.77	15.55	18.72	27.41	39.53	5.92	4.82	....
Current Transfers: Debit	78akd	−.58	−.72	−.56	−22.94	−19.00	−31.22	−30.76	−38.00	−38.26	−8.77	−9.90	....
Capital Account, n.i.e.	78bcd	26.30	37.28	31.62	4.90	−5.46	−20.86	−49.72	−23.58	−16.03	−2.29	−4.65	....
Capital Account, n.i.e.: Credit	78bad	32.04	41.45	38.33	43.38	23.75	25.44	23.94	31.88	46.07	10.59	10.45	....
Capital Account: Debit	78bbd	−5.74	−4.17	−6.71	−38.48	−29.21	−46.29	−73.66	−55.46	−62.10	−12.89	−15.09	....
Financial Account, n.i.e.	78bjd	14.53	−13.41	25.30	20.88	−16.73	17.37	56.17	19.33	12.75	20.71	39.57	....
Direct Investment Abroad	78bdd	—	—	—	....	....	....	....	....	....	−.57	−.67	....
Dir. Invest. in Rep. Econ., n.i.e.	78bed	25.97	29.79	31.04	32.73	30.23	20.38	13.40	20.26	18.00	8.85	15.45	....
Portfolio Investment Assets	78bfd	—	—	—	....	....	3.45	−1.01	.69	−4.33	−.33	2.11	....
Equity Securities	78bkd	—	—	—	....	....	....	....	....	....	....	....	....
Debt Securities	78bld	—	—	—	....	....	....	....	....	....	—	—	....
Portfolio Investment Liab., n.i.e.	78bgd	—	—	—	....	....	....	....	....	....	—	—	....
Equity Securities	78bmd	—	—	—	....	....	....	....	....	....	....	....	....
Debt Securities	78bnd	—	—	—	....	....	....	....	....	....	—	—	....
Financial Derivatives Assets	78bwd	....	....	....	....	....	....	....	....	....	....	....	....
Financial Derivatives Liabilities	78bxd	....	....	....	....	....	....	....	....	....	....	....	....
Other Investment Assets	78bhd	−27.50	−45.47	−1.59	−16.63	−23.53	5.12	29.63	−13.55	−11.41	−3.35	51.80	....
Monetary Authorities	78bod	....	....	....	....	....	....	....	....	....	....	....	....
General Government	78bpd	−.43	−.45	−.30	−.39	−.46	....	....	....	....	....	....	....
Banks	78bqd	−10.76	10.60	−2.18	−16.25	−23.07	5.89	27.05	−13.10	−14.81	....	....	....
Other Sectors	78brd	−16.31	−55.62	.89	....	....	−.77	2.59	−.45	3.40	....	....	....
Other Investment Liab., n.i.e.	78bid	16.05	2.27	−4.15	4.78	−23.43	−11.58	14.15	11.93	10.48	16.12	−29.12	....
Monetary Authorities	78bsd	.16	−.05	.18	−.12	.12	−.11	1.30	−.03	.53	....	....	....
General Government	78btd	6.60	2.17	2.21	.45	.68	10.52	5.12	16.36	3.20	—	....	....
Banks	78bud	9.29	.16	−6.54	4.46	−24.23	−20.91	8.73	−4.79	3.05	....	....	....
Other Sectors	78bvd	—	—	—	....	....	−1.09	−1.01	.39	3.70	....	....	....
Net Errors and Omissions	78cad	−22.44	−10.21	−33.38	−4.14	39.37	6.01	3.57	−.88	7.55	−5.60	−5.02	....
Overall Balance	78cbd	3.45	−6.12	5.30	−5.30	−2.16	−6.89	−23.19	−18.77	−10.27	−18.37	−11.35	....
Reserves and Related Items	79dad	−3.45	6.12	−5.30	5.30	2.16	6.89	23.19	18.77	10.27	18.37	11.34	....
Reserve Assets	79dbd	−6.70	4.86	−5.30	5.30	2.16	−8.06	3.48	.87	.62	4.85	−.93	....
Use of Fund Credit and Loans	79dcd	—	—	—	—	—	—	—	—	—	—	—	....
Exceptional Financing	79ded	3.26	1.26	....	....	....	14.95	19.71	17.90	9.64	13.52	12.27	....

Vanuatu 846

		1993	1994	1995	1996	1997	1998	1999	2000	2001	2002	2003	2004
International Investment Position							*Millions of US Dollars*						
Assets............................	79aad	....	....	....	....	....	237.57	264.79	....	....	458.94	503.20	....
Direct Investment Abroad..............	79abd	....	....	....	....	....	—	—	....	....	9.33	11.84	....
Portfolio Investment...................	79acd	....	....	....	....	....	2.93	4.42	....	....	11.79	12.19	....
Equity Securities........................	79add	....	....	....	....	....	2.00	3.49	....	....	—	—	....
Debt Securities.........................	79aed	....	....	....	....	....	.92	.93	....	....	11.79	12.19	....
Financial Derivatives.....................	79ald	....	....	....	....	....	—	—	....	....	—	—	....
Other Investment........................	79afd	....	....	....	....	....	189.99	219.01	....	....	401.30	435.10	....
Monetary Authorities..................	79agd	....	....	....	....	....	—	—	....	....	....	....	....
General Government..................	79ahd	....	....	....	....	....	—	—	....	....	—	—	....
Banks.....................................	79aid	....	....	....	....	....	189.99	164.26	....	....	....	....	....
Other Sectors...........................	79ajd	....	....	....	....	....	—	54.74	....	....	412.04	442.66	....
Reserve Assets..........................	79akd	....	....	....	....	....	44.65	41.36	....	....	36.52	44.07	....
Liabilities..............................	79lad	....	....	....	....	....	265.14	280.72	....	....	483.14	578.92	....
Dir. Invest. in Rep. Economy...........	79lbd	....	....	....	....	....	47.62	66.53	....	....	108.88	149.45	....
Portfolio Investment...................	79lcd	....	....	....	....	....	—	—	....	....	—	—	....
Equity Securities........................	79ldd	....	....	....	....	....	—	—	....	....	—	—	....
Debt Securities.........................	79led	....	....	....	....	....	....	....	....	....	—	—	....
Financial Derivatives.....................	79lld	....	....	....	....	....	—	—	....	....	—	—	....
Other Investment........................	79lfd	....	....	....	....	....	217.52	214.19	....	....	374.27	429.47	....
Monetary Authorities..................	79lgd	....	....	....	....	....	.18	1.70	....	....	....	....	....
General Government..................	79lhd	....	....	....	....	....	51.93	56.98	....	....	....	....	....
Banks.....................................	79lid	....	....	....	....	....	162.17	153.25	....	....	....	....	....
Other Sectors...........................	79ljd	....	....	....	....	....	3.25	2.27	....	....	....	....	....
National Accounts							*Millions of Vatu*						
Househ.Cons.Expend.,incl.NPISHs....	96f	11,701	12,286	12,777	....	17,473	18,399	18,727	19,376	19,407	20,035	21,085	....
Government Consumption Expend...	91f	6,765	6,903	6,916	....	6,161	6,751	7,462	7,787	7,688	7,582	7,707	....
Gross Fixed Capital Formation.........	93e	6,075	6,618	8,128	....	5,343	5,606	6,418	7,181	6,880	6,943	6,756	....
Changes in Inventories....................	93i	540	580	570	....	242	129	152	275	−65	−15	−42	....
Exports of Goods and Services..........	90c	10,772	11,796	12,041	....	15,459	14,145	12,930	14,491	13,734	13,891	14,786	....
Imports of Goods and Services (-).....	98c	12,789	14,278	14,603	....	14,945	17,543	18,630	19,087	20,119	19,200	19,829	....
Gross Domestic Product (GDP)........	99b	23,779	24,962	26,633	27,393	29,650	32,423	32,399	33,662	34,105	32,726	33,757	....
Net Primary Income from Abroad.....	98.n	−2,696	−3,021	−2,792	−2,027	−1,342	−1,055	−657	−1,784	−669	−704	−1,416	....
Gross National Income (GNI)...........	99a	21,083	21,941	23,841	25,366	28,308	33,239	32,094	33,177	33,436	31,863	32,341	....
GDP Volume 1983 Prices.................	99b.p	13,676	14,024	14,469	15,733	16,505	17,216	16,668	17,113	16,760	15,832	16,216	....
GDP Volume (2000=100)...............	99bvp	79.9	81.9	84.5	91.9	96.4	100.6	97.4	100.0	97.9	92.5	94.8	....
GDP Deflator (2000=100)...............	99bip	88.4	90.5	93.6	88.5	91.3	95.7	98.8	100.0	103.4	105.1	105.8	....
							Millions: Midyear Estimates						
Population..............................	99z	.16	.17	.17	.18	.18	.18	.19	.19	.20	.20	.20	.21

Venezuela, República Bolivariana de   299

		1993	1994	1995	1996	1997	1998	1999	2000	2001	2002	2003	2004
Exchange Rates							*Bolivares per SDR: End of Period*						
Official Rate	aa	145.102	† 248.175	431.082	685.188	680.359	794.833	889.730	911.711	958.885	1,905.027	2,374.580	2,978.673
						Bolivares per US Dollar: End of Period (ae) Period Average (rf)							
Official Rate	ae	105.640	† 170.000	290.000	476.500	504.250	564.500	648.250	699.750	763.000	1,401.250	1,598.000	1,918.000
Official Rate	rf	90.826	† 148.503	176.843	417.333	488.635	547.556	605.717	679.960	723.666	1,160.953	1,606.962	1,891.333
						Index Numbers (2000=100): Period Averages							
Market Rate	ahx	753.2	477.0	388.9	170.4	139.3	124.4	112.4	100.0	94.0	61.5	42.3	36.0
Nominal Effective Exchange Rate	nec	548.8	392.6	319.4	144.3	124.6	115.2	106.6	100.0	97.8	63.6	40.6	32.9
Real Effective Exchange Rate	rec	51.5	49.4	61.9	52.2	68.4	83.8	94.3	100.0	107.2	82.7	68.8	66.2
Fund Position							*Millions of SDRs: End of Period*						
Quota	2f.s	1,951	1,951	1,951	1,951	1,951	1,951	2,659	2,659	2,659	2,659	2,659	2,659
SDRs	1b.s	354	317	255	317	135	74	93	28	8	8	7	5
Reserve Position in the Fund	1c.s	145	145	145	145	145	145	322	322	322	322	322	322
of which: Outstg.Fund Borrowing	2c	—	—	—	—	—	—	—	—	—	—	—	—
Total Fund Cred.&Loans Outstg.	2tl	1,951	1,810	1,506	1,527	1,199	870	540	156	—	—	—	—
International Liquidity					*Millions of US Dollars Unless Otherwise Indicated: End of Period*								
Total Reserves minus Gold	1l.d	9,216	8,067	6,283	11,788	14,378	11,920	12,277	13,088	9,239	8,487	16,035	18,375
SDRs	1b.d	486	463	380	456	183	104	127	36	10	11	10	9
Reserve Position in the Fund	1c.d	199	212	215	208	196	204	442	419	405	438	478	500
Foreign Exchange	1d.d	8,531	7,393	5,688	11,124	14,000	11,612	11,708	12,633	8,825	8,038	15,546	17,867
Gold (Million Fine Troy Ounces)	1ad	11.46	11.46	11.46	11.46	11.46	9.76	9.76	10.24	10.94	10.56	11.47	11.49
Gold (National Valuation)	1and	3,440	3,440	3,440	3,440	3,440	2,929	2,887	2,794	3,056	3,515	4,632	5,122
Monetary Authorities: Other Liab.	4..d	2,180	2,142	1,784	1,875	1,006	270	228	214	194	159	140	367
Deposit Money Banks: Assets	7a.d	1,495	1,133	647	794	767	859	1,192	1,159	976	1,096	1,146	1,625
Liabilities	7b.d	634	261	181	212	209	170	131	316	433	228	101	53
Other Banking Insts.: Assets	7e.d	28	32	23	40	37	67	8	18	5	6	2	6
Liabilities	7f.d	1	1	—	—	—	—	—	—	—	1	—	—
Monetary Authorities							*Billions of Bolivares: End of Period*						
Foreign Assets	11	1,340.04	1,951.31	2,813.96	† 7,242.40	9,609.67	8,850.62	9,863.17	11,148.95	9,459.92	16,937.94	33,153.73	45,185.39
Claims on Central Government	12a	359.09	632.06	1,038.12	† 1,649.40	1,095.54	1,007.04	1,057.18	1,106.42	1,044.66	1,656.85	1,114.74	1,160.10
Claims on Nonfin.Pub.Enterprises	12c	10.05	10.05	22.18	† 9.78	.55	.55	.55	.55	.50	.50	.50	.50
Claims on Nonbank Pub. Fin. Inst.	12cg	15.47	813.15	1,355.13	† 1,372.75	1,384.14	1,386.24	1,385.64	1,389.73	1,389.34	1,391.71	1,387.85	6.39
Claims on Deposit Money Banks	12e	33.90	18.59	26.42	† 10.95	10.23	.80	.90	17.58	42.61	36.18	.53	.60
Claims on Other Banking Insts	12f	1.43	1.05	1.00	† .40	.34	.77	.77	.76				
Reserve Money	14	431.28	707.13	931.36	† 1,852.07	3,221.25	3,808.74	5,064.63	5,815.51	6,515.18	7,783.42	11,460.22	16,648.81
of which: Currency Outside DMBs	14a	136.55	278.53	355.23	† 566.73	987.34	1,235.05	1,816.79	1,997.61	2,286.26	3,795.87	4,777.52	6,506.31
Time, Savings,& Fgn.Currency Dep.	15	8.71	16.24	21.91	† 20.33	36.58	16.28	13.01	11.44	11.47	15.98	27.06	29.39
Liabs. of Central Bank: Securities	16ac	70.88	744.71	609.34	† 1,659.38	1,803.07	1,579.69	895.74	.76	.73	391.66	7,551.98	7,064.38
Foreign Liabilities	16c	514.64	811.38	1,166.48	† 1,935.92	1,320.47	842.56	627.56	291.12	147.81	221.60	223.66	702.09
Central Government Deposits	16d	119.69	222.88	192.32	† 991.45	1,739.49	727.67	684.87	2,119.13	1,081.89	786.23	3,614.10	8,321.59
Liab. to Nonbank Pub. Fin. Insts	16dg	21.96	59.60	70.09	† 98.01	15.85	10.59	3.32	12.37	16.72	29.24	644.03	542.81
Capital Accounts	17a	117.36	311.91	325.79	† 2,250.32	3,277.72	4,232.05	4,849.26	3,898.43	3,919.34	10,293.08	10,699.78	13,049.45
Other Items (Net)	17r	475.47	552.35	1,939.52	† 1,478.21	686.03	28.44	169.81	1,515.25	243.88	501.99	1,436.51	−5.55
Deposit Money Banks							*Billions of Bolivares: End of Period*						
Reserves	20	291.61	400.34	483.54	† 1,077.68	1,874.69	2,392.37	2,921.31	3,566.15	4,031.12	3,827.13	6,004.15	9,103.36
Claims on Mon.Author.:Securities	20c	13.92	354.06	252.27	† 1,043.96	783.22	802.00	390.76	—	—	380.93	7,468.14	6,746.33
Foreign Assets	21	157.92	192.57	187.51	† 377.44	385.99	484.14	771.76	809.98	743.73	1,532.11	1,828.38	3,112.56
Claims on Central Government	22a	139.48	440.70	839.70	† 721.61	765.20	777.96	1,220.47	2,511.38	2,904.51	4,364.02	5,372.99	9,523.88
Claims on State and Local Govts	22b	—	1.20	4.92	† 1.19	.12	.15	13.51	26.82	.07	.07	.07	.07
Claims on Nonfin.Pub.Enterprises	22c	79.64	136.68	179.52	† 7.76	8.21	2.79	16.04	88.69	3.34	.02	.83	.02
Claims on Nonbank Pub. Fin. Inst.	22cg				† 293.88	56.41	32.21	45.43	22.27	.01			
Claims on Private Sector	22d	859.81	797.97	1,184.61	† 2,392.28	5,287.72	6,021.81	6,655.06	8,350.97	10,310.04	10,406.55	11,494.47	22,850.13
Claims on Other Banking Insts	22f	.80	.72	.18	† 47.42	45.55	112.78	145.49	314.18	60.18	210.68	130.44	332.09
Claims on Nonbank Financial Insts	22g	—	10.75	12.79	† 24.89	46.38	57.16	179.77	409.56	129.95	118.71	379.04	599.90
Demand Deposits	24	256.54	666.18	902.56	† 2,010.16	3,616.46	3,683.59	4,211.88	5,743.23	6,821.99	7,029.87	13,651.21	20,036.51
Time, Savings,& Fgn.Currency Dep.	25	1,077.76	1,532.33	2,079.16	† 2,405.98	3,431.80	4,508.54	5,247.37	6,325.39	7,270.21	8,191.19	11,138.65	16,445.20
Money Market Instruments	26aa	—	—	—	† 32.43	63.76	15.43	50.72	94.92	103.94	80.97	44.93	155.60
Bonds	26ab	—	—	—	† 17.15	.51	3.48	8.96	10.69	28.01	6.95	14.38	9.59
Restricted Deposits	26b	—	—	—	† 47.98	63.17	68.21	94.91	168.57	226.77	259.17	306.46	438.66
Foreign Liabilities	26c	67.00	44.41	52.62	† 100.90	105.01	95.65	84.57	220.54	329.83	318.34	161.17	100.62
Central Government Deposits	26d	27.81	47.20	57.95	† 270.51	464.51	492.97	865.93	1,523.01	1,277.75	1,236.90	2,479.25	4,432.91
Liab. to Nonbank Pub. Fin. Insts.	26dg	16.17	106.12	13.42	† 41.70	51.53	52.57	109.29	138.83	64.36	87.46	88.69	2,947.73
Credit from Monetary Authorities	26g	33.04	17.73	25.57	† 1.06	—	—	13.10	41.16	84.16	971.65	21.60	40.98
Liabilities to Other Banking Insts	26i	37.02	31.05	21.87	† 208.18	287.70	283.77	267.04	400.01	297.94	94.83	52.92	310.60
Liab. to Nonbank Financial Insts.	26j	—	—	—	† 38.83	105.51	195.18	160.53	164.28	296.23	253.09	204.48	391.22
Capital Accounts	27a	146.86	90.55	330.50	† 848.76	1,271.61	1,665.67	1,877.47	2,364.81	2,937.11	3,863.99	5,175.24	7,049.79
Other Items (Net)	27r	−119.04	−200.58	−338.59	† −35.51	−208.08	−381.70	−632.18	−1,095.43	−1,555.36	−1,554.15	−660.45	−91.07

		1993	1994	1995	1996	1997	1998	1999	2000	2001	2002	2003	2004
Monetary Survey						*Billions of Bolivares: End of Period*							
Foreign Assets (Net).........................	31n	916.32	1,288.09	1,782.37	† 5,583.02	8,570.18	8,396.54	9,922.80	11,447.28	9,726.00	17,930.12	34,597.28	47,495.24
Domestic Credit.............................	32	1,318.27	2,574.26	4,387.89	† 5,259.43	6,486.16	8,178.82	9,169.12	10,579.20	13,483.77	16,126.82	13,788.40	21,719.40
Claims on Central Govt. (Net)........	32an	351.07	802.68	1,627.54	† 1,109.07	−343.25	564.36	726.85	−24.34	1,589.53	3,997.74	394.38	−2,070.52
Claims on State and Local Govts....	32b	—	1.20	4.92	† 1.19	.12	.15	13.51	26.82	.07	.07	.07	.07
Claims on Nonfin.Pub.Enterprises...	32c	89.69	146.73	201.71	† 17.53	8.76	3.34	16.59	89.24	3.84	.52	1.33	.52
Claims on Nonbank Pub.Fin.Inst....	32cg	15.47	813.15	1,355.13	† 1,666.63	1,440.54	1,418.45	1,431.07	1,412.00	1,389.34	1,391.71	1,387.85	6.39
Claims on Private Sector..............	32d	859.82	797.98	1,184.62	† 2,392.29	5,287.73	6,021.82	6,655.07	8,350.98	10,310.86	10,407.37	11,495.29	22,850.95
Claims on Other Banking Insts......	32f	2.23	1.78	1.18	† 47.83	45.89	113.55	146.26	314.95	60.18	210.68	130.44	332.09
Claims on Nonbank Financial Inst...	32g	—	10.75	12.79	† 24.89	46.38	57.16	179.77	409.56	129.95	118.71	379.04	599.90
Money..	34	407.22	974.12	1,343.96	† 2,777.65	4,917.78	5,149.17	6,412.64	8,037.22	9,287.01	10,973.46	19,055.81	27,927.25
Quasi-Money.................................	35	1,086.46	1,548.58	2,101.07	† 2,426.31	3,468.38	4,524.82	5,260.38	6,336.83	7,281.68	8,207.17	11,165.71	16,474.59
Money Market Instruments..............	36aa	—	—	—	† 32.43	63.76	15.43	50.72	94.92	103.94	80.97	44.93	155.60
Bonds...	36ab	—	—	—	† 17.15	.51	3.48	8.96	10.69	28.01	6.95	14.38	9.59
Liabs. of Central Bank: Securities.....	36ac	56.96	390.65	357.06	† 615.43	1,019.85	777.68	504.98	.76	.73	10.73	83.84	318.05
Restricted Deposits.......................	36b	—	—	—	† 47.98	63.17	68.21	94.91	168.57	226.77	259.17	306.46	438.66
Liab. to Nonbank Pub. Fin. Insts.....	36dg	38.13	165.72	83.52	† 139.70	67.39	63.16	112.62	151.20	81.08	116.69	732.72	3,490.55
Liabilities to Other Banking Insts.....	36i	37.02	31.05	21.87	† 208.18	287.70	283.77	267.04	400.01	297.94	94.83	52.92	310.60
Liab. to Nonbank Financial Insts.......	36j	—	—	—	† 38.83	105.51	195.18	160.53	164.28	296.23	253.09	204.48	391.22
Capital Accounts..........................	37a	264.22	402.46	656.29	† 3,099.09	4,549.33	5,897.72	6,726.74	6,263.24	6,856.46	14,157.06	15,875.02	20,099.24
Other Items (Net).........................	37r	344.57	349.77	1,606.49	† 1,439.71	512.97	−403.27	−507.59	398.77	−1,250.08	−103.17	849.43	−400.72
Money plus Quasi-Money..............	35l	1,493.68	2,522.70	3,445.03	† 5,203.96	8,386.16	9,674.00	11,673.02	14,374.05	16,568.69	19,180.62	30,221.51	44,401.84
Other Banking Institutions						*Billions of Bolivares: End of Period*							
Reserves..	40	12.34	22.69	27.57	† 37.95	86.71	96.01	210.86	298.50	95.38	72.54	90.90	180.98
Claims on Mon.Author.:Securities....	40c	.07	1.39	2.06	† 39.04	40.06	22.91	9.12	—	—	6.24	14.85	14.09
Foreign Assets..............................	41	2.99	5.42	6.55	† 18.89	18.50	37.55	4.92	12.84	3.60	8.20	3.72	11.21
Claims on Central Government.........	42a	32.00	103.93	88.07	† 24.77	18.34	23.50	97.10	238.45	63.42	100.84	273.92	446.37
Claims on Nonfin.Pub.Enterprises...	42c	.81	1.71	.02	† 27.96	5.07	2.31	—	—	—	—	—	—
Claims on Nonbank Pub. Fin. Inst...	42cg	—	—	—	† 16.39	10.74	4.61	5.26	5.07	.43	—	—	—
Claims on Private Sector...............	42d	361.62	326.46	430.61	† 401.52	897.44	1,007.23	1,426.40	1,581.47	527.25	354.51	278.92	503.73
Claims on Deposit Money Banks......	42e	81.30	47.11	44.77	† 110.27	101.60	137.59	172.19	138.65	106.76	81.30	126.00	64.04
Claims on Nonbank Financial Insts...	42g	—	—	—	† 4.17	7.77	6.97	21.93	40.84	19.31	71.77	15.58	23.27
Demand Deposits...........................	44	11.15	13.43	16.13	† 29.88	46.95	109.68	156.41	276.51	92.19	108.58	135.51	280.05
Time, Savings,& Fgn.Currency Dep...	45	452.53	460.63	558.42	† 300.16	613.32	686.24	1,019.00	1,155.61	260.23	265.99	353.10	604.80
Money Market Instruments..............	46aa	—	—	—	† 4.75	—	—	.05	1.06	13.01	—	—	—
Bonds...	46ab	11.03	8.49	7.04	† .77	.94	18.89	50.31	48.66	28.97	15.89	2.55	2.28
Restricted Deposits.......................	46b	—	—	—	† .28	1.19	1.27	2.40	3.75	1.36	1.26	1.50	1.75
Foreign Liabilities..........................	46c	.07	.12	—	† .06	—	—	—	—	—	1.21	—	—
Central Government Deposits...........	46d	5.27	1.03	.76	† 13.37	40.80	30.89	191.78	438.28	4.72	6.16	12.77	15.06
Liab. to Nonbank Pub. Fin. Insts......	46dg	.79	.64	.14	† 2.18	2.71	.58	3.82	8.59	1.38	37.93	80.51	80.51
Credit from Monetary Authorities.....	46g	.56	.50	.18	† .11	.02	.01	.01	—	—	5.38	3.32	
Credit from Deposit Money Banks....	46h	8.40	8.17	7.36	† 41.96	115.46	117.67	110.73	70.67	79.65	100.06	77.31	11.13
Liab. to Nonbank Financial Insts.......	46j	—	—	—	† 10.10	20.54	7.50	49.85	89.34	13.19	11.06	8.16	6.34
Capital Accounts...........................	47a	60.63	63.72	77.47	† 174.41	198.62	242.89	296.05	362.53	112.07	86.74	102.82	124.41
Other Items (Net)..........................	47r	−59.30	−48.02	−67.82	† 102.94	145.68	123.06	67.36	−139.18	209.37	55.16	26.35	117.37
Banking Survey						*Billions of Bolivares: End of Period*							
Foreign Assets (Net).......................	51n	919.23	1,293.39	1,788.93	† 5,601.85	8,588.68	8,434.09	9,927.73	11,460.12	9,729.60	17,937.11	34,601.00	47,506.44
Domestic Credit.............................	52	1,705.20	3,003.55	4,904.65	† 5,673.05	7,338.85	9,079.02	10,381.76	11,691.81	14,029.28	16,437.10	14,213.62	22,345.63
Claims on Central Govt. (Net)........	52an	377.80	905.58	1,714.85	† 1,120.47	−365.71	556.96	632.17	−224.17	1,648.24	4,092.42	655.53	−1,639.21
Claims on State and Local Govts....	52b	—	1.20	4.92	† 1.19	.12	.15	13.51	26.82	.07	.07	.07	.07
Claims on Nonfin.Pub.Enterprises...	52c	90.49	148.44	201.73	† 45.50	13.83	5.66	16.59	89.24	3.84	.52	1.33	.52
Claims on Nonbank Pub.Fin.Insts...	52cg	15.47	813.15	1,355.13	† 1,683.03	1,451.28	1,423.07	1,436.33	1,417.07	1,389.77	1,391.71	1,387.85	6.39
Claims on Private Sector...............	52d	1,221.44	1,124.44	1,615.24	† 2,793.81	6,185.17	7,029.05	8,081.47	9,932.45	10,838.11	10,761.88	11,774.21	23,354.68
Claims on Nonbank Financial Inst..	52g	—	10.75	12.79	† 29.06	54.15	64.13	201.70	450.41	149.26	190.48	394.62	623.17
Liquid Liabilities............................	55l	1,945.02	2,974.06	3,992.00	† 5,496.05	8,959.72	10,373.90	12,637.57	15,507.67	16,825.73	19,482.65	30,619.21	45,105.71
Money Market Instruments..............	56aa	—	—	—	† 37.18	63.77	15.43	50.76	95.98	116.95	80.97	44.93	155.60
Bonds...	56ab	11.03	8.49	7.04	† 17.92	1.46	22.37	59.27	59.35	56.99	22.84	16.93	11.87
Liabs. of Central Bank: Securities.....	56ac	56.89	389.27	355.00	† 576.38	979.79	754.77	495.86	.76	.73	4.48	68.99	303.96
Restricted Deposits.......................	56b	—	—	—	† 48.25	64.36	69.49	97.31	172.32	228.13	260.43	307.97	440.41
Liab. to Nonbank Pub. Fin. Insts.....	56dg	38.92	166.36	83.65	† 141.89	70.10	63.75	116.44	159.79	82.46	154.62	813.23	3,571.05
Liab. to Nonbank Financial Insts.......	56j	—	—	—	† 48.93	126.05	202.68	210.39	253.62	309.42	264.14	212.64	397.56
Capital Accounts...........................	57a	324.86	466.18	733.76	† 3,273.50	4,747.95	6,140.61	7,022.79	6,625.76	6,968.53	14,243.80	15,977.84	20,223.65
Other Items (Net).........................	57r	247.72	292.58	1,522.12	† 1,634.80	914.33	−129.89	−380.90	276.68	−830.05	−139.73	752.88	−357.74
Interest Rates						*Percent Per Annum*							
Discount Rate (End of Period)...........	60	71.25	48.00	49.00	45.00	45.00	60.00	38.00	38.00	37.00	40.00	28.50	28.50
Money Market Rate.......................	60b	....	....	....	16.70	12.47	18.58	7.48	8.14	13.33	28.87	13.23	4.38
Savings Rate.................................	60k	38.59	29.11	22.17	19.53	7.59	12.34	8.15	3.17	2.66	3.86	6.24	4.47
Deposit Rate.................................	60l	53.75	39.02	24.72	27.58	14.70	34.84	21.28	16.30	15.51	29.00	17.21	12.60
Lending Rate................................	60p	59.90	54.66	39.74	39.41	23.69	46.35	32.13	25.20	22.45	36.58	25.19	18.50
Government Bond Yield..................	61	41.03	54.73	53.38	49.09	25.41	47.88	† 31.12	21.03	22.12	38.51	32.15	15.57
Prices, Production, Labor						*Index Numbers (2000=100): Period Averages*							
Industrial Share Prices....................	62	12.8	† 23.0	24.5	73.6	130.8	79.2	76.5	100.0	112.6	100.1	208.5	418.5
Prices: Home & Import Goods.........	63	8.3	14.7	23.2	47.1	61.2	74.7	86.8	† 100.0	115.5	158.6	240.1	313.4
Home Goods.........................	63a	7.8	13.8	22.1	44.1	58.5	72.7	85.6	† 100.0	124.1	164.7	247.3	323.9
Consumer Prices............................	64	6.6	10.7	17.1	34.2	51.3	69.6	† 86.1	100.0	112.5	137.8	180.6	219.9
Crude Petroleum Production...........	66aa	78.4	83.0	92.4	95.7	103.8	104.8	94.3	100.0	98.9	....	....	....
						Number in Thousands: Period Averages							
Labor Force..................................	67d	7,546	8,027	8,545		9,507	....	....	....	11,105	11,674	....	....
Employment.................................	67e	7,103	7,626	7,667	7,819	8,287	8,711	8,717	8,822	9,405	9,699	9,759	10,234
Unemployment..............................	67c	503	687	875	1,043	1,061	1,093	1,526	1,424	1,436	1,823	2,142	1,841
Unemployment Rate (%)................	67r	6.7	8.7	10.3	11.8	11.4	11.2	14.9	13.9	13.2	15.8	18.0	15.3

Intl. Transactions & Positions		1993	1994	1995	1996	1997	1998	1999	2000	2001	2002	2003	2004
							Billions of Bolivares						
Exports	70	1,311.8	2,409.8	3,332.6	9,803.1	10,295.6	9,393.5	12,751.4	21,450.8	18,199.7	30,758.1	38,875.1	† 13,280.6
Petroleum	70a	979.9	1,751.6	2,444.8	7,844.8	8,853.1	6,557.6	9,954.5	18,102.6	14,495.3	22,497.0	30,153.6	—
Crude Petroleum	70aa	637.6	1,197.8	1,641.7	5,346.6	5,934.9	4,220.1	6,592.4	12,305.2	10,114.9	15,978.7	22,307.8	—
Imports, c.i.f	71	1,107.2	1,324.0	2,202.0	4,179.9	7,145.5	8,604.0	8,380.5	10,964.0	13,221.1	14,594.9	14,835.1	31,647.4
Imports, f.o.b	71.v	997.4	1,192.8	1,983.8	3,765.7	6,437.3	7,751.3	7,550.0	9,877.5	11,910.9	13,148.5	13,364.9	28,770.4
							Millions of US Dollars						
Exports	70..d	14,686	16,089	18,457	23,060	21,624	17,193	20,190	31,413	25,353	25,890	23,990	33,929
Petroleum	70a.d	11,030	11,473	13,739	18,520	18,186	12,021	16,295	26,485	20,122	18,839	18,552	26,829
Imports, f.o.b	71.vd	11,271	8,277	11,396	8,901	13,159	14,250	12,670	14,606	16,507	11,678	8,339	15,163
Volume of Exports							*2000=100*						
Petroleum	72a	76.6	82.5	90.8	97.3	107.5	109.6	98.6	100.0	96.9	....	....	....
Crude Petroleum	72aa	76.8	84.5	92.2	98.9	110.3	112.8	96.0	100.0	103.0	....	....	....
Refined Pretroleum	72ab	76.1	78.4	87.8	93.9	101.7	103.0	104.0	100.0	84.3	....	....	....
Import Prices (Wholesale)	76.x	10.0	18.0	27.1	58.0	70.7	81.7	91.0	† 100.0	111.2	170.8	265.2	342.4
Balance of Payments							*Millions of US Dollars: Minus Sign Indicates Debit*						
Current Account, n.i.e	78ald	−1,993	2,541	2,014	8,914	3,732	−4,432	2,112	11,853	1,983	7,599	11,448	13,830
Goods: Exports f.o.b	78aad	14,779	16,105	19,082	23,707	23,871	17,707	20,963	33,529	26,667	26,781	27,170	38,748
Goods: Imports f.o.b	78abd	−11,504	−8,480	−12,069	−9,937	−14,917	−16,755	−14,492	−16,865	−19,211	−13,360	−10,687	−17,318
Trade Balance	78acd	3,275	7,625	7,013	13,770	8,954	952	6,471	16,664	7,456	13,421	16,483	21,430
Services: Credit	78add	1,340	1,576	1,671	1,573	1,314	1,423	1,352	1,182	1,376	1,013	878	1,098
Services: Debit	78aed	−4,525	−4,672	−4,836	−4,842	−3,922	−4,072	−4,191	−4,435	−4,681	−3,922	−3,522	−4,724
Balance on Goods & Services	78afd	90	4,529	3,848	10,501	6,346	−1,697	3,632	13,411	4,151	10,512	13,839	17,804
Income: Credit	78agd	1,599	1,626	1,867	1,579	2,421	2,479	2,272	3,049	2,603	1,474	1,729	1,564
Income: Debit	78ahd	−3,314	−3,530	−3,810	−3,304	−4,938	−5,013	−3,725	−4,437	−4,623	−4,230	−4,140	−5,449
Balance on Gds, Serv. & Inc	78aid	−1,625	2,625	1,905	8,776	3,829	−4,231	2,179	12,023	2,131	7,756	11,428	13,919
Current Transfers, n.i.e.: Credit	78ajd	452	606	413	526	233	169	203	261	356	288	257	180
Current Transfers: Debit	78akd	−820	−690	−304	−388	−330	−370	−270	−431	−504	−445	−237	−269
Capital Account, n.i.e	78bcd	—	—	—	—	—	—	—	—	—	—	—	—
Capital Account, n.i.e.: Credit	78bad	—	—	—	—	—	—	—	—	—	—	—	—
Capital Account: Debit	78bbd	—	—	—	—	—	—	—	—	—	—	—	—
Financial Account, n.i.e	78bjd	2,656	−3,204	−2,964	−1,784	879	2,689	−516	−2,969	−211	−9,246	−4,942	−8,716
Direct Investment Abroad	78bdd	−886	−358	−91	−507	−557	−1,043	−872	−521	−204	−1,026	−1,318	348
Dir. Invest. in Rep. Econ., n.i.e.	78bed	372	813	985	2,183	6,202	4,985	2,890	4,701	3,683	782	2,659	1,518
Portfolio Investment Assets	78bfd	79	−22	−14	−41	−1,651	470	248	−954	397	−1,354	−812	−1,090
Equity Securities	78bkd	−1	10	−3	−11	−47	−240	72	13	138	−164	−222	5
Debt Securities	78bld	80	−32	−11	−30	−1,604	710	176	−967	259	−1,190	−590	−1,095
Portfolio Investment Liab., n.i.e	78bgd	542	275	−787	780	911	306	1,857	−2,180	710	−956	−143	−853
Equity Securities	78bmd	48	585	270	1,318	1,444	187	417	−574	31	−5	97	−170
Debt Securities	78bnd	494	−310	−1,057	−538	−533	119	1,440	−1,606	679	−951	−240	−683
Financial Derivatives Assets	78bwd	—	....	....	—	—	—	—	—	—	—	—	—
Financial Derivatives Liabilities	78bxd	—	—	—	—	—	—	—	—	—	—	—	—
Other Investment Assets	78bhd	615	−4,173	−661	−1,592	−3,748	−3,325	−4,788	−4,839	−3,919	−7,169	−4,328	−8,004
Monetary Authorities	78bod	—	—	—	—	−2	28	128	18	42	22	11	13
General Government	78bpd	−16	−27	240	57	−264	391	64	−228	−1,016	65	−718	−1,047
Banks	78bqd	−538	−932	216	−53	−17	−182	−262	−50	267	−32	46	15
Other Sectors	78brd	1,169	−3,214	−1,117	−1,596	−3,465	−3,562	−4,718	−4,579	−3,212	−7,224	−3,667	−6,985
Other Investment Liab., n.i.e	78bid	1,934	261	−2,396	−2,607	−278	1,296	149	824	−878	477	−1,000	−635
Monetary Authorities	78bsd	778	−51	−317	−289	−430	−561	−24	8	18	−4	19	250
General Government	78btd	−210	128	−262	−543	162	986	272	36	−1	170	298	−605
Banks	78bud	113	−77	52	153	36	−69	−34	197	122	−257	−141	1
Other Sectors	78bvd	1,253	261	−1,869	−1,928	−46	940	−65	583	−1,017	568	−1,176	−281
Net Errors and Omissions	78cad	−539	−281	−494	−892	−1,517	−1,662	−538	−2,926	−3,601	−2,781	−1,052	−2,959
Overall Balance	78cbd	124	−944	−1,444	6,238	3,094	−3,405	1,058	5,958	−1,829	−4,428	5,454	2,155
Reserves and Related Items	79dad	−124	944	1,444	−6,238	−3,094	3,405	−1,058	−5,958	1,829	4,428	−5,454	−2,155
Reserve Assets	79dbd	144	1,145	1,907	−6,271	−2,643	3,853	−608	−5,449	2,027	4,428	−5,454	−2,155
Use of Fund Credit and Loans	79dcd	−268	−201	−463	33	−452	−448	−450	−508	−198	—	—	—
Exceptional Financing	79ded	—	—	—	—	—	—	—	—	—	—	—	—
International Investment Position							*Millions of US Dollars*						
Assets	79aad	43,156	46,634	45,944	41,216	49,537	50,051	55,792	67,931	70,064	75,513	88,316	99,777
Direct Investment Abroad	79abd	2,447	3,124	3,427	4,595	5,209	6,176	7,143	7,676	7,894	8,732	9,548	9,204
Portfolio Investment	79acd	1,799	1,796	1,530	1,986	3,646	3,406	2,784	4,057	3,836	5,405	6,596	7,636
Equity Securities	79add	—	—	—	43	113	385	260	245	101	262	538	534
Debt Securities	79aed	1,799	1,796	1,530	1,943	3,533	3,021	2,524	3,812	3,735	5,143	6,058	7,102
Financial Derivatives	79ald	—	—	—	—	—	—	—	—	—	—	—	—
Other Investment	79afd	25,106	28,955	30,391	17,862	21,669	25,019	29,835	34,707	39,812	46,516	50,805	58,730
Monetary Authorities	79agd	—	—	—	205	340	313	186	167	125	106	96	84
General Government	79ahd	812	812	874	1,401	1,658	1,272	1,216	1,430	2,449	2,285	2,967	4,018
Banks	79aid	2,719	3,774	3,586	188	240	443	703	753	485	517	471	456
Other Sectors	79ajd	21,575	24,369	25,931	16,068	19,431	22,991	27,730	32,357	36,753	43,608	47,271	54,172
Reserve Assets	79akd	13,804	12,759	10,596	16,773	19,013	15,450	16,030	21,491	18,522	14,860	21,367	24,207
Liabilities	79lad	50,713	51,730	49,250	56,284	62,341	61,866	67,160	69,595	71,885	72,471	78,552	84,066
Dir. Invest. in Rep. Economy	79lbd	5,059	5,872	6,772	18,124	24,694	28,915	31,470	35,480	39,074	39,007	41,902	43,575
Portfolio Investment	79lcd	22,816	22,844	22,555	20,506	21,146	15,367	18,349	16,557	16,322	15,850	19,175	22,864
Equity Securities	79ldd	917	1,184	1,060	2,488	3,882	1,623	2,185	1,706	1,301	948	1,713	1,812
Debt Securities	79led	21,899	21,660	21,495	18,018	17,264	13,744	16,164	14,851	15,021	14,902	17,462	21,052
Financial Derivatives	79lld	—	—	—	—	—	—	—	—	—	—	—	—
Other Investment	79lfd	22,838	23,014	19,923	17,654	16,501	17,584	17,341	17,558	16,489	17,614	17,475	17,627
Monetary Authorities	79lgd	4,376	4,246	3,525	2,271	2,275	1,316	810	278	93	75	86	338
General Government	79lhd	8,459	8,454	8,009	3,960	3,978	5,055	5,362	5,367	5,352	5,698	6,409	6,018
Banks	79lid	1,447	1,394	1,451	294	328	261	226	423	545	290	149	149
Other Sectors	79ljd	8,556	8,920	6,938	11,129	9,920	10,952	10,943	11,490	10,499	11,551	10,831	11,122

Venezuela, República Bolivariana de 299

		1993	1994	1995	1996	1997	1998	1999	2000	2001	2002	2003	2004
Government Finance							*Billions of Bolivares: Year Ending December 31*						
Deficit (-) or Surplus.........................	80	−125.0	† −485.9	−493.8	456.5	955.5	−1,967.6	−999.8	−1,361.1	−3,941.1	....	....	....
Revenue..	81	946.0	† 1,575.1	2,242.6	5,767.8	10,241.0	9,157.1	11,251.8	16,873.5	19,326.5	....	....	....
Grants Received..........................	81z	—	—	—	—	—	—	—	—	—	....	....	....
Expenditure................................	82	1,013.8	1,666.3	2,541.5	4,964.2	8,894.3	11,014.0	12,170.0	17,860.2	22,883.8	....	....	....
Lending Minus Repayments...........	83	57.3	394.6	195.0	347.1	391.2	110.6	81.7	374.4	383.8	....	....	....
Financing													
Net Borrowing.............................	84	125.0	485.9	493.8	−456.5	−955.5	1,967.6	999.8	1,361.1	3,941.1	....	....	....
Domestic.......................	84a	131.8	530.6	476.2	−301.7	−1,359.9	1,378.4	1,623.4	3,207.4	3,640.4	....	....	....
Foreign.........................	85a	−6.8	−44.8	17.7	−154.8	404.4	589.2	−623.6	−1,846.2	300.7	....	....	....
Use of Cash Balances...................	87	....	....	....	....	....	....	....	....	....	....	....	....
National Accounts							*Billions of Bolivares*						
Househ.Cons.Expend.,incl.NPISHs....	96f	3,977.4	6,077.1	9,507.7	18,618.0	21,610.1	28,822.6	34,071.6	41,220.7	48,838.8	57,740.1	73,483.7	103,303.9
Government Consumption Expend...	91f	466.0	627.0	974.8	1,475.6	5,675.8	6,735.6	7,309.5	9,917.0	12,663.4	14,027.2	17,288.3	26,233.2
Gross Fixed Capital Formation..........	93e	1,091.1	1,528.4	2,255.6	4,645.8	10,686.2	14,289.5	14,067.3	16,740.9	21,391.6	23,644.4	20,943.6	36,430.5
Changes in Inventories....................	93i	−68.5	−300.3	223.4	227.6	920.5	1,044.6	1,669.0	2,512.2	3,090.0	−826.6	−58.6	6,957.8
Exports of Goods and Services..........	90c	1,470.3	2,677.5	3,709.8	10,748.9	12,272.2	10,463.0	13,596.9	23,693.0	20,222.3	32,819.6	45,344.7	74,956.8
Imports of Goods and Services (-).....	98c	1,482.4	1,934.5	2,985.7	6,278.3	9,221.6	11,342.4	11,369.6	14,428.0	17,260.5	19,564.5	22,784.4	41,756.8
Gross Domestic Product (GDP)........	99b	5,453.9	8,675.2	13,685.7	29,437.7	41,943.2	50,013.0	59,344.6	79,655.7	88,945.6	107,840.2	134,217.3	206,125.4
Net Primary Income from Abroad.....	98.n	−162.4	−274.6	−322.9	−665.7	−1,203.8	−1,366.8	−887.4	−947.5	−1,469.0	−3,191.7	−3,887.5	−6,162.2
Gross National Income (GNI)...........	99a	5,291.5	8,400.6	13,362.8	28,772.0	40,739.4	48,646.1	58,457.2	78,708.2	87,476.6	104,648.5	130,329.9	199,963.2
Consumption of Fixed Capital..........	99cf	422.4	625.8	927.7	1,884.4	2,309.3	3,034.7	3,544.3	4,499.8	5,367.0	7,113.0	8,284.6	12,676.7
GDP Volume 1984 Prices.................	99b.p	558.2	545.1	566.6	565.5	601.5	602.6	565.9	584.2	600.5	547.2	....	....
GDP Volume (2000=100)................	99bvp	95.5	93.3	97.0	96.8	103.0	103.1	96.9	100.0	102.8	93.7	....	....
GDP Deflator (2000=100)...............	99bip	7.2	11.7	17.7	38.2	51.1	60.9	76.9	100.0	108.6	144.5	....	....
							Millions: Midyear Estimates						
Population...............................	99z	21.15	21.62	22.09	22.55	23.02	23.49	23.95	24.42	24.88	25.35	25.82	26.28

		1993	1994	1995	1996	1997	1998	1999	2000	2001	2002	2003	2004
Exchange Rates					*Dong per SDR: End of Period*								
Market Rate	aa	14,893	16,133	16,374	16,032	16,585	19,558	19,254	18,910	18,957	20,941	23,249	24,502
					Dong per US Dollar: End of Period (ae) Period Average (rf)								
Market Rate	ae	10,843	11,051	11,015	11,149	12,292	13,890	14,028	14,514	15,084	15,403	15,646	15,777
Market Rate	rf	10,641	10,966	11,038	11,033	11,683	13,268	13,943	14,168	14,725	15,280	15,510	....
Fund Position					*Millions of SDRs: End of Period*								
Quota	2f.s	241.6	241.6	241.6	241.6	241.6	241.6	329.1	329.1	329.1	329.1	329.1	329.1
SDRs	1b.s	4.9	11.0	2.2	11.9	9.4	1.8	1.1	.3	11.6	—	1.5	.3
Reserve Position in the Fund	1c.s	—	—	—	—	—	—	—	—	—	—	—	—
Total Fund Cred.&Loans Outstg	2tl	72.5	193.4	253.8	374.6	335.3	277.9	258.7	242.6	291.2	280.2	227.9	178.6
International Liquidity					*Millions of US Dollars Unless Otherwise Indicated: End of Period*								
Total Reserves minus Gold	1l.d	....	....	1,323.7	1,735.9	1,985.9	2,002.3	3,326.1	3,416.5	3,674.6	4,121.1	6,224.2	7,041.5
SDRs	1b.d	6.8	16.1	3.3	17.1	12.7	2.5	1.5	.3	14.6	—	2.2	.5
Reserve Position in the Fund	1c.d	—	—	—	—	—	—	—	—	—	—	—	—
Foreign Exchange	1d.d	....	....	1,320.4	1,718.8	1,973.1	1,999.7	3,324.7	3,416.2	3,660.0	4,121.0	6,222.0	7,041.0
Gold (Market Valuation)	1and	....	....	55.4	77.9	112.3	98.2	97.3	93.1	90.6	110.8	135.0	144.6
Monetary Authorities: Other Liab	4..d	—	....	377.1	537.3	507.8	505.5	513.5	487.6	535.9	557.4	537.8	486.0
Deposit Money Banks: Assets	7a.d	538.3	....	869.2	1,004.2	999.2	1,347.0	2,119.0	4,221.8	5,261.4	4,589.2	3,264.2	3,746.5
Liabilities	7b.d	321.4	....	865.0	985.5	868.7	679.0	664.7	682.6	679.6	640.1	684.8	1,197.8
Monetary Authorities					*Billions of Dong: End of Period*								
Foreign Assets	11	4,381	....	15,153	20,031	25,633	29,147	48,004	50,934	56,586	65,177	99,460	113,367
Claims on General Government	12a	13,323	....	9,593	12,576	13,382	16,658	11,289	11,732	12,421	15,130	15,223	21,005
Claims on Banking Institutions	12e	6,792	....	6,779	7,693	6,776	6,521	10,312	14,234	17,776	19,182	13,565	14,400
Reserve Money	14	18,296	....	26,343	31,633	35,599	38,687	58,220	72,759	84,945	95,502	121,633	141,165
of which: Currency Outside DMBs	14a	14,218	....	19,370	22,639	25,101	26,965	41,254	52,208	66,320	74,263	90,584	109,097
Foreign Liabilities	16c	—	....	4,154	5,991	6,241	7,022	7,203	7,077	8,083	8,585	8,414	7,668
General Government Deposits	16d	4,883	....	6,575	7,383	9,348	10,340	11,089	7,410	4,390	4,005	4,553	9,729
Capital Accounts	17a	230	....	1,378	1,568	3,512	8,201	8,568	10,015	12,008	12,736	15,919	18,584
Other Items (Net)	17r	750	....	−6,791	−6,245	−7,938	−10,611	−15,475	−20,361	−22,644	−21,338	−22,271	−28,375
Banking Institutions					*Billions of Dong: End of Period*								
Reserves	20	3,709	....	7,409	9,323	9,451	9,920	16,881	20,390	18,426	20,166	30,778	31,646
Foreign Assets	21	5,836	....	9,574	11,196	12,282	18,710	29,725	61,276	79,364	70,687	51,071	59,109
Claims on General Government	22a	1,718	....	4,372	2,031	3,492	5,332	6,358	8,246	10,258	17,566	34,169	34,050
Claims on Rest of Economy	22d	7,669	....	18,199	23,942	31,220	34,889	112,730	155,720	189,103	231,078	296,737	420,046
Demand Deposits	24	4,796	....	6,870	10,213	14,682	18,241	27,106	38,781	46,089	51,066	66,441	88,891
Time and Savings Deposits	25a	3,250	....	9,622	12,445	15,194	20,091	36,191	47,462	60,251	77,387	133,617	182,408
Foreign Currency Deposits	25b	5,892	....	8,924	11,042	15,611	22,098	40,919	58,543	78,187	81,428	87,418	115,050
Bonds & Money Mkt. Instruments	26a	2,544	....	5,490	5,635	7,703	10,890	10,865	18,842	21,012	35,262	26,265	26,530
Restricted Deposits	26b	1,514	....	2,138	2,117	3,080	2,830	4,059	7,045	7,923	9,744	7,899	10,369
Foreign Liabilities	26c	3,485	....	9,528	10,987	10,678	9,432	9,324	9,908	10,251	9,860	10,715	18,898
General Government Deposits	26d	1,786	....	3,321	2,795	3,127	4,974	3,606	13,052	16,187	19,848	23,805	32,201
Credit from Central Bank	26g	6,621	....	5,793	6,133	5,565	4,249	11,576	14,427	17,753	19,250	14,491	16,679
Capital Accounts	27a	3,273	....	8,166	7,984	9,798	13,172	22,033	24,801	26,962	34,684	46,986	59,411
Other Items (Net)	27r	1,856	....	6,688	5,735	3,655	2,246	15	12,772	12,537	967	−4,881	−4,188
Banking Survey					*Billions of Dong: End of Period*								
Foreign Assets (Net)	31n	6,732	....	11,046	14,249	20,997	31,404	61,201	95,225	117,616	117,419	131,402	145,910
Domestic Credit	32	16,040	....	22,268	28,370	35,620	41,566	115,682	155,236	191,204	239,921	317,771	433,171
Claims on General Govt. (Net)	32an	8,371	....	4,069	4,428	4,400	6,677	2,952	−484	2,102	8,843	21,034	13,126
Claims on Rest of Economy	32d	7,669	....	18,199	23,942	31,220	34,889	112,730	155,720	189,103	231,078	296,737	420,046
Money	34	19,088	....	26,736	33,439	39,972	45,207	68,360	90,989	112,408	125,329	157,025	197,989
Quasi-Money	35	9,142	....	18,546	23,487	30,805	42,189	77,110	106,005	138,437	158,815	221,035	297,459
Bonds & Money Mkt. Instruments	36a	2,544	....	5,490	5,635	7,703	10,890	10,865	18,842	21,012	35,262	26,265	26,530
Restricted Deposits	36b	1,514	....	2,138	2,117	3,080	2,830	4,059	7,045	7,923	9,744	7,899	10,369
Capital Accounts	37a	3,502	....	9,544	9,552	13,310	21,374	30,601	34,816	38,970	47,420	62,904	77,995
Other Items (Net)	37r	2,804	....	−1,525	−2,398	−4,447	−8,835	−14,111	−7,236	−9,932	−19,229	−25,955	−29,862
Money plus Quasi-Money	35l	28,231	....	45,283	56,926	70,777	87,396	145,470	196,994	250,846	284,144	378,060	495,447
Interest Rates					*Percent Per Annum*								
Refinancing Rate (End of Period)	60	....	....	....	18.90	10.80	12.00	6.00	6.00	4.80	4.80	5.00	5.00
Treasury Bill Rate	60c	26.40	....	....	....	....	....	....	5.42	5.49	5.92	5.83	....
Deposit Rate	60l	22.04	....	....	....	8.51	9.23	7.37	3.65	5.30	6.45	6.62	....
Lending Rate	60p	32.18	....	....	20.10	14.42	14.40	12.70	10.55	9.42	9.06	9.48	....
Prices					*Index Numbers (2000=100): Period Averages*								
Consumer Prices	64	....	....	83.5	88.3	91.1	97.7	101.7	100.0	99.6	103.4	106.6	114.9
Intl. Transactions & Positions					*Billions of Dong*								
Exports	70..d	....	....	....	7,256	9,185	9,361	11,540	14,449	15,100	16,530	20,176	25,625
Imports, c.i.f	71..d	....	....	....	11,144	11,592	11,500	11,742	15,638	15,999	19,000	24,863	31,091

Vietnam 582

		1993	1994	1995	1996	1997	1998	1999	2000	2001	2002	2003	2004
Balance of Payments					*Millions of US Dollars: Minus Sign Indicates Debit*								
Current Account, n.i.e.	78ald	....	....	....	−2,020	−1,528	−1,074	1,177	1,106	682	−604	....	....
Goods: Exports f.o.b.	78aad	....	....	....	7,255	9,185	9,361	11,540	14,448	15,027	16,706	....	....
Goods: Imports f.o.b.	78abd	....	....	....	−10,030	−10,432	−10,350	−10,568	−14,073	−14,546	−17,760	....	....
Trade Balance	78acd	....	....	....	−2,775	−1,247	−989	972	375	481	−1,054	....	....
Services: Credit	78add	....	....	....	2,243	2,530	2,616	2,493	2,702	2,810	2,948	....	....
Services: Debit	78aed	....	....	....	−2,304	−3,153	−3,146	−3,040	−3,252	−3,382	−3,698	....	....
Balance on Goods & Services	78afd	....	....	....	−2,836	−1,870	−1,519	425	−175	−91	−1,804	....	....
Income: Credit	78agd	....	....	....	140	136	127	142	331	318	167	....	....
Income: Debit	78ahd	....	....	....	−524	−679	−804	−571	−782	−795	−888	....	....
Balance on Gds. Serv. & Inc.	78aid	....	....	....	−3,220	−2,413	−2,196	−4	−626	−568	−2,525	....	....
Current Transfers, n.i.e.: Credit	78ajd	....	....	....	1,200	885	1,122	1,181	1,732	1,250	1,921	....	....
Current Transfers: Debit	78akd	....	....	....	—	—	—	—	—	—	—	....	....
Capital Account, n.i.e.	78bcd	....	....	....	—	—	—	—	—	—	—	....	....
Capital Account, n.i.e.: Credit	78bad	....	....	....	—	—	—	—	—	—	—	....	....
Capital Account: Debit	78bbd	....	....	....	—	—	—	—	—	—	—	....	....
Financial Account, n.i.e.	78bjd	....	....	....	2,909	2,125	1,646	1,058	−316	371	2,090	....	....
Direct Investment Abroad	78bdd	....	....	....	—	—	—	—	—	—	—	....	....
Dir. Invest. in Rep. Econ., n.i.e.	78bed	....	....	....	2,395	2,220	1,671	1,412	1,298	1,300	1,400	....	....
Portfolio Investment Assets	78bfd	....	....	....	....	....	....	....	....	....	....	....	....
Equity Securities	78bkd	....	....	....	....	....	....	....	....	....	....	....	....
Debt Securities	78bld	....	....	....	....	....	....	....	....	....	....	....	....
Portfolio Investment Liab., n.i.e.	78bgd	....	....	....	....	....	....	....	....	....	....	....	....
Equity Securities	78bmd	....	....	....	....	....	....	....	....	....	....	....	....
Debt Securities	78bnd	....	....	....	....	....	....	....	....	....	....	....	....
Financial Derivatives Assets	78bwd	....	....	....	—	—	—	—	—	—	—	....	....
Financial Derivatives Liabilities	78bxd	....	....	....	—	—	—	—	—	—	—	....	....
Other Investment Assets	78bhd	....	....	....	−33	−112	−537	−786	−2,089	−1,197	624	....	....
Monetary Authorities	78bod	....	....	....	....	....	....	....	....	....	....	....	....
General Government	78bpd	....	....	....	....	....	....	....	....	....	....	....	....
Banks	78bqd	....	....	....	−33	−112	−537	−786	−2,089	−1,197	624	....	....
Other Sectors	78brd	....	....	....	—	....	....	....	....	....	....	....	....
Other Investment Liab., n.i.e.	78bid	....	....	....	547	17	512	432	475	268	66	....	....
Monetary Authorities	78bsd	....	....	....	—	—	—	—	—	—	—	....	....
General Government	78btd	....	....	....	....	....	....	....	....	....	....	....	....
Banks	78bud	....	....	....	....	....	....	....	....	....	....	....	....
Other Sectors	78bvd	....	....	....	547	17	512	432	475	268	66	....	....
Net Errors and Omissions	78cad	....	....	....	−611	−269	−535	−925	−680	−847	−1,038	....	....
Overall Balance	78cbd	....	....	....	278	328	37	1,310	110	206	448	....	....
Reserves and Related Items	79dad	....	....	....	−278	−328	−37	−1,310	−110	−206	−448	....	....
Reserve Assets	79dbd	....	....	....	−453	−274	41	−1,284	−89	−267	−435	....	....
Use of Fund Credit and Loans	79dcd	....	....	....	175	−54	−78	−26	−21	61	−13	....	....
Exceptional Financing	79ded	....	....	....	—	—	—	—	—	—	—	....	....
Government Finance					*Billions of Dong: Year Ending December 31*								
Deficit (-) or Surplus	80	−6,035p	−2,530	−1,219	−502	−5,397	−454	−6,328	−12,402	−14,130	....	....	....
Total Revenue and Grants	81y	19,265p	42,125	53,370	62,387	65,352	72,965	78,489	90,749	103,050	....	....	....
Revenue	81	18,416p	40,925	51,750	60,844	62,766	70,822	76,128	88,721	97,750	....	....	....
Grants	81z	849p	1,200	1,620	1,543	2,586	2,143	2,361	2,028p	5,300f	....	....	....
Exp. & Lending Minus Repay.	82z	25,300p	44,655	54,589	62,889	70,749	73,419	84,817	103,151	117,180	....	....	....
Expenditure	82	27,021p	44,655	54,589	62,889	70,749	73,419	84,817	103,151	117,180	....	....	....
Lending Minus Repayments	83	−1,721p	—	—	—	—	—	—	—	—	....	....	....
Total Financing	80h	6,035p	2,530	1,219	502	5,397	454	6,328	12,402	14,130	....	....	....
Domestic Financing	84a	4,449p	2,330	2,709	552	5,206	−2,814	1,491	6,110	9,086	....	....	....
Foreign Financing	85a	1,586p	200	−1,490	−50	191	3,268	4,837	6,292	5,044	....	....	....
National Accounts					*Billions of Dong*								
Househ.Cons.Expend.,incl.NPISHs	96f	106,440	133,299	168,492	202,509	225,084	255,921	274,553	293,507	312,144	348,747	406,451	465,506
Government Consumption Expend.	91f	10,279	14,738	18,741	22,722	25,500	27,523	27,137	28,346	30,463	33,390	38,770	45,715
Gross Fixed Capital Formation	93e	30,635	43,325	58,187	71,597	83,734	97,551	102,799	122,101	140,301	166,828	204,608	237,868
Changes in Inventories	93i	3,385	2,153	3,944	4,853	5,020	7,324	7,704	8,670	9,732	11,155	12,826	15,818
Exports of Goods and Services	90c	40,285	60,725	75,106	111,177	135,180	161,910	199,836	243,049	262,846	304,262	363,735	470,216
Imports of Goods and Services (-)	98c	52,582	77,591	95,925	141,016	160,706	188,281	211,254	253,927	273,828	331,946	415,023	524,216
Gross Domestic Product (GDP)	99b	140,258	178,534	228,892	272,037	313,624	361,016	399,942	441,646	481,295	535,762	613,443	713,071
Net Primary Income from Abroad	98.n	−5,345.0	−4,517.0	−2,501.0	−4,300.0	−5,748.0	−6,648.0	−5,328.0	−6,327.0	−6,440.0	−8,375.0	−9,755.0	−11,165.0
Gross National Income (GNI)	99a	134,913	174,017	226,391	267,736	308,675	354,368	394,614	435,319	474,855	527,387	603,688	701,906
GDP Volume 1994 Prices	99b.p	164,043	178,534	195,567	213,832	231,264	244,596	256,269	273,666	292,535	313,247	336,243	362,093
GDP Volume (2000=100)	99bvp	59.9	65.2	71.5	78.1	84.5	89.4	93.6	100.0	106.9	114.5	122.9	132.3
GDP Deflator (2000=100)	99bip	53.0	62.0	72.5	78.8	84.0	91.5	96.7	100.0	101.9	106.0	113.0	122.0
					Millions: Midyear Estimates								
Population	99z	70.52	71.88	73.16	74.36	75.48	76.55	77.60	78.67	† 79.77	80.88	82.00	83.12

		1993	1994	1995	1996	1997	1998	1999	2000	2001	2002	2003	2004
Exchange Rates							*Francs per SDR: End of Period*							
Official Rate..................	aa	404.89	† 780.44	728.38	753.06	807.94	791.61	896.19	918.49	935.39	850.37	771.76	747.90
						Francs per US Dollar: End of Period (ae) Period Average (rf)								
Official Rate..................	ae	294.77	† 534.60	490.00	523.70	598.81	562.21	652.95	704.95	744.31	625.50	519.36	481.58
Official Rate..................	rf	283.16	† 555.20	499.15	511.55	583.67	589.95	615.70	711.98	733.04	696.99	581.20	528.28
Fund Position							*Millions of SDRs: End of Period*							
Quota..........................	2f.s	628.6	628.6	628.6	628.6	628.6	628.6	855.8	855.8	855.8	855.8	855.8	855.8
SDRs..........................	1b.s	7.3	6.9	10.2	5.8	2.3	1.3	6.6	2.2	8.1	8.9	10.9	6.4
Reserve Position in the Fund..........	1c.s	28.0	28.1	28.2	28.3	28.5	28.5	28.6	28.7	28.9	29.0	29.3	29.5
Total Fund Cred.&Loans Outstg......	2tl	525.9	686.9	836.0	920.6	938.1	1,076.0	1,068.3	1,031.3	984.6	949.0	824.4	655.9
International Liquidity						*Millions of US Dollars Unless Otherwise Indicated: End of Period*								
Total Reserves minus Gold..............	1l.d	....	....	2,538.6	2,739.8	2,868.4	3,164.3	2,932.1	3,283.9	3,780.5	5,454.9	6,728.8	7,248.8
SDRs.........................	1b.d	10.0	10.1	15.2	8.3	3.1	1.9	9.1	2.8	10.2	12.2	16.2	10.0
Reserve Position in the Fund..........	1c.d	38.5	41.0	41.9	40.7	38.4	40.2	39.3	37.4	36.3	39.5	43.5	45.8
Foreign Exchange................	1d.d	....	....	2,481.5	2,690.7	2,826.9	3,122.3	2,883.7	3,243.6	3,734.0	5,403.2	6,669.0	7,193.1
Gold (Million Fine Troy Ounces)........	1ad	....	....	.801	.859	.902	.959	1.012	1.058	1.117	1.172	1.172	1.173
Gold (National Valuation)..............	1and	....	....	308.3	322.8	276.1	281.4	298.9	284.4	310.6	377.8	458.4	508.3
Monetary Authorities: Other Liab....	4..d	415.4	313.1	264.1	256.5	252.9	242.0	239.9	203.6	144.1	220.3	276.6	379.9
Deposit Money Banks: Assets..........	7a.d	391.4	571.1	813.5	746.7	649.1	722.1	801.0	682.4	655.7	811.6	825.0	921.2
Liabilities..................	7b.d	699.5	461.2	641.1	527.9	438.7	565.4	659.7	478.3	438.8	405.9	507.0	601.8
Monetary Authorities							*Billions of Francs: End of Period*							
Foreign Assets..............	11	....	....	1,388	1,586	1,865	1,920	2,082	2,493	3,011	3,632	3,702	3,702
Claims on Central Government........	12a	....	....	940	976	1,122	1,283	1,295	1,228	1,262	1,248	1,131	972
Claims on Deposit Money Banks.....	12e	....	....	150	146	159	179	123	91	43	16	2	1
Claims on Other Financial Insts........	12f	....	....	13	16	15	17	16	14	11	9	6	1
Reserve Money..................	14	....	....	1,251	1,284	1,428	1,534	1,589	1,773	2,194	2,647	2,596	2,633
of which: Currency Outside DMBs..	14a	....	....	1,018	1,060	1,217	1,305	1,361	1,465	1,703	2,010	1,848	1,797
Foreign Liabilities..................	16c	....	....	738	828	909	988	1,114	1,091	1,028	945	780	673
Central Government Deposits..........	16d	....	....	158	231	325	352	328	252	343	392	430	415
Other Items (Net)...............	17r	....	....	344	381	499	523	485	710	762	921	1,035	955
Deposit Money Banks							*Billions of Francs: End of Period*							
Reserves..................	20	....	....	177	178	188	175	198	280	392	534	700	829
Foreign Assets..................	21	....	....	399	391	389	406	523	481	488	508	428	444
Claims on Central Government........	22a	....	....	724	827	807	824	805	699	705	719	776	846
Claims on Private Sector..................	22d	....	....	1,819	1,998	2,204	2,377	2,407	2,665	2,835	3,010	3,223	3,501
Claims on Other Financial Insts........	22f	....	....	3	—	—	—	—	—	—	—	—	—
Demand Deposits..................	24	....	....	1,028	1,108	1,137	1,245	1,303	1,378	1,488	1,686	1,899	2,066
Time Deposits..................	25	....	....	995	1,101	1,157	1,090	1,160	1,264	1,369	1,598	1,718	1,910
Foreign Liabilities..................	26c	....	....	255	227	239	295	391	304	288	213	222	248
Long-Term Foreign Liabilities...........	26cl	....	....	59	49	24	23	40	33	39	41	41	42
Central Government Deposits..........	26d	....	....	524	624	599	663	606	706	765	778	778	765
Credit from Monetary Authorities.....	26g	....	....	162	148	159	180	114	96	44	16	2	4
Other Items (Net)................	27r	....	....	98	136	274	285	320	343	426	439	468	585
Monetary Survey							*Billions of Francs: End of Period*							
Foreign Assets (Net).......................	31n	....	....	793	922	1,105	1,043	1,101	1,579	2,183	2,982	3,129	3,224
Domestic Credit..................	32	....	....	2,831	2,978	3,243	3,501	3,608	3,670	3,727	3,839	3,957	4,175
Claims on Central Govt. (Net)........	32an	....	....	971	935	992	1,081	1,157	974	854	797	710	659
Claims on Private Sector................	32d	....	....	1,844	2,028	2,236	2,404	2,435	2,682	2,862	3,033	3,241	3,515
Claims on Other Financial Insts......	32f	....	....	16	16	15	17	16	14	11	9	6	1
Money..................	34	....	....	2,101	2,229	2,415	2,607	2,721	2,896	3,281	3,775	3,816	3,913
Quasi-Money..................	35	....	....	995	1,101	1,157	1,090	1,160	1,264	1,369	1,598	1,718	1,910
Long-Term Foreign Liabilities...........	36cl	....	....	59	49	24	23	40	33	39	41	41	42
Other Items (Net)..................	37r	....	....	469	521	752	825	788	1,056	1,222	1,407	1,511	1,534
Money plus Quasi-Money................	35l	....	....	3,096	3,330	3,573	3,697	3,881	4,160	4,650	5,374	5,534	5,823
Interest Rates							*Percent Per Annum*							
Bank Rate (End of Period)..............	60	....	....	6.00	6.00	6.00	6.00	6.00	6.00	6.00	6.00	4.50	4.00
Money Market Rate.......................	60b	....	....	4.95	4.95	4.95	4.95	4.95	4.95	4.95	4.95	4.95	4.95
Deposit Rate........................	60l	....	....	3.50	3.50	3.50	3.50	3.50	3.50	3.50	3.50	3.50	3.50
Prices							*Index Numbers (2000=100): Period Averages*							
Share Price Index..................	62	....	....	....	....	....	....	112.4	100.0	89.0	92.3	93.5	106.9
Consumer Prices..................	64	61.0	79.2	88.8	91.8	94.6	98.1	98.3	100.0	104.0	107.1	108.5	109.1
National Accounts							*Billions of Francs*							
Househ.Cons.Expend.,incl.NPISHs.....	96f	....	....	8,856.6	9,576.0	10,541.1	11,380.3	11,889.7	12,280.6	13,328.2	13,246.8	....	....
Government Consumption Expend...	91f	....	....	2,576.3	2,880.7	3,016.1	3,740.8	3,769.4	3,779.9	3,940.5	4,354.0	....	....
Gross Fixed Capital Formation..........	93e	....	....	1,947.2	2,214.7	2,525.8	2,889.6	2,919.3	2,733.1	3,049.4	3,228.3	....	....
Changes in Inventories....................	93i	....	....	288.7	−13.6	86.2	−199.4	−62.5	209.6	78.9	−195.6	....	....
Exports of Goods and Services........	90c	....	....	3,896.6	4,414.2	4,964.5	5,194.4	5,410.5	5,623.8	6,162.3	7,126.9	....	....
Imports of Goods and Services(-)......	98c	....	....	4,463.8	4,649.2	5,063.1	5,459.4	5,762.6	6,263.4	6,814.8	7,038.3	....	....
Gross Domestic Product (GDP).........	99b	....	....	13,101.5	14,422.7	16,070.0	17,546.4	18,163.8	18,363.7	19,744.6	20,722.2	....	....

		1993	1994	1995	1996	1997	1998	1999	2000	2001	2002	2003	2004
Exchange Rates						*US Dollars per SDR: End of Period (sa)*							
Market Rate.....................	sa	1.37356	1.45985	1.48649	1.43796	1.34925	1.40803	1.37251	1.30291	1.25673	1.35952	1.48597	1.55301
Monetary Authorities						*Millions of US Dollars: End of Period*							
Foreign Assets....................	11	....	....	....	....	....	181.97	184.48	275.45	259.14	273.64	374.09	401.47
Claims on Central Government........	12a	....	....	....	....	....	14.10	15.94	13.98	16.04	18.02	13.76	7.91
Claims on Deposit Money Banks......	12e	....	....	....	....	....	95.59	146.28	111.82	96.66	103.59	130.68	158.18
Bankers Deposits.........................	14c	....	....	....	....	....	266.37	321.38	372.28	338.91	357.18	479.01	530.04
Demand Deposits........................	14d	....	....	....	....	....	—	—	—	—	—	—	—
Foreign Liabilities......................	16c	....	....			....	—	—	—	—	—	—	—
Central Government Deposits..........	16d	....	....			....	—	—	—	—	—	—	—
Capital Accounts.........................	17a	....	....			....	24.95	27.42	31.48	32.41	33.87	32.18	36.97
Other Items (Net).........................	17r	....	....	....	....		.33	−2.27	−2.51	.54	4.20	7.04	.56
Deposit Money Banks						*Millions of US Dollars: End of Period*							
Reserves....................................	20	....	....	....	177.30	248.00	271.40	335.76	383.52	346.40	357.22	482.45	541.52
Foreign Assets............................	21	....	....	....	1,393.70	1,643.00	1,776.90	2,160.85	2,347.42	2,372.81	2,515.80	2,538.06	2,620.89
Claims on Central Government........	22a	....	....	....	18.63	58.00	81.63	92.03	328.87	296.87	133.83	224.95	383.30
Claims on Local Government...........	22b	....	....	....	—		.01	—	—	9.17	4.36	6.85	3.35
Claims on Nonfin.Pub.Enterprises.....	22c	....	....	....	8.62	10.00	6.76	6.19	87.80	62.86	6.61	23.18	33.88
Claims on Private Sector..................	22d	....	....	....	408.84	563.00	733.40	912.59	926.93	860.00	859.28	860.78	1,064.13
Demand Deposits.........................	24	....	....	....	552.04	562.00	614.61	685.69	815.07	761.09	779.72	1,050.77	1,213.91
Time and Savings Deposits..............	25	....	....	....	1,093.10	1,329.00	1,634.72	1,985.41	2,522.39	2,461.03	2,298.34	2,300.49	2,282.51
Foreign Liabilities.......................	26c	....	....	....	105.15	265.00	289.83	373.26	310.20	303.30	221.52	117.36	132.82
Central Government Deposits...........	26d	....	....	....	62.31	176.00	136.28	156.83	119.56	116.77	191.37	206.55	371.08
Credit from Monetary Authorities.....	26g	....	....	....	100.45	125.00	97.61	143.43	118.52	88.38	104.74	112.04	146.49
Capital Accounts.........................	27a	....	....	....	144.22	229.00	265.18	304.78	343.31	369.09	383.01	467.96	568.45
Other Items (Net).........................	27r	....	....	....	−50.19	−164.00	−168.12	−141.98	−154.50	−151.56	−101.60	−118.11	−68.20
Monetary Survey						*Millions of US Dollars: End of Period*							
Foreign Assets (Net)........................	31n	....	....	....	....	....	1,669.04	1,972.07	2,312.67	2,328.65	2,567.92	2,794.79	2,889.54
Domestic Credit............................	32	....	....	....	....	....	699.63	870.17	1,238.03	1,128.16	830.73	922.97	1,121.49
Claims on Central Govt. (Net)........	32an	....	....	....	....	....	−40.55	−48.86	223.29	196.13	−39.52	32.16	20.13
Claims on Local Government..........	32b	....	....	....	....	....	.01	—	—	9.17	4.36	6.85	3.35
Claims on Nonfin.Pub.Enterprises...	32c	....	....	....	....	....	6.76	6.19	87.80	62.86	6.61	23.18	33.88
Claims on Private Sector...............	32d	....	....	....	....	....	733.40	912.84	926.93	860.00	859.28	860.78	1,064.13
Deposit Money............................	34	....	....	....	....	....	614.61	685.69	815.07	761.09	779.72	1,050.77	1,213.91
Quasi-Money...............................	35	....	....	....	....	....	1,634.72	1,985.41	2,522.39	2,461.03	2,298.34	2,300.49	2,282.51
Capital Accounts.........................	37a	....	....	....	....	....	290.13	332.20	374.79	401.50	416.88	500.14	605.42
Other Items (Net).........................	37r	....	....	....	....	....	−170.80	−161.48	−161.55	−166.79	−96.29	−133.15	−90.81
Interest Rates						*Percent Per Annum*							
Deposit Rate...............................	60l	....	....	....	....	....	....	....	....	1.48	.89	.74	1.12
Lending Rate...............................	60p	....	....	....	....	....	....	....	....	8.36	7.97	7.56	6.92
Prices and Labor						*Index Numbers (2000=100): Period Averages*							
Consumer Prices...........................	64	....	....	....	81.5	87.3	92.2	97.3	100.0	101.2	107.0	111.7	....
						Number in Thousands: Period Averages							
Labor Force.................................	67d	....	....	....	....	....	631	672	696	681	708	....	....
Employment................................	67e	....	....	....	....	....	540	593	596	507	486	591	....
Unemployment.............................	67c	....	....	....	....	....	92	79	99	174	222	203	....
Unemployment Rate (%).................	67r	....	....	....	....	....	14.5	11.8	14.5	25.6	31.4	25.6	....
						Millions: Midyear Estimates							
Population............................	99z	2.42	2.51	2.61	2.71	2.82	2.93	3.04	3.15	3.26	3.37	3.48	3.59

Yemen, Republic of 474

		1993	1994	1995	1996	1997	1998	1999	2000	2001	2002	2003	2004
Exchange Rates						*Rial per SDR: End of Period*								
Market Rate	aa	16.496	17.533	† 74.384	† 182.492	176.023	199.447	218.366	215.749	217.754	243.368	273.879	288.658
						Rial per US Dollar: End of Period (ae) Period Average (rf)								
Market Rate	ae	12.010	12.010	† 50.040	† 126.910	130.460	141.650	159.100	165.590	173.270	179.010	184.310	185.870
Market Rate	rf	12.010	12.010	† 40.839	† 94.157	129.281	135.882	155.718	161.718	168.672	175.625	183.448	184.776
Fund Position						*Millions of SDRs: End of Period*								
Quota	2f.s	176.5	176.5	176.5	176.5	176.5	176.5	243.5	243.5	243.5	243.5	243.5	243.5
SDRs	1b.s	.5	33.5	37.0	33.3	124.1	131.6	128.5	65.0	14.7	33.0	3.3	33.0
Reserve Position in the Fund	1c.s	—	—	—	—	—	—	—	—	—	—	—	—
Total Fund Cred.&Loans Outstg.	2tl	—	—	—	84.0	185.4	238.4	297.6	243.5	297.3	283.8	270.1	242.2
International Liquidity						*Millions of US Dollars Unless Otherwise Indicated: End of Period*								
Total Reserves minus Gold	1l.d	145.3	254.8	619.0	1,017.2	1,203.1	995.5	1,471.5	2,900.3	3,658.1	4,410.5	4,986.9	5,664.8
SDRs	1b.d	.6	48.9	55.0	47.9	167.4	185.2	176.3	84.6	18.5	44.9	4.9	51.3
Reserve Position in the Fund	1c.d	—	—	—	—	—	—	—	—	—	—	—	—
Foreign Exchange	1d.d	144.6	205.9	564.0	969.3	1,035.7	810.3	1,295.1	2,815.6	3,639.6	4,365.6	4,982.0	5,613.5
Gold (Million Fine Troy Ounces)	1ad	.050	.050	.050	.050	.050	.050	.050	.050	.050	.050	.050	.050
Gold (National Valuation)	1and	2.4	2.6	2.6	18.6	18.5	15.3	15.3	14.4	14.6	18.4	21.9	23.4
Deposit Money Banks: Assets	7a.d	547.7	477.2	861.1	334.5	455.9	457.9	446.2	624.1	695.5	849.0	862.3	888.4
Liabilities	7b.d	549.4	548.1	479.1	209.8	60.8	50.2	45.6	56.5	26.9	18.7	21.7	52.6
Monetary Authorities						*Millions of Rial: End of Period*								
Foreign Assets	11	1,774	4,292	31,108	131,459	159,892	143,257	† 237,502	482,436	636,331	792,193	923,080	1,057,038
Claims on Central Government	12a	135,664	180,586	209,342	199,058	171,234	196,702	† 159,621	17,913	2,082	686	206	2,606
Claims on Nonfin.Pub.Enterprises	12c	76	57	—	10	50	1,108	† 9,026	1,821	1,540	1,513	1,650	1,767
Claims on Deposit Money Banks	12e	5	40	94	54	49							
Reserve Money	14	108,933	147,585	176,756	189,030	165,443	184,002	222,245	253,255	288,694	315,140	381,668	436,649
of which: Currency Outside Banks	14a	79,019	111,006	129,114	120,477	126,904	139,668	166,924	197,123	212,795	239,329	268,813	297,939
Other Liab. to Dep. Money Banks	14n	....	....	....	....	....	....	5,659	5,865	41,933	46,807	39,429	33,490
Time, Savings,& Fgn.Currency Dep.	15	2,352	3,881	9,440	19,966	22,193	18,978	11,932	18,531	22,112	20,267	31,902	23,040
Restricted Deposits	16b	....	....	....	....	....	....	8,388	7,935	19,858	15,090	42,623	39,184
Foreign Liabilities	16c	1,913	2,053	11,323	43,931	66,613	84,138	† 101,159	89,094	100,821	103,187	108,094	95,795
Central Government Deposits	16d	16,326	18,294	27,011	41,003	46,106	18,171	† 26,095	79,708	106,488	195,311	158,199	225,906
Capital Accounts	17a	1,077	1,100	2,738	5,835	5,673	6,323	† 35,201	24,592	65,636	91,451	143,224	180,888
Other Items (Net)	17r	6,916	12,023	13,182	30,762	24,846	29,458	† −4,526	23,190	−5,589	7,138	19,796	26,458
Deposit Money Banks						*Millions of Rial: End of Period*								
Reserves	20	25,987	32,879	44,055	59,903	28,052	35,714	43,631	45,545	50,647	55,710	87,593	112,679
Other Claims on Monetary Author.	20n	....	....	....	....	....	....	5,659	5,865	31,790	46,207	38,779	31,440
Foreign Assets	21	6,578	5,731	43,088	42,453	59,472	64,857	70,991	103,340	120,511	151,981	158,925	165,128
Claims on Central Government	22a	281	336	1,295	6,963	34,873	36,267	39,972	63,173	54,814	75,215	112,467	158,680
Claims on Nonfin.Pub.Enterprises	22c	3,395	3,401	11,011	2,237	1,641	317	649	474	674	1,066	1,303	1,943
Claims on Private Sector	22d	12,653	14,143	23,865	22,358	34,380	45,957	62,426	75,747	95,318	108,949	137,553	183,611
Demand Deposits	24	21,489	25,390	22,985	27,353	28,875	31,490	29,649	41,004	49,458	49,819	56,346	69,628
Time, Savings,& Fgn.Currency Dep.	25	17,251	19,359	71,956	88,640	106,272	130,753	155,981	204,053	252,725	328,914	405,096	485,199
Restricted Deposits	26b	1,240	1,210	1,977	3,661	3,540	3,684	4,185	4,692	5,064	9,034	12,900	18,485
Foreign Liabilities	26c	6,599	6,582	23,973	26,624	7,932	7,114	7,248	9,358	4,652	3,351	3,991	9,774
Central Government Deposits	26d	1,543	1,863	1,127	171	474	52	30	46	62	38	101	219
Credit from Monetary Authorities	26g	—	14	4	5	26	23	32	—	—	—	—	—
Capital Accounts	27a	1,997	2,829	4,601	6,669	10,762	17,615	† 22,688	23,439	28,074	32,724	36,424	48,127
Other Items (Net)	27r	−1,224	−745	−3,305	−19,203	564	−7,597	† 3,515	11,552	13,718	15,249	21,754	22,040
Monetary Survey						*Millions of Rial: End of Period*								
Foreign Assets (Net)	31n	−160	1,388	38,900	103,358	144,820	116,863	† 200,086	487,324	651,369	837,637	969,920	1,116,598
Domestic Credit	32	134,201	178,365	217,375	189,453	195,598	262,128	† 245,568	79,373	47,878	−7,921	94,879	122,482
Claims on Central Govt. (Net)	32an	118,076	160,765	182,499	164,848	159,527	214,746	† 173,468	1,331	−49,654	−119,449	−45,627	−64,839
Claims on Nonfin.Pub.Enterprises	32c	3,472	3,457	11,011	2,247	1,691	1,425	† 9,674	2,295	2,214	2,579	2,953	3,710
Claims on Private Sector	32d	12,653	14,143	23,865	22,358	34,380	45,957	62,426	75,747	95,318	108,949	137,553	183,611
Money	34	103,306	139,590	164,019	156,579	166,384	179,927	207,197	247,248	283,149	306,450	347,465	390,541
Quasi-Money	35	19,604	23,239	81,396	108,605	128,465	149,731	167,913	222,585	274,836	349,181	436,997	508,239
Restricted Deposits	36b	1,240	1,210	1,977	3,661	3,540	3,684	† 12,573	12,627	24,922	24,123	55,532	57,679
Capital Accounts	37a	3,073	3,929	7,339	12,504	16,434	23,938	† 57,889	48,030	93,711	124,176	179,648	229,016
Other Items (Net)	37r	6,821	11,784	1,544	11,461	25,292	21,712	† 87	36,208	22,628	25,786	45,156	53,604
Money plus Quasi-Money	35l	122,909	162,829	245,415	265,184	294,849	329,658	375,109	469,833	557,985	655,631	784,463	898,781
Interest Rates						*Percent Per Annum*								
Discount Rate	60	....	....	27	29	15	20	19	16	15	13	....	....
Treasury Bill Rate	60c	....	....	....	25	16	13	21	14	13	12	13	14
Deposit Rate	60l	....	....	....	24	15	11	18	14	13	13	13	13
Lending Rate	60p	....	....	....	31	23	15	24	20	18	18	18	19
Prices						*Index Numbers (2000=100): Period Averages*								
Consumer Prices	64	26.8	40.1	62.2	81.3	83.0	88.0	95.6	100.0	111.9	125.6	139.2	....
Intl. Transactions & Positions						*Millions of Rial*								
Exports	70	7,333	11,216	79,434	251,830	323,716	203,480	380,010	659,609	542,359	....	....	....
Imports, c.i.f.	71	33,883	25,070	64,591	191,862	260,331	294,510	312,749	375,783	389,638	....	....	....

Yemen, Republic of   474

		1993	1994	1995	1996	1997	1998	1999	2000	2001	2002	2003	2004
Balance of Payments						*Millions of US Dollars: Minus Sign Indicates Debit*							
Current Account, n.i.e.	78ald	−1,275.3	178.3	143.7	38.8	−68.8	−472.2	358.2	1,336.6	667.1	538.2	148.7	224.6
Goods: Exports f.o.b.	78aad	1,166.8	1,796.2	1,980.1	2,262.7	2,274.0	1,503.7	2,478.3	3,797.2	3,366.9	3,620.7	3,934.3	4,675.7
Goods: Imports f.o.b.	78abd	−2,138.1	−1,522.0	−1,831.5	−2,293.5	−2,406.5	−2,288.8	−2,120.5	−2,484.4	−2,600.4	−2,932.0	−3,557.4	−3,858.6
Trade Balance	78acd	−971.3	274.2	148.6	−30.8	−132.5	−785.1	357.8	1,312.8	766.4	688.7	376.9	817.1
Services: Credit	78add	177.2	148.0	179.4	185.7	207.6	174.4	183.2	210.9	166.4	166.2	317.7	369.7
Services: Debit	78aed	−1,043.4	−704.3	−639.3	−555.4	−677.4	−692.9	−718.7	−809.4	−847.8	−934.8	−1,003.6	−1,059.4
Balance on Goods & Services	78afd	−1,837.5	−282.1	−311.3	−400.5	−602.3	−1,303.6	−177.6	714.2	85.1	−79.9	−308.9	127.3
Income: Credit	78agd	22.0	22.0	37.4	46.8	69.6	69.0	56.7	149.6	178.5	135.0	98.9	103.6
Income: Debit	78ahd	−430.2	−553.9	−598.4	−680.7	−670.6	−413.4	−752.3	−926.7	−869.4	−900.6	−1,008.3	−1,450.1
Balance on Gds, Serv. & Inc.	78aid	−2,245.7	−814.0	−872.3	−1,034.4	−1,203.3	−1,648.0	−873.2	−62.9	−605.8	−845.6	−1,218.3	−1,219.1
Current Transfers, n.i.e.: Credit	78ajd	1,065.2	1,062.3	1,080.5	1,140.1	1,177.6	1,223.5	1,261.1	1,471.9	1,344.4	1,456.8	1,442.1	1,493.1
Current Transfers: Debit	78akd	−94.8	−70.0	−64.5	−66.9	−43.1	−47.7	−30.7	−72.4	−71.4	−73.1	−75.0	−49.4
Capital Account, n.i.e.	78bcd	....	....	....	....	4,236.2	2.2	1.5	338.9	49.5	—	5.5	163.3
Capital Account, n.i.e.: Credit	78bad	....	....	....	....	4,236.2	2.2	1.5	338.9	49.5	—	5.5	163.3
Capital Account: Debit	78bbd	....	....	....	....	....	—	—	—	—	—	—	....
Financial Account, n.i.e.	78bjd	49.5	−710.7	−858.4	−367.8	−197.6	−418.0	−415.1	−376.2	−53.5	−156.8	19.7	−68.6
Direct Investment Abroad	78bdd	....	....	....	....	....	—	—	—	—	—	—	....
Dir. Invest. in Rep. Econ., n.i.e.	78bed	903.0	15.8	−217.7	−60.1	−138.5	−219.4	−307.6	6.4	155.1	114.3	−89.1	143.6
Portfolio Investment Assets	78bfd	1.6	2.8	−3.1	.9	5.0	4.9	4.1	.1	−1.4	−5.8	−.4	−6.4
Equity Securities	78bkd	1.6	2.8	−3.1	.9	5.0	4.9	4.1	.1	−1.4	−5.8	−.4	−6.4
Debt Securities	78bld	....	....	....	....	....	—	—	—	—	—	—	....
Portfolio Investment Liab., n.i.e.	78bgd	....	....	....	....	....	—	—	—	—	—	—	....
Equity Securities	78bmd	....	....	....	....	....	—	—	—	—	—	—	....
Debt Securities	78bnd	....	....	....	....	....	—	—	—	—	—	—	....
Financial Derivatives Assets	78bwd	....	....	....	....	....	....	....	....	....	....	....	....
Financial Derivatives Liabilities	78bxd	....	....	....	....	....	....	....	....	....	....	....	....
Other Investment Assets	78bhd	−5.3	−130.9	158.8	24.0	196.3	60.1	−110.1	−177.9	5.6	−124.5	49.1	−25.4
Monetary Authorities	78bod	....	....	....	....	....	—	—	—	—	—	—	—
General Government	78bpd	−51.3	1.3	−32.5	−63.7	63.5	70.7	−119.4	—	75.6	−57.6	—	−5.7
Banks	78bqd	−4.0	67.8	141.3	7.7	−122.3	−10.6	9.3	−177.9	−70.0	−147.7	−12.8	−19.7
Other Sectors	78brd	50.0	−200.0	50.0	80.0	255.1	—	—	—	—	80.8	61.9	....
Other Investment Liab., n.i.e.	78bid	−849.8	−598.4	−796.4	−332.6	−260.4	−263.6	−1.5	−204.8	−212.8	−140.8	60.2	−180.4
Monetary Authorities	78bsd	−31.5	61.1	4.4	−.6	34.3	−3.0	−23.7	−8.1	−11.5	−22.4	−10.9	−45.7
General Government	78btd	−771.4	−656.6	−626.1	−353.2	−145.7	−250.5	27.1	−207.7	−171.6	−110.3	68.1	−165.6
Banks	78bud	−41.0	−1.4	−174.7	21.2	−149.0	−10.1	−4.9	11.0	−29.7	−8.1	2.9	30.9
Other Sectors	78bvd	−5.9	−1.5	—	—	—	—	—	—	—	—	—	....
Net Errors and Omissions	78cad	113.9	−189.2	186.5	−107.0	48.4	307.0	129.4	295.1	−110.0	43.3	156.4	53.3
Overall Balance	78cbd	−1,111.9	−721.6	−528.2	−436.0	4,018.2	−580.9	74.0	1,594.4	553.2	424.7	330.3	372.5
Reserves and Related Items	79dad	1,111.9	721.6	528.2	436.0	−4,018.2	580.9	−74.0	−1,594.4	−553.2	−424.7	−330.3	−372.5
Reserve Assets	79dbd	175.2	−207.9	−263.1	−415.7	−192.7	210.9	−482.2	−1,429.4	−761.3	−556.9	−326.3	−532.3
Use of Fund Credit and Loans	79dcd	—	—	—	122.5	139.4	72.3	79.5	−71.0	69.0	−17.2	−19.3	−41.2
Exceptional Financing	79ded	936.7	929.5	791.3	729.3	−3,964.9	297.7	328.7	−94.0	139.1	149.4	15.3	201.0
International Investment Position							*Millions of US Dollars*							
Assets	79aad	....	....	....	....	....	1,484.0	2,067.5	3,686.8	4,441.7	5,405.6	6,020.7	6,744.8
Direct Investment Abroad	79abd	....	....	....	....	....	—	—	—	—	—	—	—
Portfolio Investment	79acd	....	....	....	....	....	4.5	.4	.3	1.7	7.5	7.9	14.4
Equity Securities	79add	....	....	....	....	....	4.5	.4	.3	1.7	7.5	7.9	14.4
Debt Securities	79aed	....	....	....	....	....	—	—	—	—	—	—	—
Financial Derivatives	79ald	....	....	....	....	....	—	—	—	—	—	—	—
Other Investment	79afd	....	....	....	....	....	466.3	576.5	772.9	767.3	972.5	1,004.3	1,043.2
Monetary Authorities	79agd	....	....	....	....	....	12.0	131.4	149.1	73.5	131.0	149.9	155.6
General Government	79ahd	....	....	....	....	....	—	—	—	—	—	—	—
Banks	79aid	....	....	....	....	....	454.3	445.1	623.8	693.8	841.5	854.4	874.1
Other Sectors	79ajd	....	....	....	....	....	—	—	—	—	—	—	13.5
Reserve Assets	79akd	....	....	....	....	....	1,013.2	1,490.6	2,913.6	3,672.7	4,425.6	5,008.5	5,687.2
Liabilities	79lad	....	....	....	....	....	6,077.9	6,305.5	6,372.9	6,006.5	6,092.8	6,543.6	6,825.2
Dir. Invest. in Rep. Economy	79lbd	....	....	....	....	....	1,088.6	993.2	843.0	998.1	1,112.4	1,010.7	1,248.9
Portfolio Investment	79lcd	....	....	....	....	....	—	—	—	—	—	—	—
Equity Securities	79ldd	....	....	....	....	....	—	—	—	—	—	—	—
Debt Securities	79led	....	....	....	....	....	—	—	—	—	—	—	—
Financial Derivatives	79lld	....	....	....	....	....	—	—	—	—	—	—	—
Other Investment	79lfd	....	....	....	....	....	4,989.3	5,312.3	5,529.9	5,008.4	4,980.3	5,532.9	5,576.3
Monetary Authorities	79lgd	....	....	....	....	....	624.6	664.0	538.0	596.3	576.4	586.5	515.4
General Government	79lhd	....	....	....	....	....	4,314.4	4,602.9	4,935.3	4,385.2	4,385.2	4,924.8	5,006.4
Banks	79lid	....	....	....	....	....	50.3	45.4	56.5	26.9	18.7	21.7	52.6
Other Sectors	79ljd	....	....	....	....	....	—	—	—	—	—	—	1.9
Government Finance						*Millions of Rial: Year Ending December 31*								
Deficit (-) or Surplus	80	−29,297	−44,788	−24,907	−17,428	−13,588	−19,116f	−40,278f	....	....	....	....	....
Revenue	81	36,720	41,384	89,646	216,053	287,347	300,791f	279,418f	....	....	....	....	....
Grants Received	81z	1,201	856	1,620	1,870	4,639	5,480f	4,219f	....	....	....	....	....
Expenditure	82	65,247	85,875	111,128	215,738	290,571	309,942f	310,702f	....	....	....	....	....
Lending Minus Repayments	83	1,971	1,153	5,045	19,613	15,003	15,445f	13,213f	....	....	....	....	....
Financing													
Domestic	84a	28,804	43,838	25,976	11,860	2,696p	−7,750f	25,283f	....	....	....	....	....
Foreign	85a	493	950	−1,069	5,568	16,572p	26,866f	14,995f	....	....	....	....	....

		1993	1994	1995	1996	1997	1998	1999	2000	2001	2002	2003	2004
National Accounts							*Millions of Rial*						
Househ.Cons.Expend.,incl.NPISHs....	96f	212,249	244,753	431,346	531,423	618,701	620,429	765,695p	965,294p	1,105,217p	1,258,531p	1,551,942p	....
Government Consumption Expend...	91f	45,483	57,585	74,017	97,458	116,832	124,473	156,273p	193,322p	219,124p	244,560p	267,147p	....
Gross Fixed Capital Formation..........	93e	41,627	58,267	106,227	158,016	191,666	267,810	265,371p	251,684p	263,994p	277,593p	330,988p	....
Changes in Inventories....................	93i	6,622	6,123	6,486	12,863	29,549	8,655	13,122p	12,590p	13,894p	14,610p	19,541p	....
Exports of Goods and Services..........	90c	32,833	42,091	115,957	285,587	320,822	228,025	414,527p	645,230p	596,006p	659,824p	647,138p	....
Imports of Goods and Services (-).....	98c	99,760	98,218	217,390	351,795	398,686	405,152	442,194p	528,485p	582,290p	651,728p	735,112p	....
Gross Domestic Product (GDP).........	99b	239,054	310,601	516,643	733,552	878,884	844,240	1,172,794p	1,539,635p	1,615,945p	1,803,390p	2,081,644p	....
Net Primary Income from Abroad.....	98.n	−4,901	−6,388	−22,535	−72,365	−77,697	−23,846	−74,262p	−125,746p	−113,566p	−130,484p	−113,898p	....
Gross National Income (GNI)............	99a	234,153	304,213	494,108	661,187	801,187	820,394	1,098,532p	1,413,889p	1,502,379p	1,672,906p	1,967,746p	....
GDP Volume 1990 Prices.................	99b.p	142,818	147,106	165,040	178,293	189,450	202,393	207,320p	216,970p	227,086p	235,943p	245,411p	....
GDP Volume (2000=100)................	99bvp	65.8	67.8	76.1	82.2	87.3	93.3	95.6	100.0	104.7	108.7	113.1	....
GDP Deflator (2000=100)...............	99bip	23.6	29.8	44.1	58.0	65.4	58.8	79.7	100.0	100.3	107.7	119.5	....
							Millions: Midyear Estimates						
Population.............................	99z	13.95	† 14.60	15.22	15.80	16.34	16.86	17.39	17.94	18.51	19.09	19.70	20.33

Zambia 754

		1993	1994	1995	1996	1997	1998	1999	2000	2001	2002	2003	2004
Exchange Rates						*Kwacha per SDR: End of Period*							
Official Rate	aa	686.78	993.10	1,421.28	1,844.46	1,908.97	3,236.95	3,612.71	5,417.28	4,813.78	5,892.70	6,903.04	7,409.89
					Kwacha per US Dollar: End of Period (ae) Period Average (rf)								
Official Rate	ae	500.00	680.27	956.13	1,282.69	1,414.84	2,298.92	2,632.19	4,157.83	3,830.40	4,334.40	4,645.48	4,771.31
Official Rate	rf	452.76	669.37	864.12	1,207.90	1,314.50	1,862.07	2,388.02	3,110.84	3,610.94	4,398.60	4,733.27	4,778.88
					Index Numbers (2000=100): Period Averages								
Official Rate	ahx	693.3	408.0	357.9	255.9	233.3	167.1	128.5	100.0	85.3	71.6	64.8	64.1
Nominal Effective Exchange Rate	nec	572.2	370.5	272.7	204.4	200.9	152.6	119.7	100.0	92.4	74.5	64.0	62.3
Real Effective Exchange Rate	rec	95.8	92.2	88.3	92.4	110.7	101.1	98.8	100.0	108.7	103.1	101.3	109.5
Fund Position						*Millions of SDRs: End of Period*							
Quota	2f.s	270.3	270.3	363.5	363.5	363.5	363.5	489.1	489.1	489.1	489.1	489.1	489.1
SDRs	1b.s	—	—	8.2	1.4	.8	.6	.1	17.1	53.3	51.7	.3	16.0
Reserve Position in the Fund	1c.s	—	—	—	—	—	—	—	—	—	—	—	—
Total Fund Cred.&Loans Outstg	2tl	565.8	551.2	833.4	833.4	843.4	843.4	853.4	873.4	781.6	746.6	577.9	573.3
International Liquidity					*Millions of US Dollars Unless Otherwise Indicated: End of Period*								
Total Reserves minus Gold	1l.d	192.3	268.1	222.7	222.7	239.1	69.4	45.4	244.8	183.4	535.1	247.7	337.1
SDRs	1b.d	—	—	12.1	2.0	1.1	.8	.1	22.3	66.9	70.3	.5	24.8
Reserve Position in the Fund	1c.d	—	—	—	—	—	—	—	—	—	—	—	—
Foreign Exchange	1d.d	192.3	268.1	210.5	220.7	238.0	68.6	45.3	222.5	116.5	464.8	247.2	312.2
Gold (Million Fine Troy Ounces)	1ad	....	....	—	—	—	—	—	—	—	—	—	—
Gold (National Valuation)	1and	....	....	—	—	—	—	—	—	—	—	—	—
Monetary Authorities: Other Liab	4..d	678.7	736.0	160.0	151.7	114.4	69.7	52.4	37.0	69.1	160.6	164.7	69.3
Banking Institutions: Assets	7a.d	205.5	84.3	121.8	148.6	158.8	198.9	201.4	239.5	233.3	293.5	235.3	334.0
Liabilities	7b.d	16.8	15.6	9.8	11.2	13.5	29.2	34.9	25.9	24.5	26.0	35.0	42.9
Monetary Authorities						*Billions of Kwacha: End of Period*							
Foreign Assets	11	137.7	213.7	† 208.1	268.4	338.4	103.0	211.2	336.8	432.6	1,337.2	† 1,190.5	1,497.6
Claims on Central Government	12a	611.9	1,114.7	† 2,017.5	2,636.7	2,659.5	4,670.2	5,584.5	8,605.1	7,816.2	9,320.4	† 9,371.3	6,586.3
Claims on Nonfin.Pub.Enterprises	12c	20.2	9.1	† 1.2	1.3	1.3	5.3	7.9	69.2	195.0	30.5	† 60.8	60.9
Claims on Private Sector	12d	2.1	4.4	† 14.0	23.6	25.1	30.7	31.4	35.7	42.6	50.9	† 28.5	28.9
Claims on Banking Institutions	12e	7.8	—	† 121.8	157.2	164.9	161.4	120.9	82.4	72.9	107.7	† 263.0	206.1
Reserve Money	14	102.3	151.4	† 129.2	175.0	259.3	303.0	389.2	597.0	870.0	1,258.7	† 1,442.3	1,908.2
of which: Currency Outside Banks	14a	40.4	56.3	† 77.8	106.3	136.7	† 169.7	212.2	287.8	373.6	422.4	† 590.7	727.0
Time, Savings,& Fgn.Currency Dep	15	5.4	—	† 1.5	2.3	.7	.8	1.6	2.2	3.5	6.1	† 5.9	7.5
Foreign Liabilities	16c	727.9	1,048.1	† 1,337.6	1,731.8	1,771.9	2,890.4	3,221.2	4,885.6	4,027.0	5,095.3	† 4,754.5	4,578.4
Central Government Deposits	16d	267.8	173.6	† 545.4	895.6	955.0	1,351.6	2,011.9	2,975.3	3,112.4	3,642.8	† 4,413.5	846.1
Capital Accounts	17a	−411.6	−52.7	† 172.5	211.1	300.9	304.7	440.9	1,023.7	937.5	418.2	† 645.3	719.6
Other Items (Net)	17r	87.9	21.6	† 176.3	71.4	−98.6	120.1	−108.8	−354.6	−391.1	425.5	† −347.4	320.1
Banking Institutions						*Billions of Kwacha: End of Period*							
Reserves	20	49.8	96.1	34.6	62.8	87.8	† 134.7	175.6	322.7	475.5	731.3	† 768.1	1,111.4
Foreign Assets	21	102.8	57.4	116.5	190.7	224.6	† 457.3	530.2	995.7	893.6	1,272.1	† 1,093.2	1,593.8
Claims on Central Government	22a	71.4	84.7	202.8	216.4	222.7	† 153.0	231.6	356.7	776.9	916.3	† 1,794.4	1,789.4
Claims on Local Government	22b	—	—	—	—	—	† 2.6	.4	.4	.4	—	† .6	.5
Claims on Nonfin.Pub.Enterprises	22c	29.1	16.8	35.6	49.7	40.9	† 119.1	248.9	289.7	246.8	63.0	† 60.8	113.4
Claims on Private Sector	22d	68.9	136.0	240.0	350.2	386.1	† 392.7	522.0	825.5	902.8	958.3	† 1,346.3	2,045.0
Claims on Nonbank Financial Insts	22g	—	—	—	—	—	† 2.7	1.4	.5	.4	9.7	† 10.4	.6
Demand Deposits	24	56.8	83.8	140.2	163.1	217.2	† 243.7	299.0	472.0	637.1	912.6	† 921.2	1,131.4
Time, Savings,& Fgn.Currency Dep	25	105.8	191.0	287.6	423.4	515.6	† 679.0	883.3	1,651.0	1,714.9	2,273.7	† 2,748.6	3,771.5
Money Market Instruments	26aa	15.0	14.9	23.3	31.1	29.8	† 11.8	9.9	34.6	21.3	4.8	† —	.1
Restricted Deposits	26b						† —					† 53.6	53.6
Foreign Liabilities	26c	8.4	10.6	9.3	14.4	19.1	† 67.1	91.8	107.7	93.7	112.6	† 162.8	204.9
Central Government Deposits	26d	5.8	12.4	44.6	57.7	63.6	† 61.3	125.2	43.2	94.4	112.4	† 418.5	695.3
Credit from Monetary Authorities	26g	.2	2.7	60.2	86.6	82.5	† 21.4	78.5	39.1	30.3	23.1	† 32.9	39.4
Capital Accounts	27a	44.2	58.5	74.5	112.7	138.1	† 227.8	297.2	448.6	533.7	769.9	† 560.8	638.2
Other Items (Net)	27r	85.7	17.0	−10.1	−19.2	−103.8	† −50.1	−74.7	−4.9	171.0	−258.3	† 175.3	119.8
Banking Survey						*Billions of Kwacha: End of Period*							
Foreign Assets (Net)	31n	−495.9	−787.6	† −1,022.4	−1,287.1	−1,228.0	† −2,397.2	−2,571.6	−3,660.9	−2,794.4	−2,598.6	† −2,633.6	−1,691.8
Domestic Credit	32	530.0	1,179.7	† 1,921.1	2,324.6	2,316.9	† 3,963.3	4,491.3	7,164.4	6,774.2	7,594.0	† 7,841.0	9,083.7
Claims on Central Govt. (Net)	32an	409.7	1,013.4	† 1,630.3	1,899.7	1,863.6	† 3,410.2	3,679.1	5,943.4	5,386.3	6,481.5	† 6,333.7	6,834.3
Claims on Local Government	32b			† —			† 2.6	.4	.4	.4	—	† .6	.5
Claims on Nonfin.Pub.Enterprises	32c	49.3	25.9	† 36.9	51.0	42.2	† 124.4	256.9	358.8	441.7	93.5	† 121.7	174.3
Claims on Private Sector	32d	71.0	140.4	† 254.0	373.8	411.1	† 423.5	553.5	861.3	945.4	1,009.2	† 1,374.7	2,074.0
Claims on Nonbank Financial Inst	32g	—	—	† —	—	—	† 2.7	1.4	.5	.4	9.7	† 10.4	.6
Money	34	97.3	141.0	† 227.1	271.1	355.2	† 414.9	513.0	775.9	1,041.4	1,339.3	† 1,513.8	1,860.4
Quasi-Money	35	111.2	191.0	† 289.1	425.7	516.3	† 679.8	884.9	1,653.2	1,718.3	2,279.9	† 2,754.6	3,778.9
Money Market Instruments	36aa	15.0	14.9	† 23.3	31.1	29.8	† 11.8	9.9	34.6	21.3	4.8	† —	.1
Restricted Deposits	36b			† —			† —					† 53.6	53.6
Capital Accounts	37a	−367.4	5.8	† 247.0	323.8	439.1	† 532.5	738.1	1,472.3	1,471.2	1,188.1	† 1,206.1	1,357.8
Other Items (Net)	37r	177.9	39.4	† 112.3	−14.3	−251.4	† −73.0	−226.2	−432.4	−272.5	183.3	† −320.7	341.0
Money plus Quasi-Money	35l	208.6	332.0	† 516.2	696.9	871.5	† 1,094.7	1,397.9	2,429.1	2,759.7	3,619.2	† 4,268.4	5,639.4
Money (National Definitions)						*Billions of Kwacha: End of Period*							
Monetary Base	19ma	....	....	....	....	382.9	409.4	390.8	599.2	873.5	1,264.9	1,442.3	1,908.2
M1	59ma	....	....	....	....	382.9	409.4	513.8	795.3	1,036.6	1,328.3	1,513.8	1,860.4
M2	59mb	....	....	....	....	889.7	1,049.5	1,352.0	2,404.6	2,718.6	3,515.2	4,189.9	5,302.9
M3	59mc	....	....	....	....	901.3	1,080.2	1,396.9	2,446.4	2,747.4	3,606.2	4,268.4	5,639.4
Interest Rates						*Percent Per Annum*							
Discount Rate (End of Period)	60	72.50	20.50	40.20	47.00	17.70		32.93	25.67	40.10	27.87	14.35	16.68
Treasury Bill Rate	60c	124.03	74.21	39.81	52.78	29.48	24.94	36.19	31.37	44.28	34.54	29.97	12.60
Savings Rate	60k	77.85	44.21	25.01	31.14	24.95	7.42	10.43	10.18	9.52	8.54	7.89	6.41
Deposit Rate	60l	....	46.14	30.24	42.13	34.48	13.08	20.27	20.24	23.41	23.33	21.95	11.51
Lending Rate	60p	113.31	70.56	45.53	53.78	46.69	31.80	40.52	38.80	46.23	45.20	40.57	30.73

Zambia 754

		1993	1994	1995	1996	1997	1998	1999	2000	2001	2002	2003	2004
Prices and Production		*Index Numbers (2000=100): Period Averages*											
Share Prices....................	62	....	....	....	....	75.3	78.0	75.5	100.0	121.5	134.1	157.8	243.6
Wholesale Prices (1995=100).........	63	34.1	58.1	100.0	....	....	....	....	....	....	....	....	....
Consumer Prices......................	64	13.5	20.9	28.2	40.4	50.3	62.6	79.3	100.0	121.4	148.4	180.1	212.5
Cons.Prices (Low Inc.Househ)(1995	64a	48.1	73.6	100.0	143.8	....	....	....	....	....	....	....	....
Industrial Production (1995=100)....	66	122.0	107.0	100.0	....	....	....	....	....	....	....	....	....
Mining Production (1990=100)........	66zx	92.0	76.8	....	....	....	....	....	....	....	....	....	....
Intl. Transactions & Positions		*Billions of Kwacha*											
Exports..................................	70	374.1	620.5	898.6	1,252.7	1,203.0	....	....	....	....	....	....	....
Imports, c.i.f...........................	71	366.3	397.7	604.8	1,004.3	1,077.0	....	....	....	....	....	....	....
Balance of Payments		*Millions of US Dollars: Minus Sign Indicates Debit*											
Current Account, n.i.e.....................	78ald	....	....	....	....	−383	−573	−447	−584	....	....	....	....
Goods: Exports f.o.b.................	78aad	....	....	....	....	1,110	818	772	757	....	....	....	....
Goods: Imports f.o.b................	78abd	....	....	....	....	−1,056	−971	−870	−978	....	....	....	....
Trade Balance.....................	78acd	....	....	....	....	54	−153	−98	−221	....	....	....	....
Services: Credit......................	78add	....	....	....	....	112	102	107	114	....	....	....	....
Services: Debit......................	78aed	....	....	....	....	−282	−282	−306	−340	....	....	....	....
Balance on Goods & Services.......	78afd	....	....	....	....	−115	−332	−297	−447	....	....	....	....
Income: Credit......................	78agd	....	....	....	....	47	44	44	46	....	....	....	....
Income: Debit.......................	78ahd	....	....	....	....	−296	−258	−178	−166	....	....	....	....
Balance on Gds, Serv. & Inc........	78aid	....	....	....	....	−364	−546	−431	−566	....	....	....	....
Current Transfers, n.i.e.: Credit.....	78ajd	....	....	....	....	—	—	—	—	....	....	....	....
Current Transfers: Debit................	78akd	....	....	....	....	−19	−27	−16	−18	....	....	....	....
Capital Account, n.i.e..................	78bcd	....	....	....	....	—	203	196	153	....	....	....	....
Capital Account, n.i.e.: Credit........	78bad	....	....	....	....	—	203	196	153	....	....	....	....
Capital Account: Debit.................	78bbd	....	....	....	....	—	—	—	—	....	....	....	....
Financial Account, n.i.e..............	78bjd	....	....	....	....	−324	−264	−174	−274	....	....	....	....
Direct Investment Abroad.............	78bdd	....	....	....	....	—	—	—	—	....	....	....	....
Dir. Invest. in Rep. Econ., n.i.e.....	78bed	....	....	....	....	207	198	162	122	....	....	....	....
Portfolio Investment Assets..........	78bfd	....	....	....	....	—	—	—	—	....	....	....	....
Equity Securities....................	78bkd	....	....	....	....	—	—	—	—	....	....	....	....
Debt Securities.....................	78bld	....	....	....	....	—	—	—	—	....	....	....	....
Portfolio Investment Liab., n.i.e......	78bgd	....	....	....	....	1	1	13	−1	....	....	....	....
Equity Securities....................	78bmd	....	....	....	....	1	1	13	−1	....	....	....	....
Debt Securities.....................	78bnd	....	....	....	....	....	....	....	....	....	....	....	....
Financial Derivatives Assets..........	78bwd	....	....	....	....					....	....	....	....
Financial Derivatives Liabilities.......	78bxd	....	....	....	....					....	....	....	....
Other Investment Assets..............	78bhd	....	....	....	....	−24	−40	−2	−85	....	....	....	....
Monetary Authorities..................	78bod	....	....	....	....					....	....	....	....
General Government..................	78bpd	....	....	....	....					....	....	....	....
Banks...................................	78bqd	....	....	....	....	−24	−40	−2	−85	....	....	....	....
Other Sectors.........................	78brd	....	....	....	....					....	....	....	....
Other Investment Liab., n.i.e..........	78bid	....	....	....	....	−508	−422	−347	−309	....	....	....	....
Monetary Authorities.................	78bsd	....	....	....	....	—	—	—	−7	....	....	....	....
General Government..................	78btd	....	....	....	....	−192	−136	−259	−290	....	....	....	....
Banks...................................	78bud	....	....	....	....	19	−2	—	—	....	....	....	....
Other Sectors.........................	78bvd	....	....	....	....	−335	−284	−88	−12	....	....	....	....
Net Errors and Omissions................	78cad	....	....	....	....	−225	−37	−229	185	....	....	....	....
Overall Balance.......................	78cbd	....	....	....	....	−932	−671	−654	−520	....	....	....	....
Reserves and Related Items.............	79dad	....	....	....	....	932	671	654	520	....	....	....	....
Reserve Assets.......................	79dbd	....	....	....	....	−25	194	−1	−90	....	....	....	....
Use of Fund Credit and Loans........	79dcd	....	....	....	....	14	—	14	26	....	....	....	....
Exceptional Financing.................	79ded	....	....	....	....	944	477	642	584	....	....	....	....
Government Finance		*Billions of Kwacha: Year Ending December 31*											
Deficit (-) or Surplus........................	80	−115.6	−27.4	−136.9	−96.2	−488.5	−330.4p	−275.4f	....	....	....	....	....
Revenue................................	81	266.4	502.8	600.7	745.3	957.0	1,097.6p	1,430.4f	....	....	....	....	....
Grants Received......................	81z	....	.6	5.6	25.4	4.7	432.7	414.2	....	....	....	....	....
Expenditure...........................	82	391.1	492.2	727.5	842.7	1,313.6	1,717.1p	1,874.3f	....	....	....	....	....
Lending Minus Repayments...........	83	26.6	38.6	15.7	24.2	136.6	143.6p	245.7f	....	....	....	....	....
Financing													
Net Borrowing: Domestic.............	84a	38.0	−46.5	−351.4	−91.2	−283.9	50.2	....	....	....	....	....	....
Net borrowing: Foreign.................	85a	77.6	73.9	488.3	187.4	772.4	280.2	....	....	....	....	....	....
Use of Cash Balances...............	87	14.3	−674.3	....	....	....	....	....	....	....	....	....	....
Debt: Domestic.......................	88a	1.6	149.9	238.8	265.8	303.2	212.8p	....	....	....	....	....	....
Debt: Foreign.........................	89a	2,396.3	3,502.4	4,869.4	7,378.7	8,185.9	10,408.4p	....	....	....	....	....	....
National Accounts		*Billions of Kwacha*											
Househ.Cons.Expend.,incl.NPISHs...	96f	1,015.7	1,602.7	1,775.9	2,033.2	3,006.0	....	....	....	....	....	....	....
Government Consumption Expend...	91f	273.2	293.6	464.0	676.5	792.3	....	....	....	....	....	....	....
Gross Fixed Capital Formation.........	93e	170.0	512.1	799.4	1,719.6	1,928.6	....	....	....	....	....	....	....
Changes in Inventories....................	93i	52.9	−69.1	104.8	63.1	73.9	....	....	....	....	....	....	....
Exports of Goods and Services..........	90c	420.9	806.5	1,082.3	1,237.4	1,552.0	....	....	....	....	....	....	....
Imports of Goods and Services (-).....	98c	450.6	905.2	1,228.2	1,710.4	2,196.0	....	....	....	....	....	....	....
Gross Domestic Product (GDP)........	99b	1,482.1	2,240.7	2,998.3	3,969.5	5,155.8	....	....	....	....	....	....	....
Net Primary Income from Abroad.....	98.n	−377.2	69.0	−104.9	−13.2	−72.9	....	....	....	....	....	....	....
Gross National Income (GNI)............	99a	1,104.9	2,309.7	2,893.4	3,956.3	5,082.9	....	....	....	....	....	....	....
Net National Income.......................	99e	866.0	1,518.0	2,227.4	3,396.4	....	....	....	....	....	....	....	....
GDP Vol. 1977 Prices (Billions)........	99b.p	2.322	2.241	2.190	2.332	2.414	....	....	....	....	....	....	....
GDP Volume (1995=100)..............	99bvp	106.0	102.3	100.0	106.5	110.2	....	....	....	....	....	....	....
GDP Deflator (1995=100)..............	99bip	46.6	73.0	100.0	124.3	156.0	....	....	....	....	....	....	....
		Millions: Midyear Estimates											
Population..............................	99z	9.09	9.33	9.56	9.79	10.03	10.26	10.49	10.70	10.91	11.10	11.29	11.48

Zimbabwe   698

		1993	1994	1995	1996	1997	1998	1999	2000	2001	2002	2003	2004
Exchange Rates		*SDRs per Zimbabwe Dollar: End of Period*											
Official Rate...............	ac	.1050	.0817	.0723	.0642	.0398	.0190	.0191	.0139	.0145	.0134	.0008	.0001
		US Dollars per Zimbabwe Dollar: End of Period (ag) Period Average (rh)											
Official Rate...............	ag	.1442	.1192	.1074	.0923	.0537	.0268	.0262	.0182	.0182	.0182	.0012	.0002
Official Rate...............	rh	.1545	.1227	.1155	.1008	.0841	.0467	.0261	.0231	.0182	.0182	.0040	.0002
Fund Position		*Millions of SDRs: End of Period*											
Quota......................	2f.s	261.3	261.3	261.3	261.3	261.3	261.3	353.4	353.4	353.4	353.4	353.4	353.4
SDRs......................	1b.s	.6	—	.5	6.8	.2	.3	.8	.2	—	—	—	—
Reserve Position in the Fund...........	1c.s	.1	.1	.1	.1	.1	.2	.3	.3	.3	.3	.3	.3
Total Fund Cred.&Loans Outstg.......	2tl	205.0	257.5	310.0	304.1	285.5	289.2	268.8	215.4	208.4	206.1	202.9	188.8
International Liquidity		*Millions of US Dollars Unless Otherwise Indicated: End of Period*											
Total Reserves minus Gold..............	1l.d	432.0	405.3	595.5	598.8	160.1	130.8	268.0	193.1	64.7	83.4	....	....
SDRs......................	1b.d	.9	.1	.8	9.8	.3	.4	1.1	.2	—	—	—	—
Reserve Position in the Fund.........	1c.d	.1	.1	.1	.2	.2	.3	.4	.4	.4	.4	.5	.5
Foreign Exchange.....................	1d.d	431.1	405.1	594.6	588.9	159.6	130.1	266.5	192.5	64.3	82.9	....	....
Gold (Million Fine Troy Ounces)....	1ad	.50	.47	.76	.64	.77	.62	.73	.47	.20	.14	....	....
Gold (National Valuation)...........	1and	79.1	89.7	139.7	117.2	56.0	82.6	105.4	45.4	27.5	22.7	....	....
Monetary Authorities: Other Liab.....	4..d	291.1	76.1	36.5	28.5	224.6	335.6	229.9	99.5	59.0	82.9	119.7	292.6
Deposit Money Banks: Assets........	7a.d	79.6	321.3	275.0	299.8	314.7	179.3	156.9	163.4	146.0	230.6	219.0	147.9
Liabilities...	7b.d	518.6	579.3	814.4	827.8	623.8	458.3	245.0	169.2	126.6	186.6	97.0	103.9
Other Banking Insts.: Assets............	7e.d	1.5	1.0	3.9	6.4	1.3	.6	1.4	1.1	.7	—	—	—
Liabilities...................	7f.d	—	.2	17.0	15.4	6.8	2.4	2.6	4.0	3.0	1.8	.9	.7
Monetary Authorities		*Billions of Zimbabwe Dollars: End of Period*											
Foreign Assets.......................	11	3.55	4.15	6.70	7.71	3.99	7.94	14.24	13.13	5.16	5.84	89.65	1,634.44
Claims on Central Government........	12a	2.76	7.10	13.64	22.83	30.55	47.54	58.73	98.66	38.61	66.74	499.31	2,542.16
Claims on Nonfin.Pub.Enterprises....	12c	.10	.13	.13	.16	.19	.19	.67	.65	2.03	.64	.12	254.30
Claims on Private Sector.............	12d	.21	.18	.22	.28	.36	.81	1.09	2.04	2.26	2.65	7.20	35.58
Claims on Deposit Money Banks......	12e	.31	.45	1.33	1.34	1.40	4.37	3.23	8.07	26.62	62.85	423.73	2,914.41
Reserve Money......................	14	2.94	3.63	3.72	6.17	8.51	11.05	17.79	20.64	54.67	148.25	733.55	2,329.52
of which: Currency Outside DMBs..	14a	1.19	1.47	1.82	2.44	3.56	4.47	7.26	9.94	25.64	79.66	441.71	1,655.89
Liabs.of the Central Bank:Securities..	16ac		2.05	.92									732.29
Foreign Liabilities..................	16c	3.97	3.79	4.63	5.05	11.35	27.76	22.84	20.94	17.66	19.99	347.03	3,356.49
Central Government Deposits...........	16d	—	3.31	14.74	22.83	18.04	26.06	43.77	80.05	—	9.62	—	393.88
Capital Accounts.....................	17a	.39	.67	.87	.80	.84	1.01	1.97	1.92	5.03	6.35	12.54	1.88
Other Items (Net)....................	17r	-.38	-1.44	-2.86	-2.54	-2.26	-4.55	-8.41	-1.00	-2.69	-45.47	-73.10	566.83
Deposit Money Banks		*Billions of Zimbabwe Dollars: End of Period*											
Reserves............................	20	1.19	2.02	1.82	3.60	4.28	6.04	10.11	9.72	30.63	88.69	610.58	3,904.01
Claims on Mon.Author.:Securities....	20c	—	2.05	.58	—	—	—	—	—	—	—	—	732.29
Foreign Assets......................	21	.55	2.70	2.56	3.25	5.86	6.70	5.98	9.00	8.04	12.69	180.39	847.57
Claims on Central Government........	22a	1.46	.97	6.03	7.15	7.10	6.74	11.23	30.90	56.59	108.49	167.28	3,560.57
Claims on Local Government.........	22b	.01	.03	.03	.03	.09	.24	.27	.38	.45	.68	1.53	31.67
Claims on Nonfin.Pub.Enterprises.....	22c	1.12	.73	.63	.96	1.08	1.83	2.65	7.52	17.38	47.10	227.32	435.37
Claims on Private Sector.............	22d	9.06	11.74	15.06	18.15	27.10	36.81	41.36	62.04	101.18	293.38	2,116.63	4,981.01
Claims on Other Banking Insts........	22f	.06	.03	.19	.31	.92	.14	1.48	1.93	2.12	10.37	22.42	52.93
Claims on Nonbank Financial Insts....	22g	.03	.06	.01	.06	.04	.19	.09	.73	5.99	6.23	52.52	102.77
Demand Deposits....................	24	4.55	5.79	9.35	11.29	17.10	21.42	27.80	44.17	106.00	275.40	1,636.45	5,148.17
Time, Savings,& Fgn.Currency Dep...	25	3.47	5.75	5.24	8.14	9.76	8.25	11.51	24.98	49.24	172.33	717.10	2,377.26
Money Market Instruments..............	26aa	.59	.69	.48	.31	.89	1.27	2.55	4.10	16.66	18.65	145.07	380.53
Foreign Liabilities..................	26c	3.60	4.86	7.58	8.97	11.61	17.13	9.34	9.32	6.97	10.27	79.91	595.30
Central Government Deposits.........	26d	.51	.44	.69	1.08	1.75	1.70	1.99	5.30	6.69	23.62	53.72	267.00
Credit from Monetary Authorities.....	26g	.25	.43	1.33	1.33	.95	3.80	2.61	7.89	7.77	50.11	439.89	3,460.33
Capital Accounts.....................	27a	1.44	1.92	2.05	2.52	4.41	6.44	9.51	15.17	31.44	79.87	406.16	1,964.13
Other Items (Net).....................	27r	-.93	.43	.17	-.14		-1.33	7.85	11.29	-2.39	-62.62	-99.61	455.46
Monetary Survey		*Billions of Zimbabwe Dollars: End of Period*											
Foreign Assets (Net).................	31n	-3.47	-1.80	-2.95	-3.06	-13.11	-30.25	-11.96	-8.13	-11.44	-11.72	-156.89	-1,469.78
Domestic Credit.....................	32	14.34	17.24	20.50	26.01	47.63	67.21	71.79	119.48	219.93	503.05	3,040.62	11,335.48
Claims on Central Govt. (Net)........	32an	3.70	4.32	4.24	6.07	17.85	26.52	24.20	44.20	88.51	142.00	612.87	5,441.85
Claims on Local Government.........	32b	.01	.03	.03	.03	.09	.24	.27	.38	.45	.68	1.53	31.67
Claims on Nonfin.Pub.Enterprises....	32c	1.22	.87	.76	1.12	1.27	2.51	3.30	8.17	19.41	47.74	227.44	689.67
Claims on Private Sector.............	32d	9.26	11.92	15.28	18.43	27.46	37.62	42.45	64.07	103.44	296.03	2,123.83	5,016.59
Claims on Other Banking Insts.......	32f	.06	.03	.19	.31	.92	.14	1.48	1.93	2.12	10.37	22.42	52.93
Claims on Nonbank Financial Inst...	32g	.08	.08	.01	.06	.04	.19	.09	.73	5.99	6.23	52.52	102.77
Money..............................	34	6.26	7.40	11.27	13.87	21.32	26.33	35.47	54.40	132.09	356.64	2,086.70	6,856.61
Quasi-Money.........................	35	3.47	5.75	5.24	8.14	9.76	8.25	11.51	24.98	49.24	172.33	717.10	2,377.26
Money Market Instruments..............	36aa	.59	.69	.48	.31	.89	1.27	2.55	4.10	16.66	18.65	145.07	380.53
Liabs.of the Central Bank:Securities..	36ac	—	—	.34									
Capital Accounts.....................	37a	1.83	2.59	2.93	3.32	5.25	7.46	11.47	17.08	36.47	86.22	418.70	1,966.00
Other Items (Net)....................	37r	-1.28	-.99	-2.71	-2.70	-2.70	-6.35	-1.17	10.80	-25.98	-142.52	-483.84	-1,714.71
Money plus Quasi-Money..............	35l	9.73	13.15	16.51	22.01	31.08	34.58	46.98	79.37	181.33	528.97	2,803.80	9,233.88
Other Banking Institutions		*Billions of Zimbabwe Dollars: End of Period*											
Reserves............................	40	.68	.91	3.63	4.45	7.51	4.69	5.06	12.32	21.33	50.18	150.35	511.47
Foreign Assets......................	41	.01	.01	.04	.07	.02	.02	.05	.06	.04	—	—	—
Claims on Central Government........	42a	2.35	2.79	3.96	4.41	3.72	4.05	9.23	18.46	18.16	12.75	17.44	472.77
Claims on Local Government.........	42b	.04	.04	.06	.27	.43	.44	.44	.46	.45	.41	.41	.41
Claims on Nonfin.Pub.Enterprises.....	42c	.18	.40	2.15	.59	.86	1.08	1.47	1.70	2.01	2.25	1.62	8.11
Claims on Private Sector.............	42d	3.41	4.04	5.58	8.29	12.41	15.00	16.09	16.49	25.36	65.69	154.26	287.48
Claims on Nonbank Financial Insts....	42g	—	—	.01	2.49	.74	.03	—	—	—	.05	2.59	1.52
Time, Savings,& Fgn.Currency Dep...	45	6.70	9.35	14.89	20.68	26.02	23.96	28.52	43.50	57.35	120.34	348.02	1,105.67
Money Market Instruments...	46aa	.21	.39	.48	.46	1.36	2.74	1.88	1.63	4.89	15.24	5.29	33.12
Foreign Liabilities..................	46c	—	—	.16	.17	.13	.09	.10	.22	.17	.10	.76	4.16
Credit from Deposit Money Banks....	46h	.16	.03	.11	.07	.42	.32	.91	.43	1.28	3.38	10.20	12.72
Capital Accounts.....................	47a	.64	.69	1.05	1.50	2.14	2.04	4.04	7.46	9.26	15.45	65.64	256.94
Other Items (Net).....................	47r	-1.03	-2.25	-1.27	-2.32	-4.37	-3.85	-3.10	-3.74	-5.61	-23.17	-103.23	-130.86

Zimbabwe 698

		1993	1994	1995	1996	1997	1998	1999	2000	2001	2002	2003	2004
Banking Survey						*Billions of Zimbabwe Dollars: End of Period*							
Foreign Assets (Net)	51n	−3.46	−1.80	−3.07	−3.16	−13.21	−30.31	−12.00	−8.29	−11.57	−11.82	−157.65	−1,473.94
Domestic Credit	52	20.27	24.49	32.06	41.74	64.88	87.66	97.55	154.68	263.78	573.83	3,194.52	12,052.84
Claims on Central Govt. (Net)	52an	6.05	7.11	8.20	10.48	21.58	30.57	33.43	62.66	106.67	154.74	630.31	5,914.62
Claims on Local Government	52b	.05	.07	.09	.30	.53	.68	.71	.84	.90	1.09	1.94	32.08
Claims on Nonfin.Pub.Enterprises	52c	1.40	1.27	2.91	1.71	2.13	3.58	4.77	9.87	21.42	49.99	229.06	697.78
Claims on Private Sector	52d	12.68	15.95	20.85	26.72	39.87	52.62	58.54	80.56	128.80	361.72	2,278.10	5,304.07
Claims on Nonbank Financial Inst.	52g	.08	.08	.01	2.54	.78	.22	.10	.74	5.99	6.28	55.11	104.29
Liquid Liabilities	55l	15.76	21.58	27.77	38.24	49.59	53.85	70.45	110.56	217.35	599.13	3,001.47	9,828.08
Money Market Instruments	56aa	.80	1.08	.96	.77	2.25	4.02	4.43	5.73	21.55	33.89	150.36	413.65
Liabs.of the Central Bank:Securities	56ac	—	—	.34	—	—	—	—	—	—	—	—	—
Capital Accounts	57a	2.47	3.28	3.97	4.82	7.40	9.50	15.52	24.54	45.73	101.67	484.33	2,222.95
Other Items (Net)	57r	−2.22	−3.24	−4.05	−5.25	−7.56	−10.02	−4.85	5.57	−32.43	−172.68	−599.30	−1,885.77
Interest Rates						*Percent Per Annum*							
Bank Rate (End of Period)	60	28.50	29.50	29.50	27.00	31.50	† 39.50	74.41	57.84	57.20	29.65	300.00	110.00
Money Market Rate	60b	34.18	30.90	29.64	26.18	25.15	37.22	53.13	64.98	21.52	32.35	110.05	130.42
Treasury Bill Rate	60c	33.04	29.22	27.98	24.53	22.07	32.78	50.48	64.78	17.60	28.51	52.73	125.68
Deposit Rate	60l	29.45	26.75	25.92	21.58	18.60	29.06	38.51	50.17	13.95	18.38	35.92	103.21
Lending Rate	60p	36.33	34.86	34.73	34.23	32.55	42.06	55.39	68.21	38.02	36.48	97.29	278.92
Prices, Production, Labor						*Index Numbers (2000=100): Period Averages*							
Consumer Prices	64	14.2	17.4	21.3	25.9	30.7	40.5	64.2	100.0	176.7	424.3	....	....
Manufacturing Prod.(1995=100)	66ey	105.7	115.8	100.0	103.6	106.9	....	....	....	....	....	....	....
						Number in Thousands: Period Averages							
Labor Force	67d	....	....	....	....	4,921	....	4,963	....	....	....	....	....
Employment	67e	1,239	1,264	1,240	1,273	1,323	1,349	1,316	1,237	1,184	1,071	....	....
Intl. Transactions & Positions						*Millions of Zimbabwe Dollars*							
Exports	70	10,164.2	15,364.7	18,359.1	24,209.3	28,967.0	46,317.0	73,844.9	81,350.2	66,882.5	110,721.0	2,344,373.0	9,563,607.0
Imports, c.i.f.	71	11,798.4	18,270.6	23,048.1	38,156.4	37,646.4	66,155.6	83,407.2	81,762.1	94,507.4	128,027.9	479,308.3	10,910,182.2
Imports, f.o.b.	71.v	10,259.5	15,887.5	20,043.0	....	....	....	....	....	....	....	....	....
Balance of Payments						*Millions of US Dollars: Minus Sign Indicates Debit*							
Current Account, n.i.e.	78ald	−115.7	−424.9	....	....	....	....	....	....	....	....	....	....
Goods: Exports f.o.b.	78aad	1,609.1	1,961.1	....	....	....	....	....	....	....	....	....	....
Goods: Imports f.o.b.	78abd	−1,487.0	−1,803.5	....	....	....	....	....	....	....	....	....	....
Trade Balance	78acd	122.1	157.6	....	....	....	....	....	....	....	....	....	....
Services: Credit	78add	372.1	383.2	....	....	....	....	....	....	....	....	....	....
Services: Debit	78aed	−563.8	−711.7	....	....	....	....	....	....	....	....	....	....
Balance on Goods & Services	78afd	−69.6	−170.9	....	....	....	....	....	....	....	....	....	....
Income: Credit	78agd	35.0	27.5	....	....	....	....	....	....	....	....	....	....
Income: Debit	78ahd	−287.1	−321.2	....	....	....	....	....	....	....	....	....	....
Balance on Gds, Serv. & Inc.	78aid	−321.6	−464.5	....	....	....	....	....	....	....	....	....	....
Current Transfers, n.i.e.: Credit	78ajd	270.6	69.4	....	....	....	....	....	....	....	....	....	....
Current Transfers: Debit	78akd	−64.7	−29.8	....	....	....	....	....	....	....	....	....	....
Capital Account, n.i.e.	78bcd	−.4	284.4	....	....	....	....	....	....	....	....	....	....
Capital Account, n.i.e.: Credit	78bad	.6	285.4	....	....	....	....	....	....	....	....	....	....
Capital Account: Debit	78bbd	−1.0	−1.0	....	....	....	....	....	....	....	....	....	....
Financial Account, n.i.e.	78bjd	327.2	−25.5	....	....	....	....	....	....	....	....	....	....
Direct Investment Abroad	78bdd	—	−4.7	....	....	....	....	....	....	....	....	....	....
Dir. Invest. in Rep. Econ., n.i.e.	78bed	28.0	34.7	....	....	....	....	....	....	....	....	....	....
Portfolio Investment Assets	78bfd	—	—	....	....	....	....	....	....	....	....	....	....
Equity Securities	78bkd	—	—	....	....	....	....	....	....	....	....	....	....
Debt Securities	78bld	—	—	....	....	....	....	....	....	....	....	....	....
Portfolio Investment Liab., n.i.e.	78bgd	−5.1	50.2	....	....	....	....	....	....	....	....	....	....
Equity Securities	78bmd	—	56.9	....	....	....	....	....	....	....	....	....	....
Debt Securities	78bnd	−5.1	−6.7	....	....	....	....	....	....	....	....	....	....
Financial Derivatives Assets	78bwd	....	—	....	....	....	....	....	....	....	....	....	....
Financial Derivatives Liabilities	78bxd	....	—	....	....	....	....	....	....	....	....	....	....
Other Investment Assets	78bhd	99.9	−260.3	....	....	....	....	....	....	....	....	....	....
Monetary Authorities	78bod	....	....	....	....	....	....	....	....	....	....	....	....
General Government	78bpd	—	—	....	....	....	....	....	....	....	....	....	....
Banks	78bqd	99.9	−260.3	....	....	....	....	....	....	....	....	....	....
Other Sectors	78brd	—	—	....	....	....	....	....	....	....	....	....	....
Other Investment Liab., n.i.e.	78bid	204.4	154.7	....	....	....	....	....	....	....	....	....	....
Monetary Authorities	78bsd	−7.8	−109.9	....	....	....	....	....	....	....	....	....	....
General Government	78btd	191.0	62.0	....	....	....	....	....	....	....	....	....	....
Banks	78bud	—	—	....	....	....	....	....	....	....	....	....	....
Other Sectors	78bvd	21.2	202.6	....	....	....	....	....	....	....	....	....	....
Net Errors and Omissions	78cad	14.9	80.2	....	....	....	....	....	....	....	....	....	....
Overall Balance	78cbd	225.9	−85.8	....	....	....	....	....	....	....	....	....	....
Reserves and Related Items	79dad	−225.9	85.8	....	....	....	....	....	....	....	....	....	....
Reserve Assets	79dbd	−293.6	12.9	....	....	....	....	....	....	....	....	....	....
Use of Fund Credit and Loans	79dcd	67.7	72.8	....	....	....	....	....	....	....	....	....	....
Exceptional Financing	79ded	....	....	....	....	....	....	....	....	....	....	....	....

Zimbabwe 698

		1993	1994	1995	1996	1997	1998	1999	2000	2001	2002	2003	2004
Government Finance		*Millions of Zimbabwe Dollars: Year Ending June 30*											
Deficit (-) or Surplus.........................	80	−2,645	−2,092	−5,791	−5,147	−5,077	....	....	....	....	....	....	....
Total Revenue and Grants..............	81y	11,752	13,699	18,687	23,811	31,126	....	....	....	....	....	....	....
Revenue.......................................	81	11,152	12,776	16,998	22,808	30,670	....	....	....	....	....	....	....
Grants...	81z	600	923	1,690	1,003	456	....	....	....	....	....	....	....
Exp. & Lending Minus Repay..........	82z	14,396	15,790	24,479	28,958	36,202	....	....	....	....	....	....	....
Expenditure................................	82	12,390	14,538	22,000	29,691	36,454	....	....	....	....	....	....	....
Lending Minus Repayments.........	83	2,006	1,252	2,479	−733	−252	....	....	....	....	....	....	....
Total Financing................................	80h	2,645	2,092	5,791	5,147	5,077	....	....	....	....	....	....	....
Domestic.....................................	84a	1,279	1,733	4,802	3,973	5,168	....	....	....	....	....	....	....
Foreign.......................................	85a	1,366	359	990	1,175	−91	....	....	....	....	....	....	....
Total Debt by Residence..................	88	25,054	31,131	47,503	53,201	59,303	....	....	....	....	....	....	....
Domestic.....................................	88a	9,071	12,875	24,671	31,407	30,371	....	....	....	....	....	....	....
Foreign.......................................	89a	15,983	18,257	22,832	21,793	28,932	....	....	....	....	....	....	....
National Accounts		*Millions of Zimbabwe Dollars*											
Househ.Cons.Expend.,incl.NPISHs....	96f	29,259	31,586	36,853	57,218	78,435	92,808	146,108	223,743	....	....	....	....
Government Consumption Expend...	91f	6,350	9,375	11,100	14,492	16,653	23,764	32,423	47,907	....	....	....	....
Gross Fixed Capital Formation..........	93e	10,022	12,002	15,265	15,434	18,424	31,122	33,550	41,554	....	....	....	....
Changes in Inventories.....................	93i	−2,416	4,274	410	−253	1,971	1,531	4,278	550	....	....	....	....
Exports of Goods and Services..........	90c	13,050	19,431	23,562	30,910	....	....	....	....	....	....	....	....
Imports of Goods and Services (-).....	98c	13,784	20,509	25,216	30,747	....	....	....	....	....	....	....	....
Gross Domestic Product (GDP)........	99b	42,481	56,159	61,974	87,055	108,323	146,744	221,588	311,890	....	....	....	....
Net Primary Income from Abroad.....	98.n	−1,604	−2,405	−2,794	−2,931	−3,908	....	....	....	....	....	....	....
Gross National Income (GNI)............	99a	40,877	53,375	58,951	84,144	103,353	137,588	212,051	301,812	....	....	....	....
GDP Volume 1990 Prices................	99b.p	21,531	22,780	22,820	25,038	25,389	25,586	24,537	22,876	....	....	....	....
GDP Volume (2000=100)................	99bvp	94.1	99.6	99.8	109.5	111.0	111.8	107.3	100.0	....	....	....	....
GDP Deflator (2000=100)...............	99bip	14.5	18.1	19.9	25.5	31.3	42.1	66.2	100.0	....	....	....	....
		Millions: Midyear Estimates											
Population...............................	99z	11.38	11.61	11.82	12.01	12.19	12.34	12.48	12.60	12.70	12.79	12.86	12.94